The Encyclopedia of
Saskatchewan

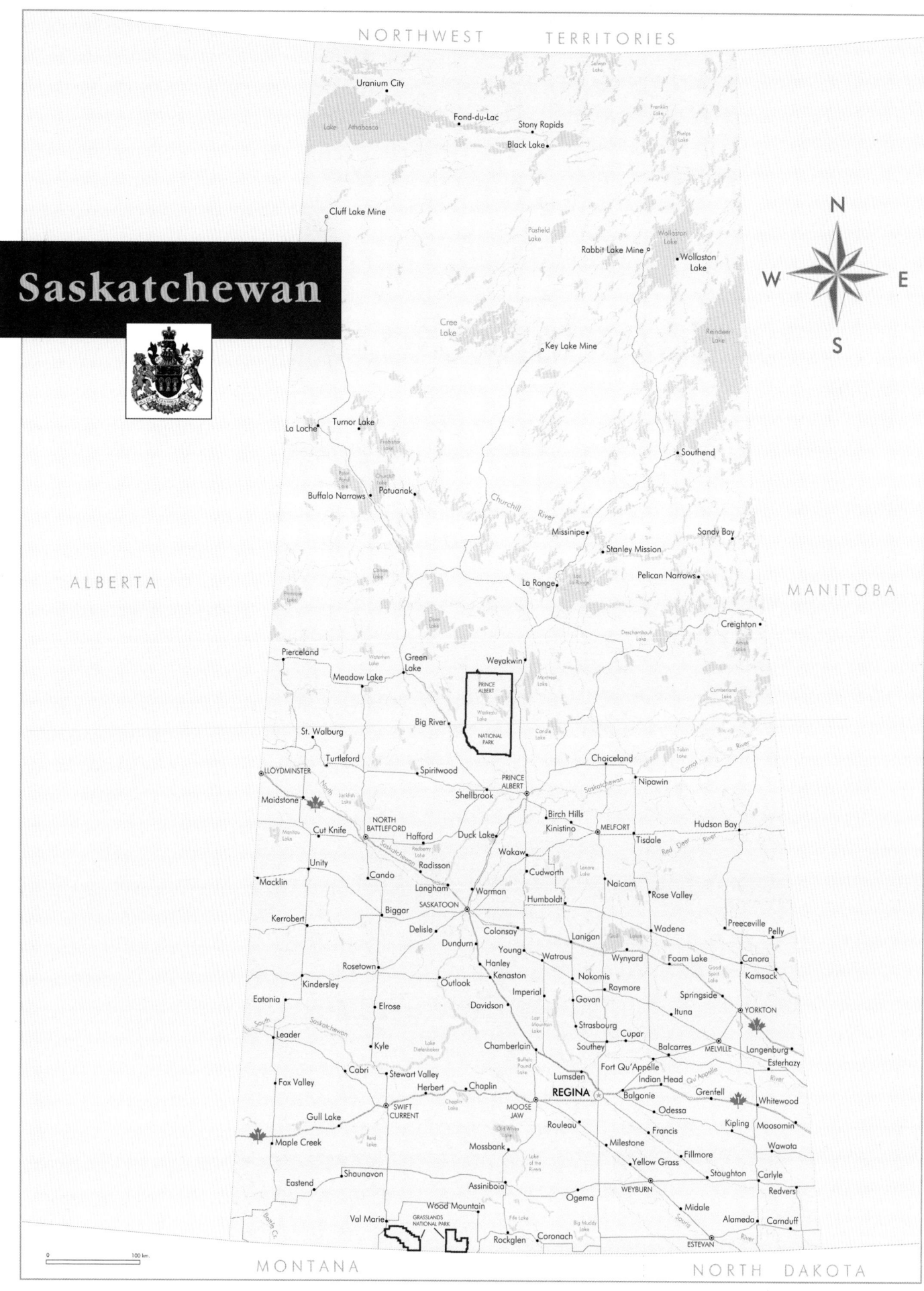

Saskatchewan

NORTHWEST TERRITORIES

ALBERTA

MANITOBA

MONTANA

NORTH DAKOTA

N
W E
S

Uranium City

Fond-du-Lac

Stony Rapids

Black Lake

Lake Athabasca

Selwyn Lake

Franklin Lake

Phelps Lake

Cluff Lake Mine

Pasfield Lake

Rabbit Lake Mine

Wollaston Lake

Wollaston Lake

Cree Lake

Key Lake Mine

Reindeer Lake

La Loche

Turnor Lake

Frobisher Lake

Southend

Buffalo Narrows

Patuanak

Peter Pond Lake

Churchill Lake

Churchill River

Missinipe

Sandy Bay

Stanley Mission

Pelican Narrows

Canoe Lake

La Ronge

Lac la Ronge

Creighton

Deschambault Lake

Amisk Lake

Pierceland

Waterhen Lake

Green Lake

Weyakwin

Cumberland Lake

Meadow Lake

Dore Lake

PRINCE ALBERT

Montreal Lake

Big River

Waskesiu Lake

Candle Lake

St. Walburg

NATIONAL PARK

Choiceland

Tobin Lake

Carrot River

LLOYDMINSTER

Turtleford

Spiritwood

PRINCE ALBERT

Shellbrook

Nipawin

Maidstone

North Saskatchewan

Jackfish Lake

Birch Hills

Saskatchewan River

Cut Knife

NORTH BATTLEFORD

Hafford

Duck Lake

Kinistino

MELFORT

Hudson Bay

Manitou Lake

Redberry Lake

Wakaw

Tisdale

Red Deer River

Unity

Radisson

Cudworth

Macklin

Cando

Langham

Warman

Lenore Lake

Naicam

Rose Valley

Biggar

SASKATOON

Humboldt

Kerrobert

Delisle

Colonsay

Wadena

Preeceville

Pelly

Dundurn

Young

Lanigan

Gull Lakes

Canora

Rosetown

Hanley

Watrous

Wynyard

Foam Lake

Kamsack

Kindersley

Outlook

Kenaston

Nokomis

Good Spirit Lake

Springside

Ituna

Eatonia

Elrose

Imperial

Raymore

YORKTON

Davidson

Govan

Last Mountain Lake

Strasbourg

Cupar

MELVILLE

Langenburg

Leader

Kyle

Lake Diefenbaker

Chamberlain

Southey

Balcarres

Esterhazy

South Saskatchewan

Fox Valley

Cabri

Stewart Valley

Herbert

Chaplin

Lumsden

Fort Qu'Appelle

Indian Head

Grenfell

Qu'Appelle River

Whitewood

Gull Lake

SWIFT CURRENT

Chaplin Lake

MOOSE JAW

REGINA

Balgonie

Odessa

Kipling

Moosomin

Red Lake

Rouleau

Francis

Milestone

Fillmore

Wawota

Maple Creek

Mossbank

Old Wives Lake

Yellow Grass

Stoughton

Carlyle

Shaunavon

Lake of the Rivers

Redvers

Eastend

Assiniboia

WEYBURN

Midale

Alameda

Carnduff

Val Marie

Wood Mountain

Ogema

Big Muddy Lake

GRASSLANDS NATIONAL PARK

Frenchman River

Fife Lake

Rockglen

Coronach

ESTEVAN

Souris River

Battle Cr.

0   100 km.

The Encyclopedia of
Saskatchewan

Published by

Canadian Plains Research Center

2005

UNIVERSITY OF
REGINA

CANADIAN PLAINS
RESEARCH CENTER

Canadian Plains Research Center
University of Regina
Regina, Saskatchewan S4S 0A2
Canada
Tel: (306) 585-4758
Fax: (306) 585-4699
e-mail: canadian.plains@uregina.ca
http://www.cprc.uregina.ca

Library and Archives Canada Cataloguing in Publication

The Encyclopedia of Saskatchewan

Includes bibliographical references and index.
ISBN 0-88977-175-8

1. Saskatchewan--Encyclopedias. I. University of Regina. Canadian Plains Research Center

FC3504.E53 2005   971.24
C2005-900762-1

We acknowledge the financial support of the Government of Canada through the Book Publishing Industry Development Program (BPDIP) for our publishing activities.

Cover and title pages by Brian Danchuk Design, Regina, Saskatchewan
Cover images and title page images courtesy of Courtney Milne

Printed in Canada by Houghton Boston, Saskatoon

To the People of Saskatchewan

Derived from a poem by the Roman poet Catullus, Saskatchewan's motto

— *Multis E Gentibus Vires*, "From many peoples strength" —

was well chosen to reflect the energy and vigour

of the province's multicultural heritage.

While there are many deserving individuals

to whom this book could be dedicated,

these are the stories of the people of Saskatchewan,

and it is therefore dedicated to them.

The Canadian Plains Research Center gratefully acknowledges the support of Saskatchewan Centennial 2005 for the Encyclopedia of Saskatchewan Project

THE WORLD could use a little more Saskatchewan, and in this exceptional book about Saskatchewan people, places and events, readers will find out why.

Saskatchewan Centennial 2005 is proud to be a partner of the Encyclopedia of Saskatchewan— a legacy project that has literally been a century in the making. This exciting centennial project is a perfect tribute to an incredible province that is proud to celebrate 100 years of heart.

Back on September 1, 1905, Saskatchewan and Alberta officially became provinces within the Canadian Confederation. On that day in Edmonton, Prime Minister Sir Wilfrid Laurier and Governor General Earl Grey officiated in inaugural ceremonies with the people of Alberta to celebrate this historic event. From Edmonton, the entourage, including the Prime Minister, Governor General and other dignitaries, journeyed by special train to arrive in Regina on September 4th for the inaugural ceremonies welcoming Saskatchewan into Confederation.

The excitement and celebration of this special day, September 4, 1905, Saskatchewan's inauguration into the Dominion of Canada, started early in the morning and extended late into the night. By all accounts, this was a grand day that left memories in the lives and minds of Saskatchewan people for many years to come.

One hundred years later, Saskatchewan celebrates the growth, progress and accomplishment as a province of Canada. It is an occasion for celebration by all Saskatchewan communities and residents.

The celebration of Saskatchewan's centennial is an opportunity to create a focal point for optimism and pride in Saskatchewan and to rally loyalty in the hearts and minds of Saskatchewan people. It is also an excellent opportunity to share Saskatchewan pride with all the people of Canada and the world.

The centennial is also an opportunity to reflect on our past accomplishments—the work of our province's pioneers and a province built on the heart of our first inhabitants—the First Nations and Métis peoples that lived here hundreds of years before Saskatchewan became a province.

From many peoples strength, Saskatchewan's official motto, explains that building Saskatchewan—building such a unique province— has been a work hundreds of years in the making. Hardworking pioneers came to this land from all over the world. With courage, determination and a dream, a province was created. Their hands built a province and their ideas influenced history.

Saskatchewan is known throughout Canada and the world as a province that has introduced countless firsts. Many combined talents have built a reputation as a global leader in many different areas. In virtually every field—from healthcare, business, arts and agriculture—Saskatchewan continues to develop the answers the world is looking for. All who have called Saskatchewan home—athletes, artists, inventors, community leaders, musicians and volunteers—have contributed to building this province.

There is no other place like Saskatchewan. With rich resources, diverse geography and a mixing of cultures not found anywhere else, those who live here or lived here before know just what makes this province special.

Known as home to hardworking, honest, trusted and trusting people—Saskatchewan is recognized for opening up its doors, rolling out the welcome mat and hosting some of the best— and largest—events in Canada and the world!

Saskatchewan's future is filled with possibility and opportunity. It's a future that will be led by the youth of this province. It's a time when their creativity and hard work will build the second century, and they will show the world it could use a little more Saskatchewan.

Happy centennial, Saskatchewan!

Commemorate. Celebrate. Saskatchewan!

The Canadian Plains Research Center gratefully acknowledges the sponsorship of the Government of Saskatchewan to the Encyclopedia of Saskatchewan.

**Government of
Saskatchewan**

Culture, Youth and Recreation

Environment

Government Relations

Industry and Resources

Learning

The Canadian Plains Research Center gratefully acknowledges the sponsorship of the following groups to the Encyclopedia of Saskatchewan.

Courtney Milne Productions Inc.

LEADER-POST

**Doug Chisholm
Woodland Aerial Photography
La Ronge, Saskatchewan**

The StarPhoenix

 University of Regina Archives and Special Collections

 University of Saskatchewan Archives

Program Grants in Aid of Publishing
Cultural Assistance Program
Community Initiatives Fund
Cultural Industries Development Fund

CONTENTS

On behalf of the Government of Saskatchewan, it is my great pleasure to welcome readers to the *Encyclopedia of Saskatchewan*.

Saskatchewan's founders had a vision of a land full of opportunity for all. Through hard work, resourcefulness and the strength of our people and communities, we have realized this dream. As we celebrate our province's centenary, our thoughts naturally turn to the many things Saskatchewan has to celebrate. We have beauty overhead and around us, and rich resources under our feet. We have fertile farmlands, bountiful forests, advanced technology, a growing manufacturing sector and an ever-increasing number of value-added enterprises. We are especially proud of our publicly funded health care system, our education system that places us among the highest-educated people in the world, and our internationally recognized social programs.

Saskatchewan Centennial 2005 is pleased to be able to support this worthy initiative. I congratulate the Director and staff of the Canadian Plains Research Center for their efforts to produce the *Encyclopedia*, truly a fitting tribute to our wonderful province on its birthday.

Welcome again, and best wishes for a centennial year filled with good health, happiness and celebration!

Lorne Calvert
Premier

Throughout 2005 we are paying tribute to the heart and spirit of Saskatchewan people. The *Encyclopedia of Saskatchewan* tells the story of many achievements of our province and the people who have made those achievements happen. It also shares information on what makes up our province—our resources, our landscape, our communities and our residents. As you read through the entries in this book, or use it as a reference guide, you'll learn many things about Saskatchewan that you may not have known.

Knowledge is a powerful gift and it is a gift worth sharing. I encourage you to spread your new understanding and appreciation of what Saskatchewan has achieved with as many people as possible. Together, we'll show the world it could use a little more Saskatchewan.

Our centennial is a unique opportunity to look at our province's past with a sense of pride and accomplishment. We can also look forward to our second century with confidence and optimism. Our province has so much to celebrate and the centennial year is a perfect time to collect these incredible stories and put them in a lasting commemorative resource book that will create a legacy of learning.

Happy centennial, Saskatchewan!
Glenn Hagel, MLA
Chair of Saskatchewan Centennial 2005

Universities have a three-fold mission: to share existing knowledge, to create new knowledge, and to use knowledge in the service of others. In managing the development and publication of the *Encyclopedia of Saskatchewan*, the University of Regina has done all three for our province in its Centennial year.

This remarkable *Encyclopedia* is a result of the work of many people, including over 800 dedicated writers and editors, and so it embodies our provincial motto—*From many peoples strength*. I would like to thank them all, especially Dr. David Gauthier, Executive Director of the University's Canadian Plains Research Center, who served as General Manager for the project, and Dr. Courtney Milne, who generously donated dozens of his awe-inspiring photographs of Saskatchewan to enliven these pages.

In a line from his poem "Abundance," Micheal O'Siadhail says, "So much is that might never have been." For Saskatchewan, this book tells us what it is that might never have been for us. With that foundation, our task now is to go forward so that there will be more social, cultural and economic richness here in the next 100 years "that might never have been."

Dr. David T. Barnard
President and Vice-Chancellor (1998–2005)
University of Regina

MESSAGE FROM THE PUBLISHER

David A. Gauthier

These are the stories of Saskatchewan, "*kisiskatchewan*," the land of the swiftly flowing river, so named by its First Peoples. From the earliest evidence of humans in Saskatchewan over 11,000 years ago, hundreds of generations have given of their strength and knowledge in overcoming great adversity to build this great province. It is no less than the natural and cultural legacy of Saskatchewan that we have tried to capture in this encyclopedia.

In celebration of Saskatchewan's centennial, *The Encyclopedia of Saskatchewan* is a gift both for and by the people of Saskatchewan of their knowledge and experience to all who would care to know of the people, places and events that have shaped this province's legacy to Canada and the world.

The clichéd image of Saskatchewan as a "flatland" fails to capture a place of unsurpassed beauty, a people of indomitable strength and compassion, and events that have influenced the world. While very few people have the opportunity to explore the breadth of space and history that Saskatchewan encompasses, our hope is that this book will act as a guide to the wealth of information about this immense and diverse province. Over 650,000 square kilometres in size, about one-half of the province is covered by forest, one-third is prairie and agricultural land and one-eighth is fresh water (two of the ten largest freshwater lakes in North America are in Saskatchewan). Caribou graze the lichen forests of the north at the same time that pronghorn antelope roam the coulees of the prairies. In these pages you can read about North America's first bird sanctuary at Last Mountain Lake or the wetlands that produce one in four ducks in North America. You can explore the lodgepole pine forests of Saskatchewan's Cypress Hills, the highest point of land in Canada between the Rocky Mountains and Labrador, or read about the richest uranium deposits in the world that occur in the northern Athabasca basin, also home to the largest area of active sand dunes north of 58 degrees found in the world. Discover caverns mined from ancient sea-beds in the southern part of the province that yield the world's second-largest production of potash.

Read about the legacy and on-going contributions of Saskatchewan's First Nations and Métis—about the leadership of Chiefs Piapot, Poundmaker and Big Bear, or the First Nations University of Canada, an independently administered university-college serving the academic, cultural and spiritual needs of First Nations' students. Read about Louis Riel, the influential Métis leader, and the 1885 Resistance and Gabriel Dumont and the Battle of Batoche.

Read about the province that gave rise to North America's first socialist government, and the second province to grant suffrage in support of women's rights. Learn about the contributions of Violet McNaughton, first president of the Women Grain Growers, in the suffrage movement. Find out about the province's leadership in the development and evolution of co-operative movements. Saskatchewan was the first province to introduce comprehensive medical insurance and the first to establish an Arts Board in North America. It is the home of Canada's longest continuously performing symphony orchestra (the Regina Symphony Orchestra) and second longest continuously running stage production (*The Trial of Louis Riel*) in Canada.

"We were educated by our grandparents and by our parents about what the true meaning of education really is, that it is life long and that it encompasses everything around us— the environment, our emotions, our intellect, our customs and our culture."

Linda Pelly-Landrie, Testimony to the Office of the Treaty Commissioner of Saskatchewan on First Nations and the Treaty Right to Education, September 14, 1992.

Learn about Saskatchewan's contributions to the arts and literature through entries on W.O Mitchell (Weyburn, SK), Buffy Sainte-Marie (Piapot Reserve, SK), Guy Vanderhaeghe (Esterhazy, SK) and many others.

Read about the achievements of Saskatchewan sports figures such as Gordie Howe (Floral, SK), Bryan Trottier (Val Marie, SK), the Ernie Richardson, Vera Pezer and Sandra Schmirler curling rinks, Ethel Catherwood, the "Saskatoon Lily," who set the world record in high jump at the 1928 Olympic Games, Catriona Le May Doan (Saskatoon), gold medal winner at the 1998 and 2002 Winter Olympics, and the 17-year-old George Genereux (Saskatoon) winning gold at the 1952 Olympics.

Discover a wealth of information about the province's contributions in science and technology such as the Canadian Light Source Project at the University of Saskatchewan, the country's largest scientific project, and the world's largest fibre optics network. In these pages you will read about the province's leadership in conducting the world's most advanced research into carbon dioxide sequestration. You will find out about innovation in Saskatchewan that has led to many technological "firsts": the first automated teller machine (ATM) in Canada, the first in-store direct debit system, the world's first heavy oil upgrader, the world's first zero-effluent pulp mill.

You will also learn about Saskatchewan's significant contributions in meeting Canada and the world's food needs. Not only the leading wheat (spring and durum) producer for Canada, it also leads in the production of lentils, canary seed, mustard, field peas, flax and canola. The majority of Canada's wild rice is grown and harvested in Saskatchewan which is also the country's largest per capita honey producer.

The facts and figures of Saskatchewan's accomplishments are embedded in an array of fascinating stories about people, places and events, for example, the Willow Bunch "Giant," Édouard Beaupré, the World Championship of "Bunnock" (Macklin, SK), and the Japanese "balloon bombs" of World War II. Learn about the Regina Cyclone of 1912, the most devastating tornado for loss of life in Canada, or the impact of the tragic 1935 Regina Riot on the country. Follow the discovery of "Scotty" of Eastend, one of the few *Tyrannosaurus rex* found in the world, or "Big Bert," a rare species of crocodile over 92 million years old from Carrot River. Explore the Wood Mountain, home to Sitting Bull and his followers after their victory at the Battle of Little Big Horn, and learn about Saskatchewan's Big Muddy Badlands. Read about the Tunnels of Moose Jaw, where notorious gangster Al Capone supposedly ran his bootleg operation during Prohibition. Find out about the creation of the North-West Mounted Police, later to become the Royal Canadian Mounted Police, whose training academy in Regina serves the nation. You will also read about the many Saskatchewan men and women who made tremendous sacrifices in defense of freedom during World War I, World War II, and the Korean War.

The above provides only a glimpse of what the *Encyclopedia* documents in terms of Saskatchewan's contributions across many diverse areas including agriculture, arts and culture, business and industry, communities, education, First Nations and Métis, geography, health, history, labour, law and justice, the military, politics and government, philosophy, population, science and technology, religion, social policy, sports, transportation, and women. Many entries celebrate Saskatchewan's contributions, nationally and internationally, and we have provided in-depth essays with detailed information on specific themes. There are also stories of individuals and events that were important in shaping Saskatchewan's communities, and entries that reflect difficult and tragic times in the history of our province.

Our intent in developing the *Encyclopedia of Saskatchewan* is that it serve as an educational resource for students, teachers, researchers and all who care about the people, places and events that have shaped Saskatchewan's legacy to Canada and the world. It is our hope that, as a permanent record of achievements, the *Encyclopedia* will increase awareness and understanding of the region's rich cultural and natural heritage and serve as a fitting and timely vehicle through which to encourage readers to reflect not only on the province's accomplishments, but on the wealth of opportunities and advantages afforded to Saskatchewan residents.

This encyclopedia, which through many years of labour we came to refer to as ESask, was created by the contributions of hundreds of dedicated individuals. Although the involvement of the Canadian Plains Research Center (CPRC) in ESask began in 1993, the idea of an encyclopedia about the province had been around for much longer. Frank Korvemaker, then with the Heritage Branch, was an early proponent of the need for a compendium of information about the province. He and Dr. John Archer, the first President of the University of Regina, encouraged support from the government of Saskatchewan for the idea. Frank, along with Garth Pugh (Manager, Saskatchewan Heritage Foundation), brought the concept to CPRC because of its role as a scholarly and educational press. Although there was general enthusiasm for the idea, the challenges of developing a provincial encyclopedia were enormous. In the early 1990s there were few examples in Canada of encyclopedias. Mel Hurtig of Hurtig Publishing had released the three-volume *Canadian Encyclopedia* in 1985. The only provincial encyclopedia that had been published by the early 1990s was the *Encyclopedia of Newfoundland and Labrador* originated by former Premier Joseph ("Joey") Smallwood; its five volumes were released between 1981 and 1994. In BC, publisher Howard White and editor Daniel Francis of Harbour Publishing undertook the development over a ten-year period of the *Encyclopedia of British Columbia*, which was published in 2000. Alberta, through the Heritage Community Foundation, is developing an online encyclopedia as a contribution to that province's 2005 centenary.

It was clear from CPRC's earliest discussions that, while we would benefit from the experiences from other places, the development of a general knowledge encyclopedia of Saskatchewan would require a blend of partnerships that reflected the volunteerism and community involvement that has so characterized the development of the province. In 1996 CPRC sought guidance from representatives of a wide group of government and non-government agencies and organizations who met with us in a workshop at the University of Regina. Mel Hurtig, Robert MacDonald (a multi-media and publishing expert), Avi Bennett (former owner of McClelland and Stewart Publishers) and Jim Marsh (editor from McClelland and Stewart) participated in the discussions. That meeting confirmed the widespread enthusiasm for an encyclopedia that could be created to celebrate Saskatchewan's centenary. It identified initial partners and resulted in the formation of an advisory committee to guide the development of a vision and concept plan for the encyclopedia. The members of that first committee were:

> Dr. John Archer (Honorary Chair)
> Dr. David Gauthier, Committee Chair, CPRC, University of Regina
> Ved Arora, Saskatchewan Provincial Library
> Denis Hosford, Saskatchewan Property Management Corporation
> Dr. Michael Jackson, Saskatchewan Provincial Secretary
> Peter Jonker, University of Saskatchewan
> Frank Korvemaker, Heritage Branch, Government of Saskatchewan

"As I sat on the rail watching and listening that day a new world was washing slowly over me, seeping in without my noticing, a slower world, and a timeless one that resonated with a sense that it must always have been there in just this way and always would be."

Sharon Butala, from *The Perfection of Morning: An Apprenticeship in Nature* (1994)

Brian Mlazgar, CPRC Publications Coordinator
Russ Moore, Saskatchewan Finance
Garth Pugh, Saskatchewan Heritage Foundation
Gail Saunders, Saskatchewan Education
Neil Sawatzky, Tourism Saskatchewan
Jocelyn Souliere, Saskatchewan Environment
Jane Turnbull-Evans, Saskatchewan Arts Board

The above individuals, in consultation with many others throughout the province, guided the development of the vision for the encyclopedia. A concept plan was produced in 1997 and its collective vision bears repeating:

> As Saskatchewan approaches its centenary in the year 2005, there is a growing recognition of the need for a substantial memorial to the people of Saskatchewan that highlights their achievements and provides a comprehensive synthesis of the people, places and events that have helped to shape the province. The *Encyclopedia of Saskatchewan* is proposed as a lasting compendium of knowledge on Saskatchewan and its place in the world. It will celebrate the many significant achievements in the history of our province through the involvement of contributors from all walks of life throughout Saskatchewan and Canada. By reaching out to all people, it will stand as a permanent legacy celebrating our rich heritage that will form a lasting province-wide memorial to future generations.

You, the reader, will be the judge of how well we have held true to that vision. We have strived for fairness, accuracy and balance. For all of the people, places and events deserving of mention that were omitted, I apologize. There were many entries developed by contributors that I regret could not be included because of limitations of time and space. I encourage you to use what you find in these pages to delve more deeply into the rich sources of information about Saskatchewan that are now at your disposal.

The *Encyclopedia* features approximately 2,300 individual entries covering all aspects of life in Saskatchewan with over 1,000 charts, graphs, maps, tables, and photographs, including dozens of stunning images by world-renowned photographer Courtney Milne, as well as photographs and illustrations from many other sources. The entries are organized alphabetically and suggested readings are provided with many of them. We have highlighted words and phrases within entries that will connect you to other entries containing related information. Also included is an index to allow you to search for subjects of greatest interest. Entries recognize the author(s) who contributed so generously of their knowledge and we have also provided a list of the names of all writers. The entries are supplemented by 21 major theme essays written by noted experts.

Following this preface are acknowledgements of those who contributed to the development of this book as sponsors, writers, editors, research assistants and as administrators. I hope that you will take the time to look at their names and, should you have the opportunity to meet them, to thank them for their commitment and generosity. I stress their generosity because so much of the content of the encyclopedia was contributed by writers and editors who volunteered their time. That this book has become a reality is a testament to their commitment to education, and to their willingness to share their time and knowledge.

While hundreds of people contributed to the *Encyclopedia*, there are key individuals without whom we could not have maintained our vision and produced the book. It is my great delight after so many years of work to be able to thank them publicly.

"If I am native to anything, I am native to this ... I can say to myself that a good part of my private and social character ... [has been] scored into me by that little womb-village and the lovely, lonely, exposed prairie of the homestead."

Wallace Stegner, resident of Eastend, Saskatchewan, 1914–20, from *Wolf Willow: A History, a Story, and a Memory of the Last Plains Frontier* (1962).

First and foremost, I want to express my deepest gratitude to Brian Mlazgar, the Publications Coordinator for CPRC, who worked with me from the start on this project; he laboured countless hours in making the *Encyclopedia* a reality and its publication is a tribute to his enormous skills. Brian was ably assisted in this by Donna Achtzehner. The layout of the book is due largely to her great talent.

In particular, I thank Dr. Patrick Douaud who so ably chaired our Editorial Board and whose awesome task was to read every entry and essay in the *Encyclopedia* to insure that standards were maintained. His years of dedication and commitment to the project are most gratefully appreciated, as is the support of the Faculty of Education at the University of Regina in allowing Dr. Douaud the time to participate in this undertaking.

I also want to express my deepest gratitude to all of our Editorial Board members, current and past, whose names are listed on subsequent pages. Within the Government of Saskatchewan, Learning also established an internal committee for the development and review of education entries. The Centre for the Study of Co-operatives at the University of Saskatchewan and the Gabriel Dumont Institute undertook the development of entries related to co-operatives and Métis, respectively. All Editorial Board members worked with writers to ensure that entries would meet the quality of content deserving of a lasting legacy of knowledge for the people of Saskatchewan. Theirs was a most challenging task in guiding what entries would best characterize the province, and in working with writers to make certain that the information was accurately and clearly expressed. I thank them for their patience and commend them for their devotion to the highest scholarly standards.

One of our objectives in developing the *Encyclopedia* was to provide opportunities for students to gain research experience by helping editorial board members and writers in gathering background information. We were able to employ twenty-two student assistants throughout the years, and I thank them all for their significant contributions.

Damian Coneghan, the ESask Project Manager, brought his excellent organizational skills to bear in leading or helping to coordinate so many aspects of the administration of the project. Coordinating the development of over 2,000 entries and of 1,000+ photos and illustrations involving hundreds of writers and contributors would have been much more daunting without his efforts. He was ably assisted by Fiona Stevenson.

The photographs that you see throughout the book were contributed from many sources listed in the acknowledgements. I thank all of them for adding a visual perspective that enhances the information in the entries.

In particular, Courtney Milne, well-known and celebrated Saskatchewan photographer, generously donated from his vast collection of photographs a variety of images that vividly capture the beauty of our province. It is his images that you see in the transitions from letter to letter throughout the book.

David McLennan provided photos and photographic research for many of the Saskatchewan communities. With information collected from many sources, Diane Perrick expertly crafted the maps and charts that add another important form of information content to the book.

Managing the office support for such a long-term and complex publishing project was most ably handled by CPRC's Office Manager, Lorraine Nelson—an amazing achievement given the many other research and publishing projects that she served while the *Encyclopedia* was being developed. I am very appreciative of the support that Bob Ivanochko, our encyclopedia librarian, brought to this project; through the generous support of the Provincial Library and of Learning, Bob was seconded to this project for five years and was instrumental in assisting us through content development and discussions with contributors. We

"Education needs courage. The very fact that education, if it is vital, leads to purposeful change, indicates the need for courage on the part of those who lead because even purposeful change is always opposed. It is opposed by those who do not understand."

Woodrow Lloyd (Premier of Saskatchewan, 1961–64), Canadian Education Association Convention, Saskatoon, 1951

would like as many people as possible to know about the *Encyclopedia* and Anne Pennylegion, CPRC's Marketing Coordinator, worked hard to communicate information about the *Encyclopedia* to sponsors, partners and the public. When the work of others is completed, that of Jeffrey Morman begins, ensuring that orders for the *Encyclopedia* are shipped in a timely fashion.

With all the contributions of our writers, editors and staff, we would still not have been able to bring you this book if it were not for the kind and generous support of our sponsors. There have been difficult times throughout the past nine years when resources were scarce. There were some not directly involved in the project who doubted that it would be possible for a comprehensive encyclopedia of the province to be completed and some who urged that we abandon it. However, it was the on-going encouragement of the many friends and supporters of the project that buoyed our spirits and efforts over the years and it is to them that we owe a great debt of gratitude.

Before the Millennium or Centennial celebrations were even being discussed in Saskatchewan, the Government of Saskatchewan Culture, Youth and Recreation (CYR) and Learning saw the important contribution of a provincial encyclopedia. They have been steadfast supporters throughout its long process of development. I greatly appreciate the encouragement and faith of former Minister Joanne Crofford and current Minister Joan Beatty of CYR as well as of Minister Andrew Thomson of Learning in the vision of this project. I also want to express my deepest gratitude to Olivia Shumski of CYR and to Gail Saunders of Learning who were tireless supporters of the project within government.

The support of the former Anniversaries Secretariat and Saskatchewan Centennial 2005 office chaired by Glenn Hagel was instrumental in helping us to complete the content of the book and have it printed.

To all of our sponsors ranging from government and non-government organizations, educational institutions, business, industry and media, I want to express my deepest gratitude for your support of education.

Finally, on a more personal note, I was born in Regina and Saskatchewan is my home place. My mother was born and raised in Rosthern, Saskatchewan, in a family descended from Ukrainian immigrants. In turn, Saskatchewan has provided the secure foundation within which my wife and I raised our son and daughter. In all of my travels throughout Canada and other countries I have not found a place that offers such unique natural beauty or a people more caring, friendly, and committed to principles of fairness and equity than in this land of flowing rivers.

The legacy of Saskatchewan is written by its people every day. Throughout its history and to the present day, the people of Saskatchewan have made great contributions and never faltered in their belief in the potential of the province. So much has been achieved in the past 100 years that serves for future generations to build upon. While there will always be challenges to face, I have no doubt in the ability of the people of Saskatchewan to work together with their neighbours to face those challenges and, in a spirit of fairness for all, to overcome them. When another hundred years have passed and Saskatchewan celebrates its bicentennial, I know that the citizens of 2105 will look back on the accomplishments of their ancestors with the greatest gratitude and pride.

David A. Gauthier
Publisher and General Manager
September 2005

"There is only one good, knowledge, and one evil, ignorance."

Socrates, from *Diogenes Laertius, Lives of Eminent Philosophers*, Athenian philosopher (469 BC – 399 BC)

HOW TO USE THE
ENCYCLOPEDIA OF SASKATCHEWAN

We have endeavoured to make the *Encyclopedia* as "user-friendly" as possible. To that end, the entries are organized alphabetically, with the entry name capitalized in boldface. We have also cross-referenced using SMALL CAPITALS words and phrases within entries that will lead interested readers to other, related entries. The name of the author appears at the end of each entry, and is italicized. Where relevant, there is a "Further Reading" section, which directs readers to more detailed information on topics they find interesting.

To avoid confusion (and with few exceptions), figures and tables for regular entries are labeled using an abbreviated form of the entry name, along with a number. (For example, the figure for the entry on Conservation Areas is labeled "Figure CA-1"; the tables for the entry on Agricultural Regions are labeled "Table AR-1" and "Table AR-2".) Within theme essays, figures and tables are simply labeled numerically.

Population figures for Saskatchewan communities, unless otherwise stated, are derived from the 2001 Census of Canada.

At the back of the book are several helps for readers. Appendix A is a list of all contributing writers. Appendix B is a list of entries organized by twenty general subject areas. Finally, beginning on page 1062 is the general index, which includes individuals who are referred to in the *Encyclopedia* but who do not have their own articles.

DID WE MISS ANYTHING?

Every effort has been made to ensure that the Encyclopedia of Saskatchewan is as comprehensive and up-to-date as possible at the time of printing (June 2005). However, it is inevitable with a project of this magnitude, given the constraints of time and space, that certain people, places or events have been left out. In other cases, although every effort was made to check facts, mistakes may have inadvertently been made. We ask you to please contact us with your comments, corrections, additions, and suggestions at:

Encyclopedia of Saskatchewan
Canadian Plains Research Center
University of Regina
Regina, SK   S4S 0A2
canadian.plains@uregina.ca

ACKNOWLEDGEMENTS

Patron of the Encyclopedia of Saskatchewan

Office of the Lieutenant-Governor of Saskatchewan

Lynda Haverstock (2000–present)

J.E.N. (Jack) Wiebe (1998–2000)

CPRC Management Team

David Gauthier   General Manager

Brian Mlazgar   Publishing Coordinator and Senior Design and Layout Editor

Patrick Douaud   Senior Content Editor and Chair of the Editorial Board

Damian Coneghan   Project Manager

Project Support

Donna Achtzehner   Assistant Design and Layout Editor

Daria Coneghan   Research Associate, Indexing

Kristine Douaud   Proofreading

Bob Ivanochko   Librarian (on secondment from Learning)

Jeff Morman   Packing and Shipping

Greg Murphy   Legal Advice

Lorraine Nelson   Office Manager

Anne Pennylegion   Communications and Marketing

Diane Perrick   Cartography and Graphs

Fiona Stevenson   Assistant to the Project Manager

Friends of the Encyclopedia

Over the course of the *Encyclopedia of Saskatchewan* project, many individuals and groups, too numerous to mention, allowed us the opportunity to examine their collections of photographs and illustrative material. Although we were not able to use all of the material offered, the support of these groups and individuals is deeply appreciated.

From the many sources to which we had access, photographs and illustrative material were selected and generously provided by the following individuals, organizations and institutions for use in the *Encyclopedia of Saskatchewan*:

Accutrak Systems Ltd.
Agriculture and Agri-Food Canada
Allen Sapp Gallery
Assiniboia and District Museum
Maureen Baker
Biggar Museum and Gallery
Birch Hills Museum
Black Box Images
Ted Bowen
Ian Brace
Mark Brigham
Cabri Museum
Robert Calder
Canada Post Corporation
Canadian Actors Equity Association
Canadian Light Source
Warren Cariou
Carleton University
Gerry Carline
Churchbridge Historical Society
City of Yorkton Archives
Climax Community Museum
Kane L. Coneghan
Coteau Books
Department of Community Resources and Employment
Ovide and Irene Desjarlais
Nancy Dill
Paul Dojack
Lillian Dyck
Eastend Historical Museum
Shannon England
Environment Canada, Canadian Wildlife Service
Esterhazy Community Museum
Estevan Art Gallery and Museum
Evangelical Lutheran Church in Canada, Saskatchewan Synod Office
Sherry Farrell Racette
Sylvia Fedoruk
Fisher Rare Book Library, University of Toronto
Folle Avoine Productions
Frank Cameron Museum
Bonnie Galenzoski
Kay Garside
Globe Theatre
Grenfell Museum
Greystone Books, a division of Douglas & McIntyre Ltd.
Don Hall
David Halstead
Claude-Jean Harel
Harold Johns Museum, Saskatoon Cancer Agency

Ninita Hautz
Norm Henderson
Heritage Resources Unit (Culture, Youth and Recreation)
Heritage Room Archives, St. Paul's Hospital, Saskatoon
R.E. Hlasny
David Hnatyshyn
Hodgson family
C.J. Houston
C.S. Houston
Gary M. Houston
Raphael Idem
Information Services Corporation, Regina
Innovation Place
International Road Dynamics
Ituna and District Museum
Tom Jackson
Tim Jones
Juventus
Connie Kaldor
Kamsack Powerhouse Museum
Donald Kerr
Kerrobert Museum
Honor Kever
Kindersley and District Plains Museum
Kipling and District Historical Society Museum
David Krughoff
Patrick Lane
James Lanigan
Therese Lefebvre Prince
Legislative Building Art Collection
Library and Archives Canada
Donald Link
Alison Lohans
Larissa Lozowchuk
Luther College
Ann Mandel
Greg Marchildon
A. Patricia Matthews
McClelland and Stewart
McKay family
David McLennan
Mendel Art Gallery
Millar Western Forest Products Ltd.
Ormond Mitchell
Joni Mitchell
Brian Mlazgar
Kim Morgan
Debra Moser
Mountney family, Moosomin
Naicam Museum
National Doukhobor Heritage Village
Saskatchewan New Democratic Party Archives

Barry Needham
Nipawin and District Living Forestry Museum
Nomadic Visions
Northern Resource Trucking
Notre Dame d'Auvergne Church Archives
Office of the Lieutenant Governor
Office of the Premier
Owen Olfert
Delia Opekokew
Natalie Ostryzniuk
Parks Canada
Petroleum Technology Research Centre
Joseph Pettick
Popowich family
Prince Albert Historical Society
Provincial Archives of Manitoba
Robert E. Redmann
Sid Robinson
Hank Roest
Roy Romanow
Doris Rowe
Saskatchewan Agriculture, Food and Rural Revitalization
Saskatchewan Arts Board
Saskatchewan Housing Corporation
Saskatchewan Provincial Secretary
Saskatchewan Sports Hall of Fame and Museum
Saskatchewan Watershed Authority
Saskatoon Public Library
Sasktel
SED Systems
Shakespeare on the Saskatchewan
Jacqui Shumiatcher
Arthur Slade
Soeurs de Notre Dame d'Auvergne
Glen Sorestad
Southwestern Saskatchewan Oldtimers' Association Museum and Archives
Bobby St. Cyr
Stoughton and District Museum
Sturgis Station House Museum
Anne Szumigalski Estate
George Tosh
Turner Curling Museum
Unity and District Heritage Museum
University of Regina Photography Department
Geoffrey Ursell
Vaccine and Infectious Disease Organization (VIDO)
Wadena and District Museum
Watson and District Heritage Museum
Winona Wheeler

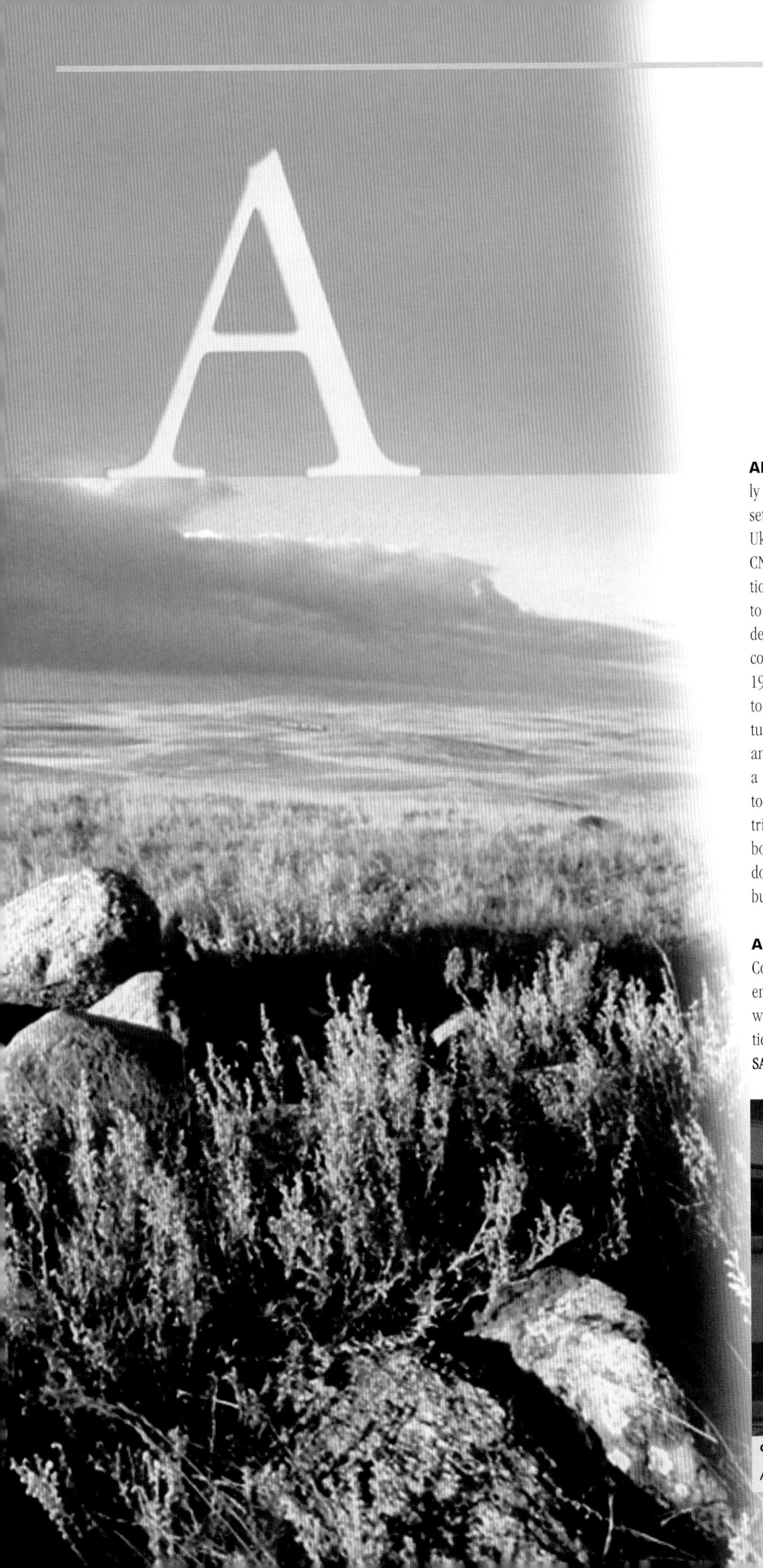

ABERDEEN, town, pop 534, located approximately 32 km NE of Saskatoon off Hwy 41. The first settlers—people of Russian, English, Scottish, and Ukrainian descent—arrived in the late 1890s. The CNR arrived in 1905, and by the 1930s the population was close to 300. While Aberdeen's proximity to the city of Saskatoon contributed to the town's decline for several decades, it has more recently contributed to renewed growth beginning in the 1970s. Many residents of Aberdeen now commute to work in Saskatoon, and local employment opportunities are found in agriculture-based industries and small business. Aberdeen Composite School has a staff of 38 and provides K–12 education to close to 400 students from the town and surrounding district. In 2003, the community received a major boost with the announcement that a multi-million dollar cultural and recreational complex would be built. *David McLennan*

ABORIGINAL ARTISTS, CONTEMPORARY. Contemporary Aboriginal art in Canada owes an enormous debt to the many Saskatchewan artists who have enriched it with their vast array of artistic expressions. Beginning with the work of **ALLEN SAPP**, a number of Aboriginal artists working in

COURTESY OF TOURISM SASKATCHEWAN

Allen Sapp.

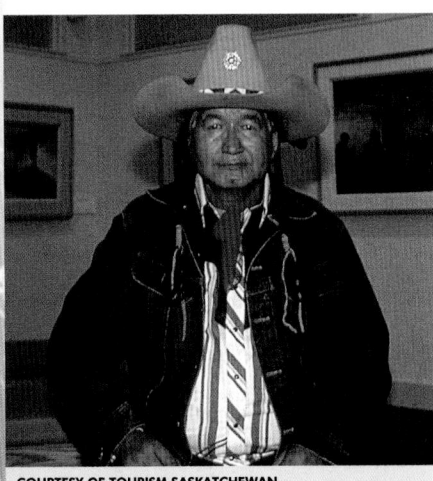

two- and three-dimensional media, installation, and performance art have created significant works of art that comment on issues related to Aboriginal people in Saskatchewan, such as politics, social concerns, and spiritual matters. These artists utilize a wide variety of artistic styles ranging from realism to abstraction. Many contemporary Aboriginal artists integrate art forms from more than one artistic medium, or collaborate with writers and dancers in their artistic endeavours. Moreover, contemporary Aboriginal artists often incorporate traditional Indigenous cultural expressions with established Western mediums and new technologies when creating their works. Through their explorations, these artists and their work become part of the process of debate and critique in questioning the boundaries constructed within the art establishment.

Allen Sapp, a Plains **CREE** artist from the Red Pheasant Reserve uses a realist style to depict life during the reservation period of his youth. Since the 1960s his painting has been internationally recognized and heralded as an important contribution to Saskatchewan contemporary art. His narrative manner has influenced other Saskatchewan artists such as Sanford Fisher, Henry Beaudry, and Michael Lonechild. In 1987, Allen Sapp was awarded the Order of Canada.

BOB BOYER was a **MÉTIS** artist whose politically charged Blanket series launched his career: he used blankets and Plains Indian designs together to comment on colonialism. Boyer was part of a newer generation of Saskatchewan artists educated in art schools, but with a knowledge of traditional Aboriginal art. His work is shown both nationally and internationally. In addition to painting, Boyer curated a number of important art exhibitions, including a retrospective of Allen Sapp's work. Boyer taught art and art history in the Indian Fine Arts department at the Saskatchewan Indian Federated College (now **FIRST NATIONS UNIVERSITY OF CANADA**) from 1980 until his death in 2004.

GERALD MCMASTER, from Red Pheasant First Nation, has worked in a variety of media to comment on issues of colonialism. In 1981 McMaster was appointed Curator of Contemporary Indian Art and subsequently became Curator-in-Charge of the First Peoples Hall at the Canadian Museum of Civilization. In this capacity, he has created a number of significant exhibitions of contemporary Aboriginal art in Canada. McMaster has shown his two- and three-dimensional art nationally and internationally.

EDWARD POITRAS, a Métis Treaty Indian from Gordon's First Nation, creates installation environments through his art. Poitras was the first Aboriginal artist to represent Canada in the Venice Biennale of 1995. He benefited from the guidance of Sarain Stump at the Saskatchewan Indian Cultural College's Indian Art program, along with other

Saskatchewan artists such as Ray McCallum. Drawing on both urban and reserve living experiences, Poitras often implies ideological conflicts through juxtapositions in his mixed-media sculptures and installations.

Jerry Whitehead, from the James Smith First Nation, paints abstractly, combining traditional forms such as powwow dancing in his art. Neal McLeod, also from James Smith First Nation, creates bold abstract expressions that incorporate traditional stories and contemporary issues, in addition to creating films and poetry. **MARY LONGMAN**, born in Fort Qu'Appelle, offers a rich story of family, loss, and rediscovery in her sculptural art. In her video and performance art, **DANA CLAXTON**, born in Yorkton, also explores issues of identity. Sheila Orr mixes traditional media such as porcupine quills and beadwork with acrylics and canvas; she teaches traditional arts at First Nations University of Canada. **SHERRY FARRELL RACETTE**'s work explores Métis history, cultural traditions and women's issues in her multimedia creations, which often include a variety of technologies such as beading and quilting.

Just as these noted contemporary Aboriginal artists have individually contributed to the history of contemporary Aboriginal art in Canada, countless others continue to be inspired and motivated to further this visual dialogue. The Fine Arts department at First Nations University of Canada provides an excellent opportunity for studying both contemporary and traditional art forms. These emerging artists are making strong connections to both the past and the future of Aboriginal art in the province.

Carmen Robertson

FURTHER READING: Acland, J.R. 2001. *First Nations Artists in Canada: A Biographical/Bibliographical Guide, 1960–1999*. Montreal: Concordia University Press; McMaster, G. 1988. "Saskatchewan Indian Art: More than Beads and Feathers," *Saskatchewan Indian* (July/August 1988): 13–14.

ABORIGINAL ARTISTS, TRADITIONAL.

Traditional Aboriginal arts have had a long and rich history in Saskatchewan. From rock art to clothing, ceremonial items, and utilitarian goods, traditional Aboriginal arts display a high level of artistry and technical adaptation to Saskatchewan geography and climate. Almost every object traditionally used by First Nations groups in Saskatchewan was decorated; the amount and type of decoration remained an important factor in determining the object's functional, ceremonial, or trade value. The five main tribal groups in this province—**CREE**, **DAKOTA**, **DENE**, **NAKOTA**, and **SAULTEAUX**—established a rich artistic history that continues today. Large numbers of Saskatchewan Aboriginal artists continue to produce traditional arts.

Rock art helps fathom the long history of tradi-

GEORGE TOSH PHOTO

The largest of three Herschel petroglyph boulders, about 2.2 m wide.

tional Aboriginal art in the province. Evidence of rock art can be found throughout Saskatchewan in the form of petroglyphs, medicine wheels, pictographs, and effigies. However, most objects of art were portable and made from organic materials. Often the expression of individual identity and achievement was conveyed through one's adornments. Men, women, and children were beautifully dressed and adorned with amulets, feathers, and other important items. Designs were painted, quilled and, after contact, beaded onto clothing to express meanings. Both men and women helped create ceremonial clothing; today, that ornate tradition is continued through the designing of powwow regalia.

In the past, Aboriginal women's artistry was often organized communally within women's artistic guilds. Large-scale tasks such as the making and raising of a tipi required the full orchestration of the group, with specialists performing particular tasks. Quillwork is a sacred art among plains First Nation's

PATRICK PETTIT/REGINA LEADER-POST

Lorraine Bear making a traditional Cree dress, February 1987.

women, and the exchange of women's quillwork was central to maintaining relations with neighbouring groups. With the introduction of glass beads, beadwork also became an important art form for women.

On the prairie, men's arts were connected to the creation of narrative scenes on buffalo-hide robes and tipis. These scenes memorialized a man's exploits in war, success in hunting, or depicted images from dreams and visions. Winter counts—records of the most important events of a year—were also important images recorded by men. This style of painting was flat and semi-abstract; during the 19th century the contemporary art form, ledger art, emerged from this tradition.

Sculpture has a long history as one of the traditional Aboriginal art forms. War clubs carved from wood and antler, pipes carved out of soft stone, and spoons and bowls made from wood or bent horn are all part of this artistic tradition. Perhaps best known are the horse effigies that were carried in dance performances. Traditional decorative designs used by First Nations groups were abstract and geometric as well as realistic. Floral designs, favoured by European traders, became more popular in the north because of earlier contacts; these designs were adopted and adapted mainly by Cree and Saulteaux artists in Saskatchewan. After contact, designs, materials, and techniques changed: beads and manufactured cloth were added to the traditional artistic materials, and European styles and designs were incorporated with traditional ones. After 1900, stylistic differences between First Nations in the province became less noticeable as traditional arts became more standardized owing to market demands for First Nations arts. *Carmen Robertson*

FURTHER READING: Berlo, J.C., and R.B. Phillips. 1998. *Native North American Art.* London: Oxford University Press; Boyer, B. 1975. *100 Years of Saskatchewan Indian Art.* Regina: Mackenzie Art Gallery.

ABORIGINAL EDUCATION. Long before Saskatchewan was a province, the original peoples who lived on this land had a commitment to learning and education. In the 19th century, this commitment was reflected in the signing of treaties that placed great importance on education and affirmed the value of learning. Over the years, Saskatchewan's education system has attempted to respond equitably to the needs of First Nations and **MÉTIS** peoples. The history of Aboriginal education in Saskatchewan has been strongly influenced by a variety of provincial policies, practices and partnerships. In the 1980s, the Department of Education's **CORE CURRICULUM** initiative endorsed the integration of First Nations and Métis content and perspectives as a foundation for provincial curriculum and resources for all students. Subsequently the 1989

BRYAN SCHLOSSER/REGINA LEADER-POST

Grand opening of the newly renovated school on the Piapot First Nation Reserve, March 2000.

framework, *Indian and Métis Education Policy from Kindergarten to Grade 12*, charted curriculum integration of First Nations and Métis content and perspectives across all required areas of study. In light of the rapidly growing Aboriginal population, the provincial government recognized the need for enhancements in the professional development of teachers, for specialized courses such as Native Studies and Indigenous languages, and for resources that reflect both the face and the voice of First Nations and Métis peoples.

Joint initiatives between the province and First Nations and Métis peoples reflect their beliefs, values and worldviews as well as those of government departments responsible for education. For example, in 1984 the Minister's Advisory Committee on Native Curriculum Review was established, and renamed the Indian and Métis Education Advisory Committee (IMEAC) in 1989. IMEAC was established to advise and make recommendations to the Department on the development, implementation, monitoring, and review of the Kindergarten to Grade 12 policy and program in Indian and Métis education. In 2000, IMEAC became the Aboriginal Education Provincial Advisory Committee (AEPAC). Based upon recommendations and action plans put forth by AEPAC (and its predecessor advisory committees), Aboriginal education in the province has been shaped with a commitment to First Nations and Métis children and youth.

Saskatchewan is nationally renowned for transforming the nature of teaching and learning in Aboriginal education. This is demonstrated in the professional roles of First Nations and Métis peoples in school systems. In partnership, this province pro-

duces an increasing number of First Nations and Métis teachers and administrators through highly regarded teacher education programs that include the **FIRST NATIONS UNIVERSITY OF CANADA** (formerly known as Saskatchewan Indian Federated College), SUNTEP (**SASKATCHEWAN URBAN NATIVE TEACHER EDUCATION PROGRAM**), ITEP (**INDIAN TEACHER EDUCATION PROGRAM**), and NORTEP (Northern Teacher Education Program). A critical lesson learned in this journey towards inclusive, responsive, and culturally affirming education indicates that our provincial motto, From many peoples, strength serves not only to inspire, but to indicate the need for partnerships in Aboriginal education. In 2003, *Building Partnerships: First Nations and Métis Peoples and the Provincial Education System* outlined a policy framework for Saskatchewan's pre-kindergarten to Grade 12 education system. Where provincial school divisions and band schools decide to combine their efforts through co-governance or co-management, such education partnerships are supported by Saskatchewan Learning. The formation of Elders' Councils to advise school administrations, and joint committees mandated to change curriculum to reflect local priorities and innovations, are examples of such partnering. The intent of the Building Partnership policy is to listen to First Nations and Métis peoples and share responsibility for decision-making in the field of education. *Maureen Simpson*

FURTHER READING: Saskatchewan Learning. 2003. *Building Partnerships: First Nations and Métis Peoples and the Provincial Education System.* Regina: Saskatchewan Learning.

ABORIGINAL EDUCATION POLICY. Prior to the Indian Act of 1876, Indigenous peoples of North America exercised full control over all aspects of life including education. Autonomous, self-governing nations exercised control over complex, holistic, and pedagogically sound systems of enculturation, in which networks of extended community, family members, and in particular Elders were (and still are) the teachers. Following the Indian Act, federal government authorities and the churches controlled First Nations' education. This involved extensive efforts to colonize First Nations peoples through social, political, economic, and educational systems designed to isolate/assimilate First Nations peoples, the effects of which still resonate.

The implementation of the Indian Act led to the establishment of church-operated residential and industrial schools. Residential schools began in 1849 and were attended by children between the ages of 6 and 14; industrial schools were attended by older students, who were trained in trades. Federal legislation obligated First Nations parents to turn their children over to RESIDENTIAL SCHOOL authorities. By 1920 it was evident to some missionaries and civil servants that the assimilation and isolation strategies of residential and industrial schools were ineffective. However, the 1927 Indian Act allowed the government to exert yet stronger control over the lives of First Nations children attending residential schools. Lack of funding had previously forced the closure of industrial schools in 1920, but residential schools remained in operation until the 1970s.

The provincial and residential school systems functioned simultaneously between 1849 and 1970. The federal government implemented a second phase of education for First Nations students in the 1950s and into the1960s, with on-reserve day schools. The federal government's 1969 *White Paper* caused concern in First Nations communities because its intent was to abolish the special legal status of Indians already entrenched by treaties; within a year, First Nations peoples rallied and responded with the *Red Paper*. Then, in 1972, the National Indian Brotherhood, predecessor to the Assembly of First Nations, released a policy statement, *Indian Control of Indian Education*, advocating control of education by and for First Nations peoples.

In the late 1960s and into the 1970s, the federal government initiated another strategy, known as the integration period, to educate First Nations children and youth. First Nations students living on reserves began attending provincial schools that were ill-prepared for this influx of new students. The integration period stymied learners, teachers, and communities as they wrestled to find mutually beneficial ways of working together. Up to this time, the relationship between First Nations people and the federal government had been strained because of contradictory positions on education. Furthermore,

the BNA Act of 1867 delegates jurisdiction for education to the provinces, while at the same time the Numbered Treaties protect rights to education for First Nations people. This jurisdictional conundrum led to First Nations children and youth "falling through the cracks" of both education systems.

While jurisdictional dilemmas led to inadequate education for First Nations children and youth, the education of MÉTIS peoples was a random proposition. In some cases, Métis children were educated through the options provided for First Nations children, while others attended provincial schools. Education for both First Nations and Métis students in provincial schools began to stabilize in the 1980s. The provincial government published the *Indian and Métis Education Policy from Kindergarten to Grade 12*, which advocates incorporating Indian and Métis content and perspectives across curricula. This positive shift in policy direction led the way to further systemic improvements. Additionally, in response to the Royal Commission on Aboriginal People's recommendations, Saskatchewan Learning is one of twelve departments involved in the Métis and Off-Reserve Strategy initiated in 2001. As well, in 2003 Saskatchewan Learning published *Building Partnerships: First Nations and Métis Peoples and the Provincial Education System—Policy Framework*, which encourages strong partnerships among First Nations and Métis peoples and the provincial education system.

In this collaborative spirit, Saskatchewan Learning refocuses its resources on working in partnership with First Nations and Métis peoples to create an education system that is not only inclusive, but also governed in innovative ways for the benefit of all Saskatchewan children and youth. In light of provincial policy enactment and supportive initiatives, Saskatchewan Learning together with First Nations and Métis peoples envisions a "shared and harmonious future."

Sandra Bellegarde and Trish LaFontaine

FURTHER READING: Royal Commission on Aboriginal People, Minister of Supply and Services Canada. 1996. *Report of the Royal Commission on Aboriginal Peoples, Volume 1: Looking Forward, Looking Back*. Ottawa; Saskatchewan Learning. 2003. *Building Partnerships: First Nations and Métis Peoples and the Provincial Education System*. Regina.

ABORIGINAL FISHING RIGHTS. The right to fish is generally considered by the Indigenous peoples of Saskatchewan as an inherent right that precedes Canadian law. These lakes and rivers have been their sources of food and transportation for thousands of years. When First Nations entered into treaties with Canada, the right to fish was guaranteed as a Treaty right. However, the traditional fishing practices of First Nations have been steadily

restricted despite Treaty promises that they would be allowed to continue hunting and fishing as before. Canada and Saskatchewan first modified this fishing right through the Constitution Act, 1930, which dictated that First Nations would retain a right to fish and hunt off-reserve, but only for subsistence rather than commercial purposes. From 1930 on, Canadian courts have recognized First Nations' right to fish, but have placed restrictions on that right by preventing them from selling or trading fish. Such restrictions have chagrined First Nations people, who expected that these rights would be protected when they signed treaties with the Crown at the end of the 19th and beginning of the 20th centuries. The most significant restriction has been the above-mentioned assertion of the courts that First Nations in Saskatchewan do not possess an Aboriginal right to fish commercially.

Other infringements include those for purposes of conservation. Aboriginal rights are subject to regulation by the province, but infringement of these rights must be justified. Justifiable infringements of the Aboriginal right to fish have included a ban on net fishing in order to conserve fish stocks. However, the burden for justifying any such infringements rests with the Crown according to the 1990 decision of the Supreme Court of Canada in the *Sparrow* case. Aboriginal fishing rights now belong to Métis as well as First Nations peoples in the province. The provincial government had recognized a limited Métis right to hunt and fish, but the 2003 decision of the Supreme Court of Canada in the *Powley* case has identified a MÉTIS right for hunting and fishing under Section 35 of the Charter. Although its implementation is ongoing, it is clear that Métis will now have rights similar to those of First Nations. *Brock Pitawanakwat*

ABORIGINAL FRIENDSHIP CENTRES OF SASKATCHEWAN. The concept of Friendship Centres originated in the 1950s with the increasing numbers of Aboriginal people moving into urban areas. The centres were created within urban settings as a way to address the needs of Indian and Métis people at the local level, providing referrals and counseling with respect to employment, housing, education, health, and liaison with other community organizations. Saskatchewan currently has thirteen Friendship Centres, with a corporate office in Saskatoon. The Centres fall under the administration of the Aboriginal Friendship Centres of Saskatchewan, which is controlled by a board of directors consisting of two representatives from each Centre and an elected executive committee. The mission of the Centres is to provide access to Elders and help Aboriginal people through friendship, harmony, cultural integrity, awareness, and sharing. The present Friendship Centres in Saskatchewan are the following: Battlefords, Buffalo

SASKATCHEWAN ARCHIVES BOARD S-SP-A23692-16, SASKATOON STARPHOENIX FONDS

This celebratory gathering of Indian and Métis graduates from Saskatoon collegiates was put on by the Saskatoon Indian and Métis Friendship Centre, 1985.

Narrows, Ile-à-la-Crosse, Kikinahk, La Loche, Moose Mountain, North West, Prince Albert, **QU'APPELLE VALLEY**, Regina, Saskatoon, Sipisihk, and Yorkton.

Rob Nestor

ABORIGINAL HEALTH. Aboriginal groups throughout the Americas experienced severe population loss after contact with Europeans. Depopulation was caused by a number of related factors such as the importation of diseases, interference with Aboriginal lifestyle by missionaries and traders, and the colonial policies of governments that aimed to change Aboriginal people through assimilation.

On the prairies, in the late 18th and 19th centuries epidemics of smallpox, measles, and influenza erupted along fur-trade routes. After about 1880, with the destruction of the bison herds and the consequent loss of food, shelter, and clothing, there was a severe population decline.

Treaties with the Canadian government in the 1870s had failed to meet basic human needs. Housing on reserves was severely overcrowded, often with fifteen people living in small one-room, mud-roofed shacks. Nutrition was likewise inadequate. The government provided rations of bacon and flour to some reserve residents, but only to those who performed farm work. The colonial policy of assimilation and abandonment of Aboriginal language, culture and spirituality was held out as the solution to the economic problems on the reserves, but also as the path to good health; thus "work for rations" not only saved money, but taught valuable civilizing lessons such as industry. Two contradictory impulses—assimilation and civilization to save Native people from themselves on the one hand, and isolation to protect Native people from

civilization on the other hand—led to increasingly coercive and repressive policies. In practice, the clearest manifestation of such policies was the erosion of health.

Insidious poverty continued, and chronic diseases became entrenched on Saskatchewan reserves. The most destructive diseases were red measles and whooping cough in children, and pulmonary tuberculosis in adults. On the File Hills and Crooked Lakes reserves, population decreased an average of 46% in the first two decades after the treaties were signed. From 1884 to 1892, the child mortality rate, one of the clearest indicators of community health, exceeded the birth rate: for 355 infants born on these reserves, 420 children died.

Industrial and residential schools, the government's primary vehicle for assimilation, were an important vector for the spread of disease, especially tuberculosis. The schools were funded on a per capita basis, therefore to send a sick child home meant a loss of money. It was reasoned that since there was so much tuberculosis in the school already, one more sick child would not make much difference. However, when death seemed imminent the school would send the child home, thus spreading the disease to the reserve. In 1907, the Department of Indian Affairs medical officer, Dr. Peter Bryce, reported that 69% of all ex-pupils at the File Hills school were dead, most of them from tuberculosis.

In the post-**WORLD WAR II** period, antibiotic treatment for tuberculosis emptied sanatorium beds across the country, but for Aboriginal people high rates of disease and death continued and were seen as a function of their "race" rather than as a symptom of their social and economic position.

Maureen Lux

FURTHER READING: Lux, M.K. 2001. *Medicine that Walks: Disease, Medicine and Canadian Plains Native People, 1880–1940.* Toronto: University of Toronto Press.

ABORIGINAL HUNTING RIGHTS. Although Indigenous economic activities varied widely across North America, many First Nations groups relied on hunting for a substantial part of their diet. Consequently, an Aboriginal right exists at common law which protects Aboriginal hunting rights. Such rights, which stem from prior occupation of traditional territories before the arrival of European settlers, were formally recognized by the British Crown in the Royal Proclamation of 1763, now embedded in the Canadian Constitution via Section 25 of the Constitution Act, which promises to protect Indigenous hunting grounds from incursion by European settlers. In Saskatchewan, Treaty agreements replaced Aboriginal hunting rights with more specific Treaty hunting rights. However, this unambiguous recognition of Indigenous hunting rights was modified by Numbered Treaties (**TREATIES 2, 4, 5, 6, 8 AND 10**) as well as the Natural Resources Transfer Agreement in 1930. The Treaty agreements cover the current provincial **BOUNDARIES OF SASKATCHEWAN**; Section 13 restricts the right to one of hunting for subsistence but not commercial purposes on all unoccupied Crown lands.

Canadian courts have protected the Crown's authority to infringe Aboriginal hunting rights for purposes of safety and conservation. However, such infringements must be justified by the Crown. For example, Aboriginal hunting is not allowed on or near public highways, and this restriction is allowed as a justifiable infringement of that right. Meanwhile, Aboriginal hunters retain the right of first allocation should conservation concerns arise.

It took significantly longer for **MÉTIS** hunting rights to be won in the courts. The northern district of Saskatchewan recognized Métis hunting rights as early as 1996 as a result of the *Morin* and *Daigneault* decisions. An economic test determined whether the hunter in question lived a "traditional lifestyle"; a Métis hunter who was a resident of the north was deemed to have an Aboriginal right to hunt. The 2003 decision of the Supreme Court of Canada in the *Powley* case has expanded this right, though its implications for Saskatchewan Métis have yet to be defined. However, it is clear that certain conditions will apply before Métis individuals will be able to obtain an Aboriginal hunting right. These criteria include self-identification, community acceptance, and links to a historical Métis community. Furthermore, unlike hunting rights for Status Indians, the Métis hunting right will be site-specific, which will restrict its use to the traditional territory of that individual's historic Métis community.

Brock Pitawanakwat

ABORIGINAL JUSTICE. Alternative measures programming was developed to deliver programming for Aboriginal people who come in conflict with the existing judicial system. Alternative measures programs provide increased options for police discretion to deal with minor offenses by way of informal cautioning, and make referrals for post-charge or pre-charge diversion. In other words, offenders are diverted away from the formal court process, both prior to and after being charged with an offence. The Crown Prosecutors' Office also has the discretion to refer a matter to alternative measures. These programs include: victim-offender mediation and diversion; youth programming; sentencing circles; family group conferencing; healing circles; crime prevention workshops; after care reintegration initiatives; section 81 initiatives; probation; and other programs that focus on healing and the use of First Nations' traditions and healing models.

This **RESTORATIVE JUSTICE** approach attempts to place the focus on the behaviour of the offender rather than on the offender himself. It also focuses on the context within which an offence took place. Accordingly, more attention may be paid to offender needs, such as treatment for alcohol or drug addiction. Shame is central to restorative justice models, and specifically family group conferences. Most people avoid culturally inappropriate behaviour because of internal and external shame. The external source of shame comes from the disapproval of one's family and peers, leading to a loss of social status and affection; the internal source of shame comes from a person's conscience, and a sense of what is right and wrong. Social disapproval from one's own community is thought to be a more effective deterrent to repeated offending behaviour than punishment meted out by state representatives.

The province of Saskatchewan has committed substantial monies to restorative justice approaches, with matching funds provided by the government of Canada. Because the design of programs is flexible and open as well, Saskatchewan may take the initiative to provide new programs, as long as they are approved by the Attorney General of Canada or by his representative. Under Sections 717 and 718 of the Criminal Code and Saskatchewan's Justice Initiative, sentencing options have expanded to include alternative measures diversionary programs. Courts have the discretion to allow for "circle sentencing" under Saskatchewan Justice's Restorative Justice Initiative, which provides further sentencing options for judges.

The restorative justice approach adopted by the province of Saskatchewan views crime as a personal matter between individuals. This approach focuses on: problem-solving; involving victims, offenders and community, as well as responding to their needs; forgiving the offender; and reintegrating the offender back into the community. The restorative

justice approach to sentencing was introduced to the province through Saskatchewan Justice (Minister's Order) under Section 717 of the Criminal Code (Canada), dated September 30, 1996. Flexibility of diversion options under Saskatchewan's initiative include: restitution/compensation (reparation for damages or loss); referral to a program such as crime prevention; referral for drug/alcohol treatment or health/mental health counseling; community or personal service work for the victim; victim-offender mediation; culturally appropriate activities for Aboriginal people; or other arrangements that may combine some of the above options.

Under Saskatchewan Justice's Restorative Justice Initiative, communities have some discretion to shape programs to fit their needs. The main alternatives include police cautioning, pre-charge diversion, post-charge diversion, victim-offender mediation, family/community group conferencing (community justice forum), and sentencing and healing circles. Aboriginal communities have the flexibility to develop diversion programs consistent with existing policing agreements and community justice programs. The agency administering the program has the discretion to determine whether an offender is suitable for their diversion program. Victim refusal to participate may exclude participation in a mediation program. However, although no criteria exist in Saskatchewan Justice's Diversion Program Policy framework for the use of surrogate victims, this has become a popular process in Saskatchewan.

Eligibility criteria for alternative measures for adults are quite broad, and include the following: the evidence is sufficient for a criminal charge to be laid; the offence can be prosecuted under the law; the offender must take responsibility for the behaviour and has not been diverted more than twice in the last three years or failed a diversion in the last six months; and the offender has no, or a minimal, past record of similar offences or recent charges.

Mediation is an informal, voluntary process in which a neutral third party facilitates parties in conflict to come to a mutually satisfactory resolution of a dispute. In victim-offender mediation, the offender must be willing to take responsibility for his/her actions and agree to be a participant. If the victim is not willing to participate, in some cases a surrogate victim may be used in his/her place. This approach is meant to restore the physical, emotional, psychological, and spiritual harmony of each person, as well as the relationships between victims, offenders, and the community.

The family/community group conferencing/community justice forum model initially came from the Maori of New Zealand, and was modified for dealing with criminal offences in Australia and North America. This model, while similar to victim-offender mediation, includes all those people directly affected by a crime, including victim(s), offend-

er(s), police officer(s), support people for victims and offenders (family, friends, etc.), community members, and facilitator(s). The major difference between the family group conference and victim-offender mediation is that the family group conference involves more people from the offender's community and acknowledges that more people have been victimized, therefore involving more participants in the process. While expressing their emotions about the impact of the crime, participants may become involved in the process of reintegrating the offender and victim into the community.

The primary goal of the family group conference is to repair damages and minimize any harm caused by the behaviour of the offender, while maximizing the achievement of social justice for all of the above parties. The assumption is that the interest of the larger community will be served by providing a venue for the families of the victim and offender, and for other members of their community to attempt to repair the harm caused by the crime. The family group conference focuses on the offence rather than the offender, and provides the offender with an opportunity to accept responsibility for his/her actions. Reparation and restitution for victims are also goals of the family group conference.

The family group conference model relies on "reintegrative" rather than "stigmatizing" shame. Stigmatizing shame can humiliate and label the person as an offender, often provoking a reaction of anger and resentment. The offender may become alienated and seek revenge, which is often thought to be the case with the Western justice approach. Reintegrative shame focuses on the behaviour, rather than the person, and the encouragement of social reintegration of the offender. While helping the offender to shed his/her label as an offender, it can also help the victim to shed his/her label as a victim. Ultimately, the hope is that offenders will begin to understand how their actions have affected others, thereby reinforcing their conscience as well as their self-control.

Sentencing circles provide a forum for community members to make recommendations to a judge regarding sentencing in cases involving an offender from that community. A sentencing circle may be requested by the offender or recommended by a judge; or in the case of First Nations communities, their Community Justice Committee may request one. Those who participate in the inner circle of a sentencing circle may include victim(s) and offender(s), family/supporters of both victim and offender, judge, defense counsel, Crown prosecutor, court recorder, police officer(s), various service workers (youth, social, drug and addictions, probation officer), and respected Elders of the community. There may also be an outer circle consisting of some of the above, plus additional community members not directly involved in the incident. Sentencing circles may differ slightly from case to case, depending on the judge or community involved. Sentencing circles differ from family group conferences in that state officials are fully involved in the process. Sentence recommendations are made to the judge and are subject to appeal through the criminal justice system. The sentencing circle allows for an informality not available in the courtroom, and may provide more thorough information from which to determine an appropriate sentence.

For a sentencing circle to proceed, there must be a finding of guilt and all facts must be agreed; the accused must be a willing participant and meet the requirements of eligibility (i.e., be eligible for suspended sentence, intermittent sentence, or minimal term of imprisonment followed by probation– not for prison terms of two years or more); the victim must be willing to participate; the community must consent to participate in the circle, as well as provide ongoing supervision and reintegration for the accused; and the case must be one in which the court is willing to allow a sentence outside the usual range.

The objectives of the sentencing circle are to make the offender aware of the impact of the offence on the victim(s) and the community, to allow the community to recommend sentencing options and engage in sharing some responsibility for decisions affecting sentencing, to focus on rehabilitation rather than punishment, and to deter further criminal behaviour. There is some similarity in the use of shame and involvement of the larger community in family group conferences and sentencing circles. The hope is that these models will provide a better justice for Aboriginal people.

Miriam Beverley Handel

FURTHER READING: McDonald, J., D. Moore, T. O'Connell and M. Thorsborne. 1995. *Real Justice Training Manual: Coordinating Family Group Conferences.* Pipersville, PA: Piper's Press; Roberts, J.V. and C. LaPrairie. 1996. "Sentencing Circles: Some Unanswered Questions," *Criminal Law Quarterly* 39: 69–83.

ABORIGINAL JUSTICE ENQUIRY. The Commission on First Nations and Métis Peoples and Justice Reform was announced on November 15, 2001, and was mandated to address concerns over the treatment of First Nations and **MÉTIS** people by the justice system and in particular police services. The Justice Reform Commission was partnered with the government of Canada, the province of Saskatchewan, the **FEDERATION OF SASKATCHEWAN INDIAN NATIONS** and the **MÉTIS NATION– SASKATCHEWAN**, and was made up of five members (Willy Littlechild, Joe Quewezance, Hugh Harradence, Glenda Cooney and Irene Fraser). The Commission submitted its final report, entitled "Legacy of Hope," on June 21, 2004, and included

122 recommendations. The report identified racism among provincial police forces as a major reason why Aboriginal people misunderstand and mistrust the justice system.

Among the recommendations were suggestions on how to eliminate racism in policing through better screening of police candidates, increased training of officers already employed and a more proactive strategy to recruit First Nations and Métis officers. Also included in the recommendations was a call for an independent complaints agency, the construction of a number of emergency detox centres, sentencing alternatives, a court to deal with issues such as addictions, fetal alcohol syndrome, and family violence, and an investigation into why incarceration rates are so high among Aboriginal youth.

Rob Nestor

ABORIGINAL LANGUAGES. The province of Saskatchewan received its name from the Cree word *kisiskâciwan*, which describes the "fast-flowing" **SASKATCHEWAN RIVER** or its "swift current." Place names of Aboriginal origin are common throughout the province, whether recorded in translation or in attempts to represent the sounds of Aboriginal languages through English or French spelling convention. It is important to note, however, that these names do not come from just one "Indian" language, nor are all of these languages closely related. The Aboriginal languages of Saskatchewan represent three distinct language families, as diverse and unrelated as English, Hungarian, and Chinese.

The Algonquian language family is the largest group of First Nations languages in North America, covering a wide area of the northeastern coast and ranging inland around the Great Lakes and westward to the Rocky Mountains. Algonquian languages are generally characterized by having a small number of distinct sounds, but a very complex morphology or word structure. Two Algonquian languages are found in Saskatchewan today: Cree and Saulteaux.

The **CREE** language has the largest speaker population of all of Canada's First Nations languages with an estimated 75,000 speakers, including dialect groups ranging from Quebec to northeastern British Columbia and into the Northwest Territories. Approximately 20,000 of these speakers live in Saskatchewan, where Cree ranks second only to English as the most commonly spoken language of the home–Cree bands making up over half of the province's seventy-four First Nations. Cree reserves range from the southeast (White Bear, near Carlyle) to southwest (Nekaneet, near Maple Creek), and northwards from east-central (Peter Ballantyne, at Pelican Narrows) to west-central (Meadow Lake) regions. Three separate dialects of the Cree language are represented in Saskatchewan, commonly divided along the lines of a diagnostic sound alternation.

Plains Cree, or the "Y" dialect, is found on the southern plains and through the central parkland; it is sometimes divided into northern and southern subdialects. Woods Cree, or the "TH" dialect, is found to the north of Plains Cree in the central, forested region of Saskatchewan. Swampy Cree, or the "N" dialect, is more prevalent in Ontario and Manitoba, but is also spoken in the region of Cumberland House on the eastern edge of the province. The dialect alternation of "Y," "TH" and "N" sounds is evident in many Cree vocabulary items, including the Cree name for their own language: *nêhiyawêwin* in Plains Cree, *nêhinawêwin* in Swampy Cree, and *nîhithawîwin* in Woods Cree. Other than this sound alternation, western Cree dialects are quite similar, all containing just seventeen distinct sounds, one of the smallest sound systems among the world's languages (this can be compared with Hawaiian, which has only thirteen distinct sounds, and with Canadian English, which has thirty-eight). Both the Plains and Swampy Cree alphabets consist of these sounds: /a, â, c, ê, h, i, î, k, m, n, o, ô, p, s, t, w, y/. Woods Cree differs only in dropping /ê/ and adding the "th" sound.

The vast majority of Saskatchewan place names of Aboriginal origin derive from Cree. This is due not only to the role the Cree played as middlemen in the fur trade and guides to westward-reaching European expansion, but also to the role that the Cree language played as a lingua franca of the prairie region, adopted and used by many other Aboriginal groups. For this reason, a very large number of Cree-derived names can be found on the map of Saskatchewan, including the name of the province itself and many of its larger centres such as Saskatoon (*misâskwatômina* "saskatoon berries"), Moose Jaw (*moscâstanisîpiy* "river of mild winds"), the Battlefords (*nôtinitosîpîhk* "at the battle river"), and an increasingly popular name around Regina, Wascana (*oskana* "bones").

Closely related to Cree is the Ojibwa language with its many dialects, found primarily to the south of Cree-speaking regions from Quebec to Saskatchewan and in the neighbouring areas of the United States. Ojibwa has the third highest speaker population of Canadian Aboriginal languages (after Cree and Inuktitut), at approximately 22,500; but this number virtually doubles when the American Ojibwa population, often referred to as Chippewa, is included. In Saskatchewan, the westernmost dialect of Ojibwa is known as **SAULTEAUX**, belying a more eastern origin and westward expansion during the fur trade. Saulteaux or nahkawêwin is the primary language of eleven bands, and is also spoken along with Cree on several other reserves. Most Saulteaux reserves are located in the southeastern region of Saskatchewan and include Cote, Fishing Lake, Keeseekoose (*kîsikônš* "little sky"), Key, Kinistin, Muscowpetung (*maskawapîtank* "he sits steadfast-

7

ly"), Muskowekwan (*maskawîkwan* "strong quill"), Pasqua, Sakimay (*sakimê* "mosquito"), Saulteaux, and Yellowquill.

There are considerably fewer Saulteaux place names than Cree ones on the Saskatchewan map; but in addition to some of the reserve names already cited, places such as Punnichy (*panacay* "fledgling bird"), Kissina (*kisinâ* "it is cold"), and Ogema (*okimâ* "chief") derive from Saulteaux. Additionally, several other Ojibwa-derived names have found their way into Saskatchewan, including Wadena (*ôtênâ* "town, village") and Nokomis (*nôkomihs* "grandmother"). As an Algonquian language, Saulteaux has a relatively small sound system, although compared to Cree it has an added important distinction among consonants, so that the standard Saulteaux alphabet uses the following symbols and digraphs for the twenty-four distinct sounds: /a, â, c, hc, ê, h, i, î, k, hk, m, n, o, ô, p, hp, s, hs, š, hš, t, ht, w, y/.

In addition to Cree and Saulteaux, some other Algonquian-speaking peoples are known to have had an historical presence in Saskatchewan. The Atsina or Gros Ventre, speakers of a dialect of the Algonquian language Arapaho, are one such group, although today Atsina is spoken only by a few Elders in Montana. Members of the Algonquian-speaking Blackfoot nations also frequented the southwestern reaches of the province historically, but Blackfoot reserves are now to be found in Alberta and Montana.

Unrelated to the Algonquian languages are those that make up the Siouan language family, which covers a large area of central and mid-eastern North America. Though most Siouan speakers live in the United States, three very closely related Siouan peoples, the **NAKOTA**, **DAKOTA** and Lakota, have representatives in Saskatchewan, where they have been more commonly known by Algonquian-derived names. The Nakota are long-time residents of our province and have several reserves at Mosquito, Carry the Kettle, Ocean Man, and Pheasant Rump, as well as sharing others, such as White Bear, with their Cree allies. The Nakota have been commonly known by the name Assiniboine, though this is, in fact, derived from the Ojibwa name *ahsinipwân* indicating "Stoney Sioux," the translation of which lends them another common name, Stoney. The term *Sioux*, often applied to both the Dakota and Lakota, is also derived from the second-last syllable of an Ojibwa word, *nâtowêhsiwak*, referring to a particular type of "snakes" or simply "enemies," and applied at various times to either Siouan or Iroquoian peoples. Thus, despite the linguistic use of the term *Siouan* for the entire language family, this is not a name favoured by "Siouan" speakers. More correctly known as the Dakota, they are more recent immigrants to Saskatchewan, arriving after the troubles of 1862 in Minnesota and settling at White Cap (Moose

Woods), Wahpeton and Standing Buffalo Reserves. The one band of Lakota at Wood Mountain is even more recent to the province, arriving with **SITTING BULL** in 1877 following the previous year's Battle of the Little Big Horn. Due to their more recent settlement in Saskatchewan, neither the Dakota nor Lakota are signatory to the Treaties.

Although the Nakota, Dakota and Lakota are considered three separate groups culturally and politically, they speak mutually intelligible dialects of a single language which have not yet reached the point of diverging into separate languages. One feature shared by all three of these Siouan dialects is their endangered status: few speakers remain in Saskatchewan, with estimates suggesting, for instance, as few as twenty-five Nakota and three Lakota speakers left. Each of these dialects also has speaker populations in the United States, where Lakota remains relatively strong; but children in Saskatchewan learn none of these dialects as their first language. Nakota in particular has very few remaining speakers and is in immediate danger of language extinction.

There are also surprisingly few Siouan names on the Saskatchewan map, although examples from Nakota, Dakota and Lakota can all be found. Given the much longer history of the Assiniboine in the province, it may seem odd that Sheho (*šio* "prairie chicken") is one of the very few Nakota words that have been used. Wawota (*wa ota* "deep snow") and Wahpeton (*waxpet?* "people of the leaves") are representative of Dakota, while even the relatively small presence of Lakota speakers in the region has yielded the names Oakshela (*hokšila* "boy") and Sintaluta (*sinta luta* "red tail"—in reference to a fox tail). The small number of Siouan-based names can be attributed in part to the more recent presence of Dakota speakers, but also to the fact that many Nakota-speakers were bilingual in the language of their close allies, the Cree. Even when Nakota names have been used, they are often found in translation owing to the relative complexity of the Siouan sound systems. In comparison to Algonquian, the Siouan languages in general have more complex sound systems, and although the number of distinct sounds is not dissimilar to English, there are many sounds and sound distinctions that are unfamiliar to English ears. The Dakota sound system, for instance, consists of 40 distinct sounds. These include important distinctions among consonants (unaspirated /t/, aspirated /th/, and ejective /t'/) and vowels (nasal /?/ versus oral /a/) not found in English. Nakota and Lakota have similar systems, with minor differences such as the /l/ found only in Lakota, and the more common use of voiced sounds (e.g., /b, d, g/) in Nakota.

Different again from Algonquian and Siouan languages is the sole representative of the Athapaskan language family found in Saskatchewan.

This is the **DENE** language, commonly known by the Cree name of Chipewyan (*cîpwayân* "pointed hide"), said to be derived from a description of their mode of dress. As a name from a completely unrelated language, however, Chipewyan is not an appellation preferred by the Dene people, who occupy the northern third of the province of Saskatchewan, as well as neighbouring areas of Alberta and Manitoba. Related Athapaskan languages cover a vast area of the northwest of North America, and can be found through much of Alaska, Yukon, the Northwest Territories and northern British Columbia, as well as in other areas comprising the Navajo and Apachean languages in the American southwest.

Dene is the second most commonly spoken First Nations language in Saskatchewan. Although the approximately 5,100 speakers in the province may appear to be a small number, this represents a fairly high language retention rate from a total Saskatchewan Dene population of approximately 6,300, whose northern location has allowed them to resist more successfully the encroachment of English and retain their own language as a first language. At this time, a relatively high percentage of Dene children still continue to learn Dene as their first language, which has the most complex sound system of all First Nations languages spoken in Saskatchewan—a common feature of Athapaskan languages in general. Not only does Dene share some of the features of Siouan languages, such as nasal vowels and ejective consonants: other distinctions also increase the number of distinct sounds in Dene to thirty-five consonants and eleven vowels for a total of forty-six distinct sounds. Additionally, Dene is unique among Saskatchewan's Aboriginal languages in that it is a tone language distinguishing between high and low tone; this means that, like in many Asian languages, the pitch at which a word or syllable is uttered can change the meaning.

Perhaps in part due to the complexity of the Dene sound system, very few official Saskatchewan place names have been adopted from Dene. Those that have are almost always found in translation (e.g., Black Lake, Stony Rapids), while many other places in Dene territory have Cree names (e.g., Patuanak, *wapâciwanâhk*) belying the more prevalent use of Cree by guides introducing these areas to European explorers and settlers.

The common use of Cree, even by First Nations of other than Cree origin, meant it was ideally suited to serve as one-half of a unique mixed language that arose upon contact with Europeans in the Red River area of Manitoba. Michif, the language of the Métis, is an interesting blend of Cree and French. Unlike many "creoles" that have arisen upon language contact throughout the world, in which the vocabulary of one language dominates and is fitted to the grammar of another, Michif mixes Cree verbs with French nouns and uses a sound system born of both parent languages. The Michif language was spread westward across the plains by buffalo hunters, and it remains an important means of communication in a number of communities as wide-ranging as Turtle Mountain (North Dakota) and Ile-à-la Crosse, Saskatchewan. However, as with other Aboriginal languages, Michif is an endangered language today, learned as a first language by few.

The future of Saskatchewan's Aboriginal languages is uncertain. Many of the languages, such as Saulteaux, Nakota, Dakota, Lakota and Michif, are seriously endangered and are now rarely if ever learned by children as their first language. Even Cree, despite its relatively high number of speakers, and Dene, despite its higher retention rate, cannot be considered safe under the global influences of mass communication and the prestige role of English. In response to the threat of language loss, language education programs and retention committees have been founded at the FIRST NATIONS UNIVERSITY OF CANADA and the SASKATCHEWAN INDIAN CULTURAL CENTRE, as well as at the Universities of Regina and Saskatchewan and other educational bodies throughout the province. Additionally, language programming is playing an increasingly more important role in First Nations' schools; and immersion programs, such as those pioneered at Onion Lake and Cumberland House, are being put in place to protect, maintain and stimulate interest in this exceptionally important part of Aboriginal heritage and the heritage of Saskatchewan. *Arok Wolvengrey*

FURTHER READING: Bakker, P. 1997. *A Language of Our Own: The Genesis of Michif, the Mixed Cree-French Language of the Canadian Métis*. Oxford: Oxford University Press; Boas, F. and E. Deloria. 1976. *Dakota Grammar*. New York: AMS Press; Cote, M. 1984. *Nahkawêwiwin (Saulteaux)*. Regina: Saskatchewan Indian Federated College; Okimâsis, J.L. 2004. *Cree, Language of the Plains/nêhiyawêwin, paskwâwipîkiskwêwin*. Regina: Canadian Plains Research Center; Wolvengrey, A. 1998. "On the Pronunciation and Spelling of First Nations Names and Languages in Saskatchewan," *Prairie Forum* 23 (1): 113–25.

ABORIGINAL MEDIA. Aboriginal media in Saskatchewan developed in the late 1960s and early 1970s with the political organizations serving as incubator. Both the Metis Society and the FEDERATION OF SASKATCHEWAN INDIANS (FSI) had newspapers which served as political house organs but in the process expanded to include news of general interest to the client group. The Metis Society published *The New Breed* and the Federation of Saskatchewan Indians *The Saskatchewan Indian*; these two news magazines are still published sporadically. The print media has since become privatized, with publications such as *Eagle Feather News* and *Saskatchewan Sage*. In the past thirty years the province's Aboriginal population has tripled, thus creating a more lucrative market for private media. In addition to print media, the FSI produced a weekly radio program called "Moccasin Telegraph"; this half-hour radio program followed in the footsteps of previous northern programming established by CKBI radio. At the same time, Harry Bird and Stan Cuthand hosted a program on CBC radio, "North Country Fair," providing news and information for two hours on Saturday afternoons. It was quite popular until CBC went to national programming in the time slot.

Later in the 1970s the Saskatchewan Indian Cultural College developed for cable in Saskatoon a television program called *The Fifth Generation*, which ran for about a year. In the late 1970s CBC broadcast "Keewatin Radio," which provided news for northern listeners one hour a day, five days a week. In the early 1980s Missinippi Broadcasting began in La Ronge as a part of the Northern Native Broadcast Access Program funded by the federal Department of the Secretary of State. Missinippi currently reaches out to communities in northern Saskatchewan; the station is now self-sufficient, sustaining its operations through bingos and advertising revenue. Programming is in three languages: CREE, DENE and English.

Television has also grown in proportion to the Aboriginal presence in the marketplace. SCN, the Saskatchewan Communications Network, provides an outlet for material produced by Aboriginal television producers, and APTN (Aboriginal People's Television Network) serves as a national broadcaster. Saskatchewan people have seen the power and influence created by the media, and the First Nations University in Regina offers the Indian Communications Arts Program (INCA), which has provided a large number of graduates who work in both the mainstream and Aboriginal media. *Doug Cuthand*

ABORIGINAL MIGRANT LABOUR FORCE: *see "GRAB-A-HOE" INDIANS*

ABORIGINAL PEOPLES AND THE WORLD WARS. During WORLD WAR I (1914–18) and WORLD WAR II (1939–45), thousands of Aboriginal men and women voluntarily enlisted in Canada's armed forces. They served in units with other Canadians, fought in every theatre in which Canadian forces took part, and more than 500 status Indian servicemen lost their lives on foreign battlefields. An estimated 800 men and women from First Nations in Saskatchewan served during the World Wars and in Korea. Although reliable statistics are not available, the official record lists more than 100 status Indians from Saskatchewan who served during World War I, including over half of the eligible adult males on the Cote Reserve. Overseas, Aboriginal soldiers were recognized as effective snipers and scouts, endowed with courage, stamina, and keen observation powers.

At home, Saskatchewan Indians also donated $17,257.90 in support of the war effort—almost double that of any other province. The File Hills community alone raised $8,562 for the Red Cross and Patriotic Funds, while Aboriginal women formed Red Cross societies, organized patriotic leagues, sewed, and knitted socks and sweaters for the troops overseas. The school children of Gordon's reserve knitted seventy-five pairs of socks and raised money for the Belgian Relief and Soldier's Tobacco Funds. A serious issue arose about the federal Military Service Act (1917), which conscripted Canadians for overseas service: although there is no reference to military service in any of the written treaties, oral assurances recorded during negotiations for Treaties 3, 6, 8 and 11 promised that Indians would not be forced to serve in foreign wars. After concerted protest, the government passed in 1918 an Order-in-Council exempting Canadian First Nation peoples from conscription.

The Department of Indian Affairs trumpeted the achievements of status Indians at war's end. And in 1920 EDWARD AHENAKEW could proclaim: "Now that peace has been declared, the Indians of Canada may look with just pride upon the part played by them in the Great War, both at home and on the field of battle. Not in vain did our young men die in a strange land; not in vain are our Indian bones mingled with the soil of a foreign land for the first time since the world began." Exposure to the broader world changed veterans profoundly—but they returned to the same patronizing society they had left. Inequitable veterans' settlement packages disadvantaged many First Nation persons, and the Soldier Settlement Board acquired more than 69,803 acres of Saskatchewan reserve land to settle non-First Nation veterans.

Despite interwar discontent, Saskatchewan's Aboriginal peoples again answered the call during World War II. More than 440 Saskatchewan Indians enlisted for military service in this conflict (including at least 22 women), with the highest enlistments from the Carlton, Crooked Lakes, and File Hills agencies. Twenty-seven of these soldiers were killed or wounded. Overall, Aboriginal enlistments from Saskatchewan were undoubtedly higher than these figures because non-status Indians and MÉTIS were not differentiated from non-Aboriginal Canadians. On the home front, women's service clubs and community groups again raised funds for the Red Cross and other war charities. Indian Affairs records indicate that many donations went directly to local organisations, and that "substantial donations of furs, clothing and other articles were made, the

A

COURTESY OF DORIS ROWE

Sergeant Harvey Dreaver, son of Chief Joe Dreaver of the Mistawasis Band, was killed in action during the battle at the Leopold Canal and is buried at Adegem Canadian War Cemetery in Belgium.

monetary value of which has not been calculated." The difficult question of Indian conscription also arose; while the federal government did not grant a blanket exemption to Indians during World War II, liberal exemption policies ensured that few if any Aboriginal conscripts were sent overseas.

Aboriginal servicemen and women had again fought overseas as equals, and returned home with a self-awareness that that they were not "second-class" persons. They sought the same principles of democracy, freedom, and equality for which all Canadians had fought and died. After the war, how-ever, First Nations veterans did not receive the same treatment as other Canadians, particularly in the limited Veterans Land Act benefits available to them. After 1950, disillusioned veterans thus took a leader-ship role in Aboriginal social and political move-ments, including the Federation of Saskatchewan Indians. The Saskatchewan Indian Veterans' Associa-tion (now the Saskatchewan First Nations Veterans' Association) was incorporated in 1982 to focus sole-ly on veterans' issues and seek restitution for discriminatory treatment. For two decades they lobbied provincial and federal agencies, and initiated court actions seeking damages. The Saskatchewan Métis Veterans' Association undertook similar actions for Métis veterans.

In recent years, Aboriginal veterans have re-ceived acknowledgment for their special service dur-ing the World Wars. In 2002, the federal govern-ment offered a redress package of $20,000 to indi-vidual First Nations veterans; in November 2004, the Federal Interlocutor for Métis and Non-Status Indians announced $100,000 in funding for Métis veterans to promote their contributions to war-time efforts. For some Saskatchewan veterans, both offers represented long overdue recognition. For others, it was too little, too late.   *P. Whitney Lackenbauer*

FURTHER READING: Dempsey, L.J. 1999. *Warriors of the King: Prairie Indians in World War I*. Regina: Canadian Plains Research Center; Gabriel Dumont Institute of Métis Studies and Applied Research. 1997. *Remembrances: Métis Veterans*. Regina: Gabriel Dumont Institute; Sweeny, A. 1979. *Government Policy and Saskatchewan Indian Veterans: A Brief History of the Canadian Government's Treatment of Indian Veterans of World War Two*. Ottawa: Tyler, Wright and Daniel.

ABORIGINAL PEOPLES OF SASKATCH-EWAN: *see essay on facing page.*

ABORIGINAL POPULATION TRENDS. There are several different ways of defining the Aboriginal population: by national census data, Indian and Northern Affairs (INAC) data (the Indian Register), health data, band rolls, membership in the MÉTIS NATION–SASKATCHEWAN, etc. Census data count Aboriginal population in at least three ways: self-identification (as Registered Indian, non-status Indian, Métis, Inuit, or undifferentiated Aboriginal); claimed Aboriginal ancestry (single or multiple responses); and people who are officially counted as Registered Indians. In the 2001 census, 130,190 res-idents of Saskatchewan self-identified as Aboriginal (13.5% of the total population of the province) (*see* Figure APT-1). Of these, 83,745 (64.3%) claimed to be only "North American Indian" (First Nation); 43,695 (33.5%) to be only Métis, and 235 only Inuit; while another 895 claimed more than one type of Aboriginal identity (likely First Nation and Métis) and 1,620 some other sort of Aboriginal identifica-tion. Examining data for people claiming Aboriginal origin, however, one can note that a slightly larger number of Saskatchewan residents (135,035) claimed to be wholly or partially of Aboriginal

descent. Of these, 70,390 (52.1%) were only of "North American Indian" origin, and another 24,045 (17.8%) partially; 12,480 (9.2%) were solely of Métis descent, compared to 19,880 (14.7%) who were par-tially so; 7,860 (5.8%) claimed other multiple Aboriginal origins; and 150 respondents claimed to be only Inuit, plus another 235 partly Inuit. The count of Registered Indians again provided different data: 84,075 divided almost equally between those living on reserve (43,715) and off reserve (40,365). In fact, there has been progressive urbanization of the entire Aboriginal population in Saskatchewan, with close to half (46.7%) now living in urban areas.

Saskatchewan now accounts for 13.3% of the total Aboriginal population of Canada, including about 15% of both the Registered Indian and Métis populations. In absolute numbers, Saskatchewan currently ranks fifth for the province having the largest number of Aboriginal residents; however, proportionate to the total provincial population it is ranked first or second (comparable to Manitoba). The Aboriginal and Registered Indian populations of Saskatchewan have grown rapidly: the Aboriginal identity population grew to 111,245 in 1996–twice what it had been in 1971–and, as already noted, to 130,190 in 2001. This rapid growth may be largely attributed to the fact that the estimated total fertility rate among Registered Indian women is higher in Saskatchewan (3.1 in 1996) than any other province or territory, while the regional patterns for both Métis and non-status Indians are similar. This growth is somewhat countered, however, by Aboriginal mortality rates which, while declining, are still higher than in the non-Aboriginal popula-tion. Certain illnesses and causes of death are still multiple times higher among Aboriginals in

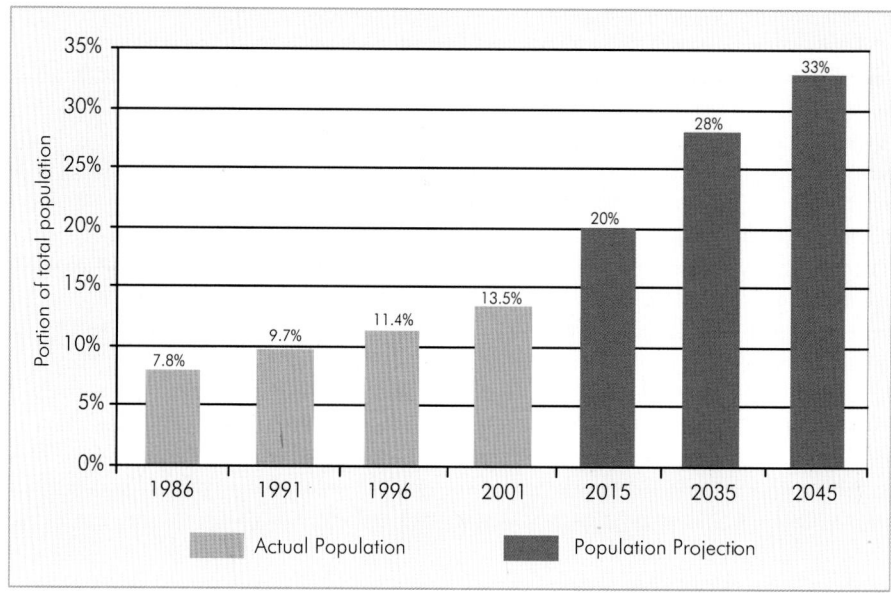

Figure APT-1. This graph shows Aboriginal population as a percentage of the total Saskatchewan population from 1986 to 2001, and population projections to 2045.

Saskatchewan than non-Aboriginals: pneumonia has long been a prominent factor in neonatal, infant, and child mortality; deaths by fire, suicide, drug and alcohol abuse, and accidental poisoning have been more prominent among Aboriginal youth; and diabetes, circulatory and respiratory system diseases, and motor vehicle accidents have ranked above the provincial norm, especially for Registered Indians on reserve.

On the whole, the Aboriginal population of Saskatchewan is much younger than the non-Aboriginal: 49.9% (in 2001) is under 20, compared to just 26.5% of the non-Aboriginal population; only 3.2% is over 65 years of age, compared to 15.9% of the non-Aboriginal population. While a large number of young Aboriginal people will soon be entering the labour force, their occupational diversity will depend on educational levels attained. On the one hand, the proportion of Aboriginal people aged 15 and above who have had less than high school education (52.6% in 2001) is disproportionately large compared to the non-Aboriginal population (37.8%). On the other hand, the proportion of Aboriginal people with a university education, trades or other higher education (39.3%) has been rapidly increasing. Today, close to 10% of the total student body at the University of Saskatchewan is Aboriginal. Opportunities for higher education have multiplied for Aboriginal students, as evidenced in increasing enrolments at the FIRST NATIONS UNIVERSITY OF CANADA (Regina and Saskatoon) and the SASKATCHEWAN INDIAN INSTITUTE OF TECHNOLOGIES (Saskatoon).

Although it lags behind the non-Aboriginal population in certain respects, the occupational diversity of the Aboriginal population will be improving. Compared with non-Aboriginals, the Aboriginal labour force is proportionately over-represented in construction (8.2% compared to 5.2%), sales and service (30.8% compared to 22.8%), and trades (19.0% compared to 14.4%); but still somewhat under-represented in finance and insurance (1.6% compared to 3.9%), real estate (1.1% compared to 1.3%), management (6.4% compared to 8.6%), business, finance and administration (12.0% compared to 15.1%), and primary industry (8.1% compared to 16.5%); and seriously under-represented in other occupational categories. The unemployment rate for the potential non-Aboriginal labour force in Saskatchewan was 4.8% in 2001, whereas among the potential Aboriginal labour force it was 23.0%, among First Nations 29.4%, and among Métis 15.5%. On-reserve average individual income has been increasing, yet it has consistently lagged behind off-reserve, particularly urban. While the gap between Aboriginal and non-Aboriginal incomes has been gradually closing, the former still remain well behind the latter. (*See also* URBAN ABORIGINAL POPULATION.) *Alan Anderson*

Aboriginal Peoples of Saskatchewan

Blair Stonechild

The Aboriginal peoples of Saskatchewan have inhabited this region for approximately 11,000 years, during which time they established self-sustaining societies. Contact with Europeans brought with it external cultural and economic forces that would dramatically affect the lives of Aboriginal people; their story has been one of adaptation and survival. During the 235 years of FUR TRADE contact (1670–1905), challenges included devastating epidemics and depletion of wildlife resources; after Canadian annexation of the North-West Territories, Aboriginal people were subjected to government policies that sought to erode their identity and rights. Today, they are recovering many of their rights, rebuilding their societies, and seeking to play a meaningful role in contemporary Canada.

European contact resulted in the common use of First Nations names that were different from the way they referred to themselves. The proper self-ascribed names of the First Nations of Saskatchewan are as follows: Nêhiyawak[1] (Plains Cree), NAHKAWININIWAK (Saulteaux), NAKOTA (Assiniboine), Dakota and Lakota (Sioux), and DENESULINE (Dene/Chipewyan). The term "First Nations" is preferred to the misnomer "Indian," and is generally used except where the latter is required in an historical context (*see also* CREE and DAKOTA/LAKOTA).

The First Peoples

Aboriginal hunter-gatherers are believed to have entered the northern plains following the retreat of the last glacier, approximately 11,000 years ago. Around 9000 BC, there is archaeological evidence of the spread of hunters using fluted spear points to hunt BISON. Archaeologist James V. Wright theorizes that eastern Early Archaic peoples migrated to the western plains

282. SUN-DANCE. INSIDE MEDICINE-LODGE.

RCMP MUSEUM, REGINA, 72.68.XIX

First Nations of the Plains possessed stable social and political institutions. At annual tribal gatherings, major ceremonies such as the Sun Dance (shown above) and major political meetings would be conducted.

A around 6000 BC, where they came into contact with the Plano peoples.[2] By 3000 BC, there is evidence of organized bison hunts on the northern plains, using more advanced spear points with distinctive rippled flaking.[3] These ancestral peoples laid the basis of the tribal cultures that were found at the time of European contact.

First Nations traditional cultures were based upon ideologies in which humans formed a part of, but were not necessarily central to, creation: humans existed within a web of life in which all entities, be they inanimate, plant, animal or natural, possessed a spiritual dimension of their own. Life was a process of developing relationships and striving for well-being within this "Circle of Life."[4] Ceremonies reflected this worldview: for example, the burning of sweetgrass represented communication with the spirit world; the vision quest a connection with protector spirits; the sweat lodge a spiritual cleansing; and the thirst (or rain) dance symbolized the process of renewal of life.[5] Closeness to the land and natural environment was central to such a belief system. (*See also* FIRST NATIONS RELIGION: OVERVIEW.) In terms of social organization, families, clans and tribes were founded upon a system of kinship and intermarriage that emphasized extended families. Political decisions tended to be based upon the reaching of consensus among families, and it was imperative to share food and other necessities. The buffalo provided virtually all of the daily needs of the plains First Nations, including food,

shelter, clothing, and tools. In the parklands and further north, fishing and gathering were important sources of nourishment, as was the hunting of large animals such as moose, elk, and caribou.

The original tribal distributions were significantly different from the pattern of Aboriginal occupation of the region today. The first White man to reach the interior of the northern plains, HENRY KELSEY, led by Nakota and Nêhiyawak guides in 1690, reported that much of present-day southern Saskatchewan area was occupied by the Atsina, (also called Gros Ventres), as well as the Nakota and Hidatsa to the southeast and the Shoshone (also called Snake) in the southwest. To the north, the area between the forks of the North and South Saskatchewan rivers and to the west was occupied by the Blackfoot.[6] The Chipewyan, a branch of the Dene, occupied areas of the northern boreal forest. The advent of the fur trade brought about dramatic changes in territorial distributions as these First Nations groups entered into competition and conflict over fur resources.

Relations during the Fur Trade

The Hudson's Bay Company (HBC) established its first fur trade post at York Factory on the shores of Hudson Bay in 1670 and named its trading territory, all of the lands draining into Hudson Bay, Rupert's Land.[7] A typical First Nation trader could bring in a hundred beaver pelts, with

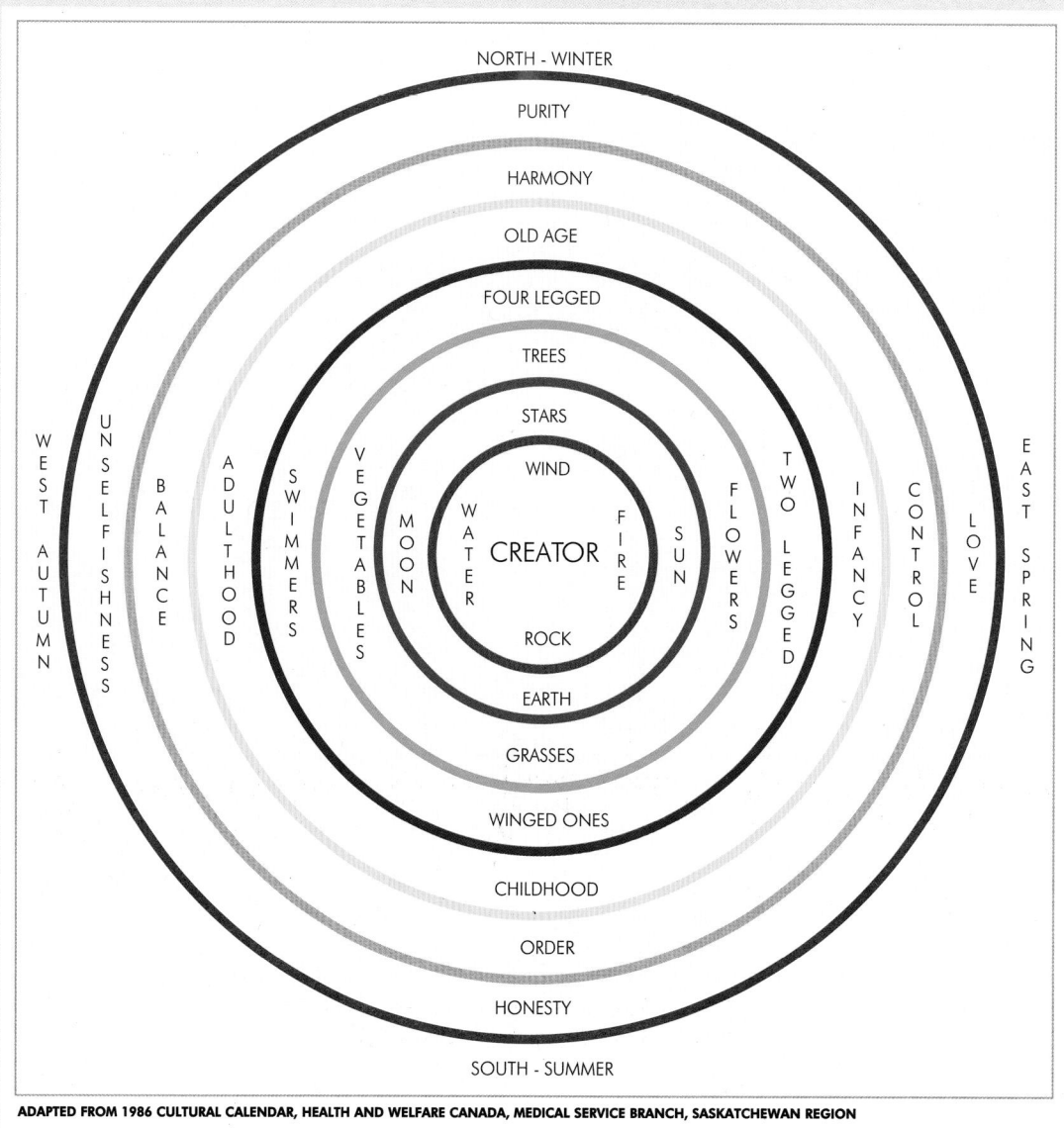

ADAPTED FROM 1986 CULTURAL CALENDAR, HEALTH AND WELFARE CANADA, MEDICAL SERVICE BRANCH, SASKATCHEWAN REGION

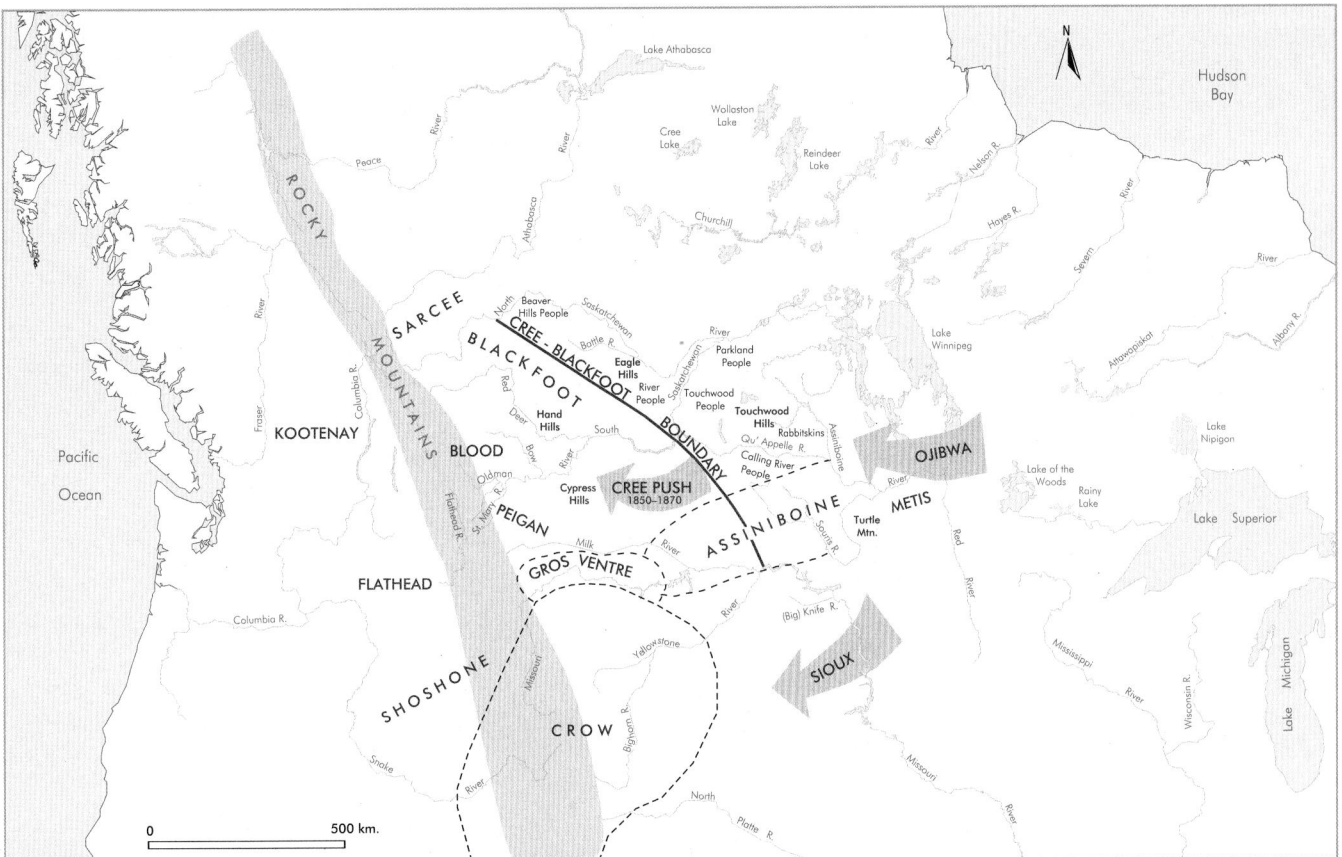

CANADIAN PLAINS RESEARCH CENTER MAPPING DIVISION/ADAPTED FROM MILLOY, *THE PLAINS CREE* (1988)

Plains Indian tribal boundaries, ca. 1850.

which he could purchase necessities such as a gun and ammunition, kettles, knives, traps, and blankets. Once the necessities were purchased, he could buy luxury goods such as tobacco, beads or liquor. The introduction of iron trade goods dramatically affected Aboriginal lifestyles, diverting much of their efforts from traditional seasonal activities to an economy based upon the harvesting of furs and bartering of trade goods to First Nations in the interior. The Nakota, whose prior habitation on the prairies eased territorial access for their Nêhiyawak trading allies, acted with the latter as middlemen who bartered trade goods for furs. The Blackfoot became early beneficiaries of trade, and with the acquisition of guns were able to drive away their adversaries, including the Shoshone and Kootenay.[8] During this period, changes in lifestyle and intertribal relations occurred as First Nations sought to use newly introduced technologies to their advantage; First Nations and fur traders also developed a relatively peaceful relationship based on reciprocal dependence, in which each side would come to the other's aid in times of need.

By the 1730s, the Cree were beginning to reside permanently on the plains, and this led to the development of a distinct tribal entity: the Nêhiyawak (Plains Cree).[9] The Blackfoot had a valuable commodity to trade to the Nakota and Nêhiyawak: horses, which had been spreading northward after being first introduced to Central America by the Spanish.[10] Despite limited equipment, First Nations became highly skilled horse riders: this, combined with the use of guns, enabled them to wield unprecedented influence. By 1787, the ruthless trading practices used by the Nakota and Nêhiyawak contributed to the breakdown of friendly relations with the Blackfoot.[11] The vanquishing of their mutual enemies, the Shoshone, Gros Ventres and Kootenay, not only removed a common foe but deprived these tribes of a vital social function: the opportunity

for young warriors to go on raiding parties in order to prove their valour. In this changed cultural landscape former allies became rivals, and over the next century the raiding between Nakota-Nêhiyawak and Blackfoot became legendary.

With the end of their alliance with the Blackfoot in 1787, the Nakota-Nêhiyawak alliance turned to the Mandan Nation's trading centre, located on the upper Missouri River, for horses. With no other providers of guns and other trade goods to compete with, the Nakota and Nêhiyawak enjoyed a tremendously strong trading position,[12] which was further strengthened when the Nahkawininiwak (Saulteaux or Plains Ojibway),[13] who traded goods originating from Montreal via the Great Lakes, joined the Nakota and Nêhiyawak. This came to be known as the Iron Alliance, the term reflecting the trade in iron goods upon which their power was built.[14] The Alliance's influence at the Mandan trading centre waned after American sources of trade goods became available around 1805.[15]

The MÉTIS, mixed-blood descendants of marriages between French fur traders and First Nations women, had come to play an important role in the trading network of the North West Company (NWC), which was established in 1779 and threatened the Hudson's Bay Company's trade monopoly.[16] Increasingly hostile relations between these two companies would eventually lead to their forced merger in 1821. When the HBC established the Selkirk Colony, consisting of Scottish farmers, to introduce agriculture to Rupert's Land, this was viewed as a threat to the NWC supply route: the Métis confronted the settlers at Seven Oaks in 1816 and killed twenty, an event that has been heralded as the birth of Métis nationalism. Over the next five decades, the Métis increased in numbers, becoming the dominant population of Red River and enjoying an economic power based upon the trade of buffalo products to the United States market.[17]

Almost two centuries of fur trade, however, were beginning to take their toll on the land and the people. Epidemics, in particular small-pox, were the greatest single killer of First Nations: the major epidemics, recorded in 1780, 1819, 1838 and 1869, carried away over half of the population each time, the Métis being affected to a lesser degree.[18] The effects of such events on the social, political and economic well-being were traumatic. Fur trade resources began to decline noticeably, first on the eastern prairies with the beaver by the 1820s and the buffalo by the 1850s.[19] In the 1820s, missionaries began to appear in Rupert's Land, and First Nations youths such as CHARLES PRATT were recruited to attend the first mission school at Red River. Other leaders such as AHTAHKAKOOP welcomed missionaries—not only for their new religious ideas, but also because of the reading, writing and arithmetic skills they could impart.[20] Missions were established earlier in the north: for example the church at Stanley Mission, constructed in 1854, is the oldest existing building in the province.

As the fur trade declined, interest in the agricultural potential of the northern prairies began to be explored by the PALLISER AND HIND EXPEDITIONS of 1859. First Nations faced increasing hardship due to the decline of their middleman role in the fur trade and to increasing inter-tribal conflict over dwindling herds of buffalo. However, as the fur trade drew to a close, the First Nations retained a strong sense of their own cultural identity, as well as a firm attachment to the land which had often been acquired through protracted intertribal struggle. The Nakota, Nêhiyawak and Nahkawininiwak of the Iron Alliance, and to a lesser extent the Métis, were forming through intermarriage a new hybrid culture loosely based upon Nakota material culture, Nêhiyawak language, and Nahkawininiwak spirituality. This legacy can be seen in the mixed tribal compositions that are found in today's First Nations.[21]

The Numbered Treaties with Canada

One of the earliest initiatives of the fledgling nation of Canada was the acquisition of Rupert's Land in 1870 (*see* RUPERT'S LAND PURCHASE). This move to expand the country west to the Pacific Ocean was sanctioned by Great Britain on the condition that treaties be negotiated with the First Nations, pursuant to the British policy enunciated in the Royal Proclamation of 1763. The Proclamation attempted to bring peace to the frontier and to secure First Nations allegiance to Britain by addressing the primary source of Aboriginal discontent: the forced loss of tradition-al land occupancy. It empowered government authorities to enter into negotiations with First Nations on behalf of the British Crown: at a public meeting, both sides had to agree to the terms upon which First Nation territory would be made accessible to settlers, and what benefits the Aboriginals would receive in return.

The treaty negotiations began with the Ojibway of the Lake of the Woods region in 1869, but a treaty in that area was not concluded until 1873 owing to stiff Indian demands. The first successfully negotiated agreements were Treaty 1 at Fort Garry in 1871, and Treaty 2, essential-ly a repetition of the terms of the earlier treaty, at Manitoba Post that same year.[22] The Nahkawininiwak of these areas drew upon the experi-ence of their eastern brethren, the Ojibway. A prominent chief, Pontiac, had led the uprising that precipitated the issuance of the Proclamation in 1763, and the Ojibway had since negotiated numerous treaties with the British authorities.

However, evidence of discontent over the process of acquiring Rupert's Land occurred first with the Métis of Red River: led by LOUIS RIEL, they protested the lack of consultation and asserted their political and land rights, ultimately establishing a Provisional Government in 1870. The forcible quelling of the Métis movement and the partial settle-ment of grievances under the Manitoba Act (1870)[23] proved insufficient to meet the aspirations of the Métis Nation, especially in terms of creat-ing a land base. Many migrated further west to the BATOCHE and Qu'Appelle areas of the North-West Territories. Continuing dissatisfac-tion over the failure to address their issues led to the NORTH-WEST RESISTANCE in 1885, again led by Riel.

Canada's strategy in approaching treaty negotiations had been to attempt to arrange a straight land transaction modeled on the 1850 Robinson Treaties negotiated by the British, as this would involve mini-mal costs or ongoing commitments. The First Nations strategy was to retain as much territory as possible, their initial request amounting to keeping two-thirds of the "postage stamp" province of Manitoba as Indian land. Treaty Commissioner Weymss Simpson conceded to his superiors that major concessions would need to be made in order to con-clude an agreement: "It was obvious therefore that we must yield some-thing, or we must be prepared to people the country, with hostile Indians hovering on our settlements, and an Indian war in the back-ground..."[24] To persuade them to drop their position on land, the Saulteaux were accorded a wide variety of concessions including agricul-tural assistance, education, and medical benefits. The vision for such a treaty relationship mirrored the relationship of mutual dependence that had previously existed between First Nations and the fur traders. The Crown's negotiators had been forced to make concessions far beyond what had been initially intended, and when some oral promises were omitted in the written text of Treaties 1 and 2, First Nations threatened to disrupt White settlement; as a consequence, Treaties 1 and 2 were revised in 1875.[25]

First Nations' retention of land would continue to be a central issue for negotiation, and larger reserve sizes were conceded in Treaty 3. The slaughter of approximately twenty Assiniboine in the CYPRESS HILLS in 1873 hastened the organizing and dispatching to the west of the North-West Mounted Police. The dispute over perceived land owner-ship claims by the Hudson's Bay Company dominated TREATY 4 talks. TREATY 5, concluded in 1875, primarily involved land in northern Manitoba but included three Saskatchewan First Nations. TREATY 6 focused primarily on broadening the scope of treaty benefits, which in 1876 expanded to include med-ical aid, taxation exemptions, and assistance in the event of famine.[26]

The treaties had come at a crucial time: the buffalo disap-peared from the prairies around 1880, and the next few years would be devastating as wide-spread starvation set in and First Nations struggled to survive. The response of the Canadian govern-ment, hampered by disorganiza-tion and lack of infrastructure, was woefully inadequate in addressing the rapidly deteriorat-ing conditions. This situation was complicated by the arrival of Sioux Chief SITTING BULL, who

SASKATCHEWAN ARCHIVES BOARD R-A5043

Sitting Bull.

Poundmaker.

Piapot (Edmund Morris painting).

A

1880s by organizing political meetings. PIAPOT, one of the principal leaders of Treaty 4, organized a meeting at Pasqua Reserve, and Treaty 6 chiefs BIG BEAR[29] and POUNDMAKER organized gatherings to air Treaty grievances in 1884.[30] The federal government, believing that such activities were worthless and only led to trouble, used North-West Mounted Police intervention and deprivation of rations to disrupt these activities; such responses resulted in near-violent confrontations on the Sakimay and Poundmaker reserves in 1884. The First Nations' political strategy sought to avoid violence, opting instead to organize a broad-based political movement in Treaties 4, 6 and 7, which would present a unified voice to Ottawa.[31]

North-West Resistance of 1885

Frustrated by the lack of progress in addressing their concerns, the Métis of the Batoche area, supported by local settlers, approached Louis Riel, then living in Montana, to lead their cause. Riel, having had some success in forcing the federal government to meet Métis demands in 1870, declared again the establishment of a Provisional Government on March 19, 1885. The only group that had not provided political support for his plans, which by this time radically called for the establishment of a New Papacy, were the First Nations. However, due to a series of circumstances beyond their control, First Nations quickly became mired in the events of the North-West Resistance of 1885.[32]

After the Resistance was quelled through the use of military force, the federal government quickly convicted 19 Métis and 33 Indians of offenses related to the uprising. Cree chiefs Big Bear, Poundmaker and One Arrow were each found guilty of treason-felony and sentenced to three years in Stony Mountain Penitentiary. A fourth chief, the Dakota leader White Cap, was acquitted of charges despite being a member of Riel's Exovedate Council[33] when a Saskatoon merchant testified on his behalf. Some leaders including Métis commander GABRIEL DUMONT evaded capture by fleeing to the United States. In the aftermath of the Resistance, the federal government instituted a series of repressive policies that enabled it to gain a firm grip over First Nations. These measures, which went against the spirit of the treaties signed a decade earlier, included forcible confinement to Indian reserves, dismantling of Aboriginal culture, and removing of children to residential schools for assimilation. A final sad note to the suppression of First Nations was when ALMIGHTY VOICE, who was reduced to illegally killing a cow for food, died in a barrage of police cannon fire in 1897[34]; his fate seemed to represent that of a once-proud and independent people. In the aftermath of the 1885 Resistance the dream of a Métis homeland again

sought refuge in Canada in 1876 following the defeat of General Custer and his troops at the Battle of the Little Big Horn in the United States. Reserve agriculture was slow to evolve: growing crops proved virtually impossible, as they succumbed to early frosts, grasshoppers, and prairie fires. The primitive form of agriculture practiced used the tools provided under treaty, and resulted in a labour-intensive and time-consuming process that was simply not viable.[27] TREATY 8, signed in 1899, occurred in response to pressure for mining and affirmed the First Nations' rights to hunt and fish. TREATY 10, whose terms resembled those of Treaty 8 signed in 1906–07, was intended to cover areas of Saskatchewan not covered by other treaties.

The First Nations' oral understanding of the Numbered Treaties varies significantly from that of the written text. First Nation elders assert that only the topsoil was surrendered for agricultural purposes, and that ownership was retained not only over their reserve land (in Cree called *iskunikan*, i.e., "land that was kept"), but also over the wildlife upon which they relied as well as all other resources including minerals.[28] While the presence of the North-West Mounted Police is sometimes cited as proof of coercion in the making of the treaties, in fact the First Nations were the dominant party who tended to view the police as potential allies rather than enemies.

First Nations responded to the emerging starvation crisis of the

Treaty Ceremony Mural at Duck Lake.

Beardy's Warriors, Duck Lake, 1885.

A

SASKATCHEWAN ARCHIVES BOARD R-A225317

St. Philippe Mission, built in 1927.

suffered a blow, but such an aspiration has provided a foundation for grievances that persist into modern times.

Policy of Assimilation

RESIDENTIAL SCHOOLS, which were not mentioned during treaty discussions, became the federal government's primary tool with respect to the assimilation of Aboriginal people.[35] The Social Darwinist belief popularly held by Canadians at the time was that Indian cultures were inferior and therefore should be replaced by British culture. First Nations children, who were the most vulnerable to influence, were removed from contact with their parents and communities to the greatest extent possible. As Prime Minister John A. Macdonald, then Superintendent General of Indian Affairs, explained:

> When the school is on the reserve, the child lives with its parents, who are savages, and though he may learn to read and write, his habits and training and mode of thought are Indian. He is simply a savage who can read and write. It has been strongly impressed upon myself, as head of the Department, that Indian children should be withdrawn as much as possible from the parental influence, and the only way to do that would be to put them in central training industrial schools where they will acquire the habits and modes of thought of white men.[36]

Indian industrial schools were initially established in 1883 at Lebret, Battleford, and High River.[37] Other schools, such as the Regina Indian Industrial School in 1890, were established at the initiative of religious denominations. More common were less costly boarding schools, which offered less in the way of training programs and were closer to their communities, but still isolated the children from their families.

Residential schools soon proved to be expensive and ineffective. Zealous religious denominations, competing for converts, built too many schools. Meanwhile enrollments were falling due to high student mortality rates caused by tuberculosis and other diseases. The denigration of their culture, homesickness, and an unimaginative curriculum resulted in a deplorable education experience, and some tried to escape. Children who finally returned to their communities found themselves alienated from both Indian and White societies. Altogether, fourteen residential schools were built in Saskatchewan.[38]

The creation in 1905 of the province of Saskatchewan, named after the Cree term for "fast flowing river," led to a boom in land speculation. A policy emerged around this time aimed at the erosion of First Nations land through the securing of Indian reserve land surrenders. While First Nations viewed their reserves as permanent homelands for their descendents, surrenders became very appealing to land speculators and government officials, who believed that the Indian population would continue to decline. Reserve lands could only be lost through a majority vote in favour of the surrender taken under the Indian Act, a piece of legislation intended to manage every aspect of First Nations life. First Nation reluctance was overcome through fraudulent dealings often involving bureaucrats at the highest levels, and by the use of coercion such as cutting off rations and offering inducements of immediate large cash payments. As a result of these actions, close to half of Indian Reserve lands in southern Saskatchewan were surrendered between 1896 and 1920.[39]

The influence of Indian agents over Indian reserves was pervasive: these individuals held total control and their authority displaced that of chiefs, many of whom had been deposed by the federal government. The agents controlled the ability of Indians to travel out of the reserve, and nothing could be bought or sold without their permission. Under the Indian Act, agents possessed broad judicial powers enabling them to lay and adjudicate charges without recourse to appeal. First Nations resistance attempted to organize politically: at a meeting on the Thunderchild Reserve in 1921, the League of Indians of Western Canada was formed, led by JOHN TOOTOOSIS.[40] Other organizations, such as the Allied Tribes representing Qu'Appelle area bands, were also formed.

Post-War Period

Uncertainty set in during the 1930s and 1940s as Indian policy was generally viewed as being a failure and no new directions were emerging. Following the end of WORLD WAR II, pressure came from ABORIGINAL VETERANS, who had volunteered in higher proportion than the general population and become sensitized to the need to be freed from oppression.[41] In 1951, the Indian Act was revised, removing some of the most archaic aspects of the old regime such as employing Indian agents. First Nations individuals were allowed to leave the reserve, although it was not until 1960 that they were granted the right to vote federally by the Diefenbaker government and could begin to enjoy the privileges of ordinary citizenship. The Hawthorne Report, a national survey of the social conditions of Indians conducted in 1963, revealed that Saskatchewan Indians were among the most poverty-stricken in Canada.[42]

The holding of provincial consultations by the CCF government under T.C. DOUGLAS made possible the formation of the first provincial organization, the Union of Saskatchewan Indians in 1946, with John

DON HEALY/REGINA LEADER-POST

About 100 Aboriginal veterans were honoured at the RCMP training grounds on June 6, 1995: World War II veteran Gordon Ahenakew on podium; Howard Anderson (foreground right) and Greg Rainville with traditional eagle staffs.

Tootoosis elected as first president[43]; this was the forerunner of the Federation of Saskatchewan Indians (later FEDERATION OF SASKATCHEWAN INDIAN NATIONS). Others, including JOSEPH LAROCQUE, CLARENCE TROTCHIE, JAMES BRADY and MALCOLM NORRIS, worked to organize the Métis politically. The Saskatchewan CCF government finally extended the provincial vote to Indians in 1960.[44]

Contemporary Aboriginal Peoples of Saskatchewan

Category Definitions

According to the current Canadian constitution, "Aboriginal Peoples" includes "Indian, Inuit and Métis peoples of Canada."[45] Treaty Indians are listed as members of First Nations who are descendants of the signatories to one of the Numbered Treaties. Non-Treaty Indians are members of First Nations, primarily the Dakota, who have reserves and are recognized as having Indian Status under the Indian Act, but were not signatories to treaties. The term "First Nations" has become commonplace following the assertion of Aboriginal political rights in the 1980s.

ROBERT WATSON/REGINA LEADER-POST

Students at Fond du Lac Dene School, January 1989.

Non-Status Indians are those First Nations who for varying reasons never signed treaties nor fell under the jurisdiction of the Indian Act. The Métis are descendants of French fathers who participated in the fur trade and of First Nation mothers, and are generally identified with origins in the Red River area. The descendants of British fathers and Aboriginal mothers have historically been referred to as half-breeds.[46]

Of the ABORIGINAL LANGUAGES, Nêhiyawêwin (Cree language), part of the Algonquian language group, is the most commonly spoken in Saskatchewan, with about 20,000 speakers. Nahkawêwin (Saulteaux language), primarily spoken on eleven First Nations mainly in southeastern Saskatchewan, is the westernmost dialect of the Ojibway language. Nakota, Dakota and Lakota are dialects of the Siouan language found mainly in the United States, but only a few fluent speakers of the latter two languages remain in Saskatchewan. There are approximately 5,100 speakers of Dene, most of whom are found in northern Saskatchewan. Michif is the unique language of the Métis, created through the blending of French and Cree words. The teaching of Aboriginal languages in First Nations and provincial schools is becoming commonplace.

Aboriginal Demographics

The Aboriginal population is growing at a higher rate than the general population of the province, and demographic projections indicate that the Aboriginal proportion will grow to 32.5% by 2045.[47] Today, Aboriginal peoples occupy an increasingly important role in the province, with 2001 census figures indicating 83,745 Status Indians, 43,695 Métis, and 190 Inuit—together amounting to 13.6% of the population. The total number of Registered Indians on the lists of the 74

Saskatchewan First Nations in 2003 was 114,248.[48] As for the MÉTIS NATION, it is believed to comprise close to 80,000 individuals.

Politics and Governance

The announcement of the Trudeau government's Indian Policy of 1969, which advocated termination of Indian treaties, rights and reserves, galvanized the First Nations of Canada to organize nationally under the National Indian Brotherhood (NIB).[49] The rejection of the Canadian government's assimilation policy signaled the first major shift in Indian policy since Confederation and ushered in the contemporary period, marked by the recovery of culture, rights, and self-determination. The NIB's first president was WALTER DEITER of the Peepeekisis Reserve.[50] Other national leaders of the NIB from Saskatchewan included DAVID AHENAKEW and NOEL STARBLANKET. Following the rejection of the 1969 policy, the Federation of Saskatchewan Indians turned its efforts toward the recovery of Treaty Rights, including redress of Indian land claims. Leaders of the provincial political organization have included SOL SANDERSON, ROLAND CROWE, and PERRY BELLEGARDE.

In 1982, the Federation of Saskatchewan Indians entered into a political convention that acknowledged the Federation of Saskatchewan Indian Nations as representing the collective interests of the province's First Nations, each of which continued to retain its inherent sovereignty. This transformation was consistent with the enhanced recognition of Aboriginal rights entrenched in the Canada Act of 1982. The FIRST NATIONS GOVERNANCE structure includes Tribal Councils—regional groupings of First Nations set up for advisory and program delivery purposes.

The focus of First Nations political activity, apart from the reclamation and protection of rights, has been the building of capacities for self-determination: for example, an agreement signed by the Meadow Lake Tribal Council with the governments of Canada and Saskatchewan acknowledges the First Nations' inherent right to self-government.[51] While First Nations are still heavily dependent on government transfer agreements, increasing emphasis is being placed on facilitating the creation of band and individual enterprises, as well as promoting greater involvement in the mainstream economy through post-secondary training and creation of employment opportunities. The Department of Indian Affairs allocates annually about $600 million for First Nations programs and services such as governance, education, housing, and economic development.

The OFFICE OF THE TREATY COMMISSIONER (OTC), created in 1989, is a unique approach devised in Saskatchewan to resolve issues surrounding Treaty Land Entitlement. The OTC was given a new mandate in 1996 to educate the general public about why treaty rights exist, and how those rights affect the general public. The Office convenes discussion tables to bring First Nations and the federal government to consider Treaty implementation measures in areas such as education, health, and justice. The province participates as an observer.[52]

Métis and Non-Status Indians

The first provincial organization to unite the Métis of northern and southern Saskatchewan was the Métis Society of Saskatchewan, formed in 1967. Under the leadership of JIM SINCLAIR, Non-Status Indian issues came to be included in 1975 under the umbrella of the Association of Métis and Non-Status Indians of Saskatchewan (see NON-STATUS INDIANS). Following the recognition of the Métis as an Aboriginal people under the Canadian Constitution in 1982, focus returned to the Métis achieving rights and self-determination; the new political organization was named the MÉTIS NATION–SASKATCHEWAN.

While most continue to live in historical MÉTIS COMMUNITIES such as Lebret, Willow Bunch, Duck Lake, St. Louis, Green Lake and Buffalo Narrows, where some MÉTIS FARMS are located, the Métis are becoming an increasingly urbanized people. MÉTIS AND NON-STATUS INDIAN LEGAL ISSUES have received greater attention, particularly since the inclusion of the former as an "Aboriginal people" in Canada's 1982 Constitution; of special concern are hunting and fishing rights, and setting aside a dedicated land base. The lack of a distinct Métis land base, apart from Métis farms, has presented great challenges to the preservation of a sense of community, as individuals commonly assimilate into the mainstream. Enumeration of the Métis population is a central issue, since no official lists have been kept historically. Mixed-blood peoples other than the Métis, such as those descended from Scottish fathers and Aboriginal mothers and historically referred to as half-breeds, as well as Non-Status Indians, who are culturally Aboriginal but are not recognized by the federal government, are represented by the Congress of Aboriginal Peoples.[53]

Political pressure for recognition of Métis rights, applied by individuals such as HARRY DANIELS and CLÉMENT CHARTIER, resulted in their recognition as an Aboriginal people under the Constitution Act of 1982: there is now a Federal Interlocutor for Métis and Non-Status Indians, whose role is to help to reaffirm the unique position of these peoples in Canada.

Aboriginal-Provincial relations

Treaty Indians were initially hesitant to engage in provincial politics, fearing that it would lead to loss of treaty rights and assimilation; however, they received some reassurance when the CCF government of T.C. Douglas granted them the provincial vote in 1960.[54] Presently, FIRST NATIONS INTERGOVERNMENTAL RELATIONS exist primarily with the federal government; the latter provided all entitlements, including those traditionally under provincial jurisdiction such as education and health. Saskatchewan played a key role in Indian policy with the Natural Resources Transfer Agreement (1930), in which the province was obligated to respect Indian hunting and fishing rights, and to provide provincial Crown lands if required for the creation of Indian reserve lands.

Provinces have hesitated to become involved in Indian policy because of the enormous costs involved in dealing with Aboriginal needs, which have become increasingly focused on urban issues of poverty, crime, adoptions, and family services. In Saskatchewan, the Department of First Nations and Métis Relations coordinates the province's dealings with Aboriginal issues and programs. Increasingly, Aboriginal people such as former Cabinet Minister KEITH GOULET are becoming involved in provincial politics.

Education

Residential schools began to be phased out in 1965 and were replaced by an imposed Joint School Agreements system, under which seats were purchased in local mainstream schools; but this policy failed because of racism and an inappropriate curriculum, and was discontinued.[55] The adoption by the federal government of the Indian Control of Indian Education poli-

cy in 1973 led to the construction of First Nations-controlled education facilities on the reserves. There was, up until the time of the CCF government in the 1940s, uncertainty about the administration of Métis affairs: the federal government had left the issue to the provinces, while the provinces expected the federal government to become involved.[56] This was particularly true in education, as both the provincial and federal governments rejected responsibility for Métis issues such as education, which resulted in phenomena such as the "road allowance people."

Responding to the high Aboriginal dropout rates, the Saskatchewan Education Department began to develop and institute an accredited Kindergarten to Grade 12 Native Studies curriculum that respects Aboriginal cultures, heritage, and rights.[57] Such changes are designed to eradicate the ignorance that underpins much of the racism that exists today. Reforms to the provincial curriculum in the mid-1980s have helped to provide, for both Aboriginal and non-Aboriginal students, accurate and culturally reaffirming portrayals of Aboriginal conditions and aspirations. Today, First Nations children have the choice of attending one of approximately 100 elementary and high schools located on reserves, or to attend a local provincial school. Given the expansion of reserve youth numbers and the decline of rural populations, non-Aboriginal students sometimes attend reserve schools, a startling reversal from a few decades ago.

In the area of post-secondary education, the SASKATCHEWAN INDIAN CULTURAL CENTRE (originally the Saskatchewan Indian Cultural College), founded in 1972, was mandated to promote the preservation of Indian culture through the production of curriculum as well as other activities. Based in Regina, with sub-campuses in Saskatoon and Prince Albert, the FIRST NATIONS UNIVERSITY OF CANADA (formerly the Saskatchewan Indian Federated College), founded in 1976, has a provincial, national and international mandate to meet the higher-education needs of Indigenous peoples. Traditional Ecological Knowledge is an example of a unique subject being taught that is relevant to modern issues—in this case the environment. As of 2004, the institution had graduated over 2,500 students. The SASKATCHEWAN INDIAN INSTITUTE OF TECHNOLOGIES (formerly the Saskatchewan Indian Community College), founded in 1976, has the mandate of providing post-secondary education in areas other than academic.

Similarly, the Métis Nation-Saskatchewan has established institutions such as the GABRIEL DUMONT INSTITUTE, which mounts higher education programs such as the SASKATCHEWAN URBAN NATIVE TEACHERS EDUCATION PROGRAM (SUNTEP) and offers post-secondary training of a technical nature.

Health Issues

In the recent past, treatment for diseases such as tuberculosis has been instrumental in improving ABORIGINAL HEALTH.[58] The nature of illness among Aboriginal peoples has been changing: diabetes and AIDS have emerged as major contemporary challenges. The well-being of Aboriginal people lags behind mainstream society, with infant mortality nearly twice and diabetes four times the national rate. The First Nations and Inuit Branch of Health Canada funds community health clinics on reserves, as well as at Indian Hospitals such as those at Fort Qu'Appelle and Battleford.

BRYAN SCHLOSSER/REGINA LEADER-POST

Fort Qu'Appelle Indian Hospital, May 1996.

Land Management and Claims

Challenges faced include finding improved ways to manage land and capital, strengthening of human resource capabilities, and diversification of the economy including greater integration with the surrounding areas. Reserve lands are held communally by the First Nations, although individual families have occupancy rights to use specific areas. The fact that lands cannot be sold places obstacles to raising capital, which may require land as collateral; under the Indian Act property is not taxable, and First Nations members cannot be sued.[59]

There are different categories of FIRST NATIONS LAND CLAIMS. Land surrenders denote the removal of portions of land from reserves that already existed. Although First Nations viewed reserve lands as *iskunikan*, homelands for future generations, land speculators actively pursued surrenders during the period of land settlement between 1896 and 1913. Surrenders were secured using tactics such as deprivation of rations, suspension of privileges, offering inducements of large amounts of money, and outright fraud: all this resulted in 576,781 acres of Indian Reserve land being surrendered on the prairies. Investigations of improprieties in these land dealings have resulted in the awarding of substantial monetary settlements.[60]

Land entitlement is lands to which First Nations were entitled under the original treaties, but which were never allocated for reasons such as punishment for alleged involvement in the North-West Resistance. Under the Land Entitlement "Saskatchewan Formula" reached in 1976, reserve land allotment would be based upon band populations as of December 1, 1976; however, only three claims were settled under this process. A more effective solution was the Saskatchewan Land Entitlement Framework Agreement in 1993, which provided $539 million for the settlement of Indian Land Entitlements to purchase lands that were still owed to First Nations under the treaty terms.[61]

Economic Development

The lack of an adequate economic base has been one of the most serious problems facing Saskatchewan First Nations. Indian agriculture has historically been a failure because of defects in government policies involving inadequate land management approaches and insufficient support for modernization of technology; as a result, agriculture has not proven to be the economic salvation that was promised under the treaties. Today, the economy of the reserves remains largely dependent on government transfer payments: opportunities remain few and unemployment remains high.

Successful FIRST NATIONS ECONOMIC DEVELOPMENT today is increasingly globalized; examples are the Kitsaki Development Corporation, as well as various Indian urban satellite reserves such as the McKnight Commmercial Centre in Saskatoon.[62] Some First Nations have funded entities such as the Saskatchewan Indian Equity Foundation, and the FIRST NATIONS BANK OF CANADA provides targeted funding for economic development ventures. As regards the Métis, Sasknative Economic Development Corporation (SNEDCO) provides loans for small business development.

Today Aboriginal business is one of the most rapidly expanding sectors of the provincial economy: over 1,000 band and privately owned businesses are in existence.[63] Gaming has become an important aspect of the Saskatchewan First Nations economy. The first casino was launched by the Whitebear First Nations in defiance of provincial wishes, and a First Nations Gaming Agreement was arrived at in 1995, leading to the creation of four First Nations-controlled casinos operated by the SASKATCHEWAN INDIAN GAMING AUTHORITY. In 2002, a 25-year Gaming

Framework Agreement was signed. Of $29.4 million in profits in 2003, 37.5% went to the provincial government, 37.5% to the First Nations Trust Fund, and 25% to community development corporations.[64]

Urbanization

Since the 1960s, there has been a general trend, encouraged originally by government assimilation policies, for First Nations individuals and families to move to urban centres in pursuit of education and job opportunities. Today, 47% of the First Nations population resides in urban centres; owing to problems of racism and lack of training, large areas of urban poverty have sprung up in Regina and Saskatoon. This phenomenon is accompanied by a high crime rate, the formation of gangs, and a high incarceration rate.[65] Indian and Métis Friendship Centres (*see* ABORIGINAL FRIENDSHIP CENTRES OF SASKATCHEWAN) started to come into existence in the 1960s to ease the transition of Aboriginal Peoples into urban areas, and began to receive federal funding under the Migrating Aboriginal Peoples program in 1972. Today, thirteen centres continue to offer social and program supports in Saskatchewan.

One of the innovations providing hope for the future is the creation of URBAN RESERVES[66]: there are now over twenty urban satellite reserves, in and around the major urban centres of Saskatoon, Regina, and Prince Albert. Urban reserves provide a unique opportunity for First Nations to participate in the larger economy, and greater employment opportunities for urban Aboriginal residents.

Socio-Economic Conditions

As a group, the Aboriginal population continues to be youthful, with a large though diminishing birthrate: 49.9% of the Aboriginal population is below the age of 20, compared to 26.5% for the general provincial population. In terms of well-being, Aboriginal people remain among the most impoverished, disadvantaged, and undereducated in society. The Aboriginal labour force unemployment is 23%, five times that of 4.8% for the non-Aboriginal population.[67] Aboriginal people continue to be severely underrepresented in professional occupations such as the medical and justice systems. In Saskatoon, 64% of the Aboriginal population falls under the Low Income Cutoff Poverty Line, compared to 18% in the non-Aboriginal population of the city. Housing is a reflection of this situation, along with crime and incarceration statistics. Mortality rates are high; adoptions and effective provision of social services are issues of concern. Disparities continue to exist in rural areas, where First Nations youth who lack employment opportunities and access to recreational facilities tend to become involved in crime. FIRST NATIONS WOMEN have also faced unique social challenges. Indian women had lost Indian Status under previous provisions of the Indian Act, but they and their children have been able to apply for reinstatement under Bill C-31 (1985). The association representing First Nations women is the Saskatchewan Indian Womens' Association.

Law and Justice Issues

Aboriginal hunting and fishing rights have been a long-standing source of dispute, as the implementation of federally protected treaty rights comes into conflict with provincial wildlife enforcement management; one compromise is to involve First Nations in their own enforcement, licensing and conservation initiatives.[68] Water rights are another controversial area, with provincial water management often impinging on Indian lands. The justice system faces challenges when dealing with Aboriginal people, as they constitute over 70% of inmates held in provincial correctional institutions. The investigation of the freezing deaths of

A

Aboriginals outside of Saskatoon, such as the Commission of Inquiry into the death of Neil Stonechild,[69] placed a focus on relations with the police. The Saskatchewan Justice Reform Commission, established in 2001 to carry out investigations, has made recommendations including the creation of an independent complaints investigation agency.[70]

One of the solutions being pursued is the development of Aboriginal policing services, with emphasis on recruitment into mainstream agencies such as the Royal Canadian Mounted Police, as well as agreements to create reserve-based First Nations police forces. Courts are also beginning to provide greater clarity about MÉTIS AND NON-STATUS INDIAN LEGAL ISSUES, hunting and fishing, and RESTORATIVE JUSTICE.

Contemporary Aboriginal Arts

Traditional Aboriginal art forms such as beading and hide work continue to thrive while contemporary Aboriginal artists such as ALLEN SAPP and GERALD MCMASTER explore new avenues within which to interpret Aboriginal experience (see ABORIGINAL ARTISTS, CONTEMPORARY and ABORIGINAL ARTISTS, TRADITIONAL). The Saskatchewan First Nations artistic community is the birthplace of internationally acclaimed singers BUFFY SAINTE-MARIE and TOM JACKSON, and of actors such as GORDON TOOTOOSIS. There is a growing interest in ABORIGINAL THEATRE: for example, the Saskatchewan Native Theatre, founded by Aboriginal cultural leaders in Saskatoon in 1999, has generated a great deal of interest and support from the community.

COURTESY OF TOURISM SASKATCHEWAN

First Nations Dancer, Wanuskewin Heritage Park.

ABORIGINAL MEDIA began to emerge in the 1960s with the establishment of news magazines such as *The Saskatchewan Indian* and *The New Breed*. There now exist radio stations and television programs dedicated to Aboriginal audiences. There is also a burgeoning community of Aboriginal writers, one of the best-known being Métis writer MARIA CAMPBELL.[71]

Aboriginal cultural tourism is attracting increasing numbers of international visitors, who can witness any one of a number of regional powwows or experience cultural settings such as WANUSKEWIN HERITAGE PARK, located on the outskirts of Saskatoon. Back to Batoche Days, held each July at the National Historic Site of BATOCHE, represent the central annual cultural and social gathering of the Métis.

The North

Over 80% of the approximately 40,000 inhabitants of northern Saskatchewan are Aboriginal. While the peoples of the north face unique challenges because of geographical isolation and small populations, Aboriginal peoples have the opportunity to become major players in areas such as resource management and environmental protection. The Prince Albert Grand Council's investment in a variety of economic ventures including hotels and office buildings, as well as corporations such as Kitsaki Management Limited Partnership owned by the La Ronge Band have made the First Nations of the north among the most prosperous and progressive in the province. Other economic activities include guiding, fishing, and harvesting of WILD RICE and berries. The Métis Nation–Saskatchewan's ongoing effort to create a Métis homeland is focused on an area of northwestern Saskatchewan.

Towards a Shared Future

Observers sometimes refer to "two solitudes" when discussing Aboriginal/non-Aboriginal relations in the province. However, when considering the degree of segregation that existed prior to the 1960s under the federal policy of isolating Indians on reserves, the changes that have occurred since then are dramatic. With improved access to health care, First Nations have made great strides in terms of overcoming health challenges, and instead of being a "dying race" are now the most rapidly expanding portion of the provincial population. Currently, close to half of children entering school age have Aboriginal heritage, and it is anticipated that by the end of the 21st century persons having some Aboriginal ancestry will be a majority.

Aboriginal peoples are in the process of successfully defending and securing their rights, an arrangement that brings hundreds of millions of federal dollars into the province. While unemployment rates remain high, educational participation has greatly increased, particularly at the postsecondary level. Other challenges, such as finding ways to vitalize rural First Nations reserve economies, will involve much imagination, commitment, and developmental support. Life has changed dramatically for Aboriginal peoples in this province—beginning with the fur trade, then moving into the reserve period, and now largely in urban centres—but the story has been one of survival, adaptation, and versatility. One hopes for a future in which, as the treaty signatories originally envisioned, both Aboriginal and non-Aboriginal societies can co-exist while respecting each other's cultures and rights. Despite the challenges facing them, Aboriginal peoples in Saskatchewan are undergoing a social and cultural renaissance. Such a society can only become richer in heritage as well as more prosperous overall when Aboriginal peoples regain control over their destinies and once again become a vital force in the lands that they rightly call their home.

FURTHER READING:

Barron, L. 1997. *Walking in Indian Moccasins*. Vancouver: University of British Columbia Press.

Barron, L. and J. Garcea. 1999. *Urban Indian Reserves: Forging New Relationships in Saskatchewan*. Saskatoon: Purich Publishing.

Campbell, M. 1973. *Halfbreed*. Lincoln: University of Nebraska Press.

Cardinal, H. and W. Hildebrant. 2000. *Treaty Elders of Saskatchewan*. Calgary: University of Calgary Press.

Beal, B. and R. McLeod. 1984. *Prairie Fire: The North West Rebellion*. Edmonton: Hurtig.

Carter, S. 1990. *Lost Harvests: Prairie Indian Reserve Farmers and Government Policy*. Montreal: McGill-Queen's University Press.

Christiansen, D. 2000. *Ahtakakoop and His People*. Shell Lake, SK: Ahtakakoop Publishing.

Dempsey, H. 1984. *Big Bear: The End of Freedom*. Vancouver: Douglas & McIntyre.

Dickason, O. 1997. *Canada's First Nations*. Don Mills, ON: Oxford University Press.

Elias, D. 1988. *The Dakota of the Canadian North West*. Winnipeg: University of Manitoba Press.

Gaffen, F. 1985. *Forgotten Soldiers*. Penticton: Theytus Books.

Grant, J. 1984. *Moon of Wintertime: Missionaries and the Indians of Canada in Encounter*. Toronto: University of Toronto Press.

Lux, M. 2001. *Medicine That Walks: Disease. Medicine and Canadian Plains Native People 1880–1940.* Toronto: University of Toronto Press.

Mandelbaum, D. 1979. *The Plains Cree: An Ethnographic, Historical and Comparative Study.* Regina: Canadian Plains Research Center.

Milloy, J. 1988. *The Plains Cree: Trade, Diplomacy and War, 1790 to 1870.* Winnipeg: University of Manitoba Press.

——.1999. *A National Crime: The Canadian Government and the Residential School System, 1879 to 1986.* Winnipeg: University of Manitoba Press.

Miller, J. 1996. *Shinguak's Vision: A History of Native Residential Schools.* Toronto: University of Toronto Press.

Newman, P. 1987. *Caesars of the Wilderness.* Markham, ON: Penguin.

Peers, L. 1994. *The Ojibway of Western Canada.* Winnipeg: University of Manitoba Press.

Pettipas, K. 1994. *Severing the Ties That Bind.* Winnipeg: University of Manitoba Press.

Ray, A. 1974. *Indians in the Fur Trade.* Toronto: University of Toronto Press.

Ray, A., J. Miller and F. J. Tough. 2000. *Bounty and Benevolence: A History of Saskatchewan Treaties.* Toronto: University of Toronto Press.

Sluman, N. and J. Goodwill. 1982. *John Tootoosis.* Ottawa: Golden Dog.

Sprague, D.N. 1988. *Canada and the Métis, 1869–1885.* Waterloo: Wilfrid Laurier University Press.

Stonechild, B. and B. Waiser. 1997. *Loyal Till Death: Indians in the North West Rebellion.* Calgary: Fifth House.

NOTES

1. The term for Cree varies according to dialect. Plains Cree are *Nêhiyawak*, Woodland Cree are *Nêhithawak* and Swampy Cree are *Nêhinawak*.
2. Olive Dickason, *Canada's First Nations* (Don Mills, ON: Oxford University Press, 1997), 11.
3. Henry Epp, *Long Ago Today: The Story of Saskatchewan's Earliest People* (Saskatoon: Saskatchewan Archeological Society), 58.
4. Blair Stonechild, Neal McLeod and Rob Nestor, *Survival of A People* (Regina: First Nations University of Canada, 2004), 2. Health and Welfare Canada, "Cultural Calendar–1986" contains detailed diagrams of the Circle of Life.
5. Katherine Pettipas, *Severing the Ties that Bind* (Winnipeg: University of Manitoba Press, 1994), 185.
6. John Milloy, *The Plains Cree: Trade, Diplomacy and War 1790 to 1870* (Winnipeg: University of Manitoba Press, 1988), 6–7.
7. Arthur Ray, *Indians in the Fur Trade* (Toronto: University of Toronto Press, 1974), 4.
8. Milloy, *The Plains Cree*, 8–10.
9. David Mandelbaum, *The Plains Cree* (Regina: Canadian Plains Research Centre, 1979), 26.
10. Ibid., 32.
11. Milloy, *The Plains Cree*, 31 and 43–45.
12. Ibid., 50.
13. Patricia Albers, "Plains Ojibway," in *Handbook of North American Indians* (Washington: Smithsonian Institution, 2001), 659; and Laura Peers, *The Ojibway of Western Canada* (Winnipeg: University of Manitoba Press, 1994), 46.
14. Albers, "Plains Ojibway," 652; and Treaty Number Four Council of Chiefs, "Treaty Four First Nations Governance Model" (October 23, 2000), 2.
15. Milloy, *The Plains Cree*, 51.
16. Peter Newman, *Caesars of the Wilderness* (Markham, ON: Penguin, 1987), 10.
17. Dickason, *Canada's First Nations*, 242.
18. Ray, *Indians in the Fur Trade*, 182–192.
19. Ibid., 203–212.
20. Deanna Christensen, *Ahtakakoop* (Shell Lake, SK: Ahtakakoop Publishing, 2000), 169.
21. Neal McLeod, "Plains Cree Identity," *Canadian Journal of Native Studies* 20, no. 2 (2000): 441.
22. Alexander Morris, *The Treaties of Canada with the Indians of Manitoba and the North West Territories* (Toronto: Coles [reprint], 1971), 43.
23. D.N. Sprague, *Canada and the Métis 1869–1885* (Waterloo: Wilfrid Laurier University Press, 1988), 94.
24. Indian Claims Commission, *Roseau River Anishinabe First Nation Inquiry Report,* 14 ICCP (Ottawa: 2001), 26.
25. Morris, *The Treaties of Canada*, 126.
26. Ibid., 178.
27. Sarah Carter, *Lost Harvests: Prairie Indian Reserve Farmers and Government Policy* (Montreal: McGill-Queen's University Press, 1990), 98–99.
28. Blair Stonechild, "The Iron Alliance and Domination of the Northern Plains, 1690–1885: Implications for the Concept of Iskunikan" (unpublished, 2002), 15.
29. Hugh Dempsey, *Big Bear: The End of Freedom* (Vancouver: Douglas & McIntyre, 1984), 126.
30. Blair Stonechild and Bill Waiser, *Loyal Till Death* (Calgary: Fifth House, 1997), 50–60.
31. Dempsey, *Big Bear*, 123.
32. Stonechild and Waiser, *Loyal Till Death*, 4.
33. Ibid., 151.
34. Frank Anderson, *Almighty Voice* (Aldergrove, BC: n.p., 1971).
35. J.R. Miller, *Shinguak's Vision: A History of Native Residential Schools* (Toronto: University of Toronto, 1996), 153; and John Milloy, *A National Crime; The Canadian Government and the Residential School System 1879 to 1896* (Winnipeg: University of Manitoba Press, 1999), 40.
36. House of Commons, *Debates*, 46 Vict. (May 9, 1883) 14: 1107–1108.
37. Miller, *Shinguak's Vision*, 103.
38. Ibid., xiv.
39. Stewart Raby, "Indian Land Surrenders in Southern Saskatchewan," *Canadian Geographer* 17, no. 1 (Spring 1973.)
40. Norma Sluman and Jean Goodwill, *John Tootoosis* (Ottawa: Golden Dog, 1982), 134.
41. Fred Gaffen, *Forgotten Soldiers* (Penticton: Theytus Books, 1985), contains detailed accounts of individual Aboriginal veterans and their experiences.
42. Harry Hawthorne, *A Survey of Contemporary Indians of Canada: Economic, Political Educational Needs and Policies*, 2 vols. (Ottawa: Queen's Printer, 1966).
43. Laurie Barron, *Walking in Indian Mocassins* (Vancouver: UBC Press, 1997), 76–77.
44. Ibid., 134.
45. *Canada Act* (1982), Section 35, 1982.
46. Peggy Brizinski, *Knots in a String* (Saskatoon: University of Saskatchewan, 1993), 10.
47. Federation of Saskatchewan Indians, *Saskatchewan and the Aboriginal Peoples in the 21st Century* (Regina: Printwest, 1997).
48. First Nations and Northern Statistics, *Registered Indian Population by Sex and Residence 2003* (Ottawa: Indian and Northern Affairs Ottawa, 2003), xviii.
49. Sally Weaver, *Making Indian Policy: The Hidden Agenda 1968–70* (Toronto: University of Toronto Press, 1981), 171.
50. Rick Ponting and Roger Gibbins, *Out of Irrelevance* (Toronto: Butterworths, 1980), 198.
51. Meadow Lake Tribal Council, Tripartite Agreement in Principle, January 22, 2001.
52. Office of the Treaty Commissioner, *Treaties as a Bridge to the Future* (Saskatoon: Office of the Treaty Commissioner, 1998), 36.
53. Brizinski, *Knots in a String*, 11.
54. James Pitsula, "The Saskatchewan CCF Government and Treaty Indians," *Canadian Historical Review* 74, no. 1 (1994).
55. Federation of Saskatchewan Indians, *Indian Education in Saskatchewan*, Vol. 2 (Saskatoon: Saskatchewan Indian Cultural College, 1973), 149.
56. Barron, *Walking in Indian Mocassins*, 36.
57. Saskatchewan Education, *Reaching Out: The Report of the Indian and Métis Education Consultations*, Regina, 1985.
58. Maureen Lux, *Medicine that Walks: Disease. Medicine and Canadian Plains Native People 1880–1940* (Toronto: University of Toronto, 2001), 213.
59. Thomas Isaac, *Aboriginal Law* (Saskatoon: Purich Publishing, 1995), 271.
60. Peggy Martin-McGuire, *First Nations Surrenders on the Prairies 1896–1911* (Ottawa: Indian Claims Commission, 1998), 27.
61. www.fnmr.gov.sk.ca/html/documents/tle/TLEFA_Schedule1.pdf. Accessed January 20, 2005.
62. Robert Anderson, *Economic Development among the Aboriginal Peoples of Canada* (Toronto: Captus, 1999), 161.
63. Ibid., 174.
64. Saskatchewan Indian Gaming Authority, *Annual Report 2002–2003*, 3.
65. Commission on First Nations and Métis Peoples Justice Reform, *Legacy of Hope: An Agenda for Change* (Regina: n.p., 2004).
66. Laurie Barron and Joseph Garcea, *Urban Indian Reserves: Forging New Relationships in Saskatchewan* (Saskatoon: Purich Publishing, 1999).
67. Saskatchewan Government Relations and Aboriginal Affairs, "Demographic Data–Aboriginal Population in Saskatchewan" (2001).
68. Isaac, *Aboriginal Law*, 234.
69. *Report of the Commission of Inquiry into Matters Pertaining to the Death of Neil Stonechild* (Regina: Queen's Printer, 2004).
70. Commission on First Nations and Métis Peoples Justice Reform.
71. Campbell is author of the award-winning autobiography, *Half-Breed*.

ABORIGINAL RESERVE AGRICULTURE TO 1900.

An understanding of the history of agriculture in the province of Saskatchewan must begin with the vital contributions of First Nations. Aboriginal people of the western plains were the true "sod-busters"—the earliest and largest group to attempt agriculture west of the Red River Settlement, beginning in the 1870s. But the history of Aboriginal agriculture goes back much further than that: in Central and South America, Aboriginal agriculture preceded the arrival of white settlers by about three millennia. Aboriginal Americans excelled in the arts of plant domestication: nearly 300 food crops were cultivated, including corn, potatoes, sunflowers, tomatoes and squash, which were all introduced to Europe following contact. Aboriginal foods of the Americas constitute 60% of the world's crops now in cultivation.

There was pre-European contact agriculture even in the northerly stretches of the plains that became Canada. Agriculture was a far more ancient and indigenous tradition on the Great Plains than equestrian culture, which was only introduced after European contact. Groups such as the Mandan, Arikira and Hidatsa maintained a flourishing agricultural economy on the upper Missouri as far north as North Dakota. There is archaeological evidence that this village and agricultural complex extended into the Canadian plains: remains have been found near the present-day town of Lockport, Manitoba, which date to 400 years before the arrival of the Selkirk settlers, often heralded as the west's first farmers. The Blackfoot were found by the earliest of European explorers to be growing tobacco, likely in what became part of Saskatchewan; each spring an elaborate tobacco-planting ceremony was conducted, with which over 200 songs were associated.

Although at the time of European contact, beginning in the 17th century, the people of the plains of Saskatchewan were primarily mobile buffalo hunters, they had extensive contact with Aboriginal agricultural products through trade, particularly with the Mandan. They also "farmed" the prairies, collecting over 180 plant species used for foods, medicines, ceremonies, and construction materials. They had a profound knowledge of the resources and climate of the west, and were thus much better equipped than White settlers to expect the extreme variations, locusts, fire, drought and frosts that discouraged so many newcomers. Several of the Aboriginal groups who moved west, including the **SAULTEAUX** (Plains Ojibway), the **ASSINIBOINE** and the Dakota, had backgrounds in Aboriginal agriculture.

Well before the treaties of the 1870s Aboriginal people had begun to raise crops and cattle in Saskatchewan. In the 1830s and 1850s, a group of **CREE** known to fur traders as the Magpies cultivated corn and potatoes. In 1857 explorer John Palliser met Cree Church of England catechist **CHARLES PRATT** in the **QU'APPELLE VALLEY**, and noted that his house was surrounded by an excellent garden. Pratt and Hudson's Bay Company employees informed members of this expedition that the Cree were anxious to try agriculture and would begin operations if they had the proper equipment. Among the people who began to cultivate and raise cattle before the treaties we find the Pasquah, Little Bones, Yellow Quill, Cote, Key, Kishikonse, and Sakimay bands. In the treaties of the 1870s, Saskatchewan's Aboriginal negotiators requested that they be provided with the means to establish an economy based on agriculture, including tools, seed and animals. Clauses in the treaties as well as oral promises assured that the necessary assistance would be given to establish an alternative economy following the disappearance of the buffalo; but the implements and livestock promised in the treaties proved inadequate: ten families, for example, were to share one plough. Government officials were reluctant to distribute even what had been promised in the treaties. Aboriginal people were expected to begin farming *before* they could receive their implements, oxen and seed; yet it was impossible to begin cultivation until they had received the promised assistance.

The first Aboriginal farmers of the 1870s to early 1880s laboured under many disadvantages—some of which they shared with all other farmers, and others unique to their situation. The seed grain that was provided in the earliest years arrived damaged and too late for sowing. Aboriginal farmers of the 1870s were issued Ontario-made ploughs that were not suitable to prairie conditions. There were no blacksmiths to attend to broken metal parts of ploughs and other equipment. Implements, carts and oxen sent to many reserves were the cheapest that could be found, and were altogether unfit for use. Wild Montana cattle were sent to many reserves. Other disadvantages of these early agriculturalists included the fact that there were no grist mills located near the reserves.

By the late 1870s, as a result of the disappearance of the buffalo and a lack of progress of reserve agriculture, starvation loomed for the Aboriginal people of Saskatchewan. The 1879 government response was to send farm instructors from the east, who were to instruct in agriculture and raise quantities of food on "home farms" to feed the hungry. This was an ill-conceived and short-lived program. It soon proved that the instructors could not raise even enough to sustain themselves and their families, and they could not both do this and instruct. The program was shelved by the early 1880s, although farm instructors remained on southern Indian agencies.

The early 1880s brought a series of natural disasters to all who tried to farm in Saskatchewan: drought, frosts, and prairie fires. While non-Aboriginal farmers left in large numbers, Aboriginal reserve farmers were obliged to stay: they could not try their luck elsewhere as they were prohibited from taking up homesteads under the Indian Act. They had fewer privileges and rights than newly arrived farmers, as they could also not sell any of their grain or other produce without a permit, and after 1885 a pass system controlled and confined movements off the reserves. Aboriginal farmers could not take out loans and they had difficulty acquiring credit from local merchants.

Despite this series of setbacks, reserve farmers in some localities began to make headway in the later 1880s, increasing their acreages and herds, raising a surplus for sale, acquiring the necessary machinery (mowers and rakes, and self-binding reapers), and competing for local markets in grain and hay. This provoked loud complaints from non-Aboriginal farmers, who alleged that government assistance gave Aboriginal farmers an unfair advantage. Non-Aboriginal settlers had the misconception that reserve farmers were lavishly provided with livestock, equipment and rations, and did not have to worry about the price at which their products were sold. The solemn promises of assistance made to them in the treaties, in exchange for sharing the land that permitted the settlers to acquire their farms, were regarded as charity. As a result of this clamour, in 1889 the federal government imposed a "peasant" farming policy. Aboriginal farmers were to reduce their acreages dramatically and to grow root crops, not wheat. They were to use the most rudimentary implements: to broadcast seed by hand, harvest with scythes, bind by hand with straw, thresh with flails, and grind their grain with hand mills. They were to manufacture at home any items they required. Aboriginal farmers were profoundly discouraged by the new rules, and the Indian agents and instructors were dismayed by the policy that robbed reserve farmers of any potential source of revenue. By the mid-1890s per capita acreage under cultivation on the reserves had fallen to about half of the 1889 level, and many serious farmers had given up farming altogether. Although this policy was shelved after 1896, Aboriginal farmers gained little ground in the early 20th century, as large tracts of arable land were "surrendered" to non-Aboriginal interests.

Sarah Carter

FURTHER READING: Carter, S. 1990. *Lost Harvests: Aboriginal Reserve Farmers and Government Policy.* Montreal: McGill-Queen's University Press; Dyck, N. 1986. "An Opportunity Lost: The Initiative of the Reserve Agricultural Programme in the Prairie West." Pp. 121–38 in F.L. Barron and J.B. Waldram (eds.), *1885 and After: Native Society in Transition.* Regina: Canadian Plains Research Center, 1986.

ABORIGINAL SPIRITUAL HEALING LODGE.

In 1997, Saskatchewan's Minister of

Corrections and Public Safety and the Prince Albert Grand Council signed a Spiritual Healing Lodge Agreement for the purpose of fostering a justice system relevant to, respectful of, and respected by Aboriginal people. The provincial department currently maintains this contract with the Prince Albert Grand Council for the operation of a Spiritual Healing Lodge that houses up to twenty-five provincial male offenders. There is also an exchange of service agreement with the Correctional Service of Canada to house up to five federal male offenders. The Spiritual Healing Lodge is located just outside of the city of Prince Albert.

The Spiritual Healing Lodge offers a holistic program that is designed according to Aboriginal cultural traditions. It is for offenders who are nearing the end of their period of incarceration and are preparing to return to their communities; they are assessed as presenting a minimal risk to public safety and likely to benefit from such a correctional program while serving a custodial sentence. In order to qualify for transfer to the Healing Lodge, an offender must demonstrate satisfactory interest in spiritual healing and express a sincere effort to overcome the problems that have led to his current and past offences. He must also develop a healing plan and demonstrate the ability to follow the program and plan during his time at the Healing Lodge. Of particular interest is the central involvement of Elders, who provide most of the traditional teaching, as well as the general Aboriginal community in the rehabilitation and reintegration of Aboriginal offenders. In addition, offenders are invited to take part in larger cultural events within the community and surrounding reservations. The Healing Lodge is staffed primarily by persons of Aboriginal descent.

Regan Hart-Mitchell

ABORIGINAL THEATRE. Andrea Menard's *The Velvet Devil* speaks to the involvement of Aboriginal peoples in the performing arts since the 1930s. Velvet, a **MÉTIS** singer who leaves her home at Batoche for the bright lights of Toronto, is not exactly a work of fiction: in the 1930s several Aboriginal women from Saskatchewan performed in small halls, on reserves, and in Métis communities across the prairies. Inspired by Pauline Johnson, they traveled with a trunk of costumes singing songs, dancing and doing dramatic recitals of Johnson's work. It is said that one show involved a woman playing the fiddle and another performing with a bullwhip; the latter would call for a male volunteer from the audience, stick a cigar in his mouth, and flick it away with her whip. Live performances came to a halt during the war years, but re-emerged later when Saskatchewan Aboriginal artists re-enacted plays such as Shakespeare's *Romeo and Juliet* (one of the few plays available in Aboriginal communities). **MARIA CAMPBELL** tells of rewriting this play,

changing the houses of Montague and Capulet to those of the **DENE** and **CREE**; performances took place outdoors in front of a log cabin, with the audience seated on benches.

JIM BRADY traveled around northern Saskatchewan, visiting families and communities; he would do dramatic readings of a scene, a chapter or a poem, usually accompanied by fiddle-playing and singing. The readings would continue over several days; when Brady left, the community would visit and share their understanding of the chapters, poems or scenes. Brady's stories were highly political, and motivated the communities to become politically involved. **HARRY W. DANIELS** was one of Saskatchewan's first Aboriginal actors; having studied under Dora Mava Moore in Toronto, he came home to Saskatchewan, did local acting in Regina, and went on to play the first Louis Riel in the *Trial of Louis Riel*. This play has been staged annually in Regina since 1967, making it Canada's second-longest continuously running stage production after *Anne of Green Gables*.

In 1967, George Rega's *The Ecstacy of Rita Joe* toured the prairies, featuring Margo Kane and Chief Dan George. As both performers were Aboriginal and it was an Aboriginal story, this was an inspiration for many Aboriginal artists who wanted to perform and write culturally relevant stories. Jim Buller, an Aboriginal artist from Saskatchewan, began his career in local high school productions and in the early 1970s went on to Toronto, where he founded the Association for Native Development in the Performing and Visual Arts (NDPVA) and later the Native Theatre School, now known as the Centre for Indigenous Theatre.

In the 1970s well-known performers began to emerge, including Joseph Charles of La Ronge and **GORDON TOOTOOSIS** of Poundmaker First Nation, who began working in mainstream theatres and film companies. In 1976, Upsasik Theatre was founded by the Rossignol High School in Ile-à-la-Crosse. This community-based theatre group produced well-known artists Maureen Belanger and Duane Favel, who are two of the founding members of the Batoche Theatre Company. In 1980 the Native Survival School in Saskatoon (currently known as Joe Duquette High School) formed the Saskatoon Native Theatre Company, which produced community theatre utilizing renowned artists Maria Campbell, Tantoo Cardinal and Floyd Favel. Favel pursued his studies at the Native Theatre School in Ontario, the Tukak Teatret in Denmark, the Suziki Company of Togi in Japan, and the Italian Theatre Centre of Grotowski. He returned to Saskatchewan and founded the Red Tattoo Theatre, and more recently the Takwakin A Performance Laboratory.

Other well-known Saskatchewan Aboriginal artists include **BERNELDA WHEELER**, Carol Greyeyes, Michael Greyeyes, Erroll Kinistino, Kennetch

Charlette, **BUFFY SAINTE-MARIE**, Winston Wuttanee, Yvette Nolan, Ken Williams, Joe Welsh, Mark Dieter, Peggy Vermette, Greg Daniels and many more. Donna Heimbecker and Kennetch Charlette founded in 1999 the Saskatchewan Native Theatre Company (SNTC), whose directors include cultural figures such as Tantoo Cardinal and Gordon Tootoosis. SNTC produces a unique blend of community and professional arts programming, with shows and events that offer mentoring, skill development training, workshops, and career opportunities. SNTC productions include: *Thunderstick*, by Kenneth Williams; *Wawatay*, by Penny Gummerson; Andrea Menard's *The Velvet Devil*; and *400 Kilometers*, by Drew Hayden Taylor. The Saskatchewan Native Theatre Company is the first Aboriginal theatre in Canada to have a 110-seat theatre facility, located in Saskatoon.

Donna Heimbecker

ABORIGINAL TREATY RIGHTS. Who has Treaty Rights? It is important to remember that all Saskatchewan residents, whether Aboriginal or non-Aboriginal, benefit directly or indirectly from the treaty relationships between First Nations and the Crown. Euro-Canadians and other immigrants, who today are the majority of the provincial population, benefit because it was through treaties that they acquired the right to settle here. These settlement rights for non-Aboriginals were granted in exchange for certain specific treaty rights to First Nations. As a result, it is generally assumed that "Treaty Rights" refers only to those held by First Nations because Canada's two other constitutionally recognized Aboriginal groups, the Métis and Inuit, were not treaty signatories here in Saskatchewan.

Several First Nations lived in what is now Saskatchewan when the Numbered Treaties were signed. The largest of these were the **CREE**, **ASSINIBOINE**, and **SAULTEAUX** in the south, and the Dene to the north. **NAKOTA** and Dakota as well as other Nations lived on the Plains region that includes the present-day northern states of North Dakota and Montana as well as the three prairie provinces of Manitoba, Saskatchewan and Alberta. The Canadian government sought to populate the area in order to prevent an incursion by the United States, which was rapidly expanding into the interior of North America. Its dilemma was that this area was already populated by tens of thousands of people who were wary of uninvited incursions into their territory. Rather than follow the United States' military western expansion against Indigenous peoples to the south, Canada relied on Treaties to open up its western territories.

After much negotiation, Canada successfully entered into Treaties with the First Nations to open the North-West Territories for Euro-Canadian agricultural settlement. Although small portions of present-day Saskatchewan include lands from Treaty 2

(1871) and Treaty 7 (1877), the five major historical or numbered treaties of this province are **TREATY 4** (1874), **TREATY 5** (1875–76), **TREATY 6** (1876), **TREATY 8** (1899–1900), and **TREATY 10** (1906–07) (*see* Figure ATR-1). These five Treaties are of enormous significance to the First Nations people of Saskatchewan, and are frequently referred to as sacred and solemn agreements that cannot be altered or broken without the mutual consent of all parties.

There is a distinction between Aboriginal and Treaty rights. Aboriginal rights are those that stem from people's prior occupation of the land and are considered to be inherent. Treaty rights, on the other hand, flow from the agreements made between the First Nations of Saskatchewan and the Crown. Treaty rights that were secured in all parts of what is now Saskatchewan include: the ability to maintain a traditional lifestyle through hunting, fishing, and gathering; medals and annuities; clothing for headmen and chiefs; building and staffing of schools; and agricultural supplies. Certain treaties contained specific promises that were not included in other agreements. For example, Treaty 6 and Treaty 8 included two provisions for a "medicine chest" as well as aid in case of famine, although only Treaty 6 had them included in the written text. This

"medicine chest" provision would later be interpreted by the courts to mean free healthcare. Unfortunately for Treaty First Nations, many of these promises were never carried or were arbitrarily altered by the federal government. One example is how the treaty promises of "schools" for First Nations children became the ethnocidal residential school policy. Treaty Land Entitlement and Specific Claims have sought to correct some of the historical injustices caused by Canada's failure to live up to its treaty promises. Today, all Treaty rights are protected legislatively in section 88 of the Indian Act and constitutionally in section 35 of the Constitution Act, 1982.

Unfortunately, the Treaties are ambiguous as to rights that are not specifically listed in the Treaty documents. For example, the right to self-government is one upon which the federal government has repeatedly attempted to legislate. First Nations have argued that the federal government has no such authority because the right to self-government was never surrendered during the Treaty negotiations. Another example of controversy has been whether First Nations have a Treaty right to economic development through gaming. This dispute has been managed with some success by the province and

Saskatchewan First Nations through the creation of the **SASKATCHEWAN INDIAN GAMING AUTHORITY** (SIGA). As a result, gaming has been a major source of economic development in the province for First Nations.

Today, the **OFFICE OF THE TREATY COMMISSIONER** plays an important role in the interpretation and implementation of the Treaties' terms. There has been a growing consensus that the treaties are complex documents that represent a commitment to developing a relationship. Therefore, reading treaties as contractual agreements involving what would effectively be real estate transactions would represent an incomplete understanding. Canadian courts have ordered that oral history must be taken into account because promises were frequently made by Canadian negotiators that were not subsequently included in the written treaty. Examples include promises of no taxation and no compulsory military service (Treaty 8), as well as of farming instruction (Treaty 4).

The Treaties are crucial to understanding the relationships between Indigenous peoples, Saskatchewan, and Canada. For the First Nations of this province, the Treaties did not signify cession or surrender to Canadian authority but rather the establishment of a nation-to-nation relationship. Indeed, many First Nations are uncomfortable with tripartite negotiations between the provincial, federal and First Nations governments because this is seen as a derogation of the bilateralism that was established when the treaties were agreed upon.

Brock Pitawanakwat

ABORIGINAL VETERANS. Approximately 1,000 Saskatchewan Aboriginal people enlisted in **WORLD WAR II**. Reasons for enlisting in the war service vary but included financial circumstances, patriotism, the lure of adventure, and the influence of friends and family.

Although the returning Aboriginal veterans had learned military skills, these skills were not transferable to civilian employment. Many veterans returned to the same semi-skilled and unskilled jobs they had had prior to the war and to the same living conditions. Some communities welcomed their veterans back with celebrations; other communities did little. Status Indian veterans were denied equal access to veterans' benefits. Other veterans who obtained benefits experienced animosity from some community members who felt veterans received special treatment. For a number of reasons, many veterans left their home communities. Some found life at home slow and uneventful and saw better opportunities elsewhere.

In the immediate post-war period Aboriginal veterans, as a group, were not actively involved in the political fight for Indian rights, but their presence represented a symbol of the "progressive

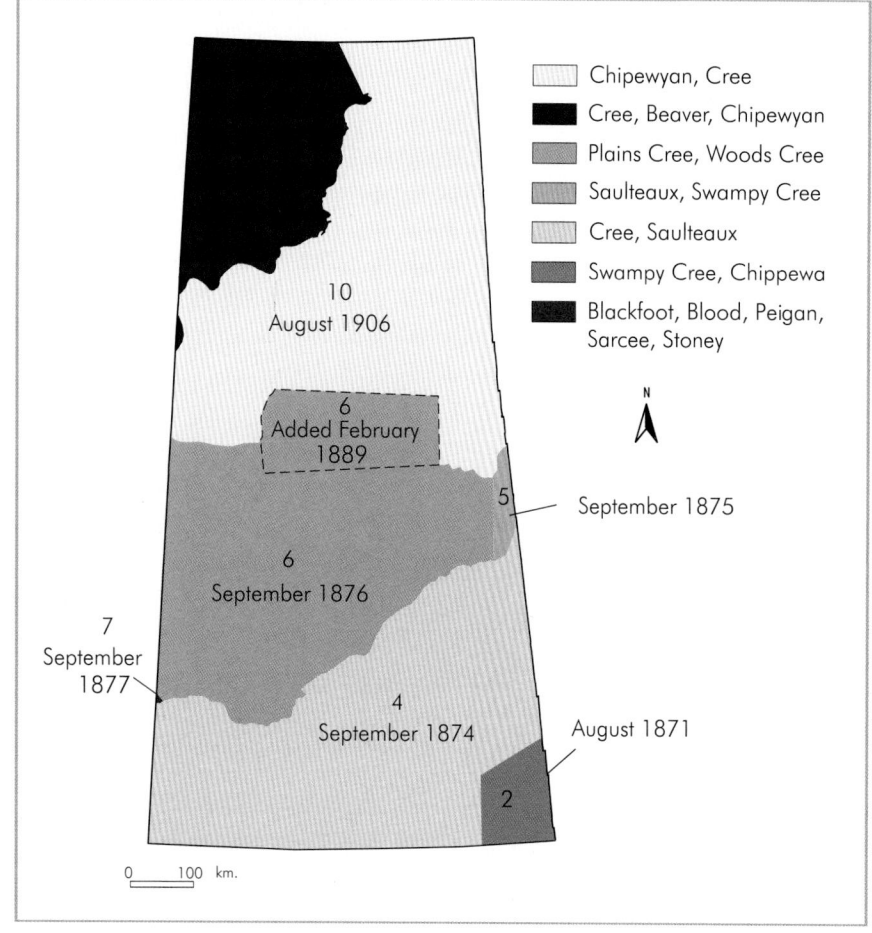

Legend:
- Chipewyan, Cree
- Cree, Beaver, Chipewyan
- Plains Cree, Woods Cree
- Saulteaux, Swampy Cree
- Cree, Saulteaux
- Swampy Cree, Chippewa
- Blackfoot, Blood, Peigan, Sarcee, Stoney

10
August 1906

6
Added February 1889

5
September 1875

6
September 1876

7
September 1877

4
September 1874

August 1871

2

0   100 km.

CANADIAN PLAINS RESEARCH CENTER MAPPING DIVISION

Figure ATR-1. First Nations historical treaties.

Indian" towards which the Canadian public was sympathetic. The veterans were, for the most part, politically inexperienced young men attempting to readjust to civilian life. As they matured, however, they assumed greater responsibilities for themselves, their families and their communities. At the beginning of the 1950s, veterans were generally still unsettled, but by the end of the decade, many were in positions of influence. The more socially and economically mobile they were, the more socially and politically active they became. All the Chiefs of the Federation of Saskatchewan Indians during the 1960s, for example, were veterans. Veterans played significant roles in the emerging urban organizations, such as the Regina Friendship Centre. Today, Saskatchewan Aboriginal veterans' sacrifice and service in the armed forces are a source of pride to the Aboriginal community in Saskatchewan.

Robert Innes

FURTHER READING: Robert Alexander Innes. 2000. "The Socio-Political Influence of the Second World War Saskatchewan Aboriginal Veterans, 1945–1960." Masters Thesis, University of Saskatchewan.

ABORIGINAL WRITERS. Saskatchewan is home to many acclaimed writers who draw on their Aboriginal cultures, languages, and histories to create their poems and plays. Hailing from Ile-à-la-Crosse, Rita Bouvier is a **MÉTIS** poet and educator whose work is connected to the land and people of the north. In her collections, *Blueberry Clouds* (1999) and *Papîyâhtak* (2004), Bouvier blends Cree and Michif languages with English to write about her life and family. **BETH CUTHAND** of the Little Pine First Nation studied poetry with Patrick Lane at the **UNIVERSITY OF SASKATCHEWAN** and was later at the University of New Mexico, where she earned an MFA in Creative Writing. Her collections *Horse Dance to Emerald Mountain* (1987) and *Voices in the Waterfall* (1992 and 1999) explore the historical and contemporary realities of Aboriginal people. Cuthand has also written a children's book, *Little Duck = Sikihpisis* (1999), in **CREE** and English with her father Stan Cuthand as translator and **MARY LONGMAN** as illustrator. A long-time resident of Saskatoon, **LOUISE HALFE** originally hails from the Saddle Lake Cree Nation in Alberta. Halfe's experiences at residential school shape her life and her poetry, and motivated her to earn a BSW from the **UNIVERSITY OF REGINA** as well as certificates in addictions and counselling from the Nechi Institute in Edmonton. Her first collection of poetry, *Bear bones & feathers* (1994), focuses on trauma and healing while her second, *Blue Marrow* (1998), gives voice to the nameless Aboriginal women whose work sustained the fur trade. Also a long-time resident of Saskatchewan, Randy Lundy was born in northern Manitoba and is a member of the Barren Lands

band; he received a BA and MA in English from the University of Saskatchewan. In his first collection of poetry, *Under the Night Sun* (1999), Lundy writes about love, loss, and longing, and then goes on an exploration of the natural world in his second collection, *Gift of the Hawk*. A member of the James Smith First Nation, Neal McLeod performs his poetry across the country in a style that combines beatnik and rap. Having edited *Coyote, Trickster and Other Stories My Family Never Told Me: An Anthology of Aboriginal Writing* in 2000, McLeod will release his own collection of poetry, *Songs to Kill a Wîhtikow*, in 2005.

Greg Daniels is a Cree Métis playwright from Regina and a member of Gordons First Nation who made his theatrical debut in 1990 with his play *3rd House from the Corner*, which he co-wrote with Eugene Stickland. After publishing *Blind Girl, Last Night* (1991) and *Percy's Edge* in *DraMétis: Three Métis Plays* (2001), Daniels is turning his attention to poetry and a collection is forthcoming. Floyd Favel Starr is a playwright, actor, and director from the Poundmaker First Nation. A fluent speaker of Cree, Favel Starr studied at the Native Theatre School in Ontario, the Tuak Teatret in Denmark, and the Ricerca Theatre in Italy. His plays include *House of Sonya* (1998), *Lady of Silences* (1998), *Governor of the Dew* (1999), and *The Sleeping Land* (2004).

Jo-Ann Episkenew

ABRAHAMSON, CAL (1930–). Calvin David Abrahamson attended Teachers' College in Moose Jaw, the University of Saskatchewan, and the Banff School of Fine Arts. He received the Canadian Drama Award in 1955, Saskatchewan Drama Festival Awards in 1956, 1960 and 1967, and many awards for community service, including the 125 Anniversary Medal "for service to compatriots, community, province and Canada." A member of the

SASKATCHEWAN ARCHIVES BOARD 71-991-50
Cal Abrahamson.

Order of Canada since 1989 in recognition of his work as executive director of Saskatchewan Community Theatre and former administrator of the Calgary Zoo, Botanical Gardens and Prehistoric Park, Abrahamson became an officer of the Order in 2002. Retiring from teaching, administration and business in 1995, Cal and his wife, Yvonne, formed the Montmartre Arts Council and Hurricane Hills Players. In 1998, he formed the "Circle of the Drum Players" at the Carry the Kettle Reserve. He wrote, directed and produced four plays based on social problems encountered on the reserve. One play was invited to a world conference in San Diego and to a North American Indian Youth Conference in New Mexico. Abrahamson was inducted into the Margaret Woodward Hall of Fame in 2002 for his contribution to theatre in Saskatchewan.

Lyn Goldman

ACCUTRAK. Accutrak successfully demonstrated in 1985 a pre-programmed, auto-steering system that allowed a tractor to pull a 30-foot cultivator over a field without a human driver. The historic test by the Regina-based company was captured on film by CBC television and broadcast nationally on

PHOTO COURTESY OF ACCUTRAK SYSTEMS LTD.
Swather.

the popular agriculture show called *Country Canada*. Since the test in a field near Southey, about 45 km north of Regina, Accutrak has continued to refine its proprietary auto-steering product with a pair of industry giants–John Deere and Caterpillar Tractor.

Steered by Ron Palmer, its founder and president, Accutrak pioneered development of the auto-steering navigational products by applying Global Positioning System (GPS) technology to farming practices. Utilizing clusters of satellites orbiting the globe around the equator, GPS can help farmers pinpoint a position in their field to within one metre. Accutrak's auto-steering products improved upon the GPS guidance systems employed in the industry by taking on the task of ensuring tractors steered along parallel lines. The operator is left only with the task of turning at the end of each field or steering around obstacles; as a result, savings of 10% or more each year amount to millions more dollars in farmers' pockets.

Joe Ralko

ACOOSE, PAUL (1885–1978).

A world-renowned long-distance runner, Acoose was born in the QU'APPELLE VALLEY "around the time when the Saskatoons bloom in the year the Half Breeds fought the government (1885)." A distinguished member of the Saulteaux First Nation, Acoose was born into a prominent family known for their prowess as runners. According to one legend, Old Acoose was out hunting in the Moose Mountain area when he sighted a number of elk. Restricted by the federal government's rations policy, he was without weapon or bullets and so chased the elk towards the Indian Agency at Crooked Lake, a distance of about 60 miles, where he was certain he could obtain a gun and ammunition. Acoose killed nine of the elk, and the people of his community were able to eat well for some time.

Paul became a professional runner in 1909, his debut marked by a victory over the famed English runner Fred Appleby. During this first race as a professional, Acoose defeated Appleby in a 15-mile race which elevated Acoose's stature to world champion because he finished it in a record time of 1:22:22. In a rematch a week later, a gambling enthusiast threw thumbtacks on the race track; and although Acoose completed the race with thumbtacks piercing his feet, he finished second. Not to be deterred by his second-place finish, he went on to run against some of the top runners in the world at Madison Square Gardens in New York City, where he placed a respectable second.

Although he ran many professional races, one of his proudest victories as a runner was when he competed against the celebrated Onondaga runner Tom Longboat. Acoose had waited a long time for a chance to run against Longboat, whom he regarded as a superb athlete and his only match. The race

SASKATCHEWAN ARCHIVES BOARD R-A14889
Paul Acoose.

was finally scheduled for March 30, 1910, and was billed as the "Red Skin Running Championship of the World." After defeating Longboat, Acoose retired from running, returning to his Sakimay Reserve home, which he shared with his wife Madeleine (O'Soup) Acoose. Together they raised nine children, supporting them though farming and gardening. Paul Acoose died in 1978.

Janice Acoose

ADAMS, HOWARD (1921–2001).

Born into poverty, Howard Adams became one of the most highly educated, outspoken, and controversial Aboriginal leaders of his time. As an educator, political leader, and writer he raised the political consciousness of Aboriginal people concerning their position in capitalist society. The single-minded purpose of his work was the struggle against the colonization of Aboriginal people in Canada and throughout the world. He was born on September 8, 1921, at St. Louis, Saskatchewan. His mother was French-**CREE** and his father English-Cree; his great-grandfather was the famed Maxime Lépine, who fought with **LOUIS RIEL** and **GABRIEL DUMONT** against the Canadian troops in the **NORTH-WEST RESISTANCE** of 1885. Growing up in St. Louis, Adams witnessed numerous acts of racism against First Nations and **MÉTIS** people, which left a lasting impression and instilled in him a passion to fight for the betterment of his people. In 1940, he completed high school and joined the **ROYAL CANADIAN MOUNTED POLICE** as a constable, a position he held until 1944. Between 1944 and 1955, he worked as a school liaison counselor for the Vancouver School Board, during which time he attended the University of British Columbia and completed a Bachelor of Arts degree in Sociology. Adams then attended the University of Toronto and received a teaching diploma in 1957. From 1957 until 1962, he taught high school at Coquitlam,

PATRICK PETTIT/REGINA LEADER-POST
Howard Adams, October 1984.

British Columbia. In 1962, he enrolled at the University of California, Berkeley and completed a doctorate in 1966 in the History of Education, thereby becoming the first Canadian Métis to acquire a PhD. In the same year, Adams returned to Saskatchewan and took up a position in the College of Education, **UNIVERSITY OF SASKATCHEWAN**. In 1975 Adams returned to the University of California, where he held a position as professor of Native American Studies until he retired in 1987. In the following year, Adams and his wife Marge moved to Vancouver, from which he returned to the University of Saskatchewan during the spring and summer to teach courses in the Department of Native Studies.

The time Adams spent at the University of California during the 1960s had a huge impact on his intellectual and political development. After listening to Malcolm X speak on the Berkeley campus, he began to draw parallels between the Métis in Canada and the Blacks in the United States: he began to view the Métis as an internally colonized group and to understand that their struggle was very similar to the struggle of Black Americans and Africans against colonization. When Adams returned to Canada in the mid-1960s, there was a growing cultural and political awakening among Aboriginal people, and Adams immersed himself in Métis politics. Before long, he became one of the most prominent leaders of First Nations and Métis people in the province and on a national level. In 1969, he was elected president of the Métis Society of Saskatchewan, a position he held until 1970. As a political leader, Adams was a master at using protests and the media to draw public attention to the struggles of Aboriginal people. He was also a gifted orator prone to espouse militant leftist views, which earned him the label of one of the most aggressive and controversial Aboriginal leaders of the time. Above all, however, Adams' political leadership during the late 1960s and early 1970s served to reinvigorate Métis pride and identity, and thereby to fan the flames of Métis nationalism that had been dormant since the post-1885 Resistance period.

Adams published his first book, *The Education of Canadians 1800–1867: The Roots of Separatism*, in 1968. Another book, *Prison of Grass: Canada from the Native Point of View*, published in 1975, thrust him into the national and international limelight. Seen as groundbreaking because it was written by a Métis scholar and from a Marxist perspective, the premise of the book was that the deplorable conditions of Indian and Métis people in Canada were the product of three centuries of colonization; Adams condemned the Canadian government's assimilationist policies towards Aboriginal people, while he also lambasted the supremacist ideology of mainstream society. In 1995, he published *Tortured People: The Politics of Colonization*, unleashing a scathing attack on the effects that racism, Euro-centrism, and neo-colonialism have had on Aboriginal people. In particular, Adams was deeply disturbed by the effects that government funding had on Aboriginal leaders—many of whom he characterized as neo-colonial collaborators and self-interested opportunists. Adams' aggressive political leadership style during the late 1960s and early 1970s symbolized the Aboriginal struggle for decolonization and self-determination. In 1999 the contributions Adams made to Aboriginal people in Canada were acknowledged when he was presented with the National Aboriginal Achievement Award. He died on September 8, 2001, in Vancouver.

Ron Laliberté

ADAMS, NANCY (1908–1998). An advocate for issues affecting rural women, Nancy Adams was born in Yorkshire, England on May 3, 1908. She immigrated to Canada with her parents at an early age, settling first in Calgary and then Saskatchewan in 1920. She received her teacher's training at Regina Normal School and a Bachelor of Arts degree from the UNIVERSITY OF SASKATCHEWAN in 1931. Adams' dedication to several women's organizations included serving as president of the Federated Women's Institute of Canada and the Associated Country Women of the World. She was also the first woman appointed to the University of Saskatchewan Board of Governors, and was awarded an honourary Doctor of Laws from the University in 1958. A recipient of the Queen's Silver Jubilee and Canada 125 medals, Nancy Adams was made a Member of the Order of Canada in 1975. She passed away on March 17, 1998.

ADASKIN, MURRAY (1906–2002). Composer, teacher, violinist, and conductor Murray Adaskin spent over twenty years in Saskatchewan and was among the first Canadians to contribute to the growth of significant musical culture outside of Toronto and Montreal. He was born into an artistic family in Toronto on March 28, 1906; two brothers, Harry and John, were musicians and another, Gordon, was a painter. He studied violin with Harry, and then with Luigi von Kunits (Toronto), Kathleen Parlow (New York), and Marcel Chailley (Paris). Initially active as an orchestral and chamber musician in Toronto (1923–36 with the Toronto Symphony Orchestra, and 1938–52 as a member of the Royal York Hotel Trio), by the mid-1940s Adaskin found his central interest shifting from performance to composition. To this end, he began

studies with John Weinzweig, Darius Milhaud, and Charles Jones.

In 1952, the Dean of Arts and Sciences at the UNIVERSITY OF SASKATCHEWAN, J. Francis Leddy, recruited Adaskin to head a restructured Department of Music. Since the university did not offer a degree in music until 1967, his courses in composition and music appreciation were developed for non-music majors. In 1966, Adaskin left the chair of the Department of Music to become composer-in-residence, the first such position in Canada. As head, Adaskin played a pivotal role in arranging for the purchase by the university of a quartet of 17th-century Amati stringed instruments from Saskatchewan wheat farmer and amateur musician Steven Kolbinson. His orchestral piece *Saskatchewan Legend*, is dedicated to Dr. W.P. Thompson, President of the University of Saskatchewan from 1949 to 1959, and his wife. During his time at the university and afterwards, Adaskin adjudicated at music festivals throughout western Canada.

Adaskin and his wife, soprano Frances James, were very involved in the Saskatoon musical and artistic communities. He conducted the SASKATOON SYMPHONY ORCHESTRA from 1957 to 1960, and initiated the practice of commissioning a new Canadian work annually. The first commission, in 1958, was given to Saskatchewan composer ROBERT FLEMING. Adaskin was responsible for bringing a number of distinguished visitors to Saskatchewan, including Benjamin Britten and Peter Pears. In 1959, he organized a six-week GOLDEN JUBILEE Music Festival to mark the fiftieth anniversary of the opening of the University of Saskatchewan. For Canada's centennial, he mounted six Exhibition Concerts, each devoted to a single Canadian composer.

After his retirement in 1973, Adaskin and his wife moved to Victoria, BC, where he was equally involved in the cultural life of the community. Although his free summers as a university professor

GORDON SISSON/UNIVERSITY OF SASKATCHEWAN ARCHIVES
A-4099

Murray Adaskin.

had allowed him time annually to compose, retirement was especially conducive to his creative muse, and over half of his total compositional output of 131 pieces was written after leaving Saskatchewan. Adaskin wrote works for band, chamber ensembles, one or two instruments, and voice. He composed an opera (*Grant, Warden of the Plains*, 1967), orchestral works, concertos for solo instruments and orchestra, numerous divertimenti and fanfares, and many educational works for beginning, intermediate, and advanced students. In addition to the many works that received their first performances in Saskatchewan, provincial organizations provided Adaskin with many commissions, including: *Saskatchewan Legend* (University of Saskatchewan Golden Jubilee Committee, 1959); *Divertimento No. 3 for Violin, Horn in F, and Bassoon* (University of Saskatchewan, Regina Campus, 1965); *Divertimento No. 4 for Trumpet and Orchestra* (Saskatoon Symphony Orchestra, 1970); *Fanfare for Orchestra* (official opening of the Saskatchewan Centre of the Arts, 1970); *Divertimento No. 8 for Concert Band* (Saskatchewan Music Educators' Association, 1986); and the *String Quartet No. 2* (University of Saskatchewan, 1994). Adaskin's musical style is characterised by the manipulation of small rhythmic cells, clear but dissonant contrapuntal textures, and a lyrical, long melodic line that is expressive but never sentimental. The influence of mid-century neo-classicism is clearly discernible. Folk material makes an appearance in works such as *Saskatchewan Legend* and the *Algonquin Symphony*. Overall, his music tends to be optimistic and upbeat, a trait that many commentators link to his personality.

Adaskin was a founder of the Canadian League of Composers, an associate of the Canadian Music Centre, and a member of the Canada Council between 1966 and 1969. He was named an Officer of the Order of Canada in 1980, and received the Lifetime Achievement Award for Excellence in the Arts from the SASKATCHEWAN ARTS BOARD in 1991. He was awarded honorary degrees from the universities of Lethbridge, Brandon, Windsor, Saskatchewan, Victoria, and Brock. For his 75th birthday, the University of Saskatchewan mounted an Adaskin Celebration in 1982. Six years later, the University of Victoria arranged a series of concerts of Adaskin's music, a conference on the arts in Canada, and an exhibition of the Adaskins' collection of Canadian painting—collectively entitled *The Adaskin Years: A Celebration of Canada's Arts*.

The libraries of both the UNIVERSITY OF REGINA and the University of Saskatchewan have complete collections of his musical scores; in addition, the latter holds several autograph manuscripts of early works. The National Library of Canada is the major repository of Adaskin's manuscripts and papers. Adaskin died on May 6, 2002. *Stephen McClatchie*

FURTHER READING: Lazarevich, G. and R. Cathcart. 2003. *Murray Adaskin: An Annotated Catalogue of His Music–A Unison of Life, Music and the Man.* Victoria, BC: Dolce.

ADOPTION ACT, 1998: *see* LEGISLATION IN SASKATCHEWAN

ADULT BASIC EDUCATION. Adult Basic Education (ABE) is an umbrella term that refers to a wide range of credit and non-credit programs. These include adult upgrading, literacy development, GED 12 Preparation, Life Skills, and English as a Second Language. For many adults, ABE programs provide them with a "second chance" to improve their education and get a credential. ABE, or BE as it is referred to in Saskatchewan in 2004, developed in Canada in the 1960s as part of the federal government's national manpower policy and efforts to promote technical/vocational training. Before that, the only way for undereducated adults to improve their education was by completing high school subjects offered by school boards to adults during evening hours (or at summer school, paying tuition and writing departmental exams).

In 1960, the Vocational Training Assistance Act greatly expanded vocational training programs in apprenticeship and trades/technical training in Canada. However, a number of candidates for training had not completed Grade 10. In 1967, the federal government passed the Adult Occupational Training Act, which funded ABE training programs and provided training allowances for adult learners. This enabled the provincial government to develop ABE programs such as BTSD (Basic Training for Skill Development), which provided upgrading for Grades 1 to 12 for adults, and Basic Job Readiness Training (BJRT) in 1973, which emphasized job search techniques and work experience, including life skills. These programs were precursors to pro-

grams like the ABE Grade 10, which served as a prerequisite to entering technical training. Adult Grades 11 and 12 courses were developed as entrance requirements for technical/vocational programs.

In the 1960s, the federal government also introduced the "Canada Newstart Program," whose original purpose was "to develop through action-research and experimentation, new methods for motivating and training adults, particularly those who are disadvantaged as to their education." Its overall aim was to facilitate uniform delivery of federally funded ABE programs across Canada. Of six Newstart Corporations set up in Canada, one was located in Prince Albert, Saskatchewan. Through Newstart, new approaches and program models were introduced; of these, only one program, Life Skills, continued in Saskatchewan's delivery system.

Between the 1960s and the mid-1970s, ABE programs in Saskatchewan were delivered by technical institutes, vocational centres, and directly by the provincial Department of Education. While the federal government provided the majority of funding for ABE, some funding was provided by the province under the Non-Registered Indian Métis (NRIM) program. With the establishment of community colleges in 1972, ABE came under their mandate, and later under regional colleges and SIAST. Many school boards, which until that time had offered adult education programs although that responsibility was not specified in the Education Act, discontinued adult programming because they ceased to have access to per-hour grants. Two institutions with specific mandates for Saskatchewan's Aboriginal population, the **DUMONT TECHNICAL INSTITUTE** (for Métis) and the **SASKATCHEWAN INDIAN INSTITUTE OF TECHNOLOGIES** (for First Nations), also offered ABE programs.

Dwindling funding as a result of shifting federal government policy in 1977 created new pressures for the province to find funding for the delivery of

ABE. One longstanding issue that the Department of Education did not address was "core funding for ABE," a matter that took many years to resolve because of complex federal-provincial cost-shared arrangements for post-secondary education. However, introduction of a new provincial initiative in 1984–the Saskatchewan Skills Development Program (SSDP), linked to welfare reform–increased the capacity for community colleges and technical institutes to provide ABE programs to recipients on social assistance.

Changes to ABE were implemented in 1997 under the *Saskatchewan Training Strategy*, which introduced a new approach to the funding, organization and delivery of literacy and basic education programs. The strategy also provided an opportunity to consolidate a number of ABE funding programs (NSIM, SSDP, Northern Training Program [NTP], and non-sponsored programs) under one fund, the Basic Education Consolidation Fund. Annual funding was provided to public training institutions and community-based organizations to deliver an array of tuition-free adult education programs. In addition, adult learners eligible for income support had access annually to provincial training allowances through a provincial fund. Changes over the next five years, beginning in 2000, included redesign of the Basic Education 10 curriculum, a review of the Adult 12 program, and development of a Provincial Literacy Strategy.

By 2004, the demand for BE had steadily increased and the evolution of non-university, post-secondary educational institutions has resulted in a diversified program delivery for Basic Education that includes credit and non-credit as well as formal and non-formal learning opportunities for about 10,000 adult learners annually. (*See* **COMMUNITY AND REGIONAL COLLEGES**) *Donna Woloshyn*

FURTHER READING: Hindle, J. 1990. *Literacy Learning in Saskatchewan: A Review of Adult Literacy Programs (1989)*. Regina: SIDRU, University of Regina; Thomas, A. 1983. *Adult Illiteracy in Canada–A Challenge*. Ottawa: Canadian Commission for UNESCO, Occasional Paper 42.

ADULT EDUCATION IN NORTHERN SASKATCHEWAN. Adult education has played a significant role in the economic, political and social developments that have shaped northern Saskatchewan. During the first half of the 20th century, few northern residents had access to formal education opportunities in their own communities. The north was cut off from southern services until roads opened it up in the 1940s. By the 1950s the northern population consisted of approximately 15,000 people of **CREE**, **DENE**, and **MÉTIS** ancestry. For many years, Anglican and Catholic missions were the only organizations to provide schooling in

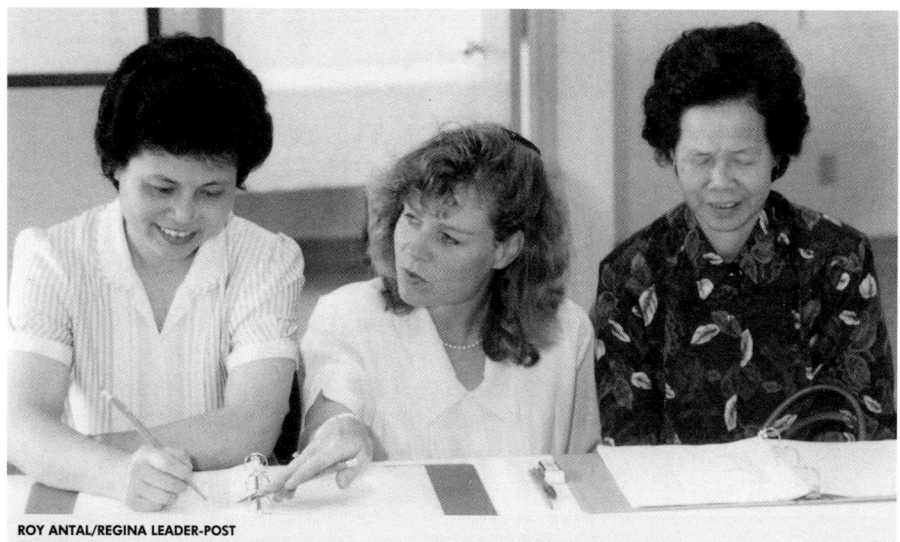

ROY ANTAL/REGINA LEADER-POST

Instructor Debra Maione (centre) helps Gail Chong (left) and Vien Trinh improve their literacy skills, August 1991.

northern communities. After **WORLD WAR II**, changing world conditions and provincial government interest in important resources (forestry, uranium and gold) found in northern Saskatchewan led to economic initiatives that brought services to the region (also referred to as the "Northern Administrative District" or NAD) in the 1950s and 1960s. With these developments came a realization that education was fundamental to the development of the north, and that an integrated approach was required to reduce socio-economic disparities between the northern and southern parts of the province.

Formal organization of adult and continuing education opportunities for northerners can be divided into three stages: pre-college (1968–72); college establishment and development (1973–86); and college amalgamation and future plans (1987 to present). The pre-college stage laid a foundation to help northerners make transitions in their lifestyles and livelihoods. Administered by the Department of Continuing Education in Regina, programming in the north focused on adult upgrading and domestic science programming (specifically for northern women), supported primarily through federal training funds. Later, programs like the Training Opportunity Program (TOP) combined English and Mathematics upgrading with technical skills to enhance the learner's ability to gain employment-related skills; adults attending these programs also received a training allowance.

Two provincial Acts had a major impact on how adult education developed and advanced in northern Saskatchewan. In 1972, the Department of Northern Saskatchewan Act established a single agency, based in La Ronge instead of Regina, to administer and facilitate delivery of all its programs and services to northern residents. Within the new department, the Northern Continuing Education Branch became responsible for organization and administration of adult education and training in the NAD. In May 1973, the Community Colleges Act created the province's first four community colleges, including one in the north. This was the beginning of the College Establishment and Development stage, in which La Ronge Region Community College (1973) was founded to provide adult education services to the central region. The overall aim was to help northerners adapt to and take a greater part in the changes that were rapidly occurring in northern Saskatchewan. Upgrading programs including Adult Basic Education 1–4, 5–10, 11–12, and GED continued to be a major focus.

The Department of Northern Saskatchewan (DNS) continued to provide for the direct delivery of adult education in areas outside the central region until West Side Community College, administered from Beauval, was formed in 1976, followed by North East Community College, administered from

Creighton, in 1981. Together, the three northern colleges continued to offer programming in the areas of adult basic education, basic job readiness, home management, and life skills. The growing demand for skilled labour in the expanding forestry and mining sectors resulted in the offering of apprenticeship trades training as well as other skill and industry-specific trainings (prospector, surveyor aide, mill operator, and diamond drilling), technical training (chemical laboratory technician, environmental monitoring technician, recreation technician), and other types of skill training (bush camp and commercial cooking, general labourer, early childhood development worker), and administrative studies. In 1983, DNS was dissolved and responsibility for adult training in the Athabasca region in the far north was transferred to La Ronge Region Community College.

The college amalgamation stage began in 1987 with the Regional Colleges Act. The three northern colleges were amalgamated into Northlands College, with headquarters in La Ronge and campuses at Buffalo Narrows and Creighton. A major focus of Northlands College was to provide employment-related training: this required Northlands College to continue to offer programming in adult basic education as well as skill and trades related training, and to include technical training and university programming in its mandate. The Northern Teacher Education Program (NORTEP), established in 1976, further increased northerners' ability to participate in the changing north. This program began as a three-year elementary teacher certificate program, and evolved to a nationally recognized teacher-education program with students earning a Bachelor of Education. NORTEP continues to be an off-campus institution accredited by the **UNIVERSITY OF REGINA**, the **UNIVERSITY OF SASKATCHEWAN** and the **FIRST NATIONS UNIVERSITY OF CANADA**. Northlands College, NORTEP, and the university access program called NORPAC provide leadership in adult education in northern Saskatchewan. Recent initiatives in which adult education played a significant role to address chronic underemployment and support human resource development in the north include the *Multi-Party Training Plan* (1993–98) and the *Northern Strategy* (1997).

Michèle Bonneau and Donna Woloshyn

FURTHER READING: Winkel, J.D. 2002. *Northern Saskatchewan–A Transformation.* Regina: Saskatchewan Northern Affairs.

ADULT EDUCATION IN THE CO-OPERATIVE MOVEMENT. In Saskatchewan, a co-operative is an organization incorporated under either provincial or federal laws. It differs in several distinctive ways from other incorporated organizations: its primary goal is to provide goods and serv-

ices to its member-owners; and it has a system of democratic control in which each member has one vote and the profits are distributed to the users on the basis of patronage. There are several kinds of co-operatives in Saskatchewan: consumer co-operatives (retail stores); producer co-operatives (e.g., **SASKATCHEWAN WHEAT POOL**); and workers co-operatives, which are businesses jointly owned and operated by the workers of the enterprise. All of the co-operatives are involved in promoting educational activities.

In 1958, the Co-operative Institute came into being at 402 Grain Building in Saskatoon; courses were offered for co-operative and credit union employees, as well as their elected officials. The facilities were inadequate, so in 1959 a permanent building site of three acres was selected near the University of Saskatchewan campus, with financial backing from large co-operatives such as Federated Co-operative Wholesale, Saskatchewan Wheat Pool, and the Credit Unions; and the name was changed to "Western Co-operative College." The college classrooms and residences were designed to encourage social gatherings for debates and the exchange of ideas, reinforcing the concept that learning is a continuous process which takes place both in and outside of the classroom. The college was administered by a board elected from representative co-operatives; the board hired the Institute's principal, who hired staff and produced programs to fit the needs of the member co-operatives. The first principal of the Western Co-operative College was Harold Chapman. He developed the principles of adult learning, whose guidelines were: problems need to be considered important to those expected to solve them; start where people are–not where we think they are or would like to be; a person cannot transfer his/her knowledge and skills to another–the person must go through his/her own learning process; significant learning takes place when facts and information are integrated into the experiences of the learner; a person feels more responsible for what he/she helps to create.

There was not one area of consumer needs that could not be fulfilled through the vast array of financial, production, or consumer co-operatives, and the college attempted to develop courses specific for these training needs. Courses gave practical training for the directors, management, staff, and other institutions, but all course groupings would include the basic tenets for a democratic organization.

The college developed two levels of adult education certificates so that all program instructors or extension teachers in local communities had a common standard in the delivery of the course materials. The **UNIVERSITY OF SASKATCHEWAN** used Western Co-operative College adult instructors to offer their adult education courses through the university's extension programs. The Western Co-operative

College adult education certificates, however, were only officially recognized within the co-operative movement.

The College was a pioneer in developing self-learning packages for northern Aboriginal people, as well as an international program which brought adults from overseas developing countries to the college to learn how to set up a consumer-owned co-operative to help balance the power of the industrial giants. In 1987, the college amalgamated with the Co-operative Union of Canada under the name of "Canadian Co-operative Association." *Ken Rodenbush*

FURTHER READING: Wright, J.F.C. 1956. *Prairie Progress: Consumer Co-operation in Saskatchewan.* Saskatoon: Modern Press.

ADVANCED TECHNOLOGY INDUSTRY.

Systems to operate satellites, detect chemical weapons and provide flight arrival/departure in airports are among the world-leading products made by Saskatchewan's advanced technology companies for almost forty years. There are only about 200 companies that work in the industry, many of which grew up around the Innovation Place cluster at the University of Saskatchewan campus.

SED Systems, considered to the province's oldest advanced technology company, began as part of the university's Institute of Space and Atmospheric Studies. Founded in 1965, the university's Space Engineering Division or SED had a mandate to design and build rocket instrumentation for upper atmospheric studies. For almost four decades, SED Systems has been providing system solutions to satellite manufacturers, operators, and service providers worldwide. SED employs 225 people in Saskatoon and has annual sales of $50 million. Customers include household names in the telecommunications, satellite and defense industries from Boeing to XM Radio Satellite.

While SED is the reference point for the start of the advanced technology industry in Saskatchewan, the $173.5-million CANADIAN LIGHT SOURCE (CLS) became the province's most visible entry into the industry when it opened in late 2004. Construction funding came from federal, provincial, municipal, industrial and academic sources. Saskatoon was selected as the location for construction of Canada's biggest scientific research facility in more than thirty years because of the experience from working with a linear accelerator in the 1960s.

A synchrotron produces extremely bright light—millions of times brighter than the sun—by using powerful magnets and radio frequency waves to accelerate electrons to nearly the speed of light. This infra-red, ultraviolet and X-ray light is shone down beam lines to experimental stations where scientists can select different parts of the spectrum to "see" the microscopic nature of matter, literally right down to

the level of the atom. Information obtained with the CLS or super microscope is expected to be used to help design new drugs, examine the structure of surfaces for developing more effective motor oils, build more powerful computer chips, and help with clean-up of mining wastes.

Another Saskatoon-based company, Scientific Instrumentation, has developed a niche market by putting advanced technologies to work. Scientific Instrumentation designs and manufactures specialized electronic instruments and equipment for scientific research, industrial, and military applications. The company's Chemical Agent Detection System (CADS II) provides advanced warning against chemical agent attack. The rugged and versatile system establishes a protective warning perimeter around military installations and can also be used to monitor chemical agents at storage and disposal sites. The United Nations used the Saskatchewan-developed system to monitor disposal of chemical weapons in Iraq.

VCom has grown since inception in 1988 as WaveCom Electronics Inc. to employ 440 people and generate $46 million in revenue. VCom is recognized as a world-leading designer and manufacturer of cable television and wireless telecommunications products.

Terminal Systems International (TSI), has been making and marketing information display systems since 1996. TSI has installed and maintained flight arrival and departure system monitors in Canadian airports from Victoria to Halifax as well as the United States (Seattle and Abilene) and southeast Asia (Singapore).

Meanwhile, a new generation of Saskatchewan companies is entering the advanced technology industry by providing intelligent systems for use in a wide range of products. Intelligent systems may be found in robotics, machine sensing, human-machine interfaces, neural networks and controls, and intelligent computation. These systems have broad applications in a number of sectors including mining, forestry, agri-food, energy, environment, manufacturing, space and aerospace, medical and information technologies, communication, and virtual reality. Intelligent systems emulate human intelligence and employ some part of the intelligent capacity of a human in performing a task.

Saskatchewan companies continue to be on the leading edge as technology is used to advance our society. *Joe Ralko*

AGRICULTURAL IMPLEMENT INDUSTRY.

As the machinery that shaped Saskatchewan agriculture was usually designed and manufactured outside of the Canadian prairie region, much of it, especially tillage equipment, was inferior and not suitable for local conditions and soil. The need for appropriate machine technology and equipment stimulated

innovation and invention. The farm equipment industry was born in the 1930s, during the DUST BOWL and the DEPRESSION. However, owing to the lack of capital, infrastructure such as electricity, and farm income to purchase equipment, the manufacturing of farm equipment on the prairies is mostly a post-WORLD WAR II phenomenon. Saskatchewan's problem in attracting investment in manufacturing was due to several factors: the province was landlocked, had a small population, and was distant from the major North American markets; in addition, national economic and trade policies including transportation and freight rates worked against prairie manufacturing.

Manufacturing of farm equipment on the prairies developed within an industry dominated by a few large corporations located outside of the region; these were known as full-line companies as they tended to manufacture a full line of equipment including power equipment such as tractors. These full-line companies in Canada and the United States grew through consolidation and merger of smaller short-line companies. Prior to 1900, all manufacturing consisted of short-line companies: full-line companies emerged primarily as a means to overcome competition. International Harvester Company (IHC), for instance, was formed in 1902 as an amalgamation of the five largest existing manufacturers of harvest equipment at the time. By 1936 there were seven full-line companies, sufficiently large to determine the conditions under which they operated, including setting prices. The price leaders of the time were John Deere and IHC. Monopoly practices in the farm equipment industry in North America would lead to numerous investigations and commissions of inquiry into marketing practices over the century. In 1915 the Saskatchewan Royal Commission on Farm Machinery recommended the development of a co-operative distribution system for farm machinery. As a result, UNITED GRAIN GROWERS (UGG) began the practice of making bulk purchases of farm machinery and selling it at a lower cost to farmers; this was abandoned when the large manufacturers put pressure on UGG. In 1939 the Saskatchewan Royal Commission on Farm Equipment recommended the formation of a distribution co-operative for farm equipment as well as a campaign to educate farmers about machinery pricing. In 1940, Canadian Co-operative Implements Ltd. (CCIL) was formed; in 1942 it took the added step of manufacturing farm equipment

Canada had two full-line companies: Massey-Harris (later to become Massey-Harris-Ferguson, and finally Massey-Ferguson) and Cockshutt, both located in the Hamilton region of Ontario. The Massey Company at one time was the world's largest manufacturer of farm equipment; however, it fell on hard times and went into receivership in 1988. Most full-line companies were in financial trouble in the

1980s: one of the problems of the farm equipment industry is the cyclical nature of purchases, which tend to follow fluctuations in farm income. The short-line prairie companies had to operate within the framework of the full-line Canadian and American companies which had developed sales, distribution, parts, and credit systems. The prairie companies focused on tillage equipment, which was the least complex to manufacture; however, some manufacturers began to produce swathers as well as haying and feed processing equipment.

There were only a few attempts at manufacturing farm equipment in Saskatchewan prior to World War II. The exceptions were farmers like the Hanson Brothers, who farmed near Regina and developed a swather in the mid-1920s. Their decision not to patent their invention provided a notable example of the problems with the patent: they were afraid that the likely court costs to defend their patent would bankrupt them as farmers. Their invention was picked up by IHC. Charles Noble in 1936 began to produce cultivators on his farm; in 1943 he established a factory at Nobleford, and by 1946 he had produced about 2,100 blade cultivators that became known as the Noble blade and were designed to leave the trash on the soil surface to reduce erosion. This equipment was developed for sound environmental reasons that would later dominate the approach to soil management. When Charles Noble died in 1957 his family carried on the business, which was sold to Versatile in 1972. In 1938 the Morris Rod Weeder Company at Yorkton began to manufacture the rod weeder, which like the Noble blade left the trash on the soil surface. In 1939 the Richardson Road Machinery Company in Saskatoon began to manufacture road equipment, and later rotary snow plows. Brandt Industries was formed in 1938 to offer welding and machine shop services; they first began to manufacture a wooden grain conveyer, followed by a grain auger, and then field sprayers and wind cones.

It was after World War II that manufacturing on the prairies took off; Table AII-1 shows the extent of this growth. Manitoba always had the major share of manufacturing due to an available labour force and being closer to steel. Saskatchewan saw notable growth, particularly after 1971 when it reached sales of $158 million in 1981. By compari-

Assiniboia implement dealer, ca. 1913.

son, Ontario had a value of shipments of $733 million in 1981. Farm equipment sales for Saskatchewan in 1991 (not shown in table) were $250 million; they were $389 million for Manitoba and $120 million for Alberta. In 2004, the number of farm manufacturers stood at 89 in Saskatchewan and at 83 in Manitoba, but no figures were available for value of shipments (sales).

It is important to make the connection between the blacksmith shop and farm equipment manufacture, as it has often been said that the innovations and progressive ideas for machinery improvements largely came from farmers. John Schulte took over his father's blacksmith shop in 1938 and began to manufacture brush cutting equipment in 1942, later expanding into rock pickers. Leon Malinowski, who took over his father's blacksmith shop at Bankend in the 1950s, began to manufacture stock troughs, fuel stands, and tank stands. He incorporated as Leon Manufacturing in 1965 and moved to Yorkton in 1967; by 1989 he had 150 employees. One of the main problems for early manufacturing on farms was the lack of electricity, which prevented the use of welders. On the basis of research at the UNIVERSITY OF SASKATCHEWAN concerning farm use of generators to produce electricity, Clem Roles modified war surplus generators that would power

welders; with his partner Tom Smith, he formed Smith-Roles Ltd. to market the welder outfit. Following rural electrification, the company began to manufacture line welders, expanding several times its manufacturing field equipment; but in the late 1980s it went into receivership.

In 1948 **PETER SAKUNDIAK** formed Sakundiak Farm Equipment. Operating initially out of a small shop in Regina, he began manufacturing a disc harrow, but production was short-lived. In 1949 he made a grain auger that proved popular. He moved his manufacturing operations to the family farm in 1955, but in 1974 transferred operations to Regina and added a line of grain bins. In 1950 the Doepker brothers, starting with a garage and repair shop, expanded into manufacturing when Francis Doepker invented the harrow drawbar. They later added a rod weeder, harrow packer, drill and swather carriers. In 1952 Emerson and Kenneth Summach started Flexi-Coil Ltd. to manufacture a land packer that grew into a multi-product firm producing air seeders, tillage equipment, field sprayers, and harrow packer drawbars. As Canada's largest farm equipment manufacturing company, their equipment is sold worldwide. In 1997 New Holland acquired a 35% interest in Flexi-Coil. At St. Brieux, Bourgault Tillage Tools Ltd. began the manufacture of a four-row cultivator in 1969; after incorporation in 1973 they expanded into a full line of dual-purpose cultivators, and in 1985 they reorganized into a cultivator division and air seeder division. **WILFRED DEGELMAN** manufactured rock pickers on his farm in 1963; in 1965 he incorporated and set up a plant in Regina, adding dozer blades, harrows, deep-tillage cultivators, and rock rakes. In 1975 Wilfred Wilger established Wilger Industries Ltd. in Saskatoon to manufacture farm field sprayers.

There are two important organizations that

Table AII-1. Value of Production and Number of Implement Plants on the Prairies, 1961–1981

	1961		1971		1981	
	# of firms	Value of shipments	# of firms	Value of shipments	# of firms	Value of shipments
Alberta	7	$2 m	18	$7 m	22	$57 m
Manitoba	15	$9 m	24	$37 m	25	$395 m
Saskatchewan	5	$1 m	23	$12 m	30	$158 m

Source: D. Wetherell and E. Corbet, *Breaking New Ground*

serve the farm implement manufacturing industry in Saskatchewan, Alberta and Manitoba. The Prairie Implement Manufacturers Association (PIMA) was formed in 1970 with its current stated mandate to provide programs and activities that inform, educate, and transfer skills to Canadian manufacturers; George Morris of Morris Rod Weeder Company was its first president. To facilitate communication amongst members and to provide information PIMA first developed a newsletter, the *Factory Action* in 1973, then the *PIMA Pulse* in 1975, and in 1990 a quarterly magazine, the *AgScene*. PIMA was instrumental in initiating the Western Canada Farm Progress Show in 1978. The other important organization is the Prairie Agricultural Machinery Institute (PAMI), with offices in Humbolt, Saskatchewan. PAMI is an applied research, development and testing organization serving manufacturers and farmers with the resources needed to compete in domestic and world markets. Its services include design, development, fabrication and evaluation of vehicles, machinery, and components. In addition to these two organizations serving farmers and manufacturers, the Agricultural Implements Act regulates farm implement dealers to ensure that parts and service are available to farmers; the Act provides legal guidelines for warranties, sales contracts, emergency parts service, and compensation claims. *Gary Storey*

FURTHER READING: Wetherell, D. and E. Corbet. 1993. *Breaking New Ground*. Saskatoon: Fifth House Publishers.

AGRICULTURAL MARKETING. Agricultural marketing can be defined as the performance of all business activities included in the flow of products from the beginning of agricultural production until they are in the hands of consumers—"from the farm to the fork." Agricultural marketing is more than just selling a commodity and receiving payment: it consists of a supply chain which combines capital items such as land and livestock, labour, purchased inputs, equipment, transportation, advertising, processing, and selling (wholesaling and retailing). This integrates the flow of goods and information in response to consumer demand, from the farm through to delivery to the consumer. Some view marketing as the most important activity that a business does; however, production and financial and human resource activities are also essential to a successful agricultural business.

Marketing functions are specialized activities performed in accomplishing the marketing process. There are three groups of marketing functions: exchange, physical, and facilitating. Exchange functions consist of buying and selling; physical functions include storage, transportation, and processing; facilitating functions are comprised of standardizing and grading, financing, risk taking, securing marketing information, and promotion and adver-

tising. As these functions of marketing are integrated throughout the supply chain, a product's raw form is converted into a finished product at a location that is convenient for the consumer. It is also available at a time when consumers want it; the transformation of a product through these processes creates a level of satisfaction for the end user; and a transfer of ownership takes place, often several times, along the supply chain. Five agricultural supply chains as seen by Saskatchewan farmers marketing their products are highlighted below.

An open market pricing mechanism exists for many agricultural products including lentil, field pea, chickpea, rye, mustard, canary seed, herbs, spices, bison and elk. These commodities priced on the open market have no formal mechanism of price discovery: they are not sold on a centralized exchange, and there is no futures or options market. The open market is freely competitive, and price is determined through open competition. There are no restrictions as to where open market commodities are sold, and the marketplace is accessible to all. Commodities sold on the open market are subject to marketplace fluctuations: for example, the price received for most open market commodities declines as production increases. Contracts are sometimes used to provide protection from this uncertainty. Commodities sold under contract may have production volumes and prices predetermined prior to delivery or even prior to the growing season. Market information may be difficult to obtain, and prices may vary for similar products on the same day.

An open market pricing mechanism, together with a corresponding futures (and options) market, exists for some agricultural products including canola, feed barley and feed wheat at the Winnipeg Commodity Exchange. A futures market also exists for wheat in the United States on three exchanges: the Minneapolis Grain Exchange, the Kansas City Board of Trade, and the Chicago Board of Trade. Cattle and hogs are dealt with at the Chicago Mercantile Exchange. These United States futures markets may be used as a price discovery and risk management mechanism for commodities produced in Saskatchewan. However, there is an added degree of risk due to fluctuations in the dollar exchange rate between the two countries and to border disruptions that may restrict the flow of commodities from Canada to the United States, thus affecting the hedge. Price risk is inherent in the production of agricultural commodities: farmers and firms involved in marketing food products are exposed to large swings in price. A futures market is not only a method of price discovery, but also a risk management mechanism: it is a centralized facility where buyers and sellers meet to buy and sell futures contracts and options. Futures contracts are legally binding contracts with the obligation to deliver (sell) or accept delivery of (buy) a specific commod-

ity at a specific place and point in time, with price as the only factor to negotiate. Futures contracts offer a marketing tool that producers and users of agricultural commodities can use to protect profit margins against unfavourable price changes. Through a process called hedging, a futures position is taken that is equal and opposite to the position held of the physical commodity. The futures position is offset prior to the settlement date at the time the physical commodity is either bought or sold: in this way, a futures market can be used as a temporary substitute for the purchase and sale of actual commodities. Some exchanges also provide an options market that offers the opportunity, but not the obligation, to obtain a futures contract by purchasing a put or call option.

Saskatchewan has a history of marketing commodities through single-desk selling agencies. These agencies take possession of the products they are marketing on behalf of farmers. For many years all hogs sold in Saskatchewan had to be marketed through a single-desk selling agency, SPI Marketing Group, which remained in effect until April 1, 1998. Since that time, producers have been free to market their hogs as they choose, either through a newly formed SPI Marketing Group Inc., or directly on the open market. Today, Saskatchewan hogs are, in effect, marketed in a dual marketing environment. Wheat and barley produced in Saskatchewan and sold for export or domestic human consumption must be marketed through a single-desk marketing board known as the Canadian Wheat Board (CWB), which markets wheat and barley for western Canadian farmers, all sales revenue being returned to farmers less marketing costs. The goal of single-desk selling is to allow farmers to sell as one entity, thus exerting a degree of market power within Canada and around the world—instead of as individual farmers competing against one another. In this way, farmers may be able to command a higher return for their grain. The CWB has a number of pricing mechanisms available to farmers. Price pooling ensures that all farmers who deliver the same grade and quality of wheat and barley anytime throughout the crop year (August 1 to July 31) receive the same price at the end of that year. Farmers receive an initial payment for part of the value of their wheat or barley upon delivery, and a final payment once the CWB has marketed all grain delivered within a crop year. The CWB also offers a number of producer payment options, allowing producers to take advantage of a number of risk-management pricing mechanisms; these include fixed price and basis contracts, early payment options, and guaranteed delivery contracts. The CWB is continually evolving as it responds to a changing marketplace and changing farmers' demands.

Supply management is a system of marketing whereby producers use quotas to control the domestic supply of a number of commodities including eggs, chickens, turkeys, and dairy products. Supply management was implemented to ensure stable domestic consumer supplies and a return to producers that covered their cost of production plus a reasonable return on investment. Through federal-provincial agreements, each province administers the production of supply-managed commodities within its borders through the use of a production quota. Provincial commodity marketing boards coordinate what individual producers are entitled to market provincially during a specific production period. A national marketing agency also regulates the volume of product marketed interprovincially and for export though the use of quota for some products. Imports are limited in these commodities by tariffs which were negotiated at the World Trade Organization (WTO).

A number of producers have responded to the uncertainty of open markets by marketing commodities through producer-led integrated marketing systems. Examples include producers of hogs, poultry and bison. Producers are moving along the supply chain (closer to the end user) in an effort to capture a greater portion of the consumer food dollar. Primary producers vertically integrate, combining with shippers, packers and processors, using a variety of business arrangements such as co-operatives, partnerships and direct buyouts. New- generation co-operatives are a recent example where farmers establish a closed co-operative to market co-operatively and own shares according to their level of production. These co-operatives represent a new effort by farmers to respond to specialized niche markets and to the challenges of deregulated agricultural markets. *Robert G. Roy*

FURTHER READING: Carter, C.A. 2003. *Futures and Options Markets: An Introduction.* Toronto: Prentice Hall; Kohls, R.L. and J.N. Uhl. 2002. *Marketing of Agricultural Products.* Toronto: Prentice Hall.

AGRICULTURAL MARKETS AND TRADE.
Exports of agricultural products are a mainstay of the Saskatchewan economy. The province is endowed with one of the world's most important agricultural resource bases. The Canadian prairies are ideally suited to dryland crop production, being characterized by a cool climatic regime that naturally controls many diseases and pests, and an adaptable to extensive mechanized agricultural production. Individual farmers enjoy high productivity. As a result, farms generally produce far more than their consumption requirements and, indeed, the consumption needs of Saskatchewan's entire population. The surplus is available for export, which can take a number of different forms. The base of Saskatchewan's agricultural production is cereal grains and oilseeds. While grains can be exported in

unprocessed form, they can also be fed to livestock that can be exported either as live animals or as processed meat products. Grains can also be processed for human consumption in the form of breads, bakery goods, and pastas. Similarly, oilseeds can be exported in bulk, or processed into vegetable oil and protein meal and then used domestically or exported. More processing and other value-adding activities prior to export lead to more employment and economic activity in Saskatchewan, fostering economic spin-offs and broad-based economic development. Consequently, it has been a long-standing public policy in Saskatchewan that adding value to agricultural products prior to export should be encouraged.

While grains and oilseeds and their respective value-added products such as beef, pork, and canola oil and meal are the overwhelming components of Saskatchewan's agricultural export base, a range of pulses, cool climate fruits and vegetables also thrive in the province, particularly in some of its micro-climates. These products enter specialty market export supply chains and are a growing segment of agricultural exports. In recent years, specialized livestock such as bison, nutraceuticals, and organic products are being produced and adding diversity to the province's exports. Saskatchewan's cold winters, however, mean that fresh fruits and vegetables are not available locally in winter months and must be imported. Of course, tropical products are also imported. The steady globalization of consumers' culinary tastes and the increasing ethnic diversity of Saskatchewan's population have led to rising imports of specialty and international foods, often in a highly processed form.

Saskatchewan is one of Canada's most successful trading provinces. Over 40% of the province's gross domestic product is derived from exports; in terms of agricultural goods and services, the contribution of exports is considerably greater. While this export success is something the farm and agribusiness sector can look on with pride, it is also a source of vulnerability for the province. Export success has also meant export dependence. In itself, export dependence is not a bad thing, but when exports are not well diversified, volatility in export markets or the decline in the relative value of key exports translates into an unstable economic environment and reductions in relative prosperity. Both tend to inhibit investment. International markets for major agricultural products, particularly prairie grains, exhibit considerable volatility. This is exacerbated by high levels of agricultural protection in some major potential markets such as the European Union, and the heavy subsidization of agricultural production and exports by Canada's competitors. As a result, the sector is often characterized as "boom or bust." This increases the risks associated with investing in not only agriculture but also the wider provincial econ-

omy. Unfortunately, the prices of most major agricultural commodities tend to move together, meaning that it is difficult to diversify the risks associated with export market volatility within the province's agricultural sector. Further, some of the province's major non-agricultural exports such as POTASH (an input to fertilizer) are also dependent on international agricultural markets.

Rapid rates of technological change in agriculture have resulted in food becoming relatively cheaper over the long run, particularly in grains. This means that, over time, Saskatchewan's grain exports are able to buy less and less imports of non-agricultural products. Thus, it is important to encourage more processing and other activities that add value in Saskatchewan prior to exporting, because highly processed products can fetch premiums in international markets.

In normal years, Saskatchewan exports nearly $2 billion in WHEAT. Wheat exports, along with international sales of BARLEY ($150 million/year) are coordinated by the Canadian Wheat Board, a uniquely Canadian state trading agency. In 2002, live animal exports exceeded $400 million, and meat products added $130 million. PULSES and VEGETABLE exports were nearly $400 million, while CANOLA exports were in excess of $400 million. *William A. Kerr*

AGRICULTURAL POLICY.
Policy is a set of guidelines, which includes ethics, economics and law, among others, agreed upon by the public through the political process. Canada has a liberal democracy, which determines the political process: thus policy is determined by elected politicians. Policies are converted, often poorly, into government programs by civil servants. Most government programs are a direct result of government legislation, which are implemented through the various economic instruments available to governments such as taxes, subsidies and regulations. The impact of government policy is the influence that government programs have on individuals or firms in the nation.

Within the Canadian Constitution both levels of government have responsibility for agricultural policy. Generally speaking the responsibilities are assigned in the Constitution so that provinces are responsible for activities that are confined within the province, with the federal government responsible for national and international issues. At times the responsibilities, such as parts of the farm income safety net, overlap. In this case there is a joint responsibility, and the two governments must work together to develop and deliver the agriculture program. One example of this joint responsibility is the crop insurance program.

To comprehend policy one must first understand what motivates government in creating policies. For example, Why did the Saskatchewan government create legislation to limit the ownership of farmland? Why does the government charge less than the market rate for government-owned land leases? Traditionally, one thinks of the government creating policies for the public good, which are then converted into programs that benefit the public. This fails to explain the many programs which transfer financial benefits to a few, at the expense of the general taxpayer. A superior explanation is that governments create the policies and programs in order to respond to both the public need for intervention and the lobbying influence of special interest groups in society.

Provincial agricultural policy originates with the Minister of Agriculture, Food and Rural Revitalization. Examples of agriculture policy include land ownership policy, subsidization of farm income, and technology use policy. The policies may come forward to the government from the general public or from the agricultural industry. When the government develops agricultural programs, it does so in order to support policy objectives which have been agreed to through the political process. One of the major provincial policies is the protection, use, and ownership of farmland.

Two of the most far-reaching farmland policy changes were introduced in the early 1970s. In the first, the **NEW DEMOCRATIC PARTY** (NDP) government introduced the "Land Bank" as a means to aid the intergenerational transfer of farmland. This policy did aid the intergenerational transfer but had the side effect of a large amount of land being accumulated by the government. When the Progressive **CONSERVATIVE** Party came into power in 1982, it abandoned the Land Bank, to which farmers had objected. The second change took place when the Farmland Security Act (FSA) was introduced in 1974 by the NDP, placing limits on who could own Saskatchewan farmland. The FSA restricted non-Saskatchewan residents to owning up to 160 acres, a figure which was later increased to 320 acres; non-Saskatchewan corporations were restricted to 10 acres. This restriction was relaxed in 2003 by a different NDP government, owing to political pressure from farmers.

An early example of a joint farm income program is Canada-Saskatchewan Crop Insurance, which subsidizes the premiums and the administration cost of crop insurance. This was followed by a large number of farm programs aimed at raising farm incomes through direct subsidization of commodity prices, production margins, and farm income programs. Initially, from 1958 to 1989, the cost of the farm income programs was borne by the federal government, with small farmer premiums after 1974. The province started to subsidize crop revenues in 1989 with the introduction of the Net Income Stabilization Account (NISA) and the Gross Revenue Insurance Program (GRIP). With the introduction of these two programs the province was

into the business of directly supporting crop farm incomes for the first time.

The province has provided both grain and livestock producers with various forms of price and revenue support. In the 1970s the Saskatchewan government introduced the Beef Stabilization Program. This program had the objective of stabilizing the revenue from cow-calf and fat cattle production. In the 1970s a hog stabilization program was introduced, which provided price support to hog producers. In the 1980s these programs were rolled into national programs known collectively as the National Tripartite Stabilization Program (NTSP). The NTSP programs were funded by federal, provincial and producer contributions. They were discontinued in the early 1990s due to countervailing actions by the United States government.

The creation of farm policy and the development of supporting programs are an ongoing process. In the future the most important question will concern the role that government sees for itself in supporting farm income through subsidization.

W. Hartley Furtan

FURTHER READING: Schmitz, A., H. Furtan and K. Baylis. 2002. *Agricultural Policy, Agribusiness, and Rent-Seeking Behaviour.* Toronto: University of Toronto Press.

AGRICULTURAL REGIONS. Agricultural regions mapped below are based on the most important type of farm in 2001 in each rural municipality, with smoothing of boundaries between regions (Figure AR-1). Statistics Canada classifies farms from data in its agricultural censuses. Farm type is determined by the single crop or type of livestock (or, if necessary, group) that provides 51% or more of total farm cash receipts. For example, a farm on which 60% of potential farm cash receipts are from **WHEAT** would be classified as a wheat farm.

Before 1996, most of Saskatchewan's farms were classified as wheat farms. However, recent years have seen a sharp percentage decline in wheat farms and a corresponding increase in grain and oilseed farms as well as beef cattle farms (Table AR-

1). The decline of wheat farms is almost entirely explained by a reduction in spring wheat. Grain and oilseed farms have dramatically increased, partly because of a rise in economic importance of cereal crops other than wheat, specialty crops and oilseeds (Table AR-2). On many former wheat farms, these crops now provide the majority of farm income. On other farms, wheat is still the main source of income but now accounts for less than 51% of farm income, so wheat earnings must be combined with income from other sources to determine a farm type. In most cases, these farms have become grain and oilseed farms. Beef cattle farms have also increased, in part because of farmers diversifying away from wheat.

Figure AR-1 shows that in 2001 beef cattle farms formed the majority or plurality (less than a majority but the main farm type) of farms in three main areas: in the southwest, aridity and rough topography favour beef cattle ranching; the eastern plurality regions are located on or flank prominent uplands, e.g., Moose Mountain; and in the northwest, climate and soils are suitable for beef cattle farms based on tame hay and feed grains.

Wheat farming, based mainly on spring wheat and durum wheat with frequent summer fallowing, is the mainstay on flatter lands in the dry south and southwest. Grain and oilseed regions dominate overall (Figure AR-1). Plurality grain and oilseed regions typically separate the majority regions of this type from wheat or beef cattle regions (Figure AR-1).

Agricultural regions based on the two main types of farms combined reveal a close relationship between these regions and the main soil zones (Figures AR-2 and AR-3). Grain and oilseed farms combined with beef cattle farms are dominant (50–75% of all farms) or predominant (76% or more of all farms) over much of the relatively cool and moist Black and Grey soil zones (Figures AR-2 and AR-3). Smaller regions occur in the drier Dark Brown and Brown soil zones, with beef cattle farms generally on the rougher lands and grain and oilseed farms on the more level land. Regions of grain and oilseed farms combined with wheat farms

Table AR-1. Types of Farms (1981-2001)									
Census Year	Total # of Farms (all Types)[1]	Wheat Farms		Grain and Oilseed Farms[2]		Beef/Cattle Farms		Other Farm Types	
		Number	%	Number	%	Number	%	Number	%
1981	64,342	41,096	63.8	10,162	15.8	7,057	11.0	6,027	9.4
1990	58,651	29,777	50.8	14,183	24.2	9,037	15.4	5,654	9.6
1996	54,979	20,192	36.7	19,928	36.3	8,952	16.3	5,907	10.7
2001	48,990	8,992	18.4	21,736	44.3	12,078	24.7	6,184	12.6

Source: Statistics Canada, agricultural censuses
[1] Statistics Canada types all farms with total gross farm receipts of $2,500 or more. These farms comprise 95% or more of all farms in Saskatchewan.
[2] Grain and oilseed farms excluding wheat farms.

Table AR-2. Value of Production[1] of the Main Grain and Oilseed Crops in Saskatchewan, 1981 to 2001 (in millions of dollars[2])

Years	Spring Wheat	All Wheat[3]	Canola	Flaxseed	Barley	Oats	Specialty Crops[4]
1982-1986	1,881	2,258	362	63	344	61	incomplete data
1987-1991	1,427	1,811	390	60	321	59	177
1992-1996	1,682	2,352	807	117	503	136	364
1997-2001	1,254	1,979	925	154	536	152	634

Source: Agricultural Statistics, Saskatchewan Agriculture, Food and Rural Revitalization
[1] Production in tonnes times farm price per tonne.
[2] Not adjusted for inflation.
[3] Spring wheat plus durum wheat and winter wheat.
[4] Includes dry field peas, lentils, mustard, canary seed and sunflowers from 1982 to 1996, and these crops plus chickpea from 1997 to 2001.

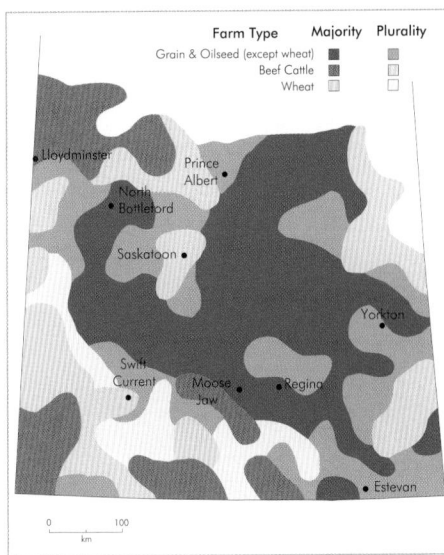

Figure AR-1. Types of farms in southern Saskatchewan.

tend to be located on the moderately moist Dark Brown soil zone as well as in adjacent and moister parts of the generally dry Brown soil zone (Figures AR-2 and AR-3). Wheat and beef cattle regions occupy small patches in the core of the Brown soil zone in areas either too dry for most cash crops except wheat, or too dry or rough for other than beef cattle.

W.J. Carlyle

FURTHER READING: Carlyle, W.J. 2002. "Cropping Patterns in the Canadian Prairies: Thirty Years of Change," *Geographical Journal* 168 (2): 97–115; —. 2004. "The Rise of Specialty Crops in Saskatchewan, 1981–2001," *Canadian Geographer* 48 (2): 137–51; Fung, K. (ed.), 1999. *Atlas of Saskatchewan.* Saskatoon: University of Saskatchewan; Statistics Canada. 1994. *Canadian Agriculture at a Glance.* Ottawa: Statistics Canada, Agriculture Division.

AGRICULTURE AND FOOD: *see essay on page 37.*

AGRICULTURE CANADA RESEARCH STATIONS. To address the problem of outdated agricultural methods, five experimental farms were established under the Experimental Farm Station Act of June 2, 1886. These were located at: Nappan, Nova Scotia; Brandon, Manitoba; Indian Head, North-West Territories; and Agassiz, British Columbia—with the Central Experimental Farm at Ottawa acting as the headquarters for the Experimental Farms System.

The Indian Head Experimental Farm opened in 1887, with Angus Mackay as superintendent, responsible for the whole of the North-West Territories. The intent of the farm was to meet the needs of new settlers for reliable information on the best farming methods and practices for local conditions. Long-term studies with field crops, animal husbandry and horticulture were initiated.

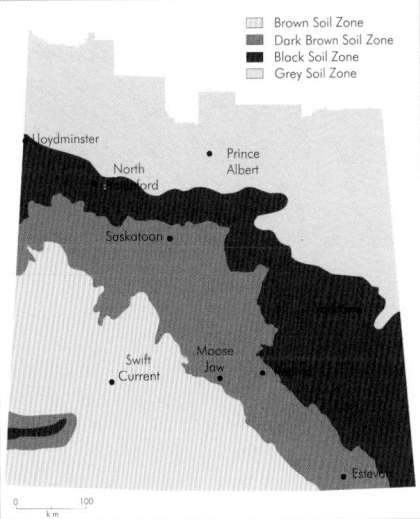

Figure AR-2. Main soil zones of southern Saskatchewan.

Because the experimental farm at Indian Head could not supply all the necessary information to immigrant farmers entering Saskatchewan, a second experimental station was established at Rosthern in 1908 to aid farmers in central Saskatchewan. A station at Scott was opened in 1911 to develop practices suited to the dry plains of the west-central region. In 1920, an experimental station was established at Swift Current to improve agricultural methods for the dry areas of southern Saskatchewan and Alberta. The Regina Experimental Substation, which became an experimental station in 1954, was opened in 1931, to work on the problems of soil drifting and weed control. In 1934 an experimental station at Melfort was started to serve the farming community of east-central Saskatchewan, an area suited to livestock production. The Experimental Farms System was also briefly responsible for the administration of the

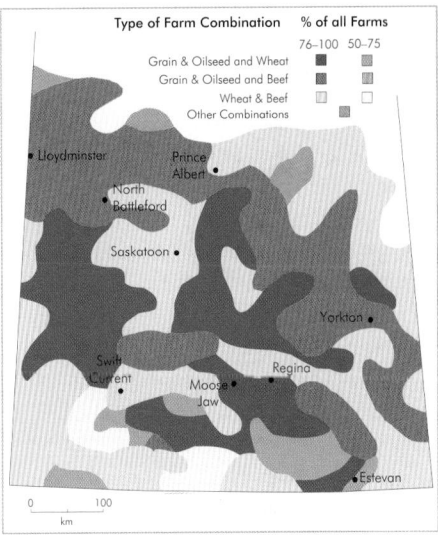

Figure AR-3. Farm combinations in southern Saskatchewan.

Dominion Forest Nursery Stations at Indian Head and Sutherland.

In 1935, the **PRAIRIE FARM REHABILITATION ADMINISTRATION** (PFRA) was established to provide for the rehabilitation of the drought-stricken areas of Manitoba, Saskatchewan and Alberta. From 1935 to 1946 the Indian Head Experimental Farm administered the PFRA program and was responsible for reclamation projects. In 1936, the PFRA financed at the Swift Current Experimental Station the Soil Research Laboratory that was to carry out studies into soil fertility, moisture conservation, and wind erosion control. The laboratory became a section of the Swift Current Station in 1957.

Amalgamation of several federal laboratories in Saskatoon resulted in the formation of the Saskatoon Research Station in 1959. The new station was entrusted to conduct research on the breeding and agronomy of oilseed, forage and cereal crops, as well as the control of plant diseases and insect pests. Changes within Agriculture Canada resulted in the closure of the stations at Scott in 1940, and at Regina in 1997. With the reorganization of the Experimental Farms System as the Research Branch in 1959, the experimental stations became research stations. In 1995, Agriculture Canada was further restructured as Agriculture and Agri-Food Canada (AAFC), with the research stations being reorganized to encourage a more interdisciplinary approach to farming and the food industry.

Currently, there are two major research centres in Saskatchewan operated by the Research Branch of AAFC. The Saskatoon Research Centre and its two associated research farms at Scott and Melfort have as their mandate a long-term commitment in crop research to the agri-food industry in western Canada. This includes programs to improve germplasm of oilseed and forage crops, crop production and pest control practices for the parkland region, and to develop processes and products that expand the utilization of prairie crops. At Swift Current, the Semiarid Prairie Agricultural Research Centre (SPARC), together with the associated Indian Head Research Farm and the Land Resources Unit in Saskatoon, carry out research on the semiarid soils of southwestern Saskatchewan and southeastern Alberta to develop agricultural practices that will support cereal, forage and field crops while conserving moisture and soil fertility.

Initially, the research stations were an essential element of rural communities, providing practical information to improve the effectiveness of local agriculture. During the 1930s, a concerted effort against the blowing topsoil by the Indian Head Experimental Farm and the stations at Regina, Rosthern, Scott and Swift Current was effective in developing tillage methods that reduced soil erosion. The post-war years saw great changes with the introduction of selective chemicals to control insects, plant diseases and weeds. Programs were set up at all stations to advise farmers on the use of these new chemicals. Nutrition and management studies at Indian Head, Melfort and Scott have done much to improve livestock production in the province. Great efforts have been made to breed crops with increased yields which are early maturing and resistant to diseases, insect pests and drought. The stations at Saskatoon and Swift Current have been particularly successful in this regard, with the canola breeding program at the former resulting in the oilseed becoming a major Canadian crop, second only to wheat production. *Allan E. Smith*

FURTHER READING: Anon. 1939. *Fifty Years of Progress on Dominion Experimental Farms 1886–1936.* Ottawa: Patenaude; Anstey, T.H. 1986. *One Hundred Harvests: Research Branch, Agriculture Canada, 1886–1986.* Agriculture Canada Historical Series, No. 27.

AGRONOMY. Agronomy, the science of field crop production and soil management, is concerned with determining the best way to grow crops and manage the soil. In Saskatchewan, agronomy has changed significantly since the land was first farmed over 100 years ago. At present the province has one of the most advanced dryland crop production systems in the world. When the Saskatchewan prairie first came under cultivation, the pioneers brought with them agronomic methods from their homelands in America and Europe. These methods included deep ploughing of the land; in addition, it was soon recognized that there was insufficient rainfall to grow a crop, and that therefore the land should lay fallow for a year to save a portion of the rainfall that fell that year. Tillage was done during this summerfallow period to control the weeds. Summerfallow allowed for more stable yields of high-quality wheat, and farmers soon gauged their management ability on their capacity to maintain their summerfallow fields as weed-free as possible.

During this initial phase of agriculture, the dust mulch system of tillage also gained popularity. Advocates of this system believed that pulverizing the soil into a fine dust with repeated tillage would allow capillary action to draw up deep moisture reserves, making them available to plants; we now know that this is not true, as plant roots are very effective at taking up moisture from deep in the soil profile. In fact, the combined effects of deep, intensive tillage and summerfallow dried the soil and left no protective layer of plant residues on the soil surface: this allowed the wind to literally blow away the topsoil in many areas. Combined with drought, this unsuitable agronomy resulted in the dust storms of the "Dirty Thirties." These dust storms were so intense that they were often known as "Black Blizzards" and often completely covered fences with soil drifts.

The **PRAIRIE FARM REHABILITATION ADMINISTRA-** TION (PFRA) was formed at this time to address the problem of soil erosion. Researchers quickly recognized that the practices of black summerfallow and excessive tillage were causing soil erosion. They learned that if the straw and plant residue from the previous year's crop was left on the soil surface, it would slow the wind and protect the land from erosion. However, tillage was required to kill the weeds, which were capable of using much of the precious soil moisture. The Noble blade was developed to allow for tillage to kill weeds but still keep plant residues on the surface. This stubble mulch system allowed for tillage but did not invert the soil, so that much of the previous crop's plant residues remained on the soil surface. The PFRA also promoted planting shelter belts of trees around agricultural land in order to reduce the wind speed and therefore soil erosion.

Through the efforts of the PFRA and others, soil erosion was reduced in Saskatchewan. However, it was not until the development of no-tillage cropping systems that the problem could be almost eliminated. No-tillage cropping systems are also known as zero-till and direct seeding. The herbicide glyphosate is applied before seeding to kill the weeds, and the farmer plants directly into the crop residue (stubble). Initially the seeders that were available were unsuitable for planting into the crop residue: plugged with straw, they could not place the seed evenly in the soil. However, Saskatchewan farmers and machinery manufacturers soon began producing seeders which allowed them to plant efficiently large areas of land directly into standing crop residue. The farm equipment produced by companies such as **FLEXI-COIL**, **BOURGAULT**, and **MORRIS** is now recognized as some of the best dryland farm equipment available worldwide. The direct seeding cropping system has allowed farmers to produce crops on large farms with very little risk of soil erosion. Other benefits to this system include a reduced reliance on

Lentils (left) and peas (right) are two recently introduced crops in Saskatchewan agriculture.

summerfallow, since this system is good at conserving water. How summerfallow is managed has also changed, as farmers can now use chemical for weed control instead of tillage operations.

The crops that are grown in Saskatchewan have changed. **WHEAT** has always been the most important crop, but its importance has diminished. The quality of wheat produced is among the best in the world in terms of protein, thanks to good wheat varieties and a semiarid climate. In the early 20th century, Saskatchewan farmers such as **SEAGER WHEELER** became famous for their world championship wheat. Saskatchewan has always produced other crops such as **OATS**, **BARLEY** and **FLAX**. However, the 1970s saw the beginnings of crop diversification with the large-scale production of rapeseed, which later became know as **CANOLA**. Following this, lentils and peas were introduced: Saskatchewan is now one of the largest lentil producers in the world, and further crop diversification has continued with the introduction of chickpeas in the late 1990s.

The management of crops has intensified in recent years. Up until the 1960s most crops were grown on land that had been summerfallowed the previous year; because of this farmers did not apply fertilizer and pesticide inputs. As decades of summerfallow have now exhausted the easily mineralized soil organic matter from the land, most farmers now apply synthetic fertilizers to increase yield. In addition, pesticides are used to control unwanted **WEEDS**, insects, and plant diseases. The farm input supply industry now employs many agronomists that assist farmers in the management of their crops. Saskatchewan is also a major producer of organic crops; in this system, synthetic fertilizers and pesticides are prohibited, and producers seek to manage the land in a more holistic manner. Increased consumer demand for organic produce has resulted in the rapid expansion of organic production.

Although modern agronomic methods have reduced environmental problems such as soil erosion, many challenges still exist. Modern agriculture is the third-largest industrial segment producing greenhouse gases. The pesticides used in agriculture have in the past damaged wildlife. Furthermore, the biodiversity of modern agriculture is very low, as one of the goals in agronomy is usually to kill all other plants except the crop; most plant ecologists, however, recognize that greater **BIODIVERSITY** allows for a better functioning ecosystem. Finally, as most annual crops have a living cover on the land for only a few months of the year, fertilizer and soil nutrients can easily be lost from the system. Through the work of scientists in the area of agronomy and ecology, these remaining challenges may be surmounted in the future. *Steven J. Shirtliffe*

Agriculture and Food

Gary Storey

Agriculture is variously defined as the science and art of farming, which is the work of cultivating the soil and raising crops and livestock; food, on the other hand, is any substance taken into the body for nourishment. The main purpose of agriculture is to produce food and fibre. Canada's food production has become very specialized, and less than 4% of the population is directly engaged in agricultural production. It is important, therefore, to think of food and fibre production as a complex system of combining resources to produce primary commodities. This system must assemble these primary agricultural commodities for processing into food and fibre products, which are distributed to consumers and users located far from the initial production source. Saskatchewan, with its abundant land base and small population, is a large surplus producer of raw and processed food products. We shall now see how this system of agricultural production was initiated, how it has evolved, and what are the consequences of this evolution.

Background to Settlement and Agricultural Development

Prior to European settlement, indigenous people occupied the land area now known as Saskatchewan. They were primarily hunters and gatherers; their numbers relative to the food resources from bison, other animals and birds, native fruit and plants did not warrant an extensive agriculture production system to provide food. This, however, does not mean that there was no agricultural production: before the treaties of the 1870s, some Aboriginal people had begun to raise crops and cattle in Saskatchewan; however, this was nothing like the transformation of the native prairie for crop production that took place following European settlement. Europeans began to emigrate to North America in the early 17th century. Louis Hébert arrived in Quebec in 1617, cleared land, and thus became the first non-indigenous farmer. But it would take almost 300 years before interest developed interest in the west as a place to live and farm. This interest came with the **FUR TRADE**. In 1670 Charles II of England granted a charter to London merchants to establish the Hudson's Bay Company (HBC), which was to trade in the territory known as Rupert's Land and comprising the territory whose rivers flowed into Hudson Bay and James Bay. Because fur trade and agriculture were incompatible, the fur trade companies portrayed an image of the west as a cold, barren, desolate, inhospitable wasteland; this image prevailed until it was expedient to portray the west in a different light.

The Canadian merchants who operated along the St. Lawrence River depended on agricultural and other commodities from the developing interior in the United States. The construction of the Erie Canal diverted commerce from the St. Lawrence to the Atlantic seaboard of the United States: Canadian merchants thus lost out to American merchants for the agricultural commerce of the interior, and this forced them to look elsewhere. Further economic development in British North America would require the exploitation of some new economic resource as a new frontier for investment. Canadian merchants became interested in what the Canadian west could offer. If the west could be developed for agriculture, the government would have to acquire Rupert's Land from the HBC and construct a transcontinental railway: these were major issues even prior to Confederation. Both the Canadian legislature and the British House of Commons debated the possibilities of agricultural settlement in the North-West Territories. Prior to Confederation, in 1857 both political offices dispatched explorations to determine the economic capability of the region. Captain **PALLISER** as head of the British expedition and Professor **HIND** as head of the Canadian expedition saw limitations to settlement and agriculture, although Hind foresaw the lack of markets as the main impediment (*see* **PALLISER AND HIND EXPEDITIONS**).

One of the first orders of business, after Confederation in 1867, was to link the territory of British Columbia to Canada and to secure the territory west of the Great Lakes for Canada. Rupert's Land was purchased in 1868 for $1.5 million, with the guarantee that 5% of the land in the fertile belt would remain with the HBC. The next step in the plan was for Sir John A.

Macdonald, Canada's first Prime Minister, to establish the National Policy, which refers specifically to the policy of tariff protection that was put in place in 1879. This policy was felt to be necessary to accomplish the economic and political objectives for which Confederation was established. Manufactured goods from textiles to farm machinery would be produced in Canada, instead of being imported from Europe and the United States. The next task was to develop a market for these manufactures. This is where the Canadian west appears, to be filled with people who would produce agricultural commodities that would flow east and down the St. Lawrence to Europe. These manufactures would be paid for from the revenue earned in export markets. The CANADIAN PACIFIC RAILWAY (CPR) Company was formed to accomplish this plan.

The CPR crossed Saskatchewan in 1884 and was completed in 1885. It was now possible to bring in settlers and move out the agricultural commodities they would produce. The CPR and the federal government provided an image of the west as a "promised land," a garden of abundance where all material wants would be satisfied. This image was used to lure immigrants from other settled areas of North America and Europe. The international economic depression of the 1890s, however, delayed settlement: the low price of grain in Great Britain, coupled with the high costs of transportation (rail and ocean freight), meant that net returns to grain production in the west would be insufficient to warrant investment. Farmers could not make a living, and infrastructure (roads, grain storage, schools, etc.) could not be financed. This lesson would be repeated several times from settlement to the present day: when net returns to farming fail to cover costs of production and marketing, the rural areas of the prairies are left with insufficient net returns to maintain infrastructure and to provide new capital for investment—let alone provide for a decent standard of living for rural people.

Settlement and the Wheat Economy

By the turn of the 20th century the conversion of wind- to steam-powered ocean freight and over-capacity had reduced rates to less than half of what they had been thirty years earlier. Low interest rates coupled with higher grain prices made the economic conditions ripe for settlement to take off. The west was settled and the native prairie was converted to cropland within a period of thirty years. WHEAT was the staple crop on which the prairie economy was built, although other crops such as OATS, BARLEY, and FLAX were produced. The establishment of the

SASKATCHEWAN ARCHIVES BOARD R-B1337

Wheat was the staple crop on which the prairie economy was built.

prairie wheat economy was accompanied by a period of economic expansion throughout the Canadian economy. The settlement of 2.5 million people in the prairies meant an enormous demand for materials for the construction of homes, schools, churches, grain storage, branch rail lines, and businesses as well as the manufacture of household goods. The National Policy of high tariffs meant that most of the manufacturing took place in Canada: it is what the eastern merchants had received under federal policy; it meant that prairie farmers had to pay higher prices for goods owing to the import tariffs.

The grain varieties in existence were not ideally suited to prairie CLIMATE and growing conditions. To facilitate development of the agricultural economy in the west and other parts of Canada the federal government passed the Experimental Farm Station Act in 1886, thus creating experimental farms largely to conduct plant breeding and research to support agricultural production (see AGRICULTURE CANADA RESEARCH STATIONS). Five stations that included Indian Head (1887) were established initially under the direction of William Saunders. It was William's son, CHARLES SAUNDERS, who discovered Marquis wheat in 1904; as it was several days earlier in maturity, Marquis quickly replaced all other

SASKATCHEWAN ARCHIVES BOARD R-A12349

Regina, October 20, 1925. Back row, left to right: J.C. Mitchell of Dahinda, three-time winner of the World's Best Wheat Prize; Manley Champlin, professor, Field Husbandry Department of the University of Saskatchewan; M.P. Tullis, Field Crops Commissioner, Department of Agriculture; James Field, Regina, winner of the World's Best Wheat Prize, 1920. Front row, left to right: Mrs. Saunders; Dr. Charles Saunders, discoverer of Marquis Wheat; F. Hedley Auld, Deputy Minister of Agriculture.

wheat varieties. Marquis also had excellent milling qualities and became the standard for all new varietal development. Another essential element for the development of the agricultural economy was the GRAIN HANDLING AND TRANSPORTATION SYSTEM. Three companies—CANADIAN PACIFIC RAILWAY, Canadian Northern Railway, and GRAND TRUNK PACIFIC RAILWAY—vied for the business of moving grain by building rail branch lines. Soon it became evident that the rail line network was over-built: by the beginning of WORLD WAR I there were three transcontinental railways, but only the CPR was financially sound. As the Grand Trunk Pacific and the Canadian Northern Railway faced bankruptcy, they were taken over, along with the Intercolonial, the Grand Trunk and the National Transcontinental, by the federal government to become the CANADIAN NATIONAL RAILWAY (CNR).

The three western railway companies encouraged American interests to build primary elevators along their railway lines; among these were SEARLE GRAIN COMPANY, NATIONAL GRAIN COMPANY, FEDERAL GRAIN LTD., and McCabe. In addition, Canadian grain companies were formed (N.M.

PATERSON AND SONS GRAIN COMPANY, PIONEER GRAIN COMPANY, and PARRISH AND HEIMBECKER GRAIN COMPANY), which still exist today. At one time there were over 100 companies in the grain business; most of these failed for financial reasons, and their assets were bought by the larger companies. How the railways and grain companies charged for their services of transportation, grain handling and storage were major issues for farmers then as they are today. In 1897 the federal government enacted the CROW'S NEST PASS AGREEMENT with the CPR, setting a maximum rail freight rate for grain moving from prairie delivery points to Fort William and Port Arthur (Thunder Bay) on Lake Superior. The freight rates became statutory in 1926, and eventually were applied to grain moving to the west coast.

Four factors determine what the farmer receives for grain delivered to the elevator: gross weight of grain delivered, dockage and shrinkage, grade, and price. Even during the initial settlement period, farmers complained of collusion between the railways and elevator companies over these factors. As a result of political action by farmers, the federal government appointed two Royal Commissions (1899 and 1904), out of which came first the Manitoba Grain Act and later the Canada Grain Act. These acts provided for regulation over the grain industry and helped solve the problems of weighing, grading, and dockage. Today the CANADIAN GRAIN COMMISSION serves to provide regulation over various elements of the grain industry.

The open-market system of pricing grain was adopted along the American model, with cash and futures markets. The Winnipeg Grain and Produce Exchange was established in 1887, first to facilitate cash trading and later to provide trading in futures contracts for wheat, flaxseed, oats and barley. The grain companies needed viable futures markets in order to hedge their grain purchases from farmers. Their bid price to farmers (street price) was based on the daily futures market price. Because futures trading allowed for (required) speculation from interests outside of the grain trade, farmers developed a distrust for this pricing system: this became a major issue for farmer organizations and the early FARM MOVEMENT. E.A. PARTRIDGE, a Saskatchewan farmer, led a movement through the Territorial Grain Growers Association (later the Saskatchewan Grain Growers Association) to form the first of several farmer-owned co-operative elevator companies. Under Partridge's leadership the GRAIN GROWERS GRAIN COMPANY (GGG) was formed in 1906; it eventually acquired and built a line of elevators across the prairie provinces.

Through their organizations, farmers petitioned the federal and provincial governments to take over the ownership of all terminal and primary elevators. In Saskatchewan the provincial government, following the recommendations of an appointed Commission, instead offered support by guaranteeing bank loans to farmers who wanted to build their own elevators. On this basis the SASKATCHEWAN CO-OPERATIVE ELEVATOR COMPANY (SCEC) was formed in 1911. In 1917 the GGG Company merged with the Alberta Co-operative Elevator Company to form UNITED GRAIN GROWERS (UGG); the Saskatchewan Co-operative Elevator Company did not join the merger. Today, UGG is known as Agricore United after merging with Agricore (Alberta and Manitoba Pools).

Farmer-owned grain companies helped to resolve many of the farmers' problems with the private grain companies, but they did not resolve the problem of price. Because of farm debt, farmers were being forced to sell their grain at harvest time, when prices tended to be low owing to gluts of grain on the market. A group of farmers, who envisioned the formation of a monopoly marketing agency operating in their interest and pooling their grain, developed a plan for a CANADIAN WHEAT BOARD (CWB). After suspending open-market trading during World War I and installing a Board of Grain Supervisors to market grain at a fixed price, the federal government instituted the CWB to market the 1919-20 crop at the end of the war. Under the CWB, farmers received an initial payment on delivery of their grain and were issued a participation certificate that qualified them for a final payment once all pooled grain had been marketed. With favourable market conditions the CWB provided farmers with the highest price for wheat that they had received to date. But the federal government did not retain the CWB, and the following year allowed the open market to return. Wheat prices fell. Farmers, ever suspicious of the open market and its speculators, began a campaign to restore the CWB.

Following a Royal Commission on the grain trade that recommended in favour of the open market, farmers developed a plan for pooling with five-year contracts. The Saskatchewan Co-operative Wheat Producers Limited was formed in 1924 to handle the marketing of the grain that was acquired under these contracts; with similar organizations in Alberta and Manitoba, it formed the Central Selling Agency in 1926 to market grain jointly. All three cooperatives eventually went into the elevator business. When the Central Selling Agency became insolvent in 1929 with the collapse of wheat prices at the onset of the GREAT DEPRESSION, pooling ceased; but the elevator component survived, later to become the SASKATCHEWAN WHEAT POOL.

Following intense political action by farmers, the federal government reestablished the Canadian Wheat Board in 1935 to market wheat in the prairie region under a pooling arrangement. At first operating as a voluntary agency, the CWB was made permanent in 1943. Trading in wheat futures was discontinued on the Winnipeg Grain Exchange. Oat and barley were added to the CWB in 1949. Feed grains for the domestic market were removed from the CWB in 1974, as was oats in 1989. The CWB has been under periodic attack from a minority of farmers, who argue for a dual market system where they could choose how they wish to market their wheat and barley. In recent years the CWB has undergone numerous changes including a new Act that has installed a producer-elected board of directors. It has also introduced marketing alternatives which allow farmers to fix the price of their grain and thus opt out of the pooling system. (*See also* AGRICULTURAL MARKETING.)

The Agricultural Economy from Settlement to the Present

Table 1 on the following page outlines the changes that have taken place in the 20th century in terms of area in Saskatchewan farms, farm numbers, land area in crops, and SUMMERFALLOW. It shows that settlement occurred quickly. The area in farms increased from 3.8 to 28.6 million acres from 1901 to 1911, the population increasing from 91,000 to 492,000 over the same period. Farm numbers increased correspondingly to 96,440 by 1911. By 1921, area in farms had increased to 44 million acres, and then to 56 million aces by 1931. Population grew to 757,000 by 1921, and to 922,000 by 1931. The number of farms reached 136,472 by 1931. Saskatchewan's population of 931,000 in 1936 was little different from what it is today. Where there were less than 1 million acres in crops in 1901, by 1911 there were over 9 million acres, and by 1921, 17 million acres. Between 1921 and 1941 an additional 16 million acres were occupied. Land in crops did not increase proportionately because the new practice of leaving land fallow for one year was adopted: summerfallow acreage increased by 8 million acres between 1921 and 1941.

A

Table 1. Saskatchewan Agricultural Land Area, in Crops and Summerfallow and Number and Average Size of Farms, 1901 to 2001

Year	Area in farms (acres)	Number of farms	Average size of farm (acres)	Land in crops (acres)*	Summerfallow (acres)
1901	3,833	13,711**	291	643	n/a
1911	28,643	96,440	297	9,257	n/a
1921	44,023	119,452	369	17,823	5,908
1931	55,673	136,472	408	22,129	7,275
1941	59,961	138,173	432	19,767	13,803
1951	61,663	112,018	550	23,706	12,855
1961	64,416	93,924	686	23,923	17,180
1971	65,057	76,970	845	27,339	16,600
1981	64,117	67,318	974	29,012	16,567
1991	66,386	60,840	1,091	33,258	14,117
2001	64,904	50,598	1,283	35,375	7,738

Sources: Census of Canada; Agricultural Statistics, Government of Saskatchewan
*   Based on addition of major crop acres.
** Other sources place this number much lower.

Table 2. Area of Major Crops Grown in Saskatchewan, 1921 to 2004, in thousand acres

Year	Spring-wheat	Durum wheat	Oat	Barley	Rye	Flax	Canola	Special Crops	Tame hay
1921	13,557	—	5,682	498	1,208	427	—	—	288
1931	15,026	—	4,295	1,375	528	509	—	—	174
1941	12,120	75	4,026	1,659	527	725	—	—	430
1951	15,163	472	3,815	2,449	710	296	7	—	572
1961	14,504	1,578	1,492	1,839	239	941	374	—	1,052
1971	11,034	1,889	1,966	5,571	528	925	2,737	246	1,646
1981	15,850	3,450	1,100	3,700	500	350	1,350	327	1,700
1991	17,253	3,925	510	3,100	225	545	3,359	1,083	2,432
2001	10,550	4,150	1,300	4,250	105	1,165	4,650	6,125	3,050
2004	9,880	4,600	2,100	4,800	170	1,400	6,150	6,175	—

Source: Agriculture Statistics

Table 3. Livestock and Poultry on Farms, 1921 to 2003, in thousands

Year	Horses and ponies	Cattle and calves	Sheep and lambs	Pigs	Hens and chickens	Milk cows	Beef cows
1921	1,078	1,296	195	420	7,474	350	n/a
1931	997	1,189	281	949	10,660	424	121
1941	801	1,241	330	944	9,731	438	106
1951	304	1,275	136	533	8,587	316	258
1961	110	2,121	189	641	6,925	241	670
1971	65	2,645	145	1,145	5,082	112	1,028
1981	60	2,418	77	574	4,411	85	946
1991	54	2,285	92	809	3,770	45	897
2001	71	2,900	149	1,129	3,618	30	1,240
2003	n/a	3,220	145	1,250	n/a	34	1,335

Source: Agriculture Statistics

After WORLD WAR II, significant changes began to take place. As compared to the stagnant economic situation through the 1930s where there was little adoption of farm machinery, farmers with higher returns began to expand their operations and become mechanized. In 1921 only 15% of farms reported having a tractor; this increased to 29% in 1931, and to 81% by 1951.

Farm numbers that stood at 138,173 in 1941 started to decline: in 1951 there were 26,000 fewer farms than in 1941, and these numbers have continued to fall, reaching 50,598 in 2001. Between 1951 and 2001 the average size of farm increased from 550 to 1,283 acres. The other significant change was the reduction in summerfallow and the corresponding increase in land in crops. This, however, has occurred particularly after 1990, with a move to continuous cropping and zero till seeding.

The changing pattern of crop production in Saskatchewan between 1921 and 2004 is outlined in Table 2. While spring wheat remains the main crop, it no longer dominates production as it once did. Durum wheat, which is grown primarily in the Brown and Dark Brown soil zones, has become an alternative to spring wheat. When much of the farming operations were done with horses, oats was grown primarily as horse feed. As horses were replaced by tractors, oat acreage declined from 5.6 million acres in 1921 to only 510,000 acres in 1991; since then, however, the renewed demand for oats as food has resulted in a partial revival of the production. With the increased demand for malt, barley acreage has increased significantly, especially since the 1970s (see MALTING INDUSTRY). RYE, never a major crop, has now become quite insignificant with less than 200,000 acres. CANOLA, originally known as rapeseed, is now rivaling spring wheat as the crop with the highest annual farm revenue. Specialty crops, which include triticale, MUSTARD, sunflowers, CANARYSEED, and the pulse crops of lentils, dry peas, and chickpeas, have increased in prominence in the last few years: there are now over 6 million acres grown (see PULSE CROPS AND INDUSTRY).

The history of livestock and poultry on Saskatchewan farms from 1921 to the present is outlined in Table 3. Horses and ponies, which numbered over 1 million when farmers required horses for farm operations, have declined to less than 100,000 today, now used primarily for recreation (see HORSE INDUSTRY). BEEF FARMING and the BEEF INDUSTRY have expanded: cattle and calves, which numbered around 1.2 million

head until 1951, have grown steadily to over 3 million head in 2003. Sheep farming has never had a prominent place in Saskatchewan agriculture, given consumers' preference for beef, pork and chicken; however, sheep numbers have grown in recent years to over 145,000 head in 2003 (see SHEEP FARMING AND INDUSTRY). HOG FARMING and the SWINE INDUSTRY have gone through a major transformation, from small-scale to large-scale intensive hog operations; actual hog marketing has increased more than what the number of hogs on farms shows, as productivity has increased significantly.

The number of milk cows has fallen from 350,000 in 1921 to just 34,000 in 2003, as DAIRY FARMING and the DAIRY INDUSTRY have gone through a major transition. A similar development has taken place in poultry farming and the poultry industry, with the number of hens and chickens on farms in 2001 about one-third of what it was in 1931 and 1941 (see POULTRY FARMING AND INDUSTRY). This in part is explained by farm specialization. In the early settlement period most farms kept cows that they milked for their household needs; they kept pigs and beef that were slaughtered for meat; and chickens were kept for eggs and meat. With increased net incomes and more women working off the farm, farm families felt they did not need to be self-sufficient any more, and they quit keeping livestock for their own food requirements. Improvements in food availability in rural Saskatchewan also had a lot to do with this transition. In addition, with the introduction of supply-managed marketing boards, only farms with quota allocations have the right to market milk, eggs, chickens, and turkeys. The marketing boards in question are the Saskatchewan Milk Control Board, the CHICKEN FARMERS OF SASKATCHEWAN, the SASKATCHEWAN TURKEY PRODUCERS' MARKETING BOARD, and the SASKATCHEWAN BROILER HATCHING EGG PRODUCERS' MARKETING BOARD. The advantage that farmers under supply management have over farmers who are dependent on the market is that under supply management farmers are guaranteed a return for their labour. The marketing board sets the level of output so that a price can be generated which covers the average cost of producing these commodities, including a return for the farmer's labour and management.

Table 4 shows the economic situation for Saskatchewan farmers over the period 1926 to 2003; all figures are averages for the periods shown. Realized net farm income represents the financial flows, both cash and non-cash, attributable to the farm business; it does not account for changes in value of inventory, which is accounted for by "total net

Table 4. Cash Receipts, Expenditures, Farm Income and Value of Farm Capital in $ millions

Year	Cash receipts (range)	Expenses and depreciation (range)	Realized net income (range)	Real realized net income*	Value of land and buildings	Value of farm capital**
1926–1930	284 (246 to 293)	157 (148 to 162)	151 (116 to 182)	1,659	n/a	n/a
1931–1940	103 (73 to 128)	110 (98 to 138)	8 (-25 to 62)	110	n/a	n/a
1941–1950	383 (157 to 579)	168 (115 to 234)	243 (60 to 401)	2,670	n/a	n/a
1951–1960	583 (438 to 732)	303 (274 to 349)	260 (173 to 465)	1,844	1,437	2,109
1961–1970	801 (612 to 973)	471 (340 to 559)	356 (173 to 461)	2,119	3,150	4,461
1971–1980	2,162 (995 to 3,332)	1,342 (591 to 2,472)	776 (382 to 1,381)	2,676	9,652	12,951
1981–1990	4,210 (3,993 to 4,498)	3,541 (3,020 to 3,835)	687 (259 to 1,001)	1,092	22,606	29,991
1991–2000	5,184 (4,127 to 5,922)	4,723 (3,823 to 5,496)	473 (239 to 735)	540	18,228	29,422
2001–2003	6,223 (5,691 to 6,496)	5,837 (5,727 to 6,091)	398 (-390 to 814)	398	22,109	32,809

Sources: Agricultural Statistics
* Deflated by consumer price index, 2000=100.
** Includes value of livestock and poultry, land and buildings, and implements and machinery.

income" (not shown here). It is revealing to place income in current dollars: realized net income was therefore adjusted using the Canadian consumer price index to generate "real" realized net income with the year 2000 set as index 100. The 1920s were good years for farmers: realized net income in the four years 1926–29 averaged $151 million, and farmers were beginning to mechanize, buying tractors, trucks and cars. This all ended with the Great Depression which started in 1929, and with the DROUGHT that gripped the prairies for most of the 1930s. As Table 4 shows, annual cash receipts only averaged $103 million in the 1930s, and realized net income averaged only $8 million; farmers were forced to cut back on expenses, and farm mechanization ceased. Farm income improved in the 1940s partly due to World War II. Realized net income averaged $243 million, ranging from $60 to $401 million. Realized net income was fairly stable through the 1950s and 1960s—with the exception of 1967 and 1968, when income fell sharply. While realized net income averaged $356 million in the 1960s, it would average $776 million in the 1970s; this large increase can be attributed to high grain prices, largely thanks to the Soviet Union entering the grain market as a major importer. The price of land increased sharply as farmers attempted to expand their operations; value of farm capital, comprising value of land and buildings, farm livestock and machinery and equipment, increased from $5.465 billion in 1971 to $31.355 billion by 1981. However, the 1980s were a complete turn-around in the farm economy: farm cash receipts remained high, but the cost of farm inputs increased, reducing farm income. This trend has increased through the 1990s to the present. In 2003, realized net income was at a record low negative $390 million.

In today's purchasing power terms, Saskatchewan farmers have been worse off in the 1990s and currently than at any time since settlement, except the 1930s. Per farm realized net income has averaged $7,900 for 2001–03, $9,890 for 1991–2000, $17,000 for 1981–90, $37,100 for 1971–80, $24,800 for 1961–70, $18,900 for 1951–60, $21,298 for 1941–50, $800 for 1931–40 and $13,000 for 1926–30. An estimate of the return to farm capital was made by taking realized net income as a percentage of the value of farm capital for each period: based on this, the return on farm capital that averaged 6% in 1971–80 fell to 2.3% in 1981–90, to 1.6% for 1991–2000, and to 1.2% for 2001–03. These figures show that farming in Saskatchewan has been an economic struggle. Facing declining real prices for grains and livestock, farmers have had to expand and diversify their operations, as well as increase efficiency by adopting new technologies in an attempt to increase output and to find cheaper means of production. While some farms have expanded into large-scale specialized farms, others have turned to off-farm income to survive: close to three-quarters of farm household income is now from non-farm sources.

Farming is thus like being on a treadmill: running harder and harder, but getting nowhere. In most industries where there are relatively few firms, firms recognize their interdependence; as a result, when the industry experiences falling net returns the solution is to reduce production, and to maintain or increase prices. The opposite typically occurs in farming: when facing declining income, the individual farm usually attempts to increase output as the only way it sees to maintain income; when all farms do this, the increased output leads to lower prices.

An increasing number of farmers are turning to organic farming, in part to reduce the costs of chemical inputs (fertilizers, pesticides, and herbicides), and in part to find a more environmentally friendly method of farming (see ORGANIC FARMING AND INDUSTRY). An organic commodity also sells for a premium over conventional non-organic commodities. These advantages are offset by lower yields; but with increased research under way on how to manage crop production without chemicals, the yield gap appears to be narrowing. Saskatchewan is the leading province in organic production, which consists mostly of cereals and oilseeds. In 2004 there were over 1,000 certified organic producers, farming approximately 560,000 acres of organic farmland. While most of Saskatchewan's organic production is exported to the United States, Europe and Japan, there is a growing organic processing sector.

With Canada's large land base and with a population of less than one million, the Saskatchewan agricultural economy is largely export-oriented: over 40% of the province's gross domestic product is derived from exports. In a normal year, Saskatchewan exports about $2 billion in wheat alone; canola and pulse exports tend to average $400 million each. In 2002 live animal exports were nearly $400 million, and meat exports represented $130 million.

Agricultural Industrialization

Saskatchewan, like the other prairie provinces, has not been noted for its manufacturing sector, which has developed primarily in relation to agriculture. The FOOD PROCESSING INDUSTRY accounts for approximately one-third of all manufacturing shipments in the province. There are approximately 300 food processors that employ over 7,000 people and have annual shipments of $2 billion. The industry is dominated by MILLING and by the processing of meat, oilseed, pulse, and dairy products. Most of the food processors are small: over 70% employ less than ten people.

The malting industry consists of only one malting plant, Prairie Malt, located at Biggar; constructed in 1975, it is currently owned by CARGILL LIMITED and Saskatchewan Wheat Pool. The plant annually processes 300,000 tonnes of barley to produce 230,000 tonnes of malt, of which over 90% is exported. The barley breeding program at the CROP DEVELOPMENT CENTRE of the University of Saskatchewan has produced several barley varieties that have contributed to the success of the prairie malting industry. The BREWING AND FERMENTATION INDUSTRY is one of the oldest agricultural industries in the province. The first fermentation process was begun in Moose Jaw and Prince Albert in 1883. Although there were several brewing companies, only one major plant exists today: GREAT WESTERN BREWING COMPANY in Saskatoon. Since 1989–90,

ALEX B. PARLEY PHOTO/SASKATCHEWAN ARCHIVES BOARD R-A7409

Hoeschen-Wentzler Brewing Company, Saskatoon, 1910.

more than nineteen brew pubs have operated in the province. Saskatchewan did have a distillery in Weyburn, McGuiness (Central Canada), which operated until 1987. The Growers Wine Company (then Jordon's Ste. Michelle) operated in Moose Jaw between 1964 and 1981. Currently there are two fruit wineries: Aspen Grove, east of Regina, and Bannach at North Battleford. A plant manufacturing white vinegar has existed since 1948, today known as Reinhart Foods.

Milling is another industry established early. With limited transportation, numerous flour mills were developed shortly after settlement. In 1915 there were at least thirty-seven flour mills, with chopping mills in an additional twenty-three towns. By 1935 there were fifty-five flour and grist mills, which had a daily combined capacity of 7,860 barrels of flour. However, most of the mills were small and were not able to survive in an increasingly competitive market: most had closed by the mid-1900s. Currently there are three large flour mills in Saskatchewan: J.M. Smucker (Canada) Inc. in Saskatoon, and Dawn Food Products mills in Saskatoon and Humboldt. Oats are milled in two plants: Can Oat at Martensville, and Popowich Milling in Yorkton. Peas and flaxseed are milled by Parrheim Foods in Saskatoon, and by Randolph and James Flax Milling in Prince Albert. Nutrasun Foods is a dedicated organic flour mill that started operations in 2000. There are numerous other small mills and processing plants milling grains and oilseeds.

The LIVESTOCK FEED INDUSTRY produces feed ingredients valued at $1.6 billion. The largest segments of this industry produce crops for processing into animal and poultry feed. The main crops used are barley, wheat, oats, field peas, and canola meal. Both complete feeds and supplements (protein, vitamin, and minerals) are manufactured. The poultry industry has relied mainly on on-farm processing. In the beef industry, only supplements are typically purchased; forages constitute over 50% of the diet of dairy, beef and other ruminants. In addition, dehydration plants process alfalfa into pellets for domestic use in the livestock industry and export.

Oilseed processing began in Moose Jaw, where an extraction plant for crushing rapeseed was constructed in 1945–initially to produce oil as a lubricant for the military (see OILSEED PROCESSING INDUSTRY). In 1946 the Saskatchewan Wheat Pool built a plant in Saskatoon to extract linseed oil from flaxseed, adding rapeseed in 1949. Both of these plants have ceased operation. In 1963 a plant was built at Nipawin to crush rapeseed; it later added a refinery and packaging plant to produce vegetable oils, margarines, and shortenings; the packaging operation was then shifted to Edmonton. Rapeseed processing did not begin to prosper until canola oil, the successor to rapeseed, was accepted as a food source. In 1996 Cargill Limited built a canola crushing plant at Clavet, which is one of the largest of its type in North America. Several smaller specialty processors (BIORIGINAL FOODS, Goldburn Valley, and Science Corporation) now operate in Saskatchewan.

On the farm input side, the AGRICULTURAL IMPLEMENT INDUSTRY was largely developed to meet the particular needs of Saskatchewan's farming conditions. Adapting technology to the land and climate occurred especially with tillage and seeding equipment. Manufacturing developed within an industry dominated by several large full-line companies such as John Deere, International Harvester, and Canada's company Massey-Harris, whose pricing and business practices were not always accepted by farmers. The government of Saskatchewan created two Commissions in 1915 and 1939 to investigate the marketing practices of these full line companies; one of the recommendations from both Commissions was to foster a co-operative distribution system for farm equipment and machinery. This led to the formation in 1940 of Canadian Co-operative

Implements Limited, which in 1942 took the added step of manufacturing farm equipment. Most of the manufacturing that developed on the prairies took place after World War II. In 1961 there were only five companies manufacturing equipment; this expanded to 23 by 1971, and to 30 by 1981, with sales of $158 million. Sales increased to $250 million by 1991. In 2004 the number of firms manufacturing equipment in Saskatchewan stood at 89; by comparison Manitoba, which had led manufacturing on the prairies, had 83 firms manufacturing equipment.

Farm Protest, Political Action and Agricultural Policy

As outlined earlier, farmers sought redress for their economic and marketing problems through political protest; this was carried out largely through farm organizations that were created primarily for this purpose. The first was the Territorial Grain Growers Association, renamed the Saskatchewan Grain Growers Association (SGGA) in 1905 when Saskatchewan became a province. When the action of the SGGA did not meet with the approval of farmers who wanted to take a more radical approach to issues, a new organization was formed in 1921: the Farmers Union of Canada (FUC). The FUC and the SGGA amalgamated in 1926 to form the United Farmers of Canada (UFC), Saskatchewan Section.

Although opposed on many issues, the Saskatchewan Co-operative Wheat Producers and the UFC managed to co-operate in efforts to establish co-operative pooling. They jointly invited Aaron Sapiro, a California lawyer who was instrumental in the United States in the formation of marketing co-operatives to assist in the campaign for pooling. Sapiro, an inspirational speaker, campaigned in Saskatchewan to get farmers to sign five-year contracts for a farmer-controlled agency to market their grain on a pooled basis, instead of selling it to the grain companies for cash on delivery. While the UFC continued to campaign for compulsory pooling after the collapse of the Central Selling Agency, they were opposed by the Saskatchewan Co-operative Wheat Producers (to become the Saskatchewan Wheat Pool). In 1931 the UFC, with an amended constitution, participated in a new political organization: the Saskatchewan Farmer Labour Group, which emerged as part of the new political party, the CO-OPERATIVE COMMONWEALTH FEDERATION (CCF), under the leadership of T.C. DOUGLAS.

As the Depression took its toll on farm organizations, the UFC struggled to maintain membership. It continued to petition governments for parity prices and compulsory pooling, which did occur with the passage of the Canadian Wheat Board Act in 1935. The UFC reorganized in 1949 as the SASKATCHEWAN FARMERS UNION (SFU), with JOSEPH PHELPS as the new president, and became a more militant organization. The SFU succeeded the UFC on the Interprovincial Farm Union Council (IFUC); with Phelps as president of the IFUC, there was a move to expand membership in Manitoba, Ontario and British Columbia. In 1960 the IFUC was renamed the National Farmers Union Council. In 1962 ROY ATKINSON became president of the SFU and chairman of the National Farmers Union Council. In 1963 the SFU launched a campaign for a producer hog-marketing plan in Saskatchewan, which would mean single-desk selling of hogs. Similar action had taken place in Ontario, Manitoba and Alberta. After several setbacks a Hog Marketing Commission was established in 1972, which after a successful producer vote became a Board selling hogs using a formula price. The provincial government cancelled the Board in the 1990s.

Declining farm incomes in 1968 and 1969 from lower grain prices and grain surpluses resulted in the SFU organizing a rally of 6,000 farmers in Saskatoon in April 1969. On July 14 a four-day demonstration was held by farmers, who clogged Saskatchewan highways with tractors; this in large part led to the founding convention of the National Farmers Union (NFU) in Winnipeg on July 30–31, 1969, as a direct membership organization.

The Canadian Federation of Agriculture (CFA) was formed in 1935 with the purpose of dealing with farm problems through one voice. Unlike the NFU, the CFA was an umbrella organization representing provincial farm organizations and commodity groups. In Saskatchewan, the existing Co-operative Council that was formed in 1928 became the SASKATCHEWAN FEDERATION OF AGRICULTURE (SFA) in 1944; its belief was that farm organizations should work together to develop and promote provincial, national and international farm policies for a better life for farm families. After 1966 the SFA had more than fifteen member organizations, which included co-operatives, marketing boards, commodity groups, and municipal and women's groups. There was a close affiliation between the SFA and the Saskatchewan Wheat Pool, with several of the Pool's vice-presidents serving as SFA presidents. The organization was a supporter of the Canadian Wheat Board and the International Grain Wheat Agreements. But not all member organizations could always agree on certain policy issues, especially marketing, and tension among member organizations led to the demise of the SFA.

The policy concerns of farmers have been represented by other general organizations. The Palliser Wheat Growers Association was founded in 1970 as a non-profit, voluntary farm organization to represent farmers' interests to governments and other sectors of agriculture. The name was changed to Western Canadian Wheat Growers Association in 1985; but with declining membership in the late 1990s the organization ceased to operate, only to be reformed in 2004. Another general farm organization is the Agricultural Producers Association of Saskatchewan (APAS), formed in 2000 as a general farm organization to provide farmers and ranchers with a democratically elected, grassroots, non-partisan producer organization based on rural municipal boundaries.

In addition to the general farm organizations there are numerous commodity-type organizations that focus on representing specific farm commodities or farm management issues, although some exist primarily to collect check-off levies used to support research and communication, and therefore do not engage in policy issues. These organizations, operating under the Saskatchewan Agri-Food Act and its Council, include: Saskatchewan Pulse Crop Development Board, Saskatchewan Flax Development Commission, Saskatchewan Canola Growers Association, Saskatchewan Winter Cereals Growers Inc, Saskatchewan Soil Conservation Association, Flax Council of Canada, Saskatchewan Bison Association, Saskatchewan Elk Breeders Association, Saskatchewan White-Tail and Mule Deer Producers Association, Saskatchewan Reindeer Association, SASKATCHEWAN ORGANIC DIRECTORATE, and others. Regarding cattle, the Saskatchewan Stock Growers Association (SSGA) is a non-profit organization established in 1913 that works to represent the cattle industry on the legislative front with a strong united voice. It is the provincial affiliate of the Canadian Cattlemen's Association (CCA), which represents Canadian cattlemen on the national scene.

As it was under the British North America Act, under the Canadian Constitution both levels of government have responsibility for agriculture policy: the province is generally responsible for policy of a local nature, while the federal government is responsible for national and international issues. Where the issues overlap the two branches must work together, as they do over most income safety net programs.

Governments tend to create the policies and programs that are a response to the public's need for intervention and to the lobbying influence of special interest groups—hence the myriad of farm organizations mentioned above. Provincial agricultural policies originate with the ministry of Agriculture, Food and Rural Revitalization; they have tended to focus on farmland ownership, providing support for farmers through loans and grants, commodity-focused programs such as income stabilization, and support for agricultural research, crop insurance, and technology use. Examples include the Farmland Security Act, introduced in 1974 to place regulations on the ownership of farm land, and the Land Bank program, introduced in the early 1970s to assist in the intergenerational transfer of land; the latter was cancelled by the Conservative government when it came to power in 1982.

An example of a joint program is Canada-Saskatchewan Crop Insurance, which subsidizes the premiums and administration costs of crop insurance. The province also engages in programs to raise farm income. These have included the Net Income Stabilization (NISA) and the Gross Revenue Insurance Program (GRIP), both of which have been phased out; they were the first programs in which the government of Saskatchewan directly supported farm income. The program replacing NISA, Canadian Agricultural Income Assurance (CAIS), was begun for the 2003–04 crop year. Another example is the Canadian Adaptation and Rural Development in Saskatchewan (CARDS) program, which has received federal funding for various development programs in Saskatchewan. Saskatchewan's first allocation of money from the federal CARDS fund was $8.8 million over four years; the second allocation was $11.3 million for 1999–2003; and the government of Canada has provided further funding to extend the CARDS program until March 2006.

The province has provided both the grain and livestock sectors with price and revenue support. Two examples, both introduced in the 1970s, are the Beef Stabilization Program and the Hog Stabilization program. In the 1980s these programs were rolled into the National Tripartite Stabilization Program; but they were discontinued in the 1990s due to countervail actions of the United States government. The FarmStart Corporation was begun in 1973 to provide credit and grants to support the further development of the livestock and poultry sectors and irrigation. FarmStart was changed to Agricultural Credit Corporation of Saskatchewan (ACS) in 1984, and the head office was moved from Regina to Swift Current. The earlier program had both a credit and advisory component, with both credit officers and agronomists working in the field; this evolved into a primarily credit function in the years prior to the government's decision in 1996 to wind down ACS (see FARMSTART CORPORATION AND THE AGRICULTURAL CREDIT CORPORATION).

Education, Research and Extension in Agriculture

Education in the agricultural subject matters in Saskatchewan has tended to be carried out at the college and university levels. Although some information on agriculture has appeared in public schooling, it has not been extensive. In 1994, Agriculture in the Classroom Saskatchewan was formed to assist Saskatchewan learners in the K–12 education system to acquire some awareness and understanding of the complexities and importance of agriculture. This has been done through partnerships with educators, agribusiness, and agriculture organizations. Agriculture in the Classroom provides resource materials for teachers: agricultural components appear in several subjects in the K–12 curriculum, and there is now an Ag 20 course in the high school curriculum.

Three colleges at the University of Saskatchewan offer programs in the agricultural area: Agriculture, Western College of Veterinary Medicine, and Engineering. The College of Agriculture was one of two colleges established in 1909; since then, agricultural teaching and research have been consistent areas of strength at the University, and the practical transfer of college research to producers has played a significant role in the development of agriculture in western Canada. There are approximately 1,000 students studying at the diploma, degree, and postgraduate levels, as well as 350 employees, including faculty, research scientists, administrative and scientific support staff. Five academic departments (Agricultural Economics, Animal and Poultry Science, Applied Microbiology and Food Science, Plant Sciences, and Soil Science) and associated research, extension and service units form one of Canada's leading training centres for agricultural science and business education. Certificate, diploma, undergraduate and postgraduate degree training is available in a wide range of specializations. The College of Agriculture operates with an annual budget of $38 million (2003–04) from a variety of sources.

In addition to research carried out through its various departments, the College has several centres for agricultural research: the CROP DEVELOPMENT CENTRE, the PRAIRIE SWINE CENTRE, the Beef Development Centre, CSALE–CENTRE FOR THE STUDIES IN AGRICULTURE, LAW AND THE ENVIRONMENT, the Saskatchewan Centre for Soil Research, and the Land Resources Centre. In addition the Food Centre, the Meat Research Laboratory, and the Prairie Feed Resources Centre offer technical and related assistance to the agricultural industry in Saskatchewan.

The Western College of Veterinary Medicine was established at the University of Saskatchewan in 1964 as a result of a decision by representatives of the University, the governments of the four western provinces, and the federal government. The first class entered the College in 1965 and graduated in 1969.

There are five departments within the College: Large Animal Clinical Sciences, Small Animal Clinical Sciences, Veterinary Microbiology, Veterinary Pathology, and Veterinary Biomedical Sciences. The College has a fully functional Veterinary Teaching Hospital, and offers courses leading to the degree of Doctor of Veterinary Medicine (DVM); in addition, all five departments offer graduate programs at the Masters and PhD level. There are currently 281 undergraduate students enrolled in the Western College of Veterinary Medicine. Research facilities include a number of individual research laboratories in all five departments: the Goodale Farm provides extensive animal facilities for cattle, horses, bison, elk and deer; the Animal Care Unit provides on-site care and housing for a wide variety of research animals, including laboratory rodents, rabbits, dogs, cats, birds, mink, sheep, horses, and cattle; the Equine Performance Centre is equipped with a high-speed treadmill and a force plate for studying locomotor and other physiological parameters of horses. In its short history, the College has gained international stature in the fields of animal reproduction, infectious diseases, toxicology, and wildlife health.

The University of Saskatchewan began offering engineering courses in 1912, and the College of Engineering was established in 1921. It has five departments: Agricultural and Bioresource Engineering, Chemical Engineering, Civil and Geological Engineering, Electrical Engineering, and Mechanical Engineering. During the 2002–03 academic year there were 1,395 undergraduate and 272 graduate students enrolled in the College of Engineering. The Department of Agricultural and Bioresource Engineering operated as the Department of Agricultural Engineering until 1992, when the name was changed to reflect its broader teaching and research program. The Department's specialty in Agricultural Mechanics, which was once a popular program in the College of Agriculture, has been discontinued.

Agricultural education program specialties exist at all four campuses of the SASKATCHEWAN INSTITUTE OF APPLIED SCIENCE AND TECHNOLOGY (SIAST). The Kelsey Campus in Saskatoon offers a program in agricultural machinery technician, biotechnology, food and nutrition management, agricultural partsperson and technician for the John Deere company, meat processing, and veterinary technology. The Wascana Campus in Regina offers programs in beef management, beekeeping, custom harvester, equine studies, and pork production technician.

Extension programs have been an important educational component of Saskatchewan agriculture and rural communities. To assist settlers in exchanging information amongst themselves, Agricultural Societies were formed under a bill introduced in the Legislature of the North-West Territories in 1884. In 1905 the first Minister of Agriculture, W.R. MOTHERWELL, initiated an extension service through the Fairs and Institutions Branch. When the decision was made to place the College of Agriculture at the University of Saskatchewan in Saskatoon, an agreement was made between the University and Motherwell in 1910, by which the University would take on educational (to include extension) work in agriculture, the province being responsible for administration and inspection. Over ninety years ago "Better Farming Trains" began bringing agricultural programs to rural Saskatchewan; over 40,000 contacts were made in the first year. The program operated between 1914 and 1922, with the trains carrying exhibitions and displays, lecture cars, and even a nursery car for small children. In 1929 the University of Saskatchewan began to offer correspondence courses so that rural students could take Grade 12 educational standing and university courses; currently, it offers a Certificate in Agriculture Program in Crop Production and Farm Business Management. Other programs include a Prairie Horticulture Certificate and a Master Garden Program. (*See* UNIVERSITY EXTENSION, UNIVERSITY OF SASKATCHEWAN.)

In 1913, in order to provide a link between settlers and the Department of Agriculture in Regina, the government hired four district representatives and stationed them in rural Saskatchewan. This program was discontinued in 1923. It was not until 1945 that the province reintroduced it through the Agricultural Representatives Act and created a branch by that name in the Department of Agriculture. The "Ag Reps," as they were called, tended to be generalists offering information and advice to farmers and rural people on various subjects related to farming and gardening, as well as information on government programs and policies. There were approximately forty Ag Reps working in rural Saskatchewan. In the mid-1970s the extension service reorganized into six regions, and three agricultural specialists were hired for each region—in farm management, soils and crops, and livestock. In addition there were six farmstead engineers, who were more closely tied to agricultural engineering (at present Agriculture and Bioresource Engineering).

The extension program has changed over the years to reflect the needs of rural people for information, and has followed the evolution of information technology. In the late 1980s, in order to facilitate a new policy to diversify the agricultural economy, the Extension Service became a partner agency in the creation of a Rural Service Network, and fifty-two Rural Service Centres were created. These Centres included other programs such as the Lands Branch and Crop Insurance; Ag Reps were renamed Extension Agrologists, and were given broader responsibilities to work toward diversification through the new Agricultural Development and Diversification Boards. In 1993 the province established the Agricultural Business Unit at the University of Saskatchewan's College of Agriculture; the objective was to commercialize new technology for the creation of increased value added enterprises in agriculture.

On March 31, 2004, the extension service that has focused on supporting agricultural production throughout rural Saskatchewan was discontinued. It was replaced with an Agricultural Knowledge Centre, located in Moose Jaw and staffed by several specialists in various fields of specialization. Replacing the existing extension service are nine Regional Centres situated in rural Saskatchewan, whose mandate is to assist in the commercialization of agriculture, and thus in the development of value-added enterprises.

Epilogue

Farming and the agricultural economy today are not what the first settlers and Saskatchewan's early leaders envisaged. What was envisaged was a very populous province with thriving rural communities: no one foresaw the development of technologies in farm equipment and machinery, coupled with chemical and biological technologies that would lead to the scale of farming we experience in the 21st century. As farm numbers have declined, so has Saskatchewan's rural population. In 1906, 82% of Saskatchewan's population was rural; in 1951 the number was 70%; and by 2001 the rural population had fallen to 36%. The highest percentage of rural towns and villages continue to experience declining populations, and as a consequence, failing businesses.

Saskatchewan was settled to be a "breadbasket" supplying Great Britain and other European countries with wheat and other grains they could not produce for themselves. In the last forty years, since the introduction of the Common Agricultural Policy in an integrated Europe, the European Union has become a major net exporter of agricultural products and has forced the other breadbasket areas of the world (United States, Australia, and Argentina) to find new markets. These new markets are in the less developed parts of the world where population growth continues, unlike the developed parts of the world where population growth has stabilized; but birth rates in the less developed parts of the world are declining making it easier for these countries to meet their growing food requirements. This raises questions for the future of the world's breadbaskets as producers of surplus food: Are there alternative uses for the surplus agricultural capacity of the breadbaskets? Will the shortage of fossil fuels mean that grains will be one of the new sources of energy?

The tragedy for farming is that while farms have expanded in size

and productivity, farm incomes have tended to decline over the last twenty-five years. With fewer numbers, farmers who once had some political influence nationally today have little political power. Government support for agriculture has continued to decline. The Crow Rate subsidy, which was worth about $400 million to Saskatchewan farmers, was eliminated by the federal government in 1995; farmers are now paying this amount in higher rail freight rates. The federal government still makes occasional special payments to agriculture; but these usually come when there is some crisis, as with BSE ("mad cow disease"), which struck the beef industry in 2004. The federal and provincial governments have not arrived at a stable policy for income stabilization and support, in comparison with that enjoyed by farmers in the United States and the European Union. Has farming in the prairies returned to the situation that existed prior to settlement, where the price of grains, coupled with costs of transportation and input costs, made settlement uneconomic? In other words, has Saskatchewan agriculture come full circle? It can be suggested that if settlement had not already occurred, it could not happen under the current economic conditions.

What then are the future prospects for Saskatchewan's agriculture? When the real purchasing price of agricultural products and foods has been declining for over 140 years on a worldwide basis, it is hard to be optimistic about a trend toward higher prices for food. Farmers are in a cost/price squeeze, as the costs of farm machinery and other energy-embedded inputs continue to increase with the rising price of petroleum. When farm prices decline, and hence farm incomes, farmers seek to expand their operations: this means a further decline in farm numbers and a further deterioration in rural communities. If the average farm size were to increase to 5,000 acres, which is quite feasible given current technology, this would result in the number of Saskatchewan farms falling to approximately 12,000 from the current approximate 50,000. With fewer farms and a smaller rural population, new ways to provide educational, health and other services would have to be found.

But within this pessimistic scenario, some farmers find ways to survive and even to thrive. They are the innovators—seeking and finding new crops to produce, establishing new enterprises, discovering new ways to cut costs, and finding new markets. This is how it has been in Saskatchewan agriculture over the last fifty years; it is difficult to see the future being much different.

FURTHER READING:

Fowke, V. 1957. *The National Policy and the Wheat Economy.* Toronto: University of Toronto Press.

Schmitz, A., H. Furtan and K. Baylis. 2002. *Agricultural Policy, Agribusiness, and Rent-Seeking Behaviour.* Toronto: University of Toronto Press.

COURTNEY MILNE PHOTO

AGUDAS ISRAEL SYNAGOGUE/JEWISH COMMUNITY CENTRE. The history of the JEWISH COMMUNITY OF SASKATOON is an important part of Saskatchewan's story. The early Jewish settlers were a very diverse group of people, primarily from Eastern Europe, and ranged in beliefs from freethinking communists to ultra-Orthodox. In 1912, the first simply constructed synagogue was built; by 1920 its members had developed a set of principles embodied in a constitution. This achievement gave official recognition to a second synagogue, built to conform to the Orthodox practices of its members: the *Aron Kodesh* (Holy Ark) was situated on the eastern wall; the reader's platform was in the centre of the sanctuary, surrounded by pews of solid oak; men prayed in this main area, while women congregants prayed in an upstairs semicircular gallery; the *Mikvah* (Ritual Bath), a kitchen and a social hall on the lower level. Many activities catering to the needs and interests of the Jewish community were coordinated by the Saskatoon Jewish Community Budget: these included the Jewish cemetery located on the old Battleford Trail and established in 1913; the *Chevra Kadisha* (Burial Society); and the Talmud Torah (Hebrew School), built in 1928.

The synagogue was the vibrant heart of the Jewish community through WORLD WAR I, the DEPRESSION, the trials of WORLD WAR II, and up to the present. World War II, in particular, had a profound effect on the Jews of Saskatoon: 111 men served in the armed forces, out of a Jewish population of 700. In the early 1950s there was a rapid increase in the size of the Jewish community, and most Jewish families moved to the east side of Saskatoon. The synagogue and Hebrew School were no longer conveniently located. The result was the purchase of property on 10th Street and McKinnon Avenue; the Saskatoon B'nai Brith Lodge #739 funded this purchase and continues its support. The sod-turning ceremony took place on May 15, 1957, and the first service was held in 1958; Mayor SIDNEY L. BUCKWOLD, the first and so far the only Jewish mayor of Saskatoon, cut the ribbon at the official opening ceremony. Religious services in the new facility no longer separated men and women; the sanctuary and social hall were located on the same floor and could be separated by moveable partitions; classrooms, library, a boardroom, and Mikvah were all located on the lower level. This synagogue/centre was designed to serve religious, educational and social needs.

In 1964, the congregation was affiliated with the United Synagogues of America and officially recognized as an adherent of the Conservative branch of Judaism. It is still a member of the United Synagogue (of Conservative Judaism) and is today fully egalitarian: it was among the very first synagogues to elect, in 1979, a woman president. In

1998, Congregation Agudas Israel celebrated the fortieth anniversary of its present building, together with the Jubilee year of the state of Israel, and produced a commemorative volume entitled *L'Dor V' Dor: Heritage and History.*

In March 2000 a schism occurred in the congregation: a number of members chose to leave Agudas Israel and to form a new congregation. For the first time in almost a century, there were two Jewish congregations in Saskatoon. In April 2002, someone threw a Molotov cocktail into the synagogue's lower level, starting a fire that totally destroyed the Rev. David Avol Memorial Library. Fortunately no lives were lost, as the building was unoccupied at the time. There was a great outpouring of outrage at this event but also overwhelming support from the general Saskatchewan community as well as individuals and organizations across Canada and the United States. The library reopened a year later.

Gladys Rose

AG-WEST BIOTECH INC. Ag-West Biotech Inc. was established in 1989 as a not-for-profit corporation funded by the provincial government with a mandate to foster agricultural biotechnology growth in Saskatchewan. In 2004, Ag-West was renamed Ag-West Biotech Inc. and agglomerated with the Saskatchewan Nutraceutical Network and Bioproducts Saskatchewan. Ag-West's contributions to the growth of agricultural biotechnology in Saskatchewan include: helping biotechnology companies get started; networking and facilitating strategic alliances; providing venture capital funding; attracting international companies; providing support for existing companies; and educating the public, the government and private organizations. Ag-West Biotech absorbed the ICAST investment portfolio in 1997, and has invested $9.1 million in start-up and expansion projects in the life science area since 1999.

Ag-West develops several publications for the biotech industry, including *AgBiotech Bulletin*, *InfoSource* and *Newtrition*, and hosts numerous seminars, conferences and workshops every year. Ag-West hosted the first Agricultural Biotechnology International Conference (ABIC) in June 1996; since then, ABIC has become a bi-annual conference held in various countries around the world. The Saskatchewan Agricultural Biotechnology Information Center (SABIC) was opened in 1997 and offered orientation programs to students and professionals in its first year. SABIC has an interactive laboratory open for public tours that allow people to learn about processes in biotechnology. Ag-West also offers regulatory assistance to companies and Canadian policy makers through the Saskatchewan Agbiotech Regulatory Affairs Service (SARAS).

Crystal Wallin

AHENAKEW, DAVID (1933–). Born on July 28, 1933, Ahenakew grew up on the Sandy Lake First Nation (now the Ahtahkakoop First Nation). In 1951 he married, but soon after joined the Canadian Army, with which he saw action in the KOREAN WAR, and served with the NATO forces in Germany and along the Suez Canal. In 1964 Ahenakew was decorated for distinguished service and good conduct, and in 1967 he retired from the military and returned to Saskatchewan. Accepting a position with the Saskatchewan government as a placement and training officer, Ahenakew began working with band councils. In 1968 he took the position of communications worker with the Federation of Saskatchewan Indians (now the FEDERATION OF SASKATCHEWAN INDIAN NATIONS), and eight months later was elected chief of the organization. He maintained that position for the next ten years. Ahenakew was a key figure in developing the Saskatchewan Indian Cultural College (now Centre) in 1972, and the Saskatchewan Indian Federated College (now FIRST NATIONS UNIVERSITY OF CANADA) in 1976. He served on the executive of both organizations for many years, and in 1976 received an honorary LLD from the UNIVERSITY OF REGINA. Ahenakew successfully negotiated between the federal, provincial, and First Nations governments for changes to curriculum content and educational opportunities for First Nations students. The 1972 report *Indian Education in Saskatchewan* suggested changes that have now been implemented and have had positive effects on the education levels attained by First Nations students.

Ahenakew helped to develop a radio and communications network for Saskatchewan's First Nations people and to establish the Special Constable Program, a First Nation contingent of the RCMP. In 1978 he became the first recipient of the

David Ahenakew.

John Stratychuk Memorial Award from the Saskatchewan Human Rights Association, and received the Order of Canada for his unswerving dedication to the advancement of First Nations rights. Ahenakew was active in the development of the National Indian Brotherhood, and when this organization became the Assembly of First Nations he was elected as its first leader in 1982. Defeated as leader in 1985, Ahenahew continued his role as senate Chair within the Federation of Saskatchewan Indian Nations until December 2002, when he was forced to resign following anti-Semitic comments he made in a speech. At that time he was also suspended from the board of the Saskatchewan Indian Federated College.   *Charlene Crevier*

AHENAKEW, EDWARD (1885–1961). Born at Sandy Lake on June 11, 1885, this grandnephew of Chief **POUNDMAKER** attended the missionary school on the Sandy Lake Reserve, and then the boarding school in Prince Albert, where he proved an able scholar and an impressive athlete. After boarding school Ahenakew returned to Sandy Lake, where he assisted his father until he was invited to teach at a missionary school on the James Smith Reserve. Wishing to continue as a missionary with his own people, he attended Wycliffe College in Toronto for two years, and then Emmanuel College in Saskatoon, from which he graduated in 1910 with a degree in theology. After his ordination, Ahenakew moved to Onion Lake and assisted the Rev. J.R. Matheson before beginning missionary work in northern Saskatchewan. He traveled by dogsled in the winter and canoe in the summer, and was warmly welcomed in the far northern communities he visited. Ahenakew also helped care for the sick who were unable to access transportation for out-

SASKATCHEWAN ARCHIVES BOARD R-B11359

Edward Ahenakew, ca. 1910.

side medical care, and following the 1918 epidemic he obtained leave from the church to enroll in the Faculty of Medicine at the University of Alberta. After three years of studies, however, he was forced to discontinue because of his own ill health, and returned to missionary work.

Emmanuel College honored Ahenakew with the Doctor of Divinity degree in 1947, an honour previously given to only one other Aboriginal person in Canada. Ahenakew worked at Fort à la Corne for several years, and he and A.S. Morton (professor of history at the **UNIVERSITY OF SASKATCHEWAN**) succeeded in locating the sites of several old fur-trading posts along the Saskatchewan River. Ahenakew collected and transcribed many legends and stories during those years, and in 1925 several were published as the *Cree Trickster Tales*. He also wrote and published a monthly magazine written in Cree syllabics, and worked with Archdeacon Faries in preparing a Cree-English dictionary. A collection of traditional tales entitled *Voices of the Plains Cree*, narrated by Chief Thunderchild and written by Ahenakew, was published posthumously in 1974. "Old Keyam," a tale of the changing world of the Cree, was another of his published works. Rev. Ahenakew passed away on July 12, 1961, while traveling to Dauphin, Manitoba to help establish a summer school.

Charlene Crevier

AHENAKEW, FREDA (1932–). Freda Ahenakew was born on the Ahtahkakoop First Nations Reserve on February 11, 1932; she married and moved to the Muskeg Lake Reserve. As **CREE** speakers, her eldest children struggled when they entered school; to prevent this occurring with her younger children, only English was spoken at home. This meant, however, that her own children were not grounded in Cree, their mother tongue. Looking for solutions to the critical cultural issue of language retention, Ahenakew completed her grade twelve and began work as the Education Liaison Worker with the Federation of Saskatchewan Indians. Wishing to further her education, she convocated from the Institute of Teachers' Education Program (1979), taught in the field, and enrolled at the University of Manitoba. She convocated in 1983 with a Master of Arts Degree majoring in Cree Linguistics. Ahenakew then taught for the **UNIVERSITY OF SASKATCHEWAN**, the Saskatchewan Indian Federated College, the University of Calgary and, until her retirement, at the University of Manitoba. She also served as director of the Saskatchewan Indian Languages Institute (**SASKATCHEWAN INDIAN CULTURAL CENTRE**). Ahenakew's thesis, "Cree Language Structures: A Cree Approach" became her first publication (1987). Others works include *kohkominawak otacimowinawawa* (*Our Grandmothers' Lives, as Told in Their Own Words*) and *Kwayaske e-ki-pe-kiskinowapahtihicik* (*Their Example Showed Me the*

Way: A Cree Women's Life Shaped by Two Cultures), which received an Alberta Award for Scholarly Book of the Year in 1988. Ahenakew received an honorary LLD from the University of Saskatchewan and was named to the World Indigenous Education Task Force; she also received the Citizen of the Year Award from the Federation of Saskatchewan Indians (1992), as well as the Order of Canada (1998) and a National Aboriginal Achievement Award in 2001.   *Christian Thompson*

FURTHER READING: Greyeyes, G. 2001. "Revival begins at Home," *Saskatchewan Indian* 31 (1): 5; La Rocque, L.A. 1992. "Citizen of the Year: An Inspiration to All," *Saskatchewan Indian* 21 (3): 1.

AHMAD, NAHID (1941–). A psychologist by training, Nahid Ahmad has made outstanding contributions in health care and in the field of immigrant women and visible minority women. Born near Bhagalpur, Bihar (British India), on July 5, 1941, and raised in Pakistan, Ms. Ahmad has been a resident of Saskatchewan since 1966. Appointed to the Royal University Hospital Foundation Board in 1995 and serving as chairperson from 1998 to 2001, she was pivotal in raising money to acquire equipment for, and support research at, this teaching hospital.

Ms. Ahmad served as a board member of the Community Clinic and of Immigrant and Visible Minority Women of Canada, and as president of the Immigrant Women of Saskatchewan (Saskatoon Chapter) from 1987 to 1990. She also served on the Immigration and Citizenship committee of the Multicultural Council of the Saskatoon Health District. Through the Islamic Association of Saskatchewan, Saskatoon Chapter, she helped three refugee families from Kosovo settle in Saskatoon. She received the Saskatchewan Order of Merit in 2002.   *Michael Jackson*

AHTAHKAKOOP (C. 1816–96). Chief Ahtahkakoop (Starblanket) led his people through the difficult transition from hunter and warrior to farmer, and from traditional Indian spiritualism to Christianity during the last third of the 19th century. A Plains **CREE**, Ahtahkakoop was born in the Saskatchewan River country in 1816. He was raised during the era when millions of buffalo roamed the northern plains and parklands, and developed into a noted leader, warrior, and buffalo hunter. By the 1860s, the buffalo were rapidly disappearing and newcomers arrived in greater numbers each year. Ahtahkakoop realized that the children and grandchildren in his band would have to adopt a new way of living if they were to survive. Accordingly, in 1874 the chief invited Anglican missionary John Hines to settle with his people at Sandy Lake (Hines Lake), situated northwest of present-day Prince Albert. Two

SASKATCHEWAN ARCHIVES BOARD R-B2837

Back row, left to right: O'Soup (Chippewa Chief) and Peter Hourie. Front row, left to right: Ah-tah-ka-koop (Starblanket), Kah-kiwistahaw (Flying in a Circle), Mistawasis (Big Child). Photo taken on October 16, 1886, on their visit for the unveiling of the Brant Memorial, October 18, 1886.

years later, Ahtahkakoop officially chose this land for his reserve. Ahtahkakoop was the second chief to sign **TREATY 6** at Fort Carlton in 1876. Supported by the chief and his headmen, Hines established a school for the children and taught their parents how to farm. The children did well in school. Two of Hines' first students, Ahtahkakoop's nephews, became qualified teachers, and two great-nephews were ordained as Anglican priests. Hines prepared the adults for baptism; gradually most families converted to Christianity. Meanwhile, the families were increasing the number of acres cultivated and sown, raising herds of cattle, and building substantial homes. Unfortunately, the crops were often destroyed by frost, hail, and drought. Hunting was poor, and the people sometimes starved despite their hard work; additionally, restrictive government policies made life difficult. Ahtahkakoop and his people remained neutral during the uprising of 1885, determined to honour the treaty signed nine years earlier. Ahtahkakoop died on December 4, 1896, and was buried on the reserve that was named after him.

Deanna Christensen

FURTHER READING: Christensen, D. 2000. *Ahtahkakoop: The Epic Account of a Plains Cree Head Chief, His People, and Their Struggle for Survival, 1816–1896.* Shell Lake, Saskatchewan: Ahtahkakoop Publishing.

AHTAHKAKOOP FIRST NATION. Chief AHTAHKAKOOP signed TREATY 6 at Fort Carlton on August 23, 1876. He wished to have a reserve adjoining Mistawasis on the Green Lake Trail at Sandy Lake, as his band already had houses and gardens there. The reserve was surveyed in the summer and fall of 1878, but when the survey was completed the reserve was neither in the location nor of the size that had been advised to the surveyors. Chief Ahtahkakoop died on December 4, 1896, and Basil Starblanket became chief. The land at Sandy Lake was fertile, and though the band suffered many hardships and setbacks, progress was made. The 1929 fall in market prices, followed by prolonged

drought, forced people off reserve as they sought employment clearing land and helping on farms. The first church was built in 1874, and Reverend Hines started the first school in 1876. The band's infrastructure includes a school, workshop, warehouse, police station, RCMP residences, fire hall, health clinic, band hall, arena, gymnasium, daycare, the Lonesome Pine Convenience Store, the Indian Child and Family Services Agency, and the Cree Nations Treatment Centre. In 2000 the band-owned Ahtahkakoop Publishing Company published its first book, *Atahkakoop: The Epic Account of a Cree Head Chief, His People, and Their Struggle for Survival, 1816–1896.* Currently there are 2,706 registered members, with 1,440 people living on their 17,347-hectare reserve 72 km northwest of Prince Albert.

Christian Thompson

AIR AMBULANCE. Air ambulance service began in the 1930s with a private company; the government-operated Saskatchewan Air Ambulance system began in 1946. On February 12, 1935, Charlie Skinner, a barnstorming pilot in Regina, received an emergency telephone call from Dr. A.C. Scott in Indian Head. The doctor had a very sick patient at Odessa, but the roads and railways were blocked with huge snowdrifts. Skinner flew his two-seat Swallow to Indian Head, took the doctor to Odessa, returned to Indian Head, and then flew back to Regina. All this took place between 2:00 and 5:45 p.m., and represented Saskatchewan's first-ever "mercy flight."

The Johnson-Murphy Funeral Home in Regina joined with Skinner's Air Service by providing a ground ambulance to meet all mercy flights into

SASKATCHEWAN GOVERNMENT PHOTOGRAPHIC SERVICES/SASKATCHEWAN ARCHIVES BOARD R-B5438

Saskatchewan Air Ambulance Service – patient being unloaded from Cessna 195 (after mercy flight) for transfer to city ambulance.

Regina. Skinner's rate was 15¢ per mile, each way. On March 15, 1936, Skinner flew down to Harptree to collect a woman with a ruptured appendix. On the return flight, after dark, the revolving beacon light, unlit for the previous four years, was turned on to guide the plane to a safe landing. At other farms, Skinner would arrange for special markers to denote the pick-up point: a pair of overalls on the top of a windmill, a large circle of hay in the snow, or a black column of smoke from a ground fire.

Speers Funeral Home then bought a Waco cabin biplane that could carry a stretcher and held the engine heat for increased patient comfort. During the late 1930s, hundreds of patients were brought to Regina, with Charlie Skinner, Steve Albulet and Harold Batty as pilots. Soon after **WORLD WAR II** the government, instigated by Keith Malcolm, introduced the Saskatchewan Air Ambulance service. The first aircraft was a Noorduyn Norseman, based at the Regina airport; and the first mercy flight was to Liberty on February 3, 1946. By the end of August, it had completed over a hundred trips, and a second Norseman was purchased. A Fairchild Husky was added in 1947; and a Cessna 195 and a two-engine Cessna Crane were added to the fleet in 1948.

DON CAMPBELL, after wartime service with the RCAF, flew for the ambulance for over thirty years. His experiences are described in his book, *Wings of Mercy* (1993), together with a list of all pilots, nurses and engineers involved. Irene Sutherland, RN, joined the air ambulance service in December 1946 and became its chief flight nurse six years later.

Regina was the sole base of operations for the Saskatchewan Air Ambulance Service from 1946 until 1953, when the Saskatoon base was added. The Regina base closed in 1994. Average trips per month increased from less than twenty-five per month in the early 1990s to over 100 by 1999, and distances increased as more patients were sent out of province to obtain specialty services not available within Saskatchewan. Beechcraft King B200 turboprop aircraft, less costly to operate, each with two-stretcher capability and seating for three medical crew, were purchased in 2001 and 2002. *Ray Crone*

AIR DEFENCE STATIONS. Throughout the period of the Cold War, the province of Saskatchewan was home to a number of air defence radar stations. These were set up to protect North America from the threat of a nuclear attack by manned bombers from the Soviet Union (USSR).

Pinetree Radar Line. In 1951 the Canadian and American governments entered into an agreement to construct 44 strategically located radar stations to counter the Soviet air threat against North America. The system, known as the Pinetree Line, entered service in 1954. The radar stations were fully manual air defence systems with both aircraft control and early warning functions. Primarily built

to defend the industrial heartland, most of these radar stations were located in eastern Canada and were manned by the United States Air Force (USAF). The Royal Canadian Air Force (RCAF) manned Saskatchewan's three Pinetree radar sites: Alsask (1963-86), Dana (1964-87), and Yorkton (1963-86).

46 Radar Squadron, Yorkton. Construction for RCAF Station Yorkton (C-51), one of the last CADIN/Pinetree stations built, began in 1961 at a location approximately 14.5 miles northwest of the city of Yorkton. The site, declared operational on October 15, 1963, was a Long Range Radar (LRR) and Ground Air Transmitter Receiver (GATR) facility. 46 Radar Squadron became a self-accounting unit in January 1963. The station, known officially as 46 Radar Squadron Yorkton, initially reported to the Minot North America Air Defence Command (NORAD) Sector, part of the 29th NORAD Region. On May 15, 1963, 46 Radar began reporting to the Great Falls NORAD Sector. 46 Radar Squadron Yorkton was renamed Canadian Forces Station Yorkton on May 12, 1967. On October 17, 1968, CFS Yorkton began to report to Central NORAD Region through the 28th NORAD Division. In August 1984, Yorkton formed part of the Canada West Region Operation Control Centre (ROCC). The site continued in its long-range radar role until it ceased operations in December 1985. On August 1, 1986, the Minister of National Defence authorized the disbanding of a number of radar stations, including Yorkton.

45 Radar Squadron, Dana. Construction of the Station (C-52) commenced in September 1961 and was completed in December 1962. 45 Radar Squadron, RCAF Station Dana received its first RCAF personnel on October 8, 1962, and was declared operational on February 3, 1964. The station was equipped with the AN/FPS 26, AN/FPS 27, AN/FPS 507 radars as well as the FTS-2 Data Processor and the obligatory GATR Site. The station was renamed 45 Radar Squadron, Dana in 1964. In February 1968 the station's name was changed to Canadian Forces Station Dana. 45 Radar Squadron originally reported to the Minot Sector, later reporting to Great Falls and the 28th NORAD Region. In 1983, the squadron began reporting directly to North Bay. The radar station at Dana, also known as Sagehill, was located 35 miles east of Saskatoon. RCAF Station Dana was supported by RCAF Station Saskatoon until it was closed in mid-1964. One of the station's height-finders ceased operation on April 1, 1975. In 1983, as a result of the Canadian NORAD Region's introduction of two Regional Operations Control Centres (ROCCs), CFS Dana became part of Canada West ROCC. 45 Radar Squadron, Dana was closed in late summer of 1987.

44 Radar Squadron, Alsask. Construction began at Alsask (C-53) in January 1961, and on November 1, 1962, RCAF Station Alsask was official-

ly established. The long-range radar unit, 44 Radar Squadron, became operational in early 1963. Equipment at the Station included the FPS-7C Search and FPS 507 and FPS 206 Height Finder radars. The site reported to the 24th NORAD Region. The Station's name was later changed to 44 Radar Squadron Alsask, and remained so until it became a Canadian Forces station in May 1967. The radar station was located at the junction of provincial Highways 7 and 44, on the border of Alberta and Saskatchewan, hence its name. The nearest community was the village of Alsask, which bordered the southern boundary of the 418-acre military facility. Alsask continued to operate until it was disbanded on August 1, 1986.

Mid-Canada Line. The Mid-Canada Line was a detection system, designed at McGill University, that was based on the doppler principle. This system was proposed as a defence line as early as 1951; however, it was not established until October 1953. Although Saskatchewan did not have any manned Mid-Canada Line sites, there were several unmanned sites situated between RCAF Cranberry Portage, Manitoba (47 km southeast of Flin Flon), and RCAF Stoney Mountain, Alberta (close to Anzac, Alberta, 32 km south of Fort McMurray).

Prince Albert Radar Laboratory. Air Defense Command (ADC) also gained the ability to track satellites with the Satellite Tracking Unit in Cold Lake and a detachment at the Prince Albert Radar Laboratory (PARL). The Satellite Tracking Unit was equipped with a Baker-Nunn tracking camera. By 1962 these units were working on a full-time Space Detection and Tracking System (SPADATS) basis. Initially these units received their "look angles" (the angle to position the camera to view a satellite) from the SPADATS Centre in Colorado Springs, but the workload on their Philco computer necessitated that units calculate their own look angles. This was done by a digital computer with information from SPADATS.

Ground Observation Corps. Many members of the Ground Observation Corps (GObC) were located in northern Saskatchewan. Before the advent of the Mid-Canada and Pinetree Radar Lines, a number of civilian volunteers reported any air movements in northern Canada to their respective headquarters. The two squadrons responsible for western Canada were 20 RCAF GObC Squadron, Edmonton and 51 RCAF GObC Squadron, Winnipeg. *Don Nicks*

AIR FORCE MEMORIAL-SASKATCHEWAN. The Air Force Memorial-Saskatchewan is dedicated to the memory of the thousands of airmen and airwomen from the province, the nation and their allies, who sacrificed their lives in defence of peace and freedom throughout the world. Planning for the memorial commenced in mid-2002, when it was decided to replace and relocate a memorial cairn previously erected at **15 WING, MOOSE JAW**. The Office of Air Force History and Heritage, 15 Wing, Moose Jaw, in consultation with the Air Force Association of Canada, decided that a general tribute to the Air Force in the form of a monument should be constructed as its replacement, and that it should also be located at 15 Wing, Moose Jaw, the last remaining active Air Force base within the province of Saskatchewan. The previous monument stood on the southwest corner of the intersection of NATO Avenue and Rideau Street on 15 Wing, adjacent to the main intersection. At the northeast corner of the memorial site is a pedestal-mounted North American Harvard Mark IV single-engine training aircraft, representing Saskatchewan's legacy as the home of military pilot training. The design of the memorial represents the "walls" that still exist to peace and freedom for people throughout the world today, while honouring the courage of all airmen and airwomen who have defended democratic values.

Construction of phase one of the memorial commenced in the fall of 2002 and saw the erection of three freestanding monoliths, which form the central aspect of the memorial. Open to the elements, these monoliths reach skywards and are meant to symbolize the words of the poem "High Flight," by Pilot Officer John Gillespie Magee of the Royal Canadian Air Force; the brass plaques from the original 15 Wing memorial cairn have been placed upon them. Phase two of the project will see the construction of a "distressed" masonry wall, divided into two distinct wrap-around elements, half-enclosing the memorial site and physically separating it from the surrounding area. This wall, symbolic of destroyed homes and buildings throughout the world, reminds us all of the stark reality of war. The pathway situated directly in front symbolizes the journey taken by countless airmen and airwomen from their homes to battlefields around the globe in defence of peace and freedom. Phase three will see the installation of benches along the pathway; these will be oriented to face the wall, offering guests an opportunity for quiet reflection or for remembering a loved one, a squadron, or a unit.

Jeff R. Noel

AIR POLLUTION. Air pollution refers to contamination of the atmosphere by gaseous or particulate substances that are harmful to plant, animal, or human health or cause damage to property or the environment. It may lead to smog or acid precipitation (rain, fog or snow) or, over longer time periods, trigger changes in climate or in the earth's ozone layer. Because Saskatchewan has a small population and little industry, air is generally good quality. Sources of air pollution can be anthropogenic (caused by human activity) or natural. Anthropogenic sources in Saskatchewan include thermal power generation (from coal and natural

gas), transportation, industrial smokestacks (pulp and paper mills, oil refineries, mining operations), and chemical pesticide application. Natural-source pollution includes particles from wind-blown soils (*see* **DUST STORMS**), road dust, pollen and spores, and smoke and ash from forest fires and burning crop residue.

Energy production causes much of Saskatchewan's air pollution. Toxic, acidic, and greenhouse gases are released by the combustion of fossil fuels (coal, oil and natural gas) in vehicles, domestic and industrial heating, and thermal power generation. Saskatchewan is a producer and consumer of fossil fuels, and relies heavily on coal for electricity. Fossil fuel combustion produces pollutants such as carbon dioxide (CO_2), sulphur dioxide (SO_2), and nitrogen oxide (NO_X). These pollutants have been implicated in possible human-induced climate change. Saskatchewan has the second highest per capita emissions rate for CO_2 in Canada. Another contributor to poor air quality is the burning of crop residues. This smoke can produce respiratory ailments as well as obstruct visibility for traffic.

Saskatchewan's air quality is monitored by Environment Canada's two nationwide air-sampling networks: the National Air Pollution Surveillance Network (NAPS) and the Canadian Air and Precipitation Monitoring Network (CAPMoN). NAPS continuously monitors levels of sulphur dioxide, carbon monoxide (CO), nitrogen dioxide (NO_2), ozone (O_3), and total suspended particulates in fifty-five urban centres across the country, including Regina and Saskatoon. Air-monitoring stations in Estevan, Prince Albert, and Lloydminster are also part of the NAPS network but are operated provincially by Saskatchewan Environment and Resource Management. CAPMoN is a rural-based network that includes one air-monitoring station in Saskatchewan, located at Bratt's Lake 50 km south of Regina. Environment Canada issues daily air quality forecasts for Regina and Saskatoon, based on the Air Quality Index, derived from measurement of ground-level ozone and particulate matter. The Air Quality Index ranges from "poor" to "excellent"; air quality in both Regina and Saskatoon consistently rates as "good."

Transboundary air pollution across the Canada–United States border is also monitored in Saskatchewan. In keeping with the Saskatchewan Clean Air Act and the 1991 United States–Canada Air Quality Agreement, the Transboundary Monitoring Network was established to measure the flow of air pollutants across the Saskatchewan–North Dakota (Burke County) border. Environment Canada, Saskatchewan Environment, SaskPower, and the North Dakota Department of Health jointly operate a network of air-monitoring stations near the Boundary Dam and Shand power stations (*see* **SOURIS RIVER**). *Iain Stewart*

FURTHER READING: Bosgoed, Charles A. 1996. *Study on Air Pollutant Emissions and Their Impacts on the Province of Saskatchewan.* Regina: University of Regina, Faculty of Engineering; Saskatchewan Environment. 1979. *Urban Air Monitoring Program–1979.* Air Pollution Control Branch; —. 2002. *Transboundary Monitoring Network: Estevan, Saskatchewan–Burke County, North Dakota. 1999–2000 Report*; Saskatchewan Environment and Resource Management. 2003. *2003 State of the Environment Report.* Regina.

AIR RONGE, northern village, pop 955, located on the W shore of **LAC LA RONGE**, on Hwy 2, across the mouth of the Montreal River from the town of La Ronge. The village is nestled between the reserve lands of the Lac La Ronge Indian Band, and the combined population of these communities is approximately 6,000. Air Ronge, as the name indicates, was for many years the location of one of the major airstrips serving northern Saskatchewan. With increasing air traffic into the area, however, a major airport was built north of La Ronge, and today much of the area of Air Ronge's old airstrip has been converted into a residential subdivision. The growing and harvesting of **WILD RICE** provides some seasonal employment. Tourism is also increasingly important to the economy, the primary attractions being fishing, hunting, camping, canoeing, snowmobiling, cross-country skiing, and the scenery. *David McLennan*

AIR SEEDERS. BOURGAULT INDUSTRIES of St. Brieux, Saskatchewan, began a revolution in the agriculture industry in 1980 by manufacturing an air seeder that could be towed behind a cultivator to provide the tractor operator with a clear view of the field. The first air seeders had been patented in Australia in 1956 and several companies had been marketing the product to farmers around the world before the Bourgault breakthrough.

However, the technology acquired by Frank Bourgault from Jerome Bechard, another Saskatchewan inventor, changed farming practices and saved producers' time: the Bechard Seeding System was the heart of the new Bourgault Air Seeder, Model 138.

Bourgault Industries manufactured seven air seeders in the first year, but the number rose to forty in 1981 to feed an increasing demand. Since then, the Bourgault Air Seeder has served as a prototype for air seeders developed for farmers around the world.

The Bourgault Air Seeder's three large floatation tires mean that it applies no more pressure to the field than a man walking across it: crop yields thus increase because of reduced damage to the seeded field. Another key advantage that the Bourgault Air Seeder offers producers is that the machinery can quickly be disconnected, freeing the cultivator for other field work. The tow-behind concept unit has since served as the concept for virtually all the tow-behind air seeders currently being produced throughout the world.

Over the years, Bourgault has continued to improve upon the original technology, and now produces air seeders that can cover more than 20 metres in a single pass. *Joe Ralko*

AIR TRANSPORT, NATIONAL AND INTERNATIONAL. National and international air transport developed in Canada immediately prior to the GREAT DEPRESSION. Western Canadian Airways, founded by Winnipeg financier James A. Richardson, launched airmail delivery flights across western Canada in 1930, with stops in Regina and Saskatoon. A decade earlier, aerial postal revenues had laid the foundation for development of a national commercial passenger airline system in the United States; the model failed in Canada, where railroads dominated transportation, and the strategy was abandoned several years later. The federal government formed Trans-Canada Airlines (TCA), with mandated national and international routes, in 1937. Regina was situated on the mainline between Montreal and Vancouver when the Crown carrier began service with 12-passenger aircraft in 1939. Trans-Canada Airlines, later Air Canada, added Saskatoon, Yorkton, and Swift Current to its national route system in 1947. Saskatchewan air service was characterized by short-distance, low-density seg-

SASKATCHEWAN ARCHIVES BOARD R-B9553

A Trans Canada Air Lines plane, the "North Star," flies over Regina (1950s).

ments that prompted complaints from travelers: for example, a trip to Ottawa required three changes of aircraft. The introduction of larger, faster aircraft enabled the flag carrier to provide direct flights to major cities with connections to international destinations. In recent years, Air Canada has emerged as a full-service flag carrier linking Saskatchewan to a world route network through a system of global code-sharing and fare alliances with other airlines.

The jet age ushered in the concept of mass air travel in the mid-1960s. Wardair pioneered economical charter flights, but not without obstacles. In support of incumbent airlines, federal regulators established "Affinity Rules," a protectionist measure which required passengers on a charter flight to be affiliated group members. Deregulation of the airline industry in the mid-1980s reduced barriers to entry, and encouraged competition and innovation in air travel. Tour operators were now able to hire aircraft and sell without restriction individual tickets on leisure charter flights from Regina and Saskatoon to a wide range of destinations. Air Canada, in the process, became a publicly listed company in 1989. Liberalized regulations allowed Canadian Airlines to attain national and international status through a series of acquisitions. Competition on domestic routes led to financial reversals that forced the integration of its operations with Air Canada, followed shortly by a merger of the two airlines. WestJet Airlines, a Calgary-based discount carrier, opened routes into Saskatchewan in 1996. The low-cost airline adopted new technology and an aggressive business model to challenge Air Canada, the dominant legacy airline, with expanded routes across the country and to the United States.

Frontier Airline opened a trans-border route between its base in Denver, Colorado and Regina and Saskatoon in 1981. The same-plane service to major United States markets ceased several years later when the carrier filed for bankruptcy. Northwest Airlines arrived in Saskatchewan in 1995, supported by a hub airport system in Minneapolis, Minnesota, which efficiently distributes passengers to North American and international destinations. The direct link to a US gateway has proven to be of benefit to Saskatchewan's tourist trade and export economy. *Merv Samborsky*

ALAMEDA, town, pop 311, located 60 km NE of Estevan and 40 km N of the US border. The first settlers in the early 1880s were of Scottish and English origins. Beginning in 1897, German settlers from Michigan began homesteading in the district. Today, mixed farming and oil field development are the major industries of the area. In 1993, the Alameda Dam, about 3 km east of the town, was opened. The reservoir, approximately 26 km long, provides a stable water supply and has created enhanced recreational opportunities. *David McLennan*

ALEXANDER, JOHN F. (1942–). Numerous amateur and professional athletic teams have benefited from the sports medicine expertise offered by Dr. "Jack" Alexander of Regina. A graduate of the UNIVERSITY OF SASKATCHEWAN College of Medicine, Alexander joined the Regina Rams as team physician in 1967 and was named to the medical staff of the SASKATCHEWAN ROUGHRIDERS two years later. His service as the team's head doctor began in 1979. In addition to practicing as a family physician, Alexander fulfilled commitments to the Rams and other teams in hockey, wrestling, volleyball, figure skating, and basketball. His work in sports medicine includes co-founding the Canadian Academy of Sport Medicine and serving as its president in 1981–82; he also has experience as an Olympic doctor. In recognition of his contributions to provincial sports, Alexander was inducted into the SASKATCHEWAN SPORTS HALL OF FAME in 1988. The Roughriders honoured him for his outstanding service to the team in 2004. *Holden Stoffel*

ALGAE. Algae encompass a diverse group of plants. The majority are microscopic (microalgae), but some larger forms (macroalgae) resemble higher plants in size. The distinction between algae and higher plants relates to a lesser degree of cell differentiation in the former. Algae include both eukaryotic (membrane-bounded internal cell structures) and primitive prokaryotic forms. For the purposes of this text, algae in five divisions are recognized: Chlorophyta, Chromophyta (seven classes), Rhodophyta, Cyanophyta, and Charophyta. Some groups contain exclusive or varied proportions of photosynthetic pigments, which impart a range of colours to particular algae in nature, through green, red, yellow and brown. The world of algae contains a vast range of cell shapes and sizes, from non-motile and motile single cells to complex three-dimensional, multicell forms. These latter colonial forms may be visible to the naked eye. Colonial forms have a greater degree of complexity in shape, ranging from branched filaments to clumps of undifferentiated cells. Some may be characterized by a fixed number of cells, while others comprise variable mass and shape, with breakaway cells forming new colonies. Interestingly, some colonial forms may lose their tendency for cellular aggregation when maintained in laboratory cultures. This speaks to the role of species interaction, competition and predation, etc., in the ecology and physiology of algae in nature. The same is true of pigment composition, which may shift in response to light regimes, temperatures, and available nutrients. The nutritional status and form dimensions of algae may influence their quality as a food source to grazers.

Biologists further differentiate algae on the basis of where they are most commonly found. The major split is into planktonic (or floating/drifting) types, and benthic (bottom dwelling) types. Benthic algae can only grow as deep as light penetration permits, whereas viable planktonic forms can occur throughout the water column, well below the boundary of critical light availability, due to mixing of the water by various turbulent forces. The species composition and abundance of algae is very cyclical in nature. Typically, one sees marked seasonal oscillation in abundance and composition of algae. A series of complex interactions sets the stage for the ecology of algae, including among others: water temperature; availability of nutrients such as carbon, phosphorus, nitrogen, silica, iron, and vitamins; salinity light; water depth and mixing regime; and zooplankton grazing. Base conditions vary seasonally, and with the type of rocks, soils, vegetation and drainages found across the landscape.

The full range of inland water types can be found in Saskatchewan. A transition of conditions extends from northern cold-water systems in the boreal Shield, to cool and warm-water systems in the southern prairies. This cline of inland water types means that species occurrence and abundance of algae is highly varied. In cases of high nutrient availability, algae may reach nuisance densities, which may interfere with desired uses such as drinking water sources, fisheries, and recreation. Many "problem" species do well in nutrient-rich warm waters, especially cyanophytes (blue-green algae, also known as cyanobacteria). Some of these species can supplement their nitrogen requirements by fixing atmospheric nitrogen—a considerable advantage. They can also regulate their buoyancy, thereby optimizing light exposure. Bloom-forming cyanophytes may produce a range of toxic compounds acting on the liver, kidneys, and nervous system of higher animals. High levels of algae may lead to wide diurnal swings in dissolved oxygen concentrations, as well as oxygen depletion during bloom die-offs.

Ken Scott

FURTHER READING: Wehr, J.D. and R. Sheath (eds.). 2003. *Freshwater Algae of North America.* San Diego: Academic Press; Wetzel, R.W. 2001. *Limnology.* San Diego: Academic Press.

ALLAN, town, pop 679, located 58 km SE of the city of Saskatoon on Hwy 397. Two structures dominate the Allan skyline: St. Aloysius Roman Catholic Church, built in 1922; and the Potash Corporation of Saskatchewan's (PCS) Allan mine, which looms over the community to the northwest. The first group of homesteaders in the area were of German origin, arriving from the US in 1903. By the mid-1920s, the population was more diverse and well over 300; it would remain stable until the early 1960s, although the town's business community dwindled as more people shopped and sought services in Saskatoon. In the mid-1960s, construction of

the potash mine at Allan began; as many as 1,000 workers were employed building the mine and bringing it into operation. Today, the PCS Allan Division's mine employs approximately 300 workers. Similarly, the Colonsay mine, begun a couple of years later, is also a large area employer. The district surrounding Allan also supports a strong agricultural industry. A number of Allan's residents commute to work in Saskatoon. *See also* **POTASH INDUSTRY**.

David McLennan

ALLEN, HILDA BUCKLEY (1906–86). Born in England, Hilda Allen began her career in the arts as a teenager in Regina, with singing lessons and competitions. In the late 1920s and 1930s, she appeared in eighteen light opera productions, but gradually turned to acting with several community groups, including **REGINA LITTLE THEATRE**, in such roles as Nora in "A Doll's House." After a summer of classes at the Banff School of Fine Arts (her only formal theatre training) confirmed her "natural flair," she joined the boards of the Saskatchewan Drama League and RLT, serving both for many years. In 1943, she turned to directing with RLT, first with one-act plays and then the full-length "Watch on the Rhine" in 1945, but also continued to act on occasion, eventually including roles in professional and film productions. On average, she directed or acted in at least one work a year until 1985, not counting her best-known achievement, *The Trial of Louis Riel*, which she staged at Saskatchewan House every summer from 1967 to 1985.

Among her proudest accomplishments was her production of John Steinbeck's *Burning Bright*, with **JOHN VERNON** in the cast, a Canadian premiere for which she received a warm letter of appreciation

REGINA LEADER-POST

Hilda Allen, 1985.

from the author. At the same time as her work for RLT, she directed several large-scale musicals for the IODE in the 1970s, appeared with the **REGINA SYMPHONY ORCHESTRA**, and actively supported many arts groups. For her work, Mrs. Allen received the Canadian Drama Award in 1950 and the Saskatchewan Order of Merit in 1985.

Richard Harvey

ALLIANCE OF CANADIAN CINEMA, TELE-VISION AND RADIO ARTISTS (ACTRA). The Alliance of Canadian Cinema, Television and Radio Artists (ACTRA) is a Canadian union of 20,000 professional performers working in English-language broadcasting, sound recording, film, commercial, and audio-visual production. Nationally, ACTRA was founded in 1940s, born from the mobilization of freelance performers and writers, working principally in CBC radio production. The first Saskatchewan founding member was actor/writer Jean Freeman; others included renowned performers and theatre innovators Sue and Ken Kramer, founders of the Regina **GLOBE THEATRE**. Saskatchewan ACTRA was tied originally to Winnipeg, but shortly evolved as an independent unit.

ACTRA represents performers' interests in negotiation and administration of agreements with producers, servicing and supervising members' contracts and production engagements, provision of benefit plans, and information and promotion; it also advocates on behalf of members and all artists. Prior to 1992, ACTRA represented writers and journalists as well as performers. However, writers separated to form the Writers Guild of Canada, and in 1993 journalists were required to join with the newly formed Canadian Media Guild. The Saskatchewan Branch of ACTRA has been a consistent advocate on behalf of Canadian artists, joining with community organizations and cultural unions to advance issues important to all artists. This advocacy has included critical support of many developments: advancement of engagement terms for artists- performers, writers, and journalists in CBC and regional programming in general; development of regional educational and private sector agreements; the Saskatchewan Motion Picture Association, SaskFilm; co-operative training and professional development initiatives, particularly in drama; the Professional Development Initiative; the Saskatchewan Sectoral Council for Culture; and Status of the Artist initiatives.

Despite the blow dealt to the Saskatchewan Branch by the division of the union in 1992-93, it has since regained strength—stimulated by the growth of the Saskatchewan film industry, between 1990 and 2003, from $5 million to over $50 million in production, and by innovative affirmative action recruitment and apprenticeship programs.

Sheila Roberts

SASKATCHEWAN ARCHIVES BOARD B4512
Almighty Voice.

ALMIGHTY VOICE (1875–97).

Almighty Voice was born in 1875 near Duck Lake, Saskatchewan. He grew up on the One Arrow Reserve, where he heard stories of his grandfather One Arrow, who had resisted taking up his reserve until 1879. On October 22, 1895, Almighty Voice was arrested by the North-West Mounted Police (NWMP) after being accused of slaughtering a government cow. While he was transferred to the jail at Duck Lake, one of the arresting officers is said to have joked that the penalty for killing a government cow was hanging. Almighty Voice seemed to have taken the joke seriously: he escaped from jail that night, and fled to his mother's home on the reserve. Initial attempts to capture him were not successful. On October 29, 1895, NWMP officer Colebrook caught up with him near Kinistino, and in the attempted arrest was shot and killed by Almighty Voice. By April 1896 there was a $500 bounty on Almighty Voice; however, he avoided the authorities until May 1897. On May 27, 1897, it was reported that Almighty Voice and two companions had shot and wounded a local Métis scout near Duck Lake. The NWMP under Inspector Allan came across Almighty Voice at the Minichnas Hills, a few miles from the One Arrow Reserve. There was an exchange of gunfire, and Allan and another officer were seriously wounded. Another force made up of both civilians and NWMP officers attempted to rush the three men, but again they were turned away by gunfire. On May 30, after

heavy gunfire including rounds from a nine-pound field gun, Almighty Voice, his brother-in-law Topean and his cousin Little Saulteaux were all found dead.

Rob Nestor

ALSASK,

village, pop 178, located just inside the Alberta-Saskatchewan border, W of Kindersley on Hwy 7. Settlement of the district began around 1909, and by 1916 the population was over 300. The 1930s hit the region hard, however, and by WORLD WAR II the town had lost a third of its citizens. In 1959, the village's fortunes changed when RCAF Station Alsask was conceived as part of an early warning radar system deemed integral to North American air defence against Soviet missiles and bombers. Construction of the 418-acre military facility adjacent to the north side of the village began in 1961, and in early 1963 the long-range radar unit, 44 Radar Squadron, was operational. The station later became known as CFD (Canadian Forces Detachment) Alsask. The base included three radar domes, housing, a school, a swimming pool, and the first cable television in the province. It was staffed by 125 service personnel, many of whom lived on site with their families, as well as 60 civilian employees. The village of Alsask was transformed by the activity and the combined population was over 800 in the early 1970s. The disbanding of the station in 1987 had a major impact on Alsask, as hundreds of people were gone within months. Few businesses remain in the community today. The one remaining radar dome, built in 1961, was designated a heritage property in 2002. Today, agriculture as well as and oil and gas are the major industries in the area. (*See also* **AIR DEFENCE STATIONS**)

David McLennan

ALTSCHUL, RUDOLPH (1901–63).

Rudolf Altschul, born on February 24, 1901, in Prague, Bohemia, graduated from the German University of Prague in 1925 with an MUDr degree. He did post-doctoral work in neurology and neuropathology in

SASKATCHEWAN ARCHIVES BOARD S-B4758
Rudolf Altschul.

the Charcot Clinic in Paris and at the University of Rome.

In 1929 he returned to Prague where he practiced neuropsychiatry and began research in the Department of Histology, German University. In September 1939 the Nazi occupation forced the Altschuls to flee to Canada. The Altschuls were aboard the S.S. *Athenia*, the first Allied ship to be torpedoed in **WORLD WAR II**. They survived, but lost all their possessions and scientific records.

In Saskatoon, Rudolph Altschul became an instructor in Anatomy at the **UNIVERSITY OF SASKATCHEWAN**, and soon established himself as a dedicated researcher and a teacher regarded with trust and affection by his students. He became Professor and, in 1955, Head of the Department of Anatomy. He resumed his study of cellular reactions in atherosclerotic blood vessels, and eventually proposed the niacin therapy for hypercholesterolemia and hyperlipemia.

Altschul published on a wide variety of topics, including three books: *Selected Studies on Arteriosclerosis* (1950), *Endothelium* (1954), and *Niacin in Vascular Disorders and Hyperlipemia* (1964, posthumously).

An enthusiastic photographer, a linguist, and a connoisseur of the arts, he was a Fellow of the Gerontological Society and of the Royal Society of Canada. He died in Saskatoon on November 4, 1963.

Sergey Fedoroff

AMALGAMATED TRANSIT UNION (ATU).

The Amalgamated Transit Union (ATU) Local 588 in Regina is the oldest of the three locals affiliated to the ATU. The other two locals are Saskatoon Local 615, representing the city of Saskatoon transit workers, and Local 1374, representing employees from the Saskatchewan Transportation Company, who were certified on August 19, 1946; these employees provide rural bus service to all areas of Saskatchewan. Currently the ATU Local 588 has approximately 220 members, who work for the city of Regina Transit Service; and there are 45 para-transit workers working for First Bus Canada, which supplies bus services to Regina's disabled community. The Saskatoon ATU Local 615 was certified on February 3, 1913; on April 24, 1947, it was officially recognized as an appropriate unit of employees for the purpose of collective bargaining by the Labour Relations Board of Saskatchewan. In August 1994, ATU Local 615 members walked off the job for ten and one-half weeks in what became known as the Saskatoon Civic Dispute—part of a common front strike which also involved four CUPE Locals and an IBEW Local also employed by the city of Saskatoon. This strike was a result of a significant dispute over wages and increased vacation time. Today, ATU Local 615 represents 275 members of the city of Saskatoon Transit Services.

John McCormick

AMERICAN DIPPER. Dippers (family Cinclidae) are small (~20 cm), stocky songbirds with short tails and stubby wings. They have the distinctive habit of living in and near mountain streams, where they feed on aquatic insects and other aquatic organisms by wading in shallow water or diving into deeper water. The family contains five species, which live in mountainous regions of the Americas, Eurasia and North Africa. The slate-grey American dipper is rarely seen in Saskatchewan and only in the **CYPRESS HILLS**, which is the only region of the province with the required high-grade streams.

Diane Secoy

FURTHER READING: Alsop, Fred J., III. 2002. *Birds of Canada*. New York: Dorling Kindersley Handbooks.

AMERICAN FEDERATION OF MUSICIANS. The American Federation of Musicians is the largest entertainment union in the world, representing professional musicians in the fields of broadcasting, commercials, films, TV, video production, symphonic and theatre work as well as casual and club date engagements. Internationally the AFM was formed in 1886, with the first Canadian Local being chartered in Toronto in 1901. There are two Locals in Saskatchewan, Regina and Saskatoon. Each Local represents roughly one-half of the province, based on an imaginary line drawn through Davidson and Yorkton, and offices are maintained in both cities. The Regina Local was chartered on February 12, 1912, as the Musicians Protective Union, AFM Local 446, Regina City; it was re-chartered on January 1, 1996, under the Regina Musicians Association as a part of the American Federations Centennial celebrations, although it has operated under this name for many years.

Both charters hang in the Local 446 office, which represents the members of the **REGINA SYMPHONY ORCHESTRA**, Canada's longest continuously performing symphony, negotiating on their behalf and administering their contracts. Additionally the Local represent musicians working with CBC and other networks doing national programming as well as during contract disputes and cancellations; it also advises on many aspects of the music business and provides access to low-cost instrument insurance and an excellent pension plan.

In recent years, Local 446 has again become more active in the trade union movement through its affiliation with the Regina and District Labour Council and the Saskatchewan Federation of Labour, and has been very active with other arts organization in encouraging the provincial government to establish enabling legislation for Status of the Artist (the first anglophone province to do so). As well, Local 446 is affiliated with the Canadian Conference of Musicians and the American Federation of Musicians of the United States and

SASKATCHEWAN ARCHIVES BOARD R-B9806/LIBRARY AND ARCHIVES CANADA C11553

This photo was published in 1906 in *The Canadian Magazine* (Toronto, Volume 26, page 131) with this description: *Settlers from the United States crossing the western prairies, heading for the wheat fields.*

Canada, and through this organization with the Fédération Internationale des Musiciens.

Brian Dojack

AMERICAN IMMIGRATION. While European migration to Saskatchewan has received considerable attention, relatively little is known about the experiences of American immigrants and the role they played in the settlement and development of the province. Before Americans crossed the border in any significant numbers, the influence of the United States had already made itself felt in the prairie region: indeed, the drive to build a transcontinental railway and settle the west was fuelled in part by the long-held fear of American Manifest Destiny. The salient features of Canadian land policy–homesteads, sectional survey, and railway land grants–were transplants from the United States. The end of the American land frontier in the 1890s precipitated the movement northwards. American immigrants—native-born and transplanted Canadians and Europeans–looked to western Canada, where free homestead land was available upon payment of a $10 registration fee, and where land was selling for as little as $2 an acre. Laurier's Minister of the Interior, Clifford Sifton, instituted a program of land promotion and sent agents throughout the United States in search of American farmers with capital. Sifton deemed the United States the greatest source of first-class settlers because American immigrants had capital, goods, and experience in prairie farming, and because Ottawa considered them ethnically desirable–at least those with white skin. No attempt was made to recruit black agriculturalists, although

a few hundred black families from Oklahoma entered Canada in 1910 and 1911, settling in Saskatchewan and Alberta.

Estimates indicate that between 1901 and 1914, over 750,000 immigrants entered Canada from the United States. Although Alberta was the most common destination for American migrants coming to the prairies, a significant number settled in Saskatchewan. During the period from 1905 to 1923, 332,155 immigrants arrived in Saskatchewan from the United States; the peak years were 1911–12 and 1912–13, when 46,158 and 45,147 immigrants respectively registered with border officials. In 1916, American-born comprised 36%, 30% and 8% of the foreign-born populations of Alberta, Saskatchewan and Manitoba respectively. When **WORLD WAR I** began, American immigration dropped considerably. While settlers who came directly from Europe tended to emigrate in large groups and settle in blocs, Americans tended to travel alone or with immediate family. As a result, their presence, while ubiquitous, was also less apparent. Although spread throughout the southern part of the province, American immigrants tended to concentrate both in the southeastern section near the major rail lines and in the southwestern part, where ranching played a major role in the local economy.

While hyphenated Americans (those born in Europe but subsequently residing in nearby states such as Minnesota and North Dakota) often joined their former countrymen in newly formed rural communities, most immigrants from the United States were generally inconspicuous, even in areas of relatively high concentration. Yet their presence was noted: Americans were valued for both their wealth and experience in farming, and were looked upon favourably by those who put stock in the fact that most Canadians and Americans shared the same Anglo-Celtic blood. Yet while appreciating American capital and labour, many native-born Canadians in Saskatchewan were uneasy about certain aspects of American society and the threat of annexation. Many of these same people expressed some regret about the weakening of the British connection, in economic as well as social terms. Yet the sheer number of Americans by the end of the first decade of the 20th century, their investment in agriculture and business, and the technological expertise they brought with them ensured that they would play a major role in developing the province. American technology such as the steel plough, barbed wire, and the self-binding reaper, along with dryland farming techniques, facilitated the move into drier regions and the development of wheat monoculture. Many Saskatchewan communities (e.g., Climax, Mankota, Willmar) were American transplants. While British and eastern Canadian capital played a major part in the development of Saskatchewan's ranching industry, recent literature asserts that cattle companies found it necessary to adopt American practices and employ American labour in order to cope with a challenging environment. A considerable number of American immigrants established their own cattle ranches in the Maple Creek area. Importation of agrarian movements such as the Patrons of Industry and the Farmers' Alliance had a major impact on the development of populist organizations and the socialist movement in the province.

While many of the original American settlers eventually left Saskatchewan, those who remained virtually disappeared into the fabric of provincial life. Yet, while their presence as a cultural group is barely discernible today, their legacy in terms of the contributions they made to the development of the province is visible in almost every facet of society. (*See also* **ETHNIC BLOC SETTLEMENTS, INTERNATIONAL MIGRATION, BLACKS: EARLY SETTLEMENTS**)

Randy Widdis

FURTHER READING: Sharp, P.F. 1947. "The American Farmer and the 'Last Best West,'" *Agricultural History* 21: 65–74; Shepard, R.B. 1997. *Deemed Unsuitable.* Toronto: Umbrella Press; Widdis, R.W. 1998. *With Scarcely a Ripple: Anglo-Canadian Migration into the United States and Western Canada, 1880–1910.* Montreal: McGill-Queen's University Press.

AMPHIBIANS. Amphibians are animals with backbones and legs, and thin, usually moist, skins. All Saskatchewan species have gilled aquatic larvae, which metamorphose into terrestrial, lunged adults. Amphibians are cold-tolerant, sometimes seen active

Table AMP-1. Saskatchewan Amphibians			
Common Name	Scientific Name	Family	Distribution
Tiger salamander	*Ambystoma tigrinum*	Ambystomatidae	prairie, aspen parklands
Plains spadefoot	*Spea bombifrons*	Pelobatidae	dry prairies of the southwest
Canadian toad	*Bufo hemiophrys*	Bufonidae	all, except northeastern subarctic woodland
Great Plains toad	*Bufo cognatus*	Bufonidae	dry prairies of the southwest
Western chorus frog	*Pseudacris triseriata*	Hylidae	all, except northeastern subarctic woodland
Wood frog	*Rana sylvatica*	Ranidae	all, except northeastern subarctic woodland
Northern leopard frog	*Rana pipiens*	Ranidae	all, except northeastern subarctic woodland

below the ice on ponds, but are not dry-tolerant. All amphibians are carnivores, feeding on arthropods and any small animal food they can find, including other amphibians.

Saskatchewan has representatives of two of the orders of amphibians: the Caudata (tailed salamanders) and the Anura (frogs and toads which lack tails as adults) (*see* Table AMP-1). The single species of salamander is the tiger salamander, a fairly large salamander which is usually olive-green with black blotches or specks. The aquatic larva, found in prairie sloughs, is also large with four well-developed legs and bushy gills. This animal is sometimes mistakenly called a "lizard."

There are six anuran species. The Plains spadefoot and Great Plains toad are limited to the dry prairies of the southwestern corner of the province. They breed in ponds, where the trilling calls of the males can be heard in the spring. As the ponds dry up, they dig down into the soil and stay inactive through dry periods. The other species are found in suitable habitats, from temporary sloughs in the prairies to small ponds in the boreal forest, in which they lay their eggs and the tadpoles can develop without predation from large fish.

Wood frog.

Some of the Saskatchewan amphibians, such as the northern leopard frog, are reduced in their distribution and numbers from earlier records. This reduction of amphibians is a world-wide phenomenon. A number of species, particularly of anurans, have recently disappeared. This loss in numbers has been blamed on several possible factors, such as increased ultraviolet radiation, the presence of parasites, the use of certain pesticides or the presence of exotic species, but no clearcut causes have been identified.

Diane Secoy

FURTHER READING: Didiuk, A.B. "Amphibians and Reptiles." Pp. 143–44 in *Atlas of Saskatchewan.* Saskatoon: University of Saskatchewan; Stebbins, Robert C. 2003. *Peterson Field Guide to Western Reptiles and Amphibians.* New York: Houghton Mifflin.

ANDERSON, JAMES THOMAS MILTON (1878–1946). J.T.M. Anderson was born in Fairbank, Ontario, on July 23, 1878. After graduation he taught for six years in Ontario and migrated to western Canada in 1906. He taught first in Manitoba, then near Melville, and finally at Grenfell. Here he met and married Edith Redgewick with whom he had a son and a daughter. In 1911 he was appointed inspector of schools based in Yorkton, a position he held for seven years. During this time he continued his own education, earning BA, MA and law degrees from the University of Manitoba and a doctorate in pedagogy from the University of Toronto. In 1918 he published his first and only book, *The Education of the New Canadian,* and the Martin government brought him to Regina as a director of education, with special responsibility to ensure that school boards and teachers in "ethnic" districts obeyed the law with respect to educating their children in English. The integrity of the public school system was a principal concern of Anderson, and he might never have turned to politics had he been allowed to remain in his post. He was, however, removed from it in 1922 and his bitterness may explain in part why he listened to the overtures

SASKATCHEWAN ARCHIVES BOARD R-A12057

J.T.M. Anderson (ca. 1908) in front of his "bachelor shack" during his early years as a teacher in the province.

from the provincial **CONSERVATIVE PARTY** two years later.

The Conservative Party in Saskatchewan in the early 1920s was in disarray with no leader, only three members in the Legislature, and surpassed in public support by both the **LIBERALS** and **PROGRESSIVES**. In these circumstances the party turned to Anderson to lead it at its convention in March 1924. Shortly thereafter, the federal party made him its paid organizer in the province, an arrangement which became the norm for most provincial Conservative leaders into the modern era. Anderson did not turn things around for his party immediately; in fact, the Conservatives again won a mere three seats in the 1925 election. Nevertheless, the party emerged from that campaign far stronger than in 1921; Anderson won his seat and the party raised its popular vote considerably. Over the next four years he would receive the help of a new Conservative newspaper in Regina and the co-operation of many of those opposed to the Liberal government. Furthermore, a number of issues arose to split the coalition which had kept the Liberals in power for over two decades.

On June 6, 1929, enough voters in Saskatchewan deviated from their traditional voting patterns to bring the Conservatives to power, albeit in coalition. The defensive campaign waged by the Liberals, the presence of the Liberal "machine" and the many scandals attributed to it, and the belief that the government had stagnated after so many years in office all contributed to the Liberal downfall. Also important was the failure of Premier **JAMES G. GARDINER** to gain control of Saskatchewan's natural resources, which had been held back by the federal Liberals in 1905. Of even greater significance was Anderson's tireless effort to ensure that the opposition vote was not split on election day. Right from the time he took on the Conservative leadership he

sought the support of every person, group and party committed to the defeat of the Liberals. Eventually the strategy paid dividends. By 1928 he had an agreement with the provincial Progressives not to oppose each other at the next election and further that a "co-operative" government consisting of representatives from all parties would be formed should the Liberals be defeated.

Of greatest importance, however, was the sudden appearance of the **KU KLUX KLAN** in Saskatchewan in 1927. Klan speakers charged that the large-scale immigration of people from central and southeastern Europe threatened the province's Anglo-Canadian way of life; that Roman Catholicism posed a danger to the public school system; and that the Gardiner government had turned a blind eye to both in order to attract the "foreign" vote to the Liberal Party. Anderson stated categorically that neither he nor his party had any formal ties to the Klan, but he did promise to promote additional immigration from Great Britain and to amend the School Act so that no one in religious garb could teach and no religious emblems could be displayed in public schools. Further, he blamed the Liberals for allowing such emotional and divisive matters to become political issues in the first place and his campaign had the desired effect. On election day Liberal representation fell by 50%—to twenty-six seats plus two elected at deferred contests. The Conservatives elected twenty-four, the Progressives five, and six constituencies returned independents opposed to the Liberals. Three months later, after all Opposition members joined to pass a want-of-confidence motion in the Gardiner government, J.T.M. Anderson became Premier.

Anderson's government, which he always referred to as a "co-operative" government, had the misfortune to come to power at the very beginning of the Depression. Although it amended the School Act, established a non-partisan public service commission, passed much-needed labour legislation, began an ambitious highway construction program, and concluded an agreement with the Bennett government which brought Saskatchewan's natural resources under provincial control, as the years went by more and more of its time had to be devoted to attempts to alleviate the worst effects of the **DEPRESSION**. To this end, it created the Saskatchewan Relief Commission to administer the province's many relief programs, declared a moratorium on sales of land to pay municipal taxes, established the Debt Adjustment Board to mediate between debtors and creditors, tried to protect the Wheat Pool, and borrowed from wherever it could to keep farms operational and to maintain minimum standards in the health and education systems. Just the same, none of this saved it at the next election. On June 19, 1934, neither Anderson nor any candidate—Conservative, Progressive or inde-

pendent—who supported his government won a seat in the Legislature.

Thus, in ten years J.T.M. Anderson took his party from the political wilderness to power, himself to the premiership, and both to near oblivion. He deserves credit for the accomplishment, and probably sympathy rather than blame for the defeat. It is most unlikely that anyone, or any set of policies, would have saved any government of Saskatchewan given the impact of the Depression. Anderson resigned as leader of the Conservative party in 1936 but continued to urge co-operation with anyone and everyone opposed to the Liberal Party, a legacy of dubious value to his successors. He went into business from 1936 to 1944, and from 1944 until his death was superintendent of the Provincial School for the Deaf. He died December 28, 1946, and is buried in Saskatoon.   *Patrick Kyba*

FURTHER READING: Barnhart, Gordon L. (ed.). 2004. *Saskatchewan Premiers of the Twentieth Century.* Regina: Canadian Plains Research Center.

ANDERSON, MATHIAS S. (1882–1974).

Mathias (Matthew) Severin Anderson was born in Hoddevik, Norway, on October 22, 1882. He homesteaded in the Bulyea district in 1905, changing his first name to Matthew at that time. As councillor (1922–30) and reeve (1930–49) of the Rural Municipality of McKillop #220, his personal studies and education of the public led to Canada's first comprehensive tax-paid medical and hospital insurance plan. Year after year, beginning in 1927, he presented his resolution for a health insurance plan at the rural municipal conventions. Failing to receive the required support, he decided to focus on his own municipality. Following consultation with several Cabinet ministers and members of the medical profession, the outlines of the plan were submitted to the voters of the municipality in 1938 and received overwhelming support.

The plan was introduced to the Legislature in March 1939 as the "Matt Anderson Plan"; the bill, officially known as An Act Respecting Medical and Hospital Services for Municipalities, was passed by Order-in-Council. This allowed municipalities to collect taxes for health services. The plan provided for residents to obtain unrestricted services of the physician of their choice (unlike municipal doctor plans), including specialist services, hospital accommodation up to 21 days, and prescription drugs (this was cancelled after sixteen months), at a cost of $5 per year, up to a maximum of $50 per family. Within a decade the plan had been adopted by a number of other municipalities. It was the forerunner of the Swift Current regional plan and the Saskatchewan medical care legislation of 1962. Matt Anderson was a successful farmer, a skilled carpenter, and with his wife Martha (*neé* Amundson, 1883–1962) he raised a family of seven children. He died in Regina on July 24, 1974.   *Marilyn Decker*

FURTHER READING: Anderson, M.S. and H. Longman. 1969. *Bold Experiment*. Regina: Commercial Printers.

ANDERSON CART. Similar in design to a **BEN-NETT BUGGY**, an Anderson Cart included a seat over the front axel of an automobile in place of an engine. The conveyance was derisively named after J.T.M. Anderson, Premier of Saskatchewan from 1929 to 1934.   *Holden Stoffel*

ANDREYCHUK, RAYNELL (1944–). Raynell Andreychuk was born in Saskatoon on August 14, 1944. She completed a BA and a law degree from the **UNIVERSITY OF SASKATCHEWAN** in 1967, and established a law practice in Moose Jaw. In 1976, she was appointed to the provincial court and helped establish the family court in Regina. Andreychuk was elected chancellor of the **UNIVERSITY OF REGINA** in 1977 and served eight years. She left the court to become associate deputy minister for Social Services in Saskatchewan.

In 1987, Andreychuk was named high commissioner to Kenya and Uganda, and Ambassador to Somalia until 1990 when she was appointed Ambassador to Portugal. During her diplomatic career she served on several United Nations committees, including the Environmental Programme and the Human Rights Commission.

In 1993 Andreychuk was appointed to the Senate, the first female senator from Saskatchewan. She has served on a number of senatorial committees. Andreychuk has also served on a number of volunteer boards. Between 1975 and 1981 she served as national president and international vice-president of the YMCA and played an active role with the United Way of Canada and Big Sisters Canada.   *Leah Sharpe*

UNIVERSITY OF REGINA ARCHIVES AND SPECIAL COLLECTIONS
78-108-29

Raynell Andreychuk.

GIBSON PHOTO/UNIVERSITY OF SASKATCHEWAN ARCHIVES
A-4716

Constantine Andrusyshen.

ANDRUSYSHEN, CONSTANTINE HENRY (1907–83). Educated as a linguist, Constantine Henry Andrusyshen dedicated his life to the development of Ukrainian studies and is considered the first Canadian-born Slavist. Born in 1907 in Winnipeg, Andrusyshen was the son of Ukrainian immigrants from what was then the Province of East Galicia. Andrusyshen received his BA in 1929, and a BA Honours a year later, specializing in French and English at the University of Manitoba. In 1930–31 he received a French government scholarship to study at the Sorbonne, at the same time completing his Master's thesis in French literature for the University of Manitoba. After five years of work in the local Ukrainian community, he enrolled at the University of Toronto in Romance languages and received his PhD in 1940.

As it was impossible to obtain employment in his field, he accepted an editorship in a Winnipeg Ukrainian weekly, where he worked until 1944. By 1943 there appeared prospects of teaching Slavic languages in Canadian universities. With the help of **GEORGE W. SIMPSON**, a professor of history at the **UNIVERSITY OF SASKATCHEWAN**, Andrusyshen did post-doctoral studies on a Rockefeller Foundation fellowship in the field of Slavistics at Harvard University in 1944–45. He received a certificate confirming his competency to teach in the newly established Department of Slavic Studies at the University of Saskatchewan, the first such department in Canada. In addition to instructing courses in Russian and Ukrainian, Andrusyshen contributed to scholarly publishing in this emerging field of study. He was the main compiler of the largest existing Ukrainian-English dictionary, whose publication in 1955 contributed greatly to the growth of Ukrainian studies in English-speaking countries. In the 1960s he continued with translations into English of Ukrainian poetry and selections of works by Taras

Shevchenko, in co-operation with Watson Kirkconnell. He received the Shevchenko Centennial Medal from the Ukrainian Canadian Committee, and was elected to the Royal Society of Canada. Andrushyshen died in Saskatoon in 1983.
                                    Victor O. Buyniak

FURTHER READING: Buyniak, Victor O. 1991. "Constantine Henry Andrusyshen: The First Canadian-Born Slavist," *Journal of Ukrainian Studies* 16 (1–2): 211–18; Kutka, J. 2000. *The Grade of Passing. Constantine H. Andrusyshen–The Odyssey of a Slavist*. Edmonton: Canadian Institute of Ukrainian Studies Press.

ANGLICAN CHURCH OF CANADA. The Anglican Church had been active in the Canadian North-West since 1820, but its missionary activity in what was to become Saskatchewan was largely confined to scattered fur-trading posts and missions. It was not until the Canadian government acquired western lands from the Hudson's Bay Company in 1869 that the missionary effort of the Church was considerably expanded among the Native population and preparations made for the expected flood of settlers. In order not to lose ground to other denominations, the Anglican Church quickly established a number of dioceses and consecrated bishops to provide the required leadership and direction. In 1874, the Diocese of Saskatchewan was created to oversee missionary activity among Native people and to minister to the colonists settling along the fertile Saskatchewan River valley. Another diocese, Qu'Appelle, was established in 1883 to meet the religious needs of immigrants moving into the agricultural lands of the prairies. Although reasonably well organized at the diocesan and provincial levels, Anglicans were not united at the national level. Furthermore, the eastern Canadian dioceses did not respond in a liberal manner to the numerous appeals for financial support and volunteers. As a result, the western Canadian dioceses relied on money and manpower from the Church of England and its missionary societies. Heavy dependency on overseas help in turn created problems for the Church on the frontier: inadequate funding by far-removed committees, party divisions, the "Englishness" of the Church, a laity not used to voluntary giving, and the failure of the clergy to adjust to frontier conditions all hurt the Anglican cause.

Not content with the existing state of affairs, bishops John McLean of Saskatchewan and Adelbert Anson of Qu'Appelle sought ways for the Church to be more responsive and effective in its ministry. They established theological colleges to train local men and provide a steady supply of regular clergy and catechists. In Saskatchewan, Emmanuel College trained **MÉTIS** and Natives as catechists and teachers, and prepared others for ordination. Throughout its history, Saskatchewan would work to develop and

St. Nicholas Anglican Church, east of Craven.

maintain a strong Native ministry. In Qu'Appelle, where the emphasis was on reaching the newcomer, both English-speaking and non-English-speaking, St. John's College and later St. Chad's Theological College served not only as divinity schools, but as centres from which services and pastoral visiting were conducted. Other means of reaching the immigrant, such as hospitals, schools and nursing programs, were established during the early years of the province's development. Both dioceses experimented with different forms of ministry, particularly in response to the massive influx of immigrants entering the province after the turn of the 20th century. Bishop Anson successfully used the brotherhood system in Qu'Appelle as a means of spiritual renewal and of ministering to a scattered membership. On a grander scale, Bishop Newnham of Saskatchewan trained and deployed sixty catechists at half the cost of regular clergy in the mission field. By far, the most ambitious project was in Qu'Appelle, where the English Church Railway Mission exploited the extensive railway network being constructed throughout southern Saskatchewan. Although relatively short-lived, brotherhoods, the catechist scheme and the Railway Mission permitted the Church to reach its members during the first few years of settlement until such time as they fell under the care of regular clergy.

Financial recession and war put an end to the expansion of the Church on the prairies, as clergy and laity left to join the "colours" or serve in the war effort. Some missions had to be closed. It was not until the mid-1920s that the two dioceses, particularly Saskatchewan, would see their finances improve and expansion occur. Under Bishop Harding of Qu'Appelle and Bishop Lloyd of Saskatchewan, missionary outreach during the 1920s was largely the responsibility of women workers through deaconesses, Bishop's Messengers, Sunday School by Post, and the Canadian Sunday School Caravan

Mission under Eva Hasell and Iris Sayle. In Regina, building on the College and Cathedral site went beyond the theological college, girls' school, Railway Mission house, and Synod Office to include Bishop's Court and a hostel for schoolteachers. Re-organization of the Diocese of Saskatchewan seemed to occupy the mind of Bishop Lloyd from the mid-1920s onwards: suggestion of a separate diocese had been discussed ever since Emmanuel College had moved from Prince Albert to Saskatoon in 1909. Despite a worldwide depression, a decision was made in 1932 to create a new diocese and raise an endowment. Controversially, not the original Diocese of Saskatchewan, but the new Diocese of Saskatoon became the continuing and senior diocese.

The ravages of drought brought untold hardship to the agricultural areas of Qu'Appelle, Saskatoon, and eventually Saskatchewan dioceses. Even though the income of the average churchgoer dropped, members made a determined effort through their weekly giving to ensure that churches were kept open and that clergy facing severe financial hardship were supported. As debt mounted and income from all sources dropped, however, consolidation of missions and often closure followed. Despite these pressures, the Diocese of Saskatchewan under Bishop Burd sought to meet the spiritual needs of newcomers migrating from the cities and drought-stricken parts of the province. As the 1930s progressed, all three dioceses embarked upon a program of financial recovery; but such a worthy objective was not to be reached until the mid-1940s. **WORLD WAR II** and the post-war years caused different problems for the Church. Men and women left their parishes once again to enlist in the armed forces or to work in factories. There was also a noticeable shift in population during the 1940s from the rural to the urban areas. At the same time, women came to play a more significant and sustained role in the affairs of the Church. The economic recovery of the 1950s led to the leadership in all three dioceses looking at ways of becoming self-supporting and embarking upon a plan of expansion. Rather than managing from one year to the next, long-range planning played a greater role in administrative and religious affairs. As worship attendance grew and membership in time-honoured church organizations such as Women's Auxiliary and the Anglican Young People's Association swelled, more clergy were trained and ordained for ministry in rural and urban areas.

The Anglican leadership in the 1960s and 1970s came to the realization that they could not continue to pour money and manpower into rural ministry when the economic base and membership were gradually declining across the province. At the same time, the larger urban centres of Regina and Saskatoon, with a growing Native population, posed different challenges to the Church. With increasing-

ly limited resources at their disposal, even cherished diocesan institutions did not escape scrutiny. In 1964, for reasons of efficiency St. Chad's Theological College was amalgamated with Emmanuel College in Saskatoon. Six years later, St. Chad's Girls' School was closed and the diocesan site sold, which allowed the Diocese of Qu'Appelle to become self-supporting. Ways of co-operating, amalgamating and sharing have been explored and implemented. While issues such as the ordination of women and same-sex blessings have created divisions in recent decades, at the same time there have been just as many issues, such as reaching a just resolution over residential schools and communion with the **EVANGELICAL LUTHERAN CHURCH** of Canada, which have brought the three Anglican dioceses in Saskatchewan together to meet the religious needs of their respective members.   *Trevor Powell*

ANTS: *see* HYMENOPTERA

APOSTOLIC CHURCH. The first recorded meeting of any size was held in an elm and maple bluff one-half mile from Trossachs in the summer of 1914, with Miss Peden and Miss Andrews as evangelists, and Frank Small, later the founder of the Apostolic Churches of Canada, as coordinator. For up to three weeks, people gathered there for two hours of teaching in the morning, two more in the afternoon, and an evening service. It is reported that thousands were in attendance on Sunday evenings. Around the same time, a young man named O.J. Lovick moved from Minnesota to Hanley, Saskatchewan, where he became a lay preacher while working for a local farmer. After studying at the Rochester Bible Training School he returned to the Swift Current area, where he attracted crowds of 500 in the Methodist Church building with his preaching and healing—the most notable of which was curing a woman diagnosed by the Mayo clinic with untreatable cancer. A church was formed with its successor, the Full Gospel Church, still existing in Swift Current.

Lovick continued his work in Regina, starting in a hall that seated 500 but soon moving to the Grand Theatre, which seated 1,200. When the Grand Theatre was no longer available, the Rex Theatre, seating only 800, was rented to continue the revival. The congregation that began from these meetings had Rev. E.W. Storie as its pastor from 1924 until 1950; it later became known as the Regina Apostolic Church, still in existence today. Lovick moved on to Moose Jaw, where in his first healing service a blind woman and a paralyzed woman also blind in one eye were healed of their blindness immediately, with the paralysis disappearing within a week. This was reported on the front page of the Moose Jaw *Evening Times* and it was soon necessary to rent the Capital Theatre to accommodate the capacity crowds. This revival lasted three months, resulting in a church which continues today as the Hillcrest Apostolic Church.

Lovick's success continued in Yorkton, where despite -25° temperatures, crowds of 500 showed up in a poorly heated building every night for three weeks. Rev. Joe Erickson took over the care of that congregation, which continues today as the Family Worship Centre. A similar series of events occurred in Saskatoon and resulted in the Saskatoon Full Gospel Church. Currently, there are thirty-one Apostolic Churches in Saskatchewan, affiliated with the Apostolic Church of Pentecost of Canada, its head office in Calgary. *M.A. Switzer*

APPRENTICESHIP AND TRADE CERTIFICA-TION. Apprenticeship is an industry-driven training process that leads to certification in a designated trade. Apprenticeship training and trade certification ensure workers develop skills that industry and society need. Apprenticeship and skilled trades training contribute to the development of a skilled labour force. Building that skilled labour force requires the co-operation of industry, both business and labour, education and training institutions, governments, and labour-market partners.

As work evolves to meet challenges within the economy, there is an increasing demand for well-educated and skilled workers. Historically, skilled trades have been viewed as physically demanding and labour intensive, and a response to the local economy. With advances in technology and global marketing systems, the trades today are involved with computerized systems, robotics, and meeting the demands of a just-in-time and "on-line" society.

The work of apprentices and tradespeople is visible throughout the community and the trades are basic to our standard of living. To address challenges brought about by the evolution in the marketplace, the apprenticeship system has designated new trades and sub-trades; reviewed and maintained relevant curricula; developed innovative and flexible training delivery; and broadened its partnerships in training and certification, provincially and nationally.

Apprenticeships are implemented when an employer wants a skilled worker and a worker wants to learn the skills of the trade. An individual must be working in a trade to access apprenticeship training. An apprentice is an employee. The employer and the individual employee sign a training agreement or contract and register the contract with the provincial government (the Saskatchewan Apprenticeship and Trade Certification Commission). The apprenticeship contract outlines the period of training and the responsibilities of the employer, the employee (apprentice), and the Saskatchewan Apprenticeship and Trade Certification Commission.

Apprenticeship training ranges from two to five years depending on the trade. While actively employed and earning a wage, registered apprentices learn the knowledge, skills and attitudes associated with the trade over the course of the apprenticeship term. Approximately 80% of apprenticeship training takes place in the workplace, where apprentices learn how to do a task from a supervising journeyperson (an expert in the trade). This practical training component is reinforced with a theoretical training component, where apprentices learn why they do the various tasks. The theoretical training component usually takes place at a technical institute and lasts six to ten weeks per year in length. Apprentices are enrolled in one of these courses each year. Most of the theoretical training is offered throughout Saskatchewan through SIAST.

Apprentices who have experienced the broad range of skills in the trade, worked the prescribed number of hours in the workplace, and successfully completed all levels of technical training are eligible to write the journeyperson trade examination. If successful, they receive a Certificate of Completion of Apprenticeship and a Journeyperson Certificate of Qualification. Employers accept journeyperson certification at face value because the industry has set the standard of performance in apprenticeship. A journeyperson certificate, with a nationally recognized "Red Seal" endorsement, offers tradespeople opportunities to work across Canada without having to recertify in other provinces or territories.

Apprenticeship is industry-driven, and based on the demand for skilled workers. Apprenticeship training is employment-based, and training and certification standards are developed and validated by industry. As a system of training in the trades, apprenticeship has had a long tradition in Canada and around the world. The system presently used in Saskatchewan, a combination of on-the-job training reinforced with periods of technical theoretical training, was initiated in 1944. At that time, thirteen trades were designated. In 2004, there were forty-nine designated trades in the province, and more than 5,200 apprentices registered in the apprenticeship system. In the first few years of the 21st century, Saskatchewan has experienced a shortage of qualified apprentices entering the trades field. Recognized trades in the province of Saskatchewan are: Agricultural Machinery Technician; Aircraft Maintenance Engineer Technician; Automotive Service Technician; Barber-Stylist; Boilermaker; Bricklayer; Cabinetmaker; Carpenter (plus a sub-trade); Concrete Finisher; Construction Craft Labourer; Cook; Cosmetologist; Crane and Hoist Operator (plus sub-trades); Custom Harvester; Drywall and Acoustical Mechanic; Electrician; Electronics Assembler; Electronics Technician (Consumer Products); Floorcovering Installer; Food and Beverage Person; Glassworker; Guest Services Representative; Heavy Duty Equipment Mechanic; Horticulture Technician; Industrial Instrument Mechanic; Industrial Mechanic (Millwright); Insulator; Ironworker Reinforcing Rebar; Ironworker Structural; Locksmith; Machinist; Motor Vehicle Body Repairer (plus a sub-trade); Painter and Decorator; Partsperson; Pipeline Equipment Operator trades; Plasterer; Plumber; Pork Production Technician (plus sub-trades); Power Lineperson; Refrigeration Mechanic; Roofer; Sheet Metal Worker; Sprinkler Systems Installer; Steamfitter-Pipefitter; Steel Fabricator; Tilesetter; Truck and transport Mechanic; Water Well Driller; Welder (plus a sub-trade). *Susan Pentelichuk*

APPRENTICESHIP AND TRADE CERTIFI-CATION ACT, 1999: *See* **LEGISLATION IN SASKATCHEWAN**

AQUACULTURE. Saskatchewan's aquaculture industry consists of about 108 licensed hatcheries and 2,000 licensed producers. Of these, eleven hatcheries and eighty production units are of commercial level. Unlike terrestrial agriculture, which is regulated by Saskatchewan Agriculture Food and Rural Revitalization, aquaculture is regulated by Saskatchewan Environment and Resource Management (SERM). SERM licenses hatcheries and fish production in aquaculture facilities within Saskatchewan.

The most important aquaculture species in Saskatchewan is rainbow trout: the province ranks third among Canadian provinces, producing about 875 tonnes per year of this species. Commercial production of rainbow trout is almost entirely from the Cangro Fish Farm on Lake Diefenbaker. This facility was started in 1993 and is owned by the Saskatchewan Wheat Pool. Cangro raises rainbow trout from hatchlings to a two-kilogram market size, which are filleted and packaged on site and sold throughout North America.

While Saskatchewan aquaculture production is relatively small, the province may have a larger impact on the international aquaculture industry as a supplier of specialty feed ingredients. Aquaculture currently relies heavily on fish meal and fish oil from the capture fisheries as the primary feed ingredients for most aquaculture species. However, the explosive growth of aquaculture around the world has so much increased demand on these commodities that shortages are expected within the next ten years. Saskatchewan crops such as canola and peas have been shown to be excellent sources of protein for the replacement of fish meal in aquaculture diets; several Saskatchewan companies are developing protein concentrates of peas and canola that further improve the nutritional value of these products as fish meal replacements. Fish oil is a rich source of omega-3 fatty acids, which enhance the nutrient value of fish to consumers. Most vegetable oils, however, are poor sources of omega-3 fatty acids. The exception to this is linseed oil produced from flax;

whole flax seed contains approximately 24% omega-3 fatty acids which, with the proper processing, is very palatable to aquaculture species. Aquaculture is a large, high-valued opportunity for the expansion of both fish and crop production in Saskatchewan.

Murray D. Drew

FURTHER READING: Office of the Commissioner for Aquaculture Development. 2000. *Current Status and Potential of the Canadian Aquaculture Industry.* Ottawa: Department of Fisheries and Oceans.

ARBORFIELD, town, pop 411, located NE of Tisdale on Highway 23, on the western edge of the Pasquia Hills and just south of the Carrot River. The first settlers cut trails into the heavily treed area of Arborfield in 1908; with timber plentiful, most homes and buildings were built of logs. The settlers had expected that a railway would soon serve the district, but in 1919 there were still no signs of construction. A delegation was chosen to travel to Ottawa to petition authorities, and they were promised a railroad in the near future. In 1929, the first train arrived. Over the following few years, more people streamed into the region from the drought-ravaged areas of the province's south. In 1950, the population was over 500 and growing. Today, farming remains the main industry in the area. Grains, lentils, hay, and cereal crops are grown; the types of animals (and insects) raised in the Arborfield district include leafcutter bees, honey bees, hogs, cattle, horses, sheep, goats, elk, wild boar, and chinchillas. A large subsidiary to the agricultural industry is alfalfa dehydration and processing. Arborfield Dehy Limited, which was established by a group of local farmers in the early 1970s, is a large area employer; the company processes alfalfa hay into feed pellets and has a large export market in Japan. Nearby Pasquia Regional Park has a trail to the site where fossilized remains of a 90-million-year-old, 6-metre-long (20 ft.) crocodile were discovered.

David McLennan

Alfalfa dehydration and processing plant, Arborfield.

ARCAND, JOHN (1942–). John Arcand, born on July 19, 1942, in Debden, Saskatchewan, is one of Canada's most accomplished fiddle players. The son of Emma and Victor Arcand, he was born into a large musical family and learned to play the fiddle at an early age. He was taught in the Red River style by his father and his grandfather Jean-Baptiste Arcand, both master **MÉTIS** fiddle players. By the age of 12, Arcand was already an exceptional musician, playing at school and community dances. To date, he has composed over 250 original fiddle tunes, and is known internationally as the "Master of the Métis Fiddle." In 1998, Arcand founded the "John Arcand Fiddlefest" in order to expose Métis fiddle music and dancing to a wider audience and to provide a venue where people can gather every summer to share their love and appreciation of old-time fiddle music. He has increasingly been recognized for his efforts to revitalize, preserve and promote Métis fiddle music. In 2003, Arcand obtained a National Aboriginal Achievement Award, and in 2004 he received the Lieutenant-Governor's Award for Lifetime Achievement in the Arts, awarded for his efforts in preserving and promoting Métis fiddling traditions. Arcand has recorded nine fiddle albums, and is regularly featured at community events such as "Back to Batoche Days."

Cheryl Troupe

ARCHAEOLOGICAL HERITAGE, MANAGEMENT OF. Saskatchewan is endowed with a rich and diverse archaeological heritage reflecting more than 12,000 years of human history. Archaeological sites and landscapes in Saskatchewan, whether ancient First Nations encampments and rock paintings, Métis wintering villages, Euro-Canadian fur trade posts, or historic pioneer settlements, are valued today for their humanistic and scientific significance. From a humanistic perspective, archaeological sites have historical, social, religious or other special symbolic or cultural value. They are preserved to be understood and appreciated, and often contribute towards a deeper sense of community identity and respect for other cultures. Scientifically, archaeological sites contain a unique body of data that bears directly upon our understanding of human behaviour and societal change over time. They also contribute to our knowledge of past environments, including changes in species, bio-geography, vegetation, and climate, and of various aspects of human biology and evolution. Today, archaeological sites are used for scholarly research, education and interpretation, land-use planning, heritage tourism, and traditional ceremonial or other cultural uses.

As physical and often inconspicuous components of the land, however, Saskatchewan's archaeological heritage is particularly vulnerable to disturbance or destruction from land use and development and natural erosion. When archaeological sites are disturbed, their value to contemporary society may be significantly diminished or lost altogether. As archaeological sites are also non-renewable and measurably finite in quantity, and, consequently, the archaeological record of Canada is gradually being erased. For these reasons, and because they are a valued public resource, Saskatchewan's archaeological sites require both responsible stewardship and legal protection (from destructive land developments, vandalism and theft, and other consumptive misuse).

Archaeological resource protection refers to the application of laws to safeguard the integrity of archaeological sites for present and future use. In Saskatchewan, archaeological resource protection is achieved through the enabling and regulatory provisions of The Heritage Property Act. Saskatchewan's Parks Act also serves to protect archaeological sites located on provincial park lands and those specifically scheduled as "protected areas." The Heritage Property Act is administered by the Department of Culture, Youth and Recreation, while The Parks Act is administered by Saskatchewan Environment. Key protection provisions are those that: require land developers whose activities may threaten archaeological sites to assess impacts and implement conservation measures; require persons to immediately cease activities that damage archaeological sites until proper assessments are completed; regulate the consumptive use of archaeological sites through an investigation permitting system; restrict access to information to prevent loss or damage to archaeological property; impose land use and development controls on heritage properties through their formal "designation," and; provide for covenants and conservation easements to protect and preserve archaeological property. The Act also affords explicit protection to archaeological burials, rock art sites, and other "sites of a special nature," and provides for Crown ownership of Saskatchewan archaeological objects to prohibit their sale or unauthorized removal from the province.

Archaeological resource management involves activities and procedures to enable the identification, scientific investigation, preservation, interpretation, economic development and sustainability, or other appropriate use of archaeological sites and objects. Resource management is often about making choices and selective decisions to balance archaeological preservation with other public interests and needs, such as resource and energy development.

The government of Saskatchewan, in its capacity to administer and enforce The Heritage Property Act, is the primary steward of archaeological heritage within the province. However, municipal governments, specifically those that designate or establish zoning to protect heritage property, are also important stewards of the resource. As well, private property owners, whose lands contain archaeological sites, and avocational archaeologists who record and report new discoveries, are often crucial partners with government in resource protection and stewardship. The government of Canada is responsible for the protection and management of sites found on federal lands within the province.

In Saskatchewan, the main goals of archaeological resource management are to: control or prevent the uncontrolled loss of archaeological sites and regulate their consumptive use; protect and preserve significant and representative sites; facilitate responsible public access to and use of the resource, and; foster greater public awareness, understanding, and appreciation of archaeological heritage.

To control resource loss, proposed land developments (such as mining, forestry, oil and gas development, Crown land dispositions, and so on) are routinely reviewed to determine their possible impact on archaeological heritage. Where adverse impacts are likely, developers are required (as a condition of project approval) to document, assess, and mitigate development-related impacts. Mitigation may entail archaeological salvage excavation, avoidance through project relocation or re-design, or selective preservation. All impact assessment/mitigation studies (as well as scientific research) that may impact the resource must be carried out by qualified personnel, under approved permits. Permits safeguard the resource by ensuring that investigators have legitimate reasons for conducting their studies, are qualified to do so, use appropriate methods of inquiry, and report their findings for the benefit of other investigators or the public in a timely manner.

While archaeological resource protection occurs through legal means, preservation is achieved through a combination of study and intervention aimed at conserving a site in its best possible condition. This may involve active physical protection, site stabilization, restoration, or site monitoring and maintenance to prevent further deterioration. Determining which sites to protect and preserve often requires systematic and thematic planning, significance assessment, comparative analysis, and other research.

Responsible public access to and use of the archaeological resource (for research, recreational, cultural, or other purpose) is achieved by developing and managing a provincial site registry, providing for the management and care of archaeological collections, developing culturally sensitive policies (e.g., those that acknowledge and respect First Nations traditions and customs), and by providing web-based information, technical advice, and liaison services. Enforcing regulations and standards, and disseminating educational materials help prevent or minimize irresponsible use of the resource.

A significant objective of archaeological resource management today is to build general public awareness and appreciation of archaeology and its contribution to society. Based on thorough research and consultation, communication efforts aim to further the public's archaeological understanding in accurate, culturally sensitive and meaningful ways. Common mediums for presenting archaeological information include museum displays, written materials, audio-visual productions, and various programs and activities. "Public archaeology" programs, in which the public is provided opportunities to participate or otherwise experience field and laboratory work firsthand, can be particularly effective in enhancing public awareness and appreciation of the archaeological past.

Archaeological resource management in Saskatchewan continues to evolve in response to new technologies, changing economic conditions, increasing public interest, and legal decisions (such as those relating to Aboriginal rights and related issues). Collaborating with First Nations and Métis (e.g., by incorporating oral history, traditional knowledge and community values in resource management and decision making), and with all sectors of the province's archaeological heritage community (including learning institutions, heritage associations, professional consultants and researchers, avocational archaeologists, land developers, and property owners) are vital ingredients for successful archaeological resource management. Through sensible administration of The Heritage Property Act and the support and active participation of heritage stakeholders and the public, Saskatchewan's archaeological heritage will continue to provide scientific, educational, social and economic benefits to present and future generations. *C. Germann*

ARCHAEOLOGY. Saskatchewan archaeology falls within the three broad philosophical assumptions central to North American anthropology: each human group has a distinctive culture; culture history has great explanatory power; and cultures cannot be ranked within a superior-inferior framework. Archaeology explains past human events via material culture remains related to environmental and cultural contexts. Within its broad definition, archaeology in Saskatchewan has seen a sequence of seven narrower, but not mutually exclusive, paradigms.

Archaeology as material culture history. Local material culture histories are developed within geographically defined areas and provide explanations for culture changes over time and space. Cultures are defined on the basis of diagnostic materials that can be identified both spatially and temporally as unified in some way (e.g., projectile points, pottery).

Swift Current Petroglyph Boulder Provincial Heritage Property.

Archaeological research excavations by students at Wanuskewin Heritage Park, near Saskatoon.

COURTESY OF HERITAGE BRANCH, SASKATCHEWAN CULTURE, YOUTH AND RECREATION

Archaeological research excavations by students at Wanuskewin Heritage Park, near Saskatoon.

COURTESY OF THE ROYAL SASKATCHEWAN MUSEUM

Archaeological research excavations at the Gull Lake Bison Drive.

Saskatchewan's contributions have been within the established North American prehistoric approximate time periods (listed in years ago or y.a.) of Early (12,000–8,000 y.a.), Middle (8,000–2,200 y.a.), and Late (2,200 y.a.-historic contact), based on projectile points, pottery, and other artifact types. Saskatchewan's contributions have been especially strong for the Middle and Late periods, often exhibiting newly defined projectile point and pottery types. Contributions to historic archaeology also have been important, and include defining the distributions of Aboriginal groups in western Canada at the time of European contact, initiated by HENRY KELSEY in 1690.

Processual archaeology. The overriding goal is to discover and explain lifeways and culture process, thereby contributing to anthropology; the emphasis is on culture rather than on individual choice as a determinant of behaviour. The use of pottery in inferring lifeways and cultural process has contributed to an especially successful anthropological archaeology of the late Late period-historic boundary in the boreal forest, with explanations of sequential distributions related to movements of peoples.

Archaeology as science. This approach provides explanations of observed phenomena by first seeking generalizations on the basis of observations (hypotheses), then testing the hypotheses for truth via verification across time and space, and finally contributing to a theory derived from verified hypotheses. Most of the archaeological theory development in Saskatchewan in the last three decades has been scientific. Culture history has figured in these endeavours more as background for temporal placement than as an explanatory frame of reference. Site and artifact distribution studies, especially of the Middle and Late Periods, have contributed to explaining cultural boundaries and subsistence strategies. Comparisons with ecological features have provided contributions to theories on preferred locations for prehistoric habitation, population movements, culture change over time and space, and population levels.

Postprocessual archaeology. During the 1980s, dissatisfaction with cultural determinism as explaining all archaeological phenomena resulted in renewed emphasis on individual choice as a behavioural determinant, promoting a more pragmatic approach to archaeological explanation. Nonetheless, the explanation of cultural process did not disappear: it became more complex, involving ecological processes and choices made in relation to these. Recent works in Saskatchewan archaeology reflect this interpretive trend, but show that it is not independent from the other paradigms. These works include testing hypotheses on specific movements of human groups in relation to environmental features and ethnic boundaries.

Postmodernist archaeology. Also in the early 1980s came a trend in the social sciences and humanities in North America called "postmodernism." Postmodernism became linked to the postprocessual influence on archaeology. Postmodernism assumes that all knowledge is relative to the person who defines it, ascribing little determining power to culture. This contrasts with the older "modernism" which expresses the hubris-laden notion that one day, via science, we can know everything. The postmodernist assumption leads to the rather startling conclusion that there is no objective reality. Alternatively, it has stimulated an awareness of political implications of archaeological investigations, resulting in increased input from the descendants of people who are being studied, and in recognition of means other than science for obtaining knowledge, including traditional knowledge. At its extreme, this trend promotes the idea that only those individuals whose ancestors have practiced a culture have the right to talk about it. Beginning in the mid-1990s, postmodernism has been rejected by leading physical scientists, and this trend is now spreading into the social sciences and humanities as well, with obvious implications for archaeology. North American, including Saskatchewan, archaeol-

ogy has seen only a limited postmodernist influence in its explanatory approaches owing to strong retention of the culture concept. As in other Canadian jurisdictions, Saskatchewan archaeologists now seek Aboriginal input into artifact and site use and protection.

Archaeology as a part of resource and environmental management. Coming from a completely different perspective than the academic paradigms, Archaeological Resource Management (ARM) began rather suddenly in the early 1970s as a part of environmental impact assessment. The main purpose of ARM was always to provide scientifically accurate information, but initially many archaeologists criticized ARM for not contributing sufficiently to archaeological explanation. Yet the data provided by ARM have added substantially to the overall information base, from which it has been possible to verify hypotheses and strengthen theory, especially explanations of cultural movements and habitation choices. Saskatchewan ARM has been unusually successful in stimulating archaeological explanations: assessments of the potential heritage impacts of proposed dams in boreal forest and prairie river basins have been especially prominent. The credit for this positive and massive addition to archaeological science is due both to the consulting archaeologists who have done the work, and to the influence of the regulatory agencies which have ensured explanatory requirements in the contractual terms for the projects.

Archaeological consilience (unity of knowledge): integration into the broader knowledge framework. Archaeology increasingly tends to borrow freely from any science that may provide a basis for explaining archaeological phenomena. Retaining the useful aspects of other archaeological paradigms, this as yet poorly defined but emerging approach is providing a renewed appreciation of theory. Incorporating recently discovered aspects of the behavioural ecology of resource animals and the concepts of landscape ecology, the new approach is beginning to contribute significantly to explanations of past land-use sequences and cultural landscapes. Within this framework, Saskatchewan archaeology has been integrating new information into extant theoretical paradigms; a currently developing theory identifies the tendency to cultural continuity in the southwest of the province, whereas in the southeast there was more cultural replacement, probably because of the proximity of forest cultures. *Henry Epp*

FURTHER READING: Dyck, I. 2000. "The Last Quarter-Century in Canadian Plains Archaeology," *Prairie Forum* 22 (2): 143–68; Epp, H. (ed.). 1993. *Three Hundred Prairie Years*. Regina: Canadian Plains Research Center.

ARCHAEOLOGY, HISTORY OF. Archaeology is the study of human history and prehistory through analysis of sites and physical remains. In Saskatchewan, archaeology began as part of a scientific expedition in the 1850s. Yet the basis was laid earlier, when fur traders/explorers, such as the La Vérendreys, **ALEXANDER HENRY**, and **DAVID THOMPSON** described the fur trade and Aboriginal cultures in the region.

Some of the early explorers noted signs of previous human existence. For example, **PETER FIDLER** recorded some fur trade posts and stone circles. Such observations established the existence of archaeological remains throughout the Western Interior, but not their antiquity. This changed during the 1800s, when it became important to determine the age of remains and changes over time.

During the late 1850s, scientific expeditions explored the region, and several earthen mounds in the east were excavated. The explorers concluded that the mounds were made by humans who predated the traditions of current Aboriginals inhabiting the region. Near the **QU'APPELLE RIVER**, the explorers observed numerous stone rings, which they correctly interpreted as sites of former tipis. Since tipis were in common use in the area at that time, expedition members decided they were of **CREE** manufacture and, believing that the Cree were newcomers to the region, concluded that tipi rings were a recent historic phenomenon. They summed up their archaeological observations as representing a recent historic Aboriginal occupation, and a somewhat older mound-building period confined to the eastern part of the region. This seemed to leave the archaeological potential of Saskatchewan and Alberta with prospects solely of historic interest.

In Manitoba, questions regarding the burial mounds became subjects of curiosity and study. Between 1879 and the mid-1880s, amateurs carried out excavations and surveys. They were able to show that the mounds were at the northwestern edge of their distribution, which seemed to be centered in the Mississippi valley. They also determined

that some of the mounds had been built several centuries before the arrival of Europeans, and that some of them had been used for burials at different times. This subject was of such interest that the Smithsonian Institution reported in 1993 that the North American burial mounds were made by historic Aboriginals or their direct ancestors. This made it appear that all archaeological remains in the Great Plains area dated to historic times, resulting in a decline in interest in their archaeology.

Nevertheless, mound investigations continued sporadically into the early 1900s, when the first of a few burial mounds in Saskatchewan was discovered. In 1907, Dr. Henry Montgomery from the University of Toronto excavated at the Halbrite mound in the southeast. His report, published in a scholarly journal, created the first real archaeological literature for Saskatchewan.

Even though archaeology had lost an important motivation—the desire to know the age of things—people continued to make discoveries. For example, in 1896 the Reverend John Maclean recorded a large boulder monument on a hill near Moose Mountain. At the centre was a cairn surrounded by a heart-shaped ring of stones. Lines of stones radiated out from the ring and ended in small cairns. However, Maclean was unable to discover the origin or purpose of this monument. In 1905, Charles Noddings, from near Beaver Hills, made another discovery, a slab-like boulder with a face carved onto one side. Noddings pressured the provincial government to protect the object, and it became the first object in the new museum's collection. It helped sustain public interest in Saskatchewan archaeology until the development of an archaeological program in the 1950s.

Until the end of the 1920s, Saskatchewan archaeology remained basically a collection of curiosities with little temporal framework. Then, a radical series of changes occurred in archaeology, including the discovery that human occupation of the Great Plains was not limited to historic times. Between 1926 and 1932, distinctive fluted spear points were found in New Mexico that were directly associated with extinct bison and mammoths, extending human occupation back 10,000 and more years. These discoveries provided Plains archaeology with a lengthy chronological framework.

A bit later, the natural and economic environments also became more conducive to archaeology. The 1930s brought drought and economic depression to the Plains. The drought caused wind erosion, which exposed formerly buried artifacts, including arrowheads, other stone tools, bone tools, and pottery. Furthermore, with opportunities for recreation limited by the economy, artifact collecting became popular. People began to ask questions: Who made these objects? When? Why? To seek answers, collectors compared their finds with one another, but the

newness of the finds meant that much Saskatchewan material was unique.

To enhance the sharing of information, in 1933 the amateur Saskatchewan Archaeological Society was formed in Regina. A Saskatoon society followed in 1935. They identified artifacts and published a newsletter, but without professional expertise and funding they lacked the means to create a reliable temporal framework. Institutional support simply was not available until after **WORLD WAR II.**

During 1951, **BOYD WETTLAUFER**, working out of the Museum of Natural History in Regina, conducted the first systematic archaeological survey in Saskatchewan, followed in 1954 by the first scientific excavation at the stratified, seven-layered Mortlach site, a bison hunters' campsite in the south. The subsequent report established a firm chronological framework reaching back 3,500 years, and described diagnostic artifacts for each layer. Later in the decade, Wettlaufer helped excavate the Long Creek site, also stratified, near Estevan, and extended the dated occupation back to 5,000 years ago. The two reports provided a scientific chronology for almost half of Saskatchewan's human history. In addition to this fundamental work, Wettlaufer also helped establish the first radiocarbon dating laboratory in western Canada at the **UNIVERSITY OF SASKATCHEWAN.**

History and archaeology first merged in Saskatchewan with studies of the fur trade. From the 1920s to the 1940s, **ARTHUR MORTON** did important work in this field. He located and identified a large number of fur trade post ruins, and arranged protection for the François-Finlay posts near Nipawin. In 1949, **JOHN ARCHER** reported on an even

UNIVERSITY OF SASKATCHEWAN ARCHIVES A-5255

Measurements of human jawbones from prehistoric site near Swift Current.

EVERETT BAKER PHOTO/COURTESY OF THE SASKATCHEWAN HISTORY AND FOLKLORE SOCIETY

Boyd Wettlaufer with his young sons, sorting buffalo bones, Mortlach, September 1954.

broader range of historic sites in Saskatchewan. Another such study was done in 1951 by Jack Herbert. Together, these reports helped launch a provincial historic sites service, which eventually got involved in historic archaeology.

The first major historic site excavation in Saskatchewan was carried out by Alice Kehoe in the mid-1960s at the François-Finlay posts. This began a trend which addressed a much broader range of historic sites and structures, including pioneer farmsteads, abandoned villages, brickyards, hospitals, battlefields, and others.

Regarding Aboriginal sites, an important event was the hiring of Thomas Kehoe as curator at the Saskatchewan Museum of Natural History (now the Royal Saskatchewan Museum) in 1959. The result was reconnaissance and excavations in both the north and the south. During the early 1960s, work also was done in the valley of the **SOUTH SASKATCHEWAN RIVER** that was scheduled to be inundated. In 1962 government responsibility for archaeological remains was bolstered by the addition of antiquities clauses within parks legislation. In 1964, the University of Saskatchewan established an Anthropology and Archaeology department with **ZENON POHORECKY** as head. This meant that students no longer had to leave the province to obtain training in archaeology, and by the late 1960s major projects were being directed out of the university.

The last three decades of the 20th century were times of consolidation and integration for Saskatchewan archaeology. There were many studies of individual cultures of particular sites and features, methods, and past culture-environment relationships. The oldest parts of the archaeological record, 5,000–12,000 years ago, began to yield their secrets.

Good, broad picture syntheses now exist as well. The Saskatchewan Archaeological Society, the Museum, and the University of Saskatchewan are more active than ever. One of the biggest recent changes in archaeology has been the enactment and enforcement of heritage legislation, beginning in 1980. Now, field archaeology is controlled by the provincial government, requiring pre-development assessments. The result is that most of the field work in archaeology now is done by consultants, whose activities are regulated by the government.

Integration has occurred in two ways. First, over the past 30 years, Aboriginal concerns and involvement have become part of archaeology. The creation of the First Nations gallery at the Royal Saskatchewan Museum, and the **WANUSKEWIN** museum near Saskatoon are exemplary in this regard. Schools, too, are beginning to integrate Saskatchewan archaeology into their curricula. Thus, over the past 150 years, Saskatchewan archaeology has developed in synchrony with the rest of the world, and is now an important ingredient in the investigation and preservation of the province's heritage.

Ian Dyck

FURTHER READING: Dyck, I. 2001. "The Last Quarter Century in Canadian Plains Archaeology," *Prairie Forum* 22, no. 2: 143-68; Montgomery. H. 1908. "Prehistoric Man in Manitoba and Saskatchewan," *American Anthropologist* 10, no. 1: 33-40; Wettlaufer, B. 1955. *The Mortlach Site in the Besant Valley of Central Saskatchewan.* Anthropological Series No. 1, Saskatchewan Museum of Natural History, Regina; Wettlaufer, B. and W.J. Mayer-Oakes. 1960. *The Long Creek Site.* Anthropological Series No. 2, Saskatchewan Museum of Natural History, Regina.

ARCHER, JOHN (1914–2004). John Hall Archer was an accomplished historian and civil servant, and the first president of the **UNIVERSITY OF REGINA**. Born on July 11, 1914, near Broadview, Archer was a teacher in Saskatchewan's rural districts from 1933 to 1940, and during **WORLD WAR II** served with the Royal Canadian Artillery in the United Kingdom, North Africa and Italy. After the war, he earned BA and MA degrees in history from the **UNIVERSITY OF SASKATCHEWAN**, and a BA in library science from McGill University. He served as Saskatchewan's legislative librarian (1951–64), assistant clerk of the Legislature (1956–61), and provincial archivist (1957–62). Archer became director of libraries at McGill University (1964–67), then archivist and associate professor of history at Queen's University, where he earned his PhD in history. He returned to his home province in 1970 as principal of the Regina campus of the University of Saskatchewan, and served as president of the University of Regina from its establishment as an independent institution in 1974 until his retirement in 1976. During and after his career he served on numerous Royal Commissions, boards and advisory councils, and was a prolific author and editor. His books include *Land of Promise* (1969), *Saskatchewan: A History* (1980), *Honoured with the Burden* (1987) and, as editor, *One Canada* (1975–78), the memoirs of John Diefenbaker. He received the Order of Canada and the Saskatchewan Order of Merit; the University of Regina's main library is named after him. John Archer passed away on April 5, 2004.

John Chaput

UNIVERSITY OF REGINA ARCHIVES AND SPECIAL COLLECTIONS
84-11-303

John Archer, 1984.

ARCHITECTURAL INFLUENCE. Many architects from outside the province have influenced the nature of architecture in Saskatchewan. Beginning in the territorial period, Dominion Architect Thomas Fuller designed **GOVERNMENT HOUSE** (1889–91) in Regina, then the capital of the North-West Territories. After the province was created in 1905, Toronto firm Darling and Pearson, well known for its bank projects, acted as provincial architects and completed the Land Titles building in Regina (1907–09) and the Moose Jaw Courthouse (1908–09).

Architectural firms from Montreal had a prominent role during the early years. In 1907, the firm of Maxwell and Maxwell was chosen through a limited competition to design the **SASKATCHEWAN LEGISLATIVE BUILDING**. Another Montreal firm, Brown and Vallance, was chosen in 1909 by the board of governors of the **UNIVERSITY OF SASKATCHEWAN** to create a master plan for the campus and act as university architects until the 1930s; they went on to design what has been identified as the finest grouping of collegiate Gothic-style buildings in Canada. They were also responsible for the first building for the Anglican Diocese of Qu'Appelle (1912), the Canada Life Assurance building (1912–14), the Sherwood Department Store (1913; now the **SASKATCHEWAN WHEAT POOL** headquarters)—all in Regina—and the Fairbanks Morse warehouse in Saskatoon (1911). The Hotel Saskatchewan, built by the **CANADIAN PACIFIC RAILWAY** in Regina and opened in 1927, was designed by the Montreal firm, Ross and MacDonald. The Bessborough Hotel in Saskatoon, last of the Chateau-style hotels, was designed by another Montreal firm, J.S. Archibald, and constructed from 1930 to 1932 for the **CANADIAN NATIONAL RAILWAY**.

Many bank buildings in the province were designed by architects from Ontario, Manitoba, and the United States. Prototypical, prefabricated wood bank buildings, designed by Darling and Pearson in the Classical Revival style for the Canadian Imperial Bank of Commerce, can be found in Watson (1906) and Nokomis (1910). Winnipeg firm Blair and Northwood designed buildings for the Northern Bank in Qu'Appelle and Regina (both 1906); and the Minneapolis firm, Lamoureax & Long, designed the Weyburn Security Bank (1910–11).

During the 1930s, Modernist architecture arrived in the province through modest buildings like the Mainline Ford auto dealership in Indian Head (1937) and the CBK radio transmitter building (1939) in Watrous. This was the start of a trend still current, where projects are designed elsewhere as prototypical buildings that could fit on any site. In 1962, the Winnipeg architectural firm, Blankstein Coop Gillmor and Hannah (later number TEN architectural group), won the design competition for the **MENDEL ART GALLERY** in Saskatoon. Also in 1962, prominent American architect Minoru Yamasaki, known as the designer of the World Trade Center in New York, was chosen as the master planner and architect for the **UNIVERSITY OF REGINA**. In 1966, the Toronto firm of John B. Parkin and Associates was chosen for their expertise in laboratories to design an extension to the Thorvaldson Building at the University of Saskatchewan.

In the 1980s, a consortium of firms including prominent Canadian architect Arthur Erickson and the Saskatoon firm Folstad & Friggstad Architects completed a design for City Hospital in Saskatoon. In 2001, Douglas Cardinal, internationally renowned First Nations architect, completed the design of the **FIRST NATIONS UNIVERSITY OF CANADA**.

Bernard Flaman

FURTHER READING: Barnhart, G.L. 2002. *Building for the Future*. Regina: Canadian Plains Research Center; Kerr, D.C. 1998. *Building the University of Saskatchewan*. Saskatoon: University of Saskatchewan.

ARCHITECTURE. Saskatchewan architecture is a reflection of a short and compressed period of European and American settlement, preceded by a long history of First Nations settlement and quickly followed by participation in a global economy.

Local First Nations did not possess a tradition of permanent construction; there is, however, evidence of semi-permanent structures such as the conical log dwelling of the northern **CREE**. The tipi (a Siouan word) has become an iconic representation of a temporary form of shelter on the prairies which utilized materials at hand: poles and bison skins. As the investigation of First Nations' past advances, more constructions are being discovered: stone circles, effigies and mounds, the meaning of which is open to debate, continue to survive and are studied from an archaeological rather than an architectural viewpoint. These constructions are often found on high ground, and oral traditions suggest that they may have been used as ceremonial places, or as orientation devices for travelers crossing the vast prairie. **WANUSKEWIN**, near Saskatoon, preserves an example of First Nations settlement and one of the earliest known subterranean dwellings in the province. The name of the Assiniboine Nation translates to "Stony Sioux" in Saulteaux (Plains Ojibwa), in recognition of their frequent use of and reverence for this material.

Fur traders and settlers brought with them building traditions imported from many places, but transformed them with construction techniques that depended on the availability of materials and expertise. Holy Trinity Anglican Church at Stanley Mission is the oldest standing building in the province, built between 1854 and 1860 utilizing a heavy timber structural frame constructed onsite, combined with **STAINED GLASS** windows, locks and hinges imported from England and floated down the Churchill River. In 1882, the arrival of the transcontinental railway caused the flow of European settlers to accelerate. Battleford, Prince Albert and Fort Qu'Appelle, settlements during the pre-railway territorial period, were comprised of modest wood-frame, log or stone build-

University of Saskatchewan, College Building, designed by Montreal firm Brown and Vallance, 1912, the centerpiece of the finest grouping of collegiate Gothic-syle buildings in Canada.

ings exemplified by the Hudson's Bay Store in Fort Qu'Appelle (1897) and Government House in Battleford (1877; lost to fire in June 2003). Grain elevators, developed in the 1880s as a solution for quickly loading grain onto railway cars and benefiting from the new technologies of "cribbed" wood construction and elevating devices, are viewed as one of the first modern building types. The town of Fleming is home to the oldest standing grain elevator in Canada, dating from 1895.

With the creation of Saskatchewan as a province in 1905, there was unbounded optimism for the future. The Legislative Building (Regina), the University of Saskatchewan (Saskatoon), the Provincial Hospital (North Battleford), and the correctional facility (Prince Albert) were then built, along with courthouses and land titles buildings throughout the province. These buildings employed substantial materials like brick and stone, and were designed by professional architects in a variety of styles (*see* **ARCHITECTURAL INFLUENCE**): Gothic, French Classicism and Georgian Classicism are examples of many "revival" styles popular at the time. The Capitol Theatres in Regina and Saskatoon, and the Towne Cinema in Saskatoon displayed lavishly decorated interiors known as "atmospheric," usually in a Spanish style. Building materials included Tyndall stone (a fossilized limestone from Manitoba), local fieldstone, and brick from over 100 small brick-making facilities or from one of the three major plants located at Estevan, Claybank and Bruno. The Regina architectural firm Storey and Van Egmond designed many early buildings. From 1915 to 1929, provincial architect **MAURICE SHARON**

designed courthouses and hospitals in the American Colonial style.

With the coming of the **DEPRESSION** in 1929, building activity slowed dramatically but the projects that were realized, mainly service stations, airports and radio stations, were built in a new style called Art Moderne, characterized by streamlined forms rendered in stucco. **WORLD WAR II** saw the construction of airplane hangars and military facilities. Metal Quonset huts, which would later become ubiquitous as farm storage sheds, appeared. The Federal Building in Regina (1935) was one of the few large institutional buildings constructed during this period; designed by Regina architect **FRANCIS PORTNALL**, it represents a transition between the "revival" styles of the previous decades and the Modernist architecture of the 1950s, 1960s and 1970s.

Since 1945, architectural developments in Saskatchewan have paralleled those in the rest of the world. The province does not have an architectural school, and graduates who choose to return after their studies or move to the province from elsewhere bring with them an international perspective that they often combine with a keen sense for local materials and a particular way of engaging the prairie terrain. Between 1960 and 1980, **JOSEPH PETTICK**, **CLIFFORD WIENS**, and the firm Holliday-Scott, Paine designed buildings in the modernist style that combined international influences with local materials; examples include the Saskatchewan Power Corporation (Regina, 1963), the Silton Chapel (1969), and the Lutheran Seminary (Saskatoon, 1968). Recent concerns in the architectural community, related to sustainable design, energy efficiency

and heritage conservation, have combined with a Saskatchewan tradition of utilizing substantial materials and engaging the landscape. "Post Modernism," where historical forms are rendered in modern materials, and "Revisionist Modernism," where a humanizing influence is brought to modernism, are two international developments that influence Saskatchewan architecture. Examples include the Saskatchewan Provincial Court (Prince Albert), the Alice Turner Library (Saskatoon), the T-Rex Interpretive Centre (Eastend), the Spinks addition at the University of Saskatchewan, and the **FIRST NATIONS UNIVERSITY OF CANADA** (Regina).   *Bernard Flaman*

FURTHER READING: Boddy, T. (ed.). 1980. *Prairie Architecture. Prairie Forum, Special Issue.* Regina: Canadian Plains Research Center.

ARCHIVES. Interest in preserving Saskatchewan's documentary heritage began soon after the first settlers arrived in the North-West Territories and gathered momentum after provincial status was achieved. Members of the early heritage movement such as Dr. **E.H. OLIVER**, **ARTHUR SILVER MORTON** and Z.M. Hamilton were instrumental in establishing societies to collect historical records, build up library collections, and mark historic sites. While citizens were engaged in preserving heritage, successive governments were much slower to act in ensuring that public records were properly preserved. In 1897, an ordinance was passed establishing the Department of Territorial Secretary to keep the archives of the government, but it never really became an archival repository. During **WORLD WAR I**, provision was made for an archives branch of the Legislative Library, but public records were never acquired.

The first piece of legislation to deal with the retention and disposal of inactive public records, the Preservation of Documents Act, was passed in 1920. Essentially, the Act allowed for the legal destruction of large quantities of records by Order-in-Council. During the period 1920-45, a total of seventy-eight orders were issued, but only two directed the transfer of records to the "archives of the province": without an official repository, valuable records were invariably lost. It was largely due to the tireless efforts of Dr. A.S. Morton of the **UNIVERSITY OF SASKATCHEWAN** that the need for the province to preserve its records was brought to the fore. With the support of the Canadian Historical Association, Morton pushed for the creation of provincial archives under the control of an archivist. The University's offer to provide space, to appoint an archivist and to cover operational costs met with a favourable response from a cash-strapped provincial government. In 1937 a Historical Public Records Office was established at the University, with Morton assuming the title and responsibility as Keeper of the Public Record.

JOSEPH PETTICK PHOTO

Saskatchewan Power Corporation building, Regina, combines local materials and colours such as a wheat-coloured brick from Estevan with a gently curved plan inspired by Brazilian modernism.

By the early 1940s Morton realized that a more formal and stable funding arrangement was required. His call for legislation met with approval from the newly elected CCF government, which was interested in establishing a public records policy. In 1945, an Act Establishing the Archives of Saskatchewan was passed. As well as formalizing the spirit of co-operation between the government of Saskatchewan and the **UNIVERSITY OF SASKATCHEWAN**, the legislation broadened the mandate of the new archives to include all types of archival records from both public and private sources.

For its time, Saskatchewan's archival legislation was on the leading edge. It established a system of accountability whereby all public records were scheduled before they could be discarded. It called for a professional archivist to select those records of historical value for permanent preservation. For several decades, Saskatchewan's archives legislation stood the test of time and occasionally served as a model for other jurisdictions. By the 1990s, new technology was being used in the workplace, more and more records were being created, access and privacy legislation was coming into force, a different and expanded client base used archival resources, and new approaches to information and records management were being introduced. In the spring of 2004, a new Act was passed updating the legislative framework under which the Saskatchewan Archives had been operating, and bringing Saskatchewan's legislation in line with that of other Canadian jurisdictions.

While the Saskatchewan Archives spearheaded the preservation of public and private records in this province, more specialized repositories have been created over the past four decades. Some archival programs such as those of the University of Saskatchewan and the cities of Regina and Saskatoon were originally created in partnership with the Saskatchewan Archives and later became independent, with paid staff; others such as archives of churches, municipalities and associations were created by their parent body and staffed by volunteers. Most of these local archives focus on collecting and preserving the records of their institutions or organizations as well as those of individuals closely associated with them. At this time, there are approximately forty archives across the province.

In the late 1980s, the Saskatchewan Council of Archives was created as part of a national archival network. Through the channeling of grants and contributions from the Canadian Council of Archives, the provincial council is responsible for directing federal funds to member institutions for control of archival holdings, preservation management, and professional development and training. As well as distributing grants, the Council has conducted needs assessments, established provincial priorities, and sponsored workshops and seminars. It

has also managed programs such as archival conservation and outreach services, which member archives could not have offered or afforded on their own. Over the past fifteen years, the Saskatchewan archival community has benefited greatly from being part of the Canadian archival system—as the growth of smaller archives, the increasing professionalism of members, and the strength of archival programs, both large and small, attest. *Trevor Powell*

FURTHER READING: Champ, J. 1991. "Arthur Silver Morton and His Role in Founding the Saskatchewan Archives Board," *Archivaria* 32: 101.

ARCOLA, town, pop 532, located just S of Moose Mountain Provincial Park, west of Carlyle on Hwy 13. The first settlers arrived in the area in 1882, and within a few years churches, schools, post offices, and stores were scattered about the countryside. By 1901, as the first trains arrived, the community was large enough to be incorporated as a village. Arcola would remain at the end of the rail line for the next few years, and thus prospered as an important link during this period of large-scale immigration and westward expansion. Many fine buildings were erected in the community in the early years; five of these have since been declared heritage properties. These well-preserved early-20th-century buildings typifying the quintessential prairie town led filmmakers to choose Arcola as the setting for the 1976 filming of **W.O. MITCHELL**'s *Who Has Seen the Wind*. Arcola is also distinguished by another literary link: **SINCLAIR ROSS** worked in Arcola between 1929 and 1933, and it is believed that during this time he began his Canadian classic, *As for Me and My House*. The Arcola area became well known for its quality livestock quite early. One of the earliest homesteaders, Isabelle Rogers Bryce, became an internationally acclaimed breeder of heavy horses: Canada's only woman exhibitor at the International Livestock Exposition at Chicago in 1924, she won a grand championship with her Clydesdale mare, "Doune Lodge White Heather," the first time in the history of the show that the prize went to a woman. Today, the oil industry is a significant part of the local economy, with pumpjacks dotting the district. Each summer, Arcola hosts an Annual Rodeo and Fair. *David McLennan*

ARGUE, HAZEN ROBERT (1921–91). Hazen Argue was born in Moose Jaw on January 6, 1921. His parents rented their Kayville farm when Argue was five and moved to Avonlea where his father operated a farm machinery business that was successful until the crash of 1929. Argue graduated from the **UNIVERSITY OF SASKATCHEWAN** in 1944 with a BSc in agriculture.

Saskatchewan's longest serving federal parliamentarian (eighteen years as a member of

SASKATCHEWAN NEW DEMOCRATIC PARTY ARCHIVES
Hazen Argue.

Parliament and twenty-five years as a senator) began his career as a member of the **CO-OPERATIVE COMMONWEALTH FEDERATION** (CCF) and ended it as a Liberal senator. He was elected to the House of Commons in 1945 at the age of 24 as the CCF member for Wood Mountain. In 1958 he was the only Saskatchewan Opposition MP to survive the **DIEFENBAKER** sweep. With the defeat of **M.J. COLDWELL**, Argue was elected House Leader. Two years later Coldwell resigned and Argue was elected CCF leader. In 1961 a union between the CCF and the Canadian Labour Congress created the **NEW DEMOCRATIC PARTY** (NDP). The leadership contest for the new party was between Argue and Saskatchewan CCF Premier, **TOMMY DOUGLAS**. Douglas won a first-ballot victory and Argue returned to his farm.

Controversy was a part of the career of "Blazin' Hazen." In 1962 Argue announced he was leaving the NDP and joining the Liberals. Argue entered the 1962 federal election as a candidate for the **LIBERAL PARTY**. He held his seat in 1962 but was badly defeated in 1963 and 1965. Lester Pearson appointed Argue to the Senate in 1966. He held this position until his death. In 1980 Trudeau named Argue Minister of State for the Canadian Wheat Board. Argue served in this capacity until the Liberal defeat of 1984. In 1982 Argue achieved national recognition by arranging a grain deal with the Soviet Union.

In 1989 Argue was accused of using Senate funds to hire research assistants and other staff to help his wife Jean attempt to win a federal Liberal nomination. Argue was charged with fraud, theft and breach of trust. The charges were dropped in 1990 when he became seriously ill. He died October 2, 1991. *Dwayne Yasinowski*

FURTHER READING: McLeod, Thomas H. and Ian McLeod. 1987. *Tommy Douglas: The Road to Jerusalem.* Edmonton: Hurtig Publishers.

ARMSTRONG, GRACE (CA. 1867–1960).

Born about 1867 in New Zealand, Grace Armstrong graduated from Otage University. In 1908 she came to Regina as did her younger sister, Nora Armstrong, a graduate nurse who became one of the first public health nurses in the city. Initially, Dr. Armstrong was in private practice, but during the war years she became a public school dentist, serving from 1917 until her retirement in 1935. A supporter of women's suffrage, she also became active in several women's organizations such as the University Women's Club, the Women's Canadian Club, and Women's Musical Club. Other involvements included the Natural History Society and the Society for the Prevention of Cruelty to Animals. She died on January 5, 1960, in Regina.   *Ann Leger-Anderson*

ARNOLD, GLADYS (1905–2002).

Gladys Arnold was the sole Canadian journalist in France at the outbreak of **WORLD WAR II**. She covered the early days of the conflict until the German occupation of Paris in June 1940. Born in Macoun on October 2, 1905, Arnold joined the *Regina Leader-Post* as an editorial assistant in 1930. Soon, she was writing editorials and feature articles. Seeking adventure in Europe, Arnold left her job in 1935 and traveled to England aboard a grain cargo ship. She found herself in Paris, where she intended to study the modern age philosophies of socialism, communism, and fascism. Arnold began submitting freelance pieces to the Canadian Press and was soon hired as their Paris correspondent. In the next four years she reported from France and Germany on the Spanish civil war, the Austrian *Anschluss* with Germany, and the Munich agreement regarding Czechoslovakia.

UNIVERSITY OF REGINA ARCHIVES, GLADYS ARNOLD FONDS

Gladys Arnold in Paris, 1938.

After the fall of Paris, Arnold returned to Canada and worked tirelessly for the Free French. From the end of the war until her retirement in 1971, Arnold headed the information service of the French embassy in Ottawa. Gladys Arnold died in Regina on September 29, 2002.   *Mark Vajcner*

FURTHER READING: Arnold, Gladys. 1987. *One Woman's War: A Canadian Reporter with the Free French.* Toronto: Lorimer.

ART, VISUAL.

There has been visual art in Saskatchewan for as long as people have lived here; but the development of painting, sculpture and printmaking has occurred since the settling of the province in the latter part of the 19th century. Once the early settlers had gained a level of stability, some began to reflect their new environment in small paintings and drawings, which tended to be amateur in nature and were influenced by their European or eastern Canadian backgrounds. The arrival from England of **INGLIS SHELDON-WILLIAMS** in 1887, **AUGUSTUS KENDERDINE** in 1907, and **JAMES HENDERSON** in 1910 gave the province three professionally trained artists who brought with them the academic style prevalent in British art schools at that time. Sheldon-Williams and Kenderdine were influential as teachers as well as painters. Sheldon-Williams taught at Regina College from 1913 until 1917, and Kenderdine went on to become lecturer in art and artist-in-residence at the **UNIVERSITY OF SASKATCHEWAN** in 1927; he then moved to Regina in 1936 to undertake the expansion of the Art Department at Regina College.

The relative economic stability and level of affluence prior to the 1930s led to an increasing interest in visual art, and a variety of arts organizations were created. Collectors of art were also emerging, the most prominent being Norman MacKenzie, a Regina lawyer, who started collecting as early as 1900. While much of MacKenzie's efforts were centred on acquiring European art, he became a supporter of Saskatchewan artists, and it was his collection that became the basis of the permanent collection of the **MACKENZIE ART GALLERY** when it opened at Regina College in 1953. The majority of visual art activities in the early years was centred in both Regina and Saskatoon. In 1926, **ERNST LINDNER** came to Saskatoon from Austria. Both a respected artist and teacher, Lindner was head of the Art Department at the Saskatoon Technical Institute from 1936 until 1962, and a catalyst for much of the art activity in the city during that time. **FRED MENDEL** arrived in Saskatoon in 1939, bringing with him a collection of 20th-century art, and he immediately began to acquire works by Saskatoon artists. A number of arts organizations came together to form the Saskatoon Arts Centre in 1944. In 1964, with the help of Mendel, the Centre spearheaded the building of the **MENDEL ART GALLERY**.

From 1950, the visual arts in Saskatchewan evolved rapidly. The **SASKATCHEWAN ARTS BOARD** had been created by the provincial government in 1948, with a mandate to provide financial support to artists through grants and by collecting their work. In 1950, **ELI BORNSTEIN** came to work and teach at the University of Saskatchewan, and **KEN LOCHHEAD** came to be head of the Art School at Regina College; in 1952, **ART MCKAY** joined Lochhead in Regina. In order to deal with the physical isolation of the province from the major art centres of the world, the two persuaded the University of Saskatchewan to organize an annual workshop at **EMMA LAKE**, with major international artists and critics as guest instructors. Starting in 1955, the workshops were to have a profound effect on art in Saskatchewan. They created international interest and recognition for artists living and working here, including Lochhead, McKay, **RON BLOORE**, **DOUG MORTON**, and **TED GODWIN**, who became collectively known as the **REGINA FIVE**, as well as **WILLIAM PEREHUDOFF** and **DOROTHY KNOWLES** of Saskatoon.

The Emma Lake workshops resulted in a new confidence in Saskatchewan art; this sentiment was strengthened by the next generation of artists and still permeates much of the work in the province. Painting has been the most prevalent discipline, the landscape being the dominant subject. Painters who have dealt with issues of abstraction have tended towards the use of colour as the primary theme, but today there are many approaches to the making of art, resulting in a wide range of imagery and styles. Three types of sculpture have dominated the three-dimensional work created in Saskatchewan: large, open, welded-steel abstract work emerged as a result of the Emma Lake workshops; ceramic sculpture developed during the late 1960s and 1970s and was influenced by the folk art of the province; and bronze casting was brought to prominence by **JOE FAFARD**. Printmaking was limited for many years to lino and wood-block prints, but silkscreen printing became popular after 1950. The first etching press was brought into the province in 1965, and printmaking became a more serious discipline in both university art schools with the arrival of respected artist printmakers as teachers.   *Paul Fudge*

ARTS AND CULTURE: *see essay on facing page.*

ASELTINE, WALTER MORLEY (1886–1971).

Walter Aseltine was born on September 3, 1886, in Napanee, Ontario and educated in Perth. He taught school in Manitoba and Saskatchewan and later obtained his BA from the University of Manitoba. In 1913, Aseltine was called to the Saskatchewan Bar, and established a law firm in Rosetown. He was made King's Council in 1930. Aseltine served on the Rosetown School Board from1920 to 1927 and from 1930 to 1934 he was the town's mayor. In 1921 Aseltine ran unsuccessfully for the **CONSERVATIVE PARTY** in the Rosetown constituency. Prime Minister R.B. Bennett appointed him to the Senate on December 30, 1933. From 1958 to 1962 he served as the leader of the government in the Senate. He performed many international duties including attending the coronation of Queen Elizabeth II as a member of the official Canadian delegation. In 1961 he was made a member of the Privy Council. For twenty-one years he served on the Senate Divorce Committee, ten of which as chairman.

While he was a member of the Senate he was still very active within his community. He resigned from the Senate in March 1971, one of the longest serving senators in Canadian history at 37 years. He died November 14, 1971.   *Trent Evanisky*

ASQUITH, town, pop 574, located on Hwy 14 W of Saskatoon. Settlers began arriving in the district around 1902. A construction boom began in 1906, and both the CPR and the CNR had come through by 1909. Sports have always played an important role in this community, and over the years Asquith has earned an enviable reputation in both baseball and hockey circles. While mixed and dairy farming have long been the economic backbone of the community, today many residents either commute to work in Saskatoon or are employed in nearby potash mines. Asquith has also become the retirement home of many area farmers.   *David McLennan*

ASSINIBOIA, town, pop 2,483, located approximately 105 km SW of Moose Jaw at the junction of Hwys 2 and 13. Named after the former district of the North-West Territories, the community serves primarily as an agricultural service centre for the surrounding region. Originally settled mainly by people of English and French origin (with smaller

numbers of Romanians, Scots, and Scandinavians), Assiniboia dates its beginnings to October 12, 1912, when the CPR put 980 lots up for sale at the Assiniboia townsite: people stood in line overnight to buy their lots, and the community rapidly sprang up on the previously barren prairie. In 1913, the population rose from roughly 400 to 1,400; a quarter of a million bushels of grain were shipped out of the five brand-new elevators that fall. During the Depression, forward-looking town officials employed out-of-work men to construct the town's sewer system, which it could not afford to operate until 1948. After **WORLD WAR II**, prosperity returned to the area and Assiniboia resumed growing at a steady rate.

Today, Assiniboia has a wide variety of businesses including agricultural equipment dealers, manufacturing companies, a tire recycling plant, grain-handling facilities, and one of the country's largest livestock auction yards. The Assiniboia District Museum features displays relating to the area's pioneer history. St. Andrew's Presbyterian Church, completed in 1920, and the Assiniboia Court House, built in 1930 and designed by Provincial Architect **MAURICE SHARON**, have both been designated heritage properties.   *David McLennan*

ASSINIBOINE: *see* **NAKOTA (ASSINIBOINE)**

ASSINIBOINE RIVER (51°17'N, 101°32'W; map sheet 62 N/5). The Assiniboine River has its headwaters just southeast of Greenwater Provincial Park in the Nut Mountain district. It flows in a southeasterly direction through Kamsack and into the Lake of the Prairies across the Manitoba border. Joined by the Qu'Appelle River at St. Lazare, the Assiniboine eventually flows eastward into the Red River in

downtown Winnipeg. Like many prairie rivers, the Assiniboine occupies a former glacial spillway, flowing through a valley far too large to have been carved by the modern-day river. The Assiniboine was an important link in the fur trade, and was probably seen by **HENRY KELSEY** on his journey into the prairies in 1691. In 1774, when **MATTHEW COCKING** traveled inland with **SAMUEL HEARNE** to establish the Hudson's Bay Company's first inland post at what became Cumberland House, Cocking's guides, members of the Sturgeon **CREE**, wanted the post located in their territory on the upper Assiniboine instead; over the years, a number of trade posts were established along the river, the town of Pelly serving as a reminder of this fur trade connection. Several First Nations reserves located along the Assiniboine, north of Kamsack, also attest to the historic importance of this region to Saskatchewan's First Nations.   *Marilyn Lewry*

ASSOCIATION CULTURELLE FRANCO-CANADIENNE.

The French constituted less than 6% of settlers in 1905 despite the diligence of the clergy and the government. French settlers were located in the four corners of the newly created province because of the diocesan structure and the dynamism of key missionaries. These factors led a few clerics, concerned about the survival of the faith, language and culture of members of their flock, to argue that a strong provincial association would protect the religious and linguistic rights of their parishioners. When the *Société du Parler Français du Canada* proposed the organization of a major convention in Quebec City for June 1912, Francophones of Saskatchewan were invited to select delegates. In February 1912, 450 regional representatives met in Duck Lake, created a provin-

RON GARNETT—AIRSCAPES

Assiniboine River, near Kamsack.

cial chapter of the society, selected fourteen delegates to attend the convention in Quebec, and elected an executive of prominent laymen and members of the clergy. The executive met in Regina that summer and created the *Association Franco-Canadienne de la Saskatchewan*. The provincial association was renamed *Association Catholique Franco-Canadienne de la Saskatchewan* in 1913 to promote the interests of French-speaking residents.

By 1914, the ACFC had more than 1,400 members paying annual dues of $1. Local chapters were spearheaded by the local curé, and at the provincial level several clerics sat on the executive committee. A parish priest, Abbé Baudoux of Vonda, even served as president of the ACFC. The ACFC focused most of its attention on education. It helped to create the Association Interprovinciale, concentrating on recruiting bilingual teachers from Quebec. It supported the creation of the Association des Commissaries d'Ecole Franco-Canadiens. It instituted in 1925 the *concours de français*, which resulted in the creation of a bilingual office of education parallel to that of the provincial ministry of education. The ACFC appointed *visiteurs d'école*, mostly clerics, to assist teachers and promote the expansion of bilingual education for the French-speaking students of Saskatchewan. The ACFC also supported activities which protected the Catholic and cultural interests of the French minority. It endorsed French radio stations across the prairies, lobbied extensively to obtain French television services, and played a vital role in the survival of such newspapers in Saskatchewan as *Le Patriote de l'Ouest* and its successor *L'Eau Vive*.

ACFC's success can be attributed to the widespread support of the clergy and the dedication of certain laymen such as Raymond Denis (president for ten years), Dr. Laurent Roy, **IRÈNE CHABOT**, **ROLLAND PINSONNEAULT**, Dumont Lepage, Albert Dubé, and others who all served as president. Their work was often facilitated by such men as Antonio de Margerie, who served as secretary of the association from 1929 to 1962. *L'Association Catholique Franco-Canadienne* became *L'Association Culturelle Franco-Canadienne* in 1962, more closely reflecting the evolution in the mandate of the ACFC to support the socio-cultural interests of the French community. By 1998, the ACFC was reorganized and renamed *L'Association Communautaire Fransaskoise* in an attempt to reach the grassroots more readily and be more accountable to its supporters and the government. (*See also* **FRENCH SETTLEMENTS**)   *André Lalonde*

FURTHER READING: Lapointe, R. and L. Tessier. 1986. *Histoire des Franco-Canadiens de la Saskatchewan*. Regina: Société historique de la Saskatchewan.

Arts and Culture

Ken Mitchell

At the time of its creation in 1905, the province of Saskatchewan was considered as alien to the development of arts as the surface of the moon. With a provincial economy based on agricultural production and resource extractions such as petroleum, forestry and minerals, the "square" province seemed a very unlikely base for the development of artistic sensibility or belles-lettres. But geography, as well as history, is an eccentric determinant of culture, and it appears that this most inhospitable of climates and most challenging of landscapes have produced an artistic harvest that in a scant hundred years has made Saskatchewan home to a most original and lively regional culture. By "culture" is meant that massive assembly of beliefs, histories, languages, and commonly held values that forms the collective consciousness (and unconsciousness) of a society—a sort of conceptual glue that binds any given group of people together. Over time, such a culture can be studied, and through analysis will define and explain the particular nature of that society, the traits and values which give it distinction. Culture is both highly abstract, being composed of evanescent ideas, attitudes, opinions, and beliefs, and reassuringly tangible, as when it is rendered through books, works of art, and architecture of stone, metal and wood. Culture is the GDP of ideas, the "cultural capital" which becomes the heritage of its citizens—sometimes valued, sometimes not—and provides the foundational knowledge they depend on to pursue their social and material goals. Culture is what people rely on to give them context as they establish individual identity and moral purpose; it is the DNA of social evolution. Most of it is transmitted through language, but much of it is visual and tactile as well.

The people who inhabited and developed this semi-arid region of North America brought with them diverse elements of their own cultural heritage from elsewhere: the Aboriginal peoples of First Nations; the early French and Scots settlers who initiated the massive migration of European land-seekers; and finally the international refugees of the latter 20th century who came as "displaced persons," political refugees, boat people, and economic migrants seeking a better life in the Canadian heartland. This hodge-podge of various cultural roots can become dissonant and conflict-ridden, or it can be hybridized, with new and marvelous patterns of rich variety: this happy process has been true of Canada generally, but becomes even more specific in Saskatchewan. Because this portion of the original North-West Territories was largely an agricultural preserve, whose initial appeal was mainly to those who herded animals or tilled the soil, it should not be surprising that the land itself, and human relationship with that land, would become one of the strongest themes in the mosaic pattern of beliefs. Of course, in most Canadian literature the landscape plays a dominant role, and reference to that landscape—whether in the oil paintings of the Group of Seven, the balladeers of Newfoundland, or the totem poles of the West Coast Aboriginals—is what defines and illustrates a great deal of Canadian art. But there are many other themes and motifs which appear in a study of a national culture.

What is distinctive about Saskatchewan culture? First, it is informed by two unique geophysical features. The primary one is the flatness of the prairie landscape, particularly in the southern half of the province; this is associated with the unrelieved horizontal plane of perception that exaggerates the intensity of the sky. As might be expected, this geographical feature, with its implications of openness and solitude, has left a distinct impression on the Saskatchewanian psyche. The second feature, no doubt related to the flatness, is its extreme climate, a climate that rages through the seasons in crescendos of natural violence that include blizzards, droughts, tornadoes, floods, dust-storms, frost, heat, and cataclysmic thunderstorms—a weather of constant and turbulent change. Nature in Saskatchewan is relentlessly threatening, and barely tolerant of human life. Such a landscape and climate naturally discouraged more people than it attracted, but many did become attracted as time went on. The people who sought their future in "The Land of Living Skies" were inclined to be enterprising groups and literal risk-takers, such as Sioux and Blackfoot hunting nomads from the south, Métis buffalo hunters from the Red River valley, or European colonists who arrived with visions of establishing utopian communities.

Extremities also interested people like the English explorer HENRY KELSEY, the first European to set foot on the Great Plains. He arrived around 1690, traveling upriver from York Factory, the Hudson's Bay Company post on the Hayes River, inland from the coast of Hudson Bay. It is perhaps significant that the introduction to his exploration journals was written in the form of a poem—in fact, the first known literary reference to the Saskatchewan plains:

...The inland country of good report hath been
By Indians but by English not yet seen
Therefore I on my journey did not stay
But making all ye haste I could upon our way
Gott on ye borders of ye Stone Indians country...
...And now will give account of that same country's soil
Which hither part is very thick with wood
Affords small nuts with cherryes very good
Thus it continues till you leave the woods behind
And then you have beast of several kind
The one is a Black a Buffillo great
Another is an Outgrown Bear wch is good meat
His skin to get, I have used all ye ways I can
He is man's food and he makes food of men
His hide they would not me it preserve
But said it was a god and they should starve
This plain affords nothing but Beasts and grass
And over it in three day's time we past

Almost two centuries later, Kelsey's poetic declaration was countermanded by the Irishman John Palliser, who was commissioned by the British government to explore the territory between the Red River and the Rocky Mountains, north of the 49th parallel. Palliser was specifically instructed to report on the agricultural potential of the region, and his 1863 report to the British Parliament was emphatically negative (*see* PALLISER AND HIND EXPEDITIONS). He recommended against construction of a transcontinental railroad through western Canada, concluding that the desert-like terrain would never be fit for human settlement. The semi-arid grassland comprising most of southern Saskatchewan and Alberta came to be known as the "PALLISER TRIANGLE." Fortunately for the future province, another Irishman, William Francis Butler, arrived in Red River as a military officer during the first Riel Rebellion, and was commissioned to report on trading posts along the Saskatchewan River as far as the Rocky Mountains. His winter journey of 2,700 miles was reported in his book, *The Great Lone Land* (1872), a classic of western exploration. His description of the "Prairie Ocean" set the tone for future waves of immigrants:

No ocean of water in the world can vie with its gorgeous sunsets; no solitude can equal the loneliness of a night-shadowed prairie: one feels the stillness, and hears the silence, the wail of the prowling wolf makes the voice of solitude audible, the stars look down through infinite silence upon a silence almost as intense... One saw here the world as it had taken shape and form from the hands of the Creator. Nor did the scene look less beautiful because

SASKATCHEWAN ARCHIVES BOARD R-H8655

Sir William Butler.

nature alone tilled the earth, and the unaided sun brought forth the flowers.

Butler was just one of the adventurous sojourners who contributed to the identity of Saskatchewan. Others of the 19th century whose literary or artistic endeavours became significant included LOUIS DAVID RIEL, the leader of the North-West Rebellion (*see* NORTH-WEST RESISTANCE), as well as pioneer feminist and writer KATE SIMPSON HAYES and her lover, NICHOLAS FLOOD DAVIN. Davin was the silver-tongued orator, poet and politician who founded the first newspaper in the North-West Territories, the Regina *Leader*, in 1884. Many among this assortment of idealists, rogues and entrepreneurs saw themselves as risk-takers on a cosmic scale, conscious founders of a new society based on utopian and artistic visions, a human paradise made possible by the vacuity of the cultural atlas. Davin, for example, put Saskatchewan on the map in many ways, not only establishing the Regina *Leader*, but also becoming Regina's first Member of Parliament, representing Assiniboia West. He was only one of many who made Saskatchewan's a political culture. He was also the first poet published in the North-West.

By the late 19th century, the treeless prairie was being settled by dispossessed crofters from Scotland and "the men in sheepskin coats," Doukhobors that the Canadian Minister of the Interior Clifford Sifton enticed from the steppes of Russia and Ukraine. The first settlers had to be very tough and adaptive people, mentally prepared to deal with the cruel logistics of human survival. Like the frontier territories in the United States, the Canadian prairies saw their share of political extremists and social outcasts, such as the colonies of Jews, Mennonites and Hutterites who followed the Doukhobors, seeking communal land in a world of religious freedom where their collective labour might pay off in material prosperity. The huge Eastern European influx (mostly Germans, Russians, and Ukrainians) brought not only tough, experienced farmers to grow wheat and other cereal crops: it also carried Eastern Orthodox culture and values into the nascent social and political system of the province. These eastern values were to have a huge and long-lasting impact on the indigenous culture. In a somewhat different way, so did the Chinese immigrants who entered North America as coolie labourers on the construction of the Canadian Pacific Railway, and moved on to Saskatchewan to operate the network of small-town cafés and laundries that became their livelihood. Various political and religious "colonies" were established by old-world migrants, such as CANNINGTON MANOR, the Saskatoon Temperance Colony and the BARR COLONISTS from England. There were colonies of Swedes, Finns, Icelanders and Romanians, who arrived on their own little enclosure of "Promised Land," bringing not only dreams of a new beginning for generations yet to come, but also esoteric cultures from the Old World. One of the best accounts of this contribution is in the book *Slava Bohu*, a history of the Doukhobor diaspora by J.F.C. Wright.

It seems natural that extreme climatic conditions can breed a culture of extremity, and might foster the evolution of extreme political ideas—and this turns out to be the case. It was evident along the SOUTH SASKATCHEWAN RIVER in March 1885, when Riel and GABRIEL DUMONT declared the "Provisional Government of the Saskatchewan" at St.

Laurent: based on the organizational principles of the buffalo hunt, this "republic" had already adopted a ten-point Revolutionary Bill of Rights to ensure equitable land distribution for farming among the Métis buffalo-hunters of the plains. The result was the North-West Rebellion and Riel's trial and execution for treason. Other communitarian philosophies were introduced by European settler groups, to be forged in the crucible of adverse climate and geography. They resulted in the rapid development of radical political parties and movements, which came to characterize the province of Saskatchewan. The Captains of Industry, the Progressives, the KU KLUX KLAN of Kanada, the Social Credit movement, UNITED FARMERS OF CANADA, the Saskatchewan-Farmer-Labour Group, and the CO-OPERATIVE COMMONWEALTH FEDERATION (CCF) were all born on the prairies and usually centred in Saskatchewan, though shared with the sister provinces of Alberta and Manitoba. This stream of "prairie radicalism" was fed by diverse branches (right wing and left), and quickly came to define the social history of Saskatchewan, making it a "politics" deeply embedded in its culture.

This historical development was related to, and perhaps dependent on, the populist convictions carried by early agricultural settlers such as the Doukhobors and Scottish crofters. Under adverse conditions, the tiny groups of settlers quickly proved in the most practical way that the strength of their community was greater than the strength of individual members. Barn-building and threshing bees, community entertainments, beef rings, and various other communal activities led to an intensification of community formation—and ultimately to early forms of co-operatives such as the GRAIN GROWERS GRAIN COMPANY and the SASKATCHEWAN CO-OPERATIVE ELEVATOR COMPANY. These agrarian movements progressed in 1923 to the creation of the SASKATCHEWAN WHEAT POOL, a remarkable farmers' co-operative (organized by the charismatic American speaker Aaron Sapiro) that became the world's largest agricultural co-operative and possibly the most successful. Many other co-operatives were established, from the Dairy Producers Co-operative to the legendary Matador Ranch (see MATADOR FARMING POOL AND THE CO-OPERATIVE FARM MOVEMENT); and there was a great proliferation of credit unions across the province as an opposition to the banking system. Ultimately such collectivist social inclinations would (and did) lead to the formation of a grass-roots socialist party, the Co-operative Commonwealth Federation. The election of the CCF in 1944 introduced North America to its first socialist government. This mid-century milestone has come to be seen as a defining moment in Saskatchewan, if not Canadian, history, and has had the effect of projecting Saskatchewan and its culture as intensely political—the "home of socialism." But in real terms, this was a "small-p" political, a collectivist identity whose strength lies in its social and community institutions. This was certainly the case in the arts, wherein Saskatchewan people came to rely on local

BERNARD FLAMAN PHOTO/COURTESY OF GOVERNMENT OF SASKATCHEWAN, HERITAGE

Prince Albert Town Hall Opera: This building is one of the few 19th-century town halls still standing on the Prairies. Built in 1892-93, it housed a variety of facilities, including a theatre, large meeting room, and the town's municipal offices.

resources and on art "made in Saskatchewan." Entertainment in most communities was self-generated, rather than imported, so there was relatively little instruction or encouragement from the top down, or from external institutions and teachers. In an agricultural economy, there was little support for academies, art schools, or professional theatre companies.

Yet many of these burgeoning prairie towns competed to plan and erect their own "opera house," determined as they were to take part in the development of high culture (see OPERA). These old heritage buildings remain in use in towns like Wolseley, Biggar and Hanley. They and dozens of others were home to a wide variety of touring musicians and theatre groups who enlivened the early years of Saskatchewan, bringing culture from the centres of civilization beyond the borders. The CHAUTAUQUA movement—a traveling "tent show" of arts and entertainment—introduced live music and recitation to hundreds of towns and villages, often incorporating local artists into the program. This was the most popular form of access to the performing arts in early Saskatchewan; it generated many talented artists who developed in later years. This highly democratic form of entertainment died out in the 1930s under the impact of radio and recording technology, which could more easily bring music, theatre and comedy into rural living rooms.

Most of the small farming towns and villages that blossomed throughout Saskatchewan in the pioneer years have perished in the last half-century. The industrializing economy and transportation systems caused the demise of railway lines. Hundreds of little communities that survived even the Depression years—the Dirty Thirties so mythologized in Saskatchewan lore and history—have gone the way of the prairie bison. But loyalty and commitment to the community have remained an important part of Saskatchewan culture. The strongest have survived and grown—little towns like Arcola and Livelong and Wynyard. That Saskatchewanians value their communities can be seen in the sheer volume of local histories published and circulated through the province's extensive library system. Saskatchewan—"the heartland of Canadian football"—came to be so identified because of the unparalleled success and province-wide support for its community-owned team, the SASKATCHEWAN ROUGHRIDERS: football became an important element of Saskatchewan culture.

The first historically significant arts group was probably the Regina Literary and Musical Society, initiated in the capital in 1885 by the peripatetic Kate Simpson Hayes. Only a year before, the village of tents and shacks was known as Pile of Bones Creek. Mrs. Simpson Hayes recruited troops from the North-West Mounted Police headquarters to perform as choristers in the operettas and musical concerts she produced. This fledgling group anticipated the formation of the Regina Orchestral Society, which presented its first concert in the city in 1908.

The **REGINA SYMPHONY ORCHESTRA** now makes the proud claim of being the oldest continually operating symphony orchestra in Canada. A second important agency, the **SASKATCHEWAN MUSIC FESTIVAL ASSOCIATION**, was also established in 1908, and the following year produced the first provincial music festival in Regina, featuring musical groups and choirs from around the province. The annual festival then rotated to the other cities each year: Saskatoon, Moose Jaw, and Prince Albert. It turned out to have great influence on the development of musical arts in the coming years, so that there are now as many as fifty local festivals taking place each year, which send musicians from Saskatchewan to the national competition.

As for visual art, there was very little creative production in the early years of the century. Art exhibitions, where they occurred at all, were associated with agricultural exhibitions and fairs—even rodeos and horse sales. Prizes were awarded for painting, photography and various crafts, with local artists producing work to appeal to the tastes and standards of their community, not for the critical audience in the centres of civilization. It should not be surprising that the subject and themes of such artistic creation would be focused on the agricultural landscape and on the human interaction associated with it. However, various folk arts like furniture making, weaving, quilting and woodworking—any craft that had a practical value—thrived.

The importance of geography in Saskatchewan culture is perhaps most easily demonstrated in the literary arts. The prairies of Saskatchewan were the setting for a number of Canada's earliest writers, whose work became best-sellers. For example the evangelical novelist, Rev. Charles Gordon (*nom de plume*, Ralph Connor), wrote about the hard life of homesteaders in epics like *The Sky Pilot: A Tale of the Foothills* (1899) and *The Patrol of the Sundance Trail* (1914) while serving as a Presbyterian church minister in Winnipeg. Similarly, Nellie McClung, a Manitoba writer who became a champion of women's rights, presented her populist views in literature, particularly in her autobiographical *Clearing in the West* (1935). Her first novel, *Sowing Seeds in Danny* (1908), was an account of small-town prairie life that created a huge readership in Saskatchewan. Other Manitoba writers who popularized the agricultural settlement life on the prairies included Robert Stead with his impressive novel *Grain* (1926), depicting the life of the young farmer Gander Stake, and the German-born immigrant Frederick Philip Grove, with his epic accounts of agricultural survival on the prairies, *Settlers of the Marsh* (1925), *Fruits of the Earth* (1933), and his celebrated "autobiography" *In Search of Myself* (1946).

But one expatriate Saskatchewan writer had even greater influence on the cultural identity of the province: the American novelist **WALLACE STEGNER**, whose semi-autobiographical account *Wolf Willow* (1955) was "a history, a story, and a memory of the last plains frontier." The book tells the history of the **CYPRESS HILLS** area of southwestern Saskatchewan, in particular Stegner's boyhood community of Eastend. This is how he describes the Saskatchewan landscape and its effect on people:

"Desolate? Forbidding? There was never a country that in its good moments was more beautiful. Even in drouth or dust storm or blizzard it is the reverse of monotonous, once you have submitted to it with all the senses. You don't get out of the wind, but learn to lean and squint against it. You don't escape sky and sun, but wear them in your eyeballs and on your back. You become acutely aware of yourself. The world is very large, the sky even larger, and you are very small. But also the world is flat, empty, nearly

abstract, and in its flatness you are a challenging upright thing, as sudden as an exclamation mark, as enigmatic as a question mark.

It is a country to breed mystical people, egocentric people, and perhaps poetic people. But not humble ones. At noon the total sun pours on your single head; at sunrise or sunset you throw a shadow a hundred yards long. It was not prairie dwellers who invented the indifferent universe or impotent man. Puny you may feel there, and vulnerable, but not unnoticed. This is a land to mark the sparrow's fall." (p. 8, *Wolf Willow*, Viking Compass edition, 1962)

Similar insights mark the literary production of the province's most-celebrated authors, **W.O. MITCHELL** and **SINCLAIR ROSS**. It is no exaggeration to refer to them as Saskatchewan's literary giants, for by the mid-20th century their novels and short stories came to be seen as the ultimate expression of Saskatchewan culture.

James Sinclair Ross (1908–96) was the first native-born writer whose work reached an international audience. He is now best known for the short stories he wrote during the 1930s and 1940s, later gathered in the collection *The Lamp at Noon and Other Stories* (1968). These stories are dramatic tales which portray the brutalization and occasional human triumph of rural people beset by the hostile Saskatchewan landscape: in "The Painted Door" a young farmer dies in a blizzard; in "The Lamp at Noon" a young housewife goes mad in a dust-storm; in "A Field of Wheat" a family survives a violent hail-storm. Ross's influence on Canadian writing has been deep and pervasive, especially through his early novel *As For Me and My House* (1941), now recognized as a masterpiece of Canadian literature. The novel is a first-person diary account of a year in the life of Mrs. Bentley, a church minister's wife, who with her husband Philip, a failed artist, experiences deep intellectual isolation in the fictional Saskatchewan village of Horizon during the drought of the 1930s. Among the many features of the book is the impact of the surrounding landscape on the lives of its people. For all its brilliant insights and critical acclaim, Ross's work is little known to most Saskatchewan people. Although his short stories appear in international literary anthologies, there are no copies of his books on the library shelves of the town of Shellbrook, where he was born. After his death, however, the town of Indian Head, where he lived and attended school in the 1920s, commissioned a bronze statue by sculptor **JOE FAFARD** and dedicated it to Ross. It stands in front of the Indian Head library.

William Ormond Mitchell, born in Weyburn in 1914, was a more popular literary figure than Ross, and for the last half of the 20th century was the voice of Saskatchewan. His reputation came about largely

W.O. Mitchell.

through his series of farm-life stories *Jake and the Kid*, first written for CBC Radio, later published and then adapted as a popular television series. Mitchell had a gift for reconstructing Saskatchewan dialect in comic modes, and became perhaps better known as a public storyteller than as a writer. Nevertheless, his first novel, *Who Has Seen the Wind* (1947), was a literary gem, extensively reprinted in many editions and widely taught in the educational system. It is a beautifully written account of a boy growing up in a small town and coming to grips with the mysteries of life and death. Like Ross, Mitchell made poetic use of the prairie environment, and in the opening words of the novel wrote, "Here was the least common denominator of nature, the skeleton requirements simply, of land and sky—Saskatchewan prairie." Mitchell and Ross were, of course, expatriate Saskatchewanians by the time their work was published. Although he had left Saskatchewan as a young man, W.O. Mitchell occasionally returned from Toronto and High River, Alberta, to conduct writing workshops for the SASKATCHEWAN ARTS BOARD. Ross lived mostly in Montreal, later in Greece and Spain, though he continued to write primarily about his Saskatchewan background.

SASKATCHEWAN ARCHIVES BOARD R-A4657

Chautauqua at Manitou Lake, July 1922.

Other important authors of the mid-century included R.D. (BOB) SYMONS, an Englishman who immigrated to become a cowboy and wrote several accounts of ranch life, such as *Where the Wagon Led*. EDWARD MCCOURT, a well-published novelist and professor of English at the University of Saskatchewan, wrote an important book on regional literature, *The Canadian West in Fiction* (1949), as well as three novels set in Saskatchewan. The best, *Music at the Close* (1947), is a tragic account of a young farmer who goes to university, becomes a poetic member of "the lost generation," and dies on the beaches of Normandy in WORLD WAR II. Saskatchewan literature and its preoccupation with the landscape were effectively illustrated and satirized by Paul Hiebert, a University of Manitoba professor and writer. He created SARAH BINKS, the "Sweet Songstress of Saskatchewan," a tongue-in-cheek biography of the fictitious young woman who proclaimed the farming society's enthusiasm for poetry and other high culture.

Visual art began making its impact with the emergence of a number of landscape artists who had emigrated from Europe, most with some degree of classical training. These included AUGUSTUS KENDERDINE, INGLIS SHELDON-WILLIAMS, ILLINGWORTH KERR, JAMES HENDERSON, and the Austrian-born ERNEST LINDNER. Also working in Saskatchewan in the early years was the "primitive" folk artist JAN WYERS, from his home in Windthorst. These early painters were patronized to a great extent by the wealthy collector NORMAN MACKENZIE, a Regina lawyer whose legacy to the city and the province led to the first public art gallery, established in 1953 at Regina College (*see* MACKENZIE ART GALLERY). This important institution was matched in Saskatoon by the (equally wealthy) philanthropist and art collector FRED MENDEL in 1964, when he helped the Saskatoon Arts Centre build the MENDEL ART GALLERY. MacKenzie mostly collected landscape painting, a genre that dominated his legacy. In one letter, he said "...you will remember that in marine scenes I like storms, and in landscapes I like rugged heavy pictures, not the little delicate shrubs, grass and trees that you so often see..." The early painters of Saskatchewan all worked in this tradition. Their paintings tended to reflect, as they did for later generations, the powerful effect of the dominant sky and its spectacular flood of light. They had a great influence on the style and quality of subsequent painting, which tended to emerge from the art programs at the UNIVERSITY OF SASKATCHEWAN and Regina College (*see* UNIVERSITY OF REGINA). Sheldon-Williams taught painting at Regina College from 1913 to 1917; Kenderdine taught art at the University of Saskatchewan in Saskatoon from 1927 to 1936, when he moved to the expanded Art Department at Regina College; and Lindner was hired in 1936 as head of the Art Department at the Saskatoon Technical Institute and had a wide-ranging effect on the development of local artists.

Following the decline of touring repertory companies and traveling shows, the amateur "little theatre" movement began developing in the major cities and towns of Saskatchewan. They were probably influenced and encouraged by the CHAUTAUQUA community tent shows that were popular in the 1920s. The Saskatoon Little Theatre was established in 1922, and REGINA LITTLE THEATRE in 1926; the latter still produces full seasons of drama, making it the oldest continuously operating amateur theatre in Canada. Soon smaller towns and even villages were creating their own theatrical entertainments as the province's "do-it-yourself" culture grew through the Depression years. They were supported by the Saskatchewan Drama League (formed in 1933), backed by the University of Saskatchewan. The university itself, located in Saskatoon, created the first drama department at a Canadian university in 1946. THEATRE SASKATCHEWAN, the amateur theatre umbrella organization, currently has 86 member groups scattered throughout the province.

With these developments in art, music, theatre and literature, it was clear that the fine arts were setting down roots in Saskatchewan. In 1948, a key event occurred that was to have long-ranging implications. During its first term in office, T.C. DOUGLAS' CCF government created the Saskatchewan Arts Board through an Order-in-Council. Premier Douglas was quoted as saying, "The people of the Prairies are hungry...for things of the mind and the spirit: good music, literature, paintings and folk songs" (the folk songs were apparently his personal addition to the usual trinity of arts). The arts board was said to be modeled after the British Arts Council, and broke ground in Canada as the first formal government program in support of the arts. It preceded the creation of the Canada Council of the Arts by thirteen years, and was in many respects its prototype. The first chair was Dr. STEWART BASTERFIELD, then dean of Regina College. The board was proclaimed to be "responsible for formulation of policies designed to make available to the citizens of the province greater opportunities to engage in creative activities in the fields of drama, visual arts, music, literature and handicrafts, with qualified guidance and leadership, and to establish and improve the standards for such activities in the province."

The Saskatchewan Arts Board thus set out to challenge the conventional wisdom that Saskatchewan was a cultural wasteland: "The form...was tempered by western Canadian conditions, the comparative smallness of the cities, the thinly spread population and the various limitations due to distances. Rather than the Old Country Plan of having panels for each of the Arts, it was considered best to have each of the Arts Board members contribute to the whole field of interest in order to strengthen the Board's plans and projects" (W.A. Riddell, *Cornerstone for Culture*, p. 6).

A

The Regina Five, left to right: Ron Bloor, Art McKay, Doug Morton, Ken Lochhead, Ted Godwin.

Half a century later, the results of this far-seeing creation have become evident. The annual allocation of arts grants by the board has risen from its original sum of $4,400 in 1949 to over $5.3 million in 2004. More important than its support of individual artists, however, was its development and support of dozens of arts organizations and companies, such as the ORGANIZATION OF SASKATCHEWAN ARTS COUNCILS (OSAC), an umbrella group comprising the dozens of local arts councils throughout the province. It also fostered the creation of professional theatre companies, film producers, and dance companies like Saskatchewan Dance Theatre in Saskatoon and Regina Modern Dance Works in Regina. The impact of the Saskatchewan Arts Board was most clearly felt at first in the visual arts. In 1950, the board organized the first in a series of annual juried all-Saskatchewan art exhibitions. One of its earliest accomplishments was the establishment of the Norman MacKenzie Art Gallery and its permanent collection of art (painting, sculpture and craft art) at the Regina College campus. This was complemented by the hiring of KENNETH LOCHHEAD as director of the college's art school in 1950. He was soon joined by ARTHUR MCKAY, who along with RONALD BLOORE, DOUGLAS MORTON and TED GODWIN became known as the "REGINA FIVE" as they embraced modernist styles. They approached the University of Saskatchewan to set up an annual workshop at Emma Lake in northern Saskatchewan, with important international artists and critics imported as instructors. Other artists who became part of this annual workshop were DOROTHY KNOWLES and WILLIAM PEREHUDOFF.

Another innovation was the establishment of the Summer School of the Arts. It evolved out of a series of summer workshops in drama by FLORENCE JAMES, which began in 1951 and later expanded into music, writing and art. In 1967, the board inaugurated the SUMMER SCHOOL OF THE ARTS at Fort San, a former tuberculosis sanatorium in

Saskatchewan Centre of the Arts, Regina.

the Qu'Appelle Valley. In this scenic setting, writers, artists, musicians, photographers, and actors would gather during the summer months for specialized workshop classes with instructors from throughout the world. The summer school operated until 1989, when it was closed due to rising costs. In the meantime, its multi-disciplinary fervour had shaped the lives of an entire generation of Saskatchewan artists.

One of the clearest successes of the arts board was its role in establishing the province's professional theatre companies, 25TH STREET THEATRE and PERSEPHONE THEATRE in Saskatoon, and the GLOBE THEATRE in Regina. Before 1960, there was no professional theatre production in the province, although there were many touring performances from eastern Canada and abroad. In 1966, Ken and Sue Kramer established the Globe, primarily for school performances; but in 1969 their first season of professional theatre was under way in Regina. 25th Street Theatre began operations in 1972, and Persephone Theatre in 1974, under the guidance of Brian Richmond and members of Saskatoon's theatrical Wright family (actors Janet, Susan, John and Anne Wright). A few years later, SHAKESPEARE ON THE SASKATCHEWAN began producing summer tent shows of Shakespearean plays under the direction of Henry Woolf.

Nineteen sixty-seven was a milestone year, not only in the Saskatchewan arts, but across Canada as well. It was Canada's Centennial, and in the general festivities and celebrations it was clear that a new generation of artists was appearing throughout the country. The provincial government initiated the funding for two huge Centennial auditoriums in Regina and Saskatoon, a long-awaited development to put major performing arts centres in the province's principal cities. These became the Centennial Auditorium in Saskatoon, and the Saskatchewan Centre of the Arts in Regina. Not only in Saskatchewan, but also across the land, a new spirit began to rise in the arts communities, as Canada advanced into its second century. The Canada Council's years of investment in developing artists was about to pay off.

Before 1967, there was very little literary production coming from Saskatchewan. The only publisher at the time was Modern Press, the Saskatchewan Wheat Pool's publishing wing, which marketed homesteader reminiscences and a few historical accounts. Then in 1969, the Saskatchewan Arts Board invited a number of the province's writers to a conference at Fort Qu'Appelle. This conference resulted in the creation of the SASKATCHEWAN WRITERS GUILD, the first provincial writers' organization in Canada, preceding by a couple of years the establishment of the Writers' Union of Canada. The guild began with the declared purpose of advocating on behalf of writers, promoting opportunities for publication, and developing "professional attitudes toward the craft." Its development, along with the ongoing programs of the Summer School of the Arts, ignited an explosion of literary activity that continues to generate international attention. A literary movement seemed to reach critical mass as a number of poets, novelists, playwrights, and non-fiction writers began to reach out to the world. Writers associated with this movement include the poets ANNE SZUMIGALSKI, ELI MANDEL, ANDREW SUKNASKI, and JOHN HICKS, and novelists KEN MITCHELL and Robert Kroetsch. There was a growing realization among Saskatchewan writers that they could pursue their craft at home, rather than emigrating to literary centres such as Toronto or New York.

By 1973, the guild and the arts board had initiated the province's first literary magazine, *Grain*; there followed the development of a system of artists' colonies, and a theatrical offshoot, the Saskatchewan Playwrights Centre, to promote the professional development of play scripts. Several literary presses were soon established: Coteau Books in Regina, and Thistledown Press and Fifth House Publishers in Saskatoon. Modern Press in Saskatoon created a literary imprint, Greystone Books. Chief among them was Coteau Books, which originated in Moose Jaw as Thunder Creek Publishing Co-operative and capitalized on the energy of its team of founding writers, all from Moose Jaw: GARY HYLAND, ROBERT CURRIE, GEOFFREY URSELL and BARBARA SAPERGIA. They published not only their own works, but also a wide range of literary and children's titles, and led Coteau to become one of the largest and most successful regional publishers in Canada.

Many successful literary careers were born in Saskatchewan in the 1970s. Writers such as LORNA CROZIER, Bonnie Burnard, DAVID CARPENTER, DON KERR, BYRNA BARCLAY, GLEN SORESTAD, GERTRUDE STORY, MARIA CAMPBELL, SHARON BUTALA, and GUY VANDERHAEGE had become internationally known and reviewed by the end of the century. More recent new voices include BRENDA BAKER, ART SLADE, DAVE MARGOSHES, and Chris Fisher. Similar development occurred in music and the visual arts, with the continuing support of the Saskatchewan Arts Board. In addition to the symphonies, bands and choral groups, popular musical groups like Humphrey and the Dumptrucks of Saskatoon were performing and recording their music around the province, and singer/songwriters like JONI MITCHELL, BUFFY SAINTE-MARIE, CONNIE KALDOR and Don Freed were making waves internationally. They were followed quickly by blues musicians such as COLIN JAMES and Jack Semple. The francophone group Hart Rouge enjoyed a national following. Recent successes have included singer Brad Johner and the band of Jason Plumb and the Willing. Independent art galleries opened and thrived in various centres of the province, marketing the work of the new galaxy of artists. These included the ceramicists Joe Fafard, JACK SURES, and VIC CICANSKY of Regina, painters BOB BOYER and DAVID THAUBERGER, sculptor BILL EPP of Saskatoon, and the brothers Huang Zhongyang and Huang Zhongru, immigrants from China. Of these, the best known is Joe Fafard, a francophone artist from Ste. Marthe, whose bronze cows and clay portraits appear in cityscapes and private collections around the world.

An important later development has been the establishment of film production and film-making in Saskatchewan, which until the 1970s had only been a consumer of film entertainment. The only bright spot in this landscape was the long-running YORKTON SHORT FILM AND VIDEO FESTIVAL, first presented in 1947. In 1976, a cinematic adaptation of *Who Has Seen the Wind* was shot by Alan King in and around Arcola; and three years later appeared the Genie-winning feature, *The Hounds of Notre Dame*, about Père ATHOL MURRAY and the founding of Notre Dame College at Wilcox. These major film productions helped develop a professional complement of film technicians, producers, directors and actors which led to an outburst of cinematic enterprise in the 1980s and

JEAN-FRANÇOIS BÉRUBÉ PHOTO/COURTESY OF FOLLE AVOINE PRODUCTIONS

Hart Rouge, 1997.

1990s. In short order, the Saskatchewan Film Development Corporation and a production unit of the National Film Board were established in Regina. KEVIN DEWALT's Mind's Eye Pictures began a long and impressive production of feature films, television series, and commercial film-making. In recent years, the Canada Saskatchewan Production Studios, with a complete sound stage, was established in Regina. There a hit television series, *Corner Gas*, featuring Saskatchewan actors like Brent Butt, Janet Wright and Eric Peterson, has been produced to record the foibles of small-town community life. Saskatchewan culture and artists suddenly seem to have reached a new level of international recognition.

As in most other parts of Canada, the late 20th century saw the development of major community arts festivals: the Festival of Words in Moose Jaw (which led directly to the creation of a Moose Jaw Cultural Centre), the Saskatoon Fringe Festival, the Regina Folk Festival, the North Battleford Crafts Fair, Regina's Cathedral Village Arts Festival, and the Fort Qu'Appelle Midsummer Arts Festival. The Regina Arts Commission was established in 1979, the province's first municipal arts agency, with the goal of generating more artistic activity in the capital: this led fairly directly in 2004 to the city being declared a Cultural Capital of Canada by the federal government, and receiving a generous grant to promote even more art projects, in time for the province's centennial. By the end of the 20th century, Saskatchewan culture had experienced an artistic coming of age, and though its population growth in 2005 appears to be in a holding phase, the richness of its culture remains an important feature as the province celebrates the centenary of its birth.

FURTHER READING:

Archer, J.H. 1965. *Footprints in Time*. Toronto: House of Grant.

Black, N.F. 1913. *History of Saskatchewan and the North West Territories*. Regina: Saskatchewan Historical Company.

Hawkes, J. 1924. *Saskatchewan and its People*. Chicago-Regina: S.J. Clarke Publishing.

DAVID MCLENNAN PHOTO

Brent Butt on set in Rouleau (Dog River), Saskatchewan.

ASSOCIATION OF TRANSLATORS AND INTERPRETERS OF SASKATCHEWAN (ATIS).

Incorporated in 1980, ATIS is a non-profit professional association committed to fostering and promoting translation and interpretation in the province. It is an affiliate of the Canadian Translators, Terminologists and Interpreters Council (CTTIC), which itself represents Canada in the *Fédération internationale des traducteurs* (FIT), a worldwide organization of translators' associations from more than fifty countries. ATIS gives users of translation services access to a body of competent professionals, and provides a collective voice for its members, ensuring that they conform to its Code of Ethics. The Association deals with a wide variety of languages including French, Cree, Spanish, Serbo-Croatian, Chinese and Japanese among many others, as well as American Sign Language.

Patrick Douaud

ASSOCIATION OF UNITED UKRAINIAN CANADIANS.

The Association of United Ukrainian Canadians (AUUC) was founded in Winnipeg as the Ukrainian Labour Temple Association (ULTA) in 1918. By 1928 it had 167 branches across Canada, including Saskatchewan. These Labour Temples became a home for immigrants and their children when discrimination against Eastern Europeans began to intensify in Saskatchewan. They offered a wide range of folk activities as well as English language classes for adults and children. As no form of medicare was available, ULTA founded the Workers Benevolent Association (WBA) in Winnipeg in 1922, with branches and membership rapidly spreading throughout Canada; it even extended its membership to all workers, irrespective of ethnic origin. The AUUC was at the forefront of assistance to Ukraine after **WORLD WAR II**; it later fought for ties with that country and sponsored Canadian artists, writers, and choreographers to go there—at times under very difficult conditions, especially during the Cold War. A lasting tribute to the AUUC's dedication to its literary heritage was the establishment of a monument to the great Ukrainian poet Lesya Ukrainka, a gift from Ukraine, on the grounds of the University of Saskatchewan in 1976.

Alex Lapchuk

ASTROBLEMES.

Astroblemes are the physical scars produced by the impact of asteroids or comets with the Earth's surface. The dynamic nature of earth processes (weathering, erosion, deposition, and orogenesis) means that impact structures are rarely preserved. Five astroblemes are known in Saskatchewan. The largest, 35 km in diameter, is the deeply eroded multi-ring Carswell structure, located in northwest Saskatchewan. It has an 18 km-diameter core of Precambrian gneisses, which rebounded at the time of impact about 2 km from

DOUG CHISHOLM PHOTO
Gow Lake and Calder Island.

their original depth, just as a column of water rises up after a stone has been dropped in water. The core is surrounded by successive rings of highly disrupted and tilted sediments of the Athabasca Group; irregular bodies of impact-related breccias occur mainly in the central core. The Carswell astrobleme, created by a 0.5 to 1 km-diameter asteroid, is about 478 million years old.

Gow Lake, about 160 km north-northeast of La Ronge, is a 5 km-diameter circular lake with a central island, Calder Island, upon which impact melt rocks and fall-back breccias are preserved. Gow Lake is one of the smallest impact structures to have a central uplift, and is about 210 million years old.

Deep Bay, near the south end of **REINDEER LAKE**, is 11 km in diameter and up to 220 m deep. Partially surrounding the bay is a ridge up to 100 m above the lake, with a maximum diameter of 13 km, which probably represents the outer rim of the crater. Deep Bay has a low, but totally submerged, central uplift. Cretaceous sediments on the bottom of Deep Bay provide an age estimate of 100 ± 50 million years.

The completely buried, 2 km-diameter Viewfield impact structure, located east of Weyburn, was first identified by seismic surveys in the early 1970s during petroleum exploration. Subsequent drilling revealed a 100 m-deep circular feature excavated into the Mississippian bedrock and surrounded by a raised rim of breccia, the ejecta blanket, formed at the time of impact approximately 190 million years ago. The rim breccia has produced substantial quantities of oil and gas.

The Maple Creek structure, discovered in the early 1990s south-southeast of Maple Creek, has a 6 km diameter and is barely recognizable at the surface. It has a central uplift of strongly disrupted

Cretaceous sediments, which indicates an age of about 75 million years (*see also* **METEORITE DISCOVERIES**).

Charles Harper

ATHABASCA SAND DUNES

59° N, 109° W; Mapsheet 74 N. The Athabasca Sand Dunes are a unique geological feature located in northwest Saskatchewan on the south shore of Lake Athabasca. The region of dunes stretches for 100 km in a narrow strip along **LAKE ATHABASCA** from the Alberta border east to Richards Lake. The dunes reach heights of 30 metres and vary in length from 400 to 1,500 metres. The Athabasca Sand Dunes comprise the largest area of active sand dunes in North America, and are the most northerly active dunes in the world. The dunes were formed roughly 8,000 years ago during the last glacial period. When the ice-sheet retreated from the area, meltwater channels and spillways (such as the valleys of the present-day William and MacFarlane rivers) washed great volumes of sand and sediment into Glacial Lake Athabasca. As the lake receded, these deposits were exposed and through years of wind action have been shaped into the spectacular and expansive dune formations of today. Considerable portions of the Athabasca Sand Dunes are unstable: the dunes gradually move with the prevailing wind direction and encroach on the adjacent forest. Within the Athabasca Sand Dunes region, a variety of depositional and glacial landforms can be found including braided river channels, beach ridges, inland river deltas, desert pavement, moraines, eskers, and kettle lakes. The ecology of the region is unique and varied. It supports as many as seventy rare plant species, ten of which are endemic (i.e., found nowhere else in the world). Active dunes have been colonized by field chickweed (*Cerastium*

COURTESY OF TOURISM SASKATCHEWAN

Athabasca sand dunes.

arvense), felt-leaved willow (*Salix silicicola*), Mackenzie hairgrass (*Deschampsia mackenzieana*), Tyrrell's willow (*Salix planifolia* ssp *tyrrellii*), and fluccose tansy (*Tanacetum huronense* var. *floccosum*)—all endemic species—in addition to common grasses and fescues. Habitat on stabilized dunes is characterized by low shrubs, herbs, and grasses interspersed with open sand patches and stands of jack pine. In 1973, the Saskatchewan government protected the Athabasca Sand Dunes as a Crown Reserve. In 1992, after nearly two decades of consultation, the Reserve was given Provincial Park status. The Athabasca Sand Dunes Provincial Wilderness Park encompasses 1,925 square kilometres, and is deemed by Parks Canada to be one of the most significant natural areas in the country. Although the park has no road access, services, or communities, guided interpretative trips are available into the park to explore the dunes on foot or by boat.

Iain Stewart

FURTHER READING: Karpan, R., and A. Karpan. 1998. *Northern Sandscapes–Exploring Saskatchewan's Athabasca Sand Dunes.* Saskatoon: Parkland Publishing; Saskatchewan Environment and Resource Management.1998. *The Ecoregions of Saskatchewan.* Regina: Canadian Plains Research Center.

ATHOL MURRAY COLLEGE OF NOTRE DAME.

Notre Dame College of Wilcox, Saskatchewan was and is inseparable from the name of its founder, Father (Père) **ATHOL MURRAY.** James Athol Murray was born in Toronto in 1892; his father was a prominent industrialist and a founder of the Canadian Chamber of Commerce; his Roman Catholic mother died when Athol was four. He attended private French Canadian Catholic schools in Montreal, Toronto, and Quebec City. After graduation he began to study Law. He ended his

studies, however, and quit his newspaper job to enter Toronto's St. Augustine's seminary. He was ordained to the priesthood in 1918, and came west to Regina in 1922. In addition to his duties as chancellor of the archdiocese, he formed a sports club made up of a group of Protestant boys who had been caught stealing candy from a church basement. Murray convinced his colleagues to drop criminal charges in return for the youngsters joining a sports club under his supervision. This became known as the Regina Argos Club and helped many boys find direction in their lives.

In 1927, Père Murray was assigned to the village of Wilcox, south of Regina, and took many of his young Argos with him. He began to school them, first in the existing Notre Dame collegiate, founded by the Sisters of Charity of St. Louis in 1920, then in

BRYAN SCHLOSSER/REGINA LEADER-POST

Father Norman Fitzpatrick blesses the coats of arms of the provinces during dedication ceremonies of Canada Park at Athol Murray College of Notre Dame, October, 1993. The park symbolizes Notre Dame's support for Canadian unity and honours the spirit of "Pere" Athol Murray.

abandoned buildings acquired during the **GREAT DEPRESSION**. Murray officially established Notre Dame in 1933 as a classical college affiliated with the University of Ottawa. Students came from nearby farms and from across North America–many without the ability to pay tuition. Murray's only admission requirement was a willingness to learn or to compete on one of his teams. The Notre Dame Hounds became well known in the west, winning many provincial titles in hockey, football and baseball, and traveling throughout North America to compete. The college became known nationally and began to send many young hockey players to the top junior leagues and the NHL.

Père Murray consorted with Canadian politicians, and corresponded with Winston Churchill, Theodore Roosevelt and other contemporary leaders. He received the Order of Canada in 1968 and was inducted into both the Canadian Sports Hall of Fame and the Hockey Hall of Fame. He died in 1975, and in 1983 the name of the college was officially changed to "Athol Murray College of Notre Dame." Over the years the college has developed into an institution which combines academics, athletics, and spiritual growth. Its motto, chosen by Athol Murray, is *Luctor et emergo*, "I struggle and come through." The College has been associated with the **UNIVERSITY OF REGINA** since 1976; in addition to its co-educational high school programs offered to day and residential students who increasingly come from around the world, it delivers a number of courses for university credit and is a site for off-campus credit classes.

Margaret Sanche and James McNinch

ATKINSON, ISABEL (1891–1968).

Born in Bramley, England on July 22, 1891, Isabel Atkinson moved with her widowed mother to Waterbury, Connecticut when she was 14. She worked in a factory, and became a women's rights' activist. In 1914 she came to Saskatchewan to live with her mother and brother on the latter's farm near Strasbourg, and to assist on the farm. In 1919 the two women moved to Kerrobert, where Isabel worked as a bookkeeper for twenty-five years. She helped found the local library and avidly studied social issues, especially public health. Four years after her mother's death, she moved to Saskatoon. Her concern for housing, public health, and social services led her to travel abroad to study programs in Commonwealth countries in 1948–49. She wrote about them in a series of articles published in the *Star-Phoenix* and other newspapers. The *Winnipeg Free Press* later published selected articles in booklet form.

Active in the Consumers' Association of Canada (CAC), Atkinson became provincial president in 1954, and was national president of this Ottawa-based organization from 1956 to 1960. After returning to Saskatoon, she continued to do research for the CAC. Her other involvements included the

Saskatoon Council of Women (for which she received a life membership) and the Liberal Party. She died in Saskatoon on August 11, 1968.

Bob Ivanochko

FURTHER READING: Pratt, F. 1985. "Isabel Atkinson." *Western People*, a supplement to *The Western Producer*.

ATKINSON, PATRICIA (1952–). Patricia Atkinson, born in Biggar on September 27, 1952, graduated from the UNIVERSITY OF SASKATCHEWAN with degrees in Arts and Education. She worked for the Radius Community School in Saskatoon as a teacher therapist and as school principal. Her father, ROY ATKINSON, was a prominent Saskatchewan farmer, active in farm organizations. Pat Atkinson became involved in variety of organizations too, most notably on the board of the Saskatoon Community Clinic. In 1982 she was defeated as the NDP candidate in Saskatoon Nutana in the Conservative sweep, but in 1986 she won the seat and became the opposition health critic. Re-elected in 1991, Atkinson was appointed Minister of Social Services in 1992. A year later she was appointed Minister of Education, a post she held for five years. The Community School program was expanded, she introduced a pre-kindergarten program for children at risk, and she restructured the school divisions. Atkinson was moved into the Department of Health in 1998, where she dealt with the increasing strife between the health sector unions and government over wage demands. The situation deteriorated in 1999 when the nurses' union went on strike and defied back-to-work legislation. Re-elected in 1999, Atkinson remained Minister of Health until February 2001, when she was appointed Minister of Highways and Transportation in the first CALVERT Cabinet. Atkinson left Cabinet in October 2001, but returned in 2003 as Minister of the Crown Management Board after she was successfully re-elected in Saskatoon Nutana.

Brett Quiring

SASKATCHEWAN NEW DEMOCRATIC PARTY ARCHIVES

Pat Atkinson.

ATKINSON, ROBERT ROY (1924–). Roy Atkinson is an activist farmer who has devoted a major part of his life to lobbying governments and providing leadership in the Canadian farm movement. He was born on February 17, 1924, in the Springwater-Landis area on a farm his grandfather had homesteaded in 1905. Atkinson was president of the SASKATCHEWAN FARMERS UNION from 1962 to 1969, and president of the National Farmers Union from 1969 to 1978. He served on the Economic Council of Canada in 1966 and 1967, for eight years was a member of the Canadian Council for Rural Development, and served on the board of directors of Federated Co-operatives Ltd. Atkinson was a member of the Canadian Wheat Board Advisory Committee from 1965 until 1994, and its chair from 1980 to 1985. From 1985 to 1994 he served as an elected SASKATCHEWAN WHEAT POOL delegate. From 1998 until 2001 he served as co-chair of Prairie Alliance for the Future, a western Canadian organization dedicated to creating a regional grain collection and transportation system. Atkinson brought a new dimension to farm lobbying, using public demonstrations to attract wide attention to the causes he was advancing. His objective was to improve the economics of farming, and he worked to ensure the continuation of the family farm as a way of life in western Canada. In 1990 he was inducted into the Saskatchewan Agricultural Hall of Fame, and in 2002 was invested into the Order of Canada.

AURORA BOREALIS (NORTHERN LIGHTS). Named in honour of the Greek goddess of the dawn, the transient green and red arcs, rays and nebulous glows that distinguish an auroral display are produced in the Earth's ionosphere at heights of between 100 and 400 km. Auroral displays occur when high-energy electrons, captured from the Sun's solar wind, interact with the Earth's magnetic field and excite through collisions atmospheric atoms. The excited atoms, mainly atomic oxygen and nitrogen, characteristically de-excite by emitting a photon; it is those photons with wavelengths corresponding to visible light that produce the observed auroral display. The green and red auroral colours are the result of the de-excitation of oxygen atoms; the rare blue auroral colour is produced by the de-excitation of molecular nitrogen (N_2). Auroral displays are commonly seen from latitudes between 60° and 75° (corresponding to the auroral oval), favouring northern Saskatchewan for the best viewing, but they can on less frequent occasions be seen at much lower latitudes. The times at which aurora displays might be seen at lower latitudes is largely unpredictable, but auroral activity is strongly correlated with the Sun's 11-year sunspot cycle, with greater numbers of displays being recorded at the time of sunspot maximum.

Martin Beech

AUTOMATED TELLER MACHINES. The first automated teller machine and the first debit card transaction in Canada were developed by Saskatchewan credit unions. Under the direction of its vice-president, Ed Gebert, Sherwood Credit Union introduced its first Automated Teller Machine (ATM), also known as Automated Banking Machine (ABM), in 1977. Sherwood, now known as Conexus Credit Union, worked with Co-operators Data Services (now called CGI), Credit Union Electronic Transaction Services (CUETs), and Credit Union Central of Saskatchewan to create the ATM system. Initially, the ATMs at the Sherwood Credit Union's two branches in Regina provided service eighteen hours a day, seven days a week, with a maximum withdrawal of $200. Since then the system has sprawled across the country, and over 36,000 machines are available from coast to coast.

The next logical step in the evolution of electronic banking was the introduction of debit cards. The MasterCard payment card, a forerunner of today's debit card, was introduced to Canadians by Saskatchewan credit unions in 1982; called MasterCard II, it allowed credit union members to pay for purchases directly at the point of sale without running up credit card interest charges. Now called the Global Payment MasterCard, the credit unions' card can be used at 14 million locations around the world. The first true debit card was piloted in May 1985 by credit unions in the Swift Current area, and involved the installation of a point of sale system at twenty-eight Co-op outlets. The one-year trial was successful, but credit union members demanded cards that could be used with merchants in addition to just the Pioneer Co-op.

At about the same time, the Interac Association was being formed to promote the concept of sharing access to ATMs among various financial institutions in order to allow people to access their money more readily across the country. This led to the recognition that debit cards would also work if merchant terminals were shared; this concept led to the introduction of debit cards in the early 1990s. Now nearly half of all purchases in Canada are made with a debit card, and in 2003 about 19 million Canadians (86% of the population) had debit cards. *Joe Ralko*

AUTOMOBILES. In the early 1900s automobiles quickly appeared in Saskatchewan and brought profound changes to the social and economic conditions of the province: they improved access to rural areas, provided relief from rural isolation, facilitated the movement of agricultural commodities, eased access to medical services, and generated new businesses and recreational choices for Saskatchewan residents. Early demand for automobiles was greatest in the frontier regions of Canada, and in particular Saskatchewan, where agriculture and resource development drew large numbers of immigrants.

Official automobile registration in Saskatchewan dates back to 1906; twenty-two motor vehicles were registered that year under the new provincial legislation. Automobiles and drivers were initially registered by the Provincial Secretary's Department; but as the number of motor vehicles in the province grew, additional government agencies assisted in administering this new form of transportation. After 1910, vehicle registrations increased dramatically, exceeding 10,000 by 1915. During **WORLD WAR I**, extraordinary growth in automobile ownership continued, with annual registrations climbing to 60,000 by 1920. Automobile use sustained rising popularity until the Great Depression, when vehicle registrations declined from 128,000 in 1929 to 91,000 in 1934. It was not until the end of **WORLD WAR II** that motor vehicle registrations would rebound to the level witnessed in 1929.

The large-scale adoption of automobile use in Saskatchewan after World War I can be attributed to mass production and promotion, falling automobile prices, improvements to the safety and reliability of vehicles, and rising farm incomes (in 1926, nearly 60% of all motor vehicles registered in Saskatchewan were farm vehicles). From 1915 to 1923, Saskatchewan ranked second only to Ontario in its number of registered automobiles. By the early 1930s a tremendous growth in vehicle ownership had begun in small towns, villages, and rural areas across the province, as trucks were fast replacing horse drawn wagons for hauling agricultural commodities from farms to railheads. Beyond the obvious benefits to rural farming and freight delivery, automobiles were prized in cities by business people, police and fire departments, and pleasure drivers of the urban middle class. The most common make of motor vehicle in Saskatchewan prior to World War II was Ford (the only real competitor on the provincial market was General Motors). Following World War II, gas rationing ended, roads improved, farm incomes rose, automobiles were modernized and weather-proofed, and society as a whole became more affluent: these conditions ushered a continued rise in vehicle ownership for decades to come. In 1964, nearly 400,000 vehicles were registered in the province, a figure that doubled to more than 800,000 by the 1990s. The number of registered motor vehicles in Saskatchewan has remained relatively steady since the 1990s. *Iain Stewart*

FURTHER READING: Bantjes, R. 1992. "Improved Earth: Travel on the Canadian Prairies, 1920-1950," *Journal of Transport History* 13 (2): 115–40; Bloomfield, G.T. 1984. "'I Can See a Car in That Crop': Motorization in Saskatchewan 1906–1934," *Saskatchewan History* 37 (1): 3–24.

AUTONOMY BILLS (1905). The Autonomy Bills created the provinces of Saskatchewan and Alberta, but precipitated bitter debates over party politics, the division of federal-provincial powers, and French-English rights in Canada. A **LIEUTENANT-GOVERNOR** for the North-West Territories had been appointed in 1876 and empowered to govern in co-operation with, and on the advice of, an appointed Legislative Council. Over the next decade the Council grew to include elected members, and its authority slowly increased to include most areas of provincial jurisdiction. In 1888, the Legislative Council was replaced by the Legislative Assembly of the North-West Territories. Responsible government was granted in 1897, with **FREDERICK W.G. HAULTAIN** as the first Premier. The government was responsible for education, roads, and other services in the Territories. By 1901, the Assembly was vested with the full powers of a provincial Legislature, with the exception of the ability to raise revenue by direct taxation and the management of Crown lands. Parliament voted a yearly grant-in-aid to compensate for these omissions, but when the federal government repeatedly failed to provide a grant large enough to cover the territorial government's growing expenses, Haultain demanded that the North-West Territories be given provincial autonomy.

In 1903, Haultain proposed to Prime Minister Wilfrid Laurier that one large province, stretching from Manitoba to British Columbia, replace the Territories. When the Saskatchewan Act and the Alberta Act were introduced in the House of Commons in 1905, however, they proposed two provinces of approximately equal size and population. Haultain maintained that the region's integrated economy and shared history pointed to the practicality of one province; but Laurier feared that in light of the rapid population growth on the prairies one province stretching from Manitoba to British Columbia to the Arctic Ocean would become unmanageably large. Other Liberals were concerned about the power such a large province could potentially wield in Parliament. Two clauses in the Acts initiated a storm of controversy across the country. In their original form, the bills reinstated the educational system outlined in the North-West Territories Act, 1875, which guaranteed linguistic and religious minorities the right to manage their own schools. Anglo-Canadians were outraged; Haultain objected strongly to the provision; and Clifford Sifton, the Minister of the Interior, resigned rather than support the measure. It was felt that the school system should be used to assimilate immigrants to the English language and British culture rather than to encourage plurality of religion and language. Many Franco-Canadians, led by MP and journalist Henri Bourassa, objected to what they saw as an attack on the French culture and the Catholic faith, arguing that the western provinces should be bilingual and bicultural, like Manitoba. Laurier struck a compromise by reinstating the 1901 educational system, which gave minorities the right to maintain separate schools but required them to teach the provincial curriculum.

The Acts also reserved the management of Crown lands and natural resources to the federal government; without this authority, Parliament would have lost control over the dispersal of homesteads, and thereby over western settlement. The two new provinces were awarded yearly transfer payments to compensate for losses in revenue, but their lack of control over resources hindered economic growth. The provision, both at the time and since, has been cited as an insult to western equality and one of the root causes of western alienation. The Saskatchewan Act received Royal Assent on July 20, 1905, and the proclamation creating the province was issued by the Governor General during a ceremony in Victoria Park in Regina on September 4. Canada's first protest party, the Provincial Rights Party, was formed in response to the failure of the federal government to give Saskatchewan equal jurisdiction with the original provinces. Headed by Haultain, it served as opposition to Saskatchewan's Liberal government, led by Premier **WALTER SCOTT**, until 1912. Their objections did little, however, and power over resources and land were not returned to Saskatchewan and Alberta until 1930.

Erin Millions and Michael Thome

FURTHER READING: Brennan, J.W. 1980. "The 'Autonomy Question' and the Creation of Saskatchewan and Alberta, 1905." Pp. 43–63 in H. Palmer and D.B. Smith (eds.), *The New Provinces: Alberta and Saskatchewan*. Vancouver: Tantalus Research; Lingard, C.C. 1978. *Territorial Government in Canada: The Autonomy Question in the Old North-West Territories*. Toronto: University of Toronto Press.

AVALOKITESVARA BUDDHIST TEMPLE SOCIETY. The Avalokitesvara Buddhist Temple Society Inc. was incorporated in July 1997 in Saskatoon. It came about as a result of a long-time desire within Saskatoon's Asian community to have a Buddhist monk living and teaching in the city. In May 1997, several hundred people attended a celebration of the Buddha's birth, which was organized by the society and held in the Union Centre. A commercial building owned by a member had been rented to the society under a legal lease with an annual rent of $1 for a ten-year period. In October 1998 the Avalokitesvara Buddhist Temple relocated to a larger facility in order to accommodate the rising number of members. The society provides spiritual guidance and services according to Buddhism. The mission and objectives of the society are to: promote Buddhism; enrich the quality of life of all members through the practice of Buddhist principles; provide a facility for members to study, meditate and think in tranquillity; arrange for Buddhist monks and practitioners to lecture at spiritual retreats for members and interested individuals; help support local and visiting Buddhist monks and nuns when appropriate; establish a library of Chinese and English Buddhist resources, as well as cultural and other educational materials specializing in Buddhist philosophy; maintain contact with other Buddhist groups for mutual association; provide Buddhist charitable programs; help and support other charities with similar concerns; provide cultural programs such as English and Chinese language training, and the study of Confucianism and Taoism; provide instructional programs such as vegetarian cooking and horticultural classes; and collect donations from members and the public. *Theresa Mui*

AVIATION. The first experiments in aviation in what would become Saskatchewan took place in the early 1890s, when William Wallace Gibson wondered if the kite he often flew could somehow be mated with an engine. Gibson maintained his interest in this subject. After reading of the Wright brothers' successful 1903 flights he accelerated his experiments by launching a large paper glider from the roof of his Balgonie hardware store in June 1904, and also designed a man-carrying machine and a gasoline engine to power it. These Saskatchewan experiments bore fruit on September 8, 1910, when Gibson (by then living in Victoria) flew his "Twinplane," the first aircraft designed and built in Canada, and powered by a Canadian-designed engine. Although a few Saskatchewanians also built flying machines, the first powered flight in the province was made on May 19, 1911, when American barnstormer C.W. Shaffer flew his biplane over Saskatoon; he made another flight in Regina on August 5.

Desultory experiments by aviation enthusiasts and summer flights by touring aviators made up the extent of flying in Saskatchewan for the next eight years. The end of **WORLD WAR I** saw the return of military pilots and ground crew, notably **ROLAND GROOME**, who gained a place in Canada's aviation history in the spring of 1920 when the federal government's new Air Board, which was traveling across western Canada, issued Canadian commercial pilot's licence No. 1 to him. Groome's business partner, Robert McCombie, received aero engineer's licence No. 1; their airfield (in Regina's Lakeview district) became Canada's first licensed "air harbour"; and their Canadian-built JN-4 (Can) Canuck was registered G-CAAA—the first licenced aircraft in Canada. An airport in Saskatoon received licence No. 2.

Aviation in Saskatchewan waned as the 1920s passed; but in 1927 the federal government, wanting a pool of trained aviators, offered light aircraft to flying clubs across the country. Thus were formed clubs in Regina, Moose Jaw and Saskatoon, setting the stage for sustained development. The two former clubs co-operated with Western Canada Airways in the first prairie airmail service; members of Saskatoon's Aero Club formed M&C Aviation, a northern air service headquartered in Prince Albert. Saskatchewan flying clubs nurtured two other enterprises. Prairie Airways, an airline organized by Moose Jaw Flying Club members, began operation in 1934 and four years later bought two Beech 18 airliners for north-south routes in the province. In Regina, the RCAF's 120 (Auxiliary) Squadron, was recruited mostly from Regina Flying Club members; its role was training ground crew and aircrew—presaging one of Saskatchewan's most important contributions to the Allied effort during **WORLD WAR II**, as it was home to twenty training schools under the

BRITISH COMMONWEALTH AIR TRAINING PLAN (BCATP). Though some existing airports were used for BCATP schools, most were created from scratch during summer building campaigns in 1940 and 1941.

As had happened after World War I, the arrival of peace in 1945 brought a boom in the innovative use of aircraft. The provincial government in 1946 started an air ambulance service that used specially equipped aircraft with trained crews to take patients to hospitals. To develop the northern half of the province, the government purchased M&C Aviation to create Saskatchewan Government Airways (SGA) in 1947. SGA was a Crown corporation that operated scheduled and charter services in the north, and also recruited "smokejumpers," specially trained men who parachuted to fight forest fires. In the private sector, the postwar years saw the use of aircraft for recreation, transport, and specialized purposes like pipeline/powerline patrol and the application of agricultural chemicals. Trans-Canada Airlines (TCA), serving Regina since 1939, upgraded its service with new aircraft and started service to Saskatoon in 1947. Canadian Pacific Airlines flew between Regina and Edmonton.

In 1947, Saskatoon became home to an RCAF auxiliary, or reserve, squadron, and from 1951 to a military air training school. A parallel school was created in 1952 at Moose Jaw, which two years later was the site of the worst aviation accident, to that point, in Canadian history: on April 8, 1954, an RCAF Harvard trainer collided over the city with a TCA North Star, killing 31 passengers, the TCA crew of four, the Harvard's pilot, and a woman on the ground. The military air base at Moose Jaw gave birth in 1970 to an air demonstration team called the Snowbirds. Operation of the base itself was taken over in 2000 by a civilian consortium headed by the Bombardier aerospace group, though military personnel remain as instructors. *Will Chabun*

FURTHER READING: Crone, R. 1975. "Aviation Pioneers in Saskatchewan," *Saskatchewan History* 23: 9–28; Holman, R.F. 1995. *Best in the West–The Story of Number 2 Canadian Forces Flying Training School and Flying Training In Canada*. Moose Jaw: Big 2 Fund.

AZEVEDO, E.N. (TED) (1916–). Born in Strasbourg in 1916, Ted Azevedo promoted issues relating to Saskatchewan senior citizens such as home care, pensions, preventive health, activity centres, and housing. In 1977, he was appointed chairman of the Saskatchewan Senior Citizens Provincial Council. He served as president of the Saskatchewan Senior Association from 1981 to 1989 and was first vice-president of the National Pensioners and Seniors Foundation of Canada. Azevedo received the Saskatchewan Order of Merit in 1989.

Groome and McCombie's JN-4 Canuck—the first airplane in Canada to be licensed for commercial purposes. The sign on the side of the building behind the plane reads: "Aeroplane Ride over city. Flights At Any Time. $10.00."

BAHÁ'Í. The Bahá'í faith originated in Iran in the mid-19th century. Following several decades of intense persecution, its progressive teachings began to attract interest in the West. The unity of humankind, global governance, the importance of science and education, and the equality of men and women have attracted Saskatchewanians from diverse backgrounds. Though still a small community, the Bahá'í faith has been a presence in Saskatchewan for ninety years. William Sutherland Maxwell, a prominent Canadian Bahá'í, designed the Legislature Buildings in Regina and the Shrine of the Báb at the Bahá'í World Centre in Haifa, Israel. Today, some 2,459 Saskatchewan Bahá'ís reside in 236 different municipalities and First Nations reserves. The first Canadian Bahá'í, **WILLIAM HENRY JACKSON** (also known as Honoré Jaxon), lived in Prince Albert during the late 19th century and worked to integrate the arriving settlers, local First Nations peoples, and **MÉTIS**. For a time, he

SASKATCHEWAN ARCHIVES BOARD R-A2443

W.S. Maxwell, a prominent Canadian Bahá'í, who designed Saskatchewan's Legislative Building.

served as **LOUIS RIEL**'s secretary. He encountered the Bahá'í faith in the early 1890s in Chicago, where it had been introduced to North America at the World Parliament of Religions, an adjunct of the Chicago World's Fair.

Edward W. Harris (1871–1922), homesteader at Gull Lake, became a Bahá'í in 1913 and Saskatchewan's first resident Bahá'í. Bahá'ís from the United States and eastern Canada traveled to Saskatchewan in the 1930s and 1940s, giving talks at hotels and meeting with community organizations. In May 1944, a broadcast on CKRM informed the Regina public about the Bahá'í faith; Saskatoon elected its first Local Spiritual Assembly in 1953. Saskatchewanians began to show interest in the Bahá'í faith: Harry Takashiba joined with six other Regina residents in 1945; two other Regina Bahá'ís from that year, Mabel and Leslie Silversides, were the first non-Aboriginal Bahá'ís in Canada to move to a reserve. Saskatchewan First Nations have shown considerable interest in the Bahá'í faith's teachings: currently, over 1,100 Aboriginal Bahá'ís reside in Saskatchewan. Saskatchewan Bahá'ís were prominent in the emergence of the Canadian Bahá'í Community and of the Bahá'í International Community. The two universities in Regina and Saskatoon have had active Bahá'í groups since the late 1960s. During that time, hundreds of young Saskatonians attended Bahá'í meetings; they expanded the community's membership rolls there and in Regina. By the early 1970s, Saskatoon and Regina had communities of several hundred. Many of these young Bahá'ís traveled all over Canada; some worked in other countries, several contributing to development projects, especially in agriculture. Socio-economic development is an important focus of Bahá'í attention, and agriculture is considered the basis of any sound economy.

Gerald Filson and Valerie Warder

BAKER, BRENDA (1959–). Brenda Baker, a multifaceted artist, is one of Saskatchewan's best loved children's entertainers. Born in Saskatoon on April 6, 1959, Brenda graduated from the **UNIVERSITY OF SASKATCHEWAN** with a BFA in Visual Arts and continued to study theatre and creative writing, eventually becoming a "writer-performer." Between 1989 and 1994, she toured regularly to folk clubs and festivals, performing for adults. She was a guest on such national CBC programs as *Morningside*, *Gabereau*, *Swinging on a Star*, and *Basic Black*. She has recorded five albums (two for adults, three for children) of mostly original music. Currently, she makes her living from school and festival concerts for children. She has also produced a theatrical story-song show and CD entitled *The Old Elephant's Christmas*. In 1999, she hosted the pre-school TV series *Prairie Berry Pie with Brenda Baker* (Global/SCN). Among several awards is a nomina-

JERRY HUMENY / BLACK BOX IMAGES
Brenda Baker.

tion for Best Children's Album 2003 Canadian Independent Music Awards and the 1999 **SASKATCHEWAN BOOK AWARD** for Fiction for her short story collection, *The Maleness of God*. A dedicated volunteer, Brenda served as Saskatchewan's UNICEF Ambassador for a year, and received the Saskatoon YWCA Woman of Distinction Award in 2001. Brenda is married to writer Arthur Slade and resides in Saskatoon. *Richard Belford*

BAKER, EVERETT (1893–1981). Everett Baker was born in Minnesota and immigrated to Canada in 1916. He settled in Aneroid, Saskatchewan, and took up farming there. He worked for the Saskatchewan Grain Growers Association; served as

SASKATCHEWAN ARCHIVES BOARD R-A22215
Everett Baker (right) with Mr. Preece, Loon Lake, June 1938.

the Aneroid Co-operative Association's store manager from 1924 to 1935; and worked for the **SASKATCHEWAN WHEAT POOL**, traveling across the province to recruit individuals, until his retirement in 1957. In the late 1930s, Baker began to record everyday scenes on Kodachrome slide film, both as a hobby and for professional purposes. At his death, he left 10,000 slides—now the property of the **SASKATCHEWAN HISTORY AND FOLKLORE SOCIETY**, of which he became the first president in 1957. Baker's slides are of exceptional quality: the colours are still vivid; people's poses and expressions are natural and unaffected; and there is a truly artistic flair for composition. Taken at a time when black-and-white photography was still the rule, conditioning the modern viewer to a rather dull view of the past, these slides constitute a remarkably realistic document on the landscapes, farms, towns, and Aboriginal populations of Saskatchewan in the 1940s and 1950s. A sample of them has been gathered in the 3rd Eye Media Productions video, "Everett Baker's Saskatchewan." *Patrick C. Douaud*

FURTHER READING: Anderson, F. 2002. "A Glimpse into the Past Through the Eye of Everett Baker (1893–1981)." Pp. 89–91 in P. Douaud and B. Dawson (eds.), *Plain Speaking: Essays on Aboriginal Peoples and the Prairie.* Regina: Canadian Plains Research Center.

BAKER, HAROLD R. (1927–). Harold R. Baker directed the Consulting Division of the Centre for Community Studies from 1958 to 1963, served as director of University Extension from 1963 to 1973, and continued as professor of Extension and administrator of the Community and Rural Development Program (1974–94) at the **UNIVERSITY OF SASKATCHEWAN**. His research and teaching interests included agricultural extension, community planning, and rural development. During his tenure, changes took place in extension administration, adult education, community development, and professional education. Starting in 1963, the university extension function was broadened from agriculture and home economics to all university colleges. Baker was instrumental in initiating the first courses in Extension Administration and in Program Planning for extension and community development practitioners. He administered an interdisciplinary Master of Continuing Education degree program (College of Education) and created the Saskatchewan Committee for Rural Area Development, a collaborative, inter-organizational approach to community development training and action, forerunner to the Saskatchewan Council for Community Development (SCCD). Following a term as president of the International Community Development Society (CDS) and the hosting of the CDS international conference in Saskatoon in 1991, the Community Development Society of Saskatchewan (CDSS) was

Harold Baker, 1960.

formed. Baker also pioneered educational events on Inter-community Collaboration, on the Business Incubator, and on the Community Development Corporation (CDC). (*See also* **UNIVERSITY EXTENSION, UNIVERSITY OF SASKATCHEWAN**) *James McNinch*

BAKER, HENRY HAROLD PETER (1915–2004). Baker was born in Lipton on November 24, 1915, and educated in Lipton and Regina. He enrolled in the Regina Teachers' College and taught from 1934 until the outbreak of **WORLD WAR II**. He served two years in the RCAF training Commonwealth aircrews. Baker completed a business course in Chicago and was appointed secretary of the Saskatchewan Public Service Commission in 1944.

Henry Baker.

Baker was elected to Regina City Council in 1955. He was elected mayor three years later and re-elected the next three terms until Harry Walker defeated him in 1970. Baker was elected as a CCF member of the Legislative Assembly in 1964 and re-elected three times as an NDP MLA. In 1973 Baker was elected mayor again and re-elected in 1976, the longest serving mayor of Regina.

During his tenure as mayor, Regina undertook several major projects such as the construction of the Ring Road, the Centre of the Arts and the new City Hall. He was criticized for serving both as mayor and an MLA at the same time. Baker ran in the 1982 election but was defeated, ending his twenty-seven year career representing Regina. In 1997, the city of Regina re-named the city council chamber in his honour. Henry Baker died in Regina on March 4, 2004. *Brett Quiring*

BAKER, LUCY (1836–1909). Lucy Baker, the first Presbyterian single woman to work with Canadian Aboriginals, devoted her life to missionary work. Born in Summerstown, Ontario in 1836, she was adopted by her aunt after her mother's death, and lived in Dundee, Quebec. She was educated there and at nearby Fort Covington, New York. She taught in the United States, but returned home when the Civil War erupted. On October 28, 1879, she arrived in Prince Albert, where she taught until the Resistance of 1885; at this time her house became a hospital for the wounded. She then resumed teaching, and when Nisbet Academy opened in 1887 she taught there until it burned down in 1890.

Subsequently Baker opened a school for refugee Sioux from the United States, who had settled across the river from Prince Albert. Her learning their language won the respect of Chief Tomas. In 1895 she was instrumental in establishing the Wapeton Reserve (Round Plain Reserve), about thirteen miles from the Prince Albert settlement: a mission house and a log school were built, and she lived and worked there until retirement in 1905. Baker returned east and died on May 30, 1909, in Montreal. In 1954 Baker Lake was named in her honour. *Phyllis Carlson*

BAKER, MARY (1918– 2003). Born in Regina on July 10, 1918, Mary Baker (*née* George) was internationally renowned as an outstanding softball player. Since major league baseball was postponed during **WORLD WAR II**, Chicago Cubs owner P.K. Wrigley started the All-American Girls' Professional Baseball League, which Baker joined in 1943. She played back catcher for the South Bend Blue Sox in Indiana and was a three-time all-star. Baker played nine seasons in the league (1943–50, 1952) and in 1950, she became the league's only full-time female player-manager for the Kalamazoo Lassies. Noted

An outstanding catcher, batter and base runner, Mary Baker epitomized the AAGPBL's image of athleticism and wholesome glamour.

for her attractive appearance and softball skills, Baker was the league's most publicized player and was referred to as "Pretty Bonnie Baker" by the press. She later returned to Regina and led the city's Legion softball club to provincial, Western Canadian, and World Ladies Softball titles. In addition, Mary Baker worked for Regina's CKRM in 1964–65, becoming the first female sports broadcaster in Canada. She also managed the Wheat City Curling club for twenty-five years. She is a member of the **SASKATCHEWAN SPORTS HALL OF FAME**, the Saskatchewan Baseball Hall of Fame, the Canadian Baseball Hall of Fame, and the Baseball Hall of Fame in Cooperstown, New York. Baker died on December 17, 2003. *Daria Coneghan and Holden Stoffel*

BAKER, WILLIAM B. (1919–69). W.B. (Bill) Baker was born at Verigin, Saskatchewan in 1919 and was raised on his parents' farm. He graduated from the **UNIVERSITY OF SASKATCHEWAN** School of Agriculture in 1940 and from the College of Agriculture (with Distinction) in 1944. His primary fields of study included sociology, rural sociology, and social psychology. His broad interest was adult education, with a special interest in group process. He was the director of the School of Agriculture and professor of rural education, University of Saskatchewan, from 1946 to 1956. In this role he pioneered a number of adult education methods in campus instruction. From 1952 to 1956, he was

William Baker, ca. 1952.

director of the Royal Commission on Agriculture and Rural Life; this was the first commission to implement broad public participation in its data collection process, resulting in fourteen benchmark reports. Following the Commission, he was named director of a newly formed Centre for Community Studies, a position he held from 1957 to 1964. From 1966 until his death in 1969 he was president of the Canadian Centre for Community Studies, located in Ottawa.

During his career, Baker worked on a variety of rural and community development projects, as well as on issues related to adult education, including agriculture, co-operative research, the rural church, and aging and long-term illness. He believed that if adults had access to information they would make wise decisions, and strove to improve the methods and processes used to involve the public in decision making. Baker's sociological and adult education contributions extended into numerous international arenas, including the United States, Australia, India, Venezuela, and the United Nations. His many honours included a Doctor of Laws degree from North Dakota State University in 1964. *Harold R. Baker*

BALCARRES, town, pop 622, located NE of Fort Qu'Appelle and served by Hwys 10, 22, and 310. Settlers, mainly of British origin, began arriving in the area in advance of the CPR in the early 1880s. In 1884 the Balcarres post office was established, named after the postmaster in Indian Head, from where the mail was hauled. In 1903, the CPR was working westward north of the QU'APPELLE VALLEY, and the townsite of Balcarres was established. Today the economic base of the Balcarres area remains agriculture, and a number of the town's businesses and services cater to the industry. Terminal 22, just west of Balcarres on Hwy 10, is a 50/50 joint-venture grain company comprised of local area farmers and CARGILL LIMITED; a state-of-the-art facility, it has

a storage capacity of 32,000 tonnes, the ability to handle over 400,000 annually, and can load 112 rail cars with product cleaned and ready for export. It is the first inland facility in western Canada to be certified under internationally recognized standards. Just to the northeast of Balcarres, four First Nations communities (Little Black Bear, Star Blanket, Okanese, and Peepeekisis) occupy a large block of land and, with a combined population of over 900, contribute to the town's economy and social fabric. Balcarres has a large modern hospital, a special care home, an RCMP detachment, and Balcarres School, which provides K-12 education to close to 500 students. *David McLennan*

BALDWIN, MILDRED (1908–99). An enthusiastic educator, Mildred Baldwin was born in North Dakota in 1908 and later made Yorkton the centre of her life's work. Beginning in 1933, she taught numerous grades and was principal of Fairview School. Outside the classroom, Baldwin was involved in the Girl Guides organization, the University Women's Club, and Westview United Church, serving as Clerk of Session. Although Baldwin ended her thirty-five-year teaching career in 1969, she volunteered in Zambia for a year-and-a-half, teaching English to Zambian women. She also developed a tutoring project in Yorkton. In 1985, Mildred Baldwin received the Saskatchewan Order of Merit and was chosen as Yorkton's citizen of the year.

BALGONIE, town, pop 1,239, located approximately 24 km E of Regina on Hwy 1. The Balgonie post office was established in 1883, named after the

14th-century Balgonie Castle in the county of Fife, Scotland. While Scots did settle in the Balgonie area from the 1880s, large numbers of English from both eastern Canada and Great Britain also took up land in the area, together with a significant population of Germans from eastern Europe and southern Russia (see **GERMAN SETTLEMENTS**). The economy developed around agriculture, particularly the large-scale production of wheat. The completion of the **TRANS-CANADA HIGHWAY** in the late 1950s ushered in a period of significant growth. During the 1970s substantial residential development began, and today construction of new subdivisions continues as Balgonie further develops into a bedroom community for people who commute to work in Regina. One of the oldest remaining buildings in Balgonie is the former United Church: a stone structure built in 1901 for the community's Presbyterian congregation, the building was designated a heritage property in 1987 and most recently has served as a community museum and heritage centre. Balgonie was also home to one of Canada's pioneers in aviation. During the first years of the 20th century, while the Wright brothers were experimenting with their own heavier-than-air aeroplane, William Wallace Gibson, also known as the "Balgonie Birdman," was building a four-cylinder, air-cooled engine for an aircraft he was designing; he worked in secret and tested his model airplanes in the early morning hours to avoid ridicule from sceptical neighbours. Gibson built the first Canadian-made aircraft engine and installed it in an aircraft of his own design, which he successfully flew in Victoria in 1910, the first completely Canadian-built aircraft. Gibson has been the subject of both an animated short film produced by the

First aeroplane engine built near Balgonie, 1905.

National Film Board of Canada, and a 60-minute documentary produced by the Regina-based film and video production company, Partners in Motion.

David McLennan

BALLANTYNE, TOM (1924–). Tom Ballantyne, first president of the Saskatchewan Forestry Association, was born in Kapuskasing, Ontario, in 1924. After graduating from the University of New Brunswick with a BSc in Forestry in 1950, he worked first for the Spruce Falls Pulp and Paper Company in Kapuskasing, then for Kimberly-Clark in Longlac, Ontario. In 1966 he moved to Prince Albert to be the first general logging superintendent for the newly formed Prince Albert Pulp Company (PAPCo). He became vice-president of woodlands for PAPCo in 1972, and remained there until his retirement in 1984. Throughout his career, Ballantyne emphasized the need for public education about forestry, particularly in Saskatchewan, which, despite its reputation as a prairie province, is more than half forested. He was involved in the Prairie Provinces Forestry Association until its dissolution in 1972, followed by the formation of the Saskatchewan Forestry Association (SFA) in 1973. He was president of the SFA from 1973 until 1980. During this time he was also the Saskatchewan representative on the Canadian Forestry Association (CFA), serving as president in 1979–80. He was instrumental in the establishment of the CFA program Forestry Capital of Canada (FCC), and in the awarding of the first FCC designation to Hudson Bay, Saskatchewan, in 1975; since then, Prince Albert has been FCC in 1985, and Meadow Lake in 1995. In retirement, Ballantyne remained active in the SFA, serving continuously on its board of directors for more than thirty years. In 1991 he received the SFA Friend of the Trees Award for his continuing efforts in promoting forestry awareness and education in Saskatchewan. He was also active in the formation of the Farm Woodlot Association of Saskatchewan in the late 1980s, serving on its board of directors for several years. He was chair of the TREEmendous board of directors, and was involved with the Prince Albert Model Forest and the steering committee for Saskatchewan Forestry Expo.

Andrea Atkinson

BALOGH, MARY (1944–). Best-selling author Mary Balogh (née Jenkins) was born March 24, 1944, in Swansea, Wales. A prolific novelist, Balogh is known primarily for her Regency romances, romance novels set in 19th-century England during the regency of George, Prince of Wales.

Balogh attended the University of Wales at Cardiff, studying first English language and literature, then education. She moved to Kipling, Saskatchewan in 1967 for a two-year teaching contract. She settled in Kipling after marrying Robert Balogh, with whom she has three grown children.

Balogh began writing in her spare time while raising her children and working as a high school principal and English teacher. Her first novel, *A Masked Deception*, was published in 1985 by Signet, earning her the New York–based *Romantic Times Magazine*'s Best New Regency Author award. Many more awards followed, and in 1988 her success allowed her to retire from her twenty-year career as an educator to commence writing full-time.

In 1999, Balogh signed with Dell, who published her first hardcover novel, *More Than a Mistress*, in 2000. Since then, several of her novels have appeared in the *New York Times*' top-35 best-sellers list and in the *Publishers Weekly* top 15.

Justin Messner

FURTHER READING: Clemence, Verne. 2000. "Romance for Everyone: Saskatchewan Writer Puts to Rest Reader Stereotype." *Saskatoon StarPhoenix* (December 2), E4; Froese, Christalee. 2003. "A World Away from Regency England." *Regina Leader-Post* (May 24), G1.

BALTZAN, DAVID MORTIMER (1897–1983). Baltzan was born on May 10, 1897, in Bessarabia, a province of Tsarist Russia, now Moldova, and came to Canada with his parents in 1905. David's father started up the Saskatchewan Hide and Fur Company in Saskatoon. David excelled at school, and was the first in his family to become a doctor. He graduated from McGill University in 1920, completed his practical experience in New York, and then studied internal medicine in Edinburgh, London, Vienna and, finally, at Johns Hopkins in Baltimore. He eventually chose Saskatoon as the site for his ground-breaking practice, fired by the need for modern innovations in internal medicine. Against all advice he eschewed surgery, which was making others rich, to invest in a portable electrocardiograph (ECG) and an X-ray machine for his office.

In spite of predictions that he could not succeed, he created the Baltzan clinic, enticed his three sons to join him, and stayed active for fifty years. David Baltzan was in the top ranks of medicine in Canada. Among other contributions, he was a member of the **HALL COMMISSION**, which created the blueprint for public health care in Canada. He died in Saskatoon on June 15, 1983.

Verne Clemence

FURTHER READING: Clemence, V. 1995. *David M. Baltzan, Prairie Doctor*. Toronto: Fitzhenry and Whiteside.

BALTZAN, MARC A. (1929–2005). Born in Saskatoon on October 31, 1929, Marc Baltzan obtained his MD CM degree from McGill University in 1953, and trained in Internal Medicine at Johns Hopkins University. His main research interest is renal dialysis, of which he was a pioneer in 1960, and renal transplantation. The first of the latter operations was performed (the second in Canada) on December 11, 1963. Baltzan was the internist, "captain" and the longest-serving member of the transplant team, which included urologists and surgeons. Thirty-one of the world's first 330 cadaveric renal transplants (using kidneys removed from deceased patients) were performed in Saskatoon, where the survival rate was well above the world average. A review in 1992 showed that Saskatoon had more twenty-year survivals (six) than any other centre in the world; 930 kidney transplants were done by this team to the end of 2003. Baltzan was president of the **SASKATCHEWAN MEDICAL ASSOCIATION** in 1966–68, and of the Canadian

Left to right: Marc Baltzan, Dick Baltzan, David Baltzan, and Don Baltzan, June 1959.

Medical Association in 1982–83. He was made an Officer of the Order of Canada in 1995, and received the Saskatchewan Order of Merit in 1999 and an Honorary D. Sc. from the **UNIVERSITY OF SASKATCHEWAN** in 2004. Marc Baltzan died on January 1, 2005.

C. Stuart Houston

BAMFORD FLETCHER, JOAN (1918–79). In 1945 Regina's Joan Bamford Fletcher captured headlines in Canada and Britain after shepherding some 2,000 Dutch civilian captives from a Japanese prison camp through the Sumatra jungle to safety: while commanding seventy vanquished but armed Japanese soldiers she guided the evacuees through territory swarming with hostile Indonesian rebels. This remarkable feat earned her an MBE, a Samurai sword, and public renown. Born in Regina in 1918, Bamford Fletcher came from a family of prosperous cotton merchants in England. After early years spent on their dairy farm near Regina, she attended boarding school in England in the 1920s, and took further schooling in Belgium and France. After the outbreak of **WORLD WAR II** Fletcher first trained as a driver in the Canadian Red Cross transport section, then traveled to Britain around December 1940 and joined the First Aid Nursing Yeomanry (FANY). In Scotland she worked as a driver for the exiled Polish army. At war's end she was sent to Sumatra, where her rescue feat took place. Later she was posted to the British Embassy in communist-held Poland, but eventually returned to Canada, where she died in 1979.

Ruth Wright Millar

FURTHER READING: Millar, R.W. 2004. *Saskatchewan Heroes and Rogues.* Regina: Coteau Books.

BANDS. Saskatchewan's first wind bands were modeled on prototypes brought by British immigrants in the late 1800s: industrial brass bands, and military brass and reed bands. The North-West Mounted Police organized the earliest, first at Fort Walsh in 1878, with others following at Fort Qu'Appelle (1880), Battleford (1882), and Regina (1883). The Prince Albert Cornet Band, established in 1883, was probably the first civilian band. Before the turn of the century, similar aggregations were assembled in Regina, Moose Jaw, Grenfell, Qu'Appelle, Indian Head, Moosomin, Whitewood, Kolin, and conceivably elsewhere. Brass bands were also formed in Indian residential schools at Lebret (1892) and Regina (1894). The number of "town bands" or "citizens' bands" increased steadily from the turn of the 20th century to the outbreak of **WORLD WAR I**. Bands were frequently the first large concert ensembles established in prairie towns and villages, providing music for all civic occasions: sports days, sporting events, special ceremonies, public skating, ice carnivals, fairs, and parades.

The two World Wars and the **GREAT DEPRESSION**

SASKATCHEWAN ARCHIVES BOARD R-B7425

Regina's first Brass Band, 1886.

adversely affected civilian bands. During the Depression, funding shortages often forced bands to stop operations. Similarly, many civilian bands ceased during the wars, as musicians and bandmasters left to serve overseas. Concurrently, the number of militia, cadet, and military bands increased. Service organizations such as Kinsmen, Kiwanis, Lions, and Elks clubs assumed a major role in sponsoring the bands re-established after **WORLD WAR II**. Unlike the earlier town bands, the majority of these post-war community groups were "junior" or youth bands. By the early 1960s, an increasing number of school bands were also active. However, it was a program introduced by the Department of Education in 1966 specifically to encourage the creation of school bands that triggered their general proliferation. This initiative was highly successful, and by 1975 bands were an established component of Saskatchewan's educational system. Though the specific details of Saskatchewan's "school band movement" are unique, general trends mirrored those across North America.

Many community bands disbanded or reorganized as school bands when funding became available through the Department of Education. Some community bands such as the Regina Lions Band continued to flourish outside the school system, while others devised idiosyncratic arrangements between service clubs and school boards (e.g., Melfort Kinsmen School Band). Since the early 1970s, band proponents worldwide have striven to elevate the wind band as an artistic medium, particularly through improvements in the quality of the repertoire. However, owing to trends in both popular culture and art music, the wind band's role at the dawn of the 21st century remains primarily educational.

Edwin B. Wasiak

FURTHER READING: Wasiak, E.B. 2000. "School Bands in Saskatchewan, Canada: A History," *Journal of Historical Research in Music Education* 21: 112–31.

BANNATYNE-CUGNET, JO (1951–). Best-selling children's author Jo (Elizabeth Jo-Anne) Bannatyne-Cugnet was born on July 19, 1951, in Estevan and grew up in that city. She completed a BSc in Nursing at the **UNIVERSITY OF SASKATCHEWAN** in 1974, and started work in Weyburn as a public health nurse. Bannatyne-Cugnet wrote to learn for herself and to teach her four sons about life on a prairie farm. She has been most successful in collaboration with Yvette Moore of Moose Jaw, the illustrator for *A Prairie Alphabet*, *A Prairie Year*, and *Heartland, A Prairie Sampler*, which have sold nearly half a million copies and won several awards. Other books include two novels for young children, one of which was translated into French, and a picture book on new Canadians. Regina composer **ELIZABETH RAUM** was inspired by Bannatyne-Cugnet's work to write a symphony for children, "A Prairie Alphabet Musical Parade," which has been recorded by the **REGINA SYMPHONY ORCHESTRA**. Following early retirement from nursing in 1994, Bannatyne-Cugnet continues to write but spends considerable time doing volunteer work for community, social service and arts organizations.

Bob Ivanochko

BAPTIST GENERAL CONFERENCE. The Baptist General Conference (BGC) churches in Saskatchewan have their roots in Sweden. In 1847, F.O. Nilsson was deported after imprisonment for charges of heresy; moving to the United States, he was involved in establishing the First Swedish Baptist Church in Rock Island, Illinois. The organization then searched out Swedish immigrants in North America, and planted Baptist churches where there were sufficient numbers. In 1894 their first church was founded in Canada: the Scandinavian Baptist Church in Winnipeg, now Grant Memorial Baptist. By 1905 the Central Canada Baptist Conference was organized. The oldest church in Saskatchewan is First Baptist in Midale (est. 1903). All the original churches followed the Swedish immigrant settlement patterns: the large cities in Saskatchewan were left thus out. The 1920s and 1930s were a transitional period for the churches as they began to hold services in English. Also, some of the small rural churches were closed or combined with other churches as roads and transportation improved.

A new vision for missions and church planting was born in the Baptist General Conference in 1944, as the ethnic era was completed and the Conference launched into a period of tremendous growth. In the 1950s, the largely rural church community in Saskatchewan faced the migration of people from the farm to the city. Soon there was an attempt to plant churches in the major centres: two successful examples of church plants have been Ebenezer Baptist in Saskatoon (est. 1954) and Hillsdale Baptist in Regina (est. 1957). Evangelism has always been part of the Baptist heritage, and many missionaries have been sent from the Saskatchewan churches over the last hundred years. One example is Ruby Eliason, who left Wadena in 1955 to work in India, and then served for years in Cameroon; after retiring she continued to serve her former mission fields, and died in a car accident in Ethiopia in 2000.

In 1977 an ad hoc meeting was organized in Calgary to explore the possibilities of working together, as at that time the BGC existed as three independent districts directed from the central office in the United States. In April 1981 a meeting in Regina was held to consider forming the Baptist General Conference of Canada; the motions passed, with more than 95% of the delegates voting in favour. There are three primary reasons why the Baptist Conference of Canada was born. The first and initial motivation was the desire for fellowship across the three districts: prior to 1977, the only time any of the Canadian conference members would see each other was at the BGC function in the United Sates. A second issue, entirely external, was the new regulation on the part of Revenue Canada that required Canadian charities to organize and control their funds. And the third issue had to do with a perceived responsibility to Canada as a nation: the three districts had been provincial in outlook; it was now time to become more knowledgeable about the spiritual state of the nation.

Allan Ramsay

BAPTIST UNION OF WESTERN CANADA.

The history of the Baptist Union of Western Canada (BUWC) has its roots in the missionary efforts of the Baptist Missionary Convention of Ontario, which in 1869 sent two Baptist ministers to what was then called the North-West. Four years later they sent Alexander (Pioneer) MacDonald as a missionary to Winnipeg with the mandate to preach the Gospel and maintain the ordinances. During the ten years that MacDonald remained the primary Baptist figure in the North-West, he helped to establish ten churches, all in Manitoba. The work of pioneering Baptist ministers soon extended into what is now Saskatchewan, resulting in the establishment of a church in Moose Jaw in 1883, Moosomin two years later, and Regina in 1891.

By the time the Baptist churches in western Canada joined to form their own Convention (1907), Saskatchewan churches had been established in Yorkton (1900), Prince Albert (1903), Saskatoon (1904), Asquith (1906) and Weyburn (1906). Others soon followed: Estevan (1908), Droxford (Bingham) (1910), Congress and Kipling (1912), Shaunavon (1913), and Leask (1916). While some of this growth was due to the work of the Home Mission Superintendents who were employed by the newly formed Convention (called the "Union" in 1909), individual churches also established daughter churches in neighbouring towns or other parts of the same city. In the 1920s the rate of growth dropped off considerably, as only four new churches were started in the province during that decade, and no more until the 1950s. The latter half of the 20th century saw the establishment of a few new churches and the re-establishment of what were once active churches. Swift Current, for example, initially began in 1956 but then collapsed, to be reorganized only in 1995. The most prominent Baptist churches in several cities in Saskatchewan were called "First" churches to distinguish them from other Baptist churches in the community and to establish visibility and prominence in the city.

While the large majority of these churches were English, the Baptist churches in the province also included German, Hungarian, Scandinavian, Ukrainian, Czech and Slovak churches. Already in 1889 there were three German Baptist churches, at Edenwold, Lemberg and Ebenezer (north of Yorkton), begun by Rev. F.A. Petereit, a Home missionary of the BUWC, whose task was to minister to German immigrants. At least sixteen more were established between 1890 and 1934, but by then the German Baptist churches had severed their relationship with the BUWC and joined the North American Baptist Conference. Similarly, the Swedish Baptist churches in western Canada, which for many years had had a close working relationship with their American counterparts, joined the Baptist (Swedish) General Conference of America in 1948, severing their long connection to the BUWC. The loss of these two large ethnic groups was significant for the BUWC, and was certainly felt by the Saskatchewan Baptist churches as they were two of the most vigorous in the Union. Other groups such as the Ukrainians, Hungarians, Czechs and Slovaks continued to remain under the Baptist Union umbrella, and today have either died out or become anglicized. The only remaining "ethnic" church is the Ukrainian Baptist Church in Saskatoon, which still has some of its services in the Ukrainian language.

Among the distinguishing features of the local Baptist Churches that are associated with the BUWC is their emphasis on freedom for the individual, both in terms of human rights and religion. Growing out of their historical roots in the Puritan-

First Baptist Church, Regina, 1961.

Independent movement in England, they have shied away from any overarching structure that might curtail their freedom. It has also been the conviction among those Baptists who were part of the BUWC that ministers need to be well educated, and thus even in the early 20th century ministers often had a liberal arts as well as a seminary degree. An educational institution designed for the express purpose of training ministers was begun in Brandon in 1898, while McMaster University in Hamilton trained Baptist ministers long before that. In addition, there was the sense that the Baptist Church was a key member of the community. As a result, well-known Baptists include Prime Minister **JOHN DIEFENBAKER**, of the Prince Albert Baptist Church, and **T.C. DOUGLAS**, pastor of Calvary Baptist Church in Weyburn before he entered politics. Members have also engaged in public service and taken part in Canada's war efforts.

The Union Church is somewhat less conservative regarding a variety of social, political, and theological issues. While not immune from the tensions created by the liberalism/fundamentalism debate that took place in the 1920s and 1930s, the Baptist Union churches maintained what might be termed an "open evangelical" position. They, for example, have allowed for the ordination of women since 1959 and have had several women as presidents of the Union; they have also shied away from having new members sign formal statements of faith. As of 2003, there are nineteen BUWC churches in Saskatchewan, the largest being Westhill Park and First Baptist in Regina, Emmanuel in Saskatoon, and the Community Baptist Church in Swift Current. Administratively, the churches in Saskatchewan and Manitoba form the Heartland Area, one of three administrative districts that exist in the BUWC. They are served by an Area Minister and an Area Board which, although having limited authority, oversee two camps in this province (Katepwa Baptist Kamp and Christopher Lake Bible Camp), supervise "mission" churches, facilitate the ordination and licensing of pastors, and provide some resources as well as pastoral support to the churches in the Area.

Henry Friesen

FURTHER READING: Harris, J.E. 1976. *The Baptist Union of Western Canada: A Centennial History, 1873–1973*. Saint John, NB; Renfree, H.A. 1988. *Heritage and Horizon: The Baptist Story in Canada*. Mississauga.

BARBER, CLARENCE LYLE (1917–2004). A Canadian economist of international stature, Clarence Lyle Barber was born on May 17, 1917, on a farm near Wolseley, Saskatchewan. Growing up during the **GREAT DEPRESSION**, Barber became interested in economic problems. After studying economics at the **UNIVERSITY OF SASKATCHEWAN**, he did graduate work at Clark University and the University of

Minnesota. Barber served in the Canadian Air Force until 1945, then joined the faculty at the University of Manitoba in 1949, where he worked until his retirement in 1983. He was instrumental in convincing Manitoba, through his work on the Royal Commission Flood Cost-Benefit from 1957–59, to build the crucial protective floodway. He also implemented the Canadian Royal Commission on Farm Machinery, which reported in 1971. His seminal work on Canadian tariff policy, unemployment, and welfare economics earned him an international following. Barber was a member of the Royal Society of Canada, the Order of Canada, and the Order of Manitoba. He passed away in Victoria on February 26, 2004.

Merle Massie

BARBER, LLOYD (1932–). Lloyd Barber has been a key figure in the educational and economic development of Saskatchewan. Born on March 8, 1932, in Regina, Barber specialized in business and commerce, receiving an undergraduate degree from the **UNIVERSITY OF SASKATCHEWAN**, as well as graduate degrees from the University of California (Berkeley) and the University of Washington. He has held positions as professor of commerce with the University of Saskatchewan (1955–76), as member of the Northwest Territories Council (1967–70), and as Indian Claims Commissioner for Canada (1969–77). From 1976 until his retirement in 1990, he served as president and vice-chancellor of the **UNIVERSITY OF REGINA**. Lloyd Barber is credited with expanding both the size and scope of that university; he was instrumental in establishing the Saskatchewan Indian Federated College (now **FIRST NATIONS UNIVERSITY OF CANADA**) in 1976, and in developing international university relations between the University of Regina and Chinese educational institutions in Hunan province. The Dr. Lloyd Barber Academic Green at the centre of the university commemorates his contributions to higher education in Saskatchewan. In recognition of his work advancing the social and economic development of First Nations peoples, Barber was made an honorary Saskatchewan Indian Chief in 1980 and was awarded the Aboriginal Order of Canada in 1985. He received the Saskatchewan Order of Merit (1995) and the Vanier Medal from the Institute of Public Administration of Canada (1979). Invested as an Officer of the Order of Canada in 1978, he was later promoted to Companion of the Order in 1993.

Lauren Black

BARCLAY, BYRNA (1940–). Byrna Barclay, born on October 8, 1940, has nurtured a lifelong love affair with reading and writing. She has authored novels, collections of short stories, poetry, and a play. Her work has appeared in numerous literary magazines and anthologies. Publications include *Girl at the Window* (2004), *Searching for*

the Nude in the Landscape (1997), *Crosswinds* (1996), *Winter of the White Wolf* (1985), *The Last Echo* (1983), *From the Belly of a Flying Whale* (1988), and *Summer of the Hungry Pup* (1982). In 2004, she published *The Room with Five Walls*, a poetic drama in two acts, which won the Regina Book Award. Barclay has served as president of the **SASKATCHEWAN WRITERS GUILD**, vice-chairman of the **SASKATCHEWAN ARTS BOARD**, and as a board member of the Saskatchewan Playwrights' Centre. Editing experiences include: fiction editor of *Grain* (1988–90); editor-in-chief of *Transition* (1983–2002); and founding editor of *Spring* (2000). Her awards include: Prairie Fire's Long Short Story Contest (1999); the Saskatchewan Culture Distinguished Service Award (1998); the Saskatchewan Book Best Fiction Award (1996); and the Saskatchewan First Novel Award (1982). She was awarded the Saskatchewan Order of Merit in 2004. Barclay is also a strong advocate for mental health reform, and has served on related boards.

Christian Thompson

BARD, FREDERICK GEORGE (1908–89). Fred Bard was a pioneer and leader in wildlife conservation who worked at the Saskatchewan Museum of Natural History for forty-five years. Bard was born in Granum, Alberta on August 1, 1908. He began his distinguished career at the museum in Regina in 1924, at the age of 16. From 1947 until his retirement in 1970, Bard served as director of the museum, now called the **ROYAL SASKATCHEWAN MUSEUM**.

Through years of field work in collecting museum specimens, documenting the flora and fauna of Saskatchewan, bird banding, photography, film making, public-speaking engagements, and designing museum exhibits, few people had a broader knowledge of the province's natural history than Bard.

In the 1940s, Bard was one of the first in North America to bring the plight of the endangered whooping crane to the public's attention; he was the Canadian leader in the international effort to save

SASKATCHEWAN ARCHIVES BOARD R-A11982

Frederick Bard.

the whooper from extinction. Another example of his major efforts in conservation was his work in the 1950s in bringing the Canada goose back to the Canadian prairies, after it had all but vanished owing to hunting and habitat destruction.

In 1953, Bard obtained a pair of captive geese from the late Ralph Stueck of Abernethy. From this meager beginning the Wascana Canada Goose Flock was established, which soon numbered in the hundreds and was plentiful enough to be used for restocking. Offspring from this flock were reintroduced throughout southern Saskatchewan and in several provinces and states.

Saskatchewan celebrated its 50th anniversary as a province in 1955. With the support of naturalists, the Saskatchewan Golden Jubilee Committee, and dedicated staff, Bard was successful in completing the present day Royal Saskatchewan Museum for the official opening by His Excellency, the Right Honourable Vincent Massey, Governor-General of Canada on May 16, 1955. The museum, with its lifelike and detailed exhibits, was viewed at its opening as one of the best natural history museums on the continent.

Bard was active in many organizations and recognized on a number of occasions for his lifetime commitment to conservation and to the museum. In 1967, he received the Canadian Centennial Medal. He was inducted as a Fellow of the Canadian Museum Association, and in 1970 he received an Honorary Doctor of Laws degree from the UNIVERSITY OF SASKATCHEWAN, Regina Campus.

Following his retirement from the museum, Bard and his wife Philomene retired to Surrey, British Columbia, where he died on September 23, 1989.
Lorne Scott

BARLEY. Barley (*Hordeum vulgare* L.) is the second most widely grown cereal crop in Canada after WHEAT. It contributes significantly to the world supply of livestock feed, malt products, and human food. Cultivated barley in Canada is an annual plant with spring or winter growth habit; in the prairie region, only the spring type is commercially produced. Barley has a spike inflorescence and is recognized as of either a two-rowed or a six-rowed type: in the case of two-rowed barley, only one of the three florets at each rachis node is fertile, whereas all three florets are fertile in the six-rowed type. Barley and other small grain cereals were brought to Canada in the early 17th century by European colonists. The barley was two-rowed and was targeted for the malting market; the first Canadian brewery was built in Quebec City in 1668. In the mid- to late-1800s, an active export market into the United States developed for Canadian malting barley; this essentially came to a halt when the American government imposed stiff import taxes.

Cereal crops were introduced to the prairies in

PHOTO COURTESY OF AGRICULTURE AND AGRI-FOOD CANADA 97-08-024

Barley.

the mid-1700s as trading posts became established in western Canada. As settlement occurred in the 1800s, the majority of the barley crop was grown as livestock feed. When the malting barley trade came to a halt in the late 1800s, and with increased usage for feed, there was less impetus to renew and improve seed stocks–which ultimately tarnished the image of barley. This changed in 1918 when a National Barley Committee was established to promote the development of the crop: this led to concerted efforts in barley improvement through research and development. Currently, Canada is a major exporter of malt and malting barley, with large markets in the United States and China. In western Canada, barley improvement efforts were initiated at agricultural colleges and experimental farms in the prairie provinces. Efforts were targeted at two-rowed and six-rowed malting and feed types. Currently, three barley breeding programs contribute to Saskatchewan production. They are located at the Crop Development Centre of the UNIVERSITY OF SASKATCHEWAN; the Agriculture and Agri-Food Canada Research Centre at Brandon, Manitoba; and with a joint program in Lacombe, Alberta with Alberta Agriculture, Food and Rural Development, and Agriculture and Agri-Food Canada.

Saskatchewan statistics for barley acreage over the last twenty years show a slight rise, in spite of increased cropping options such as pulses and oilseeds. The upward trend is likely due to improving demand for both malting and feed barley. The 1998–2002 five-year average harvested acres and production for Saskatchewan were 4.1 million acres

and 4.2 million tonnes respectively. Generally, farmers have two marketing options: malt and feed. Cultivars are developed specifically for these purposes. Approximately 75% of acres sown to barley in Saskatchewan are malting type, in hope of capturing the premium malting market price. However, less than 20% of production is actually selected for malting, with the remainder sold as feed. In addition to the conventional malting and feed markets, breeding efforts are targeting specialty markets: hull-less barley cultivars are available for the poultry and hog industries, and cultivars with high beta-glucan content and/or waxy types (special starch composition) are available for specialty food markets. In western Canada, the marketing of barley was placed under the authority of the Canadian Wheat Board in 1949. In 1974, as part of a new domestic feed grain policy, the federal government removed feed barley for the domestic market from the sole authority of the Board, which continues to market malting barley domestically, and malting and feed barley for export. (*See also* MALTING INDUSTRY)
Blaine Recksiedler

FURTHER READING: Metcalfe, D.R. 1995. "Barley." Pp. 82–97 in A.E. Slinkard and D.R. Knott (eds.), *Harvest of Gold*. Saskatoon: University of Saskatchewan Extension Press.

BARMBY, MARJORIE (1904–89). Marjorie Barmby's many involvements included church work, the Council of Women, and the co-operative movement. Born Marjorie Wight in Nebraska in 1904, she moved with her family to a farm near Regina in 1911. She attended NORMAL SCHOOL, then taught at country schools and at Lang, where she married a farmer, Walter Barmby. After farming for twenty-five years, they and their four children moved to Regina in 1942, and to Saskatoon in 1955. Barmby joined the Co-operative Women's Guild in 1943, later becoming president. She was on the Sherwood Co-operative Board and, while a member of the Co-op Union Board, participated in province-wide co-op education programs. She was active at local–namely Saskatoon and Regina–and provincial levels with the Council of Women, and the Saskatoon and Provincial Councils awarded her life memberships. Active also in the United Church, she was a Life Member of the Salvation Army Advisory Board.

Work on behalf of children included piano teaching (at Lang) and establishment of a kindergarten in her home from 1957 to 1961. Barmby also sought to preserve Saskatoon's first school, Little Stone. By babysitting and making stuffed toys, she raised money to help overseas children. As well, she directed the United Church Junior Girls' Camp at Manitou Beach for six years. She died in Saskatoon on September 11, 1989.
Bob Ivanochko

FURTHER READING: Saskatoon Business and Professional Women's Club. 1976. *Some Outstanding Women: They Made Saskatoon a Better Community.*

BARNARDO CHILDREN. In the late 19th century, charitable organizations in the United Kingdom dispatched Britain's surplus children to Canada to meet the soaring demand for cheap agricultural and household labour. One of the best-known figures of child emigration was Thomas John Barnardo, Irish-born philanthropist and founder of Dr. Barnardo's Homes. His organization sent roughly 30,000 children to Canada between 1882 and 1939. Typically, young boys and girls, most of whom were age 8 to 16, were taken first to receiving homes established in Ontario. From there, boys were apprenticed as farm labourers and girls as domestic servants.

With the expansion of the Canadian West, Barnardo opened the Industrial School for Barnardo Boys near Russell, Manitoba, in 1887. The youths selected for the industrial farm received an eight-month apprenticeship in all areas of agriculture, after which they began homesteading. Although the Industrial School closed in 1908, subsequent child emigration to the prairies, including Saskatchewan, was administered from Barnardo's Winnipeg Receiving and Distributing Home. As might be expected, the practice of sending young children from Britain to Canada was highly controversial. In 1925, the Canadian Immigration Branch prohibited voluntary immigration societies from bringing children under 14 years of age to the country. All child emigration schemes were halted in 1939.

Holden Stoffel

FURTHER READING: Bagnell, Kenneth. 2002. *The Little Immigrants: The Orphans Who Came to Canada.* Toronto: Dundurn Press; Corbett, Gail H. 1997. *Nation Building: Barnardo Children in Canada.* Toronto: Dundurn Press.

BAROOTES, EFSTATHIOS WILLIAM (1918–2000). "Staff" Barootes was born in Saskatoon on November 15, 1918. He obtained his BA from the UNIVERSITY OF SASKATCHEWAN in 1940 and his MD from the University of Toronto in 1943, then served two years as medical officer with the Toronto Scottish regiment. Following specialty training in Toronto, he practised urology in Regina. After serving as a member of the Thompson committee in 1960–61, he became president of the SASKATCHEWAN MEDICAL ASSOCIATION in 1962, presiding over the twenty-three-day DOCTORS' STRIKE. Because of his financial expertise, he served six years as treasurer of the Canadian Medical Association (CMA), and one year as its deputy president, for which he received the Association's prestigious Medal of Service. Barootes was president of the Medical Council of Canada in 1972–73. He was appointed by

SASKATCHEWAN ARCHIVES BOARD R-B2871

Dr. E.W. Barootes (left) appeared with Alex Jupp (centre) and T.C. Douglas (right) on CKCK-TV's "Opinions Unlimited" on March 20, 1960. Not surprisingly, the topic under discussion was the government-sponsored pre-paid medical care program.

Prime Minister Mulroney to the Canadian senate from 1984 to 1993. In an article written in 1991 he admitted that his early fears that doctors would be conscripted to civil service had been unfounded, since MEDICARE had not destroyed the sacred doctor-patient relationship nor professional self-government. He recommended that health professions should be forbidden to strike by law, provided that binding arbitration be available instead. Barootes died on July 30, 2000. *C. Stuart Houston*

BARR COLONY. Located in the region of present-day Lloydminster, the Barr Colony was an all-British settlement founded by Reverend Isaac M. Barr in 1903. His colonizing scheme attracted almost 2,000 eager Britons, most of whom lacked the necessary farming experience to survive on the Canadian prairie. On March 31, the colonists sailed from England on the SS *Lake Manitoba*, a ship originally built to accommodate 550 passengers. A rough ocean voyage, numerous delays at the port of Saint John, New Brunswick, and an uncomfortable railway journey to Saskatoon turned many hopeful immigrants against Reverend Barr.

The long wagon trip from Saskatoon to North Battleford proved too much for those colonists who had no experience driving oxen and wagons. Some turned back but the majority persevered. By May, however, the colonists deposed Barr, having accused him of profiteering and misleading them about conditions on the prairies. Control of the colony passed to Reverend George Exton Lloyd and twelve advisors. Homesteading began as soon as the colonists reached the reserve. Despite the initial hardships, the settlement survived and began to prosper. Its first village, Lloydminster, was named in honour of George Lloyd. As for Reverend Barr, he lived for several years in the United States and eventually immigrated to Australia. *Holden Stoffel*

FURTHER READING: Bowen, Lynne. 1992. *Muddling Through: The Remarkable Story of the Barr Colonists.* Vancouver: Douglas & McIntyre; Foster, Keith. 1982. "The Barr Colonists: Their Arrival and Impact on the Canadian North-West," *Saskatchewan History* 35 (3): 81-100; Wood, Christie. 2003. "Celebrating the Arrival of the Barr Colonists." *Saskatchewan History* 55 no. 1: 40-43.

RCMP MUSEUM, REGINA, 1997.47.3

Barr colonists, camped at Saskatoon, 1903.

BASEBALL. Settlers from the United States and eastern Canada brought baseball with them when they moved west in the decades after Confederation. The first recorded game in the North-West Territories took place near Fort Battleford on May 31, 1879. One of Saskatchewan's first notable players was **WALTER SCOTT**, a pitcher on Moose Jaw and Regina teams of the 1880s and 1890s, who would become the province's first Premier in 1905. By the turn of the century, dozens of towns boasted their own men's, and in some cases women's, teams. Independent professional and semi-pro leagues have come and gone throughout the province's history, but only the Western Canada League (1909–11, 1913–14, 1919–21) has operated in Saskatchewan as a fully sanctioned member of the National Association of Professional Baseball Leagues. Regina (Bonepilers originally, Red Sox after 1912) and the Moose Jaw Robin Hoods (1909–21) were in the league throughout its existence, while Saskatoon (Berrypickers at first, Quakers after 1912) joined in 1910. Moose Jaw won the pennant in 1911 and 1913, Saskatoon in 1914 and 1919.

Baseball's popularity has fluctuated but left a legacy of participation and achievement that bridges communities, race and gender. Many past and future major-leaguers have played for or against Saskatchewan clubs. Barnstorming teams, particularly those featuring Satchel Paige and other great "Negro" ballplayers, frequented the province from the 1920s through the 1960s. During and after **WORLD WAR II**, twenty-five women from Saskatchewan played in the All-American Girls Professional Baseball League, easily the largest provincial contingent of the sixty-three Canadians in that institution. Spectator interest in men's baseball peaked in the 1948–56 period when several leagues flourished and tournaments with thousands of dollars in prize money were held annually, most notably in Saskatoon and Indian Head.

Amateur baseball, regulated by the Saskatchewan Baseball Association, has sustained itself over the decades but has not attained the widespread popularity of hockey, curling or football–

partially because of the few months conducive to baseball, but also because it competes with softball for participants.

TERRY PUHL of Melville is certainly the best baseball player who was born in the province. Puhl, who holds the major-league career record for fielding percentage by an outfielder (.993), spent fourteen seasons with the Houston Astros (1977–90) and one with the Kansas City Royals (1991). Other Saskatchewan-born major-leaguers are catcher Joe "Stubby" Erautt of Vibank (Chicago Cubs 1950–51) and pitchers Ralph Buxton of Weyburn (Philadelphia Athletics 1938 and New York Yankees 1949), Aldon "Lefty" Wilkie of Zealandia (Pittsburgh Pirates 1941–42, 1946), Ed Bahr of Rouleau (Pittsburgh 1946–47), Reggie Cleveland of Swift Current (four teams, 1969–81) and Dave Pagan of Nipawin (four teams, 1973–77). *John Chaput*

FURTHER READING: Hack, P. and D. Shury. 1997. *Wheat Province Diamonds*. Regina: Saskatchewan Baseball Association.

BASTEDO, FRANK LINDSAY (1886–1973). Born in Bracebridge, Ontario in 1886, Frank Bastedo received his law degree from the University of Toronto in 1909. In 1911 he joined a Regina law firm. He was appointed King's Counsel in 1927 and argued cases before the Supreme Court of Canada and the Judicial Committee of the Privy Council in London. He served as president of the Regina federal Conservative Association from 1921 to 1924 but declined to stand for nomination.

Frank Bastedo was appointed eleventh **LIEUTENANT-GOVERNOR** of Saskatchewan in 1958 by the federal government of **JOHN DIEFENBAKER**. He placed great emphasis on the dignity of the office, going against the trend of reduced formality since the closure of **GOVERNMENT HOUSE** in 1945. On April 8, 1961, during the CCF administration of **WOODROW LLOYD**, Frank Bastedo made history by reserving royal assent for the Governor-General on Bill 56, The Alteration of Certain Mineral Contracts, because he had doubts about its validity and whether it was in

SASKATCHEWAN ARCHIVES BOARD R-B5532-1

Frank Bastedo.

the public interest–the first case of reservation in Canada since 1937, the only example in the history of the province, and the last in the country. Mr. Bastedo had not consulted the federal government, and the Diefenbaker government passed an Order-in-Council giving the legislation royal assent. *Michael Jackson*

FURTHER READING: Eager, Evelyn. 1980. *Saskatchewan Government: Politics and Pragmatism*. Saskatoon: Western Producer Prairie Books; Hryniuk, Margaret and Garth Pugh. 1991. *A Tower of Attraction: An Illustrated History of Government House, Regina, Saskatchewan*. Regina: Government House Historical Society/Canadian Plains Research Center; Leeson, Howard A. (ed.) 2001. *Saskatchewan Politics: Into the Twenty-first Century*. Regina: Canadian Plains Research Center.

BASTERFIELD, STEWARD (1884–1954). Steward Basterfield, chemist and administrator, was born in England in 1884. He studied at the Universities of Birmingham and London, where he received a BSc in 1908. In 1913 he came to Canada and undertook an appointment as instructor in chemistry at the **UNIVERSITY OF SASKATCHEWAN**. Subsequently he completed his PhD at the University of Chicago and was appointed professor at the University of Saskatchewan, a position he held from 1920 to 1940. He was dean of Regina College (precursor of the **UNIVERSITY OF REGINA**) from 1940 until his retirement in 1950. Basterfield became dean shortly after the college was moved to make way for RCAF training. After the war he oversaw the college move back to its own buildings. As enrolment expanded, courses were added, and for the first time the curriculum included first year engineering, commerce, and pharmacy. In recognition of his research in organic chemistry, he was made a Fellow of the

Little League play, Regina, May 1998.

Steward Basterfield.

Royal Society of Canada in 1933. Basterfield died in 1954. The Steward Basterfield Lectureship at the University of Regina is named in his honour.

Mark Vajcner

BATOCHE. Batoche is a National Historic Site and an annual **MÉTIS** cultural gathering place, 44 km southwest of Prince Albert. On May 9–12, 1885, Batoche was the site of the last pitched battle on Canadian soil, when approximately 300 Métis, **CREE** and **DAKOTA**, led by **GABRIEL DUMONT**, clashed with Frederick Middleton's 900 Canadian volunteers. A former Métis wintering (*hivernant*) community, Batoche (or "St. Laurent Settlement," as it was originally known) was founded in 1871 by Métis émigrés from Manitoba. After 1873, the community gradually became known as Batoche in honour of the Batoche family, whose patriarch, Xavier Letendre *dit* Batoche, opened a general store at the nearby crossing on the **SOUTH SASKATCHEWAN RIVER**. Today, Batoche is home to "Back to Batoche Days," an annual cultural celebration which occurs during the week of July 24 (on St. Joseph's Day, the Métis patron saint). During "Back to Batoche Days," thousands gather to celebrate Métis culture and heritage and reconnect with old friends. The modern festival originated in 1970; however, its antecedent, "St. Joseph's Day," ran from 1884 to the early 1930s. For the Métis, Batoche is more than a place to celebrate their culture: it is also a sacred place, where their ancestors resisted marginalization. It is the Saskatchewan equivalent of the Plains of Abraham or Queenston Heights. All that remains at the site are the remnants of the Métis' rifle pits, a church, a rectory, and a cemetery containing the graves of nine Métis killed during the Battle of Batoche.

Darren R. Préfontaine

FURTHER READING: Payment, D.P. 1990. *The Free People–Otipemisiwak: Batoche, Saskatchewan, 1870–1930*. Ottawa: National Historic Sites, Environment Canada;

–. 1996. "La vie en rose?' Métis Women at Batoche, 1870–1920." Pp. 19–37 in C. Miller and P. Churchryk (eds.), *Women of the First Nations: Power, Wisdom and Strength*. Winnipeg: University of Manitoba Press.

BATS. Bats are the only **MAMMALS** capable of true flight; others, such as "flying" squirrels, only glide. Their wings have little or no fur while the rest of their bodies are well furred. The eight species found in Saskatchewan are members of the family Vespertilionidae or smooth-faced bats. They have large ears and small eyes and they eat nothing but insects, mostly flying ones. Bats are small; those in Saskatchewan range in mass from 6 to 30 g.

Bats are active at dusk, dawn and/or night. They can navigate in complete darkness by using sound, a system called echolocation. The intense sounds they produce are high pitched, usually above the range of human hearing. Echoes from these calls bounce off objects, providing bats with information about size, shape and distance and whether the object is a potential meal or an obstacle. Bats eat a variety of insects, but different species tend to have preferences. Little brown bats mainly eat small, soft-bodied insects such as midges, often hunting over calm bodies of water. Hoary and big brown bats, which are larger, stronger fliers and have more powerful jaws, eat harder-bodied prey such as bee-

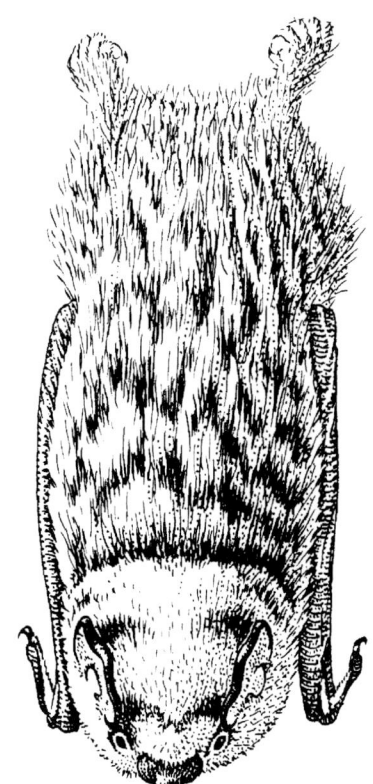

Hoary bat.

tles. Saskatchewan bats have two options to cope with winter when insects are unavailable. Some, like the red, hoary and silver-haired bats, migrate south while others hibernate in shelters such as caves or abandoned mines. Few hibernation sites are known in Saskatchewan.

Bats' rear legs are small, with five clawed toes on each foot, used when they hang upside down in roosts with their wings folded against their bodies. Bats are able to conserve their fat stores by lowering their body temperatures while roosting. While most small mammals reproduce often over a short life, bats tend to have few young and live long. Thirty-year old little brown bats have been caught. Most species give birth to a single pup, although twins occur and red bats may have litters of four. Young bats fly and begin foraging approximately four to six weeks after birth.

There are many myths about bats; but they are not blind, do not fly into people's hair, and do not suck blood. The most terrifying aspect for many is the assumption that most are rabid. Bats can indeed succumb to this disease, and any bat lying on the ground should not be touched. However, the vast majority of bats are healthy.

Raccoons, weasels, cats, snakes, hawks and owls occasionally catch bats, but humans inflict the most damage. Because many bat species are colonial, large numbers can easily be destroyed. If hibernating bats are disturbed they awaken, which costs energy and increases the possibility that the bat's stored fat will be insufficient to keep it alive all winter.

Mark Brigham

FURTHER READING: Nagorsen, D.W. and R.M. Brigham. 1993. "Bats of British Columbia." In *Royal British Museum Handbook, Vol. 1: The Mammals of British Columbia*. Vancouver: UBC Press.

BATTEN, MARY JOHN (1921–). Born August 30, 1921, in Sifton, Manitoba, Mary John Batten (*née* Fodchuk) was educated in Saskatchewan in Calder, Ituna, and Regina. Attending the **UNIVERSITY OF SASKATCHEWAN** she earned degrees in both arts and law. Articling under future Prime Minister **JOHN DIEFENBAKER**, she was accepted to the Saskatchewan bar in 1945. She settled in Humboldt and became involved in a variety of community organizations.

Batten ran in 1956 in the constituency of Humboldt for the Liberals, defeating CCF Cabinet Minister Joseph Burton. As the Liberals' only elected lawyer, Batten served as Justice critic. A vocal critic of party leader **HAMMY MCDONALD**, Batten was instrumental in precipitating McDonald's resignation, which led to the leadership convention that elected **ROSS THATCHER**.

Re-elected with a large majority in 1960, Batten served out the term before being appointed to the Court of Queen's Bench. She was the second woman

Mary Batten (right), delegate to the Provincial Liberal Convention, November 28, 1961.

appointed to the court. In the 1960s she chaired two provincial Royal Commissions—in 1966 on accounting practices, and in 1968 on the cost of living. In 1983, Batten was appointed Chief Justice of the Court of Queen's Bench, the first female chief justice in Saskatchewan history. Batten remained on the bench until her retirement from the court in 1990, having spent twenty-six years as a judge.

Brett Quiring

BATTLEFORD, town, pop 3,820, located halfway between the cities of Saskatoon and Lloydminster on the Yellowhead Hwy (No. 16). The historic former capital of the North-West Territories, Battleford sits on a high plateau across from the city of North Battleford, on the south side of the **NORTH SASKATCHEWAN RIVER**, near its confluence with the Battle River. Fur trading activity in the area dates to the later 1700s. Permanent settlement began in the mid-1870s, a few years after the route for the CPR was surveyed across the northern plains and along the south banks of the river. A station was established as the telegraph line was being built westward from Winnipeg to Edmonton, and the location was chosen to be the site of the capital of the North-West Territories. The name Battleford was selected after a nearby ford of the Battle River. In 1876, Fort Battleford was established as an NWMP post; in the same year, construction of **GOVERNMENT HOUSE**, the first permanent residence of the **LIEUTENANT-GOVERNOR**, began. The settlement developed rapidly. A post office and the Battleford Land Registry Office were opened in 1877, and in 1878 the first newspa-

per in what is now the province of Saskatchewan, the *Saskatchewan Herald*, was begun by **PATRICK GAMMIE LAURIE**. That same year, the first meeting of the Territorial Council, under Lieutenant-Governor **DAVID LAIRD**, took place at Government House.

As the capital, Battleford appeared to have a bright future. But in 1881 the community's destiny was altered with the federal government's abrupt decision to alter the route of the trans-continental railway to cross the southern plains: as a consequence, the territorial capital was officially transferred to Regina in 1883. Battleford remained of strategic importance, however, for in 1885 it was the scene of significant events during the **NORTH-WEST RESISTANCE**. Approximately 500 people were sheltered within the fort's stockade during the weeks of unrest. On November 27, 1885, the largest mass hanging in Canadian history took place within the fort's walls as eight Aboriginal men were publicly hanged. Despite the destruction caused during the Resistance, and despite being by-passed by the railway, the community continued to grow. The CPR had reached Swift Current in 1883, 300 km due south of Battleford, and this opened up a new trading route which substantially cut down the cost of bringing in food and other supplies (see **BATTLEFORD TRAIL**). But Battleford was to suffer yet another blow when in 1905 the Canadian Northern Railway built its line en route to Edmonton on the opposite side of the river. North Battleford quickly surpassed the older community in size and importance, and gained city status in 1913.

Battleford would be somewhat compensated, however: in 1907–08, a new Land Titles Building and the Court House (still in use) were constructed; and over the next few years, the Post Office, the Town Hall/Opera House, and a number of impressive homes were built. These structures, dating from the 1870s until about 1912, give Battleford one of the finest collections of period architecture and heritage properties in the province. In 1907–08, rail and road links from North Battleford were also completed. The twin spans built across Finlayson Island in the North Saskatchewan River in 1908 comprise the oldest existing highway bridge in the province, and the longest of its type. Despite population growth in the early decades of the century (from 609 in 1901 to nearly 1,500 by 1916), Battleford was in financial trouble owing to over-zealous municipal spending in anticipation of an expansion which never came. The population fell during the 1920s and the 1930s, and the community languished until after **WORLD WAR II**. Battleford's debts were finally cleared in 1959; the 1950s also brought improvements to water and sewer systems, as well as better highway connections.

Battleford's population more than doubled in the years between 1961 and 1981, increasing from 1,627 to 3,565. Today, Battleford is an agricultural

service centre with a dynamic manufacturing sector. Tourist attractions in the community include the Fort Battleford National Historic Site, which showcases the role of the NWMP in the development of the Canadian West (*see* **ROYAL CANADIAN MOUNTED POLICE**). Additionally, the Fred Light Museum houses one of the most comprehensive collections of firearms in western Canada: flintlocks, matchlocks, muzzleloaders, as well as swords, bayonets, and military uniforms are on display. Battleford is also home to the Saskatchewan Baseball Hall of Fame. Unfortunately, Battleford's Government House was burned to the ground on June 7, 2003.

David McLennan

BATTLEFORD LIGHT INFANTRY. A Saskatchewan-based Canadian military unit, the Battleford Light Infantry (BLI) was formed on July 3, 1905, as the 16th Mounted Horse. At the outbreak of **WORLD WAR I**, the 16th Mounted Horse was combined with seven other **MILITIA** cavalry units to form the 5th Battalion (Saskatchewan). Throughout the war, the 5th Battalion was consistently reinforced by men from northern Saskatchewan. The 5th Battalion served in France with the 2nd Infantry Brigade, 1st Canadian Division from February 14, 1915, until the Armistice. Following the war, the Saskatchewan militia was reorganized, and from 1920 to 1924 all infantry soldiers in northern Saskatchewan were part of the North Saskatchewan Regiment. In 1924, three city-based infantry units were established: The Saskatoon Light Infantry (SLI); the Prince Albert Volunteers (PAV) and the Battleford Light Infantry (BLI). On September 1, 1939, the BLI was placed on active service for local protective duty. The BLI was disbanded in November 1945. In 1958, the BLI amalgamated with the SLI and the PAV to become the 1st and 2nd Battalions of the North Saskatchewan Regiment. In 1969, the 1st and 2nd Battalions of the North Saskatchewan Regiment amalgamated to form the North Saskatchewan Regiment "A" Company, headquartered Saskatoon, and "B" Company, headquartered in Prince Albert.

Peter Borch

FURTHER READING: Bercuson, David J. 1994. *Maple Leaf against the Axis: Canada's Second World War.* Don Mills, ON: Stoddart; Blackburn, George G. 1996. *The Guns of Victory: A Soldier's Eye View, Belgium, Holland, and Germany, 1944-45.* Toronto: McClelland & Stewart; Worthington, Larry. 1965. *Amid the Guns Below: The Story of the Canadian Corps, 1914-1919.* Toronto, Montreal: McClelland and Stewart.

BATTLEFORD-RED DEER FORKS TRAIL. First Nations, settlers, merchants, and traders used this trail well into the late 19th century. The trail's northern terminus was Fort Battleford; its southern terminus was the junction of the Red Deer and

SOUTH SASKATCHEWAN rivers, approximately 25 km west of present-day Leader, Saskatchewan. The trail stretched for more than 200 km over southern prairie and parkland, linking the North and South Saskatchewan river systems. It was used extensively until the turn of the century, when surveyed roads replaced wagon trails throughout the province.

James Winkel

BATTLEFORD-SWIFT CURRENT TRAIL. The Battleford-Swift Current Trail was a vital supply link between two very important geographical regions. First Nations used the route as a supply line between the Saskatchewan and Missouri River systems; merchants used it as one of many overland trading routes in the North-West Territories in the early 1880s. The 192-mile (309 km) trail ran between Fort Battleford and Swift Current, crossing the SOUTH SASKATCHEWAN RIVER north of Swift Current. The arrival of the CANADIAN PACIFIC RAILWAY (CPR) in Swift Current (the closest overland transportation route to Fort Battleford) in 1883 heightened trail activity: from then on settlers, traders, and government officials began to use it extensively. The North-West Mounted Police (NWMP) used the trail during the NORTH-WEST RESISTANCE of 1885. A stagecoach was also established, transporting passengers, mail and goods between the two locations. The completion of a rail line from Regina to Prince Albert, via Saskatoon, after the turn of the 20th century marked the end of the Battleford-Swift Current Trail. The closest overland route to Fort Battleford became Saskatoon, making the trail obsolete.

James Winkel

BEAR, ANGUS (1907–88). For nearly four decades, Angus Bear contributed to the growth of mining and hydro-electric power in northeastern Saskatchewan as a guide and labourer. Born at Mari Lake in 1907, Bear was hired by Hudson Bay Mining and Smelting to bring work crews and provisions to the Island Falls Power dam site. He was also an important presence in his own community of Sandy Bay where he helped record the history of the hydro-electricity industry at Island Falls and preserve the oral traditions of the CREE. Angus Bear received the Saskatchewan Order of Merit in 1987. He passed away in 1988.

BEARDY'S AND OKEMASIS FIRST NATION. Chief Beardy's Willow Plains Cree hunted and trapped throughout the Duck Lake area prior to signing TREATY 6 on August 28, 1876, at Fort Carlton. Beardy (Kahmeeyistoowaysit) was so named because of his beard, an unusual feature for Aboriginal men during that period. He chose land for both himself and Chief Okemasis (Sayswaypus) west of Duck Lake, and began building small log houses and cultivating gardens. After Beardy died in

1889, his reserve was without a chief until 1936. On June 21, 1953, a monument was built on the outskirts of Beardy's Reserve acknowledging the lives lost in the 1885 Resistance. In 1991, Beardy's and Okemasis First Nation and Saskatchewan Provincial Parks entered into a joint agreement creating the Tipi Encampment at Fort Carlton, a Hudson's Bay Company post, 30 km west of the reserve. More recently, the Beardy's and Okemasis First Nation developed a justice program that provides alternative measures in community-based justice, organizing sentencing and healing circles as well as supervising offenders, in which Elders play a major role. The Willow Cree Healing Lodge, opened in 2003 as an important step toward rehabilitation, is the second healing lodge in the province. Currently there are 2,738 registered band members, 1,073 of whom live on reserve. Their 18,368.5-hectare land base is located approximately 58 km southwest of Prince Albert.

Christian Thompson

BEAUPRÉ, ÉDOUARD (1881–1904). On January 9, 1881, Willow Bunch's most famous resident was born. Édouard Beaupré, the Willow Bunch Giant, would grow to a height of 2.5 m (8'3") and a weight of 170 kg (375 lbs.), and would be touted as the world's tallest man before his untimely death at age 23 at the St. Louis World's Fair in 1904. His family was unable to afford to have his body returned home, and for years it was put on exhibit, before ending up at McGill University in Montreal to be studied for research purposes. The family fought unsuccessfully for years to recover his body; finally, in 1989, the university conceded. Beaupré's remains were cremated, and on July 7, 1990, 86 years after Édouard Beaupré's death, his ashes were interred in front of a life-sized statue dedicated to him at the Willow Bunch Museum. Four hundred people attended the memorial mass.

David McLennan

DAVID MCLENNAN PHOTO

Édouard Beaupré's headstone, Willow Bunch.

BEAUVAL, northern village, pop 843, located SE of Ile-à-la-Crosse on Hwy 165. The community is situated in a beautiful setting overlooking the Beaver River Valley. Beauval's origins date to the beginning of the 20th century, and are associated with the founding of a Roman Catholic mission and a resi-

dential school. The area has a history of trapping, freighting, commercial fishing, and forestry. For many years area roads were simply wagon trails, but eventually a paved highway was constructed from Meadow Lake. In 1969, local residents were given the power to govern their community through an elected council which had the authority to collect taxes, provide services, and oversee bylaws under the Northern Administrative District Act. Beauval was incorporated as a northern village in 1983. The predominantly Métis community has grown rapidly over the past two decades, with an average age of just over 21 years. Valley View School provides K–12 education to close to 400 students. Economic opportunities include tourism, commercial fishing, trapping, and work in mines, local businesses and the school.

David McLennan

BEAVER LUMBER. Beaver Lumber, once Canada's leading supplier of lumber, building materials and related products and services, began in 1883 as the Banbury Bros. Lumber Company in Wolseley, Saskatchewan. Banbury Bros. Lumber Company bought its local rival, Gibson Lumber, in 1904 and two years later joined with the Regina Lumber and Supply Co., creating a business with twelve lumber yards. A thirst for expansion resulted in the Banbury brothers striking a deal with some Winnipeg lumber yards. A new name was needed that was in some way connected to wood, so when Erwin Banbury suggested "Beaver," the company identity was created and would become an institution in parts of Canada for another ninety years.

Beaver Lumber was a community-based business and focused on building relationships with its customers. The company eventually operated 130 stores across the country. Molson, the Montreal-based brewing giant, bought Beaver Lumber in 1972 and sold the retail chain to Home Hardware in 1999.

The first store opened by Erwin and his brother, Robert, was sold to the Wolseley Museum Association in 1980 and continues to be open to the public.

Joe Ralko

BEEF FARMING. Beef production is one of Saskatchewan's most important agricultural sectors, generating approximately $1 billion in annual farm cash receipts. Census data indicate that in 2001, 25.7% of all farm operators in Saskatchewan were involved with cattle. In any given year, there are 3.3 million acres of tame or seeded pasture and 13 million acres of natural land for pasture. This land base supported 1.5 million beef cows in 2004, or approximately 28% of Canada's cow herd.

The industry is comprised of purebred and commercial cow-calf operations, and stocker and finishing operations. Cow-calf operations tend to be mixed farming or extensive RANCHING operations. While there are over twenty-five breeds of cattle in use, the

Origin of Cattle Marketed in Saskatchewan, 2001 and 2000		
Crop District*	2001 Total	2000 Total
1a	48,390	48,100
1b	84,430	87,280
2a	26,330	27,480
2b	72,490	70,070
3a-s	71,810	68,930
3a-n	40,250	36,870
3b-s	67,770	51,830
3b-n	74,970	72,860
4a	91,820	82,370
4b	38,520	30,520
5a	82,450	83,130
5b	60,000	62,760
6a	109,260	111,760
6b	101,400	96,060
7a	30,850	24,750
7b	62,430	59,330
8a	38,970	38,650
8b	32,480	33,860
9a	129,480	130,820
9b	144,230	139,880
Saskatchewan	1,408,330	1,357,310
Other Provinces	82,790	70,750
Total	1,491,120	1,428,060

Source: Saskatchewan Agriculture, Food and Rural Revitalization—Cattle Marketing Report—Annual 2001, Table 2

* see accompanying map for location of Crop Districts.

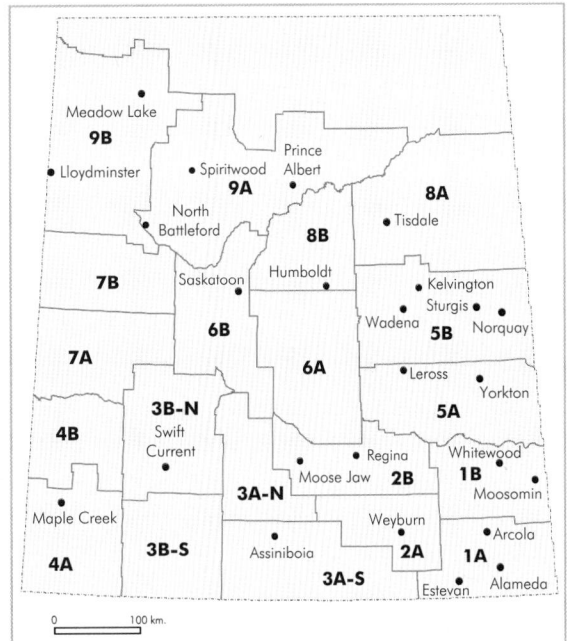

Saskatchewan Crop Districts and Livestock Inspection Points at Weekly Auctions

Figure BI-1. Origin of Cattle Market (table left and map above).

REGINA LEADER-POST

Commercial cattle show held in Stockman's Arena at Canadian Western Agribition, November 2001.

majority of the commercial cow herd is comprised of cross-bred animals, the norm being crosses between "British" and/or "Continental" breeds. Most of the cow herd is bred to calve in the spring; the calves are weaned in the fall. The majority are sold at weaning, and typically exported to Alberta, Ontario or the United States. Calves that remain in the province are back-grounded in stocker operations or finished in feedlots. A typical winter back-grounding program would involve feeding 230 kg steers to 385 kg, gaining 1 kg per day. These cattle are marketed in the spring as "short yearlings." An alternative program is to grow the animals at a slow rate of gain over the winter (0.7 kg per day), and then grass the cattle over the subsequent summer. Such animals are typically marketed in the fall as "long yearlings."

Intensive feedlot operations range in size from 500 to 30,000 head, and are filled with weaned calves and/or yearling cattle. Most are finished on barley-based diets. Common finishing weights are 500 kg for heifers and 580 kg for steers. A typical yearling finishing program would consist of feeding a 375 kg steer to 580 kg at a rate of 1.6 kg per day. Targeted carcass characteristics include high lean meat yield, a minimal marbling score of traces (Canada A), firm, white fat cover, and a bright, cherry-red colour to the meat. At present, there is one major beef processor in the province, XL Foods, Inc. at Moose Jaw. There is also growing interest in natural and organic beef production. Although currently under severe stress due to the "BSE" crisis, the beef industry is one agricultural sector that holds significant promise for expansion and job creation in rural Saskatchewan. (*See also* **BEEF INDUSTRY**)

John McKinnon

BEEF INDUSTRY. Cattle for milking, meat and locomotion accompanied the earliest European settlers, and from that basis developed one of the major economic drivers of the Saskatchewan rural economy. Herds were present in the Red River Valley by 1824, and by 1864 had spread into the North-West Territories as far as Fort Edmonton. Canada was committed to settlement by homesteaders and opposed to an open-range policy. But in 1881 the Macdonald government reluctantly allowed for some very large leases across what would become southern Alberta and into southwestern Saskatchewan, stocked with longhorn cattle from the United States. Unlike the farmers who stored winter feed for their stock, the ranchers from the south expected the cattle to graze all winter. A series of devastating winters for cattle, the incursion of the **CANADIAN PACIFIC RAILWAY** (which was given every other section of land along the right-of-way through ranching country), and the **NORTH-WEST RESISTANCE** (fought over Métis land claims) convinced the government to end the large ranch period after less than two decades.

Marketing of beef beyond the farm gate was initially for government contracts to supply the Natives, and for church missions and police outposts. Soon, however, a marketing centre was established in Winnipeg for shipment of live cattle to eastern Canada and the United States. This brought pressure for an improved quality of the animal: so first the Shorthorn, and then the Aberdeen Angus and Hereford breeds were introduced. The first system of marketing involved dealers and drovers who went from farm to farm, buying cattle on a per-head basis and then moving them by train to Winnipeg. In 1918 the farmers began building scales in local centres to make the pricing more transparent. Some of these centres, such as Prince Albert, Moose Jaw and Saskatoon soon became established as collection yards. All centres were federated in 1926. Eventually these centres built a slaughter facility in Saskatoon. Later these centres and slaughter facility became the Livestock Division of the **SASKATCHEWAN WHEAT POOL**, which was more recently purchased by the Nilsson Bros. Group of Companies.

As the Saskatchewan beef industry evolved from shipping live cattle to transporting swinging carcasses and then boxed beef (cuts), there was increasing interest in quality standards; grades were therefore created to reward excellence. To supply the bulls demanded by commercial cow/calf operators, the purebred organizations thrived and the exhibitions and bull sales grew in number and sophistication. The Western Canada Agribition held each fall in Regina is rated as one of the leading beef shows in the world. Grading shifted from assessing live animals to examining the dressed carcass, and finally to measuring the rib eye (a cross section between the eleventh and twelfth ribs). Selection pressure for highly muscled carcasses led to a dramatic reduction in carcass size, corrected by introducing programs of selection for growth rate and by the importation from continental Europe of several larger breeds for crossbreeding, such as the Charolais and Simmental.

In the 1950s the development of the feeding industry in the United States soon spread to Saskatchewan. This produced uniform, well-finished carcasses with efficiencies not available to small farm feeders. The Saskatchewan industry has been slow to develop, but is based on feeding **BARLEY**, and to a lesser extent feed **WHEAT**. The increasing population of beef cattle in Saskatchewan is expected to generate an increased beef feeding industry. Logically, at some point there will be a new beef cattle processing plant built.

So long as there was a tariff structure for beef and beef cattle between Canada and the United States, the natural flow was from western Canada to Toronto and Montreal. Since the tariffs were all removed and a free border entrenched in NAFTA, the flow has been from Saskatchewan south. The movement can be either as feeder cattle, finished cattle for processing, or processed beef, depending upon price. A secondary market for feeder and finished cattle is to the processing plants and feedlots concentrated in southern Alberta. *See* Figure BI-1 (table and map) on page 97. (*See also* **BEEF FARMING**)

C.M. Williams

FURTHER READING: Williams, C.M. 1992. "Always the Bridesmaid: The Development of the Saskatchewan Beef Production System, Parts 1 & 2," *Saskatchewan History* 42 (1989) and 44 (1992).

BEEKEEPING. Beekeeping and the production of honey have been an important industry in Saskatchewan since the early 1900s. In 2003, honey production was estimated to be worth $35 million to the provincial economy. Beekeeping is a part-time activity for some 1,000 producers and a full-time career for 150. The migration of honeybees into Saskatchewan coincided with the coming of the first settlers from eastern Canada and the United States. The first records of honeybees in the province date back to 1900; by 1922 there were about eighty-fuve beekeepers who produced 24,000 pounds of honey. Most of these beekeepers were located in the southern and eastern parts of the province. Interest in producing honey was aroused at this time by a growing demand as well as by increasing prices, due in part to the shortages and high prices of sugar which occurred during and immediately after **WORLD WAR I**.

BRYAN SCHLOSSER/REGINA LEADER-POST
Beekeeper Henry Peters, August 1995.

The Saskatchewan Beekeepers Association was organized in 1923 with John Hubbard of Grenfell as the first president and Thomas Mack of Lumsden as the first vice-president. Hubbard held the first organized beekeeper meeting in 1920 at his apiary in Grenfell, assisted by Robert Hamilton of Aylsham. Organized research and extension work in beekeeping had their beginning at the **UNIVERSITY OF SASKATCHEWAN** in 1923 under the direction of Dr. **C.F. PATTERSON**, head of the Horticulture Department. The first pamphlets on beekeeping were "Possibilities of Beekeeping in Saskatchewan," by J. Hubbard, in 1922, and "Beekeeping, A New Industry for Saskatchewan," by C.F. Patterson, in 1924. The first bulletin "Beekeeping in Saskatchewan," by R.M. Pugh, was published in 1929. A five-day course was held at the University of Saskatchewan in February 1926, while the first regular course in beekeeping offered there was given during the academic year 1926–27 and is still offered each year.

The Apiaries Act which now governs the beekeeping industry in the province came in 1924. The first office to look after beekeeping was set up in the Field Crops Branch, with A.I. Smith, a Regina beekeeper, in charge of the work. The first Provincial Apiarist, R.M. Pugh, took office in 1927 and continued in that capacity until 1948. **WORLD WAR II** caused a further expansion of beekeeping because of sugar rationing and by 1947 there were over 10,000 registered beekeepers in Saskatchewan. The Saskatchewan Honey Producers Co-operative Association was organized in 1939, with its first packing plant at Yorkton. For a time, the Apiary Branch of the Department of Agriculture and the offices of the Beekeepers Association and Honey Producers Co-operative were located at Fort Qu'Appelle. The Association was then credited as having the largest membership of any beekeeping organization in the world. The president, from 1940 to 1951, was P.C. Colquohoun, beekeeper, rancher and farmer from Maple Creek.

The Beekeepers Association and the Honey Producers Co-operative became separate entities in the 1950s, and the Co-operative amalgamated with the Manitoba Honey Producers Co-operative in the 1970s. The Saskatchewan Beekeepers Association continues as an organization dedicated to the support and success of the industry in the province, and functions to educate the membership and represent the industry at the provincial and national government levels. In 2004, provincial beekeepers operated approximately 100,000 colonies of bees, and produced a honey crop of close to 20 million pounds. The per-colony honey production in Saskatchewan is consistently higher than in any other Canadian province.

John Gruszka and Ray Ambrosi

BEES: *see* **HYMENOPTERA**

BEETLES. Beetles are the order of insects known as "Coleoptera," which means "sheath wings." The underwings are membranous and used for flight, while the outer wings are hard and known as elytra; the latter act as shields to cover and protect the wings and the body while beetles are at rest. Beetles differ from bugs by having a chewing rather than a sucking mouth. They undergo complete metamorphosis, with a soft-bodied larva. There are more species of beetles in the world than any other group in the animal kingdom. Over 2,000 species of beetles of 81 families are known in Saskatchewan, but there are many others still to be found. More species are being added as they are discovered; and others are being added as they are named by scientists doing research work on certain groups.

The province's smallest beetles are some of the feather-winged beetles, and the clambid beetles. They are barely over one-half a millimetre in length. Our largest beetle is a water scavenger beetle, *Hydrophilus triangularis*, which reaches 39 millimetres in length. Our beetle family with the greatest number of species so far is that of the carabid beetles (Carabidae), which comprises 322 species of ground beetles and tiger beetles. The tiger beetles often have brilliant colours, with paler stripes and markings; they run around on bare earth or sand, and fly so readily that they have to be caught with a net.

Every environment has its own particular kind of beetles. Predacious diving beetles, water scavenger beetles, whirligigs, and crawling water beetles live in the water. Carrion beetles, burying beetles, and some of the hister beetles can be found on dead animals. Dung beetles and some of the hister beetles live in cow dung. Certain species of dung beetles, hister beetles and mammal-nest beetles are found in the burrows and nests of mammals. Various kinds of fungus beetles live on fungi. The larvae of metallic wood-boring beetles and long-horned beetles live in the trunks of dead and dying trees. Bark beetles live under the bark, making peculiar engravings with their tunnels. Leaf beetles feed on leaves, and some of the weevils on fruit. Sap-feeding beetles are found on rotting fruit. The larvae of May beetles feed on the roots of various plants.

Numbers of leaf-eating beetles and weevils are destructive to our crops and gardens. The turnip flea beetle has become a serious pest, attacking garden plants of the mustard family. Some species of cucujid beetles and of darling beetles are destructive to the food stored in cupboards and in granaries. All beetles are not destructive, however: some are decidedly beneficial. Seventy-five species of lady beetles, which feed on aphids that do a lot of damage to plants, are known in Saskatchewan. They are very colourful—most are orange with various arrangements of spots. The seven-spotted lady beetle was introduced to this continent from Europe to help

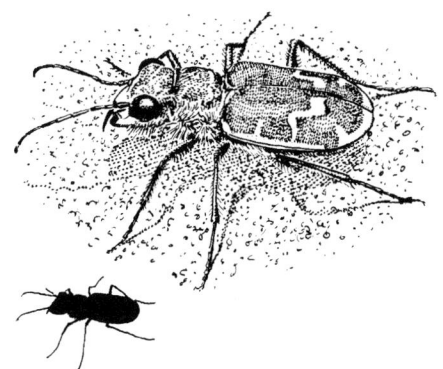

ILLUSTRATION BY PAUL GERAGHTY/COURTESY OF THE ROYAL SASKATCHEWAN MUSEUM

Tiger beetle.

control pests. Since it has reached Saskatchewan it is taking over the native species, many of which are becoming scarcer.

If we pay attention we will find a whole beetle world about us. They are not to be feared: they do not sting, although some can give a sharp pinch. The rove beetles, for instance, have long, bare abdomens which they bring forward over their backs in scorpion-like fashion, but they are only bluffing. Beetles are of great interest, and much can be learned from them and about them.

Ronald R. Hooper

BEGAMUDRÉ, VEN (1956–). A writer of novels, short stories, science fiction, fantasy, poetry, biography, and memoir, Ven Begamudré has made Regina his home base since 1978. He was born in Bangalore, India on March 13, 1956, lived two years in Mauritius (1957–59), and moved to Canada at the age of six. During his youth he lived in Ottawa, Kingston, and Bethlehem (Pennsylvania) before completing high school in Vancouver. He received a BA (Honours) in public administration from Carleton University (1977) and an MFA in Creative Writing from Warren Wilson College in Asheville, North Carolina (1999). He has also studied at the Banff Centre for the Arts as well as the SASKATCHEWAN SCHOOL OF THE ARTS. After moving to Regina, he worked in various departments of the provincial civil service on the basis of his training in public administration; but over time, and with the help of positions as writer-in-residence or part-time positions with various writing or arts councils, he has been able to devote more of his time to writing. His books include two novels (*Van de Graaff Days* and *The Phantom Queen*), two story collections (*A Planet of Eccentrics* and *Laterna Magika*), and a biography (*Isaac Brock: Larger Than Life*). Although these books and his many publications in literary journals manifest a wide variety of genres, narrative styles, settings and themes, Begamudré's works consistently demonstrate his interest in liter-

ary experimentation. He has experimented with narrative and poetic techniques, with literary forms such as mythic realism, speculative fiction, the postcard story or essay, prose-poetry, and bio-fiction. He has also set up comparative themes such as cross-cultural migration in his Indian-Canadian fiction as well as in his historical-fantasy writing, and even intergalactic migration in his science fiction. Consistently, the figure of the outsider recurs in his writing. Begamudré has received the F.G. Bressani Literary Prize for Prose, the City of Regina Writing Award, and prizes for fiction and creative non-fiction from various literary magazines. His second story collection, *Laterna Magika*, shared the City of Regina Book Award and was a best book finalist in the Canada-Caribbean region for the 1998 Commonwealth Writers' Prize. In addition to his own books, Begamudré has edited *Lodestone: Stories by Regina Writers* and co-edited *Out of Place: Stories and Poems*; he has also been a generous sponsor and contributor to the writing community. He was the founding president of the SAGE HILL WRITING EXPERIENCE, has served in a variety of capacities including the presidency of the SASKATCHEWAN WRITER' GUILD, and has given workshops and served as a mentor for the Saskatchewan Writers Guild and the Saskatchewan School of the Arts. He has been much sought after as a writer-in-residence, having been selected for the University of Calgary's Markin-Flanagan Distinguished Writers Programme, the University of Alberta's Department of English, the Canada-Scotland Exchange, the Regina Public Library, McMaster University's Department of English, and the Yukon Public Libraries. *Daniel Coleman*

FURTHER READING: Casey, Allan. 1991. "A Life in Revolution." *Books in Canada* 20 (9): 16–18; Coleman, Daniel. 1996. "Writing Dislocation: Transculturalism, Gender, Immigrant Families: A Conversation with Ven Begamudré." *Canadian Literature* 149: 36–51.

BEGG, ROBERT WILLIAM (1914–82). Born at Florenceville, NB, on December 27, 1914, Bob Begg obtained his MD from Dalhousie in 1942 and his DPhil from Oxford in 1946. His lifelong military career began with Cadets in 1929, continued with service in the First Canadian Parachute Battalion during WORLD WAR II, and ended as Commander of 21 Militia Group in the northern half of Saskatchewan in 1963. Begg held an appointment as Honorary Physician to the Queen; he taught and conducted research at Dalhousie University from 1946 to 1950, and at the University of Western Ontario from 1950 to 1957. He was the first Head of the Department of Cancer Research at the UNIVERSITY OF SASKATCHEWAN in 1957, Dean of Medicine in 1962, Principal of the Saskatoon Campus in 1967, and President of the University of

Robert Begg, March 1962.

Saskatchewan in 1975, retiring in 1980. A cheerful and practical man, he kept the College of Medicine out of the **MEDICARE** crisis in 1962 and steered the Saskatoon campus through seven years of a one-university, two-campus system. During his presidency the University acquired two research farms; as well, the University Studies Group, the **MEEWASIN VALLEY AUTHORITY**, the **POS PILOT PLANT**, Innovation Place, and the exchange program with Chernivtsi University in Ukraine came into being. Begg became an Officer of the Order of Canada in 1976, and died in Saskatoon on March 2, 1982. *Merle Bocking*

BELANEY, ARCHIBALD: *see* **GREY OWL**

BELCHER, MARGARET (1920–2003). Margaret Belcher was a university professor, author and ornithologist, as well as a lover of literature, nature, and the prairies. Born at Dilke on December

Margaret Belcher.

19, 1920, she was educated there and at Luther College, Regina. She then studied at the **UNIVERSITY OF SASKATCHEWAN** and at Toronto. Belcher taught high school in Rosetown. Subsequently she became a professor of French at Regina College, where she was for a time Dean of Women, and at its successor, the University of Saskatchewan, Regina Campus, now the **UNIVERSITY OF REGINA**. Her book, *Bird Imagery in the Lyric Poetry of Tristan L'Hermite* (1987), combined her two main interests: French literature and ornithology. Member, president, and recording secretary of the Saskatchewan Natural History Society, Belcher wrote its history, *The Isabel Priestly Legacy* (1996). For twenty-one years she was associate editor of the Society's quarterly, the *Blue Jay*, and also authored *The Birds of Regina* (1961, 1980). Margaret Belcher was honoured by the Regina Soroptomist Club in 1988, and named a Fellow of the Saskatchewan Natural History Society in 1989. In 1997 she was invested with the Saskatchewan Order of Merit, and in 2003 received the Queen's Golden Jubilee Medal. She died on June 29, 2003. *Brian Rainey*

BELL, CAROL GAY. Regina native Carol Gay Bell has dedicated most of her life to the performing arts, communications, and broadcasting. A graduate of the University of Manitoba and Ryerson Polytechnical Institute, Bell was educated in radio and television arts and began her journalism career in Saskatchewan. She was the first female staff announcer for CBC radio and television, the first female producer of musical variety on CBC television, and the first female jazz disc jockey in Canada. Bell established the **SASKATCHEWAN ROUGHRIDERS** cheerleading team and directed the squad for seventeen years. In 1980, she formed Saskatchewan Express, a nationally-recognized touring musical review, and served as the group's first general manager and artistic director. Bell received the Saskatchewan Order of Merit in 1997.

BELL, JOHN MILTON (MILT) (1922–98). Milt Bell joined the faculty of the Department of Animal Husbandry at the **UNIVERSITY OF SASKATCHEWAN** in 1948. He served as Department Head from 1954 to 1975, then as Associate Dean from 1975 to 1980, and finally as the Burford Hooke Research Chair until his retirement in 1990.

He earned a BSc in Agriculture at the University of Alberta in 1943, an MSc from McGill University in 1945, and a PhD at Cornell University in 1948, specializing in nutrition. In his productive research career, Bell's favourite research models were the laboratory mouse, Yorkshire swine, and Holstein calf. These led to three notable contributions. First, as chairman of the Subcommittee on Laboratory Animal Nutrition (National Research Council of the United States) from 1954 to 1979, he was responsi-

ble for developing the first mouse nutrition guide that formed the basis for feeding the 20 million mice used annually in biomedical research in North America. Second, he led the introduction of the lean Yorkshire nutrition standards into the (US) National Research Council Guide. And third, he developed the first commercially practical dairy-calf milk replacer.

Milt Bell was an active member of a small team of plant breeders, nutritionists and chemists that developed **CANOLA** as a major crop for Canadian farmers. His work with rapeseed, begun in the early 1950s, involved basic nutritional research but also branched into toxicology and the mechanism of action of goitroigens and glucosinolates in swine and mice. He worked co-operatively with plant breeders and other animal nutritionists in defining the detrimental characteristics in rapeseed, which eventually gave rise to the development of canola and the effective utilization of canola meal in livestock rations. Other research areas of interest in which he was active included mineral utilization and deficiencies, water quality, the nature of plant fibre in animal nutrition, and dairy cow housing.

Bell served as president of the Canadian Society of Animal Science in 1952, also serving on the editorial board of the *Journal of Nutrition*, the *Canadian Journal of Animal Science*, and the *Journal of the European Association of Animal Production*. In recognition of his many contributions, he received more than twenty major awards including Fellow of the Agriculture Institute of Canada (FAIC), Fellow of the Royal Society of Canada (FRSC), Doctor of Science (McGill University), and Officer in the Order of Canada. He was invested into the Saskatchewan Agricultural Hall of Fame. His dedication to the field of animal nutrition was demonstrated by his response to receiving the James McAnsh Award from the Canola Council of Canada; this prestigious award carries with it both a cash component and a specially minted medallion. Bell, the first recipient of this award, chose not to accept the cash award, and directed that the money be used to establish the J.M. Bell Post Graduate Scholarship in Animal Nutrition at the University of Saskatchewan. This scholarship program continues to fund the education of young scientists and future industry leaders. *Philip Thacker*

BELLEGARDE, PERRY (1962–). Born at the Fort Qu'Appelle Indian Hospital on August 29, 1962, Perry Bellegarde is a member of the Little Black Bear First Nation. He attended elementary school in Goodeve, and following graduation from the Balcarres high school (1980) attended the Saskatchewan Indian Federated College (now **FIRST NATIONS UNIVERSITY OF CANADA**). In 1984 he became the first First Nations person to earn a Bachelor of Administration degree from the **UNIVERSITY OF REGINA**, after which he became director of personnel for the **SASKATCHEWAN INDIAN INSTITUTE OF TECHNOLOGIES** (1984–86). From 1986 to 1988, Bellegarde was vice-president/assistant tribal council representative for the Touchwood–File Hills–Qu'Appelle (TFHQ) Tribal Council; and from 1988 to 1998 he was president/tribal council representative. As president, Bellegarde was instrumental in negotiating a transfer agreement for the federally operated Fort Qu'Appelle Indian Hospital to First Nation-owned-and-operated status; he initiated and implemented the First Nation urban service delivery centre which continues to operate in Regina today; and with the guidance and assistance of Elders he aided in regaining the original grounds of **TREATY 4** to First Nations control as reserve land.

In May 1998, Bellegarde became the ninth Grand Chief of the **FEDERATION OF SASKATCHEWAN INDIAN NATIONS** (FSIN), a position that carries with it the seat of vice-chief of the Assembly of First Nations. Perry Bellegarde is the third member of his family to be elected to this position. Grand Chief Bellegarde supported First Nations veterans in their struggle for compensation for post-war injustices, aiding them in receiving a compensation package in 2003. He signed a 25-year gaming agreement with the government; advanced outstanding issues regarding the 1930 Natural Resource Transfer Agreement; worked in areas of inherent and treaty rights; was a strong advocate for the advancement of women; made presentations on the Declaration on the Rights of Indigenous Peoples to the United Nations; and was involved in the International Study of Treaties. Throughout his years in the political system, Bellegarde persistently pursued his vision of equal opportunity and participation in all sectors for the First Nations people of Saskatchewan. It is his firmly held belief that the treaties were meant to ensure that all people could live in "mutual respect and peaceful co-existence."

Charlene Crevier

BELTED KINGFISHER. Kingfishers are medium-sized (10–45 cm) birds with stocky, brightly-coloured bodies and large heads with strong bills. Despite their names, they feed on a variety of prey other than fish. The family of approximately ninety-five species (family Alcedinidae, order Coraciiformes) are found on all continents other than Antarctica. They are most numerous in the tropics.

The belted kingfisher occurs throughout North America. It is a summer resident of Saskatchewan, wherever there are sufficient large freshwater bodies to support populations of fish. They are seen sitting on tree branches and telephone wires above the water before they dive down for fish, then flying off to feed their young in their nest burrows in river or lake banks. Their distinctive large head with the loose crest of feathers and their slate-blue back and chesnut breast make them easily recognizable.

Diane Secoy

FURTHER READING: Alsop, Fred J., III. 2002. *Birds of Canada*. New York: Dorling Kindersley Handbooks; Godfrey, W. Earl. 1986 (revised edition). *Birds of Canada*. Ottawa: National Museum of Natural Sciences.

BENEDICTINES OF ST. PETER'S ABBEY (OSB). This Roman Catholic Benedictine monastic community had its origins in the Benedictine community in Wetaug, Illinois. Prior Alfred Mayer led the community to Muenster, SK in May 1903, and named it St. Peter's Priory, after Abbot Peter Engel of St. John's Abbey, Minnesota. The priory became the heart of St. Peter's Colony in Saskatchewan. In 1911 the priory became an abbey, and Bruno Doerfler, OSB, was appointed its first abbot. Subsequent abbots were Michael Ott (1919–26), Severin Gertken (1926–60), Jerome Weber (1960–90), and Peter Novecosky (1990–).

St. Peter's Abbey had over sixty monks at its zenith in the mid-1960s. The Benedictines' work involved founding parishes and parish schools, establishing a press, publishing Catholic newspapers (*St. Peter's Bote* [1904] and *Prairie Messenger* [1922]), engaging in mixed farming, and establishing St. Peter's College.

Monastic prayer remains an essential part of Benedictine daily life. The monks stop their work five times a day and gather to chant the Divine Office, and once a day they celebrate the Eucharist. Catholic lay people participate in the work and spirituality of the Benedictine community as oblates, and the abbey monastery continues to play a significant role in the community as a place of hospitality and retreat.

Peter Novecosky

FURTHER READING: Fitzgerald, C. 2003. *Begin a Good Work: A History of St. Peter's Abbey, 1903–2003.* Muenster, SK: St. Peter's Press.

BENGOUGH, town, pop 401, located on Highway 34, just north of the **BIG MUDDY VALLEY** and badlands. These sub-marginal tracts are primarily suited for ranching, and lands formerly utilized for crop production have been returned to grazing pasture. Land nearer the town itself supports mixed farming as well as ranching operations. Wheat, durum, barley, and oats are the main crops; lentils and peas are increasingly grown. The Bengough district was originally settled between 1905 and 1913. The drought years of the 1930s hit Bengough hard, but after **WORLD WAR II** the community witnessed an unprecedented period of prosperity. By the mid-1960s, 700 people called the town home. Today Bengough, the "Gateway to the Big Muddy," has an RCMP detachment, a health centre and special care home, a volunteer fire department, and a K–12 school. Each year the town hosts amateur and professional rodeos, a horse show, and a summer fair. Recently, Bengough and district schoolchildren accompanied

palaeontologists from the **ROYAL SASKATCHEWAN MUSEUM** into the Big Muddy Valley to uncover the remains of a 55-million-year-old crocodile. The rare fossil is one of only a few known to exist in the world.

David McLennan

BENJAMIN, LESLIE GORDON (1925–2003). Les Benjamin was born on April 29, 1925, in Medicine Hat, Alberta. He was raised in southwestern Saskatchewan and southeastern Alberta. Benjamin enlisted in the air force during **WORLD WAR II**, but spent much of his time in the armed forces fixing the Alaskan Highway. He worked for the CPR as a telegrapher, station agent and manager. As a CCF activist, Benjamin made two unsuccessful runs for provincial office in the riding of Maple Creek. By 1961 he had become the provincial secretary for the **NEW DEMOCRATIC PARTY**, a position he held until 1968.

That year Benjamin ran for federal office in the riding of Regina–Lake Centre. He won, beginning a twenty-five-year political career. While in the House of Commons, Benjamin worked on the transportation committee. "Boxcar Benjamin" was an outspoken critic on the subject of grain transportation. He resigned from his seat in 1993.

Benjamin was married twice: in 1950 to Marjorie Kathleen McKinnon (Kay), and then to Constance Freisen in 1976. He had three children and two stepchildren. Les Benjamin lost his battle with cancer on June 16, 2003. The city of Regina has honoured Les Benjamin by naming a crescent in his honour.

Dana Turgeon

FURTHER READING: Benjamin, Les and James Warren. 1997. *Rolling in the Grass Roots*. Ottawa: Doculink International.

BENNETT BUGGY. Named for Prime Minister R.B. Bennett, a Bennett Buggy was a popular mode of transportation for impoverished prairie farmers. Unable to afford gasoline, farmers removed the extraneous engine from an automobile chassis and used horses to pull it. The Bennett Buggy became a symbol of disenchantment associated with the **DEPRESSION** and the Prime Minister of the time.

Holden Stoffel

BENTHAM, DOUGLAS (1947–). Douglas Wayne Bentham was born in Rosetown, Saskatchewan and has resided in Saskatoon since 1959. He received his BFA in painting from the **UNIVERSITY OF SASKATCHEWAN** in 1969 and his MFA (sculpture) in 1989. With over forty solo exhibitions and over 100 group exhibitions in public and commercial galleries, his work has gained national and international recognition. Selected solo exhibitions (with publications) include: **MACKENZIE ART GALLERY**, 1975; Art Gallery of York University, 1976 (toured); **MENDEL**

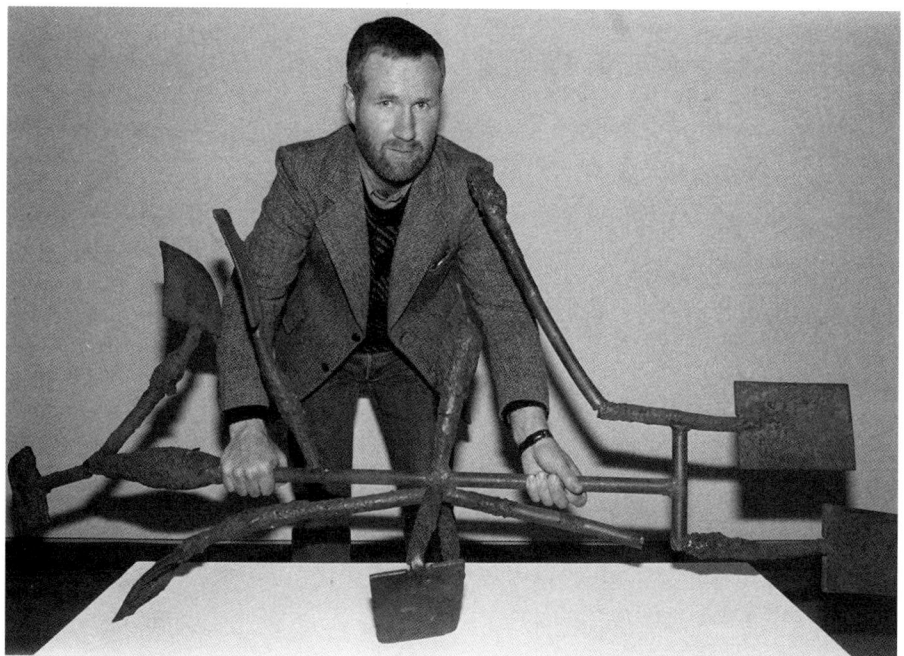

ROBERT WATSON/REGINA LEADER-POST

Doug Bentham and "Mudra I", April 1985.

ART GALLERY, 1984 (toured); Dunlop Art Gallery, 1985; Edmonton Art Gallery, 1993; and Mendel Art Gallery, 2004. He has executed numerous public sculpture commissions in Canada, including those at the National Science Library, Ottawa, 1973; the Government of Canada Building, Calgary, 1981; and Innovation Place, Saskatoon, 1989. His sculpture is in many major public collections in Canada, and in private collections throughout North America and Europe.

Bentham works "in and around the constructivist process, i.e., an additive/subtractive approach to collaging." He often works in concurrent series, with one series based on and affecting the other. His earlier work was usually made from plate, sheet or rod steel that was cut and welded into abstract forms. His concerns in his early work with linear framing, surface contrasts, human scale and gesture, and the exploration of "drawing in space" persist to the present. By the mid-1980s, he felt the need to explore the expressive qualities of other materials and began to incorporate such things as found metal objects, wood, Plexiglas, etc., into his work. Bentham often finishes his sculpture with a variety of surface treatments such as high-gloss enamel, patinating with ferric and copper nitrate on the brass and bronze, hand-rubbing or coating with various substances, in order to produce painterly surface effects and bring out the inherent qualities of light and colour of his material. While he has been influenced by such prominent modernist sculptors as David Smith and Sir Anthony Caro, as well as the critical writing of Clement Greenberg, he has also been significantly informed by his interest in the material culture of the west: such items as

Mennonite and Ukrainian furniture, handmade toys, Navajo blankets, and items of popular culture have influenced his approach to sculpture. By incorporating found objects with an inherent history (wheels, tools, etc.) into his work, he synthesizes the formal aspirations of high modernism while encouraging a narrative interpretation concerned with time and change.

Bentham has had a prolific and distinguished career. He has participated in numerous international workshops including the Emma Lake Artists' Workshops (in 1977 he was the co-leader with British sculptor Sir Anthony Caro), the Triangle Workshop (Pine Plains, NY), and the Hardingham (England) Sculpture Workshop. He is a founding member of Canadian Artists Representation (later CARFAC). He was elected a member of the Royal Canadian Academy in 1976, and was the recipient of the Lynch-Staunton Award from the Canada Council in 1981.

Dan Ring

BENTLEY BROTHERS: DOUGLAS (1916–72), MAXWELL (1920–84). Despite their small stature, Douglas and Maxwell Bentley of Delisle distinguished themselves as accomplished players in the National Hockey League. Born on September 3, 1916, Douglas played most of his minor hockey with the Moose Jaw Millers. Maxwell was born on March 1, 1920, and played junior hockey in Saskatoon and Drumheller. Beginning in the 1939–40 season, Douglas made the roster of the Chicago Black Hawks while Maxwell joined the club a year later. Their youngest brother, Reggie, played briefly for the Black Hawks during the 1942–43 season, marking the first time in NHL history that three brothers

constituted an entire forward line. In 1946, the Bentleys anchored the high-scoring "Pony Line" with Bill Mosienko. Although he missed one year while tending the family farm during **WORLD WAR II**, Douglas Bentley remained with the Black Hawks through the 1952–53 season. He spent his final year in the NHL with the New York Rangers and was briefly reunited with his brother. He won the Art Ross Trophy as the league's highest scorer in 1943 and was named to the First All-Star Team in 1943, 1944, and 1947. He finished his career with 543 points.

Shortly after the start of the 1947–48 season, Maxwell Bentley was traded to the Toronto Maple Leafs, with whom he won the Stanley Cup in 1948, 1949, and 1951. He was awarded the Lady Byng Trophy for sportsmanship in 1943, the Hart Trophy as league MVP in 1946, and the Art Ross Trophy in 1946 and 1947. He was selected to the First All-Star Team in 1946. He, too, finished his career with the New York Rangers after tallying 544 NHL points. Douglas and Maxwell Bentley were inducted into the Hockey Hall of Fame in 1964 and 1966 respectively. The brothers entered the **SASKATCHEWAN SPORTS HALL OF FAME** one year later. Douglas passed away on November 24, 1972; Maxwell died on January 19, 1984.

Daria Coneghan and Holden Stoffel

SASKATOON PUBLIC LIBRARY 2717-1

After completing their National Hockey League careers in 1954, Doug (left) and Max Bentley became teammates with the Saskatoon Quakers of the senior Western Hockey League.

BERGTHALER MENNONITE CHURCH. The name *Bergthaler* is derived from the Bergthal Colony in the Ukraine, the origin of many of the original Saskatchewan Bergthaler. They came to southern Manitoba in the 1870s and were among the first Mennonites who settled at Rosthern in 1891–92. Kornelius Epp was ordained as the first elder in 1902 and served until 1908, when he

Bergthaler Mennonite shopkeeper, Gruenthal, Saskatchewan, 1986.

August 28, 2001: Jacqueline Berting speaking at the unveiling of "The Story Wall" at the Saskatchewan Legislative Building; the work was commissioned by the Saskatchewan Legislature as a gift for the Nunavut Legislative Assembly.

formed his own church. He eventually moved to Mexico with Herbert-area Sommerfelder Mennonites. Those remaining were led by Elder Aron Zacharias until 1926, when he migrated to Paraguay with a small group of followers. Zacharias, like Epp, left Canada because the Canadian government broke its promise of allowing Mennonites to operate their schools in the language of their choice. The remaining nucleus united under Elder Cornelius Hamm. The 1930s economic depression exhausted the "Waisenamt" (widows and orphans fund), and many Mennonites resettled in northern Saskatchewan. A Sunday School program started in the 1940s, and the language of the worship services became Low instead of High German.

Bergthaler migrations from Saskatchewan include Paraguay (1948), Honduras (1951), and Bolivia (1962). Education has been a key factor in these migrations. In Saskatchewan, two private schools have been established: one at Reinland in 1979, now closed, and Valley Christian Academy, west of Osler, which opened in 1986 and is thriving. There have been three major splits in the Bergthaler church—in 1979, 1983 and 1992. The issues of concern have been language and accommodations to the world. There are presently 1,800 people attending the Bergthaler churches in Saskatchewan, located at Warman, Martensville, Gruenthal, Blumenheim, and Reinfeld. Presently, the worship services are primarily conducted in English, and music is accompanied by instruments. *Leonard Doell*

BERTING, JACQUELINE (1967–). Berting was born in St. Gregor, Saskatchewan on August 9, 1967. She attended Red Deer College in 1987, and Sheridan College in Oakville, Ontario from 1987 to 1990, where she majored in glass art. She also studied iron art and blacksmithing at the Penland School of Arts in North Carolina in 1990. She has

since formed Berting Glass in Cupar, Saskatchewan, where she works with her husband, James Clark. Jacqueline Berting's most famous work to date is *The Glass Wheatfield*, encompassing 14,000 waist-high glass wheat stalks standing in a 36-square-metre "field." Each piece was painstakingly hand-cut and lamp-worked. It is her personal salute to the Canadian farmer and is housed at the Regina Plains Museum. In 1996, she and her husband created *The House of Perception*, a clear-glass and iron house consisting of 400 sand-cast glass panels. Berting Glass supplies gifts to over 100 gift shops and galleries. Berting's work has been commissioned by the UNIVERSITY OF REGINA, the Legislative Assembly in Nunavut, and the city of Weyburn. *Daralyn Fauser*

BERZENSKY, STEVEN M. (MICK BURRS) (1940–). Steven Michael Berzensky was born on April 10, 1940 in California. He graduated with a BA in English, and came to Canada in 1965. He moved to Regina in 1973, and in 1985 took a position as the first writer in residence in Yorkton, where he lives today. He has published five books of poetry and twenty-four chap-books of his work, which has also appeared in nearly 40 anthologies and many literary periodicals. He founded the "Warm Poets for Cold Nights" gatherings in 1975, co-founded the Parkland Writers' Alliance in Yorkton in 1985, and created of the literary page for *Yorkton This Week*. He has received awards from the SASKATCHEWAN WRITERS GUILD, and won the SASKATCHEWAN BOOK AWARD for Poetry in 1998 for his *Variations on the Birth of Jacob*. His most recent book is *The Names Leave the Stones: Poems New and Selected*, which was published in 2001. *Daralyn Fauser*

BETH JACOB JEWISH COMMUNITY. There were nine Jewish residents living in Regina as early as 1891. This number declined to one in 1901,

before rising to 130 in 1911. There are three key elements that signify a sense of permanence for a Jewish community: a Talmud Torah, or school of Jewish religious study; a synagogue; and a Jewish cemetery. The first synagogue was built in Regina in 1913; the Regina Jewish cemetery, although officially deeded to the Jewish community by the city of Regina in 1915, had been operating since 1905. In fact, the *Chevra Kaddisha* (Jewish Burial Society) was officially formed in 1904. To emphasise the founding of the *Chevra Kaddisha* is not to deny the importance of either the building of the first Regina synagogue or the organizing of the Talmud Torah, both of which were certainly signal developments in the emergence of a functioning community: what is significant is that the priorities were Jewish priorities—building a community meant standing together and supporting each other in death as in life, from generation to generation. In that sense we may take 1904 as an appropriate date for the founding of a sense of community amongst Regina Jewry.

The first *Minyan* or prayer meeting took place in 1905 in a private home and shortly after that a group gathered at the home of Jacob Shachter to organize a Jewish community. It was then passed by all members that since the gathering took place at Jacob's home, the congregation be called Beth Jacob Congregation. By 1910 the House of Jacob congregation had hired a ritual slaughterer and established regular weekly worship services. By 1912 the community numbered twenty families, and Samuel Pearlman had become its first president. In 1912 the community organized its first building committee; an active canvas of the Jewish community was undertaken, and in the spring of 1913 the foundation stone was laid in the presence of the LIEUTENANT-GOVERNOR and the Mayor. The raising of funds proceeded apace with the building operations, and the new "Beth Jacob" synagogue was completed

Beth Jacob Synagogue, Regina.

and ready for worship on Rosh Hashanah, free of all debt or encumbrance. In 1913 the founders of the House of Jacob synagogue opened a Talmud Torah in rented quarters, with forty children and two teachers. Within a year the congregation had rented a double lot on St. John Street, moved a two-storey frame building onto the site, and renovated it for use as a Hebrew school. The community now had a Chevra Kaddisha, a name, a synagogue, a Talmud Torah, and legal title to its own cemetery; it had also grown substantially in size, numbering by now almost 400 persons.

By 1931 the population of the Jewish community peaked at 1,010, and although the **GREAT DEPRESSION** took its toll, they still numbered 944 in 1941 and continued to be an active part of the larger Regina community. In 1937 the Credit Union Act received royal assent, and on August 2, 1937, the Regina Hebrew Savings and Credit Union Limited received charter number one and became the first credit union incorporated under the law. The Depression of the 1930s precluded plans to build a larger synagogue to accommodate the growing needs of the community, and the war years saw the community preoccupied along with the rest of Regina in the war effort. Finally, in April 1948, the decision was made to build a new synagogue, and on September 3, 1950, the building was officially opened.

From a religious perspective, the synagogue has undergone changes over the years that are reflective of the changing make-up of the community: it has shifted from orthodox to conservative in its outlook, and embraced equality between men and women in the ritual aspects of religious Jewish life. The Beth Jacob Jewish community continues to be a strong and active partner in the larger Regina community.

Jeremy Parnes

BETHANY COLLEGE. Bethany College, initially known as Bethany Bible Institute, was started in 1927 in Hepburn—one of over twenty Bible schools started by the Conference of Mennonite Brethren Churches in Canada. The first of eight Mennonite Brethren Bible school initiatives located in southern Saskatchewan was Herbert Bible School, which was started in 1913. This precedent, along with the proximity of the German-English Academy in Rosthern, stimulated interest among the Mennonite Brethren in central Saskatchewan to have their own "Bible-centred school," which could help preserve the German language, teach the Bible to their young people, and prepare leaders for their churches. After experimenting with itinerant Bible classes for several years, the public school building in Hepburn was purchased in 1927 and a permanent school was established.

Despite numerous commonalities with other Mennonite Brethren schools, Bethany was unique in at least three respects. First, it experienced a comparatively rapid transition from German to English, the language of instruction quickly becoming a mixture of German and English during the 1930s as pressure for a bilingual curriculum mounted from students. Second, the school promoted evangelism and missions: in 1935, the Bethany Prayer League Children's Mission was formed as an outreach extension of the school and sent hundreds of Bible school students into rural communities across northern Saskatchewan to conduct summer Vacation Bible Schools for children. Third, it was the first Mennonite Brethren school to experiment with offering a "college" program: a two-year program of study was expanded to three years in 1932, to four years in 1934, and then to five years in 1941. Although the fifth year was discontinued in 1945, this signaled an interest in higher education within the denomination that came to fruition more fully in 1944 with the start of the Mennonite Brethren Bible College in Winnipeg.

Advances in communication and transportation eventually prompted the denomination to consolidate its educational institutions. In 1957, Herbert Bible School amalgamated with Bethany. After the closure of Alberta Mennonite Brethren Bible

Institute, the Conference of Mennonite Brethren Churches in Alberta joined together with the Mennonite Brethren in Saskatchewan in 1968 as co-sponsors of Bethany. The school has never been a large enterprise: its enrollments reached 100 near the end of the 1930s, plummeted during the early 1940s, and gradually increased during the late 1950s, peaking at nearly 200 in the early 1980s. With the financial support of an ever-expanding constituency, the school successfully completed numerous building projects to expand campus facilities. In 1995, the Saskatchewan Conference of Evangelical Mennonite Mission Churches joined the Mennonite Brethren as a third sponsor of Bethany College. Full accreditation with the Accrediting Association of Bible Colleges was obtained in 2000.

Bruce L. Guenther

FURTHER READING: Guenther, B.L. 2002. "'Wrenching Our Youth Away from Frivolous Pursuits': Mennonite Brethren Involvement in Bible Schools in Western Canada, 1913–1960," *Crux* 38 (4): 32–41.

BEUG, LORNE (1948–). A long-time Regina resident, Lorne Beug has practiced as a visual artist for over thirty years. He studied anthropology and psychology at the **UNIVERSITY OF REGINA**, obtaining his BA with Great Distinction in 1969. Following graduation, he worked as a clinical psychologist at the Weyburn Mental Hospital. In 1972, he enrolled in the University of Regina's ceramics program, where he studied with **MARILYN LEVINE** and **JOE FAFARD**. While informed by the Folk/Funk tradition of those artists, Beug was also influenced by his academic background. Typical is "Patterned Ground," which was commissioned by the city of Regina for installation at the Fieldhouse: this ceramic mural depicts an aerial view of a "patchwork quilt" prairie landscape underlaid by layers of geological strata. In the late 1980s, Beug shifted to photo-collage, using images of architectural detail on existing buildings to construct his own edifices. While it was tempting for critics to read the collages as the ruins of a great civilization that had succumbed to the ravages of time, Beug preferred to regard them as articulating an alternative civic history. Most recently, he has been using digital technology to create artist's books and panoramic scrolls on a similar architectural theme.

Gregory Beatty

BIBLE SCHOOLS AND COLLEGES. More Bible schools and colleges have been started in Saskatchewan than in any other province in the country. Although the first Bible school in Canada was launched in 1885, it was not until 1909 that the Holiness Movement Church started the first school in western Canada: Western Holiness Bible School, initially located in Crystal City, Saskatchewan. More than fifty additional schools have had their origins

Table BSC-1. Bible Schools/Colleges in Saskatchewan (Historical)				
Name of School	**Location**	**Origin**	**Closure**	**Denominational Affiliation**
Western Holiness Bible School	McCord	1909	1953 - moved	Holiness Movement Church
Herbert Bible School	Herbert	1913	1957	Mennonite Brethren
Regina School of Theology	Regina	1917	1919	Church of the Nazarene
Glad Tidings Bible Training School	Saskatoon	1929	1930?	Full Gospel Missions
Saskatoon Pentecostal Bible School	Saskatoon	1924	1925	Pentecostal Assemblies of Canada
Bethany College	Hepburn	1927	Still operating	Mennonite Brethren
Millar College of the Bible	Pambrun	1928	Still operating	Transdenominational
Tabor Bible School	Dalmeny	1928	1954	Mennonite Brethren
Bible School	Aberdeen	1930	1937?	Mennonite Church Canada
German Baptist Winter Bible Schools	Itinerant	1930	1945	North American Baptist
Saskatoon Bible College	Saskatoon	1931	1953?	Transdenominational
Western Christian College	Regina	1932	Still operating	Church of Christ
Rosthern Bible School	Rosthern	1932	1957	Mennonite Church Canada
Glenbush Bible School	Glenbush	1932	194?	Mennonite Brethren
Bible School	Yorkton	1932	1934?	Full Gospel Missions
Central Pentecostal College	Saskatoon	1935	Still operating	Pentecostal Assemblies of Canada
Briercrest College	Caronport	1935	Still operating	Transdenominational
Nipawin Bible Institute	Nipawin	1935	Still operating	Transdenominational
Fundamental Bible College	Grenfell	1935	1939 - moved	Apostolic Church of Pentecost
International Bible College	Moose Jaw	1936	Still operating	Church of God (Cleveland, Tennessee)
Marpeck School of Discipleship	Swift Current	1936	1996	Mennonite Church Canada
Speedwell Bible School	Speedwell	1937	1942?	Mennonite Brethren
Pioneer Mission Bible School	Meadow Lake	193?	194?	Likely transdenominational
Bible School	Aberdeen	193?	193?	Mennonite Brethren
Midale Bible Institute	Itinerant	193?	1938?	Norwegian Lutheran Church
Woodrow Bible School	Woodrow	1938	1940	Independent Holiness Congregation
Bible School	Eigenheim	1938	1945	Mennonite Church Canada
Regina Bible Institute	Regina	1938	1947	Evangelical Church in Canada
Drake Bible School	Drake	1939	194?	Mennonite Church Canada
Bible School	Silberfeld	1939	1945	Mennonite Church Canada
Queen City Bible School	Regina	1939	1940	Full Gospel Missions
Lutheran Collegiate Bible Institute	Outlook	1939	1986	Evangelical Lutheran in Canada
Prince Albert Bible School	Prince Albert	1939	1942	Evangelical Free Church
Aldersgate College	Moose Jaw	1940	1995	Free Methodist Church
Canadian Bible College	Regina	1941	2003 - moved	Christian & Missionary Alliance
Covenant Bible College	Prince Albert	1941	1995 - moved	Evangelical Covenant Church
Bible School	Hochfeld	1942	1944	Mennonite Brethren
Apostolic Missionary Training Institute	Saskatoon	1943	1953	Apostolic Church of Pentecost
Meadow Lake Bible Institute	Meadow Lake	1943	195?	A local interdenominational effort
Russian Bible School	Arlee	1943	1945?	Mennonite Brethren
Ukrainian Bible Institute	Saskatoon	1944	1958	Ukrainian Baptist Conference
Full Gospel Bible Institute	Eston	1944	Still operating	Apostolic Church of Pentecost
Bible School	Duval	194?	194?	Independent Christian Tabernacles
Berean Bible School	Tribune	194?	194?	Grace Gospel Mission
Sharon Bible School	North Battleford	1947	1952	New Order of the Latter Rain
PCTC - Calling Lakes Centre	Fort Qu'Appelle	195?	Still operating	United Church of Canada
La Ronge Bible School	La Ronge	1956	1970	Northern Canada Evangelical Mission
Full Gospel Indian Bible School	Fort Qu'Appelle	1963	Still operating	Apostolic Church of Pentecost
Canwood Indian Bible School	Canwood	1963	19??	Pentecostal Assemblies of Canada
Into His Harvest Training School	Regina	1977	Still operating	Harvest City Church
Faith Alive Bible College	Saskatoon	1981	Still operating	Faith Alive Ministries
Canadian Baptist Theological College	Saskatoon	198?	198?	Southern Baptist
Dr. Jessie Saulteaux Resource Centre	Fort Qu'Appelle	1984	198? - moved	United Church of Canada
Revelation College	Prince Albert	1994	Still operating	Prince Albert Family Church
Faith College Training Centre	Saskatoon	1995	Still operating	Saskatoon Christian Centre
Fountain of Life School of Ministry	Prince Albert	1997	Still operating	Apostolic Church of Pentecost
Weyburn Faith Family Bible School	Weyburn	2002	Still operating	Weyburn Faith Family Church

Note: This chart identifies schools by their last known name and location in Saskatchewan; many schools had multiple names and locations, with several relocating from or to other provinces. While all the major initiatives have been included, it is possible that there are still some other short-lived Bible schools that have inadvertently been omitted.

in Saskatchewan (*see* Table BSC-1), representing almost 20% of all the Bible schools and colleges in Canada. Half of the Bible schools in the province were started during the economically depressed decade of the 1930s, with another 25% during the 1940s. The decade following 1950 marked a significant watershed for the Bible school movement: advances in transportation and communication resulted in the closure and consolidation of 80% of the Bible schools before the end of the 20th century. With the exception of a handful of schools started by several Pentecostal and charismatic groups, relatively few new Bible schools were started in the second half of the 20th century.

The majority of Bible schools and colleges in the province were initiated by a diverse range of more than twenty incoming immigrant groups and new evangelical Protestant denominations, most of which had relatively few members during the first half of the 20th century. Two different Mennonite groups account for fourteen schools alone: the Mennonite Brethren with eight, and Mennonite Church Canada with six. In total, the Mennonites were responsible for starting more than forty Bible schools across Canada. The driving force behind their educational endeavours was a passionate concern for finding new ways to provide both religious instruction and preserve aspects of the Mennonite heritage and identity. Another nineteen schools were started by a cluster of ten different Pentecostal denominations or independent congregations. At least six schools can be categorized as transdenominational, that is, without direct affiliation to any denomination. Influenced by a larger fundamentalist network within North America, these schools emphasized a common understanding of doctrine and mission without necessarily discouraging participation in denominations. Briercrest College, started in 1935, and currently located in Caronport, has become the most prominent transdenominational school in the province; it is also currently the largest Bible college in the country, with a college enrollment of approximately 800 students.

Bible schools typically offered a Bible-centred, intensely practical, lay-oriented program of theological training. As educational institutions, they operated in a zone between the upper years of secondary education and the undergraduate years of post-secondary education. About 70% of Bible schools in Saskatchewan were located in rural communities. During the early years, most schools organized the term of study to accommodate the winter lull in farm work (late October to mid-April). Bible schools intentionally developed an environment for encouraging spiritual formation, for teaching Bible knowledge, and for learning the disciplines and practical skills for a lifetime of Christian discipleship and ministry. For many decades facilities were austere, and students were required to help out in order to keep

Table BSC-2. Post-Secondary Religious Training Institutions in Saskatchewan	
Institution	Location
Bethany Bible Institute	Hepburn
Briercrest Bible College	Caronport
Campion College	University of Regina, Regina
Central Pentecostal College	Saskatoon
College of Emmanuel and St. Chad	Saskatoon
Full Gospel Bible Institute	Eston
International Bible College	Moose Jaw
Luther College	University of Regina, Regina
Lutheran Theological Seminary	Saskatoon
Miller College of the Bible	Pambrun
Nipawin Bible Institute	Nipawin
St. Andrew's College	Saskatoon
St. Peter's College	Muenster
St. Thomas More College	Saskatoon
Western Christian College	Regina

Note: These religious institutions are either federated or affiliated with the University of Regina or the University of Saskatchewan, or otherwise are generally recognized under the Saskatchewan Student Loans Program.

schools operating. Bible schools offered students the opportunity to meet members of the opposite sex—hence the facetious, but occasionally justifiable, title "bridal institute" that has been applied to many schools.

Bible schools can be differentiated from Bible colleges, which confer accredited degrees, offer courses recognized by other colleges and universities, and whose curricula include significantly more liberal arts or general education courses alongside course offerings in theological studies (*see* Table BSC-2). During the 1960s, Bible school leaders gradually became more interested in obtaining a new level of respectability and recognition for their schools. Four of the Bible schools started in Saskatchewan have managed to become accredited colleges with full membership status with the Accrediting Association of Bible Colleges, an organization designed to clarify and establish standards within Bible schools and colleges. In addition, two schools, **CANADIAN BIBLE COLLEGE** (now located in Calgary) and Briercrest College, started graduate degree programs in 1970 and 1983 respectively. Not all schools pursued accreditation: some were unable to afford the additional costs; others deliberately avoided it, fearing that the addition of liberal arts courses in the curriculum would dilute the traditional emphasis on the study of the Bible.

The influence of Bible schools and colleges has been extensive. By 1950, the cumulative enrollment in all Bible schools in Saskatchewan was over 1,000; this represents a substantial contribution to the overall educational landscape of the province, partic-

ularly when one considers the fact that 55% of Bible school students have been women (as a point of comparison, university enrollment in the province in 1950 was less than 2,600, of whom only 20% were women). Bible schools prepared thousands of Protestant men and women as church workers, pastors and missionaries who have been scattered to every corner of the country and beyond. A Bible school training offered many young people an opportunity for improving their social status. Missionary work required international travel, and both missionaries and pastors were (and often still are) given special recognition in many evangelical communities. Still others experienced the influence of these schools by attending annual missionary and Bible conferences, listening to radio broadcasts, and reading the printed material regularly distributed by these schools. Sixteen Bible schools and colleges remain in operation in the province, with a cumulative enrollment exceeding 1,400 students. Today these schools struggle to maintain their "market share" of students by highlighting the unique strengths of small schools, adjusting and diversifying curriculum, and modernizing facilities. They wrestle too with defining their place within Christian higher education as the demand for seminary-trained leaders increases within evangelical denominations and missionary organizations, and as more Bible colleges become liberal arts colleges. Despite the challenges, they remain important centres of influence, having made substantial contributions to many of the evangelical Protestant denominations in Saskatchewan. *Bruce Guenther*

B

FURTHER READING: Guenther, B.L. 2001. "Training for Service: The Bible School Movement in Western Canada, 1909–1960." Ph.D. Dissertation, Montreal: McGill University; McKinney, L.J. 1997. *Equipping for Service: A Historical Account of the Bible College Movement in North America.* Fayetteville: Accrediting Association of Bible Colleges.

BIENFAIT, town, pop 786, located approximately 14 km E of Estevan on Hwy 18. People began arriving in the area in the 1890s. The first viable **COAL** mine was established a few kilometres south of the Bienfait town site at **ROCHE PERCÉE** in 1891. Although the **PALLISER-HIND EXPEDITIONS** noted coal along the **SOURIS RIVER** in 1857, quantities had been thought too insubstantial to warrant development. It was decades before the extent of the coal beds was realized and the first lignite in the area was mined by individual entrepreneurs and small-time operators. In the early 1900s, the CPR started Bienfait Mines Ltd. and soon more mines were opened in the area. Many local farmers used coal mining income to help them establish their farms. In 1922, the only murder ever associated with Saskatchewan's illicit liquor trade with the United States took place in Bienfait (*see* **PROHIBITION AND TEMPERANCE**). The population grew rapidly in the early 1900s as people of many diverse nationalities flocked to the area: from 245 in 1916, to well over 500 in 1931. That same year, Bienfait coal miners joined the Mine Worker's Union of Canada and went on strike to try to force mine owners to recognize their union and to restore wages that had been cut (*see* **ESTEVAN COAL MINERS STRIKE**). The Depression years hit the coal mining industry hard, but another development which was to affect miners significantly was the beginning of surface "strip" mining by electric shovels. Originally, all mining operations had been underground, but by 1956 a six-decade era of underground coal mining had come to an end. Today, some of the world's largest mining equipment is operated in the Bienfait area. The coal mining industry and its role in the development of Bienfait have been commemorated in a museum, formerly the CPR station built in 1907. A vintage steam locomotive used by the Manitoba and Saskatchewan Coal Company is also displayed at the north end of the town's main street.

David McLennan

BIG BEAR (MISTIHAI-MUSKWA) (CA. 1825– 88). Born near Jackfish Lake around 1825 to an Ojibwa chief named Black Powder (Mukitoo), Big Bear spoke Cree as a first language, but also Ojibwa. Contracting smallpox in 1837, he survived with disfiguring facial markings that he commonly referred to in jest, shouting happily "Now I feel very handsome!" He was a capable and uncompromising leader; but his adherence in traditional customs made him appear stubborn in the eyes of the federal government. Big Bear hesitated to sign **TREATY 6**, and became the leader of the First Nations who remained outside of it. He led his followers to the **CYPRESS HILLS**, where they faced starvation from lack of game and the withholding of food rations, as the federal government attempted to coerce them to sign treaty and move onto reserves. Big Bear still refused to sign. He and his followers moved to Montana, where he spent time with **SITTING BULL** and **LOUIS RIEL**, discussing a means to perpetuate their way of life. Big Bear realized that if all the tribes of the North-West Territories spoke with a united voice they could achieve more in their negotiations with the federal government. Faced with another winter of starvation, he grudgingly signed Treaty 6 in 1882, but as he did not choose a location for his reserve his people did not receive rations. In the summer of 1884 he met Riel at Duck Lake but failed to be swayed by Riel's plans. Big Bear waited to choose a reserve in the spring of 1885, but his decision drew much criticism from his band. As his authority declined, Wandering Spirit gained influence over the more militant band members. Big Bear continued his attempts to reach a peaceful resolution but was unsuccessful. The arrival of troops from eastern Canada squelched the Métis resistance, and First Nations people including Wandering Spirit, Miserable Man, Four-Sky-Thunder, and Big Bear surrendered. Big Bear was tried in Regina on September 11, 1885, on four counts of treasonfelony and was imprisoned in Stony Mountain Penitentiary, Manitoba. When he was freed two years later, his integrity remained intact but he was broken in health and spirit. He died in the winter of 1887–88.

Christian Thompson

FURTHER READING: Dempsey, H. 1984. *Big Bear: The End of Freedom.* Vancouver: Douglas & McIntyre; Stonechild, B. and B. Waiser. 1997. *Loyal Till Death: Indians and the North-West Rebellion.* Calgary: Fifth House.

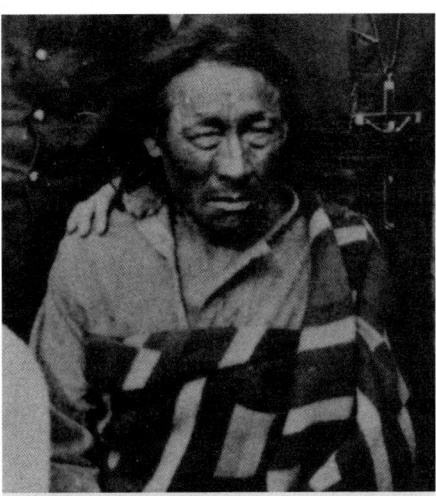

RCMP MUSEUM, REGINA, 1953.31.3

Big Bear, September 1885.

BIG BEAR FIRST NATION. BIG BEAR (*mistihaimuskwa*), born around 1825 near Jackfish Lake, was recognized as a leader by the early 1860s and was the leading chief of the Prairie River People in 1871. Big Bear was present during the **TREATY 6** (1876) negotiations, but refused to sign until destitution and starvation forced him to sign an adhesion on December 8, 1882. In the 1880s he attempted to create an Indian territory in the North-West by encouraging bands to choose reserves in an adjacent line; however, fearing the concentration of that many Indians in one area, the government refused to grant them contiguous reserves. According to official reports, Big Bear and his band arrived at Fort Pitt in August 1883 and promised to take a reserve; but they failed to do so, traveling instead to the Battleford district. In June 1884 Big Bear hosted a Thirst Dance (**SUN DANCE**) on the Poundmaker Reserve; when the North-West Mounted Police arrived to disperse them, Big Bear and **POUNDMAKER** were barely able to avert violence. Big Bear began to lose influence over his band's warrior society, and on April 2, 1885, his son Ayimâsis and a war chief named Kapapamahchakwew (Wandering Spirit) killed nine people at Frog Lake. Big Bear did not participate in the 1885 Resistance, but was held accountable for the actions of his band. He surrendered at Fort Carlton in July of that year; tried in Regina on September 11, he was sentenced to three years at the Stony Mountain Penitentiary. Upon his release he settled on the Poundmaker Reserve, where he died on January 17, 1888. Reports from 1886 reveal that Big Bear's band had scattered following the Resistance, together with people from the Thunder Child, Poundmaker, and Little Pine Reserves (amongst others). The Big Bear Band has not been reconstituted.

Christian Thompson

"BIG DIG". The city of Regina's Wascana Lake was created in the 1900s as a reservoir fed by Wascana Creek. In recent years, sediment had been collecting at the bottom of the lake, reducing its depth by 35% to 1.5 metres on average. The excavation of the lake started on January 6, 2004. During the excavation, 1.3 million cubic metres of earth were moved by 200 workers working 24 hours a day, and trucks made about 96,000 trips out of the lakebed. Upon the completion of the excavation, the lake reached depths of over 5.5 metres. The Wascana Lake project also included the creation of a new promenade and pedestrian way at Albert Street, a new pedestrian underpass at the Broad Street Bridge, the creation of Discovery Island, a new island in the east lake federal migratory bird sanctuary, the enlargement of Willow Island and Spruce Island, and a new floating fountain north from the Legislative Building. The excavation of the lake was completed on March 21, 2004, with further enhancements and landscaping continuing until

November of that year. The cost of the project, which reached $18 million, was shared by city, provincial, and federal governments.

Dagmar Skamlová

BIG ISLAND LAKE FIRST NATION (JOSEPH BIG HEAD). Cree Chief Joseph Bighead signed an adhesion to **TREATY 6** on June 25, 1913, and requested that his band be allowed to continue to hunt and fish in the region of Lac des Iles. In 1916 the Big Head Reserve, No. 124, was surveyed. It was noted that the cattle owned by the band were some of the finest in the country, but that they were not increasing in number as quickly as the Department of Indian Affairs would have liked. Agriculture has remained an important aspect of their economy, with a potato plantation that has expanded to include the sale of other vegetables while employing sixty people seasonally. This is further supplemented by gas and oil revenue. The community's infrastructure includes a band office, warehouse, school, band hall, and community maintenance facility buildings. The 851-member band controls 4,700 hectares; 559 people live on their reserve, located 35 km east of Cold Lake, Alberta. *Christian Thompson*

BIG MUDDY VALLEY (49°03' 00"N, 104°51' 00"W; Map sheet 72 H/2). Located 200 km south of Regina, in one of the driest, most rugged environments in the province, the banks of the Big Muddy Valley are so far apart that its floodplain is 3 km wide in places. Some 60 km in length and up to 160 metres deep, the Big Muddy was part of an ancient glacial melt water channel that carried vast quantities of water southeastward at the end of the last ice age. The waters that carved the Big Muddy were then considerably more abundant than the many ephemeral creeks and springs that now grace this landscape of sandstone cliffs and buttes. Hidden away from any public roads, shallow and alkali Big Muddy Lake sits 140 m below the surrounding landscape, as the only reminder of times when waters flowed more generously through the valley.

The Big Muddy may have been visited by Plains nomadic societies as early as 10,000 years ago. Occupation and buffalo kill sites indicate that the landscape has long sustained human occupation. The variety of stone circles, and turtle and buffalo effigies in the area suggests that this badlands region was associated with ritualistic events or ceremonies. What drew them there? Resources such as **BISON** and berries, sheltered areas, abundant fresh water and fuel, and a likely central position in the worldviews of local indigenous populations made the Big Muddy a favoured destination throughout the cycle of seasons.

The aesthetic qualities of this extraordinary landscape may have inspired ranchers and early settlers to come here, as much as the relative freedom of living in a remote area. Ironically, the level of isolation also contributed to less savoury activities. Because of its location near the American border, the Big Muddy attracted bandits and horse thieves needing a refuge north of the 49th parallel. Patrolling the region was a challenge for the North-West Mounted Police because local ranchers, who wanted no trouble from these ruffians, often turned a blind eye to illegal activities. Contemporary visitors enjoy less intrusive activities such as observing the blooming prickly pear cactus and hiking around the base of Castle Butte, which reaches 60 m in height and is known informally as the flagship attraction of the Big Muddy Valley. *Claude-Jean Harel*

FURTHER READING: Eaglesham, I. 1970. *The Big Muddy Valley*. Regina: Saskatchewan History and Folklore Society.

CLAUDE-JEAN HAREL PHOTO

Castle Butte, Big Muddy Valley.

BIG RIVER, town, pop 741, located approximately 135 km NW of Prince Albert, just W of **PRINCE ALBERT NATIONAL PARK**. The community is situated overlooking the southern end of the long and narrow Cowan Lake, which was created in 1914 by the damming of the Big River, from which the community derives its name. In 1908, William Cowan built there the first sawmill. By 1911, the Big River Lumber Company was operating what was reportedly the largest sawmill in the British Empire, with the capacity to produce one million board feet of lumber every 24 hours. The mill, as well as the work in the bush, provided employment for over 1,000 men. Big River soon became a boomtown with a population estimated at over 3,000. In 1914, the Big River Lumber Company sold the entire "town" to American interests, and in the summer of 1919 an enormous forest fire swept through the area, eventually completely surrounding the town. Women and children were evacuated, while the men remained behind to battle the flames. The fire eventually burnt itself out; even though the countryside was blackened and scorched almost as far north as Green Lake, the townsite remained unscathed. However, with most of the area's timber gone, the community's future looked bleak. Faced with unemployment, many people moved on; those who remained turned to homesteading, fishing, freighting, and trapping. The community entered an economic slump which was to last for years. By the 1940s, as roads improved to areas of forest that the fire had spared, the Saskatchewan Timber Board decided to rebuild the lumber industry in the village. The population of Big River nearly doubled in five years: from 502 in 1946 to 901 in 1951. Today, Big River is a dynamic community with a diverse array of businesses and services. The Canadian Northern Railway Station, built in 1910, has been designated a heritage property. Tourism is a developing industry; the area has become home to a significant artistic community; and the Ness Creek Music Festival features musicians from across North America and draws audiences from across western Canada. *David McLennan*

BIG RIVER CREE FIRST NATION. Big River First Nation is located 98 km northwest of Prince Albert and 19 km southwest of the village of Debden. It is uncertain when the original Indigenous populations began to settle on the banks of the long, narrow Oklemow-Cee-Pee River (Big River), but the Cree Chief See-See-Way-um signed **TREATY 6** on September 3, 1878, and for the next twenty years his band remained self-sufficient as they continued to hunt, trap, and fish the bountiful resources of the area. Kenemotayoo was the second chief, and one of the oldest trails in the district was named after him. The 11,964.8-hectare Big River Cree reserve land consists of farmland, natural meadows, an abundance of trees, and lake waters. Economic development opportunities include agriculture, forestry, trapping, tourism, and commercial fishing and hunting camps. A popular historic site is the buffalo jump on the outskirts of Victoire, where buffalo herds were stampeded over the hilltop. Another attraction is the remnants of the **CARLTON TRAIL**, which during the days of the fur trade provided a link between Edmonton and Winnipeg. Facilities available in the community include a band office, Mistahi Sipiy Elementary School, Se-se-wahum High School, the Whitefish Arena, an Internet access site, a carpentry shop, an arena, laundromat, health clinic, and Elders' Hall. There is a current band population of 2,700 members, with 1,918 people living on reserve. *Christian Thompson*

BIG SKY FARMS. Big Sky Farms Inc., was established in 1995, by four Saskatchewan businessmen who together have more than sixty years experience in the hog industry. The company's mandate is to own and operate fully modern, farrow-to-finish hog production facilities in Saskatchewan using the most advanced production methods available. In response to soaring global consumption of pork (an increase of 15 million tonnes between 1993 and 1999), Big Sky Farms expanded rapidly and set an aggressive goal of producing two million hogs per year by 2008. It owns and operates production units in the Humboldt, Goodeve, Kelvington, Lintlaw, Preeceville, Sturgis, Ogema, Rama and Porcupine Plain areas, and is one of the largest producers in western Canada. The company employs 385 people and reports annual sales of almost $90 million. *Joe Ralko*

BIGGAR, town, pop 2,243, located 93 km W of Saskatoon at the junction of Hwys 4, 14, and 51. The town is famous for its slogan "New York is Big, But This is Biggar"; local legend has it that an early survey crew had too much to drink one night and wrote the famous phrase on the town's sign as a prank. Evidently, the townspeople liked the slogan and adopted it. The railway has played a major role in Biggar's prosperity. In 1910, the **GRAND TRUNK PACIFIC RAILWAY** (GTP) decided to establish Biggar as a divisional point on its line, sparking both a construction boom and population growth. A roundhouse was built and Biggar's station was, reportedly, one of the largest in the Canadian west, boasting an all-night restaurant. By the mid-1920s, the population exceeded 2,000 and remained fairly stable for several decades. The 1950s saw renewed growth. While the railroad is still a significant employer today, Biggar's economy is more reliant now on agriculture and other industries. In total, Biggar has over 100 commercial enterprises, among them the community's weekly newspaper, the *Biggar Independent* (in business since 1909), Saskatchewan's largest greenhouse, the province's second-

KEVIN BRAUTIGAM PHOTO/COURTESY OF BIGGAR MUSEUM AND GALLERY, WITH THE PERMISSION OF THE CANADIAN ACTORS' EQUITY ASSOCIATION

This photograph was taken to promote the theatrical production "New York is Big, but this is Biggar–The Musical," which ran at the Biggar Majestic Theatre from July 27 to August 11, 2000, as a part of the community's Millennium celebrations. In front of the town's famous logo are Angie Tysseland of Saskatoon, who composed the original music for the production, and Tom Bentley-Fisher, a playwright and director born in Swift Current, who now divides his time between Canada and San Francisco. Bentley-Fisher wrote and directed the performance.

largest turkey producer, a sodium sulphate plant, a transport company with a fleet of over fifty trucks, a manufacturer of environmentally safe containment tanks for petroleum, chemicals, and other hazardous materials, and a producer of malt which exports to markets around the world. Community attractions include the Biggar Museum and Gallery, Roger Martin's Homestead Museum, and **SANDRA SCHMIRLER** Olympic Gold Park, established in honour of the Canadian and Olympic curling champion who was born and raised in the town. *David McLennan*

BILINGUALISM. The debate over bilingualism in Saskatchewan concerns essentially the relationship of Canada's two official languages in the spheres of government, the courts, and education. Its roots predate the establishment of the province. It involves the continuing attempts of Saskatchewan's French-speaking population, the Fransaskois, to maintain their language rights; and also the impact that federal bilingual initiatives, as expressed in the Official Languages Act (1969) and the Canadian Charter of Rights and Freedoms (1982), has had on provincial support for the French language. When the **NORTH-WEST TERRITORIES ACT** was amended in 1877, section 110 stipulated that "either the English or the French language may be used by any person in the debates of the Legislative Assembly of the Territories and in proceedings before the courts." An 1886 amendment gave the Assembly the power to "regulate its proceedings and the manner of recording and publishing the same"; such regulations would come into force once proclaimed and published by the **LIEUTENANT-GOVERNOR**. In 1892, the Assembly

resolved that its proceedings be recorded and published in English only. This amendment, however, never received royal assent, and when Saskatchewan became a province in 1905 and the provisions of the North-West Territories Act remained in force, French remained theoretically an official language.

By 1911, however, less than 5% of the population was French-speaking. English was increasingly regarded as a unifying factor, and **WORLD WAR I** increased attacks against other languages: this attitude was reflected especially in education, and from 1918 a series of anti-French, anti-Catholic measures, culminating in 1931, saw English legislated as the sole language of instruction, and religious garb and symbols banished from the classroom. French might still be taught as part of the curriculum for one hour a day if a school district requested it, but Francophones had to resort to their own resources in order to preserve French language and culture. This was rendered more difficult by rural depopulation and increasing school centralization. Not until the new federal emphasis on bilingualism and biculturalism in the late 1960s did attitudes begin to change. In 1967, an amendment to the Education Act restored French as a language of instruction for one hour a day. This provision was broadened in 1973 and again in the 1978 Education Act, which provided for schools to be designated in which French would be used as the principal language of instruction, thus opening the possibility of Francophone and immersion schools. To facilitate the organization and curricula of the new designated schools, the Official Minority Language Office (OMLO) was established in 1980.

Since 1982, a number of important developments have taken place. In 1987, the Saskatchewan Court of Appeal decided that Francophones had a right to a trial in French, and in the following year it was ruled that they could manage and control their own school system. The Fransaskois had been campaigning for this since 1984, based on Article 23 of the Charter. The Saskatchewan government stalled, however, and it was not until 1993 that the Romanow government amended the Education Act, thus allowing the Fransaskois to manage their own schools. Provincial government action had already been taken in 1988 when the Supreme Court of Canada, ruling on the Mercure case, found that Section 110 of the North-West Territories Act was still valid in Saskatchewan and that all statutes enacted only in English were thus invalid. However, it also recognized that the government of Saskatchewan could exercise its legislative power, which it did, enacting the Language Act (1988). This declared all existing laws valid, even if enacted in English only, and provided for certain language rights that apply to the judicial system. Saskatchewan did not, therefore, become an officially bilingual province, but it did enter into an agreement with Canada to provide increased support for French-language education at all levels. Two years later, the Office of French-language Co-ordination was set up to assist in the provision of services in French. In 2004, the government of Saskatchewan defined its French-language services policy, recognizing that "linguistic duality is a fundamental characteristic of Canada and that Saskatchewan's Francophone community is an important component of that linguistic duality."

General opinions of non-Francophones on bilingualism in the province have been divided. Many continue to object to the perceived imposition of a federal and provincial policy that they consider unnecessary and wasteful. Others, such as CANADIAN PARENTS FOR FRENCH, have welcomed new opportunities in education and championed French immersion schools as a means to ensure future bilingualism and biculturalism. The last few decades have then seen progress, but with a declining Francophone population and a current provincial bilingualism rate of 5.1% it must be concluded that in the 21st century official bilingualism in Saskatchewan faces an uncertain future. *Brian Rainey*

BILL 2. After five consecutive successful elections and twenty years of governance, the left-wing CO-OPERATIVE COMMONWEALTH FEDERATION (CCF) was defeated by ROSS THATCHER and the LIBERAL PARTY in April 1964. Thatcher's two-term reign would last until 1971, during which time he made major changes to industrial relations in Saskatchewan. The Liberals were more attuned to the business community than the CCF, which most of the labour

movement had supported. The first move that the new government made concerned changes to the province's TRADE UNION ACT, first introduced by the CCF in 1944. Bill 79 was to weaken the Act and undermine the rights of workers previously provided for. Bill 79 allowed employers to interfere in union organizing drives, and restricted the inclusion of "professional" employees into unions. But Bill 79 was just the seed of much more oppressive legislation that was introduced under Bill 2.

The Essential Services Emergency Act, Bill 2, was introduced on September 12, 1966, in response to a strike by the Oil, Chemical and Atomic Workers (OCAW) at the provincially owned SASKATCHEWAN POWER CORPORATION. The Bill allowed the provincial Cabinet to end a strike in the public service if it deemed those services essential to life, health or property. Compulsory arbitration could be imposed if Cabinet so chose, and a union could be decertified if it defied the legislation. OCAW and later the CANADIAN UNION OF PUBLIC EMPLOYEES (CUPE), representing health care workers, would be targets of the new legislation. The scope of Bill 2 was expanded in 1970 to cover the construction industry, which was involved in a protracted strike with its unions. It was further expanded in early 1971, to allow Cabinet to establish compulsory arbitration in any industrial dispute in the province, whether it was in the public or private sector.

Bill 2 was the most comprehensive Act undermining the principles of free collective bargaining ever to be introduced in Saskatchewan. It would cast a shadow over all collective bargaining and strengthen the hand of employers at the negotiating table. The United Church in Saskatchewan declared Bill 2 a "dangerous piece of legislation," which "tends to move us away from the democratic ideal." The Liberal government called for a provincial election on June 23, 1971. The successor to the CCF, the NEW DEMOCRATIC PARTY (NDP) led by ALLAN BLAKENEY, soundly defeated the Liberals and quickly revoked Bill 2. Thatcher's Bill 2, however, was to set a precedent for future governments to use legislation to intervene in the collective bargaining process, particularly when it involved their own employees. *Doug Taylor*

FURTHER READING: Eisler, D. 1987. *Rumours of Glory: Saskatchewan and the Thatcher Years*. Edmonton: Hurtig.

BINKS, SARAH. Known to Canadian culture as the "Sweet Songstress of Saskatchewan," Sarah was the fictional creation of Paul Hiebert, professor of chemistry at the University of Manitoba. Though fictitious, she became one of the best-known poets in Saskatchewan after her first appearance in Hiebert's "biography" *Sarah Binks*, published in 1947. It won the Leacock Medal for Humour, and remains in

print as a much-quoted satirical classic of Canadian literature.

Professor Hiebert claimed that Sarah was a simple country girl from Willows, Saskatchewan who showed a precocious genius for poetic insight in, for example, "The Hired Man on a Saturday Night," or "Hi Sooky Ho Sooky." The latter, inspired by her neighbour Steve Gryczlkaeiouc's courtship of her best friend Mathilda Schwantzhacker, initiated the long "Grizzlykick Symphony" of ultra-romantic poems. Hiebert became known for reading the poems and discussing Sarah's life on CBC Radio, so that to many fans she came to be remembered as a living poet.

Hiebert published a sequel in 1967, *Willows Revisited*, in which a group of Sarah's poetic disciples, known as the Saskatchewan School of Seven, congregated to celebrate her memory and carry on the great Binksian tradition. *Sarah Binks*

FURTHER READING: Paul Hiebert. 1947. *Sarah Binks*. Toronto: Oxford University Press; —. 1967. *Willows Revisited*. Toronto: McClelland and Stewart.

BINNIE-CLARK, GEORGINA (1871–1947). Georgina Binnie-Clark was a farmer (associated with the Union Jack Farm Settlement), women's rights' supporter, and author. Born on April 25, 1871, in Dorset, England, she became a journalist. In 1905 she and her sister visited their brother, a remittance man and homesteader near Fort Qu'Appelle. Binnie-Clark decided to remain, and purchased land for farming. Subsequently she wrote a travel book, *A Summer on the Canadian Prairie* (1910). In 1914 *Wheat and Woman* appeared; in it she included a discussion of her experiences as a greenhorn single woman farmer on the prairies, a critique of discriminatory homestead laws that worsened economic woes, and her conviction that farming was a suitable occupation for women. Binnie-Clark became a leading spokeswoman for the (unsuccessful) campaign to amend homestead legislation so that single women could secure homesteads. She had also established a training station for prospective women farmers from England in 1909; this program ended when WORLD WAR I erupted and the British Minister of Labour asked her to return to England and organize Anglican women for farm work so that male labourers could enter the military. Binnie-Clark eventually came back to her farm, but frequently travelled to England, leaving her sister in charge. By WORLD WAR II she was residing in England, where she died on April 22, 1947. *Lisa Dale-Burnett*

FURTHER READING: Binnie-Clark, G. 1979 (1914). *Wheat and Woman*. Toronto: University of Toronto Press.

BIODIVERSITY. Biodiversity, an indicator of biological complexity, can be measured at the species level, with a catalogue of the number of types of organisms present. In order to understand the importance of biodiversity, diversity both above and below the species level must also be known. At the ecosystem level, diversity of habitat and functional types must be recognized. Within a species, long-term ecological health requires diversity at the genetic level: for instance, not only must there be a large number of BEETLES, but the beetles must not all be bark-borers and there must be genetic flexibility within the species, in order for the species to survive in the changes found within a natural environment.

An area with a high biodiversity has a large number of species of organisms, from microbes to mammals and flowering plants; there are many biological communities, not large tracts of a few species; and there are large numbers of individuals from different gene lines within any species. Natural communities are made up of a number of species: these species fill a number of niches or functions within the communities; and species which reproduce sexually will have genetic diversity if their populations are large enough. On the other hand, in agriculture, a field contains a single species of plant, and other species are discouraged by various practices. In Saskatchewan, this field may cover a considerable amount of land; it is the product of commercial seed in which a number of traits have been selected, resulting in reduced genetic variability. Thus, agricultural settings are characterized by very low biodiversity.

Natural communities differ in their level of biodiversity. Saskatchewan has relatively low biodiversity due to its high latitude position, the absence of mountains, the absence of an ocean coast, low precipitation, and the large scale of its landscape, resulting in only four ecozones and eleven ECOREGIONS. Higher biodiversity is found in areas such as Peru, which is at a low latitude, benefits from the foothills and mountains of the Andes, borders on the Pacific Ocean, and has areas of high and low rainfall as well as a variable landscape. If we contrast the well-known bird faunas of the two areas, we see that Saskatchewan has 300 regularly occurring species while Peru, at only twice the area, has 1,800 species. These include a number of types of birds, such as fish-eating seabirds and fruit-eaters, which do not occur in Saskatchewan. Research has shown that areas of low biodiversity may be particularly vulnerable to species loss with the occurrence of any perturbation, such as human processes and climate change. Conservation is the process where groups and agencies attempt to maintain biodiversity at as high a level as possible, for the good health of the environment in which all the species, including humans, live.   *Diane Secoy*

FURTHER READING: Bocking, S. 2000. *Biodiversity in Canada*. Peterborough: Broadview Press; Wilson, E.O.

1992. *The Diversity of Life*. Cambridge, MA: Harvard University Press.

BIODIVERSITY ACTION PLAN. The Biodiversity Action Plan (BAP) was developed by a consortium of Saskatchewan government departments in order to ensure the maintenance of a healthy biodiversity within the province. These agencies, ranging from Environment through Agriculture, Highways, and Industry and Resources, recognize the importance of acting to preserve and enhance biodiversity at all levels: genetic diversity within species, which is only possible with healthy sizes of populations; species diversity, or the number and variety of types of organisms; and ecosystem diversity, or the variety of habitats in which organisms live. Loss of diversity at any level decreases the health of the world in which humans live. The goals of the plan for the government are: to conserve biodiversity and biological resources in a sustainable manner; to improve our understanding of ecosystems and increase our resource management; to promote an understanding of the need to conserve biodiversity and use biological resources in a sustainable manner; to develop a set of initiatives and legislation supporting the conservation of biodiversity and sustainable use of biological resources; and to co-operate with other jurisdictions (international, federal, provincial, municipal, and First Nations as well as MÉTIS people) having policy responsibility and/or program interests to conserve biodiversity and use biological resources in a sustainable manner. These goals require research to catalogue and monitor biological diversity, development of educational plans to inform the community of the needs for biodiversity, and negotiation with the various agencies and groups to promote the goals.   *Diane Secoy*

FURTHER READING: 2004. *Caring for Natural Environments: A Biodiversity Action Plan for Saskatchewan's Future*. Regina: Government of Saskatchewan, Saskatchewan Environment.

BIOFILTRATION WATER TREATMENT SYSTEM. The Yellow Quill First Nation in east-central Saskatchewan was able to lift a boiled-water advisory after nine years in 2004 because of the efforts by the Safe Drinking Water Foundation, a non-profit organization based in Saskatoon. Hans Peterson and his group designed a water treatment system that first filters water through biofiltration, then treats it a second time by reverse osmosis. The foundation also recommended that Yellow Quill change its source of water from the Pipestone Creek to a deep-water well. Solving the water problems at Yellow Quill became urgent when crises in other parts of Canada occurred after the original boiled-water advisory was issued in 1995: seven people died and hundreds became ill in Walkerton, Ontario,

when the town's drinking supply became contaminated with E. coli in May 2002; a year later, in April 2003, thousands of people in North Battleford became ill after their drinking supply was contaminated by cryptosporidium. Groups from several countries, including China, with large rural populations and drinking water problems have shown interest in Hans Peterson's simple and relatively inexpensive water treatment solution.   *Joe Ralko*

BIORIGINAL FOODS. Bioriginal Food & Science Corp. has grown from a Saskatoon company selling bee pollen in 1993 to become the world's leading supplier of Essential Fatty Acid (EFA) oils. Bioriginal was built on science and is recognized as an industry pioneer with more than 200 products now available through a distribution network on six continents from offices in Canada, China and Europe. The company, which employs almost 100 people, obtains its raw materials from flax, evening primrose, borage, black currants and fish. Merchandise ranges from bulk oil and capsules to finished, manufactured products. The extensive product lines serve five key markets: nutritional supplements, functional foods, cosmetics, pet and veterinary products and over-the-counter pharmaceuticals. Products are exported from Canada to customers in countries such as Argentina, Australia, China, Germany, Japan, Mexico, Netherlands, Taiwan and the United States. Bioriginal has a sophisticated resource management system that ensures product traceability and is registered with the Food and Drug Administration (FDA) in compliance with the United States Bioterrorism Act. The company received the 2003 ABEX Business of the Year Award as well as the ABEC Export Award. The Saskatchewan Chamber of Commerce sponsors the Achievement in Business Excellence Awards (ABEX). Bioriginal also was named a Canadian Innovation Leader by the National Research Council in 2003.   *Joe Ralko*

BIOTECHNOLOGY. Saskatchewan, situated at the centre of Canada's agriculture belt, is home to more than 47% of Canada's suitable land mass available for animal production or farming operations. It has 20% of all farm capital in the country, and consistently leads all other provinces in grain production as the major supplier of Canadian cereal and CANOLA crops for the world market. Prairie farmers have struggled for prosperity in an uncompromising landscape, a climate striking in its extremes, and at great distances from international markets. Yet it is this very dependence on agriculture production that has made Saskatchewan the logical site and Canada's leader in agricultural biotechnology. The history of agricultural achievement in the prairie economy is a story of tenacious adaptation: prairie people making use of science and technology to triumph over the environment and the market.

From its earliest years, Saskatchewan has been a fertile ground of agriculture science. Research farms and the **UNIVERSITY OF SASKATCHEWAN**'s College of Agriculture have worked to develop new farming techniques and food and feed crops. Ground-breaking research resulted in new hardy **WHEAT** varieties such as Marquis and Thatcher, changed the economic prospects of the province, and validated agricultural research as a tool to enhance the rural economy. The 1970s witnessed the real triumph of plant science: Saskatchewan laboratories created an entirely new crop from rapeseed: canola, which is the second most important crop on the prairies. The success of canola meant that many foresaw the possibilities of the emerging science of agriculture biotechnology.

The 1980s were to become years of intense energy for agriculture science in Saskatchewan and Canada. Nationally, science was being identified as the driver of the future economic prosperity; in Saskatchewan, the government introduced a new Department of Science and Technology, with the province's first biotechnology strategy as its showpiece. Emerging was a deep commitment and investment in the province's researchers and scientific infrastructure. Partnerships between levels of government, provincial universities, and provinces played a strong role in advancing the biotechnology agenda. Canada's first technology incubator, Innovation Place, emerged in 1977; that same year, a partnership of the governments of Canada, Alberta, and Saskatchewan, and of private industry established the **POS PILOT PLANT** Corporation.

The University of Saskatchewan (U of S) College of Agriculture was an early leader in agriculture biotechnology through its emphasis on and support for science, research, and extension services. One such outcome in 1975 was the **VACCINE INFECTIOUS DISEASE ORGANIZATION** (VIDO), which went on to patent one of the world's first biotechnology-based animal vaccines; later, VIDO and the U of S together created Biostar (1983), one of the province's first university biotechnology spin-off companies.

Other key components of Saskatchewan's agriculture biotechnology industry were the National Research Council's (NRC) Plant Biotechnology Institute (PBI) and Agriculture and AgriFood Canada (AAFC). NRC-PBI, along with University of Manitoba and AAFC, developed canola from rapeseed. NRC-PBI took over the national mandate in plant biotechnology in 1983; AAFC moved its research activity to Saskatchewan along with a national mandate for plant research. Both these organizations have led the Canadian plant and agriculture science research agenda. **AG-WEST BIOTECH INC.**, the first biotechnology industry-government association in Canada, was formed in 1988 as a federal-provincial government-industry partnership; it was charged with expanding biotechnology research and industry in Saskatchewan. Proximity to the field and to research attracted numerous national and multi-national companies to Saskatchewan, and local start-ups as well as university spin-offs blossomed in this environment.

Saskatchewan is home to between 30 and 40% of the Canadian agricultural biotechnology sector: from three companies in 1982, to over 30 in 1999 and 35 in 2002, an estimated 50 companies today are part of this sector. Private and public institutions provide over 400 research and technical positions and 700 supporting jobs in Saskatoon. Total employment in the sector is estimated at between 1,300 and 1,500. Direct product sales have also grown steadily: in 1999 Saskatchewan farmers planted approximately 3.6 million acres of genetically modified canola; today, more than half of the canola grown in Saskatchewan is genetically modified to be herbicide-resistant. A key industry in Canada's innovation program, biotechnology is one of the priority areas identified by the Saskatchewan government. Support for this technology in Saskatchewan has come through investment in infrastructure (**CANADIAN LIGHT SOURCE**, VIDO, etc.), in support for industry (R & D Tax Credits), and in agriculture research funding. Over $100 million per year of public and private investment supports science and agricultural research activity, and today over $1 billion is invested in science-based infrastructure.

Quality research excellence is a driving force behind agricultural biotechnology in Saskatchewan. Scientists, the research infrastructure and activities of the U of S, NRC-PBI, and AAFC Saskatoon Research Centre, in combination with the province's public organizations and private industry, have created a world-leading research environment. Expertise exists in basic biotechnology research all the way through to commercial product and company development; most importantly, these activities are carried out in close consultation with farmers, agri-services and agri-industry, and with the public. Ultimately, agriculture biotechnology serves the needs of prairie farmers, adding a valuable option to their production toolbox. *Cheryl Loadman*

BIPHASIX™. Marianna Foldvari, a **UNIVERSITY OF SASKATCHEWAN** pharmaceutical scientist, has developed a unique microscopic delivery system that could replace needles in administering proteins and genes to people. Called Biphasix™, this system is the first technology in the world that administers large protein molecules in a pharmaceutical cream applied on the skin, rather than by an injection or any other device. PharmaDerm Laboratories Ltd., set up in 1991 to market the system, was acquired in 2003 by Helix Biopharma Corp., an Ontario company that specializes in non-injection drugs and vaccines. Helix focused on developing three products: an insulin patch for the treatment of diabetes; interferon—a cream for the treatment of topical viral infections such as genital warts; and a vaccine delivery system. An insulin patch and HPV (human papilloma virus) cream are expected to be on the market by 2008. *Joe Ralko*

BIRCH HILLS, town, pop 957, located approximately 38 km SE of Prince Albert at the junction of Hwys 3 and 25. Fur traders had plied the **SOUTH SASKATCHEWAN RIVER** north of the community since the latter half of the 18th century, and the origins of Birch Hills date to the 1880s, when settlement of the district began. After the Canadian Northern Railway came through the area in 1905, new settlers began to pour into the district. They came from Ontario, the United States, Scandinavian countries (predominantly Norway), and other areas of Europe. By 1917 the population was approximately 250, and the district surrounding the community was proving to be some of the finest agricultural land in Saskatchewan. By the 1950s, the population of Birch Hills was over 500. It is one of the few rural communities in Saskatchewan not to have experienced a decline over the past few decades. The community's proximity to Prince Albert has led to the creation of new residential subdivisions in recent years. Its commercial sector consists of approximately ninety businesses and services, including a health centre, a modern airport, a K–12 school, a weekly newspaper, and numerous recreational facilities. *David McLennan*

BIRCH NARROWS DENE FIRST NATION. The Birch Narrows Dene Band signed Treaty 10 on August 28, 1906. They were originally part of the Peter Pond Band, but separated in 1972 into the Birch Narrows and Buffalo River Dene Nations; most of the Birch Narrows Dene Nation Reserve adjoins that of the Buffalo River Dene Nation. The present settlement was created when the residents of the old village on Churchill Lake relocated to have Churchill road access. Half of the community is non-status (many are related to First Nation people): because of the difference in the status of the two populations as it relates to treaty rights, jurisdictional conflicts have been common. Community infrastructure includes a taxi service, candy store, band store, a health clinic, youth centre, learning centre, justice program, educational complex, day care, post office, fire truck and fire hall. Economic development opportunities involve a fish plant, forestry, hunting and trapping, and tourism and adventure tours that include opportunities to learn about Dene culture if so desired. The band's three reserves at Churchill and Turnor Lakes total 2,693.6 hectares; Turnor Lake (193B), located 124 km northwest of Ile-à-la-Crosse, is the smallest and most populated site. The band has a membership of 586 people, but only 321 live on reserve. *Christian Thompson*

Ada Bird.

BIRD, DICK (1892–1986) AND ADA (1917–2003).

Born in Leamington Spa, Warwickshire, England on August 16, 1892, Dick Bird was an adventurer with a keen and inquisitive personality. At age 15, he arrived in the United States and eagerly learned photography and cinematography. He then travelled widely, documenting events and life in the United States, Canada, Mexico, China, Japan and Korea. In 1921, he came to Saskatchewan to make documentary films for the government and continued to shoot newsreels for Pathescope and produce industrial films. He filmed the dedication of the Albert Street Bridge in Regina, the opening broadcast of Saskatchewan's first radio station CKCK in 1922, the first drilling for oil and gas, as well as the visits of various dignitaries including Lord Baden Powell, Lord Tweedsmuir and Prime Minister **MACKENZIE KING**. He captured images of **ETHEL CATHERWOOD** training for the Olympic high jumping event that won her a gold medal in 1928. As tensions mounted and escalated into the Regina Riot of 1935, Bird was there with his camera (*see* **ON-TO-OTTAWA TREK AND THE REGINA RIOT**).

In the 1930s, Bird's interests turned to the world of nature. He became a dedicated conservationist, and in 1937 was elected president of the Regina Natural History Society and produced a weekly *Camera Trails* broadcast on CKCK. He also published *The Camera Trailer*, illustrated with his own photographs, for distribution to the radio audience.

Bird's first wife, Pansy Nix, died in 1937. In 1947 Dick married school teacher Ada Bovee (born December 21, 1917), and they became a successful filmmaking team. In the late 1940s and 1950s, the Birds gained international prominence for their nature movies; an executive of Eastman Kodak called them "probably the most outstanding photographers of birds and wildlife in North America." They travelled extensively on the lecture circuit, where they were in great demand. For a number of years, the Audubon Society sponsored these tours, and their audiences included Harvard, the National Geographic Society, and the Smithsonian Institute. During the early 1950s, they shot footage for Walt Disney's *True Life Adventure* series. Much of their work has been preserved at the Saskatchewan Archives and the National Archives of Canada.

In 1919 Dick Bird became the first president of the Canadian Press Photographers Association. Lacking formal education, he earned letters after his name the hard way. He was a Fellow of the Zoological Society of London, a Fellow of the Photographic Society of America, an Associate of the Photographic Society of Great Britain, and he received an honorary Doctor of Laws degree from the **UNIVERSITY OF REGINA**. After a career that spanned more than six decades, Dick Bird died on September 28, 1986. Ada Bird passed away on October 3, 2003. *Krzysztof Gebhard*

BIRDS. Birds are members of the class Aves, one of the classes of vertebrates or animals with backbones. They are specialized for flight with forelimbs developed as wings; feathers which insulate and function as lift surfaces and rudders; hollow bones and lack of teeth to reduce weight; brains with well-developed centres for coordination of visual information, balance and muscle activity; an extremely efficient lung with no dead air space; and the levator of the wing attached to the sternum rather than the vertebral column, which lowers the centre of gravity. Like **MAMMALS**, birds have a high body temperature, which maintains their brains and muscles at a high activity level but requires a considerable amount of food. Birds can reduce their food requirements by migrating to a warmer climate after the breeding season is completed, when they have fed themselves and their growing young on the abundant insects and rodents of the northern summer. A few birds such as nightjars are able to lower their body temperatures, which reduces their food requirements; but this condition is not as well developed or as common as the hibernation of mammals. All birds are oviparous, usually laying their eggs in a nest. They have complex behavioural patterns, particularly associated with the breeding cycle. Their behaviours are based on the senses of sight and audition. Birds evolved from small feathered reptiles, perhaps dinosaurs, during the Jurassic approximately 150 million years ago. They are considered by many to be a group of reptiles specialized for flight, rather than a separate class.

Birds are found on all continents; they inhabit a variety of habitats, from the richest rain forests to the sparsely vegetated tundra and deserts. Their diversity is highest in the rain forests. They can be generalist feeders, such as the widely distributed herring gulls and crows, or highly specialized nectar feeders whose bills may allow them to feed on only a few species of plants.

Saskatchewan has records for 364 of the more than 10,000 modern species of birds. Of these, 300 species occur regularly and are ecologically important. There are representatives of 17 of the 28 living orders: Gaviiformes (loons), Podicipediformes (grebes), Pelecaniformes (pelicans, cormorants), Ciconiiformes (ibis, vultures), Anseriformes (ducks), Falconiformes (falcons, hawks), Galliformes (grouse), Gruiformes (cranes, rails), Charadriiformes (shorebirds, gulls), Columbiformes

Dick Bird and young cormorant.

Sharp-tailed grouse, Saskatchewan's provincial bird.

(pigeons), Cuculiformes (cuckoos), Strigiformes (owls), Caprimulgiformes (nightjars), Apodiformes (swift, hummingbirds), Coraciiformes (kingfisher), Piciformes (woodpeckers), and Passeriformes (all others). The affinities of the avifauna are cosmopolitan (peregrine, osprey), with Eurasia (thrushes, crows, owls), or with the rest of the New World (vulture, warblers, tyrant flycatchers, warblers); there are no species unique to Saskatchewan.

There are a number of species which have been introduced to North America for purposes of sport or to bring in familiar garden birds. Successful introductions which have spread into Saskatchewan are: gray partridge, ring-necked pheasant, wild turkey, rock dove/pigeon, Eurasian collared dove, European starling, house finch, and house sparrow. The turkey and finch are native to North America. Some of these introductions, particularly the sparrow and starling, have had a considerable negative impact on the native avifauna owing to competition for nesting sites and food.

Species have also been lost. Passenger pigeons were found in the eastern woodlands until the late 19th century. Lost by a combination of overhunting and destruction of the extensive woodlands that the species needed for nesting, it exemplifies the effects of human action on the biota of North America. A number of species have been reduced in numbers since the major settlement period. The trumpeter swan, whooping crane and Canada goose were hunted in great numbers for market, sport and feathers until by the early part of the 20th century their numbers were greatly reduced—in the case of the swan and crane, to near extinction. With agriculture, prairie sparrows and ground-nesting songbirds lost their nesting and feeding habitat. By the middle of the 20th century, concern about these and other species led to a variety of programs to conserve our natural heritage (*see* **BIODIVERSITY, CONSERVATION, CONSERVATION AGENCIES**).

There are also species which have benefited from the changes brought about by human action, such as the increased vegetation of town sites. Besides the introduced species, some of which have become very numerous, some native species, especially those of the forest edge such as American robins, have taken full advantage of the fruit trees and hedges of the towns. If the apparent warming trends continue, we can expect to see more birds which before never came as far north as Saskatchewan.

The provincial bird symbol is the sharp-tailed grouse, a prairie inhabitant. The largest bird is the trumpeter swan; the smallest is the ruby-throated hummingbird.

Diane Secoy

FURTHER READING: Godfrey, W.E. 1986. *The Birds of Canada*. Ottawa: National Museum of Natural Sciences; 2002. *National Geographic Field Guide to the Birds of North America*. Washington, DC: National Geographic Society; Sibley, D.A. 2001. *The Sibley Guide to Bird Life and Behavior*. New York: Knopf; Smith, A.R. 1996. *Atlas of Saskatchewan Birds*. Regina: Nature Saskatchewan Special Publication No. 22.

BIRDSELL, SANDRA (1942–). Sandra Louise Birdsell, one of Canada's most significant writers, was born in Hamiota, Manitoba on April 22, 1942, of **MÉTIS** and **MENNONITE** heritage. From her first collection of short fiction, *Night Travellers* (1982), Birdsell was recognized as a rare new literary voice. *Ladies of the House*, a second short story collection, followed in 1984; the two collections were subsequently published in the single-volume *Agassiz Stories*. Birdsell's first novel, *The Missing Child* (1989), which won the W.H. Smith/Books in Canada First Novel Award, was an evocative magic realist portrait of the fictional town of Agassiz.

Sandra Birdsell has been nominated twice for the Governor General's Award for Fiction (for the novel *The Chrome Suite* in 1992, and the short story collection *The Two-Headed Calf* in 1997) and she was the recipient of the Marion Engel Award in 1993. Birdsell lived in Winnipeg for thirty years before moving to Regina in 1997. In 2001, she published *The Russländer*, a novel that explores events in revolutionary Russia that led to the emigration of Mennonites to Manitoba in the 1920s. *The Russländer* won three **SASKATCHEWAN BOOK AWARDS** and was shortlisted for the Giller Prize.

Sandra Birdsell has served as writer-in-residence at numerous universities; her books have been translated into Spanish, French, and German, and her stories have been much anthologized. She is the author of film scripts, radio dramas and a children's book, but is best known for the originality, stylistic range, and humanity of her fiction.

Joan Thomas

Sandra Birdsell and Shep, Oman's Creek, Winnipeg.

BISON. The American Bison (*Bos bison*) is the only wild member of the cattle family (Bovidae) in Saskatchewan. The family of approximately 125 species occurs in the Northern Hemisphere, Africa, and Asia; five species are found in North America. The family contains ruminant animals with cloven hooves, permanent horns over bony lateral processes on the skull, and no upper incisors or canines. Adult male American Bison are the largest land animals in North America; at nearly 1,000 kg in weight, they are larger than grizzly or polar bears. The females are considerably smaller, at about 600 kg. The body shape of heavy forequarters and smaller hindquarters give a distinctive outline and a rocking gait when galloping. The heavy forequarters are due

DAVID KRUGHOFF PHOTO

Bison, just off Highway #48 near Glenavon, fall 2004.

to the large flat-faced skull and the long spines on the thoracic vertebrae which support the large muscles that move the skull. The heavy mane of wooly dark-brown fur over the shoulders and head, along with the beard, emphasizes the heaviness of the head and chest. The coat on the rest of the body is shorter and lighter brown. The coat of the single calf, born in the spring, is light brown.

Bison are gregarious, staying in small family groups that may join others to form larger herds. Before European settlement, bison were found throughout North America from the East Coast to the Rocky Mountains—in small groups in the woodlands and in large migratory herds on the prairie grasslands. Bison were the dominant animal in the grasslands ecosystem, cropping the grasses, breaking the soil with their hooves, and dunging as they moved over the landscape; they also fed on flowering plants, including young trees and shrubs, preventing their growth and replacement of the grasses.

With European settlement, the bison were killed for food and sport, for their hides, to prevent their interbreeding with imported domestic cattle, and to remove them as competitors for pasture for domestic livestock. In the prairies, in particular, they were slaughtered to remove them from possible use by the local First Nations, who were dependent on them for food and other uses. By the end of the 19th century, the species was almost eliminated; only deliberate and continuing conservation efforts have maintained its survival. Even so, the species is found only in controlled environments such as parks or private herds; there are no free-ranging animals. The closest relative of the American Bison, the European bison (*B. bonasus*), has approximately the same history and is now found only in park herds in eastern Europe.

Diane Secoy

FURTHER READING: Banfield, A.W.F. 1974. *The Mammals of Canada*. Toronto: University of Toronto Press.

BLACK, DONALD W. (1947–). Born in Regina on February 18, 1947, Donald Black has shown distinguished leadership in the Canadian financial services sector and in his own community. Since his graduation from the UNIVERSITY OF REGINA, Black has occupied various posts with a number of large corporations. He served as president and chief executive officer of SASKATCHEWAN GOVERNMENT INSURANCE from 1982 to 1985 and as Director and chair of Farm Credit Corporation for five years beginning in 1995. He is currently deputy chair and chief executive officer of Greystone Capital Management Inc. Black has also devoted his time and expertise to a variety of community organizations including the United Way of Regina and the Hospitals of Regina Foundation Inc. He was made a Member of the Order of Canada in 2002.

BLACK LAKE DENESULINE FIRST NATION. The ancestors of the Black Lake Denesuline Nation (Stony Rapids Band) signed an adhesion to TREATY 8 in July 1899 under Chief Maurice Piche (also known as Moberley) at Fond du Lac. In 1949 Maurice's band split (officially) into the Fond du Lac and Black Lake Bands. The Black Lake Denesuline Nation has three reserves on the east and west sides of Black Lake about 170 km southeast of Uranium City, the most populated being Chicken 224. Following treaty, the Denesuline continued to hunt, fish, and trap as they always had, spending extended periods in the Northwest Territories. The Denesuline bands are in the process of a claim against the federal government for deterioration of harvesting rights in the Northwest Territories. Economic development for this band includes hunting, fishing and trapping as well as commercial fishing, sawmill, mining, and tourism. Community infrastructure includes air service, all-weather road, radio and television communication, a school and teacherage, day care, band office, church, health clinic, band store, gas station, hotel, fire hall, and other community maintenance facilities. The band's 32,219.7 hectares of reserve land is home to 1,351 of the 1,683 registered members.

Christian Thompson

BLACKBIRDS. The general name "blackbirds" is given to perching birds of the family Icteridae. These are medium-sized birds of open habitats or forest edges, which are often of shiny or dull black plumage; some also have other melanin-based colours such as orange or yellow. Many have ringing, distinctive calls as they announce their territories. They feed on insects, fruits and seeds. This New World family contains approximately 103 species, of which 23 are found in North America. Eleven species are known from Saskatchewan, all of which are migratory. One of the species is the only Saskatchewan songbird that is a nest parasite, i.e., it lays its eggs in the nest of other species, which then raise the young. The brown-headed cowbird (*Molothrus ater*) parasitizes songbirds such as warblers; the young cowbirds usually out-compete the young of the host species and cause their death. A bird of the grasslands at the time of the great American bison herds, cowbirds have expanded north into the southern regions of the boreal forest.

Two of the species nest mainly in marshy vegetation. The red-winged blackbird (*Agelaius phoeniceus*) is very common in the marshes and larger sloughs of the southern half of the province, and is found nesting in lower numbers up to the northern border. Populations of this species can be very large, causing considerable impact on the cultivated areas in which they feed. The yellow-headed

COURTESY OF SASKATCHEWAN ENVIRONMENT

Yellow-headed blackbird.

blackbird (*Xanthocephalus xanthocephalus*) is more limited in its distribution, being more likely to use wetlands with deeper water in the southern half of the province.

Other species, such as the bobolink (*Dolichonyx oryzivorus*), are found in grainfields and grasslands. Brewer's blackbird (*Euphagus cyanocephalus*) nests in open grasslands country, but is also willing to make use of the shrubby vegetation of townsites. The Western meadowlark (*Sturnella neglecta*) is a common sight of the summer grasslands as it gives its cheery song from a fence post or small shrub; the bright yellow belly and black cravat are obvious on a frontal view, but the ground-nesting bird disappears when it turns its camouflaged brown-striped back. The rusty blackbird (*Euphagus carolinus*) and common grackle (*Quiscalus quiscula*) both nest in the boggy areas of the middle southern boreal region; the grackle is also a successful breeder in the settled sites of the agricultural grasslands.

Three species of the colourful orange and black orioles nest here. The most common is the Baltimore oriole (*Icterus galbula*), whose flute-like song is heard in woodlots and wooded town sites in the southern half of the province. There are a few records, mostly from the southwestern corner, of Bullock's oriole (*I. bullocki*), the western counterpart of the Baltimore oriole. The first record of the orchard oriole (*I. spurius*), in 1972, indicated the spread of this eastern woodland species into the province. Since then, it has been recorded and found breeding, usually in the southeast, but as far north and west as Saskatoon and the **CYPRESS HILLS**.

Diane Secoy

FURTHER READING: Alsop, F.J., III. 2002. *The Birds of Canada.* New York: Dorling Kindersley.

BLACKS: EARLY SETTLEMENTS.

Following the American Civil War (1861–65), thousands of African Americans exercised their newly won freedom by moving west. One of their destinations was the Indian Territory which had been set aside by the United States as a place to settle First Nations displaced by advancing White settlement. The area was particularly attractive to African Americans because they had the opportunity to obtain land, and because their civil and political rights would be protected thanks to the federal administration. However, White Americans were also attracted to the Indian Territory, and when it became the state of Oklahoma in 1908 they dominated the new state government. The majority of Oklahoma's White population, having come from the older southern states, quickly began implementing the racial segregation policies which characterized their region until the civil rights movement of the 1960s and 1970s. In 1910 the White majority took away the

Blacks' right to vote in Oklahoma in a statewide referendum.

Canada began advertising for settlers in Europe and the United States shortly after it obtained the Canadian plains region as part of its purchase of the Hudson's Bay Company lands. Some of these advertisements found their way into African-American newspapers in the Indian Territory and Oklahoma. Canada's appeals found many eager listeners among Oklahoma's Black population who had moved west to escape discrimination and found themselves engulfed in it once again. The available land in what became Saskatchewan attracted some Black settlers even before Oklahoma began its racist policies. As early as 1905, a few Black homesteaders settled near what became Maidstone, Saskatchewan. A short time later the Lafayette brothers from Iowa settled near Rosetown. The appearance of these early settlers did not attract much attention; this changed dramatically when trainloads of Black men, women and children began arriving on Canada's border, having been driven north by Oklahoma's implementation of segregation and disenfranchisement.

White Canadians reacted overwhelmingly against the Black migration. Farmers' organizations and womens' groups joined Boards of Trade across the region in demanding that the federal government halt the movement. The issue was debated several times in Parliament, and the Department of the Interior began an investigation. Eventually the federal government sent an agent, a Black doctor from Chicago, to Oklahoma to work against the movement; in effect countering its own advertising. His work was successful, and by 1911 the Black migration from Oklahoma was ending. Initially unaware of their Black agent's success, the Canadian federal Cabinet of Wilfrid Laurier approved an Order-in-Council barring anyone of African descent from entering Canada. When the agent's accomplishments became clear, the order was quietly withdrawn.

The majority of the Black settlers who made it over Canada's immigration barriers headed to Edmonton and established a number of settlements in an area around the Alberta capital. The largest settlement in Saskatchewan was north of Maidstone, along the **NORTH SASKATCHEWAN RIVER**, in what became known as the Eldon district. By 1912 the Shiloh Baptist Church, which still stands, had been erected, giving form and substance to the community. The Eldon settlers also tried to create a school district so that their children could obtain an education in their new country. They encountered an inordinate number of delays and obstructions until it was revealed that the White settlers of the area refused to send their children to school with Blacks. While eventually resolved, the dispute meant that a racially segregated school existed in Saskatchewan for several years.

As with so many rural areas across the

Canadian plains, the Eldon district began losing its young people to the economic lure of the region's cities during and after **WORLD WAR II**. They encountered racial prejudice there, and many were forced to take menial jobs. Young Black men were particularly discriminated against. One of the few occupations open to them was as porters and baggage handlers on the railroads; the more lucrative and prestigious position of conductor was closed to them for many years. A significant result of this discrimination was that Blacks from the Canadian plains region were scattered to railroad centres across the country. Today, African-Canadian families from Vancouver to Montreal have roots in the prairies due to the northward migration of African Americans nearly a century ago. *See also* **BLACKS: RECENT IMMIGRATION, AMERICAN IMMIGRATION, ETHNIC BLOC SETTLEMENTS.**

Bruce Shepard

FURTHER READING: Shepard, R.B. 1997. *Deemed Unsuitable.* Toronto: Umbrella Press; Winks, R.W. 1971. *The Blacks in Canada: A History.* Montreal: McGill-Queen's University Press.

BLACKS: RECENT IMMIGRATION.

Black residents of Saskatchewan have come from many different countries, at different times, and for different reasons, and their experiences have been just as diverse as their places of origin. The term "Blacks" is used here to denote people of African descent in Canada. The category is made up of three subgroups: Canadian-born descendants of Blacks who came from Africa during the slave trade; descendants of Black Loyalists, refugees, fugitives and settlers who migrated during the American Civil War; and those who migrated mostly from the Caribbean and Africa after World War II, in search of a better socio-economic and political environment. It should be noted, however, that Statistics Canada uses the term "Blacks" in its categorization of race in the Canadian census. Until the 1966 census, Canadians were not officially disaggregated into races: it was thus difficult to procure empirical data on Black Canadians. As a consequence, some pre-1996 data used in this entry are mostly approximations derived from a variety of sources.

In 1865, following the defeat of the South in the American Civil War, slavery was abolished; but a new era of political and social segregation ensued. Blacks in Oklahoma, who were technically free to own property and be subject to the same law as everyone else, faced impossible constraints and economic disadvantages. They began to move to the Canadian prairies in search of equity in the early 20th century. One of their earliest settlements in Canada was Maidstone, Saskatchewan. Despite this initial move, it was not until half a century later that Blacks started to arrive in Saskatchewan in larger numbers. Since the 1960s, as a result of changes in

Canada's immigration policy, the country has witnessed a major immigration of Blacks, primarily from the Caribbean and to a lesser extent from tropical Africa. Black migration has continued to increase, although at a much lower pace than other visible minority migrants. Most of the recent Black immigrants from Africa within the last ten years have come from Somalia, Eritrea and, more recently, the Sudan. *See also* BLACKS: EARLY SETTLEMENTS, VISIBLE MINORITIES, IMMIGRANT INTEGRATION.

Patience Elabor-Idemudia

FURTHER READING: Mensah, J. 2002. *Black Canadians: History, Experiences, Social Conditions.* Halifax: Fernwood Publishing.

BLAINE LAKE, town, pop 508, 80 km N of Saskatoon at the junction of Hwys 12 and 40. Although there was some settlement in the area as early as the 1880s, it was in 1899 with the arrival of the Doukhobors that significant numbers of people settled the region. Within a few years, they were joined by French people from Brittany and eastern Canada, and still others coming northward from the United States. Within ten to fifteen years, the communal villages of the Doukhobors were largely abandoned, as many had moved on to colonies in eastern Saskatchewan or to British Columbia. Those who remained in the area became independent landowners, and the town of Blaine Lake and the district today still reflect a strong Doukhobor heritage. Today, the town is the major trading centre in the district. Area attractions include the Doukhobor Settlement Caves, temporary riverbank dwellings constructed in 1899, and the Popoff Tree, reputedly Saskatchewan's largest tree, with a girth of 4.9 metres (16 ft. 1 inch). *See also* DOUKHOBOR SETTLEMENT. *David McLennan*

BLAIR, ALLAN WALKER (1900–48). Allan Walker Blair was born on November 28, 1900, at Brussels, Ontario, and was 11 when his family moved to Regina, where he attended Victoria School and Central Collegiate. He earned a BA from the UNIVERSITY OF SASKATCHEWAN in 1924, and MD CM degrees from McGill University in 1928. Blair taught Pathology at the University of Alabama School of Medicine in Tuscaloosa (1929–34), and studied surgery in Winnipeg in 1934–35. He was the first Canadian awarded a Rockefeller Fellowship to study cancer at New York Memorial Hospital, in 1935–36; he also visited cancer centres in Great Britain, France, Belgium, Sweden and Germany in 1936–37.

Blair was an associate in Radiotherapy at the Toronto General Hospital for two years before returning home to Regina to take charge of Radiotherapy in 1939. When the 1944 Cancer Control Act entitled Saskatchewan patients to free diagnosis and treatment, he became director of

SASKATCHEWAN ARCHIVES BOARD R-B11015
Allan Walker Blair.

Saskatchewan Cancer Services and the Regina Cancer Clinic. After his death from coronary thrombosis on November 9, 1948, the new cancer clinic building was named in memory of Allan Blair's inspired leadership and contributions to cancer care. The *Regina Leader-Post* recognized him as a great healer, adding that "his wit was delightful, the twinkle in his eye constant." *Pat Krause*

BLAKE, JOYCE (1931–). Joyce Blake's dedication to her professional career and years of volunteer service have earned her numerous awards and honours. She was director of Personnel Services at the UNIVERSITY OF REGINA for several years and president of the Soroptimist International of the Americas, a federation of women's service clubs. In addition, Blake served as president of the Regina YWCA and was the first women to act as people's warden of St. Paul's Cathedral. A recipient of the "Living Legacy Award" from the Women's International Centre, Joyce Blake was invested as a Member of the Order of Canada in 1986.

BLAKENEY, ALLAN E. (1925–). Allan Emrys Blakeney was Premier of Saskatchewan between 1971 and 1982. Born in Bridgewater, Nova Scotia on September 7, 1925, he was a gold medalist in law school at Dalhousie University in Halifax. He won a Rhodes Scholarship to Oxford University, where he studied economics, modern history and philosophy.

Following his return to Canada, Blakeney went to work for the government of T.C. DOUGLAS. He married Molly Schwartz in Halifax just prior to moving to Regina in 1950. She was to die suddenly in 1957, and Blakeney was remarried in 1959 to Anne Gorham.

Blakeney occupied increasingly senior posts in the civil service, then in 1960 he won election as an MLA and was soon appointed to Cabinet. In 1962, the CCF government introduced North America's

first public, tax-financed health care system. Most doctors were opposed, and on July 1 they went on strike. Blakeney played a key role in the negotiations, and when the crisis ended he was appointed Minister of Health.

Blakeney succeeded WOODROW LLOYD as NDP leader in 1970. Premier ROSS THATCHER called an election for June 1971 and campaigned on his record. The NDP offered a detailed program called New Deal for People, and on June 23 won 45 of 60 seats. Blakeney turned quickly to improving health and social programs—a dental program for children, a prescription drug program, subsidized housing, home care, and a guaranteed income supplement to improve the lot of the elderly poor. The centerpiece of the agriculture program was a Land Bank (*see* AGRICULTURAL POLICY), where the government purchased land, usually from older farmers, and leased it back to others, most often family members.

By 1975, Blakeney had concluded that the key to diversification and prosperity lay in Saskatchewan's burgeoning mineral sector. He created new CROWN CORPORATIONS, such as SASKOIL, that became vehicles for government to become a major player in resource development. When potash companies balked at paying increased royalties and refused to pay their taxes, Blakeney responded by buying out half of the industry and creating the Potash Corporation of Saskatchewan to operate the government's mines.

On the national stage, Blakeney played a significant role in the constitutional debates of the 1980s. Prime Minister Trudeau made known his intention to bring Canada's constitution home from Great Britain, and to add to it a Charter of Rights. Blakeney was apprehensive about Trudeau's charter, which he believed would remove power from elected legislators and hand it to appointed judges. He played a pivotal role in negotiating a compromise where provinces accepted a Charter of Rights, but one that could be overridden by elected Legislatures.

Blakeney seemed poised in 1982 to win a fourth election. His was a clean and competent administration, and one that delivered an unbroken string of budget surpluses despite an activist government agenda. The Conservatives offered both lower taxes

SASKATCHEWAN ARCHIVES BOARD R-A26551

Allan Blakeney, as premier, discusses agricultural issues with a Saskatchewan farmer.

and more spending, a program that was popular but was later to almost bankrupt the province. The NDP suffered a resounding defeat in 1982, retaining a mere eight seats in the Legislature. Blakeney felt he had an obligation to rebuild the party, and he led the NDP into the 1986 election, which the NDP lost despite receiving marginally more votes than the Conservatives. Blakeney resigned in 1987, and was replaced by **ROY ROMANOW** as leader.

Blakeney and his wife Anne then spent two years in Toronto, where he occupied the Bora Laskin Chair in Public Law at Osgoode Hall. Later, they settled in Saskatoon, where he accepted the Law Foundation Chair at the **UNIVERSITY OF SASKATCHEWAN** then remained as a visiting scholar at the College of Law. Blakeney has remained active, serving on numerous boards of directors and volunteer associations, but his most intense engagement has been with South Africa, where he helped to develop the structures for democratic government following the dismantling of apartheid.

Tommy Douglas, summarizing the contributions of his successor, said that Blakeney had proved social democracy is a practical program and not just an impossible dream. He brought to his task as Premier an extraordinary mix of intellect, stamina and experience. He was a principled pragmatist, a decent, extremely capable man who provided good, honest and compassionate government, a most valuable contribution in any age. *Dennis Gruending*

FURTHER READING: Blakeney, Allan. 1980. *The Future of Canada: Speeches and Interviews by Hon. Allan Blakeney in the Course of a Trip to Ontario and Quebec, April 1980.* Regina: Government of Saskatchewan; Blakeney, Allan and Sandford Borins. 1992. *Political Management in Canada.* Whitby, ON: McGraw-Hill Ryerson; Gruending, Dennis. 1990. *Promises to Keep: A Political Biography of Allan Blakeney.* Saskatoon: Western Producer Prairie Books.

SASKATCHEWAN ARCHIVES BOARD R-A4983
Thomas Blakiston.

BLAKISTON, THOMAS WRIGHT (1832–91). Born in Lymington, Hampshire, England, on December 27, 1832, Blakiston served with the Royal Artillery in the Crimea. Appointed as magnetic observer to the **PALLISER EXPEDITION** in 1857, Blakiston traveled inland from Hudson Bay to reach Cumberland House on October 4 and Carlton on October 23, 1857. He carried out daily magnetic and meteorological observations at Carlton from November 12, 1857, to April 16, 1858. In addition, he recorded 129 species of birds, taking specimens of 100 of them. He wrote down the world's first record of the nests (with four and five eggs) of the ferruginous hawk near the Anerley lakes on April 29 and 30, 1858. He left Carlton about June 10 and Fort Pitt, in what is now Saskatchewan, at the end of June. On his return from surveys of Rocky Mountain passes, he stayed at Carlton from October 23 to December 27, 1858, and then walked on snowshoes to the Red River in Manitoba. From 1861 to 1884, he was the foremost expert on the birds of Japan. He moved to California in 1884 and died at San Diego on October 15, 1891. *C. Stuart Houston*

BLONDEAU, MELANIE (MALANEH) (1866–CA. 1932). Melanie Blondeau was a **MÉTIS** woman who played a prominent role in the preservation and evolution of traditional Indigenous arts. She was born on April 9, 1866, on the Little Saskatchewan. The last of the plains buffalo hunters, the Blondeaus settled near the Qu'Appelle mission on Lake Katepwa. Following her father's death, Melanie supported her elderly mother and aunt with her skills in beadwork, quillwork and embroidery. In 1913 she came to the attention of the Canadian Handicraft Guild. Melanie's excellent work and personal qualities resulted in the guild's urging the Department of Indian Affairs to hire her at the local residential school; as a result, the Qu'Appelle school was the only residential school in Canada to employ a full-time craft instructor. She was employed from 1914 to 1931, working for $20 a month and never earning more than $240 annually. In the 1930s **CREE** Elders identified floral designs like those she used as a relatively new phenomenon, the result of Métis influence. Teaching hundreds of girls during her career, Melanie Blondeau played a significant role in both the preservation of traditional arts and the evolution of 20th-century First Nations beadwork. She died around 1932. *Sherry Farrell Racette*

BLOORE, RON (1925–). Ronald Langley Bloore was born on May 29, 1925, in Brampton, Ontario. After studying art and archaeology at the University of Toronto, New York University, and Washington University in St. Louis, he traveled to Europe to continue his studies in Brussels, Antwerp, and London. He lectured in art history at the University of Toronto before coming to Regina as instructor of art and archaeology at Regina College, and as director of the Norman **MACKENZIE ART GALLERY**. Bloore was based in Regina for only a brief period of time, from 1958 to 1966; but while there he made a deep and

SHERRY FARRELL RACETTE PHOTO/GLENBOW MUSEUM AR 12
Melanie Blondeau, tea cozy, floral quillwork on leather, © 1913.

HANK ROEST PHOTO
Ronald Bloore's Sign #5, oil on masonite, 1961.

lasting impression. As director, he was noted for his energy and determination in bringing the art world to the prairies: he sponsored and contributed to the infamous "Win Hedore" exhibit, along with **TED GODWIN** and **KEN LOCHHEAD**, where car parts and buckets of sand challenged viewers' notions of art; and he acquired for the gallery the sculpture "Mother and Child" by Jacques Lipchitz—a bold and farsighted move at the time.

Bloore, who constantly painted while studying and teaching as an art historian, finally painted fully non-representational works soon after arriving in Saskatchewan. In Regina, he produced such works as "White Sun-Green Rim" (1960), "Double Sun" (1960), "Byzantium" (1961), and the "White Line Series" from 1963 to 1965. With a few notable exceptions, these mark the beginning of Bloore's entry into white. Asked if the prairie winter landscape influenced this move, Bloore answered that while the prairie affected his vision of light, texture and space, the shift to white was inspired by Egypt and Greece. In 1961, in conjunction with the annual meeting of the Canadian Museums Association, Bloore mounted a show of local contemporary art called simply "The May Show." The National Gallery of Canada remounted the exhibit in Ottawa, without the architect **CLIFFORD WIENS**, as "Five Painters from Regina," and then travelled the show across Canada. Bloore, Ken Lochhead, **ART MCKAY**, Ted Godwin, and **DOUG MORTON**, made a lasting impression on the Canadian art scene; by 1966, however, the **REGINA FIVE** had gone their separate ways.

Bloore left Regina in 1966 to teach visual art and art history at York University in Toronto, where he remained for the rest of his academic career. He now employs his retirement to paint full time.

Mark Vajcner

FURTHER READING: Heath, T. 1991. *Ronald L. Bloore: Not Without Design*. Regina: MacKenzie Art Gallery; Verrall, K. 1999. "Five Painters in Ottawa: The Governance of Exhibitionary Spaces." MA Thesis, York University.

BLUE, GRACE E. (1891–1992). Grace Blue (maiden name unknown), an educator and prominent volunteer worker, played an important role in the establishment of the provincial Home and School movement that sought to enhance co-operative teacher-parent relationships. Born in Emerson, Manitoba in 1891, she graduated from Winnipeg Normal School, then taught in rural, town, and city schools. She married A.M. (Monty) Blue; they had two sons. After her marriage, she moved to Saskatoon. In 1926 she founded the **HOME AND SCHOOL** movement and served as first president of the Buena Vista Home and School Association. Blue helped to organize the first citywide council in Saskatoon, and also participated in the organization and leadership of the Association provincially and

nationally. Blue was the first woman elected to the High School Collegiate Board in Saskatoon. She served on the first advisory committees for the **SALVATION ARMY** and the School for the Deaf, was president for the Women's Canadian Club, and became a life member of the Saskatoon Council of Women. During **WORLD WAR II** she did extensive voluntary work to support the war effort, and served in leadership positions with wartime women's committees in Saskatoon. She had an honorary membership in the **SASKATCHEWAN TEACHER'S FEDERATION**, and received the Canadian Red Cross Society Badge of Service and a Centennial Medal. Grace Blue died on August 7, 1992 in Saskatoon. *Daria Coneghan*

FURTHER READING: Younger, M. (ed.). 1976. *Some Outstanding Women: They made Saskatoon a Better Community*. Saskatoon: University of Saskatchewan Printing Services.

BLUEBIRDS: *see* **THRUSHES AND BLUEBIRDS**

BOER WAR. Fought from October 12, 1899, until May 31, 1902, the Boer War, also known as the South African War, was an Imperialist-Nationalist conflict between Britain and the Afrikaner-populated regions of Southern Africa. The first major overseas expedition by Canadian troops occurred during the Boer War. During the course of the war, four contingents of Canadian troops were mustered. The first contingent of Canadian volunteers was infantry, but subsequently the British requested mounted troops. As a result, the Second Mounted Rifles was mustered in Regina with the majority of recruits coming from British Columbia, Manitoba, and the North-West Territories. The Second Mounted Rifles was dominated by members of the NWMP and all of the regiment's officers were NWMP. The Second Mounted Rifles departed from Regina in January 1900. Two additional regiments were created: in 1901, the Lord Strathcona's Horse, under the command of Col. **SAM**

STEELE; and in the spring of 1902 a fourth recruitment drive was held, but these troops were not deployed due to the cessation of hostilities. Of the 8,372 Canadians who participated in the Boer War, 89 were killed in action, and 181 died from accidental causes and disease. A further 252 Canadians were wounded during the Boer War. *Peter Borch*

FURTHER READING: Hawkes, John. 1924. *The Story of Saskatchewan and Its People*. Chicago: Clarke; Nasson, Bill. 1999. *The South African War, 1899–1902*. London: Arnold, 1999; Pakenham, Thomas. 1979. *The Boer War*. New York: Random House.

BOLD EAGLE. Bold Eagle, a unique program for Aboriginal youth developed by the Canadian Department of National Defence in partnership with First Nations organizations from across western Canada, originated with the **FEDERATION OF SASKATCHEWAN INDIAN NATIONS** in 1988 and has expanded to include participation by Aboriginal youth from all four western provinces and northwestern Ontario. The goals of the program are to develop self-confidence, self-discipline, physical fitness and teamwork skills. Bold Eagle consists of two parts: the development of cultural awareness through participation in a four-day "culture camp," and military recruit training. To participate in Bold Eagle, candidates must be of Aboriginal or **MÉTIS** background, be at least 16 years of age, and have completed Grade 10 or equivalent. Participants are enrolled as recruits in the Canadian Forces at the beginning of the program.

The purpose of the culture awareness aspect is to ease the transition for the participants from civilian to military life. The culture camp is conducted by Elders of different First Nations and Aboriginal groups, and focuses on common spiritual beliefs. Participants and their friends and families have the opportunity to attend a powwow as part of the program. The provision of Aboriginal cultural awareness is a key component of Bold Eagle; it

Recruits for the Bold Eagle program, July 1991.

differentiates the program from all other military training programs of the Canadian Forces. Participants also attend the standard five-week Army Reserve basic military training course, held at Wainwright (Alberta) during the months of July and August. Taught by military personnel, the course includes general military knowledge, weapons handling, drill first aid, as well as navigation and survival skills. At the conclusion of the course, successful graduates are eligible to enroll in the Regular or Reserve components of the Canadian Forces.

Stewart Mein

BOLDT, ARNOLD (1957–). Despite losing his right leg in a farm accident at age 3, Arnold Boldt excelled as a disabled high jumper and athlete. Born in Osler, Saskatchewan on September 16, 1957, Boldt became interested in track and field at elementary school and was told by his prosthetist about athletics for amputees. He competed at the 1976 Toronto Paralympiad, where he won two gold medals and set world records in high jump and long jump. He also won a gold medal in volleyball and a bronze in the 100-metre breaststroke. Boldt was a gold medalist in the jumping events at the 1977 and 1978 Canadian Games for the Physically Disabled. At the Olympiad for the Disabled in July 1980, he broke his world record in high jump with a mark of 1.96 metres; he also won a gold medal in the long jump. He capped off his career with a gold medal in the high jump at the 1992 Barcelona Paralympic Games. Boldt's best jump stands at 2.08 metres. He was inducted into the Canadian Sports Hall of Fame in 1977 and the SASKATCHEWAN SPORTS HALL OF FAME in 1980. *Daria Coneghan and Holden Stoffel*

BOLEN, MEL (1947–). Since 1977, Mel Bolen has worked full-time as a ceramic artist from a home studio located in a converted church near Humboldt. Born in Regina, Bolen studied engineering at the UNIVERSITY OF REGINA in1966–67, before switching to the Bachelor of Fine Arts program. Following graduation in 1971, he worked as a pottery instructor for the city of Regina for one year, before becoming head of the University of Regina's Extension Pottery Department from 1972 to 1976. After one year at the UNIVERSITY OF SASKATCHEWAN, where he taught off-campus credit classes in ceramics, he established his current practice in Humboldt. A long-time member of the Saskatchewan Craft Council, Bolen is best known for his functional ware—bowls, platters, planters—which he and his partner, Karen Holden, market through their company, North Star Pottery. Bolen has periodically obtained SASKATCHEWAN ARTS BOARD and Canada Council grants, which have permitted him to take sabbatical leaves from his commercial practice to produce more personal, non-functional items in the vein of ceramic sculpture. Freed from the dictates of

the marketplace, Bolen then experiments with various clay mixtures, glazes and firing techniques. During Expo 86 in Vancouver, he served as a demonstrator and exhibitor at the Saskatchewan Pavilion.

Gregory Beatty

BONNEAU, SOLOMON (1888–1976). A lawyer and pillar of the town of Gravelbourg, Solomon Bonneau was born in Winnipeg on July 18, 1888. Educated at St. Boniface College and the University of Manitoba where he received his LLB, Bonneau came to Gravelbourg and was called to the Saskatchewan Bar in 1918. Besides practicing law, he purchased a printing plant in 1927 and published several weekly newspapers in French and English throughout the 1930s. He was the town's mayor for seven years and performed numerous public, administrative, cultural, and athletic functions. Solomon Bonneau was awarded the Centennial Medal in 1967, and the Order of Canada shortly before his death on September 29, 1976.

BORNSTEIN, ELI (1922–). Eli Bornstein, artist and educator, was born on December 28, 1922, in Milwaukee, Wisconsin. He received a BSc from the Milwaukee State Teachers' College in 1945, after briefly studying at the Art Institute in Chicago in 1943. He was an instructor at the Milwaukee Art Institute from 1943 to 1947, and taught design at the University of Wisconsin, Milwaukee in 1949. He was appointed head of the new Department of Fine Arts at the UNIVERSITY OF SASKATCHEWAN in 1950. During summer breaks from his university commitments, Bornstein studied at art academies in Paris and completed an MSc at the University of Wisconsin, Madison in 1954. He resigned as head of Fine Arts in 1971, but continued to teach art at the University of Saskatchewan until his retirement in 1990.

Bornstein is best known for the three-dimensional structurist reliefs that he started doing in 1957. His previous drawings, paintings, prints and sculptures were based on nature but used abstract and cubist techniques. His first commission was for "Growth Motif," an abstract welded aluminum sculpture for the SASKATCHEWAN TEACHERS' FEDERATION in 1956. During a sabbatical spent in Italy and Holland in 1957, Bornstein experimented with reliefs; the works progressed in complexity using colour, form, and space, with multiplaned bases which create varying shadows as the light changes. Major works are now in the International Air Terminal in Winnipeg (1962), the WASCANA CENTRE AUTHORITY building in Regina (1982), and on the CANADIAN LIGHT SOURCE Building in Saskatoon (2004). Bornstein has had solo and group shows in Canada, the United States, and Europe. Several private and public galleries include his work.

In 1960 Bornstein founded the journal *The*

Structurist, which reflects his interdisciplinary interest in the artist as builder using the forms and processes of science, technology, and nature. Since its inception, the journal has appeared annually or biannually. Each issue of the journal is focused on a theme such as Continuity and Connectedness, Transparency & Reflection, or the Artist. Bornstein is particularly interested in nature and ecological themes. *Bob Ivanochko*

FURTHER READING: Karpuszko, K. 1982. *Eli Bornstein: Selected Works/Oeuvres Choisies, 1957–1982.* Saskatoon: Mendel Art Gallery.

BOTHWELL, GEORGE R. (1916–96). Born in Winnipeg on June 4, 1906, George Bothwell combined careers in journalism and advertising with a life-long dedication to volunteer service. From 1932 to 1943, he worked as a journalist in Regina, and following WORLD WAR II, as an advertising and publicity manager for SASKATCHEWAN GOVERNMENT INSURANCE. Numerous civic, provincial, and national organizations benefited from Bothwell's leadership as a volunteer. He chaired the board of the Regina Public Library for thirty years, served as director of the SASKATCHEWAN ROUGHRIDERS Football Club for two decades, and was a forty-year member of the Kiwanis Club. In recognition of his service to the province, George Bothwell received the Saskatchewan Order of Merit in 1992.

BOTHWELL, JESSIE ROBSON (1883–1971). Jessie Bothwell was born in Regina on June 17, 1883. After receiving a certificate in library sciences from McGill University in 1931, she became legislative librarian and held this position for twenty-three years. In 1944, as the first female to head a branch of government, she became provincial librarian in charge of legislative, open shelf, and traveling libraries in Saskatchewan. In 1945, she became involved with the establishment of

SASKATCHEWAN ARCHIVES BOARD R-A2916-2

Jessie Robson Bothwell, 1951.

regional libraries. As a result of her efforts the Regional Library Act was passed, and in 1950 the first regional library on the prairies, the North Central Regional Library in Prince Albert, was established. During her civic service, she was also a member of the board of the Regina Public Library and worked as secretary of the Saskatchewan Library Council, formed to study the needs of regional libraries in Saskatchewan. She was made a life member of the Canadian Library Association. Bothwell was also appointed to the Minimum Wage Board and served on the Regina Public School Board. Bothwell Crescent in Regina is named after her and her husband, Austin Bothwell, in recognition of their contribution to the community. She died on November 10, 1971.   *Dagmar Skamlová*

BOUCHER, JOHN B. Born in St. Louis, Saskatchewan, John B. Boucher is a Senator of the **MÉTIS NATION–SASKATCHEWAN**. Since the 1960s, Senator Boucher has been active in **MÉTIS** politics as an advocate of Métis rights, self-governance, and fair land claim settlements. Other organizations that have benefited from his guidance are the St. Louis Métis Local, the Aboriginal Advisory Board for the RCMP, and the Métis National Council. Senator Boucher was made a Member of the Order of Canada in 2002.

BOULDER MONUMENTS. Boulder monuments are patterns traced upon virgin prairie utilizing glacial till boulders to define a desired outline pattern. The boulders most commonly used range from 10cm (4 inches) to 40cm (16 inches) in diameter. In Saskatchewan the boulders are most commonly smooth quartzite or granite cobbles, although some dolomites (limestone) and feldspar stone varieties have been used. In Saskatchewan these monuments extend from the Alberta border to the Manitoba border and from the Prince Albert area south to the international boundary. An additional 200–300 of these monuments have been recorded on the Great Plains beyond Saskatchewan's borders. Their extent across the northern Great Plains ranges from the Rocky Mountain foothills in Alberta, Montana and Wyoming east to Manitoba, Minnesota and Iowa. In Alberta and Saskatchewan they extend south from the region of the 53rd parallel into central Nebraska. Additional boulder outline designs have been recorded as far away as the northern Baja peninsula, southeastern Texas, and central Ontario; however, none of those patterns are deemed to relate to the monuments recorded within the Great Plains/shortgrass prairie environment.

The monuments commonly depict the location of a specific sacred ceremonial activity (see figure, image at left: medicine wheel near Oxbow), an environmental site marker (see figure, image second from left: salamander outline near Mankota), an offering between an individual and his Creator (see figure, image second from right: human figure near Mantario), or the location of a specific ceremony (see figure, image at right: ceremonial circle near Claybank). Currently, 167 of these monuments have been recorded in Saskatchewan; however, only 33 have been mapped. The mapped examples include 11 medicine wheels, 10 ceremonial circles (circles too large in diameter to be considered habitational/tipi ring structures), four human effigies, five animal effigies, and three geometric designs (special ceremony patterns). Medicine wheels are monuments that resemble a wheel pattern; the radiating lines of the pattern are referred to as the spokes. Associated piles of rock are called cairns, while circular patterns of stones are referred to as circles; these latter patterns may be transected by the spokes, or form an encompassing exterior boundary to the monument. Additional research has further subdivided medicine wheels and ceremonial circles into more categories that have been compared with specific First Nations' cultural ceremonies, although the different categories may reflect many different cultural groups. The four medicine wheel designs may identify: burials—a central cairn with a minimum of four radiating spokes; surrogate burials—the location where a leader died but was not buried is represented by four spoke lines, without a central cairn structure; medicine hunting structure—a large central cairn with a minimum of four radiating spokes which dissect an encompassing boulder circle, where the spokes terminate at small cairns; and a fertility symbol—a small central cairn with a minimum of four radiating spokes that all terminate at an encompassing boulder circle.

Ceremonial circles are either too large to be tipis (which range in size from 4m to 6m in diameter) or have features that identify them as separate from tipi rings. The four ceremonial circle designs theoretically represent a buffalo fertility symbol (a large central cairn with a pathway extending out to, or beyond a large encompassing boulder circle); a meeting circle, where the boulder circle measures between 18m up to 44m in diameter; a burial (a large central cairn encompassed by a boulder circle); or a ceremonial/dance oval (6m wide and 18m long transected by an interior boulder line, which ends within 2m of one edge). The four human effigies can be positively identified as two males and two females. The animal effigies are identified as two turtles, a badger, a bison and a salamander. The geometric figures record a special sacred site, a resource marker and a raiding shelter.

The first of these outlines was recorded in what is now Saskatchewan in 1864 by William Clandening, an explorer from eastern Canada. The second discovery was mapped and excavated by Henry W. Montgomery, of Illinois, in 1907. Beginning about 1954, the Saskatchewan Museum of Natural History, now the **ROYAL SASKATCHEWAN MUSEUM** (RSM), began a program of detailed mapping and recording of all the known boulder monuments. This practice was continued into the late 1980s, when the recording aspects were transferred

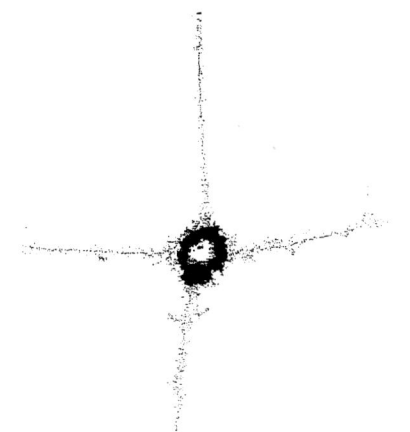   

IMAGES COURTESY OF IAN BRACE

Left to right: Oxbow Medicine Wheel; Mankota Salamander; Cabri Lake Human Effigy; Claybank Ceremonial Circle.

to the Heritage Resource Management branch of the Department of Culture, Youth and Recreation. Only one of the two excavated medicine wheels in Saskatchewan has supplied datable samples: the Moose Mountain medicine wheel has tentatively been dated as about 1,300 years old. Additionally, three Alberta medicine wheels have been tentatively dated as 1,600 years old, 120 years old, and 60 years old. The latter two dates record a possible tradition continuance. The two earliest dates were based upon radiocarbon dating analysis, while the two recent dates were recorded by recent oral history. A lichenometric dating attempt was initiated by the RSM in 1980; however, as lichen diameters increase extremely slowly, that analysis may not produce results for another twenty years. *Ian Brace*

BOULTON'S SCOUTS. Boulton's Scouts were an ad hoc military mounted troop formed at Fort Qu'Appelle during the 1885 **NORTH-WEST RESISTANCE**. The troop was recruited from Boulton's Mounted Corps, which had been raised in the Russell-Birtle district of Manitoba by Major Charles A. Boulton. At its inception, the total strength of Boulton's Mounted Corps consisted of five officers and 123 men; the unit was formed to be the advance guard for General **MIDDLETON**'s column of militia. Middleton's column set out northward from Qu'Appelle to engage Métis forces led by **LOUIS RIEL** and **GABRIEL DUMONT**. Boulton's Scouts fought at Fish Creek and **BATOCHE**; the unit was disbanded in September 1885. *Peter Borch*

BOUNDARIES OF SASKATCHEWAN. The Saskatchewan Act, passed by the Canadian Parliament on September 1, 1905, created the contemporary boundaries of Saskatchewan. The international boundary along the 49th parallel was demarcated first. Internal boundaries–along the 60th parallel in the north; 110° W in the west; and between 60° N, 102° W and 49° N, 101°30' W in the east–were designated between 1881 and 1905.

The 49th parallel was first established as the international boundary by the Treaty of Utrecht in 1713, reinforced by the Treaty of Paris in 1783 and ultimately designated by British-American Convention in 1818. The boundary was initially surveyed between 1872 and 1875.

The Dominion Lands Survey was established in 1868 by a federal Order-in-Council, although events in Red River in 1869 and 1870 prevented its widespread application until 1871. The Dominion Lands Survey enabled the division of western lands among the Hudson's Bay Company (HBC), the **CANADIAN PACIFIC RAILWAY** (CPR) and homesteaders, and set aside two sections in each township for the future of local education. Except in the extreme south, most prairie lands between 50° and 55° north, were surveyed by the end of 1883.

With Canada's purchase of Rupert's Land (the former HBC territory; *see* **RUPERT'S LAND PURCHASE**) and the North-Western Territory from the British in 1870, the region came under the political, social and economic aegis of the Dominion of Canada. Ottawa exerted complete control over the shape, dissemination and regulation of land.

Before the creation of the province of Manitoba, the most important regions of the west had been the HBC's fur-trade districts. As population and administrative demands grew, Ottawa and the territorial governments deemed more internal divisions necessary. The North-West was divided into different units, for different purposes. With the creation of the "Postage Stamp" province of Manitoba in 1870, the internal organization of the North-Western Territory began to change, beginning with its renaming to North-West Territories. In 1878 the administrative centre of the territory was moved from Fort Livingstone to Battleford. Each centre had a land registration office and two more were opened in Westburne and Dufferin. That same year four judicial districts were created. In 1884, these were divided into seven judicial districts, four of which (Regina, Medicine Hat, Calgary and Fort Macleod) were located in the south where the North-West's population was growing rapidly.

By 1880, population numbers warranted the creation of three electoral districts to meet the Canadian standard for representation in the Territorial Assembly. However, in 1881 the province of Manitoba was enlarged by Ottawa (Dominion Act, July 1, 1881) to include the electoral districts of Wallace and Moosomin, North-West Territories. This Act established the ultimate eastern boundary of the province "on the centre of the road allowance between the twenty-ninth and thirtieth ranges west of the Principle Meridian."

In May 1882, four "provisional districts" were created (Figure BSK-1 on facing page). Later, in 1886, Assiniboia was divided into eastern and western districts. These "provisional" districts were not legally defined Canadian provinces, nor were they legal territories, but before 1905 they were the North-West's clearest internal boundaries with the potential to become provinces.

As early as 1872, J.S. Dennis, the Surveyor General of Dominion Lands, had advanced proposals to divide the west into provinces. Plans were reiterated in 1882 and thereafter regularly put forward to the Ottawa government. Before 1905 scenarios for four, three, two and one province had been proposed (Figure BSK-2). The Canadian government only considered those that would result in one or two provinces, with the latter being preferred.

The ruling Liberals (and most vociferously Prime Minister Laurier) cited two reasons for dividing the North-West Territories. The first involved the relative sizes of then contemporary provinces. To

Laurier, it was obvious that a North-West Territories of 1,791,168² km was much too large compared to other provinces. Second, Laurier argued there was a certain economic *raison d'être* for separateness: Alberta was ranching country; Saskatchewan was farming. Provinces would thereby simply be based on land-use patterns and similarities in lifestyles. The actions of Laurier's government to create two provinces, separated along the fourth initial meridian, were consistent with those of Sir John A. Macdonald, who had often emphasized the paramount power of the federal government. However, those boundaries, created on paper in 1905 when Saskatchewan became a province, were not surveyed in their entirety until the end of the 1960s. *Ben Moffat*

FURTHER READING: Brennan, J.W. 1985. "The 'Autonomy Question' and the Creation of Alberta and Saskatchewan, 1905." Pp. 262–379 in R.D. Francis and H. Palmer (eds.), *The Prairie West: Historical Readings.* Edmonton: Pica Pica; Nicholson, N.L. 1979. *The Boundaries of Canada: Its Provinces and Territories.* Ottawa: Carleton Library; Nicholson, N.L., et al. 1990. Plate 2 in "Territorial Evolution," in D. Kerr and D. Holdsworth (eds.), *Historical Atlas of Canada*: Volume III. Toronto: University of Toronto Press.

BOUNDARY SURVEY TRAIL. The Boundary Survey Trail in Saskatchewan was established in 1873-74. The trail was used by both the Dominion and American governments to survey accurately the international boundary (49th parallel) as determined by the London Convention of 1818. The Canadian government commissioned the legal survey after acquiring Rupert's Land (*see* **RUPERT'S LAND PURCHASE**) from the Hudson's Bay Company in 1870. The Boundary Commissioners, consisting of Canadian and American surveyors, first met in Pembina, North Dakota in September 1872. After spending the first winter near Willow Bunch, the party left its winter post in the spring of 1874 and headed for Waterton Lake, where a boundary marker signifying the end of the Pacific-Rocky Mountains survey was already erected. On August 8, 1874, the boundary commission party reached Waterton Lake, erecting the last boundary marker and completing the difficult task of legally surveying the border between Canada and the United States. *James Winkel*

BOUNDARY SURVEYS. Saskatchewan's boundaries were not all surveyed at the same time. The 49th parallel, claimed by the Hudson's Bay Company as the southern limit of its territory in the early 18th century, was agreed in principle as the border between British North America and the United States in 1818. However, it was not surveyed until after the purchase of Rupert's Land (*see* **RUPERT'S LAND PURCHASE**) in 1869; this survey took place in

Figure BSK-1: Provisional Districts.

Assiniboia was split into two regions, East and West, in 1886.

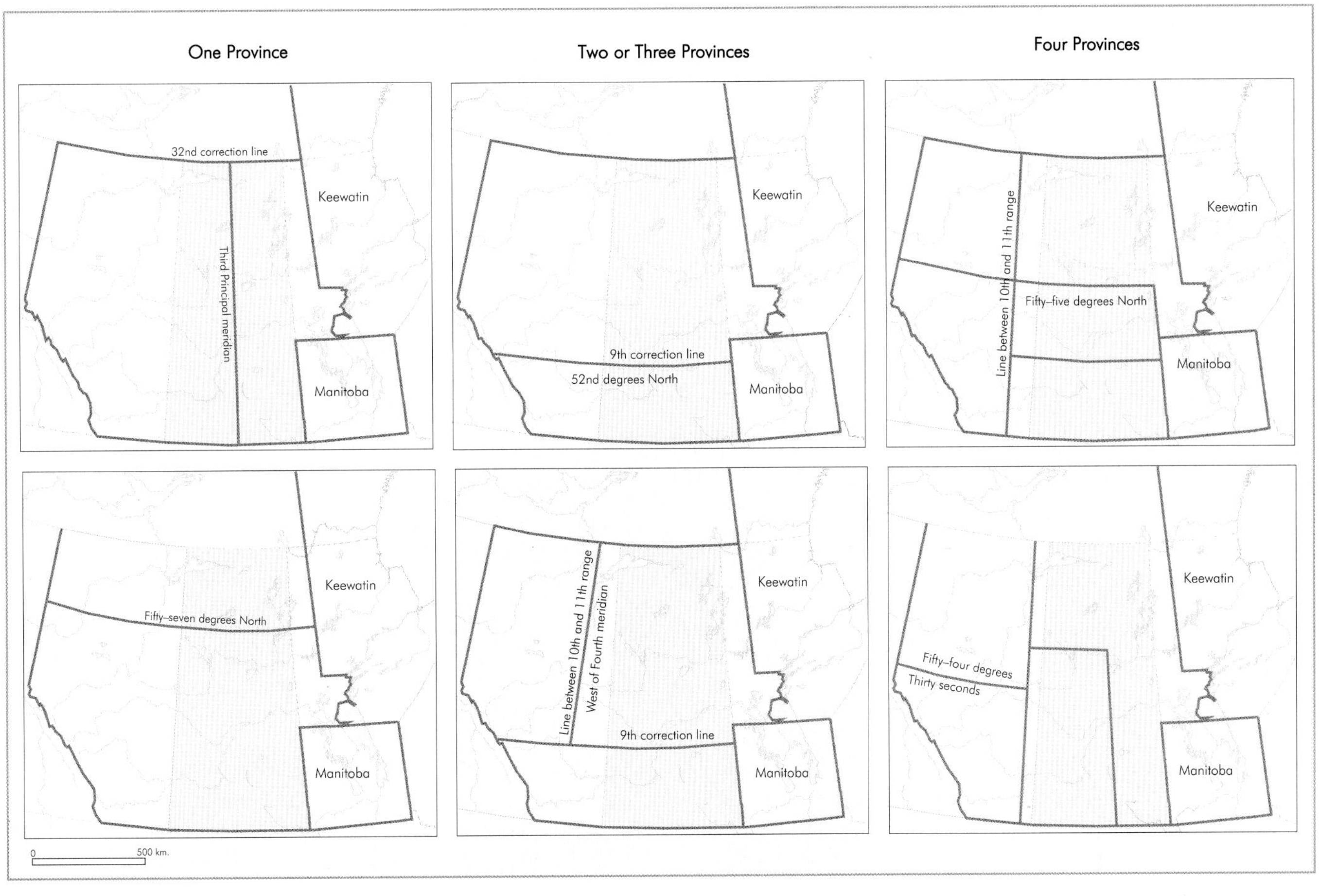

Figure BSK-2: Provincial proposals.

B

1873–74 (*see* **G.M. DAWSON**), with the Saskatchewan section of the international border extending for 630 km from east to west.

After considerable debate over the number and organization of provinces in the west (*see* **BOUNDARIES OF SASKATCHEWAN**), the present-day internal boundaries were designated in 1905 when Saskatchewan became a province. As Alberta and Saskatchewan were both designated as provinces at the same time, the border between them was easily established; it is located along 4th initial meridian at 110°W, and is 1,225 km long.

The eastern border with Manitoba is more complex. Manitoba first became a province in 1870, but was much smaller than today. It was enlarged in 1882, and its western boundary with the adjacent North-West Territories later became part of the Saskatchewan/Manitoba border. This boundary was located along the centre of the road allowance between ranges 29 and 30, west of the prime meridian and intersecting the US border at 101°30'. Because of the use of "correction lines" at the second and every fourth township north of the Canada/US border, this part of the boundary forms a series of north/south segments offset from one another towards the west. In 1905 Saskatchewan's eastern neighbours were Manitoba in the south and the District of Keewatin (NWT) in the north, the border between them being at approximately 52°47' N. Before 1930, only sections of that border had been surveyed. In 1912 Manitoba's borders were extended to the 60th parallel, and in the following years some additional sections were surveyed. The southern, segmented portion of the border extends to the 22nd baseline at 56°20' N. Northward of this it follows the 2nd meridian (approximately 102°W) to the 60th parallel. This northern section of the Saskatchewan/Manitoba boundary was first surveyed in 1961–62; the remaining border was surveyed or resurveyed between 1961 and 1972.

Saskatchewan's northern border, some 445 km long, runs along the 60th parallel. Surveying began in December 1954 and was completed in March 1958. On August 15, 1963, a ceremony was held at the junction between Saskatchewan, Manitoba and the Northwest Territories to celebrate completion of both the interprovincial boundary and the survey along the 60th parallel from the Alaska Panhandle to Hudson Bay. An aluminum obelisk, containing letters addressed to government officers in the year 2063, marks the intersection of these borders.

Marilyn Lewry

FURTHER READING: Nicholson, N.L. 1954. The Boundaries of Canada, its Provinces and Territories. Ottawa: Department of Mines and Technical Surveys.

BOURGAULT INDUSTRIES. Bourgault Industries is an innovative agricultural implement manu-

facturer based in St. Brieux, Saskatchewan. In 1973, Frank Bourgault, an area farmer and skilled mechanic, established Bourgault Industries to design and market a durable, high-quality cultivator better able to break the notoriously stony soils of the St. Brieux region. In 1974, with a local workforce of ten and a 4,000-square-foot production facility, Bourgault Industries began rapid production of Bourgault's prototype cultivator. Within five years, Bourgault Industries had produced and sold nearly 1,000 cultivators and 9,000 harrow units, while increasing its workforce to seventy-five. From such modest beginnings, Bourgault Industries has become a world leader in the design and production of leading-edge agricultural equipment, most notably air seeders, cultivators, plows, drills, bale movers, and grain carts. Today, Bourgault Industries owns and operates manufacturing plants in Canada, the United States and Australia, and continues to probe new market areas in Eastern Europe and Asia. Bourgault Industries maintains a staff of over 350 and operates 250,000 square feet of production space in St. Brieux. In 2001, Bourgault Industries was inducted into the Saskatchewan Business Hall of Fame for its longstanding commitment to the economy and people of Saskatchewan. *Iain Stewart*

FURTHER READING: Sinkewicz, P. 1998. "St. Brieux Partnership More Than Business," *Saskatoon StarPhoenix* (April 9): C12.

BOWEN, GAIL (1942–). One of Canada's most popular crime writers, Gail Bowen is the author behind the Joanne Kilbourn mystery series. Born Gail Bartholomew in Toronto, she was educated at the University of Toronto, where she received a BA in 1964, and at the University of Waterloo, where she graduated with an MA in 1975. Bowen undertook post-graduate studies at the **UNIVERSITY OF SASKATCHEWAN** from 1975 to 1979. She married Ted

PHOTO BY TED BOWEN

Gail Bowen.

Bowen in 1968 and lives with her family in Regina. Bowen's first book, *1919: The Love Letters of George and Adelaide* (1987), was a novella written in collaboration with Ronald Marken, a University of Saskatchewan professor. The first title in the Kilbourn series, *Deadly Appearances* (1990), was nominated for the W.H. Smith/Books in Canada award for best first novel. It was followed by *Murder at the Mendel* (1991), *The Wandering Soul Murders* (1992), *A Colder Kind of Death* (1994), which won the Arthur Ellis Award for best crime novel, *A Killing Spring* (1996), *Verdict in Blood* (1998), *Burying Ariel* (2000), and *The Glass Coffin* (2002). A new novel in the series, *The Last Good Days* was published in 2004.

Set in Saskatchewan, the Kilbourn mysteries focus on a **UNIVERSITY OF REGINA** professor who finds herself reluctantly aiding the police in solving various local murders. The series has been popular locally, nationally, and internationally with the novels being translated into various languages. The first six novels in the series have also been adapted for television and star actress Wendy Crewson as Joanne Kilbourn. Bowen has also written several plays which have been produced at theatres throughout Canada. An associate professor and head of the English department at the **FIRST NATIONS UNIVERSITY OF CANADA**, Bowen began her teaching career at the University of Saskatchewan and the Saskatchewan Indian Cultural College in Saskatoon before moving to Regina in 1979. There, she taught at the University of Regina and the Saskatchewan Indian Federated College, the forerunner to the First Nations University. Besides teaching and writing, Bowen has contributed to CBC radio both locally and nationally as an arts columnist and political commentator. In the role of guest lecturer, she has delivered speeches and readings in Vancouver, Calgary, Ottawa, and extensively throughout Saskatchewan. She holds memberships in the **SASKATCHEWAN WRITERS GUILD** and the Writers' Union of Canada. *Mark Vajcner*

BOWMAN, LILLIE (1894–1969). Born in Ontario on October 16, 1894, Lillie Bowman came to Saskatoon in 1909. She married Aden Bowman, pioneer businessman and city councillor (1941–52); they had four children. As city councilor from 1955 to 1964, she served on several boards: police commission, transit (as chair), parks and recreation, municipal library, hospital, and assessment. She was also on the housing and centennial committees, and involved with the Playgrounds Association. While councillor she supported construction of the **MENDEL ART GALLERY** and of new municipal buildings. She also served on the Saskatchewan Urban Municipalities Association executive. Bowman was a board member for the **SALVATION ARMY**, YMCA, and Saskatoon Branch of the Canadian National Institute for the Blind. Concerned about victims of addiction, she was a director of the Saskatoon Alcoholism Association, led the **WOMEN'S CHRISTIAN TEMPERANCE UNION**, and helped establish Hope Haven (Saskatoon). Other interests included Bethany Hospital, United Church Women's Missionary Society, Saskatoon Council of Women, and the Board of Trade industrial promotion committee. In 1963 Bowman was recipient of the Saskatoon Quota Club Woman of the Year Award. She died on August 21, 1969.   *Ruth Wright Millar*

BOYER, BOB (1948–2004). Bob Boyer was a painter, installation artist, powwow dancer, social activist, educator, author of several art catalogues and reviews, curator of a significant number of art exhibitions, and a national and international exhibitor. He was born on July 20, 1948 in Prince Albert of **MÉTIS** heritage. In 1971, he received a BEd (Arts Education) from the **UNIVERSITY OF REGINA**, and upon returning to Prince Albert began teaching at St. Mary's High School. In 1977, Boyer was hired as program consultant for the Saskatchewan Indian Federated College's (now the **FIRST NATIONS UNIVERSITY OF CANADA**), Department of Indian Fine Arts. He was Department Head between 1979 and 1997, and was a highly respected art and art history instructor.

Boyer's career as a professional artist began in 1971 and was recognized as a critical element in the development of contemporary First Nations art. His artistic versatility enabled him to move from one medium and technique to another, incorporating Northern Plains First Nations geometric design to reflect personal experiences, social issues, and spirituality. Boyer was best known for his politically

charged "blanket statements," which critically reviewed the effects of non-First Nation influence on First Nations people and land. He painted these accounts on blanket canvasses representing the distribution of Hudson's Bay blankets infected with smallpox, and each piece marks how colonialism impacted the Aboriginal and Métis people. In 1994 Boyer's work underwent a change in direction, and although he continued to use traditional symbols, motifs and icons, his art began to exhibit a place of spiritual calm from which he celebrated First Nations' cultures, peoples and events.

Boyer's artistic influence and teaching have provided direction and understanding to First Nations and non-First Nation students alike for First Nations' art and art history. Bob Boyer died on August 30, 2004.   *Christian Thompson*

BRABANT LAKE, northern settlement, located 172 km NE of La Ronge on gravel Hwy 102, amidst the forests and lakes of the **PRECAMBRIAN SHIELD**. This small community is situated just north of the lake from which it derives its name. The population is predominantly **CREE**. The 2001 Census recorded 102 permanent residents; more recent estimates, however, put the number closer to 70. Trapping, fishing, guiding, some construction work, and mining provide employment, much of which is seasonal. In the late 1990s, a significant archaeological discovery was made on the southwest shore of Brabant Lake after forest fires exposed campsites and artifacts which indicated people have lived in the area for at least 2,500 years; non-indigenous clays and stone materials revealed travel and contact with other areas; evidence of ceremonial activity was also found.   *David McLennan*

DON HEALY/REGINA LEADER-POST
Judy Bradley, March 2001.

BRADLEY, JUDY LLEWELLYN (1952–). Born in Regina on October 18, 1952, Judy Bradley (*née* Bratt) grew up on the family farm in the Milestone-Gray area. She earned a BSc and a BEd from the **UNIVERSITY OF REGINA**, taught biology at Sheldon Williams Collegiate in Regina, and later returned to Milestone to teach elementary and special education. In 1973 she married Gary Bradley, a farmer and carpenter, with whom she has three children. Bradley was elected in Bengough-Milestone in the 1991 general election, and re-elected in 1995 to represent the newly redistributed riding of Weyburn-Big Muddy. In 1997 she was appointed Minister of Highways and Transportation as well as Minister responsible for the Status of Women. As the first female Minister of Highways and Transportation, she steered the department through a tumultuous period: road conditions became a major political issue, as the department implemented a policy of returning some minor highways to gravel roads. Bradley was also a strong advocate for bringing short-line railways to rural communities. Defeated in the 1999 provincial election, she returned to Milestone and resumed her teaching career.   *Derek de Vlieger*

BRADSHAW, JOHN ERNEST (1866–1917). John Bradshaw was born on the Isle of Wight on December 13, 1866. He immigrated to Canada with his family as a teenager. In 1891 he joined the Hudson's Bay Company which appointed him manager of its branch in Prince Albert where he met and married Agnes Thompson in 1894. They had five children. Bradshaw left the HBC in 1900 to establish an insurance business in Prince Albert. He served as alderman from 1895 to 1905 and became mayor of

ROY ANTAL/REGINA LEADER-POST
Bob Boyer at Cumberland Gallery in the Saskatchewan Legislative Building, November 7, 2001.

the city in 1906. A year later he ran unsuccessfully for the Provincial Rights (Conservative) Party in a by-election in Prince Albert, but defeated the sitting member, **W.F.A. TURGEON**, in the general election of 1908. He won the seat as a Conservative in other elections. He raised the question of votes for women in the Legislature in 1912 and kept pressing it until the **SCOTT** government introduced enabling legislation in the 1916 session. He accused Liberal Cabinet Ministers and backbenchers of accepting bribes. He demanded and won three Royal Commissions to investigate his charges. By the time they reported Premier Scott and four Liberal members had resigned and two others had been expelled from the Legislature. In the election of 1917, Conservative representation at Regina dropped, and Bradshaw himself was defeated in part due to the national Conservative's determination to introduce conscription. Bradshaw's recruitment of an infantry battalion during the war and his willingness to act as its colonel, did him no good politically. He died on Christmas day, 1917.   *Patrick Kyba*

FURTHER READING: Smith, David E. 1998. "Bradshaw, John Ernest." *Dictionary of Canadian Biography*. Toronto: University of Toronto Press; Saskatchewan Archives Board. J.E. Bradshaw Papers. A-35. Saskatoon; Ward, N. and D.E. Smith. 1990. *Jimmy Gardiner: Relentless Liberal*. Toronto: University of Toronto Press.

BRADY, JAMES PATRICK (1908–67?). MÉTIS leader and prospector James Brady was born on March 11, 1908, at Lac St. Vincent, Alberta. He was the son of James Brady Sr., a well-respected non-Aboriginal storekeeper, and Philomena Archange, a nurse. At an early age, Brady was influenced by family members—particularly his maternal grandfather, Laurent Garneau—who were strong social advocates for **MÉTIS** identity and social equality. During the 1920s Brady worked as a labourer, and through reading and life experience began to understand the inner workings of politics, socialism, and the labour movement. In response to the adverse social conditions facing Alberta's Métis, Brady became a social and political activist; and in 1939, with the help of **MALCOLM NORRIS** and Joseph Dion, he founded L'Association des Métis de l'Alberta. When **WORLD WAR II** broke out, Brady enlisted, but was at first refused because of his Communist affiliations. In 1943, he was admitted into the Royal Canadian Artillery. Brady's war experience greatly impacted his world view, making him further aware of the Métis' oppression in western Canada. In 1947 he moved to northern Saskatchewan, where he worked as a prospector and, for a time, for the Department of Natural Resources under the new socialist CCF government. In the north, Brady and Norris were reunited and began organizing the northern Métis and Non-Status Indians through the Métis Associa-

tion of Saskatchewan. In June 1967, Brady and fellow prospector Abbie Halkett disappeared while on a prospecting expedition in the Foster Lakes area. An extensive RCMP search ensued, but they were never found. Many believe that the two men were murdered for political reasons.   *Cheryl Troupe*

BRANDT, ELISABETH H. (1922–99). Born in Austria on May 29, 1922, and educated in the United States, Dr. Elisabeth Brandt specialized as a speech language pathologist with an expertise in communications disorders. Along with her husband, Brandt moved to Regina in 1968. She is best remembered for her role in developing SCEP Centre, a non-government organization that offered unconventional speech-language therapy for difficult children. Students in medicine, social work, nursing, psychology and education that received training at the centre also benefited from Brandt's influence. In 1981, she was named YWCA Woman of the Year and in 1994 was given a Woman of Distinction Award from the Saskatchewan Branch of Soroptimist International. Dr. Brandt received the Saskatchewan Order of Merit in 1995. She died in 1999.

BRANDT INDUSTRIES LIMITED. Brandt Industries Limited was founded in 1938 by Abram Peter Brandt of Regina, Saskatchewan, under the name Brandt Electric. The company is well known for its innovative products, including one of the first grain augers available in Canada. Brandt has expanded to become the fourth largest private company in Saskatchewan, with over 800 employees throughout Canada in 2003, 350 of whom are employed in Saskatchewan. Brandt has markets in Canada, the United States, Europe, Australia, and Asia. Brandt Industries Limited is comprised of five independent divisions. Brandt Agricultural Products Ltd. manufactures spraying equipment, heavy harrows, a versatile bale processor, and a complete line of grain handling equipment. Brandt Tractor Ltd. is the exclusive John Deere Construction and Forestry Equipment Dealer for Manitoba, Saskatchewan, Alberta and the Northwest Territories, with eight dealerships in Winnipeg, Regina, Saskatoon, Calgary, Red Deer, Edmonton, Grande Prairie and Fort McMurray. Brandt Tractor Ltd. is the largest privately held John Deere Construction and Forestry Equipment Dealer in the world. Brandt Engineered Products Ltd. designs and builds a wide range of custom manufacturing equipment. The companies' products include pipe and material handling equipment, research equipment, specialized railroad equipment, cranes, and large-scale structural equipment. Brandt Equipment Inc. has six industrial and turf equipment dealerships in western Canada, and sells Ditch Witch® trenching as well as a wide range of turf equipment from Textron and Grasshopper. Brandt Road Rail Corporation manufactures and markets

the Brandt Power Unit® at its custom manufacturing facility in Regina. The Brandt Power Unit is a railcar mover that is legal on both road and rail and can shunt up to fifteen 100-ton railcars on a tangent track. Brandt has received many performance and service awards, including the Top 50 Best Managed Private Companies in Canada Award (1994, 1995, 1996); Abex Award for the Saskatchewan Business of the Year (1993); and the John Deere Partner in Excellence Award (1997), which is given to the top seven dealerships in North America.   *Jessica Pothier*

ROY ANTAL/REGINA LEADER-POST
Eleanor Brass, August 1987.

BRASS, ELEANOR (1905–92). Eleanor Brass (*née* Dieter) was born on the Peepeekisis Reserve on May 1, 1905. Her ancestors included two treaty signers, Chief Gabriel Cote and Chief Okanese. She attended high school in Canora, but went to work before graduation, and in 1925 married Hector Brass, also from Peepeekisis. Concerned about the difficulties facing First Nations people, Brass sought to redress them and to educate the White public. In 1944 she became the first woman executive to serve as the secretary-treasurer of the Association of Indians of Saskatchewan; she also helped to establish and run groups like the Indian Friendship Centre in Regina. For several years she was employed by the provincial government to advance Native employment. After retirement, she worked in Alberta, becoming Director of the Peace River Friendship Centre and serving as correspondent for Alberta Native Communication. Her writing career had begun in 1949 when "Breaking the Barriers" appeared in the *Regina Leader-Post*. She wrote extensively in magazines and newspapers, including columns in the *Leader-Post* and the *Melville Advance*. She authored two books: *Medicine Boy and Other Cree Tales* (1979) and the autobiographical *I Walk in Two Worlds* (1987). In 1991 the University of Toronto gave Brass an honorary degree in Literature. She died on May 20, 1992, in Regina.   *Daria Coneghan*

BRASS, OLIVER JOHNSTON (1944–97). Oliver Brass was born in the Fort Qu'appelle Indian Hospital on March 4, 1944. Also known as Thunder Bird Sitting First, he was devoted to his family and to the education of his people. He grew up in a Christian family on the Peepeekesis reserve, and after completing high school earned a Bachelor of Theology (1965) from Aldersgate College in Moose Jaw. On a trip home to give a service at the Free Methodist Church, he met his future wife Sheila, who was teaching on the reserve; they married in 1965 and moved to Broadview, where Brass ministered to area reserves while Sheila taught adult upgrading. Having moved to Regina they both began attending university in 1969, and after graduation returned to Peepeekesis. Brass farmed for three years while serving as band councilor and on the board of the band school. Moving back to Regina, he served as a Free Methodist minister, and family life revolved around the church. Brass again took university classes, and in 1979 began teaching at the Saskatchewan Indian Federated College in the Department of Indian Studies. In 1980 he became a deacon in the Methodist Church; he also served as a pastor of the Big Sky Native Church, and was the director of Native ministries for the Methodist Church of Canada (1983–86). In 1985 he earned his PhD in Canadian Plains Studies from the **UNIVERSITY OF REGINA**, making him the first Status Indian in Saskatchewan to obtain a doctoral degree.

Oliver Brass, February 1990.

In the early 1980s Brass began attending First Nations ceremonies, and after attending his first "Winter Sing" he realized he had come to the heart of Indian culture. In 1986, one year after becoming president of the Saskatchewan Indian Federated College (1985–90), he wrote a letter to the superintendent of the Canada West Free Methodists asking why the "good of the old way" could not be interrelated with the "goodness of the cross." One month later he resigned from the ministry. Brass learned his **SAULTEAUX** language, and by assisting in ceremonies was drawn closer to the inner circle of Saulteaux ceremonialists. He became recognized as a senior servant (*scapiwis*), and having undergone the piercing ceremony four times he had the authority to conduct piercing unassisted. He learned dozens of sacred songs, some of which he sang when he began to hold **SWEAT LODGES** in the summer of 1996. At each step of his spiritual evolution his wife and five children were with him. He died on March 1, 1997.   *Bernard Selinger*

BREDENBURY, town, pop 354, located roughly halfway between Yorkton and the Saskatchewan/ Manitoba border on the Yellowhead Hwy (No. 16). The district began to be settled in the 1880s, mainly by people of British and Icelandic origin. The Manitoba and Northwestern Railway (later taken over by the CPR) came through en route to Yorkton in the late 1880s, and by May 1911 Bredenbury had grown large enough to be incorporated as a village; two years later, the community attained town status. Major employers are the CPR in Bredenbury, and the IMC Kalium potash mines near Esterhazy. A manufacturer of semi-trailers provides additional employment, and the district surrounding Bredenbury sustains a combination of crop and livestock production. Many residents of the community also commute to work in Yorkton, and in recent decades Bredenbury has become somewhat of a bedroom community. Children attend school in Saltcoats until Grade 8, and then travel to Yorkton for high school. A nine-hole golf course is maintained by local volunteers, and Bredenbury is well known for its elaborate displays during the Christmas season.   *David McLennan*

BREITKREUZ, GARRY W. (1945–). Born in Yorkton on October 21, 1945, Breitkreuz was raised near Springside. He obtained a BEd from the **UNIVERSITY OF SASKATCHEWAN** and worked within that field for twenty-four years. Breitkreuz was elected to the House of Commons in 1993 as Reform member for Yorkton-Melville, in 1997 and 2000 for the Canadian Alliance, and in 2004 for the Conservatives. He served as the Deputy Whip of the Opposition between 2000 and 2003, spending four months as Chief Opposition Whip. Breitkreuz was the Opposition's Deputy House Leader in 2004, and

the Firearms and Property Rights Critic, remaining a vocal opponent of the firearms registration scheme throughout his years in office. He sat on the House of Commons' Procedure and House Affairs Standing Committee as deputy critic of the Solicitor General, and of Aboriginal Affairs, and was critic for Unemployment Insurance. Breitkreuz was vice-chair of the Standing Committee on Procedure and House Affairs, and served on the Agriculture and Agri-Food, Justice and Human Rights, and Public Safety and Emergency Preparedness Standing Committees. He introduced a series of private member's motions that reflect his pro-life views, and in March 2004 introduced Private Member's Motion M-560, hoping to change the criminal code to protect unborn children in cases of violence against pregnant women.   *Teresa Welsh*

BREWING AND FERMENTATION. Brewing, the longest and most successful fermentation process in Saskatchewan, began in 1883 in Moose Jaw and Prince Albert, in 1887 in Regina, and in 1915 in Saskatoon. The most enduring ventures were the Moose Jaw Brewing and Malting Company (1906–36); Prince Albert Breweries (then Sick's Prince Albert Brewery, Molson Saskatchewan Brewery) (1924–86); Regina Brewery (then Sick's Regina Brewery, Molson Regina Brewery, Molson Saskatchewan Brewery) (1907–2002); Adenac Brewing Co. (then Drewry's Regina Brewery, Blue Label Brewery, Carling Breweries, Carling O'Keefe Breweries) (1928–80); the Saskatchewan Brewing Co. (then Labatt's Saskatchewan Brewery) (1915– 93); and Hub City Brewing (then Western Canada Brewing, Drewry's Ltd., Western Canada Breweries, O'Keefe Brewing Co., Carling-O'Keefe Breweries of Canada, Molson Breweries, and finally Great Western Brewery) (1928–present). The latter is the only "large" brewery existing today in Saskatchewan—in part due to the elimination of provincial boundary restrictions on production of beer. Since 1989–90, more than nineteen brew pubs operate in Saskatoon, Regina, Moose Jaw, Humboldt and Swift Current following changes in provincial legislation.

Brewing begins with a good source of water which is filtered to remove particulates and any bacteria. Activated charcoal is applied to remove residual chlorine and phenolics. The water is demineralized to remove salts, and the resulting softened water is adjusted by addition of food grade salts to enhance flavour.

Malted **BARLEY** such as that manufactured by Prairie Malt in Biggar is the primary raw material for brewing. Malt is carefully dried to preserve the activity of the enzymes formed in malting that convert starch to sugars, proteins to amino acids, and facilitate dissolution of cell walls and other complexes in the malt. Because malt is high in starch-degrading enzymes, it is possible to use non-malted grains in brewing as a secondary source of starch. For this, milled corn, **WHEAT**, rice, unmalted barley, other grains or syrups replace some of the malt. Cereal adjuncts are heated in water in a cereal cooker in the presence of about 10% of the milled malt. Temperatures rise from ~40°C to close to 100°C to gelatinize the starch making it more soluble. Viscosity is reduced by enzyme action. Hot cereal is added slowly to the rest of the malt in water in a mash cooker where the temperature is allowed to rise to 50°C followed by an increase to near 67°C which provides optimal degradation of starch to sugars by the alpha and beta amylases. The temperature is then raised to 75–80°C and the "wort" can then be clarified and separated from the barley husks in a unique vessel called the "lauter tun" (slotted false bottom) where the malt husks create a filter bed. Residual grain components are then rinsed, and taken for animal feeding. The mashing process results in the dissolving of low molecular weight salts, sugars, protein derivatives, and production of fermentable sugars. Large proteins are denatured and removed from the wort. Clear wort is taken via the "grant" to the kettle where it is boiled one to three hours to inactivate enzymes, concentrate the wort to fixed sugar levels, denature proteins, increase and standardize colour, lower wort pH, extract hops, and remove volatile materials. The prepared wort is then clarified removing precipitated "trub," cooled, analyzed and pumped to sterilized fermentors.

Specially selected yeasts are then added. Fermentation initiates as the yeasts grow in the wort using the nutrients provided by malt. Yeasts ferment the sugar to ethanol and carbon dioxide. The level of initial sugars dictates the level of ethanol which can be attained. At the end of fermentation, the yeasts are removed by sedimentation or centrifugation. Primary aging then occurs followed by clarification and a secondary storage. The beer matures during this time, and is then given a final filtration so that it is brilliantly clear. Packaging and in most cases pasteurization then takes place to provide a longer product shelf life.

It should not be forgotten that the McGuiness (Central Canada) distillery in Weyburn operated until 1987 and a winery, Growers Wine Company (then Jordan's Ste. Michelle), operated in Moose Jaw from 1964 until 1981. Today, two cottage wineries located near Regina (Aspen Grove) and Battleford (Bannach) make wines out of local berries and rhubarb. Co-op Dairy (now Saputo Foods) and Palm Dairies (then Parmelat, now closed) have produced traditional fermented dairy products. In addition, a white vinegar manufacturing plant (capacity ~5 million L/year) has existed in Saskatoon since 1948. This plant, originally Vinegars Ltd, was acquired by Canada Vinegars, Campbell Soup, Fleischmann's (Burns Philp), and operates today as Reinhart Foods.

POUNDMAKER AG-VENTURES at Lanigan began production of fuel ethanol and the feeding of distillers wet grain and thin stillage to cattle in their feedlot complex in 1991. Saskatchewan is poised (January 2004) to foster a significant expansion in fuel alcohol capacity with two major projects: Shaunavon's Cyprus Agri-Energy and Belle Plaine's Prairie Sun Energy Products facilities (both on hold and waiting for funding). Other locations considered for fuel alcohol use are Yorkton, Tisdale, Swift Current and the old Weyburn distillery. Most are envisioned to be seven- to tenfold larger than the twelve to 13 million L/yr Lanigan plant. The Applied Microbiology and Food Science fermentation lab in the Agriculture College, **UNIVERSITY OF SASKATCHEWAN** has provided research support to this industry.

Fuel alcohol production here begins with slurried ground wheat using heat and industrial microbial amylases to convert starch to sugars. The fermentation is similar to brewing except that stronger "beer" is distilled to 95% alcohol with the last 5% of water removed by a molecular sieve so that the alcohol is free of water and capable of being blended with gasoline for automobiles. Ethanol is an octane enhancer, a fuel extender, an oxygenated fuel, and a liquid fuel made via agriculture that enhances farm income. It reduces importation of foreign oil, and is greenhouse gas friendly. These motives and the fact that it can be made profitably and produced with a net energy balance of 1.34 provide the reasons for extensive recent expansions of the industry in North America. The by-products of this process are distillers' dried grain and carbon dioxide. Residual thin stillage is an animal feed.

Successful use of fermentation technology to produce bioinoculants and bioherbicides is carried out in Saskatoon by Philom Bios Inc. and Becker Underwood. The Saskatchewan Research Council operates a fermentation pilot plant which is available for contract research and for small-scale production of biological products using scale-up propagation. *William Michael Ingledew*

FURTHER READING: Ingledew, W.M. and D.W. Hysert. 1994. "Brewing Technology." Pp. 315–26 in *Encyclopedia of Agricultural Science*; Jacques, K.A., T.P. Lyons and D.R. Kelsall. 2003. *The Alcohol Textbook*. Nottingham University Press.

BREWSTER, ELIZABETH (1922–). Elizabeth Brewster, the poet and writer, was born on August 26, 1922, in Chipman, New Brunswick. She earned a BA from the University of New Brunswick in 1946, a Masters from Radcliffe College (Harvard) in 1947, a library science degree from the University of Toronto in 1953, and a PhD from Indiana University in 1962. She worked in a number of university libraries (Carleton, Indiana, Mount Allison, Alberta) and at the New Brunswick Legislative Library

RICHARD MARJAN PHOTO/ SASKATCHEWAN ARCHIVES BOARD S-SP-A20070-4, SASKATOON STARPHOENIX FONDS

Elizabeth Brewster, 1983.

between 1953 and 1970. She taught English at the University of Victoria (1960–61), the University of Alberta (1970–71), and then at the **UNIVERSITY OF SASKATCHEWAN** from 1972 until her retirement in 1990. She is currently a Professor Emerita and lives in Saskatoon.

Brewster has been writing and publishing, mainly poetry, for more than fifty years. Her poems appeared in early issues of *The Fiddlehead*, and her first chapbook, *East Coast*, was published by Ryerson in 1951. She published seven books of poems, a novel, and a short story collection before moving to Saskatoon and has since published ten more books of poetry and five works of prose, principally by Oberon Press. Brewster has published three selections of her poetic work: *Passage of Summer: Selected Poems* (1969); *Selected Poems of Elizabeth Brewster, 1944–1984* in two volumes (1985); and *Footnotes to the Book of Job*, which includes new poems as well as selected poems from three books published after 1985. She has also published two novels: *The Sisters* (1974) and *Junction* (1982), as well as two poetic memoirs, *The Invention of Truth* (1991), and *Away from Home* (1995). She identifies with the east in her memories of her past; her writings of the prairies are from the perspective of an outside observer seeking reference points. Brewster is a member of the Order of Canada, received the award for Lifetime Excellence in the Arts from the **SASKATCHEWAN ARTS BOARD**, and is a Life Member of the League of Canadian Poets. *Bob Ivanochko*

BRIDGES. Bridges allow the movement of people and transported goods to cross over obstacles and hazards, thereby saving considerable time and expense as well as ensuring safety. The railway, with its transcontinental and local lines, required numerous bridges to cross major rivers and minor streams. These early bridges, made of timber, were usually rebuilt using steel. North Battleford and Nipawin are examples of major railway bridges; Swift Current is an example of a community developed at a site of the railway bridge on the CPR mainline. Railway companies are responsible for the safety and maintenance of their bridges. The Department of Highways is responsible for the con-

SASKATCHEWAN ARCHIVES BOARD R-A24051
University Bridge in Saskatoon, September 14, 1919.

struction and maintenance of 850 bridges on the provincial highway network. There are an additional 2,200 bridges on rural and urban municipal roads in Saskatchewan; most of these are short, but about 20% are larger span bridges. Several bridges are located at former ferry sites. Saskatoon has become known locally as the City of Bridges: in 1908 it had three railway bridges and one for vehicles; now there are two railway bridges and five vehicle bridges, with two more proposed for a future transportation corridor.

Bob Ivanochko

BRIERCREST SCHOOLS. Briercrest Schools began first with the Briercrest Bible Institute (now known as Briercrest College) in the small village of Briercrest during the economically depressed 1930s. The idea for a school was conceived by a diverse group of people including Annie Hillson, Isabel Whittaker, and the latter's husband, Sinclair Whittaker, a local entrepreneur and former Conservative member of the provincial Legislature. Together they organized Bible studies and conferences in the area, and initiated a small independent congregation. Through their connections to an emerging fundamentalist network in western Canada, they met **HENRY HILDEBRAND**, a young Mennonite immigrant and recent graduate from the Winnipeg Bible Institute; they invited him to pastor the newly formed Briercrest Gospel Assembly and to help them start a Bible school.

With Sinclair Whittaker as chair of the Board and responsible for facilities, Hildebrand organized in 1935 a course of studies patterned after the curriculum of the Winnipeg Bible Institute, intentionally steering the school in a transdenominational and evangelical direction. Without a denominational constituency from which to draw students, the school made effective use of radio broadcasts and annual conferences to develop a loyal following. The

school's central purpose was to train men and women for effective Christian service in both lay and professional roles. Hildebrand's moderate Calvinism, mixed with a strong biblicism, dispensational premillennialism, Keswick Holiness teaching, and a passion for evangelism and foreign missions converged to make the school an institutional embodiment of fundamentalist beliefs. For decades the school functioned as a kind of regional headquarters for a network of independent churches and missionary organizations in western Canada. Hildebrand remained as principal of the school until 1977, and then as chancellor until 1996; the longevity of his tenure at the school contributed considerably to its growth and stability.

A steady increase in students set the stage in 1946 for the purchase of the Caron airport (later renamed Caronport), located fifteen miles west of Moose Jaw. This ready-made, self-contained campus offered ample room for the expansion of residential facilities and for the development of a more multifaceted operation. By 1948, enrollment in the Bible school neared 250. The addition of a high school in 1946 was followed by a general store, a post office, an elementary school, and a farm operation. The routing of the **TRANS-CANADA HIGHWAY** across the front of its property during the 1950s, and the addition of a motel, service station and restaurant enhanced the visibility of the school. The centrepiece of the extensively developed campus is the 3,500 seat Hildebrand Chapel, the largest auditorium in the province.

Reflecting post-war trends towards more education and higher vocational standards, the school encouraged faculty to enhance their academic credentials. By 1974 the Briercrest Bible Institute was given authority to grant degrees, and in 1976 the school was accredited by the Accrediting Association of Bible Colleges. A graduate division, now known as

Briercrest Seminary, was initiated in 1983 and was granted full membership in the Association of Theological Schools in 1998. Briercrest College is currently the largest Bible college in Canada; its 19,000 alumni are active throughout Canada and in over 80 countries. Cumulative enrollment in the various Briercrest schools numbers 1,400 annually.

Bruce L. Guenther

FURTHER READING: Budd, H.H. 1986. *Wind in the Wheatfields: A Pictorial History of Briercrest Bible College, 1935–1985.* Caronport, SK: Briercrest Bible College; Guenther, B.L. 2001. "Training for Service: The Bible School Movement in Western Canada, 1909–1960." Ph.D. Dissertation, Montreal: McGill University.

BRITISH COMMONWEALTH AIR TRAINING PLAN. Representatives from Canada, Great Britain, Australia, and New Zealand signed the British Commonwealth Air Training Plan (BCATP) on December 17, 1939. Canadian Prime Minister **W.L.M. KING** supported the training of aircrew for allied air forces in the war against Germany, expecting this contribution to offset any further land force commitments by Canada to the war effort and thereby reduce the risk of having to implement national conscription. Canada agreed not only to provide approximately 80% of the pilot, observer, and wireless operator-air gunner recruits, but also to cover 80% of the training plan's costs. Canada also agreed to graduate 520 elementary pilots, 544 advanced pilots, 340 observers, and 580 wireless operator-air gunners each month. The BCATP in Canada was organized into four Training Commands: schools in Alberta and southern Saskatchewan were part of No. 4 Training Command, with headquarters originally in Regina and later in Calgary; schools in Manitoba and central Saskatchewan were under the jurisdiction of No. 2 TC, headquartered in Winnipeg. Each Command had its own recruiting, manning, supply, and repair depots.

From 1940 to 1945, 120 training schools were constructed across Canada, twenty of which were located in Saskatchewan (*see* Table BCATP-1). These schools trained aircrew for the Royal Canadian Air Force, the Royal Air Force, the Royal Australian Air Force, and the Royal New Zealand Air Force (*see* Table BCATP-2). Many volunteers from the United States and from the occupied nations of Europe also participated in the aircrew training plan. Contrary to popular belief, held both during **WORLD WAR II** and still by some, the selection of BCATP aerodrome sites was based solely on technical merit—not on the intensity of a community's lobbying effort or on the political affiliation of the constituency. Patronage played little role in the process: what was important in a location was a flat piece of land with few obstacles to be removed. Quick and economical developments were determining factors, as were the

129

B

Table BCATP-1. British Commonwealth Air Training Plan Schools in Saskatchewan

School	Location	Dates in Operation
Manning Depots		
#2 MD	Swift Current	May–August 1944
Initial Training Schools		
#2 ITS	Regina	July 1, 1940–Nov. 30, 1944
#7 ITS	Saskatoon	Dec. 30, 1941–June 30, 1944
Elementary Flying Training Schools		
#6 EFTS	Prince Albert	July 22, 1940–Nov. 15, 1944
#15 EFTS	Regina	Nov. 11, 1940–Aug 11, 1944
#23 EFTS	Davidson/Yorkton	Nov. 9, 1942–Sept. 15, 1945
#33 EFTS	Caron	Jan. 5, 1942–Jan. 14, 1944
#34 (later #25) EFTS	Assiniboia	Feb. 11, 1942–July 28, 1944
Service Flying Training Schools		
#4 SFTS	Saskatoon	Sept. 16, 1940–Mar. 30, 1945
#8 SFTS	Weyburn (from Moncton)	Jan. 24–June 30, 1944
#11 SFTS	Yorkton	April 10, 1941–Dec. 1, 1944
#13 SFTS	North Battleford (from St. Hubert)	Feb. 25, 1944–March 30, 1945
#32 SFTS	Moose Jaw	Dec. 9, 1940–Oct. 17, 1944
#35 SFTS	North Battleford	Sept. 4, 1941–Feb. 25, 1944
#38 SFTS	Estevan	April 27, 1942–Feb. 11, 1944
#39 SFTS	Swift Current	Dec. 15, 1941–March 24, 1944
#41 SFTS	Weyburn	Jan. 5, 1942–Jan. 22, 1944
Bombing and Gunnery Schools		
#2 BGS	Mossbank	Oct. 28, 1940–Dec. 15, 1944
#5 BGS	Dafoe	May 26, 1941–Feb. 17, 1945
Air Observer Schools		
#3 AOS	Regina	Sept. 16, 1940–Sept. 12, 1942
#6 AOS	Prince Albert	March 17, 1941–Sept. 11, 1942

Table BCATP-2. British Commonwealth Air Training Plan Graduates by Nationality

Nationality	Number of Graduates, April 1940 to March 1945
Royal Canadian Air Force	72,835
Royal Australian Air Force	9,606
Royal New Zealand Air Force	7,002
Royal Air Force*	42,110
Naval Fleet Air Arm**	5,296

* Includes 448 Poles, 677 Norwegians, 800 Belgian/Dutch, 900 Czechs, 2,600 Free French.
** Also trained at BCATP schools.

proximity of water and electricity supplies, gravel deposits, transportation routes (rail and highway), and communication lines (telephone and telegraph). The air training schools could not be built near forests, mountains, or densely populated areas. Saskatchewan's topography and demography made the province an excellent choice for BCATP bases: consequently, it had the second highest number of schools built in any province; only Ontario, with thirty-six, had more.

New recruits, enlisting at various air force recruiting centres such as those in Regina or Saska-toon, were introduced to air force life at a Manning Depot. There were seven main depots in Canada; No. 2 Manning Depot was transferred from Brandon to Swift Current in 1944. After about four weeks there, recruits moved to an Initial Training School (ITS). No. 2 ITS was located at Regina College and the adjacent Regina NORMAL SCHOOL. Both buildings still stand on College Avenue: the former houses the Conservatory of Music, while the latter has been converted to a sound stage for the movie industry. No. 7 ITS had its living quarters and classrooms in the Saskatoon Normal School and Bedford Road

Collegiate. ITS lectures covered theory of navigation, mathematics, armaments, meteorology, Morse code, aircraft recognition, aerodynamics, drill, and physical instruction.

Trainee pilots next joined an Elementary Flying Training School (EFTS), where they began flying Tiger Moths, Fleet Finches, or Fairchild Cornells. Civilian staff, mostly from flying clubs, managed each EFTS; many of the instructors were former bush pilots, crop dusters, or WORLD WAR I pilots. EFTS graduates then trained at a Service Flying Training School (SFTS) on more advanced aircraft such as twin-engine Ansons, Cranes, and Oxfords, or single-engine Harvards. Finally, SFTS graduates were posted to an Operational Training Unit (OTU), either in Britain or Canada, to gain operational experience. Only two SFTS in Canada exceeded the number of pilots trained at Saskatoon (2,966): No.1 SFTS Camp Borden (3,083) and No.2 SFTS Ottawa (3,156).

After ITS, student air observers spent two months at an Air Observer School, six weeks at a Bombing and Gunnery School (BGS), and four weeks at an Air Navigation School. The final stage was an OTU posting. In March 1942, air bomber and navigator specialties were created to separate the roles of navigating and bombing. Air gunners received twelve weeks of ground training and air-firing practice at a BGS. Wireless operator/air gunners went directly from Manning Depot to Wireless Training School for twelve weeks, followed by six weeks of gunnery training. Flight engineers on heavy bombers trained on aero engines, but also learned the rudiments of flying in case the bomber pilot was killed or injured. Most flight engineers trained in the United Kingdom, but 1,913 engineers trained in Canada under the BCATP.

Saskatchewan's contribution to World War II was significant. From a population of approximately 896,000, 23,070 men and 2,461 women joined the RCAF. Of the 131,533 Commonwealth aircrew graduating in Canada, 20,359 attended Saskatchewan schools.

Training aerodromes had a significant economic and social impact on Saskatchewan. Devastated by the GREAT DEPRESSION in the 1930s, Saskatchewan communities lobbied their provincial and federal representatives with great fervour: they wanted the financial benefits accruing from employment during the construction phase, employment in civilian jobs on the base, and the spending of pay cheques by construction workers and air force personnel in local businesses. Air force personnel and local residents intermingled at countless social events hosted by the training schools: open houses, sports days, dances, and graduation ceremonies. Local citizens welcomed visiting recruits into their homes, and communities put on variety shows and supplied books for unit libraries. Airmen even helped farmers during harvest. The romances between Canadian women and BCATP personnel–including recruits from Britain, Australia, and New Zealand–attest to the cordial integration of stations into local communities: approximately 3,750 Canadian women married members of visiting allied air forces; many of these airmen returned to live in Canada after the war.

Although most BCATP bases have been abandoned, leaving buildings and runways derelict, many structures were moved after the war to local communities and are still in use today. Regina's Turvey Centre uses a former Mossbank hangar; a hangar from Assiniboia serves as the Saskatchewan Transportation Company's Regina garage; and the nursing home in Leroy was formerly the Dafoe base hospital. The former No. 32 SFTS at Moose Jaw has been modernized, and is now home to 15 **WING CANADIAN FORCES** and the NATO Flying Training in Canada program. *Rachel Lea Heide and Ross Herrington*

FURTHER READING: Douglas, W.A.B. 1986. *The Official History of the Royal Canadian Air Force, Volume II: The Creation of a National Air Force.* Toronto: University of Toronto Press; Hatch, F.J. 1983. *Aerodrome of Democracy: Canada and the British Commonwealth Air Training Plan, 1939–1945.* Ottawa: Canadian Government Publishing Centre.

BROADVIEW, town, pop 669, located on the **TRANS-CANADA HIGHWAY** and the **CANADIAN PACIFIC RAILWAY** (CPR) main line, approximately 155 km E of Regina and 80 km W of the Saskatchewan-Manitoba border. The foundations of Broadview date to 1882, with the construction of the trans-continental railway across eastern Saskatchewan. The CPR designated the site to be the divisional point between Brandon and Moose Jaw because of its location and ample supply of good water. For many years, the railway was the economic backbone of the community; despite mechanization, it long remained a major employer in the town. In 1885, the RCMP set up a division in the community. A brick-making plant was established in 1906; reportedly, 165,000 bricks manufactured in Broadview were used in the construction of the **SASKATCHEWAN LEGISLATIVE BUILDING**. The population of Broadview peaked at over 1,000 from the mid-1950s through the 1960s. Today, Broadview still has many businesses, services, and active community groups. The Broadview Museum houses a collection of heritage buildings and pioneer artifacts, as well as a display honouring Saskatchewan's most famous goat, **SERGEANT BILL.** *David McLennan*

BROCKELBANK, JOHN HEWGILL (1897–1977). He was born June 25, 1897, in Grey County, Ontario. He moved west in 1911 with his parents, who homesteaded near North Battleford. In 1917 he enlisted in the army and served in Europe. Upon

John Hewgill Brockelbank, August 1947.

return, he began farming near Bjorkdale. Along with Sandy Nicholson, he laid the foundation for the CCF organization in northeastern Saskatchewan. In 1938 he was elected to the Legislature from the constituency of Tisdale and was re-elected in every election until his retirement in 1967. He became the CCF's primary legislative tactician. In 1941, when CCF leader **GEORGE WILLIAMS** enlisted in the military, Brockelbank became leader of the Opposition. Upon the CCF's victory in 1944, he was appointed to **DOUGLAS**' first Cabinet as Minister of Municipal Affairs. After the 1948 election, he was appointed Minister of Natural Resources, a post he held for fourteen years. During his time as Minister, both the potash and oil industries of the province would begin significant growth. His tenure as Minister marked the change in the CCF's focus away from government-administered development of natural resources towards encouraging development by the private sector. In 1962, the new Premier, **WOODROW LLOYD**, appointed Brockelbank Provincial Treasurer and Deputy Premier, positions that he held until the CCF's defeat in 1964. Brockelbank remained active within the NDP's organization until his death on May 30, 1977. *Brett Quiring*

FURTHER READING: Saskatchewan Archives Board. John H. Brockelbank Papers. R-907. Regina; Richards, John and Larry Pratt. 1979. *Prairie Capitalism: Power and Influence in the New West.* Toronto: McClelland and Stewart.

BRONFMAN FAMILY. The Bronfman family is known the world over for its business acumen and its substantial holdings in the global economy–with controlling interests in the Seagram Company, which employs over 30,000 people and is the largest distributors of spirits and wine in the world. While

the Bronfman family business holdings have grown to a huge number of international conglomerates, their history is deeply rooted in the social fabric of Saskatchewan during the prohibition era.

The Bronfman family immigrated to Canada after fleeing Czarist Russia in 1889, the year Samuel Bronfman was born. His first foray into the business world was as a horse trader in rural Saskatchewan and Manitoba. By the early 1920s, Samuel and his brothers Harry, Abe, and Allan were owners of a successful "booze-by-mail" business. Samuel acquired the House of Seagram during the prohibition decade. The Bronfmans' success in the liquor industry came at a time when social gospel proponents James S. Woodsworth, Salem Bland, Nellie McClung, and Emily Murphy spread the word about the evils of alcohol. Reflecting the spirit of entrepreneurship and adventure, the Bronfmans' history is coloured with the resistance to social mores that defined the 1920s in North America: Samuel's brother-in-law was shot to death at the **CANADIAN PACIFIC RAILWAY** station in Bienfait, Saskatchewan; Harry Bronfman was jailed for attempted bribery and witness tampering; and the four Bronfman brothers were charged with fraud and income tax evasion–although nothing was ever proven against them.

Despite controversial beginnings, the financial success of the Bronfman family from the 1920s to the new millennium is well charted in the annals of Canadian business. The Bronfman brothers' sojourn in Saskatchewan will remain a colourful saga that helped build Saskatchewan's social and economic communities. Liquor-runs to the States, back-street deals, and legends about using the famous tunnels in southern regions of the province make the Saskatchewan connection a permanent fixture in the lives of one of the most successful and powerful families in Canadian history. *Michael Cottrell*

FURTHER READING: Marrus, M.R. 1991. *Mr. Sam: The Life and Times of Samuel Bronfman.* Toronto: Viking; Newman, P.C. 1979. *King of the Castle: The Making of a Dynasty: Seagram's and the Bronfman Empire.* New York: Atheneum.

BROWN CREEPER. The brown creeper belongs to the family Certhiidae (seven species) of tiny (12–18 cm) songbirds which glean insects from the bark of coniferous trees. They are found in the temperate areas of the Northern Hemisphere. The Saskatchewan bird belongs to a species (*Certhia americana*) found throughout North America. It nests in the coniferous or mixed forests of the centre, and is seen as a migrant in the wooded areas of the Grasslands. It is difficult to see with its camouflage of brown-striped back and head as it hugs to trees with its tiny feet and short legs. Its small size, striped plumage and down-curved bill may confuse it with a wren or nuthatch, but its habit of feeding around a tree from the bottom to the top and then flying to the base of the next tree, makes it distinctive.   *Diane Secoy*

FURTHER READING: Alsop, Fred J., III. 2002. *Birds of Canada*. New York: Dorling Kindersley Handbooks.

BROWN, GEORGE WILLIAM (1860–1919).

The Honourable George W. Brown, Saskatchewan's second LIEUTENANT-GOVERNOR, was born May 30, 1860, at Holstein, Grey County, Ontario. Educated at Mount Forrest High School, Brantford College, and the University of Toronto, he journeyed west in 1882 and settled at Rose Plain, a community ten miles north of Regina. Although he experienced some success as a farmer, Brown moved to Regina in 1889 to article in law. Three years later he joined Norman Mackenzie in what was to become a flourishing legal practice.

An ambitious and able leader, Brown was elected as a Liberal member of the Territorial Assembly in 1894, but illness forced him to withdraw from politics in 1903. His debilitation, however, was short-lived. As the partnership with Mackenzie prospered, Brown invested in Métis SCRIP and amassed a considerable holding in land that he later sold for profit. His firm foothold in Regina's business and professional realm resulted in appointments to various boards and directorships. Brown's official appointment as Lieutenant-Governor on October 14, 1910, came at the recommendation of WALTER SCOTT, his good friend and frequent travelling companion.

Brown, his wife Annie, and their two children moved into GOVERNMENT HOUSE in December 1910. The vice-regal residence was the focal point of numerous social functions throughout Brown's tenure, including popular New Year's Levees. With the onset of WORLD WAR I, however, the Browns became more visible outside Government House, attending benefit concerts, visiting wounded soldiers, and supporting the war effort. George William Brown's term as Lieutenant-Governor ended on October 17, 1915. He remained a resident of Regina until his death on February 17, 1919.   *Holden Stoffel*

FURTHER READING: Hryniuk, Margaret and Garth Pugh. 1991. *"A Tower of Attraction": An Illustrated History of Government House, Regina, Saskatchewan*. Regina: Government House Historical Society/Canadian Plains Research Center, 1991.

BROWN, JACOB A. (1926–92).

Jacob Brown was a very influential agricultural economist with both the provincial government and the UNIVERSITY OF SASKATCHEWAN. He was born at Beechy, Saskatchewan on July 12, 1926. He received his BSA in Agricultural Economics at the University of Saskatchewan in 1951 and his MS degree from North Dakota State University, and undertook

SASKATCHEWAN ARCHIVES BOARD R-A11499-1

Jacob Brown.

further studies toward his PhD at the University of Minnesota. From 1957 to 1967 he was employed with the Saskatchewan Department of Agriculture, where he worked in farm management and later headed the Economics and Statistics Branch. He came to the University of Saskatchewan, where he taught Agricultural Economics and was Dean of Agriculture from 1974 to 1984.

Public service played an important role in Brown's career. He served on numerous boards and committees such as the Economic Council of Canada, the Canada West Foundation, the Saskatchewan Farm Ownership Board, and the Saskatoon District Planning Commission. His two terms as Dean coincided with the development of innovative/university research funding leading to increases in research program and staff in the College of Agriculture, as well as with the Research Park at the University. Awards include Fellowship in the Agricultural Institute of Canada, the Saskatchewan Order of Merit, and induction into the Saskatchewan Agricultural Hall of Fame; in 1987 Brown was appointed a Member of the Order of Canada for leadership in agricultural education. It was in his second term as Dean that he was diagnosed with cancer, a disease he fought with courage for fifteen years. He passed away on July 6, 1992.   *Gary Storey*

BROWN, LARRY (1948–).

Larry Brown was born in Gravelbourg, Saskatchewan in 1948 and raised on a farm near there. He became an important figure in the Saskatchewan labour movement and later in the national labour movement. Brown began his social activism at the UNIVERSITY OF SASKATCHEWAN, where he was active in the Student's Union and became president of the Saskatchewan Federation of Students. While articling with a Saskatchewan law firm, Brown was hired by the ALLAN BLAKENEY NDP government as executive secretary to the Task Force on Workers' Compensation, and later as executive assistant to the Deputy Minister of Labour. He was instrumental in drafting precedent-setting occupational health and safety legislation, which included the right of workers to refuse dangerous work.

In 1974, Brown was hired as executive secretary of the Saskatchewan Federation of Labour, where he served until 1979 and provided important leadership in protests against wage controls. He also was labour's representative on task forces on workers' compensation and provincial rent controls. In 1979 he became the chief executive officer of the SASKATCHEWAN GOVERNMENT AND GENERAL EMPLOYEES' UNION. Brown became one of the most recognizable figures in Saskatchewan's labour movement, particularly during one of Saskatchewan's largest public service strikes in 1979.

In 1986, Brown was elected as secretary-treasurer of the National Union of Public and General Employees, based in Ottawa. He continues to be an outspoken and progressive voice for workers across the country, speaking out in favour of the value of public services and challenging the merits of free trade agreements and globalization. Brown is also President of the Canadian Centre for Policy Alternatives, Canada's leading progressive research/policy organization.   *Doug Taylor*

BROWNE, JEAN ELIZABETH (1885–1973).

Jean Browne was born in Parkhill, Ontario, on May 11, 1883, and graduated from the Toronto General Hospital. As the first public health nurse in Saskatchewan she organized the first school health program, developed the School Hygiene Branch for the Department of Education, and served for five years as its director. She chaired the committee that successfully drafted the Saskatchewan Registered Nurses Act in 1917, and serve as the first President of the Saskatchewan Nurses' Association from 1917 to 1919, an office she filled again in 1921–22. She served as the first Saskatchewan representative to the Canadian Nurses' Association, and was its president from 1922 to 1926. In 1929–30 she was secretary for the Survey of Nursing Education in Canada.

She developed and organized the Canadian Junior Red Cross, served as National Director, and represented the organization internationally. She was the recipient of the Florence Nightingale Medal in 1939 for outstanding nursing service. She received the George VI Coronation Medal in 1938, the George V Jubilee Medal in 1939, and the Canadian Nurses' Association's Snively Medal for her outstanding contributions to the ideals of nursing and service. Browne retired in 1950 and married Dr. W.A. Thomson. She died in Regina on October 7, 1973.

Karen Wright

BRUNO, town, pop 571, located approximately 90 km E of Saskatoon, 7 km N of Hwy 5. The area terrain is gently rolling; about 80% of the land is farmed; and the remainder consists of aspen groves, wetlands, and prairie. The community is named for its founder, Rev. Bruno Doerfler, a Benedictine Father who immigrated to the area in 1902 with a small number of German families from Minnesota. The next year, more German American settlers arrived at the fledgling religious colony, and after the railway was completed in 1905 settlers poured into the district. On the eve of **WORLD WAR I**, as convents in Germany were being taken over by the government for military use, a number of **URSULINE SISTERS** sought refuge in Canada and, upon Doerfler's urging, eventually settled in Bruno. An Ursuline convent was opened in 1919, and St. Ursula's Academy in 1922. During the 1960s, it is estimated that there were more than a hundred Ursuline Sisters in the community. The Academy, closed in 1982, was temporarily managed as a satellite campus of the **UNIVERSITY OF SASKATCHEWAN** between 1999 and 2004, and has since been returned to the Ursuline Sisters. The primary economic base of the Bruno area has long been agriculture, which today involves grains, oil seeds, hogs, cattle and turkeys. Potash mines at Colonsay and Allan provide additional employment. (*See also* **GERMAN SETTLEMENTS**)

David McLennan

BRYANT, JAMES FRASER (1877–1945). J.F. Bryant was born in Glen Allan, Ontario, on May 19, 1877, and educated at Upper Canada College, Queen's University, and the University of Manitoba, graduating with a Master's degree in Classics and a Bachelor of Laws. He became a partner in the Regina law firm Allan, Gordon, Bryant and Gordon in 1907 and a year later married Myra Boyd, also of Regina. He chaired the Regina Public School Board and later served as president of the Saskatchewan School Trustees. In 1917, he established the Bryant Oratorical Competition which introduced thousands of high school students to the art of public speaking. Also during his presidency, the Trustees came out in opposition to religious teaching and in favour of English as the sole language of instruction in the province's public schools—issues which Bryant brought with him when he entered politics in the mid-1920s.

A lifelong Conservative, Bryant served the party in several capacities in Regina and eventually as provincial president from 1922 to 1925. He ran unsuccessfully in the 1925 provincial election but, over the next four years, continued to raise the issues of sectarianism in the public school system

SASKATCHEWAN ARCHIVES BOARD R-B3067
James Bryant.

and corruption in government. Such attacks helped defeat the Liberals in the 1929 election; Bryant won a seat at Lumsden, and Premier **J.T.M. ANDERSON** gave him two portfolios—Public Works, and Telephones and Telegraphs—in his new administration. Bryant established himself as one of the most important members of the Cabinet. He helped rewrite the School Act to ban religious symbols from public schools and to strengthen the position of English as the language of instruction and administration. He worked on the agreement which gave the province control over its lands and natural resources held back by Ottawa since 1905. As well, he led the government's attempts to create a less corrupt public service.

Bryant lost his seat in 1934 and accepted an appointment to the bench as a judge of the District Court in Saskatoon, a position he held until his death on September 18, 1945.

Patrick Kyba

B-SAY-TAH, resort village, located along the S shore of Echo Lake on Hwy 210, between Fort Qu'Appelle to the E and Echo Valley Provincial Park to the W. Development first began along the beachfront in the early 1900s, and B-Say-Tah was incorporated in 1915. Recent decades have seen substantial development. The fish hatchery at B-Say-Tah, which was begun in 1913, produces a wide range of native and exotic species, and distributes 40 to 50 million fish per year in over 200 bodies of water throughout Saskatchewan. The hatchery plays a major role in the province's fisheries resource, helping to support more than 3,400 jobs in the commercial and sport fishing industries. Over the years, the hatchery has stocked provincial waters with more than 2 billion fish.

David McLennan

BUCKLE, WALTER C. (1886–1955). Walter Clutterbuck Buckle, Minister of Agriculture in the Co-operative government of **J.T.M. ANDERSON** from 1929 to 1934, was born in Gloucester, England in 1886. Following his education at Sir Thomas Rich's School and Brentford College, he immigrated to Canada in 1905 and settled in the Tisdale area five years later, homesteading and later operating a farm implement business. Buckle became mayor of Tisdale in 1921, a position he held until his election to the Legislature in 1925. As one of only three Conservatives elected that year, he served as his party's agriculture critic and became Minister of Agriculture after the defeat of the **GARDINER** government in 1929. His career as Minister followed a pattern common to most of his colleagues in the Anderson Cabinet: first, attempts to discover and halt corrupt practices in his Department inherited from the previous Liberal regime; then, introduction of legislation designed to improve the lot of Saskatchewan's farmers; and finally, frustration as the **DEPRESSION** deepened and the understanding grew that no money would be available for anything other than keeping people alive on their farms and safe from foreclosure. Thus in 1930 Buckle initiated an audit of the Farm Loan Board which showed misappropriation of funds and political interference with the Board's operations under the Liberals, and these he stopped. The same year he also announced a series of measures aimed at increasing farm revenues, ranging from fruit growing to moisture conservation. Within two years, however, further investigation of the Liberals seemed pointless and new programs proved unaffordable as the government tried to cope with the appalling effects of drought, pestilence, and declining revenues both private and public. Saskatchewan simply did not have the means to withstand the catastrophe, and departments such as Agriculture gave way to new non-partisan institutions such as the Relief Commission and the Debt Adjustment Board. The length and severity of the Depression altered the expected course of the Anderson government completely, and left it in a vulnerable position from which to campaign for re-election. In fact, not a single supporter of the Co-operative government won a seat in 1934. Buckle went down to defeat in Tisdale and never made it back to the Legislature as a Member. In 1946 he retired from business and moved to Victoria, where he lived until his death in 1955.

Patrick Kyba

BUCKWOLD, SIDNEY L. (1916–2001). A respected and progressive public servant, the Honourable Sidney L. Buckwold was born in Winnipeg on November 3, 1916, and settled in Saskatoon with his family in 1925. He earned his Bachelor of Commerce degree from McGill University, graduating with Great Distinction in 1936, and later served as an officer with the

Canadian Army Service Corps. Credited with revitalizing Saskatoon's downtown area, Buckwold was the city's mayor from 1958 to 1963 and again from 1967 until 1971 when he was appointed to the Canadian Senate. He retired from the upper house in 1991 and was appointed an Officer of the Order of Canada in 1995. Sidney Buckwold died on June 27, 2001.

SASKATCHEWAN ARCHIVES BOARD R-4814

Henry Budd.

BUDD, HENRY (1812–75). Henry Budd was the first First Nation person in North America to be ordained in the Anglican Church. Reverend Henry Budd's contribution to the Canadian west centred on his ministry and his teaching of **CREE**. An orphan, Budd entered a missionary school as part of a Hudson's Bay Company initiative providing Christian education for Rupert's Land First Nations and **MÉTIS** children; he left the mission school to train as a Hudson's Bay Company clerk in 1827, and remained in the Company's employ until 1837. He and his wife Betsy settled in the Red River area, where he taught at the St. John's parish school. He spent the next thirteen years in W'passkwayaw (The Pas, Manitoba), where he taught school and conducted Anglican Church services.

In June 1840, Budd began a new school for First Nations children in the Cumberland House district. Following his ordination as an Anglican priest in 1850, Budd was assigned to the Mission at Nepowewin (Nipawin), where he remained until 1867. Budd's last assignment sent him and his family back to The Pas; there he resumed teaching, as well as ministerial duties that included overseeing the communities of Nipawin, Cumberland House, and Carlton. Known for his eloquence, Henry Budd was also a gifted organizer. He was methodical, neat, thrifty, and was seen as an important role

model for the communities where he taught. Budd was well known for translating Anglican scripture and prayer books into the Cree language. He was buried in the Pas, Manitoba; the road into Stanley Mission, Saskatchewan is named in his honour.

Elizabeth Mooney

FURTHER READING: Heeney, B. (ed.). 1920. *Leaders of the Anglican Church, Vol 2.* Toronto: Toronto Mission, Project Canterbury.

BUFFALO NARROWS, northern village, pop 1,137, located in NW Saskatchewan between the communities of Ile-à-la-Crosse and La Loche on Hwy 155. Buffalo Narrows is situated on the channel or "narrows" between Peter Pond and Churchill Lakes. Prior to the establishment of a permanent settlement, the area was an ancient hunting site that provided a bottleneck into which Aboriginal hunters could drive wood **BISON**, or "buffalo." Aboriginal people had also long come to the narrows to catch and dry fish during the summer months, and in the 1790s the first fur trading posts were established in the area. While the first people to settle permanently at Buffalo Narrows arrived in 1895, the settlement developed very slowly. After **WORLD WAR I**, and through the 1930s, there was an influx of people—many Norwegian, German, and Scottish—who came to work in commercial fishing operations and to trap. People also relocated to the district from the communities of Ile-à-la-Crosse and La Loche. A school was established in 1934, and a post office in 1936. An economy based on resources—fishing, trapping, some logging operations, and mink ranching—peaked from the 1950s to the 1970s. From the 1940s until 1965, the Department of Natural Resources had administered the community; but then local government was established, and through the 1970s community infrastructure was greatly improved: better homes were built, long-distance telephone service was introduced, a new airport capable of handling small jets was opened, and in 1980 a bridge across the narrows was opened, finally linking the community to the provincial highway system. Although by this time, trapping, commercial fishing, and mink ranching were in serious decline, the infrastructure that had been put into place meant that the community was positioned to be a significant regional centre providing government and commercial services to the northwest of the province. Buffalo Narrows was incorporated as a northern village in 1983. Today, the population is largely comprised of people of **CREE**, **DENE**, and European origins; the community's **MÉTIS** population is estimated at between 80 and 90%. The median age is just over 25, while the average age in Saskatchewan is close to 37. Government offices and services are significant employers, as are businesses in the areas of tourism, mining, forestry, construc-

tion, fishing, and wild rice harvesting. While the economy is diverse, unemployment remains high: 19.8%, compared to 6.3% for the province. Economic development is high on the community's agenda. Buffalo Narrows has a pre-school and a day-care centre. The K–12 school has 322 students, and Northlands College offers programs and services for adult learners. Buffalo Narrows also has its own radio station, an RCMP detachment, and a community health centre.

David McLennan

BUFFALO RIVER DENE FIRST NATION. The Buffalo River Dene Nation (Peter Pond Lake) signed **TREATY 10** on August 28, 1906. Research indicates that the Dene people were encouraged by the Hudson's Bay Company to move southward toward the **CHURCHILL RIVER** in the mid-1700s to trap beaver. Before settling at Buffalo River, the Band is thought to have lived at Buffalo Narrows for a period of time in the 1890s. In 1972, the Peter Pond Band was divided into the Turnor Lake (Birch Narrows First Nation) and Buffalo River First Nations. Their 8,259.7-hectare reserve is located about 84 km northwest of Ile-à-la-Crosse, and the largest community is at Dillon. Of a total of 1,090 band members, 567 live on their reserve. The Buffalo River First Nation hunted and trapped around Watapi Lake, and thus became one of the many First Nations bands filing claims for land and economic development losses through the creation of the Primrose Lake Air Weapons Range in 1954; in addition to the value of this land for food harvesting, the prohibition to utilize the rangelands hindered their ability to travel to meet their relatives at Cold Lake. Economic resources include trapping, fishing, and timber; economic potential exists in oil, gas, platinum, uranium, diamonds, and water. Community infrastructure includes a band office, school and teacherage, fire hall, band hall, arena, gas station, and community maintenance facilities.

Christian Thompson

BUGS (HEMIPTERA). Hemipterans, the true bugs, belong to an order of insects (Hemiptera) having a jointed proboscis or beak comprised of four sharp stylets for piercing-sucking their food. In many Hemipterans, the front wings are partly thickened, hard and leather-like, and partly membranous, giving the order the name Hemiptera, from the Greek words *hemi*, meaning half, and *pteron*, meaning wing. The systematics of the Hemiptera is in some disarray. Traditionally, the group was divided into two orders, the Heteroptera, or true bugs, and the Homoptera—aphids, leafhoppers, and related insects. Research has shown that the Homoptera are not a natural phylogenetic group. Morphological and molecular evidence, however, indicates that the Homoptera and Heteroptera are related at the order level.

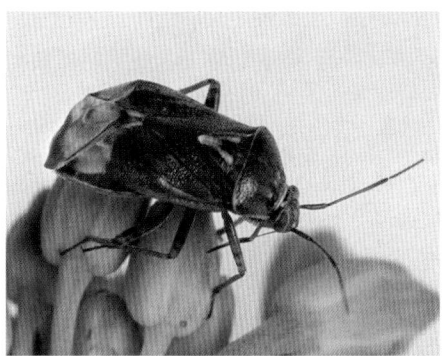

Tarnished plant bug (*Lygus lineolaris* L.) adult on a canola inflorescence. Note piercing-sucking mouthparts, characteristic of Hemiptera.

There are several suborders in the order Hemiptera, the most common of which are: the Sternorrhyncha, comprising aphids, psyllids, whiteflies, and scale insects; the Auchenorrhyncha, including cicadas, leafhoppers, froghoppers, treehoppers, and planthoppers; and the Heteroptera, the true bugs, including plant bugs, seed bugs, and stink bugs. There are over 80,000 named species of Hemiptera worldwide, with literature records of 1,012 species in Saskatchewan, and an estimated 200 to 300 more hemipteran species likely occurring in the province.

The Hemiptera are the most successful of the hemimetabolous insects. These are insects with incomplete metamorphosis, whose young resemble wingless adults. Instead of developing from egg to larva, to pupa, to adult, as do insects with complete metamorphosis, Hemiptera develop from eggs to nymphs to adults. The morphology of Hemiptera reflects the diverse habitats to which they have become adapted. They vary in size from minute external parasites of birds to giant water bugs 50 mm long. The antennae of the Heteroptera comprise four or five segments, while those of other Hemiptera may be reduced and bristlelike, or long and filamentous. A main feature of the order is its piercing-sucking mouthparts, wherein the mandibles and maxillae form two pairs of piercing needlelike stylets that contain both feeding and salivary tubes, all contained in a flexible sheath derived from the labrum or upper lip.

All Sternorrhyncha and Auchenorrhyncha, and many Heteroptera, feed on plant vascular tissues or nutrients of developing seeds, and the order is one of the most economically destructive groups of insects. Piercing-sucking feeding results in localized injury, including discoloration, wilting, distortion, weakening or stunting of plant parts, or in some cases the formation of galls. Heavily infested plants may be killed. While some Hemiptera such as certain aphids have plant hosts restricted to one species or group of related species, others, such as the tarnished plant bug, *Lygus lineolaris* L., may have over 300 host plant species. Several families of Hemiptera, particularly aphids and leafhoppers, are vectors of plant pathogens such as barley yellow dwarf virus and plum pox virus.

Not all Hemiptera are plant pests. Several heteropteran families include species that are predators of other arthropods. Families such as the assassin bugs (Reduviidae), ambush bugs (Phymatidae), damsel bugs (Nabidae), and minute pirate bugs (Anthocoridae), play an important role in the biological control of a variety of insects, many of which are economically damaging. There are several families of aquatic hemipteran predators, including water boatmen (Corixidae), water striders (Gerridae), water scorpions (Nepidae), and giant water bugs (Belostomatidae) that prey on aquatic insects such as mosquito larvae. And a few hemipteran species affect humans directly: bed bugs, in the family Cimicidae, are ectoparasites of birds and mammals, including humans; Chagas' disease is transmitted to humans by conenose bugs in the genus Triatoma.

Economically important Hemiptera that occur in Saskatchewan include aphids such as pea aphid, English grain aphid, and green peach aphid, and others such as spruce gall adelgid, pine needle scale, tomato psyllid, greenhouse whitefly, aster leafhopper, alfalfa plant bug, tarnished plant bug, and black grass bug. As exemplified by the range of families and habits of the order, Hemiptera are a fascinating and diverse group of insects. *Juliana Soroka*

FURTHER READING: Maw, H.E.L., R.G. Foottit, K.G.A. Hamilton and G.G.E. Scudder. 2000. *Checklist of the Hemiptera of Canada and Alaska.* Ottawa: NRC Research Press; Dolling, W.R. 1991. *The Hemiptera.* 1991. London: Oxford University Press.

BULLER, ANNIE (1896–1973). Annie Buller was an important figure in the development of the militant, radical wing of the Canadian labour movement and the Communist Party of Canada. She was briefly, but significantly, involved in the ESTEVAN COAL STRIKE of 1931. Annie Buller was born in Montreal in 1896 to a working class family. At age 13, she went to work in a tobacco factory, 12 hours a day and six days a week. She later worked in retail and department stores until she was in her late teens. While still a teenager she joined the Socialist Youth Movement, which was active in campaigns to promote world peace and keep working-class young men out of conscripted military service.

During WORLD WAR I, Annie Buller enrolled in the Rand School of Social Science in New York, a centre for the study of Marxist theories, where she developed an interest in and sympathy for the Russian Revolution and trade union organizing. Upon returning to Montreal, Annie, now a confirmed Marxist, set up the Montreal Labour College with a small circle of like-minded friends to instruct progressive people as the Rand School was doing. The College started in 1920 and operated for a number of years.

Annie Buller was one of the founding members of the Communist Party of Canada. Beginning in the 1920s she traveled extensively throughout the country promoting the Party and revolutionary trade unionism. In 1929 the Communist Party set up the WORKERS' UNITY LEAGUE (WUL) as a trade union central. Annie Buller became an organizer of a WUL affiliate in the needle trades industry; she organized in Quebec and Ontario, as well as in Winnipeg. In the summer of 1931 wage cuts, unsafe working conditions, and squalid company housing caused the coal miners of southeastern Saskatchewan to approach the WUL affiliate, the Mine Workers Union of Canada (MWUC). The MWUC organized the miners and tried to bargain with the mine owners. The mine owners refused to negotiate, forcing a strike at the end of the first week of September. The WUL

Annie Buller addressing a crowd in Bienfait two days prior to the Estevan Riot.

B

asked Annie, who was in Winnipeg, to go to Bienfait and offer support and encouragement to the miners' wives and families.

On September 27, 1931, Annie spoke to a mass meeting of union miners, family members, and supporters in Bienfait. Her remarks dealt with the inadequate wages and terrible living conditions of the miners. Two days later, during a peaceful motorcade through Estevan, the municipal police and RCMP provoked a confrontation with the strikers and shot three of the picketing miners dead. Annie Buller was arrested for inciting a riot, unlawful assembly, and rioting. She was tried in February 1932 in the Estevan court-house and convicted. She was sentenced to one year of hard labour at the Battleford Jail and a $500 fine; she served the sentence in solitary confinement.

Annie Buller worked with organizations for the unemployed during the 1930s, and campaigned against fascism in the 1940s. She also devoted considerable time to left-wing and labour publications such as *The Worker* and *The Tribune*. In 1955 she visited the USSR with her husband, Harry Guralnick. In the 1960s she was active in opposition to the Vietnam war.

Annie Buller died on January 19, 1973. Perhaps the best description of her appeared in a police report following the 1931 Estevan Coal Strike. It read: "Age: 36; height: 5'10"; weight: 140 lbs; build: medium; hair: dark brown; eyes: brown; wears heavy dark-rimmed spectacles; religion: loyalty to the working class. Is a very powerful speaker; very well liked. Dangerous agitator." *Garnet Dishaw*

BULYEA, GEORGE (1859–1929). George Hedley Vicar Bulyea was born February 17, 1859, in Gagetown, New Brunswick and graduated from the University of New Brunswick with honours. He married Annie Blanch Babbitt in 1885 and they had one son, Percy, who died in his fifteenth year. Bulyea taught school in New Brunswick from 1878 to 1882, rising to principal, and sometimes worked as a surveyor and undertaker. In 1892 he moved to Winnipeg and in 1893 to Qu'Appelle, Assiniboia, where he ran a general store. He also wrote a pamphlet for the Canadian government extolling the virtues of the North-West Territories to potential settlers.

Bulyea lost the 1891 Territorial election but was elected to the Legislative Assembly of the North-West Territories from South Qu'Appelle in 1894. He joined the first Cabinet in 1897 as Territorial Secretary and Commissioner of Agriculture. In 1903 he relinquished these positions to become Commissioner of Public Works. He was the unofficial leader of the Liberals in the Assembly by 1903, second only to Premier **FREDERICK HAULTAIN** in influence. He served as a special commissioner for the North-West Territories to the Yukon in 1897.

SASKATCHEWAN ARCHIVES BOARD R-B3198
George Bulyea.

Bulyea resigned in 1903 due to Haultain's Conservative partisanship, but was persuaded to rejoin the Cabinet. He became a key member of the Cabinet sub-committee that represented Territorial interests in Ottawa in negotiating the creation of Alberta and Saskatchewan as provinces. During the provincial elections of 1905, the Liberal "machine" that Bulyea created was one of the keys to the Liberal victory in both provinces.

Laurier appointed Bulyea the first Lieutenant-Governor of Alberta and he served until 1915. Bulyea died on July 28, 1928, at Peachland, BC, and is buried in the Qu'Appelle Cemetery in Saskatchewan.

Michael Thome

FURTHER READING: McDougall, D. Blake, et al. 1991. *Lieutenant-Governors of the Northwest Territories and Alberta, 1876–1991*. Edmonton: Alberta Legislative Library.

BUNNIE, SAMUEL (1945–2004). Born on the Sakimay Reserve on June 2, 1945, Samuel Bunnie promoted education and self-government for First Nations people. In 1964, he received his Grade 12 diploma from Regina's Scott Collegiate, a rare accomplishment for an Aboriginal person at the time. He then returned to the Sakimay Reserve near Grenfell and served as Chief of the Sakimay Indian Band for twelve years. In addition, Bunnie chaired the Education Commission of the **FEDERATION OF SASKATCHEWAN INDIAN NATIONS** and served on the boards of the Saskatchewan Indian Federated College and the **SASKATCHEWAN INDIAN INSTITUTE OF TECHNOLOGIES**. He was instrumental in negotiating a $6.3 million Alternative Funding Agreement for the Sakimay Band and a $3.9 million land claim settlement. Having improved the quality of life for his

band members and others, Samuel Bunnie received the Saskatchewan Order of Merit in 1992. He died in June 2004.

BUNTINGS AND ALLIES. The New World family Cardinalidae consists of about forty-three species of medium-sized, brightly-coloured songbirds with large seed-eating beaks; of the thirteen species found in North America, six occur in Sakatchewan. They are all migratory. The only species which is common is the well-named rose-breasted grosbeak (*Pheucticus ludovicianus*) which nests in the southern boreal forests and aspen parklands region. This boldly black-and-white marked bird with its contrasting rosy breast is seen regularly as a migrant in the grasslands and townsites. The others are rare. The black-headed grosbeak (*P. melanocephalus*) is a regular summer resident throughout the south, as far north as Saskatoon. The western lazuli bunting (*Passerina amoena*) breeds in the brush and shrubs of coulees and river valleys in the south, including the Qu'Appelle system, where it may hybridize with its eastern counterpart, the indigo Bunting (*P. cyanea*), which is known only from the southeast. The dickcissel (*Spiza americana*) is now rarely seen. This dry-grasslands denizen, which looks much like a miniature meadowlark, was reported more commonly in the dry years of the 1930s. The distinctive Northern cardinal (*Cardinalis cardinalis*) is vagrant, with the unusual pattern of many winter records, rather than spring or fall transients. *Diane Secoy*

FURTHER READING: Alsop, F.J., III. 2002. *Birds of Canada*. New York: Dorling Kindersley.

BURAK, WILLIAM JAMES (1905–76). William Burak was born at Goodeve on April 1, 1905. In 1943 or 1944, as municipal secretary of RM Pittville at Hazlet, he learned of the "**MATT ANDERSON**" Health Plan at RM McKillop at Strasbourg, visited Strasbourg, and initiated a similar plan for RM Pittville.

In August 1945, Dr. Mindel Sheps came to Swift Current. She conveyed Premier **T.C. DOUGLAS**' desire that the Swift Current region become the regional demonstration unit for preventive medicine only; Burak instead proposed that the region offer "complete medical, surgical and hospital services." A "mover and shaker," as Lester Jorgenson called him, Burak was appointed a committee of one to sound out the adjacent municipalities. At his own expense, never reimbursed, he sent out information, visited weekly newspapers and municipal councils, and called a meeting for September 15, 1945, attended by representatives from 48 RMs, towns, and villages. On November 26, 1945, residents of the southwest voted for Burak's more comprehensive plan. The Douglas government somewhat reluctantly acceded to this "fast-tracking" of universal hospital and medical care for the region. It came into force on July 1, 1946, two full years in advance of Great Britain's National Health Insurance Plan. Burak was not appointed secretary of Swift Current Health Region #1. Disappointed, he moved to Ogema, Aberdeen, and Hafford as municipal secretary. He died in Saskatoon on June 8, 1976. *C. Stuart Houston*

BURGESS, MARY ELLEN (1895–1984). Born on January 4, 1895, in Chatham, Ontario, the daughter of a Presbyterian missionary, Mary Ellen Morrison spent her formative years in rural areas and graduated from Regina Normal School in 1912. While her rural teaching career inspired a lifelong interest in young people, she also became involved in community theatre with Jack Thomson, her first husband. Widowed in 1923 with two sons, Allan and Harry, her return to teaching ended with her marriage to George Burgess in 1928 and the birth of a third son, Orrison. Between 1928 and 1944, she became increasingly active in community theatre as an adjudicator, director and executive member of the **REGINA LITTLE THEATRE** and Saskatchewan Drama League.

Widowed again in 1944, Burgess became the drama consultant for the Division of Fitness and Recreation, Department of Education. Between 1944 and 1961 she travelled extensively across Saskatchewan advising teachers, assisting on school productions, and adjudicating festivals. Her work focused mainly on school theatre, especially with drama becoming a curricular subject in 1946. However, acting on her belief that educational theatre and community theatre were closely linked, she also reached a wider audience through lectures, broadcasts, articles, workshops, and summer

LES ROBINSON PHOTO/ SASKATCHEWAN ARCHIVES BOARD
PS57-116-01

Mary Ellen Burgess, June 1957.

SASKATCHEWAN ARCHIVES BOARD R-B5327-7

Saskatchewan Government Airways Norseman airplane at Cree Lake. The Norseman planes were used for freight hauling, and also for smoke jumping.

schools. In 1977 she received an honorary doctorate from the **UNIVERSITY OF SASKATCHEWAN**, Regina Campus, for her outstanding pioneering work in Canadian drama. Mary Ellen Burgess died on December 12, 1984. *Moira Day.*

FURTHER READING: Lyn Goldman File R-1647. Saskatchewan Archives Board. Regina, Saskatchewan; Regina Little Theatre R-135 Saskatchewan Archives Board. Regina, Saskatchewan.

BURRS, MICK: *see* **BERZENSKY, STEVEN**

BURSTALL, town, pop 388, located SW of Leader, just inside the Saskatchewan-Alberta border, on Hwy 321. In the first half of the 20th century, Burstall, like many other Saskatchewan communities that sprang up along rail lines, was an agricultural centre. Its population remained fairly stable at around 200. However, since construction of the TransCanada Pipeline began near Burstall in 1956, the natural gas industry has been a dominant area employer. By 1963, both the new industry and Burstall's population were booming. Today, Burstall is a modern town with a diverse business community and extensive recreational opportunities. In autumn, the area is popular with hunters. In 1976, a notable event took place near Burstall: a few kilometres east of the town, excavation work for the laying of a pipeline unearthed evidence of a prehistoric human settlement. The subsequent archaeological dig revealed evidence of a culture dating back roughly 5,000 years. *David McLennan*

BUSH PILOTS. It was in August 1924 that the first aerial survey pilots flew into northern

Saskatchewan. The challenge they faced was to photograph the uncharted areas of the **CHURCHILL RIVER** and **REINDEER LAKE** in open cockpit Royal Canadian Air Force (RCAF) flying boats. Many of these early bush pilots in northern Saskatchewan received their wings with the Air Force in **WORLD WAR I**. However, aircraft that flew north in the 1920s and 1930s were often mechanically unreliable and not well designed for the task: with no radio communication, reliable maps or weather reports, bush pilots relied on their ingenuity to fly into northern regions. By 1940, many of the early bush pilots were recruited by the RCAF to train young pilots for service in **WORLD WAR II** through the **BRITISH COMMONWEALTH AIR TRAINING PLAN** (BCATP). After the war, many among this next generation of pilots headed north to participate actively in the growth of mineral exploration and resource development in Saskatchewan. Improved aircraft reliability and radio communication provided the opportunity to fly in better conditions and open up new areas of the north. *Doug Chisholm*

BUSHELL, CHRISTOPHER (1914–41). Squadron Leader Christopher Bushell, a fighter pilot, was one of over 3,800 servicemen from Saskatchewan who lost their lives during the **WORLD WAR II**. Bushell was born in Fort Qu'Appelle on September 24, 1914, and raised there. He was in his second year of studies as a "Gentleman Cadet" at the Royal Military College of Canada in Kingston, Ontario when he enlisted in the Royal Canadian Air Force (RCAF), shortly after war broke out in 1939. Following his pilot training, Bushell was sent overseas in February 1940, where he served in an army co-operation squadron. In June 1941, he was reassigned as second-in-command of No. 412 (Fighter)

Squadron, RCAF. Bushell flew the Supermarine Spitfire on combat operations against the German *Luftwaffe* during the Battle of Britain; he was promoted to the rank of Squadron Leader and appointed Commanding Officer of No. 412 Squadron on November 1, 1941. While leading his squadron on a fighter sweep over occupied France on November 8 of that year, Bushell was shot down and killed. He was buried at Runnymede Memorial near Egham, England. On June 1, 1952, a housing area at RCAF Station Moose Jaw was established as part of a large-scale expansion of existing World War II facilities at the base. On September 19, 1954, the locale was officially named Bushell Park in honour of Squadron Leader Christopher Bushell. Encompassing an area of 28.84 hectares, Bushell Park continues to house Air Force personnel and their families. *Jeff R. Noel*

BUSHELL PARK, pop 379, located 5 km S of the city of Moose Jaw on provincial highway 363 and adjacent to the Canadian Air Forces 15 WING, MOOSE JAW-Air Vice-Marshal CM McEwen Airfield. Part of a large-scale expansion of existing WORLD WAR II facilities at the airbase when it was reactivated as a Royal Canadian Air Force Station in 1952, the community was organized to provide housing for Air Force personnel and their families. On September 19, 1954, Sybil Bushell of Fort Qu'Appelle, Saskatchewan, cut a ribbon at the main entrance to the community, officially naming it Bushell Park in memory of her son, Squadron Leader Christopher "Kit" Bushell, a World War II fighter pilot who was killed in action during the war. *Jeff R. Noel*

FURTHER READING: Office of Air Force History and Heritage, 15 Wing Moose Jaw: *CFB Moose Jaw Base History, 1939–1985*.

BUSINESS AND PROFESSIONAL WOMEN'S CLUBS.

Professional and business women in Saskatchewan started to organize service and support groups in the early 1930s. The first Business and Professional Women's Clubs (BPW) were formed in Saskatoon (1930) and Regina (1933). Membership included women prominent in business and in local legal and education systems.

Initial club activities addressed local needs such as helping female students with tuition; but upon affiliation with the Federated Business and Professional Women of Canada, local topics shared space with national and international concerns. During the late 1930s, for example, clubs studied subjects such as "Economic Problems of Germany," established a Peace Study Group, and donated funds to the Women's Disarmament Committee. During the war, BPW members knitted and collected salvage for the war effort, as did other women's groups, but remained advocates for women in business and public life. In the post-war reconstruction

era they were foremost among those who lobbied for greater female representation on public boards and committees.

In 1946, Regina club member RUTH MCGILL became president of the Federated Business and Professional Women of Canada. This, and the success of a national conference held in Regina, energized existing clubs in Prince Albert, Regina and Saskatoon, and spurred the creation of new ones in the Battlefords, Kamsack, Rosetown, Shaunavon, and Swift Current. A Moose Jaw war service club and a Yorkton Business Girl's Club became Business and Professional Women's Clubs. The BPW concern for women's rights began to consume more energies in the 1950s, 1960s and 1970s. In briefs to royal commissions and in meetings with elected officials, the clubs addressed subjects such as equal pay for work of equal value, matrimonial property rights, family planning, day care, and the involvement of women in politics. Although some clubs have folded and membership has declined, remaining clubs continue to work for women's advancement and greater opportunities in business, professions, and the industry. In July 2004 Regina hosted the national convention. *Lisa Dale-Burnett*

BUTALA, SHARON (1940–).

Sharon Butala was born on August 24, 1940, in Nipawin, Saskatchewan. She attended the UNIVERSITY OF SASKATCHEWAN to obtain a Bachelor of Fine Arts and a Bachelor of Education, and then worked as an educator of special needs teenagers in Saskatoon. In 1976 she left academia to live with her husband, Peter Butala, on a ranch near Eastend; she also began her writing career, which focused on the

character of the land and the personalities of ranchers and small-town people. Butala first wrote short stories, such as: "The Perfection of the Morning: An Apprenticeship in Nature" (1994), "Coyote's Morning Cry: Meditations and Dreams from a Life in Nature" (1995), "Wild Stone Heart" (2000), and "Old Man on His Back" (2002). She has also written several plays including *Natural Disasters* (1986), *A Killing Frost* (1988) and *Rodeo Life* (1993).

Although Butala found the move to her new rural home difficult at first, she eventually came to embrace the vastness of her surroundings and used it as inspiration for her writing. However, the underlying theme in all her work has been understanding and exposing the female soul. She is also active in preserving the Saskatchewan landscape: in 1996, she and her husband turned over a portion of their 13,000-acre ranch to the Nature Conservancy of Canada; this land now makes up the Old Man on His Back Prairie and Heritage Conservation Area, a vast expanse of mixed-grass prairie that is to remain undisturbed. Also committed to preserving historical sites, she recognized the importance of WALLACE STEGNER's accomplishments in literature and ensured that his home in Eastend was declared a historical site and made into an artists' retreat.

Since the beginning of her writing career over twenty years ago, Butala has been recognized numerous times for her work. Awards include the Marian Engel Award for a Woman Writer in Mid-Career in 1998; the Non-Fiction Award and Spirit of Saskatchewan Award from the SASKATCHEWAN BOOK AWARDS in 1994; and in 1991 both the SASKATCHEWAN WRITERS GUILD Member's Achievement Award and a Silver Award for Fiction from the National

DUANE PRENTICE PHOTO, NOMADIC VISIONS, VICTORIA, B.C.

Sharon Butala.

Magazine Awards. She was also shortlisted for the Governor General's Award for Non-Fiction in 1994 for "The Perfection of the Morning," and for Fiction in 1986 for *Queen of the Headaches*, as well as for the Commonwealth Writers' Prize, Canada-Caribbean Section, for *Fever* in 1992. Butala has also received awards for her commitment to preserving Saskatchewan ecology and her contributions to the literary world; these include an honorary degree from the **UNIVERSITY OF REGINA** in 2000, the Queen's Jubilee Medal in 2002, and an honorary degree from the University of Saskatchewan in 2004. She was invested as an Officer of the Order of Canada in 2002. *Melanie Neuhofer*

FURTHER READING: Butala, S. 2002. *Old Man on His Back: Portrait of a Prairie Landscape*. Toronto: Harper Collins.

BUTT, BRENT (1966–). Brent Butt was born on August 3, 1966, in Tisdale. He decided to be a stand-up comic at the age of 12 after watching the *Al Hamel* television show. When he was 20, he moved to Saskatoon to pursue a career in humour, and eventually was offered a tour on the road. After a year he was headlining in Toronto, and after four years he participated in an international comedy festival, Montreal's Just For Laughs. He received several Gemini Nominations, and at the 2001 Canadian Comedy Awards was named Best Male Stand-Up in Canada. In 2004, he won two Canadian Comedy Awards and was nominated for an International Emmy Award. Brent Butt is the creator, star, and executive producer of the comedy series *Corner Gas*; he has appeared in numerous Canadian television programs, and in several American shows such as *X-Files* and *Millennium*. Brent lives in Vancouver; between seasons of *Corner Gas*, he tours across the country. *Dagmar Skamlová*

BUTTERFLIES AND MOTHS. Butterflies and moths belong to the order of insects called "Lepidoptera," which means "scale-wings." They are named thus because their wings are covered with coloured scales that are arranged in rows, like shingles on a roof. The arrangement of these scales pro-

COURTESY OF THE ROYAL SASKATCHEWAN MUSEUM
Vashti sphinx moth.

J. PEPPER PHOTO/© SASKATCHEWAN ENVIRONMENT/SKCDC, 2001. ECOSYSTEM IMAGE INFORMATION SYSTEM
Speyeria hesperis lais, Northwestern Fritillary.

duces many beautiful patterns in the various species. Lepidopterous larvae are called caterpillars; they undergo complete metamorphosis and later pass through a pupa stage, from which they emerge as adult butterflies or moths. Butterflies are diurnal (day-fliers); some moths are also diurnal, although most are nocturnal. Most butterflies are very colourful, and so are many of the moths. The most noticeable difference between butterflies and moths is that butterflies have enlargements, known as clubs, on the ends of their antennae.

So far, 160 species of butterflies have been found in Saskatchewan. The skippers have stout bodies and curled antennal clubs. Eight species of the swallowtail family have been recorded in Saskatchewan; these usually have a false eye-spot at the outer corner of each hind wing, and also a tail which acts as a false antenna—both being a means of protection that diverts the attention of their enemies away from more vulnerable areas.

The pure white butterflies are called whites. We have several species of yellow butterflies known as sulphurs. There are three species of marbles, which have green marbling underneath. The gossamer-winged butterflies are small and dainty. The hairstreaks have hair-like tails on their hind wings. The coppers often have bright coppery colours and are found in wet areas. Seventeen species of blues have been observed in Saskatchewan—more than in any other province.

The harvester is North America's only known butterfly whose caterpillars feed on other insects instead of leaves. The metalmarks are a tropical family, the Mormon metalmark being the only Canadian species. Our largest butterfly family, the brushfooted butterflies, comprises the fritillaries, crescents, checkerspots, anglewings, tortoiseshells, admirals, and ladies. The meadow browns have fif-

teen known species in Saskatchewan. They vary in colour from tan (ringlets) to dark brown (wood nymphs).

Saskatchewan's largest butterfly is the monarch, orange with black veins, and with a wing expanse of up to 10 centimetres. It reaches Saskatchewan as a migrant in late June, and produces a brood on milkweed, which emerges in August and goes south to Mexico for the winter. Early in the spring the monarchs move northward and produce a brood that then continues on to Canada.

There are nearly 1,500 species of moths known to occur in Saskatchewan, and a few additional species are discovered annually. These moths are divided into two groups: the Macrolepidoptera contain the biggest specimens, the black witch moth that strays here from the southern United States being the largest species; the Microlepidoptera, on the other hand, comprise many tiny species as well as some marginally larger ones—the only big moths in this group being the ghost moths.

Moths of the Macrolepidoptera normally have heavy bodies, with the exception of the geometrid moths. Their caterpillars are called "measuring worms": lacking any semblance of legs in the centre of their bodies, they loop themselves up and then stretch forward as they are crawling. Our six species of silk moths are up to 10 centimetres across. The caterpillars spin silken cocoons. The adults do not eat, and live only a few days. The males find the females by picking up the scent with their feather-like antennae. Our twenty-six species of sphinx moths have long, narrow fore wings, and hover over flowers while feeding. Moths of the clearwing species fly in bright sunshine with the butterflies; the caterpillars do not spin cocoons, but the pupae hibernate in the ground. The tiger moths spin silken cocoons; the colourful adults have a variety of spots and stripes.

Saskatchewan's largest family of moths is that of the owlet moths. A number of species are destructive cutworms, but most are not plentiful enough to be serious pests. The most colourful owlet moths are the underwings, with red, pink, or orange hind wings. *Ronald R. Hooper*

BUTTERS, M. ISABELLE (1929–). M. Isabelle Butters, an influential figure in Weyburn's commerce and community development, has received international, national, and provincial recognition. Born in Weyburn, April 22, 1929, she attended a rural school, then Weyburn Collegiate, and business school. In 1945, she began a forty-six-year career with the Weyburn Co-operative Association, serving as General Manager, 1978–91. Elected to city council in 1963, she served until 1976. In that year Butters became the second Saskatchewan woman to be elected mayor; she served until 1982.

PATRICK PETTIT/REGINA LEADER-POST
Isabelle Butters, October 1998.

Prominent in numerous organizations, she has been president of the Saskatchewan Library Trustees Association, the Arthritis Society, the Heart and Stroke Foundation, and the Special Care Homes Corporation. She has served on the Weyburn Arts Council, the Weyburn Community Health Council, the Chamber of Commerce, the Weyburn Union Hospital Board and Executive, the Community Development Committee, the Aid for the Aging Committee, the Saskatchewan Centre of the Arts Board, and the Public Service Appeal Board. Other involvements have included Quota Club (local and international), Rebekah Assembly of Saskatchewan, and the United Church.

The first of numerous awards came in 1979 when Butters was named a Member of the Order of Canada. In 1980 she received the Weyburn Citizen of the Year (Chamber of Commerce). In 1998 she was given the Saskatchewan Order of Merit, and in June 2004 she received the Saskatchewan Library Trustees Association Merit Award.   *Lauren Black*

BUTTERWORTH, MARJORIE SINCLAIR (1902–2004).
Marjorie Sinclair Butterworth was born on November 27, 1902 in Regina, North-West Territories, to Reverend John and Laura (McCutcheon) Sinclair. She had three siblings, James, Watson, and Helen. A lifelong resident of Regina, she attended Connaught Elementary School and Central Collegiate, graduated with a Bachelor of Science in Commerce at the University of Iowa in

1935, and then taught in the Regina Public School System from 1924 to 1967. She was a commercial teacher at Scott Collegiate from 1924 to 1930. In 1930 she was a charter staff member of Balfour Technical School, where she was the stenography department head until her retirement in 1967. She introduced the Wiese-Coover method of teaching touch typewriting that resulted in thousands of highly successful speed typists at Balfour and in the province. In the 1930s Butterworth coached her students for national and international typewriting contests in which they won several championships. She instigated the Alpha Tau Club and Awards at Balfour—incentives for high achievement in typewriting and shorthand throughout the 1900s.

Butterworth pioneered work experience, career counselling, and student employment services in high schools, and mentored many of her students in the teaching profession, several of whom returned to teach at Balfour. She influenced Business Education in Saskatchewan through her successful teaching and provision of professional methods courses for teachers. After retirement, she taught and developed Business Education teacher training courses for the Ministry of Education in Kenya in the early 1970s, and sponsored African students' post-secondary education in Saskatchewan universities and at SIAST. During her lifetime, she received numerous honours for her outstanding contribution to education, including the Canada Commemorative

ROBERT WATSON/REGINA LEADER-POST
Marjorie Sinclair Butterworth, June 1990.

125 Medal (1992), the Saskatchewan Order of Merit (1993), and the Regina YWCA Women of Distinction Award in Education (2003). Educators, friends, and hundreds of her students expressed their appreciation at her 100th birthday celebration on November 27, 2002, at the Saskatchewan Centre of the Arts. She died on April 29, 2004.   *Dorothea Schrader*

BYERS, BARBARA (1951–).
Barbara Mary Byers, born in Saskatoon in 1951, became one of the most influential women in the Saskatchewan and Canadian labour movement, beginning in the 1980s and moving into the 21st century.

Byers began her career as a social worker for Saskatchewan Social Services, where she worked for over seventeen years. She became active in the Saskatchewan Government Employees' Association prior to their major strike in 1979, and became the first Woman president of the union in 1984. As SGEU President for five terms, she effectively fought for members against the anti-labour policies of the **GRANT DEVINE** Progressive Conservative Government. In 1988 she became the president of the **SASKATCHE-WAN FEDERATION OF LABOUR** (SFL); during her tenure she continued her opposition to the Devine government's initiatives such as the "Fair Share" program, which would have decentralized the provincial civil service, and fought against privatization and in support of public services. Byers even spent a day in jail after demonstrating in support of Massey Ferguson workers for a better contract. Her convictions and principles ensured that the Saskatchewan media paid attention to labour issues and that the Saskatchewan public associated her as the voice of workers, unionized or not.

She was a defender of women's rights and advocated on behalf of other disempowered groups —gays and lesbians, men and women of colour, and Aboriginal people—and encouraged young people to get involved in the labour movement. She sought to build links with farm groups, churches, students, women's groups, and other social justice groups.

During her term in office at the SFL, Byers helped in the development of a summer camp sponsored by SFL/CLC (Canadian Labour Congress) to introduce the sons and daughters of union members to the principles of social justice and the labour movement. She served as president of the SFL from 1988 to 2002, when she was elected executive vice-president of the Canadian Labour Congress, the first Saskatchewan woman to hold this position in the history of the CLC.   *Doug Taylor*

C

CABRI, town, pop 483, located approximately 65 km NW of Swift Current on Hwy 32, and 60 km N of Gull Lake via Hwy 37. In 1908 settlers were arriving in the Cabri district, and the village grew quickly. By 1918, an impressive string of nine grain elevators lined the railway tracks, and by 1921 Cabri had a population of over 500. Low precipitation in the 1930s discouraged many area farmers, who left. But after **WORLD WAR II** Cabri, like many other Saskatchewan communities, entered a period of unprecedented prosperity and growth. Agricultural technology had improved, and with irrigation, fertilizers and herbicides the heavy clay gumbo produced higher yields. Oil was discovered in the region in the early 1950s; the TransCanada Pipeline, constructed in 1956, ran just a few kilometres from town. By 1971, the town's population had swollen to 737. In subsequent decades, however, with improved roads, fewer people farming the countryside, and the abandonment of passenger rail

COURTESY OF THE CABRI MUSEUM

An early resident of Cabri was Woo Sing, who arrived in 1913, a tailor by trade. For the next 55 years, he worked mainly as a tailor in the community, with dry cleaning as a side line.

service, the population returned closer to the community's historic average. Although agriculture and its subsidiary activities remain the backbone of the district, the recent discovery of large reserves of natural gas in the area has injected money into the local economy and provided some off-farm employment. Today, Cabri remains an important centre in the district, with many businesses, services, and recreation opportunities. The Cabri Brass Band became renowned throughout the province; one of its members, Bobby Gimby (1919–98) later gained national attention as the composer of the 1967 Centennial song "Canada"; he received the Order of Canada for his contribution to the country's national identity.

David McLennan

CADBURY, GEORGE WOODALL (1907–95).

Born and raised in Birmingham, England, Cadbury was the eldest grandchild of the Quaker founder of the famous chocolate dynasty. In the 1920s, Cadbury attended King's College at Cambridge to study economics, where John Maynard Keynes was his supervisor. Afterwards, he studied at the Wharton School of Business at the University of Pennsylvania.

Cadbury accumulated years of experience as a managing director of two sizeable food processing enterprises in England. He was lent to the Ministry of Aircraft Production where he was the deputy director of production for three years during **WORLD WAR II**. He then worked for the British Air Commission in Washington, DC. Cadbury had close links with the British Labour Party and was well known in Fabian Society circles. He got to know a number of Canadian socialists including David Lewis, the future leader of the NDP. Lewis suggested

SASKATCHEWAN ARCHIVES BOARD R-A11291-1
George Cadbury.

that Cadbury pay a visit to see the newly elected CCF government in Saskatchewan. In the summer of 1945, Cadbury met with officials in the Saskatchewan government, was invited to observe a Cabinet meeting, and was offered a job.

Cadbury arrived in December, soon joined by his wife Barbara, also a committed socialist with much experience in the co-operative movement, along with their two daughters. **T.C. DOUGLAS** needed Cadbury to bring order to the group of enterprises purchased or set up in its first few months of government. Douglas also wanted an effective system of long-term economic planning. Cadbury established the Economic Advisory and Planning Board, a committee of Cabinet with himself as chair, to provide advice to Cabinet on improving performance of government enterprises. With experts recruited from all over Canada, the Planning Board soon became the brains trust for the new government. Two additional central agencies were created which had a great impact on the evolution of government in Saskatchewan. The Budget Bureau pioneered a more collective approach to expenditure control and acted as an advisory body on the machinery of government. The Government Finance Office, later known as Crown Investments Corporation, was a holding company and treasury board for the growing number of Crown corporations in the province.

Through these agencies, Cadbury put Saskatchewan at the cutting edge of innovative government in the world. By the end of the decade, Cadbury felt that the creative part of his job had been completed and he left the province for a long career in the United Nations as an advisor to various developing countries. After retirement, he moved to Ontario and returned to political life as the chairman, and later president, of the national NDP. He was also active with his wife in the International Planned Parenthood Federation. He died on February 28, 1995.

Gregory P. Marchildon

FURTHER READING: Cadbury, George. 1971. "Planning in Saskatchewan." Pp. 51–64 in Laurier Lapierre et al. (eds.), *Essays on the Left*. Toronto: McClelland and Stewart; —. 1981–82. Transcription of oral interview. Saskatchewan Archives Board, R-8343 to R-8345; McLaren, Robert I. 1995. "George Woodall Cadbury: The Fabian Catalyst in Saskatchewan's 'Good Public Administration'," *Canadian Public Administration* 38 (3): 471–80.

CADETS. The history of the Cadet movement in Saskatchewan begins with the creation of the Prince Albert Cadet Corps under the authority of a militia order in February 1903. Although that particular Army Cadet Corps was disbanded two years later, the Cadet movement has thrived in the province, with sixty-four corps and squadrons and more than 2,300 Sea, Army and Air Cadets at the end of 2003. Cadets are taught citizenship and personal disci-

pline, as well as general military knowledge. National Defence Canada co-sponsors the Cadet movement, along with the civilian sponsoring bodies, the Navy League, the Army Cadet League, and the Air Cadet League. Officers with the Cadet movement are members of the Cadet Instructors Cadre, the largest component of Canada's Reserve forces. Logistical support and oversight for Saskatchewan Cadet units are provided through Regional Cadet Support Unit (Prairie) Detachment in Regina. The Cadet program accepts young people between the ages of 12 and 19.

There are currently seven Royal Canadian Sea Cadet Corps in Saskatchewan, the oldest being RCSCC *Impregnable* in Regina, founded in 1922. Sea Cadets learn about naval tradition, as well as sailing and seamanship. Although some Sea Cadet Corps had accepted female members of the Navy League beginning in 1972, female Cadets were first enrolled in Cadet corps in 1975.

There are currently twenty Army Cadet Corps in Saskatchewan, including the oldest cadet unit in the province, No. 155, Royal Regina Rifles Cadet Corps in Regina. Army Cadets learn about army tradition, as well as basic orienteering and field camping skills.

There are thirty-seven Air Cadet Squadrons in Saskatchewan, the oldest being RCACS #17 in Yorkton. Air Cadets learn the traditions of the Air Force as well as basic air navigation, and can take training leading to a civilian pilot qualification.

The Navy League of Canada also offers a modified Cadet program for young people ages 10 to 12. There are six Navy League Cadet Corps in Saskatchewan, the oldest being NLCC W.K. Reed in Prince Albert. The programming is similar to the Sea Cadets.

Malcolm French

CALDER, JAMES ALEXANDER (1868–1956).

James Calder was born on a farm in Oxford County, Ontario on September 17, 1868. At age 13, Calder moved with his family to Winnipeg and took high school there. Calder's father died accidentally shortly after and the Calder children all found jobs to keep the family together. Calder attended Manitoba College and University of Manitoba, graduating with a BA in Science in 1888. He received a teaching certificate from **NORMAL SCHOOL** and taught in various rural schools until he became principal of the Moose Jaw High School in 1891. Three years later, he became a school inspector. While he was within the school system, he began to study law. He was called to the Bar but he never assumed an active law practice.

From 1901 to 1905, Calder was Deputy Commissioner (Deputy Minister) of Education in the North-West Territories under the premiership of **FREDERICK HAULTAIN**. When the province of Saskatchewan was formed in 1905, **WALTER SCOTT**

James Calder.

became Premier and Calder was the Commissioner (Minister) of Education and Provincial Treasurer in the first Cabinet. Calder was elected in South Regina in the first general election on December 13, 1905. He was defeated in the 1908 election in Milestone, but won a by-election in Saltcoats a few months later. He was re-elected in 1912 and 1917. In 1912, Calder became the Minister of Railways, Telephones and Highways. Scott was out of the province for up to six months of every year and Calder served as Deputy Premier in Scott's absence. Scott generated big ideas and long term plans, while Calder was the "detail man" and administrator.

In 1917, Calder resigned his seat in the Legislative Assembly and joined Borden's Union government at the national level. He was elected to the House of Commons representing Moose Jaw and assumed the Immigration and Colonization portfolios. In 1921, Calder was appointed to the Senate as a Conservative, where he served until 1956.

He married Eva Mildred Leslie in 1910 and they had one son, James Alexander. Calder devoted nearly his entire life to public service. He served the people of Saskatchewan and Canada for 62 years. Calder died on July 20, 1956.   *Gordon Barnhart*

FURTHER READING: Saskatchewan Archives Board. J.A. Calder Papers. Personal recollections. M2-file #63, Saskatoon.

CALDER, JAMES FRANKLIN ARCHIBALD (1913–88). Jake Calder was born in Regina on September 11, 1913; but his Anglican clergyman father moved to London, Ontario when he was an infant. He was a journalist with the *Toronto Star*, served with the Princess Patricia Light Infantry during WORLD WAR II, and then joined the staff of the

Prince Albert Herald. He arranged for a speaker to come to Prince Albert to inform the public about alcoholism, and as a result Alcoholics Anonymous groups were formed in the Saskatchewan Penitentiary and the Men's Correctional Centre. Calder's tireless advocacy for a provincial approach to the problems associated with alcoholism resulted in the formation of the Bureau on Alcoholism in October 1953. He was the first employee, providing educational services. ANGUS CAMPBELL was hired two years later to work directly with alcoholics and their families. The Bureau became, over time, the Saskatchewan Alcohol and Drug Abuse Commission, providing a complete range of services to addicted persons and their families across Saskatchewan. Calder resigned from the Bureau in 1963 to take a position with the National Council on Alcoholism in New York City. After two years there, he returned to journalism in New Jersey and Toronto until his retirement. The Calder Centre in Saskatoon is named for him. He died in Toronto on February 22, 1988.   *Al Hergott*

CALDER, ROBERT L. (1941–). Robert Lorin Calder is an award-winning author and an accomplished scholar of modern British literature at the UNIVERSITY OF SASKATCHEWAN. Born in Moose Jaw on April 03, 1941, he grew up in Saskatoon and completed his honours and master's degrees in English at the University of Saskatchewan. In 1970, after earning a PhD from the University of Leeds in England, he returned to the University of Saskatchewan to become a professor of English and a specialist in 20th-century British fiction and drama. As a writer, Calder has distinguished himself through numerous books. He is also considered a world authority on W. Somerset Maugham, about whom he has authored two books: *W. Somerset Maugham and the Quest for Freedom* (1972), and *Willie: The Life of W. Somerset Maugham* (1989). The latter work is an award-winning biography that earned Calder the Governor General's Literary Award for Non-Fiction. He is also well known for his expertise in British and Canadian wartime literature. His recent books, *A Richer Dust: Family, Memory*

Robert Calder.

and the Second World War (2004) and *Beware the British Serpent: The Role of British Propaganda in the United States, 1939–1945* (2004), reflect on the social impacts of WORLD WAR II. In 2003, *A Richer Dust* won the John V. Hicks Manuscript Award for excellence in literary non-fiction and in 2004, *Beware the British Serpent* won two SASKATCHEWAN BOOK AWARDS. Calder also co-authored the popular 1984 book on the SASKATCHEWAN ROUGHRIDERS, *Rider Pride: The Story of Canada's Best-Loved Football Team.*   *Iain Stewart*

Jessie Caldwell and Louis St. Laurent.

CALDWELL, JESSIE (1901–90). Born in Manchester, England on October 17, 1901, Jessie Rowles immigrated with her parents to Crandall, Manitoba, in 1910. She was one of five high-profile siblings including EDITH SIMPSON and P. Winifred Rowles. After graduating from NORMAL SCHOOL and the UNIVERSITY OF SASKATCHEWAN, she married Dr. A.L. Caldwell in 1924; they had one son. After a period in Cabri, the family moved to Saskatoon in 1941. Caldwell was the first woman to serve on the University of Saskatchewan senate (1929–50) and on the board of the National Film Board (1950–56), and was the first vice-president of the United Nations Association of Canada. In 1953 she was an alternate delegate to the UN General Assembly. She held top posts in the local, provincial and national COUNCILS OF WOMEN. Also prominent in the Liberal Women's Association, she ran (unsuccessfully) for office in the 1952 provincial and 1958 federal elections. Her honours include local and provincial citizens' awards, life memberships in several organizations, an honorary Doctors of Laws degree (University of Saskatchewan), and inclusion in the *Canadian Who's Who*. Caldwell died on February 17, 1990.   *Ruth Wright Millar*

CALL CENTRES. Saskatchewan's telephone call centre industry has emerged as a dominant force in the provincial economy. The number of people working for call centres in Saskatchewan has dramatically increased over the past five years, with more than 8,000 people drawing pay cheques from 150 companies. Service provided through the call centres ranges from accepting catalogue shopping orders to activating cellular telephones and processing credit card inquiries.

The call centre market is fiercely competitive. Incentives to lure a company to a community often involve a financial package that includes training and tax breaks. In addition, a 2004 study by the KPMG consulting firm concluded Saskatchewan was one of the most cost effective locations to do business in North America. The same report also concluded that Saskatchewan has one of the most productive and reliable labour forces in Canada. Saskatchewan job tenure–or the measurement of how long an employee remains with a company–consistently exceeds the Canadian average by 25%.

The KPMG study results are reflected in the experience of Staples, an office supply company, since moving to Saskatchewan. Staples began with 100 call agent positions and grew to over 750 jobs in just four years.

Regina became StarTek's fourth Canadian location and complements other StarTek facilities in Colorado, Oklahoma, Tennessee, Texas, Wyoming, the United Kingdom and Singapore. Forbes magazine named StarTek one of America's top 200 Best Small Companies for 2002. StarTek's clients are predominantly in the software, Internet, E-commerce, technology and communications industries. In 2003, StarTek retrofitted the third floor of the former Eaton's department store in the Cornwall Centre in Regina and installed 520 workstations at a cost of $5 million.

In 2004, GC Teleservices Canada Corporation established a 250-job call centre in Saskatoon. GC Teleservices and StarTek are both predicting an increase from their initial employment numbers.

Joe Ralko

CALVERT, LORNE ALBERT (1952–). Lorne Calvert was born on December 24, 1952, in Moose Jaw. Given his deep commitment to community and Saskatchewan roots, it is not surprising that he has followed two paths in his public life: religion and politics. Furthermore, his religious background helps to explain the strong social orientation he has brought to his work as an elected official.

After high school, Calvert obtained a BA in economics at the **UNIVERSITY OF REGINA** and a Bachelor of Divinity in theology at Saint Andrew's College in Saskatoon. In 1976, he was ordained in the United Church of Canada. Calvert served congregations in various towns in Saskatchewan, including Perdue,

COURTESY OF THE PREMIER'S OFFICE
Lorne Calvert.

Gravelbourg, Bateman, Shamrock, Coderre and Palmer. In the late 1970s, he returned to Moose Jaw to serve as a minister of Zion United Church. He remained in that position until 1986, when he was first elected to the Saskatchewan Legislative Assembly as the **NEW DEMOCRATIC PARTY** (NDP) representative for the riding of Moose Jaw South. His decision to join the Saskatchewan NDP was in part influenced by his father who had been a long-time supporter of the **CO-OPERATIVE COMMONWEALTH FEDERATION**.

Subsequently, Calvert was re-elected twice as the NDP representative for Moose Jaw Wakamow. Between 1992 and 1995, he was appointed to several important Cabinet positions: Associate Minister of Health and Minister responsible for the Wakamow Valley Authority (1992), Minister responsible for SaskPower and SaskEnergy (1992–93), and Minister of Health (1995). In the fall of 1995 he became Minister of Social Services. In that capacity, Calvert had to address issues relating to the Public Service Commission, seniors, and eventually disabilities.

In the late 1990s, Calvert decided to take a break from politics to spend more time with his family. After a two-year hiatus, he returned to politics in 2001 to contest the leadership of the Saskatchewan NDP. The leadership convention took place at the end of January in Saskatoon. For the first time in its history, the party was to use a direct form of voting (allowing all registered party members, as opposed to party delegates, to vote) to select its new leader. After four rounds of voting, Calvert finally defeated six challengers, including **NETTIE WIEBE**, an ethics professor at Saint Andrew's College, and Chris Axworthy, the Minister of Justice in **ROY ROMANOW**'s government. In the last round of voting, he defeated Axworthy with 10,289 votes (or 57.6% of the vote). Calvert officially assumed the duties of Premier of Saskatchewan on February 8, 2001, and won Roy Romanow's former seat of Saskatoon-Riverdale one month later.

When Calvert became Premier of Saskatch-

ewan, the NDP government was in a coalition with the **LIBERAL PARTY**. As a result of the 1999 provincial election, the NDP found itself with 29 seats, the **SASKATCHEWAN PARTY** with 26 seats, and the Liberal Party with 3 seats. Eluding the legislative majority by one seat, the NDP then formed Saskatchewan's first coalition government in almost seventy years with the Liberal Party. Liberal MLAs **JIM MELENCHUK**, Ron Osika, and Jack Hillson were given positions in the Romanow government. After Romanow's retirement from politics, Calvert was able to renew the coalition by appointing Jim Melenchuk as Minister of Education and maintaining Ron Osika as the Speaker of the Legislative Assembly. He later moved Melenchuk to Finance and Osika to Government Relations.

Although Saskatchewan's fiscal situation had dramatically improved since Romanow first became Premier in 1991, Calvert's approach to government finances has been cautious. In keeping with his NDP predecessors beginning with **T.C. DOUGLAS**, he launched several social initiatives while keeping a close eye on the province's finances. Consequently, during his tenure as Premier, funds were provided for agricultural revitalization, highway repairs, childcare spaces, training and education opportunities, health care, and renewable energy projects. At the same time, measures such as government restructuring and tax increases on cigarettes and alcohol were implemented in order to ensure that budgets would remain balanced. Under Calvert's leadership, the NDP won 30 seats in the November 2003 provincial election and formed the government with the Saskatchewan Party forming a strong opposition with 28 seats. *Jocelyne Praud*

CAMECO CORPORATION. Cameco Corporation is the world's largest producer of **URANIUM**, generating roughly one-fifth of the total uranium output in the Western world. Cameco's principal source of uranium is the McArthur River mine in northern Saskatchewan, known to be the world's largest high-grade deposit of uranium. Production from this deposit is processed at the Key Lake milling operation. Cameco also has significant uranium operations at Cigar Lake, Saskatchewan, in the United States (Wyoming, Nebraska), and in Central Asia (Kazakhstan). Cameco sells its uranium–and its services to convert uranium into fuel for nuclear power reactors–to companies throughout the Americas, Europe, and Asia. It is also partnered with North America's largest nuclear electricity generating facility, located in southern Ontario, to refine and convert uranium for sale as fuel. Cameco's refining and conversion facilities are located at Blind River and Port Hope, Ontario. Although Cameco's primary focus is the production of uranium and the generation of nuclear electricity, it is also involved in gold mining and exploration, with large operations in Mongolia and the Kyrgyz Republic in Central Asia. Cameco generates annual sales in excess of $700 million and employs a workforce of over 3,200. Since its creation in 1988 through the merger of Eldorado Nuclear Limited and the Saskatchewan Mining Development Corporation (two former Crown corporations), Cameco has maintained its corporate headquarters in Saskatoon. *Iain Stewart*

FURTHER READING: Martin, P. 2003. "Saskatchewan's Top 100," *Saskatchewan Business* 24: 17–26.

CAMERON, ALEXANDER C. (1907–96).

Alex Cameron was born in Avonhurst on June 30, 1907. After receiving his education at CAMPION COLLEGE in Regina and the UNIVERSITY OF SASKATCHEWAN, Cameron taught in several schools in southwest Saskatchewan. He ended up in Richmound, where he was principal and active in the SASKATCHEWAN TEACHERS FEDERATION. He operated a garage in Richmound with his brother from 1941–60. Cameron was Richmound's mayor, organized credit unions, and was involved in the SWIFT CURRENT HEALTH DISTRICT. In the 1948 Saskatchewan election Alex Cameron won the Maple Creek seat for the Liberals. Cameron ran for leadership of the LIBERAL PARTY in 1959 but was defeated by ROSS THATCHER. In 1964 Premier Thatcher appointed Cameron Minister of Mineral Resources, which he held until the Liberals lost the 1971 election. In 1965 Cameron was also appointed Minister of Telephones. During his term as Mineral Resources Minister, Alex Cameron worked closely with the private sector, encouraging exploration and the development of the industry, especially with petroleum and potash. His department introduced telephone service to Saskatchewan farms still without telephones in the 1960s, while Mineral Resources developed a cost-

SASKATCHEWAN ARCHIVES BOARD R-A10450-3

Alexander Cameron.

sharing program to encourage mining in the North. He lost his seat in 1971. Cameron died on January 16, 1996. *Maryanne Cotcher*

FURTHER READING: Eisler, Dale. 1987. *Rumours of Glory: Saskatchewan and the Thatcher Years*. Edmonton: Hurtig Publishers.

CAMERON, DAN (1880–1963).

Dan Cameron's residence in the Modern Apartments in Regina mirrored the man: stuffed with books, redolent with cigar smoke, and with rum always on hand. He was never far from his vocal studio or the editorial offices of the local *Regina Leader*, for which he wrote music columns, book reviews, articles on international affairs, and whimsical notes. Indeed at the age of 74, after thirty years at the Regina Conservatory, he became a full-time worker for the paper.

Born on August 7, 1880, in Ottawa of Scottish parents, he lived in Winnipeg and became a singer, pianist and organist. His teaching at Albert College (Belleville, Ontario) revealed his passion for the broader cultural education of his pupils, whom he took to restaurants for fine food and to Toronto for Shakespeare. Respected for good music, good thinking, good food and wine, and the appreciation of the truth, he was to prove "a teacher of living." Commissioned in 1917 after two years in the Expeditionary Force, Cameron won the Military Cross and then worked in Veterans Affairs. Studies with eminent New York teachers Herbert Witherspoon, Oscar Saenger, Carl Odell, and George Sweet led him to the headship of voice teaching in Regina and a career as a linchpin of the city's musical life.

A leader in the Amateur Operatic Society, the Philharmonic Society, and the Orchestral Society, he was also conductor of the Bach Ladies' Choir, the founding conductor of the Male Voice Choir (1926–46), and the director of music at Knox Church. He challenged this choir not only with anthems, but also with concert versions of opera. Convinced of the need for fellowship among teachers, he helped found the Regina Music Teachers' Association and became national vice-president of the Canadian Federation of Music Teachers, whose news bulletin he edited. He loved to maintain contact with the Conservatory students and teachers, writing about them and the city's musical life in a student bulletin, which he began in 1933. During WORLD WAR II, as Director of the Conservatory, he kept city music alive by urging young students to enroll in what was largely an adult training institution and sponsoring the symphony orchestra. Successive professors of music at the UNIVERSITY OF SASKATCHEWAN thought he kept too much control in his own hands and were critical, but the testimonial dinner given in his honour in May 1962 showed the deep affection in which

UNIVERSITY OF REGINA ARCHIVES AND SPECIAL COLLECTIONS 80-1-5

Dan Cameron.

he was held. That year, he fulfilled a lifetime ambition to attend the Bayreuth Festival in Germany. On November 13, 1963, this most cosmopolitan of men collapsed at work in the press office, smoking a large cigar, at the age of 83. *Robin Swales*

FURTHER READING: Pitsula, J. M. 1988. *An Act of Faith*. Regina: Canadian Plains Research Center; *Encyclopedia of Music in Canada*, 2nd ed., 1992.

CAMERON, EARL (1915-2005).

Earl Cameron, born in June 1915, held several jobs prior to distinguishing himself as a national newscaster. His career started at CHAB Radio in his home town of Moose Jaw, where he went on to become the station's chief announcer and commercial manager. In 1943, he worked for the Manitoba government station in Winnipeg, which was an important production centre for the Canadian Broadcasting Corporation (CBC). Cameron joined the CBC staff a year later and was transferred to Toronto, where he won the coveted assignment of reading the evening national news. Canadians quickly recognized Cameron for his steady and genuine delivery of the news. In 1959, he left radio to anchor the CBC television news at 11:00 p.m. Seven years later, he switched to the supper-hour TV report while also reading the 10:00 p.m. national news to radio audiences in the Maritimes, Quebec, and Ontario. Later in his career, Cameron hosted the *Viewpoint* series and provided the voice-over for the famous "Look Ma, no cavities" Crest toothpaste commercials. Having retired in 1976, Earl Cameron died in Barrie, Ontario, on January 13, 2005. *Holden Stoffel*

CAMERON, ELIZABETH (1875–1959).

Elizabeth Gow Cameron was born in Scotland in 1875. At the age of 18 she received the Lady Literate in Arts (LLA) degree with distinction from the University of St. Andrews. In 1911 she married W.F. Cameron; they had two children. In 1914, they moved to Saskatchewan, first to Saskatoon, then to

Davidson, and finally in 1930 to Regina. Becoming active in the **HOMEMAKERS' CLUBS** of Saskatchewan, Cameron served two terms as president (1918–20 and 1921–23) and was editor of *Retrospect and Prospect*, a history of the first twenty-five years of the Homemakers' Clubs; in recognition of her many contributions she was given a life membership. A founder of the Federated Women's Institutes of Canada (1919), she served as convention secretary at the organizational meeting and became national president from 1929 to 1933. Cameron was also a lifelong member of the University Women's Club, Regina Council of Women, **WOMEN'S CHRISTIAN TEMPERANCE UNION**, and the United Church Women's Missionary Society. Because of her active involvement with women's organizations in Saskatchewan and Canada, she was awarded the Queen's Medal. Cameron died on May 9, 1959 in Regina. In 1973, she was inducted into the Saskatchewan Agricultural Hall of Fame.

Dagmar Skamlová

CAMP DUNDURN. The Canadian Forces training area known as Camp Dundurn is located about 35 km south of Saskatoon in what is primarily a raw prairie region of sand, sprinkled with poplar bluffs. The area was first used as early as 1928 for **MILITIA** exercises. For the first few summer militia exercises, men slept in tents because there were no permanent structures for habitation or operations. The land began to be cleared for a permanent militia training camp by local labour in 1930. Camp Dundurn was also used as an ammunition storage depot. During the **GREAT DEPRESSION**, a relief camp was established at Dundurn under the authority of the Department of National Defence; there, men worked for 20¢ a day plus meals, tobacco, lodging and work clothes. The relief camp included barracks-style accommodation for up to 2,000 men, a hospital, a recreation hall, and a fully functional water system. There was unrest at Camp Dundurn when 200 men went to Regina to join the **ON-TO-OTTAWA TREK**, until it was quashed at the **REGINA RIOT** of July 1, 1935. Dissatisfaction simmered at Dundurn, and a strike began on December 12, 1935, when two men were evicted. Despite calls from camp and other authorities to apply forceful measures, a peaceful settlement to the strike was negotiated on January 22, 1936. Federal relief camps were phased out in the summer of 1936.

With the outbreak of **WORLD WAR II** in 1939, Camp Dundurn was transformed into a bustling military base, the largest in Saskatchewan. Facilities were expanded to accommodate an armoured corps training school, an engineer training unit, a large hospital, a nurses' residence, a Canadian Women's Army Corps barracks, a fire hall, and an extended training area. More than 50,000 soldiers trained at Camp Dundurn before being assigned to duty over-

REGINA LEADER-POST

Live-firing exercise at Camp Dundurn, April 1995.

seas. Reserve soldiers who were exempt from active service also went through compulsory training there. Since World War II the camp has remained in military hands, and it operates today as Canadian Forces Detachment Dundurn. Permanent personnel have been reduced to less than 200, but the site maintains its role as an ammunition storage and training area. Activity peaks in the summer, when cadet and reserve army units arrive for extended training exercises.

John Chaput

FURTHER READING: Archer, J.A. 1980. *Saskatchewan: A History.* Saskatoon: Western Producer; Chisholm, D. 2001. *Their Names Live On: Remembering Saskatchewan's Fallen in World War II.* Regina: Canadian Plains Research Center; Dundurn and District History Committee. 1982. *Dundurn Memories.* Altona, MB: Friesen.

CAMPBELL, ANGUS (1917–2002). Born on August 12, 1917, in Swift Current and educated at Norden school near Kinistino, Angus Campbell played a key role in education and rehabilitation in the field of alcohol and drug abuse. He raised public awareness and made major contributions to alcoholism programs in Corrections, Aboriginal organizations, health education, and industry. The first counsellor in the Saskatchewan Bureau of Alcoholism in 1953, he did pioneer research and public education on alcohol dependency. After graduating from the Yale School of Alcohol Studies in 1959, he founded the Saskatoon Alcoholism Society; this led to the establishment of the multidisciplinary in-patient Calder Centre, which he directed from 1967 to 1975. From 1975 until 1983, he was director of community services with the Alcoholism Commission of Saskatchewan. In 1976 the Moose Jaw intervention and recovery facility was named the Angus Campbell Centre. His history of Saskatchewan's alcohol rehabilitation efforts, *The*

Grand Vision, was awarded the medallion of distinction by the Canadian Centre on Substance Abuse. He was awarded the Saskatchewan Order of Merit in 1996 and named a Member of the Order of Canada in 1998. He died in Penticton, BC on March 22, 2002.

Michael Jackson

CAMPBELL, CONSTANTINE (1934–). A respected authority on soil science, Constantine Campbell was born in Jamaica on January 18, 1934, moved to Canada in 1955, and studied at the Ontario Agricultural College. Having obtained degrees in agricultural chemistry and soil science, Campbell earned his PhD from the **UNIVERSITY OF SASKATCHEWAN** in 1965. He headed the soils and environment section and was program leader for the soil management and conservation program at Agriculture Canada Research Centre in Swift Current. His main interest was soil research relating to dry-land farming and his findings have increased the productivity and sustainability of farming on the Canadian prairies. A Fellow of the Agricultural Institute of Canada and the American Society of Agronomy, Dr. Campbell was made a Member of the Order of Canada and received the Saskatchewan Order of Merit in 1998.

CAMPBELL, DONALD (1919–2001). Don Campbell, born on December 22, 1919, was the first pilot to fly for the Saskatchewan Air Ambulance Service, which was created by the **CO-OPERATIVE COMMONWEALTH FEDERATION** (CCF) government in 1946 to provide reliable service to every region of the province. It was the first air service of its kind in North America and the Commonwealth. Campbell flew a variety of aircraft through his years for the service, one of which was the Noorduyn Norseman (CF-SAM) that remains on display today at the **WESTERN DEVELOPMENT MUSEUM** in Moose Jaw. He died on June 18, 2001.

James Winkel

CAMPBELL, MARIA (1940–). Maria Campbell is a community worker, storyteller, and filmmaker whose best-selling autobiography *Halfbreed*—an important document on racial relations in Canada—encouraged many First Nation people to become writers. Of **CREE**, French, and Scottish descent, she was born on April 26, 1940, eighty miles northwest of Prince Albert, in Park Valley, an impoverished Road Allowance community. The oldest of eight, Campbell quit school at age 12, after her mother died, to help her father, a **MÉTIS** trapper, raise the children. At 15 she married a White man, largely in an attempt to keep the family together; but he became abusive, reported her to the authorities, and the children were placed in foster homes. After she moved to Vancouver with her husband he deserted her, and she entered a life of alcohol, drugs, and prostitution. She attempted suicide twice, suffered a

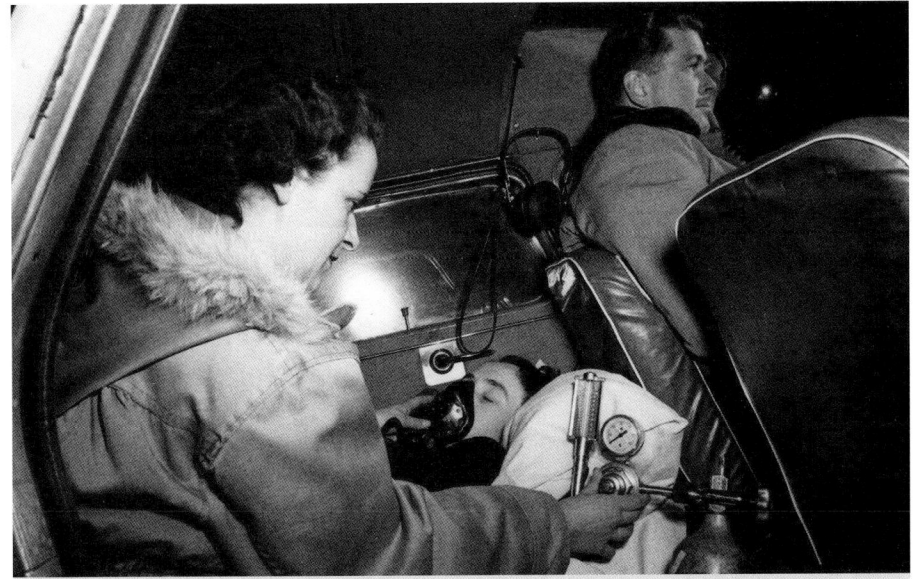

A Saskatchewan Air Ambulance nurse administers oxygen to a patient while Don Campbell pilots the plane, January 1952.

Progressive in the Liberal stronghold of Mackenzie. In the House of Commons, Campbell became a leading speaker for the Progressives on such issues as the proposed Hudson Bay railway, unfair freight rates, and transportation issues generally. Campbell was re-elected in 1925 with an increased majority. The small Progressive caucus had enormous influence in a minority government. Re-elected in 1926, he became closely involved with the Labour group under Woodsworth. Re-elected a final time in 1930, he believed the Bennett government more apt to rectify the west's grievances. He was appointed to the Tariff Advisory Board in 1933. Campbell served out his ten-year term before retiring from public life. He retired to London, Ontario, where he died on November 11, 1965.   *Brett Quiring*

FURTHER READING: Thomas, Lewis. 1976. "Milton Campbell-Independent Progressive." In Carl Berger (ed.), *West and the Nation*. Toronto: McClelland and Stewart.

nervous breakdown and was then hospitalized, at which time she joined the Alcoholics Anonymous program. To keep from drifting back to the street, she began writing *Halfbreed* (1973), which recounts the first thirty-three years of her life.

Campbell's other publications include: *People of the Buffalo: How the Plains Indians Lived* (1976); *Little Badger and the Fire Spirit* (1977); *Riel's People* (1978); *Achimoona* (an anthology, 1985); *The Book of Jessica: A Theatrical Transformation* (1989), co-authored with Linda Griffiths; and *The Road Allowance People* (1995). She has also written or directed stage plays, films, and videos. Campbell has been guest speaker at numerous conferences and universities across Canada, the United States and Australia on issues related to justice, women and youth in crisis, and community development. She has also been a visiting professor and writer-in-residence at various Canadian institutions.

Maria Campbell at a book reading, March 1980.

She holds honorary doctorates from Athabasca University, York University, and the UNIVERSITY OF REGINA. Currently an associate professor at the UNIVERSITY OF SASKATCHEWAN, she helps operate the Gabriel Crossings Foundation, a First Nation arts school committed to preserving traditional culture and arts; she also works with women in prison at the Pine Grove institute and with the Saskatchewan Native Theatre Company in Saskatoon. Her most recent work has been concerned with how people retain their identity when they have lost their homeland; for Campbell, identity is shaped by the land, and from that shape come narrative and song. If there is a theme that runs through her life and work, it is that inner peace and social justice can only be found by returning to the kind of spirituality—practiced by the early people of the plains—that regards humans and animals as interdependent, and that encourages people to listen to the guiding voices of the Grandmothers and Grandfathers.

Bernard Selinger

FURTHER READING: Campbell, Maria. 1973. *Halfbreed*. Toronto: McClelland and Stewart.

CAMPBELL, MILTON NEIL (1881–1965).

Milton Campbell was born in Greenvale, PEI, on January 21, 1881. He graduated from Prince of Wales College in 1902 and worked as a telegraph agent for the Canadian Northern Railway in Ontario, then transferred to Humboldt. In 1905 he settled in Kamsack where he remained until 1933. Campbell and two of his brothers went into business in Kamsack and Pelly. He was active in the local community, serving ten years as chairman of the Pelly School Board and as a town councillor from 1912 to 1920. Campbell was elected federally as a

Milton Campbell.

CAMPION COLLEGE, UNIVERSITY OF REGINA.

Established in Regina in 1917 by the Jesuit Fathers of Canada, Campion College started as a Catholic boys' residential school of the "classical college" model. It first offered only Grade 9; but the program extended upward each year to include a full program of university-level BA courses by 1926. Although it became a junior college of the UNIVERSITY OF SASKATCHEWAN in 1923, only the first two years were recognized: Campion thus affiliated with St. Boniface College in Manitoba so that its students could receive degrees.

In 1964, the university portion of Campion College became federated with the University of Saskatchewan, Regina Campus (since 1974 the UNIVERSITY OF REGINA), and a full university Arts program was offered in 1966. The new Campion building was opened on the university campus in

January 1968. Campion College is a Catholic community of learning in the Jesuit tradition: it provides a liberal arts education for the whole person—intellectual, social, spiritual—within the requirements of contemporary society. As a federated college, Campion offers students access to the resources of the university as well as the unique qualities of personal attention which a small college can offer.   *Joanne Kozlowski and Kenneth McGovern*

CAMPUS SASKATCHEWAN. Campus Saskatchewan, a partnership among Saskatchewan's post-secondary institutions and the Department of Learning, was established in 2002. The partners work together to use technology-enhanced learning to increase opportunities for people in Saskatchewan to access high quality education and training, at times and in places that best meet their needs. Charter members of Campus Saskatchewan were the **UNIVERSITY OF REGINA**, the **UNIVERSITY OF SASKATCHEWAN**, the **SASKATCHEWAN INSTITUTE OF APPLIED SCIENCE AND TECHNOLOGY**, Carlton Trail Regional College, Cumberland Regional College, Cypress Hills Regional College, Northlands College, Parkland Regional College, Prairie West Regional College, North West Regional College, Southeast Regional College, **FIRST NATIONS UNIVERSITY OF CANADA**, the Saskatchewan Indian Institute of Technologies, **GABRIEL DUMONT INSTITUTE**, **DUMONT TECHNICAL INSTITUTE**, and Saskatchewan Learning.

Through Campus Saskatchewan, post-secondary institutions coordinate development of courses and programs using technology that respond to student demands as well as provincial economic and social needs. The Campus Saskatchewan partnership provides a forum for the institutions to work together to coordinate services to support students. The members review and revise institutional academic and administrative policies to make it easier for students to take courses using alternate formats from more than one institution. The institutions also coordinate professional development and support for faculty in the integration of technology into teaching practice. The partners have established a web site (www.campussaskatchewan.ca) that provides a one-stop location for information, announcements and links related to technology-enhanced learning. The web site houses a comprehensive directory of Saskatchewan post-secondary credit courses delivered in alternative formats, including online, televised, off-campus classes, independent studies, and other multimedia technologies.   *Kathy Stedwill*

CANADIAN ACTORS' EQUITY ASSOCIATION. Canadian Actors' Equity is the professional association of performers, directors, choreographers, fight directors and stage managers in English Canada who are engaged in live performance in theatre, opera and dance. Recognizing that the arts are vital to life and that artists make an important contribution to our society, the association supports the creative efforts of its members by seeking to improve their working conditions and opportunities. The business of Equity is to negotiate and administer collective agreements, provide benefit plans, information and support, and act as an advocate for its membership.

For many years, exploitation in the theatre was a condition of employment, and there were no standard agreements. Dismissal was possible without cause or notice, and productions could suddenly close with no payment to the artists. In May 1913, a group of actors in New York drafted a constitution for the first Actors' Equity Association. It took six years of fighting and a thirty-day strike in 1919, led in part by Canadian actor Marie Dressler, before the theatre managements finally recognized Equity as the actors' rightful bargaining agent. Another strike in 1960 won the right of a pension for actors. By 1954, professional theatre in English Canada was coming into its own to the point where there was enough activity to justify a Canadian Equity office. On February 13, 1955, the Canadian Executive Committee held its first official meeting. It represented fewer than 200 artists. In 1976, after an amicable separation, Canadian Actors' Equity Association became a completely separate organization, operating under its own constitution and by-laws. Today it represents more than 5,000 active members from coast to coast. In Saskatchewan, Equity members are engaged in professional theatre, dance and opera at the **GLOBE THEATRE**, Opera Saskatchewan, **PERSEPHONE THEATRE** and **SHAKESPEARE ON THE SASKATCHEWAN**. In 1998, to commemorate the 75th anniversary of the **SASKATCHEWAN ARTS BOARD**, Canada's first, Equity met in Saskatoon—the first national members meeting outside of Toronto.
Darlene Bullard

CANADIAN ARTISTS REPRESENTATION/ FRONT DES ARTISTES CANADIENS (CARFAC) SASKATCHEWAN. CARFAC Saskatchewan was organized in 1983, amalgamating two groups of artists centred around Regina and Saskatoon who had met informally since the 1970s to address the concerns of artists. CARFAC Saskatchewan is a non-profit provincial cultural organization. Its board of directors comprises practicing visual artists, and its membership includes students, practicing visual artists, artists from other disciplines, museums and art galleries, educational institutions, and other individuals and organizations with an interest in visual art. Full membership, which includes voting privileges, is reserved for professional visual artists resident (or normally resident) in Saskatchewan. The International Association of Artists (IAA) defines a "professional artist" as one who earns a living through art-making; possesses a diploma in an area considered to be within the domain of the fine arts; teaches art in a school of art or applied art; whose work is often seen by the public or is frequently or regularly exhibited; or is recognized as an artist by consensus of opinion among professional artists. CARFAC Saskatchewan membership includes membership in CARFAC National, the national voice of visual artists across Canada.   *Patrick Close*

CANADIAN AUTO WORKERS (CAW/TCA). The origin of the Canadian Auto Workers in Saskatchewan dates back to August 16, 1955. Local 820 was chartered to the International Automobile, Aircraft, and Implement Workers of America (UAW/CIO) in Regina. The founding members of this local were employed by Ford Motor Company of Canada working in a parts distribution centre. Local 820 was to remain a small local (around fifty) throughout its history, but did acquire new members as time went on, owing to some activities in organizing. Canadian Aviation Electronics Ltd, Chrysler of Canada, and Massey Ferguson workers were to become members of the amalgamated local. The local no longer exists today as none of the companies it represented have workplaces in the province. In 1985 the United Autoworkers in Canada were going through changes which led to differences of opinion and approach to collective bargaining within the structure of the international union; the Canadian section of the union wanted more control over its destiny when bargaining with international corporations in Canada.

The result of all this was the formation of the National Union, United Automobile, Aerospace and Agricultural Implement Workers of Canada (UAW/ Canada) at a founding convention held on September 4, 1985, in Toronto, Ontario. The name was amended at subsequent conventions to National Automobile, Aerospace, Transportation and General Workers Union of Canada (CAW-Canada). The membership grew across the country through traditional organizing and through a number of mergers with other Canadian unions in industries, workplaces, and jurisdictions not represented by the autoworkers; membership in Saskatchewan also increased. The CAW now represents approximately 1,100 workers in the airline, railway, hospitality and trucking industries as well as other workplaces in the province.   *Barry Farrow*

CANADIAN BIBLE COLLEGE/CANADIAN THEOLOGICAL SEMINARY. The Canadian Bible Institute began in 1941 with a student body of fifty. It was established under the founding leadership of Gordon Skitch, superintendent of the Western Canadian District of the Christian and Missionary Alliance (C&MA), Willis Brooks, pastor of the Regina Alliance Tabernacle and well-known radio pastor, and George Blackett, who had served as the principal of Winnipeg Bible Institute and became the first principal, then president, of the Institute. The Institute was established to meet the growing need for ministers in the churches of the C&MA in western Canada, but over the years it also met similar needs in other denominations and para-church organizations. Its graduates were soon serving throughout Canada, the United States, and many countries overseas.

With modest beginnings at the Alliance Tabernacle on Osler Street in Regina, then occupying the old Clayton Hotel on Broad Street, the Institute relocated in 1956 to 4400 Fourth Avenue under the leadership of its second president, William McArthur. In 1957 its name was changed to Canadian Bible College (CBC), now offering programs leading to bachelor's degrees. In 1961, the Accrediting Association of Bible Colleges accredited the College and, in later years, transfer agreements were established with the UNIVERSITY OF REGINA. In 1970 Canadian Theological College (CTC), a professional program leading to master's degrees in divinity, Christian education and missiology, was established. The original enrollment of the College was twenty, under the leadership of president Alvin Martin and vice-president/academic dean Samuel Stoesz. Although continuing to share a president and board with CBC, CTC was granted a separate charter by the Saskatchewan Legislature in 1973. In the same year, CTC was approved for affiliation with the University of Regina, offering six classes at the University in Hebrew, Greek and biblical literature, with its president serving on the University Senate. In 1982, during the administration of the fifth president, Rexford Boda, CTC became Canadian Theological Seminary. In 1989, after the inauguration of the sixth president, Bob Rose, CTS achieved full accreditation with the Association of Theological Schools and began offering a program leading to a Doctor of Ministry degree. George Durance was elected the seventh president of CBC/CTS in 1997. The combined enrollments of CBC/CTS reached a high of approximately 700 full- and part-time students by the 1980s. On July 1, 2003 the College and Seminary relocated to Calgary, Alberta.

Rexford A. Boda

CANADIAN CATHOLIC ORGANIZATION FOR DEVELOPMENT AND PEACE.

The Canadian Catholic Organization for Development and Peace (CCODP or simply Development and Peace) was set up by the bishops of Canada in 1967, following the Second Vatican Council, with a dual mandate: to fund development projects in the Third World, and to make Canadians aware of the problems facing people in the developing countries. In Saskatchewan, CCODP took root at the parish level from the very beginning, with key priests and lay people promoting the organization's work and encouraging support for both fund raising and education campaigns. The first full-time provincial animator was hired in 1976 to build committees at the diocesan level and to increase links with other like-minded organizations in the province.

Today CCODP remains strong in Saskatchewan, with diocesan councils in Prince Albert, Regina and Saskatoon. A network of lay volunteers across the province carries out two annual campaigns: Share Lent (February to April) and the Fall Campaign (September to December). In addition, CCODP regularly arranges exposure tours for its activists to travel to countries in which there are Development and Peace partners (e.g., Mexico, Brazil, El Salvador), and brings to Saskatchewan spokespersons from the overseas partner organizations.

Michael Murphy and Susan Eaton

CANADIAN FEDERATION OF UNIVERSITY WOMEN (CFUW).

Committed to the pursuit of knowledge, promotion of education, encouragement of culture, improvement of women's status and human rights, participation in public affairs, and advancement of international friendship, the CFUW has had a strong Saskatchewan presence. Open to university graduates, and formerly known as University Women's Clubs, Saskatchewan groups emerged during WORLD WAR I. In 1915 a club was organized in Regina, and in 1918 the Saskatoon University Women's Club was founded; both predated establishment of the Canadian Federation (1919). Early topics of interest included women's suffrage and education, but members also presented educational programs on numerous topics. Two additional clubs were founded in the early 1930s: Swift Current (1930) and Prince Albert (1931). Reflecting economic and environmental challenges of the DEPRESSION, University Women's Clubs took particular interest in socio-economic issues: they raised money for Welfare Bureaus and established Milk Funds, but also sought to effect broader structural change. WORLD WAR II brought renewed club involvement in typical patriotic activities such as sewing and knitting for the Red Cross, conserving food, and supporting international relief. The 1950s and 1960s saw extensive development. Existing groups grew larger, and new ones in Weyburn and Yorkton received charters (1954). Clubs were very effective at fundraising during this time, and used the extra money to increase existing scholarships and create new ones. Activities during this era included lobbying for, and establishing, public libraries. Club interests during the 1970s reflected changing times: the Saskatchewan groups, like the national organization, placed renewed emphasis upon women's rights. In 1979 the youngest club in the province was organized in Estevan. As of 2004, there were approximately 300 members in seven clubs in Saskatchewan.

Lisa Dale-Burnett

CANADIAN GIRLS IN TRAINING.

Founded in 1915 by the YOUNG WOMEN'S CHRISTIAN ASSOCIATION (YWCA) and major Protestant denominations, Canadian Girls in Training (CGIT) sought to address the needs of teenage girls from a Christian perspective. It reflected then-modern concepts in Protestantism, including historical criticism of the Bible and the SOCIAL GOSPEL, as well as progressive education. CGIT emphasizes cherishing health, seeking truth, knowing God, and serving others. Affirming ideals of progressive education, volunteer leaders worked with small groups of girls to select and plan a wide range of programs and activities in a democratic environment. The exact date of CGIT's entry into Saskatchewan is unclear, but YWCA board minutes show initial organization occurring in Regina in March 1918. The movement proved popular with teenage girls and helped many to develop leadership skills and self-confidence. During the 1920s groups sprang up in communities across the province. CGIT survived the drought and economic depression of the 1930s, but membership numbers declined in the course of the second half of the century. As of 2004, CGIT groups continue to exist in Saskatchewan, though greatly diminished in number.

Lisa Dale-Burnett

CANADIAN GRAIN COMMISSION.

The Canadian Grain Commission, known from 1912 to 1971 as the Board of Grain Commissioners, is a regulatory body overseeing the activities of the Canadian grain industry through the administration of the Canada Grain Act. As Canada's most important grain producers, Saskatchewan farmers have always had a major stake in the activities of the Commission. The Canada Grain Act of 1912 and the Board of Grain Commissioners were the result of grievances on the part of western farmers, who lobbied effectively for their resolution. Politicians like Prime Minister Wilfrid Laurier and Premier WALTER SCOTT of Saskatchewan were anxious to please the grain growers of the west who, as western agriculture developed, became a potent force in politics and the economy. As the influx of settlers picked up in the 1890s, the growing western farming region produced larger and larger crops each year. By 1911, Saskatchewan alone had 28 million acres in production—more farmland than Manitoba and Alberta combined. As the western prairies came under the plough, Canada's WHEAT production grew apace from 42 million bushels in 1890 to 231 million in 1911, and an astounding 393 million bushels in 1915.

In the late 1890s western grain farmers and their organizations, such as the Territorial Grain Growers, were not happy with the treatment they received when they came to sell grain at many country elevators. They felt that they were often cheated on weights and grades, and that prices were being illegally fixed by Winnipeg grain companies; they suspected that further cheating took place in the large terminal elevators at the Lakehead. There was some truth in these charges and, in the time-honoured Canadian way, the first of many Royal Commissions was set up to look into the grain industry. The resulting Manitoba Grain Act of 1900 was the cornerstone of the regulatory framework that was finally consolidated in the Canada Grain Act of 1912. The leaders of the organized farmers, such as **E.A. PARTRIDGE** of Sintaluta and **W.R. MOTHERWELL** of Abernethy, had tremendous influence on the development of the legislation. The 1912 Act set up a board of three grain commissioners who would oversee the regulation of the movement of grain from the country elevator to the point where it was loaded for export or processed within Canada. Today, the 700 Grain Commission staff continue to arbitrate disagreements over grade and weight, inspect grain passing into and out of terminal elevators, and license and regulate elevators and grain companies.

Perhaps the most important function of the Board and now the Commission has been the administration of the Canadian grading system: Canadian grades are trusted and respected throughout the world because of the uncompromising honesty and thoroughness with which the Commission has always administered them. Grades like Number 1 or Number 2 Canadian Western Red Spring Wheat correspond to established specifications based on measures such as the percentage in the shipment of damaged or broken kernels, of other kinds of seeds, and of foreign matter such as dirt—as well as moisture content and weight of the grain. The grades assigned by the Grain Commission are under the control of the Western and Eastern Grain Standards Committees, which meet and make decisions about any changes or additions to the grades which may be necessary because of changing market and crop conditions. Each year they also establish standard samples for each grade.

Over the years the quality testing of Canadian crops and the publication of the findings has been another important support provided to the industry, as well as a key source of information for customers who wish to have a clear idea of what they are getting when they purchase from Canada. The Commission's Grain Research laboratory has, since its founding in 1914, produced useful, reliable and increasingly sophisticated information about crop quality, publishing its findings on factors like milling and baking quality, as well as moisture and protein content. Since 1927 the Laboratory has conducted surveys of western wheat crops for protein content. High-protein wheat brings a premium in the marketplace, and farmers in districts producing it, such as south and central Saskatchewan, naturally wanted it taken into account in grading; it was

not, however, until the 1970s that customer demand and the development of simple and fast techniques for establishing protein levels led to Canada offering, at a higher price, cargoes of wheat segregated by protein levels. Since 1912, the Canadian Grain Commission has changed a great deal in order to accommodate changes in the industry, new crop varieties, automation of procedures, and shifts in government policy. Its basic functions, however, remain the same: the regulation of the grain industry to ensure the continued high quality and orderly marketing of its crops. *James Blanchard*

CANADIAN LIGHT SOURCE. The Canadian Light Source (CLS), located on the **UNIVERSITY OF SASKATCHEWAN** campus, is Canada's largest science research initiative in over 30 years. The first visible light from the facility was recorded on December 10, 2003, in a diagnostic beamline. Once fully operational, it will be one of the most powerful, third-generation synchrotrons in the world with over 30 operational beamlines. The $173.5-million project is a unique national facility that will provide numerous opportunities for science and innovation. The CLS, wholly owned by the University of Saskatchewan, is funded by federal, provincial, municipal, industrial and academic sources.

A synchrotron functions like a microscope with an extremely bright light—millions of times brighter than sunlight. Electrons are accelerated in a synchrotron at nearly the speed of light for an extended period in a closed system. The beamlines fit into groups of wavelengths including infrared, soft X-ray, and hard X-ray beamlines. Many components make a synchrotron operational: electron gun, linear accelerator (LINAC), booster ring, storage ring, synchrotron light, beamlines, optics hutch, experimental hutch, and work stations. The process involves injecting 220keV electrons into an ultra-high vacuum tube, then accelerating the electrons to nearly the speed of light. The electron beam is then transferred to the booster ring, where microwaves increase the energy to 2.9 giga-electron volts (GeV). From there, the electron beam is transferred to the storage ring at a current of 500 milli-amps, and bending magnets are used to accelerate and bend the beam many times to produce synchrotron light, which is then manipulated to investigate the structure of molecules.

There are many applications of synchrotron science: developing designer molecules for drugs; cancer research; studying the functionality of proteins, hormones, metabolic enzymes, bacteria, genes and viruses; creating materials such as hybrid metal alloys; trace-metal fingerprinting to manage natural resources; and developing micro-sensors and micromachines for drug delivery systems. *Jessica Pothier*

CANADIAN NATIONAL RAILWAY. Canadian National Railway (CNR), incorporated on June 6, 1919, took form through a series of mergers between 1917 and 1923, uniting several older and financially troubled railways, many of which had been built between 1850 and 1880. In 1918 the federal government combined the operations of the government-owned Canadian Government Railways and the privately owned Canadian Northern Railway, bringing CNR into existence. CNR then took control of the **GRAND TRUNK PACIFIC RAILWAY** in 1919, and of its parent company, the Grand Trunk Railway (eastern Canada's largest and oldest railway company), in 1923. Out of these amalgamations

PHOTO COURTESY OF CANADIAN LIGHT SOURCE

Synchrotron.

emerged Canada's most extensive railway system, with over 35,000 km of track linking the country from coast to coast and with the United States. As one of Canada's first **CROWN CORPORATIONS**, the CNR experienced significant growth in the late 1920s, especially on the prairies. Through the vision of its new president, Sir Henry Thornton, CNR expanded its reach in the prairie west in hopes of populating the uninhabited lands along many of its lines, increasing its passenger and freight traffic, and tapping further into the region's forest, fish, mineral, and agricultural resources.

Between 1927 and 1930, CNR constructed more branch lines in Saskatchewan than in any other Canadian province, accumulating a total of 6,730 km of track. CNR also operated 575 stations and shelters, 1,551 elevators, 653 loading platforms, and 437 stock yards in the province. CNR Immigration and Colonization Department offices in Saskatoon, Winnipeg, and Edmonton recruited thousands of settlers to the west. In Saskatchewan, the districts of Prince Albert, Kelvington, Henribourg, and St. Walburg (all located in the parkland region) were direct targets of CNR's settlement policy and branch line expansion. In the latter half of the 20th century, the face of CNR began to change: many prairie branch lines closed after 1945; the passenger service was terminated in 1978; and in 1995 CNR was privatized after more than seventy-five years as a government-owned railway. Now called Canadian National (CN), the corporation has as its focus in western Canada the bulk transport of coal, potash, sulfur, grain, and forest products; its holdings include marine operations, hotels, telecommunications, and resource industries. *Iain Stewart*

FURTHER READING: Landry, N. 1990. "The CNR and Western Settlement, 1925–1930," *The Archivist* 17 (3): 14–16; MacKay, D. 1992. *The People's Railway: A History of Canadian National Railway.* Vancouver: Douglas & McIntyre.

CANADIAN NAVY. The Canadian Navy has long had a close connection to Saskatchewan despite the province's geography; indeed, one of the first naval engagements involving Canadian forces occurred in Saskatchewan during the **NORTH-WEST REBELLION**. During the battle of **BATOCHE**, the **MÉTIS** and First Nations under **GABRIEL DUMONT** attacked the riverboat *Northcote*, which had embarked members of the North-West Mounted Police under General **MIDDLETON**. A ferry cable strung across the river damaged *Northcote*'s smokestack and wheelhouse, effectively scuttling the waterborne portion of Middleton's battle plan.

On May 4, 1910, the Liberal government of Sir Wilfrid Laurier created the Royal Canadian Navy. The Royal Canadian Naval Volunteer Reserve was created by Order-in-Council on January 31, 1923,

with twenty-four Divisions across Canada, including Half Companies in Regina and Saskatoon. The Regina and Saskatoon Half Companies both went through a series of homes in their early years, and both faced a number of challenges training prairie sailors; pay was minimal for ratings and non-existent for officers. During the **GREAT DEPRESSION**, the Regina Half Company established a training facility at Last Mountain Lake to ensure that no naval reservist would have to go on relief.

During **WORLD WAR II**, both units became recruiting and training centres for the Royal Canadian Navy. Naval custom has long designated shore-based training establishments as ships. In 1942, the Saskatoon Half Company was commissioned as HMCS *Unicorn*, in honour of one of the first ships to sail into Hudson Bay, while the Regina Half Company became HMCS *Queen*, in honour of Queen Elizabeth (subsequently the Queen Mother). HMCS *Queen* was closed between 1964 and 1975.

Today, Canada's Naval Reserve is responsible for Maritime Coastal Defense, Port Security, and Naval Co-operation and Guidance to Commercial Shipping. In recent years, Saskatchewan Naval Reservists have served with every part of Canada's Navy, and in operations as diverse as the Gulf War and peacekeeping missions from Cyprus to Bosnia. *Malcolm French*

CANADIAN PACIFIC RAILWAY. The Canadian Pacific Railway (CPR) Company was incorporated on February 16, 1881. Primarily serving only a small portion of Canada at the time, it became nationally significant after the company purchased the Canada Central Railway on June 9 of the same year: this 409-km addition connected the CPR to Ottawa, giving it

a dominant presence in eastern Canada. Once it was firmly established in the east, the CPR planned to expand in the west. Much of the CPR's success in this regard has been attributed to its first president, William Cornelius Van Horne: while he was working in the United States, the CPR offered Van Horne $15,000 a year to become the corporation's general manager and oversee the expansion of the CPR into the west; he accepted the offer and managed the CPR into a nationally recognized carrier.

The CPR line ran through what is now Saskatchewan in 1883. In addition to its mainline running from east to west, the CPR branched northward: it accomplished this by purchasing the Qu'Appelle-Long Lake and Saskatchewan Railroad and Steamboat Company. The Regina to Prince Albert line was completed in 1889–90. In answer to persistent demands by settlers and businesses from communities adjacent to the railway, the CPR proceeded cautiously, building feeder lines only when there were prospects for profitable returns—if not immediately, then at least in the foreseeable future. The CPR linked Canada from east to west when the last spike was driven by Donald A. Smith (later Lord Strathcona and Mount Royal) at Craigellachie, British Columbia on November 7, 1885. In later years the CPR became involved in land sales, communications, shipping, hotels, insurance, irrigation, manufacturing, mining, pulp and paper, trucking, and even waste management. In 1941 the CPR became involved in commercial aviation by acquiring and amalgamating ten commercial aviation companies into Canadian Pacific Airlines (CPA). Today the CPR operates and maintains over 22,500 km of rail line in Canada, hauling grain, fertilizer, automobiles and freight to numerous destinations throughout the country. *Ted Regehr*

Construction of the CPR "Empress Line," northwest of Swift Current, ca. 1911.

CANADIAN PAPERWORKERS UNION LOCAL 1120.

In 1967, the International Brotherhood of Pulp, Sulphite and Paper Mill Workers granted a charter to Local 403 to represent workers at the Prince Albert Pulp Mill. In 1972, these workers came under the jurisdiction of the United Paperworkers International Union (UPIU) as local 1120. In 1974, the majority of the Canadian locals who belonged to UPIU formed the Canadian Paperworkers Union. Finally, in 1992, the local became part of the Communications, Energy and Paperworkers Union after a merger of workers in the energy sector and the communications field. In 1985, the local spearheaded a drive to clean up asbestos contamination in its plant and assisted the Department of Labour, Occupational Health and Safety Division to set up a program to clean up, monitor, test and remove asbestos from worksites.

Victor Gignac

CANADIAN PARENTS FOR FRENCH.

Canadian Parents for French (CPF) is the national network of volunteers which values French as an integral part of Canada and which is dedicated to the promotion and creation of French second-language learning opportunities for young Canadians. The organization has volunteer-operated chapters in communities across Canada. A small professional staff located in provincial or territorial branch offices and in the national office in Ottawa provides support to volunteers, members, educators, partner organizations, and the public at large by collecting and disseminating information about French second-language education; it also assists volunteer board members in the planning and delivery of extracurricular programs designed to enhance the French second-language learning of young people.

CPF was established following a March 1977 parents' conference on French language and exchange opportunities, organized by Canada's first Commissioner of Official Languages, Keith Spicer. Dr. William Chermenkoff and Mrs. Vivianne Fior from Saskatoon were the Saskatchewan representatives present at the founding meeting. In October 1977 Marcel de la Gorgendière, a Saskatoon lawyer, was elected as the first director from Saskatchewan to the national organization. One of the first chapters in the country was established in Regina in 1978 under the leadership of Jos Craven Scott—who shortly thereafter moved to Ottawa, where she served as the organization's National Executive Director for many years. The Saskatchewan Branch of CPF, which was incorporated in 1980, provides services to the entire province from its office in Saskatoon.

Karen Taylor-Browne

CANADIAN PLAINS RESEARCH CENTER.

CPRC is the longest serving research institute at the UNIVERSITY OF REGINA with a broad mandate to

Official opening of the Canadian Plains Research Center, February 5, 1974. Left to right: Hon. R.L. Hanbidge, former Lieutenant-Governor of Saskatchewan; Dr. W. Don Stewart, CPRC's first director; Dr. J.W, Spinks, President of the University of Saskatchewan; and Dr. J. Archer, Principal, University of Saskatchewan, Regina Campus.

develop an understanding and appreciation of the Canadian Plains region. The Center also co-operates with United States scholars on issues relevant to the broader North American Great Plains.

CPRC works to develop a community of students of the region, including staff from prairie universities, governments, and other institutions, and members of an interested public. It provides services to prairie institutions and researchers to study and help solve problems of the region, its people, and its resources. CPRC has a role to initiate, undertake, encourage, and support research and scholarly work on all aspects of prairie life.

It delivers four specific programs. The Canadian Plains Studies Program is a graduate student program facilitating interdisciplinary studies of masters and doctoral students on topics relevant to the Canadian Plains. Over 35 students have been supported through the program. CPRC's Research Fellow Program, established in 1983, has provided support to over 40 scholars conducting studies relevant to the Canadian Plains. CPRC's Publication Division is a university press established in 1973 and publishes about eight to ten scholarly books per year, with a total of over 130 titles. The Press also publishes *Prairie Forum*, a multidisciplinary journal on topics of relevance to the Canadian Plains region. CPRC's Geographic Information Systems Division is a grouping of research and technical staff and facilities supporting education and research in the spatial distribution of resources, both physical and cultural.

As part of its original and continuing education and community outreach mandate, CPRC also organizes, facilitates or partners with other organizations in delivering numerous conferences, symposia, workshops, lectures, meetings and seminars.

CPRC also administers the Woodrow Lloyd Occasional Seminar Series in which leading scholars present on topics relevant to the Canadian Plains as well as a Trust Fund dedicated to advancing communication and education about conservation issues in Saskatchewan.

David A. Gauthier

CANADIAN UNION OF POSTAL WORKERS.

The first letter carrier delivery started in Regina in 1903, and mail delivery began in Saskatoon and Moose Jaw in 1911. As the postal service began to expand, post office workers joined national staff associations organized for their particular craft. The Federated Association of Letter Carriers (FALC) was the first federal employee association to view itself as a trade union and to join the Dominion Trades and Labour Congress. Responding to poor working conditions and rising prices during World War I, the first strike in the federal civil service took place in the post office in 1918. The ten-day strike was largely a western Canadian event. Letter carriers and postal clerks in Regina, Saskatoon and Moose Jaw joined the strike. In Saskatoon the metal trades and railway workers began a sympathy strike. A general strike in the west in support of the post office workers was a real possibility until the leadership of the Trades and Labour Congress withheld support.

The Federation of Western Postal Workers held its first convention in Saskatoon in February 1919. Delegates changed the name to the Amalgamated Postal Workers, hoping to build a strong national organization for all workers in the post office. In 1950 the employee associations began a campaign for collective bargaining rights. In 1965 a two-week postal strike led to this right being established for federal government employees. The Canadian Union of Postal Workers emerged from the Canadian

Postal Employees Association (CPEA, 1931–65), as did the Letter Carriers Union of Canada (LCUC, 1966–89) from the Federated Association of Letter Carriers (FALC, 1891–1966). The two unions negotiated together with their employer through the Council of Postal Unions. In 1968, a 22-day strike ended with a first collective agreement.

After years of campaigning by postal unions and the CLC, and on the heels of a 42-day summer strike, the Post Office Department was converted to a Crown corporation on October 16, 1981. A review of the postal bargaining units by the Canada Labour Relations Board began in 1985, ending with a winner-takes-all certification vote between CUPW and LCUC in 1988. CUPW won the vote by 51%, doubling in size in January 1989. The LCUC's last national convention took place in Saskatoon in July 1987. Today CUPW represents 1,400 members in Saskatchewan, grouped into twelve Locals. In 2003 CUPW won employee status and a first collective agreement for 6,000 rural and suburban mail contractors, 170 of them in Saskatchewan.

Keith Jeworski

CANADIAN UNION OF PUBLIC EMPLOYEES. The Canadian Union of Public Employees (CUPE) was established in 1963 through a merger of the National Union of Public Service Employees (NUPSE) and the National Union of Public Employees (NUPE). The merger brought together service-providers, white-collar workers, technicians, labourers, skilled trades people, and professionals from a variety of sectors into one large public sector union. The new union emphasized grassroots democracy in autonomous locals, which directed their own affairs. CUPE Saskatchewan, the political and policy arm of the union in the province, was established the following year to protect and advance the welfare and economic security of public employees. George Cairns was elected as its first president.

As the public sector expanded in the 1960s, CUPE increased its membership substantially, bringing women into the labour movement in large numbers. The growth in membership was aided by the ability to negotiate contracts ensuring that public sector workers obtained significant wage increases, benefits, and other contract improvements. These contract gains were curtailed with the imposition of wage and price controls by the federal Liberal government of Pierre Trudeau in 1975. CUPE and other unions in Saskatchewan were incensed when NDP Premier **ALLAN BLAKENEY** supported the wage controls by implementing the provincial Public Sector Price and Compensation Board.

The relationship between public sector unions and the NDP reached a new low in 1982 when Blakeney legislated 5,000 striking CUPE hospital employees back to work. The Premier proceeded to call an election the next day. Angered by the attack on the fundamental right to strike, CUPE Saskatchewan urged its members to back an independent labour candidate, the Aboriginal Peoples' Party (which opposed the back-to-work legislation), or to spoil their ballots in other ridings. The subsequent defeat of the NDP by **GRANT DEVINE**'s Progressive Conservatives sparked an intense debate within CUPE over political strategy. In the end, CUPE Saskatchewan endorsed a direction of independent political action and education, and "selective support for those NDP and other candidates who publicly endorse labour's political principles and objectives."

This commitment to independent political action led CUPE Saskatchewan to work closely with the **SASKATCHEWAN COALITION FOR SOCIAL JUSTICE** in protests against Devine's agenda of privatization and assault on labour rights and the welfare state throughout the 1980s. CUPE's social unionism also found expression in the fight against free trade agreements, regressive tax reform and attacks on the medicare system, as well as in strong support for international solidarity projects. The election of **ROY ROMANOW**'s NDP in 1991 found CUPE fighting a new round of cutbacks and wage restraint as the government focused on reducing the debt of the Devine years. As the province's financial situation improved, a renewed militancy took hold from 1999 to 2004 with CUPE strikes in the health, education, and library sectors.

As women make up about 60% of its membership, CUPE has been at the forefront in the fight for pay equity. CUPE has also pioneered a new representative workforce strategy in Saskatchewan to increase employment for Aboriginal people. Today, CUPE remains the largest union in Saskatchewan, representing over 24,000 members employed in hospitals, nursing homes, school boards, municipalities, universities, libraries, and community-based organizations.

Guy Marsden

CANADIAN UNION OF PUBLIC EMPLOYEES HOSPITAL STRIKE. On March 26, 1982, the government of Premier **ALLAN BLAKENEY** ordered about 5,000 striking non-medical hospital workers back to work and passed legislation making any strike illegal during election campaigns. One day later, as angry workers demonstrated outside NDP headquarters in Regina, Blakeney announced that a general election would be held on April 26. The first province-wide hospital strike in Saskatchewan history had begun on March 11, when 420 workers at two Prince Albert hospitals, represented by the **CANADIAN UNION OF PUBLIC EMPLOYEES** (CUPE), walked out. The strike escalated within two weeks until almost 5,000 hospital employees were walking picket lines.

This strike was the product of years of frustration by health care workers, who felt they were

REGINA LEADER-POST

Demonstrating CUPE members with Manitoba premier, Howard Pawley, March 1982.

underpaid and undervalued, pointing out that their wages were 27% less than the Saskatchewan average. The back-to-work order only added to that feeling, and created cynicism and bitterness towards a government supposedly supportive of working people. The provincial division of CUPE decided to run one of its members, Carol Stadnyk, as an independent candidate in Saskatoon against cabinet minister Herman Rolfes; recommended voting for Aboriginal People's Party candidates in ten ridings; and urged its members in other ridings to spoil their ballots by writing in Stadnyk's name. If the Blakeney government's back-to-work decision was an attempt to garner public sympathy and win it another term in office, it failed miserably: the Tories, led by **GRANT DEVINE**, won 55 seats while the NDP was reduced to only nine members.

The strike and subsequent actions by CUPE officials caused divisions within both the party and the union. Some CUPE members blamed their fellow health care colleagues for going on strike at that time; some even suggested that their actions and the subsequent decision not to support the NDP were responsible for the election defeat. *Clare Powell*

CANADIAN WHEAT BOARD. The Canadian Wheat Board (CWB) is the single desk marketer for **WHEAT** and **BARLEY** growers in the provinces of Manitoba, Saskatchewan, Alberta, and the Peace River district of British Columbia. The mission of the CWB is to maximize market returns for prairie farmers. The CWB derives its mandate from federal government legislation, but is controlled by a board of directors, the majority of whom are elected by prairie farmers.

The CWB's roots can be traced back to wartime conditions in the early 20th century. Prior to **WORLD WAR I** the Canadian Council of Agriculture had submitted a plan to the federal government for a Canadian Wheat Board that would market grains on a pooled basis. It would have a monopoly over the marketing of prairie grains. Due to wartime demands and to crop failures in 1916, the futures markets for wheat were oversold in both Canada and the United States, and governments in both countries were forced to suspend futures trading in the summer of 1917. In Canada the government established the Board of Grain Supervisors, which assumed complete control over the purchase, sale and pricing of wheat for export. When the marketing of the 1918 wheat harvest was completed, the Board of Grain Supervisors was terminated. In July 1919, under pressure from the private trade, the government allowed the Winnipeg Grain Exchange to resume trading in wheat futures; but when erratic speculative behaviour occurred, the government required the Exchange to cease trading ten days later. In its place the government by Order-in-Council established the Canadian Wheat Board to market the 1919 crop.

Unlike its forerunner, this CWB did not sell at export prices determined by the government; rather, its mandate was to pool farmers' sales for the entire crop year (August to July) and to sell wheat in export markets at prices in accordance with world levels. With pooling, the CWB could not determine the final value of wheat marketed on behalf of producers until its sales for the entire crop year had been complete. To manage this uncertainty the CWB implemented a two-payment system. Farmers received an initial payment when they delivered their wheat to elevators, and were issued a participation certificate entitling them to a final payment at the end of the marketing year once the financial results of the sale for the 1919 wheat crop were known. The initial payment functioned as a floor price guaranteed by the federal government, which would absorb any deficit. Because the crop's total sales value was higher than the initial payment, the difference less marketing costs was returned to farmers in the form of a final payment. Farmers received $2.63 per bushel (#1 Northern basis Fort William), the highest price they had ever received; it would be the highest price received until the early 1950s.

This first CWB was disbanded in 1920, although the concept had won solid support from the prairie farm co-operative movement and farm organizations. They pressed the federal government to re-establish the CWB. When the government declined to

reverse its decision, these groups were instrumental in forming the Alberta, Saskatchewan and Manitoba Co-operative Wheat Producers organizations which became known as the "Wheat Pools." They operated a system of pooling and payment similar to that established by the 1919-20 CWB, but lacked government guarantees for the pool accounts. In 1924 they formed the Central Selling Agency for the purpose of joint marketing. The organization enjoyed some success during its first six years of operations, but when world wheat prices collapsed in 1929 and the **GREAT DEPRESSION** began in the 1930s, it experienced serious financial difficulties. Operating on bank loans, the prairie Wheat Pools were threatened with foreclosure by the banks when the open market wheat price fell below the initial payment. The federal government was once again called upon, and this time it responded. It provided a guarantee of borrowings by the Central Selling Agency and later, through Act of Parliament, re-established the CWB as a voluntary marketing agency for wheat. The Canadian Wheat Board Act received royal assent on July 5, 1935.

Over the years the jurisdiction of the CWB in the grain market has varied. At first, the deliveries to the CWB were only voluntary and it handled only wheat. This was a difficult period for the CWB, as deficits and lack of deliveries plagued the organization. During **WORLD WAR II**, the CWB was empowered to market all Canadian grains, including oilseeds and Ontario corn. The CWB was made permanent by the government in 1943. After the war the CWB returned to marketing only wheat. In 1949 Parliament expanded the CWB to include oats and barley. In 1974, interprovincial sales of wheat, oats and barley for animal feed were removed from the CWB's sole jurisdiction. In 1989 oats marketing was also removed from the CWB, leaving it responsible for marketing wheat and barley for export and for domestic human consumption. In the 1998–99 crop year, one of the most significant changes in the history of the CWB took place: on December 31, 1998, the CWB changed from being a federal Crown corporation led by federally-aappointed commissioners to being a shared-governance corporation where

a fifteen-member board of directors assumed control of the organization.

This board of directors consists of ten farmers, elected by their farming peers from districts across western Canada, and five directors appointed by the federal government. One of the farmer-elected directors is selected each year by the board of directors to be the chair. The board of directors is responsible for the overall governance of the corporation and its direction. Farmer control of the CWB has led to significant changes to pricing and payment options available to farmers. In addition to the system of government-guaranteed initial and final payments through the pooling system, farmers can now sign a number of producer payment option contracts, which enable farmers to access more of the value of their grain early in the crop year, or price grain based on US grain futures contractsmarkets. This increased flexibility allows farmers more control over managing their income and the marketing of their grain.

Gordon Gilmour

FURTHER READING: Morris, W.E. 1987. *Chosen Instrument: The Canadian Wheat Board*. Winnipeg: Canadian Wheat Board; —. 2000. *Chosen Instrument II: The Canadian Wheat Board*. Winnipeg: Canadian Wheat Board; Wilson, C.F. 1978. *A Century of Canadian Grain: Government Policy to 1951*. Saskatoon: Western Producer Prairie Books.

CANADIAN WOMEN'S ARMY CORPS. The Canadian Women's Army Corps (CWAC) was created on August 13, 1941, as a women's auxiliary to the Canadian army in order to free trained male soldiers for active military duty. On August 26, 1941, a CWAC unit was organized in Saskatchewan; this Military District 12 unit, of platoon strength, was designated as "O" Company, CWAC, and headquartered in Regina. On March 1, 1942, the CWAC became a corps of the Active Militia and was placed on active duty. Throughout **WORLD WAR II**, the CWAC were employed in more than fifty trades and served throughout Canada and overseas. By the end of the war, there were 636 officers and 13,326 women of

SASKATCHEWAN ARCHIVES BOARD R-B12169

The 42nd Company, Canadian Women's Army Corps, Canadian Army Overseas, 1940s.

COURTESY AGRICULTURE AND AGRI-FOOD CANADA

Canaryseed.

EVERETT BAKER PHOTO/COURTESY OF THE SASKATCHEWAN HISTORY AND FOLKLORE SOCIETY

Cannington Manor church, built 1885; photo taken September 1956.

other ranks in the Canadian Women's Service. The CWAC was demobilized at the end of World War II, but was re-activated in 1951 as a corps of the Canadian Army Reserve Force. The CWAC was again disbanded when in later years women were recruited directly into the Canadian Armed Forces and the need for a separate corps disappeared. *Peter Borch*

FURTHER READING: Bruce, J. 1985. *Back the Attack! Canadian Women During the Second World War–At Home and Abroad.* Toronto; Macmillan; Conrod, W.H. 1984. *Athene, Goddess of War: The Canadian Women's Army Corps–Their Story.* Dartmouth: Writing and Editorial Services; Pearson, R.R. 1986. *"They're Still Women After All": The Second World War and Canadian Womanhood.* Toronto: McClelland and Stewart.

CANARYSEED. Canaryseed (*Phalaris canariensis*), or annual canarygrass, is a major component of feed mixtures for caged and wild birds. The seedlings resemble green foxtail or corn seedlings; they are finely leafed, and purple to red at the base of the stem. Mature plants are approximately one metre in height and have small compact heads. The major canaryseed producing countries are Canada, the USA, Hungary, and Argentina. World canaryseed production has ranged from 150,000 to 347,000 tonnes in recent years. World exports ranged from 148,000 to 233,000 tonnes during the period from 1992 to 2002. Plantings in Canada have ranged from 95,000 to 247,000 ha in the past ten years, with over 90% grown in Saskatchewan.

Saskatchewan is the largest producer and exporter of canaryseed in the world, and provides over one-half of total annual world production and world trade. Fluctuations in production of canaryseed in Saskatchewan can have a major impact on world price, and the market is characterized by large price swings. Birds are popular pets for apartment dwellers, and large markets exist in countries with high urban populations such as the USA, Belgium, Spain, Italy, Mexico, and Brazil.
Ray McVicar

CANCER TREATMENT: *See* HIGH-ENERGY CANCER TREATMENT

CANDLE LAKE, resort village, pop 503, is a rapidly developing resort community located 77 km NE of Prince Albert off Hwy 120. The community is situated at the south end of the large lake which gave it its name, originating with a CREE legend that a mysterious light can sometimes be seen on the lake's surface. As the resort area is comprised of approximately 2,000 cottages, the temporary summer population can far exceed the permanent population cited above. Numerous subdivision developments continue to be built. Candle Lake Provincial Park, which includes approximately 300 campgrounds, also encompasses much of the lake's shore. Commercial fishing and trapping in the area date to around 1912; people were permanently settling in the area in the 1920s; the post office was opened in 1936; and tourism began to develop in the late 1940s. Candle Lake was incorporated in 1977.
David McLennan

CANNINGTON MANOR. Cannington Manor is located 26 km southeast of Moose Mountain Provincial Park. Captain Edward Michell Pierce, a failed English gentleman who came to Canada to revive his fortunes, established Cannington Manor in 1882. After building a log farmhouse to accommodate his wife and eight children, Pierce established an agricultural college in an effort to teach English gentlemen how to farm. The "pups," as his pupils were known, came from the privileged classes in England where they had failed to live up to strict aristocratic expectations. For £100 a year, they were given room and board at Cannington Manor along with lessons in farming. However, many of the wealthy English were not serious agriculturalists. Instead, they lived the leisurely life of country gentlemen, playing tennis and cricket and participating in numerous social events.

When Pierce died on June 20, 1888, Cannington Manor had grown to include an Anglican church, a grist mill, the Mitre Hotel, blacksmith's shop, sawmill, and general store. More than 200 people lived there by the mid-1890s, many of whom contributed to the cultural and recreational life of the community. Ultimately, however, the struggle to maintain the social customs of Victorian England on the Canadian prairie proved too much, and the village of Cannington Manor was abandoned by 1900. Today, original and reconstructed buildings at Cannington Manor Provincial Historic Park recreate this distinctive experiment in the development of western Canada. *Holden Stoffel*

FURTHER READING: 1965. *Cannington Manor Historic Park: A Saskatchewan Historic Site.* Regina: Saskatchewan Diamond Jubilee and Canada Centennial Corp.; Humphrys, Ruth. 1982. "Edward Michell Pierce: The Founder of Cannington Manor." *The Beaver* 313 (2): 12–21.

CANOE LAKE FIRST NATION. The Canoe Lake First Nation came into existence when Chief John Iron, Headmen Baptiste Iron, and Jerome Couilloneur signed TREATY 10 on September 19, 1906. These CREE speakers occupied a very large region with varied resources. Able-bodied band members lived mostly by hunting and trapping, while the older or feebler members depended upon fish as their primary food source. Their traditional way of life still prevailed in 1954, when the creation of the Primrose Lake Air Weapons Range removed 75% of their most productive lands. The community had not undergone any major change or development since the time of treaty, and even commercial fishing was comparatively recent because of poor access to markets. In 1975, the Canoe Lake Cree Nation (among others) submitted a claim for the loss of their traditional territory; and in 1995 the government accepted the claim, stating that it had no legal obligation but acknowledged there was a need to improve the economic and social circumstances of the community. The claim was settled in June 1997. The band's population currently sits at 1,764 persons, with 755 residing on their 14,172.6 ha of reserve land (the most populated of which is 37 km southwest of Ile-à-la-Crosse). The band's economic development includes hunting, fishing, trapping, lumber, a sawmill, and handicraft business. The infrastructure includes an arena, school, handicraft building, sawmill, band office, teacherages, band hall, café, service station, laundromat, and recreation building/pool hall. *Christian Thompson*

CANOEING. Since **WORLD WAR II**, canoeing has become a major pastime and sport in Saskatchewan. Most participants are recreational canoeists who spend a few hours or days paddling in the province's extensive lakes and rivers, although canoe racing has become a major sport in recent years. There are also whitewater canoeists who enjoy the challenge posed by the many rapids of northern Saskatchewan—as on the **CHURCHILL RIVER**, a drawing card for whitewater enthusiasts from many other parts of Canada as well as overseas. Canoe outfitters and ecotourist operators located in northern Saskatchewan as well as the province's major cities now provide an array of services for local and visiting canoeists. Just over 1,000 of Saskatchewan's more avid paddlers now belong to one or more of the province's thirteen canoe clubs; this compares with a total membership of only 238 in 1995. First established in 1976, the Saskatchewan Canoeing Association is the

umbrella organization for the province's canoe clubs and administers four divisions: recreational, whitewater, marathon, and flatwater. Of these, flatwater (Olympic) racing clubs have grown the most rapidly, with a membership now constituting well over half of canoe club membership in the province.

Greg Marchildon

CANOES. Before the fur trade, Aboriginal peoples used canoes to navigate the rivers, streams and lakes of northern Saskatchewan. Made entirely of local materials, these small birchbark canoes were light enough to portage the rapids and land connecting these rivers and lakes. With the arrival of the Europeans and the fur trade, these Aboriginal canoes were enlarged to deliver large payloads of trade goods and furs. At this time, the average fur trade *canot du nord* was eight metres long, weighed about 135 kg empty, and could support up to 2,000 kg of weight including a crew of between four and six voyageurs. Even with the introduction of heavy wood rowboats known as York boats in the 19th century, the fur trade version of the birchbark canoe continued to ply Saskatchewan's smaller streams and lakes. By the 20th century the fur trade had waned in importance, and the introduction of the motorboat increasingly replaced the working canoe. After **WORLD WAR II**, however, recreational canoes that were larger than the early Aboriginal canoes but smaller than fur trade canoes became more common. They were first made out of different types of wood, but aluminum, plastic and more space-age materials have since been used to construct these canoes. *Greg Marchildon*

CANOLA. Canola is the name given to the nutritionally enhanced seed, oil and meal produced by the conventional genetic modification of Argentine and Polish type rapeseed (*Brassica napus* L. and *B.*

rapa L., respectively), and more recently tame mustard, *B. juncea* (L.) Czern. Although rapeseed and tame mustard were ancient oilseed crops of Asia and the Indian subcontinent, they are a recent introduction to Canada. Development of the Canadian rapeseed/canola crop is frequently referred to as a Cinderella story. The crop has undergone a great metamorphosis in nutritional quality and productivity since it was first grown on a few acres in 1942 as a **WORLD WAR II** emergency measure. At that time rapeseed oil was considered an essential lubricant for steam engines, since it clings to water- and steam-washed surfaces better that any other oil. As the war cut off all supplies from Europe and Asia and all trains and ships of the time were steam-powered, Canada was asked to undertake rapeseed production. Seed of *B. napus* was imported from Argentina, and an immigrant farmer from Poland provided the original *B. rapa* seed; thus the common names, Argentine and Polish, came into common use.

Both species proved to be well adapted to the prairie climate and required only slight modifications to existing grain growing and handling systems. Under a guaranteed price support program the crop area expanded. However, the crop almost disappeared in 1950 because of the rapid conversion from steam to diesel power and the elimination of the support price. Fortunately, Canadian entrepreneurs sought and established new markets, first in Europe and then in Japan.

From the outset researchers realized that oilseed rape could become a major source of edible oil for Canada, which until that time had to import about 90% of its edible oil needs. However, two characteristics limited the domestic market for rapeseed oil and meal. First, the fatty acids which constitute some 98% of a vegetable oil differed from other vegetable oils in having a high proportion of

Removing birch bark for a canoe, 1935.

Birch bark canoe, October 1943.

Canola plant.

long carbon-chain fatty acids called eicosenoic and erucic. These fatty acids were determined to be nutritionally undesirable. Second, the seed and meal contained high concentrations of anti-nutritional sulfur compounds called glucosinolates. Although this family of compounds imparts the desired flavour to related vegetables such as cabbage, radishes and mustard, when such high concentrations as are found in rapeseed meal are fed to swine and poultry, growth and feed efficiency are adversely affected.

To solve these problems, fast and accurate methods of detection and measurement of the offending compounds were needed. Chemists at the National Research Council's Saskatoon laboratory developed the necessary methods, and plant breeders at the AAFC Research Centre in Saskatoon and the University of Manitoba applied them in their successful search of the world's rapeseed germplasm for plants with low levels of the undesirable compounds. Additional plant-breeding work produced the first low erucic varieties, Oro (*B. napus*) and Span (*B. rapa*), and later the first varieties with both low erucic and low glucosinolate, Tower (*B. napus*) and Candle (*B. rapa*). The first tame mustard variety (*B. juncea*) with canola quality was grown in 2003.

The development of the low erucic, low glucosinolate varieties and their rapid adoption by producers and the industry greatly expanded both the domestic and export markets for the seed, oil and meal. A new name was required to distinguish the superior nutritional quality of the "double low" materials from the old rapeseed, and a committee of the then Rapeseed Association proposed the name "canola," derived from "can" for Canada and "ola" because it sounded like oil. Canola varieties in Saskatchewan have a growing season similar to wheat and grow about 1–1.5 m tall. The *B. rapa* species, because it matures ten to fourteen days earlier, was initially grown on the greatest area; but with the introduction of effective herbicides, the later but higher yielding *B. napus* species now dominates. Each canola flower has four bright yellow petals, and upon fertilization by insects and wind a

pod develops with fifteen to forty small round seeds arranged in two rows. Ripe seeds may be black, brown or yellow, and contain 41% to 44% oil and 36% to 40% high-quality protein in the oil-free meal.

Canada's success is reflected in its production record. In 1951 there were only 2,600 ha of rapeseed planted in Saskatchewan; by 1960 there were 220,000 ha. Canola peaked in 1994, when 2.6 million ha were planted–generating for the first time a million- dollar canola crop.   *R. Keith Downey*

FURTHER READING: Downey, R.K. 1988. "Canola: A Quality Brassica Oilseed." Pp. 211–15 in J. Janick and J.E. Simon (eds.), *Advances in New Crops: Proceedings of the 1st National Symposium on New Crops*. Portland: Timber Press.

CANORA, town, pop 2,200, located 48 km due N of Yorkton at the junction of Hwys 5 and 9, first settled in the late 19th century by Doukhobors, Romanians, and Ukrainians. The town's name is derived from a combination of the first two letters of each word in Canadian Northern Railway, which laid steel through the area in 1904. The community experienced early rapid growth; population levels remained stable even through the Depression, and peaked at 2,734 in 1966. Canora's continued viability is due in large part to its location at the corners of four adjacent rural municipalities which constitute a trading area of approximately 15,000 people in a district well suited to successful crop and livestock production. Additionally, Canora is situated in a parkland setting surrounded by several lakes and parks including Crystal Lake, Good Spirit Provincial Park, and Duck Mountain Provincial Park. Tourism is also bolstered by the proximity of the nearby National Doukhobor Heritage Village, the grotto at Rama, and the sites of forts Pelly and Livingstone; Canora is situated on Via Rail's trans-continental line and on the rail link to Churchill, Manitoba and its beluga whale and polar bear tours. The town's 1904 rail station still remains the oldest operating station of its type in the province. Canora has a wide range of businesses, services, and recreational facilities. Saskatchewan's first woman Lieutenant-Governor, **SYLVIA FEDORUK**, was born in Canora in 1927.   *David McLennan*

CAPELING-ALAKIJA, SHARON (1944–2003). Sharon Capeling-Alakija served with CUSO and headed three United Nations organizations. Born on May 6, 1944 and adopted by a Moose Jaw family, she received a BEd degree from the **UNIVERSITY OF SASKATCHEWAN** in 1966, and taught in Saskatoon for a year. Seeking adventure, she joined CUSO in 1967. After teaching overseas, Capeling held several positions in CUSO administration in Canada from 1972 on. Then, in 1981, she headed its West Africa program, based in Togo.

There she married, and became widowed from, Nigerian Robin Alakija.

In 1989, Capeling-Alakija became the director of the UN Development Fund for Women. She brought a high profile to, and raised millions of dollars for, the organization. She set up the UN Development Program's office of evaluation and strategic planning in 1994, and was the executive coordinator of Bonn-based United Nations Volunteers from 1997 until her death on November 4, 2003. While with UNV, she oversaw 3,000 volunteers and organized the highly successful 2001 International Year of the Volunteer. Capeling-Alakija received an honorary doctoral degree from the University of Saskatchewan in 1998, and was appointed an officer in the Order of Canada in 2003.   *Carol Cooper*

FURTHER READING: Cooper, C. 2003. "Canada's champion volunteer." *Globe and Mail* (December 8).

CAPITAL CITY, SELECTION OF. The 1875 **NORTH-WEST TERRITORIES ACT** stipulated that the **LIEUTENANT-GOVERNOR** of the North-West Territories must reside in the region, thereby necessitating the establishment of a territorial capital. Prince Albert was the only sizeable settlement in the region in 1875, but, in what has been called one of the great mysteries of western Canadian history, Fort Livingstone was named the first territorial seat of government. Located near present-day Pelly, and populated by more snakes than people, the fort served as the headquarters of the North-West Mounted Police when **DAVID LAIRD** was appointed Lieutenant- Governor in November 1876. The first session of the North-West Council was subsequently held there the following March.

The NWMP headquarters moved when Laird left Fort Livingstone in August 1877 to establish a new capital at the more centrally located Telegraph Flat, later renamed Battleford. **GOVERNMENT HOUSE**, which stood until it was destroyed by fire in 2003, was erected to serve the purposes of the Lieutenant-Governor and his staff. The settlement's prestige was bolstered by a visit from the Governor General of Canada (and son-in-law of Queen Victoria), the Marquis of Lorne, in the fall of 1881. A permanent capital, authenticated by official buildings and royal visits, and an administrative body helped reinforce the Canadian government's rather precarious authority over the North-West.

EDGAR DEWDNEY succeeded Laird in December 1881. Battleford had originally been selected with the belief that the **CANADIAN PACIFIC RAILWAY** would pass through the town, but by 1881 the railway route been had altered to a more southern path. Dewdney, in consultation with Prime Minister John A. Macdonald and W.C. Van Horne, the general manager of the Canadian Pacific Railway, decided in June 1882 to move the territorial capital to Regina, effective March 1883. The fact that Dewdney himself owned land in Regina was likely a factor in the process. In 1905, Regina, as the territorial capital, was the logical choice for the location of the new provincial capital as well. *Erin Millions*

FURTHER READING: Waiser, Bill. 2005. *Saskatchewan: A New History*. Calgary: Fifth House, 2005.

CARBON DIOXIDE STORAGE. A four-year multidisciplinary study released in 2004 concluded that carbon dioxide–a greenhouse gas–can be stored safely underground in geological formations such as the Weyburn oil fields in southeastern Saskatchewan. The Petroleum Technology Research Centre (PTRC) in Regina conducted the study under the auspices of the International Energy Agency Greenhouse Gas (IEA GHG) Research and Development Programme and in close collaboration with EnCana Corporation of Calgary, which operates the 50-year-old Weyburn oil field. This was the first large-scale study ever conducted of geological storage of carbon dioxide in a partially depleted oil field. The Weyburn oil field was selected for the study because detailed geological records and core samples, as well as almost 50 years of production history, were readily available; some 380 million barrels of oil have been produced from the field since it was discovered in 1954.

About 5 million tonnes of carbon dioxide were stored in the Weyburn oil field over the life of the study–the equivalent to taking about one million cars off the road for one year. The carbon dioxide was supplied for the experiment via a 325-km pipeline from the Dakota Gasification Company's coal-gasification plant at Beulah, North Dakota. During the study, researchers conducted a long-term risk assessment, completed geological and seismic studies, matched reservoir modeling against actual results, and performed frequent sampling to understand chemical reactions occurring in the reservoir. Utilizing seismic equipment, they were able to "see" the carbon dioxide mix with oil and follow the flow through the ground into nearby pump jacks. The $40 million funding for the Weyburn project came from Natural Resources Canada, the United States Department of Energy, Saskatchewan Industry and Resources, Alberta Energy Research Institute, and the European community. Altogether, the project involved 24 research and consulting organizations in Canada, the United States, and Europe. *Joe Ralko*

CARGILL LIMITED. Cargill is a large, diversified international company which got its start in the grain business when William Cargill, a Scottish immigrant, bought his first elevator in Iowa. In partnership with his brother Sam, he began purchasing elevators in 1870 in Minnesota, and later in North and South Dakota on the new Great Northern Railroad. The Cargill company became active in Canada in 1930 when it began to purchase and export Canadian grain. In 1960 it acquired and began to operate a grain transfer elevator at Baie Comeau, Quebec. In 1975 it entered the primary elevator business with the acquisition of National Grain Limited from the Peavey interests, a major competitor in the United States. With headquarters in Minneapolis, Minnesota, Cargill has become the largest grain trader/exporter, with 25% of the world market. In addition it is the world's largest cotton trader, largest feed manufacturer of livestock feed (Nutrena Mills), second largest US wet corn miller, second largest US soybean crusher, and third largest US pork slaughterer/packer. It also has interests in poultry production, in river, lake and ocean transport, and in rail hopper cars. Cargill and its subsidiaries operate 800 plants, and have 500 US offices and 300 foreign offices, with approximately 100,000 employees in sixty-one countries. The combined Cargill and MacMillan families, who own Cargill, are one of the ten richest families in the US, worth about $5.1 billion US in 1995.

In Canada, Cargill is one of the largest agricultural processors and merchandizers: in addition to its grain handling and merchandizing, it has investments in meat, egg, malt and oilseed processing, and livestock feed, salt and fertilizer manufacturing. It has $1.2 billion in assets and annual sales of $3.5 billion. In 2004, Cargill had thirty-three primary licenced elevators, including fifteen in Saskatchewan with a capacity of 158,640 tonnes. In the province it operates, as a joint venture with farmers, Mainline Terminal Ltd. in Langbank, North East Terminal in Wadena, South West Terminal near Gull Lake, and Terminal 22 at Balcarres. It also operates, as a joint venture with the government of Saskatchewan, Saskferco Products Inc., a fertilizer plant at Belle Plaine, completed in 1992 at a cost of $435 million. In 1998, Cargill became joint venture partner in Prairie Malt in Biggar. The company owns a 2,400 tonne per day canola processing plant at Clavet; the largest soft seed oil processing plant in North America, it produces canola oil as well as canola meal for the North American and world markets. *Gary Storey*

FURTHER READING: Anderson, C.W. 1991. *Grain: The Entrepreneurs*. Winnipeg: Watson and Dwyer Publishing; Wilson, C.F. 1978. *A Century of Canadian Grain*. Saskatoon: Western Producer Prairie Books.

CARLTON TRAIL. The Carlton Trail was an overland transportation route connecting Fort Garry (Winnipeg, Manitoba) to Fort Carlton, Saskatchewan. The trail was used extensively in the early 19th century when First Nations and **MÉTIS** began to trade with both the Hudson's Bay and North West Companies. The trail became a vital transportation link for these companies at the height of the fur trade in the North-West Territories. The 700 km trail entered Saskatchewan southeast of Melville, meandering northwest near the present-day communities of Wynyard, Lanigan and Humboldt; it crossed the **SOUTH SASKATCHEWAN RIVER** at **BATOCHE** before reaching Fort Carlton. A southern section, originating in Humboldt, was established in the mid-19th century to accommodate traders in the Humboldt-Bruno region. It crossed the South Saskatchewan River at Gabriel's Crossing (operated by **GABRIEL DUMONT**) to join up again with the original trail west of Batoche. The trail continued west another 980 km from Fort Carlton to Fort Pitt before terminating at Fort Edmonton. *James Winkel*

CARLTON TRAIL RAILWAY. The Carlton Trail Railway (CTRW) is a regional railway operating the Meadow Lake, Big River, and Blaine Lake subdivisions, from Meadow Lake to Speers Junction. CTRW also operates the Warman subdivision from a point north of Prince Albert to Warman, and the part of the Tisdale subdivision from Prince Albert to Birch Hills. In addition, it operates the Arborfield subdivision in the northeast grain belt. In all, CTRW operates 475 km of track in Saskatchewan; all of these lines were formerly CN branch lines. CTRW, a subsidiary of Denver-based OmniTRAX, began its Saskatchewan operations in December 1997. Its major customers are the forest products companies around Prince Albert and Meadow Lake, which move pulp, paper, oriented strand board, and lumber. For the agriculture industry, CTRW serves grain elevators, producer car loading sites, and grain processing plants scattered across all its lines. OmniTRAX also owns the Hudson Bay Railway, which operates to the prairie port of Churchill; grain for Churchill comes mostly from northeastern Saskatchewan. *Paul Beingessner*

CARLYLE, town, pop 1,260, located S of Moose Mountain Provincial Park and the White Bear First Nation at the junction of Hwys 9 and 13. Early settlers to the district were of mainly British descent. The name Carlyle was chosen by the first postmaster (the post office opened in 1883) to honour the niece of the Scottish historian and essayist, Thomas Carlyle: his niece and her husband settled in the Arcola district, and farmed and raised a family there. Trains were running though the town site in 1901, and the population increased from 23 that year to nearly 400 in 1906. In 1941, Carlyle still had around this number, but by 1956 the population had surged to 829. Subsequently, and uniquely for a smaller community in Saskatchewan, Carlyle's population has slowly but steadily continued to climb. Traditionally, the area economy had been largely based upon agriculture; however, in recent decades the oil industry has become increasingly significant.

Additionally, Carlyle is an important centre for tourists as it benefits from its proximity to Moose Mountain Provincial Park and Kenosee Lake, the casino and resort at White Bear Lake, and Cannington Manor Provincial Historic Park. Each December, Carlyle hosts its premier annual event, the Dickens Village Festival. The entire town adopts a Victorian theme, and features live stage productions and lighted parades at dusk.   *David McLennan*

CARNDUFF, town, pop 1,017, located on Hwy 18, 32 km W of the Manitoba border, and 20 km N of the International Boundary. The first settlers arrived in the Carnduff district, primarily from Ontario, in the early 1880s. It was not until the fall of 1891 that the CPR's Brandon-Estevan branch line reached the Carnduff area. Until the 1950s, the town had a widely fluctuating population. After that, the community experienced rapid growth, doubling in size by the 1970s, and then the population stabilized. Agriculture and oil production are the main industries in the area. The sandy loam land around Carnduff is used mainly for mixed farming, and many of the family farms in the district date back to the homestead era. Since there are several hundred producing oil wells in the region, a number of companies in the industry have offices in the town. Carnduff provides a full range of businesses, services, and recreational facilities. This community also has the distinction of being the birthplace of Ernest C. Manning (1908–96), who served as Premier of Alberta from 1943 to 1968.   *David McLennan*

CARNIVORES. The members of the mammalian order Carnivora are distinguished by having shearing teeth (the last upper premolar bites past the first lower molar), a reduced clavicle, fused carpal bones in the wrist and, in all families except the hyenas, a baculum or penis bone. The approximately 230 species are found on all continents except for Antarctica. They range from strict meat-eaters (the cats), through omnivores which feed on whatever is available (bears, raccoons, wolverines), to herbivores (panda). Carnivores hunt and communicate mainly by scent produced by skin glands, such as enlarged anal glands. They are important in the environment as predators of herbivores such as insects, rodents, and ungulates. Many of the species are shy, so their numbers are difficult to assess. The order contains a number of species which, because of their size, power and intelligence, figure in human myth, ritual and art throughout the world. The coyote is a trickster figure in many North American Aboriginal stories, and wolves and bears often symbolize the wild.

Saskatchewan now has twenty native species of carnivores, in five families (*see* Table CAR-1). Two species have been exterminated in the province since settlement: the grizzly bear (*Ursus arctos*) and

Table CAR-1. Saskatchewan Carnivores			
Common Name	Scientific Name	Family	Distribution
Coyote	*Canis latrans*	Canidae	All but the extreme northeast
Wolf	*Canis lupus*	Canidae	Northern two-thirds
Arctic fox	*Alopex lagopus*	Canidae	Extreme northeast
Red fox	*Vulpes vulpes*	Canidae	Throughout province
Swift fox	*Vulpes velox*	Canidae	Reintroduced to southwest
American black bear	*Ursus americanus*	Ursidae	Northern two-thirds
Raccoon	*Procyon lotor*	Procyonidae	Southern two-thirds
American marten	*Martes americana*	Mustelidae	Boreal regions
Fisher	*Martes pennanti*	Mustelidae	Boreal regions
Short-tailed weasel	*Mustela erminea*	Mustelidae	Throughout province
Least weasel	*Mustela nivalis*	Mustelidae	Throughout province
Long-tailed weasel	*Mustela frenata*	Mustelidae	Prairies; southern boreal plain
American mink	*Mustela vison*	Mustelidae	Throughout province
Wolverine	*Gulo gulo*	Mustelidae	Northern half
American badger	*Taxidea taxus*	Mustelidae	Prairies; southern boreal plain
Striped skunk	*Mephitis mephitis*	Mustelidae	All but far north
River otter	*Lutra canadensis*	Mustelidae	Northern two-thirds
Cougar	*Puma concolor*	Felidae	Southern half
Canadian lynx	*Lynx canadensis*	Felidae	Forests and woodlands
Bobcat	*Lynx rufus*	Felidae	Prairie wild lands

the black-footed ferret (*Mustela nigripes*). Many other species of carnivore, especially larger forms such as the wolf, have been reduced as they have been hunted for furs, sport and protection of domestic animals. As a result, many of these species are absent from the more heavily settled prairies and parklands but remain in the boreal forest. They are now protected, and their trapping and killing controlled by wildlife legislation. They can develop and spread rabies.

The canid family has five representatives. The coyote is a medium-sized (13 kg) predator of small rodents, ground birds, and other prey in the prairies and parklands. Like the smaller red fox, it is tolerant of human settlement and has been able to maintain healthy populations throughout most of the province. Wolves are pack predators on deer species in the north. The two remaining smaller species are more limited in their distribution, and rarer: the arctic fox is found in the subtundra of the northeast; and the swift fox, limited to the dry short-grass prairie, was extirpated but has been released back into the area by conservation programs.

The American black bear is the only bear now in the province. It is found in the boreal and aspen woodlands but may wander south, particularly in dry years which reduce wild fruits. It is omnivorous, and makes use of whatever foods are available during that season, from fish and insects to honey combs. It reduces its need for food in the winter by denning up and entering a deep sleep, during which the cubs are born.

The raccoon is the only member of its family in Canada; the others are found in South America and Asia. The raccoon is increasing its distribution northward, which may be due partly to post-glacial climate

change and partly to its unspecialized food habits: as an omnivore it is able to make use of small animal prey, fruit, farm produce, and human garbage.

The weasel family is the largest carnivore family in North America. The ten species in Saskatchewan range from the large wolverine to the very small short-tailed weasel. They are generally long-bodied and short-legged. The weasels are mainly rodent predators, but the wolverine can kill prey as large as deer. The marten and fisher are mainly arboreal; the smaller marten feeds on squirrels and other small rodents, while the fisher is one of the few predators which can successfully hunt porcupines. The American badger is a prairie burrower, specializing in hunting ground squirrels. The three small weasels change their coat colour in winter to

COURTESY OF THE ROYAL SASKATCHEWAN MUSEUM
American badger.

COURTESY OF TOURISM SASKATCHEWAN

Coyote.

white, with a black-tail tip—thus becoming "ermine." They feed on a variety of small prey, from mice to insects. The river otter is found in larger streams and rivers, living in burrows in the banks and feeding on fish and other aquatic prey. Mink are also often found denning and feeding on a variety of prey along the shores of lakes and other wetlands. Striped skunks are carnivores with large anal glands producing a noxious secretion which they use to defend themselves; their white stripes on a black back also exhibit a warning pattern. They have a habit, also found in the porcupine, of standing and turning their back on a potential predator, in order to present their first defense rather than fleeing; this habit causes them to be often struck by cars.

Cats, with their short face and strong bite, are the purest meat-eaters. Their solitary, shy nature makes it difficult to ascertain details of their distribution or population size. The cougar is the largest cat in the province, with its distinctive long tail and uniform colour in the adult. The kittens are spotted. Cougars will hunt a variety of mammalian and bird prey, but are particularly predators on the species of deer found in the prairies and southern woodlands. The other two cats are both members of the *Lynx* genus, with large tipped ears, large feet, short tails, and one less molar tooth in the jaw than other cats: the small bobcat is a predator of small prey in the prairies and coulees of the aspen parklands; the larger lynx is more common and trapped in the boreal forests for its luxurious winter fur. The latter preys mainly on snowshoe hares, and its numbers cycle with those of the hare.
Diane Secoy

FURTHER READING: 2001. *Natural Neighbours: Selected Mammals of Saskatchewan.* Regina: Canadian Plains Research Center.

CARPENTER, DAVID (1941–). Author David Carpenter's work is imbued with a profound sense of the need for compassionate commitment

between characters, and to the natural world. Born on October 28, 1941, in Edmonton, Alberta, to middle-class parents from Saskatchewan, Carpenter spent much time in the outdoors with his father and grandfather, hunting, fishing, and camping. That early ease and enjoyment of nature has been a continuing influence in his work. He earned both a BA (1962) in modern languages (French and German) and a BEd (1964) from the University of Alberta, where he was also so influenced by Henry Kreisel that he altered his career direction, earning an MA in English (1967) at the University of Oregon and then returning to the University of Alberta for a PhD (1973). Following a two-year postdoctoral position at the University of Manitoba, Carpenter joined the faculty of English at the UNIVERSITY OF SASKATCHEWAN in 1975.

His creative writing career was similarly serendipitous, initiated in 1976, both with poetry and, more importantly, with a lengthy unpublished novel. Particularly adept at the short story, novella and essay, Carpenter writes with compelling clarity and affection. His first published fiction may be read as a single interconnected work: *Jokes for the Apocalypse, Jewels,* and *God's Bedfellows* were all published between 1985 and 1988. A revised edition of *Fishing in the West,* a non-fiction work on a topic close to Carpenter's heart, was published in 1995. Two collections of his essays are also notable: *Writing Home,* published in 1994, and *Courting Saskatchewan,* an exploration of place or, more appropriately, an exploration of the definition of home, which was published in 1996. His first novel, *Banjo Lessons,* was published in 1997. His first collection of poetry, *Trout Stream Creed,* was published in 2003.

Carpenter has received critical acclaim and numerous awards for his work: *Jokes for the Apocalypse* was runner-up for the Lampard Award

HONOR KEVER PHOTO

David Carpenter.

for best first work of fiction in Canada, and *The Ketzer* was winner of the Canadian novella contest. It was reworked into a longer novella and published as a book in 2004. Carpenter left the University in 1998 to pursue writing full time. He is married to artist Honor Keever, and they reside in Saskatoon.
Cheryl Avery

CARR, DENNY (1939–99). Born in Vancouver on June 16, 1939, Denny Carr was a renowned Saskatoon radio personality and a tireless community volunteer. His broadcasting career began in British Columbia, and after a brief stint with CKSA Lloydminster, Carr joined CFQC Saskatoon in 1961. He remained at CFQC until it was sold in 1991, and later worked at CJWW. Carr was responsible for the Salvation Army's Secret Santa Campaign, a long-standing annual program that provides toys for less-fortunate children. In recognition of his professional and community service, Denny Carr received the Order of Canada in 1999 prior to his untimely death on July 22 of that year.

CARRIER, LORNE (1959–). Born on the Piapot First Nation on November 5, 1959, Lorne Carrier has led several initiatives designed to promote First Nations cultures, traditions, and heritage. Educated at the Saskatchewan Indian Federated College and the University of Victoria, Carrier created and was curator of the TREATY 4 Keeping House and Archives in Fort Qu'Appelle. He has a committed interest in the handling and reinterment of ancient burials and the repatriation of sacred First Nations artifacts. He works as Community Development Manager with the Saskatchewan Museums Association and is currently developing a Certificate in Aboriginal Museum Studies. Lorne Carrier was awarded the Saskatchewan Order of Merit in 2004.

CARRY THE KETTLE FIRST NATION. Upon signing an adhesion to TREATY 4 on September 25, 1877, the Assiniboine wanted a reserve west of the Cypress Mountain. Initially progress was made in that direction, but in June 1882 they were moved to Indian Head. The survey of their reserve was completed on June 5, 1885, 11 km south of Sintaluta. Their leader, Long Lodge, was succeeded by Man Who Took the Coat and then by Carry the Kettle in April 1891. The band's farmers took many prizes at exhibitions in Regina and Indian Head; they developed a fine herd of cattle and kept sheep for wool. Over the years women sold Seneca root, knitted socks, mitts, gloves and mufflers for their own use and for sale, and worked as housekeepers. The men sold firewood and hay, worked as wage labourers, and built and repaired implements for themselves and for sale. Current band enterprises involve school, health centre, healing lodge, store-gas station, and an eco-tourism business. Of the 2,188 band members, 757 live on the 16,590-ha reserve 80 km east of Regina. The band also owns 192.4 ha 21 km northeast of Sintaluta. *Christian Thompson*

SASKATCHEWAN ARCHIVES BOARD R-A9579-4

Nellie Carson (right) and Grace Hutchison, the first two licensed female pilots in the province, with a Gypsy Moth belonging to the Saskatoon Aero Club.

CARSON, NELLIE (1900–49). Nellie Carson, born in Yorkton in 1900, was the first woman in Saskatchewan to receive her commercial pilot's license: on October 12, 1929, she qualified for her license and immediately marked the occasion by breaking a new altitude record of 16,000 feet without an oxygen mask. Grace Hutchinson became the next female pilot to receive her license in the province, qualifying immediately after Carson on the same day. Nellie Carlson died on July 11, 1949, and is buried in Saskatoon's Woodlawn Cemetery. *James Winkel*

CARROT RIVER, town, pop 1,017, located SE of Nipawin on Hwy 23, 10 km N of the river from which the community derives its name–a derivation of the Cree word meaning "the river of wild carrots." The first homesteaders crossed to the north side of the river in 1911; however, since the land was wet and heavily wooded, little development occurred before the CNR penetrated the region in 1931. A large number of those who took up homesteads in the area were Mennonites; others were from eastern Canada and from the drought-stricken regions of southern Saskatchewan. The community prospered following **WORLD WAR II**, and the population jumped from 223 in 1946 to 801 in 1951. In the 1980s, the construction of many new public facilities was undertaken. Today, the area economy, although

largely dependent on agriculture, is diversified. The district's agricultural output includes cattle, hogs, lamb, elk, leaf cutter bees, alfalfa, and honey, in addition to the high-quality oil seed and cereal grain crops produced. The economy is otherwise supplemented by a sawmill, peat moss harvesting and processing, and seed processing. Tourism is gaining increasing importance as the town is situated near Tobin Lake and Pasquia Regional Park, the recent site of the discovery of a 92-million-year-old fossil of a crocodile-like sea dweller that lived during the Cretaceous period. Nicknamed "Big Bert," the remains found along the banks of the Carrot River are one of only four such fossils found in North America. Numerous other prehistoric marine fossils have also been found, an interpretive centre has been established, and the location has been declared a provincial heritage site because of its palaeontological significance. A Big Bert cancellation stamp is put on all mail leaving the Carrot River post office. *David McLennan*

SASKATCHEWAN ARCHIVES BOARD S-SP-A9787-2, SASKATOON STARPHOENIX FONDS

Mary Carter, 1976.

CARTER, MARY YVONNE (1923–). Mary Carter has had a long and distinguished career as lawyer, magistrate, and judge. She was born Mary Munn on October 11, 1923, in Cromer, Manitoba, where her father was employed by the United Grain Growers. The family moved to Saskatoon in 1938, and she graduated from Nutana Collegiate in 1941. She received two degrees from the **UNIVERSITY OF SASKATCHEWAN**: a BA (with Distinction) in 1944, and an LLB in 1947. She married **ROGER CARTER** in 1947. After articling with the law firm of Caswell, Whitmore and Stokan, she practiced with her husband in the firm of Makaroff, Carter and Carter from 1948 to 1953, leaving practice when the first of her six children was born. In 1960, she became the second woman to be appointed a magistrate in

Saskatchewan. In this role, her work often concerned matrimonial disputes, child support and child custody, and cases under young offender legislation; these were the areas that came to be most closely associated with her judicial career. Carter was elevated to Saskatchewan's District Court in 1978, where her work was part of the pilot project for a Unified Family Court. In 1981, when the courts were amalgamated, she became a judge of the Court of Queen's Bench, where she sat until her retirement in 1998. *Beth Bilson*

CARTER, ROGER C. (1922–). Born on March 23, 1922, Roger Colenso Carter of Moose Jaw, an innovator in legal education for Aboriginals, completed his law degree at the **UNIVERSITY OF SASKATCHEWAN** and his master's degree at the University of Michigan. Having practiced law in Saskatoon for sixteen years, Carter joined the College of Law at the University of Saskatchewan. He served as dean of the college from 1968 to 1974 and opened the Native Law Centre a year later. The Centre has developed Aboriginal law in Canada and administers the summer Program of Legal Studies for Native People, an initiative created by Carter to prepare Aboriginal people for the study of law. He received an honorary doctorate of laws from Queen's University and became the first non-Aboriginal person to be named a Companion of the Order of Gabriel Dumont. In 1998, Carter received the Saskatchewan Order of Merit and was made an Officer of the Order of Canada in 2001.

CATHERWOOD, ETHEL (1908–87). Ethel Catherwood is the only Canadian female athlete to have won an individual gold medal in Olympic track and field. Born in North Dakota on April 28, 1908, Catherwood and her family settled in Scott, Saskatchewan and moved to Saskatoon in 1925. Within a two-week period in 1926 she equaled the Canadian women's high-jumping record, then broke the world record. At the 1928 Olympic Games in Amsterdam she won the gold medal in the women's high jump. Known as the "Saskatoon Lily,"

© CANADA POST CORPORATION (1996); REPRODUCED WITH PERMISSION

This stamp honouring Ethel Catherwood was issued by Canada Post in 1996.

Catherwood gave up competitive jumping and moved to the United States in 1929. She is a member of the Canadian Olympic Hall of Fame (1949) and the Canadian Sports Hall of Fame (1955). Catherwood was one of the original inductees to the **SASKATCHEWAN SPORTS HALL OF FAME** in 1966. She died at Grass Valley, California in 1987.

Daria Coneghan and Holden Stoffel

FURTHER READING: Ransom, D. 1988. "'The Saskatoon Lily': A Biography of Ethel Catherwood," *Saskatchewan History* 41 (3): 81–98.

CATHOLIC HEALTH CARE.

In Saskatchewan, Catholic health care began when communities of religious women arrived in the region (North-West Territories). The first group, the **SISTERS OF CHARITY OF MONTREAL** (Grey Nuns), came to the Ile-à-la-Crosse mission in 1860 and cared for the sick in their convent or in the people's homes.

Between 1907 and 1952, religious congregations established hospitals in many communities which otherwise would have been without such services, namely St. Paul's, Saskatoon*; Grey Nuns', Regina; Holy Family, Prince Albert; Notre Dame, North Battleford; St. Elizabeth's, Humboldt*; Providence, Moose Jaw; Gabriel, Ponteix; St. Joseph's, Macklin; St. Margaret's, Biggar; St. Theresa, Tisdale; St. Michael's, Cudworth; St. Joseph's, Ile-à-la-Crosse*; St. Joseph's, Gravelbourg*; St. Michael's, Broadview; St. Joseph's, Lestock; St. Joseph's, Estevan*; St. Anthony's, Esterhazy*; St. Peter's, Melville*; St. Martin's, LaLoche; Union, Leoville; Notre Dame, Val Marie; Community, Radville; Notre Dame de l'Assomption, Zenon Park (an asterisk indicates those still operating in 2004).

Care of the elderly was a concern, and over the years thirteen "Seniors' Homes" were established in Whitewood, Regina (two), Moose Jaw, Marcelin,

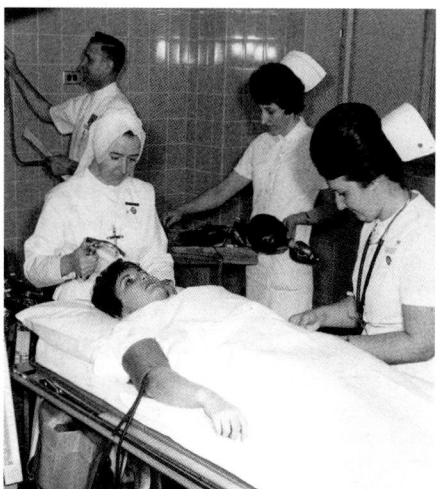

Operating room of St. Paul's Hospital, Saskatoon, ca. early 1960s.

Weyburn, Prince Albert, Radville, Saskatoon (two), Ponteix, Gravelbourg, and North Battleford.

The Catholic Hospital Conference of Saskatchewan was formed on May 27, 1943, under the direction of **EMMETT M. HALL**, with seventeen member hospitals and three long-term care facilities, for a total of 2,007 beds. Membership grew to twenty-four hospitals and ten long-term care facilities. By 2004, seven hospitals, eight long-term care facilities, and two health centres were still operating as Catholic institutions; the Macklin and Radville hospitals were converted to Health Centres.

A name change to the Catholic Health Association of Saskatchewan (CHAS) occurred in 1986 to reflect the reality that health care now included long-term care. In the early 1990s, as health care began to focus on the community, the Association published a manual entitled *Parish Home Ministry of Care*. CHAS sponsors workshops, seminars and education conferences for its members and the general public, on topics relating to Mission, Ethics, Spiritual Care, Palliative Care, Spirituality, and other areas that impact on the Catholic health system. A newsletter, *Communiqué*, is published four times a year.

The Saskatchewan Catholic Health Corporation, founded in 1977 as the Catholic Health Council, is an ownership/sponsorship group under the direction of the Catholic Bishops of Saskatchewan. The Corporation provides leadership and direction in carrying forward the mission and identity of Catholic health care in facilities that have been transferred to it by religious congregations.

Sister Anne Collins

FURTHER READING: CHAS. 1993. *Our Roots, A Promise: The Catholic Health Association of Saskatchewan, 1943–1993*. Saskatoon: CHAS; Cellard, A. and G. Pelletier. 1990. *Faithful to a Mission: Fifty Years with the Catholic Health Association of Canada*. Ottawa: Catholic Health Association of Canada.

CATHOLIC MINISTRY TO FIRST NATIONS PEOPLE.

"Bringing to," "doing for," and "walking with": these are three phrases which best describe the stages of Roman Catholic ministry among the First Nations and **MÉTIS** people of Saskatchewan.

The first or missionary stage ran from the mid- to late-1800s and was characterized by missionaries living with the people and learning the language, but in general evangelizing with a Eurocentric sense of superiority and a cultural bias that was seen as "bringing the gospel" to a largely pagan people. The second or institutional stage ran from the late 1800s to the early 1900s. This stage was characterized by the establishment of mission complexes and a spirit of "doing for" or offering services for the people, in places such as hospitals and Indian Residential schools, as well as providing for elements of Church

life in worship and sacraments. Then came the social and cultural upheaval of the 1960s and 1970s, which heralded the beginning of a post-institutional stage of ministry. The Second Vatican Council fostered a view of the Church as "People of God" as well as a greater appreciation of world religions, the power of inculturation, and interreligious dialogue.

In 1973, indigenous peoples from South, Central and North America gathered with Oblate missionaries in Guatemala. They asked the Oblates not to abandon them now, but to "walk with them" in their struggle for justice, land, political independence, cultural identity, and spiritual revival—a request that became symbolic for many. This new attitude of "walking with" has influenced Native ministry in Saskatchewan over the last thirty years, at least from a Roman Catholic perspective. It has taken the form of greater sensitivity to First Nations culture and spirituality, language learning for some, participation in First Nations ceremonies such as the **SWEAT LODGE**, dances, and pipe ceremonies, as well as entering into respectful interreligious dialogue with First Nations elders. Initiatives imbued with this attitude are the Circle Project in Regina; Valley Native Ministry in the Qu'Appelle valley; Guadalupe House in Saskatoon; Kateri Ministry in Prince Albert; the Keewatin Renewal Team that traveled the diocese of Keewatin-Le Pas from 1987 to 1990; and the Roman Catholic First Nations ministry team in the Battlefords—not to mention the individual efforts by clerical, religious, and lay missionaries. More recent initiatives are the creation of a diocesan First Nations circle in Prince Albert, the language and culture-based Cree Nation Oblate community in Makwa, and a team approach in northwest Saskatchewan.

Some significant events and persons contributing to this "walking with" approach were the Oblate-sponsored Summer Leadership Institutes from 1975 to 1985 across Canada; Fr. John Hascall, a Capuchin Ojibway priest from the United States, who shared his understanding and example of inculturation (Christian faith expressed within the heart of First Nations culture and spirituality); the "Faith Family Festivals" in Northern Saskatchewan from 1983 onwards; the Lebret Oblate 1988 conference, which articulated a new vision for First Nations ministry; the Lebret Task Force (1988–98), which sought to implement that vision; Four-Day Fasts in Alberta (1984–88 and 1993–97); the orientation sessions for Native ministry at Lac St. Anne, Alberta (1995–98); and most recently, an annual First Nations retreat held at Queen's House in Saskatoon. The annual pilgrimage at the St. Laurent shrine in the diocese of Prince Albert now includes a Cree Eucharist that integrates both the sweet grass and pipe ceremonies.

Some of the programs and movements that became part of this transition are the Christopher Leadership course; addictions awareness workshops;

Marriage and Engaged Encounter; Search weekends for youth; and more recently, Cursillo, Red Road to Recovery, 12 Step Pilgrimages, a Basic Ecclesial Community approach, and also "Return To Spirit," a three-stage approach for fostering healing from the Residential School experience. Much of this "walking with" ministry includes hearing the stories and healing the wounds of life's hurts in a variety of ways.   *Sylvain Lavoie*

CATHOLIC SHRINES AND PILGRIMAGES. A devotional practice which has become a tradition for many Saskatchewan Catholics and their families over the years is participation in a pilgrimage during the summer months. Pilgrimages usually take place at a church or shrine, where pilgrims gather for the day or in some cases camp for a few days, around the time of a special feast day. Pilgrimages usually involve a journey of some sort, with some pilgrims walking for long distances to the pilgrimage site, then praying and singing together, receiving the sacraments of Reconciliation and Anointing of the Sick, celebrating Eucharist, participating in candlelight rosary processions or the Way of the Cross, hearing talks or homilies on religious topics, and sharing food and stories with relatives, friends and fellow pilgrims. Most of the shrines and pilgrimage sites are dedicated to the Virgin Mary, although some are dedicated to saints or local holy people.

Some Saskatchewan shrines and pilgrimage sites, with the year each was established or the first pilgrimage was held:

Our Lady of Lourdes, St. Laurent, 1879
Our Lady of Sorrows, Cudworth, 1911
Our Lady of Perpetual Help, Yorkton, 1915
Our Lady of Lourdes, Kronau, 1917
Sacred Heart Shrine, Lebret, 1919
Our Lady of Lourdes Redemptorist Shrine, Yorkton, 1921

EVERETT BAKER PHOTO/COURTESY OF THE SASKATCHEWAN HISTORY AND FOLKLORE SOCIETY

Pilgrimage grotto, St. Laurent, September 1950.

Our Lady of Mount Carmel, Carmel, 1922
Our Lady of La Salette, Forget, 1922
St. Therese of the Child Jesus, Wakaw, 1925
St. Therese of the Child Jesus, Lisieux, 1930
Our Lady of the Holy Rosary, Reward, 1932
Calvary Shrine, Candiac, 1934
Our Lady of Sorrows, Ponteix, 1934
Our Lady of Sorrows, Blumenfeld, 1936
Our Lady of Lourdes, Rama, 1941
Our Lady of Lourdes, Kaposvar, 1942
Mary, Queen of All Hearts, Lestock, 1942
Immaculate Conception, Ile-à-la-Crosse, 1944
Our Lady of Lourdes, Lake Lenore, 1947
Our Lady of Lourdes, La Loche, 1954
Our Lady of Lourdes, Cochin, 1955
Our Lady of Lourdes, Battleford, 1957
Our Lady of Lourdes, Dillon, 1957
Our Lady of Lourdes, Yorkton, 1958
Our Lady of Good Counsel, Saskatoon, 1965
Our Lady of Lourdes, Wollaston Lake, 1981
Our Lady of Lourdes, St. Walburg, 1981
Mary, Mother of God, Cole Bay Mission, 1981
Our Lady of the Prairies, Saskatoon, 1982
Blessed KateriTekakwitha, File Hills, 1983
                                        Margaret Sanche

FURTHER READING: Lozinsky, J. and H. Leir. 1987. *Mary as Mother: The Pilgrimage Shrines to the Blessed Virgin Mary in Saskatchewan: A Pictorial and Historical Approach.* Muenster, SK: St. Peter's Press.

CATHOLIC WOMEN'S LEAGUE (CWL) OF CANADA. The Catholic Women's League is a national organization of Catholic lay women. With its roots in England, the first Canadian council was founded by a group of Edmonton women in 1912. Initially, their goal was to work together to assist immigrants, but this expanded to include a wide variety of works for church, community and society at large. The League was organized nationally in 1920 with the motto "For God and Canada." In Saskatchewan, the first council was formed in the archdiocese of Regina at Holy Rosary Cathedral in 1919, and their first work was the establishment of a Catholic women's hostel, later named Rosary Hall. CWL councils were formed in many parishes in the ensuing years. The first Regina CWL diocesan convention was held in 1923, and the diocesan council of Prince Albert and Saskatoon was formed in 1924. By 2003, Saskatchewan had 9,100 CWL members in 179 parish councils. Over many years, Saskatchewan CWL members have offered their service–locally, provincially, and nationally–in the areas of health care, family, agriculture, education, the environment, farm safety, genetics, social justice, child poverty, human dignity, ecumenism, evangelization, spirituality, church teachings, and faith.
                                        June Krogan

CENAIKO, FREDERICK T. (1926–). Cenaiko was born on March 21, 1926, at Chestohorb, Ukraine. An immigrant at age three, he grew up on a homestead near Quill Lake, the fourth of seven children. He met his wife, Helen Manchur, while teaching in Watson; he then enrolled in pre-medical courses at the UNIVERSITY OF SASKATCHEWAN, graduating with his MD from the University of Alberta in 1954. Upon completion of internship at St. Paul's Hospital, Dr. Cenaiko arrived in Wakaw in 1955, despite pressure from classmates to stay in Saskatoon. He can tell stories of house calls on bitter winter nights, of carrying pre-op patients upstairs, and of being paid in chickens and potatoes. He has experienced the pain of pronouncing friend's deaths and the joy of delivering three generations of babies. Endurance is exemplified by his service as an admired general practitioner in rural Saskatchewan for forty-eight years.

Dr. Cenaiko has served as school board chair and as mayor. Religious faith has prompted his work in the local Baptist Church, "holiday" medical mission trips to Honduras, and humanitarian work in Ukraine. In 1990 he was awarded the Saskatchewan Order of Merit.   *Linda Baker*

CENNON, J.J. (1922–). A well-known broadcaster and community member, J.J. (Jack) Cennon was born in Saskatoon on October 13, 1922. From 1936 to 1941, he worked as a radio announcer with CFQC Saskatoon before serving with the Royal Canadian Signal Corps during WORLD WAR II. Later, Cennon moved to Prince Albert and was production manager of CKBI. Interested in penal reform, he volunteered at the Saskatchewan Penitentiary for forty years, serving on several committees and the parole board. Cennon was made a Member of the Order of Canada in 1980.

CENTRAL BUTTE, town, pop 439, located approximately 42 km N of Chaplin at the junction of Hwys 19 and 42. The Riverhurst ferry, which crosses the south arm of LAKE DIEFENBAKER, lies to the northwest. The name of the community dates to the years prior to settlement when the region had been entirely devoted to ranching. The district has three large hills and, according to local lore, at round-up time the central butte became the most convenient landmark for all to converge. Homesteaders, largely of British, German, and Scandinavian origins, began arriving in the area in 1905–06. In 1926–27, a number of Mennonite families also moved into the region. The Central Butte post office and school were established in 1907 and 1908 respectively, both at separate locations within a few kilometres of the present townsite; after the arrival of the railway from Moose Jaw in 1914 and the establishment of the townsite, they were moved into the fledgling community. Central Butte's population was 122 in

1916; it grew fairly steadily until the mid-1960s, at which point it levelled off, just shy of 550. The population of the town remained stable until 1996, when the rail line through the community was abandoned. Today, Central Butte has a diverse core of businesses and services, several being related to the district's agricultural industry. *David McLennan*

CENTRAL PENTECOSTAL COLLEGE.

Central Pentecostal College traces its origins back to the initiative of George Hawtin, a Pentecostal pastor who began a small school in his church in Star City, Saskatchewan, in 1935. Two years later, he moved the school, then known as Bethel Bible Institute, to Saskatoon. In the mid-1940s, the school officially became the property of the Pentecostal Assemblies of Canada. Shortly thereafter, conflict over management decisions and theological differences between school administrators and denominational leaders made the school a focal point of a theological controversy that resulted in one of the most serious schisms in the denomination's history: in 1947 several faculty members, including the founder, and a significant proportion of the student population started Sharon Bible School in North Battleford, which became a centre for the Latter Rain Movement. Despite low enrolments, the Bethel Bible Institute managed to survive and rebuild its support during the 1950s under the leadership of Robert Argue and Carl H. Stiller. During the 1960s the school purchased the former Lutheran Theological Seminary building and some land. With the erection of a new residence in 1969, capable of housing seventy-six students, the Institute began to develop a campus more suited to its needs and purposes. In 1972, an agreement was negotiated with the Lutheran Theological Seminary whereby qualified students could study at Central and earn credit towards a graduate-level theological degree program. The school was granted affiliate college status by the UNIVERSITY OF SASKATCHEWAN in 1983, and obtained full accreditation with the Accrediting Association of Bible Colleges in 1997. A significant percentage of its graduates from the ministerial training program have chosen professional ministry and missionary careers. *Bruce Guenther*

FURTHER READING: Miller, T.W. 1994. *Canadian Pentecostals: A History of the Pentecostal Assemblies of Canada*. Mississauga, ON: Full Gospel Publishing House.

CENTRE FOR COMMUNITY STUDIES.

The Centre for Community Studies was established at the UNIVERSITY OF SASKATCHEWAN in 1957 following a recommendation of the Saskatchewan Royal Commission on Agriculture and Rural Life. Governance was invested in a Board appointed by the Minister of Education and the President of the University. WILLIAM B. BAKER, who had directed the Royal

Commission, was appointed the Centre's director.

The primary work of the Centre was to accumulate and communicate tested knowledge about community phenomena, in order that the effectiveness of rural communities as contributors to social and economic development might be increased. The Centre was organized into research, consulting, and training units, each one complementing the others. The Consulting Division was to establish contacts with selected communities and to open up opportunities for training and research. In 1957, communities in the province were invited to apply for partnership with the Centre, and in 1958 six co-operating or demonstration communities, differing in history and nature, were selected. They included Hudson Bay, Rose Valley, Beechy, Cabri, Esterhazy and Wawota. Each community established a "Community Development Council" made up of representatives of community organizations. A community consultant from the Centre, who would visit the community for one week each month, was assigned to each of these communities. One result of this consulting was the publication of a series of practical pamphlets entitled "Key to Community." Later, this series was distributed widely throughout North America.

The Centre's Training Division focused on leadership roles including helping professional and community leaders to work more effectively on the development of their communities, and helping field workers in government and voluntary agencies improve their understanding of the process of supporting community efforts. Workshops and seminars were held on such topics as "The Role of the Social Sciences in Rural Development," "The Role of the Rural Church," and "Learning and Behavioural Change." The Centre's Research Division projects, such as a major study of the establishment of a potash mine in Esterhazy, were undertaken within the co-operating communities. Other studies focused on topics of more general interest to communities: voluntary associations, leadership, the role of extension agencies, population migration, declining communities, the farmers' movement, citizen education in member-controlled organizations, and settlement policy as a factor in economic development.

In spite of what many considered to be much good work completed by the Centre, its history was greatly changed by the politics of the time. The Liberal opposition questioned the purpose and nature of the Centre's work, arguing potential interference in the lives of those asked to provide information. Supporters of the Centre countered that social research was being confused with socialism. Conflict also arose in the University between the role of the Centre and the newly formed Department of Sociology. The Centre's core budget of between $150,000 and $200,000, provided by the government under the university/government partnership,

was annually under threat. A responding strategy of the Centre's administration and Board was to focus more on contract research as a means of gaining financial independence.

Structural arrangements that would ensure a long-term future for the Centre for Community Studies did not materialize. In 1966, it was incorporated as a national non-profit corporation with a central office in Ottawa; Bill Baker moved there as the president of the National Centre. The Saskatoon office remained open for work in the western region. There was promise of federal contracts, but sufficient work did not materialize. Then Baker suffered ill health and had to give up his leadership role, and in 1968 the Centre closed and its assets were liquidated. Much has been said about the contribution of the Centre to Saskatchewan and beyond. Aside from research reports, many of its contributions consisted of extensive and creative adult education activities. Continuing support came from local community leaders and from the agency staff members who received training from it. Some have argued that the Centre, as a social experiment in community development, had been ahead of its time. *Harold R. Baker*

FURTHER READING: Baker, H.R. 1991. "The Centre for Community Studies." Pp. 191–209 in H.R. Baker, J.A. Draper and B.T. Fairbairn (eds.), *Dignity and Growth: Citizen Participation and Social Change*. Calgary: Detselig.

CENTRE FOR CONTINUING EDUCATION, UNIVERSITY OF REGINA.

In 1965, a Department of Extension Services (subsequently named Centre for Continuing Education) opened at the UNIVERSITY OF SASKATCHEWAN, Regina Campus. The new department was responsible for degree classes held off-campus and outside regular hours, and for expansion of certificate courses in administration. University Extension, as it became known in 1981, offered non-credit programs designed for personal and professional development. These courses, held on campus, brought learning opportunities to a wide range of people in the areas of business and management, professional development, personal growth, fine arts and humanities, languages, communications, and the environment. In 1977–78, when the Seniors' Education Centre was established, it was the only year-round centre for seniors on a Canadian university campus. Another aspect of Extension programming, English as a Second Language, began in the mid-1970s; foreign visa students travelled to the University to study English, many in preparation for undergraduate studies at the UNIVERSITY OF REGINA. In 1986–87, University Extension was granted responsibility for the Conservatory of Music.

A few memorable initiatives have included

university degree classes held in French in the town of Gravelbourg, in collaboration with the Faculty of Education and **COLLEGE MATHIEU**; a "Back to Nursing" refresher course offered in co-operation with the **SASKATCHEWAN REGISTERED NURSES' ASSO-CIATION**; a forum with Parti Québecois leader René Levesque and associate editor of *Le Devoir*, Claude Lemelin, drawing a crowd of 800 in 1970; and a lecture series in 1972 featuring distinguished Canadian artists who had at one time lived in the province, including **W.O. MITCHELL**, Farley Mowat, and Paul Hiebert.

When an end to non-credit programs and closure of the College Avenue campus was proposed in 1984–85, public protests evidenced the valued position of Extension programming in the wider community. The protests resulted in increased government funding to ensure the future of the area. In a report to the University's Board of Governors in 1992, University Extension, expressing the philosophy of "lifelong learning," advised that a university education should be more than training for employment: it should satisfy, throughout life, the broader thirst for knowledge, and expose people to the perspectives and ideas of others. In order to meet diverse learning needs and to provide maximum access for Saskatchewan people, University Extension diversified its response; the flexibility of the approach reflected the use of both traditional and non-traditional delivery modes. In addition to programs offered on campus, considerable efforts were made to deliver these courses to other communities, using local and travelling instructors, correspondence, and televised instruction. Effective collaboration with other institutions of post-secondary education and the use of evolving online technology have allowed the steady advancement of distance learning to the present. (*See* **CAMPUS SASKATCHEWAN**)

A review in 1999–2000 resulted in restructuring and in a name change to Centre for Continuing Education (CCE) to reflect more accurately contemporary operations. Led by a director, the CCE is organized into six divisions: Credit Studies, Distance Learning Division, Conservatory of Performing Arts, Seniors' Education Centre, English as a Second Language, and Business and Professional Development Programs. The current vision of the Centre for Continuing Education is to be a contributor to the intellectual, economic, social and cultural development of the communities it serves by fulfilling the University of Regina's commitment to respond to the needs of lifelong learners. CCE's mandate is to meet lifelong learning needs by offering to learners of all ages high-quality, accessible, innovative and responsive education and training programs that build on the strengths and resources of the community and the University. *Marilyn Miller*

CENTRE FOR STUDIES IN AGRICULTURE, LAW AND THE ENVIRONMENT (CSALE).

CSALE is an interdisciplinary research institution located on the **UNIVERSITY OF SASKATCHEWAN** campus in Saskatoon. Established in January 1996 as a joint venture between the Colleges of Law and Agriculture, the Centre consists of a group of university faculty, staff and graduate students who integrate the life sciences, social sciences and legal knowledge in order to better understand environmental change and legal issues related to agriculture. CSALE conducts research on the relationships between ecosystem health and agricultural production and distribution. Researchers at the Centre investigate the assumptions of environmental analysis, stimulate discussion concerning the legal regulation of markets and the environment, propose integrative policy frameworks, and communicate with researchers, policy makers and industry participants. Core activities include the training of undergraduate and graduate students, and the distribution of research results through websites, conferences, workshops, manuscripts and publications in peer-reviewed journals. CSALE's Fellows program allows a diverse group of researchers from the University of Saskatchewan and elsewhere, who are interested in law, agriculture and the environment, to connect with each other.

Researchers at the Centre monitor trends in agricultural policy and alterations to biophysical and economic conditions emphasizing issues affecting prairie and Canadian agriculture. The Centre has established itself as one of the key locations for greenhouse gas research in Canada. CSALE Fellows participated in the national "tables" that prepared the launch of the National Action on Climate Change program. Graduate students with CSALE were among the first in Canada to focus on climate change, pursuing a variety of projects on associated economic and policy options and publishing the *Climate Change Handbook 2000*. CSALE has since produced materials on a wide range of issues including papers that analyze carbon emission trading schemes and large-scale agro-forestry projects, food safety, animal welfare, and environmental sustainability of agricultural production and marketing. Researchers at the Centre are interested in rural revitalization and in partnering with Saskatchewan communities to examine issues in need of attention to those communities. *Murray Fulton*

CENTRE FOR THE STUDY OF CO-OPERA-TIVES.

The Centre for the Study of Co-operatives is an interdisciplinary teaching and research institute at the **UNIVERSITY OF SASKATCHEWAN**. Established in 1984, the Centre is supported financially by the University of Saskatchewan, by major provincial co-operatives, and by the government of Saskatchewan. The objectives of the Centre are to develop and offer university courses that provide an understanding of co-operative theory, principles, development, structures, and legislation; to undertake original research into co-operatives; to publish co-operative research, both that of Centre staff and that of other researchers; and to maintain a resource centre of co-operative materials that supports the Centre's teaching and research functions. The Centre has five faculty members who teach undergraduate and graduate courses in their respective disciplines: History, Agricultural Economics, Management and Marketing, Sociology, and Political Studies. Co-operative theory and models are incorporated into courses to increase students' understanding of co-operatives and to foster an appreciation for the significant role co-operatives have played, and continue to play, in economic and social development. The Centre also works with community groups to provide educational programs about co-operatives.

Although co-operatives are an integral part of Canadian economy and society, their special contributions and potential are often not fully understood. The Centre undertakes scholarly, often interdisciplinary, research about co-operatives and political, social, and economic issues relating to them. Its research flows from, draws on, and leads into the practical work of partner organizations in the co-operative sector, particularly in Saskatchewan and in Canada, although it is also networked to researchers around the world. Connections to co-operatives and communities stimulate the research questions it pursues; and it not only welcomes, but also requires collaboration and interaction with co-operatives to succeed in the work it does. Projects are supported by the Centre's own resources, by external funds from research funding agencies, or by organizations commissioning particular studies. The Centre sponsors a Visiting Research Fellows program, which is designed to encourage and promote research that focusses on co-operatives. Financial support is provided to both academic scholars and co-operative practitioners who undertake a specific short-term project that would benefit from concentrated study in a research milieu and from access to extensive academic resources. While at the Centre, researchers typically develop a research paper, present one or two seminars geared for the public, give a more in-depth presentation to Centre staff, and provide guest lectures in classes taught by Centre faculty.

The Centre also encompasses a category of associates known as CSC Scholars, who are actively involved in teaching, theoretical or applied research, and/or extension education concerning co-operatives. The scholar model gives the Centre an opportunity to involve more faculty members at the University of Saskatchewan in its activities, to broaden the base of its interdisciplinary teaching and research, and to create linkages with external organizations and other universities. The Resource Centre, housed with the Centre's offices, is a specialized library offering an extensive collection of journals, books, reports, and videos that focus on co-operatives and related social, political, and historical topics. It offers information and research support to anyone interested in studying co-operatives. The Centre publishes research results in various forms—books, professional journals, its own series of occasional papers, booklets, research reports—and this increasingly through electronic means. *Nora Russell*

CEYLON, village, pop 105, located on Hwy 6, 110 km due S of Regina, and 50 km N of the Canada-US border. The first homesteaders began arriving in the area in 1905, although it was not until the railroad was being built through the district in 1910 that Ceylon had its beginnings. A number of Ceylon's standing architectural landmarks, including the hotel built in 1912, date to the community's early years. In 1922, in the early morning hours of Wednesday, September 27, the most notorious event in the village's history occurred: armed thieves used explosives and a fast get-away car to rob the Bank of Montreal of about $16,000 worth of cash, securities, and bonds. One theory is that the thieves knew the bank's vault would house the proceeds of the illegal liquor trade going on in the area at the time. The brazenness of the theft and the fact that the Union Bank in Moosomin had been robbed the same night caused news of the robberies to capture provincial headlines for days. In quieter times, Ceylon serves as a trading centre for the surrounding mixed farming and ranching district. A small percentage of the area economy relates to OIL AND GAS development. *David McLennan*

CHABOT, IRÈNE (1930–). As a result of her leadership role in local, provincial, and national francophone organizations, Irène Chabot (née Fournier) has contributed to the advancement of French-speaking women in Saskatchewan. Born on August 25, 1930, in Montreal, Quebec, she was the eldest child of a Ferland-based business couple. In 1950 she married Alfred Chabot, a Ferland grain buyer and farmer; the couple raised five children. Irène Chabot served on the Directorate of CFRG, southern Saskatchewan's French radio station, from 1958 to 1970. She co-operated with her mother, Pearl Fournier, in the expansion throughout western Canada of a national women's organization, the *Fédération des Femmes Canadiennes-Françaises*, serving as national vice-president in the late 1970s. She was the first woman president of the *Association Culturelle Franco-Canadienne de la Saskatchewan*, serving three consecutive terms from 1977 to 1983, and was a member of the board and the executive of the *Fédération des Franco-*

ROY ANTAL/REGINA LEADER-POST
Irène Chabot, August 1978.

phones Hors-Québec, a lobby group for francophones outside Québec. She also served as member of the Canadian Advisory Council on the Status of Women. As well, Chabot was president of the Board of Gravelbourg's Collège Mathieu from 1983 to 1996. Widely respected for her lifelong commitment to the preservation of francophone culture in Saskatchewan, she has received numerous honours from provincial, national and international bodies. In 2004 she became a Member of the Order of Canada. *Richard Lapointe*

CHACACHAS FIRST NATION. Chief Chacachas signed TREATY 4 on September 15, 1874, at Qu'Appelle, as did Chief Kakisheway. Adjacent reserves were surveyed on the south side of Round Lake and the QU'APPELLE RIVER in 1876, and when Kakisheway requested to be relocated in 1881 surveyor John Nelson placed both Calling River bands (Kakisheway and Chacachas) on one reserve. Members of both bands were away when this occurred and were upset when they returned to Crooked Lakes in 1882 to find they no longer had separate reserves. About forty-five Chacachas band members joined Kakisheway's band; others, including Chacachas, remained stragglers. In 1884 Kakisheway died and his son Ochapowace succeeded him, becoming the first chief of the amalgamated bands. From that day on, the reserve became known as Ochapowace Reserve Number 71, enforced by an Order-in-Council on May 17, 1889. In 1886 Chief Chacachas took some of his people across the Canadian-American border to find former band members and bring them back to Canada, as he struggled to have his reserve separated from that of Kakisheway. He died while in the USA, and those who had followed him did not return to Canada. Attempts by Chacachas band members to learn why they were amalgamated were made in 1911, when a delegation went to Ottawa to interview the

Superintendent General of Indian Affairs, and in 1928 when band members consulted a lawyer to write a letter to Ottawa seeking information about a possible claim for compensation. Today, much of the old Chacachas Reserve has been purchased and re-designated reserve land (Ochapowace) through Treaty Land Entitlement, and descendants wait on the federal government to decide if they will be re-established as a separate band and reserve once again. *Christian Thompson*

CHAKASTAPAYSIN FIRST NATION. Chakastapaysin and four headmen signed TREATY 6 in August 1876 at Fort Carlton. Their band resided in an area around Fort à la Corne in the late 1880s, but the Department of Indian Affairs alleged that all of the Chakastapaysin Band members had moved off their reserve by 1898 and that their names had been added to the pay lists of other bands. The government claimed that they had ceased to exist as a band from that point, and their reserve was sold. Proceeds were credited to the bands to which Chakastapaysin Band members were transferred. In December 1998, members of the James Smith Cree Nation, descended from Chakastapaysin Band members, launched a claim against the federal government arguing that the Chakastapaysin Reserve had been unlawfully surrendered and sold. In May 1999 the Indian Claims Commission was asked to conduct an inquiry into the rejection of this claim; Canada has not raised a challenge to the inquiry, although it remains unsettled. The Chakastapaysin Band is thus recognized at some level by various First Nations organizations and government departments, but it has not been re-established.

Christian Thompson

CHAN, ERNEST C.F. (1909–90). Ernest C.F. Chan devoted much of his life to teaching science and fostering Saskatoon's folkarts, theatre, and Chinese immigrant communities. Born near Canton, China on June 25, 1909, Chan immigrated to Canada in 1928 and earned a degree in Mechanical Engineering from the UNIVERSITY OF SASKATCHEWAN in 1937. Two years later, he began a long and distinguished teaching career at Saskatoon's Technical Collegiate, becoming the first Chinese person to teach in a public school system in Canada. Active in his community, Ernie Chan served as president of the Saskatoon Rotary Club, the Saskatoon Highland Dancing Association, and the Saskatoon Folk Arts Council. He was also a founder of the city's popular Folk Festival. In 1984, Chan was made a Member of the Order of Canada. He died on December 12, 1990.

CHARTIER, CLÉMENT (1946–). Clément Chartier, born in 1946 at Ile-à-la-Crosse, Saskatchewan, is a Métis lawyer, activist and politician. Raised in Buffalo Narrows, Chartier received his law degree from the UNIVERSITY OF SASKATCH-EWAN in 1978 and was called to the Saskatchewan Bar in 1980. In the late 1960s, after leaving a position with the provincial Department of Social Services, Chartier became a political activist after realizing that government was not serious about addressing the adverse social conditions faced by the Métis. During his political career, Chartier has held a number of executive positions in Métis and Indigenous political bodies, including: Native Youth Association of Canada (executive director in the 1970s); Association of Métis and Non-Status Indians of Saskatchewan (AMNSIS) (vice-president, 1982–85); Métis National Council (MNC) (chairperson, 1983 and 1985; ambassador, 1993–96; president, 2003); World Council of Indigenous Peoples (president, 1984–87; vice-president, 1993–97); MÉTIS NATION–SASKATCHEWAN (MN-S) (president, 1998–2003). A strong advocate for Métis rights, Chartier worked with other Métis activists to dissolve the AMNSIS in 1988 and create a Métis-only political body, the reformulated Métis Society of Saskatchewan. He was the plaintiffs' lawyer in *R. v. Grumbo* (1996), which briefly granted Métis Aboriginal hunting rights in Saskatchewan, and in *R. v. Morin and Daigneault* (1996), which provided Métis living in Saskatchewan with "Indian" fishing rights. He also served as MNC counsel for the 2003 Supreme Court of Canada decision *R. v. Powley*, which granted Métis in Ontario Aboriginal hunting rights. *Darren R. Préfontaine*

FURTHER READING: Chartier, C. 1999. "Aboriginal Self-Government and the Métis Nation." Pp. 112-129 in John H. Hylton (ed.), *Aboriginal Self-Government in Canada*. Saskatoon: Purich Publishing; Teillet, J. 2004. *Métis Law Summary, 2004*. Vancouver: Pape & Salter.

Clem Chartier, February 1984.

CHASE, LILLIAN (CA. 1894–1987). Lillian Alice Chase, a pioneer in treating diabetes, practiced in Regina from 1925 to 1942. Born in Nova Scotia about 1894, she received her BA from Acadia University in 1916. In 1922 she graduated from the University of Toronto Medical School, where she witnessed the first human trial of insulin, which had just been discovered there. While interning at Toronto General Hospital, she participated in the newly founded diabetic clinic. She also interned in Philadelphia. Dr. Chase established a general practice in Regina, where she lectured nursing students and gave talks to women in the area. Active in local and provincial medical organizations, she was elected president of the Regina General Hospital medical staff in 1932, likely the first woman to hold that position in Canada. In 1937 she published a benchmark study on the prevalence of diabetes in Saskatchewan. In 1942 Dr. Chase joined the Royal Canadian Army Medical Corps. After WORLD WAR II she held appointments at Toronto hospitals, and in 1948 became a specialist in internal medicine. She was a founding member of the Canadian Diabetes Association, and in 1967 was named a Senior Member of the Canadian Medical Association. Dr. Chase died in Ottawa on August 28, 1987. Chase Crescent in Regina is named after her. *Fay Hutchinson*

CHAUTAUQUA. A project by a Methodist minister and businessman to train Sunday School teachers at a summer camp at Lake Chautauqua, New York in 1874 captured the imagination of rural and urban America. Quickly it grew into a multitude of local "summer fairs" featuring music, drama, comedy, and lectures with the expressed purpose of enhancing democracy, co-operation, community, and political discussion. By WORLD WAR I some 8,000 communities in the United States hosted chautauqua summer programs put on by private "chautauqua" companies. In 1916 chautauquas came to Canada, organised by J.M. Erickson, backed by a chautauqua businessman from Chicago, and encouraged by the United Farmers of Alberta. With its head office in Calgary, the company put on chautauqua events in communities in British Columbia, the three prairie provinces, Ontario, Quebec, and Alaska from 1917 to 1935. Companies in New England took chautauquas to the Maritime provinces.

Typically the company would sign a contract with local sponsors to host the next year's summer event—week-long in larger centres and three days in smaller communities. The company would recruit the theatre troupes, musicians and vocalists, comedians and lecturers, sending them on the circuit to appear in each contracted community in sequence. The task of staging each local event fell to the "superintendents," most often young women who were university students or recent graduates. The "Chautauqua lady" arrived in town a week before the event; she handled the financing, did advertising, sold tickets, got the sponsors on-side, supervised putting up the tent, coordinated the artists and lecturers, was the master of ceremonies for the actual event, and then collected any shortfall in the contracted amount from the sponsors, who often had to make it up out of their own pockets. In smaller centres it was not uncommon to find her delivering a Sunday sermon or umpiring a ball game. By 1935 a combination of the radio, better transportation, and especially widespread poverty in rural communities during the Depression, finally brought an end to the chautauquas, although imitations lingered on and the tradition was revived in Battleford in 1974.

At their height during the 1920s, chautauquas served an important need, especially in isolated rural communities. Residents were delighted—indeed brought to tears in some accounts—by the musicians and singers, enthralled by the stage plays, and thoroughly engaged by the lecturers. The chautauqua message, one of progress and democracy coupled with an aura of the Social Gospel emanating from its Methodist roots, fitted well with the populist era in prairie politics and arguably helped to develop community solidarity and social consciousness, and to raise morale in prairie communities. *Bob Stirling*

CHERRY, EVELYN SPICE (1906–90). Evelyn Spice Cherry was a pioneering documentary filmmaker. A producer, director, scriptwriter, and editor, she was a driving force at the National Film Board of Canada (NFB) in the 1940s. With her husband, cameraman Lawrence Cherry, she formed her own company, Cherry Film Productions Ltd., in Regina in 1961. She made over 100 films between 1929 and 1979. Born in Yorkton, Cherry taught public school before earning a journalism degree from the University of Missouri in 1929. She worked briefly at the *Regina Leader-Post*, and in 1931 travelled to London, England. Working for John Grierson at the GPO Film Unit—the only woman and the only Canadian—she produced *Weather Forecast* (1934), an acclaimed poetic treatment of forecasting methods, and *Prairie Winter* (1935). In London, she married Yorkton expatriate, Lawrence Cherry, and they worked there until war was declared in 1939. Returning to Canada as independents, they joined the NFB at Grierson's invitation in 1941. As Head of the Agricultural Unit, Spice Cherry produced films for the war effort and the co-operative farm movement, and brought prairie life to national and international consciousness. The Cherrys were also key figures in the development of the Yorkton Film Council in 1947 and the distribution circuits that brought films to rural areas. As a filmmaker, Spice Cherry's achievement was to make the art of social documentary a populist vehicle for the voice of Saskatchewan people and their communitarian energies. *By Their Own Strength* (1940) is remarkable in the way it depicts class conflict in a bold, agit-prop montage style, foregrounding the contributions of working people to larger social and economic systems. Other films include *New Horizons* (1940), *Windbreaks for the Prairies* (1942), *That They May Live* (1942), *Soil for Tomorrow* (1945), *Land for Men* (1945), and *Water for the Prairies* (1950).

In 1950 Evelyn Spice Cherry left the NFB, disillusioned by accusations of Communist infiltration. She taught English and attempted to set up a day-care centre for working mothers in the 1950s. In 1958 the Cherrys returned to Regina to establish a film section for the Saskatchewan government, and in the early 1960s they produced films on environmental topics and Aboriginal issues. Lawrence died in 1966, but with her youngest son, Bill, Spice Cherry continued as an independent filmmaker and activist. In the 1970s and 1980s, she continued her involvement with the Yorkton festival, and played a key role in the Regina movement for nuclear disarmament. Evelyn Spice Cherry retired to Cortes Island, British Columbia in 1985 and died in Victoria.   *Christine Ramsay*

FURTHER READING: Morris, P. 1984. *The Film Companion.* Toronto: Irwin; Ramsay, C. 2003. *Canadian Film Encyclopedia Online*; Wise, W. 2001. *Take One's Essential Guide to Canadian Film.* Toronto: University of Toronto Press.

CHICKADEES. Chickadees belong to the family Paridae, with approximately fifty-three species worldwide. These small perching birds are found on all continents except Australia and Antarctica. Of the seven species native to North America, two are common in Saskatchewan and one is a rare, irregular visitor. All chickadees are small, active birds with relatively long tails and short, strong bills. Mostly non-migratory, they nest in tree cavities. The black-capped chickadee (*Parus atricapillus*) is the best-known Saskatchewan chickadee, common in the southern boreal forest, the parklands, and the **CYPRESS HILLS.** Its neat uniform of gray back, black cap and bib, and pale underparts is easily recognized. Immensely social, they come readily to feed trays and will often alight on one's hand to pick up food. One of the most admired local birds, they are adaptable, fearless, skilled at evading predators, and capable of withstanding the rigours of a prairie winter.

The boreal chickadee (*P. hudsonicus*) inhabits the boreal forest to the northern limits of the province. In winter it occasionally moves south to the parklands, but is almost never seen on the prairies. Partial to coniferous trees, it is somewhat more elusive and less gregarious than its black-capped cousin. It is easily recognized by its mouse-brown cap, brown flanks, and rather nasal *chick-a-dee-dee.* The mountain chickadee (*P. gambeli*), similar to the black-capped chickadee but with a strik-

J. BROMPTON PHOTO/© SASKATCHEWAN ENVIRONMENT/ SKCDC, 2001. ECOSYSTEM IMAGE INFORMATION SYSTEM

Black-capped chickadee (*Poecile atricapillus*).

ing white eyebrow line, is a rare visitor from the Rocky Mountains. Two summer records in the Cypress Hills (1980, 1989) suggest the possibility of breeding in that area.   *J. Frank Roy*

FURTHER READING: Alsop, J.F., III. 2002. *The Birds of Canada.* New York: Dorling Kindersley.

CHICKEN FARMERS OF SASKATCHEWAN. Chicken meat production is one of the agriculture sectors that operate under a supply managed system. The management of production in Saskatchewan is carried on through a quota system; control of the quota is the responsibility of a board of elected producer directors of a provincial organization called Chicken Farmers of Saskatchewan (CFS). This body sets provincial policy and negotiates at the national level to determine production levels for Canada as well as Saskatchewan's share of Canadian chicken production. The national market requirement is determined by the national body, Chicken Farmers of Canada. Saskatchewan's ninety-eight licensed operators produced about 41,370,000 kg of chicken over 6.7 production cycles in 2003, at an average price of $1.23 per kg. Chicken meat production takes place in large open barns where the birds have access to feed and water lines running the length of the building. Approximately two-thirds of the farms are within an 80 km radius of Saskatoon; the remainder are situated close to Wynyard.   *Van Stewart*

CHILD AND FAMILY SERVICES ACT: *see* **LEGISLATION IN SASKATCHEWAN**

CHILD-CARE AND PRESCHOOL CO-OPERATIVES. Co-operatives play an important role in providing adequate and affordable child-care and preschool services. While private firms may be inclined to enhance profitability by charging higher prices, member-owned child-care and educational facilities are more likely to place emphasis on providing more spaces at prices that members can afford. The total number of co-operatives in this sector remained remarkably consistent throughout the 1990s—around 120—although the number of active

members fell by 16%. While there was a slight drop in the number of people employed by these organizations overall, the wage bill increased, suggesting better salaries, and there was a steady decline in liabilities. Assets, revenue, and member equity also rose consistently over the decade, indicating good financial health in this sector.

Unlike other types of co-operatives in the province, child-care facilities are located mainly in larger urban centres. There are approximately fifty child-care centres in Saskatchewan, employing a total of about 375 people and managing a wage bill of nearly $7 million. Healthy rises in revenue, surplus, assets, and member equity indicate ongoing successful financial management and a consistent demand for co-operative services in this area.

In contrast to child-care facilities, preschools do not receive a high level of government funding, and as a result tend to rely more heavily on donations and fund-raising drives to bolster revenues. Relative to their numbers, preschools have far fewer paid employees than child-care centres (80 as opposed to 375), which is probably a reflection of their smaller size and a greater reliance on volunteer labour. Preschools maintained a consistent presence of more than seventy organizations in Saskatchewan during the 1990s, although active membership declined by almost 13%. Assets rose by 83% over the same period, while liabilities increased even more dramatically, from $23,000 in 1989 to $182,000 at the end of the next decade. On the positive side, both revenues and member equity increased as well, and although the total number of employees dropped from 106 to 80 individuals, the wage bill rose. While this indicates improved salaries in these organizations, they still lag considerably behind those of their child-care counterparts.   *Nora Russell*

FURTHER READING: Fulton, Murray, et al. 1991. *Economic Impact Analysis of the Co-operative Sector in Saskatchewan*, Research Report Prepared for Saskatchewan Department of Economic Diversification and Trade; Herman, Roger and Murray Fulton. 2001. *An Economic Impact Analysis of the Co-operative Sector in Saskatchewan: Update 1998*; Ketilson, Lou Hammond, et al. 1998. *The Social and Economic Importance of the Co-operative Sector in Saskatchewan*, Research Report Prepared for Saskatchewan Department of Economic and Co-operative Development.

CHILDREN. When Saskatchewan became a province in 1905, its population included 108,755 children, the majority of whom were part of larger families and living in rural areas. In 2001 there were over 280,000 children in Saskatchewan, the majority living in urban settings, and in smaller families on average. Children are considered a resource to be nourished and supported by families and communities, both as children and as future

PATRICK PETTIT/REGINA LEADER-POST

Four-year-olds play in the sandbox at their playschool, January 1993.

adult citizens. While parents have always had the primary responsibility for raising children, even in the early days of the province communities rallied to provide services to children, such as basic education, that were beyond the means of most parents.

In 1905, however, Saskatchewan children's future was usually on the farm, and few completed a high school education. Today's children face a more diverse future in a much more complex society, and most will need substantial education and training to be successful in the modern economy. Government services and supports have gradually increased over the years to help parents raise children effectively. Education programs have been significantly enhanced, particularly for children with disabilities. Public health measures such as vaccinations have reduced the risk of epidemic disease that formerly affected child populations. More attention is devoted to protecting the rights of children and to ensuring their input into decisions affecting their lives. The *United Nations Convention on the Rights of the Child* set out basic rights for children in 1992.

Both the provincial and federal governments are involved in programs to benefit children. The Saskatchewan government is responsible for education, child welfare, and health services. National programs such as the Canada Child Tax Benefit provide income support and supplementation directly to low- and middle-income parents. The federal government also assists with the costs of a variety of provincial services like early learning and care, as well as helping individual youth and young adults with access to post-secondary education. Until recently, professional models for children's services focused on children themselves, and child-centred approaches were common in areas such as education and child welfare. More recently, it has been recognized that better results are achieved when children's needs are considered within the context of their families. New models are under development which, for example, increase parent involvement in schools, or offer support to parents and

extended families to reduce the need for intensive child welfare services.

One in four children in Saskatchewan is Aboriginal, and that proportion is expected to rise. Historically, Aboriginal children have been less likely than the mainstream population to be healthy, to complete their education, and to grow up to participate in the labour force. Communities and governments are devoting specific attention to improving the educational success of Aboriginal children in order to ensure their full participation as adults in the economic and social life of the province.

In the decades prior to the 1970s, it was relatively common for one spouse, usually the woman, to stay home to care for young children. As a result, public investment was focused on the needs of children as they reached "school age": investment in younger children was limited, on the presumption that a parent was available to provide the needed care and support to the child. Changes in the labour force participation of women and the increased incidence of single parenthood have focused more attention on the need for support from outside the family to meet children's needs before they reach school age. While support for preschool age children remains relatively inconsistent and incoherent, parents, communities, and governments are gradually moving towards approaches that support children along their whole developmental path from birth to adulthood.

What makes children healthy and able to grow up to be productive citizens? Many things determine optimal health and development, some inherited and others a result of the child's environment. A debate has long centred on how some children thrive despite being raised in difficult circumstances, while others struggle despite many advantages. Factors related to poverty—parental unemployment, inadequate nutrition and housing—are frequently associated with problems in children's health and development. Parents and experts agree that children need to feel safe and secure as well as to be

loved and respected, protected from harm, and stimulated to encourage healthy mental and physical development within their capacities. Research confirms that a positive relationship with a nurturing adult, good parenting skills, and a supportive community have a tremendous impact on the health and development of a child. *Janet Mitchell*

CHILDREN'S LAW ACT, 1997: *see* **LEGISLATION IN SASKATCHEWAN**

CHILEAN COMMUNITY. The presence of resident Chilean nationals in Saskatchewan was almost non-existent before 1973. However, as a result of the American-sponsored, violent overthrow of the democratically elected socialist government of Salvador Allende on September 11, 1973, more than a million Chileans fled their country seeking refuge from persecution. Several thousand came to Canada, and a few hundred settled in Saskatchewan. The most recent Census (2001) reports that there are 845 Chileans living in Saskatchewan: 285 in Regina and 290 in Saskatoon. The political reasons behind their immigrating characterized the activities by which Chileans would become known in the local community. Provincial press reports (particularly from Regina, Saskatoon and Moose Jaw) show that from the mid-1970s until the end of the military dictatorship in the early 1990s, Chileans, with the support of many Canadian churches, trade unions, students, political activists, human rights organizations and individuals, staged hunger strikes, educational conferences, vigils, picket lines, and marches. These protest activities denounced the systematic violation of human, labour, political and civil rights taking place in Chile. Although the repression of the Chilean people was taking place thousands of kilometres away, it had a profound impact on the hearts and minds of the new Saskatchewan residents.

The history of Saskatchewan's small Chilean community also reveals significant developments in art and sport. The Regina and Saskatoon Chilean Association Folklore Groups, Mamma Llajta, the Salvador Allende Folklore Group, Raíces Chilenas (Chilean Roots), and Desde el Sur (From the South) are examples of old and new performing artists whose live singing and dancing enable Chilean and Latin American folklore and music to be enjoyed by audiences throughout the province. Chileans have supported the growth of soccer in Saskatchewan: Barrabases in Regina and Arauco in Saskatoon are two of the most successful teams at the provincial level in their respective divisions, and both had a large contingent of Chileans over the years. The solidarity, cultural, athletic, and educational organizations created by Chilean arrivals to Saskatchewan helped many of them to rebuild their social and professional identities. The fact that every day across Saskatchewan hundreds of Chileans work in many different professions is a testament to the resilience of a community whose members overcame the trauma of a military coup at home, and quickly adjusted to the realities of a new society, a new language, and a new climate. *Miguel Sanchez*

CHIMNEY SWIFT. Swifts are small, insectivorous birds known for their swift flight. The long, narrow wings make them very maneuverable in their habitat in forests and cliff faces. Members of the family (family Apodidae, order Apodiformes), containing approximately 100 species, are found on all continents except Antarctica.

The Chimney Swift is an uncommon summer resident, which breeds in wooded areas near the Manitoba border and is sometimes seen in the southern half of the province. It has a distinctive shape, described as a cigar with wings, with a small head and short tail propelled by the sickle-shaped wings. Their buzzy, rasping call is often heard before they are seen flying rapidly in pursuit of their small insect prey. *Diane Secoy*

FURTHER READING: Alsop, Fred J., III. 2002. *Birds of Canada*. New York: Dorling Kindersley; Godfrey, W. Earl. 1986 (revised edition). *Birds of Canada*. Ottawa: National Museum of Natural Science; National Audubon Society. 2001. *The Sibley Guide to Bird Life and Behavior*. New York: Alfred A. Knopf.

CHINESE COMMUNITY. Chinese settlement in Saskatchewan dates back to the late 1880s, when the Canadian Pacific Railway (CPR) was completed. Early Chinese immigrants arrived in Saskatchewan mainly through British Columbia. There were only forty-one Chinese in Saskatchewan in 1901, according to the 1901 Canadian census. With the growing hostility towards the Chinese in British Columbia at the turn of the century, Chinese immigrants began moving eastward. Moose Jaw was initially one of the largest Chinese communities in Saskatchewan, with over 160 Chinese and over twenty businesses by 1911. Other Chinese communities were in Regina, Swift Current, Battleford, and Saskatoon. According to the Canadian census, the total Chinese population in Saskatchewan had grown to 957 by 1911.

The growth of Saskatchewan was closely linked with the building of the CPR and Chinese immigrants immediately settled in the new railway towns. In 1882, Moose Jaw was chosen as the divisional point of the CPR and developed quickly into a booming town with the largest Chinese population: by 1910, a small Chinatown with a population of about 150 had emerged on River Street, and in 1913 Moose Jaw had about 450 Chinese men and two women, thirty-five to thirty-eight Chinese laundries, and three Chinese restaurants. As in other Chinese communities, the introduction of steam laundry and the Depression put many Chinese laundries out of

business: the Chinese population in Moose Jaw dropped steadily, from 320 in 1921 to 260 in 1941; its Chinatown was, in effect, extinct by the 1940s.

In Saskatoon the Chinese population was merely 228 in 1921, but increased to 308 in 1931. A short-lived Chinatown consisting of a few stores was established, and the population grew from 225 in 1951 to 499 in 1961. After the mid-1960s, a few Chinese restaurants and stores opened, and by November 1986 Saskatoon's New Chinatown consisted of about twenty Chinese businesses. Regina did not have a Chinatown, partly due to the small Chinese population and partly because of the mutual agreement made among early Chinese immigrants that they would avoid competition by not setting up businesses close to each other. In 1907, for example, there were four Chinese laundries, two Chinese restaurants, and one Chinese grocery store in Regina, scattered throughout the city's downtown area. The Chinese population in Regina was only eighty-nine in 1911. By 1914, the number of Chinese laundries had increased to twenty-nine, but there were only two Chinese grocery stores and restaurants. As in Moose Jaw, Chinese hand laundry businesses in Regina declined after the 1920s, so that by 1940 only eight laundries remained. In 1941, Regina had a Chinese population of only 250.

Historically, Chinese immigrants in Canada experienced racial discrimination. In 1885, the first federal anti-Chinese bill was passed to impose a head tax of $50, with a few exceptions, on all persons of Chinese origin entering the country. It was increased to $500 in 1903, which at the time was the equivalent of two years' wages. The Chinese in Saskatchewan were disenfranchised in 1908. The small Chinese community in Moose Jaw was particularly affected in 1912, when a Chinese restaurant owner was arrested after his employee, a White waitress, filed an assault complaint against him. The case was widely publicized and prompted an act by the Saskatchewan Legislature disallowing the employment of White females in restaurants and other businesses kept or managed by the Chinese; any Oriental who violated the act would be fined $100. The act was repealed in 1918, only to be replaced by the **FEMALE EMPLOYMENT ACT**, which required Chinese businessmen to obtain a special licence from the municipality in order to hire a White female. In 1923, the Canadian Parliament passed the Chinese Immigration Act, preventing Chinese from entering the country and controlling those already here; this Act remained in effect for twenty-four years. Since Chinese men could not bring their wives and children into Canada, the sex imbalance in the Chinese community remained the highest among ethnic groups in Canada.

In the decade between 1937 and 1947, Canada and China were allies in **WORLD WAR II**, and it was during this time that the Chinese made another sig-

KANE L. CONEGHAN PHOTO

Sifu Curtis Kautzman and the Canadian Hung Kuen Association perform the lion dance for the Chinese Benevolent Association for Year of the Rooster, 2005.

nificant contribution to Canada. After the establishment of a Resistance and National Salvation Association in Regina in 1937, its small Chinese population of about 175 observed the memorial days, wired the Chinese government to keep up the fight, and used tag days and other devices to solicit funds. Despite a small Chinese population of only 300 in Saskatoon and 260 in Moose Jaw, these two cities achieved fame for their high level of bond purchases by the Chinese in the early years of the war. These contributions greatly helped to improve White Canadian attitudes towards the Chinese: this made possible, by 1947, enfranchisement of the Chinese in Saskatchewan as well as major improvements for the Chinese immigration policy in Canada.

In 1947, two years after the war, the Chinese Immigration Act was repealed, allowing for the reunion of many families. The Chinese population in Saskatchewan started to increase: in 1941 it stood at 2,249; by 1961 it had increased to 3,660. Since 1967, a fairer immigration policy based on the point system has been adopted in Canada. The universal point system, applied to all prospective immigrants irrespective of country of origin or permanent residence, allowed Chinese immigrants to come to Canada from mainland China and other Asian regions including Taiwan, Hong Kong, Malaysia, Singapore, and Vietnam. As a result, between 1971 and 2001 the Chinese population in Saskatchewan doubled, from 4,605 to 9,280. According to the 2001 census statistics, the Chinese community represented the largest visible minority group in Saskatchewan (29%), and about 1% of the total population. Today most of the Chinese in Saskatchewan live in Saskatoon (48%) and Regina (30%).

The Chinese community in Saskatchewan is now a heterogeneous group with diverse cultural, professional and social backgrounds: unlike their predecessors, who toiled mainly in restaurants and laundries, the Chinese in Saskatchewan have moved into a wide range of professions and gained their rightful place in the multicultural society. (*See also* **VISIBLE MINORITIES, ETHNIC BLOC SETTLEMENTS, URBAN ETHNIC DIVERSITY**) *Li Zong*

FURTHER READING: Chuenyuan Lai, D. 1988. *Chinatowns: Towns Within Cities in Canada*. Vancouver: University of British Columbia Press; Li, P. 1998. *Chinese in Canada*. Toronto: Oxford University Press; Wickberg, E. (ed.). 1982. *From China to Canada: A History of the Chinese Communities in Canada*. Toronto: McClelland and Stewart.

CHINESE LABOUR IN MOOSE JAW. The Tunnels of Moose Jaw Passage to Fortune tour correctly acknowledges that its characters, including a demanding White laundry owner and his foreman, are fictitious. The historic reality is quite different. As in other cities, Chinese workers in Moose Jaw's early years were mainly self-employed, or employed by other Chinese workers. Many had constructed the CANADIAN PACIFIC RAILWAY, but did not find work where they later settled. They established themselves in service work such as laundries or restaurants. Their success later led the dominant society to seek legislative means to protect "White" businesses. Trade unions were also involved in the campaign for laws to curb the Chinese workers' success, seeing cheap Chinese labour as a threat to their status.

In 1912, Saskatchewan became the first jurisdiction to prohibit the employment of White (Caucasian) women by Oriental employers. Shortly after, Moose Jaw was the site of the first conviction under this law: Quong Wing and Quong Sing pleaded not guilty at their trial, but lost; each was fined $5, and they were required to fire the three "White" staff. With the help of the Chinese community, they challenged their conviction in the Saskatchewan Court of Appeal and subsequently at the Supreme Court of Canada. They lost both times. The legislation remained in effect until 1969, although it was not enforced in later years. *Martha Tracey*

FURTHER READING: Backhouse, C. 1996. "The White Women's Labour Laws: Anti-Chinese Racism in Early Twentieth-Century Canada," *Law and History Review* 14: 315–68; Li, P.S. 1988. "Capitalist Expansion and Immigrant Labour: Chinese in Canada." Pp. 101–26 in B. Singh Bolaria and Peter S. Li (eds.), *Racial Oppression in Canada*. Toronto: Garamond Press.

CHIROPRACTORS' ASSOCIATION. The Chiropractors' Association of Saskatchewan was created following an Act of the Saskatchewan legislature in 1943 (revised in 1994), which set the rules for licensing all chiropractors in the province and defined what chiropractic is, what it does, and how it relates to society. It is a self-governing professional association, and there are controls and penalties for non-compliance. Successful candidates for practice must be graduates of an institution approved by the Canadian Examining Board, and must have passed a national board exam and a subsequent provincial exam. Continuing education is required by all mem-

bers as a condition for continued licensure. Chiropractic practices can be solo, group, multidisciplinary, or specialty (e.g., sports, rehabilitation, assessment). Chiropractic care is paid for partly by medicare, partly by the patient, and also by third parties such as insurance companies and Workers' Compensation. The Chiropractors' Association of Saskatchewan is dedicated to providing quality care of the neuromusculoskeletal system, and strives to co-operate with all providers of health care for the benefit of the patient. *J. Kenneth Goldie*

CHOICELAND, town, pop 370, located 42 km NW of Nipawin, just N of the junction of Hwys 6 and 55. Choiceland is situated in the forest fringe of the northernmost agricultural region of eastern Saskatchewan. The beginnings of the Hanson Lake Road and Narrow Hills Provincial Park are located north of the town. Settlement of the area began in the early 1920s, the first arrivals being primarily of British origin. As the community developed, it became somewhat cosmopolitan as people of German, Ukrainian, Polish, Dutch, and Chinese descent arrived. Schools and a post office were established in the district in the late 1920s; however, with the arrival of the railroad in 1932, the post office relocated to the newly established townsite and a new school was then built in the burgeoning community. Today, the community has a number of businesses and services, many of which are involved with the district's agricultural industry. Choiceland has a library, a museum, three churches, a K–12 school, and a volunteer fire department. Recreational facilities include a curling rink, an indoor arena, ball diamonds, a campground, a paddling pool, and a community hall. The Wapiti Valley Ski Area, 25 km south of Choiceland on the SASKATCHEWAN RIVER, offers 90 vertical metres of skiing with runs over a kilometre long. *David McLennan*

CHOIRS. In 1914, A.S. Vogt (founder of the Mendelssohn Choir) claimed that Saskatchewan's

excellent choral work was one benefit of the province's isolation and corresponding need to create its own art. The province not only had church and school choirs as well as glee clubs which had developed by the early 1890s: it also had substantial choral societies in the larger cities, male voice choirs (including a Welsh group in Saskatoon, which agreed to add English members in 1913!), and an annual music festival. At the first festival in 1909, 400 singers assembled from eight centres, and 200 of them combined to perform Mendelssohn's *Festgesang* and Bennett's *May Queen*. In 1914, Moose Jaw alone sent 65 children and 310 adults to the festival in Saskatoon in eight rail cars. In cities, the choral societies, with 80 to 250 members, were performing Mendelssohn's *Elijah and St. Paul*, Haydn's *Creation*, and the complete *Messiah*. Among groups in other centres were the Beethoven Choir in Moose Jaw and a Philharmonic Society in Indian Head, which exchanged performances with the Regina Philharmonic Society (1906–08).

After WORLD WAR I, choirs for women were founded and flourished. Church choirs often numbered over 60 members, and many provincial communities raised their standards to compete successfully in the music festivals: the Biggar Choral Society won the Grand Challenge Shield in 1931; and a school chorus from Sedley, conducted by Jean Graham, gained a mark of 98 from no less a figure than Sir Hugh Roberton. It was, however, the growth in the school choruses that kept the music festivals buoyant in the late 1930s. During the war, morale was boosted in Regina by the Victory Choir, approved by city council and formed in July 1942, which consisted of 82 men and 191 women representing every choral unit and denomination in the city.

More recent times have seen large choral works regularly performed with the city symphony orchestras, with smaller ad hoc groups in centres like Swift Current, and in summer workshops with distinguished visiting conductors (John Alldis and Wayne

ROYAL STUDIOS PHOTO/COURTESY OF JUVENTUS
Regina's "Juventus" is just one of the youth choirs active in the province.

Riddell, for example). Youth choirs in Prince Albert, Saskatoon, North Battleford, Moose Jaw and Regina have been highly successful in local, national and international competitions. The Saskatchewan Choral Federation, founded in 1978, has promoted choral music throughout the province and organizes annual camps for young singers. Chamber choirs in Outlook, Humboldt, Rosthern, Saskatoon, Regina, and in the universities have made it possible for audiences to hear the entire choral repertoire. Meanwhile, the groups that formed the base of the earlier tradition—church and school choirs—have been less numerous and less adventurous.   *Robin Swales*

CHRISTENSEN, DAVID A. (1936–). David Christensen has had a wide-ranging influence on Canadian agriculture. His impact has resulted from teaching nutrition and dairy management to undergraduate, graduate, vocational and veterinary students at the **UNIVERSITY OF SASKATCHEWAN**. He has also been widely sought as an international consultant in over twenty countries in Africa, Asia, Central America, and the Middle East. Christensen's international development activities were recently recognized when he was awarded the International Animal Agriculture Award in 1998 in Seoul, Korea by the World Congress of Animal Production, and by the J.W. George Ivany Internationalization Award in 1999 from the University of Saskatchewan. Christensen earned a BSA at the University of Saskatchewan in 1948 specializing in Animal Science, an MS in Agriculture in 1952 at the University of British Columbia, and a PhD from Oregon State University in 1955. Early in his career, he helped establish the principles of feed testing in Saskatchewan, bringing scientific nutrition information and ration formulation to the farm. In response to the enormous growth in the use of corn silage in the United States, he developed ensiling techniques and feeding systems for dairy and beef cattle based on cereal silage, which have been widely adopted in western Canada. In the late 1970s, Christensen was one of the first nutritionists to appreciate the economic impact of trace mineral deficiencies in western Canada: trace mineral supplementation is now widespread, primarily as a result of a ten-year research program.

The dehydrated alfalfa industry in western Canada developed markets and expanded production based on Christensen's research and recommendations for use of "dehy" in ruminant rations. More recently, Christensen has been active in the development of new, high-value feedstuffs based on Canadian feed ingredients for use in domestic and international markets. His research and expertise in this area were critical to the development of new export markets for such sectors of Canadian agriculture as the **CANOLA**, **FLAX**, alfalfa and sunflower industries. In 2001, Christensen received the

Distinguished Researcher Award from the University of Saskatchewan. In addition to teaching, research and extension activities, Christensen has served Canadian agriculture by participating on numerous boards and committees such as the Saskatchewan Dairy Association, British Columbia Department of Agriculture Dairy Project, Prairie Feed Resource Centre, Dairy Farmers of Canada, the Agricultural Institute of Canada International Development Committee, Saskatchewan Livestock Association, Saskatchewan Advisory Committee on Animal Nutrition, and Canadian Society of Animal Science. He is a Fellow of the Agricultural Institute of Canada.
Philip Thacker

CHRISTIAN AND MISSIONARY ALLIANCE CHURCH. The Christian and Missionary Alliance (C&MA) Church in Saskatchewan is part of an international fellowship of over three million members in eighty countries. It began as an interdenominational movement led by Canadian Presbyterian Albert B. Simpson, who graduated from Knox College in Toronto in 1865 and served Presbyterian churches in Hamilton, Ontario, Louisville, Kentucky and New York City. When confronted with the spiritual needs of the New York masses, he left his prestigious Presbyterian pulpit in 1881 and began an independent church known as the Gospel Tabernacle. Out of this local ministry, two organizations were established in 1887; they merged in 1897 as the Christian and Missionary Alliance. The Alliance remained an interdenominational society during those early years as Simpson was joined by men and women of many backgrounds who remained in their churches. They included Methodists, Presbyterians, Congregationalists, Anglicans, Baptists, Brethren, Salvationists, and people from other groups. Cross-denominational involvement has given the Alliance a depth of biblical and theological insight from the Puritan and Pietistic traditions; the writings of its well-known preacher and author, A.W. Tozer, draw on the works of the medieval mystics.

A similar movement concurrently developed in Canada under the leadership of a former Methodist turned Congregationalist, Rev. John Salmon. In February 1889, Salmon and his associates met with Simpson; this meeting resulted in the union of their ministries in Canada as the "Dominion Auxiliary of the Christian Alliance," with William Howland, former mayor of Toronto, as its first president. The 1920s saw the beginning of an ongoing C&MA ministry in Saskatchewan. To address the spiritual needs of isolated prairie residents, gospel teams of students were sent out to minister throughout the summer months in camps and tent meetings. Alliance leaders also recognized that to support an ongoing ministry on the prairies, churches needed to be established in key cities: in 1924 the C&MA thus moved toward

establishing churches throughout the province, so that now there are nine C&MA churches in Regina as well as in Saskatoon. These, and the other Alliance churches in the towns and villages of Saskatchewan, serve as a strong support base for local, national and international Alliance ministries.

The C&MA has a long history of ministering to a variety of ethnic groups throughout the world. In 1932 Ruby Johnston began gospel work with the Chinese in Regina: this ministry led to the organization of the Regina Chinese Alliance Church in 1961 and the calling of Rev. Augustus Chao from Hong Kong as pastor; this fellowship became the "mother church" of the more than 140 Chinese Alliance churches in North America. Radio programming has also played a significant role in reaching the people of the prairies. In 1935, Rev. W.H. Brooks, the Saskatoon pastor, started a Sunday evening radio broadcast, *Glad Tidings Half Hour*, over station CFQC and received great public response. Rev. Roy McIntyre in the 1940s and Rev. A.H. Orthner in the 1950s also reached out to the population on radio in Moose Jaw. After eighty years of ministry, the C&MA has now forty-nine churches in Saskatchewan, with a membership of 11,000. They are served by approximately 125 official workers and support missionaries in fifty-two countries of the world.
Rexford A. Boda

CHRISTIAN REFORMED CHURCH IN NORTH AMERICA. The Christian Reformed Church in North America (CRCNA) is a bi-national denomination in Canada and the United States. As of 2004 it had 747 congregations and ministries in the US and 256 in Canada—three of which are in Saskatchewan. The CRCNA entered Saskatchewan first during the opening up of the prairies between 1905 and 1912. Immigrants of Dutch descent, arriving direct from Holland or by way of the mid-western US, were gathered in the colonies of Edam and Cramersburg (in the Leader/Cabri area). They brought with them their Christian faith, drawn from the Calvinist branch of the Protestant Reformation of the 16th century. The flow of immigration was short-lived, however, as the prairie hardships were intense. A Reformed congregation in Cramersburg lasted from 1912 to 1923, when the last remaining deacon moved back to the US because of sustained drought. The Dutch population of Edam assimilated into the Anglo-Canadian culture quite rapidly, joining the Presbyterian Church and lending strength to the newly formed United Church of Canada from the 1920s onward. When Dutch immigration resumed after **WORLD WAR II**, those arriving settled mostly in Saskatoon and Regina, or were placed as workers on farms in the vicinity. The CRCNA Synod, based in Grand Rapids, Michigan, assigned itinerant ministers to serve the immigrant groups, and congregations were established in the two cities in 1952 and 1954. Both congregations grew through continued immigration from the Netherlands and other parts of Canada; they have also suffered from extensive out-migration, and currently number about 100 persons each.

The main focus of the Christian Reformed Church is to bring the Christian message into the neighbourhoods and communities it serves. This denomination has also been instrumental in establishing Christian schools, which have far outpaced their founding churches in influence within their communities. Reformed Christians have had an abiding concern for the disadvantaged: they give consistent support to alleviating world hunger through the federal Canada Food Grains Bank, and through active participation in refugee aid and resettlement programs. There has also been a deep concern for Aboriginal Canadians: the Indian Métis Christian Fellowship in Regina, a ministry of the CRCNA started in 1978, has been a leader in combining Christian faith with cultural integrity in a Native context. It is also at the forefront of addressing awareness and justice issues in the inner-city sex trade, and partners with Aboriginal groups and government to seek social, family and individual healing in Aboriginal settings. *Charles Kooger*

CHRONIC PAIN. In 2003 Gordon Asmundson, of the Faculty of Kinesiology and Health Studies at the **UNIVERSITY OF REGINA**, received a $1.1 million grant from the Canadian Institute of Health Research to help his inter-university team study Post-Traumatic Stress Disorder (PTSD). Now known as the Traumatic Stress Group, the team includes five other researchers from the University of Regina, as well as members from the University of British Columbia, the University of Manitoba, York University, and the University of California. The Traumatic Stress Group study ranges from genetic pre-disposition to the

PHOTOGRAPHY DEPARTMENT, UNIVERSITY OF REGINA

Dr. Gord Amundson, University of Regina Psychology, conducting chronic pain research.

strong relationship between PTSD and chronic pain. PTSD is a chronic condition that usually develops after exposure to a situation or an event that is or is perceived to be highly threatening to an individual's well-being; symptoms range from nightmares to emotional numbing. People who are exposed to war, who have been injured in the workplace, or who have been physically assaulted can develop the disorder.

Asmundson estimates that about 90% of the population in Canada will be exposed to an event in their lifetime that is perceived to be traumatic, while about 8% will develop PSTD. *Joe Ralko*

CHURCH OF JESUS CHRIST OF LATTER-DAY SAINTS (MORMONS). The Church of Jesus Christ of Latter-day Saints established itself in the valley of the Great Salt Lake in 1847, and in the next fifty years began to establish colonies in much of the Rocky Mountain area of western North America, including colonies in what was to become southern Alberta. No such colonies were established in Saskatchewan, but those established in southern Alberta had a significant impact on the development of the Church of Jesus Christ of Latter-day Saints in this province.

Growth in the Church in Saskatchewan has come from people being converted and from Church members from other areas, primarily Alberta, coming to the province for employment or other economic reasons. The growth of the Church in Saskatchewan has been gradual. There have been members of the Church of Jesus Christ of Latter-day Saints in Saskatchewan since early in the 20th century. The earliest record of a baptism is that of George Gordon Whyte: records show he was baptized in the Moose Jaw Creek on August 17, 1913 by Valentine Knechtel, who had joined the Church and been ordained an Elder when he lived for a time in Alberta. The day after his baptism, Whyte moved to Regina, where he found employment with the **SASKATCHEWAN CO-OPERATIVE ELEVATOR COMPANY** until he retired. He became the anchor around which the Church grew in Regina.

The first branch of the Church of Jesus Christ of Latter-day Saints in Saskatchewan was organized in Regina on April 23, 1934 with about forty members. Whyte was the branch president. Branches were organized in Saskatoon in 1944, Moose Jaw in 1945, Silver Park (which later became the Melfort Branch) in 1947, Swift Current in 1952, Weyburn about 1957, Prince Albert in 1959, Yorkton in 1966, Carry-the-Kettle in 1966, and the Kindersley Branch in 1967. The Saskatoon Saskatchewan Stake, a regional organization including all of the members in Saskatchewan, was set up on November 5, 1978. Noel Burt (of Saskatoon) was called as president, with Kent Cahoon (of Saskatoon) and Kenneth Svenson (of Regina) as counsellors. There were five

wards (larger, more mature congregations) and seven branches. The wards were Saskatoon First, Saskatoon Second, Regina First, Regina Second, and Moose Jaw; the branches were Swift Current, Kisbey (Weyburn), Yorkton, Melfort, Prince Albert, North Battleford, and Kindersley. Later, the Flin Flon Branch was added. The Saskatoon Saskatchewan Stake was divided in October 2001, and the Regina Saskatchewan Stake was formed to oversee all units of the Church in southern Saskatchewan while the Saskatoon Saskatchewan Stake retained jurisdiction over all units in northern Saskatchewan. Eric Slocombe of Saskatoon was called as president of the Saskatoon Saskatchewan Stake and E. Gregg Wood of Regina was called as president of the Regina Saskatchewan Stake.

Gordon B. Hinckley, president of the Church of Jesus Christ of Latter-day Saints, visited Regina on August 3, 1998 and announced that a temple was to be built in Regina. For members of the Church, the temple is a holy place set apart from the world, whereas the meetinghouse or chapel is filled with weekday activities and Sunday worship services. In the temple sacred ordinances of the gospel of Jesus Christ are performed. Therefore, Latter-day Saints view the temple as a spiritual centre. At the time of the announcement there were only two other temples in all of Canada: one in Toronto and one in Alberta. The Regina Temple was constructed over the next year and was dedicated on November 14, 1999.

One of the most widely known community contributions of the Church of Jesus Christ of Latter-day Saints worldwide is the collection of genealogical records. Following this trend, the Church of Jesus Christ of Latter-day Saints operates family history centres in Saskatoon, Regina, Moose Jaw, Kindersley and Prince Albert; these are open to the public, and make available locally all the genealogical records that have been collected by the Church worldwide. *Kenneth Svenson*

CHURCH OF THE NAZARENE. The Church of the Nazarene is an evangelical Wesleyan denomination with its roots in the United States. The denomination was officially formed at Pilot Point, Texas, in 1908, and spread largely by the amalgamation of various small denominations throughout the United States and Canada. In 1913 Tomas Bell held a revival meeting in the Pleasant Ridge community, south of Ernfold. This was the first penetration of the province by the denomination. The Saskatchewan District was officially organized in August 1916; but prior to this, churches had been organized by the Rev. C.A. Thompson in Regina and Luseland. In order to establish a base along the main line of the **CANADIAN PACIFIC RAILWAY**, a church was organized at Morse in the fall of 1916 or early 1917. In April 1917 the Bestville church was organized with thirteen charter members. Over the next eight years a number of preaching points were begun, and by the District Assembly of 1921 there were ten organized churches in the province, which expanded to twelve by 1923. The Saskatchewan District became a part of the newly formed Canada West District (Alberta, Saskatchewan and Manitoba) in 1948, bringing 454 members into the new district. At the present time there are five active congregations in Saskatchewan: Prince Albert, Saskatoon, Regina, Wapella, and Yorkton.   *Douglas L. Cooney*

FURTHER READING: Parker, F. 1971. *From East to Western Sea*. Kansas City: Nazarene Publishing House.

CHURCHBRIDGE, town, pop 796, located approximately 54 km SE of Yorkton and 31 km NW of the Saskatchewan-Manitoba border at the junction of Hwys 16 (the Yellowhead) and 80. The district began to be settled in the mid-1880s. Settlers of German and Icelandic origin took up land in the area, and Churchbridge was founded by English settlers who were sponsored by the Anglican Church. Incorporated as a village in 1903, the community grew as a small agricultural service centre; however, the development of the K1 potash mine south of Churchbridge in the late 1950s/early 1960s had a profound effect on both the area economy and the community. The population jumped from 257 in 1956 to 914 in 1966. Churchbridge attained town status in 1964, and today the majority of the community's workforce is employed at the K1 and K2 sites. Churchbridge serves the area with a variety of businesses and services, recreational facilities, a volunteer fire department, a number of churches, and a K–12 school. Community attractions include an enormous replica of the 1992 $1 coin which commemorated the country's 125th anniversary of Confederation; the Royal Canadian Mint held a design competition for the special edition coin, and the entry submitted by local artist Rita Swanson was selected among hundreds from across the country.   *David McLennan*

CHURCHILL RIVER (55°52'N, 102°02'W; map sheet 63 M/16). The Churchill River drains most of north-central Saskatchewan into Manitoba and on into Hudson Bay via the Nelson River. The Churchill Basin is estimated to be 20% covered by water–over double that of typical drainage basins in southern Saskatchewan. The Churchill River itself is generally made up of a series of lakes of various sizes, interconnected by numerous series of rapids. Its headwaters are in the interior plains of east-central Alberta and in the Boreal Plains and Boreal Shield of west-central Saskatchewan. The vast majority of the flow originates as snowmelt in May, reaches a maximum in July, and gradually recedes to a relatively constant flow from December to April. The significant lake

storage in the basin serves to attenuate flows, generally resulting in flow throughout the entire year. A significant portion of flow in the Churchill River at the Manitoba-Saskatchewan border comes from the **REINDEER RIVER**, which drains Wollaston and Reindeer lakes. Flow in the Reindeer River is controlled by the Whitesand Dam, located at the outlet of Reindeer Lake. The only other significant dam is Island Falls Dam on the Churchill River near Sandy Bay; but it has a relatively small reservoir storage capacity, and as a result has only a minor impact on the flow in the Churchill River at the border. The mean annual flow volume for the Churchill River near Sandy Bay is 21,620,000 dam^3. (*See also* **HYDROLOGY, EXPLORATION, FUR TRADE**)

Martin Grajczyk

CHURCHILL ROUTE. The Churchill Route was opened to world grain markets in September 1931. The first rail shipment consisted of approximately 500,000 bushels of Saskatchewan wheat hauled over the Hudson Bay Railway. The route promised improved economic conditions throughout Saskatchewan and western Canada through lower shipping costs and better access to markets in northern Europe and Latin America. The Port of Churchill is located at the mouth of the **CHURCHILL RIVER** on the western shore of Hudson Bay. It is Canada's only northern seaport, and the most northern point reached by regularly scheduled passenger train service on the North American continent (excluding the isolated railroads of Alaska); it is also the northern terminus of the Hudson Bay Railway, which extends

816 km from The Pas to Churchill, Manitoba. Distances from many grain delivery points in Saskatchewan and Manitoba to this seaport are shorter than delivery to Vancouver, Prince Rupert, or Thunder Bay. The port of Churchill not only provides an economical alternative for prairie producers, it also serves as a supply terminal for arctic communities. However, it has an operating season of only thirteen weeks–which has given rise to a debate about its efficiency. The volume of traffic going through the port is affected by two factors: only boxcars may be used on the line because of weight restrictions; and transportation trends are shifting from European to Asian markets, which are better served from ports in British Columbia.   *Daria Coneghan*

CICANSKY, VIC (1935–). Vic Cicansky, who works also in wood and steel, is one of Saskatchewan's best-known ceramic and bronze sculptors. He was born in Regina on February 12, 1935, the eldest son of Romanian parents. He grew up in Regina's east end, quit school in grade nine, and became a carpenter like his father. Later, he completed matriculation at Regina College, received a BEd from the **UNIVERSITY OF SASKATCHEWAN** in 1965, and a BA from the University of Saskatchewan, Regina Campus, in 1967. He taught in primary and high school for seven years, before gaining an MFA at Davis Campus, University of California, in1970; he also taught at the **UNIVERSITY OF REGINA** in the Faculty of Education and the Visual Arts Department from 1970 to 1993.

Cicansky's work falls into three phases: the

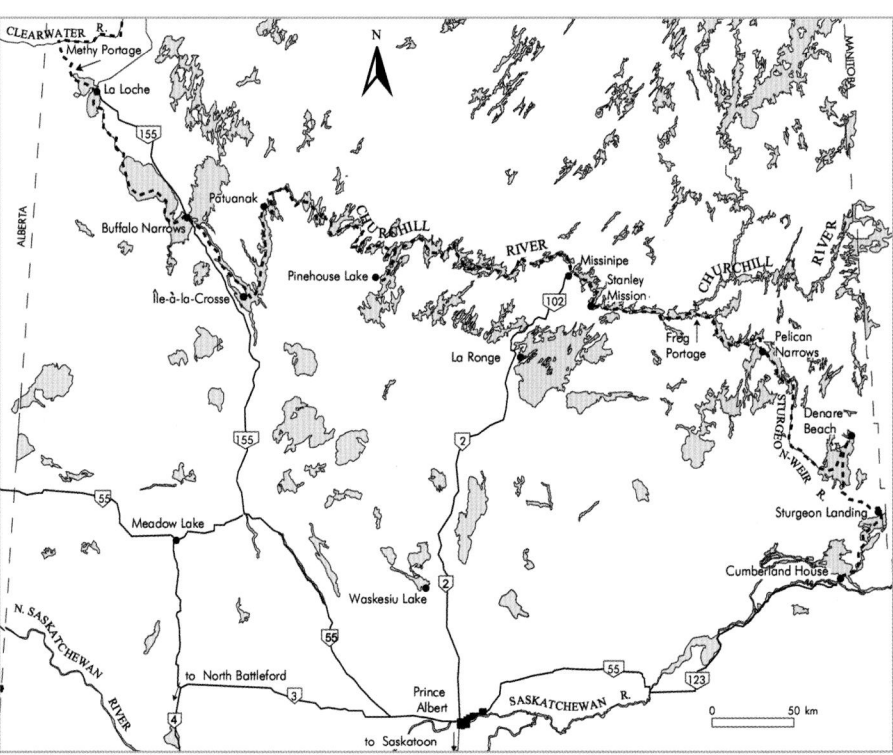

CANADIAN PLAINS RESEARCH CENTER MAPPING DIVISION

Churchill River.

early funk work at Davis and in Regina, followed by his outhouse series and his Volkswagen series; his jars and pantries, starting in 1978 (the jars have remained his trademark); and the bronze work, especially that which follows the random processes of nature in the tables and bonsai trees. Almost all of his work follows processes of nature, whether domestic or wild, orderly or random. He is also a populist, making art that can be enjoyed by anyone, and a regionalist who often celebrates prairie life.

Cicansky has a provincial, national and international reputation, with a major show at the **MACKENZIE ART GALLERY** in 1983 and one-man shows in commercial galleries in Regina, Edmonton, Vancouver, and Toronto every two years since the 1980s. He has been part of many international shows in the United States, and received the Saskatchewan Order of Merit in 1997. In his late 60s, he remains the art worker he has been all his adult life, spending time in his studio every day of the week and making the joyous work for which he is known.   *Don Kerr*

FURTHER READING: Kerr, D. 2004. *Victor Cicansky, the Garden of the Mind.* Calgary: University of Calgary Press.

CINEMAS, INDEPENDENT. Independent cinemas have ranged from small, local film clubs to free-standing theatres. These groups generally premiere independent or foreign films, which are often not shown at commercial movie houses in Saskatchewan. Up to the late 1960s, movie buffs formed film clubs that ordered foreign movies from specialty distributors–a practice that gave way to more dedicated venues in the 1970s, particularly in Regina and Saskatoon. The **UNIVERSITY OF REGINA** screened foreign films and Hollywood classics for students and the general public. An eighty-seat theatre opened in the basement of Regina's downtown public library in 1975. Filmmakers such as Guy Maddin, Lynne Stopewich, and Patricia Rozema have discussed their movies there. Elsewhere in Regina, the Saskatchewan Film Pool screened Canadian movies through its "Hidden Cinema" program in the early 1980s. In 1988, the short-lived "Paradise Theatre" showed classic movies in a rented warehouse. The **ROYAL SASKATCHEWAN MUSEUM** held weekend screenings of cult and classic movies in 1996–97.

The Place Riel Theatre opened to students and the public at the **UNIVERSITY OF SASKATCHEWAN** in 1975; it closed in 1998 because of competition from discount commercial theatres. In 1984, former Place Riel programmer, Chris Jones, became co-owner of Saskatoon's Broadway Theatre. The new owners restored the theatre's dignity, replacing its soft-core adult fare with artier films. It closed its doors briefly in 1993, and then reopened as a community-owned and operated, heritage-designated enterprise. In 2002, the Toronto International Film Festival made independent and foreign films available to movie fans in Moose Jaw through its "Film Circuit" program. Swift Current, Yorkton and Shaunavon soon followed.   *Mike O'Brien*

CIPYWNYK, DMYTRO (1927–2003). Dmytro Cipywnyk was born on a farm near Brooksby on April 15, 1927. He obtained his MSc at McGill University and his MD from the **UNIVERSITY OF SASKATCHEWAN** (U of S) in 1963, before becoming a Psychiatry Fellow at the Albert Einstein College of Medicine. He taught psychiatry at the U of S from 1971 to 1992, and was medical director of the Saskatchewan Alcohol and Drug Abuse Commission from 1983 to 1992. He was also president of the Saskatchewan and National Councils of the Ukrainian Canadian Congress, and of the Ukrainian World Congress. He chaired the Advisory Committee on Saskatchewan-Ukraine relations and co-chaired the Prairie Centre for Ukrainian Heritage. He was president of the Canadian Ethnocultural Council, and sat on the U of S Senate and the Canadian Council of Christians and Jews. Appointed a Member of the Order of Canada in 1992, he also received an honorary doctorate in Canon Law from St. Andrew's College, Winnipeg in 1995, and received the Order "For Merit" of Ukraine in 2002. Cipywnyk died in Saskatoon on March 9, 2003.   *Paul Cipywnyk*

CITIZENS CONCERNED ABOUT FREE TRADE (CCAFT). CCAFT is a national, non-partisan group dedicated to fighting what it regards as the threat to Canadian sovereignty posed by international trade agreements such as the Canada-United States Free Trade Agreement (FTA), the North American Free Trade Agreement (NAFTA), and the proposed Multilateral Agreement on Investment (MAI). CCAFT was founded in 1985, shortly after Canada and the United States agreed to begin negotiations to attempt to achieve a bilateral free-trade agreement. It was created by a small group of activists including David Orchard, a farmer from Borden, Saskatchewan, who became its president, and Marjaleena Repo, a native of Finland with a history of involvement in political organizing and activism, who became its chief organizer. The group held its first public meeting in Saskatoon, at the Frances Morrison Library, on December 12, 1985. By late 1988 it was reported to have around 3,000 members, though Orchard has asserted that the actual number was closer to 10,000. Whatever the case, if CCAFT was not the largest anti-free-trade group operating in Canada during the late 1980s–a distinction that would have to go to the national organization then known as the Pro-Canada Network (PCN)–it was among the most visible, with active branches across the country in cities such as Vancouver, Edmonton, Winnipeg and Thunder Bay.

In December 1987 it successfully organized one

PATRICK PETTIT/REGINA LEADER-POST

David Orchard speaking on behalf of CCAFT, September 1992.

of the largest public meetings on free trade in Saskatchewan, a debate between Orchard and Bob Andrew, the Saskatchewan Minister of Economic Development, which attracted some 1,500 people to the Centennial Auditorium in Saskatoon. CCAFT members also attracted national media attention when several of them were charged in cities across Canada under municipal bylaws prohibiting the posting of notices on city property, such as telephone and hydroelectric utility poles. Although many were convicted, two members charged in Toronto were acquitted, a decision upheld by the Ontario Court of Appeal in a 1994 ruling stating that such bylaws were "disproportionately invasive" of the right to freedom of expression as guaranteed under the Charter of Rights and Freedoms. This reinforced a ruling by the Supreme Court of Canada in a similar case in 1993, thus establishing a further precedent for the "right to poster." CCAFT maintains its headquarters in Saskatoon, and estimates that it currently has an active membership base of about 20,000 people.   *Tim Krywulak*

FURTHER READING: Orchard, D. and CCAFT. 1988. *Free Trade: The Full Story.* Saskatoon: Patriots Press.

CIVIL SERVICE. The Civil Service is the body of permanent employees who serve the government of Saskatchewan as the executive branch; their ranks range from the Deputy Ministers down to the lowest clerks. They have traditionally numbered no more than 15,000 people throughout the province, and usually far fewer; at present, there are approximately 10,000 provincial civil servants. Since 1906, the Civil Service in Saskatchewan has also been known as the Public Service.

The Civil Service has not always received equal trust and support from its political superiors. For the period from 1905 through **WORLD WAR II**, it was con-

175

sidered as simply a patronage-ridden group of supporters of the dominant Liberal Party. However, this image was completely reversed when **T.C. DOUGLAS** became Premier in 1944: for the next twenty years, the Saskatchewan Civil Service was considered one of the most meritorious in all of Canada. But the days of the leadership of **ROSS THATCHER** in the 1960s saw its reputation plummet again as his dominance forced good employees to leave. Premier **ALLAN BLAKENEY** revived the reputation in the 1970s by encouraging meritorious people to be recruited, but Premier **GRANT DEVINE** lowered it again in the 1980s through whole scale dismissal of these same people. Since then, the overall reputation has been that of a competent body of employees.

Saskatchewan civil servants are usually expected to conduct themselves according to the Westminster model. They are expected to be hired on the basis of merit; leave policy-making to the politicians and simply implement what these decide; serve any government by offering objective advice in a non-partisan manner; remain anonymous and allow the Minister to deal with the public; and as a result, be hired for a career and thus provide continuity to the government and the citizens. However, this traditional model was probably never followed exactly and is certainly under attack nowadays as some civil servants are being urged to become innovative, policy-making problem-solvers.

The key concern is whether the employees are being hired on the basis of merit or because of their loyalty to a political party—patronage. There is nothing to say that an employee could not be hired for both reasons, but the stigma of a patronage appointment, no matter how meritorious the person is, usually leads to that person's dismissal if the government changes after an election; then the desired continuity is lost. Through all its ups-and-downs, the Saskatchewan Civil Service has been plagued by charges of patronage; the main mechanism to try and defeat patronage is the **PUBLIC SERVICE COMMISSION**.

In one area—industrial relations—the Civil Service of Saskatchewan has been a leader. Saskatchewan was the first province in Canada, and indeed the first government, to allow its employees to unionize. This occurred in 1944 at the first session of the new government of Premier Douglas: he believed that civil servants should have the same rights as employees in the private sector and should not be "second-class" citizens. As a result, in any given year about 80% of Saskatchewan civil servants are union members. Although the Legislature of Saskatchewan is located in Regina, less than half of the Civil Service is located there. Some of the reasons for the dispersal of civil servants across the province are the implementation of programs for specific citizens such as Aboriginals, or for areas such as highways; the inspection of situations where operations

have been regulated, such as in education or in commerce; and the need for research facilities and other institutions such as hospitals and prisons.

Robert McLaren

FURTHER READING: McLaren, R.I. 1998. *The Saskatchewan Approach to Public Administration in Historical Perspective.* Lewiston, NY: Mellen; Pitsula, J.M. and K.A. Rasmussen. 1990. *Privatizing a Province.* Vancouver: New Star.

CLARKE, BILL (1932-2000). Born in Regina on November 25, 1932, Clarke played junior football with the **REGINA DALES** before turning professional with the **SASKATCHEWAN ROUGHRIDERS** in 1951. Over fourteen seasons with the Riders, he was a two-time nominee for most valuable Canadian and a two-time Western Football Conference All-Star.

Following his retirement, Clarke embarked on a second career as a public servant. Beginning in 1966, he was executive director of Sport and Recreation for the province. From 1982 to 1987, he served as Deputy Minister of what is now the Department of Culture, Youth and Recreation. He was a member of numerous boards and committees including the Saskatchewan Games Council, the Canada Games Council, and Hockey Canada. An advocate for the Special Olympics and the United Way, Bill Clarke also organized charity curling bonspiels and golf tournaments to raise money for Parkinson's disease research, an affliction from which he suffered.

Clarke was admitted to the **SASKATCHEWAN SPORTS HALL OF FAME** in 1979 and the Canadian Football Hall of Fame in 1996. He was inducted to the Roughriders' Plaza of Honour in 1988 and received an honourary Doctorate of Law from the **UNIVERSITY OF REGINA** in 1995. The Bill Clarke Scholarship Fund was created in his memory. Bill Clarke died on December 20, 2000.

Daria Coneghan and Holden Stoffel

FURTHER READING: Davis, Darrell. 2000. "Clarke's Generosity Remembered." *Regina Leader-Post* (December 21); 1980. *Saskatchewan Sports Hall of Fame.* Regina: The Board of Directors, Saskatchewan Sports Hall of Fame.

CLAUDE RESOURCES. In 1982 entrepreneur Bill MacNeill gained control of Claude Resources Inc., which has grown to become Saskatchewan's largest gold mining company. Claude Resources has a strong balance sheet, experienced management and a unique mix of long-term revenue generating assets including the Seabee gold mine in Saskatchewan and interests in property in northern Manitoba and Ontario. The Seabee mine, 125 km northeast of La Ronge, has produced more than 650,000 ounces of gold since it went into production 1991.

In addition to the mining operations, Claude

Resources also owns interests in several large oil and natural gas properties, most of which are located in the province of Alberta. These properties typically generate $9 million in gross revenues annually.

Joe Ralko

CLAXTON, DANA (1959–). Dana Claxton, born in 1959 in Yorkton, is socially committed to her work as a photographer, illustrator, performance artist, film maker, and teacher. Her artistic production is resonant in symbol and addresses issues connected to colonization and identity. Her Lakota Sioux heritage has been a strong inspiration for much of her work. *Buffalo Bone China* is a piece of Claxton's performance art that incorporates video footage and Claxton smashing fine bone china, made with buffalo bone from the prairies. Claxton has been the recipient of numerous awards and scholarships from Canada Council and Heritage Canada, and in 1999 she received the Simon Wilson Memorial Trust Scholarship, presented by the National Aboriginal Achievement Foundation, for her commitment to Aboriginal film and video.

Carmen Robertson

CLAYBANK, organized hamlet, pop 20, located approximately 16 km W of Avonlea on Hwy 339 at the foot of the Dirt Hills. The community takes its name from the rich hillside clay deposits found in the area, and is well known for its historic brick plant (*see* **CLAYBANK BRICK PLANT**). In 1902–03, large numbers of settlers, predominantly German Catholics, began arriving in the area. Construction of the plant began in 1912. Many of the people who lived in the community worked there, and Claybank reached its peak around the mid-1930s and into the 1940s. Subsequently, the community declined. Although the brick plant closed in 1989, it remains one of Canada's finest examples of early 20th-century industry and has been declared a national historic site.

David McLennan

CLAYBANK BRICK PLANT. The Claybank Brick Plant is one of the best North American examples of an early 20th-century brickmaking complex. All of the key structures erected during the site's development from 1912 to 1937 and much of the original brickmaking equipment and archival records survive. Using clay mined on site, the plant became a major manufacturer of fire brick and other refractory products for the railway, oil refining, power and metallurgical industries across Canada and beyond. Situated 60 km southwest of Regina, it operated between 1914 and 1989. Prominent buildings faced with the distinctive buff-coloured brick include the Bessborough Hotel in Saskatoon, the Roman Catholic Cathedral in Gravelbourg, and the central tower of Quebec City's Chateau Frontenac.

During **WORLD WAR II**, Claybank was declared

an essential war service industry, and its production focused exclusively on fire brick to line the boilers of new air-training bases and for boilers in the Corvettes and Destroyers under construction in Canada's shipyards. After the war, new synthetic products and better steel reduced the demand for both face and fire brick, while the plant's outdated equipment limited its production capabilities. In 1992, the abandoned complex was donated to the Saskatchewan Heritage Foundation, which has partnered with Parks Canada and the Claybank Brick Plant Historical Society to preserve and interpret this industrial heritage site. It was designated as a National Historic Site in 1994. *Frank Korvemaker*

FURTHER READING: Korvemaker, F. and S. Algie. 1998. *Claybank Brick Plant National Historic Site: Conservation and Presentation Plan*. Winnipeg: Parks Canada.

CLEARWATER RIVER (56°42' N, 110°00' W; map sheet 74 D/9). Located in northwestern Saskatchewan, 50 km north of La Loche, the Clearwater River is exceptional in that it flows westward, joining the Athabasca River at Fort McMurray. En route the river carves its way through Precambrian and Phanerozoic rocks into a gradually deeper, cliff-lined valley with spectacular canyons of Devonian age dolomitic limestones. By the time it exits the province into Alberta, this river (187 km long) has displayed Class II to Class IV+ rapids and one breathtaking set of tightly knit waterfalls. A number of ancient pictographs or Aboriginal rock paintings along the water's edge of the upper section of the Clearwater attest to the area's pre-European occupation, which could be as old as 5,000 years. The river was also an important communication channel for Canada's early explorers and fur traders. The likes of **DAVID THOMPSON**, Sir Alexander Mackenzie, **PETER POND**, and Sir **JOHN FRANKLIN** all came across Methy Portage, a 19-km overland link on the Churchill-Clearwater-Athabasca route which ultimately linked Hudson Bay to the Arctic, allowing travelers to bypass the more difficult route across Precambrian rock formations further east. As early as 1778, Methy Portage provided the first major overland connection for what was to be the only route between east and west for almost forty years.

In 1986, the Clearwater earned a federal Canadian Heritage River System designation for its heritage and cultural significance. That same year, the provincial government turned most of the Saskatchewan portion into the 200,000-ha Clearwater River Wilderness Park. Visitors traveling by canoe or on foot can encounter a variety of rare plants, as well as animals such as bald eagles, black bear, moose, and many species of boreal songbirds and waterfowl. As the current takes travelers into the ancient glacial spillway, it assumes the shape of 30 m high gorges dominated by trees and nesting raptors that bear witness to the impregnable quality of the river as an obstacle to land-based journeys. Some of the landscape features worthy of attention include Gould Rapids and the spectacular Smoothrock Falls, which even those traveling by raft must portage. Further west lies Skull Canyon, also known as Bald Eagle Gorge, where a towering island of rock splits the river into two dramatic channels that lead into a calmer and wider body of water. In the lower portion of the Clearwater, it is easier to discern the dimensions of the valley, which reaches 3 km in width and over 100 m in height.

Claude-Jean Harel

FURTHER READING: Engstrom, E. 1984. *Clearwater Winter*. Edmonton: Lone Pine Press; Marchildon, G. and S. Robinson. 2002. *Canoeing the Churchill: A Practical Guide to the Historic Voyageur Highway*. Regina: Canadian Plains Research Center.

CLEARWATER RIVER DENE BAND. The Clearwater River Dene (Big "C," La Loche) First Nation occupies three La Loche Reserves located 11 km southwest and 24 km east of La Loche, and 24 km northwest of Buffalo Narrows. Ancestors of this band signed **TREATY 8** in 1899, and chose the La Loche area for their reserve as it was thick with vegetation and wildlife. The language spoken by the Clearwater River Nation is Dene. The band controls 9,511 ha of land and has a membership of 1,418 people, 619 of whom live on reserve. La Loche Landing (located between La Loche and Buffalo Narrows) is the most populated reserve area, but most of the Band's members live in the town of La Loche. Facilities available on the reserve include a band office, a school, a group home, a drop-in centre, a fire hall, a health clinic, and community maintenance structures. The band's economy is based mainly on trapping and fishing, with potential for timber and mining development. *Christian Thompson*

CLEVELAND, REGGIE (1948–). Reggie Cleveland earned the distinction of being the first ever Canadian-born pitcher to start a World Series game in 1975. Born on May 23, 1948, in Swift Current, Cleveland played Little League baseball in Moose Jaw and Junior ball in Cold Lake, Alberta. He pitched in the Southern Saskatchewan Senior League for the Swift Current Indians before signing as an undrafted free agent with the St. Louis Cardinals in 1966. Cleveland spent three years in the minor leagues before joining the Cardinals in 1969. Despite having his best season in 1973, he was traded to the Boston Red Sox the following year and remained with the club until midway through the 1978 schedule. A short stint with the Texas Rangers was followed by three seasons with the Milwaukee Brewers before Cleveland announced his retirement. He continued his involvement in baseball as a coach in the Toronto Blue Jays' farm system from 1991 to 1995. In a thirteen-year major league career, Reggie Cleveland posted 105 wins, 106 losses, and 25 saves in 428 appearances; he pitched 57 complete games and had 12 shutouts. His career earned-run average was 4.01 in 1,809 innings with 930 strikeouts. Cleveland was inducted into the Canadian Baseball Hall of Fame in 1986 and the **SASKATCHEWAN SPORTS HALL OF FAME** in 2002. *Daria Coneghan and Holden Stoffel*

DOUG CHISHOLM PHOTO
Road 955 crosses the Clearwater River at Warner Rapids.

CLIMATE. The climate of Saskatchewan is characterized by its extremes. Its position near the centre of the continent, a relatively high latitude, and great distance from the moist and moderating influence of oceans largely determine its atmospheric environment. It is generally considered a continental climate, with temperatures varying greatly between seasons. Precipitation is also variable both seasonally and inter-annually; average amounts are sufficient to support grasslands in the south and forests in the north. Extremes of temperature and precipitation are to be expected and form an integral component of the climate. Other factors are variable winds throughout the year, an abundance of sunshine, and possible severe weather in both summer and winter. The climate resources are usually sufficient for an agrarian economy, but sometimes impose constraints on these and other enterprises.

The temperature climate of Saskatchewan is extreme. It is common for temperatures at any point to vary more than 65°C within any year. The average values shown in Table CL-1 suggest a great seasonal variation but do not show the inherent variability. Latitudinal differences typically explain most of the 6–8°C difference in mean annual temperature across the province. However, extremes are still possible, no matter the latitude. The south Saskatchewan town of Midale had the highest temperature recorded in Canada at 45°C, and many sites have had record low temperatures of at least -50°C. These extremes of temperature are usually attributed to the province's mid-continental position: the thermal character of the vast North American landmass heats and cools extremely well seasonally. It is also strongly influenced by the West Coast mountains, which inhibit the passage of moderating air from the west. The lack of terrain impediments to cold, Arctic air from the north is also a strong factor.

Saskatchewan has a relatively dry climate with a strong seasonal character. As with most mid-continental locations in mid latitudes, the majority of the precipitation is summer rainfall; but because of the coolness of winter temperatures, long-surviving snow pack is also an important factor. Year-to-year fluctuations in precipitation make for a challenging agricultural environment. The summer (May to September, inclusive) is the wet season, with usually two-thirds of the precipitation falling. Depending on the latitude, either June or July is the peak, with the more northerly locations having the later maximum. Most precipitation falls as a result of passing mid-latitude cyclones when their most favoured path crosses the region. Significant amounts can also result from convective systems (**THUNDERSTORMS**) at a variety of scales. Table CL-2 shows this seasonal character for stations spread across Saskatchewan.

Interannual variability is usually great. For example, Muenster has experienced annual totals

Table CL-1. Mean temperature (°C) at selected locations

	J	F	M	A	M	J	J	A	S	O	N	D	YEAR
Coronach	-13	-9	-3	5	11	16	19	18	12	5	-4	-11	3.8
Indian Head CDA	-16	-12	-5	4	11	16	18	18	11	5	-5	-13	2.6
Muenster	-18	-14	-7	3	11	15	17	17	11	4	-7	-15	1.5
Island Falls	-23	-19	-11	0	8	14	17	16	9	2	-10	-20	-1.5
Collins Bay	-24	-21	-14	-3	5	11	15	13	7	-1	-13	-22	-4.0

Table CL-2. Mean annual total precipitation (mm) at selected locations

	J	F	M	A	M	J	J	A	S	O	N	D	YEAR
Coronach	18	15	26	27	65	68	58	42	34	21	19	21	414
Indian Head CDA	20	16	24	25	56	79	67	53	41	24	17	25	447
Muenster	21	14	19	24	45	77	71	48	36	25	16	20	414
Island Falls	22	16	19	21	45	71	88	65	65	41	29	26	508
Collins Bay	24	17	26	32	42	69	102	74	63	46	33	24	552

between 229 and 639mm in its over 70 years of record; these values are typical of most other places in Saskatchewan.

An important feature of the climate of Saskatchewan is the frequent clear skies and the resulting sunny conditions. The province's position in the lee of the Rocky Mountains and in the middle of the continent means that high surface pressure is frequently experienced. This high pressure in part explains the general aridity of the climate but also has other effects. One is the abundance of bright sunshine hours: many places in Saskatchewan have considerably more than 2,000 hours of bright sunshine each year, and Estevan, in the southeast, is known as the "sunniest place in Canada," with an average of 2,435 hours of bright sunshine each year. The clear skies and general lack of humidity, along with frequently unmitigated winds, allow for large potential evapotranspiration (PET). This exacerbates the aridity and dictates that the climate can only support grasslands in the southern third of the province. In the north, where PET is lower, woody vegetation can grow. This is often a greater determinant of natural vegetation than the slight difference in total precipitation from north to south. (*See also* **METEOROLOGY, HAIL, TORNADOES**)   *Mark Cote*

CLIMATE CHANGE: THE FUTURE. The evolution of climate is dependent upon the energy balance of the earth-atmosphere-ocean system, which is in turn dependent on the composition of the atmosphere, in particular on the concentration of gases and aerosols, which may absorb or reflect long-wave and short-wave radiation. The atmospheric concentration of these constituents is dependent on their emission into the atmosphere from both natural and man-made sources. The increase in the man-made component of these emissions since the beginning of the Industrial Revolution and the

effect this is having, and will have, on climate are cause for concern. Global climate models (GCMs) have been developed to determine the climate response to changing atmospheric composition, and have been used in the simulation of both past and future climates. GCMs are complex three-dimensional mathematical models of the earth-atmosphere-ocean system, able to reproduce successfully the spatial patterns of global climate. At more regional scales, however, there are differences, or biases, between model-simulated and actual current climate conditions, which affect how this information is used. In order to overcome these biases, changes in the simulated climate between some future time period, e.g., the 2050s, and the GCM's baseline climate period, currently 1961–90, are used rather than the model output directly from the climate change experiments. There are many GCMs available for use; each one gives slightly different results because of differences in the way in which they are formulated.

To simulate future climate, GCMs require information about future atmospheric composition, which is dependent on a scenario of future emissions of radiatively active gases into the atmosphere. Since future emissions are dependent on such things as future population and economic growth, energy use, technological development and land use change, the uncertainty associated with estimates of future emissions increases over time. There are, therefore, any number of future emissions scenarios which are plausible and could be used as the basis for GCM climate change experiments. However, the cost of running GCMs precludes their use for simulating climate for many emissions scenarios: instead, a small number of plausible emissions futures have been selected by the Intergovernmental Panel on Climate Change (IPCC) and have been used by the international global climate modelling community.

All experiments indicate warmer future conditions for Saskatchewan, with the largest increases in mean temperature occurring in winter and spring as a result of snow and ice cover change. There is also a general tendency for increases in precipitation, particularly in winter and spring, although about half of the experimental results indicate decreases in precipitation in the summer. Business-as-usual emissions scenarios indicate that climate may change in the future if little is done to reduce greenhouse gas emissions. Most GCMs project increases in winter average temperature of between about 2° and 4°C by the 2050s, although some GCMs indicate changes less than or in excess of this range. Changes in summer precipitation are much more variable, being less coherent spatially and also differing much more from GCM to GCM; this is partly due to the difficulty in modelling the precipitation process, which occurs at spatial scales smaller than a global climate model can resolve directly. However, there is a general trend for decreases in summer precipitation in southern Saskatchewan, which will lead to decreases in soil moisture content. Soil moisture deficits are likely to increase even where precipitation increases are projected, since the warmer conditions will lead to increased evapotranspiration.

Elaine Barrow

CLIMATE CHANGE: THE PAST. Global climate changes, and their consequences for human populations, are known from studies of the climate of the recent geological past. Instrumental climate records generally do not capture the full range of climate variability and long-term trends (i.e., climate change) because they are mostly confined to the past 150 years. This period is shorter than many cycles of climate variation and corresponds to the interval of time during which human activities have significantly increased the atmospheric concentrations of greenhouse gases. Proxy climate data span millions of years and thus define what is possible in terms of natural climate change and variability, providing the context for the current global warming. A plot of Northern Hemisphere temperatures for the past millennium, reconstructed mainly from tree rings, is one of the most convincing and widely used illustrations of the unusual rate of recent warming. It demonstrates that the 1990s was the warmest decade of the past millennium, and 1998 the warmest single year. The past 200 years have also seen the coldest years of the past several millennia because the earth recently emerged from the Little Ice Age (approximately 1450 to 1850 CE). The climate system is extremely complex, with many factors interacting over a range of time scales and with teleconnections over long distances. Over millions of years, the earth's climate history is related to the drifting of continents and resulting changes in the configuration of the continents and ocean basins.

Periodicity in the position of the earth relative to the sun is a dominant cause of shorter-term climate variation over thousands of years, the scale of ice ages. Superimposed on these long cycles of solar irradiance are shorter-term fluctuations in the sun's energy (sunspot cycles) and climate fluctuations caused by the effects of volcanic eruptions on the composition of the atmosphere. Annual to decadal climate variation, the time scale of most relevance to humans, is sensitive to internal oscillations in the climate system such as fluctuations in sea surface temperatures associated with ocean circulation anomalies like ENSO (El Nino Southern Oscillation).

Past climate is inferred from geological and biological archives, which preserve a measurable response to climate; the longest paleoclimate records are derived from glaciers and ocean sediments. In continental interiors like Saskatchewan, the common sources of proxy climate data are the minerals and the plant and animal fossils that accumulate in lakes. Other archives include tree rings, buried soils and terrestrial sediments, and ground temperatures. While these proxies record different types of climate signal, a general picture of post-glacial climate emerges that includes an interval of warmer drier climate about 5,000 to 7,500 years ago, in the middle of the Holocene (the last 10,000 years), and the cooler conditions of the Little Ice Age of the past millennium. In Saskatchewan, variations in climate over the past several millennia are reflected in the migration of the boundary between grassland and forest, and fluctuations in the level and salinity of lakes. Tree rings record prolonged droughts prior to Euro-Canadian settlement; these long droughts affected sand dunes activity, the fur trade, and the health of Aboriginal people. The tree rings and other climate proxies suggest that the climate of the 20th century was relatively favourable for the settlement of Saskatchewan because it lacked the sustained droughts of preceding centuries.

David Sauchyn

FURTHER READING: Mann, M.E., R.S Bradley and M.K Hughes. 1999. "Northern Hemisphere Temperatures During the Past Millennium: Inferences, Uncertainties and Limitations," *Geophysical Research Letters* 26: 759–62; Sauchyn, D.J., E. Barrow, R. F. Hopkinson and P. Leavitt. 2002. "Aridity on the Canadian Plains," *Géographie physique et quaternaire* 56: 247–59; Sauchyn, D.J., J. Stroich and A. Beriault. 2003. "A Paleoclimatic Context for the Drought of 1999–2001 in the Northern Great Plains," *The Geographical Journal* 169: 158–67.

CLINE, ERIC (1955–). Cline was born August 12, 1955. He was raised and educated in Saskatoon, earning degrees in political science (1976) and law (1979) at the **UNIVERSITY OF SASKATCHEWAN**. He practiced law with Mitchell, Taylor, Romanow and Ching. He married Pauline Melis in 1988. Cline ran in Regina South in 1975 but was defeated. He was elect-

DON HEALY/REGINA LEADER-POST
Eric Cline, March 2000, on budget day.

ed MLA for Saskatoon Idylwyld in 1991, was re-elected from Saskatoon in 1995, 1999, and 2003. **ROMANOW** appointed him to Cabinet in 1995 as Minister of Health. This post required that he manage the consequences of healthcare cutbacks and reforms implemented during the Romanow government's first term. He was appointed Minister of Finance after the 1997 provincial budget. In the 2000 budget, Cline introduced the largest income-tax cuts in Saskatchewan's history. He sought to make Saskatchewan more competitive with other provinces in attracting and retaining high-income individuals and business investment. He recovered about half the cost of these cuts by applying the sales tax to more goods. Early in 2003, **CALVERT** moved Cline from Finance and appointed him Minister of Justice and Attorney General, and Minister of Industry and Resources. After the 2003 election, Cline was re-appointed only to Industry and Resources.

Erin M.K. Weir

CLUN, YEE. In 1912 the Saskatchewan Government enacted the anti-Asian Act to Prevent the Employment of Female Labour in Certain Capacities. This Act, sometimes called the "white women's labour law," barred Asian men from employing White women in businesses such as restaurants, rooming houses, and laundries. The Act was supported by Protestant moral reformers and various women's groups, who embellished racial stereotypes and created an atmosphere of fear. The Act strangled the Asian business community, who could ill afford the higher wages demanded by White men, and had few other labour resources. The next year the Act was amended so that it only applied to Chinese, and in 1919 a further amendment deleted all reference to race. The right to employ women was referred to municipalities, which, upon application, could license businesses on an individual basis.

Long-time Regina resident, activist, and Chinese entrepreneur Yee Clun tested this race-neutral amendment in 1924, applying to Regina City Council for a special permit to hire White women workers. His application set off a storm of protest and debate at council and in the newspapers about race, discrimination, and the moral standing of the Chinese community. Both racial and gender stereotypes were hurled about, with frequent reference to narcotic use and gambling among Chinese, as well as women's essential weaknesses and need for "protection." Under the influence of both leading women's activists and business leaders, the application was rejected.

Yee Clun then decided to appeal to the courts. In the Court of King's Bench Judge Phillip Mackenzie heard the arguments of the municipality —which he called "fallacious" and "absurd"—and despite public sentiment, forced council to issue the license. It was a short-lived victory, however, as legislators passed a statute allowing municipalities to ignore the court ruling. It is not known if Regina revoked Clun's license, but his case marked a milestone in Canadian legal history and legally empowered racism. The offensive law was finally repealed in 1969, because it was seen to be unfair to women.

Merle Massie

FURTHER READING: Backhouse, C. 1994. "White Female Help and Chinese-Canadian Employees: Race, Class, Gender and Law in the Case of Yee Clun, 1924," *Canadian Ethnic Studies* 26 (3): 34–40; —. 1999. *Colour-Coded: A Legal History of Racism in Canada, 1900–1950*. Toronto: University of Toronto Press.

COAL. Coal is a solid hydrocarbon made up of plant and vegetable matter that has been buried for millions of years and transformed through various chemical changes, heat, and pressure. The main component in coal is carbon. The four classes or grades of coal in Saskatchewan (classed primarily on the basis of the amount of water within it) are: lignitic, sub-bituminous, bituminous, and anthractic. The province has mainly high-quality lignitic coal, which provides low heat value but is environmentally friendly owing to the low percentage of sulphur emitted when it is burned. Lignitic coal found in Saskatchewan typically contains about 35% water. The earliest records of coal mining in Saskatchewan date back to 1857. Since then the industry has grown tremendously, and the province is now the third largest producer of coal in Canada. There are five operating mines in the province, near Estevan, Willowbunch, Wood Mountain and Shaunavon. The Ravenscrag formation in southwestern Saskatchewan is of current interest due to attractive reserves. The province consumes around 90% of the total value mined annually, and exports the remaining coal to Manitoba and Ontario. Over 70% of the

DON HEALY/REGINA LEADER-POST

Bienfait mine: a giant dragline strips away the dirt so miners can get at the coal seam that lies 110 feet below the surface.

province's domestically produced electricity comes from coal used in SPC power stations at Boundary Dam.

Julie L. Parchewski

COAT OF ARMS. In 1986 Queen Elizabeth II granted a Royal Warrant augmenting into a full coat of arms the Saskatchewan shield of arms granted by King Edward VII in 1906, which displays a red lion on a horizontal gold band and three gold wheat sheaves on a green background. The crest above the shield displays the golden helmet of sovereignty, signifying Saskatchewan's co-sovereign status as a province in Confederation; and a beaver, Canada's national animal, holding a western red lily, the province's floral emblem. The Crown represents the link with the Sovereign through the LIEUTENANT-GOVERNOR. The wreath and mantling surrounding the helmet are in Canada's national colours, red and white. On either side of the shield are a royal lion and a white-tailed deer, the provincial animal emblem of Saskatchewan, wearing collars of prairie Indian beadwork and badges in the form of the stylized lily of the Saskatchewan Order of Merit. The

COURTESY OF SASKATCHEWAN PROVINCIAL SECRETARY

Saskatchewan's Coat of Arms.

badge on the lion displays Canada's emblem, the maple leaf, while that on the deer displays the western red lily. The base is formed of western red lilies and features the province's motto, *Multis E Gentibus Vires*, Latin for "From Many Peoples Strength," which expresses the ethnic diversity of Saskatchewan's population.

Michael Jackson

FURTHER READING: Jackson, M. 2002. *Images of a Province: Symbols of Saskatchewan*. Regina: Government of Saskatchewan.

COCHIN-GREEN LAKE TRAIL. This 150-km trail was used extensively by missionaries, traders, and the North-West Mounted Police (NWMP). One of the more prominent missionaries using the trail was Father Louis Cochin, who in 1884 established the Thunderchild Mission at Cochin, the southern terminus of the trail, 36 km north of North Battleford. The trail connected the mission to settlements such as Birch Narrows and Chitek Lake; its northern terminus was Green Lake, approximately 200 km northwest of Prince Albert. The Hudson's Bay Company post at Green Lake was one of the more prominent posts in north-central Saskatchewan since it connected many overland trails with the CHURCHILL RIVER, an integral waterway of the fur trade era. The NWMP also patrolled the trail extensively during the NORTH-WEST RESISTANCE of 1885.

James Winkel

COCKING, MATTHEW (1743–99). Matthew Cocking, a Hudson's Bay Company employee, was the last European to record his daily travels with CREE wintering on the northern Saskatchewan plains. In 1772, he was sent from Hudson Bay to obtain information on the Montreal traders who were moving up the SASKATCHEWAN RIVER. Cocking went with Pegogamaw Cree, who met their families at the well-known rendezvous at present James Smith First Nation; there they began walking a 500 km-long circuit which took them west to the Eagle Hills, then to the Thickwood Hills, and finally to a bison pound near Red Deer Hill, south of Prince Albert. In 1774, following Cocking's recommendations, the HBC sent SAMUEL HEARNE to establish their first inland post at Cumberland House. Cocking was to help Hearne, but his Sturgeon Cree guides wanted the post in their own lands; consequently, he was forced to winter near Good Spirit Lake, west of Canora. He commanded Cumberland House in 1775 and 1776, then remained at the Bay until he retired to England in 1782; unlike others, he provided for the three daughters he left behind; a grandson, the famous Rev. HENRY BUDD, was the first ordained Christian Cree. Cocking kept detailed journals during his two journeys, but only a shortened version of his 1772–73 account has been published.

Dale Russell

FURTHER READING: Burpee, L.J. (ed.). 1908. "An Adventurer from Hudson Bay: Being the Journal of a Journey Performed by Matthew Cocking, 1772–1773," *Proceedings and Transactions of the Royal Society of Canada* 2 (2): 91–121; Meyer, D. and D. Russell. 2004. "So Fine and Pleasant, Beyond Description: The Lands and Lives of the Pegogamaw Nehiyawaks," *Plains Anthropologist* 49 (191): 217–52.

COCKS, WILLIAM E. (1877–1961). William Cocks was born into a working-class family in London, England in 1877. He came to Regina in 1904 and apprenticed as a painter. He had some understanding of trade unions from his father, a member of the Steam Engineers Union, and helped organize the painters, carpenters, and bricklayers unions in Regina. Cocks was a member of the Painters Union. On February 9, 1907, a group of trade unionists met in his house and organized the Regina Trades and Labour Council (RTLC). Tom Molloy was the first president, and Cocks the first secretary and later president of the council for two years. Cocks was a socialist, and also a practical and committed trade unionist. His organizing led to 95% of the painters in Regina joining Local 509 by 1909. The painters went on strike in 1910, 1912, 1916, and 1919. He was actively involved in the formation of the Regina Labour Temple in 1912, and held many of the offices, including managing director from 1946 until his death. He was one of four labour candidates for city council in 1914, but all lost. Cocks represented the Dominion Congress of Working Men, and accompanied a delegation of about 100 women who presented a petition on women's suffrage to the provincial legislature in 1915. He was active in the RTLC protests against privately run streetcars in Regina, and caused a vote that initiated a public service. Cocks also helped establish the Workmen's Compensation Board. He died on June 12, 1961. *Bob Ivanochko*

FURTHER READING: Makahonuk, G. 1985. "Painters, Decorators and Paperhangers: A Case Study in Saskatchewan Labourism, 1906–1919," *Prairie Forum* 10 (1): 189–204.

COGEMA RESOURCES INC. COGEMA Resources Inc. is one of the world's leading URANIUM exploration, mining and milling companies. From its head office in Saskatoon, it is active in the development of large-scale, high-grade uranium deposits in northern Saskatchewan. Since beginning exploration in the 1960s, COGEMA Resources has invested more than $1 billion in exploration, construction and operations in the north. It is wholly owned by the French AREVA Group, the world leader in nuclear power and connectors.

COGEMA Resources is the operator and majority owner (70%) of uranium mining and milling facilities at McClean Lake, and is the sole owner and operator of the Cluff Lake mine. The company also operates the proposed Midwest uranium project (54.8% owner), and holds interests in the Cigar Lake (37.1%), McArthur River (30.2%), and Key Lake (16.7%) operations. All of these mines are located in the Athabasca Basin, 600-700 km north of Saskatoon; about half of the mine site workers are residents of northern Saskatchewan, primarily of Aboriginal descent.

Corporate involvement in Saskatchewan began in the 1960s through MOKTA, which discovered the Cluff Lake uranium deposits. AMOK was later created to develop and operate the project. In 1984 COGEMA Canada Ltd. arrived in Saskatchewan, and three years later bought out MOKTA's shares in AMOK. The company moved its head office from Montreal to Saskatoon in 1991, and changed its name to COGEMA Resources Inc. in 1993, becoming the sole owner of the Cluff Lake mine. It also became the operator and 70% owner of Minatco, the original owner of the McClean Lake project. Following the Cluff Lake Board of Inquiry, also known as the Bayda Commission, the Cluff Lake mine began production in 1980. By the time production ceased twenty-two years later, the mine had produced over 28 million kg of uranium oxide (U_3O_8) and some gold. Following an extensive environmental review and public discussion, Cluff Lake is entering a decommissioning phase to return the site to a safe and productive natural state suitable for future uses. Discovery of the McClean Lake uranium deposits occurred in 1979. Following change of majority ownership and operatorship to COGEMA Resources, as well as extensive environmental studies and public and regulatory reviews, McClean Lake began mining and site development in 1995. The uranium mill at McClean Lake is the most innovative in the world: it is capable of processing low- to high-grade uranium from a series of on-site mines as well as the Cigar Lake and the proposed Midwest mines. The first uranium concentrate was produced in 1999. In late 2000, McClean Lake's environmental management system achieved ISO 14001 certification In mid-2004, COGEMA Resources had 210 employees at the McClean Lake and Cluff Lake mine sites; its 2003 revenues totaled about $230 million. *Alun Richards*

COHEN, SAUL (1921–). Saul Cohen was born in Toronto on January 29, 1921. He came to Saskatchewan in 1946 following medical service in the Canadian Army, and was in family practice in Melville until he moved to Regina in 1954. In 1959 he became a consultant to the Bureau on Alcoholism and continued his teaching and research in the field. Dr Cohen was a founder of the Physicians at Risk Committee, the author of the *Physician's Manual on Alcoholism*, and a charter member of the teaching program on chemical

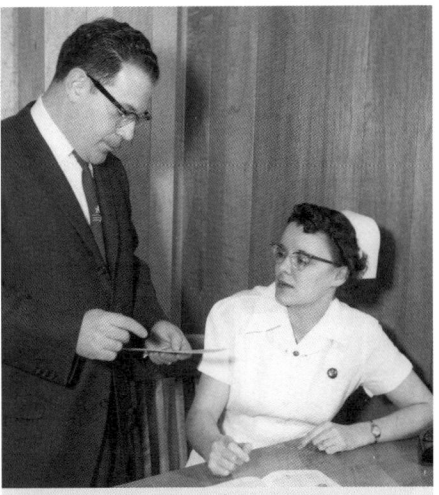

Dr. Saul Cohen and Audrey Hamilton, Alcoholics Referral Centre, Regina, circa 1959.

dependencies at the College of Medicine, UNIVERSITY OF SASKATCHEWAN. He was chairman of the board of the Saskatchewan Alcohol and Drug Abuse Commission. He was named Fellow of the College of Family Medicine of Canada. In 1986 he was awarded the Saskatchewan Order of Merit and senior life memberships in the College of Physicians and Surgeons of Saskatchewan and in the Canadian Medical Association. Dr. Cohen, through his publications, research, practice and counselling, placed Saskatchewan in the forefront of alcohol and drug abuse treatment and rehabilitation. He retired to Toronto. As of March 10, 2004, he was active as a medical consultant, two days a week, at an addiction centre in Mississauga, Ontario. *Michael Jackson*

COLD LAKE (PRIMROSE LAKE) AIR WEAPONS RANGE, 4 WING COLD LAKE. Cold Lake (or Primrose Lake) Air Weapons Range (CLAWR) straddles the Saskatchewan-Alberta border along the 55th parallel, covering an area of 11,753.5 km^2; 54% (totaling 1.6 million acres) of the range is situated in Saskatchewan, and 46% is in Alberta. The heavily forested terrain of this facility resembles European topography. With its unrestricted airspace, and equipped with state-of-the-art targets, Cold Lake Air Weapons Range is considered to be one of the finest combined air operations training ranges in the world. It contains an instrumented aerospace testing and evaluation range, a manned air-to-ground range (including a high explosive range), and an air-to-air gunnery range.

Construction of RCAF Station Cold Lake, located southwest of the range in Alberta, began in 1952. It became a major Cold War facility after 1954, eventually housing an establishment of more than 2,000 service personnel. In operational terms, an air armament division of the Central Experimental and Proving Establishment (CEPE) was formed at Cold

Lake, and evaluation facilities were constructed on the accompanying range so that fighter pilots could test armament systems and fire their guns at various altitudes. During the 1950s, the No. 3 (All-Weather) Operation Training Unit moved to the site to train crews up to operational standard with the CF-100 all-weather interceptor. When this aircraft was phased out in 1961, the military created operational training units to convert pilots to Starfighter, CF-5, and later CF-18 aircraft.

In 1953, the federal government signed agreements with the governments of Saskatchewan and Alberta to perpetually lease the range. The leases, originally established for a twenty-year period, have been renewed continuously since 1954. The latest agreements between the federal and provincial governments are automatically renewed on an annual basis until the federal government chooses to cancel them. In return, the federal government provides annual compensation to the provinces for loss of revenue from forest resources, fur, fish, and recreational, agricultural and related purposes.

Although the range was laid out to avoid First Nations reserves, it encompassed traditional Aboriginal and treaty areas. Five First Nations were affected by the creation of the CLAWR, including the Canoe Lake Cree Nation in Saskatchewan, who in 1975 and 1985 submitted land claims alleging inadequate compensation for the disruption to their rights and livelihoods. In 1993, an Indian Specific Claim Commission inquiry recommended that the federal government negotiate an agreement for breaching treaty guarantees and its fiduciary duty by inadequately compensating and rehabilitating Aboriginal groups. In 1997, the federal government reached with the Canoe Lake Cree a final settlement that provided an estimated $12 million in compensation, as well as controlled access for traditional activities (hunting, fishing, trapping, and gathering), commercial fishing, and cultural heritage activities. Several other Saskatchewan First Nations and Métis communities continue to push for monetary compensation, access, and support for economic development.

Non-military use of the CLAWR has increased over the last decade, and will continue to grow as various sectors vie for access to airspace, land and resources (such as natural gas, commercial fishing, and logging) in and around the range. 4 Wing controls land-based access to ensure that safety, operational and security requirements are met. Recently, the province of Saskatchewan has established three environmental protected areas on the CLAWR, allowing 4 Wing Cold Lake and its clients to sustain the tempo and full scope of flying training on the CLAWR. The mission of 4 Wing is to train, deploy and support world-class tactical fighter forces to meet Canada's defense needs. Two operational CF-18 Squadrons and two training squadrons, as well as

numerous support units, make 4 Wing Canada's largest and busiest fighter wing. Every year Cold Lake hosts Exercise Maple Flag, an international air combat exercise promoting leadership, initiative, and self-discipline in the air; it provides air crew with realistic training in a modern, simulated air combat environment, combining large-scale operations with airborne and ground-based electronic threats. Since 2001, Phase IV of the NATO Flying Training in Canada (NFTC) program has been conducted at Cold Lake.

The relatively unrestricted Cold Lake Air Weapons Range represents one of the largest live-drop training ranges in the world and is the largest low-level flying area in North America. It continues to provide the air force with an unparalleled training environment. In 2004, the Cold Lake base reached a momentous milestone with 50 years of operation and service to the Canadian Forces—a testament to the enduring partnership between the armed forces and the provinces of Saskatchewan and Alberta.   *P. Whitney Lackenbauer*

COLDWELL, MAJOR JAMES (1888–1974).
M.J. Coldwell was born in Seaton, England, on December 2, 1888. Educated in England, Coldwell arrived in Canada in 1910 to take up his first teaching appointment in Alberta. The next year he was hired as a principal in Sedley. Later he was a school principal in North Regina and Regina until 1934. Active in several teachers' federations from the mid-1920s until the mid-1930s, he served as president of the Saskatchewan Teachers' Alliance and president of the Canadian Teachers' Federation. Coldwell became an alderman in 1921 and served four terms until 1932.

In 1925 Coldwell was a federal candidate for the **PROGRESSIVE PARTY** and also ran in 1934 as a provincial candidate for the Saskatchewan Farmer-Labour Party. A year later, Coldwell, campaigning for the federal CCF in Rosetown-Biggar, was victorious and would go on to win four subsequent elections in 1940, 1945, 1953, and 1957, until losing in the Tory landslide of 1958.

In 1931 Coldwell was president of the Independent Labour Party and was selected the first leader of the Saskatchewan Farmer-Labour Party in 1932, which was renamed the **CO-OPERATIVE COMMONWEALTH FEDERATION** in 1934. **GEORGE WILLIAMS** replaced him as provincial leader after the 1934 election.

Following Woodsworth's death in 1942, Coldwell was elected the national CCF's leader and remained in the post until 1960. Under Coldwell's tenure, the CCF achieved its greatest gains federally in seats and vote in 1945. Later, the aging and ill Coldwell was no match for the prairie populism of **JOHN DIEFENBAKER** and the party's vote and seats fell dramatically in 1958. Following this setback, social

M.J. Coldwell, February 1963.

democracy would be reborn as the NDP.

Coldwell was respected by his peers in other political parties and was offered Cabinet posts in provincial and federal governments, Speakership of the House of Commons and a Senate seat. He served as a member of the Canadian delegation at the creation of the United Nations. Coldwell was named to the Privy Council (1964) and made a Companion of the Order of Canada (1967). The Douglas-Coldwell Foundation, a left-wing educational organization, is named after two remarkable Saskatchewan political figures.

Coldwell's distinguished record of public service was achieved while caring for an invalid wife for two decades. Coldwell died in Ottawa on August 25, 1974.   *Alan Whitehorn*

FURTHER READING: Coldwell, M.J. 1945. *Left Turn Canada*. New York, Toronto: Duell, Sloan and Pearce; Stewart, Walter. 2000. *M.J: The Life and Times of M.J. Coldwell*. Toronto: Stoddart.

COLLÈGE MATHIEU DE GRAVELBOURG.
Le Collège Mathieu de Gravelbourg, Saskatchewan, founded by Reverend Olivier Elzéar Mathieu, Archbishop of Regina, obtained its charter on December 15, 1917. The institution opened its doors in December 1918 for boys only. Collège Mathieu has taken the leadership to enunciate the aspirations put forth by the French-speaking community. Plans and efforts to create a French radio station and numerous French associations in Saskatchewan would not have been realized had it not been for the initiatives, leadership, and support of the staff and administrators of Collège Mathieu. They actively supported the introduction and the establishment of French public schools in Saskatchewan and across Western Canada. Since 1970, the College has been a co-ed institution. Sports have an important place in the life of the school, and performing arts are of great interest to the students. In Saskatchewan and

elsewhere in French-speaking communities outside Quebec, Collège Mathieu's cultural program is recognized for its variety and quality. The college also offers room and board to students from outside the immediate area. Life in residence at Collège Mathieu is a central aspect of the institution's activities. This is where a sense of belonging to the college culture is created and developed. In 1986, the college set out to offer new educational services to the French-speaking community by creating the Franco-Saskatchewan adult education service (*Service fransaskois d'éducation aux adultes–SEFFA*) and *Le Lien*, a French cultural and educational resource centre. In 1998, the College went on-line with the opening of the Franco-Ouest Virtual School (transferred in 2003 to the Official Minority Language Office-Saskatchewan Learning). Collège Mathieu is also part of a national French-language education network (*Réseau national d'éducation universitaire francophone–RNEUF*) providing long-distance post-secondary education through tele-conferencing. In 2002, Collège Mathieu's *SEFFA* established an Entrepreneurship program in partnership with other educational institutions. In 2003, Collège Mathieu partnered with the *Division scolaire francophone #310*. The Francophone School Board now assumes responsibility for the Grade 8 to 12 academic program. *James McNinch and Margaret Sanche*

COLLEGE OF MEDICINE, UNIVERSITY OF SASKATCHEWAN.

A medical college was part of President **WALTER MURRAY**'s design for the new **UNIVERSITY OF SASKATCHEWAN**, and was consistent with his view that the university should serve the needs of the province. In 1926 a School of Medical Sciences was established, which provided the first two years of medical training. Between 1928 and 1954, 605 students completed the course and then went elsewhere in Canada for the clinical years.

In 1944, a survey of the health needs of the province (Sigerist Report) recommended that the

SASKATCHEWAN ARCHIVES BOARD R-A19777

Le College Mathieu.

School be expanded to a "complete Grade A Medical School" and that a University Hospital of 500 beds be constructed for scientific teaching, clinical instruction, and research. A medical building was completed in 1950, a four-year degree-granting College was inaugurated in 1953, and University Hospital opened in 1955.

The College admits sixty medical students per year, supervises the training of 200 residents, and provides basic science training to 330 students in Arts/Science. The aim of the program is to produce a "basic" or undifferentiated doctor capable, with further training, of becoming a family practitioner, specialist or research scientist. Between 1953 and 2003, the College of Medicine has graduated 2,134 MDs, of whom 30.5% were women. *Louis Horlick*

COLLEGE OF PHYSICIANS AND SURGEONS OF SASKATCHEWAN.

The College of Physicians and Surgeons of Saskatchewan continued the work of its North-West Territories predecessor in 1905. The College regulates the practice of medicine in the public interest. This is accomplished through licensure of physicians, setting standards for their work, receiving complaints, and dealing with aberrant physicians in an educational or disciplinary fashion. The major committees, established under the bylaws, are the Advisory Committee on Medical Imaging, the Anaesthetic and Operative Deaths Study Committee, the Complaints Resolution Advisory Committee, the Perinatal and Maternal Mortality Study Committee, and the Health Care Facilities Credentialling Committee.

In carrying out its duties, the College interacts provincially with a number of agencies such as Saskatchewan Health, Regional Health Authorities, the **SASKATCHEWAN ASSOCIATION OF HEALTH ORGANIZATIONS** (SAHO), the **SASKATCHEWAN MEDICAL ASSOCIATION**, and a number of national and international organizations.

In recent years the College has become more proactive in its efforts to prevent patient harm by extracting information from complaints or critical incidents. This information is then applied to prevent future adverse outcomes. *Lowell Loewen*

COLLINGWOOD, ARTHUR (1880–1952).

Norman Palmer, secretary to the Saskatchewan Association of Music Festivals, opined to President **MURRAY** that the appointment of Collingwood in October 1930 to the first Chair of Music at the **UNIVERSITY OF SASKATCHEWAN**, funded by the Carnegie Corporation, was "one of your frequent masterstrokes." Born on November 24, 1880 in Halifax, Yorkshire, and trained as an articled organ pupil in Manchester and London, Collingwood obtained his ARCO at the very early age of 15 and his Fellowship in 1904, by which time he was in Aberdeen. His versatility and enthusiasm for music education gained him posts in a church, in two outstanding schools, at Marischal College, University of Aberdeen, and as conductor of the Aberdeen Choral Union, the Madrigal Choir, the Male Choir, and the local BBC Choir.

Collingwood was no stranger to Canada, because his son-in-law was Dean of Graduate Studies at McGill University and he had himself adjudicated widely there in 1929. Collingwood's achievements until he retired in 1947 included adjudicating throughout Saskatchewan and across Canada, introducing music options into the BA and developing a Bmus, supervising the Conservatory of Music in Regina, inspiring the founding of the Western Board of Music (he tried hard to get a national system), conducting the newly formed **SASKATOON SYMPHONY ORCHESTRA**, establishing string ensembles in all Saskatoon collegiates, gaining credit in school for music examinations taken through outside boards, obtaining several thousand dollars from the Carnegie Corporation for equipment and a large record collection for use by students and teachers in the province, and successfully soliciting donations of scores from publishers.

Described by himself as "a propagandist" and by others as "the layman's musician," Collingwood promoted music and the university in talks to service clubs (he had been the president of the Rotary Club in Aberdeen) and musical organizations. His Friday talks on CFQC illuminated set pieces for examinations, and he was instrumental in the links created between that station, CKRM, and the CBC. Almost every summer, Collingwood traveled to England. He conducted broadcasts of the BBC Symphony Orchestra, and in one summer went to twenty concerts and operas in London, Paris and Monte Carlo. In New York he saw *Showboat* with Paul Robeson and admired the "ever bright lights of Broadway." He was the highest paid teacher, except for President Murray, and clearly earned his $5,500 salary. His compositions for piano, voice, schoolroom use, and choirs are listed in the Catalogue of Canadian Music. He died in Montreal on January 22, 1952.

Robin Swales

FURTHER READING: Kallmann, H. 1992. *Encyclopedia of Music in Canada*, 2nd edition.

COLLVER, RICHARD LEE (1936–). Dick Collver was born in Toronto on February 13, 1936. He earned an arts degree in economics, University of Alberta, and articled as an accountant for Price Waterhouse in Calgary. In 1965 Collver moved to Saskatchewan, and in 1972 ran for public office contesting the Saskatoon mayoralty. Although defeated, his campaign impressed many people and he was approached to lead the troubled Saskatchewan Progressive Conservative party. Gaining the leadership (1973), Collver set out to expand a party that had achieved less than 3% of the vote the previous provincial election. His effort paid off when the party won seven seats with over 28% of the vote in the 1975 election. They became the official opposition after winning two by-elections and convincing two Liberal MLAs to abandon their party. Collver was convinced the Conservatives would win the 1978 election, and although they won over 38% of the vote and elected 17 MLAs his disappointment led to his resignation of the party leadership. He left the party in 1980 to create the Unionest party. Following the 1982 election Collver purchased a ranch in Wickenberg, Arizona and left Saskatchewan. Although unsuccessful in his own bid for the premiership, he had laid the foundation for the Conservative victory in 1982.

Brett Quiring

COLONSAY, town, pop 426, located 55 km E of Saskatoon on Hwy 16. The community as well as many of its streets are named after islands off Scotland's west coast. The area was settled around 1905, and the beginnings of the village date to 1907–08 with the construction of the CPR line from Lanigan to Saskatoon. By the early 1920s, the population was around 200; it remained at that level for the next few decades. With the construction of the potash mine at Colonsay in the latter years of the 1960s, the community's numbers significantly increased: by 1971, the population had reached 526. Although employment at the mine remains highly important (about 300 people from a number of communities are employed there), agriculture also contributes significantly to the economy. A variety of crops and livestock are produced in the area. The SASKATCHEWAN WHEAT POOL (SWP) sells fertilizers, herbicides, pesticides, and seed products at Colonsay; however, in April 2002 Colonsay's SWP elevator was demolished, superseded by the ever larger inland terminals established in the region. Colonsay retains a small core of essential businesses and services.

David McLennan

SASKATCHEWAN ARCHIVES BOARD S-SP-A10969-42, SASKATOON STARPHOENIX FONDS

Dick Collver delivers an election speech in Nipawin, September 27, 1978.

COMMERCIAL FISHING: *see* **FISHING, COMMERCIAL**

COMMISSION ON FIRST NATIONS AND MÉTIS PEOPLE AND JUSTICE REFORM: *see* **ABORIGINAL JUSTICE INQUIRY**

COMMONWEALTH, THE. *The Commonwealth* is the official paper of the **NEW DEMOCRATIC PARTY** (NDP) and its predecessor the **CO-OPERATIVE COMMONWEALTH FEDERATION** (CCF). The paper was founded in 1936 under the name *The New Era*, but the name was changed to *The Commonwealth* in 1938 to avoid confusion with a Ukrainian paper of the same name. At various points in its history it also served as the official paper of both the Alberta and Manitoba CCF and NDP, although its primary focus has always been on Saskatchewan. Originally established as a monthly, it increased its circulation in 1944, becoming a weekly paper and remaining so until 1970. After 1970 the paper became a bi-weekly and was later reduced to a monthly; in 1999 it was reduced again to a quarterly as a party cost-cutting measure.

Brett Quiring

COMMUNICATIONS, ENERGY AND PAPER-WORKERS UNION OF CANADA. The Communications, Energy and Paperworkers (CEP) Union of Canada is the newest union in Canada, yet it has a history that goes back more than 150 years. The CEP was created at a founding convention in November 1992 when the Communications Workers of Canada (CWC), the Energy and Chemical Workers Union (ECWU), and the Canadian Paperworkers Union (CPU) merged forces after a year of discussions. The new CEP membership would exceed 150,000, making it the fourth-largest private sector union in Canada and the eighth-largest union in the Canadian Labour Congress.

CEP has an active history in the trade union movement in Saskatchewan. The presidents of the founding organizations all played key roles in the development of the labour movement in the province. Don Holder, president of the CPU, was responsible for organizing workers at the peppermill in Prince Albert, a local that has over 700 members today. Fred Pomeroy, an employee of SaskTel, was the treasurer of the Saskatchewan Federation of Labour and the president of the CWC in Saskatchewan prior to taking on the national presidency of the CEP.

Additional strength came from fifty-year activist Ralph Wyatt, who retired from CEP in 1994. Wyatt negotiated for SaskTel employees for many years. Cy Palmer, a cableman from Saskatoon assisted with the organization of the Saskatchewan Federation of Labour in the 1930s and 1940s. He later became a director in the Canadian Labour Congress.

The ECWU leader Neil Reimer, an employee of the Co-op Refinery, went on to become the national president of the ECWU. He was followed by Reg Baskin, from Churchbridge, an employee of SaskPower who worked his way up to be president of ECWU as well and executive vice-president of CEP prior to his retirement.

Ron Carlson

COMMUNITIES OF SASKATCHEWAN. Communities listed in the Saskatchewan Municipal Directory include towns, villages, resort villages, organized hamlets, northern towns, northern villages, northern hamlets, northern settlements, and one municipal district. Those listed in the table on the following six pages appear in the on-line directory as of May 9, 2005. Additionally, non-organized hamlets have been included in the table if they serve as the administrative centre of a rural municipality. An asterisk at the end of the community name indicates there is an entry on the place in the encyclopedia. The location column indicates a community's position within either a rural municipality (e.g. Argyle No. 1), a Municipal District (e.g. District of Katepwa), or the Northern Saskatchewan Administration District (NSAD). Not listed on the table are other types of Saskatchewan communities such as First Nations reserve centres, Hutterite colonies, and former Doukhobor villages, which are addressed separately within the body of the encyclopedia. Population figures (unless otherwise stated) are from the 2001 Census of Canada. Population figures for resort villages, organized hamlets that are resort areas, and the communities that comprise the District of Katepwa are based upon the number of permanent year-round residents. The population of these areas, however, can fluctuate greatly depending on the season. The former resort villages of Katepwa Beach, Katepwa South, and Sandy Beach are listed in the table since their names are familiar, although all three were dissolved on July 24, 2004, and together were reincorporated as the District of Katepwa.

David McLennan

Saskatchewan's Communities

Community	Type	Population	Location
Abbey	Village	137	Miry Creek No. 229
Aberdeen*	Town	534	Aberdeen No. 373
Abernethy	Village	213	Abernethy No. 186
Admiral	Village	25	Wise Creek No. 77
Air Ronge*	Northern Village	955	NSAD
Alameda*	Town	311	Moose Creek No. 33
Albertville	Village	132	Garden River No. 490
Alice Beach	Resort Village	55	Sarnia No. 221
Alida	Village	117	Reciprocity No. 32
Allan*	Town	679	Blucher No. 343
Alsask*	Village	178	Milton No. 292
Alta Vista	Organized Hamlet (resort)	20	McKillop No. 220
Alvena	Village	86	Fish Creek No. 402
Amsterdam	Organized Hamlet	25	Buchanan No. 304
Aneroid	Village	56	Auvergne No. 76
Annaheim	Village	217	St. Peter No. 369
Antler	Village	45	Antler No. 61
Aquadeo	Resort Village	62	Meota No. 468
Arborfield*	Town	411	Arborfield No. 456
Archerwill	Village	215	Barrier Valley No. 397
Arcola*	Town	532	Brock No. 64
Ardill	Organized Hamlet	0	Lake Johnston No. 102
Arlington Beach	Organized Hamlet (resort)	20	Last Mountain Valley No. 250
Arran	Village	55	Livingston No. 331
Asquith*	Town	574	Vanscoy No. 345
Assiniboia*	Town	2,483	Lake of the Rivers No. 72
Atwater	Village	30	Fertile Belt No. 183
Avonlea	Village	412	Elmsthorpe No. 100
Aylesbury	Village	50	Craik No. 222
Aylsham	Village	106	Nipawin No. 487
Balcarres*	Town	622	Abernethy No. 186
Balgonie*	Town	1,239	Edenwold No. 158
Balone Beach	Organized Hamlet (resort)	5	Hoodoo No. 401
Bangor	Village	48	Fertile Belt No. 183
Bankend	Organized Hamlet	15	Emerald No. 277
Barrier Ford	Organized Hamlet (resort)	10	Bjorkdale No. 426
Battleford*	Town	3,820	Battle River No. 438
Bayard	Organized Hamlet	10	Terrell No. 101
Bayview Heights	Organized Hamlet	15	Meota No. 468
Bear Creek	Northern Settlement	47	NSAD
Beatty	Village	79	Flett's Springs No. 429
Beaubier	Organized Hamlet	25	Lake Alma No. 8
Beauval*	Northern Village	843	NSAD
Beaver Creek	Organized Hamlet	138	Corman Park No. 344
Beaver Flat	Resort Village	34	Excelsior No. 166
Beechy	Village	295	Victory No. 226
Belle Plaine	Village	70	Pense No. 160
Bellegarde	Organized Hamlet	40	Storthoaks No. 31
Bengough*	Town	401	Bengough No. 40
Benson	Hamlet	95	Benson No. 35
Bethune	Village	380	Dufferin No. 190
Bienfait*	Town	786	Coalfields No. 4
Big Beaver	Organized Hamlet	20	Happy Valley No. 10
Big River*	Town	741	Big River No. 555
Big Shell	Resort Village	16	Spiritwood No. 496
Biggar*	Town	2,243	Biggar No. 347
Birch Hills*	Town	957	Birch Hills No. 460
Bird's Point	Resort Village	66	Fertile Belt No. 183
Birsay	Hamlet	53	Coteau No. 255
Bjorkdale	Village	229	Bjorkdale No. 426

Community	Type	Population	Location
Black Point	Northern Settlement	47	NSAD
Bladworth	Village	67	McCraney No 282
Blaine Lake*	Town	508	Blaine Lake No. 434
Blumenthal	Organized Hamlet	44	Rosthern No. 403
Borden	Village	225	Great Bend No. 405
Brabant Lake*	Northern Settlement	102	NSAD
Bracken	Village	35	Lone Tree No. 18
Bradwell	Village	156	Blucher No. 343
Brancepeth	Organized Hamlet	35	Birch Hills No. 460
Bredenbury*	Town	354	Saltcoats No. 213
Briercrest	Village	113	Redburn No. 130
Broadview*	Town	669	Elcapo No. 154
Brock	Village	130	Kindersley No. 290
Broderick	Village	83	Rudy No. 284
Brownlee	Village	55	Eyebrow No. 193
Bruno*	Town	571	Bayne No. 371
B-Say-Tah*	Resort Village	177	North Qu'Appelle No. 187
Buchanan	Village	233	Buchanan No. 304
Buena Vista	Village	397	Lumsden No. 189
Buffalo Narrows*	Northern Village	1,137	NSAD
Bulyea	Village	107	McKillop No. 220
Burgis Beach	Organized Hamlet	45	Good Lake No. 274
Burstall*	Town	388	Deer Forks No. 232
Cabri*	Town	483	Riverside No. 168
Cactus Lake	Organized Hamlet	0	Heart's Hill No. 352
Cadillac	Village	95	Wise Creek No. 77
Calder	Village	109	Calder No. 241
Camsell Portage	Northern Settlement	37	NSAD
Candiac	Organized Hamlet	25	Montmartre No. 126
Candle Lake	Resort Village	503	Paddockwood No. 520
Cando	Village	102	Rosemount No. 378
Cannington Lake	Organized Hamlet (resort)	5	Moose Mountain No. 63
Canora*	Town	2,200	Good Lake No. 274
Canwood	Village	374	Canwood No. 494
Carievale	Village	254	Argyle No. 1
Carlyle*	Town	1,260	Moose Mountain No. 63
Carmichael	Village	20	Carmichael No. 109
Carnduff*	Town	1,017	Mount Pleasant No. 2
Caron	Organized Hamlet	120	Caron No. 162
Caronport	Village	1,040	Caron No. 162
Carrot River*	Town	1,017	Moose Range No. 486
Casa Rio	Organized Hamlet	229	Corman Park No. 344
Cathedral Bluffs	Organized Hamlet	78	Corman Park No. 344
Cedar Villa Estates	Organized Hamlet	139	Corman Park No. 344
Central Butte*	Town	439	Enfield No. 194
Ceylon*	Village	105	The Gap No. 39
Chamberlain	Village	89	Sarnia No. 221
Chaplin	Village	292	Chaplin No. 164
Chelan	Organized Hamlet	52	Bjorkdale No. 426
Chitek Lake	Resort Village	174	Big River No. 555
Choiceland*	Town	370	Torch River No. 488
Chorney Beach	Resort Village	15	Foam Lake No. 276
Chortitz	Organized Hamlet	16	Coulee No. 136
Christopher Lake	Village	230	Lakeland No. 521
Churchbridge*	Town	796	Churchbridge No. 211
Clavet	Village	357	Blucher No. 343
Claybank*	Organized Hamlet	20	Elmsthorpe No. 100
Clemenceau	Organized Hamlet	5	Hudson Bay No. 394
Climax	Village	206	Lone Tree No. 18
Cochin	Resort Village	136	Meota No. 468

Saskatchewan's Communities

Community	Type	Population	Location
Coderre	Village	50	Rodgers No. 133
Codette	Village	237	Nipawin No. 487
Cole Bay	Northern Village	161	NSAD
Colesdale Park	Organized Hamlet (resort)	0	McKillop No. 220
Coleville	Village	313	Oakdale No. 320
Collingwood Lakeshore Estates	Organized Hamlet	8	McKillop No. 220
Colonsay*	Town	426	Colonsay No. 342
Congress	Organized Hamlet	36	Stonehenge No. 73
Conquest	Village	163	Fertile Valley No. 285
Consul	Village	91	Reno No. 51
Corning	Organized Hamlet	30	Golden West No. 95
Coronach*	Town	822	Hart Butte No. 11
Coteau Beach	Resort Village	20	Coteau No. 255
Courval	Organized Hamlet	10	Rodgers No. 133
Craik*	Town	418	Craik No. 222
Crane Valley	Organized Hamlet	40	Excel No. 71
Craven	Village	264	Longlaketon No. 219
Crawford Estates	Organized Hamlet	50	Edenwold No. 158
Creelman	Village	85	Fillmore No. 96
Creighton*	Northern Town	1,556	NSAD
Crooked River	Organized Hamlet	64	Bjorkdale No. 426
Crutwell	Organized Hamlet	77	Shellbrook No. 493
Crystal Bay-Sunset	Organized Hamlet (resort)	0	Mervin No. 499
Crystal Lake	Organized Hamlet (resort)	55	Keys No. 303
Crystal Springs	Organized Hamlet	25	Invergordon No. 430
Cudsaskwa Beach	Organized Hamlet (resort)	10	Hoodoo No. 401
Cudworth*	Town	766	Hoodoo No. 401
Cumberland House*	Northern Village	632	NSAD
Cupar*	Town	602	Cupar No. 218
Cut Knife*	Town	556	Cut Knife No. 439
Dafoe	Village	15	Big Quill No. 308
Dalmeny*	Town	1,610	Corman Park No. 344
Darlings Beach	Organized Hamlet (resort)	10	Lac Pelletier No. 107
Davidson*	Town	1,035	Arm River No. 252
Davin	Organized Hamlet	50	Lajord No. 128
Day's Beach	Organized Hamlet (resort)	27	Meota No. 468
Debden	Village	355	Canwood No. 494
Delisle*	Town	884	Vanscoy No. 345
Delmas	Organized Hamlet	112	Battle River No. 438
Demaine	Organized Hamlet	20	Victory No. 226
Denare Beach	Northern Village	784	NSAD
Denholm	Village	79	Mayfield No. 406
Denzil	Village	161	Eye Hill No. 382
Descharme Lake	Northern Settlement	42	NSAD
Dilke	Village	70	Sarnia No. 221
Dinsmore	Village	337	Milden No. 286
Disley	Village	62	Lumsden No. 189
Dodsland	Village	211	Winslow No. 319
Domremy	Village	135	St. Louis No. 431
Dore Lake	Northern Hamlet	27	NSAD
Dorintosh	Village	125	Meadow Lake No. 588
Drake	Village	248	Usborne No. 310
Drinkwater	Village	80	Redburn No. 130
Dubuc	Village	80	Grayson No. 184
Duck Lake*	Town	624	Duck Lake No. 463
Duff	Village	40	Stanley No. 215
Dundurn*	Town	596	Dundurn No. 314
Duval	Village	103	Last Mountain Valley No. 250
Dysart	Village	210	Lipton No. 217

Community	Type	Population	Location
Eagle Ridge Country Estates	Organized Hamlet	84 (2005 est.)	Corman Park No. 344
Earl Grey	Village	292	Longlaketon No. 219
Eastend*	Town	576	White Valley No. 49
Eatonia*	Town	474	Chesterfield No. 261
Ebenezer	Village	147	Orkney No. 244
Echo Bay	Resort Village	24	Spiritwood No. 496
Edam	Village	429	Turtle River No. 469
Edenwold	Village	226	Edenwold No. 158
Edgeley	Organized Hamlet	40	South Qu'Appelle No. 157
Elbow	Village	298	Loreburn No. 254
Elbow Lake	Organized Hamlet (resort)	0	Hudson Bay No. 394
Eldersley	Organized Hamlet	40	Tisdale No. 427
Elfros	Village	161	Elfros No. 307
Elrose*	Town	517	Monet No. 257
Elstow	Village	97	Blucher No. 343
Endeavour	Village	154	Preeceville No. 334
Englefeld	Village	245	St. Peter No. 369
Ernfold	Village	50	Morse No. 165
Erwood	Organized Hamlet	68	Hudson Bay No 394
Esterhazy*	Town	2,348	Fertile Belt No. 183
Estevan*	City	10,242	Estevan No. 5
Eston*	Town	1,048	Snipe Lake No. 259
Etters Beach	Resort Village	5	Big Arm No. 251
Evergreen Acres	Organized Hamlet (resort)	17	Mervin No. 499
Evergreen Brightsand	Organized Hamlet (resort)	10	Mervin No. 499
Eyebrow	Village	136	Eyebrow No. 193
Fairholme	Organized Hamlet	20	Parkdale No. 498
Fairlight	Village	45	Maryfield No. 91
Fairy Glen	Organized Hamlet	25	Willow Creek No. 458
Fenwood	Village	48	Stanley No. 215
Fife Lake	Organized Hamlet	46	Poplar Valley No. 12
Fillmore	Village	246	Fillmore No. 96
Findlater	Village	62	Dufferin No. 190
Fiske	Organized Hamlet	96	Pleasant Valley No. 288
Flaxcombe	Village	128	Kindersley No. 290
Fleming*	Town	95	Moosomin No. 121
Foam Lake*	Town	1,218	Foam Lake No. 276
Forget	Village	40	Tecumseh No. 65
Fort Qu'Appelle*	Town	1,940	North Qu'Appelle No. 187
Fort San	Resort Village	239	North Qu'Appelle No. 187
Fosston	Village	55	Ponass Lake No. 367
Fox Valley	Village	326	Fox Valley No. 171
Francis*	Town	172	Francis No. 127
Frenchman Butte	Organized Hamlet	74	Frenchman Butte No. 501
Frobisher	Village	149	Coalfields No. 4
Frontier	Village	302	Frontier No. 19
Furdale	Organized Hamlet	195	Corman Park No. 344
Gainsborough	Village	286	Argyle No. 1
Garrick	Organized Hamlet	30	Torch River No. 488
Garson Lake	Northern Settlement	34	NSAD
Gerald	Village	159	Spy Hill No. 152
Girvin	Village	25	Arm River No. 252
Gladmar	Village	45	Surprise Valley No. 9
Glaslyn	Village	375	Parkdale No. 498
Glen Ewen	Village	158	Enniskillen No. 3
Glen Harbour	Resort Village	43	McKillop No. 220
Glenavon	Village	207	Chester No. 125
Glenside	Village	63	Rudy No. 284
Glentworth	Hamlet	88 in 1996	Waverley No. 44

Saskatchewan's Communities

Community	Type	Population	Location
Glidden	Hamlet	48 in 1996	Newcombe No. 260
Golden Prairie	Village	56	Big Stick No. 141
Good Spirit Acres	Organized Hamlet	92	Good Lake No. 274
Goodeve	Village	70	Stanley No. 215
Goodsoil	Village	284	Beaver River No. 622
Goodwater	Village	25	Lomond No. 37
Govan*	Town	274	Last Mountain Valley No. 250
Grand Coulee	Village	366	Sherwood No. 159
Grandview Beach	Resort Village	15	Sarnia No. 221
Gravelbourg*	Town	1,187	Gravelbourg No. 104
Gray	Organized Hamlet	106	Lajord No. 128
Grayson	Village	210	Grayson No. 184
Green Lake	Northern Village	498	NSAD
Greig Lake	Resort Village	15	Meadow Lake No. 588
Grenfell*	Town	1,067	Elcapo No. 154
Griffin	Organized Hamlet	70	Griffin No. 66
Gronlid	Organized Hamlet	70	Willow Creek No. 458
Guernsey	Village	108	Usborne No. 310
Gull Lake*	Town	1,016	Gull Lake No. 139
Hafford*	Town	401	Redberry No. 435
Hagen	Organized Hamlet	41	Birch Hills No. 460
Hague*	Town	711	Rosthern No. 403
Halbrite	Village	109	Cymri No. 36
Handel	Village	25	Grandview No. 349
Hanley*	Town	495	Rosedale No. 283
Harris	Village	232	Harris No. 316
Hawarden	Village	57	Loreburn No. 254
Hazel Dell	Organized Hamlet	30	Hazel Dell No. 335
Hazenmore	Village	71	Pinto Creek No. 75
Hazlet	Village	126	Pittville No. 169
Hendon	Organized Hamlet	25	Lakeview No. 337
Hepburn	Village	475	Laird No. 404
Herbert*	Town	812	Morse No. 165
Herschel	Village	35	Mountain View No. 318
Heward	Village	25	Tecumseh No. 65
Hitchcock Bay	Organized Hamlet (resort)	15	Coteau No. 255
Hodgeville	Village	175	Lawtonia No. 135
Hoey	Organized Hamlet	50	St. Louis No. 431
Holbein	Organized Hamlet	92	Shellbrook No. 493
Holdfast	Village	190	Sarnia No. 221
Horseshoe Bay	Organized Hamlet (resort)	25	Mervin No. 499
Hubbard	Village	38	Ituna Bon Accord No. 246
Hudson Bay*	Town	1,783	Hudson Bay No. 394
Humboldt*	City	5,161	Humboldt No. 370
Hyas	Village	131	Clayton No. 333
Ile-à-la-Crosse*	Northern Village	1,268	NSAD
Imperial*	Town	339	Big Arm No. 251
Indian Head*	Town	1,758	Indian Head No. 156
Indian Point-Golden Sands	Organized Hamlet (resort)	31	Parkdale No. 498
Insinger	Hamlet	20	Insinger No. 275
Invermay	Village	284	Invermay No. 305
Island View	Resort Village	35	McKillop No. 220
Ituna*	Town	709	Ituna Bon Accord No. 246
Jans Bay	Northern Village	198	NSAD
Jansen	Village	158	Prairie Rose No. 309
Jasmin	Organized Hamlet	5	Ituna Bon Accord No. 246
Kamsack*	Town	2,009	Cote No. 271
Kandahar	Organized Hamlet	15	Big Quill No. 308
Kannata Valley	Resort Village	98	Longlaketon No. 219
Katepwa Beach*	Municipal District	189	District of Katepwa
Katepwa South	Municipal District	44	District of Katepwa
Kayville	Organized Hamlet	15	Key West No. 70
Keeler	Village	15	Marquis No. 191
Kelfield	Hamlet	5 in 1996	Grandview No. 349
Kelliher	Village	317	Kellross No. 247
Kelvington*	Town	1,007	Kelvington No. 366
Kenaston	Village	282	McCraney No. 282
Kendal	Village	83	Montmartre No. 126
Kennedy	Village	243	Wawken No. 93
Kenosee Lake	Village	182	Wawken No. 93
Kerrobert*	Town	1,111	Progress No. 351
Ketchen	Organized Hamlet	10	Preeceville No. 334
Killaly	Village	91	Grayson No. 184
Kincaid	Village	161	Pinto Creek No. 75
Kindersley*	Town	4,548	Kindersley No. 290
Kinistino*	Town	702	Kinistino No. 459
Kinley	Village	40	Perdue No. 346
Kipling*	Town	1,037	Kingsley No. 124
Kisbey	Village	199	Brock No. 64
Kivimaa-Moonlight Bay	Resort Village	42	Mervin No. 499
Kopp's Kove	Organized Hamlet (resort)	36	Mervin No. 499
Kronau	Organized Hamlet	196	Lajord No. 128
Krydor	Village	25	Redberry No. 435
Kuroki	Organized Hamlet	74	Sasman No. 336
Kyle*	Town	478	Lacadena No. 228
Kylemore	Organized Hamlet	56	Sasman No. 336
La Loche*	Northern Village	2,136	NSAD
La Ronge*	Northern Town	2,727	NSAD
Lacadena	Hamlet	15 (2004 est.)	Lacadena No. 228
Lady Lake	Organized Hamlet	30	Preeceville No. 334
Lafleche*	Town	446	Wood River No. 74
Laird	Village	236	Laird No. 404
Lake Alma	Village	35	Lake Alma No. 8
Lake Lenore	Village	314	St. Peter No. 369
Lakeview	Organized Hamlet (resort)	20	Meota No. 468
Lampman*	Town	650	Browning No. 34
Lancer	Village	75	Miry Creek No. 229
Landis	Village	161	Reford No. 379
Lang	Village	189	Scott No. 98
Langbank	Organized Hamlet	35	Silverwood No. 123
Langenburg*	Town	1,107	Langenburg No. 181
Langham*	Town	1,145	Corman Park No. 344
Lanigan*	Town	1,289	Usborne No. 310
Lanz Point	Organized Hamlet (resort)	41	Meota No. 468
Laporte	Organized Hamlet	5	Chesterfield No. 261
Lashburn*	Town	783	Wilton No. 472
Leader*	Town	914	Happyland No. 231
Leask	Village	447	Leask No. 464
Lebret*	Village	207	North Qu'Appelle No. 187
Lemberg*	Town	306	McLeod No. 185
Leoville	Village	343	Spiritwood No. 496
Leross	Village	59	Kellross No. 247
Leroy*	Town	413	Leroy No. 339
Leslie	Village	30	Elfros No. 307
Leslie Beach	Resort Village	15	Foam Lake No. 276
Lestock	Village	226	Kellross No. 247
Liberty	Village	94	Big Arm No. 251
Limerick	Village	146	Stonehenge No. 73

Saskatchewan's Communities

Community	Type	Population	Location
Lintlaw	Village	187	Hazel Dell No. 335
Lipton	Village	331	Lipton No. 217
Lisieux	Organized Hamlet	20	Willow Bunch No. 42
Little Fishing Lake	Organized Hamlet (resort)	10	Loon Lake No. 561
Little Swan River	Organized Hamlet (resort)	0	Hudson Bay No. 394
Livelong	Organized Hamlet	93	Mervin No. 499
Lloydminster*	City	7,840† / 20,988††	Britannia No. 502 (Sask. portion)
Lone Rock	Organized Hamlet	87	Wilton No. 472
Loon Lake	Village	318	Loon Lake No. 561
Loreburn	Village	143	Loreburn No. 254
Love	Village	71	Torch River No. 488
Lucky Lake	Village	354	Canaan No. 225
Lumsden*	Town	1,581	Lumsden No. 189
Lumsden Beach	Resort Village	0	Lumsden No. 189
Luseland*	Town	602	Progress No. 351
MacDowall	Organized Hamlet	136	Duck Lake No. 463
Macklin*	Town	1,330	Eye Hill No. 382
MacNutt	Village	85	Churchbridge No. 211
Macoun*	Village	170	Cymri No. 36
MacPheat Park	Organized Hamlet		McKillop No. 220
Macrorie	Village	96	Fertile Valley No. 285
Maidstone*	Town	995	Eldon No. 471
Main Centre	Organized Hamlet	5	Excelsior No. 166
Major	Village	81	Prairiedale No. 321
Makwa	Village	101	Loon Lake No. 561
Manitou Beach*	Resort Village	212	Morris No. 312
Mankota	Village	248	Mankota No. 45
Manor	Village	305	Moose Mountain No. 63
Mantario	Village	10	Chesterfield No. 261
Maple Creek*	Town	2,270	Maple Creek No. 111
Marcelin	Village	167	Blaine Lake No. 434
Marengo	Village	47	Milton No. 292
Margo	Village	106	Sasman No. 336
Markinch	Village	67	Cupar No. 218
Marquis	Village	94	Marquis No. 191
Marsden	Village	276	Manitou Lake No. 442
Marshall	Village	633	Wilton No. 472
Martensville*	Town	4,365	Corman Park No. 344
Martinson's Beach	Organized Hamlet (resort)	35	Meota No. 468
Maryfield	Village	359	Maryfield No. 91
Mayfair	Organized Hamlet	48	Meeting Lake No. 466
Maymont	Village	164	Mayfield No. 406
Maymont Beach	Organized Hamlet (resort)	10	Meota No. 468
McCord	Organized Hamlet	45	Mankota No. 45
McLean	Village	271	South Qu'Appelle No. 157
McTaggart	Village	126	Weyburn No. 67
Meacham	Village	90	Colonsay No. 342
Meadow Lake*	Town	4,582	Meadow Lake No. 588
Meath Park	Village	204	Garden River No. 490
Medstead	Village	144	Medstead No. 497
Melfort*	City	5,559	Star City No. 428
Melville*	City	4,453	Cana No. 214
Melville Beach	Resort Village	16	Grayson No. 184
Mendham	Village	40	Happyland No. 231
Meota	Village	293	Meota No. 468
Merrill Hills	Organized Hamlet	72	Corman Park No. 344
Mervin	Village	146	Mervin No. 499
Meskanaw	Organized Hamlet	20	Invergordon No. 430

† population in Saskatchewan
†† total population

Community	Type	Population	Location
Metinota	Resort Village	69	Meota No. 468
Meyronne	Village	35	Pinto Creek No. 75
Michel Village	Northern Hamlet	70	NSAD
Midale*	Town	496	Cymri No. 36
Middle Lake	Village	300	Three Lakes No. 400
Mikado	Organized Hamlet	55	Sliding Hills No. 273
Milden	Village	196	Milden No. 286
Milestone*	Town	542	Caledonia No. 99
Minton	Village	95	Surprise Valley No. 9
Missinipe	Northern Hamlet	38	NSAD
Mistatim	Village	104	Bjorkdale No. 426
Mistusinne	Resort Village	31	Maple Bush No. 224
Mohr's Beach	Organized Hamlet (resort)	5	McKillop No. 220
Montmarte	Village	465	Montmartre No. 126
Moose Bay	Organized Hamlet (resort)	16	Grayson No. 184
Moose Jaw*	City	32,131	Moose Jaw No. 161
Moosomin*	Town	2,361	Moosomin No. 121
Morse*	Town	248	Morse No. 165
Mortlach	Village	241	Wheatlands No. 163
Mossbank*	Town	379	Lake Johnston No. 102
Mowery Beach	Organized Hamlet	14	Mervin No. 499
Mozart	Organized Hamlet	40	Elfros No. 307
Muenster	Village	379	St. Peter No. 369
Mullingar	Organized Hamlet	5	Meeting Lake No. 466
Naicam*	Town	761	Pleasantdale No. 398
Neilburg	Village	366	Hillsdale No. 440
Nesslin Lake	Organized Hamlet (resort)	0	Big River No. 555
Netherhill	Village	35	Kindersley No. 290
Neuanlage	Organized Hamlet	141	Rosthern No. 403
Neudorf	Village	304	McLeod No. 185
Neuhorst	Organized Hamlet	135	Corman Park No. 344
Neville	Village	70	Whiska Creek No. 106
Nipawin*	Town	4,275	Nipawin No. 487
Nokomis*	Town	436	Wreford No. 280
Norquay*	Town	485	Clayton No. 333
North Battleford*	City	13,692	North Battleford No. 437
North Colesdale Park	Organized Hamlet (resort)	15	McKillop No. 220
North Grove	Resort Village	44	Dufferin No. 190
North Portal	Village	136	Coalfields No. 4
North Shore Fishing Lake	Organized Hamlet (resort)	46	Sasman No. 336
North Weyburn	Organized Hamlet	51	Weyburn No. 67
Northside	Organized Hamlet	48	Paddockwood No. 520
Nut Mountain	Organized Hamlet	15	Sasman No. 336
Odessa	Village	242	Francis No. 127
Ogema*	Town	292	Key West No. 70
Okla	Organized Hamlet	35	Hazel Dell No. 335
Orkney	Organized Hamlet	5	Val Marie No. 17
Ormiston	Organized Hamlet	35	Excel No. 71
Osage	Village	25	Fillmore No. 96
Osler*	Town	823	Corman Park No. 344
Otthon	Organized Hamlet	56	Cana No. 214
Ottman-Murray Beach	Organized Hamlet (resort)	15	Sasman No. 336
Oungre	Organized Hamlet	15	Souris Valley No. 7
Outlook*	Town	2,129	Rudy No. 284
Oxbow*	Town	1,132	Enniskillen No. 3
Paddockwood	Village	171	Paddockwood No. 520
Pangman	Village	255	Norton No. 69
Paradise Hill	Village	486	Frenchman Butte No. 501

Saskatchewan's Communities

Community	Type	Population	Location
Parkland Beach	Organized Hamlet (resort)	5	Mervin No. 499
Parkside	Village	130	Leask No. 464
Parkview	Organized Hamlet (resort)	30	Marquis No. 191
Parry	Organized Hamlet	20	Caledonia No. 99
Pasqua Lake	Organized Hamlet (resort)	220	North Qu'Appelle No. 187
Patuanak	Northern Hamlet	72	NSAD
Paynton	Village	172	Paynton No. 470
Pebble Baye	Resort Village	15	Leask No. 464
Peebles	Organized Hamlet	20	Chester No. 125
Pelican Cove	Organized Hamlet (resort)	20	Leask No. 464
Pelican Narrows*	Northern Village	690	NSAD
Pelican Point	Organized Hamlet (resort)	45	Meota No. 468
Pelican Pointe	Resort Village	18	McKillop No. 220
Pelican Shores	Organized Hamlet (resort)	18	Fertile Belt No. 183
Pelly*	Village	303	St. Philips No. 301
Pennant	Village	150	Riverside No. 168
Pense	Village	533	Pense No. 160
Penzance	Village	41	Sarnia No. 221
Percival	Organized Hamlet	15	Willowdale No. 153
Perdue	Village	372	Perdue No. 346
Phillips Grove	Organized Hamlet (resort)	5	Big River No. 555
Piapot	Hamlet	55	Piapot No. 110
Pierceland	Village	449	Beaver River No. 622
Pilger	Village	85	Three Lakes No. 400
Pilot Butte*	Town	1,850	Edenwold No. 158
Pinehouse	Northern Village	1,038	NSAD
Pleasantdale	Village	98	Pleasantdale No. 398
Plenty	Village	147	Winslow No. 319
Plunkett	Village	75	Viscount No. 341
Ponteix*	Town	550	Auvergne No. 76
Porcupine Plain*	Town	820	Porcupine No. 395
Powm Beach	Organized Hamlet (resort)	20	Mervin No. 499
Prairie River	Organized Hamlet	30	Porcupine No. 395
Preeceville*	Town	1,074	Preeceville No. 334
Prelate	Village	164	Happyland No. 231
Primate	Village	45	Eye Hill No. 382
Prince	Organized Hamlet	50	Meota No. 468
Prince Albert*	City	34,291	Prince Albert No. 461
Prud'homme	Village	203	Bayne No. 371 / Grant No. 372
Punnichy	Village	317	Mount Hope No. 279
Qu'Appelle*	Town	648	South Qu'Appelle No. 157
Quill Lake	Village	439	Lakeside No. 338
Quinton	Village	107	Mount Hope No. 279
Rabbit Lake	Village	87	Round Hill No. 467
Radisson*	Town	401	Great Bend No. 405
Radville*	Town	735	Laurier No. 38
Rama	Village	90	Invermay No. 305
Raymore*	Town	625	Mount Hope No. 279
Redvers*	Town	917	Antler No. 61
Regina*	City	178,225	Sherwood No. 159
Regina Beach*	Town	1,039	Lumsden No. 189
Rhein	Village	175	Wallace No. 243
Riceton	Organized Hamlet	75	Lajord No. 128
Richard	Village	20	Douglas No. 436
Richmound	Village	193	Enterprise No. 142
Ridgedale	Village	85	Connaught No. 457
Riverhurst	Village	143	Maple Bush No. 224
Riversedge	Organized Hamlet	43 (2004 est.)	Corman Park No. 344
Riverside Estates	Organized Hamlet	221 (2004 est.)	Corman Park No. 344
Rocanville*	Town	887	Rocanville No. 151
Roche Percee*	Village	162	Coalfields No. 4
Rockglen*	Town	450	Poplar Valley No. 12
Rockhaven	Village	30	Cut Knife No. 439
Rose Valley*	Town	395	Ponass Lake No. 367
Rosetown*	Town	2,471	St. Andrews No. 287
Rosthern*	Town	1,504	Rosthern No. 403
Rouleau*	Town	434	Redburn No. 130
Ruddell	Village	25	Mayfield No. 406
Runnymede	Organized Hamlet	28	Cote No. 271
Rush Lake	Village	65	Excelsior No. 166
Ruthilda	Village	20	Grandview No. 349
Saltcoats*	Town	494	Saltcoats No. 213
Sand Point Beach	Organized Hamlet (resort)	40	Marquis No. 191
Sandy Bay	Northern Village	1,092	NSAD
Sandy Beach	Municipal District	83	District of Katepwa
Sarnia Beach	Organized Hamlet (resort)	17	Sarnia No. 221
Saskatchewan Beach	Resort Village	120	McKillop No. 220
Saskatoon*	City	196,811	Corman Park No. 344.
Sceptre	Village	136	Clinworth No. 230
Scott*	Town	110	Tramping Lake No. 380
Scout Lake	Organized Hamlet	20	Willow Bunch No. 42
Sedley	Village	322	Francis No. 127
Semans	Village	267	Mount Hope No. 279
Senlac	Village	50	Senlac No. 411
Shackleton	Village	10	Miry Creek No. 229
Shamrock	Village	35	Shamrock No. 134
Shaunavon*	Town	1,775	Grassy Creek No. 78
Sheho	Village	148	Insinger No. 275
Shell Lake	Village	172	Spiritwood No. 496
Shellbrook*	Town	1,276	Shellbrook No. 493
Shields	Resort Village	142	Dundurn No. 314
Shipman	Organized Hamlet	15	Torch River No. 488
Silton	Village	94	Longlaketon No. 219
Simmie	Organized Hamlet	10	Bone Creek No. 108
Simpson	Village	194	Wood Creek No. 281
Sintaluta*	Town	145	Indian Head No. 156
Sled Lake	Northern Settlement	35	NSAD
Sleepy Hollow	Organized Hamlet (resort)	16	Meota No. 468
Smeaton	Village	178	Torch River No. 488
Smiley	Village	55	Prairiedale No. 321
Snowden	Organized Hamlet	30	Torch River No. 488
Sorenson's Beach	Organized Hamlet (resort)	10	McKillop No. 220
South Lake	Resort Village	47	Marquis No. 191
Southend	Northern Settlement	35	NSAD
Southey*	Town	693	Cupar No. 218
Sovereign	Village	52	St. Andrews No. 287
Spalding	Village	261	Spalding No. 368
Speers	Village	71	Douglas No. 436
Spiritwood*	Town	907	Spiritwood No. 496
Spring Bay	Organized Hamlet (resort)	5	McKillop No. 220
Spring Valley	Hamlet		Terrell No. 101
Springside*	Town	525	Orkney No. 244
Springwater	Village	20	Biggar No. 347
Spruce Bay	Organized Hamlet (resort)	10	Spiritwood No. 496
Spruce Lake	Village	70	Mervin No. 499
Spy Hill	Village	213	Spy Hill No. 152
St. Benedict	Village	109	Three Lakes No. 400
St. Brieux	Village	505	Lake Lenore No. 399
St. George's Hill	Northern Hamlet	102	NSAD
St. Gregor	Village	121	St. Peter No. 369

Saskatchewan's Communities

Community	Type	Population	Location
St. Isidore-de-Bellevue	Organized Hamlet	95	St. Louis No. 431
St. Joseph's	Organized Hamlet	68	South Qu'Appelle No. 157
St. Louis	Village	474	St. Louis No. 431
St. Walburg*	Town	672	Frenchman Butte No. 501
Stanley Mission*	Northern Settlement	124	NSAD
Star City*	Town	482	Star City No. 428
Stenen	Village	110	Clayton No. 333
Stewart Valley	Village	101	Saskatchewan Landing No. 167
Stockholm	Village	303	Fertile Belt No. 183
Stony Rapids	Northern Hamlet	189	NSAD
Stornoway	Village	10	Wallace No. 243
Storthoaks	Village	99	Storthoaks No. 31
Stoughton*	Town	720	Tecumseh No. 65
Strasbourg*	Town	760	McKillop No. 220
Strongfield	Village	42	Loreburn No. 254
Sturgis*	Town	627	Preeceville No. 334
Success	Village	51	Riverside No. 168
Summerfield Beach	Organized Hamlet (resort)	26	Meota No. 468
Sun Valley	Resort Village	111	Marquis No. 191
Sunset Beach	Organized Hamlet (resort)	21	Grayson No. 184
Sunset Cove	Resort Village	24	McKillop No. 220
Sunset View Beach	Organized Hamlet (resort)	35	Mervin No. 499
Swan Plain	Organized Hamlet	15	Clayton No. 333
Swift Current*	City	14,821	Swift Current No. 137
Sylvania	Organized Hamlet	56	Tisdale No. 427
Tadmore	Organized Hamlet	30	Buchanan No. 304
Tantallon	Village	110	Spy Hill No. 152
Taylor Beach	Organized Hamlet (resort)	32	North Qu'Appelle No. 187
Tessier	Village	30	Harris No. 316
Theodore	Village	381	Insinger No. 275
Thode	Resort Village	133	Dundurn No. 314
Timber Bay	Northern Hamlet	108	NSAD
Tisdale*	Town	3,063	Tisdale No. 427
Tobin Lake	Resort Village	45	Moose Range No. 486
Togo	Village	143	Cote No. 271
Tompkins	Village	191	Gull Lake No. 139
Torquay	Village	231	Cambria No. 6
Tramping Lake	Village	85	Mariposa No. 350
Trevessa Beach	Organized Hamlet (resort)	15	Meota No. 468
Tribune	Village	35	Souris Valley No. 7
Trossachs	Organized Hamlet	30	Brokenshell No. 68
Tuffnell	Organized Hamlet	15	Foam Lake No. 276
Tugaske	Village	116	Huron No. 223
Turnor Lake	Northern Hamlet	155	NSAD
Turtle Lake Lodge	Organized Hamlet		Parkdale No. 498
Turtle Lake South Bay	Organized Hamlet (resort)	16	Mervin No. 499
Turtleford*	Town	465	Mervin No. 499
Tuxford	Village	97	Marquis No. 191
Tway	Organized Hamlet	15	Invergordon No. 430
Uhls's Bay	Organized Hamlet (resort)	5	McKillop No 220
Unity*	Town	2,243	Round Valley No. 410
Uranium City*	Northern Settlement	201	NSAD
Usherville	Organized Hamlet	15	Preeceville No. 334
Val Marie	Village	134	Val Marie No. 17
Valparaiso	Village	20	Star City No. 428
Vanguard	Village	187	Whiska Creek No. 106
Vanscoy	Village	345	Vanscoy No. 345
Vantage	Organized Hamlet	0	Sutton No. 103
Veregin	Village	83	Sliding Hills No. 273
Vibank	Village	381	Francis No. 127
Viceroy	Organized Hamlet	35	Excel No. 71
Viscount	Village	272	Viscount No. 341
Vonda*	Town	322	Grant No. 372
Wadena*	Town	1,412	Lakeview No. 337
Wakaw*	Town	884	Hoodoo No. 401
Wakaw Lake	Resort Village	30	Hoodoo No. 401
Waldeck	Village	333	Excelsior No. 166
Waldheim*	Town	889	Laird No. 404
Waldron	Village	15	Grayson No. 184
Wapella*	Town	354	Martin No. 122
Warman*	Town	3,481	Corman Park No. 344
Waseca	Village	169	Eldon No. 471
Watrous*	Town	1,808	Morris No. 312
Watson*	Town	794	Lakeside No. 338
Wawota*	Town	538	Wawken No. 93
Webb	Village	51	Webb No. 138
Wee Too Beach	Resort Village	20	Sarnia No. 221
Weekes	Village	65	Porcupine No. 395
Weirdale	Village	90	Garden River No. 490
Weldon	Village	219	Kinistino No. 459
Welwyn	Village	108	Moosomin No. 121
West End	Resort Village	10	Fertile Belt No. 183
West Chatfield Beach	Organized Hamlet (resort)	10	Meota No. 468
Westview	Organized Hamlet	53	Stanley No. 215
Weyakwin	Northern Hamlet	183	NSAD
Weyburn*	City	9,534	Weyburn No. 67
White Bear	Organized Hamlet	15	Lacadena No. 228
White City*	Town	1,013	Edenwold No. 158
White Fox	Village	436	Torch River No. 488
Whitewood*	Town	947	Willowdale No. 153
Wilcox	Village	322	Bratt's Lake No. 129
Wilkie*	Town	1,282	Buffalo No. 409
Willow Bunch*	Town	395	Willow Bunch No. 42
Willowbrook	Village	47	Orkney No. 244
Windthorst	Village	228	Chester No. 125
Wiseton	Village	111	Milden No. 286
Wishart	Organized Hamlet	121	Emerald No. 277
Wollaston Lake	Northern Settlement	129	NSAD
Wolseley*	Town	766	Wolseley No. 155
Wood Mountain*	Village	40	Old Post No. 43
Wroxton	Hamlet	49 in 1996	Calder No. 241
Wymark	Organized Hamlet	148	Swift Current No. 137
Wynyard*	Town	1,919	Big Quill No. 308
Yarbo	Village	93	Langenburg No. 181
Yellow Creek	Village	55	Invergordon No. 430
Yellow Grass*	Town	422	Scott No. 98
Yorkton*	City	15,107	Orkney No. 244
Young	Village	299	Morris No. 312
Zealandia*	Town	111	St. Andrews No. 287
Zelma	Village	40	Morris No. 312
Zenon Park	Village	231	Arborfield No. 456 / Connaught No. 457

COMMUNITY AND REGIONAL COLLEGES.
The community colleges in Saskatchewan were the forerunners of what are known today as the province's regional colleges. In 1969 an advisory committee chaired by Ron Faris toured the province to obtain input from people on a so-called "middle-range educational program." The recommendation of the Faris Report was to establish a grid of community centres of learning where local facilities, local instructors, and local resources would be utilized to provide learning opportunities as determined by the people themselves. It was a community development approach to adult education previously unseen in Canada. Based in many respects on the "folk schools" of Europe, these colleges eventually had 500 volunteer groups called the "local college committees," which surveyed the region and told the colleges what the people wanted. Programs varied from university and technical school credit classes to courses of general interest, such as arts and crafts and local history.

The colleges program began in November 1972 when the Department of Continuing Education hired four developers: John Oussoren for the Yorkton-Melville area; Ken Rodenbush for the Humboldt area; Jake Kutarna for LaRonge and the northern area; and Stewart McPartlin for the Swift Current and southwest area. These were considered pilot projects: the developers were to nominate members for the first community college boards, make recommendations on the size of the regions to be served, and establish volunteer groups to advise on programs to be offered.

The Community Colleges Act was passed in May 1973, and the first four colleges went into operation. Rev. Bud Harper, a member of the first Faris Advisory Committee, chaired in 1974 a colleges review committee that launched the new series of five rural colleges. In 1975, the urban colleges in Moose Jaw, Regina, Saskatoon, and Prince Albert were officially created, and boards were appointed. In the case of Prince Albert, the Prince Albert Regional Community College, under the chairmanship of Bishop Short of the Anglican Church and Principal Lorne Sparling, was brought into the provincial college structure. In the north, the La Ronge Regional Community College was divided into three distinct college regions in 1975, adding the West Side Community College (Buffalo Narrows) and North East Regional College (Creighton). In 1976, the governments of Saskatchewan and Alberta agreed on a college centred in Lloydminster, the Lakeland College. This brought the total number of community colleges to fifteen. The Saskatchewan Indian Community College was officially created in 1976–the first such Aboriginal post-secondary learning institution in Canada–and later was renamed the Saskatchewan Institute of Indian Technologies. The last area in the province in which the govern-ment provided direct delivery programming for adults, the Athabasca region, was transferred in 1983 from the Northern Continuing Education Branch to La Ronge Regional College. In 1987, the three northern colleges were amalgamated under "Northlands College."

A count of program offerings and attendees at courses in 1976 indicated over 100,000 adults enrolled in over 10,000 courses. The informal motto of the college system was "The community is the college and the college is the community."

In 1979, the Saskatchewan Community Colleges Trustees Association undertook a review of the community college system. The resulting report, *A Better Tomorrow*, recommended that government significantly expand the role of colleges. In 1986, articulation of a renewed policy framework for adult education in Saskatchewan, *Preparing for the Year 2000: Adult Education in Saskatchewan*, implemented several new initiatives to provide increased access to adult education programming. In 1987, the Regional Colleges Act replaced the Community Colleges Act (1972), changing the name of the colleges to "Regional Colleges"; with the change in name came changes in mandate. The new Act enabled colleges to offer: university and technical institute courses provided by way of a contract; programs that prepare individuals or provide education with respect to health or social issues; programs paid wholly or partly by business, non-government organizations, or government agencies; career services; adult basic education, and literacy and upgrading programs; and other educational activities that the Lieutenant-Governor-in-Council may prescribe in the regulations.

The new mandate for colleges excluded general interest and recreation courses, and enabled the colleges to offer credit programs near rural residences, thereby altering the philosophy of colleges. More employment and skill training courses were to be offered, and interest programs were to be cost-recovered by tuitions. The influence for this change came largely from then Education Minister Lorne Hepworth's consultations on post-secondary education, carried out in 1986, which identified credit offerings on a decentralized basis as a priority. Community organizations were encouraged to take on general interest courses previously offered by community colleges.

The new legislation provided for eight regional colleges: Carlton Trail Regional College, Cumberland Regional College, North West Regional College, Prairie West Regional College, Parkland Regional College, North East Regional College, Southeast Regional College, and Northlands College. One other significant change in 1987 resulted in the amalgamation of four urban colleges in Regina, Moose Jaw, Saskatoon, and Prince Albert with the technical institutes in those cities. These four urban institu-tions became known as campuses of the **SASKATCHEWAN INSTITUTE OF APPLIED SCIENCE AND TECHNOLOGY** (SIAST). Today, regional colleges play a vital role in providing adult and post-secondary training opportunities across Saskatchewan. They offer a wide range of programs and services including adult basic education, work-based training, and credit programs, some of which are brokered through SIAST and Saskatchewan's two universities. Increasingly, more people across Saskatchewan have access to a variety of educational programs without leaving their home communities.

Jake Kutarna

COMMUNITY CLINICS. Saskatchewan's community clinics were born amid turmoil and controversy in July 1962. Most of the province's doctors withdrew services on July 1, and Saskatchewan was plunged into a bitter 23-day strike. The CCF government had introduced North America's first public, tax-financed health insurance system, and the medical profession was opposed.

As the strike loomed, however, some doctors and consumers organized to provide health care during the crisis. In Saskatoon, doctors Margaret Mahood and Joan Whitney-Moore began to see patients on July 3 in a threadbare room in an office building. Dr. **SAMUEL WOLFE**, an internationally known physician and researcher, and a professor of medicine at the **UNIVERSITY OF SASKATCHEWAN**, resigned his academic post to work at the clinic and was later to become its first medical director. Similar community health associations were organized in twenty-five centres, including Regina, Moose Jaw, Nipawin, Biggar and Wynyard. In Prince Albert, Dr. Orville Hjertaas was a pioneer and enduring presence in the community health clinic. The strike ended with the signing of the Saskatoon Agreement on July 23. Under terms of that agreement, doctors were to be paid on a fee-for-service basis. That created immediate difficulties for the co-operative clinics, which would have preferred global budgets, encouraging a different relationship between medical professionals and their consumer boards.

There were continuing strained relations between doctors who had opposed **MEDICARE** and those who supported it, particularly those who chose to work in the clinics. A number of physicians new to the province, including Dr. Reynold Gold of the Saskatoon clinic, were denied hospital privileges for months.

Despite these and other difficulties, community clinics have provided health services for forty years, and continue to exist in five Saskatchewan centres. They offer a comprehensive range of services to 85,000 people in settings where medical professionals work in formal co-operation with citizen boards.

This type of practice has frequently been lauded by governments, but less often supported financially. With the endorsement of primary health care in 2003 by two prestigious government reports (the so-called Romanow Report, and the Senate report popularly known as the Kirby Report), community health centres or their equivalent may come into their own at last.

Dennis Gruending

COMMUNITY DEVELOPMENT CO-OPERATIVES.
Falling commodity prices on the world market and Saskatchewan's dependence on agricultural exports resulted in calls to diversify the province's economy in the 1980s. The subsequent formation of Small Business Loans Associations (SBLAs) and Rural Development Corporations (RDCs) were attempts to address these rural development issues. SBLAs raise investment capital to establish new businesses in their communities. The number of these associations grew rapidly after the program's inception in May 1989. Within a year there were eighty-nine of them, and by 1996 the number of co-operative SBLAs stood at 147. There was a massive rise in assets over the same period–from $107,000 to $3.2 million. Since that time there has been a gradual decline in numbers, assets, revenue, and member equity, although large numbers of these organizations continue to operate in Saskatchewan communities. Spin-off benefits of SBLA activity include the creation and maintenance of jobs in areas where employment opportunities are limited. At their peak in 1996, there were a total of 488 jobs created and maintained in smaller communities around the province.

Rural Development Corporations are the other type of co-operative found within the community development sector. Their role has been to assist member organizations with the identification, promotion, and implementation of development projects in rural areas. Although 65% of them were co-operatives in the mid-1990s, there has been since then a lack of growth in numbers, revenues, and assets that can be explained by their declining role in economic development as they are gradually replaced by Regional Economic Development Authorities. REDAs are voluntary, community-owned organizations designed to assist regional development. Although they generally function as co-operatives, maintaining the principle of one member, one vote, they do not have a formal co-operative structure. It can be expected that most, if not all, RDCs will eventually disappear as they give way to the REDA model.

Nora Russell

COMMUNITY ECONOMIC DEVELOPMENT.
Community economic development is an approach through which communities can work together to build capacities to pursue common economic, social and environmental objectives. Community economic development strategies attempt to link solutions to the economic needs of individuals with the broader

well-being of the community as a whole.

"Community" may mean a specific geographical community, or a group sharing a common interest or set of values. Community economic development processes help community members develop leadership, articulate a common vision, and develop the individual and collective skills necessary to implement that vision. Successful community strategies are able to create broad-based, sustainable partnerships of stakeholders within and around the local community. Community-based economic development processes respect the character of specific communities as well as their belief systems and social and cultural values. For example, community economic development organizations have been active since the 1990s in inner-city areas of Regina, Saskatoon and Prince Albert to help local citizens develop and implement solutions to the social and economic problems of their neighbourhoods.

Saskatchewan's long tradition of community economic development is rooted in the co-operative movement that gave the province's producers and consumers a greater voice in the decisions that impacted both on their interests and their local communities. Like the co-operative movement, commu-

nity economic development operates on principles of local ownership and decision making, self-determination, inclusiveness, autonomy, and governance of initiatives by the community itself. Saskatchewan may be unique in its reliance on a blend of individual enterprise and initiative with co-operative and collective community action.

Rob Watts

COMMUNITY PASTURES.
In Saskatchewan, a large portion of the land has been classified as protected lands. Some of these lands are designated as national and provincial parks, others are organized as community pastures. In fact, both federal and provincial governments have established such pastures to promote environmental and agricultural sustainability, in addition to provide grazing and breeding opportunities to agricultural producers. In 2001, there were sixty federal and fifty-six provincial community pastures in Saskatchewan (*see* Figure CP-1). They occupied 2.57 million acres (1.04 million hectares) of land, most of which is under native pastures. These lands are used primarily for grazing cattle. In fact, federal community pastures have served 2,540 producers with 73,000 cattle and 72,000 calves, per annum, on average. Similarly, on

CANADIAN PLAINS RESEARCH CENTER MAPPING DIVISION / ADAPTED FROM PASTURES BRANCH, SASKATCHEWAN AGRICULTURE AND FOOD, 2002

Figure CP-1. Provincial community pastures.

provincial community pastures 2,500 producers had 68,000 cattle and 53,000 calves during the summer grazing period. In addition, producers also pasture ewes, horses and colts on these facilities.

These community pastures create a number of benefits to producers. The cattle brought by producers receive professional herd management, through the expertise of experienced pasture managers and riders. These staff members have access to the latest information on livestock research and technology. Herd health related issues are dealt with quickly and in a professional manner. For small producers, these pastures provide a vehicle for enjoying economies of size without having to incur a large capital investment. Through releasing producers' time for managing their cattle herd, this program also helps diversify farm operations, particularly for the small-sized operations.

Community pastures provide major benefits. Although benefits to producers, as noted above, have long been recognized, other benefits occurring to society at large have not been. In addition, various levels of the governments also benefit from such activities. Community pastures are protected areas and economic activities are regulated to the point

that environmental benefits are not compromised. These provide pristine environment on a large contiguous tract of land. This enables the federal government to fulfill the commitment made under international treaties related to protected areas and biodiversity. Community pastures, being a natural (or semi-natural) ecosystem, are multifunctional in nature. This multi-functionality is present through provision of ecological functions, such as life-support functions, economic functions leading to many commercial activities, and social functions including information through scientific research and educational roles, and through meeting spiritual needs of the society. A recent study identified and estimated value for some of the above functions of the community pastures. Five categories of social benefits were identified: pasture-use related activities; provision of social goods; improving economic development of local and surrounding areas; provision of ecosystem functions; and protection of a natural and social resource base. In addition, pursuit of various commercial activities has been permitted on these community pastures, making them a source of revenue to the federal government.

The pasture-use related activities included soil

conservation, conversion of land use from cropland to grazing land, and improvement in the health of animals. On the issue of health improvement for cattle grazed on community pastures, it was concluded that such benefits are not significant. This was based on interviews of federal community pasture managers, and patrons of such pastures.

Total economic benefits of community pastures were estimated to be $2,248 per 100 acres or almost $22 per acre (Table CP-1). Of these, almost half are in terms of private benefits—received for grazing cattle and other animals, and for breeding services. These benefits were in the neighborhood of $11 per acre. A portion of total benefits also accrue to the governments, either through direct revenues generated by other activities on these pastures, or through reduced amount spent on subsidies to producers.

Society benefits from community pastures in several ways. Soil conservation can reduce many social costs, and therefore preserves a valuable resource to society. Many members of society use these community pastures for outdoor recreation and wildlife related recreational activities. Since they are under better management, community pastures can sequester more soil carbon; this becomes a valuable resource, particularly in the context of climate change. In total, social benefits add up to $982 per 100 acres. Thus, community pastures are a valuable resource both in terms of providing benefits for grazing and breeding for producers, but also in terms of bringing benefits to society at large through creating many streams of direct and indirect benefits.

The existence of private, social and fiscal benefits from community pastures has a number of important implications. First and foremost is the implication for establishing user fees for private benefits. If a portion of the total benefits from a natural ecosystem (such as the community pastures) is received by society at large, it would be unfair to charge all costs to the private users only. The level of social and fiscal benefits should be taken into account in estimating user fees for grazing and breeding. A second implication of these results is for privatization of such resources. In the past suggestions have been made to privatize the breeding and grazing services. If such were to happen, the question of continuation of social benefits from these ecosystems might be in jeopardy. Preservation of large contiguous spaces under these federal and provincial community pastures has an intrinsic value that should not be sacrificed for reducing government expenditures. *S.N. Kulshreshtha*

COURTESY OF AGRICULTURE AND AGRI-FOOD CANADA

Community pasture program.

FURTHER READING: Kulshreshtha, S.N., and G.G. Pearson. 2002. *Estimation of Cost Recovery Levels on Federal Community Pastures under Joint Private and Public Benefits. Research Report.* Saskatoon: Department of Agricultural Economics, University of Saskatchewan.

Table CP-1. Benefits from Federal Community Pastures in Saskatchewan per 100 acres

Type of Benefits	Value $ per 100 acres		
	Private	Society	Fiscal
Grazing and Breeding	$1,127		
Soil Conservation, Land Use		$182	$20
Wildlife and other recreation		$144	
Community Development		$217	
Carbon sequestration, Biodiversity and Habitat preservation		$434	
Ecosystem Protection		$5	
Commercial Activities			$119
TOTAL	$1,127	$982	$139

COMMUNITY SCHOOLS. The Community Schools program was introduced by the province of Saskatchewan in 1980. Community Schools were part of a strategy to address Aboriginal poverty and to provide enhanced educational opportunities for First Nation and **MÉTIS** peoples. Other elements of the strategy included: teacher education (*see* **SASKATCHEWAN URBAN NATIVE TEACHER EDUCATION PROGRAM**), curriculum development, teacher in-service, and equity programs. Initially, eleven elementary schools were designated in the core areas of Regina, Saskatoon and Prince Albert in the highest need areas of these cities according to Statistics Canada census data. The objective was to provide additional supports and opportunities to elementary schools, and to encourage communities and families to become more involved in their children's education, helping them to stay in school and achieve success in life.

Throughout the 1980s and into the mid-1990s the Community Schools program experienced moderate growth and expansion. In 1996, a new policy framework, *Building Communities of Hope*, was released; it affirmed the comprehensive, holistic Community Schools model and philosophy, and resulted in the incremental expansion of schools designated as "Community Schools." The Community Schools approach received affirmation with the 2001 Role of the School Task Force Report recommendation that all Saskatchewan schools should adopt the Community Schools philosophy. This led to a doubling of the number of Community Schools, and to enhanced community education funding to the Northern Community Schools program.

Designated Community Schools have continued to expand and comprise over 12% of the provincial schools in Saskatchewan. As of 2004, ninety-eight Community Schools have been established across the province. A number of additional school divisions and schools are adopting the Community Schools philosophy and choosing–without official designation or recognized funding from the province–to implement this model in their school community.

Pat Erhardt

COMMUNITY SERVICE CO-OPERATIVES. Community service co-ops meet a variety of needs, including health care, fire protection, funeral services, water systems, and adult education. Saskatchewan was home to forty-eight of these co-operatives at the end of the 1990s, with a total membership of nearly 33,000. This sector experienced a growth in numbers of more than 23% over that decade, mainly in health care and water systems; it is financially healthy, with significant increases in membership, assets, members' equity, number of employees, and capital investment.

Total membership grew by nearly 14% over the decade, while assets for the sector stood at $6.9 mil-

lion, up from the $4.9 million reported in 1989. Member equity nearly doubled over the same period, from $2.2 million to $4.1 million, and the number of employees grew by 20%. With an increase in the wage bill of only 3.8%, however, the average salary actually fell from $24,693 to $21,369. Revenues increased by more than 28% during the 1990s–to $15.6 million–while capital investment rose even more impressively, from $279,000 in 1989 to $1.3 million ten years later.

There were thirteen health care co-operatives registered with the Department of Justice at the end of the 1990s, up from the eight reporting in 1989. Total membership grew from 24,845 to 28,658 people, most of whom were accounted for by the three largest community clinics–those in Regina, Saskatoon, and Prince Albert. Revenues rose over the decade from $11.2 million to $14.1 million, while assets increased by nearly 19%–to $4.7 million–and liabilities decreased by 14%–to $2.2 million. At $239,000, the surplus in the late 1990s was 17% higher than that reported in 1989, and employment climbed as well, from 242 to 312 paid positions. With the wage bill remaining virtually unchanged over the decade at about $6.6 million, however, this resulted in a decrease in the average annual wage from $27,272 to just over $21,000.

The number of fire protection co-operatives remained small but consistent over the 1990s, dropping by only one–from nine to eight–while membership over the same period increased from 2,170 to 2,536. Revenues increased by 54%–from $112,000 to $173,000–while the surplus dropped from $21,000 in 1989 to a $32,000 loss at the end of the next decade. The number of employees increased from six to seven part-time workers, and the wage bill rose from $12,000 to $19,000; the low average wage indicates that few working hours are necessary to maintain these co-operatives. Capital investment and liabilities in fire protection co-operatives remained extremely low over the decade, while both assets and member equity rose, by 29% and 28% respectively.

Never an area of high activity in the province, funeral co-operatives declined by 50% during the 1990s–from four to two–and membership fell by more than 70% during the same period. Wages, revenue, surplus, assets, and member equity all dropped significantly as well, indicating the low priority for this type of co-op in Saskatchewan.

Although water supply co-operatives are not numerous in Saskatchewan, their numbers increased significantly during the 1990s, from four in 1989 to seventeen a decade later, indicating growing interest in this area. Membership also increased, from 71 to 250 individuals. Assets held by the water system co-operatives during the same period at first increased dramatically, from $53,000 in 1989 to $919,000 in 1996, and then fell off to $681,000 by the end of the

decade, while liabilities climbed from $47,000 to $87,000. Capital investment fell from $52,000 to a mere $1,000, suggesting minimal maintenance costs to existing systems purchased earlier in the decade. Revenue was reported at only $3,000 in 1989, but by the end of the 1990s that figure had grown to $73,000, and member equity increased even more significantly, from $5,000 in 1989 to $594,000 ten years later. Interestingly, these businesses operated throughout the 1990s with only volunteer labour.

Adult education organizations operate in a number of areas, including co-operative education and development, promotion of the arts, and preservation of culture. The number of adult education co-operatives in the province remained consistent at five throughout the 1990s, although membership decreased by 31% from 417 to 286. The number of employees increased from six to twelve, but the drop in the wage bill from $115,000 to $6,000 suggests that by the end of the 1990s the term "employee" was being used quite loosely and that these individuals were receiving honorariums rather than wages. Revenues dropped as well, from $308,000 to $268,000, while assets plummeted from $259,000 to $37,000. There was a corresponding fall in liabilities and member equity, which dropped from $199,000 to $31,000 over the course of the decade.

Other community services consisted of only three co-operatives at the end of the 1990s–a drop of one from ten years earlier–which provided support to those with mental disabilities as well as services to enhance the quality of life for disadvantaged individuals. Despite their small number, these organizations enjoyed significant increases in membership, revenue, assets, and member equity during the decade; but they also saw a large rise in liabilities. Membership rose by 31%, from 826 to 1,085 people, while revenue more than quadrupled, from $210,000 to $957,000. Assets grew almost five times–from $96,000 in 1989 to $463,000 at the end of the 1990s–and member equity increased from $91,000 to $373,000 over the same period. Although liabilities also increased significantly, at $90,000 they were still relatively low and did not adversely affect the financial health of these organizations.

Nora Russell

FURTHER READING: Fulton, Murray, et al. 1991. *Economic Impact Analysis of the Co-operative Sector in Saskatchewan*, Research Report Prepared for Saskatchewan Department of Economic Diversification and Trade; Herman, Roger and Murray Fulton. 2001. *An Economic Impact Analysis of the Co-operative Sector in Saskatchewan: Update 1998*; Ketilson, Lou Hammond, et al. 1998. *The Social and Economic Importance of the Co-operative Sector in Saskatchewan*, Research Report Prepared for Saskatchewan Department of Economic and Co-operative Development.

COMMUNITY SOCIAL SERVICES. Saskatchewan has evolved from a rural society with relatively stable communities and family relationships, to a much more urbanized province in which citizens are mobile, time-pressured, and faced with numerous challenges to everyday life as individuals and families. Over time, a number of social services have developed or been organized in order to help people address some of the challenges of life. In Canada there are very few direct social services that are operated by the federal government. The government of Saskatchewan offers a significant range of services such as income support for individuals, employment programs, child protection services, etc. These tend to be programs where uniform standards of service from community to community are important, or where programs have elements of enforcement that may not be appropriate for governments to delegate to neighbours and communities.

The majority of non-mandatory social services are organized within individual communities, and tailored to some degree to the specific needs of those communities. Where uniform service is not critical to good outcomes for citizens, local social service organizations and providers have certain advantages over government: services may be more easily tailored to local circumstances, and local volunteer resources may be engaged in management and governance, thus increasing the effective value of public investment in such services. In many cases community social services are operated by a non-profit organization governed by a board of directors. Boards of directors are legally responsible for the affairs of the organization, including hiring and supervision of a senior staff member, usually an executive director, who in turn hires and manages the other staff of the agency.

There are several possible funding sources for community social services. Most social service organizations receive at least a portion of their funding, directly or indirectly, from federal, provincial, or municipal governments. Other sources of funds include private charities and foundations, donations from members or the general community, fund raising, community events, and user fees for service. Some community social agencies are affiliated with provincial or national organizations that provide a recognized organizational name, infrastructure, and full or partial funding. Some may also take part in local fund-raising, co-operative groups such as the United Way.

The range of social services available in Saskatchewan varies considerably from community to community. One service that is widely provided is support for children and adults with disabilities. Such services may range from residential services to rehabilitation support, developmental activities, training, and employment initiatives. Examples of this type of service are Cosmopolitan Industries in Saskatoon, the Redvers Activity Centre, or Estevan Diversified Services.

Most major centres have a women's shelter, like Transition House in Moose Jaw or Shelwin House in Yorkton for women leaving abusive domestic relationships. Most urban centres also have personal counseling services such as Family Service Regina or Saskatoon's Catholic Family Services. Some communities have after-hours social service and crisis intervention services such as Swift Current's Southwest Crisis Services or Regina's Mobile Crisis Services. Larger centres have services to help in the readjustment of those who have been in conflict with the law—the major organizations being the **JOHN HOWARD SOCIETY** for men, and the **ELIZABETH FRY SOCIETY** for women.

Most larger communities have a food bank or similar organization that gathers, organizes, and distributes surplus local food supplies and collects cash or food donations from the public to help lower-income people meet their food needs. Examples of this type of services are the Regina Food Bank and the Moose Jaw & District Food Bank. Some food banks are co-located with meal services, clothing thrift shops, budget counseling, and other supports to people managing on low and modest incomes.

There are a number of community social service agencies that serve the needs of children and youth. Early childhood development programs exist in most major centres. Agencies like the Rainbow Youth Centre in Regina or the Lashburn Teen Wellness Centre provide help to youth experiencing difficulties. In a number of communities, Big Brothers and Big Sisters organizations match adult volunteers with children and youth to provide mentoring and personal guidance. Local social service organizations play important roles in the management and administration of public housing assets and programs, and in capacity-building services like employment preparation, job referral, and workplace support.

Certain social services that are otherwise provided by the province are offered by community social service agencies in First Nations communities. First Nations child and family service agencies, for example, were organized initially to provide child welfare services to reserve communities that are beyond the province's jurisdiction. These agencies now also work co-operatively with provincial agencies when community members live off-reserve. First Nations governments are expanding the range of social services they provide to members of their communities, both on and off-reserve.

Some community social service agencies define at least part of their mandate as advocacy on behalf of low-income or disadvantaged people. One example would be Regina's Welfare Rights Centre that provides financial trusteeship services, helps individuals with income support problems, and advises government on income support policy issues. Other agencies like the Saskatchewan Association of Rehabilitation Centres act in part as advocates for systemic change in government and community approaches to disability supports. Some agencies act as umbrella organizations for a variety of programs and services. Yorkton's Society for the Involvement of Good Neighbours (SIGN), for example, is involved in the operation of group homes, and coordination of services such as budget counseling, sexual assault services, early childhood intervention programs, child and youth mentoring, and other responses to community needs. This agency is also involved in mental health supports, family/school programs, parent education and other services, and is often a leader in community development initiatives.

Since most community social services receive some form of support from government, changes in government approaches to helping citizens can affect the organization of services in communities. One emerging trend is individualized, self-managed help for individuals to purchase services, as opposed to subsidies to service providers. This approach supports self-reliance and independence, and gives the service consumer more choice and power in controlling service quality and outcomes.

In some service areas private social service providers play a role. Private service providers are active, particularly in larger centres, in some aspects of disability support, and private suppliers also operate some types of residential care service. The vast majority of out-of-home child-care services purchased by Saskatchewan families is supplied by private individuals and small businesses. As a general trend, governments are moving gradually away from direct provision of services to citizens by government employees. As a result, the community social service sector has grown significantly in the past few decades. To the extent that social services are developed further in the future, this is likely to take place in most cases through local agencies and service providers.

Because public funds flow to these services, governments, acting on behalf of taxpayers, are looking for ways to ensure that services are efficient and appropriate, without unduly interfering in the details of the management of local social services. One emerging approach is for government and service providers to agree on strategic goals and on measurable outcomes that can be tracked to assess the effectiveness of the service. While there is progress to be made in the coordination and focus of the overall sector, there is little doubt that locally organized social services and personal supports, whether provided by private or non-profit operations, are important to the quality of life of communities and their members. *Rick August*

COMMUNITY SUPPORT FOR PEOPLE WITH INTELLECTUAL DISABILITIES.

At the time the province of Saskatchewan was formed, people with intellectual disabilities, then referred to as "mentally retarded," were treated in the same way as those with psychiatric disabilities. The provincial Mental Health Act of 1936 was the first recognition of a distinction between intellectual deficiency and mental illness. In the mid-20th century it was common to house, educate, and care for people with intellectual disabilities in institutions. In 1947, the Saskatchewan Training School for people with intellectual disabilities opened in Weyburn as a temporary facility, until in 1955 it moved to Moose Jaw, where it is now known as Valley View Centre. By 1961 the Saskatchewan Training School was filled beyond capacity, and a second facility was opened in Prince Albert.

Even in this period of institutionalization, parent groups were beginning to organize to develop educational services for children with intellectual disabilities. In 1955, parents formed the Saskatchewan Association for Retarded Children (now known as Saskatchewan Association for Community Living or SACL), with an initial focus on children's education. Through the 1960s parent groups expanded their focus to include the development of community organizations to support adults with intellectual disabilities. A network of sheltered employment workshops and activity centres, group homes, and developmental centres emerged as communities experimented with alternatives to the institutionalization of people who were labeled mentally retarded.

During the 1950s and 1960s, the federal government increased its financial support to provincial social programs. Among the areas of expansion was the Vocational Rehabilitation of Disabled Persons (VRDP) Act of 1961, which for the first time provided federal cost-sharing to help the province develop programs for people with disabilities that were "rehabilitative" with respect to employment and daily living. In 1968, the Saskatchewan Association of Rehabilitation Centres (SARC) was formed by eight community agencies operating vocational workshops for people with intellectual disabilities. Over the years SARC has expanded its membership and significantly increased the services, supports, and employment opportunities available to people with intellectual disabilities in Saskatchewan communities. One of its most notable achievements is the development of SARCAN Recycling, a substantial non-profit business venture that is now a major employer of Saskatchewan people with disabilities.

An important work by Wolf Wolfensberger (1972), *Normalization*, was influential on directions for federal and provincial investment, and on how the provincial government organized its services and supports. A single provincial administration

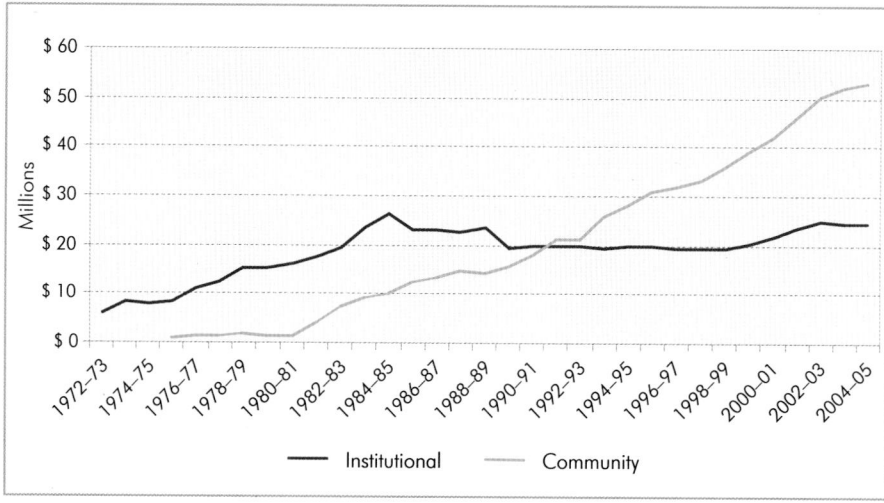

Figure CSID-1. Trend in provincial residential and support expenditures for people with intellectual disabilities, 1974-2005.

was created in 1972 to coordinate and strengthen government health, social service, and education services to people with intellectual disabilities, with a focus on community-based options. During this period, government and community agencies expanded training on the job programs to provide people with disabilities with more opportunities to develop their labour market attachment. By the 1980s, communities had demonstrated significant capacity and willingness to accommodate the needs of people with intellectual disabilities. A trend towards deinstitutionalization was well established, and many people who were previously seen as lifetime residents of institutions were moving into communities. An emerging focus on the potential of each individual resulted in further development of individualized community program options for people with disabilities. In 1985, the Canadian Charter of Rights and Freedoms explicitly recognized persons who were mentally retarded as full citizens.

The decade of the 1990s saw continued growth and development of community-based services for people with intellectual disabilities, with a continued focus on supported employment programs and services. There were also advances in research and policy development, and milestones in recognition of people with intellectual disabilities as citizens, workers, and members of communities. As the province enters its second century, our perspective on people with intellectual disabilities continues to evolve. The *Disability Action Plan*, proposed by the Saskatchewan Council on Disability Issues in 2001, expresses a vision of "a society that recognizes the needs and aspirations of all citizens, respects the right of individuals to self-determination, and provides the resources and supports necessary for full citizenship." Mainstream service systems are now becoming more inclusive of people with intellectual disabilities.

In 1974 there were about 1,200 individuals with

significant intellectual disabilities living in institutional settings, compared with approximately 1,400 living in community settings. Twenty years later the estimated number of people with intellectual disabilities living in communities had increased to over 3,200, and the number in institutions had declined to fewer than 400. Trends in institutional versus community living attest to the success of Saskatchewan communities at developing supports for people with intellectual disabilities. (*See* Figure CSID-1 above.)

James Sanheim

FURTHER READING: Federal/Provincial/Territorial Ministers Responsible for Social Services. 1998. *In Unison: A Canadian Approach to Disability Issues*. Ottawa: Human Resources Development Canada, catalogue number SP-113-10-98E; Saskatchewan Council on Disability Issues. 2001. *Saskatchewan's Disability Action Plan*.

COMPETITIVE GAMES.

Competitive games simulating the Olympics have become part of Saskatchewan's cultural fabric since Canada's centennial year of 1967. The inception of the nationwide Jeux Canada Games has been followed by more regional and specialized gatherings: Western Canada Summer Games, Saskatchewan Games, and North American Indigenous Games. Jeux Canada Games are staged for both summer and winter sports, each in four-year cycles; Winter Games began in 1967, and Summer Games in 1969. Athletes from all ten provinces and Canada's territories converge on the host site to compete in a variety of individual and team sports, usually those contested in the Olympics. Maximum age limits ranging from 17 to 23 are enforced; rather than give elite athletes an opportunity to compete, the Jeux Canada Games strives to give promising young competitors the experience of a multi-sport competition in a provincial team context. In addition to striving for medals within their own sports, athletes also collect points for their province: the province that earns the most points is awarded the Canada Games flag, while the province or territory that shows the greatest improvement from the past four years receives the Centennial Cup. Saskatchewan has never placed in the top three of team standings, but it won the Centennial Cup at the 1983 Winter Games in Saguenay/Lac St. Jean, Quebec and at the 1989 Summer Games in Saskatoon. Among the Saskatchewan athletes who have used the Jeux Canada Games as a springboard to international success are pentathlete **DIANE JONES KONIHOWSKI**, speed skater **CATRIONA LE MAY DOAN**, and hockey player **HAYLEY WICKENHEISER**. Saskatoon played host to the second Winter Games in 1971 despite the lack of an acceptable facility for Alpine events. This was overcome with the creation of Mount Blackstrap, a man-made mountain created from landfill, 32 km south of Saskatoon near Dundurn. Saskatoon was also the venue for the 1989 Summer Games. Regina will play host to the 2005 Summer Games, which are expected to draw 4,500 athletes and support staff from August 6–20, with some events to be staged at Moose Jaw, Lumsden, and Last Mountain Lake.

Western Canada Summer Games (WCSG) are held every four years in the odd-numbered year between Jeux Canada Summer Games. Athletes from the four western provinces and three Canadian territories take part. The WCSG's primary goals are to provide a competition that supports the provincial and territorial sports organizations' development plans, and to prepare athletes for the Jeux Canada Games and other athletic gatherings. From 2,200 to 2,400 competitors and support staff take part in Olympic sports for individual medals and team points. Four of the first eight WCSG have been staged in Saskatchewan: Regina, 1975 and 1987; Saskatoon, 1979; and Prince Albert, 1999.

Regina and Saskatoon are ineligible to stage the Saskatchewan Games in order to promote province-wide involvement and to afford smaller communities the benefits of new or upgraded facilities. The Saskatchewan Games, begun in 1972, maintain a similar schedule to the Canada Games in that both summer and winter games are staged in four-year cycles. Saskatchewan Summer and Winter Games now occur in the same years as their Olympic counterparts. Summer Games have been held in Moose Jaw (1972), Swift Current (1976), Estevan (1980), North Battleford (1984), Melfort (1988), Prince Albert (1992), Moose Jaw (1996), Yorkton (2000), and Weyburn (2004). Winter Games have been held in North Battleford (1974), Moose Jaw (1978), Prince Albert (1982), Yorkton (1986), Melville/Ituna (1990), Kindersley (1994), Nipawin (1998), and Humboldt (2002). Athletes, coaches, managers and trainers number from 1,700 to 2,000; the team concept is achieved by dividing the province into nine zones.

The North American Indigenous Games (NAIG) are to resume in 2005 in Buffalo, NY, after an eight-year hiatus. NAIG were held in Edmonton in 1990, Prince Albert in 1993, and Victoria, BC in 1997. The 1999 event slated for Fargo, ND was cancelled. Participation grew from about 3,000 athletes and officials in 1990 to 5,000 in 1993 and 8,000 in 1997. Sports are contested in four age groups: Bantam (13 and under), Midget (14 to 15), Juvenile (16 to 17) and Senior (18 and over); heavy emphasis is also placed on the concurrent cultural festival. Prince Albert drew representation from all ten Canadian provinces, the Yukon and Northwest Territories, as well as eight American states. *John Chaput*

COMPLEMENTARY/ALTERNATIVE MEDICINE. Complementary/ alternative medicine (CAM) encompasses therapies, healing systems, and self-help practices which do not currently have widespread acceptance within the conventional medical system. They are referred to as *alternative* when they are used instead of conventional treatments, and *complementary* when they are used in conjunction with conventional treatments. Many CAM therapies have their roots in ancient healing traditions which include acupuncture, Traditional Chinese Medicine (TCM), homoeopathy, massage therapy, natural health products (such as herbal remedies), Reiki, yoga, taiji, shiatsu, and meditation. Traditional Aboriginal Healing is a distinctive and unique health system that has much in common with CAM.

The National Institute of Health classifies CAM treatments into the following categories: *Physical*, e.g., massage therapy; *Biological*, e.g., herbal remedies; *Psychological*, e.g., meditation; *Energetic*, e.g., Reiki; and *Complete healing systems*, e.g., Traditional Chinese Medicine. The best available estimates suggest that CAM therapies are used by roughly 25% to 50% of the population in most western industrialized countries, including Canada. Rigorous research into CAM has accelerated sharply over the past decade, funded by Health Canada, the Canadian Institutes for Health Research (CIHR), and other

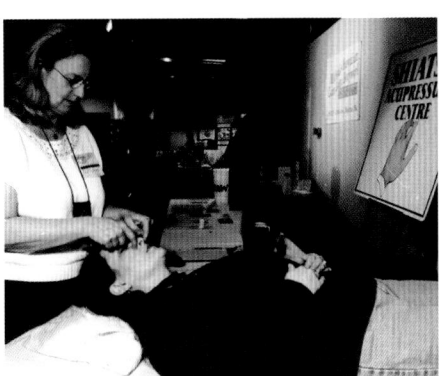

Susan Cooke administers Shiatsu treatment to Alison MacDonald of Regina, January 1999.

major granting agencies. Preliminary conclusions regarding the safety and efficacy of some CAM treatments for specific conditions are now available.

Until recently, most CAM practices have lacked reliable mechanisms for quality assurance, such as professionalization, standards, accreditation, formal credentialling, licensing, and self-regulatory bodies. This in turn has made it difficult to differentiate between legitimate, credentialled providers and those who are incompetent or fraudulent. Several CAM therapies will likely achieve status as self-regulating professions in the coming decade. In Saskatchewan, techniques have been disseminated primarily through informal channels, and have been modified through accumulated experience. Some therapies have their roots in Aboriginal healing systems; others derive from European folk-healing traditions.

Some evidence now suggests that each system of health care has its relative strengths: conventional medicine for acute conditions, infectious diseases, and emergency treatment; complementary/ alternative medicine for the prevention and treatment of many chronic conditions involving pain, fatigue, anxiety, depression, and sleep disturbance. Integrative medicine, involving the selective incorporation of evidence-based CAM therapies in conjunction with conventional medicine, is currently the focus of several national, provincial, and local initiatives involving research, education, and clinical practice. *Michael Epstein*

COMPUTER-GENERATED PLANT ANIMATION. A former **UNIVERSITY OF REGINA** computer science professor, Przemyslaw Prusinkiewicz, received international acclaim for a model, called L-system, which he developed with several of his graduate students at the University of Regina. It incorporates the biological principles of plant growth to achieve a realistic simulation of plants and flowers, and their growth patterns, for computer animations. A practical application of the computer model was used in the movie *Toy Story*. The Association for Computing Machinery bestowed the 1997 SIGGRAPH Computer Graphics Achievement Award upon Prusinkiewicz for his cutting-edge work "pertaining to modeling and visualizing biological structures," and recognized him for making complex natural environments a visible part of computer graphics. As a result of his research, plants can be modeled with unprecedented visual and behavioural fidelity to nature. Przemyslaw Prusinkiewicz now teaches computer science at the University of Calgary. He began his work on plant modeling at the University of Regina, and held visiting professorships at Yale University and the École Polytechnique Fédérale de Lausanne. He was also a visiting researcher at the University of Bremen and the Centre for Tropical Pest Management in Brisbane. *Joe Ralko*

CONGREGATION OF THE MOST HOLY REDEEMER (REDEMPTORISTS).

The Congregation of the Most Holy Redeemer, commonly called Redemptorists and indicated by the Latin acronym "CSSR," is a religious community of Catholic priests and brothers founded by Saint Alphonsus Liguori in Naples in 1732 to preach to the destitute. The first Redemptorists arrived in North America from Austria in 1832 and in Canada soon after. In 1904, Belgian Redemptorist Achille Delaere, a Roman Catholic priest working in St. Augustine's, Brandon, Manitoba, established St. Gerard's monastery in Yorkton to care for the large Galician (Polish and Ukrainian) population in Saskatchewan's and Manitoba's prairie parkland. In 1906, convinced that Greek Catholics, Ruthenians and, later, Ukrainian Catholics required services in their own language and rite, he persuaded his superiors to allow him to adopt the Byzantine rite, to preach in Ukrainian, and to use Old Church Slavonic instead of Latin as the liturgical language.

When the French Canadian, Belgian, and Ukrainian-speaking Redemptorists transferred the care of St. Gerard's to the English Canadian Redemptorists (1913–91), the latter, under the influence of Father George Daly, CSSR, expanded their activities to care for Holy Rosary Cathedral in Regina (1915–27) and then St. Joseph's in Moose Jaw (1927–2001). A Montreal-born Redemptorist, Gerald Murray, became the first Roman Catholic bishop of Saskatoon and invited the Redemptorists to take over St. Mary's there (1935). At present, the Roman Catholic Redemptorists maintain their monastery in Saskatoon, and give religious and spiritual missions, retreats, and conferences on moral theology and medical ethics throughout the prairies.

Other Belgian Roman Catholic Redemptorists had joined Delaere, and together they left St. Gerard's to establish St. Mary's Ukrainian Catholic Church in Yorkton (1913). They invited other religious communities to Yorkton to help in building the church. The identification of Yorkton with the Eastern-rite Redemptorists was completed by the establishment in 1961 of the Yorkton Province, a distinct unit within the world-wide Redemptorist Congregation. The Yorkton Redemptorists also founded monasteries in Ituna (1919), Saskatoon (1954), and Wynyard (1966), and cared for other parishes when needed. While the number of Ukrainian Catholic Redemptorists has always been low—now no more than two dozen members—several priests have been appointed to exarchates and eparchies (bishoprics) in the Ukrainian Catholic Church in England, France, Germany, Australia, the United States, as well as Canada.

The Eastern-rite Redemptorists' influence on Ukrainian Catholic life and thought in Saskatchewan was strengthened by the hundreds of thousands of items of religious literature published by the Redemptorist-owned Redeemer's Voice Press in Yorkton from 1922. The Roman Catholic Redemptorists had their own press in eastern Canada (1928-68), but now support their American Redemptorist confreres at Liguori Publications in Missouri. Saskatoon and Yorkton have become the two main centres of Redemptorist activity in Saskatchewan. *Paul Laverdure*

CONSERVATION.

Conservation is the process whereby groups and agencies attempt to maintain BIODIVERSITY at as high a level as possible, for the good health of the environment in which all the species, including humans, live. It is a combination of protection of present-day natural habitats and of restoration of some disturbed and simplified environments to as close to their original natural state as possible. The conservation movement began as a 20th century reaction to the impact of human population growth and 19th century industrial practices. At first, it centered on individual species, usually BIRDS or MAMMALS, which had been seen to diminish from large populations to near extinction, often within the lifetime of one human: the American BISON nearly became extinct, and the passenger pigeon did. Now conservation recognizes that it is the habitat or natural community, made up of a large number of species, which must be protected. The recognition that natural habitats throughout the world were being lost led to the development of natural reserves, such as Canada's National Park system, and to a variety of government agencies and citizens' groups (*see* CONSERVATION AGENCIES). Conservation activities range from private individuals who retain wetlands on their farm (rather than filling and plowing them) in order to preserve the breeding habitat of a wide range of plants and animals, to international treaties on cessation of whaling.

Saskatchewan, like many jurisdictions, began its conservation activities in reaction to the visible reduction in numbers of migrating birds. The province is on one of the major migratory pathways between the breeding grounds of the arctic tundra and boreal forest, and the wintering grounds further south. The Last Mountain Lake National Bird Sanctuary is located at the north end of the lake, a staging area for large flocks of migrating waterfowls and other species. It was established in 1887, when the flocks began to be reduced by hunting pressure. It is one of the oldest public sanctuaries in the world, the first in Canada, and now the home of the LAST MOUNTAIN BIRD OBSERVATORY. The Migratory Bird Protection Act, between Canada and the United States, was the first international treaty for the protection of wild species.

In Saskatchewan, areas designated as reserves or parks offer a range of protection to habitats. These are the province's Protected Areas. This pro-

tection varies, since the areas are often also used for recreation, grazing, or mineral exploration and exploitation. These areas range from international projects (e.g., the Chaplin Shorebird Sanctuary; Nature Conservancy of Canada sites), through national initiatives (the two national parks; national wildlife areas; national bird sanctuaries), to provincial lands (ecological reserves; provincial forests; provincial parks; provincial wildlife areas) and lands protected by local groups such as Nature Saskatchewan or by municipalities. A number of these sites are recognized by the International Union for Conservation of Nature (IUCN). *Diane Secoy*

FURTHER READING: Gollop, B. 1999. "Protected Wildlife Areas." Pp. 167–68 in *Atlas of Saskatchewan*. Saskatoon: University of Saskatchewan.

CONSERVATION AGENCIES.

Conservation, or activity to preserve or reconstruct the diversity of natural habitats, is the work of many people. It ranges from the individual working alone to combined efforts by national and international agencies. Ranchers who maintain natural grasslands pastures, and city gardeners who plant gardens with local species which support native birds and insects are small-scale conservationists who are important because of their numbers. Many communities have natural history and horticultural societies which are active in preserving habitats that support native plant species. At the provincial level, Nature Saskatchewan, the Native Plant Society, the Saskatchewan Econetwork and the SASKATCHEWAN WILDLIFE FEDERATION raise funds for projects to protect and study specific habitats, such as wetlands, which support a large number and variety of species. The provincial government's Wetlands Corporation as well as Saskatchewan Environment and Resource Management study the management of the health of the habitats. National bodies, such as the Nature Conservancy of Canada, act to conserve native grasslands and wetlands. Saskatchewan also is the site for projects funded by international bodies such as Ducks Unlimited and the World Wildlife Fund. There is an increasing tendency for these various levels of agencies to co-operate in funding and overseeing conservation and restoration. For example, the important Bird Area of Chaplin Lake, a major staging area for migrating tundra-nesting shorebirds, is supported by the town, the province, the federal government, and international agencies. *Diane Secoy*

CONSERVATION AREAS.

Last Mountain Lake Sanctuary in Saskatchewan was created in 1887 and was the very first wildlife area not only in Canada but also in North America. Since that time Saskatchewan's network of conservation areas has expanded to ensure that representative areas of the province's natural and cultural heritage are sustained for present and future generations. Areas are conserved for a multitude of purposes including sustaining ecological goods and services, biodiversity conservation, providing areas for scientific study and research, as benchmarks or control sites for ecological health monitoring, the provision of areas of public use for recreation, education and interpretation, and spiritual and aesthetic fulfillment. To fully represent the varied roles of protected areas and to address threats to biodiversity, Saskatchewan committed in 1997 to the development of a Representative Areas Network (RAN) that would serve to conserve samples of the range of biodiversity found in Saskatchewan, and as benchmarks or long-term reference points against which the impact of management practices being applied outside of the network could be compared.

Approximately 9% (57,600 km²) of Saskatchewan's territory is managed under 30 different types of conservation categories. Almost 70% of those lands are within provincial conservation categories and 23% are federal lands (*see* Figure CA-1). The majority of conservation areas (57,553 km²) are included with Saskatchewan's Representative Areas Network (RAN).

Over the past 100 years, human perception of the vastness and apparent inexhaustibility of resources of the province has fundamentally changed. The lessons learned include: interactions between the environment (air, water, land and biota) and human activities (social, cultural and economic systems) are inseparable parts of an ecosystem; the importance of critical connections at the continental and macro ecosystem scales; the realization that what was happening elsewhere outside of a region such as the prairies, a province and, at times, a nation could have critical impacts within the region; the thresholds and breaking points of critical ecosystems and habitats could be breached under the pressure of human-generated stresses; that seemingly minor or negligible by-products of humans activities could accumulate in ecosystems and have significant negative long-term impacts on

habitats and species (for example, that pollution levels and impacts of land use could reach such inordinate levels of magnitude)—that is, humans through their activities and decisions are a major driving force of ecological change; that entire ecosystems could become so extensively degraded and altered at the continental and macro ecosystem scales; that wildlife and habitats would reach unexpected degrees of economic and social importance; and that to protect species, it is critical to conserve their habitats and the ecosystems that contain those habitats.

From those lessons learned, it has become clear that conservation can only be accomplished if humans think, plan and act in terms of ecosystems. Ecosystem-based management is a practice and philosophy aimed at integrated management of natural landscapes/seascapes, ecological processes, physical and biological components and human activities to maintain ecological health and integrity of an ecosystem. Saskatchewan has adopted an ecosystem planning approach in which land/water management is conducted according to geographic areas (ecozones and **ECOREGIONS**) defined by their ecosystem structure and functions. Conservation areas are distributed throughout Saskatchewan's four ecozones and eleven ecoregions. Approximately 3% of the Boreal Shield ecozone is contained within a park or conservation area, most notably the Athabasca Sand Dunes (*see* **GREAT SAND HILLS**), **LAC LA RONGE** and **CLEARWATER RIVER** provincial parks. Approximately 8% of the Boreal Plain ecozone is managed within parks and conservation areas, principally national and provincial parks and Wildlife Habitat Protection Act lands. These include **PRINCE ALBERT NATIONAL PARK** and Duck Mountain, Greenwater Lake, Narrow Hills, and Meadow Lake provincial parks. Just under 9% of the Prairie ecozone is in some form of park or conservation area. Canada's only national park dedicated to the conservation of grasslands, **GRASSLANDS NATIONAL PARK**, occurs in this zone.

David A. Gauthier and Lorena Patino

FURTHER READING: Acton, D., G.A. Padbury, C.T. Stushnoff, L. Gallagher, D. Gauthier, L. Kelly, T. Radenbaugh and J. Thorpe. 1998. *The Ecoregions of Saskatchewan.* Saskatchewan Environment and Resource Management, and the Canadian Plains Research Center, Regina, Saskatchewan; Gauthier, D.A. and L. Patino. 1998. "Saskatchewan's Natural Heritage: Provincial and Federal Lands Classified by International Conservation Management Categories." Poster map. CPRC Press, University of Regina, Saskatchewan; Hammermeister, A.M., D. Gauthier and K. McGovern. 2001. *Saskatchewan's Native Prairie: Statistics of a Vanishing Ecosystem and Dwindling Resource.* Native Plant Society of Saskatchewan Inc., Saskatoon, Saskatchewan; Saskatchewan Environment. 2002. *Saskatchewan's Representative Areas Network–Progress Report.* Fish and Wildlife Branch, Government of Saskatchewan, Regina, Saskatchewan.

CONSERVATIVE PARTY OF CANADA. The Conservative Party, a right-wing federal political party, was formed on December 8, 2003, with the merger of the Canadian Alliance and the Progressive Conservatives. The merger represented the uniting of the major factions of Canadian conservatism. In the 2004 election, the party, led by former Canadian Alliance leader Stephen Harper, improved on the results of both parties, electing 99 members of Parliament. In Saskatchewan they captured 13 of the province's 14 seats.

Brett Quiring

CONSERVATIVE PARTY OF SASKATCH-EWAN. The Conservative Party has played a significant role in Saskatchewan politics since the beginning, although it has rarely been successful electorally; in fact, it has won only three of twenty-four elections since 1905, has suffered through decades as a "third" party in a competitive two-party province, and has changed its name several times in an attempt to broaden its appeal. Quite often it has been leaderless, without enough candidates or money to provide credible competition to its rivals, and today is one short step from oblivion. The history of the party falls into three distinct eras, which describe not only its electoral competitiveness but also the major changes in its philosophy and policies. The first of these, from 1905 to 1934, was the party's "traditional" period, during which it focused its attention on issues of major concern to conservatives all across the west: immigration, education, and natural resources. Indeed, those three sections of the federal legislation which brought Saskatchewan into Confederation so upset the first Conservative leader, **FREDERICK HAULTAIN**, that he changed the name of the party to "Provincial Rights," and fought the 1905 and 1908 elections promising to rewrite these sections more in Saskatchewan's interests. Although the party reverted to the name "Conservative" for the 1912 election, Haultain and the two men who followed him as leader—**WELLINGTON WILLOUGHBY** and **DONALD MACLEAN**—continued to campaign for greater provincial control over immigration as well as the province's resources and education system. However, neither these issues nor any others could shake the Liberal party's grip on power and the Conservatives' share of seats in the Legislature dwindled from 32% to 5% over the five elections held between 1905 and 1921.

It was not until the party chose **J.T.M. ANDERSON** as its leader in 1924 that Conservative fortunes began to brighten. Anderson was prepared to cooperate with anyone opposed to the Liberals, and by the election of 1929 had united the most important of these groups behind single candidates in several constituencies. At the same time he was also able to use the racial and religious animosity created by the **KU KLUX KLAN** to bring the customary Conservative

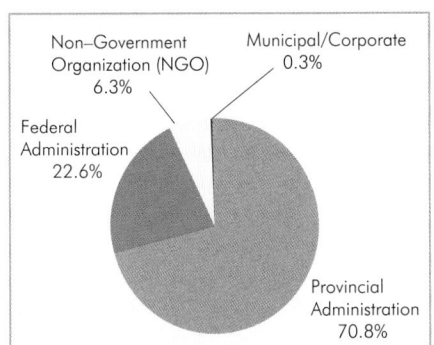

Figure CA-1. Managed conservation areas in Saskatchewan (does not include private stewardship lands).

issues of immigration and education to the forefront of the campaign, as well as attack the Liberals for their continued failure to gain control of the province's resources. The Conservatives did not win the most seats in 1929, but they won enough to defeat the Liberals in the Legislature with the help of the Progressive and Independent MLAs. Once Premier, Anderson negotiated within a year a transfer of the province's resources from Ottawa to Regina, and also altered the School Act to ensure the predominance of English and the non-sectarian nature of Saskatchewan's public schools. Unfortunately for the Conservative party, Anderson's "Co-operative government" took office just as the **GREAT DEPRESSION** began: when they faced the electorate in 1934, not a single Conservative nor any supporter of the government won a seat.

Thus began the second period in the history of the Conservative party of Saskatchewan–one of frustration, decline, and unremitting electoral defeat. In the nine elections held between 1938 and 1971, the Conservatives elected only one member (in 1964) and the party sank as low as 2% of the popular vote. Nevertheless, this also proved to be the most "progressive" era in the party's history. Forced to meet the growing threat from the new CCF, the Conservatives adopted in the late 1930s a radical platform which called for state intervention in a host of areas ranging from protection of the family farm to the provision of **MEDICARE**. Anderson's successor, **JOHN DIEFENBAKER**, first used the new platform in the 1938 election; it continued to be used, adapted to changing circumstances, by all the leaders who followed him until the end of the period: Rupert Ramsay, **ALVIN HAMILTON**, **MARTIN PEDERSON**, and Ed Nasserden. During this time, however, despite changing its name to "Progressive" Conservative, the provincial party was no longer a viable contender for power: it had been supplanted by the CCF, and elections were now fought between the Liberals and the CCF (later the NDP). The Conservative party was no longer seen as a realistic alternative to either of its rivals.

Several factors led to a resurgence of the Conservative Party in the 1970s–the beginning of the third period in its history. The success of the national party in the 1950s and 1960s finally spilled over into provincial politics, and Saskatchewan Liberals suffered from their links to the Trudeau government in Ottawa, which showed itself unresponsive to western concerns. Internationally, the philosophy of less government and more private enterprise achieved some success in Margaret Thatcher's Britain and Ronald Reagan's America; and two new, dynamic leaders of the provincial party–**DICK COLLVER** and **GRANT DEVINE**–adopted this "neo-conservatism" wholeheartedly. Collver rejuvenated the party and made it the major alternative to the ruling NDP by the late 1970s. Devine built on

this success, led the party to an overwhelming victory in 1982, winning over four-fifths of the seats in the Legislature, and held on to power, albeit with a reduced majority, in 1986. By 1991, however, a steady diet of privatization and cuts to social programs, together with an ever-increasing provincial debt, alarmed sufficient voters to defeat the government. Shortly thereafter, many former Ministers and Conservative MLAs were charged with fraud and misuse of public funds, and several were convicted. Neither of Devine's successors, Rick Swenson or William Boyd, could convince voters that the Conservative party deserved another chance at power, and at the 1995 election only five of fifty-eight Conservatives won seats. Two years later, a party conference decided to cease all activities for the next two provincial elections, after which time a further judgment would be made as to whether the party should be revived. In these circumstances, Boyd and the remaining Conservative MLAs joined with a like number of disaffected Liberal members to form the Saskatchewan Party. The success or failure of this experiment will most probably determine the fate of the Conservative party in Saskatchewan in the foreseeable future. *Patrick Kyba*

FURTHER READING: Pitsula, J.M. and K. Rasmussen. 1990. *Privatizing a Province: The New Right in Saskatchewan.* Vancouver: New Star Books.

CONSTRUCTION INDUSTRY LABOUR RELATIONS ACT, 1992: *see* **LEGISLATION IN SASKATCHEWAN**

CONSUMER AND DOCTOR-SPONSORED MEDICAL CARE ASSOCIATIONS. Consumer and doctor-sponsored medical services associations offered pre-paid medical care to Saskatchewan residents prior to the establishment of **MEDICARE** in 1962. In order for Saskatchewan's urban residents to obtain pre-paid health services, the Mutual Medical and Hospital Benefit Association Act was passed in 1938, enabling any ten or more persons to incorporate a health insurance plan. The first association to organize under the Act was a co-operative headed by H.L. Fowler, manager of Consumer's Co-operative Refineries, which in 1939 began collecting 80 cents a month from its members for the provision of medical care. The association attempted to hire doctors to work on salary, but switched to a fee-for-service basis to accommodate local doctors. Similar associations were established in Saskatoon, Prince Albert and Melfort. They were important participants in the debate on the form that a provincial medical services plan should take in the 1940s. In their submissions to the 1944 **SIGERIST COMMISSION** they opposed fee-for-service remuneration and insisted on a substantive role for ordinary citizens in the administration of health services, arguing that a

provincial scheme should be financed predominantly from personal contributions rather than from general revenues. With the exception of the Saskatoon association, which rendered medical services up until 1962, the consumer plans either died or merged with the more successful doctor-sponsored plans.

The consumer-sponsored medical services associations were both the forerunners of Saskatchewan's **COMMUNITY CLINICS** and also an important impetus to the establishment of the doctor-sponsored insurance schemes. The Regina District Medical Society organised Medical Services Incorporated (MSI) under the Companies Act in 1939 to compete with the Regina medical co-operative. MSI offered patients free choice of physician and remunerated doctors on a fee-for-service basis. It was the first doctor-sponsored insurance scheme established outside of Ontario, and was modeled on Dr. J.A. Hannah's Toronto-based Associated Medical Services Incorporated. In 1949 MSI and the Regina Mutual Medical Benefit Association merged to form Group Medical Services (GMS).

The Saskatoon District Medical Society established Medical Services Incorporated (Saskatoon) in 1946, to deter the plans of the thriving Saskatoon Medical and Hospital Benefit Association to expand to larger rural centres, and to establish a group practice clinic in Saskatoon with 40 salaried physicians. When in 1959 the Douglas government announced its plans to implement medicare, MSI provided medical services to 217, 000 persons in both urban and rural Saskatchewan, and GMS had an enrollment of 91,000 persons. Of the consumer-sponsored plans, only the Saskatoon mutual remained, but its enrollment had declined to less than 5,000 persons.

The success of the doctor-sponsored plans, which they viewed as a viable and preferred alternative to a government-controlled medical care scheme, emboldened organized medicine to withdraw its support for a state-financed medical services plan in 1950. Although the last of the consumer-sponsored medical care plans were superseded by the implementation of Medicare, their enabling legislation–the Mutual Medical and Hospital Benefit Association Act–permitted the organization of community clinics during the 1962 doctors' strike. *Gordon S. Lawson*

CONTRACEPTIVE PATCH. Research methodology developed in 2000 by Dr. Roger Pierson, a **UNIVERSITY OF SASKATCHEWAN** professor of obstetrics and gynecology, helped establish the contraceptive patch as a more effective means of birth control than the contraceptive pill. Johnson and Johnson now market the patch under the Ortho Erva brand name. Dr. Pierson's methodology was subsequently adopted as a standard for measuring birth control effectiveness in Europe and the United States. There were two key phases of the testing: comparing the effectiveness of the patch with traditional oral contraceptives, and determining the most effective size and dose. A problem with oral contraceptives is that the release of hormones fluctuates dramatically throughout the day; by comparison, the patch releases a steady flow of hormones throughout the entire week. Because the hormone dose is constant, follicle growth in the ovaries is halted much sooner; while follicles may be reduced to 17 mm or more with some pills, with the contraceptive patch they are inhibited to a size of only 6 mm, making the release of an egg that much more unlikely. Another problem with the pill is that is must be taken every day at the same time; unlike oral contraceptives, the patch does not require daily attention, and is simply placed on the body once a week. *Joe Ralko*

COOPER (HUNT), MARJORIE (1902–84).
Marjorie Lovering was born in Winnipeg on May 28, 1902, and moved to Regina in 1907. At the age of 17 she began a teaching career in a one-room schoolhouse in McCord. In 1925 she left teaching and married Ed Cooper. She spent the following three decades raising two daughters and volunteering for several organizations. Cooper served as president of the Regina YWCA (1941–43) and the Regina COUNCIL OF WOMEN (1946–48). Cooper was appointed to the Labour Relations Board in 1945 and the Public Service Commission in 1951. In 1952 Cooper won a seat in the provincial Legislature for the CCF. She was the third female member of the Saskatchewan Legislative Assembly, served four terms, and retired from politics undefeated in 1967. Although never appointed to Cabinet, Cooper acted as an unofficial women's advocate and sat on numerous committees including Crown Corporations, Cabinet

SASKATCHEWAN ARCHIVES BOARD R-A 5352

Marjorie Cooper.

Planning, Health and Welfare, Public Accounts, and the Law Amendments Committees. Her life and career provide clear examples of some of the ways in which women promoted change between the two waves of the feminist movement in Canada. Predeceased by her husband, Marjory Cooper married Wilfred Hunt. She died September 12, 1984, in Regina. *C. Marie Fenwick*

FURTHER READING: Fenwick, C. Marie. 1999. "A Political Biography of Marjorie Cooper Hunt, 1902–1984," MA Thesis, University of Regina; —. 2002. "Building the Future in a Steady but Measured Pace: The Respectable Feminism of Marjorie Cooper," *Saskatchewan History*, 54 (1): 18–34.

CO-OPERATIVE COLLEGE OF CANADA.
Based in Saskatoon from 1973 to 1987, the Co-operative College of Canada (CCA) was a national centre for co-operative education and research. It was established to provide co-op business training and to teach co-op principles. Although the CCA itself was short-lived, its formative years in Saskatchewan go back to the late 1930s and early 1940s, when there was a strong push and a practical need for an educational link to the co-operative movement. In 1955, a small centre called the Co-operative Institute was opened in Saskatoon; by 1959, the Institute had evolved into the Western Co-operative College. In the early 1970s the College faced financial uncertainty, and hoped that securing national memberships, building stronger partnerships with regional members, and extending its programs beyond the West would bring much-needed stability. Thus in 1973 the Western Co-operative College was reincorporated as the Co-operative College of Canada. The CCA focused intently on developing regional outreach and extension programs while gradually expanding its curriculum to include manager training, youth and Aboriginal programs, and courses for international students. In a short time the CCA became a national research centre for Canada's co-operative movement. For more than a decade it produced volumes of publications, research, and outreach programs. Yet the CCA could not escape the economic realities of the time: its co-operative members began to drift away from traditional co-op values and practices; competition from other adult-education programs in Canada increased; and the struggle to survive in a developing global economy became increasingly difficult. In 1987 the Co-operative College of Canada merged with the Co-operative Union of Canada to form the Canadian Co-operative Association. *Iain Stewart*

FURTHER READING: Crewe, J. 2001. *An Educational Institute of Untold Value: The Evolution of the Co-operative College of Canada*. Saskatoon: Centre for the Study of Co-operatives, University of Saskatchewan.

CO-OPERATIVE COMMONWEALTH FEDERATION (CCF).
The Co-operative Commonwealth Federation (CCF) had a significant impact on Saskatchewan in the 20th century. Its history can be divided into three parts: the GREAT DEPRESSION years of the 1930s; the DOUGLAS era during the 1940s and 1950s; and the move into the NEW DEMOCRATIC PARTY (NDP) in the early 1960s. The Saskatchewan CCF was born amidst the devastation of the Great Depression. In 1932 the United Farmers of Canada, Saskatchewan Section (UFC) and the provincial Independent Labour party (ILP) met jointly in Saskatchewan and created the Farmer-Labour party. Its program emphasized protection against foreclosures, socialization of finance, and a public health system. In 1934 it became a part of the newly formed national CCF and was now the Saskatchewan CCF. The party was unsuccessful in the 1934 and 1938 provincial elections. During this formative stage, the CCF was primarily a radical agrarian response to an economic crisis that left an indelible imprint on the province. M.J. COLDWELL, a labour spokesman, was the party's first provincial leader, but the UFC was the focus of party activity. GEORGE WILLIAMS, FRANK ELIASON and LOUISE LUCAS played especially critical roles; in 1935 Williams became CCF leader.

Support for the CCF in Saskatchewan increased after 1940. A comprehensive policy was formulated, and party organization was strengthened. The abilities of the new leader, T.C. Douglas, became especially apparent in the 1944 election as he led the CCF to a landslide win. Four more electoral victories followed, in 1948, 1952, 1956 and 1960. Under Douglas the CCF faced the realities of power, and moved beyond the combination of despair and idealism which had given rise to the party in the 1930s. Both public and private enterprise played important roles as resources were developed, electricity brought to farms, and a system of social services established. CCF leaders such as the provincial treasurer, C.M. FINES, typified the Douglas era, as did a group of indispensable public servants including A.W. JOHNSON, TOMMY SHOYAMA, and ALLAN BLAKENEY. The Douglas years drew to a close with plans to implement universal public health insurance in Saskatchewan.

The national CCF became a part of the New Democratic Party in 1961. Premier Douglas left Saskatchewan to lead the new party. Although the Saskatchewan CCF supported the move into the NDP, it did so with reluctance and hesitancy; to preserve its identity it temporarily maintained the CCF name, and candidates ran under that label in the 1964 provincial election. The party, led by WOODROW LLOYD, was defeated, and the CCF era in Saskatchewan thus ended. However, the party was not gone: the Saskatchewan NDP, in all but name, was the old CCF. Also, during the next generation many would identify the NDP with Canadian medicare, a program conceived and delivered by the Saskatchewan CCF. *George Hoffman*

FURTHER READING: Johnson, A.W. 2004. *Dream No Little Dreams: A Biography of the Douglas Government of Saskatchewan, 1944–1961*. Toronto: University of Toronto Press; Lipset, S.M. 1950. *Agrarian Socialism: The Co-operative Commonwealth Federation in Saskatchewan*. Berkeley: University of California Press; McLeod, T.H. and I. Mcleod. *Tommy Douglas: The Road to Jerusalem*. Edmonton: Hurtig.

CO-OPERATIVE FISHERIES LIMITED. Co-operative Fisheries Limited (CFL) was created in 1959 by an Act of the Saskatchewan Legislature to provide fish processing, marketing and other services to northern Saskatchewan fishermen, mostly of First Nation and MÉTIS descent. CFL initially was a transitional organization, created out of an existing provincial CROWN CORPORATION (the Saskatchewan Fish Marketing Service) and, as part of the northern co-operative development program of the CCF provincial government, was mandated to become a true co-operative. Through the 1960s CFL had fish sales of about $1.5 million a year, with about eighteen local fishermen's co-operatives as members, which in turn had about 1,500 member producers. In 1966 its debt to the provincial government was repaid in full, and several government-appointed board members were replaced by elected fishermen board members. In 1971, CFL became a true co-operative, being fully owned and controlled by its members.

When CFL experienced financial problems in the 1970s, its functions were taken over by a federal Crown corporation, the Freshwater Fish Marketing Corporation (FFMC). Members decided to dissolve CFL in 1981. They used their share capital to set up a lobbying group, the Saskatchewan

Commercial Fishermen's Co-operative Federation Limited (SCFCFL), and in 2003 nine locals remain active, marketing through FFMC. The impact of CFL was significant both economically and socially: CFL was not only a source of millions of dollars of revenue for northern people as fish producers and fish plant workers, it was also a training ground for democracy, a vehicle through which people participated in making decisions related to managing their business and resources. *Dan Beveridge*

CO-OPERATIVE ORGANIZATIONS, LEGISLATION RELATING TO. Legislation providing for the incorporation of co-operatives dates back to 1930. The co-operative movement in Saskatchewan began to gain momentum in the 1920s, and it was deemed that legislation to facilitate the self-help goals of people with mutual economic and social interests was desirable. Unlike the United States, there was virtually no tradition in Saskatchewan, or indeed in Canada, of unincorporated co-operative organizations. Thus, the advent of law allowing independent corporate status to co-operatives marked the beginning of the major development of co-operatives in the province. There were numerous acts which provided the necessary legal machinery to incorporate co-operatives. They can be divided into three categories.

The first category of legislation was designed to enable and regulate co-operatives engaged in many general economic activities. The most general of these acts was the Co-operative Associations Act; and the slightly more focused were the Co-operative Marketing Association Act and, later, the Co-operative Production Associations Act. Ultimately these three acts were folded into one: the Co-operative Associations Act.

The second category of co-operative legislation was directed to financial co-operatives, primarily

George and Mary Farnsworth proudly display Co-op products, Admiral, Saskatchewan, August 1950.

credit unions. These included the Credit Union Act and the Co-operative Guarantee Act. The Credit Union Act, in addition to enabling the incorporation of credit unions, contained a high degree of regulatory provisions appropriate to control organizations which were the trustees of peoples' savings. The earlier general co-operative legislation was also quite regulatory compared to current-day legislation, but still fell far short of the control mechanisms in credit union legislation, which is similar to banking legislation.

The third category of Saskatchewan co-operative legislation was composed of acts passed to incorporate specific co-operatives. Saskatchewan passed more specific co-operative legislation than any other province; the most notable of this category was legislation to specifically incorporate the SASKATCHEWAN WHEAT POOL and Federated Co-operatives. Other examples include an Act to Incorporate Canadian Co-operative Implements Ltd. and the Consumer's Co-operative Refineries Act.

The activity of the Saskatchewan legislature surrounding co-operatives in the past seventy-five years has been impressive. It was the result both of responding to the needs and desires of the people of Saskatchewan, and of the government of the province taking a leadership role in the encouragement and development of co-operatives. *Dan Ish*

CO-OPERATIVE TRUST COMPANY OF CANADA. Co-operative Trust Company of Canada is a financial services institution owned by Canadian credit unions. The company was incorporated in 1952 by special act of the Saskatchewan Legislature, and continued in 1967 under a federal charter. Co-operative Trust is the only national financial institution with its headquarters in Saskatchewan. The company maintains eight regional Relationship Management & Sales Offices across the country, and employs over 200 people nationwide. Assets under administration are currently about $12.4 billion,

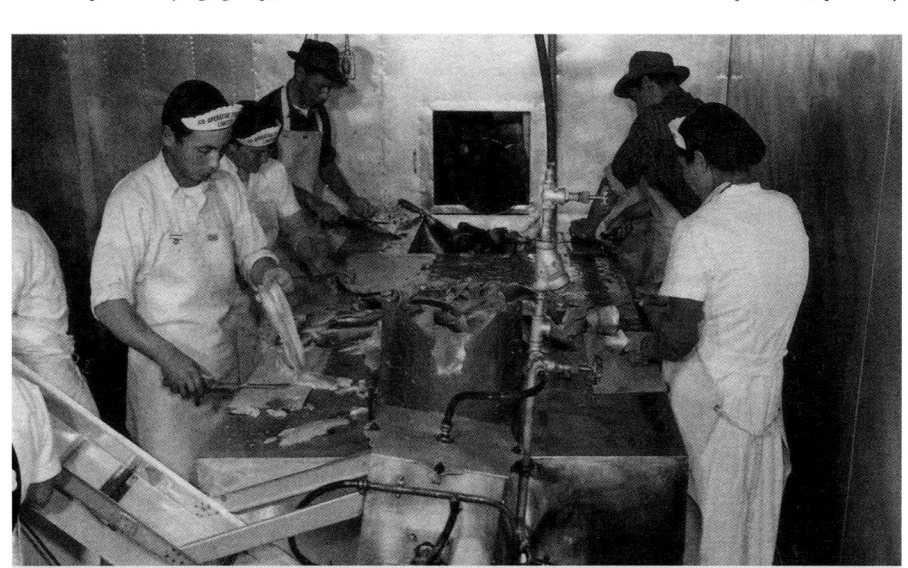

Co-operative Fisheries Limited, October 1959.

and corporate assets approximately $1.3 billion. Co-operative Trust is a national trust company specializing in business-to-business financial and trust services for credit unions and varied corporations across Canada. Initially, Co-operative Trust was created by credit unions and other co-operatives in order to expand member services, predominantly in personal trust services and mortgage funding. In the 1950s credit unions concentrated on short-term lending and needed a special vehicle to offer long-term credit. As credit unions expanded, there was a need for Co-operative Trust to provide a more diverse range of services. In response to changing needs, the company expanded services to include financial intermediary and trusteeship services nationwide. Because Co-operative Trust's activities connect with and have sometimes overlapped the functions of other financial co-operatives and centrals, it has had to be flexible, collaborative, and innovative within the co-operative financial sector.

The company sees itself as founded on co-operative values emphasizing teamwork and community development. The staff and company are actively involved in community initiatives, giving time as volunteers, as well as monetary support to charities. Commitment to the community is seen as part of the corporate culture and as one of the benchmarks by which corporate success is measured. In 2004, for the fourth consecutive year, Co-operative Trust was again designated as one of Canada's Top 100 Employers. As well, due to Co-operative Trust's commitment to best practices, operational excellence, innovative culture, and strong financial achievements, the company was named one of Canada's fifty best-managed companies for 2004 and 2005. With a willingness to change as part of its success, Co-operative Trust is presently reinventing itself in partnership with Credit Union Central of Saskatchewan. This restructuring will include the creation of two new organizations: Concentra Financial and Concentra Trust. Once implemented, the Co-operative Trust name will be retired and these two new organizations will work together to provide an expanded line of financial intermediation and trust services. The goals of this initiative are to offer significantly expanded commercial banking capability nationwide, and promote growth in the Canadian Credit Union System.   *Karen Zemlak*

FURTHER READING: Purden, C. 1980. *Agents for Change: Credit Unions in Saskatchewan.* Regina: Credit Union Central of Saskatchewan.

CO-OPERATIVES. Like its counterparts in England and Europe, the co-operative movement in Canada arose from a sense of exploitation. On the prairies, farmers were frustrated by the high prices being charged by bankers, railroads, elevator companies, implement manufacturers, and shopkeepers.

Individuals had little control over what they paid for goods and services, or the prices they received for their products. The formation of the first co-operatives was thus fuelled by the desire of farmers to gain control over their local economies, coupled with a shared sense of the necessity for collective action.

While agitating for change in the political arena, farmers at the same time began to use co-operatives to supply themselves with goods and to help them take control of handling and marketing their produce. They formed buying clubs to make bulk purchases of farm supplies and basic commodities, and in 1906 banded together to establish the **GRAIN GROWERS' GRAIN COMPANY** to market their grain. In 1911, farmers launched the Saskatchewan Co-operative Elevator Company, with the aim of building an elevator system owned and controlled by farmers.

The heightened demand for Canadian produce during **WORLD WAR I** created a favourable environment for the growth of producer and consumer co-ops, but although hundreds of co-operative associations were formed over the next few years, many did not survive the post-war depression. The successful formation of the **SASKATCHEWAN WHEAT POOL** in 1924 encouraged livestock, dairy, and poultry producers to form their own marketing organizations a few years later.

Surprisingly, the hardships of the 1930s strengthened the co-op movement, and co-operative methods were used to meet a wide variety of needs, including marketing, banking, insurance, the refining of oil, and provision of farm implements. That decade witnessed the birth of Consumers Co-operative Refineries, credit unions, and Canadian Co-operative Implements, at its peak one of North America's largest farm machinery co-ops. It was also during the 1930s that the Saskatchewan Wheat Pool gave up its marketing function to the Wheat Board and developed its expertise in grain handling.

The sector made major strides during the next decade, beginning in 1940, when the western co-op wholesales came together to form Interprovincial Co-operatives Limited (IPCO). IPCO facilitated the marketing, under the familiar CO-OP label, of commodities produced and processed by co-operatives throughout the sector. In 1941, the Saskatchewan Co-operative Credit Society (today's Credit Union Central) became English Canada's first central credit union system. In 1944, the provincial government created the Department of Co-operation and Co-operative Development to support new and existing co-ops. That same year witnessed the amalgamation of the Co-op Refinery and Saskatchewan Co-op Wholesale into a single organization known as Saskatchewan Federated Co-operatives Ltd. (SFCL). This merger was an important step towards the establishment of an integrated co-operative retail system.

Like the 1914–18 conflict, **WORLD WAR II** brought expanded opportunities for all types of co-operatives. Farm production co-ops were formed by veterans returning from the war. Ventures that had taken root during the **DEPRESSION** grew stronger and diversified, often through amalgamations. SFCL merged with the other western wholesales to form Federated Co-operatives Ltd. (FCL); the western wheat pools became members of IPCO; the Saskatchewan Wheat Pool began to diversify through joint ventures with other co-ops; and the Dairy Pool and Saskatchewan Co-op Creameries came together to form Dairy Producers Co-op. The formation of the Co-op Life Insurance Company, Co-op Trust, and the expansion of the credit union system contributed to substantial growth in the co-operative financial sector over this period. During the 1960s, health care and other community-service-based co-ops took on a more formalized structure, and by the 1980s there were co-operative organizations in almost every sector of the economy.

Although urbanization has eroded its rural base, the co-operative movement in Saskatchewan remains strong, vibrant, and innovative. And as they have done since their earliest stages, co-operatives continue to play an integral role in the social and economic development of the province. Initial forms of co-operation have evolved into an extensive network of co-operatives engaged in a wide range of activities, including agriculture and resources, community development, recreation, child care and education, wholesale and retail, financial and community service, housing, and employment.

Co-operatives play an important role at every level of the economy. A major statistical analysis done in 1998 revealed that the 1,306 co-operatives in Saskatchewan generated revenues of nearly $7 billion and controlled assets of more than $10 billion. Capital investment totalled $372 million, and they had a surplus amounting to $208.9 million. In addition, co-operatives employed 15,046 people and paid wages of $458.7 million.

Two of Saskatchewan's three largest businesses are co-operatives, as are four of the province's top twenty firms. Large organizations, such as the Saskatchewan Wheat Pool (SWP), Federated Co-operatives Limited (FCL), and Credit Union Central (CUC) wield significant economic power in the provincial economy. Although smaller co-operatives seem insignificant in comparison, they are major players at the community level, and two of the largest—FCL and CUC—exist primarily to serve the needs of a network of smaller retail and financial co-operatives.

Saskatchewan is home to a broad range of co-operative organizations that vary greatly in size, scope, and operational focus. Not surprisingly, agricultural and resource-based co-operatives comprise more than one-quarter of the total. Other areas in which co-operatives play a major role include retail and wholesale, finances, community development, recreation, child care and preschool, and community service. There is a small group of other types of co-operatives that provide services to members in areas such as housing, real estate development, employment, publishing, film production, and transportation.

The diverse nature of the organizations that are able to function successfully according to co-operative principles is a testament to the flexibility of this business model. Co-operatives clearly possess characteristics that have enabled them to address problems experienced by their members and the communities in which they live. Their impact on communities is substantial, especially in the smaller centres, where the co-op may be one of the few remaining businesses in town. In these cases, co-ops supply not only a wide range of goods and services that might not otherwise be provided, but also employment, thus contributing significantly to the survival of the most vulnerable communities. Co-operatives have a long track record in Saskatchewan and are engaged in organizational renewal that will allow them to continue to make crucial contributions to sustainable economic development in the province. *Nora Russell*

CO-OPERATIVES, AGRICULTURAL AND RESOURCE-BASED. Since the inception of co-operatives in the early years of the 20th century, farmers in Saskatchewan have perceived them as an effective means of growing, processing, and marketing their produce. Over the past decade, agriculture and resource-based co-operatives have comprised approximately one-quarter of the co-operative organizations in the province. Correspondingly, they also account for nearly 25% of co-op employees, about the same percentage of co-op wages, and more than 60% of the revenues generated by co-operatives in Saskatchewan. Co-operatives in this category include farming, feeder, grazing, breeding, seed cleaning, farmers' markets, soil conservation, fishing, **SASKATCHEWAN WHEAT POOL**, Dairyworld (until December 2000), and other agricultural-based organizations.

The roots of farming and machinery co-operatives in Saskatchewan can be traced to the mid-1940s, when the rehabilitation of returning war veterans became an issue and existing farmers were beginning to face the challenges of increased mechanization and high capital investment. In response, the CCF government of the day facilitated the establishment of farming co-operatives; and although most of them, struggling in an environment and an economic and legal system dominated by the family farm, eventually failed, co-operative farming enterprises continued to be formed into the 21st century. At the time of writing the financial health of these organizations was relatively good, although com-

pared to the many farms operating in Saskatchewan their numbers–fewer than forty–remain quite small.

Feeder co-operatives began appearing in the mid-1980s with the formation of the Feeder Association Loan Guarantee Program, which assisted farmers with feeding and marketing their cattle. Each association was required to deposit 5% of the funds borrowed under government loan guarantees in an assurance fund. The number of feeder co-operatives peaked in the mid-1990s and has gradually dropped off since that time. At the time of writing there were about 4,500 active members in somewhat over 100 feeder co-operatives, which provided employment for around 140 individuals.

Grazing co-operatives enable farmers to rent grazing land on a collective basis. While the number of co-operatives has remained relatively stable over the past fifteen years–around 135–there has been a decrease in the number of active members, which now totals about 1,400 individuals. Although assets and revenues have also declined over the past few years, the number of individuals employed in grazing co-operatives and consequently the wage bill have increased by about 23% and 17% respectively.

In addition to the services provided by grazing and feeder co-operatives, livestock farmers have also formed breeding co-operatives to supply artificial insemination services. Although there are fewer than twenty of these organizations in the province, breeding co-operatives have nevertheless been increasing in numbers and in active members over the past fifteen years. A low level of reporting from this sector makes it difficult to be conclusive about overall changes.

Seed-cleaning co-operatives are in a similar situation to breeding co-ops, although it is known that their number has remained consistent at ten since 1989. The employment they provide has remained relatively stable, while active membership has increased slightly.

Dispersed throughout the province, farmers' markets provide an avenue for the direct marketing of a wide variety of farm produce. The majority of these businesses operate on a break-even basis, and revenues consist mainly of charges to members for co-ordination services and table rentals. The number of co-operatives, the number of active members, assets, revenues, and the employment provided by this sector have declined slowly but consistently over the past fifteen years, leaving about forty farmers' markets with approximately 1,300 active members at the time of writing.

In keeping with concerns about sustainable agricultural practices, soil-conservation co-operatives began to spring up in the mid-1980s. Several of these received substantial funding from the **PRAIRIE FARM REHABILITATION ADMINISTRATION**, with which they embarked on conservation projects such as the

establishment of shelter-belts, conservation tillage, and continuous cropping. The number of these co-operatives declined substantially from a peak of fifteen in 1989 to only three at the turn of the 21st century. Total membership declined likewise, from more than 200 to less than 40.

All but one of the ten fishing co-operatives in Saskatchewan are in the north of the province. The primary service provided by these co-ops to their members is the rental of fishing equipment, and most operate on a break-even basis while relying on volunteer labour. Although the number of fishing co-ops has been consistent over the past few years, active membership has fallen significantly to fewer than 400 individuals.

Established in 1924 as a central marketing organization for grain producers, the Saskatchewan Wheat Pool (SWP) now ranks as the largest Saskatchewan-based corporation. It is also Canada's largest grain-handling company, but while this accounts for almost half of its operations it is also deeply involved in the farm supply sector, agri-food processing, livestock marketing, and, until 2001, publishing. The Pool underwent a significant change in its ownership structure in 1996, which allowed it to be listed as a publicly traded company and to issue Class B non-voting shares, an unusual move for a co-operative in Canada. Although it has struggled with serious financial difficulties over the past number of years, SWP employs more than 2,500 people and manages a wage bill of over $100 million, which makes a significant contribution to the economy of the province.

While Saskatchewan no longer has a dairy co-operative, this sector was active in the province for more than 100 years, beginning with the organization of a number of creameries during the 1890s. Dairy Producers Co-operative, established in 1972, was the result of a merger between the Saskatchewan Co-operative Creameries Association and the Dairy Pool. After that amalgamation, Dairy Producers handled the majority of the province's milk and cream shipments, and while milk and milk products made up the largest proportion of its sales, the co-op also handled other products such as poultry, eggs, and juice. In 1996 Dairy Producers amalgamated with a number of other dairy co-operatives in western Canada to form Agrifoods International Co-operative, which marketed its products under the name of Dairyworld Foods. In December 2000, Agrifoods sold its Dairyworld assets to an Italian dairy multinational, Saputo, which brought an end to the co-operative dairy sector in western Canada.

Agricultural and resource-based co-operatives in the "other" category cover a wide variety of enterprises, including wild-rice producers, organic growers, a greenhouse, Christmas-tree growers, pheasant and rabbit producers, as well as livestock and sheep marketers. While there are fewer than twenty of these miscellaneous co-operatives, and incomplete data collection makes comparisons difficult, it is known that the number of co-ops in this category has increased slightly over the past few years and that the number of employees has grown dramatically.   *Nora Russell*

FURTHER READING: Fulton, Murray, et al. 1991. *Economic Impact Analysis of the Co-operative Sector in Saskatchewan*, Research Report Prepared for Saskatchewan Department of Economic Diversification and Trade; Ketilson, Lou Hammond, et al. 1998. *The Social and Economic Importance of the Co-operative Sector in Saskatchewan*, Research Report Prepared for Saskatchewan Department of Economic and Co-operative Development; Herman, Roger and Murray Fulton. 2001. *An Economic Impact Analysis of the Co-operative Sector in Saskatchewan: Update 1998.*

CO-OPERATIVES, FINANCIAL. A lack of financial services on the prairies during the Depression led to the establishment of the co-operative financial sector. During the 1930s, the number of bank branches in Saskatchewan declined by 40%. The banks were also accused of setting high interest rates and operating conservative loan policies, factors that led to a determination to develop locally based and locally responsive financial institutions. The financial co-operatives detailed here include the credit unions and Credit Union Central, The Co-operators Group (a holding company for nine financial services organizations), and Co-operative Hail Insurance. Figures for the Co-operative Trust Company of Canada are included with those for Credit Union Central of Saskatchewan.

At the end of the 1990s, there were 154 financial co-operatives in the province, most of which were credit unions, with 560,000 active members and $7.5 billion in assets. Active membership for this sector overall declined by about 4% during the 1990s, but the number of employees rose slightly and the wage bill increased by nearly 60%, from $116 million to $186 million. Assets rose during the same period by 9%, and member equity grew from $157 million to $563 million.

The first credit union in Saskatchewan was organized in Regina in 1937. By 1996, the credit union system in Saskatchewan had grown to include 340 credit union outlets and almost $7 billion in assets. Local ownership and control, combined with the establishment of a large, province-wide, central organization, allowed members to take advantage of the efficiencies provided by economies of scale while maintaining responsiveness to local needs. Firms that were locally owned and controlled could continue to provide services in communities where it was no longer profitable for a private firm to do so. Local ownership also meant that the money deposited locally was more likely to remain in the community.

Originally established around a rural population with limited mobility, the credit unions are now undergoing a consolidation process common to many institutions within the province. Trends towards greater urbanization and reduced economic activity in the smaller towns and villages have heightened the need for the reinvestment of savings back into the community. And the globalization of financial services finds the credit unions increasingly in competition with the traditional banking system, as well as with other financial institutions.

At the end of the 1990s, 339 credit union locations representing 151 credit unions reported assets totalling $6.5 billion, up from the $5 billion reported a decade earlier. Over the same period, the number of employees rose by nearly 14% and the wage bill by 59%. Although revenues dropped from $587 million to $482 million, savings rose from $26 million to $37 million and member equity grew at an astonishing rate, from $14 million to $430 million.

The credit unions own Credit Union Central (CUC), which serves the system by providing financial services, information technology support, and consulting services. As part of its efforts to support the credit unions, CUC has developed a number of alliances and partnerships. Insurance products for credit union members are provided through the Co-operators Group and CUMIS Insurance Company. Financial planning and trust and estate services are offered through MemberCARE Financial Services and the Co-operative Trust Company of Canada. A variety of products and services are available through a number of other joint ventures, such as CU Electronic Transaction Services and Credit Union Payment Services.

It is important to note that the data for Credit Union Central reported here include Co-op Trust's activities, which had been considered separately by the Department of Justice until the late 1990s. For comparative purposes, CUC and Co-op Trust data from earlier in the decade have been added together. CUC assets at the end of the 1990s were $2.4 billion, as compared to $1.7 billion ten years earlier. Revenues fell considerably, from $226 million in 1989 to $185 million at the end of the 1990s, while member equity rose from $121 million to $137 million. The number of people employed fell slightly, while the wage bill more than doubled, to $31 million. Even more remarkable was the increase in capital investment from $3.7 million to $31.2 million.

Substantial growth in the co-operative sector during the 1940s generated a demand for long-term loans that could not be adequately met by the small localized credit unions that existed at the time. Co-operative Trust was established in 1952 to provide individuals with trust services and to extend long-term loans to co-operative organizations. In 1967, Co-operative Trust expanded beyond the boundaries

of Saskatchewan to become a national firm. Although it is governed by a board representing credit union systems across Canada, Credit Union Central holds a majority of the voting shares, and financial and other statistics generated by the trust company, as noted above, are included with CUC data.

Co-operators Group Limited is a national firm owned by thirty co-operatives across Canada. In Saskatchewan, ownership consists of Federated Co-operatives, Credit Union Central, and Saskatchewan Wheat Pool. Co-operators Group is the holding company for the following wholly owned companies: Co-operators Life Insurance, Co-operators General Insurance, COSECO Insurance Company, The Sovereign General Insurance Company, Co-operators Financial Services Limited, Co-operators Investment Counselling, Co-operators Development Corporation, Federated Agencies Limited, and HB Group Insurance Management Limited.

The Co-operators Group owned assets worth $172.6 million in Saskatchewan at the end of the 1990s, dramatically up from the $22 million reported in 1989. Revenue from Saskatchewan over the same period was down by about 7%, and employment fell from 973 to 620 individuals; but the wage bill over the same period increased from $28 million to nearly $39 million.

First organized in 1947 by a group of farmers in the Edenwold district of Saskatchewan, Co-operative Hail Insurance, now based in Regina, has members and policy holders in Saskatchewan and Manitoba. Statistics reported here reflect Saskatchewan's share of this economic activity. At the end of the 1990s, Saskatchewan farmers accounted for more than 77% of the co-operative's membership, which remained stable over the course of the decade, rising only 3% from 70,095 to 72,173 individuals. Although the number of policies written in the province fell during the same period, revenues increased by 36% to $16.3 million. The value of assets grew by about the same percentage, to $30.9 million; and member equity rose as well, from $22.8 million to almost $27 million. The number of employees increased dramatically, from ten full-time and six part-time positions in 1989 to seven full-time and ninety-two part-time positions ten years later. Although the wage bill increased from $254,000 to $475,000, the average salary dropped from $15,875 to $4,798, reflecting the large number of part-time workers at the end of the decade.   *Nora Russell*

FURTHER READING: Fulton, Murray, et al. 1991. *Economic Impact Analysis of the Co-operative Sector in Saskatchewan*, Research Report Prepared for Saskatchewan Department of Economic Diversification and Trade; Ketilson, Lou Hammond, et al. 1998. *The Social and Economic Importance of the Co-operative Sector in Saskatchewan*, Research Report Prepared for

Saskatchewan Department of Economic and Co-operative Development; Herman, Roger and Murray Fulton. 2001. *An Economic Impact Analysis of the Co-operative Sector in Saskatchewan: Update 1998.*

CO-OPERATIVES, NORTHERN. Northern Saskatchewan has the third largest concentration of Aboriginal co-operatives in Canada after the Northwest Territories/Nunavut and Nunavik in northern Quebec. Most are survivors of the extensive program of northern co-operative development undertaken by the Saskatchewan CCF government during the 1950s and 1960s. The first northern co-operative in Saskatchewan was the fishers' co-op at Kinoosao on **REINDEER LAKE**, incorporated in 1945; the number of co-operatives grew to a high of 62 in 1971. In 1969 there were 57 co-operatives, including 18 local fishers' co-operatives and a central fish marketing co-operative, 15 local retail stores and a central consumer co-operative, 2 credit unions, and co-operatives for electric power, wood products, recreation, handicrafts and fur production. They had 4,900 members, and represented $2.5 million in annual sales and services. In 2003 there were 25 co-operatives reported, including 9 fishers' co-operatives, 4 retail (store) co-operatives, and 2 credit unions. Pinehouse, a **MÉTIS** settlement, has a successful co-operative store and a fishers' co-operative; Stanley Mission is one of several First Nations settlements with co-operative stores.

Many of the northern co-operatives grew out of two northern **CROWN CORPORATIONS** formed in 1949: the Saskatchewan Fish Marketing Service, which purchased and marketed fish; and Saskatchewan Government Trading, which sold equipment and supplies to fishers. Whereas the Crown corporations succeeded in involving northern people in the commercial fishing industry, co-operatives were intended to involve them in business decision-making. So the two northern Crowns were transformed in 1959 into two convertible corporations. Initially placed under one government-appointed central board of southern co-operative leaders, they were intended to become true co-operatives as soon as the members were ready to own and operate them. The Saskatchewan Fish Marketing Service became **CO-OPERATIVE FISHERIES LIMITED** (CFL), initially with 12 local fishers' co-operatives, fish processing plants, and other assets (*see* Figure CN-1). In 1966 the $225,000 debt to the provincial government for the assets transferred was repaid in full, and in 1971 CFL became a true co-operative.

Similarly, Saskatchewan Government Trading transferred its six trading stores and other assets to Northern Co-operative Trading Services Limited (NCTSL). Co-operatives with local boards of directors were formed. By 1966, two-thirds of the initial $275,000 debt had been repaid and two stores had paid their debts in full. NCTSL was dissolved in

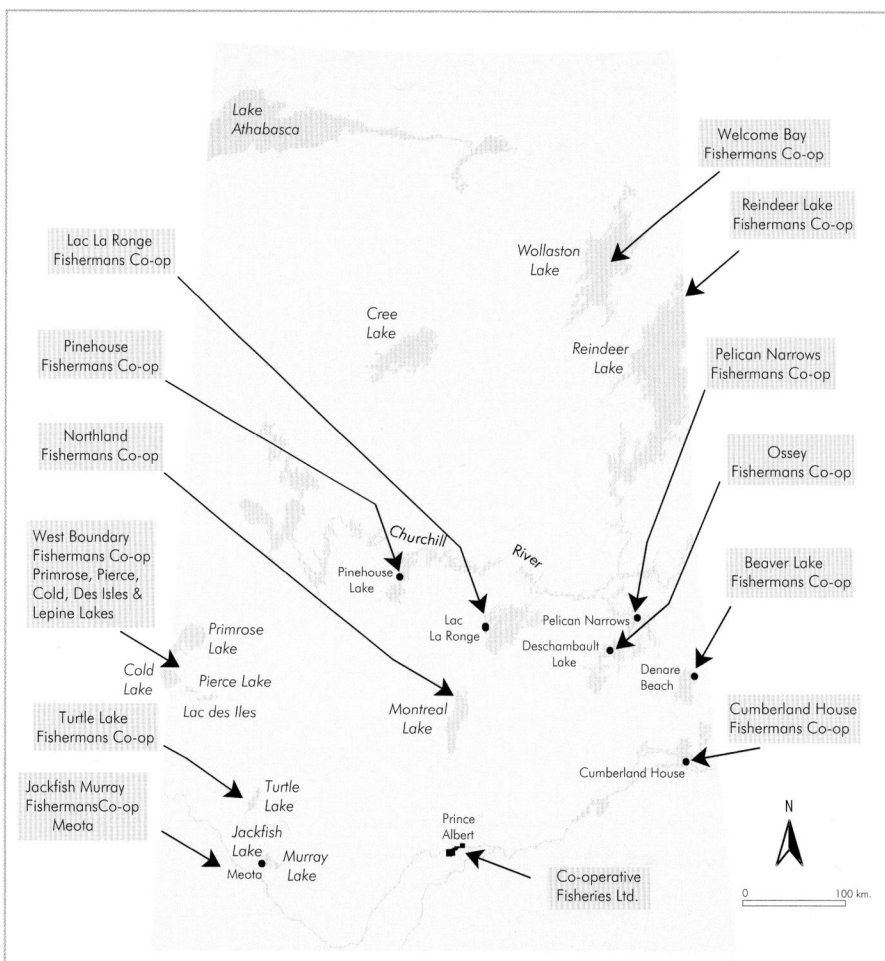

Figure CN-1. Locations of the local fishers' co-operatives that made up Co-operative Fisheries Limited.

1978. A key element in establishing and supporting new northern co-operatives through the 1960s was co-operative management advisors, who worked in the north both to oversee the economic aspects and to help the people learn the skills needed to manage and control their own businesses. Also important were a "learn by doing" approach and a strong educational component at membership and board meetings. The impact of northern co-operatives was both economically and socially significant, particularly with Aboriginal people, and greatly contributed to developing skills in leadership and decision-making. (*See also* **CO-OPERATIVES**; **CO-OPERATIVES, OTHER**)

Daniel M. Beveridge

CO-OPERATIVES, OTHER. This category of co-operatives includes organizations involved in areas such as housing, real estate development, employment, publishing, and other unrelated activities. Since it does not represent any particular activity or industry, there is little point in comparing aggregate data. Comparisons are limited instead to the five types of co-operatives identified.

Housing co-operatives represent the largest cat-

egory in this sector in terms of numbers and financial activity. As is the case with child-care co-operatives, collective ownership of housing units can help increase the number of affordable units available. At the end of the 1990s there were twenty-six housing co-operatives with 1,145 active members, up from the twenty-two co-ops and 1,045 members reporting to the Department of Justice a decade earlier. Although assets fell by $4.4 million, liabilities declined by an even greater extent—$9.1 million—resulting in a decrease in the debt-to-asset ratio, an indication of general financial health. There was a large increase in member equity over the same period, from $2 million to $6.6 million, and although revenues dropped considerably over the decade, there was a surplus of $79,000 in the late 1990s, in contrast to a negative $202,000 reported in 1989. Housing co-operatives employed forty people at the end of the 1990s, up from the thirty-two reported a decade earlier, although the wage bill dropped by 14%, reflecting the large percentage of part-time workers.

Real estate development includes co-operatives that deal with the building of non-residential facilities, as well as the purchase of land and the regulation of development in various communities. The enterprises reporting as real estate developments are primarily cottage and resort co-operatives. Although the number of co-operatives increased from eight to ten over the decade, membership decreased by 27%, dropping from 528 to 384 individuals. And while assets decreased from $1.6 million to $0.9 million—nearly 47%—liabilities fell even more remarkably, from $1.3 million to $0.2 million, resulting in a lower debt-to-asset ratio. Revenues decreased as well, but the surplus more than doubled over the decade, from $83,000 to $168,000. At the same time, member equity increased by 114%, from $334,000 to $715,000. Real estate co-operatives reported no employees in 1989; but by the end of the next decade they were employing twenty-one people, albeit with a modest wage bill of $74,000. Capital investment appears as zero at both the beginning and the end of the decade, which probably means it was simply not reported.

One response to high levels of unemployment has been the formation of employment co-operatives, with the primary focus of providing jobs for their members. Although data for most of the employment co-operatives was unavailable at the end of the 1990s due to a low level of reporting, some general observations are possible. The number of co-operatives declined by three—from eight to five—since 1989, although membership more than quadrupled, to 546 individuals. The number of people employed fell from forty-nine positions in 1989 to eighteen at the end of the next decade, and although the wage bill dropped by 56%, the average wage paid out increased.

The number of publishing co-operatives increased over the decade, from three to five, but membership fell significantly, from 210 to 89 individuals. Although both the number of employees and the wage bill decreased as well, the average wage went up for those who kept their jobs. Both assets and liabilities increased, resulting in a decreased debt-to-asset ratio, while member equity fell by nearly 6%. At $752,000, revenue was 24% higher at the end of the 1990s, while the surplus of $39,000 compared favourably to the $28,000 deficit reported in 1989. Capital investment fell from $7,000 to zero during the decade, which again may reflect a lack of reporting in this area.

The co-operatives listed as miscellaneous comprise a varied collection of enterprises, including snowploughs, crafts, a railway, and film production companies. Of the thirteen listed as active at the end of the 1990s, few provided any data at all to the Department of Justice, and none of it allowed for effective analysis. *Nora Russell*

FURTHER READING: Fulton, Murray, et al. 1991. *Economic Impact Analysis of the Co-operative Sector in*

Saskatchewan, Research Report Prepared for Saskatchewan Department of Economic Diversification and Trade; Herman, Roger and Murray Fulton. 2001. *An Economic Impact Analysis of the Co-operative Sector in Saskatchewan: Update 1998*; Ketilson, Lou Hammond, et al. 1998. *The Social and Economic Importance of the Co-operative Sector in Saskatchewan*, Research Report Prepared for Saskatchewan Department of Economic and Co-operative Development.

CO-OPERATORS LIFE INSURANCE. The Co-operators Life Insurance Company is one of the top ten life insurance organizations in Canada. Based in Regina, it employs 750 people, manages $3 billion in assets, and offers a wide portfolio of life and health insurance as well as retirement savings products. Co-operators Life Insurance Company is the second largest subsidiary of the Canadian-owned Co-operators Group Ltd. Consisting of twenty-eight member co-operatives, the Co-operators Group of companies specializes in insurance and financial security products, property development and management, and investment counseling. The Co-operators Group has a combined membership of 4.5 million, assets of over $5 billion, and a workforce of 4,000. The idea of a co-operative insurance company was inspired by the **GREAT DEPRESSION** of the 1930s and Canada's co-operative movement. In 1945, a group of Saskatchewan wheat farmers pooled their resources to form the first insurance co-operative in Canada, which flourished through the years to become the Co-operators Group, the largest Canadian-owned multi-product insurer in the country. Co-operators Life Insurance Company consistently ranks among Saskatchewan's top companies and has been named by MediaCorp as one of Canada's top 100 employers for three consecutive years. Co-operators Life Insurance Company has also received numerous awards for its outstanding support of community programs such as the United Way, the Food Bank, and the Hospitals of Regina Foundation. *Iain Stewart*

FURTHER READING: 2004. "Co-operators Life Posts Record Revenues," *Regina Leader-Post* (April 16): B4.

REGINA LEADER-POST

The Co-operators Life Insurance Company building, Regina.

CORDIS, LEORA L. (1929–2000). LeOra L. Cordis, born in 1929 in Thedford, Nebraska, received a Bachelor of Education degree from Chadron State College in 1964, followed by Master of Education and Doctor of Philosophy degrees from the University of Oregon in 1972. She accepted a position in the Faculty of Education at the **UNIVERSITY OF REGINA** in 1972, continuing until 1994. As a professor of Early Childhood Education in the 1970s, Cordis held key roles as a researcher and in-service consultant during the implementation of kindergarten programs throughout the province. Later, in 1977, she designed the Daycare Staff Development Program for the Saskatchewan Community College. While serving as director of the Children's Centre from 1981 to 1987 in the Faculty of Education, Cordis developed the Teacher Development Program for in-service teachers and the Aide Training Program preparing people to work as classroom assistants. Upon her retirement, she initiated the LeOra Cordis Elementary Education Fund to help sustain a commitment to equity and social justice issues in teacher education. Recognizing her contributions to the well-being of young children, the Canadian Association of Young Children presented the Friends of Children Award to LeOra Cordis in 1995. She died in 2000.

Caroline D. Krentz

CORE CURRICULUM. In the early 1980s, Saskatchewan undertook a review of its K–12 education system. As a result, a report entitled *Directions* (1984) listed sixteen recommendations that formed the blueprint for the K–12 educational reform known as Core Curriculum introduced in 1987. Core Curriculum outlines a K–12 continuum of seven required areas of study: English language arts, mathematics, science, social studies, health education, physical education, and arts education. In addition, Core Curriculum identifies six Common Essential Learnings (CELs) for all students: communication, numeracy, critical and creative thinking, technological literacy, personal and social values and skills, and independent learning. The CELs assist students in acquiring the knowledge, values, skills, and processes that make up their school subjects; they also develop the abilities needed to function as rational, responsible, and productive members of society.

To meet community and student needs at the local level, provision is made within Core Curriculum to offer locally determined options. Such options can be provided through the selection of provincially developed courses or through courses developed at the local level. Some schools, for example, offer bilingual education in French or Ukrainian; some offer religious instruction at all grades; some offer English as a Second Language programs; and many offer specialized arts programs, practical and applied courses such as welding and wildlife management, or sports or cultural programs to reflect local interests and community contexts. In recognition of the diverse needs of students, provision is also made for teachers to adapt their instruction, materials, and environment in order to help students achieve curriculum objectives. Adaptations are tailored to students' strengths, needs and interests and are applied within all programs of instruction (i.e., regular and alternative programs). This adaptive dimension addresses the importance of providing varied ways for students to learn and for assessment to take place. In addition to these components, Core Curriculum includes various initiatives that guide the development of teaching materials as well as instruction in the classroom. These initiatives include: resource-based learning, Indian and Métis content and perspectives, gender equity, multicultural education, career education, instructional approaches, and evaluation practices.

Jane Thurgood Sagal

CORE FRENCH EDUCATION IN SASKATCHEWAN.

In a Core French program, daily instruction time is similar to that given to the other school subjects. While the immersion approach to language study is relatively recent, dating from the 1960s, the study of second languages has been part of education systems for a very long time. Latin and Greek were studied to provide access to literature written in those languages and as an academic discipline. Later, modern languages were studied for much the same reasons; Core French, or French as a subject, thus took its place in the curriculum.

With **WORLD WAR II**, people in North America began to see a need to communicate with other cultures, and communication became a goal of core language programs. In an effort to meet this objective, Core French programs underwent a series of changes in methodology—from grammar-translation to a direct method, to a structural approach, to a communicative approach. In spite of teachers' and students' best efforts, students did not become bilingual. With the publication of the Gillin Report (1976), expectations changed because Gillin estimated that it takes approximately 5,000 hours of time on task to become fluent in a second language. Because of the limited time factor, bilingualism is not a realistic goal of a Core French program. There are, however, many good reasons to study French as a subject in school.

The Core French program enables students to increase, within realistic limits, their ability to communicate in French and allows them to take advantage of some vocational and leisure opportunities and to meet post-secondary eligibility requirements.

Like immersion, Core French programs are now built on a sound theoretical and research base, and based on recommendations from the National Core French Study (1990) as well as on the Core French Curriculum Model provided by the Canadian Association of Second Language Teachers (CASLT). The multidimensional curriculum which resulted from these two initiatives provides a rich educational experience for Core French students. Core French educators have learned much from the success of immersion programs and have incorporated aspects of that approach to language learning. Today's Core French programs begin earlier, taking advantage of young children's ability to imitate a good French accent, and provide much more time on task. The programs use an oral communicative approach, and through experiential learning, create a need to use French in a meaningful way. Some 70,000 students are enrolled in Core French programs in Saskatchewan.

Harvey Châtlain

FURTHER RESEARCH: Canadian Association of Second Language Teachers. 1994. *The National Core French Study–A Model for Implementation.* Ottawa: Canadian Association of Second Language Teachers; Gillin, R. 1976. *French Language–Study and Teaching.* Toronto: Ontario Institute for Studies in Education.

CORMAN, JOHN WESLEY "JACK" (1884–1969).

Jack Corman was born on a farm at Stoney Creek, Ontario, on August 2, 1884. In 1912 he graduated from the University of Toronto with a BA in political science. He moved west that year to pursue legal studies, articling in Moose Jaw and was called to the Bar in 1915. For the next twenty years he built his legal practice and was active in the **LIBERAL PARTY**. In 1937 he was one of five aldermen elected as part of a Civic Progressive Association slate. Corman ran as a Social Credit candidate in the 1938 provincial election but lost. In 1939 Corman was elected mayor of Moose Jaw and served for four and a half years. Corman agreed to run for the CCF in 1944 with the promise of a Cabinet post and legisla-

John Corman.

tion to reduce municipal debt. Corman was sworn in as Attorney General in the first **DOUGLAS** Cabinet. Highlights of Corman's tenure included the Farm Security Act in 1944 and the Saskatchewan Bill of Rights in 1947. Corman was well known for his political radio broadcasts between 1946 and 1950. He was twice re-elected to the Saskatchewan Legislature and he remained Attorney General until he retired in 1956. He died in Moose Jaw on April 29, 1969.

Robert Allan

FURTHER READING: Whelan, Ed and Pemrose Whelan. 2002. *Run It by Jack: Tommy Douglas' First Attorney General, J.W. Corman.* Regina: Whelan Publications.

Double-crested cormorant (*Phalacrocorax auritus*).

CORMORANTS.

Cormorants form the family Phalacrocoraidae of the order Pelecaniformes. Like the pelicans, they have a completely webbed foot; they differ in having a much smaller throat pouch and dark or pied plumage. Of the approximately thirty species of cormorants in the world, the double-crested cormorant (*Phalacrocorax auritus*) is the only species found in Saskatchewan. They are most often found nesting on islands in association with other colonial nesting species such as pelicans, herons, gulls, and terns. They build their nests either on the ground or in trees. Cormorants will use and add to the same nest structure each year, with some of the nests reaching a height of 2 m or more. The cormorant is an opportunistic feeder that preys mostly on fish but will also eat invertebrates, crayfish, and salamanders. It dives underwater for its prey, propelled by its totipalmate feet (its four toes being connected by a web). A hook at the tip of the upper bill helps the cormorant grasp its prey. As the cormorant's uropygial gland does not produce much water-proofing oil, after diving it will perch with wings outstretched in order to dry its feathers.

Cormorants were recorded for Saskatchewan in 1892. The population of the double-crested cormorant has been steadily increasing in the province since the late 1960s. Being fish-eaters, they are often persecuted by commercial and recreational fishermen.

Keith Roney

FURTHER READING: Alsop, F.J., III. 2002. *Birds of Canada*. New York: Dorling Kindersley; Macoun, J. 1900. *Catalogue of Canadian Birds, Part I: Water Birds, Gallinaceous Birds, and Pigeons*. Ottawa: Geological Survey of Canada.

CORONACH, town, pop 822, located due S of Moose Jaw on Hwys 18 and 36, 19 km from the Canada-US border. The area landscape is one of gently rolling hills, which are underlain by substantial deposits of lignite **COAL**. The land supports grain farming, particularly red spring wheat, and livestock production. The region only began to be settled between 1908 and 1914. Like most communities in the province, Coronach was hit hard by the **DEPRESSION** and drought of the 1930s, but it rebounded in the post-war era. Also, while many communities again began to decline in the 1960s and 1970s, here the downturn was halted by a pivotal moment in Coronach's history: although coal had been mined in the area since the early 1900s, it was not until the mid-1970s that the significance of the resource was realized. The richness of the coal seams in the area was a determining factor in SaskPower's decision to locate a new major power-generating station and coal mine in the immediate vicinity of the community. Within a few years, the village of just over 300 mushroomed into a bustling business centre with a population of over 1,000. The Poplar River Power Station and the Poplar River Coal Mine employ approximately 300 people today. The community hosts an agricultural fair in July and the Poplar River Indoor Rodeo in September.

David McLennan

CORPS OF COMMISSIONAIRES. The Saskatchewan Corps of Commissionaires was established in 1859 in Great Britain by Captain Edward Walter to help British veterans make the transition back to employment in civilian life. A similar organization was developed in Canada in 1915 by then Governor General, the Duke of Connaught, whose goal was to assist former servicemen and women who were unemployed in obtaining quality jobs and pensions. In 1925, upon federal charter approval, the first Canadian Corps of Commissionaires Companies were designated in Toronto, Montreal, and Vancouver. In Saskatchewan, the Corps developed throughout the 1940s, dividing into north and south sectors, with head offices in Saskatoon and Regina respectively. Today they are a leading provider of security-related services to business, government, industry, and individuals, with services including alarm monitoring, security patrolling, airport screening, court guard services, and traffic control.

Lauren Black

CORRECTIONS. "Corrections" is a generic term now used for what is sometimes termed the third

Saskatchewan Penitentiary, Prince Albert.

segment of the criminal justice system—the first two being courts and police. Its meaning is quite broad and encompasses probation and parole services, prisons, and community-based services that can be provided to achieve preventive, ameliorative or integrative goals. Prior to 1870 only prison services were provided, and these were located either in England or, later, in the eastern parts of British North America. After 1870, North-West Mounted Police guardhouses served as detention centres and also as prisons for offenders serving sentences of less than two years. Guardhouses existed at police barracks in locations such as Maple Creek, Battleford, Prince Albert, Yorkton and Regina; and for most of the territorial period (1870–1905) they were the region's only prison facilities. Territorial jails were eventually built in Regina and Prince Albert, and many, though not all, of the prisoners held by the Mounted Police were transferred to them. Persons sentenced to two years or more, however, were commonly sent to Stony Mountain Penitentiary, a federal facility located in Manitoba. This was because at the time of Confederation in 1867, it had been decided that although provinces would be responsible for maintaining prisons for persons sentenced to less than two years, the national government would take responsibility for persons sentenced to two years or more. In 1905 Saskatchewan assumed full responsibility for those prisons located within the new provincial boundaries.

The objective of penal policy until 1946 was custody and punishment. Punishment was assumed to reform offenders and prevent their re-offending. From 1946 to 1966 the orientation, based on the

Penal Reform Commission's recommendations, shifted to treatment and then in 1966 to rehabilitation. Rehabilitation and re-integration of offenders into society continued to be the orientation until 1982, and Saskatchewan was at the leading edge of prison and correctional reform and development from 1946 to 1982. From 1982 to 1992 there was a return to a modified custody and punishment orientation. This was largely the result of an influential book by Dr. Martinson (an American criminologist), who suggested that the new initiatives did not work to reduce recidivism. His views appealed to the province's Conservative government, and as a result there was a significant increase in the custody and safety orientation of provincial correction. But although there was retrenchment, the vision for community-centred approaches to corrections and reintegration of the offender was not entirely lost, and the construction in corrections facilities and programs reflected this orientation. In 1992 the decision was taken to once again emphasize rehabilitation and reintegration, although Saskatchewan is no longer considered to be in the forefront of correctional development.

The current mission of Adult Corrections is to promote safe communities by providing a range of controls and reintegration opportunities for offenders. The vision is to respect offenders as individuals, support them in victim/community reparations, and advocate community participation in corrections programs. The guiding principles include the use of the least restrictive controls because offenders retain all rights as members of society except those removed or restricted by law, and the duty to act fairly and have victims consulted in planning regarding offenders.

Federal penal policy also went through a process of reform after 1950, and a Federal Mission Statement identified five core values: the dignity of individuals, the rights of all members of society, and the potential for human growth and development; the offender has the potential to live as a law-abiding citizen; staff and human relationships are the cornerstone of the Mission's endeavour; ideas, knowledge, values and experience must be shared nationally and internationally to achieve the Mission; and Federal Corrections must be managed with openness, integrity and accountability.

Guiding principles and objectives have flowed from this, and include placing a strong emphasis on the reintegration of offenders into the community, ensuring the safety of the community, and providing a milieu in which offenders have the highest possibility of personal development.

There are four provincial correctional centres: three for men, located in Prince Albert, Saskatoon and Regina; the centre for women is Pine Grove, in Prince Albert. In addition, there are two community correctional centres, the Battlefords Community Correctional Centre and the Buffalo Narrows Centre, and two correctional camps, at Besnard Lake and Saskatoon.

In 1885, plans were announced for construction of the "Regina Jail and Lunatic Asylum." It was built on the shores of Wascana Lake and contained twenty-eight cells for male inmates, a ward for female prisoners, and a ward each for male and female "insane." The building, however, stood empty for several years owing to poor construction, and did not admit prisoners until 1891. In 1905, Regina Jail was transferred from federal jurisdiction to the province, and served to house prisoners sentenced to less than two years. In 1906, legislation empowered the Department of Public Works to maintain the buildings and the provincial Attorney General to provide operational supervision. It appears that the Attorney General did not provide input, and in 1915 full responsibility for jails was given to Public Works.

In 1915 a new Regina jail opened, with accommodation for 150 prisoners; it was built northeast of Regina (its present site). The quality of construction was vastly superior to the previous building, and it included a 640-acre farm, since farming was a major activity for inmates and was seen as an important element in reforming prisoners. The 1946 Penal Commission recommendations had a major impact on the Regina Jail, as it did for the other institutions. It became known as the Regina Correctional Institution (later renamed Centre), with treatment and reeducation as its major objective. The transition was slow, but in the 1950s vocational training shops were built and a treatment staff unit added.

Treatment staff consisted of social workers and a psychologist. A work camp was created at Kenosee as an initiative to assist in the movement of offenders back into the community. Leg irons, organ boots (iron boots used for prisoners who were likely to escape), the paddle, and other such items of corporal punishment were not allowed to be used after the Penal Commission recommendations were accepted. Guards had been armed, and this policy was also changed after the Commission recommendations. Stronger initiatives to move into a community corrections model were taken in 1967. A new Corrections Act made it possible for the development of community-based half-way houses, expansion of probation services, and involvement of volunteers in rehabilitation. New units were built at the Centre that were self-contained with a central living area. The objective was to develop within each unit a sense of community that would enhance the socialization of offender and assist in reintegration.

The change of government in 1982 was accompanied by a strong shift to more punitive and restrictive policies in human services, and this had a major impact on correctional centres. Resources for rehabilitation were more restricted, and focus shifted to greater emphasis on custody and security, even though the rehabilitation model was not withdrawn. Additional security fences were constructed, and the use of razor wire increased significantly. At the same time, vocational training facilities were cut back, as was programming for inmates. The shift to a less conservative orientation in the 1990s had only a slight effect on the policy focus, which continued to be more on security than on rehabilitation and reintegration of the offender.

The facility is located three miles northeast of Regina. The original design provided for the typical bank of cellblocks, and these continue in use for offenders on remand and new admissions. Administrative offices are still located in the old section of the Centre. Presently there are three cottage-like structures that are the most modern units in the Centre, and this is where the majority of sentenced inmates are housed; inside, individual cells encircle a common room where there is a pool table and several other leisure time facilities. The Centre offers programs and services such as courses on anger management, AA meetings, and addictions counseling. An Elder is available for Aboriginal inmates who desire Native spiritual services; and a chaplain is on contract to conduct services, Bible study, and personal counseling. Recreational and social programming is limited. At present (2004), over half the population of the Centre is of Aboriginal origin.

Prince Albert Jail was the second territorial jail that was built in what is now Saskatchewan. It was constructed in 1886, but was not open for reception of prisoners until 1898. The building served as both a jail and courthouse, and consisted of twenty cells.

A new provincial jail was constructed in Prince Albert in 1921, on its present site, and included a farm of 272 acres. There was both a female and male section in the prison. Gallows and death row were part of the original prison construction; executions occurred in the provincial prisons since this was seen as a sentence of less than two years. With the shift to a treatment model after the Penal Commission, the government determined that they would not be obligated to carry out the death sentence in a provincial facility, and informed the federal government that they would not carry out such orders in a provincial prison. The gallows was finally dismantled in 1962.

From 1930 to 1941, women were moved from the Prince Albert jail to a renovated high school in Battleford because there had been an influx of women prisoners due to the **DOUKHOBOR** troubles, and more space was needed than the Prince Albert jail could provide. Women were moved back to the Prince Albert jail in 1941, however, and a women's unit continued there until a new facility for women was built in 1967. In 1970, much of the farmland was sold to the city for city expansion. In 1981, a new prison was opened, based on the modern philosophy of cottages rather than cell blocks to house prisoners, and the old 1921 building was demolished. Programs and services are similar to those available at the Regina Centre; however, the potential for positive rehabilitation and reintegration of offenders into the community—to which the building design lends itself—has not been entirely utilized.

A provincial jail was built in Moosomin in 1908 for male offenders only. It also had a farm attached. It was unique in that it had an orchard where apples and plums were grown. It was closed during the period of reform ushered in by the province's CCF government.

The Saskatoon Correctional Centre has the shortest history in that it was established in 1981. Similar to the Prince Albert Centre, it was built on the latest ideas of good correctional policy. Again, programs that are available are similar to those in the other two Centres, and do not maximize the potential. Political orientation in the 1980s in Saskatchewan was reflected in Corrections policy by shifting emphasis towards custody and safety; inertia has meant that reorientation towards a greater focus on reintegration has been slow.

The development of Community Training Residences and other "halfway house" resources was first initiated in the late 1960s. At present there are three such residences operated by the Saskatchewan Government, and other community-based residences have been established.

Correctional Services Canada has developed a system of maximum-, medium- and minimum-security institutions across Canada. It has also developed

Community Correctional Centres from which it is easier for offenders to reintegrate into society in a positive way. In Saskatchewan the federal government has one medium-security institution (Saskatchewan Penitentiary, in Prince Albert, which was a maximum-security institution at one time), a minimum-security facility (the Farm Annex, also at Prince Albert), and a Community Correctional Centre (Oscana Centre in Regina). The regional headquarters of the Correction Service of Canada is located in Saskatoon, as is the Regional Psychiatric Centre operated by the Correction Service of Canada. This Centre is a fully accredited psychiatric facility; it is used for sentenced offenders from the prairie region who have mental disorders. In addition, there are parole offices in Prince Albert, Saskatoon and Regina.

"Stony" is the federal penitentiary located northwest of Winnipeg, Manitoba. During the nineteenth century it housed prisoners from the North-West Territories (which included Saskatchewan at the time) who had been sentenced to two years or more. Stony Mountain Penitentiary continued to be used for more serious offenders from the North West Territories and, after 1905, from Saskatchewan. After 1911, when the Saskatchewan Penitentiary was built in Prince Albert, more serious offenders from the province were sent to that facility.

The Saskatchewan Penitentiary, with a high surrounding wall and gun turrets at each corner, immediately became a major landmark at the western edge of Prince Albert. After its completion Saskatchewan persons sentenced to two years or more were no longer sent to Stony Mountain in Manitoba, but served their sentence here. The institution has served both maximum- and medium-risk offenders, and is presently rated with a capacity of 64 for maximum- and 499 for medium-security inmates. Early on the prison developed a farm to produce grain, beef, and dairy products, and the farm was used as a work and skill development place for inmates. Workshops for trades training were also built, and a variety of educational programs have been developed. When classification of prisoners became formal, the part of the institution which housed female prisoners was split from the main institution and became a separate entity, called Riverbend Institution.

Riverbend Institution is a minimum-security institution which allows for more flexibility and freedom of movement of inmates. It became a separate institution in 1962 and has a capacity of 126. It produces good quality agricultural products that provide dairy and beef for correctional institutions in the prairie region.

The Regional Psychiatric Centre in Saskatoon is a federal penitentiary and also a licensed psychiatric facility. It is part of the Correctional Service of Canada system, and provides a secure facility for prisoners who have psychiatric disorders or who need psychiatric assessment. It provides services for the Federal Prairie Region, and also has agreements signed with the three prairie provinces so that prisoners from any of them can obtain services from the Centre. It serves both men and women.

The Okimaw Ohci Healing Lodge (near Maple Creek) is a federal institution and was designed as a special facility for female Aboriginal offenders. An Aboriginal healing approach is used to assist the women to move back into the community. It was built in 1995 at a rated capacity of 28.

Nipisikopawiyiniwak Nanapawihokamik Healing Lodge, a healing lodge similar to Okimaw Ohci, was built for men on Beardy's First Nation at Duck Lake. It became operational in 2003.

Oscana Centre in Regina was opened in 1972. It is a community residence operated by the Correctional Service of Canada for offenders who are in the process of moving back into the community. Many inmates have day parole, and thus can go into the community to find employment. They can also attend educational programs in the community. Oscana is the last institutional phase of an offender's process of reintegration into the community and full parole. It is located on the edge of downtown Regina, close to most community services. There is a very active program of reintegration for each inmate, facilitated by a close working relationship between Oscana staff and parole service staff.

Prior to the introduction of probation services, when the offence was minor or when the judge deemed the offender did not need imprisonment the sentence would be suspended, although a number of conditions might be imposed; and if after a specified time the offender had not re-offended, the case would be closed. However, consistent with current corrections policy, Saskatchewan now has a probation service, and 80% of convicted offenders are sentenced to probation or to a range of community services. Probation services were initiated in Saskatchewan as a result of the Penal Commission recommendations. In the early 1950s the service began with one probation officer in Saskatoon, and one in Regina. Presently probation is available in the whole province. Other community-based sentences such as electronic monitoring and community service have also been developed

Parole services are provided by the federal government through the Correctional Service of Canada. Persons serving sentences are eligible to apply for parole after having served one-third of their sentence. If parole is granted—there is no guarantee that it will be—offenders are placed under the supervision of a parole officer, to whom they must report and be accountable for their actions. If offenders do not abide by the conditions of parole, it can be revoked and offenders sent back to prison. Almost one-half of offenders presently serving a sentence of two years or more are under parole supervision.

Community-based correctional services have proliferated since 1975. There are several important factors that promoted these developments. One is the momentum restorative justice has been gaining in society (see RESTORATIVE JUSTICE and ABORIGINAL JUSTICE). Another is the study of victimology, which became a sub-discipline of criminology in the 1970s. A third element is the increased initiatives, particularly by Christian faith groups, in developing services based on their faith mandate; this was enhanced by the revitalization of chaplaincy services in the Correctional Service of Canada that provided leadership in developing community-based correctional services. The concept of rehabilitation, and particularly integration of offenders back into the community, has contributed immensely to community corrections initiatives.

Two organizations that have worked for decades with offenders in the community are the JOHN HOWARD SOCIETY and the ELIZABETH FRY SOCIETY. These non-profit agencies have worked tirelessly with offenders released from prison, and also play an important advocacy role in calling on public institutions and governments to address corrections issues in society.

The SALVATION ARMY has also played a historic role both in prisons and in the community by responding to the needs of offenders and ex-offenders. This service has taken many forms: providing lodging, clothing, food and other services on an emergency basis; operating facilities and services such as halfway houses; advocating for improved services; and providing spiritual services.

Other non-governmental organizations and church denominations provide volunteer services both in the institutions and in the community. Such services include personal visitation of long-term offenders who have no personal community or family contact, supporting chaplaincy service in and outside institutions, and providing support groups for ex-offenders. Examples of this include: the Person to Person Program, which was developed and maintained to provide visits by a person or a couple to long-term offenders at the Saskatchewan Penitentiary, and is of great help in eventually reintegrating prisoners into society; community chaplaincy services in Saskatoon and Prince Albert, which provide services for persons returning to those centres and also provide an ongoing location for socialization and contact; "Friends on the Outside," which provides a support base and friendship in Regina for persons coming from a prison; friendship centres, which provide an important support service for Aboriginal persons; and residences such as Waterton House, in Regina, which is maintained by the Salvation Army.

Circles of Support and Accountability are being

developed for high-risk offenders who have served their sentences and are returning to the community. These circles were initiated in Ontario in the early 1990s, and have been developed in Prince Albert, Saskatoon and Regina since 1998. By 2004, twelve circles had been established in these centres, many of which are still functioning. A high-risk person returning to the community from prison can request that a circle be formed for him or her in the community. The principles on which Circles of Support and Accountability are based are quite straightforward. At the outset, an agreement or covenant is signed by the core member (the person returning from prison) and the group of persons in the circle. It outlines the expectations and responsibilities of the core member and the other members. There are generally four to seven persons in one Circle, and Circles have been found to have a profound effect on successful reintegration into the community. The reason for this success is not difficult to find: everyone in society has a circle of family, friends and workmates—often augmented by church, club or society associations—so it is only logical that a person returning from prison, who either has no support base or a very negative base, needs a group of people who will be supportive and assist in accountability.

Otto H. Driedger

COTE FIRST NATION. Gabriel Cote's Cree-Saulteaux band signed **TREATY 4** on September 15, 1874, and a reserve was surveyed in 1877. In 1904, land was surrendered for the Canadian Northern Railway station and the town site of Kamsack. Between 1905 and 1907 additional land was surrendered, the northern sections of which were returned to reserve status. In 1913 a further two-mile strip of land on the southern boundary was surrendered, but returned in 1915 when concern was raised that the band had lost too much of their best agricultural land. In 1963, further acres surrendered in 1905 were also reconstituted as reserve land. The interest in and surrender of land from the reserve's southern boundary—nearest the Kamsack town site—resulted in part from speculation of its value for settlement. The surrender and then reconstitution of the reserve's land hardly produced an environment favourable to the community's economic development. Of the 2,819 registered band members, 721 live on their 8,088-ha reserve just north of Kamsack. The band has a day care centre, band office, community hall, health station, and arena, as well as the Saulteaux Healing and Wellness Centre, Cote United Church, and Chief Gabriel Cote Education Complex.

Christian Thompson

COTE-LERAT, MARGARET (1950–). Margaret Cote-Lerat, born on August 2, 1950, was the first person in Saskatchewan to teach a First Nations language in a public school. She enjoyed a diverse work experience before her employment with the Indian Language Program of the Saskatchewan Indian Cultural College (1979), where she assisted in developing the Saulteaux language curriculum guides. After teaching at Brandon University and at the Kamsack Junior High School, Cote-Lerat joined the **FIRST NATIONS UNIVERSITY OF CANADA** in Regina. Her publications include *Nahkawewin–Saulteaux, Ojibway Dialect of the Plains* (1984), Nahkawewin Workbook, a *Saulteaux Syllabics Book*, sixteen children's books (entitled *Saulteaux Talking Books*), and a songbook (*Anihsinape-Apinoci Naka-mowinan: Children's Saulteaux Songs and Nursery Rhymes*). Cote-Lerat has translated stories for Pebble Beach Interactive Fiction Inc. (Saskatchewan Education), and aided by her parents has recorded lessons from "Nahkawewin" in Saulteaux and written *First Edition Saulteaux Dictionary*.

Christian Thompson

COUNCILS OF WOMEN. Inspired by formation of the International Council of Women in 1888, women created local councils across Canada during the 1890s. They were umbrella organizations that brought together women's societies and associations. In 1893 the National Council of Women of Canada was founded; it brought together nationally organized associations, and saw itself as the reform-oriented, organized voice of Canadian womanhood. In 1895, Regina women founded a Local Council of Women; in 1916 others followed in Saskatoon, Prince Albert and Moose Jaw; and in 1918 one was founded in Swift Current. In 1919, the Provincial Council of Women in Saskatchewan was organized; its president was **W.C. (CHRISTINA) MURRAY**, wife of the University of Saskatchewan president and western vice-president of the National Council of Women. In 1923 local councils were formed in Estevan and Weyburn; in 1945 one was organized in Mossbank; and a final one appeared in Yorkton in 1965.

Women's groups could affiliate with the organization at any or all of the local, provincial or national levels, and included church groups, political associations, professional associations, ethnic societies, and service clubs. Representatives of affiliated groups attended council meetings and sat on the executive or committees. The councils offered members a chance to tackle women's issues in a coordinated way. Though some affiliated groups had conflicting ideologies, the councils helped them to find common elements in their mandates and coordinated work towards common goals that concentrated upon community betterment. The Provincial Council of Women was a powerful force in mobilizing Saskatchewan women. One of its first major projects was raising funds for tuberculosis sanatoria; within six years it had raised $50,000, an impressive amount for 1926. Over the decades particular projects undertaken by the councils have varied, but the over-riding themes—improving women's and children's lives and addressing social issues—have endured.

Lisa Dale-Burnett

FURTHER READING: Griffiths, N.E.S. 1993. *The Splendid Vision: Centennial History of the National Council of Women of Canada, 1893–1993.* Ottawa: Carleton University Press.

COUPLAND, ROBERT THOMAS (1920–2002). Bob Coupland was born in Winnipeg, Manitoba in 1920 and lived there until 1941, when he moved with his parents to a farm near Eriksdale. He won a Dominion-Provincial Youth Training Scholarship to take a vocational course in Agriculture at the University of Manitoba, and completed a BSA degree in Agriculture in 1946. During summers he worked at the Experimental Station, Canada Department of Agriculture, Swift Current. He earned a PhD at the University of Nebraska in 1946, studying with J.E. Weaver.

In 1948 Dr. Coupland was appointed assistant professor and Head of the Department of Plant Ecology at the **UNIVERSITY OF SASKATCHEWAN**. As a specialist on **WEEDS**, he served as a member of the National Weed Committee and as its chairman in 1954 and 1955, when he began issuing research reports. He was also a member of the Saskatchewan Advisory Weed Council, chairing it in 1963 and 1964. From 1948 to 1954 he was a member of the Grassland Subcommittee of the National Pasture Committee. He was chairman of the Saskatchewan Committee on Ecology and Preservation of Grasslands from 1953 to 1964.

By 1957 he had become professor of Plant Ecology at the University of Saskatchewan. Bob Coupland was science editor of the *Canadian Journal of Plant Science* from 1959 to 1963 and a member of the editorial board of *Ecology* from 1962 to 1964. He was an exchange scientist to the Soviet Union in 1961, carrying out discussions on Soviet grassland ecological problems. During that year, he chaired a symposium at the 10th International Botanical Congress.

Coupland's major contribution to science was as director of the Centre of the International Biological Program Grasslands Studies, Matador, Saskatchewan, from 1966 to 1976. This was a major world project utilizing many scientists who produced an extensive list of publications. During his university career from 1948 to 1985, he became internationally recognized as an expert on grassland ecology. He wrote five books, edited four others, and wrote many other publications; he was also considered an excellent teacher. A major article concerning him appears in the fifteenth edition of the *Encyclopedia Britannica*.

Dr. Coupland was awarded the Canadian

Centennial Medal for service to Canada. In 1976 he was made a Fellow of the Linnean Society of London. He received the Certificate of Merit in 1985 from Environment Canada for his work on prairie grasslands. Upon retirement he was appointed Emeritus Professor, Department of Plant Science and Ecology, University of Saskatchewan. He continued making contributions as Honorary Visiting Professor, Northeastern Normal University, Changchun, People's Republic of China in 1984–85. He was further recognized by being appointed an Officer in the Order of Canada in 1995.

Bob Coupland had married Irene Butterworth. He died in Saskatoon in 2002.   *U. Theodore Hammer*

FURTHER READING: Coupland, R.T. 1974. "Conservation of Grasslands in Canada." Pp. 93–111 in J.S. Maini and A. Carlisle (eds.), *A Conspectus*. Ottawa: Environment Canada; —. 1979. *Grassland Ecosytems of the World: Analysis of Grasslands and Their Uses*. Cambridge: Cambridge University Press; —. 1992. *Natural Grasslands: Introduction, Western Hemisphere*. Amsterdam: Elsevier.

COVINGTON, ARTHUR EDWIN (1913–2001).

Arthur Covington was born in Regina on September 21, 1913. After graduate education, he was employed at the National Research Council in Ottawa as an astronomer from 1946 until his retirement. He studied the cycle of solar activity, and made the first Canadian measurements of microwave emissions by sunspots relative to the rest of the sun. He established a long-term study of solar radiowave activity and solar flares which enhanced the prediction of the interruptions of long-range radio and other transmissions. His work expanded the activities of Canadian astronomers and enhanced the reputation of Canadian scientific research in the period after **WORLD WAR II**. Covington died on March 17, 2001.   *Diane Secoy*

COWESSESS FIRST NATION.

Chief Cowessess (Ka-wezauce, "Little Boy") adhered to **TREATY 4** on September 15, 1874, on the Hudson's Bay Company reserve, at the southeastern end of Echo Lake, with his **SAULTEAUX**, **CREE**, and **MÉTIS** followers. They remained nomadic until 1878–79, when they began farming near Maple Creek in the **CYPRESS HILLS**, and in 1880 a reserve was surveyed for them at Crooked Lake. While several band members settled there under O'Soup, Cowessess and his followers remained in the Hills until the spring of 1883. Education was always a priority: the first log school house was built in 1880 by the Oblate fathers; Cowessess Indian Residential School opened in 1898; and Lakeside Day School was built in 1934. The Roman Catholic Mission was called Crooked Lake Mission until the community was granted a post office under the name Marieval in 1908. The

21,488-ha Cowessess Reserve is 13 km northwest of Broadview, and an additional 257.1-ha reserve (73A) is situated 31 km west of Esterhazy. There are 3,266 band members, 597 of whom live on reserve.   *Christian Thompson*

COWLEY, ELWOOD LORRIE (1944–).

Born August 2, 1944, Cowley was raised in Kinley, near Perdue. In 1961 he began studies at the **UNIVERSITY OF SASKATCHEWAN**, completing a BEd in 1965 and a BA shortly thereafter. Cowley first taught in Assiniboia and later at Thom Collegiate in Regina. Cowley was president of the NDP youth at university and also the provincial NDP youth wing. Cowley was a key organizer for **ROY ROMANOW** in the 1970 leadership campaign, and at the leadership convention was elected party treasurer. Cowley was elected in 1971 in Biggar and appointed to Cabinet in 1972 as Minister of Finance. In 1975, Cowley was moved to the portfolio of Provincial Secretary but was also assigned the responsibility to form the Saskatchewan Potash Corporation. He introduced controversial legislation to nationalize a portion of Saskatchewan's **POTASH INDUSTRY**. As Minister of Mineral Resources, he expanded the role of government in the oil sector through **SASKOIL** and in the uranium industry through the Saskatchewan Mining Development Corporation. He was a central member of Cabinet's political committee and exercised considerable influence on the government's priorities and strategy. In 1982 Cowley was defeated along with the NDP government and returned to teaching before he found work as an investment broker in Saskatoon. In 1989 he established his own consulting company in Saskatoon.   *Brett Quiring*

FURTHER READING: Gruending, Dennis. 1990. *Promises to Keep: A Political Biography of Allan Blakeney*. Saskatoon: Western Producer Prairie Books.

SASKATCHEWAN ARCHIVES BOARD R-A24786
Elwood Cowley.

COWLEY, RETA (1910–2004).

Reta Cowley was born on April 1, 1910. Her paintings are renowned for their remarkable ability to capture the experience of being in the Saskatchewan prairies–evoking the expanse of space and depth of colour found only by a sensitive understanding of the light of the region. Cowley's ability to communicate this breathtaking environment was achieved through a lifetime dedicated to studying, teaching and practicing art.

Born Reta Madeline Summers in Moose Jaw, Cowley spent her childhood years near Truax and in Yorkton before graduating from the **NORMAL SCHOOL** in Saskatoon and beginning her teaching career in 1930. She taught at various rural schools through the difficult 1930s, moving to a permanent job in Yorkton from 1938 to 1946.

Having a lifelong interest in painting, Cowley began receiving formal training in 1937 when, encouraged by her sister, she attended the **UNIVERSITY OF SASKATCHEWAN** Summer School at Emma Lake, established the previous year by **AUGUSTUS KENDERDINE**. She returned every summer until 1940, studying art history under Dr. Gordon Snelgrove and painting with Kenderdine, from whom she adopted the *plein-air* tradition of the Barbizon school, painting from nature on the spot rather than in the studio. From 1941 through 1944, Cowley spent her summers at the Banff School of Fine Arts, focusing her practice on watercolours under the guidance of Walter J. Phillips. In 1945, she married Fred Cowley and was able to leave her teaching position and move to Saskatoon. She attended night classes at the University of Saskatchewan, studying with **ELI BORNSTEIN** and Nicolas Bjelajac, and absorbing the influence of modern art, particularly Cézanne and John Marin.

While Cowley did not share Bornstein's preference for avoiding reference to the natural world in her paintings, she did gain an understanding of how to structure her paintings according to form and colour and develop a patterning in her brush strokes. By the late 1960s, Cowley's mature style had emerged, capturing the space and light of the landscape in a style informed by modernism. She taught at the Emma Lake Summer School in the early 1950s (and again in the mid-1980s), and attended the seminal 1963 workshop as a participant. She received her Bachelor of Arts from the University of Saskatchewan in 1966, and served there as a sessional lecturer until 1972. She continued to teach public school, retiring in 1975 to paint full-time.

From the 1950s on, Cowley has been honoured with more than twenty solo exhibitions of her work and has been in numerous important group exhibitions. Her work is held in collections across Canada. In 1990, she received the **SASKATCHEWAN ARTS BOARD**'s Lifetime Award for Excellence in the Arts and the Saskatchewan Order of Merit. Cowley died on November 23, 2004.   *Christine Sowiak*

FURTHER READING: Dillow, Nancy E. *Reta Cowley.* Regina: Mackenzie Art Gallery, 1975; Ring, Dan. 1986. *Reta Cowley: A Survey.* Saskatoon: Mendel Art Gallery.

CRAFTS. Saskatchewan has a rich and largely unexplored history of craft practice. Some Aboriginal peoples used a range of craft skills, including pottery, to produce articles for personal adornment, domestic and ceremonial use, and trade. Materials were found locally, or obtained through the extensive trade networks which covered the Americas and which also provided for an exchange of cultural ideas, motifs and fashions. Knowledge of these artifacts comes from archaeological finds, and the accounts and acquisitions of the Europeans traders who first travelled through the prairie regions in the 17th century.

Comparable networks of cultural trade and exchange existed throughout Eurasia; craft knowledge was used to produce items for the same range of use, albeit using different materials and techniques. The great wave of European immigration to the prairies, which started in the late 19th century, included craftspeople who had learned their skills as apprentices in the small factories and craft industries of Europe, as students in art and craft schools, and informally from craftspeople within their family or their community. In Saskatchewan they confronted a very different situation from their densely populated homelands, where they had an established clientele in the villages and cities, a common vocabulary of inherited designs, colour preferences and social use, and access to materials suppliers and marketing networks. These immigrant craftspeople became part of a widely dispersed, poor and unstable homesteading population with its patchwork of ethnic groups.

Ever creative, craftspeople adapted. Cabinetmakers set up small businesses producing everything from furniture to coffins, until they were overwhelmed by mass-produced, mail-order furniture from eastern Canada. A few potters dug clay, built wheels and kilns, and carted or sledged along prairie trails to market their fragile wares; goldsmiths and blacksmiths plied their trade; but many skilled craftspeople found no market for their craft. Women continued to spin, embroider, knit, crochet, and to a lesser extent weave garments and household necessities, including those articles of personal and household adornment considered essential to their time and culture. They also contributed to the growing communities through selling their crafts to raise money for the building of churches and other community services, and produced tons of knitwear for the combatants and victims of the two World Wars.

Saskatchewan women started societies to nurture craft activity. The most important were the Saskatoon Arts and Crafts Society (SACS) and the Ukrainian Women's Association of Canada (UWAC),

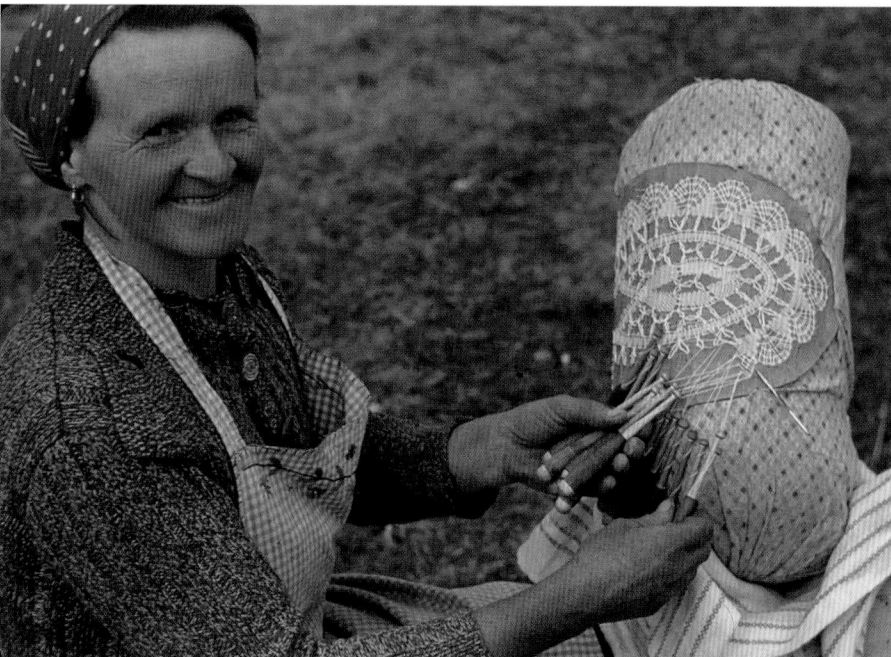

EVERETT BAKER PHOTO/COURTESY OF THE SASKATCHEWAN HISTORY AND FOLKLORE SOCIETY

Making lace, May 1943, at Bright Sand.

which ran education and exhibitions programs and collected craftwork—predominantly textiles. SACS marketed the work of rural "New Canadian" women, mainly from Eastern Europe, through a national network of craft shops. UWAC documented, taught and published books on Ukrainian embroidery, and established the Museum of the Ukrainian Women's Association of Canada in 1941, the first Ukrainian museum in North America.

Another first was the **SASKATCHEWAN ARTS BOARD** (SAB), established in 1948, which also supported craft activity through staff-run education programs and craft festivals. Several of SAB's employees, with its support, were instrumental in founding and staffing new national craft organizations in the 1960s. In 1975, the Saskatchewan Craft Council was formed to further the marketing, education, and promotion of provincial craftspeople, particularly those making a living from their crafts.

By the last half of the 20th century, Saskatchewan's population was increasingly stable, affluent, and concentrated in urban centres offering markets and patrons to a new generation of studio craftspeople. The distinctive crafts forming part of the ethnic heritage of the original settlers were overwhelmed by a new wave of internationalist studio crafts. The **UNIVERSITY OF REGINA** (and for a short time the **UNIVERSITY OF SASKATCHEWAN**) had notable ceramics departments, giving rise to a vigorous provincial ceramics scene and internationally known ceramists, such as **JACK SURES**, **JOE FAFARD**, **VIC CICANSKY** and **MARILYN LEVINE**. Among other internationally and nationally known Saskatchewan craftspeople are tapestry weavers Kaija Sanelma Harris (five times recipient of the government of Saskatchewan

Premier's Award) and Anne Newdigate Mills; furniture makers Michael Hosaluk, Jamie Russell and Don Kondra, who were responsible for a series of wood, now multimedia, conference/workshops attracting national and international participants; luthier David Freeman, who teaches his skills to international students; and the late William Hazzard, who won the national Sadye Bronfmann Award for Excellence in the Crafts for his bird carvings.

Quilters, embroiderers, spinners and weavers, blacksmiths, potters, furniture makers, woodturners, knife-makers, stained glass craftspeople and others have formed single media guilds to advance their knowledge. Comprising professional and leisure craftspeople, they form a lively network linking communities across the province and beyond.

Sandra Flood

FURTHER READING: Saskatchewan Craft Council fonds and Saskatoon Arts and Crafts Society fonds, Saskatchewan Archives; Silverthorne, J. 2003. *Ingrained Legacy: Saskatchewan Pioneer Woodworkers 1870–1930.* Regina: Spiral Communications.

CRAIG, ALBERT M. Albert M. Craig of North Battleford was a rancher who helped improve cattle breeding, especially Hereford cattle. He was invested as a Member of the Order of Canada in 1980. He died on November 1, 1981.

CRAIK, town, pop 418, located about mid-way between Regina and Saskatoon on Hwy 11. Although the Qu'Appelle, Long Lake & Saskatchewan Railway was running between Regina, Saskatoon, and Prince Albert in 1890, the Craik district was not really settled until the early 1900s. The majority of those who arrived in the area were of British origin. Craik had a peak population of 607 in 1956. Today, the town has a range of businesses and services, including a health centre and special care home, a K-12 school, and a local RCMP detachment. The Craik Community Archives and Oral History Society is located in the 1913 building which previously had housed the town hall, opera house, and fire hall. The Craik Prairie Pioneer Museum site includes a collection of pioneer artifacts housed in an assembly of heritage buildings. The most significant development in the community in recent years has been the Craik Sustainable Living Project: this initiative aims at advancing the local use of ecologically sound technologies by presenting viable alternatives related to land use, food and fibre production, energy generation and conservation, shelter, recycling, and water and waste management. Through the recently completed Eco-Centre, the development of an Eco-Village, and outreach and education programs, it is believed the project will stimulate socio-economic revitalization in the community.   *David McLennan*

CRANES. Cranes are long-legged, long-necked omnivorous birds found in water-edge and grass-lands habitats throughout the world, except for South America and the Antarctic. Although they look very similar to herons and storks, they are more closely related to rails. They are usually grey or white in plumage, often with red patches of skin or feathers on the head. They have elaborate "dancing" behaviours, which have often been imitated by the people who live near the cranes. They are ground-nesters, having small broods of one or two eggs. There are 15 species of cranes (Family Gruidae, Order Gruiformes); two of these occur in North America, including Saskatchewan. Many of the crane species are considered to be vulnerable or endangered.

The Whooping Crane (*Grus americana*) is the largest bird which occurs in the province and is the tallest bird on the continent, at 130 cm. This tall white bird with black wingtips and red forehead and cheek bred in the province before the end of the 19th century but is now only a rare, but regular, transient between its breeding grounds in northern Alberta and the wintering grounds along the Texas coast. It can be seen in migration in the centre of the province, particularly around the north end of **LAST MOUNTAIN LAKE**. The Whooping Crane was once found widely within the central regions of North America. By the 1940s, the population had been reduced by hunting and the drainage of its beeding sites to around 15 birds. Heroic efforts to conserve it from extinction have resulted in the present population of about 160 birds. The threat of the loss of this stately species, along with other significant species such as the **BISON**, have given impetus to the **CONSERVATION** movement, which is concerned with the health of the natural world, including individual species such as this crane.

The Sandhill Crane (*G. canadensis*) has much larger populations, but is also under pressure from habitat loss. The Sandhill Crane is somewhat smaller than the Whooping Crane, but is still a tall bird of over a metre in height. The grey adult has a red crown, while the juveniles are sandy in plumage. The species is presently a rare breeding bird at several marshes, scattered throughout the province. These local breeding birds are joined by large numbers of Arctic tundra breeders to form the large migrant flocks which are so visible, particularly in the fall. These large flocks stop to feed at several places in central Saskatchewan, such as the Quill lakes and **LAST MOUNTAIN LAKE**, providing a natural spectacle.   *Lorne Scott and Diane Secoy*

FURTHER READING: Alsop, Fred J. III 2002. *Birds of Canada*. Toronto: Dorling Kindersley.

CRAWFORD, ROY DOUGLAS (1933–). Roy Crawford was born on June 6, 1933, in Saskatoon. He completed a BSA in Poultry Husbandry at the **UNIVERSITY OF SASKATCHEWAN** in 1955 and received an MSc in Animal Genetics from Cornell University in 1957. From 1957 until 1964, Crawford was a research officer in Agriculture Canada, with postings in Ottawa, Charlottetown and Kentville. During this period, he returned to school and received his PhD in Poultry Genetics from the University of Massachusetts in 1963. In 1964, he accepted the position of professor of Poultry Science at the University of Saskatchewan, which he held until he retired on June 30, 1991. He taught in the areas of poultry genetics, breeding and husbandry, but has also made significant contributions in teaching introductory Animal Science and Animal Genetics courses. He taught in the College of Agriculture, Western College of Veterinary Medicine, College of Graduate Studies and Research, and the School of Agriculture. When the College of Agriculture established the award of Professor of the Year, Crawford received the initial honour in 1977. Similarly, he was named the first University of Saskatchewan Master Teacher in 1984, and on two occasions was designated Professor of the Year in the College of Veterinary Medicine. In 1981, he was presented with the Ralston Purina Teaching Award by the Poultry Science Association.

Crawford published over sixty papers in refereed journals, presented or was a co-author on a similar number of papers at scientific meetings, as well as giving numerous invited lectures. One of his most important contributions was the discovery of a mutation which caused epileptiform seizures in chickens; this mutation is still an important animal model in the study of the grand mal form of epilepsy in humans. Upon the request of the Poultry Science Association, in 1989–90 he edited and wrote five chapters of *Poultry Breeding and Genetics*, the first comprehensive review of this topic since F.B. Hung published "Genetics of the Fowl" in 1949. This text is already considered a classic contribution to our knowledge of poultry science. A world leader in the area of animal genetic conservation, Crawford published in 1968 the first catalogue of poultry stocks held at teaching and research institutions in Canada, and continued to publish this document on an annual basis until 1981. Thereafter, the catalogue was included in the document "Research Animals in Canada," which was produced in co-operation with

One immature and two adult Whooping Cranes.

the Canadian Council on Animal Care. Crawford was an active member of the FAO/UNEP Expert Panel on Genetic Resources Conservation, and has lectured extensively on the philosophy and technical aspects of germplasm preservation. Currently, he is a member of an ad hoc planning committee for Rare Breeds International, a new organization for the global coordination of national rare breeds conservation groups, and an executive member of the American Minor Breeds Conservancy. He was named a Fellow of the Agricultural Institute of Canada in 1986, and of the Poultry Science Association in 1991. *Philip Thacker*

CREDIT UNION ELECTRONIC TRANS-ACTION SERVICES. Credit Union Electronic Transaction Services (CUETS) is a supplier of credit card–related products and services for credit unions, banks, and other financial services providers. CUETS is a member of MasterCard International and services about 500 MasterCard-affiliated organizations across Canada, reaching millions of cardholders through national and international network connections. CUETS is based in Regina, where it employs about 350 people; an additional 150 are employed at the CUETS MasterCard service centre in Winnipeg. CUETS has regional offices in Vancouver, Calgary, Toronto, and Moncton. In the late 1970s, Credit Union Central of Saskatchewan and Credit Union Central of Alberta (the current joint-owners of CUETS) identified a need within the Credit Union system to provide its members with a card product. The MasterCard brand was chosen, and in 1982 CUETS was incorporated as an operations centre to manage the MasterCard services program for its affiliated members. The first card was issued by Sherwood Credit Union in Regina in 1982; by the late 1980s CUETS had issued over 200,000 cards to credit unions and co-operative financial institutions in nearly every Canadian province. Throughout the 1990s CUETS greatly diversified its services and expanded its product line, earning a reputation as one of Saskatchewan's fastest growing companies and ranking among the top 100 employers in Canada. In 2003, CUETS reported sales of $140 million. *Iain Stewart*

CREE. The term *"Cree"* is derived from the French renderings (*Kristineaux, Kiristinous, Kilistinous*) of the Ojibway term *kinistino*. The proper term in the Plains Cree language is *nêhiyawak*. The Cree occupy a large area of Saskatchewan, from the northern woodlands areas to the southern plains. While being one people, there is a great variation amongst the different regional groups. One of the main differences is in terms of dialect, of which there are three main ones: "th" Woodlands, "y" Plains, and "n" Swampy Cree. There are also important differences in terms of culture: the **SUN DANCE**,

for example, is practiced only in the southern areas. Despite those variations, the Cree are bound together by a shared collective memory, worldview, religious practices, and experience of colonialism.

The *nêhiyawak* began to move onto the prairies with the fur trade in 1740. The Cree in the south were part of the Iron Confederacy, an alliance with the Saulteaux and Assiniboine; they were middlemen in the fur trade, trading with the English and the French, as well as with other Indigenous groups. As the *nêhiyawak* began to move onto the prairies in greater numbers, they slowly adapted from using canoes to using horses; the latter also replaced dogs as pack animals. Despite these changes, the *nêhiyawak* retained many of their Woodland beliefs and practices. In their worldview, it is believed that humans are intimately linked with the world around them: for instance, hunters would have *pawâkanak* (dream helpers) to guide people towards game; the *pawâkanak* would also help the person in times of need. Furthermore, one of the key values of the Cree was sharing: game was shared as well as any other resources. Another key concept was *wâhkotowin* (kinship), important not only for the way in which people were related, but also in terms of peoples' connection to the land. An important part of *nêhiyawak* oral tradition is reflected in the stories of *wîsahkêcâhk*, commonly referred to as the "trickster." *wîsahkêcâhk* links humans to the rest of creation (e.g., other animals), makes the world safe for humans, teaches humans many things, and also is a joker who often gets caught up in his own jokes. These stories, which taught children lessons about life, are referred to as *âtayôhkêwina* (sacred stories).

In the 1870s, the Canadian government began to expand westwards and initiated a Treaty process with the Indigenous people, including the *nêhiyawak*. One major difference between the English and Cree accounts is that the latter understood the deal as *tipahamâtowin* (rent), whereas the former understood it as land surrender; also, the Cree used the pipestem to invoke the powers of the land (*asotamâkêwin*: a sacred vow). Some leaders such as *mistahi-maskwa* (**BIG BEAR**) were skeptical of the process. He did not stand against the Treaty process, but rather against the way in which the Crown was handling matters. He tried therefore to organize his people peacefully, but the Resistance of 1885 brought trouble; and despite Big Bear's efforts to avert trouble, many people lost their lives. While this series of events is called the **NORTH-WEST RESISTANCE** (or Rebellion) in English, in Cree it is referred to as *ê-mâyihkamikahk*, which means "when it went wrong."

The Cree of the woodland and northern areas entered into Treaty through later adhesions. There was also less pressure for European settlement in their territories, and as a result they were able to

GERALDINE MOODIE PHOTO
Cree family, Battleford, June 1895.

maintain their traditional hunting and trapping much longer than the southern Cree. The Cree are today the most numerous Indigenous group in Saskatchewan. Many efforts are made to revive the language through immersion programs, writing of dictionaries, and increased use of Elders in the classrooms. Cree people have revived many ceremonies which were banned for a long period of time, and social gatherings such as powwows and round dances enjoy popularity amongst many people. *nêhiyawak* are becoming more and more significant in the culture and economy of Saskatchewan. *Neal McLeod*

FURTHER READING: Dion, J.F. 1979. *My Tribe the Crees*. Calgary: Glenbow Museum; Mandelbaum, D.M. 1979 (1940). *The Plains Cree*. Regina: Canadian Plains Research Center.

CREE COSMOLOGY. The Cree, or *nêhiyawahk*, are a group of people with homelands and territories dotting the country from east to west. Although the continuity of Cree existence is largely unwritten in any text, it is indelibly etched in memory and within the oral tradition of linguistic and spiritual observances of song, dance, art, and ritual still maintained in many communities. This identity and the practice of Cree-being is most fully expressed within the contexts of individuals, families, extended families and multiple other relationships that comprise the essence of every Cree community. Like any other culture, the Cree people recount their origins and sacred beginnings to creation time. According to the narrative, the beginning of time started without form: darkness shrouded the void of nothingness, where stillness encapsulated the potential of what was to follow. In the opening moments of the sacred beginning, a light shone forth and the potential started to unfold as the universe came into being in its designed order: the heavens opened up, and the universe with all the stars, the worlds and Mother Earth herself came into being. With the establishment of the firmament the elements of life took hold, and eventually human life itself came into existence.

The coordinates of Cree existence locate the creation narrative as the archetype of its spiritual foundation, the events and sequence of the unfolding universe being the basis of the Cree belief system. In time, other sacred narratives of Cree mythology speak of the emergence of a cultural hero who changed the chaotic myth-world into the ordered creation of today: this trickster, *wîsahkêcahk*, named and organized everything that existed in the Cree lifescape, and made the flora and fauna, earth, and heavens harmonious and safe in preparation for the arrival of the Cree people. The Cree corpus of tribal narratives represents the archives of centuries of learning and the synthesis of human, ecological, and spiritual knowledge. In many cases, Cree knowledge is only accessible through the understanding of a complex nexus of sacred oral narratives and communal spiritual practices that are reenactments of the creation time. The whole scheme of creation and mythological beginnings, along with a complex array of peoples' experiences since ancient times, contributes to what traditional Cree people consider the truth of existence. (*See also* **CREE**; **CREE RELIGIOUS ETHOS**)

Willie Ermine

FURTHER READING: Ahenakew, F. and H.C. Wolfart. 1998. *The Counselling Speeches of Jim Kī-Nīpitêhtêw*, Winnipeg: University of Manitoba Press; Christensen, D. 2002. *Ahtahkakoop: The Epic Account of a Plains Cree Head Chief*. Shell Lake: Ahtahkakoop Publishing; Young, D., G. Ingram, and L. Swartz. 1989. *Cry of the Eagle: Encounters with a Cree Healer*. Toronto: University of Toronto Press.

CREE LAKE (57°30'N, 106°30'W; Map sheet 74 G/7). Cree Lake, 81 km long and 57 km wide, covers some 1,434 km². It is located in the northern Saskatchewan Shield, about 300 km northwest of La Ronge. It drains northward via Cree River into Black Lake. There is also access southward via portage into the Mudjatik and Churchill rivers. Cree Lake is a remnant of a much larger lake formed by meltwaters of the retreating continental ice-sheet about 8,700 years ago. While the present shoreline lies at 487m, strand-lines of the former pro-glacial lake are elevated at 520 m. Glacial Cree Lake initially drained southward through glacial spillways into the **CHURCHILL RIVER**, but isostatic rebound elevated these southern outlets and the lake spilled northward into a succession of spillways leading into **LAKE ATHABASCA**.

DOUG CHISHOLM PHOTO
Cree Lake.

A sandy area at the south end of Cree Lake was historically a Dene wintering ground. Today, a reserve and a small settlement are found there. In spite of the isolation, a fur-trade post was located on the lake around 1803. In the 1920s and 1930s the area was used by white trappers seeking a living during the **GREAT DEPRESSION**. Today, fly-in fishing camps on the lake provide southern tourists with the chance to catch trophy specimens of northern pike, lake trout, Arctic grayling and walleye.

Marilyn Lewry

FURTHER READING: Karras, A.L. 1970. *North to Cree Lake*. New York: Trident Press; Schreiner, B.T. 1984. *Quaternary Geology of the Precambrian Shield, Saskatchewan*. Regina: Saskatchewan Energy and Mines Report No. 221.

CREE RELIGIOUS ETHOS. The Cree community is the microcosm and representation of the entire Cree nation. The whole system of relationships includes not only the family and extended family, but also the alliances with natural and supernatural entities. These relationships extend to the participation level, where everything in the world takes part in the experience that the spirit of things is all one. The community is a structure of support mechanisms that emphasizes reciprocity: not only is the collective to be upheld, respected and protected, but conversely the nature of personhood is to be honoured and clearly identified. The community is the primary expression of a natural context and environment where personhood can aspire and achieve what it is meant to be: movement within this community context allows individuals to discover all there is to discover about one's self.

In Cree communities it is the older people who keep the stories and who relate the teachings of good thought and action to the children: they tell the children how the world and their people came to be and what it means to be one of the people. The Cree community can be thought of as a living organism which has its vital components and functioning units, such as the mind, heart, soul, and all the attributes that give essence and character to a living being. Like any living organism, the communal soul needs to be nurtured in order for it to be healthy and vital. One can conceive of the many separate units functioning together and appropriately for the benefit of the whole living entity. As an example, particular people in the communities perform the role of the mind for the organism: it is their compulsion to sit long hours thinking, calculating, anticipating and charting the best course for the community to follow. There are also some within the community who represent the eyes of the organism: gifted with second sight, they foresee the future and mobilize the conditions necessary for the community to negotiate that future.

The most important parts of this organism are the heart and the soul. The heart of the community may be represented by the many people who engage in work dedicated to health and well-being. Their work is done with no expectation of recognition or reward, but they are models for others to follow. The sacredness of communities may well be expressed by the wholeness of the people, but it is the spiritual leaders who remind others of the sacred connections: these are the people who rise with the dawn and silently pray that only good may come to all.

The community ethos is the inviolable spirit of the collective. It acts as the dynamic blueprint for families to adjust and live in the varying contexts imposed by time.

The Elders and spiritual people of the Cree meditate about the meaning of existence and about the relationship between human inner space, the natural world, and the mysterious life force that permeates creation. This practice of Cree metaphysics provides insight into the origin and nature of knowledge, with the result that there is a deeper understanding of the natural order; this spiritual understanding and connectedness is the foundational principle of the Cree ethos. The earth, plants, animals, elements and everything in nature exhibit an intelligence that is perceptible and responsive to human endeavour. Within this perspective, dividing the universe into living and non-living things has no meaning: animate and inanimate matter is inseparably interwoven, and human life is also enfolded in the totality of the universe. The attitude of a personal relationship with the spiritual and natural worlds is moulded into a systematic code of conduct and behaviour and includes agreements with the spirits of creation. In each Cree territory, covenants were established with land, water, plant-life, animals, etc., which would act as spiritual agreements of reciprocity dictating how all life would co-exist in mutual protection, benefit, and continuity. This reciprocity is maintained through the various ceremonies, songs, narratives, and personal sacrifices of Cree spirituality.

The accumulated knowledge of the Cree people is embedded in the ethos of the community as a representative form of the collective. In this sense, additional insights and understandings about Cree existence are obtained through close observation and participation in communal ceremonies and ritual, teachings and inheritance, connectedness to the dream world, and the affirmation and study of sacred oral narratives. Language is also a part of the Cree ethos because it describes the worldview, the spiritual consciousness, and narratives of that consciousness. The language of the Cree describes and makes understandable the processes governing Cree reality; it works as a system of knowledge where it becomes possible to identify the human actions congruent with the flowing wholeness in nature. Every Cree community holds the religious ethos of the entire Cree nation: this heritage not only informs the people of their roots and of the rights to a tradition entrusted to Cree society, but also reminds them that the future is collectively negotiated.

Willie Ermine

CREIGHTON, northern town, pop 1,556, located in northeastern Saskatchewan near the Saskatchewan-Manitoba border. Situated almost at the 55th parallel within the Precambrian Shield, Creighton is one of only two municipalities with town status in northern Saskatchewan (the other is La Ronge). By road, Creighton is accessed via Hwy 106 (the Hanson Lake Road) or, on the Manitoba side, by Hwy 10 from The Pas. Highway 167, lead-

ing south from Creighton, gives access to Denare Beach and Amisk Lake, the south end of which was the scene of Saskatchewan's first and little-known gold rush, which occurred between 1914 and 1918. Creighton had its beginnings in the 1930s after the Department of Natural Resources built a road from Flin Flon to Amisk Lake. People began to settle along this road; after **WORLD WAR II**, a townsite was surveyed and lots were made available for residential and business development. Many servicemen returning from overseas came to the area, and in 1952 the community was incorporated as a village. Creighton attained town status in 1957. It is named after Tom Creighton, whose prospecting discoveries in 1915 were largely responsible for the development of mining operations at Flin Flon. Today, the Hudson Bay Mining & Smelting Company is the largest employer in the area, producing zinc, copper, and gold. Other economic activities are based in forestry and tourism.

David McLennan

CROATIAN AND SERBIAN SETTLEMENTS. People of Croatian origin began to settle in the Kenaston area in 1904, concentrating in homesteads to the east of Hanley and Kenaston, and in the Smales district between Kenaston and Bladworth. These settlers had come from Lovinac and surrounding villages in a valley across the coastal mountain range to the east of the port city of Zadar, in Croatia. The first to arrive were the Pavelic(h)(k), Prpic(k), Masic(h), and Tomljenovic/Tomlenovich/Thompson families. In the next ten years they were joined by other families including Sekulic(h), Brkic(h), Vrkljan, Matevic(h), P(e)rsic(h), Sarich, Zdunich, K(e)rpan/Krypan, Rupcich, Stromatich, Yelich, and Obrigavi(t)ch. Already by 1914 Croatians occupied forty-one homesteads in the settlement. By the late 1920s, Croatian farmers had accumulated some 50,000 acres of land–a remarkable contrast with their recent background in the mountains of Croatia, where their families were poor illiterate farmers and family farms seldom exceeded forty acres (some were as small as one or two acres); the migrants had been forced to sell their shares of family farms to pay for their passage to North America. The first to leave were younger men escaping overcrowding on these small farms. In the mountain villages young men were accustomed to having to find physical work. In North America they took whatever manual labour they could find: these first settlers around Kenaston had worked in railroad section gangs in Oklahoma, Kansas, Arkansas, and other midwestern states, and as coalminers in the Crowsnest Pass in Canada, before hearing of homesteads in the prairies. So they initially arrived in Saskatchewan as single young men before being joined by wives and other family members; some temporarily returned to Croatia to find wives.

Typically, men in the mountain villages of

Croatia were limited to only four years of formal education; but they were used to hard work, and had come to Saskatchewan to develop farms their predecessors back in Croatia could hardly imagine. When they first settled they made their own handsewn clothing. Mixed subsistence farming soon became large-scale grain farming. Farm buildings were concentrated, in keeping with the *zadruga* communal tradition, at the centre of four converging blocs of land in order to enhance mutual cooperation. *Susjed*–helpful neighbours–were highly valued: this co-operative tradition was reflected in strong support of the **UNITED GRAIN GROWERS**, **SASKATCHEWAN WHEAT POOL**, and Co-operative Association. Country schoolhouses quickly familiarized Croatian children with the English language; in turn, children assisted parents and even grandparents to learn some English. Within one generation English given names–and even an occasional surname–were adopted. Strong rural communal life was evident in the religious calendar (Kenaston had an active Roman Catholic parish which the Croatians shared with other Slavs), especially at Christmas and Easter, school concerts, various fairs, church bazaars and harvest suppers, homemakers meetings and sports events, as well as at the weddings, baptisms and funerals marking the passage of life. While the Kenaston area remained the best-defined Croatian settlement in Saskatchewan, smaller numbers of Croatians did settle in other areas such as near Leask and, together with their Serbian neighbours, also from Yugoslavia, in several other locations. Holy Trinity Serbian Orthodox Church, founded in Regina in 1916, was the first Serbian Orthodox parish in Canada. (*See also* **ETHNIC BLOC SETTLEMENTS**) *Alan Anderson*

CROFFORD, JOANNE SHARON (1947–). Joanne Crofford (*née* Elkin) was born in Regina on October 29, 1947. After graduating from the **UNIVERSITY OF REGINA** in Communications and Social Studies, she moved to La Ronge, where she did personnel work for the Department of Northern Saskatchewan and was business manager of the Kikinahk Indian and Métis Friendship Centre. She also served on the provincial Environment Impact Assessment Secretariat. After twelve years, Crofford returned to Regina, and worked for Rainbow Youth Centre and as research coordinator for the Faculty of Social Work at the University of Regina. Crofford was elected in 1991 as the NDP MLA for Regina Lake Centre, and re-elected in 1995 and 1999. In 1995, Crofford was appointed Minister for Saskatchewan Property Management Corporation and the Liquor and Gaming Authority. She served as minister of several portfolios: Status of Women; Indian and Métis Affairs; Culture, Youth and Recreation; Provincial Secretary; Post-Secondary Education and Skills Training; Labour; Wascana Centre Authority; and the

Joanne Crofford, January 2001.

Information Highway. In 2001, Crofford was one of seven candidates who ran in the NDP leadership race to replace ROY ROMANOW. She was re-elected in Regina Rosemont in 2003, and was appointed Minister of Community Resources and Employment. Crofford has been active in cultural, human rights, community service, youth, labour, and business organizations. In 2000, the World March of Women honoured Crofford for her commitment and dedication to social justice. She is a recipient of the Canada 125 and Queen's Golden Jubilee medals. *Jenn Ruddy*

CROP DEVELOPMENT CENTRE. The Crop Development Centre (CDC) was established at the UNIVERSITY OF SASKATCHEWAN in 1971 through collaboration between the University, the National Research Council (NRC) and the Saskatchewan Department of Agriculture. The NRC funded the sci-

entists and support staff for the first three years. The government of Saskatchewan has provided the Centre's core staff and operational funding through its Department of Agriculture since that time. The original mandate of the CDC was to expand research and breeding in winter and spring wheat, feed grains, and new crops. Later expansion of the program provided capacity for research on weed control, CONSERVATION tillage, and BIOTECHNOLOGY. The current research focus is on plant breeding in WHEAT (winter, spring and durum), BARLEY (malting, feed and food), OAT (feed and food), FLAX (linseed and solin) and pulse crops (peas, lentils, chickpeas and dry beans), as well as pulse crop pathology.

The Centre has access to extensive research facilities that include a very large land base, controlled environment growth facilities, and laboratories and equipment that are unmatched in Canada. Besides the core and project funding provided by the provincial government, the CDC receives significant financial support from several producer groups and private industry. Royalties on the sale of pedigreed seed of CDC crop varieties as well as the sale of breeder seed and commercial grain are also important revenue sources. With excellent facilities and staff and strong government and industry support, the CDC has made significant contributions to the agricultural economy of Saskatchewan and the rest of western Canada.

Since 1977, the Centre has released 222 new crop varieties of twenty-two different crop types. Scientists in the Centre were instrumental in the development of the Saskatchewan pulse crop industry. The area planted to pulses has increased from a few thousand acres in 1971 to nearly five million acres in 2004. Lentil, flax, winter wheat, oat and barley varieties developed at the Centre occupy

major portions of the area seeded to these crops in western Canada, and in many cases they set the quality standards for those crops. Harrington barley was registered in 1981 and is recognized throughout the world as the quality standard for two-row malting barley. Laird- and Eston-type lentils enjoy similar stature in export markets. Scientists at the Centre have also made significant contributions to improvements in crop production and pest-management techniques, and have played a major role in providing Saskatchewan farmers with up-to-date crop production information. With a solid record of success and strong support from farmers and funding agencies, the Centre continues to develop improved crop varieties and crop-management practices for Saskatchewan. *Frederick A. Holm*

CROP PESTS. Agricultural insect pests are a diverse group: they include herbivores, stored grain pests, and livestock pests. There are also insects that act as vectors of disease organisms. The primary factors that influence insect population growth include weather (temperature, moisture and wind), food supply, availability of habitat, and natural enemies. Many pest insects are invasive species that have been introduced into Canada from other countries, especially Europe. However, some of our most chronic pests are native to the Canadian prairies. Although there has been an increase in the area seeded to oilseed and pulse crops in Saskatchewan, cereal crops still dominate. There are some twenty species of insect pests that attack cereal crops; the predominant species, and those most frequently in need of control, are grasshoppers and wheat midge. Other pests include wireworms, cutworms, wheat stem sawfly, and aphids.

Of the seventy or so grasshopper species native to Saskatchewan, there are only a small number (a few *Melanoplus* species) that are of economic importance to crop production. The occurrence and distribution of these species are generally associated with the GRASSLAND ecozones in Saskatchewan, although isolated outbreaks can also occur in the parkland ecozone where the soil is lighter in texture. Grasshoppers remain a chronic pest problem in the province primarily because they are so well adapted to conditions on the Canadian prairies. Most species overwinter as eggs in the soil, insulated by snow cover. Grasshoppers emerge in spring in response to temperature; higher temperatures result in faster development of the eggs and nymphal growth. Hot, dry weather conditions favour population increase, while cool moist conditions slow population growth. Although there is a guild of natural enemies (predators, parasites, diseases), they generally do not reduce grasshopper populations sufficiently during outbreaks.

Wheat midge, *Sitodiplosis mosellana*, is native to Europe. Since it was discovered in Saskatchewan

Barley research in a greenhouse at the University of Saskatchewan Crop Development Centre, 1980.

OWEN OLFERT PHOTO
Wheat midge adult.

in 1983, the insect has spread to most of the wheat-growing areas of the prairies. Larvae feed on developing wheat kernels, reducing grain yield and quality. At low levels, wheat midge populations may go unnoticed for several years; however, under favourable conditions, these populations can reach epidemic levels within one or two years. Moist conditions in May and June favour larval development and emergence of adults; warm, calm conditions in July favour egg-laying. There is one natural enemy, the pteromalid wasp *Macroglenes penetrans*, that plays a significant role (30% to 40%) in reducing wheat midge infestations. Other pest management practices include rotating wheat with resistant crops (oilseeds or pulses) to discourage buildup of wheat midge populations.

Saskatchewan produces a major share of oilseed crops in the prairie region. This shift away from cereal crops has also been accompanied by a change in the insect pest complex of prairie field crops. Some thirty species of insect pests attack oilseed crops; the predominant species are flea beetles and bertha armyworm. Other pests include diamondback moth, root maggots, red turnip beetle, plant bugs, red-backed cutworm, beet webworm, cabbage looper, imported cabbageworm, and painted lady butterfly.

Eight flea beetle species are known to damage canola, mustard and rapeseed crops. However, only the crucifer flea beetle, *Phyllotreta cruciferae*, and the striped flea beetle, *P. striolata*, are economically important. Both species were introduced into Canada from Eurasia. Adult beetles overwinter in plant litter, become active early in spring, and cause severe damage to newly emerging crops. Planting oilseed crops early and using large seeds to maximize seedling vigour produces plants that can tolerate flea beetle injury. Natural enemies do not significantly suppress flea beetle populations.

Bertha armyworm (*Mamestra configurata*), a type of climbing cutworm, is native to North America. Severe infestations on oilseed crops can occur throughout Saskatchewan, but they occur more frequently in the parkland ecozone. The adult emerges in early summer and is strongly attracted to its host plants when they are in bloom. The larvae mature rapidly and cause severe damage in the last two larval stages. In most years, bertha armyworm populations are suppressed by unfavourable weather conditions and by natural enemies, which include a nuclear polyhedrosis virus, an ichneumonid wasp, and a tachinid fly. However, when these natural regulators fail, populations tend to increase dramatically in just a few seasons.

As the dominant land animals, it is not surprising that some insects have a negative impact on agricultural production. However, it has been estimated that insects that function as decomposers, pollinators, predators and parasites, provide five to ten times more benefits to agricultural production than the damage caused by pest species. *Owen Olfert*

FURTHER READING: Doane, J., M. Braun, O. Olfert, F. Affolter and K. Carl. 2001. "*Sitodiplosis mosellana*, Orange Wheat Blossom Midge (Diptera: Cecidomyiidae)." Pp. 246–49 in P.G. Mason and J.T. Huber (eds.), *Biological Control Programmes in Canada, 1981–2000*. Oxford: CABI Publishing. Olfert, O. 1986. "Insect Pests of Wheat in Western Canada and Their Control." Pp. 415–30 in A.E. Slinkard and D.B. Fowler (eds.), *Wheat Production in Canada–A Review*. Saskatoon: University of Saskatchewan.

CROSS, JOHN VALENTINE (1940–). Born in the village of Budworth, Great Britain on February 14, 1940, John Valentine Cross has become a model for Saskatchewan entrepreneurs. He obtained his Bachelor of Chemical Engineering degree in 1963 from the University of Bradford in England. He immigrated to Canada in 1963 and furthered his education at the University of Western Ontario with a Master's of Engineering Science in 1965. Cross worked in the Food Research Division of John Labatt from 1965-75 in Saskatoon. In 1975, he became the founding director of the **POS PILOT PLANT** Corporation. Partnering with George Khachatourians and John Schaw in 1980, John Cross began building the foundations of **PHILOM BIOS**, which today is the leading inoculant company in western Canada. In the early 1980s he was also involved in the dog food business, developing novel grain-handling systems, and consulting in the food and agricultural sectors. He has served on numerous national bodies over the past 25 years, including the National Biotechnology Advisory Committee, the National Research Council of Canada, and the Pest Management Advisory Committee. In Saskatoon he has served as director and chairman of Saskatchewan Research Council, and as a member of several Boards: **AGWEST BIOTECH INC.**, the Saskatoon and Region Economic Development Authority (SREDA), the International Centre for the Advancement of Science and Technology (ICAST), and the Advanced Technology Training Centre at the Kelsey campus of SIAST. Cross was recognized as Canadian Entrepreneur of the Year for the Prairie Region for Science and Technology; in 1998 he was awarded the first Agri-business Leadership Award by the Saskatoon Chamber of Commerce; and in 2003 he received the AgWest Biotech BioScience Award for Entrepreneurial Leadership and Vision. The Saskatchewan Institute of Agrologists recognized John Cross with an Honorary Life Membership in 2002. *Tara L. Procyshyn*

CROW FAMILY. The members of the family Corvidae include crows, ravens, jays and magpies. These large, gregarious, intelligent perching birds have strong feet and stout, straight beaks which enable them to feed on any available food. The larger species are often predators on smaller birds and rodents. Most plumages are black, gray or white, with only the jays being more colourful. There are approximately 118 species, found on all continents except Antarctica. Twenty of these are in North America, with seven found in Saskatchewan. Several species, such as the American crow, common raven and black-billed magpie, were reportedly common in the grasslands in the days of the great bison herds. With the destruction of the herds, the populations of these scavengers declined, but they are now recovering and expanding.

Four of the species are permanent residents. The gray jay (*Perisoreus canadensis*), a soft-plumaged small crestless jay, is a permanent resident of the boreal and mixed wood forests which comes into the townsites and wooded areas of the grasslands. The common raven (*Corvus corax*), distinguished from the very similar American crow by its heavier beak and wedge-shaped tail, resides permanently in the north, coming into the southern regions in the winter. The blue jay (*Cyanocitta cristata*), with its bright blue plumage and noisy chatter, is a common sight in the middle of the province and is seen occasionally in the townsites of the grasslands; the populations are higher in the summer, and this species has both resident and

COURTESY OF SASKATCHEWAN ENVIRONMENT
Blue jay.

migratory populations. The black-billed magpie (*Pica hudsonia*) is again a common resident of the southern half of the province, increasingly found in townsites as well as wooded natural areas. The American crow (*Corvus brachyrhynchos*), a species found earlier in the forested areas, is increasingly a resident in the older, heavily treed townsites. The arrival of the crows in April and May is a sure sign of spring.

Two species, the Clark's nutcracker (*Nucifraga columbiana*) and Steller's jay (*Cyanocitta stelleri*) are rare strays from the Rocky Mountains.

Diane Secoy

FURTHER READING: Alsop, F.J., III. 2002. *The Birds of Canada.* New York: Dorling Kindersley.

CROWE, ROLAND (1943–). Roland Crowe, born in 1943, is a member of the Piapot First Nation and resides in Regina with his wife Brenda and their children. Over the years Crowe has worked in a variety of occupations including farming, construction, guard (Provincial Correctional Centre), and public office. His career in public office began in the 1960s when he accepted the wishes of his people, standing for two years as band councilor and six years as chief. His political career continued in the 1980s when he was first elected vice-chief of the FEDERATION OF SASKATCHEWAN INDIAN NATIONS (FSIN), followed by two terms (over eight years) as FSIN chief. In 1995 he returned home to his farming operation, and was once again elected band chief in 1997. From 2000 to 2003 Crowe served as spokesperson of the TREATY 4 Council of Chiefs and chairperson of the Treaty 4 Executive Council, and was appointed to the FSIN Senate (2000). During his time of service with the FSIN, Roland Crowe made numerous and significant accomplishments. As vice-chief he dedicated himself to improve housing conditions and saw 1,000 low-income housing

units built in urban centres through the creation of off-reserve housing corporations. He also played a key role in the development of new training and employment strategies, including the creation of local Indian Management Boards. As FSIN chief, Crowe forged important new protocols and inter-governmental arrangements, spearheading the 1992 Treaty Land Entitlement Agreement that saw an additional 1.6 million acres added to the First Nations' land base; he saw the completion of the Hunting-Fishing-Trapping-Gathering Act, an important step in the application of First Nations Treaty rights, jurisdiction and management in the area of wildlife resources; and as one of his last achievements he helped develop a foundational agreement with the province on gaming, which resulted in over 1,100 jobs for First Nations people in the gaming industry and major wealth creation for First Nations communities.

Brenda Crowe

CROWN CORPORATIONS. Crown corporations are companies owned by the Saskatchewan government on behalf of the people of the province. Public enterprises in the form of Crown corporations were established in Saskatchewan to provide certain essential services that were either not offered by private companies or not available to all residents on an equitable basis. The four guiding principles of the Crowns were that the services they provided should be universal (available to everyone), reliable, of high quality, and offered at a reasonable cost. As the Crowns have grown, they have been required to balance these public policy objectives with commercial and financial objectives by contributing to the economy and providing a return on investment to their shareholder, the government, on behalf of the people (*see* Table CC-1).

Saskatchewan's earliest public enterprise was begun four years before Saskatchewan joined Confederation in 1905. In 1901, the Territorial

Government sold hail insurance. In 1906, three commercial creameries were established by the new provincial government. A year later, the Eagle Lake coal mine was developed. The predecessor of SaskTel was established in 1908 as the Department of Railways, Telephones and Telegraphs; it was given the authority to create and operate local and long-distance telephone lines in an effort to provide cost-effective service to as many farms, homes and businesses as possible. In 1929, the predecessor of SaskPower was established as the Saskatchewan Power Commission to provide safe, reliable, and cost-effective power to all Saskatchewan people. The Saskatchewan Government Insurance Office (now SGI) was established in 1945, while the SASKATCH-EWAN TRANSPORTATION COMPANY started the following year to ensure that as many communities as possible had access to reasonably priced transportation and freight service from a fleet of buses. The Government Finance Office (predecessor of Crown Investments Corporation of Saskatchewan) was formed in 1947 as a holding company for the province's commercial Crown corporations; besides being a holding company, it developed broad policy control, directed investment, and routed dividends from the Crowns into the government's consolidated fund.

Over the years, various Crowns have been established in the province's resource sector. Saskatchewan Oil & Gas Corporation (SASKOIL) was formed in 1973 to explore for, develop, produce, and market crude oil and natural gas. SaskOil's status as a Crown was ended in 1985, and a year later the majority of its shares were sold to the public. SaskOil was renamed Wascana Energy Inc. in 1996, and in 1997 the government's remaining minority interest in the company was sold to Canadian Occidental Petroleum (now Nexen). The Potash Corporation of Saskatchewan (PCS) was formed in 1975 to allow the government to exert greater influence on Saskatchewan's potash resources. The company's status as a Crown corporation was ended in 1989, and the majority of its shares were sold to the public in two share offerings in 1989 and 1990.

Saskatchewan Mining Development Corporation (SMDC) was established in 1975 to explore for minerals in northern Saskatchewan. In 1988, SMDC and the federally owned Eldorado Nuclear merged to form the CAMECO CORPORATION, and in 2002 the province sold its remaining shares in the company. CAMECO is now one of the world's largest uranium mining companies. Crown Investments Corporation of Saskatchewan (CIC) is the holding company for Saskatchewan's commercial Crown corporations. CIC's 11 wholly owned subsidiary Crowns in 2004 were: Information Services Corporation of Saskatchewan (ISC), a Crown formed in 2000 to administer the province's land titles and survey legislation, and to automate and operate a computer-

TREVOR SUTTER/REGINA LEADER-POST

Left to right: Ovide Mercredi, National Chief of the Assembly of First Nations; Roland Crowe, Chief of FSIN; Phil Fontaine, Grand Chief of the Assembly of Manitoba Chiefs, November 1991.

Table CC-1. Contribution to Saskatchewan's Economy by the Crown Sector, 2003[1]	
CIC's total holdings account for:	15% of Saskatchewan's Gross Domestic Product
	9% of total employment in Saskatchewan
CIC's Assets	$7.9 billion
Employees in CIC's subsidiary Crown corporations	More than 9,500
Dividends to the General Revenue Fund (2003)	$200 million
Dividends and equity repayments since 1995	More than $1.8 billion
Debt at year end	$3.36 billion
Debt reduction during 2003	$165 million
Debt reduction since 1991	More than $2 billion
Debt ratio[2]	51%
Earnings	$347.4 million
Return on equity[3]	11%

[1] All numbers are for the fiscal year ending December 31, 2003.
[2] Ratio of consolidated debt to debt plus equity.
[3] Ratio of earnings to the average amount of shareholder's equity.

ized land titles system; Investment Saskatchewan Inc., a Crown formed in 2003 to manage the portfolio of publicly owned investments formerly held by CIC; Saskatchewan Development Fund Corporation, established in 1974 to act as trustee, custodian and manager of the Saskatchewan Development Fund, an open-end investment trust; Saskatchewan Government Growth Fund Management Corporation (SGGFMC), started in 1989 to create and manage subsidiary fund companies which raise venture capital from new Canadian immigrants; SASKATCHEWAN GOVERNMENT INSURANCE (SGI), which sells a complete line of home, personal, and auto insurance protection and administers the Saskatchewan Auto Fund, the province's compulsory auto insurance program; Saskatchewan Opportunities Corporation (SOCO), established in 1994 to support economic growth and job creation through investments in businesses and infrastructure. In 2002, SOCO's investment portfolio was transferred to CIC (and subsequently to Investment Saskatchewan Inc. in 2003). SOCO continues to operate the Regina Research Park and the Innovation Place research park in Saskatoon; SASKATCHEWAN POWER CORPORATION (SaskPower); Saskatchewan Telecommunications (SASKTEL); Saskatchewan Transportation Company (STC), established in 1946 to provide passenger transportation and freight service with a fleet of buses; Saskatchewan Water Corporation (SaskWater), begun in 1984 to manage, administer, develop and protect the water and related land resources in Saskatchewan; and SaskEnergy Incorporated (SASKENERGY), which was formed in 1988 to provide natural gas transmission and distribution services across the province.

Each of CIC's subsidiary Crown corporations has its own board of directors and minister responsible, through whom they report to the CIC Board of Directors. The CIC Board, made up of provincial Cabinet Ministers, is a key committee of the provincial government's Cabinet. The Board makes decisions in its own right, and forwards recommendations to Cabinet for consideration. The Board's responsibilities include: approving CIC's strategic direction, operating plans and budget; monitoring and evaluating the performance of subsidiary Crown corporations; allocating capital within the Crown corporation sector; and approving CIC's annual financial statements.

CIC and its subsidiary Crown corporations are required to appear annually before the Standing Committee on Crown Corporations. This committee is made up of members of all parties in the Saskatchewan Legislative Assembly. Each Crown is also required to table an annual report with the Legislature. (*See also* CROWN CORPORATIONS AND PUBLICLY OWNED ENTERPRISES)   *Karen Schmidt*

CROWN CORPORATIONS AND PUBLICLY OWNED ENTERPRISES. Pragmatism and ideology both influenced the history of CROWN CORPORATIONS in Saskatchewan. Early Crowns concentrated on meeting needs not met by the private sector. The province of Saskatchewan inherited hail insurance and creamery businesses from the North-West Territories; other Crowns soon extended agricultural credit and mined coal. Provincial ownership of telephone systems began in 1908 through the Department of Railway, Telephones and Telegraphs. Involvement with electrical service dates from the 1928 creation of the Saskatchewan Power Commission; municipal and private systems also continued. Following its election in 1944, T.C. DOUGLAS' CO-OPERATIVE COMMONWEALTH FEDERATION (CCF) government greatly expanded the role of Crown corporations: the Crown Corporations

Act of 1945 and new structures followed; ministers chaired advisory boards, while Cabinet retained final responsibility. To increase coordination and planning for the Crowns, the Economic Advisory and Planning Board began in 1946, chaired by British economist GEORGE W. CADBURY. The Government Finance Office (GFO) began in 1947 as a holding company and coordinator of Crown operations; it also reinvested profits and paid monies into provincial coffers. To monitor matters, the CCF established the Crown Corporations Committee.

Motivated by socialist ideology, the CCF created numerous new Crowns. JOE PHELPS, Minister of the new Department of Natural Resources and Industrial Development, led the charge into public ownership. Saskatchewan Government Insurance Office (SGIO, later SGI) began in 1944. New Crowns in 1945 included Saskatchewan Wool Products, Saskatchewan Leather Products, and Saskatchewan Clay Products. Expropriation following a labour dispute added the Prince Albert Box Factory. Some Crowns proved popular and successful, while others met resistance: for example, many residents opposed government production of woollens, shoes, bricks, and boxes. Success greeted the 1946 acquisition of a sodium sulphate plant at Chaplin, the creation of SASKATCHEWAN TRANSPORTATION COMPANY (STC), and the Swift Current horse plant, which gathered unwanted horses for slaughter. Provincial involvement with telephone and electrical services also expanded under the CCF: Saskatchewan Government Telephones, later renamed SaskTel, was given responsibility for telephone service in 1947. SASKATCHEWAN POWER CORPORATION (SPC) began in 1949; rural electrification followed in southern Saskatchewan, where SPC soon also distributed natural gas. The Industrial Development Fund and Saskatchewan Economic Development Corporation (SEDCO) encouraged private investment by 1963; one notable success involved aiding IPSCO to locate in Saskatchewan.

In northern Saskatchewan, the CCF used Crown corporations to take over industry and control resources. SASKATCHEWAN GOVERNMENT AIRWAYS, later renamed SaskAir, began in 1947 with the purchase of a private company; rapid expansion followed, although efforts to develop a monopoly over northern commercial flying failed. A new Crown, Saskatchewan Fur Marketing Services, raised strong resistance from northern trappers, who opposed compulsory marketing of furs to the Crown; faced with increasing opposition, the compulsory fur program ended in 1955. Saskatchewan Lake and Forest Products Corporation and its divisions, Saskatchewan Forest Products and the Fish Board, operated sawmills, lumberyards, and fish plants; following controversial losses for the Fish Board, a new Crown, Saskatchewan Fish Marketing Services, processed fish. In another effort to displace capitalist enterprise, the CCF retailed goods through Government Trading Services, until stores were transferred to Northern Co-operative Trading Services.

Following the 1964 election of **ROSS THATCHER**'s Liberals, free-enterprise ideology dominated and the influence of Crown corporations declined. Thatcher eliminated government monopolies in insurance, timber, and natural gas, and sold SaskAir and the brick plant. Seeing a role for Crowns, the Liberals continued the most popular corporations. A major expansion of government enterprise followed the 1971 election victory of **ALLAN BLAKENEY** and the **NEW DEMOCRATIC PARTY** (NDP). Ideology again determined policies. The Saskatchewan Mining Development Corporation (SMDC) brought government into uranium mining. Controversially, the NDP added the pulp mill at Prince Albert to the Crown group and cancelled plans for a second pulp mill. SaskOil began after private companies slowed exploration to protest increased royalties. Beginning in 1975, the Potash Corporation of Saskatchewan assumed about one-half of Saskatchewan's potash production. A new Crown Corporation Act in 1978 replaced the GFO with the Crown Investments Corporation (CIC), whose assets totalled about $5 billion by 1981.

A reduction in the role of Crown corporations followed the election of **GRANT DEVINE** and the Conservatives in 1982. Sales of SaskOil, the pulp mill, the Potash Corporation, and SMDC took place. New Crowns included the Saskatchewan Water Corporation; and SaskEnergy came from a 1988 split of SaskPower. After the return of the NDP in 1991, Premier **ROY ROMANOW** adopted a moderate course in relation to Crown corporations. In addition to various smaller Crowns, the stalwart SaskPower, SaskEnergy, SaskTel, STC, and SGI continued. Privatization of the Crowns became a key issue in the 2003 provincial election, and the narrow victory of the NDP indicated the continued support for public ownership among the Saskatchewan electorate.
David M. Quiring

FURTHER READING: Archer, J.H. 1980. *Saskatchewan: A History.* Saskatoon: Western Producer Prairie Books; Eager, E. 1980. *Saskatchewan Government: Politics and Pragmatism.* Saskatoon: Western Producer Prairie Books; Quiring, D.M. 2004. *CCF Colonialism in Northern Saskatchewan: Battling Parish Priests, Bootleggers, and Fur Sharks.* Vancouver: UBC Press.

CROWN CORPORATIONS, LEGISLATIVE HISTORY OF. The Crown Corporations Act, S.S. 1945. c. 17 was introduced in 1945 by the **DOUGLAS** government. Although the province had government corporations operating prior to 1945, this Act was the first piece of legislation that aimed to define the powers and governance structure of provincial **CROWN CORPORATIONS**. It empowered the provincial government to appoint Crown corporations "to operate any designated industrial or commercial enterprise, or undertaking, the operation of which, on behalf of the province is deemed advisable for the public good" (s. 2). It also enabled members of Cabinet to purchase controlling interests in publicly traded corporations and transfer those interests to be administered by a Crown corporation (s. 10).

The 1945 Act gave Crown corporations the power to run their business ventures (s. 3), including purchasing and disposing of land with the consent of the government (s. 3), expropriating land (s. 8), borrowing money (s. 14 and 15), and acquiring insurance (s.17). Accountability of the corporations was achieved through making them responsible to a Minister of the government (s. 12), requiring government approval for certain land and financial transactions (s. 3, s. 15) and submitting annual reports (s. 19).

The 1945 Act was repealed two year after its enactment, and replaced by the Crown Corporations Act, S.S. 1947, c. 13. The 1945 Act had been deficient in only providing for the formation of Crown corporations to serve industrial and commercial purposes. The 1947 Act expanded this scope, allowing for the establishment of financial and public works Crown corporations (s. 2). This amendment allowed for the establishment of the Government Finance Office (GFO) on April 2, 1947 (Order-in-Council 535/47)–the precursor to our present day Crown Investments Corporation (CIC).

The GFO became responsible to the Provincial Treasurer (s. 21) for the financial operations of all government departments, offices and Crown corporations. The GFO actively supervised Crown corporations by establishing financial rules and regulations for the business of the Crowns, giving advice to the directors of the Crown corporations, and having access to their books (s. 22). The 1947 Act also established the Industrial Development Fund (IDF), enabling the government to borrow money for industrial development projects and allowing the funds to be controlled by the GFO (ss. 30-33). In 1950, (c. 11) amendments to the 1947 Act further enabled the GFO to acquire controlling interest in publicly trade corporations in Saskatchewan, which ability was previously reserved only to Crown corporations (ss. 3).

In the 1950s and 1960s various other significant amendments to the 1947 Act were introduced, including retroactively subjecting Crown corporations to tort liability (1951, c. 11, s. 2), repealing the ability of Crown corporations to expropriate property without consent (1957, c. 13, s. 1), dispensing with Cabinet approval for acquisition of property over $5,000 (1958, c. 86, s.2), and enabling Crown corporations to form pensions for employees

(s. 1964, c. 59, s. 1). In 1966, all property invested in the GFO was transferred to the Saskatchewan Economic Development Corporation (SEDCO), and Part III of the 1947 Act was repealed (1966, c. 5, ss. 1 & 3). In 1973-74, the governance structure of the GFO was significantly changed: it was no longer responsible to the Provincial Treasurer, but required to report to the Minister of Finance (1973-74, c. 18).

The 1947 Act was repealed in 1978, and the Crown Corporations Act, R.S.S.1978 (supp.) c. C-50.1 was enacted. The governance structure of the Crown Boards was clarified, setting out the ability of Cabinet to appoint Board members (s. 6) and granting to the Boards the ability to appoint advisory and executive committees for more effective governance of the Crown corporations (s. 7). The GFO was continued under a new name, Crown Investment Corporation of Saskatchewan (CIC) (s. 23), with the Minister of Finance designated as the minister responsible for CIC. Vested in CIC was also the authority to regulate audits of the financial transaction of the Crowns (s. 19). In 1980-81, amendments to the 1978 Act provided for the payment of dividends to the Saskatchewan Heritage Fund (c. 48, s.7)–although this provision was subsequently repealed with the repeal of the Heritage Fund (Sask) Act in 1992 (c. 53). It further provided for CIC to be subject to an audit by the Provincial Auditor or other audit firm appointed by Cabinet (s. 8).

In 1992, the Crown Employments Contracts Act (c. C-50.11) was enacted, deeming all Crown employment contracts public documents (s. 4) and requiring the filing of employment contracts by senior Crown executives, with the Clerk of Executive Council (s. 5). It further voided all Crown employment contracts that provided for payments of benefits and compensation upon termination or expiration of the contract, and prohibited any rights of action against the government for violating such contracts (s. 6). In 1993, the Crown Corporations Act, 1993, S.S. c. C-50.101, the current governing legislation, was introduced. It created a new classification for all Crown corporations by dividing the Crowns into CIC, CIC Crown Corporations, or Treasury Board Crown Corporations (s. 11). CIC is designated as the holding company for all subsidiary Crown corporations, and is responsible for making and administering the investments authorized by the Act on behalf of the government (s. 5). CIC Crown Corporations are subject to the orders and directives of CIC, while Treasury Board Crown Corporations are subject to the orders and directives of the Treasury Board (s. 14). The governance structure also changed on the Crown Boards. The Cabinet was required to appoint the Minister responsible for CIC as Chair of the CIC Board, and other members of Executive Council responsible for the subsidiary Crown Corporations were required to be Chairs of the Boards of Directors for each respective

Crown. (s. 23). The 1993 Act further articulates the duties of care and good faith expected by directors of Crown corporations, and provides a statutory indemnity from liability if those duties are met (s. 46).

Since 1998, a significant amendment to the Board of Directors structure of Crown Corporations Boards has operated to depoliticize the governance structure of the Crown corporations by eliminating the requirement for the Minister responsible to be a Director and Chair of the Board and by opting for these positions to be filled by appointment of the Minister (1998, c. 20, s. 23). An amendment in 2000 has further removed the responsibility of CIC to report to Cabinet on matters of budgets and programs of the subsidiary Crown corporations, but has confirmed responsibility for reporting on the goals, revenues, expenses, expenditures, investments and operating results of subsidiaries (2000, c. 39, s. 5(2)).   *Heather Heavin*

CROW'S NEST PASS AGREEMENT. On September 6, 1897, Ottawa agreed to provide a $3.4 million subsidy to **CANADIAN PACIFIC RAILWAY** (CPR) to build a rail line through the Crow's Nest Pass, from Lethbridge, Alberta to Nelson, British Columbia. This subsidy allowed CPR to compete directly against American railroad companies transporting minerals out of the Kootenay region of British Columbia; in return, the CPR was obligated to fixed grain transportation rates in perpetuity for western Canadian farmers hauling to the port of Thunder Bay. These rates, known as the Crow's Nest Pass Agreement and Rates, were based on the distance between specific delivery points to Thunder Bay. In the early 1920s, legislation was passed extending the rate set in 1897 to all shipping points on the prairies, to all railways, and to additional destination points. This legislation changed the system from one governed by a two-party agreement between the federal government and CPR, to one where parliament unilaterally imposed a national policy by statute.

By the 1960s, the cost of shipping exceeded the revenue railways were seeking. As a result, the railways began to defer investment in grain transportation infrastructure, and the lines in western Canada were less able to support the demands of increased grain exports. Between 1972 and 1985, provincial and federal governments attempted to alleviate the situation by purchasing or leasing more than 15,000 covered, steel hopper cars for the railways to use in the movement of grain. In addition, the provincial governments of Alberta and Saskatchewan each purchased 1,000 hopper cars, and the Canadian Wheat Board another 2,000. The 19,120 publicly owned cars were augmented by cars owned and leased by the railway. The purchase of these hopper cars was an attempt by all parties to alleviate some of the

increasing financial burden that railway companies were experiencing.

The Crow's Nest Pass Agreement rates were finally eliminated following the passage of the Western Grain Transportation Act (WGTA) in 1983. The WGTA increased the freight rates so that the railways would have enough revenue to maintain the grain transportation system. The Act committed Ottawa to paying a share of grain rates, with farmers paying a gradual increasing proportion of the costs. The federal government's portion of the payment to the railways came to be known as the Crow benefit; it too was eliminated in 1995, leaving the responsibility of grain transportation rates to the producer.   *Daria Coneghan*

CROZIER, LEIF NEWRY FITZROY (1846–1901). Born in Newry, Ireland on June 11, 1846, Leif Newry Fitzroy Crozier served as a militia officer and North-West Mounted Police (NWMP) officer. The Crozier family settled in Belleville, Upper Canada in the 1860s. Despite articling as a lawyer and training as a doctor, Crozier pursued a military career and was appointed a sub-inspector of the newly created mounted police force in 1873. He rose rapidly through the ranks and was one of six NWMP superintendents by 1876.

In the fall of 1878, Crozier was given command of Fort Walsh, the most important and volatile NWMP post, as **SITTING BULL** and 5,000 Sioux were camped roughly 150 miles to the east. He urged the refugees to return to the United States on several occasions, but they ignored his instructions. Shortly before Sitting Bull's eventual surrender, Crozier was transferred to Fort Macleod. In May 1884, he took command of the detachment at Battleford where dissatisfaction and militancy were growing among the area's **MÉTIS** and **CREE**.

Leif Newry Fitzroy Crozier.

On March 13, 1885, Crozier warned Lieutenant-Governor **EDGAR DEWDNEY** about the likelihood of a Métis rebellion. On March 26, he ignored approaching reinforcements and led a group of about 100 Mounted Police and volunteers out of Fort Carlton. Crozier and his men encountered a superior force of Métis on the Carlton Trail north of Duck Lake, which led to the opening engagement of the North-West Resistance. Crozier's force suffered serious casualties during the short battle as nine volunteers and three police were killed. Despite his impetuous leadership, Crozier was promoted to assistant commissioner of the NWMP on April 1. He returned to his post at Battleford and was transferred to headquarters in Regina in 1886.

Crozier resigned from the NWMP in June 1886 after being passed over for the position of commissioner. He later moved to the United States where he established a general store at Cushing, Oklahoma. Leif Crozier died there on February 25, 1901, and was buried in Belleville.   *Holden Stoffel*

FURTHER READING: Dunn, Jack. 1994. *The Alberta Field Force of 1885.* Winnipeg: The Author; Light, Douglas W. 1987. *Footprints in the Dust.* North Battleford, SK: Turner-Warwick Publications; Stanley, George F.G. 1961. *The Birth of Western Canada: A History of the Riel Rebellions.* Toronto: University of Toronto Press; Stonechild, Blair. 1997. *Loyal till Death: Indians and the North-West Rebellion.* Calgary: Fifth House.

CROZIER, LORNA (1948–). Lorna Crozier, described by Margaret Laurence as "a poet to be grateful for," was born in Swift Current, Saskatchewan. She holds a BA from the **UNIVERSITY OF SASKATCHEWAN** (1969) and completed an MA in English at the University of Alberta in 1980. A high school English teacher for several years, Crozier has held teaching positions or given creative writing workshops in a number of institutions including the Banff School of Fine Arts, Red Deer College, the Saskatchewan Summer School of the Arts, the **SAGE HILL WRITING EXPERIENCE**, and the Sechelt Summer Writing Festival. She has been a writer-in-residence at the Cypress Hills Community College, the University of Toronto, and the Regina Public Library. Currently Professor of Poetry and Chair of the Department of Writing at the University of Victoria, Crozier has received numerous awards for her work, including the Canadian Authors' Association Award for Poetry, the Governor General's Award for Poetry, two Pat Lowther Awards for the best book of poetry by a Canadian woman, and the National Magazine Awards Gold Medal. She has been invited to take part in various writers' festivals in Canada and abroad, and for a time worked as a CBC arts show host. In 2004, the **UNIVERSITY OF REGINA** bestowed an honorary Doctor of Laws degree on Crozier, whose collected papers are housed in the archives of the University.

Not only a writer of poetry but a theorist as well, Crozier describes her writing experience as a woman: "I throw out the poem like a net and pull things together with the threads of language that need mending, that need new patterns to catch the light, this is my woman's work, pulling these threads through my voice." Her books include *Inside is the Sky* (1976), *Crow's Black Joy* (1979), *Humans and Other Beasts* (1980), *No Longer Two People* (with Patrick Lane, 1981), *The Weather* (1983), *The Garden Going on Without Us* (1985), *Angels of Flesh, Angels of Silence* (1988), *Inventing the Hawk* (1992), *Everything Arrives at the Light* (1995), *A Saving Grace* (1996), *What the Living Won't Let Go* (1999), *Apocrypha of Light* (2002), and *Bones in Their Wings: Ghazals* (2003). Crozier has also edited two collections of essays: *Desire in Seven Voices* (2000), and *Addicted: Notes from the Belly of the Beast* (with Patrick Lane, 2001).   *Ellen J. Chapco*

PHOTOGRAPHY DEPARTMENT, UNIVERSITY OF REGINA

Lorna Crozier, June 2004.

CRUICKSHANK, ELIZABETH (1895–1989).
Elizabeth Cruickshank (Liz Roley) was a Regina-based journalist, naturalist, and community leader. Born Elizabeth Kierstead on August 25, 1895 in New Brunswick, she was educated at Fredericton Normal School. Arriving in Regina in January 1916, she soon met and married Warburton Kerr Cruickshank; they raised two children. Active in the Westminster Church, and their representative to the Local Council of Women (LCW) in 1935, she became LCW liaison to the ON-TO-OTTAWA trekkers, participating in the trekkers' delegation that met with Premier GARDINER. She was LCW president (1936–38) and provincial Council of Women president (1939–42). Her many other activities involved operation of Regina's Community Chest sewing room (1932). Her extensive wartime work—including provincial chairman of Women's Activities for the National

BOB HOWARD PHOTO/SASKATCHEWAN ARCHIVES BOARD R-B12710

Elizabeth Cruickshank, 1973.

War Finance Committee (1942)—led to her naming to the Order of the British Empire (1948).

Prominent in the Saskatchewan Natural History Society, she proposed the creation of the Museum of Natural History to honour Saskatchewan pioneers. She wrote for the *Blue Jay*, and scripted Department of Education nature broadcasts for CBC radio. She was best known as *Leader-Post* columnist "Liz Roley," and was the author of *A Second Look: Liz Roley's Nature Notes* (1976). Cruickshank was active in the Regina Canadian Women's Press Club, receiving a Centennial Medal for Women in Journalism in 1967 and an Honorary Degree of Laws from the UNIVERSITY OF REGINA in 1980. She died on May 31, 1989.   *Anthony Jo*

FURTHER READING: Belcher, M. 1991. "Elizabeth Roley Cruickshank, 1895–1989," *Blue Jay* 49 (1): 55.

CUCKOO, BLACK-BILLED.
This is the only member of the order Cuculiformes, family Cuculidae confirmed for the province. This family of approximately 142 species is found on all continents except Antarctica, with greater diversity in the Old World. These long-tailed, slim birds take insect prey with their long, slender, down-curved bills. Their zygodactylous (two toes forward and two toes backward) foot gives them a good grip on branches. A number of species are brood parasites; the black-billed cuckoo is not. The moderate-sized (approximately 30 cm) black-billed cuckoo (*Coccyzus erythropthalmus*), a bird of the eastern hardwoods, is migratory, breeding in the lower half of the province, up into the southern margins of the boreal forest. It is more common in the eastern portion of the province. It feeds particularly on tent caterpillars. It is hard to detect, sitting quietly within vegetation. When seen, its brown back and white underparts, along with its long tail and red eye-ring, are distinctive.   *Diane Secoy*

FURTHER READING: Alsop, Fred J., III. 2002. *Birds of Canada*. New York: Dorling Kindersley.

CUDWORTH,
town, pop 766, located S of Wakaw on Hwy 2 in the Minichinas Hills. The first pioneers came to the Cudworth area in 1899. In 1903, German immigrants settled at nearby Leofeld (*see* GERMAN SETTLEMENTS). The community would eventually come to be comprised of families of Ukrainian, German, and French origins. Other than a slight slump experienced during the Depression, the community developed at a steady rate until the early 1980s, reaching a peak population of 947 in 1981. Major employers in the area include livestock industries and a biomass energy producer. With approximately 60 local businesses, Cudworth is a retail and service centre for the surrounding rural population. A few kilometres south of Cudworth, the Shrine of Our Lady of Sorrows, which includes a chapel and the Stations of the Cross, draws large numbers of people during an annually conducted pilgrimage. Other annual events hosted by the community include a fair held in July. Cudworth's former CNR station, built in 1925, has been declared a heritage property and has recently been converted into a museum which features German and Ukrainian pioneer artifacts.   *David McLennan*

CULLITON, EDWARD MILTON (1906–91).
Ted Culliton was born April 9, 1906, in Grand Forks, Minnesota, but his family immigrated to Canada and he grew up on a farm near Elbow. After graduating from the UNIVERSITY OF SASKATCHEWAN, Culliton was accepted into the Saskatchewan Bar in 1930 and established his practice in Gravelbourg. In 1935, Culliton was elected to the Legislative Assembly for Gravelbourg as a Liberal. In 1938, he was re-elected and selected Provincial Secretary by Premier PATTERSON. He enlisted in the Canadian Army in

SASKATCHEWAN ARCHIVES BOARD R-B7904

Edward Culliton.

1941 and served overseas for the duration of the war. He continued to serve in the provincial Cabinet as Minister without portfolio, but lost his seat in the 1944 provincial election. Culliton contested the provincial Liberal leadership in 1946 but was defeated by **WALTER TUCKER**. He was re-elected in Gravelbourg in 1948 and served as Liberal finance critic until he left politics in 1951 when he was appointed to the Saskatchewan Court of Appeal. In 1952 Culliton was recruited by CCF Premier **T.C. DOUGLAS** to serve as chair of the Saskatchewan Golden Jubilee Committee. In 1962 he was made Chief Justice for Saskatchewan and held this position until his retirement in 1981. After leaving the bench he chaired a commission on freedom of information and on provincial electoral boundaries. He was also the first chair of the Advisory Council of the Saskatchewan Order of Merit. He served on many boards and associations as a dedicated volunteer. Culliton was named a Companion of the Order of Canada and received the Saskatchewan Order of Merit and an honourary degree from the University of Saskatchewan as well as other awards. Culliton died on March 14, 1991. *Mike Fedyk*

CUMBERLAND HOUSE, northern village, pop 632, located 163 km NE of Nipawin at the end of Hwy 123. Cumberland House is the oldest permanent settlement in Saskatchewan and western Canada. Although today the community is remote in terms of access by land, historically it had a central location in terms of water-based travel: during the **FUR TRADE** era, it served as a key transportation hub and supply depot as waterways led north and northwest to the fur-rich Churchill and Athabasca regions, east to Hudson Bay, and southwest onto the plains. Situated on an island which separates Cumberland Lake from the **SASKATCHEWAN RIVER**, Cumberland House was established in 1774 by **SAMUEL HEARNE** for the Hudson's Bay Company. Named for Prince Rupert, the Duke of Cumberland, who was the first governor of the Hudson's Bay Company, it was the company's first inland trading post. In 1840, an Anglican mission was established at Cumberland House by catechist **HENRY BUDD**, a Swampy **CREE**, who later became the first ordained minister of First Nations ancestry. Following the Red River insurrection in 1870, a number of Manitoba **MÉTIS** came to the Cumberland district and a Roman Catholic mission was established to serve these newcomers. In 1875, the Cumberland House First Nation, whose reserve lands are located southeast of the village, was a signatory to **TREATY 5**. Between 1874 and 1925, Cumberland House was an important centre for the steamboat traffic on the Saskatchewan River systems. The remains of the S.S. *Northcote*, which was involved in the battle at **BATOCHE** in 1885, are today situated in a park at Cumberland House.

The 20th century progressively saw fewer people making their living off the land, and more settling in the community. Outlying settlements in the district disappeared as Cumberland House grew. In 1966, an all-weather road was built into the district, giving residents a new connection with the outside world; however, it stopped at the south shore of the **SASKATCHEWAN RIVER**, necessitating reliance on a seasonal ferry service. The construction of the Squaw Rapids (now E.B. Campbell) Dam in 1962 adversely affected the traditional livelihoods of many in the area. A lawsuit launched in 1976 resulted in the awarding of a compensation package worth an estimated $23 million for the community and the neighbouring Cumberland House First Nation. In 1996, a bridge was built across the Saskatchewan River; no longer were people reliant on the seasonal ferry service, and no longer were hazardous river crossings necessary when the ferry was unusable. Today, the combined population of the northern village and the adjacent reserve totals approximately 1,500 persons. Together they comprise one of Saskatchewan's principal Métis communities. Unemployment is a problem for this remote community, and many rely on government assistance. Some income, as well as food, is still derived from trapping, hunting and fishing, and a number of outfitters and guides accommodate hunters from all over North America each fall. Logging, cattle raising, **WILD RICE** harvesting, and the production of maple syrup provide additional opportunities. Notable people from Cumberland House include **KEITH GOULET**, Saskatchewan's first Métis Cabinet Minister; Judge **GERALD M. MORIN** of the Saskatchewan Provincial Court; and Solomon Carriere, a four-time world marathon canoeing champion. *David McLennan*

CUMBERLAND HOUSE FIRST NATION. The Cumberland House **CREE** signed an adhesion to **TREATY 5** in September 1876, and a reserve was surveyed for them in 1883. This initial survey included an island (named Chief's Island) on which the chief, a councilor, and a number of the band's members resided. A lay reader and the Reverend Davis also lived within the community. Before the surveyor left the area, the chief requested that a reserve be laid out for himself and his people near Fort à la Corne, knowing that there was better agricultural land in that region; however, the government would not grant reserve land outside of their own treaty area. The band's attempt at growing potatoes, cabbage, turnips, carrots, onions and lettuce was successful, but their grain production was not. The soil of Chief's Island is of fair quality, ranging from stony areas to small hay marshes, wetlands, and timberland. Band members still rely on hunting, fishing and trapping, while the forestry industry, tourism, guiding, and hunting camps contribute to furthering their economic development. Their community infrastructure includes a school and gymnasium, teacherage, health clinic, band office, and community maintenance facilities. The Cumberland House Reserve totals 2,145.8 ha; while their total band membership sits at 957 people, only 535 members live on the reserve, 160 km northeast of Nipawin. *Christian Thompson*

CUMMINGS, NORA (1938–). Born in Saskatoon on January 1, 1938, Nora Cummings has roots in the historic **MÉTIS** community of Round Prairie. She became politically and socially active in the Métis community in the late 1960s, and has been involved at the local, provincial and national levels. In 1969, with the encouragement of her uncle **CLARENCE TROTCHIE**, Cummings helped to form Métis Local 11 in Saskatoon; in 1970 she became the first woman fieldworker for the Métis Society of Saskatchewan. In 1971–72, she was instrumental in organizing the Saskatchewan Native Women's Association, serving as its president from 1972 to 1975 and from 1976 to 1978. In 1974 she was one of the founding members of the Native Women's Association of Canada, and sat on its board of directors for two years. In the late 1970s, she was a family worker and employment councilor for Métis Local 11 and was actively involved with the Saskatoon Indian and Métis Friendship Centre. In 1975, she was honoured as one of fifty Saskatoon women who had made an outstanding contribution to the city. From 1986 to 1993 she served as president of Métis Local 11, stepping down in 1993 to sit on the **MÉTIS NATION–SASKATCHEWAN** Senate, where she served as Chair of from 1994 to 2003. In 2002 she helped establish the Métis Elders Council of Saskatchewan, and today she continues to sit on the MNS Senate and to work with youth in restorative justice circles. In 2003 she received the Saskatchewan Volunteer Medal for her commitment to the Métis community. *Cheryl Troupe*

CUPAR, town, pop 602, located 21 km E of Southey on Hwy 22; Fort Qu'Appelle lies approximately 45 km to the southeast. Settlers began arriving in the late 1800s and early 1900s. Prior to the turn of the century, these were of largely Scottish, English, and Irish descent; afterwards, many came from Eastern Europe, particularly the historic polyglot province of Bukovina (now split between Romania and Ukraine). A significant number were Hungarian, but there was also a small quotient of Romanian Jews who settled in the district around 1906. Named after Cupar, Fife, Scotland, the community developed into a significant service and trading centre for the surrounding agricultural district, growing steadily from the time of its inception until about the mid-1970s, at which point the population stabilized around its current level. Cupar has curbed paved streets, tree-lined boulevards and a museum, as well as a range of businesses and services, many of which cater to the area's agricultural industry. Cupar was the home of **EDDIE SHORE**, famous defenseman with the Boston Bruins, Stanley Cup champion, and an inductee into the NHL Hall of Fame. His father, T.J. Shore, financed the first enclosed rink in Cupar in 1911. The town's main annual event is the "Cupar Gopher Drop," devised as a community fund-raising event in 1993. Residents purchase tickets on stuffed facsimiles of the rodent. The numbered gophers are dropped from a hot air balloon, and prizes are awarded according to their landing in proximity to target gopher holes.   *David McLennan*

CURLING. Curling provides a distinctive piece in the social history of Saskatchewan: from modest beginnings to its present complex levels, it has been associated with almost every aspect of prairie life. Curling was seen in Saskatchewan as early as 1879, with the first reported match played on January 17, 1882, in Prince Albert. In 1892, the Regina Curling Club held the first bonspiel in the North-West Territories, with rinks participating from Qu'Appelle, Indian Head, Calgary and Regina. In 1904 the Assiniboia Branch of the Royal Caledonian Curling Association was formed in Regina, changing its name to the Saskatchewan Branch in 1905, when it held its first bonspiel in Regina. In 1910 the Saskatchewan Branch of the Royal Caledonian Curling Association officially became the Saskatchewan Curling Association. The first quarter of the 20th century marked a time of significant growth in the number and popularity of bonspiels in Saskatchewan. As communities competed to demonstrate who could host the largest and greatest bonspiel, one of the most important aspects of the game –its intrinsic sociability–was reinforced. "Smokers," featuring variety shows and imported cigars, were often the most popular event. It was in Saskatchewan in 1947 that the era of carspiels began: Nipawin put up four Hudson automobiles as prizes; the carspiel attracted over 500 curlers, as well as international attention for being the first bonspiel to offer such prizes. The carspiel lasted eight years and was widely copied throughout western Canada; it eventually gave way by the 1970s to the cashspiel as the dominant spectator attraction next to the Canadian men's championship, popularly known as the Brier.

By 1952–53, Saskatchewan had 511 affiliated clubs with 18,973 curlers, making it the province with the most curlers per capita. From the 1950s to the end of the 1970s was a time of unmatched growth for curling in Saskatchewan, which claimed the finest curlers and most victorious bonspiels and championships. The province boasts many curling legends. Its first Brier win was in 1955 at Regina by brothers Garnet, Don, Glen and Lloyd Campbell of Avonlea. Garnet Campbell became the first man to

SASKATCHEWAN ARCHIVES BOARD R-B3796

Winners of the 1909 Regina Bonspiel, the province's most prestigious curling event at the time. The team was especially noteworthy in that all four players were members of the Legislature. Clockwise from top left: J.A. Sheppard of Moose Jaw, Dr. R.M. Mitchell of Weyburn, G.A. Scott of Davidson and J.D. Stewart of Arcola.

SASKATCHEWAN ARCHIVES BOARD R-B1159

Action at the 1955 Macdonald Brier Canadian men's curling championship at Exhibition Stadium, Regina. The Saskatchewan team, wearing white sweaters and skipped by Garnet Campbell of Avonlea, is playing on Sheet D. Campbell and brothers Don, Glen and Gordon won all 10 of their games to give Saskatchewan its first Brier championship.

compete in ten Briers, and was renowned for his bonspiel successes and sportsmanship. Inspired by Campbell's triumph, the Richardsons of Regina took up the sport in earnest to capture four Brier titles and four of the first five world championships in 1959, 1960, 1962 and 1963; **ERNIE RICHARDSON** was the first skip to win four Canadian men's championships. Saskatchewan has won the Brier only twice since then. Harvey Mazinke of Regina led Billy Martin, George Achtymichuk and Dan Klippenstein to the 1973 title, only to lose the subsequent world championship final before a home-town crowd when conditions produced sloppy ice and an extra-end victory for Kjell Oscarius of Sweden. Rick Folk of Saskatoon, with Ron Mills, Tom Wilson, and Jim Wilson won the Brier and world championships in 1980. Folk and Wilson also teamed up with different female team mates to win 1974 and 1983 Canadian mixed championships.

Curling for women began later in the province than it did for men; while women always played a vital role in organizing for curling bonspiels, ladies' events were not instituted until 1923. By 1947 the Saskatchewan Ladies' Curling Association was founded, which amalgamated with the men's organization fifty years later in 1997. In 1952 the Western Canadian Ladies' Curling Association was established in Winnipeg. The first provincial championship for women was held in 1948. The first Western Canadian Women's Championship was held in Regina in 1953, won by Janet Perkin of Regina. Women began national competition in 1960 and world championships in 1979. Joyce McKee of Saskatoon, with **SYLVIA FEDORUK**, Donna Belding, and Muriel Coben won the first Canadian women's title, a showdown between eastern and western champions in 1960. A year later the team—with Fedoruk, Barbara McNiven and Rosa McFee—went undefeated to earn the first Canadian championship. McKee would win four more national titles: as a skip in 1969 and as second on **VERA PEZER**'s three-time champions from 1971–73. With Dorenda Schoenhals (1970) and Emily Farnham (1974) also leading their teams to ultimate victory, Saskatoon claimed six consecutive Canadian women's championships from four different skips from 1969-74. Regina picked up the women's winning habit in 1980 when **MARJ MITCHELL**'s rink swept the Canadian and world crowns. Later, **SANDRA SCHMIRLER**, Jan Betker, Joan McCusker and Marcia Gudereit became the most accomplished women's team in history, earning national and world titles in 1993, 1994 and 1997, as well as a gold medal at the 1998 Winter Olympics in Nagano, Japan. Schmirler's death from cancer at the age of 36 in 2000 was mourned across Canada.

Saskatchewan has also produced a number of successful junior men and women curlers. Thirteen Saskatchewan rinks have won the Canadian Junior

Men's Championship since 1950. The Saskatoon foursome of Steve Laycock, Christopher Haichert, Michael Jantzen, and Kyler Broad won both the Canadian Junior Mens and World Junior Men's titles in 2003. Repeating this feat in 2005 was the Regina rink of Kyle George, Justin Mihalicz, D.J. Kidby, and Chris Hebert. On the women's side, nine Saskatchewan rinks have claimed the Canadian Junior Women's Championship since 1971. Most recently, Saskatoon's Marliese Miller, Teejay Surik, Janelle Lemon and Chelsey Bell won the 2003 Junior national and world titles.

Today, the Saskatchewan Curling Association (SCA) is the provincial governing body. Clubs in the province who wish to participate pay an affiliation fee by facility. While there are clubs that are not affiliated, in 2003-04 there were 207 clubs that were. In 2003-04 the complete membership was 35,724 people; there were 669 sheets of artificial ice, and thirty-two of natural ice. The SCA receives the majority of its funding from SaskSport, but has many corporate sponsors as well. Curling's popularity in Saskatchewan may reflect the need to find competitive and enjoyable entertainment to endure harsh winters. It enjoys the advantage of being accessible to people of both genders, almost any body type, the competitive sportsperson as well as the recreational player, and virtually all ages. Men's, women's and some mixed provincial championships are contested from Juvenile (under-18) through Masters (over-60) levels. Curling has gained considerable attention for Saskatchewan as both a host for major championships and for the province's competitive success. As curling has become an important part of the social, political, and economic make-up of Saskatchewan, the provincial Legislature recognized curling as the official sport of the province on April 24, 2002.

Karen Zemlak

FURTHER READING: Lefko, P. 2000. *Sandra Schmirler: The Queen of Curling*. Toronto: Stoddart Publishing; Pezer, V. 2003. *The Stone Age: A Social History of Curling on the Prairies*. Calgary: Fifth House; Scholz, Guy. 1999. *Gold on Ice: The Story of the Sandra Schmirler Curling Team*. Regina: Coteau Books.

CURRIE, BALFOUR WATSON (1902–81).

Balfour Currie was born in Montana in 1902 and grew up on his parents' homestead near Kindersley, Saskatchewan. He received a BSc with High Honours in Physics, followed by an MSc in 1927 from the **UNIVERSITY OF SASKATCHEWAN**. He was appointed an assistant professor at the University of Saskatchewan in 1930, following completion of his PhD at McGill. From 1932 to 1934 he was granted leave to spend the Second International Polar Year at Chesterfield Inlet in the Arctic as a meteorologist with the Canadian Weather Service. He became professor in 1943, Head of the Department of Physics in

UNIVERSITY OF SASKATCHEWAN ARCHIVES A-8622
Balfour Watson Currie, ca. 1940.

1952, Dean of the College of Graduate Studies in 1959, and Vice-President (Research) of the University of Saskatchewan in 1967.

Currie was a dedicated teacher. As an administrator, his efforts resulted in the formation of the Institute of Atmospheric Physics, from which evolved the **SPACE ENGINEERING DIVISION** (later SED Systems). He published sixty scientific papers on topics such as auroral heights and spectra, and later, when radar became available, on radio reflections from the aurora and on scattering of radio waves by the ionosphere. Later he published a series of reports on climatic trends in the prairie provinces and the Northwest Territories.

Balfour Currie received many honours during his career. In 1947 he was elected a Fellow of the Royal Society of Canada. He strongly supported the objectives of the Society, and frequently represented it on national and international committees. In June 1972, Dr. Currie was appointed a Companion of the Order of Canada, in recognition of his outstanding contributions as a distinguished university teacher, as a highly respected research scientist, and as an able administrator. He was elected a Fellow of the Royal Meteorological Society of Great Britain, and a Fellow of the Arctic Institute of Canada. He also served as President of the American Geophysical Union and the Canadian Association of Physicists, which in 1962 awarded him the Gold Medal for "Achievement in Physics." In 1967 the Canadian Meteorological Society awarded him the Patterson Medal for his notable contribution to meteorology. He received an honorary LLD from the University of

Saskatchewan in 1975 and an honorary DSc from York University in 1977.

Currie retired in 1974 but continued as research advisor to the President of the University of Saskatchewan. From 1975 to 1980 he served as coordinator of Canadian research activities in the International Magnetospheric Studies. He was also President of the University of Saskatchewan Alumni Association.

Dr. Currie had married Elva Washington in 1934; they had two daughters and one son. He died in Saskatoon in 1981. *U. Theodore Hammer*

FURTHER READING: Currie, B.W. 1980. *Canada's Participation in the International Magnetospheric Study, 1976–1979*. Ottawa: National Research Council Canada; Currie, B.W. and W.C. Kendrew. 1955. *The Climate of Canada: Manitoba, Saskatchewan, Alberta and the Districts of Mackenzie and Keewatin*. Ottawa: The Queen's Printer.

CURRIE, GORDON (1923–). Gordon Currie has been an inspiration to youth both as educator and coach. Born in Semans, Saskatchewan on May 20, 1923, Currie began his teaching career at Balfour Technical School, where he also coached the football team. Over fourteen years, Currie led the Balfour Redmen to nine city championships, eight southern Saskatchewan titles, and eight provincial titles. He also coached the school's hockey team to three provincial championships. In 1965, Currie joined the Regina Rams football club as head coach. During his tenure with the junior team, he guided his players to six national titles in twelve seasons. In 1975, he was named the Canadian amateur coach of the year. He retired as Rams' head coach following the 1976 campaign, having amassed a record of 108 wins in 135 games. Gordon Currie returned to teaching at Balfour before becoming principal of

Gordon Currie.

Campbell Collegiate. A Member of the Order of Canada since 1979, his many honours and awards include the establishment of the Gordon Currie Foundation, membership in the SASKATCHEWAN SPORTS HALL OF FAME, and an honorary degree from the UNIVERSITY OF REGINA.

Daria Coneghan and Holden Stoffel

CURRIE, ROBERT (1937–). Robert Currie was born on September 21, 1937 in Lloydminster to Duncan and Jean Currie. As a youth growing up in Moose Jaw, he was published in *The Canadian Boy* (a United Church paper), but decided to pursue a career in pharmacy after graduation. While attending the College of Pharmacy at Saskatoon, he wrote much of the college paper and was influenced in his decision to intern at Saskatoon's University Hospital partly by the opportunity to write for *The Hospital Pharmacist*. After accepting a sessional lecturer position Currie discovered he loved teaching, but decided to teach a subject he loved and returned to the UNIVERSITY OF SASKATCHEWAN, where he earned a BA in 1964, an Honours English diploma in 1965, and a BEd in 1966. Upon graduating in 1966 he returned to Moose Jaw, where he began a thirty-year career as an English teacher.

In 1965 Currie purchased his first book of poetry, and this sparked his lifelong passion for the medium. In 1969, he was editing and publishing *Salt*, a small magazine that published numerous writers long before their first books appeared. His own first published volume, *Quarterback #1* (Montreal's Delta Press), consisted of only six poems, but was quickly followed by *Sawdust and Dirt* (1973), *The Halls of Elsinore* (1973), and *Moving Out* (1975). Beginning in 1972, Currie spent five summers teaching and studying at Fort San, where he was inspired by KEN MITCHELL, ANNE SZUMIGALSKI, Robert Kroetsch, ELI MANDEL, and Rudy Wiebe. In 1973 he was elected chairman of the SASKATCHEWAN WRITERS GUILD; and two years later he, GARY HYLAND, BARBARA SAPERGIA, and GEOFFREY URSELL founded Coteau Books.

Three times during his teaching career Currie took unpaid leaves-of-absence to write full time; and on each occasion, books and awards followed. He retired from teaching in 1996 and now writes full time. Over the years, he has received three first-place awards (twice for poetry, once for children's literature) and two second-place awards from the Saskatchewan Writers' Guild, as well as a third prize for poetry in the CBC National Literary Awards (1980). Together with Eli Mandel, Ken Mitchell, W.O. MITCHELL, JOHN NEWLOVE, SINCLAIR ROSS, and Anne Szumigalski, he was honoured with a Founder's Award from the Saskatchewan Writers Guild in 1984. Examples of publications by Currie are *Diving into Fire* (1977), *Yarrow* (1980), *Night Games* (1983), *Learning on the Job* (1986), *Klondike*

Fever (1992), *Things You Don't Forget* (1999), and his first novel *Teaching Mr. Cutler* (2002).

Christian Thompson

CUT KNIFE, town, pop 556, located 50 km W of the Battlefords on Hwy 40. The Little Pine, Poundmaker, and Sweet Grass First Nations are situated north and east of the community. The name Cut Knife was derived from Cut Knife Hill (now Chief POUNDMAKER Hill) on the Poundmaker reserve. The hill was named for a Sarcee chief, whose name was roughly translated to "Cut Knife" and who was slain near the location during a skirmish with the Cree in the 1840s. Cut Knife Hill was also the location of Colonel Otter's encounter with, and retreat from, Chief Poundmaker's forces during the NORTH-WEST RESISTANCE. When settlers of European origin arrived in the district in the early 1900s, they adopted the name for their community. In 1952, Governor General Vincent Massey unveiled a cairn erected by the Historic Sites and Monuments Board of Canada, which memorializes the heroism on both sides of the 1885 conflict and pays tribute to Chief Poundmaker for restraining his men from slaughtering Otter's troops during their retreat. Homesteaders began arriving in 1903–04, and the community came to be comprised of British, Italian, Ukrainian, and Scandinavian people, as well as members of the Aboriginal population. Cut Knife was incorporated as a village on May 17, 1912, and, other than a slight decline in its population during the 1930s, the community grew steadily. In 1981, it reached a peak population of 624. Today, the community serves a trading area of approximately 4,000 people, and grain farming and cattle ranching largely form the basis of the regional economy. The oil and gas industry, however, is becoming increasingly significant. Cut Knife is the site of a tourist attraction described as "the world's largest tomahawk": perched upon a 9-metre-high tepee, the tomahawk sculpture was erected in 1971 as a part of Saskatchewan's Homecoming celebrations, and was built to symbolize unity and friendship between the area's populations. *David McLennan*

CUT KNIFE HILL, BATTLE OF. The Battle of Cut Knife Hill, fought on May 2, 1885, was an encounter between the CREE forces under chief POUNDMAKER (*pîhtokahânapiwiyin*) and the Battleford Column of the Canadian Militia Field Force commanded by Lieutenant-Colonel William Otter. The action ended in the defeat and withdrawal of the militia; the engagement was prevented from turning into a slaughter of the militia force only by the personal intervention of Poundmaker. Otter had arrived at Fort Battleford on April 24, 1885, with a force of 500 men and orders from Major-General FREDERICK MIDDLETON to defend the garrison from attack by Cree and Stoney (Assiniboine) Indians. Otter, con-

Lieutenant-Colonel William Otter.

trary to his orders, instead adopted an aggressive approach and left the fort on the afternoon of May 1 with 325 soldiers and policemen, and two anti-quated field guns and a Gatling gun, in search of Poundmaker's camp. After a 60-km overnight march in freezing weather, the militia stopped at dawn for breakfast on a hill bounded by rolling, bushy terrain on each side and a ravine beneath. Otter had blundered into a poor tactical position. Poundmaker's camp lay just over a hill on the other side of the ravine; however, neither side was aware of the other's proximity. Jacob, a Cree elder who habitually began his day with a horseback ride before anyone else arose, detected the militia and hurried back to rouse the camp.

The engagement began when Otter's men detected the Cree camp and directed cannon fire at it. Cree war chief Fine Day divided his force into groups of four or five men, which he directed through the bush from a high ridge with signals from a hand mirror. The militia, quickly pinned down in open ground, overestimated their enemy's numbers because of the rapidity with which the Cree and Stoney groups moved. Otter's gun carriages virtually fell apart, rendering his cannon useless, and the Gatling gun was ineffective at the 100-metre range that separated the combatants. Late in the morning, Otter organized a retreat that cleared the battlefield but left his men open to pursuit. Warriors were about give chase on horseback when Poundmaker intervened; although authority during battle was in the hands of Fine Day as war chief, Poundmaker persuaded his people to take no aggressive action. Canadian casualties numbered eight dead and fourteen wounded. Because of the speed and intensity with which they were out-flanked, the soldiers and police thought they were facing up to 600 warriors and that they had killed

anywhere from 26 to more than 100; in fact, Fine Day triumphed with a force of fewer than 100 men, sometimes reduced to as few as 50 as others left to guard the evacuation of the camp's women and children. Cree casualties were nine in number: six killed and three wounded. The skirmish at Cut Knife Hill was carried by the clever guerrilla tactics of Cree war chief Fine Day, and marked the last time government forces were defeated during the NORTH-WEST REBELLION. *John Chaput*

FURTHER READING: Beal, B. and R. Macleod. 1984. *Prairie Fire: The 1885 North-West Rebellion*. Edmonton: Hurtig.

CUTHAND, BETH (1949–). Beth Cuthand was born in La Ronge in 1949. She earned a Bachelor of Arts in sociology from the UNIVERSITY OF SASKATCHEWAN, and an MFA in Creative Writing from the University of Arizona. A supporter of First Nations education, Cuthand has taught at the FIRST NATIONS UNIVERSITY OF CANADA (Regina and Saskatoon), En'Owkin International School of Writing (Penticton), and the Nicola Valley Institute of Technology (Merritt). She has also mentored many young First Nations writers and poets. Cuthand has given readings across North America, and was writer-in-residence at Kenyon College in Gambier, Ohio (1993). She is currently working on her Master of Divinity at the College of Emmanuel and St. Chad (University of Saskatchewan). The major themes of Cuthand's writing reflect both voices from her ancestral past and the lives of contemporary Native women. Her poems and other writings appear in anthologies and magazines, the most notable being: *An Anthology of Canadian Native Literature in English, 2nd ed.*; *Native Poetry in Canada*; and *Reinventing the Enemies' Language: Contemporary Native American Women's Writings of North America*. Cuthand collaborated with Stan Cuthand and Mary Longman on a bilingual Cree-English children's book entitled *The Little Duck*, and recently published a collection of poetry entitled *Voices in the Waterfall*. *Christian Thompson*

CYPRESS HILLS (49°40'N, 109°30'W: map sheet 72 F/11). The Cypress Hills are located in the southwestern corner of Saskatchewan, where elevations rise more than 600 m above the surrounding plains over a distance of less than 50 km. This historic landscape consists of three "blocks" spanning an area of about 2,500 km² between Eastend in Saskatchewan and the "head of mountain" west of Elkwater, Alberta. The East Block is rangeland and home to the Nekaneet First Nation. Most of the Centre and East Blocks are within the boundaries of Cypress Hills Interprovincial Park. They are separated by "the Gap," an area of hummocky moraine and native mixed grassland. Westward, the Cypress Hills

become higher and more rugged. The West Block, straddling the Alberta-Saskatchewan boundary, rises to the highest elevation in Saskatchewan (1,392 m); in Alberta it reaches 1,466 m, the highest point in Canada from the Rocky Mountains to Labrador and the Appalachians. The Cypress Hills were created from the floor of a broad river valley. Sands and gravels transported by rivers from the Rocky Mountains now cap this elevated plateau. The topography was reversed as the rivers of the late Tertiary period gradually removed layers of rock, lowering the northern Great Plains to its present level. A few erosional remnants survived as flat-topped uplands or plateaux. The Cypress Hills survived, mostly because of their location midway between the South Saskatchewan and Missouri rivers. They now form a continental drainage divide between these two major river systems. During the Pleistocene glaciation, the Laurentide ice sheet was unable to flow over this prominent upland. Consequently, about 300 km² of the West Block was probably a *nunatak* or island in the ice. Meltwater, trapped between the uplands and the ice sheet, flowed through and around the Cypress Hills, eroding large glacial melt-water valleys. "Underfit" streams such as Battle Creek and the Frenchman River now occupy these valleys. The large valleys and incised tributary valleys remain active, with slumping of the valley sides and shifting of the streams during floods.

Because of their higher elevation, the Cypress Hills are cooler and wetter than the adjacent plains. The local climate varies with changing aspect. This influences vegetation, which ranges from dry grassland to humid forested slopes. Mixed grassland, native to the surrounding plains, occurs at lower elevations and on dry south-facing slopes in the Cypress Hills. John Palliser described the Hills as "a perfect oasis in the desert." Wetlands are common: there are numerous springs and ponds, especially in the hummocky terrain of the landslides. White spruce forest grows in the cool, moist conditions near springs and on north-facing slopes. Balsam poplar and trembling aspen can occur at these sites, but also as groves on the plateaux or along moist creek beds extending out onto the prairie. Lodgepole pine grows in the drier areas and above the other forests, while fescue prairie is found at the highest elevations. Fescue grassland and the lodgepole pine forest are considered montane vegetation; the closest similar plant communities are in the Rocky Mountain foothills. This disjunct flora of the Cypress Hills includes many plants that are rare in Saskatchewan, and several, such as orchid species, that are rare in general. This island forest in the midst of grasslands is sensitive to human activities and to small perturbations in climate. It has been highly valued for economic, cultural, spiritual, and environmental reasons. The woodlands are habitat for a large variety of birds including the hairy wood-

Cattle drive in the Cypress Hills.

pecker, great horned owl, ruffed grouse, mountain bluebird, yellow-breasted chat, turkey vulture and wild turkey. They also provide shelter for red squirrels, porcupines, chipmunks, deer, elk, moose, bobcats, and the occasional lynx.

Artifacts from archaeological sites in the Cypress Hills represent more than 7,000 years of human history. Accounts of European contact with Aboriginal people suggest that the Hills were a buffer zone among the various tribes who followed bison and elk as they retreated to the woods during winter months. The name Cypress Hills originated with **MÉTIS** settlers of the early 19th century, who mistook the lodgepole pine for jack pine, or *cyprès* in French. The next wave of settlers, primarily from the United States and eastern Canada, settled in the Cypress Hills region starting in the 1880s; they established the **RANCHING** industry that has dominated the land use ever since. A historical event of national significance was the **CYPRESS HILLS MASSACRE** of 1873, when over twenty deaths resulted from a disagreement between American wolfers and a group of Assiniboine (**NAKOTA**) over lost horses. When news of the massacre reached Ottawa, the government of Sir John A. Macdonald established the North-West Mounted Police (NWMP). The following year, the (NWMP) established Fort Walsh on Battle Creek; this site is now a popular national historic site. *David Sauchyn*

FURTHER READING: Hildebrandt, W. and B. Hubner. 1994. *The Cypress Hills: The Land and its People.* Saskatoon: Purich Press; Nelson, J.G. 1973. *The Last Refuge*. Montreal: Harvest House.

CYPRESS HILLS MASSACRE. The intensely competitive trade for buffalo robes, furs, and the attendant trade in whiskey ultimately produced the volatile conditions responsible for the Cypress Hills Massacre of June 1, 1873. It was the theft of some horses from a party of American wolfers by the **CREE** that set in motion the chain of events that culminated in the massacre of a group of **ASSINIBOINE** a few weeks later in the **CYPRESS HILLS.** For the Assiniboine, led by Chief Manitupotis (Little Soldier), the winter of 1872–73 was a hard one as food supplies were becoming increasingly scarce on the prairies. At the end of May 1873, the Assiniboine were camped in a valley alongside the north fork of the Milk River; there they were joined by another small band of Assiniboine under Chief Inihan Kinyen. The camps of Little Soldier and Inihan Kinyen together consisted of 300 people, fifty of whom were soldier-warriors.

Close by the camp were two small log forts belonging to wintering White traders representing American companies from Fort Benton: on the west side of the creek was Abel Farwell's post, and on the other side, a few hundred metres to the northeast, was that of Moses Solomon. The Assiniboine had accused Solomon of cheating them and had fired shots into his post; they threatened to "clear out" the traders and kill them all if they resisted. The tension between the Assiniboine and Solomon might have ended without incident had it not been for events that had taken place two weeks earlier in Montana. A group of about a dozen wolfers were returning with their season's take and were only a day's journey from Fort Benton when forty of their horses were stolen. Their large herd of animals had not

been closely guarded, as the wolfers had not expected a raid on their camp so close to Fort Benton. After noticing that their horses were missing, Thomas Hardwick, alias the Green River Renegade, and his men attempted to give chase; but recognizing the futility of pursuit, they headed for Fort Benton instead.

The wolfers arrived in the Cypress Hills on the last day of May. They searched for their horses, but Farwell assured them that Little Soldier's band was poor and had very few animals of their own. The gang spent the evening drinking with recently arrived **MÉTIS** freighters; having no particular business the next day, they began this again early in the morning, with Solomon joining in the festivities. Around noon the situation reached a climax when George Hammond's horse went missing. Cursing in both English and French, he began shouting that the Assiniboine had stolen it, suggesting that they thought they would be rewarded with whiskey if they returned it. Hammond went across to Solomon's and asked the wolfers to join him in seizing some Assiniboine horses in retaliation. These men needed little encouragement: they grabbed their rifles and proceeded toward the Assiniboine camp along with some Métis freighters, all of them sodden with drink. Alexis Labombarde in the meantime had discovered that Hammond's horse had only wandered off, and shouted this to the men rushing toward the Assiniboine camp. Unfortunately it was too late: by this time there were few level heads willing to listen.

It is difficult to ascertain what happened next. Farwell later said that he tried to dissuade the angry men from becoming violent, and that when this failed he waded across the river to the Assiniboine camp. He claimed that there he found an Assiniboine headman and struck a deal by which he would take two Assiniboine horses as security until the missing horse could be found. Farwell knew little or no Assiniboine, but swore afterwards that he had made himself understood and that the headman had agreed. About then, a Métis ran across to the camp to warn the Assiniboine of the approaching danger, and people began to run from the camp.

As some of the Indians spoke to Farwell, Hammond attempted to take two horses from the Assiniboine camp but was stopped by Bighead, an armed warrior. Hammond returned to the wolfers and some of the freighters, who by this time had lined the edge of a coulee that faced the exposed Assiniboine camp on two sides. From the protection of the bush surrounding the coulee, these men were virtually unseen. Fearing the worst, Farwell told the Assiniboine to scatter. Then, according to his own testimony, he went to speak to the wolfers and tried to find Labombarde, who by this time had recovered Hammond's horse; but it was too late. Someone, possibly Hammond, fired a shot, which was followed by indiscriminate fire at the unprotected Assiniboine camp. With Winchester and Henry repeating rifles, the men in the sheltered coulee fired volley after volley into the camp. The Assiniboine tried to fight back, but as they had few modern weapons their situation was hopeless: men, women and children fled from the camp. Most headed for some timber fifty metres to the east; others hid in the bushes lining the coulee or crossed the river. Many were shot as they fled, including Inihan Kinyen. From distant cover, the Assiniboine attempted to return fire, but to no avail. Approximately twenty Assiniboine died in the fighting. This event, one of the most violent episodes in the Canadian west, is generally credited with prompting the federal government's decision to create the North-West Mounted Police to police the region.

Walter Hildebrandt

FURTHER READING: Hildebrandt, W. and B. Hubner. 1994. *The Cypress Hills: The Land and Its People.* Saskatoon: Purich Publishing.

CZECH AND SLOVAK SETTLEMENTS. Czech and Slovak settlement in Saskatchewan began in 1884, when four Czech families Pangrac, Junek, Dolezal, and Skokan) from Bohemia settled in the Kolin district near Esterhazy. Count **PAUL ESTERHAZY** brought Slovaks to his primarily Hungarian colony of Huns' Valley, west of Minnedosa, Manitoba in 1885, then to the new Esterhazy colony in Saskatchewan the next year. Bohemian Czechs from the Volhynia region in Ukraine settled around Gerald, just northeast of the town of Esterhazy, in 1898: so the entire region around Esterhazy had small concentrations of Czechs and Slovaks, outnumbered by Hungarians. In 1901 George (Juraj) Zeman, an American Slovak, was appointed as a CPR colonization agent. Anxious to help get his people out of dangerous, unhealthy work in mines, mills and refineries (especially in Pennsylvania) and back into farming, he introduced Czech and Slovak families to the central region in Saskatchewan around Davidson, Kenaston, Hanley, Glenside, Broderick, Hawarden, Strongfield, and Milden. Other Czech families settled further west around Marriott in the Valley Centre district in 1902.

COURTESY OF BRIAN MLAZGAR

The family of Michael and Anna Salamon, Slovak immigrants who settled in Lebret in 1909. Photo ca. 1922.

Beginning in 1905, several Slovak families (Mlazgar, Tomecko, Beros, Mantyak, Pletz, Krafchek, Tkach) emigrated north from Minnesota and homesteaded in the Lipton area. Other related families (Salamon, Ondic) followed, settling in and around Lebret and Balcarres. Much later, large numbers of ethnic Germans from Sudetenland would settle around St. Walburg, Brightsand Lake and Loon Lake, to the northeast. Most of the early Czech and Slovak settlers were Roman Catholics. They tended not to form separate parishes in Saskatchewan but to join their Ukrainian, Hungarian, Polish and Croatian neighbours; undoubtedly this facilitated intermarriage. But some Czechs and Slovaks were Lutheran, Reformed or other Protestant; Hus Chapel in Glenside was named after the progenitor of the Hussite or Moravian Brethren movements.

Despite their relative isolation, Czechs and Slovaks in rural Saskatchewan became integrated into ethnic networks uniting them with their co-ethnics across North America. The earliest Czech organizations in Canada were local community associations at Kolin and Esterhazy in 1912, which were responsible for a Czech cultural revival in these enclaves during the 1930s. Kolin also had a service club called the Good Companions, led by the Czech minister of the United Church in Esterhazy, with the aim of promoting Czech culture and language in the next generation. A national Czech Benevolent Association was founded in Winnipeg in 1913, connected with the Bohemian National Alliance in the United States. Similarly, Slovaks founded local

benevolent associations which became federated into the Canadian Slovak Benevolent Society in 1946. Czechs and Slovaks were united in Sokal, a sports and recreational society with many local chapters in Canada and the US; one early chapter was established at Goldburg, Saskatchewan. The Canadian Slovak League was formed in 1932. The National Alliance of Slovaks, Czechs, and Subcarpathian Ruthenians, established in 1939, later became the Czechoslovak National Alliance of Canada, then in 1960 the Czechoslovak National Association of Canada. There have been wide variations in counting Czechs and Slovaks in Canadian census data. While the earliest concentrations were found in the prairies and British Columbia, later they were far outnumbered by co-ethnics in central Canada. The most recent census (2001) data counted 4,735 residents of Saskatchewan who claimed Czech ethnicity; 950 of them claimed to be only of Czech origin, compared to 3,785 who also claimed other ethnic origins. In 1991 only 615 people in Saskatchewan claimed Slovak ethnicity. (*See also* **ETHNIC BLOC SETTLEMENTS, HUNGARIAN SETTLEMENTS, GERMAN SETTLEMENTS, ROMANIAN SETTLEMENTS**)

Alan Anderson

FURTHER READING: Gellner, J. and J. Smerek. 1968. *The Czechs and Slovaks in Canada.* Toronto: University of Toronto Press; Schilling, R. 1989. *Sudeten in Saskatchewan: A Way to be Free.* Saskatoon: Saskatchewan German Council and St. Walburg German Club.

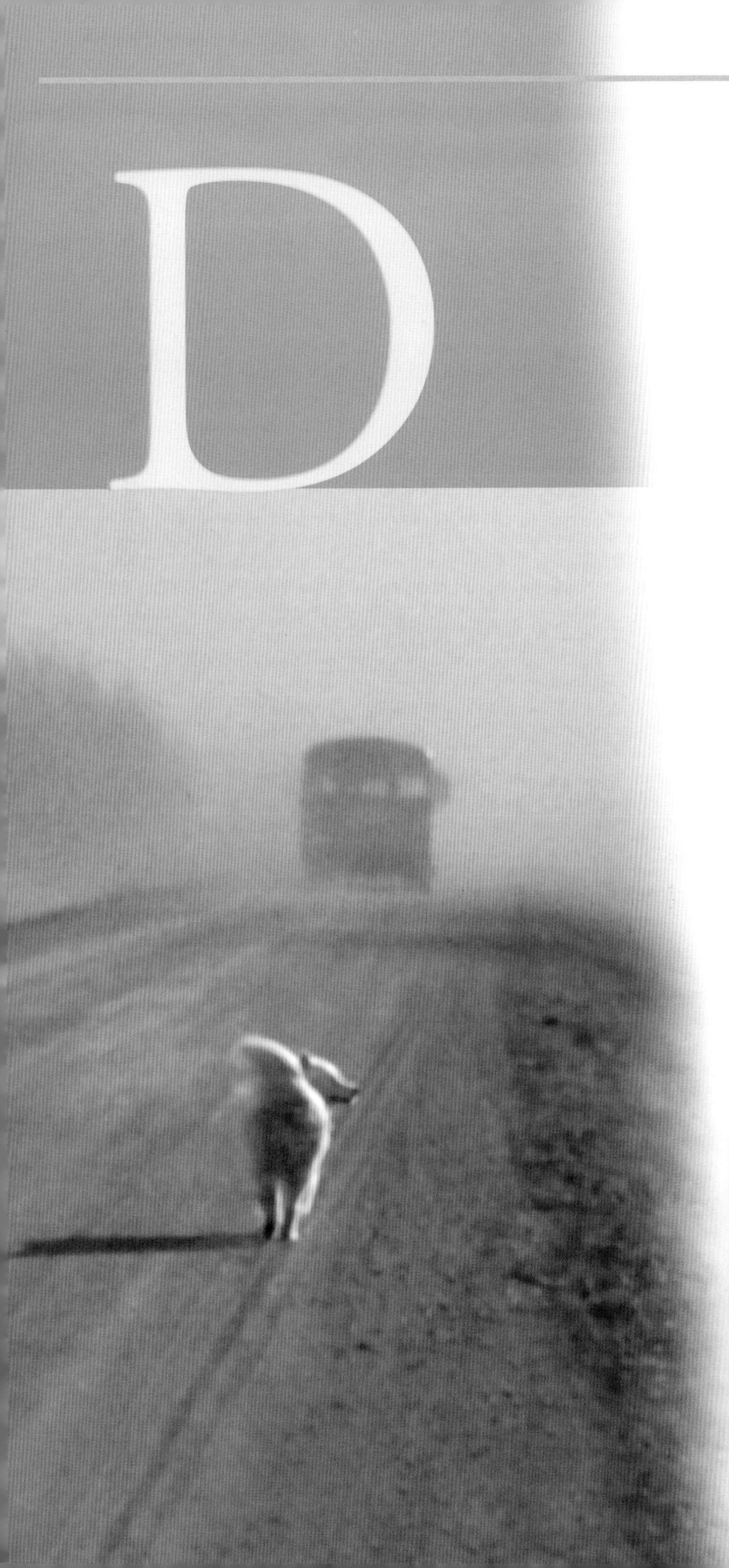

D

DAGNONE, ANTONIO (1941–). Born in Civitanova, Campobasso, Italy, on August 4, 1941, Tony Dagnone came to Simpson, Saskatchewan in 1949. He attended Scott Collegiate in Regina, studied Commerce at the **UNIVERSITY OF SASKATCHEWAN**, and completed post-graduate studies in Hospital Administration at the University of Toronto. In 1967, Dagnone embarked on an illustrious healthcare career at University Hospital in Saskatoon. At age 36, he became the hospital's executive director, and subsequently its president and CEO. During his 25-year tenure at Saskatchewan's major teaching hospital, renamed **ROYAL UNIVERSITY HOSPITAL** in 1990, Dagnone directed expansion projects in excess of $70 million and facilitated the development of new tertiary care programs, including Saskatchewan's first CT scanner and magnetic resonance imager (MRI); the latter necessitated a $4.2 million provincial fund-raising campaign. Dagnone was instrumental in developing outreach and community-based healthcare services, including Kinsmen Children's Centre, Ronald McDonald House, and the Geriatric Assessment Unit/Day Hospital, first of its kind in Canada. Known for his high energy and community commitment, Dagnone was Chair of *Century Saskatoon*, marking the 1982 city centennial. In 1989, he presided over

SASKATCHEWAN ARCHIVES BOARD S-SP-A19574-14, SASKATOON STARPHOENIX FONDS

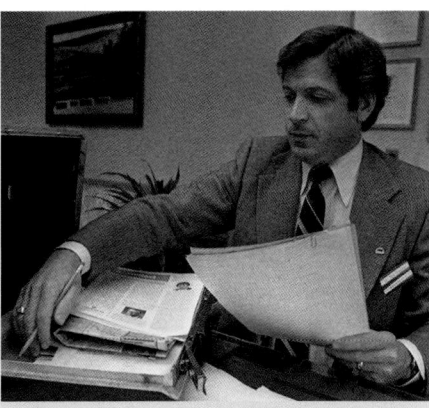

Tony Dagnone, January 1983.

Saskatoon's Canada Summer Games. Dagnone was named a Member of the Order of Canada in 1991. The following year, he left Saskatoon for London, Ontario, where he is president and CEO of the London Health Sciences Centre.   *Kathryn J. Ellis*

DAIRY FARMING. Milk production for sale to processing plants began in Saskatchewan in the late 1890s. The number of dairy cows in Saskatchewan peaked at 590,000 in 1935, and has declined steadily since that time. In 1935 most of the milk produced was used to make butter; the skim milk was kept on the farm and used as a protein and vitamin source for pigs and poultry. As refrigeration and transportation systems improved, cream production was gradually replaced by sale of whole milk to processing plants with improved sanitary and product quality standards. By 2003 the number of milk cows had declined to 31,000, and cream shipping had been phased out. Rural electrification, which took place mainly in the 1950s, had a significant impact on the dairy industry. Bulk handling milk began in Ontario in 1953, and was introduced into western Canada soon after that.

The technology to freeze semen was developed in the 1950s, which greatly expanded the use of artificial insemination (AI) in dairy cattle. The 1950s also saw the development of computer programs for record keeping and analysis of the production of daughters of bulls. This new technology allowed identification and widespread use of superior bulls. The first barns in western Canada housed cows in individual stalls; but in the 1950s group

housing in the free stall system was introduced, with cows being moved from the stalls to a milking parlour. There was a gradual evolution of mechanization and housing systems in the 1970s and 1980s: new types of housing were introduced in the mid-1990s which greatly improved barn ventilation through use of much higher roofs and the adoption of natural updraft ventilation.

In 2002 there were just over one million milk cows in Canada, on 18,600 dairy farms. About 81% of these dairy farms are located in Ontario and Quebec; 14% are in the western provinces, and 5% in the Atlantic provinces. In 2002 the dairy farms in Saskatchewan numbered 300. There is a continuing decline in the number of dairy farms, accompanied by an increase in number of cows and milk production per cow. Average production per cow is now 9,000 kg annually, or twice the 1960 level. The genetic improvement of dairy cattle for milk production as well as physical soundness and removal of genetic defects is a joint effort involving Agriculture and Agri-Food Canada, the breed associations, and a number of organizations that are members of the Canadian Dairy Network. About 95% of the dairy cattle in Saskatchewan belong to the Holstein breed. There are also small numbers of Ayrshire and Jersey dairy cattle in the province, but very few of other breeds such as Guernsey, Brown Swiss, or Shorthorn. The reason for the popularity of the Holstein breed is its high milk production and the pricing system which favours the low-fat composition of Holstein milk. Bull calves from the Holstein breed enter the feedlot system and are finished for

market at a slightly heavier weight than traditional beef breeds.

All dairy animals are individually identified, and detailed milk production composition and physical type characteristics are recorded on many dairy farms. Most dairy herds have adopted a mixed-ration feeding system in which forages and concentrate ingredients are blended, and sufficient water or wet feeds are included to increase the moisture content to about 45%. In Saskatchewan the main forages are whole-plant barley silage and alfalfa hay or silage. The main cereal grain used in the concentrate is barley, and the protein supplements include canola meal, soybean meal, corn gluten meal, and wheat distillers grain. Trace mineral supplementation suitable for specific regions has been developed.

In the year 2000 total Canadian farm cash receipts from the dairy sector amounted to $4.1 billion, with about $130 million in Saskatchewan. Canada exports dairy cattle and other genetic material in the form of embryos and semen. In addition to the Canadian Dairy Commission, there are a number of important organizations involved in the dairy industry. These include Dairy Farmers of Canada, which is a national policy, lobby, and dairy product promotion organization; individual farm milk production quotas are set by provincial regulatory boards according to Canadian Dairy Commission guidelines. The Canadian Dairy Network is involved in the genetic evaluation of Canadian dairy bulls and cows. This function was previously carried out by Agriculture and Agri-Food Canada, but was formed as a private organization in 1995 with the board of directors from the artificial insemination industry, the breed associations, and the milk recording agencies. (*See also* **DAIRY INDUSTRY**)   *David A. Christensen*

FURTHER READING: Martin, J., R.J. Hudson and B.A. Young. 1993. *Animal Production in Canada*. Edmonton: University of Alberta.

DAIRY INDUSTRY. Saskatchewan's dairy industry evolved from its early beginnings during the settlement of the province to its current form and structure as a significant sector within the agricultural economy. The development of the Saskatchewan dairy industry was an integral part of national settlement policy aimed at diversifying and stabilizing prairie agriculture, which was highly dependent on volatile grain markets. In Saskatchewan, early attempts to establish a viable dairy industry met with considerable success (although below initial expectations) through a government development program consisting of loans and other incentives to build plants and market butter and cheese, with milk supplied by local farmers. In spite of the many challenges facing the industry, dairy production expanded and prospered. At its peak, it repre-

RON GARNETT—AIRSCAPES
Dairy farm near Leroy.

EVERETT BAKER PHOTO/COURTESY OF THE SASKATCHEWAN HISTORY AND FOLKLORE SOCIETY

Edwin Cowie's dairy herd, Shaunavon, June 1956.

sented an important aspect of early farm production and diversification, with about 100,000 farmers shipping cream and milk to numerous processing plants located throughout rural Saskatchewan for manufacturing into fluid milk products and butter.

The Saskatchewan dairy industry has undergone dramatic change due to technological improvements and market trends. No longer is cream shipped in cans by rail by thousands of producers to processing plants. Innovations such as refrigeration, pasteurization and bulk handling have greatly impacted on industry productivity and structure. Today, milk is produced on about 300 large, specialized dairy farms and delivered by bulk tankers to one large processing plant which produces fluid milk, yogurt and cheeses for the western regional and national markets. Throughout the production/transportation/processing chain, the most advanced technical and sanitary practices are employed to ensure consumers receive a high-quality product.

While the dairy farms have decreased in number, the volume and value of milk and milk products continue to grow. Average herd size in 2003 stood at 85 cows per farm, with productivity per cow increasing almost threefold over the last half-century, owing largely to improved housing, feeding, and breeding practices. Producers now market over 210 million litres of milk annually, valued at $130 million. The Saskatchewan dairy industry makes a significant contribution to the provincial economy in terms of value-added processing and job creation, ranking third behind beef and hog production.

The dairy industry has undergone a major shift in the products manufactured, in response to changing consumer attitudes and product demand. The trend to consuming lower fat in diets has resulted in a shift to dairy products with high protein/low fat content. Demand for fluid products has shifted from regular homogenized milk to lower fat and flavoured milk options. Growth in demand is strong for high-value products such as various cheese vari-

eties (4–5% annually) and for yogurt (9–10% annually). On the other hand, the demand for butter is flat because of its high fat content and strong competition from vegetable oil-based alternatives.

Product quality is maintained at a high standard by the enforcement of various health and sanitary regulations applied at the producer, processor, and retail levels of the industry. At the provincial level, production and marketing are governed by regulations under the Animal Products and Public Health Acts. At the national level, regulations under the Food and Drug Act set out the definitions for various dairy products and measures to safeguard consumer interests. All milk destined for processing is tested for antibiotics before entering the plant. If a load tests positive, it is automatically rejected. In addition, all milk entering the plant is first pasteurized before processing into any end-use product. At the Provincial Dairy Laboratory, producer milk samples undergo comprehensive testing for bacteria and other contaminants, as well as analysis of milk components (butterfat, protein, and other solids). The component analysis provides the information required for producer payments.

Producers and governments addressed the need to improve industry stability by creating a national orderly marketing and supply management system for milk. A milestone agreement among the provinces and the federal government was the formation of the National Milk Marketing Plan (1984). This agreement provided producers with countervailing power in the market for milk to balance the growing concentration of market power in the hands of national and multinational processors and grocery chains. Under this agreement, national quotas were established at levels to serve market needs, and prices were set for various classes of dairy products. The Canadian Dairy Commission is responsible for marketing milk used for industrial (processing) purposes, while the provincial marketing boards were made responsible for allocating quotas to pro-

ducers within their boundaries, and for the marketing of milk used for fluid purposes (milk and cream). In Saskatchewan, the Milk Control Board is responsible for managing the milk supply through a system of quota allocations to producers, and for the transportation, pricing and marketing of all milk produced under the supply management system. The Board works closely with the CDC and other provincial boards in managing the system on a national basis to ensure that market needs are met, and that consumers receive high-quality products at reasonable prices.

Pooling of revenues generated from the sale of milk used in various dairy products is a very important aspect of the orderly marketing structure established to maintain industry stability. Milk used for processed products serves a national market. Milk revenues from this source are pooled nationally, and administered by the Canadian Dairy Commission. Until recently, fluid product revenues were pooled and administered by each provincial marketing board in their respective jurisdictions. In response to changing processing circumstances, it was in the interest of producers to broaden the market for fluid milk products and to establish two regional milk pools: in 1997, the Western Milk Pool and the P5 Pool (in central and eastern Canada) were created to better serve the needs of both processors and consumers. These regional pools established common prices for all milk and milk products marketed with the regional revenues pooled and distributed among all producers on a common basis, regardless of location and product produced. Dairy producers had the opportunity to participate in provincial and national agriculture policy development through the Dairy Farmers of Canada, a producer-funded advocacy organization, and through the Dairy Farmers of Saskatchewan at the provincial level. Both organizations are also heavily involved in promoting milk and milk products to various consumer groups. (*See also* **DAIRY FARMING**)   *Gerald Gartner*

FURTHER READING: Church, G.C. 1985. *An Unfailing Faith: A History of the Saskatchewan Dairy Industry*. Regina: Canadian Plains Research Center.

DAKOTA/LAKOTA. Dakota peoples emerged from a long history linked to the demise of Hopewell and later Mississippian archaeological cultures, and arrived in Minnesota/Wisconsin taking advantage of the region's mosaic of forests, lakes and prairies. The ancestral Dakota were associated with the specific mid-western Woodland archaeological complexes: the Initial (c. 200 BC–AD 500) and the Terminal (c. AD 500–1680) traditions. Concentrated at the Mississippi River headwaters in the parkland transitions zones between forest and prairie, the Dakota exploited the plentiful resources of these ecotones. Linguistically part of the Siouan language family, dialects emerged to distinguish the Dakota proper (Mdewakanton, Wahpeton, Sisseton, and Wapakute) and middle division (Yanktonai and Yankton) from the western division Lakota (Teton).

Dakota expansions onto the eastern prairies in the mid-17th century were a response to the population increases that came with access to French trade goods, including firearms. In the early 18th century, as Ojibwa-Dakota conflict increased over control of hunting territories and access to traders in the Mississippi watershed, the Lakotas moved west onto the prairies, crossed the Missouri to the high plains, and continued their expansion westward to control the Black Hills. As horses came through the trade networks, Lakotas expanded in number and flourished because of the abundant game resources. Their expansions were composed of forays into neighbouring regions that comprised the border regions and territories of their enemies: Lake of the Woods and Rainy Lake, Turtle Mountains/Pembina Hills, as well as the Souris, White Earth, and Missouri-Yellowstone Rivers regions.

The Dakota, once abandoned by the French in the early 18th century, became allies of the British and were increasingly bound to them by treaties and trade alliances, involving fighting as British allies in the War of 1812. From the arrival of the Americans with the Pike expedition to the upper Mississippi in 1805, uneasiness characterized relations for much of the next decades. While the French had been acculturated as kinsmen, the English replaced these roles imperfectly; and when the Americans arrived, they did not grasp the importance of reciprocity for the Dakota. Treaties of friendship and trade gave way to extorted land cessions; the American appetite for land and resources was never satiated. By the 1850s the Dakota were left with reservations upon which they were allowed to reside only at the discretion of the President of the United States. This dependency left them vulnerable and periodically destitute. Minnesota became a territory in 1849 and a state in 1858, surrounding them and filling up their former lands. While less circumscribed, the Lakota and Yankton-Yanktonai participated in the 1851 Fort Laramie Treaty that began a process of fixing the boundaries of tribal territorial domains, with pledges of annuities for cessation of intertribal warfare. However, as the United States drifted toward civil war, promises to Indians were all but forgotten amidst the graft and corruption in the Indian service.

The collision of events and circumstances that led to the Dakota outbreak were numerous. The breaking point was reached between August and December of 1862, when young men refused to watch their families starve any longer. With the onset of fighting, the diaspora of many Dakota began as vast numbers fled onto the prairies of eastern Dakota Territory, then north into Canada—first

to the vicinity of the Red River settlement, then westward into present-day western Manitoba. Standing Buffalo led his followers back into Montana Territory, where he was killed in battle on June 5, 1871. His son, taking his father's name, led part of this group back into Canada, eventually settling on the Standing Buffalo reserve in 1878. White Cap had led followers into Manitoba and eventually into what became Saskatchewan, but when forced by the Métis to join in the fighting in 1885, White Cap's group was punished; however, once rehabilitated they were given a reserve at Moose Woods. A group led by Hupa Yakta, previously affiliated with White Cap in 1890, asked for a reserve at Round Plain, which came to be called Wahpeton. Most of the followers of **SITTING BULL** went south and preceded his surrender to US authorities on July 19, 1881; however, a small group of Lakota remained and struggled for survival at the edges of Moose Jaw, and were finally granted a reserve at Wood Mountain in 1910. While reserves at Oak River, Birdtail, and Oak Lakes had been established for Dakota in the 1870s, and others for the Portage la Prairie bands in 1886 in Manitoba, the Dakota communities in Saskatchewan and Manitoba remained extremely isolated.

The contemporary Dakota/Lakota communities in Saskatchewan have remained outside of treaty, and have had differential relations with the various jurisdictions among which they must deal. A contemporary movement among the Sioux in Saskatchewan is pressing for treaty adhesions to bring them into full status and equal relations with Canada, as are the other First Nations within Saskatchewan.   *David Reed Miller*

FURTHER READING: Elias, P.D. 1988. *The Dakota of the Canadian Northwest: Lessons for Survival*. Winnipeg: University of Manitoba Press; White, R. 1978. "The Winning of the West: The Expansion of the Western Sioux in the Eighteenth and Nineteenth Centuries," *Journal of American History* 6 (2): 319–43.

DAKOTA/LAKOTA SPIRITUALITY. For the Dakota, all of creation has been accomplished by the Creator and is beautiful, powerful and sacred. Everything in the universe possesses a kind of power that it is capable of transferring or sharing with other birds, animals and humans. Mother Earth is a living, nurturing, evolving being; all things in the Universe are connected; and anything that happens somewhere affects something somewhere else. In the natural order of things, humans—because they can reason, scheme, rationalize, lie, etc.—are not always as close to the Creator as other parts of the universe such as birds, animals, trees, etc., which do exactly what the Creator wants them to do. Humans are the only ones who disturb things; animals or birds are therefore used as messengers or conduits to take petitions to the Creator, and to bring the

responses back to humans. The Dakota also believe that the spirits of relatives who have gone to the spirit world still care about them: if these departed relatives are petitioned properly they will help, guide, and give wisdom to those beseeching them.

In general, Dakota people place a great deal of faith in the power of prayer. There is also a greater faith in the power of collective thought: persons about to pray, for instance, will ask everyone to help them pray in their own way. Dakota people regard ceremonies as re-enactments of sacred moments in their tribal memories when something worked for them as a people. They are very observant, not only of what things happen, but of patterns, sequences, and types of logic that result in something happening: this is often referred to as the natural order of things. It is reflected in the liturgy that one sees in Dakota ceremonies. The Dakota also believe that when people are born they are given a task to do on this earth: it is their responsibility to find out what that task is. Traditionally, this was the motivation for the vision quest, a period of isolated fasting, meditation, and prayer in the hope that one would be given a sign regarding the proper direction to follow.   *Ken Goodwill*

DALMENY, town, pop 1,610, located 24 km NW of Saskatoon on Hwy 305. The district began to be settled in the early 1900s; many of the early homesteaders were Mennonites. A Mennonite Brethren Church was built at Dalmeny in 1901. With the arrival of the Canadian Northern Railway in 1904-05, the townsite developed. In 1906, the post office opened, the first grain elevator was built, and a general store was established. The community was named after Dalmeny, Scotland. The village grew slowly but steadily until the 1960s, having developed into a service centre for the surrounding farming population. Beginning in the 1970s, Dalmeny began to attract people who worked in Saskatoon but wanted to live in a smaller community. Young professionals and their families augmented the village's population from 417 in 1971 to 1,064 a decade later. In 1983, Dalmeny attained town status. While there is a small core of essential businesses, residents benefit from the employment opportunities, services, and amenities that nearby Saskatoon has to offer. Dalmeny's two schools provide K–12 education to over 500 students, and there is a library, a municipal police service, a fire department, a special care home, and a new community complex with a rink for hockey and skating.   *David McLennan*

DANCE. Since the days of the earliest settlers, dance has been a vibrant part of the cultural mosaic of this province. Languages have struggled to survive, but dance in all its forms has not only survived but flourished. First Nations dancers, with their traditional pow-wow, were the earliest dancers; but the art form was soon to embrace highland flings, hopaks, jigs, polkas, etc. Cultural dance activity at the grass-roots level is widespread, with some groups aspiring to professional standards. Many have toured to their European homelands, to critical acclaim.

Traditional dance forms like ballet, jazz, and tap are taught in all the major centres in Saskatchewan as well as in smaller towns and villages. Dance Saskatchewan, the umbrella organization for dance in the province, currently lists over 120 dance schools. Earliest records of dancers and teachers in the province in the 1930s include Gail Grant, Nellie Smith, Jean Gauld, Lillian Stevens, Jean Botkin, Shirley Whittet, and Marjorie Matchett. The following generation included teachers who have had a remarkable impact on dance in Saskatchewan: Doris Sitter in Moose Jaw, Lucia Pavlychenko and Juliette Perry-Perez in Saskatoon, and Maureen Johnson in Regina. Most of the dance schools and organizations in the province can trace their roots back to one of these teachers. Other notable teachers include Reg Hawe (Conservatory of Music, **UNIVERSITY OF REGINA**) and Petre Bodeutz (Regina Modern Dance Works).

There are several dance festivals held throughout the province annually. The first and largest of these, the Moose Jaw Festival of Dance, was founded in 1960 by a committee headed by Helen Tait; Arnold Spohr (Royal Winnipeg Ballet) assisted with adjudication. On a professional level, Saskatchewan has been home to four dance companies since its inception as a province. The first of these, Saskatchewan Dance Theatre (SDT), was created by Lucia Pavlychenko in Saskatoon in 1973. The original company was composed of five dancers: Michele Presly, Jim Green, Elaine Loo (Hanson), Paul Jaspar, and Kathryn Greenaway. It expanded in its second season to include four more dancers; in its third and final season, three of the original dancers were replaced. During its short life, SDT was a successful company, touring throughout Saskatchewan to critical acclaim. Financial problems and tensions within the company led to its demise in December 1976.

Meanwhile, another company was being formed in Regina under the direction of Marianne Livant and Maria Formolo. Regina Modern Dance Works was incorporated in 1974, with seven dancers in the company: Livant and Formolo, with Patrick Hall, Pearl Louie, Allan Risdill, David Weller and Belinda Weitzel. Later additions to the company included Connie Moker Wernikowski, Marnie Gladwell, Susan McKenzie, Stephen Karcher, Kim Sachaw and Keith Urban. Livant resigned in 1976 as a result of artistic differences, and Urban took on the role of co-artistic director with Formolo. Maestro Petre Bodeutz was hired as ballet master/choreographer for the company in 1977. At the height of its success (1976–78) the company was offering full-length productions in Regina, as well as touring nationally to critical acclaim. By October 1979, how-

ever, the company was in trouble both financially and artistically. Formolo and Urban were the only two dancers remaining by the final season, and Regina Modern Dance Works folded in February 1982.

Marie Nychka (director of the Boyan School of Dance and Tavria Ukrainian Ensemble) dreamed of creating a touring ballet company, and soon convinced fellow dancers Lorne Matthews and April Chow to join her in creating Saskatchewan's third professional dance company, Saskatchewan Theatre Ballet, in March 1982. Five dancers were hired as apprentices: Suzanne Stewart, Darleen Schlademann, Cheryl Tweet, Sheryl Gardner and Darla Thompson. Eventually, the company grew to twelve dancers (six of them apprentices). Although popular with rural audiences, the company was unable to attract Canada Council funding, and financial difficulties were experienced throughout its six-year history. General Manager Jean Botkin was forced to resign in February 1986 due to illness. After four months on the job, her replacement disappeared, having embezzled the company's meager funds. Dancers and board members rallied to finish off the season, taking out personal loans to pay for the final tour and ending operations in October 1988. Two years earlier, another very different company had been formed in Regina. Under the artistic direction of Robin Poitras and Dianne Fraser, **NEW DANCE HORIZONS** produced its first season of contemporary dance in 1986. This company remains vibrant.

Barb Cameron

FURTHER READING: Cameron, B. 1998. *A History of the Professional Dance Companies that have Existed in Saskatchewan Since 1905*. Saskatoon: Dance Saskatchewan.

DANIELS, HARRY W. (1940–2004). A MÉTIS leader, social activist, author, and actor, Harry Daniels was born on September 16, 1940, in Regina Beach, Saskatchewan. One of Canada's most visible and charismatic modern Aboriginal leaders, Daniels spent over forty years in the national and international Aboriginal political arenas, fighting for the rights of Canada's Aboriginal peoples. Influenced by the labour movement and the civil rights movement, Daniels was one of the founding members of both the Métis Society of Saskatchewan (MSS) and the Native Council of Canada (NCC). He served as vice-president of the Métis Nation of Alberta and helped to organize the Métis Association of the Northwest Territories. From 1976 to 1981, Daniels served as NCC president; as the national spokesman for the Métis and Non-status Indians, he was primarily responsible for negotiating the constitutional recognition of the Métis into the Constitution Act, 1982. He was also chair of the Canadian Aboriginal Justice Council, and commissioner on the Métis and

REGINA LEADER-POST

Harry Daniels and Mireille Deyglun on the set of *Madeleine* at Lower Fort Garry, June 1986.

Non-Status Indian Crime and Justice Commission as well as the Métis and Non-Status Indian Constitutional Review Commission. From 1997 to 2000, he served as president of the NCC's successor, the Congress of Aboriginal Peoples, calling on the United Nations to pressure the Canadian government to meet its obligations to the country's Aboriginal peoples. Daniels was an accomplished author who wrote three books on Métis rights, as well as numerous papers, articles, and submission papers relating to the Constitution and Aboriginal rights. A talented film and stage actor, he held an undergraduate degree from the **UNIVERSITY OF SASKATCHEWAN**, a graduate degree from Carleton University, and an honorary doctorate in Law from the University of Ottawa. He died in Regina on September 6, 2004.

Cheryl Troupe

DANIELSON, GUSTAF HERMAN (1883–1971). Born in Sweden in 1883, Danielson immigrated to the United States in 1901 and to Saskatchewan in 1904 and homesteaded south of Elbow. Danielson was active in community organizations. He was a Wheat Pool delegate and served on the board of the Davidson Co-operative Association for over forty years. Danielson was elected to the RM council for seven years and an additional eight years as reeve. He spent seven years on the school board and thirty-eight years on the Davidson Hospital Board. Danielson was elected to the Saskatchewan Legislature in 1934 as part of the Liberal sweep of the province. In 1938, he narrowly won re-election, defeating Conservative leader **JOHN DIEFENBAKER**. In 1944 he was one of five Liberals elected and one of only three with previous legislative experience. His attacks on **T.C. DOUGLAS**' policies and his length of service in the Legislature made him a prominent figure in the province. In 1964, Progressive

SASKATCHEWAN ARCHIVES BOARD R-A692
Gustaf Danielson.

SASKATCHEWAN ARCHIVES BOARD R-B6179
James Darling.

SASKATCHEWAN ARCHIVES BOARD R-A11176-4
William Gwynne Davies (right) at Canadian Congress of Labour meeting, March 1949.

Conservative leader **MARTIN PEDERSEN** defeated Danielson. Ironically, it was the election that saw the Liberals returned to power after twenty years in opposition. In July 1971 Danielson died at his home in Davidson. With thirty years in the Legislature, Danielson still remains the chamber's longest serving member.   *Brett Quiring*

DANISH SETTLEMENTS. Recent census data (2001) reveal that 9,375 residents of Saskatchewan claimed that they are of Danish ethnic origin, of whom 86.9% (8,155) also claimed other ethnic origins; only 13.1% (1,225) claimed only Danish origin. Most people of Danish origin, unlike people of other Scandinavian origins, concentrated in cities, particularly Saskatoon, where they pioneered the Saskatoon Scandinavian Club. Small numbers or individual families settled among other Scandinavians in several rural settlements, or in mixed areas where they were not sufficiently numerous to constitute a settlement of their own. Only a single, small specifically Danish settlement came into existence in Saskatchewan: the Redvers area in the southeastern corner, where Danish families settled around 1910 and formed the Dannevirke Danish Lutheran congregation in 1923. Today the town of Redvers is little more than 10% Scandinavian, as is the surrounding Antler RM; altogether there could be some 200 people of Scandinavian origin (mostly Danes) in this area. (*See also* **ETHNIC BLOC SETTLEMENTS, SCANDINAVIAN SETTLEMENTS, NORWEGIAN SETTLEMENTS**)

Alan Anderson

DANUBE SWABIANS. According to the 2001 census, Germans make up the largest ethnic group in Saskatchewan. Many people assume they came from Germany, but the vast majority came from German communities in Eastern Europe, and a significant number of Saskatchewan's Germans are descendants of *Banat Donauschwaben* (Danube

Swabians from the Banat region, divided today between Romania and Serbia). After the Austro-Hungarian Empire had driven the Ottoman Turks out of the Danube basin in the years before and after 1700, it resettled the depopulated area with ethnic Germans from southern Germany, where one of the provinces was known as Schwaben (Swabia). Many also came from farther west in Alsace and Lorraine, and farther south from Austria and Switzerland (part of which was historically included in Swabia); but all came to be known as Danube Swabians. The term was first used in 1922 by Professor Robert Sieger in Austria to differentiate the "Swabians" of southeastern Europe from those still in the Swabian area of Germany. There were two principal areas of settlement, each several thousand square miles: Banat, north of Belgrade and east of the Danube, was largely Roman Catholic, whereas Batschka, west of the Danube, was largely Lutheran. In these areas the Germans made up about one-third of the population, mixing with Hungarians, Serbs, Romanians, and other ethnic groups.

As a minority group with little political influence, the Danube Swabians felt threatened by the political unrest that eventually led to the outbreak of **WORLD WAR I** in 1914. This instability, combined with a shortage of affordable land and a lack of industrial opportunity, caused many Danube Swabians to emigrate to North and South America in search of new opportunities. After World War I, the Danube Swabian homeland was divided among Hungary, Romania, and Yugoslavia; the ethnic Germans were now even more isolated and politically impotent. Immigration to the New World resumed until interrupted by **WORLD WAR II**, during which the Nazi Germans treated the Serbian people harshly. After the War the Yugoslavian government responded by stripping the ethnic Germans of their property and citizenship and interning the population in camps, where a large percentage died of starvation, disease, and exposure to the elements. After about

five years, the survivors were released. Some were able to relocate to Germany, which was already overflowing with refugees including many Romanian and Hungarian ethnic Germans. Some of these displaced persons continued on to Saskatchewan, where they had family and friends, and some bypassed Germany entirely owing to the overcrowding.

Saskatchewan's Danube Swabians are concentrated in the southern part of the province. Concentrations of Banat Germans are found in Regina, around Odessa/Vibank/Kendal, in an area encompassed by Weyburn, Parry, Bengough, and Minton, and in pockets around Rouleau/Drinkwater, Qu'Appelle/Indian Head, Rockglen/Fife Lake, Quinton/Raymore, Luseland, Holdfast, Humboldt, Alameda/Steelman/Lampman, and Hodgeville/GlenBain/Gravelbourg. Some Banat villages that sent significant numbers of families to Saskatchewan include Zichydorf, Georghausen, Setschan/Setschanfeld, Glogon, and Gross-Zsam. Early immigrants from Zichydorf (also known as Zichyfalva and Mariolana), a village of about 3,000 people 70 km northeast of Belgrade, founded Zichydorf Colony south of Regina in 1897 at the site of an artesian well which they dug 3.5 km south of present-day Highway 1 and 4 km east of Highway 6. The founding of this colony inspired an exodus from Zichydorf in the ensuing years to the Regina area. When it became clear that the village would not be served by a hoped-for railroad line, the colony began to disintegrate, and by 1910 all the families were living on their homesteads or in the city.

Although the colony did not survive, the immigration of Zichydorfers to Saskatchewan continued. Most first came to Regina's "Germantown," working to accumulate capital to begin homesteading. Many put down roots in Regina, so densely populating part of east Regina that it was known as "Little Zichydorf." Many others later moved on to farm near other communities. Today numerous descendants of the Zichydorf pioneers live in Regina, in southern Saskatchewan, and across Canada. They have become anglicized and their history is largely forgotten: few realize that they share a common ancestry with some of their social and business associates. (*See also* ETHNIC BLOC SETTLEMENTS, GERMAN SETTLEMENTS)

Glenn Schwartz

FURTHER READING: Anwender, B. 1996. "Zichydorf Colony: A Brief History," *Saskatchewan Genealogical Society Bulletin* 27 (3): 103–05; Lehmann, H. 1986. *The German Canadians, 1750–1937*. St. John's, Newfoundland: Jesperson Press.

DARLING, JAMES ANDREW (1891–1979).

Darling was born in Shotts, Scotland, on May 21, 1891, into a family of industrialists. Darling emigrated to Manitoba in 1908 and worked as a farm hand before purchasing a farm near Colonsay in 1911. He served on the Elstow agricultural society, the Colonsay municipal council, the school board, and the local telephone board. He was also active with the SASKATCHEWAN WHEAT POOL. Darling was caught up in the farmers' protest movement and helped the Progressives. He joined the CCF shortly after its inception and was elected in Watrous in 1944. Re-elected in 1948, he was appointed to Cabinet as the Minister of Public Works and as Minister of Telephones. In 1949 the SASKATCHEWAN POWER CORPORATION was formed to purchase the province's electrical facilities and electrify Saskatchewan's farms and reduce the cost to consumers. Saskatchewan's telephone system was expanded in a similar way. After his re-election in 1952, Darling fostered the development of the natural gas network in Saskatchewan. Re-elected in 1956, Darling resigned from Cabinet and was elected Speaker of the House until his retirement from politics in 1960. Darling retired to Saskatoon and died there on October 18, 1979.

Brett Quiring

FURTHER READING: White, Clinton. 1976. *Power for a Province: A History of Saskatchewan Power*. Regina: Canadian Plains Research Center.

DAUGHTERS OF PROVIDENCE (LES FILLES DE LA PROVIDENCE, FDLP).

On May 15, 1897, six members of the religious congregation of the Daughters of Providence arrived in Prince Albert from Brittany, France, at the invitation of Bishop Pascal, in order to teach the children of the Catholic families in the area. The first teachers attended NORMAL SCHOOL in Regina in 1903. In the early years they helped to establish St. Patrick's Orphanage in Prince Albert, a special school and home for needy children. To meet the needs of rural families, the Sisters established boarding schools for girls in Prud'homme, St. Louis, St. Brieux and Prince Albert. Many of the young women who were educated in

these schools joined the ranks of teachers and nurses in Saskatchewan. Signatures of the Daughters of Providence can be found in the school registers of St. Louis, Prince Albert, Domremy, Prud'homme, Viscount, Vonda, St. Brieux, St. Front, Perigord, Muenster, Leoville, Victoire, Saskatoon, Cabri, Ile-à-la-Crosse, Little Red River Reserve, Whitefish Reserve School, Patuanak, and Pine Lake. Today the remaining Sisters are retired from teaching.

Mary Ryan

DAVIDSON, town, pop 1,035, located about midway between Regina and Saskatoon on Hwy 11. The railway through the area was built in the late 1880s. Trains were running the distance from Regina through Saskatoon and on to Prince Albert in 1890. The first residents of the Davidson area were the Meshen family. Charles Meshen was a section foreman for the railroad; between 1899 and 1902, he and his family spent the summer months living out of a boxcar just south of the present townsite. The location was known as Finsbury, and while Meshen spent his days seeing to the maintenance of the track through the area, the vast region was still deemed to be a desert-like wasteland. In 1902, at the urging of the Canadian government, Colonel Andrew Duncan Davidson formed the Saskatchewan Valley Land Company and began aggressive campaigns to promote immigration to the area. As much of Davidson's advertising was aimed at Americans, his marketing strategy included naming some of the townsite's streets after former US presidents. Andrew Davidson was immensely successful: the first few settlers arrived in 1902, but in 1903 waves of homesteaders began pouring into the region. The Meshens built a house in town that year, the post office was established, and by early 1904 about 15 businesses were in operation–largely in makeshift shacks. Two years later, the population of the community was over 500, and on November 15, 1906, Davidson became a town. It developed into a trading centre for a large area that included the Watrous, Long Lake, Elbow, and Outlook districts, and soon earned the nickname "The Midway Town" because of its location between the cities of Saskatoon, Regina and Moose Jaw. Today, Davidson serves an immediate trading area of over 10,000 people and has a wide array of business providing a variety of goods and services. Davidson is also one of the province's major grain handling points and agricultural service centres. Its weekly newspaper, the *Davidson Leader*, was established in 1904. Because of the community's central location, it has become established as a meeting place for businesspeople and a variety of organizations from Saskatchewan's major cities. Its 7.3-metre-high coffee pot, situated on the highway, symbolizes the town's position as a hospitality centre.

David McLennan

DAVIDSON, AGNES (1900–96). Agnes Davidson (*née* McKechnie) played a prominent role in Regina for several decades. Born in Wolseley on July 6, 1900, she taught science at Battleford High School until her 1926 marriage to Robert J. Davidson; they had four daughters. Her interests included women's rights, mental health, and immigrant and Aboriginal concerns. Davidson was a central figure in numerous organizations. Her first involvement began in 1927 with the Local COUNCIL OF WOMEN in Regina: she headed numerous committees, served as president, and was named a life member of it and of the Provincial Council of Women. She was active in the Canadian Mental Health Association (CMHA) locally, provincially, and nationally. In 1972 she was instrumental in establishing what became the Saskatchewan Action Committee on the Status of Women, and was made its first life member (1977). Davidson also served on the Saskatchewan Advisory Council on the Status of Women. Davidson's awards included a YWCA Woman of the Year Award (1981) and the Governor General's Person's Award for advancing the equality of women (1981). She was made a Member of the Order of Canada in 1982. She died on October 30, 1996, in Regina.

Lisa Dale-Burnett

DAVIES, WILLIAM GWYNNE (1916–99). Bill Davies was born on February 11, 1916, at Indian Head, Saskatchewan. He took his early schooling there, then moved with his family to Regina at age 7. Bill Davies was a good student, but the death of his father forced him to abandon his studies and go to work to help support his siblings and mother. His first job was as an office boy at the *Regina Daily Star*, which paid him $25 a month. He was interested in political causes from an early age, and attended his first socialist meeting at the age of 16. He was also present at the Regina Riot, where he was tear-gassed by the police.

A long career in the labour movement began when Davies was working at the Swift Canadian slaughterhouse in Moose Jaw in the 1940s: Davies, HUB ELKIN and others organized the plant for the United Packinghouse Workers of America. In 1944 Davies was a leader in the effort to establish the first SASKATCHEWAN FEDERATION OF LABOUR (SFL), which was affiliated to the Canadian Congress of Labour. He was named to the Federal Wartime Labour Relations Board and the Saskatchewan Labour Relations Board, where he served for almost two decades. Before the Saskatchewan Federation of Labour had a full-time president, the most prominent labour leader in the province was the executive secretary of the Federation, a position Bill Davies held for twenty-five years. During that time he wrote hundreds of submissions, briefs and policy papers on behalf of organized labour and working people; he, more than anyone else, laid the philosophical and structural groundwork for modern, industrial trade unionism in Saskatchewan.

In the early 1950s, when Pat Conroy retired as the top staff person with the Canadian Congress of Labour, its president Aaron Mosher and others offered this important national post to Davies; but he declined, preferring to remain in Saskatchewan.

Bill Davies also had a successful political career, first as a member of Moose Jaw City Council from 1948 to 1956, and then as a CCF member of the Legislative Assembly for Moose Jaw from 1956 to 1971. During his tenure in municipal government he was instrumental in establishing the first low-cost housing program in the province. He was also appointed to the provincial health committee, which recommended a universal, publicly funded medical care plan. He was appointed to Cabinet from 1960 to 1964, serving as Public Works minister and as minister of Public Health during the introduction of medicare. Davies' calm, sensible leadership during the three-week doctor's strike in July 1962 was a significant factor in the successful implementation of medicare: he recruited physicians from abroad, and kept the hospitals open until an agreement could be worked out with the SASKATCHEWAN MEDICAL ASSOCIATION.

Davies was an advocate for the conservation of the natural landscape, and an avid walker with a keen interest in archaeology and Aboriginal culture. He also wrote poetry, and published a book of verse entitled *The Buffalo Stone*. Bill Davies and Murray Cotterill of the Steelworkers Union spent many years researching and writing an extensive history of the Saskatchewan trade union movement. He was awarded an honorary doctor of laws degree from the UNIVERSITY OF SASKATCHEWAN in 1978, and was named a member of the Order of Canada in 1975.

Davies was strongly committed to his leftist and pro-labour principles–yet he was also an accomplished negotiator and often managed to achieve compromises. Just days before he died, he wrote a letter of encouragement from his hospital bed to 190 locked-out packinghouse workers on a picket line in Moose Jaw; it was an inspirational message which, when read at an SFL convention a few days later, received a standing ovation from the 600 delegates. Bill Davies died on November 9, 1999.

Garnet Dishaw

DAVIN, NICHOLAS FLOOD (1840–1901).
Baptized Nicholas Francis, Davin was born in Kilfinane, Ireland in 1840. After law studies and journalistic experience in Ireland and London, he came to Toronto to work for the *Globe* in 1872, having already acquired an impressive knowledge of classical and modern languages and literature. In Toronto Davin was noticed as an orator and a writer. In his lengthy *The Irishman in Canada* (1877), he praised the role played by his country-

SASKATCHEWAN ARCHIVES BOARD R-A6665
Nicholas Flood Davin.

men in establishing the new nation. As a Conservative he was narrowly defeated in the 1878 election. Two years later, his brilliant, though losing, defence of the assassin of George Brown led to a patronage post. Davin came to Regina as secretary to the Royal Commission on the Pacific Railway in October 1882. Davin established a Conservative newspaper, the *Regina Leader*, which began publication on March 1, 1883. In financial difficulty, he appealed to John A. Macdonald to obtain the post of secretary to the Royal Commission on Chinese Immigration. The 1885 NORTH-WEST RESISTANCE and the subsequent trial of LOUIS RIEL brought national attention to him and the *Leader* when he disguised himself as a priest and interviewed Riel in his cell. In Regina, Davin was involved in all aspects of civic, political, legal, and cultural life. In 1887 he won the new constituency of Assiniboia West as a Conservative. He was re-elected in 1891 and 1896. WALTER SCOTT, to whom he had sold the *Leader* in 1895, defeated him in 1900. His *Eos: An Epic of the Dawn and other Poems* (1889) was the first volume of poetry published in the North-West Territories. The rest of his published work consists mainly of his own speeches. His legal career did not progress and other problems compounded his difficulties. Davin had a relationship with KATE SIMPSON HAYES but married Eliza Reid in 1895. He died by his own hand in Winnipeg in 1901. However, Davin left his mark on the province and remains the only politician after whom a locality, a school, and a street have been named, and who, fittingly, is the subject of a biography, a play, and an opera.

Brain Rainey

FURTHER READING: Koester, C.B. 1980. *Mr. Davin, M.P.* Saskatoon: Western Producer Prairie Books; Thompson, John Herd. 1994. "Davin, Nicholas Flood." Pp. 249–53 in *Dictionary of Canadian Biography* vol. 13. Toronto: University of Toronto Press.

DAVIS, ERNEST F.H. (1897–?). Ernest Francis Hartley Davis became a fighter "ace" during WORLD WAR I. Born on July 12, 1897, he was raised in Oxbow and enlisted in the Canadian Expeditionary Force's 249th Battalion in 1916. He later trained as a pilot and was posted from October 31, 1917, until July 21, 1918, to No. 41 Squadron of the Royal Flying Corps (renamed the Royal Air Force on April 1, 1918). He has been credited with seven victories while flying the SE.5A Scout in aerial combat, and was himself downed four times without serious injuries. He finished the war in Britain, test-flying new aircraft. Davis received Canadian commercial pilot's licence No. 405 on September 27, 1928, and the next spring helped found in Saskatoon the short-lived National Airways, which intended to market the American-built Monocoupe light aircraft.

Will Chabun

DAVIS, THOMAS CLAYTON (1889–1960).
Davis was born on September 6, 1889, in Prince Albert. His father, Thomas Osborne Davis, served two terms as a member of Parliament and then several years in the Senate before his death. Davis was educated in Prince Albert before completing university at St. Johns' College in Winnipeg and law school at Osgoode Hall in Toronto. He returned to practice law in Prince Albert where he began his political career in 1916 as a city alderman, serving two terms. Davis won the mayoralty in 1921 and served until 1924. Davis won the 1925 provincial election for the Liberals in Prince Albert. When JAMES GARDINER replaced CHARLES DUNNING as Premier, he appointed Davis as the province's first Minister of Municipal Affairs. His contribution was mainly as Gardiner's Minister for Northern Saskatchewan. When Prime Minister W.L.M. KING lost his seat in

SASKATCHEWAN ARCHIVES BOARD R-B8266
Thomas Davis.

1926 and chose to run in Prince Albert, Davis was instrumental in convincing King to establish the **PRINCE ALBERT NATIONAL PARK**. In the 1929 election, Davis narrowly fought off a challenge from a young Prince Albert lawyer, **JOHN DIEFENBAKER**. The government fell and Davis was vocal in Opposition. In 1934, he was again re-elected and was appointed Attorney General in the new Liberal government. He remained as Attorney General in the **WILLIAM PATTERSON** government. Re-elected in 1938, Davis resigned in 1939 to take an appointment on the Saskatchewan Court of Appeal. His term on the bench was short-lived as the next year he was appointed Deputy Minister of War Services with the federal government. In 1943, he received his first diplomatic appointment as Canadian High Commissioner to Australia. He would serve in several diplomatic posts in China, Japan and West Germany until his retirement in 1957. Retiring to Victoria, he died on January 21, 1960. *Brett Quiring*

FURTHER READING: Ward, Norman, and David Smith. 1990. *Jimmy Gardiner: Relentless Liberal.* Toronto: University of Toronto Press.

DAY STAR FIRST NATION.

Prior to signing **TREATY 4** on September 15, 1874, Chief Day Star (Kii-si-caw-ah-chuck) and his people hunted near the south branch of the **SASKATCHEWAN RIVER**. A reserve was surveyed in September 1876, with alterations made to the boundary in 1881 and 1888. Day Star remained chief until his death in 1892. Initially, cultivation was done using spades and hoes, and a plot known as the "community garden" was maintained by the whole reserve. The community developed a fine herd of cattle, each farmer keeping his herd until they numbered 10 to 12 animals, then giving half of them to someone else who could then get started. After the band received walking ploughs they began to grow wheat, barley, and oats, and with the arrival of the railway in Lipton in 1905 an outlet was created for the sale of their produce. In 1946 Chief Kinequon and Willie Buffalo purchased the first tractor, and as more modern equipment appeared, people began to farm as individuals. Social events involved a variety of games including football for men and lacrosse for women, as well as horse racing, rodeos, and powwows; after a hall was built in 1938, dances and bingo parties were also held. In 1953 a hockey team was organized,and bingo parties were held to raise money for equipment. The 6,724-ha reserve is located 16 km north of Punnichy, with land also near **LAST MOUNTAIN LAKE**. There are 426 members of this band, 130 of whom live on reserve. *Christian Thompson*

DAWSON, GEORGE MERCER (1849–1901).

George Mercer Dawson, born on August 1, 1849, in Pictou, Nova Scotia, was the son of Sir John William

LIBRARY AND ARCHIVES CANADA 48487
George Dawson.

Dawson, a prominent academic and scientist who became principal of McGill University in 1855. George spent a year at McGill before going to the Royal School of Mines, in London, where he studied under Professors Huxley and Ramsay. He is known for his work in British Columbia and the Yukon, but his chief reputation was made following his appointment in 1873 as geologist and botanist to Her Majesty's North American Boundary Commission. During the **BOUNDARY SURVEY** he collected specimens and made extensive notes on the geology and natural history of land along the international border. His findings were published in 1875 in the *Report on the Geology and Resources of the Region in the Vicinity of the 49th Parallel from the Lake of the Woods to the Rocky Mountains.* During his work with the Commission he discovered dinosaur bones on the southern flank of the **CYPRESS HILLS** and mapped the Tertiary lignites (coal) noted by James Hector during the Palliser Survey of the 1850s. He also made notes on the occurrence of locusts in the southern prairies in the years 1874 and 1875, publishing his observations in the *Canadian Naturalist.*

In 1875 Dawson was hired as paleontologist and chief geologist to the Geological Survey of Canada; he became assistant director of the Survey in 1883, and was made director in 1895. He worked throughout western Canada, including a survey in 1883 (assisted by **J.B. TYRRELL**) of the area between Maple Creek and the Milk River. He was taken ill in his Ottawa office on February 28, 1901, and died two days later on March 2. *Marilyn Lewry*

DE LINT, WILLEM B.C. (1933–).

An award-winning architect whose creativity can be seen in several Regina landmarks, Willem B.C. de Lint was born in Breda, Netherlands on January 10, 1933, and immigrated to Canada in 1954. A graduate of the University of Manitoba School of Architecture, he practiced in Prince Albert before moving to Regina

in 1967. Some of de Lint's most notable commissions have been the **MACKENZIE ART GALLERY**, the former **PLAINS HEALTH CENTRE**, and the Neil Balkwill Civic Arts Centre. An active member in the community, de Lint has served at the local, regional, and provincial levels of the Boy Scouts of Canada. In 1989, he was appointed as the Honorary Consul of the Netherlands for Saskatchewan. Willem de Lint was made a Member of the Order of Canada in 1995.

DE PAUW, RONALD (1944–).

Internationally recognized for his contributions to agriculture research, Dr. Ronald De Pauw of Kamsack was born on February 21, 1944. He earned his doctorate in plant genetics and pathology from the University of Manitoba. Working as a plant breeder and research scientist for Agriculture and Agri-Food Canada, DePauw helped develop varieties of wheat and other cereal crops that established new standards of grain yield, protein content, and resistance to disease. He played a leading role in the introduction of Canadian Prairie Spring, a new class of wheat that has expanded the market for western Canadian farmers. In 1991, Ronald DePauw received the Saskatchewan Order of Merit. He was made a Fellow of the Agricultural Institute of Canada in 1994 and a Member of the Order of Canada in 2004.

DECOTEAU, ALEX (1887–1917).

Born on the Red Pheasant Reserve near Battleford in December 1887, Alex Decoteau attended the Battleford Indian Industrial School, where he excelled in soccer and running. His first competitive race was a one-miler

SASKATCHEWAN ARCHIVES BOARD R-A17343
Alex Decoteau and Alex Latta, ca. 1908.

at Fort Saskatchewan on May 24, 1909, where he came in second. On July 1, 1909, he set a new western Canadian record (27.45.2) for the five-mile Mayberry in Lloydminster; he also won the Hon. C.W. Cross Challenge Cup Race (26.34.4) in Edmonton later that summer. Decoteau won a ten-mile race in Fort Saskatchewan in 1910–eight minutes faster than his nearest competitor–and then entered and won the half-mile, one-mile, two-mile and five-mile races on July 1 in Lethbridge. Decoteau moved to Edmonton to work in his brother-in-law's machine shop, and raced competitively with the Irish-Canadian Athletic Club. In 1911 he joined the Edmonton City Police force as the first Aboriginal to serve on the force, and was one of the first motorcycle policemen in the city. Decoteau was promoted to desk sergeant of the South Side Police Station in 1914, and continued to run competitively under the colours of the Edmonton Police Association. On Christmas day in 1910 Decoteau set the record for the *Calgary Herald*'s annual 6.33 mile race (on a snow-covered course) at 34 minutes, 19 seconds. He continued to win this race every time he entered it; with his record unbeaten, the cup was permanently presented to him in 1915.

Decoteau tried out for the Canadian Olympic team in 1912 (10,000-metre), but withdrew because of a leg cramp; he competed in the 5,000-metre race, winning easily but with a time not considered good enough for the Olympics. The Canadian Olympic Committee ordered a race between Decoteau and the favourite from Vancouver; Decoteau set a new Dominion record at 15.27.4 and became the only athlete from Alberta to participate in the games. In Stockholm, Decoteau placed second in the 5,000-metre and sixth in the final, and was awarded an Olympic Merit Diploma and a medal for his performance. In 1916 Decoteau resigned from the police force and joined the Canadian Army, winning several races while stationed in England. He was killed near Passchendaele Ridge in France on October 30, 1917. Decoteau was elected to the Edmonton City Police Hall of Fame (where his many of his medals, cups, and photos are displayed), and has been inducted into both the Alberta Sports Hall of Fame and the Saskatchewan Indian First Nations Sports Hall of Fame. *Christian Thompson*

DEER. The deer family, Cervidae, consists of approximately thirty-five species of long-legged browsers with deciduous bony antlers on the frontal bones of the skull of males, and glands on the face before the eye. They occur on all continents except for Australia and Africa, south of the Sahara. They are usually found in woodlands or the edges of forests. Saskatchewan has five species of deer. Several of the species have burgeoning populations, particularly the white-tailed deer, following the killing off of their natural predators. Others have

COURTESY OF TOURISM SASKATCHEWAN
Moose.

reduced populations owing to the contraction of their former habitats with settlement and opening of the boreal forest. Hunting is allowed of those species with healthy populations.

The largest, with a 1.8 m shoulder height for a large male, is the moose (*Alces alces*). This marsh-feeding deer with broad, spatulate antlers is found in wooded areas of the boreal plains and in the boreal forest, including the boreal remnants in the Moose Mountain and **CYPRESS HILLS** areas. The other large species, the elk or wapiti (*Cervus elaphus*), with branching antlers, is mostly found in the Boreal Plains Ecozone of the centre of the province, with small populations in some wooded areas in the prairies, such as Moose Mountain and the Cypress Hills. Unlike moose, in which the male stays with and defends a cow while she remains in breeding

condition, the male elk gathers a harem of females in the fall, which he defends from rival males.

The white-tailed deer (*Odocoileus virginianus*), a small, lightly built deer, is the most common and widespread species, found from the southern boundary to the **CHURCHILL RIVER**. While the white-tailed deer is found throughout temperate North America, except for the southwestern deserts, the mule deer (*O. hemionus*) is a western deer. Mule deer are more abundant in the southwest, although they may be found in other areas of the grasslands and parklands. The males of both species have branching antlers and do not form harems. Members of the genus *Rangifer* are the only deer in which females develop antlers; these are smaller than those of the males. The caribou (*R. tarandus*) are midway in size between the smaller deer and the elk. During the fall breeding season males gather a number of females, which they defend against other males. The barren-ground populations form large herds which migrate over their sparsely vegetated feeding grounds in the northern boreal forest and Taiga Shield regions of the extreme north of the province. The woodlands population is found in small, static groups in the boreal forest, where they feed on lichens and flowering plants. *Diane Secoy*

FURTHER READING: 2001. *Natural Neighbours: Selected Mammals of Saskatchewan*. Regina: Canadian Plains Research Center.

DEGELMAN, WILFRED (1930–). An entrepreneur known for his creative inventions and modifications of farm machinery, Wilfred Degelman was born in Raymore, Saskatchewan on August 7, 1930. Neighbours purchased the young man's specialized equipment, invented and perfected in his father's shop. Degelman's pivotal invention is the Degelman

COURTESY OF TOURISM SASKATCHEWAN
Elk (Wapiti).

Stone King rockpicker, first manufactured in 1963. Two years later, Degelman Industries was established in Regina as the demand for the implement increased. Since then, it has upgraded and expanded its facilities many times: in addition to the rockpicker, the company has diversified its output to include bulldozer blades, rock rakes, harrows, and tillage machines. Although the operation continues to be family-run, the workers joined the United Steelworkers Union in 2000 and initiated a successful strike in 2004, much to the company's surprise. Degelman still takes an active role as president of the company, working on new designs and flying in his airplane to help customers. *Merle Massie*

FURTHER READING: Wetherell, D.G. and E.A. Corbet. 1993. *Breaking New Ground: A Century of Farm Equipment Manufacturing on the Canadian Prairies.* Saskatoon: Fifth House Publishers.

DEITER, WALTER PERRY (1914–88). Deiter was a Cree-Saulteaux from the Peepeekisis Reserve. He served as the chief of the Federation of Saskatchewan Indians (FSI) from 1966 to 1969, and was the founding president of the National Indian Brotherhood (1968–70). Deiter was a major figure in the development of Indian lobby groups across Canada, including the Manitoba Indian Brotherhood, the Indian Association of Alberta, the Indian Veterans Association, and the Native Alcohol Council. He also led the fight in 1969 against the federal government's plan to terminate the special status of Indian people and their lands. Deiter's contribution to Aboriginal political development has served as a fulcrum for contemporary organizations and their effectiveness in the granting of collective rights through treaties, as well as their continuing battle toward self-determination within Canadian society. In 1977 Deiter moved back to Peepeekisis and served a term as band councilor; in 1978 he organized Indian veterans to establish lobby groups to pressure for compensation parity. He served as the founding president for the National Indian Veterans Association and as president of the southern region of the Saskatchewan Indian Veterans Association; he also accepted an appointment to the FSI Senate. In 1980, Deiter was honoured as an Officer of the Order of Canada in recognition of his outstanding achievements and services.

Walter Deiter has great historical importance in the political development of the First Nations people of Canada. He was the first Canadian Indian leader to organize successfully national and regional Indian political aspirations into forums that could be understood by mainstream society. His leadership style encouraged unity among First Nations people while establishing a credible presence to the general public. His approach was to confront colonialism in the federal government and to assert the potential of First Nations people to help themselves. He provided leadership at a time when funds for First Nations political movements were non-existent, and his willingness to use his personal funds demonstrated his belief in his people. He was single-minded in his efforts to liberate First Nations peoples, awakening them to new opportunities, empowering them through example, and unifying them towards a goal of self-determination. *Patricia Deiter*

FURTHER READING: Ponting, J.R., and R. Gibbins. 1980. *Out of Irrelevance: A Socio-Political Introduction to Indian Affairs in Canada.* Toronto: Butterworth; Weaver, S.M. 1981. *Making Canadian Indian Policy: The Hidden Agenda 1968–70.* Toronto: University of Toronto Press.

DELISLE, town, pop 884, located approximately 40 km SW of Saskatoon at the junction of Hwys 7 and 45. Settlers began taking up land in the area in the first few years of the 20th century, and by 1905 a small village had begun to appear a few kilometres south of the present townsite. A post office was established that year, taking its name from the first postmaster, John Amos Delisle. The town developed primarily as an agricultural community until a potash mine was opened to the north in 1969; it boosted the local economy by providing a large number of well-paying jobs. While Delisle's economy remains largely based on agriculture and mining, the town is also increasingly becoming a bedroom community for a number of people who commute to work in Saskatoon. The community is well known in curling circles as over the years both women's and men's teams have won numerous provincial championships. Delisle was also the hometown of NHL hockey legends **MAX AND DOUG BENTLEY**, who have both been inducted into the Hockey Hall of Fame. *David McLennan*

DELURY, ABIGAIL (1872–1957). Abigail DeLury, born in 1872, was raised in Manilla, Ontario. She trained as a teacher at Port Perry Model School and Toronto Normal School. In 1904, she enrolled at Macdonald Institute, Ontario Agriculture College, and in 1906 received her Diploma in Home Economics. After graduating, she first taught at Macdonald College at McGill University and later moved to Moose Jaw. During the summers of 1911 and 1912, DeLury was employed by the University of Saskatchewan to speak to women about forming **HOMEMAKERS CLUBS**. In 1913, she was appointed the first Director of Women's Work at the University. Through lectures, demonstrations, short courses, conferences and conventions she and her staff provided a wide range of homemaking programs for rural women in such areas as nutrition, cooking, gardening, dressmaking, and home nursing. She also trained judges for fairs. She was the author of

Abigail Delury (centre), Director of Women's Work (Homemaker's Clubs), ca. 1920.

the University's first home economics extension bulletins, as well as of *History of Homemakers' Clubs of Saskatchewan* and *Handbook for Homemakers' Clubs.* DeLury was also an advocate of school health programs and community libraries. In 1930 she returned to Manilla after her retirement, and died there on June 10, 1957. She was inducted into the Agricultural Hall of Fame in 2005. *Gwenna Moss*

FURTHER READING: Rowles, E.C. 1964. Home Economics in Canada, *The Early History of Six College Programs: Prologue to Change.* Saskatoon: University of Saskatchewan.

DENE: *see* **DENESULINE**

DENESULINE (DENE). The Denesuline (pronounced Dene-su-lee-neh,), Dene or Chipewyan people occupy territory in northern Saskatchewan from **LAKE ATHABASCA** in the west to Wollaston Lake in the east. The Athabascan First Nations Denesuline live primarily in three communities: Fond-du-Lac, located on the northeast shore of Lake Athabasca at 59°20' north latitude and 107°20' west longitude; Black Lake, located at 59° north latitude and 105°40' west longitude; and Wollaston, located at 58°5' north latitude and 103°15' west longitude. The Denesuline of the Athabascan Basin hunt over a vast area, often extending their winter range of hunting camps northward into the Northwest Territories. The northern Athabasca Basin consists of four Denesuline bands, and the northwestern **CHURCHILL RIVER** Basin accommodates the remaining four. The Athabascan region comprises the Fond-du-Lac, Hatchet Lake, Black Lake, and Stoney

Rapids First Nation bands; and the Churchill River Basin includes the Buffalo River, English River, Birch Narrows, and Clearwater River First Nations.

The fort at Churchill River was established in 1717, and the Dene First Nations began direct trade with the European settlers—soon after the peace mission to end hostilities with the northern **CREE** (this mission was led by a Denesuline woman, Thanághelttver, who had been taken as a slave by the Cree). The Denesuline population of the Churchill River Basin includes treaty First Nations, living in the community of Dillon, and non-treaty First Nations, living in the nearby settlements of St. George's Hill and Michel Village. These three Denesuline villages are located on the southwest shore of Big Buffalo Lake near the mouth of the Buffalo River at 55°50' north latitude and 109° west longitude. The Buffalo River Dene Nation inhabitants hunt, trap, and fish an area of about 2,500^2 km (965^2 miles) just south of Dillon.

Denesuline of northern Saskatchewan live in a vast territory characterized by relatively consistent sub-arctic conditions with limited regional variation in climate, physiography, and plant and animal life. Yet, regional distinctions exist between the Upper Churchill River district and the Athabasca Basin, reflected in different sociocultural expressions or regional adaptations. Major differences between the two regions are found in the gradual depletion of forest cover that occurs from the southwest towards the northeast following the Precambrian configuration. The special shift from full boreal forest towards a sparse and underdeveloped transitional forest is accompanied by a change in animal species and numbers of animals across the region. Although most animal species are found commonly throughout the territory, fur-bearing animals are more numerous within the full boreal woodland area. The animal resources of the Athabascan Basin and the forest-tundra margin further to the north are varied, and some species are seasonally abundant. Fur-bearing animals that are consistently trapped are beaver, muskrat, squirrel, marten, mink, weasel, fox, rabbit, and otter; other, rarer species include wolf and lynx; fisher, wolverine, and bear are also found in the region. Although beaver was once very important to trappers during the early fur trade, it has declined in importance over the years.

Moose are also found in abundance throughout the Athabascan region, particularly in marshland areas containing black spruce trees under-grown with willow. While moose is an important source of meat for the Denesuline, the most important large-game animal is the barren-ground caribou. Not only is the caribou economically important, it also helps to create a Dene identity in terms of social organization, territoriality, and way of life. A major difference in animal resources between the Churchill River district and the Athabasca Basin is the season-

al availability of barren-ground caribou in the farthest northern zone: while barren-ground caribou are available with some regularity in the Athabasca Basin, they are not often seen along the Churchill River. Wood **BISON** were found in earlier times along the Upper Churchill River and as far north as Great Slave Lake, and likely played a significant role in defining local patterns of resource procurement and identity for regional Indian bands. Today, wood bison do not enter into the ecological strategy of Denesuline in northern Saskatchewan. Varying renewable resources across the territory play a role in defining Dene adaptations and identity change.

The Denesuline people continue their traditional way of life to some extent: the hand game is still performed in the northern regions of the province; the traditional tea dance is still part of social gatherings; and feasts are an everyday practice. Drums made out of caribou hide are very popular, and prized among both the old and the young. The Athabascan language group consists of about 23 languages, Denesuline being one of them. Because the Denesuline communities are so spread out across the province, there exist variations in the way the language is spoken.

Elaine Hay

FURTHER READING: Kerry, A. 1993. *Drumsongs: Glimpse of the Dene History.* Montreal and Kingston: McGill-Queens University Press.

DENESULINE WORLDVIEW. Like many First Nations, the Denesuline have a very close relationship with the land. For traditional Denesuline people this relationship is intertwined with everything in their daily living; children learn about it in two ways: through observation of the adults around them, and through oral stories. Denesuline children learn to be respectful of the land by observing the manner in which the adults properly look after the bones and other parts of the animals and birds they gather for survival. In this way people will survive with the assistance of the animals which have been shown respect; if there is no respect, the living animals will go away and not allow themselves to be used by humans.

Like other First Nations people, the Denesuline present this relationship with the land in the metaphorical form of oral stories, which talk about the need to have a helper who is one of the animals inhabiting their surrounding world. To obtain this animal guide, Denesuline youth are required to go into the bush for a song. Amongst most Dene, the song thus acquired is a private matter, not to be discussed with others. They hold to this belief very strongly: to break this privacy is a violation of the person's right to learn about the world in which they live.

William Asikinack

DEPRESSION: *see* **GREAT DEPRESSION**

Grant Devine, October 1989.

DEVINE, GRANT (1944–). Grant Devine was born July 5, 1944, in Regina, and was raised on a farm that his grandfather had homesteaded near Lake Valley, not far from Moose Jaw. After high school he enrolled at the **UNIVERSITY OF SASKATCH-EWAN**, where he earned a BSc in Agriculture. He pursued post-graduate studies and completed a PhD in Agricultural Economics at Ohio State University in 1976. He joined the faculty of the University of Saskatchewan, where he taught Agricultural Marketing and Consumer Economics.

Devine was drawn to politics at a time when the fortunes of the Saskatchewan Progressive Conservative Party were rising. **DICK COLLVER**, who was elected leader in 1973, argued that the Liberals were a spent force provincially and that the only way to dislodge the NDP government was to build an anti-socialist coalition around the Conservatives. His brand of right-wing populism appealed to voters. In the 1978 election, the PCs displaced the Liberals as the official opposition.

The election marked Grant Devine's entry into electoral politics. He contested the constituency of Saskatoon Nutana and was soundly defeated. When Collver stepped down as leader, Devine put his name forward and cruised to victory at the November 1979 convention. He led the party into the provincial election called for April 26, 1982. It soon became evident that the NDP was vulnerable. Interest rates were at 18% and there was a feeling that Allan Blakeney's eleven-year-old government was out of touch with the people. On the first day of the campaign, Devine announced that he would eliminate the provincial tax on gasoline. This was followed by a commitment to guarantee home mortgage rates at 13.25%. The Conservatives rolled to victory, winning 54.1% of the popular vote and 55 out of 64 seats in the Legislature.

One of the first actions of the new administration was to organize an "Open for Business" conference in October 1982 to advertise the fact that the "socialist" era was over, and private investment and free enterprise were welcome in Saskatchewan. As an incentive to the oil industry, the government introduced a three-year royalty holiday for new wells and reduced royalties for existing wells. Drilling increased markedly, but at the sacrifice of a lower royalty revenue share of the value of production. The expansion of **CROWN CORPORATIONS** was curtailed, but there was no large-scale effort to sell them. A notable exception was the Land Bank, which the NDP had set up to facilitate the inter-generational transfer of land. Devine said the government should not be in the business of owning land, and he dismantled the Land Bank (*see* **AGRICULTURAL POLICY**), replacing it with 8% loans to enable farmers to purchase their own land.

The government ran consecutive deficit budgets, accumulating a debt of over $1.5 billion its first four years in office. Sensing that he might lose the 1986 election, Devine opened the coffers, giving farmers production loans at 6% and homeowners $1,500 home-improvement matching grants. The strategy worked. Although he narrowly lost the popular vote to the NDP, Devine won a second term with 38 seats, against 25 for the NDP and one for the Liberals. In doing so, the PCs ran up a deficit of over $1.2 billion in 1986–87, a far cry from the deficit figure of $389 million that had been presented in the pre-election budget.

The fiscal crisis led to cutbacks in services, cancellation of programs, and firing of employees. The government launched a privatization crusade, disposing of a wide array of Crown corporations from the $15 million SaskMinerals to the Potash Corporation, valued at well over $1 billion. When the government broke its promise not to sell utilities and placed the natural gas division of SaskPower on the block, the NDP brought the Legislature to a halt by letting the bells ring for seventeen days. The public sided with the NDP, and the government backed down from the sale.

Although he pledged to get government out of business, Devine gave loans, subsidies, guarantees and other incentives to private business. The results were impressive: two heavy oil upgraders, a fertilizer plant, a paper mill, a pulp mill, and a bacon-processing plant. The Rafferty-Alameda Dams were built as a public works megaproject. However, the government was never able to control the debt it had incurred in its first term. By the end of the 1980s it was running a surplus on operating expenses excluding debt charges, but interest payments drove the province deeper into debt each year. By 1991–92 the accumulated debt was over $15 billion, and annual interest payments exceeded $500 million, the third-largest item in the budget after health and education.

On the national scene, Devine reversed the old rule of Saskatchewan politics: pick a fight with Ottawa at election time. He was a staunch supporter of Prime Minister Brian Mulroney and gave whole-hearted support to Mulroney's two main initiatives, the Meech Lake Accord and the Free Trade Agreement with the United States. Mulroney responded with deficiency payments to Saskatchewan farmers who were suffering drought and record-low grain prices. Farmers were not the only beneficiaries: the billion-dollar assistance package announced days before the 1986 provincial election was a key element in Devine's victory.

Devine sought to undo the legacy of CCF/NDP socialism in Saskatchewan and build a pro-business, entrepreneurial culture. His government carried out a massive privatization program, reduced social assistance payments, and curbed the power of labour unions, but private enterprise continued to rely heavily on government financial assistance. The greatest failure of the Devine years was the accumulation of an unprecedented debt, much of it attributable to tax cuts and unwise election spending. The government lost power in 1991, winning only 10 seats and 25% of the popular vote. After the election, a scandal came to light, resulting in the conviction of several former Conservative MLAs on fraud charges. Despite setbacks, Devine remained an eternal optimist holding fast to his free enterprise principles and his belief in the potential of Saskatchewan. In 2004, Devine attempted a political comeback, but lost in his effort to win a seat in Parliament in the federal election of that year.

James M. Pitsula

FURTHER READING: Biggs, Leslie, and Mark Stobbe (eds.). 1991. *Devine Rules in Saskatchewan: A Decade of Hope and Hardship.* Saskatoon: Fifth House; Pitsula, James M., and Ken Rasmussen. 1990. *Privatizing a Province: The New Right in Saskatchewan.* Vancouver: New Star.

DEWALT, KEVIN (1957–). Kevin DeWalt is a groundbreaking film entrepreneur. In 1986 he formed Minds Eye Pictures in Regina, which for several years was the biggest privately held film entertainment company in western Canada. As CEO and chairman of Minds Eye he has produced many award-winning films and television series, and he was a catalyst in the building of Regina's state-of-the-art Canada Saskatchewan Production Studios in 2002. He is a founding member of the Saskatchewan Motion Picture Association, and has served on the board of directors of SaskFilm and the National Screen Institute, and as vice-president of the International Quorum of Film and Video Producers.

Born in Moose Jaw, DeWalt studied music at the **UNIVERSITY OF REGINA**. However, what began as a student's working holiday in Australia led him on an odyssey across many countries, and his passion shifted from music toward the power of moving images. He filmed his exotic and sometimes harrowing experiences on a shoestring budget as a personal document for family and friends; but seeing

ROY ANTAL/REGINA LEADER-POST

Kevin DeWalt, Minds Eye Pictures, and Virginia Thompson, Vérité Films, with the 2000 Gemini award for Best Children's or Youth Program for "Incredible Story Studio."

Richard Attenborough's epic movie *Ghandi* in Bombay inspired a growing desire to move people and have an impact on the way they think. The result was his first production, a touring multimedia travelogue of his adventures titled *Namaste*. This led to work producing corporate videos and to the formation of Minds Eye in 1986, which within two years grew to employ 27 people. In 1989 Minds Eye produced its first television drama, *The Great Electrical Revolution*, based on a **KEN MITCHELL** short story. Since then, the company has built a reputation producing high quality television series for youth and family audiences, such as *Mythquest*, *2030 CE*, *My Global Adventure*, and the Gemini Award-winning *Incredible Story Studio*, which has been seen in more than 400 million homes in seventy-five countries. Minds Eye has also branched into feature film production and has made more than ten dramatic features since *Decoy* in 1994, including *Lyddie* (1995), *My Lost Daughter* (1996), *Without Malice* (1999), *The Unsaid* (a.k.a *Sins of the Father*, 2000), and *Betrayed* (2002). In 2002, Minds Eye's feature, *Falling Angels*, was the first film completed in the Canada Saskatchewan Production Studios. It garnered rave reviews and brought Minds Eye Pictures the distinction of being included in Canada's Top Ten list for 2003, compiled by the Toronto International Film Festival Group.

Christine Ramsay

FURTHER READING: Ramsay, C., and K. Wilson. 2002. "Minds Eye: Kevin DeWalt's Big Adventure," *Take One* 10 (36): 31-33.

DEWAR, PHYLLIS (1916–61). An outstanding freestyle swimmer during the 1930s, Phyllis Dewar was born in Moose Jaw on March 5, 1916. Dubbed the "Moose Jaw Mermaid" by the press, Dewar recorded the best performance of any Canadian at

Phyllis Dewar.

the 1934 British Empire Games in London, England. She won gold medals in the 110- and 440-yard freestyle, the 330-yard medley, and the 4 x 110-yard relay. Chosen as Canada's female athlete of the year in 1934, Dewar set new national records in the 100-, 400-, 1,000-, and 1,500-yard freestyle and one-mile event in 1935.

Although the flu hampered Dewar's performance at the 1936 Berlin Olympics, she returned to the medal podium at the 1938 British Empire Games in Sydney, Australia. She won her fifth gold medal as a member of the Canadian 4 x 110-yard relay team and later retired from competitive swimming. After the death of her husband in 1954, Dewar's health deteriorated and she died in Toronto on April 8, 1961. She was posthumously inducted into the SASKATCHEWAN SPORTS HALL OF FAME (1967), the Canadian Sports Hall of Fame (1971), and the Canadian Olympic Hall of Fame (1972).

Holden Stoffel and Karen Zemlak

FURTHER READING: 1971. "Hall of Fame Honours Given to 14 Persons." *Regina Leader-Post* (May 28); McDonald, David. *For the Record: Canada's Greatest Women Athletes.* Toronto: Mesa Associates, 1981

DEWDNEY, EDGAR (1835–1916).

Edgar Dewdney was born in Bideford, Devonshire, England on November 5, 1835, to a prosperous family. Arriving in Victoria in the Crown Colony of Vancouver Island in May 1859 during a gold rush, he spent more than a decade surveying and building trails through the mountains on the mainland. In 1872, shortly after British Columbia's entry into Confederation, he was elected MP for Yale and became a loyal devotee of John A. Macdonald and the CONSERVATIVE PARTY. In Parliament he pursued

the narrow agenda of getting the transcontinental railway built with the terminal route via the Fraser Valley, where he happened to have real estate interests.

In 1879 Dewdney became Indian commissioner of the North-West Territories (NWT) with the immediate task of averting mass starvation and unrest among the First Nations following the sudden disappearance of the buffalo. Backed by a small contingent of Indian agents and Mounted Police, he used the distribution of rations as a device to impose state authority on the First Nations population. Facing hunger and destitution, First Nations people were compelled to settle on reserves, adopt agriculture and send their children to mission schools. These measures to bring about self-sufficiency and cultural assimilation appeared to be working, but provoked a sullen resentment that could not be repressed in the spring of 1885. Dewdney has often been blamed for the NORTH-WEST RESISTANCE, but in truth much of the responsibility lay in policies devised in Ottawa by men unfamiliar with western conditions. He had warned his superiors of the dangers and urged them to resolve First Nations and MÉTIS grievances, but to little avail. He did succeed, however, in limiting Indian involvement in the hostilities by acts of unprecedented generosity with food and presents. Following the Resistance, a policy of strict surveillance and coercive tutelage was imposed, and it endured as his legacy to First Nations administration in the region.

In 1881 Dewdney was appointed LIEUTENANT-GOVERNOR of the NWT, a position he held in conjunction with that of Indian commissioner. One of his first significant acts in this role was the selection of Regina as the new territorial capital in 1882. He happened to own land in the vicinity and was widely criticized by Liberal politicians and the press for his attempt to profit from the decision. As Lieutenant-Governor, he exercised real executive power and his authority was independent of the

Edgar Dewdney.

North-West Council, a partly elected, partly appointed body that served as an incipient popular assembly for the region. As the settler population grew, the elected Council members became increasingly insistent on a larger role in decision-making. They demanded a responsible executive, representation in Parliament and ultimately provincial status. The Lieutenant-Governor's policy, in accordance with Prime Minister Macdonald's wishes, was to keep these demands in check while gradually conceding democratic reforms.

In 1888 Dewdney resigned his two positions in Regina and entered Macdonald's federal Cabinet as Minister of the Interior. His connection with the prairie region remained, in that he was now MP for Assiniboia East and his portfolio included the administration of the NWT. In connection with this, his policy was as before: the gradual devolution of political powers to the Territorial Assembly (which had replaced the North-West Council in 1888) while resisting the creation of a responsible executive.

Dewdney left Parliament and his Cabinet post in October 1892 to become Lieutenant-Governor of British Columbia, something he had long coveted. His new position was mainly social and ceremonial in nature, and he enjoyed it immensely. Upon completion of his term of office in 1897, he stayed on in Victoria in semi-retirement, pursuing his passion for investments in real estate, mining and railways. He died on August 8, 1916. He was married twice and there were no children from either relationship.

Edgar Dewdney was a representative of a class of immigrant adventurers who saw in the western Canadian frontier an opportunity for self-aggrandizement. He viewed public office as a means to personal wealth and acquired a reputation as a speculative fortune hunter. Yet his dream of sufficient wealth to lead a life of gentlemanly leisure continued to elude him. He was also noted for his intense loyalty to the Conservative Party—a man who readily used his public offices to dispense an enormous array of patronage appointments and government contracts to the party faithful. One of the main thoroughfares in Regina is named in his honour.

Brian Titley

DIAMONDS.

Diamonds are a crystalline form of carbon. They are the hardest known minerals and have several uses once they are mined. Diamonds are formed in volcanic rocks called kimberlites and lamproites, located as far as 150 to 200 km below the earth's surface. There are various techniques used to extract the diamonds from the kimberlites or lamproites, such as crushing, blending with water and passing over grease, or passing the crushed mixture through an x-ray sorter. Diamonds can be used as gems, or for various industrial purposes such as drilling bits or surgical equipment. In 2004, there were no operating diamond mines in

A diamond drill in operation in the Beaverlodge area of northern Saskatchewan, August 1956.

Saskatchewan. There are, however, several sites that have been set up to test the ground for prospective development. Areas of interest for exploration in the province include the Choiceland, Fort à la Corne, Pasquia Hills, Molanosa Arch, Candle Lake, Sturgeon Lake, Smoothstone Lake and Wapawekka Lake areas. The first discovery of kimberlite in Saskatchewan was made in 1988 in the Sturgeon Lake area. Several micro-diamonds (less than 0.5 mm) have been found in the province since then; larger diamonds (macro-diamonds) have also been found during some exploratory drilling, but there have been no signs of large stones or sites. The most promising site would appear to be Fort à la Corne, located approximately 65 km west of Prince Albert. Kimberlites were first discovered there in 1989, and the area is now known to be the largest diamond deposit in the world. To date, the largest diamond to come out of the Fort à la Corne area weighs 10.23 carats. Entities that have invested in this collaborative effort of exploration include **CAMECO CORPORATION**, De Beers Canada Exploration Inc., Kensington Resources Ltd., and UEM Inc.

Julie L. Parchewski

DICKSON, BRIAN (1916–98).

Canadian Supreme Court Chief Justice Robert George Brian Dickson was born in Yorkton on May 25, 1916. After attaining an LLB from the University of Manitoba in 1938, he enlisted in the armed forces and served overseas in **WORLD WAR II**. Wounded in 1944, Dickson returned home to practice and lecture in law. After serving on both Manitoba's Court of Queen's Bench and Court of Appeal, he was appoint-

ed in 1973 to the Supreme Court of Canada, and became its Chief Justice in 1984. Dickson presided over some of the most important and controversial judicial decisions of late 20th-century Canada, including: striking down part of Quebec's language law (Bill 101) in 1988, a move circumvented when Quebec invoked the notwithstanding clause; the 1985 ruling that Cabinet decisions were subject to judicial review; the decision to remove abortion from the Criminal Code in 1988; and the landmark 1989 ruling that a fetus cannot be legally recognized as a person.

Upon retirement in 1990, Dickson continued to work for legal, military, political and civil reform. He chaired committees and advised on Aboriginal rights, military justice, the North American Free Trade Agreement, and civil justice. Dickson was still working, attending meetings even in ill health, when he died on October 17, 1998.   *Merle Massie*

FURTHER READING: Macdonald, M. 1999. *The Dam the Drought Built*. Regina: Canadian Plains Research Center.

DIEFENBAKER, JOHN GEORGE (1895–1979).

John Diefenbaker was born in Neustadt, Ontario, on September 18, 1895. He was the eldest of the two sons of William T. Diefenbaker and his wife Mary (*née* Bannerman). The family moved to the Fort Carlton district in 1903 because the doctors of the era recommended the dry prairie climate to help his father's breathing problems. In 1905, the family moved to Hague, and in 1906 relocated to a homestead near Borden.

In 1910, the Diefenbaker family moved to Saskatoon so that John and his brother Elmer could attend high school. Diefenbaker graduated from what is now Nutana Collegiate in the spring of 1912, and entered the **UNIVERSITY OF SASKATCHEWAN** as a member of the first class to be educated on the new campus. He studied economics and politics for his BA, and began graduate work on an MA. In 1916, he volunteered for service in **WORLD WAR I**, and was granted his MA in absentia. He was sent to England for training, but was removed from service as an invalid and returned to Canada in 1917. He returned to the University of Saskatchewan to study law, graduating in 1918.

John Diefenbaker was called to the Saskatchewan Bar in 1919, and opened his own law office in Wakaw on July 1, 1919. He had always been interested in politics, and in 1920 won election as an alderman in Wakaw. In 1922, he won a decision protecting French language rights in Saskatchewan in the case of *Boutin et al. vs. Mackie*.

In 1924, Diefenbaker opened a new law office in Prince Albert, beginning his long association with that city. He ran as a Conservative in the federal elections of 1925 and 1926 and in the provincial election of 1929, but was defeated each time. On June 29, 1929, he married Edna Mae Brower, a school teacher who had grown up in Langham.

Diefenbaker ran for mayor of Prince Albert in 1933, but was defeated. He became leader of the provincial **CONSERVATIVE PARTY** in 1936 and ran in the provincial election of 1938, but lost again. He considered abandoning politics, but was persuaded to run one last time in the federal election of 1940. He won the constituency of Arm River and was elected to every federal Parliament thereafter, although he did switch to the Prince Albert riding in 1953.

He ran for the Conservative Party leadership in 1942, but came third to John Bracken, who insisted that the party become the Progressive Conservatives. He again ran for leader in 1948, but lost to George Drew. He lost his wife Edna to leukemia in 1951.

John Diefenbaker married Olive Freeman Palmer on December 8, 1953. He won the leadership of the Progressive Conservatives in 1956. In 1957, he led his party to a surprising election victory, although it was a minority government.

In 1958, Parliament was dissolved and Diefenbaker led his party to the largest election victory in Canadian political history. His government lost its majority in the federal election of 1962, but continued as a minority government. In 1963, Lester Pearson led the Liberals to a minority government, and Diefenbaker became leader of the Opposition. He continued in that role until 1967 when he gave way to Robert Stanfield, who had been elected leader of the party the year before. Diefenbaker continued to serve as a member of Parliament until his death in 1979.

EVERETT BAKER PHOTO/COURTESY OF THE SASKATCHEWAN HISTORY AND FOLKLORE SOCIETY

John Diefenbaker at Batoche, June 1961.

The governments led by John Diefenbaker are notable for a number of accomplishments. Diefenbaker was a champion of human rights, and his government passed Canada's first Bill of Rights in 1958. He also appointed the first First Nations senator, James Gladstone of Alberta, and extended the right to vote to First Nations people. Diefenbaker criticized the Soviet Union for its repression of minorities. He headed the movement for racial equality in the Commonwealth, which led to South Africa leaving that organization.

Having grown up on a pioneer farm, Diefenbaker knew the difficulties faced by the agricultural industry. His government brought in an Agricultural Stabilization Act in 1958 which provided for flexible support and minimum prices on commodities. The Diefenbaker government also began wheat sales to China, which opened a huge new market for Canadian farmers. Diefenbaker supported the construction of the South Saskatchewan Dam at Outlook (later named the **GARDINER DAM**). The lake it created was named **LAKE DIEFENBAKER** in his honour.

A controversial decision of the Diefenbaker government, which still resonates, was the cancellation of the Avro Arrow airplane. This jet had been developed to intercept Soviet bombers over the Arctic should North America ever be attacked. When the Russians launched *Sputnik* it was evident that they had missiles which could reach across the world, and the Arrow's task was over before it really began. The Americans and British, who had similar aircraft under development, cancelled their programs in favour of missile systems. After failing to find other customers or uses for the airplane, the Diefenbaker government cancelled the Arrow in 1959.

The defence crisis created by the Soviet missile threat was a contributing factor to the end of the Diefenbaker government. The military insisted on a

missile defence system, but the only one available was the already obsolete American Bomarc missile. It was designed to be equipped with a nuclear warhead, and this created a controversy in Canada, which had never had nuclear weapons. John Diefenbaker's government divided on the issue, and he lost the confidence of Parliament. This defeat led to the election of 1963, won by the Pearson Liberals.

Diefenbaker lost his second wife Olive in 1976. He was re-elected to Parliament for a record thirteenth time in 1979. He passed away at his home in Ottawa on August 16, 1979. A state funeral was held in Ottawa, and his body was transported by train across the country, stopping many times for Canadians to pay their respects. He is buried, with Olive, beside the Diefenbaker Canada Centre on the campus of the University of Saskatchewan in Saskatoon.

R. Bruce Shepard

FURTHER READING: Diefenbaker, John G. 1972. *One Canada* (3 vols.). Toronto: Macmillan; Shepard, R. Bruce and D.C. Story (eds.). 1998. *The Diefenbaker Legacy: Canadian Law, Politics, and Society Since 1957*. Regina: Canadian Plains Research Center; Smith, Denis. 1995. *Rogue Tory: The Life and Legend of John G. Diefenbaker*. Toronto: Macfarlane, Walter and Ross.

DIEPPE RAID. A small city located on the northwestern coast of France, Dieppe is 60 km northeast of Le Havre, and approximately 100 km south of the English coast. On August 19, 1942, during **WORLD WAR II**, Dieppe was the site of a raid code named Operation Jubilee, an Allied assault designed to probe Nazi defenses in preparation for the establishment of a second European Front.

The raid was carried out by a force consisting of 1,073 British commandos, 50 American Rangers, and 4,963 Canadian soldiers of the 2nd Canadian

Division under the command of Major-General J.H. Roberts, the force commander. The assault lasted nine hours and involved landings on five separate beaches along a 16-km front. Although the troops carried out their duties in an exemplary fashion, they did not have a chance against the well-fortified shore defenses of the Germans; overall, the raid disintegrated into a disaster for the Allied troops. As a result of the operation, 907 Canadian soldiers were killed, 1,400 were wounded, and 1,946 were taken prisoner by German forces.

The South Saskatchewan Regiment (SSR), commanded by Lt.-Col. C.C.I. (Cecil) Merit, one of the units of 2nd Canadian Division, landed on "Green Beach" at Pourville, 4 km west of Dieppe. The Regiment's objectives were to capture the village, destroy a German radar site, and disable all local enemy artillery instillations. Of the 523 SSR soldiers who landed at Pourville, 84 were killed, 89 were captured, and 166 were wounded; only 184 returned to England unharmed. Lt.-Col. Merit was awarded the **VICTORIA CROSS** for his actions during the raid.

Peter Borch

FURTHER READING: Buchanan, G.B. 1958. *The March of the Prairie Men: A Story of the South Saskatchewan Regiment*. Weyburn: South Saskatchewan Regiment Regimental Association; Campbell, J. 1993. *Dieppe Revisited: A Documentary Investigation*. Portland: Frank Cass; hristie, N. 2001. *The Suicide Raid: The Canadians at Dieppe, August 19, 1942*. Ottawa: CEF Books.

DIETRICK, LORNE E. (1915–). The success of the co-operative movement in Saskatchewan is in large part due to the efforts of people like Lorne Dietrick. Born in Saskatoon on November 3, 1915, Dietrick was the first manager of the LeRoy Co-operative Association. Following his service in the Royal Canadian Navy, he received a diploma in agriculture and helped establish the Matador Co-operative Farm, serving as its first chairman. In 1948, Dietrick spearheaded the creation of the Saskatchewan Federation of Production Co-operatives. Dietrick is also recognized for his work on Canada-China relations. Although China was a closed society, he visited the country on four occasions to study co-operatives and advise on farming methods. He also founded the Canada-China farmers' exchange program, which further strengthened relations between the two nations. Dietrick was awarded the Saskatchewan Order of Merit in 2000.

DISABILITY, CITIZENSHIP, AND PUBLIC POLICY. Disability is a normal part of the human condition. Some people are born with a disability; others develop a disability through the course of life owing to an accident, illness, aging; still others have disabilities that reoccur throughout their lives. Many people experience more than one condition that could be considered a disability.

Disability occurs as a result of the interaction of health conditions such as disease or injury, personal factors such as age, gender or cultural identity, and one's social environment. Not all disabilities result in significant limitations or restrictions on everyday life and work. For example, eyeglasses are a common intervention that effectively eliminates the impact of poor vision. Most people who wear eyeglasses would not consider themselves disabled, but without this intervention they might not be able to drive an automobile or pursue other aspects of their lives without limitation. Disability is usually important only when it affects a person's ability to function with normal independence and self-sufficiency.

The Participation and Activity Limitation Survey (PALS) is conducted by Statistics Canada every ten years to collect information on disability in the country. According to PALS, the overall rate of disability in the general Saskatchewan population in 2001 was 14.5%. The survey reported that 3% of children from birth to 14 years of age, 11% of individuals from 15 to 64 years of age, and 44% of individuals age 65 and older have one or more disabilities. Because disability and aging are closely connected, it is important to plan to address the needs of individuals throughout their life cycle.

There are a number of perspectives reflected in current public attitudes and policies for people with disabilities. The charity model is the oldest and still most prevalent approach—one that views people with disabilities as unfortunates or victims of circumstance, whom society must care for as a moral responsibility. While this approach may enrich benefits and services for people with disabilities, the charity model tends to under-emphasize the capacities of people with disabilities to participate more fully in work and community life.

The medical model views disability primarily from the perspective of health conditions, and emphasizes rehabilitation, restoration or repair of an abnormality or defect. While medical approaches are important for stabilization and treatment of conditions, they tend to focus on deficits rather than capacities, with less emphasis on the individual's capacities to function in his or her social and physical environment.

The social and human rights model sees disability as society's failure to meet the needs of an individual with a disability, and to recognize his or her inherent rights as a human being. This model is based on the premise that if the environment is adapted to the person, the effects of a disability can be reduced or eliminated. Its advocates focus on public policy measures to address physical, attitudinal, and social barriers to participation in society.

The functional limitation model emphasizes the capacity of the individual to perform typical tasks and social roles, and pursues interventions through which that capacity may be strengthened. The functional limitation model blends a focus on measures that support individual capacity for daily living with a concern for the physical and social environment and its capacity to accommodate needs specific to disability.

The Canadian Charter of Rights and Freedoms prohibits discrimination based on mental or physical disability, but the Charter contains no definition of disability. The concept is not easy to define because the range of possibly disabling conditions is very broad and their impact can differ from individual to individual. The practical impact of the Charter on disability issues is evolving slowly through legal precedent.

In Saskatchewan a significant array of supports exist to help people with disabilities. These range from income support to health services, employment supports, and other benefits or services. Sometimes eligibility for disability programs is established on the basis of diagnosis or functional impact assessment alone. Other programs combine disability criteria with other criteria such as the individual's personal income or assets. Choices in eligibility criteria affect the accessibility of programs and services to individuals, as well as the capacity of public programs, with limited budgets, to address the full scope of need in the population.

In recent years, governments and advocates have begun to view people with disabilities in a different way. *Saskatchewan's Disability Action Plan*, a position paper released by the Saskatchewan Council on Disability Issues in 2001, describes a vision of a society in which "individuals with disabilities are citizens in the full sense of the term. They have the same rights and responsibilities as other citizens to be included and to participate fully in society." This integrative vision represents a great step forward from the early days of the province, when people with disabilities were often isolated from the mainstream of life. Consistent with this view, Saskatchewan public policy is moving toward a functional impact model of disability, with more focus on impact than on diagnosis, and greater recognition of the relationship between an individual's disability and his or her environment, resources, skills, and personal support network.

Many past failures of disability policy were rooted in a simplistic view of disability, and a tendency to segregate people into "disabled" program categories. Public policy is evolving towards recognition of disability as a quality all humans share in some measure. Approaches are emerging that will gradually minimize the practical effect of disabilities on citizens' lives. Such developments have the potential to improve the quality of life of individuals with disabilities, and to strengthen the social and economic fabric of the province as a whole.

Tara Truemner

FURTHER READING: Bickenback, J.E. 1993. *Physical Disabilities and Social Policy*. Toronto: University of Toronto Press; Saskatchewan Council on Disability Issues. 2001. *Saskatchewan's Disability Action Plan*.

DISTANCE EDUCATION AND TECHNO-LOGY-ENHANCED LEARNING.

Technology-enhanced learning has its roots in correspondence education, an instructional practice in which teacher and students who were separated by distance used various modes of technology to supplement print-based materials and enhance communication and learning outcomes. This approach later came to be known as distance education, and remains an important method of extending access to learning opportunities. Today, technology-enhanced learning encompasses a variety of information and communication technologies to support learning at a distance and in traditional instructional settings.

A range of technological enhancements has been used to augment print-based materials, from radio broadcasts during the 1930s to audiocassette and videocassette tapes in the 1970s. Rapid advances in telecommunications technology during the 1980s facilitated real-time communication among teachers and learners through audio and video. Audio-conferences and slow scan video used the telephone system to transmit voice and video images, while fibre optic and cable networks added televised instruction and videoconferences to the technologies available to educators and their learners.

During the early 1980s, the Saskatchewan Tele-learning Association Inc. (STELLA) pioneered a network of thirty-five receiving sites across the province, where students gathered to participate in live televised instruction delivered by satellite. This led to the creation of the Saskatchewan Communications Network (SCN) in 1989, a provincial educational broadcasting authority which continues to operate a network of over 200 receiving sites across the province. Students view their instructors on the receiving site's monitor and communicate by telephone, facsimile, or e-mail. Today, SCN's network also provides Internet access via satellite to small rural and remote facilities.

The 1990s witnessed an explosion in digital technology. Computers and the Internet have revolutionized the use of technology in learning and created flexible and enriched opportunities for learners. In 2001, Saskatchewan launched a second major provincial initiative called CommunityNet, which established a high-speed digital network across the province, providing access to the Internet and a network of electronic educational resources and services.

With the variety of communication tools now available, educators are integrating technologies with traditional instructional methods to enhance interaction and course content in ways that best meet the needs of their learners. Learners in the classroom, in their homes, at work, and across the globe are able to participate in on-line courses and take advantage of a rich array of learning resources via the Internet. *Lynn Oliver*

DIXON, SOPHIA (1900–94). Sophia Dixon was a progressive thinker, writer, educator, and political activist. Born Sophia Rossander on April 1, 1900, in Denmark, she immigrated in 1911 with her family to homestead near Kerrobert. She later attended NORMAL SCHOOL, taught for a time, and married a farmer in 1921. Her life of activism included involvement in the Progressive Party, the United Farmers of Canada (UFC) (Saskatchewan Section), the Farmers' Union, the State Hospital and Medical League, the Women's International League for Peace and Freedom, the co-operative movement, the credit union movement, and the CO-OPERATIVE COMMONWEALTH FEDERATION (CCF). Leadership roles included serving as woman president of the UFC (Saskatchewan Section) and on the first federal council of the CCF. In 1952 Dixon became the first woman returning officer for Saskatoon. She was also a pioneer supporter of birth control, writing and speaking in favour of free dissemination of birth control information in the 1920s and 1930s.

In 1954 a difficult period began. She was asked to wind up a company, Western Export Import Co., Ltd (WEICO), which had ties with SGIO and the CCF government. Accused of making profits from disposal of tractors the company had imported to sell to farmers, she was sued by the company. Dixon's reputation suffered, but the Saskatchewan Court of Appeals and, eventually, the Supreme Court of Canada (in 1976), found in her favour. In 1979 Dixon was one of the first five women in Canada to receive the Person's Award in recognition of her work for women and the co-operative movement. Subsequently she wrote, and spoke, for social justice. She died on April 14, 1994. *Elaine Hamm*

FURTHER READING: Clemence, V. 2004. *Saskatchewan's Own: People Who Made a Difference*. Calgary: Fifth House; Taylor, G. 1980. "Sophia Dixon–Progressive Always–Indifferent Never," *Saskatoon History* 1: 25–31.

DMYTRUK PETER (1920–43). Peter Dmytruk was born in Radisson, Saskatchewan on May 27, 1920. He joined the Royal Canadian Air Force in July 1941, and in 1942, after graduating from Bombing and Gunnery school, was assigned as Flight Sergeant to No. 405 "City of Vancouver" Bomber Squadron, flying from the bases of Topcliffe and Leeming, Yorkshire, England. On March 12, 1943, during a mission over France, a German fighter attacked the Lancaster on which Dmytruk was the rear gunner. He survived the crash of his plane and

The monument in Martres-de-Veyre to the memory of Peter Dmytruk (Demytruck)– "Pierre le Canadien."

eventually escaped to the Auvergne region. He later served in the French Resistance for ten months, hijacking ammunition trucks, stealing supplies, blowing up railroads, and hiding Allied airmen who had been shot down. Dmytruk was captured and executed on December 9, 1943, in the village Les Martres-de-Veyre after being stopped at a German roadblock. He remains a local and national hero to the French, who in 1947 awarded Dmytruk the Croix de Guerre; in Les Martres-de-Veyre a street was named after him, and the French have erected a monument on the spot where he was killed. In Saskatchewan, Dmytruk Lake was named in his honour. In 1999 he was posthumously awarded the Nation Builders Award, which celebrates the contributions of outstanding Ukrainian Canadians from the province of Saskatchewan. *Dagmar Skamlová*

FURTHER READING: Chisholm, D. 2001. *Their Names Live On: Remembering Saskatchewan's Fallen in World War II*. Regina: Canadian Plains Research Center.

DOCTORS' STRIKE. In July 1962, doctors in Saskatchewan began a provincewide general strike

that marked the peak of a conflict between organized medicine and its allies against the government's MEDICARE bill. One of the great crucibles of provincial history, the issues surrounding the strike divided communities and even families. Since it led to a national debate on the merits of universal health insurance, interest in the strike went far beyond the province, and for three weeks national and foreign media focused on the strike in Saskatchewan.

The origins of the strike lay in Premier T.C. DOUGLAS' promise, in a by-election speech in Birch Hills, Saskatchewan, in April 1959, to introduce a pre-paid, universal and publicly managed system of primary physician care. Commonly known as "medicare," this initiative was to complement universal hospital insurance introduced the decade before with the support of most doctors. In the 1950s, however, organized medicine in Saskatchewan became more opposed to universality. A new generation of more ideologically conservative doctors, some of whom were refugees from the National Health Service in Britain, along with a successful foray by organized medicine into the health insurance business (which the doctors wished to extend provincewide), translated into a strong opposition to any extension of universal health care coverage.

In an effort to mitigate physician opposition to medicare, Douglas established in April 1960 an Advisory Planning Committee on Medical Care with nominees from organized medicine, government, business and labour under the chairmanship of WALTER P. THOMPSON. Delaying its establishment and then delaying its ultimate report, the nominees of the COLLEGE OF PHYSICIANS AND SURGEONS bought time for more organized opposition to the government. The medicare bill was introduced just before Douglas left the premiership to become leader of the federal New Democratic Party. It was left to his suc-

Protesting the implementation of medicare, July 11, 1962.

cessor, **WOODROW LLOYD**, to implement the bill by April 1962. In March, however, Lloyd decided to extend the deadline to July in a last-ditch effort to find a compromise with the province's physicians. However, the delay, along with the sharp drop in electoral support for the NDP in Saskatchewan in the federal election of June 18, simply served to strengthen the hand of the more militant doctors who concluded that the government would eventually back down. Threatening to leave the province if the bill was implemented, they helped establish numerous "Keep our Doctors" (KOD) committees throughout the province.

Despite the defection of his own ex-minister of Health to the Liberals in May and a threatened general strike by physicians, the Lloyd government proceeded with implementation on the July 1 deadline. The same day, the physicians began a strike which would last twenty-three days. Its high point was a demonstration in front of the Saskatchewan legislature in Regina on July 11 that attracted about 4,000 people, about one-tenth the number hoped for by the organizers. The strike officially ended twelve days later when Lord Stephen Taylor of the United Kingdom earned the trust of both sides and mediated what became known as the "Saskatoon Agreement." This compromise ultimately set the terms for medicare in Saskatchewan (and Canada) by ensuring physician autonomy and fee-for-service remuneration in exchange for the provision of publicly administered, universal physician services for all residents.   *Gregory P. Marchildon*

DOG SLEDDING. Dogs were used by First Nations as pack animals for transporting hunting supplies and for moving camp. The dogs sometimes carried supplies in packs on their backs; loads were increased by having the dogs pull a travois on the plains, and sleds or toboggans in the northern forests. Horses gradually replaced dogs for transport, as they became more available on the northern plains in the 18th century. In the late 19th century,

J. CAMERON PHOTO/ SASKATCHEWAN ARCHIVES BOARD R-B3499

Three dog teams transporting small carrioles on a northern lake, 1917; the photographer labeled the photograph "In the Cree country."

as dog sledding became more common, breeding with European dogs increased the size of the animals; the numbers of dogs per team also increased. Traditional and non-traditional settlers in remote northern areas used dog teams until they were replaced by the snowmobile in the 1960s. Today, dog sledding is primarily a recreational activity and a competitive sport.   *Bob Ivanochko*

DOGS: *see* **WORKING FARM DOGS**

BILL ROSE PHOTO/PHOTO COURTESY OF PAUL DOJACK

Paul Dojack, Canadian Football League referee, 1962.

DOJACK, PAUL (1917–). One of the longest serving officials in the Canadian Football League, Paul Dojack was born in Winnipeg on April 24, 1917. His family established a retail music business in Regina, and Dojack began playing football at a local school ground. His enthusiasm for sport led to the formation of the Dales Athletic Club, an organization that supported numerous sports teams including the **REGINA DALES** Football Club. Dojack played for the Dales, but his greatest success came as the team's coach: under his guidance, the Dales appeared in four consecutive western Canadian championships and won the 1938 Canadian junior football title. Paul Dojack's 29-year officiating career began in 1941. He worked in 546 CFL games including fourteen Grey Cup finals, and was head referee in eight championship games. Dojack presided over two record-setting games: the only Grey Cup final to have gone into overtime in 1961, and the 1962 "Fog Bowl" played over two days. Several of his judgement calls have since been adopted into the CFL rulebook. He is a member of the Canadian Football Hall of Fame and the Canadian and **SASKATCHEWAN SPORTS HALL OF FAME**. In addition to working as a

referee, Dojack helped troubled youth and served as recreation director of the Saskatchewan Boy's Training School from 1965 to 1975. A decade later, the school was renamed the Paul Dojack Youth Centre.   *Daria Coneghan and Holden Stoffel*

DOMINION LANDS ACT/HOMESTEAD ACT. The Saskatchewan landscape changed as the Dominion Lands Act/Homestead Act came into effect in 1872. While Saskatchewan would not become a province until 1905, settlers arrived during the mid- to late 1800s because of promises of land grants by the government. The Dominion Lands Act of 1872 outlined the provisions for granting homesteads to settlers: free homesteads of 160 acres were offered to farmers who cleared ten acres and built a residence within three years of a registered intent to settle a specific land claim. The Dominion Lands Act imposed a standard measure for surveying, subdividing and settling the prairies: land had to be located through cadastral surveys; individuals had to show that their land was improved upon and had increased in value or use by constructing a dwelling or cultivating the land; letters patent would then be issued to settlers by a Dominion Lands Board which screened and validated all applications.

While the availability of land helped to entice settlers, the Dominion Lands Act also ensured that inhabitants would have no control over the land and other resources: the Dominion would hold this control until 1930, when the federal government transferred responsibility of land issues to the provinces. The 1879 amendments to the Dominion Lands Act acknowledged previously unsettled claims and addressed the claims of First Nations and **MÉTIS** in the west; section 42 of the Act indicated recognition and protection of Aboriginal rights, limiting settlement of the land by homesteaders until title was extinguished by Métis and other Aboriginal inhabitants. However, while criteria regarding land claims for settlers were clearly defined under section 31 of the Manitoba Act, the stipulations applying to Métis in the North-West Territories before joining the Dominion as Saskatchewan in 1905 were not: section 125 of the Dominion Lands Act of 1879 empowered the federal government to grant persons who established undisturbed occupation and peaceable possession of the land, occupancy of that land.   *Elizabeth Mooney*

DONALDSON, MARY (1908–66). Mary Elizabeth Donaldson was born in Brandon, Manitoba in 1908. She received a BA from the University of Alberta in 1928 and a BSc in Library Science from the University of Toronto in 1929. She began her professional career as a cataloguer in Toronto and Edmonton Public Libraries, as well as at the **UNIVERSITY OF SASKATCHEWAN**, where she served briefly as chief cataloguer before transferring to Saskatoon Public Library as chief assistant librarian in 1945.

In 1948, she headed a group of Canadian librarians attending the International Summer School for Librarians in Manchester, England; thereafter she maintained a keen interest in library development throughout the world. From 1951 until her death in 1966, she held the position of Provincial Librarian for Saskatchewan. In addition, she served as president of the Canadian Library Association from 1956 to 1957, and was an American Library Association (ALA) councillor at the time of her death. To honour her memory, the SASKATCHEWAN LIBRARY ASSOCIATION established the Mary Donaldson Trust and the Mary Donaldson Award of Merit.

Judith Silverthorne

DONISON BROTHERS: LEE (1928–), DANNY (1932–), SEBASTIAN "BUTCH" (1937–). The Donison brothers of the Avonlea district had outstanding athletic careers in amateur wrestling and boxing. Born on March 9, 1928, Lee Donison excelled at both wrestling and boxing. He was Provincial Heavyweight wrestling champion four consecutive times beginning in 1953. As a boxer, he was a two-time light heavyweight and five-time heavyweight provincial champion and the 1963 Canadian Light Heavyweight Champion. He was chosen as an alternate for the Canadian Boxing Team that competed at the 1954 British Empire and Commonwealth Games in Vancouver. Lee is the only Canadian athlete to have won provincial titles in both boxing and wrestling four times. He also enjoys an enviable reputation as a healer.

Danny Donison was born on August 12, 1932, and began wrestling at the Regina YMCA in 1950. Between 1953 and 1968, he won six provincial championships in the lightweight, welterweight, and middleweight categories, and was Canadian Lightweight Champion in 1955. In addition to competing, Danny Donison coached at the Regina Wrestling Club and chaired the wrestling committee for the Saskatchewan branch of the Amateur Athletic Union of Canada. He promoted amateur and free-style wrestling across the province, and served as secretary-treasurer of the Regina Boxing and Wrestling Club.

The youngest Donison brother, "Butch" was born on September 26, 1937, and is the only Canadian wrestler to have participated in every weight class in provincial competition. He amassed numerous titles between 1953 and 1967, including thirteen provincial titles, Canadian titles in the featherweight and middleweight categories, and a silver medal in the light heavyweight competition at the 1966 British Empire and Commonwealth Games. He retired after winning his last Canadian title in 1967, and later coached at the Regina Wrestling Club and the University of Regina.

Lee, Danny, and Sebastian Donison were inducted into the SASKATCHEWAN SPORTS HALL OF FAME in 1982. *Daria Coneghan and Holden Stoffel*

DORVAL, ONÉSIME (1845–1932). Onésime Dorval is Saskatchewan's first officially certified teacher, and her work and service marked the establishment of French and English education in the province. Born and raised in St. Jérôme, Quebec, Dorval had wanted to join the order of the Sisters of Good Shepherd in New York, but owing to her frail health she was not allowed to make her final vows. During her postulate and noviciate, she learned English and remained determined to serve the Church. She responded to the call of Bishop Vital Grandin, OMI, of St. Albert, who was recruiting resourceful women as housekeepers and teachers for Roman Catholic missions of the North-West. In 1877, Dorval journeyed west to teach in the Red River settlement of Fort Garry. In the summer of 1880, she made another arduous journey by RED RIVER CART to St. Laurent de Grandin. Between 1881 and 1883 she made her way to St. Albert, next to Ste. Anne, and then back to St. Laurent de Grandin, which was soon to be Saskatchewan territory. She spent many hours teaching and performing religious duties with the MÉTIS and French communities of St. Albert (Alberta), St. Laurent (Saskatchewan), and Ste. Anne (Manitoba). Her kindness, piety and great memory won her the admiration of many; she was also a resourceful teacher, who loved and respected her Métis students. While in St. Laurent, she contributed to the establishment of a grotto to Our Lady of Lourdes.

She then moved to Battleford and started another school, where she taught until 1896. She moved again, and taught in a one-room school in the Batoche No. 1 School District from 1896 until 1914. In 1913, St. Michael's School held a celebration to mark her fifty years of teaching. During this time, she also worked as a housekeeper and provided board for children who lived outside walking distance to school. From there, Dorval taught in Aldina for one year before returning to St. Laurent de Grandin, as French teachers there were in short supply. After retiring from teaching in 1921 with the Sisters of Presentation in Duck Lake, she continued her community and missionary activities and wrote her memoirs. She died in Rosthern on December 10, 1932, at the age of 87, and is buried in the cemetery of St. Michael's School in Duck Lake.

The government named four small islands in her honour in the NORTH SASKATCHEWAN RIVER near North Battleford. In 1954, Dorval was designated a person of national historic significance by the National Historic Sites and Monuments Board of Canada. In commemoration of her life and work, a bronze plaque was presented to the Batoche Museum. In 1994 the *Division scolaire francophone #310* (*see* FRENCH EDUCATION) instituted its first *Prix Onésime Dorval*, and since then the *Association des directions d'écoles fransaskoises* has annually recognized its teachers who have exemplified the hard work and dedication of Onésime Dorval. When Parks Canada made women's history a priority, another plaque in her honour was unveiled in Duck Lake on October 29, 2002. *Estelle D'Almeida*

FURTHER READING: Lapointe, R. 1988. *100 noms: Petit dictionnaire biographique des Franco-Canadiens de la Saskatchewan*. Regina: Société historique de la Saskatchewan.

DOUGLAS, JAMES MOFFAT (1839–1920). James Moffat Douglas was born in Linton, Scotland, on May 26, 1839, and emigrated to Upper Canada in 1851. He was ordained a minister of the Presbyterian Church of Canada in 1867, after studying at the University of Toronto and the Princeton University Seminary. He served congregations in Ontario and was a missionary to central India. In 1882 he was assigned a parish in Manitoba. Later he served in Brandon, then in Moosomin from 1890 to 1893. He established a homestead called Tantallon (later to serve as the name for the village) in the North-West Territories in 1883 with his son John Douglas, but he did not permanently reside there until 1893.

In 1894 he was nominated as a candidate for the Patrons of Industry, an agrarian political movement. He won the seat of Assiniboia East in the federal election of 1896 as a Patron-Liberal. He was deeply involved in agricultural legislation. He proposed a bill in 1898 to end the perceived monopoly on the grain trade that led to the creation of a commission to examine the trade. This commission recommended the basis for the Manitoba Grain Act of 1900. He was re-elected in 1900 and appointed to the Senate in 1906 where he served as chairman of the Senate's committee on agriculture. He died August 19, 1920. *Jeremy Mohr*

DOUGLAS, JOHN TAYLOR (1892–1976). John Taylor Douglas was born at Cumberland, Ontario, on October 28, 1892. In 1906, John traveled west with his parents to the Laura district in Saskatchewan. He received an agriculture degree from the UNIVERSITY OF SASKATCHEWAN and began farming near Laura. Douglas became secretary of the Rosetown constituency Progressive Association. As the movement evolved into the CCF, Douglas supported the policies of the new party. In 1935 he managed the campaign that elected M.J. COLDWELL to the House of Commons. From 1936 to 1941 Douglas served on the CCF Saskatchewan council and became the party's provincial organizer in 1941. When the CCF swept to power in 1944, he was elected to the Legislative Assembly. Douglas would

SASKATCHEWAN ARCHIVES BOARD R-A11520

John Taylor Douglas.

REGINA LEADER-POST

Shirley Douglas addressing Saskatchewan Federation of Labour on the status of Medicare, November 2002.

EVERETT BAKER PHOTO/COURTESY OF THE SASKATCHEWAN HISTORY AND FOLKLORE SOCIETY

T.C. Douglas (right) with part of his Cabinet, at the Matador Co-op Farm, July 1947.

win three more elections and serve a total of sixteen years in the **T.C. DOUGLAS** administration. In 1944 John Douglas was named Minister of Highways and Transportation and Minister of Public Works. In 1946 he set up a Royal Commission on Penal Reform and organized the **SASKATCHEWAN TRANSPORTATION COMPANY** into a **CROWN CORPORATION**. When he took on the job of Highways Minister Douglas made it a priority to upgrade the highway system. He retired in 1960. Douglas died on February 19, 1976. *Dwayne Yasinowski*

FURTHER READING: McLeod, Thomas H. and Ian McLeod. 1987. *Tommy Douglas: The Road to Jerusalem.* Edmonton: Hurtig Publishers; Saskatchewan Archives Board. Interview with J.T. Douglas, tapes R-6086, R-6087.

DOUGLAS, SHIRLEY (1934–). Born in Weyburn in April 1934, Douglas is the daughter of Irma and **T.C. DOUGLAS**, former Saskatchewan Premier. She attended the Banff School of Fine Arts, then studied at the Royal Academy of Dramatic Art in London, and acted in British television and theatre. She returned to Canada in 1957, married, and had her first child. She remarried, to actor Donald Sutherland, and had twins. Douglas has had a life-long commitment to social activism. Having moved with her family to California in the late 1960s, she became involved in protest movements, first opposing the Vietnam War and then focusing upon the oppression of immigrants and women. She was later refused a work permit because of protest activities, so after her divorce from Sutherland she returned to Canada in 1977. Douglas continued to develop her acting career after her return to Canada. She is also a national spokesperson for the Canadian Health Coalition, an organization dedicated to preserving public health care. She has received numerous awards, including membership in the Order of Canada (2003). *Lisa Dale-Burnett*

DOUGLAS, THOMAS CLEMENT (1904–86). Premier and national party leader Tommy Douglas was Saskatchewan's most notable and influential politician. He led the CCF to victory in 1944 and led an administration that transformed the role of government in Saskatchewan and across the country.

Douglas was born in Falkirk, Scotland, on October 20, 1904, and grew up in a working-class family. The Scottish Independent Labour Party had heavily influenced his father Tom, and that set the tone for Douglas' political education. Douglas moved with his family to Winnipeg in 1910. At the time, Winnipeg was the centre of a strong working class and social gospel movement. He became active in the Labour party and by the early 1920s decided to devote his life to social reform through Christian ministry. He attended Brandon College in 1924, a training ground for Baptist ministers, and started his first ministry in 1927. In 1929, he accepted a full-time ministry at Calvary Baptist Church in Weyburn. While preaching, Douglas finished his BA in 1930 and MA from McMaster by correspondence in 1933. He began a doctorate at the University of Chicago but failed to complete all the requirements, preferring to remain ministering in Weyburn.

For Douglas, religion was closely connected with politics. He believed the best way to serve God was to create a better, more just society. He founded a branch of the Independent Labour Party in Weyburn and was active in the formation of the CCF. In 1934, he unsuccessfully ran in the provincial election. Douglas tried again in 1935, running in the federal riding of Weyburn, and was narrowly elected.

One of seven CCF MPs in the House of Commons, Douglas soon established himself as potent weapon for the party through his oratorical and debating skills. After his re-election in 1940, many Saskatchewan CCF activists called for Douglas to return to provincial politics and lead the provincial CCF. The local party was embroiled in internal strife as party leader **GEORGE WILLIAMS'** style alienated him from a large section of the party. Douglas challenged Williams for the party presidency in 1941 and won. A year later he won the party leadership over Williams' supporter, MLA **JOHN H. BROCKELBANK**.

After becoming leader, Douglas set about toppling the Liberal government. Party membership expanded and the CCF became more organized. In 1944, Douglas swept the province, winning 47 of 53 seats and capturing over 53% of the vote. During the first term of the government, Douglas put forward an ambitious program of reform. Labour standards were greatly improved, the educational system was consolidated, legislation was introduced to expand the co-operative sector of the economy and bills were enacted to protect farmers from foreclosure. The government established many social welfare programs and began to set the foundation of socialized medicare. The CCF began to play a larger role in the economy through a number of business ventures such as a shoe factory, a box factory, and a brick plant. These ventures attracted a great deal of opposition, and after 1948 the government largely retreated from non-utility business ventures.

The Douglas government was re-elected four times in 1948, 1952, 1956, and 1960. It was largely responsible for the modernization of Saskatchewan by using **CROWN CORPORATIONS** to expand electricity and telephone service throughout the province, using natural gas as a heating source, and expanding the province's highway system.

Douglas' contribution was most significant in the field of health care. The government provided a province-wide hospitalization program in 1947, established a medical school at the **UNIVERSITY OF SASKATCHEWAN**, and increased the mental health budget. After contesting the 1960 general election on the issue of universal state-run health insurance, Douglas began to set up the parameters of the **MEDICARE** system. After a heated consultation process and substantial opposition from the doctors, Douglas moved the Medicare legislation into the Legislature. However, Douglas never saw the legislation passed.

In 1961, Douglas returned to the federal arena to lead the **NEW DEMOCRATIC PARTY**, which had been created after the CCF and the Canadian Labour Congress entered into a political alliance. Douglas first ran for the party in 1962 in the riding of Regina City but, facing the brunt of the doctors' strike over the Medicare issue, he lost. He subsequently won a by-election in the British Columbia riding of Burnaby-Coquitlam and returned to the House of Commons. Douglas continued to lead the federal NDP but would never again represent a Saskatchewan riding. He was re-elected in 1963 and 1965 in Burnaby and, after defeat in 1968, he ran in Nanaimo and won in 1969, 1972, and 1974. In 1972 Douglas resigned as NDP leader, but continued to be a prominent party spokesman until he retired from politics in 1979. On February 24, 1986, Douglas died in Ottawa.   *Brett Quiring*

FURTHER READING: McLeod, Thomas H. and Ian McLeod. 1987. *Tommy Douglas: The Road to Jerusalem.* Edmonton: Hurtig Publishers; Shackleton, Doris French. 1975. *Tommy Douglas.* Toronto: McClelland and Stewart; Thomas, Lewis. 1981. "The CCF Victory in Saskatchewan, 1944," *Saskatchewan History* 34 (1): 1–16.

DOUKHOBOR PHILOSOPHY. Saskatchewan Doukhobors are an integral part of the 7,500 Russian dissidents from Transcaucasia who, in 1899, emigrated to Canada because of their pacifist and anti-church beliefs. In the face of English assimilation and secularization, these Saskatchewan citizens (15,000 out of 40,000 in Canada) have survived remarkably well. Their *sobranies* (gatherings of people for religious, social, and business purposes) in community homes still persist in Kamsack, Verigin, Blaine Lake, Langham, and Saskatoon. Unique *a cappella* singing can be heard in these homes. A museum and heritage village in Verigin has been designated as a National Heritage Site; it attracts visitors and serves as a focal point for the annual Peace Day, commemorating the 1895 arms burning in Tsarist Russia.

With the pull of the university, along with good leadership and student initiatives (e.g., holding seminars and publishing the monthly journal *The Inquirer*, and later *The Dove*), Saskatoon has become a magnet for Doukhobor activities in the province. Beginning in the early 1950s, Doukhobors constructed their own community centre, and established a pioneer dwelling and a successful brick oven bread-baking project at the Western Development Museum. Every year, during the city's week-long exhibition, local volunteers produce thousands of loaves of freshly baked bread; their sales bring in enough money to finance national and international causes.

Doukhobors do not believe in creeds—nor do they rely on any formal church, the Bible, priests, or sacraments. The sole exception is the appearance in official religious and business functions of a loaf of bread, a bowl of salt, and a jug of water. These emblems are simply meant to affirm the slogan "Toil and Peaceful Life." In a manner similar to the Quakers, Doukhobors believe in the Spirit Within or the God Within. Because people have the spark of divinity in them, they argue, it is wrong to kill another human being. As an expression of their inner values, Saskatchewan Doukhobors continue to commemorate the annual Peace Day, take part in peace marches, and support petitions for nonviolent action. Their values of hospitality, kindness towards others, co-operation, creativity, compassion, and hard work persist to this day.   *Koozma J. Tarasoff*

FURTHER READING: Palmieri, A. 1915. "The Russian Doukhobors and Their Religious Teachings," *Harvard Theological Review* 8: 62–81; Tarasoff, K.J. 2002. *Spirit Wrestlers: Doukhobor Pioneers' Strategies for Living.* Ottawa: Legas Publishing and Spirit Wrestlers Publishing.

DOUKHOBOR SETTLEMENT. Canada's nation-building policy of creating a healthy industrial economy involved the settlement of the west through vigorous immigration promoted by Clifford Sifton, Minister of the Interior. Sifton's coup came in 1899 when he attracted 7,500 Russians to western Canada as the largest single group to emigrate to this country. Known as Spirit-Wrestlers/Doukhobors, these people were dissidents from southern Russia who were persecuted by the Tsarist government and the Orthodox Church for their refusal to go to war and for their rejection of the formal church. They attracted the attention of Leo Tolstoy, who saw in them the practical expression of the morality in which he believed, as well as of the English Quakers, who were sympathetic to their cause (*see* **DOUKHOBOR PHILOSOPHY**). After arriving in eastern Canada on four cattle boats and travelling across the country by rail, the new settlers stopped in immigration halls in Winnipeg, Selkirk, Brandon, Dauphin, Yorkton, and Prince Albert, until in early spring they moved to temporary block houses. Awaiting them were three reserves of land in the North-West Territories (now Saskatchewan), totaling nearly 750,000 acres of pristine prairie land dotted with trees, shrubs and creeks. This was a magnificent endowment set aside by the Canadian government for the Doukhobors' sole use.

Two of the reserves were in the northeast corner of Assiniboia Territory. The North Colony (Thunder Hill) was located 112 km from Yorkton and contained six townships. The South Colony, with an annex called Devil's or Good Spirit Lake Colony and containing fifteen townships, was situated 48 km from Yorkton, which, located on the north line of the **CANADIAN PACIFIC RAILWAY**, served as a shipping and trade centre for the colonists in the two reserves. The third reserve, 320 km to the northwest, was the Prince Albert or Saskatchewan Colony; its southern part lay 32 km northwest of Saskatoon.

The first year in Canada tested the strength of the Doukhobors. It witnessed the building of fifty-seven Old World villages, surrounded by scattered plots of tilled land and connected by rudimentary roads and trails. While able-bodied men were away working for wages on railway construction and in neighbouring farms, women, children and elder men built the villages, some twenty houses in each, in the summer and fall of 1899: thirteen villages in the North Colony; twenty-four in the South Colony and another ten in the Annex; and ten in the

COURTESY OF NATIONAL DOUKHOBOUR HERITAGE VILLAGE

Given the absence of oxen and horses, members of the community were often forced to haul basic necessities dozens of miles from larger centres to their villages.

Provincial heritage property, the Doukhobor Prayer Home in Veregin, was built in 1912 as a home for Peter Verigin, an early leader of the Doukhobor movement in Canada.

Saskatchewan Colony. Women's determination was evidenced when they hitched themselves to ploughs and cultivated the first gardens.

With no more than fifty families each, these single-street villages followed tradition and belief. They resembled the peasant commune or *mir*–the settlement of generations of Doukhobors and other Russians–as well as the first-century Christian belief of holding all things in common, which leader-in-exile **PETER V. VERIGIN** had recently revived among the Doukhobors. Log dwellings luted with clay were common in the North Colony, while sod and clay houses were constructed in the South and Prince Albert colonies. The more individualistic settlers in the Saskatchewan Colony built traditional house-barn combinations. Later, many of the early dwellings were replaced with brick or wooden structures. Some villages erected a separate meeting house or dom. In all, ninety villages were established in Saskatchewan. Grain elevators, flourmills, and brick factories soon arose in several central locations such as Verigin, near Kamsack. An ideal community had begun.

Like Tolstoy, Doukhobors looked at land rights as a basis for expressing equality and morality. The old Russian *mir* system embraced land as a common resource to be used by those working on it: land was therefore not a commodity to be sold. When the Russians arrived in Canada in 1899, the Canadian government agreed to agricultural villages because twenty-five years earlier it had accommodated the Mennonites immigrating to southern Manitoba. The Hamlet Clause in the Dominion Lands Act allowed communal-minded settlers to live in a village within three miles (4.83 km) of the homestead quarter section (160 acres, or 64.8 ha) instead of living on each quarter. Clifford Sifton, Minister of the Interior, reaffirmed this arrangement

in February 1903 when he allowed a committee of three to make entry on behalf of all the Doukhobors. By November 1904, 422,800 acres representing approximately 2,640 homesteads had been entered.

An abrupt end to the period of agreement came in 1906 when the new Minister of the Interior, Frank Oliver, overruled the cultivation and residence concession granted by Sifton. Instead he accepted a recommendation by Reverend John McDougal, Land Commissioner, to cancel the reserves, and threatened eviction if they did not individually comply to make new entries for the land and if the people did not become citizens. The new policy thus stamped out communal competition in favour of free enterprise. Taking the oath, a requirement of naturalization towards obtaining citizenship (a fulfilment of the Homestead Act), was a technicality to which the

Doukhobors would have objected to had they known it before coming to Canada: many feared the oath as a negation of their exemption from military service, which was secured under an Order-in-Council. On June 1, 1907, these regulations were enforced and some 2,500 homesteads, representing approximately 400,000 acres of land, were cancelled. To soften dislocation, the government set up for the Community Doukhobors temporary reserves around each village, based on fifteen acres of land for each villager. These village reserves dwindled from year to year, and in 1918 the land remaining was sold.

The loss was a major blow to the Doukhobor community and immediately caused splits into three camps. Those in conscience who would affirm rather than take the oath were able to maintain their homesteads and remain in Saskatchewan; known as Independents, they were suspicious of hereditary leadership. Today, practically all of the estimated 15,000 Doukhobors in Saskatchewan are Independents. A large party of 5,000 Community Doukhobors, led by Peter V. Verigin, settled in the interior of BC in 1908; privately, the group purchased 21,600 acres of land. The third group, the Zealots (also known as the Sons of Freedom), comprising a minuscule percentage of the Doukhobor population, took to heart the dictum that land is God's and that Christian teaching cannot be taken piecemeal: initially they sided with their Community brethren and moved to BC.

The outcome of all these developments was an unprecedented land rush and a major loss to the Doukhobor community of some $11 million. James Mavor of the University of Toronto, who assisted the Doukhobors in negotiations with the government, called this a "breach of faith." The officials would not listen, and to this day 40,000 Canadian

Mealtime on the prairies.

Doukhobors remember this as a deliberate betrayal of government to break up their co-operative structure, their traditional way of looking at morality, and their anti-military social movement.

Koozma J. Tarasoff,

FURTHER READING: Tarasoff, K.J. 2002. *Spirit Wrestlers: Doukhobor Pioneers' Strategies for Living.* Ottawa: Legas Publishing and Spirit Wrestlers Publishing; Tracie, C.J. 1996. *"Toil and Peaceful Life": Doukhobor Village Settlement in Saskatchewan 1899–1918.* Regina: Canadian Plains Research Center.

DOVES AND PIGEONS. The familiar rock dove and mourning dove are members of the family Columbidae, order Columbiformes. Birds of this family are characterized by their small feet and head and their plump bodies with soft plumage. They are the only birds able to drink water with their heads down; all other birds must fill their mouth and tip their heads back to swallow. There are over 300 species, found everywhere except the polar regions; diversity is highest in the tropics, where there are plentiful supplies of the fruits and seeds on which the members of the family typically feed.

There are five species on the provincial bird list: two native, two introduced, and one recently extinct. The native species are the mourning dove (*Zenaida macroura*), whose long-tailed silhouette and soft gray-brown plumage, with its whistling wings and sobbing coo, are a familiar sight and sound in summer in the southern half of the province, along with the band-tailed pigeon (*Columba fasciata*). This western forest-edge bird, first seen in 1970, has been seen a few times since, mainly in townsites in the southern third of the province.

The extinct species is the passenger pigeon (*Ectopistes migratorius*), an eastern forest species which nested in the river valleys of the province. It was numbered in the millions when first encountered by European settlers. Hunting pressure and destruction of the hardwood forests in which it nested in colonies resulted in its extinction by the beginning of the 20th century. The introduced species are the rock dove (*Columba livia*) and the Eurasian collared dove (*Streptopelia decaocto*), an escaped cage-bird species. The multi-coloured domestic form of the rock dove is a common permanent resident in the southern half of the province, often to pest proportions. The collared dove has recently been recorded in the southern margins of the province, as an invasive species.

Diane Secoy

FURTHER READING: Alsop, Fred J., III. 2002. *Birds of Canada.* New York: Dorling Kindersley Handbooks.

DOWLING, DONALDSON BOGART (1858–1925). Born in Ontario on November 5, 1858, Dowling graduated from McGill University with a Bachelor of Applied Science in 1883. He joined the Geological Survey in 1884 and worked there until his death. Initially employed as a topographer, he developed into a well-respected geologist.

In the late 19th and early 20th centuries he worked extensively in Saskatchewan, as well as in northern Manitoba, Ontario and Alberta. **J.B. TYRRELL**, his party chief in northern Saskatchewan during the 1890s, described him as "positively brilliant." In 1899 Dowling was the first to recognize the mineral potential of the future Flin-Flon/Sherridon mining district, but he is best known for his geological mapping of **COAL** and other mineral resources of the **WESTERN CANADA SEDIMENTARY BASIN**. His 1914 publication on the coalfields of Manitoba, Saskatchewan, Alberta and eastern British Columbia was considered a seminal work. He was also a lead author in the four-volume *Coal Resources of the World*, compiled for the Twelfth International Geological Congress in 1913.

Dowling, active in academic circles, was elected fellow of the Royal Geographical Society in 1912 and president of the Canadian Institute of Mining and Metallurgy in 1918. He served as advisor to several government organizations. Particularly important to western Canada was his 1915 discovery of artesian water in southern Alberta. He died on May 26, 1925.

Marilyn Lewry

FURTHER READING: Allan, J.A. and S.E. Slipper. 1931. "Donaldson Bogart Dowling," *Bulletin of the American Association of Petroleum Geologists* 10: 1123–28; Dowling, D.B. 1914. *Coalfields of Manitoba, Saskatchewan, Alberta and Eastern British Columbia.* Geological Survey of Canada Memoir No. 53.

DOWNEY, RICHARD KEITH (1927–). Keith Downey, known as the "Father of Canola," is a plant breeder who was largely responsible for transforming rapeseed into **CANOLA**. This crop, first grown on the prairies during **WORLD WAR II** for industrial oil, now is a major vegetable oil crop, rivalling wheat as the leading money-maker for Saskatchewan farmers. Born in Saskatoon in 1927, Keith Downey earned a BSc and MSc in Agriculture at the **UNIVERSITY OF SASKATCHEWAN**, and a PhD at Cornell University. In 1952 he was appointed head of alfalfa breeding at Agriculture Canada's Lethbridge Research Station; he was co-developer of the alfalfa variety Beaver. In 1958 Downey transferred to the Saskatoon Research Station to direct the oilseed breeding program. He became the breeder or co-breeder of thirteen rapeseed/canola varieties and five condiment mustard varieties, many of which dominated the Canadian production area for oilseeds. He was a leader in the drive to develop rapeseed varieties with low ratios of potentially harmful erucic acid and glucosinolates; with the transformation, rapeseed was renamed canola. When this objective was achieved, he sought earlier maturing varieties with higher oil content. In recent years he has been involved in developing improved canola varieties through genetic engineering.

In 1963 Downey received the American Oil Chemists' medal for work on the biosynthesis of rapeseed fatty acids. In 1973 the Agricultural Institute of Canada presented him with the Grindley medal for contributions to agriculture. Then, in 1975, he shared the Royal Bank Award with Dr. Baldur Stefansson of the University of Manitoba for their success in rapeseed breeding. Downey was named an officer of the Order of Canada in 1976 and a Fellow of the Royal Society of Canada in 1979; he is also a Fellow of the Agriculture Institute of Canada and an honorary life member of the Canadian Seed Growers Association and of the Saskatchewan Rapeseed Association. He received an honorary Doctor of Science degree from the University of Saskatchewan in 1994 and the Eminent Scientist Award at the Ninth International Rapeseed Congress in 1995. In 1996 he was inducted into the Saskatchewan Agricultural Hall of Fame, and in 2002 into the Canadian Agricultural Hall of Fame. He served a term as president of the Saskatchewan Institute of Agrologists and of the Canadian Society of Agronomy. Downey's expertise has been in demand around the world: in Europe, as well as in Chile, Japan, Hong Kong, Singapore, the Philippines, Algeria, Egypt, Ethiopia, and Pakistan. At present he manages brassica oilseed improvement programs in both China and India.

DRAGONFLIES. Dragonflies belong to the order Odonata, derived from the Greek meaning "toothed-jaw." Odonata as a taxonomic order of class Insecta is divided into two suborders: damselflies (Zygoptera) and dragonflies (Anisoptera). Dragonflies and damselflies are closely related but show some physical differences. Damselflies are much smaller in body size and are more delicately structured; dragonflies are larger, swift-flying insects with voracious appetites. Another distinguishing feature is the difference in which the two groups position their wings when at rest. Dragonflies hold their wings outstretched at right angles to their body while damselflies fold their wings roof-like together, parallel to the body. There are many taxonomic divisions further along until we finally get to the individual species, but on the whole dragonflies and damselflies together are known as *dragonflies*, or in scientific language *Odonata*.

Adult dragonflies are among Saskatchewan's most beautiful insects. Since they fly only during daylight times, the sun accentuates the colours of their bodies and their beautifully patterned wings when they hover or fly. Saskatchewan has a variety of aquatic environments ranging from alkaline lakes, sloughs and rivers, to acidic boreal bogs, fens

DAVID HALSTEAD PHOTO

Black meadowhead (*Sympetrum danae*), a common late summer inhabitant of small marshes and ponds throughout Saskatchewan.

and ponds. While large in extent, the range of wetlands in Saskatchewan is relatively low in diversity; therefore the species diversity of dragonflies is also low: the province has sixty-eight species of Odonata—twenty-two species of damselflies and forty-six species of dragonflies—as compared to approximately 650 species for the rest of North America. However, in this large area of wetlands, Saskatchewan's low diversity is countered by the sheer volume of dragonflies on the wing. These all-important wetlands are where the dragonfly's life begins and ends, and where most of their activities take place.

Dragonflies are strong fliers because the flight muscles are directly attached to four individual net-veined wings. This individual wing attachment is found in only a few groups of insects. Dragonflies have mastered the use of their muscled wings and they are able to hover, fly backwards and go from a full-stop position to rapid speeds almost instantly. Dragonflies have had a very long time to evolve such specialized flying techniques, considering that their fossil records go back over 300 million years to the Carboniferous Period.

Dragonflies begin their life cycle as "nymphs." When hatched, these nymphs are squat, flattened, gill-breathing creatures that crawl in aquatic vegetation, mud or sand. They may stay in this nymph stage from one to five years. When the nymphs are ready to transform into adults, they pick a lily pad, a tall cat-tail plant or other object to crawl out of the water, and then shed their final outer exoskeleton and become fully winged adults. This process takes several hours to complete, and as dragonflies are very prone to dangers at this time, they usually emerge at night or in the early morning.

Once their wings have hardened enough to support flight, they take to the air with their newly found aerial freedom. As they grow, they shed their skin ten to fifteen times; these stages are called "instars." The nymphs feed on all types of aquatic invertebrates including tadpoles and small fish, which may be done by either ambushing or stalking their prey. Even as nymphs, these "swimming drag-

ons" possess deadly equipment for capturing their prey: they are endowed with an extendible lower toothed lip that shoots out, grasps, and then retracts the prey back to awaiting jaws.

Dragonflies are very beneficial to humans as they feed upon mosquitoes, black flies, and other blood-sucking insects usually found at fresh water sites; but these "dragons of the airways" are not discriminatory in their taste and are known to feed on other beneficial insects, including each other. After spending years as mud-crawling nymphs, they may last only days before being eaten by birds or smashed on vehicle windshields; but if they are able to continue on their own, they may last up to six or eight weeks, patrolling over wet lands or hawking over nearby open fields. The males patrol the shores of these waters in anticipation of finding a receptive female to mate with and renew the cycle once again. The females stay away from the water except to oviposit their eggs and to mate, never actively patrolling near aquatic environments. *Gordon Hutchings*

FURTHER READING: Dunkle, Sidney W. 2000. *Dragonflies Through Binoculars: A Field Guide To Dragonflies of North America.* Oxford: Oxford University Press; Parker, Dale. *The Saskatchewan Aquatic Insect Pages.*

DROUGHT. Lying in the rain shadow of the great Rocky Mountains, the province of Saskatchewan is susceptible to frequent and often severe droughts. Especially vulnerable to drought is the semi-arid **PALLISER TRIANGLE** region in the south of the province. In meteorological terms, a drought is an extended period of below-normal precipitation (rain or snow). A drought may last for several months or for many years; it may affect a single municipality or the entire province; and it may occur in any season. Saskatchewan has had many droughts since instrumental climate records began in the 1880s. Southwestern Saskatchewan experienced severe drought for six years between 1917 and 1926. This was soon followed by the "**DUST BOWL**" conditions of 1929 to 1937, which gave rise to one of the most

REGINA LEADER-POST

A drainage ditch west of Osage, Saskatchewan, April 1988.

destructive prairie drought periods of the 20th century. However, the size and intensity of the 1961 drought exceeded even that of the Dirty Thirties. In 1961 the driest parts of the province received only 45% of normal precipitation. Rivaling the desert-like conditions of the 1930s, the late 1980s were also extremely dry and warm: in 1988 southern Saskatchewan received only 50% of normal precipitation and recorded one of its hottest summers ever. The most recent drought period was 2000–03; Saskatchewan recorded its driest year in more than a century in 2001. Scientists claim that 20th century droughts were relatively moderate and short-lived compared to those of previous centuries. Analyses of historical proxy data from tree-rings and lake sediment cores indicate that severe and prolonged drought periods (i.e., up to several decades) occurred on the southern prairies in the early 1600s, late 1700s, and mid-1800s. These so-called super-droughts are characteristic of a dry, continental-type climate, and thus future drought events of similar magnitude are likely to occur in Saskatchewan. The social and economic implications of drought in the province are wide-ranging. Droughts threaten wetlands and waterfowl, diminish municipal water supplies, heighten the risk of forest fires, reduce crop yields, and disrupt livestock production. Due to the importance of agriculture in Saskatchewan, economic losses from drought can be crippling. In 1961—generally considered Saskatchewan's worst drought year—losses to prairie wheat production alone totaled $668 million. The 1986–88 drought also triggered staggering losses (e.g., a $4 billion drop in grain exports) to Canadian agriculture. Saskatchewan farmers have adopted a range of water and soil moisture conservation strategies to combat the effects of drought. During periods of below-normal precipitation, irrigation systems, wells, dugouts, and reservoirs provide farmers with a stable water supply; and shelterbelts, grass barriers, stubble mulching, minimum tillage, and reduced summer fallow help farmers retain valuable soil moisture. *Iain Stewart*

FURTHER READING: Environment Canada. 1992. *Drought: Fact Sheet.* Downsview: Atmospheric Environment Service; Fung, K.I (ed.). 1999. *Atlas of Saskatchewan.* Saskatoon: University of Saskatchewan; Nemanishen, W. 1998. *Drought in the Palliser Triangle.* Regina: Prairie Farm Rehabilitation Administration; Sauchyn, D.J. and A.B. Beaudoin. 1998. "Recent Environmental Change in the Southwestern Canadian Plains," *Canadian Geographer* 42 (4): 337–53.

DRUG PLAN. Since 1945, public drug benefits have been an area of notable Saskatchewan innovation and change. In the post-war period, public drug benefits existed for certain population groups (social welfare recipients), for certain chronic conditions (cancer, mental health, tuberculosis), and for particular types of treatment (acute care). However, the introduction of the service on a universal basis was opposed due to financial considerations and "the extremely difficult problems of cost control." At the national level, three major studies–the report of the Restrictive Trade Practices Commission (1963), the Hall Royal Commission on Health Services (1964), and the final report of the House of Commons Special Committee on Drug Costs and Prices (1967)–presented a common finding with respect to the excessively high costs of prescription drugs. In addition, the Hall Commission highlighted the need for drug benefits within a national health system. These national investigations resulted in the introduction of federal compulsory licensing legislation in 1969. The legislation had the effect of encouraging generic drug products and lowering prescription drug prices.

In Saskatchewan, the report of the Advisory Planning Committee on Medical Care (1961), chaired by **W.P. THOMPSON**, recommended the establishment of a universal medical care insurance plan, but rejected the introduction of a comprehensive drug program due to concerns regarding predicted high and escalating drug costs. Resolutions were, however, endorsed at the Saskatchewan **NEW DEMOCRATIC PARTY** (NDP) annual conventions during the period 1963–69 in support of a prescription drug plan; and the 1971 election program committed the party to the establishment of a drug program upon assuming office. Two provincial studies–a 1966 study of prescription drug costs incurred by Weyburn area residents and a 1973 review of provincial prices and prescribing practices–revealed an uneven distribution of drug use and cost among residents, as well as the existence of "unacceptably high" drug prices.

Against this background, the Saskatchewan Prescription Drug Plan came into effect on September 1, 1975. The Drug Plan provided coverage to all Saskatchewan residents, with consumers paying a maximum of $2 for each drug. Use of a product formulary, bulk purchasing of drug products, and creation of a standard dispensing fee were the other main features of the new provincial program. A 1983 review of the program concluded that "the Plan had, in most instances, met its original objectives," and that any changes in the Plan were not recommended "given the Plan's popularity among the general public, its qualified approval by professionals and its cost advantages in comparison to other drug programs." However, provincial funding in support of the program increased dramatically, with expenditures growing by an average annual rate of 41% over the period 1976 to 1986. On July 1, 1987, the Drug Plan was changed to a deductible arrangement, whereby most consumers paid the full cost of drugs and then submitted claims for an 80%

reimbursement of amounts over an initial deductible level of $125 per family. Significant increases to the deductible level and co-payment arrangements were made in subsequent years. By 2002, Saskatchewan's public drug programs provided benefits almost exclusively to those residents with the most pronounced health needs–individuals with low income, high drug costs, or a combination of these two conditions.

Daniel Hickey

DRUMMOND, THOMAS (1790–1835). Drummond was born in Scotland about 1790, and trained there as a botanist. In 1825, he was appointed assistant naturalist to Dr. **JOHN RICHARDSON** on the Second **FRANKLIN** Arctic Land Expedition. Drummond was at Cumberland House, June 27 to August 20, 1825; at Carlton, August 29 to September 1; and left present-day Saskatchewan about September 9 to spend a year and a half in the Rocky Mountains collecting specimens near the present site of Jasper, Alberta.

Drummond returned in the spring of 1827, entered Saskatchewan in the last week of March, and collected about 103 bird specimens at Carlton between April 5 and July 15. These included the world's first described and illustrated specimen, and the first-ever nest, of Swainson's hawk; the first specimens of the spotted towhee on May 19 and July 1, 1827; and the first nest (with six eggs) and first specimen of the plains subspecies of the loggerhead shrike in June. Finally, on July 18, when he was about fifty miles upstream from Cumberland House (where he stayed until August 8), he collected the first specimen of Forster's tern.

Drummond subsequently collected plants in the United States, especially Texas, from 1831 to 1834. He died in Havana, Cuba, in early March 1835.

C. Stuart Houston

DUCK FAMILY. The cosmopolitan family Anatidae of approximately 154 species is varied, but its members usually have large heads with flattened bills, short tails, and legs with the three forward-pointing toes webbed together. They occupy a variety of aquatic habitats. Saskatchewan has records of thirty-eight species (*see* Table DS-1), which fall into three groups: geese are broad-billed grazers with both sexes of similar plumage; swans are large white, long-necked browsers on underwater vegetation; and ducks are smaller, water-feeding birds in which the sexes have dissimilar plumage (sexual dichromatism). They are often seen in large numbers during migration, when their calls can be heard throughout the day and night. All species migrate, although there are individuals that overwinter on open water.

The only goose which breeds in the province is the Canada goose. It has gone from a species limited to nesting on larger water bodies to a very com-

COURTESY OF THE ROYAL SASKATCHEWAN MUSEUM

Northern shoveler pair.

mon bird of the sloughs and town ponds throughout the southern half; it is less common in the north. There are three separate races in the province: the large prairie race is the one which has adapted very well to human habitats and which regularly overwinters on open water in the cities; a medium-sized race nests in the north; while the small Arctic race is a transient. The other geese are regular and fairly common transients (greater white-fronted and snow geese) or uncommon transients (Ross' goose, brant).

The tundra swan is a common transient to and from its breeding grounds in the Arctic tundra. The larger trumpeter swan still breeds in the **CYPRESS HILLS** and Greenwater Lake. This once-widespread bird was nearly extinguished by hunting for feathers and sport in the late 19th century, but now has several successful populations in North America.

There are eleven genera of ducks. Their size ranges from the small ruddy duck and bufflehead to the large canvasback. Their bills reflect their food habits: from the deep-based bill of the canvasback, which feeds on the tubers of rooted aquatic plants; through the flattened bill of shovelers, which helps them sift material on the surface; to the serrated-edged, narrow bill of the fishing mergansers. The eleven species of the genus *Anas* include some of the most common ducks which nest in the province, particularly in the small sloughs and potholes of the glaciated grasslands. These are the green-winged and blue-winged teal, mallard, Northern pintail, gadwall, Northern shoveler, and American wigeon. The American black duck, cinnamon teal, garganey and Eurasian wigeon are uncommon to rare and occasional in the south. The members of this genus are called "dabblers" because of their habit of sitting on the surface and tipping over, feeding underwater.

The other common genus is *Aythya*, which contains five species; these are "divers," which dive from the surface to feed underwater. The Roman-nosed canvasback and the smaller redhead are fairly common prairie nesters, although their populations have been reduced recently with drainage of the wetlands. The ring-necked duck and lesser scaup nest in the boreal regions as well as the prairies, although they are more common in migration in

Table DS-1. Ducks in Saskatchewan

Common name	Scientific name	Distribution	Abundance
Greater white-fronted goose	Anser albifrons	Transient	Common
Snow goose	Chen caerulescens	Transient	Very common
Ross' goose	Chen rossii	Transient - west	Uncommon
Canada goose	Branta canadensis	Province wide	Very common
Brant	Branta bernicla	Transient	Rare, irregular
Trumpeter swan	Cygnus buccinator	Cypress Hills	Very rare
Tundra swan	Cygnus columbianus	Transient	Common
Wood duck	Aix sponsa	Southeast - rivers	Rare
Gadwall	Anas strepera	Prairie nester	Common
Eurasian wigeon	Anas penelope		Straggler
American wigeon	Anas americana	Grasslands; parklands	
American black duck	Anas rubripes	Southern half	Uncommon
Mallard	Anas platyrhynchos	Province wide	Very common
Blue-winged teal	Anas discors	Province wide	Common on prairies
Cinnamon teal	Anas cyanoptera	Southern half	Uncommon; local
Northern shoveler	Anas clypeata	Southern half	Common
Northern pintail	Anas acuta	Province wide	Common to uncommon
Garganey	Anas querquedula		Rare straggler
Green-winged teal	Anas crecca	Parklands; boreal	Common
Canvasback	Aythya valisineria	Southern half; deep water	Common to uncommon
Redhead	Aythya americana	Southern half; deep water	Common to uncommon
Ring-necked duck	Aythya collaris	Boreal regions nester	Locally common
Greater scaup	Aythya marila	Transient	Uncommon
Lesser scaup	Aythya affinis	Boreal nester	Locally common
King eider	Somateria spectabilis		Rare straggler
Common eider	Somateria mollissima		Rare straggler
Harlequin duck	Histrionicus histrionicus		Uncommon straggler
Surf scoter	Melanitta perspicillata	Northern nester; transient	Uncommon
White-winged scoter	Melanitta fusca	Province-wide	Uncommon
Black scoter	Melanitta nigra	Scattered	Rare
Long-tailed duck	Clangula hyemalis	Province-wide	Rare visitant
Bufflehead	Bucephala albeola	Province-wide	Common to uncommon
Common goldeneye	Bucephala clangula	Province-wide	Common
Barrow's goldeneye	Bucephala islandica	Southern half	Rare; regular
Hooded merganser	Lophodytes cucullatus	Mainly in wooded south	Uncommon; local
Common merganser	Mergus merganser	Province-wide	Can be fairly common
Red-breasted merganser	Mergus serrator	Province-wide	Can be locally common
Ruddy duck	Oxyura jamaicensis	Parklands nester	Common

the south than as nesters. The greater scaup is an uncommon transient, with a few breeding records in the northern boreal forest. Several other species are common nesters. The little white-faced, blue-billed ruddy duck, with its tail cocked up during its courtship, is common on prairie potholes and permanent sloughs. The common merganser, bufflehead and common goldeneye are common boreal lake nesters and common transients further south. Others, such as the wood duck, surf scoter, white-winged scoter, hooded merganser, and red-breasted merganser are uncommon nesters in the deeper lakes and marshes of the parklands and boreal forests. The remaining species are transient or rare visitants. *Diane Secoy*

DUCK LAKE, town, pop 624, located 88 km NE of Saskatoon and 44 km SW of Prince Albert at the junction of Hwys 11 and 212. The Beardy's and Okemasis First Nation lands and the **NORTH SASKATCHEWAN RIVER** are located to the west of the community; the **SOUTH SASKATCHEWAN RIVER** lies to the east. To the north of Duck Lake is the vast wilderness of the Nisbet Provincial Forest. The name of the town is taken from a body of water immediately southwest of the community, which was long known to the indigenous population of the area as a significant stopping place for migratory waterfowl. The community of Duck Lake is situated in a region of historic importance: within a short drive from the town is the Batoche National Historic Site, the Battle of Fish Creek National Historic Site, the historic site of the Battle of Duck Lake, Fort Carlton Provincial Historic Park, Our Lady of Lourdes Shrine at St. Laurent, and the Seager Wheeler Farm National Historic Site. Within the town are the 1890s NWMP jailhouse in which **ALMIGHTY VOICE** was imprisoned, an 1890s Anglican church, and a 1914 school, which was one of only two Protestant separate schools in Saskatchewan. All three of these buildings have been designated heritage properties. The **CARLTON TRAIL** passed by Duck Lake, and Red River **MÉTIS** established temporary camps in the area, from which to pursue the **BISON** as the herds moved further westward. In 1870, following the Red River Rebellion, there was an influx of Métis settlers to the Duck Lake area, and hence the beginning of a permanent settlement. Over the ensuing decades, not only was Duck Lake at the centre of events at the beginning of the **NORTH-WEST RESISTANCE**, it was also a hub of a burgeoning pioneer society. Substantial numbers of French settlers were among those who came to the area. The railway to Prince Albert was completed in 1890, and Duck Lake became a point of disembarkation for many pioneers venturing out into the prairie. Today, tourism focusing upon the history of the First Nations, Métis, and pioneer societies of the area has developed into a major industry for the town; the Duck Lake

Regional Interpretive Centre, opened in 1992, now draws several thousand visitors a year. The town also has eleven large and colourful outdoor murals depicting the history of the region. An additional community attraction is the gallery of a notable Saskatchewan artist, Glen Scrimshaw. Annual events include a three-day powwow, held in late August, and a rodeo hosted by the Duck Lake Métis Society. Back-to-Batoche Days and two pilgrimages to the St. Laurent Shrine draw each summer thousands of people.

David McLennan

DUCK LAKE, BATTLE OF. On March 26, 1885, the opening engagement of the **NORTH-WEST RESISTANCE** began west of the settlement of Duck Lake on the Carlton Trail. Dissatisfaction and militancy among the area's **MÉTIS** and **CREE** had been growing since the return of **LOUIS RIEL** from his Montana exile in July 1884. North-West Mounted Police (NWMP) Superintendent **LEIF CROZIER** had been monitoring the situation from his post at Battleford. In early 1885, he urged Ottawa to come to terms with Riel and the Métis, but the government of Sir John A. Macdonald ignored his request. As the predicament intensified, Crozier moved with about twenty-five men from Battleford to Fort Carlton, which was nearer to Riel's base of operations at **BATOCHE**. On March 13, Crozier warned Lieutenant-Governor **EDGAR DEWDNEY** about the likelihood of a Métis rebellion. Five days later **GABRIEL DUMONT**, Riel's military commander, learned that a group of mounted policemen intended to arrest him and Riel. Accompanied by sixty to seventy supporters, both men responded by ransacking two stores, confiscating arms and ammunition, and seizing two prisoners near Batoche. On March 19, Riel proclaimed his provisional government and appointed his "exovedate" or council of fifteen men, including Dumont.

Needing supplies for his troops, Dumont ransacked a store at Duck Lake on March 25 and prepared his defences against the expected NWMP attack from Fort Carlton. Early the next morning, Crozier sent Sergeant Alfred Stewart and a small party of police and volunteers to seize the goods and arms at the Duck Lake store. Stewart's force encountered Dumont and his men on the **CARLTON TRAIL**. A noisy confrontation ensued, and the police retreated. Although reinforcements were approaching, Crozier impetuously led a force of 100 mounted police and special constables out of Fort Carlton, where they confronted Dumont and 300 Métis on the Carlton Trail. A Cree emissary and a police interpreter scuffled during a brief parley, setting off gunfire and the first battle of the rebellion. Although the battle of Duck Lake lasted only thirty minutes, Crozier's force suffered severe casualties: twelve were killed and eleven were wounded, as compared to the Métis who lost only five men. The police and volunteers

might have been annihilated had Dumont not suffered a head wound that prevented him from continuing to command his men; in fact, Riel prevented the slaughter of the government forces by ordering the fighting to stop.

Holden Stoffel

FURTHER READING: Flanagan, T. 1999. *Riel and the Rebellion: 1885 Reconsidered*. Toronto: University of Toronto Press; Klancher, D.J. 1999. *The North-West Mounted Police and the North-West Rebellion*. Kamloops, BC: Goss Publications; Morton, D. 1972. *The Last War Drum: The North West Campaign of 1885*. Toronto: Hakkert; Woodcock, G. 2003. *Gabriel Dumont: The Métis Chief and His Lost World*. Peterborough, Ontario: Broadview Press.

DUCK MOUNTAIN (51°38'N, 101°38'W; Map sheet 62 N/12). Duck Mountain is located in east-central Saskatchewan, straddling the Manitoba border about 25 km east of Kamsack. It is an upland region, rising 240 m above the surrounding plain. Only one-fifth is located in Saskatchewan; the rest is in Manitoba. It is one of several Saskatchewan uplands (Pasquia Hills, Porcupine Hills) that form part of the Manitoba escarpment, developed from eroded Cretaceous rocks, dipping gently to the southwest. The landscape is characterized by rolling topography formed during glacial deposition under stagnant, melting ice. Ecologically, Duck Mountain represents a southern extension of the boreal forest: white spruce, aspen and birch grow, but there are also boggy areas along creeks, and pockets of native grassland on drier, south-facing slopes. More than 180 bird species (e.g., bald eagles, grouse, woodpeckers) and 35 animal species (e.g., moose, fox,

mink) have been recorded–many normally found in the boreal forests to the north. Developed for timber in the early part of the 20th century, much of the present-day aspen forest is over ninety years old. The centre portion of the upland includes Duck Mountain Provincial Park, which covers some 26,000 ha and offers a variety of recreational services for both summer and winter visitors.

Marilyn Lewry

DUMONT, GABRIEL (1837–1906). Gabriel Dumont–the name conjures up a host of images: the diminutive but courageous *chef métis* who led his people in armed struggle against the Dominion of Canada; the 19th-century Che Guevara passionately concerned with his people's self-governance; the quintessential *homme de prairie* who lived freely as a **BISON** hunter and entrepreneur; and the humanitarian who shared his bounty with the less fortunate. Gabriel Dumont was a man of action, whose many admirable qualities, including his selflessness, courage, sense of duty and love of his people, have inspired generations of **MÉTIS**.

Despite being so lionized, little is known of Gabriel Dumont prior to the 1870s. He was born in December 1837 in St. Boniface, Red River Settlement, the third child of Isadore Dumont and Louise Laframboise. Alongside other Métis from St. François-Xavier, Red River, Dumont participated in the bison hunt in present-day North Dakota for the first time in 1851; in time, the boy who embraced this activity with so much gusto would become an excellent buffalo hunter. Another event happened in 1851 that would profoundly impact upon young Dumont's psyche: on July 13–14, he and 300 other

RON GARNETT—AIRSCAPES
Duck Mountain Provincial Park.

SASKATCHEWAN ARCHIVES BOARD R-A6277

Gabriel Dumont.

Métis decisively defeated, through disciplined marks-manship and the use of barricaded rifle pits, a much larger party of Yankton Dakota at the Battle of Grand Coteau. The ease of the Métis victory, with only one fatality, made a huge impression upon Dumont; however, when he used the same defensive rifle pit system in 1885, he would be less successful.

Dumont's life as a young adult was typical of other Métis. In 1858, he married Madeleine—daughter of Jean-Baptiste Wilke, a Métis bison hunt leader and trader—at St. Joseph (Walhalla), in present-day North Dakota. They had a warm, loving relationship, although they had no children of their own. The couple's early years were spent on the hunt, constantly moving between the **NORTH SASKATCHEWAN RIVER** and the rich bison-hunting grounds of the Dakotas. By the 1860s, the great herds of bison which provided many Métis with their livelihood were rapidly dwindling. Seeking new economic opportunities, Dumont operated a ferry service at "Gabriel's Crossing" and owned a general store. Dumont had become the leader of several hundred Métis living in and around St-Laurent de Grandin, in what is now central Saskatchewan. The Métis community, which was steadily being augmented by émigrés from Manitoba, elected him Chief of the Hunt in the 1860s, and President of the St. Laurent Council in 1873. Dumont presided over the Council until 1878, when the North-West Mounted Police (NWMP) disbanded it after it attempted to levy a fine against those Métis who contravened the conservation measures of the Law of the Hunt.

Gabriel Dumont's role as the Métis' military leader during the 1885 Resistance is where he is best remembered. Under his leadership, throughout the 1870s and 1880s, the **BATOCHE** area Métis anxiously sought redress from the federal government, particularly regarding their land tenure. However, being unlettered and uncomfortable with Euro-Canadian politics, Dumont knew his limitations: therefore he, Michel Dumas, and Alexander Isbister brought **LOUIS RIEL** back to Canada from Montana in order to negotiate with the federal government. Riel then became the undisputed political leader, and Dumont the military commander. However, once the resistance broke out, Dumont knew that his force of 100 to 300 men could not defeat the Dominion's larger, better-equipped army, backed ultimately by the might of the British Empire. Despite successfully employing guerrilla tactics and superior marksmanship at Duck Lake against the NWMP and Prince Albert Volunteers on March 26, and at Fish Creek on April 24 against General **MIDDLETON**'s forces, the Métis resistance was doomed. On May 9–12, the Métis fought an entrenched battle at Batoche against a larger, well-armed force. Tired and out of ammunition, the Métis succumbed to a swift charge by Canadian volunteers. Thus ended Gabriel Dumont's role as military leader.

After 1885, Dumont lived a varied existence: as a political exile in the United States, a Wild West Show performer, a political speaker in French-Canadian nationalist circles (where his tenure was brief), and a raconteur of the events of 1885 (which he dictated in January 1889). He was also a farmer—he received land-scrip in 1893—and a hunter and trapper. Madeleine had died of tuberculosis in 1886; Gabriel Dumont died suddenly on May 19, 1906 at Bellevue, Saskatchewan, probably of a heart attack.

Darren R. Préfontaine,

FURTHER READING: Barnholden, M. 1993. *Gabriel Dumont Speaks.* Vancouver: Talon Books; Stanley, G.F.G. 1949. "Gabriel Dumont's Account of the North West Rebellion, 1885," *Canadian Historical Review* 30 (3): 249–69; Woodcock, G. and J.R. Miller (eds.). 2003. *Gabriel Dumont.* Peterborough, ON: Broadview Press.

DUMONT, MADELEINE (1840–86). Madeleine Dumont (*née* Wilkie) was a prominent Métisse, and wife of **GABRIEL DUMONT**, a leader in the resistance of 1885. Born in 1840 in Pembina, Dakota Territory, she was the daughter of Isabella Azure and Jean-Baptiste Wilkie, a buffalo hunt leader and trader. She married Gabriel Dumont in 1858; they adopted two children. Theirs was a close relationship, and evidence suggests that Dumont greatly respected her.

They spent their early years on the prairies moving between the **NORTH SASKATCHEWAN RIVER** and the Dakotas. On several occasions Madeleine Dumont was believed to have traveled alone from

BATOCHE to Winnipeg, selling her husband's furs. By 1872, they settled in the Batoche-St. Laurent area, where her husband ran "Gabriel's Crossing," a ferry service across the North Saskatchewan River. Hospitable and compassionate, she was an educator to the community's children.

With the outbreak of resistance in 1885, Dumont, like other Métisses, fled from home, camped in tents and makeshift dugouts, nursed the sick and wounded, cared for the children and elderly, and distributed to the men whatever meager rations and supplies were available. Following 1885, she sought refuge with Dumont's father, Isadore, who lived in the Batoche area. Her husband sought refuge in the United States. After Isadore's death, she joined her husband in Montana but died in October 1886 at Lewistown, from tuberculosis and from complications following a fall from a horse and buggy.

Cheryl Troupe

DUMONT TECHNICAL INSTITUTE. The Dumont Technical Institute (DTI), the **GABRIEL DUMONT INSTITUTE** (GDI)'s largest program, began operations in 1992 in order to serve the basic education, upgrading, technical, and vocational training needs of Saskatchewan's **MÉTIS**. DTI is affiliated with the **SASKATCHEWAN INSTITUTE OF APPLIED SCIENCE AND TECHNOLOGY** (SIAST), and delivers programs in partnership with the Métis Employment and Training of Saskatchewan Inc., Human Resources Development Canada (through the "PATHWAYS" program), Saskatchewan's Provincial Training Allowance program, the **SASKATCHEWAN INDIAN INSTITUTE OF TECHNOLOGIES**, and the province's regional colleges. DTI's administration is based in Saskatoon, but its programming is province-wide. DTI's origins can be traced back to 1983 with the creation of the Saskatchewan Training for Employment Program or STEP, which was a partnership between GDI, Employment and Immigration Canada, and the provincial Department of Advanced Education and Manpower. Through STEP, GDI offered SIAST-accredited human resource development, early childhood development, business administration, electronics, and mechanics programs, with counseling and Native Studies components. In 1987, GDI and SIAST signed an agreement creating the Native Services Branch, which provided counseling services to SIAST's Aboriginal students. Through the late 1980s and early 1990s, the Native Services Branch delivered a variety of courses tailored to meet the socioeconomic and cultural needs of the province's Aboriginal population. However, by the early 1990s the increasing demand for basic education as well as vocational and skills training delivery within the Métis community necessitated the creation of an independent Métis technical institution. As a result DTI signed in 1994 a formal affiliation agreement with SIAST. *Darren R. Préfontaine*

ROY ANTAL/REGINA LEADER-POST

Joan Duncan, April 1985.

DUNCAN, JOAN HEATHER (1941–). Joan
Duncan (*née* Tratch), along with Patricia Smith,
were the first female Cabinet Ministers appointed in
Saskatchewan history. Born October 30, 1941, in
Cudworth, Duncan was educated at the UNIVERSITY
OF SASKATCHEWAN. Before entering politics she
owned and operated a drug store in Maple Creek. In
1978, Duncan was elected for the Progressive Conservatives in Maple Creek. Duncan soon took a
prominent role as the only woman elected to the
Legislature that term. She was a key member of the
Progressive Conservative revitalization and a strong
supporter of GRANT DEVINE's campaign for party
leader. Easily re-elected in the Conservative sweep of
1982, Duncan was appointed to Devine's first
Cabinet as Minister of Government Services. She
held a variety of Cabinet positions during her term
and spearheaded several initiatives and programs.
As Minister responsible for Northern Saskatchewan,
she shaped the Devine government's policy on the
region and oversaw the construction of the La
Loche-Fort McMurray road. While Tourism Minister,
the government invested significantly in developing
the industry through local initiatives and by building
a tourist infrastructure throughout the province. In
1989, Duncan was dropped from Cabinet and did
not contest the 1991 election.   *Brett Quiring*

DUNDURN, town, pop 596, located a 20-minute
drive S of Saskatoon on Hwy 11. Canadian Forces
Detachment Dundurn occupies approximately 902
km just to the west and northwest of the town.
While there were a few pioneering ranchers in the
region in the 1880s, the origins of the town date to
1902. Much credit for the founding of Dundurn is
given to Emil Julius Meilicke and his sons, German
immigrants from Minnesota. Meilicke was an entrepreneur who had served in the state senate; he was
successful in inducing a number of his fellow
Americans to settle in the Dundurn area. The
Meilickes established a lumber and machinery busi-

ness at Dundurn, and built a number of homes, four
of which are still standing. By 1903, settlers were
arriving in the Dundurn district in droves. Adding to
the German component were people of British origins–both from eastern Canada and overseas–as
well as a few BARR COLONISTS, who abandoned that
group in Saskatoon to come to the Dundurn area. In
1924, Mennonites would also arrive. Dundurn developed largely as an agricultural community; however-
er, as the military base developed (it has origins dating to 1927), many residents found employment
there. Today, many of its facilities and programs are
available to the citizens of the town. In recent
decades, Dundurn has also become home to a number of people who commute to work in Saskatoon.
Three buildings in Dundurn–the Northern Bank
building built in 1906, the Moravian Brethren
Church built in 1910, and the former school built in
1916–have all been designated heritage properties.
David McLennan

DUNNING, CHARLES AVERY (1885–1958).
Charles Dunning was born July 31, 1885, in
Leicestershire, England. He came to Canada to farm
in 1902 when he was 16, penniless, with little formal education, and no knowledge of agriculture. He
spent a year working as a farm labourer around
Yorkton before establishing a homestead near
Beaverdale and eventually formed a farming partnership with his father. He married Ada Rowlatt in
1913 and they had two children.

Dunning was disillusioned with the treatment
of farmers and became involved with the Territorial
Grain Growers Association, and later with the
Saskatchewan Grain Growers Association (SGGA)

local. A natural speaker, Dunning was elected district director at the 1910 SGGA convention in Prince
Albert and vice-president in 1911. He was charged
with investigating the country elevator system in
Saskatchewan and different grain-handling options
to remedy faults in the current system. His report led
to the establishment of the Saskatchewan Co-operative Elevator Company. Dunning was appointed to
the board of directors of the co-op and was selected
its first general manager. Within four years the co-
op became the largest grain-handling company in
the world. By 1916, the co-op had built 230 elevators
and handled over 28 million bushels of various
crops. During this time Dunning served on two
Royal Commissions dealing with Saskatchewan agriculture. The Grain Market Commission had little
lasting influence but the Agricultural Credit
Commission eventually led to government experiments in farm credit during Dunning's later political
career.

In 1916 Premier WALTER SCOTT was suffering
from ill health and his government was under siege
in a corruption scandal. Scott resigned and Regina
MP WILLIAM MARTIN took over as Premier. He asked
Dunning to come into government as Provincial
Treasurer for his business expertise and to bolster
the Liberal Party's ties to the farm movement.
Dunning won a by-election in the constituency of
Kinistino by acclamation. In 1919, he was given
added responsibility for the Department of
Agriculture and he expanded the duties and responsibilities of the Labour Bureau. He used the bureau,
created in 1911, to expand Saskatchewan's resource
base. Dunning promoted the first commercial
extraction of SODIUM SULFATE reserves, established

SASKATCHEWAN ARCHIVES BOARD R-B29

During a trip to Great Britain in 1924, Charles Dunning visited the foundry where he had worked as a boy before
coming to Canada in 1902.

the first experimental **COAL** plant near Estevan, and undertook the first extensive prospecting for mineral resources in northern Saskatchewan.

The Saskatchewan Liberals officially severed ties with the unpopular federal party to avoid the creation of a farmers' party in Saskatchewan. Premier Martin later openly supported federal Liberal candidates in the 1921 federal election, upsetting many in the farmers' movement. A senior Minister resigned and with the SGGA openly discussing the option of forming a third party, Martin's authority was undermined and he resigned. The Liberals chose Dunning as Premier to reduce agrarian unrest. Dunning met with the SGGA directly to convince them that he still represented farmers and was not Prime Minister **MACKENZIE KING**'s pawn. A series of provincial by-elections resulted in Liberal victories over independent progressive candidates. In 1924 the SGGA rescinded their call for a new farmers' party and the Liberals won the 1925 election. As the federal **PROGRESSIVE PARTY** began to wane, Dunning became more actively involved in federal politics and was eventually able to re-establish formal ties between the provincial and federal levels of the **LIBERAL PARTY**.

As Premier, Dunning's main concern was the falling price of **WHEAT** due to the post-war depression. He supported farmers in their opposition to the abolishment of the Canadian Wheat Board by the federal government and worked for its reestablishment. Dunning tentatively supported the idea of voluntary pooling. After a rough start, the **SASKATCHEWAN WHEAT POOL** was established in 1924. The Wheat Pool then sought to buy the Saskatchewan Co-operative Elevator Company, a move that was supported by Dunning, who passed legislation allowing the sale to take place. This proved to be his last act as Premier.

Dunning was invited to become Saskatchewan's representative in the federal Cabinet and won a by-election in Regina in March 1926. The successive Liberal and Conservative minority governments fell and in September 1926 Dunning was re-elected in the general election. Dunning was appointed Minister of Railways and Canals in the Liberal majority government. He was instrumental in the construction of the Hudson's Bay Railway with Churchill as its terminus. In 1929, he was promoted to Minister of Finance until the Liberal defeat in 1930. Dunning suffered a personal defeat in Regina.

In 1930 Dunning returned to the business world until Prime Minster King pressured him to return to government when the Conservatives lost the 1935 election. The MP for Queen's County, PEI resigned, allowing Dunning easy access to the House of Commons. Dunning reassumed his post as Minister of Finance. In 1938, he suffered a heart attack; although his actions were severely limited, he struggled to continue in his post, but finally resigned in July 1939. He went to England to recuperate but returned to Canada just before **WORLD WAR II**.

Dunning was appointed chair of the National War Loans Committee, which raised money for the war effort. He also was named chair of Allied Supplies Limited, the company established by the federal government to administer and bolster production of munitions and explosives for the British government. He was appointed chancellor of Queen's University and continued at this post until his death. After the war Dunning continued his connection with the business community, serving on the board of directors of several companies. Although he had interests in several Saskatchewan farms, Dunning retired to Montreal. He usually returned to Regina once a year until his death. He died October 1, 1958.   *Brett Quiring*

FURTHER READING: Brennan, J.W. 1968. "The Public Career of C. A. Dunning in Saskatchewan." M.A. thesis, University of Saskatchewan; —. 1969. "C.A. Dunning and the Challenge of The Progressives: 1922–1925," *Saskatchewan History* (Winter): 1–12; Smith, David E. 1975. *Prairie Liberalism: The Liberal Party in Saskatchewan 1905–1971.* Toronto: University of Toronto Press.

DUPERREAULT, MARIE-ANNE (1885–1976). Despite her heavy obligations as farm wife and mother of twelve, Marie-Anne Duperreault was able to chronicle the main events of life on a farm in the **PALLISER TRIANGLE** between 1910 and 1940. Born Marie-Anne Boucher on September 25, 1885, in the Laurentian village of St. Damien de Brandon, she was a school teacher when she married Joseph Duperreault in 1904. The couple settled on a home-

SASKATCHEWAN ARCHIVES BOARD R-A24117

Joseph Duperreault and Marie-Anne Duperreault ("Perrette"), at their first home, Willow Bunch district, 1924–25.

stead near Willow Bunch in 1907. She became local correspondent for Saskatchewan's French-language newspaper, *Le Patriote de l'Ouest*, soon after it was launched in 1910, and chose the pseudonym "Perrette" from one of La Fontaine's fables. Despite often harsh living conditions, the naturally optimistic Duperreault described, with style and verve, various aspects of farm and community life, and celebrated the beauty of the land. She dealt with education, religion and politics, as well as with the threat faced by the French minority in Saskatchewan. She served as women's page editor, always without pay, until the *Patriote* was moved to Manitoba in 1941. Many of her articles were assembled in a book published in 1969. She was also active in local French-language literary, drama, choral, and women's groups. After the death of her husband in 1971, she retired to Vancouver and died there on January 6, 1976.   *Richard Lapointe*

FURTHER READING: Lapointe, Richard. 1988. "Marie-Anne Duperreault." Pp. 145–48 in *100 noms: Petit dictionnaire biographique des Franco-Canadiens de la Saskatchewan*. Regina: Société historique.

DUST BOWL. The name given to the Great Plains of North America, including the southern prairies of Canada, that suffered ecological devastation throughout the 1930s. High prices for wheat and the needs associated with **WORLD WAR I** caused farmers to cultivate land formerly used only for grazing. The soil, disturbed by plows and parched by drought, blew away in immense clouds of dust. (*See also* **GREAT DEPRESSION**)   *Holden Stoffel*

DUST STORMS. Dust storms are atmospheric disturbances with moderate to strong winds, blowing soil particles, and visibility reduced to one kilometre or less at eye level. Dust storms are serious climatic hazards for Saskatchewan, resulting in environmental, health and economic costs. These include soil erosion, vegetation damage, respiratory problems, and fatalities. The semi-arid to sub-humid climate, topography, vegetation, soil conditions and land use in agricultural Saskatchewan provide an ideal setting for dust storms. Dust storms begin after a period of dry weather, when the wind speed is greater than the threshold value needed to lift and transport vulnerable soil particles, or when moving particles bombard an area. Land management practices such as cultivation and over-grazing increase dust storm risk because they loosen soil particles and reduce the protective vegetation cover.

Spring, especially April, is the time of peak dust storm occurrence. A weak secondary peak may occur during August. This spring maximum likely results from the combination of peak wind speed and lack of vegetative cover. Canada's dust storm bowl is located in south-central Saskatchewan. This area has

COURTNEY MILNE PHOTO
Dust storm.

the second highest annual dust storm frequency in North America. An improved understanding of the nature of the dust storm hazard is crucial to improving the sustainability of the prairie ecosystem.

E.E. Wheaton

FURTHER READING: Wheaton, E. and A Chakravarti. 1990. "Dust Storms in the Canadian Prairies," *International Journal of Climatology* 10: 829–37; World Meteorological Organization (WMO). 1983. *Meteorological Aspects of Certain Processes Affecting Soil Degradation–Especially Erosion, Technical Note No. 178.* Geneva: Secretariat of the WMO.

DUTCH SETTLEMENTS. In 2001, 32,300 residents of Saskatchewan claimed to be of Dutch origin: 6,445 completely and 25,860 partially. Close to a million Canadians are entirely or partially of Dutch descent. However, in Saskatchewan far fewer people have ever claimed to be Dutch-speaking than to be of Dutch origin, at least partly due to the fact that many Mennonites, who traditionally have spoken a German dialect, have claimed Dutch origin (Menno Simons, the progenitor of the Mennonite faith, lived in the Netherlands). In 2001, only 1,930 Saskatchewan residents recognized Dutch as their mother tongue. In 1892–93, Frisian farmers arrived in Winnipeg, the vanguard of a larger group of Dutch immigrants assisted by the Christian Emigration Society to homestead around Yorkton, although only a small number actually made it to their destination—most remaining in Manitoba. By 1904 Dutch immigrants, primarily from Iowa and Montana but including some directly from the Netherlands, settled in southern Alberta around Granum, Nobleford, and Monarch (where their settlement was named Nieuw Nyverdal after their place of origin in Overyssel). Subsequently a Dutch Catholic settlement developed around Strathmore,

also in southern Alberta, in 1908, and a Dutch Calvinist settlement, Neerlandia, near Barrhead in northern Alberta, in 1912. These successful settlements would encourage further Dutch settlement in all three prairie provinces.

In Saskatchewan, Dutch Americans settled near Moose Jaw in 1908, then in the Cramersburg rural district in the RM of Miry Creek near Abbey in 1910. The first settlers (named De Vries, Veltkamp, Vry, Van der Wall, Leep) were men who lived in tents while building wooden houses and barns, before being joined by their wives and families. The railway arrived in nearby Cabri in 1912, facilitating settlement. However, this settlement started to break up in 1919-23 due to drought, influenza, hard winters, light crop yields, and low grain-buying prices; several families returned to the United States. Meanwhile, Edam, near Turtleford, became a post office in 1908, continued to be settled in 1914-17, and became a bicultural Catholic community shared with French neighbours. Other rural Dutch concentrations emerged around Leoville and Morse, while Dutch immigrants continued to arrive in Saskatoon, where they established a Dutch (now Christian) Reformed congregation which has long been served by Dutch-origin pastors. (*See also* **MENNONITES; MENNONITE SETTLEMENTS**) *Alan Anderson*

FURTHER READING: Ganzevoort, H. 1988. *A Bittersweet Land: The Dutch in Canada, 1890–1980.* Toronto: McClelland and Steward.

DUWORS, MAUREEN (1938-). Maureen DuWors (*née* Rever) has represented Saskatchewan and Canada as a track and field athlete, coach, official, and administrator. Born in Regina on July 21, 1938, she attended Luther High School and held both the Saskatchewan Open and high school all-around track and field titles. DuWors was also the

1955 Canadian champion in the 60-yard and 100-yard events. Throughout her career as a track and field athlete, she held the Canadian record for 50-yard, 60-yard, and 100-yard sprint events and the Canadian Juvenile Long Jump record. Internationally, DuWors competed in the 100-metre, 200-metre, and 4x100 metre relay at the 1956 Melbourne Olympics. She earned bronze medals in the 4x100 metre relay at the Pan American Games, and at the British Empire and Commonwealth Games. DuWors' accomplishments off the track are equally as impressive. She became a respected coach and administrator, and an internationally rated official. She served as an executive member of the Saskatchewan branch of the Athletic Association of Canada and as director of the Saskatoon Track and Field Club. Maureen DuWors was inducted into the **SASKATCHEWAN SPORTS HALL OF FAME** in 1977.

Daria Coneghan and Holden Stoffel

DYCK, LILLIAN EVA (1945-). Lillian Dyck was born in North Battleford in 1945 to an Aboriginal mother and a Chinese father. After earning a PhD from the **UNIVERSITY OF SASKATCHEWAN** in 1981, she became a neurochemist and a professor in the Neuropsychiatry Research Unit. Her research has included the impact upon neurotransmission of antidepressants and antipsychotics, as well as alcohol metabolism in Saskatchewan First Nations and other races. She has been on a research team to develop drugs that may be useful in treating Parkinson's disease, schizophrenia, and Alzheimer's disease. She also writes and speaks about topics such as equity for women and First Nations people in the sciences. Dyck's many awards include the National Aboriginal Achievement Award for Science and Technology (1999) and a Saskatchewan First Nations Women of the Dawn Award for Science and Technology (2000). In March 2005, Lillian Dyck was appointed to the Canadian Senate.

Daria Coneghan

PHOTO COURTESY OF LILLIAN DYCK
Lillian Dyck.

E

EAGLES: *see* **HAWKS AND EAGLES**

EAGLESHAM, ISABELLE (1915–). Isabelle Eaglesham (*née* Hilliar) is a Weyburn-based writer, local historian, community worker, and business-woman. Born in 1915, she married Dr. Fergus Eaglesham in 1939; they had two children. From 1958 to 1978 she wrote a thirty-minute weekly program for CFSL radio that featured children's stories and historical sketches. She has published numerous children's stories and poems. Reflecting her twin loves of writing and local history, she wrote a book about Weyburn and its people entitled *The Night the Cat Froze in the Oven*. Eaglesham has also been active in a broad range of organizations: the Soo Line Historical Museum, the IODE, the SASKATCHEWAN HISTORY AND FOLKLORE SOCIETY, the SASKATCHEWAN WRITERS GUILD, the Schizophrenia Society, and the Saskatchewan LIBERAL PARTY. Her numerous awards include Canada's first Heritage Award in Communications, Saskatchewan Culture and Recreation's Heritage Preservation Award, the Weyburn Chamber of Commerce Golden Spike Award, and a volunteer Award from the Wheatland Souris Regional Recreation Association.

Lisa Dale-Burnett

SASKATCHEWAN ARCHIVES BOARD R-A19106

Isabelle Eaglesham at Fort Livingstone cairn, ca. 1960s.

265

EARLY CHILDHOOD DEVELOPMENT PRO-GRAMS. The early years of a child's life represent a period of intense learning. Babies and preschool children only gradually learn to walk, talk and comprehend language, to feed, clothe and toilet themselves, and to behave appropriately. Early childhood experiences affect learning, behaviour, and health throughout the lifetime. Early childhood programs support healthy child development, provide opportunities for playing and socializing with other children, and ensure that children are ready to learn. Parents may also make use of programs to facilitate adult activities such as employment, education, volunteer participation, or social and recreational activities. Good early childhood programs can improve life outcomes and quality of life for both children and parents.

Saskatchewan has a tradition dating back to the 19th century of public involvement in the care and learning of "school-age" children. Until recently, however, raising preschool children in Saskatchewan was considered the business of parents, with limited public intervention or support. Early childhood programs that did exist were typically run by charities, independent non-profit organizations, or individuals. As the public becomes more aware of the importance of early childhood to school success and life outcomes, public support for early childhood are gradually becoming more extensive and coherent.

Kindergarten is one form of early childhood program that has been available in most communities for many years. Kindergarten is made available through school systems at no cost to parents, and most 5-year-olds are enrolled. Boards of Education also offer early entrance supports to preschool children with disabilities to ensure they will be ready for school along with their age-mates. A system of licensed child care services was introduced in Saskatchewan in 1974, along with a subsidy designed to cover a portion of fees for low-income families. Licensed child care is intended to have both a custodial and developmental aspect. This system represents a relatively small proportion—about 10%—of care and learning services used by parents.

Many publicly funded early childhood programs in Saskatchewan are targeted to children at risk owing to poverty or disability. The Early Childhood Intervention Program (ECIP) helps children at risk of developmental delay. The KidsFirst program provides high-risk families with home visits, early learning opportunities, child care, and other family supports. About 100 prekindergarten programs have been set up in designated "community schools," and the federal government provides similar programs for Aboriginal children, both on and off-reserve.

Preschool programs have become popular among parents of 3- to 5-year-olds. In 2001, more than 40% of all Saskatchewan children in this age group were enrolled in a preschool (sometimes called play school or nursery school) even though these private or non-profit early childhood programs receive no direct public funding. Many parents also take advantage of popular community programs, such as story hours at the public library or swimming lessons. Economists and business leaders are becoming more aware of the importance of early childhood to school success and the successful transitions of children to adulthood and the labour force. Families, communities, and governments continue to work towards sustainable early childhood services that respect parents' needs and choices, and that result in verifiable benefits to young children in Saskatchewan.

Janet Mitchell

EARLY CHILDHOOD EDUCATION. Early childhood education (ECE) in Saskatchewan now includes provincially funded educational programs for children aged 3 to 8 years. At the beginning of the 20th century, however, early childhood schooling was delivered through private kindergarten programs usually located in urban areas such as Regina, where the first early schooling was established. Interested parents operated fee-paying kindergartens while the provincial Department of Education focused on establishing the grade one to twelve system. By the 1950s, a provincial kindergarten curriculum guide was available for sale to private kindergartens. Provincial superintendents made periodic safety checks of these private kindergarten programs, but no program quality standards were in effect.

During the 1960s, the interest in early childhood education grew, with the result that the Department of Education began to fund kindergarten programs in Regina and Moose Jaw public school systems; 1969 brought partial funding to other local boards for these programs. In 1972, the *Report of the Minister's Committee on Kindergarten* provided a plan for publicly funded kindergarten programs throughout the province. The kindergarten program goal was to promote self-actualization, socialization, and a commitment to learning through a variety of individual and group activities. The early childhood program was to be separate from Division One (grades one to three), but articulation for continuous progress through the early school years was paramount. Half-days in urban settings or full-days every other day in rural communities were common attendance patterns. Integrated kindergarten and grade one, two, or three groups reflected the economic realities of rural school divisions.

Saskatchewan recognized that the most important component in an early childhood setting is the teacher: qualified teachers with specialized training in early childhood education were essential in the implementation of kindergartens. Several approaches were introduced. The need to prepare new kindergarten teachers fell to the province's two teacher education programs in the Universities of Regina and Saskatchewan. Each program developed a series of early childhood courses for their four-year programs, and offered summer school courses on both campuses over the ensuing years. The UNIVERSITY OF SASKATCHEWAN eliminated its ECE specialty in the early 1980s.

Summer school bursaries for kindergarten teachers were instituted in 1974 by the Department of Education. The UNIVERSITY OF REGINA offered an Early Childhood Education Institute described as a seminar-work-study experience in early childhood education to teachers in 1974, 1975, and 1976. The Saskatchewan Teachers' Federation provided a one-week course in its annual kindergarten sessions. The Department of Education and some local school divisions also provided consultative services. A review of kindergarten programs in 1981–82 revealed a need to clarify the purpose of the program: educators were interpreting the program either as education for school readiness, or as education for child development. In 1991, a survey assessing program needs identified a continuing confusion about program direction and supports for successful maintenance of the program.

A kindergarten curriculum guide, *Children First*, was developed in 1974, then revised in 1978 and 1994. The most recent curriculum guide emphasizes the provision of a strong foundation from which students can grow to become active participants in lifelong learning. In 1997, Saskatchewan Education introduced a pre-kindergarten program as part of the Community Schools initiative. Pre-kindergarten is a prevention and early intervention program for children who would benefit from early school-based experiences. This holistic education program is intended to nurture 3- and 4-year-old children's socio-emotional, intellectual, and physical development. A handbook based on the kindergarten curriculum, *Better Beginnings, Better Futures: Best Practices Policy and Guidelines for Pre-kindergarten*, provides a conceptual framework that promotes a high-quality early childhood experience. This framework stresses the enhancement of children's positive self-esteem, speech and language development, and communication skills through direct family involvement, community partnerships, and integrated social and health services.

In pre-kindergarten programming, qualified early childhood education teachers partner with teacher assistants who are familiar with the community context to provide a half-time education program for up to sixteen children for twelve hours weekly. Family liaison and education programming complement the children's educational experiences.

To complement the pre-kindergarten focus, the Faculty of Education at the University of Regina instituted an early childhood education section in the Elementary Teacher Education program in 2002. Consisting of ECE courses focused on teaching children between the ages of 3 and 8, this program prepares teachers who are knowledgeable about the importance of appropriate early learning experiences and environments for very young children. In addition, the program offers practicum opportunities in pre-kindergarten classrooms in Community Schools, where these pre-service teachers also participate in family and community activities.

Caroline D. Krentz

FURTHER READING: Kratzmann, A. n.d. *Kindergarten and Early Childhood Education in Western Canada.* OECD. Review of Educational Policies in Canada, Study No. 3; Saskatchewan Education. 1997. *Better Beginnings, Better Futures: Best Practices Policy and Guidelines for Pre-kindergarten in Saskatchewan Community Schools.* Regina: Saskatchewan Education.

EARLY CHILDHOOD EDUCATION TRAINING. The education and training of Saskatchewan people working with children between the ages of birth and 5 years did not begin until the last half of the 20th century. Day care centres and some training of workers began during World War II in more industrialized parts of Canada, but because of the essentially agricultural economy this did not happen in Saskatchewan. Early Childhood Education training in the province became more prominent in the 1960s, with social activists calling for more support for families who needed quality care for their children during the work day. Some private day cares and preschools appeared, mostly funded by parent fees. The Canada Assistance Plan of 1966 made it possible for the provincial government to become financially involved in establishing child-care policy and providing support to address needs. A call for

quality standards in child care by advocacy groups such as Action Child Care led the provincial government in 1980 to initiate the Day Care Review, which looked into issues related to child-care spaces, cost, and quality. Among other findings, the Day Care Review found that day care staff lacked specialized training. Although a 42-hour course had been implemented for day care centre staff under the Day Care Regulations of 1975, it was considered inadequate and a two-year training program was introduced by the Department of Education. An Advisory Board was then formed, and guidelines developed for the Child Care Worker Program.

In September 1980 a team at Kelsey Institute in Saskatoon began to develop the curriculum for the two-year program. Led by Margaret Neil, a modular curriculum was produced. In September 1981, twenty students enrolled in the first Child Care Worker Program. The program was to prepare graduates to work in a variety of early childhood settings, and with this in mind the name was changed in 1983 to Early Childhood Development Program. This program included a one-year certificate and a two-year diploma. Over the next ten years, curriculum development occurred and manuals were prepared for each course. This made it possible for the program to be offered through distance education as well as extension courses. Since 2002, candidates with experience in the early childhood field can, through Prior Learning Assessment and Recognition, challenge courses by demonstrating that they have learned and practiced the content while working with children.

By the 1990s the Early Childhood Development program was offered at Woodland Campus in Prince Albert and Wascana Campus in Regina, as well as at the Kelsey Campus where it was originally developed. This followed the 1986 amalgamation of community colleges to form the **SASKATCHEWAN**

INSTITUTE OF APPLIED SCIENCE AND TECHNOLOGY (SIAST). In 1994, the program changed its name once more, to Early Childhood Education Program. The three programs work closely together, graduating over 100 students each year from their Certificate and Diploma programs. These students are employed in day care centres and homes, preschools, schools, hospitals, and early intervention programs. The SIAST Early Childhood Education program works with Regional Colleges throughout Saskatchewan to deliver the program to a wider rural area, especially in the north. Private colleges have also brokered the SIAST Early Childhood Education Program. Other partners such as the University of Alberta and the University of Victoria have articulation agreements with the SIAST Early Childhood Education Program, which grant SIAST students one or two years of credit towards an Early Childhood or Child Studies degree.

Other programs in Early Childhood Education have evolved within Saskatchewan. Particularly noteworthy is a program partnership between the Meadow Lake Tribal Council and the University of Victoria, which began in 1990; this project suited the needs of First Nation people in the area. Since 1994 the **SASKATCHEWAN INDIAN INSTITUTE OF TECHNOLOGIES** has delivered this program in such places as Pine House Lake, La Ronge, and North Battleford. After finishing the two-year diploma, students may enroll in the third year of the University of Victoria Child and Youth degree; the northern community of Onion Lake has successfully run the complete degree program in partnership with the university in the past few years. *Susanne McElhinney*

EASTEND, town, pop 576, located in the Frenchman River Valley 33 km SW of Shaunavon on Hwy 13. The Eastend area is rich in history and geology, and rife with archaeological and palaeontological sites. In the mid-1880s, as **BISON** populations were being decimated on the eastern plains, the area became an increasingly important hunting ground for the animals, and Indian tribes to the east and west of the territory regularly fought over the essential resource. A **MÉTIS** settlement developed (ca. 1860s) to the north of Eastend, and in the early 1870s the Hudson's Bay Company had a post in the location. The post, however, lasted only a season due to hostilities between the Assiniboine and Blackfoot peoples, and perhaps because of competition from independent traders selling whiskey. Many years later, the site came to be known as Chimney Coulee—the name being derived from the remnants of the stone chimneys that had been built in the Métis homes. In the mid- to late 1870s, the NWMP established a satellite detachment of the newly built Fort Walsh at the site, which they dubbed East End because of its location at the east end of the **CYPRESS HILLS**. When the Mounties moved

PHOTO COURTESY OF NANCY DILL

First graduating class of the Early Childhood Education Diploma program, 1983.

NWMP Post at East End, 1878.

to the vicinity of the present townsite years later, the name endured. The first ranch was established in the area around 1883. A ranch house built at Eastend in 1902, the community's first residence, remains occupied to this day. Huge ranching operations started to give way to homesteaders and crop production, and in 1914 the CPR built the railway through the area; the village of Eastend (East End originally) was incorporated, growing steadily over the next decades. Over the winter of 1951–52, a record amount of snow fell in the area and extremely warm spring temperatures caused the snow to melt within three days, causing the dam above the community to wash out on April 15. The entire valley was flooded and Eastend had to be evacuated. Subsequently, a dike and a new dam were constructed to prevent such an occurrence from happening again. Today, the economy of the town is driven by agriculture, oil and gas, and tourism. Another of the area's natural resources is the white mud clay mined from deposits in the district hills. In the early 1950s, a ceramics course was offered in Eastend with the purpose of stimulating interest in developing a local industry; today, Eastend artisans utilize the resource to produce pottery. Tourism has developed substantially in recent years, following the discovery in 1991 of one of the few *Tyrannosaurus rex* skeletons ever found in the world. Although prehistoric fossils had been unearthed in the region for over a century, the find, made by local school principal Robert Gebhardt, made history and led to the opening of a palaeontological interpretive centre and research station at Eastend. The T-Rex Discovery Centre, opened in May 2000, now hosts several thousand visitors a year. Additional Eastend attractions include the **WALLACE STEGNER** House, the boyhood home of the Pulitzer Prize–winning author best known to Saskatchewan residents for his 1955 book, *Wolf Willow*. Also in Eastend is one of the few observatories open to the public in western Canada. The Wilkinson Memorial Observatory was founded by Jack Wilkinson, a blacksmith who built his own telescopes and hand-ground his own lenses. When he died in 1953, the community took over maintenance of the observatory, which is located on top of one of the valley hills and features an 11-inch (28-cm) Celestron telescope. The museum in Eastend houses additional palaeontological specimens, as well as artifacts and exhibits relating to the town's early history. The Eastend area is also home to writer **SHARON BUTALA**, who became an Officer of the Order of Canada in 2002.   *David McLennan*

EATON INTERNMENT CAMP. Under the provisions of the War Measures Act (1914), 8,579 enemy aliens–nationals of countries at war with Canada–were interned in Canada during **WORLD WAR I** as prisoners of war. The result of a severe economic recession that coincided with the outbreak of the war, widespread indigence became a major factor leading to the internment of immigrants of Ukrainian and other East European nationality from the Austro-Hungarian and German Empires. Sent to prisoner of war camps located in the Canadian hinterland, the civilian internees were used as military conscript labour, working on federal and provincial public work projects as well as for private industry, including railway companies. As the economy expanded and the labour market contracted, internees were gradually released into Canadian society. The scaling back of the internment operations in 1917 led to the dismantling of some camps and the consolidation of others to which a number of the remaining prisoners were relocated.

With the closure of the Morrissey Internment Camp (Fernie, British Columbia) in October 1918, sixty-five internees were relocated to Munson, Alberta on the Goose Lake Railway Line. Quartered in railway cars which served as a base of operations, the internees were put to work repairing and laying new track for six months. However, an outbreak of the 1918 Spanish Influenza and a disastrous train wreck affected the morale among internees and military guard alike, resulting in the relocation of the Munson camp to a hastily constructed camp on the site of the railway siding at Eaton, Saskatchewan. The move on February 25, 1919, did little to placate the inmate population; rather, the growing truculence of the internees, who refused to do any further work on the railroad, an undisciplined military guard anxious to return home from the war, and a successful prison escape prompted authorities to abandon the Eaton siding location for more secure facilities. On March 21, twenty-four days after the facility had been established, the internees were transported by rail to a military installation at Amherst, Nova Scotia. The Eaton Internment Camp was dismantled shortly after that.

One of twenty-six internment facilities created in Canada to accommodate prisoners of war during the period 1914-20, the Eaton Internment Camp was the only facility of its kind in Saskatchewan. Renamed Hawker in 1919, the Eaton siding is located at the junction of Highway 60 and the Canadian National Railway, 4 km southwest of Saskatoon.

Bohdan S. Kordan

FURTHER READING: Kordan, B. 2002. *Enemy Aliens, Prisoners of War: Internment in Canada during the Great War.* Montreal-Kingston: McGill-Queen's University Press.

EATONIA, town, pop 474, located 44 km SW of Kindersley at the junction of Hwys 21 and 44. For decades, Eatonia's slogan has been "the Prairie Oasis," as tree-planting efforts led by the community's first doctor resulted in the early beautification of the town. The first settlers began arriving in the Eatonia district around 1906. With the advent of rail lines through Kindersley to Alsask (in 1910–11) and south of the river to Leader (in 1913), larger numbers of people began to arrive in the region. Settlement was interrupted by **WORLD WAR I**, but resumed through the 1920s. In 1918, as the railway progressed westward from Eston toward the Alberta border, the townsite of Eaton (Eatonia's original name) was established. Businessmen began erecting buildings, and people from the German settlement to the south began relocating to the new community. That same year a weekly newspaper, the *Eatonia Enterprise*, first went to print (it was absorbed by the *Kindersley Clarion* in 1965). In 1920, the village of Eaton was incorporated, its name honouring the family of the Canadian retailers, the T. Eaton Company. The name of the community was changed to Eatonia in 1921 to avoid confusion with the community of Eston, some 50 km to the east. Other than a setback experienced during the 1930s, the village grew steadily, and in 1954 was incorporated as a town. From the late 1950s through to the early 1970s, Eatonia had a population of over 600.

Today, Eatonia is a trading centre for a region whose economy is largely based upon grain farming, ranching and hogs, with some oil production occurring to the northwest. Eatonia's CNR station, built in 1924, is now a heritage property.

David McLennan

ECONOMIC STRUCTURE OF SASKATCH-EWAN COMMUNITIES. The agricultural settlement of Saskatchewan occurred in the context of late 19th-century technology. Railroads were the primary means of intercity and interprovincial movement of goods and people: products destined for distant markets departed by train, and products imported for local consumption arrived by rail. The principal export from Saskatchewan was wheat, which was collected in country elevators that were spaced at approximately ten-mile intervals by the end of the settlement era. The origin of most of Saskatchewan's communities can be traced to the elevators and the businesses, schools, churches and offices that clustered around them. By the end of the settlement era, in the early 1930s, there were over 900 communities in Saskatchewan; they ranged in size from Saskatoon and Regina at 43,000 and 53,000 respectively, down to more than 400 villages with an average population of 50.

Even as the agricultural settlement era was nearing completion, however, technological advances were being made in production, transportation, distribution, and communications systems that would render obsolete the occupational and spatial patterns that were being put into place. Only the **GREAT DEPRESSION** of the 1930s and **WORLD WAR II** postponed the inevitable structural and spatial adjustments that otherwise would have begun just as the settlement phase ended. With the end of World War II, the adoption and implementation of new technologies accelerated during the 1940s and

have continued to the present, with only occasional and temporary interruptions.

In agriculture, the new technologies led to the substitution of machinery for labour and to the consolidation of farms. The farm population has fallen from nearly 600,000 in the mid-1930s, to approximately 125,000 in 2004. At the same time, the number of farms decreased from nearly 150,000 to just over 50,000. The total rural population became smaller as well, falling from approximately 650,000 to 350,000.

As the rural population moved away and primitive roads became all-weather highways, rural communities began a long process of adjustment as well. Rural infrastructure was consolidated into fewer, but larger, facilities in larger communities. Rural businesses either consolidated or closed. Large communities prospered both by capturing virtually all the employment generated in the expanding service-producing industries, as well as through attracting businesses and services which were previously provided from smaller places. As larger communities expanded their offerings of goods and services, rural shopping patterns shifted to focus on these centres, bypassing local rural communities.

By the 1960s, the number of communities with populations of 50 or more numbered approximately

600; over 100 places had expired in the previous 25 years, and 200 had populations of less than 50 in 1961.

The experience of the 598 Saskatchewan communities which had populations of 50 or more in 1961 has been carefully traced over the 40 years from 1961 to 2001. To accomplish this, each community was classified into a functional category based upon the number and type of businesses and public services offered at five different dates. The classifications proceed from the Primary Wholesale-Retail category (PWR), which has included only Saskatoon and Regina, down to the Minimum Convenience Centre (MCC) level, which includes the smallest communities offering a very limited array of commercial and public facilities. Table ESSC-1 provides a summary of the experience of these 598 centres from 1961 through 2001. A process of continuous downward filtering is revealed for communities in the four lower categories between 1961 and 1981. Between 1981 and 2001, communities in the lower three categories have continued to filter downward, while the centres in the upper three classifications have experienced stability in their classifications.

The structure of the trade-centre system as it existed in 2001 is shown in Table ESSC-2, arrayed

Table ESSC-1. Functional Classification, Saskatchewan Centres, 1961–2001

Community Level	1961	1981	1990	1995	2001
Primary Wholesale-Retail	2	2	2	2	2
Secondary Wholesale-Retail	8	8	8	8	8
Complete Shopping Centre	29	22	6	7	8
Partial Shopping Centre	99	30	46	22	6
Full Convenience Centre	189	136	117	59	72
Minimum Convenience Centre	271	400	419	500	502
Total	598	598	598	598	598

Table ESSC-2. Average Number of Businesses, Various Types, Saskatchewan Trade Centres, 2001

Count	502	72	6	8	8	2
Functional Classification	Minimum Convenience	Full Convenience	Partial Shopping	Complete Shopping	Secondary Wholesale-Retail	Primary Wholesale-Retail
Population	168	1,083	2,233	4,364	18,361	187,024
All consumer services	5.65	36.89	101.82	131.70	392.71	3,181.50
All producers	0.97	7.97	17.67	30.03	97.27	994.50
Public Infrastructure						
Clinics[1]	0.01	0.03	0.00	0.13	0.38	1.00
Health Centres[1]	0.06	0.39	0.00	0.00	0.00	0.50
Doctors[2]	0.06	1.51	2.67	7.00	33.5	503.50
Hospital Beds	.14	7.74	20.50	38.50	103.88	742.00
Special Care Beds	1.55	34.83	49.33	93.00	206.88	1,372.50
HS Enrollment	12.78	94.29	186.83	317.00	1,212.25	9,174.00
ES Enrollment	42.44	263.11	487.00	885.75	3,230.13	26,839.00

1 For this variable the presence or absence of the function is measured.
2 Where a doctor is present for one day a week, for example, this is counted as 0.20.

according to the characteristics that define the functional categories. At the top of the system, the PWR centres of Saskatoon and Regina have five to ten times as many consumer services as the next classification, the Secondary Wholesale-Retail category (SWR), which includes centres such as Yorkton, Prince Albert and Swift Current. The PWR centres have an even greater advantage in producer services, producers and public infrastructure: Saskatoon and Regina are major province-serving communities while those centres in the SWR classification are region-serving communities. The eight centres in the Complete Shopping Centre (CSC) category, exemplified by Meadow Lake, Humboldt, Kindersley and Assiniboia, provide an area-serving function, essentially filling in geographical niches between the PWR and the SWR centres.

At the Partial Shopping Centre level (PSC), communities provide a very local service somewhat like the smallest neighbourhood shopping centres in a major urban area. There were six communities in this group in 2001: Maple Creek, Moosomin, Outlook, Rosetown, Shaunavon, and Unity.

The 72 centres in the next lower classification, the Full Convenience Centre category (FCC) provide a limited array of only the most basic everyday functions—somewhat like those offered by 7-11 stores in an urban setting. Communities in this group include places such as Biggar, Davidson, Leader, Oxbow, and Wynyard.

The MCC category, with 502 places, has, by far, the largest number of communities. As can be seen from Table ESSC-1, the number of centres in this classification has continuously increased as it is the residual category for descending communities. The 502 communities in the MCC category, as a group, no longer perform a coherent role in the trade centre network; there is no single function that is present in all communities. While the average MCC will have approximately six consumer-service outlets, they consist of an eclectic combination of functions left over from a time when they did perform a well-defined role in Saskatchewan's trade-centre network. *M. Rose Olfert and Jack Stabler*

ECONOMICS AND DEVELOPMENT. Economics is the study of choices made by individuals, institutions and societies in the use of resources to satisfy wants or needs. The discipline was first taught when the University of Saskatchewan opened in 1911, and an Economics Department was established in 1914. Both the University of Saskatchewan and the University of Regina now offer undergraduate and graduate programs in economics to a large number of students.

The staple theory, first developed by Toronto economists, was very influential in Saskatchewan as a framework for understanding western Canadian economic development. The staple theory held that

agriculture was exploited as a sector to help build the manufacturing industries in central Canada, and thus that the country was being built on the backs of western farmers. This belief, in a form of colonialism by central Canadian commercial interests, fuelled populist and radical political movements that had a significant effect on the economic development of Saskatchewan. Wheat producers felt exploited by central Canadian monopolies. Initiatives by grain producers and others led to the creation of the **SASKATCHEWAN WHEAT POOL** in 1924 and to an extensive co-operative network across the province.

The devastation of **DEPRESSION** and drought in the 1930s led to demands for more government intervention in the economy. In 1932 the **CO-OPERATIVE COMMONWEALTH FEDERATION** (CCF) was founded, and in 1944 formed a social democratic government in Saskatchewan. The province developed stronger health and social programs, pursued initiatives to diversify the provincial economy through resource development and industrialization, and developed infrastructure such as roads and electricity systems.

A historical scepticism towards capitalism, the atypical type of development associated with staple-based economies, and the relatively radical nature of Saskatchewan politics resulted in a distinct type of economic organization for the province. It was based on a network of public and quasi-public agencies to encourage and direct economic development, comprehensive social programs, and an independent and activist civil service willing to extend government's reach into the economic lives of its citizens. Among the civil servants who led this transformation of the Saskatchewan economy were David Cass-Beggs (**SASKATCHEWAN POWER CORPORATION**), **THOMAS SHOYAMA** (Economic Advisory and Planning Board), **GEORGE CADBURY** (Premier's Office), and Charles Schwartz (who designed the first public crop insurance plan in the early 1960s).

As of the 1996 Census, there were approximately 120 economists, economic policy researchers, and analysts working in Saskatchewan, primarily in the public sector, more than half of whom were based in Regina. There were an additional 630 people employed in related professions: business development officers, marketing researchers, and consultants, with about two-thirds of these jobs located in Regina and Saskatoon. *Gary Tompkins*

ECONOMY OF SASKATCHEWAN: *see essay on page 273.*

ECOZONES AND ECOREGIONS. The ecoregion concept grew from the realization that **CONSERVATION** and recognition of human effects on the natural world required that we think at the level of ecosystems and biological communities, rather than at the single species level. The earlier single species

approach concentrated on mammals and birds, often recognizing other organisms only as prey, predator or nesting site. The present approach recognizes the complexity and interactions of the physical, as well as the biotic, aspects of the environment. Ecoregions are described by the basal physical features of the environment: geological structure and chemistry, the landforms which have developed on the geological underpinnings over time, and climate. The interactions of these physical factors determine the development of the soil in which the plant and other producer or autotrophic organisms can live. Only after the autotrophs have become established can animal species, completely dependent on the producers for food and shelter, become a sustainable part of the community. The ecoregion concept also includes the effects of human actions on communities. Some ecoregions have been affected more than others; in Saskatchewan, the ecoregions within the Prairie Ecozone have been modified to a far greater extent than those of the Taiga Shield. As a result, some of the affected areas, especially where the ecosystem is vulnerable, have been declared Endangered Spaces, which need recognition and protection. Implicit within the concept is the realization that ecoregions will shift and change over time. Physical processes such as erosion and accumulation of water-borne materials will change watercourses. Long-term climate change, as well as short-term changes in weather patterns, will shift the position of plant communities. Warmer, drier climate will shift the ecoregions to the northeast; cooler, moister climate will shift them to the southwest.

The ecoregion concept is hierarchical. It consists of three levels of communities. The first, or ecozone, level is the largest in scale. It is at the subcontinental level, describing extensive, major ecosystems and ignoring political boundaries. The ecozones have a northwest to southeast alignment across the province, reflecting the precipitation gradient. The ecoregion subdivisions of the ecozones constitute distinctive communities, set apart by climatic or landform factors. The ecodistrict subdivisions of the ecoregions reflect local differences in factors such as climate, soil, relief and water availability, which result in distinctive vegetation. The

SOURCE: ECOREGIONS OF SASKATCHEWAN (1998)

Fungi growing on a lichen-covered forest floor, Selwyn Lake Upland Ecoregion.

Shallow rapids are common throughout the Tazin Lake Upland Ecoregion.

more southerly ecoregions have more ecodistricts, in relation to the more finely developed drainage systems. Saskatchewan is part of four ecozones: the Taiga Shield, the Boreal Shield, the Boreal Plain, and the Prairie. These are all extensive, being found in a number of contiguous provinces and states. They are divided into eleven ecoregions, ranging from two to four within a zone (*see* Figure ECO-1 on page 272).

Taiga Shield: Underlain by the crystalline rocks of the Precambrian Shield, with poor soil development, covered in areas by glacial drift, in low relief, this is the northernmost ecozone of the province. The poor drainage and rolling post-glacial topography result in numerous lakes, including Lake Athabasca. The long, very cold winters and low precipitation limit the vegetation to lichen woodlands on higher elevations, and bogs in the lowlands. The limited vegetation results in a low number of animal species—the lowest of any ecozone in the province. This is the only area in the province in which arctic and subarctic species such as the arctic fox, caribou, and rock ptarmigan predominate. The human population of the region has apparently always been low. There is virtually no agriculture possible, but mineral exploration and exploitation have had some effect.

Selwyn Lake Upland: This ecoregion is found in the extreme northeast. The relief is low, and the landscape is dominated by moraines and till plains. The area is drained by the Churchill and Nelson rivers. The ecodistricts, differing in soil development, relief, and plant cover are: Dunvegan Lake Upland, Eynard Lake Upland, Robins Lake Upland, Striding River Upland, Nueltin Lake Plain, and Seale River Plain.

Tazin Lake Upland: An area of higher relief than the Selwyn Lake Uplands, where moraines are less well developed and the surface is often bare rock outcrops. There are black spruce-jack pine forests with a more specious vegetation, reflecting the somewhat less harsh climate. The ecodistricts, differing in relief and soil development, are: Uranium City Upland and Territories Upland.

Boreal Shield: This largest ecozone, which at 18.7 million hectares comprises nearly one-third of the province, is a region of extensive boreal forest lying on the Canadian Shield. Bedrock alternates with glacial tills; as in the Taiga, glaciation resulted in a rolling topography containing numerous lakes of various sizes. The climax vegetation of much of the region is dense black spruce with moss ground cover. In more protected and open areas, there are birch and trembling and balsam poplar, as well as jack pine and tamarack. This more diverse vegetation supports a larger fauna than further north. Several species of the deer family as well as a number of carnivores such as wolf, marten and mink, are residents. Bird such as ravens, barred owls and boreal chickadees are also to be found, while a large number of insectivorous birds are summer residents, raising their young on the numerous insects of the short summer. This region has been the site of extensive mining.

Athabasca Plain: This ecoregion is on sandstone bedrock along the Alberta border, south of **LAKE ATHABASCA** and east to Wollaston Lake. The landscape is a patchwork of glacial and waterborne deposition, with moraines, eskers and sand dunes resulting from erosion of the underlying sandstone. The ecodistricts are: Athabasca Dunes, Carswell Plain, McTaggert Plain, MacFarlane Upland, Livingstone Plain, Squirrel Lake Plain, Fond du Lac Lowland, Lower Cree River Plain, Pasfield Lake

Smooth shorelines and sandy beaches, such as we see along Lake Athabasca, can be attributed to the sandy nature of the Athabasca Sandstone bedrock which prevails in the Athabasca Plain Ecoregion.

Plain, Pine River Plain, Cree Lake Upland, and Wheeler Upland.

Churchill River Upland: Based on Precambrian crystalline bedrock, this is the eastern section of the ecoregion. It is the largest single ecoregion of the province; at 11.3 million hectares, it comprises 17% of the province. The area has a thinner glacial deposit and less soil development than the softer rock of the Athabasca Plain. The lack of erosion materials leads to the clear water of the lakes and their lower productivity. The ecodistricts are: Black Birch Plain, Frobisher Plain, Pinehouse Plain, Foster Upland, Highrock Lake Plain, Wollaston Lake Plain,

Reindeer Lake Plain, Macoun Lake Plain, Sisipuk Plain, Flinflon Plain, and Reed Lake Plain.

Boreal Plain: The Boreal Plain is an area of rolling plain based on sedimentary rock and covered by thick glacial deposits, interspersed by lakes and glacial kettles. The warmer climate of the ecozone, in relation to those further north, supports a greater variety of vegetation. The forest is mixed hardwood and coniferous species that include white and black spruce, jack pine, aspen, white birch, and balsam poplar. Lowlands near water may have American elm, green ash, and willows and sedges, along with a variety of flowering plants. More than fifty of the province's seventy-two mammal species have been identified here, with most of the species in the southern areas of the zone; these include a number of carnivores which have been extirpated in the more heavily settled grasslands. Bird species richness is also high, with a number of migrants breeding in the area. Human activities in the region include forest-based hunting, fishing, trapping, and logging. Most of the pelts taken by trapping in the province are from this area. Approximately 16% of the land is devoted to agriculture, along the southern margins; this includes grain production, as well as the raising of livestock.

Mid-Boreal Upland: This region, consisting of rolling uplands and plains, is discontinuous. The main northwestern block is the largest single region of the zone. Other districts of this region lie to the south and east. Thirty ecodistricts have been delineated, ranging from the Firebag Hills in the northwest to Porcupine Hills and Duck Mountain in the east.

Mid-Boreal Lowland: This region is the lower-lying area of the region, along the Manitoba border. The low relief area is dominated by fens and peat bogs, with less wooded land. The ecodistricts are: Mossy River Plain, Namew Lake Upland, Saskatchewan Delta, and Overflowing River Lowland.

Boreal Transition: As noted by the name, this is an area of transition between the boreal forest and the southern grasslands. The gently rolling landscape is covered by a deciduous boreal forest with a higher percentage of trembling aspen,

Black Bear are common in the Boreal Plain Ecozone.

interspersed with native grassland species. In uncultivated areas, grasslands have been reduced with the suppression of the natural fires which once controlled the margins of the forest. Twenty-three ecodistricts have been named, based mainly on drainage patterns. These range from the Beaver River Plain, between the Beaver and Waterhen river drainages along the western border, to the Swan River Plain along the Assiniboine River.

Prairie: This is the Saskatchewan section of the great North American grasslands of the centre of the continent. The grasslands are separated from the boreal forest by a band of aspen parkland, with grasslands dotted by aspen bluffs. It is a zone of rolling plains with eroded uplands, with the **CYPRESS HILLS** unglaciated uplands as a prominent feature in the southwest. Thick glacial deposits cover the surface, with development of the chernozemic soils characteristic of grasslands. It is these soils which made the area so attractive to grain farmers. The

thick glacial sediments and other features support the many aquifers of the zone. It has the most equable climate of the province, although there are still long, cold winters and short, often hot summers. The vegetation is mostly of grasses, with a number of flowering plants and shrubs found in the lower, moister areas. The wildlife species of the region are fewer in number; this is due partly to the specialized nature of the vegetation, with fewer trees for nesting and shelter, and partly to a reduction of habitat and hunting by the larger human population. There are a number of grasslands specialist burrowers and runners, such as the pronghorn, badger, ground squirrel, and burrowing owl. The bison, once the dominant member of the natural ecosystem, has been to some extent replaced by domestic cattle, although these are not migratory and therefore do not have the same effects on the ecosystem.

The Prairie, being the predominant area of agri-

cultural production, is the provincial ecozone most modified by human action. There is considerable activity to explore for, and extract, various nonrenewable resources such as lignite, natural gas, and petroleum. Reservoir development, with attendant dams, has modified the precipitation-evaporation cycle, as well as the natural erosion-deposition which affects the natural changes in waterways. This is the most heavily settled area: over 80% of the province's population lives in this zone. This combination of activities has resulted in the greatest amount of reduction of native vegetation. A number of protected areas, including the **GRASSLANDS NATIONAL PARK**, have been developed by various conservation groups in an attempt to preserve what little native grasslands remain. (*See also* **PRAIRIE**.)

Aspen Parkland: This zone of transition between the aspen woodlands of the Boreal Transition and the prairie grasslands forms a band across the province, angling to the southeast. Aspen

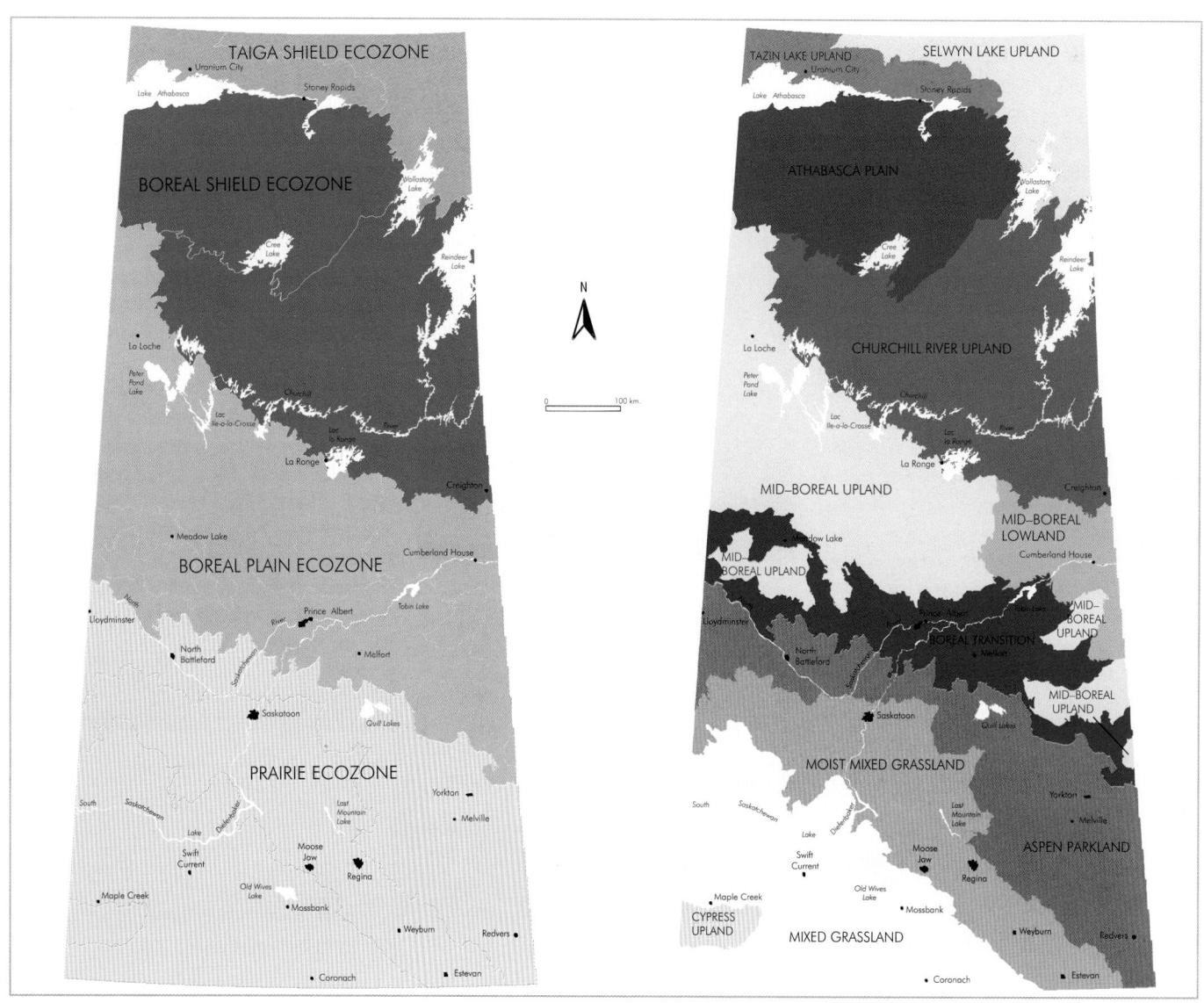

Figure ECO-1: Left, Saskatchewan's 4 ecozones, and right, Saskatchewan's 11 ecoregions.

SOURCE: ECOREGIONS OF SASKATCHEWAN (1998)

The black chokecherry is common to edges of wooded areas and coulees of the Aspen Parkland Ecoregion.

groves are found in the moister north-facing slopes and low-lying depressions, while fescue grasslands are found on the drier south-facing slopes and hillocks. There are twenty-two ecodistricts in the region, from the Lloydminster Plain in the west to the Oak Lake Plain in the east. They include Moose Mountain, an unglaciated upland with a remnant boreal forest ecosystem.

Moist Mixed Grassland: This ecoregion lies to the south of the Aspen Parkland band, echoing its angle across the province. It is drier than the parkland and consequently has fewer trees and shrubby vegetation, although they occur along stream courses and permanent sloughs. There are twenty ecodistricts in the region, ranging from the Neutral Hills in the west to the Souris River Plain in the east.

Mixed Grassland: The semiarid grasslands region is found in the southwest of the province. It is a dry grassland with a mixture of mid-grasses, such as wheatgrasses, and short-grasses, such as blue gramma. Because of the lower precipitation in the area, it has not been broken for agriculture to the same extent as the more humid Moist Mixed Grassland. There are twenty-five ecodistricts in the region, from the Kerrobert Plain, through the **GREAT SAND HILLS**, to the Wild Horse Plain.

Cypress Upland: This unglaciated plateau, with the erosional dissection typical of an older landscape, is a very distinctive and easily recognized ecoregion. The higher elevation supports a forest associated with the montane forests further west, with lodgepole pine, white spruce and aspen. The bird fauna also reflects this, with western species such as Steller's jay and MacGillivray's warbler. There are only two ecodistricts, the Cypress Slope of moraine on the northern face of the hills, and the Cypress Hills themselves.

Diane Secoy

FURTHER READING: Acton, D.F., G.A. Padbury and C.T. Stushnoff. 1998. *The Ecoregions of Saskatchewan.* Regina: Canadian Plains Research Center; Jonker, P. 1997. "Endangered Spaces." Pp. 163–66 in *Atlas of Saskatchewan.* Saskatoon: University of Saskatchewan.

Economy of Saskatchewan

E

Peter Phillips

Saskatchewan is the fifth largest Canadian province in terms of area, with a land mass of 651,900^2 km, divided about one-third each in Precambrian rock and agricultural land, 23% in commercial forest, and 12% in lakes and rivers. As such, the province makes up about 6.5% of the area of Canada and 0.4% of the world. In 2001, close to one million people lived in the province, a number almost unchanged since the 1930s. Approximately 53% of the population lives in the thirteen cities, and another 16% in towns; the remaining 31% of the population lives on farms, in small rural villages, or on Indian reserves.

Economic History

Most of the development in Saskatchewan until this past decade was based on the production and export of natural resources. The first phase of development in western Canada occurred in the late 1800s after a number of conditions were met. First came the political and legal systems. In 1867 Canada acquired Ruperts' Land from the Hudson's Bay Company (*see* RUPERT'S LAND PURCHASE) and introduced a legitimate form of government in the Territories (leading to provincial government in 1905); also, in response to the political strife between the Indigenous peoples and the first European settlers, the North-West Mounted Police force was formed in 1885 and introduced to the west. The second phase of development was the result of two key factors. In 1885 the Canadian Pacific transcontinental rail link was completed, providing the means to move people into the west and ship products to markets (*see* CANADIAN PACIFIC RAILWAY). A massive migration then was triggered after the turn of the century by the development of the Marquis strain of WHEAT and the opening of new grain markets in the United Kingdom: this new wheat produced a higher yield and matured earlier than existing varieties, which turned the latent potential of the virgin prairie into a valuable economic resource ripe for development.

From a base of only a few thousand in 1885, the population of the province rose to 91,300 in 1901 and then surged to 921,800 by 1931. People migrated from eastern Canada and Europe, attracted by free land and virtually unbounded economic potential. The industries that serviced these new farmers followed close behind. By 1929, Saskatchewan had a vibrant developing economy. The third phase of economic development followed the decision in 1930 of the federal government to transfer control and ownership of the land and its natural resources to the provincial government: from Confederation until 1930 the land and resources of Saskatchewan had been owned by the federal government and developed according to federal priorities. Halted during the GREAT DEPRESSION, development resumed after WORLD WAR II with the discovery of rich natural resource deposits below the ground and the growth of export markets for these products. New technologies led to the discovery of oil, potash and uranium reserves; the growth of energy-intensive economic systems in North America and Europe created the opportunities. By the 1980s the Saskatchewan economy was highly specialized and competitive. As production and export capacity increased, demand increased for specialized business as well as community and personal services. Primary production of wheat, oilseeds, livestock, oil and gas, potash, uranium, and timber naturally led to the development of firms supplying inputs to these industries (e.g., IPSCO), and of firms processing the raw products further (e.g., flour mills, oilseed crushers, slaughter houses, oil refineries, and pulp and paper plants). As these industries developed and expanded, a select few rural and urban communities grew as industrial and regional service centres. (*See* Table 1.) (*see* FORESTRY, OIL AND GAS INDUSTRY, POTASH INDUSTRY and URANIUM)

The Modern Saskatchewan Economy

The production and export of natural resources and their refined products is the backbone of the Saskatchewan economy. About 95% of all goods produced in the province directly depend on its basic resources (grains, livestock, oil and gas, potash, uranium and wood, and their refined products). In addition, the individuals and firms involved in these industries make

E

Table 1. Stages in resource-based economic development

Natural Resources	Processed Products	Services
Agriculture (1900–40)		
• wheat	• flour; malt	• towns & villages
• oilseeds	• canola oil	• farm machinery
• livestock	• bacon	• transportation
Mining & forestry (1940–90)		
• oil and gas	• refineries/IPSCO	• pipelines
• potash	• hopper cars	• finance
• uranium	• machinery	• northern towns
• timber	• pulp & paper	• trucking

purchasing decisions that drive the rest of the economy; farmers, mining companies, and the manufacturers processing primary products purchase the bulk of the non-resource manufactured output and business services produced in the province. Two factors fundamentally influence the provincial economy. First, given its orientation on primary and resource extraction and processing, the provincial economy is heavily dependent on financial markets to provide attractively priced financial resources to sustain heavy annual investments in gross fixed capital formation; on average, in the 1993-2002 period, more than 21% of the annual output was invested in new infrastructure and capital. Second, trade access and international market growth are vital to the future: the province's grains, CANOLA, livestock, oil, potash and uranium producers are leaders in their fields and produce many times more than local demand could use. More than 90% of the grains and oilseeds produced in the province are sold to other Canadians or offshore; all of the potash and uranium is used outside the province; 83% of the oil pumped is shipped to other markets; and 30% of the goods processed in the provincial manufacturing industry are exported (e.g., wood pulp and paper from WEYERHAEUSER, pipes from IPSCO INC., canola oil). At the same time, the provincial economy could never produce enough goods at competitive prices to feed, house, clothe and transport the population in its accustomed style: the province thus imports the vast majority of consumer goods such as automobiles, fresh fruit and vegetables during the winter, clothes, and household equipment and appliances.

There are a number of means of measuring the scope and scale of the economy. The conventional method is to look at distribution of

value-added activity by sector. The provincial economic accounts show that the province has moved rapidly from an agrarian and resource-based economy into a services-propelled region. This transformation has been mirrored by the shift of employment between those sectors. (*See* Table 2).

This approach overstates the shifts of activity away from the commodity market drivers. The move from goods to services production is at least partly the result of greater specialization. For instance, as farmers use more inputs and out-source more of their trucking and financial management, the value and employment created are now counted as manufacturing, transportation, wholesale trade, finance, or business services. The final market for many of the new processing or service jobs remains as embedded value in exported commodities: in agriculture, for example, only about 40% of the export value of our products is added on-farm. If this is consistent across the primary sector, the all-in estimate of both value-added and employment based on supply chain relationships between final markets and primary producers, input suppliers, output processors and related services would suggest that the primary sectors drive not only the 25% in the core sectors, but rather more than 60% of the total economy. After more than a century of commercial development, the provincial gross domestic product in 2002 was $34.5 billion, equal to about 3% of the Canadian economy. The average per capita income was approximately $34,700, equal to about 94% of the national average. The provincial average per capita income in 2002 was more than three times the global average and would earn Saskatchewan a position among the most affluent regions in the world.

Key Sectors

The goods-producing sectors in the province directly contributed about 32% of the provincial gross domestic product in 2002. Agriculture remains the single largest sector, even though it has been significantly restructured in recent years. Saskatchewan, with 202,400 km² of improved agricultural land, equal to 44% of Canada's farmland, is a major producer of crop products. In 2001, 50,600 farms involved 66,200 operators and employed an estimated $33 billion of capital. The sector accounted for about 50% of Canada's wheat production, 80% of its durum production, 33% of its BARLEY production, and 43% its canola production. Saskatchewan alone accounted for 10% of world trade in

Table 2. Saskatchewan's evolving industrial structure, 1976 and 2002–03

Sector	% GDP at factor cost		% of labour force	
	1976	2002	1976	2002
Agriculture	24.0	6	24.7	9.7
Forestry, fishing and mining	6.2	15	2.1	3.7
Construction	5.8	4	6.2	5.0
Manufacturing	5.8	7	6.0	5.8
Transportation, storage, communications & miscellaneous utilities	9.9	12	8	5.8
Wholesale & retail trade	9.8	12	17.1	15.9
Finance, insurance and real estate	13.7	16	3.9	5.6
Community, business and personal services	17.7	21	24.4	43.0
Public Administration	7.0	6	7.5	5.6
Total	$7.3 B	$28.1 B	385,000	486,800

Source: Saskatchewan Bureau of Statistics Provincial Economic Accounts (1976 GDP), Statistics Canada, 15-203 (2002 GDP) and Statistics Canada Labour Force Survey

wheat, 60% in durum, and 40% in canola. The province is also a significant producer of red meats, especially feeder and slaughter cattle and hogs. The domestic market consumes about 43% of the slaughter cattle, and keeps just less than that percentage of the feeder cattle. The major export markets for slaughter cattle, in order of importance, are the US, Alberta, and Manitoba; over 40% of the feeder cattle produced in the province are exported to Alberta, with only small amounts shipped to Ontario, the US, and Manitoba. The hog market is more domestically driven, with more than 80% of the production being sold to the two main slaughterhouses, some of which is then sold elsewhere as processed meat products. The US makes up about 5% of the slaughter animal market; the rest is exported (often through confidential contracts) to Alberta and Manitoba.

Saskatchewan is also endowed with an abundant supply of natural resources. As a result of having been submerged under a prehistoric ocean, the province has an estimated 75% of the world's potash reserves: exploration in the 1950s revealed the existence of huge potash beds underlying most of the southern region. The first potash mine in Saskatchewan was completed in 1958, but promptly flooded. Potash production, however, has been continuous since 1962. There are ten potash mines spread throughout the province, and four producing companies with a total capital investment of over $2.5 billion. Only about 5% of the potash produced in Saskatchewan is consumed in Canada. Saskatchewan also has large deposits of a relatively high grade of uranium, which is mined and processed into yellowcake for international markets. Canada has a significant portion of known uranium resources in the world, and the bulk of these resources are located in Saskatchewan: these large, high-grade uranium deposits, which can be extracted at production costs below those in many other parts of the world, are sufficient for more than forty years at current rates of production. Saskatchewan is now the largest uranium-producing region in the world, accounting for 25% of annual world uranium production in 2002. There are currently three uranium mining and milling operations in the province: Rabbit Lake, Cluff Lake and Key Lake produced 15.6 million kgs U3O8 in 2002, earning revenues from sales of $593 million, about two-thirds from sales to the rest of Canada and one-third from sales to the world.

Saskatchewan is a small but significant producer of crude oil, natural gas, and coal and electrical energy, with about 10% of Canada's reserves for oil and 25% of its gas reserves. The province's crude oil, discovered in 1944, varies from light sweet crude to heavy sour crude. Saskatchewan is the second largest oil producer in Canada after Alberta, accounting for more than 20% of the total Canadian oil production: cumulative oil production up to December 31, 2002 was 622 million cubic metres. Remaining recoverable reserves on December 31, 2002, were estimated to be approximately 183 million cubic metres. There are an estimated 25 billion barrels of heavy oil in-place in the west-central region of the province, which represents the greatest potential for future development. About 20% of Saskatchewan's production is currently used within the province, 10% in the rest of Canada, and about 70% is exported to the US. Saskatchewan natural gas producers account for more than 6.5 billion cubic metres annually, earning on average about $1 billion per year in the 2000-02 period, while coal producers produced 11.3 million tonnes of coal in 2002, earning $180 million.

Non-energy mineral production in Saskatchewan has risen significantly in recent years. In 2002, the province produced 11.7 million kg of copper, 4.6 million kg of zinc, 1,678 kg of gold, 1,344 kg of silver, 921,000 tonnes of salt, 184,000 tonnes of sodium sulphate, and a variety of other metals and minerals. In aggregate, the total value of mineral sales (net of oil, gas, coal, potash and uranium) was $156 million in 2002 (see MINING).

With 23% of the land mass covered by commercial forest, the province is a small but competitive producer of pulp, paper and wood products for domestic and international markets; it has commercial softwood production of balsam fir, black spruce, jack pine, tamarack and white spruce, and hardwood operations for balsam poplar, trembling aspen, and white birch. The aggregate forestry sector generates about $750 million annually in revenue, divided among about 300 forestry industry firms and 9,000 workers.

The construction sector in Saskatchewan is devoted to delivering approximately $8.9 billion of new and renovation construction annually; there were an estimated 24,200 construction workers in the province in 2003. In terms of manufacturing, there were 1,044 firms in Saskatchewan in 2001, most of which either process primary produce from the agricultural, forestry, mining and energy sectors, or produce intermediate goods for use in those sectors. In aggregate, these firms produced $7.2 billion in manufacturing receipts in 2001, and employed 28,300 workers. Only a small portion of the firms and value added in the manufacturing sector produce consumer goods or equipment for direct export. The bulk of the revenues and value added in the sector is in the two heavy-oil upgraders and the oil refinery, the various wood, pulp and paper operations, and in a variety of food processing and agrichemical ventures. The $1.8 billion food processing industry includes more than 160 processors and 5,000 employees. About 300 firms in the machinery, transportation and industrial equipment sector employ about 12,000 employees and generate about $2.2 billion in annual sales.

The service-producing parts of the economy have grown significantly faster than the goods-producing sectors, accounting for about 62% of the total gross domestic product in 2002. A small number of very large employers—governments, health and school boards, utility corporations—employ a large portion of the workers in the service-producing economy. In 2002, the federal, provincial and local governments, combined, employed 27,200 workers, or about 5.6% of the total workforce; in addition, the publicly funded and managed health and education sectors employed in aggregate more than 87,000 in 2002. Crown Investments Corporation of Saskatchewan (CIC) owns or manages enterprises that account for 15% of the province's gross domestic product, employs assets totaling $8.1 billion, and directly employs 9,500 people. CIC's eleven wholly owned subsidiary CROWN CORPORATIONS span the commercial services sector, providing electricity, natural gas distribution, telephones, water, automobile and general insurance, intercity bus service, computer services, and a variety of investment funds and services.

A large number of independent and chain wholesale and retail operations facilitate $9 billion of retail trade in the province annually, equal to approximately $9,100 per capita. In conjunction with more than 22,000 accommodation outlets, restaurants, caterers, taverns, and attractions operators, these firms also support a $1.3 billion tourism industry, which serves more than 3.5 million tourist-day visits by residents, and an estimated 3.4 million Canadian and 0.1 million foreign tourists annually. For tourism purposes, the trip expenditures are most important: Saskatchewan residents account for 45% of expenditures by those making trips of one or more nights in Saskatchewan, while other Canadians account for 35%, United States visitors for 17%, and those from overseas for 3%.

Finally, a large number of small- and medium-sized firms offer an array of services. The finance, insurance and real estate sector and commercial transportation operators account for more than 20% of the province's economic activity and employ more than 11% of its work force. Furthermore, there are thousands of firms offering business and personal services, employing more than 100,000 workers in what is increasingly becoming the backbone of the commercial and public activity; among those are more than 20,000 professional, scientific, technical and managerial service providers such as lawyers, accountants, computer supply firms, and engineers.

The Labour Market

In 2003 the province had a total labour force of 515,800, which varied by as much as 25,000 between the months with the highest and lowest activity. On average 68% of adults (aged 15+) were in the active labour force in that year, a percentage slightly higher than the national average. Participation rates rise sharply, depending on the education level: only about 26% of adults with less than a Grade 8 education were in the labour market, while 84% of adults with post-graduate training were active in the workforce.

An estimated 486,800 people were employed on average during 2003, approximately 80% in full-time jobs and 20% in part-time work; 68% of all employed workers had some formal education beyond high school (26% with university degrees), 24% simply had high school, and 19% had not completed high school. The average weekly earnings, including overtime, for employed workers in Saskatchewan was about $610–about 10% less than the national average. In total, 29,000 workers on average were unemployed over the year, representing 5.6% of the provincial labour force; those unemployed people were without work for about 18 weeks. The provincial unemployment rate was the third lowest rate of any province, marginally behind Alberta and Manitoba, and significantly lower than the national average. However, one of the reasons why the province has a low unemployment rate is that unemployed workers tend to migrate to other provinces for jobs: over the 1994-2003 period, about 5,000 more people migrated each year to other provinces than arrived.

Labour force surveys focus primarily on individuals actively engaged in paid employment or in self-employment that is done with an expectation of a profit. Three important socio-economic groups are generally excluded from any detailed analysis. First, those individuals that are 15 years or older and in full-time education are for the most part not included in the analysis: about 90,000 Saskatchewan residents were 15-24 years old in December 2003, a majority of whom were in high school or some post-secondary education or training program. Second, about 16,000 of the 134,000 elderly (aged 65+) were active in the labour force. Third, a significant number of women do not work for pay outside the home and are therefore excluded from analysis in the labour force survey: in 2003, about 35,000 women in the prime working ages of 25-64 were not active in the labour market; many of these were stay-at-home wives and mothers. Each of these groups adds significant uncounted value to the economy, both directly in terms of acquiring education and maintaining homes and families, and indirectly as volunteers and contributors to the social fabric of the province. In 2000, 42% of Saskatchewan residents, both those employed and those outside the labour market, volunteered to a range of educational, social, cultural and community non-profit organizations and ventures, according to the National Survey of Giving, Volunteering and Participating: this was the highest rate of volunteerism in Canada for that year. In all, 323,000 Saskatchewan people volunteered 49.7 million hours in 2000, or on average 154 hours of their time each, which is the equivalent of 26,000 full-time jobs. (*See* VOLUNTARY SECTOR.)

Saskatchewan Business

In 1997, Saskatchewan had approximately 30,000 firms registered to operate with province-based headquarters; 27,000 sole proprietorships; and 8,000 firms with out-of-province headquarters but registered with Saskatchewan Justice to undertake business in the province. Urban-based firms employed 76% of provincial workers, northern firms about 0.8%, and rural firms about 23%. Looking at the top 100 grossing companies in the province in 2003, Saskatoon had the head offices of 35 commercial enterprises while Regina had 31 commercial headquarters and the head offices of eleven Crown corporations. The other cities each had one or two headquarters, for a total of ten firms. The other private companies are scattered around the smaller centres. Over 86% of all domestic firms have fewer than twenty employees; the 5% of all firms that employ more than 100 workers accounted in 1993 for 52% of all jobs and more than 60% of the provincial payroll. As a result of the small average size of Saskatchewan firms, the average net profit per firm is 16% lower than the national average. At the same time the average equity per firm was about 25% below the national average, and only 24 firms with Saskatchewan-based headquarters have raised equity capital on Canadian stock exchanges. Many firms compensate for shortages of capital by leveraging their equity to a greater extent than their national counterparts; as a result, the average firm in Saskatchewan has a higher debt to equity level and is more at risk to changes in financial conditions than many other firms. Out-of-province firms are significant actors too. Only about 68% of gross revenues by firms operating in Saskatchewan are controlled by private Canadian firms; firms controlled by government–federal, provincial and local–are responsible for about 19% of gross business revenues in the province; and foreign-controlled firms contribute about 12% of gross revenues.

Economic Challenges in the 21st Century

Diversification has been a key priority for Saskatchewan. Given the international orientation of the provincial economy, the primary and secondary export industries are forced to remain globally competitive, which often leads to new capital infrastructure replacing some jobs. Pulp and paper mills, computerized business services, heavy oil upgraders, irrigation projects, and many new food processing plants all add essential new diversified layers to the economy and thereby increase value added, employment, and incomes. One benefit of the diversifying economy has been a moderation in the annual swings in economic activity. In the decade leading up to 1962, the real (inflation-adjusted) gross domestic product was extremely volatile: on average, the economy changed by almost 14% between years, with contractions of up to 26.7% in some years and expansions of as much as 23.4% in other years. In contrast, during the decade leading up to 2003, the economy changed by an average of only 2.5% each year, the largest contraction being 0.8% and the largest expansion only 4.7%. Although considerable progress has been made over the past few decades, the gains from diversified production have barely been sufficient to offset the jobs lost from agriculture. High real interest rates, volatile financial markets, international trade wars, changing world-wide demand for primary products, and a long-term decline in real prices for resource exports have been key features of the operating environment since the 1970s and are likely to continue into the foreseeable future, challenging the provincial economy to remain dynamic and growing.

Education

Ken Horsman

Frederic Edmunds.

EDMUNDS, FREDERIC HARRISON (1898–1965). Born in Flintshire, Great Britain on January 27, 1898, Frederic Edmunds served in the Royal Engineers from 1917 to 1919, and then obtained a BscHons and MSc in a combined program of chemistry and geology at the University of Liverpool. In 1925, he immigrated to Canada and took a position at the **UNIVERSITY OF SASKATCHEWAN** in the Soils Department. In 1929, he became the first professor in the newly developed Department of Geology (later Geological Sciences), of which he became Head in 1961. He married Mabel Workman; they had three sons. In his early work with the Soils Department, Edmunds participated in the soil surveys of the province from 1925 to 1930. His knowledge of the surface deposits of the province gave him an interest and expertise in the effects of glaciation on the landscape. His surveys and mapping of the Cretaceous strata and the oil deposits in them laid the groundwork for the explorations and later development of the petroleum industry. His influence on the growth of the provincial geological community through his students, fieldwork, and participation on boards such as the Saskatchewan Oil and Gas Conservation Board was profound. This was recognized by awards such as Fellow of the Royal Society of Canada, Fellow of the Geological Society (London), and member of the governing bodies of professional geological societies. He was recognized not only as a knowledgeable and hardworking field geologist, despite permanent physical damage from a war injury, but also as a dedicated teacher and helpful associate. Edmunds died in Saskatoon on February 28, 1965. *Diane Secoy*

EDUCATION: *see essay on this page.*

Education in Saskatchewan Before Confederation

Prior to the missionary schools, First Nations followed traditional customs: there were no special educative institutions; the social group as a whole was the school; and the tribal education system involved imitating the adults. Children were seen not as belonging to their parents, but rather as on loan from the Creator; they did not experience corporal punishment, and were rarely punished or scolded. Celebration and spiritual practice were an important part of the education and maturation process for children. **HENRY BUDD**, the first Aboriginal person in North America to be ordained in the Anglican Church, established the first school in 1840 at Cumberland House. From then until 1884, when an Ordinance Providing for the Organization of Schools in the North West Territories was passed, education was a combination of First Nations custom, missionary education, and a few schools established by settlers.

Treaty 2, **TREATY 4** and **TREATY 6** were signed in 1871, 1874, and 1876 respectively and covered about the southern half of what is now Saskatchewan; **TREATY 8** and **TREATY 10** were signed in 1899 and 1906, and covered most of the northern part of the province. These Treaties contained clauses that committed the federal government to the provision of schools on reserves; this commitment was slowly implemented, but soon was not the preferred direction of the government of Canada in Saskatchewan or elsewhere. The promise of education for First Nations then became a commitment to church-run industrial boarding schools, which were modified in 1923 and became known as **RESIDENTIAL SCHOOLS**. Although the French first established industrial schools in Canada in the early 1700s, it was an 1879 report by **NICHOLAS FLOOD DAVIN** that is generally credited with the adoption by Sir John A. Macdonald of the policy of supporting the establishment of industrial schools in Canada. Davin's *Report on Industrial Schools for Indians and Half-breeds* also advocated including the **MÉTIS** in these federal schools, but this policy was unevenly implemented, and in 1910 the federal government stopped the practice.

Industrial schools were established to provide academic learning, practical everyday skills, socialization, and religious training. The academic skills emphasized the English language; school staff were involved outside of the classroom ensuring that students did not speak their first language. Other academic studies included history, music, drawing, and arithmetic as well as reading and writing. Practical courses for girls included cooking, cleaning, tailoring, and dairying; for boys, the practical portion of the day taught skills such as carpentry, shoemaking, agriculture, blacksmithing, and printing. English culture was emphasized to the detriment of Aboriginal culture. The role of industrial and residential schools in pulling First Nations children

Industrial School, Battleford, ca.1895.

EDUCATION IN SASKATCHEWAN TIMELINE

1670 The Hudson's Bay Company is founded.

1763 The Royal Proclamation of October 7 recognizes that the Indian Nations on land west of the established colonies should not be disturbed by settlement.

1774 The first trading post is established in Saskatchewan at Cumberland House.

1816 The School Act provides property owners in Upper Canada with the ability to meet, hire a teacher, and be eligible for government grants.

1820 Sir Peregrine Maitland brings forward the idea of Indian residential schools in British colonial Canada.

1840 The first school in Saskatchewan is established at Cumberland House by Henry Budd.

1840 The Act of Union unites Upper and Lower Canada into a British colony called the Province of Canada.

1841 The Common School Act provides for one central Chief Superintendent of Education for Canada East and Canada West.

1843 The Education Act repeals the Common School Act of 1841 and re-establishes Canada East and West as responsible for education. It continues to provide for separate schools in Canada West and dissentient schools in Canada East.

1844 The Bagot Commission Report recommends Indian residential, manual or industrial schools for First Nations students.

1846 Egerton Ryerson is hired as the Chief Superintendent of Education for Canada West; he holds that position until 1876.

out of their cultural milieu and establishing a process of acculturation and assimilation remained in place and expanded from 1879 until well after 1948. In June of that year, a committee of the Canadian House of Commons and the Senate concluded that First Nations children would receive better care in their parent's home, and better education in schools with non-Aboriginal children; however, it took another 38 years, until 1986, before the involvement of the federal government in residential schools would end.

The government of Canada policy of using Indian residential schools as a tool for education and assimilation was replaced in 1948 with a policy of integration. The new policy of integrating First Nations children into provincial schools required the establishment of joint school agreements with existing provincial school boards, in which provincial school boards provided educational services to First Nations in return for tuition and capital payments from the federal government. Although the operation of federal on-reserve day schools remained a possibility and the operation of residential schools continued, integration of First Nations students into provincial schools became the preferred approach. The policy of integration into provincial schools was replaced in the 1990s with a program of building schools on reserves.

The British North America Act of 1867 and Education Law to 1905

The British North America Act of 1867 (BNA Act) established Canada as an independent country in the British Empire. With respect to education it did three things. First, it allocated responsibility for First Nations people to the federal government (Section 91); second, the Act made education a provincial responsibility (Section 93); third, it placed limits on provincial laws with respect to denominational, separate, and dissentient schools (those disagreeing with the majority or official view). The BNA Act also gave the Parliament of Canada the power to overturn provincial laws that were seen to violate the right of these schools to exist (Section 93).

Saskatchewan was not one of the founding provinces of Canada, and remained part of federal responsibility until 1905. In 1875, Canada passed the NORTH-WEST TERRITORIES ACT, which provided for a territorial government comprised of the North-West Territories Council and a Lieutenant-Governor; the Council and Governor were given responsibility for education. The Act also established electoral districts (but not school districts), provided for the majority of ratepayers to establish schools, for the minority of ratepayers either Catholic or Protestant to establish separate schools, and for ratepayers to make assessments on themselves to operate schools. Teaching could be in English or French according to the wishes of the ratepayers.

In 1881, schools in the North-West Territories with a minimum daily attendance of fifteen students were paid one-half of the teacher's salary from the Parliament of Canada. This was the first financial support to education from government in the North-West Territories: prior to this time churches, parishes or ratepayers bore all of the costs of education.

The first Territorial school law, called An Ordinance Providing for the Organization of Schools in the North West Territories, was enacted in 1884 and provided for the organization of school districts as unique entities separate from electoral districts. Each school district was to be a minimum of 36 square miles in area, and it was to have a minimum of ten school-age children. The first school districts established in 1884 were Moose Jaw (#1), Qu'Appelle (#2), Prince Albert (#3), and Regina (#4). A Territorial Board of Education was also established, comprised of two sections, one Catholic and the other Protestant. These two sections had respectively the power to administer the Catholic and the Protestant schools in the Territory. This meant that they had power over the administration of the districts, teacher certification, textbooks, and school inspectors; the school district boards hired the teachers and raised taxes. In 1892 the Board of Education was redesigned and renamed the Council of Public Instruction, and in 1901 it was again modified to become the first Department of Education headed by a member of the Territorial Council and supported by the Education Council. By the time Saskatchewan joined Confederation as a province on September 1, 1905, the basic elements of the elementary and secondary education system had been laid. Based largely on the Ontario model, the foundations of the Saskatchewan education system included: education as a provincial responsibility; school districts established for a small geographic area; locally elected boards of trustees who raised taxes, hired teachers and operated the school; and a central professional administrative structure, now called the Department of Learning, the purpose of which was to determine what was taught, provide funding, and maintain an administrative and governance system. During the 1800s the role of schools was to provide a basic education and social influence, and to develop the British culture in Canadians, while acknowledging and in some ways coping with ethnic diversity. Little post-secondary education development had occurred prior to 1905.

Language and Religion in Elementary and Secondary Education

The role of religion and language in school had been a matter for debate since before Canada became a British colony. The nature of the education system in Saskatchewan was strongly influenced by what became known as the Manitoba school question: owing to the nature of the population in Manitoba and the provisions of the British North America Act, the Manitoba Act of 1870 had established the province and granted official status to the French and English languages and to denominational schools. With migration, the population of Manitoba quickly became less Catholic and less French-speaking; this happened so rapidly that by 1890, only twenty years after the province was established, Manitoba abolished separate denominational schools and French as an official language. This action became a national controversy, and a compromise was reached through the involvement of Prime Minister Sir Wilfrid Laurier. The compromise provided Catholics with the opportunity to establish separate private schools, but it did not allow for publicly supported separate schools; it provided for instruction in French if ten or more students spoke French, or any language other than English.

Saskatchewan and Alberta prepared to join Confederation in 1905. Because of the Manitoba experience, Catholics made such strong representations to the federal government that the Saskatchewan Act of 1905 provided for separate Catholic and Protestant schools, as had the Ordinance of 1884. The Secondary Education Act of 1907 did not provide for separate schools at high school level, and was not amended in this respect until 1963. With respect to the language of instruction, the passage of the Saskatchewan Act in 1905 retained the right of instruction in a language other than English, but there was no provision for publicly funded, francophone-governed education. Over time, legislation was changed to be more restrictive of the use of languages other than English in school. By 1918, legislation was passed that made English the sole language of instruction, except for French-speaking students during their first year of attendance at school. It permitted school districts to offer French as a subject, but did not permit any other language as the language of instruction. Additional restrictions came about in 1931, when legislative changes withdrew the right to use French as a language of instruction during the first year of attendance; this legislative arrangement remained in place until 1967, when a series of amendments were introduced between then and 1978. Among other things, the changes provided for French immersion classes and for designated schools, operated by existing school divisions, where French was the language of instruction. The federal Official Languages Act of 1969 and the provision of financial support by the federal government largely precipitated the change. With the financial support of the federal government, enrolments in French immersion programs and designated schools grew rapidly during the 1970s and early 1980s. Instruction in other languages, including Ukrainian and some First Nations languages, began to develop as well. As a consequence of guarantees for minority language rights embedded in the 1982 Canadian Charter of Rights and Freedoms of the Constitution Act, the government of Saskatchewan undertook to implement a francophone minority school system. In 2005, over 1,000 students were enrolled in twelve schools or programs operated by the *Division scolaire francophone*.

Elementary and Secondary Education

Prior to 1907 education in Saskatchewan used the terminology of "standard" to indicate the level a student had obtained. The following chart compares today's grade system with that used in previous years.

Comparison of Standard Education Levels			
Pre-1907	1907 to 1918	1918 to 1924	Post-1924
Standard	Grade/ Form	Grade	Grade
I	1 & 2	1 & 2	1 & 2
II	3 & 4	3 & 4	3 & 4
III	5 & 6	5 & 6	5 & 6
IV	7 or 7 & 8	7 or 7 & 8	7 or 7 & 8
V	8	8	8
VI	Junior Form	First and Second Year	9 & 10
VII	Middle Form	Third Year	11
VIII	Senior Form	Fourth Year	12

1867 Confederation of Canada, July1. Section 93 of the British North America Act establishes the current basis of a publicly funded and provincially controlled school system; it protects the rights of separate and dissentient schools that existed prior to Confederation.

1870 North Western Territory and Rupert's Land transfer from the Hudson's Bay Company to the Dominion of Canada.

1870 The province of Manitoba is formed, with denominational schools and French and English as official languages.

1871 August 21, Treaty 2 is signed; it covers a small portion of southeastern Saskatchewan.

1874 September 15, Treaty 4 is signed; it covers most of Saskatchewan south of the South Saskatchewan River. The federal government commits to provide schools on reserves.

1875 The North-West Territories Act is passed; it provides for local governments to operate schools, and maintains the rights of Catholic and Protestant separate schools.

1876 The North-West Territories Act is proclaimed, and provision is made for education.

1876 September 9, Treaty 6 is signed; it covers much of Saskatchewan north of the South Saskatchewan River and south of Lac La Ronge.

1879 Nicholas Flood Davin's *Report on Industrial Schools for Indians and Half-Breeds* advocates for residential schools.

1881 North-West Territories schools with a minimum daily attendance of 15 students are paid one-half of the teacher's salary from the Parliament of Canada. This is the first financial support to education from government in the North-West Territories.

During the late 1800s most students completed Standard II or III (Grades 3 to 6). Teachers were classified according to their level of education: third-class teachers had achieved Standard VI (roughly Grade 9), second-class teachers Standard VII (Grade 10), and first-class teachers Standard VIII (Grade 11). The education system in the 1880s was thus largely preoccupied with providing basic education to as many children as possible and using older students as teachers.

The School Ordinance of 1888 was the first to use the term "high school" and to prescribe under what conditions high school education should take place. This Ordinance made grants available to schools that met a number of conditions related to class size, teacher qualifications, and the ability of students to pass the Board of Education entrance examination. It also permitted two adjacent school districts to establish "Union Schools." The two districts would jointly operate the school: this arrangement would enable the districts to bring together enough students to be eligible to receive the high school grant. The first two Union Schools in the territories were established in Regina and Calgary in 1889.

By 1895 agriculture had become a component of education, and that year the Council of Public Instruction adopted a Programme of Studies that included a course called "Nature Study and Agriculture" for students in Standards I to V. This course included topics from the simple observation of nature, in the lower Standards, to preparation of the soil for seed, feeding and care of animals, destruction of noxious weeds, use of fertilizer, and other practical topics in the upper Standards. A subject called "Manual Training," offered in a few settings, included woodwork, cardboard or Bristol board cutouts, and clay modeling. By 1901 just over 2% of the school population, or 514 students, were in high school grades. Grants encouraged the provision of high school education, but Saskatchewan was still an agricultural community: the main purpose of high school education was seen to support the preparation of teachers, or to cater for the intellectually gifted or wealthy who might go on to university or professional school. High school enrolments therefore remained low.

School District Consolidation

When schools offered only elementary education, the challenges were manageable and thousands of school districts and thousands of schools sprang up across the province. However, as soon as high school or secondary education became an interest, school district consolidation began. The first mention of high schools was made in the legislation in 1888. That same legislation permitted the establishment of Union Schools, made up of two or more existing school districts and established to facilitate high school education. The Secondary Education Act, passed two years after Saskatchewan became a province, provided grants to aid high schools and collegiate institutes; rural and village schools could provide high school education in continuation rooms, but did not have the status of high schools or collegiate institutes. This organizational arrangement and the grant structure at the time created a disincentive to provide secondary education outside of the larger centres. From 1906 to 1911 the number of school districts in Saskatchewan grew from 1,190 to 2,546, and to 3,873 by 1916. The secondary education legislation, the growth of elementary enrolments, and the pioneer environment resulted in the percentage of the school population attending high school declining between 1906 and 1911; and even by 1916, less than 6% of the school population was in high school.

In 1917, the School Attendance Act made school attendance compulsory: if children had not graduated from Grade 8, attendance was required for those aged 7 to 12 and living within 2.5 miles of school, and for those aged 13 and 14 and living 3.5 miles from school. In 1964 the age of attendance was raised to 16. A crisis in education occurred before Saskatchewan was a decade old. At that time, throughout North America many held the view that education was not keeping pace with the advancing needs of a modern society; this concern grew, and Saskatchewan Premier WALTER SCOTT declared June 30, 1916, a public holiday so citizens could discuss the issue. The government went on to hire Dr. Harold W. Foght, a specialist in Rural School Practice, Bureau of Education, Washington, DC, to conduct a survey of the Saskatchewan educational system. Foght filed his report on January 20, 1918; it contained 53 recommendations covering all aspects of the elementary-secondary system, including teacher education. The recommendations called for sweeping changes, including a call for the consolidation of school districts on the basis of municipalities rather than school districts, the expansion of high school education to all aspects of the public education system, a reduction in the examination system, and the modification of the curriculum to include vocational education. Foght's school consolidation recommendations were not immediately acted upon, but the issue did not go away: throughout the 1920s and beyond, teachers pressed for the reorganization of the school districts. The government encouraged school district consolidation through legislation in 1912, 1928, and 1940, but little occurred.

Following the election of the CO-OPERATIVE COMMONWEALTH FEDERATION (CCF) government, with WOODROW LLOYD (a former SASKATCHEWAN TEACHERS' FEDERATION president) as Minister of Education, the Larger School Units Act was passed in late 1944. It moved away from a voluntary approach and empowered the Minister of Education to establish larger school units. The basic unit of governance and administration of schools was changed to a larger school unit comprised of several school districts. Although the government softened its position to accommodate exceptions, forty-six larger school units had been formed by 1946, and a map had been drawn that called for the establishment of sixty larger units in rural Saskatchewan. The 1944 Larger School Unit Legislation appeased the calls for consolidation. The baby boom, the growth of the school age population during the 1950s and 1960s, and the greater availability of secondary education turned educational discussion toward other matters for nearly forty years. However, enrolments began to decline in the early 1970s, and calls for changes to the governance of education grew in the late 1970s and early 1980s. The reality of education in Saskatchewan from 1970 to 1990 was one of declining enrolments, and increased expectations and cost; as a consequence, the government appointed Murray Scharf, Dean of Education at the University of Saskatchewan, and Hervé Langlois, deputy director of education, Saskatoon School Division #13 to review school finance and governance.

Their 1991 report recommended greater equity in the school finance system and a reduction in the number of school divisions to about one-third of the 1990 number. The government continued to proceed cautiously, and after extensive consultations it announced in 1996 a restructuring policy that created the expectation that school boards should amalgamate, but this remained voluntary. Under the policy a number of school divisions did amalgamate, and the number of school divisions declined from 120 in 1996 to 82 in 2004. In 2003, the government established the Boughen Commission to examine the high level of property taxation; it recommended a reduction in property taxes and in the number of school divisions. In May 2004 the Minister of Education announced the intention to restructure school divisions, and established a task force to draw a new map of school division boundaries. The task force, chaired by Fred Herron, filed its report in November 2004; the Minister of Learning accepted its recommendation to reduce the number of school divisions to 34, and set in motion the processes necessary for this to be accomplished by January 1, 2006. Restructuring of the minority faith school (Roman Catholic separate) divisions will likely bring that number to below 30 school divisions by that time.

Teacher Education

The 1888 Ordinance that provided grants for Union high schools also permitted Union Schools to set up Normal departments for the training of teachers. Prior to this there was no formal teacher-training program, and the supply of teachers came from outside of the Territories or from upper-level students who were pressed into service. The name NORMAL SCHOOL is an adaptation of the French *École Normale*, a place where students learn the *norms* necessary to teach. In Saskatchewan, the opportunity to establish Normal departments in Union Schools was actually the opportunity to dedicate a room in the school where students were taught to be teachers. The first such classes were offered as "The Science of Teaching" and "School Law" in 1888. There was a large demand for teachers, and the Board of Education decided in September 1890 to offer Normal School classes, called "Local Sessions," in any centre where ten or more students requested these classes. Once underway, Local Sessions were typically operated for a couple of months a year, and targeted students entering the third-class certificate program (the lowest level, about equivalent to Grade 9). Often taught by school inspectors, these sessions were offered in nearly a dozen centres throughout the province and served to provide at least some training as the demand for teachers grew. The last local session was offered in 1928. Teacher shortages gave way to teacher surpluses in the 1930s, and the concern with shortages did not return until the 1950s. By the 1960s, teachers were once again being recruited from overseas.

In the fall of 1893, the Normal School in Regina commenced offering classes out of Alexandra School. A new facility was opened in January 1914, by which time the Saskatoon Normal School had already opened (1912). The Moose Jaw Normal School opened in 1927. The Regina Normal School closed in 1944, but opened again in 1957 to absorb the students from Moose Jaw as the latter's Normal School closed to accommodate the Saskatchewan Technical Institute. In 1953, the Normal Schools in Saskatoon and Moose Jaw were changed to Teachers' Colleges, and in order to

1893 The first Normal School is established in Regina. In April, David J. Goggin is appointed principal of the North-West Territories Normal School; he becomes Superintendent of Education in December.

1897 The Manitoba Schools Question is resolved through the involvement of Prime Minister Laurier. The compromises allow for instruction in French if 10 or more students speak French; Catholic schools are not publicly funded.

1899 June 21, Treaty 8 is signed.

1901 The first Department of Education is established.

1903 On November 19 the Legislature of the North-West Territories under the leadership of F.W.G. Haultain seeks a university for the Territories.

1905 The Saskatchewan Act is passed and the province of Saskatchewan is formed.

1906 August 28, Treaty 10 is signed.

1907 The Secondary Education Act, formally known as An Act to Provide for the Organization and Maintenance of Secondary Educational Institutions, is passed. The Saskatchewan Educational Association is formed. The University Act creates the University of Saskatchewan. Chief Justice Edward L. Wetmore is the only nominee for the post of first chancellor of the University of Saskatchewan.

1908 On August 20, Walter Murray is appointed the first president of the University of Saskatchewn.

1909 April 7, Saskatoon is chosen as the location of the University of Saskatchewan. The board of governors approves the College of Agriculture as a fundamental founding part of the new university. Emmanuel College is affiliated with the University of Saskatchewan. September 29, is the first day of classes at the U of S.

1910 Law classes are first offered at the University of Saskatchewan. The practice of including Métis children in Indian residential schools is ended.

1911 The Methodist Church registers the first students in Regina College.

1912 The first edition of the University of Saskatchewan student newspaper *The Sheaf* is published. The first earned degrees are awarded at the University of Saskatchewan: seven Bachelor of Arts degrees; five are awarded to men, and two to women. The first classes in Agriculture begin. The Association Franco-Canadienne de la Saskatchewan is formed. Canada passes the Agricultural Aide Act, which provides agricultural education and aide to farmers. Saskatoon Normal Schools offers its first classes. Canada passes the Agricultural Instruction Act giving financial support to instruction in Agriculture.

1913 Saskatchewan amends the School Act to provide for manual and industrial training.

1914 The Saskatchewan Union of Teachers is formed, a forerunner to the STF.

1915 The Saskatchewan School Trustees' Association is formed.

1916 Premier Walter Scott declares June 30 a provincial holiday to discuss the lack of quality in the Saskatchewan education system.

1917 The School Attendance Act is passed.

1918 Harold W. Foght files his report, *A Survey of Education in the Province of Saskatchewan*. The Association des Commissaires d'Écoles Franco-Canadiens is formed. English becomes the sole language of instruction, except for French-speaking students during their first year of attendance at school.

SASKATCHEWAN ARCHIVES BOARD R-B4594

Normal School, Regina, 1915.

bring a more university-based teacher education system, the Act Respecting the Education and Training of Teachers was passed in 1964. This Act eliminated the term Teachers' College and integrated all teacher education programs into the University of Saskatchewan College of Education at the Saskatoon and Regina campuses; this remained the situation until First Nation and Métis teacher education programs were developed in 1972.

University Development

Many believe that no university existed in Saskatchewan until the University of Saskatchewan was established in Saskatoon in 1907. Technically, this view is not correct: in 1883 the government of Canada had provided Bishop McLean, of the Anglican Archdiocese of Saskatchewan in Prince Albert, with a dominion charter which established the University of Saskatchewan. The Anglican Church also operated Emmanuel College in Prince Albert, which was to be a part of the new University of Saskatchewan; but the charter obtained by Bishop McLean never developed into a university. In 1903, F.W.G. HAULTAIN, Premier of the North-West Territories, proposed the establishment of a single, secular, and state-supported university; he believed that Saskatchewan could only support one university, funded by the government but free from government control. Haultain also held the view that denominational bickering had not helped the cause of scholarship in the predominantly denominational university system of eastern Canada, and was adamant that the University of Saskatchewan be non-denominational. Haultain made the establishment of the UNIVERSITY OF SASKATCHEWAN an issue in the election of 1905, and although he did not win, Walter Scott, the winner, also made this a priority.

In July 1907 the University Act came into effect, providing for one university with the exclusive right to grant university degrees, except in theology. The exception for theology was to accommodate Emmanuel College in Prince Albert: as the College technically held the charter for the University of Saskatchewan, the Anglican Church and Emmanuel College retained religious degree-granting status while giving up their hold on the charter for the University as a whole. By 1909, Emmanuel College had moved to Saskatoon and become the first theological affiliated college with the new University of Saskatchewan. Some of the first steps in establishing the University were to elect a senate (the first meeting was on November 13, 1907) and choose a president: WALTER MURRAY was appointed and commenced work on August 20, 1908.

Early in its deliberations, the board of governors recognized that the economic base of the province was agriculture and that this should be emphasized; this focus was intense and long lasting. Walter Murray was president during the developmental years from 1908 to 1937. After defining the foundational character of the University, his next task was to determine the location: this was controversial, with Regina, Saskatoon, Prince Albert, Indian Head, North Battleford, and Moose Jaw among the contenders. Regina was Walter Murray's personal choice; but on April 7, 1909, the board of governors chose Saskatoon. The Methodist Church had wanted to enhance its status among the other denominations in the province; this desire, combined with the need for secondary education in Saskatchewan and the bitterness about the University going to Saskatoon, led to the establishment of Regina College by the Methodist Church in 1911. The Saskatchewan Methodist Church proposed such a college at its annual meeting in 1909, and by the fall of 1911 the first students were registered. The basic idea was to provide secondary education to rural Saskatchewan students who did not have such an opportunity. Regina College became noted for its conservatory of music, which made it a musical centre for Regina and the surrounding area.

As the province grew, secondary education became available to more communities. By the early 1920s Regina College, under the leadership of ERNEST W. STAPLEFORD, president from 1915 to 1934, realized that there was little future for such a secondary school, and Stapleford developed a plan to transform the College from a secondary school to a university. He reasoned that providing university courses in Regina was a way to keep Regina College open and to meet the need of the people of southern Saskatchewan for a university closer to home. In 1925, Regina College became affiliated with the University of Saskatchewan. The GREAT DEPRESSION of the 1930s brought financial difficulties to both the University of Saskatchewan and Regina College; the College ran out of money, and on July 1, 1934, the University of Saskatchewan took it over. The establishment of a second university in Saskatchewan had been averted; but Regina College continued to offer the first two years of university, the conservatory of music, and a fine arts program. With the growing demand for greater access to university education that followed World War II, the University of Saskatchewan decided in 1959 to implement an arts and science degree at Regina College: on July 1, 1961, Regina College was renamed University of Saskatchewan, Regina Campus.

The establishment of a degree program did not dissipate the demands for an independent university in Regina; in fact, the difficulties of managing the Regina Campus from Saskatoon may have exacerbated the problems between the two locations. Those problems grew to such proportions that efforts to create a workable one-university system failed. In 1973 the government established the HALL COMMISSION to find a solution. Retired Chief Justice EMMETT HALL filed his report in December 1973, and by the next summer the government had acted on its recommendation for a two-university system. In July 1974, legislation passed that established two universities in Saskatchewan: the University of Saskatchewan and the UNIVERSITY OF REGINA.

In Regina, Campion College had been established in 1917; it was given Junior College status in 1923 and initially affiliated with St. Boniface College in Manitoba in order to provide degree-granting status; finally, in 1964 Campion College was granted federation with the University of Saskatchewan, Regina Campus. Similarly, Luther College, established in 1914 in Melville, began offering University classes in Regina in 1926 through an affiliation with Capital University in Ohio; it became officially affiliated with the University of Saskatchewan, Regina Campus in 1968. The affiliation of Campion College and Luther College continued with the University of Regina when it was established in 1974 (*see* CAMPION COLLEGE, UNIVERSITY OF REGINA and LUTHER COLLEGE, UNIVERSITY OF REGINA). In 1976, the University of Regina and the FEDERATION OF SASKATCHEWAN INDIAN NATIONS entered into a federation agreement creating the Saskatchewan Indian Federated College (SIFC), an independently administered university college. On June 21, 2003, National Aboriginal Day, the College was renamed the FIRST NATIONS UNIVERSITY OF CANADA; it provides an opportunity for students to learn in an environment of First Nations culture and values.

During the 1990s, the government of Saskatchewan initiated a number of efforts to address matters of quality, accessibility, and accountability at the universities. The Johnson Report of 1993 and the MacKay report of 1996 are particularly noteworthy in the continuing efforts by the universities and government to provide efficient university education in Saskatchewan.

Teachers and Trustees

The Saskatchewan Teachers' Federation (STF) and the SASKATCHEWAN SCHOOL BOARDS ASSOCIATION (SSBA) have played significant roles in Saskatchewan's education system (prior to 2003 the SSBA was known as the Saskatchewan School Trustees' Association or SSTA). Although the provincial government is constitutionally responsible for education, over the years it delegated substantial responsibility to locally elected, fiscally responsible school boards. Because of their important role in education and the expertise they bring, teachers have also had a significant impact on the development of the education system in the province. In many ways the Trustees' Association and the Teachers' Federation grew out of a May 1908 conference of teachers, trustees, and department officials that was called to address the issue of the large number of students who could not speak English; this conference became a regular event, and the group became known as the Saskatchewan Education Association. By 1915, out of these meetings the trustees formed the SSTA, which in 1917 held a convention and passed a resolution calling for instruction in English only. Consequently, in 1918 the French-Canadian school trustees broke away from the SSTA and formed their own group, the *Association des Commissaires d'Écoles Franco-Canadiens*. Similarly, the trustees' convention of

1919 Canada passes the Technical Education Act, providing direct training for young people and using conditional grants to encourage technical education in the provinces. The Saskatchewan Union of Teachers changes its name to Saskatchewan Teachers' Alliance. The Regina Collegiate Board introduces the first adult education programs.

1920 Saskatchewan passes the Vocational Education Act in 1920, enabling school boards to establish schools aimed at training students in industrial programs.

1921 The first teachers' strike in Saskatchewan occurs in Moose Jaw.

1925 Regina College becomes affiliated with the University of Saskatchewan. The Outpost Correspondence School is established to serve settlers and trappers.

1926 The School of Medicine is founded at the University of Saskatchewan. It provides the first two years of medicine, then students must complete medical school at another university.

1927 The School of Education is opened at the University of Saskatchewan.

1930 The Outpost Correspondence School is reorganized to establish the Saskatchewan Government Correspondence School. The Teachers' Superannuation Act is passed.

1931 Grants for the school year are based on 200 rather than 210 days. French as a language of instruction during the first year of school is removed. The first radio school broadcasts are transmitted to support correspondence school courses.

1932 The R.J.D. Williams Provincial School for the Deaf is opened in Saskatoon. The Rural Teachers' Association is established.

1933 The Saskatchewan Book Bureau opens.

| 1934 | January 1, the Saskatchewan Teachers' Federation is formed. Regina College becomes part of the University of Saskatchewan. |

1934 January 1, the Saskatchewan Teachers' Federation is formed. Regina College becomes part of the University of Saskatchewan.

1935 An Act Respecting the Teaching Profession is the first in the English-speaking world to require all teachers to belong to a teachers' organization, in this case the Saskatchewan Teachers' Federation.

1937 Walter Murray retires as first president of the University of Saskatchewan.

1938 The School of Nursing is established at the University of Saskatchewan.

1939 Canada passes the Youth Training Act, providing capital and operational funding for the training of skilled and unskilled workers in the war industries. The Trade School Regulation Act governing Saskatchewan private vocational schools comes into force.

1940 The School Act is amended to provide a minimum wage of $700 per year for teachers.

1944 The Normal School in Regina closes. The Larger School Units Act is passed. The Department of Education establishes the first Adult Education Branch.

1945 A voluntary provincial salary schedule is distributed to all school districts. Canada passes the Vocational Schools Act, which leads to the establishment of a number of Composite Schools in Saskatchewan. The province passes the first Saskatchewan Apprenticeship Act, which provides a system for the training and certification of apprentices and the trades.

1946 The School of Medicine at the University of Saskatchewan becomes a full-fledged College of Medicine. The forerunner to the Saskatchewan Association of School Business Officials is established.

1920 adopted a resolution calling for the abolition of separate schools. Almost immediately, the Catholic trustees formed the Catholic School Trustees' Association of Saskatchewan. To some extent, these early divisions continue to be manifested in trustee organizations in 2005.

The Saskatchewan Teachers' Federation grew out of a 1914 meeting of Premier Walter Scott with exam markers. He asked them for suggestions on what should be done to improve the education system, and these teachers came up with a number of suggestions, most of which addressed improvements to the working conditions of teachers. This was not what the Premier was looking for; but the teacher examiners, undeterred, called teachers to a meeting at the Normal School in Regina with the intent of establishing a teachers' organization. At the meeting in July 1914 the Saskatchewan Union of Teachers was formed; starting with less than twenty members, the organization had as its purpose to improve the situation of teachers and upgrade professional standards. Many teachers did not like the term "Union," so the name was changed to the Saskatchewan Teachers' Alliance in 1919; this name change, combined with reductions in teachers' salaries following WORLD WAR I, provided an environment conducive to the growth of an organization concerned with working conditions, salaries, and benefits for teachers. The status of female teachers was very low during the early 1900s: as a consequence the women teachers of Saskatoon began to meet, and formed the Saskatoon Women Teachers' Association (SWTA) in 1918. They limited their membership to female grade school teachers, and their aim was to advance the welfare of Saskatoon women teachers. Under the leadership of VICTORIA MINERS, a founding member of the SWTA, they addressed the poor salaries for women as well as the policy, common throughout North America, of discriminating against married women teachers.

The first teacher strike in Saskatchewan occurred in 1921 in Moose Jaw. Although the strike was short, teachers felt it was a symbolic victory for the Alliance because the Board recognized the right of teachers to negotiate with boards through representatives. During the 1920s the Alliance grew in membership and was instrumental in lobbying the government to pass in 1930 the Teachers' Superannuation Act, which provided pension benefits to teachers. The early 1930s witnessed reductions in teachers' salaries, and poor working conditions. Teachers in rural parts of the province felt these changes most severely: disenchanted with the Alliance, which they considered dominated by teachers in urban centres, they formed in 1932 a rival teachers' organization, the Saskatchewan Rural Teachers' Association. In October 1933, through a series of discussions a group of independent teachers from the Balcarres and Fort Qu'Appelle area called a teachers' meeting in Regina. At this meeting the concept of one Saskatchewan teachers' organization was supported, and on January 1, 1934, the two existing teachers organizations combined to form the Saskatchewan Teachers' Federation (STF). Over the next year, the STF lobbied government for support and made it an issue in the 1934 election. These efforts were successful, and on February 21, 1935, royal assent was given to An Act Respecting the Teaching Profession, which was the first in the English-speaking world to recognize a teachers' organization and to make membership in its federation compulsory and a condition of employment.

Meanwhile, the Saskatchewan School Trustees' Association spent most of the 1920s and 1930s providing administrative and educational services to school districts. The Bryant Public Speaking Contest established in 1920, the School Supply Bureau established in 1925, the development of a co-operative school insurance plan, and support to high school drama competitions were but a few of the activities in which the SSTA was engaged during its first thirty years of existence.

During the 1930s the STF focused its energies on the improvement of teachers' salaries, but its efforts were unsuccessful. However, in March 1940, with the support of teachers, government, and the SSTA, the School Act was amended to provide for a minimum wage for teachers of $700 per year. Beginning in 1922, teachers had advocated for their employment by the provincial government and for being paid according to a provincial salary schedule. Their efforts to establish a provincial salary schedule were unsuccessful for over seventy years: although during the late 1940s a number of provincial salary schedules were circulated, the use of these schedules was on a voluntary basis. In 1944 the province emerged from the Depression and the government had a mandate for change in education; the Minister of Education, WOODROW LLOYD, was an advocate for larger school units, teacher collective bargaining, payment of teachers according to a salary schedule, and for a co-operative approach to decision-making in education. By the end of the 1940s, the SSTA, the STF and the government had largely agreed to proceed with the Larger School Unit Act of 1944, the distribution of a voluntary provincial salary schedule of 1945, and the passage of the Teachers' Salary Negotiations Act of 1949. The latter required teachers and trustees to bargain when requested to by either side, and placed the onus on reaching a final agreement with the negotiating parties. In keeping with Woodrow Lloyd's emphasis on working together, this legislation was agreed to by the teachers and the trustees, and was passed unanimously in the Legislature. In 1952 the Teacher Tenure Act, providing greater job security for teachers, was passed; through it, teachers with two years of service with a school board, if terminated on June 30, could appeal to a non-binding board of conciliation for a review of the circumstance, and the board would have to defend its reasons for the termination.

Teacher supply and teacher qualifications had been a frequent concern, shared by both trustees and teachers, for the province's schools. Prior to the 1930s teacher shortages were the order of the day, and teacher qualifications and training were very rudimentary. During the 1930s, the economic downturn brought many former teachers back to teaching, and school boards received numerous applications for a single position; salaries dropped, and in many cases teachers were not paid for years. It was not until the 1940s that the issue of teacher qualifications and certification began to re-emerge. This matter became a first order of business in the 1950s as concerns about the quality of education grew and shortages of teachers returned. Discussions between the Department of Education, trustees and teachers about teacher education programs continued until 1964, when An Act Respecting the Education and Training of Teachers was passed.

Teacher bargaining was one area where the relationships between teachers and trustees were strained. Under the Teacher Salary Negotiation Act of 1949 disagreements that required conciliation and mediation steadily increased, until in 1965 the government appointed a committee headed by Judge Ben Moore to recommend a solution. In 1968, the Teachers' Salary Negotiations Act was replaced by the Teachers' Salary Agreements Act; the features of this new Act included salary agreements negotiated by teacher and school board area committees that included a number of school units, provision for the Minister to appoint a conciliator, and limiting the scope of agreements to salaries and allowances. The government changed in 1971 and a new Teacher Collective Bargaining Act was passed at the 1973 spring session of the Legislature, providing for bi-level bargaining: at the provincial level, teacher representatives bargained with the trustees and the government representatives on matters of salaries, some allowances, and major benefits; at the school division level, local teacher representatives bargained with local school board representatives. With a small number of changes, this bi-level bargaining process remains in place. With the exception of collective bargaining, the co-operative relationships between teachers and trustees continued to build on the base established by Woodrow Lloyd. In the later part of the 20th century, the superintendents and directors of education (under the auspices of their organization, the League of Educational Administrators, Directors and Superintendents, or LEADS), the school board financial officers (under the auspices of their organization, the Saskatchewan Association of School Business Officials, or SASBO), and the parent association (the Saskatchewan Association of School Councils, or SASC) became part of the semi-official group which had an influence on policy developments in the Kindergarten to Grade 12 education sector. These organizations did not always agree and often engaged in very independent directions, but they remain a force in the educational policy-making process of Saskatchewan.

K-12 Educational programs

In the early years of the 20th century, the Department of Education provided teachers with *Courses of Study for the Public Schools of Saskatchewan*; the 1913 course of studies for all elementary grades and subjects was thirty-seven pages long. The topics to be covered by teachers included morals and civics, physical culture and hygiene, reading and literature, composition, arithmetic, history, geography, nature study, writing, drawing, and music. In two or three small paragraphs an outline of the purpose of the subject was provided, and a few pages were devoted to each grade, with a very brief summary of the content to be taught in each subject. The last three pages listed the content of manual training as well as sewing and cookery, and the texts for music. The Department also published a *Course of Studies for High Schools and Collegiate Institutes*; the 1913 version was twelve pages long. The subjects listed included reading, English composition and rhetoric, history, algebra, geometry, trigonometry, chemistry, biology, physical science, as well as Latin, Greek, French, and German. Separate sections of the course of studies defined the content of "commercial" as including bookkeeping, shorthand, typewriting, and a special agricultural course on soil and its treatment, plant life, farm management, and construction. In 1913, the Department of Education also provided a three-page listing of reference books for teachers and school libraries; by 1929 this document was eight pages long, the course of study for elementary schools had grown to fifty-six pages, and the secondary course of study was fifty-one pages long. Compared to today's

1948 A committee of the Canadian House of Commons and the Senate concludes that the placing of First Nations children in residential schools should end.

1949 The passage of the Teachers' Salary Negotiations Act requires teachers and trustees to bargain.

1951 The Catholic School Trustees' Association of Saskatchewan amalgamates with the SSTA.

1952 The Teacher Tenure Act is passed. The first National Conference on Apprenticeship in Trades and Industries provides a stimulus for the development of the Red Seal program.

1953 The University Act is amended to eliminate reference to Normal Schools and to replace it with references to Saskatchewan Teachers' Colleges.

1956 The Royal Commission on Agriculture and Rural Life, chaired by W.B. Baker, director of the School of Agriculture, files its report on rural education.

The Moose Jaw Teachers' College closes to make way for the Saskatchewan Technical Institute; the Regina Teachers' College reopens to accommodate teachers in training from Moose Jaw. As a result of the Royal Commission on Agriculture and Rural Life report, the University and the provincial government establish the Centre for Community Studies, with W.B. Baker as director; its purpose is to study the characteristics of changing social and economic life in the province and to explore effective adaptations.

1959 Saskatchewan's first technical school, the Saskatchewan Technical Institute, opens in Moose Jaw. The University of Saskatchewan offers for the first time an Arts and Science degree at Regina College.

1960 Canada passes the Technical Vocational Training Act, which provides 75% of the funding for the construction and equipping of Comprehensive High Schools in Saskatchewan.

1961 July 1, Regina College is renamed the University of Saskatchewan, Regina Campus.

1963 A Plan for the Reorganization of Instruction in Saskatchewan Schools is adopted by the Department of Education. A second technical institute, the Central Saskatchewan Technical Institute, opens in Saskatoon. Amendments to the Secondary Education Act permit the establishment of Separate High School Districts.

1964 An Act Respecting the Education and Training of Teachers is passed; it integrates all teacher education into the University of Saskatchewan, with colleges in Regina and Saskatoon.

1965 The federal government passes the Adult Occupational Training Act, which terminates federal financial support to high school vocational programming and focuses federal training on adults.

1967 The Joint Committee on Higher Education recommends the establishment of a committee to examine the need for community colleges for Saskatchewan.

1968 The Teachers' Salary Agreements Act is passed, establishing area bargaining for teachers and trustees.

1969 The Parliament of Canada passes the Official Languages Act.

1970 The Prince Albert Regional Community College is established as a non-profit corporation.

standards, these teacher support documents were remarkably brief.

By the mid-1920s other supports to education developed. In 1926, the government established the Outpost Correspondence School, through which students in remote areas of the province were supplied with courses via the postal system. During its initial years, C.E. SHELDON-WILLIAMS headed the Outpost Correspondence School; this branch of the department soon became the SASKATCHEWAN GOVERNMENT CORRESPONDENCE SCHOOL. In 1931 radio broadcasts were instituted to support the School; during the first year, lessons covered English, history, science, Latin, and German. Originally, the lessons were one-half hour long and broadcast at 6:00 P.M. The difficult times of the 1930s caused the cancellation of the programs in 1938, but through the co-operation of the Canadian Broadcasting Corporation (CBC) and the four western provincial departments of education, school radio broadcasts were reintroduced in the fall of 1941. These broadcasts remained a mainstay of provincial educational programming until 1982, when they were terminated. Following the reintroduction of radio broadcasts, school broadcasts were expanded to include educational television in the mid-1950s.

During the late 1920s, under the leadership of R.J.D. Williams, petitions were made to government drawing attention to the educational needs of deaf children. At that time, deaf students were sent to Manitoba or Montreal; this caused hardship for the families, and Premier J.T.M. ANDERSON announced in the fall of 1929 that Saskatoon would be the site of a residential school for the deaf. The school opened in September 1932 with R.J.D. Williams as the Dean of Residence, a position he held until his retirement in 1963. The school, called the R.J.D. Williams Provincial School for the Deaf, provided kindergarten to Grade 12 programming for 3- to 21-year-old deaf or deaf-blind students. During the 1970s and 1980s, as it became more common to integrate deaf students into regular classrooms, enrolments in the school declined and on June 30, 1991, the school ceased to operate.

Toward the end of 1933, the SASKATCHEWAN BOOK BUREAU was established to coordinate the supply and handle the distribution of authorized textbooks, reference books, and library books at a uniform price throughout Saskatchewan; the demand for its services decreased in the late 1990s, and in 2003 it ceased operating. The Correspondence School, school broadcasts, the School for the Deaf, and the Book Bureau are only some of the examples of efforts by the government and the community to meet educational needs. Other programs included: the provision of public library and school library services; the development of a film library; the establishment of SaskMedia in 1974; the development of Western Canadian Curriculum Protocols and of a Pan-Canadian Science Curriculum Framework in the 1990s; the purchase of database licenses; the establishment of a virtual resource centre; the formation of an Educational Technology Consortium; and the establishment of CommunityNet in the first years of the 21st century.

Technical and Vocational Education

Prior to the turn of the century, little post-secondary or adult education existed in Saskatchewan. Some school boards offered what might be called technical vocational programs, such as manual training, bookkeeping, agriculture, and household science. However, the enrolment in these courses was limited, and until the entry of the federal government into the technical vocational education arena very little was accomplished. Although the provincial government was responsible for education, section 91 of the British North America Act of 1867 made the federal government responsible for the economic growth and well-being of Canada: with this mandate, the need to improve agricultural practice, and the pressures of the rapidly industrializing world, Canada passed legislation in 1912 and 1919 that supported education in agriculture and technical education. This legislation made federal money available to provinces for development in these areas. Saskatchewan responded by passing the Vocational Education Act of 1920, which gave school boards the authority to establish schools for the purpose of training youth in industrial programs, and made grants available for the construction of such facilities. The scattered population prevented most school districts from taking advantage of the opportunities presented by the Vocational Education Act, but the legislation led to the construction of three technical schools: Balfour Technical Collegiate, which opened in Regina in 1930; Moose Jaw Technical School, which opened in 1931; and the Technical Collegiate Institute in Saskatoon, which opened in 1932. As with other initiatives, however, little growth occurred in technical and vocational education during the 1930s.

World War II is sometimes considered to mark the beginning of an adult emphasis in technical and vocational education. This emphasis arose in part because of the needs growing out of the war, and in part as a response to the employment issues experienced in the 1930s. In 1944 the

Department of Education created the first Adult Education Branch, which within its first year of operation produced several publications and sponsored a number of adult education activities, including Lighted School classes (community-based evening classes covering art, sewing, wood work, and St. John's Ambulance), Basic English and Citizenship (a precursor to English as a Second Language programs), and Study-Action conferences. In some ways the Branch was a forerunner of the community college system which developed in the 1960s and 1970s, and whose objectives spoke to community life, co-operative citizen action, literacy, and issues confronting society. As the 1940s advanced, the increased industrial activity and the training needs of the returning armed forces caused the federal and provincial government to establish, under the Vocational Training Agreement, vocational training centres in Regina, Moose Jaw, Saskatoon and Prince Albert. However, by 1948 the demand for such programs had declined and all but the Saskatoon program closed; the Canadian Vocational Training School in Saskatoon became the first long-term non-university Saskatchewan facility with a mandate to provide adults with training to improve their technical and vocational employment skills.

Through the Vocational Schools Assistance Act of 1945 the federal government encouraged the construction of a number of composite secondary schools that offered academic courses as well as vocational and technical training. The federal Technical Vocational Training Assistance Act of 1960 provided 75% of the funding for approved provincial expenditures for technical or vocational education at high school level; this led to the construction and equipping of another set of schools placed strategically throughout Saskatchewan: the Comprehensive High Schools, which were to provide a broad range of courses designed to meet the needs of all high school students. Most of these schools were completed and in operation by the late 1960s.

Over the years, federal technical and vocational education initiatives in secondary schools in Saskatchewan led to the establishment of the three secondary technical schools around 1930, of composite schools in the 1940s and 1950s, and of the comprehensive high schools in the1960s. This leadership ended in 1965 when the federal Parliament passed the Adult Occupational Training Act, which terminated all programming for vocational high schools and replaced it with a focus on adult basic skill development, upgrading skills, language development for new Canadians, and apprenticeship training.

Apprenticeship training made little progress until 1944, when the provincial government, in response to the needs that grew out of the war period, established formal training programs for apprentices. The passage of the Saskatchewan Apprenticeship Act in 1945 and the first National Conference on Apprenticeship in Trades and Industries in 1952 provided a stimulus for advances in apprenticeship programs. As a consequence of the conference, the federal government developed a series of occupational analyses that enabled an educational process based on standard curricula and exams for apprenticeship. As individuals met the training and certification standards of the inter-provincial system, they received the Red Seal designation; this national recognition provided for the inter-provincial movement of trained workers. (*See also* APPRENTICESHIP AND TRADE CERTIFICATION).

In Saskatoon, the Canadian Training Vocational School had been operating since the 1940s

A carpentry class building a cabin at the Canadian Vocational Training School, Saskatoon, March 1954.

1971 Amendments are made to the School Act, requiring School Units to provide appropriate educational programs for disabled children. The Minister of Education establishes the Minister's Advisory Committee on Kindergarten to examine the feasibility of implementing a publicly funded Kindergarten program in Saskatchewan.

1972 The Indian Teacher Education Program (ITEP) is established at the University of Saskatchewan. A new foundation operating grant is implemented, linking grants to class size. Chaired by Ron Faris, the Minister's Advisory Committee on Community Colleges is established to develop a plan for community colleges in the province. The Department of Continuing Education is established to coordinate post-secondary education in Saskatchewan. The Faris Report recommends the establishment of community colleges in Saskatchewan. The Saskatchewan Institute of Applied Arts and Sciences is established in Regina.

1973 The Community Colleges Act is passed, establishing the community college system in Saskatchewan. The Hall Commission, consisting of Emmett Hall, Stewart Nicks and Gordon Sout, is established to examine the need for a university in Regina. The Teacher Collective Bargaining Act is passed, establishing bi-level provincial bargaining between teachers and a government-trustee team.

1974 Legislation is passed establishing the University of Regina. Funding for Kindergarten is provided.

1976 The Saskatchewan Indian Community College is established; in 1985 it is renamed the Saskatchewan Indian Institute of Technology. The Saskatchewan Indian Federated College is established at the University of Regina.

1977 The Northern Teacher Education Program (NORTEP) is established.

1978 The School Act and several other education-related pieces of legislation are consolidated in a new Education Act.

1980 The Gabriel Dumont Institute of Native Studies and Applied Research is established. The Trade Schools Regulation Act (1939) replaces by the Private Vocational Schools Regulation Act.

1981 The Minister of Education establishes the Curriculum and Instruction Review Committee to make recommendations on improving the educational system.

1982 The Canadian Charter of Rights and Freedoms in the Constitution Act guarantees official language and minority language rights in Canada. School radio broadcasts are terminated.

1984 The Directions report is filed, calling for long-term changes to curriculum in the province.

1986 Prince Albert's Northern Institute of Technology opens its doors, with a mandate to use a competency-based model to provide technical education to northern Saskatchewan. The last Indian residential school closes.

1988 Saskatchewan passes the Regional Colleges Act, renaming the community colleges regional colleges, reducing their number, and restructuring them with the Saskatchewan Institute of Applied Science and Technology. February 15: Justice Wimmer of Saskatchewan Court of Queen's Bench rules that some provisions of the Education Act are inconsistent with Section 23 of the Charter of Rights and Freedoms.

1989 The Coordinating Committee for the Governance of Francophone Schools by Francophones is established and files its report.

with a mandate to train and rehabilitate war veterans. To support the province's technology, industrial and apprenticeship needs, Saskatchewan's first technical institute, the Saskatchewan Technical Institute, was established in Moose Jaw in 1959. With the increased demand for a skilled labour force, a number of programs were moved in 1963 from the Canadian Training Vocational School to a new Central Saskatchewan Technical Institute in Saskatoon, which became the Kelsey Institute of Applied Arts and Sciences in 1974. A Regina Institute was added in 1972 with the opening of the Saskatchewan Institute of Applied Arts and Sciences (SIAAS), whose initial mandate was to provide Dental Nursing, Diploma Nursing, Psychiatric Nursing, and Nursing Assistant programs. Following the move to new facilities in 1973, the Institute was renamed the Wascana Institute of Applied Arts and Sciences. It took until 1986 before the Northern Institute of Technology in Prince Albert opened its doors, whose mandate was to provide technical education for northern Saskatchewan using a competency-based model; given the popularity with adults of a self-paced, performance-based and learner-driven model, the competency-based model expanded to other programs over the years.

Regional and Community Colleges

During the 1960s, technical and vocational needs were met in the technical institutions in Moose Jaw and Saskatoon; however, in rural Saskatchewan interest grew for training closer to home. The Royal Commission on Agriculture and Rural Life had filed its report in 1956, and one entire volume was devoted to rural education: critical of the adult education services of the government and the university in rural Saskatchewan, the report turned decision-makers' minds to the question of how rural Saskatchewan could be provided with better adult education services.

In Prince Albert, community members came together in 1964 to discuss post-high school education in basic literacy, trades skill training, technology training, university transfer, and leisure studies. These discussions led to the formation in 1970 of the first Saskatchewan Community College. Established as a nonprofit corporation, the College was operated by a council of community groups including the chamber of commerce, the local teachers' association, the school boards, city council, a number of agencies of the federal government, and representatives of First Nations and Métis groups.

At the provincial level, the University of Saskatchewan and the Minister of Education established in May 1965 a Joint Committee on Higher Education to examine all aspects of higher education; the committee, chaired by JOHN W.T. SPINKS, filed its *First Interim Report* in 1967. Following an election, the government also created a new Department of Continuing Education in 1972; on the basis of Ron Faris' 1972 report, the Community Colleges Act was passed in 1973; and by 1976 fourteen regional community colleges had been established, covering adult education for the entire province. The new community colleges were mandated to identify the adult education needs of the community and the local or provincial resources to meet those needs, and to coordinate and facilitate the delivery of programs. In 1988, the Regional Colleges Act was passed, in which the name of the colleges was changed from community to regional colleges. The focus of the colleges was directed away from the provision of leisure and hobby programming and toward occupational, labour market, and employment preparation; the delivery mechanism continued to be achieved by brokering courses through the universities and the institutes. The four urban community colleges and the technical institutes were amalgamated in 1988 to form the new SASKATCHEWAN INSTITUTE OF APPLIED SCIENCE AND TECHNOLOGY (SIAST). The establishment of SIAST began the process of moving away from the four independent institutes in Moose Jaw, Saskatoon, Regina, and Prince Albert, and toward one institute with four program centres. During the 1990s the colleges and institutes evolved as they tried to better meet the labour market needs of the province: these needs were growing, and a variety of methods for delivery expanded to include distance education, partnerships with employers, and linkages to the federal government.

Post-Secondary First Nations and Métis Education.

During the 1960s, the move away from residential schools was gaining momentum and the education system was beginning to recognize that treating First Nations and Métis students in the same way as non-Aboriginal students was not equitable. In 1972, the INDIAN TEACHER EDUCATION PROGRAM (ITEP) at the University of Saskatchewan was established, funded through a contribution agreement between Indian and Northern Affairs Canada and the University of Saskatchewan. Also in 1972, the Federation of Saskatchewan Indian Nations established the SASKATCHEWAN INDIAN CULTURAL CENTRE, which serves as a centralized resource centre through which First Nations languages, culture and traditional arts are preserved and revitalized. The Saskatchewan Indian Community College, established in 1976, had a well-defined geographic area: the land made up by all of the reserves and Crown land occupied by First Nations. None of the other colleges entered those land areas without the invitation of the Saskatchewan Indian Community College, and all adult education services were contracted with the College. The Indian Community College grew quickly, and in 1985 its name was changed to the SASKATCHEWAN INDIAN INSTITUTE OF TECHNOLOGIES (SIIT). Initially, SIIT delivered adult academic upgrading, as well as introductory skills and trades programming, but the program offerings grew to a broad array of vocational and technical training, and on July 1, 2000, the provincial legislation in Saskatchewan recognized SIIT as a post-secondary institution.

In 1980 the Métis, and those then known as non-registered and non-status Indians, established the GABRIEL DUMONT INSTITUTE (GDI) and the SASKATCHEWAN URBAN NATIVE TEACHER EDUCATION PROGRAM (SUNTEP). The provincial government funded the Institute, and SUNTEP established programs providing teacher training for students of Métis ancestry in Saskatoon, Regina, and Prince Albert. By 2005, well over 400 teachers had graduated from the program.

The Gabriel Dumont Institute of Native Studies and Applied Research grew to become the designated official educational arm of the MÉTIS NATION-SASKATCHEWAN; it offers accredited educational, vocational, and skills training opportunities in partnership with the Universities of Saskatchewan and of Regina, the Saskatchewan Institute of Applied Science and Technology (SIAST), and the regional colleges. One of the more innovative developments of the 1970s was the establishment in 1977 of the Northern Teacher Education Program (NORTEP). Based in La Ronge, the program is funded by the Northern Lights School Board and the northern Indian bands, and provides teacher education to northern students so that they can become teachers in their home communities across the north. It also offers a broad range of classes in Native Studies, Science, English, and the Cree and Dene languages.

When the Saskatchewan Indian Federated College first opened in the fall of 1976, it had nine students. In 2004, after becoming the First Nations University of Canada it had an enrolment of over 1,200, with students from every province and territory in Canada. It offers programs and services on three campuses in Regina, Saskatoon, and Prince Albert, and has ten academic departments, as well as community-based and distance education programs. Saskatchewan is now home to First Nations and Métis educational organizations that are fundamental to the education of students and the retention of Aboriginal culture and languages.

Curriculum and Instruction

In 1944, the appointment of Henry Janzen as the director of curriculum with the Department of Education marked a new beginning for curriculum development in the province. Prior to his appointment, teachers in a classroom might have a textbook in addition to the very general program of studies, but mostly they had to develop materials for their classrooms.

Beginning in the mid-1940s, curriculum began to change: more subject-specific curricula were developed for high schools, with improved textbooks and greater teacher participation in the development process. Enrolments in high school remained low, and about one-quarter of the students reached Grade 12: to improve the situation, programs were expanded to include more supports for teachers and students; these programs included guidance, instructional materials, and school broadcasts. In 1963 the Department of Education adopted a *Plan for the Reorganization of Instruction in Saskatchewan Schools*, which reorganized the grades into four divisions. The *Plan* was based on the principles that grade skipping, grade failure and repetition were not appropriate; rather, it advocated that teachers give students more time to learn the material and master the learning objectives. Average students would take three years to master the material in a division; a more gifted student might take two years; and a more challenged student might take four years. Division I comprised Grades 1, 2, and 3; Division II Grades 4, 5, and 6; Division III Grades 7, 8, and 9; and Division IV comprised Grades 10, 11, and 12. This was referred to as the continuous progress system.

On October 13, 1971, the Minister of Education established the Minister's Committee on Kindergarten Education, charged with examining the feasibility of implementing a publicly supported Kindergarten education program in Saskatchewan. In June 1972 the committee filed its report recommending the establishment of a half-day, non-compulsory, publicly funded Kindergarten program; the program was implemented as recommended, and remains essentially the same as it was in the early 1970s. Also during that period, public pressure on the education system grew. In the 1960s, at the high school level, more courses were added in order to retain students: the idea was to provide courses of interest to non-university bound students so that they would obtain a high school education. Parents and other members of the public expressed concern that education was

1991 June 30, the R.J.D. Williams Provincial School for the Deaf ceases to operate. In December, the Scharf-Langlois Report on Educational Finance and Governance files its report calling for school division restructuring and reform of the school grant system.

1992 The Dumont Technical Institute is established to serve the educational and technical needs of Saskatchewan's Métis, as the adult upgrading and technical training arm of the Gabriel Dumont Institute of Native Studies and Applied Research.

1993 The province of Saskatchewan announces its Saskatchewan Action Plan for Children. As Chair of the University Program Review Panel, A.W. Johnson delivers to the government his report, *Looking at Saskatchewan Universities: Programs, Governance, and Goals.*

1995 The Private Vocational Schools Regulations Act (1980) is repealed and replaced by the Private Vocational Schools Regulation Act, 1995 and the Private Vocational Schools Regulations, 1995.

1996 Harold H. MacKay files his report on universities, in which he proposes methods to enhance collaboration between the two institutions.

1998 The Minister of Education appoints the Special Education Review Committee to identify concerns and recommend improvements.

1999 The Apprenticeship and Trade Certification Act, 1999 is passed to establish the Apprenticeship and Trade Certification Commission. The Minister of Education establishes the Task Force and Public Dialogue on the Role of the School.

2000 The Saskatchewan Indian Institute of Technologies Act is passed to establish the Saskatchewan Indian Institute of Technologies, which provides adult basic education, post-secondary training programs, and related educational programs. In January, the Special Education Review Committee files its report, *Directions for Diversity: Enhancing Supports to Children and Youth with Diverse Needs.* In October, the Minister of Education files his response and action plan, called Strengthening Supports, for implementing the Special Education Review Committee's recommendations.

2001 The Task Force and Public Dialogue on the Role of the School files its final report, *SchoolPLUS: A Vision for Children and Youth.* Commonly referred to as the Role of School Report, it recommends that all services for children and youth be delivered in an integrated school-linked/school-based fashion. In April, the government announces KidsFirst, the cornerstone of the province's early childhood strategy; funded by the federal government, the purpose of the program is to enhance the capacity of vulnerable families to nurture their children.

2002 The Premier releases the government's response to the Role of School Report, *Securing Saskatchewan's Future: Ensuring the Wellbeing and Educational Success of Saskatchewan's Children and Youth,* which endorses the *SchoolPLUS* report and agrees that schools have two primary roles: to educate children and youth, and to support delivery of other human services such as health, social services and justice. Campus Saskatchewan is established to expand the use of technology-enhanced learning in the post-secondary sector.

watered down, and there was a call for a return to the basics. This sentiment was widespread across North America, and was one of the forces that led the Minister to establish in 1981 a Curriculum and Instruction Review Committee to make recommendations to support schools in meeting the students' and the public's needs. The Committee filed its report, called *Directions*, in 1984; the Minister supported its findings and established an implementation plan. The report launched the Department of Education and the education system into a collaborative effort to strengthen education through improvements to the curriculum and instructional practices. Through a set of goals, the design of a core curriculum, and the development of a resource-based learning policy, changes were supported; this direction would dominate educational developments for over twenty years.

At about the same time as the Department of Education embarked on the Curriculum and Instruction Review, it implemented new programs to address the needs of First Nations and Métis students and students living in poverty. These programs included the provision of more accurate First Nations and Métis content in the curriculum, and the establishment of the Community Schools Program, which provided a closer connection to the community, the provision of nutrition programs, and the engagement of teacher associates to work in classrooms. Sixteen community schools were established in the early 1980s; in addition, St. Paul's Roman Catholic School Division established the Saskatoon Native Survival School, later to be named Joe Duquette High School. These initiatives complemented a variety of other programs developed by school boards across the province.

Since at least the 1950s, concerns increased throughout North America about the ability of the education system to meet individual differences. Although the School for the Deaf had provided an institutional environment for deaf students in Saskatchewan, other students with special needs were frequently left with little or no opportunity to gain an education, or were educated in institutional settings. During the 1950s the department began to support school units as they established classes for gifted students or children with special needs. In the mid-1960s the trend changed from specialized, segregated classes to integrated classes where needs were met in the regular classroom. This inclusive approach made a major step forward with the passage of legislation in 1971, an amendment to the School Act which required school boards to provide appropriate educational programs for children with disabilities; the principle was that children must be provided with an education in the least restrictive environment. The integration of special needs students into regular classrooms received widespread support, but also encountered resistance from teachers, parents and students. Even with additional support programs, teachers found it difficult to teach children with severe special needs, and at the same time provide a quality education for other students; at times, some students and parents felt that the quality of non-special needs programs was being compromised. However, a Special Education Review that completed its work in 2000 confirmed inclusion as the appropriate philosophy of education; it made recommendations for supporting the inclusive philosophy, accelerating integrated services, enhancing accountability, and increasing resources. These recommendations were implemented.

School^PLUS

The connection between the well-being of school students and that of the communities served by the schools has been recognized since the first school was established in Saskatchewan in 1840. SCHOOLS AND COMMUNITY DEVELOPMENT have always been closely linked in the province: this helps to explain why declining school-age populations, increasingly larger school divisions, and the closure of schools have meant the demise of some communities. Such challenges led the Saskatchewan School Trustees' Association to hold a symposium on the "Role of the School" in 1992, the purpose being to provide a forum for examining the expanding role of the school and to develop a forward-looking and commonly supported understanding of that role. The 1984 *Directions* report had recommended that the government departments of Health, Education and Social Services establish mechanisms for the coordination of their services. Social issues including rural depopulation, cross-cultural problems, family changes, and youth violence began to overtake the service providers and their clients, particularly students. In response to such concerns, the government released its Action Plan for Children in 1993. In late 1998, educational stakeholders approached the Minister of Education seeking a review of the role of schools. The Minister established the Task Force and Public Dialogue on the Role of the School, with Michael Tymchak as Chair; its mandate was to engage the community at large in a discussion of the role of the school and to identify the extent to which there was a gap between the expectations of the school and the school's ability to meet those expectations. In February 2001 its report, *School^PLUS: A Vision for Children and Youth*, was submitted to the Minister.

On the basis of similar principles, the federal government and the province of Saskatchewan recognized that improved early childhood services would help break the cycle of poverty. The province had been involved in an Early Childhood Development policy since the unveiling of Saskatchewan's Action Plan for Children in 1993. The value of early childhood (prenatal to Pre-Kindergarten) programs to prevent such problems as Fetal Alcohol Syndrome was recognized by all provinces: as a result, in September 2001 Canada's First Ministers issued an "Early Childhood Communiqué" outlining the commitment of federal, provincial, and territorial governments to work together to address the early developmental needs of all Canadian children. The federal government committed to fund the program, and Saskatchewan established the *KidsFirst* program, which began operation in September 2002 in eight communities in southern Saskatchewan and in all the communities in the northern part of the province.

Meanwhile, the School[PLUS] report had concluded that there was a gap between the capacity of the school and the expectations of the community; further, it recommended that the role of the school should be expanded to serve as a centre for addressing social issues: all schools should take on additional responsibilities, and in that sense become School[PLUS]. In 2002, the government's response was released under the signature and commitment of six Ministers of the government with a covering message from the Premier: it endorsed the recommendations of the report and launched a government commitment to the School[PLUS] concept. In a major policy statement, the government acknowledged that the role of the school had changed and that it now carries two functions: to educate children and youth, and to serve as a community centre for the delivery of appropriate social, health, recreation, culture, justice and other services for children and their families.

Conclusion

The history of education in Saskatchewan is filled with endeavours at the local, provincial and national levels to meet the learning, training and community needs of the many dimensions of the province's society. Those efforts faced the challenge of people living across vast areas, in isolated communities, from various cultural, religious and language traditions, and from various socio-economic circumstances. Throughout the history of Saskatchewan, education has been viewed as the foundation needed for people to reach new and better opportunities.

FURTHER READING:
Campbell, E. 1996. *Reflections of Light: A History of the Saskatoon Normal School (1912-1953) and the Saskatoon Teacher's College (1953-1964).* Saskatoon: College of Education, University of Saskatchewan.
Deiter, C. 1999. *From Our Mother' Arms: The Intergenerational Impact of Residential Schools in Saskatchewan.* Toronto: United Church Publishing House.
Gallant, E. 1989. *A Fransaskois Component for the Saskatchewan School System.* Regina: Saskatchewan Education.
Hayden, M. 1983. *Seeking a Balance: The University of Saskatchewan, 1907-1982.* Vancouver: University of British Columbia Press.
Joint Committee on Higher Education. 1967a. *First Interim Report.* Regina: Saskatchewan Education.
——. 1967b. *Second Interim Report, Volume 1.* Regina: Saskatchewan Education.
——. 1968. *Second Interim Report, Volume 2.* Regina: Saskatchewan Education.
Kojder, A.M. 1979. "The Saskatoon Women Teachers' Association: A Demand for Recognition." Pp. 177-191 in D.C. Jones, N.M. Sheehan, and R.M. Stamp (eds.), *Shaping the Schools of the Canadian West.* Calgary: Detselig.
Lambert, R.S. 1963. *School Broadcasting in Canada.* Toronto: University of Toronto Press.
Lapointe, R., and L. Tessier. 1988. *The Francophones of Saskatchewan: A History.* Regina: Campion College, U of R.
Mandelbaum, David G. 1979 (1940). *The Plains Cree: An Ethnographic, Historical, and Comparative Study.* Regina: Canadian Plains Research Center.
McLachlan, E. 1999. *With Unshakeable Persistence: Rural Teachers of the Depression.* Edmonton: NeWest.
Milloy, J.S. 1999. *A National Crime: The Canadian Government and the Residential School System, 1879 to 1986.* Winnipeg: University of Manitoba Press.
Noonan, B. 1998. *Saskatchewan Separate Schools.* Muenster, Saskatchewan: St. Peter's Press.
Peck, J. 1988. *Post-secondary Education in Saskatchewan: An Institutional History.* Regina: Saskatchewan Learning.
Pitsula, J.M. 1988. *An Act of Faith: The Early Years of Regina College.* Regina: Canadian Plains Research Center.
Poelzer, I. 1990. *Saskatchewan Women Teachers, 1905-1920: Their Contributions.* Saskatoon: Lindenblatt and Hamonic Publishing.
Ray, A.J., J. Miller and F. Tough. 2000. *Bounty and Benevolence: A History of Saskatchewan Treaties.* Montreal: McGill-Queen's University Press.
Riederer, L.A. 1991. *A History of the Saskatchewan Community Colleges.* Regina: University Extension, Seniors Education Centre.
Thorson, L.I. 1985. *70 Years of SSTA: A Short History of the Saskatchewan School Trustees' Association, 1915-1985.* Regina: Centax of Canada.
Tyre, R. 1968. *Tales Out of School.* Saskatoon: W.J. Gage.
Young, J., and B. Levin. 2002. *Understanding Canadian Schools: An Introduction to Educational Administration.* Scarborough, Ontario: Thomas Nelson.

2003 The Learning Resources Distribution Centre, formerly the Book Bureau, is closed. In May, the government announces the appointment of the Boughen Commission to examine the funding of K-12 education, with particular emphasis on the role of property taxation. On June 21, National Aboriginal Day, the Saskatchewan Indian Federated College is renamed the First Nations University of Canada. In December, the Boughen Commission files its report, *Finding the Balance.*

2004 In May, the Minister of Learning announces the response to the Boughen Commission and establishes a task force to draw new school division boundaries. In November, the Minister of Learning releases the new school division boundaries, to be effective on January 1, 2006.

COURTESY OF ITUNA AND DISTRICT MUSEUM

Miss Hilda Olson, teacher, File Hills School, 1914.

EDUCATION ACT, SS. 234–269: *see* LEGISLATION IN SASKATCHEWAN

Patti Dillistone is teacher-mom to daughters Nicole (left) and Kimberley (right), 1993.

EDUCATION, HOME-BASED. Home-based education in Saskatchewan was predominantly distance education for children who could not attend school; the Saskatchewan Correspondence School was established in 1925 to serve this group. Nowadays, some parents are choosing to educate their children at home for ideological reasons. While there exists a broad continuum of perspectives among home-based educators in Saskatchewan, three major perspectives prevail: child-initiated learning; late introduction to academic learning; and a traditional back-to-basics approach to learning, with a Christian philosophical base. Saskatchewan's home-based education parents are educating their children at home in a new legal climate, represented by the Canadian Charter of Rights and Freedoms, 1982. The powers and responsibilities of provincial governments with respect to both independent schools and home-based education were clarified in 1987, when the Supreme Court of Canada rendered its decision in the 1986 Alberta case, *Jones v. The Queen*.

When parents choose to educate their children at home, they are exercising a constitutional right to educate their children in accordance with their conscientious beliefs. No rights, however, are absolute. In particular, the right of parents to educate their children in accordance with their conscientious beliefs must be balanced against both the right of every child to an education and the com-

pelling interest of the state in the education of all children. This balance, envisaged by the Supreme Court of Canada in *Jones v. The Queen*, required a new legal framework for home-based education. In 1987, the provincial government appointed Gordon Dirks to examine both private or independent schools and home-based education in Saskatchewan. The Minister of Education released the *Review of Private Schooling in Saskatchewan* in 1987; it announced that home-based education would continue to be permitted, but with stronger supervisory procedures to ensure that home-schooled children receive a good education.

In 1989 the Minister of Education established an Independent Schools Branch, which was given administrative responsibility to develop new legislation, regulations, and policies with respect to independent schools and home-based education.

Saskatchewan has long had a reputation for the development of education policy through a collaborative process. In keeping with this collaborative process, the Minister then appointed independent schools and home-based education advisory boards to make recommendations concerning regulations, policies, and procedures governing the operation of Independent Schools and home-based education. The Home-Based Education Advisory Committee was established in 1990; chaired by Ernie Cychmistruk and representing all the major educational organizations, it submitted its report to the Minister in 1992. The report included recommendations and a new legal framework that acknowledged rights, freedoms, and legal principles regarding home-based education.

Implementation of the new legal framework involved amending the Education Act and establishing the *Home-Based Education Program Regulations* in 1993. In 1994, the *Home-Based Education Policy Manual* and *Home-Based Education Parent Handbook* were released.

While the new regulations and provincial-level policies provided a constant policy framework for home-based education in the province, boards of education retained local autonomy to administer this framework according to their own local circumstances. Boards of Education were given the responsibility for registering, monitoring, and providing services to home-based education students. As a result of this delegated responsibility, school divisions receive 50% of the per-pupil recognized expenditure for home-based education pupils. Home-based education student enrolment as a percentage of total provincial student enrolment is 1%; this enrolment increased from 1,021 in 1994 to 1,798 in 2003. The Minister of Education also established a Home-Based Education Review Board in 1993 to review the implementation of the new legal framework. This Review Board has met annually since 1993.   *Eugene Hodgson*

EGNATOFF, JOHN G. (1914–). Born in the Perdue-Arelee region of Saskatchewan on August 18, 1914, Dr. John G. Egnatoff has devoted his career to teacher training and education administration. Having earned his BPaed from the University of Toronto, Egnatoff taught in Saskatchewan rural and urban schools from 1935 to 1958. In the early 1960s, he served as an advisor on teacher training to the federal ministry of education in Nigeria. He was professor and head of the department of educational administration at the **UNIVERSITY OF SASKATCHEWAN** from 1968 to 1975, and was later named Professor Emeritus of Education. Dr. Egnatoff has also been active in political and community life as Liberal member of the Legislative Assembly for Melfort and a member of the First Baptist Church in Saskatoon. His many honours include the Queen's Silver Jubilee Medal and the Order of Canada in 1981.

1885 REBELLION: *see* **NORTH-WEST RESISTANCE; ABORIGINALS AND THE NORTH-WEST RESISTANCE**

ELIASON, FRANK (1883–1956). Frank Eliason was born January 13, 1883, in Sweden. In 1902 he emigrated to the United States and lived in Minneapolis until 1910. His American experiences led him to conclude that the producers of wealth, the labourers and the farmers, should unite to build a co-operative society. In 1910 Eliason came to Wynyard. Soon he was secretary of the Saskatchewan Grain Growers Association local. He coordinated bulk buying for local farmers, supported the organization of the wheat pool and in the 1920s was active in the **PROGRESSIVE PARTY**. In 1929 Eliason became the provincial secretary of the United Farmers of Canada (Saskatchewan Section), the successor to the SGGA. From its office in

Frank Eliason.

Saskatoon he administered the UFC during the Great Depression. His salary, with which he supported eight children whom he raised alone after the tragic death of his wife in 1921, was greatly reduced. In 1932 the UFC and the Saskatchewan Independent Labour Party met in Saskatoon and created the Farmer-Labour Party, the forerunner of the Saskatchewan CCF. Eliason served a dual role as secretary of both the new party and the UFC and directed day-to-day activities from UFC headquarters. The CCF was created at the 1932 Calgary conference, and Eliason's draft document was accepted as the basis for the program the party adopted. At the first CCF convention in 1933 Eliason moved the motion that the REGINA MANIFESTO be adopted as a whole. Eliason continued as secretary of the UFC until it was reorganized as the SASKATCHEWAN FARMERS UNION in 1949. He died March 22, 1956.

George Hoffman

FURTHER READING: Eliason, Frank. n.d. "Biography of a Swedish Emmigrant" [*sic*]. Typescript. Saskatchewan Archives Board; Hoffman, George. 1979. "The Saskatchewan Farmer-Labour Party, 1932–1934: How Radical Was It at Its Origins?" Pp. 210–24 in D.H. Bocking (ed.), *Pages from the Past: Essays on Saskatchewan History*. Saskatoon: Western Producer Prairie Books.

ELIZABETH FRY SOCIETY OF SASKATCHEWAN.

The Elizabeth Fry Society of Saskatchewan (EFSS), incorporated in 1981, is one of twenty-five sister agencies that comprise the Canadian Association of Elizabeth Fry Societies (CAEFS)–the first of which was established in Vancouver in 1939. EFSS is the only organization in the province that works with young and adult women involved with the criminal justice system; its programs and services aim to end recidivism and support crime prevention. Emphasis is upon a social development approach, not costly incarceration, in the belief that the most effective and humane solutions are community-based.

EFSS operates the Women's Community Training Residence (WCTR) in Saskatoon, the only facility of its kind in Saskatchewan. It has room for fourteen women, and small children sometimes live with their mothers. Women-staffed, the facility is open to provincially sentenced women, federally sentenced women on day parole, women on probation, women serving conditional sentences, women serving intermittent sentences, and women on bail supervision. They work or study in the community; in-house programming focuses upon women's concerns. The organization is culturally sensitive, as a disproportionate number of these women are Aboriginal: a staff Elder provides support and guidance, and encourages them to develop links, or reconnect, with their Aboriginal cultures.

Ailsa M. Watkinson

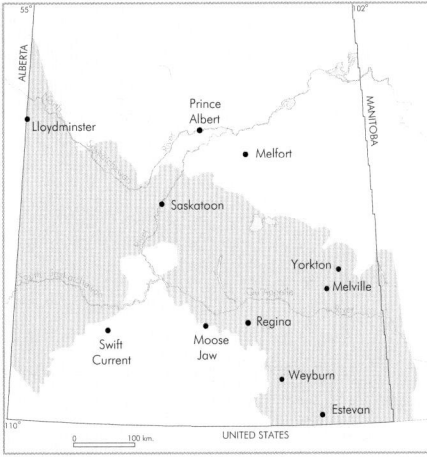

CANADIAN PLAINS RESEARCH CENTER MAPPING DIVISION

Figure EPS-1. Present extent of prairie evaporite salt in Saskatchewan and Manitoba.

ELK POINT SEA. The Elk Point Sea was a shallow waterway that extended southeastward from the present Northwest Territories to the Williston Basin of North Dakota, southwestern Manitoba and southeastern Saskatchewan. The inland sea persisted for much of mid-Devonian time, approximately 375 to 400 million years ago. For some millions of years the growth of organic reefs in the area from Great Slave Lake to the Yukon limited circulation into the embayment from open ocean to the northwest. The result of this restriction, along with a hot and arid climate, was that as much as 215 m of prairie evaporite–mostly halite (sodium chloride), anhydrite (calcium sulphate) and potash (mostly potassium chloride)–were precipitated (*see* Figure EPS-1 above). In southern Saskatchewan four zones of potash near the top of the evaporite unit are buried to a depth of 900 m to 2750 m. Eight underground mines and two subsurface solution projects in Saskatchewan which produce from the potash zones account for a third of the world's commercial production; in 2000, potassium chloride production approximated fourteen million tonnes, with an export value of about $1.6 billion (*see* MINERAL RESOURCES; MINING).

Laurence Vigrass

ELKIN, HUB (1916–). Hub Elkin was among the most active, influential and longest-serving trade union leaders and industrial relations administrators in Saskatchewan history. Hubert Samuel (Hub) Elkin was born in Moose Jaw on February 11, 1916, and took his education there. He nearly completed grade eleven, then left school to go to work. Elkin began employment at the Swifts Canadian meat-packing plant in Moose Jaw in 1934, and was a leader in organizing the workforce into the Packinghouse Employees Federal Union #75, an affiliate of the craft union federation, the Trade and Labour Congress of Canada (TLC). He was president of the local, and bargained the first collective agreement with the company in Moose Jaw in 1941. The

following year, with industrial unionism sweeping North America under the banner of the Congress of Industrial Organizations (CIO), Elkin again led the effort to shift his local out of the TLC and enroll his co-workers in the Packinghouse Workers Organizing Committee (PWOC), a CIO-affiliated organization.

Beginning in 1942, Hub Elkin undertook organizing and union staff work for the PWOC in Saskatchewan and eastern Canada, financed by the United Packinghouse Workers of America, the United Steelworkers, and the Canadian Congress of Labour. He was instrumental in founding the first Saskatchewan Federation of Labour–established by the Canadian Congress of Labour, which represented the CIO unions in Canada. He served as the first president of the SFL in 1944–45. From 1945 to 1964 Hub Elkin was employed by the newly formed provincial Department of Labour as a conciliation officer, then as executive officer of the Labour Relations Board, and from 1949 to 1964 as deputy minister of Labour. In 1963 he graduated with great distinction from the Labour College of Canada, the trade union movement's post-secondary training institute located in Ottawa. From 1964 to 1970 he was executive secretary of the SASKATCHEWAN FEDERATION OF LABOUR–the most senior trade union staff person in the province.

In 1970 Elkin became a union representative with the CANADIAN UNION OF PUBLIC EMPLOYEES (CUPE); he bargained contracts, settled grievances, and handled arbitration cases for the CUPE membership for the next eleven years. While on leave from CUPE from 1971 to 1974, he acted as an industrial relations advisor for the International Labour Organization in the Netherlands Antilles. From 1976 to 1983, Elkin was also an employee representative on the Workers' Compensation Board.

For most of his life Hub Elkin was involved in political issues, supporting democratic-socialist causes. He was a longtime member of the CO-OPERATIVE COMMONWEALTH FEDERATION, the NEW DEMOCRATIC PARTY, and the Council of Canadians.

SASKATCHEWAN ARCHIVES BOARD R-PS57-459-01

Hub Elkin.

By the late 1990s, Hub Elkin was widely respected for his six decades of service to the labour movement. In 2002 he revived a stalled project to research and write a comprehensive history of working people and unions in Saskatchewan; that work took more than two years to write, and became a very well-regarded account of labour in the province. *Garnet Dishaw*

ELLIOTT, MOSES (1854–1939). Moses Elliott, a prominent ranching pioneer in the Maple Creek area, was born in Carleton County and later lived at St. Marys, Ontario, where as a young man he worked as a clerk in Timothy Eaton's original store. By 1881 Moses Elliott was managing a hotel at Little Saskatchewan in the Manitoba Extension. With a solid understanding of **CREE** he joined the Indian Affairs Department as an interpreter, accompanying various officials on their travels across the prairies. In January 1888, while working as a farming instructor at the Duck Lake Indian Agency, he was fired over a misunderstanding over his weekend use of the government horse and sleigh to attend his wedding. Elliott and his wife then moved to Maple Creek, where his father Andrew had preceded them. At Maple Creek Moses and Emily began ranching and raised a family of one son and three daughters. The family then moved out to the sandhills at Cross, northeast of Maple Creek, where he continued to raise cattle and horses. There he served on the local school board, and in 1914 obtained the position of postmaster, which he held until he disappeared in 1939. When neighbours and relatives noticed the 85-year-old was missing from the post office, they became suspicious of a drifter named John Zalenko, whom Moses had taken in. Nephew Vernal Elliott called in the RCMP; when questioned, Zalenko claimed that Moses had hanged himself. After Zalenko showed them where he had buried the body, he was charged and later convicted of murdering Moses with an axe. Declared insane, Zalenko spent the rest of his days in the Weyburn Mental Hospital. *David R. Elliott*

ELLIOTT, ROBERT LAWTON (1928–). Robert Lawton Elliott, grandson of pioneer **ROBERT WILSON ELLIOTT**, was born in 1928 to Percy Elliott and Elsie Shaw and raised on a farm near Vibank, southeast of Regina. After graduating in political science and history from the University of Saskatchewan in 1949, he worked as a radio news editor and broadcaster before joining the British Colonial Service. He took further studies for a year at London University and the London School of Economics, and was then sent to West Nigeria as a District Officer with the British Colonial Service. In 1956 he joined the Canadian Department of External Affairs and was assigned to the Middle East Division, where he helped formulate policy during the Suez Crisis. In

1957 he was appointed vice-consul in Beirut, Lebanon, where he remained until 1960. His next posting was in Ottawa, where he worked in the Africa and Middle East Division of External Affairs; this involved him in the Congo Crisis.

From 1963 to 1966, Elliott served as the Canadian High Commissioner to London, and in 1966 he was transferred to Lagos, Nigeria, to deal with the Biafran Crisis. In 1970, after the civil war ended, he organized Canadian government CIDA relief for Nigeria's post-war reconstruction. Elliott returned to Ottawa to become director of the Middle East Division. In 1973 he was appointed as Canadian Ambassador to Algeria. In 1976 he was transferred to Paris, working at the Canadian Embassy as Minister Plenipotentiary for four years. In 1980 Robert Elliott became the Canadian Ambassador to Egypt and the Sudan. He was on the reviewing stand with Anwar Sadat in 1981 when Sadat was assassinated, but was unhurt himself. Returning to the External Affairs headquarters in Ottawa in 1983, Elliott became Director General for the Middle East until he was named Ambassador to Hungary in 1985. He left Budapest in 1988 to become the Canadian High Commissioner to Nigeria, and remained there until 1991.

After he returned to Canada in 1991, Elliott was loaned by External Affairs to the University of Saskatchewan as a visiting professor. He retired from External Affairs in 1992 after serving that department for thirty-seven years. During those years he had three temporary postings (1961, 1962, 1974) with the Canadian Permanent Mission to the United Nations. In recognition of Robert Elliott's diplomatic and humanitarian work, the University of Saskatchewan awarded him an Honorary Doctor of Laws degree in the spring of 1997 when he delivered the convocation address. *David R. Elliott*

ELLIOTT, ROBERT WILSON (1830–1912). Robert Wilson Elliott was born in Ireland in 1830, and emigrated to Canada West in 1850, where he was a shoemaker in Waterloo and Haldimand counties. During the Fenian raids he served in the local militia. After a short stay in Huron County, where he had moved to care for his orphaned nephews, he and his enlarged family joined the western migration about 1882, sojourning for a while at Brandon. In 1883 he took up a homestead southwest of Balgonie in the District of Assiniboia. For the first year he lived in a "soddy" before building a frame house.

He was active in the Methodist Church, the Orange Lodge, and local politics. As president of the local Conservative riding association, Elliott supported **NICHOLAS FLOOD DAVIN**, the MP and editor/publisher of the *Regina Leader*, and successfully campaigned to have the community named in honour of Davin. R.W. Elliott was appointed Justice of the

Peace by the Territorial Government and also held the position of postmaster at Davin from 1890 to 1900. He gave up the postmaster's title following the death of his wife Isabella, who had actually run the post office from their home at 16-16-16 W2.

In 1901 Robert Wilson Elliott resigned as Justice of the Peace and moved to Maple Creek where his daughter Emily and her husband Moses lived. There he resumed his trade as a shoe and boot maker, catering to the needs of the local ranchers, residents, and Mounties. He died in Maple Creek in 1912. *David R. Elliott*

UNIVERSITY OF SASKATCHEWAN ARCHIVES A-1695

Kathleen W. Ellis on the occasion of the granting of her honorary doctorate, 1955.

ELLIS, KATHLEEN WILHELMINA (1887–1968). A nursing leader and the first professor and director of the School of Nursing, **UNIVERSITY OF SASKATCHEWAN**, Kathleen Ellis was born in Penticton, BC on June 16, 1887. Well educated and experienced in administration, she was executive-secretary and registrar of the Saskatchewan Registered Nurses' Association from 1937 to 1950. She instituted changes in conditions of nursing, and regulated schools, curriculum, and teaching. Under her aegis, the small but highly regarded degree program was established at that university in 1938. During the war she also served as Emergency Nursing Advisor to the Canadian Nurses' Association, determining the use of federal funds to sustain services and education during **WORLD WAR II**. The nursing profession emerged strengthened and improved.

With unusual insight, sound judgment, seemingly boundless energy, and the ability to mobilize others, she made a permanent imprint on nursing in Saskatchewan. In 1955, the University of Saskatchewan awarded her an honorary Doctor of Laws degree for her "lifetime of responsibility and service in the nursing profession." She was a dignified and gracious lady, independently wealthy, the embodiment of *noblesse oblige*. Kathleen Ellis retired in 1950, and died in Vancouver, BC, on March 9, 1968. *Lucy Willis*

ELLISON, ALBAN CEDRIC (1889-?). In the aftermath of the REGINA RIOT and the continued stranglehold of the DEPRESSION, Regina citizens turned to the Labour Party for new ideas. Alban Cedric Ellison, a former councilor born in England in 1889, was elected mayor in late 1935 along with six fellow Labour Party councilors in one of the largest Labour sweeps in Canadian civic politics. Ellison, a young lawyer and naval reserve officer, was popularly known as Regina's "sailor mayor" for his continuing interest in the navy. He defeated Henry Black in the 1937 civic elections, and won by acclamation in 1938. In 1939, he reluctantly ran again under the Labour banner, but with the easing of the Depression Labor support had dwindled and reputedly fallen to more radical elements. Defeated by JAMES GRASSICK, Ellison returned to active duty with the navy in WORLD WAR II. *Merle Massie*

ELROSE, town, pop 517, located 38 km S of Rosetown on Hwys 4 and 44. The area was largely settled between 1909 and 1912, and the townsite was surveyed in 1913. Elrose grew rapidly until the beginning of the 1930s; it then experienced a substantial loss of population during that decade, from which it did not recover until after WORLD WAR II. In 1951, the town's population was close to 700. The basis of the regional economy was, and remains, agriculture; however, in recent years oil and gas production has become an increasingly important industry. The town has a number of suppliers and services which cater to the agricultural industry, as well as financial and professional services, recreational facilities, and cultural institutions.
David McLennan

EMBLEMS OF SASKATCHEWAN. Saskatchewan's first emblem was the shield of arms granted by King Edward VII in 1906. In 1986 it became part of the Saskatchewan coat of arms granted by Queen Elizabeth II. The Saskatchewan FLAG was adopted in 1969. Official symbols are defined in the Provincial Emblems and Honours Act (*see* Table ES-1 below).
Michael Jackson

FURTHER READING: Jackson, M. 2002. *Images of a Province: Symbols of Saskatchewan*. Regina: Government of Saskatchewan; Swan, C. 1977. *Canada: Symbols of Sovereignty*. Toronto and Buffalo: University of Toronto Press.

EMBURY, JOHN FLETCHER LEOPOLD (1875-1944). Brigadier General J.F.L. Embury, CB, CMG, VD, was born on November 10, 1875, in Thomasburg, Ontario. He completed his law studies at the University of Toronto's Osgoode Hall in 1902, and the following year moved to Regina, where he established a thriving practice and was appointed King's Counsel in 1913. He was also a militia officer in the Regina Company of the 95th (Saskatchewan) Rifles. On its mobilization, Embury was appointed commanding officer the 28th (North-West) Battalion, CEF. The Battalion embarked overseas to Britain in 1915, and then to France as part of 2nd Canadian Division. Embury was wounded in September 1916. After a period of convalescence, he returned to active duty in January 1917 and was appointed commander of 2nd Canadian Brigade. He finished the war as a brigadier general, commanding the Canadian section at British General Headquarters, where in 1918 he oversaw the demobilization of all Canadian troops in France. Returning from overseas in 1918, Embury was appointed a judge of the Saskatchewan Court of King's Bench, He continued in that appointment in Regina until his sudden death from pneumonia on August 13, 1944. At his death, Embury was the senior officer in charge of military registration in Regina, and chairman of the National War Services Board.
John Chaput

EMERGENCY SOCIAL SERVICES. Every year a variety of natural, technological and human-caused disasters such as floods, fires, tornadoes, storms, blizzards, hazardous chemical spills, transportation and industrial accidents strike communities across Canada. They can strike anywhere and at any time. Along with the damage and destruction they cause to the physical environment, disasters primarily affect people: people may be killed or injured, homes or properties damaged or destroyed, utilities interrupted or severely damaged, and families dislocated. In some disasters such as toxic fires, floods, or forest fires, people may have to evacuate temporarily their homes or communities.

Individual citizens and families have a responsibility to educate and prepare themselves and their households for emergencies. Individual and family preparedness may help tip the scales between being a survivor or a victim in a disaster. At the same time, communities and governments are expected to plan for emergencies to protect their citizens and provide services to reduce the impacts of emergency situations. People may require immediate assistance with basic needs such as food, clothing, emergency shelter, medical assistance, transportation, emotional support, and information. In Saskatchewan, authority for emergency planning and response is derived from the Emergency Planning Act. The Saskatchewan Emergency Plan details emergency response

Table ES-1. Official Emblems of Saskatchewan

Adopted	Emblem	Description/Details
1906	Shield of Arms	Granted by Royal Warrant of King Edward VII, August 25, 1906. Red lion on gold background in upper third, three gold wheat sheaves on green background in lower two-thirds.
1906	Great Seal	Authorized by Order-in-Council, November 26, 1906. Shield of arms surrounded by legend "The Great Seal of the Province of Saskatchewan".
1941	Floral Emblem	Western Red Lily (*Lilium philadelphicum L. var. andinum*)
1945	Bird Emblem	Sharp-tailed Grouse (*Pedioecetes phasianellus jamesi*)
1961	District Tartan	Registered with the Court of Lord Lyon, King of Arms, in Edinburgh in 1961. Two-block tartan with seven different shades.
1969	Flag	Selected by competition and dedicated in the Legislature September 22, 1969. Horizontal bands of green and gold, displaying the Shield of Arms and the Western Red Lily.
1977	Logo	Wheat sheaf logo adopted for visual identity of executive government.
1986	Coat of Arms	Complete armorial bearings granted by Royal Warrant of Queen Elizabeth II on September 16, 1986. Shield of Arms augmented by supporters, crest, and motto.
1988	Tree Emblem	White Birch (*Betula papyrifera*). Adopted in *The Provincial Emblems and Honours Act*, 1988.
1991	Great Seal	Adopted by Proclamation, November 1, 1991. Armorial bearings surrounded by legend "Elizabeth II. Queen of Canada. The Great Seal of the Province of Saskatchewan".
1997	Mineral Emblem	Potash (Sylvite). Selected by school competition in 1996 and adopted by legislative amendment in 1997.
1997	Dress Tartan	Variant of the District Tartan. Registered with the Court of Lord Lyon King of Arms and adopted by legislative amendment in 1997.
2001	Grass Emblem	Needle-and-Thread Grass. Proposed by environmental groups in 1999 and adopted by legislative amendment in 2001.
2001	Animal Emblem	The White-Tailed Deer (*Odocoileus virginianus*). Appeared on the 1986 armorial bearings; adopted by legislative amendment in 2001.
2001	Official Sport	Curling. Adopted by legislative amendment in 2001. Permits Saskatchewan Curling Association to use Shield of Arms.

structures, procedures, and responsibilities of both the municipal and provincial governments.

The first level of government responsible for dealing with an emergency is the local authority for the area affected. When the capacity of the local authority is exceeded or is likely to be, a second level of intervention is activated which involves the provision of resources from adjacent or neighbouring communities through formal or informal mutual aid or other agreements. When these two combined levels of responses are exceeded or are in danger of being exceeded, the local authority may request assistance from the provincial government. The province may, if it deems necessary, also call on the federal government for assistance. In a large-scale disaster the volume, urgency, and intensity of human needs and the degree of social disorganization are usually such that regular community social service resources are unable to cope. The situation requires implementation of an emergency social service response system to meet the urgent physical and personal needs until regular community social services or recovery services are again operational.

In Saskatchewan, as elsewhere in Canada, emergency social services organizations may be called into action in an emergency situation to help provide the basic services essential to meet the non-medical needs of people affected by a disaster. Emergency social services include a variety of measures. Where necessary, people may be evacuated from an affected area. Safe, temporary lodging may be required for people displaced from their homes, along with clothing and food. Food, lodging, and other services may also be required for volunteers and other emergency responders. Good organization is a key to effective emergency social services. Emergency responders frequently need to set up a reception centre in a facility such as a school gymnasium, church hall or arena, where services can be organized for people affected by the emergency. Reception centres also facilitate registration and inquiry processes, so that people can be accounted for and families reunited. People affected by an emergency disaster may also have to adjust to major changes in their lives. Illness or injury, and even loss of life may accompany an emergency. Personal services associated with the emergency response are made available where necessary to help people deal with personal, family and job issues, to grieve for losses, and to begin recovering homes and property affected by the event. A key goal for emergency social services is to help people regain their independence as soon as possible after a disaster.

Theo Tibo

EMMA LAKE KENDERDINE CAMPUS. Emma Lake Kenderdine Campus is a 55-acre boreal forest summer research retreat and art campus of the **UNIVERSITY OF SASKATCHEWAN.** It is situated on

Murray Point at the northern edge of Okema Beach on Emma Lake. Since it was founded in 1936 by **AUGUSTUS KENDERDINE,** then head of the University of Saskatchewan Department of Art, with the support of then-president of the university, **WALTER MURRAY,** the campus has been developed as an art school. Despite initial economic difficulty the original site, named the Murray Point Art School, flourished. Over the years, well-known Canadian and international artists associated with the school (1936–73) and the Emma Lake Artists' Workshops (1955 to present) have enabled the site to achieve national and international renown. Since the mid-1960s, under the auspices of the University of Saskatchewan Department of Biology, the site has also been a provincial research area for biologists and other researchers interested in botany, zoology, limnology, and the environment in general. The campus and the associated Fairy Island biology station provide the requirements for field courses in natural history because the geographical area offers a variety of ecological habitats, along with living and working facilities. It is the most northerly field station in Saskatchewan, and one of the few sites in Canada that specifically examine the boreal forest. The site was declared a game preserve in 1962.

In the early 1980s the campus also became a venue for the men's team artistic gymnastics program sponsored by the University of Saskatchewan College of Physical Education, and for boys and girls gymnastics clubs. Over the years the artists, biologists and gymnasts have collaborated on programming. The Emma Lake Kenderdine Campus has also been the site of a variety of community arts programs for the Extension Division of the University of Saskatchewan. Since the early 1990s, these program offerings have expanded in number and duration, and provide an extensive slate of offerings on an annual basis. Over the years, the site has also been available to a variety of other university departments and various user groups for such programs as Leadership Training, Life-Skills Coach Training, the Emma Lake Fiddle Camps of the Saskatchewan Cultural Exchange Society, the Saskatchewan Craft Council Woodworkers' Biennial Conference, SIAST art workshops, and the Writers and Artists Colony of the **SASKATCHEWAN WRITERS GUILD.** The facilities themselves form part of the site's heritage too—especially Kenderdine 9 (the founder's first studio-cabin) and Cabin 4 (his homestead). These buildings reflect the stages of the site's development, and the visions of its various users.

During the 1970s the University of Saskatchewan entered into an agreement with the Prince Albert Regional Community College (PARCC), whereupon PARCC operated what was then the Emma Lake Art Camp through a partnership with the university. In 1988, PARCC amalgamated with the Northern Institute of Technology to form the

Woodland Campus of SIAST. Part of the amalgamation agreement stipulated that Woodlands continue all programs of both institutions. In 1989, the University of Saskatchewan and Woodlands signed a ten-year agreement by which Woodlands was responsible for the management and operation of the newly named "Kenderdine Campus at Emma Lake." In 1995, the Kenderdine Campus board of directors undertook a study of the operation and potential uses of the Kenderdine Campus at Emma Lake; the final document recommended actions designed to position the Kenderdine Campus to play a sustainable role in the future. On November 30, 1998, the partnership between the University and SIAST was completed, and the University of Saskatchewan took sole responsibility for site management and renewal.

Kate Hobin

EMPLOYMENT SUPPORTS AND SERVICES. The term "employment supports" refers to the range of programs and services available to individuals to help them participate and remain in the paid labour force, and to employers to help them recruit and retain the skilled labour they need. Saskatchewan, like all other Canadian jurisdictions, is faced with an aging workforce, a negative birth rate, and a need to ensure that all its citizens of labour force age (15 to 64 years) can and do participate as fully as possible in the labour market. To help ensure that this happens, industry, government, public post-secondary institutions, non-government agencies, and individuals must work collaboratively toward the common goal of helping the individual maximize self-sufficiency through employment. Employment supports, funded primarily through the provincial and federal governments, are one way this is accomplished.

In Saskatchewan, individual employment supports are targeted to those who have difficulty

Training and employment support programs respond to the demand for skilled labourers.

finding and keeping employment. This group includes low-income individuals, many of whom are single parents, as well as those with a disability, older workers, youth, Aboriginal people, or recent immigrants. Supports are also targeted to Saskatchewan people who are eligible for Employment Insurance (EI). Employment supports have been developed to help employers locate, hire, and retain the labour they need to successfully operate in Saskatchewan's changing labour market and economy. They can be used to help employers manage the costs of providing wages and/or training on-the-job to newly hired employees.

The key to designing effective employment supports lies in developing the right kind of support to meet the needs of individuals at the time and in the quantity needed. Often, the most important employment support is information. In Saskatchewan, this information is readily available on-line, through the SaskNetWork internet site. Developed by the province, with significant contribution from the federal government under the terms of the Canada-Saskatchewan Labour Market Development Agreement, this service offers information to job seekers, employers, adult learners, apprentices, students, parents, and instructors. The site gives up-to-date information related to career planning, job search, labour market information, resumé writing, and available jobs. It is organized around the categories of job seekers, employers, youth, entrepreneurs, and learners. Exploring the site enables individuals to explore options for employment and to review the training and experience required. Because it is internet-based, the SaskNetWork site is available to job or employee searchers in any geographic location; it is linked to national and international sites as well.

Other employment supports are provided through programs that offer a temporary, targeted wage subsidy to an employer to offset the costs of hiring an individual who has limited labour market experience, or who does not yet have the full skill set required to do the job. The wage subsidy is negotiated with the employer, who enters into a contract with the government agent that provides it, agreeing to terms and conditions aimed at ensuring that the individual and employer both benefit from the arrangement. Wage subsidy programs have been used for a number of years in Canada and other industrialized countries. Targeted wage subsidies are most appropriate to individuals who have had some labour market experience (for example, someone receiving Employment Insurance) or who are employment-ready. Individuals who lack labour market experience (for example, young single parents) or are without essential workplace skills may require special employment supports, such as a job coach. A job coach is assigned to an individual for a defined period of time to help that person adjust to working set hours and performing the tasks

required. The coach also identifies areas where the individual may need additional help or specific training to effectively meet all job requirements, or additional supports such as child care. The coach may work to identify a job mentor who will help the individual sustain her or his employment. Sometimes, in conjunction with a job coach, job carving is done: the employer works with the support agency to identify areas of a job that the individual is expected to do, with remaining areas assigned to others in the work unit.

The Saskatchewan government provides employer supports primarily through the Department of Community Resources and Employment. Local service centres around the province provide employers and job seekers with career and workforce planning information, with labour market information, and with employment-related and community-based employment support services. Employers can post jobs electronically and get help with posting, screening, and interviewing processes as well. Employment supports are an important part of Saskatchewan social programs that are oriented towards employment, self-reliance, and reduced reliance on social assistance and Employment Insurance.   *M.W. Buckley*

ENDANGERED SPECIES: *see* **SPECIES AT RISK**

ENEMY INTERNMENT CAMPS: *see* **EATON INTERNMENT CAMP**

ENERGY-EFFICIENT HOUSES. An energy-efficient home built in northwest Regina in 1977 is believed to be one of the first conservation demonstration houses constructed in North America. Over the years, more than 30,000 people toured the two-storey structure, roughly cubicle in shape, airtight, and equipped with a heat recycling system. It had no furnace; instead, the house was heated with a solar heating system designed specifically for Saskatchewan's extreme climate. The **SASKATCHEWAN RESEARCH COUNCIL** was the project manager for this

REGINA LEADER-POST

Saskatchewan Conservation House, Regina, ca. 1977.

conservation home; other partners included the Saskatchewan Housing Corporation, the **SASKATCHEWAN POWER CORPORATION**, the National Research Council's division of building research, and the engineering faculties at the **UNIVERSITY OF REGINA** and the **UNIVERSITY OF SASKATCHEWAN**. Land was provided by the city of Regina.

Energy consumption was 85% less than it would have been if conservation techniques had not been applied. The house was designed to expose a minimum amount of exterior surface area per square foot of floor space; there was no basement. The exterior finish was dark-brown cedar siding: as dark colours absorb heat from the sun, this enabled the house to act as a giant solar collector. The landscaping was also designed to increase thermal efficiency: deciduous trees on the south side of the house provided shade in summer and allowed solar heat to enter the windows in the winter. There were energy-efficient kitchen appliances and a water-conserving toilet. Hot water was recycled with an experimental heat recovery system consisting of three basic parts: solar collects, which collected radiation from the sun and converted it to heat; a large storage tank which stored the heat in water; and a distribution system which utilized the stored heat to provide warm air and hot water as required.

After the initial scientific monitoring period ended, the house was sold and a family moved in. A garage was added at the back of the property, and the solar thermal collectors were removed because the manufacturer was no longer providing servicing. The Regina energy-efficient house had a large impact on the house-building community: the Canadian R-2000 program now has a requirement for air tightness that recognizes this important technique as demonstrated in the 1977 home. The use of an air-to-air heat exchanger for ventilation was a pioneering effort: these types of heat exchangers are now produced in the tens of thousands each year in North America. In addition, the use of passive solar heating has become incorporated into the mainstream of construction techniques by advanced designers. Higher levels of insulation have virtually doubled to 140 mm from the 62 mm common in the late 1970s; however, this is still less than half the amount of wall insulation (300 mm) applied to the Regina house.   *Joe Ralko*

ENGLISH RIVER FIRST NATION. This reserve emerged from the signing of **TREATY 10** on August 28, 1906, under Chief William Apisis. Prior to and succeeding treaty, the economy revolved around the fur trade, but later turned to commercial fishing. The band's name originates from the area in which the Poplar House People resided seasonally, for instance when treaty payments were made; it was also known as the Grassy Narrows Reserve. The people of the English River Band chose land around the lakes to be assured of wildlife, fish, and thick vegetation. There are seven different reserves registered under the Chipewyan- speaking English River Band. These include La Plonge, Wapachewunak (the most populated reserve site), Ile-à-la-Crosse, Elak Dase, Knee Lake, Dipper Rapids, and Primeau Lake. All are found in the far northern region of Saskatchewan and make up a total of 17,509.5 ha. They have a current population of 1,277 band members, with 663 people living on reserve. The economy is based on trapping, fishing, agriculture, tourism, and forestry; the community infrastructure includes a store, post office, arena, RCMP office, clinic, airport, youth centre, schools, teacherages, a band office, arena, band hall, fire hall, and numerous community maintenance structures. *Christian Thompson*

ENGLISH SETTLEMENTS. The "English" population in Saskatchewan included not only large numbers of Anglo-Canadians who moved here from Ontario and neighbouring Manitoba, as well as Anglo-Americans, but also many immigrants direct from England. The early English immigrants tended to be romantic idealists who mostly lacked any farming experience, yet viewed the Canadian west as a wild colonial frontier of the British Empire. They came to escape industrial unemployment, poverty and class inequity, religious discontent, and agrarian depression in England. Several early utopian settlements were established. In 1882 Cannington Manor, named after a village in Somerset, was founded by Capt. E.M. Pierce (1832-88) and his four sons; the colony attracted English aristocrats, businessmen, and landowners. Mutual visits were exchanged between these and French aristocrats at St. Hubert: together they went hunting with horses and hounds. All Saints Anglican Church and Beckton Place manor house on the Didsbury Stock Farm were prominent features of the colony. Cannington Manor thrived for two decades, yet it was all but deserted by 1905: five years earlier the new railway line had missed the community by more than ten miles.

As Cannington Manor was developing in the southeastern region, other utopian settlements came into existence elsewhere in what would become Saskatchewan. Methodists from Toronto formed the Temperance Colonization Society, which founded the Temperance Colony in 1882 on the east side of the river flowing through Saskatoon. The East London Artisans settled in the Wapella-Moosomin area in 1884; the York Farmers Colonization Company commenced a prosperous farm settlement centred on Yorkton in 1885; and the Church Colonization Land Company attempted—with limited success—to settle urban immigrants on preplanned homesteads around Saltcoats in 1887. The Barr Colony, an extensive settlement centred on Lloydminster, was established in 1903 by Rev. Isaac

M. Barr. He was assisted, and soon replaced as leader, by Rev. George Exton Lloyd (1861–1940), a Canadian who accompanied the colonists from England; later he became principal of the Anglican Theological college in Saskatoon, and Bishop of Saskatchewan (1922–23).

As the English—and more generally British—population of Saskatchewan grew, it controlled political, economic and social interests: "Anglo-conformity" was emphasized in urban and rural schools, which ensured the dominance of Anglo-Canadian culture and a strong resistance to "foreign" immigrants. The total British proportion of the Saskatchewan population (i.e., the areas which would be included within the province of Saskatchewan in 1905) could be estimated at 57%, just over half of the total population in 1901. A British majority was maintained until 1941 (49.7%), after which the British proportion continued to decline to the present quarter of the population. In fact, in 1941 Saskatchewan became the only province in Canada (besides Quebec) lacking a British-origin majority; yet English and British-origin residents have been pervasive throughout much of the province, outnumbering other ethnic groups in numerous communities. Today, out of a total Saskatchewan population of 963,150 (2001), 235,715 residents (24.5%) claim to be of English ethnic origin; 41,815 claim English-only origin, and 193,895 partially English origin. A total of 561,155 residents claim various British origin—70,535 solely, and another 490,605 partially. However, there is considerable overlap between these categories (English, Scottish, Irish or Welsh). People claiming to be specifically of English origin (in whole or in part) are outnumbered only by people claiming German origin. (*See also* **SCOTTISH SETTLEMENTS, IRISH SETTLEMENTS, WELSH SETTLEMENTS**)

Alan Anderson

FURTHER READING: Barry, B. 1997. *People Places: Saskatchewan and Its Names*. Regina: Canadian Plains Research Center.

ENS, GERHARD (1863–1952). Ens was born on December 28, 1863, in Ekaterinoslaw, then in the southern part of the Russian Empire. He received his education and was married in Russia, emigrating to Canada in 1891. Ens settled in the Rosthern area and many consider him to be the town's founder. He was instrumental in bringing settlers to the Rosthern area, especially settlers from Mennonite communities, although Ens himself became a Swedenborgian. While farming and becoming president of the Rosthern Realty Company, Ens worked as an Immigration Agent for the Canadian government for nine years. In 1905 Rosthern elected Ens, running for the Liberals, as its first member of the Legislative Assembly. Ens was Saskatchewan's first

Gerhard Ens.

MLA to be neither Anglo-Saxon nor Canadian-born. He became the government whip, and remained in the Legislature until 1913. After leaving provincial politics, Ens continued to help the Mennonite community. In the early 1920s he worked to have the ban on Mennonite immigration lifted. This ban had been put in effect by an Order-in-Council as a result of Mennonite pacifism during World War I. Gerhard Ens died on January 2, 1952. *Maryanne Cotcher*

ENVIRONMENTAL PROTECTION LEGISLATION. In 1972, inspired by the rise of environmental consciousness in this country, the province of Saskatchewan created the Department of Environment. Since its inception the department has changed title on several occasions, from Saskatchewan Environment and Public Safety (1988) to Saskatchewan Environment and Resource Management (1993) to Saskatchewan Environment (2002). The objects and purposes of the Department of Environment remain fundamentally the same as when it was first established: to co-ordinate, develop, promote and enforce policies and programs to protect and enhance the environment in a manner that promotes the physical, economic and social well-being of the people of Saskatchewan today and in the future; and to co-ordinate, develop, promote and enforce policies and programs relating to the conservation, preservation, management, protection and development of fish, wildlife, air, water, forests, resource lands, parks, and other renewable resources in Saskatchewan, including urban parks. This mandate has been reflected in nearly two dozen statutes and numerous supporting regulations. Although the Environmental Management and Protection Act, 2002 is the primary piece of environmental legislation in the province, it is complemented by other important statutes including the Wildlife Act, 1998, the Environmental Assessment Act, the Watershed Authority Act, the Forest Management Resources Act, and the Parks Act (see below). In addition, smaller statutes such as the Litter Control Act and the Groundwater

Conservation Act complement the environmental management regime. In accordance with statute, since 1991 the province has prepared a biannual State of the Environment Report (S.S. 1990-91. c.S-57. as amended by S.S. 1994, c.21; S.S. 1996, c.F-19.1). This report outlines the current condition of the environment in Saskatchewan, and the relationships between the condition of the environment and the economy of Saskatchewan. The report is tabled in the Legislative Assembly and made available to the public for examination.

Environmental Assessment Act. S.S. 1979-80. c.E-10.1 (effective August 25, 1980) as amended by S.S. 1983 c.77; 1988-89 c.42 and c.55; 1996 c.F-19.1; and 2002, c.C-11.1. Environmental assessment (EA) is the systematic description and evaluation of the impacts of a development on all environments prior to irrevocable decision-making. EA can promote environmental sustainability by mitigating negative effects of our activities and, in cases where the impacts are significant, stop the initiative completely. Initially, Saskatchewan adopted an EA policy to assess large-scale proposals in the province, such as the Cluff Lake uranium project and the Nipawin Dam proposal. The system was fairly successful, and as a result the Environmental Assessment Act was passed in 1980 to enshrine the policy in statutory form. The process requires the assessment of "developments"–those projects, operations or activities which trigger any one in a list of criteria within the legislation. These criteria include: affecting a rare, unique or endangered feature of the environment; substantial use of a provincial resource which pre-empts the use for other purposes; and causing widespread public concern due to the potential environmental changes. Once labeled a development, the proposal cannot proceed without the approval of the Minister. The proponent of the development must prepare an environmental impact statement (EIS) outlining the details of the project, the host environment, as well as the mitigable and non-mitigable impacts of the development on all environments (biophysical, economic, social, aesthetic, cultural, etc). This EIS is submitted to the EA Branch of Saskatchewan Environment, and if determined to be substantially complete it is circulated to the public for a thirty- to sixty-day comment period.

As a matter of policy, public information meetings are often held during this period by the proponent, and if deemed necessary the Minister may also order a public inquiry in association with any development review. (There has only been one inquiry to date, concerning the Rafferty Alameda Dam project.) Once satisfied that all requirements of the Act have been met, the Minister decides whether or not the project may proceed, or if it may proceed subject to conditions. Since passage there have been only minor amendments to the legislation. Of the 1,928 proposals received by Saskatchewan Environment,

some 170 developments have been assessed since passage of the Act: 114 ultimately received ministerial approval; three were denied as proposed; forty-five projects were deferred; and three are currently under review.

Environmental Management and Protection Act, 2002. S.S. 2002 c.E-10.21 (effective October 1, 2002) as amended by S.S. 2003, c.29. The Environmental Management and Protection Act, 2002 (EMPA, 2002) empowers the Minister of Environment with primary responsibility for all matters respecting the enhancement and protection of the provincial environment; as such, it is the primary piece of legislation in the environmental field. Among other topics the statute addresses contaminated sites, unauthorized discharges, protection of water quality, drinking and waste water regulation, and halocarbons. In addition to these substantive areas, EMPA sets out rules relating to orders, permits, emergency action, and general matters respecting administrative powers and the powers of environmental officers. EMPA includes fines of up to $1 million and/or three years of imprisonment for those convicted under the statute, and incorporates a "polluter pay" approach to environmental damage.

Saskatchewan Watershed Authority Act S.S. 2002. c.35.02 (effective October 1, 2002). The Saskatchewan Watershed Authority was created as a direct result of the recommendations of the North Battleford Water Inquiry (the Laing Report) of 2002, combining the objectives of the former Saskatchewan Wetland Conservation Corporation with many of the tasks of the Saskatchewan Water Corporation. In turn, the Water Corporation Act was revamped (S.S.2002, c.35.01 (effective October 1, 2002)) to reflect the corporation's narrower mandate to construct, acquire, manage or operate works or services associated with the provision of water or sewage disposal. Under the Watershed Authority Act, the corporation is charged with a broad range of water-related responsibilities, which include the management, development, control and protection of water, watersheds and related land resources in the province. Consistent with water history on the prairies, the legislation reiterates the right of the provincial Crown to the use of all ground and surface waters within Saskatchewan borders. As agent for the Crown, the Authority is empowered to regulate the flow of water, license water uses and water works, control drainage, and undertake activities which enhance the quantity, quality, and availability of water in the province. In keeping with good environmental practices the authority is also mandated to promote conservation programs, and has broadened its approach to highlight watershed management. The Authority is also the agent for the province in extra-provincial consultations with the Prairie Provinces Water Board, and assists in both national and international issues

relating to water use that may have implications within Saskatchewan.

Wildlife Act, 1998. S.S. 1998. c. W-13.12 (effective March 6, 2000 except s.87 effective April 1, 1999) as amended by S.S. 2000 c.51 and 65. The property in all wildlife in Saskatchewan rests with the provincial Crown. Pursuant to the Wildlife Act, 1998 the province has established a scheme for the management of wild animals, with special emphasis on the protection of endangered species within the province's borders. As a result, individuals may gain title in wildlife only if they are in licensed possession of that vertebrate animal and have not otherwise violated the Act. In addition to provisions for the administration of the system, the Act outlines licensing, hunting and trapping regulations, prohibitions and offenses, and penalty provisions. It is noteworthy that there are special provisions in relation to the rights of First Nations people within the Act. Prohibitions in the Wildlife Act, 1998 range in scope from hunting while intoxicated to trafficking in wildlife. Penalties within the Act vary according to the offense, with $100,000 and two years imprisonment as the maximum penalty under the statute.

Of particular interest are the provisions dealing with protection of species at risk, including extirpated, endangered, threatened or vulnerable wild species. The categories within the Act are the same as those used by the Committee on the Status of Endangered Wildlife in Canada (COSEWIC). With very limited exception, if an animal is designated by the Minister as within one of the categories, it may not be disturbed, killed, captured, exported or otherwise trafficked. In making his decision regarding the status of any species, the Minister may use both scientific and community-based advice provided by advisory committees contemplated in the legislation. In addition, the Minister may see the preparation and implementation of a recovery plan to assist in the recovery and conservation of any designated species. At present fifteen species at risk are listed under the provincial regulation.

Forest Resources Management Act. S.S. 1996, c.F-19.1 as amended by S.S. 1997, c.W-13.11; 1998, c.W-13.12; 2000, c.46 and 50; and 2002, c.31. The purpose of the Act is to promote the sustainable use of forest land for the benefit of current and future generations by balancing the need for economic, social and cultural opportunities with the need to maintain and enhance the health of forest land. Forest land is defined as any Crown land where a forest ecosystem is the predominant ecosystem. The provincial forest consists of those Crown lands designated by regulation and which are to be managed in a sustainable manner for the purposes of conserving, developing, enhancing, maintaining, managing, protecting and utilizing the forest resources on that land. The allocation of forest resources is regulated through the use of forest management agreements, term supply licenses, and forest product permits. The Act requires the preparation of integrated forest land use plans before forest management agreements are finalized. In addition, these plans require approval under the Environmental Assessment Act. The Act also mandates the preparation of a report on the state of the provincial forests at least once every ten years.   *Marie-Ann Bowden*

EPP, WILLIAM HAROLD (1930–95).

Bill Epp was born on June 12, 1930, in Glenbush, Saskatchewan and grew up on a farm; his father was a blacksmith. At a very early age, Epp used his creative mind to make toys from available pieces of wood and metal, influenced by the machinery that he saw around him. In 1948–49, he attended the Saskatoon Teachers' College, where he studied art with **WYNONA MULCASTER**. Later, he took courses at the Banff Summer School and the Winnipeg School of Art, and studied with **ELI BORNSTEIN** at the **UNIVERSITY OF SASKATCHEWAN**, where he received his BA in 1968. From 1949 to 1967, he taught at schools in Saskatchewan. In 1967, he joined the Art Department at the University of Saskatchewan, teaching sculpture, drawing, design, and art history. He retired in 1993, having influenced and inspired many students. Epp had varied styles—mainly figure and portrait—and he worked in welded steel, wood, clay, fibreglass, stone, and bronze. When he began working in bronze casting, he built his own foundry on his farm near Martensville.

His work was shown in many solo and group exhibitions, and is represented at the University of Saskatchewan, the **MENDEL ART GALLERY** and the **SASKATCHEWAN ARTS BOARD**, as well as in private collections. Early in his career, Epp received grants for travel and materials from the Canada Council and the Saskatchewan Arts Board. He was a founding member of the Prairie Sculptors' Association in Saskatoon, and in 1991 was made an honorary member of the Saskatchewan Society for Education Through Art. Several of his public statues can be seen in Saskatoon, notably "Spirit of Youth," done for the 1989 Jeux Canada Summer Games, and that of Sir Wilfrid Laurier and a young **JOHN DIEFENBAKER**, completed in 1990. His statues of Lieutenant Harry Colebourn and Winnie-the-Bear are displayed at the Assiniboine Park Zoo in Winnipeg and in the London Zoo. Epp died on September 4, 1995.   *Margaret A. Hammond*

ERASMUS, PETER (1833–1931).

Peter Erasmus was a **MÉTIS** trader, guide, hunter, translator, Indian agent, farmer and mission worker involved in many of the notable historical events in western Canada in the late 1800s. Born in 1833 to Danish-**CREE** parents, he was well educated and worked with his uncle the Reverend **HENRY BUDD** at The Pas, translating Scripture. It is recorded that Erasmus was fluent in

SASKATCHEWAN ARCHIVES BOARD B597

Peter Erasmus, left.

six Aboriginal languages in addition to English, Latin, and Greek. Because of these skills Erasmus was recognized as an able translator and played this key role in many critical cross-cultural encounters. He assisted a number of Christian missionaries, especially the Methodists, and was also chosen by the Earl of Southesk and by Captain John Palliser as official translator for their famous expeditions. These travels gave him an intimate knowledge of the entire land and of the Aboriginal groups between Lake Superior and the Rocky Mountains. In the early 1860s Erasmus married Charlotte Jackson, a young Métis woman, and they had six children before her death in 1880.

In 1876 Cree Chiefs Mistawasis and **AHTAHKAKOOP** hired Erasmus to interpret for them at the **TREATY 6** negotiations at Fort Carlton. He was subsequently hired by the Canadian government's Treaty Commissioner, Alexander Morris; this left him open to charges of sharp dealing. Erasmus was privy to some of the deliberations among the Aboriginal leadership, noting the authority of Mistawasis and Ahtahkakoop and their support for the treaty; he further recorded that **POUNDMAKER** and The Badger spoke strongly against signing. Erasmus also made it clear that he personally supported the treaty. Erasmus subsequently worked in a number of capacities for the Indian Department, and attempted to play a mediating role in the events leading to the 1885 conflict in **BATOCHE**. He settled near Whitefish Lake in what would become Alberta, continuing to trap and trade as well as farm until his death in 1931 at the age of 97. At age 87, Erasmus told his story to a Métis journalist and the resulting manuscript found its way to the Glenbow Archives. Published in 1976 as *Buffalo Days and Nights*, it is a critical first-hand historical source for this period of great change in the Canadian west.   *Michael Cottrell*

FURTHER READING: Erasmus, P. 1976. *Buffalo Days and Nights: As Told to Henry Thompson.* Calgary: Fifth House Publishers.

ESSENTIAL SERVICES EMERGENCY ACT: *see* **LEGISLATION IN SASKATCHEWAN**

ESTERHAZY, town, pop 2,348, is located SE of Melville at the junction of Hwys 22 and 80. The town was named for Count Paul Oscar Esterhazy (*see* **ESTERHAZY, PAUL**), who settled the first 35 Hungarian families in the area, establishing what came to be known as the Kaposvar Colony. Other settlers to the area included English, Scandinavian, and German immigrants. After initial hardships, the settlement flourished and its success helped publicize the agricultural viability of the region to later waves of immigrants. The development of the potash industry in the late 1950s and early 1960s had a dramatic impact on Esterhazy's progress. International Minerals and Chemicals Corp. (IMC) began construction of the world's largest potash mine, K1, which became fully operational in 1962; a second mine, K2, was finished in 1967. The workforce required at these huge enterprises had a drastic effect on Esterhazy's population: by 1966, it had reached 3,190. No longer just a farming community, Esterhazy had become one of the bigger and more modern rural communities in Saskatchewan, with all the facilities and amenities of a larger urban centre.

Today, the area potash mines employ approximately 800 people; but agriculture remains important to the economy, with district farms growing wheat, canola and flax, and raising cattle. Just south of the town is the Kaposvar Historic Site, featuring the Our Lady of Assumption Roman Catholic Church, built in 1906–07, which was constructed of large stones hauled to the site by the early Hungarian pioneers and is the location of a traditional annual pilgrimage. (*See also* **HUNGARIAN SETTLEMENTS**, **POTASH INDUSTRY**)   *David McLennan*

ESTERHAZY COMMUNITY MUSEUM

Clements' Store, Esterhazy, was a pioneering retail firm operated by several generations of the Clements family.

ESTERHAZY, PAUL (1831–1912). Paul Oscar Esterhazy, an immigration agent, was also founder of the Esterhaz Colony, the first Hungarian settlement in Saskatchewan. Esterhazy was born Johannes Packh in Esztergom, Hungary in 1831. He left Hungary after the failed war for independence of 1848–49, in which he served as a rebel soldier; during the following decade, Packh served in the British army. He adopted the Esterhazy name about 1867 when obtaining an Austrian passport in Munich. His reasons for adopting the name are unknown, and while he never concealed or changed any details of his past he steadfastly maintained his claim of relationship to the Esterhazy family, one of the wealthiest and most prominent in Hungary. By 1868 he was residing in New York City under the name of Paul Oscar Esterhazy; his name often appears with the title "Count" before it.

Esterhazy took a keen interest in the fate of his fellow countrymen. In the late 19th century many immigrants from Hungary, ethnic Hungarians and Slovaks, migrated to the United States and found work in the coalmines of Pennsylvania. In 1885 and 1886 Esterhazy arranged the migration of a group from the United States, first to Manitoba and later to the Qu'Appelle valley near what is today the town of Esterhazy. In 1888 a second group of peasants came directly from Hungary to the same district. Esterhazy continued to aid immigration from his homeland to western Canada, and remained keenly interested in the success of his colony for the remainder of his life. (*See also* HUNGARIAN SETTLEMENTS, CZECH AND SLOVAK SETTLEMENTS)
Mark Vajcner

FURTHER READING: Kovacs, M.L. 1974. *Esterhazy and Early Hungarian Immigration to Canada*. Regina: Canadian Plains Research Center.

ESTEVAN. The city of Estevan (pop 10,242), named after the registered telegraphic address of George Stephen, the original president of the CANADIAN PACIFIC RAILWAY, was incorporated on March 1, 1957. It is a regional service centre 186 km SE of Regina at the junction of Highways 18, 39 and 47 on the northeast bank of the Souris River. The exposures of coal, the hardwoods flanking the Souris River, and numerous buffalo herds steadily drew various First Nations hunting and trading groups to the area during the past 10,000 years. On La Vérendrye's 1734 "Map of the West," a trade and hunting corridor called the Warriors Trail was marked in the vicinity of Estevan. European fur traders adopted the trade routes established by the Aboriginal people. By 1805, when Lewis and Clark scouted along the Dakota stretch of Long Creek, the Assiniboine had replaced the Mandan/Hidatsa as the dominant people of the area. Years later, James McKay, the Factor of Fort Ellice, led John Palliser and geologist James Hector to a point near what

MÉTIS hunters called "la ROCHE PERCÉE," about 25 km southeast of Estevan; Indians made offerings to Manitou when they passed this site. In 1873 the British-American Boundary Commission established a survey camp at Woodend, near the junction of Long Creek and the Souris River, so named because there was no firewood to be found north or west of this area for many kilometres. The following year, Commissioner G.A. French of the North-West Mounted Police led a force of 275 policemen, 114 Red River carts with 20 Métis drivers, and 310 horses to Woodend, on their march to the mountains. In 1894 the Soo Line was completed through Estevan, linking Minneapolis-St. Paul and Moose Jaw. The Territorial Government of the North-West Territories incorporated Estevan as a village on November 2, 1899. By 1905 the population was 596, and Estevan was proclaimed a town on March 1, 1906. Growth was accelerated by the centralization of electrical power production and the development of coal and oil resources in the area: Estevan Generating Station was constructed in 1930, Boundary Dam Generating Station between 1957 and 1970, and Shand Generating Station in 1992. The population doubled to 8,500 within two years of the intense development of the local oil fields in 1955. Local events of national significance include the coal miners' strike and riot in 1931 (*see* ESTEVAN COAL STRIKE); the crash of a Dakota Mk III, which killed twenty-two people in 1946; the survival story of Brent Dyer and Donna Johnson in 1979, as documented in PETER GZOWSKI's *The Sacrament*; and the controversy surrounding the construction of the Rafferty and Alameda dams in 1989. Natural resources in the area include agricultural products, clay, coal, fly ash, flare gas derivatives, natural gas, and oil. The two coal-fired electrical generating plants produce 50% of Saskatchewan's electricity. Estevan is a regional service centre in the automotive, education, government, medical, recreation, retail, and tourism sectors.
G.C. Salmers

ESTEVAN COAL STRIKE. In the summer of 1931, 600 men and boys worked in the almost two dozen underground mines of the Souris Coal Fields of southeastern Saskatchewan. They laboured ten hours a day in subterranean coal seams sometimes not big enough to allow a miner to stand up. In the Crescent Mine and Eastern Collieries, one to two feet of water routinely collected in the work areas. Western Dominion Collieries was notorious for not replacing damaged or rotted timbers, and roof cave-ins were frequent. Many of the underground mines had totally inadequate ventilation; smoke from blasting hung in the air like a fog. "Black damp"—high concentrations of carbon dioxide—plagued many of the mines and regularly made the workers seriously ill. "Refuge holes," which offered miners some protection during a fire or cave-in, were few and far from the coal face.

For working in these harsh and dangerous conditions miners were paid 25¢ for each ton of coal that they dug, hand-loaded on coal cars and pushed to the main shaft. An experienced miner working hard for the whole of his ten-hour shift could earn $1.60. Dockage for rocks, clay and small-sized coal further reduced his take-home pay. Miners were also obliged to do extra work such as laying track, timbering, pumping water, and clearing up roof falls, for which they were not paid. Coal miners' wages in Alberta and British Columbia exceeded those paid in Saskatchewan by 50% in the decade between 1921 and 1929. Despite this, the Estevan–Bienfait area mine owners implemented sizable wage cuts in 1931.

Living conditions were as bad as the work environment. Only two mines had shower facilities. The company houses and "bachelor bunkhouses" were tar paper shacks with no insulation or indoor plumbing; as often as not, these dwellings were infested with lice, bedbugs and cockroaches. The larger mines had "company stores" where employees were expected to buy everything from food and clothes to miners' supplies.

SASKATCHEWAN ARCHIVES BOARD R-A18508

Estevan Coal Miners' Strike, 1931.

In July and August 1931 miners from several collieries met in secret to talk about organizing. They decided to contact the **WORKERS' UNITY LEAGUE** (WUL), a militant, left-wing labour federation centred in Toronto. The WUL affiliate with jurisdiction over mining was the Mine Workers' Union of Canada (MWUC). The WUL sent organizers Martin Forkin and Sam Scarlett into the Souris Coal Fields, and a sign-up got underway.

Scarlett addressed a crowd of 1,200 miners and family members at a union picnic at Taylorton on August 23. Two days later, MWUC president James Sloan spoke to a meeting of over 1,000 in Estevan and announced that the union had obtained a 100% sign-up. The mine owners, however, absolutely refused to deal with their employees' choice of union, citing as their reason the fact that the leaders of the MWUC were Communists. The MWUC had negotiated with coal operators in Alberta; but the Saskatchewan mine owners repeatedly refused to recognize the union, even when the Deputy Minister of Labour tried to get negotiations started. Finally, with no other real option, the miners voted to strike and walked off the job at midnight, September 7, 1931. The mine owners still refused to bargain, and instead brought in scabs (replacement workers) to reopen three of the biggest mines on September 16. Mass picketing by hundreds of striking miners sent the scabs away, and the mines once again closed.

On September 28, the strikers decided to hold a parade through coal country from Bienfait to Estevan to dramatize the miners' plight and encourage public support. In the early afternoon of September 29, the motorcade set off with miners, their wives and children, all packed into old cars and on the backs of trucks. As the cavalcade entered Estevan, they unfurled Union Jack flags and banners reading "We will not work for starvation wages," "We want houses, not piano boxes," and "Down with the company store." Before the motorcade reached the centre of town it was stopped by a cordon of two dozen Estevan police. An argument erupted when the police insisted that the peaceful demonstration must disperse. When the strikers refused, police chief McCutcheon grabbed striking miner Martin Day and tried to pull him down from the truck. This set off a pushing and shoving match, during which the police summoned the fire brigade, apparently to hose down the demonstrators. When the fire truck arrived, McCutcheon began ordering arrests and the struggle escalated. Strikers and their family members began throwing stones and wielding picket signs. The police, bolstered now by RCMP officers, began firing their guns in the air or into the ground in front of the demonstrators.

A group of strikers climbed on the fire truck, and one was shot dead by the police. Two other miners were killed by police bullets. Eight more unarmed strikers, four bystanders, and one RCMP officer were wounded by police gunfire. Those fatally wounded were Peter Markunas, Nick Nargan and Julian Gryshko. The following morning, police raids on homes led to the arrest of thirteen strikers on charges of rioting; others were apprehended later. A number, including several of the leaders of the union, were convicted and sentenced to as much as a year of hard labour.

Even with the death of three co-workers, the miners refused to give in. On October 6, the mine owners finally agreed to implement an eight-hour day, a minimum wage of $4 a day, payment for timbering, a reduction in the rent for miners' houses and the price of blasting powder, the appointment of check weighmen, and an end to the company store monopoly. Because of the employers' stiff opposition towards the Mine Workers Union of Canada, the miners dropped their demand for union recognition. It was not until the end of **WORLD WAR II** that the United Mine Workers were able to establish a lasting trade union presence in the Souris Coal Fields.

Garnet Dishaw

ESTEVAN POLICE SERVICE. The Estevan Police Service is one of twelve municipal police forces in Saskatchewan. The Estevan police are responsible for enforcing federal, provincial, and municipal laws applicable in the city of Estevan. Policing in Estevan began in 1906, the year Estevan was incorporated as a town; the first police officer to serve the townspeople was officer S. Dryden. Prior to 1906, laws in the village of Estevan were enforced by the North-West Mounted Police (NWMP). In 1886, NWMP inspector J.A. McGibbon came to the Estevan area from Regina. Accompanied by sixteen men and twenty-five horses, McGibbon established summer headquarters at Alameda, with a detachment at Wood End, eight miles south of Estevan; and by 1892, an NWMP detachment had been set up in Estevan. Through the 1920s and 1930s Estevan's police force consisted of a chief and a single constable. In 1957, Estevan was proclaimed a city and its municipal police force had grown to nine officers. Today, serving Saskatchewan's eighth largest city and a population of over 10,000, the Estevan Police Service maintains a staff of twenty-six, including twelve constables, five sergeants, and a chief of police. *Iain Stewart*

ESTEY, JAMES WILFRED (1889–1956). James Estey was born in Keswick Ridge, New Brunswick, on December 1, 1889. After graduating from the University of New Brunswick in 1910 he studied at Harvard, earning a law degree. Estey came to Saskatchewan in 1915 to lecture in law and economics at the **UNIVERSITY OF SASKATCHEWAN**, a position he held for ten years. In 1917 he helped establish a law practice until he was appointed Crown Prosecutor in Saskatoon from 1921 until 1929. In 1929, Estey first ran for the Liberals in the constituency of Saskatoon City but was defeated by Conservative leader **J.T.M. ANDERSON**. Estey was successful in 1934 as the Conservatives were swept out of office. He was appointed Minister of Education and over his term, which ended in 1941, the issues of school grants, collection of property taxes, and payment of teachers were gradually dealt with as the economy rebounded and government revenue increased. Estey took on the responsibility of Attorney-General in 1938. He redrafted the Debt Adjustment Act to give greater protection to debtors who faced seizure of property, particularly farm land, as a result of the effects of the **DEPRESSION**. Estey was defeated in the CCF electoral sweep in June 1944. In October he was appointed to the Supreme Court and served for eleven years until his death on January 22, 1956. Estey's son, Clarence Estey, would follow in his father's footsteps, also becoming a Cabinet Minister and judge.

Brett Quiring

ESTEY, WILLARD (1919-2002). Willard Zebedee Estey was born in Saskatoon on October 10, 1919. He was the son of **JAMES WILFRED ESTEY**, a Supreme Court of Canada Justice, and Muriel Baldwin. He graduated from the **UNIVERSITY OF SASKATCHEWAN** with a BA in 1940 and an LLB in 1942. After serving in **WORLD WAR II**, Estey went to Harvard Law School and completed an LLM in 1946. He taught at the University of Saskatchewan for a year, and in 1947 joined a Toronto law firm. In 1973 he was appointed to the Ontario Court of Appeal; in 1975 he was named Chief Justice of the High Court of Justice of Ontario; he became Chief Justice of Ontario in 1976; and he was appointed to the Supreme Court of Canada on September 29, 1977. Estey received an honorary doctor of laws degree from Wilfrid Laurier University in 1977 and served as that university's sixth chancellor from 1990 to 1995. In 1985 Estey chaired the Commission of Inquiry into the Collapse of the Canadian Commercial Bank and Northland Bank, and his report absolved the government of blame. In 1990, Estey was appointed to the Order of Canada by Governor General **RAY HNATYSHYN**. Justice Estey served on the Supreme Court for eleven years, and had the distinction of writing the Supreme Court's first ruling under the Charter of Rights and Freedoms in 1984. He also headed numerous government inquires and was named a companion to the Order of Canada. Justice Estey retired on April 22, 1988 and died on January 25, 2002.

Daria Coneghan

ESTON, town, pop 1,048, located SE of Kindersley on Hwys 44 and 30. The **SOUTH SASKATCHEWAN RIVER** and Eston Riverside Regional Park lie 23 km south of the town. The Eston area was opened to homesteaders in 1906, and settlers arrived from eastern Canada, the USA, and the British Isles. From 1914 to 1984, Eston experienced steady growth; then began a period of decline and challenges. Community leaders reacted with a series of successful locally based initiatives and economic development strategies which helped stabilize the population, create employment, and enhance the quality of life in the town. Today, the area economy remains based upon agriculture—the production of a wide variety of cereal grains and specialty crops, as well as cattle, bison, and elk—and Eston has a number of services and suppliers catering to the agricultural industry. Eston also has an RCMP detachment, banking, shopping, a weekly newspaper, and a K–12 School with approximately 225 students. Annual events in Eston include an indoor rodeo, the "World Super Gopher Derby," Christmas lights, and "Communities in Bloom" competitions.   *David McLennan*

ETHNIC BLOC SETTLEMENTS: *see essay on page 305.*

EVANGELICAL FREE CHURCH OF CANADA. The Evangelical Free Church of Canada (EFCC) has its roots in the Danish-Norwegian Evangelical Free Church, which sent missionaries from the United States to Canada, beginning in 1912. Historically, the first recognized Canadian Evangelical Free Church began in Enchant, Alberta, planted by Rev. Carl Fosmark (a prominent leader for sixty years) in 1917. In small Norwegian communities of eastern Saskatchewan, revival tent meetings were held during the Depression by Rev. Olai Urang. The Fosston revival meetings, with Professor L.J. Pedersen of Minneapolis, resulted in Saskatchewan's first EFC, Elim Evangelical Free Church, pastored by pioneer evangelist John Has-Ellison, in autumn of 1932. A total of twenty-one Evangelical Free Churches were established in Saskatchewan over the next seventy-one years. Thirteen remain active (asterisks indicate the three largest): Big River EFC, Lashburn EFC, Osler Community Church*, Buffalo Narrows Community Fellowship Church, Parkland EFC (Kamsack), Elim EFC, Manitou EFC (Neilburg), Quill Lake EFC, Herbert EFC, EFC of Meadow Lake*, EFC of Regina, EFC of Mt. Nebo, and Saskatoon EFC*.

Provincial contributions include: the community support ministry "The Door of Hope"(Meadow Lake); camps sponsored by Big River, Fosston, Quill Lake, Meadow Lake and Kamsack EFC churches; and international involvement by Saskatchewan individuals in Bolivia, Venezuela and elsewhere through the EFCC Missions organization. In 1950, the Danish-Norwegian EFC and the Swedish EFC merged, forming the Evangelical Free Church of America (EFCA), of which the EFCC became independent in 1984, with national headquarters based in Langley, BC—also the location of an EFCC institution, Trinity Western University (TWU).   *Pam Franklin*

FURTHER READING: Hanson, C.B. 1984. *From Hardship to Harvest.* Edmonton: EFCC.

EVANGELICAL LUTHERAN CHURCH IN CANADA. The Evangelical Lutheran Church in Canada, otherwise known as the ELCIC, was organized as an autonomous Lutheran Church in Canada at the constituting convention in Winnipeg in May 1985. The ELCIC is made up of five synods spanning the country from the Atlantic to the Pacific: the Eastern Synod extends from the Atlantic ocean to western Ontario; the Manitoba Synod includes Manitoba and northwestern Ontario; the Saskatchewan Synod includes all of that province; the Synod of Alberta and the Territories is comprised of Alberta and the western Territories; and the British Columbia Synod is inclusive of the entire province, including Vancouver Island and the Queen Charlotte Islands. The total membership of the ELCIC is about 200,000 members, with the Saskatchewan Synod accounting for 36,000. The first bishop of the ELCIC was the Rev. Dr. Donald Sjoberg; the present bishop is the Rev. Raymond Schultz. The first bishop of the Saskatchewan Synod was the Rev. Telmor Sartison, and the present bishop is the Rev. Cynthia Halmarson.

The ELCIC came into existence as a result of a merger of the Canadian constituencies of two of the largest bodies of Lutherans in North America. In 1962 the Lutheran Church in America was formed in a merger of four antecedent Lutheran churches: the United Lutheran Church of America (largely German background); the Augustana Lutheran Church (Swedish origin); the Suomi Synod (Finnish); and the American Evangelical Lutheran Church (Danish in background). At the time of the formation of the Lutheran Church in America, a Canada section was also formed to represent Canadian interests. The chair of that section was the Rev. Robert Binhammer. The second of those merging bodies was the American Lutheran Church, constituted in 1960 by a merger of four other antecedent Lutheran churches: the American Lutheran Church (of largely German background); the United Evangelical Lutheran Church (Danish origin); the Evangelical Lutheran Church (primarily Norwegian background); and the Lutheran Free Church (also of Norwegian origin).

When the American Lutheran Church (ALC) was formed in 1960, a Canada District of that church was also organized to represent the Canadian constituency. That Canadian District subsequently organized itself in 1967 as an autonomous Lutheran church in Canada under the name "Evangelical Lutheran Church of Canada." Its first presiding officer was the Rev. Dr. Karl Holfeld, who had been the District president of the Canada District of the American Lutheran Church. The smaller Lutheran churches that united to become

COURTESY OF THE EVANGELICAL LUTHERAN CHURCH IN CANADA SASKATCHEWAN SYNOD OFFICE

Reverend Cynthia G. Halmarson, bishop of the Saskatchewan Synod, on the occasion of her installation as the first female bishop of the Evangelical Lutheran Church in Canada.

larger Lutheran synods were all formed initially from the large flow of European immigration in the 19th century. As the immigrants settled in various parts of North America they tended to congregate in ethnically homogeneous communities. The formation of the first congregations and their eventual organization into synods reflected those ethnic origins. In the early years of immigration from the "old country," worship was conducted in the language of each particular ethnic group. As the congregations grew, however, taking in members from many other ethnic origins, English gradually replaced the German and Scandinavian languages. There is no longer a dominant ethnic group in either the national church or the provincial synods, even though some traditions still reflect the early origins.

The Saskatchewan Synod is the third largest of the five Canadian synods of the ELCIC; this is reflective of the very large immigration from Europe in the formative years of the province. Many of the congregations were established in rural areas in the early days. Today, in spite of the urbanization of the population, many of those rural congregations still exist. Because of the depopulation of smaller centres, some of the congregations have had to disband or enter into co-operative arrangements with other Lutheran churches, and in some cases with churches of other denominations. The ELCIC continues to make a strong contribution to the religious culture in Canada, and also globally, through its mission and service agencies throughout the world.

Roger Nostbakken

EVANGELICAL MENNONITE CONFERENCE.

The Evangelical Mennonite Conference, initially known as the *Kleine Gemeinde*, had its beginning in the Molotschna Mennonite Colony of southern Russia in 1812. Approximately 200 *Kleine Gemeide* families emigrated to North America during the 1870s as one part of a larger Mennonite migration. Approximately eighty homesteaded in southern Manitoba, with a smaller group settling in Nebraska. In 1952 the *Kleine Gemeinde* in Canada changed its name to Evangelical Mennonite Church, and in 1959 to Evangelical Mennonite Conference. While the majority of its Canadian membership still remains in Manitoba, the Evangelical Mennonite Conference now has congregations scattered throughout five provinces in Canada. In 1949 the group organized its first two congregations in Saskatchewan in the communities of Kamsack and Canora. Four more were started during the 1950s (Pelly, Weekes, Heron, and Wymark).

These initiatives took place as a result of significant transitions within the denomination, which included a gradual language change from German to English, the geographical dispersion of its membership, and the influence of evangelical Protestantism, which awakened an interest in missionary activity both in Canada and abroad. The Evangelical Mennonite Conference maintains a theological identity that blends emphases from 16th-century Anabaptism and evangelical Protestantism in North America. The denomination has started a total of fourteen congregations in Saskatchewan, of which six have closed, two have affiliated with other denominations, and six remain in active operation (Pelly, Wymark, Creighton, Hudson Bay, Swift Current, and Endeavour). Membership within the six Saskatchewan congregations is less than 500, which represents approximately 7% of the Canadian membership. *Bruce L. Guenther*

FURTHER READING: Plett, H. 1996. *Seeking to be Faithful: The Story of the Evangelical Mennonite Conference*. Steinbach, MB: Evangelical Mennonite Conference.

EVANGELICAL MENNONITE MISSION CONFERENCE.

The Evangelical Mennonite Mission Conference (EMMC) began as a division within the Sommerfeld Mennonite Church in southern Manitoba in 1937. Initially known as the Rudnerweider Mennonite Church, the group adopted its current name in 1959 to signal its evangelical identity and its interest in missionary activity. Through the evangelistic activity of its ministers during the late 1930s among Old Colony Mennonites north of Saskatoon, several small congregations were organized in Saskatchewan during the mid-1940s. By the middle of the 1960s, the denomination had organized six congregations in the province, located in Hague, Warman, Hepburn, Saskatoon, Wynyard, and Blumenhof. One of the more prominent leaders emerging out of Saskatchewan was John D. Friesen who, as a young man, was elected to serve as a minister in the first EMMC congregation in this province, and who became both a popular conference evangelist as well as the primary voice of an international Low-German radio ministry called *Die Evangelische Botshaft* ("The Gospel Message"), based in Saskatoon.

Like most other Mennonite groups in western Canada, the EMMC have faced many challenges: language transition; remaining a peace witness during times of war; internal reorganization; urbanization; and a transition towards a more professionalized ministry. Despite its aggressive emphasis on evangelism and missions, which has facilitated international expansion in countries such as Bolivia, Belize and Mexico, the group only managed to hold its own in Saskatchewan during the last three decades of the 20th century. While the majority of its approximately 4,100 Canadian members are located in Manitoba, membership within the six Saskatchewan congregations numbers nearly 400, which represents approximately 9% of the denomination's membership in Canada. In 1995, the Saskatchewan EMMC congregations joined with the Mennonite Brethren in the sponsorship of Bethany College in Hepburn. *Bruce L. Guenther*

FURTHER READING: Heppner, J. 1987. *Search for Renewal: The Story of the Rudnerweider/EMMC, 1937–1987*. Winnipeg, MB: Evangelical Mennonite Mission Conference.

EVANS, ARTHUR "SLIM" (1890–1944).

Born on April 24, 1890, in Toronto, Arthur H. "Slim" Evans left school at the age of 13 to help support his family. He sold newspapers, drove a team of horses and learned the carpentry trade. He came west in 1911, working at various jobs on the prairies before moving from Winnipeg to Minneapolis, Minnesota. He was sentenced to three years imprisonment for participating in a free speech demonstration by the International Workers of the World (IWW): his "crime" was reading aloud the Declaration of Independence. He was released in 1912 after leading a jail strike of political prisoners. A year later, he was present at the massacre of workers and their families in Ludlow, Colorado and was hospitalized with leg wounds from a machine-gun bullet. During this period, Evans fraternized with such famous labour leaders as "Big Bill" Haywood, Frank Little, and Joe Hill. He then left for Kimberly, BC, where he became organizer for the IWW. He led the ONE BIG UNION miners in a strike at Drumheller, Alberta in 1919–20 and was sentenced to three years in prison—allegedly for using United Mine Workers of America (UMWA) funds for a wildcat strike without permission. He secured an early release because of a petition from the miners he supposedly robbed.

As an organizer for the Communist Party in BC, he was expelled for fighting the corrupt leadership of the United Brotherhood of Carpenters and Joiners in Vancouver. In 1932, he organized the National Unemployed Workers Association and won increased rates for relief work. Having helped the coal miners of Princeton strike for higher wages, Evans was imprisoned for eighteen months in Oakalla after police worked in collusion with the KU KLUX KLAN to frame him. To protest the welfare of unemployed single men in Prime Minister R.B. Bennett's "slave camps" in the early 1930s, Evans conceived and later led the most substantial labour protest in Canadian history, the ON-TO-OTTAWA TREK. After the trek was stopped in Regina on orders from the Prime Minister, Evans led a delegation invited to Ottawa on June 22, 1935, to meet with him. When Bennett called him a thief, Evans shot back, "Bennett, you're a liar!"

The RCMP and Regina City Police were ordered to arrest the Trek leaders. On July 1, 1935, police armed with clubs, tear gas and guns broke up an open-air meeting, sparking the REGINA RIOT. Evans was arrested under Section 98 of the criminal code; the charges were later withdrawn as there was not enough evidence to proceed to trial. Two years later, he helped organize workers at the Consolidated Mining and Smelting Company in Trail, BC. The same year, he led a campaign for a medical fund to support the Canadian Mackenzie-Papineau Battalion fighting the Facist Franco regime in Spain.

Evans died on February 13, 1944, after being struck by a car. *Clare Powell*

FURTHER READING: Waiser, B. 2003. *All Hell Can't Stop Us: The On-to-Ottawa Trek and Regina Riot*. Saskatoon: Fifth House.

EVANS, LYLE (1907–92).

Lillian Lyle Evelyn (Evans) King, known to most people as Lyle Evans, is responsible for the growth of school library services in Saskatchewan through her initiative, enthusiasm, and efforts to interest school boards, superintendents, principals, teachers, and teacher librarians in the need for better school library service in the province. Following NORMAL SCHOOL, Evans taught from 1930 to 1939 in both elementary and secondary schools. She obtained a BA in 1940 from the UNIVERSITY OF SASKATCHEWAN, a BLS in 1942 from the University of Toronto, and an MLS in 1952 from Columbia University. She worked in the Toronto Public Library and then the Graham-Eckes Private School in Palm Beach, Florida from 1942 to 1945. She returned to Saskatchewan in 1946 to become the first Supervisor of School Libraries in the province as well as the first appointed in Canada.

Miss Lyle Evans, Supervisor of School Libraries, June 1948.

She developed at the Normal School a course in the organization, administration, and use of the school library which in time became part of the College of Education program.

Lyle Evans was instrumental in establishing school library demonstration projects, from the first locally supported project in Cupar School Unit #28 in 1947 to the more elaborate Saskatchewan School Library Demonstration Project at Columbia School in Yorkton. Her efforts ensured that in 1947–48 the school curriculum included provision for school library services, including personnel, materials, programs, and standards of actual space for a library. She lectured at the College of Education, assisted in the production of radio programs, film, and book displays, and authored numerous articles and pamphlets. In 1962, she was appointed Associate Professor at the College of Education of the University of Saskatchewan, Regina Campus, where she was responsible for the program in school library service until 1974.

Some of Evans' other achievements involved being president of the Saskatchewan Library Association (1950–51); chair of the Canadian Library Association (CLA) Committee on Education for School Librarianship (1952); organizer for the first annual workshop on School Library Services in the province (1953); chair of the CLA Young People's Section; director of the American Association of School Librarians (1958–60); chair of the organizing committee of the Saskatchewan Association of School Librarians (SSLA), in 1959; council member (1961–63) and later president (1969–70) of the Canadian School Library Association (CSLA); and CSLA's Margaret B. Scott Award winner in 1978. *Gail Saunders*

Ethnic Bloc Settlements

Alan Anderson

Since the opening of western Canada to homesteading in 1872, much of the prairie (grassland and parkland) area of Saskatchewan has been settled by ethno-religious groups who formed their own bloc settlements. A bloc settlement may result from the consolidation of a larger territory initially settled by a particular ethnic group which now finds itself in a minority position within the region: such was the case of the MÉTIS, who resisted by armed conflict (the NORTH-WEST RESISTANCE of 1884–85). Again, a bloc settlement may result from importation of a similar form of social organization from Europe by immigrants who formerly occupied a minority position there as well: such was the case of the MENNONITES, HUTTERITES, DOUKHOBORS, and many German Catholics. Or a bloc settlement may result from colonization schemes of the federal government and an ethnic or religious agency: such schemes introduced to Saskatchewan German Catholics from the American Midwest; French from France, Quebec, and New England; Ukrainians, Poles and other ethnic groups from Eastern Europe; and Scandinavians from Scandinavia and the American Midwest. We may speculate that their decision to settle here rather than to immigrate into, or stay in, the United States possibly revealed a dislike for a "melting-pot" attitude in that country and a preference for a Canadian "cultural mosaic," a belief that Canada would be more tolerant of ethnic minorities holding unique beliefs (such as an emphasis of pacifism), or an appreciation of less expensive and more readily available farmland in Canada.

Regarding the reasons for migration, we may distinguish between the factors pushing the migrant from a place of origin and those pulling the migrant to a new destination. The principal "push" factors were overpopulation, impoverishment, political discontent, and persecution (perhaps leading to forced migration or mass expulsion) in the sending country. Among the most significant "pull" factors were the recruitment of immigrants by the government of the new country to offset low internal migration, recruitment by agencies seeking cheap labour, the influence of settlers writing home, and the transportation of immigrants as a lucrative business. Admittedly, certain factors considered as "push" from one standpoint may be seen as "pull" from another: for example, Canada engaged in purposeful commercial colonization to exploit natural resources and to extend its political influence by importing continental European immigrants as pioneering grain farmers who would ensure stabilization of the restive Métis and First Nations in the west. Virtually all of the "push" and "pull" factors affected migration into the bloc settlements of the prairie provinces.

Immigration may be seen as primarily, though not entirely, an individual undertaking or collective drift rather than as an organized group movement. Yet whole villages have been known to migrate to another country; moreover, governments regulate, direct, and encourage or discourage the migration process. What exactly were the Canadian government's policies on immigration during the decades when the vast majority of settlers arrived? Towards the end of the 19th century, in competition with the then fairly open American immigration policy, the Canadian campaign for immigrants intensified. In 1891, census results had indicated an unsatisfactory increase in population during the previous decade. When Clifford Sifton became Minister of the Interior in 1896, he immediately began to encourage immigration. Agents were appointed throughout Europe, even though most European countries had strict laws against emigration; the quest for migrants was publicized through circulars, exhibits, and advertisements; and transportation companies were federally subsidized. Moreover, the flow of Central and Eastern European migrants to the Canadian prairies was, no doubt, soon enhanced by the imposition of American quota restrictions.

Every sort of device was employed to attract immigrants—including those who had first settled in the United States—to the Canadian prairies. Many of the 160,000 initial continental settlers in Saskatchewan were by 1911 secured through the efforts of the North Atlantic Trading Company, which had held an agreement with the Canadian government since 1899. The company was obligated to spend a minimum of $15,000 annually to secure immigrants from various parts of continental Europe: the Low Countries (the Netherlands and Belgium), the predominantly German countries (Germany, Luxembourg, and Switzerland), Scandinavia (Denmark, Norway, Sweden, and Finland), and Eastern Europe (Austria-Hungary and Russia). The company was to be paid £1 for every farmer who settled. The contract was renewed in 1904 for ten years, but cancelled only two years later due to the hostility of European governments towards clandestine immigration propaganda and manipulation of finances. With regard to the latter, apparently payments had been made for immigrants who had come into Canada under other auspices. But by 1906, the company had already received immense sums from the Laurier government.

The Sifton policy of fairly open immigration from continental Europe was not without its critics. In the first place, the provincial government's attitude toward immigration differed markedly from that of the federal government: provincial financial difficulties were only augmented by the immigrant influx resulting from the immigration polices of the federal government, as continued and accelerating immigration created demands for heavy expenditures in educational facilities, public works, and other provincial government services. Moreover, Sifton's policy conflicted sharply with the desire of the province's population of British origin to preserve Saskatchewan "for English-speaking peoples." Resentment against uncontrolled immigration, especially from Eastern Europe, grew steadily after World War I. At the hearings conducted by the Saskatchewan Royal Commission on Immigration and Settlement in 1930, numerous briefs opposing open immigration were submitted. The Saskatchewan section of the United Farmers of Canada suggested that immigration of farmers was to be stopped until the native-born were better provided for; that there should be no solicited or assisted immigration; and that a quota system should be put in place, controlled to some extent by the provincial government. The Saskatchewan Command of the Canadian Legion believed that immigration from continental countries should not exceed immigration from "within the Empire." The Saskatoon Labour Trades Council advocated selective immigration where assimilation was a certainty. The Regina Assembly of the Native Sons of Canada opposed assisted immigration, whether sponsored by Canada, the immigrant's country of origin, or group inter-

ests; special homesteading concessions to immigrants; and granting Canadian citizenship before five years of residence in Canada had elapsed. The KU KLUX KLAN in Saskatchewan desired that immigration from "non-preferred" countries in central, eastern, and southern Europe be stopped entirely for at least five years; after which a rigid quota of 2% of the 1901 census would be imposed, except for British, French and Scandinavian immigrants; that "trained" British and Scandinavian families be allowed to settle on the land; that all handling of immigration be removed from religious organizations; and that any ethnic group settlement be prevented. The Provincial Grand Lodge of the ORANGE ORDER in Saskatchewan advocated Anglo-Saxon predominance, speaking out against the "unwise" policy of bringing in more immigrants than could be easily assimilated "to those British ideals which are fundamental to our national existence."

While the Saskatchewan Royal Commission on Immigration and Settlement did not appraise the situation in 1930 as negatively as did many of the organizations submitting briefs, it did recognize that the development of such isolated bloc settlements was not readily conducive to an integrated Canadian society:

> Throughout the province will be found many group settlements, representative of diverse racial stocks. While group settlement has many good features, nevertheless there are grave objections to its further development... . Doubtless these groups do add diversity and elements of richness to the cultural life of the community; and also doubtless by this very diversity there is greater opportunity to adapt newcomers to the new environment. This, in turn, may result in their more rapid economic progress. The warm welcome that may be expected from a racial brother, the overcoming of the nostalgia resulting from separation from the homeland, as well as other aids, are factors that appear to support group settlement. On the other hand, it is the rooted conviction of many of our people that group settlement tends to create blocks, thus preventing those intimate contacts without which it is impossible to create a sound citizenship.

The Commission concluded that "homesteading should be discontinued and remaining Crown lands should be sold, preferably to residents of this province; as a second choice to other Canadians; thirdly to British settlers; and lastly to other immigrants." Therefore the period of establishing bloc settlements in Saskatchewan extended primarily from the advent of Sifton's policy in 1896 to the Commission's report in 1930.

The process of settlement on the land and into bloc settlements was a rather complicated one. The homesteading system was first established in the Canadian prairies in 1872, in accordance with the Land Act, Section 33:

> Every person who is the sole head of a family and every male who has attained the age of 18 years and is a British subject or declares his intention of becoming and British subject, is entitled to apply for entry to a homestead. A quarter-section may be obtained as a homestead on payment of an entry fee of $10 and fulfillment of certain conditions of residence and cultivation. To qualify for the issuing of the patent, the settler must have resided upon his homestead for at least six months of each of three years, must have erected a habitable house thereon, and must have at least 30 acres of his holding broken, of which 20 acres must be cropped. A reduction may be made in the area of breaking where the land is difficult to cultivate on account of scrub or stone.

SASKATCHEWAN ARCHIVES BOARD R-B3667

Saskatchewan Royal Commission on Immigration and Settlement, 1930.

The federal government's settlement schemes were closely integrated with the railways' schemes, and the latter in turn with those of ethnic and religious organizations. The federal government subsidized settlement through the Colonization Department of the CPR, which had offices in Britain and France. A similar CNR department was not organized until 1923, to settle immigrants on vacant lands adjacent to its lines. The Canada Colonization Association (CCA) was a CPR subsidiary; it chiefly placed continental immigrants with insufficient capital, and was backed by loan and banking companies as well as wealthy individuals and landowners, suggesting some sympathy for continental immigration. Besides the CCA, the railways operated through ethnic and religious subsidiary organizations interested in establishing bloc settlements; these organizations were financed by the railways to some extent ($5 per each adult in a family settled or $1 per single agricultural worker).

The development of ethnic enclaves is not unusual, according to sociological literature on ethnic relations. Competition for space often results in the formation of segregated ethnic islands, each of which develops a distinctive culture. Members of each minority group tend to congregate in areas where they can speak their own language, practice their religion, and follow their own customs. Immigrants were sometimes made to feel the hostility of the larger society and were segregated into well-defined areas. Many immigrants wanted to be among their co-ethnics, with whom they could identify and sympathize. Once such colonies come into existence, moreover, other people of a given ethnic group tend to gravitate toward them.

Four principal types of bloc settlements could be noted. First, planned bloc settlements were organized and settled by specific ethnic or ethno-religious groups through the work of group agents and associations. Second, the Canadian government as well as transportation and settlement companies were responsible for recruiting settlers of particular ethnic and religious groups. Third, bloc settlements came into existence gradually as the result of chain migration, a process whereby people from a certain place of origin settled in a new locality in Saskatchewan, then established linkages with their relatives, friends or other contacts back home, thereby inducing further emigration from the place of origin. Fourth, bloc settlements formed through a process of gravitation when migrants were drawn together by forces of mutual attraction such as common origin, language, religion and culture.

The original character of the settlement may change in time, and some settlements may be offshoots from earlier ones. The bloc settlements of Saskatchewan conformed to all of these types. The Jewish, Mennonite, Hutterite, and Doukhobor settlements—as well as some German Catholic, German Protestant (mostly Lutheran), British, French, and Hungarian settlements—may be described as primarily of the organized type, whereas the Scandinavian, Ukrainian, Polish, and Black settlements tended to be more representative of the chain or gravitation types. The establishment of ethno-religious bloc settlements in Saskatchewan was, in sum, due partly to organized colonization schemes and partly to rather coincidental gravitation of co-ethnics.

The effect of these settlement processes on the population of the prairies was profound. Since the opening of Canadian prairie land to homesteading in 1872, most of the prairie grassland and parkland areas of Saskatchewan had been settled within little more than half a century by diverse ethno-religious groups that had formed their own settlements. The population and extent of each bloc settlement could vary from the immediate land around a single small community to a vast area inclusive of many towns and villages; yet it must be emphasized that most rural communities in Saskatchewan are located within such settlements.

Despite an immigration policy favouring immigrants only from "desirable" countries, by the 1920s Saskatchewan had twice as many immigrants of non-British as of British origin. Vast areas of the prairie regions of this province had been incorporated into bloc settlements, some of which included over thirty towns and villages. Moreover, the Canadian prairies had received the diversion of unskilled Eastern European farm labour from the United States. Ethnic enclaves had become a prominent feature of the prairies, helping to turn Canadian society into a "cultural mosaic" largely lacking the strong national identity and melting-pot consciousness emerging in the US. These enclaves were characterized by isolation from other enclaves of different ethnic origins and religious affiliations, and from the larger society. Social organization was extremely localized, and most bloc settlements used the dialects, customs and traditions of particular areas in Europe.

Adding to the existing early francophone Métis settlements widely scattered throughout Saskatchewan, French-speaking immigrants direct from Europe (not only many regions in France, but also Belgium and Switzerland) were joined by migrants from Quebec (even including some who were ultimately of Acadian descent), as well as from Manitoba and the United States, to establish thirty-two distinct French settlements and over 100 parishes. In a few cases these settlements were expansions of an original nucleus established by Métis; however, most were completely new settlements. The linguistic diversity was pronounced: one could hear Mitchif, country Québecois, many French dialects brought from France and Belgium, and even Breton (the Celtic language of Brittany). The French settlements ranged from larger settlements of over 3,000 people of French origin living in and around several towns and villages, to smaller settlements consisting of only 200 or

Andrzej Wojcik family, Kelvington, ca. 1931.

300 French around a single village or hamlet. The pattern of settlement which developed was unique: sixteen across southern Saskatchewan, and an equal number across the central region. The impact of French settlement on the Saskatchewan prairies has been an important part of the French diaspora across Canada.

SASKATCHEWAN ARCHIVES BOARD R-B10323

Wedding at Cannington Manor, before 1897.

Immigrants of Scandinavian and Finnish origins also tended to concentrate in their own settlements. Norwegians, both as immigrants direct from Norway and as migrants from neighbouring American states, concentrated in certain rural areas scattered throughout the Saskatchewan prairies, starting in 1894. Swedes founded the New Stockholm colony as early as 1885, then concentrated in at least five other widely

Settlers of British origin collectively constituted the largest proportion of the Saskatchewan population, so one might assume that there were no distinctly British settlements as the British-origin population was simply equated with the "general population." This would be an incorrect assumption, as distinct English, Scottish, Irish and Welsh settlements were founded. Several English colonies—CANNINGTON MANOR, the East London Artisans Colony, the York Farmers Colony, Churchbridge, the BARR COLONY—were established as utopian ventures by immigrants from England, whereas the Temperance Colony at Saskatoon was originally settled by migrants from Ontario. The many Scottish settlements included several established as colonies of Highland crofters, Orkney Islanders, Lowland Scots, and Scottish-Canadians from Ontario and Nova Scotia. There were concentrations of Irish, and at least one distinct "Irish Colony." A Welsh colony was established by immigrants who came not directly from Wales, but from Argentina. Until the 1940s, settlers ultimately of British (including Irish) origin constituted a majority of the Saskatchewan population, and today their descendants remain omnipresent throughout the province.

The origins of German-speaking settlers were remarkably diverse. They came mainly from ethnic German colonies in Eastern Europe, as well as from large German settlements in the neighbouring American states. Their settlements in Saskatchewan tended to be founded by specific religious affiliations. Often the origins of German settlers were very specific: the settlements established by Danube Swabians from the border region of present-day Serbia, Romania and Hungary are a case in point. Two extensive Mennonite settlements developed respectively to the north of Saskatoon and south and east of Swift Current. Hutterites did not begin to establish colonies in Saskatchewan until 1949; yet their colonies have proliferated since then, new ones having been founded almost every year. People of German ethnic origin have settled many areas of the prairie portion of the province; today their descendants, together with more recent German immigrants, outnumber any other ethnic group in the province. While people of Dutch origin have concentrated mainly in cities, they did establish two distinct rural settlements near Swift Current in 1910, and near North Battleford in 1914.

SASKATCHEWAN ARCHIVES BOARD R-A23868

Leopold and Anna Amon, Danube Swabian settlers, ca. 1902.

dispersed areas. Icelanders were also among the earliest settlers, developing three distinct colonies—Thingvalla-Logberg near Churchbridge, Valar-Holar near Tantallon, and the extensive Quill Lakes settlement centred on Wynyard and Foam Lake during the 1880s and 1890s. The first Finnish colony was New Finland near Whitewood in 1887, followed by the Rock Point and Turtle Lake settlements in 1908–10. People of Danish origin tended to be urban; however, Dannevirke, a distinctly Danish parish, was established at Redvers by 1910. Today many rural farming areas of Saskatchewan remain predominantly populated by people of Scandinavian (including Finnish) origins, continuing to form a significant part of the Saskatchewan mosaic.

Numerous settlements were developed by Eastern European ethnic groups. The largest Ukrainian settlements all had their beginnings within a short time period, from 1896 to 1906. The majority of these settlers were immigrants from neighbouring districts in Galicia and Bukovina. Today their descendants constitute the second largest non-British and non-Aboriginal ethnic group in Saskatchewan (after people of German origin), and very extensive rural areas are included within Ukrainian settlements. Polish concentrations often developed within Ukrainian settlements, although several distinctly Polish settlements did come into existence between 1896 and 1906. Russian Doukhobors first arrived in 1899 and were settled in four colonies: the North or Swan River Colony, the South or Veregin Colony, the Good Spirit Lake Annex, and the north and south sections of the Saskatchewan or Prince Albert Colony. Jews arrived from Eastern Europe to settle in eight farm colonies: New Jerusalem near Moosomin in 1882, the Oxbow area in 1894, north of Wapella in 1886, Hirsch west of Estevan in 1892, Sonnenfeld or Hoffer and Edenbridge in 1906, and Montefiore in the Alsask area and across the Alberta border by 1910. Hungarians developed their own settlements over two decades, between 1886 and 1908. Czechs and Slovaks concentrated at Kolin, Gerald, Glenside, and Valley Centre in 1884–1902, and the Lipton area after 1905. Croatians settled around Kenaston in 1904, and Serbs founded the first Serbian Orthodox church in Canada in Regina in 1916, while Romanians founded the first Romanian Orthodox church in Canada in Regina in 1902 as well as five widely scattered rural settlements. People of non-European ethnic origins have settled mainly in the larger cities, especially in recent decades; yet Chinese have long been widely dispersed in rural communities as café owners, Syrians/Lebanese have long been found in southern Saskatchewan communities, and Blacks from Oklahoma settled in the Eldon district near Maidstone in 1909.

Ethnic or ethno-religious bloc settlements are still today, or hitherto have been, significant forms of social organization within the Canadian context; yet this significance is changing, and thus should not be viewed as static. Bloc settlements may persist or they may be in a gradual process of dissolution; moreover, rural ethnic identities may be reinterpreted. While it is possible to discern factors contributing to persistence or dissolution, considerable variation may be noted in comparing the settlements of particular ethnic groups. In general, assimilation may be viewed as a re-orientation of ethnic group members from an orientation primarily toward the ethnic group to one primarily toward the general (Canadian) society. More specifically, assimilation refers to identity change. But what exactly is changing? Which factors comprise identity? How do demographic-ecological conditions such as vital statistics (age, generation, gender, occupation, and education), community differences (in terms of size, homogeneity, and location), community decline and mobility (rural depopulation and physical mobility, social mobility, and "de-localization" or the eradication of rural focal points) relate to identity change? And to what extent has a re-orientation of group members been apparent in intermarriage across ethnic or religious lines?

This pattern of ethnic settlement has effectively reduced the opportunity for intermarriage between ethnic or religious groups, although attitudes toward such intermarriage have progressively become more open. Religious intermarriage has long tended to be more evident than ethnic or especially racial intermarriage: thus German Catholics, for example, have intermarried with Polish, Hungarian, French, and other Catholics. Yet people of relatively similar ethnic origins have also tended to mix: for example, Ukrainians with Poles or Russians. A steadily increasing proportion of Saskatchewan residents now claim more than a single ethnic origin. It is likely that as the population becomes more mixed, emphasis on ethnic identities may decrease. Locally, it is becoming increasingly common, especially in mixed communities, to find people of one particular ethnic origin with spouses of a different ethnic origin—hence people with surnames indicative of one ethnicity may speak the language of a different ethnicity.

This raises the question of language retention, a highly variable phenomenon. For example, the Fransaskois community has tended to emphasize strongly the ability to speak French—an attitude reinforced by French's official language status in Canada, by schools and broadcasting in the French language, and by meetings of provincial organizations conducted in French. Yet less than half of the French-origin population still speaks French, and a decreasing number of formerly francophone parishes still offer services primarily, much less exclusively, in French. Eastern European ethnic groups have tended to retain their traditional languages from generation to generation more than people of German or Scandinavian origins, for various reasons including better defined bloc settlements, strong ethnic cultures, and degree of perceived social differentiation from other Saskatchewan people. People of Scandinavian origins have tended not to use Scandinavian languages very often nor to resist intermarriage with the larger population of British origin. The former importance of German culture in Saskatchewan was dealt a harsh blow during two world wars, triggering a sharp decrease in ability to speak German by the second or third generation. Yet to some extent, this trend has been reversed with the immigration of German speakers to the cities in postwar years, so that there has been a re-emphasis of German language and culture through the Saskatchewan German Council. In general, language retention rates tend to be highest among recent immigrants, who are almost exclusively urban residents. In the rural population, familiarity with traditional languages has inexorably declined; the only group not affected by this generalization has been the Hutterites.

Whatever may have been the ability to maintain ethnic traditions and promote knowledge of the history of ethnic settlements in Saskatchewan, the influence which these settlements have had on the cultural geography of Saskatchewan could hardly go unnoticed. While it is unfortunate that many rural churches have been closed, abandoned or even removed over the years, together with country schoolhouses and community halls which were once the very focus of community life, Saskatchewan still retains numerous examples of ethnic architecture such as the many onion-domed Ukrainian churches which dot the countryside. Even patterns of settlement may occasionally have tended to be unique to specific ethnic groups, such as the Strassendorf line villages of Mennonites (and formerly of Doukhobors), the rang or riverlot pattern of settlement which characterized the Batoche and St-Laurent-Grandin Métis settlement, and the orderly arrangement of buildings in Hutterite colonies. (*See also* CROATIAN AND SERBIAN SETTLEMENTS, CZECH AND SLOVAK SETTLEMENTS, DANISH SETTLEMENTS, DANUBE SWABIANS, DOUKHOBOR SETTLEMENTS, DUTCH SETTLEMENTS, ENGLISH SETTLEMENTS, FINNISH SETTLEMENTS, FRENCH AND METIS SETTLEMENTS, FRENCH SETTLEMENTS, GERMAN SETTLEMENTS, HUNGARIAN SETTLEMENTS, HUTTERITE COLONIES, ICELANDIC SETTLEMENTS, IRISH SETTLEMENTS, JEWISH RURAL SETTLEMENTS, MENNONITE SETTLEMENTS, NORWEGIAN SETTLEMENTS, POLISH SETTLEMENTS, POPULATION TRENDS, RURAL POPULATION, RURAL SETTLEMENT PATTERNS, SCANDINAVIAN SETTLEMENTS, SCOTTISH SETTLEMENTS, SWEDISH SETTLEMENTS, UKRAINIAN SETTLEMENTS, URBAN ETHNIC DIVERSITY, VISIBLE MINORITIES, WELSH SETTLEMENT.)

SASKATCHEWAN ARCHIVES BOARD R-B10101

Pioneer celebrations at Hryhoriw, south of Preeceville, 1937.

EXPLORATION TRAILS. Early exploration trails in southern Saskatchewan (formerly the North-West Territories) were largely established by scientists and observers hired by the Dominion government. These people took a natural inventory of the region to determine whether it was suitable for agricultural settlement. Although several explorations were conducted, some of the more notable ones were completed by John Palliser, Henry Youle Hind and **JOHN MACOUN.** John Palliser first explored the region from 1857 to 1870; his exploration trails originated near Roche Percee and continued north to Fort Qu'Appelle, west to Moose Jaw Creek, and north across the **SOUTH SASKATCHEWAN RIVER.** Palliser's initial exploration led to further expeditions by Henry Youle Hind (1857–58) and John Macoun (1879–81) (*see* **PALLISER AND HIND EXPEDITIONS**). Palliser and Hind concluded that the region extending along the 49th parallel between 100°W and 114°W longitude, with its apex at 52°N, was unfit for agricultural settlement; Macoun disagreed, claiming that the region represented great agricultural potential.

Exploration trails in northern Saskatchewan were primarily conducted by geologists and surveyors, who reported to the Geological Survey of Canada (GSC). This agency, created in 1842, was responsible for obtaining scientific data on the country's natural resources. Among the first such surveyors were **JOSEPH TYRRELL,** William McIness and Frank Crean. Tyrrell assessed the geologic potential of the Wollaston, Cree, and Reindeer lake regions of northern Saskatchewan from the late 1880s to the early 1890s. William McIness, a survey geologist, explored geological formations from the **CHURCHILL RIVER** basin to Manitoba from 1907 to 1910. Frank Crean, a civil engineer, was hired by the Department of the Interior to assess the agricultural potential of land in Saskatchewan's north-central region; he conducted explorations from Prince Albert towards present-day **PRINCE ALBERT NATIONAL PARK,** and northwest to La Loche in 1908 and 1909.

James Winkel

EXPLORERS. The history of the exploration of Saskatchewan has not been well documented. The contribution of Aboriginal people is largely unacknowledged, although all explorers depended upon their knowledge, skills and experience. By 1810, **DAVID THOMPSON** and **PETER FIDLER** had compiled maps of nearly all the major waterways; nevertheless, the mapping of Saskatchewan was not completed until the mid-1940s.

European traders arrived on the western shore of Hudson Bay in 1682, but for over 70 years the only description of the northern plains was **HENRY KELSEY**'s brief nine-week journal of 1691. The La Vérendryes reached the mouth of the **SASKATCHEWAN RIVER** in 1741, and their immediate successors established posts further upriver and on

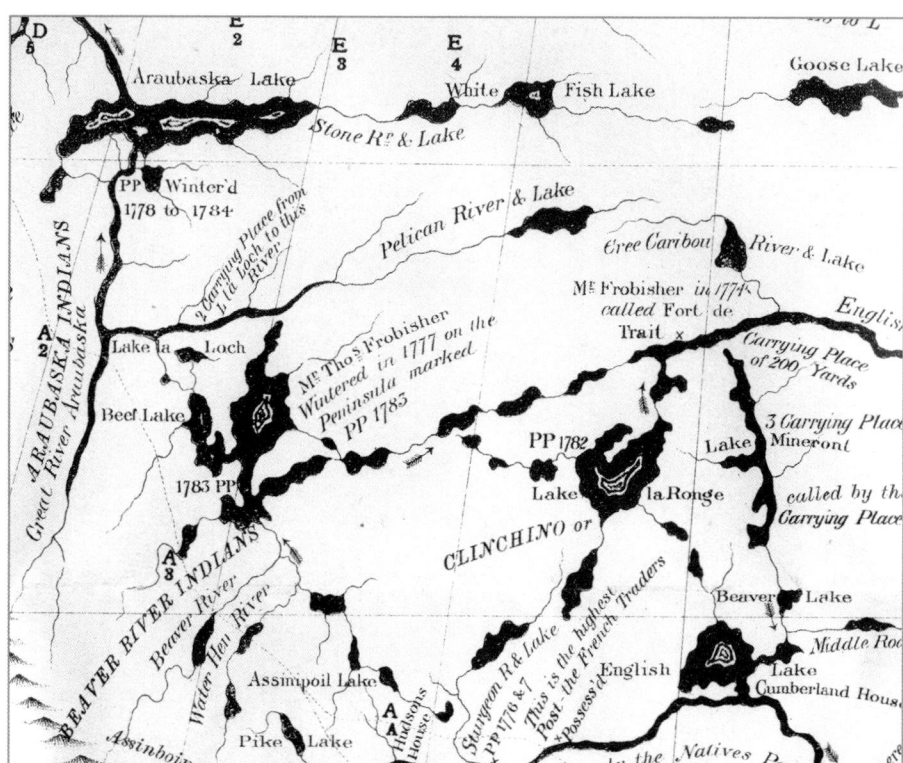

Detail of "Peter Pond's May 1785"—as it appears in *Peter Pond: Fur Trader and Adventurer* by Harold A. Innis (Irwin & Gordon, 1930).

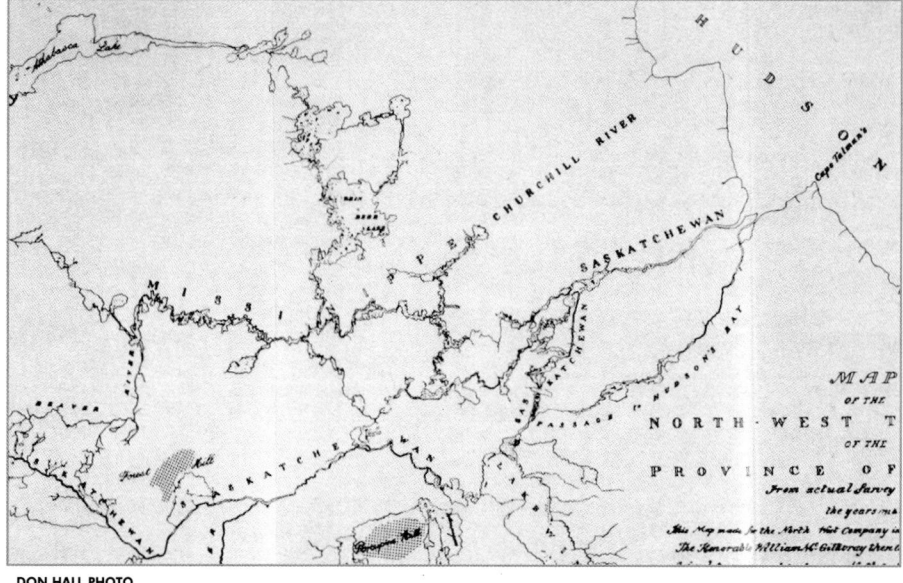

DON HALL PHOTO

Detail of David Thompson's "Map of the North-West Territory of the Province of Canada." Reproduced from *David Thompson's Narrative 1784-1812*, published by the Champlain Society, 1962.

the Red Deer River, but they did not describe the Saskatchewan landscape. Between 1754 and 1774, the Hudson's Bay Company (HBC) at York Factory sent men inland to winter with **CREE** people on the northern plains. Journals from four of these men survive; unfortunately, they seldom identified specific geographical features, and their routes are difficult to retrace.

The first crude maps of the interior were drawn by **PETER POND** in the 1780s. In 1790, while at Cumberland House, David Thompson and Peter Fidler were taught surveying skills by Philip Turnor. These two men mapped all the main provincial waterways except for the region west of **REINDEER LAKE.** Their information was used in the famous Arrowsmith maps of North America published between 1791 and 1857. Most of their records remain unpublished, including Fidler's copies of the few surviving Aboriginal maps of Saskatchewan.

In 1801, Alexander Mackenzie published a best-selling account of his journeys to the Arctic and Pacific Oceans, including a detailed description of the CHURCHILL RIVER. Daniel Harmon, Gabriel Franchère and other traders then began publishing their experiences. More importantly, in 1819 the British government sponsored JOHN FRANKLIN's four-year expedition to the Arctic. Franklin's account included several chapters describing the Cumberland and Fort Carlton areas. Later travelers into the far northwest, including George Back, Richard King and JOHN RICHARDSON, also published their accounts but contributed little that was new. The increased publicity of the West and the development of the CARLTON TRAIL attracted adventurers such as the Earl of Southesk, Viscount Milton, W.B. Cheadle, George Grant, William Butler, and Thomas McMicking. However, their accounts all lack detailed geographical observations.

By the 1850s, interest developed in the resource and settlement potential of the northern plains. In 1857–60, the British government sent John Palliser (see PALLISER AND HIND EXPEDITIONS) to explore the area between the Assiniboine River and the Rocky Mountains. Skilled expedition members collected a wide range of information while Palliser's large, detailed map remained the basis for later maps for many years. In 1858, the Canadian government sent Henry Youle Hind and Simon J. Dawson to explore the area between Lake Winnipeg and the SOUTH SASKATCHEWAN RIVER. Hind lacked personnel, and his account is somewhat superficial. The last major

mapping expedition across the south was the British-American Boundary Commission of 1872–74, which resulted in a detailed geological report by G.M. DAWSON. In 1872, JOHN MACOUN began evaluating agricultural potential with a series of expeditions across central Saskatchewan which were initially part of the railway and telegraph surveys carried out under Sandford Fleming. Then, between 1877 and the 1920s the Dominion Land Survey carried out a massive program, mapping over 3,000 individual townships across the southern half of the province. This resulted in the series of "sectional maps" which were the first accurate maps of the settled portion of Saskatchewan.

By the late 1800s, the Geological Survey of Canada began focussing on the potential for mineral resources. J.B. TYRRELL, the last of the great inland explorers, mapped the country west of Reindeer Lake in 1892, and later crossed into the Barrens. Finally, between 1907 and 1910 William McInnes mapped the region between the Churchill and Carrot Rivers, while Frank Crean explored the forested area to the west. These ended the large regional surveys, although geologists still continue today to map and describe smaller units of land. The first aerial photography surveys began in 1924, eliminating the need for ground mapping. They resulted in the present topographic maps at a scale of 1.25 miles/inch. Satellite coverage became generally available after 1972. Today, satellites offer a wide range of imagery, which can be updated on a daily basis, providing much environmental data for scientific analysis. To this day, however, the only descriptions of many landscapes throughout the province are those made by Thompson and Fidler, 200 years ago.

Dale Russell

FURTHER READING: Ingles, E.B. and N.M. Distad (eds.). 2003. *Peel's Bibliography of the Canadian Prairies to 1953.* Toronto: University of Toronto Press; Russell, D. 1999. "Fur Trade Journeys: 1691-1808." In K.I. Fung (ed.), *Atlas of Saskatchewan.* Saskatoon: University of Saskatchewan; –. 1999. "Organized Expeditions: 1819-1910." In K.I. Fung (ed.), *Atlas of Saskatchewan.* Saskatoon: University of Saskatchewan; Thomson, D.W. 1966. *Men and Meridians: The History of Surveying and Mapping in Canada.* Ottawa: Queen's Printer; Warkentin, John and Richard I. Ruggles. 1970. *Manitoba Historical Atlas; A Selection of Facsimile Maps, Plans, and Sketches from 1612 to 1969.* Winnipeg: Historical and Scientific Society of Manitoba.

EXTRA-PARLIAMENTARY POLITICS. Extra-parliamentary politics has fundamentally shaped Saskatchewan. The 19th-century uprising of the Red River MÉTIS and settlers in the west led to the creation of provinces, including Saskatchewan in 1905, out of the North-West Territories. The Saskatchewan Grain Growers, with the slogan "in union is

strength," organized in Sintaluta that year to challenge the CPR's monopoly; they used rallies, the courts, and direct action such as rail blockades. In the 1920s farmer groups went on to build their own economic organizations. Since 1949 the SASKATCHEWAN FARMERS UNION has used extra-parliamentary actions in support of such things as the Crow rate and the Wheat Board, and to oppose GMO crops.

In 1931 Estevan coal miners worked sixteen hours per day with wage cutbacks and were dependent on company stores. A general strike demanding recognition of the Mine Workers' Union lasted nearly all of September; on September 29, "Black Tuesday," several strikers were killed by police who tried to stop a parade which had gone ahead without receiving a permit from the town. This extra-parliamentary action helped advance workers' right in Saskatchewan. The drought and low grain prices in the "Dirty Thirties" forced thousands of single, unemployed men into government relief camps; these men built Regina's Albert Street bridge and Wascana Lake. The ON-TO-OTTAWA TREK started in BC as a rebellion against the restrictions of these early "work for welfare" camps, and as a demand for work and wages. Prime Minister R.B. Bennett ordered police to stop the protest en route to the capital, and the REGINA RIOT resulted on July 1, 1935: this event catalyzed forces supporting social policy reforms across Canada.

First Nations and Métis peoples have used extra-parliamentary protest in their continuing struggle for self-determination. Not having a vote until the 1950s, Indian people often had no recourse but passive resistance to their continued colonial status. Reserve Indians sometimes had to choose between starvation and breaching Indian Affairs regulations by killing livestock. Some Indian people rebelled against the "pass laws" which restricted their movement off reserve. Indian children in residential schools sometimes risked death from the elements trying to escape to return to their families. As the migration to towns and cities accelerated in the 1960s, protests against racist practices, including police brutality, became more common. The right to engage in First Nations spiritual or healing practices was partly won when First Nations inmates refused to obey rules in provincial jails.

Northern Aboriginal people have resorted to civil disobedience to gain more control of traditional lands. Roads have been blocked to protest everything from corporate clear-cutting to uranium mining. There was a prolonged campaign, including blockade of the road to the Rabbit Lake uranium mine at Wollaston Lake in 1984–85. Such protests continue: in August 2004 the Clearwater Dene blocked the highway going through their reserve to COGEMA's Cluff Lake uranium mine, in protest of exploration on their traditional land. Since the early

Henry Youle Hind, from a picture in the *London Illustrated News*, October 2, 1858.

1980s there have been regular campaigns by environmental coalitions, including several "Survival Gatherings" in the North, a Greenpeace campaign against the Cigar Lake uranium mine, and picketing of companies shipping uranium yellowcake on Saskatchewan highways. Perhaps the most notable was the province-wide coalition that stopped a uranium refinery at the Mennonite town of Warman.

Saskatchewan people have done solidarity work in support of campaigns elsewhere. Farm and labour unions supported the sixteen-year boycott of California table grapes waged by the United Farm Workers, which ended in 2001 after farmers won concessions including the banning of toxic chemicals. While civil disobedience has been less common on the prairies than in some other jurisdictions, broad-based community protest has played an important role in righting wrongs ignored by political elites. Many mainstream institutions resulted from "rebellions" against the marketplace and the politicians who supported it: co-ops, credit unions, marketing boards, and non-governmental organizations (NGOs) to meet human needs and expand human rights—all have roots in extra-parliamentary politics.

Extra-parliamentary action can, of course, be used for many political purposes. In 2002 a resolution supporting civil disobedience against the Federal Firearms Act on gun control was passed by the Wildlife Federation, but nothing other than refusal to register guns materialized. Some farmers wanting to bypass the Canadian Wheat Board and sell grain directly to US companies have tried to drive across the border in breach of Canadian law. The law criminalizing the use of marijuana for any purpose, including medical, has deliberately been broken as an act of protest, and arrests at "pot rallies" still lead to the jailing of some conscientious objectors. During the **MEDICARE** crisis in the mid-1960s, the "Keep Our Doctors" group engaged in its own form of civil disruption on behalf of private health-care interests across North America; some hospital boards controlled by anti-medicare doctors refused hospital privileges to pro-medicare physicians. But that led to another wave of community action, in the spirit of Saskatchewan's progressive extra-parliamentary tradition, and the **COMMUNITY CLINIC** movement was born.   *Jim Harding*

EYRE, IVAN (1935–). Ivan Eyre was born in Tullymet, northeast of Regina. The Eyre family lived in Red Deer, Alberta, and Turtleford, Southey and Ituna, Saskatchewan before moving to Saskatoon in 1946. Ivan subsequently studied art at the Saskatoon Art Centre, the Saskatoon Technical Collegiate, and the **UNIVERSITY OF SASKATCHEWAN**. In 1953 he began studies at the School of Art, University of Manitoba. He graduated in 1956, married fellow art student Brenda Fenske, and pursued graduate work at the University of North Dakota, where he also taught. In 1959, he returned to the School of Art to teach drawing. He retired in 1992, and was named Professor Emeritus in 1994.

While a student, Eyre exhibited in the annual *Winnipeg Show* at the Winnipeg Art Gallery (WAG). His first solo drawing exhibition was held in 1962 at the University of Manitoba, followed by a one-man exhibition of paintings at the WAG in 1964. Since that time, Eyre has had over sixty-five one-person exhibitions and has participated in over 250 group shows. His work has achieved national prominence and has toured internationally. Highlights of his exhibiting career include the 1980 Robert McLaughlin Gallery's *Ivan Eyre: Exposition*, which toured Canada, Great Britain and France, and the 1988 WAG exhibition *Ivan Eyre: Personal Mythologies*, which became the first contemporary Canadian solo exhibition at the new National Gallery in Ottawa.

Eyre is a consummate draughtsman, using drawing to translate the figure in sensitive, realistic and imaginary ways, and to explore small abstract compositions that he makes out of materials. These drawings appear in his figurative paintings, which utilize the conventions of realism and illusionism to create magical and mythical spaces and events, which some commentators have linked to Surrealism. While the young artist was open to many art historical precedents, the artist's mature style employs its own lexicon of highly developed symbolism, compositional devices, and reoccurring imagery. Eyre is known for large-scale, breathtaking and imaginative landscapes, which are built up slowly with subsequent colour layers in acrylic. The landscapes are not based on exact geographic referents, yet many viewers insist on finding resemblances to specific points across the globe. The vast skies, spaces, built environment, and Gothic undercurrent of the prairies have influenced his landscapes and figurative works.

Eyre's work is included in most public collections in Canada and many private ones. His work is featured in a permanent installation at the Pavilion Gallery in Winnipeg's Assiniboine Park; the Ivan Eyre drawing archive, which includes more than 4,000 drawings, is part of this collection.   *Amy Karlinsky*

F

FAFARD, JOSEPH (1942–). Born on September 2, 1942, at Ste. Marthe, Saskatchewan, and raised on a farm in a French and MÉTIS community, Joe Fafard was dubbed by his family "the great French Canadian artist." One of twelve children, his talent was encouraged by his mother, Julienne, a folk artist who made papier-mâché cows and who was a descendant of a Quebec wood carver, Louis Jobin,

Joe Fafard, "The Politician," 1987, bronze, paint and patina, 107 x 35 x 24 cm, MacKenzie Art Gallery, University of Regina Collection.

Joe Fafard, January 1973, with figurines inspired by his parents.

whose church statuary was collected by the National Gallery of Canada. Supported by his family, Fafard completed a BFA at the University of Manitoba in 1966 and an MFA at Pennsylvania State University in 1968.

When in 1968 he returned to teach art at the UNIVERSITY OF SASKATCHEWAN, Regina Campus, Fafard's work bore the influence of trends he had witnessed in New York, including minimalism and kinetic sculpture. However, it was an encounter with California Funk ceramicist David Gilhooly, with whom he taught from 1969 to 1971, which proved decisive. Gilhooly's irreverent attitude and rambunctious storytelling approach, epitomized by his "Frog World" sculptures, served as a catalyst for Fafard, freeing him to create work out of his own personal experience. He resumed making figurative sculpture, starting with plaster caricatures of art world colleagues. A sculpture of 107-year-old immigrant Michael Haynee marked the beginning of his clay portraiture. This work led him to embark on a series of portraits of family members as well as of neighbours from the nearby village of Pense, where he moved in 1971. Sculptures of cows formed another important subject, allowing Fafard to reconnect with his rural upbringing. The choice to work in small scale distinguishes this period of his work, marking a concern with memory and communal narratives.

It was not long before Fafard's work met with critical and popular success. In 1973, he was chosen to represent Canada, along with fellow Regina ceramicists VICTOR CICANSKY, Gilhooly, Ann James, MARILYN LEVINE, and RUSSELL YURISTY, in *Canada Trajectoires '73* at the Musée d'art moderne de la Ville de Paris. In the same year, he was the subject

of a nationally televised National Film Board documentary, *I Don't Have to Work That Big*. Fafard left teaching in 1974, in part because his regionalist values and accessible work left him at odds with the modernist ideology still prevalent in the academy. Throughout the late 1970s and 1980s, Fafard continued to develop his portraiture. His choice of subjects reflects an expanded notion of community, encompassing self-taught Saskatchewan artists (JAN WYERS, Harvey McInnis), First Nations and Métis leaders (BIG BEAR, GABRIEL DUMONT), politicians (Sir John A. Macdonald, TOMMY DOUGLAS), and artistic luminaries (Robert Arneson, Pablo Picasso). In 1979, the Edmonton Art Gallery showed twenty of his figures in an exhibition that toured eleven Canadian cities. Cows and bulls offered Fafard subjects for formal experimentation with material, volume, and scale. In 1980, after returning from a year teaching at the University of California, Davis, he began to play with perspective—and the modernist dictum of "flatness" in painting espoused by New York critic Clement Greenberg—by foreshortening cows and producing portraits in low relief. A series of flattened portraits of Vincent van Gogh explored the intersection of painting and sculpture by treating van Gogh's famous brushwork as a sculptural surface. Fafard's continual investigation led him to work in bronze and laser-cut steel, media which allowed a greater flexibility in producing large works with thin, unsupported forms, including tables and other furniture.

In 1985, Fafard received a major commission from Cadillac Fairview for the Toronto-Dominion Centre. *The Pasture*, which features seven oversized bronze cows, allowed Fafard to make a statement about the importance of regional realities in the

heart of Toronto's financial district. Drawing on the experience gained through this commission, Fafard built a commercial foundry in Pense, Julienne Atelier, where he produces limited-edition bronze sculptures. Other important commissions include: *Oskana-Ka-Ashteki*, a large plasma-cut steel buffalo in three sections for Regina Market Square in 1997; *Bonnie Buchlyvie*, a large work-horse installed in 1999 at the University of Saskatchewan; and *Claudia*, a bronze oversized cow for the grounds of the Montreal Museum of Fine Arts in 2003. Fafard has been recognized as one of Canada's leading visual artists in solo exhibitions, including: *Joe Fafard: Cows and Other Luminaries 1977–1987*, co-organized by the MENDEL ART GALLERY and Dunlop Art Gallery in 1987-88; and *Joe Fafard: The Bronze Years*, organized by the Montreal Museum of Fine Arts in 1996–97.

Among many awards, Fafard was named an Officer of the Order of Canada in 1981, given the Architectural Institute of Canada Allied Arts Award in 1987, awarded an Honorary Doctorate from the UNIVERSITY OF REGINA in 1989, and named to the Saskatchewan Order of Merit in 2002. His work is represented in the collections of the National Gallery of Canada, Montreal Museum of Fine Arts, Vancouver Art Gallery, Glenbow Museum (Calgary), Edmonton Art Gallery, Winnipeg Art Gallery, Art Gallery of Hamilton, Agnes Etherington Art Centre (Kingston), MACKENZIE ART GALLERY, Mendel Art Gallery, SASKATCHEWAN ARTS BOARD, and several corporate collections.   *Timothy Long*

FALCONS. Falcons are streamlined birds of prey with long pointed wings and long tails. During flight, wing beats appear rapid and shallow as the wings are designed for speed, not sustained soaring. All falcons belong to the order Falconiformes and the family Falconidae. There are five falcon species found in Saskatchewan: American kestrel (*Falco sparverius*), merlin (*F. columbarius*), prairie falcon (*F. mexicanus*), peregrine (*F. peregrinus*) and gyrfalcon (*Falco rusticolus*). Falcons do not build their own nests, and females are larger than males. They possess a tomial tooth, or tooth-like structure on the upper beak which is used to dispatch their prey by dislocating their neck vertebrae.

The American kestrel is the most numerous, widespread and smallest of our falcon species. This colourful falcon is sexually dichromatic, i.e., the sexes differ in their colour patterns. Males have blue-grey wings and a rufous tail with a single broad black band, while the females have rufous tails and wings with black bars across their lengths. American kestrels hunt predominantly rodents in open areas. They are secondary cavity nesters and can be found breeding throughout the entire province. Merlins are slightly larger than kestrels. Prairie merlins are lighter in colour than merlins which nest in forested areas. Adult males have blue-grey backs and black-banded tails. Females and immature birds have dusky brown backs and brown tails with buff-coloured bands. Both sexes have cream-coloured underparts with light brown streaks and yellow legs. Merlins use abandoned crow and magpie nests in deciduous and coniferous trees throughout the province, and are also very common in cities in Saskatchewan. The merlin's main food consists of small birds, and in urban areas they are particularly fond of house sparrows.

The prairie falcon is a crow-sized bird, with sandy-coloured back and tail which contrast with its creamy white underparts. The breast, belly, and legs are streaked with darker markings. At close range, its distinguishing mark is its white face with a narrow, dark "moustache." In flight, its underside is whitish with a black patch under each wing at its base. Prairie falcons establish a nesting territory where there is a ledge or crevice on a cliff or embankment that faces open grassland areas, as in the southern badlands. The most common food item during the prairie falcon's breeding season (summer) is the Richardson's ground squirrel (*Spermophilus richardsonii*). In winter prairie falcons depend heavily on small passerine birds, but they will also eat other prey such as ducks, rabbits and hares, as well as small mammals such as mice.

The peregrine is one of the most widely distributed warm-blooded terrestrial vertebrate species. Indeed, the name peregrine means "wanderer," and peregrines can be seen throughout Saskatchewan during the spring and fall migration periods. Peregrines have bluish-gray backs and whitish, grayish or buffy underparts with variable amounts of spotting and barring. Peregrines hunt a wide variety of other birds. Somewhat ironically, the best places to observe peregrines in Saskatchewan are in our larger urban centres of Saskatoon and Regina, as these provide ideal breeding habitat in the form of inaccessible cliffs (skyscrapers) and a ready supply of prey (mostly in the form of rock pigeons, *Columba livia*). Observing peregrines in these locations may diminish their image as a symbol of

R.J. LONG PHOTO/© SASKATCHEWAN ENVIRONMENT/SKCDC, 2001. ECOSYSTEM IMAGE INFORMATION SYSTEM

Prairie falcon (*Falco mexicanus*).

wilderness, but it does not detract from their amazing abilities as one of nature's pre-eminent aerobatic performers.

The gyrfalcon, our largest falcon, is also the fastest falcon in level flight. Its colour is highly variable and can range from a dark slate-grey to white. Gyrfalcons typically nest on cliffs in the more remote areas of the Arctic and make their way into Saskatchewan during the late fall and winter months in search of prey. Often the birds seen in Saskatchewan are sub-adults. These large raptors can hunt a variety of prey, but are best adapted to kill other large birds such as ducks and grouse. At times, however, they will take rabbits and hares. As is to be expected with a bird of this size, and also given the nature of its preferred breeding habitat, it has never been a very common bird in Saskatchewan.

Rick Espie

FURTHER READING: Alsop, F.J., III. 2002. *Birds of Canada*. New York: Dorling Kindersley; Cade, T.J. 1982. *The Falcons of the World*. Ithaca, NY: Cornell University Press.

FAMILIES. Families are groups of people who consider themselves a unit based on ties of birth, adoption, or mutual consent. Commonly, when people speak of a family unit they are referring to one or more adults who are raising children; but the definition could also include vulnerable adults residing with parents, children living with a custodial adult in another home, and children living with extended family.

According to Statistics Canada, there were 265,620 families (defined as one or more adults and at least one child aged 0 to 19) in Saskatchewan in 2001. While the "traditional" family constellation of mother, father, and several children is still the most common family form, over 42,000 families (roughly 16% of the total) are headed by a single parent. About 38,000 families involve a grandparent raising the children. In 2001, same-sex partners were raising 95 children in Saskatchewan.

When Saskatchewan became a province, most families lived in rural areas and families were larger than they are today. In those days, when families faced economic hardship or other problems, they generally relied upon other family members, neighbours, charitable organizations, and churches for support. Communities focused on providing the most basic support to families, such as an elementary-level education for the children. Gradually, however, as social and economic relations became more complex, the public came to accept a partial role in the well-being of families because of their value to a healthy society. Over time, a larger role in family matters evolved for governments at all levels.

One way that governments help families is through direct or indirect financial benefits to help with the costs of raising children. The first significant government recognition of children's needs was a tax deduction for children introduced along with Canada's first income tax system in 1918. Since 1945, when the Family Allowance was established, the federal government has provided a monthly benefit for children. Federal child benefits are now provided through the Canada Child Tax Benefit in a system that has replaced basic social assistance for children in Saskatchewan, and which provides income for children's needs to both low and moderate-income families. The Canada Child Tax Benefit acts as an anti-poverty measure for families and children, and by offsetting some child-related costs helps families get by on employment earnings and avoid dependency on social assistance.

Saskatchewan also provides a number of family benefits, most targeted to lower-income families. These may be cash benefits, such as the Saskatchewan Employment Supplement, or in-kind programs such as Family Health Benefits, which reduce health costs for children in low-income families. Often a family, particularly with a young child, faces difficult choices with respect to work and parenting: most parents want to care for their own children, but must balance this option with building careers and supporting the family economically through employment. Every family situation is unique, and families have different resources to support parenting choices—including a choice by either or both spouses to care for children themselves and not take part in employment outside the home. Personal resources, government children's benefits, the earnings of one spouse, or Employment Insurance parental benefits may help a family finance a period of stay-at-home care.

For most parents, at-home care of children is a temporary phase in family life. Nearly as many women as men are engaged in the labour market, and the majority of women with children, including those with preschool children, are in paid employment. Parents who work or go to school must often rely on others to care for their children at least part of the time. Research shows that most parents in Saskatchewan prefer care by family members, neighbours, or other private arrangements, but will consider more structured child care services if necessary. School-based and private early learning programs have also become extremely popular with parents of children in the 3- to 5-year-old age group. Balancing work and family can be more than just an income issue. Family-friendly employment policies are becoming more widespread, as many employers provide options for flexible hours and family leave to enable staff to balance work with the responsibilities of raising children or caring for aging relatives. The trend towards family-friendly workplaces is expected to grow over time.

Very few families can function well in isolation: most parents rely, to some degree, on support from friends, relatives, and community social services. Families meet their needs through a mix of their own resources, community resources, and investment by governments in families' purchasing power and in services such as family service bureau and community recreation programs. The school system in Saskatchewan is also playing an increasing role in supporting families. While all families need some outside help, most get by without specific government intervention beyond mainstream benefits and services such as the Canada Child Tax Credit or school systems. A certain proportion of families, especially low-income families, may need more public support, particularly to afford child care or early learning services, so that parents can work and children will be well cared for. Some families may also require modest parenting supports as well to ensure good life outcomes for children.

Very small proportions of families have high levels of need for family supports. For teenage mothers in particular, it is important to encourage participation in school or work, as well as effective parenting. Research evidence suggests that living in a family with at least one parent attached to the labour market results in better outcomes for children, and employment usually means the difference between poverty and self-sufficiency for the parent and the children. Some families also face more serious parenting or child development issues. In Saskatchewan, governments support services like the Canada Prenatal Nutrition Program, KidsFirst, or Aboriginal Head Start provide help to families and children with significant needs.

This targeted approach to family support has been successful to a point, but targeted programs are inherently limited in the scope of their impact. Experts with the Organization for Economic Cooperation and Development (OECD) and others suggest that more broadly based social investments in families, enhanced by targeted programs for those in vulnerable situations, are more likely to achieve the best overall outcomes for children and families. Although governments are increasingly involved in family matters, parents have first responsibility for their own children. Effective parenting is critical to healthy child development: supportive, responsive, and consistent parents cause children to have better learning and behavioural outcomes. However, the pressures of balancing responsibilities at home, at work, and in the larger community can be difficult, and good parenting is often a challenge. Evidence of good parenting is not typically reported publicly, and governments tend to measure poor parenting only by the number of families involved with child welfare programs. Most families involved with child welfare are low-income, but evidence from Canadian research suggests that family challenges cut across income groups. In fact, because of the size of the middle class, most children

suffering inadequate parenting come from middle-class families—not poor families, as is commonly believed.

Supportive communities are an important aspect of successful parenting and healthy families. The degree to which communities take care of their own members is important to creating safe and inclusive communities that help parents provide the healthy family environments allowing children to develop into responsible adult citizens. (*See also* **CHILDREN**) *Janet Mitchell*

FAMILY MAINTENANCE ACT, 1997: *see* LEGISLATION IN SASKATCHEWAN

FAMILY PROPERTY ACT, 1997: *see* LEGISLATION IN SASKATCHEWAN

FARM LABOURERS. The first grain was shipped from Manitoba to an international market in 1878; this was the beginning of an agricultural economy on the Canadian prairies. The National Policy of the Macdonald government opened the prairies to rapid settlement with the construction of the **CANADIAN PACIFIC RAILWAY**. Agricultural development required a large workforce and a massive amount of capital. The Canadian government worked with immigration agents and transportation companies to attract North American and European migrants to become agricultural settlers on land recently acquired from the Hudson's Bay Company, and surveyed for settlement after signing treaties with Aboriginal tribes. Many of the settlers arrived from eastern Canada and the United States; they were attracted by the opportunity to improve their status and independence. British and northern Europeans arrived along with eastern Europeans who came for free land.

Saskatchewan had the largest agricultural land base, and the population grew from 90,000 in 1900 to 930,000 by 1930. The majority lived or worked on farms. The most successful farmers started with some capital for farm equipment and animals, building materials, and supplies. Many migrants, having come without money, worked for more established farmers and gained experience until they could afford their own farms. The agricultural workforce

included farmers, their sons, and paid workers; farm women and their daughters also provided labour. Farm work was seasonal, with peaks during spring seeding and especially during harvest. There were ongoing chores to look after farm animals; horses were used for work and required care and skills to manage. Summer jobs included summerfallowing, hay production, and breaking new land. Workdays were long, and the workers, isolated on dispersed farms, had to operate a variety of machines. Wages varied by season, by job, and by region. Living conditions and food were often poor, as farmers reneged on paying wages. Politicians, sensitive to the large farm vote, initiated many programs to assist the farmers. Working with railways and steamship lines, the government organized **HARVEST EXCURSIONS** to transport unemployed workers from the Maritime provinces, the United States, and Britain to the prairie farms. During **WORLD WAR I** military men were granted 30 days' furlough to work on prairie farms. Farm workers were exempt from most labour legislation and fell under the Masters and Servants Act.

By 1920, all the homesteads were taken and the farm economy was depressed by renewed agricultural production in Europe. Most farmers' sons and paid workers no longer had the possibility of starting their own farm. Without this option as potentially independent farmers, their status dropped; many drifted into cities, where unemployment was also high and workers were being influenced by union organizers and radical politics. In the early 1920s the Industrial Workers of the World tried to organize Canadian farm workers. The federal government harassed and arrested potential organizers, and turned back harvest workers from the United States who were suspected of being "Wobblies."

During the **DEPRESSION** of the 1930s the federal government started work camps for unemployed urban workers. It also worked with provincial governments, particularly in Saskatchewan, to organize farm employment plans to match unemployed farm workers with farmers requiring help, but with no money to pay workers. After 1935, the new Liberal government expanded this program but tried to restrict it to urban workers when they closed the

SASKATCHEWAN ARCHIVES BOARD R-B3514

Farm labourers at harvest time.

labour camps. After **WORLD WAR II**, increased mechanization on the farms reduced the need for labour and workers were able to move on to higher-paying jobs in cities, and to work in mines and lumber camps. With increasing numbers of corporate farms, especially in livestock operations, the need for farm workers is increasing. They have been exempted from most labour legislation, but have unionized a few hog barns and have had extended strikes in operations near Biggar and Purdue.   *Bob Ivanochko*

FURTHER READING: Danysk, C. 1994. "No Help for the Farm Help: The Farm Employment Plans of the 1930s in Prairie Canada," *Prairie Forum* 19 (2): 231–51; —. 1995. *Hired Hands: Labour and the Development of Prairie Agriculture, 1880–1930.* Toronto: University of Toronto Press.

FARM MACHINERY AND EQUIPMENT.
When the first Europeans came to North America in the early 1600s, they brought with them their seeds and equipment to grow crops. Almost 300 years later, when settlers came west to farm they did the same; but farming technology had changed, and it was to undergo even greater changes over the next hundred years. Several key technologies were in existence at the time of prairie settlement: the self-scouring steel plough, developed by John Deere in 1837, was critically important for breaking prairie soils; in 1831 Cyrus McCormick invented the reaper, which was commercialized in 1847; Jethro Tull had invented the mechanical seed drill in 1701, and the threshing machine had been patented in 1788. Although harnessing steam had been investigated by the Greeks of Alexandria, it would take almost 2,000 years before a ground-driven steam tractor would be developed; the J.I. Case Company in Racine, Wisconsin made the first steam engine for agricultural application in 1869. While the steam engine was beneficial in reducing manual labour and releasing the reliance on horses, it was cumbersome and difficult to adapt to farm tasks. One of the biggest problems with steam engines was the need for engineers to operate them: many of the engineering schools in the US had their origins in filling this need. The big steamers (Case 110 hp, American Abell 110 hp, Reeves 120 hp) broke much of the prairie land, turning about five acres per hour, compared to the one-quarter acre per hour possible with horses.

Recognizing the problem inherent in steamers, J.I. Case introduced the first gasoline-powered successor to the steam engine in 1892. However, it took several years to perfect it: the early gas tractors were nothing more than big stationary engines mounted on wheels and with a crude transmission, of which IHC Titan and Mogul are good examples. It was the Hart Parr company that coined the name "tractor." The first mass production of tractors began in 1917

EVERETT BAKER PHOTO/COURTESY OF THE SASKATCHEWAN HISTORY AND FOLKLORE SOCIETY

This Case steam engine, described as "Grandmother of them all" was on display at "Pionera" in Saskatoon in July 1955.

with the Fordson, by the Ford Motor Company; the power take off (PTO) was introduced about the same time—a significant development as all equipment up until then had to be ground driven, which limited the size and effectiveness of much farm equipment. But even though mechanical power existed, much of the task of breaking up the prairie was done by oxen and particularly by horsepower. This was especially true in the case of small homestead operations; only the larger farmers relied more on heavy machines.

Tillage equipment was the main area that needed development. The role of the local blacksmith was important in transforming equipment to meet the conditions of prairie soils; it was in this area that Saskatchewan farmers made their mark. The tilling methods used in the early days in Saskatchewan were developed in other areas, under different climatic conditions, on different soils. The results in Saskatchewan were disastrous under drought conditions, and contributed greatly to the **DUST BOWL** years of the "Dirty Thirties." It took many years to develop suitable tillage systems that would leave a protective vegetative cover on the soil throughout the crop production process. The first approach to dealing with inadequate water was to **SUMMERFALLOW**: this meant preventing the growth of any vegetation in a field for one year, thereby allowing water to accumulate in the soil to facilitate the growth of a good crop the following year. Unfortunately, this worsened the problem of wind erosion and blowing dust during the fallow year. One solution to this problem was the Morris rod weeder, which used a rotating rod pulled sideways through the soil to cut

weed roots while minimizing disturbance of the soil surface.

Eventually, by the last third of the 20th century, machines were developed which could seed through the trash left in the fields from the previous harvest. Much of this equipment was developed by small local manufacturers who were the descendants of local blacksmiths. Together with the development of more drought-resistant crops, these new practices virtually ended the **DUST STORMS** which had begun in the 1930s. While these methods reduced soil surface disturbance, they also resulted over time in increased compaction of the lower soils, which were never loosened by tillage; the Noble cultivator, with a very wide blade operating deep in the soil, then used to loosen the subsoil, while again minimizing surface disturbance. The early no-till seeders were small and proved inadequate for the large Saskatchewan farms. By the late 1970s new machines called air seeders were developed, which used pressurized air and hoses to distribute seed from a large tank to soil openers over a width of up to sixty feet. These machines could seed over 300 acres a day, but required powerful tractors to pull them: again, Saskatchewan farmers needed the biggest, most expensive tractors available.

Although the first self-propelled combine had been invented in 1896, it was the stationery threshing machine powered by a steam engine that dominated threshing until after the **GREAT DEPRESSION**. Hovland developed a "Travelling Threshing Machine" in Minneapolis in 1910; some of these appeared in the province and inspired the development of the swather by Hanson Brothers of Lajord,

Saskatchewan. Protection from weeds and insects required pesticide sprayers. The small sprayers used in the first half of the 20th century were not up to the task, so faster sprayers were needed: this resulted in the use of aerial sprayers as well as large tractor-mounted and self-propelled sprayers on modified truck chassis, with large flotation (balloon) tires to reduce soil compaction. Large machinery ultimately meant large farms and large fields: this in turn demanded large, high-capacity combines. While traditional manufacturers scaled up their combines, Western RotoThresh in Saskatoon designed a new combine from the ground up, using a rotary drum and a pneumatic grain cleaner instead of the traditional straw walkers and shoe. This company also had its roots in the blacksmith/local machine builder tradition.

Handling the large volumes of grain from these harvesters required large augers and other elevating devices. Again, local shops developed machines and grew into larger companies driving local economies (e.g., Wheatheart, GrainVac). Transporting the grain from the farm to elevators was another process undergoing change. As local rail lines and elevators were closed, grain had to be hauled greater distances: this meant bigger trucks, first semi-trailers, then truck trains. Again, local manufacturers built the trailer bodies. This increase in heavy truck traffic has had serious consequences for a road system designed for cars and light trucks. One interesting response to the growing cost of field machinery has been a return to the "old" ways. McLeod Harvesting Equipment has developed machinery based on the old principle of harvesting in the field and threshing in the farmyard. In this instance, the wheat heads are clipped off in the field and hauled to a central yard, where a stationary thresher/cleaner processes the grain; straw is left in the field or baled into large bales for sale. Balers have also undergone change over the years: from the traditional 100 lb. square bale to round bales, which may be loose-centered (600 lb.) or solid-centered (up to 2,000 lb.), to large square bales (750 lb.)—all of which require special handling equipment. While the balers are imported from the USA, local manufacturers are beginning to produce the handling equipment.

Livestock farming has also seen many changes. As the industry has grown, so have the needs for manure disposal: while the traditional manure spreader is still in use for spreading relatively dry manure on land, new practices using lagoons and pits for manure collection, as well as the encroachment of residential areas around livestock operations, require different methods and different equipment. Typical of these new methods is the soil injection of liquid manure: this method uses a tank truck on which is mounted a set of soil openers through which the manure is pumped into the soil while the truck drives through a field.

One of the most significant changes to have taken place over the first century of farming in Saskatchewan has been the increased size of equipment. The early gasoline tractors developed between 25 and 40 hp. Today a common tractor on medium to large farms generates from 240 to 300 hp, with some exceeding 400 hp. Combines today are capable of threshing over 200 acres per day; air seeders are typically about 40 feet in width. As farms have become bigger, machines have become bigger—or is it the other way around? *Ron Ford and Gary Storey*

FURTHER READING: Carroll, J. 2002. *The World Encyclopedia of Tractors and Farm Machinery.* London: Hermes House; Wetherell, D. and E. Corbet. 1993. *Breaking New Ground: A Century of Farm Equipment Manufacturing on the Canadian Prairies.* Saskatoon: Fifth House.

FARM MOVEMENT (1901–49). Agricultural settlement was well advanced before the formal creation of the province of Saskatchewan in 1905. Wheat was king: this reality had not escaped the attention of the open-market trade members of the Winnipeg Grain Exchange, who, in collaboration with the **CANADIAN PACIFIC RAILWAY** (CPR), were unchallenged in actively exploiting export grain buying opportunities. Farmer grievances began to build over complaints of unfair grading practices, excessive dockage, short weights, and unreasonable and monopolistic pricing and shipping practices. Farmer anger had been building when **W.R. MOTHERWELL** and Peter Dayman called a general meeting in Indian Head for December 18, 1901. It was unanimously resolved that united action was needed; and after drafting a constitution and by-laws, the Territorial Grain Growers Association (TGGA) was organized. Following a rapid expansion in membership, the first convention of the TGGA was held on February 12, 1902, where Motherwell was elected president and John Miller secretary. The fledgling organization soon had its first court challenge against the CPR agent in Sintaluta, who had refused to honour a "Car Order Book" provision under the Manitoba Grain Act, whereby a farmer might independently obtain a grain car, and load and ship his grain to market. The organization won the case, which was then appealed to the Supreme Court by the CPR; the Supreme Court upheld the lower court's decision, establishing for all time the farmers' right to the use of the Car Order Book. The Sintaluta trial represented the first major victory for the organized movement.

At the fourth annual convention of the TGGA held in Regina in 1904, **EDWARD A. PARTRIDGE** of Sintaluta was delegated to go to Winnipeg to learn about the grading of grain cars and about grain marketing in general. In January 1905, he reported his findings to a mass meeting of farmers and out-

lined a plan to form a joint stock company to be known as the **GRAIN GROWERS' GRAIN COMPANY** (GGGC). After strong opposition from members of the Winnipeg Grain Exchange and against legal challenges, the GGGC was accorded on the Exchange a seat that permitted it to trade. When Saskatchewan became a province in 1905, the TGGA was renamed the Saskatchewan Grain Growers Association (SGGA). W.R. Motherwell became the province's first Minister of Agriculture in the government of Premier **T. WALTER SCOTT**.

The concept of orderly marketing of grain was, as early as 1907, being advanced by Partridge. Congestion and a shortage of grain storage were major problems. Prairie farmers had petitioned provincial governments to take over the country elevators, and the federal government to take over the terminals. Partridge promoted the idea that the whole trade be brought under the management of one agency, and suggested an independent commission be nominated by the SGGA and appointed by government. The Saskatchewan government appointed a three-man Commission of Enquiry in February 1910; two of its members were SGGA executive members. It recommended that the government support a co-operative elevator system, which it did by guaranteeing bank loans so that farmers could construct an elevator. The **SASKATCHEWAN CO-OPERATIVE ELEVATOR COMPANY** Ltd. resulted in 1911. Although the SGGA executive was appointed as its provisional directorate, it never operated as a true co-operative. In 1913–14, the federal government storage elevators were constructed in Calgary, Saskatoon, and Moose Jaw as a direct result of farmer agitation.

The February 1913 Annual Convention of the SGGA was highlighted by the formation of the Women's Section of the SGGA, which broadened the organization to a farm family movement. It was active in the promotion of social and educational, as well as economic issues; **ANNIE HOLLIS** was its first president. **VIOLET MCNAUGHTON**, who served as secretary of the Women's Section and later as its president, campaigned for the establishment of municipal hospitals and was active in the Women's War Conference in 1918 and in the **PROGRESSIVE PARTY** in 1921. The GGG had assisted the Alberta government in the establishment of the Alberta Co-operative Elevator Company. Wartime demand for export wheat accelerated greatly, and a move was made to amalgamate the three farmer-owned companies. The GGG and the Alberta Co-operative Elevator Company did so in 1917 to form the United Grain Growers Ltd.; however, the Saskatchewan Co-operative Elevator Company declined to participate.

The SGGA established a Trading Department in 1914, enabling its farmer members to co-operatively purchase in bulk such items as coal, lumber, binder twine, and farm fuels at wholesale prices. In 1929, it amalgamated with the Saskatchewan Co-op Wholesale Society (a forerunner of present day **FEDERATED CO-OPERATIVES LIMITED**). **WORLD WAR I** had brought about major disruption in world grain trade and commerce. The federal government undertook direct intervention in the marketing of wheat in 1917 by appointing a Board of Grain Supervisors, which set fixed wheat prices for the succeeding two crop years, 1917–18 and 1918–19. It appointed a Canadian Wheat Board to market the crop of 1919, but restored open marketing for the 1920 crop year; this caused a great outcry within the farm community, as the Canadian Wheat Board had given producers the highest wheat price they had seen to date, as well as pooling. Discussions on forming a producer co-operative marketing pool for wheat began to emerge, but sentiment among many SGGA members for a 100% compulsory wheat pool remained strong.

On December 17, 1920, a new, more radical farm group was established at Ituna, Saskatchewan, with Joseph Thompson as president and N.H. Schwarz as secretary. On July 1, 1921, the Ituna group joined with like-minded farmers in Kelvington under the leadership of L.P. McNamee, resulting in the formation of the Farmers Union of Canada (FUC). Many farmers favoured the compulsory pooling concept promoted by the FUC, which launched a drive to sign up farmers for a five-year compulsory pooling contract. The rivalry between the FUC and the SGGA became increasingly divisive.

In April 1923, FUC secretary N.H. Schwarz wrote a letter of invitation to Aaron Sapiro, a California lawyer and expert in co-operative marketing, to come to western Canada to discuss the marketing issue. Sapiro agreed to attend a joint conference in Saskatoon of all stakeholders on August 6, 1923, which was followed by a large public meeting the following day. Sapiro strongly emphasized the need for unity between the organizations if a pooling effort was to succeed. Further mass meetings followed in Regina, Moose Jaw and Swift Current. Sapiro's presence triggered the formation of a joint Provisional Wheat Pool Committee of the FUC and SGGA to conduct a province-wide campaign to gain contract signers. As a result of a successful sign-up program, the Saskatchewan Co-operative Wheat Producers was incorporated in August 1923. By April 1924, more than 6.2 million contract acres had been signed up, thereby enabling the Saskatchewan Co-operative Wheat Producers Ltd. (later to become the **SASKATCHEWAN WHEAT POOL**, or SWP) to enter into export marketing. On August 2, 1926, the Pool acquired the grain elevators of the Saskatchewan Co-operative Elevator Company.

Sapiro continued his efforts to unify the SGGA and the FUC. On July 15, 1926, a joint convention was held in Saskatoon. With Sapiro's presence and urging, agreement was attained: the historic amal-gamation resulted in the formation of the United Farmers of Canada (Saskatchewan Section), or UFC (SS); J.A. Stoneman was elected its first president. The UFC (SS) resumed in 1927 the campaign to gain a 100% compulsory Pool by legislation. They were strongly opposed by Saskatchewan Wheat Pool president **A.J. MCPHAIL**, who considered that co-operation and compulsion were incompatible. This disagreement created a rift between the UFC (SS) and SWP at the official level, although UFC members continued to deliver their grain to the Pool. The economic crash of 1929 seriously disrupted the Pool's marketing efforts. An initial price of $1 per bushel had been advanced to farmers, when wheat fell to 50¢ a bushel on the Winnipeg open market: an overpayment on the 1929 crop of $13,752,000 resulted. The province, with a federal loan guarantee, covered the shortfall; but this meant the end of pooling.

The shattering of hope for a compulsory producer Pool caused the UFC (SS) to consider taking political action. In 1931, it amended its constitution to remove the non-political clause and participate in the launching of the Saskatchewan Farmer Labour Group (SFLG). The UFC (SS) actively promoted the new political movement. In 1932 the SFLG emerged as part of the **CO-OPERATIVE COMMONWEALTH FEDERATION** (CCF) under the leadership of Reverend **T.C. DOUGLAS**. At its 1935 annual convention, the UFC (SS) restored the "non-partisan in politics" section to its constitution. By this time it had become increasingly impoverished, and the **GREAT DEPRESSION** had the farm community in its grip. The UFC's policy differences with the Wheat Pool, and the divisive foray into partisan politics, left it with a depleted treasury and struggling to maintain membership. It continued to call upon governments for parity prices and compulsory single-desk central marketing of grain. Depressed market prices and large world wheat carryovers eventually resulted in the passage of the Canada Wheat Board Act, 1935, which restored orderly marketing and the fixing of minimum government-guaranteed initial prices.

The UFC (SS) continued to struggle for economic survival during the mid-1930s and throughout World War II. In 1945 its president, Frank Appleby, and his executive met with the executives of the labour and teacher organizations to form the Saskatchewan Occupational Group Council, which was to serve as a liaison and educational group between the three organizations. The UFC (SS) met with officials of the Alberta Farmers Union in 1945 to discuss the feasibility of a farm strike if grievances on farm prices and marketing problems could not be solved. The Interprovincial Farm Union Council was created. A ten-point joint submission was drafted and presented to the federal cabinet in Ottawa on August 26, 1946. It included calls for the establishment of parity prices for farm products, tax reform, and revision of freight rate policy. With less than satisfactory response from the federal Cabinet, the first farm strike was called to commence at midnight on September 6, 1946. It was scheduled to run for thirty days. The strike action was both unifying and divisive within the farm community and the business community. After twenty-one days, federal Agriculture Minister **J.G. GARDINER** invited the farm leaders to return to Ottawa for further discussions. Certain concessions were gained, such as $1 acreage payments; a floor price for hogs; removal of a three-cent-per-gallon wartime tax on farm fuel; and removal of an 87.5¢ domestic wheat subsidy to flour millers.

Synonymous with the UFC (SS) during most of its history had been the name of **FRANK ELIASON**, who became its secretary in 1929 and laboured for twenty years throughout the difficult years of the Depression and its accompanying poverty, farm debt, and loss of land. It was widely expected that the November 1949 convention of the UFC (SS) would be its last; but after long soul-searching and discussion, it was agreed that the movement must stay alive. The name of the organization was changed to **SASKATCHEWAN FARMERS UNION**, and **JOSEPH L. PHELPS** was elected as its first president.

Stuart A. Thiesson

FURTHER READING: Gleave, A.P. 1991. *United We Stand: Prairie Farmers 1901–1975.* Toronto: Lugus Publications; Wright, J.F.C. 1956. *Prairie Progress: Consumer Co-operation in Saskatchewan.* Saskatoon: Modern Press; Yates, S.W. 1935. *The Saskatchewan Wheat Pool: Its Origin, Organization and Progress, 1924–1925.* Saskatoon: United Farmers of Canada, Saskatchewan Section.

FARM ORGANIZATIONS. The history of farm organizations is the story of farmers' attempts to work collectively to better their social and economic position. Prior to the formation of the province of Saskatchewan, farmers attempted to better their situation by four main forms of collective action: education, non-partisan policy groups, direct political action, and buying and selling arrangements. This early collective action was influenced by the agrarian protest movements known to settlers from the United States, and by the trade unionism and co-operative approach brought by settlers from Great Britain and continental Europe. The National Policy for the 1878 federal election set out a number of objectives for the nation. One was to develop the western agricultural hinterland and integrate the area into the national economy; this was a natural follow-up to the homestead policy introduced in 1872 to attract people from eastern Canada, the United States and overseas to settle the North-West Territories. The essence of the National Policy was to make Ontario and Quebec the core area for industry, finance and commerce, leaving the west to produce staples for export and import consumer goods produced in central Canada. The Policy provided the basis for farmer grievances, mainly concerning the grain-marketing system: it was the beginning of **WESTERN ALIENATION**.

The farm organizations prior to 1905 served to heighten awareness and "class consciousness" respecting economic and social issues facing farmers. Organizations like the Farmers' Unions, the National Grange, and the Patrons of Industry all laid the cornerstone for a strong co-operative movement and for the general farm organizations which were dominant farm policy lobbies to governments for most of the 20th century. By 1936 the number of farms and farm population had peaked, and most farms could be described as "mixed," producing a variety of field crops, animal and poultry products: it was therefore appropriate for both the farm unions and the farm federations to represent most farmers on a wide variety of farm policy issues. After **WORLD WAR II**, tractor power rapidly replaced horsepower. As farm population declined, farms continued to become larger. They also became more specialized in what they produced, and more diversified: new kinds of field crops and animals were introduced. As a result, from the 1950s there was a phenomenal increase in the formation of specialized commodity groups; this was in contrast to the period 1870–1950, when mergers between farm organizations and organizations ceasing to exist were commonplace.

Saskatchewan has produced strong farm organization leaders, who along with their counterparts in Alberta and Manitoba have formed interprovincial and national farm lobby groups, as well as two general farm organizations: the Canadian Council on Agriculture (and its successor the Canadian Federation of Agriculture) and the National Farmers Union. Soon after farmers began settling on the land, educational groups improved methods of production and enhanced the fabric of rural living. These groups included agricultural societies, horticultural societies, boys and girls clubs and the 4-H movement, homemaker clubs and women's institutes, and more recently the women's agricultural network. Several farm organizations also established women's sections or auxiliaries to address the policy concerns of rural women. In addition to policy concerns, the various livestock and field crop commodity groups have an educational component.

At the beginning of the 21st century there are a large number of farm commodity groups, and three general farm policy organizations: the **SASKATCH-EWAN ASSOCIATION OF RURAL MUNICIPALITIES**, which develops farm policy in addition to municipal policy; the Agricultural Producers of Saskatchewan, with a municipal membership base; and the National Farmers Union, headquartered in Saskatoon. There

is also a provincial government body known as the Action Committee on the Rural Economy, whose goal is to revitalize rural communities and develop a strong, viable agricultural sector. Speaking with one united voice on policy issues has often eluded farm organizations: different social, economic and political philosophies among farmers have created internal tension and dissention in their organizations and between farm organizations. Organizations that attempt to represent all commodities are often faced with internal conflict, as policies and programs that are beneficial to one group (e.g., livestock producers) are not beneficial to another group (e.g., grain producers). Failures to agree have weakened the opportunities to become a viable and recognizable sector in the economy of the nation. *Gary Carlson*

FARMER LABOUR TEACHER INSTITUTE. The first Farmer Labour Teacher Institute (FLTI) was held at Watrous from June 28 to July 1, 1947. The institutes continued to be held annually over a summer long weekend at different locations around the province, although often at the Qu'Appelle Valley Centre after it was opened in 1949. The Institute was organized by the Saskatchewan Occupational Group Council (SOGC) and assisted by the Adult Education Division of the provincial government. The SOGC was created in 1947 by the United Farmers of Canada, the **SASKATCHEWAN TEACHERS FEDERATION**, and the **SASKATCHEWAN FEDERATION OF LABOUR**, with input from the Trades and Labour Congress of Canada. The FLTI brought members of these organizations together to discuss current social, political and economic issues, to foster an understanding of varying points of view, and to reach resolution on future action. Later the Co-operative Union of Canada, Saskatchewan Federation of Agriculture, and the **SASKATCHEWAN WHEAT POOL** sent delegates to the FLTI. The last FLTI was held in 1981. The SOGC executive met periodically until 1984 but was inactive until 1991, when their remaining funds were turned over to the Saskatchewan Coalition for Social Justice, which had a broader-based organization. *Bob Ivanochko*

FARMING. Farming was synonymous with the economic development of Saskatchewan in the early decades of the 20th century. As a result of the national government's land disposal schemes (1872), the building of a transcontinental railroad (completed in 1885), and the 1897 **CROW'S NEST PASS AGREEMENT** establishing low freight rates "in perpetuity," Saskatchewan was Canada's fastest-growing province during the first three decades of the 20th century: between 1900 and 1930, it boasted 303,000 homestead entries. The territory that became the province of Saskatchewan in 1905 saw its population increase from 91,000 in 1901 to 932,000 in 1936. During this interval the number of

farms grew from 13,000 to 142,391; the farm population reached 573,894 in 1936, representing 88% of the rural and 62% of the total population in the province. Communities developed, usually where none had existed before, to serve the agricultural industry and the farm population.

The number of farms in Saskatchewan, as well as the farm population, peaked in 1936. New technologies facilitated the substitution of capital for labour, expanding farm size and making it possible for fewer farmers to produce the same, or even a growing, volume of output. Between 1936 and 1956, the number of farms declined by about 40,000 and the farm population by about 210,000; average farm size increased by 50%, from 400 to 600 acres.

The continuing decline in the number of farms and farm population has persisted through good times and bad in the agricultural sector, even as some level of diversification from the wheat economy took hold. New technologies available to farmers led to economies of size and scale in agriculture—the larger the size of the operation, the lower the per unit costs of production. With output prices falling over the long run, and costs of production rising, it was essential to access the most cost-efficient technologies: as the size of operations increased, given a relatively fixed land base, fewer and larger farms were the result. Diversification into livestock has not solved the population decline problem since economies of size were present here too; although the income levels and stability may have been positively affected, the farm population size has not.

The farm population has proven innovative and adaptable, both in terms of their farming operations and their participation in the broader economy. On-farm adjustments have consisted of the adoption of new technologies from mechanization to biotechnology, and the use of the latest information-intensive management and marketing techniques. The extremely narrow margins in most farm production, combined with the lack of producer influence on output prices, have required farmers to continually search for the lowest-cost means of production. Acquiring the newest machinery and equipment, expanding farm size, and participation in the latest education and training are all ways in which farmers are continually modifying farming operations.

On-farm adaptation has included both specialization and diversification. While the small mixed farm is still present to some degree, production is increasingly concentrated in large-scale specialized farms: 35,000-head feedlots, 5,000-sow hog barns, 17,000-acre grain farms, 1,500-cow-calf operations, 225,000-bird poultry operations, and 500-head dairy farms. These are large, complex and highly specialized businesses requiring major capital investments and sophisticated business skills, but the directly associated employment is relatively minor.

TOP AND MIDDLE: EVERETT BAKER PHOTOS/COURTESY OF THE SASKATCHEWAN HISTORY AND FOLKLORE SOCIETY; BOTTOM: COURTNEY MILNE PHOTO

Developments in technology have meant increases in farm size and decreases in number of farms and farm population.

At the other end of the spectrum are relatively small farms where the family is highly dependent on off-farm income. Especially in locations where there is easy access to urban-based employment, it sometimes makes sense to make the farming operation as routine and simple as possible so that substantial (often full-time) participation in other employment is possible. Urban and strong rural communities provide a range of employment opportunities for farm household members in education and health, public administration, and the growing private services sector. Rural areas provide sources of off-farm employment in the form of work in the oil and gas, mining, transportation, construction, forestry, and rural manufacturing sectors. Farm women participate in off-farm employment at about twice the rate of their male counterparts. As the rural population becomes sparser and more widely dispersed, the jobs are fewer and farther away, leading to longer commuting distances. While off-farm employment may consist of a full-time work-day, farm responsibilities are still a major time commitment and responsibility, especially at peak times of the year.

For some farming operations, diversification ventures consist of incorporating new crops and new varieties, often initially on a small scale, as part of the farming operation. In some cases, labour-intensive crops such as herbs and spices are grown for niche markets. Specialty livestock (bison, llamas, elk, angora goats, Vietnamese pigs) is another form of on-farm diversification. Some of these turn out to be no more than a novelty; but others have real long-term commercial value, becoming mainstream enterprises.

Farming is thus very diverse. The 50,598 farms in Saskatchewan reported in the 2001 Census include the large sophisticated businesses, the moderately sized family farms, and the small lifestyle/hobby farms. Farming as the major source of employment comprises about 13% of the provincial labour force. Average farm household income exceeds the average provincial household employment income for all farm size categories: this is the result of creative and varied means of adaptation on the part of farm families—specialization, diversification, expansion, increasing efficiency, off-farm employment, and involvement in non-farm businesses. Close to three-quarters of farm household income is from non-farm sources, illustrating how closely the farming community is integrated into the rest of the provincial economy. *M. Rose Olfert*

FURTHER READING: Fowke, V.C. 1957. *The National Policy and the Wheat Economy*. Toronto: University of Toronto Press; Stabler, J.C. and M.R. Olfert. 2001. "Public Policy in the 21st Century: Is Prairie Agriculture Becoming Like Any Other Industry? Does it Matter?" *Canadian Journal of Agricultural Economics* 48: 385–95.

FARMSTART CORPORATION AND THE AGRICULTURAL CREDIT CORPORATION.

Saskatchewan FarmStart Corporation was established in 1973 by the Saskatchewan government to assist in the expansion and development of the province's agriculture industry. The three primary objectives of the new Corporation were: to provide low income and low equity farmers or potential farmers with an opportunity to develop viable farm units by intensifying production through livestock production; to encourage diversification of the agricultural industry, thereby adding stability to the economy; and to encourage employment in the province by providing a larger base of livestock production that had the potential of being processed locally. Program administration was handled through a team approach using both agrologists and loans officers. Agrologists scrutinized loan applications in order to assess farm viability, while the loans officer assessed credit worthiness and security requirements. Final approval for loans could be granted by either field staff or head office staff in Regina.

To reach these objectives, a Loan and Grant Program was established which made credit available to producers who were either establishing or expanding a livestock enterprise. The program was targeted through its eligibility criteria. Applicants were required to have a net worth of less than $60,000, a net income of less than $10,000 per year, and a value of applicant's productive agricultural assets of less than $100,000. The eligibility criteria were expanded in subsequent years as income and net worth increased.

In conjunction with the Loan and Grant Program, FarmStart offered operating loan guarantees to its customers who could not otherwise obtain operating credit. A number of special assistance programs were also administered by FarmStart to provide short-term credit relief for livestock producers.

A significant change for the Corporation was the replacement of FarmStart with the Agricultural Credit Corporation of Saskatchewan (ACS) effective January 1, 1984. The purpose of ACS was similar to FarmStart, but the change provided the Corporation with "a new start with a broader client base and streamlined operating procedures." In conjunction with the expanded mandate, the head office of ACS was established in Swift Current; field offices were maintained throughout the province. Under ACS a major expansion of the Loan and Grant Program, then called the Capital Loan Program, came in 1989 when home quarter and debt settlement financing became eligible purposes. Following this, the Corporation expanded its ability to refinance its own customers' existing ACS debt into a Capital Loan. ACS also administered the Guaranteed Vendor Mortgage program to assist with intergeneration transfers, and the Investment Loan Program to expand the hog and feedlot industries.

The Livestock Cash Advance Program was introduced by ACS in 1985 in response to a drought that threatened livestock herds because of a lack of feed supplies. Initially advances were available only for beef and dairy cattle, but the program was expanded in later years to include other livestock species. In 1986, production loans were provided to individuals, partnerships, corporations or co-operatives to assist with the expenses associated with seeding the 1986 crop. Loans were provided for up to $25 per eligible acre; the maximum loan per individual was $100,000. For a multiple operator unit the maximum was $200,000. Loan applications were available through rural elevators, and required only verification of acreage from their 1985–86 Canadian Wheat Board permit book. Loan repayment was scheduled for three years. In 1987, an extension was available whereby customers could pay interest only and postpone any repayment of the principal until 1988. In 1988, customers were given the option of extending the loan over ten years.

The Saskatchewan Spring Seeding Loan Program was an operating loan guarantee administered by ACS and disbursed by banks and credit unions in the spring of 1990. Loans of up to $50,000 were available to individuals, and $100,000 to multiple operator units. Loans were originally to be repaid by January 15, 1991; any unpaid loans were transferred to ACS, with banks and credit unions drawing on the government guarantee. On March 28, 1996, in the province's budget speech, the winddown of ACS was announced: no new lending would occur after that date, with the exception of limited refinancing of existing ACS loans. In March 2000, the Financial Programs Branch was created within Saskatchewan Agriculture and Food. The remaining ACS employees were rolled into this branch on January 1, 2001; they continue to manage the winddown of the ACS portfolio.

David Boehm

FARRELL RACETTE, SHERRY.

Sherry Farrell Racette lives in Regina where she is Associate Professor at the **FIRST NATIONS UNIVERSITY OF CANADA**. She is of First Nations and Irish descent and a member of Timiskaming First Nation in Quebec. She received a BFA (1974) and a Secondary Certificate in Education (1975), both from the University of Manitoba. She earned an MEd from the **UNIVERSITY OF REGINA** (1988) and received a doctorate degree in the Interdisciplinary Program in Anthropology, History and Native Studies at the University of Manitoba (2004).

Using both visual and literary art forms, Farrell Racette contributes to a better understanding of **MÉTIS** and First Nations history. In 1985, she wrote and illustrated the book, *The Flower Beadwork People*, in commemoration of the 100th anniversary of the Métis (or Riel) Resistance of 1885 and pub-

COURTESY OF THE REGINA LEADER-POST

Sherry Farrell Racette.

lished subsequently by the **GABRIEL DUMONT INSTITUTE** in 1991. In her role as book illustrator, her visual vocabulary captures the intrinsic essence of the author's texts and brings the words to life. She has worked closely with numerous writers, such as **MARIA CAMPBELL** on *Stories of the Road Allowance People* (1995), **FREDA AHENAKEW** on *Wisahkechak Flies to the Moon* (1999), and Ruby Slipperjack on *Little Voice* (2001). She also contributes to scholarly publications as one of the growing number of First Nations intellectuals. Her essays on the history of Métis women's art and on Louis Riel are included in numerous anthologies published in 2001.

Farrell Racette maintains an active artistic practice in addition to her role as writer and educator, exhibiting frequently in venues throughout Saskatchewan. Solo exhibitions include *Illustrative Images*, **MACKENZIE ART GALLERY** (travelling 2002-04); *Building Community*, a mural installation, the Plains Museum, Regina (2001); *Dolls for Big Girls*, Rosemont Art Gallery, Regina (2000); *Stories of the Road Allowance People*, Harbour Centre Gallery, Vancouver and **WANUSKEWIN HERITAGE PARK** Gallery, Saskatoon (1995); and *The Flower Beadwork People*, Dunlop Art Gallery, Regina (travelling 1992–94). Recent group exhibitions include *Animate Objects: The Grammar of Craft in First Nations Contemporary Art*, Sakewewak Artists Collective, Regina (2002); *Rielisms*, Winnipeg Art Gallery, Winnipeg (travelling 2001); *Mark Makers: First Nations Graphics+*, MacKenzie Art Gallery, Regina (travelling 1997–99); *Here and Now*, Dunlop Art Gallery, Regina (1997); *Returned Gifts: Saskatchewan Based First Nations Artists*, Neutral Ground, Regina (1997); and *Separate Identities: Six Artists of Aboriginal Ancestry*, The Little Gallery, Prince Albert (travelling 1993–94).

Her artwork is included in the collections of the Regina Plains Museum, the MacKenzie Art Gallery, the Dunlop Art Gallery and the **SASKATCHEWAN ARTS**

BOARD. Farrell Racette is a board member of the Saskatchewan Arts Board, the Saskatchewan Heritage Foundation and Sakewewak First Nations Artists' Collective, Regina. She was a member of the Visual Arts Advisory Committee of the Canada Council for the Arts (1998) and of the Indian and Métis Education Advisory Committee, Saskatchewan Education (1994–97). (*See also* ABORIGINAL ARTISTS, CONTEMPORARY)
Lee-Ann Martin

FEDERAL GRAIN LTD. Federal Grain became Canada's largest private line elevator company; it eventually encompassed twenty original companies before it was sold in 1972. The "father" of Federal Grain, John C. Gage, arrived in Winnipeg in 1903 at the age of 27. That year, along with his father and Arthur Andrews he formed the Andrew-Gage Grain Company, which became the International Grain Company in 1905. In 1906 he formed Consolidated Elevator Company, with Alex Reid of the Western Elevator Company, for the primary purpose of building a terminal at Fort William. In 1922, Gage was joined by Henry Sellers and N.L. Leach, of the Searle-Peavey group, to form the Northland Elevator Company with Gage as president; Sellers' grandfather and father were involved in the early grain trade, specifically as terminal managers.

Federal Grain Ltd was formed in 1929 to take over several companies: Federal Grain Company, International Elevator Company, McLaughlin Elevator Company, Brook Elevator Company, Consolidated Elevator Company, Northwestern Elevator Company, Stewart Terminals, Union Grain Company Ltd, and Topper Grain Company Ltd. Federal also acquired Maple Leaf Milling Company, which had fifty-four elevators, and Gold Grain Company, which had fourteen elevators. Federal then had 355 elevators and a terminal: this compared closely with the Alberta Pacific Grain Company, which had 353 elevators. The three key players in the formation of Federal were James Gage, Henry Sellers and James Stewart. James Stewart, with K.B. Stoddart and William Herriot, had formed in 1912 Federal Grain Company Ltd. (*not* Federal Grain Ltd); born in Scotland, he had entered employment with the CANADIAN PACIFIC RAILWAY (CPR) and joined the Western Grain Company in 1906. Considered by many the shrewdest and ablest grain man in Canada, he served on the Board of Grain Supervisors and became Chairman of the first Canadian Wheat Board when it operated in 1919–20.

By 1929 Gage, Sellers and Stewart had through their share holdings a commonality of ownership and control of these companies. There was economic pressure to combine to improve their competitive position vis-à-vis the farmer-owned co-operatives. There was also interest in expansion, and with the large grain production and the rising stock market of the late 1920s, Federal went public and listed shares on the Toronto Stock Exchange to raise capital. The directors of Federal were closely linked with Maple Leaf Milling Company and the Alberta Pacific Grain Company, as James Stewart was president of all three companies and, through his own Stewart Grain Company, was responsible for hedging and trading operations. But Stewart made a colossal error. In 1929 there was great optimism that prices would rebound from the record wheat harvest in Canada which had driven prices lower: Stewart was so bullish on prices that he decided not to hedge the grain that the companies were buying, placing the companies in a risky speculative position. Instead of rising, prices began to fall, creating huge losses for the three partners. As he felt responsible for bringing Federal and the other companies to the brink of bankruptcy, Stewart sold his house and distributed most of his assets to the three firms. Twenty-three elevators of Stewart Grain went to Federal, and Stewart's shares went to Alberta Pacific Grain, giving it almost controlling interest in Federal Grain.

Gage became president of Federal and Alberta Pacific, but he died within a year, and Sellers became president of both companies. James Murray, who later became chief commissioner of the Canadian Wheat Board, was appointed manager of Alberta Pacific. Although the 1930s were not good years to make money in the grain trade, by the mid-1930s Sellers and Murray had placed the companies on a sound financial footing. In 1940 the Bawlf Grain Company was purchased by Federal (getting twenty-one elevators) and Alberta Pacific (getting seventy-two elevators); in 1943, Federal purchased Alberta Pacific with its 800 elevators. In 1967 the SEARLE GRAIN COMPANY, Federal Grain Ltd. and Alberta Pacific amalgamated as Federal Grain Ltd.; the company had more than 1,150 elevators and terminals–making it the largest private grain company in Canada.

In the 1970s there was growing concern over rail line abandonment, which would force many elevator closures and compel all grain companies to build new facilities if they were to maintain their market share of the grain business. So George Sellers (son of Henry Sellers) and his associates decided to sell Federal Grain. But who could purchase such a large company? Only the three Prairie Pools were capable of the purchase: this they did in 1972 for $30 million. Only four private line companies remained in business: National, N.M. Paterson and Sons Ltd, Parrish and Heimbecker, and Pioneer.
Gary Storey

FURTHER READING: Anderson, C.W. 1991. *Grain: The Entrepreneurs*. Winnipeg: Watson and Dwyer Publishing; Fowke, V. 1957. *The National Policy and the Wheat Economy*. Toronto: University of Toronto Press; Wilson, C.F. 1978. *A Century of Canadian Grain*. Saskatoon: Western Producer Prairie Books.

FEDERATED CO-OP REFINERY AND NEWGRADE UPGRADER. The Federated Co-op Refinery (FCR) was established in Regina in 1935 as a small 500-barrel/day refinery, in response to concerns about the buying up of independent oil refineries in Saskatchewan by major oil companies in 1933 and 1934, which led to price increases of 3¢/gallon. Expanded many times over the past sixty years, the Co-op refinery had a capacity of 80,000 bbl/day at the end of 2003.

BRYAN SCHLOSSER/REGINA LEADER-POST
Federated Co-op Refinery, August 1988.

The refining industry in Saskatchewan and western Canada in general began in the first half of the 20th century. In Saskatchewan alone, in 1951, there were nine refineries ranged across the province: three in Moose Jaw, two in Regina, and single refineries in Saskatoon, Rosetown, Prince Albert and Kamsack. Many of the refineries were very small, unsophisticated operations with production of only a few hundreds or thousands of barrels a day. The second half of the 20th century saw large consolidation and shut-down of refinery operations across the region, with the result for Saskatchewan that, except for FCR, the nearest refineries are now near Edmonton; the next Canadian refinery to the east of Regina is roughly 2,000 km away in Sarnia, Ontario. Besides products from the FCR, refined petroleum products are also transported from the Edmonton area to Saskatchewan and Manitoba.

FCR has an associated operation, the NewGrade Upgrader, located next to the refinery which transforms heavy oil from the Loydminster deposits into light synthetic oil. The NewGrade Upgrader began operations in 1988 and has a capacity of 55,000 barrels/day. The NewGrade refinery received substantial financial investment from the federal and the Saskatchewan governments, which had not been recovered as of 2004 because of initial operational difficulties and because the price differential between heavy oil and light synthetic oil was often too small during the 1990s to cover the cost of the upgrading process. The Newgrade Upgrader and the Bi-provincial Upgrader at Lloydminster, owned by Husky Energy, provide an important source of demand for heavy oil. Both operations have made a substantial contribution to encouraging the development of Saskatchewan's heavy oil resources by raising the expected value of heavy oil. *David Hanly*

FEDERATED CO-OPERATIVES LIMITED.

Federated Co-operatives Limited (FCL) is a central wholesaling, manufacturing, and administrative organization uniting 300 locally owned retail co-operatives in western Canada. In Saskatchewan alone FCL administers 165 retail co-ops, with over 300,000 members and 5,700 employees. Together, FCL and its member retail co-operatives comprise the Co-operative Retailing System, which employs 15,000 people across western Canada. FCL, through the Co-operative Retailing System, provides over one million members in 500 communities with a variety of goods and services, such as food, petroleum products, general merchandise, farm supplies, hardware, and building materials. The co-operative system began in 1928 when local co-ops joined together, establishing provincial wholesales with increased buying power. In 1955, wholesales in the four western provinces united to form FCL. FCL has its head office in Saskatoon and numerous regional offices

and distribution centres across the prairies. It also owns and operates feed plants and propane distribution centres throughout western Canada, a sawmill and plywood production facility in British Columbia, a food wholesaler and retailer in Edmonton, and an oil refinery (Consumers' Co-operative Refineries Ltd) in Regina. With 3,000 employees and revenues of $3.31 billion in 2002, FCL was the top-ranked non-financial co-operative in Canada and the top-ranked company in Saskatchewan. *Iain Stewart*

FURTHER READING: 2003. "Co-operative System Stronger than Ever," *Saskbusiness* 24: B3; Martin, P. 2003. "Saskatchewan's Top 100," *Saskatchewan Business* 24: 17–26.

FEDERATION OF SASKATCHEWAN INDIAN NATIONS (FSIN).

The Federation of Saskatchewan Indian Nations (FSIN) is the representative body of Saskatchewan's seventy-four First Nations, committed to honouring the spirit and intent of the provincial treaties made with the First Nations in the 1870s. The FSIN is a complex organization consisting of the Chiefs-in-Assembly, a Senate, an Elders Council, an Executive, an Executive Council, and an Indian Government Commission. Other aspects include an Auditor General, Treasury Board, and five major commissions: Lands and Resources, Economic and Community Development, Education and Training, Health and Social Development, and Justice. Members of the Cree, Saulteaux, Assiniboine, Dakota/Sioux, and Dene Nations form the FSIN, which recognizes the autonomy and jurisdiction of each of Saskatchewan's First Nations. Ten tribal councils and eleven independent First Nations are also affiliated.

The history the FSIN dates back to 1946 and the merger of the League of Indians of Western Canada, the Protective Association for Indians and their Treaties, and the Association of Saskatchewan Indians into the Union of Saskatchewan Indians (USI). Saskatchewan Premier **T.C. DOUGLAS** (CCF) promoted the union, anticipating that the USI would encourage First Nations integration into Canadian society; but First Nations leaders were more concerned with establishing on-reserve day-schools, accessing higher education and old-age pensions, and fostering improved treatment of First Nations war veterans. **JOHN TOOTOOSIS** was elected president, John Gambler and Ernest Goforth elected first and second vice-presidents; Mistawasis Chief and **WORLD WAR I** veteran Joe Dreaver's daughter, Gladys, was selected as secretary-treasurer. A new constitution was struck, identifying six key issues requiring resolution: the protection of treaties and treaty rights; the fostering of progress in First Nations economic, educational and social endeavours; co-operation with civil and religious authorities; constructive criticism and thorough discussion on all matters; the

adherence to democratic procedure; and the promotion of respect and tolerance for all people.

The year 1946 was a watershed for First Nations politics in Canada, following the federal government's invitation to the USI and several other First Nations political organizations to testify before the Special Joint Senate-Parliamentary Committee (SJC) investigating the Indian Act. Little came of the SJC; the USI concerned itself more with provincial political issues, and in 1958 changed its name to Federation of Saskatchewan Indians (FSI). The FSI continued its work at improving First Nations socio-economic conditions through regular interaction with provincial officials. In an age of limited communication, various strategies to keep members informed were devised, ranging from annual meetings to publishing *Indian Outlook* (1960–63), which was analogous to published conference proceedings.

The catalyst leading to the emergence of FSI was Prime Minister Pierre Trudeau's 1969 proposal to eliminate treaty rights and abolish reserves. FSI leadership fought implementation of what became popularly known as the "White Paper," initiating a long period of political growth and influence. Agitation led the federal government to offer financial support for the FSI's community development program in 1972, a year in which organization delegates agreed that the FSI's constitution should be registered under the Canadian Companies Statute. The FSI also took a significant leadership role in First Nations education in 1970s: the Saskatchewan Indian Cultural College (currently **SASKATCHEWAN INDIAN CULTURAL CENTRE**), the Saskatchewan Indian Federated College (currently **FIRST NATIONS UNIVERSITY OF CANADA**), the Saskatchewan Indian Equity Foundation, as well as the **SASKATCHEWAN INDIAN INSTITUTE OF TECHNOLOGIES** were all established in succession, in an attempt to meet the increasing educational needs of the provincial First Nations.

The FSI is perhaps best known for its work intensifying the First Nations self-government debate when, in 1977, it formally articulated the principles of self-government in a position paper entitled *Indian Government*. Sovereignty was presented as both "inherent and absolute" since First Nations governments traditionally exercised the powers of sovereign nations. A second paper in 1979, *Indian Treaty Rights: The Spirit and Intent of Treaty*, expanded upon the idea of self-government and prescribed the recognition of treaty rights in return for ceding certain "Indian" lands for use and settlement. The FSI held firm to the belief that during treaty negotiations, First Nations leaders were guaranteed all powers of Indian nationhood and accompanying jurisdiction, the right to be born and live Indian, and socio-economic rights.

A reorganization effort in the early 1980s-resulted in the FSI evolving from a longtime provincial non-profit governing body into the FSIN, described as a true federation of nations. On April 16, 1982, following an agreement to form Canada's first Indian legislative assembly, the chiefs gained formal control of the executive and administrative functions of Saskatchewan First Nations government at the band, tribal council, and provincial levels. A resolution known as the Provisional Charter of the Federation of Saskatchewan Indian Nations (Convention Act) was adopted, outlining the FSIN's governing structure; and the first Chiefs' legislative assembly was held one year later, on October19, 1983.

The FSIN to this day remains an influential political organization. The FSIN and the Canadian government, for instance, established the **OFFICE OF THE TREATY COMMISSIONER** (OTC) in 1989 to aid in determining the restitution owed to twenty-five First Nations in lieu of improper land surrenders; the OTC was renewed in 1996 for a five-year term with expanded terms of reference. Ever concerned with economic development, the FSIN also signed two agreements with Saskatchewan in 1995, initiating Aboriginal gaming: the *Gaming Framework Agreement (GFA)* and the *Casino Operating Agreement (COA)*. The stated goal behind gaming was to engage in an economic venture to aid in ameliorating poor on-reserve socio-economic conditions. The prevalent theme throughout this brief history of the FSIN is the push toward self-governance by strengthening the internal authority of bands through the reassertion of traditional institutions. Self-governance in this instance is not considered irreconcilable with promoting cross-cultural dialogue with representatives of the federal and provincial governments; in fact, it is deemed a necessity if a nation-to-nation relationship is to flourish once again.   *Yale D. Belanger*

FEDOROFF, SERGEY (1925–). Sergey Fedoroff was born in Daugavtils, Latvia, on February 20, 1925. After the war he interrupted his medical studies at the University of Tubingen to come to Canada. He joined the Department of Anatomy at the **UNIVERSITY OF SASKATCHEWAN** as an assistant animal keeper, obtained his PhD in 1958 and his DSc in 1984, and was head of the department from 1964 to 1987.

In 1950 he became involved in the incipient field of tissue culture, developed a world-class tissue culture and neurobiology research program, and for over thirty years offered a unique summer course in tissue culture that markedly enhanced the research careers of persons from all over the world. This led to the presidency of the Tissue Culture Association and its Lifetime Achievement Award, and to the presidencies of the Canadian Federation of Biological Societies and the PanAmerican Association of

UNIVERSITY OF SASKATCHEWAN ARCHIVES A-8856

Sergey Federoff, 1964.

Anatomists. Fedoroff edited fifteen books on tissue culture, contributed twenty-six chapters to other books, and published over 100 papers in peer-reviewed journals. He remains highly involved in the Saskatchewan Neuroscience Network.

W. Earle DeCoteau

FEDOROWICH, RUDY (1906–2002). Rudolph Fedorowich was born on October 25, 1906 in the town of Lemberg in the old Austro-Hungarian Empire, which is now the western Ukraine. As a young man, he experienced **WORLD WAR I** raging around his home, saw the rise of the Bolshevik Revolution, and heard Leon Trotsky speak. He also fought for Ukrainian independence and witnessed the formation of the Soviet Union. In 1922, Fedorowich immigrated to Regina and finished his schooling at Central Collegiate, where he trained to be a mechanic.

During the **GREAT DEPRESSION**, Fedorowich, along with tens of thousands of other young unemployed men, was forced into a "relief camp" in Alberta, where make-work projects were the order of the day. He joined the Relief Camp Workers Union (RCWU), an affiliate of the Workers Unity League and a Communist-led trade union federation. In 1935, he joined the **ON-TO-OTTAWA TREK** and returned to Regina "riding the rails" with the Trekkers. After the Depression, Fedorowich joined the Canadian army and served during **WORLD WAR II**. He stayed in the military after the war, married in 1949, served in the **KOREAN WAR**, and raised five children.

After retiring from the army in 1956, he worked with the **CORPS OF COMMISSIONAIRES** in Regina for thirty-two years. Rudy Fedorowich was one of the most decorated veterans in the province. He was also proud of his association with the early labour movement and the radical union protests of the 1930s. He died on June 24, 2002.   *Garnet Dishaw*

FEDORUK, SYLVIA OLGA (1927–). Born in Canora May 5, 1927, and educated at the **UNIVERSITY OF SASKATCHEWAN**, Sylvia Fedoruk pursued a distinguished career in medical physics, specializing in radiation therapy for cancer patients. For thirty-five years she was associated with the Saskatoon Cancer Clinic, where she served as chief medical physicist, and the Saskatchewan Cancer Foundation, where she was director of Physics Services. Fedoruk held the positions of professor of Oncology and associate member in Physics at the University of Saskatchewan. At the end of 1986 she took early retirement. Fedoruk was involved in the development of the world's first Cobalt 60 unit and one of the first nuclear medicine scanning machines. She was the first woman member of the Atomic Energy Control Board of Canada. She also served as a consultant in nuclear medicine to the International Atomic Energy Agency in Vienna. An avid sportswoman and curler, Sylvia Fedoruk was inducted into the Canadian Curling Hall of Fame in 1986. She was Chancellor of the University of Saskatchewan from 1986 to 1989. In 1986 she was voted Saskatoon's YWCA Woman of the Year and was appointed to the Saskatchewan Order of Merit. In 1987 she was named an Officer of the Order of Canada. She was the first woman **LIEUTENANT-GOVERNOR** of Saskatchewan, from 1988 to 1994. Sylvia Fedoruk faced the issue of the use of special warrants by the Progressive Conservative government of **GRANT DEVINE**. She came under pressure to refuse her signature to the warrants but concluded that it was up to the electorate to render final judgement. Continuing as Lieutenant-Governor during the NDP administration of **ROY ROMANOW**, she and the Premier agreed that they would hold regular monthly meetings; Saskatchewan thus became the only province where the practice existed.

Michael Jackson

COURTESY OF THE OFFICE OF THE LIEUTENANT GOVERNOR

Sylvia Fedoruk.

325

FURTHER READING: Hryniuk, Margaret and Garth Pugh. 1991. *A Tower of Attraction: An Illustrated History of Government House, Regina, Saskatchewan.* Regina: Government House Historical Society/Canadian Plains Research Center; Leeson, Howard A. (ed.). 2001. *Saskatchewan Politics: Into the Twenty-first Century.* Regina: Canadian Plains Research Center.

FEMALE EMPLOYMENT ACT. In the early decades of the 20th century, many Saskatchewan citizens regarded Chinese immigrants to the province with suspicion and hostility. The labour movement supported legislation which would restrict the employment of Chinese workers, and community leaders expressed anxiety about the dangers of social contact. One of the responses to this current of public opinion was An Act to Prevent the Employment of Female Labour in Certain Capacities, enacted by the Saskatchewan Legislature in 1912, which prevented the employment of White women or girls in any "restaurant, laundry or other place of business or amusement owned, kept or managed by any Chinaman." A Chinese businessman, **YEE CLUN**, convicted of violating the statute challenged the Act on the grounds that it impinged on his right as a naturalized Canadian citizen to operate his business. The majority of the Supreme Court of Canada, though acknowledging that it did affect his rights, held that the essential purpose of the statute was to protect women and girls in a labour context, and that it therefore lay within the power of the provincial government to enact such legislation. In subsequent legislation, the Female Employment Act, the direct prohibition of employment of White women by Chinese men, was replaced by provisions which required any employer to obtain a license from the municipality to employ women; municipalities did on occasion use these provisions to prevent Chinese employers from hiring White female employees. These provisions were in place until 1969, when the statute was repealed as part of the consolidation of the Labour Standards Act. (*See also* **CHINESE COMMUNITY**; **CHINESE LABOUR IN MOOSE JAW**)

Beth Bilson

FEMINISM: CONSCIOUSNESS AND ACTIVISM SINCE THE 1960S. Modern feminism in Saskatchewan falls into three periods. In the 1960s and 1970s, Saskatchewan feminists grappled with the question of whether an autonomous women's movement was necessary. From the late 1970s to the early 1990s, feminist activists formed issue-based advocacy groups; the three issues that dominated in this period were reproductive rights, child care, and employment equity—in particular pay equity. In the period from the early 1990s to the present, feminism has little public presence; activism involves working to maintain women's organizations such as rape crisis lines and university women's centres, and trying to voice feminist issues within political parties and other groups.

In the late 1960s and early 1970s, Saskatchewan women's groups often focused on consciousness raising, but early on many feminists saw the need for creating more lasting institutions for women. Women students, some with no previous political connections, created women's liberation groups on the two university campuses, which by the early 1970s had women's centres. The Royal Commission on the Status of Women led to the formation of the Saskatchewan Action Committee on the Status of Women (SAC) in 1972. By the mid-1970s, feminists were playing central roles in creating women-centred institutions such as shelters for abused women and rape crisis centers in urban centres.

Throughout the 1980s, issue-oriented advocacy groups were the primary face of Saskatchewan feminism. The Women's Action Collective on Health Care, Saskatchewan Working Women, Immigrant Women of Regina, and many other groups had a strong public presence, while students and faculty at the province's two universities began to develop Women's Studies programs. No one form of feminism dominated this era. Some feminists saw an autonomous women's movement as essential, while others argued that it was important to raise feminist issues within mainstream organizations. Feminism had a quasi-official face as well, since the federal government provided funding to many women's groups, including substantial funding to SAC.

In the 1990s, Saskatchewan feminism entered a period of ambivalence, less about the importance of feminist goals than about whether it was still necessary to fight for them, and if so, how. Partial victories in child care, reproductive rights, and employment equity made activism seem less urgent; yet continued cutbacks in government funding for advocacy groups such as SAC and for institutions such as shelters demonstrated how easily gains could be lost. Many people believed that the women's movement had won its battles, even while many activists had to focus their energies on keeping endangered women's institutions afloat. The ambivalence of Saskatchewan feminism has partial roots in the relation of feminist activism to elected governments. Starting in the 1970s, the federal government funded women's groups, and the provincial government played an essential role in supporting women-centred organizations such as shelters, sexual assault centres, and daycares. Both levels of government treated SAC as a semi-official voice of women. All of this led many feminists to develop a sense of entitlement to government support, and when governments began to cut back this support in the mid-1980s, they treated the loss of entitlement as an issue.

Saskatchewan feminism became a public force under an NDP government (1971–82) that eliminated some of the most egregious forms of discrimination against women in pensions, matrimonial rights, and other areas. Yet the NDP leadership was not supportive of women who stepped outside auxiliary roles, and was ambivalent about such important issues as access to abortion and support for daycare. The many feminists with some loyalty to the NDP seldom knew whether they should try to work with government or oppose it. The Conservative government that was elected in 1982 appointed the first female Cabinet ministers in the history of the province and established a Women's Secretariat, but shelters and rape crisis centres became prime targets of Conservative budget cutting, and feminist ideas became ideological targets. There was little incentive to try to work with this government, and Saskatchewan feminism became more overtly oppositional than it had been.

The return of the NDP to power in 1992 did not clarify the context of feminist activism. Feminist ideas had become part of mainstream politics, and women were part of the Cabinet, which made oppositional feminism seem ungrateful. Yet it is clear that feminist victories are not secure: women still face major problems in access to child care, abortions, and other services. Even so, in 2002, the NDP government eliminated the Women's Secretariat; at the same time, changes in federal programs have effectively eliminated funding for SAC. Saskatchewan feminist consciousness and activism persist, but the directions they must take are far from clear.

Alison Hayford

FERGUSON, ROBERT GEORGE (1883–1964). Ferguson was born on September 12, 1883, near South Joliette, North Dakota. In 1906, after his father's death, George moved his mother to a farm one mile south of Yorkton, Saskatchewan, and ran this farm each summer while in winter he obtained his BA and MD degrees in Winnipeg.

In 1917 Dr. **MAURICE SEYMOUR** hired Ferguson as the first medical doctor at the Fort Qu'Appelle Sanatorium. As secretary of the Saskatchewan Anti-tuberculosis Commission in 1921–22, Ferguson was able to gather statistically valuable information about the prevalence of tuberculosis, and to plan his lifetime campaign against the disease: under his gentle guidance, individuals, service clubs, municipalities, and the provincial government worked together to lead Canada in a costly but effective grassroots fight against what was at that time the number one health problem.

On January 1, 1929, Saskatchewan was by eight years the first jurisdiction in North America to provide free tuberculosis diagnosis and treatment. Ferguson completed two landmark scientific studies: the first BCG (*Bacillus Calmette-Guérin*) prophylaxis in Aboriginal infants, and the first BCG prophylaxis in student nurses. He organized the first

SASKATCHEWAN ARCHIVES BOARD R-A17042
Robert George Ferguson.

photofluorographic survey in North America. His 1955 book, *Studies in Tuberculosis*, remains a classic. He died in Regina on March 1, 1964. (*See also* TUBERCULOSIS CONTROL)   *C. Stuart Houston*

FERGUSON, ROBERT R. (1917–). An agriculturist and WORLD WAR II air ace, Robert Ferguson, son of Dr. R.G. FERGUSON, was born on May 13, 1917, in Winnipeg but his family moved to Fort Qu'Appelle while he was still an infant. The war interrupted his studies at the UNIVERSITY OF SASKATCHEWAN, but Ferguson distinguished himself with the Royal Canadian Air Force, retiring in 1945 with the rank of squadron leader. After the war, he completed degrees in arts and agriculture. Recognized for his community leadership, Ferguson served the rural municipality of North Qu'Appelle in various capacities for thirty years. He is a former member of the Boards of Governors of the Universities of Saskatchewan and Regina. For his service to the university community, Ferguson received an honorary doctorate of law from the UNIVERSITY OF REGINA in 1984, and a distinguished graduate award in agriculture from the University of Saskatchewan in 1986. Named a Member of the Order of Canada in 1987, Robert Ferguson received the Saskatchewan Order of Merit in 1994.

FERRANTI PACKARD 6000. In 1962, the SASKATCHEWAN POWER CORPORATION bought the largest of only five FP6000 computers ever built by the Canadian firm, Ferranti Packard. The FP 6000, an innovation in the relatively new area of general-purpose computers, was one of the first to offer time-sharing and multiprogramming in a mid-sized computer, which allowed SaskPower to run engineering calculations alongside a customer billing program. The computer filled a room and required its own air conditioner; however, the size of its memory was nearly 10,000 times smaller than what is available on a laptop computer today. The home-

grown expertise that created the FP 6000 began with work on the Royal Canadian Navy's DATAR (Digital Automated Tracking and Resolving) project in 1949. The rights to the FP 6000 computer were sold by its British parent company to International Computers and Tabulators (ICT), who recognized the potential for the machine and quickly made it the foundation for their 1900 series, from which thousands were sold in Europe. The FP 6000 became the ICT 1904; a proposal to design and manufacture ICT's 1905 and 1906 computers in Canada was not successful, putting Ferranti Packard–and Canada– out of the computer business. The FP 6000 has been compared to the Avro Arrow; ironically, the two companies were neighbours in Malton, Ontario. The SaskPower system, after being in use for eighteen years, was donated to the Saskatchewan WESTERN DEVELOPMENT MUSEUM in 1983.   *Daryl Hepting*

FERRIES AND BARGES. Ferries played a significant role in the early settlement and development of Saskatchewan. They not only provided transportation over the rivers, but also played a part in developing the economy by moving goods and providing employment: ferry service required operators and construction crews to undertake annual repairs and maintenance during the spring thaw when ice jams and flood waters damaged the ferries and riverbank landings. Saskatchewan's first known river ferry was operated and owned by the Hudson's Bay Company (HBC) near Fort Carlton in the 1860s. It was primarily responsible for hauling trade goods and HBC

employees across the NORTH SASKATCHEWAN RIVER during the summer months. In 1871 the first commercial ferry service was established by Xavier Letendre at BATOCHE on the SOUTH SASKATCHEWAN RIVER. It was also during this time that GABRIEL DUMONT, who later became famous for his participation in the NORTH-WEST RESISTANCE, started ferry service on the same river just south of Batoche, at a location appropriately named Gabriel's Crossing.

All ferry operators in Saskatchewan required a licence by 1875. Initially the licensing was granted through competition to the highest bidder, who received a three-year permit. This system resulted in expensive tolls, inefficient and unreliable service, and unsafe operating conditions. In 1898 the newly created Department of Public Works took over jurisdiction of ferry operations; operators were paid a salary, and set fees were established for the vessel's use. When Saskatchewan became a province in 1905, ferry service fell under provincial jurisdiction; by 1926 there were 47 ferries operating in the province. Many of these ferries were replaced by bridges during the 1930s and 1940s. Today, Saskatchewan Highways and Transportation operates and maintains twelve ferries and one barge. All ferry operations are seasonal, but generally take place from mid-April to mid-November depending on ice conditions. Ferry service is free; all ferries, except Wollaston and Riverhurst, are river crossings which operate from 7:00 a.m. to midnight (CST), predominantly in southern Saskatchewan (*see* Table FB-1).

Table FB-1. Saskatchewan Ferries and Barges			
Ferry	**Location**	**Load Limit**	**Capacity**
Estuary	North of Estuary on Grid Road	37 tons (33.6 tonnes)	6 cars
Lemsford	North of Lemsford	37 tons (33.6 tonnes)	6 cars
Lancer	North of Lancer between Highways 30 and 32	37 tons (33.6 tonnes)	6 cars
Riverhurst	Highway 42	100 tons (90.7 tonnes)	15 cars
ClarkBoro	Between Warman and Aberdeen on Grid 784	38 tons (34.5 tonnes)	6 cars
Hague	East of Hague from Highway 11	32.5 tons (29.5 tonnes)	6 cars
St. Laurent	East of Duck Lake on grid road between Highway 11 and 225	38 tons (34.5 tonnes)	6 cars
Fenton	Between Highway 25 and 3 on grid road	38 tons (34.5 tonnes)	6 cars
Weldon	Between Highway 3 and 302 north of Weldon	38 tons (34.5 tonnes)	6 cars
Paynton	Between Highway 16 and 26 on Grid 764	38 tons (34.5 tonnes)	6 cars
Wingard	East of Marcelin on grid road between Highway 40 and 11	30 tons (27.2 tonnes)	6 cars
Cecil	Between Highway 302 and 55 east of Prince Albert	38 tons (34.5 tonnes)	6 cars
Wollaston Barge	Hwy 905 to Wollaston Lake community	30 tons (27.2 tonnes)	depends on vehicle size

Source: Saskatchewan Highways Ferry Service Information.

EVERETT BAKER PHOTO/COURTESY OF THE SASKATCHEWAN HISTORY AND FOLKLORE SOCIETY

Carleton ferry at Fort Carleton, Saskatchewan, October 1945.

Beyond road's end in northern Saskatchewan, a number of communities have had to rely on water transport as their means of receiving fuel, heavy goods (such as construction materials), and a wide range of retail supplies. As with communities along the Mackenzie River in the Northwest Territories, Saskatchewan settlements on the Athabasca River system (including Uranium City, Fond du Lac, Stony Rapids, and Black Lake) were serviced by barges pulled or pushed by tug boats; as many as four of these tug boats were used each season during the height of uranium and gold exploration and development in the 1950s. They were operated by Northern Transportation Company Limited (NTCL), a subsidiary of Eldorado Mining and Refining Company Ltd. (Eldorado had been created as a federal Crown corporation in 1944 to oversee strategic **WORLD WAR II** interests related to uranium; it assumed ownership of a private mining company that included NTCL operations). NTCL was originally based at Waterways, Alberta (near present day Fort McMurray), where it could load barge freight targeted for both the Mackenzie and Athabasca river systems.

The silting waters of the Athabasca River were a constant source of grief for NTCL mariners and for the Canada Coast Guard, which was responsible for navigation aids and dredging on the northern river systems. Since 1997, the federal government has discontinued its dredging and navigational aids support for the Athabasca system; instead of maintaining the *west-to-east* Athabasca route for commercial water transport, it agreed to contribute to the cost of constructing a seasonal road from Points North (end of Highway 905) to Stony Rapids to provide an alternative re-supply route to the area. The seasonal road was completed in 2000, constructed and maintained

by Saskatchewan Highways and Transportation. Winter ice roads and limited summer barge services from Stony Rapids are now used to ship goods *east-to-west* from Stony Rapids to Fond du Lac, Uranium City, and Camsell Portage. In 1982, Eldorado closed its operations at Uranium City: this resulted in a major reduction in freight shipping to the area. Since 1986, limited barge transport services to the area have been provided by private firms using smaller barges.

Barge service is also provided to the community of Wollaston Lake from Highway 905 during the summer and early fall. The community is situated on the eastern side of the lake, beyond the existing northern highway system. The motorized barge service was initiated by Co-op Fisheries Ltd. in 1974, primarily to enable trucks to haul fish from the company's Wollaston Lake packing facility to a processing plant in La Ronge. The service became used for general freight and vehicle transport, ownership being transferred to the provincial government in 1980. Saskatchewan Highways and Transportation has a contract with the Hatchet Lake First Nation to operate and maintain several transportation services for the community of Wollaston Lake, including the community airport, the continuing barge service, and a winter ice road across Wollaston Lake.

Brian Cousins and Daria Coneghan

FIDLER, PETER (1769–1822). Peter Fidler, a lifetime employee of the Hudson's Bay Company (HBC), has yet to be fully recognized for his skills as an explorer, cartographer and naturalist. In large part this is because so little of his material has been published, although much survives in the HBC archives; unlike **DAVID THOMPSON** he never wrote an account of his experiences, and his large map of the

North-West appears to be unfinished. Fidler kept detailed notes of the surveys he made along all the major waterways of present-day Saskatchewan from **LAKE ATHABASCA** south to the Assiniboine River. Ironically, except for the South Saskatchewan, these same water routes were also surveyed by David Thompson. Fidler recorded his wintering with a Peigan group in southern Alberta and, later, with a **DENESULINE** group north of Lake Athabasca. Of the few surviving Aboriginal maps of the west, most are in Fidler's papers. He established Chesterfield House in 1800, the only post on the upper **SOUTH SASKATCHEWAN RIVER**, where he collected much information on plains groups. His later posts were undermanned, and he often suffered extreme hardships at the hands of his North West Company rivals. In 1812 he was transferred to the Red River Colony, and died in 1822 at Dauphin Lake House. Fidler formally married Mary, his Muskeko wife, with whom he had eleven surviving children.

Dale Russell

FURTHER READING: MacGregor, J.G. 1966. *Peter Fidler, Canada's Forgotten Surveyor, 1769–1822.* Toronto: McClelland and Stewart.

15 WING AIR RESERVE FLIGHT, MOOSE JAW. The Air Reserve is an integral part of the Canadian Air Force. Air Force reservists are citizens who volunteer to devote a portion of their free time to military service. They augment and serve alongside members of the Regular Force, performing the various roles required to maintain an effectively functioning Air Force base. Reservists are involved in a wide variety of Air Force activities including surveillance and control of Canadian airspace, worldwide airlift of Canadian Forces personnel and material, support to the navy and army, support to other government departments, search and rescue, and humanitarian operations. 15 Wing Air Reserve Flight, Moose Jaw is the only air reserve unit currently operating in Saskatchewan. *Lillian Mein*

15 WING, MOOSE JAW. 15 Wing, Saskatchewan's only military base, is located 6 km south of the city of Moose Jaw. The base and its operations provide approximately 1,000 jobs and a $30-million payroll to the area. With its clear prairie skies and almost perfect flying conditions, it has proven to be an ideal training site for the thousands of pilots who have earned their wings at the base over the years. Military aviation in Moose Jaw began in the 1920s with the creation of a local flying club. During the early days of **WORLD WAR II**, the Moose Jaw Flying Club was contracted to train student pilots for wartime service with the Royal Canadian Air Force (RCAF). Within months, this program was replaced by the greatest aircrew training program of all time, the **BRITISH COMMONWEALTH AIR TRAINING PLAN**, which was implemented in 1940. This necessitated the expansion of the facilities at Moose Jaw into a massive airbase. During the period 1940 to 1945, over 130,000 Commonwealth and Allied aircrew were trained in Canada. Late in 1940, No. 32 Service Flying Training School (32 SFTS) of Britain's Royal Air Force took up residence at the new airbase following its transfer from England. For the next four years, until it was disbanded in 1944, 32 SFTS graduated 1,207 pilots for the Air Forces of Canada, New Zealand and Britain. Although it served for a short time as an aircraft maintenance depot for the RCAF, the airbase was deactivated in 1946 and its facilities turned over to the city of Moose Jaw for use as a civilian airport.

From 1950 to 1959, in reaction to the mounting pressures of the Cold War, Canada hosted the NATO Air Training Plan through which about 4,000 pilots and navigators from Belgium, Denmark, France, Germany, Italy, the Netherlands, Norway, Portugal, Turkey and the United Kingdom were trained. Under the program, RCAF Station Moose Jaw was reactivated in 1952, becoming the new home of **2 FLYING TRAINING SCHOOL (2 FTS) RCAF**, which had been transferred from the airbase at Gimli, Manitoba. On May 4, 1953, 2 FTS began flight operations using North American Harvard single-engine trainers and Canadian-built CT-133 Silver Star advanced jet-training aircraft. Both of these types of aircraft became a familiar sight in the skies over Moose Jaw throughout the 1950s. The NATO Air Training Plan evolved into four bilateral training agreements in the late 1950s. February 1968 saw the unification of the Air Force, Army, and Navy into the Canadian Forces. This caused the renaming of RCAF Station Moose Jaw to Canadian Forces Base (CFB) Moose Jaw. On April 1, 1993, the Canadian air force adopted the Wing concept and CFB Moose Jaw officially became 15 Wing. 15 Wing underwent a major change in 2000 when the first wave of allied military pilots started training under the NATO Flying Training in Canada (NFTC) program. The base is also home to 15 Air Traffic Control Squadron and to Canada's goodwill ambassadors, 431 (AD) Squadron, better known as the Canadian Forces **SNOWBIRDS**.   *Jeff Noel*

5TH (WESTERN CAVALRY) BATTALION.
At the outbreak of **WORLD WAR I** in 1914, cavalry units from western Canada sent contingents to Camp Valcartier, Quebec, to form the 5th (Western Cavalry) Battalion, Canadian Expeditionary Force. Lieutenant-Colonel (later Brigadier-General) **GEORGE STUART TUXFORD** became the battalion's first commanding officer. The 5th Battalion, later known as the "Red Saskatchewans" because of its red divisional shoulder patch and the high percentage of Saskatchewan men in its ranks, served with 2nd Brigade, 1st Canadian Division, on the Western

COURTESY OF THE SASKATOON PUBLIC LIBRARY (LOCAL HISTORY ROOM)
5th (Western Cavalry) Battalion soldiers, 1918.

Front in France and Flanders, from February 14, 1915, until the Armistice on November 11, 1918. On April 22, 1915, the 5th Battalion was one of twelve Canadian infantry battalions assigned to the front line at the Second Battle of Ypres. On April 24, the allies came under chlorine gas attack; this affected about 10,000 troops, half of whom died of asphyxiation almost immediately. Of those who lived, 2,000 were captured as prisoners of war. Despite having to use urine- soaked handkerchiefs in place of proper respirators, the 5th Battalion held the line while other allies retreated. By May 10, almost half of the Battalion's officers were dead and one-third of its men had either been wounded or killed.

During the battle of Festubert (May 15–25), Tuxford was evacuated from the battle because of serious illness. Every other officer as well as and the majority of the senior non-commissioned officers (NCOs) were either killed or wounded, leaving the junior NCOs of the Battalion to fill the vacant leadership positions. Despite these heavy losses, the 5th Battalion was able to capture a German strongpoint and 130 yards of enemy trench. The Battalion held its position until it was relieved on May 25, becoming the only unit of the brigade to achieve its mission during the battle. At the Battle of Mount Sorrel (June 2–13, 1916), the 5th protected the flank of the 1st Division and supported the 3rd Division, enabling the Canadians to retake and hold Mount Sorrel. The Battles of the Somme resulted in the loss of 58,000 British troops, one-third of them killed, on the first day of the battle, July 1, 1916. The 5th Battalion, however, was one of the few units to make appreciable gains during the battle when the Canadian Corps succeeded in taking the Flers-

Courcelette defensive position and the Thiepval Ridge.

In April 1917, the 5th Battalion was part of the assault on the Pimple, the highest point on Vimy Ridge, during which the Canadian Corps successfully captured that position. Following the victory at Vimy Ridge, the 5th Battalion formed the left flank of the 1st Division's attack on the town of Arleux-en-Gohelle. The Battle at Arleux-en-Gohelle was the only allied success during the advance on Hill 70, a critical position needed to defend the Canadian line. In August 1917 the Battalion, as part of the 2nd Canadian Brigade, was successful in taking the hill and holding it despite suffering heavy casualties. During the Second Battle of Passchendaele, officially known as the Third Battle of Ypres, the 5th Battalion fought the enemy in close combat over a 17-day period. On November 12, 1917, after three months of fighting, Passchendaele was finally taken. In late August 1918, a member of the 5th Battalion, Sgt. Raphael L. Zengel, won the **VICTORIA CROSS** for his actions during the Battle of Amiens. The Battalion was present at Mons when the armistice was declared. The present-day North Saskatchewan Regiment perpetuates the 5th (Western Cavalry) Battalion.   *Daria Coneghan*

FIGURE SKATING.
Fancy skating, as it was then called, began in the 1880s on both outdoor and indoor rinks, with competitions held at winter carnivals. The first figure skating club began in Saskatoon in 1929, attracting both adults and children. In 1934, the Wascana Winter Club in Regina opened a rink dedicated exclusively to this sport; skaters took lessons and competed in singles, pairs,

SASKATCHEWAN ARCHIVES BOARD R-B10854

Senior figure skaters in Davidson.

and dance events. Competitions consisted of both figures, which were patterns traced on the ice, and free skating events, which featured spins and jumps. Regina skater William Thomas won the national junior men's title in 1942. Skating became extremely popular among young girls in the 1950s. The two large city clubs served as centres of activities, with their better skaters traveling to smaller communities to give lessons and organize carnivals. Local people became qualified figure skating judges who officiated at competitions–among them Margaret Sandison, who judged for over fifty years. The province hosted interprovincial competitions, and in 1955 staged the North American Championships in Regina.

Figure skating continued to grow during the 1960s and 1970s, with local organizers affecting the sport at the national as well as the provincial level. From 1965 to 1967, Bert Penfold of Regina was president of the Canadian Figure Skating Association (CFSA), in which capacity he worked to increase television coverage of national events. On the ice, the province's skaters competed at national championships and in the Canada Winter Games, winning three bronze and three gold medals during this period. In the 1980s, organizers both nationally and provincially started two new programs to increase participation in the sport. One of these was CAN-SKATE, a program designed to teach preschoolers the basics of the sport. The second was precision skating, in which teams of from twelve to twenty skaters, usually women, execute well-synchronized routines to music. Doug Steele of North Battleford,

who served as CFSA vice-president from 1986 to 1992 and president from 1992 to 1994, helped initiate precision skating competitions.

Saskatchewan figure skaters continued to do well at national competitions. In precision skating, a team from Wynyard won the national championship in 1988. In novice and junior events, several skaters took silver and bronze medals; and two, Trudy Treslan and Herb Cherwoniak, both of Saskatoon, won gold medals in 1984 and 1991 respectively. In 1996, the nature of competition changed because the CFSA did away with the figures that had given this sport its name.

Sandra Bingaman

FURTHER READING: Bingaman, S. 2000. *Figure Skating: Spinning into the Spotlight; Figure Skating in Saskatchewan, 1883–1996.* Regina: Saskatchewan Figure Skating Association and Saskatchewan Sports Hall of Fame and Museum.

FILM LOAN SERVICES FOR SCHOOLS.

During the 1930s there was a growing awareness of the potential of educational audio-visual resources to support instruction. The Audio Visual Instruction Branch of the Department of Education was formed in 1941 for the purpose of establishing a provincial Visual Aids Library with resources that could be used by schools in the province, and for developing educational radio programs. At this time a grant was also provided for every school district that purchased projectors or radios for schools; Morley P. Toombs became head of the branch. The library that was set up included both silent and sound 16 mm

films that supported curricula. The films were loaned to schools free of charge, although schools were required to pay for the costs of transportation. Later, the Branch also assumed responsibility for making available other types of resources such as filmstrips, slides, maps, charts, pamphlets, bulletins, and pictures: the rural schools of the province were thus able to access a broader range of materials for teaching.

In January 1942, the Audio-Visual Instruction Branch assumed responsibility for supervising the National Film Board's public information programs throughout the province; six circuits were set up, and in each circuit there were twenty communities where a program was presented every four weeks. Later that year the number of circuits was expanded, and the Branch worked with the **SASKATCHEWAN WHEAT POOL** to offer the service to a broader range of communities. Approximately 300 communities received this service at the time. The National Film Board projectionist often provided assistance in showing educational films in cases where the school did not have a projector, and service was provided to both adult and school audiences. This arrangement with the National Film Board continued until the 1954–55 school year, when the NFB established its own office in Regina for distribution of its films in Saskatchewan.

In the 1944–45 school year, there were several changes to the organization of the Department of Education: Henry Janzen became director of Curricula, with audio-visual services as one of his areas of responsibility; Morley Toombs left the Department to work for the NFB; and E.F. Holliday assumed responsibility for audio-visual loan services as supervisor of the Visual Education Branch. The Branch included services related to production and distribution of audio-visual aids and accompanying teacher guides, as well as to the organization of rural circuits and the presentation of film programs for the National Film Board. J.W.Kent became supervisor of School Broadcasts. The audio-visual loan service proved to be very popular with teachers, and by the 1945–46 school year plans were in place to set up film circuits and smaller film libraries within the larger school units in order to meet the increasing need; these smaller libraries were intended to draw from the central collection based at the Department offices in Regina. Schools were encouraged to build up their own libraries of 2" x 2" slides and 35 mm filmstrips, as these were comparatively inexpensive.

By the 1945–46 school year, about 20 school units had established circuits for the use of audio-visual aids, coordinated by teachers who presented films as curriculum support resources. These travelling teachers, with the use of portable power units, carried the audio-visual service to the rural schools, under the supervision of the superintendent.

The teacher education programs in the province provided support for audio-visual instruction, and in 1948 an audio-visual course was offered at the **UNIVERSITY OF SASKATCHEWAN** Summer School. Twelve scholarships of $50 each were given by the Department of Education; in 1962–63, two scholarships were awarded in the amount of $150 each. In 1959–60, projectionist courses were offered to teachers in the province, and students in attendance at Teachers Colleges in Regina and Saskatoon were trained to operate projectors. Libraries of films and filmstrips were set up at the Teachers Colleges for use by the students.

As time passed, the loan service for filmstrips and other lower-cost resources was discontinued, but the educational film loan service continued for many years. Anne Davidson assumed the position as supervisor of Visual Education in the 1964–65 school year, replacing E.F Holliday; she continued to be responsible for educational film acquisition until 1981, when she was promoted to associate director of the Instructional Resources Unit with responsibility for film loan services, school broadcasts and telecasts, school library consultative services, and the Department's Resource Centre. Diane Neill assumed responsibility as educational consultant responsible for educational film services at that time, and served in this capacity until 1987. The service operated from Saskatchewan Education offices until 1976, when it was transferred to SaskMedia. The Department continued to have responsibility for evaluation and purchase of programs.

In 1983, the service was transferred back to the Department when SaskMedia was dissolved. The Educational Media Services Unit handled the distribution of films while purchasing decisions were made by the educational consultant in the Instructional Resources Unit. In 1989, operation of the loan aspect of the service was contracted to an independent service provider, with film titles still being purchased by the Department of Education. In 1997, with a stronger emphasis on video and electronic formats, the film loan service was discontinued.

Delee Cameron

FILM, VIDEO, AND NEW MEDIA. Since the 1920s, Saskatchewan people have been producing moving images; and while that movement began with documentaries, the field has become rich and diversified with today's award-winning practitioners working across documentary, art and experimental, feature fiction, and new media forms.

The most important figure in Saskatchewan's early film history was **DICK BIRD**. His films, *Nation Building in Saskatchewan: The Ukrainians* (1920) and *This Generation: A Prairie Romance* (1932), depict respectively the history of eastern European immigration to the prairies and the importance of education and technology to the farm economy. Bird also produced what is considered Canada's first musical, *Youth Marches On* (1937). When the National Film Board of Canada (NFB) was established in 1939, two Saskatchewan filmmakers, **EVELYN SPICE CHERRY**, a director, writer and producer, and her husband, cinematographer Lawrence Cherry, played a leading role. During their careers, they produced over 100 documentary films on agricultural and environmental themes. The most important of these is *By Their Own Strength* (1940), about the rise of the co-operative farm movement. The Cherrys were also inspirational in the formation of the Yorkton Film Council (established in 1947) and the distribution circuits that brought films to rural areas; this activity was important in developing a film culture in Saskatchewan, and led to the creation in 1950 of the Yorkton Short Film Festival (*see* **YORKTON SHORT FILM & VIDEO FESTIVAL**)—the first film festival in Canada and the longest running film festival in North America.

When the NFB tried to expand beyond the genres of documentary and animation to produce fiction features in the early 1960s, one of its first efforts was *The Drylanders* (1964), a film that told the story of two generations of settlers in southwestern Saskatchewan. However, unlike the cases of Manitoba and Alberta, the NFB did not establish an office to encourage filmmaking in this province. A film production program was nevertheless set up at the **UNIVERSITY OF REGINA** in the early 1970s, and what began as a handful of courses has grown into a full-fledged university program.

Several feature films were made in Saskatchewan in the 1970s and early 1980s, including *The Hounds of Notre Dame*, a story about Père **ATHOL MURRAY** and his work at the College of Notre Dame in Wilcox in the 1930s. However, the filming of *Who Has Seen The Wind* in 1977 in Arcola was a critical moment in the development of Saskatchewan's film industry. **JEAN OSER**, an internationally known film editor who was teaching at the University of Regina, convinced the film's director, Canadian auteur Allan King, to hire six of his students for the film's crew. Inspired by their experience, they established what became the Saskatchewan Filmpool Co-operative in Regina in 1977. The Filmpool has become central in the creation of the province's independent film scene. Filmpool members have since produced some of the province's most critically successful features, including *Wheat Soup* (1987) and *Solitude* (2000), as well as experimental films, shorts, and documentaries that have won international awards.

With the creation of SaskFilm in 1989, a commercial industry began to take shape in Saskatchewan. Over forty feature-length dramas and television movies have been produced in the last decade, including *Paris or Somewhere* (1993), *Conquest* (1997), *Dinosaur Hunter* (1999), and *Falling Angels* (2002), along with internationally distributed children's television series such as *International Story Studio* and *Prairie Berry Pie*. With the opening of the new Canada Saskatchewan Production Studios in Regina in 2002, more films and television series are in development. There are now thirty companies and independent producers operating in the province. Six of these are the most prolific: Regina-based Cooper Rock Productions, Minds Eye Pictures, Partners in Motion, and West Wind Pictures; and Saskatoon's Edge Entertainment. Documentarists continue to make their mark, winning prestigious Gemini (*They Live to Polka* in 2001) and Emmy (*13 Seconds: The Kent State Shootings* in 2002) awards. Meanwhile, Aboriginal communities are beginning to produce important film and television work such as the animated film *Christmas at Wapos Bay* (2002) and the television series *Moccasin Flats* (2003).

Since 1992, the economic impact of the film, television and new media sector in Saskatchewan has increased dramatically, from $2.5 million to $60 million, making it one of the province's strongest growing industries and one of its most important resources for promoting its cultural identity.

Christine Ramsay

FURTHER READING: Horne, G. 1997. "Interpreting Prairie Cinema," *Prairie Forum* 22 (1): 135–49; Morris, P. 1978. *Embattled Shadows: A History of Canadian Cinema 1895–1939*. Montreal and Kingston: McGill-Queen's University Press; Petty, Sheila. 1998. *(Re)Positioning the Unstable Frame: Early Cinematic Visions of the Canadian Prairies*. Saskatoon: Mendel Art Gallery; Wise, W. (ed.). 2001. *Take One's Essential Guide to Canadian Film*. Toronto: University of Toronto Press.

FINCHES. Finches (family Fringillidae) are small to medium seed- and insect-eating songbirds with relatively pointed wings, often with white wingbars, and with conical bills and notched tails. They perch in the open, and their cup-shaped nests are built in trees or shrubs. Finches give distinctive calls, and their flight is high, strong and undulating. Many species are gregarious and frequent backyard feeders. The plumage is dimorphic, with brightly coloured adult males and relatively drab females. Globally, there are about 150 species of finches, twelve of which have been recorded in Saskatchewan.

The pine grosbeak (*Pinicola enucleator*) breeds in the stunted coniferous forests of the subarctic ecoregion and is a winter resident in southern Saskatchewan. The adult male has reddish tipped plumage on head, back, and rump and uppertail coverts. Evening grosbeaks (*Cocothraustes vespertinus*) breed in mixedwood and coniferous stands in the southern boreal and **CYPRESS HILLS** ecoregions, and are uncommon winter residents in southern Saskatchewan. Adult male evening grosbeaks have a black crown on brownish head and nape, yellow eyebrow and forehead, are dark brown and yellow overall, and have a prominent white patch on black wings.

The purple finch (*Carpodacus purpureus*) is most commonly found in the southern boreal ecoregion in mature mixedwood stands, but does breed at Fort Qu'Appelle, Moose Mountain and **LAKE ATHABASCA**. Adult male purple finches have a distinctive rosy plumage. The introduced house finch (*C. mexicanus*) has been expanding its range in Saskatchewan after the first confirmed nest in Regina in 1992. Male house finches have orange to red bibs, and brown heads and bodies with white streaking.

The two species of crossbills are conifer specialists. Their beaks have crossed tips, which allows them to remove seeds from cones. Red crossbills (*Loxia curvirostra*) breed in jack pine stands in northern Saskatchewan and lodgepole stands in the Cypress Hills. They are brick-red overall, while the white-winged crossbills (*Loxia leucoptera*), which breed in coniferous and mixedwood stands in northern Saskatchewan and periodically irrupt southward in winter, are pink with white wingbars.

The two redpolls are arctic birds which winter irregularly in Saskatchewan. The small common redpoll (*Carduelis flammea*) has an orange or red cap, black chin, and whitish plumage with brown streaking and bright rose pink breast and sides, while the hoary redpoll (*C. flammea*) is generally paler.

The pine siskin (*C. pinus*) is a small brown bird with white lower and yellow upper wing bars. It breeds in the boreal forest and Cypress Hills, and occasionally in aspen parkland.

American goldfinches (*C. tristis*) are commonly found breeding in open and semi-open areas, including cultivated areas in central and southern Saskatchewan. These bright yellow birds with black tail, cap and wings with double white wingbars are often called "wild canaries." The gray-crowned rosy finch (*Leucosticte tephrocotis*), with its brown body, black bill, black cap on a gray head and pinkish wings and rump, is an uncommon and irregular winter resident of the Cypress Hills and grasslands.

The orange and black Eurasian brambling (*Fringilla montifringilla*) is a straggler species in Saskatchewan. *Robert Warnock*

FURTHER READING: Alsop, Fred J., III. 2002. *Birds of Canada*. New York: Dorling Kindersley.

FINES, CLARENCE MELVIN (1905–93).
Clarence Fines was born August 16, 1905, in Darlingford, Manitoba. Initially a school teacher, Fines became involved with the newly formed CCF

SASKATCHEWAN ARCHIVES BOARD R-A2889-1
Clarence Fines.

Party, chairing the CCF's organizing convention in 1932 in Calgary and later becoming the Saskatchewan CCF president in 1942. As party fundraiser, he played a key role in the fledgling party. Fines made his first entry into politics as a city alderman for Regina in 1934. He decided to run in the provincial election in 1944 and both he and the party emerged victorious. He was appointed Minister of Finance and succeeded in shoring up Saskatchewan's credit rating and was able to bring down a balanced budget in his first year as treasurer, while continuing to finance increased social spending. Fines brought down sixteen consecutive balanced budgets in his tenure as Provincial Treasurer, a record unparalleled by any other province at this time. Fines also had an important role in creating the Saskatchewan Government Insurance Office (SGIO and later SGI). He was the Minister responsible for SGIO from 1948 to 1960. For this work the SGI head office building in Regina on 11th Avenue, erected in 1979, is named after him. He retired in 1960 to Florida where he died on October 27, 1993, the last surviving member of **T.C. DOUGLAS'** original 1944 Cabinet. *Jay Kasperski*

FINNISH SETTLEMENTS.
Three isolated rural areas may be discerned where Finns have concentrated. The New Finland colony was founded by a small number of "Church Finns" affiliated with the Suomi (Finnish) Lutheran Synod in 1887 in the backcountry Clayridge district, northeast of Whitewood in southeast Saskatchewan. Today their descendants in the area number less than a hundred. In 1910, more people of Finnish ethnic origin arrived from earlier Canadian and American colonies to settle in a second backcountry district, Rock Point, about 40 km southwest of Outlook in central Saskatchewan. This settlement was divided between the fundamentalist Laestadian sect, concentrated in the Rock Point district to the east, and left-

ist "Red Finns," concentrated in the King George district to the west. Repression of Communists in Saskatchewan during the 1930s led to the emigration of some of these leftists to Karelia in the Soviet Union. Finns in the Rock Point district held socials to support the Finnish Relief Fund in 1939. Today an estimated 300–400 Finns remain in the settlement, inclusive of the former Finland school district and extending toward Macrorie, Dunblane, Birsay, Lucky Lake, and Dinsmore. Despite rural depopulation, these descendants still retain a strong sense of Finnish identity, evidenced in many folk traditions. Finns from this latter settlement gradually began to obtain summer cottage property in the Turtle Lake area, northwest of North Battleford. Some eventually settled there on a more permanent basis, so that now there may be as many as 300–400 Finns and Scandinavians in the area, in resort colonies around the lakes and in the nearby communities of Turtleford and Mervin. Recent census data (2001) indicated that 3,675 people in Saskatchewan claimed Finnish ethnic origin, of whom 20% (745) claim to be only Finnish and 80% (2,930) partly Finnish. (*See also* **ETHNIC BLOC SETTLEMENTS**, **SCANDINAVIAN SETTLEMENTS**) *Alan Anderson*

FURTHER READING: New Finland Historical and Heritage Society. 1982. *Life in the New Finland Woods: A History of New Finland, Saskatchewan*. Edmonton: Ronalds Western Printing; Warwaruk, L. 1984. *Red Finns on the Coteau*. Saskatoon: Core Communications.

FIRST NATIONS BANK OF CANADA.
In 1993 the **FEDERATION OF SASKATCHEWAN INDIAN NATIONS** (FSIN) proposed the creation of a First Nations bank and approached a number of financial institutions for support. In 1994 the Saskatchewan Indian Equity Foundation Incorporated (SIEF) accepted a successful bid from the Toronto-Dominion Bank (TD). In that year negotiations began, and on September 16, 1996, the Toronto Dominion, SIEF, and the FSIN announced their intention to create the First Nations Bank of Canada. November 19, 1996, saw the First Nations Bank of Canada being granted Letters of Patent, and on December 4, 1996, the Bank's application for membership in the Canadian Deposit Insurance Corporation received regulatory approval. On December 9, 1996, the Toronto Dominion, SIEF, FSIN partners officially unveiled the First Nations Bank of Canada. The Bank was created with an investment of $2 million from SIEF, which is owned by the FSIN member Nations, and an investment of $8 million from the TD Financial Group. The next three years saw the opening of three branches: the first in Saskatoon in early 1997; the second in Chisasibi, Quebec (James Bay) in July 1998; and the third branch, purchased from the TD in March 1999 at Walpole Island, Ontario. In 2002 the Bank had assets of $98.4 mil-

lion and a net income of $557,000. The First Nations Bank of Canada offers a wide range of lending and investment services in both the personal and business sectors.   *Rob Nestor*

FIRST NATIONS ECONOMIC DEVELOPMENT.

In Canada and elsewhere around the world Indigenous peoples are struggling to rebuild their "nations" and improve their socioeconomic circumstances. Many see economic development as the key to success: this is certainly true for Indigenous people in Canada, who see participation in the mainstream globalized economy through entrepreneurship and business development as a path toward economic improvement and nation rebuilding. Aboriginal people want this participation in the mainstream, globalized economy to be on their own terms and for their own purposes. The Aboriginal approach to economic development can be described as a predominantly collective one, centred on the community or "nation" for the purposes of ending dependency through attaining economic self-sufficiency, controlling activities on traditional lands, improving socioeconomic circumstances, and strengthening traditional culture, values and languages. This approach is achieved by means of creating and operating businesses that can compete profitably over the long run in the global economy, forming alliances and joint ventures among themselves and with non-Aboriginal partners.

It is important to note two things about the Aboriginal approach to development: first, it involves active participation in the global economy on a competitive business-based basis; second, this participation—in terms of both process and objectives—has a distinctly Aboriginal character. Indigenous people in Canada are rejecting what is imposed on them from the outside, in favour of development strategies originating in the Indigenous community with the sanction of Indigenous culture. The key to Indigenous success lies in recognizing in each culture those forces conducive to development and in designing plans accordingly.

In 2004 a survey was conducted to try and determine how many First Nations businesses exist in Saskatchewan, how old they are, how big, at what market scale they operate, and which forms of ownership are prevalent. The research also explored those factors that might contribute to the capacity of First Nations communities to develop businesses: size, location with respect to urban centres, general geographic location, education level, presence of an economic development office, and approach to business development. In addition, the survey explored whether First Nations are adopting an approach oriented toward non-local as opposed to local markets, involving alliances and partnerships with others, or favouring community versus individual ownership. The survey found that out of a total population of

Table FNED-1. The Kitsaki Companies					
Name of Business	LRIB	Other Aboriginal	Non Aboriginal	Total Work Force	% Ownership
Athabasca Catering	40	89	38	167	20
Canada North Environmental	0	13	15	28	100
First Nations Insurance	1	7	1	9	91
Kitsaki Management Limited Partnership	8	0	2	10	100
Northern Lights Foods	15	3	2	20	100
Keewatin Procon	0		0.5	0.5	22
La Ronge Industries	1	0	0	1	51
La Ronge Motor Hotel	52	7	41	100	100
La Ronge Wild Rice Corporation	5	0	2	7	25
Northern Resource Trucking	5	8	78	91	0
Wapawekka Lumber	n/a	n/a	n/a	52	16.3
Woodland Cree Logging	2	4	9	15	33
Total	129	131	188.5	448.5	

45,261 for thirty-four responding First Nations, 23,057 people live on reserve. The average size of each community is slightly less than 11,000 ha, with 85% of the communities located in the southern agricultural area of the province and 15% in the northern boreal forest. The total number of businesses owned by the thirty-four communities is 488, an average of 14.4 businesses per community; of this number, 142 or 29% are five years old or less. The businesses employ 1,969 people for an average of four jobs per business, or 57.9 jobs per community. Males account for 58.4% of the employees, and 85.7% of the employees are Aboriginal; 49% of the businesses serve the local market, 39% the regional market, and 8% have their focus on the international market. Privately owned businesses account for 34.4% of the total, community-owned (non-partnership) for 37.2%, and community-owned (partnership) for 4.3%.

There is great variation among Saskatchewan First Nations with respect to business activity. The five most active of the thirty-four responding First Nations accounted for 33% of the total businesses and 14.5% of total employment, while the five least active First Nation communities accounted for 2.6% of the total businesses and 2.3% of the total employment. However, it cannot be conclusively stated that there are specific capacity variables that explain the reason for economic growth in one First Nation over another. For example, both the top five and bottom five communities had similar averages for levels of education (15.2% and 16.1% respectively), defined as trade certificate or diploma, other non-university education with a certificate or diploma, and university degree. Similarly, there is no differentiation with respect to geographic location, as 80% of the communities are located in the southern portion of the

province and 20% in the northern portion. The same holds true for relative proximity to larger urban centres.

The survey suggests, however, that the business development strategy of the most active and least active communities differed in several respects. The most active communities had a higher proportion of businesses that focused on the national and international market than the least active. The more active communities had 40% of their businesses targeting non-local markets, while 23% of the businesses located in the less active First Nation communities concentrated on non-local markets. As well, the largest businesses in the active communities are considerably larger relative to the larger businesses in the smaller, less active communities. The largest businesses in the most active communities employ an average of seventeen people, whereas the largest businesses in the least active communities employ an average of six people. However, the active communities both had a higher proportion of businesses in partnership with others than the inactive. Finally, the most active and least active groups showed a higher proportion of community-owned versus privately owned businesses.

A good example of successful Aboriginal business initiatives is offered by the Kitsaki Development Corporation (KDC), based in La Ronge. From its creation in 1981 the KDC's strategy for improving the socioeconomic circumstances of the La Ronge Indian Band (LRIB) has been to form sound, secure partnerships with other Aboriginal groups and successful world-class businesses in order to generate revenue for Kitsaki and employment for band members. Implementing this strategy, between 1981 and 2004 the KDC created a number of business ventures (*see* Table FNED-1). These businesses now employ almost 450 people (an average of thirty-eight per business) and have an annual payroll of almost $6 million. In addition, an estimated 300 LRIB members were paid $120,000 for picking wild mushrooms, and 200 other Aboriginal people were paid $80,000. As well, 300 LRIB members were paid $637,000 to harvest wild rice, and 200 other Aboriginal people were paid $275,000. Combining these payments with the payroll, the Kitsaki companies paid out a total of $7 million in salaries and contract payments annually.

The activities of the Kitsaki Development Corporation, now renamed the Kitsaki Management Limited Partnership, have made a decisive impact over the two decades from 1981 to 2001. With a 116% increase in the potential labour force and a 6.3% increase in participation rate, which together resulted in a 153% increase in the actual labour force, the LRIB unemployment rate fell by 2% and the employment rate increased by 5%; the number of LRIB people employed increased by 410. This is a considerable achievement, especially when compared to the figures for the neighbouring community of La Ronge for the same period. The La Ronge potential labour force grew by only 10%, while the actual labour force increased by just 7%. The numbers employed increased by only seventy, resulting in an increase of 1% in the unemployment rate and a 3% decrease in the employment rate. Several similar business success stories could be quoted as evidence of the changing nature of Aboriginal communities and of their growing importance in the economy of the province. *Robert B. Anderson*

FURTHER READING: Anderson, R.B. 1999. *Economic Development among the Aboriginal Peoples of Canada: Hope for the Future.* Toronto: Captus University Press; Robinson, M., and E. Ghostkeeper. 1987. "Native and Local Economies: A Consideration of Economic Evolution and the Next Economy," *Arctic* 40 (2): 138–44.

FIRST NATIONS GOVERNANCE. Governance can be defined as the stewardship over the processes guiding everyday life. Despite this seemingly straightforward definition, First Nations governance is a complex matrix of relationships involving Aboriginal law, politics, administration, financial management, community and natural resource development and maintenance, as well as individual and community-based entrepreneurship. Canadian officials understand it to be a delegated authority to direct federal programming at the community level. The FEDERATION OF SASKATCHEWAN INDIAN NATIONS (FSIN) and the provincial First Nations, however, view each First Nation in Saskatchewan as an independent sovereign nation with a pre-existing right to self-government that is both inherent and absolute.

The Liberal government under the leadership of

Prime Minister Jean Chrétien established the Inherent Rights Policy in 1995, thereby committing itself to realizing First Nations governance. Self-government agreements would be negotiated; however, the degree of sovereignty was not considered enough from the First Nations perspective, which demands jurisdiction over a full range of institutions in social, economic, cultural, spiritual and educational spheres, as well as over First Nations lands. The federal government would be responsible for providing resources for education and other services, under the authority and direction of First Nations governments.

Beyond the larger self-government debate, First Nations governance is a complex reality. There are a number of mechanisms of First Nations governance in Saskatchewan, including the FSIN, seventy-four band councils, and ten tribal councils. The FSIN is the representative body of all of Saskatchewan's First Nations, committed to honouring the spirit and intent of the provincial treaties struck during the 1870s. Its role is to protect Treaties and Treaty Rights, to foster progress in economic, educational and social endeavours, to co-operate with civil and religious authorities, to offer constructive criticism and thorough discussion on all matters, and to maintain democratic procedure while promoting respect and tolerance for all people.

Tribal councils are made up of bands which join together to provide advisory and/or program services to member bands. In 1984 the Tribal Council Program was established; its goal was to provide funding to tribal councils to enable them to offer advisory services to First Nation members. Agreements to establish program and service delivery can also be struck with Indian and Northern Affairs Canada (INAC) and other government agencies. Funding for tribal council advisory services and administrative overheads is determined by a formula which takes into account the services delivered, the number of First Nations forming the tribal council, the on-reserve population of member First Nations, and the geographic location of the tribal council office. Finally, each band considers itself to be a sovereign nation, vested with the ability to govern its people and territory under its own laws and customs. A band is a First Nation that has established its own governing council, usually consisting of a chief and several councilors. Community members select the chief and councilors by either election or custom. These officials are chosen for two- or three-year terms to carry out band business, which may include: education; water, sewer and fire services; by-laws; community buildings; schools; roads; and other community businesses and services.

The recent proliferation of First Nations populations in urban centres has resulted in a call for the realization of urban governance. First Nations demands for increased influence and jurisdiction

over urban services such as employment and cultural institutions have further heightened the debate. The complexity of urban issues suggests that many communities and leaders will need to become involved, including First Nations political organizations and Aboriginal service providers. First Nations are attempting to improve self-sufficiency through a variety of strategies such as the establishment of Aboriginal gaming. The Federation of Saskatchewan Indian Nations, and the governments of Canada and Saskatchewan, are working with the OFFICE OF THE TREATY COMMISSIONER (OTC) to develop an understanding on jurisdiction in the areas of child welfare, education, shelter, health, justice, treaty annuities, hunting, fishing, trapping, and gathering, in the constantly evolving process known as First Nations governance. *Yale D. Belanger*

FIRST NATIONS INTERGOVERNMENTAL RELATIONS. There is a long history of diplomatic relations between Saskatchewan First Nations and the Canadian government, initiated by treaty negotiations in the 1870s. Determined to expand and assert ownership over the prairie region, federal negotiators were dispatched to finalize treaties with the Cree, Saulteaux, and Assiniboine. By 1876, Treaties 4, 5, and 6 were concluded; and the Cree and Dene signed Treaties 8 and 10 by the end of the century. First Nations leaders believed that they were establishing a nation-to-nation relationship with Crown officials, as opposed to engaging in simple land transactions. As independent sovereign nations with a pre-existing right to self-government, they felt therefore entitled to engage the Crown diplomatically. By the early 1880s it was apparent to First Nations leaders that federal officials were reneging on treaty promises. Cree leader POUNDMAKER unsuccessfully attempted to form political councils consisting of various First Nations leaders to lobby Canadian officials for change; in response, federal officials employed the Indian Act of 1876 to dissuade First Nations political activity. Following the NORTH-WEST RESISTANCE of 1885, further measures were instituted to isolate First Nations on reserves, making it illegal to participate in ceremonies and rendering leaders politically impotent to contend with federal directives.

Unwavering in their belief in the nation-to-nation relationship, First Nations leaders continued to lobby the government for change. By the 1940s the Union of Saskatchewan Indians (USI), representing the provincial First Nations, was invited to testify before the Special Joint Senate-Parliamentary Committee (SJC) investigating the Indian Act. Also during this period, CCF Premier T.C. DOUGLAS began to work closely with First Nations leaders, hoping that he could promote First Nations integration into mainstream society. The leaders took advantage of this opportunity to unite politically and gain influence over the development of First Nations policy and legislation. Following Prime Minister Pierre Trudeau's ill-fated 1969 "White Paper" policy proposing the elimination of First Nations status, treaties, and reserves, the Federation of Saskatchewan Indians (FSI) became increasingly involved in federal politics, traveling to Ottawa to meet with members of Liberal, Progressive Conservative, and New Democratic Party caucuses. FSI Chief **DAVID AHENAKEW** expressed his frustration at the lack of programs for Saskatchewan First Nations people, galvanizing Prime Minister Trudeau to hold meetings regarding the protection of treaty rights.

Following a restructuring in 1982, the newly named **FEDERATION OF SASKATCHEWAN INDIAN NATIONS** (FSIN) moved toward implementing First Nations self-government. The Canadian government and the FSIN established the Office of the Treaty Commissioner (OTC) in 1989 to provide an impartial forum to advance treaty discussions; its original mandate was to review treaty land entitlement and education. The OTC was renewed in 1996 with an expanded mandate to facilitate a common understanding between the FSIN and Canada on treaty rights and/or jurisdiction in the areas of child welfare, education, shelter, health, justice, treaty annuities, hunting, fishing, trapping, and gathering. The purpose was to expand upon the Treaty relationship in an attempt to foster a First Nations/federal/ provincial tripartite dialogue rather than negotiations. Cognizant of the need to boost economic development, the FSIN began investigating gaming as a tool of economic growth in the late 1980s. By 1993, Saskatchewan First Nations and Premier **ROY ROMANOW** concluded that gaming revenues could aid in ameliorating First Nation socioeconomic conditions. Two years of protracted negotiations followed, culminating in the province and the FSIN signing two agreements to formally establish a provincial/First Nations gaming partnership. To resolve highly contentious jurisdictional issues surrounding gaming activities on reserves, two incorporated bodies were established to function as agents of the partnerships: the Saskatchewan Liquor and Gaming Authority (SLGA) and the **SASKATCHEWAN INDIAN GAMING AUTHORITY** (SIGA). This partnership was renewed in 2002 for an additional 25-year period. First Nations intergovernmental relations also occur at the community level: between bands and tribal councils; and between bands, tribal councils, and the federal and provincial governments. The unprecedented growth of urban First Nations populations has resulted in increased involvement with municipal officials and in a sphere of interaction previously unknown. *Yale D. Belanger*

FIRST NATIONS LAND CLAIMS. There are three major types of claims in Saskatchewan: specific, surrender, and land entitlement. A specific claim

arises when a First Nation alleges that the federal government has not lived up to its obligations under treaty or other agreement or legal responsibility (*see* Table FNLC-1). According to Canada's land claim policy, a valid specific claim exists when a First Nation can demonstrate that Canada has an outstanding lawful obligation as follows: the non-fulfillment of a treaty or agreement; a breach of an Indian Act or other statutory obligation; the mishandling of Indian funds or assets; or an illegal sale or disposition of Indian land. Canada will also consider claims that go beyond what is considered to be a lawful obligation, usually including failure to compensate a band for reserve land taken or damaged under government authority; or fraud by federal employees in connection with the purchase or sale of Indian land.

Surrender claims are a form of specific claims that refer to the surrender of reserve lands that were taken improperly by Canada. These types of specific claims occur when there has been a technical breach of the Indian Act (meaning that the proper regulations within the Indian Act were not followed), or if there has been a fiduciary breach of the government's obligation (meaning that the surrender was not in the best interests of the First Nation).

A Treaty Land Entitlement claim occurs when a First Nation alleges that the Canadian government did not provide the reserve land promised under treaty. For some, this means that no reserve land was received; for others, that the correct amount was not received. Between 1871 and 1921, eleven numbered treaties were signed in Canada, six of

which were within the boundaries of Saskatchewan. These treaties resulted in the Canadian government gaining access to large tracts of lands, in exchange for smaller parcels of land (reserves) and a number of benefits including education, health care, hunting and fishing rights, as well as assistance in making the transition to a farming economy. Treaties 2 and 5 allowed for 160 acres for each family of five, or 32 acres per person; Treaties 4, 6, 8 and 10 allowed for one square mile for each family of five, or 128 acres per person. Although the Numbered Treaties were clear on what formula was to be used to determine the size of reserves, they were silent as to when the land should be set aside and thus what population figure would be used to determine the amounts of acreage for reserves. It is this issue in particular that has resulted in the need for Treaty Land Entitlement in Saskatchewan.

By the early 1930s, both the federal and provincial governments were aware of this issue, and under the terms of the Natural Resources and Transfer Agreement the province of Saskatchewan was obligated to negotiate in Treaty Land Entitlement arrangements. Under paragraph 10 of the Agreement, the province agreed to provide unoccupied Crown lands, or to share in the cost of providing money for bands to purchase land if no suitable Crown lands were available. In 1976 the issue was revisited and it was agreed that the cutoff for resolving outstanding entitlements would be the population as of December 31, 1976: as a result, the entitlement would be based on the population of the band

Table FNLC-1. First Nations Claims Settlements			
Specific Claims Settlements			
First Nation	Year of Settlement	Value	Acres
White Bear	1986	$16,165,000	47,104.00
Island Lake	1991		10,561.00
Kahkewistahaw	1991	$404,000	27.50
Kawacatoose	1991	$3,020,000	8,266.00
Sakimay	1991	$3,940,000	6,000.00
Piapot	1993	$11,530,000	17,529.00
Ochapowace	1994	$13,000,000	18,223.40
Little Black Bear	1996	$6,079,770	12,462.00
Fishing Lake	2001	$34,500,000	13,190.00
Mistawasis	2001	$16,338,000	18,155.00
Kahkewistahaw	2002	$94,676,770	28,500
Thunderchild	2003	$53,000,000	5,000
Moosomin	2003	$41,000,000	0
Totals:		**$293,676,770**	**185,017.90**
Special Claims Settlements			
Treaty Four	1995	$6,600,000	1,300.00
Totals:		**$6,600,000**	**1,300.00**

at December 31, 1976, multiplied by 128 acres, minus the number of acres the band had already received. This became known as the Saskatchewan Formula. Owing to the unavailability of suitable unoccupied Crown land, to the province wanting compensation from the federal government, and to third party interests in land, only three entitlements were resolved under the Saskatchewan Formula. In 1987 both levels of government revisited the issue of

shortfall acres and decided to examine population numbers at the date of first survey of reserves: shortfall acres would therefore be based on only those individuals who were not accounted for at the time the reserve was surveyed. This meant that many bands were to receive fewer acres than under the Saskatchewan Formula, and resulted in five First Nations taking legal action against both levels of government.

In 1989 the **OFFICE OF THE TREATY COMMISSIONER** (OTC) was created as an alternative to litigation and to seek agreement on a fair and equitable way to deal with the shortfall issue. Under the leadership of **CLIFFORD WRIGHT**, the OTC was mandated by the Federation of Saskatchewan Indian Nations and the federal government to develop a model for settling recognized shortfalls. In 1990 the OTC submitted a report with what has become

Table FNLC-2. First Nations in Saskatchewan — Entitlement				
Entitlement First Nations	Shortfall Acres	Equity Acres	Honour Acres	Settlement Value
TLE FRAMEWORK AGREEMENT				
Little Pine	30,720.00	92,870.31	0.00	$ 25,732,066.54
Mosquito	20,096.00	33,153.33	0.00	$ 9,596,792.38
Ochapowace	44,928.00	54,160.59	0.00	$ 16,222,124.14
Onion Lake	25,984.00	108,550.57	0.00	$ 29,630,152.01
Piapot	39,073.02	81,081.41	0.00	$ 23,017,020.47
Poundmaker	13,824.00	47,687.44	0.00	$ 13,125,250.38
Star Blanket	4,672.00	11,235.58	0.00	$ 3,156,095.85
Thunderchild	38,464.00	120,816.41	0.00	$ 33,407,734.61
Yellow Quill	11,801.60	101,470.62	15,803.38	$ 29,376,731.13
First Nations that have achieved their shortfall Acres:				
Beardy's and Okemasis	11,648.00	71,137.51	0.00	$ 19,175,704.22
Canoe Lake	6,885.00	49,973.33	0.00	$ 13,412,333.43
English River	13,040.70	37,646.66	0.00	$ 10,457,408.21
Flying Dust	6,788.00	33,910.08	0.00	$ 9,196,342.56
Keeseekoose	7,552.00	48,676.75	34,523.25	$ 17,998,139.46
Moosomin	24,960.00	75,355.43	0.00	$ 20,880,639.82
Muskeg Lake	3,072.00	13,385.62	35,219.05	$ 8,642,228.85
Muskowekwan	18,121.26	51,555.52	0.00	$ 14,332,798.27
Okanese	6,905.60	14,337.58	0.00	$ 4,069,921.10
One Arrow	10,752.00	58,615.79	0.00	$ 15,852,313.21
Pelican Lake	5,961.60	35,714.68	0.00	$ 9,632,302.71
Peter Ballantyne	22,465.56	234,248.85	0.00	$ 62,428,657.03
Red Pheasant	20,118.00	72,331.77	0.00	$ 19,869,976.46
Saulteaux	16,845.13	56,144.17	0.00	$ 15,478,470.77
Sweetgrass	8,192.00	23,914.02	0.00	$ 6,638,656.96
Witchekan Lake	7,923.00	32,442.60	0.00	$ 8,862,660.29
INDIVIDUAL AGREEMENTS:				
Cowessess	53,312.00	189,367.00	0.00	$ 46,662,314.00
Carry The Kettle	24,320.00	86,491.00	0.00	$ 21,393,564.00
Kawacatoose	7,872.00	68,406.00	34,570.00	$ 23,191,969.00
First Nations that have achieved their shortfall Acres:				
Nekaneet	16,160.00	27,327.00	0.00	$ 7,963,993.00
Totals (Framework and Individual Agreements)	522,456.47	1,932,007.62	120,115.68	$539,404,360.86
Total (=Equity + Honour Acres)		2,052,123.30		

Source: Saskatchewan First Nations & Metis Relations
Note: Honour Acres is the difference between Equity Acre formula in the existing TLE Agreements and what the First Nations would have received pursuant to the formula agreed to in 1976. Equity Acres plus Honour Acres is the maximum amount of land eligible for Entitlement Reserve Status.

known as the Equity Formula. Under the formula, the OTC examines what percentage of band members did not receive land, then takes the present population and bases the acreage on that percentage: for example, if a band was made up of 100 people in 1880 and only 60 were present when the reserve was surveyed, then 40% of the band was not accounted for when the reserve was surveyed; using the Equity Formula, one would take 40% of the current population, multiply it by 128 acres, and subtract the amount of land first surveyed.

In September 1992, twenty-five First Nations, the province of Saskatchewan and the Canadian government signed the Saskatchewan Treaty Land Entitlement Framework Agreement (*see* Table FNLC-2). Under the terms of the agreement, the First Nations with outstanding entitlements will receive approximately $539 million over twelve years to purchase just over two million acres of land. As of February 2004, 596,010 acres had attained reserve status. When the TLE process is completed, reserve land will account for just over 2% of the provincial land base. Presently about 1% of the land base is reserve land, but the status Indian population constitutes about 10% of the province's population.

Rob Nestor

FIRST NATIONS RELIGION: OVERVIEW.

Given the great diversity of the sacred ways of First Nations' peoples, an outline of sacred beliefs and ceremonies of a selected number of First Nations peoples is all that can be attempted here. In Saskatchewan, there are three major language families: Algonquian, which includes languages such as Cree, Saulteaux (also called Ojibwa, Ojibwe, Chippewa, Bungi, or Anishinabe), and Blackfoot (in Alberta); Athapascan or Dene, which includes languages such as Chipewyan, Dogrib, Hare, and Beaver (in the Northwest Territories); and Siouan, which includes Dakota, Lakota, and Nakota (Assiniboine).

Ceremonies that have come to public knowledge include the Sweat Lodge, the Pipe Ceremony, and smudging. Another major ceremony done by many First Nations of the plains is called the **SUN DANCE**, Rain Dance or Thirst(ing) Dance, depending on who is hosting the ceremony. Observing and reporting about the sacred beliefs as followed by traditional First Nations peoples must always be done respectfully, taking care not to intrude on the practice, role, or observance of those beliefs. One of the greatest difficulties is to define the sacred belief systems of First Nations people in terms of religion, because they encompass much more than just religious ritual. Those who practice these sacred beliefs do so in a holistic manner: attempts to isolate them from First Nations cultures make them basically meaningless. These sacred beliefs have become what can be called the total life-way of the people.

William Asikinack

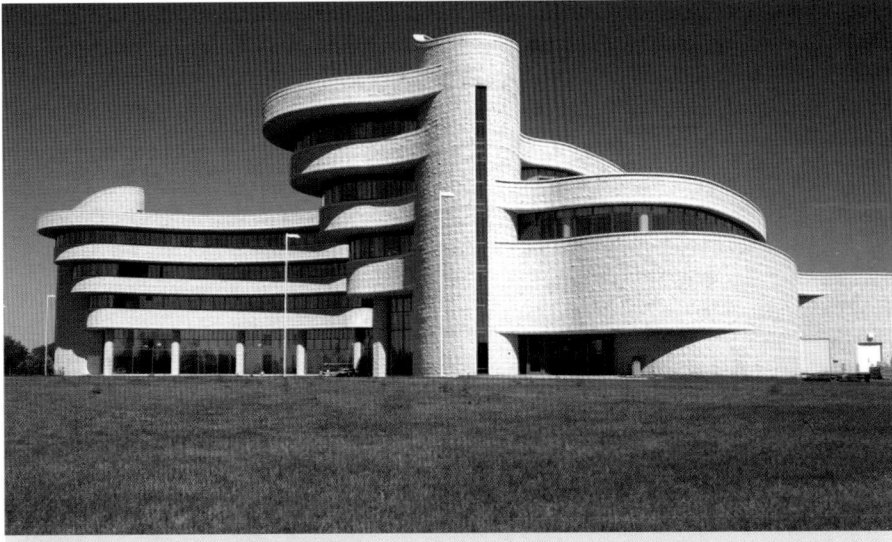

PHOTOGRAPHY DEPARTMENT, UNIVERSITY OF REGINA

First Nations University of Canada, Regina.

FIRST NATIONS UNIVERSITY OF CANADA.

The First Nations University of Canada began as the Saskatchewan Indian Federated College (SIFC) in 1976, with an agreement between SIFC and the **FEDERATION OF SASKATCHEWAN INDIAN NATIONS** (FSIN). This agreement initiated the independently administered university college, whose mandate serves the academic and cultural needs of First Nations students. Enrolment in campuses at Regina, Saskatoon, and Prince Albert grew steadily over the years, and it became apparent that a larger facility was needed. Construction of the First Nations University of Canada was subsequently initiated in the spring of 2001, and the University was officially opened on June 21, 2003, coinciding with Canada's National Aboriginal Day. Designed by architect Douglas J. Cardinal, it is the first accredited First Nations university in North America. In 2004, approximately 2,000 students were enrolled, 400-500 of them on a full-time basis. With over 2,500 alumni, the university is host to a number of departments, including the School of Business and Public Administration and the National School of Dental Therapy, as well as various programs in education, social work, science, and languages, all taught with special reference to the First Nations perspective.

Lauren Black

FIRST NATIONS WOMEN IN SASKATCH-EWAN.

"First Nations women" refers to a specific group of Aboriginal women, namely registered/status Indians, as distinct from Métis and Inuit women, and sometimes also distinguished from those descendants of North American Indians not recognized as Indians under the federal Indian Act. First Nations women are also identified by tribal or national affiliations. In Saskatchewan we have *nehiyawak* (also *nehithawak*: Plains and Woodland **CREE**), **DENESULINE** (widely known as Chipewyan), **DAKOTA/LAKOTA/NAKOTA** (Sioux/ Assiniboine or Stoney), and Anishnabe (**SAULTEAUX/** Ojibway). In Saskatchewan, First Nations or registered/status Indians are generally also "Treaty Indians." As well, the Constitution denotes them as Aboriginal People, whose Aboriginal and Treaty Rights are recognized and affirmed. In October 2004, Amnesty International championed the human rights of Indigenous women of western Canada and censured Canadian and provincial governments for neglect of their plight. The report reveals that Indigenous women face harsh conditions and that their disappearances are rarely investigated properly. As a result of this attention, the First Nation Chiefs of Saskatchewan have declared 2005 the Year of the First Nations Woman.

Abuse of First Nations women in Saskatchewan and elsewhere in western Canada has a history that goes back to the early days of White settlement. In their pre-colonial societies First Nations women generally enjoyed egalitarian status, as their productive and reproductive roles were essential to the well-being of the people. When European fur traders arrived, First Nations women became their wives and helpmates. With the advent of White settlement, they were marginalized: White society began to look down on First Nations women and made them scapegoats for the deteriorating conditions of Indigenous people after reserve settlement. The women suffered the effects of racism, compounded by sexism and poverty; such discrimination continues today, regardless of legislative efforts to curb it. After confinement on reserves and implementation of strict measures by Canada, women found it increasingly difficult to supplement their families' incomes. Through hard work and determination, however, they found ways of surviving. As men learned agriculture in the south, women assisted them while maintaining traditional skills—hunting and snaring small game, picking berries, fishing, tanning hides, and making moccasins and other crafts for sale. In the early industrial and residential schools, women learned many Euro-Canadian homemaking skills that assisted reserve life.

By the 20th century the government and churches pursued rigorous policies of assimilation that involved wholesale removal of First Nations children from their mothers to attend residential schools. In the 1960s and 1970s, child welfare authorities removed children to non-Aboriginal foster homes and institutions. This prolonged assault on families and culture is manifest today in generational cycles of dysfunction among many. An issue that attracted international attention in the late 20th century was the penalty paid by First Nations women who married non-Natives or non-status Indians: Indian Act provisions meant that these women and their children lost their status and their rights to live on a reserve or benefit from education and health programs for Treaty and Status Indians. The Act was amended in 1985 to conform to the Charter of Rights and Freedoms; more than 113,000 people nationally (approximately 13,000 in Saskatchewan) were subsequently re-registered as Indians. The change was brought about largely by women's political activism.

While Saskatchewan First Nations women have not generally been involved with national women's political groups, a province-wide association has existed for the last thirty-five years: the Saskatchewan Indian Women's Association (SIWA) was formed in 1971 with close ties to the mainly male FEDERATION OF SASKATCHEWAN INDIAN NATIONS (FSIN). Changes over the years have resulted in an FSIN Women's Commission. In 2004 there were seven women Chiefs of First Nations in Saskatchewan, and many more councillors. Underrepresented in the larger political arena, First Nations women are nevertheless leaders in tackling grassroots issues affecting children and families in cities or reserves. Of 114,248 members of seventy-four First Nations in Saskatchewan in 2003, women comprised 50.7% (57,887). While 28,168 women lived on reserves in the province, 29,719 lived off reserve, according to Department of Indian Affairs records. The First Nations population is extremely young, with high rates of single parenthood, unemployment, and poor housing. SIWA established three shelters for victims of domestic violence. One focus of the current FSIN Women's Commission is child prostitution in our cities. Gangs, addictions, violence and murder concern women in isolated northern areas as well as in urban centres. While teenage pregnancy is still a major cause of school dropout rates for girls, women often return and successfully complete educational programs later in life, determined to improve their children's quality of life.

Miriam McNab

FURTHER READING: Acoose, J. 1995. *Iskwewak: Kah' Ki yaw Ni Wahkomakanak: Neither Indian Princesses nor Easy Squaws*. Toronto: Women's Press; Carter, S. 1997. *Capturing Women: The Manipulation of Cultural Imagery in Canada's Prairie West*. Montreal: McGill-Queen's University Press; Ouellette, G. 2002. *The Fourth World: An Indigenous Perspective on Feminism and Aboriginal Women's Activism*. Halifax: Fernwood Publishing.

FISH CREEK, BATTLE OF. At the onset of the NORTH-WEST RESISTANCE in 1885, the Canadian government reacted to the news of the fighting at DUCK LAKE (March 26, 1885) and the FROG LAKE MASSACRE (April 2, 1885) by sending a force of militia under the command of Major-General FREDERICK MIDDLETON to the North-West Territories. The task of the North-West Field Force was to restore order by extinguishing the growing resistance of the Métis and the Cree to government policies for the region. Upon reaching the Territories, the Force was divided into three columns, each of which was to march north from starting points along the newly constructed prairie section of the Canadian Pacific Railway. On April 6, 1885, the main column of the force, under direct command of General Middleton and led by BOULTON'S SCOUTS, left Qu'Appelle to began its march north towards the headquarters of LOUIS RIEL's MÉTIS provisional government at BATOCHE, over 200 miles away. On the morning of April 25, Middleton's column reached the area of Fish Creek, a small stream flowing at right angles into the SOUTH SASKATCHEWAN RIVER. As Middleton's column approached, his scouts found farmhouses that had been raided, and evidence of a recent Métis encampment.

The Métis chose to face Middleton's troops at a heavily wooded coulee where the trail crossed Fish Creek, known to the Métis as Tourond's Crossing. They hid themselves and their horses in the bushes and, when Middleton's scouts approached, the Métis who were in the coulee opened fire. Rather than pursuing the Métis forces into the coulee, the scouts dismounted and returned fire. When the main body of Middleton's force arrived, they took up positions on the bluffs on the west side above the coulee and engaged the Métis from distances of 50 to 100 yards across the creek. When the militia attacked, they moved forward in the open, at the top of the coulee, where they became easy targets; many of them were killed. The Métis were on the east side of the coulee, using the natural brush cover by the stream and up on the eastern plateau. The west plateau is slightly higher than the east plateau, and Middleton's gunners had a difficult time depressing their guns low enough so that they could fire into the lower banks of the coulee. The Métis started brush fires in order to create panic and screen their attempts to outflank Middleton.

Meanwhile, the part of Middleton's force which was on the opposite bank of the South Saskatchewan River crossed the river on a barge. Now Middleton had fresh troops; but seeing that he was taking too many casualties, he did not renew the attack. A drizzle that had begun in the morning had, late in the afternoon, turned to sleet as Middleton's cold, wet soldiers withdrew from the battle. The Métis and Indians began to slip away from the coulee, returning to their homes to prepare to defend them against the coming assault by Middleton's forces. Finally, there were only about 47 Métis left in the coulee, facing over 400 militia. After six and a half hours, the battle drew to a close with the withdrawal of all the Métis to Batoche. Middleton's forces had suffered 10 deaths and 40 wounded. The Métis casualties were four dead and one wounded; they also lost over 50 horses.

After the skirmish at Fish Creek, Middleton consolidated his column on the east side of the South Saskatchewan River. As his untried soldiers had performed poorly in their first encounter with the enemy, he delayed continuing his advance in order to train his troops for the main assault on Batoche. After waiting for two weeks, Middleton resumed his march to Batoche on May 8, 1885. The battle of Fish Creek was also significant in that it was the first time that war photography was practiced in Canada, the first photos being taken by Captain James Peters of Middleton's artillery. On the whole, Middleton tolerated the war correspondents and photographers accompanying his campaign; but when they reported the defeat and the retreat of his force at Fish Creek, his relationship with the press began to deteriorate. Subsequently Middleton, during the initial stages of the fighting at Batoche, did not allow any news reports to be dispatched until the fighting had ceased.

Daria Coneghan

FURTHER READING: Hildebrandt, W. 1985. *The Battle of Batoche: British Small Arms Fire and the Entrenched Métis*. Ottawa: Parks Canada; Stanley, G. 1992. *The Birth of Western Canada: A History of the Riel Rebellions*. Toronto: University of Toronto Press; Wallace, J. 1998. *A Trying Time: The North-West Mounted Police in the 1885 Rebellion*. Winnipeg: Bunker to Bunker Books.

FISHES OF SASKATCHEWAN. The term *fish* refers to a number of aquatic and marine animals ranging from jawless creatures with cartilaginous skeletons to sharks and bony, ray-finned fishes. They share backbones, fins and gills, and are typically described as cold-blooded. All but one (the chestnut lamprey) of the fish species of Saskatchewan are bony fishes. Fishes first appear in the fossil record in the late Cambrian period; but the first ray-finned fishes (in the form of sturgeon-like fish) do not appear until the late Silurian, with most present forms not being found until the Eocene. Presently, there are 58 species of fishes from 15 families considered native to Saskatchewan (*see* Table FOS-1), with 11 extant species of exotic fishes from three families which have invaded or been introduced (*see* Table FOS-2). Most familiar are the larger-bodied fishes such as northern pike, walleye or lake trout; but more than half of the species are smaller, many of which are members of the minnow family (*see* Figure FOS-1). The most recent addition to Saskatchewan's list of native fishes is the prairie minnow, which was discovered in Rock Creek in 2003.

Initial colonization is thought to have followed closely upon glacial recedence and to have followed three main routes: southern entry via the Missouri and Red River systems (the Mississippi and Montana refugia); and northern and eastern entry from Arctic refugia via the Mackenzie, Churchill and Nelson drainages (the Atlantic, Beringia and Nahanni refugia). This contributed to the cold water assemblage still present in many of the northern lakes. Some freshwater-adapted marine species, such as the deepwater sculpin, colonized during this period of marine inundation. Further colonization occurred as waters warmed, ecosystem diversity increased, and organisms dispersed from their more southern glacial refugia. Individuals travelled through connected waters or where floods formed new connections. It is through these mechanisms that the majority of the aquatic biota of Saskatchewan was established. There is speculation that the channel catfish and rock bass may have immigrated more recently: this supposition arises as they are currently expanding their range in Saskatchewan, and confirmed collections are restricted to the past half-century.

The majority of Saskatchewan's fishes are spring spawners, although a number of the salmonids are fall spawners whose eggs over-winter before hatching in spring. The diet of fishes ranges from plankton to other fishes, with the adult lamprey perhaps being strangest in attaching to other fish and consuming both body fluid and tissue through its sucker mouth. The rarest native fishes appear to be the central mudminnow (Carrot River drainage), mountain sucker (headwaters of the Frenchman River), hybognathid minnows and stonecat (Frenchman and Assiniboine Rivers), and shortjaw cisco (**REINDEER LAKE** and **LAKE ATHABASCA**). The shortjaw cisco is listed as a threatened species, and the status of both the lake sturgeon and bigmouth buffalo is under review. Having only been found once in Saskatchewan, the central mudminnow was thought to be an accidentally occurring species; it was found again during a survey in 2004. Exotic fishes are species intentionally and officially introduced to Saskatchewan, regardless of their capacity to establish (many are reintroduced as populations wane). There are also fishes which have invaded and established after an intentional or accidental introduction elsewhere in North America.

Table FOS-1. Native Fishes of Saskatchewan

Common Name	Scientific Name	Family
Arctic grayling	*Thymallus arcticus*	Salmonidae
bigmouth buffalo	*Ictiobus cyprinellus*	Catostomidae
black bullhead	*Ameiurus melas*	Ictaluridae
blackfin cisco	*Coregonus nigripinnis*	Salmonidae
blacknose dace	*Rhinichthys atratulus*	Cyprinidae
blackside darter	*Percina maculata*	Percidae
blacknose shiner	*Notropis heterolepis*	Cyprinidae
brassy minnow	*Hybognathus hankinsoni*	Cyprinidae
brook stickleback	*Culaea inconstans*	Gasterosteidae
brown bullhead	*Ameiurus nebulosus*	Ictaluridae
burbot	*Lota lota*	Gadidae
central mudminnow	*Umbra limi*	Umbridae
channel catfish	*Ictalurus punctatus*	Ictaluridae
chestnut lamprey	*Ichthyomyzon castaneus*	Petromyzontidae
cisco (lake herring)	*Coregonus artedi*	Salmonidae
common shiner	*Luxilus cornutus*	Cyprinidae
creek chub	*Semotilus atromaculatus*	Cyprinidae
deepwater sculpin	*Myoxocephalus thompsoni*	Cottidae
emerald shiner	*Notropis atherinoides*	Cyprinidae
fathead minnow	*Pimephales promelas*	Cyprinidae
finescale dace	*Phoxinus neogaeus*	Cyprinidae
flathead chub	*Platygobio gracilis*	Cyprinidae
golden shiner	*Notemigonus crysoleucas*	Cyprinidae
oldeye	*Hiodon alosoides*	Hiodontidae
Iowa darter	*Etheostoma exile*	Percidae
johnny darter	*Etheostoma nigrum*	Percidae
lake chub	*Couesius plumbeus*	Cyprinidae
lake sturgeon	*Acipenser fulvescens*	Acipenseridae
lake trout	*Salvelinus namaycush*	Salmonidae
lake whitefish	*Coregonus clupeaformis*	Salmonidae
logperch	*Percina caprodes*	Percidae
longnose dace	*Rhinichthys cataractae*	Cyprinidae
longnose sucker	*Catostomus catostomus*	Catostomidae
mooneye	*Hiodon tergisus*	Hiodontidae
mountain sucker	*Catostomus platyrhynchus*	Catostomidae
ninespine stickleback	*Pungitius pungitius*	Gasterosteidae
northern pike	*Esox lucius*	Esocidae
northern redbelly dace	*Phoxinus eos*	Cyprinidae
pearl dace	*Margariscus margarita*	Cyprinidae
plains minnow	*Hybognathus placitus*	Cyprinidae
quillback	*Carpiodes cyprinus*	Catostomidae
river shiner	*Notropis blennius*	Cyprinidae
rock bass	*Ambloplites rupestris*	Centrarchidae
round whitefish	*Prosopium cylindraceum*	Salmonidae
sand shiner	*Notropis stramineus*	Cyprinidae
sauger	*Sander canadense*	Percidae
shorthead redhorse	*Moxostoma macrolepidotum*	Catostomidae
shortjaw cisco	*Coregonus zenithicus*	Salmonidae
silver redhorse	*Moxostoma anisurum*	Catostomidae
slimy sculpin	*Cottus cognatus*	Cottidae
spoonhead sculpin	*Cottus ricei*	Cottidae
spottail shiner	*Notropis hudsonius*	Cyprinidae
stonecat	*Noturus flavus*	Ictaluridae
tadpole madtom	*Noturus gyrinus*	Ictaluridae
trout-perch	*Percopsis omiscomaycus*	Percopsidae
walleye	*Sander vitreus*	Percidae
white sucker	*Catostomus commersoni*	Catostomidae
yellow perch	*Perca flavescens*	Percidae

Table FOS-2. Exotic Fishes of Saskatchewan

Common Name	Scientific Name	Family
Atlantic salmon	*Salmo salar*	Salmonidae
brook trout	*Salvelinus fontinalis*	Salmonidae
brown trout	*Salmo trutta*	Salmonidae
common carp	*Cyprinus carpio*	Cyprinidae
cutthroat trout	*Oncorhynchus clarki*	Salmonidae
grass carp	*Ctenopharyngodon idella*	Cyprinidae
largemouth bass	*Micropterus salmoides*	Centrarchidae
rainbow trout	*Oncorhynchus mykiss*	Salmonidae
smallmouth bass	*Micropterus dolomieu*	Centrarchidae
splake	*Salvelinus fontinalis* x *Salvelinus namaycush*	Salmonidae
tiger trout	*Salmo trutta* x *Salvelinus fontinalis*	Salmonidae

American eel, Arctic char, Atlantic salmon, brook trout, brown trout, coho salmon, cutthroat trout, grass carp, kokanee, largemouth bass, rainbow trout, and smallmouth bass have been introduced by various provincial, federal, and private agencies. Each of these introductions was deemed successful, at least in terms of initial adult survival. Several of these species did not establish breeding populations and may no longer be extant. All of the grass carp currently stocked in Saskatchewan are effectively sterile (triploid) animals. All attempts to introduce black crappie, bluegill, rainbow smelt, and white crappie have been unsuccessful. Two types of hybrid fish have been, and continue to be, stocked by the province: the splake and the tiger trout. The common carp invaded and became established in Saskatchewan after its introduction to North America; records indicate an invasion prior to 1955.

There are several species for which there is insufficient evidence to determine if an established population exists. Two dead freshwater drum specimens were taken from the banks of Swift Current Creek in 1953. Nine western silvery minnows were collected from Tobin Lake in 1966 during a survey by the Royal Ontario Museum. No other confirmed specimens of this species have been taken from Saskatchewan waters. Fish taken from the Frenchman River, previously identified as western silvery minnows, have been determined to be brassy minnows upon re-examination of the collections. At various times goldfish, piranha, and oscar have been reported; most are found in sloughs, dugouts, and storm retention ponds. Undoubtedly, there have been other unrecorded instances of species once resident to aquaria being "stocked" to Saskatchewan's waters.

In the future, climate changes may lead to an expansion in the range of some species and to the restriction or extirpation of others: for example, warm water fish such as channel catfish, largemouth bass and common carp may extend their ranges; but cold water species such as lake trout may be extirpated from the edges of their range. The recent (post-1940) loss of some lake trout populations from the more southerly portions of their former range in Saskatchewan has been attributed to over-harvest; however post-glacial climatic warming and isolation of watersheds through isostatic rebound may be at the root of these animals' susceptibility to extirpation. Aquatic biota tend to be more vulnerable to extirpation since they are islandized by topography and further confined to river corridors for movement. These restricted corridors may be rendered temporarily or more permanently impassable due to man-made structures, unsuitable flows, depths or temperatures, and other obstacles such as beaver dams.

Kevin Murphy

FURTHER READING: Atton, F.M. and J.J. Merkowsky. 1983. *Atlas of Saskatchewan Fish*. Regina: Saskatchewan Parks and Renewable Resources, Fisheries Technical Report 83-2; Page, L.M. and B.M. Burr. 1991. *A Field Guide to Freshwater Fishes: North America North of Mexico*. Boston: Houghton Mifflin; Scott, W.B. and E.J. Crossman. 1973. *Freshwater Fishes of Canada*. Ottawa: Fisheries Research Board of Canada, Bulletin 184.

FISHING, COMMERCIAL. There are three primary uses of fishery resources in Saskatchewan: recreational angling; First Nations subsistence fishing; and commercial fishing. Commercial fishing dates back to 1885, when rail transport first came to the QU'APPELLE VALLEY in what was then part of the North-West Territories. Regulated and managed from Ottawa, and based largely on whitefish, the commercial fishing industry was dominated by southern businesses and commercial interests in Alberta and Manitoba, with most exports going to eastern Canada and, until the 1930s, the United States. By 1930, Saskatchewan had taken over regulation of the industry, and improvements in rail transportation had facilitated expansion to the north of the province. Fish-processing plants were soon established across northern Saskatchewan—in places such as Big River, Dore Lake, and Buffalo Narrows—with other species such as pike, walleye, and lake trout becoming increasingly important to the industry. Over the course of the next few decades, the commercial fishing industry expanded rapidly, so that by the mid-1960s annual commercial fish production amounted to 6.8 million kg.

By the mid-1990s, however, the delivered weight of commercially caught fish had fallen by more than 60%, in part because of declining prices, and in part because of new provincial regulations (such as limiting the total number of fish that can be harvested from a given lake) imposed to halt

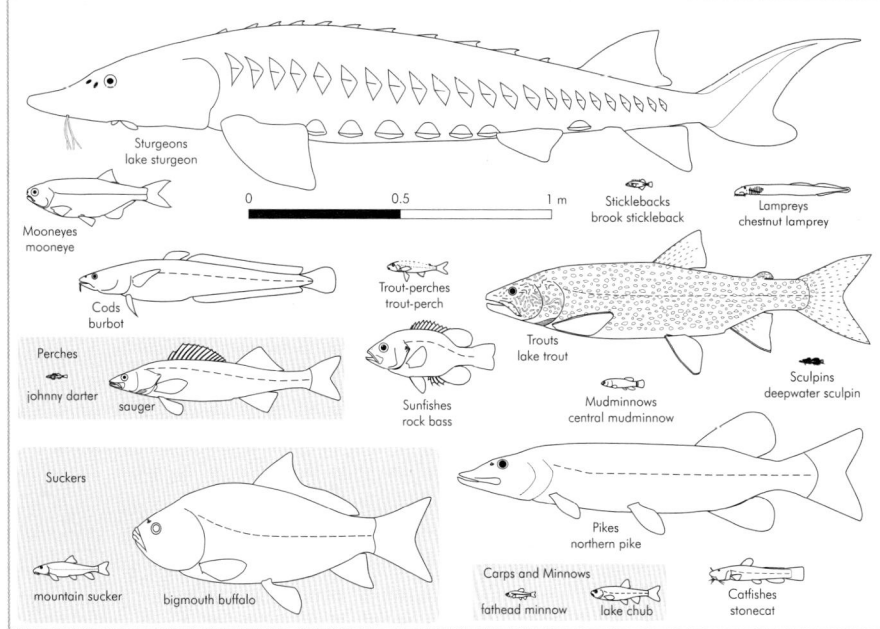

ILLUSTRATIONS BY R.E. HLASNY

Figure FOS-1. Representative fishes from each of Saskatchewan's native fish families showing relative sizes.

depleting fish stocks. In response to this decline, the provincial government launched a five-year strategy beginning in the late 1990s to revitalize the industry through a number of initiatives, including planned construction of a new $4 million fish processing plant in Prince Albert, provision of $1 million to upgrade existing northern co-op processing facilities under the Northern Saskatchewan Fisheries Infrastructure Program, and continuation of annual transportation subsidies of $300,000 to help northern fishermen offset transportation costs. Although the government's goal of doubling the annual value of production has not been met, the five-year average from 1998–99 to 2002–03 was $5.14 million–34% higher than the five-year average of $3.83 million during the 1993–94 to 1997–98 period. In 2004, there were approximately 500 licensed commercial fisherman in northern Saskatchewan. The average commercial fisherman earns less than $6,000 per year; 82% of the people working in the industry are of Aboriginal ancestry.

All commercial fish for export are marketed through the Fresh Fish Marketing Corporation (FFMC), a Schedule III Crown corporation established in 1969 to promote the sale of fish from Alberta, Saskatchewan, Manitoba, Ontario, and the Northwest Territories. Saskatchewan is the second largest freshwater fish producer of the five areas served by the FFMC. The corporation is managed by an eleven-member board of directors composed of a chairman, president, four directors appointed by the federal government, along with one director from each participating jurisdiction. The board is supported by an advisory committee appointed by the federal government. The FFMC purchases and markets all fish for export. It sets guaranteed prices in advance of each fishing season, and returns profits to fishermen at the end of the year. Northern fishermen may also sell their catch or a portion of it directly to consumers or to licensed fish processing plants within Saskatchewan. However, fish may not be sold outside the province—by fishermen or fish processors—without an export license from the FFMC.

Damian Coneghan

FURTHER READING: Snook, M. 2004. *Fishing Saskatchewan: An Angler's Guide to Provincial Waters.* Regina: Canadian Plains Research Center.

FISHING LAKE FIRST NATION. Chief Yellow Quill and two headmen, Kenistin and Ne-Pin-awa, signed an adhesion to **TREATY 4** on August 24, 1876, at Fort Pelly. In September 1881 reserves for the Yellow Quill Saulteaux Band were surveyed at Fishing and Nut Lakes, and in 1900 a reserve was surveyed for Kenistin. In 1907 approximately 13,190 acres (representing more than 60% of the Fishing Lake First Nation's land base) were secured by the Department of Indian Affairs and sold by public auc-

tion. The band submitted a claim to the Specific Claims Branch in April 1989, and years of negotiations began. As the claim progressed, discussion evolved around whether the people living on the Fishing Lake, Nut Lake, and Kinistin reserves were distinct bands (as they considered themselves to be). The creation of the three reserves by the Department validated that assertion. In 2001 a Settlement Agreement was ratified, allowing the band to purchase 13,190 acres of land that would again be given reserve status. Of the 1,439 registered band members, 404 live on the 3,906.6-ha reserve, located approximately 119 km north of Fort Qu'Appelle.

Christian Thompson

COURTESY OF TOURISM SASKATCHEWAN
Saskatchewan's provincial flag.

FLAG. The first Saskatchewan flag, created in 1964 for the province's diamond jubilee in 1965 and the Canadian centennial in 1967, and designed by Sister Imelda of St. Angela's Convent in Prelate, was divided into two equal horizontal bands of red and green, and displayed a stem of wheat and the province's shield of arms. A design by Anthony Drake of Hodgeville was selected by a legislative committee and proclaimed the official provincial flag on September 23, 1969. Divided into two equal horizontal bands of green and yellow, it featured the western red lily and the shield of arms. *Michael Jackson*

FLAX. Flax (*Linum usitatissimum*) is a traditional oilseed crop in Saskatchewan that was grown in the area for a number of years prior to the establishment of the province in 1905, and continuously since then. It can be regarded as the first special, or non-cereal field crop, to be grown in the region. Flax is grown in Canada on an average of 638,000 ha annually. Today, 70% of the Canadian flax area is in Saskatchewan, with an average production of 500,000 tonnes and an average harvested yield of 1,230 kg/ha. Flax is an annual plant with a growing time similar to spring wheat. Flax flowers have five, usually blue, petals. They appear each morning during the flowering period, and the petals are shed in the early afternoon. The seed boll contains up to ten small, flattened and ovate seeds; seed colour is usually brown but may be yellow; mature seed contains

43% to 45% oil, and 21% to 25% protein.

The oil of flaxseed is rich in linolenic fatty acid (58%), which is known by a number of different names. The largest proportion of the crop is crushed to produce linseed oil. Linseed oil is an industrial drying oil used in the production of oil-based paints, stains and inks, as well as in the manufacture of linoleum flooring. When crushed for the small human health-food market, it is known as flaxseed oil and is used because of its high concentration of omega-3 fatty acid (linolenic acid). Another type of flax that is grown in Saskatchewan is solin. Solin was developed in the late 1980s and its oil has a linolenic fatty acid concentration of 2%, and a linoleic fatty acid concentration of 70%. This makes solin oil very similar to traditional sunflower oil, and it is marketed as an edible vegetable oil. The meal remaining from the crushing of both flax and solin is used as a livestock feed.

In recent years there has been great interest in the utilization of flax seed and its components in healthy food/feed or as a nutraceutical. The outer layer of the seed coat is made of mucilage, which is a polysaccharide. Mucilage makes up about 5% of the seed and is thought to impart the laxative properties to flax. Lignans are another type of fibre which is found in a deeper layer of the seed coat. The lignan concentration of flax is many times greater than in other plant foods, and lignans may have anticancer properties. The high level of alpha-linolenic fatty acid (omega-3) found in flaxseed is also believed to have therapeutic properties: this essential fatty acid has been implicated in reducing blood pressure and modifying the immune system. *Gordon. G. Rowland*

FLEMING, town, pop 95, located 6 km W of the Saskatchewan-Manitoba border on Hwy 1. Moosomin, 14 km northwest, is the nearest major centre. The spring of 1882 brought the arrival of both the CPR main line and settlers to the district. The first settlers were primarily from Ontario and Great Britain; later, a number of Mennonites would also settle the Fleming area. In 1884, the Fleming post office opened, its name honouring Sir Sandford Fleming (1827–1915), the country's distinguished engineer, surveyor, and inventor of standard time. The main thoroughfare in the young community was named Sandford Street. Fleming developed into a service centre for the surrounding mixed farming district, and Saskatchewan's oldest surviving grain elevator was built there in 1895. In 1916, Fleming reached its peak population of 310. In 1954, a view of the town appeared on the back of the Canadian $1 bill–a quintessential vista of a small prairie town that would be familiar to Canadians for years. As the decades passed, Fleming was increasingly overshadowed by Moosomin. In June 1975, after almost 90 years, Fleming's school was closed for good. Today, most Fleming residents in the work force are employed in Moosomin, while a smaller percentage engage in farming. Clarence Campbell, president of the National Hockey League from 1946–77, was born in Fleming in 1905. The town has also been the home of two heroes. In 1958, 8-year-old John Wiebe rescued a younger boy who was badly burned by a live wire at a high voltage transformer, and was subsequently awarded a medal for his courage in dangerous circumstances. And in 1995, volunteer Fire Chief Doug Van De Kerckhove risked his life attempting to rescue another man, who had been overcome by noxious fumes and had fallen down a well; after spending weeks in intensive care recovering from hydrogen sulphide gas poisoning, he received the Governor General of Canada's Medal for Bravery in 1996. *David McLennan*

FLEMING, ROBERT JAMES BERKELEY

(1921–76). Born in Prince Albert on November 12, 1921, Fleming began his musical studies in Saskatoon. In 1937, he traveled to England, studying at the Royal College of Music with Arthur Benjamin (piano) and Herbert Howells (composition). Returning to Saskatchewan, he gave his debut concert at Darke Hall, Regina (1940), followed by a recital tour of the province. He continued piano studies with **LYELL GUSTIN** in Saskatoon and later, on Canadian Performing Rights Society scholarships, studied at the Toronto Conservatory of Music with such national luminaries as Healey Willan (composition). In 1946 he joined the National Film Board of Canada, eventually becoming music director (1958). He remained there until 1970, when he took a position at Carleton University, Ottawa, lecturing on Canadian composers and 20th century music.

Robert Fleming was well known for his many compositions encompassing not only hundreds of

Robert Fleming at the pipe organ of the National Art Centre, Ottawa (Carleton University convocation, early 1970s).

Flexi-Coil Air Seeder.

film scores but a large body of musical works for orchestra, chamber ensemble, solo instrument, voice, choir, ballet, theatre and liturgical music for the Anglican church. *The Confession Stone* (1967), his internationally known song cycle, shows Fleming's dedication to fine craftsmanship and detailed attention to text. Throughout his career, he had an ongoing influence on many young musicians, and to this day his melodic pieces are regularly heard at the Saskatchewan Music Festival. Fleming died on November 28, 1976. *J.H. Fleming*

FURTHER READING: 1981. *Encyclopedia of Music in Canada.* Toronto: University of Toronto Press; Thistle, Lauretta. 1977. "Robert Fleming: A Tribute to One of Canada's Best-loved Composers." *The Canadian Composer* 118: 10–18.

FLEXI-COIL. Flexi-Coil was founded in 1952 by Emerson and Kenneth Summach of Saskatoon, as a family-owned and operated business. The company's corporate office is located in Saskatoon; other offices are in Minot, North Dakota, and Ames, Iowa; in Perth, Western Australia, and Toowoomba, Queensland; and in York, England. Flexi-Coil had revenues of approximately $67 million in 1999. The first product to be introduced by Flexi-Coil was the coil packer, which revolutionized the seeding process. For over fifty years, the company's research and development focus led to the development of equipment used in seeding, planting, tillage, and chemical application. They design and manufacture a wide range of dryland products including air carts, precision seeding tools, tillage machinery, sprayers and harrows. Flexi-Coil also offers a precision line of Row Crop products, which include precision planting tools, air carts and nurse systems, tillage machinery, sprayers and harrows. Innovative technology has enabled Flexi-Coil to gain an international reputation for superior product service, quality and design, and allowed the company to expand to

markets around the world. One of Flexi-Coil's innovative products includes Flexi-Coil air seeding systems, which are used in over 20 countries. Another is FlexControl™ task controller, which allows for automated variable rate application of seed, fertilizer or spray using GPS control, and was recognized as a 1999 Outstanding Innovation in product or systems by the American Society of Agricultural Engineers. In 1997, through an agreement with New Holland, Flexi-Coil agreed to sell a majority stake in the company over an undisclosed period of time. New Holland initially purchased 35% of Flexi-Coil in December 1997. On January 4, 2000, CNH Global N.V., the company created through a merger of Case Corporation and New Holland, acquired all of the shares of Flexi-Coil Ltd. *Jessica Pothier*

FLOODS AND FLOOD CONTROL. There have been numerous well-documented floods in Saskatchewan since Euro-Canadian settlement began. They have usually been caused by large snowmelt spring runoffs or large summer rainfall events. In rare cases, flooding may result from a significant ice jam or from several consecutive high-flow years. Illustrated (below) is the 1952 flood in Eastend, caused by a rapid melt of a large snow pack. Severe flooding also occurred at Fishing Lake near Wadena, caused by successive high-runoff years in the 1990s. Fishing Lake lacks an effective outlet channel, which restricts outflow from the lake. Several years with high spring runoff and summer rainfall caused Fishing Lake to rise to flood stage and remain so for a prolonged period, causing significant damage.

From the 1970s through the 1990s, the governments of Saskatchewan and Canada entered into an agreement and program aimed at reducing flood damage. Twenty-six communities participated in the Flood Damage Reduction Program (FDRP). Design floods were calculated and flood plains were mapped; communities were encouraged to develop

Pool elevator and stockyards during Eastend flood, April 15, 1952.

bylaws restricting development on flood plains. In at least one community, dykes were constructed to protect existing properties and homes; in other communities, funds were set aside to purchase flood- prone properties in the flood plains. Saskatoon, Estevan and Oxbow are located downstream from major multipurpose dams which are used to reduce flood impacts.

Saskatchewan Watershed Authority also runs the River Forecast Centre (RFC), which monitors stream flows and water levels throughout the province and forecasts flows and water levels during critical periods. Information is gathered from a stream flow gauging network of approximately 300 hydrometric stations, owned and operated by the Authority or by Environment Canada; meteorological information is obtained from Environment Canada. Flood warnings and flow forecasts are important components of flood operations.

Doug Johnson

FLOWERING PLANTS. The flowering plants, or Angiosperms as botanists refer to them, are a vast cosmopolitan assemblage dominating plant life on earth today and comprised of approximately 250,000 species. Not only do their attractive flowers and overall beauty aesthetically enrich our lives, but flowering plants are vital to human existence as the biosphere's primary producers and sources of our sustenance, shelter, and other necessities. The name angiosperms originated from a combination of the Greek words *angeion* (vessel) and *sperma* (seed): angiosperms can thus be defined as seed-bearing vascular plants, with true flowers having the ovules (immature seeds) borne enclosed in a hollow ovary. While the cones of gymnosperms, the other seed-bearing plants, are basically equivalent to angiosperm flowers, their ovules (seeds) are borne naked (i.e., uncovered) on surfaces of cone scales. Angiosperms also differ from gymnosperms in having vessels (large tubes) in their conducting (vascular) system, and an endosperm (nutriment for the embryo

in the seed) developing after rather than before fertilization. Non-seed bearing vascular plants such as ferns, horsetails, and club-mosses, and non-vascular plants such as mosses and liverworts, have sporangia (spore-cases) in which single-celled spores develop, to be eventually released and dispersed, and to germinate on suitable substrate to grow into new plants.

Angiosperms evidently originated from a cycad-like line of gymnosperms as early as the Jurassic Period, but did not appear on the world scene in sizable numbers until the early-mid Cretaceous Period about 112 million years ago, when already quite diverse. Their early evolutionary history has posed some riddles owing to a fragmentary fossil record. By the end of the Cretaceous Period, about 65 million years ago, angiosperms had overwhelmingly replaced gymnosperms as the dominant plants on earth. They successfully adapted to and colonized most available habitats as they spread over the face the earth.

Angiosperms have evolved into an amazing array of life-forms, ranging in size from minute floating plants 1-2 mm in diameter (e.g., Watermeal, *Wolffia* spp.) to tall trees reaching heights of 100 m for some Australian eucalyptus species, although seldom over 30 m for Saskatchewan hardwood trees. In general life-form, angiosperms are broadly categorized as either woody plants (trees, shrubs, and some vines) with persistent aerial stems, or herbaceous (non-woody) plants with aerial stems dying back to ground level at the end of each growing season. Trees are the larger woody plants, often defined as over 3.5 m tall, with mostly single main trunks, in contrast to the shorter and usually multi-stemmed shrubs. Herbaceous plants are categorized by their longevity as: annuals, living for a single growing season; biennials, living for two seasons to flower the second; and perennials, living for several to many seasons and producing new flowering shoots from their bases each season.

Flowers are the distinctive reproductive struc-

tures of angiosperms. They vary greatly in size, from microscopic in duckweeds to nearly a metre broad in some tropical blossoms. A typical complete angiosperm flower consists of a receptacle (enlarged tip of flower stalk) that bears four basic sets of floral parts. These floral sets, from the outermost inward, are sepals (collectively calyx), petals (collectively corolla), stamens (collectively androecium), and pistils (collectively gynoecium). The reproductively essential floral parts are stamens (male structures) and pistils (female structures). An ovary containing the ovules forms the basal part of a typical pistil, with a stalk-like style atop the ovary and terminated by a pollen-receptive stigma. Stamens typically consist of stalk-like filaments bearing terminal anthers containing pollen sacs in which pollen is produced. The often conspicuous and colourful petals of flowering plants seemingly evolved for the purpose of attracting pollinating insects. Sepals, the outermost floral parts, are characteristically leaf-like and generally function to envelop and protect the immature flower in bud stage, and later lend support for the other floral parts.

Pollination is the transfer of pollen from the anthers of stamens to the stigmas of, mostly, other flowers. This is usually accomplished by insects and other animals, less frequently by wind, or occasionally by water. Upon their conveyance onto a stigma, pollen-grains form pollen-tubes that grow downward through the style to the ovary and thence to the ovules within, where male sperm cells are inserted to fertilize the contained eggs. A fertilized egg develops into an embryo within the ovule, which eventually matures as a seed, and its enveloping ovary as the fruit. After dispersal and often a dormant period, seeds may germinate in suitable sites to produce seedlings that grow into new plants.

Much variation exists among angiosperm flowers with respect to the basic parts, including number, size, fusion, texture, colour, the presence or absence of whole floral sets, and the flower-symmetry. Complete flowers have all four floral sets, while

Red wood lily.

incomplete flowers are missing one or more whole sets of parts. Both functional stamens and pistils are present in bisexual (or perfect) flowers, but the absence of either results in unisexual (or imperfect) flowers. Monoecious plants have both staminate (male) and pistillate (female) flowers present on the same individuals (e.g., birches and cattails); but they are borne on different plants in dioecious plant groups, resulting in separate male and female individuals in a population (e.g., willows and poplars). Those flowering plants that are pollinated by insects tend to display more conspicuous corollas (e.g., lilies, orchids, roses, milkweeds, snapdragons), while wind-pollinated plants generally have quite inconspicuous and often much-reduced flowers (e.g., birches, maples, goosefoots, grasses, sedges). While the term *wildflowers* often seems used to refer only or mainly to the more conspicuously flowered herbaceous plants in nature, the flowering plants include all species with true flowers, whether these are conspicuous or not, and whether the plants are herbaceous or woody. The many diverse character combinations of floral structures and other plant attributes among angiosperms serve to distinguish the numerous species and higher groupings.

Common (or vernacular) names for flowering plants originated independently in many places over the world, resulting in a multiplicity of names differing among regions, cultures, and languages. As the science of botany developed, professional botanists, to avoid confusion, established a worldwide, standardized, scientific naming system governed by internationally accepted rules, the International Code of Botanical Nomenclature (ICBN). The scientific names for plant species are in Latin form and consist of two parts: a genus name and a species epithet.

In modern plant classifications, the flowering plants are recognized as a major group within the Plant Kingdom, usually at the division or subdivision level, and comprised of two large subgroups, the monocotyledons and dicotyledons. Approximately a quarter-million species of angiosperms exist worldwide, which are grouped by botanists into about 300 plant families of various sizes. Globally, the largest flowering plant families in number of included species are: the orchid family (Orchidaceae), with over 17,000 species; the aster family (Asteraceae), with about 13,000 species; the legume family (Fabaceae), with about 12,000 species; and the grass family (Poaceae), with about 10,000 species.

Listed for Canada are 141 naturally occurring families of flowering plants, including 891 genera and 4,006 species. The largest angiosperm families in Canada in number of included species are: the aster family, with 525 species; the grass family, with 312 species; the sedge family (Cyperaceae), with 358 species; the rose family (Rosaceae), with 207 species; the legume family, with 192 species; and the mustard family (Brassicaceae), with 177 species. About 78%

DEAN NERNBERG PHOTO/COURTESY OF ENVIRONMENT CANADA, CANADIAN WILDLIFE SERVICE

Needle-and-thread grass.

of Canadian species are native (i.e., indigenous or original), and 22% naturalized (i.e., exotic introductions becoming naturally established).

Recognized for Saskatchewan are 127 families of flowering plants, including 600 genera and 1,625 species. The largest families in Saskatchewan in number of included species are: the aster family, with 240 species; the grass family, with 197 species; the sedge family, with 150 species; the mustard family, with 78 species; and the legume family, with 56 species. Following closely, with about 50 species each, are the rose family, goosefoot family (Chenopodiaceae), and pink family (Caryophyllaceae). The sedge genus, *Carex*, with 168 species, is the largest in Saskatchewan in number of species and is distantly trailed by: the willow genus, *Salix*, with 31 species; the milkvetch genus (*Astragalus*), with 24 species; the rush genus, Juncus, with 22 species; and the violet genus, Viola, with 20 species. About 80% of Saskatchewan's flowering plants are native, and 20% are introduced and naturalized.

It is impossible to describe the whole spectrum of Saskatchewan flowering species in a brief account. They range from the many brightly coloured wildflowers and less conspicuously flowered plants of prairies, woodlands, and byways to sundry trees and shrubs, aquatic plants, sedges and grasses. Possibly surprising to those who do not envisage such plants at this latitude, there are 10 species of carnivorous (insect-eating) plants, 25 orchid species, and three cactus species native to Saskatchewan.

It is noteworthy that flowering plants are particularly well represented among Saskatchewan's official emblems, including not only the official provincial flower, the red wood lily (*Lilium philadelphicum* var. *andinum*), but also the provincial tree, the white birch (*Betula papyrifera*),

and the provincial grass, the needle-and-thread (*Heterostipa comata*). *Vernon L. Harms*

FURTHER READING: Harms, Vernon L. 2003. *Checklist of the Vascular Plants of Saskatchewan, and the Provincially and Nationally Rare Native Plants in Saskatchewan*. Saskatoon: University of Saskatchewan Extension Press; Scoggan, H.J. 1978. *The Flora of Canada, Part 1*. Ottawa: National Museum of Natural Sciences; Willis, J.C. 1973. *A Dictionary of the Flowering Plants and Ferns*, 8th edition. Cambridge: Cambridge University Press.

FLYCATCHERS. Saskatchewan flycatchers are of the New World family Tyrannidae, usually called the "tyrant flycatchers," to distinguish them from other families of small songbirds with the habit of sitting on an exposed perch and sallying out in pursuit of a single insect. All of these are called "flycatchers." The tyrant flycatchers make up a large family of about 420 species, with thirty-seven occurring in North America. They are large-headed, with broad bills, and sit erect at the ends of branches or other open perch. They often have a small crest. Many look very similar, making their identification difficult; it is often necessary to hear their call rather than judging by their appearance. Their habit of fiercely protecting their territory from other birds, including larger ones, gives them their common name of "tyrant" flycatcher. Thus, we often see kingbirds chasing hawks, crows, robins, and other species.

Saskatchewan has confirmed records of fourteen species; all are migratory. The regularly occurring species belong to five genera. The genus *Contopus* contains the olive-sided flycatcher (*C. borealis*), a fairly common breeding species in the boreal forests, and two species of pewees: the Western wood-pewee (*C. sordidulus*), a regular breeder in the southern boreal forest and prairie woodlots; and the Eastern wood-pewee (*C. virens*), a rare breeder in the southeast. Both pewees are drab greyish-brown birds with wingbars, and they are distinguished by their calls.

The genus *Empidonax* contains five species of small (12–13 cm) flycatchers which are so similar that many birders simply identify them by the genus. The most abundant is the little least flycatcher (*E. minimus*), nesting throughout most of the province except for the north; its ringing chee-bek is a familiar sound. The alder flycatcher (*E. alnorum*) is also fairly common through the centre, while the more strongly marked yellow-bellied flycatcher (*E. flaviventris*) is occasionally seen and heard in the bogs of the boreal region. The willow flycatcher (*E. traillii*), closely related to the alder flycatcher, is apparently limited to the river valley woodlands of the south. The dusky flycatcher (*E. oberholseri*), a western species, has been identified only in the CYPRESS HILLS.

The Eastern phoebe (*Sayornis phoebe*) is a dark-backed light-bellied bird which is a fairly common nester in the middle of the province, nesting near water. Say's phoebe (*S. saya*) is more brightly coloured, with a grey back and head, black tail, and light orange chest and belly; it nests in the southwest and is occasionally seen further east and north. The great crested flycatcher (*Myiarchus crinitus*) is a larger (24 cm) brown bird with tawny outer primaries and tail, which nests in the transition deciduous woodlands of the south-central region. The kingbirds, which are about the same size, are more common birds. The yellow-bellied, grey-backed Western kingbird (*Tyrannus verticalis*) is a common nester in farm shelterbelts and other areas of plantings in the grasslands. The Eastern kingbird (*T. tyrannus*), with its dark grey back and head, white belly and white terminal tail band, is common in the shrubs, tree stands and coulee trees of the south. In the north it is less common, nesting in shrubby open areas. The distinctive scissor-tailed flycatcher (*Tyrannus forficatus*) is a straggler from the southern United States.   *Diane Secoy*

FURTHER READING: Alsop, F.J., III. 2002. *Birds of Canada*. New York: Dorling Kindersley.

FLYING DUST FIRST NATION. Chief Kopahawakemum, as leader of the Meadow Lake First Nation, signed TREATY 6 on September 3, 1878, at Fort Carlton. A reserve immediately north of Meadow Lake was settled in 1889 by this Cree nation. Annuity payments were received at Fort Carlton between 1899 and 1904, at the Battleford Agency between 1905 and 1948, and in June 1948 the Meadow Lake Agency was formed. It is unknown when Chief Kopahawakemum passed away, but Aypaspik was noted as chief in 1899. On July 3, 1909, James Bear became chief, and remained in office until 1918. Matchee (Good Little Hunter) was born about 1863 on the Stony Point Reserve in northern Manitoba and moved to Pasqua-Se-Kee-Ha-Gan (Meadow Lake) when he was 17. He became chief when he was 60 years old in 1923, and as a hereditary chief was not replaced until he passed away. Initially the forest provided the band with building materials, game, fish, and berries, and as they became agriculturally productive they were able to sell livestock, dairy and poultry products. The band controls 5,254.8 ha of reserve land (.2 in the town of Meadow Lake); of the 1,000 band members, 396 people live on reserve.   *Christian Thompson*

FOAM LAKE, town, pop 1,218, located SE of Wynyard at the junction of Hwys 16 and 310. The first family of settlers in the region arrived in the early summer of 1882; the Milligans named a shallow body of water in the region Foam Lake, as a froth often developed along its shores. The first

Icelanders arrived in the district in 1892, and during the first decade of the 20th century many Ukrainians arrived to take up land. Settlement of the area was greatly hastened by the arrival of the railway at Sheho in 1904; three years later, as the CPR was pushing westward again, the townsite of Foam Lake was established. The first buildings were erected in 1907, and in 1908 the fledgling community was incorporated as a village. By the early 1920s, the population was well over 400, and in 1924 Foam Lake attained town status; it became the major service and distribution centre for the surrounding agricultural district. Town and area attractions include: the Foam Lake Museum, housed in the former 1926 town hall; the 1915 Douglas Heritage House; and the Foam Lake Heritage Marsh, an important staging area for migratory birds.   *David McLennan*

FOLK, RICK (1950–). Born on March 5, 1950, in Saskatoon, Rick Folk is a world champion men's curler. Folk's Saskatoon rink won the 1970 Saskatchewan Junior Men's championship, while his mixed curling teams captured five provincial (1974–75, 1981–83) and two Canadian (1974, 1983) mixed championships. His rinks won three consecutive Saskatchewan Men's titles (1978–80), and both the Canadian Brier and the Air Canada Silver Broom as world curling champions in 1980. Consisting of Folk, Ron Mills, Tom Wilson, and Jim Wilson, the team brought Canada its first world title since 1972. Folk moved to British Columbia in the late 1980s and skipped his Kelowna-based rink to four provincial crowns (1989, 1993–95), and to the 1994 Brier and World Curling Championship. Folk's Silver Broom foursome were inducted into the SASKATCHEWAN SPORTS HALL OF FAME in 1980 and the Canadian Curling Hall of Fame in 1985. His 1974 and 1983 mixed rinks were inducted into the Saskatchewan Sports Hall of Fame in 2004.
Daria Coneghan and Holden Stoffel

FOLLICULAR WAVES. In 2003 a UNIVERSITY OF SASKATCHEWAN research team funded by the Canadian Institutes of Health Research uncovered evidence suggesting that the traditionally accepted model of the human menstrual cycle is wrong. This discovery, initially published in the scientific journal *Fertility and Sterility*, may lead to the design of new, safer and more effective contraception, and may improve success with assisted reproductive technology for women who are having trouble conceiving. Dr. Roger Pierson, head of the university's Reproductive Biology Unit, received the 2003 Women's Health Hero Award from *Chatelaine* magazine for the discovery; in addition, *Discover* magazine ranked the results among the top 100 science stories of the year.

Previous research had shown that a group of 15–20 follicles grew during the menstrual cycle, and

that one follicle from the group was selected to ovulate while the others died off. The new research found that this process occurs in waves: in response to hormone surges, women experience two to three periods of follicular development each month, although only one egg is selected for ovulation. As a result, it is estimated that up to 40% of women may not be able to use natural family planning methods: for women who experience two or three waves of dominant follicle growth per month, there is no "safe" time to have intercourse during the cycle, as there may always be a follicle capable of ovulating. The study, involving sixty-three women with normal menstrual cycles who underwent ultrasound every day for a month, was the culmination of a long-term collaboration between Roger Pierson, veterinarian Gregg Adams, and biologist Angela Baerwald.
Joe Ralko

FOND DU LAC DENESULINE FIRST NATION. The Dene-speaking Fond du Lac Desenuline First Nation signed an adhesion to TREATY 8 in July 1899 as part of Maurice Piche's band. They hunted, fished, and trapped in order to live—as they continue to this day. The Chipewyan word "Denesuline" translates as "people of the barrens"; they are also referred to as "*Ethen-eldeli*" or "caribou-eaters." In the 1930s, government officials began discussing the possibility of setting aside reserves for the Denesuline. By 1944 the band was anxious to have a reserve set aside in northeastern Saskatchewan and the Northwest Territories, but it was not until January 11, 1960, that the Department of Indian Affairs acknowledged an outstanding treaty land entitlement for the band and allowed land selections to be made. Economic development for this community includes commercial fishing, trapping, and mining. The infrastructure comprises an airstrip, band office complex, school and teacherage, fisherman's cold storage plant, fire hall, senior citizen centre, arena, nursing station and nursing staff residency, day care, and various community maintenance facilities. The main community area of the Fond du Lac Denesuline First Nation Reserve is located on the northeast side of Lake Athabasca. The band has a total land base of 36,812 ha; there are a total of 1,576 band members, with 869 people residing on reserve.
Christian Thompson

FOOD PROCESSING INDUSTRY. Saskatchewan's agricultural industry is best known for the production and export of cereal grains, oilseeds, pulses and livestock—hence the long-held stereotype of its being the "wheat province." Less well known is that Saskatchewan boasts a small yet rapidly growing food processing industry. According to Saskatchewan Agriculture, Food and Rural Revitalization, in 2002 the largest processing and manufacturing sector in the province was the food

Table FPI-1. Value of Food and Beverage Product Exports from Saskatchewan, 1995–2000 (in millions of dollars)			
Year	Food products	Beverage products	Total Export
1995	$1,107	$64	$1,172
1996	$1,263	$81	$1,344
1997	$1,534	$104	$1,638
1998	$1,665	$88	$1,754
1999	$1,628	$89	$1,718
2000	$1,716	$91	$1,807

Source: Government of Saskatchewan Agriculture, Food and Rural Revitalization

and beverage industry, which accounted for approximately one-third of all manufacturing shipments. Over the period 1995-2000, the value of food and beverage shipments increased by 54%, from $1,172 million to $1,807 million (see Table FPI-1). More than fifty processors actively export processed food products from the province. Total exports from the sector increased by 125% between 1995 and 2001 (from $14.6 million to $32.9 million). The United States, Japan, the Pacific Rim and Mexico are key markets for food and beverage exports. Recent information (2004) from the Saskatchewan Food Processors Association reveals that the approximately 300 food processors in Saskatchewan employ more than 7,000 people, have an annual payroll of more than $225 million, and post annual shipments in excess of approximately $2 billion.

The food and beverage processing sector is characterized by having a high proportion of very small companies, with over 70% employing fewer than ten people, and approximately 40% fewer than five. More than half of the processors are located in rural Saskatchewan; but a few large meat processing companies, a similar number of cereal, oilseed and pulse processors, and a large dairy products manufacturer, mostly located in or near Saskatoon, dominate the industry with respect to the number of employees and the value of total shipments. Although Saskatchewan will remain distant from major markets for processed products, if it can develop a stronger entrepreneurial and value-added processing culture it can look forward to continued growth in both the size and the complexity of its food processing industry. Its pristine environment and access to a wide variety of high-quality raw materials, combined with relatively low production costs, support industry development. To assist in this development, the Food Centre was established in 1997 at the UNIVERSITY OF SASKATCHEWAN. It is a partnership between the government of Saskatchewan, the University and the Saskatchewan Food Processors Association. Its mandate is to work with small and intermediate-sized processors to develop

food products and assist in business development, including processing technologies and marketing.

Robert Tyler

FOOD RETAILING AND WHOLESALING. Food retailing and wholesaling is an important sector in the Saskatchewan economy. Saskatchewan consumers spend about 10.7% of their disposable income on grocery (food, non-food, and alcoholic beverages) items; this generates $2 billion in sales annually. There are over 1,100 retail stores in Saskatchewan, employing 13,500 people. The food retailing industry in Canada is dominated by a small number of large firms. Market shares for food retailers in Manitoba/Saskatchewan in September 2003 were: Westfair (a subsidiary of Loblaw Companies Ltd.; stores include Extra Foods and Superstore)—27.8%; Canada Safeway (a subsidiary of Safeway Inc.)—20.3%; Federated Co-operatives Ltd—16.2%; Wal-Mart—8.7%; others (including IGA and Garden Market IGA and also independent retail stores—28%. The market shares change continually as firms merge, existing firms decline, and new competitors emerge. Wal-Mart has been rapidly increasing its market share in Canada.

The large grocery retailers carry a diverse array of food and household products; on average, these grocery stores carry 24,000 different items. Most of them operate their own wholesaling divisions, and own wholesale distribution depots throughout western Canada. There are also a number of small, independent food retail stores. While some of these are general grocery retailers carrying a range of food items, many more specialize in the retailing of meat, fish or other fresh items. Organic foods, although still a small component of total food demand, are growing rapidly: there are several small specialized organic food stores, and the major retail stores are carrying an increasing number of organic food items.

Food retailing has developed into a high-technology business. The major food grocery chains utilize barcoding and scanner technology as an integral part of their supply chain management practices. The barcodes attached to individual items are read by electronic scanners at the checkout, and enable the company to manage its inventory more accurately. As items are sold, new items can be ordered automatically from the company's distribution centres; advertising and promotion can be based on this information. Retailers are responsible for ensuring that food products are labelled appropriately: In January 2003, the Canadian government passed a new law requiring mandatory nutrition labeling for food products. The retailing sector participates in industry consultations with the federal government on food labeling regulations and food standards through the Canadian Council of Grocery Distributors (CCGD). CCGD members account for over 80% of grocery distribution in Canada.

Jill E. Hobbs

FOOTBALL. Football, as it has come to be known in Canada, evolved from the game of rugby in the late 19th and early 20th centuries. Members of the North-West Mounted Police are reported to have played the game as early as 1886 and engaged in inter-city contests by 1890. Rugby was played sporadically for the next two decades, primarily as part of the festivities on holidays or at local fairs. The staging of the first Grey Cup in Toronto in 1909 evidently inspired the organization of a men's amateur rugby league in 1910; but of the five original cities who were to take part, only Moose Jaw and Regina fielded teams. Moose Jaw swept the four games, but the Regina Rugby Club would win 21 of 22 provincial championships between 1911 and 1935.

Resistance to western participation in the Grey Cup kept the "national" championship an all-eastern affair until 1922. Regina reached the Grey Cup final six times from 1923 to 1934, but lost every time. Known as the Roughriders from 1924 on, the team was a western powerhouse—but not equal to the elite squads in Ontario and Montreal. Meanwhile, the province was making swifter inroads in junior football. Saskwanis, an essentially self-coached Saskatoon squad, won two western titles and all but one game from 1921 to 1923, but was shut out of the national championship by an "East-only" policy that prevailed until 1925. The Regina Pats broke through to a Canadian junior title in 1928 with an 8–6 triumph over the St. Thomas (Ontario) Tigers. Ten years later the REGINA DALES, a ragtag group from the "wrong side of the tracks" coached and managed on a shoestring budget by PAUL DOJACK, went on to become one of the Canadian Football League's most accomplished teams.

The Roughriders went through a prolonged slump until 1951, when quarterback Glen Dobbs was signed to a contract and led the team to first place and its first Grey Cup appearance in 17 years, only to fall 21–14 to the Ottawa Rough Riders. Now renamed the SASKATCHEWAN ROUGHRIDERS, the team followed the nationwide trend to import top players from the United States but rely on Canadians to fill most of the roster. Many of the team's most reliable veterans in the 1950s and 1960s were Canadian. Two junior programs, the Saskatoon Hilltops and Regina Rams, were established in 1947 and 1954 respectively; Saskatoon won its first of twelve Canadian championships in 1953, while the Rams won fifteen times from 1966 to 1998, after which the organization was integrated into the UNIVERSITY OF REGINA. In addition, the UNIVERSITY OF SASKATCHEWAN Huskies, moribund from 1950 to 1958, were resurrected in 1959. Many of the players from these teams would go on to play for the Roughriders in the 1960s, including defensive linemen Ron Atchison and BILL CLARKE, linebacker Wayne Shaw, defensive backs Dale West and Ted Dushinski, receiver Gordon Barwell and centre Ted

SASKATCHEWAN ARCHIVES BOARD R-A27624-42

Western Interprovincial Football Union action at Park De Young (later renamed Taylor Field), 1947. A Regina Roughriders ball carrier tries to elude two opponents.

FURTHER READING: Kelly, G. 2001. Green Grit: *The Story of the Saskatchewan Roughriders*. Toronto: HarperCollins.

FORAGE CROPS. Forage crops are grass and legume plant species that are grown for livestock feed as well as land conservation and reclamation. It is the vegetative portion of the plant, mainly leaves and stems, which is consumed by livestock. Forage crops are fibrous in nature; ruminant livestock, such as cattle and sheep, require this fibre in their diet for proper digestion. They also obtain nutrients such as protein, minerals, and vitamins from forage crops. As forage plants mature, they become more fibrous and have lower concentrations of essential nutrients. Forage crops can be grazed directly by animals in pastures, or conserved for winter feeding as hay or silage.

In Saskatchewan, forage crops are grown on close to three million hectares (Census of Canada, 2001), second only to wheat. Most forage crops are consumed by livestock on the same farm on which they were produced. However, a certain portion of the seeded forage area is used for the production of high-quality alfalfa pellets and cubes, most of which are exported. There is also a growing baled hay industry in the province, serving both the domestic and export markets.

Both annual and perennial plant species are used as forage crops, but perennials are much more commonly utilized. Alfalfa (*Medicago sativa* L.), a legume, is the most important forage crop in Saskatchewan. It offers high productivity, excellent quality, drought tolerance, and the ability to fix and utilize atmospheric nitrogen—thus not requiring the addition of nitrogen fertilizer. Saskatchewan is the

Urness. The Roughriders' greatest stars, however, were running back **GEORGE REED** and quarterback **RON LANCASTER**, who joined Saskatchewan in 1963 and would play thirteen and fifteen seasons respectively. Reed's career record of 16,116 yards stood until 2004, while Lancaster was the first professional quarterback to pass for more than 50,000 yards. The 1963–76 period became known as the era of the "Jolly Green Giants," when the Roughriders always made the playoffs, finished first five times, played in the Grey Cup game five times, and won it for the first time in 1966 with a 29–14 decision over Ottawa.

Immediately afterward came a period of futility in which the Roughriders failed to make the playoffs for eleven straight seasons (1977–87), followed by an unexpected Grey Cup victory in 1989 in what is frequently called "the greatest CFL game ever played," a 43–40 thriller against the Hamilton Tiger-Cats. Since then, the Roughriders have struggled through more bad times than good, with only one Grey Cup appearance (1997) and no regular-season finish higher than third place since 1988. Fan support has remained fairly constant, with attendance averaging about 25,000 in Taylor Field, where capacity has yet to reach 28,000 (seating was temporarily boosted to slightly more than 50,000 for the hosting of the Grey Cup game in 1995 and 2003). Although CFL rosters are essentially half American and the "draft" system of obtaining Canadian players has reduced the convenience of stocking home-grown players, Saskatchewan players continue to stand out on the Roughriders: guard Roger Aldag of Gull Lake was enshrined in the CFL Hall of Fame for his superb career (1976–92), and Gene Makowsky

of Saskatoon was the league's outstanding offensive lineman in 2004. The Roughriders have been "community-owned" since 1951: individuals can buy memberships and have a say in the selection of the board of directors, which monitors the team's finances and is responsible for the hiring and firing of the team's general manager and chief executive officer. The general manager selects the head coach, and either directs or delegates the management of all football operations. The chief executive officer oversees office management and day-to-day business operations.

University football has been a success story for the province's two teams, who compete in the Canada West conference of Canadian Interuniversity Sports (CIS). The Saskatchewan Huskies earned the Vanier Cup as national champions in 1990, 1996 and 1998 and were runners-up three times since 1988. Regina's performance has been sporadic since entering CIS competition in 1999, but it gained distinction as the national runner-up in only its second season. On the high school level, the SHSAA maintains competitive balance by dividing the province into twelve-man 4A, twelve-man 3A, nine-man, 2A six-man and 1A six-man leagues. Regina and Saskatoon league teams with more than 326 male students in Grades 10–12 are classified 4A. Other Regina and Saskatoon league teams, in addition to all Moose Jaw schools, are classified 3A. Schools with 86 to 250 boys in Grades 10–12 play nine-man football. Six-man football (played on a slightly smaller field) is designated 1A for schools in the lower half of enrollments of Grade 10–12 boys (maximum 43), and 2A for the upper half (maximum 85).

John Chaput

AGRICULTURE AND AGRI-FOOD CANADA 93-07-054

Alfalfa is the most important forage crop in Saskatchewan.

world's largest producer of alfalfa seed, with markets across Canada and in many other countries.

The most widely grown grass species are smooth bromegrass (*Bromus inermis* L.), meadow bromegrass (*Bromus riparius* Rehm.), and crested wheatgrass (*Agropyron cristatum* L.). These grasses, which are the principal species seeded in pastures, show high productivity, winter hardiness, and drought tolerance, and are commonly mixed with alfalfa in fields for hay production. There are a large number of other grass and legume species used as forage crops, giving Saskatchewan producers a choice of species adapted to almost any soil and climatic condition. Forage legumes and grasses, because of their wide adaptability and long-lived perennial nature, are frequently used for revegetation of disturbed areas such as roadsides and mines, as low maintenance turf species, and for wildlife habitat preservation. *Bruce Coulman*

FURTHER READING: Barnes, R.F., D.A. Miller and C.J. Nelson. 1995. *Forages: An Introduction to Grassland Agriculture, Vol. 1*. Ames, Iowa: Iowa State University Press.

FOREST FRINGE SETTLEMENT. The southern dust-bowl of the 1930s forced farmers to seek land in the drought-free forest fringes of northern Saskatchewan. Urban relief recipients also participated in this "back-to-the-land" scheme, all hoping for a better life. An estimated 45,000 people migrated north between 1930 and 1936. Government policy and control of this migration varied. Federal and provincial settlement schemes tried to place migrants onto abandoned homesteads or otherwise improved land; loans averaging $300 were available. The SASKATCHEWAN RELIEF COMMISSION would pay to move settlers' effects on boxcars, but local history books suggest politics decided who did and did not qualify for these schemes: as a result, many settlers moved north without government help, purchasing land or squatting wherever possible. The intense migration pressure meant that families took homesteads on any available land, suitable for agriculture or not. Conditions in the north were harsh: subsistence crops and gardens grown on land hacked from the bush faced fire, frost, and rust; prairie animals died of swamp fever. Cash made from cutting cordwood and railway ties, fishing, hunting, and trapping helped, but most settlers still needed direct relief. This desperate situation forced the creation of the NORTHERN SETTLERS RE-ESTABLISHMENT BRANCH (Department of Municipal Affairs) in 1935 to provide relief and bring self-sufficiency to the forest fringe. Its program relocated farmers, converted unsuitable farmland back to public land, broke and drained arable land, and constructed roads. These measures, combined with the abandonment of unworkable homesteads dur-

ing and following WORLD WAR II, improved conditions in the north for White settlers. For Aboriginal peoples, the arrival of these migrants led to competition for already scarce resources and to further marginalization. *Merle Massie*

FURTHER READING: Powell, T.J.D. 1977. "Northern Settlement, 1929-1935," *Saskatchewan History* 30 (3): 81–98; McDonald, J. 1981. "Soldier Settlement and Depression Settlement in the Forest Fringe of Saskatchewan," *Prairie Forum* 6 (1): 35–55.

FOREST NURSERY STATIONS: *see* **PRAIRIE FARM REHABILITATION ADMINISTRATION (PFRA) SHELTERBELT CENTRE**

FORESTRY. The federal government controlled forestry in Saskatchewan prior to 1930. The first legislation applicable to the area's forests, the Dominion Lands Act of 1872, permitted the designation of timber districts and forest reserves. Ottawa continued to regulate forestry administration until the Natural Resources Transfer Agreement of 1930 transferred natural resources and Crown lands to Saskatchewan. Forestry has long served as a major part of Saskatchewan's economy: early logging and wood processing operations concentrated in the southern fringe of the commercial forest zone; large sawmills operated at Prince Albert, Big River, Crooked River, and Prairie River by 1900; timber sawn by a large mill at The Pas, Manitoba also came mainly from Saskatchewan. Over-cutting of accessible forests and forest fires led to the closure of many early mills. During the 1930s, The Pas Lumber Company carried out one of the largest operations in Saskatchewan, with six camps and about 1,200 men working. A shift from the use of axes, cross-cut saws, and horses to power saws and mechanized skidding and hauling eliminated many forestry jobs.

Over-cutting of accessible stands again increased during WORLD WAR II. The appointment of the Saskatchewan Royal Commission on Forestry in 1945, the imposition of strict limits on cutting, and the launching of the first general forest inventory in 1947 brought unprecedented planning to forestry. An upward revision of the estimated available resource took place, preparing the way for a greatly expanded forest industry: utilization of the forest increased, from 12% of the sustainable supply in 1965 to 61% in 1995. A local pulp and paper industry took a long time to develop in Saskatchewan. Prior to construction of a local pulp mill, whole logs suitable for pulp production were exported. The first, and for many years the only, pulp mill began operating at Prince Albert in the late 1960s. WEYERHAEUSER took over the Prince Albert mill in 1986, adding a paper mill in 1988; a second pulp mill began production in 1992 when the Millar Western mill opened at Meadow Lake. Relatively

large sawmills and plywood, waferboard, and oriented strand board plants have also proven important to the industry. A shift towards operations using smaller trees and hardwood species also occurred. Meadow Lake, Big River, Prince Albert, and Hudson Bay serve as centres for wood processing. Over the decades, hundreds of small mills also operated, utilizing timber from Crown and private lands. Fire and fire control continue to determine many details of what happens in the forests.

Various companies have entered into Forest Management Agreements with Saskatchewan, designed to allow sustainable yields and benefits from the forests. More than 90% of Saskatchewan's forests grow on Crown land; nine provincial forests, designated by the Forest Act, cover about 35.6 million hectares or 54.5% of the province. Today's commercial forest zone lies largely south of the CHURCHILL RIVER; it includes about 14.4 million hectares, of which about 6.4 million hectares are available for production of forest products. In the past, centres near the southern fringe of the forest benefited most from the jobs and other benefits that flowed from forestry. A recent estimate suggests that the value of Saskatchewan's forest production can double within a decade; the challenge is to extend the benefits from forestry to the high-unemployment areas and especially the Aboriginal communities located deep in the forest. *David M. Quiring*

FORESTS. There are four types of forest in Saskatchewan: urban forests, agro-forests, commercial forests, and northern forest. They all have their importance, and each should be considered as a valuable resource. Due to the nature of the prairies and the fires which occurred regularly, there were few trees in the southern parts of the province to greet settlers, except in coulées and along river banks. Because of the short growing season and the priorities of raising farm crops, attention to trees centred mainly around using current timber for living needs. When trees were planted, it was to provide shelter from the prairie winds and the summer sun, forming the urban forest in each community. The importance of these continues to be recognized: Regina alone, for instance, has over 300,000 trees, 40% of which are elm. As agriculture developed, especially in the parklands where there were already trees, woodlands were left for shelter, fuel production, and aesthetics. Although most of these were for "own use," some of the larger areas have been used as "commercial" woodlots. From the early years the federal Department of the Interior encouraged planting: the Indian Head Forest Nursery (now the Shelterbelt Centre) was developed in 1901, and through the years has supplied over 150 million seedlings–first for the forest reserves, and later to farmers. In the 1960s the provincial Department of Natural Resources (DNR) had a woodlot program to

This forest in the Boreal Plain has trembling aspen (in fall colour) and black spruce and tamarack.

encourage management of trees on private land. There is currently increasing interest in agro-forestry, partly as another diversification avenue for farmers: the Saskatchewan Forestry Centre estimates that there are 1.9 million hectares of land highly suitable for poplar production in the agricultural zone.

Through the years the areas set aside for commercial operations have varied. In the early years there were forests scattered around the south, some of which are now provincial parks. There are today nine provincial forests forming the Northern Provincial Forest, which is well defined in, protected by, and designated in the Forest Resources Management Act (FRMA). The northern provincial forest falls in the Boreal Plain and Boreal Shield ecozones; it consists of 54.5% of the total provincial area—some 35.6 million hectares. Another 3% occurs as tree cover on private land, and another 1% on federal land. The commercial forest zone (CFZ), in the southern portion of this area, is managed by Forest Management Agreement (FMA) holders under the control and direction of the provincial Forest Service; it falls between the forest boundary on the south and the Clearwater/Churchill systems in the north, and consists of 14.5 million hectares. The area has a number of tree species such as "hardwoods" (Angiosperms, or broad-leafed trees) and "softwoods" (Gymnosperms, or conifers). The softwood species are jack pine (*Pinus banksiana* Lamb.), white spruce (*Picea glauca [Moench] Voss*); black spruce (*Picea mariana [Mill.] B.S.P.*), balsam fir (*Abies balsamea* [L] Mill.), tamarack (*Larix laricina [Du Roi] K. Koch*); and in the CYPRESS HILLS lodgepole pine (*Pinus contorta* Dougl). The hardwoods include trembling aspen (*Populus tremuloides* Michx), black poplar (*Populus balsamifera* L.), white birch (*Betula papyrifera* Marsh.), and minor populations of white elm (*Ulmus americana* L.), green ash (*Fraxinus pennsylvatica var.subintegerrima [Vahl] Fern*), and Manitoba maple (*Acer negundo* L.). In the south are bur oak (*Quercus macrocarpa* L.) and plains cottonwood (*Populus deltoides var occiden-*

talis Rydb.), with several varieties and hybrids of *P. deltoides*. Current estimates of sustainable harvest are at 7.9 million cubic metres/year, and the harvest is at 4.5 million. Calculations show that this could be increased substantially by increased fire protection and by greater production from agro-forestry sources. In addition, there is potential for using an estimated 1.5 million m³ of mill residues produced by current industry.

Saskatchewan's forest resources have been in provincial hands since the Natural Resources Transfer Act of 1930, and are administered under the provincial Forest Act of 1931. The current Forest Resources Management Act allocates timber through Forest Management Agreements (FMA), Term Cutting Licences, and Timber Permits. The industry includes one BCTMP pulp mill, one bleached kraft mill, one paper mill, two OSB (oriented strandboard) mills, one plywood mill, and several sawmills and treatment plants. It employs 24,000 people, (7,990 of whom are direct employees), and its wages represent $280 million. The primary wood products sector includes lumber (mainly white spruce), treated products such as posts, poles, rails and lumber (mainly pine), plywood, OSB, pulp and paper. The value of primary forest products shipped in 2000 was almost $900 million. Primary products are exported mostly within North America; 28% leave the continent. Traditional market patterns have shown the USA to be a major market, accounting for about 30-35% of lumber, 10-15% of treated products, and 50% of the pulp and paper. The value of secondary products totals about $100 million and includes mainly engineered building components, and cabinet and other mill-work. Most of this is sold in Saskatchewan, and the remainder in eastern Canada. While it can be seen as merely consisting of trees and wood, the forest has other uses and values—aesthetic and spiritual—as well as a potential for fishing, game, trapping, and outdoor recreation. "Non-consumptive" activities such as hiking, kayaking, and photography are increasingly pursued.

Fires are a major threat to the commercial forest, and everything is done to hold fires to a manageable size wherever possible. Historically the natural boreal forest was renewed regularly by fire, and harvest is not a perfect substitute to natural replacement. This, together with the fact that full harvest levels have never been attained, has resulted in the forest becoming generally older, especially the parts which were not as economically desirable; the susceptibility to fire and insects has therefore increased. Pest management has become an important part of forest protection, and programs have been mounted to counter mountain pine beetle (*Dendroctonus ponderosae [Hopkins]*) in the lodgepole pine forest of the Cypress Hills, and to counter spruce budworm (*Choristoneura fumiferana [Clemens]*) in the boreal forest. The latter, dif-

ficult to control, expanded rapidly during the early 1990s. Heaviest infestations are sprayed with the naturally occurring biological insecticide *Bacillus thuringiensis var Kurstaki* (Bt.K), which reduces the populations. More periodic outbreaks occur of forest tent caterpillar, jack pine budworm, and several insects of younger stands and plantations. The responsibility for forest renewal has now been handed over to the industry. The Prince Albert Nursery is the only nursery which grows for the industry; it has been leased out to PRT Inc., a private producer which now produces 13 million greenhouse grown container seedlings annually. The Shelterbelt Centre (now under PFRA) produces twenty-nine hardy tree and shrub species, and annually distributes over 5 million trees and shrubs to 10,000 prairie clients, predominantly to land owners for shelterbelts in the Agro-forestry area. The urban forest is served by several private tree nurseries which have developed varieties suitable for the Saskatchewan climate.   *Murray Little*

FORGET, AMÉDÉE EMMANUEL (1847–1923).

Born November 12, 1847, at Marieville, Canada East, where he was educated, Amédée Forget made his career in the North-West Territories. For more than forty years he sat close to the centres of non-elected power. Secretary to the Territories' governor, clerk of its Council, a commissioner of MÉTIS land claims (1885) and, later, assistant and then commissioner of Indian Affairs for Manitoba and the NWT, he was named LIEUTENANT-GOVERNOR of the Territories in 1898. His appointment as Lieutenant-Governor of Saskatchewan was controversial as he was in a privileged position to influence the compo-

Amédée Forget.

sition of the province's first government. The *Mail and Empire* termed Forget's appointment "A Crime Against the West," because he was "an instrument in the hands of Sir Wilfrid Laurier," an assertion the appointment of **WALTER SCOTT** as Premier did nothing to counter. Forget and his wife, Henriette (*née* Drolet), established the routine of vice-regal events and ceremonies that their counterparts a century later still follow: hosting, welcoming, presenting, swearing-in and laying cornerstones. Forget was Lieutenant-Governor between September 1, 1905, and October 13, 1910. He was called to the Senate in May 1911, a position he held at the time of his death on June 8, 1923.   *David E. Smith*

FURTHER READING: Hryniuk, Margaret and Garth Pugh. 1991. *A Tower of Attraction: An Illustrated History of Government House, Regina, Saskatchewan.* Regina: Government House Historical Society/Canadian Plains Research Center.

FORT À LA CORNE–CUMBERLAND HOUSE TRAIL. The trail between Fort à la Corne and Cumberland House was an important alternative travel route for the two posts during the winter months. During the summer the **NORTH SASKATCHEWAN RIVER** provided an important means of conveyance between Cumberland House, the oldest settlement in Saskatchewan (1774), and Fort à la Corne, established near the North and **SOUTH SASKATCHEWAN RIVER** forks in 1753. However, when the river froze each winter, travelers between the two posts relied on the Fort à la Corne-Cumberland House Trail. The trail generally followed the North Saskatchewan River east of the forks for more than 200 km to Cumberland House.   *James Winkel*

FORT CARLTON-GREEN LAKE TRAIL. This trail was a vital link between two very important Hudson's Bay Company trading posts during the fur trade: Fort Carlton and Green Lake. The Green Lake post was established in 1781, and Fort Carlton in 1795; the forested and often marshy regions between the two posts made travel difficult. The 176-km trail was considered by many as one of the more efficient overland routes to northern Saskatchewan via the Green, Beaver and Churchill river systems. Fort Carlton became the company's distribution centre for the entire northwest, and Green Lake was the closest post that connected overland trails to the **CHURCHILL RIVER**.   *James Winkel*

FORT CARLTON-TOUCHWOOD TRAIL. This trail was widely used by First Nations and Métis traders during the early stages of the fur trade. Once Fort Carlton was established in 1795, its main provisional supply cache became Fort Touchwood. The trail was approximately 240 km long; the western terminus was Fort Carlton, and the eastern terminus

Fort Touchwood, near present-day Punnichy. The Fort Carlton-Touchwood Trail became a common patrol route for the North-West Mounted Police after the **NORTH-WEST RESISTANCE** in 1885.   *James Winkel*

FORT ELLICE–WOOD MOUNTAIN TRAIL. The Fort Ellice-Wood Mountain Trail was a provisional route used primarily in the late 18th century. Although many of Saskatchewan's earliest trails were used to haul fur, there were also those that carried provisions. The Fort Ellice-Wood Mountain Trail was widely known for its use as a pemmican supply route from 1757 until the 1850s. The trail was longer than most (approximately 400 km), and it connected Fort Ellice (near present-day St. Lazare, Manitoba) and Wood Mountain, Saskatchewan. It also became the primary route to Moosomin after the establishment of the **CANNINGTON MANOR** agricultural settlement in the mid-1880s.   *James Winkel*

FORT PITT. Founded in 1829 and located at a large bend in the **NORTH SASKATCHEWAN RIVER**, Fort Pitt was the Hudson's Bay Company's major trading post between Fort Carlton and Fort Edmonton. From 1829 to 1876 Fort Pitt's main role in the fur trade was to supply provisions such as dried meat, buffalo grease, and furs. In 1876, Fort Pitt and Fort Carlton were chosen to co-host the signing of **TREATY 6**. Fort Pitt was also to play an important part in the **NORTH-WEST RESISTANCE** of 1885. On March 26, 1885, the **MÉTIS** uprising and victory over government forces at **DUCK LAKE** encouraged the **CREE** in the western region of Saskatchewan to confront the government. On April 2, 1885, Cree warriors of **BIG BEAR**'s band, led by Wandering Spirit, killed nine people and took several hostages at **FROG LAKE**. After the massacre, 250 Cree warriors moved from Frog Lake to camp on a hill overlooking Fort Pitt, the closest fort to Frog Lake. Not having enough horses or wagons to allow them to escape, the people in Fort Pitt prepared for a siege. There were 67 people in the fort at the time, including approximately 23 NWMP stationed there under the command of Inspector Francis Dickens, son of Charles Dickens, the British author. The fort, built for trading, provided very little protection for the police and the other occupants. On April 13, 1885, Dickens sent Constables Clarence Loasby, David Cowan and Henry Quinn out of the fort to try to locate Big Bear's camp.

The next morning W.J. McLean, Chief Trader for the Hudson's Bay Company, met with Big Bear, Imasees and Wandering Spirit to negotiate a peaceful settlement to the siege. McLean and Big Bear were able to convince Wandering Spirit to let the police leave safely if the Hudson's Bay employees gave themselves up to Big Bear. The three scouts sent out the previous day were returning to the fort when they unexpectedly came upon the Indian

camp. The Indians, believing that they were being attacked, opened fire. Cowan was killed immediately; Quinn escaped, but was captured the following day; Loasby, seriously wounded, was nevertheless able to ride to safety. The negotiations at the Cree camp were concluded: while the police were allowed to escape by boat down the North Saskatchewan River to Battleford, the 44 civilians of the fort became prisoners of the Cree. Once the police had left, the fort was looted and burned by the Cree. On May 25, General Strange and the Alberta Field Force used the fort as the militia's battle headquarters until the campaign ended in July 1885. Fort Pitt was partially rebuilt in 1886, and then closed in 1890.   *Daria Coneghan*

FORT QU'APPELLE, town, pop 1,940, located in the **QU'APPELLE VALLEY** 70 km NE of Regina between Echo and Mission Lakes. The community is served by Hwys 10, 22, 35, 56, and 210. Named for the **QU'APPELLE RIVER**, Fort Qu'Appelle was the crossroads of a number of historic trails that traversed the North-West Territories. An Anglican mission was established in 1854 and the Hudson's Bay Company built a post at Fort Qu'Appelle in 1864. After 1870, there was an influx of Métis from Red River. Cree and Saulteaux peoples signed **TREATY 4** at Fort Qu'Appelle in 1874, followed somewhat thereafter by the establishment of a NWMP post. Chief **SITTING BULL** and a party of Sioux travelled to Fort Qu'Appelle from Wood Mountain in 1881 to secure provisions, and to negotiate with Superintendent James Walsh in a last-ditch effort to remain in Canada. A post office was established at Fort Qu'Appelle in 1880; settlers began to appear and the homesteading era began in earnest. At least a dozen businesses had been established by 1882. On April 6, 1885, General **MIDDLETON** marched out of Fort Qu'Appelle en route to **BATOCHE**. As the fur trade waned and the district became increasingly settled, agriculture came to play a significant role in the expansion of the community. Shortly after the province of Saskatchewan was formed, Fort Qu'Appelle, along with several other communities, vied to become the new provincial capital; however, Premier **SCOTT** was unswayed and the seat of government remained at Regina. Significant development of Fort Qu'Appelle occurred in the years prior to World War I as the railway came through the valley. The recreational potential of the district began to be exploited and numerous cottages began to appear on the area lakes. In 1913, construction began on a fish culture station near Fort Qu'Appelle and, to date, the facility has supplied more than 2 billion fish to stock water bodies throughout the province. Construction began on the Fort Qu'Appelle Sanatorium (Fort San) for tuberculosis patients in 1912, though wartime exigencies delayed its opening until 1917. Fort Qu'Appelle experienced steady growth and, on January 1, 1951, the community attained town status. The population that year was 878 and the town continued growing until the early 1980s, at which point the population stabilized close to its current level. Today, Fort Qu'Appelle is a shopping, service, and institutional centre serving the surrounding farming community, neighbouring resort villages, cottagers and summer vacationers, as well as several area First Nations reserves, the nearest of those being the Standing Buffalo and Pasqua First Nations. A Treaty 4 Governance Centre was completed at Fort Qu'Appelle in recent years, housing administrative and educational offices for the 34 bands that comprise the Treaty 4 First Nations. The facility also includes an archives, a museum, and a cultural centre, and a striking feature of the building is the Legislative Council Chamber, designed in the form of a large contemporary teepee. The former Hudson's Bay Company store in Fort Qu'Appelle, built in 1897, remains a community landmark, as does the 1911 Grand Trunk Pacific Railway station.

David McLennan

FORT WALSH. In response to the **CYPRESS HILLS MASSACRE** of June 1, 1873, Sir John A. Macdonald passed a bill establishing a police force to be known as the North-West Mounted Police (NWMP). The force's mandate was to bring law and order to the North-West Territories by suppressing the illegal whiskey trade, asserting Canadian sovereignty, and peacefully encouraging the First Nations to sign treaties. After 1869 the Hudson's Bay Company had seldom ventured into the **CYPRESS HILLS** area, allowing Americans to trade whiskey and bison robes without competition or interference. By 1873, at least four trading posts were operating along Battle Creek, which runs through the Cypress Hills. Two of the posts, one owned by Moses Solomon and the other by Abel Farwell, were located near the scene of the Cypress Hills Massacre.

On June 1, 1873, a group of American "wolfers" were staying at Farwell's camp. The wolfers wrongly believed that the group of Assiniboine Indians camped nearby had stolen forty head of horses from them; after much drinking, the wolfers set out to take revenge. When the battle was over, nearly 30 Assiniboine and one White man had been killed. In June 1875, Inspector James Morrow Walsh and about 30 men of "B" troop, NWMP, were dispatched to the Cypress Hills region; there they built Fort Walsh, a short distance from where the massacre occurred. The NWMP investigation of the Cypress Hills Massacre showed that illegal whiskey trading by American "wolfers" and horse thieving had led to the event. Even though the police were unsuccessful in convicting any of the participants in the massacre, the First Nations people appreciated their efforts. The good relationship that developed between the police and the First Nations of the area aided in the implementation of the Canadian Indian policy. Adhesions to **TREATY 4** were signed at Fort Walsh in 1877, and to **TREATY 6** in 1879 and 1882.

The importance of Fort Walsh reached its peak during the Lakota refugee crisis, when **SITTING BULL** and 5,000 Lakota Sioux followers took refuge from the US Army after the battle of the Little Big Horn in 1876. After the Lakota refugees arrived in the area, Fort Walsh was reinforced and in 1878 it was made NWMP headquarters. All NWMP communication went through Fort Walsh, and new recruits received their basic training there. Inspector Walsh and his men were to ensure that Canadian law was enforced, that the Sioux did not conduct raids on the Americans, and that peace was kept between the Canadian and American First Nations. Walsh and his American counterparts were able to convince the majority of the Sioux refugees to return to the US by late 1879. The Lakota crisis finally ended when Sitting Bull and his followers were delivered to US authorities on July 17, 1881. The sixty Lakota who remained in the area were finally granted a small reserve in 1913.

During this same period, the buffalo declined to a point of near distinction, and First Nations peoples were forced to moved onto reserves where they could learn to farm to support themselves. The Cypress Hills no longer needed the presence of such a large force: in 1882 the headquarters were moved to Regina, where the territorial government and a railway station were located. Fort Walsh was closed in 1883. In 1942, the **ROYAL CANADIAN MOUNTED POLICE** bought the site of the old fort and constructed the RCMP Remount Ranch, where the force's internationally recognized black horses were bred and raised. At three years of age, the horses were sent to Regina for training. The RCMP discontinued mandatory equitation training in 1966, and the breeding program was moved to Rockcliffe, Ontario. The Remount Ranch and a portion of its lands were transferred to Parks Canada in 1968. Fort Walsh is now a national historic site. *Daria Coneghan*

49TH PARALLEL. At just over 630 km, the 49th parallel separating Saskatchewan from North Dakota and Montana is one of the longest continuous boundary lines in the world. First established in an 1818 treaty between Great Britain and the United States, and stretching from the Lake of the Woods in the east to the Pacific Coast in the west, this particular segment of the international border was ignored by the buffalo and by the Native peoples, Métis, and Whites who hunted them. Settlement and economic development occurred for the most part elsewhere in North America: this part of the continent remained largely unsettled even after the boundary line was delineated in 1874 by a joint British and American commission. Yet the effects of this geopolitical creation were soon felt. The border cut across the hunting grounds of Native peoples and Métis, and erased their former territories. When the flow of peoples, goods and ideas from the United States into Canada increased after the building of the Soo Line and the completion of agricultural settlement in the American west, the boundary acquired greater significance as it became the focus for changing relations taking place within the Great Plains and prairies borderland region of which it was a part.

By the turn of the 20th century, American immigrants, both native-born and transplanted Europeans, had an impact on western Canadian settlement that was disproportionate to their numbers. Although Alberta was the most common destination

Fort Walsh.

for American migrants, a significant number settled in Saskatchewan, particularly in the southwestern part of the province, where ranching played a major role in the local economy. In 1916, American-born comprised 36%, 30% and 8% of the foreign-born populations of Alberta, Saskatchewan and Manitoba respectively. While settlers who came directly from Europe tended to immigrate in large groups and settle in blocs, Americans tended to travel alone or with immediate family, and were dealt with individually. As a result, their presence, while ubiquitous, was also less apparent.

Americans were valued for both their wealth and experience in farming, and were looked upon favourably by those who put stock in the fact that most Canadians and Americans shared the same Anglo-Celtic blood. Yet, while appreciating American capital and labour, many native-born Canadians in Saskatchewan were uneasy about certain aspects of American society and the threat of annexation. Many of these same people expressed some regret about the weakening of the British connection, in economic as well as social terms. However, the sheer number of Americans by the end of the first decade of the 20th century, their investment in agriculture and business, and the technological expertise they brought with them in relation to machinery and dry-land farming ensured that they would play a major role in developing the province.

While integration within this trans-national region occurred to some extent at the turn of the 20th century because of a common hinterland, divergence between Saskatchewan and its American neighbours was ensured by several factors: migration flows, diffusion of technology and ideas, evolution of capitalist relations across the border, east-west flow of trade and migration paralleling the CANADIAN PACIFIC RAILWAY and the Great Northern Railroad, different settlement histories, different political cultures, different urban systems, and different core-periphery relations. Whatever economic or cultural linkages developed between peoples and places on both sides of "the line," the simple fact remains that a very real boundary, a border that cannot be ignored, existed between them. Today, the 49th parallel continues to function as a matrix for Canadian culture for all Canadians, including Saskatchewanians, even in the face of new technologies, globalization, and "time-space compression" which challenge the traditional view of the border as a territorial symbol of sovereignty and separation.

Randy Widdis

FURTHER READING: Sharp, P.F. 1947. "The American Farmer and the 'Last Best West,'" *Agricultural History* 21: 65–74; Widdis, R.W. 1998. *With Scarcely a Ripple: Anglo-Canadian Migration into the United States and Western Canada, 1880–1920.* Montréal: McGill-Queen's University Press.

46th Battalion

46TH CANADIAN INFANTRY BATTALION, CEF.

At the outbreak of WORLD WAR I the Minister of Defence, Sir Sam Hughes, ordered the raising of units for overseas service. Scrapping the existing mobilization plan, he ordered the formation of numbered battalions: as a result the 46th Battalion, headquartered in Moose Jaw and commanded by Lieutenant Colonel Herbert Snell, came into being on February 1, 1915. The 46th traveled to Camp Sewell, Manitoba on May 28, 1915, for basic training before entraining for Halifax and overseas service. The battalion arrived in England on November 1, 1915, with a strength of 36 officers and 1,115 other ranks. Many of the original soldiers of the battalion were then transferred to other units, and new men took their place; the winter of 1915–16 was spent re-establishing the cohesion of the unit as the new men were moulded into the battalion.

The 46th embarked for France on August 10, 1916, becoming an integral part of the 10th Infantry Brigade, 4th Canadian Division, from August 11, 1916 until the Armistice. During its active service the battalion fought in every major victory attributed to the Canadian Corp, suffering 1,433 killed and 3,484 wounded (a 91.5% casualty rate) and earning the title of "Suicide Battalion." Sergeant Hugh Cairns was awarded the VICTORIA CROSS posthumously for his actions at Valenciennes on November 1, 1918; he was the last Canadian to win this distinction in World War I. Two former members of the 46th Battalion were also awarded the Victoria Cross posthumously: Private William Johnstone Milne while serving with the 16th Canadian Scottish; and Sergeant Arthur Knight, of Regina, while serving with the 10th Battalion. On March 24, 1919, in preparation for its return to Canada, the battalion was presented with Colours bearing the sixteen Battle Honours that it had earned in the twenty-seven months of combat. On April 26, 1919, the battalion began its homeward journey. It arrived in Moose Jaw on June 9, 1919, and after a brief reception paraded to the Armoury to be demobilized. The 46th Canadian Infantry Battalion is perpetuated by the Saskatchewan Dragoons of Moose Jaw.

Gerry Carline

FURTHER READING: McWilliams, J. and R.J. Steel. 1978. *The Suicide Battalion*. Edmonton: Hurtig.

FOSSIL RECORD. Saskatchewan's fossil record, extensive and diverse, covers the last 1.8 billion years. During this immense span of time, life evolved from relatively simple organisms such as bacteria and algae to the vast variety of plants, animals and other organisms living today. In the process, various groups, including dinosaurs, huge marine lizards called mosasaurs, and many others evolved and thrived, only to become extinct. Our knowledge of ancient natural history is necessarily incomplete. For an organism's remains to be fossilized and preserved for later discovery they must be buried quickly by sediments. In other words, fossils normally form only in locations where sediment is being deposited, such on a lake bottom, but not where erosion predominates, such as on the side of a mountain. Also, most fossils are only discovered when they become exposed at the earth's surface. Most of Saskatchewan is covered by sediments deposited by the glaciers of the last 2 million years; most of the older rocks that preserve the largest part of fossil history are hidden beneath these recent sediments, and are only exposed in river valleys where erosion has cut down into those older sediments.

The oldest fossils found in the province come from uranium-bearing beds near Uranium City. These 1.8 billion-year-old fossils are stromatolites, which consist of mounds of calcareous material produced by blue-green algae. These organisms are still with us today, and the modern stromatolites they produce can be found in intertidal flats off Australia and other locations in the southern hemisphere. The southern two-thirds of Saskatchewan are part of a large sedimentary basin that filled during the last 500 million years. For much of this period Saskatchewan was covered by shallow seas, and as a result the fossils that are preserved are the remains of marine organisms. Approximately 65 million years ago the shallow seas retreated from Saskatchewan for the last time, so that the most recent fossils are of terrestrial and freshwater organisms.

Multicellular life forms became plentiful and diverse by about 600 million years ago. Rocks from the earliest portion of this period are deeply buried in Saskatchewan and poorly known, but limestone rocks from the Ordovician Period (450 million years ago) are exposed at the surface in the Amisk Lake area. These rocks preserve inhabitants of the shallow tropical sea that covered Saskatchewan at that time. Both solitary and colonial corals were present, but the latter did not form the huge reefs found elsewhere. Shelled animals included clams, snails, brachiopods and nautiloids. The nautiloids were predators that are distantly related to the modern octopus and squid; they had straight or slightly curved shells, and a head and tentacles that resemble those of the squid. The sedentary sea lilies (crinoids) might be mistaken for plants with their supportive stalk and branch-like "arms"; in fact, these animals are echinoderms, relatives of the starfishes. The limestones also include lines of darker rock that are interpreted as the burrows of marine worms. These Ordovician-aged limestones are quarried in Manitoba and are used as building stones; this "Tyndall Stone" and the fossils it contains can be seen on the exterior of many buildings in Saskatchewan, including the **SASKATCHEWAN LEGISLATIVE BUILDING** and the **ROYAL SASKATCHEWAN MUSEUM**, both in Regina.

The subsequent Devonian Period was characterized by the continuation of shallow marine conditions. Massive coral reefs developed in the middle Devonian, but by the late Devonian the water had become too saline to support most forms of life; the conditions were ideal, however, for the deposition of Saskatchewan's potash. The absence of rocks of latest Palaeozoic age (up to 250 million years ago) suggests that the marine seas had by then retreated from this area. The Mesozoic Era (250–65 million years ago) that followed is often called the Age of Dinosaurs because this group evolved early in the era and dominated terrestrial ecosystems until its extinction 65 million years ago. Although the dinosaurs existed for approximately 150 million years, for much of this time Saskatchewan was again covered by shallow continental seas that would not be expected to preserve fossils of terrestrial animals. Saskatchewan's dinosaurs come from rocks in the southwest portion of the province that are dated at 75–65 million years ago, when the shallow marine seas were finally starting to retreat from the centre of North America.

Rocks from the last 30 million years of the Mesozoic are exposed in various areas of southern Saskatchewan: as a result we have a good record of the faunas of this time period. Rocks that are approximately 90 million years old are exposed in the Pasquia Hills area just west of the Manitoba border. At that time this area was close to the eastern shore of an inland seaway that extended down the middle of North America. One of the most spectacular fossils recovered from this area is the almost complete skeleton of a 7.5-metre-long crocodile known as "Big Bert." Big Bert came from sediments along the Carrot River near Pasquia Regional Park; it is the best known example of the species *Terminonaris robusta*, a member of an extinct group of crocodiles. The sediments in the area preserve other marine reptiles, various fishes including sharks and the 4-metre-long *Xiphactinus*, and a variety of toothed birds.

Beginning approximately 80 million years ago, some terrestrial sediments were deposited in the western portion of the province. 75 million-year-old sediments containing the remains of horned and carnivorous dinosaurs, fish, lizards, and other terres-

trial or freshwater animals are exposed near Unity and at Saskatchewan Landing Provincial Park. By 70 million years ago Saskatchewan was again covered by a shallow sea. Fossils of the shelled invertebrate animals that inhabited this sea are quite common. The coiled ammonites and straight-shelled baculites are extinct relatives of the octopus and the pearly nautilus, and a variety of large and small marine clams are also preserved. The most impressive fossils from this sea are the marine reptiles. The plesiosaurs, which tend to resemble most people's image of the Loch Ness monster, include both long- and short-necked species. A well-preserved skeleton of a short-necked plesiosaur was discovered near the town of Herschel, west of Rosetown, whereas an elasmosaur, a long-necked plesiosaur, was excavated from a site near Ponteix. Recent research on these two skeletons established that both represent plesiosaur species that are new to science. The other common marine reptiles of this time period are the mosasaurs; closely related to lizards, they had long crocodile-like heads, limbs modified into flippers, and long laterally compressed tails. A very large skeleton of a mosasaur called *Tylosaurus* was excavated from the southern shore of Lake Diefenbaker near Herbert Ferry in the mid-1990s.

By 68 million years ago the sea began to retreat from southwestern Saskatchewan, and rocks in the area dated to approximately 65 million years preserve the province's best record of dinosaurs and their contemporaries. Herbivorous dinosaurs include the horned *Triceratops*, the duck-billed *Edmontosaurus* and the armoured *Ankylosaurus*. A variety of carnivorous dinosaurs are known, such as the smaller dromaeosaurs, *Troodon*, the ostrich-like ornithomimids, and the largest known meat-eater, *Tyrannosaurus rex*. Although isolated remains of *T. rex* had been collected for many years, Saskatchewan's one partial skeleton of this dinosaur, known as "Scotty," was discovered in the **FRENCHMAN RIVER** Valley in 1991. Subsequent excavations recovered approximately 65% of the skeleton. The geology and plant fossils at the site suggest a mild climate with forested lowlands that included palms and cypress-like conifers. The rocks of this age preserve a variety of other animals such as garfish, salamanders, lizards, soft-shelled turtles, crocodiles, the crocodile-like champsosaurs, birds, and mammals. Among the mammals, small opossum-like marsupials and the rodent-like multituberculates predominate. Although mammals remained small until after the extinction of the dinosaurs, sites in Saskatchewan may contain ancestral species of some of the mammal groups that dominated later terrestrial ecosystems.

An extraterrestrial impact event 65 million years ago marks the end of the dinosaur era. Because this event, and the intervals both immediately before and after that event, are recorded in sed-

iments in southwestern Saskatchewan, this area is one of the best places to study the faunal and floral changes that occurred during this period of Earth's history. Saskatchewan's fossil record of the subsequent Tertiary Period (65–2 million years ago) is the best in Canada. Rocks of Palaeocene age (65–55 million years ago) are exposed in various locations across the southernmost portion of the province. The occurrence of coal and plant fossils of horsetails, ginkgo, cypress, and various broadleafed plants indicates a warm, wet environment of lowland forest and cypress swamps. Animal fossils are less common but record the survival by various fish, salamanders, crocodiles, champsosaurs, and turtles of the extinction event that marked the end of the Mesozoic. Mammal fossils document the beginning of the diversification of this group. Although they were diverse, mammals remained small during the age of dinosaurs, but our Palaeocene rocks include fossils of herbivores that were over two metres in length. Early members of modern mammal groups such as primates, carnivores and ungulates are also present. Earlier groups, such as the marsupials and multituberculates, also persisted; a rare skeleton of a multituberculate was discovered in sediments of this age near Estevan.

The next 12–13 million years of earth history do not appear to be preserved in the province, suggesting that this was a time of erosion rather than deposition of sediments. Deposition of sediments began again about 42 million years ago, and much of the next 30 million years is preserved in sediments in southwestern to south-central Saskatchewan. The fossils document the changes to faunas that occurred as the climate became cooler, drier and more seasonal. During this period closed-canopy forests slowly gave way to open woodland savanna and grassland habitats. The earliest stage of this transition is recorded at a 42 million-year-old site southeast of Swift Current. The habitat was probably still dominated by woodlands, but with some grassy areas. By this time early members of modern mammal groups, including rodents, rabbits, bats, horses, and rhinos, are present, together with members of groups such as multitiberculates that are now extinct. Mammal faunas of approximately 35 million years ago are well preserved in the **CYPRESS HILLS** area northwest of Eastend. Fossil sites in this area tend to include the broken up remains of many animals rather than complete skeletons. The Calf Creek locality contains specimens representing over 70 mammal species, giving us a very detailed picture of the mammal fauna at the time. This fauna includes many rodents, rabbits, three-toed horses, rhinos, saber-toothed cats, early fox-sized dogs, the pig-like entelodonts, and the massive rhino-like horned brontotheres. The site also includes one of the last records of the rodent-like multituberculates. Although skeletons are rare, two partial brontothere skeletons have been discovered, one near the Calf Creek locality, and one near Simmie. The last known chapter of this 30-million-year period is recorded in localities in the Wood Mountain area near Rockglen. The habitat was probably largely grassland, and the mammals include larger three-toed horses, early prong-horns, camels, and rhinos. The fauna also includes extinct relatives of the modern elephants, a group that had recently arrived in North America. Other vertebrates include extremely large land tortoises. The last 12 million years (14–2 milllion years ago) of the Tertiary Period are not preserved in Saskatchewan sediments.

The last 2 million years of Saskatchewan's geological history are dominated by a series of ice sheets that advanced and retreated across the province, eroding older rocks and depositing new layers of sediment. A site in Wellsch Valley, northeast of Swift Current, preserves fossils from early in the ice age. The fauna is a mix of animals living today (prairie dog, coyote) and others that are now extinct (mammoth, giant ground sloth, shrubox). Other sites, such as several in the Qu'Appelle Valley, are more recent and contain animals characteristic of the later ice age, such as wooly mammoth and giant bison. A partial skeleton of a wooly mammoth was unearthed near Kyle, north of Swift Current in the 1960s. The ice associated with the last glaciation retreated from Saskatchewan between 17,000 and 8,000 years ago. Most of the land forms we see today are the result of that glaciation. Fossils from this last glaciation, such as bison and mammoth, have been found in many locations throughout the province. Fossils are an important component of Saskatchewan's rich geological history. They are significant clues to the events of the past, and are the only direct evidence we have of the extinct organisms that once lived here. This irreplaceable heritage resource is protected through the Heritage Property Act. *Harold N. Bryant*

FURTHER READING: McAnally, L. (ed.). 1997. *Upper Cretaceous and Tertiary Stratigraphy and Paleontology of Southern Saskatchewan. Canadian Paleontology Conference Field Trip Guidebook No. 6.* St. John's: Geological Association of Canada; Storer, J. 1989. *Geological History of Saskatchewan.* Regina: Government of Saskatchewan.

406 SQUADRON, RCAF. First formed on May 10, 1941, 406 Squadron was a night fighter squadron and remained so until November 27, 1944, when it was renamed 406 Intruder Squadron and converted to offensive operations over Europe. It was disbanded in England on September 1, 1945. On April 1, 1947, 406 (Intruder) Squadron was reformed at RCAF Station Saskatoon as 406 Tactical Bomber Squadron (Auxiliary). The squadron flew B-

25 Mitchell aircraft in a light bomber role, as well as Harvard and T-33 Silver Star aircraft in an army co-operation role. It was renamed "City of Saskatoon" Squadron on September 3, 1952. In March 1958, 406 Squadron was reassigned to a light transport and emergency rescue role, and re-equipped with Expeditor and Otter aircraft. A reduction in the RCAF's Auxiliary Force resulted in 406 "City of Saskatoon" Squadron (Auxiliary) being disbanded on April 1, 1964. Today, 406 Maritime Helicopter Squadron is the Helicopter Operational Training squadron for the Sikorsky CH-124 Sea King. *Stewart Mein*

4-H CLUBS. The 4-H Clubs and their predecessors, Boys and Girls Clubs, have been a part of rural life in Saskatchewan since 1918. Administered by the Agricultural Extension Department of the **UNIVERSITY OF SASKATCHEWAN**, these clubs were a means of actively engaging youth in the development of farm products and promoting a rural lifestyle. Early clubs focused on one area of agriculture such as beef, grain, or homecraft; but "Multiple Clubs" that combined different projects started to emerge in the 1950s. In 1952 Boys and Girls together with Homecraft Clubs across Canada adopted the name 4-H (from the motto "heads, hearts, hands and health"). As well as learning about agricultural topics through their individual projects, club members gained valuable experience in running meetings and organizing community events such as the annual Achievement Day. Saskatchewan 4-H members and leaders have long been involved in national activities. Even before 1918, farm boys and girls attended farm camps that were held in conjunction with agricultural exhibitions. They learned how to

prepare, show and judge agricultural produce; and top participants often represented their province at larger fairs, competing with youths from other provinces or even countries. Though still focused on traditional topics such as beef and sewing, current 4-H projects reflect the diverse range of activities undertaken in rural Saskatchewan, from photography to llama production. *Lisa Dale-Burnett*

FOURNIER, MARGUERITE (1919–2000). "Margo" Fournier devoted her life to fostering the musical and athletic talents of many generations of Prince Albert's youth. Born Marguerite Helen Leblond on August 16, 1919, she grew up in Rosthern and Prince Albert. An accomplished singer and dancer, she joined the RCAF as an entertainer during **WORLD WAR II**, touring bases in Canada, Britain, and continental Europe. She married Prince Albert's L.J. "Pluke" Fournier, of the Canadian Auxiliary Corps, in Glasgow, Scotland, on May 5, 1945, and the couple raised a family of seven. Margo Fournier became known as a take-charge music teacher and conductor of boys and girls, student nurses, church and local penitentiary inmates' choirs. As well, she founded the local Music Festival Association and, in the early 1960s, helped organize and was president of the local Jeunesses Musicales group. In September 1965, she was named to the Saskatchewan Youth Review Committee. She was best known as the founder and director of the Prince Albert Boys' Choir, which received national and international recognition. With her husband's guidance, she also taught and coached swimming and diving. A local multi-purpose recreation centre was named after her. In 1983 she was invested as a Member of the Order of Canada. She died on July 22, 2000. *Richard Lapointe*

EVERETT BAKER PHOTO/COURTESY OF THE SASKATCHEWAN HISTORY AND FOLKLORE SOCIETY
4-H Jubilee, August 5, 1955, Admiral.

FOURNIER, PEARL (1907–82). Pearl Fournier (*née* Kemp) was the main organizer and first president of the Saskatchewan branch of the national organization, Fédération des Femmes Canadiennes-Françaises. Born on April 26, 1907, in Montebello, Quebec, Pearl Miella Kemp was educated at a convent in Montreal before attending Normal School. Recruited by the Association Catholique Franco-Canadienne de la Saskatchewan, she attended Regina **NORMAL SCHOOL** to obtain her provincial teaching certificate, and accepted a position at Ferland in June 1929. On New Year's day in 1930 she married local homesteader Aristide Fournier. During the 1930s, while raising a family of eight, she helped her husband operate a post office and a small store. In the mid-1960s, in the wake of the upheaval caused by Vatican II, she founded a parish-based women's organization, the Fédération des Franco-Canadiennes, in the Catholic diocese of Gravelbourg, and sought affiliation with a national group, the Fédération des Femmes Canadiennes-Françaises. Its mandate was to help French-speaking Catholic women play a more active role in preserving their religious, linguistic, and cultural values. Fournier was soon named regional president of the national federation, and went on to organize a large number of local branches in Saskatchewan, Alberta, Manitoba, and British Columbia. She died on January 6, 1982. *Richard Lapointe*

FURTHER READING: Lapointe, Richard. 1988. "Pearl Fournier." Pp. 163–68 in *100 noms: Petit dictionnaire biographique des Franco-Canadiens de la Saskatchewan*. Regina: Société historique.

14th Canadian Hussars

IMAGE COURTESY OF GERRY CARLINE

14TH CANADIAN HUSSARS. The 14th Canadian Hussars were originally organized as the 27th Light Horse on April 1, 1910, in Moose Jaw. The unit was formed by officers and senior non-commissioned officers of D Squadron, 16th Light Horse, which was previously located in that city. Lieutenant-Colonel **GEORGE STUART TUXFORD** commanded the newly formed regiment. At the outbreak of **WORLD WAR I**, the 27th Light Horse contributed contingents to the 5th (Western Cavalry) Battalion,

CEF. After the war, the headquarters of the 27th Light Horse were moved to Swift Current. The Regiment was designated the 14th Canadian Light Horse on March 15, 1920; it was renamed the 14th Canadian Hussars on August 1, 1940. The regiment was mobilized on January 26, 1941, and converted to an armoured regiment. It was redesignated the 8th (Reserve) Reconnaissance Battalion (14th Canadian Hussars) in April, and the 8th (Reserve) Reconnaissance Regiment (14th Canadian Hussars) in June of 1942. The unit went overseas and participated in several significant campaigns in northwestern Europe. In 1947, the unit was renamed the 8th Armoured Car Regiment (14th Canadian Hussars) to reflect its role as a reconnaissance regiment during **WORLD WAR II**. This name was reversed in 1949, then shortened in 1954, and reverted to the 14th Canadian Hussars on May 19, 1958. The regiment was finally disbanded on March 1, 1965, and placed on the Supplementary Order of Battle.
Holden Stoffel

FOWKE, EDITH FULTON (1913–96). Canada's pre-eminent scholar of English-language traditions, Edith Fowke published more than twenty books of and about folklore, mainly traditional songs, stories, and games of Canada. Born on April 30, 1913, in Lumsden, Saskatchewan, she wrote poems and stories for the *Regina Leader-Post*'s Saturday magazine during adolescence, and collected Saskatchewan oral traditions that five decades later appeared in her *Folklore of Canada* (1976). While studying at the **UNIVERSITY OF SASKATCHEWAN** (BA, English and History, 1933; MA, English, 1937), Fowke met J.S. Woodsworth and became actively involved in the CCF, editing the party's newsletters, and later a selection of Woodsworth's essays (1948), before breaking with the party in the early 1950s. Also, as a young Saskatchewan schoolteacher, she edited the *Western Teacher* from 1937 to 1944. On marrying and moving to Toronto, she used her private collection of folksong recordings as the basis of her CBC radio shows *Folk Song Time* (1949–63) and *Folk Sounds* (1963–74). From the mid-1950s to the mid-1960s, Fowke collected in rural Ontario and among Toronto children most of the folklore for her anthologies and recordings. Meanwhile, she had become a major and highly energetic figure in the North American folk music revival, was appointed to York University's English Department as a folklore specialist (1971), and founded and edited the *Canadian Folk Music Journal* (1973–96). Nonetheless, she still took time during this period to write and publish *Saskatchewan: The Sixtieth Year–Historical Pageant*, a set of short musical plays for schools, theatre groups, and community organizations. She also helped Barbara Cass-Beggs's early efforts at collecting Saskatchewan folksongs, and compiled with her the first comprehensive

reference list for Canadian folksong research (1973).

A recipient of several honorary doctorates (Brock, Trent, York, Regina), Fowke became a Fellow of the American Folklore Society (1974), a Companion of the Order of Canada (1978), a Fellow of the Royal Society of Canada (1983), a life member of Canadian Folk Music Society (1984), and was posthumously honoured by a Lifetime Achievement Award from the North American Folk Music and Dance Alliance (2000). Although her main folksong collecting had been concluded by the late 1960s, she continued to publish scholarly studies of previously collected items and to do fieldwork with her favourite Canadian singer, LaRena Clark, which resulted in her last book, *A Family Heritage*, published when she was 81. She died in Toronto on March 28, 1996. *Jay Rahn*

FURTHER READING: Fowke, E. 1976. *Folklore of Canada*. Toronto: McClelland & Stewart.

FRANCIS, town, pop 172, located approximately 60 km SE of Regina on Hwy 33 and 50 km N of Weyburn on Hwy 35. First settled around 1900 by Scots from the historic Glengarry County, Ontario, Francis was incorporated as a village in 1904, the same year that the CPR had trains running between Arcola and Regina. Two years later, in 1906, Francis attained town status. The community had a peak population of 263 in 1911, but its numbers have hovered roughly around the current level since the early 1920s. The basis of the area economy is agriculture–largely a combination of grain and livestock production. Francis has a small business community, consisting mainly of farm suppliers; there are two grain elevators. Francis School is a K–6 facility, which had 66 students enrolled in the fall of 2004; students attend Grades 7–12 in the neighbouring village of Sedley. The community has indoor rinks for skating and curling, and three churches.
David McLennan

FRANCIS, EMILE (1926–). Emile Francis' association with the game of hockey lasted for over four decades. Born in North Battleford on September 13, 1926, he played goal for junior hockey teams in his hometown, Moose Jaw, and in Regina. His professional career lasted fourteen seasons with a number of teams, including ninety-five regular season games with the NHL's Chicago Black Hawks and New York Rangers. During the 1945–46 season, he experimented with a first baseman's glove, adding a cuff to provide extra support and protection; the modification was a huge success and became the prototype for the glove used by net minders all over the world today. After his playing career ended in 1960, Francis coached the Guelph Royals junior team and joined the New York Rangers in 1962. He coached

COURTESY OF SASKATOON PUBLIC LIBRARY 3933-1

Emile Francis with the senior Western Hockey League's Saskatoon Quakers, 1955.

the Rangers on three separate occasions, in addition to serving as general manager from 1964 to 1975. A year later, Francis became executive vice-president, general manager, and coach of the St. Louis Blues until 1983. He was president and GM of the Hartford Whalers until his retirement in 1993. Emile Francis credits his success in hockey to his experience in the Reserve Army and his leadership role as a non-commissioned officer just as **WORLD WAR II** was ending. In addition to his duties as coach and team executive, he established hockey scholarships throughout Canada and won the Lester Patrick Trophy in 1982 for his contributions to the sport. Emile Francis was inducted into the Hockey Hall of Fame in 1982 and the **SASKATCHEWAN SPORTS HALL OF FAME** in 2002.

Elizabeth Mooney

FRANCISCAN SISTERS OF ST. ELIZABETH (OSE). Three Franciscan Sisters of St. Elizabeth came to St. Peter's Colony from Klagenfurt, Austria in 1911. They were responding to a request made by Abbot Bruno Doerfler, Prior of the Benedictines of Muenster, for a community of Sisters to establish a hospital to look after the sick among the German settlers.

The Sisters established and operated three hospitals in Saskatchewan: St. Elizabeth in Humboldt; St. Michael in Cudworth; and St. Joseph in Macklin. They also administered and cared for the seniors at St. Anne's Home in Saskatoon and St. Mary's Villa in Humboldt. Home Care Services were developed in the Humboldt district upon the initiative of St.

Elizabeth Hospital. Sisters of St. Elizabeth supported the work of the Benedictines at St. Peter's College, Muenster for almost seventy-eight years, as well as the Oblates at St. Charles Scholasticate, Battleford and St. Thomas College, North Battleford, and the Franciscans at St. Michael's Retreat House, Lumsden.

Presently the congregation comprises forty-nine members. It continues to operate St. Michael's Haven, an assisted-living facility in Cudworth, and St. Joseph's Health Centre, a long-term care facility in Macklin. The Franciscan Forest Sanctuary, established in 1997, operates as a retreat centre at Christopher Lake.

Sr. Viola Bens

FRANCOPHONES. In the early 1880s there were less than 3,000 people claiming French origin scattered throughout the entire North-West Territories (which then comprised most of western Canada and all of northern Canada, excluding British Columbia and a small central portion of Manitoba). However, according to some estimates, as many as half the total population of the Territories may have been at least partially francophone, for French—or a mixture of French with various Native languages—was widely spoken by the omnipresent **MÉTIS**. In 1882, the Districts of Assiniboia, Saskatchewan, Athabasca and Alberta were created out of the western portions of the North-West Territories; the southern or prairie portion of present-day Saskatchewan occupied most of the Districts of Saskatchewan and Assiniboia. By 1891 just over 900 residents counted in the Districts of Saskatchewan and Assiniboia had been born in

Quebec, while almost 100 had immigrated directly from France. During the next decade immigration from Quebec continued, with the establishment of francophone settlements across the prairies: by 1901, the number of Québecois had tripled to almost 2,700. However, immigration direct from France was only a trickle: 167 by the turn of the century. A more substantial flow from francophone Europe (France and Belgium, and to a minor extent Luxembourg and Switzerland) during the next decade lessened this Québecois dominance; in fact, many of the thirty-two French settlements in the new province of Saskatchewan (founded in 1905) had been established primarily if not exclusively by French-speaking immigrants direct from Europe.

In 1941, census data indicated that a high proportion (87%) of the 50,530 people in Saskatchewan claiming French ethnic origin (excluding the 4,250 claiming Belgian ethnic origin) were Canadian-born. Migration into Saskatchewan from other Canadian provinces, the United States, and Europe had virtually ceased. Almost two-thirds (63%) of French Canadians in Saskatchewan had been born in this province, compared to about 14% who had migrated from Quebec, almost 6% from the other western provinces (particularly Manitoba), and just over 4% from Ontario and the other eastern provinces. But a substantial, if lessening, proportion were immigrants from Europe and the United States: approximately 13%. Prior to the 1981 Census, respondents to the question on ethnic origin could claim only a single ethnic origin through the male lineage. Thus the French-Canadian population of Saskatchewan, for example, was actually counted as people with a French father (hence presumably a French surname), regardless of whether the mother, or any other female predecessor, had been French or not—whereas people with a French mother but not a French father could not claim French origin. So it is conceivable that, on the one hand, the actual French-Canadian population of the province was under-counted in each census; on the other hand, it may have been over-counted because intermarriage had not been taken into consideration. The 1981 Census attempted to correct this situation by permitting respondents to claim multiple ethnic origin.

In 1981 almost 47,000 people claimed to be only of French descent, plus almost 3,000 of Belgian, over 1,000 Swiss, and a small number of Luxembourg origin (note, however, that in these latter three countries, French is not the mother tongue of most people). Another 15,000 people claimed Métis origin; yet it is not clear how many of these people would be more specifically of Franco-Métis descent, or speaking a Franco-Métis dialect such as Mitchif (while a majority of Métis in Saskatchewan are probably of part-French origin, a substantial proportion could be of other Euro-Canadian ethnicity—especially Scottish—mixed with Aboriginal origin).

Of the more than 22,000 people estimated to be of part-French origin (apart from those claiming only Métis origin), the largest number–more than 9,000–also claimed British origin; almost as many–over 8,000–claimed other non-Aboriginal origins; while another 4,000 combined French origin with British plus other non-Aboriginal origins. Relatively few (just over 1,000) people who did not identify themselves exclusively as Métis claimed to be of part-French, part-Aboriginal origin. Adding up all of these data, we arrive at an absolute maximum figure for possible French or part-French origin of almost 89,000 (that is, including all people of Belgian, Swiss, Luxembourg and Métis origins). Obviously, a far lower number would be French-speaking.

In 1901, there were very few people of French origin (2,634), and still fewer of Belgian origin, living in what would soon become the province of Saskatchewan. However, during the first decade of the 20th century the French population would increase tenfold (to 23,251 in 1911), then again double in the second decade (to 42,152 in 1921). Much of this rapid increase was doubtless due to large-scale migration of Francophones from Quebec and other Canadian provinces, as well as from French settlements already established in American states such as Minnesota, and particularly from many regions in France and to a lesser extent Francophone regions in Belgium and Switzerland. During the 1920s this influx slowed, and with the exodus from French settlements in Saskatchewan due to the **DEPRESSION** and repeated droughts, the French population of the province remained quite static after 1931 (50,700 in 1931; 50,530 in 1941; 51,930 in 1951), reaching a peak in 1961 (59,824), and then slowly declining again (to 56,200 in 1971). With the change in census definitions in 1981, 46,915 people claimed to be solely of French origin, yet by then an increasing proportion of French were intermarried, so that their children were claiming mixed ethnic origins. Recent census data (2001) revealed that 109,800 Saskatchewan residents (11.4% of the total population) claimed French origin, making them the sixth largest ethnic group in the province. However, only 13.7% (15,040) of them claimed to be only of French origin, compared to 86.3% (94,755) who also claimed other ethnic origins besides French.

During the past several decades, the urbanization of the French population of Saskatchewan has been dramatic. Back in 1941, 70% of that population was living in rural areas, whereas by 1981 this proportion had fallen to 45%. Moreover, through the 1960s most of the rural French population consisted of farming families, whereas today most are non-farming rural families. In 1971 (the last census in which detailed, complete data on ethnicity in rural communities are available) there were thirty-nine incorporated communities in Saskatchewan where Francophones comprised at least 10% of the total community population; yet only thirteen of these communities had a Francophone majority. Francophones made up between one-third and one-half of the population in another eight communities; between 20% and one-third in seven communities; and 10–19% in the remaining eleven communities. It must also be noted that people claiming French ethnic origin made up a majority in fifteen communities, 33–49% in eleven, 20–32% in six and 10–19% in six. Of course, the difference between those two sets of data is due to the fact that not all those of French origin in these communities were still speaking French as their primary mother tongue. Yet there were some striking discrepancies: in five communities, Francophones outnumbered people claiming French origin; and in one rural community, residents claiming to be of French origin outnumbered those who recognized French as their mother tongue four to one. The small village of Ferland had both the highest proportion of French origin (94.1%) and French speakers (90.9%); the largest predominantly French community was Gravelbourg.

Examination of demographic data since 1971 in thirty substantially Francophone communities in Saskatchewan reveals that seventeen communities have been consistently declining, although the rate of decline has varied from slow to rapid. Most of the rapidly declining communities are located in the southwestern region, which is more prone to drought; but the other sixteen communities have been increasing. Given the variation, any generalization about overall population trends is difficult. It could be pointed out, though, that seven of the smallest communities (with less than a hundred residents) are declining and seem destined to become virtual ghost towns. Moreover, besides these incorporated communities, most of the many francophone communities which are unincorporated small villages and hamlets have experienced rural depopulation more severely.

The proportion of French-origin population in Saskatchewan speaking French as their primary mother tongue has declined markedly over the past several decades. Back in 1921, 91.7% of the French-origin population over ten years of age was French-speaking, whereas by 1961 little more than half of the French population was speaking French as their mother tongue. Yet, as this proportion has remained more or less constant since then, linguistic assimilation may have been slowed more effectively in recent decades, perhaps due to the increased availability of French language media and education. By 1981, within the population claiming only French origin, for every person speaking primarily French at home, four were speaking English . Approximately half of those claiming exclusively French origin were bilingual; the other half spoke only English. Moreover, almost two-thirds of the bilingual population of exclusively French origin preferred to speak English at home; similarly, of the total Francophone (French mother tongue) population in Saskatchewan, almost two-thirds preferred to speak English at home. Every one in ten of these people claiming French mother tongue reported that they speak only English; the vast majority were bilingual; very few–only several hundred–could speak only French. On the other hand, there were almost 800 people in the province claiming English as their mother tongue, yet speaking primarily French at home. However, with the rapid rise in the number of French language immersion programs throughout Saskatchewan since the 1980s, there were twice as many people bilingual in French and English as there were bilingual French-Canadians; apparently, familiarity with the French language was increasing among people who were not French-Canadians, although still only a small proportion of these non-French were bilingual in French and English. While less than half of the people claiming only French origin are Francophone, to this French-speaking, French-origin population may be added people speaking French as their mother tongue who are either partly of French origin, or claim other ethnic origins.

Does French tend to be spoken by a higher proportion of the French-origin population in urban or in rural areas? Clearly, French Canadians in rural Saskatchewan (especially the farming population) have consistently been more likely to retain French. Moreover, a far higher proportion of the rural francophone population has continued to speak French at home than the urban Francophone population (42.5% compared to 29.9% in 1981). Yet, with the steady shift of French population from rural into urban areas, there are now more Francophones of French origin in urban than in rural areas, although there are more people speaking French at home in rural areas than urban, in absolute numbers. In 2001, 17,775 residents of Saskatchewan considered French to be their mother tongue; another 1,375 considered both French and English; and 8,280 considered French plus another language other than English.

Age and generation differences in ethnic language retention in Saskatchewan, including among French-origin population, are noteworthy. Retention, and particularly actual use of the French mother tongue, declines markedly from first generation through third or fourth, and from older age cohorts to younger. The age structure of French-Canadians in Saskatchewan is distributed quite evenly, both in urban and rural areas; but patterns of language use are not. Far higher proportions of French language use in the home, and exclusive use of French are found in the very youngest (pre-school) and oldest (post-retirement) age cohorts.

The demographic trends discerned are not indicative of a strong survival of the French minority in Saskatchewan. Ethnic origin will continue to become more complex with increasing intermarriage; concomitantly, the number of Saskatchewan people claiming only French origin continues to decline. The proportion of French-origin population resident in urban areas has steadily been increasing at the expense of the rural proportion, and it is in the urban areas that the greatest decline in actual use of the French language has occurred. There are numerous communities in Saskatchewan with substantial proportions of French residents; however, most of them have been losing population. There has been a marked decline, over the past several decades, in the proportion of people of French origin still speaking French as their primary mother tongue. The steady drift into English language use may have been slowed down in recent years by the increased availability of French language programs and immersion classes, French media, and organized activities conducted in French; but examination of the age structure and language use would seem to indicate that as a whole younger-generation French Canadians in Saskatchewan are not significantly reversing the trend of linguistic assimilation. Even among young adults who claim to be francophone, only about one in five is actually speaking French more than English at home.

Committed French-speaking French residents of Saskatchewan represent only a relatively small and declining proportion of the total population in the province claiming, in whole or in part, French origin. While familiarity with the French language has increased somewhat among the non-French population, the vast majority of Saskatchewan people are not familiar with the French language, as are more than half of the people claiming to be of French descent. Yet the historical impact of French settlement in Saskatchewan has been most significant, represented in the many French communities scattered across the province. (*See also* **FRENCH SETTLEMENTS**, **FRENCH AND MÉTIS SETTLEMENTS**)

Alan Anderson

FRANKLIN, SIR JOHN (1786–1847). Born on April 16, 1786 at Spilsby, Lincolnshire, Franklin entered the Royal Navy and served at the battles of Copenhagen (1801), Trafalgar (1805), and New Orleans (1814). During a period of peace in 1801–03, he served under his cousin Matthew Flinders on the first circumnavigation of Australia. After the battle of Waterloo, when the Royal Navy began to use part of its huge fleet for exploration and mapping, Franklin was given his first command, of the brig *Trent*, in 1818 to attempt to reach the North Pole between Greenland and Spitzbergen. This led to his being ordered to map the northern coast of North America from the mouth of the

LIBRARY AND ARCHIVES CANADA/C-001352

John Franklin.

Coppermine River to the east. His group, which included Dr. **JOHN RICHARDSON** and Lt. George Back, explored and surveyed the area, including what is northern Saskatchewan, in three hard years from 1819 to 1822. His second voyage (1824–27) surveyed the northern coast, from the mouth of the Mackenzie to the west. He was governor of Tasmania from 1836 to 1843. In 1845, the British government decided on a third expedition to attempt to find a navigable Northwest Passage. Franklin was assigned *Erebus* and *Terror*, two ships especially designed for polar exploration, which had been used by Ross for the exploration of the Antarctic. He sailed through the Bering Strait and was last seen in Lancaster Sound on July 26. When he failed to report, the Royal Navy sent out a number of unsuccessful rescue attempts from 1846 to 1857. A number of artifacts from the expedition have been found, including writings which tell of the hardships endured by the men. These include a journal recording Franklin's death on June 11, 1847.

In accounts of Franklin's voyages of exploration the last fatal, well-publicized failure tends to overshadow the earlier, successful voyages which provided a great deal of information about northern Canada.

Diane Secoy

FURTHER READING: Beattie, O. and J. Geiger. 1987. *Frozen in Time: Unlocking the Secrets of the Franklin Expedition*. Saskatoon: Western Producer Prairie Books.

FREE METHODIST CHURCH. There are several Free Methodist Churches throughout the province, which enjoy fellowship with each other but have no political alliance. The denomination had its origins in Saskatchewan in the 1920s as a result of the work of Rev. Lotta Babcock, who had been preaching in the East Ontario Conference and had moved to Estevan with Edith Abbott of Kitchener, Ontario as her companion and helper. Babcock, with her

booming voice and ability to preach powerful sermons, enjoyed great success in various revivals and was appointed in 1920 as Conference Evangelist, with Regina as her main focus. At first, meetings were held in an empty store on Dewdney Avenue, and prayer meetings in homes in three different parts of the city. A congregation was finally organized, with John Low as the first member. Babcock left Regina in the spring of 1921. District Elder R.H. Hamilton, another effective evangelist who had helped Babock, completed the year for her until the conference appointed Rev. and Mrs. Fred Wees to pastor the Regina church. In 1972, Gordon and Bonnie Hallett began working with the Aboriginal people of Regina, using the Free Methodist Church facilities to hold meetings. Over fifty people attended their first Sunday School class. More teachers were soon recruited, and the ministry grew. The Halletts left in 1973, but in September 1977 **OLIVER BRASS** and his wife became the first full-time appointees to this ministry. The Sherwood Drive Church shared its facilities with the new ministry, and by October 1979 the group was self-sufficient enough to move to its own church building on Elphinstone Street.

Bryan Hillis

FREIGHT SWINGS. Freight swings in Saskatchewan can be traced back to the turn of the 20th century. The establishment of the rail lines in the 1880s and the network of branch lines established throughout the 1920s allowed for freight delivery to many communities in the south. For northern Saskatchewan the absence of a rail network made freight hauling much more difficult. The northern terminus of Saskatchewan's rail network in the early 20th century was Big River, and many freight swings originated from this location; others originated further north out of La Ronge, Flin Flon, and Ile-à-la-Crosse. Because freight hauls were extremely large and heavy, horse-drawn sleighs were the most reliable form of transportation: for the next decade horse-drawn caravans, from six to ten sleighs in length, traversed across the frozen lakes and rivers of Saskatchewan's north during the winter. The northern freighting industry boomed in northern Saskatchewan during the 1920s, owing in large part to the growth of the commercial fishing industry. Freighters would gather their horse teams in communities such as Big River and La Ronge and pull numerous wooden sleighs north with supplies; they would return two or three weeks later with loads of fish from commercial fisheries scattered throughout the north. The freight swings went as far north as La Loche, Cree Lake, and Brochet Lake.

By the late 1930s and throughout the 1940s, mechanized equipment was replacing the horses, and tracked vehicles began to pull the freight swings. These "cat swings," as they were often called, were more efficient and comfortable than the horse-drawn

Freight swing.

sleighs: they could travel day and night; needed only a three- or four-man crew; contained a heated caboose for the driver and crew; and could pull much more freight than a team of horses. By the 1950s, overland roads began to reach some communities served by the freight swings; trucks were much faster, more efficient, and could travel to northern communities year-round. Those communities without road connections at the time were serviced by aircraft. By 1960, the freight swings that had served Saskatchewan's north for forty years had thus become obsolete.   *James Winkel*

FRENCH AND MÉTIS SETTLEMENTS. The settlement of French-speaking people in the regions which today comprise the province of Saskatchewan occurred in three distinct stages. First, during the era of the fur trade, from the mid-18th to the mid-19th century, numerous trading posts were established on the principal river systems by *voyageurs* of French or part-French extraction. Second, from the mid-19th century until the **NORTH-WEST REBELLION** in 1885, many small **MÉTIS** (mixed French-Indian) communities came into existence, some on the old river routes but most widely scattered across the southern prairies. Third, for half a century after the rebellion, French-speaking immigrants from Quebec, Europe and the United States arrived in large numbers to establish bloc settlements on the prairies. Yet the French were not alone in settling by this time: wide varieties of other ethnic groups were also establishing their own settlements, and soon greatly outnumbered the French. No longer was the French language the most widely spoken lingua franca in the region. French settlement in Saskatchewan, however, compared to settlement by most other ethnic groups, covered a relatively long period of time. Although the proportion

of French-speakers declined, the absolute number of them greatly increased. By the 1930s numerous settlements, communities and parishes had been founded in which French was spoken.

Following the exploration of the **SASKATCHEWAN RIVER** by de la Vérendrye in 1737–41, Fort-à-la-Corne was the first European agricultural settlement in what would later become Saskatchewan. However, the area had been claimed by England since 1670 as the hinterland to the Hudson's Bay Company's territory of Rupert's Land, a claim supported by the explorations of **HENRY KELSEY** in 1690–91. With the collapse of Nouvelle France in 1763, a monopoly of the Hudson's Bay Company (HBC) in the North-West might have seemed imminent, but from 1763 to 1779, independent traders based in Quebec established two trading posts on the Saskatchewan river systems for every one built by the Hudson's Bay Company. Between 1779 and 1787, with the gradual consolidation of independent interests into the North West Company, based in Montreal, the HBC posts remained outnumbered by their rivals. In the years remaining until the turn of the century, the HBC increased its efforts to counter the Quebec concerns, especially in the north and upper Assiniboine area: half of the new posts were HBC ones. Competition between the two companies became so acute that a merger was forced in 1821, giving the HBC its long-sought monopoly of the fur trade.

Some eighty-six main trading posts had been established in what would become Saskatchewan between 1763 and 1821, though only about a dozen of them—mostly in remote northern areas—were to remain as permanent settlements. The French-speaking traders based in Quebec had constructed the majority of these. Approximately one-third of these posts were on the Churchill and other northern rivers, while two-thirds were on the North and

South and lower Saskatchewan rivers, on the upper Assiniboine, and on the Qu'Appelle. Despite the impermanency of most of the posts, the era of the *voyageur* should be considered a significant chapter in the history of French settlement in Saskatchewan. Many of the posts established by the Quebec-based traders were given French names. However, French-speaking *voyageurs* had also worked for, or traded with, the arch-rival Hudson's Bay Company, and some instances of HBC posts with French names could be noted prior to the merger of 1821. Métis communities grew around the northern posts after the merger, as well as around new posts established by voyageurs on the prairies. At this point, though, the initial stage of French settlement in Saskatchewan was ending, and a second stage was beginning. The mostly impermanent posts established by the *voyageurs* had, after more than a century, contributed relatively little French population. It was more the development of fairly permanent Métis communities which would lay a firmer base for French settlement.

The designation of "Métis" was originally applied to persons of mixed French and First Nations descent, while the term "half-breed" applied to persons of mixed descent who were not French-speaking Catholics but English-speaking Protestants, mostly of Scottish origin (later, the term Métis would be applied to both groups). Both groups were found in adjacent settlements along the Red River in Manitoba after 1812, with the French-speakers around St. Boniface and the English-speakers around Selkirk. The descendants of both groups were to move westward into Saskatchewan to establish new settlements. By 1870, the census of the North-West Territories and Manitoba listed 5,770 French-speaking Métis, 4,080 English-speaking Métis, and only 1,600 "European" settlers. But considerable numbers of the French-speaking Métis were at least partly of Scottish origin, as had been their *voyageur* predecessors. It was not uncommon for French-speaking Métis to have Scottish surnames. The first Francophone Métis settlements in Saskatchewan grew around the more permanent trading posts in the north, notably Ile-à-la-Crosse, La Loche, Buffalo Narrows (Lac-de-Boeufs), Green Lake (Lac-Vert), Beauval, and Meadow Lake (Lac-des-Prairies). After an exploratory visit by Br. Thibeault in 1844, the mission of St-Jean-Baptiste was founded at Ile-à-la-Crosse in 1846 by two Oblate priests, **PÈRE TACHÉ** and Br. Laflèche. With the arrival in the community of three Soeurs de la Charité (**SISTERS OF CHARITY** or "Grey Nuns," based in Quebec) in 1860, a school, convent and medical clinic were established under the supervision of Bishop Grandin.

During the 1850s and the 1860s small bands of French-speaking Métis buffalo hunters settled on the prairies to the south: at Chimney Coulee in the **CYPRESS HILLS**, in the **FRENCHMAN RIVER** Valley, at

Mr. and Mrs. Michel Bouvier, early Metis settlers at Ile-à-la-Crosse, ca. late 1890s. The descendents of the Bouviers still live in the community.

Lac-Pelletier and Vallée-Ste-Claire, around Montagne-de-Bois (Wood Mountain) in the Big Muddy Valley, on the **MISSOURI COTEAU**, in the Souris River Valley, in the Qu'Appelle River Valley, and at La Prairie Ronde (Round Prairie), south of present-day Saskatoon. These settlements were linked to each other and to similar settlements in Manitoba by a network of wagon trails. In 1864 Fort Qu'Appelle, established by Pierre Hourie, a Métis from the Red River settlement in Manitoba, became a focal point for distant outlying Métis settlements. In 1866 Père Ritchot began to serve a mission near this fort, which had been established by Archbishop Taché of St-Boniface. Named St-Florent a couple of years later by two Oblate priests, Pères de Corby and Lestanc, it was soon renamed Lebret by Senator Girard after an early missionary, Père Lebret. The influential Père Hugonard continued to serve the Métis and Indians of Lebret and area from 1874 until his death in 1917.

A considerable influx of both French-speaking and English-speaking Métis from Manitoba resulted from the Red River Rebellion of 1869–70. These Métis had been concerned about the survival of their culture and settlements. The transfer of the Hudson's Bay Company's lands to Canada being imminent in 1869, the Métis feared that their traditional landholding system of river lots, which was in turn patterned after the *rangs* of the St. Lawrence and Richelieu valleys in Quebec, would be disrupted. The arrival of Canadian government land surveyors confirmed their suspicions, with the result that under the leadership of **LOUIS RIEL** the Métis organized their own provisional government to protect their traditions and their title to the river lots. While open conflict was generally averted and the province of Manitoba was created in 1870 as a part of

Canada, the restive Métis still did not feel secure, in view of the banishment of Riel and the continuing deprivation of Métis landholdings.

The French-speaking Métis who left the Red River settlements trekked westward up the Assiniboine River Valley, then split up, some heading southwest to Wood Mountain, others following the Qu'Appelle past St. Lazare, Marieval, and Lebret, then heading over the Touchwood Hills to the South Saskatchewan River. Forty families, largely from St-Francois-Xavier and Pembina, settled around La Coulée-Chapelle and La Coulée-des-Rochers, respectively a few kilometres northwest and north of Willow Bunch in the Wood Mountain area. An equal number of families moved to the banks of the **SOUTH SASKATCHEWAN RIVER** to found the short-lived community of La Petite Ville, situated several kilometres southeast of Duck Lake. The settlement soon shifted east across the river and several kilometres to the north with the foundation of the communities of **BATOCHE** and St-Laurent-Grandin by 1871, in a more favourable locale.

The St-Laurent settlement developed rapidly with the arrival of more families from the Red River settlements. They came from the St-Francois-Xavier, Rivière-Rouge, and Rivière-Seine settlements, respectively west, south and southeast of St-Boniface. Clergy immigrated directly from France to assist in the process of converting hard-living Métis buffalo hunters into sedentary, docile agriculturalists. The initial mission at La Petite Ville had been founded by Père Moulin, who had immigrated from Dinan in northern Brittany. Père Moulin and Père Bourgine of St-Laurent both also visited the mission of St-André-de-la-Prairie Ronde in 1870 and 1873. In 1874 Père André took charge of the church at St-Laurent-Grandin; he came from Guipavas, in Brittany. Other parishes were soon founded in the settlement: St-Sacrement-de-Duck-Lake in 1876, St-Eugene in 1880, St-Antoine-de-Batoche in 1881, and St-Louis-de-Langevin in 1882. Assisting in this effort were a couple of priests from the Maine region in western France: Pères Vegreville and Fourmond, as well as Père Lecoq (who had already founded the parish of Ste-Rose-du-Lac in Manitoba). River ferries came into service at Batoche in 1874 and at Gabriel's Crossing three years later, started by Batoche Xavier Letendre and **GABRIEL DUMONT**, two of the most influential men in the settlement. By the 1880s, the St-Laurent settlement included four communities of forty to sixty families each (largely from St-Norbert in the Rivière-Rouge settlement), eight separate schools instructing in French, at least seven churches and missions, several post offices and stores, a fire brigade, a grist mill, and at least one saloon. Although the settlement was then situated within Canada's North-West Territories, it was the seat of a self-declared Métis provisional government patterned after its predecessor in the Red River settlements.

Yet the stability of this settlement should not be overemphasized. The priests from France found it difficult to divert the Métis buffalo hunters from their nomadic ways, from using a Mitchif dialect infused with Indian words, and from a traditional mistrust of the clergy, education, alcoholic temperance, and European morality. In the opinion of the priests, then, the adaptation to farming went very slowly. Some Métis were becoming increasingly apprehensive about the likelihood of a repetition of a struggle with the Canadian government over the question of land titles, as the government had already announced its intention to resurvey the river lots and impose a grid system of land ownership. The Métis, assisted by the church hierarchy, demanded more representation in the administration of the North-West Territories and the courts. By 1883 some Métis were already selling their land to non-Métis farmers: reluctant to lead a sedentary life, they exhibited little enthusiasm for developing their lots, and chose to seek the charity of the church as they became progressively impoverished.

In 1884 Gabriel Dumont and a small Métis delegation brought Louis Riel back into Canada from exile in Montana, and during the spring of 1885 the frustrations of the Métis in the St-Laurent settlement erupted into armed conflict with Canadian troops. However, the **NORTH-WEST RESISTANCE** only served to increase rather than alleviate the difficulties of the Métis: it was not entirely supported by all Métis, nor backed completely by the clergy, and it resulted in an increasing exodus from the settlement, more destitution, and an identity crisis. The defeat and humiliation of the Métis marked the end of a fairly short period of Métis settling and predominance in the prairies. Many Métis were scattered, some moving to more isolated communities up north, some merging into larger surrounding French settlements, and others moving eventually into cities. La Prairie Ronde was dissolved soon after the Rebellion; yet nearby Frenchman's Flats was resettled in 1902–12, only to find the last Métis families moving out again (mostly to Saskatoon) by 1939. (*See also* **FRENCH SETTLEMENTS, ETHNIC BLOC SETTLEMENTS**) *Alan Anderson*

FURTHER READING: Anderson, A.B. 1985. "French Settlements in Saskatchewan: Historical and Demographic Perspectives," Research Report No. 5, Research Unit for French-Canadian Studies, University of Saskatchewan.

FRENCH EDUCATION IN SASKATCHEWAN.

French education has been an integral part of the linguistic history of our province since before 1905 and encompasses a rich and challenging past. The history of French education begins with the linguistic and education rights promised to French Canadians outside of Quebec which led to the development and implementation in 1995 of Saskatchewan's only francophone school division, *la Division scolaire francophone No. 310*. It offers a complete Pre-K–12 curriculum in a highly varied program tailored to meet the academic, cultural, and linguistic needs of francophone students throughout the province.

The **NORTH-WEST TERRITORIES ACT** of 1875 granted the establishment of separate schools to minority Protestant or Catholic ratepayers in the North-West Territories based on religious practice. Instruction could be in French or English according to the wishes of the majority of the ratepayers. By 1885, four Catholic public schools were in operation: Duck Lake, Bellevue, St. Louis, and St. Laurent, all within the future confines of our province. These four schools were effectively French Catholic. A subsequent law promulgated in 1888, however, limited French instruction by obliging schools to teach in English at the primary levels. In 1892, allowance for French instruction was reinstated, but French-Canadian Catholics no longer had the right to manage their own schools.

When Saskatchewan became a province in 1905, it followed in principle the tenets of section 93 of the British North America Act which had confirmed that French was one of the two official languages of Canada and that minority education rights would be protected. In 1905, however, there were no provisions concerning French education. It was a law called *La Loi de la Saskatchewan* that provided for the establishment of separate schools. The federal government under Sir Wilfrid Laurier, using the rights of Catholics under existing laws, tried to re-establish a religion-based education system when Alberta and Saskatchewan became provinces. However, under heavy protest by radical lobby groups such as the Orange Order, and the weakening of the government position with the resignation of Clifford Sifton, Laurier's Minister of the Interior, the provisions of 1892 were retained.

Four years after becoming part of Canada, English was the only language of instruction in Saskatchewan with French instruction limited to the primary grades even though French, among other languages, was present in many communities. It was only in 1915 that provincial laws actually stated that French could be taught. Again, in 1917 these laws were amended to limit French instruction to Grade 1. The French community protested and the ensuing lobby resulted in a further modification of the law so that in 1918, only one hour of French instruction per day was allowed. Subsequently, in 1925, the ACFC (*Association catholique franco-canadienne de la Saskatchewan*) assumed full responsibility for the French program by establishing a curriculum, purchasing and distributing textbooks and supplies, carrying out periodic evaluations of its program, instituting a system of annual examinations, awards, and diplomas, and ensuring a supply of qualified teachers, all without any government support until the mid 1960s.

During these early years, the negative reactions of the **KU KLUX KLAN** (KKK) were severely affecting the French-Catholic community. By 1925, the KKK had many followers in Saskatchewan who protested against religious dress of nuns and brothers who taught in ACFC schools, the use of religious images and symbols, and the use of the French language.

In 1931, the provincial government led by Premier **J.T.M. ANDERSON** declared English to be the only language of instruction in the entire province. The Education Act still allowed for one hour of French instruction per day but practically the language of instruction had to be English. In school districts where school trustees adopted the appropriate resolutions, the French course could be taught during the school day. In some cases, it was taught after school, on weekends, in parish halls, and usually on a volunteer basis.

By 1944, French-Catholic communities faced another challenge with the adoption of the Larger School Unit Act which forced the amalgamation of school districts, and consequently, French Catholics found themselves in a minority situation in all school units. Though French Catholics were still a majority in a large number of school districts in areas where they had been established, they did not control a single Larger School Unit in the whole province. Assimilation took root and numbers of French-language speakers dwindled. As a result, some French communities disappeared as linguistic entities.

It was not until 1965 that the tide would change with Saskatoon French-Catholic students going on strike, fighting for catechism to be taught in French. Following this public demonstration, the Department of Education established the Tait Commission to investigate the problem, and also created a supervisor position within the Department responsible for French instruction. One year later, the Education Act was amended to allow the use of French as the language of instruction for the one hour per day and the half hour of religious instruction. In 1968, another revision allowed for the establishment of designated schools: Type "A" schools that could now teach as much as 80% in French, and Type "B" schools that offered a variable amount of teaching time in French (usually about 50%). It was also during this decade that the term "francophone" came into use when referring to French Catholics or those of French descent.

In this same year, the federal government recognized French and English as the two official languages of Canada. This would have far-reaching consequences on the Education Act and its regulations in Saskatchewan. First, in 1972 the Department of Education named a second French-language consultant, and in 1976 the Ready Commission presented its recommendations regarding the teaching of languages in Saskatchewan.

More importantly, the 1978 amendments to article 180 of the School Act provided for Area Minority Language Schools which could offer programs using any minority language as the language of instruction. The right to education in the minority language was later spelled out in the Federal Charter of Rights in 1982.

These events resulted from Canada-wide lobbying and a number of challenges before the Courts on the part of the francophone community and most notably the ACFC, now called the *Association Communautaire Fransaskoise de la Saskatchewan*. Their efforts, along with those of local francophone school boards, were pivotal in creation of the Official Minority Language Office in Saskatchewan within the Department of Education. This office, formed in 1980, would be responsible for all French education in the province. Following this, the early 1980s witnessed symposiums regarding the needs of French education. In time, the province would witness the implementation of the particulars of Section 23 of the Canadian Charter of Rights and Freedoms that guaranteed to all official language minorities the right of instruction in one's mother tongue. Also instrumental in this process were the francophone parents who used a Court challenge in 1987 to obtain their rights because they felt that the Charter of Rights had not been respected. In the mid-1980s, the Department of Education published in French the policies on Core Curriculum followed by the development and implementation of French curricula until about 1998.

During the implementation of Core Curriculum, important legislation was being drafted concerning francophone schools. Saskatchewan's francophone parents issued a Court challenge in late 1987 at the Court of Queen's Bench to obtain control of their own school board. The Court's decision, rendered the following year, recognized the francophone community rights to French education and granted them control over their own school system. Additional challenges were met and finally amendments to the Education Act in 1994 created a third public and legal entity of education in the province (in addition to the public and separate school divisions), to administer francophone education. Nine regional francophone boards were established, which in 1999, for optimum efficiency, grew into one single provincial school division called *la Division scolaire francophone No. 310*. Core Curriculum was implemented in French beginning in 1988. As part of this initiative, the particular needs of francophone students were considered. Since 1994-95, the notion of integrating and developing the Fransaskois culture and identity has become an important focus for curriculum development and implementation at the Official Minority Language Office.

In 2004 in the francophone school division, there were twelve schools, with a student population of about 1,039. The school division administers pre-schools in all of its jurisdictions and before and after-school daycares in many others. One main area of focus from pre-school to Grade 12 is the nourishing of French identity, language, and culture as they pertain to students, parents, and the teaching community living in a minority milieu. It is the undying determination and political action of the francophone community and fellow stakeholders that has made French language education a reality for francophone students in Saskatchewan.

The needs and rights of francophones were etched into Saskatchewan's linguistic history. Most notably, the Official Languages Act of 1968 would be equally instrumental in providing a bilingual education for students outside of the francophone school community. (*See* CORE FRENCH EDUCATION; FRENCH IMMERSION EDUCATION). This law declared Canada to be an officially bilingual country, and as previously indicated, the provinces would continue to have jurisdiction over education. Soon after the passing of this law, Saskatchewan would see the establishment of French immersion schools and formal Core French programs. The administration of these three programs continues to be managed by the Official Minority Language Office at Saskatchewan Learning. (*See also* COLLÈGE MATHIEU).

Estelle D'Almeida

FURTHER READING: Office of the Commissioner of Official Languages. 2001. *Canadian Linguistic Facts and Figures: Manitoba and Saskatchewan.* Ottawa: Minister of Public Works and Government Services Canada; Martel, Angéline. 2001. *Rights, Schools and Communities in Mimority Contexts: 1986-2002.* Ottawa: Minister of Public Works and Government Services Canada.

FRENCH IMMERSION EDUCATION. Saskatchewan was the second province in Canada to implement a French Immersion program in the public education system for non-francophones. In 1968, Saskatchewan and British Columbia opened their first publicly funded French Immersion programs. The Saskatoon Catholic school board, at the request of parents, opened the first early Immersion program. In 1969, a second program opened in Regina under the jurisdiction of the Regina Catholic School Board. The teaching of 50% to 100% of the curriculum in French to grade one children who did not speak French is known internationally as an innovative Canadian experiment. Research continues to support this approach to the teaching of French as a second language as the most effective in achieving functional bilingualism by the end of high school.

The growth of the program in the 1970s and 1980s was attributable to the proclamation of Canada's first Official Languages Act (1969), as well as to the commitment and support of communities willing to try this approach to learning French.

In 1970, federal funds became available to support provincial French second-language programs; in Saskatchewan, the federal government support has continued since that time. These funds have translated into consultant support, curriculum development opportunities for French second-language teachers and administrators, the Official Languages Monitors Program, and student bursaries. Saskatchewan's Education Act (1978) enabled instruction in publicly funded schools to be conducted in a language other than English. An Official Minority Languages Advisory Committee was formed in the 1977–78 school year, and by 1980 the Official Minority Language Office was established to support the development of French language education in Saskatchewan.

The first Saskatchewan graduates of a French Immersion program received their diplomas in 1981 with the introduction of the "bilingual mention" qualification on the student high school transcripts in the fall of 1992. The number of students in French Immersion or bilingual programs increased annually by over 20% in the first half of the 1980s. A unique French teacher education program at the UNIVERSITY OF REGINA responded to the growing demand for bilingual teachers trained in second language teaching and Immersion methodology. The number of kindergarten to grade twelve students in French Immersion programs in the province of Saskatchewan continued to increase until 1990; some large urban school divisions had as many as 30% of their kindergarten students enrolled in French Immersion programs during the late 1980s.

With the development and introduction of

ROY ANTAL/REGINA LEADER-POST

Grade 1 and 2 students learn about the 14 new street signs and squares that have gone up in St. Mary's School, a French immersion elementary school in Regina.

Saskatchewan Core French curricula for grades one to twelve in the late 1980s, a number of school boards introduced the new Core French program in their schools. Core French is defined as the study of French as a second language for 120–150 minutes per week, with various entry points from grade one to grade seven. The numbers of students in French Immersion declined as this alternative means of second language learning became more readily available By the 1993–94 school year, 6.6% of all the children in the province were enrolled in French Immersion or bilingual programs. In 1994–95, the Fransaskois school boards were formed, and over 1,000 students were transferred from French Immersion programs in anglophone school boards to the newly formed jurisdiction. Approximately 5.6% of the students in the province remained in French Immersion programs.

The political unrest that characterized Quebec-Canada relations during the 1990s is thought to have been one of the factors in a significant decline in the percentage of students enrolling in French Immersion in the province: from 1996 to 2001 the percentage of "bilingual" 15–19-year-olds decreased from 10.7% to 9.9%, producing one of the lowest rates of provincial bilingualism in Canada. The first non-francophone parents to advocate for and choose French Immersion for their children tended to be university-educated persons who believed in the value of a second language in the education of a child; but they also were likely to be committed to a bilingual Canadian nation. By the year 2000, the children in French Immersion represented a more typical cross-section of the diverse school age population. Over the thirty-seven years of French Immersion in Saskatchewan, parents' motivation evolved from choosing French Immersion for their child in support of the linguistic duality of Canada and future employment advantages, to a search for a more challenging academic program and the acquisition of the cognitive benefits of bilingualism; in some cases, it is also a result of their awareness of the increasing globalization of our world.

Mary E. Reeves

FRENCH SETTLEMENTS. Three explanations for the establishment of series of French bloc settlements across the prairies after the NORTH-WEST RESISTANCE can be suggested. First, the immigration of large numbers of French-speaking farmers to the prairies could serve to stabilize the restive, semi-nomadic MÉTIS. The Métis would be provided not only with the opportunity to improve their farming, but also to intermarry with French-speakers and to incorporate their stigmatized half-breed identity into a broader French-Canadian identity. Many Métis, however, chose to retreat further into isolation rather than have their mixed identity viewed unfavourably.

Second, the establishment of specifically French bloc settlements should be seen as only one element in the general context of prairie settlement: many other ethnic groups rapidly developed their own bloc settlements throughout the prairies due to immigration schemes of the federal government and specialized agencies, often operating in close connection with the railways, which were anxious to settle profitable grain farmers along their rights of way. Moreover, with the emergence of the bloc settlement as the typical pattern in this region of Canada, the gravitation of co-ethnics to appropriate settlement areas was likely: people of French origin would settle in one of the new French settlements rather than in an area which had been settled predominantly by people of other ethnic origins.

Third, most of the French settlements resulted from a planned attempt to maintain a significant proportion of French-speakers in the west. French clergy played a vital role in such colonization schemes. Most of the French settlements which developed in southeastern Saskatchewan were founded by Mgr. Jean Gaire during the 1890s, while most of those in the south-central and southwestern regions were established by Pères Royer and Gravel in 1906–10. Many of the immigrants from France and Quebec who settled areas adjacent to the St-Laurent settlement after the 1885 Rebellion arrived under the auspices of the Société d'Immigration Française, centred in Montreal and supervised by Auguste Bodard, the secretary-general, himself an immigrant from Brittany. The society had been formed to encourage immigration from France, Belgium and the "Suisse romande" (French Switzerland) to French settlements throughout the west. Bodard believed that such immigration would re-establish equilibrium between French speakers and English speakers in the west, at least in the rural areas. Bodard saw the chances for survival in Saskatchewan and Manitoba as better than in Ontario, pointing out that already the Franco-Manitobans had priests, parishes, and schools everywhere.

Many of the tens of thousands of "Fransaskois" (Saskatchewan French) live in francophone communities and parishes located within thirty-two distinctly French rural settlements. Two series of French bloc settlements were organized in Saskatchewan, one across the northern part of the prairies (note that the prairies constitute only the southern half of the province as a whole, however) and the other across the southern part; these two series were separated by a central belt in which no French settlements were organized. With the arrival of the French immigrants after the 1885 Rebellion, the Métis settlement of St-Laurent became the nucleus of one of the largest French settlements in the prairies, despite the scattering of the Métis. While a few immigrants from France settled in the BATOCHE

COURTESY OF BRIAN MLAZGAR

The family of Napoléon Pilon, ca. 1910, who homesteaded near Patrick, Saskatchewan.

area as early as 1881 and 1884, the main influx commenced in 1886 when settlers arrived in the St-Louis area. They came from Poitou, Brittany, Maine, Savoy, and Picardy. The small community of Hoey was first settled at about the same time by immigrants from Belgium, Paris, and the Saintonge region. The village of Domrémy was established in 1892 by settlers from Ste-Anne-de-la-Pérade and Ste-Geneviève-de-Batiscan, Quebec; in 1894–95 they were joined by immigrants from France, chiefly from Brittany but also from Poitou. In 1896 the Abbé Barbier came from St-Louis to organize a new parish, Ste-Jeanne-d'Arc. At St-Isidore-de-Bellevue the francophone population included Métis families who had settled in the district by the early 1880s, followed by descendants of Acadian exiles who had resettled in Quebec before coming to Bellevue in 1883–94, Québécois families from communities in the Eastern Townships and other regions of Quebec, several families from a French-Canadian (originally Québécois) settlement in Minnesota, and a few families who came directly from France.

While these communities immediately east of the St-Laurent settlement of the Métis were developing, the historic Métis village of Duck Lake (Lac-aux-Canards) was being reinforced as a French-speaking centre in 1894–95 by immigrants from Poitou, Brittany, Paris, Normandy, Savoy and Franche-Comté. West of Duck Lake, the parishes of Ste-Anne-de-Titanic and St-François-de-Carlton were established in 1902 to serve the newly arrived immigrants from Brittany, Poitou, and Belgium.

Southeast of Domrémy, immigrants from Franche-Comté and Dauphiné had settled by 1899 around Bonne-Madone and Reynaud; they were served by Père Voisin, himself an immigrant from the Jura area on the Swiss frontier, as well as the Abbé Barbier from St-Louis. Virtually all of the communities in this settlement remain predominantly French.

A second French settlement to develop in the north-central region of the province was situated about 40 km east of Saskatoon. The settlement began to develop in 1897 with the first establishment of the community successively called Marcotte Ranch, Lally Siding (since 1904), Howell (since 1906), and finally Prud'homme (after the bishop of the French-language diocese of Prince Albert, since 1922). The initial settlers were from Nantes in Loire-Atlantique, and Arras, in Artois, France; some arrived after first settling in Ste-Rose-du-Lac and Grande-Clairière, Manitoba. In 1910 they were joined by immigrants from the Belgian province of Hainaut. The Abbé Bourdel, born in Brittany, arrived in 1904 to establish the parish of Sts-Donatien-et-Rogatien; he was succeeded in 1931 by Maurice Baudoux, a son of one of the families from Belgium, who was destined to become Bishop of St-Paul, a French-language diocese in Alberta, then Archbishop of St-Boniface. A second parish in the settlement was St-Philippe-de-Néri, established at Vonda in 1907. The parish of St-Denis, due south of Vonda, came into existence in 1910; it had been settled first by immigrants from Saintonge, Poitou, Brittany, Flanders and Hainaut, and then by families brought out from

Quebec by the Abbé Bérubé. The Abbé Mollier, the first resident parish priest, came from the Rhône Valley in southern France. Today there are over 1,000 people of French origin in this settlement, inclusive of the town of Vonda, the incorporated village of Prud'homme, and the hamlet of St-Denis.

To the northeast of Prince Albert, the White Star area was settled in 1904 by Breton immigrants. Originally this locality was called Edouardville (after Br. Edouard Courbis, the director of an orphanage in Prince Albert, who was originally from the Guyenne region in southwestern France). The adjoining area to the east was soon settled by immigrants from Guyenne, Brittany, and Normandy. The parish of St-Jacques became the focal point for the small settlement, which today has a French population of about 600 in and around the hamlets of Albertville and Henribourg, originally Morinville (named after Henri Albert Morin, as influential first settler). In 1904 a large Breton settlement began to develop at St-Brieux, about 35 km southwest of Melfort, with the arrival of several families from St-Brieuc, Brittany, led by Père Le Floch. A second church, Notre-Dame-de-la-Nativité, was constructed at nearby Kermaria in 1906. The mission of St-Philippe (1930) serves a mixed French and Hungarian population in the Little Moose district west of St-Brieux. Today the settlement has a French population numbering about 900, and St-Brieux remains predominantly French. There are also another 300 people of French origin in the Omand district near Meskanaw, about 35 km northwest of St-Brieux.

French and Belgian colonists from Manitoba had settled in three areas in the northeastern region of the Saskatchewan prairies by 1910: St-Front (about 50 km southeast of St-Brieux); Perigord (40 km east of St-Front); and Veillardville (immediately west of the town of Hudson Bay). They were joined by immigrants from Savoy, Limousin, and Beauce at St-Front; by immigrants from Auvergne, Poitou, Savoy, and Picardy at Perigord; and by Québecois in all three settlements. The parish of St-Front (1926) was first served by the omnipresent Abbé Barbier; other early French parishes were St-Athanase-de-Perigord and the mission of Pré-Ste-Marie (30 km north of Perigord). The French population in each of these three settlements may be estimated to number at least 300. Zenon Park (named after Zenon Chamberland, an early settler) had been settled by Québecois by 1910; centred on the parish of Notre-Dame-de-la-Nativité, it remains solidly French (close to 90% of the residents claim French origin). There are approximately 500 people of French extraction in the immediate area.

While French settlements were developing in the northeastern region of the Saskatchewan prairies, others began to develop in the northwestern region. During the early 1880s, Père Cochin established missions to serve Indians and Métis at

Cut Knife, Delmas, Cochin, and Meadow Lake. **ONÉSIME DORVAL**, who was to become the best known and most respected French-language teacher in the settlements on the northern plains, arrived in Battleford in 1880, having come to the Red River settlement in Manitoba from Quebec three years previously; in 1896 she moved to Batoche, and in 1914 to Duck Lake. The Prince brothers, one of whom was to become a senator, began farming in the country immediately west of the Battlefords in 1888, having immigrated from St-Grégoire, Quebec. By 1907, immigrants from France had settled at Delmas and Jackfish Lake and had joined Québecois at Vawn. Today people of French origin number some 1,500 on the north side of the river, around the communities of Vawn, Edam, Cochin, and Jackfish Lake (parish of St-Léon); and they number about 800 on the south side of the river around Delmas (parish of St-Jean-Baptiste-de-la-Salle). In 1971 they constituted a large majority at Delmas and Jackfish Lake, and almost half of the population of Vawn and one-quarter of Edam.

A second French settlement to develop in the northwestern region was the one centred on the village of Marcelin, about midway between North Battleford and Prince Albert. In 1899 Antoine Marcelin immigrated from North Dakota to settled in the Moon Hills (part of the Coteau), west of the present village of Marcelin; later he purchased land where the village now stands. Breton immigrants soon settled in the area, and a French school as well as the parish of St-Albert (1902) were organized by Père Lejeunesse. During the 1930s families from French settlements in the southern regions of the province, driven north by drought and the search for pastures for their livestock, settled among immigrants from France, Quebec, and Michigan in the hills west of Marcelin. People of French origin in the Marcelin and Coteau settlement today number close to 1,000, but now comprise less than half of the population of Marcelin.

The most extensive French settlement in the northwestern region began to develop in 1909, when labourers immigrated from Quebec and New England to work in the new pulp mills at Big River. By 1912 many French-Canadian families were settling around Debden. At the same time Spiritwood was named by its first postmaster, Rupert Dumond, after his former hometown in North Dakota. Several families from the Prud'homme-St-Denis settlement near Saskatoon settled in the Laventure district north of Spiritwood in 1911, as well as in the Lac-Bérubé district southwest of Debden in 1914. With the construction of a railway west through Spiritwood, immigrants from Bapaume, France, settled in a district of the same name immediately west of town in 1929. The Québecois followed the construction of another line west from Debden in 1930–31 to settle around Ormeaux, Victoire, Pascal,

Morneau, Capasin, and Léoville. Meanwhile, other adjacent districts had been settled, uniting all of these communities into an extensive French settlement. Today there are six French parishes in this general region: Notre-Dame-du-Sacré-Coeur at Big River (1909), St-Bonaventure at Laventure (1911), St-Jean-Baptiste at Debden (1912), Sacré-Coeur at Spiritwood (1912), Notre-Dame-des-Victoires at Victoire (1914), and Ste-Thérèse-de-l'Enfant-Jésus at Léoville (1930). People of French origin comprise approximately two-thirds of the population of Debden and a quarter of the population of Spiritwood. Today there are close to 3,000 French people in this settlement as a whole.

Two other, smaller French settlements in the northwestern region remain to be considered. There are some 1,600 French in the Meadow Lake area; almost a third of them live in the town of Meadow Lake itself, where they are served by the parish of Notre-Dame-de-la-Paix; about 400 of them are in the vicinity of Makwa, where they are served by the parish of St-Thomas-Apôtre; and the remainder are scattered around the bush districts to the southeast of Meadow Lake. There are also some 700 French in the Paradise Hill area. This settlement developed in 1910–14 with the arrival of French-speaking settlers from southwestern France, Brittany, and even the Yukon goldfields; focal point for the settlement was the rural district of Butte-St-Pierre, where the parish church of St-Pierre was originally located; it was eventually moved into the village of Paradise Hill.

The earliest French settlements in southern Saskatchewan developed in the southeastern region. A French-speaking aristocrat from Alsace, Dr. Rudoph Meyer, arrived in Whitewood in 1884, accompanied by several counts from Alsace and Paris; together they developed the St-Hubert settlement southwest of Whitewood. The parish of Ste-Jeanne-d'Arc was organized, and imposing houses were constructed. Whole families were imported from France to work for the aristocrats: house domestics, gardeners, craftsmen, horse grooms, and tenant farmers. Horse racing days, held in conjunction with nearby Cannington Manor, where English gentry had settled, were especially popular social events. When the French counts visited their English counterparts, they did so in coaches accompanied by coachmen and footmen wearing top hats. In lieu of fox hunting, coyotes were hunted with imported purebred dogs and thoroughbred horses; expensive wines and foodstuffs were also imported. However, this curious colony was not without its problems: cattle, sheep and horse ranching was largely unsuccessful, as were brushmaking and cheese factories, and chicory and sugar beet farming. Meyer, disillusioned, returned to France within five years, followed by the other aristocrats, the last of whom left in 1913. But their entourage did remain, to be joined by settlers from many parts of France and Belgium as well as from the Fannystelle area in Manitoba. Other immigrants, from the Lyon region in France, settled around Dumas (about 35 km southeast) with the arrival of the railway in 1906. Today there are approximately 600 people of French origin in these two small settlements and in nearby towns and villages, where they comprise a small minority.

Many of the French bloc settlements in the southeastern region were formed due to the colonization schemes of Mgr. Jean Gaire, who immigrated from Alsace to St-Boniface in 1888. After visiting the Wolseley area in southern Saskatchewan, he returned to France the following year to recruit potential settlers. Responding to advertisements in French journals, French and Belgian immigrants first established the small colony of Grande-Clairière in Manitoba in 1890, then the communities of Cantal (parish of St-Raphael) and Bellegarde (parish of St-Maurice) in Saskatchewan, respectively in 1892 and 1893. The settlement, situated in the southeastern corner of Saskatchewan, expanded to include Wauchope (parish of St-Francois-Régis) by 1901–03, Storthoaks (parish of St-Antoine) and Alida by 1912–13, and finally Redvers (where the parish of Notre-Dame-de-Fatima was not organized until 1950). The original settlers included a few Métis families, but most immigrated directly from Belgium (Belgian Luxembourg) and France (Brittany, Lorraine, Provence, Auvergne, and Burgundy); later settlers arrived from Quebec. Today the settlement includes about 1,500 people of French origin. The hamlets of Bellegarde and Cantal remain wholly French (in fact, the former has been called "la capitale du Petit-Québec"); French people comprise about three-quarters of the population in Wauchope, half at Storthoaks, less than a third at Alida, and about a quarter at Redvers and Antler.

In 1892 Mgr. Gaire also founded the settlement of Forget (named after the first **LIEUTENANT-GOVERNOR** of Saskatchewan). The first settlers arrived from many regions in France, particularly from Lorraine and Dauphiné; there are about 300 people of French origin in this small settlement today, yet they comprise only a quarter of the population in the small village of Forget itself. The next year the settlement of Montmartre (parish of Sacré-Coeur) began to develop some 25 km southwest of Wolseley. The settlers came from Montmartre, today an integral part of Paris, as well as from other regions in France and from Quebec. Today the settlement includes about 600 French living in and around the village of Montmartre, which is little more than one-third French, the hamlet of Candiac, and the surrounding rural districts. Another 300 French live about 50 km to the west, around the village of Sedley (parish of Notre-Dame-de-Grâce) and the rural district of Bechard. Residents of French origin now constitute a very small proportion of the population of Sedley: they claim that they are "pas

forts, mais pas morts" ("not strong, but not yet dead"). French Canadians continued to supplement the Métis in the Qu'Appelle Valley. The mission at Lebret was established in 1866, and Mgr. Gaire founded the parish of Ste-Anne-du-Loup at Wolseley in 1888. The French proportion in Lebret has fallen only a little, and in other towns and villages of the area the French constitute a small minority; but people of French origin in this general area today may be estimated to number at least 1,000.

Another 400 are found downriver where the river crosses into Manitoba. Yet the settlement around Ste-Marthe-Rocanville (named after A.H. Rocan Bastien, the first postmaster) is actually an adjunct to the larger St-Lazare settlement across the border, inclusive of over 1,000 French and Francophone Métis. St-Lazare dates back to Métis settlement; the Métis were joined by French immigrants (served by a priest from Reims) in 1904. In the Souris River Valley west of Estevan, the Métis were joined by immigrants from Auvergne and Languedoc. The town of Radville (named after Conrad Paquin, an original homesteader) had its beginnings in 1905. About 1,000 people of French origin are found today in the Radville area, yet the French constitute little more than a third of the total population of Radville.

After the foundation of French settlements throughout the southeastern region, similar settlements rapidly came into existence in the south-central and southwestern regions, so that by 1910 a continuous series of French settlements stretched across southern Saskatchewan. Again, the clergy played a key role in this colonization process. The Abbé Marie-Albert Royer, curé of the parish of Ponteix in Auvergne, immigrated to St-Boniface in 1906, then set out to serve a small French-speaking community in Saskatchewan, Gauthierville or Villeroy, on Rivière-la-Vieille (Wood River). He moved further west that same year due to the arrival of the Abbé Louis-Pierre Gravel (born in Princeville, Nicolet, Quebec) with Québecois colonists from the Eastern Townships at nearby Ste-Philomène (later Gravelbourg). The Abbé Gravel had impressive credentials: he had been appointed "missionary-colonizer" of southern Saskatchewan by Archbishop Langevin of St-Boniface and was reportedly a personal friend of Prime Minister Laurier, who materially aided his colonization schemes. He was further assisted by his brothers Émile and Henri, who led the colonists in by wagon train from Moose Jaw. The Abbé Gravel supervised the expansion of the settlement to include the parishes of Ste-Radegonde at Laflèche in 1906–08, Mazenod in 1907–08, and Notre-Dame-de-Lourdes at Meyronne in 1908. Gravelbourg itself grew into a major French centre, gaining a "collège classique" (Collège Mathieu) in 1918, a large convent in 1919 and monastery in 1926, then the cathedral of Ste-Philomène in 1930,

a seminary in 1931, and a couple of French-language radio stations in 1952. The diocese has always maintained close links with French Canada; the first bishop, Bishop Villeneuve, became Archbishop of Quebec and a cardinal, and later bishops became the Archbishops of Moncton, New Brunswick, and Ottawa. Today there are over 2,000 French Canadians in the Gravelbourg area.

While Gravelbourg was first coming into existence in 1906–07, settlers from St-Gabriel-de-Brandon and L'Acadie, Quebec, were joining the Métis at Willow Bunch, about 80 km to the southeast. Within ten years the settlement had expanded to include an extensive area. Today there are more than 2,000 French and Francophone Métis in this settlement; they constitute a majority in the town of Willow Bunch and in the hamlets of Lisieux and St-Victor, and in the surrounding rural districts. Francophone parishes and missions in this settlement have included St-Ignace-des-Saules at Willow Bunch (1906), St-Victor (1906), the mission of La Rivière-aux-Trembles at Little Woody (1907), Christ-Roi at Fife Lake (1908), St-Georges at Assiniboia (1913), Ste-Thérèse-de-l'Enfant-Jésus at Lisieux (1916), St-Jean at Rockglen, Notre-Dame-de-Lourdes at Verwood, and l'Assomption-de-la-Ste-Vierge at Maxstone.

The Wood Mountain (Montagne-de-bois) area, south of Gravelbourg and west of Willow Bunch, began to develop when Québecois from Ste-Clair in Dorchester County founded the community of Ferland. This settlement, centred on the parish of St-Jean-Baptiste at Ferland, founded in 1909, continued to expand with the establishment of new parishes and missions at Glentworth (St-Marcel) in 1929, Fir Mountain in 1939, and Wood Mountain in 1955. While Ferland remains almost completely French, the neighbouring villages of Glentworth and Wood Mountain have only small French minorities. All told, some 600 people of French origin are found in the general area. A small French settlement developed about 40 km northeast of Gravelbourg when the hamlets of Courval (parish of St-Joseph) and Coderre (parish of St-Charles) originated respectively in 1908 and 1910. The settlers came from the Eastern Townships in Quebec as well as from North Dakota; today their descendants number about 400–500.

The town of Ponteix, about 70 km west of Gravelbourg, had its origins when Père Royer arrived in 1907. First called Notre-Dame-d'Auvergne, it was renamed Ponteix after Père Royer's home parish near Clermont-Ferrand, France. The first settlers came from Auvergne as well as from Belgium. At Lac-Pelletier (where the parish of Ste-Anne was founded in 1906), to the northwest, the Métis were joined by Québecois in 1906–07, then by immigrants from France in 1910. To the north of Ponteix, Vanguard (where the

Les quatre religieuses:
Sr. Marie Emmanuelle
Sr. Marie du St. Sacrement
Sr. Marie de la Croix
Angèle Auteroche
XXXXXXXXXXXXXXXXXXXXXXXXXXXXXX

1913 - Premier Couvent
First Convent
N. Dame d'Auvergne

NOTRE DAME D'AUVERGNE CHURCH ARCHIVES

First convent at Ponteix, 1913.

FRENCHMAN RIVER (49°00' 107°18'; Map sheet 72 G/3). The Frenchman River rises in Cypress Lake and is fed by streams flowing off the southern flank of the **CYPRESS HILLS**. It flows eastward across southwestern Saskatchewan before turning south across the 49th parallel and into the Milk River in northern Montana. Approximately 341 km long, it is one of the few Saskatchewan rivers that lie within the Mississipi drainage basin. Christiansen and Sauer (1988) have shown that the valley originated as glacial meltwater channel, draining water from an ice-lobe that flowed around the southern edge of the Cypress Hills. Meltwaters carved a channel up to 180 metres deep between the ice and the unglaciated uplands. The modern valley ranges from 30 to 106 metres deep, much of it infilled by debris from ancient landslides.

The Frenchman flows through the West Block of the **GRASSLANDS NATIONAL PARK**. Its flow is highly variable, and early ranchers trapped floodwaters for irrigation. After the **DEPRESSION**, the PFRA developed irrigation reservoirs at Eastend and Val Marie. The origin of the name is uncertain but both Métis and francophone settlers occupied the region in the early 1900s. The Frenchman River is known locally as the Whitemud River, after the white clays common to the area. The region is immortalized in Wallace Stegner's *Wolf Willow*.   *Marilyn Lewry*

FURTHER READING: Christiansen, E.A. and E.K. Sauer. 1988. "Age of the Frenchman Valley and Associated Drift South of the Cypress Hills, Saskatchewan, Canada." *Canadian Journal of Earth Sciences* 25: 1703–08; Stegner, W. 1962. *Wolf Willow*. New York: Viking Press.

FRENCHMAN'S BUTTE, BATTLE OF. After General **MIDDLETON** and his 5,000-man North-West Field Force arrived from Ottawa to quell the 1885 Resistance, the force split into three columns. The main one, commanded by Middleton, marched on **LOUIS RIEL**'s self-proclaimed capital of **BATOCHE**. A

---

parish of St-Joseph was established in 1908) and Pambrun were settled partly by French-speaking farmers from the Eastern Townships in Quebec, from the United States, and from Belgium and France in 1908–09. To the southwest, the hamlet of Frenchville (where the parish of St-Joseph came into being in 1909) was settled in 1909–10 by immigrants from France and Belgium. To the west, the settlement expanded to include the Gouverneur district and the village of Cadillac (named after Antoine de Lamothe Cadillac, governor of Nouvelle France), where the parish of Notre-Dame-de-la-Confiance was organized in 1914. To the south, the settlement expanded into ranching grasslands. Today there are approximately 1,500 people of French origin in these areas. The town of Ponteix remains largely French, whereas in the small villages of Cadillac, Pambrun, and Vanguard the French are a minority.

Meanwhile, other French settlements had developed in the southwestern region. In 1908–10, the community of Valroy (later Dollard, named after Adam Dollard des Ormeaux, a Quebec hero in 1660), 70 km west of Cadillac, was established by settlers from Quebec and various French settlements on the prairies as well as by some Belgian families. Today their descendants number about 500 in the predominantly French community of Dollard, where the parish of Ste-Jeanne-d'Arc was founded in 1908, in the nearby towns of Eastend and Shaunavon, and in the surrounding rural districts at the eastern end of the **CYPRESS HILLS**.

Almost 50 km south of Cadillac, Val-Marie, originally a Métis settlement, developed in 1910 when immigrants from France were brought in by Père Passaplan, who also contributed to the settlement of Lac-Pelletier; today their descendants number about 500, and approximately half of the population is French. The central parish is La-Nativité-de-Val-Marie (1910); later a second church, Notre-Dame-de-la-Présentation (1938), was organized in the neighbouring Masefield area, settled in 1926.

Approximately one-third of all the French-origin population in Saskatchewan lives in the northern tier of settlements, an almost equal number in the southern tier, and the remaining third in the major cities and in ethnically mixed areas not included within settlements. By 1971 there were almost 20,000 people of French origin in the six largest urban centres. Yet these urban minorities are proportionately insignificant within the total urban population, and they tend to be quite anglicized, the majority speaking English as their mother tongue (54% in urban areas, compared to 34% in rural areas in 1971). They are served by only five French-language parishes, although by 1977 six of the fifteen "écoles désignées" (designated schools offering French-language instruction in a variety of subjects) and both bilingual university programs were in the larger urban centres. Saskatoon and Regina have the largest *number* of French people, whereas Prince Albert and North Battleford have the highest *proportion*. (*See also* **FRANCOPHONES**)   *Alan Anderson*

FURTHER READING: Frémont, D. 1980. *Les Français dans L'Ouest canadien*. St-Boniface: Les Editions du Blé; Lapointe, R. and L. Tessier. 1986. *Histoire des Franco-Canadiens de la Saskatchewan*. Regina: Société historique de la Saskatchewan.

RCMP MUSEUM, REGINA, 32.20.CXLIV

Major-General Strange.

EVERETT BAKER PHOTO/COURTESY OF THE SASKATCHEWAN HISTORY AND FOLKLORE SOCIETY
Frenchman's Butte, September 1947.

second column, commanded by Colonel William Otter, moved against **POUNDMAKER**'s band. The third, under Major General Thomas Bland Strange, marched north from Calgary and turned east along the **NORTH SASKATCHEWAN RIVER,** where Strange hoped to trap **BIG BEAR**'s Cree warriors. On May 28, Strange's column of 300 men caught up with the 250 Cree warriors at Frenchman's Butte and launched an initial attack; after several hours of fighting, both sides withdrew their forces with neither side suffering any fatalities. On June 3, Middleton arrived with 200 more troops and assumed command of Strange's column. By that time, Big Bear had withdrawn into the swampy northern wilderness, taking seventy White hostages with him. On June 18, the Indians released some White prisoners with a message pleading for "our Great Mother, the Queen, to stop the Government soldiers and Red Coats from shooting us." Soon afterwards the Cree began turning themselves in at **FORT PITT**, and on July 2, 1885, Big Bear and his 12-year-old son surrendered themselves at Fort Carlton.

Peter Borch and Daria Coneghan

FURTHER READING: Dunn, Jack. 1994. *The Alberta Field Force of 1885.* Winnipeg: Hignell; Light, D. 1987. *Footprints in the Dust.* North Battleford: Turner-Warwick; Stonechild, B. and W.A. Waiser. 1997. *Loyal Till Death: Indians and the Northwest Rebellion.* Calgary: Fifth House.

FRENCH'S SCOUTS. It was at Fort Qu'Appelle that General **MIDDLETON** commenced the real preparations for the campaign against the **MÉTIS** during the 1885 Resistance. Middleton empowered Captain French, an Irish officer who had been in the North-West Mounted Police (NWMP), to raise a mounted force in the vicinity of Fort Qu'Appelle. French had served in various military establishments before he joined the NWMP and received many honours for his horsemanship. This mounted troop, known as French's Scouts, joined the 10th Royal Grenadiers from Toronto and the Winnipeg Field Battery under the command of artillery officer Lieutenant-Colonel C.E. Montizambert, to form the west-bank column that would march from Qu'Appelle to Batoche. French's Scouts, along with the rest of Montizambert's, column was about two miles away on the left bank of the river when Métis attacked Middleton's forces. By the time the column arrived, the battle was over.

On May 12, 1885, Captain John French was killed in combat. Following his death, French's Scouts were re-named Brittlebank's Scouts after Lieutenant William Brittlebank. Brittlebank's Scouts were disbanded in September 1885.

Peter Borch and Daria Coneghan

FURTHER READING: Light, Douglas. 1987. *Footprints in the Dust.* North Battleford: Turner-Warwick; Stanley, George. 1961. *The Birth of Western Canada.* Toronto: University of Toronto Press.

FRIGGSTAD, OLAF (1921–). Olaf Friggstad, farm machinery innovator and manufacturer, was born at Frontier on June 29, 1921. In May 1970, Olaf and two of his sons founded Friggstad Manufacturing Ltd. Their mainstay product was the Friggstad cultivator, designed to cope with stony land and trash cover; the cultivator's unique design allowed flexibility between the sections, assuring even penetration. The Friggstad product line gained such respect in western Canada, the United States and Australia that within twelve years production staff at the Frontier plant grew from six to 180. The presence of the Friggstad plant greatly helped the economy of Frontier and southwest Saskatchewan. The company's other two plants in Havre (Montana) and Fargo (North Dakota) had 100 employees. The firm diversified into rock pickers, bale wagons, land levellers, tine harrows, and air seeders. When Saskatchewan agriculture was forced into rapid retrenchment by the recession of the 1980s, the Friggstad firm went into receivership; however, its assets, including advanced machinery designs, were purchased for use by Flexi-Coil.

Olaf Friggstad served as reeve of the Rural Municipality of Frontier, board member of the Prairie Implement Manufacturers Association, chairman of the Frontier Credit Union, chairman of the Wheat Pool Committee, chairman of the Frontier Co-operative, Sunday school superintendent, deacon of the Bethel Lutheran Church, and zone leader of Gideons International. For thirty-five years he travelled extensively as a lay evangelist to churches, conferences, and Bible camps. In 1981 he was named an honorary life member of the Saskatchewan Institute of Agrologists in recognition of his contributions to the farming industry of the province. In 1982 he was installed as a Member of the Order of Canada. In 1988 he was made an honorary life member of Gideons International in Canada, and in 1997 he was inducted into the Saskatchewan Agricultural Hall of Fame.

FURTHER READING: Friggstad, O. 1997. *Faith When Dreams Die.* Altona, MB: Friesen Printers.

FROG LAKE MASSACRE. Although it was not a military engagement, the incident known as the Frog Lake Massacre proved to be one of the most influential events associated with the **NORTH-WEST RESISTANCE**. Incited by hunger and mistreatment rather than political motives, a breakaway element of the Plains Cree murdered nine White men on the morning of April 2, 1885, in Frog Lake (now Alberta), North-West Territories. **BIG BEAR**, chief of the Plains Cree in the region, sought improved conditions for Treaty Indians through peaceful means and unity among the tribes. However, the food shortage that followed the virtual extinction of the buffalo left his people near starvation and weakened his authority. Disaffection focused upon Thomas Quinn, an Indian agent who treated the **CREE** with harshness and arrogance. Before dawn on April 2, a party of warriors captured Quinn at his home. The Cree, led by war chief Wandering Spirit (Kapapa-

Burial site of the victims of the 1885 Frog Lake battle; names are inscribed on the large cross in the middle, which is surrounded by smaller unmarked wooden crosses.

mahchakkew) and Ayimâsis, Big Bear's son, took more prisoners as they occupied the village. Shortly before 11 a.m., the prisoners were ordered to move to an encampment about 2 km from Frog Lake.

When Quinn obstinately refused, Wandering Spirit shot him in the head. In the short minutes of panic that followed, eight more prisoners were shot dead: sawmill operator John Gowanlock, farming instructor John Delaney, Catholic priests Rev. Leon Fafard and Felix Marchand, clerk William Gilchrist, trader George Dill, carpenter Charles Gouin, and John Wolliscroft, Father Fafard's lay assistant. Cree women hid William Cameron, a Hudson's Bay clerk, beneath a large shawl and thereby saved his life. Cameron, Theresa Delaney and Theresa Gowanlock, widows of two of the slain men, their families, and others from the settlement, numbering 70 in all, were taken as captives. The Cree then moved on to occupy **FORT PITT**. At the conclusion of the 1885 Resistance, six Cree men were tried and sentenced to death for their roles in the Frog Lake Massacre: Bad Arrow (Manchoose), Iron Body (Nahpase), Little Bear (Apischaskoos), Miserable Man (Kitah-wahken), Walking the Sky (Pahpahmekeesick), and Wandering Spirit. They, and two Cree men condemned for a murder committed on March 29, just before the Siege of Battleford, were hanged on November 27, 1885, at Fort Battleford, in the largest mass execution in Canadian history. *John Chaput*

FURTHER READING: Beal, B. and R. Macleod. 1984. *Prairie Fire: The 1885 North-West Rebellion.* Edmonton. Hurtig.

FRUIT INDUSTRY. At first glance, the prairie environment does not appear conducive to fruit production, but in fact the people of Saskatchewan have a long tradition associated with fruit usage and production. Historically, native fruit species were important to indigenous peoples and, subsequently, European settlers. The explorer **DAVID THOMPSON** suggested in 1787–88 that the saskatoon ought to be cultivated in Canada and England. The first professor of horticulture at the **UNIVERSITY OF SASKATCHEWAN**, **C.F. PATTERSON**, included an entire chapter in his 1936 book on native fruits that merited cultivation. Saskatchewan native fruit species include the saskatoon, choke cherry, pin cherry, buffaloberry, highbush cranberry, blueberry, bog cranberry, wild grape, hawthorn, lingonberry, beaked hazelnut, and wild rose. The saskatoon has now overtaken the strawberry as the most important fruit crop on the prairies. A wide range of domesticated fruit species also can be successfully produced in Saskatchewan. The domesticated small and tree fruits include strawberries, raspberries, black and red currants, gooseberries, bush cherries, apples, pears and plums. U-Pick strawberries have long been a part of a typical prairie summer. Apples have always been popular with gardeners in Saskatchewan, but fruit size and quality have been limited by the harsh climate.

The fruit industry in Saskatchewan is spearheaded by the Saskatchewan Fruit Growers' Association, an organization comprised of both growers and processors. The industry grew from about eight ha in 1980 to over 600 ha in 2002. In 2002, the Saskatchewan fruit industry had 328 growers, with a total of 613 ha of fruit. There were 240 saskatoon growers (366 ha), 94 strawberry growers (86 ha), and 59 fruit growers (62 ha) of other fruit crops (raspberry, apple, choke cherry, sour cherry, sea buckthorn, plum and cherry plum, black currant, highbush cranberry). An average of 1.5 million pounds of saskatoons were produced in both 2001 and 2002; 500,000 pounds of saskatoons

Harvesting saskatoon berries—one of Saskatchewan's most popular native fruit species—at North Battleford, August 1943.

were processed in 2001 (a $5 million value) by ten processors marketing fresh, frozen and processed products. The total value of the saskatoon crop (fresh and processed) in 2001 was $6.5 million. The Saskatchewan fruit industry employs approximately 300 people, full or part-time.

Fruit production in Saskatchewan is both challenging and rewarding. The short growing season, late-spring and early-fall frosts, lack of sufficient rainfall, strong winds, severe winter temperatures, and lack of winter snow cover, along with the high cost of labour for harvesting, sorting/cleaning and transport, and the sparse population, place significant limits on fruit production. In general, only relatively few, adequately hardy varieties of the domesticated fruit species are suitable for the harsh local climatic conditions. Most Saskatchewan commercial fruit operations involve hardy small fruit species. Good management practices, including site selection and preparation, variety selection, irrigation, fertilization, and weed, insect pest and disease control, are essential to successful fruit production in the province. Because of high labour costs, mechanical harvesting is becoming a more common practice. The relatively low incidence of insect pest and disease problems has inspired many fruit growers to adopt organic production practices. The warm, sunny, dry prairie summers enhance fruit quality and help decrease the incidence of disease.

Increasingly widespread cultivation of fruit species in small orchards, shelterbelts and hedgerows is contributing to the diversification and health of the prairie agricultural economy by enhancing alternative agricultural production, by promoting the development of mixed cropping operations, and by providing a more substantive base for a processing industry. Both native and domestic fruits are characterized by a variety of traits that allow substantial versatility of use. Their multipurpose function includes use as ornamentals for landscaping purposes, wildlife habitat improvement, shelterbelts and hedgerows, and as edible fruits that help balance and diversify our diets, and make eating a pleasure. Some fruits like the saskatoon and blueberry can be eaten fresh. Processed fruit products include jams, jellies, sauces, syrups, juices, ice cream, yogurt, chocolates, muffins, pies, tarts, cookies, pancakes, wine and liqueurs, raisins, fruit leathers, water-reduced purees, flavour concentrates, and dyes.

Research and industry development is associated with the Native Fruit Development Program and the Domestic Fruit Program in the Department of Plant Sciences at the University of Saskatchewan, in conjunction with the Saskatchewan Fruit Growers' Association and the Government of Saskatchewan–Saskatchewan Agriculture, Food and Rural Revitalization. The Native Fruit Development Program at the University of Saskatchewan is a pro-

gram of industry development oriented to the biology, culture and improvement of native fruit species, the primary goal being to help develop some of our native fruit species into new horticultural crops and thus contribute to agricultural diversification within the province.

The Native Fruit Development Program has made substantial contributions to the development of the saskatoon industry in particular, with the creation of disease-resistant varieties, improved methods of propagation, improved crop management practices, and improved post-harvest practices. The main funding for this program was terminated in 2004. However, some components of the fruit research are being pursued. The Domestic Fruit Program at the University of Saskatchewan is focussing on the further development of hardy sour cherry, raspberry and apple varieties with good fruit quality. New cultivars developed and released have included SK Prairie Sun apple, the new sour cherry cultivar SK Carmine Jewel, and the higher-yielding and more cold-hardy summer-bearing raspberries SK Red Mammoth and SK Red Bounty.

Richard St-Pierre

FURTHER READING: 2003. *Fruit Production in Saskatchewan*. Saskatoon: Saskatchewan Fruit Growers Association.

FUR FARMING AND INDUSTRY. Fur farming is a small industry in Saskatchewan which raises primarily fox. The majority of the pelts exported from the province are harvested from the wild; the Canadian ranch-raised fur production is located in the eastern and Atlantic provinces. Most of the Canadian fur garment manufacturing industry is centred in Montreal, representing approximately 80%, and in Toronto. The major fur-dressing facilities are located in Winnipeg and Montreal, with the three largest Canadian fur auction facilities being located in Toronto, North Bay and Vancouver. In Saskatchewan, an annual license is required from the Department of Agriculture in order to establish or operate a fur farm, or trade in fur animals or products. Licensed operators are required to follow the provisions of the Fur Farming Regulations. Trapping wild fur-bearers is regulated by Saskatchewan Environment.

Various national producer associations have established codes of practice and grading systems for their respective species. These rancher associations are also involved in sales coordination, promotion, education, and industry advocacy. Most fox and mink used in the fur trade are raised on farms; these animals have been raised for decades, generation after generation, like other domestic livestock. Feed for farmed mink and fox is either a prepared ration, produced by commercial animal feed companies, or produced with leftovers from abattoirs, fish plants,

and other food processing sectors along with grains, depending upon availability and location.

Diets vary according to the season and breeding cycle of fur-bearers. To make birthing easier, a low-fat diet is fed in the spring when the animals are breeding, and kept low through gestation until whelping in May-June. The diet of nursing females is made richer to encourage milk production and subsequently improve the growth rates of their litter. In the fall, fat is added once again to the diet to improve fur-growth. The litter size varies with the species; however, there are typically four or five kits born. Breeding occurs in the early spring (February-March), and the kits are born in early summer (May–June). The young are weaned after about six to eight weeks, and are then vaccinated. They moult in early fall in preparation for the winter, and begin developing their winter fur. The pelts are harvested in mid-winter when prime (November–December). Fur ranching is complementary with other agricultural operations. The majority of work occurs during the winter months when other farm work is typically reduced. Straw from crops can be used as bedding and cage insulation, while the accumulated manure may be used as a fertilizer. *Raymond Nixdorf*

FUR HARVESTING. Saskatchewan has a rich history of harvesting and marketing its wild fur resources. The industry began in what is now Canada's Northwest Territories 175 years before Saskatchewan became a province, and preceded settlement of the land for farming by 150 years. At least 55 fur trading posts operated for varying periods between 1774 and 1890. Saskatchewan historically also had a thriving ranched fur industry, but changing economic conditions eventually put the local commercial operators out of business.

Saskatchewan has 25 species of wild mammals with marketable pelts, of which 22 are officially recognized as furbearers under provincial regulations (the exceptions are the three species of rabbits that are taken). The only provincial furbearer species that cannot be harvested is the endangered swift fox. The most important species taken in terms of their economic contribution to the industry are coyote and beaver. Lynx, otter, marten and fisher also contribute significantly. Muskrats are taken in large numbers, but their cash value is significantly less than in other species. The province has the regulatory authority for managing furbearers to ensure the long-term sustainability of populations. For management purposes the province is divided into two major management zones: the Northern Fur Conservation Area (NFCA) covers approximately the two-thirds of the province north of the forest fringe and is further divided into 88 blocks, each of which has its own trapper membership; the South Saskatchewan Trapping Area (SSTA) covers the predominately agricultural land of southern Saskatchewan.

Fur harvesting as a commercial venture is dependent on international demand for fur products. The number of licensed trappers fluctuates with the market demand for furs, ranging from a high of 26,100 in 1979-80 to a low of 2,700 in 1999-2000. The numbers of trappers tend to fluctuate far more in the SSTA, where the price of coyote and red fox fur establishes the degree of interest in the resource. In the NFCA—where there is greater species diversity, the majority of trappers are of Aboriginal descent, and trapping has a traditional value apart from monetary returns—the numbers have tended to be more stable.

Anyone wishing to sell fur in Saskatchewan must have a provincial trapper's license and must be a Saskatchewan resident. Trappers in Saskatchewan can market their pelts directly to the large fur auction houses in North Bay, Toronto or Vancouver; they can also sell to local dealers or they can market the pelts privately.

The value of the fur industry to the provincial economy fluctuates greatly with market demand, but in general its importance has decreased over time. From 1915 to 1960 there were rarely fewer than one million pelts marketed annually. The value of these pelts peaked at $3.7 million in 1954–55, but had already exceeded $2 million in 1917–18. There was also a period from 1976–77 to 1987–88 when annual cash values exceeded $5 million, peaking at the historical high of $10.1 million in 1978-79. By comparison, in the last 20 years the pelts marketed peaked at 488,400 in 1987–88 and have been below 100,000 in the last five years. Cash value during this period peaked at $7.6 million in 1986–87, but has generally ranged between $1 and 2 million in each of the last 10 years.

While the trapping industry is no longer a key component in the provincial economy, it is still important for its role in helping to foster and maintain traditional values in the northern Aboriginal community. It is also an important source of additional income for many people, particularly in the rural areas of southern Saskatchewan.

Trappers and the trapping industry also make a significant contribution through their role in helping to regulate populations of many species that might otherwise cause significant conflicts. Predator attacks on livestock as well as flooding and infrastructure damage caused by beaver can be kept to acceptable limits when populations are actively harvested. As a participant under Canada's signature in the Agreement on International Humane Trapping Standards, Saskatchewan continues to promote improved trapping technologies and methods through ongoing trapper education and through establishment of equipment standards. *Mike Gollop*

FURTHER READING: Runge, W. 1995. *A Century of Fur Harvesting in Saskatchewan*. Saskatoon: Wildlife Technical Report No. 5, Saskatchewan Environment.

FUR TRADE. Long before European traders arrived on Hudson Bay in 1682, Aboriginal groups had developed long-distance trade networks. Plains groups made expeditions to Aboriginal trading centres to the south and brought back goods to trade at smaller local gatherings. Exotic goods, even seashells, were traded from group to group. Trading rituals involved formalized speeches, pipe ceremonies, and the exchange of gifts. European traders were quickly absorbed into this system and adopted its rituals. For many years, Aboriginal groups held

the upper hand. Local leaders who organized groups to travel to the posts were also middlemen and traded their goods with other groups further inland. Thus it was important for the traders to maintain good relations with these men. More importantly, European traders depended on local groups not just for furs but also for provisions. The early English and French traders developed different methods. In 1670, the Hudson's Bay Company (HBC) had been granted ownership of Rupert's Land, all the territory drained by rivers flowing into Hudson Bay. The HBC established large posts on the coast at York Factory and later at Fort Churchill. There they remained, depending on Cree, Assiniboine and Dene groups to make annual trading trips to the Bay. Traders, based in Montreal, were often organized in partnerships that sent out men to build small posts among Aboriginal groups. The French reached the mouth of the **SASKATCHEWAN RIVER** in 1741, and by the early 1750s were on the lower Red Deer River in Manitoba and below the Forks of the Saskatchewan, their furthest western post.

The French intercepted groups going to the Bay, skimming off the best furs. In 1754, the HBC began to send men inland to winter with the Cree and persuade them to continue their annual trips to the Bay. Although the French left after the Seven Years War (1756–63), English-speaking Montreal traders quickly returned guided by former French employees. By the late 1760s, these traders had returned to the Red Deer and Saskatchewan Rivers. They were so successful in intercepting Aboriginal groups traveling to the Bay that the HBC was forced to move inland, establishing Cumberland House in 1774. Traders rapidly moved up the **NORTH SASKATCHEWAN RIVER**, while in 1778 **PETER POND** was guided across **PORTAGE LA LOCHE** to the vast Athabasca country. Beginning in 1776, Montreal traders began joining forces to form the North West Company (NWC). Finally the XY Company joined in 1804, leaving only two trading firms: the NWC and the HBC.

The years between 1776 and 1821 were marked by intense, often vicious competition-especially at the hands of NWC traders, who had no central authority to control their actions. The HBC often suffered because their posts were under-manned. However, the main victims were Aboriginal people, who were often coerced into trade: they were no longer able to maintain advantageous trading conditions, and their role as middlemen largely disappeared with the establishment of small, localized trading posts. The situation was so bad that in 1821 the British government pressured the two companies to combine under the HBC. Governor **GEORGE SIMPSON** streamlined the company, eliminating many small posts in favour of several large ones. Redundant employees, often **MÉTIS**, were let go—many settling at Red River. There they became involved with the annual **BISON** hunt, supplying

Bringing in furs from spring trapping, Lac La Ronge.

pemmican and, later, hides to the trade. However, the short-lived monopoly of the HBC after 1821 was broken in 1849 when Red River traders interpreted a court case as allowing them the right to trade. These free traders quickly moved west, reaching Ile-à-la-Crosse by 1862.

In 1870, Rupert's Land was sold to Canada (*see* **RUPERT'S LAND PURCHASE**). In the south, the fur trade lost importance with the disappearance of the bison in the mid-1880s, the confinement of Aboriginal groups onto reserves, and the arrival of settlers. However, the trade remained important in the north, where First Nations continued to occupy traditional lands. New competing firms appeared, such as Revillon Frères, Lamson and Hubbard, the Northern Trading Company, and Stobard and Company. These either failed or were absorbed by the HBC, the last being Revillon Frères in 1936. However, independent traders continued to compete in northern communities. Then, in 1985 the HBC sold off its northern posts, ending its 300 years of fur trade in the West. The period left a complex legacy. For over 200 years the fur trade was the basic economy in the West; it resulted in the exploration of the province; it forced peaceful relations between Aboriginal groups and Euro-Canadians; it led to a further elaboration of Aboriginal plains cultures; and it resulted in the Métis nation.   *Dale Russell*

FURTHER READING: Foster, J. 1985. "Fur Trade after 1760." Pp. 705–07 in *The Canadian Encyclopedia*, Volume II. Edmonton: Hurtig; Morton, A.S. 1973. *A History of the Canadian West to 1870–71*. Toronto: University of Toronto Press; Ray, A.J. 1974. *Indians in the Fur Trade: Their Role as Trappers, Hunter, and Middlemen in the Lands Southwest of Hudson Bay 1660–1870*. Toronto: University of Toronto Press.

FUR TRADE POSTS. Most of the hundreds of trading posts in Saskatchewan resulted from two periods of intense competition: from 1774 to 1821, and again from the 1880s to the 1920s. Over 350 posts are known, but from the latter period only the Hudson's Bay Company (HBC) posts have been documented. The posts varied greatly, ranging from a large, stockaded multi-building complex to a simple cabin used for only one winter, to an Aboriginal family dwelling in a small, isolated bush community. After the mid-1800s, major posts included an HBC trader, one or more competing traders, and a mission. In the north, these complexes formed the core for Aboriginal settlements, which began developing in the late 1800s. Since the traders depended on water transport, posts were built along rivers and lakes, often on traditional Aboriginal gathering grounds.

Typically, the traders arrived from the east with new stocks of goods in late fall. Aboriginal families had already gathered in expectation of their arrival,

SASKATCHEWAN ARCHIVES BOARD S-B8970

Revillon Frères fur trading post at Ile-à-la-Crosse, 1908.

and after obtaining their supplies on credit quickly left for their wintering grounds. They seldom returned until spring, when they brought their winter furs, paid off their debts, and traded for the remaining merchandise. Immediately after break-up, the traders left with their cargoes of furs. During the summer, posts were abandoned or were maintained by only several men. Then, in the fall, the cycle repeated itself. People seldom came to the posts to trade during the winter. Instead, they sent word for traders to come and fetch their furs, or employees were sent out on short trips with a small stock of goods, traveling from one wintering camp to another. After missionaries arrived in the 1850s, people began to come to the mission for Christmas and Easter, and traded at the nearby posts. By the late 1800s, Aboriginal men were often subcontracted to take goods to their wintering cabins, where they would trade with their neighbours. Others were hired as seasonal freighters. Consequently, by 1900 most posts had only two or three employees–unlike earlier times when they might have over 40 men.

In the south, much of the trade focused on obtaining **BISON** provisions from large camps of **ASSINIBOINE** or **CREE** who spent most of the year on, and at the edge of, the northern plains. Several times a year, large groups would arrive at the post bringing hundreds of pounds of pemmican and bladders of fat. Increasingly, **MÉTIS** from Red River participated in this trade, traveling out onto the plains on annual hunts. As the bison retreated west after the mid-1800s, the Métis followed, often with their own itinerant traders, moving into the Wood Mountain area in the south and to Moose Woods, south of present-day Saskatoon. Consequently, small temporary posts began to be established well out on the plains.

Following the merging of the NWC and HBC in

1821, Governor **GEORGE SIMPSON** imposed cost-cutting methods by closing many posts. Métis employees were increasingly barred from advancement. Simpson tried to centralize operations at several regional posts–although he soon found it necessary to re-establish several small posts, especially in the north. The larger posts were prominent during the 1800s; however, they were not centred on trapping grounds. Instead, they became important stops along the rapidly developing travel routes leading west to the Pacific and north to the Arctic. Cumberland House (est. 1774), the oldest community in Saskatchewan, retained its importance since it adjoined two crucial transportation routes: the **SASKATCHEWAN RIVER**, leading west, and the Sturgeon-weir, leading to the Athabasca country by way of the **CHURCHILL RIVER**. **CARLTON HOUSE** (est. 1810) and **FORT PITT** (est. 1829), on the **NORTH SASKATCHEWAN RIVER**, began as provisioning posts, but both became important way-stops on the newly developing **CARLTON TRAIL** between Red River and Fort Edmonton. Fort Pelly (est. 1824), on the upper Assiniboine River, was the gateway for the trade on the northeastern plains, but it became a backwater as the bison retreated further west. The focus shifted to Fort Ellice (est. 1831), near the junction of the Assiniboine and Qu'Appelle Rivers, which became important for both travelers on the Carlton Trail and for Métis who were traveling out onto the plains. Ile-à-la-Crosse (est. 1776), the only major post in northern Saskatchewan, and the second-oldest community, was an important stop along the **PORTAGE LA LOCHE** route and the terminal for the Green Lake Trail, by which pemmican was brought from the south.   *Dale Russell*

FURTHER READING: Brown, J.S.H. 1980. *Strangers in Blood: Fur Trade Company Families in Indian Country.*

Vancouver: University of British Columbia Press; Ray, A.J. 1988. "The Hudson's Bay Company and the Native People." Pp. 335-50 in W.E. Washburn (ed.), *Handbook of North American Indians, Volume Four: History of Indian-White Relations*. Washington, DC: Smithsonian Institution; Russell, D., and D. Meyer. 1999. "The History of the Fur Trade ca. 1682–post-1821; Trading Posts pre-1759–post-1930." Pp. 33–35 in K.I. Fung (ed.), *Atlas of Saskatchewan*. Saskatoon: University of Saskatchewan.

FYKE, KENNETH J. (1940–). Kenneth Fyke has had a long and distinguished career as an administrator, manager and consultant on health issues both in Canada and internationally. He chaired the Saskatchewan Commission on Medicare, otherwise known as the **FYKE COMMISSION**, which in 2001 issued its report, *Caring for Medicare: Sustaining a Quality System*.

Born in Moosomin on September 11, 1940, Fyke earned a degree in pharmacy from the **UNIVERSITY OF SASKATCHEWAN** in 1962. His first day of work coincided with the beginning of the doctors' strike over the introduction of **MEDICARE** in the province. He later earned a Masters of Health Services Administration from the University of Alberta.

Fyke served as Deputy Minister of Health in Saskatchewan and British Columbia, as CEO of the Greater Victoria Hospital Society and CEO of the Capital Health Region in Victoria, as founding Chair of the Board of Directors for the Canadian Blood Services, and as a member of the British Columbia Royal Commission on Health Care and Costs (1991). He represented Canada at the World Health Assembly in Geneva, Switzerland and at the Pan-American Health Conference in Washington, DC.

Fyke's work is notable for its focus on health service integration and regionalization. He received national and international recognition for his innovations in community-based care in Victoria, where he now lives. He also received an honorary doctorate from Royal Roads University, the Lieutenant Governor's Silver Medal for Excellence in the Public

REGINA LEADER-POST
Kenneth Fyke, March 2001.

Service, and the Award for Distinguished Service given by the Canadian Healthcare Association.

Tom McIntosh

FYKE COMMISSION, 2000–01. In June 2000, **KENNETH J. FYKE** was commissioned by the Saskatchewan government under **ROY J. ROMANOW** "to identify the key challenges ... in reforming and improving medicare," and "to recommend an action plan for delivery of health services ... that embodies the core values of medicare."

Following an interim report in October 2000, the final report, *Caring for Medicare: Sustaining a Quality System*, was presented in April 2001 to Romanow's successor, **LORNE CALVERT**.

The Commission occurred at an important juncture in the ongoing evolution of Canada's health care system. In the midst of reduced federal transfers, significant technological and medical innovation, and increasing pressure to balance their budgets, provincial governments were struggling to deal with the mounting costs and declining public confidence in the system. Hence the Fyke Report was preceded by the Clair Report in Quebec and followed by the Mazankowski Report in Alberta. Shortly after Fyke completed his work, Romanow himself headed up the federally appointed Commission on the Future of Health Care in Canada.

The Fyke Report insisted that the measure of the system's success be its ability to provide high-quality services in a sustainable manner. Without significant reform, Fyke warned, the quality of the services would continue to decline. The report laid out a detailed plan for the reorganization of health services in the province, beginning with integrated primary health care teams at the local level, increasingly sophisticated services at the regional level, and high-end diagnostic, complex and tertiary care in Regina, Saskatoon and Prince Albert.

Although the government's response was muted at first, it did eventually follow through on some of Fyke's recommendations. In 2002–03, the Health Services Utilization and Research Commission (HSURC) was divided into the Saskatchewan Health Research Foundation (SHRF) and the Health Quality Council, a body designed to assess the system's performance and to recommend further changes as needed. The province's thirty-three health districts were also amalgamated into twelve health authorities in order to better coordinate service delivery on a regional basis. But many of Fyke's more sweeping recommendations for a new approach to primary health care and service integration have yet to be realized. However, Fyke's model of "putting quality first" remains an important benchmark for measuring the success of health care reform in Saskatchewan and in the nation.

Tom McIntosh

GABRIEL DUMONT INSTITUTE. The Gabriel Dumont Institute of Native Studies and Applied Research (GDI), the official educational affiliate of the **MÉTIS NATION–SASKATCHEWAN** (MN–S), is directed by a twelve-person Board of Governors representing the MN-S regions. GDI offers a variety of accredited educational, vocational and skills training opportunities for the province's Métis in partnership with the **UNIVERSITY OF REGINA**, the **UNIVERSITY OF SASKATCHEWAN**, the **SASKATCHEWAN INSTITUTE OF APPLIED SCIENCE AND TECHNOLOGY** (SIAST), the **SASKATCHEWAN INDIAN INSTITUTE OF TECHNOLOGIES** (SIIT), the province's regional colleges, and Métis Employment and Training of Saskatchewan.

GDI, the only Métis-controlled educational and cultural institution of its kind in Canada, provides a wide range of programs and services to the province's Métis, including the **SASKATCHEWAN URBAN NATIVE TEACHER EDUCATION PROGRAM** (SUN-TEP), which has graduated more than 700 teachers through centres in Prince Albert, Saskatoon and Regina. Gabriel Dumont College (GDC), another affiliate, delivers the first two years of a University of Saskatchewan Bachelor of Arts and Science degree (in Saskatoon and Prince Albert). The **DUMONT TECHNICAL INSTITUTE** (DTI) develops and

ROY ANTAL/REGINA LEADER-POST

Dan Hamilton's class at Gabriel Dumont Institute, October 1990.

implements Adult Basic Education, skills training, as well as vocational and cultural programs. GDI's library services possess a substantial Métis-specific library collection, and the Publishing Department has developed more than seventy-five Métis-specific resources. In addition, the Institute administers various scholarship and cultural development funds on behalf of the Métis community.

GDI was founded in 1976 at an Association of Métis and Non-Status Indians (AMNSIS) cultural conference. However, it took four years of hard bargaining, protests and even sit-ins at the Legislative Building by AMNSIS and community activists before the provincial government allowed for GDI's creation. In 1980, it began operations in Regina with the signing of an affiliation agreement between itself, the University of Regina, and Advanced Education and Manpower. In 1980, the Institute's programs included SUNTEP, Curriculum Development and Research, a Library/Resource Centre, and a Field Liaison Program. That year the Institute had its first of fourteen consecutive annual cultural conferences, where the Métis and Non-Status Indian community celebrated Aboriginal culture. In 1983, the Institute began offering federally sponsored technical and vocational programs through the Saskatchewan Training for Employment Program (STEP). In 1985, GDI played a lead role in preparing cultural content for the 1885 Resistance Centenary celebrations at BATOCHE.

Darren R. Préfontaine

GALLAGHER, PATRICIA MARIE (1939–).
Patricia Gallagher (*née* Young) was born in Vanguard, Saskatchewan on November 20, 1939. Her family moved to Moose Jaw, where her father was a member of the United Packing House Workers of America at the Swift Canadian packing plant. In 1959–60 she was a schoolteacher for the Regina Public School Board. Gallagher first became involved with the union movement in 1964, when she was working at the UNIVERSITY OF REGINA; she was elected to the union negotiating committee and was on the union executive and grievance committee. In 1976, Gallagher was hired by the SASKATCHEWAN FEDERATION OF LABOUR as the executive assistant. Six years later she became the education officer with the SASKATCHEWAN GOVERNMENT EMPLOYEES UNION (SGEU); in 1987 she was appointed director of membership services, and became the executive director of operations in 1996. She retired from SGEU on March 31, 2001.

Gallagher was instrumental in protecting SGEU members' collective bargaining rights when the Progressive Conservative government moved the four technical schools and urban community colleges into the newly created SASKATCHEWAN INSTITUTE OF APPLIED SCIENCE AND TECHNOLOGY (SIAST). She successfully argued SGEU's case for successor rights before the Labour Relations Board.

Gallagher was a prominent and progressive defender of the rights and unions of working people. She was an active member of SASKATCHEWAN WORKING WOMEN, a grassroots feminist group. She served as co-editor for the alternate news magazine, *Next Year Country*, and, in the early 1970s, was the legislative reporter for *The Commonwealth*. In retirement, Gallagher serves as a labour representative on the Labour Relations Board.

George Rosenau

GALLAWAY, MARGUERITE (1929–).
Marguerite Gallaway has made accessible the finest music, dance, theatre, and fine arts in Saskatchewan. Born in Birsay on May 13, 1929, Gallaway completed her education and arts degrees at the Universities of Saskatchewan and Regina respectively. In 1974, she became executive director of the Organization of Saskatchewan Arts Councils, and over the next thirteen years developed it into one of Canada's strongest artistic networks. Gallaway was also on the board of the Saskatchewan Centre of the Arts, a member of the Saskatchewan Talent Selection Committee of SaskExpo 86, and president of the Saskatchewan Council of Cultural Organizations. In 1988, she received the Saskatchewan Order of Merit and was made a Member of the Order of Canada two years later.

GARDINER DAM.
The Gardiner Dam, located 25 km downstream from Elbow on the SOUTH SASKATCHEWAN RIVER, was the world's largest earth-filled dam when it was officially opened on June 21, 1967. On September 1, 1958, a federal-provincial agreement to develop the South Saskatchewan River had received unanimous approval by Parliament. The PRAIRIE FARM REHABILITATION ADMINISTRATION (PFRA), a federal government agency, accepted the

engineering challenge. Construction took eight years to complete and 64 million cubic metres of earth to fill; it created a dam 64-metres high and 5,000 metres in length. The Gardiner Dam, which opened in conjunction with the Qu'Appelle River Dam, helped establish Lake Diefenbaker, a 225 km-long reservoir that was designed as a multi-purpose source of water for irrigation, industry, human consumption, and recreation. It is named for JAMES GARDINER, a Liberal Premier of Saskatchewan who continued to advocate for the need of a reliable water supply when he was elected to the House of Commons and then became Canada's Minister of Agriculture in 1944.

The Gardiner Dam is used to moderate the flow of water on the South Saskatchewan River with its 1 km-long spillway, made from 250,000 cubic metres of concrete, able to discharge 7,500 cubic metres of water per minute. It stores and releases water to serve a variety of needs: irrigating 37,000 hectares of agricultural land, providing water to 45% of the Saskatchewan population including the cities of Regina, Moose Jaw, and Saskatoon; and helping three power stations generate electricity.

LAKE DIEFENBAKER boasts a shoreline of almost 800 km, virtually the distance from Regina to Calgary, which provides an abundance of recreational opportunities. The South Saskatchewan River system also supplies water to more than 450 Saskatchewan farmers, who irrigate WHEAT, BARLEY, alfalfa, CANOLA, corn, potatoes and a variety of pulse crops. Ownership of the project was transferred to the province of Saskatchewan in 1969, but PFRA continued to perform on-site duties until 1997, when the province assumed all responsibilities for the South Saskatchewan River project. Those duties now are the responsibility of the Saskatchewan Watershed Authority.

Joe Ralko

COURTESY OF SASKATCHEWAN WATERSHED AUTHORITY

Gardiner Dam.

SASKATCHEWAN ARCHIVES BOARD R-B7146-4

When this photo was taken in 1957, James G. Gardiner had served as federal minister of Agriculture for 22 years. He retired the following year.

GARDINER, JAMES GARFIELD (1883–1962).

Gardiner, born November 30, 1883, on a farm near Farquhar, Ontario, was one of a legion of southern Ontarians who came west (in his case by harvest excursion in 1901) and left their political mark on the Canadian prairies. First elected in a provincial by-election in 1914, Gardiner spent two decades in office in Regina and, after entering MACKENZIE KING's Cabinet and later Louis St. Laurent's as Minister of Agriculture, another twenty-two years in Ottawa. Nonetheless, his heart remained rooted in agriculture. He bought his farm at Lemberg during WORLD WAR I, and supervised its operation under his son or a close associate for more than four decades. When he was defeated in the general election of 1958, he returned to the farm, and it was there that he died January 2, 1962.

Gardiner's agrarian interests permeated his politics, most certainly during the unprecedented span in which he held one federal portfolio. The Prairie Farm Assistance Act (1939), which recognized federal government responsibility for the economic well-being of prairie grain farmers, proved to be the forerunner of a score of national agricultural initiatives with the same objective. The disruption to overseas markets caused by World War II demanded immediate and continuous adjustments in all areas of agriculture over all regions of Canada. Following the war, Mackenzie King announced that he would step down as leader of the Liberal Party of Canada. Gardiner sought but lost the leadership in 1948, coming second to St. Laurent.

Gardiner's reputation, established in Saskatchewan first as a backbencher, then Minister and finally as Premier, was as that of a relentless partisan who would brook no compromise. Following the cleavage in the Liberal Party over Union Government and conscription, events which saw Gardiner and a tiny minority of Liberals stand by Laurier and against the Military Service Act (1917), Gardiner took com-

mand of the LIBERAL PARTY organization in Saskatchewan and made it a near invincible electoral force. Between 1914 and 1958, Gardiner personally won every election contest he entered, except the last. The provincial party, between 1914 and the CO-OPERATIVE COMMONWEALTH FEDERATION victory in 1944, won every election except that of 1929, although even then it won more seats and votes than any other party. In addition to its provincial prowess, Gardiner's organization saw that Mackenzie King won the federal seat of Prince Albert in a by-election in 1926 and that he kept that seat in five more contests until 1945. Prince Albert was the only seat in King's political career that he retained as an incumbent.

The Liberal Party organization under Gardiner entered the realm of myth as "the machine" largely due to an academic article written by Escott Reid. Reid's depiction downplayed the extent of popular participation by rank-and-file Liberals that made the organization so successful. In his capacity as Highways Minister and then as Premier, Gardiner stood at its head overseeing a platoon of government "inspectors" who, while on the public payroll, had the interests of the party as their priority. But the party required more than a leader to make it succeed, as its slow deterioration once Gardiner departed from Regina demonstrated.

Gardiner's administrative and organizational skills explain his electoral and departmental achievements. They did not contribute to an outstanding career in public policy, either as a provincial Cabinet Minister or as Premier. He succeeded CHARLES DUNNING as Premier in 1926. Between then and the Liberals' defeat in 1929, the economy was good, and there were no decisions in which Gardiner had a hand that exercised long-term influence on the province. Similarly, after he led the Liberals back to power in 1934 (thereby becoming the only Saskatchewan Premier to hold the office twice), his eyes were on a federal Cabinet appointment. Except for undoing the Co-operative government's civil service reforms and disbanding its Relief Commission, in both instances handing power back to the politicians, where he believed it belonged, depression and drought limited any policy initiative Gardiner might have attempted.

The singular event of Gardiner's first ministry was the electoral defeat of 1929. That election saw the KU KLUX KLAN play a determinative role in coalescing previously fragmented opposition to the Liberals. For the anti-Liberals, the major issue was the government's purportedly loose administration of the separate schools and excessive influence exercised by the Roman Catholic Church. Gardiner attempted to refute the charges with statistics and by appeals to tolerance for minorities. For the first time (and the last until 1999), a coalition, on this occasion composed of Conservatives, Progressives and

Independents, formed a government under J.T.M. ANDERSON as Premier. In his long career Gardiner never willingly relinquished power; however, he maintained until the end of his life that the outcome of that contest was "an honourable defeat" and that the Liberal Party emerged the stronger for its electorally unpopular position. *David E. Smith*

FURTHER READING: Barnhart, Gordon L. (ed.). 2004. *Saskatchewan Premiers of the Twentieth Century.* Regina: Canadian Plains Research Center.

GATHERCOLE, FREDERICK (1908–93).

In recognition of his lifetime of service to the education profession, Dr. Frederick Gathercole of Broadview was awarded the Saskatchewan Order of Merit in 1985. Trained as a teacher at the Regina NORMAL SCHOOL, Gathercole furthered his education with degrees from Queen's University and the University of Manitoba, and a doctorate from the University of Toronto. He taught in classrooms across the province before becoming superintendent of Saskatoon's public elementary schools from 1950 to 1966. Then, he was director of education for the city's elementary and secondary schools until 1973. Gathercole also served as chairman of the Board of Governors of the University Hospital in Saskatoon and chairman of the Saskatchewan Alcoholism Commission. In addition to his Saskatchewan Order of Merit, Dr. Gathercole was named Saskatoon's citizen of the year in 1973. Born on April 12, 1908, he died on December 23, 1993.

GAULEY, DAVID E. (1922–).

Respected for his dedication to the profession of Law, David Eldon "Tom" Gauley was born in Unity, Saskatchewan on October 15, 1922. Having earned an LLB from the UNIVERSITY OF SASKATCHEWAN in 1943, Tom was called to the Saskatchewan Bar and founded his first law firm two years later. Appointed Queen's Counsel in 1956, he helped organize the first Bar Admission Course as a Bencher of the LAW SOCIETY OF SASKATCHEWAN. He has given generously of his time and leadership to the University of Saskatchewan, serving as member and chair of its Board of Governors. He is the recipient of numerous awards from the legal profession and was made a Member of the Order of Canada in 2003.

GAY AND LESBIAN ACTIVISM.

Saskatchewan is not a place one commonly associates with gay and lesbian activism—and with good reason, for, with its small population base, larger percentage of rural and small-town dwellers, and ample number of religious adherents, it would not appear to have the necessary ingredients for such activism. This is a stereotype that needs revision. Not only did Saskatchewan have pockets of activism and produce gay and lesbian activists who would become

DAVID MCLENNAN PHOTO

Gay pride parade, Regina, 2003.

prominent nationally, but for a time in the mid-1970s, it appeared that Saskatchewan would lead the way for Canadian recognition of sexual diversity.

Formal gay activism, as opposed to informal lesbian and gay socialization networks, had existed since the end of **WORLD WAR II** and arrived in the province in March 1971. Saskatoon's Gens Hellquist placed an advertisement for "Saskatoon Gay Liberation" in Vancouver's alternative publication *The Georgia Straight*. Slowly, a few men and one lone woman wrote to Hellquist asking for information. This group, supplemented with other members of Hellquist's social circle (a diverse group that included **UNIVERSITY OF SASKATCHEWAN** professors, university students, professionals, and a few working-class men and women) met to formally discuss plans to organize the city's gay community. These discussions led to the creation of the Zodiac Friendship Society, an umbrella organization that would be devoted to gay political issues (or "liberation" as it was known in the 1970s), education, counselling and support groups, and, most popular of all, a social club—the Gemini Club. The money generated at the weekly dances, initially held at the Unitarian Centre, eventually resulted in sufficient funds to open a Gay Community Centre in March 1973. The Saskatoon Gay Community Centre was located on prime downtown real estate. The only other Canadian city to have a dedicated gay centre then was Toronto, and Saskatoon's achievement was a point of considerable pride for local activists.

In the early years, a number of short-lived activist groups, including Saskatoon Gay Alliance Toward Equality (GATE) and Gay Students Alliance, had existed in the city. These were eventually amal-gamated into Saskatoon Gay Action (SGA), which sought to "bring about the total liberation of the gay community." Regina activists launched GATE Regina and the University of Saskatchewan Homophile Association (Regina Campus), but these proved very short-lived and struggled for membership. That pattern would be repeated throughout the next twenty years, as Regina groups came and went, while Saskatoon's core group demonstrated remarkable continuity. The primary focus of the Regina gay and lesbian community's energy was its social club, which was created in 1973. Originally called the "house on Smith Street," the Gay Community of Regina (GCR), a co-operative, has successfully run a social club until the present day, earning the distinction of operating the longest serving gay social organization in the country.

In 1973, members of Saskatoon Gay Action met with the Saskatchewan Human Rights Commission (SHRC) to present a brief outlining homosexual discrimination which urged them to recommend the inclusion of sexual orientation into the human rights code. Favourably impressed by the brief and convinced of the importance of including sexual orientation in the code, the Commission recommended to the Attorney General, **ROY ROMANOW**, that sexual orientation be added. Building on this success, SGA delegates were offered a meeting with Romanow's assistant. Press reports indicated that the Attorney General "felt positively" about this document. Had the legislative change occurred then, in 1973–74, the **BLAKENEY** NDP government would have led the way for Canadian gays and lesbians. However, in the fall of 1974 the government began backtracking, worried about the impact such changes would have upon the rural areas, and upon more conservative voters. Instead, the first province to amend its provincial human rights code was Quebec, in December 1977.

Another key step in Saskatchewan gay activism was the publicity given to the **DOUG WILSON** case at the University of Saskatchewan. The positive media portrait of Wilson's struggle against the discriminatory practice of the administrators was an important educational opportunity for the province's gay activists. It marked a turning point, where it became evident that people's attitudes and awareness were beginning to change with respect to the treatment of lesbians and gays. Wilson leveraged such goodwill in a host of volunteer and paid political roles. In March 1977, he was one of the leaders of a 125-member protest rally at the legislature, where chants of "gay rights now" and "talk is cheap" amplified the urgency of the written document which demanded the immediate addition of sexual orientation to the human rights code. The success of this rally led Wilson and others to begin discussions about a provincial group, and in December 1977 Saskatchewan Gay Coalition (which included members from Regina, Saskatoon, Prince Albert and Moose Jaw) was formed. In SGC's four years in existence, its monthly newsletter, *Gay Saskatchewan*, was sent to people throughout the province, concentrating on the small towns and the countryside. This was an important act of grassroots politicizing that would, eventually, assist in demonstrating province-wide support for change. SGC presented a brief to the government in January 1979. Additionally, the Attorney General met with gay activists to receive the document and to hear firsthand of the need for human rights protection. Whatever goodwill the NDP Cabinet had towards the issue was nullified by a letter-writing campaign initiated by the evangelical churches, which successfully pressured the government not to officially recognize "sinful" behaviour.

The election of the Progressive Conservative government, under Premier **GRANT DEVINE**, was a blow to provincial gay activism. The years 1982–91 represent an interregnum, when few overtly gay organizations or activists risked public exposure to counterbalance the frequently homophobic pronouncements from members of the government, the media, and their supporters. One exception was a small group called the Coalition for Human Equality (CHE), which was founded by Don McNamee. Initially CHE was a coalition of gay and lesbian activists from Saskatoon and Regina, but when the Regina contingent left to join the national gay lobbying group, EGALE, the Saskatoon activists continued. CHE members worked tirelessly, lobbying individual NDP MLA's and holding fund-raising socials, as well as exchanging information and strategy with their counterparts in Alberta and Manitoba.

Within the national context, by the time the NDP government, led by Roy Romanow, returned to office in 1991 the situation was dramatically different than in 1979. By 1991, four provinces (Quebec, Ontario, Manitoba and Nova Scotia) and the Yukon territory had recognized sexual orientation in their human rights codes owing primarily to successful court challenges originating from the 1982 Charter of Rights and Freedoms. New Brunswick and British Columbia would both amend their codes in 1992. So, in 1993, when the Saskatchewan government introduced and eventually passed Bill 38, which included sexual orientation in its rights code revisions, this reflected not only the twenty years of gay and lesbian activism in Saskatchewan, but also the changed Canadian legal realities. As the seventh province to include sexual orientation as a protected category in its human rights code, Saskatchewan began the process of official, legislative recognition of gays and lesbians that members of the Saskatoon Gay Coalition first requested in 1973. Subsequently, in the ensuing ten years the province has begun a process of complying with and quickly ratifying any subsequent federal legislative changes regarding lesbian and gay "rights," including same-sex pensions, common-law recognition, and adoption rights. Most recently, Premier **LORNE CALVERT** has offered a positive endorsement of the federal government's decision to recognize same-sex marriage. While precedents elsewhere might appear to drive Saskatchewan decisions on such matters, it is important to realize that provincial gay and lesbian activism has played an important role in lobbying and educating Saskatchewan residents to the invisible minorities in their midst.   *Valerie J. Korinek*

FURTHER READING: McNinch, James, and Mary Cronin (eds.). 2004. *I Could Not Speak My Heart: Education and Social Justice for Gay and Lesbian Youth*. Regina: Canadian Plains Research Center.

GENEREUX, GEORGE (1935–89). An exceptionally talented trapshooter, George Genereux was born in Saskatoon on March 1, 1935. As a teenager, he won numerous provincial, national, and international trapshooting titles. At the Grand American Trap Shoot in Vandalia, Ohio, Genereux captured the 1951 Junior Clay Target Championship, the 1952 Junior Champion of Champions title, and the 1956 Champion of Champions crown. This latter achievement made him the first Canadian to win a major championship at such a prestigious event. In 1951, he was a silver medalist in world championship competition at Oslo, Norway. The pinnacle of his amateur career came at the 1952 Helsinki Olympics, where he claimed the gold medal in the trapshooting event. Following his departure from the shooting world, Genereux earned a doctorate in medicine from McGill University; he later worked as

a radiologist at **ROYAL UNIVERSITY HOSPITAL** in Saskatoon. Genereux is a member of the Canadian Sports Hall of Fame and was an original inductee to the **SASKATCHEWAN SPORTS HALL OF FAME** in 1966. He died in Saskatoon on April 10, 1989.

Daria Coneghan and Holden Stoffel

GEOGRAPHIC EDUCATION AND RESEARCH. Geography is a spatial science that seeks to understand why phenomena are located where they are and how they interact with one another in a spatial context. It is a discipline with practical application in fields such as geomatics, rural and urban planning, resource management, and many others. Although the social science and science components of K–12 education have significant geographic content, geography as a discreet discipline is not currently taught as part of the core curriculum in Saskatchewan schools; it is, however, chosen by about 2% of students as a high school elective. Both of the provincial universities have departments of geography in which they train graduates able to work in a wide range of careers.

The teaching of geography began at the **UNIVERSITY OF SASKATCHEWAN** in 1959 with the appointment of J.H. Richards. In 1960–61, 257 students were enrolled in a total of three geography classes. Currently, thirteen full-time faculty teach fifty different classes in the general areas of physical, human, technical, and regional geography. More than 3,500 students a year take classes in geography through the department, including off-campus students. Geography instruction at the Regina campus of the University of Saskatchewan began in 1965 when Victor Dojcask was employed to teach an evening class. Currently, the Department of Geography at the **UNIVERSITY OF REGINA** has eight full-time faculty members and three half-time instructors, teaching a total of fifty-two classes. In 2004,1,350 students were registered in geography courses offered by the department. Classes are taught around four basic themes: physical, environmental, human, and regional geography. Both provincial departments offer graduate studies, including a PhD program at the University of Saskatchewan. In addition to teaching, each faculty member is free to follow individual research interests. At the University of Regina these are as varied as the geography of business and industry, the reconstruction of paleo-environments, cartographic semiotics, or the study of Canadian-American borderlands. The research activities of faculty at the University of Saskatchewan are reflected in the more than 120 Masters and twenty-five PhD candidates who have successfully defended thesis topics in areas such as regional science, spatial modeling, environmental science and management, geomatics, and social geography.

Linkages with other institutions, faculties and

organizations are an essential part of geographic education and research at both universities. Geographers at the University of Saskatchewan have developed strong links with Environment Canada's National Water Research Institute, while researchers at the University of Regina are affiliated with a number of provincial and federal government departments through the Prairie Adaptation Research Collaborative (PARC). Geographers at the University of Regina are playing a major role in investigating rural sustainability and social cohesion in order to help communities in southern Saskatchewan survive and prosper in an era of globalization. The Department of Geography at the University of Saskatchewan, by contrast, has placed particular emphasis on problems of northern development. This includes an association with the University of the Arctic, which attracts students from as far afield as Greenland, Scandinavia and Russia.

In addition to numerous scholarly publications by faculty members at both universities, the Department of Geography at the University of Saskatchewan must be especially recognized for its commitment to portraying the geography of the province through the *Atlas of Saskatchewan*. Published in 1968, and edited by J.H. Richards and K.I. Fung, this provided a comprehensive portrait of the physical, historical, population, economic, and urban geography of the province at a time of dramatic social and economic transformation. In 1999 a new edition of the *Atlas* was published. While the *Atlas* provides two distinct snapshots of the province taken some thirty years apart, geographers at the University of Regina are currently developing a book that will provide a broader perspective on the province's geography. It will not only examine present-day spatial organization, but also explore the way in which the province has changed over time. Authors from both departments have contributed chapters for this book.

Marilyn Lewry, W.O. Archibold and Randy Widdis

GEOGRAPHICAL MEMORIAL TRIBUTES. Geographical memorial tributes preserve the names of the many servicemen who lost their lives during **WORLD WAR II**. Those names are shown on topographic maps of northern Saskatchewan. The mapping of the north was greatly advanced after World War II, when extensive aerial survey mapping was completed through vertical aerial photography. As a consequence of that process, geographic features across the north are now documented on thirty-five 1:250,000 (one centimetre representing four kilometres) maps and on the 560 more detailed 1:50,000 maps (two centimetres representing one kilometre). As post-war mineral exploration and other economic activities expanded across northern Saskatchewan, officially gazetted names appeared as geographic locations on these topographic maps, identifying many thousands of lakes, islands, bays, creeks and rapids—all unique geographic features. There are over 14,000 geographic features represented on provincial maps by officially gazetted names; this collage of names represents part of Saskatchewan's heritage.

Some 3,862 of these geographic features in northern Saskatchewan were named in memory of the province's servicemen who lost their lives in World War II. Between 1939 and 1945, a total of 91,000 men and women from Saskatchewan enlisted in the war effort; more than 4,000 of these did not make it home again. The naming of geographic features in their honour was a fitting tribute by the province.

Letters written to the families of these men and women by the provincial government in the 1950s and 1960s acknowledge the sacrifice they had made during World War II. These letters and signed certificantes describe how specific geographic features were named as a perpetual sign of our collective indebtedness to those who gave their lives in defence of democratic ideals. Although the provincial government tried to contact the families of all those so honoured, many families remained unaware of this until recent years. In 1997 Doug Chisholm, a bush pilot in La Ronge, started to research the location of these features and has recorded on aerial photos most of the nearly 4,000 geo-memorial sites. The names of those memorialized, along with their hometowns, their casualty dates, and the location of the geographic feature named in their memory are now found in the book *Their Names Live On.* Over the years, many families have taken the initiative to visit these specific geo-memorial sites or have made arrangements to have permanent memorial markers placed there.

Doug Chisholm

FURTHER READING: Chisholm, Doug, and Gerald Hill. 2001. *Their Names Live On: Remembering Saskatchewan's Fallen in World War II.* Regina: Canadian Plains Research Center; Fung, K.I. 1999. *Atlas of Saskatchewan.* Saskatoon: University of Saskatchewan.

GEOGRAPHY OF SASKATCHEWAN: *see essay on facing page.*

GEOLOGY. The geology of Saskatchewan is complex. The province is underlain throughout by crystalline Precambrian rocks of the stable North America Craton. In the north, these are exposed as part of the Canadian Shield. In the southern two-thirds of the province, the Precambrian basement is overlain by unmetamorphosed younger Phanerozoic sedimentary rocks. Thick ice sheets covered almost the entire region during the Pleistocene, leaving behind a variety of sculpted and deposit-strewn features. (*See* Figure GEO-1.)

Precambrian Shield. The Shield region is generally rugged and forested, with many bedrock exposures and lakes. The region has been divided geologically into a number of distinctive domains or terranes. In the past thirty years or so, detailed mapping and ever improving structural, geochemical and radiometric isotope techniques have been used to refine understanding of these terranes in terms of their age, origin, and assembly through plate tectonic and other processes.

The oldest rocks found so far, dated at about 3.4 Ga. (billion years), occur north of Lake Athabasca. The Hearne and Rae geological provinces comprise rocks of late Archean/Early Proterozoic age, mostly in the range 2.7 to 2.2 Ga. Many of these are of high metamorphic grade (granulite through amphibolite facies), produced in deeply buried crust at the roots of mountain ranges similar to the Alpine ranges of today, and now exhumed. The Wollaston belt to the southeast comprises mainly foreland basin sediments overlying Archean basement remobilized in Proterozoic times. The Reindeer Zone in the southeast is a collage of juvenile Proterozoic greenstone volcanics, greywacke and granitic rocks dated

approximately 1.9 to 1.75 Ga. These greenstone belts are associated with the major base metal mine at Flin Flon, as well as gold deposits. The domains are generally bounded by major shear zones, such as the Needle Falls shear zone and the Snowbird line, which accommodated extensive translational movement during assembly of the terranes. Unmetamorphosed sandstones and other sediments of the Athabasca basin, which overlie much of the north-central part of the Shield, have been dated at about 1.7 Ga. Saskatchewan's world-renowned uranium deposits are related to the weathered regolithic interface between the Athabasca Group and the underlying basement.

Subsurface Precambrian of the South. The Precambrian basement surface declines gradually from the Shield edge towards the south, taking a deeper plunge from about Regina southeastwards, to a maximum depth of about 3,300 m. Regional geophysical airborne surveys, deep seismic probing, and samples from oil wells have enabled mapping of domains, similar to those of the Shield area, in Precambrian basement rocks underlying the Phanerozoic rocks to the south.

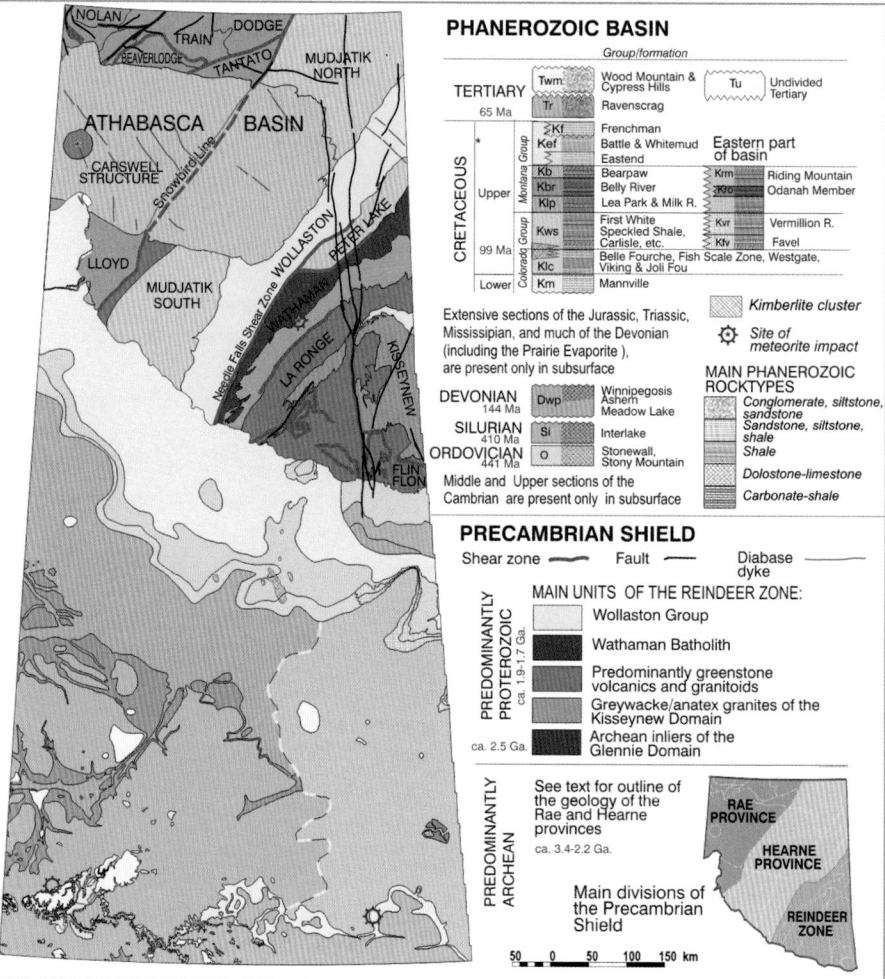

Figure GEO-1. Saskatchewan Bedrock Geology.

Phanerozoic Geology. The wedge of Phanerozoic sediments overlying the Precambrian basement are part of the **WESTERN CANADA SEDIMENTARY BASIN**. Although rarely exposed, these sediments have been studied extensively at subsurface from extensive oil well drillings by the oil industry. The lower sedimentary sequences formed during an initial Cambrian to Middle Jurassic passive-continental margin phase, and comprise basal clastics, platform carbonates and evaporites, including the major potash deposits of the Prairie Evaporite. These were succeeded by a Middle Jurassic to Eocene convergent-margin phase that produced a foreland basin with thick accumulations of largely clastic sediment derived from the emerging Cordilleran Mountain Belt to the west. Tertiary sands and gravels, along with extensive kaolin deposits, are exposed mainly in the US border region.

The basin is affected by episodic downwarping of the intracratonic **WILLISTON BASIN** in the south, block tectonic movements due to reactivation of basement structures, and eustatic sea-level changes. These factors, together with post-depositional folding and evaporate dissolution effects, have largely governed the distribution of the important resources of oil, natural gas, coal, and potash.

Other features. The largest known cluster worldwide of kimberlite volcanoes, with intact fallback deposits, a potential major source of diamonds, occurs mainly in the Fort à la Corne area, by the Saskatchewan River. These were extruded in shallow marginal Cretaceous seas about 100 million years ago. Major meteorite impact structures (**ASTROBLEMES**) include the Carswell, Deep Bay and Gow Lake in the Shield, and the Viewfield, Elbow and Maple Creek structures in the south.

Glacial Geology. At least eight periods of glacial advance and retreat are recorded in Saskatchewan during the Middle to Late Pleistocene, affecting all but small areas of the **CYPRESS HILLS** and Wood Mountain which stood above the ice sheets. Whereas the Shield is primarily a region of **GLACIAL EROSION** and scour, the Phanerozoic outcrop is largely a region of glacial deposition, with till sequences as much as 100 m or more thick in many places. Strong movements of the ice sheets produced thrust-stacked sequences of the glacial deposits and bedrock in some places.

R. Macdonald

FURTHER READING: Saskatchewan Geological Survey. 2003. *Geology, and Mineral and Petroleum Resources of Saskatchewan.* Saskatchewan Industry and Resources, Miscellaneous Report 2003-7; Geological Highway Map of Saskatchewan, Saskatchewan Geological Society Special Publication 15.

Geography of Saskatchewan

Randy Widdis

The view of Saskatchewan held by many Canadians is dominated by a number of images: wheat-filled elevators overlooking flat fields of grain; children with toques pulled over their ears playing a game of shinny on a frozen slough in -30° weather; parents standing at their small town's bus depot with their eyes full of tears, waving goodbye to a departing coach as it carries their child off to build a life elsewhere. While these symbols represent selected features of the place, they are illusory in the sense that they convey an image of a society that is as simple and amorphous as the horizontal landscape with which many people also associate Saskatchewan. But Saskatchewan is a more heterogeneous place than many people think, and geography serves as an insightful disciplinary canvas upon which to paint a more compelling picture of the province. This is an overview of the geography of Saskatchewan, identifying its major physical and cultural components but also examining the evolving connections between place and identity, in order to develop a more dynamic understanding of the province as it has transformed over time.

Place, Region and Identity

Geography seeks to understand the nature of place. Geographers systematically analyse the social, economic, political, and environmental processes operating in a place in order to provide an integrated understanding of its distinctiveness or character. The answer to the question, "What makes Saskatchewan unique?" requires a geographical approach that focuses on integration in place and interdependencies among places. In this context, it is important to consider interactions taking place over time within the province, and also those relations developing *between* Saskatchewan and the rest of Canada and the world.

Traditionally, the nature of and identification with this place have been built on the linked characteristics of rurality, agriculture, and isolation. However, the traditional culturally identifiable references—small towns and a wheat monoculture—are diminishing in importance: indeed, the iconography of the province, so dominated by a rural agricultural sector, experiencing decline in the face of global restructuring, is increasingly irrelevant. This raises the question, "What is this place becoming?" and emphasizes the need to shift conceptions of the province from an image mostly connected with a rural Euro-Canadian past to a present and future in which Aboriginal presence, urban dominance, and an evolving economy can be meaningfully articulated.

Spatial isolation resulting from physical barriers such as the Canadian Shield and the Rocky Mountains as well as great distances have combined with cultural separation to act as divisive forces within Canada, and have fostered attachments to province and region. The role played by geography is significant: Saskatchewan as region/place has evolved from the constant re-creation of society through human actions and interactions with a changing environment. These were carried out in historically and geographically specific contexts, but the transformations that took place also occurred in wider contexts of political, economic and social relationships with the rest of the country and the larger world.

Location

A central tenet of geography is that location is key to understanding a wide variety of processes. Social and geographical isolation has historically played a role in the development of the province and, arguably, still functions to make this place unique. Its relative location within Canada, far from the largest markets, has always hindered the development of secondary manufacturing and, for many years now, has discouraged the in-migration of other Canadians and foreign-born alike. In a larger context, Saskatchewan is part of a greater North American international region (the Great Plains) that is primarily extractive, economically limited by its peripherality, and politically under-represented because of its small population[1] (Figure 1). While geographical isolation continues to affect the pace of development, revolutions in trans-

379

G

Figure 1. This map shows Saskatchewan's geographical isolation. The Great Plains region, outlined in black, stretches from Canada's Northwest Territories through the mid-United States and into eastern Mexico.

portation and communication technology have reduced the costs associated with relative inaccessibility and generated scope for the development of high-tech and location-free industries. These include BIOTECH-NOLOGY and petroleum-based research, linked to the traditional agricultural and petroleum industries already prominent in the province.

The Physical Environment

Geographic research on the distinctiveness of place also focuses on the nature of relationships between humans and their physical environment. Saskatchewan has a number of distinct physical environments, and their peopling at different times has resulted in variable settlement experiences. Many Canadians are unaware of this diversity because most of those who pass through the province travel along the TRANS-CANADA HIGHWAY, across a part of the province that is flat: this reinforces the common perception of Saskatchewan as a place dominated by horizontal and monotonous landscapes. Those who take the time to explore the province know differently.

Geographers apply the concept of ecozone, defined as a spatial unit that describes particular biophysical features and underlying relationships, to illustrate the regional variety of physical environments. Saskatchewan has four ecozones—the PRAIRIE, BOREAL PLAINS, BOREAL SHIELD, and TAIGA SHIELD—and three natural vegetation regions—grassland, parkland, and forest.[2] The Shield is comprised of ancient, mostly crystalline rocks of Precambrian age (see PRECAMBRIAN GEOLOGY). Younger sedimentary rocks cover this crystalline basement in the WESTERN CANADIAN SEDIMENTARY BASIN that underlies the southern portion of Saskatchewan. The relatively flat landscape of this region is referred to as the Interior Plains. Prairie and boreal plains ecozones cover this region. (See ECOREGIONS).

Grasslands dominate the drier prairie with trees only growing near rivers where they can get enough moisture. The prairie is divided into tall and short grasses, the latter now concentrated in the drier southwestern part of the province. The parkland, a transitional zone

separating the grassland and boreal forest, is covered with trees interspersed with grassland. Deciduous trees (aspen, poplar and birch) dominate in the south; conifers (spruce and pine) are more prevalent in the north. The parkland merges into the southern boreal forest as areas of grassland diminish and finally disappear. Black and brown soils often derived from glacial deposits left during the last ice age are ideal for the cultivation of crops in the grassland and parkland. (*See also* GRASSES AND GRASSLANDS, NATIVE; TREES; SOILS).

The southern part of the boreal forest lies within the Interior Plains; but to the north lies the Precambrian Shield, comprising crystalline basement rocks and the somewhat younger sedimentary rocks of the Athabasca Basin, which together represent more than three billion years of Earth history. GLACIAL EROSION scoured this land, creating a poorly drained region dotted with thousands of lakes, rivers and bogs. Agriculture is almost impossible because of thin grey soils, rocky and swampy terrain, and short growing season. Hardier coniferous trees prevail in this region. The taiga shield in the far northeastern part of the province is a transitional zone between the boreal forest to the south and the treeless Arctic tundra to the north. The black spruce and jack pine in this cold environment are widely spaced.

The entire province, with the exception of the CYPRESS HILLS in the extreme southwest, was affected by GLACIATION. GLACIAL DEPOSITION during the retreat of the ice sheets left behind a landscape of moraines, glacial spillways (e.g., the Qu'Appelle Valley), drumlins, and other related landforms. The last ice cap left a moraine-capped escarpment (the MISSOURI ESCARPMENT) running from 100 km west of the Manitoba border, angling northwestward to Swift Current and then north-northwest into Alberta. In many parts of the prairie are deposits formed on the floor of former PROGLACIAL LAKES, creating the large expanses of flat land so prominent in southern Saskatchewan.

The Cypress Hills, a plateau bypassed by the glaciers, reach as high as 1,392 metres, the highest point in Canada between Labrador and the Rockies. Cooler temperatures and greater precipitation than the surrounding prairies produce a mixture of wet grasslands, aspen parkland and fescue prairie, as well as aspen, lodgepole pine and white spruce forest. Other distinctive landforms include the badlands of south-central Saskatchewan, characterized by unusually shaped rocks, sandstone bluffs, and cliffs. The ATHABASCA SAND DUNES, along the south shore of

SOURCE: ECOREGIONS OF SASKATCHEWAN (1998)

The Cypress Hills are the highest point in Canada between Labrador and the Rockies.

LAKE ATHABASCA in the northwest, form the largest dune fields in Canada. Other sand dune areas occur in the GREAT SAND HILLS, Douglas Provincial Park, and Good Spirit Lake.[3]

Saskatchewan's CLIMATE can be classified a number of different ways. Generally, the southern areas (especially the southwest) are drier, while the north has cooler summers and colder winters. The province's continental position and the unencumbered invasion of cold Arctic air masses from the north and warm Gulf of Mexico air masses from the south usually ensure both long cold winters and hot dry summers. The prevailing westerlies that come from the Pacific are dry because they lose most of their moisture in the form of orographic precipitation as they cross the Rockies.

Because Saskatchewan depends so much on agriculture, it is understandable that climate is a subject that engenders much discussion. In this context, the issue of climate change is one that attracts considerable attention. Most climate change scenarios for the prairie provinces, predicated on increased atmospheric carbon dioxide, indicate a rapid increase in temperatures, a reduction in soil moisture because of higher evapo-transpiration, and a greater incidence of extreme climate events. While predicted increases in temperature would lengthen the growing season, higher temperatures and lower soil moisture could adversely affect agriculture, particularly in the drier regions of the province. The potential impact of climate change on agriculture, forest ecosystems, RECREATION AND TOURISM, wildlife and biodiversity, AQUATIC ECOSYSTEMS, water supply and demand, and other aspects of Saskatchewan's economy and environment, is a topic for debate. The perceived inevitability of this change, regardless of its nature and dimensions, is something that concerns many. (*See* CLIMATE CHANGE: THE FUTURE).

Historical Geography

Widely divergent soil types, vegetation, and surface features at the local and regional scales as well as significant differences in climate between north and south produced a variable setting for the historical evolution of the province. In the far north, the last glacier receded about 9,000 years ago. As the ice disappeared the land was colonized by plants, animals, and people. The early forest cultures that followed established hunting and gathering societies based on moose, woodland caribou, beaver, waterfowl, and fish. In the sub-Arctic climate zone of the taiga shield, people hunted the barren ground caribou as they migrated between the Arctic tundra in the summer and the northern edge of the boreal forest in the winter. In the south the glaciers had receded several thousand years earlier. The first grasslands peoples, belonging to the Clovis material culture, hunted Pleistocene species such as mammoth, prehistoric bison and horses during the period 11,500 to 10,500 years before present (*see* ARCHAEOLOGY). A number of cultures followed, and with the extinction of the Pleistocene species the subsistence economies of these groups became focused on BISON. The development of the bow and arrow facilitated large-scale, communal bison hunts during the Late Plains Indian period (2,000 to a little over 300 years ago).[4]

It is generally believed that HENRY KELSEY, a Hudson's Bay Company (HBC) agent who followed the SASKATCHEWAN RIVER from HUDSON BAY in 1690–91, was the first European to enter present-day Saskatchewan. At that time, the DENESULINE (Dene) were the only cultural group in the far north. Woodland peoples belonging to the CREE culture lived in the boreal forest. Atsinas (Gros Ventre) inhabited the grasslands of west-central and southwestern Saskatchewan, while NAKOTA (Assiniboine) bands occupied the eastern half of the grasslands at that time.[5] The Dene are believed to have obtained some European

goods as early as the 1620s, procuring them from Cree who lived further south and east. By 1682 the HBC had established a post at Port Nelson on Hudson Bay, and endeavoured to establish permanent trade with the Dene. In 1717, Fort Churchill was built at the mouth of the CHURCHILL RIVER and Dene from northern Saskatchewan came to trade there. Following SAMUEL HEARNE's travels to Lake Athabasca in 1769–72, PETER POND in 1779 supervised the construction of the first HBC trading post in the region, about 50 km from the mouth of the Athabasca River. Ten years later, this post was replaced by Fort Chipewyan, which was built on the southwestern shore of LAKE ATHABASCA.[6]

The Plains Cree were originally a woodland group who adopted the horse-bison culture when they moved into central and southern Saskatchewan in the early 18th century. With the beginning of trade with the English and French on James Bay and Hudson Bay in the late 17th century, the western Cree and Nakota of present-day northwestern Ontario and Manitoba no longer had to rely on the Ottawa and Ojibwa for European goods (e.g., steel traps, guns) they wanted. Almost immediately, the Nakota and western Cree began building trading networks toward the grasslands/parkland region.[7] By this time, the horse had been reintroduced to the North American plains from New Mexico, and was quickly integrated into the economic and social life of the Indians of the region.

Firearms and the fur trade had an indelible impact on the Plains Cree and the Dene. Within a short period of time, Natives prized European goods for both utilitarian purposes and as new forms of wealth. They exchanged furs (beaver and buffalo) and meat for trade goods, and gradually adopted more of the Europeans' food, clothing and technology. While western Aboriginal peoples originally travelled to Hudson Bay to trade, they eventually persuaded both the French and the English to establish trading posts in their territories: Cumberland House was built in 1774 to include the Saskatchewan area.

Recent research challenges the traditional interpretation of this trade, which assumes that First Nations peoples fell into a subordinate and dependent relationship vis-à-vis the Europeans. The revisionist position is summarized by Thistle, who states:

> Natives in the region were numerically superior and knowledgeable enough to maintain a significant degree of control over their participation in the production of fur and in the transportation and provisioning systems, as well as the strategic balance of power. The social and political systems of First Nations peoples clearly served as the basis for the structuring of the early fur-trade periods as it is apparent that changes in the Native material culture was predicated on their own needs and world views. On the other hand, it was Europeans who adapted themselves [...] to the "customs of the country." During the period from 1690 to 1840, Europeans were clearly unable to impose their own conditions on the relationship with Native peoples and, therefore, found it necessary to adapt themselves to the existing social, political, technological, and economic systems of the First Nations peoples of the regions.[8]

Despite the efforts of the French and English to manipulate the conditions of trade and rival bands to their advantage, Native peoples took advantage of the rivalries between the Europeans before 1763, and between the trading companies after that date, to attain as advantageous a position as possible within the system. Over time, however, the continued expansion of the fur trade resulted in differing paths of development and relationships with the trading companies. Parkland Cree and Nakota intensified their hunting of bison to meet the growing provision requirements of the HBC and North West Company, and consequently became less dependent on the trapping and trading of furs to obtain goods. This transition from a woodland- to a grassland-based economy gradually reduced their reliance on the trading companies, as they found that the bison would meet many of their requirements for survival. Those groups remaining in the forests, however, faced a different situation. Over-hunting meant that the Woodland Nakota, Cree, and Ojibwa had to rely increasingly on trapping—in spite of the fact that the fur resource was declining. Increased trapping intensified their dependence on European ammunition, axes, traps, cloths, blankets, and other equipment.[9]

Yet eventually, the parkland and grassland tribes would lose their advantage. Missionary activity challenged traditional forms of leadership, and Native peoples concentrated around permanent settlements. The impact of disease and the near extinction of the buffalo had a devastating effect on Native groups. It was at this time that the nature of the relationship with Europeans changed from that of parity and, arguably, control, to dependence.[10] The HBC was not prepared to replace the bison with another food source for the Plains Indians: instead, the Canadian government provided sustenance, but required these nomadic hunters to relocate and settle on reserves.[11]

During the mid-19th century, British and Canadian expeditions, the former led by John Palliser and the latter by Henry Youle Hind and Simon Dawson respectively (see PALLISER AND HIND EXPEDITIONS), explored the prairies. Both expeditions divided the western interior into two zones: a fertile belt appropriate for agricultural settlement, which loosely followed a trajectory along the NORTH SASKATCHEWAN RIVER from the Red River Settlement to the Rockies; and an arid area (PALLISER'S TRIANGLE) south of that arc which was seen as suitable only for grazing. Both parties failed to explore the far southwestern part of present-day Saskatchewan, choosing instead to make second-hand references to this area as the northern extension of the Great American Desert.[12] The impact of these expeditions and the subsequent and more favourable report of JOHN MACOUN were significant. The region was no longer viewed as a wilderness suitable only for the fur trade, but as an area with great potential for agriculture. Indeed, as one historian maintains, the information contained in their reports "provided the basis for the redefinition of the geography of the North West."[13]

In 1868, legislation was passed enabling the Crown to accept the surrender of Rupert's Land (see RUPERT'S LAND PURCHASE). This was followed in 1870 by an Order-in-Council that set out the details of transfer to the Dominion government and the entry of Manitoba into Confederation, after which the lands of present-day Saskatchewan and Alberta were administered as territories (see BOUNDARIES).[14] After the exile of their leader LOUIS RIEL, disillusioned MÉTIS from southern Manitoba began to settle land along the SOUTH SASKATCHEWAN RIVER. Métis buffalo hunters previously had temporary camps throughout southern Saskatchewan, including the Qu'Appelle Valley, DUCK LAKE and BATOCHE areas, and later returned to these places, establishing permanent agricultural settlements to supplement traditional hunting. It was as this time that the Canadian government began negotiation of treaties with the Native peoples in preparation for an expected influx of settlers.

The salient features of Canadian land policy in the west—homesteads, land survey, and railway land grants—were transplants from the United States. The sectional survey system, with its geometrical design, was intended to get settlers on the land as cheaply and quickly as possible. Although western Canada's first Homestead Act was passed in 1872, the region failed to attract the hundreds of thousands of Europeans and North Americans moving westward. Between 1870 and 1896, adjacent American lands were filling up while the Canadian prairies remained largely empty of White settlement. The lack of rail connections to export points limited development before 1879, but the completion of the CANADIAN PACIFIC RAILWAY in 1886 and the extension of its subsidiary, the SOO LINE RAILWAY, to the Canadian border removed this barrier. Yet settlement still proceeded slowly: less than 170,000 people settled in the three North-West Territories (Assiniboia, Saskatchewan, Alberta) between 1881 and 1886.[15]

The Métis of the Saskatchewan Valley had settled the land before the survey was begun, and dreaded the prospect of White settlement. Appeals to the government to have their river lots legally recognized were only partially successful: established lots were acknowledged, but new areas needed for expansion would only be surveyed under the sectional system. The Métis believed the land was theirs by right of their Indian parentage, and objected to having to wait three years for title as immigrants did.[16] They asked Louis Riel to return to Canada to lead the protest for land rights. Ottawa ignored their demands, and in 1885 the Métis and their Indian allies proclaimed a provisional government. Following an armed skirmish at Duck Lake between the Métis, Natives, Mounted Police and White volunteers, Ottawa sent an armed force under General F.D. MIDDLETON to quell the revolt. They eventually succeeded, Riel was executed, and the Métis were forced to live under the new order.[17]

Only by 1896, when lands to the south had largely filled and the worldwide recession of the 1890s was ending, did significant numbers of settlers begin to flow into the region. The British were the largest immigrant group (N=562,054) between 1900 and 1910, although the numbers of Americans (N=497,249) and, to a lesser extent, continental Europeans (N=394,088) increased dramatically at the end of the decade. While many of the British were attracted to the developing industrial heartland of Ontario and Québec, Americans and continental Europeans were more responsive to the opportunities presented by settlement in the west. Between 1897 and 1910, 32% of arrivals from continental Europe and 42% of arrivals from the United States made homestead entry in western Canada.[18] This influx of population and the development of an economy based primarily on agriculture played a direct role in the creation of Saskatchewan as a province in 1905.

A basic fact of immigrant life in Saskatchewan and in the west

EVERETT BAKER PHOTO/COURTESY OF THE SASKATCHEWAN HISTORY AND FOLKLORE SOCIETY

Eight-horse One Way, June 1947.

was the inherent tension between the centrifugal forces of new social patterns on the one hand, and the centripetal attractions of nucleated settlement and cultural retention on the other. The RURAL SETTLEMENT PATTERNS of the region as well as the associated URBAN GEOGRAPHY were influenced by a variety of factors including soil quality, land availability, and access to markets and railways. But for large numbers of Europeans and transplanted European migrants from the United States, settlement was also shaped by social factors: kinship and kith affiliation, and ethnic congregation were primary migratory forces. Communities in the west were centred on ethnic institutions that served as a basis for social ties. In the resultant ETHNIC BLOC SETTLEMENTS, family, church and community structured local society and relationships.

Despite the competing pulls of the novel and the familiar, allegiances both to the new nation and to transplanted cultural traditions could coexist in Saskatchewan, although at times this relationship was uneasy. Ethno-cultural groups were influenced by Anglo-conformity, but also by transplanted and re-institutionalized cultural practices. While the availability of "free"[19] homestead land enabled cultural groups to congregate in space, it also created economic opportunities which reduced the potential for conflict that arises from scarcity. Thus, while segregation did occur to some extent in Saskatchewan and the west, evidence shows that "neighbourly contacts with families of different ethnicity but from the same region, as well as interaction with English-speaking groups in the marketplace, precluded the emergence of mono-cultural blocs... Bloc settlement could thus be regionally homogeneous but ethnically diverse."[20]

Other factors—the NATIONAL POLICY (1879) and low freight rates established under the 1897 CROW'S NEST PASS AGREEMENT, and the new strains of wheat developed to grow in the harsh climate of the prairies—also played a role in developing the economy and attracting settlers to Saskatchewan. During the first three decades of the 20th century, Saskatchewan was Canada's fastest growing province: between 1900 and 1930, there were 303,000 homestead entries. The population grew from 91,000 in 1901 to 922,000 in 1931, and during this interval the number of farms increased from 13,000 to 136,000.[21] A linear pattern of service centres emerged across the prairies, controlled and directed by the railways: stations with grain elevators were established 8–18 km apart, thus easily accessible to most farmers. Other services were soon established, catering to the farmers' needs. Those centres most favourably situated, chosen as the location of government or commercial enterprises, or benefiting from the energy and acumen of local leaders, moved quickly to the top of the urban hierarchy.

The development of the province and the western region in general, both during the fur trade and agricultural settlement periods, occurred in wider contexts of political, economic and social relationships that Swainson contends were characterized by dependence and exploitation:

> The area and its resources were controlled from outside, for the benefit of several distant centres, whose relative importance changed from time to time. London, Montreal and Toronto, the major and competing metropolises, were flanked by such lesser competitors as Minneapolis-St. Paul, Benton and Vancouver. A prime result of this pattern of development has been a continuing resistance to outside controls. At the same time, the character of western people and institutions has been heavily influenced by forces outside western control.[22]

For example, Potyondi argues that during the fur trade era, Native peoples and Métis were "in the vanguard of the assault on the very resources that gave their cultures meaning. In turning their profound knowledge of the regional ecosystem to monetary advantage, they quickly depleted the natural resources of the plains to satisfy a far-off, metropolitan-based demand that they scarcely understood."[23]

External influences on development were also evident in the federal control of public lands and natural resources in the three prairie provinces, which lasted for twenty-five years after Saskatchewan and Alberta achieved provincial status. Ironically, the three provinces gained control of their lands and resources just as the GREAT DEPRESSION brought dreadful conditions for western grain farmers, already heavily indebted to eastern banks and trust companies. Thousands declared bankruptcy, and anger was directed towards federal policies that prevented farmers from taking advantage of cheaper American farm machinery and consumer goods during a time when their grain was sold on world markets at abysmally low prices. This frustration translated into the creation of social movements and political parties (PROGRESSIVE PARTY, the United Farmers of Canada, the CO-OPERATIVE COMMONWEALTH FEDERATION, SOCIAL CREDIT PARTY) which assailed eastern capitalists and politicians.[24] During the 1930s, Saskatchewan experienced drought, falling grain prices, out-migration, farm consolidation, the beginning of rural-urban migration, and the decline of rural communities. Although economic conditions improved during the war years with increasing yields and grain prices, the population continued to decline, falling by more than 100,000 during the 1930s and 1940s.[25]

A notable feature of Saskatchewan is the prevalence of co-operatives across different economic sectors (see CO-OPERATIVES IN SASKATCHEWAN). The first co-operative was organized by wheat farmers in the early 1900s to help market and distribute crops. The largest today is the now publicly traded SASKATCHEWAN WHEAT POOL, which operates grain elevators and terminals, livestock yards, and many other facilities. Other co-operatives are active in retailing, wholesaling, housing, banking, and other service industries. This co-operative consciousness also made its way into politics. The socialist Co-operative Commonwealth Federation (CCF), which was organized in 1933 during the nadir of the Depression, emphasized the need for government intervention in the economy in general and the importance of CROWN CORPORATIONS specifically. The party designated health care and agriculture as the primary issues in the 1944 election, and swept to power on the basis of overwhelming rural support. The first "socialist" government in North America put into place policies that have persisted, in spite of changing administrations.

FORESTRY, the OIL AND GAS INDUSTRY, the POTASH INDUSTRY and URANIUM mining spurred economic growth in the 1950s and 1960s. This, in turn, triggered the development of the service sector. As a consequence, agriculture, although still the most important industry in the province, gradually decreased in terms of its primacy. International trade of primary resources continued to be the lifeblood of the Saskatchewan economy during the last few decades of the 20th century, but gradually the economy diversified.

Human Geography

Population

Any consideration of population in Saskatchewan has to take into account the context of socio-economic trends such as increased farm size and mechanization, declining farm incomes due to agricultural restructuring and decreasing prices, increasing loss of community

G

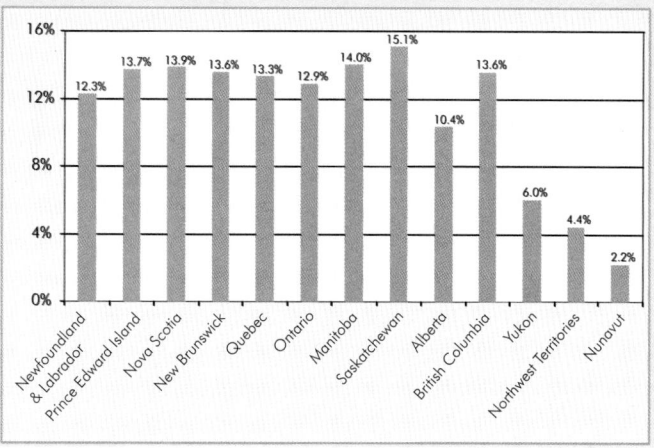

Source: Statistics Canada

Figure 2. Percentage of Population 65+, Canada, provinces and territories, 2001.

services, and greater mobility resulting from improvements in the transportation system. The population of the province has displayed only minimal growth since the middle of the 20th century, and most projections maintain that growth will continue to be slow in the immediate future. Among the provinces, only Newfoundland and Labrador exhibited lower growth than Saskatchewan during the period 1981–2001. Compared with the other provinces, Saskatchewan has the highest elderly dependency ratio (Figure 2)[26]: this is a consequence of a declining fertility rate and a significant out-migration of the young. INTERPROVINCIAL MIGRATION has resulted in a net population loss for most of the last thirty years, as both young and old leave the province in record numbers. The result will be fewer people in the workforce, more people collecting pensions, and greater demands on the health care system. Saskatchewan also has relatively low attraction and retainment of immigrant rates when compared to other provinces.[27]

Yet, while the overall population of Saskatchewan is experiencing slow growth, the same cannot be said for the Aboriginal sector of the province. Registered Indians, living on and off reserves, increased to 90,797 in 2000 from 74,095 in 1996—an increase of 23%. In January 2001, approximately 143,000 registered and non-registered Aboriginals comprised about 14% of Saskatchewan's population of just fewer than one million people. The net growth of this population sector is currently about 5% per year,[28] and projections made of the Aboriginal population in 2045 range from 434,000 to just less than one million. Even using the lower estimate, Aboriginals are expected to make up approximately 32.5% of Saskatchewan's population at that time, compared to 13.3% in 1995.[29]

Northern Saskatchewan's population differs from the south in that the relative proportions of First Nations (Cree and Dene) and Métis are greater. Yet Aboriginal people from both northern and southern reserves and communities are joining non-Natives in-migrating to the province's largest cities. In 2001, Saskatoon was the country's youngest metropolitan area, due primarily to the fertility of its large Aboriginal population. Regina also had a much younger population than most other cities in Canada, for the same reason.[30]

The Saskatchewan Chamber of Commerce has identified population growth as a priority for the province. Migrants tend to be young, skilled, and in their family-raising years. Depopulation creates a vicious downward spiral that erodes the foundation of rural communities: those who remain are proportionately older and poorer than urban populations, and struggle to maintain basic services. Fewer people mean fewer

businesses, fewer tax dollars, and a deteriorating infrastructure. These conditions combine to repel both businesses and people from locating in these centres, and drive out those who would seek better prospects elsewhere. Many are also pulled to neighbouring provinces by the promise of a better living standard: in 2001, Alberta and Manitoba had better job creation records than Saskatchewan (64,787, 17,499, and 4,268 respectively). Saskatchewan's greater dependence on agriculture, primary resources and a less diversified economy means that the province feels the effects of poor markets and low commodity prices more than the other prairie provinces.[31] (*See also* POPULATION TRENDS.)

A struggling farm economy and resultant community decline have fuelled rural-urban migration within Saskatchewan: more and more, people are moving to the larger centres, particularly Saskatoon and Regina, where greater opportunities for employment exist. In addition, improved TRANSPORTATION has increased the attraction of larger communities, and shopping patterns for rural people have shifted from nearby rural communities to regional shopping centres, where more businesses, greater variety, and lower prices are available. This circumvention of small- and mid-sized communities discourages new commercial development from locating in these centres, and hastens their decline.

Economic Geography

The economy of the province remains highly export-oriented and includes the traditional resource-based industries (agriculture, FORESTRY and mineral extraction), a limited manufacturing base, and a small but growing high-tech sector focusing on industries such as biotechnology, aerospace, and petroleum-based research. As is the case elsewhere, non-industrial sectors of the economy have expanded more than industrial sectors. The prices for primary products fluctuate significantly, but increasing diversification of the economy has served to offset somewhat the downturns in primary prices and sales that occur from time to time. The relative prosperity of the 1950s, 1960s and 1970s, a period that witnessed some declines but was generally characterized by modest growth, gave way in the 1980s to more severe recessions: "World overproduction of small grains, coupled with the failure of GATT to restore order in international grain markets, resulted in several successive years in which prices received were at or below the cost of production."[32] Smaller subsidies, a leaner safety net, and the termination of the Crow Rate, which resulted in a substantial increase in the cost of shipping grain, hurt agriculture. All this took place within the context of a global restructuring of the industry, resulting in a shift away from grain farming to a more diversified crop and livestock base.

In most rural communities, agriculture is no longer the major direct employer, and farm mechanization and amalgamation have substantially reduced the demand for farm labour. The number of farms has decreased; average values of farmland have fallen; farm income has shrunk relative to the average income per worker in other sectors; farm debt has risen; and wheat prices have declined. Rural communities in general and farmers in particular are desperately trying to adapt to new institutional arrangements of global restructuring. While the 1990s were kinder to Saskatchewan, particularly because of the emergence of a new economy made possible by agricultural diversification, limited manufacturing growth and the expansion of new technologies especially in Saskatoon and Regina, hundreds of rural communities experienced significant decline and some even became extinct. Saskatchewan enjoys a low unemployment rate—5.6% in January 2004, the third lowest in the country—but this figure is tempered by the out-migration of those people who might otherwise find it difficult to gain employment.[33]

Table 1. Saskatchewan Exports Outside of Canada ($ millions) by Industry and Total, 1995 to 1999

Industry	Years					Average Annual Change
	1995	1996	1997	1998	1999	1995-1999
Primary Agriculture	4005.17	4146.97	4968.85	4152.25	3630.71	-1.40%
Mining Industries	1539.6	1364.67	1606.95	1898.44	2004.88	7.50%
Crude Petroleum and Natural Gas	1682.47	1855.38	1912.69	1428.76	1647.46	0.80%
Other Primary Industries	1.59	2.19	3.38	5.53	7.52	47.90%
Total Manufacturing	1601.54	1903.89	2264.7	2358.17	2524.79	12.30%
Chemical and Chemical Products	381.07	382.06	413.59	342.88	386.98	1.10%
Clothing and Textiles	0.79	2.59	2.93	6.17	6.27	88.70%
Electrical and Electronic Products	92.41	171.96	172.01	295.43	367.64	45.60%
Fabricated Metal Products	9.47	18.73	29.25	24.07	41.84	52.50%
Food and Beverage	219.37	428.89	482.11	481.08	476.2	26.70%
Furniture and Fixtures	0.32	0.5	1.59	2.12	2.75	84.10%
Machinery (except electrical)	163.14	207.61	221.63	191.24	190.1	4.90%
Non-Metallic Mineral Products	3.66	3.82	5.53	6.29	11.48	36.30%
Paper and Allied Products	399.19	270.88	412.61	444.18	460.8	7.90%
Plastic Products	9.25	15.86	16.49	14.58	23.21	30.70%
Primary Metal	121.28	90.98	82.7	132.21	92.45	-1.10%
Refined Petroleum and Coal Products	89.63	119.63	136.29	97.02	104.44	6.60%
Transportation Equipment	37.78	44.24	54.21	58.59	54.03	10.00%
Wood	54.49	130.28	211.69	233.4	278.35	57.80%
Other Manufacturing	19.68	15.87	22.08	28.9	28.25	12.10%
Total SK Exports Outside Canada	8882	9349	10832	9944	9948	3.20%

Source: Strategis, Industry Canada

Despite some modest diversification, the Saskatchewan economy is still reliant on primary exports and therefore remains strongly affected by global trends (Table 1). In 2001, total exports of $22 billion accounted for 73% of Saskatchewan's Gross Domestic Product (GDP), a figure that sustained and/or created 220,000 jobs. The largest trading partner for both Canada and Saskatchewan is the United States: in 2002, the province shipped $6.9 billion worth of products to the US.[34] The most important exports–non-durum and durum wheat, oats, barley, and canola seed–are sold primarily to the West Coast (California, Oregon and Washington) and the Midwest (Illinois and Minnesota). Saskatchewan Agriculture is attempting to expand its markets in Europe, particularly Germany and the United Kingdom, and in Japan.[35] Drought, a higher Canadian dollar, and BSE (Mad Cow Disease) have recently reduced agri-food exports; but exports still increased by 5% between 2002 and 2003 owing to export sales of energy, minerals, industrial goods, forestry products, and machinery and equipment.[36] In total, mineral resources now account for a larger proportion of export value than agriculture. In the future, agriculture will further diversify, with greater emphasis on cattle and hog raising; processing grains into foods, feeds, alcohol and ethanol; and the development of nutraceutical and dermaceutical industries (organic food, vitamins and minerals, herbs).

Saskatchewan's strongest inter-provincial trade ties are with Ontario, the neighbouring prairie provinces, and Québec. With the exception of the Atlantic region and the Territories, Saskatchewan had trade deficits in the 1990s with every major region of Canada, a point that reflects the relatively underdeveloped state of the province's manufacturing sector. Between 1992 and 1998, Ontario was the province's primary domestic trading partner, accounting for $2.1 billion (33%) of total inter-provincial exports and $3.9 billion (37%) of inter-provincial imports. Major imports from Ontario include automobiles, pharmaceuticals, food products, and computers.[37]

As agriculture declines in relative terms, OIL AND GAS extraction is playing a greater role in the economy of southern Saskatchewan: in January 2004, some 400 companies employed 22,000 people directly or indirectly in this sector. Saskatchewan is the second-highest oil-producing province, with 20% of all Canadian crude oil and equivalent production. It is also the third-highest gas-producing province. Refineries in Regina and Lloydminster upgrade the heavy, viscous oil that is dominant in Saskatchewan.[38] In addition, the province is the largest world producer and exporter of potash.

Mining and forestry, so important in the northern half of the province, have also been features of the post-war economy. Saskatchewan is the world's largest URANIUM producer; this is the most important export from the north, but there has also been extraction of base metals such as copper, nickel, and zinc, as well as of GOLD, silver, and other precious minerals. Exploration for DIAMONDS could generate future mines. Total mineral sales in 2001 were $2.4 billion, about 6% of the provincial GDP.[39] During the 1960s, the increasing demand for paper and other wood-based materials resulted in the expansion of forestry: more than half the province is forested, and in 2003 the industry put more than $750 million into the provincial economy.[40]

The development of forestry and mining in the north disrupted the land base of Aboriginal peoples, and precipitated a change in the relations between traditional hunting and gathering societies and non-Natives representing both provincial and external capital interests. Increasingly, First Nations, Métis and non-Natives, both northerners and from elsewhere, were employed as wage labourers in a resource sector. In addition, many new businesses have been created in the service sector through government, First Nations and corporate investment. However, wages in these industries are generally low.

A relatively rapid transition from a hunting and gathering periphery to an extractive industrial periphery has occurred in northern Saskatchewan. Unfortunately, forestry and mining are subject to the vagaries of the world market: this fact, combined with the significant multiplier leakage associated with these industries, results in high rates of unemployment and dependency. This dependency is exacerbated by the reality that external interests control the primary flows of capital into and out of the region. Despite the traditional importance of resource extraction and production, it is the TOURISM industry that many northern communities look to as the key to development, notwithstanding the considerable obstacle presented by geographical isolation.

As the First Nations population increases relative to the rest of the population, its role in the provincial economy is becoming more crucial. Treaty Land Entitlement (TLE) agreements are slowly providing the capital needed by First Nations to purchase land and engage in economic activities, a significant development in light of the fact that the Aboriginal population is growing faster than the Aboriginal employment rate. The funding received as a result of these agreements is often invested in a manner that reflects a collective approach to economic development. This approach, according to Robert Anderson, serves three purposes: "the attainment of economic self-sufficiency as a necessary condition for the realization of self-government at the First Nation level; the improvement of the socio-economic circumstances of the people of the First Nations; [and] the preservation and strengthening of traditional culture, values and languages, and the reflection of the same in development activities."[41] Yet while many advocate a collective approach, there is disagreement among First Nations people regarding economic development, especially in areas of forestry and gaming. Those who are business- and politically minded want to take charge of economic opportunities that exist in the larger society. Others oppose this type of development, which they view as essentially foreign to Indian culture, preferring instead to leave the land in its natural state and strive for alternative forms of growth.

Culture and Landscapes[42]

Landscapes reveal and evoke the personality of a place. Geographers argue that landscape is more than the visible, concrete elements associated with human occupation: it may also be conceptualized as a metaphorical text which, like a book, can be read and written by individuals and groups for different purposes and with many different interpretations. Geographers contend that landscapes reveal much about alienation, power relations, and dependency.

There are a number of cultural landscape images that give us lasting connections to the place called Saskatchewan—symbols and metaphors that dominate artistic expressions of the province in a vari-

ety of media. The visible and perceptual imprint of humankind that is most associated with the province, both within and without, is the agricultural landscape, a landscape where the sectional survey ensures that geometry triumphs over geography, at least in the south. Traditionally, southern Saskatchewan was dominated by the isolated, dispersed farmstead: the product of a settlement pattern created by a survey system designed to get people on the land quickly, with little regard for the isolation that it produced. However, the countryside was and still is interspersed with pockets of clustered farm settlements, where various ethnocultural (e.g., UKRAINIANS, GERMANS) and ethno-religious (e.g., HUTTERITES, MENNONITES) groups have located together in order to maintain their culture and communal ways of life.

Saskatchewan is made up of people from more than fifty ethnic and racial origins. In the 2001 Census, 963,150 Saskatchewanians reported ethnic ancestry in the groups shown in Table 2. The imprints

Table 2. Saskatchewan's Ethnic Ancestry, 2003			
	Total Responses	Single Responses	Multiple responses
Total Population	963,150	481,230	481,920
Ethnic origin			
German	275,060	84,280	190,785
Canadian	240,535	111,745	128,790
English	235,715	41,815	193,895
Scottish	172,300	16,600	155,700
Irish	139,205	11,155	128,045
Ukrainian	121,735	40,710	81,025
French	109,800	15,040	94,755
North American Indian	102,285	70,390	31,900
Norwegian	60,510	9,135	51,370
Polish	51,445	7,275	44,170
Métis	40,110	12,475	27,630
Dutch (Netherlands)	32,300	6,445	25,860
Swedish	29,900	3,400	26,500
Russian	27,695	3,640	24,050
Hungarian (Magyar)	24,340	5,875	18,465
Austrian	14,450	2,055	12,400
Welsh	13,935	965	12,965
American (USA)	11,280	795	10,485
Romanian	10,290	1,930	8,360
Danish	9,375	1,225	8,155
Chinese	9,275	7,015	2,260
Belgian	8,090	1,155	6,940
Italian	7,565	1,690	5,875
Icelandic	6,110	805	5,305
Czech	4,735	950	3,785
Swiss	4,050	455	3,600
British, not included elsewhere	3,825	965	2,860
Finnish	3,675	745	2,930
Filipino	3,275	2,365	910

Source: Statistics Canada, Census of Population (last modified: April 29, 2003)

Ukrainian Greek Orthodox Church of St. Elia, built in 1953, is a long-recognized landmark in east central Saskatchewan. Located in Wroxton, approximately 40 km east of Yorkton, the traditional onion-domed design of the church clearly reflects the ethnicity of the community.

of this ethnicity on the cultural landscape—sometimes striking, more often subtle—are revealed in the architecture, language, RELIGION, and dress, as well as the settlement pattern, of Saskatchewan's ethno-cultures. With a few exceptions, ethnicity is more visible in rural parts of the province, where sites and buildings closely associated with particular ethnic groups stand out because of lower surrounding densities.

While the rural portion of southern Saskatchewan is defined largely by the agricultural landscape, despite the significance of potash mining and the growing importance of the energy sector its counterpart to the north is characterized by a more rugged natural environment and a small, dispersed population. Yet the human imprint is still very much evident in the boreal forest. Northern Saskatchewan is varied topographically, and challenges the clichés of the flat prairie. Forestry and its associated pulp and paper production, and uranium and other mining activities have given rise to structures and communities that sometimes have a limited life span (e.g., URANIUM CITY). The exploitation asso-

ciated with this primary activity has profoundly affected the natural landscape, but there is also evidence of the more recent efforts of humans to inject sustainable principles into their development.

Community as place and value is the symbol most associated with the rural landscape. Yet the rural landscape is no longer secure, and is increasingly marred by an imposed *relic landscape of abandonment*: see-through houses litter the landscape; barns, churches, schools, businesses, and train stations stand empty of both people and animals.

The cities present a number of different cultural landscapes that reflect successive phases of capitalist development. Both Regina and Saskatoon grew rapidly as service centres, and neither developed much of an industrial base: as a result, the industrial landscape so prominent in other major centres in North America is not much in evidence in either city. Notable exceptions include the oil refinery and steel mill in Regina. In both Regina and Saskatoon, the present cityscape bears evidence of what has been termed the post-Fordist era of capitalism, in which factories are small and more flexible in their methods of production. In addition, research and development are carried on in RESEARCH PARKS present on university campuses in both cities.

These changes in the cityscape prompt reflection upon what these places are becoming. Certainly, there is much evidence of the construction of landscapes that are increasingly distant from the environment and the history of the region. It seems that all cities, not just those in Saskatchewan, are being taken over by developments (e.g., strip malls, fast food and clothing chains) that are built on a national and very often American-based model, and are insensitive to local cultural and visual traits. Efficient they may be, particularly in this automobile-dominated society, but to many they are blight on the landscape. The continuing expansion of capitalism is accompanied by countervailing tendencies towards homogenization; a trend most clearly expressed by the large "box" businesses (e.g., Wal-Mart, Home Depot) that now dominate the landscape of the suburbs. This kind of development is occurring at the expense of the central business districts, and decay in the form of vacant buildings is very much evident in Saskatchewan's cities.

The most significant paradox evident in the cultural makeup of Saskatchewan is that which exists between Native and non-Native societies. The immense social changes that indigenous peoples have experienced are reflected in both the rural and urban landscapes. The Indian reserve can be interpreted as a *landscape of segregation*, the result of a colonial process of subjugation and a cultural ideology of racism; alternatively, it can be viewed as a *landscape of congregation*, a place where cultural identity is ensured, ironically, by geographical and social isolation. No matter how it is interpreted, the reserve, with a few exceptions, is a place of poverty: the reserve system isolates people from the

Old bank and fire hall in Liberty, Saskatchewan, are an example of the province's "relic landscape of abondonment."

Research Park, University of Regina.

larger economy, and the result for the most part has been disastrous poverty and social ills.

Increasingly, Saskatchewan Native groups have left impoverished reserves to find jobs in cities, so that today over 50% of Aboriginal people in the province reside in urban areas. Yet while cities and towns are home to the majority of Native and Métis people, there is little in the urban landscape that is reflective of their traditional rural-based ways of life. While many who left the reservation have enjoyed the "benefits" of city life—better employment and education prospects, improved housing, better transportation and communication, and so on—for others, the cycle of poverty continues as much in the city as it did on the reserve. Standards of Aboriginal housing are often below what is required for basic health, safety and comfort, and Aboriginals frequently find themselves segregated within urban ghettos. Yet the Native urban landscape is undergoing change: Treaty Land Entitlement has resulted in the purchase of a number of urban reserves that present greater opportunities for economic development. The newly constructed campus of the FIRST NATIONS UNIVERSITY OF CANADA in Regina bears witness to this change, and serves as a symbol for a new kind of place-making in which Aboriginal people no longer feel alienated.

Conclusion

This overview has emphasized to a considerable degree the complex and dynamic nature of Saskatchewan, a place of varied landscapes and ecosystems with a society where different races and cultures overlap. The real Saskatchewan is no longer rural, dominated by flat fields of wheat and by small towns; it is a place undergoing economic, social, cultural and political transformations. The traditional icons associated with the province no longer reflect the place that it is becoming. It is a place of dualities: Native/non-Native, urban/rural, grasslands/forest, north/south. Within this context the historical myth of an unlimited future, promised in the propaganda images of "A Garden of Eden" and "The Last Best West," must be juxtaposed against a present and future reality of a province whose development has been, and will continue to be, confronted by geographical, demographic, economic, social, and political challenges.

NOTES

1. Joel Garreau, in his book *The Nine Nations of North America* (Boston: Houghton Mifflin, 1981), included southern Saskatchewan within a greater North American nation that he identified as the "Bread Basket," and the rest of the province within an international nation called the "Empty Quarter." In the former, southern Saskatchewan was linked with the American northern plains, the upper Midwest states, southern Manitoba and southern Alberta, on the basis that each region within this "nation" is based on a renewable economy and a productive agricultural sector. In the latter, the rest of the province is linked with the central and northern parts of Manitoba, Alberta and the mountain west states of America on the basis of small populations, rich energy resources, and vast wilderness.

2. David Gauthier and Ed Wiken, "Ecoregions of Saskatchewan." In Peter Jonker, John Vandall, Lawrence Baschak and David Gauthier (eds.), *Caring For Homeplace: Protected Areas and Landscape Ecology* (Saskatoon and Regina: University Extension Press and Canadian Plains Research Center, 1997), 4.

3. Information on the physical environments of Saskatchewan comes primarily from: Gauthier and Wiken, "Ecoregions of Saskatchewan"; Jeffrey Thorpe, "The Life: Vegetation and Life Zones." In Henry Epp (ed.), *Three Hundred Prairie Years: Henry Kelsey's "Inland Country of Good Report"* (Regina: University of Regina, Canadian Plains Center, 1993), 11–16.

4. David Meyer, "People Before Kelsey: An Overview of Cultural Developments." In Epp, *Three Hundred Prairie Years*, 54–73.

5. Ibid., 70–71.

6. "Human History in Far Northern Saskatchewan" (February 17, 2004): 2–4. Canoe Saskatchewan Site: http://www.lights.com/waterways/.

7. Arthur J. Ray, "Some Thoughts About the Reasons for Spatial Dynamism in the Early Fur Trade, 1580–1800." In Epp, *Three Hundred Prairie Years*, 115.

8. Paul Thistle, "Dependence and Control: Indian-European Trade Relations in the Post-Kelsey Era." In Epp, *Three Hundred Prairie Years*, 128–29.

9. Arthur J. Ray, *Indians in the Fur Trade: Their Role as Hunters, Trappers and Middlemen in the Lands Southwest of Hudson Bay, 1660–1870* (Toronto: University of Toronto Press, 1974), 147.

10. Thistle, "Dependence and Control," 129.

11. James Dempsey, "Effects on Aboriginal Cultures Due to Contact with Henry Kelsey." In Epp, *Three Hundred Prairie Years*, 135.

12. Barry Potyondi, *In Palliser's Triangle: Living in the Grasslands, 1850–1930* (Saskatoon: Purich Publishing, 1995), 39.

13. Douglas Owram, *Promise of Eden: The Canadian Expansionist Movement and the Idea of the West, 1856–1900* (Toronto: University of Toronto Press, 1992), 65. An insightful treatment of the British and Canadian Scientific expeditions is presented by John Warkentin, who in his book entitled *The Western Interior of Canada* (Toronto: McClelland and Stewart, 1964), includes excerpts from the journals of Palliser and both Hind and Dawson as well as from other accounts and reports written by explorers of the western interior of Canada between 1612 and 1917.

14. Much of this discussion of settlement is drawn from R.W. Widdis, *With Scarcely A Ripple: Anglo-Canadian Migration into the United States and Western Canada, 1880–1920* (Montreal and Kingston: McGill-Queen's University Press, 1998), 290–336.

15. John Culliton, "Assisted Emigration and Land Settlement," *National Problems of Canada*, Economic Studies 9 (Montréal: McGill University, 1928), 23.

16. John Archer, *Saskatchewan: A History* (Saskatoon: Western Producer Prairie Books, 1980), 81.

17. Ibid., 84–98.

18. Minister of the Interior, *Immigration Facts and Figures* (Ottawa: King's Printer, 1910).

19. Homesteaders had to pay a $10 settlement fee and clear a minimum number of acres within the first three years of settlement before they were awarded title to land.

20. Dirk Hoerder, *Creating Societies: Immigrant Lives in Canada* (Montréal and Kingston: McGill-Queen's University Press, 1999), 158.

21. Jack C. Stabler and M. Rose Olfert, *Saskatchewan's Communities in the 21st Century: From Places to Regions* (Regina: Canadian Plains Research Center, 2002), 1.

22. Donald Swainson, "Canada Annexes the West: Colonial Status Confirmed." In R. Douglas Francis and Howard Palmer (eds.), *The Prairie West: Historical Readings* (Edmonton: Pica Pica Press, 1985), 120.

23. Potyondi, *In Palliser's Triangle*, 42.

24. Tom Flanagan, "From Riel to Reform: Understanding Western Canada." Working paper of the fourth annual Seagram Lecture, McGill Institute for the Study of Canada (1999), 2.

25. Stabler and Olfert, *Saskatchewan's Communities*, 2.

26. The elderly dependency ratio is the population aged 65 and over expressed as a proportion of the total population.

27. Doug Elliott, *Demographic Trends in Saskatchewan* (Regina: Saskatchewan Intergovernmental and Aboriginal Affairs, 2003), v–viii.

28. Mario DeSantis, "The Aboriginal People are our Forgotten People" (2001): http://www.ftlcommm.com.

29. No author, "The Impact of Saskatchewan's Growing Aboriginal Community." *Saskatchewan Indian* 30, no. 2 (2000): 18. http://www.sicc.sk.ca/saskindian.

30. Andrew Ehrkamp, "Aboriginal Population Growing." Regina *Leader-Post* (Wednesday January 22, 2003).

31. Ibid.

32. Stabler and Olfert, *Saskatchewan's Communities*, 3.

33. Government of Saskatchewan, *The Saskatchewan Economy* (February 16, 2004): http://www.ir.gov.sk.ca

34. Ibid.

35. Saskatchewan Agriculture, *Food and Rural Revitalization* (Regina: Saskatchewan Agriculture, 2002): http://www.agr.gov.sk.ca

36. Export Development Canada, http://www.edc/ca/docs/news/2003.

37. *Trade Patterns and the Economy of the Northern Great Plains: A Baseline Report* (2000): http://www.tnt.ngplains.org.

38. Government of Saskatchewan, *The Saskatchewan Economy*.

39. Customs Brokers, *International Trade Bulletin* (February 17, 2004): http://www.pcb.ca

40. Ibid.

41. Robert Anderson, *The Business Economy of the First Nations in Saskatchewan: A Contingency Perspective* (Regina: School of Business and Public Administration, Saskatchewan Indian Federated College, n.d.), 310–11.

42. Much of this discussion comes from Randy Widdis, "Place, Placelessness, and Placemaking as Evidenced in Saskatchewan's Cultural Landscape." In Jonker et al., *Caring For Homeplace*, 19–26.

GEOMATICS. Geomatics is the application of digital technologies to solve spatial problems. In-car navigation systems, precision farming, and satellite imaging are all examples of geomatics applications. Geomatics encompasses three closely related disciplines: geographic information systems (GIS), global positioning systems (GPS), and remote sensing systems. A GIS lies at the heart of many geomatics functions. GISs can be used to discern spatial relationships among different map data: for example, between urban population density and income, or between variation in precipitation and diversity among vegetation communities. Maps are among the primary data sources for, and products of, a GIS. When new maps need to be created for inaccessible areas or when up-to-date information is needed about a region, images of the Earth from space can be invaluable. Remote sensing is the acquisition and processing of data about the Earth obtained at a distance; most remote sensing is in the form of satellite images, but it can also include techniques such as airborne aeromagnetic or ground-based seismic surveys.

A GPS is a tool that can tell you exactly where you are on the Earth. GPS coordinates are most useful when they are used in conjunction with a GIS. For example, a GPS reading can be used to ask, "I am here now; which way should I go next?" or for putting new information into a map database, as in "I made the observation at this location." Location is the glue that binds these components together: everything analyzed or interpreted by geomatics is identified (in part) by its locational coordinates (e.g., latitude and longitude).

Saskatchewan is showing leadership in geomatics by integrating its information flow from top to bottom: from corporate objectives to public data sharing. The centrepiece for the government's initiatives is the Information Services Corporation of Saskatchewan (ISC). This provincial Crown corporation is home to one of the most advanced land registry systems in North America. ISC's LAND (Land Titles Automated Network Delivery) system can handle a title change instantly—a huge improvement over traditional methods. The LAND system is a specialized GIS with digital cadastral maps for every property in the province. In addition to land registry, ISC maintains and distributes all of Saskatchewan's mapping, surveys, aerial photos, and GIS data. Other provincial agencies, such as Saskatchewan Environment, SaskPower and SaskTel, as well as many municipalities, use geomatics for managing land and water resources, planning new routes for power and telephone lines, and for urban planning. The province's emergency response service is endowed with a GIS database that has information about every highway and farm access lane in the province.

Saskatchewan's private sector, particularly resource-based industries, also use geomatics technologies. A GIS is at the core of decision support systems used by forestry companies for silviculture management. It allows the companies to determine which tree stands in their inventory will produce the best harvest in one, five, or ten years, based not only on projected timber volumes, but also incorporating other environmental and economic factors. Many other organizations use geomatics as the basis for their corporate facilities mapping. The oil and gas industry uses geospatial data for exploration, inventory, and pipeline route planning. Environmentalists also use geomatics. For example, a GIS can be asked to highlight the most environmentally sensitive areas on the basis of a weighted combination of geology, hydrology, soils, vegetation, landform, and land ownership of an area.

Precision farming is an innovative application of geomatics that is beneficial to one of Saskatchewan's largest economic sectors: cropland agriculture. Precision farming combines remote sensing imagery with other map and GPS information, and is processed in a specialized GIS mounted in a tractor; as the tractor travels across a cultivated field, its precise location is obtained from an on-board GPS. A recent remotely sensed image is automatically referenced to determine current crop health. The GIS compares the current crop information with the previous year's crop yields and other data (e.g., soil types) to create a prescription for the type (e.g, fertilizer or pesticide) and quantity of inputs that should be applied to the field at that point. The task is fulfilled by the variable-rate applicators that are attached to the tractor. Precision agriculture saves the farm operator money since the chemical inputs are only applied at a variable rate where they are needed, instead of a fixed amount everywhere across the field. It benefits the environment by reducing the amount of chemicals artificially introduced into the ecosystem.

In Saskatchewan, geomatics training and research falls within the domain of higher-education institutions. The **SASKATCHEWAN INSTITUTE FOR APPLIED SCIENCE AND TECHNOLOGY** (SIAST) offers GIS training for resource management at its Woodland Campus. The Geography departments at both the Universities of Regina and Saskatchewan have geomatics education and research specializations.

Joe Piwowar

GEORGE GORDON FIRST NATION. The Cree and Ojibway band under George Gordon signed **TREATY 4** in 1874, and in 1876 their reserve was surveyed on the western edge of the Little Touchwood Hills, 61 km northwest of Fort Qu'Appelle, where they had already commenced farming. By 1884 half of the families belonging to the band were farming, and this development continued for many years. The Church of England located a mission on this reserve in 1886 under Reverend Gilbert Cook, and a school was opened—a full ten years after it was first requested by the band. The George Gordon Reserve boasts a modern medical clinic, an education centre, a computer centre, an arena and a day care, as well as the Gordon Retail Centre and the Buffalo Ranch Project. Programs that are offered to band members include the Residential School Recovery and Wellness Centre, Brighter Futures, and Gordon Social Development. Other community infrastructures involve band office, pre-fab plant, fire hall, teacherage, gymnasium, warehouse, water treatment plant, and machine shed. Gordon First Nation has a total membership of 2,788 people, 1,004 of whom live on the 14,946-ha reserve. In addition, the band has shares in the 37-ha Treaty 4 Reserve Grounds near Fort Qu'Appelle. *Christian Thompson*

GEREIN, CLAYTON (1964–). Clayton Gerein has established an impressive record as a wheelchair athlete. Born in North Battleford on May 24, 1964, Gerein is a six-time Paralympian with an outstanding record in international competition: he won three gold medals at the 1988 Paralympic Games, two gold medals at the 1992 Paralympics, a gold, silver, and bronze medal at the 1996 Paralympics in Atlanta, and the gold medal in the marathon at the Sydney Paralympics in 2000. Gerein has received numerous honours, including the 2001 Fred Begley Award for Outstanding Off Track Athlete and the Canada 125 Medal for exceptional contributions to Canadian sport. He was named Saskatchewan Sports Athlete of the year in 1987, 1996, and 2001. In addition to competing, Gerein coaches other wheelchair athletes and is the athletics coordinator for the Saskatchewan Wheelchair Sports Association. He has volunteered with Prairie Assistance Dogs Inc., and has served on the board of the National Sports Centre in Saskatchewan. *Elizabeth Mooney*

GERMAN SETTLEMENTS. A considerable proportion of German immigrants came directly from German colonies in Russia, or indirectly via Russian-German settlements in the United States. Following her direction of the Russian conquest of Turkish-held territories north of the Black Sea from 1763 to 1774, Empress Catherine II wished to rapidly resettle Russia's new annexations with agricultural people loyal to her. As a result, an invitation was extended to farmers in Central Europe to establish ethnic colonies in Russia, on condition that they would enjoy religious freedom, no taxation for ten years, freedom from serfdom, and permission to emigrate from Russia after paying all debts to the Crown. The first colonies in Russia were organized on the Volga by Germans from the largely Protestant region of Hessia between 1764 and 1778. These "Wolga-Deutsche" (Volga Germans) were to be distinguished from the "Schwarzmeer-Deutsche" (Black Sea Germans) who settled later north of the Black Sea. In this latter region, colonies were founded by German and Swedish Lutherans from the Baltic coast (1787–1804); German Catholics and Lutherans from predominantly Protestant Prussia, and from mixed Catholic-Protestant Alsace-Lorraine, Rhineland, Baden-Wurttemberg, Switzerland, Silesia, Bohemia, Posen, and central Poland (1789–1855); Mennonites from East and West Prussia (1790–1854); Hutterites of Austrian and Moravian origin (1843); Jews (1809–50); as well as Bulgarians and other ethnic groups.

Among the specific factors causing Germans to emigrate from their colonies in Russia may be mentioned: the progressive deprivation of rights and privileges granted by Catherine II, particularly the *ukase* of June 4, 1871, which subjected Russian-Germans to military service, removed their right to extensive political autonomy, and increased pressure toward Russification in community schools. Germans were forced to emigrate from their colonies in other regions in Eastern Europe—including Bessarabia (today in Moldavia and Ukraine), Dobruja (now in Romania), Bukowina (Ukraine), Galicia (Ukraine), Volhynia (Ukraine), Transylvania (Romania), and Banat (Romania and Yugoslavia)—for similar and other reasons. For example, in Dobruja, a severe drought in 1884 and the imposition of military service the previous year added to the existing problem of land shortage.

The German influx into the United States from Eastern Europe may have reached 200,000 annually during the early 1880s. Large areas of the Dakotas and Minnesota were converted into replicas of the Russian-German colonies. Until the notion of German separatism became *passé* with the assimilated third and fourth generations and with the surge of anti-German feeling during **WORLD WAR I**, the homes, schools, ethnic press, voluntary associations, and churches in these settlements all collaborated in an attempt to preserve German identity, promote a segregated German lifestyle, and prevent intermarriage with non-Germans. Even political separatism was persistently encouraged, and as late as 1862 attempts were made to have German become an official language.

As for the Germans who then migrated into Saskatchewan from the United States (many of whom had previously moved from Europe, particularly Eastern Europe, within the same generation), the increasing problem of finding large tracts of good agricultural land caused many to look north at the rapidly developing Canadian west. Germans, from whatever specific origin, were lured to Saskatchewan because of: the ready availability of inexpensive, good farmland; solicitation by Canadian immigration authorities and agencies; the promise of exemption from the military service

feared in so many European regions; the encouragement of prominent Germans invited to tour the west and to organize large colonies (notably Count Hohenlohe-Langenburg, president of the German Colonial Association, and F.J. Lange, a founder of the Catholic Colonization Society); the successful precedent set by the earliest German settlers; and the influence of German newspapers and writers.

Most of the Germans who settled in Saskatchewan did not immigrate directly from Germany. In 1916 only 15,328 residents of the prairie provinces gave Germany as their country of birth, whereas 101,944 indicated that German was their mother tongue. According to one estimate, only 12% of the ethnic German immigrants who arrived in western Canada before 1914 were Reichsdeutsche (homeland Germans) from Germany; the remainder were mostly Volksdeutsche (ethnic Germans) from Eastern Europe—44% from Russia, 18% from the Austrian Empire (Austria-Hungary), 6% from Romania—and another 18% came from the United States. Among the reasons why relatively few immigrants from Germany came to Saskatchewan were ignorance of Canada, fear of the northern climate, and the German government's discouragement of emigration.

Some of the German settlements in Saskatchewan were homogeneous in both religious affiliation and precise regional origin (such as those founded by immigrants from a specific religious colony in, for example, southern Russia); but other settlements revealed mixed origins yet common religion, or conversely common origin yet mixed religious affiliations. On the whole, though, German Catholics, Lutherans, Baptists, **MENNONITES**, and **HUTTERITES** tended to form their own settlements or colonies. Many of the German immigrants concentrated in their own bloc settlements; many others did not, electing to settle in ethnically heterogeneous areas. Some settlements were planned; other German concentrations came into existence gradually through chain migration.

German Catholic Settlements

Four major settlements of German Catholics developed in Saskatchewan: St. Joseph's Colony near Balgonie, immediately east of Regina, and the adjoining Katharinental, Kronau-Rastadt, and Odessa colonies, in 1886–1904; St. Peter's Colony, centred on the town of Humboldt in north-central Saskatchewan, in 1902–12; a second St. Joseph's Colony, in the west-central region, in 1905–10; and a series of adjoining colonies in the area around Prelate in southwestern Saskatchewan, in 1907–13.

St. Joseph's Colony, Katharinental Colony, Kronau-Rostadt, and Odessa (1886–1904). St. Joseph's Colony near Balgonie originated in 1886 with the arrival of families who had migrated from the Josephstal Colony near Odessa in South Russia

or Ukraine, founded by Catholics from Alsace and southwestern Germany in 1804. The settlers decided in June 1898 to organize a *dorf* (communal village clustered around a church) in Russian-German style, remnants of which still exist. Between 1890 and 1893, more families arrived from the communities of Rastadt and Munchen (founded in 1809 in the Beresaner colonies northwest of Nikolayev, by immigrants originally from the Palatinate, Baden and Alsace), as well as from Klosterdorf (founded in 1805 by Catholic settlers from Austria, Swabia, and southwestern Germany). These *Schwarzmeerdeutsche* (Black Sea Germans) settled south of St. Joseph's Colony, establishing St. Peter's parish by 1894. Some of these Russian-German immigrants decided to form *dorfs* similar to St. Joseph's: Rastadt-Dorf, Katharinental (named after the original community of Katharinental in the Beresaner colonies), and Speyer (named after another community in the same area in South Russia). The villages of Davin, Rastadt, and Kronau came into existence, the latter two named after communities in South Russia (the Kronau colony in South Russia, west of Nikopol, had been founded in 1870 mostly by Baden-Wurttembergers).

This Russian-German Catholic settlement in Saskatchewan expanded rapidly southeast to Vibank, Odessa (named after the principal port-city on the Black Sea), and Kendal, as well as south toward Sedley and Francis. By 1896 there were already more than 200 German families in this region, almost all of them Catholic immigrants from German colonies in south Russia. From 1971 census data, we may discern that of the seven incorporated towns or villages within the settlement, four had German majorities (60–80%)—Kendal, Vibank, Odessa, and White City—while Francis, Sedley and Balgonie had substantial German minorities (between a quarter and almost half of the total population).

St. Peter's Colony (1902–). The settlers of St. Peter's Colony came largely from the American states. With the rapid opening of Saskatchewan to settlement during the 1890s, German settlers from the closest American states began to move north; in many instances they sent petitions to their former parishes for further immigrants to found new colonies. One such petition was received by a Benedictine priest in Minnesota, who then persuaded his superior, the abbot at St. John's Abbey in Collegeville, Minnesota to establish a German Catholic colony in Saskatchewan. This abbey was in the heart of a large German Catholic colony. An exploration party was sent to Saskatchewan, headed by Rev. Bruno Doerfler and consisting of representatives from several parishes. Upon their return to Minnesota, the decision to establish the colony was made and the Volksverein German-American Land Company was founded. In 1902 this company, in conjunction with the priests of the Order of St. Benedict and the Catholic Settlement Society of St.

FRANK KORVEMAKER PHOTO/COURTESY OF HERITAGE BRANCH
St. Peter's Cathedral, Muenster, constructed 1909.

Paul, Minnesota obtained colonization rights to a vast area in north-central Saskatchewan: fifty townships, covering 1,800 square miles. The German-American Land Company was responsible for buying 100,000 acres of railroad lands in the district selected and for selling it to settlers desiring more than the usual quarter-section homestead. The priests were to develop parishes and be primarily responsible for the expansion of the settlement. The Catholic Settlement Society extensively advertised the venture and assisted the settlers in filing for their homesteads.

With the arrival of the Benedictines from Cluny Priory, Wetaug, Illinois in the new colony in 1902, and from Collegeville, Minnesota the following year, settlement was under way. By the end of 1903, over a thousand homesteads had been filed and eight parishes established: St. Peter's monastery and parish at Muenster, St. Boniface (Leofeld), St. Benedict, Englefeld, Annaheim, Bruno, St. Joseph (Old Fulda), and Marysburg. Within five years after the commencement of settlement, there were over 6,000 German Catholics in the colony. Most were second- or third-generation German-Americans whose forefathers had immigrated from the *Reich* and who arrived from Minnesota, the Dakotas, Wisconsin, Iowa, Nebraska, and Kansas; but some were from Russian-German colonies from the Banat region (today in Yugoslavia and Romania). The Order of St. Benedict in the colony had been incorporated in 1904 as a complex organization of governing schools, associations, and whole communities. A German-language newspaper, *Der Bote*, began publication at Muenster the same year. Humboldt was being converted from a "wilderness of sloughs and bluffs" into the largest town in the region (with a population of over 2,000 by 1914). A

dozen more parishes had been added in 1904–07: Lake Lenore and St. John Baptist (Willmont; Humboldt, Watson, St. Martin, St. Scholastica, St. Patrick's, and St. Oswald Immaculate Conception; and Dana, St. Gregor, and St. Bernard (Old Pilger).

During the next few years the colony continued to expand and its German identity was further ensured. Another four parishes came into being in 1908–12: St. Leo (St. Meinrad), St. Gertrude, Carmel, Peterson, and Cudworth. The first *Katholikentag*, a conference of German-Catholics, was held at Muenster in 1908, with delegates from various settlements in Saskatchewan as well as from Minnesota and Manitoba; other *Katholikentage* were held at Humboldt in 1910 and 1914. In 1909 the *Volksverein*, a German-Catholic voluntary association, was formed in Winnipeg; it was to play an active role in St. Peter's Colony for many years. It was during this period that two women's religious orders were imported from Europe: in 1911 a few Sisters of St. Elizabeth, from Klagenfurt, Austria, immigrated to Humboldt, where they founded the first of a series of hospitals; and a couple of years later Ursuline nuns left their convents at Cologne and Hasseluene, Germany, to organize a convent and St. Henry's School at Marysburg, and in 1919 moved to Bruno, where they established a large convent and Ursuline Academy. In spite of the effect of World War I on discouraging the preservation of the German identity, the colony continued to maintain a distinctly Catholic, if not German, character and to expand. In 1922 *Der Bote* became an English language publication, the *Prairie Messenger* (*Der Bote* had been defunct since 1918 due to legislation against printing in German). The last important *Katholikentag* was held at Muenster in 1933. By

1951–52, the remnants of the *Volksverein* were merged with the Catholic Immigration Society for western Canada. But progress as a colony was also evident. In 1921 the settlement was declared an "abbacy nullius," equivalent to an autonomous bishopric. St. Peter's College was founded at Muenster in 1920, and new parishes continued to be established in 1925–36: Naicam and Holy Family Mission, St. Benedict, Pilger, St. James, and Middle Lake.

Relatively few of the settlers of St. Peter's Colony had immigrated directly from Europe: they came primarily from Minnesota and the Dakotas, although some of these German-Americans were first generation. Today the German Catholic population of St. Peter's Colony, one of the largest German bloc settlements in Saskatchewan, is estimated at close to 19,000. Included are three towns (Humboldt, Cudworth and Bruno), seven incorporated villages (Lake Lenore, Middle Lake, Muenster, Annaheim, Englefeld, St. Gregor, and St. Benedict), four unincorporated villages and hamlets (Carmel, Pilger, Fulda, and Mayrsburg), and over a hundred named localities. In addition to the German Catholics of St. Peter's Colony proper, there are several thousand people of German origin in the adjacent areas to the south and east. In 1971 the German proportion in communities within St. Peter's Colony ranged from approximately half (in Humboldt) to well over 80% (e.g., at Pilger).

St. Joseph's Colony at Kerrobert (1905–10). Only a couple of years after the inception of St. Peter's Colony, plans were already being made for the establishment of an even larger German Catholic colony. F.J. Lange, a founder of the Catholic Colonization Society, conceived the idea of a vast German Catholic colony covering 200 townships—about four times as large as St. Peter's Colony. During the summer of 1904, Lange selected the Tramping Lake area in west-central Saskatchewan as the focal point for a new colony. The resulting St. Joseph's Colony covered a larger land area than St. Peter's Colony, making it the largest German Catholic settlement in Saskatchewan in this sense; but it never attained the population of its predecessor. Lange's high expectations were not entirely fulfilled, and government officials agreed to the bloc purchase by the Catholic Colonization Society of seventy-seven townships, of which fifty-five (equivalent to the extent of St. Peter's Colony) eventually had German majorities. As in St. Peter's Colony, the Catholic Colonization Society collaborated with a religious order—in this case the Oblate Order from Hunfeld, Germany—in the planning, development and settling of St. Joseph's Colony. The first settlers arrived in the Tramping Lake area in early summer 1905. The colony did not develop quite as rapidly as St. Peter's Colony, but by 1911 it included over 5,000 people of German origin, and an estimated 7,000–8,000 by 1914. Most of these settlers were

COURTESY OF THE WATSON AND DISTRICT HERITAGE MUSEUM

Interior of Sacred Heart Roman Catholic Church, Watson.

Black Sea Germans, many of the first arrivals in 1905-08 migrating after first settling in the Dakotas, whereas later arrivals in 1908-10 tended to come directly from South Russia.

The parishes comprising St. Joseph's Colony were St. Paschal (Leipzig), St. Michael (Tramping Lake), St. Franziskus (Ulrich), Our Lady of the Assumption (Handel), Our Blessed Lady of Mount Carmel (Karmelheim), Broadacres, St. Francis Regis/The Assumption of Our Lady (Kerrobert), Sacred Heart (Denzil), St. Henry (Leibel), St. Anthony (Grosswerder), St. Peterskirche/St. Peter's and St. Donatus (near Cactus Lake), St. Elizabeth (Primate), St. Mary (Macklin), St. Johannes/St. John, Holy Rosary/Rosenkranz (Reward), St. Charles/Selz (Revenue), Our Lady of Fatima (Landis), Holy Martyrs (Luseland), St. Joseph (Scott), St. Peter (Unity), and St. James (Wilkie). Beyond the original boundaries of the colony were to be found Our Lady of Lourdes (Coleville), Our Lady of Grace (Dodsland), Immaculate Conception (Major), and an early mission at Ermine. Within or at the periphery of St. Joseph's Colony there are today six towns and thirteen villages. Among towns, in 1971 Macklin had the highest proportion of German population (almost 70%); Luseland, Wilkie and Scott had proportions in the 40–49% range; while in Unity and Kerrobert about one-third of the population was of German origin. Among villages, there was wide variation in the German proportion: seven villages were predominantly German, with the highest proportions (80–100%) at Leipzig, Primate, and Tramping Lake.

The Prelate Colony (1907–13). As the settle-

ment process in St. Joseph's Colony was nearing completion, a fourth major German Catholic colony–or rather a series of colonies–developed around Prelate in southwestern Saskatchewan. As early as 1889 a large Russian-German settlement of migrants from Volhynia and Galicia began to develop just across the border in Alberta; eventually a very extensive expanse of territory on both sides of the border (between Leader, Maple Creek and Medicine Hat) would be settled primarily by Russian-Germans. Beginning in 1908, Russian-German Catholics established a series of colonies and parishes on the Saskatchewan side, which included: the original parishes of Sts. Peter and Paul at Blumenfeld (1908); St. Francis Xavier at Prelate (1910); Prussia Colony, centred on Leader (1919); St. Anthony, serving Mendham and the Speyer district (1914); Immaculate Conception at Krassna (1911); Sacred Heart at Liebenthal (1914); St. Mary at Rosenthal (1913); St. Mary at Richmond (1912); Sacred Heart at Lancer (1918); St. Joseph at Shackleton (1916); St. Joseph at Josephtal (1915); Holy Trinity at Rastadt (1922); and Maple Creek (1913). Later parishes included St. Mary at Fox Valley (1929), St. John at Johnborough (1943), St. Mary at Lemsford (1948), Golden Prairie (1949), and St. Michael at Burstall (1969).

Liebenthal was named after Liebenthal, Kansas, from which some of the settlers had migrated; this Russian-German colony in the United States had been established by migrants from the Liebenthal group of Catholic colonies immediately west of Odessa, founded in 1804–06 largely by migrants from Alsace and southwestern German regions.

Germans from a variety of regions had settled in central Poland between 1795 and 1806, then moved to establish colonies in the southern Bessarabian region southwest of the Liebenthal colonies after 1814. These Bessarabian colonists were the forefathers of the settlers of the Krassna, Rastadt and Rosenthal districts in Saskatchewan; the original Krassna Colony had been founded near Akkerman (Belgorod Dnestrovskiy) in Bessarabia in 1815. While these adjoining colonies around Prelate were predominantly Catholic, they included several pockets of strongly Protestant settlement. In 1971 people of German origin comprised a majority of the population at Leader; villages having the highest German proportions were Mendham (82.9%), Richmound (76.2%), Lancer (73.2%), Prelate (64.3%), and Fox Valley (60.4%). Besides these rural parishes, there are other districts in the region with substantial German proportions: Krupp, Rosenfeld, Sagathun, and Kuest. Rural depopulation has taken a severe toll on the rural parishes comprising the settlement. One by one, country churches have been closed and occasionally even removed or demolished, such as at Rosenthal in 1943, Krassna in 1944, Josephstal and Rastadt in 1962, Shackleton in 1963, Johnsborough in 1967, Lemsford in 1982, and Speyer in 2001.

Smaller Catholic Settlements. While the four major German Catholic settlements were developing, a number of smaller Catholic concentrations came into existence. One of the earliest was the Grayson-Killaly area immediately south of Melville, settled largely by Volksdeutsche from Bukovina, Bessarabia, Galicia, and Poland. Grayson, first settled in 1896, was first called Nieven, but was renamed in 1903. The Mariahilf Catholic Colony outside Killaly was founded in 1900. The Killaly Catholic parish came into being in 1910, and Grayson and Goodeve (northwest of Melville) also had Catholic churches. In 1971 two-thirds of the population of Grayson were of German extraction, compared to about 70% in Killaly.

Another small German Catholic colony, St. Aloysius, developed around the town of Allan in 1903-07; approximately half of the population of Allan is of German descent. All across the southernmost regions of Saskatchewan small German Catholic concentrations soon came into existence. To the southwest, German Catholics began to settle near Shaunavon in 1907-08, and established a strongly German Catholic parish in 1914, assisted by German religious orders; in 1971, about one in five people in Shaunavon was of German origin. Another four German Catholic parishes or missions were established in this region between 1910 and 1921.

In the south-central region, Russian-Germans founded Billimun Colony in 1910, near Mankota. Hungarian Germans founded St. Elizabeth Colony in 1908 near Glen Bain. German Catholics also settled in 1908–14 around numerous communities in this region; many of them came from the midwestern United States, particularly from German-American settlements founded by immigrants from the original German colonies in Russia. But in all of these communities, people of German origin now constitute only a minority. In the northwestern region of the Saskatchewan prairie, the St. Walburg area was first settled between 1901 and 1912 by people of German origin, primarily Catholics from the *Reich*, Bavaria, Austria, and Luxemburg. German settlement in this region developed gradually in several stages. German Catholics settled around Goodsoil, about 100 km north of St. Walburg, during the 1920s, and later around the neighbouring community of Peerless, as well as further west with Mennonites around Pierceland, near the Alberta border. In 1929, immigrants arrived directly from Germany (mostly from Thuringen, but also from Holstein, Westfalen, Mecklenburg and the Baltic coast) to establish the Loon River settlement between St. Walburg and the more northerly communities mentioned. These immigrants, as well as the Germans around Goodsoil, apparently were ardent nationalists: Goodsoil boasted the strongest Deutscher Bund chapter in the entire province; and strong *Ortsgruppen* (chapters having at least fifteen members) were organized at Loon River, St. Walburg, and Paradise Hill, as well as a Stützpunkt (chapters having from five to fifteen members) at Blue Bell near Pierceland. In view of their strong pro-National Socialist sentiments, the Loon River Germans decided in 1939 to return *Heim ins Reich*—home to the *Reich*. However, a German presence in this particular district was maintained, the return migrants being replaced in 1938-39 by German refugees from the Sudetenland, newly annexed to the Reich. In 1971, people of German origin constituted little more than a quarter of the population of St. Walburg, but almost two-thirds of Goodsoil and a majority of the population in the Barthel-Loon River district. Finally it should be noted that throughout Saskatchewan substantial Lutheran minorities often developed within predominantly Catholic German settlements.

German Protestant Settlements

Lutherans, Baptists and Adventists of German descent established four principal colonies plus numerous smaller concentrations. The major Protestant settlements (excluding Mennonites and Hutterites) were established almost simultaneously: Neu Elsass (1884), Hohenlohe (1885), Edenwold (1885), and the Volga German Colony (1887).

Neu Elsass Colony (1884–). The Neu Elsass (New Alsace) Colony was the first German colony to develop in Saskatchewan. In 1884 twenty-two families took up homesteads around Strasbourg, approximately 80 km north of Regina; they were led by

D.W. Riedl, an enterprising German immigration agent from Winnipeg. This community may have been named after Strasbourg, the principal city of the German-speaking province of Alsace in France; however, it is more likely that both community and colony were named after the communities of Strassburg and Elsass, within the Kurtschurgan colonies northwest of Odessa, in South Russia, which had in turn been established by Alsatian migrants back in 1808–09. Still another possibility is that, given the fact that some of the settlers in this colony in Saskatchewan came from Russian-German colonies in the United States, the Alsatian nomenclature may have been imported into Saskatchewan from any of several American colonies, founded by immigrants ultimately of Alsatian origin (in Kansas and the Dakotas).

The original bounds of Neu Elsass Colony (ca. 1885) included Strasbourg, Duval, Bulyea, Earl Grey, Gibbs, Silton, Dilke, Holdfast, Penzance, and Liberty–in other words, the region around the central and southern portion of Last Mountain Lake. But the area of German settlement expanded into surrounding areas, in effect doubling its territory. The settlement remains predominantly Lutheran; some communities and districts are strongly Lutheran, such as Strasbourg, Markinch, and the Fairy Hill district; and Lutherans also settled around Duval, Govan, Earl Grey, Southey, Cupar, and Lipton. Baptists concentrated around Serath, Gregherd, Southey, Earl Grey (where a Baptist congregation actually had been founded originally not by Germans but by Swedes in 1906), Nokomis, and later Strasbourg. Yet certain communities west of Last Mountain Lake were strongly Catholic. In

Strasbourg itself, a Lutheran church was built in 1907, followed by a Baptist one in 1927, a Catholic one in 1943, and an Adventist in 1953. The highest German-origin proportion is found at Markinch, where in 1971 three-quarters of the population claimed German descent, and at Southey, where two-thirds claimed German descent. Chamberlain, Earl Grey, Holdfast, and Lipton were predominantly German, while people of German origin comprised 40% at Duval and approximately one-third at Strasbourg, Nokomis, Aylesbury, and Quinton.

Hohenlohe Colony (1885–). The Hohenlohe Colony began to develop around Langenburg, close to the Manitoba border, at the same time that the Neu Elsass Colony was developing. It was named after Count Hohenlohe-Langenburg, president of the German Colonial Association, who had toured the West and encouraged German settlement. Under the guidance of D.W. Riedl (the immigration agent also instrumental in the founding of Neu Elsass Colony), German Lutherans began to settle around Langenburg in 1885, in the Landshut, Hoffenthal, Hoffnungsthal, Berisena, and Landestreu districts; they came not only from Germany, but also from "Russian" colonies (actually in Ukraine). While the colony retained a Lutheran majority, in 1889 Catholics from Bavaria and the Black Sea colonies arrived. The Russian-German proportion here was further augmented with the arrival of settlers from the Bessarabian colonies in 1891; by 1896 the colony included fifty to sixty Russian-German families, with approximately 300 members. A unique self-help organization which came into being in this colony in the early pioneering years was the Germania Mutual Fire Insurance Company of

COURTESY OF NINITA HAUTZ

These German Lutherans (the Adam and Dietrich families) immigrated in the 1890s and settled in the Landestreu district near Langenburg. This 1911 photo shows the new home of the Adam family.

Langenburg, first advocated in 1909 by George Haas, a prominent farmer in the Hoffenthal district, who had migrated from Menno, South Dakota. Today both the town of Langenburg and the village of MacNutt retain German majorities.

The Volga German Colony North of Yorkton (1887–). Only a couple of years after the Hohenlohe and Neu Elsass Colonies first began to develop, Baptist immigrants from the Volga colonies in Russia (*Wolgadeutsche*) settled around Ebenezer. The Russian colonies from which they emigrated had been founded in 1764–68 near Saratov, mostly by Protestant and Catholic migrants from Hessia. A strong Volga Baptist colony grew in the area around Ebenezer, Gorlitz, Hampton, Rhein, and Springside; whereas to the east, Volga Lutherans concentrated around Rhein, Stornoway, Runnymede, and Togo, where they merged with the German Lutherans of the Hohenlohe Colony to the south. A Lutheran parish was first organized at Runnymede in 1917; this congregation joined with the Togo Lutherans in 1921, and both were served by an itinerant pastor based at Rhein. In addition to these Volga Germans of Baptist or Lutheran religion, Volhynian Germans settled in Yorkton. Expansion of the vast Ukrainian settlement around Yorkton has steadily diminished the German proportion in these communities: none of them now retain German majorities, although in 1971 almost half of the residents at Rhein and Ebenezer claimed German origin.

Edenwold Colony (1885–). In 1885 a group of Baptist immigrants from the region of Dobruja, in Romania, founded the colony of New Tulcea (later renamed Edenwald, then misspelled Edenwold), northeast of the city of Regina. Migrants from the German colonies near Odessa in Bessarabia had resettled in Dobruja during the 1840s-50s. During the 1860s, Baptist missionaries from the Danzig congregation in Russia were responsible for creating a Baptist majority in Kataloi colony and a significant Baptist proportion in the other two Protestant colonies, Atmagea and Cincurova. Religious quarrels as well as difficult economic and political conditions (Dobruja became part of Romania in 1878, bringing about revoking of privileges, restriction of landholdings, and state control of schools) resulted in the emigration of Germans from Dobruja to North Dakota in 1884 and Saskatchewan in 1885. Gradually, the Saskatchewan colony became more heterogeneous in terms of both the origins of its German population and their religious preferences. The colony's name was changed by German immigrants from Bukovina; other Germans arrived from German colonies in Poland, Galicia, and Russia, and from Germany. A strong Lutheran congregation had been formed by 1893, and Adventists concentrated in the area of Edenwold village. Two-thirds of the population of Edenwold were still of German origin in 1971. The other communities in the settlement

(Frankslake, Zehner, and Avonhurst) are unincorporated hamlets.

Other German Lutheran Concentrations. A variety of other, smaller German Lutheran settlements developed across Saskatchewan. In southeastern Saskatchewan, a concentration of German Lutherans and other German Protestants plus some Catholics, developed around Lampman and nearby communities. Yet none of the unincorporated communities in this area still retain a German majority: Germans constituted a third of the population at Lampman in 1971 and less than a quarter in Estevan, but only a smaller minority at Alameda, Roche Percee, Bienfait, Oxbow, Benson, Stoughton, and Arcola. Volga Germans settled in the Arcola area. German and Norwegian Lutherans settled together in a number of communities in southern Saskatchewan, such as at Torquay, Oungre, Tribune, Bromhead, Minton, Lake Alma, Gladmar, and Regway, to the west of Estevan; at Midale, between Estevan and Weyburn; and at Ibsen and Lang near Yellow Grass, northwest of Weyburn. In all of these mixed communities, German population comprised only a small minority in 1971; the highest proportion was attained at Torquay, where a quarter was German. Volhynian Germans, mostly Lutherans but including some Catholics, settled around Yellow Grass as early as 1895; there their descendants made up a little over a quarter of the village population in 1971.

German concentrations in the south-central region tended to be predominantly Catholic, but small concentrations of Lutherans were found in the Spring Valley-Ormiston area, as well as at Pangman, Mossbank, Assiniboia and Coronach. Further west, a predominantly Lutheran settlement of Volga Germans emerged around Hodgeville; German Lutherans mixed with Mennonites at Hodgeville, Kelstern, St. Boswells, Vogel, and with both Mennonites and Adventists at Flowing Well. Lutheran settlement extended north to the Chaplin-Ernfold-Uren area, and Lutheran minorities were found within extensive Mennonite settlement in the Swift Current and Vermillion Hills regions (Swift Current, Waldeck, Herbert, Stewart Valley, Central Butte). Further west, in southwestern Saskatchewan, German Lutherans settled around Gull Lake-Simmie-Illerbrun (named after an early settler from North Dakota in 1907), and Maple Creek; and Russian-Germans settled south of the CYPRESS HILLS around Consul-Vidora-Robsart. North of Maple Creek, within a predominantly Catholic settlement, Burstall was a largely Lutheran community; a Lutheran congregation came into existence at Mendham in 1914 and an Evangelical one the next year; while Leader had Lutheran, Apostolic, and United Brethren churches in additions to its strong Catholic parish.

Just across the SOUTH SASKATCHEWAN RIVER to

the north from Leader, the Eatonia-Dankin-Glidden area was settled by Lutherans as well as by Catholics, Mennonites, and most recently Hutterites. A majority of the residents of Glidden are German, as are over a third of Eatonia's. Within St. Joseph's German Catholic Colony, occupying most of west-central Saskatchewan, Lutherans were concentrated around Luseland, Kerrobert, and Wilkie. Further north a strongly German Lutheran church was established at St. Walburg in 1937; another German Lutheran congregation in this region was founded at Meadow Lake. In central Saskatchewan, small concentrations of German Lutherans developed within or near Mennonite settlements, such as at Hague (where Volhynian migrants settled). The Dundurn district was settled by German Lutherans (a couple of decades before Mennonites settled in this area), under the leadership of E.J. Meilicke, who brought German-American homesteaders.

German Lutherans settled in the Lanigan area, at Lanigan, Leroy, Watrous, Jensen, Esk, and Dafoe. In 1971 approximately two-thirds of the residents in the village of Jensen were German; their predecessors were Russian-Germans; those in the nearby hamlet of Dafoe were Volga Germans. In the east-central region, a small but cohesive German Protestant settlement developed west of Melville (where in 1971 over 30% of the population was of German origin). The village of Neudorf (over 70% German) was settled as early as 1890 by Russian-German Lutherans. The neighbouring community of Lemberg (where people of German origin predominate) was settled by German Lutherans from Galicia (Lemberg is the German name for Lviv, the principal city of Galicia in the western Ukraine). As in most Galician, Black Sea, and Bessarabian German colonies and their offshoots in Saskatchewan, in Lemberg the Germans spoke a Swabian dialect because their forefathers had migrated to the Russian colonies from Swabia and other southwest German regions. German Lutheran congregations were also established in the predominantly Catholic villages of Killaly (where three-quarters of the residents were German in 1971) in 1926, as well as at Waldron (over a third being German). Both Lutherans and Mennonites settled around Duff (over two-thirds German), while German Baptists settled at Fenwood (over a third German), and with Catholics at Goodeve.

German Lutherans were also scattered throughout the region to the south across the QU'APPELLE VALLEY. The Whitewood area was settled by German-Swiss as well as *Reichsdeutsche* from Hannover; the small village of Oakshela, between Broadview and Grenfell, was settled by *Volksdeutsche* from Galicia and Volhynia. Polish-Germans, specifically from the Tomaszow-Mazowiecki and Wengrow areas in Poland, settled around Wapella in 1928 and built their Lutheran church in 1936. Other Germans settled around Fairlight, Kennedy, and Kipling; yet in 1971, Germans constituted only a small minority in those communities. Windthorst was named after Ludwig Windthorst, one of the organizers and leaders of the Centrist Party in Germany and an able opponent of Count Bismark; it was settled around 1909 by Lutheran Russian-German immigrants from the Vladimir-Volynskiy area north of Lemberg (Lviv) and other Volhynian-Galician German communities. Further west, substantial pockets of Lutheran settlement developed within the large Catholic colony between Odessa and Balgonie as early as 1891, when Lutherans arrived from the Black Sea and Bukovinian colonies. They organized a Lutheran congregation at Vibank in 1909, later affiliated with others at Kronau and Davin, and another at Francis.

Recent German Settlement. Most of the Germans who have immigrated into Saskatchewan since **WORLD WAR II** have tended to come from Germany rather than ethnic German colonies in Eastern Europe, although shifting international boundaries during the immediate postwar years have continued to bring ethnic Germans to western Canada as refugees. Today the German population of Saskatchewan numbers at least 275,060 (according to 2001 census data), almost a third of whom (30.6%, 84,280) claimed to be solely of German origin whereas over two-thirds (69.4%, 190,785) claimed to be only partially of German origin. People of German origin (in whole or part) have become the largest ethnic component—28.6%—of the total provincial population. Yet 32,515 people, representing only about 12% of the population claiming German origin, reported German as their mother tongue, reflecting the fact that a large proportion of the descendants of earlier (pre-war) ethnic German settlers no longer speak German. (*See also* **ETHNIC BLOC SETTLEMENTS, AMERICAN IMMIGRATION, MENNONITE SETTLEMENTS, HUTTERITE COLONIES, DANUBE SWABIANS**) *Alan Anderson*

FURTHER READING: Anderson, A.B. 1990. *German Settlements in Saskatchewan*. Saskatoon: Saskatchewan German; Giesinger, A. 1974. *From Catherine to Krushchev: The Story of Russia's Germans*. Battleford, Saskatchewan: Marian Press.

GERRARD, JOHN WATSON (1916–). The son of a missionary physician, John Gerrard was born in Kasenga, Rhodesia, on April 14, 1916. He graduated from Oxford University in 1941, served in the British Army, then undertook pediatric training and doctoral research (DM) at his *alma mater*, before studying pediatric endocrinology at Johns Hopkins School of Medicine. In 1953, the **UNIVERSITY OF SASKATCHEWAN**'s College of Medicine recruited Gerrard as the first Head of Pediatrics. During his sixteen-year tenure as department head (1955–71) and until his retirement in 1983, he helped achieve pediatric health care excellence in Saskatchewan.

Dr. Gerrard was admired as an astute and dedicated physician who provided compassionate care to generations of Saskatchewan children. Students and colleagues benefited from his clear and precise teaching. An acclaimed researcher, he approached scientific endeavours with irrepressible enthusiasm and exemplary scholarship. For his work in developing treatment for children with phenylketonuria, he was co-recipient of the prestigious John Scott medal from the American Philosophical Society in 1962. He is also an Officer of the Order of Canada, 1999.

Alan M. Rosenberg

GERVAIS, ALICE (1897–1996). *La reverende soeur* Alice Gervais promoted education, culture, and bilingualism across Saskatchewan for over half a century. Known as Sister Eliza of Mary, she was born in St-Thomas de Compton, Quebec in 1897. Gervais moved to Duck Lake, Saskatchewan with her family in 1905 and entered the Roman Catholic order, Sisters of the Presentation of Mary in 1914. Her career as a teacher took her to Duck Lake, Marcelin, Bellevue, Debden, and Prince Albert before she retired in 1970. She spent the next twenty years working as a librarian in the provincial house in Prince Albert. Gervais was awarded the Order of Canada in 1973. She died on March 16, 1996.

GERWING, ALPHONSE MATHIAS (1923–). Born in 1923, Alphonse Gerwing has devoted his life to bringing music appreciation to rural communities in Saskatchewan and Alberta. His teaching and enthusiasm for music have benefited both children and adults. In addition, Gerwing has advocated the cause of social justice for street kids in Brazil. Through the Alphonse Gerwing Charitable Foundation, he has worked tirelessly to raise funds, educate people about social justice, and liaise on behalf of two Alberta-based non-government organizations. Gerwing was made a Member of the Order of Canada in 1989.

GIBBINGS, CHARLES WILLIAM (1916–). Charles Gibbings was born on a farm near Rosetown on August 10, 1916. After earning a BSc in Agriculture at the **UNIVERSITY OF SASKATCHEWAN**, Gibbings taught for the School of Agriculture there and conducted youth training programs across the province, all the while continuing to farm. In 1946 he became a delegate to the **SASKATCHEWAN WHEAT POOL**, and in 1960 became its first Saskatchewan-born president. In that capacity Gibbings hired its first general manager and reinforced the management team by hiring employees who had been trained in accounting and other management skills. The Farm Service Division, which dealt with production supplies and services, was added, and agrologists were hired to work directly with farmers—an

Charles Gibbings receiving honorary Doctor of Laws, spring 1971.

innovation in the grain elevator business. Gibbings worked hard to knit the four prairie grain elevator co-operatives into one: it was his view that the Alberta, Saskatchewan, and Manitoba Wheat Pools and the **UNITED GRAIN GROWERS** should amalgamate to better serve prairie farmers. He did not succeed in this endeavour, but there is evidence of some collaboration: all four organizations became members of X-CAN Grain Limited, a company established to market grains not covered under the Canadian Wheat Board; furthermore, the Pools joined with Federated Co-operatives in the manufacture and supply of fertilizers and agricultural chemicals.

Gibbings advised Canadian delegations involved in negotiating terms of international agricultural trade. He served as a commissioner on the Saskatchewan Royal Commission on Agriculture and Rural Life, and was a member of the University of Saskatchewan Senate. He was president of Co-operative Fire and Casualty, and served on the boards of the Regina Exhibition and **SASKATCHEWAN RESEARCH COUNCIL**. He was also chairman of the Advisory Committee to the Canadian Wheat Board. Gibbings left his position as Pool president in 1969 to become a commissioner of the Canadian Wheat Board; in this role he travelled the world helping negotiate sales of prairie grains. Among the many honours he received was the Canada Centennial Medal in 1967. He was also named a Fellow of the Agricultural Institute of Canada in 1967, and awarded an honorary Doctor of Laws degree by the University of Saskatchewan in 1971. He was inducted into the Saskatchewan Agricultural Hall of Fame in 1986.

J.G. Braidek

GILBEY, BILL (1911–90). Bill Gilbey was born in Winnipeg to middle-class, conservative parents who taught him from an early age that hard work, honesty and perseverance were the means to success. However, the family was hit hard by the coming of the **GREAT DEPRESSION**, and a search for answers led to Bill becoming a lifelong Communist. He was later to comment, "I knew that all the things happening to people during the thirties, the hunger, the unemployment, the arrests and deportations were not an accident of history; they were the consequence of the deliberate actions of a small group of people."

Bill's first union-related job was also during the early Depression years. He worked with the **WORKERS' UNITY LEAGUE** organizing a number of trade unions, and was also instrumental in the formation of the Relief Camp Workers' Union (RCWU). The relief camps had been created by the Bennett government as a means of controlling an estimated 70,000 young unemployed men in Canada. Conditions within the camps were very bad, and it was the intent of the RCWU to improve them.

In 1939 Gilbey returned to Winnipeg and became involved with organizing the needle trades (sometimes known as the garment industry) in that city. He joined the Canadian military in **WORLD WAR II**, but after the war he returned to Winnipeg, taking on a temporary job as representative and organizer for a small local of retail clerks. A year later, he returned to the needle trades. As was frequently the case with union activists during the late 1940s and early 1950s, Bill and his wife Anne became targets for the prevailing anti-Communist hysteria of the McCarthy era. In Gilbey's words, they survived the period "bloodied but unbroken." Unfortunately, the public fear during the McCarthy era severely limited the ability of union activists to do any serious organizing. Gilbey therefore had to be content with doing his job as a cutter in the needle trades. However, in 1958, a chance meeting with two friends who were employed by the Oil, Chemical and Atomic Workers Union (OCAW) led to Bill's appointment to the position of executive secretary for the largest local of the OCAW in Saskatchewan.

Gilbey remained with the OCAW for nine years. During this time he was also elected president of the **SASKATCHEWAN FEDERATION OF LABOUR** and held the position of vice-president of the Canadian Labour Congress. He later moved to the **RETAIL, WHOLESALE AND DEPARTMENT STORE UNION**. In 1967, he joined the Grain Services Union, holding the position of secretary-general manager until his retirement in 1973. One of Gilbey's principal areas of interest was occupational health and safety. He was successful in having the Workers' Compensation Board recognize the dangers of grain dust to worker's lungs as a compensable industrial disease. His position on the issue of grain dust is described in his book *Grain Handling: Dollars versus Health and Safety.*

Barrie Anderson

GILLIES, CLARK (1954–). Recognized for his leadership abilities at the amateur and professional levels of hockey, Clark Gillies was born in Moose Jaw on April 7, 1954. He played three seasons of junior hockey with the Regina Pats and led the club to the

PATRICK PETTIT/REGINA LEADER-POST

Clark Gillies.

1974 Memorial Cup championship. Drafted by the New York Islanders, Gillies made the club's roster following an impressive NHL training camp. He played twelve seasons with the Islanders and won four consecutive Stanley Cup championships beginning in 1980. A left-winger, he was teamed with Mike Bossy and fellow Saskatchewanian Bryan Trottier on a high-scoring forward line. As the Islander dynasty made way for the up-and-coming Edmonton Oilers, Gillies was claimed in 1986 by the Buffalo Sabres with whom he remained for two seasons before retiring in 1988. Over fourteen NHL seasons, Clark Gillies tallied 697 points in 958 games. He was named to the First All-Star Team in 1978 and 1979, and was a member of Team Canada at the 1981 Canada Cup. In recognition of his four Stanley Cup wins and his contributions as an Islander, Gillies' number "9" was retired in 1996. He was inducted to the **SASKATCHEWAN SPORTS HALL OF FAME** and the Hockey Hall of Fame in 2002.

Daria Coneghan and Holden Stoffel

GILROY, DOUG (1915–2003). Through his "Prairie Wildlife" columns in the *Western Producer* newspaper from 1954 to 2000, Doug Gilroy was a

ROY ANTAL/REGINA LEADER-POST

Doug Gilroy, 1986.

household name in 160,000 farm homes across western Canada. Born on October 20, 1915, and raised on a dairy farm along Boggy Creek a few miles northwest of Regina, Gilroy farmed until his retirement in 1973.

A self-taught naturalist and an accomplished wildlife photographer, Gilroy's columns on birds, plants, mammals, insects and all aspects of nature were illustrated by detailed photographs of his subjects. Gilroy's column served as a communications link for bird banders and researchers requesting the public's assistance on reporting their observations, such as rare sightings of whooping cranes.

Gilroy's 1,594 columns over a period of forty-seven years promoted an interest and appreciation of wildlife and generated thousands of responses from readers.

Gilroy was active in several conservation organizations. He served as president of the Saskatchewan Natural History Society in 1951 and 1952. In 1954, Gilroy received the society's annual conservation award for his exceptional ability as a nature photographer, columnist and lecturer. In 1990, Gilroy received the Gordon Lund Conservation Award from the **SASKATCHEWAN WILDLIFE FEDERATION** for his untiring efforts in writing the "Prairie Wildlife" column.

Gilroy was the author of four books, all from Western Producer Prairie Books: *Album of Prairie Birds* (1967), *Prairie Birds in Colour* (1976), *Parkland Portraits* (1979), and *Prairie Wildlife: The Best of Doug Gilroy's Nature Photography* (1985). He died at Regina Beach on October 19, 2003.

Lorne Scott

GIRL GUIDES. Girl Guides, an organization that emphasized physical, moral and spiritual training, was founded in England in 1909 as a counterpart to Boy Scouts. Among its many activities, outdoor camping has come to be seen as an especially important vehicle of personal development. One of the first two Canadian companies was established in Moose Jaw in 1910; then more were set up in Saskatoon, Weyburn, Outlook, Cabri, Regina, and Prince Albert. In 1922 a provincial Girl Guide Council was organized. Meetings were often held in Protestant churches, but the movement was not exclusively Protestant: by the early 1920s at least one Jewish Guide company existed in Saskatchewan. Gradually groups for several age categories developed: Brownies, Rangers, Cadets, Sparks, and Pathfinders. Saskatchewan Guides sold the first Girl Guide cookies in Canada in 1927; they were successful even during the Depression, and by 1936 they were commercially produced. The Saskatchewan Girl Guide movement blossomed during the 1950s and 1960s: in 1955 there were about 4,000 Guides, Brownies and leaders in communities throughout the province; by 1967 it was estimated that there

Girl Guides, April 1999.

were 10,000 Guides in Saskatchewan. Reflecting broader demographic changes, provincial membership numbers declined in the late 20th century: by 2000, there were approximately 4,500 Guides in about 400 units.

Lisa Dale-Burnett

GITZEL, TIM (1962–). Born and raised in Saskatchewan, Tim Gitzel has held appointments as first vice-president of the Saskatchewan Mining Association, and as a member of the boards of directors of SaskEnergy Corporation and the Royal University Hospital Foundation. In 1990 Gitzel joined the Saskatoon law firm of MacPherson Leslie and Tyerman, where he served as an associate lawyer for two years. In 1992–93 he served as ministerial assistant to **DWAYNE LINGENFELTER**, the Deputy Premier and Minister of Economic Development for Saskatchewan. He then joined **COGEMA RESOURCES INC.** (part of the French AREVA group, a world leader in **URANIUM** mining, with major operations in northern Saskatchewan) as counsel in 1994, and was appointed a director of the corporation in 1995. He was appointed senior vice-president and corporate counsel in 1997, and assumed the role of president and CEO in September 2001. In June 2004 he was appointed executive vice-president of the Mining Business Unit in charge of AREVA's worldwide mining operations, including those in Saskatchewan, and is now chairman of COGEMA Resource's board of directors. He moved to Paris, France, as part of a restructuring of the AREVA group.

Alun Richards

GJESDAL, JOSEPH HARVEY (1922–). An innovative and dedicated agriculturist, Joseph Gjesdal was born in the Birch Hills district on January 4, 1922. Since 1963, he has worked as a select seed

grower and has served as director of both the Saskatchewan Seed Growers and Canadian Seed Growers Association. Gjesdal has also contributed to prairie agriculture methods by improving, designing, and building over twenty farm implements. His most notable inventions include a rotary snowplow, rotary mower, seed cleaner, and tillage cultivator. His knowledge regarding farm policy matters has been sought by agricultural and governmental organizations, and he has provided leadership to community associations such as **4-H**. A recipient of the Canadian Centennial Medal in 1967, Gjesdal was invested as a Member of the Order of Canada in 1993.

GLACIAL DEPOSITION. Glacial deposition occurs during **GLACIATION**. It refers to the various means by which materials carried by a glacier can be released from the ice and deposited on underlying surfaces or in surrounding areas. Glacial deposition can occur directly from the glacier itself or from several associated processes involving glacial meltwater. Saskatchewan has evidence of glacial deposition throughout the province, although deposits south of the Precambrian Shield tend to be thicker and more continuous. Glaciers can erode, transport and deposit materials that range in size from the finest clay particles to blocks of rock hundreds of metres in size. Thus there is a wide range of glacial depositional landforms in the province, the most prominent of which include eskers, former lake beds, deltas, and various types of moraines from ridged to flat to hummocky plains.

Material deposited directly from glacial ice is called glacial till. Till typically has undergone little or no sorting by meltwater, so the resulting deposit is poorly sorted and contains a wide range of particle sizes, from grains of clay to boulders, jumbled together. Till forms the basis of many Saskatchewan landforms and can develop with ice advance and retreat, and in periods of stagnation. Till plains develop from materials deposited directly from the ice with the steady retreat of the glacier, while rolling landscapes called hummocky moraines are thought to form during ice stagnation. Recessional moraines, which appear as ridges of thicker deposits, developed along the ice margin during periods of glacial standstill. Erratics appear as isolated boulders or chunks of bedrock deposited directly from glacial ice often hundreds of kilometres away from their origin. Saskatchewan has several spectacular examples of erratics, such as that near Young, which is composed of rocks from the northern area.

Sediments can be deposited through the medium of glacial meltwater. In Saskatchewan these processes primarily relate to glacial meltwater stream and glacial lake deposits, referred to in the literature as glaciofluvial and glaciolacustrine deposits respectively (*see* **PROGLACIAL LAKES**). In this

case, deposits from the glacier can be built up hundreds of kilometres from the actual glacier margin. Deposits from meltwater streams or in proglacial lakes tend to be sorted into layers with respect to the grain size of the particle: thus discrete layers of sands, silts and clays may be observed. These sorted deposits are often highly valued in the aggregate industry. Other glacial deposits include eskers, which were former channel beds of meltwater streams that formed inside or at the base of a glacier. When the glacial ice melted, the stream channel was deposited on the underlying surface, appearing as a ridge on the landscape. Deltas formed at the end of these streams when they entered proglacial lakes.

Janis Dale

FURTHER READING: Christiansen, E.A. 1979. "The Wisconsinan Deglaciation of Southern Saskatchewan and Adjacent Areas," *Canadian Journal of Earth Sciences* 116: 913–38; Sugden, D.E. and B.S. John. 1976. *Glaciers and Landscape*. London: Edward Arnold.

GLACIAL EROSION. Glacial erosion refers to a group of processes that wear down land surfaces from the action of glacial ice or glacial meltwater. Particles are picked up and transported away, denuding underlying surfaces and often leaving a variety of recognizable erosional features. Glacial erosion can be subdivided into three main categories: glacial abrasion, glacial plucking, and glacial meltwater erosion. All three forms of erosion are evident in Saskatchewan, although they are especially well developed on exposed bedrock surfaces in northern Saskatchewan.

Glacial abrasion refers to the ability of debris-rich glacial ice to act like a sheet of sand paper as it moves over underlying surfaces. The size, concentration and hardness of entrained debris in the ice, the hardness of the underlying substrate, and the velocity of the moving ice control the type of erosional feature produced on the underlying surface. High concentrations of sand-sized particles in the ice can polish bedrock, leaving a shiny surface, while pebbles or boulders embedded in the moving ice can create fine scratches called striae (singular: striation), or larger features called glacial grooves on bedrock surfaces. The significance of striae and grooves is that they record the direction of glacial ice movement. Materials in the ice can also chip or fracture the underlying bedrock to form features like crescentic gouges, or leave a line of nested crescentic fractures called chattermarks.

Glacial plucking occurs when portions of bedrock become frozen in the overlying glacier. As the glacier advances, these blocks can be plucked or lifted out of the bedrock as with a car jack. A *roche moutonée* is a bullet-shaped erosional feature that shows both abrasion and plucking processes. The up-ice side is smoothed and abraded by the advancing ice, while the down-ice side is ragged in appearance from blocks plucked from the bedrock.

From time to time, substantial amounts of meltwater can be released catastrophically from a glacier. The combination of water flowing at high velocity and large loads of sediment being carried along makes glacial meltwater highly erosive. Various landforms have been recognized in Saskatchewan, including potholes and winding channels eroded into bedrock.

A combination of glacial erosion processes results in features from a few centimetres to hundreds of metres in size. Areal scouring and whalebacks are common erosional features in Saskatchewan's Precambrian Shield, where exposed bedrock has been eroded into a variety of smoothed shapes that form islands and ridges aligned in the direction of ice action. There is less evidence of glacial erosional landforms in southern Saskatchewan, as most bedrock surfaces have been covered with glacial sediments, although striae can be observed on rocks in these deposits. *Janis Dale*

GLACIATION. Glaciation describes time periods in which extensive ice sheets developed over large continental areas and extended even into temperate mid-latitude zones. Glacial periods appear to be related to times of global cooling, whereas interglacial periods describe periods of global warming, when the large ice sheets shrink and exist only in polar areas or areas of high elevation. At present, the Earth is in an interglacial period, but it is likely that glaciation has occurred throughout the entire history of the Earth. Over the last 2 million years (Quaternary Period), the global climate has fluctuated repeatedly: this has resulted in a series of continental-sized glaciers that advanced and retreated over most of the northern hemisphere. During the Quaternary, four major periods of glaciation have been identified in North America, although there were several advances and retreats of the ice during these periods. From oldest to youngest, these glacial periods are the Nebraskan, Kansan, Illinoian, and Wisconsinan—separated by interglacials called, from oldest to youngest, the Aftonian, Yarmouth, and Sangamon. In southern Saskatchewan, there is evidence for at least eight glacial advances during the Quaternary Period.

The last glacier that advanced over the province was called the Laurentide ice sheet and occurred during the Wisconsinan glacial period. This ice sheet reached its maximum size some 18,000 years before present (BP) when it covered most of Canada. At that time, a thick layer of glacial ice a kilometre in depth covered most of Saskatchewan; it is now believed that a few areas called *nunataks* escaped ice cover, for example sites of high elevation in the CYPRESS HILLS and around GRASSLANDS NATIONAL PARK. After 18,000 years BP the Laurentide Ice sheet

gradually retreated northeastward, present only in the far northeast corner of Saskatchewan around 8,000 years BP, with the last vestige of ice likely gone by 6,000 years BP.

Today, much of the present landscape of Saskatchewan owes its origin to GLACIAL EROSION and GLACIAL DEPOSITION of the Laurentide Ice Sheet. The effects of this glacier can be conveniently separated between the north and south of the province using the edge of the Precambrian Shield as a boundary. The hard exposed bedrock of the Precambrian Shield and proximity to the ice centre of the Laurentide ice sheet in Hudson Bay resulted in a landscape dominated by glacial erosional features in the north. As the ice sheet advanced it eroded and transported rocky materials southward, leaving an erosional surface behind: areal scouring, *roches moutonées*, whalebacks, and striae are common erosional landforms. The most common depositional landforms in the north are the eskers that extend hundreds of kilometres and illustrate the southward movement of materials during glacial retreat in the many meltwater channels that developed in the glacier.

In southern Saskatchewan glacial deposition is more evident, although several erosional features are apparent. It is believed that the softer Phanerozoic bedrock of the south was initially eroded and deposited by the earlier continental glaciers; but it appears that subsequent glacial advances were unable to remove all of these deposits and erode down to the bedrock each time. Instead, sizeable deposition of materials called drift and defined as deposits of glacial origin appears to have occurred in the southern part of the province: after each glacial advance, another layer of drift was laid down over the underlying deposit. Thus in most areas south of the Precambrian Shield, the bedrock is covered by a thick deposit of glacial drift ranging from 50 to 300 m in thickness. It was into this drift that several spectacular glacial meltwater spillway valleys have been carved to form such features as the FRENCHMAN RIVER Valley in the southwest corner and the QU'APPELLE VALLEY in central Saskatchewan. The Qu'Appelle Valley runs hundreds of kilometres and is some 130 m in depth; it has a U-shaped cross-section with wide flat floors and steep sidewalls, now subject to mass wasting processes. The valley floors typically contain glaciofluvial and fluvial deposits of fine clays and silts, conducive to intensive cropping. Elsewhere, evidence of glacial deposition includes proglacial lake deposits, eskers, deltas, and moraines of various types. *Janis Dale*

FURTHER READING: Benn, D.I. and D.J.A. Evans. 1998. *Glaciers and Glaciation*. London: Edward Arnold.

GLOBE THEATRE. The Globe Theatre was founded in 1966 by Ken and Sue (Richmond) Kramer,

who were inspired by their involvement in Brian Way's theatre for children in London, England. Introduced as Saskatchewan's first professional theatre since 1927, it was also one of Canada's earliest and most visionary theatres devoted to young audiences. Functioning as a touring company with a province-wide mandate, it gradually increased grants from the SASKATCHEWAN ARTS BOARD, the Canada Council, and the Department of Education, until its 1975–76 season covered a 20,188 km school touring circuit including 142 towns, 290 performances over 32 weeks, and an audience of 80,894 students and adults—or 9% of the provincial population and one-third of its school-aged children. The philosophy behind the company emphasized participation and access for all young people regardless of their location, economic means or initial interest in theatre. The early school repertoire featured the work of Brian Way; but in 1972 Rex Deverell began writing plays for the young people's company, and in 1975 the Globe formally established a writer-in-residence position (the first theatre to do so in western Canada) which he would hold for fifteen years (Canada's record for the longest serving playwright-in-residence).

Beginning in 1967, the Kramers also mounted individual shows for adults, and after two short seasons provided through the Regina Public Library they formally extended the theatre's mandate to include an adult season of six plays in 1970. Tragedy struck the theatre in 1978 when Sue Kramer died after a battle with cancer, but under Ken Kramer's ongoing artistic direction it maintained an audience of approximately 10% of the provincial population. After a variety of temporary spaces, in 1981 the Globe moved into Regina's old City Hall and a new 400-seat arena theatre unique among regional theatres in Canada. Within a year subscriptions soared to 5,652 (97% capacity), and in 1984 the theatre received the Vantage Arts Academy Award for the high calibre of its professional work and its contribution to the Canadian theatre scene. Having begun with a budget of $10,000, by 1985 the Globe had a $1 million budget—36% of which is derived from box office receipts. The adult season initially toured to five locations in southern Saskatchewan, so Kramer's sets and costumes remained modest despite the fact that the repertoire regularly included both period classics such as Shakespeare and modern classics. However, the Kramer years have become best known for the numerous new plays premiered by writers such as Carol Bolt, KEN MITCHELL, Rod Langley, Len Peterson and especially Rex Deverell. Rooted in the region's populist culture, many of these works responded directly to the immediate social and political concerns of the theatre's audience, and together with the school tour repertoire they provided many actors with stepping stones to successful careers.

CALVIN FEHR PHOTOGRAPHY/COURTESY OF THE GLOBE THEATRE

Fusion, a theatre-making process with high school and university students conceived and directed by Joey Tremblay, was performed as part of Globe Theatre's Shumiatcher Sandbox Series in February 2005. With the T.S. Elliot poem, "The Love Song of J. Alfred Prufrock," and an original score by Jason Cullimore as the starting points, the eight actors, a young designer, and two stage managers still in the midst of their training created a performance piece that was original, eclectic, non-text based and entirely engaging.

Susan Ferley took over as Artistic Director in 1989. In the first year she managed to eliminate a substantial deficit she had inherited; but because of cuts in available grants she struggled to maintain the school tours, and eventually went to touring only on alternating years with a radically reduced circuit, which in 1995–96 encompassed only fifty-seven communities and seventy-seven performances over nine weeks. However, she was able to secure funding to initiate one of Kramer's long-term ambitions: a second stage satellite series for new dramatic work whose form or content had a more limited appeal than the main stage programming. Although without a writer-in-residence after 1990, Ferley featured new work by **GAIL BOWEN** and provided modest commissions to encourage new work by other local writers, such as Greg Nelson's *Speak* and Ken Mitchell's *The Great Electrical Revolution*. During her term, the theatre secured the patronage of His Royal Highness Prince Edward–the first and only time he had bestowed patronage in Canada–and in 1994 it hosted its first royal visit.

In 1997, Ruth Smillie succeeded Ferley as Artistic Director. A successful capital campaign begun by Ferley enabled the Globe to complete over $1 million worth of renovations, including improvements to its second stage space. The school tour was finally dropped completely, increasing emphasis being placed on the family Christmas show (40% of box office revenue) and school matinees (which in 2003 accounted for more than twice the revenue of 1998). With a production budget that has more than doubled since 1998, Smillie has placed greater emphasis on set and costumes than her predecessors. Operating grant revenue has remained reasonably stable at around $600,000, but box office and corporate revenue have risen to approximately 55%

of a $2 million budget in 2003–04. Smillie has featured Floyd Favel's new work, in particular his *Governor of the Dew*, which played before Prince Edward's second visit to the Globe in 2003. Current initiatives include renovations to accommodate a theatre school, something that had been part of the Theatre's early mandate before its suspension in 1980.

Mary Blackstone

GOCKI, ANTHONY J. (1900–87). An inspiration within the church and in the community at large, Monsignor Anthony J. Gocki was born in North Dakota in 1900. Settling with his family in Cedoux, Saskatchewan, Gocki later studied classics and philosophy in Michigan and theology in Montreal. Ordained as a priest in 1922, he worked in Moose Jaw and Candiac before coming to Regina in 1931. Gocki founded St. Anthony's, the city's first Polish-speaking Roman Catholic parish, and later established Camp Monahan in the **QU'APPELLE VALLEY**. Fluent in Polish and other Slavic languages, he helped recent immigrants adapt to life in Canada. Gocki was a proponent of physical activity and he served as an advisor on fitness and recreation to premiers **T.C. DOUGLAS**, **WOODROW LLOYD**, and **ALLAN BLAKENEY**. For his tireless dedication to all people, Monsignor Gocki was invested as a Member of the Order of Canada in 1975. He died on June 4, 1987.

GODWIN, TED (1933–). Born in Calgary, Alberta, on August 13, 1933, Ted Godwin graduated from the Southern Alberta Institute of Technology and Art in 1955. He joined the **UNIVERSITY OF SASKATCHEWAN**, Regina Campus in 1964 to teach in what was then known as the Faculty of Art. Major influences in his early career included artists John Ferren, Jules Olitski, Barnett Newman and Lawrence

Alloway, with whom he studied at the Emma Lake Artists' Workshops from 1959 to 1965. A member of the group of Regina painters later known as the **REGINA FIVE**, Godwin broke onto the Canadian art scene with the group's 1961 exhibition, *Five Painters from Regina*, at The National Gallery of Canada. Throughout his teaching and professional careers, he has exhibited his paintings at public and commercial galleries across Canada and in the United Kingdom. His works are represented in major public collections including the National Gallery of Canada, the Art Gallery of Ontario, the Canada Council Art Bank, the CBC, and the **UNIVERSITY OF REGINA**.

Honoured for his work by the Royal Canadian Academy, to which he was elected in 1974, he was, along with other Regina Five members **KEN LOCHHEAD**, **RON BLOORE**, **DOUG MORTON** and **ART MCKAY**, awarded an honorary Doctorate of Laws degree from the University of Regina in 2001. That same year he received the Alberta College of Art Award of Excellence. Retired from teaching since 1985, Godwin maintains an active professional career. His most recent exhibition, *The Newfoundland Suite*, opened in 2003 in Calgary. His book, *Messages from the Real World: A Professional Handbook for the Emerging Artist* (republished in 2002 as *The Studio Handbook for Working Artists: A Survival Manual*), won a 1999 **SASKATCHEWAN BOOK AWARD**. Not unlike the writer Virginia Woolf, whose collection of essays *A Room of One's Own* (1929) points up the need for the woman writer to have a dedicated space of her own in which to create literary works, Godwin particularly recognizes the emerging artist's need of a room of his or her own, a space "where you make art and only art." Godwin is also the author of *Lower Bow: A Celebration of Wilderness, Art and Fishing* (exhibition catalogue, 1992), and *Ted Godwin: The Tartan Years 1967–1976* (exhibition catalogue, 1999). While Godwin has spent most of his life in the Canadian prairies, his paintings reflect a rich thematic palette of styles and subjects. His most

COURTESY OF THE SASKATCHEWAN ARTS BOARD

Ted Godwin's "Said the Spider to the Fly", 1965; oil, acrylic on canvas.

recent landscapes, some of which are large works, portray the play of light on water in the Canadian forest wilderness. *Ellen J. Chapco*

GOLD. Gold, a dense, malleable and ductile yellow metal, is an excellent conductor of heat and electricity. It is also somewhat rare, and therefore is highly desirable as a medium of exchange, as a monetary reserve, and for use in jewellery. In Canada gold is found in three main forms: free flakes, grains, or nuggets. In terms of value, gold is measured by troy weight; when mixed with other metals it is defined in terms of carats, typically ranging from 10 carats to pure gold which is measured at 24 carats. Since 1985 the price of gold has seen dramatic fluctuations ranging from approximately US $300/oz that year to a peak of US $500/oz in 1988. On January 1, 2004, the price of gold was US $416.25 /oz. The first discovery of gold in what is now Saskatchewan took place in 1859 in the **NORTH SASKATCHEWAN RIVER**, near Prince Albert. In the 1920s and 1930s, gold discoveries were also reported in the La Ronge area. Many of the earlier attempts were focused on dredging operations in rivers. Gold was discovered in the Lake Athabasca and Amisk Lake regions in the early 20th century. Considerable amounts of gold were then located on the Crackingstone Peninsula, and in smaller quantities near Prince Albert and Flin Flon.

More recently, the province experienced a gold boom in the late 1980s when over $50 million was spent on gold exploration. During this period, exploration focused on the Precambrian Shield—especially the La Ronge metavolcanic belt, the Glennie Domain and the Beaverlodge District—and a number of deposits were found and have been successfully developed. For the most part, gold occurrences in these areas fall into the class of mesothermal vein deposits of gold or orogenic lode gold deposits. Since 1987, five new gold mines have begun. Saskatchewan's largest primary gold producer is Claude Resources Inc., based in Saskatoon, whose largest project is the Seabee mine, located 125 km northeast of LaRonge. The project, in operation since 1991, has produced over 600,000 ounces of gold and continues to be a successful venture for the Saskatchewan company. *Julie L. Parchewski*

GOLDEN JUBILEE. In 1955, Saskatchewan marked its fiftieth anniversary as a province. A Golden Jubilee Committee, spending a modest half-million dollar budget, promoted several important provincial projects that set the standard for future anniversaries: building the Saskatchewan Museum of Natural History in Regina; commissioning two provincial histories (*The Story of a Province* and *Saskatchewan: The History of a Province*) and an anthology of Saskatchewan prose and poetry (*Saskatchewan Harvest*); publishing a historical map; and placing markers at historic points across the province. These official initiatives were strengthened by the response of municipal Jubilee committees who, encouraged by the provincial committee, planned and executed a year-long celebration that included homecoming fairs and parades, traveling exhibits, building projects, historic site preservation, and tourism and publicity promotion. Participation and support for these activities were enthusiastic as Saskatchewan people reflected on past and possible future achievements and paid respect to those who worked hard to build the province. The Department of Education's 1955 curriculum included a blueprint for students to research a school or community history book as a Jubilee project. Hundreds of histories were produced and even published, touching off the provincial preoccupation with local history book production which has continued to this day.

Merle Massie

FURTHER READING: Archer, J. 1954. *The Fiftieth Year: A Speaker's Handbook About Saskatchewan and its Jubilee*. Regina: Saskatchewan Golden Jubilee Committee; Smith, D.E. 1982. "Celebrations and History on the Prairies," *Journal of Canadian Studies* 17 (3): 45–57.

GOLDMAN, DOROTHY (1904–96). Born in New York City on July 24, 1904, and educated there, Dorothy Cohen came to Regina when she married Leon Goldman, a businessman, in 1926. A Red Cross volunteer during **WORLD WAR II**, she then served on the executive for forty-two years; and for twenty-three years she was area captain for the United Way. Goldman's work in the Jewish community—locally, regionally, and nationally—was honoured by the Hadassah Organization of Canada. The first woman to receive the Good Servant Award from the Canadian Council of Christians and Jews, she was a president and Life Member of the Women's Canadian Club of Regina. A patron of the arts, she supported the Norman **MACKENZIE ART GALLERY**, Dominion Drama Festival, **REGINA LITTLE THEATRE**, Regina Musical Club, Regina Opera Guild, and **REGINA SYMPHONY ORCHESTRA**. She was a patron of the Saskatchewan Music Festivals Association, the Canadian Opera Company, and the Metropolitan Opera seasons in Minneapolis for fifty years. She sponsored various scholarships at the **UNIVERSITY OF REGINA** for the Conservatory of Music, Journalism Program, and English Department. Her many honours included the Rotary Club's Heritage Award (1989) and Doctor of Laws degree from the University of Regina (1991). Dorothy Goldman died on February 16, 1996, in Regina, a year after her husband's death. *Lyn Goldman*

REGINA LEADER-POST

Dorothy Goldman, November 1989.

GOLF. Golf began in Saskatchewan at the Regina Golf Club, founded in 1899. In 1913, male golfers organized the Saskatchewan Golf Association (SGA) to run competitions and enforce the rules of the game; in 1926, female players formed their own association, the Saskatchewan branch of the Canadian Ladies Golf Union. Provincial championships began in 1908 for men and in 1914 for women. By 1926, there were 100 golf courses, most with nine holes and sand greens, and the SGA estimated that there were over 8,000 golfers in the province.

The **DEPRESSION** and **WORLD WAR II** caused a shortage of equipment and a severe drop in the number of players, but the game rebounded after 1945. The largest clubs, those in cities, installed watering systems for fairways as well as greens. Caddies almost disappeared, as many players pulled their clubs around the courses on carts. More competitions were held, including those restricted to younger golfers. In the 1950s, Saskatoon hosted both the men's and the women's Canadian championships. Also, Saskatoon golf professional Pat Fletcher won the Canadian Professional Golfers Association title in 1952, and the Canadian Open in 1954.

In the 1960s, new golf courses were opened, such as the municipal courses in Regina and Saskatoon, and more existing courses added watering systems. Partly because of these better facilities, more Saskatchewan golfers began to have success outside the province. Joanne Goulet of Regina was a semifinalist in the British Open Championships in 1964, and Barbara Turnbull of Saskatoon reached the Canadian women's final in 1969. These two women dominated the provincial championships for more than twenty years. Also, a four-man provincial team won the men's national championship, the Willingdon Cup, in 1964.

Golf continued to expand, with 203 courses in the province by 1987. In 2003, the SGA had a mem-

ALLAN MILLS PHOTO/COURTESY OF TOURISM SASKATCHEWAN

Golfing at Harbour Golf Club near Elbow, Saskatchewan.

bership of approximately 16,000 men and women of all ages. Equipment became much more sophisticated and expensive, with clubs made of steel or titanium instead of the traditional wood. Also, many players rode in carts instead of walking. Saskatchewan golfers continued to win national events: in both 1985 and 1990, a team of four women won the Canadian Seniors Championship (for players over age 50). Saskatoon's Dana Kidd was the best junior golfer (under age 19) in Canada in 1992.

Sandra Bingaman

FURTHER READING: Bingaman, S. 1997. *Golf: Breaking 100: A Century of Women's Golf in Saskatchewan*. Regina: Canadian Ladies Golf Association and Saskatchewan Sports Hall of Fame and Museum; Boyle, M. 1987. *Ninety Years of Golf: An Illustrated History of Golf in Saskatchewan*. Regina: Centax.

GOODALE, RALPH EDWARD (1949–). Ralph Goodale was born on May 10, 1949, and was raised on a farm near Wilcox. In 1972 he received a law degree from the UNIVERSITY OF SASKATCHEWAN. After working as a special assistant to federal Justice Minister OTTO LANG, Goodale was elected as a Liberal in Assiniboia in the 1974 federal election. He was defeated in the 1979 and 1980 federal elections, switched to provincial politics, and was elected leader of the provincial LIBERAL PARTY in 1981.

With no seats in the provincial Legislature, the Liberal vote plummeted in the 1982 provincial election and again they were shut out. Goodale campaigned on fiscal responsibility in the 1986 election. Although the Liberals remained in third place, their popular vote improved and Goodale was elected MLA for Assiniboia–Gravelbourg.

Goodale resigned in 1988 to contest the constituency of Regina-Wascana in the federal election. He lost and temporarily left politics to work in the private sector. He was elected in the 1993 federal

election and was appointed Minister of Agriculture and Minister responsible for the Canadian Wheat Board by Prime Minister Jean Chrétien. Under Goodale's guidance the Crow Rate was eliminated. In spite of an upswing in support in Saskatchewan for the Reform (Canadian Alliance) (Conservative) Party, Goodale was re-elected with comfortable margins in the 1997, 2000, and 2003 elections.

Goodale was shifted from Agriculture to Natural Resources in 1997 while retaining responsibility for the Wheat Board. Goodale continued as Natural Resources Minister until 2002, when he briefly became government House Leader. Later in 2002, however, Chrétien moved Goodale into the Department of Public Works and Government Services to deal with a scandal that involved inappropriate rewarding of government tendering and

ROBERT WATSON/REGINA LEADER-POST

Ralph Goodale, November 1986.

advertising contracts. Goodale's fortunes continued to rise in 2003 when Paul Martin succeeded Chrétien as leader of the federal Liberals and Prime Minister. Goodale, a long-time ally of Martin, was appointed Minister of Finance, a position that made him the most powerful Saskatchewan politician in the federal government since JOHN DIEFENBAKER.

Mike Fedyk

GOODWILL, JEAN CUTHAND (1928–97). Jean Cuthand Goodwill was born August 14, 1928 and raised on the Little Pine First Nation. In the 1940s she contracted tuberculosis and spent three years as a patient at the Prince Albert Sanatorium. Once recovered, she remained at the sanatorium as a nurse's aid and later went on to study nursing at the Holy Family Hospital in Prince Albert. In 1954 became the first Aboriginal Woman to finish a nursing program in Saskatchewan. Following graduation, Goodwill worked with the Indian and Northern Health Services in Fort Qu'Appelle, and then as head nurse at the La Ronge nursing station, where she often attended emergencies by bush plane or dog team. After two years, she moved to Bermuda where she worked for another two years. Upon her return to Canada, she got involved in developing Aboriginal organizations. In 1962 she became executive director of the Indian and Métis Friendship Centre in Winnipeg. In 1965 she married Ken Goodwill and together they raised two adopted daughters. In 1966 they moved to Ottawa where Jean became co-editor of *Indian News* and helped to develop *Tawwow*, a magazine that encouraged First Nations people to write about their own affairs.

In 1974, Jean co-founded the Indian and Inuit Nurses of Canada (now known as Aboriginal Nursing Association of Canada) and served as President from 1983 until 1990. In 1978, she became a nursing consultant for the Medical Services Division and an advisor to Assistant Deputy Minister D. Lyall Black at Aboriginal Affairs. In 1981 she became the first Aboriginal woman in the federal public service to be appointed as special advisor to the minister of National Health and Welfare, Monique Bégin. Thereafter she was named to the Department of Indian Affairs and Northern Development.

Upon retirement from government, she moved to Standing Buffalo reserve and became department head of the Indian Health Studies at the Saskatchewan Indian Federated College of the UNIVERSITY OF REGINA (now FIRST NATIONS UNIVERSITY OF CANADA).

An active member in her community, Jean was a member of the Board of Directors for the Canadian Public Health Association, a founding member and past president of the Aboriginal Women's Association of Canada and president of the Canadian Society for Circumpolar Health. She helped develop the National Native Access to

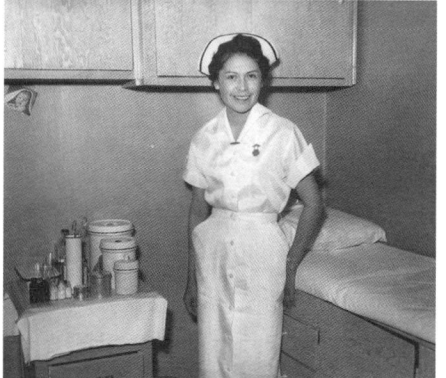

SASKATCHEWAN ARCHIVES BOARD R-B6805

Jean Cuthand (Goodwill), head nurse at the Indian health nursing station at La Ronge, January 1958. She was the first Indian nurse to hold this position in northern Saskatchewan.

Nursing Program at the **UNIVERSITY OF SASKATCH-EWAN** and the Indian Health Studies Department at the Saskatchewan Indian Federated College at the University of Regina.

In 1982 Goodwill co-wrote a book about her father entitled *John Tootoosis: A Biography of a Cree Leader*. Goodwill received the Jean Goodwill Award in 1981, created in her honour by the Manitoba Indian Nurses Association. Queen's University gave her an Honorary Doctorate of Law in 1986; in 1992 she received the Order of Canada; and in 1994 she received a national excellence award from the National Aboriginal Achievement Foundation. Jean Goodwill died in Regina on August 25, 1997.

Doug Cuthand

GOPLEN, HENRIETTA (1932–). A lifelong competitor and coach of speed skating, Henrietta Goplen was born in Saskatoon on July 14, 1932. At age 10, she joined the Saskatoon Lions Speed Skating Club and over the years participated in numerous city, provincial, and national championships. A freelance Home Economist by profession, Goplen devoted much of her time to coaching and developing some of Canada's best competitive speed skaters. She served as president of the Canadian Amateur Speed Skating Association and was a founding member and director of the Saskatoon Hall of Fame. In recognition of her contributions to amateur sport, Goplen was made a Member of the Order of Canada in 2003.

GORDON, PERCIVAL H. (1884–1975). An influential member of the Saskatchewan Court of Appeal, the Honourable Percival H. Gordon was born in Qu'Appelle, North-West Territories on January 27, 1884. Between 1905 and 1909, he earned three degrees and was a noted university athlete despite having lost his right arm in a hunting accident. Appointed King's Counsel in 1927, Gordon represented the federal government on the Saskatchewan

Relief Commission in 1930–31 and the provincial government before the Dysart Commission on natural resources in 1933–34. A year later, he was appointed to the Court of Appeal where he remained until his retirement in 1961. He continued to practice law and was one of the council who sought to have **MEDICARE** legislation declared invalid in 1962. Gordon served as chancellor of the Anglican diocese of Qu'Appelle from 1921 to 1942 and as executive chairman of the Canadian Red Cross. He was appointed an Officer of the Order of Canada in 1968. Percival Gordon died on April 6, 1975.

GOSSELIN, ROSA (1890–1964). Rosa Gosselin, given the religious name of Sister Eleonore, spent fifty years in the field of French Catholic education in southern Saskatchewan. Born on December 16, 1890, in St. Malo, Manitoba, she was educated in part by the Filles de la Croix, one of many Catholic teaching congregations which had come to western Canada from France after being forced out of the French school system by anti-clerical legislation. In 1910, she left for the congregation's training convent in France, returning to Canada in 1912 to attend Regina Normal School. In October 1914 Sister Eleonore came to the newly constructed Willow Bunch convent. Unable to return to France in 1917 because of **WORLD WAR I**, she professed final vows in Manitoba. Sent to Laflèche in 1922, she returned to Willow Bunch in 1937 when operations at the Laflèche convent were scaled back because of unfavourable economic conditions. She continued to teach in Willow Bunch, while taking on the additional tasks of parish sexton, then of convent bursar. Forced to give up teaching because of deafness in 1948, she retained her other duties for the rest of her life. Struck by cancer in the late 1950s, she underwent a series of operations. She died on August 20, 1964, in St. Boniface, Manitoba.

Richard Lapointe

FURTHER READING: Lapointe, Richard. 1988. "Rosa Gosselin (soeur Éléonore, F.d.l.C.)." Pp. 192–96 in *100 noms: Petit dictionnaire biographique des Franco-Canadiens de la Saskatchewan*. Regina: Société historique.

GOULET, JOANNE (1935–). For over a half-century, Joanne Goulet has been a fixture of Saskatchewan amateur **GOLF**. Born on May 7, 1935, she started golfing at age 14; since then, she has won dozens of local, national, and international championships. Goulet has won the city of Regina women's golf title thirty-two times. She is a two-time Saskatchewan Junior Women's champion, a nine-time Saskatchewan Amateur Women's champion, and a six-time Saskatchewan Senior Women's champion. She was also part of the Saskatchewan Senior Women's team that won the Canadian championship in 1985 and 1990. In 1964, Goulet participat-

DON HEALY/REGINA LEADER-POST

Joanne Goulet.

ed in the British Open and won the Commonwealth Trophy as a semi-finalist. She holds course records at the Royal Regina Golf Club, the Wascana Country Club, and the Riverside Country Club. In 1993, she became the first woman in Canada to have a golf course named in her honour: the Joanne Goulet Golf Course in Regina. She was installed in the **SASKATCHEWAN SPORTS HALL OF FAME** in 1980.

Daria Coneghan and Holden Stoffel

FURTHER READING: Bingaman, S. 1997. *Breaking 100: A Century of Women's Golf in Saskatchewan*. Saskatoon: Canadian Ladies' Golf Association-Saskatchewan.

GOULET, KEITH (1946–). Keith Goulet, born in 1946 in Cumberland House, Saskatchewan, is a Swampy Cree-Métis educator and politician. Raised in Cumberland House in a large traditional and entrepreneurial family, Goulet received his secondary education in his home community and in Prince Albert, before completing a BEd at the **UNIVERSITY OF SASKATCHEWAN** and an MEd at the **UNIVERSITY OF REGINA**. As a professional educator, he was a schoolteacher, a curriculum developer, a university lecturer, a program coordinator with NORTEP, a community college principal in La Ronge, and in 1984–85 an executive director at the Gabriel Dumont

Keith Goulet being sworn in as first Aboriginal Cabinet minister.

Institute. Goulet instructed the province's first university-level Cree language classes (University of Saskatchewan), and in 1976 developed the first teacher education program in northern Saskatchewan, NORTEP. A lifelong New Democrat, Goulet began his political career in 1986 when he was elected for the northern constituency of Cumberland; he was a member of the Legislative Assembly until 2001. In 1992, Goulet became the province's first Aboriginal Cabinet minister, holding several Cabinet portfolios including Saskatchewan Government Insurance, Education, Training and Employment (associate minister), and Northern Affairs. Goulet was also the first person to speak Cree in the Legislative Assembly and to have it recorded in the *Hansard*. In Cabinet, Goulet was a strong advocate for the province's Aboriginal peoples and the north. He provided Aboriginal educational programs with more autonomy, worked directly with the Treaty Land Entitlement process and the Saskatchewan Indian Gaming Authority, implemented The Métis Act, and ensured that Aboriginal people were better represented in the northern economy, particularly in mining.

Darren Prefontaine

FURTHER READING: Hodgson-Smith, Kathy. 2002. "Keith Goulet: A Proud Métis and A Leader for the People of Saskatchewan," *New Breed Magazine* (July/August): 5–7.

GOVAN, town, pop 274, located E of the N end of **LAST MOUNTAIN LAKE**, mid-way between Strasbourg and Nokomis on Hwy 20. The first known settler in the area arrived in 1903, and by around 1906 all of the available homesteads were occupied. Govan developed as a farming community with the construction of the railway from Strasbourg to Lanigan. The townsite was surveyed in 1906, and in 1907 Govan was incorporated as a village, its name honouring Walter Govan, one of the area's early settlers. The Canadian Museum of Civilization in Gatineau, Quebec, has a model depicting Govan at about this time as an example of a typical early prairie town. In 1916, the community reached a peak population of 500. In 1967, Govan's senior men's baseball team won the Western Canadian Baseball Championships; they were subsequently inducted into the **SASKATCHEWAN SPORTS HALL OF FAME**. Today the community is best known for hosting the Govan Old Tyme Fiddle Festival and the Saskatchewan Fiddlers Championships. The concurrent events, held the first weekend in July, have been running for over 20 years and draw competitors and fans from across North America.

David McLennan

GOVERNMENT HOUSE. Designed by Thomas Fuller, architect of the Parliament Buildings in Ottawa, Government House in Regina opened in 1891 as residence, office and entertainment facility for the Lieutenant-Governors of the North-West Territories. After 1905, it was the residence of the Lieutenant-Governors of Saskatchewan. In 1945 the CCF government of **T.C. DOUGLAS** closed the House as an economy measure; from 1946–57 the property was leased to the federal government as a centre for disabled war veterans; and from 1958, as "Saskatchewan House," the facility was used by the province for adult education. It was designated a National Historic Site in 1968. A volunteer "Saskatchewan House Committee" (later the Government House Historical Society) campaigned for preservation of the House, which was declared a provincial historic site in 1971. Restoration by the province between 1978 and 1980 converted the facility into "Government House Heritage Property": a museum of the 1900 period under Lieutenant-Governor **AMÉDÉE FORGET**, and a hospitality facility for government and non-profit organizations. In 1984 the Office of the Lieutenant-Governor returned. Construction of a visitor/administration centre and coach house and restoration of the grounds to the 1905 Edwardian gardens were undertaken for the provincial centennial in 2005.

Michael Jackson

Above: Government House, with newly-completed addition, May 9, 2005.

Inset: Government House, before addition.

FURTHER READING: Hryniuk, M. and G. Pugh. 1991. *"A Tower of Attraction": An Illustrated History of Government House, Regina, Saskatchewan.* Regina: Government House Historical Society/Canadian Plains Research Center.

"GRAB-A-HOE INDIANS." An aspect of Saskatchewan's labour history that receives little attention is the seasonal migration of Aboriginal workers to the southern Alberta sugar beet industry. Yet, Aboriginal workers have migrated annually to southern Alberta to hoe, weed and harvest sugar beet crops since the mid-1900s. Shortly after WORLD WAR II, the sugar beet industry experienced extreme difficulty in procuring workers to meet its labour requirements; it was then that Aboriginal workers, particularly First Nations people from reserves in northern Saskatchewan, were recruited to fill the labour gap. Prior to World War II, farmers in southern Alberta had hired European immigrant workers to hoe, weed, and harvest their sugar beet crops; even during the war, when labour was in short supply, farmers were able to utilize Japanese Canadians held in internment camps. At the end of the war, once again European immigrants were recruited for sugar beet work. By the early 1950s, however, the flow of unskilled immigrants to Canada dwindled, and sugar beet farmers experienced a severe labour shortage. The sugar beet industry, with the assistance of the Dominion-Provincial Farm Labour Committee (DPFLC) and the Department of Indian Affairs, then turned to recruiting Aboriginal workers to perform the labour formerly done by European immigrant workers.

In 1953, the Aboriginal labour force consisted of only 120 workers. By 1962, however, 551 farmers in southern Alberta employed over 2,100 Aboriginal workers. In 1966 this labour force reached its highest point when over 3,000 Aboriginal workers were hired on a seasonal basis to cultivate and harvest sugar beet crops. Although Métis and non-status Indian workers comprised a significant portion of the labour force, the majority were First Nations workers from reserves in northern Saskatchewan, some of whom traveled over 1,000 km to get to the sugar beet fields in southern Alberta. Many, for instance, came from the Montreal Lake, Lac La Ronge, Sandy Bay and Pelican Narrows reserves. During the 1960s it was not uncommon for about 95% of the population of some northern reserves, including men, women and children, to migrate to southern Alberta during May and June for six to eight weeks, or even longer.

In the post-World War II period, when immigrant labour could no longer be procured, the DPFLC and the Department of Indian Affairs used a number of tactics to recruit, mobilize and retain Aboriginal workers for sugar beet work. For instance, letters and application forms requesting workers were sent to the Chief and Band Council on reserves; chartered buses were sent to northern reserves and Métis communities to transport workers to a reception centre in Lethbridge, Alberta; and social assistance benefits were even cut off to induce workers to migrate. The Alberta Sugar Beet Growers Association and the Federal-Provincial Agricultural Manpower Committee (FPAMC), formerly the DPFLC, sought to retain the workers by providing housing and work training programs, and by inviting workers as guests to the annual stampedes in sugar-beet country. During the period when the pool of First Nations workers was recruited and mobilized by the FPAMC and the Department of Indian Affairs, it was referred to as the "sponsored movement." By the mid-1970s, however, First Nation workers migrated to southern Alberta on their own to seek employment opportunities.

Aboriginal workers comprised the largest component of the labour force in the southern Alberta sugar beet industry until the early 1980s. By that time farmers had increased mechanization and the use of chemical weed controls to such an extent that their need for hand labour was significantly reduced. Also, in the late 1970s farmers began to augment their Aboriginal labour force with Mexican Mennonite workers, who before long became the major labour force in the industry. Nevertheless, in 2004 it was found that 15% of the sugar beet crops grown in southern Alberta used seasonal hand labour for weed control purposes, and that a significant portion of the workers were Aboriginal—mainly from reserves in northern Saskatchewan: Island Lake First Nation, Onion Lake First Nation, Thunderchild First Nation, Witchekan Lake First Nation, and Big River First Nation. The importance of Aboriginal labour to the success of the southern Alberta sugar beet industry is unquestionable. During the period when they comprised the largest component of the labour force, few non-Aboriginal people sought to work there because it was low-paying, back-breaking work during long hot summer days. The workers coped through their sense of humour, some jokingly referring to themselves as the "grab-a-hoe Indians."

Ron Laliberté

FURTHER READING: Laliberté, R. and V. Satezwich. 1999. "Native Migrant Labour in the Southern Alberta Sugar Beet Industry: Coercion and Paternalism in the Recruitment of Labour." *Canadian Review of Sociology and Anthropology* 36 (1). 65–85.

GRAHAM, MARION MARGARET (1903–95). Born in Crossland, Ontario on August 25, 1903, Graham came to Saskatchewan with her family in 1907. She graduated from Saskatoon Normal School at the UNIVERSITY OF SASKATCHEWAN, and in 1928 began teaching in Saskatoon. There Graham spent most of her career, her work including pioneering involvement in special education. Promoting education and library development, she played a central role in many organizations, became a Saskatchewan library trustee, and was a member of the Saskatoon school board from 1965 to 1980. During WORLD WAR II Graham was among the first women to join the RCAF and to receive a commission; her postings across Canada included No. 4 Service Flying Training School in Saskatoon. She retired as a Squadron Leader in 1945. Later she became first woman president of the Saskatchewan RCAF Association, and received the Order of Merit from the national RCAF. After a postwar stint as national supervisor of women's training with the federal Department of Labour, she returned to Saskatoon, again teaching and engaging in community service. Among her many awards was having a high school, a school library, and an air cadet division named after her. She was named a Member of the Order of Canada in 1977. Graham died on April 23, 1995 in Saskatoon.

Ruth Wright Millar

GRAIN ELEVATORS. To understand the purpose and the form of grain elevators is to understand the grain economy which formed the basis of prairie settlement. In order for settlement to be successful there had to be efficiency in production and marketing of grain to world markets, and this meant having a system to assemble and store grain from farms and move it forward to port position for shipment overseas. This system consisted of farm hauling (horse and wagon, and later truck), roads, railway, and the grain elevator. The earliest form of grain storage was the flat warehouses built alongside the rail line which received grain, mainly in sacks. A typical flat warehouse might hold about 4,000 bushels. Bins would be located on each side of a central alley that gave access to loading and unloading the bins; this was done by shoveling grain into hand carts, and from there into wooden rail box cars. It took about one full day to load a box car this way: this system was too slow and labour-intensive. The invention of the vertical leg by which grain could be elevated and stored in vertical bins was to solve this problem. The elevator had its origins in Buffalo, New York; the design was adopted and spread across the great plains of North America and into the Canadian prairies, where it gave birth to a name for these vertical wooden facilities: "Prairie Sentinels."

The earliest grain elevators were built to a standard set by the CANADIAN PACIFIC RAILWAY (CPR) in order to obtain a licence to construct an elevator along its track; the minimum size stipulated by the CPR was 25,000 bushels. To fully understand the characteristic shape of the wooden elevator one needs to understand how it works. Figure GE-1 shows a cross-section of the standard elevator and its main working components. This drawing is of a

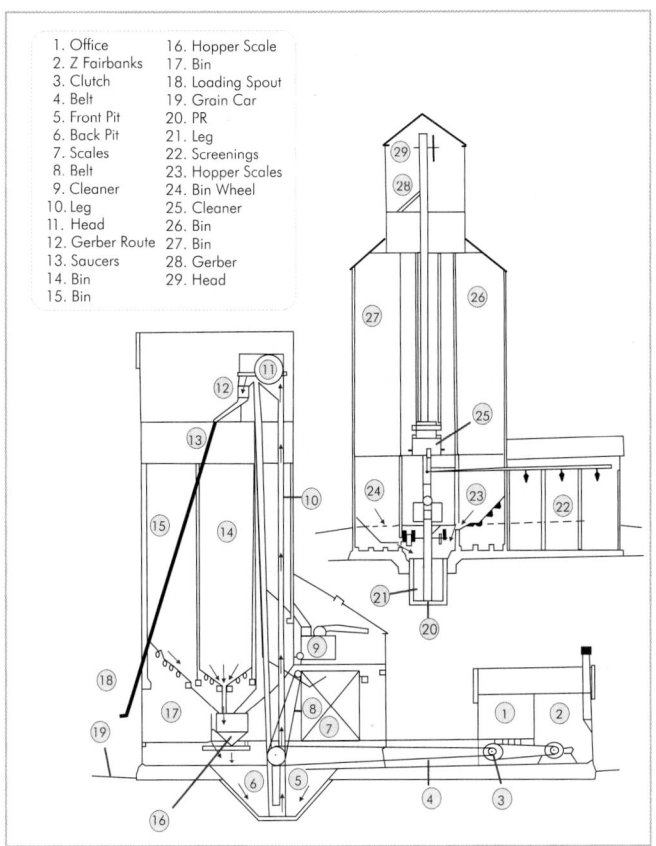

Figure GE-1. Standard Grain Elevator.

1. Office	16. Hopper Scale
2. Z Fairbanks	17. Bin
3. Clutch	18. Loading Spout
4. Belt	19. Grain Car
5. Front Pit	20. PR
6. Back Pit	21. Leg
7. Scales	22. Screenings
8. Belt	23. Hopper Scales
9. Cleaner	24. Bin Wheel
10. Leg	25. Cleaner
11. Head	26. Bin
12. Gerber Route	27. Bin
13. Saucers	28. Gerber
14. Bin	29. Head
15. Bin	

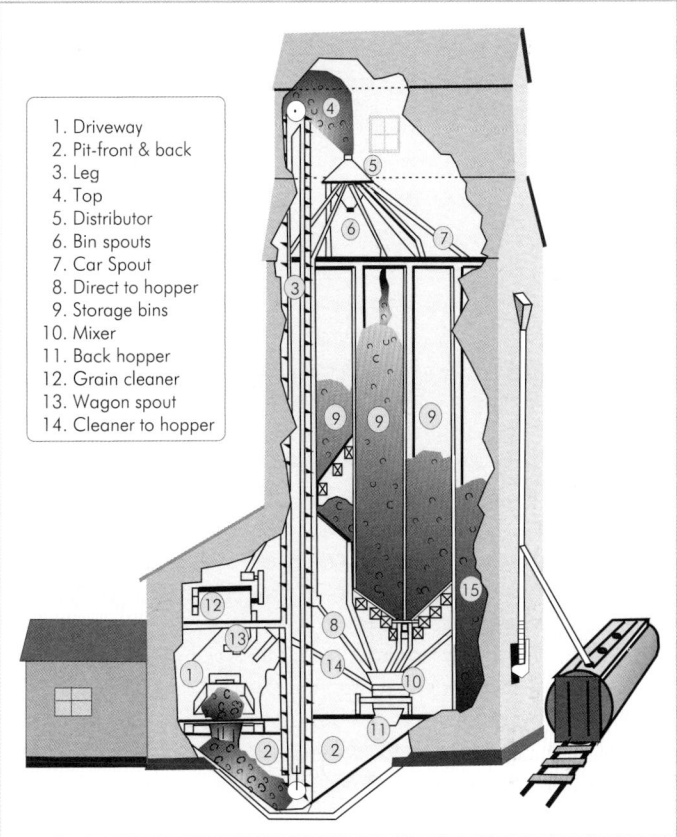

Figure GE-2. Standard Grain Elevator with Grain Movement.

1. Driveway
2. Pit-front & back
3. Leg
4. Top
5. Distributor
6. Bin spouts
7. Car Spout
8. Direct to hopper
9. Storage bins
10. Mixer
11. Back hopper
12. Grain cleaner
13. Wagon spout
14. Cleaner to hopper

1935 elevator with a 30,000 bushel capacity powered by a Model Z Fairbanks one-cylinder engine located in the basement of the office building; the motor runs a long drive belt to a pulley in the elevator which provides power to run the leg. The vertical leg consists of a belt with grain cups, which moves the grain from the front pit to the top of the elevator, where grain is allocated to different bins or to a box-car by a spout over the track. Grain is received into the driveway and weighed on the scale before being dumped into the front pit. The empty truck (a wagon in the days before the truck) would be weighed to determine the weight of grain delivered. To load a car from a bin, grain would be dropped into the hopper scale, weighed and then dumped into the back pit and elevated up the leg to the gerber at the top of the elevator. From there the grain would travel down the loading spout and into the boxcar (hopper car today). Figure GE-2 shows another view of the elevator with a focus on how grain was received, stored and loaded into grain cars.

The Saskatchewan Elevator Commission reported in 1910 that the cost of a standard 25,000-bushel elevator was $6,200, and that of a 60,000-bushel unit was $11,000: this placed the costs of construction at between 18.3 and 24.8¢ per bushel. In the early 1930s the estimated costs for a 30,000-bushel elevator was between $10,000 and $12,000: this means that the costs had risen to approximately 37¢

per bushel. Using the consumer price index as the basis for inflation, an elevator costing $6,200 in 1910 would cost approximately $106,000 in 2004. This would be $4.25 per bushel, compared to 25 cents in 1910: the cost is therefore now about seventeen times that of 1910.

There were ninety elevators in western Canada in 1890, with a total storage capacity of 4.3 million bushels. In terms of numbers, a peak was reached in the 1930s when settlement was mostly complete: there were close to 6,000 primary elevators. The average capacity, which had remained at approximately 30,000 bushels, also began to increase: it had doubled by 1960, and more than doubled again by 1990 to reach 168,000 bushels. By 1997, average capacity was seven times what it was in the early era; but between 1930 and 1997 the number of primary elevators had shrunk by 80%.

The history of elevators can be broken into three periods: up to 1910, when private companies dominated the trade; from 1911 to 1990, when farmer-owned co-operatives came to dominate the business; and from 1990 to the present, with the transformation of the co-operative sector and the entry of new firms. In the period leading to 1910, the early elevator business was represented by flour-milling companies with head offices outside of the prairies: the Ogilvie Milling Company, with head-quarters in Montreal, which had built the first eleva-

tor at Gretna, Manitoba in 1881; the Lake of the Woods Milling Company, founded in 1887 and partly funded by George Stephens and Sir William Van Horne of the CPR; Robin Hood Mills, an American milling company; and the Western Canadian Flour Mills, owned by the Mackenzie and Mann operations, which were building the Canadian Northern Railway.

When the Canadian Northern Railway was opened in 1900, Mackenzie and Mann actively solicited American interest in elevator construction. The British-American Company was consequently formed in 1906; the US-based **SEARLE GRAIN COMPANY** also entered the Canadian market and operated on Northern Railway lines; and in 1909 the Peavey interests of Minneapolis formed the **NATIONAL GRAIN COMPANY**, which operated on CPR lines. Many other companies were formed and also entered the elevator business, such as Alberta Pacific Grain Company, **PIONEER GRAIN COMPANY**, Norris Grain Company, British Co-operative Wholesale Society, Scottish Co-operative Wholesale Grain Company, **PARRISH AND HEIMBECKER**, McCabe Brothers Grain Company, Pioneer Grain, and **N.M. PATERSON AND SONS**.

The period from 1911 to 1990 was dominated by the growth of farmer-owned co-operatives. The term "line elevator companies" was associated with privately owned companies which owned a number of elevators along a single line of railway track. In the early period farmers fought the monopolization of the grain business by these companies, which were referred to as the "syndicate of syndicates" for their alleged collusive practices in fixing prices. After the first decade of settlement, farmers were so convinced that monopoly elements dominated the grain trade that they were ready to replace private monopoly with public monopoly. They petitioned the federal government to take over all terminals, and the provincial government to take over all country grain elevators. Although governments resisted this policy, there were exceptions: the government of Manitoba, for example, purchased a number of primary country elevators in 1910–which proved to be unprofitable.

The Saskatchewan government appointed a commission to look into the problems farmers were facing in marketing their grain, and recommended against the government going into the elevator business. Receiving little help from the federal or provincial government, the farmers turned to direct action. One solution was for them to raise the capital and build their own elevators, and in 1899 there were twenty-six locally farmer-owned elevators on the prairies. The Saskatchewan Elevator Commission, investigating these farmer-owned elevators, found them lacking in performance–partly because farmers did not support them even though they were shareholders. The first major action by farmers was the formation of the GRAIN GROWERS' GRAIN COMPANY in 1906 under the leadership of E.A. PARTRIDGE of Sintaluta, Saskatchewan. It operated as a marketing agency for farmers selling grain in world markets, the profits returning to farmers. In 1912, the Manitoba government leased its elevators to the Grain Growers' Grain Company: it was now in the elevator business.

In Saskatchewan the government supported the idea of a line of elevators owned and operated by farmers. The plan was for the provincial government to advance 85% of the capital for the construction of local elevators, the loan being repayable in twenty years; local farmers were to raise the other 15%. This led to the formation of the SASKATCHEWAN CO-OPERATIVE ELEVATOR COMPANY. A similar plan was followed in Alberta, resulting in the formation of the Alberta Farmers' Co-operative Elevator Company, which merged in 1917 with the Grain Growers' Grain Company to form UNITED GRAIN GROWERS (UGG). The Saskatchewan Co-op chose to remain independent; UGG was to build a line of elevators in Saskatchewan.

When the government resisted all pressures to restore the Canadian Wheat Board (CWB), which had been put in place by the federal government to market the 1919 crop, farmers set up their own marketing agency, which operated on pooling principles. Farmers in each prairie province were to form the Manitoba, Saskatchewan, and Alberta

Wheat Producers Limited. These organizations then formed the Central Selling Agency to jointly market wheat obtained from farmers under contract. These three organizations became known as the Wheat Pools, and each set up a fund to build its own elevators. In Saskatchewan the Wheat Pool took over the Saskatchewan Co-operative Elevator company in 1926. In 1925–26, the three Pools owned 100 elevators, but by 1926–27 they owned 658. The mergers which took place in the private grain trade resumed after WORLD WAR II. FEDERAL GRAIN was formed from the merger of the Searle Grain Company and Alberta Pacific Grain Company in 1967; in 1927 Federal Grain had sold its 1,000 elevators to the three Pools. The other main change was the sale of National Grain (267 elevators) to CARGILL in 1975. In 1975 the private trade owned 892 elevators, and farmer-owned companies had 3,272 or 79% of the total number.

The structure of the elevator business has undergone a massive change. The "Prairie Sentinels" have mostly been torn down or sold to local farmers, and replaced by larger concrete facilities, some of which have been financed by farmers (e.g., WEYBURN INLAND TERMINAL). This has been driven by the condition of the old wooden elevators, but mostly by changes in technology (larger farms and farm trucks) and by the rationalization of the rail network with the possibilities of moving grain in unit trains. One of the more important changes is the re-entry of the large American and international grain companies to the Canadian prairies. Prior to its merger with Agricore, UGG was 45% owned by Archie Daniel Midland (ADM). The last several years have seen the entry of several of the international grain companies such as Bunge Canada (two elevators), ConAgra Limited (three elevators), and Louis Dreyfus Canada Limited (one elevator). The SASKATCHEWAN WHEAT POOL changed its ownership structure and is now a stock traded company. One can regret the reality of "progress," which has meant larger grain farms, fewer rural people, fewer communities, and longer distances for grain to be hauled and for farm children to attend schools. What the future holds is not clear, but we do know that the landscape will never be the same when the last of the "Prairie Sentinels" is gone from rural communities.

In 1950 there were 3,035 primary elevators in Saskatchewan, with storage capacity of 283 million bushels and twenty-two licenced buyers. Twenty years later, in 1970, there were 2,750 elevators, with storage capacity of 225 million bushels. After that the number of elevators declined tremendously, so that by 2004 there are only 197 primary licenced elevators, with a storage capacity of 2.8 million tonnes (100 million bushels). Although there are only six major grain companies as buyers, there are now approximately fifteen terminals owned by

farmers–wholly or in some joint venture with a major grain company.   *Gary Storey*

FURTHER READING: Anderson, C.W. 1991. *Grain: The Entrepreneurs*. Winnipeg: Watson and Dwyer Publishing; Fowke, V. 1957. *The National Policy and the Wheat Economy*. Toronto: University of Toronto Press; Wilson, C.F. 1978. *A Century of Canadian Grain*. Saskatoon: Western Producer Prairie Books.

GRAIN GROWERS' GRAIN COMPANY. The Grain Growers' Grain Company (GGGC), established in 1906, was the first large-scale co-operative of prairie farmers; it expressed their ambition to control grain trading. E.A. PARTRIDGE, a farmer from Sintaluta, played a leading role in its organization. The GGGC was the ancestor of UNITED GRAIN GROWERS (UGG) and of today's Agricore United. It emerged from the early grain growers' movement. The Territorial Grain Growers' Association (TGGA) had been organized at Indian Head in what is now Saskatchewan in 1901, with the purpose of lobbying the government to ensure enforcement of the 1900 Manitoba Grain Act. Partridge was a leader among those who did not believe that government regulation alone would solve the abuses and injustices they perceived in the grain trade.

Early in 1905 Partridge made a trip to observe the activities of the Winnipeg Grain Exchange. He wrote about what he had seen, and argued that farmers needed to unite if they were to achieve fair returns in the face of other interests in the economy. He proposed a farmer-owned joint-stock company for this purpose and promoted the idea at farmers' meetings in 1905 and 1906. A meeting at Sintaluta in January 1906 is taken as the first organizing meeting of the new company. GGGC took shape in the summer, and was officially launched on September 5, 1906, with Partridge as president. It purchased a seat on the Exchange in order to participate in trading, but in November 1906 it was ejected in response to protests from other grain companies. The rules of the Exchange were interpreted as forbidding the co-operative practice of paying patronage refunds to farmers. The company had to be reorganized along less explicitly co-operative lines in 1907, and Partridge stepped down as president. His successor, T.A. Crerar of Manitoba (later a well-known Progressive politician), remained president from 1907 to 1917 and then became the first president of UGG.

Meanwhile, the company was growing rapidly: from 1907 to 1912 the number of shareholders went from 1,800 to over 27,000, while grain volume grew from 2.3 million to nearly 28 million bushels. One of the other activities of the new company was to publish, in conjunction with the grain growers' associations, the *Grain Growers' Guide* (1908), the most important publication of the early farm movement; Partridge was editor of the first issue. As a grain-trading enterprise, the GGGC bought farmers' grain and sold it on a commission basis on the Exchange, returning profits to its farmer-investors. It did not, at first, have its own grain elevators to handle the grain, working instead through arrangements with elevator companies; nor did it make much effort to bypass the grain-exchange system and sell directly to overseas purchasers. Its cautious business practices eventually drew criticism from activist farmers like Partridge.

The GGGC began to diversify in 1912, acquiring its first terminal elevator at Fort William, starting a farm-supply business, leasing the country elevators owned by the Manitoba government since 1910, and beginning to build elevators in Saskatchewan and Alberta. It developed close relations with the Alberta Farmers' Co-operative Elevator Company created in 1913, eventually leading to the merger of the two organizations in 1917 under the name United Grain Growers (UGG). The GGGC brought into the merger 60 elevators in Manitoba and Saskatchewan (additionally it operated 137 Manitoba government elevators), 133 coalsheds and flour warehouses, farm-supply warehouses (including one in Regina), terminal elevators, and of course the *Guide*.

The **SASKATCHEWAN CO-OPERATIVE ELEVATOR COMPANY** participated in the merger discussions, but declined to join with the other farmer organizations, preferring independence. By that time, Partridge and other radical farmers had broken with the GGGC, criticizing it as too conservative, too tied to existing interests, and insufficiently co-operative. While they moved on to other co-operative projects, the GGGC's successor organizations continued to develop as farmer-owned businesses. *Brett Fairbairn*

FURTHER READING: Rea, J.E. 1997. *T.A. Crerar: A Political Life.* Montreal: McGill-Queen's University Press; Knuttila, M. 1994. *"That Man Partridge": E.A. Partridge, His Thoughts and Times.* Regina: Canadian Plains Research Center.

GRAIN HANDLING AND TRANSPORTATION SYSTEM. The main task of the grain handling and transportation system (GHTS) is to get grain from field to final market destination. The main physical functions of this system are transportation, handling, storage, and processing (cleaning). On the prairies the main transportation infrastructures are roads and rail lines; in Saskatchewan, primary elevators are the main storage, handling and cleaning infrastructure. Changes in technology have greatly affected the nature of the GHTS. The development of the network of rail lines, which took place in the settlement period, was not a planned system but one that developed through competition between rival railway companies: the first was the **CANADIAN PACIFIC RAILWAY** (CPR), which was completed in Saskatchewan in 1884; others were the Canadian Northern Railway and the **GRAND TRUNK PACIFIC RAILWAY**. When these companies faced bankruptcy, they were taken over by the federal government and amalgamated into the **CANADIAN NATIONAL RAILWAY** (CNR), which also incorporated the Intercolonial, the Grand Trunk, and the National Transcontinental Railways. This meant there were only two railways competing for grain business.

When the prairies were first settled, the main means of grain movement from farm to elevator was by horse and wagon. Most farms, then as today, had to provide sufficient farm grain storage for almost their entire production, because they could not rely on the elevator system to be able to take their grain directly from the field. Storage space at grain elevators was used primarily to allow for loading several rail grain cars. Few primary grain elevators in the country were equipped to clean grain for export: this was carried out at port terminals. Most elevators, however, had small cleaners used to clean farmers' grain for seeding. There were over 100 grain companies that built elevators during the early years of settlement; however, most of these companies were small. Many of the main line companies were initially owned by American interests (e.g., **NATIONAL**, Federal, McCabe, **SEARLE**); the large Canadian companies were **N.M. PATERSON AND SONS**, **PIONEER** (Richardson and Sons), and **PARRISH AND HEIMBECKER**. While none of the American-owned companies exists today, all three Canadian companies are still in business.

The spacing of grain delivery points along the rail lines was to allow a farmer located furthest from the rail line to be able to deliver a load of grain by horse and wagon and return home in one day. The number of rail branch lines and elevators was suitable to 1900 technology; but sixty years later, with better roads and large trucks capable of hauling up to about 1,500 bushels of grain, as well as better railway power equipment and grain steel hopper cars instead of wooden boxcars, the rail and elevator system was overbuilt. What followed from the 1980s was the abandonment of rail branch lines and the replacement of decaying wooden elevators with larger inland cement terminals.

How the grain elevators and railways charged for their transportation, handling, cleaning and storage services became a key policy issue for farmers and hence for government, and it remains so today. The choice for government was (and is) to allow the free market to determine freight rates and elevator charges. In 1897 the federal government enacted the **CROW'S NEST PASS AGREEMENT**, which set a maximum rail freight rate for moving grain from delivery point to the lakehead ports of Fort William and Port Arthur (today Thunder Bay). This rate structure was later applied as well to West Coast movement of grains; but by the 1950s the railways claimed to be incurring losses. As the rate structure was distance-related, it was not possible for the railways to apply variable rates in order to provide an incentive for grain companies to carry out multiple car loadings

Inspecting grain.

SASKATCHEWAN ARCHIVES BOARD R-A2048

Empty grain wagons leaving the elevator, ca. 1913.

which would increase the efficiency in grain rail movement. What ensued was a deterioration in the rail line system and especially the fleet of rail cars required to move grain, as the railways refused to invest capital unless they were allowed to charge higher rates for moving grain, or unless the federal government compensated them for their losses.

The federal government initiated a series of commissions to investigate the situation and recommend solutions. These included: the MacPherson Royal Commission in the 1960s; the Hall Commission on Grain Handling and Transportation in 1975–77; the Snavely Commission on railway costing in 1975–77; and the Prairie Rail Action Committee, which was appointed to recommend on the undesignated rail lines from the Hall Commission. The Gilson Report on Western Grain Transportation came out in 1982; this led in 1983 to Bill C-155 and then to the Western Grain Transportation Act (WGTA), which came into effect on August 1, 1984. In 1985 there followed the G.C. Hall Report on the Committee of Inquiry on Crow Benefit Payment.

A political battle took place over maintaining the Crow Rate structure. Some farm groups (e.g., National Farmers Union) as well as some farmer-owned grain companies (e.g., **SASKATCHEWAN WHEAT POOL**) argued that the Crow rate was historic and was signed to remain in perpetuity. Other farm groups and grain companies supported a change in the freight rate structure, as they foresaw that the federal government would not provide the funding necessary to modernize the GHTS without allowing at least some increase in rail freight rates. It was the latter view that prevailed, and the WGTA was passed to replace the Crow Rate structure. The WGTA contained provisions to allow for the application of a lower freight rate than what was allowed under a

strictly distance basis. The CNR, **CARGILL** Grain, and Northern Sales applied for selected lower rates for the 1985–86 crop year. Following public hearings the application was disallowed, as CNR refused to disclose confidential information that was needed to substantiate the cost-efficiency gains claimed by the applicants.

Whereas under the WGTA rail freight rates were raised, the federal government took on the responsibility for sharing the increased cost of moving grain. The federal share was known as the Crow Benefit; it was initially set at $659 million, but the WGTA contained the provision that further rail cost increases would be shared jointly by the federal government and farmers. In 1992 the subsidy was worth approximately $720 million. It was clear politically that the federal government was looking for an excuse to get out of its obligations; the opportunity came about with passage of the General Agreement on Tariffs and Trade (GATT) in 1994, when the Liberal government claimed that the Crow Benefit was a subsidy to farmers and was not allowable under the new international trade agreement. The federal government passed Bill C-76 (Budget Implementation Act), which eliminated the WGTA and with it the Crow Benefit, placing grain transportation under the National Transportation Act; this left the farmer largely to pay for the entire freight cost.

In February 1995, the federal government introduced the Canadian Transportation Act (CTA), which redefined the regulatory framework on the prairies. The CTA replaced the Crow subsidy with regulated maximum freights (rate cap). The federal government provided a one-time compensation payment of $1.5 billion for farmers directly affected by the regulatory changes. The result of the change was that the cost to farmers of rail shipments more than doubled; the WGTA also allowed for the aban-

donment of rail branch lines. The general dissatisfaction with the "rate cap" system led to the federal government's Estey-Kroeger review in 1997-99, which resulted in the revision of the CTA in the form of Bill-34. The government replaced the rate cap with a revenue cap on grain shipment. This decision allowed the railways complete freedom to set rates as long as the total freight revenue is below the defined cap; it represented a complete change of philosophy toward the GHTS by the federal government and industry—from one of regulation over the freight rate structure to one of rate-setting freedom.

The allocation of rail grain cars has been another area of controversy historically. In the early settlement period farmers complained about collusion between the grain companies and the railways. These complaints led to several Royal Commissions, two of which in 1899 and 1904 led to the passage of the Manitoba Grain Act and later the Canada Grain Act, under which the Board of Grain Commission (today the Canadian Grain Commission) regulated certain aspects of the GHTS. The Manitoba Grain Act provided for the provision of a car order book that each railway agent had to keep. Previously farmers had complained that the railways discriminated against their loading their own grain cars, which many wanted to do to avoid paying the elevator companies storage and handling charges; the order book now allowed farmers to order cars on an equal footing with the grain elevator companies.

The delivery process was generally seen to be haphazard and inequitable. In 1941 the federal government introduced the mechanism of quota books, through which grain by type would be called for delivery, thus making the system more efficient and equitable. From that time to the present, numerous changes to the quota delivery system and method of calling in grain have occurred. The challenge has been to provide equitable treatment to farmers and to encourage greater efficiency. Throughout most of the period the **CANADIAN WHEAT BOARD** (CWB) had most of the power over rail car allocation, as it was responsible for the shipment of most of the grain produced on the prairies; this led to years of complaints by shippers of non-Board grains of discrimination over rail car allocation. Under Bill C-34 the CWB was required to tender a minimum of 25% of its primary grain deliveries and logistical services by a bidding process involving the grain companies. This process has led to further commercialization of the GHTS. The allocation system now in place is known as the Advance Ordering System; it allows for freight rate discounts for shippers who can commit to certain volumes or rail shipment in advance. There are also incentives for large unit trains: in 2002–03 over 60% of prairie grain was moved in unit trains of more than fifty cars.

The rail line network peaked in Saskatchewan at approximately 16,679 km; approximately 4,000 km have been abandoned. In 1975 there were 818 delivery points with one of more primary elevators; this number had declined to 455 delivery points by 1999, and 147 in 2004. There were 2,309 primary licenced elevators in 1975, but only 197 by 2004: this represents a decrease of over 90% in about thirty years. Primary elevator capacity was 5.1 million tonnes in 1975, 3.5 million tonnes in 1999, and 2.8 million tonnes in 2004. The road network consists of 26,100 km maintained by Highways and Transportation, and 159,000 km maintained by rural municipalities.

The ratio of grain handling to elevator capacity, which is a measure of the efficiency of the elevator/rail system, has improved from two to over five over the last twenty-five years. While the efficiency of this component of the system has improved, with fewer rail lines and fewer delivery points the transportation costs have shifted from railways and elevators to roads and trucks: it is therefore clear not clear whether the new system is overall less costly. The cheapest way to move grain over land is by rail, not truck; but roads have alternative uses whereas most branch lines on the prairies only served to move grain. Whether a GHTS under regulation versus one governed by market forces leads to greater efficiency and thus lower costs is also not clear: only time and effective cost studies of the evolving GHTS will tell.   *Gary Storey*

FURTHER READING: Fowke, V. 1957. *The National Policy and the Wheat Economy.* Toronto: University of Toronto Press; Storey, G.G. and S.N. Kulshreshtha. 1999. "Transportation and Marketing." In *Atlas of Saskatchewan.* Saskatoon: University of Saskatchewan Press.

GRAIN SERVICES UNION. The Grain Services Union was created in Saskatchewan in 1936; today it has 1,200 members across western Canada, working in agriculture and other sectors.

Many employees of the new **SASKATCHEWAN WHEAT POOL** were strong co-op supporters; they also believed they should co-operate as workers. Pool elevator agents tried in the early 1930s to form an association, but the **DEPRESSION** set back their organizing efforts. Finally, in late 1936 a group of Pool head office employees organized the Saskatchewan Wheat Pool Employees' Association (SWPEA).

Among its early accomplishments, SWPEA reversed the salary cuts of the Depression and bargained a pension plan in 1943 (the Canada Pension Plan did not exist until 1966, so without a company pension workers faced poverty in old age). Similarly, through the 1950s and 1960s SWPEA bargained basic working conditions such as the five-day work week, because Canada had no national labour standards until 1965.

Rank-and-file members wanted SWPEA to be more outspoken. In 1969 **BILL GILBEY** was hired as its new secretary-manager; he was a dedicated Communist who had organized relief-camp workers during the Depression. Gilbey joined SWPEA's battle against grain dust in the elevators. Dust-control equipment existed, but companies refused to acquire it; in the meantime, elevator workers were falling ill from breathing dust. In 1971, SWPEA and Wilbert Chambers, the elevator agent in Macrorie, overturned a workers' compensation board ruling that grain dust had not damaged his lungs. In 1973, the Pool agreed to install dust-elimination systems in some old and in all new elevators. By 1977, the

union's lobbying resulted in a federal commission of inquiry. Following the commission's report, the government ordered all grain companies to install dust-control units in 1981.

SWPEA renamed itself the Grain Services Union (GSU) in 1974, after Manitoba Pool Elevators employees had joined. In 1979, GSU led the first grain-elevator strike in the prairies, against Manitoba Pool Elevators. Western Canadian agriculture faced major changes in the 1980s and 1990s, and companies responded by cutting jobs and closing elevators. GSU members had never struck Saskatchewan Wheat Pool—a result of mutual respect. But in 1994 Pool management demanded major cuts to the collective agreement, and GSU members launched a twelve-day strike which successfully resisted most of management's demands. In 1999, GSU general secretary Hugh Wagner led a successful campaign to end special hours of work for elevator workers: as of February 1, 2001, unionized and non-unionized elevator workers were entitled to paid overtime and to the eight-hour day, after decades of having to work extra hours without pay. In 1999, GSU organized in Perdue the first industrial hog-barn in western Canada, and lobbied to include hog-barn workers under the **LABOUR STANDARDS ACT**.   *Adriane Paavo*

GRAND TRUNK PACIFIC RAILWAY. Constructed between 1905 and 1914, the Grand Trunk Pacific Railway served as a western extension to the Grand Trunk Railway that operated in Quebec, Ontario, and the northeastern United States. The 4,800-km rail line stretched from Winnipeg to Prince Rupert, via Melville and Edmonton, and provided Canada with an alternative transcontinental route to the **CANADIAN PACIFIC RAILWAY**. The Grand Trunk Pacific Railway was incorporated in 1903 as a subsidiary of the Grand Trunk Railway. Both the Canadian Pacific Railway and Canadian Northern Railway had extensive networks of branch and feeder lines across the prairies. In order to compete with these companies and provide much-needed rail service to the west, the Grand Trunk Pacific Railway spanned the prairies and crossed British Columbia to reach the Pacific Coast. The main branch passed through southern Saskatchewan following a northwesterly course, with Melville and Biggar its two main divisional points. The railway entered Saskatchewan from Manitoba just southeast of Spy Hill, and progressed through Melville, Watrous, Biggar, and on to Edmonton. At Melville, branch lines went north to Canora, southwest to Regina, and further south through Weyburn to the Saskatchewan-United States border. An additional branch continued west from Regina through Moose Jaw. Branch lines also broke away from the main line at Young, going north to Prince Albert, and at Biggar, where additional lines went south to Calgary and north to Battleford.

In September 1994, members of the Grain Services Union marched the picket line in the first-ever strike at the Saskatchewan Wheat Pool.

By 1920 the Grand Trunk Pacific Railway had extensive operations in Saskatchewan, with 97 depots, 138 loading platforms, 23 warehouses, and 50 stockyards. When completed on April 9, 1914, the Grand Trunk Pacific Railway had more than 1,800 km of track in Saskatchewan. Several Saskatchewan communities along the main line bear the names of Grand Trunk Pacific Railway executives: Biggar is named for the Railway's general counsel William H. Biggar; Melville for president Sir Charles Melville Hays; and Watrous for vice-president and general manager Frank Watrous Morse. An unexpected drop in western Canadian rail traffic—owing to a world-wide economic depression and a slowdown in western Canadian immigration during **WORLD WAR I**— and high construction costs ultimately led to the demise of the Grand Trunk Pacific Railway. With its parent, the Grand Trunk Railway, it eventually went bankrupt and in 1919 the federal government nationalized the troubled company. By 1923, the Grand Trunk Pacific Railway, the Grand Trunk Railway, and the National Transcontinental merged with the Canadian Northern Railway to form the new **CANADIAN NATIONAL RAILWAY**.   *Iain Stewart*

FURTHER READING: Mika, N. and H. Mika. 1972. *Railways of Canada: A Pictorial History.* Toronto: McGraw-Hill Ryerson; Talbot, F.A. 1912. *The Making of a Great Canadian Railway: The Story of the Search for and Discovery of the Route.* London: Seeley, Service & Co.

GRANT, GORDON BURTON (1910–2001).

Gordon Grant was born in Regina on September 13, 1910. He received a BA from the **UNIVERSITY OF SASKATCHEWAN** in 1933, and with his wife Eileen had three children, Donald, Sharon, and Linda. Grant worked as an insurance broker and was president of Walter M. Logan Company. He was active in the Regina community and became the first native-

Gordon Grant.

born mayor of Regina in 1952. Following his years on the Regina City Council, Grant was elected to the Saskatchewan Legislature in 1964, 1967, and 1971 as a Liberal candidate for Regina Whitmore Park. He served as Minister of Highways and Transportation from 1964 to 1966, and as Minister of Industry and Commerce until 1967. Grant also served as Minister in charge of SaskPower Corporation and Minister of Telephones, and held the portfolio for Public Health from 1966 to 1971. During his tenure as Minister of Public Health, the Liberal government introduced utilization or deterrent fees for hospital and medical services in what has been referred to as the Black Friday Budget. Grant also oversaw the decision to close eleven rural hospitals. Following the defeat of the Liberal government in 1971, Grant served as Opposition whip from 1971 to 1975. He retired to Kelowna, BC, and died on January 16, 2001.

Roberta Lexier

FURTHER READING: Eisler, Dale. 1987. *Rumours of Glory: Saskatchewan and the Thatcher Years.* Edmonton: Hurtig Publishers; Grant, Gordon. Papers. R45. Saskatchewan Archives Board, Regina.

GRASSES AND GRASSLANDS, NATIVE. The

native grasslands of Saskatchewan are part of the Grassland Biome that once stretched from the prairie provinces as far south as Mexico. These grasslands developed under the influence of major interacting forces: climate, fire, and large grazing animals. The typical grassland climate is characterized by a strong early summer peak in precipitation, a pronounced moisture deficit in late summer, precipitation/evaporation ratios of less than 1.0, and periodic droughts. In Saskatchewan, grassland composition changes in moving from the relatively hot, dry southwest to the northeast, which has similar precipitation but lower temperatures and less evaporation. The typical soil that developed under grassland vegetation is the Chernozem type, with organic matter accumulation in the black or brown A horizon. Grassland ecosystems are composed of plant communities, along with animals, microorganisms, and environmental factors, all of which interact. Grassland plant communities are dominated by grasses and graminoids (grass-like plants such as sedges). Trees are absent from climatically determined grassland (steppe), but small shrubs (half-shrubs) can be common. Non-graminoid herbaceous plants (forbs) are also present in grasslands, and sometimes are seasonally dominant. *Prairie* is a term generally considered synonymous with *grassland*. Parkland is a mixture of grassland and scattered clumps of trees that occurs in the transitional region between grassland and forest.

The first written description of Saskatchewan grassland is that of **HENRY KELSEY**, an employee of the Hudson's Bay Company who traveled from York

Factory as far inland as the Canadian prairies in 1690 and 1691. Passages from his journal, some written in rhyme, describe encounters with bison and plains grizzly bears. On August 20, 1691, he wrote: "Today we pitch to ye outermost Edge of ye woods. This plain affords Nothing but short round sticky grass a Buffillo & a great sort of Bear wch is Bigger than any white bear & is Neither White nor Black But silver haired..." Fur trade post journals made frequent reference to wildfires in the grasslands, and to the large number of bison and other wildlife species. For example, October 30, 1836, at Carlton House: "Indians indicate that plains are burnt to a very great extent and that buffalo are very far off." Captain John Palliser (*see* **PALLISER AND HIND EXPEDITIONS**), exploring the Canadian prairies in 1857–59, described the region as "bare and arid, with the herbage of the plains nearly worthless, and buffalo very numerous, and have eaten the grass down considerably, and have not left much for the horses." Although these early descriptions of the grassland region provide evidence of the important role played by fire, climate and grazing, the scientific study of grasslands did not begin until the 20th century, with the development of the discipline of ecology.

Some of the earliest work on grassland ecology in Saskatchewan was done by **ROBERT T. COUPLAND**, professor of Plant Ecology at the **UNIVERSITY OF SASKATCHEWAN** (1948–2002). His classification of the natural grasslands of the prairie provinces remains in widespread use. He directed the Matador Project (1967–72), which involved an interdisciplinary team of ecologists and other scientists working under the International Biological Programme, and analysed the structure and functioning of a grassland ecosystem east of Kyle, Saskatchewan. Coupland continued to contribute to the understanding of grassland ecosystems in Canada and abroad well into the 1990s.

Grasses have growing buds located at or just below the soil surface, protecting them from removal by grazing animals and fire, and from desiccation. Grasses are classified by height: short grasses (< 0.3 m), mid-grasses (0.3-1.0 m), and tall grasses (>1.0 m). They are also separated on the basis of growth habit into perennial bunchgrasses, perennial sod-forming grasses, and annual grasses. Species differ in the optimum temperature for plant processes such as photosynthesis. Warm-season grass species do best at temperatures about 10°C higher than cool-season species, and therefore grow during the warmer part of the growing season, or on warmer sites within the landscape (e.g., south-facing hillsides). Each plant species in a grassland community fits into a particular niche (i.e., it has its own place in time, space or functional relationships relative to other species). A single grassland community can have as many as two dozen plant species. Grassland plant species have well-developed root sys-

ROBERT E. REDMANN PHOTO

Fescue grassland in the Cypress Hills.

tems. Up to 80% of the plant biomass (weight of material produced by plants) is found below ground. The biomass of consumer and decomposer organisms is also concentrated below ground: much of the structure and functioning of grassland ecosystems is therefore hidden away beneath the soil surface. Species in the same community can have different niches, based on depth of rooting: some species have roots as deep as two metres, others have roots concentrated near the surface.

Grassland climate and vegetation favour fire. Plant growth during moist parts of the growing season produces herbage growth that dies back during dry periods, yielding a fine fuel. Before settlement the area of continuous flammable vegetation could be huge, especially during late summer and fall, as well as in dry years. Thunderstorms, sometimes with "dry" lightning (a large number of strikes, but low precipitation) ignited fires. There was also deliberate burning by Aboriginal peoples to improve grassland for forage or to drive game. Some grasses are more sensitive to fire than others: rough fescue, for instance, is sensitive because its buds are located higher than most grass species. Burning reduces the cover of woody species, which have their buds well above ground. In moister grasslands, fire can increase primary productivity by destroying heavy cover of dead plant residue (litter or mulch). In some cases, burning increases forb cover by removing excess mulch. Fire produces a fertilizer effect in some communities by releasing nutrients tied up in litter, and by producing conditions favourable for nitrification. Fire also has negative effects. Although most mineral nutrients are deposited in the ash, nitrogen compounds are subject to distillation and loss at temperatures reached during the fire. Fire can lower the water infiltration into soils due to the removal of litter and humus, and thus increase runoff and erosion. Burned sites have higher soil temperatures because the blackened surface absorbs radiation. Removal of the litter layer leads to drying of the soil surface. Burned sites have reduced snow-trapping in winter, and this also causes drier soil conditions.

Mixed Prairie is the largest grassland association in Saskatchewan and in North America. It extends from the prairie provinces to Texas, between Tall Grass Prairie in the east and the Rocky Mountains in the west. In western Canada it is bordered on the north by Aspen Parkland and Fescue Prairie. Mixed grassland is drier than Tall Grass Prairie and Fescue Prairie. The major proportion of precipitation comes in spring and early summer; late-season drought is typical. Mid-grasses dominate in wet periods of climatic cycles, short grasses in dry periods (the mixture of short and mid-grasses gives Mixed Prairie its name). Grazing also causes Mixed Grassland to shift toward dominance by shorter grasses and other species that increase with grazing (e.g., pasture sage, *Artemisia frigida*). There is often strong variation in species composition over the landscape, depending on topography, slope position, and substrate. Dozens of forb species, many with attractive flowers, can be found throughout the Grassland; prairie crocus (*Anemone patens*) is a favourite early-spring forb.

The composition of Mixed Grassland in Saskatchewan changes from the moister northeast to the drier southwest. Moist Mixed Grassland on loamy soil is dominated by northern wheatgrass (*Agropyron dasystachyum*) and western porcupine grass (*Stipa spartea* var. *curtiseta*). To the southwest, dominance of the grassland community shifts to needle-and-thread (*Stipa comata*), blue grama (*Bouteloua gracilis*), and western wheatgrass (*Agropyron smithii*). A mat of low clubmoss (*Selaginella densa*) is typical of dry Mixed Prairie. The driest part of the Mixed Prairie is found north and south of the **CYPRESS HILLS**. Grasslands in sand-hills, located in several parts of the province, are dominated by needle-and-thread, blue grama, and sand reed grass (*Calamovilfa longifolia*). Clayey soils like those on the Regina Plain and in the Rosetown-Elrose district support a distinctive grassland made up of northern wheatgrass and Junegrass (*Koeleria macrantha*). This grassland type has virtually disappeared because of widespread cultivation.

Fescue Prairie extends from the eastern foothills of the Rocky Mountains through central Alberta and Saskatchewan. It is also prominent at elevations above Mixed Prairie in the Cypress Hills. Fescue Prairie is the most typically Canadian of all the grassland associations, with only limited distribution in the United States. The climate is cooler and moister than in Mixed Prairie, and the ratio of precipitation to evaporation is relatively low: for example, the precipitation/evaporation ratio at Saskatoon (northern edge of the Mixed Prairie) is 0.35; at Prince Albert (in the Parkland) it is 0.65. The dominant grass in Fescue Prairie in Saskatchewan is plains rough fescue (*Festuca hallii*), which has a weaker bunch growth habit than mountain rough fescue (*Festuca campestris*), which occurs in the Rocky Mountain foothills. Common associates are awned wheatgrass (*Agropyron subsecundum*),

ROBERT E. REDMANN PHOTO

Wheatgrass-Junegrass grassland at the Matador Field Station east of Kyle, Saskatchewan. The area in the foreground was protected from grazing for 25 years. The low shrub is winterfat (*Eurotia lanata*), which decreases with grazing.

western porcupine grass (*Stipa spartea* var. *curtiseta*), and Hooker's oatgrass (*Helictotrichon hookerii*). Idaho fescue (*Festuca idahoensis*), timber oatgrass (*Danthonia intermedia*), and shrubby cinquefoil (*Potentilla fruticosa*) are associates in the Cypress Hills; slender wheatgrass (*Agropyron brachycaulum*), mat muhly (*Muhlenbergia richardsonis*), and sedges (*Carex stenophylla* and *C. pensylvanica*) are associated species in the Parklands. The diversity of forb species can be very high. Aspen (*Populus tremuloides*) forms groves, usually around wet depressions in the landscape.

Human settlement, particularly agricultural cultivation starting in the late 1800s, drastically reduced the area of natural grasslands in Saskatchewan. Even prior to this, over-hunting of large herbivores like the bison as well as other human activities had started the disintegration of the Grassland Biome. The Fescue Prairie has been reduced to less than 5% of its original area; only about 25% of the original Mixed Prairie of Saskatchewan survives today. Nearly all grassland on arable soils has been ploughed up: the wheatgrass-Junegrass type, for example, has been almost obliterated. Most remaining grasslands are in hilly terrain and on sandy, rocky or saline soils that are unsuitable for cultivation. Relatively large areas of native grassland can still be found in southwestern Saskatchewan, notably in Grasslands National Park and the Cypress Hills. Many parks, wildlife refuges, community pastures, and ecological reserves, as well as private land throughout the province contain native grasslands. Restoration ecologists are improving their ability to re-establish native grassland species in areas where the original grassland has been destroyed. Natural grasslands are important economically for grazing by domestic livestock, as wildlife habitat, and for the preservation of species diversity. The discipline of range management aims at balancing grazing and other uses of native grasslands in order to maintain grassland health and productivity. The complete exclusion of grazing and fire can lead to excessive litter build-up and cause the degradation of grassland. The invasion of exotic plant species such as brome grass (*Bromus inermis*) is another threat. Grassland conservation efforts like the Prairie Conservation Action Plan have expanded greatly in recent years as people appreciate more fully the value of their natural grassland heritage. *Robert E. Redmann*

FURTHER READING: Coupland, R.T. 1992. *Natural Grasslands: Introduction and Western Hemisphere. Ecosystems of the World 8A.* Amsterdam: Elsevier; Romo, J.T. 2003. "Reintroducing Fire for Conservation of Fescue Prairie Association Remnants in the Northern Great Plains," *Canadian Field-Naturalist* 117: 89–99; Trottier, G.C. 2002. *Conservation of Canadian Prairie Grasslands.* Edmonton: Environment Canada.

GRASSHOPPERS. Grasshoppers belong to the insect order Orthoptera ("straight wing"), a group whose major characteristic is long hind legs, adapted for jumping. Another distinguishing feature is the presence of short antennae; this separates the order from a related order, Grylloptera (crickets, katydids, mole crickets and camel crickets), sometimes confusingly referred to as the "long-horned" grasshoppers. They have incomplete metomorphosis, with eggs giving rise to wingless nymphs, then to winged adults. In Saskatchewan and neighbouring provinces the most common orthopteran family is Acrididae, which is dominated by three major subfamilies: Oedipodinae (banded-winged grasshoppers), Gomphocerinae (slant-faced grasshoppers), and Melanoplinae (spine-breasted grasshoppers). Collectively these comprise approximately eighty different species that vary in shape, size, colour, and behaviour. Most species belonging to the first two subfamilies are noticeable by their distinctive sounds or vivid "flash" wing colorations displayed during courtship. These features, along with morphology, help to identify particular species. In contrast, members of Melanoplinae are virtually silent, and species are generally identified by examining male genitalic characters. Diets also vary. A few species such as the sage grasshopper, *Hypochlora alba*, feed almost exclusively on one plant genus, *Artemisia* in this case. Most grasshoppers, however, are mixed feeders, with some (e.g., the migratory grasshopper, *Melanoplus sanguinipes*) showing a preference for leafy plants and others (e.g., the clear-winged grasshopper, *Camnula pellucida*) for grasses. The majority of species (e.g., the migratory grasshopper) overwinter as eggs; a few (e.g., the speckled rangeland grasshopper, *Arphia conspersa*) as nymphs.

The migratory grasshopper, two-striped grasshopper (*Melanoplus bivitattus*), Packard's grasshopper (*Melanoplus packardii*), and clear-winged grasshopper are routinely counted among five major grasshopper pests on the prairies; in outbreak years they cost tens of millions of dollars in annual crop damage. In the 19th century, this list included the legendary Rocky Mountain grasshopper, *Melanoplus spretus*, whose numbers in 1877 were estimated in the trillions. The species' extinction in 1902, an unprecedented phenomenon in the history of agriculture, remains a mystery—although a plausible explanation centres on the destruction of egg-laying habitats in riparian areas (their preferred oviposition habitat), brought about by the introduction of agriculture. Grasshopper outbreaks occur approximately every ten to twelve years, with some local infestations lasting a few years. The Research Branch of Agriculture and Agri-Food Canada, together with their provincial counterparts, regularly monitor grasshopper infestations and produce annual reports and maps (on their web-site) that predict levels of risk for different regions of the prairies. This is a complex exercise that takes into account factors both abiotic (e.g., weather, snow cover, moisture levels) and biotic (e.g., last year's numerical abundance, resource availability).

Despite economic concerns, there is an increasing awareness of the role of grasshoppers as grazing herbivores in grassland communities. As part of the prairie landscape, many nesting birds (e.g., burrowing owl, horned lark, American kestrel, and Swainson's hawk) and small mammals (e.g., mouse, shrew, vole, Richardson's ground squirrel) include grasshoppers in their daily diets. While grasshopper control may be necessary from an agricultural viewpoint, eradication of this important and fascinating group of insects could have untold

OWEN OLFERT PHOTO/AGRICULTURE AND AGRI-FOOD CANADA

Migratory grasshopper life cycle.

effects on the prairie landscape. In certain societies, grasshoppers are consumed as food; some keep them as pets. Grasshoppers have even been personified in literature and poetry. In Regina, a large metal sculpture of "Reginald the Grasshopper," designed by prairie artist **WILF PERRAULT**, adorns the corner of Albert Street and Leopold Crescent.

William Chapco

FURTHER READING: Chapman, R.F. and A. Joern (eds.). 1990. *Biology of Grasshoppers*. New York: J. Wiley and Sons; Cranshaw, W. 1992. *Pests of the West: Prevention and Control for Today's Garden and Small Farm*. Golden, CO: Fulcrum.

GRASSICK, JAMES (1868–1956). James Grassick was born at Fergus, Ontario, on March 2, 1868. At the age of 14, he arrived with his father in what was about to become Regina. In 1885 he was the youngest of 100 teamsters hauling supplies to Prince Albert during the **NORTH-WEST RESISTANCE**. He would later be active in its veterans' association. Grassick was active in many lines of business, from hauling milk and running a livery to founding the Capital Ice Company. In 1897 he married Jessie Ann Beattie, from Ontario. They had three children. Grassick held nearly every civic office in Regina, from the Exhibition, school, and hospital boards to two terms as mayor (1920–22, 1940–41). He was a founding member and long-time office holder of Knox Presbyterian Church. In 1929 Grassick was elected as a Conservative to the Saskatchewan Legislature. **CONSERVATIVE PARTY** leader Dr. **J.T.M. ANDERSON** formed a "Co-operative government" with the support of Progressive and Independent MLAs. A partisan Tory, Grassick opposed the creation of an independent civil service commission and at times voted against his own government's

SASKATCHEWAN ARCHIVES BOARD R-A3591

James Grassick.

legislation. In 1934, like every other member of the Co-operative government, Grassick was defeated. He died in a traffic accident on August 4, 1956.

Peter A. Russell

GRASSLAND: *see* **GRASSES AND GRASS-LANDS, NATIVE**

GRASSLANDS NATIONAL PARK. Grasslands National Park consists of two blocks. The West Block is based in the **FRENCHMAN RIVER** Valley, and the East Block in the Killdeer Badlands of the Wood Mountain Uplands, along the 49th parallel. The area is characterized by a mixed short grass prairie, intersected by coulees with exposed hillsides and shrubby vegetation protected in places from the strong winds. Some low-lying areas support wetland meadows. The major grass species are blue grama, needle-and-thread, and western wheatgrass. There are myriad native wildflowers.

The short grass prairie is home to a number of animal species, some of which are prairie specialists. The most obvious are such large mammals as the pronghorn and coyote, as well as the black-tailed prairie dog, which is found only here in Canada. Birds such as ferruginous hawk, burrowing owl, sage grouse and other dry grasslands birds, are seen. The threatened Western rattlesnake is known to have a number of denning sites in the coulee slopes and can be seen in the summer moving across the prairie as it hunts small rodents.

The short-grass prairie habitat was once of considerable expanse in southern Saskatchewan. During the plowing of the prairie for agriculture, it was broken up into smaller blocks and began to be greatly reduced. With the breaking of the prairie, the complex plant communities were replaced by single-species crops, along with attendant European weed species. This loss of the plants meant the loss of many herbivorous insects and rodents, with attendant loss of the carnivores. In 1956, the Saskatchewan Natural History Society recommended the establishment of a National Park to preserve remnants of this grasslands ecosystem. In 1981, Canada and Saskatchewan agreed to establish Grasslands National Park; final agreement was signed in 1988. Land acquisition continues by purchase on a willing seller/willing buyer basis. The planned park, on completion, will encompass 900 km². The effectiveness of the conservation of the short-grass prairie is increased by programs of several other bodies to purchase adjoining remnants of prairie, and by property owners willing to retain lands in their natural state or to reclaim land by seeding with natural species. The establishment of the park also affords protection to the fossil sites in the area, where dry conditions and exposed hillsides allow access to the Cretaceous seabed and shoreline strata.

Diane Secoy

FURTHER READING: 2000. *Grasslands National Park Field Guide*. Prairie Wind and Sage–Friends of Grasslands National Park.

GRAVELBOURG, town, pop 1,187, located SW of **OLD WIVES LAKE** at the junction of Hwys 43 and 58. Gravelbourg was founded by Father Louis-Joseph-Pierre Gravel (1868–1926), a missionary colonizer, and his five brothers and a sister who settled at the location in 1906. On behalf of both the Canadian government and the Roman Catholic Church, Fr. Gravel encouraged Francophones in eastern Canada and New England to come west. With the arrival of the railway in 1913 the community developed rapidly, attaining town status on November 1, 1916. Although settlers of various origins (including German Lutherans and Irish Catholics) would settle in the community over the years, Gravelbourg developed over the next decades as a bastion of both the French culture and the Roman Catholic Church in Saskatchewan. In 1918, the Convent of Jesus and Mary and the **COLLÈGE MATHIEU** were built, followed in 1919 by the construction of the cathedral, which has a seating capacity of over 1,500. More recently, the Centre Culturel Maillard, constructed in 1985, was established to ensure the preservation of the community's French language and culture; it houses a French language bookstore, as well as the offices of the Association Communautaire Fransaskoise de Gravelbourg and the Association Culturelle Franco-Canadienne de la Saskatchewan. With over 100 businesses, Gravelbourg remains a service centre for the surrounding agricultural region, which produces staple crops such as **WHEAT**, durum, and **BARLEY**, as well as pulse crops such as peas and lentils. Gravelbourg has a professional French Canadian dance ensemble, *Danseurs de la Rivière de la Vieille*, and in 2003 the CRTC approved the licencing of Gravelbourg's first francophone community radio station. Several of the community's buildings have been designated heritage properties. The cathedral, the former convent school, the Bishop's residence, the post office, the court house, and the Canadian Northern Railway station are notable community landmarks, and a completely restored 1946 theatre houses two of the oldest movie projectors in Saskatchewan.

David McLennan

GREAT DEPRESSION. The province of Saskatchewan experienced extreme hardship during the Great Depression of the 1930s. **GRASSHOPPERS**, **HAIL** and **DROUGHT** destroyed millions of acres of wheat. The drought caused massive crop failures, and Saskatchewan became known as a **DUST BOWL**. The term "Dirty Thirties" described the prairies, creating pessimistic perceptions and negative stereotypes about life in Saskatchewan. In 1928, the net farming income was $363 million; by 1933, it dropped to $11

Drifted soil near Cadillac, 1937: a common sight during the Great Depression.

million; and by 1937, two-thirds of the farm population of Saskatchewan was destitute. Relief costs for the Saskatchewan government escalated to $62 million, which was higher than its total revenues. At least 250,000 people left the prairie provinces between 1931 and 1941. While the federal and provincial governments struggled to address the desperate conditions of poverty and unemployment in Saskatchewan, aid came from across the country. Media accounts alerted the rest of Canada to the hardships faced by farmers: photographs of massive dust storms, huge Russian thistles, and the bleached bones of Saskatchewan cows dominated Canadian newspapers.

Local Girl Guide and Boy Scout organizations helped Winnipeg citizens collect clothing to send to Saskatchewan; carloads of cheese and codfish were shipped to the province from the east coast by rail car; canned goods arrived from Niagara Falls and Aylmer, Ontario; carloads of canned milk, apples, turnips, and fish were sent from the Maritimes. The federal government ordered 100 railway cars filled with fruit from the Annapolis Valley, and 35 cars of fish from Halifax were sent to Saskatchewan communities. Newspapers carried human-interest stories about the generosity of Canadian citizens; journalists compared the arrival of the goods in rural communities to being like Christmas for the families. Almost every community received one or more railway cars of food through government relief schemes, the churches, and volunteer donations. Of great interest to the Canadian public were the photographs and descriptions of conveyances used to collect the supplies from the railway stations: "**BENNETT BUGGIES**," baby buggies, old cars, wheelbarrows, wagons—anything that could be started, rolled, or pushed delivered goods to the homes of over 1,000 Saskatchewan families.

The **ROYAL COMMISSION ON DOMINION-PROVINCIAL RELATIONS** stated that although the Great Depression caused severe repercussions for each province, the conditions were the most disastrous in Saskatchewan, which was described as the most economically vulnerable area in Canada. It indicated

that the Dominion of Canada was responsible for not protecting farmers during the financial conditions that led to the Stock Market crash in 1929, as the drop in demand for Canadian grain and other products had devastated the economy of Saskatchewan. Lack of trade with the rest of the Western world greatly affected Saskatchewan's export-oriented economy. The Canadian government asked for a reciprocity arrangement with the United States, only to be met with higher trade tariffs as the American government imposed barriers to protect its own economy. While the federal government attempted to salvage national and international relationships in the aftermath of the Depression, individuals and communities in Saskatchewan demanded a stronger voice in the political issues that most concerned them.

The Great Depression altered the way westerners viewed the federal and provincial governments, and in the late 1930s the **CO-OPERATIVE COMMONWEALTH FEDERATION** (CCF) became a prominent "voice of the people" in Saskatchewan. It insisted on protection for the family farm, supported organized labour, and demanded insurance programs to cover illness, old age, accidents, and unemployment. The CCF believed that the whole of society should benefit from economic gain, rather than the few interests which controlled the capitalist system. In its **REGINA MANIFESTO**, the CCF demanded equal opportunity for all citizens, basic level of services, and equal access to the market place. Its subsequent representation in Saskatchewan and in Ottawa gave rise to political change in Canada: at least for the time being, all provinces and municipalities without economic sustainability expected that federal and provincial governments would help them cope with economic hardships.   *Elizabeth Mooney*

GREAT SAND HILLS (50°30'N, 109°00'; map sheet 72 K/11). The Great Sand Hills cover an area of 1,911 square km. They are situated about 50 km west of Swift Current in a triangular region defined by the **TRANS-CANADA HIGHWAY** to the south, the **SOUTH SASKATCHEWAN RIVER** to the north, and Highway 21 to the west. If many travelers seeking

the Sand Hills have difficulty finding them, it is perhaps because active sand dunes represent only about 0.5 % of the total area. They comprise the largest uninterrupted area of sand dunes in southern Canada, and are one of several areas of dune formation in southwest Saskatchewan. Most are parabolic sand dunes, derived from glaciofluvial and glaciolacustrine deposits that can reach 30 m between base and summit, although most rise less than 15 m above the surrounding plain. Most of the dunes are stabilized by vegetation, but active dunes are still migrating eastward as the wind pushes loose sand across their crest and over pre-established vegetation; thus, previously buried colonies of trembling aspen and ground juniper are revealed, as desiccated trunks emerge from displaced sand.

That the region has been used extensively by past indigenous nomadic societies is evidenced by the numerous finds made by archaeologists and, often, ranchers turned amateur archaeologists. Ranching has been central to the area's economy since Euro-Canadian settlement, partly as a result of many long-term Crown land leases; oil and gas exploration has also taken place for some time. Since the early 1990s, the Great Sand Hills have been the subject of numerous studies assessing the economic potential and impact of additional mineral resource development. An abundance of rare plants and animal species characterizes this ecologically sensitive region of more or less continuous deposits of unconsolidated sands. Some of these species, such as the ferruginous hawk, burrowing owl, and Ord's kangaroo rat, are threatened. Others, found in abundance elsewhere, have adapted well to this environment: they include mule deer, and the bank swallows that dwell in the sandy outcrops. How future stewardship will affect the Great Sand

Great Sand Hills.

Hills remains to be determined. Community involvement will help ensure that environmental considerations and the needs of the local population will be balanced in ways acceptable to all. The more immediate pressure might come from outside visitors wishing to extend their access to the Great Sand Hills beyond the small portion south of Sceptre that is currently open to the public. *Claude-Jean Harel*

FURTHER READING: David, P.P. 1993. "Great Sandhills of Saskatchewan: An Overview." Pp. 59–81 in D.J. Sauchyn (ed.), *Quaternary and Late Tertiary Landscapes of Southwestern Saskatchewan and Adjacent Areas*. Regina: Canadian Plains Research Center; Epp, H.T. and L. Townley-Smith (eds.). 1980. *The Great Sand Hills of Saskatchewan*. Regina: Saskatchewan Environment.

GREAT WESTERN BREWING COMPANY. The Great Western Brewing Company, located in Saskatoon, is Saskatchewan's sole continuing provincial brewing company. It was opened in 1928 by Hub City Brewing, and was later sold to Carling O'Keefe. Molson's took over the company as part of a merger with Carling O'Keefe in 1988, and decided to close the plant. A group of sixteen employees and management were determined to keep the brewery open; with assistance from the government, the employees (who acquired 80% of the equity) bought the facility and its assets from Molson in late 1989, and renamed the company the Great Western Brewing Company. In August 2002, Crown Investments Corporation (CIC) sold its interest in Great Western Brewing Company to three private investors for $4 million. The sixteen founding shareholders maintained a 20% share of the company and were given the option to maintain, increase, or sell their shares. Shares were also offered to employees who were not current shareholders. The compa-

Don Elash, one of Great Western Brewing Company's original shareholders, 1990.

ny currently has 80 employees, and markets beer throughout western Canada.

Great Western started with two initial brands, and expanded by 2004 to include eleven different brand names. The company has contracts with various marketers to produce beer and other beverages in the facility, and also sells other company's product lines for a commission. Great Western Brewery has been the recipient of a range of entrepreneurial and product awards, including the Saskatchewan Chamber of Commerce "Business of the Year" and "New Venture Awards" in 1991. The company has also won awards for its varieties of beer: Western Premium Light was a Gold Medal winner at the Midwest Brewers Festival in 1999 and a Bronze Winner at the 2000 World Beer Cup; Western Premium Lager was a Gold Medal winner at the Midwest Brewers Festival in 2000, and a 2001 Gold Medal winner at the Monde Selection in Belgium.

Jessica Pothier

GREAT WESTERN RAILWAY. The Great Western Railway (GWR) is one of a number of short-line railways that grew out of the closure of small country elevators and the desire by the main line railways to consolidate their systems. GWR began operations in September 2000 on four former CP branch lines in southwest Saskatchewan when Wescan Rail, a rail contracting company from Abbotsford, British Columbia, purchased these lines from CP. These were the Notukeu, Altawan, Shaunavon and Vanguard subdivisions—a total of 320 miles (514 km) of track. In 2002, GWR discontinued service on the 22-mile (35 km) portion of the Notukeu subdivision from Val Marie to Bracken, due to a lack of traffic; the line was then removed. GWR serves customers in the grain industry, primarily producer car loading sites, but also some remaining grain elevators and pulse crop facilities. It also handles some incoming traffic including fertilizer and corn. In 2003, Wescan Rail indicated it wished to sell the short line. A group of local investors including farmers and municipal governments formed a company to negotiate the purchase of the branch lines, so that GWR could remain in operation. *Paul Beingessner*

GREBES. Grebes (family Podicipedidae, order Podicipediformes) are small to medium-sized water birds with lobed toes on legs set far back on the body. Like in the loon, this leg position is efficient for swimming but makes the bird awkward on land. They feed on fish or other aquatic life. This is an ancient group of birds, known as fossils from 80 million years ago. The family of twenty species is found on all continents except Antarctica. Many species have elaborate courtship rituals of bobbing or dancing on the water surface. Of the seven species found in North America, six are found in Saskatchewan; they are all migratory.

Red-necked grebe (Podiceps grisegena).

Grebes are typically found in the larger sloughs and permanent waters of the southern half of the province; they may nest on the shore or construct colonies of floating nests of vegetation. There are three small grebes in the province: the pied-billed grebe (*Podilymbus podiceps*), with its brown body and small head, is distinguished by the vertical bar on its bill; the horned grebe (*Podiceps auritus*), with its large yellow patch at the side of the head and ruddy neck, can be seen throughout the province; and the closely allied eared grebe (*P. nigricollis*) has a thinner yellow patch on the cheek and a black neck.

Among the larger grebes we find the red-necked grebe (*P. grisgena*), which is often seen on the lakes and rivers of the centre of the province and is distinguished by the white cheek patch under the black cap as well as the rufous neck. The Western grebe (*Aechmophorus occidentalis*) and Clark's grebe (*A. clarkii*) are very similar in appearance, with grey bodies, long white necks and long bills. Clark's grebe has the white on the head extending above the eye, and a yellow rather than an olive-green bill. Because these last two species can be difficult to distinguish, their exact distribution in the province is not certain. *Diane Secoy*

FURTHER READING: Alsop, Fred J., III. 2002. *Birds of Canada*. New York: Dorling Kindersley.

GREEK COMMUNITY. Greek settlement in Saskatchewan dates back at least to the turn of the 20th century. Influential early pioneers of Greek origin in Saskatoon included Kostas Valaris in 1901, as well as Gus Thanagen and Gus Golf respectively in 1909 and 1910. The first permanent Greek settler in Regina was likely Gus Trihas in 1903, who ran a coffee shop and candy store. However, most early settlers of Greek origin arrived during the1930s. George Kangles in Regina and the Girgulis family in Saskatoon were particularly responsible for encouraging chain migration from the Peloppónnisos region (the southernmost region of mainland Greece), especially Kastri in Arkadia and later Nafplion in Argolis. "Uncle Bill" Girgulis owned the Elite Café in Saskatoon with his brothers Sam and James; Sam's wife Cleo, or "Nouna" (godmother), earned her nickname by participating in many baptisms. Throughout Canada, the Greek population increased substantially after **WORLD WAR II** due to crop failures, excessive taxation, escalating inflation, widespread unemployment, hunger, and continuing civil unrest in postwar Greece. In these years a large proportion of Greek immigrants were single males, who initially lived in shared apartments and rooming houses. Once established and employed in Canada, they were joined by women and children whom they sponsored.

Greeks tended to develop restaurants in Saskatchewan cities: there were more than forty Greek-owned restaurants in Saskatoon alone by the 1970s, most operated by relatives and/or immigrants from the same areas in Greece. Although these restaurant businesses were by definition competitive, they were largely established through the strong Greek tradition of mutual help. A close familial and geographical link prevailed in the Greek communities of Saskatoon and Regina. Greek restaurant owners eventually became investors in prime urban real estate, condominiums and apartment buildings, the stock market, and many business ventures. They tended to view the restaurant business as intermediary toward improving the financial and social status of the next generation. While the educational level increased with each generation—many second and third generation Greek-Canadians entered university—efforts were made to preserve the Greek cultural heritage in Canada: Greek language schools had been established in Saskatchewan cities by 1970, which served to familiarize the younger generation with Greek history, literature and drama, to teach non-Greek partners in mixed marriages, and to cement bonds between Greek children.

While Eastern Orthodox churches had long existed in Saskatchewan, specific Greek Orthodox congregations were not established in Regina until 1961, and in Saskatoon until 1964. In Regina a larger new church (St. Paul's) was constructed in 1976. In Saskatoon a former German Protestant church was purchased in 1976 through fund-raising by AHEPA (American Hellenic Educational Progressive Association). The first priest, Fr. Kakavalakis, himself an immigrant from Greece, held a conservative view of the traditional role of the church in the Greek community; he was replaced by a Canadian-educated priest, Fr. Nikolaou, who attempted to maintain age diversification in the parish rather than simply to cater to the now-elderly immigrants.

Services, which had originally been in ancient Greek, now accommodated an increasing demand for modern Greek and for English.

A chapter of AHEPA was established in Saskatoon in 1930. Through the 1980s differences between a more traditionalistic church and the more secular and modernistic AHEPA led to a split in the Greek community, with rival duplication of community services. The church had its Saturday "Greek school" and Sunday school, while AHEPA had its own language school. Both the church-oriented community and AHEPA organized separate pavilions at Folkfest for several years. The Women's Auxiliary of AHEPA (founded in 1938) had its counterpart in the Philoptochos Society ("friends of the poor") in the church. The AHEPA junior orders, the Sons of Pericles and Maids of Athena, had their counterparts in GOYA, the international Greek Orthodox Youth Association. While some more secular Greek-Canadians have tended to view as intrusive the church's efforts to become more involved in sociocultural aspects of the Greek community, the third generation have become more interested in compromise. By the 1960s the Saskatoon Greek Society had been founded. Today, meetings of Greek community organizations are usually conducted in English. A previously high degree of ethnic endogamy has gradually been replaced by increasing exogamy; in Saskatchewan this is to be expected, given the relatively small size of the Greek population compared to many other ethnic groups: approximately a thousand people claim Greek ethnicity in whole or part.

Alan Anderson

FURTHER READING: Gavaki, E. 1977. *The Integration of Greeks in Canada.* San Francisco: R&E Associates; Chimbos, P.D. 1980. *The Canadian Odyssey: The Greek Experiment in Canada.* Toronto: McClelland & Stewart.

GREEN, JOHN (1915–). A lawyer who pioneered automobile legislation, John Green was born in Yorkshire, England in 1915 and immigrated to Canada twenty years later. With law degrees from the **UNIVERSITY OF SASKATCHEWAN** and Berkeley, Green began his career with **SASKATCHEWAN GOVERNMENT INSURANCE OFFICE** in 1945 as a legal advisor. He drafted the Automobile Accident Insurance Act of 1945 and introduced the first compensation plan for personal injury regardless of fault. The Act would later develop into the first comprehensive insurance plan in North America. In 1973, he became general manager of SGIO, a position he held until his retirement seven years later. Green's accomplishments are even more remarkable considering he was visually impaired. In recognition of his efforts, Green was named a Member of the Order of Canada in 1980 and received the Saskatchewan Order of Merit in 1998.

GREEN CERTIFICATE PROGRAM. The Green Certificate is an on-farm training program in agricultural production and management. The program's objectives are to create awareness among farm managers of the importance of human resource development, to train individuals to fill competently key roles in the farming industry, and to provide a means of certifying the achievement of skills through formal testing. The program was brought into Saskatchewan in May 1995 thanks to the efforts of Walter Jess, then MLA for Redberry. Introduced as a pilot project, the Green Certificate Program has now been recognized in the province by the agricultural industry and Saskatchewan Education. After positive evaluations of a two-year pilot project in some communities and schools, the program was incorporated as a service offered by Saskatchewan Agriculture, Food and Rural Revitalization in 1997. The Green Certificate Program was initially administered through the Department's Sustainable Production Branch; as of July 2001, it became part of the Livestock Development Branch. As of September 2003, the classroom version of the Green Certificate (Agricultural Production Technician, APEC) has been accepted province-wide as an elective through the practical Applied Arts Curriculum in Grades 10–12. Saskatchewan Education reviewed and modified the Green Certificate Program in 1996-97 so that it can be used in Saskatchewan as agricultural courses in Grades 10–12. *Irene Attrux*

GREEN LAKE, northern village, pop 498, located 49 km NE of Meadow Lake at the junction of Hwys 55 and 155. Situated at the north end of a long, narrow lake from which it derives its name, Green Lake serves as a gateway to a number of communities further north. It is predominantly a Métis community with a history dating back to the late 1700s and the fur trade. In the 1870s, a Roman Catholic mission was established and an ox cart road was hewn from Fort Carlton on the North Saskatchewan River to Green Lake. From Green Lake freight could then be transported over water to Ile-à-la-Crosse, reducing the amount that had to come over the voyageur highway from **CUMBERLAND HOUSE**. Through Green Lake much pemmican that would fuel the northern fur brigades was transported. By the 1890s, Green Lake's population was steadily increasing and a post office was established in 1901. In the 20th century, farming and forestry began to dominate the Green Lake area economy. In 1939, the provincial government established farming operations to assist and train people in agriculture. In the 1940s, the **SISTERS OF THE PRESENTATION OF MARY** arrived to provide education and medical services. The Sisters also oversaw the running of a cannery, carpentry and sewing shops through which people could acquire trade skills. A sawmill was established at Green

Lake, becoming a major community employer. Green Lake was incorporated as a northern village in 1983. Today, there are two community-owned businesses: Green Lake Metis Wood Products Ltd., and Green Lake Metis Farms Ltd. Tourism is also an important, albeit seasonal, industry in the area, and there is an expanding cottage development at Green Lake. Green Lake faces several challenges as it moves forward into the 21st century. The population has been slowly falling and unemployment currently hovers around 20 per cent. *David McLennan*

Dorothy Greensmith.

GREENSMITH, DOROTHY (CA. 1890–1951). Born in England about 1890, Greensmith arrived in Canada in 1912 and settled in Regina, where she began to work in the provincial Treasury Department. In the 1920s she was working in the Attorney General's Department and studying law. She finished her legal studies at the **UNIVERSITY OF SASKATCHEWAN** in 1925, and was admitted to the bar that year. In the meantime she had begun to handle administration of soldiers' estates, doing so until the early 1930s (and again after **WORLD WAR II**). By the early 1930s she was a provincial Law Officer, remaining so until her death. In 1948 she was appointed a King's Counsel. Involved in the Civil Service Association, especially in its sports programs, Greensmith was an active member of the Regina Civil Service Tennis Club and of the Wascana Winter club. She was also concerned about women's rights and women's place in the community, and often spoke to women's organizations in the province. She died in Regina on May 20, 1951.
Ann Leger-Anderson

GREENWOOD ANDREWS, NELLIE (1864–1958). Nellie Greenwood Andrews, the first woman in Canada to receive a Bachelor of Science degree, was active in many women's organizations in Regina. Born Nellie Greenwood on April 21, 1864, in Farmington, Maine, she moved to Ontario with her family and in 1880 became the first woman stu-

dent to enroll in Victoria College. Graduating in 1884, she taught school before marrying Methodist minister Wilbur W. Andrews in 1887; they had three children. When the family moved to Sackville, New Brunswick, she taught at Mount Allison College for two years and served on the Board of Regents for four. The Andrews moved to Regina in 1911 when her husband was named head of the new Regina College. As President of the Saskatchewan W**OMEN'S CHRISTIAN TEMPERANCE UNION** from 1912 to 1917, she was a leader in the women's suffrage campaign—participating in debates, chairing the first meeting of the Provincial Equal Franchise Board, circulating petitions, and addressing the legislature on woman suffrage in 1915. In 1921, she was elected to the Regina Collegiate Board, the first woman in Saskatchewan elected to such a position. Andrews served in leadership positions in the local and provincial **COUNCILS OF WOMEN**, and was founding president of the University Women's Club in Regina. Her other activities included the Social Science Council of Saskatchewan, the Women's Musical Club, and the Women's Missionary Society of her church. She died in Regina on February 19, 1958.
Elizabeth Kalmakoff

GRENFELL, town, pop 1,067, located half-way between Regina and the Saskatchewan-Manitoba border at the junction of Hwys 1 and 47. A service centre for the surrounding farming community, Grenfell had its beginnings in 1882 as the first settlers began arriving in advance of the railroad. By the following spring, numerous shacks and tents dotted the townsite. The first settlers were mainly from the British Isles and eastern Canada; later, Germans would settle the Grenfell area. The post office was established in 1883, and the town's name honours Pasco du Pre Grenfell, a railway company official. Grenfell was incorporated as a village in 1894 and reached town status in 1911. Grenfell has a wide range of businesses, a significant number of which service the district's agricultural industry. The Grenfell Museum is located in a large Queen Anne revival-style house. The surrounding trading area has a population of approximately 6,000. Grenfell was the birthplace of **WILLIAM J. PATTERSON**, Premier of Saskatchewan from 1935 to 1944 and Lieutenant-Governor of the province from 1951 to 1958.
David McLennan

GREY OWL (ARCHIBALD STANSFIELD BELANEY) (1888–1938). Born in England on September 18, 1888, Archie Belaney became interested as a child in stories about North American Aboriginals. At 17, he came to Canada and lived with a group of Ojibwas in northern Ontario and learned their way of life; he claimed that he was the child of a Scotsman and an Apache woman, and began to use the name Grey Owl. He enlisted and

Grey Owl.

served in **WORLD WAR I**, then returned to Canada. In the early 1930s, he came to the recently established **PRINCE ALBERT NATIONAL PARK** to run a program on beaver conservation. The beavers, which had been the basis for the fur trapping industry in central Canada for centuries, had been greatly reduced in numbers. He wrote three popular books on the importance of maintaining the species: *Pilgrims of the Wild*, *The Adventures of Sajo and her Beaver People*, and *Tales of an Empty Cabin*. The public interest in his books and talks paved the way for programs stressing the importance of **CONSERVATION** of species and their habitats. Grey Owl died at Prince Albert on April 13, 1938. At his death, it was discovered that his claims of Native ancestry were false. For a number of years, the story of his subterfuge overshadowed the importance of his conservation work.
Diane Secoy

GREYEYES, DAVID G. (1914–96). A prominent Aboriginal athlete, soldier, and federal public servant, David Greyeyes was born on the Muskeg Lake Reserve on December 31, 1914. An outstanding serviceman with the Canadian Army during **WORLD WAR II**, Greyeyes earned several decorations including the Greek Military Cross for his efforts in the Italian campaign. Upon returning home, Greyeyes farmed with his family on the Muskeg Lake Reserve and became its chief in 1958. Two years later, he began his fifteen-year career with the federal public service. He held a number of senior positions within the Department of Indian and Northern Affairs, and was the first Indian to be named regional director of the department. In 1977, Greyeyes was inducted into the **SASKATCHEWAN SPORTS HALL OF FAME** and was named a Member of the Order of Canada. He received the Saskatchewan Order of Merit in 1993.

GREYSTONE MANAGED INVESTMENTS

(GMI). The Investment Corporation of Saskatchewan (ICS) was created from the privatization of the Finance Department's debt management unit in 1988. The company changed its name to Greystone Capital Management in 1994, and is now Greystone Managed Investments (GMI). The Regina-based investment firm initially had twenty-five Saskatchewan-based clients mostly represented through employee pension funds; currently with more than 700 clients from all over North America, it has offices in Edmonton and Winnipeg. Assets exceed $19.2 billion and Greystone Managed Investments boasts a spot among the top 4% of Canadian investment companies.

Greystone Managed Investments focuses on managing large and small business pension funds. Charities, workers compensation programs, pensions for private foundations, cultural organizations, religious orders and trade unions are under the GMI umbrella.

Employees own 55% of the company shares; the remainder is owned by the Saskatchewan Teachers' Fund, Saskatchewan Government Insurance Corp., and the Capital Pension Plan. *Elizabeth Mooney*

GROOME, ROLAND (1897–1935).

Regina's Roland Groome, born on July 10, 1897, was the first licensed commercial pilot in Canada: the Canadian Air Board (CAB) granted Groome his commercial license in April 1920. Groome enlisted in the Royal Air Force in March 1917 and completed his World War I service as a flying instructor at Camp Mohawk, Ontario. When he returned to Regina after the war, Groome and his plane attracted some atten-

Roland Groome.

COURTESY OF THE ROYAL SASKATCHEWAN MUSEUM
Sharp-tailed grouse.

tion by making the first delivery of a morning newspaper by air route in Canada. The *Morning Leader* was first delivered to Moose Jaw by air on May 27, 1919. A founding director of the Regina Flying Club (1927) and a popular instructor, Groome flew into northern Saskatchewan and throughout western Canada. Groome and one of his students were killed when they crashed near Regina on September 20, 1935. *James Winkel*

GROUSE AND ALLIES.

These chicken-like, ground-nesting birds with precocial young can be found in all regions of Saskatchewan. Grouse are members of the subfamily Tetraoninae, family Phasianidae, order Galliformes. There are seventeen species of grouse, distributed across North America, Europe, and northern Asia. Six species of grouse are currently found in this province: greater sage grouse, sharp-tailed grouse, ruffed grouse, spruce grouse, rock ptarmigan, and willow ptarmigan. Greater sage grouse (*Centrocercus urophasianus*), the largest grouse species in North America (total length: males: 65–75 cm, females: 50–60 cm), are found in silver sagebrush (*Artmesia cana*) communities of southwestern Saskatchewan. Males perform elaborate courtship displays on dancing grounds or leks. Populations have declined by 80% since 1987. Currently there are about 500 individuals in Canada, and the species is considered endangered. Sharp-tailed grouse (*Tympanuchus phasianellus*) (41–47 cm total length), the provincial bird, is most common in the grassland and parkland, but is also found in openings in the boreal forest. Males of this species perform courtship displays on leks. Provincial populations are thought to have declined as a result of cultivation of native grasslands. Ruffed grouse (*Bonasa umbellus*) (total length: males

43–50 cm, females: 40–43 cm) are found in poplar (*Populus* spp.) forests, and it has been introduced into the CYPRESS HILLS in southwestern Saskatchewan. Males beat their wings in a drumming display which is often performed from a stump or log. Ruffed grouse populations are cyclic, with peaks in abundance occurring every eight to eleven years. Spruce grouse (*Falcipennis canadensis*) (total length: 38–43 cm) are found in coniferous forests, typically jack pine or white spruce. Males perform aerial displays, usually in open areas of the forest between tree branches and the ground. Harvest estimates suggest that population cycles are correlated with those of ruffed grouse. Plumage is sexually dimorphic; males have blackish plumage, whereas females have brownish plumage. Willow ptarmigan (*Lagopus lagopus*) (total length: 35–45 cm) spend the breeding season in birch (*Betula*) or willow (*Salix*) shrub habitat. They migrate into the boreal forest of this province from the Northwest Territories during the winter. The rock ptarmigan (*L. mutus*) is a rare winter visitant to the area near LAKE ATHABASCA. Among the grouse species, only ptarmigan have a white plumage in the winter and have feathered feet. The red grouse and willow grouse found in Europe are of the same species as willow ptarmigan. Population cycles which peak approximately every ten years have also been recorded for this species.

Prior to 1880, the range of greater prairie chickens (*Tympanuchus cupido*) was contained only within the continental United States. However, in the late 1800s its range expanded into this province; by the turn of the century numbers started to decrease, and by the1970s this species was considered extirpated from Saskatchewan. Range expansion probably occurred from the increased availability of cultivated grain, which enhanced the winter survival of greater prairie chickens. Range contraction probably occurred as native prairie, the habitat used for nesting and brooding, decreased in the landscape. Several other species of gallinaceous birds have been introduced into the province for hunting. These are the ring-necked pheasant (*Phasianus colchius*) and gray partridge (*Perdix perdix*) from Europe, and the wild turkey (*Meleagris gallipavo*) from the east. Only the gray partridge, which is found throughout the southern half of the province, has large populations.   *Don McKinnon*

FURTHER READING: Alsop, F.J., III. 2002. *Birds of Canada*. New York: Dorling Kindersley.

GRUCHY, LYDIA E. (1894–1992). Lydia Emélie Gruchy was the first woman to be ordained in the United Church of Canada, the initial major denomination to affirm ordination of women. Born near Paris in 1894, and raised in France and England, she came with her family to Strasbourg, Saskatchewan, in 1913. She attended NORMAL SCHOOL, taught school, and in 1920 received her BA from the UNIVERSITY OF SASKATCHEWAN. In 1923 she graduated from Presbyterian Theological College (now St. Andrew's College) in Saskatoon. For thirteen years she served as a rural lay minister—at Verigin, Wakaw, and Kelvington. In 1926 she sought ordination in the newly formed United Church of Canada. She renewed the request repeatedly until 1936, when the United Church approved women's ordination. Having obtained a position on the staff of St. Andrew's United Church in Moose Jaw, she was ordained there on November 4, 1936.

She later served in national church administration and theological education in Toronto. Returning to Saskatchewan in 1943, she served pastoral charges at Naicam, Simpson, Cupar, and Neville until her retirement in 1962. In 1953 she became the first Canadian woman to receive the Doctor of Divinity degree, from St. Andrew's College. Gruchy died in British Columbia on April 9,1992. In 1994 the College established the Lydia Gruchy Chair of Pastoral Theology in her memory, and in 2003 the chapel at St. Andrew's United Church (Moose Jaw) was named the Lydia Gruchy Chapel. *Peter J. Calhoun*

FURTHER READING: Hallett, M. 1986. "Lydia Gruchy—The First Woman Ordained in the United Church of Canada," *Touchstone* 4 (1): 18–23.

GULL LAKE, town, pop 1,016, located 56 km SW of Swift Current at the junction of Hwys 1 and 37. It is believed the community's name is derived from explorer and naturalist JOHN MACOUN's translation of an Indian name for a small nearby lake (perhaps now dried up), which was frequented by gulls, and that surveyors for the railroad adopted this name for the area in 1883. The townsite of Gull Lake is situated on what was once part of the 76 Ranch, established in 1887. The 76 Ranch House, built in 1888, is one of southwestern Saskatchewan's oldest existing buildings. The 10,000-acre 76 Ranch at Gull Lake was one of several massive ranches established by Sir John Lister-Kaye's Canadian Agricultural, Coal and Colonization Company. By the early 20th century, however, the company was suffering financial losses and land was becoming more profitable for grain farming. In 1905 the Gull Lake block was sold to American millionaire developers, Conrad and Price; they surveyed the townsite and put up the lots for sale. Settlers began to pour in, and between 1906 and 1912 Gull Lake was booming. By 1911, the population was over 600 and the community attained town status. In 1912, Gull Lake had a well-established school, many businesses and services, a doctor, a hospital, and a newspaper, *The Gull Lake Advance*. Established in 1909, the paper is still in business. After the initial rush of settlers and the building boom, development levelled off and, in the early 1950s, the population was somewhat over 700. With the discovery of oil and gas in the region during the decade, Gull Lake's population jumped to over 1,000 and it has remained relatively stable since. Today, farming, ranching, and oil and gas form the basis of the economy; there are two massive grain handling facilities; and numerous oil pump jacks, gas wells, and battery sites dot the landscape. Wind power is another energy resource that is being developed in the Gull Lake area.

David McLennan

GULLS AND TERNS. Gulls are members of the cosmopolitan family Laridae, of the order Charadriiformes, along with the terns and jaegers. Saskatchewan has records of twenty-three members of the approximately 104 species worldwide. Members of the family are short-legged, short-necked, webbed-footed birds found around water, particularly on the coasts. They are ground nesters, often in colonies; the sexes have similar plumage. The gulls are typically grey-backed, white-bellied birds with strong bills, feeding on a variety of plant and animal material. The terns are also usually grey and white, with crests in breeding plumage, and long pointed bills used for catching small fish by diving into the water. In both groups the plumage of different species can be very similar, and they can be challenging to identify. The gulls have taken advantage of human habitats and are often very abundant around harbours, garbage dumps, and city lakes. They follow farm machinery, catching insects and small rodents startled up by the movement of the machinery. Most species are migratory in Saskatchewan, although some individuals may remain on open water over winter.

The common gulls are of two types: the black-headed and the white-headed. The black-headed gulls are Franklin's gull (*Larus pipixcan*), a common prairie species, and Bonaparte's gull (*L. philadelphia*), which nests in trees in the boreal regions and is a transient in the south. The most common white-headed gull is the ring-billed gull (*L. delawarensis*), named for its identifying characteristic. Other common gulls are the California gull (*L. californicus*) and the large herring gull (*L. argentatus*). The mew gull (*L. canus*) breeds in the north. Other regular transients are: the parasitic jaeger (*Stercorarius parasiticus*), a predatory gull-like bird; the very pale Iceland gull (*L. glaucoides*); and the glaucous gull (*L. hyperboreus*).

The terns are seen hovering and diving over

Franklin's gull.

large marshes, lakes and rivers. The common tern (*Sterna hirundo*) nests throughout the province, commonly on the islands and sandbars of the larger lakes, reservoirs, or rivers. Forster's tern (*S. forsteri*) is a very similar, but less common, bird seen around deeper-water marshes of the south; it is best told by having a deeper-voiced call than the common tern. The black tern (*Chlidonias niger*) is a marsh nester in the southern two-thirds of the province; its numbers appear to be decreasing with periodic drying and draining of the wetlands. The Caspian tern (*S. caspia*), a large, red-billed cosmopolitan species, is rare and sporadically distributed; the Arctic tern (*S. paradisaea*) nests in the far north and is seen only rarely farther south.

A number of marine stragglers have also been reported: pomarine jaeger (*Stercorarius pomarinus*), long-tailed jaeger (*S. longicaudus*), little gull (*L. minutus*), lesser black-backed gull (*L. fuscus*), slaty-backed gull (*L. schistisagus*), great black-backed gull (*L. marinus*), Sabine's gull (*Xema sabini*), black-legged kittiwake (*Rissa tridactyla*), and least tern (*Sterna antillarum*).   *Diane Secoy*

FURTHER READING: Alsop, Fred J., III. 2002. *Birds of Canada*. New York: Dorling Kindersley.

GUSTIN, LYELL (1895–1988).

Pianist, teacher and adjudicator, Lyell Gustin was born on May 31, 1895 in Fitch Bay, Quebec. In 1912, he graduated with the highest marks in Canada from Stanstead Wesleyan College. He moved with his parents to Saskatoon, where for four years he studied piano with Blanche St. John-Baker. He then went to Chicago to study with Canadian-born Jeanette Durno, and on to London and New York. In 1920,

LINDA HOLOBOFF PHOTO/SASKATCHEWAN ARCHIVES BOARD
S-SP-A10724-6, SASKATOON STARPHOENIX FONDS

Lyell Gustin, June 1978.

he returned to Saskatoon to establish the Lyell Gustin Piano Studio. For over sixty years he taught individuals, held monthly interpretation classes, monthly soirées, ensemble rehearsals, special programs, and social events; and for thirty years he instructed his own summer schools.

In 1924 Gustin founded the Saskatoon Musical Art Club, and in 1930 he was a founding member of the Saskatchewan Registered Music Teachers Association. He served as president of the Canadian Federation of Music Teachers (CFMT) from 1941 to 1946, during which time he established the Young Artists Series. In 1967, he received the CFMT centennial citation for outstanding teaching. Gustin served as examiner for the Toronto Conservatory of Music (1944–70), lectured at Regina College (1936–47), and occasionally at the UNIVERSITY OF SASKATCHEWAN and the Royal Conservatory of Music summer schools. He was chairman of the music committee of the SASKATCHEWAN ARTS BOARD (1952–64). In 1975, CFQC-TV broadcast a two-part documentary, *A Man and His Music*; and in 1976, CBC radio presented a documentary on his life and work. Many of his former pupils have acquired national and international reputations as concert pianists.

Gustin received many honours, including the University of Alberta National Music Award (1955) and the Canadian Music Council Medal (1973). He was an honorary Fellow of Trinity College, London (1978), and received the Canadian Council of the Arts *Diplôme d'honneur* (1983). He was also awarded an honorary degree from the University of Saskatchewan (1969), as well as the Saskatchewan Order of Merit (1986). He died on February 7, 1988.   *Isabelle M. Mills*

GUY, ALLAN RAY (1926–).

Allan Guy was born in the farming community of Senlac on May 18, 1926. Guy worked on the family farm before attending Saskatoon Teacher's College and the UNIVERSITY OF SASKATCHEWAN. After teaching for a number of years, he became a school principal in La Ronge. Guy was active in the SASKATCHEWAN TEACHERS' FEDERATION and the La Ronge Chamber of Commerce. He married Sylvia Evangeline Harach of Radisson in 1951, with a second marriage to Marjorie Hastings in 1967. Guy has three children.

First elected as the Liberal candidate from Athabasca to the Saskatchewan Legislature in 1960, Guy acted as the Opposition critic for Northern Affairs and Indian issues. He was re-elected in 1964, 1967, 1971, and in a by-election in 1972. He also ran as a candidate for the Rosthern constituency in 1975 but was defeated. Guy served in the Cabinet of ROSS THATCHER as Minister of Public Works from 1967 to 1970. He was then appointed Minister of Municipal Affairs and Minister of the Department of Indian and

© M.WEST, REGINA, WEST'S STUDIO COLLECTION/
SASKATCHEWAN ARCHIVES BOARD R-WS568-712-2

Allan Guy.

Métis Affairs, a new department established to address issues of poverty facing First Nations reserves throughout Saskatchewan with particular focus on the north. He held these positions until 1971, when the Liberal government was defeated.   *Roberta Lexier*

FURTHER READING: Eisler, Dale. 1987. *Rumours of Glory: Saskatchewan and the Thatcher Years*. Edmonton: Hurtig Publishers; Saskatchewan Archives Board. Allan Guy Papers. R9171–R9173, Regina.

GZOWSKI, PETER (1934–2002).

Born on July 13, 1934, Gzowski began his professional career as a journalist in Saskatchewan. From the time he moved to Moose Jaw in the spring of 1957, Gzowski had a long association with that city and the province. A job offer from the managing editor of the *Moose Jaw Times-Herald* brought him west from a stint as editor of the University of Toronto's student paper, *The Varsity*. He served as city editor of the paper until his departure seven months later. During that short time, Gzowski formed a strong bond with the city. He was active in the local theatre group, and while directing a play met Jennie Lissaman, who was to become his first wife.

Forty years later, after he had become a national icon as a CBC broadcaster, Gzowski chose to broadcast his final *Morningside* radio show from Moose Jaw and to make the occasion a fund raiser for the Festival of Words, a unique Moose Jaw group that promotes lifelong reading and literacy. Gzowski further supported literacy programs in the province by hosting the Peter Gzowski Invitational Golf Tournaments, which raised more than $7 million. Fittingly, the 2003 Festival of Words was dedicated to Peter Gzowski. Gzowski died on January 24, 2002.   *Gary Hyland*

H

HADASSAH-WIZO. Hadassah-Wizo is a worldwide, non-political women's volunteer Zionist organization. In both Israel and Canada, Hadassah raises money to support education, career training and health care, as well as women, child, and youth services. Hadassah-Wizo was founded in Canada in 1917; the Regina Chapter was organized in 1921, with Saskatoon following in 1923. Historically there have also been chapters in Melfort, Melville, Moose Jaw, and Yorkton. Regina and Saskatoon are the only chapters still active, with approximately 35 members in the former and 40 in the latter.

Karen Zemlak

HAFFORD, town, pop 401, located 65 km E of North Battleford, at the junction of Hwys 40 and 340. The town, situated in beautiful rolling countryside on the southern edge of the Aspen parklands, is a service centre for a predominantly agricultural district. In the early 1900s, the region was populated by one of the largest block settlements of Ukrainians in Saskatchewan (*see* **UKRAINIAN SETTLEMENTS**). The community grew rapidly, and although much of the business district was destroyed by fire in 1950, the village was rebuilt and had a population of nearly 600 by the late 1960s. Hafford today has a wide array of businesses and services. While most of its residents are employed in

DAVID MCLENNAN PHOTO
Street signs in Hafford.

agriculture, small business, health, administration, and education, a small number commute to work in Saskatoon. Hafford's rich Ukrainian heritage is still very much in evidence: the town's street signs are in both Ukrainian and English, and a number of the community's annual events have Ukrainian themes.

David McLennan

HAGUE, town, pop 711, located approximately 45 km NE of Saskatoon and 95 km SW of Prince Albert on Hwy 11. The Hague Ferry crosses the **SOUTH SASKATCHEWAN RIVER** 12 km due east of the town. Hague is situated on the rail line which was completed by the Qu'Appelle, Long Lake & Saskatchewan Railway in 1890, linking Regina, Saskatoon, and Prince Albert; and the community derives its name from a railway engineer who worked on the line. In the mid-1890s, large numbers of Mennonite settlers began arriving in the district. The Hague post office was established in 1896, and by 1903 the small agricultural community had grown large enough to gain village status. In 1905-06, a future prime minister of Canada, **JOHN DIEFENBAKER**, attended school in Hague, as his father had been employed to teach at the village's one-room school. The population of the community at the time was approaching 300, and its numbers remained roughly around this level until after **WORLD WAR II**, at which time the community experienced another period of growth, reaching over 400 by the mid-1960s. In the mid-1970s, a housing boom was spurred by people who worked in Saskatoon but wanted to live in a smaller community. While residents benefit from easy access to the employment opportunities, services, and amenities that Saskatoon has to offer, the town maintains a varied business community and the area economy is still agriculturally based. A major attraction in the community is the Saskatchewan River Valley Museum: located on a three-acre site, it houses over 3,000 artifacts and includes a number of heritage buildings, among them a rare Mennonite house-barn dating to 1908. Additionally, Hague is home to one of the few existing railroad water towers remaining in Saskatchewan.

David McLennan

HAI DUC BUDDHIST PAGODA, REGINA.

Hai Duc Buddhist Pagoda is a Mahayana Buddhist temple. The first one was established in 1990 when there were about twenty people from Vietnam in the Regina area—refugees from the Vietnam War. In 1996 they built a new temple, and now about 200 people come for the most important ceremonies, most of them of Vietnamese or Chinese background. There is no monk staying in the temple on a regular basis. Hai Duc Buddhist Pagoda plays an important role in the community: it is a religious centre where believers can celebrate Buddhist holidays; it is also a cultural centre where people celebrate various

A procession moves toward the Hai Duc Buddhist Pagoda in Regina prior to its official opening, September 1996.

festivals. The temple plays an important role for the families who come here to remember dead ancestors; and the leader of the temple offers special prayers for the recently diseased before or after the funeral during Sunday services.

The language used for prayers and chanting is Vietnamese; the Buddhist texts used are in Vietnamese or Chinese. The disciples of the Hai Duc Buddhist Pagoda are vegetarians. Every Sunday after the rituals, they share the food brought in by the members: it is the time to share their religious feelings and their life stories as well. The members place flowers and food in front of the statues of the Buddha, Bodhisattva Guan-yin, and Ksitigarbha; they also offer some food to the dead ancestors of their families. Besides these communal activities, individuals can practice by themselves. Even though there is no full-time monk, there are some devoted disciples who have become the organizers and administrators of the temple. Every year, this temple shares some activities with others in Saskatoon, providing spiritual support to people from Vietnam, China, and other Asian countries.

Yuan Ren

HAIL. Summertime thunderstorms in Saskatchewan frequently generate hail. Hailstones are pieces of ice, usually roughly round but sometimes formed in other shapes, which grow in the strong updrafts of air (convection currents) found in the mature cells of a thunderstorm. Such cells extend well into the below-freezing levels of the lower atmosphere, 10 km or more above ground. Hail season runs from May to September. Severe hailstorms, often accompanied by strong winds at ground level, can do great damage, especially to mature crops, roofs, siding, windows, and vehicles. These storms, travelling at

30–80 km per hour, often track substantial distances across Saskatchewan, leaving long (up to several hundred kilometres) and narrow (from 5–40 km) hailswaths. Within these swaths there is usually a narrower band of damaging hail 3–20 km wide.

The largest hailstone reported in Saskatchewan, and indeed in Canada, fell near Cedoux, north of Weyburn, on August 27, 1973; it weighed about 250 gm and was 10 cm in diameter. This particular storm, and others such as the Pilot Butte storm of

Heavy hail demolished Steve Heck's crops, July 1990.

August 26, 1995, destroyed many crops ready for harvest. Urban areas are sometimes hit hard too: a storm with baseball-sized hailstones hit Prince Albert on August 14, 1982, producing an estimated $14 million property loss. Many farmers purchase hail insurance on their crops, in addition to general crop insurance. Crop hail-risk underwritten usually amounts to half a billion dollars or more annually; premiums collected and losses paid average $20 million a year.

Alec Paul

HALFE, LOUISE (1953–). Born on April 8, 1953, on the Saddle Lake Reserve in Two Hills, Alberta, Halfe was sent In 1959 to the Blue Quills Residential School in St. Paul, Alberta, where she stayed until the age of 16. She continued her studies at St. Paul's regional high school and began writing about her experiences. Afterwards, she attended the University of Regina, where she earned her Bachelor of Social Work, and the Nechi Institute, where she earned certificates in Addictions. Halfe's first work was published in 1990, in *Writing the Circle: Native Women of Western Canada*, an anthology of writing by Native women. Her first book, *Bear Bones & Feathers*, was published in 1994. The book received the Canadian People's Poet Award and was a finalist for the Spirit of Saskatchewan Award. In 1998 her second book, *Blue Marrow*, was published; it was a finalist for the Governor General's Award for Poetry, the Pat Lowther Award, the Saskatchewan Book of the Year Award, and the Saskatchewan Poetry Award. Halfe's work has appeared in various

COURTESY OF COTEAU BOOKS

Louise Halfe.

anthologies and in magazines such as *NeWest Review*. In 2005, Louise Halfe was named as Saskatchewan's new Poet Laureate.

Dagmar Skamlová

FURTHER READING: *Saskatchewan Writers: Lives Past and Present*. 2004. Regina: Canadian Plains Center.

HALL COMMISSION. This is the name applied to the 1973 provincial Royal Commission on University Organization and Structure. Regina College, established in 1911, had been affiliated with

the **UNIVERSITY OF SASKATCHEWAN** since the 1920s. The great expansion in enrolments and the growing costs of post-secondary education that occurred in the 1960s and 1970s led to the appointment in May 1973 of a commission to report on the organization and structure of university education. Headed by former provincial chief justice **EMMETT HALL**, the commission held meetings throughout the province during June, July and August. After a prolonged debate on the future status of the University of Saskatchewan, the commission submitted its report to premier **ALLAN BLAKENEY** on December 22, 1973.

Citing the need for university education in the southern part of the province and the fact that the Regina Campus had a complete academic structure that could be easily developed into a new university, the report suggested that the one-university, two-campus system then in existence in Saskatchewan be replaced by two independent universities. Further recommendations called for the creation of a Universities Commission to co-ordinate funding and to act as a buffer between the universities and government. The Hall Commission also included recommendations on the structure of university governance and the re-establishment of a degree program in engineering at Regina which had been curtailed some years before. The report became the basis of the University of Regina Act that was passed by the Legislature in the spring of 1974 and officially established the **UNIVERSITY OF REGINA** on July 1, 1974.

Mark Vajcner

HALL, EMMETT (1898–1996). Emmett Mathew Hall was born into a poor Irish family on November 9, 1898 at St. Colomban, north of Montreal. The family moved west to Saskatoon in 1910, and young Emmett was in the audience that summer when Sir Wilfrid Laurier laid the cornerstone for the **UNIVERSITY OF SASKATCHEWAN**. Hall studied law at the University of Saskatchewan along with **JOHN DIEFENBAKER**, and graduated in 1919. In his thirty-five years of practice, he developed a reputation as an eminent and hard-nosed counsel. He was named a King's Counsel, played an active role in the provincial and national bar associations, and was respected for his work on the local Catholic school and hospital boards. He sought elected office twice for the Conservatives, but he was defeated on both occasions.

In 1957, the Diefenbaker Conservatives won enough seats in the general election to form a minority government, and Hall was offered a position as Chief Justice on Saskatchewan's Court of Queen's Bench. Hall, then 58, launched into a national career at an age when most of his contemporaries were planning retirement. In January 1961 he was asked to lead a Royal Commission into health care, and in 1962 was appointed to the Supreme Court of Canada. Hall's assignment to lead the health care

RICHARD E. TONE/UNIVERSITY OF REGINA

Proceedings of the Royal Commission on University Organization and Structure (Hall Commission); commissioners were (l. to r.) Gordon South, Emmett Hall, and Steuart Nicks.

commission arose during a pitched controversy in his home province. Saskatchewan had introduced tax-financed hospital care in 1947, and in the election of 1960 Premier T.C. DOUGLAS had announced that a similar plan would be introduced to pay for visits to doctors. Hall brought his legal training and judicial bearing to the work, assembling the evidence and closely questioning hundreds of witnesses to appear before him in public hearings. He was struck by the obvious gaps in the health care system, the inequitable access to services, and the generally poor health of many Canadians.

When he reported in 1964, Hall stunned the country by proposing a publicly financed and administered health plan similar to the one in Saskatchewan, not only for medical and hospital care but also for a wide range of other health services including prescription drugs and dental care for children. The Liberal government of Lester Pearson, after some indecision, passed enabling legislation in 1966, and Hall became known as a father of medicare. Soon after, he accepted an appointment by Premier William Davis to lead a commission into education in Ontario. Hall and co-chairman Dr. Lloyd Dennis delivered a report promoting child-centred education and a flexible curriculum, and opposed the separation of handicapped children and slow learners from other students.

Hall spent ten years on the Supreme Court, where he was known as a hard-working and decisive judge, respected for his practical experience as a trial lawyer, his strength of character, his integrity, and his intellect. His eloquent minority judgment in the Nisga'a land claims case in 1973 is credited with convincing then Prime Minister Pierre Trudeau to open negotiations with Aboriginal peoples. Hall's judgment was also a catalyst for the entrenching of rights of Aboriginals in the Canadian Constitution in 1981. After his retirement from the Supreme Court in 1973, he returned to live in Saskatoon, where he was soon called on to lead a commission into the structure and organization of the University in Saskatchewan. Later he served as an arbitrator and mediator in strikes by national railway workers, grain handlers, and air traffic controllers.

Between 1975 and 1977 Hall led a Royal Commission into the rail transportation of grain in western Canada. In 1979, the federal government asked him to conduct a review of the health care system. Hall was still in good health in November 1993, when hundreds of people gathered at a dinner in Saskatoon to celebrate his 95th birthday; but he suffered a stroke not along after, and died in Saskatoon on November 12, 1996. Hall was a study in contradictions: an Establishment man, but one more interested in justice than in privilege; and a member of the elite, but one who never forgot his own humble origins or the needs of the ordinary people that he encountered during his long life.

Historian J.L. Granatstein has described Hall as the most important Canadian judge of the 20th century.

Dennis Gruending

FURTHER READING: Granatstein, J.L. and H. Rawlinson. 1997. *The Canadian 100: The 100 Most Influential Canadians of the 20th Century.* Toronto: Little Brown and Company; Gruending, D. 1985. *Emmett Hall: Establishment Radical.* Toronto: Macmillan.

HALL, GLENN (1931–). A model of consistency as a professional goaltender, Glenn Hall played eighteen NHL seasons and rarely missed a game. Born on October 3, 1931, in Humboldt, Hall spent his junior career with the Humboldt Indians and the Windsor Spitfires before signing with the Detroit Red Wings in 1951. Despite playing for the Wings a mere eight times prior to 1955, Hall perfected his goaltending style while in the minors; he was a pioneer of what is known today as the "butterfly style." The 1955–56 campaign was Hall's first full season in the NHL. He recorded thirty wins and twelve shutouts in seventy games for the Red Wings, and won the Calder Trophy as the league's top rookie. Hall was equally consistent the following year, but was traded to the Chicago Black Hawks with teammate Ted Lindsay in July 1957. He spent the next ten seasons with the Hawks, winning the Stanley Cup in 1961 and playing in 502 consecutive regular-season games before an injury ended his streak. The St. Louis Blues claimed Hall in the 1967 Expansion Draft, and he backstopped the new team all the way to the Stanley Cup final. Despite losing to Montreal in four games, he was awarded the Conn Smythe Trophy as playoff MVP. Hall retired at the end of the 1970-71 season. He was named to the First All-Star Team on seven occasions, and was a three-time joint-winner of the Vezina Trophy for fewest regular season goals allowed. Hall was elected to the Hockey Hall of Fame in 1975 and the SASKATCHEWAN SPORTS HALL OF FAME in 1991.

Daria Coneghan and Holden Stoffel

FURTHER READING: Podnieks, A. et al. 2002. *Kings of the Ice: A History of World Hockey.* Richmond Hill, Ontario: NDE Publishing.

HALLAM, DONALD GEORGE (1942–2001). Born on October 27, 1942, Don Hallam was a lifelong resident of Regina, where he attended Sacred Heart Elementary School and Campion College High School. His father, who was recording secretary of the United Transportation Union (UTU) from 1924 to 1967, taught him the values and principles of trade unionism. While still attending high school, Hallam began working part-time at Sherwood Co-op and later became a full-time employee. During this period, he was active in the RETAIL, WHOLESALE AND DEPARTMENT STORE UNION (RWDSU), and in 1965 was hired as a RWDSU representative. Hallam was a strong social activist who fought for many causes in a dedicated and humorous way. He was active with a Catholic social action group in the early 1960s in support of California farm workers, promoted union history and global peace and, along with Regina city councilor Joe McKeown, raised money to replace the Peace Pole at Grant Road School, which had been vandalized. Don Hallam died on December 29, 2001.

Don Anderson

HALPIN, HENRY ROSS (1856-1930). Henry Ross Halpin was born in Ireland in 1856. His father's family was made up of prominent journalists and clergy; his mother's family was related to the Ross family, who had strong Hudson's Bay Company (HBC) connections. He moved to Canada in 1864 when his father, the Reverend William Henry Halpin, was hired as professor of Classics and Mathematics at Huron College, the original college of the University of Western Ontario. Young Henry Halpin had a great fascination with Canada's Native peoples, and in 1872 he joined the Hudson's Bay Company as an apprentice postmaster at Fort Garry. He served the HBC at Norway House, Nelson River Post, Oxford House, across the prairies, and in the Peace River District before taking over the HBC operation at Cold Lake, a branch post of FORT PITT, in 1884. Although he lacked higher education, Halpin had an inquiring mind and was an amateur anthropologist. His lively memoirs reveal a deep understanding of Native life and the varied aspects of the fur trade; a friend of BIG BEAR, he was fluent in CREE.

In April 1885, just after the FROG LAKE MASSACRE, Halpin was held captive for 62 days by members of Big Bear's camp. During the capture of Fort Pitt, Halpin served as Big Bear's secretary and wrote letters to the North-West Mounted Police inside the fort, asking them to retreat in order to avoid further bloodshed. Later, with the help of Big Bear, Halpin and the other prisoners were able to escape at Frenchman's Butte. He then joined the Alberta Field Force as a scout, looking for those who had taken him prisoner. During Big Bear's treason trial Halpin testified on behalf of his friend, stating that Big Bear was as much a prisoner as he himself had been, and was innocent of the murders at Frog Lake. Around the time of the trial Halpin was hired by the Indian Affairs Department as a translator. He worked at the Muscowpetung Reserve near Fort Qu'Appelle, and became friends with local MP NICHOLAS FLOOD DAVIN and with Robert Wilson Elliott, the local Justice of the Peace. He married Elliott's daughter Annie and named his first son after Davin. Later, Halpin was the Indian Agent at Moose Mountain, and in 1901 he was living at CANNINGTON MANOR. After his wife died, he rejoined the HBC and worked at Fort Alexander in Manitoba, where he married a Métis woman, Flora Leask, and

Henry Ross Halpin, 1928.

had a second family. He remained in the Libau, Manitoba area, and served as Justice of the Peace until 1928. He died in 1930 in Winnipeg.

David R. Elliott

HAMILTON, ALVIN (1912–2004). Francis Alvin George Hamilton, leader of the Progressive Conservative Party in Saskatchewan from 1949 to 1957 and Cabinet Minister in the DIEFENBAKER government, was born in Kenora, Ontario, on March 30, 1912. Orphaned at the age of 15, he was taken in by his father's family in Delisle, where he completed his high school education. He attended the UNIVERSITY OF SASKATCHEWAN from 1934 to 1938, graduating with degrees in both Arts and Education. He taught at Nutana Collegiate in Saskatoon until 1941, when he enlisted in the Royal Canadian Air Force. He served as a navigator in Canada, Britain and the Far East, and after the war returned to teaching for three years until he accepted the position of Director of Organization for the national Progressive Conservative Party in Saskatchewan in 1948. A year later the provincial party elected him leader, and he continued in this dual capacity for eight years. As head of what had become a "third" party in a very competitive two-party province, Hamilton faced enormous difficulties during his leadership; but he managed to keep the Conservatives alive through two elections, and laid the groundwork for the eventual success of the party a generation later.

Hamilton's victory in Qu'Appelle at the federal election of 1957 took him to Ottawa and to the position of Minister of Northern Affairs and National Resources in the first Diefenbaker government. His early work there produced the "New National Policy," a development program designed to foster economic prosperity and social justice in all regions of the country. This became the "Vision" of Canada which Diefenbaker used to obtain his huge majority in the 1958 election. Under its auspices the government constructed "roads to resources"; built the South Saskatchewan River Dam and a regional power grid in the Atlantic provinces; initiated programs which opened the north to mining and oil and gas exploration; created Canada's first Department of Forestry; passed the Agricultural Rehabilitation and Development Act (ARDA) and the Prairie Farm Rehabilitation Act (PFRA); and hosted the Resources for Tomorrow Conference which established the Canadian Council of Resource and Environmental Ministers—an intergovernmental policy coordination mechanism which remains important today.

In 1960 Diefenbaker moved Hamilton to the Department of Agriculture to tackle the manifold problems of Canada's farm population and to restore the Conservative party's fortunes among the rural electorate. The massive grain sales to China which followed quickly on his appointment, and increased exports to other Communist countries despite the opposition of the United States, made his task on the prairies relatively easy. ARDA addressed the difficulties of the farm population on a national scale, and as Hamilton's personal popularity rose, especially in the west, so did that of his party. Known as "the best Minister of Agriculture in Canadian history," he left a legacy of support for the Progressive Conservative party in rural Canada which lasted for three decades, as well as the window to China which he helped open in the early 1960s and which remains open to Canadian business today.

Hamilton remained active in national politics for another quarter of a century after the defeat of the Diefenbaker government in 1963. He served as Opposition critic for agriculture, then finance, in the mid-1960s as well as chairman of the Caucus Policy-Making Committee. He ran for the leadership of the party in 1967, but lost to Robert Stanfield. He also lost his parliamentary seat to "Trudeaumania" in 1968, but returned to the House in 1972 and remained the member for Qu'Appelle-Moose Mountain through three more elections until he decided to retire prior to the election of 1988. During these sixteen years he acted as his party's energy critic, continued to pave the way for Canadian business through his contacts in China, and supported a former assistant, Brian Mulroney, in his attempt to replace Joe Clark as leader of the Progressive Conservative Party. Hamilton did not receive a post in Mulroney's first Cabinet, but used his status as mentor and friend to advance his views on the proper direction of national policy in a host of areas. Alvin Hamilton was a "career" politician: he spent six years in the federal Cabinet, twenty-seven years as a member of Parliament, and more than forty years in the service of his party at both the provincial and national levels. He died on June 29, 2004.

Patrick Kyba

FURTHER READING: Kyba, P. 1989. *Alvin: A Biography of the Hon. Alvin Hamilton, P.C.* Regina: Canadian Plains Research Center; Smith, D. 1995. *Rogue Tory.* Toronto: Macfarlane Walter & Ross.

Alvin Hamilton speaking at the opening of the 4th Provincial Boy Scout Jamboree, 1960.

SASKATCHEWAN ARCHIVES BOARD R-B431

Charles Hamilton.

HAMILTON, CHARLES MCGILL (1878–1952).

Born on January 17, 1878, in Whitechurch, Ontario, Hamilton came with his family to farm in Saskatchewan in 1895. In 1901 Hamilton homesteaded near Weyburn, after four years of teaching. He served on several organizations, like Saskatchewan's Western Municipal Hail Insurance Association, and the Western Municipal council. He was president of his local of the Saskatchewan Grain Growers Association, and for seven years was the president of the **SASKATCHEWAN ASSOCIATION OF RURAL MUNICIPALITIES**. He was briefly a director for the Canadian Northern Railway. The Weyburn constituency elected Hamilton as a Liberal to the provincial Legislature in a 1915 by-election. One year later Premier **CHARLES DUNNING** appointed Hamilton as Minister of Agriculture. During his time in the provincial Cabinet, Hamilton also held the positions of Minister of Municipal Affairs, Minister of Highways, and Minister of the Child Welfare Act. Hamilton worked to help provide relief for the farmers seeking assistance, both as Minister of Agriculture and Minister of Municipal Affairs. Hamilton was defeated in the 1929 provincial election. He accepted a place on the Board of Grain Commissioners and served for nineteen years. Hamilton retired in 1948 and died on May 3, 1952, in Winnipeg. *Maryanne Cotcher*

FURTHER READING: Blanchard, J. 1987. *A History of the Canadian Grain Commission*. Winnipeg: Canadian Grain Commission; Brennan, J.W. 1976. "A Political History of Saskatchewan, 1905–1929." PhD dissertation, University of Alberta; Saskatchewan Archives Board. C.M. Hamilton Papers. Saskatoon.

HAMILTON, DOREEN ELLEN (1951–).

Doreen Hamilton (*née* Munholland) was born in Regina on May 17, 1951. She attended the **UNIVERSITY OF REGINA** and then taught in Southey. In 1972, she married Robert Gordon Hamilton and moved to British Columbia, where she taught kindergarten in Burn Lake until she returned to Saskatchewan in 1975. Hamilton was elected to Regina City Council in 1985 and re-elected in 1988. She was chairperson of the Mayor's Task Force on Women's Issues and a member of the Mayor's Board of Inquiry on Hunger. She served as interim mayor of Regina for one month in 1988, a position that no woman had previously held. She was elected as the NDP MLA for Regina Wascana Plains and has retained her seat since then. In 1998, Hamilton was appointed Minister of Saskatchewan Liquor and Gaming, and Minister responsible for the Saskatchewan Property Management Corporation, the Public Service Commission, and the Wascana Centre Authority. After NDP leader **LORNE CALVERT** assumed the duties of Premier in February 2001, Hamilton held these ministerial positions until October 2001. In April 2003, she was appointed as legislative secretary to Premier Calvert and as chair of his Voluntary Sector Initiative, which was established to strengthen the relationship between the public and volunteer sectors in Saskatchewan.

Jenn Ruddy

ROY ANTAL/REGINA LEADER-POST

Doreen Hamilton, March 2001.

HAMMER, ULRICH THEODORE (1924–).

Born in Maple Creek in 1924, Ted Hammer engaged in farming and ranching activities with his father and obtained an MSc at the University of Montana in 1959. During the spring and summer of 1959 he worked for the Saskatchewan Department of Natural Resources doing a limnological study of Buffalo Pound Lake, with an emphasis on fish pop-

ulations. Over the next few years he researched blue-green algae at the **UNIVERSITY OF SASKATCHEWAN**, where he was awarded a PhD in 1963. He was the first to show that blue-green algae grow more abundantly as phosphorus increases; as a result of these studies, the sewage treatment plant in Regina began to remove phosphorus from sewage effluent passing into the **QU'APPELLE RIVER** system. During this time, Hammer was involved in eutrophication problems and gave public and scientific presentations worldwide on the harmful effects of eutrophication and pollution. He organized the Second International Saline Lakes Conference, which was held in Saskatchewan in 1982. In 1984 he reviewed worldwide saline lake literature, published in many languages and going back to the early 1900s. The comprehensive review volume published in 1986 established Hammer as an international authority on world saline lakes.

Ted Hammer acquired many honours during his career. The positions he held include the following: chairman, Advisory Committee on the Algae Problem in the Qu'Appelle River Basin, 1963–68; president, Canadian Society of Fishery and Wildlife Biologists, Saskatchewan Branch, 1963–64; chairman of the Saskatchewan Water Studies Institute from 1967–69. He was a member of the Canadian International Biological Program Committee on Freshwater (IBP-PF), National Research Council, 1968–73; he was also Saskatchewan Co-Chairman, International Biological Program Committee on Conservation of Terrestrial Ecosystems (IBP-CT), 1968–73. He retired from teaching in 1991.

Jeff Hudson

HANBIDGE, ROBERT LEITH (1891–1974).

Robert Leith ("Dinny") Hanbidge was born in Southampton, Ontario, on March 16, 1891. Educated in Ontario, he moved to Regina in 1909 to article in the law firm of Sir Frederick Haultain. Hanbidge played for the Regina Rugby Club, forerunner of the Roughriders. On completion of his legal studies he joined his brother Jack's law firm in Kerrobert in 1914. A year later he married Jane Mitchell of Francis with whom he had four daughters and a son.

Hanbidge served first on the council and later as mayor of Kerrobert. He won a seat in the Legislature in 1929 and acted as **CONSERVATIVE PARTY** whip throughout the Anderson government's five-year term of office. Defeated in 1934, he returned to his law practice but continued to participate in Conservative Party activities. In 1945, he lost the Kindersley seat for the new Progressive Conservative Party in the federal election. One prominent friend and constant correspondent was **JOHN DIEFENBAKER**, who urged Hanbidge to join him in Ottawa. In 1958, Hanbidge won in Kindersley and repeated in 1962. While a member of Parliament he represented

Robert Hanbidge.

Canada at NATO and Commonwealth conferences.

He accepted Diefenbaker's invitation to become **LIEUTENANT-GOVERNOR** of Saskatchewan, a position he filled with distinction for an unusual seven-year term (1963–70). The **UNIVERSITY OF SASKATCHEWAN** awarded him an Honorary Doctorate in 1968. He died on July 25, 1974. *Patrick Kyba*

FURTHER READING: Eager, E. 1980. *Saskatchewan Government.* Saskatoon: Western Producer Prairie Books; Leeson, H. (ed.). 2001. *Saskatchewan Politics: Into the Twenty-first Century.* Regina: Canadian Plains Research Center.

HANLEY, town, pop 495, located 56 km SE of Saskatoon on Hwy 11. The first settlers in the district arrived in 1901, and in 1902 the first buildings began to appear on the townsite. Although settlers arriving in the district were of diverse backgrounds (there were people from eastern Canada, the British Isles, and the mid-western United States), two large bloc settlements of people took up land in the Hanley area: Norwegians in 1903, and Mennonites in 1924. While many young Saskatchewan communities suffered devastating fires, Hanley seems to have weathered more than its share. Significant blazes occurred in 1912, 1929, 1935 and 1947, each with a number of properties lost. One community landmark that did survive the flames could not survive the wrecking ball. For decades, the Hanley Opera House, completed in 1914, served as a centre of cultural activity for a wide area; but by 1982 it was dilapidated beyond repair, unsafe, and was therefore demolished. Today, Hanley has a core of essential businesses and services. Slightly more than 25% of Hanley's population is over the age of 65, and a small percentage of residents commute to

work in Saskatoon. Agriculture continues to be the basis of the area's economy. *David McLennan*

HANSON, WILLIAM (1925–). As a federal public servant, Bill Hanson promoted Aboriginal employment both provincially and nationally. Born in Cormorant Lake, Manitoba, in 1925, Hanson served with the Royal Canadian Air Force during **WORLD WAR II**. He then returned to Winnipeg and was educated at the Manitoba Technical Institute. In 1954, he began his career with the National Employment Service, becoming its youngest manager and the only one of Aboriginal ancestry. Later, Hanson worked as the northern Saskatchewan area manager, special projects officer, and advisor on Aboriginal issues for the federal government. Following his retirement in 1981, Hanson helped create the Interprovincial Association on Native Employment Inc. and served as its executive coordinator. He was awarded the Saskatchewan Order of Merit in 2000.

HANWAY, MABEL (1893–1968). Mabel Hanway (*née* Brigden) was a Regina-based activist and the first woman to run for mayor. Born in Manitoba in 1893 and educated there, she was the sister of socialist-feminist Beatrice Brigden. During **WORLD WAR I** she began to teach in Saskatchewan, and subsequently married Thomas V. Hanway, a salesman; she had a stepson. In 1946, Hanway, a widow since 1940, began to work for the Department of Social Welfare, from which she retired in 1958. She sought to improve socio-economic conditions and advance women's rights. Convenor of the Local Council of Women's (LCW) Trades and Professions for Women Committee from 1926 to 1931, she also participated in the Trades and Labour Congress and the Women's Labour League. After **WORLD WAR II**, she was president of the Regina Housewives' Association. Hanway engaged in pro-labour political activism, and helped organize the Independent-Labour party (later a CCF component). In 1932, she sought a city council seat—one of the first two women to do so—but lost. In the 1940s and 1950s she ran several times, never successfully, on labour-oriented slates as an aldermanic or school board candidate. In 1950 she ran for mayor, but was defeated. A lifelong peace activist, she supported the League of Nations Society and, later, the United Nations Association. At mid-century she became an organizer and leader in the Regina and provincial Peace Councils, and was a delegate to the World Peace Council (1959). In the 1960s she engaged in anti-Vietnam protests. Hanway died on July 6, 1968, in Regina. *Ann Leger-Anderson*

HARBUZ, ANN (1908–89). Ann Alexander Harbuz was born on July 25, 1908, in Winnipeg, the daughter of Mike and Maria Napastuik. A self-taught

artist, she became renowned for painting folk art. Her subject matter depicted a 20th-century Canadian Ukrainian rural (prairie) perspective. Her reinterpretations are autobiographical, historical and cultural events specific to her community and life experiences. Her childhood was spent near Whitlow, Saskatchewan. When Harbuz was 12 her mother died, and she cared for five siblings. Ann then moved to Richard, Saskatchewan, where she lived for twenty years raising her own family with her first husband. After her divorce she married Mike Harbuz, a cabinet-maker, in 1945. They lived in North Battleford for ten years, raising their daughter. In 1955 they moved to Ponoka, Alberta, where they managed a bargain store. In 1967, Ann moved back to North Battleford and took painting lessons. During her career she was commissioned to do a painting for the 1976 Montreal Olympics, and presented a painting to T.C. Douglas. Her work is exhibited across Canada and collected in numerous private and permanent collections including the **MENDEL ART GALLERY**, the **SASKATCHEWAN ARTS BOARD**, and the **MACKENZIE ART GALLERY**. She died in North Battleford on April 29, 1989. *Patricia Deadman*

HARES AND RABBITS. These animals are members of the mammalian order Lagomorpha. They have gnawing, constantly growing incisors, with a second pair of incisors directly behind, no canines, a long space between the incisors and premolars, well-furred feet, and nostrils which can be closed by surrounding muscles. They are herbivores and make more efficient use of their food by the process of reingestion, in which the defecated plant material, which is only partly digested in its first passage through the gut, is eaten and more thoroughly processed. They have several often large litters a year, and their populations can, if unchecked by predators or disease, grow very quickly. The order of approximately fifty-eight species is found naturally on all inhabitable continents except Australia. The four lagomorph species found in Saskatchewan are all members of the family Leporidae—the rabbits and hares, which have fairly long ears and long hind limbs.

The two species of rabbits are the uncommon Eastern cottontail (*Sylvilagus floridanus*), found in the southeast corner, and the more common Nuttall's cottontail (*S. nuttalli*) of the dry short-grass prairies of the southwest. Rabbits are smaller and shorter-legged than hares; their young are born naked and helpless, and are kept in burrows until their hair and eyesight have developed. The two species of hares are the snowshoe hare (*Lepus americanus*) and the larger white-tailed jackrabbit (*L. townsendi*). Hares, particularly the jackrabbits, are longer-legged and longer-eared than rabbits; their young are precocious, born with fur and their eyes open. Both species are common; the snowshoe

COURTNEY MILNE PHOTO
Cottontail rabbit.

hare is more widely distributed throughout the province, apparently absent only in the **CYPRESS HILLS** area. Both species change coats between winter white and summer brown.   *Diane Secoy*

FURTHER READING: Banfield, A.W.F. 1974. *The Mammals of Canada.* Toronto: University of Toronto Press; Saskatchewan Environment. 2001. *Natural Neighbours: Selected Mammals of Saskatchewan.* Regina: Canadian Plains Research Center.

HARMONY INDUSTRIAL ASSOCIATION. In June 1895 two brothers, Will and Ed Paynter, convened a meeting at the schoolhouse in Beulah, Manitoba. The group discussed clause by clause the Constitution for a community to be called the Harmony Industrial Association. The Constitution set out the financial conditions for membership as well as the rules and regulations of the proposed colony. The Prospectus castigated the existing capitalist system as being one of greed and exploitation, and proposed its co-operative system as a model to show how human beings should live together in peace and harmony. They called their prospective colony Hamona, a biblical name from the Book of

Ezekiel; the site was in the **QU'APPELLE VALLEY**, north of Moosomin. The colony was slow to get started because the **DOMINION LANDS ACT** required settlers to live on their own quarter-sections rather than in communal villages. The problem was eventually solved by an amendment, and the Hamona colonists began to arrive in 1897–98. With between 50 and 60 members, the colony existed for two years before it disbanded in 1900. In addition to farming on land near the colony and back in Beulah, the colonists raised cattle, produced butter which was sold in Moosomin as "Hamona Butter," and made lime for cement and whitewash, also sold in Moosomin. The lime was produced by burning limestone rocks in earthen kilns dug into the Qu'Appelle hillside. Social life at the colony included tobogganing on the hillside, topical discussions, and sing-songs in the school-house on Sunday afternoons.

There are two possible explanations for the demise of the Harmony Industrial Association: one is that the railway did not come through as expected; the other is that there was some dissension in the membership because some people wanted the colony to become fully communal, with communal kitchens and free love. In any case, a meeting was held and those present voted to discontinue the experiment; some members moved away while others settled in the nearby towns of Tantallon and Spy Hill. The two Paynter brothers who founded the colony went on to be farmers, businessmen, leaders in co-operative organizations, and utopian writers. (*See also* **UTOPIANISM**)   *Alex MacDonald*

FURTHER READING: MacDonald, A. 1995. "Practical Utopians: Ed and Will Paynter and the Harmony Industrial Association," *Saskatchewan History* 47 (1): 13–26.

HARRIS, MARGARET (1921–). Margaret Harris (Gibb) was born on February 15, 1921, in Galt (now Cambridge), Ontario, and received her early schooling there. She continued her education at the Saskatoon Continuing Education Centre and the

LINDA HOLOBOFF PHOTO/SASKATCHEWAN ARCHIVES BOARD
S-SP-A9044-6, SASKATOON STARPHOENIX FONDS
Margaret Harris, December 1975.

UNIVERSITY OF SASKATCHEWAN. She married Dr. Art Harris in 1946; they have two children. Her volunteer work began with the Home and School Association; she also played a leadership role in organizations such as the Saskatoon City Hospital Auxiliary, Social Planning Council of Saskatoon, and Planned Parenthood Association. In 1965 Harris began involvement with the Council of Women, serving as national president from 1982 to 1984, and was named a life member of local, provincial, and national councils. She was a member of the Canadian delegation to a 1974 United Nations seminar dealing with women's equality issues, and was chair from 1974 to 1978 of the recently established Saskatchewan Advisory Council on the Status of Women. In 1979 Harris helped form the Saskatchewan Coalition for Women's Pensions, and lobbied for change. Her awards include the Queen's Silver Jubilee Medal (1977) and Saskatoon's Certificate of Distinguished Community Service (1979), as well as a Governor General's Persons Case Award (1987) and membership in the Order of Canada (1988).   *Erin Legg*

HARVEST EXCURSIONS. Before the introduction of the combine, prairie harvests required large numbers of workers for short periods of time. Between 1890 and 1930, harvest excursion trains brought workers from Europe and Great Britain to western Canada; the peak year was 1908, when about 14,000 arrived. The railways offered harvest tickets for $15 one way or $20 return from anywhere in Canada. Excursion trains were crowded and offered crude accommodation. Delays, crowding and drunkenness on occasion led to riots. In the 1920s, the railways demanded and got RCMP personnel on the trains to keep order.

Regular harvesters were paid about $1.75–$2.25 for a 10–12 hour day, while a threshing crew made $2–$3.25 a day with board. There were no

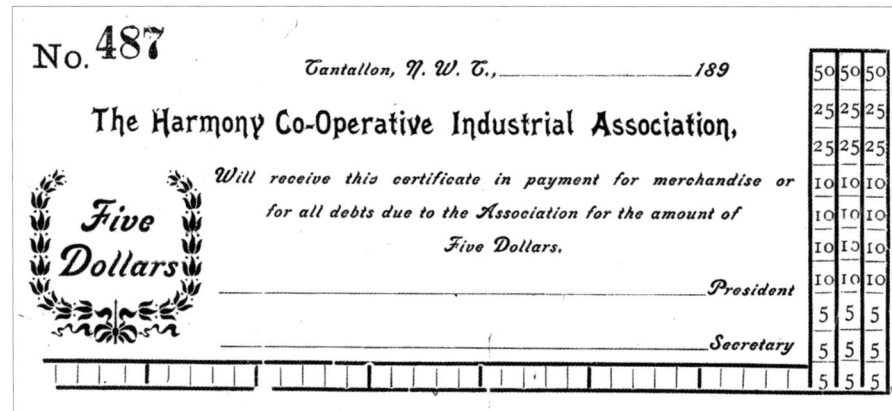

No. 487

Tantallon, N. W. T.,_____189__

The Harmony Co-Operative Industrial Association,

Five Dollars

Will receive this certificate in payment for merchandise or for all debts due to the Association for the amount of
Five Dollars.

President

Secretary

50	50	50
25	25	25
25	25	25
10	10	10
10	10	10
10	10	10
10	10	10
5	5	5
5	5	5
5	5	5

SASKATCHEWAN ARCHIVES BOARD R-A2299
Harmony Co-Operative Industrial Association scrip.

other benefits, and the work only lasted about 15 days. Despite this, many were attracted by the prairies and decided to return permanently to homestead. The collapse of the wheat economy, and new technology such as the introduction of the combine in 1930, ended the era of the harvest excursion.

Clare Powell

HASSETT, YVONNE JOAN (1933–). Yvonne Joan Hassett was born on July 2, 1933, in Admiral, Saskatchewan. After qualifying as a registered nurse at Moose Jaw Union Hospital, she nursed in Swift Current and in Jamaica. She then spent several years as a public health nurse in the Maple Creek area, working with Aboriginal people, the disabled, the elderly, and with schools. She lived on the family farm near Maple Creek and raised four daughters.

In 1984, Hassett began a second career as a volunteer. Active in the Canadian Cancer Society, she became a prime mover in CanSurmount, which offers counselling and support to cancer patients and their families. She arranged fund raising, speakers, educational and support meetings, and hospital and home visiting. On her own time and at her own expense she also visited seniors, shut-ins, and the bereaved. Widely admired for her generosity and kindness, she was an inspiration and support to countless persons suffering from cancer and terminal illness and to their families. She received the Saskatchewan Order of Merit in 1991.

Michael Jackson

HATCHET LAKE DENESULINE NATION (LAC LA HACHE). On August 19, 1907, Commissioner Borthwick met with the Denesuline of the Lac la Hache at Lac du Brochet on the north end of Reindeer Lake to negotiate an adhesion to **TREATY 10**. Three days later, after selecting their chief and headmen, they reassembled with the Treaty Commissioner and signed. The reserve was surveyed on the east side of Wollaston Lake, 354 km north of Flin Flon in the fall of 1965, and set apart as the Lac La Hache Indian Reserve on September 23, 1970. Wollaston "Post," the home community of the Hatchet Lake Denesuline Nation, is on the southeastern shore of Wollaston Lake. This lake was known as Axe Lake—hence the name "Hatchet." The Hatchet Lake Dene lived a mostly nomadic life until about 1960, when their children began to attend school regularly. It was then that the community started to develop. The Dene are still active hunters, fishermen and trappers, and those involved in a wage economy participate as time allows. Chief and council are responsible for the administration of the many programs that keep the band organized, and Elders sit on committees and assist in the band's governance. Outside of positions within the band's infrastructure and administration, there are a band-owned store (Hatchet Lake Economic Development Corporation,

2001) and a commercial fish plant. There are a total of 1,311 band members, with 1,026 people living on their 11,020-ha reserve.

Christian Thompson

HAUGHTON, WILLA A. (1908–2004). Minnesota-born Willa Haughton moved to Saskatchewan in her early childhood and was a dedicated volunteer for numerous organizations based in Regina. For over forty years, she served on various committees for the Red Cross and received the organization's Distinguished Service Award in 1973. Haughton also volunteered her time to the Regina United Way, Regina Symphony Board, Catholic Women's League, and Pasqua Hospital Auxiliary. She was active in sports and served as president of the Saskatchewan Provincial Golf Association. In 1989, Haughton received both the Lieutenant-Governor's Award and the Saskatchewan Order of Merit. She died on November 3, 2004.

HAULTAIN, FREDERICK (1857–1942). Frederick William Gordon Haultain was born near Woolwich, England, on November 25, 1857. In 1860, his family immigrated to Peterborough, Upper Canada. In 1861 his father, Frederick Haultain, a retired officer in the Royal Artillery, was elected to the Legislature of the Province of Canada, as a supporter of George Brown's Clear Grits.

The younger Haultain graduated from the University of Toronto in 1876 and after pursuing a law degree was called to the Ontario Bar in 1882. Haultain practiced law in Toronto and Kingston before moving to the North-West Territories in 1884. Haultain established his practice in the frontier town of Fort McLeod in the District of Alberta. By 1887 the Fort McLeod area's population was sufficient to be entitled representation in the Territorial Assembly. Haultain won the election to represent the constituency in Regina, the Territorial capital. He won or was acclaimed in every Territorial election after this and represented the riding until the creation of the provinces of Saskatchewan and Alberta in 1905.

The Territorial Assembly had very little authority because control over the Territorial budget rested in the hands of the federal government in the person of the **LIEUTENANT-GOVERNOR**. Haultain, nominally a Conservative, became the recognized leader of the Liberal and Conservative majority in the Assembly that manoeuvred, lobbied and pressured the federal government to grant responsible government. In 1897 the Lieutenant-Governor was excluded from the executive committee (Cabinet) and control over the Territorial budget was turned over to the Assembly. Haultain's efforts were widely credited with the achievement of responsible government and after 1897 he became the first Premier of the North-West Territories.

Haultain selected an executive committee with both Liberal and Conservative members and advo-

cated non-partisanship in Territorial matters. The financial demands caused by rapidly increasing settlement, in particular the need for more roads and schools, challenged Haultain's administration and led to a call for provincial status for the North-West Territories. The issue proved problematic as a unifying force. Some people favoured two or more provinces being created out of the Territories and Haultain faced opposition, most notably from the Calgary area, where leaders hoped their city could become the capital of one of the new provinces.

The non-partisan unity was further undermined as Haultain increasingly became identified with the **CONSERVATIVE PARTY**. In 1903, he accepted an honourary position with the Territorial Conservative Association and campaigned for the Conservatives in the federal election that year. Following the re-election of the Liberals, Haultain was shut out of all planning related to provincial status. In 1905 the federal Liberal government passed legislation that created two provinces, allowed the federal government to retain control over each province's natural resources, and guaranteed minority (Roman Catholic) rights through a separate school system. Haultain attacked the legislation, arguing that two provinces weakened the North-West's position within Confederation and that the natural resources and the separate school provisions were an intrusion on provincial rights as established in the British North America Act.

Haultain was not appointed as provisional Premier for either of the provinces and was not acknowledged in the ceremonies marking their creation. He chose to live in Saskatchewan instead of Alberta because he had lived in Regina for most of his time in the North-West. Haultain transformed the Conservative Party into the Provincial Rights Party and challenged the provisional Liberal Premier, **WALTER SCOTT**, in the 1905 Saskatchewan

SASKATCHEWAN ARCHIVES BOARD R-A12114-1

Frederick Haultain.

provincial election. Haultain portrayed the Provincial Rights Party as non-partisan and attracted a number of prominent Liberals as candidates. He campaigned against what he considered the federal government's intrusion into provincial affairs but his position on education was interpreted as anti-Catholic, which alienated a significant number of voters. The Provincial Rights Party lost the popular vote by a narrow margin and Haultain, who was elected in the riding of South Qu'Appelle, became Saskatchewan's first leader of the Opposition.

Haultain contested the 1908 election as the leader of the Provincial Rights Party and the 1912 election as leader of the Conservative Party. In both elections he made a strong showing, but was not able to defeat Scott and the Liberals. In 1912 he retired from politics and was appointed the Chief Justice of Saskatchewan. He held that position until his retirement in 1937. He was knighted in 1916 and served as Chancellor of the **UNIVERSITY OF SASKATCHEWAN** from 1917 until 1939. He received honourary degrees from the University of Toronto and the University of Saskatchewan and was made an honourary **CREE** chief. Haultain retired to Montreal where he died on January 30, 1942.

Mike Fedyk

FURTHER READING: Bocking, D.H. 1964. "Saskatchewan's First Provincial Election," *Saskatchewan History* 17 (2): 41–54; MacEwan, Grant. 1985. *Frederick Haultain: Frontier Statesman of the Canadian Northwest.* Saskatoon: Western Producer Prairie Books; Stanley, Gordon. 1981. "F.W.G. Haultain, Territorial Politics and the Quasi-party System," *Prairie Forum* 6 (1): 1–15; Thomas, Lewis. 1970. "The Political and Private Life of F.W.G. Haultain," *Saskatchewan History* 23 (2): 50–58.

HAVERSTOCK, LYNDA MAUREEN (1948–).

Lynda Haverstock was born in Swift Current on September 16, 1948. She left high school before completion, but returned to finish as an adult. She attended the **UNIVERSITY OF SASKATCHEWAN**, earning a BEd and MEd and completed a PhD in clinical psychology. She worked as psychologist in private practice and as a lecturer for both the Universities of Saskatchewan and New Brunswick. She worked for the Centre for Agricultural Medicine in Saskatoon, specializing in farm stress, and edited a book on the subject.

Her brother, Dennis Ham, served two terms as a Conservative in the Legislature. Haverstock, however, was active in the **LIBERAL PARTY** in the 1980s, and was elected leader in 1989 when the party had no seats in the Legislature and was the first woman to lead a Saskatchewan political party. In the 1991 election, Liberal support more than doubled to over 23% of the total vote, but the Liberals failed to elect any MLAs besides Haverstock, who won in Saskatoon-Greystone.

DON HEALY/REGINA LEADER-POST

Lynda Haverstock addressing a gathering at the Estevan constituency office, September 1991.

During the term, NDP MLA Glen McPherson crossed the floor to the Liberals and they won a 1994 by-election. In the 1995 election the Liberals captured eleven seats, and increased their vote to almost 35%. Nevertheless, Haverstock was forced out as leader shortly after the election but remained in the Legislature for the rest of the term as an independent. She did not contest the 1999 election, and began a short career as a radio talk show host. In 2000, Prime Minister Jean Chrétien appointed her as Saskatchewan's **LIEUTENANT-GOVERNOR**. *Brett Quiring*

FURTHER READING: Haverstock, Lynda. 2001. "The Saskatchewan Liberal Party." Pp. 199–250 in Howard Leeson (ed.), *Saskatchewan Politics: Into the Twenty-first Century.* Regina: Canadian Plains Research Center.

HAWKS AND EAGLES. Hawks and eagles belong to the family Accipitridae, along with ospreys, kites, harriers, and Old World vultures. These medium-sized to very large day-flying predatory birds are found throughout the world. They are all distinguished by their strong beaks and feet, used for catching and tearing apart their prey, but are quite diverse. This is one of the families of birds in which the females are larger than the males; in eagles they may be as much as 30% larger. Hawks are distinguished from falcons by their generally broader wings and lack of "tooth" on the upper beak. Saskatchewan has 13 of the 24 species which regularly occur in North America; all are migratory, except for the northern goshawk. The accipitrids found in Saskatchewan are of six distinctive types: ospreys, eagles, buteos, accipiters, harriers, and kites. The osprey (*Pandion haliaetus*), sometimes called "fish hawk," nests in large structures on dead trees or telephone poles, which the pair uses annually. In the boreal forest and northern parklands this large dark-backed, white-bellied bird with a black eye mask breeds near the water where it feeds; it is seen in migration in the grasslands.

There are two types of eagles in the province. The bald eagle (*Haliaeetus leucocephalus*) is one of the fish-feeding eagles found around water; the adults, with their distinctive white heads and tails, nest throughout the boreal forest, on the edges of lakes and rivers. The dark-brown golden eagle

COURTESY OF THE ROYAL SASKATCHEWAN MUSEUM

Male northern harrier.

(*Aquila chrysaetos*) feeds on small mammals; it usually nests on cliffs, and will be seen in the summer in the southern badlands, along some of the large river valleys, and near **LAKE ATHABASCA**. Both eagles are seen in migration farther south.

Five broad-winged buteos occur in the province; these common and widely distributed hawks are typically predators of small mammals. As they can occur in a number of colours of plumages, they are very confusing to identify. The red-tailed hawk (*Buteo jamaicensis*), a widespread hawk which is a common nester in the aspen parklands, has a dark phase, a light phase and the typical red-tailed, white-chested form. The smallest buteo, about the size of a crow, is the broad-winged hawk (*B. playpterus*), a fairly common nester in deciduous woodlands near water, and transient elsewhere. The brown-chested Swainson's hawk (*B. swainsoni*), which preys on ground squirrels, is one of the common grasslands hawks. The other is the ferruginous hawk (*B. regalis*), a handsome bird with white belly and chest, and reddish legs and wings; this species is apparently recovering from a population crash and is seen more often than several decades ago. The rough-legged hawk (*B. lagopus*) is a common transient to and from its northern breeding grounds; being one of the few buteos which hover while hunting, it can be identified by that habit and by the dark wrist patches in the underside of the wing.

Three accipiters, or bird hawks, occur in Saskatchewan. These are highly maneuverable fliers, with pointed wings and long tails. They are also an example of the size scaling which can be seen in hawks occupying the same habitat. The smallest is the sharp-shinned hawk (*Accipiter striatus*), found through much of the province in the wooded areas in which it nests. The medium-sized Cooper's hawk (*A. cooperi*), which also has a dark cap and thin chesnut bars on the underside, is characteristic of the wooded areas of the grasslands and aspen parklands. The larger northern goshawk (*A. gentilis*) breeds in the coniferous forests of the north and in the **CYPRESS HILLS**, but winters farther south; it shares the dark cap of the other accipiters, but has gray barring and a gray back.

The northern harrier (*Circus cyaneus*) is a common sight over the open areas of the province, particularly in the south. This ground-nesting hawk, with its long tail and broad wings, flies low over the grasses and crops in search of small rodents and other prey; the gray male and brown female are often mistaken for different species. The last species of hawk known from the province is the rare stray Mississippi kite (*Ictinia mississippiensis*), distinctive with its long pointed wings and notched tail.

Diane Secoy

FURTHER READING: Alsop, Fred J. III. 2002. *Birds of Canada*. Toronto: Dorling Kindersley.

SASKATCHEWAN ARCHIVES BOARD R-A21488
Kate Simpson Hayes.

HAYES, KATE SIMPSON (1856–1945). One of the earliest woman authors and journalists in western Canada, Kate Simpson Hayes was born in New Brunswick in 1856. She arrived at Prince Albert, North-West Territories in 1879 and, following a failed marriage, moved to Regina with her two children in the mid-1880s. She soon met **NICHOLAS FLOOD DAVIN**, owner of the newspaper *The Leader*, and their nine-year relationship resulted in the birth of two children out of wedlock. Hayes first owned a millinery shop and then worked as librarian for the legislature of the North-West Territories. As "Mary Markwell," Hayes wrote for *The Leader* and penned plays and comedic sketches that were performed in a number of prairie towns. Her first book, *Prairie Pot-Pourri*, was published in 1895. In 1900 Hayes moved to Winnipeg, where she edited the women's page of the *Manitoba Free Press*. Her writings reveal conservative social views, including opposition to **WOMAN SUFFRAGE**. Hayes also worked for the **CANADIAN PACIFIC RAILWAY**, promoting the emigration of woman domestics from Britain. She was a charter member of the Canadian Women's Press Club, and club president in 1906. Hayes continued to write until well into her seventies. She died in Victoria, BC on January 15, 1945.

Constance A. Maguire

FURTHER READING: Maguire, Constance A. 1998a. "'Leaving the Hearth Fire Untended': Women and Public Pursuits in the Journalism of Kate Simpson Hayes," *Prairie Forum* 23 (1): 67–92; —. 1998b. "Kate Simpson Hayes, Agnes Agatha Hammell, and the 'Slur of Illegitimacy,'" *Saskatchewan History* 50 (2): 7–23.

HEALTH, DETERMINANTS OF. "Health is the crown worn by the well, but visible only to the ill": this ancient saying speaks to how much we take our health for granted until faced with a crisis. Saskatchewan has a unique place in Canada's histo-

ry as not only the first jurisdiction to introduce **MEDICARE**, but also for its demonstration of how a combination of social, political and cultural attitudes and practices can successfully influence the average health of citizens. The notion that we can intervene to prevent illness and disability is a relatively modern one: whether it be the use of citrus juice to prevent scurvy in the British Navy, the symbolism of John Snow's removing the pump handle to prevent the spread of cholera in London, or the major advances in immunization and epidemiology of the past century, these are the products of relatively new knowledge concerning our relationship to the world around us and the nature of disease, ill health and well-being.

For much of human history, disease has been viewed more as the result of the fates or some resident evil than the outcome of circumstances over which we have influence. Thus Jean-Jacques Rousseau in the 18th century was able to say without much debate: "one half of children die before their eighth year; this is Nature's law, why try to contradict it?"

Our understanding that many diseases are in large part preventable and to some extent manageable continues to increase. With the developing sciences of epidemiology, population and public health, we have come to understand that much of what ails us has known causal pathways, and that there are a number of interventions which have the potential to avoid premature death or disability. Much of our improvement in health has been a result of dramatic reductions in infectious diseases, due to better housing, food and water safety, immunization, and smaller families. During the past century chronic diseases such as cancer, lung and heart disease and diabetes became the biggest killers in the developed world. Global warming and climate change, air and water pollution—all are newer challenges to health. The current and developing burden of chronic disease and injury, as well as the uncertainty of new infectious diseases such as severe acute respiratory syndrome (SARS), provide an insidious threat to health system sustainability. Strategies must be applied to address not only the obvious current concern but also the underlying determinants.

Since the mid 1800s, governments have established public health services to protect the public from the spread of infectious disease and health hazards. During the later part of the 20th century, governments became involved in ensuring access to medical services. Health and social policies have the ability to encourage improvements in basic underlying determinants of health through adequate food, shelter, employment and income, education, safer work environments, and the inclusion of all segments as active participants in society. Building community participation, support for and involvement in the arts, maintaining a healthy and active lifestyle, volunteerism, and maintaining social connections: all have been shown to be part of ensuring healthier communities.

Saskatchewan in its development was notable for its high levels of political, sports and cultural involvement, including high rates of participation in amateur sports and theatre. The province has also been an innovator in its approaches to addressing health care problems, whether they be community clinics based on the co-operative model, support for treatment of persons with tuberculosis in the 1920s and 1930s, or the development of medicare in the 1960s. Saskatchewan and Canada, however, have since fallen behind other jurisdictions and countries as the policy and funding focus in the 1980s and 1990s became more preoccupied with the struggles of the expanding treatment system, and less on the health of the public. The result of budget pressures and of this shorter-term focus has been a diminished capacity in education, housing, culture, social programs, and basic civic infrastructure, as well as a reduced ability of society to influence the other determinants of health. More recently, a renewed interest in understanding how all aspects of health care and society inter-relate to promote health and well-being bodes well for a healthier future. As Benjamin Disraeli remarked, "The health of the public is the foundation upon which is built the happiness of the people and the well-being of the nation."

David Butler-Jones

HEALTH CARE: *see essay on facing page.*

HEALTH ECONOMICS. Health economics is a subset of economics which looks at the resource allocation, efficiency, and distributional aspects of the health sector. The first textbooks in the United States, when no economists yet described themselves as health economists, appeared in 1964 and 1965. Since no "analytical infrastructure" existed for the economic dimension of this sector, the response of the HALL COMMISSION (1961–64) was to undertake an extensive research program under the guidance of the late Dr. MALCOLM TAYLOR, culminating in publications that were to become standard references. In Saskatchewan, health economics may be said to have begun with J.A. Boan's work with the Hall Commission, which he carried over into his research and teaching at the UNIVERSITY OF REGINA. Testable hypotheses from available theories were subjected to rigorous empirical analyses. The findings in the published reports, subjected to rigorous standards of external review, became part of the received wisdom that finds its place in introductory textbooks.

Beginning in the 1970s, important analyses of user fees, the socio-economic determinants of utilization, price and income elasticities, and insurance

risk bearing, were conducted by R.G. Beck and J.M. Horne at the UNIVERSITY OF SASKATCHEWAN. This work pioneered accessing administrative health databases and developing linkages between them. The work on user fees motivated important public policy legislation at both the federal and provincial level. As a byproduct of this research, both the University of Saskatchewan and the University of Regina began to attract graduate students, many of whom later occupied research and policy positions in the health sector across Canada.

J.A. Boan convened a meeting in Regina in 1983, at which the Canadian Health Economics Research Association (CHERA) was born. Since then he has served unstintingly on its executive and in other capacities. This early pioneering work should have resulted in the formation of a health research institute at one or both of Saskatchewan's universities, since the province of Saskatchewan had the most comprehensive and extensive health data sets. Proposals for such an institute were put forward, some under the notable mentorship of Dr. VINCENT MATTHEWS, with active support of Boan, Beck, Horne, Carl Darcy, and others. Unfortunately, nothing materialized.

Some of the reasons for the failure to exploit Saskatchewan's comparative advantage include the fact that scholarly work involves unpredictable outcomes and can result in criticism of programs and governments. Both politicians and bureaucrats have ambivalent affections for health care research. Governments often pay lip service to the need for research; this interest has reached a crescendo in the current infatuation with evidence-based decision-making. For example, when the analysis of the effects of user fees on physician services was completed and publicly defended as a doctoral thesis, the ministry's initial response was that it was fundamentally flawed. Soon there was an election with a change in government; user fees were abolished, and the health ministry then found it convenient to treat the analysis as thorough and authoritative.

From the early 1980s onward, Saskatchewan's research community received very little access to databases. This situation was exacerbated because custody of government databases had been placed in the hands of a private corporation, and government itself began to enjoy significant revenue from fee-for-service data access to pharmaceutical companies. When research institutions were established, they were creatures of government. Their proponents would claim that they were held at arm's length—but close examination would suggest that if so, this was a short arm. Few, if any, of their conclusions criticized government policy. Further, independent scholarly research became increasingly crowded out by community-based action research, some of it advocacy research with a predictable outcome. There is clearly a synergy between action research,

knowledge transmission, and evidence-based decision making. Royal commissions have also changed and become primarily media events, organized around public hearings. Their research is largely, if not entirely, advocacy research, drawing heavily on focus groups. These reports stress "public values" rather than extensive independent scholarly analyses. Their contribution to public discourse is modest.

Health economics, as a discipline with an "analytical infrastructure," has grown enormously in Canada and internationally. Now Canada has many health economists and several university-based health economics research centres. However, in research as in health, quality control remains an ever-present challenge.

R. Glen Beck

HEALTH LABOUR RELATIONS REORGANIZATION ACT: *see* **LEGISLATION IN SASKATCHEWAN**

HEALTH SERVICES PLANNING COMMISSION, 1944–50. The Health Services Planning Commission (HSPC) was created in November 1944 to serve as a central health planning and advisory body to the new CO-OPERATIVE COMMONWEALTH FEDERATION (CCF) government of T.C. DOUGLAS. The CCF had come to power in 1944 with the intention of creating a comprehensive system of socialized health services in Saskatchewan. Under the leadership of Douglas and the HSPC, the new government was to realize much of its goal in its first term in office from 1944 to 1948.

The Commission had been one of the "recommendations for immediate action" made by Dr. Henry E. Sigerist, professor of Medical History at Johns Hopkins University and recognized expert in public health and "socialized medicine," whom Douglas had recruited to conduct a review of health conditions in the province and to make recommendations that would serve as an outline for the government for future reform.

By 1944, Saskatchewan had already seen several innovations in health care such as municipal doctor and union hospital schemes, which collectively allowed a large number of people access to pre-paid hospital and medical care. These ideas, and others, had evolved over time as a result of local initiative, not of a central government plan. The Department of Public Health had focused primarily on public health activities and not on planning a comprehensive public health, medical and hospital scheme for the province.

A small Commission allowed for a concerted effort to transform the system. Douglas staffed the Commission with reform-minded individuals instead of relying on the more traditional Department of Public Health. The Commission was, in some ways, a continuation of Sigerist's work, with the initial three members—C.C. Gibson, an experienced hospital administrator, **T.H. MCLEOD**, economic advisor to the government, and Dr. M.C. Sheps, secretary and member—each having served in some capacity with Sigerist's survey. Selection of a permanent chairperson for the Commission did not occur until 1946, when Dr. **F.D. MOTT**, former Assistant Surgeon General for the United States, assumed the role. But the Commission did not wait for a chairperson to begin; the reforms came quickly and the list was impressive.

The Commission proved instrumental in launching a series of initiatives including a program of medical and hospital care for residents receiving various forms of social assistance (January 1945); division of the province into health regions to deliver public health and preventative services (launched in 1945); plans for these same health regions to provide hospital and medical services (by July 1, 1946, Weyburn, Health Region No. 3, had a full hospitalization scheme, and Swift Current, Health Region No. 1, had complete medical and hospital care); development of a model contract (including full medical and preventive care) and financial support for municipal doctor plans (1945); a system of grants to support hospital construction (March 1945); construction of a new medical school and a university hospital (begun in 1946); efforts to attract and retain needed health care professionals; the launch of the Air Ambulance Service (1946); and, of course, the implementation of Saskatchewan Hospital Services Plan on January 1, 1947, providing the first provincewide, universal, pre-paid hospital insurance plan in Canada.

By 1948 the HSPC was increasingly occupied with administration of its many reforms. At the same time, the CCF determined to slow the pace of social reform and concentrate on economic matters. The need for a compact planning body focused on health reform had diminished, and on April 1, 1950, the operational programs of the HSPC were moved to a reorganized Department of Public Health. The Commission reverted to its original role as a planning and advisory body, and continued to exist until 1963—but in a much diminished capacity, and without the influence or importance it held from 1944 to 1948.

The HSPC had its detractors, in particular the organized medical community who would have preferred an "independent commission," and its plans were sometimes modified or postponed (for example, plans for local health centres based on salaried physician practices were not implemented); but between 1944 and 1948, the HSPC had provided the government with advice and programs needed to eliminate many of the hardships evident in 1944 and to set the stage for the next major reform, medicare, which would come more than a decade later. (*See also* **SIGERIST COMMISSION**)

Duane Mombourquette

Health Care

Saskatchewan's Leadership

C. Stuart Houston and John A. Boan

Although most Canadians are aware that Saskatchewan was a leader in establishing national **MEDICARE**, few people, even in Saskatchewan, know how the province came to take on its leadership role. The story of how a thinly settled, often impoverished province became a global leader in universal health care is a remarkable one. The following account describes the evolution of community health care and highlights some of the impressive contributions made by Saskatchewan health care professionals and civic leaders.

Municipal Doctors and Municipal Hospitals

In Saskatchewan, an early step toward medicare was the creation of the first **MUNICIPAL DOCTOR** and municipal **HOSPITAL** schemes in North America. In 1915, the people of the Rural Municipality (RM) of Sarnia at Holdfast learned that the doctor in the nearby community of Craik was about to join the army when a delegation of Craik people tried to entice Dr. H.J. Schmitt to move from Holdfast to Craik. To retain Schmitt, RM Sarnia voted $1,500 to pay him a retainer, and thus invented a new use for tax dollars. **DR. MAURICE SEYMOUR**, the equivalent of a Deputy Minister of Health, responded quickly: he drafted an amendment to the Municipalities Act to make it legal to pay municipal doctors from taxation funds. A municipal hospital act was passed in 1916; eventually there were 173 municipal doctors in Saskatchewan.

Tuberculosis Control

Tuberculosis was at the time the leading cause of morbidity and mortality. **DR. R.G. FERGUSON**, the head of the Saskatchewan sanatorium near Fort Qu'Appelle, persuaded the government to appoint the Saskatchewan Anti-tuberculosis Commission in 1921–22, the first in any state or province in North America to assess the prevalence of tuberculosis in non-Native and Native children and adults. Ferguson was named the commission's secretary; by directing the research and writing the report, he produced a blueprint for combating tuberculosis across the province. Research for this report included the first representative cross-sectional studies of school children. Twelve of the twenty-one commission recommendations were implemented, resulting in new sanatoria at Saskatoon and Prince Albert, and in the creation of the first traveling TB clinics. Dr. Ferguson next campaigned for the commission's ultimate proposal: universal diagnosis and treatment of tuberculosis at public expense. After three failed attempts, he finally gained unanimous support for this revolutionary idea from the most influential organization in the province, the **SASKATCHEWAN ASSOCIATION OF RURAL MUNICIPALITIES** (SARM), at their annual meeting in May 1928. The government lost no time: at the next legislative session in December 1928, the necessary legislation was passed. It came into effect on January 1, 1929—eight years ahead of the next province (Alberta). The provincial government and the rural municipalities each paid half the cost of universal "free" treatment; some municipalities thus spent more tax dollars on one disease, tuberculosis, than they did on roads.

Under Ferguson, Saskatchewan's tuberculosis research and treatment garnered impressive grassroots support, particularly from farm women and rural municipalities, and led all of North America. Ferguson used controversial BCG vaccination to cut the TB infection rate among Indian infants and student nurses to between a quarter and a fifth of the previous rate, and his published scientific reports remain landmarks. With a made-in-Saskatchewan miniature photofluorography system, the province was the first jurisdiction in North America to embark on general surveys of asymptomatic people to detect early tuberculosis while it was still easily curable, and had the lowest tuberculosis death rate in Canada. It was also the first province to have sufficient TB beds: three per TB death. The close relationship between physicians and their communities helped Saskatchewan to be a healthcare leader in this fight

H against tuberculosis. Payment for the expensive treatment of tuberculosis, which typically required sanatorium stays of one to three years, set a precedent which more than a decade later greatly facilitated T.C. DOUGLAS' task of introducing medicare.

The Matt Anderson Health Plan

The next innovation was by the reeve of the RM of McKillop #220, MATHIAS S. ANDERSON, who after thirteen years of campaigning consulted with Dr. J.M. UHRICH, Minister of Health, and with REG PARKER, Minister of Municipal Affairs. Together they devised a plan whereby each resident of the RM (1,230 people), the town of Strasbourg (430), and the villages of Bulyea (107) and Silton (70), would receive medical care from Dr. Elden Hitsman, their municipal doctor, and on referral to any medical doctor of their choice in Regina. This free choice of consultant doctor was strikingly different from most other municipal plans, where care was given only by the salaried municipal doctor. Led by Dr. E.K. Sauer, members of the Regina District Medical Society agreed to accept 50% of the provincial schedule of fees as payment in full for medical services rendered to people in the McKillop/Strasbourg district.

A vote taken in the proposed area during the municipal elections of November 1938 passed with a plurality of 96%. Implementation required a special act, the Municipal and Hospital Services Act, referred to by some as the Matt Anderson Act. It was passed quickly by the Legislature in March 1939, and "Health District #1" began operation on June 1, 1939. Before long, similar plans were implemented by the RMs of Caledonia, Chester, Lajord, Lumsden, and Longlaketon. By late 1940, a fledgling doctor-sponsored health insurance plan, Medical Services Incorporated, sent doctors' bills to the RM McKillop office for services provided by Regina doctors, and the following year to the other five municipalities which had followed the Anderson plan. Municipal leaders and doctors had once again developed an innovative plan to serve the needs of the community.

Sigerist Commission

Within two days of his election in 1944, Premier T.C. DOUGLAS, with the support of his medical advisor, DR. HUGH MACLEAN, asked DR. HENRY SIGERIST, professor of medical history at Johns Hopkins University, to prepare a report on health care in Saskatchewan. Sigerist's report, produced after only three weeks of hearings and study, provided the "blueprint" for medical care in Saskatchewan for the next half century. Sigerist's recommendations included district health regions for preventive medicine, rural health centres of eight to ten maternity beds, universal hospitalization (at a projected cost of $3.60 per person per annum), and the establishment of a medical college at the University of Saskatchewan. Douglas followed MacLean's advice to assume the health portfolio, so that he as Premier could personally direct the development of health plans.

Social Assistance Medical Care Plan

When the CCF took office in 1944, there was no organized provision of medical care for the province's indigents. T.C. Douglas quickly reached an amicable, province-wide deal with the medical profession to provide care for the province's estimated 30,000 indigents, such as widows and the blind, for $9.50 per person per year. The agreement was advantageous to both sides, as the government could budget for a fixed annual

SASKATCHEWAN ARCHIVES BOARD R-B12052

Woodrow Lloyd and Tommy Douglas, fathers of Medicare in Saskatchewan.

sum for the entire province, while the doctors were paid fee-for-service and policed the system.

Swift Current Health Region

The Swift Current area was slated to be the demonstration unit for preventive medicine. The RM of Pittville at Hazlet already had a health scheme, devised by WILLIAM J. BURAK, whereby its residents received both medical and hospital care for just under $11 per person per year. Wishing to add the Pittville method of full medical care to the preventive program planned for the southwest, Burak wrote at his own expense to each municipality, town and village, visited each weekly newspaper editor, and called a public meeting to press for a full medical and hospital plan. When a vote of all ratepayers was held on November 26, 1945, a majority voted in favour of a full regional health plan.

The Saskatchewan government, manoeuvred by Burak into initiating a more comprehensive scheme than the preventive medicine program it had planned, passed an Order-in-Council on December 11. The region's hospitalization and health care scheme took effect on July 1, 1946–a full two years before Great Britain's "cradle to the grave" health care plan was implemented. Within the SWIFT CURRENT HEALTH REGION (Saskatchewan's Health Region #1) the residents felt empowered, and the region assembled statistical data on the costs of health care that were unrivalled in Canada. The regional scheme flowered when DR. VINCE MATTHEWS, the public health officer, provided seamless integration of preventive work and medical care, a first in Canada. There was a high level of rapport between the local administration, the constituent municipalities, patients, and physicians: Stewart Robertson, the administrator, Dr. Vince Matthews, and Dr. Cas Wolan, president of the district medical association, met informally most days for coffee. In 1951, Swift Current created the first regional hospital board in Canada.

Hospital Services Plan and First Province-wide Universal Hospitalization

In 1945, Saskatchewan became the first province to provide capital grants for hospital construction. Federal funding became available for such purposes in 1948, but the province lost out by having already spent most of its hospital construction funds, which thereby did not qualify for federal matching. Next came provincial hospitalization, capably organized by an American, Dr. FRED D. MOTT, a McGill medical graduate who had married a Winnipeg girl. Mott was lured away from his public health position in the United States, where he had assisted low-income farmers and migratory workers. He masterminded an efficient province-wide hospital plan with low overhead; the nominal fee of $5 per Saskatchewan resident covered 70% of the provincial hospital expenses in the first year (1947). Almost all doctors welcomed the new freedom to admit patients to hospital without concern for ability to pay.

Mental Health Services

Saskatchewan was a leader in psychiatric concepts and practice in many ways. In 1908, Dr. David Low of Regina recommended small, humane psychiatric hospitals, but his forward-thinking advice was overruled on the advice of a Toronto psychiatrist. Instead, two large institutions were built in North Battleford and Weyburn. At the former, Dr. J.W. MacNeill did his best to administer the large complex as compassionately as possible. He removed the bars from windows, forbade the use of mechanical restraints, substituted the word "hospital" for "asylum," provided meaningful therapeutic work on the farm and grounds of the North Battleford Hospital, and treated patients as human beings with illnesses in need of help. A 500-hour psychiatric nurse training program was developed at Weyburn in 1947.

Led by Dr. Sam Lawson, the Saskatchewan Plan, a comprehensive proposal for all phases of emotional or mental treatment to be given within a health region, without recourse to a remote large mental hospital, was developed in the 1950s. A team would provide continuity of care within each region. Between 1960 and 1963, Dr. D.G. MCKERRACHER at UNIVERSITY HOSPITAL, Saskatoon, showed that all types of mentally ill patients, including some psychotics, could be cared for in a small open psychiatric ward in that hospital, where selected, interested family practitioners were allowed to treat their own patients. Drs. Abram Hoffer and Humphrey Osmond, who incidentally coined the word "psychedelic," were among the first to explore the biochemical basis of mental disease, and experimented with hallucinogens and nicotinic acid in treatment.

High Energy Radiation Cancer Treatment

As part of an effort to catch up with other provinces in offering radium treatment of cancer, Saskatchewan went even farther and established the first cancer control agency in Canada in 1930. This agency set up, in Regina and Saskatoon, the first government-sponsored cancer clinics in North America; this public service later evolved into a position at the forefront of world clinical radiation science. In 1945, the Saskatchewan Cancer Commission and the University of Saskatchewan jointly hired Dr. HAROLD JOHNS, Canada's first full-time cancer physicist; in 1949, Johns began the first concerted clinical use of the high-energy betatron in the world. Given funding and *carte blanche* approval by Premier Douglas, Dr. Johns and Dr. ALLAN BLAIR, radiation therapist in Regina, next developed treatment with a new modality, cobalt-60. Dr. Johns and graduate student SYLVIA FEDORUK, later chancellor of the University and subsequently Saskatchewan's Lieutenant-Governor, calibrated the cobalt machine in eleven weeks. The first patient was treated on November 8, 1951, for an advanced carcinoma of the cervix, deemed unlikely to be cured by any treatment regimen previously known. The patient received a precise dose to an exact area, was cured, and lived to the age of 90.

Why was Saskatchewan the Leader?

Why was Saskatchewan the leader in so many areas of health? Why did a member of Parliament from Prince Albert, JOHN DIEFENBAKER, appoint in 1961 Mr. Justice EMMETT HALL, Chief Justice of Saskatchewan , to head up the Royal Commission on Health Services, which recommended universal medical care for the rest of Canada? Why was a former Premier of Saskatchewan, ROY ROMANOW, chosen to lead the one-man Royal Commission on the Future of Health Care in Canada, which reported in November 2002? In fact, the province got off to a slow start. In the 1890s, a resident of what is now Saskatchewan had to go west to Medicine Hat or Calgary, or east to Brandon or Winnipeg, to obtain hospital care and to see most medical specialists other than surgeons. But there was unlimited faith in future prospects: when, in the early years of the 20th century, small hospitals were built, a number of them quickly developed nursing training schools. Medical practitioners settled in almost every town and village with a population of 200, and their lives intertwined with their chosen community. Their dedication gained them much respect, providing them with authority and community support to suggest and introduce many health care innovations.

There were six main elements that contributed to Saskatchewan's pre-eminence in the healthcare field. First, the visionaries mentioned above acted as catalysts. Second, the citizens showed a co-operative spirit, trust, and a willingness to help one another that was perhaps developed to a higher and more practical degree than in any other province. Rarely did people have surplus cash, but there was an abundance of good will, of trust in one another, a willingness to help, and a sense that lives could be improved through communal effort. Mutual co-operation among settlers was more the rule than the exception: it was better to do things together than separately. If a family had to build a barn, neighbours came to help raise the rafters; the entire community would turn out to build a curling rink; and the same philosophy applied to creating and nurturing community services and institutions.

Third, municipal politicians were forward-thinking and innovative, using the municipal structure to full advantage. The manager, then known as the secretary-treasurer, knew every farm and every farmer; he might or might not have a "stenographer" and a man to run a road grader and do odd jobs. The hospital was managed by the nursing matron, who would also rush a bedpan to a patient in need. Things were done efficiently, with a tremendous "bang for the buck." Survivors of the DEPRESSION, severe drought, and dust storms of the Dirty Thirties, Saskatchewan's residents were more frugal than many other groups, and much effort was voluntary—without pay. Fourth, rather than appointing commissions whose reports often gathered dust where they were shelved, provincial governments responded quickly to needs, often passing appropriate legislation at the next session of the Legislature.

Fifth, medical doctors in general were altruistic, with service to sick patients as their primary goal and money only a by-product. In private practice, through the 1930s, doctors collected for less than half of their services. Except for holidays and an occasional refresher course, most were on call 24 hours a day, seven days a week. Queues were non-existent. Hospitals were patient-oriented and lacked multiple layers of bureaucracy. Through the 1950s, it was the rule (as it was in Great Britain, at least until the 1970s) that once a patient's name was placed on the morning's operating "slate," the doctors and nurses stayed until every surgery was completed, even if they ran into difficulty and ran several hours late. No one was "bumped." A patient requiring a consultation with a specialist was almost always seen that same week. If there were no beds in the wards, the patient was promptly placed in a bed in a hospital ward corridor. Laboratory and x-ray examinations were done and reported within the week. Sixth, economic hardship, particularly during the 1930s, meant that virtually everyone was in the same predicament: there was rarely a discretionary dollar to spend, but most people did not perceive themselves as poor. An egalitarian spirit of co-operation and altruism formed the cohesive social fabric that helped to drive Saskatchewan's leadership role. (*See also* TUBERCULOSIS CONTROL)

FURTHER READING:

Boan, J.A. (ed.). 1994. *Proceedings of the Fifth Canadian Conference on Health Economics.* Regina: Canadian Plains Research Center.

Houston, C.S. 2002. *Steps on the Road to Medicare: Why Saskatchewan Led the Way.* Montreal: McGill-Queen's University Press.

——. 2003. "A Medical Historian Looks at the Romanow Report," *Saskatchewan Law Review* 66: 539–547.

Johnson, A.W. 2004. *Dream No Little Dreams: A Biography of the Douglas Government of Saskatchewan, 1944–1961.* Toronto: University of Toronto Press.

McLeod, T.H. and I. McLeod. 1987. *Tommy Douglas: The Road to Jerusalem.* Edmonton: Hurtig.

Romanow, R. 2002. *Building on Values: The Future of Health Care in Canada.* Saskatoon: Commission on the Future of Health Care in Canada.

LIBRARY AND ARCHIVES CANADA/ C-020053

Samuel Hearne.

HEARNE, SAMUEL (1745–92). Samuel Hearne joined the Hudson's Bay Company (HBC) in February 1766 at the age of 21. He began his exploration of what is now northern Saskatchewan in 1768 in search of a Northwest Passage to the copper mines of the arctic regions. Hearne was the first European to view and cross Great Slave Lake. Although unintentionally, Hearne proved that a Northwest Passage via Hudson Bay did not exist. He also became the first European to formally document the overland travel routes north of Hudson Bay. In 1770, Hearne met and traveled with **DENESULINE** leader Motonabbee; although he was skilled at snowshoeing, it was Montonabbee who taught him the life-saving skills that enabled him to survive in the vast north. Hearne set up the HBC's first western inland post in 1774; following the advice of the local chiefs, he chose a site that connected to the **SASKATCHEWAN RIVER** trade route and the **CHURCHILL RIVER** system and established Cumberland House, the first permanent settlement in Saskatchewan's history.

Recognizing Hearne's vast experience with exploration and his positive relationship with local Native people, the London Committee encouraged him to initiate more sophisticated trading practices. Hearne developed an early model of the York boat so that the HBC would extend inland trade; he became chief factor at the Churchill River's Prince of Wale's Fort in 1776. By 1782, the fur trade had fallen off drastically and smallpox and starvation had decimated local First Nations communities. Out of favour with the London Committee and the HBC, Hearne wrote and published chronicles about the local Denesuline and the northern environment, describing their hunting methods, kinship systems,

and the roles of women in the communities. His book became the standard text across Canada and Europe: unlike the majority of HBC journals, missionary accounts and official government sources, Samuel Hearne's pragmatic historical analysis questioned whether Saskatchewan First Nations people actually benefited from the fur trade. He died in November 1792 at the age of 47. *Elizabeth Mooney*

FURTHER READING: McGoogan, K. 2003. *Ancient Mariner: The Amazing Adventures of Samuel Hearne, the Sailor Who Walked to the Arctic Ocean*. Toronto: Harper Flamingo Canada.

HEAVY OIL UPGRADERS. Canada's first heavy oil upgrader opened in Regina in 1988, and the second began production near Lloydminster four years later. Saskatchewan is the country's second largest oil producer after Alberta, accounting for about 20% of Canada's production. The province's oil fields have a full range of crude oil, from light sweet to heavy. Viscous crude oil is described as heavy oil and needs special equipment so that the petroleum can be refined for use as gasoline or diesel fuel for vehicles and other products including home heating oil. The Regina project involved loans and equity provided by the federal and provincial governments to build the NewGrade Energy upgrader adjacent to the Consumers' Co-operative Refinery Limited (CCRL). Announced in 1983 with a price tag of $600 million, the Regina upgrader finally opened in 1988 and produces about 55,000 barrels of synthetic oil per day. NewGrade, now a 50-50 joint venture between CCRL and the province of Saskatchewan, completed a $300 million expansion in 2003. The $1.2 billion Bi-Provincial Upgrader, which opened in 1992, produces about 70,000 barrels of oil a day from heavy oil; it is now a business unit of **HUSKY ENERGY** after shares of the commercial operation were sold by the Alberta, Saskatchewan, and federal governments. *Joe Ralko*

HEMIPTERA: *see* **BUGS**

HENDAY, ANTHONY (1725–?). Anthony Henday is the first known European to have crossed the northern plains. In 1754, he was sent to persuade the northern plains groups to bring their furs to York Factory instead of trading with French traders who were advancing up the **SASKATCHEWAN RIVER**. Henday and Connawapa, a local **CREE**, were taken inland by Attickasish (or Little Deer), a Pegogamaw Cree leader. After visiting the French post at Basquia (The Pas, Manitoba), the group met their families up the Carrot River near modern Red Earth First Nation. They continued westward on foot, crossing the South Saskatchewan in make-shift canoes. Henday gives few details about the local geography, and is especially vague after they

reached the Elbow of the **NORTH SASKATCHEWAN RIVER**. Seemingly they followed the Battle River westward, perhaps to the Red Deer area, where they met a large camp of over 200 tents of "Archithinue," an anglicized Cree term used for anyone other than Cree or Nakota. In the spring, the group built their canoes east of Edmonton. Henday gives few details of his return trip down the Saskatchewan, except to describe the French post near Fort à la Corne. No journal survives of Henday's second journey inland in 1759–60.

Henday's account presents many problems since his original journal is lost: there are four copies, each differing from the others. Although one version was published in 1908, the other three and his daily log were not published until 2000. *Dale Russell*

FURTHER READING: Henday, A. 2000. *A Year Inland: The Journal of a Hudson's Bay Company Winterer* (B. Belyea, ed.). Waterloo, Ontario: Wilfrid Laurier University Press; Meyer, D. and D. Russell. 2004. "So Fine and Pleasant, Beyond Description: The Lands and Lives of the Pegogamaw Crees," *Plains Anthropologist* 49 (19): 217–52.

HENDERSON, JAMES (1871–1951). James Henderson, born on August 21, 1871 in Glasgow, Scotland, is considered to be Saskatchewan's pre-eminent first-generation artist. An early aptitude to sketch and draw led to an apprenticeship in lithography, complemented by night courses at the Glasgow School of Art, where he was influenced by the resident and then-popular Scottish Impressionists. Following employment in London as an engraver and lithographer, Henderson immigrated to Winnipeg in 1909 and in 1910 moved to Regina, where he engaged in commercial art assignments. Periodic visits to the picturesque **QU'APPELLE VALLEY** appealed to his artistic sensibilities and resulted in relocation to Fort Qu'Appelle in 1916.

At his peak, Henderson was widely known as a painter of First Nations portraits expressive of innate dignity. He exhibited portraits at the 1924 and 1925 British Empire Exhibitions at Wembley, the same venues where Canada's acclaimed Group of Seven first achieved international recognition. (In critical retrospect, many of the portraits are now considered more important as historical records than for their artistic merit. Very few were painted after 1932.) Fort Qu'Appelle's Standing Buffalo Reserve named Henderson as Honorary Chief *Wiciteowapi Wicasa*, "the man who paints the old men."

Henderson is best remembered for the artistic mastery of his landscapes, particularly those in which he captured the charm of his beloved Qu'Appelle Valley in all its moods and seasons: the rebirth of spring, the glory of summer, the finality of autumn, and the bleakness of winter–spanning all times of day and night. He also painted land-

James Henderson's "Road to the Lake," oil on canvas, ca. 1935.

scapes in British Columbia, Alberta, and Ontario's Muskoka Lakes region. Henderson was a Member of the Ontario Society of Artists; he periodically exhibited in Toronto, Ottawa and Montreal, and in 1936 with the Royal Canadian Academy (although he was never elected as a member). A career highlight was the National Gallery of Canada's acquisition of one portrait and two landscapes from 1928 to 1932.

In the annals of Saskatchewan art history, Henderson was the first to make a living solely from creating art, without depending upon teaching income, and he was the first to gain national and international recognition. For his achievements, he received an honorary Doctor of Laws degree from the **UNIVERSITY OF SASKATCHEWAN** in 1951. Henderson died on July 5, 1951, in Regina, and was buried overlooking the valley at Fort Qu'Appelle.

James E. Lanigan

FURTHER READING: Hayworth, A. 1958. "James Henderson of the Qu'Appelle Valley," *Saskatchewan History*: 59-66.

HENRY THE ELDER, ALEXANDER (1739–1824).

Alexander Henry the Elder spent his long career as a fur trader and merchant in the east, but he did make one trip into the west. In 1775, with Joseph and Thomas Frobisher and forty men, he built the first post north of the **SASKATCHEWAN RIVER** on Amisk Lake. In January 1776, he walked up the Saskatchewan River to Isaac's House, a Montrealers' post above Nipawin. From there, he visited a large Nakota camp across the open plains to the south before returning to Amisk Lake. After spring break-

up, the traders traveled up the Churchill River, where they intercepted a large group of **DENESULINE** canoeing downstream to trade with the Hudson's Bay Company. After obtaining their furs and hearing of the Athabasca district, the traders returned to Montreal. Shortly after, in 1778, **PETER POND**, using this and other information, crossed Portage la Loche to open the Athabasca fur trade. Henry made a large map showing his travels, in which only a few features are identified. Much later, in 1809, he published his memoirs, which included an account of

Alexander Henry, the Elder.

his experiences in the west. Although his narrative is sometimes confusing and exaggerated, Henry wrote a sketch of the Denesuline and one of the most detailed descriptions of a Nakota wintering camp.

Dale Russell

FURTHER READING: Henry the Elder, A. 1969. *Travels and Adventures in Canada and the Indian Territories between 1760 and 1776.* Edmonton: Hurtig; Marchildon, G. and S. Robinson. 2002. *Canoeing the Churchill: A Practical Guide to the Historic Voyageur Highway.* Regina: Canadian Plains Research Center.

HENRY THE YOUNGER, ALEXANDER (FL. 1791–1814).

To avoid confusion, Alexander Henry is known as the Younger while his uncle, also named **ALEXANDER HENRY**, is the Elder. Henry the Younger began his career as a North West Company (NWC) trader in southern Manitoba, then lived at various posts along the Alberta portion of the **NORTH SASKATCHEWAN RIVER** and ended up at Fort George at the mouth of the Columbia River, where he drowned in 1814. Unlike many of his fellow NWC traders, Henry kept a lengthy journal throughout his career. Although the original is lost, the existing copy is 1,642 pages long and has been published twice. His journal is not a simple diary: it includes meteorological tables and lists of employees, as well as vocabularies and detailed descriptions of the major plains tribes, especially the **CREE**. He was also the only trader to name the various Nakota bands across the northern plains. Henry spent little time in what is now Saskatchewan, yet his account of travelling up the Saskatchewan and North Saskatchewan Rivers in August 1808 contains detailed descriptions of those valleys, providing both natural and historical observations.

Dale Russell

FURTHER READING: Gough, B.M. (ed.). 1992. *The Journal of Alexander Henry the Younger, 1799–1814.* Toronto: Champlain Society.

HENRY, EMMA (1881–1968).

Emma Henry (Sister St. Victor) belonged to the *Filles de la Providence* congregation, one of the teaching orders forced from France by then rising anti-clerical sentiment, and spent most of her sixty-five-year-long religious life in Saskatchewan. Born in Brittany on February 11, 1881, she came to western Canada in 1903. Here she and other women religious who had fled France found refuge, as well as a new source of novices, within the deeply religious French minority of western Canada and the rapidly expanding Catholic immigrant population. Sister St. Victor spent two years in Prince Albert and Regina, learning English and studying at Normal School. She was then assigned to Howell (as Prud'homme was then called), and taught in a small boarding convent. Soon she was sent to St. Louis, where the congregation was building a large convent. In 1919 she went to France for a short rest period, and then moved to the congregation's training convent in Vegreville, Alberta. In 1929, she was named Mistress of Novices in Prud'homme, a few years after the training convent was transferred there. In 1941 she was appointed Provincial Superior. In 1955, age and illness forced her to take a less demanding position in St. Brieux. Later retiring to the St. Louis convent, she died there on March 1, 1968.   *Richard Lapointe*

FURTHER READING: Lapointe, R. 1988. "Emma Henry (soeur Saint Victor, F.d.l.P.)." Pp. 208–10 in *100 noms: Petit dictionnaire biographique des Franco-Canadiens de la Saskatchewan*. Regina: Société historique.

HERBERT, town, pop 812, located 45 km NE of Swift Current on the Trans-Canada Hwy. The Herbert area began to be settled in the early 1900s, predominantly by Mennonites, but also by people of British and Scandinavian origins. Originally, their point of disembarkation was at a boxcar railway station with the name "Herbert" posted on it—the name honouring Sir Michael Henry Herbert, a British diplomat. In 1904, the foundations of the village were established. Within months, a boarding house, livery stable, hardware and grocery store, lumberyard, implement dealer, and post office were in business. The district was quickly settled: by 1911, the population had grown to 559. From 1916 to 1926, Ford Model Ts were assembled at a garage in Herbert for distribution in the region. From the late 1950s to the early 1980s, the community's population remained fairly stable at around 1,000. Herbert's economy continues to be largely based on agriculture (a combination of crop and livestock production), and a number of the town's businesses and services cater to the industry. To the north of the town, on Lake Diefenbaker, lies Herbert Ferry Regional Park, with opportunities for boating, fishing, and camping. Herbert's museum is located in the community's former CPR station, built in 1908 and now a heritage property. *Faspa* (a low-German term used to describe a late afternoon lunch put together for unannounced visitors) is served in the former station agent's quarters throughout the summer, following a traditional Mennonite custom. Other heritage properties in Herbert include two stately homes dating to 1912 and 1913, and St. Patrick's Roman Catholic Church, built in 1912, now a private property. The Herbert area has produced a number of people of note, among them: JACK WIEBE, former LIEUTENANT-GOVERNOR of Saskatchewan and former member of the Senate of Canada; Don Wittman, the CBC Sports commentator; and Homer Groening (born in Main Centre, northwest of Herbert), father of Matt Groening, creator of *The Simpsons*.   *David McLennan*

HERBS AND WILD MUSHROOM INDUSTRY. The herb industry in Saskatchewan has expanded relatively quickly since the early 1990s, and has focussed on production of a range of medicinal and aromatic herbs for the culinary, nutraceutical, and cosmeceutical industries. Several organizations were created to support industry development (networking, production, processing, marketing, research), provide regulatory information, and raise public awareness of the importance of nutraceuticals, functional foods, and cosmeceuticals. The Saskatchewan Herb and Spice Organization currently has 300 members and supplies information on specific crops through its links; it also provides a voice in the National Herb and Spice Coalition. The Saskatchewan Nutraceutical Network represents the nutraceutical, functional food, and cosmeceutical industry in the province and provides an on-line newsletter (*Nutra News*), market and research information, and links to over 450 national and international web sites. Research and development work on herb crops is being conducted at the University of Saskatchewan, the National Research Council-Plant Biotechnology Institute, Agriculture and Agri-Food Canada, and the Prairie Farm Rehabilitation Administration (Canada-Saskatchewan Irrigation Diversification Centre; Outlook and Shelter Belt Centre, Indian Head), as well as in private industry. In April 2003 the first Saskatchewan Natural Health Products (NHP) Research Society meeting was held in Saskatoon to network researchers in applied and basic areas of study; this network is envisioned to expand into a national base.

The Saskatchewan wild mushroom industry began about fifteen years ago and is concentrated mainly in areas north of 54°N latitude, with some harvesting in the Nipawin region. As mushroom-harvesting sites in Europe and Japan become scarce, demand for North American-sourced mushrooms has markedly increased and the majority of Saskatchewan-harvested wild mushrooms are exported to these countries. The wild mushrooms of major commercial value include chanterelles (*Cantharellus cibarius*), pine mushrooms (*Tricholoma magnivelare*), and morels (*Morchella* sp.). The wild mushroom industry has grown to a value of about $1 million, directly provided to the 400–500 pickers in 1999; it consists of harvesters, buyers, brokers, processors, exporters (which may include foreign importers), wholesalers, distributors, and retailers. The harvesters are usually Saskatchewan residents, who are becoming increasingly concerned about the loss of good mushroom habitat. Significantly, this industry provides diversified income to other segments of the forestry industry including loggers, fire crews, students, homemakers, and Aboriginal peoples.   *Karen Tanino*

Elwin Hermanson, November 2001.

HERMANSON, ELWIN NORRIS (1952–). Elwin Hermanson was born August 22, 1952, in Swift Current. Raised near Beechy, Hermanson attained a three-year diploma from the Full Gospel Bible Institute in Eston. He took over the family grain and beef cattle farm that he continues to operate. Hermanson and his wife Gail have three children. From 1979 to 1994 Hermanson served on the board of the Full Gospel Bible Institute, and was chair from 1987 to 1991. He was also on the Beechy-Demaine Economic Development Committee.

In 1988, Hermanson ran as one of the first REFORM PARTY candidates in Canada. He served three terms on the Reform Party's National Executive Council and was elected as the MP for Kindersley–Lloydminster in 1993. He served as Agriculture critic as well as Reform House Leader from 1993 to 1995. Hermanson lost his federal seat in the 1997 election, but quickly moved into provincial politics. He took leave from his job as the federal Reform Party's national election readiness manager to serve as one of the initial members of the Saskatchewan Party Steering Committee. In 1997, the SASKATCHEWAN PARTY was given the status of Official Opposition.

Hermanson was elected the first leader of the Saskatchewan Party in 1998. In the 1999 provincial election the Saskatchewan Party captured 26 of 58 seats, receiving more of the popular vote than the governing NDP. Hermanson was elected MLA for Rosetown-Biggar and became leader of the Opposition to the NDP and Liberal coalition. The Saskatchewan Party narrowly lost the 2003 election. The party's inability to win urban seats proved to be its downfall. Although he was re-elected, after two narrow defeats, Hermanson resigned as leader.   *Winter Fedyk*

HERONS. The family Ardeidae, in the order Ciconiiformes, is a family of long-legged, long-beaked birds with short tails. Their habit of flying with their head pulled back distinguishes them from cranes. During courtship the males develop specialized plumes for display; it was these plumes which led to the near-extinction of several species by feather-hunters when the feathers were in demand for decorating women's hats and men's military dress hats. The family of approximately sixty-five species is found on all continents except Antarctica; thirteen species occur in North America. They are usually found in or near wetlands, where they feed on a variety of invertebrate and vertebrate prey.

Ten species have been reported for Saskatchewan; all are migratory. The most common and largest is the great blue heron (*Ardea herodias*), which occurs south of the boreal forest. This large bird (~120 cm in length) is often seen standing at the edge of a river or lake, waiting until it can spear a fish. It usually nests in colonies which are found in the tops of tall trees along water margins. The other widespread and often encountered species of the southern half of the province is the black-crowned night heron (*Nycticorax nycticorax*), a smaller species with black crown and back, which is found around permanent marshes. A species which was once more widespread and heard more often than seen is the American bittern (*Botaurus lentiginosus*). It was seldom seen, hiding in the reeds and cattails of marsh edges in the southern half of the province and giving its "pump-handle" call. Its presence in the reeds is hard to discover owing to its camouflage pattern of brown stripes the colour of dead cattails. Its recent decline may be due to habitat change by draining of wetlands or to the reduction in population numbers of large frogs.

The great egret (*Ardea alba*) occurs regularly but rarely in the wetlands of the southern third of the province. It is nearly as tall as the more common great blue heron, but white with a yellow bill. A recent entrant is the white cattle egret (*Bubulcus ibis*), an African species which became established naturally in northern South America in the late 1800s and has since successfully colonized Central and North America. It was first reported in Saskatchewan in 1974 and can be expected, with climate change, to continue to expand its range and numbers.

Five small herons rarely appear in the province; since the reports are of single individuals along the southern border, they are considered strays, off-course during migration. These are the least bittern (*Ixobrychus exilis*), snowy egret (*Egretta thula*), little blue heron (*Egretta caerula*), green heron (*Butorides virescens*), and yellow-crowned night heron (*Nyctanassa violacea*).   *Diane Secoy*

FURTHER READING: Alsop, Fred J., III. 2002. *The Birds of Canada*. New York: Dorling Kindersley.

HERZBERG, GERHARD (1904–99). Gerhard Herzberg was one of Canada's and the world's great scientists. Born and educated in Germany, he became recognized internationally by age 30 as one of the pioneers of molecular spectroscopy and structure. With the deteriorating conditions in Germany under the Nazi regime, he found a safe haven at the **UNIVERSITY OF SASKATCHEWAN** thanks to **JOHN W.T. SPINKS** and the far-sighted **WALTER C. MURRAY**. During his ten years there, Herzberg set up an impressive laboratory, was invited to speak at universities and conferences across Canada and the United States, and published forty research papers and three outstanding texts on atomic and molecular spectra. In 1946, he joined the Yerkes Observatory of the University of Chicago for three years and developed techniques that became standards in laboratory studies of planetary spectra. However, Herzberg was homesick for Canada, and in 1948 he accepted an invitation to establish a major research laboratory at the National Research Council (NRC) in Ottawa. His famous spectroscopy laboratory at the NRC became a Mecca for hundreds of scientists around the world and helped to bring Canadian science to international prominence. Along with his research, Herzberg completed the trilogy *Molecular Spectra and Molecular Structures*, which became a bible for physicists, chemists, and astronomers working in spectroscopy. For his many accomplishments, especially his basic discoveries of spectra of free radicals, he was awarded the 1971 Nobel Prize in Chemistry. He continued

UNIVERSITY OF SASKATCHEWAN ARCHIVES A-3234

Gerhard Herzberg.

in active research at the NRC until his official retirement in 1994. After a brief illness, he died at home on March 3, 1999. Herzberg has been honoured in many ways, including scholarships and the Nobel Plaza at the University of Saskatchewan, a park in Saskatoon, the Herzberg Institute of Astrophysics in Victoria, and laboratories across Canada, along with Canada's most prestigious research award ($1 million), the annual Gerhard Herzberg Canada Gold Medal for Science and Engineering.

Boris Stoicheff and Diane Secoy

HICKS, JOHN VICTOR (1907–99). Dubbed "Canada's most neglected poet" by Earle Birney, John V. Hicks nonetheless left a legacy that included ten books and numerous accolades. Born on February 24, 1907, in London, England, he immigrated to Canada with his parents while still an infant. After living in New Brunswick, Quebec, and Alberta, he settled in Prince Albert, where he resided until his death.

Hicks began writing poetry while working as an accountant, but did not publish his first book until in his seventies. *Now is a Far Country* (Thistledown, 1978) was the culmination of years of publishing poems in journals across Canada and the United States. Other collections from Thistledown Press soon followed, including: *Winter Your Sleep* (1980), *Silence Like the Sun* (1983), and *Rootless Tree* (1985). These collections reflect the influence of writers like T.S. Eliot, W.B.Yeats, and Walter de la Mare, although the combination of playfulness and tradition is one aspect that distinguishes Hicks's work from predecessors.

Music and religion were inseparable from the man and his work. He served as the organist at St. Alban's Cathedral in Prince Albert for more than sixty years, and was married to composer and music teacher Marjorie (Kisbey) Hicks. His poems demon-

COURTESY OF TOURISM SASKATCHEWAN

Great blue heron.

strate a love of music in subject matter, structure, and tone. Carefully chosen language, rhythms, and silences reinforce the underlying themes of his work. Much of Hicks's work explores the devotional aspects of love and faith in both secular and religious contexts. Series such as "Love's Hours" and "The 'Orphic Thread' Poems" (*Sticks and Strings*, Thistledown, 1988) show the complex intersection of spirituality and music. Several Canadian composers, including **ELIZABETH RAUM**, have produced music based on his poetry.

A regular guest on **PETER GZOWSKI**'s CBC program *Morningside*, Hicks was well respected in the literary community. He was the recipient of an Honorary Doctorate in Literature (**UNIVERSITY OF SASKATCHEWAN**, 1987), a Lifetime Award for Excellence in the Arts (**SASKATCHEWAN ARTS BOARD**, 1990), and the Saskatchewan Order of Merit (1992). His collection of short essays, *Side Glances: Notes on the Writer's Craft* (Thistledown, 1987), is still considered to be one of the best books of its kind. His later work betrays a more contemplative mind reflecting on life and loss. Hicks unofficially served as Prince Albert's Poet Laureate until his death on June 16, 1999.

FURTHER READING: Bidwell, P. 1988. "Introduction." Pp. 9–15 in Paul Bidwell (ed.), *Sticks and Strings: Selected and New Poems by John V. Hicks*. Saskatoon: Thistledown Press.

HIGH-ENERGY CANCER TREATMENT. Saskatchewan has been a world leader in the fight against cancer. The Saskatchewan Cancer Commission Act, passed by the Conservative government of **J.T.M. ANDERSON** in 1930, established the first cancer control agency in Canada in 1930. North America's first government-sponsored, government-equipped, part-time diagnostic and treatment clinics were staffed by radiologists: Dr. Earle E. Shepley at the Saskatoon City Hospital, and Dr. Clarence M. Henry at the Regina General Hospital. Patients were treated with "high-voltage" machines, operating at 400 kilovolts peak, and with radium. In 1931, Dr Shepley visited Dr. Ellice McDonald (who had been raised at Fort Qu'Appelle, Saskatchewan, and had graduated in medicine from McGill University in 1901) at the Cancer Institute in Philadelphia, as well as Dr. James Ewing at the New York Memorial Hospital. On Shepley's return, the Saskatchewan government allocated $115,000 for the purchase of radium. From a radon plant at the **UNIVERSITY OF SASKATCHEWAN**, Dr. Ertle Harrington distributed radon to both cancer clinics in small gold tubes or "seeds."

In 1939, Regina-born Dr. **ALLAN W. BLAIR**, a graduate of McGill University and a radiotherapist at the Toronto General Hospital, became director of the Regina cancer clinic. The first session of the CCF leg-

islature in October 1944 passed the Cancer Control Act, which provided all services necessary for the diagnosis and treatment of cancer without charge. Dr. Blair recognized that a full-time radiation physicist was needed. In 1945, Dr. **HAROLD E. JOHNS** was hired jointly by the Saskatchewan Cancer Commission and the university, and thus became Canada's first full-time cancer physicist. A 24-MeV betatron, manufactured in Wisconsin, purchased for $80,000, was installed at the University of Saskatchewan, and nine months were spent in its meticulous calibration before the first patient was treated on March 29, 1949. Over the next seventeen years, 301 patients were treated. They were delivered a high dose of radiation, without appreciable damage to overlying skin and with few side effects, but the operating costs of the betatron were high. This represented the first concerted clinical use of the betatron anywhere.

Most important of all, Saskatchewan initiated the first use of calibrated cobalt-60 in the world. In July 1949, after visiting the Chalk River Experimental Nuclear Reactor Facility in Ontario, Dr. Harold Johns asked University of Saskatchewan president **WALTER P. THOMPSON** for 1,000 curies of cobalt-60, about 100 times the activity of any radium unit. After gaining the assent of Premier and Health Minister Douglas, Johns applied for Chalk River's first cobalt source, 2.5 cm in diameter, 1.25 cm thick, with an approximate strength of 1,000 curies. The 0.9 tonne Saskatoon unit, designed by Johns and Lloyd Bates and built by Johnny MacKay, was installed in the newly constructed cancer wing of University Hospital on August 17, 1951. McKay also built the collimation apparatus—interchangeable lead plugs—to direct the radiation to a precise area. Rigorous measurements were continued until November 8, 1951, when the first patient was treated by Watson (*see* Table HCT-1 below).

The first patient treated at Saskatoon had advanced carcinoma of the cervix at age 40. She received a precise dose to an exact area, carefully calibrated. Not only was she cured of her cancer, but she lived to the age of 90 in Victoria, British Columbia. The first formal publication giving details of cobalt therapy was written by H.E. Johns, L.M. Bates, E.R. Epp, D.V. Cormack, and **S.O. FEDORUK**, all from Saskatchewan, with three University of Saskatchewan physics graduates (A. Morrison, W.R. Dixon, and C. Garrett) working at the National

Research Council in Ottawa. The depth-dose charts compiled by Epp, Fedoruk, and Johns were used in active radiotherapy departments throughout the world.

MacKay's small firm in Saskatoon produced over 100 collimators for Picker Cobalt units that were distributed internationally. The original Saskatoon cobalt-60 unit treated 6,728 patients over the age of 21, until finally it was replaced by a commercial AECL cobalt-60 machine in 1972. Saskatchewan had been first in this effective and more economical method of treating cancer, still so inexpensive that Cobalt-60 remains widely used in less affluent countries.   *C. Stuart Houston and Sylvia O. Fedoruk*

FURTHER READING: Houston, C.S. 2002. "High-voltage Cancer Treatment." Pp. 105–23 in C.S. Houston (ed.), *Steps*

COURTESY OF HAROLD JOHNS MUSEUM, SASKATOON CANCER AGENCY, SASKATOON

Betatron: first concerted clinical use in the world was at the University of Saskatchewan, March 29, 1949.

COURTESY OF HAROLD JOHNS MUSEUM, SASKATOON CANCER AGENCY, SASKATOON

Harold E. Johns, Charles C. Burkell, and Sylvia Fedoruk, with Cobalt-60 unit.

Table HCT-1. First cobalt-60 treatments in the world, 1951		
	Saskatchewan	W. Ontario
Cobalt-60 source delivered	July 30	October 16
Unit installed	August 17	October 23
Calibration	11 weeks	—
First patient treated	November 8	October 27

on the Road to Medicare: Why Saskatchewan Led the Way. Montreal: McGill-Queen's University Press.

HIGHWAY NETWORK. Saskatchewan's highway network consists of 26,250 km of roads, or roughly 14% of the province's entire rural road network. Saskatchewan's highway and municipal road networks together constitute the largest rural road system in Canada, totaling over 190,000 km. In 1905, the province assumed responsibility for its roads from the federal government. Development of rural roads was moderate through the 1920s (the government had completed 4,200 km of provincial highway by 1927), but virtually non-existent through the DEPRESSION. Roadway construction boomed in the 1950s, propelling Saskatchewan's rural road network into national distinction as Canada's most extensive provincial road system. In 1950 the province signed the Trans-Canada Highway Act, which provided funding for constructing the local portion of the proposed transcontinental highway paralleling the CANADIAN PACIFIC RAILWAY main line. Seven years later, on August 21, 1957, Premier T.C. DOUGLAS officially opened Saskatchewan's new 650-km east-west stretch of the TRANS-CANADA HIGHWAY. The Yellowhead Highway soon after became eligible for federal assistance, as did Highways 6, 7, 11, and 39. Each of these provincial highways was an important link in the national highway system, and was therefore entitled to funding under the National Highways Project.

Saskatchewan Highways and Transportation is responsible for planning and developing transportation policy and for constructing, maintaining, operating, and regulating the province's highway network. In the past 50 years, the department has made significant progress in converting highway surfaces from gravel to thin pavements and asphalt; this conversion increases the highways' capacity to accommodate greater traffic volumes, especially truck traffic. Until 1960 the majority of Saskatchewan's highways were gravel; by 1980, pavements and dust-free surfaces had become the dominant surface types. Today, roughly 51% (13,460 km) of Saskatchewan's highway network is paved; 26.5%

(6,960 km) has been treated with a thin-membrane dust-free surface; 22% (5,700 km) remains gravel; and 0.5% (131 km) is ice road.

Saskatchewan's highways are traditionally classified into four categories: major arterial, minor arterial, collector, and local. Traffic volumes and construction standards are generally based upon these classifications. Major arterial highways move large volumes of provincial and international traffic at high speeds and under free-flowing conditions, serve urban centres of more than 10,000 people, and accommodate more than 1,000 vehicles per day. Minor arterial highways link cities and towns of 1,000 to 5,000 people, and are distributed across the province in proportion to population density. Collector highways are of inter-municipal rather than provincial importance, and link towns and villages with populations of less than 1,000. Local highways provide access to adjacent land.

A second and more recent categorization scheme groups all provincial highways and municipal roads into seven classes based on their social, economic, and connective function. Classes 1 and 2 carry the highest traffic volumes, and connect major cities and regional service centres with populations greater than 1,000. Classes 3, 4, and 5 link communities with populations of less than 1,000, and give access to large parks and industrial sites. Classes 6 and 7 carry the least traffic and provide access only to individual residences, small parks and industrial sites, farmland, and other properties. Approximately 38% of Saskatchewan's highways are designated as class 1 or 2, and 62% as class 3, 4, or 5.

Saskatchewan's primary highways are numbered 1 through 40, have speed limits ranging from 90 to 110 km/hr, and connect all of the province's major cities. Principal east-west arterial routes include: Highway 1 (Trans-Canada) across southern Saskatchewan, through Regina, Moose Jaw, and Swift Current; Highway 16 (Yellowhead) through the province's parkland region, via Yorkton, Saskatoon, North Battleford, and Lloydminster; Highway 3 from the Manitoba border to Melfort and Prince Albert; Highways 7 and 14 from Saskatoon to the Alberta border; Highway 10 east from Balgonie

to Yorkton and the Manitoba border; Highway 13 from Manitoba to the Alberta border via Carlyle and Weyburn; and Highway 40 from Prince Albert to North Battleford.

Major north-south arteries include: Highway 6 from Montana to Regina and Melfort; Highway 11 from Regina to Saskatoon and Prince Albert; Highway 4 from Montana to Swift Current and North Battleford; Highway 2 from Moose Jaw to Prince Albert and La Ronge; Highway 9 from North Dakota to Yorkton and Hudson Bay; Highway 35 from North Dakota to Weyburn; and Highway 39 from Moose Jaw to Weyburn, Estevan, and the US border. Only Highways 1, 11, and 16 have sections of divided highway. The Trans-Canada Highway (#1) is twinned from Wolseley to the Alberta border; Highway 11 from Regina to Saskatoon; and the Yellowhead route (#16) from Saskatoon to North Battleford, and from Maidstone to Lloydminster. The twinning of the Trans-Canada Highway in Saskatchewan is scheduled for completion in 2007.

Iain Stewart

HILDEBRAND, HENRY PETER (1911–). A devoted Christian educator, Henry Peter Hildebrand was born in Steinfeld, Russia on November 16, 1911. He immigrated to Canada in 1925 and a decade later founded Briercrest Bible Institute in Briercrest, which under his guidance has grown into the Briercrest Family of Schools. Hildebrand also served as director of the Canadian Sunday School Mission and president of the Association of Canadian Bible Colleges. He was made a Member of the Order of Canada in 1979 and named Chancellor Emeritus of Briercrest Family of Schools in 1996.

HILL, FREDERICK W. (1920–). Frederick Hill was born in Regina on September 2, 1920. Following his distinguished war service with the United States Air Force, Hill embarked on a career in business that eventually included holdings in real estate, broadcasting, oil and gas, and insurance. A graduate of the University of Saskatchewan and the Harvard Business School, he developed Regina's first private residential subdivision, the aptly named Hillsdale. As chairman and director of McCallum-Hill company, he was instrumental in redeveloping Regina's downtown with the addition of five office towers. Beside his business interests, Hill is a prominent benefactor to the Athol Murray College of Notre Dame in Wilcox. Awarded the Order of Canada in 1986, Frederick Hill received the Saskatchewan Order of Merit in 1999, and in 2005 was granted an honorary doctor of laws from the University of Regina.

HILL FAMILY. For more than a century, the Hill family of Regina has owned and operated one of the most successful family-run real estate development

DON HEALY/REGINA LEADER-POST

Highway 11 near Lumsden.

companies in Canada. In 1903, the patriarch of the Hill dynasty, local school teacher Walter H.A. Hill, and his business partner E.A. McCallum, founded McCallum Hill Ltd. of Regina. Specializing in insurance and real estate, McCallum Hill Ltd. was best known for its development of the historic Lakeview subdivision in south Regina. By 1912, the company had become the largest land developer in Western Canada. Ownership of McCallum Hill Ltd. fell entirely to the Hills following the death of the McCallum partners in the 1930s. In 1953, Walter's son, **FREDERICK W. HILL**, took over the family business. Frederick led the company through impressive growth, developing the first post-war residential subdivisions (Hillsdale and Normanview) in Regina, purchasing the CKCK television station, and acquiring numerous Canadian and American companies in real estate, broadcasting, oil and gas, and insurance. As director and chairman of the Hill Companies (formerly McCallum Hill Ltd.), Frederick Hill redefined Regina's downtown skyline with the addition of five office towers—each built, owned and managed by the Hill Companies. The centrepiece of the family empire is the Hill Centre, Regina's twin tower office complex that stands on the site of the former McCallum Hill Building—Saskatchewan's tallest building (ten stories) for many years after its construction in 1914. In 1976, Frederick's son, Paul J., became the third generation of Hills to run the family business. He is president and CEO of the Hill Companies and its primary operating entity, Harvard Development Inc. Paul was instrumental in coordinating the 1991 relocation of Crown Life's head office from Toronto to Regina. Paul's daughter, Rosanne, the youngest generation in the Hill dynasty, is vice-president of Harvard Development's commercial portfolio. *Iain Stewart*

FURTHER READING: Hughes, Bob. 2003. "Regina's 'Royal Family' Celebrates 100 Years in Town," *Regina Leader-Post* (May 7): A2; Martin, P. 2003. "100 Years Old and Still Not Over the Hill," *Saskbusiness* 24: 22.

HIND, HENRY YOULE: *see* **PALLISER AND HIND EXPEDITIONS**

HINDU COMMUNITIES. Hindu communities have been a part of the Saskatchewan demography since the early 1960s. These early immigrants came in their 30s, with high levels of education, mostly to occupations in teaching, medicine and engineering. Two-thirds of the wives worked either part- or full-time in various support occupations. The human capital value they added to the province thus ran into millions of dollars. Coming as emigrants to the province from India, the UK, Uganda, and the Caribbean, they mostly settled in Regina and Saskatoon. They adapted to the environment and are well integrated into the wider culture, with

REGINA LEADER-POST

Hindu Temple, Regina.

many achieving not only professional recognition and awards but also broader societal and citizenship awards at national, provincial and municipal levels. New entrants in recent years have largely come as university students, short-term contract employees, or for interim employment.

The ranks of the early settlers have thinned as many retired persons have followed their grown children who are pursuing careers elsewhere in Canada or the USA. While a majority of the early settlers spoke Hindi, Gujarati or Punjabi, English became the language used at home in about half the families; this language loss is of concern to the community. Other concerns revolve around cultural issues such as arranged and mixed marriages, religious faith, conservative sexual mores, and accompanying changes. Concerns also exist as to whether children will have the same economic opportunities as their parents, and whether new economic realities will be accompanied by religion or race prejudices. Many of the community's children attend the heritage language (Hindi and Gujarati) classes offered by the Multilingual Association of Regina, as well as Indian dance classes. The community supports the University Departments of Religious Studies in Regina and Saskatoon, which put ample focus on Hinduism in their teaching and research. The **UNIVERSITY OF REGINA**'s Language Centre has also offered summer courses in Hindi for executives and managers.

Hindu religious beliefs are private and cannot be defined in terms of outward behaviour. A central belief is that all genuine religious paths lead to God and thus deserve tolerance and understanding. Informal gatherings in private homes evolved to become more formal organizations for the pursuit of deeper spiritual practices and observation of rituals conducive to growth, harmony and understanding of Hinduism (more correctly called *Sanatana Dharma*). An ISKCON-sponsored Hare Krishna Temple was established in Regina in 1977. The Vedanta Society of Saskatchewan, incorporated in

1977, established the Lakshmi Narayan Temple in Saskatoon in 1985; the Society changed its name in 1986 to Hindu Society of Saskatchewan. In Regina, many groups such as the Gita Study Group, Amrit Vani, Satya Sai Centre, and Himalayan Yoga/ Meditation Centre led to the formation of the Hindu Samaj of Southern Saskatchewan in 1987. They established the **HINDU TEMPLE** in Regina which opened in 1990. Many members of the community are members of more than one of these temples: some also affiliate with the Sikh Society's Gurudwara as well as the multi-faith Satya Sai Centre. A majority of the community members also affiliate with secular culture groups such as the India Canada Association of Saskatchewan (ICAS) and the Gujarati Samaj. City Councils in Regina and Saskatoon have erected statues of Mahatma Gandhi in their cities. *Kalburgi Srinivas*

FURTHER READING: Srinivas, K.M. and S.K. Kaul. 1987. *Indo-Canadians in Saskatchewan: The Early Settlers.* Regina: Indo-Canada Association of Saskatchewan.

HINDU TEMPLE, REGINA. A majority of the immigrants to Regina from India came after the independence of that country in 1947. They were professionals with training in various fields—not labourers as was the case a century earlier on the Canadian West Coast. Due to the lack of ethnocultural organizations in Regina, most of these immigrants kept their faith through daily or weekly worship in their homes, or by regular reading of Hindu scripture. In the early 1960s, as the number of the Hindu families increased in the city of Regina, Hindus started to gather in their homes. These gatherings were primarily social and ethnocultural in flavour. In the early 1970s, Ramesh Aire initiated and kept alive the religious get-togethers in the form of satsangs (devotional singing); occasionally, such weekend satsangs were taken to surrounding towns in rural Saskatchewan. He was instrumental in organizing the celebrations of various Hindu festivals at such Regina venues as the Odd Fellows' Temple or other similar community centres. Organizations such as India Association, India Canada Association, Indo-Canada Cultural Organization, ISKCON Temple, Gujrati Samaj, Gita Study Circle, Regina Yoga and Meditation Centre, and Sri Satya Sai Centre assisted Hindus in keeping their faith.

On May 24, 1987, six local Hindu organizations joined forces to establish a Hindu temple. The new organization was named Hindu Samaj of Southern Saskatchewan (Hindu Society of Southern Saskatchewan). Under the direction of Dr. **KRISHNA KUMAR**, the board members worked hard to raise funds from across southern Saskatchewan for the construction of the temple. In the summer of 1989, Dr. Usharbudh Arya conducted the Bhoomi Pooja (sod turning ceremony); the following year construction started, and the doors of the new temple opened to devotees in September 1990 on Vijya Dashmi Day. Murthi Sthapana (installation of the deities) took place in October 1993 under the direction of Dr. Shreedhar Jachak.

Presently, *satsang* is observed every Sunday. The resource centre is used for Hindu Vidyalaya (Sunday school) and Bhavan (basement hall) for congregational feasts and other non-religious activities. In order to create better understanding of the Hindu faith, the Hindu Samaj organizes open houses for public viewing, and lectures on spirituality are given by visiting swamies from India; the Hindu Samaj also offers a student scholarship at the University of Regina for the study of Hinduism. Hindu Samaj is a founding member of the Regina Multi-Faith Forum. (*See also* **HINDU COMMUNITIES**)

Krishan C. Kapila

HINITT, ROBERT N. (1926–). Born on June 24, 1926, in Winnipeg, Bob Hinitt lived in Calgary and Blucher, Saskatchewan, before moving to Saskatoon

in 1935. His mother, a former costume-maker, supported him and his sister as a milliner/ seamstress, while he completed an Honours BA in French and English (1947), MA (1949), and BEd (1952) at the **UNIVERSITY OF SASKATCHEWAN**.

In 1950, Hinitt embarked on a 44-year teaching career in French, English and Drama, which included 31 years of high school teaching (1950–81) and thirteen years of sessional work (University of Saskatchewan, 1981–94). Influenced by the addition of Drama to the school curriculum and by the work of **MARY ELLEN BURGESS**, Hinitt soon began translating a high school interest in acting and an earlier training in art (**ERNST LINDNER**) and sculpture (**ELI BORNSTEIN**), into a lifelong passion for designing, directing and teaching theatre.

Between 1950 and 1958, Hinitt directed plays for City Park Collegiate, taking awards in provincial drama festivals (1956–58). In 1958, he joined Aden Bowman Collegiate, where his work contributed to Drama becoming curricular for grades nine to twelve (1972). Asked by founding principal Charles Mair to design a theatre for the school, Hinitt, who spent part of his sabbatical (1962) working in Stratford's set, property and design shop, responded with Castle Theatre. The 600-seat theatre, in a circular design loosely modeled after the Stratford Festival stage, was completed in 1966, and remains unique as a flexible, intimate theatre space for community and school productions.

Hinitt, whose eclectic range included world classics as well as contemporary British, Canadian and American work and musicals, also served as an award-winning director/designer in the community theatre. A founding member of the **SASKATOON GATEWAY PLAYERS** (1965–) and the Saskatoon Summer Players (1964–) Hinitt participated in the DDF finals in Kitchener (Molière's *Tartuffe*, University of Saskatchewan, 1963) and in Windsor (Wycherley's *Country Wife*, Gateway, 1968), pro-

duced shows for Gateway for over twenty years, and directed the annual musical for the Summer Players (1964–81). He also served on the first Board of Directors for **PERSEPHONE THEATRE** (1974). Since retirement (1981), he has continued teaching and directing on a part-time basis and designing an annual Christmas display at his home.

Honoured with the Order of Canada (1983) and the Saskatchewan Order of Merit (2000), Hinitt was inducted into the Woodward Theatre Hall of Fame (2001) as "an educator whose passion for theatre and design nurtured generations of theatre-goers, practitioners and artists, and whose vision included the creation of Castle Theatre." *Moira Day*

FURTHER READING: Taylor, Mark. 2003. "Displays Legendary Tradition: Bob Hinitt's Creations Have Been Enjoyed By All Since 1947." *StarPhoenix* (December 23), A3, A7

HISPANIC COMMUNITY. Before the great migration of Chileans after the 1973 *coup d'état* there, and of Central Americans, especially Salvadoreans, who fled the civil war of the 1980s, there were few Hispanics in Saskatchewan, although some had immigrated to Saskatchewan and left their mark, as attested by occasional Spanish place names: Buena Vista, Lake Alma, Valparaiso, and Alameda ("poplar grove," named thus by an English priest who had spent some time at Alameda in Spain). Saskatchewan's two major urban centres, Regina and Saskatoon, absorbed most of the province's Hispanic and Latin American immigration, although a few Latin Americans are scattered in the smaller cities and even in towns such as La Ronge. Census figures of 2001 state that there were 2,005 Latin Americans in the province. Hispanics and Latin Americans in Saskatchewan tend to form social circles of their own nationalities; however, there are organizations such as Círculo Hispánico in Saskatoon, in which Spaniards, Argentineans, Chileans, Salvadoreans, Peruvians, and others participate.

The recent wave of Latin American immigration has produced a significant cultural impact: supermarkets now offer the ingredients for typical Latin dishes; restaurants serving Latin foods are popular; Latin dances are well attended; and classes in Spanish language and Hispanic literature have grown more popular. The Hispanic community makes a vibrant annual contribution to the annual multicultural festivals: Folkfest in Saskatoon, and Mosaic in Regina. There have been more subtle impacts as well. In the 1970s and 1980s many of the immigrants worked actively in solidarity with the oppressed in their homelands, which increased international awareness in Saskatchewan. Churches, human rights organizations and social activist organizations were strengthened by the immigrants,

Bob Hinitt, constructing an ice castle for the Meewasin Valley Authority's winter carnival, February 1983.

among whom there were many professionals who have made significant contributions to the province. (*See also* VISIBLE MINORITIES, URBAN ETHNIC DIVERSITY, SASKATCHEWAN INTERCULTURAL ASSOCIATION)

Rodolfo Pino

HISTORIANS AND HISTORIOGRAPHY.

Historiography refers to the analysis of historical writing and is mainly concerned with changes in subject matter, interpretation, methodology, terminology, and thematic constructs created over time by historical debate. In a brief overview of the writing of Saskatchewan history what is especially striking is the extent to which major Canadian historical themes–among them the fur trade, treaties and Native relations, rebellion, prairie politics, immigration and pioneering, ethnicity, gender relations, the DEPRESSION, MEDICARE, and the concept of WESTERN ALIENATION–have been shaped and defined by events in the province of Saskatchewan. It is also clear that the way in which historical investigation is conducted has changed dramatically, as have the purposes and uses to which that investigation have been put.

One of the first recognizable local histories was N.F. Black's *A History of Saskatchewan and the Old North West*, published in Regina in 1913. Now a collector's item, this volume reflects a Eurocentric bias and an interest in the history of "great men" typical of most historical writing of the time. Black's work lacks rigorous argument or debate, and the story weaves previously unpublished documents and excerpts from private diaries, letters, and government records with a general narrative. The result is more a chronicle than an interpretive history. Black argues that "true history is the most reliable kind of prophecy," suggesting that in this case a historian's role is to map out the province's past, providing direction for the future. Another collector's item, *The Story of Saskatchewan and Its People*, was published in 1924 by John Hawkes, Saskatchewan's legislative librarian. Like Black's work a decade earlier, it is a presentation of documents, interviews and excerpts, with a biographical appendix of "great men"; it suffers from a similar lack of investigative rigour. However, Hawkes has a different view of the role of history in society: whereas Black believed that a historian's primary function was that of a chronicler, Hawkes viewed historians, and by extension their work, as agents of citizenship and civilization. He sought to cultivate a "Saskatchewan tradition" of depth and heroism, romance and achievement as part of the British Empire. What is interesting is that Hawkes' idea of citizenship placed provincial identity before national identity–a rather forthright assertion for the time.

Saskatchewan's GOLDEN JUBILEE in 1955 prompted the first of what has become a tradition: an official provincial history sponsored by the government as part of the celebration. Jim Wright wrote *Saskatchewan: The History of a Province*, a mass-produced book intended for a general audience. Less detailed but with a more cohesive narrative than earlier histories, Wright's work gives precedence to models of economic, social and co-operative prosperity and progress, painting a rosy picture of Saskatchewan's future. The book is infused by the concept of pioneers, a Saskatchewan rendering of F.J Turner's frontier thesis. This essentially agricultural theory depicts Anglo-European men and women wresting homes and livelihood, communities and a province from a wild and empty land under extreme conditions. As such, the model emphasizes life in southern Saskatchewan, creating a serious imbalance in our province's history. To create the pioneer narrative, Wright relegates First Nations history to the historical past: First Nations history ends when the pioneers arrive, which divides the book between the historical past, which has little effect on modern Saskatchewan, and the pioneer past, a history in which everyone except the First Nations community can share. Wright believes that history is about memory and acts as a living connection to the past, hence the focus on the semi-universal pioneer story.

JOHN ARCHER's *Saskatchewan: A History* was written for the Celebrate Saskatchewan festivities of 1980. It accesses the ground-breaking work of social historians from the 1960s and 1970s, particularly the "Limited Identities" schools that developed thematic categories of history corresponding to concepts of race, gender, class, regionalism and regional discontent. This allowed Archer to include some new and previously silenced voices from the provincial past. Fully referenced, with chapter endnotes and an important bibliographic essay, Archer's work marked a new regard for the rigorous methodology of professional historiography. However, it also rested on the pivotal axis of the strong Saskatchewan pioneer myth and again depicted Saskatchewan as rural, agricultural, and in debt to its pioneers. In the end, Archer simply presents a more detailed version of Wright's work, complete with similar chapter divisions and titles; there are few innovative or original arguments, and no commentary on the purpose of history.

As we head toward the province's 100th anniversary celebrations, historian Bill Waiser has written *Saskatchewan: A New History*. The rural, agricultural, and pioneer concepts that permeated the previous two provincial histories give way to a more inclusive and integrative perspective, particularly in describing the tension and interplay between south and north, rural and urban, and Aboriginal and non-Aboriginal peoples in shaping the province of Saskatchewan. Whereas both Wright and Archer argue that Saskatchewan is still "next year country," on the verge of greatness, Waiser argues that the future is here, and Saskatchewan is not ready. He paints a clear picture of the changes in Saskatchewan society and provides penetrating commentary, particularly on the last fifty years. Moving back to the idea of the historian as an agent of change or cultural influence, Waiser's work will force a new discussion regarding an evolving Saskatchewan identity.

Through these five classic studies of Saskatchewan history, major changes in the evolution of historical writing are apparent. Mirroring national trends, Saskatchewan historians moved from a "top-down" history of great men and major political events such as those presented by Black and Hawkes, to a gradually more inclusive history. Wright integrated local communities and everyday people; Archer delved into social history to introduce concepts of race, class, gender and ethnicity more fully into the Saskatchewan story; Waiser brings the solitudes of Saskatchewan (rural and urban, north and south, Aboriginal and non-Aboriginal) into perspective. In conjunction with these provincial histories, Saskatchewan has witnessed an explosion of local, community, church, business and family histories since the early 1950s (*see* LOCAL HISTORY). These popular histories, generated by and for individual communities, have captured names, voices, and experiences of ordinary individuals who have shaped this province. Most are from rural Saskatchewan, and until recently they reflected the preeminence of the pioneer narrative. These books display history in its simplest forms: as expressions of memory, pride and identity.

A major step in the preservation of Saskatchewan's past was the creation of a provincial archive in 1945, followed by the establishment of its journal, *Saskatchewan History*, in 1948. Parts of the extensive archival photo collection have been published in coffee-table style histories such as Ted Regehr's *Remembering Saskatchewan* and D.H Bocking's *Saskatchewan: A Pictorial History*. The SASKATCHEWAN HISTORY AND FOLKLORE SOCIETY, particularly through its journal, *Folklore*, has been an important and popular forum for ordinary Saskatchewan people to relate their stories. Regional historians and writers have successfully crossed arbitrary provincial boundaries in pursuit of a homogenized western experience, and their work includes important information for Saskatchewan scholars. Good introductory bibliographic essays which list important source documents, key books, and articles can be found in Archer's *Saskatchewan: A History* or Gerald Friesen's *The Canadian Prairies: A History*.

History is not always written. All cultures, even written ones, use oral history, storytelling and legends, art, music, and dance to define and transmit aspects of their past. New recognition and understanding of the importance of oral and cultural history reveals a different and valuable perspective on the provincial past. In Saskatchewan, history has been preserved through rock art and hieroglyphics, community storytellers, and Aboriginal legends and sacred stories. School aids and junior histories, classroom activity books and atlases, business and family histories, political speeches and pamphlets, advertising campaigns, tourism brochures and promotions have served the same purpose. Oral history projects, legal documents and decisions, historic markers and sites, public memorials, university graduate theses, art, music, theatre and dance, and historical fiction all provide ways of accessing the past.

Scholars are exploring and deconstructing the purpose and cultural function of history. It is now understood that there is a difference between history as it happens, as it is interpreted and studied by academic historians, and how it is disseminated, used, and changed for public consumption. The range and diversity of Saskatchewan's historical inscription highlights two fundamental truisms: for every historical event, there are multiple narratives, perspectives, and layers that must be acknowledged and studied; and each narrative or story must be placed in the context of author, audience, and purpose of the history. *Merle Massie*

FURTHER READING: Archer, J.H. 1980. *Saskatchewan: A History*. Saskatoon: Western Producer Prairie Books; Black, N.F. 1913. *A History of Saskatchewan and the Old North West*. Regina: Saskatchewan Publishing Company; Hawkes, J. 1924. *The Story of Saskatchewan and Its People*. Chicago-Regina: S.J. Clarke Publishing Company; Kaye, F. 2003. *Hiding the Audience: Viewing Arts and Arts Institutions on the Prairies*. Edmonton: University of Alberta Press; Waiser, B. 2005. *Saskatchewan: A New History*. Calgary: Fifth House Publishers; Wright, J. 1955. *Saskatchewan: The History of a Province*. Toronto: McClelland and Stewart.

HISTORIC SITES. From time to time people and leaders pause to recognize publicly the achievements of their ancestors or the occurrence of important events, and to mark places of major significance. In 1965, on the occasion of Saskatchewan's 60th anniversary as a province, J.W. McCaig, chairman of Saskatchewan's Diamond Jubilee Committee, provided the rationale for preserving historic sites: they should remind everyone that "here history was made." Since that declaration, hundreds of sites and structures have been preserved or developed as places of historic significance to the people of Saskatchewan. First Nations people left tangible remains in places of importance to them: carved or painted stones, and monuments such as medicine wheels, sacred circles, and human or animal effigies. St. Victor Petroglyphs Provincial Park in south-central Saskatchewan, which includes carvings dating between 500 and 1750 AD, is an excellent exam-

FRANK KORVEMAKER PHOTO/COURTESY OF GOVERNMENT OF SASKATCHEWAN, HERITAGE

Keyhole Castle, Prince Albert.

ple of this kind of heritage site. By now, over 1,000 sites have been established in the province, belonging to the following categories:

First Heritage Conservation Site: The first documented heritage site preservation project in Saskatchewan occurred in 1911, when people in Saskatoon determined to preserve their vacant 24-year-old stone school-house from demolition: Victoria School, erected in 1887, represented the pioneer era of settlement in Saskatoon, and the introduction of public education in the community. The "old" stone school was carefully documented, dismantled, and re-erected on the grounds of the new University of Saskatchewan.

National Historic Sites: In 1923, the Historic Sites and Monuments Board of Canada designated five Saskatchewan sites of national importance and erected a stone cairn with an ornate bronze plaque at each location. By 2004, an additional seventy-six heritage sites had been recognized for their national significance, including the Keyhole Castle (Smith Residence) in Prince Albert, and the Addison Sod Farm House near Kindersley.

Provincial Historic Sites: The government of Saskatchewan passed legislation under the Archives Act of 1938 to mark historic sites. The first plaque under this program was erected in 1943 at the South Branch House fur trade post site, near Duck Lake. A more concerted effort to commemorate provincial historic sites was made in the early 1950s, when fifty-six more sites were designated in time for the 1955 Jubilee celebrations. Many of these, especially the historic trails, were accompanied by a replica of a **RED RIVER CART**. By 2004, 164 provincial historic sites had been designated, and generally marked by a small stone cairn and a bronze or alu-

minum plaque in the shape of the province.

Local Historic Sites: Since 1966, the demand for recognizing sites of local significance has also resulted in the creation of a large number of local historic sites, erected jointly by the province and a local organization—or, since 1988, through the joint efforts of the **SASKATCHEWAN HISTORY AND FOLKLORE SOCIETY** and local groups. Approximately 475 aluminum plaques can be found throughout the province, including one in Eastend at the boyhood home of Pulitzer Prize author **WALLACE STEGNER**.

Designated Heritage Properties: Over 750 sites and structures have been designated as either Municipal or Provincial Heritage Property under the Heritage Property Act. Many of these have also been publicly recognized through placement of some form of plaque and/or inclusion in a walking or driving tour of heritage sites in the community or region. The **ALLEN SAPP** Art Gallery, located in the former North Battleford Public Library, is an example of a municipally designated site; while the Doukhobor Prayer Home, Verigin, has been recognized for its provincial significance (*see* **DOUKHOBOR SETTLEMENT**).

Although initial designations were for fur trade or military posts, political leaders and historic trails, in more recent times greater efforts have been made to include also other aspects of heritage relating to women, Aboriginal people, and industrial and cultural sites. The **BERTHOLD IMHOFF** Art Studio, near St. Walburg, is an example of a site designated for its association with an important Saskatchewan artist. Heritage sites help inform visitors about the people, places and events that have shaped the province. Some sites include historic structures, others provide exceptional natural vistas; yet others speak of the

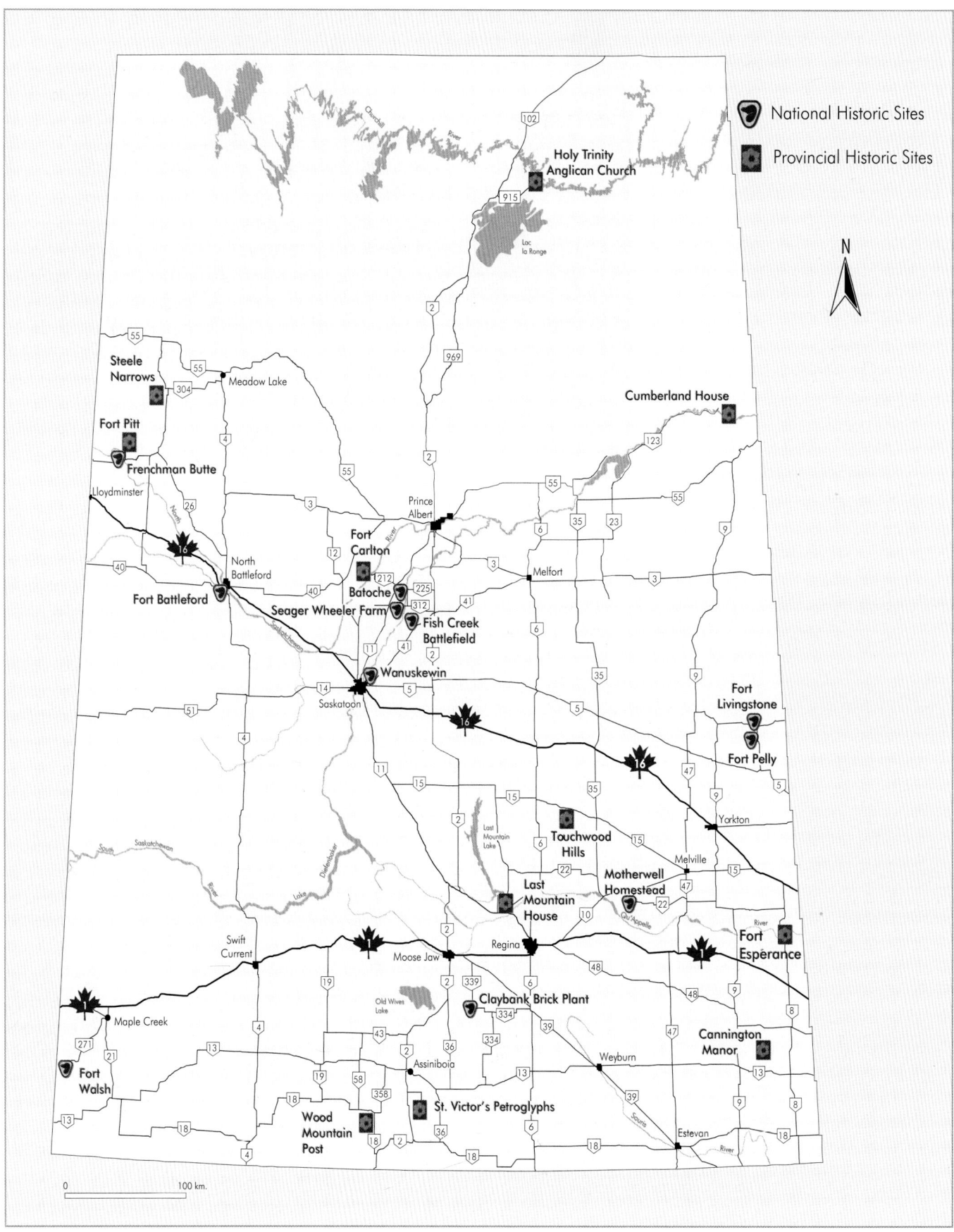

Figure HS-1. Saskatchewan Historic Sites.

evolution of society and sometimes of its conflicts—as at **BATOCHE** in 1885 or Estevan in 1931 (*see* **ESTEVAN COAL STRIKE**). (*See* Figure HS-1 opposite.)

Frank Korvemaker

HISTORY OF SASKATCHEWAN: *see essay this page.*

Orville K. Hjertaas.

HJERTAAS, ORVILLE K. (1917–98). Orville Hjertaas was a leading figure in the development of the health services in Saskatchewan, and is recognized as one of the fathers of **MEDICARE**. Born in Wauchope on May 31, 1917, he obtained his qualifications in medicine and surgery at the University of Manitoba (1943) and in Edinburgh. As a member and, briefly, secretary of the Health Services Planning Commission, he helped organize the province's first two experimental health regions in the Swift Current and Weyburn areas in 1945-46. He then served briefly as the **SWIFT CURRENT HEALTH REGION**'s first medical health officer before settling permanently in Prince Albert, where he established a successful private practice.

Hjertaas played an instrumental role in the implementation of medicare in Saskatchewan in 1961–62. As one of only two physicians who were willing to accept appointments to the Medical Care Insurance Commission, he served as its vice-chairman. In response to the doctors' strike, which he refused to join, Hjertaas helped establish the first of the province's community clinics; under his directorship, the Prince Albert community clinic pioneered group practice arrangements as well as an approach to health care delivery which emphasized prevention. Hjertaas received the Saskatchewan Order of Merit in 1993 and became a Member of the Order of Canada in 1997. He died in Prince Albert on May 23, 1998. *Gordon S. Lawson*

History of Saskatchewan

H

Michael Cottrell

The province of Saskatchewan, incorporated in 1905, is a relatively recent creation; but the history which underlies that political and social construct encompasses the countless stories engendered by all those who for millennia have made their homes in the vast plains, parklands and boreal forests of the northern fringes of the North American continent. Told by a variety of cultural groups in many different languages, these stories nevertheless share a common theme: the human struggle to come to terms with an exceptionally challenging environment, characterized by great climatic extremes over enormous expanses of land, geographically remote from the continent's larger population concentrations. At its most basic, the history of Saskatchewan is the collective story of human groups adapting to harsh weather and an expansive landscape in order to survive and prosper. It is this history which has forged a distinctive identity among those who call this place home, and the same fundamental reality will likely continue to shape the collective destiny of the province's residents long into the future.

Aboriginal peoples insist that their ancestors have inhabited the land we now call Saskatchewan since "time immemorial" (*see* **ABORIGINAL PEOPLES OF SASKATCHEWAN**), and archaeologists point to evidence of human activity beginning with the Paleo-Indians or Big Game Hunters about 9,500 BCE (*see* **ARCHAEOLOGY**). Both oral history and archaeological records attest to a process of constant human change and adjustment in response to dramatic shifts in climate, flora and fauna over many millennia. Flexibility and ingenuity were required to develop and adapt technologies, economic systems, forms of political organization, and spiritual and cultural practices to cope with these changes and to enhance the quality of human life. The southern plains and parklands proved most hospitable to settlement, and the huge **BISON** herds provided food, clothing, and shelter for the early occupants. The northern boreal forests attracted fewer people, but caribou, moose and fish were able to support small scattered bands perhaps as early as 3,000 BCE.

Ancestors of the modern Aboriginal occupants began to assert their presence in the region centuries before the arrival of the Europeans. The **NEHIYAWAK** or **CREE** were by far the largest group, with the Swampy and Woodland bands occupying the shield and boreal forests from what is now northern Quebec to northern Alberta, and the Plains bands beginning to move into the parkland and plains south of the North Saskatchewan River. The Nehiyawak enjoyed close relations with the **NAKOTA** (Assiniboine) who occupied the southern region of Saskatchewan and relied almost exclusively on the buffalo for subsistence. As allies, the Nehiyawak and Nakota traded with the Mandan south to the Missouri River, and occasionally made war on the **LAKOTA** (**SIOUX**), **DAKOTA** (Sioux) and Atsina (Gros Ventre) to the southeast and southwest. To the east of these groups were the **NAHKAWEWIN** (**SAULTEAUX**), who moved from their original homes in the Great Lakes area to what is now east-central Saskatchewan after the arrival of the Europeans. To the west was the Siksika, Kaini, and Peigan (Blackfoot) confederacy, which claimed the longest presence on the plains and whose territory extended from the Eagle Hills west to the Rocky Mountains. The Nehiyawak, Nahkawewin, Siksika, Peigan and Kaini all spoke languages belonging to the Algonquian linguistic group, possibly suggesting a common origin (*see* **FIRST NATIONS LANGUAGES**). What is now northwest Saskatchewan was originally home to the Athapaskan-speaking **DENESULINE** (Dene, Chipewyan) bands, who occupied territory far to the north and west. Conflict between the Denesuline and the Nehiyawak was endemic and continued into the post-contact period. The successful adaptation of Aboriginal peoples to the challenges of these environments required developing an extremely close relationship with the land and an intimate understanding of the animals upon which they depended for survival. Another vital aspect of their adjustment was the development of a communal ethos, where the values of redistribution and reciprocity were strongly encouraged to ensure collective survival. Although their numbers remained small and their material cultures simple in contrast to larger Aboriginal population concentrations elsewhere, plains people lived well on their own terms; they were also nurtured by a deep spirituality and rich ceremonial life.

Aboriginal peoples' sole occupation of the northern plains and boreal forests came to an end in the 17th century when the overseas expansion of European powers led to the establishment of British and French colonies in eastern North America. The lucrative fur trade was the primary motivation for this colonization; the monarchs also claimed title to the land since they denied that Aboriginal occupation constituted true ownership (see FUR TRADE IN SASKATCHEWAN). Acting on this assumption, King Charles II of England issued to the Hudson's Bay Company in 1670 a charter which granted it ownership and exclusive trading rights to a vast area in the North American interior known as Rupert's Land. Totalling 7,700,000 km², the territory included most of modern day Saskatchewan. For the next century the Company adopted a relatively passive strategy of constructing posts on the shores of Hudson Bay and waiting for Aboriginal peoples to bring their furs to trade. In a rare departure from this policy, the young HENRY KELSEY was send inland in 1690 to persuade more Native people to bring their furs to the Bay. Guided by Aboriginal people, he was the first recorded European to see the great plains of what is now Saskatchewan (see EXPLORERS).

Centuries-old European rivalry between France and England spread to North America, and the French refused to recognize the exclusive claims of the English company. The voyageurs of the Montreal-based French trade expanded west of the Great Lakes, utilizing pre-existing Aboriginal trade routes in the late 1600s and early 1700s to find new sources of fur and new Aboriginal trading partners. Pierre de La Vérendrye reached the lower SASKATCHEWAN RIVER in the early 1740s, and in the next decade de Niverville and de la Corne established posts further up the Saskatchewan River within the boundaries of present-day Saskatchewan (see FUR TRADE POSTS). The French withdrew from the West after the conquest of 1760, but two decades later their place was taken by the North West Company. Directed by Anglo-American merchants based in Montreal and staffed by experienced French-Canadian voyageurs, North West Company explorers pushed west and north through the Saskatchewan and CHURCHILL RIVER systems to exploit new fur-rich territory. Faced with this competition, the Hudson's Bay Company was forced to adopt a more aggressive strategy and established its first inland post at CUMBERLAND HOUSE in 1774. Intense rivalry over the next decades led to the construction of a chain of posts across the West, and by the time the two companies amalgamated in 1821 the area that would become Saskatchewan was home to more than fifty trading centres, many of them located at traditional Aboriginal gathering places.

It was critically important to cross-cultural relations that the initial encounters between Aboriginal and European people in this particular space occurred within the context of trade. Despite European notions of superiority, the reality of the situation dictated a significant level of dependence on the original inhabitants. Traders relied on Aboriginal people to supply them with furs, and their unfamiliarity with the climate and topography forced the newcomers to seek Aboriginal assistance for survival and exploration. The trade context also dictated that the first Europeans to arrive were exclusively male, and many of these young men established liaisons with Aboriginal women. These relationships had advantages for both parties: the women provided both practical assistance and critical cultural knowledge to their Europeans partners, and in the process cemented economic and social ties between traders and Aboriginal communities. By incorporating Europeans into their kinship systems, Aboriginal people also expected to enjoy preferential trade terms and various forms of assistance, including access to post provi-

sions in times of need. Over time the mixed-blood offspring of these marriages developed a unique syncretic identity and a distinctive sense of nationality as MÉTIS people.

For at least the first century and a half after contact, therefore, the fur trade produced a mutually beneficial relationship. The European presence was small and posed little threat to Aboriginal culture and sovereignty. Aboriginal people demonstrated flexibility and ingenuity in adapting to European economic systems, carving out a variety of roles in the fur trade as trappers, middlemen and provisioners; they furthermore were able to benefit from new technology while controlling their own destinies. Metal goods such as axes, knives, pots, scrapers, fire-steels and muskets were readily adopted, reducing labour—especially for women (see FIRST NATIONS WOMEN)—and thereby enhancing quality of life and overall security in a harsh environment. The more efficient technology and increased leisure also enhanced the aesthetic expressions and ceremonial life of Aboriginal peoples.

SASKATCHEWAN ARCHIVES BOARD S-A97

Traders and aboriginal people, Fort Pitt, 1880s.

Over time however, involvement in the fur trade brought profound changes to the regions' original inhabitants. The introduction of horses and guns revolutionized plains cultures, greatly increasing mobility but also exacerbating inter-tribal conflicts. Fierce competition between the Hudson's Bay Company and the North West Company in the early 1800s led to over-trapping and gradual depletion of fur-bearing animals. The demand for pemmican produced by the dramatic increase in the number of trading posts in this period altered the basis of buffalo hunting from a subsistence to a commercial pursuit, beginning the depletion of the herds and increasing conflict over hunting territories. DISEASES such as smallpox, influenza, whooping cough and measles caused widespread mortality, especially in the 1780s, 1830s and 1860s. Alcohol was also introduced by unscrupulous traders; as consumption increased, so also did its demoralizing effects.

The fur trade was the first staple industry to dominate the economic development of what would become Saskatchewan. Although it brought short-term wealth, the precariousness of relying on one resource became evident in the mid-19th century when changes in fashion resulted in a dramatic decline in the demand for furs. As local resources were severely depleted and Aboriginal labour was no longer critical to the creation of wealth, the collapse of the fur trade represented a significant blow to Aboriginal hegemony. The latter was further endangered by information generated by the PALLISER-HIND geological expeditions of the late 1850s: boasting the latest in scientific expertise, these surveys concluded that while portions of the southern prairies were semi-arid desert, a rich fertile belt suitable for large-scale agricultural settlement also existed, extending from the Red River Valley west to the Rocky Mountains. This discovery transformed outsiders' perceptions of the region from that of a frozen wasteland to a potential agricultural Eden, and had profound implications for the future of the West and its inhabitants. The news was immediately seized upon by politicians and businessmen from central Canada, who saw in the redefined West an opportunity to realize their larger ambitions. By opening up the prairies to settlement and integrating it with the metropolitan centres of Toronto and Montreal, the emerging central Canadian élite came to believe that a new transcontinental nation, with a self-sufficient national economy, could be created to rival the United States. The Confederation of the four original provinces in 1867 was the first step to fulfilling this larger dream. Federal representatives immediately opened negotiations with the Hudson's Bay Company, and an agreement was reached in 1869 whereby Rupert's Land was sold to the federal government. In 1870, after the creation of the province of Manitoba, all of Rupert's Land was incorporated into the Canadian Confederation as the North-West Territories (*see* RUPERT'S LAND PURCHASE).

Canada's approach to its new western territory was unabashedly imperialistic, with federal officials viewing the prairies as a colony or hinterland to be exploited for the national benefit. The NATIONAL POLICIES of the 1870s and 1880s included a cheap homestead system, a territorial police force, construction of a transcontinental railway, a protective tariff, and a political structure which permitted little local control. These policies encouraged some early White settlement, primarily from Ontario; like all charter groups, these settlers sought to mould the new society in their own image. Loyalty to the British Empire and Protestant religion, confidence in British parliamentary and legal institutions, and faith in the virtues of hard work, self-reliance, thrift and sobriety were some of the guiding principles of the first White settlers. A strong attachment to their new environment also developed quickly, and critical to the emergence of this early regional identity was a belief that the burden of federal policies—especially those relating to settlement, transportation and tariffs—fell disproportionately on the West. From the beginning of White settlement, therefore, the western Canadian regional identity was shaped by a sense of grievance against the federal government, central Canada, and ill-defined "eastern interests"—all of which were perceived to benefit unfairly from the Confederation arrangement at the expense of the residents of the West.

The difficulties faced by early White settlers paled in comparison with the challenges faced by western Aboriginal peoples, who sought to control their own destinies in the face of the profound changes con-

fronting them in this period. The purchase of Rupert's Land by Canada greatly alarmed the indigenous population, especially since they were not consulted about the disposition of what they considered their traditional territories. Métis protests against the Canadian takeover led to the creation of the province of Manitoba in 1870; but irregularities with the distribution of scrip as well as tension with the incoming settlers forced many Métis to flee west to the Saskatchewan River valleys, where they sought to continue their traditional mixed farming and buffalo-hunting economy. The federal government assumed jurisdiction over Aboriginal peoples in the British North America Act and continued the pre-Confederation practice of treaty negotiation. Seven numbered treaties were negotiated with Plains First Nations between 1871 and 1877; two of these, Treaties 4 and 6, covered the southern half of what would become the province of Saskatchewan. Faced with the collapse of their traditional economy because of the disappearance of the buffalo and the influx of White settlers, Aboriginal leaders saw these agreements as a means of establishing with the Crown a relationship which would guarantee the assistance they required to make the transition to a new settled and agricultural lifestyle, in return for the peaceful settlement of their lands. In particular, the chiefs identified collective access to education, health care, emergency assistance, practical farming aid, and guaranteed hunting rights as critical to the survival of their communities. Despite the rhetoric of the treaty negotiations, the federal government had a more limited view of the treaties, seeing them primarily as a mechanism for extinguishing Aboriginal sovereignty and land title, and as a means of segregating Aboriginal people on reserves in order to facilitate White settlement of the region. These conflicting interpretations of the treaty agreements became evident almost immediately, and ensured that the cross-cultural harmony which had generally characterized the fur trade era would not long extend into the new settlement period.

The immediate post-treaty years were thus extremely traumatic ones for Aboriginal peoples in the West: the complete disappearance of the buffalo in 1879 resulted in widespread starvation, and government parsimony in providing the assistance promised in the treaties made the transition to agriculture very difficult. The challenges of adjusting to life on reserves were compounded by the often high-handed behaviour of the Indian agents, who exercised extensive supervisory powers under the INDIAN ACT of 1876. In an attempt to retain their sovereignty, chiefs such as BIG BEAR, POUNDMAKER and PIAPOT sought to unite all Plains groups behind the demand for contiguous reserves and renegotiation of the treaties on more generous terms. This disaffection of the First Nations coincided with a growing sense of grievance among the Métis, who also suffered from the disappearance of the buffalo and whose efforts to embrace commercial agriculture were frustrated by their inability to secure title to the lands on which they settled. After repeated failure to secure redress of their grievances and to forge a common front with First Nations and disgruntled White settlers, the Métis took up arms under their charismatic leader LOUIS RIEL. Despite some initial success and remarkable gallantry, the Métis were overwhelmed by Canadian forces after a three-day pitched battle at BATOCHE in May 1885 (*see* NORTH-WEST RESISTANCE).

The 1885 Resistance (or Rebellion) was a dramatic turning point in the history of what would become the province of Saskatchewan. Métis efforts to carve out a niche on their own terms in the new society emerging on the prairies symbolically ended with the execution of Louis Riel in November 1885. For much of the next century the Métis would occupy the marginalized position of Road Allowance People, in a legal and cultural limbo between First Nations and White societies. The

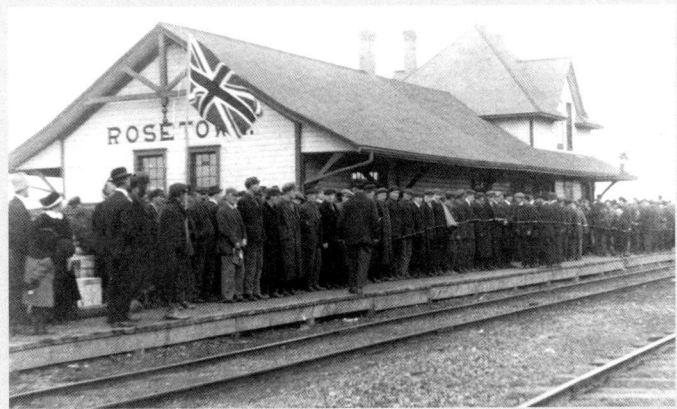

SASKATCHEWAN ARCHIVES BOARD S-B6936

The railway comes to Rosetown.

SASKATCHEWAN ARCHIVES BOARD S-8573

Louis Riel.

H

Resistance also had serious implications for the First Nations, as the federal government became increasingly coercive in its colonization policies and the gulf between Aboriginal groups and settlers became more pronounced. Chiefs such as Big Bear and Poundmaker were imprisoned, and other bands suspected of disloyalty were stripped of their chiefs. Aboriginal mobility continued to be curtailed by the PASS system, and additional restrictions were imposed by a Permit system which regulated financial transactions as part of an attempt to impose small-scale peasant farming on reserves. Federal agents, often in collaboration with Christian missionaries, launched an assault on traditional Aboriginal spirituality through a ban on the SUN DANCE and other ceremonial practices. Education also became a critical tool in controlling and transforming Aboriginal people, as the federal government, in co-operation with various Christian churches, created a system of RESIDENTIAL SCHOOLS across the country. Designed to fulfill the government's treaty obligation to provide education and practical training, these institutions had the additional objective of segregating Aboriginal children from their families in order to eradicate their culture, language and spirituality as a prelude to their assimilation into Euro-Canadian society. Although these institutions were not without some benefits, there has been growing evidence of widespread abuse, and many Aboriginal people today describe them as vehicles of cultural genocide. As part of a wider campaign to remake Aboriginal people in the image of White society, residential schools caused significant intergenerational trauma. One manifestation of this was a dramatic decrease in population; for a time, it seemed as if the predictions of Aboriginal people becoming a vanishing race would be confirmed.

The shift from Aboriginal to non-Aboriginal hegemony in the West envisioned in the National Policies was finally confirmed in the 1890s with a massive influx of White settlers. A variety of global factors, including the closing of the American frontier as well as industrial upheaval and ethnic tension in parts of Europe, all contributed to this enormous mass movement of people. The completion of the CANADIAN PACIFIC RAILWAY, advances in farming techniques and technology, and an increase in the price of WHEAT also enhanced western Canada's attractiveness as a

destination for those seeking agricultural opportunities. More than any other factor, however, it was the vigorous advertising and recruitment campaign undertaken by Clifford Sifton, the energetic Minister of the Interior appointed by Prime Minister Wilfrid Laurier in 1896, which made the Canadian prairies the "Last Best West." Determining that the settlement of the West with farmers was the main priority of his department, Sifton dispatched dozens of agents and circulated a huge volume of pamphlets in traditional sources such as Great Britain and the United States; but central and eastern European countries were also targeted for the first time, on the assumption that these "sheepskin people" would make ideal candidates for homesteading in the West.

The results were remarkable: the population of Saskatchewan grew from less than 20,000 in 1880 to almost 258,000 by 1906 and over 492,000 by 1911. About half of these were born in Canada, but the remainder was characterized by tremendous cultural diversity. This heterogeneity was reinforced by the tendency of many groups to form BLOC SETTLEMENTS when they arrived in Saskatchewan. Each of the British national groups was present with the English settling at Lloydminster, Qu'Appelle, and Churchbridge; the Irish at Young and Sinnett; the Welsh at Bangor, and the Scots in Moosomin. Americans were the largest source of foreign-born immigrants after the British, and although they were dispersed across the province many settled at Craik and Davidson as well as in the dry southwestern corner around Maple Creek. Hungarians congregated near Bekevar, Wakaw and Lestock; Rumanians at Balgonie; Belgians at Forget; Austrians at Ebenezer; and German pockets emerged around Humboldt, Tramping Lake, Melville, Grenfell and St. Walburg. Scandinavians were concentrated in the east-central parkland, from Naicam to the Manitoba border, and the Ukrainians also showed a preference for land with tree cover: a series of Ukrainian settlements developed across the parkland from Yorkton north-west to Edmonton. Most distinctive of all were the religious sects granted exemptions from the HOMESTEAD ACT to farm their land communally. Mennonites settled north of Saskatoon in Dalmeny, Hague and Osler, south of Swift Current, and in the Carrot River area. Doukhobors formed cells north of Yorkton and around Blaine Lake, while Hutterites congregated in colonies at Gull Lake, Rosetown and Riverbend.

Bloc settlements by these and the many other ethnic groups which migrated to Saskatchewan were seen initially as a mechanism for easing settlers' adjustment to the harsh prairie environment. An unintended consequence was their tendency to allow different groups to maintain their ancestral languages and cultures in their new home. The province, consequently, was characterized by a high degree of cultural diversity from the settlement period; this caused tremendous uneasiness among those, especially the early settlers from eastern Canada, who expected all newcomers to conform to Anglo-Canadian norms. This tension between proponents of cultural homogeneity or heterogeneity, reflecting a deep-seated conflict about the kind of culture and society to be created on the prairies, would form one of the major cleavages in Saskatchewan politics over the next decades.

Virtually all who settled, however, were in agreement on the desirability of owning land, and the fulfillment of these dreams was reflected in the dramatic increase in homestead entries and cultivated land: from less than 1,500 farms and 70,000 cultivated acres in 1886, Saskatchewan could boast of 56,000 farms and 3.3 million cultivated acres by 1906. This extraordinary accomplishment was the work of those collectively referred to as pioneers; their experiences, distilled into a series of myths, have had a profound influence on the creation of a Saskatchewan identity (see PIONEERS). Pioneer stories of back-breaking work, isolation, loneliness, racism, devastation and failure are juxtaposed with stories of self-reliance, perseverance, neighbourliness, community-building and success. From these stories emerged an archetypical pioneer figure, usually characterized as rugged, honest, hard-working, entrepreneurial and resourceful. One of the most common themes to emerge from pioneer stories was the limit of individual capacity and the necessity to engage in collective and co-operative action in order to survive and prosper in the strange environment and unforgiving elements which the newcomers faced. Despite this, however, and the popular myth that the pioneer story was largely a common experience, the reality is that the settlement frontier in Saskatchewan was far from an egalitarian one: the experiences of groups and individuals varied greatly depending on the timing of their arrival, the location in which they settled, the resources they brought with them, and their ethnicity and gender. Overall, there were almost as many losers as winners in the homesteading gamble. Despite their subordinate legal and political status, it is evident that the presence of women was one of the most important determinants of success in the settlement of the province (*see* WOMEN IN SASKATCHEWAN). It is clear also that First Nations and Métis people were systematically excluded from full participation in that settlement process and from the mythology which it engendered.

SASKATCHEWAN ARCHIVES BOARD S-B125

A typical pioneer home, southern Saskatchewan, 1906.

Rapid population growth resulting from the influx of pioneers transformed virtually all aspects of Saskatchewan society and intensified the demand for political control over local matters. Although too slow to satisfy local ambitions, political change actually came relatively quickly. Governed directly from Ottawa with an appointed council under the 1875 NORTH-WEST TERRITORIES ACT, the West was granted a TERRITORIAL ASSEMBLY in 1888, and this body secured responsible government in 1897. Westerners, however, were determined that their region should assume its rightful provincial status within Confederation, and in the early 1900s intense negotiations developed around what shape that would assume. The final decision to create two new provinces under the AUTONOMY BILLS of 1905 was dictated by Ottawa; it reflected the fears of federal politicians that a single western province would upset the equilibrium of Confederation by conferring too much power on the West.

The new province of Saskatchewan came into existence on September 1, 1905, amid great fanfare and some controversy. Huge resentment was generated by the federal government's retention of control over lands and resources—an issue that would bedevil relations between Saskatchewan and Ottawa for a generation. The Anglo-Protestant segment of the population was also infuriated by the provision in the Autonomy Bill for publicly funded separate schools where French and other non-English languages might be used in instruction.

These interrelated issues of education, religion and language aroused deep passions and dominated provincial political discourse for more than thirty years (*see* BILINGUALISM).

Unbridled optimism, however, was the dominant emotion at the creation of the new province, supported as it was by the spectacular growth occurring on all sides. With a population approaching half a million in 1911, Saskatchewan was close to becoming the third most populous province in Canada; it was also home to some of the fastest growing cities in North America. As the provincial capital, Regina benefited from the presence of the machinery of government and took great pride in its SASKATCHEWAN LEGISLATIVE BUILDING, officially opened by the Governor General in 1909. The other major urban centres also prospered through the acquisition of public institutions. Saskatoon won the right to construct the UNIVERSITY OF SASKATCHEWAN in 1909; Prince Albert received the federal penitentiary; and North Battleford became home to the provincial asylum. In addition to these major centres, over 500 small towns appeared in the southern part of the province in this period, directly related to the spread of railways. At the time of World War I, Saskatchewan was serviced by three major national railways and over 1,000 miles of branch lines. In the same period the entire administrative, educational and communications infrastructure of the province, including a system of rural municipalities, roads, schools, courts and hospitals, was built virtually from scratch.

During these formative years the province was dominated by agriculture, and the cultivation of wheat was clearly the most important agriculture pursuit: in 1911 over 80% of the population lived in rural areas, and more than 75% of the work force identified farming as their primary occupation. The LIBERAL PARTY, which governed the province without interruption until 1929, owed its dominance primarily to its close relations with farmers and its sensitivity to agricultural interests. Agriculture dictated the pace and direction of railway construction because the railways were built primarily to transport agricultural commodities. Towns grew up around grain elevators and these edifices, which were often the only vertical structures in the vast flat land, became vital landmarks and symbols of the pioneer presence. Agriculture also dictated the further growth of urban centres from villages to towns to cities, because these too emerged to service the needs of the surrounding farming communities. Progress in the province was measured primarily by wheat yields (over 50 million bushels in 1906), and Saskatchewanians revelled in their newly acquired reputation for creating the "bread-basket of the world." However, this single-minded commitment to the cultivation of wheat also prompted some questionable developments. One of these was the decision in 1908 to open up for homesteading the dry land in the southwest which had previously been reserved for ranchers; the folly of attempting cereal cultivation in this area became all too obvious in the 1930s. Motivated by the same desire to make more land available for White settlers, the Department of the Interior in the first two decades of the 20th century arranged for the sale of thousands of acres of Indian reserve land, often by fraudulent means. Along with the restrictions under which they already laboured, the loss of so much prime agricultural land was a crippling blow to the efforts of many bands to establish themselves in the wheat economy.

In retrospect, the settlement of Saskatchewan represented a collision between natural and human forces on a grand scale. The conversion of the environment from native prairie and parkland to a surveyed, fenced and intensively cultivated landscape constituted an enormous ecological transformation. Biodiversity was compromised by the reduction or elimination of natural predators to make way for cattle and horse ranching, and the tendency to over-graze on fenced-in ranches in turn altered the vegetational composition. Told from the settlers' perspective, this was a story of progress and dominance, represented by clearing, breaking and opening the land. Sooner or later, however, the settlers learned that there were natural limits to progress and ecological consequences for their dominance.

The first great boom in Saskatchewan lasted until 1912, but the recession which followed tempered the confidence of the boosters in the limitless potential of the new province. The outbreak of World War I in 1914 soon brought a return to prosperity, however, and also left other marks on the province. The war was initially greeted with a great outpouring of patriotic fervour as young men from across the province rushed to enlist; over 42,000 Saskatchewan residents served in the conflict, and 4,400 gave their lives for the Allied cause. Enlistment rates were highest among those of British origin, but many of the recent immigrants from eastern Europe seized on the opportunity to demonstrate their patriotism. Aboriginal people also volunteered in impressive numbers. While the war initially served as a unifying force, it also intensified prejudice against Slavic groups, especially Ukrainians, many of whom were now designated as Enemy Alians because they had originated in the Austro-Hungarian Empire. Approximately half of the 8,000 who were interned came from Saskatchewan. Germans, previously seen as ideal settlers, also became targets of persecution; Anglo conformists also used the emotionalism of the war to restrict French and other minority groups' linguistic rights in the province.

The assault on minority cultures represented the dark side of the SOCIAL GOSPEL movement which flourished in Canada during the war. Seeking to purify national society through the application of Christian principles, Social Gospellers called for a wide variety of reforms, including the PROHIBITION of alcohol and the extension of voting rights to women (see WOMAN SUFFRAGE). It is perhaps not surprising, given the crucial contribution of women to pioneer society and the strength of women's organizations, that Saskatchewan in 1916 became the second province to grant women the vote and the third to prohibit the sale and consumption of alcohol.

Saskatchewan benefited little from the enormous expansion of Canadian manufacturing prompted by wartime demand for munitions. But it was a very different story with agriculture: ranchers responded to increased demand and prices by tripling beef production between 1914 and 1918, and wheat farmers were similarly motivated by patriotism and the desire for profit. With the encouragement of the federal government, especially after the establishment of the Board of Grain Supervisors in 1917 set a fixed price for grain, the number of acres devoted to wheat increased from just over 6 million in 1914 to 10.5 million by 1918. The total volume of wheat harvested increased by 15%, despite a series of poor crops. This emphasis on wheat production by the federal government during the war years undermined the efforts of provincial officials to diversify agriculture and reinforced the Saskatchewan trend towards cereal monoculture. This accentuation of the province's extremely narrow economic base would prove to be a costly legacy of World War I.

The winds of change which blew across the country in the postwar period affected the wheat province also. In fact, some of these changes originated in Saskatchewan. Drawing on the co-operative traditions forged during the pioneer phase and motivated by a growing sense of regional grievance, Saskatchewan farmers helped to create the agrarian-based PROGRESSIVE PARTY, which formed the official opposition in the 1921 federal election. Although short-lived, the initial success of this major third party to emerge in Canada attested to the willingness of Saskatchewan voters to embrace independent and experimental political action. It also reflected a growing sense of western alienation, stemming from the perception that the interests of the region were being ignored by the federal government. This spirit of independence and experimentation also manifested itself in the economic sphere. Building on earlier co-operative initiatives in elevator ownership, farmers created the SASKATCHEWAN WHEAT POOL in 1924 to assert greater producer control over the marketing of their commodity. Organized labour, never very strong in Saskatchewan because of the province's small industrial base, also began to flex its muscles in support of the Winnipeg General Strike. An important short-term gain was the passing of minimum wage legislation in 1919. Aboriginal people too began to engage in collective action for the first time since the 1880s, and two new organizations were formed in the 1920s. Métis people later followed this lead, forming the Half-Breeds of Saskatchewan in 1935.

Ironically, these various recourses to collective action occurred against a backdrop of deepening cultural tension within the larger Saskatchewan society. The extraordinary, albeit short-lived, popularity of the KU KLUX KLAN in the province in the late 1920s was a testament to the bitterness of these cleavages, as the American White-supremacist organization was able to exploit Anglo-Protestant fear that they were losing control of the province's institutions to French Canadians, Slavs, and Roman Catholics. The Conservative Party also benefited from these concerns and was able to combine with the Progressives to finally defeat the Liberals in 1929. The new Premier, J.T.M. ANDERSON, moved quickly to reduce minority linguistic and educational rights and to restrict immigration from non-British sources. Anderson also secured provincial control of natural resources in the Natural Resources Transfer Agreement of 1930.

In the midst of these cultural convulsions, Saskatchewan's economy continued to expand. Over 150,000 new immigrants arrived in the 1920s, pushing the settlement frontier further north. For the first time since the signing of TREATY 10 with northern bands in 1905, the economic potential of the natural resources of the province's vast boreal forests and freshwater lakes began to attract the attention of southern entrepreneurs. A significant increase in mining, logging and commercial fishing occurred in the 1920s, but the interests of the Aboriginal population were of very little concern in these developments. Despite these developments the province's economy still rested almost exclusively on wheat, and peoples' confidence and faith in the land seemed to be rewarded again in 1928 when Saskatchewan farmers produced the largest harvest on record: 321 million bushels, almost 40% of the entire world's wheat supply. The province was a prosperous place, with automobiles, radios and other consumer luxuries becoming commonplace, farmers investing in new machinery to replace horse and steam power, and many farmers expanding their operations beyond the initial quarter section. All of this changed dramatically in the following decade.

Since the settlement boom of the 1890s Saskatchewan farmers had gambled their future on wheat, based on the premise that the land would continue to sustain them profitably. The folly of this gamble became evident in the 1930s. The GREAT DEPRESSION which gripped Canada and most of the industrial world after 1929 was compounded in Saskatchewan by nine successive years of drought and crop failure. Even when a crop could be harvested, the collapse in international demand for wheat drove prices to their lowest levels in memory. The result was financial disaster for thousands of Saskatchewan farmers; with agriculture accounting for more than three-quarters of the provincial economy,

Making a new start in the Dirty Thirties, Meadow Lake, 1935.

all other sectors of society were similarly impacted. Between 1928 and 1933, per capita income in Saskatchewan declined by more than 70%—the greatest loss of any region of the country—and by 1933 an estimated one out of every three people in the province was depending on government relief for survival. The great Saskatchewan dream of limitless profit from mining the land was shattered, driving thousands out of the province; many who remained were compelled to embrace even more radical political experimentation in order to survive and prosper.

Like most other administrations, Saskatchewan's Anderson government was overwhelmed by the scope of the catastrophe which confronted it. Widespread destitution forced the government to establish a Relief Commission in 1931: nearly $35 million was distributed in direct or indirect assistance over the next four years. Worst hit was the PALLISER TRIANGLE in the southwest, where nature and the elements seemed to conspire through drought, dust storms and grasshopper plagues to test human endurance. There the Depression was experienced as the "Dirty Thirties," leaving close to 20 million acres of land denuded of topsoil. By 1934 homesteads in the region were being abandoned en masse, some families moving north to the forest fringe to start over, others departing the province for good (see NORTHERN SETTLERS RE-ESTABLISHMENT BRANCH). The collapse of the farm economy soon spilled over into the manufacturing, retail, processing, construction, and transportation sectors, causing massive province-wide urban unemployment. Married male heads of families were given priority in the allocation of relief; women were generally considered to be the responsibility of their families, and single unemployed men, many of them transient, were warehoused in relief camps. On numerous occasions during the 1930s, Saskatchewan's urban centres saw violent eruptions stemming from the anger and frustration produced by this unprecedented unemployment and dislocation (see ON-TO-OTTAWA TREK).

The Depression was a watershed in the province's development. The inherent vulnerability of the wheat economy was graphically revealed, as were the disastrous environmental consequences of many traditional farming techniques. The limits of individual agency when confronted by forces outside of human control were also placed in sharp relief and produced a general recognition of the desirability of government intervention to solve economic and social problems. Initially steadfast in his defence of limited government, Prime Minister R.B. Bennett ultimately acknowledged the need for unconventional approaches, and two aspects of the "Bennett New Deal" of 1935 were particularly significant for Saskatchewan: the CANADIAN WHEAT BOARD, a federally operated, centralized marketing agency, set a floor price for wheat and restored some measure of control and security for producers; and the

PRAIRIE FARM REHABILITATION ADMINISTRATION, established initially to deal with soil erosion, soon moved beyond this limited mandate. The latter encouraged collaboration between farmers, federal officials and experts from universities and experimental farms, and had an enormous influence on the development and dissemination of a more rational and scientific approach to all aspects of prairie agriculture in subsequent decades.

These initiatives were symptomatic of a new consensus on the desirability of government exercising its power in non-traditional areas. The same impulses contributed to the birth of the CO-OPERATIVE COMMONWEALTH FEDERATION (CCF) in 1932. Drawing heavily on the co-operative and reformist traditions of earlier pioneer society, the party was also influenced by a deeply engrained hostility to large financial inter-

First CCF picnic at Crystal Lake (no date).

ests, sharpened by the more radical class analysis that gained currency during the Depression. In these circumstances it made increasing sense to beleaguered farmers to make common cause with other exploited classes, especially wage labourers, in order to create a political movement to build a better society. From the perspective of those experiencing the widespread devastation of the early 1930s, that utopia was characterized by a regulated economy operating on the principles of co-operation and public ownership, and by a society where human dignity was guaranteed by an extensive array of social welfare measures provided by the state. Combining the Utopian impulses of the pioneers and the deep-seated craving for security and control engendered by the Depression, CCF ideology may be seen as a distinctively Saskatchewan creation. More than any other single factor, the ideology and policies of this party—and of its successor the NEW DEMOCRATIC PARTY (NDP)—would shape the province for the remainder of the 20th century.

The CCF strengthened its local organization during the 1930s and came to power in Saskatchewan in 1944, at a time when wartime demand had restored some prosperity (see WORLD WAR II). Determined to use the power of government to modernize the province, the charismatic new Premier, T.C. DOUGLAS, embarked on an ambitious legislative program which set Saskatchewan on a very different course from its prairie neighbours. Over the next twenty years the CCF government sponsored measures to protect family farms and workers' rights; it created an array of publicly owned utilities which facilitated, among other developments, extensive rural electrification; it consolidated rural schools and improved roads and other rural infrastructure; it increased funding for public libraries, archives and arts activities; and it greatly expanded social welfare measures (see CROWN CORPORATIONS). The CCF's most notable accomplishment was perhaps the introduction of

MEDICARE, the first system of socialized medicine in North America, in 1962. It also sought to expand and diversify the province's economic base, and initially looked to the exploitation of natural resources to generate wealth. OIL, GAS, POTASH, URANIUM, FORESTRY, DIAMOND mining and TOURISM all saw remarkable growth in the half century after World War II, as the province slowly shifted from its exclusive reliance on agriculture to a more broad-based and resilient economy.

In power for forty of the fifty years after World War II, the CCF-NDP could boast of many accomplishments which dramatically improved the lives of ordinary people in Saskatchewan and also provided inspiration for the establishment of numerous national social programs. But despite a commitment to scientific planning, it is clear also that many of these policies had entirely unanticipated and undesirable consequences. In retrospect it is evident that consolidation of rural schools and improvements in rural roads and other services, all of which were designed to enhance the quality of life of rural residents and protect family farms, actually had the opposite effect. The ONE-ROOM SCHOOLS were the heart of rural society: once these were closed, it was only a matter of time before other service and supply functions, and ultimately railway lines and grain elevators, were also shifted to larger urban centres. The CCF-NDP was powerless to reverse the consolidation and mechanization of agriculture, which saw fewer people operating a shrinking number of larger and more intensive farms. As a result, the RURAL DEPOPULATION which began during the Depression continued and even accelerated after the war. Even periods of agricultural prosperity, such as those stemming from the farm support programs and massive foreign wheat sales which Prime Minister JOHN G. DIEFENBAKER produced for his home province in the late 1950s and early 1960s, saw little change in out-migration. Material wealth was itself a factor in rural decline, as the introduction of electricity and access to television, automobiles, airplanes and university education exposed prairie

SASKATCHEWAN ARCHIVES BOARD R-A5729-4

Tommy Douglas.

people to a larger global consensus. The profound changes in the family that accompanied widespread use of birth control, increased divorce rates, and higher employment rates for women also manifested themselves in Saskatchewan in the post-war years. The result was a growing determination on the part of many rural people, especially the young, to head to the cities or leave the province entirely in search of greater economic opportunities and a different quality of life.

Initiatives in northern Saskatchewan also produced a range of unintended consequences. The CCF was one of the first provincial administrations to include the north in its provincial vision, since its planners saw northern resources and tourism as central to the diversification of the economy and to the provision of expanded social welfare programs. They were also determined to modernize the north through the secularization of community leadership, the creation of a model socialist economy, and the assimilation of Aboriginal peoples to provincial norms. In many cases, however, even more serious problems resulted from these initiatives. Better health care facilities, for example, contributed to a dramatic population increase, worsening unemployment and poverty. New roads built to facilitate economic development brought additional social problems related to alcohol. Government intervention discouraged some existing local businesses, while the introduction of social assistance undermined self-sufficiency and encouraged dependency. Enormous wealth was thus extracted over time from the north; but in many respects living conditions among the First Nations and Métis people of the region deteriorated as they moved from trap lines into new settlements.

Aboriginal people in the south also experienced profound changes in this period, as rapid population growth was accompanied by increased political assertiveness and heightened concern for cultural revitalization. By the end of the century, Aboriginal people constituted approximately 15% of the provincial population; under the auspices of organizations such as the FEDERATION OF SASKATCHEWAN INDIAN NATIONS, they were pushing the resolutions of LAND CLAIMS and asserting the right to self-government both on and off reserve. Métis people also shared in this Aboriginal renaissance, and although not as cohesive or influential as the FSIN, the MÉTIS NATION–SASKATCHEWAN established itself as the main advocate for Métis people and succeeded in securing funds for various programs.

Nevertheless, by tempering an early radicalism in favour of social democratic pragmatism, the CCF and its successor the NDP established themselves as the province's natural governing parties. In the process they aroused tremendous hostility, especially among members of the province's business community who believed that government wielded undue influence at the expense of the private sector. A two-party system marked by deep ideological polarization came to characterize Saskatchewan politics in the second half of the 20th century, and when voters rejected the NDP in the 1960s and 1980s they were rewarded with dramatic alternatives. The Liberals under ROSS THATCHER from 1964 to 1971 and the Progressive Conservatives under GRANT DEVINE from 1982 to 1991 were unabashedly free-enterprise in their orientation, and sought to reduce significantly the influence of government as a force in provincial society. Both had some success in attracting new investment, especially in the energy and manufacturing sectors, with

SASKATCHEWAN ARCHIVES BOARD S-B4828

John and Olive Diefenbaker, October 1958.

SASKATCHEWAN ARCHIVES BOARD S-B5014

SASKATCHEWAN ARCHIVES BOARD S-SP-A18265

Ross Thatcher.

Grant Devine.

business-friendly policies; but the Progressive Conservatives especially were confronted with a serious recession, and unsustainable borrowing left the province's public finances in a critical state.

Significantly, both of these administrations disappointed their bedrock rural supporters by failing to reverse the decline of rural Saskatchewan. The trend towards capital intensification in agriculture accelerated from the 1970s onwards; but despite increasing diversification into cattle and hog production and the development of a wide variety of new crops to supplement wheat, farmers increasingly found themselves caught in a cost-price squeeze. The removal of the CROW RATE and the appearance of heavily subsidized competition from Europe and the United States further eroded the profit margins of Saskatchewan farmers in the 1980s. The result of these trends by the end of the 20th century was the virtual disappearance of the family farm, the cornerstone of the rural society created by the pioneers. It had been replaced by agribusiness: vast, multi-section holdings relying on extensive mechanization and heavy utilization of chemicals to produce maximum yields from seed that increasingly was subjected to genetic modification. With less than 10% of Saskatchewan's population directly involved in agriculture by 2001, and with agricultural commodities accounting for less than 20% of provincial GDP, it was clear that Saskatchewan's economy was now tied to the harvest more by sentiment than by reality.

As rural Saskatchewan haemorrhaged people, the major beneficiaries were the province's larger towns and cities. North Battleford, Prince Albert, Lloydminster, Moose Jaw, Yorkton, Swift Current, Humboldt, Melfort and La Ronge all saw significant growth after 1950; in the same period both Saskatoon and Regina evolved into major regional metropolitan centres: Saskatoon's population almost tripled between 1951 and 2001, surpassing its rival in the process. With this growth came a corresponding expansion in facilities for retail, entertainment, artistic, health care and post-secondary education services. These centres also took on a more multi-ethnic flavour with the arrival of small numbers of immigrants from Asia, Africa, South America, eastern Europe and the Caribbean. More significant, however, was the huge Aboriginal influx as Native people too shared in the growing preference for urban residence: by 2001 almost 50% of the province's Aboriginal population lived in urban centres, where they constituted the single largest visible minority. Many of these migrants simply traded rural for urban poverty and racism; but the creation of urban reserves, the expansion of Aboriginal educational institutions, and the proliferation of Aboriginal businesses provided growing evidence that Native people were both adjusting to and transforming the Saskatchewan urban milieu.

Although smaller than rivals such as Winnipeg, Calgary or Edmonton, by the end of the century both Saskatoon and Regina were offering their residents all of the amenities typical of other like-sized North American cities. Moreover, Saskatchewan's cities were no longer merely appendages to the province's agricultural sector. A huge expansion in resource extraction, modest growth in manufacturing, and the development of intensive commercial research activities associated with the universities meant that the urban economies now operated largely independent of the farm sector. As a consequence, increasing numbers of urban dwellers had no direct ties to agriculture or to rural areas. This widening chasm between urban and rural Saskatchewan was clearly reflected in hardening political polarization, as the NDP came to be increasingly identified with urban Saskatchewan and the opposition SASKATCHEWAN PARTY found most of its support in rural areas. A testament to the newly found dominance of urban Saskatchewan is the fact that the NDP was able to maintain power in the early 21st century with virtually no rural representation.

As Saskatchewan prepared to celebrate its centennial in 2005, its people were still confronted with geographic isolation, a sparse population, and tremendous climatic extremes. These were the chief determinants of the province's history, as each human group which entered the area was forced to come to terms with the environment in order to survive and prosper. From the vantage of the early 21st century it seems evident that the people who call this place home have met that challenge. In the process of adjusting to the land, they created a distinctive North American community whose enigmatic political culture came to exercise a significant influence beyond its own borders. Their efforts also produced great material wealth, dynamic cities and towns, and noteworthy intellectual, cultural, artistic and athletic accomplishments. Challenges remain—in particular the need to bridge the gulf between urban and rural areas, between Aboriginal and non-Aboriginal peoples, and between northern and southern residents. Protecting and enhancing the status of the province within the Canadian federation and as part of a larger North American and global community will also require careful stewardship. In meeting these and other demands, the people of Saskatchewan can look to their historical legacy of struggle, sacrifice and success for both guidance and inspiration.

FURTHER READING:

Archer, J. Saskatchewan: A History (Saskatoon: Western Producer Prairie Books, 1980).

Brennan, J.W. Regina: An Illustrated History (Toronto: Lorimer, 1989).

DeBrou, D., and A. Moffat (eds.). Other Voices: Historical Essays on Saskatchewan Women (Regina: Canadian Plains Research Center, 1995).

Epp, R., and D. Whitson (eds.). Writing Off the Rural West: Globalization, Governments and the Transformation of Rural Communities (Edmonton: University of Alberta Press, 2001).

Fairbairn, B. Building a Dream: The Co-operative Retailing System in Western Canada (Saskatoon: Western Producer Prairie Books, 1989).

Kerr, D. and S. Hanson. Saskatoon: The First Half Century (Edmonton: NeWest Publishers, 1982).

Leeson, H. (ed.). Saskatchewan Politics into the Twenty-First Century (Regina: Canadian Plains Research Center, 2001).

Morrow, D. (ed.). A Concise History of Sport in Canada (Toronto: Oxford University Press, 1989).

Quiring, D. CCF Colonialism in Northern Saskatchewan: Battling Parish Priests, Bootleggers, and Fur Sharks (Vancouver: University of British Columbia Press, 2004).

Ray, A.J., et al. Bounty and Benevolence: A History of Saskatchewan Treaties (Montreal: McGill Queen's University Press, 2000).

Waiser, W. Saskatchewan: A New History (Calgary: Fifth House Publishers, 2005).

Wheaton, E.E. But It's a Dry Cold: Weathering the Canadian Prairies (Calgary: Fifth House Publishers, 1998).

HMCS QUEEN. HMCS *Queen* is the Royal Canadian Naval Reserve Division in Regina. The "Regina Half Company" of the Royal Canadian Naval Volunteer Reserve was established in Regina in 1923. The Division was renamed HMCS *Queen* in 1942; it was closed from 1964 to 1975, when it was re-commissioned. Today, as one of five naval reserve units on the prairies it serves as a training facility for naval reservists. It features a drill deck, classrooms, and workshops for training in various naval trades and occupations. *Lauren Black*

HMCS REGINA. The original HMCS *Regina* was commissioned into the Royal Canadian Navy in January 1942. When its outfitting was completed in April 1942, the Revised Flower Class corvette was placed on convoy escort duty, escorting numerous convoys and rescuing survivors from torpedoed ships. In February 1943, she attacked and sank the Italian submarine *Avorio*. After renovations and refitting from June 1943 to February 1944, HMCS Regina was one of nineteen Canadian corvettes that participated in the invasion of Normandy. On August 8, 1944, HMCS *Regina* went to the aid of an American merchant ship, the *Ezra Weston*, which had reportedly struck a mine near the shores of Normandy. While assisting with rescue operations, HMCS *Regina* was torpedoed by the German submarine *U-667* and sank within 30 seconds. Thirty of her crew were killed, and sixty-six were rescued. A

second-generation HMCS *Regina* was commissioned in 1994, a powerful "Halifax Class" Canadian Patrol frigate which is about twice the size and speed of the original; with home port in Esquimalt, British Columbia, HMCS *Regina* currently serves as a high-readiness unit with the Canadian Navy's Canadian Pacific Task Group. *Lauren Black*

HMCS SASKATOON. HMCS *Saskatoon* was commissioned in December 1998, and is the second Canadian warship to carry the name. This Kingston Class Maritime Coastal Defense Vessel carries out various roles such as search and rescue missions, mine countermeasures, training, and coastal patrols. It features ultra-modern engineering, allowing power and versatility in maneuvering and operations. HMCS *Saskatoon*'s home port is Esquimalt, British Columbia. The ship keeps many ties with the city of Saskatoon: areas on the ship are named after Saskatoon landmarks, such as Cranberry Flats for the captain's level, and Idylwyld for one of the main hallways.

The original HMCS *Saskatoon* was built in Montreal as a Flower Class Corvette and was commissioned into the Royal Canadian Navy in June 1941. The ship spent much of its career on patrol and escort duties on the east coast of North America, having at various times home ports in Halifax, St. John's, Boston and New York. In carrying out her work, HMCS *Saskatoon* gained a reputation for being a steadfast and hardworking vessel. Perhaps the most noteworthy event of her career was the escorting of the German submarine *U-889* back to a Canadian port after its surrender. After the war, the HMCS *Saskatoon* was decommissioned and sold to a private buyer. *Lauren Black*

HMCS UNICORN. HMCS *Unicorn* is the Canadian Naval Reserve Division in Saskatoon. It was first established in April 1923 as the Saskatoon Half Company, Royal Canadian Naval Volunteer Reserve. Naval custom has designated shore-based training establishments as ships, and in 1942 the

Saskatoon Half Company was commissioned a "stone frigate" as HMCS *Unicorn* in honour of one of the first ships to sail into Hudson Bay. The name has belonged to a long line of Royal Navy ships, going back to the 16th century. HMCS *Unicorn* has served both the community of Saskatoon and Canada for over eighty years. During **WORLD WAR II**, it operated as a recruiting centre, enlisting over 3,500 men and women into the Royal Canadian Navy. It also developed a University Naval Training program. Today, HMCS *Unicorn* remains a vital part of navy operations; naval reservists are trained for maritime coastal defense, navigation, and mine countermeasures. *Lauren Black*

HNATYSHYN, HELEN (1909–93). Helen Hnatyshyn (*née* Pitts) was a teacher, community activist, and human rights leader in the Ukrainian Canadian and mainstream communities. Born in Wroxton, Saskatchewan on July 12, 1909, she completed schooling in Yorkton, and then obtained her teaching certificate from **NORMAL SCHOOL** in Saskatoon. After teaching for several years, she settled in Saskatoon with her husband John; they had four children. Hnatyshyn's many activities included a prominent role in the **COUNCIL OF WOMEN**: she was a leader on local, provincial, national, and international levels. In 1973 she was appointed to the Advisory Council on the Status of Women, and traveled across Canada. She also served on the Saskatchewan Human Rights Commission, and her

HMCS *Regina*, at Esquimalt, July 1994.

Royal Canadian Sea Cadets at HMCS *Unicorn*, Saskatoon, May 1985.

PHOTO COURTESY OF DAVID HNATYSHYN

Helen Hnatyshyn.

volunteerism included extensive (local) participation in organizations such as the YWCA, Red Cross, and United Appeal.

In the Ukrainian Canadian milieu, she was president of the Ukrainian Women's Association of Canada (Saskatoon branch) and its provincial executive. She also helped to establish the Ukrainian Canadian Women's Committee in Saskatoon. Her numerous awards for outstanding service included an honorary Doctor of Law degree and the Governor-General's Persons Award. Hnatyshyn died in Saskatoon on December, 9, 1993. To honour a project she had made before, the National Council of Women sponsored a woman from Ukraine to attend the International Council of Women Triennium in Paris in 1994. *Natalie Ostryzniuk*

HNATYSHYN, RAMON JOHN (1934–2002). Born in Saskatoon on March 16, 1934, Ramon (Ray) Hnatyshyn followed in his father

John's footsteps and entered the legal field. John Hnatyshyn, a lawyer by trade, was also Canada's first Ukrainian-born senator. Ray graduated from the **UNIVERSITY OF SASKATCHEWAN** in 1956 and was called to the Saskatchewan Bar in 1957. He practiced privately for two years, but moved to Ottawa to work as an executive assistant to the government's Senate leader. In 1960 Hnatyshyn returned to Saskatoon, married Gerda Andreasen, and resumed the practice of law. After unsuccessfully running as a Conservative in the 1964 provincial election he taught law at the University of Saskatchewan for ten years.

In the 1974 federal election Hnatyshyn was elected in Saskatoon-West. When the Progressive Conservative Party won a minority government in 1979, Hnatyshyn was appointed to the Energy, Mines and Resources portfolio and was Minister of State for Science and Technology. In 1984, in the Brian Mulroney majority government, Hnatyshyn was appointed Government House Leader. Hnatyshyn was named president of the Privy Council in 1985 and Minister of Justice and Attorney General in 1986. In 1988 Hnatyshyn was defeated. He worked with a law firm where he specialized in trade law and mediation. That year Hnatyshyn was appointed Queen's Counsel (QC) for Canada and, one year later, he was granted an honorary life membership with the **LAW SOCIETY OF SASKATCHEWAN**. Mulroney appointed Hnatyshyn as Governor General in January 1990. He reopened Rideau Hall's doors to the public, and specifically opened grounds and rooms of the official residence of the Governor General to public events, activities, and tours. He founded the Governor General's Awards for the Performing Arts in 1992, and the Ramon John Hnatyshyn Award for Voluntarism in

the Arts. Hnatyshyn returned to his law firm in 1995 as a senior partner. At the time of his death on December 18, 2002, Hnatyshyn was serving as Chancellor of Carleton University. *Teresa Welsh*

REGINA LEADER-POST

Jackie Hoag, 1988.

HOAG, JACKIE (1911–2000). Born Violet Margaret Jackson on September 11, 1911, in Manitoba, Jackie Hoag moved in 1938 to the Regina office of Ducks Unlimited. In 1939 she married Dr. John Hoag, a dentist; they had three children. During the war she worked with Women's Voluntary Services and then chaired the Regina War Brides' Committee. Involved with the Local **COUNCIL OF WOMEN**, she chaired its housing committee. Her interest in mid-century housing problems led to extensive involvements. She became the first woman in Canada to chair (for over a decade) a city planning commission, spearheading drives for low-rental housing and senior citizens housing facilities, serving on the Regina local housing authority, heading Pioneer Village Corporation, and being vice-chair of the provincial zoning appeal board. In 1966 Hoag was appointed to the Canadian Housing Design Council. Her other concerns included mental health issues and education of the mentally retarded. In the 1950s she chaired the Standing Committee on Migration and Citizenship of the National Council of Women of Canada. In 1958 supporters urged her to seek a mayoralty nomination. She was unsuccessful, but her effort garnered national attention because of her prominence. In 1967 she became the first woman councillor since 1955, but resigned to run (unsuccessfully) for mayor. Hoag founded Old Fashion Foods in 1965, and she received the Saskatchewan Order of Merit in 1968. She died on November 6, 2000, in Regina. *Ann Leger-Anderson*

BRYAN SCHLOSSER/REGINA LEADER-POST

Ramon Hnatyshyn, June 1991.

HOCKEY. Unlike sports with British or pastoral roots like cricket, rugby, football (soccer) and baseball that were played frequently in the 1880s, hockey did not arrive in the Assiniboia or Saskatchewan sections of the North-West Territories until the following decade. The first reported competition was a series between teams from Regina and Moose Jaw in 1894, with Regina winning two of the three games. By the end of the 19th century, competitive men's teams had sprung up in Prince Albert, Moosomin, Saskatoon, Rosthern, Indian Head, Qu'Appelle, and many more towns located along the railroad lines. Organized league play escalated in the first decade of the 20th century, and was consolidated in 1906 with the formation of the Saskatchewan Amateur Hockey Association or SAHA (now Saskatchewan Hockey Association) as the sport's provincial governing body. As early as 1908 the SAHA was confronted by rumours (often true) of covert professionalism. When the Prince Albert Mintos were declared professional in February 1911, they became the first Saskatchewan team to compete for the Stanley Cup; they lost 12–9 to the Port Arthur, Ontario Bearcats in a two-game, total-goals series to decide an opponent for the defending champion Ottawa Senators. Port Arthur defeated the Saskatoon Wholesalers 12–6 in a similar series in 1912. Most of Saskatchewan, however, was focused on the pursuit of the Allan Cup, emblematic of amateur hockey supremacy in Canada. The Regina Victorias won the trophy in 1914 and were succeeded in 1915 by the Melville Millionaires, who held the national title for only a few weeks before being dethroned by the Winnipeg Monarchs. The 1940-41 Regina Rangers have been Saskatchewan's only Allan Cup champions since then.

Massive enlistment in the military during **WORLD WAR I** caused both a decline in senior hockey and the emergence of the junior game. The latter was acknowledged with a national championship, the Memorial Cup, begun in 1919 and featuring the Regina Pats (named after the Princess Patricia Light Infantry regiment) as western Canada's first representatives. Although the Pats lost to the University of Toronto, Regina would rebound with Memorial Cup triumphs in 1925 (Pats), 1928 (Monarchs), and 1930 (Pats). While both junior and senior hockey thrived, the 1920s were most notable for the short life of the Western Canada Hockey League (WCHL), a major-league professional organization of equal calibre to the National Hockey League and whose champions competed for the Stanley Cup against the NHL's best teams. The Regina Capitals won the WCHL's first championship in 1921–22 and remained for four seasons, while the Saskatoon Crescents (sometimes called "Sheiks") were on hand until the league dissolved after the 1925–26 season.

Teams and leagues struggled to survive the **GREAT DEPRESSION** and **WORLD WAR II**, but individual stars emerged from a variety of backgrounds. Gordie Howe, the NHL's scoring champion and most valuable player six times in a career that spanned 34 years, honed his skills in Saskatoon by playing in as many as six youth leagues at once. Metro Prystai was recruited from Yorkton to be a scoring sensation with the junior Moose Jaw Canucks. Rural Saskatchewan produced talented individuals like brothers Max and Doug **BENTLEY** (Delisle), Elmer Lach (Nokomis), and Sid Abel (Melville). Notre Dame College in Wilcox, under the leadership of Père **ATHOL MURRAY**, moulded several NHL veterans. Professional hockey had a resurgence after World War II with the Regina Caps (later Capitals) and Saskatoon Elks (later Quakers) of the Western Hockey League, but those minor-league franchises died out in 1956. Junior hockey gradually took over

as the pre-eminent spectator attraction, with leagues and teams constantly realigning along lines of population, geography, and facilities. The Regina Pats dominated the 1950s through the citywide network of Parks League teams and elite Pee Wee, Bantam and Midget clubs that fed the junior roster. Facing little competition within the province, the Pats represented western Canada in the Memorial Cup final five times from 1950 through 1958, but lost every series.

Junior hockey, at its elite level, shifted from a provincial to a regional concern in 1966 with the creation of the Canadian Major Junior Hockey League (later the Western Canada Hockey League and the Western Hockey League, the professional circuit of that name having gone defunct). Spanning the three prairie provinces, the league originally included the Pats, Moose Jaw Canucks, Saskatoon Blades, Estevan Bruins, and Weyburn Red Wings. A sixth Saskatchewan team, the Swift Current Broncos, joined in 1967; but within eight years only the Pats and Blades remained, as the other teams were relocated outside the province in larger cities with greater economic potential. By 1986, however, staunch fan support in small cities helped Saskatchewan boost its Western Hockey League membership back to five with the Moose Jaw Warriors, the Prince Albert Raiders and the return of the Swift Current Broncos. Memorial Cup championships came to Regina in 1974, to Prince Albert in 1985, and, most dramatically, to Swift Current in 1989, two-and-a-half years after a highway bus accident killed four Broncos.

The formation and growth of the CMJHL/ WCHL/WHL led to the Saskatchewan Junior Hockey League's transition to a Tier 2 league: since 1972, the SJHL has been a stable entity, always operating with at least ten teams, except for four seasons in

Kerrobert, Goose Lake Hockey League champions, 1913–14.

A pick-up game of hockey on an outdoor rink—still a common sight in the province.

the mid-1980s when its membership fell to as low as eight. Seven national Tier 2 champions have come from the SJHL: the Prince Albert Raiders (in 1977, 1979, 1981 and 1982) before they moved up to the WHL; the Weyburn Red Wings (1984); the Notre Dame Hounds (1988); and the Humboldt Broncos (2003). Notre Dame has also produced two (1980 and 1986) of the province's seven Canadian midget champions since that title was established in 1979, lining up alongside the Regina Pat Canadians (1989, 1994, 1999), Yorkton Mallers (1993), and Tisdale Trojans (2002).

Saskatchewan's contributions to Canada's international hockey success have also been significant. The Saskatoon Quakers, 1933 Allan Cup runners-up, represented Canada at the 1934 world championship in Milan and won the gold medal. Canada's 1955 world champions, the Penticton (BC) V's, boasted nine players with Saskatchewan connections, including player-coach Grant Warwick and his brothers, Billy and Dick. Jackie McLeod, a Notre Dame alumnus and NHL veteran, coached the 1968 national team that won a bronze medal as the last wholly amateur team to represent Canada in the Olympics; seven of its players hailed from Saskatchewan. More recently, the province produced four members of Team Canada's women's squad, which won the 2002 Olympic gold medal. HAYLEY WICKENHEISER of Shaunavon, arguably the best female player in the world, went on from that triumph to become the first woman to play regularly as a professional when she logged twenty-three games for Salamat of the Finnish Second Division in the 2002–03 season. In doing so, Wickenheiser expanded on Saskatchewan's tradition of supplying elite players from virtually every populated section of the province. EDDIE SHORE–born in Fort Qu'Appelle and raised in Cupar–was the NHL's finest defenceman with the Boston Bruins in the late 1920s and throughout the 1930s. GORDIE HOWE was the game's most inexorable offensive force except when checked by defensive standout Bert Olmstead (Sceptre). GLENN HALL (Humboldt) and Johnny Bower (Prince Albert) proved themselves among the finest goaltenders of all time in the 1950s and 1960s. BRYAN TROTTIER (born in Redvers, raised in Val Marie) was a superb two-way centre of the NHL's post-expansion era and a member of six Stanley Cup championships. Wendel Clark (Kelvington) was an exceptional player among a new generation of Notre Dame prodigies. Altogether, Saskatchewan has produced more than 425 NHLers, the highest per capita output of any Canadian province, American state, or European country. *John Chaput*

FURTHER READING: Coleman, J. 1987. *Hockey is Our Game: Canada in the World of International Hockey.* Toronto: Key Porter; Lapp, R.M. and A. Macauley. 1983. *Local Heroes: A History of the Western Hockey League.* Madeira Park, BC: Harbour; Zeman, B. 1983. *88 Years of Puck-Chasing in Saskatchewan.* Regina: WDS Associates.

HODGINS, GRANT MILTON (1955–). Grant Hodgins was born July 22, 1955, in Prince Albert. After completing high school in Melfort, he attended the UNIVERSITY OF SASKATCHEWAN, completing a degree in Commerce. Hodgins was elected for the Progressive Conservatives in the Tory sweep of 1982 in the traditionally NDP seat of Melfort. In 1985, Hodgins was appointed to Cabinet as Minister of Highways and Transportation. Easily re-elected in 1986, Hodgins was given added responsibility by taking on the Indian and Native Affairs portfolio. In 1989, Hodgins was moved out of Highways and took over as Minister of Environment. He was also given the added responsibility of government House Leader, piloting the government's legislation through the Legislature. In 1991, Hodgins became upset with government policy, in particular the program called "Fair Share Saskatchewan." This rural revitalization program, which would have seen the dispersal of government offices from Regina to various centres across Saskatchewan, was a highly contentious proposal. In protest, Hodgins resigned from the government and served out the legislative session as an independent. Hodgins did not seek re-election in 1991, choosing instead to take over the family auctioneering business in Melfort. *Brett Quiring*

HODGSON, CHRISTINE WILNA (1935–2003). "Willy" Hodgson was a psychiatric nurse, social worker, church worker and CREE elder, who rose from humble beginnings to become an influential bridge builder between the province's Aboriginal and non-Aboriginal peoples.

She was born Christine Wilna Pratt on October 20, 1935, on the Sandy Lake (now Ahtahkakoop) Indian Reserve west of Canwood, Saskatchewan. After living on various air force bases in Quebec and Alberta, she settled in Moose Jaw in 1967 with her husband, Bill Hodgson, and their four children. In

BILL HODGSON PHOTO/COURTESY OF THE HODGSON FAMILY

Christine Wilna Hodgson.

the 1970s she studied social work and human justice at the UNIVERSITY OF REGINA, then worked as a social worker with the provincial government, and later helped coordinate Native employment programs.

She was active in groups as diverse as the Interprovincial Association of Native Employment, victim services and race relations committees, and the Anglican Church's council for Native ministries. In 1996 the Saskatchewan government appointed her to the LAW SOCIETY OF SASKATCHEWAN as a lay-bencher. Her awards included a Women of Distinction Award from the City of Moose Jaw in 1998, the Saskatchewan Order of Merit in 1994, and the Order of Canada in 2002. She died of cancer in Moose Jaw on February 14, 2003. *Bruce Dyck*

HOG FARMING. Domesticated pigs are derived from varying proportions of European and northern Asia wild boar (*Sus scrofa*) and pot-bellied pigs of subtropical Southeast Asia (*Sus vitatus*). Domestic pigs are raised throughout the southern half of the province for their ability to produce pork meat efficiently, for both domestic consumption and export sales. In 2004 there were 647 pork-producing farms in Saskatchewan, marketing approximately two million hogs each year. In 1990 there were 3,292 farms producing 948,095 market hogs. The shift from farms with mixed agricultural commodity production to fewer specialized farms with greater production per farm is evident in all provinces and for all commodities. This specialization and consolidation has resulted in the disappearance of pork farms in Saskatchewan, in a way comparable to other jurisdictions in North America. Over the same time period, herd size has increased–typically growing from 100-plus sows to 600 sows, with some barns housing as many as 5,000 sows.

Four production systems in Saskatchewan operate a total of 64,000 sows and market about 65% of the hogs. Production from Hutterite colonies, four breeding stock companies, and many independent farms account for the other 35% of hogs sold. The proportion of hogs produced by large farms across Canada has increased since 1992, when the top eight farms accounted for 5% of Canadian production: today, the top eight farms account for over 20% of the pork produced.

Pork is the world's most popular meat protein, and Saskatchewan exports 10% of its production as live animals for processing directly to the United States. Saskatchewan, Alberta, and Manitoba pork processors export over 50% of the pork processed. Per capita consumption of pork has remained constant for over twenty-five years in Canada at 25 kg (live carcass weight) per capita. Hog marketing can be conducted through direct sales to the packing company, or via a sales agent. Farmers have the option of taking current cash pricing or using a number of forward-contracting tools to determine prices at time of marketing. In Saskatchewan, 57% of the hogs produced are processed here, with 33% and 10% respectively being marketed in Alberta/Manitoba and in the United States.

Pork farms use a number of breeding stock suppliers, each of which combine several traditional breeds to produce the female (sow) and male (boar) progeny for the commercial pork farm. Females are selected for their ability to produce large litters, and boars are selected for their carcass (meat) characteristics. Sows have a gestation period of 115 days and will give birth to a litter of ten or eleven piglets. With an average of 2.2 litters per year, a sow will produce twenty-two to twenty-six pigs a year. A mature female weighs from 170 to 250 kg; mature boars exceed 300 kg.

The farm may be organized along two basic production system types. The first is known as farrow-to-finish: the breeding, farrowing (birthing), and growing to market weight all occur on the same farm, and typically within specialized rooms of the same barn. Bur more recently, increasing farm size as well as desire to specialize farm activity and limit the risk of possible disease outbreak have led to the development of the multi-site farm, which has farrowing, nursery, and growing operations each on their own separate farm site.

Saskatchewan pork producers take advantage of the low pig population density to enforce strict farm entry procedures to ensure good health. Biosecurity is the name given to procedures designed to reduce the risk of disease being carried into the pig barn: this is desirable, as the presence of disease reduces performance of the animal, could cause loss of animal life, increases management time and costs, and can affect meat quality. For these reasons, pork farms limit entry of live pigs, equipment, and people to their facilities. For live pigs, a quarantine period serves the purpose, and when combined with a strategy for introducing new genetics through artificial insemination, significantly reduces the risk of disease entry.

Lee Whittington

HOLLIS, ANNIE (1871–1941).

Born in England in 1871, Annie Hollis (*née* Snaith) taught there for seventeen years. In 1909 she joined the suffragette Women's Social and Political Union. In March 1914, she and two sisters accompanied their parents to Saskatchewan, where they homesteaded near Shaunavon. In 1915 she began teaching at Anglo School until her 1926 resignation to devote her time to the farmers' movement. Hollis became a leader in the Saskatchewan Grain Growers' Association Women's Section: in 1922 she was elected a member of its executive, in 1924 vice-president, and in 1926 president. In the meantime she had become convener of the new Education Committee and of the Legislation Committee which sought to improve married women's property rights and

called for joint farm ownership. Hollis also helped to ensure women's voice in the United Farmers of Canada (UFC), an amalgamation of the Saskatchewan Grain Growers' Association and the Farmers Union of Canada, and she became the UFC's first woman president. She was involved in founding the Saskatchewan Farmers Political Association, and ran in the Maple Creek riding in the 1930 federal election. Hollis wrote a weekly column in the W*estern Producer* from 1924 to 1929; during the 1930s she also wrote a column in the *Saskatchewan Farmer.* She died on June 26, 1941, near Shaunavon.

Cathy Holtslander

HOME AND SCHOOL.

Mabel Hubbard Bell, wife of Alexander Graham Bell, assisted in organizing the Parents Association of Baddeck Schools, Nova Scotia, in 1895: thus began the Canada-wide organization known for years as "Home and School." The Canadian National Federation of Home and School was founded in Toronto in 1927; in 1951 this became the Canadian Home and School and Parent-Teacher Federation, and was incorporated as a nonprofit organization. Over the years it has been shown that a parent's involvement with a child's education will greatly enhance that child's achievement: an enlightened adult can give the child a reason to want to learn. Saskatchewan's first Home and School Association began in 1926 at the Buena Vista School in Saskatoon, and soon Home and School groups were forming throughout the province. In the village of Gainsborough, for example, the group paid expenses for various grades to enter the annual Music Festival, sponsored the formation of a **4-H CLUB**, discussed discipline and safety on school buses, celebrated the graduation of Grade 12 students, sponsored gun safety and snowmobile safety courses, organized talks by RCMP for both students and parents on drug and alcohol abuse, gave prizes for students at public speaking evenings, etc. It is thanks to their efforts, too, that the opening of a branch library took place nearly forty years ago.

In 1996 the Saskatchewan Home and School Association became the Saskatchewan Association of School Councils (SASC) and was in a better position to become the umbrella organization for the upcoming school councils. Nowadays, SASC members assist in classrooms and libraries, raise funds, and help with decision-making in many areas. From the very start of Home and School, all this has been voluntary work. The organization, which represents about one-third of Saskatchewan's schools, strives to fulfill its vision statement: "Providing a provincial voice for every parent on behalf of every child."

Sheila Stevenson

HOMEMAKERS' CLUBS AND WOMEN'S INSTITUTES.

The Homemakers' Clubs of Saskatchewan (HMCS) and the Saskatchewan

Women's Institutes (SWI), which replaced the Homemakers in 1972, have played an important part in the lives of rural women. Both were affiliated with the Federated Women's Institutes of Canada (FWIC), founded in 1919, and with the Associated Countrywomen of the World (ACWW), founded in 1933, and Saskatchewan delegates regularly attended their meetings. The Homemakers and the Women's Institutes were the first of three main streams of the farm women's movement in the province, along with the second stream, the Women Grain Growers (WGG) and its successor organizations that came into being in 1913 and 1914, and the third stream, the Saskatchewan Women's Agricultural Network, established in 1985 and now inactive. Founded in 1911, the Homemakers' Clubs were patterned on the Women's Institutes in Ontario. In Saskatchewan they were affiliated with the Extension Division of the **UNIVERSITY OF SASKATCHEWAN**, which was both a strength and a problem for the Homemakers: they were at times constrained by the middle-class male administrators of the University, but on the other hand benefited from their affiliation with the University. For instance, the University hired Winnipeg agrarian journalist Lillian Beynon Thomas to organize clubs, and her work was partially responsible for the existence of the Homemakers. In later years the HMCS held an annual Homemakers' Week on the campus of the University.

The HMCS and the SWI, which were made up of numerous groups at the local level, attracted large numbers of rural women. Women often joined the Homemakers in order to overcome their loneliness on isolated farms, but many women in small towns also joined the local organizations. Both groups focused on education and homemaking skills, shunning involvement in political questions. The HMCS, for example, did not participate in the women's suffrage campaign because its constitution barred what was considered partisan action. Some farm women, however, belonged not only to a Homemakers' Club, but also to the local WGG club and the Local of the Grain Growers, which focused on economic and political questions. As well, the HMCS and the WGG co-operated in as many areas as possible. During the newcomer settlement period, for instance, both the Homemakers and the WGG believed that farm mothers, their babies and their families needed better medical aid, and both believed that by united action the WGG and the Homemakers could help to secure improved medical care for farm people.

The Homemakers also worked closely with the Victorian Order of Nurses to improve the health care available to rural women and their families. In 1914 they also urged the provincial government to give a grant of $25 to every needy mother who gave birth in the province, $15 of which was to go to the doctor who delivered the baby. These grants, which

Emma Ducie, shown here in 1976, was an active member of the Homemakers' Club.

and passed her enthusiasm on to her daughters: the elder, Rose, who worked for the *Western Producer*, promoted the Homemakers and other farm women's activities in the newspaper; the younger, Emmie Oddie, was active in the Homemakers and the SWIs at the local, district, and national level, and was also involved in the ACWW. The number of local Women's Institutes declined during the final decades of the 20th century, but there are still some throughout the province. SWI members have also continued to co-operate with other organized farm women on specific issues such as rural childcare in order to improve the lives of rural women and their families.

Georgina M. Taylor

FURTHER READING: Saskatchewan Women's Institutes. 1988. *Legacy–A History of Saskatchewan Homemakers' Clubs and Women's Institutes, 1911–1988*. Saskatoon: Saskatchewan Women's Institutes.

HOMESTEAD ACT: *see* **DOMINION LANDS ACT**

HONOURS AND AWARDS. Saskatchewan has four official honours: an order, a decoration, and two medals. The Saskatchewan Order of Merit, established in 1985, recognizes outstanding achievement and contributions to the public good. The Provincial Emblems and Honours Act of 1988 confirmed the status of the Order as an honour of the provincial Crown. Amendments to the Act in 1995 created the Saskatchewan Volunteer Medal, a decoration for the volunteer sector. In 2003 the Legislature approved two medals: the Saskatchewan

Saskatchewan Order of Merit.

Protective Services Medal, for twenty-five years of exemplary service in provincial and federal agencies such as police and firefighters; and the Saskatchewan Centennial Medal for presentation to deserving citizens during 2005. Honours are presented in the name of the Crown by the **LIEUTENANT-GOVERNOR**; their insignia include medals, lapel pins, and certificates. With a few exceptions, eligibility for provincial honours is restricted to Canadian citizens who are present or former long-term residents of Saskatchewan. The provincial government established the Saskatchewan Distinguished Service Award in 1997 for non-residents who have made a substantial contribution to the province, and the Premier's Award for Excellence in the Public Service in 2003 as part of an employee recognition program. Awards are presented by the Premier.

Michael Jackson

FURTHER READING: Blatherwick, J. 2003. *Canadian Orders, Decorations and Medals*. Toronto: Unitrade Press; Jackson, M. 2002. *Images of a Province: Symbols of Saskatchewan*. Regina: Government of Saskatchewan.

were to continue for decades, were seen as necessary prior to the implementation of medicare. The HMCS and WGG had many other common interests. Both wanted better libraries, better schools, restrooms in small towns where weary farm women could rest, and other services in rural areas.

Although thousands of Saskatchewan women were involved in the Homemakers and the Women's Institutes, one family in particular illustrates the way enthusiasm for them was often passed from one generation to another. Emma Ducie organized the Coates Homemakers' Club in 1913, was active at a local level for thirty-seven years, was provincial president of the Homemakers from 1926 to 1929,

HORLICK, LOUIS (1921–). Louis Horlick was born in Montreal on December 2, 1921. He obtained his MD and much of his post-graduate training at McGill University. His renowned career as an atherosclerosis researcher began at Michael Reese Hospital in Chicago. In 1954, he moved to Saskatchewan as the first fully trained subspecialty cardiologist at the new degree-granting medical school. He quickly established an outstanding reputation as a bedside clinical cardiologist and researcher with exceptional sensitivity to the needs of the whole person. From 1968 to 1975 he was chairman of the Department of Medicine. After formal retirement in 1989, he became enthusiastically involved in the field of geriatric medicine and continued to practice until 2000. He has published numerous medical arti-

Executive of Saskatchewan Homemakers' Clubs, elected at Saskatoon, June 1929.

Lou Horlick.

cles, plus two books on the history of the **UNIVERSITY OF SASKATCHEWAN** Medical School. He received the Saskatchewan Order of Merit in 1991 and was made an Officer of the Order of Canada in 1994. He and his wife Ruth are also well known in Saskatoon as loyal patrons of the arts. *W. Earle DeCoteau*

HORLICK, RUTH (1919-). Ruth Horlick (*née* Hood) was born in Toronto on September 25, 1919, and educated at Queen's University and Montreal General Hospital School of Nursing. She took post-graduate training in psychiatric nursing at the Royal Victoria Hospital in Montreal, in Denver and in Washington, DC, before moving to Saskatoon in 1954. While she raised her family of four sons, she became involved in psychiatric group therapy on a volunteer basis at the **UNIVERSITY OF SASKATCHEWAN** and in the McKerracher Centre, a psychiatric day-care unit, and then resumed her career in 1977 at the Royal University Hospital. She helped form the Association for Children with Learning Disabilities, and was a volunteer tutor at the Regional Psychiatric Centre as well as a board member of the Crocus Co-op for ex-psychiatric patients.

Ruth Horlick's volunteer commitments included: honorary patron of the Saskatoon Crisis Nursery; president of the Royal University Hospital Auxiliary; first president of the Saskatoon Symphony Volunteers; and board member of the Meewasin Foundation. She received a National Volunteer Award in 1988, a YWCA Woman of Distinction Award in 1989, and the Saskatchewan Order of Merit in 2000. *Michael Jackson*

HORNED LARK. Larks (family Alaudidae) are small (15–25 cm) songbirds found in open habitats of prairies and **GRASSLANDS**, where they feed on small insects and seeds. They walk and run on short legs with long hind claws. Most of the approximately ninety species are found in Eurasia and Africa.

The horned lark (*Eremophila alpestris*), the only species found in the New World, breeds from Alaska to Mexico, with an isolated Columbian population. In Saskatchewan, the prairie population breeds throughout the grasslands; the arctic population breeds around **LAKE ATHABASCA**. It is one of the earliest migrants, arriving before the snow melts. The horned lark is one of the more brightly coloured larks, with its black chest band, black and yellow facial pattern, and small black feathered "horns"; but in the Saskatchewan populations, the bird is paler in colour. *Diane Secoy*

FURTHER READING: Alsop, Fred J., III. 2002. *The Birds of Canada*. New York: Dorling Kindersley.

HORNER, WILLIAM HAROLD (1911–). Harold Horner was born in 1911 on a farm near Creelman. He graduated from the **UNIVERSITY OF SASKATCHEWAN** with a BSc in Agriculture in 1933 and an MSc in 1936, specializing in genetics and plant breeding. In July 1937 he joined the staff of the Dominion Experimental Station at Scott, where he was in charge of soil erosion and snow conservation experiments. In 1939 he moved to the Dominion Forage Crops Laboratory in Saskatoon, where he worked on improving crested wheatgrass and sweet clover. Horner served in the Canadian army during **WORLD WAR II** and was discharged in 1946 with the rank of captain. That same year he was appointed assistant director of agricultural representatives for Saskatchewan, and in 1947 became field crops commissioner.

In 1951 he was named Deputy Minister of Agriculture for Saskatchewan, and served in that role for twenty-one years. In that capacity he initiated the Family Farm Improvement Branch and the Economics and Statistics Branch. Horner was also instrumental in the development of the Veterinary Services Act, the Agricultural Development and Adjustment Act, and the South Saskatchewan Irrigation Act; and he oversaw policies relating to community pastures and conservation-earned assistance. He took an active role in the Gardiner Dam Irrigation Project, and the development of the Western College of Veterinary Medicine and the Saskatchewan Veterinary Diagnostic Laboratory. He served as chairman of the Prairie Agricultural Machinery Institute's three-province council from 1974 to 1980.

In 1972 the Saskatchewan government appointed Horner as executive advisor of Grain Handling and Transportation Systems Rationalization. In 1977 the Canada West Foundation appointed him chairman of a task force to produce a booklet, *Western Canadian Agriculture to 1990*, which was published in 1980. He received an honorary life membership in the Saskatchewan Agricultural Graduates Association in 1970, and in 1973 the

Saskatchewan Institute of Agrologists presented him with its first Distinguished Agrologist Award. In 1984 the University of Saskatchewan conferred on him an honorary Doctor of Laws degree, and in 1988 he received the Saskatchewan Order of Merit. In 1992 Harold Horner was inducted into the Saskatchewan Agricultural Hall of Fame.

HORSE INDUSTRY. The horse has been resident in Saskatchewan for over 200 years. While the current horse population is only about 10% of its peak, the horse has been rapidly growing in popularity; as a result, Saskatchewan has a burgeoning horse industry. Horses first came to the region around 1770 when Spanish horses introduced by the Conquistadores spread north from Mexico and the southwestern United States and were acquired by the Assiniboine tribe. These horses provided the backbone of agricultural power for the first settlers to the area in the late 1800s and early 1900s, as the latter yearned for horses to replace the slower and often recalcitrant oxen that were then the norm.

In 1919, the government of Saskatchewan imported purebred Clydesdale stallions from Scotland at the request of the Saskatchewan Horse Breeders Association, in order to improve the quality of the farm horses. Later, Percherons and then Belgians were brought to the province to further enhance the quality of the resident draft horse population. Government-purchased stallions were kept by the **UNIVERSITY OF SASKATCHEWAN**. The Canadian horse population peaked in 1921 at about 3.6 million head, with almost one million head in the farms of Saskatchewan. With the advent of the tractor, draft horses became redundant and the population started to decline in the late 1920s. In 1944, the Western Horse Marketing Co-operative built a slaughter plant for horses in Swift Current to help deal with the problem of surplus horses. Horse meat from the slaughter plant was exported to Europe for the armed forces.

The demise of the draft horse was essentially complete by 1960. However, the recreational use of horses has increased considerably. From 1990 to 2001, the Saskatchewan horse population rose from 62,500 head to 95,000 head. Approximately 25% of the horses are used as breeding stock, with about one-third of these being used in the pregnant mares' urine (PMU) industry. Quarter horses make up 40% of breeding mares, followed by Belgians at 15%, and Arabians and Percherons at 10% each.

Competition horses account for 17% of the population, and 15% of the horses are used for recreational riding and driving. There is a wide range of competitive equestrian sports. There are two racetracks, with thoroughbreds racing at Marquis Downs in Saskatoon and Standardbreds at Queensbury Downs in Regina. Numerous rodeos are

COURTNEY MILNE PHOTO
Draft horses.

staged throughout the province. Jumping and dressage competitions are found around Regina, Saskatoon and Prince Albert. The Saskatchewan Team Penning Association boasts the fastest growth of any horse sport in the province. From small town gymkhanas happening throughout the summer to the Summer Masters and the Canadian Arabian and Half-Arabian Championships, there are levels and types of competition available for everyone.

D.C. Winkelman-Sim

HOSPITAL AUXILIARIES. Hospital auxiliaries were composed of volunteers—nurses, wives of doctors, civic employees, and others—who performed services of a social nature. They escorted patients to different areas of the hospital, brought goods in a cart to sell to convalescing patients, and raised money through bake sales, teas, and a gift shop. In the early days when money was scarce, members would buy yard goods and make sheets, pillow slips, operating room linens, and drapes. At the ROYAL UNIVERSITY HOSPITAL in Saskatoon, the auxiliary members also staffed the library and brought patients to the chapel for Sunday services. They supplied toys at Christmas for the Pediatric ward, and arranged for a memorial service every three months for people who had died in the hospital. With changing economic conditions auxiliaries have largely disappeared, except in the larger cities. A conspicuous exception in rural Saskatchewan is Gainsborough, where the "Ladies Hospital Auxiliary" was formed in 1948. Even with the conversion of the hospital to the Gainsborough and District Health Centre, the auxiliary is still very much alive, and recently raised money for a special mattress for palliative care patients.

John A. Boan

HOSPITAL SERVICES PLAN. One of the major recommendations of the SIGERIST COMMISSION in 1944 was that universal hospitalization be provided for Saskatchewan residents. As a preliminary step, Saskatchewan was the first province in Canada to provide funds for capital construction of hospitals. Between March 16, 1945 and March 1, 1949, the Saskatchewan government provided $653,714 in outright construction grants and $173,500 in loans. The National Health Grants Programme in 1948 added substantial federal funds to support hospital construction. Unfortunately, Saskatchewan's position ahead of other provinces was a detriment to receiving matching federal funds for new construction, since many of its hospitals had already been built and hence did not qualify for federal reimbursement. The new CCF government's plan to introduce the first hospitalization insurance program in North America required a master administrator; Henry Sigerist suggested to Premier T.C. DOUGLAS that Dr. FRED D. MOTT might be that man. Mott was a graduate of McGill Medical School and a senior officer with the United States Public Health Service. He became chairman of the Saskatchewan Health Services Planning Commission on September 1, 1946. A man of integrity and action, Mott moved with remarkable speed and efficiency to bring provincewide universal hospitalization into effect on January 1, 1947.

The Saskatchewan Hospital Services Plan (SHSP) broke new ground. New administrative machinery had to be invented. A new uniform hospital accounting system was finalized. Tax collection procedures were agreed upon with the municipalities. Scores of clerical, secretarial, and tabulating personnel were appointed and trained. A massive

publicity program was mounted to encourage early registration and tax payment. The only office space available was in an ancient, vacated store building. Clerks sat elbow-to-elbow in front of long rows of plywood-on-trestles, processing the registration and tax collection payments. The annual hospital premium was $5 for each adult and child, with a maximum of $30 per family; each municipality received a 5% commission for collecting the premium. Premier Douglas favoured a premium for two reasons: the cash-strapped province needed the money, and he felt such a payment would be a psychological "buy-in" for members of the public, who would thereby feel greater responsibility for their plan. Patients no longer had to pay for in-patient hospital services. The doctors in Saskatchewan enthusiastically and almost unanimously supported the plan, because they could now admit patients to hospital whenever necessary, without concern for cost.

The hospitalization costs for the first year—$7,560,763, a per capita cost of roughly $7.56—were almost exactly twice Sigerist's original forecast. The $5 per person hospital tax nevertheless covered 60% of the cost, leaving only 40% to be paid from general revenues. This efficiency was possible because municipalities collected the premiums, and administrative costs were only 5% of the total.

Per capita costs of hospitalization then rose rapidly in subsequent years, to $9.69 in 1947, $11.41 in 1948, and $13.59 in 1949. As MALCOLM TAYLOR says, "The tax collection system was successful to a degree unexpected for a regressive 'poll' tax." In Saskatchewan, the annual premium was dispensed with for seniors on January 1, 1972, and for the entire population on January 1, 1974.

Other provinces were slower to jump on the hospitalization bandwagon. British Columbia's hospitalization plan, the second in Canada, followed in 1949 but, lacking Saskatchewan's organization, suffered horrendous problems. By 1961, all provinces were participating, but only after each had sent administrators to Regina to learn how to do it right. And cost-sharing by the federal government for 45% of the hospital plan, starting on July 1, 1958, now provided the Saskatchewan government with the funds it needed to undertake its long-sought goal of MEDICARE.

C. Stuart Houston

FURTHER READING: Houston, C.S. 2002. "Provincewide Hospitalization." Chapter 8 in *Steps on the Road to Medicare*. Montreal: McGill-Queen's University Press.

HOSPITALS. The first hospital in what is now Saskatchewan was at Ile-à-la-Crosse; it was founded in 1873, thirteen years after the arrival of the first three Grey Nuns. North-West Mounted Police hospitals followed, at Fort Walsh in 1875, Qu'Appelle in 1881, Regina and Maple Creek in 1883, and Battleford and Prince Albert in 1884. During the

SASKATCHEWAN ARCHIVES BOARD R-A1679-2

Victoria Hospital, Prince Albert, Saskatchewan, ca. 1905–07.

NORTH-WEST RESISTANCE in 1885, temporary military hospitals were operated at Moose Jaw and at Saskatoon.

The first public hospital in the newly settled south opened at Saltcoats in 1897 but was short-lived. It was followed by the Victorian Order of Nurses (VON) cottage hospital in Regina in 1898, and the Victoria Hospital in Prince Albert in 1899. As the year 1900 dawned, southern Saskatchewan had two hospitals, each with seven beds, to serve about 90,000 people. The Regina Victoria Hospital opened in September 1901, and began a nursing training school at once; it has been the largest hospital in Saskatchewan ever since. The Moosomin hospital and the Queen Victoria Hospital at Yorkton opened in 1902, Maple Creek in 1904, and Indian Head in 1905—all three with nursing training schools. Nursing training continued until 1925 at Indian Head, 1935 at Maple Creek, and 1969 at Yorkton.

In 1906, hospitals opened in Moose Jaw, Lloydminster and Wakaw, followed in 1907 by the Grey Nuns hospital in Regina and the Lady Minto hospital in Melfort, in 1909 by Saskatoon City Hospital, in 1910 by Holy Family Hospital in Prince Albert, in 1911 by Notre Dame Hospital in North Battleford, and in 1912 by Swift Current, Weyburn, St Elizabeth's in Humboldt, and Providence Hospital in Moose Jaw. The number of rural hospitals increased slowly after the advent of the Municipal Hospital Act in 1916 and the Union Hospital Act in 1917, and more quickly in 1945 when Saskatchewan became the first province to provide grants for hospital construction, followed by federal grants for the same purpose in 1948. The number of beds per thousand population increased from 4.8 in 1946 to 6.5 in 1951, and peaked at 8.46 in 1977–78—more than in any other province. By 1984–85 the ratio had dropped to 7.00, falling below Quebec and Alberta.

On April 15, 1993, Health Minister LOUISE SIMARD announced the impending closure of fifty-two hospitals in rural Saskatchewan: Arborfield, Beechy, Bengough, Birch Hills, Borden, Cabri,

Climax, Coronach, Craik, Cupar, Cut Knife, Dinsmore, Dodsland, Eatonia, Edam, Elrose, Eston, Fillmore, Gainsborough, Goodsoil, Grenfell, Gull Lake, Imperial, Invermay, Ituna, Kincaid, Lafleche, Lampman, Langenburg, Leoville, Loon Lake, Lucky Lake, Macklin, Mankota, Milden, Montmartre, Neilburg, Nokomis, Norquay, Oxbow, Pangman, Ponteix, Radville, Rockglen, St. Walburg, Smeaton, Spalding, Theodore, Vanguard, Watson, White Bear, and Whitewood. Twenty-eight closed on September 30, and the other twenty-four early in 1994. At the same time, all large hospitals were downsized. The number of acute care beds (a more restricted definition than for the examples given in previous years) dropped to 2.54 beds per thousand by March 2002.

In Saskatoon in March 2003, 638 acute care beds were divided as follows: ROYAL UNIVERSITY HOSPITAL, 315; St. Paul's Hospital, 175; Saskatoon City Hospital, 148. In Regina, 520 acute care beds are divided between the Regina General, 322, and the Pasqua, 198. The Plains Hospital, built in the early 1970s, was decommissioned in 1998. Six regional hospitals include: Prince Albert, 98 beds; Moose Jaw, 85; Yorkton, 85; Swift Current, 79; North Battleford, 75; Lloydminster, 48. Nine district hospitals are Estevan, 53; Weyburn, 40; Melfort and Humboldt, 39 each; Nipawin and Meadow Lake, 32 each; Melville, 30; Tisdale, 24; Kindersley, 19.

Forty-two community hospitals are: Rosthern, 30 beds; Moosomin, 27; Leader, 22; Esterhazy and Kamsack, 20 each; Wakaw, 19; Broadview, Maidstone, Maple Creek and Shellbrook, 18 each; Kipling and Wolseley, 17 each; Rosetown and Shaunavon, 16 each; Indian Head and Kelvington, 15 each; Canora, 14; Biggar, Herbert and Loon Lake, 13 each; Assiniboia, Fort Qu'Appelle and Wadena, 12 each; Arcola and Redvers, 11 each; Big River, Hudson Bay, Outlook, Preeceville and Unity, 10 each; Gravelbourg, Lestock, Paradise Hill, Porcupine Plain and Spiritwood, 9 each; Wynyard, 8; Balcarres, Central Butte and Kerrobert, 6 each; Lanigan and Watrous, 4 each; Davidson, 2.

Four northern hospitals are: La Ronge, 29 beds; Ile-à-la-Crosse, 20; La Loche, 11; Stony Rapids, completed late 2003, with closure of the Uranium City hospital. Three hospitals operating as health centres are Foam Lake, Hafford, and Wawota.

C. Stuart Houston

FURTHER READING: Houston C.S. 2002. *Steps on the Road to Medicare: Why Saskatchewan Led the Way.* Montreal: McGill-Queen's University Press; Taylor, M. 1978. *Health Insurance and Canadian Public Policy: The Seven Decisions that Created the Canadian Health Insurance System.* Montreal: McGill-Queen's University Press.

HOUSE SPARROW. The house sparrow (sometimes called the English sparrow) is an Old World

sparrow brought to eastern North America in the 1850s. It has since spread throughout North America, coming into Saskatchewan in 1899, and is now a common resident in the south and middle of the province. It is not migratory, and in the spring takes up nest sites which are then not available for the native migrants, thus preventing them from breeding. As a non-native non-game species, it is not protected.

The Old World sparrows (family Passeridae) of Eurasia and Africa are a small family of songbirds comprising about thirty-six species. They are stout-bodied, short-legged seed eaters, with a special bill for cracking seed coats. They have very simple songs, which helps distinguish them from the native sparrows. The males, with their black bibs and masks as well as fluttering courtship behaviour and cheeping call, are very visible and audible in the early spring.

Diane Secoy

FURTHER READING: Alsop, Fred J., III. 2002. *Birds of Canada.* New York: Dorling Kindersley.

HOUSING INDUSTRY. The housing construction industry encompasses new and renovation residential construction. Housing is important from both a social and an economic perspective. From a social perspective, housing is the foundation for community development as it contributes directly to the health, social, and educational well being of people and communities. From an economic perspective, the construction and maintenance of housing creates businesses and jobs in a variety of sectors such as manufacturing, retail, construction, legal, and financial. Over the past 30 years, new residential construction activity has experienced wide fluctuations. New-home construction reached its highest level in Saskatchewan in the mid-1970s. From 1971 to 1988, new housing starts totaled 131,367 units; starts peaked in 1976, when more than 13,000 new homes were constructed in the province. A prime determinant of the demand for new housing is the underlying pattern of demographics and household growth. The housing boom in the 1970s is mainly attributed to the aging of the large number of "baby boomers" born during the 1940s and 1950s. In the period following 1988, lower fertility rates, reduced real income growth, volatile interest rates, and recessions reduced the demand for new housing units in the province.

New housing construction and land development are very conspicuous. However, the less noticeable renovation activity and expenditure generally exceeds new-home construction expenditures. Strength in the resale market, robust housing starts, and the effects of a strong job market typically drive renovation spending. Housing has a tremendous impact on the economy, and because of the multiplier effect of residential construction activity on the rest of the economy, there is a strong relationship between housing and employment. In addition to the direct employment generated in the actual design and building of the housing units, there is indirect labour involved in the supply of goods to manufacturers of residential building products, and in the trading and transportation of materials to the contractors and construction sites. Canada Mortgage and Housing Corporation (CMHC) estimates that for every $1 million spent directly on new housing construction, 5.4 person-years of direct employment are created and a further 18.2 person-years are indirectly created in other sectors of the economy.

The share of Gross Domestic Product (GDP) accounted for by residential construction expenditures is an indication of the direct contribution that residential construction makes to the economy. Since 1970, the share of total GDP accounted for by total residential construction expenditures in Saskatchewan has ranged between 1.7% and 6.6%, the highest shares being recorded in the years 1976 and 1977. In Saskatchewan, a large number of small- and medium-sized firms, and only a handful of large-sized firms, characterize the residential construction industry. In a 1993 study, the SASKATCHEWAN HOME BUILDERS' ASSOCIATION (SHBA) estimated that there were more than 700 residential contractors in Saskatchewan. Based on the survey respondents, only 10% of residential contractors had six or more full-time employees. The existence of a large number of small firms reflects the fragmented nature of the residential construction industry as well as the ease of entry into the industry, since small firms may enter the industry when demand is buoyant, and withdraw when demand is slack. *Alicia McGregor*

FURTHER READING: Denhez, M. 1994. *The Canadian Home: From Cave to Electronic Cocoon.* Toronto: Dundurn Press.

HOUSING POLICY. Housing is a basic human necessity, and housing quality is considered by many as an important indicator of individual and community well-being. Because housing is an expensive commodity to purchase (costing roughly four years of a typical household's earnings), it can be a challenge to ensure that all citizens have adequate and affordable housing. The vast majority of housing in Saskatchewan is produced and distributed through private markets, with government involvement limited to general regulations to maintain quality standards and protect consumers and communities. The private housing market adequately meets the needs of most Saskatchewan households and the people of this province are, on average, at least as well housed as other Canadians. Over 70% of Saskatchewan households own their own dwelling, and most of these households are consid-

The Remote Housing Program is a home ownership program in northern non-market communities.

ered adequately housed. However, at any given time some Saskatchewan households experience housing problems. There may be an insufficient supply of adequate housing in specific communities or in reasonable proximity to work opportunities. An adequate supply of housing may be available, but at a cost that consumes a disproportionate share of the household's income, making it difficult to meet other basic needs like food and clothing. Some households experience both an accessibility and affordability issue.

For individual households, poor housing may result in unacceptable living conditions for adults and children. Poor housing can affect adults' employability and credibility in the community, and housing instability can negatively affect children's school achievement. Poor housing also affects the overall quality of life in neighbourhoods and cities; extreme housing problems like overcrowding or homelessness can in fact be life-threatening. Because inadequate housing is a detriment both to individual households and the community as a whole, the public expects governments to develop policies and programs to reduce the incidence and impact of housing problems.

Governments have two basic ways to influence housing outcomes. The first is through measures that increase the supply of adequate housing in particular regions or communities. This may involve construction of publicly owned housing, or various forms of subsidy to private or non-profit builders to stimulate construction of new housing units or rehabilitation of existing homes. In some cases these supply programs are accompanied by on-going subsidization of operating costs to ensure that these housing units remain affordable to lower-income households. The second means to influence housing outcomes is by increasing households' income resources so that they can afford to rent or purchase better housing. Since most households get their income for housing and other needs from employment or self-employment, government supports and incentives to labour market attachment can be an important element of housing income support.

Governments may also make cash benefits available to lower-income families to help with the cost of housing.

While the emphasis on either supply or demand measures may change over time, governments generally rely on a balance of both approaches. Supply measures alone can rarely make a significant impact on widespread housing problems. Large-scale public housing programs are very costly, can cause secondary social problems, sometimes distort private housing markets, and can create inequities between people who do or do not receive subsidized housing. Demand measures alone, on the other hand, are not likely to be effective if adequate housing is in short supply; and carelessly designed income support programs may trigger housing cost increases in private markets, without necessarily improving housing outcomes. Views on the appropriate role for governments in housing policy are changing. As in other Canadian provinces and territories, the government in Saskatchewan has historically concentrated on expanding the province's stock of publicly owned or non-profit "social housing" units. While social housing has benefited some people in housing need, this approach is costly to the public and is not effective for households who already have physically adequate housing but have inadequate income to pay the market price for it. In recent years, housing social policy has begun to be seen as a broader set of measures that incorporates, in addition to social housing, a number of more market-sensitive policy instruments that help citizens address their housing needs.

In the Saskatchewan government, housing policy is the responsibility of the Department of Community Resources and Employment, which also has provincial jurisdiction for employment, income support, and other social programs. The department's strategy is to encourage self-reliance, independence, and strong connections to communities in housing and in other aspects of everyday life. Where an individual or a family requires government assistance to achieve self-sufficiency, the department addresses these issues through a partnership approach involving government, individual citizens, communities, and businesses. The department and the community agencies it supports own and manage the province's public and non-profit housing stock through the Saskatchewan Housing Corporation, a provincial CROWN CORPORATION. These relatively high-cost public assets are a housing resource for high-needs individuals, a transitional resource for families moving towards greater housing self-sufficiency, and a resource to help lower-income seniors maintain their independence.

In addition to social housing, programs are available to help lower-income households buy and maintain affordable housing. Support is available to homeowners, and in some cases landlords, to repair and maintain housing that is at risk of deterioration. Programs are also in place to help low-income families and people with disabilities achieve better housing outcomes in private rental markets. Programs and services that support employment of low-income people also help households acquire enough income for adequate housing and other necessities. As governments shift towards more active social policies, housing programs in Saskatchewan have become more closely integrated with other public policies that support economic and social inclusion. Public housing policy is one of the tools governments may use to improve the lives of individual adults and children, and to create stronger neighbourhoods and communities.

Rupen Pandya and Alicia McGregor

FURTHER READING: Mullins, P. and J. Western. 2001. *Examining the Links between Housing and Nine Sociocultural Factors.* Melbourne: Australian Housing and Urban Research Institute, Queensland Research Centre; Pomeroy, S. 2001. *Toward a Comprehensive Affordable Housing Strategy for Canada.* Ottawa: Caledon Institute of Social Policy.

HOUSTON, CLARENCE J. (1900–86). Born in Ottawa on March 18, 1900, and raised on a farm near Tyvan, Saskatchewan, C.J. Houston obtained his MD from Manitoba in 1926 and practiced in Yorkton until the age of 75. In 1943 the Health Insurance Committee of the College of Physicians and Surgeons endorsed a proposal submitted by C.J. Houston and R.A. Dick of Canora calling for a universal provincial health plan, governed by an independent commission. Houston was a member of the council of the **COLLEGE OF PHYSICIANS AND SURGEONS OF SASKATCHEWAN** as well as its president in 1947, the year that hospitalization was introduced. He was one of two doctors on the Saskatchewan Health Survey Committee from 1949 to 1951, and one of three physician nominees on the Saskatchewan Health Services Planning Commission (the Thompson Committee). While a strong supporter of hospitalization, Houston insisted on a commission for **MEDICARE** that would be independent of the provincial government—which led him to join three others on the Thompson Committee in a dissenting report. He published a number of scholarly articles and served as president of the Medical Council of Canada for one term. He died in Saskatoon on May 21, 1986.

Gregory P. Marchildon

HOUSTON, CLARENCE STUART (1927–). Stuart Houston (OC, SOM, DLitt, DCnL, MD, FRCPC), son of Drs. Clarence J. and Sigga Houston, was born in Williston, North Dakota on September 26, 1927, and grew up in Yorkton, Saskatchewan. After obtaining an MD from the University of Manitoba in 1951, he practiced medicine with his parents from

1951 to 1960. Stuart married Mary Belcher in 1951, and they have four children. Moving to Saskatoon in 1960, he began training in Diagnostic Radiology. After graduating with a FRCPC in 1964, he joined the **UNIVERSITY OF SASKATCHEWAN** and became Head of Radiology from 1982 to 1987, before retiring in 1996. His published works in medicine and the history of medicine include five books, thirteen book chapters and sixty-six scientific articles, as well as numerous book reviews, abstracts and editorials.

In addition to medicine, Houston has been involved in ornithology and natural history since his early teens. Beginning as a bander of ducks for Ducks Unlimited, he is now recognized as one of the leading authorities on birds in Canada. He has published six books, thirty-three book chapters, 251 original papers, 123 book reviews, and numerous abstracts and editorials in this field. He and his wife Mary have banded over 126,000 individuals of 206 species, with 3,191 recoveries—the largest list for a private bander in North America. He has served in several capacities in the American Ornithologists' Union, of which he was named a Fellow in 1989.

Stuart Houston is a recognized authority on the Franklin expeditions, on the factor-naturalists of the Hudson's Bay Company, and on the medical history of Saskatchewan. The first of three books on the **FRANKLIN** expedition, *To the Arctic by Canoe, 1819–1821, The Journals and Paintings of Robert Hood*, was published in 1974; his latest books are *Steps on the Road to Medicare* (2002) and *Eighteenth-Century Naturalists of Hudson Bay* (2003) (with M. Houston and T. Ball). Houston's activities have won him a variety of awards, including honorary doctorates for literature, the Roland Michener Conservation Award from the Canadian Wildlife Federation, the Saskatchewan Order of Merit, and the Order of Canada.

J. Frank Roy

UNIVERSITY OF SASKATCHEWAN ARCHIVES A-7248

Stuart Houston, 1983.

REGINA LEADER-POST

Gordie Howe.

HOWE, GORDIE (1928–). Recognized as "Mr. Hockey," Gordie Howe had a five-decade career as an NHL player. Born on March 31, 1928, in Floral, Saskatchewan, Howe made his professional debut in the 1946–47 season as a member of the Detroit Red Wings. He played right wing on the "Production Line" with Ted Lindsay and Melville native Sid Abel. The less time Howe spent in the penalty box the more his point production improved. He led the league in scoring six times over his career, and helped the Red Wings to four Stanley Cup championships. Gordie Howe retired at the end of the 1970-71 season as arthritis in the wrist forced him to the sidelines after twenty-five years with Detroit. Yet his absence from hockey was short-lived: in 1973 he signed as a free agent with the Houston Aeros of the World Hockey Association (WHA) and joined his sons, Mark and Marty, on the team's roster. The Howe trio played three seasons in Houston before moving to the New England Whalers in 1977. Two years later, the WHA merged with the NHL, and Gordie Howe played in one final, complete season as a Hartford Whaler. Although Wayne Gretzky would eventually break many of Howe's records, Mr. Hockey's NHL career remains second to none. In 1,767 NHL regular season games, Howe scored 801 goals and added 1,049 assists for 1,850 points. His playoff totals stand at 157 games played, 68 goals, and 92 assists for 160 points. Known for his toughness, Howe amassed 1,685 regular season penalty minutes. He is a six-time Hart Trophy winner as league MVP, and the 1967 Lester Patrick Trophy recipient for service to hockey in the United States.

Named to the First All-Star Team twelve times, Gordie Howe was inducted to the **SASKATCHEWAN SPORTS HALL OF FAME** in 1971 and the Hockey Hall of Fame one year later. *Daria Coneghan and Holden Stoffel*

FURTHER READING: Podnieks, A. et al. 2002. *Kings of the Ice: A History of World Hockey.* Richmond Hill, ON: NDE Publishing.

HUDEC, MARGARET (1921–2004). Born on October 21, 1921, Margaret Hudec was a prominent volunteer for the **GIRL GUIDES** of Saskatchewan and Canada. She started out as a Brownie, then became a young leader, and was the guide lieutenant and a member of the Saskatchewan Council of Girl Guides beginning in 1948. Between 1950 and 1979, she held six different positions on the Council including provincial commissioner. In addition, Hudec spent three years as an independent member of the national council of the Girl Guides of Canada. In 1967, she helped establish Camp Can-ta-ka-ye, a provincial Guide camp on Lake Diefenbaker. For her outstanding service to the Girl Guides, Hudec received the Canadian Centennial Medal and the Order of Canada in 1981. She died on November 12, 2004.

HUDSON BAY, town, pop 1,783, located 116 km E of Tisdale, nestled in the Red Deer River valley between the Pasquia and Porcupine Hills. The community is situated at the junction of Hwys 3 and 9, 50 km west of the Saskatchewan-Manitoba border. The immediate area encompassing the town consists of farmlands surrounded by vast tracts of forest wilderness. Fur trading activity in the area dated to the latter half of the 1700s. The Canadian Northern Railway entered the district from Manitoba in the first years of the 20th century. In 1907, the Village of Etoimami (the community's original name, of **CREE** origin) was incorporated; a hotel built that year is still in business. In 1909, the name of the community was changed to Hudson Bay Junction for its position as the starting point for the on-again off-again Hudson Bay Railway to Churchill, Manitoba, which was not completed until 1929. For many years, logging and railway work were the primary occupations in the district, but in the 1920s agriculture began to develop when areas of the surrounding forest reserves were opened for settlement by soldiers who had served in **WORLD WAR I.** The 1930s saw increasing settlement of the district as people moved north fleeing the drought-ravaged southern plains. It was not until the late 1930s and early 1940s that the first roads began to be built into the region. In 1946 the community attained town status, and in 1947 the word "Junction" was dropped from its name. In 1948 the first plywood plant in Canada was built at Hudson Bay, followed in 1961 by a waferboard plant. The latter opera-

tions, sold to **MACMILLAN BLOEDEL** in 1965, were purchased by **WEYERHAEUSER** Ltd in 1999. Today, Weyerhaeuser operates both the plywood and the OSB plants (OSB, oriented strand board, is the successor to wafer or particle board). The development of these facilities spawned a building boom in Hudson Bay, and the population grew from 793 in 1946 to 1,957 in 1966. The railroad was still employing about 100 people in the mid-1960s; however, as that workforce was reduced over the following years, agriculture and especially forestry became the community's economic mainstays. A wide range of crops are grown in the valley; locally grown alfalfa enables Hudson Bay Dehydrators to process 10,000 tonnes of alfalfa pellets annually for local and export markets. Another factor in Hudson Bay's economy is tourism, particularly as it relates to big game hunting. There are approximately 130 businesses in Hudson Bay, providing a wide array of goods and services. *David McLennan*

HUMBOLDT. Humboldt, city, pop 5,562, was named after Baron Alexander von Humboldt, a famous 19th-century German naturalist. The city is located in central Saskatchewan, approximately 113 km E of Saskatoon and 231 km N of Regina. The Humboldt area was established as far back as 1878, when it was landmarked by the Dominion Telegraph Station, along the **CARLTON TRAIL** route from Fort Edmonton to Fort Garry, which became known as the Humboldt Telegraph Station and operated until 1923. In 1903, a group of Benedictine Fathers from Minnesota received rights for colonizing approximately fifty townships around Humboldt and became an integral part of the initial population in the area. The construction of the Canadian Northern Railway line in 1904 between Regina and Rosthern encouraged further settlement; on April 7, 1907, with a population of 425, Humboldt was officially incorporated as a town. Humboldt was declared Saskatchewan's thirteenth city on November 7, 2000. The city continues to grow, both in population and industry: manufacturing, agriculture and agriculture-related services are key economic activities in the Humboldt area. As a mixed farming region, the Humboldt district is part of the largest hog-producing regions in Saskatchewan. The Humboldt community is home to St. Peter's Cathedral and Abbey, whose design and artwork highlight the region's German heritage. Other attractions include the Humboldt and District Museum and Gallery, which features exhibits of the telegraph station, the railway station, and prairie pioneer homes. *Lauren Black*

HUMMINGBIRDS. Hummingbirds (family Trochilidae), limited to the Western Hemisphere, are small to tiny birds with short tails, long bills, and long primaries used for hovering flight. Many

species have iridescent plumage. Most are forest species, but all congregate at flowering plants and feeders. All species feed primarily on nectar, but also on tiny insects gleaned from vegetation or caught in flight. Nests are small cups made of spider webs, lined with moss and lichen and placed on a horizontal tree branch or in a fork of tree branches.

In North America, there are eighteen species of hummingbirds in twelve genera. The ruby-throated hummingbird (*Archilochus colubris*) is the only breeding hummingbird in Saskatchewan, found nesting in the southern boreal forest, aspen parkland, and the **CYPRESS HILLS**. The adult male has a black face and a deep red to orange throat; both sexes have iridescent green crowns and backs, and pale underparts. In late summer, this hummingbird is seen in the flower gardens and at feeders in southern Saskatchewan. In the spring, they follow woodpeckers to access tree sap.

Four other hummingbird species normally found in the western mountains of North America have been recorded in Saskatchewan. The orange and green rufous hummingbird (*Selasphorus rufus*) has been recorded a number of times in southern Saskatchewan. Rarer are the black-chinned hummingbird (*Archilochus alexandri*) (Regina, Weyburn), Anna's hummingbird (*Calypte anna*) (Raymore), and the tiny Calliope hummingbird (*Stellula calliope*) (Shaunavon). *Robert Warnock*

FURTHER READING: Alsop, Fred J., III. 2002. *Birds of Canada*. New York: Dorling Kindersley.

HUNGARIAN SETTLEMENTS. Over a quarter of a century, beginning in 1885, Hungarian immigrants developed at least ten named settlements in three regions of Saskatchewan. In the eastern region, Esterhaz colony (*Esterhaz Magyar Kolonia*) was planned by Count **PAUL OSCAR ESTERHAZY**, who adopted his name from a wealthy land-owning family in Hungary and, acting as a Canadian Pacific immigration agent, obtained 125,000 acres in 1885. He succeeded in persuading Hungarian, Czech and Slovak miners from Pennsylvania to move to the Canadian prairies, where abundant farmland was available at minimal cost. After some were settled in Huns' Valley (originally Hungarian Valley) west of Minnedosa, Manitoba in 1885, larger numbers arrived in Esterhaz colony in 1886. As Hungarian settlement quickly spread southward toward the **QU'APPELLE RIVER**, by 1888 the extended colony became known as Kaposvar, after the Hungarian city where the Esterhazy family estates were located. By 1902 Esterhazy and Kaposvar had a population of over 900 settled on 200 homesteads, and 14,000 acres were under cultivation.

Hungarian settlement was further extended westward to Stockholm, a Swedish colony founded

SASKATCHEWAN ARCHIVES BOARD R-A6204
Gathering in honour of the visit of Count Esterhazy at Esterhazy, 1903.

in 1886, when the priest at Esterhazy promoted the settlement of some fifty Hungarian families in what they called Sokhalom ("many hills"), an obvious play on words; it also spread northward toward Yarbo and Zeneta, and eastward toward Gerald. In 1894 the Hungarian colony of Otthon ("home"), located between Melville and Yorkton, was founded by Rev. Janos (John) Kovacs, a minister of the Hungarian Reformed Church in Pennsylvania. This small colony attracted immigrants both directly from Hungary and via the United States. The Bekevar colony around Kipling began to develop in 1902 after Janos Szabo, having read about the success of Rev. Kovacs at Otthon, decided to establish another Reformed colony. The focal point of the colony was the large double-steepled Reformed (later Presbyterian) church, although soon a smaller rival Hungarian Baptist congregation was very active, conducting baptisms in a slough. The Reformed church had its *Bekevari dalarda* (choir), Christmas concert called *Viragfakardas* ("blossoming time"), and an annual picnic. The initial settlers came from Botragy, northeast Hungary, which had a strong Reformed congregation. Bekevar colony grew rapidly to include four school districts: Kossuth, Magyar, Rakoczi, and Little Mountain.

Many Hungarian immigrants settled in the north-central region of Saskatchewan. The town of Wakaw became virtually surrounded by Hungarian settlements around the turn of the century. To the north, Buda school district was founded by Hungarian settlers, but today they are outnumbered by Ukrainians. Hungarian settlers were also found in the Ens district to the west (together with Ukrainians, Germans, and French) and in the Lone Pine district to the east (with Ukrainians). To the west of Wakaw, the Dunafoldvar district was settled by immigrants from Dunafoldvar, Hungary; today their descendants share the district with Ukrainian farmers. South of Wakaw Lake, the *Matyasfold* ("land of Matthias") settlement developed under the original guidance of Zoltan Rajcs. The Crooked Lake

and Bukovina districts (including the hamlet of Lepine) were mixed Hungarian and Ukrainian. Further east, Hungarians mixed with French in the Belmont and Bonne Madone districts (including Reynaud). Hungarian settlement eventually extended continuously far to the east and northeast, around Basin Lake, Little Moose Lake (where French priests from St-Brieux served a largely Hungarian congregation at St-Philippe Mission), and Meskanaw. To the southwest, between Wakaw and Prud'homme, St. Laszlo colony developed in 1900–05, receiving overflow from Matyasfold and Dunafoldvar; in fact, many original settlers such as the extended Miskolczi family arrived from Dunafoldvar, Hungary. Eventually this Hungarian settlement spread southeastward around Muskiki Lake, where Hungarians mixed with Ukrainian and German neighbours, and southward toward predominantly French Prud'homme. St. Laszlo church, constructed in 1911, long remained a focal point of Hungarian communal activity, together with the school and community hall. However, throughout the north-central region, the very dispersion of Hungarian settlement into districts also settled by Ukrainians, Germans, and French would inevitably hasten assimilation through intermarriage, especially as these Germans and French shared their Catholic religion with Hungarians.

Finally, two other Hungarian settlements developed in the south-central region. *Szekelyfold* ("land of the Szekelys," Carpathian Magyars), in the hills southwest of Lestock, commenced in 1906 and included the Magyar, Zala, and Arbury districts; homesteads were constructed in traditional Szekely style; Szekely immigrants from six villages in Bukovina were joined by ethnic Hungarians and Romanians from southern Bukovina. The Pinkefalva colony near Plunkett was founded in 1908 by Imre Pinke, an immigrant from western Hungary via the United States who attracted settlers by writing about homesteading in Hungarian-American newspapers. The Hungarian population in Saskatchewan grew to

8,946 in 1921, 13,363 in 1931, and 14,576 in 1941; it then declined to 12,470 in 1951. The most recent census data (2001) reveal a total 24,340 people claiming Hungarian ethnic origin, of which 24% (5,875) claimed Hungarian-only origin, compared to 76% (18,465) who also claimed other ethnic origins. (*See also* ETHNIC BLOC SETTLEMENTS, CZECH AND SLOVAK SETTLEMENTS, ROMANIAN SETTLEMENTS)

Alan Anderson

FURTHER READING: Dreisziger, N.F. 1982. *Struggle and Hope: The Hungarian-Canadian Experience.* Toronto: McClelland and Stewart; Kovacs, M.L. 1974. *Esterhazy and Early Hungarian Immigrants to Canada.* Regina: Canadian Plains Research Center.

HUNT, NADINE (1926–93). Nadine Hunt, born in 1926, grew up in Regina. A lifelong progressive, one of her early memories, in June 1935, was of being sent by her mother, Leita Nelson, to deliver a package of sandwiches through the fenced-in Regina Exhibition Grounds for the young unemployed men of the ON-TO-OTTAWA TREK. In 1964, she was left with three small children to raise after the death of her husband, and she went to work as a secretary at the UNIVERSITY OF SASKATCHEWAN, Regina Campus—now the UNIVERSITY OF REGINA. Almost immediately, Hunt began to take an interest in union activities, representing the clerical and support staff as a shop steward and then as a vice-president of the University of Saskatchewan Employees Union Branch 54, a directly chartered local of the Canadian Labour Congress, which later became Local 1975 of the Canadian Union of Public Employees. After serving her local for six years, Hunt became secretary of the Regina and District Labour Council, which she later represented on the SASKATCHEWAN FEDERATION OF LABOUR (SFL) executive.

In the 1970s, she was a vice-president and later secretary-treasurer of the SFL. In 1978 she made history by being elected president of the SFL, the first woman in Canada to lead a provincial federation of

DON HEALY/REGINA LEADER-POST
Nadine Hunt, October 1988.

labour; she was re-elected to that position for the next ten years. During her time as head of the SFL, she worked for the unity of the two dozen affiliated unions, and was a strong spokesperson for better occupational health and safety legislation and worker-friendly labour laws. Hunt campaigned tirelessly for better training and education for workers, an effort that resulted in the establishment of the Labour Studies Program at the College of Commerce at the University of Saskatchewan.

In 1988 Nadine Hunt retired from the SFL, but remained active: she was involved with Amnesty International, the Ranch Ehrlo Society for troubled youth, the United Way, and the Saskatchewan Human Rights Commission. In recognition of her commitment to worker education, the SFL established three scholarships in her name, to be awarded annually to working people furthering their learning. Nadine Hunt died in Regina on August 6, 1993. *Garnet Dishaw*

HUNT, TALMAGE EVELYN (1921–2004).

Tal Hunt was born at Sunderland, Ontario on April 11, 1921. He obtained his MD degree from Toronto in 1944, then qualified as a specialist in Internal Medicine and subsequently in Rheumatology. In 1955 he became the first head of Rehabilitation Medicine at the UNIVERSITY OF SASKATCHEWAN. Full of inspiring ideas, and a gentle innovator, he led the way in his field. He was the president of the Canadian Association of Physical Medicine and Rehabilitation and an examiner for the Royal College of Physicians and Surgeons of Canada. Hunt showed great anticipation of future medical care models when he established a course in Physical Therapy at the University of Saskatchewan; at first within the department of Rehabilitation Medicine, it later became the School of Physical Therapy. After twenty-two years as department head, Hunt turned to Geriatric Medicine, where he showed the same originality and soundness of judgement. He died in White Rock, BC, on September 9, 2004. *J. Leszczynski*

HUNTER, WILLIAM DICKENSON (1920–2002).

William Dickenson Hunter, better known as "Wild" Bill, was a hockey coach, team owner, and promoter. He was born in Saskatoon on May 5, 1920, and educated at Notre Dame College in Wilcox. In 1966, Hunter was among a group of team owners who established what is now the Western Hockey League. Although he later failed in his bid to buy the NHL's Pittsburgh Penguins and was denied an expansion franchise, Hunter and two American promoters formed the World Hockey Association (WHA) in 1971. Twelve teams participated in the WHA's inaugural 1972-73 season, including Hunter's franchise, the Alberta Oilers (later the Edmonton Oilers). The league folded in 1979, but the Edmonton Oilers were one of four WHA clubs

COURTESY OF THE SASKATOON STARPHOENIX
Bill Hunter, 1983.

accepted into the NHL. Ironically, Hunter had sold the Oilers in 1976. In 1983, Hunter made his final bid for an NHL team by attempting to move the St. Louis Blues to Saskatoon. He found backers to build an 18,000-seat arena and sold more tickets than seats, but the NHL refused to transfer the Blues to a small market like Saskatoon. Despite this failure, Hunter turned to promoting curling and spent his finals years in Edmonton. He was a member of the Order of Canada, the Canadian Sports Hall of Fame, and the SASKATCHEWAN SPORTS HALL OF FAME. Bill Hunter died on December 16, 2002.

Daria Coneghan and Holden Stoffel

FURTHER READING: Hunter, B. and B. Weber. 2000. *Wild Bill: Bill Hunter's Legendary 65 Years in Canadian Sport.* Red Deer, Alberta: Johnson Gorman Publishers.

HURLEY, ROBERT NEWTON (1894–1980).

Robert Hurley was widely recognized in Canada for his watercolour paintings of the prairie landscape. Hurley's intimate relationship with Saskatchewan's landscape lasted more than forty years and spawned thousands of paintings. He has been called Saskatchewan's "sky painter" for his effective use of watercolour to illuminate the prairie sky, a dominant motif throughout his collection. Born on March 26, 1894, in London, England, Hurley was intrigued by art–particularly watercolours–as a teenager and often visited London's famous galleries. He worked as an apprentice printer-compositor until he was summoned for duty in WORLD WAR I. In 1923, after returning from the war, he immigrated to Canada to work on the CANADIAN PACIFIC RAILWAY near Milden, Saskatchewan. Later that year, Hurley moved north to Saskatoon and found seasonal employment in local gardens and lumber camps. Inspired by the unadorned prairie landscape, he began his career as a professional artist. During

the Depression, he could not afford sketching paper or paint, and instead used newspaper print, toothbrushes, and berry extract to render his first sketches of the river valley near Saskatoon. Uncomfortable with the irregularity of the valley terrain, Hurley turned to the open plain and embraced its geometric simplicity. By 1940, his numerous landscape paintings had garnered national attention: he had quickly distinguished himself in Saskatchewan and Canada for his portrayals of prairie light and space, and for his flat, linear treatment of the landscape. He used broad colour washes to illustrate a vast prairie sky and explicit linearity to depict grain elevators, telephone poles, roads, railways, and the horizon–classic prairie elements that appear in most of his works. Hurley was a self-taught painter fulfilling a beloved pastime. His only formal training was from 1933 to 1935 at the Saskatoon Technical College, where he studied under prominent Austrian-born painter ERNEST LINDNER. Hurley's watercolours have been featured in exhibitions and collections across Canada, including the 1971 *Watercolour Painters from Saskatchewan* exhibit at the National Gallery of Canada. He retired in 1958 and moved to Victoria in 1963. A prolific artist throughout his lifetime, he continued to paint until his death on March 24, 1980. *Iain Stewart*

FURTHER READING: Moppett, G. 1986. *Robert Newton Hurley: A Notebook.* Saskatoon: Mendel Art Gallery; Rees, R. 1984. *Land of Earth and Sky: Landscape Painting of Western Canada.* Saskatoon: Western Producer Prairie Books.

REPRODUCED WITH PERMISSION OF DOUGLAS & MCINTYRE LTD./MENDEL ART GALLERY 1985.16.1

Robert Newton Hurley, "Untitled," ca. 1933, watercolour on paper, 28.3 x 20.8 cm, collection of the Mendel Art Gallery, gift of Mr. and Mrs. Les Pragnell in memory of Bart Pragnell, 1985.

HUSKY ENERGY. Husky Energy, founded in 1938 by Glenn Nielson, has been involved in the Saskatchewan oil industry since the beginning of commercial production in the Lloydminster area in the 1940s. A refinery in Wyoming was disassembled and moved in 1946–47 to Lloydminster; since then, Husky has focused on the production and processing of heavy oil into products such as lubricants, bunker fuel, and asphalt. Heavy oil production in Saskatchewan has been challenged to find suitable markets for production. Heavy oil trades at a significant price discount to light oil, and only a limited number of refineries have the capability of processing heavy oil. In addition, heavy oil must be mixed with a diluent to ship through pipelines, making it more costly to transport. One solution to this problem, offered by Husky, was to upgrade heavy oil into a synthetic light crude through carbon removal, coking and/or hydrogen addition from natural gas. After many years of discussion, Husky Energy entered into a joint venture with the Alberta, Saskatchewan and Canadian governments to build a **HEAVY OIL UPGRADER**. The Bi-Provincial Upgrader in Lloydminster began operations in 1992, becoming the second heavy oil upgrader in western Canada after the NewGrade Upgrader in Regina, operated by Federated Co-operatives. Similar facilities exist in the oilsands near Fort McMurray (Alberta) to create synthetic light oil from mined bitumen (a super-heavy oil). The Bi-Provincial Upgrader, built with the provision that it would source heavy oil equally from both Saskatchewan and Alberta, had an initial design capacity of nearly 55,000 barrels/day but has expanded its capability through investments in process improvements to be currently able to process 77,000 barrels/day of heavy oil and refinery tops.

In January 2000, Husky Oil brought on-line a large co-generation project, the Meridian Co-generation plant, with a capacity of 210 megawatts to supply electricity to Saskatchewan through a long-term contract with **SASKPOWER**. The co-generation plant operates in conjunction with the Bi-Provincial Upgrader. As with the NewGrade Upgrader in Regina, the Bi-Provincial Upgrader at Lloydminster faced a number of periods in the early 1990s when the price differential between heavy oil and synthetic light crude was too low to cover the costs of processing heavy oil into light synthetic crude. After encountering a series of operating losses, in 1994 the Alberta and Canadian governments wrote off their investments in the Upgrader and transferred equity to Husky and the Saskatchewan government, in return for modest buy-out payments, an end to liability for future losses, and provision for a specific claim on future profits. In 1998, with improved operating margins, the Saskatchewan government sold its interest in the Upgrader to Husky Oil and recovered its investments. Husky has announced an intention to expand the Upgrader in the next ten years to increase its processing capacity to 150,000 barrels/day.

David Hanly

HUTTERITE COLONIES. Both the **MENNONITES** and the **HUTTERITES** trace their origins to the Swiss Anabaptist movements of the 16th century; and both groups immigrated, directly or indirectly, to the Canadian prairies from German colonies in South Russia, as had most of the German Catholics. But in the intervening period of over two centuries, their histories were quite distinct. While the Mennonite group was forming in the Netherlands, another communal Anabaptist group was developing in the South Tyrol (then in Austria, now in Italy), as well as later in southern Germany and Moravia (now within the Czech Republic). In 1528 the first real *bruderhof* (communal village or colony) was established in Moravia; five years later they were joined by a South Tyrolean preacher, Jacob Hutter, from whom the sect acquired its name. Despite repeated persecution (Hutter was burned at the stake in 1536), by the end of the century there were as many as 70,000 Hutterites and over ninety *bruderhofe*. Reduced in numbers by the Austro-Turkish and Thirty Years Wars, by 1622 they had all been driven from Moravia; some 20,000 had emigrated to Slovakia, Hungary, and Transylvania (now in Romania), where they had established over thirty new colonies. However, persecution continued, particularly by Jesuits seeking to convert them in Slovakia, and they were further decimated. A small number were briefly re-established at Kreutz, Transylvania, in 1763–70; caught in the midst of the Russo-Turkish Wars, 123 of them trekked to Russia (present-day Ukraine) to found the Vishenka and Radichev colonies.

Finally, their rather unsettled existence in Europe was terminated altogether in 1874 when all of them, numbering nearly 800, moved to South Dakota along with Mennonites and other Russian-German Protestant groups escaping the repeal of their military exemption by the Russian government. The *Schmiedeleut*, *Dariusleut*, and *Lehrerleut* sects separately founded three initial colonies between 1874 and 1877. But about half of the Hutterites decided to homestead individually rather than communally, thus becoming *Prairieleut* and eventually merging with the Mennonites who settled in the same area. **WORLD WAR I** hastened the exodus of *Dariusleut* and *Lehrerleut* from the United States to Alberta, and of *Schmiedeleut* to Manitoba.

Each Hutterite colony averages approximately 100 men, women and children. Hutterites have tended to have a high, but recently declining, birth rate and a large family size; when a colony's population grows well beyond the average, new "daughter" colonies are founded, usually about every fifteen years. Thus the Hutterite population as a whole and the number of colonies have grown quite rapidly. Prior to 1949 there were no Hutterite colonies in Saskatchewan; since then more than fifty colonies have been established, about equally divided between *Dariusleut* and *Lehrerleut*.

Hutterite colonies have tended to be concentrated in western regions of Saskatchewan, although they are becoming increasingly widespread. In the southwestern region, there are five colonies in the immediate vicinity of Maple Creek: Cypress (1952), Spring Creek (1956–58), New Wolf Creek or Downey Lake (1958), Box Elder (1960), and more recently Dinsmore (1976). Further east, another seventeen colonies are found in the **CYPRESS HILLS** and around Swift Current: Bench (1949–52) west of Shaunavon was the very first colony in Saskatchewan and the initial *Lehrerleut* colony. During the 1950s and 1960s it was soon followed by Tompkins (1952–54), West Bench (1960), Simmie (1961), Waldeck (1962–63), Main Centre (1963), Sand Lake (1964), and Hodgeville (1969–71); then during the 1970s by Ponteix (1970–71), Swift Current (1976) and Vanguard (1979–80); during the 1980s by Carmichael (1983), Bone Creek (1988), Webb (1988), and Butte (1989); and most recently New Spring Creek (1993). Six colonies have been established in the Regina and Moose Jaw area: first Arm River (1964–68); then Baildon (1967–68), Huron (1968–69), Lajord (1977), Belle Plaine (1981), and Rose Valley (1985).

In the Sand Hills area north of Maple Creek, four colonies have been founded: Estuary (1958), Haven (1966–67), Abbey (1970–71), and Wheatland (1987). Sixteen colonies are widely scattered through the west country further north: Hillsvale (1960–61), Glidden (1962–63), Smiley (1966–68), Fort Pitt (1968–69), Sanctuary (1969–

EVERETT BAKER PHOTO/COURTESY OF THE SASKATCHEWAN HISTORY AND FOLKLORE SOCIETY

Hutterite children, North Fork, July 1954.

70), Lakeview (1970), Rosetown (1970), Willow Park (1977), Beechy (1978), Golden View (1978), Spring Water (1979), Big Rose (1980), Eagle Creek (1981), Eatonia (1985), Sunny Dale (1988), and Springfield (1989). Several other colonies have been developed to the north and south of Saskatoon: Leask (1953–57) and Riverview (1956) were the earliest *Dariusleut* colonies in the province, followed by Hillcrest (1969) and Clear Springs (1969–71). Finally, to the northeast two colonies have been established: Quill Lake (1975) and Star City (1978).

All Hutterites continue to live in their own colonies, which are small in population yet often control extensive farmland. Although they sell their produce (grain, livestock, poultry, vegetable crops) on the public market, they live within sequestered colonies where strict conformity is ensured in unique dress, religious education (together with limited "public education" from an outside teacher at the colony school), language (they converse in an archaic German dialect), authority (each colony is ultimately headed by a male boss), occupational specificity (male and female jobs are assigned even before adulthood), holding property in common, and an orderly lifestyle (for example, preparing meals and dining together; buildings arranged in rectangular order). Because Hutterites own their farmland and machinery in common, their farming is usually a profitable venture. However, the rapid expansion of Hutterites' territorial acquisitions has resulted in contested legislation in the prairie provinces, restricting concentration and expansion of the colonies. Moreover, Hutterites have traditionally tended to be non-political, to buy farm machinery on a wholesale rather than localized basis, and to claim tax exemptions as a religious organization, which has further caused problems in their relations with neighbouring local communities. Today, however, Hutterites are respected as prosperous farmers and as an interesting part of Saskatchewan's rural population. (*See also* **ETHNIC BLOC SETTLEMENTS, GERMAN SETTLEMENTS**) *Alan Anderson*

FURTHER READING: Anderson, A.B. 1999. *German Settlements in Saskatchewan*. Saskatoon: Saskatchewan German Council.; Hostetler, J.A. 1974. *Hutterite Society*. Baltimore: Johns Hopkins University Press.

HUTTERITES. The Hutterian Brethren (commonly called Hutterites) are named after Jakob Hutter, an Anabaptist leader in Moravia (part of what is now the Czech Republic) during the Protestant Reformation of the 16th century. Hutterites are pietist Christians believing in adult baptism and pacifism, as do other Anabaptists such as the **MENNONITES**, the Amish, and the Brethren in Christ; yet they also follow biblical texts enjoining strict community of goods. They follow Peter Rideman's

Confession of Faith (c. 1540–44) to refuse political office, bear weapons, take oaths, pay taxes for military purposes, and insist on austerity in life and conduct. Such beliefs were contrary to government demands and brought the Hutterites to leave Moravia for Hungary, Romania, Ukraine, and finally, in the 19th century, the United States and Canada. There are now twice as many Hutterites in Canada as in the United States, partly because Canada was more tolerant and receptive to Hutterite ideas of co-operation and pacifism, and more eager to obtain agricultural settlers for Canada's prairies.

Hutterites have maintained their German dialect as well as vestiges of Reformation dress (black clothes for men, and polka-dotted kerchiefs and ankle-length dresses for women); and they practise egalitarianism, division of labour based on gender, endogamy, patriarchy, and self-government through the vote of all baptized men. They function therefore as an ethnic group as well as a sectarian branch of what is called "Radical Christianity." Prompted to leave Alberta by laws restricting new colonies and imposing obstacles to land purchases, the first colonists arrived in Saskatchewan in 1949 and the first stable colony was established in 1952. Similar legal problems in South Dakota brought in further colonies, although many of these had their origins in Alberta, too. The colonies were at first founded about 50 km apart in southwestern Saskatchewan—close enough to maintain communications, yet far enough to avoid complaints from non-Hutterites, since the Hutterites' refusal to assume any political responsibility or positions could become a problem for local government. (Rarely do Hutterites even participate in elections.)

When colonies began arriving in Saskatchewan, the provincial government established in Regina a committee that Hutterites were to consult to help them find land in a district where local reaction would be favourable and, later, where Hutterite colonies were not already numerous. With better transportation, recent colonies are on average situated between 100 and 300 km apart. Hutterites have adapted 16th-century communal principles to become highly rational entrepreneurs using successful co-operative agricultural management and economies of scale to survive the semi-arid challenges of prairie farming. Such success has sometimes created resentment among non-Hutterite farmers, as Hutterites can outbid small holders for land and survive difficult years without claiming government assistance or joining with non-Hutterites in other co-operative ventures. They see themselves as a model Christian community, keep aloof from the rest of the world, and do not proselytize except by personal example.

Three Hutterite branches now exist in North America—*Dariusleut*, *Lehrerleut*, and *Schmiedenleut*—differing in minor externals such as dress, and

in their degree of acceptance of modern technology; yet these three groups agree fundamentally and recognize each other as fully Christian brethren, although marriage across branches is rarely practised. Of the fifty-four colonies registered in 1993, Saskatchewan is home to two branches: the *Dariusleut* (28 colonies) and the *Lehrerleut* (26). Eight colonies were established in the 1950s, and since then on average fifteen colonies have been established every decade. A colony splits vertically when the population approaches 100 members, although there is a tendency to earlier fission, because much of Saskatchewan's land cannot support larger colonies. From a low of forty-five to a high of 125 members, colonies are noticeably smaller than in the past, now only representing a few families each. Predominant family names are Entz, Hofer, Wipf, and Kleinsasser. Although Hutterites accept modern technology and have been known to establish manufacturing communes in the United States and Europe, Canadian Hutterites believe that agriculture is better for maintaining their lifestyle and beliefs. Southwest Saskatchewan has the majority of the colonies, although with time and colony fission more colonies have been established in farming municipalities farther north.

The distinctive communities appear as clusters of long buildings, often at a short distance from a main highway or road. They are constituted of row-houses, a German school and church, a large communal kitchen at the heart of the community yard, a laundry, a slaughterhouse, an electrical building, a waterworks building, shops, garages, barns, and grain bins. Most are incorporated under the Non-profit Corporations Acts. In 1993, about 5,000 Hutterites in 900 nuclear families occupied over half a million acres of land. They presently own over 2% of all agricultural land while representing 0.5% of Saskatchewan's total population. Since their population and their land are in rural municipalities, their importance to Saskatchewan's rural life is growing steadily. *Paul Laverdure*

HYDROGEN DIESEL TRUCKS. The world's first modified pickup truck fueled by a combination of hydrogen and diesel fuel was unveiled at a Regina event in 2004. Money for the $463,000 research project was provided by the federal and provincial governments as well as by Ecce Energy Corporation, a Saskatchewan company for which the Saskatchewan Research Council conducted a feasibility study. The proprietary hydrogen systems developed in Saskatchewan constitute a critical bridging technology as the transportation industry moves towards the fuel cell vehicles of the future. A fuel cell is similar to a battery, and uses hydrogen and oxygen to create electricity. This unique modification of existing vehicles to use hydrogen with conventional fuel provides the opportunity to reduce greenhouse gas emissions at the lowest cost and greatest flexibility to the vehicle operator. The first prototype was a General Motors heavy-duty pickup truck with a 6.6-L turbocharged diesel engine: the vehicle can be operated on diesel fuel alone, or on a combination of hydrogen and diesel fuel; performance and drivability are considered excellent; and there is no power loss when using hydrogen. The next step in testing will involve adapting the technology to fuel an automobile by a combination of hydrogen and gasoline.

Joe Ralko

PHOTO COURTESY OF RAPHAEL IDEM

Research staff of HTC Hydrogen Thermochem Corp in the Greenhouse Gas Technology Centre at the University of Regina: left to right, Prashant Kumar, Yanping Sun and Ahmed Aboudheir.

HYDROGEN PRODUCTION. The UNIVERSITY OF REGINA has become the first university in the world to develop "appliance size," environmentally sustainable processes for producing ultra-pure hydrogen for fuel cell applications from hydrocarbons and oxygenated hydrocarbons.

Based in the $13-million Greenhouse Gas Technology Centre, researchers developed a stable catalytic process for hydrogen production by dry-reforming gas and liquid fossil fuels. The university was also the first to economically produce hydrogen from crude ethanol. Work on the small-sized fuel cell began in 2003 as a collaborative effort between the University of Regina and Hydrogen Thermochem Corp., a local company; the objective was to build reformers the size of a filing cabinet to produce hydrogen for fuel cell use. Fuel cells are devices that produce electric power and heat; because the feed to the fuel cell is hydrogen, the by-product of power production is water instead of greenhouse gases such as carbon dioxide. The reformer needed to be able to supply sufficient hydrogen to a household for its electricity and heating needs, as well as a hydrogen refueling station for electric cars: this is how the description "appliance size" originated. Commercialization of the hydrogen fuel cell is expected to be a natural progression of the project once intellectual property protection is obtained and fine tuning has been completed.

Joe Ralko

HYDROLOGY. Hydrology is the study of water in and upon the Earth. Water movement in Saskatchewan is governed by the hydrologic cycle,

as shown in Figure HYD-1 (facing page). The dominant components are precipitation, evapotranspiration, infiltration, and runoff. Precipitation includes rain, snow, sleet and hail. Evapotranspiration is a combination of evaporation from open water bodies and soil surfaces, and transpiration from plants. Infiltration is the movement of water downward through the soil profiles.

Annual precipitation and seasonal distribution vary considerably across the province. Figure HYD-2 displays the mean annual precipitation: it is less than 350 mm in southern parts of the province, while it exceeds 500 mm in the CYPRESS HILLS or in northeastern Saskatchewan. Most areas receive at least 70% of the annual precipitation during the period April through October. Generally, less than 30% of the annual precipitation occurs during the winter period—except in the north, where the winter precipitation may be higher. The accumulation of snow is important to the hydrology of Saskatchewan, in that the melt rates and total accumulation cause higher flows during spring runoff.

Evapotranspiration is difficult to measure. Estimates have been calculated for gross evaporation from surface water bodies. In southern portions of the province, annual gross evaporation can exceed 1,000 mm, while in the north the gross evaporation may be in the order of 500 to 600 mm. Evaporation is affected by direct sunshine, wind, and air and water temperature. Estimates of soil surface evaporation and transpiration from plants are much less readily available. However, evapotranspiration is the largest component or output of the hydrologic cycle.

Infiltration is influenced by the coarseness of the soil, soil moisture, and pressure gradients. For example, sandy soils have higher infiltration rates than soils with high clay content. Surficial gravel deposits have higher infiltration rates than sandy soils. If soil moisture levels are low, infiltration rates will generally be higher. Practically, infiltration rates are difficult to determine for specific locations without significant instrumentation. Typically, infiltration is in the same order of magnitude as surface runoff.

Runoff is the combination of overland flow, interstitial flow from the soil profile, and ground water discharge from below the water table. Runoff is monitored at approximately 300 locations throughout Saskatchewan at hydrometric stations run by the provincial and federal government. The median annual runoff expressed in millimeters is shown in Figure HYD-3. As can be seen, runoff is generally small compared to annual precipitation (usually much less than 50% of the annual precipitation for the prairie portion of the province). Generally runoff increases as one moves northward or eastward in the province.

The major river basins in Saskatchewan are illustrated in Figure HYD-4. Starting in the south-

west part of the province, the Missouri River basin drains southward into the Mississippi River and the Gulf of Mexico. Old Wives Lake basin is an internal drainage basin, with no outflow. The Souris, Qu'Appelle and Assiniboine rivers drain primarily eastward into the Red River/Lake Winnipeg basin, and then northward to Hudson Bay. Similarly, the Saskatchewan and Churchill river basins drain eastward and northward to Hudson Bay. The MacKenzie River basin, which includes all the drainage into Lake Athabasca, drains northward into the Arctic Ocean. (*See also* CLIMATE.)

Doug Johnson

HYLAND, FRANCES (1927–2004). Born in Shaunavon on April 25, 1927, Frances Hyland won her first award for acting at 13, playing the title role in Oscar Wilde's *The Birthday of the Infanta*, directed by MARY ELLEN BURGESS. She studied at the UNIVERSITY OF SASKATCHEWAN with Professor Emrys Jones and received a BA with distinction in 1947, before receiving a scholarship to the Royal Academy of Dramatic Art (RADA) in London, England. She graduated with the coveted silver medal, and made her professional debut in London in *A Streetcar Named Desire* in 1950. She performed throughout Great Britain during the following four years.

Hyland returned to Canada in 1954 to the newly formed Stratford Festival, where she played Isabella opposite James Mason in *Measure for Measure*, as Portia in *The Merchant of Venice*, Olivia in *Twelfth Night*, Desdemona in *Othello*, Goneril in *King Lear*, and other leading roles over eight seasons. She also helped establish the Shaw Festival during three seasons, and starred on Broadway, in Chicago, in Toronto, and at England's Chichester Festival in between. "She built her career within the emerging network of companies across the country and over the years played all the leading theatres ... starring in CBC television and radio dramas and films, and generously sharing her talent and indomitable artistic values."

Hyland has performed on the stages of every Canadian province and in many Canadian television and radio productions. She also starred in *The*

SASKATCHEWAN ARCHIVES BOARD S-B4899

Frances Hyland.

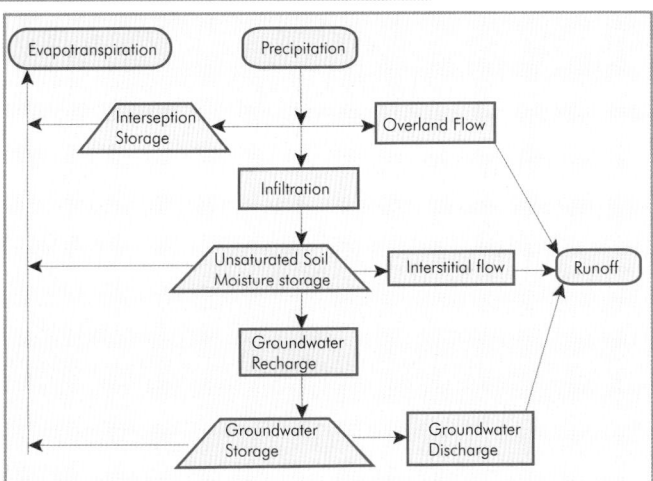

Figure HYD-1. The hydrologic cycle.

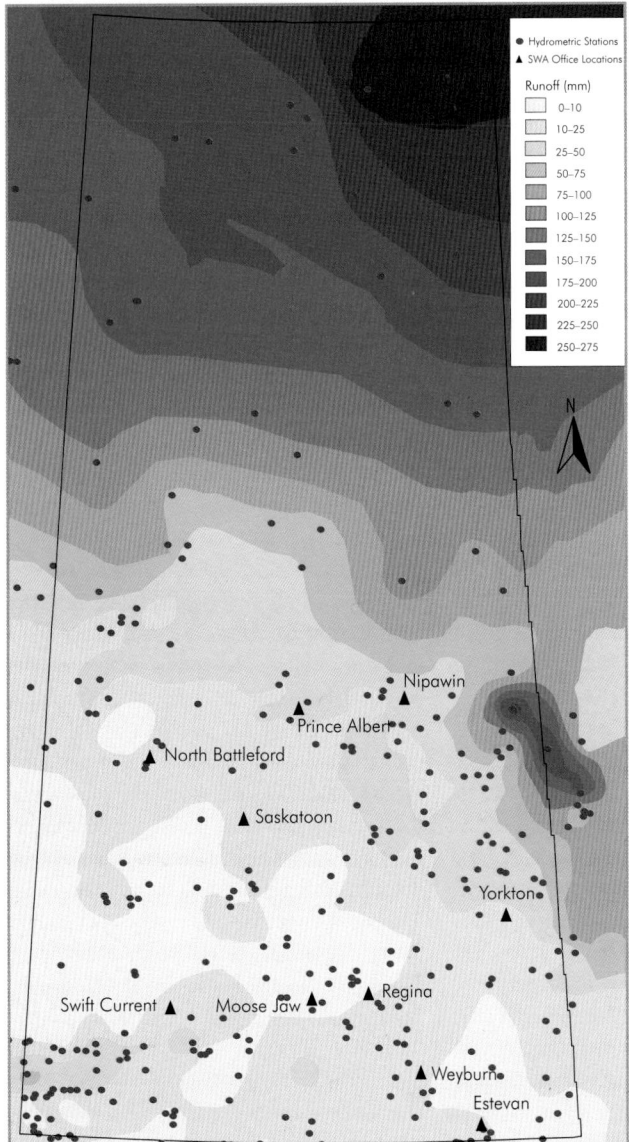

Figure HYD-3. Mean annual runoff.

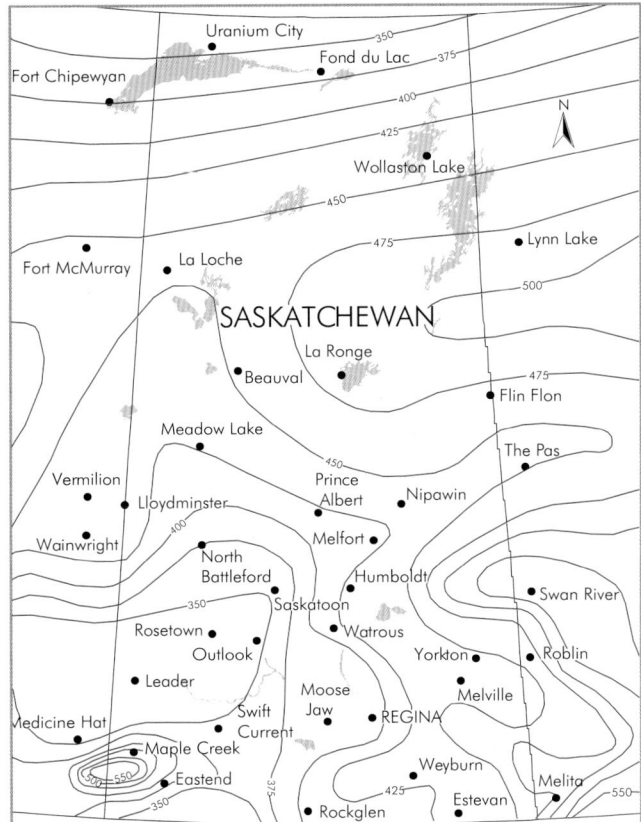

Figure HYD-2. Mean annual precipitation.

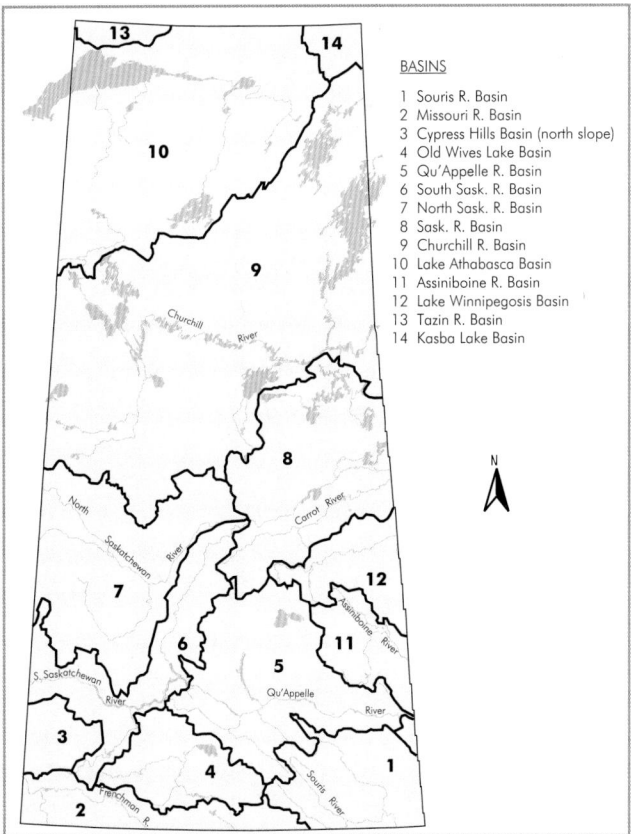

BASINS

1 Souris R. Basin
2 Missouri R. Basin
3 Cypress Hills Basin (north slope)
4 Old Wives Lake Basin
5 Qu'Appelle R. Basin
6 South Sask. R. Basin
7 North Sask. R. Basin
8 Sask. R. Basin
9 Churchill R. Basin
10 Lake Athabasca Basin
11 Assiniboine R. Basin
12 Lake Winnipegosis Basin
13 Tazin R. Basin
14 Kasba Lake Basin

Figure HYD-4. Major drainage basins.

Drylanders, the first feature film made by the National Film Board. She was awarded the Service Medal of Canada in 1971, and in 1972 received an honorary Doctor of Laws from the University of Saskatchewan, where she was appointed professor of drama in 1975.

Hyland directed the Canadian premiere of Beverley Simons' *Crabdance* and the 1979 Stratford production of *Othello*. However, "she regards her performance in the title role of George Ryga's seminal Canadian play, *The Ecstasy of Rita Joe*, as her most meaningful achievement."

She has received the John Drainie Award for Distinguished Contribution to Broadcasting (1981) as well as a 1994 Toronto Arts Award for lifetime achievement. She is a recipient of the Governor General's Lifetime Achievement Award, and is an Officer of the Order of Canada. In 2003, Frances Hyland was inducted into the Margaret Woodward Theatre Hall of Fame in Regina. Francis Hyland died on July 11, 2004.   *Lyn Goldman*

FURTHER READING: *Encyclopedia of Canadian Theatre*. 2003. Edmonton: Athabasca University.

HYLAND, GARY (1940–).

A prominent Saskatchewan poet, educator and volunteer, Gary Hyland has contributed greatly to the Saskatchewan writing community. Born in Moose Jaw on November 25, 1940 to Kenneth Hyland and Iris Frances Bourassa, he grew up in Moose Jaw's South Hill area. After graduating from St. Louis College in 1958, Hyland spent a year studying at **CAMPION COLLEGE** in Regina. He then went to the **UNIVERSITY OF SASKATCHEWAN** and graduated with a BA in 1962 and a BEd two years later. In 1962, Hyland married Linda Bell, with whom he had three sons. Upon completion of his BEd, he returned to Moose Jaw to take a position teaching English at Riverview Collegiate. Hyland and his first wife divorced in 1984, and he married Sharon Nichvalodoff in 1988. After his retirement from teaching in 1994, he instructed English classes for both SIAST and the **UNIVERSITY OF REGINA.**

Hyland began publishing poetry in various journals and magazines in the late 1960s, shortly thereafter publishing the chap-books *Poems from a Loft* (1973) and *Home Street* (1974). He has published four full-length collections, entitled *Street of Dreams* (1984), *Atlantis* (1992), *White Crane Spreads Wings* (1996), and *The Work of Snow* (2003). His poems have appeared in various literary magazines and have been collected in a number of poetry anthologies. In addition to his own writing, Hyland has co-edited several collections, including the Saskatchewan poetry anthologies *Number One Northern* (1977) and *A Sudden Radiance* (1987), and the humour collections *100% Cracked Wheat*

(1983) and *200% Cracked Wheat* (1992).

Hyland has been an active member of the Saskatchewan writing community for many years and was instrumental in the creation and survival of several organizations devoted to Saskatchewan writers. He has been a member of the **SASKATCHEWAN WRITERS' GUILD** since 1972, and is a founding member of the Moose Jaw Movement. Along with **ROBERT CURRIE**, **GEOFFREY URSELL**, and **BARBARA SAPERGIA**, he founded the Thunder Creek Publishing Co-op and Coteau Books in 1975. One of his most prominent contributions has been as founder of the Saskatchewan Festival of Words, with which he still serves as artistic coordinator.

Hyland has won several awards for both his poetry and his community involvement. He was named Moose Jaw Citizen of the Year in 1998. In 2001, he was awarded the Saskatchewan Volunteer Medal by the province of Saskatchewan and was named, along with Robert Currie, lifetime Poet Laureate of Moose Jaw. He has won several Saskatchewan Writers' Guild awards for his poetry, and in 2003 he obtained the inaugural Thistledown Press-sponsored John V. Hicks Memorial Award for *The Work of Snow*. He was awarded the Lieutenant-Governor's Arts Award for Leadership in 2004. He was named to the Order of Canada in 2005; the same year, he was granted an honorary doctor of laws from the University of Regina.   *Justin Messner*

FURTHER READING: Hillis, D. 1988. *Plainspeaking: Interviews with Saskatchewan Writers*. Moose Jaw: Coteau Books.

HYMENOPTERANS.

Hymenopterans, such as ants, bees, and wasps are an economically and ecologically significant group of animals. Although these insects are found throughout Saskatchewan, from the mixed-grass prairie in the south to the taiga shield in the north, their biology is poorly understood. Some of the major hymenopteran families in Saskatchewan include the Vespidae (the true wasp family, including yellow jackets), the Apidae (bumble-bees and the introduced honey bee), and the Formicidae (ants). Nearly 103,000 species of Hymenoptera have been identified globally. In Canada, 6,042 species have been identified, and another 10,637 species have been found but not yet described. The number of hymenopteran species in Saskatchewan is unknown, owing to an unfortunate lack of research on this important insect order.

Ants and bees are insects; therefore they have three body parts: head, thorax, and abdomen. The head bears a pair of antennae, the eyes and chewing mouth parts. The thorax bears two pairs of wings and three pairs of legs. The abdomen may bear an appendage called an ovipositor. An ovipositor is a specialized elongated organ that deposits eggs and

can also function as a sting. Hymenopterans undergo complete metamorphosis. An individual must go through larval and pupal stages before becoming an adult. Bees feed on pollen and nectar, whereas ants and wasps are omnivorous. They eat other insects, arachnids, seeds, and other pieces of vegetation.

Some bees and wasps are solitary, but many species of hymenopterans are social in nature. Honey and bumble-bees, paper wasps, and ants live in colonies that are comprised mostly of females. Within a single colony, various castes perform specific functions. Depending on the age and size of the hymenopteran colony, each egg a queen lays develops into a worker (female), a virgin queen, or in the case of social bees and wasps, a drone (non-worker male). Generally, male hymenopterans do not perform daily tasks but are essential for the establishment of new colonies because they fertilize virgin queens. Hymenopteran colonies have complicated social systems that rely heavily on pheromones for communication. Pheromones are natural chemicals that evoke a behavioural response from other members of the same species. By brushing their antennae against another individual, ants or bees can recognize others within the colony as either friend or foe. If an intruder is identified, it is communicated to the rest of the colony and the individual is attacked and removed. Honey bees also communicate through physical movements. After returning to the hive from a new source of nectar, individual bees perform a "dance" for the rest of the colony; this dance identifies the type of flower as well as the direction and distance from the hive.

Although physically small in size, hymenopterans play a large role in maintaining healthy ecosystems. Parasitic and predacious hymenopterans act as a natural control of pest species. Not only do bees provide us with honey, they are also essential for the pollination of many plants, including field crops, vegetables and fruits that we and other animals rely on for food. Wildflowers and urban flower gardens are also dependent on insect pollinators. Other hymenopterans such as ants are essential in nutrient recycling. Depending on the species, underground ant colonies may have tens to hundreds of thousands of individuals. These "super organisms" are very effective at turning over soil and cycling nutrients as animal and plant matter is digested and transported throughout the colony. The large number of diverse activities in which hymenopterans play a role illustrates what an important part of Saskatchewan's biodiversity they represent.

Jeanette Pepper

FURTHER READING: Borror, D.J. and R.E. White. 1970. *A Field Guide to the Insects of America North of Mexico*. Boston: Houghton Mifflin; Holldobler, B. and E.O. Wilson. 1990. *The Ants*. Cambridge, MA: Harvard University Press.

I

IBIS. Ibises (family Threskiornithidae) are a family of long-legged stork-like wading birds found throughout the tropical and temperate areas of the world. The approximately thirty-three species of ibis and spoonbill feed in wetlands, probing in water and mud for invertebrates. The white-faced ibis (*Plegadis chihi*) occurs sporadically in the province as far north as **LAST MOUNTAIN LAKE** as a wanderer. This medium-sized wader occurs in the same habitat as shorebirds and herons, but can be distinguished by its overall dark body and long down-curved thin bill. *Diane Secoy*

FURTHER READING: Alsop, Fred J., III. 2002. *Birds of Canada*. New York: Dorling Kindersley.

ICE ROADS. The current operational infrastructure for Saskatchewan Highways and Transportation (the government department responsible for the operation and preservation of the province's transportation system) includes more than 131 km of ice roads. The majority of these roads are located in northern Saskatchewan. The only major exception is the Riverhurst Crossing, an ice road constructed each year at Riverhurst and allowing vehicles to cross **LAKE DIEFENBAKER**. The northern ice

PHOTO COURTESY NORTHERN RESOURCE TRUCKING

Ice road.

roads allow winter access to the communities of Wollaston Lake, Fond du Lac, and Uranium City. During the summer these communities are accessible by either watercraft or aircraft. Many other ice roads previously existed in northern Saskatchewan, but are no longer in commercial use. They included an extension of Highway 955 (Semchuk Trail) to Uranium City, built in 1955–56 by Martin Semchuk, John Midgett and Jonas Clarke; and an ice road from Flin Flon to Reindeer Lake, built by the Sigfusson Transportation Company (Winnipeg) in 1945.

James Winkel

ICELANDIC SETTLEMENTS. In 1872, some 300 Icelanders immigrated to western Canada to found the New Iceland colony along the west shore of Lake Winnipeg in Manitoba. They declared their colony an independent republic in 1878, with its own constitution, laws and government, and Icelandic as the only official language. It lasted almost a decade before the Canadian government abolished it in 1887. In the meantime, Icelandic settlers had continued to move westward, eventually establishing a series of colonies across the prairies as far west as Alberta. The first Icelandic colony to develop in present-day Saskatchewan was the Thingvalla and Logberg colony in the Concordia district between Churchbridge and Calder, in 1886. Today Churchbridge is less than 10% Scandinavian, but there are an estimated 400 people of Scandinavian (mostly Icelandic) origin in the immediate area. A second colony, Valar and Holar, soon developed about 40 km south of Churchbridge, outside of Tantallon and Spy Hill, in 1887. Few people of Scandinavian origin live in these neighbouring villages (although a Norwegian Lutheran congregation came into existence in Spy Hill); but there are an estimated 300 people of Scandinavian origin in the immediate area.

Those initial colonies were always very small, but a large Icelandic settlement grew in the Quill Lakes region in central Saskatchewan after 1891. None of the three main towns in the region (Wynyard, Wadena, Foam Lake) are predominantly

Scandinavian today, the dominant population being of British or Ukrainian origin. Icelanders and other Scandinavians form little more than a third of the residents in the incorporated village of Elfros, and a slightly higher proportion in the neighbouring unincorporated village of Mozart. Yet Icelanders, preferring the family farm, settled heavily in many rural districts around these communities: this is by far the largest Icelandic colony in Saskatchewan, with an estimated 2,000 people of Scandinavian origin (mostly Icelanders) in the region.

In 1998, the Vatnabyggd Icelandic Club of Saskatchewan unveiled in Elfros a $60,000 memorial to Icelandic pioneers; it includes a bronze of a young Icelandic couple, information on the first Icelanders to move to the Vatnabyggd, murals of Iceland in the 1880s, the voyage to Canada, and Vatnabyggd then and now. To recognize the contribution of Icelandic pioneers, the main trails in the Foam Lake Marsh portion of the Quill Lakes Birding Project are named "Vatnabyggd," and the two minor loop trails have been given Icelandic names for local birds or animals. According to recent census data (2001), people of Icelandic origin in Saskatchewan numbered 6,100, of whom the overwhelming majority, 88.6% (5,405) also claimed other ethnic origins, compared to just 13% (805) claiming only Icelandic origin. (*See also* **ETHNIC BLOC SETTLEMENTS**, **SCANDINAVIAN SETTLEMENTS**)

Alan Anderson and Joan Eyolfson Cadham

FURTHER READING: Lindal, V.J. 1967. *The Icelanders of Canada*. Winnipeg: National and Viking.

ILE-A-LA-CROSSE, northern village, pop 1,268, located in NW Saskatchewan, SE of Buffalo Narrows off Hwy 155. The community is situated upon a peninsula that juts into an expansion of the upper Churchill River, called Lac Ile-à-la-Crosse. The name of the village and of the surrounding lake originates with early French fur traders observations of the game of lacrosse being played on a nearby island. The voyageurs had come to know the game as la

crosse, because the sticks used to play it resembled a bishop's crozier or *crosse*. Although the current name of the community has long been in use, it is still referred to as "Sakitawak," derived from the Cree term for "the place where the rivers meet." To the regularly visiting Dene, it is called "Kwoen," meaning "a place where people stay" or "a village." Ile-à-la-Crosse became the hub of much activity and competition during the fur trade due to its strategic location. To the north, via Methy Portage and the Clearwater River, lay the vast and fur-rich Athabasca region; and, from the south, pemmican, the fuel of the fur trade, could be brought to Ile-à-la-Crosse from the plains via the Beaver River. Heading back east down the Churchill, traders could head for Hudson Bay or Montreal. It was Montreal-based fur traders who established the first trading post at Ile-à-la-Crosse in 1776, making the village Saskatchewan's oldest continually inhabited community next to Cumberland House. Rival posts were set up with varying degrees of success in the following years including one set up in 1885 by Alexander Mackenzie. The Hudson's Bay Company tried to establish a footing at Ile-à-la-Crosse in 1799, but were initially thwarted by fierce competition from the North West Company. After the merger of the companies in 1821, Ile-à-la-Crosse became the headquarters for the Hudson's Bay Company's operations in the territory. In 1846, Father **ALEXANDRE-ANTONIN TACHÉ** (later Bishop) and Father Lafleche (for whom the southern Saskatchewan town is named) arrived from St. Boniface to establish the first Roman Catholic mission in what is present-day Saskatchewan. In 1860, Sisters Agnes, Pepin, and Boucher founded a convent, bringing medical services, education, and Western culture to the community. Around the Hudson Bay Company post and the mission a growing settlement developed comprised of the Metis descendents of the fur trade. Louis Riel's paternal grandparents were married in Ile-à-la-Crosse and his sister, Sara Riel, worked at the convent and is buried in the community's cemetery. Although a few men still voyage into the bush to trap each winter, the economy of Ile-à-la-Crosse has changed. A landing strip was built in the late 1940s; in the late 1950s an all-weather road was built to the community. Today, a modern highway runs from Ile-à-la-Crosse. Commercial fishing, forest fire fighting, forestry, wild rice harvesting, and work at the hospital and the school provide jobs. Additional employment is found in local and provincial government offices and many people work in northern uranium mines, being flown in on a "week in/week out" basis. The natural splendour of the community's location also gives rise to increasing tourism. The community's former newspaper editor and mayor, Buckley Belanger, was born in Ile-à-la-Crosse, and is currently the Government of Saskatchewan's Minister of Northern Affairs. *David McLennan*

Icelandic Celebrations, Churchbridge, ca. 1930s.

SASKATCHEWAN ARCHIVES BOARD R-A5648

Berthold John Von Imhoff.

IMHOFF, BERTHOLD JOHN VON (1868–1939). Count Berthold Von Imhoff was born into nobility in 1868 in Mannheim, Germany. He studied art, married in 1891, and with his wife Mathilda Johner and their children left Germany in 1900 to settle in Reading, Pennsylvania. There he established a reputation as a religious artist and fresco painter. In 1913 the family moved to a Saskatchewan farmhouse in the St. Walburg district; free from distractions, Berthold built a studio and began to paint. Throughout the 1920s and 1930s, he created massive paintings for many churches, Catholic and otherwise, throughout the province. He became known for his generosity as well as for his art: for example, when he was commissioned in 1918 to decorate the ceilings and sanctuary of St. Peter's Cathedral at Muenster, he refused payment for the 80 life-sized figures and frescoes. In 1939, Berthold suffered a stroke and died at the age of 71. Some sixty years later, in 1998, the community of St. Walburg erected a statue in his honour. Examples of Imhoff's works can be seen in churches in St. Walburg, Muenster, St. Benedict, Bruno, Denzil, Reward, St. Leo, Humboldt, Paradise Hill, and North Battleford. His restored studio, near St. Walburg, contains over 200 paintings. *Margaret Sanche and Pat Brassard*

IMMIGRANT INTEGRATION. Despite the fact that Saskatchewan today has one of the lowest proportions of new immigrants for any Canadian province, immigrants continue to add to the ethnic diversity of the province; immigrant integration into Canadian life thus remains an important service. The Saskatoon Open Door Society (SODS) was founded in 1980, soon after the Regina Open Door Society, to serve the growing needs of refugees (mostly from Vietnam, but also from Poland, Bulgaria, Hungary, and Ethiopia). The mission of Open Door has been "to welcome and assist refugees and immigrants to become informed and effective participants in Canadian society and to involve the community in their hospitable reception and just acceptance." Open Door has assisted refugees and immigrants from numerous countries in Latin America, Africa, the Middle East, South Asia, East Asia, Southeast Asia, and Europe. SODS, with a staff of over forty (not including board members and many volunteers), now assists over 1,600 clients a year, including more than 200 government-assisted refugees (almost a third of whom in 2002-04 were from Sudan, a quarter from Afghanistan, plus others from Sierra Leone, Columbia, Burma, Iran, Ethiopia, Pakistan, Burundi, Eritrea, Congo, etc.). Together, staff and volunteers speak some forty languages.

This agency currently offers language training to about 200 immigrants and refugees a year from at least twenty-five countries (not counting casual "drop-ins"), or as many as ninety people on a busy day. Between 400 and 500 people a year are assisted in finding suitable employment.

SODS also offers many other programs and services: multicultural child care, youth programs, refugee reception and resettlement, family and parenting programs, men's and women's programs, social and recreational activities, employment services, community outreach and home visits, civic orientation, interpretation services, personal counselling, etc. SODS and the Regina Open Door Society are part of an extensive network of agencies assisting with immigrant integration, such as the Saskatoon Refugee Coalition, Immigrant Women of Saskatchewan, Global Gathering Place, the Saskatchewan Intercultural Association, plus a broad range of health, family, youth and children services. (*See also* SASKATCHEWAN INTERCULTURAL ASSOCIATION)

Alan Anderson

IMMIGRANT, REFUGEE, AND VISIBLE MINORITY WOMEN OF SASKATCHEWAN (IRVM). In the mid-1980s, immigrant women around the country started forming organizations to do advocacy work in their respective provinces. In Saskatchewan, the provincial organization, IRVM (formerly Immigrant Women of Saskatchewan), has played a leading role in organizing educational and outreach programs to address needs and concerns of immigrant, refugee and visible minority women. As the name change suggests, the organization has evolved to reflect the changing concerns of the membership. The organization has also engaged in several research projects; its most recent publication has been *Women and Post Traumatic Stress Disorder: Moving Research to Policy*. Local chapters have been present in Moose Jaw, Prince Albert, Regina, Saskatoon, and Yorkton. While the Yorkton and Prince Albert chapters are no longer active, the Regina and Saskatoon chapters continue outreach, educational, and research work; the Moose Jaw chapter continues to provide work to newcomers. In Swift Current, immigrant and refugee women have set up an informal network to provide support to one another. Local IRVM chapters, like other nonprofit women's organizations, have faced debilitating budget constraints, and the struggle to survive has led to tremendous staff turnover and irregular work hours. The fact that the organizations continue to maintain a presence is a reflection of their belief in the value of their work. *Judy White*

FURTHER READING: Immigrant, Refugee, and Visible Minority Women of Saskatchewan. 2003. *Post Traumatic Stress Disorder: Moving Research to Policy.* Winnipeg: Prairie Women's Health Centre of Excellence.

C. FEHR PHOTO/HERITAGE BRANCH, SASKATCHEWAN CULTURE, YOUTH AND RECREATION

Imhoff Studio and decorative archway.

IMPACT STRUCTURES: *see* **ASTROBLEMES**

IMPERIAL, town, pop 339, located approximately 37 km S of Watrous, off Hwy 2. The north end of **LAST MOUNTAIN LAKE** and the Last Mountain Lake National Wildlife Area lie about 10 km to the east. Homesteaders began taking up land in the district in 1903; for a number of years, before the railway was built through the area, much of the transportation of people and freight into the region was by water. The Wm. Pearson Company established on the lake a "port of call" for its barges and steamer, the SS *Qu'Appelle*–to the east of present-day Imperial, at a location known as Watertown. In 1910, as the railway approached, businesses from Watertown and other areas moved to the rail line, and the first structures began to appear on the Imperial townsite. The rail line was constructed several kilometres west of the lake in order to maximize the amount of agricultural land on either side. The name of Imperial fits the pattern of names given to other communities established along the line–such as Holdfast, Stalwart, and Liberty–and reflects the traits and glory associated with the British Empire. Many of Imperial's tree-lined streets further the theme with names such as King, Queen, Prince, and Princess. The area economy is based on agriculture, and Imperial is home to a major manufacturer of agricultural machinery as well as to a crop processing plant. For a number of years, the community has hosted successful dinner theatres and has sponsored an ice-fishing derby on Last Mountain Lake.

David McLennan

IMPERIAL ORDER DAUGHTERS OF THE EMPIRE (IODE). The Imperial Order Daughters of the Empire (IODE) was organized in Montreal during the **BOER WAR** (1900) for women of the Empire who wanted to do war work in the course of that struggle. After the conflict in South Africa, the Order poised itself to play a key role in any future imperial war. Drawing its ranks from the upper echelons of Canadian society, the IODE designed a highly organized and efficient society of women who were anxious to serve their country and King. The first seven Saskatchewan chapters of the IODE were organized in 1909 in Battleford, North Battleford, Moose Jaw, Prince Albert, Saskatoon, Regina, and Grenfell. When Canada became embroiled in **WORLD WAR I** in 1914, the IODE was eager and able to make significant contributions, and IODE membership increased dramatically during the war years. Saskatchewan chapters had increased in number to thirty-three by war's end. Members became expert fund raisers and contributed financially toward large-scale wartime fund-raising projects. The IODE believed that its most important war work was putting all the time, money and effort that it could muster into caring for servicemen and their

SASKATCHEWAN ARCHIVES BOARD R-A20948-1
Imperial Order Daughters of the Empire, ca. 1920s.

dependents–before the men left, after they departed, and after they returned from active service. One legacy is the tens of thousands of pairs of socks that IODE members knitted to supply the men in the trenches.

Ironically, World War I proved to be the zenith of the IODE's existence as a patriotic women's organization: the war brought to a close the imperialist Edwardian era in Canada, and the organization's imperial zeal was undermined. Nonetheless, the IODE did serve in another world war from 1939 to 1945, and to the present day undertakes philanthropic, educational, and citizenship endeavours to improve the quality of life for children, youth, and those in need.

Nadine Charabin

FURTHER READING: Small, Nadine. 1988. "Stand By the Union Jack: The Imperial Order Daughters of the Empire in the Prairie Provinces During the Great War, 1914–1918." MA thesis, University of Saskatchewan.

INCOME SECURITY. In Saskatchewan, the majority of people get the income they need to live from paid employment or self-employment. In an ideal labour market, there would be work for everyone who needs income, wages would be high enough to provide a living for workers and their dependents, and employees would be able to save enough during their working life to provide income in old age. But in the real world of the labour market there are always imperfections: involuntary unemployment, skill or opportunity mismatches, gaps between earnings and needs, etc. Dependents, including children, share the economic risks of workers. There are also some adults, such as people with severe disabilities, who may not have the capacity to be fully self-sufficient. Even for those who can provide adequately for

current needs, it may be difficult to plan enough savings to provide an income in old age.

All societies establish a balance between the individual's responsibilities and the protection that society offers its members. Income security policies and programs are one of the means that societies can use to protect citizens from some of the economic risks that an individual is exposed to in a market economy. Because citizens are expected to be as self-reliant as possible, good income security policy provides protection, but also encourages people to act in their own and the community's best interests. When Saskatchewan was formed in 1905, governments had limited involvement in income security. Families were expected to take care of their own members; and where that was not possible, religious and charitable groups frequently responded to hardship and need. As the province developed, however, governments were called on to make more formal arrangements for the well-being of citizens.

The involvement of governments in income security has increased in stages as public attention and sympathy have focused on particular social issues. The first benefit plan for widows and dependent children, for example, began in Saskatchewan in 1916 during **WORLD WAR I**. Long-standing concerns about elderly people in need were first addressed through the Saskatchewan Old Age Pension of 1928–the first major social program cost-shared between the provincial and federal governments. While governments gradually addressed the needs of groups of people who were generally seen as blameless and worthy of public support, there was less consensus on how to respond to "able-bodied" people who found themselves in need owing to unemployment or other circumstances. At the end of the 1920s, programs for the health and welfare of able-bodied people in need were still organized and funded by municipal governments. The onset of the **GREAT DEPRESSION** in 1929, however, quickly overwhelmed the resources of these local governments to respond to rapidly growing demand for assistance.

The Depression was deeper and more prolonged in Saskatchewan because the global economic downturn coincided with a prolonged and severe **DROUGHT** on the prairies. Between 1929 and 1933 Saskatchewan's per capita income dropped by 72%, compared to 48% for Canada as a whole, and the per capita relief burden in Saskatchewan was more than three times the national average. The Great Depression demonstrated the vulnerability of individuals and governments to broad economic forces. While the onset of **WORLD WAR II** solved the unemployment crisis, greater economic and social justice became part of the Western allies' war aims. The Atlantic Charter, a joint statement of Churchill and Roosevelt in 1941, promised that victory would secure "for all, improved labour standards, economic advancement, and social security." Although there was essentially no unemployment during the war, a modest national unemployment insurance was enacted in Canada in 1941 in anticipation of future needs. In 1943, Dr. Leonard Marsh's *Report on Social Security for Canada* outlined a post-war vision: an economy managed for full employment; benefits for children to fight family poverty; and comprehensive social insurance to protect income in the case of unemployment, illness, or lack of resources in old age.

Except for the Family Allowance, introduced in 1945, most of Marsh's ideas were not acted upon immediately. However, federal financial support for income security programs continued to grow. The federal share of national social welfare costs, figured at 52% in 1933, had climbed to 84% by 1960. Much of this increased federal spending was for cost-sharing of provincial programs to help categories of needy persons such as the elderly, blind persons, disabled persons, and finally in 1956, those in need owing to unemployment. Between 1966 and 1971 there were major changes in national social programs, involving publicly funded health care, the contributory Canada Pension Plan, the Guaranteed Income Supplement for low-income seniors, an expansion to unemployment insurance, and other measures. In Saskatchewan, a new provincial social assistance plan replaced most municipal and categorical provincial welfare programs. Of all the changes of this period, the most effective pertained to public and private pension reform; they have drastically reduced the depth and incidence of poverty among older citizens.

These reforms came after more than two decades of growth and prosperity. The economy had been strong, and was assumed to be able to support a comprehensive social security system. Beginning with the early 1970s, these positive labour market conditions began to change: international oil crises, low growth, unemployment, and inflation increased financial pressures on governments and citizens and brought social reform to a halt. The economic events of the 1970s were the first signals of economic restructuring towards more open international trade and more global competition for lower-skilled labour. At the same time, western society was undergoing a rapid change in family relations and the status of women. One impact of this change was an increase in the number and proportion of single-parent families, generally more at risk because they have only one earner and more likely to incur child-care costs. These factors combined to push many households, especially those headed by single parents, out of the work force and onto social assistance. By the early 1990s, social assistance caseloads represented almost 12% of the population in Saskatchewan and across the country. By some measures, over 20% of Canada's children were living in poverty.

While some social advocates called for higher social assistance benefits as a response to family poverty, Saskatchewan instead chose to focus on supports to employment. The first reforms in this direction occurred within the context of the National Child Benefit, Canada's first significant new national social program since the 1960s. The National Child Benefit initiative has both federal and provincial/territorial components. The federal component is a new benefit to replace social assistance for children in lower-income families. Because the benefit is available whether a parent is working or on welfare, it increases disposable income of employed parents and encourages low-income parents to work. Parallel reforms under Saskatchewan's *Building Independence* initiative increased cash and in-kind supports to low-income working families, and strengthened employment supports provided with social assistance and other public benefits.

Many observers believe that the child benefit reforms that occurred in the late 1990s were a step forward in the evolution of Canada's social security system. Until that time there was very limited support to low-income families with children outside of the social assistance programs. Under pressure from labour market conditions, many families were drawn towards social assistance and out of the labour market, even though employment income was these families' best hope for escaping poverty. By helping both parents on social assistance and low-income working parents with children's needs, the new approach arguably allows governments to provide direct benefits for children without systematically discouraging work by low-income parents. Programs such as social assistance, which provide for the needs of adults, are more controversial because the availability of benefits is often viewed as a disincentive to work.

Proposals have been put forward over the years for a "guaranteed income" provided by government to all working-age citizens. No such plans have been implemented because of concerns about cost and work incentives. Governments and communities are still working towards the right balance between individual incentives and security of income. A perfect system would encourage individual effort and enterprise, while still ensuring that the overall wealth of society is distributed fairly enough to prevent both undue hardship and extremes of inequality. The search for this balance in income security policy continues.   *Rick August*

FURTHER READING: Grauer, A.E. 1939. *Public Assistance and Social Insurance: A Study Prepared for the Royal Commission on Dominion-Provincial Relations.* Ottawa: King's Printer; Guest, D. 1997. *The Emergence of Social Security in Canada.* Vancouver: UBC Press.

INDEPENDENT SCHOOLS. Independent schools have always existed in Saskatchewan, having been established at different times for different reasons. The first generation of independent schools are now referred to as the "historical high schools," established in the early 1900s at a time when public high schools were not always available. These historical high schools include Luther College High School, the Mennonite school at Rosthern, and the Athol Murray College of Notre Dame in Wilcox. To accommodate their unique religious beliefs, the Seventh-day Adventists started their first school in 1924, and evangelical Christian schools began in the mid-1970s. In the 1970s, other alternative schools were established to provide an education for disabled or disadvantaged students.

Roman Catholic schools in Saskatchewan, as a result of the British North America Act (1867), are considered public schools and funded accordingly, but in many other provinces they are independent schools. While independent schools were in existence in Saskatchewan for a century, regulations, policies and procedures that clearly defined their legal status had not been developed. In 1986, the powers and responsibilities of provincial governments regarding the operation of independent schools were clarified when the Supreme Court of Canada rendered its decision in the Alberta case *Jones v. the Queen*.

The Saskatchewan provincial government announced in 1987 that Gordon Dirks would conduct a study on private schooling examining quality of education, funding, taxation, attendance requirements, and parent rights. In 1988 the government announced it would establish a comprehensive system for the regulation and registration of independent schools through the Department of Education. In 1989 the Minister of Education established an Advisory Board on Independent Schools, chaired by Alec Postnikoff. Chris Gerrard was appointed head of a newly formed Independent Schools Branch in the Department of Education. In 1989, amendments to the Education Act were passed, and legislation and policies provided for regulation and registration of Independent Schools in Saskatchewan. In 2004 there were forty-eight registered independent schools, with a student population of 4,388 located in every region of the province. Such schools fall into four broad categories: religiously based, alternative, private, and other programs.

The first category, religiously based schools, makes up approximately 80% of all independent schools. Schools named after according to religious affiliation are Seventh-day Adventist, Mennonite, and Muslim. Historical high schools were founded by Lutherans, Roman Catholics, and Mennonites. The Saskatchewan Association of Independent Church Schools represents various Evangelical Christian groups. Society schools are operated by a

Luther College, Regina.

group of parents as opposed to a specific church. Associate schools refer to religiously based schools that enter into an operating agreement with a local public school division.

The second category of independent schools comprises the alternative schools, which offer special needs programs for disabled or disadvantaged students. Schools such as the Joe Doucette School in Saskatoon, which serves Aboriginal students, fall into this category. The third category consists of private schools. These include off-shore schools, which were created in 1995 when Saskatchewan Education indicated its intent to register non-profit, religiously based schools in other countries; in 2004 there were off-shore schools in Hong Kong and Venezuela. Another category of private school is referred to as for-profit school: private schools operating in Saskatchewan that cater to international students seeking Saskatchewan high school credentials fall into this category. Finally, the fourth category of independent schools concerns Montessori schools, which offer a unique student-centred program based upon the Montessori educational philosophy.

Saskatchewan's education system is a publicly funded system designed to meet the needs of the vast majority of students, with provision for parents to opt out for reasons of faith or educational belief. While historical high schools, associate schools, and alternate schools are eligible for provincial funding, private schools are not. Independent schools in Saskatchewan provide an education from a specific philosophical or religious perspective different from that of the public education system. Parents enrol their children in independent schools in order to achieve objectives that may not, or cannot, be satisfied within the public education system.

Eugene Hodgson

INDIAN HEAD, town, pop 1,758, located approximately 70 km E of Regina on Hwy 1. Indian Head had its beginnings in 1882 as the first settlers, mainly of Scottish origin, pushed into the area in advance of the railroad, most traveling by ox-cart from Brandon. The Indian Head post office was established that year, as well as a large-scale farming enterprise, the Bell Farm. Conceived of and managed by Major W.R. Bell of Ontario, the farm consisted of over 50,000 acres and was run like a military operation. Although the enterprise experienced some success, poor crops in the middle of the decade, as well as the settlers' preoccupation with the NORTH-WEST RESISTANCE resulted in the farm's failure. The need for agricultural research in the west was recognized by the federal government, and in 1887 an experimental farm was established at Indian Head (*see* AGRICULTURE CANADA RESEARCH STATIONS). Development in the young community was slow at first, but after 1900 settlers began arriving in droves. By the outbreak of WORLD WAR I, Indian Head was a thriving agricultural service centre with a population of over 1,200. Some of the province's largest wheat shipments were passing through the Indian Head elevators. The research farm at Indian Head remains to this day, as does the PRAIRIE FARM REHABILITATION ADMINISTRATION (PFRA) Shelterbelt Centre, which had its origins in 1902. Today, both operations are major community employers. Indian Head is also home to the Orange Home and Orange Home Farm. Started by the Orange Benevolent Society, the homes have provided safe and secure shelters for children experiencing family stress or turmoil since 1923. Indian Head has a range of professional services and tradespeople, financial institutions, and a large number of retail establishments.

David McLennan

INDIAN POLICY AND THE EARLY RESERVE PERIOD.

Early government policy for First Nations in Saskatchewan was administered under the Indian Act, with the goal of training First Nations people to become farmers and assimilating them into the greater Canadian society. Through the Indian Act and an assimilationist policy based on social Darwinism, attempts were made to dispossess First Nations of their land and identity: the rationale behind the reserve system was to place them on pieces of land isolated from white settlement, where policies could be more easily applied and monitored. Once reserves had been selected and surveyed, Indian agents were sent to administer them; they had sweeping powers ranging from control of First Nations' movement to control of agricultural equipment and expenditures by the band.

The most restrictive policies and legislation came after the events of the 1885 NORTH-WEST RESISTANCE, when the government of Canada concentrated its efforts on breaking up the tribal system and assimilating First Nations people. Three officials were most prominent in the development and implementation of Indian policy: Sir John A. Macdonald, EDGAR DEWDNEY, and Hayter Reed. After the events of 1885 Hayter Reed, then Assistant Indian Commissioner of Indian Affairs, drafted a lengthy "Memorandum on the Future Management of Indians," which would become a template for Indian policy in Saskatchewan; it was approved by Dewdney as Commissioner of Indian Affairs, and by Macdonald as Prime Minster and Superintendent General of Indian Affairs. Reed promoted a "peasant farming" approach, central to which were the pass, permit, and Birtle system, and severalty.

The pass system was at first to be issued only to "Rebel Indians"; however, Macdonald insisted that the system should be applied to all First Nations. In early 1886, books of passes were issued to Indian agents, and subsequently First Nations people could not leave their reserve unless they had a pass signed by the Indian agent and describing when they could leave, where they could go, and when they had to return. The pass system, however, was never passed into legislation and as a result was never legal– although it was enforced well into the 1940s.

The permit system was instituted to control the selling and buying of goods by First Nations people. If a First Nations farmer wanted to sell any produce, he had to secure a permit signed by the Indian agent. In a similar fashion, if non-First Nations people wanted to come onto the reserve to sell goods, they also had to obtain a permit from the agent.

The Birtle system was a cattle loan program whereby a First Nations farmer would be given a cow: at the end of a year, he had to return either the cow or its offspring. The belief was that if an Indian person had a vested interest in an animal, success would be more likely; however, the system failed owing to the lack of any real control by First Nations over their stock.

The severalty or subdivision of reserve land was also central to the peasant farming policy. Beginning in 1889, Indian reserves were to be divided approximately in two: one-half would be surveyed into 40-acre lots upon which individual families were to farm; the other half was to be held in common as hay and timber land. Reed's belief was that an Indian farmer was to become self-sufficient, but was not to compete in the marketplace. The pass and permit systems, as well as severalty, restricted how successful Indian farmers could be and ultimately contributed to the failure of agriculture on First Nations reserves.   *Rob Nestor*

FURTHER READING: Carter, S. 1990. *Lost Harvests.* Montreal: McGill-Queen's University Press.

INDIAN TEACHER EDUCATION PROGRAM (ITEP).

The Indian Teacher Education Program of the College of Education at the **UNIVERSITY OF SASKATCHEWAN** was established in 1972–73 as a two-and-a-half-year program leading to a two-year Standard A certificate. That first year, twenty students were selected to participate in what was then an innovative concept. Since then more than 650 students have graduated from the program, which has evolved to a four-year Elementary and Secondary Program leading to a BEd and a Professional "A" certificate. ITEP is funded through a contribution agreement between Indian and Northern Affairs Canada and the University of Saskatchewan. The success of ITEP is reflected in the number and quality of its graduates, who have taken leadership roles in teaching, administration, and band governance in their communities.

Cross-cultural education is incorporated into course work: community Elders are called on, and all student-teachers study an Aboriginal language. Academic and personal support is provided by the ITEP counselling and instructional staff. ITEP attributes its success to the strong network of students who are experts in the delivery of cross-cultural education. Three-quarters of band schools in Saskatchewan have ITEP graduates teaching in them; and since ITEP has been running for more than thirty years, it is not uncommon for today's student-teachers to be children of those from the first graduating classes. While most ITEP graduates in the past majored in elementary education, the emphasis in the 21st century is on preparation for teaching in secondary schools, where there is an even greater need for First Nations teachers and role models.   *James McNinch*

INDO-CANADIAN COMMUNITY.

Indian and other South Asian immigrants started coming to Saskatchewan in the early 1960s. They originated from different parts of the world such as India, Pakistan, Uganda, the Caribbean, and the United Kingdom. These early settlers came with high levels of education and into occupations in medicine, engineering, and teaching. They mostly settled in Regina and Saskatoon, with a few living in smaller towns. Many were young families, or started their families in Saskatchewan. A majority of the wives, also highly educated, worked either part- or full-time in various occupations. All had English language skills and quickly adapted to their new environment. Many achieved professional recognition in their careers, and many have received broader societal and citizenship awards at national, provincial and municipal levels.

The majority of these settlers acquired Canadian citizenship, but maintained links with their roots and periodically traveled back home to visit family, relatives and friends, and to maintain cultural links for their children. While a majority spoke Hindi, Gujarati or Punjabi, English became the language used at home in about half the families. This loss of mother tongue for their youths is of concern to the community, and Hindi and Gujarati classes are offered with the aid of multicultural associations in the province. In addition, Indian dance classes offered locally as well as by visiting professionals have helped to retain Indian culture.

The communities showcase their cultural arts and cuisine at annual multicultural festivals such as Folkfest in Saskatoon and Mosaic in Regina. The communities have erected statues of Mahatma Gandhi in the cities of Regina and Saskatoon; they also support the Shastri lecture series at the two universities in the province. The ranks of the early settlers have tended to become thin, as many retired persons have followed their grown children who have chosen to pursue careers elsewhere in Canada or the United States. But new immigrants have come to replace them, and the Indo-Canadian communities are continuing their presence in the province. The new immigrants fit into an increasingly diverse occupational spectrum. The numbers of Indo-Canadian students at the two universities have also been increasing. The religious faiths of Indo-Canadians consist mainly of Hinduism, Islam, Sikhism, and Christianity. The province now has a few Hindu temples, Muslim mosques and Sikh gurudwaras, all of which belong to the multi-faith forums in Regina and Saskatoon. The unique architectural style of these various houses of worship has added richness to the provincial landscape. A majority of the community members also affiliate the secular India-focused culture groups such as the India-Canada Association of Saskatchewan and the Gujarati Samaj. Eastern religious-philosophical thinking has also introduced a number of non-denominational meditation and yoga centres into the province. (*See also* **HINDU COMMUNITIES; SASKATCHEWAN INTERCULTURAL ASSOCIATION**)

                                Kalburgi Srinivas

FURTHER READING: Buchignani, N., D.M. Indra and R. Srivastiva. 1985. *Continuous Journey: A Social History of South Asians in Canada.* Toronto: McClelland and Stewart; Srinivas, K.M. and S.K. Kaul. 1987. *Indo-Canadians in Saskatchewan: The Early Settlers.* Regina: India-Canada Association of Saskatchewan.

INDUSTRIAL WOOD AND ALLIED WORKERS OF CANADA.

Like their working-class counterparts across the country, lumber workers in Saskatchewan were swept up in the labour militancy during **WORLD WAR II** and the immediate postwar period. Glen Thompson, a representative from the Trades and Labour Congress (TLC), organized about eighty workers in the Prince Albert Woodworkers Union in 1944. A year later, this new union

ROBERT WATSON/REGINA LEADER-POST
Fashion Show rehearsal for "Indian Night," March 1994.

DONNA PERKINS PHOTO/SASKATCHEWAN ARCHIVES BOARD
S-SP-A7831-4, SASKATOON STARPHOENIX FONDS

IWA union workers on the picket line at Domtar, January 1973.

was chartered directly by the TLC. In 1953 the Prince Albert Woodworkers Union became Local 184 of the International Woodworkers of America (IWA). The IWA became a national union, IWA Canada, in 1985. To reflect its changing membership in 1997, the IWA adopted the name Industrial Wood and Allied Workers-Canada (IWA-Canada). Today, Local 1-184, the Saskatchewan Local with jurisdiction over the entire province, has a membership of about 1,000 men and women who work in many different sectors of the provincial economy including sawmilling, secondary manufacturing, and services.

IWA represents sawmillers of all kinds, aspen harvesting crews, a peat moss harvesting operation, cabinet shops, rafter manufacturing, mobile home manufacturing, a town maintenance crew, and garage and service station outlets. Today, the IWA faces great challenges in representing workers, as merging companies become more powerful and hold the menace of unbalanced corporate agendas. In 2002 the United States escalated the softwood lumber dispute, with countervailing duties and anti-dumping charges as high as 27%. This ongoing dispute has put pressure on unions and companies as this industry struggles to stay competitive. *Harry Groenen*

FURTHER READING: Neufeld, A., and A. Parnaby. 2000. *The IWA in Canada: the Life and Times of an Industrial Union*. Vancouver: IWA-Canada and New Star Books.

INGHAM, ANNA GERTRUDE (1912–).

Born in 1912, Yorkton's Anna Gertrude Ingham has shared the gifts of reading and writing with thousands of children through her Blended Sound-Sight Method of teaching. Beginning in the 1930s, she taught in several one-room schoolhouses throughout Saskatchewan. In 1967, she published *The Blended Sound-Sight Program of Learning*, a textbook that outlined her system of rich phonetic

instruction with the sight method of reading. Since then, the successful instructional book has gone through five editions. In recognition of her innovation teaching methods, Anna Ingham was invested as a Member of the Order of Canada in 1995.

INTERDEPARTMENTAL COMMITTEE ON MEDICARE, 1959.

On April 27, 1959, two days after announcing his government's intention to introduce universal medicare in a by-election speech, Premier **T.C. DOUGLAS** and his Cabinet established the Interdepartmental Committee to Study a Medical Care Program. This committee of officials—some of the most brilliant civil servants of the era—would produce a blueprint for the Saskatchewan program that later became the national model for medicare. In addition to the chair, deputy minister of health Dr. Burns Roth, the committee included deputy provincial treasurer **A.W. JOHNSON**, Cabinet's chief policy guru **THOMAS SHOYAMA**, and municipal policy experts Meyer Brownstone and William Harding. In addition to reviewing the current state of health services in the province and providing detailed recommendations on the administration and financing of medicare, the committee provided advice on the formation and structure of the more public Thompson Committee on medicare.

The Interdepartmental Committee on Medicare submitted its report to the Douglas Cabinet on November 20, 1959. It recommended that a comprehensive system of universal medical care coverage be introduced in two stages. In the first and immediate stage, **MEDICARE** would include a broad range of prevention services as well as a full range of outpatient physician and diagnostic services. It was hoped that home care services could be put on a "hospital-centred" basis and cost-shared with the federal government under the recently negotiated system of national hospitalization. The Committee recommended extending coverage to prescription drugs, and optical, dental and chiropody services at a later stage, only after the government had sufficient administrative expertise and the comprehensive information required for effective cost control. Finally, the Committee recommended a combination of general tax revenues with a premium (equal in value to the hospitalization premium) to finance medicare—a system that remained in place until premiums were removed on January 1, 1974. *G.P. Marchildon*

FURTHER READING: Johnson, A.W. 2004. *Dream No Little Dreams: A Biography of the Douglas Government of Saskatchewan, 1944–1961*. Toronto: University of Toronto Press/IPAC.

INTERNATIONAL ALLIANCE OF THEATRICAL STAGE EMPLOYEES (IATSE).

The International Alliance of Theatrical Stage Employees and Moving Picture Technicians, Artists and Allied Crafts of the United States, its Territories and Canada began in 1893, when show business was confined almost entirely to the stage. The union has become well known within the entertainment business throughout North America as the IATSE or the IA. Motion pictures became an industry in the first decade of the 20th century and, beginning in 1908, film projectionists across the continent gained IATSE charters. During the 1920s the IATSE became the representative for technicians within the Hollywood studio system and the network of film exchanges throughout the United States and Canada. Today there are 12,000 members within 450 Locals, representing a complete coverage of the crafts of stage, screen and television.

The IATSE Local 295 in Regina and Local 300 in Saskatoon were granted IATSE individual charters on July 10, 1913, for stage workers and film projectionists, with sixteen names appearing on the Saskatoon charter. Stage-work was the predominant craft in Saskatchewan into the 1930s, when motion pictures became a more accessible and popular form of entertainment. Since the 1960s, Saskatoon Local 300 has been representing film production technicians. The Local maintains a membership of around 100, covering thirty craft departments in the film, stage, and projection areas of work. *Greg McKinnon*

INTERNATIONAL BROTHERHOOD OF ELECTRICAL WORKERS.

The International Brotherhood of Electrical Workers (IBEW) has been in Canada since 1899, with locals in Saskatchewan as early as 1907. Local 2067, which currently represents workers at SaskPower, Luscar and the city of Swift Current, grew out of Local 21 of the Civic Employees Association which at the time represented electrical workers for the city of Regina. In February 1950, the Electrical Utilities Employees Union (EUEU) Local 9 was certified as the bargaining agent for all workers employed in the city of Regina electrical system.

A strike that occurred July 23, 1950, left dissatisfaction within the membership and the Canadian Labour Congress encouraged workers from EUEU Local 9 to select an appropriate union operating in their field. A vote was held between the IBEW, the National Union of Municipal Employees and the Oil Chemical and Atomic Workers Union (OCAW). The IBEW won and thus IBEW Local 2067 was chartered on November 1, 1959, with C.C. McVeigh becoming the first president/business manager.

In 1965, the **SASKATCHEWAN POWER CORPORATION** (SPC) purchased the electrical-generating plant and distribution system from the city of Regina. Along with these facilities came the workers and their union, IBEW Local 2067. In 1966, after a representational struggle between OCAW and IBEW at SPC, 900 electrical workers joined IBEW Local 2067.

Although organized since 1907, IBEW Local 319 was not chartered by IBEW until 1927. It received a Labour Relations Board certification order in 1951 granting it the right to represent all electrical workers at the electrical utility and the communications department for the city of Saskatoon.

The two construction locals of IBEW, Locals 2038 (chartered in 1959) and 529 (chartered in 1947), represent workers in the southern and northern sections of the province. Their jurisdiction covers all outside and inside electrical work.

Local 2067 members were legislated back to work in January 1975, and again in 1976, after a strike occurred to protest a wage roll back under the federal government wage controls legislation. In 1998, the government legislated an end to a lockout by SaskPower. *Mike Kaytor*

INTERNATIONAL IMMIGRATION. With the exception of the Aboriginal population, all of Saskatchewan's residents are either immigrants or the descendants of immigrants: the province, and indeed the country, was largely populated by those born in other countries.

Figure INIM-1 shows the proportion of Saskatchewan residents who were born outside Canada (the definition of "immigrant" used in these data). The number of immigrants in Saskatchewan has been declining as a percentage of the population. In 1911, a few years after Saskatchewan became a province, just under 50% of the province's 492,000 residents were immigrants. By 2001 the population had doubled, but there were fewer than 50,000 immigrants living in Saskatchewan. Although some of this decline is a result of the natural aging of the population, a good deal is explained by the fact that the province is not able to

retain recent immigrants: estimates vary, but it seems that only 50–60% of immigrants who come to Saskatchewan eventually make their home here.

In Canada, immigrants make up 18% of the population. The proportion is as high as 27% in Ontario and 26% in British Columbia, but Saskatchewan has one of the lowest proportions with 5% of the residents born outside Canada. This is higher than in the four Atlantic provinces, but lower than the 12% in Manitoba and the 15% in Alberta. Whereas most of the early immigrants to Saskatchewan were from Europe, recent immigrants tend to come from Asian countries: among those who moved to Canada from 1991 to 2001 and who were living in Saskatchewan in 2001, 42% were born in Asian countries–typically China or the Philippines. Other countries that are common birthplaces among recent immigrants include the United States (11%), the various countries of the former Yugoslavia (9%), and South Africa (4%).

Among current Saskatchewan residents 15 years of age and older, 7% were born outside Canada but another 22% are "first generation" Canadians in the sense that at least one of their parents was born outside Canada. The province may be ready for a new generation of immigrants. Labour market trends indicate that there will be a surge in retirements over the next ten to fifteen years: immigrants may be able to help meet the demand for workers. (*See also* **POPULATION TRENDS**; **URBAN ETHNIC DIVERSITY**, **VISIBLE MINORITIES**) *Doug Elliott*

INTERNATIONAL ROAD DYNAMICS. International Road Dynamics (IRD) was established in 1980 by **UNIVERSITY OF SASKATCHEWAN** engineering professor Dr. Arthur Bergen. IRD is a Saskatoon-based high-tech company that develops and integrates highway traffic management products and information gathering systems for the transporta-

tion industry. IRD's cutting-edge products, systems, and solutions are able to solve transportation problems worldwide and improve highway efficiency and safety for users and operators. Technologies developed by IRD include truck weigh systems, toll systems, traffic control and data collection systems, traffic safety and advisory systems, and vehicle location systems based on wireless communications and GPS technology. IRD has installed these systems (known as Intelligent Transportation Systems) throughout Canada and in a host of countries around the world. IRD maintains sales and services offices in the United States, India, Brazil, and Columbia. In 2003, IRD employed 160 people and reported sales revenues of nearly $30 million, with roughly 90% of its sales generated through exports to the United States. *Iain Stewart*

FURTHER READING: Martin, P. 2003. "Saskatchewan's Top 100," *Saskatchewan Business* 24: 17–26.

INTERNMENT CAMPS: *see* **EATON INTERNMENT CAMP**

INTERPROVINCIAL MIGRATION. The comment is often heard that Saskatchewan's most valuable export is its young people. There is more than a grain of truth in this: the province's population has been kept at or near one million by the large number of Saskatchewan residents who move to other provinces.

Interprovincial statistics are best examined on a net basis–the number of people who move to the province relative to the number who leave. This is because Saskatchewan is a destination as well as a source for interprovincial migrants.

Figure IPM-1 shows interprovincial migration over the past thirty years (the most recent years are preliminary estimates). Several observations can be

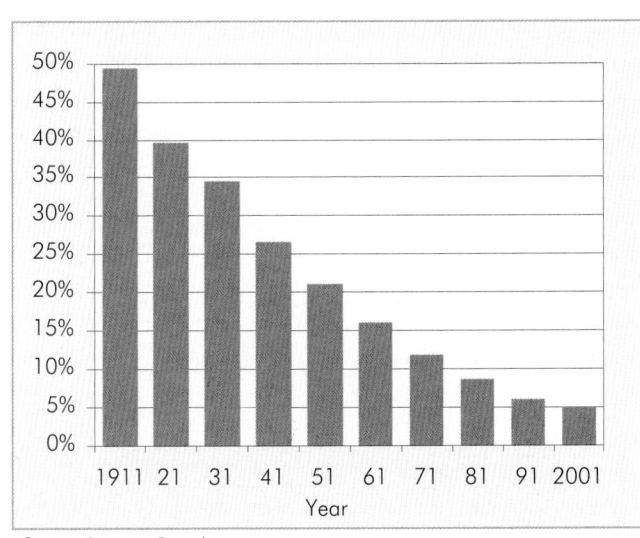

Source: Statistics Canada

Figure INIM-1. Percentage of Saskatchewan residents born outside Canada 1911 to 2001.

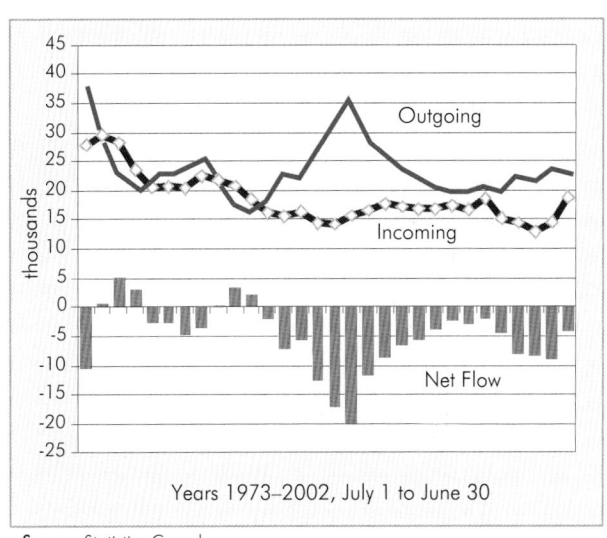

Source: Statistics Canada

Figure IPM-1. Interprovincial Migration to/from Saskatchewan, 1973-74 to 2002-03.

made about the flows, the most obvious one being that the net flow has only been positive for six of those thirty years. In and out migration were roughly in balance in the first ten years of the period, that is until the mid-1980s. The net outflow averaged just over 1,000 people per year, compared with an average of 9,000 per year from the mid-1980s to the mid-1990s. Out-migration has slowed in the last ten years, with an average outflow of 5,000 people per year.

Most of the province's interprovincial migrants –both those who come and those who leave–are young adults because they are the most mobile and arguably the most drawn to opportunities away from home: in the most recent ten years, 40% of those who left the province and 39% of those who came were in the 20–34 year age group. Alberta is the destination of choice for Canadian interprovincial migrants, and Saskatchewan is no exception. Indeed, the proximity of Alberta may be one of the reasons for the province's perennial migration outflow: over the most recent ten years, 55% of out-migrants have gone to Alberta. British Columbia is a distant second with 18% of out-migrants. Alberta is also the most common origin for people moving to Saskatchewan: over the same ten years, 46% of those moving to Saskatchewan from other provinces came from Alberta.

Saskatchewan is not the only province that loses people to interprovincial migration, although it is a major concern here. The young people who leave are the source for future population growth and major contributors to the economy as they work, build homes, and send their children to schools. They also tend to be the ones with the highest level of the education and often the most willing to accept change and do things differently. The province is therefore poorer without them. (*See also* **POPULATION TRENDS**) *Doug Elliott*

INTER-UNIVERSITY NETWORK. The first computer network connection between the two provincial universities began in the early 1980s, with the goal of enabling inter-library access to on-line catalogues. The connection speed at that time was 2,400 bits per second. By the mid-1980s, both universities helped to create NetNorth, the first national academic network with financial help from IBM Canada, which provided connections, at speeds of 9,600 bits per second, to BETNet in the United States and EARN in Europe. In 1989, the two universities built the Sask*net network and brought the internet to Saskatchewan as part of the national CA*net network. The connection speed available then was 56,000 bits per second. In the early 1990s, Canada's advanced internet organization (CANARIE) was formed; in 1994 it built the first national test network, CA*net1, which allowed the simple transfer of e-mail files. CA*net2, established in 1997, permitted sharing of web applications and large files.

Saskatchewan connected to CA*net3 in 2001, then the world's fastest internet backbone. CA*net4 was deployed in 2004: it is eight times faster than its predecessor, providing connection speeds of 10 billion bits per second. Universities, research organizations and businesses in the province are connected to the Canadian network though SRnet (Saskatchewan Research Network). SRnet provides the physical link between Saskatoon and Regina which permits direct access between the two universities. Their libraries are now interconnected with all other library resources in the province as part of a multitype library system. *Bob Kavanagh and Daryl Hepting*

IPSCO INC. The company known today as "IPSCO Inc.," one of the world's leading producers of steel plate and pipe, began its corporate life in Regina, Saskatchewan on July 13, 1956, as "Prairie Pipe Manufacturing Company Ltd." It was founded by a group of western Canadian businessmen led by **J.W. (BILL) SHARP**, the company's first president. The provincial government had completed an extensive amount of development work on a potential steel pipe plant that they had been pitching to German and American businessmen. When the foreign investors lost interest, Bill Sharp was asked to take up the project in May 1956. By mid-July his new company had been incorporated, with plans to build a small-diameter pipe mill primarily to serve the Saskatchewan market for welded line pipe. The project received no government subsidies and no loan guarantees, but as an incentive the govern-

ment-owned **SASKATCHEWAN POWER CORPORATION** agreed to purchase all its tubular requirements from Prairie Pipe between 1957 and 1960, and one-half of its needs for several years thereafter.

Prairie Pipe was successful from the start, and for a while its stock traded on the Winnipeg stock exchange. Some of its backers believed, however, that it would need its own steel supply to be successful: consequently, in 1957 many of the original pipe company investors formed a new enterprise named "Interprovincial Steel Corporation" and proceeded to build a small steel mill on property adjacent to Prairie Pipe, supported in this case by provincial government-backed loan guarantees. While the pipe company's success continued, the steel company ran into financial difficulties, and in 1959 Prairie Pipe purchased all the assets of Interprovincial Steel Corporation, which consisted of a partially built steel mill and significant liabilities. The merger of the two businesses resulted in the government of Saskatchewan becoming a minor shareholder in the enlarged company (this interest was disposed of in the mid-1980s). Prairie Pipe changed its name to "Interprovincial Steel and Pipe Corporation," and in 1960 began production of steel; the company soon came to be known as "IPSCO," and in 1984 this became its formal name.

By the mid-1960s Bill Sharp was no longer actively involved in the day-to-day business, and in 1965 **JACK TURVEY** was made president. He and his successor, Jim Maclennan, ran IPSCO from the early 1960s until 1982, during which time the company

Rolling mill, IPSCO, February 1960.

became the major producer of pipe and steel in western Canada through a combination of its own internal growth (four new furnaces, a new rolling mill, and major large-diameter pipe capacity using a new and innovative "spiral pipe" technology from Germany) and the purchase of various pipe mills (Canadian Phoenix Steel and Pipe Ltd. mills in Edmonton, Alberta and Port Moody, BC, as well as a number of smaller manufacturing facilities in the three western provinces). In 1982 ROGER PHILLIPS succeeded Jim Maclennan as president and CEO. In 1981, the company had produced 389,000 ingot tons of steel; when Phillips retired almost twenty years later, the company's steel-making capacity had reached 3.5 million tons. A number of developments contributed to growth. The first was development of a continuous caster and reheat furnace at the Regina steel mill, which radically improved the quality and capacity of the steelworks. Subsequent to that, the company purchased a number of downstream facilities (primarily in the United States) to provide markets for steel from the expanded Regina facility. In the early 1990s, the company began to build a revolutionary new plate mill in the United States, incorporating much of the technology developed in Regina with some of the ideas for thinner slab casters and in-line production which had spawned the mini-mill sheet revolution in the US; this new plate mill enabled IPSCO to improve plate product at a significantly lower cost. The first such mill was built between 1994 and 1997 in Iowa, and a second twin mill was erected between 1999 and 2001 in Alabama.

When the company began this expansion, Stelco, US Steel and Bethlehem Steel were dominant forces and major suppliers of plate steel in the North American steel industry. By 2004, the first two had vacated the plate market and the third had gone bankrupt, although its facilities were still in production under a different owner. Over the same period, IPSCO became the premier supplier of plate in the North American steel industry. To round out the company's steel processing facilities, new cut-to-length and temper lines were installed in new manufacturing plants in Toronto and Houston, and upgraded processing facilities were added in Regina and Surrey. During this growth phase, the company expanded its tubular facilities with a new plant in Blythville, Arkansas, and upgraded facilities at several other locations in both Canada and the United States. At the turn of the century, most of IPSCO's assets and customers were located in the US, leading the company to establish its operational headquarters in the suburbs of Chicago. However, IPSCO remains a Canadian company, with its registered office and significant manufacturing facilities in Regina. In early 2002, David Sutherland, a native of Moose Jaw, assumed the role of president and CEO. IPSCO's shares in 2004 were widely held and traded on both the Toronto and New York Stock Exchanges. *John Comrie and Roger Phillips*

IRISH SETTLEMENTS. Irish place names in Saskatchewan do not necessarily indicate Irish settlement: for example, Limerick has been settled by Romanians; Meath Park by Ukrainians; and Shamrock and Wynyard by Icelanders. Other Irish place names include the Enniskillen district near Oxbow, Erinferry near Big River, and the Connaught district near Tisdale. Street names in North Portal are northern Irish: Belfast, Ulster, Antrim, Clair—revealing the origin of the first station agent. Some communities have been named after Irish-Canadian politicians of renown, such as D'Arcy and McGee (after Thomas D'Arcy McGee, a father of Confederation), and Davin (after Irish-born NICHOLAS FLOOD DAVIN, who founded the *Regina Leader* and later served as a member of Parliament). People of Irish origin tended to scatter throughout Saskatchewan; yet Irish settlers concentrated in Shamrock RM 134, north of Gravelbourg, and Erinvale SD no. 3271.

The "Irish Colony" around Sinnett was originally founded in 1905 by Fr. John Sinnett, a secular priest at the time. Born in Ridgetown, Ontario in 1855, he had served in the Jesuits from 1884 to 1894, during which period he was the priest in Sheenboro, a strongly Irish area in Quebec across the Ottawa River from Pembroke, Ontario. He later returned to recruit Irish-Canadian settlers to form an Irish colony in Saskatchewan, together with Irish settlers from Prince Edward Island and immigrants directly from Ireland. Fr. Sinnett was an influential and active priest, who served in Regina before becoming Rector and Vicar-General of the Prince Albert Diocese. He established the parish of St. Ignatius in 1906 (a new church was constructed in 1915, replaced by a larger church in 1928), then St. Patrick's in 1908. Fr. Sinnett returned to Ontario in 1922 to rejoin the Jesuits, and died in 1928 without seeing the new church. Among Irish family names of homesteaders were Laverty, McEachern, Devine, McDonald, Hearn, Coughlin, Sullivan, Bevan, McGuire, and Doyle (including "Scots-Irish" originally from Northern Ireland). A railway line passed through Sinnett in 1921, and stores and grain elevators were established there and in nearby Leroy. Today, the railway closed and elevator gone, Sinnett has all but disappeared, and Leroy is dormant. Of 139,205 people in Saskatchewan claiming Irish origin (2001 Census), 11,155 (8%) claimed Irish-only origin and 128,045 (92%) partly Irish origin.

Alan Anderson

FURTHER READING: Barry, B. 1997. *People Places: Saskatchewan and Its Names*. Regina: Canadian Plains Research Center; Coughlin, J. 1995. *The Irish Colony of Saskatchewan*. Scarborough, Ontario: Lochleven Publishers.

IRRIGATION. Irrigation is the age-old agricultural practice of supplying water to land through artificial means. Irrigation increases crop yields and reduces the risk of crop failure for producers.

The first irrigation schemes in Saskatchewan pre-date the Northwest Irrigation Act, which was passed in 1894 by the Dominion government to regulate use of water for irrigation. Late 19th-century settlers near Maple Creek in the province's southwest used canals to divert water from streams on to adjacent hay lands. In 1930, the federal government transferred authority over water resources to the provinces. The Saskatchewan government immediately put much larger and more advanced irrigation systems into place in the province's drought-ravaged southwest. Between 1935 and 1950, the federal PRAIRIE FARM REHABILITATION ADMINISTRATION assisted the province in its rehabilitation of the southwest by constructing irrigation works near Val Marie, Eastend, Consul, Maple Creek, and Swift Current. Today, nearly 350,000 acres of land are irrigated in Saskatchewan, mostly in the southwest and west-central regions of the province. These regions have reliable sources of quality water (e.g., the SOUTH SASKATCHEWAN RIVER, FRENCHMAN RIVER, Swift Current Creek) that make irrigation development feasible. The province's most extensively irrigated region is around LAKE DIEFENBAKER, a large reservoir formed by the Gardiner and Qu'Appelle River dams. More than 100,000 acres of cultivated land near Lake Diefenbaker benefit from irrigation. In Saskatchewan, irrigation is used largely for forage and cereal crops, but also for oilseeds, pulses, horticulture, herbs and spices.

REGINA LEADER-POST

Sprinkler irrigation system.

Irrigation has made possible in Saskatchewan the successful production of non-traditional crops such as beans, potatoes, timothy hay, and native fruit. Water for irrigation is extracted primarily from surficial sources such as streams, rivers, lakes, dugouts, reservoirs, and wetlands. Groundwater from aquifers provides a secondary source. Irrigators in Saskatchewan use two methods of application: sprinkler and surface. Sprinklers deliver water to farmer's fields via above-ground high-pressure sprayers; surface, or "flood," irrigation uses dykes, ditches, and furrows to channel and confine water to a field. Irrigation has played a valuable role in stabilizing crop production and diversifying Saskatchewan's economy. In 1986, the Canada-Saskatchewan Irrigation Diversification Centre was established at Outlook, near Lake Diefenbaker. The Centre is a joint federal-provincial agency that promotes economic development and rural sustainability through its extensive irrigation research programs.

Iain Stewart

FURTHER READING: Fung, K. (ed.). 1999. *Atlas of Saskatchewan*. Saskatoon: University of Saskatchewan.

IRVIN, JAMES DICKINSON, JR. (DICK) (1932–).

Born in Calgary in 1932, Irvin was educated in Regina and later received his BComm from McGill University in Montreal, where his father, Dick Irvin Sr., was coach of the Canadiens hockey team. Following a short career with Shell Oil, Irvin was hired as assistant sports director for Montreal's CFCF-TV and CFCF Radio in 1961. He was promoted to sports director one year later, and remained in that position until his retirement in 1991. While working for the CTV affiliate in Montreal, Irvin Jr. joined CBC-TV's *Hockey Night in Canada* as a freelance broadcaster in 1966. To viewers of the program, Irvin is best known for his play-by-play coverage of the Montreal Canadiens. He also broadcast the teams' non-televised games on CFCF Radio from 1969 to 1997. Although he retired from *Hockey Night in Canada* in 1999, Irvin continues to host special sporting events for the public network. The author of six books on hockey, Dick Irvin is a 1988 media honouree of the Hockey Hall of Fame.

Elizabeth Mooney

FURTHER READING: Irvin, D. 2001. *My 26 Stanley Cups: Memories of a Hockey Life*. Toronto: McClelland & Stewart.

IRVINE, ACHESON GOSFORD (1837–1916).

Acheson Gosford Irvine was born in Québec in 1837. He joined the militia in 1864 and served with the Québec Rifles in Manitoba on the Red River Expeditionary Force in 1870. Following the Red River Rebellion, Irvine remained in Manitoba, where he was the provincial infantry commander. After

being promoted to Lieutenant Colonel in 1872, Irvine joined the North-West Mounted Police (NWMP) in 1875, was appointed Assistant Commissioner in 1876, and became the NWMP's fourth Commissioner from 1880 to 1886. On March 26, 1885, Commissioner Irvine led a force of 83 NWMP members and 25 civilian volunteers from Prince Albert to Fort Carlton to relieve the forces of Superintendent **LEIF CROZIER**. Before the relief column arrived, Crozier engaged in battle at **DUCK LAKE** with the **MÉTIS** forces of **GABRIEL DUMONT**. Twelve of his men were killed, and eleven were wounded; four Métis and one Indian were killed, and three were wounded before Crozier's men could retreat to Fort Carlton. The following day, Commissioner Irvine decided to abandon Fort Carlton. During the pullout, a fire broke out in the hospital, which spread to engulf the entire fort, burning it to the ground. The combined forces of Irvine and Crozier successfully retreated to Prince Albert on March 28, 1885. Irvine was criticized for his inaction during the 1885 Resistance and forced to resign in 1886. Irvine also served as a member of the Executive Council of the North-West Territories from 1882 to 1886. Following his retirement in 1886 he became warden at Stony Mountain Penitentiary in Manitoba until 1913, and then warden of Kingston Penitentiary from 1913 to 1914. He was awarded the Imperial Service order in 1902. He died in Quebec on January 9, 1916.

Daria Coneghan and Peter Borch

FURTHER READING: Klancher, D.J. 1999. *The North-West Mounted Police and the North-West Rebellion*. Kamloops, BC: Goss Publishers; Wallace, J. 1998. *A Trying Time: The North-West Mounted Police in the 1885 Rebellion*. Winnipeg: Bunker to Bunker Books.

ISLAND LAKE BAND (MINISTIKWAN INDIAN RESERVE).

With no recognized chief when they entered **TREATY 6** in 1876, this Cree band was erroneously considered part of Seekaskootch's band (Onion Lake) and received a reserve allotment

there. In 1907 the Ministikwan people petitioned the Department of Indian Affairs for their own reserve, and they obtained satisfaction in 1909. Their request that the reserve completely follow the lake's shoreline to protect their fish stock from depletion by fishing companies was not heeded when Indian Affairs created the Island Lake Reserve on August 3, 1911, for the people from Ministikwan, Makwa, Horse Lake, Hollow Lake and Lac des Isles. Without the consent of either party, the Bighead and Loon Lake Bands were also included, and when they refused to locate at Island Lake, 10,279 acres were removed from the reserve in 1914. Lacking sufficient viable farmland, people continued to trap, fish, and hunt, supplementing this with gardens and employment with the lumber industry. The 11,120.6-ha reserve is located 161 km northwest of North Battleford; 807 of the 1,139 band members live on reserve.

Christian Thompson

ITUNA, town, pop 709, located 55 km NW of Melville on Hwys 15 and 310. The first settlers began making incursions into the area in the 1880s and 1890s; however, in the first few years of the 20th century a wave of people of British origins began to take up homesteads in the district. With the construction of the **GRAND TRUNK PACIFIC RAILWAY** through the region in 1907–08, the townsite began to develop. The railway brought to the district an influx of Ukrainian settlers, who would enrich the community with their cultural heritage. The Ituna post office was established in 1909, and in 1910 the young community was incorporated. Ituna developed as the major distribution and service centre for the surrounding agricultural district; in 1966, it reached a peak population of 975. Agriculture remains the basis of the Ituna area economy, and two grain companies and numerous trucking services handle agricultural exports. A variety of crops are grown in the district, and cattle and hog operations add diversity to the area's agricultural production.

David McLennan

COURTESY OF THE ITUNA AND DISTRICT MUSEUM

Ituna, 1911. Ituna's first postmaster, S.A. Veals, is in the wagon with two horses in the centre of the photo. Buildings in the background include, from right to left, the Ituna Livery Stable, the hardware store (with the staircase-shaped roof), the post office (with veranda), the Bank of British North America, and the pool room (with sign visible).

J

JACKSON, TOM (1948–). Born on October 27, 1948, on the One Arrow Reserve and raised in Winnipeg, Tom Jackson quit school at 15 and chose to live on Winnipeg's back streets, where he developed his skills as a multi-talented entertainer and entrepreneur. He became a household name with his role as Chief Peter Kenidi in *North of 60*, and has appeared in a number of other series including *Sesame Street*, *Street Legal*, *Star Trek: the Next Generation*, *Shining Time Station*, and the *Longhouse Tales*. Theatre and acting roles include *The Ecstasy of Rita Joe*, *Dry Lips Oughta Move to Kapuskasing*, *Medicine River*, *The Diviners* (Gemini nomination), *Loyalties* (Genie nomination), *Grizzly Falls*, and *Water Giant*. Jackson's strong bass baritone is widely recognized as the narrator, among others, of *The Snow Eater*, *Great Canadian Rivers*, *Chiefs*, and *500 Nations*. As a singer and songwriter he has recorded twelve albums (two of which have received Juno nomina-

PHOTO BY BILL BORGWANDT

Tom Jackson, in concert.

tions), but claims that while music is his first love he feels his true calling is helping people whose plight is ignored by the larger society. Jackson is well known for organizing the Huron Carole benefit concerts which for the past sixteen years have raised money for the Canadian Association of Food Banks (CAFB); in addition to donating his time, Jackson offers his share of sales from his seventh album, *That Side of the Window*, to the CAFB.

His continued desire to help others is inspirational, and many individuals and organizations donate their time and facilities in support of his initiatives. Further examples are the Red River Relief Benefit (1997), for flood relief in Manitoba; Say Hay (2002), for drought-stricken prairie farmers; his collaboration with Calgary-based industries to create Beef Relief (2003), which provided cash and beef contributions for the Calgary Inter-Faith Food Bank; and his many appearances on Saskatchewan's Kinsmen Telemiracle. Jackson came face to face with a tragic event in October 1996 when a fellow *North of 60* cast member committed suicide: in response, Jackson initiated the Dreamcatcher Tour, a sixteen-stop tour delivering a message of empowerment to communities suffering the loss of life to suicide. So great was the response that the tours continued for the next eight years. Jackson's urge to help others has earned him the David Crowchild Award, the C.F. Martin Humanitarian Award, the Saskatchewan Country Music Association International Achievement Award, the Saskatchewan Distinguished Service Award, and the National Aboriginal Achievement Award. He has been appointed an Officer of the Order of Canada (2000), has received the Queen's Jubilee medal (2002), and was named one of Canada's prominent activists by Time Magazine. Jackson has received honorary degrees from several Canadian universities.

Christian Thompson

JACKSON, WILLIAM HENRY (1861–1952).

William Henry Jackson was born in Ontario in 1861. He studied Classics at the University of Toronto for three years, and in 1882 followed his parents to Prince Albert. As one of the most well-educated men in the district, Jackson became the secretary of the local Farmer's Union, and in this capacity met **LOUIS RIEL** in the summer of 1884. Jackson became convinced that the grievances of the **MÉTIS** were legitimate and, sympathetic to their cause, moved to **BATOCHE**, where he acted as Riel's secretary. He converted to Roman Catholicism and subsequently accepted Riel's reformed Christianity. Once fighting broke out, however, the Métis became concerned about his loyalty and placed him under arrest following the clash at **DUCK LAKE** in March 1885. Ironically, the Canadian forces also arrested Jackson when they captured Batoche six weeks later.

Charged with "treason-felony," Jackson was found not guilty by reason of insanity, in a trial that lasted less than half an hour. Committed to the "Selkirk Asylum," he escaped two weeks before Riel's execution, and fled to the United States. There, he presented himself as a Métis, and in 1886 changed his name to Honoré Jaxon (the French pronunciation of "Jackson"). Settling in Chicago, he became involved in the labour movement.

In 1907 Jaxon, as he was now known, returned to Saskatchewan and ran for Parliament as an Independent the following year; he was overwhelmingly defeated. He was active for a short time in Saskatoon labour issues, and was an early and enthusiastic convert to the **BAHÁ'Í** faith. Discouraged with life in Canada, however, he returned to Chicago, where he sank into obscurity. At some point in the 1920s he moved to New York, and began to collect books, newspapers and pamphlets, becoming in the process somewhat of a local curiosity who was referred to in the New York dailies as a "human packrat." He acted as a janitor for an apartment building, but was evicted on December 13, 1951. His personal library was packed into boxes—forming a pile 2 metres high, 3 metres across, and 11 metres long—and was hauled away and burned. Jaxon himself died a few weeks later on January 10, 1952, in New York at the age of 90, his role in the **NORTH-WEST RESISTANCE** all but forgotten.

Brian Mlazgar

FURTHER READING: Smith, Donald B. 1986. "Rip Van Jaxon: The Return of Riel's Secretary in 1884–1885 to the Canadian West, 1907–1909." Pp. 211–23 in F. Laurie Barron and James B. Waldram (eds.), *1885 and After: Native Society in Transition*. Regina: Canadian Plains Research Center.

JAMES SMITH CREE NATION. James Smith

arrived in 1875 from the St. Peter's Reserve in Manitoba and signed **TREATY 6** on August 23, 1876. In 1884 a reserve was surveyed for the band 58 km east of Prince Albert. After the 1885 Resistance, the Big Head Band under Chief Saddle Water asked permission to join James Smith, and it was granted. There are currently three specific claims by descended members of the James Smith, Chakastaypasin, and Peter Chapman bands against the federal government. The first claim concerns the surrender of the Chakastaypasin Reserve (IR 98): in 1898, members of the Chakastaypasin Band were added to other bands (including James Smith) when the federal government removed their reserve from reserve status; Chakastaypasin descendants want the re-establishment of their band and reserve, claiming it was never formally surrendered. The second claim concerns the Peter Chapman Band, also known as Cumberland Band (IR 100A), which was amalgamated with the James Smith Cree in 1902: while part of the 100A was surrendered on October 14,

part was also used to enlarge the James Smith Reserve. This leads to the third and final claim by the descendants of the original James Smith Band: that they did not receive sufficient acres when their reserve was surveyed in 1884, whereas the government argues that the land added from the 1902 amalgamation of the Peter Chapman Band more than makes up for any discrepancy. In the meantime, the band's infrastructure includes 15,099.5 ha of land, on which there are a band office, fire hall, teacherages, arena, the Bernard Constant Community School, and the Margaret Turner Health Centre. Economic development has involved land lease revenue, agriculture and ranching, while some of the more recent programs include the James Smith Daycare, Sakwatamo Lodge, and James Smith Health Clinic. There are 2,692 band members, of whom 1,742 live on the reserve. *Christian Thompson*

JAMES, COLIN (1964–). From blues to swing to

rock and roll, Colin James, who once failed his high school music program, has become an institution in Canadian music culture. Born Colin Munn in Regina on August 17, 1964, James was drawn to folk and blues in his early teens, took up the guitar, and attended Sheldon-Williams Collegiate in Regina before quitting school to pursue his musical dreams with his first band, The Hoodoo Men. The group went on to perform at the Winnipeg Folk Festival, and also at clubs for blues artists ranging from John Lee Hooker to George Thorogood. In 1983, Munn moved to Vancouver and caught his big break with a band called The Night Shades. After opening a show for Stevie Ray Vaughan in Saskatoon, so impressed was Vaughan with Munn's guitar wizardry that he enlisted him to open the remainder of

BRYAN SCHLOSSER/REGINA LEADER-POST

Colin James, in concert, August 1994.

his Canadian tour, talked him into changing his last name to James, and encouraged him to start his own band.

In 1988, James finally released his self-titled debut on the Virgin/EMI label; on the strength of singles such as "Voodoo Thing," "Chicks and Cars," and "Five Long Years," it became the fastest-selling debut in Canadian music history. He followed this with the album "Sudden Stop" in 1990, before his first foray into swing and jazz with "Colin James and the Little Big Band" in 1993. The latter became a double-platinum smash, which led to several opening slots on the Rolling Stones' Voodoo Lounge tour in 1994. After exploring the heavy driving blues which dominated the "Bad Habits" album in 1995 and the spare, bare-bones collection of Delta blues classics that marked 1997's "National Steel," James revisited his love of 1940s and 1950s swing with "Colin James and The Little Big Band II" in 1998. In 2004, he released "Traveler," which offers a more contemporary jazz sound. He tours extensively during the summer jazz, folk and rock festival season, and lives in Vancouver. *Gerry Krochak*

SASKATCHEWAN ARCHIVES BOARD R-B5706

Florence James.

JAMES, FLORENCE (1892–1988). Born on October 27, 1892, in Pocatello, Idaho to Irish immigrants, Florence James studied elocution at Emerson College, Massachusetts. Her marriage to Burton James in 1917 produced a daughter, Maryjo, and a more than thirty-year theatrical partnership.

Fleeing the commercialism of the New York theatre, the couple taught at the Cornish School (1923–28) and University of Washington, Seattle (1930s). They also founded the Seattle Repertory Playhouse (1928–50). The founding of the Negro Repertory Theatre group (1934–39) and a school-touring program (1936–39) furthered the Playhouse's reputation for quality in-house training as well as innovative, socially active programming. The Jameses also

frequently visited western Canada (1933–51) to adjudicate and teach summer school (University of British Columbia and Banff).

Losing the theatre in 1950 and widowed in 1951 during the McCarthy era, James worked between New York and Saskatchewan (1950–53). Her work as guest director/teacher for the Regina Little Theatre and Summer School of the Arts led to her appointment as first drama consultant for the **SASKATCHEWAN ARTS BOARD** (1953–68). Concentrating more on community drama, James travelled throughout Saskatchewan teaching, adjudicating and assisting. She also served as dramaturge/consultant for the **GLOBE THEATRE** (1968–78). Drawn by the opportunity to do pioneering theatrical work within a socialist system, James strongly assisted the transition from community to professional theatre in Saskatchewan. James died on January 18, 1988.

Moira Day

FURTHER READING: James, Florence Bean. "Fists Upon a Star." Unpublished autobiography. Florence James papers, University of Washington, Department of Special Collections. Seattle, Washington, USA; Florence James Papers.University Archives and Special Collections. University of Regina, Regina, Saskatchewan.

JAMES, GERRY (1934–). Born in Regina on October 22, 1934, Gerry James was one of the last Canadian athletes to compete simultaneously in two professional sports. At age 17, he signed with the CFL's Winnipeg Blue Bombers and joined the roster for the 1952 season. The first recipient of the Schenley All-Canadian Award in 1954, he won the trophy a second time in 1957 after sitting out the previous season. James helped the Blue Bombers to Grey Cup titles in 1958, 1959, 1961 and 1962. He missed the 1963 CFL campaign, and played his last season of professional football with the **SASKATCH-EWAN ROUGHRIDERS** in 1964. He holds the CFL record for most post-season games played with thirty-six. Beginning in 1951, James played four seasons of junior hockey with the Toronto Marlboros, winning the 1955 Memorial Cup championship over the Regina Pats. He earned a spot on the roster of the Toronto Maple Leafs from 1955 to 1957, but split the following year between Toronto and the Rochester Americans minor league team before returning to the Blue Bombers. Although he missed the entire 1958-59 NHL season due to an injury sustained in a September 1958 CFL game, James won the 1959 Grey Cup with the Bombers and later helped the Maple Leafs reach the Stanley Cup final in April 1960. He became the only player in history to participate in the Grey Cup and Stanley Cup championships in the same season. After five seasons with the Leafs, James coached HC Davos in Switzerland and the Yorkton Terriers (1972–74, 1980–84), Melville Millionaires (1975–80), and Estevan Bruins

(1984–87). He was also the Terriers' owner from 1980 until 1984, and coach of the Western Hockey League's Moose Jaw Warriors in 1987–88. Gerry James was inducted into the Canadian Football Hall of Fame in 1981 and the **SASKATCHEWAN SPORTS HALLS OF FAME** in 1994.

Daria Coneghan and Holden Stoffel

FURTHER READING: Podnieks, A. et al. 2002. *Kings of the Ice: A History of World Hockey.* Richmond Hill, ON: NDE Publishing.

JAPANESE BALLOON BOMBING. In the final year of **WORLD WAR II**, Japan developed a new weapon for use against the Allies in a last-ditch attempt to retaliate for her losses. Between November 1944 and July 1945, Japan released over 9,000 bomb-bearing balloons against the continental United States and Canada. Each paper balloon carried one high-explosive bomb and several incendiary devices designed to start massive fires in the forests of North America. Once released, these balloons drifted eastward on the prevailing winds and jet stream, crossing the Pacific Ocean in approximately sixty hours. Air Force pilots, stationed on the west coast and in the Aleutian Islands, shot down many balloons but over 1,000 reached their targets, some drifting inland as far as Michigan. Many were never found; but out of the 285 incidents recorded by the Smithsonian Institute of Washington, eight bombs descended in Saskatchewan. All reports of sightings were immediately suppressed by strict military censorship. Six more balloons landed in Manitoba.

Confirmed sites in Saskatchewan and the dates (all in 1945) were recorded as follows: Stoney Rapids (January 1), Minton (January 12), Moose Jaw (February 9), Porcupine Plain (February 22), Camsell Portage (March 21), Consul (March 30), Ituna (March 31), Kelvington (May 15).

There were no reports of serious damage at any of the sites in Saskatchewan or elsewhere in Canada. In the United States, however, five youths and an adult were killed when a group of picnickers detonated a live Japanese bomb that had come down in a forested area of Oregon. Ironically, a balloon bomb also destroyed the power source to an atomic research plant in Washington State; this power outage briefly interrupted production of the two atomic bombs which were being prepared for delivery to Hiroshima and Nagasaki. *Harold J. Fenske*

JAQUES, EDNA (1891–1978). Lecturer, author and poet, Edna Jaques was a popular figure throughout Canada. Her poems sometimes depicted the harsh beauty of the prairies, but above all they celebrated the daily experiences of domestic life. Born in Collingwood, Ontario, on January 17, 1891, she moved with her family to a homestead southeast of Moose Jaw in 1902. Her education included business college in Vancouver; in 1921 she married Ernest Jamieson, and they had one daughter. The family later homesteaded in the Tisdale area; but after four years Jaques returned south, and she and her daughter lived at various places in Saskatchewan and elsewhere. Jaque's reputation as a popular poet grew rapidly during the 1930s. She had always loved poetry, and at 14 had first published poems in the *Moose Jaw Times*. In 1932 this newspaper produced her first two poetry collections, which sold quickly. Subsequent volumes did well too, and her poems appeared in newspapers across Canada; her best-known poem, "In Flanders Now," was placed in the chapel at Arlington Cemetery near Washington, DC. She also wrote newspaper and magazine articles. A popular speaker, Jaques's first appearance was at the Moose Jaw Women's Canadian Club (1929); her touring ventures, often supported by the Women's Canadian Club, burgeoned, and she spoke regularly to diverse audiences across Canada. She died on September 13, 1978, in Toronto.   *Lisa Dale-Burnett*

FURTHER READING: Jaques, E. 1977. *Uphill All the Way*. Saskatoon: Western Producer Prairie Books.

JAQUES, LOUIS B. (1911–97).

Born in Toronto on July 11, 1911, Jaques received his PhD from the University of Toronto in 1941, as a member of the research team of Dr. Charles H. Best. He came to the UNIVERSITY OF SASKATCHEWAN in 1946 as professor and head of the Department of Physiology, a post he held until 1971.

His world-renowned research group studied various aspects of blood clotting, in particular the chemistry and biology of heparin as an anticoagulant. They demonstrated great variability in the chemical and biological properties of heparin preparations, and were instrumental in the development of the first International Heparin Standard. Jaques' tireless efforts led to trials of intrapulmonary administration of heparin, thus avoiding the discomfort of repeated injections in patients requiring prolonged therapy. His group also pioneered the cellular pool hypothesis, the concept that heparin is stored in cells and is released slowly into the blood—providing an explanation for its prolonged clinical effectiveness. After retirement in 1979, Jaques continued to bring new ideas to the heparin story, in particular the possibility of oral administration.

Because of the work of this distinguished pioneer in medical science, many lives were saved, for without heparin the development of open-heart surgery would have been impossible.

Jaques was the author of 220 scientific articles. In 1952 he was elected a Fellow of the Royal Society of Canada, and in 1977 he was awarded the Heart Foundation of Canada Outstanding Service Award as well as a Certificate of Appreciation by the Canadian Hemophilia Society. He died in Toronto on May 16, 1997.   *Armin Wollin*

JAXON, HONORÉ: *see* JACKSON, WILLIAM HENRY

JENSEN, ELEANOR (1940–).

Eleanor Jensen (*née* Haslam) of Saskatoon excelled as Canada's best woman sprinter in the late 1950s. Born on September 11, 1940, Jensen represented Canada at the 1956 Melbourne Olympiad. The following year, she was rated the nation's best 60- and 100-yard sprinter, and second-best 220-yard runner. 1958 was Jensen's most outstanding year in track and field: she won five gold medals at the Western Canada Games, and placed first in three events at the British Empire and Commonwealth Games trials in Saskatoon. Jensen also set new Canadian records in the 100- and 220-yard races. At the games in Cardiff, Wales later that year, she anchored the 440-yard relay team to a bronze medal and was a finalist in the 220-yard sprint. She set a new Canadian record in the 100-yard event and was named Canada's Outstanding University Athlete at the end of the year. Jensen was a member of the Canadian Olympic team at the 1960 Rome Olympiad. She posted Canada's best times in the 100-, 200-, and 800-metre women's events. Jensen was installed in the SASKATCHEWAN SPORTS HALL OF FAME in 1974.

Bob Ivanochko and Holden Stoffel

JEROME, HARRY (1940–82).

Born in Prince Albert on September 30, 1940, Harry Jerome was the first man to hold both the 100-metre and 100-yard world track and field records. As a student at the University of Oregon in 1960, Jerome ran the 100-metre sprint in 10.0 seconds, tying German Armin Hary's world record; two years later, he ran the 100 yards in 9.2 seconds, equaling the mark set by Frank Budd and Bob Hayes. At the 1960 Olympic Summer Games in Rome, Jerome suffered a pulled muscle during the 100-metre qualifying heats and failed to win a medal. A torn thigh muscle kept him off the medal podium at the 1962 Commonwealth Games. Despite these serious injuries, Jerome won a bronze medal in the 100-metre event at the 1964 Tokyo Olympics. Later that year, he broke two more world records, first as part of the University of Oregon relay team, then finishing the 60-yard dash in six seconds flat. In 1966, he improved his world record time in the 100-yard event to 9.1 seconds, and won gold at the Commonwealth Games, an achievement he repeated at the 1967 Pan American Games. He competed in his last Olympic Games in 1968. Harry Jerome went on to join Sport Canada as a teacher and consultant. Awarded the Order of Canada and inducted to the Canadian Sports Hall of Fame in 1971, he died of a brain aneurism on December 7, 1982. The city of Prince Albert named the track complex built for the 1992 Saskatchewan Summer Games in honour of Harry Jerome. *Elizabeth Mooney*

JEWISH COMMUNITY, SASKATOON.

Saskatoon's Jewish community has been productive and colourful ever since 1907, when William and Fanny Landa, Saskatoon's first Jewish family, moved into their dugout along the South Saskatchewan River bank. Other Jewish people followed. In spite of difficult pioneering conditions, formal religious services began around 1908. In 1910, the community hired its first religious slaughterer and a Hebrew teacher.

DIVISION OF AUDIO-VISUAL SERVICES PHOTO/UNIVERSITY OF SASKATCHEWAN ARCHIVES A-10398

L.B. Jaques (behind), Linda Hiebert (left), and technician Sandra Wice study a slide showing endothelial cells and heparin.

Classes were held in the Cahill Block; a year later, the community moved the classes to a permanent Talmud Torah. Land was also purchased for a Jewish cemetery; the following year, 1912, a synagogue was built. Saskatoon's early Jewish residents were a very diverse group of people with little or no money and few skills. Some were Americans, the progeny of families who had emigrated from Europe to the United States. Some, like the Landa family, homesteaded first, then moved to the city. Most, however, had immigrated from many eastern European countries to Saskatchewan's larger cities. With the exception of the Americans, very few spoke English on their arrival. They spoke Yiddish; some never learned to speak English fluently, and the Americans rarely learned to speak Yiddish. They ranged in religious belief from free-thinking communists to ultra-orthodox. While the members of the new community came from different parts of Europe and the United States and integrated in the society-at-large in different ways, they not only helped but sometimes also supported one another financially. On the other hand, their differences on occasion created tensions within the community.

Perhaps it was these tensions and the diversity which gave energy to the community. As early as 1912, Jewish organizations mushroomed. Despite their small number, the American English-speaking members exerted considerable influence. During the earliest days, social life was centred in the Jewish community itself, in the homes and the synagogue. With time, entertainment, both home-grown and imported, became significant: for example, in 1915 the B'nai Brith produced minstrel shows. Sports also played a prominent role in the lives of young Jewish men: the Jewish hockey team was part of Saskatoon's "Church League," and during the 1930s and 1940s the Young Men's Hebrew Association had a very successful softball team. The dominant society's attitude towards Jews was restrictive: the Bay, for instance, did not hire Jews. However, some non-Jewish businesses and organizations had their "token Jew" on staff.

Married women who wished to work outside the home faced anti-Semitism. Nevertheless, Saskatoon's Jewish women have always been involved in many fund-raising ventures: the Talmud Torah's Ladies' Aid had a bazaar in 1922 in support of the Talmud Torah and other charities; the Hadassah bazaar was a mainstay in Saskatoon for many years; and Clare Boothe's play "The Women" was presented in 1956 by the Greystone Theatre of the UNIVERSITY OF SASKATCHEWAN, with the co-operation of the Saskatoon Section of the National Council of Jewish Women. In more recent times the annual Silver Spoon Dinner, sponsored by the Saskatoon Jewish community and Saskatoon Hadassah-Wizo, has presented the Silver Spoon Sterling Award to a woman from Saskatoon and

area for her voluntary contribution and service. Their proceeds are divided between the Saskatoon Crisis Nursery and Interval House to combat prejudice against married women participating in the workforce. Many Jewish women worked with their husbands in family businesses. Knowing from the time of their arrival what conditions prevailed, most Jewish people in Saskatoon either worked for other Jews or opened their own small businesses. **WORLD WAR II** had a profound effect on the Jews of Saskatoon: there was hardly a home which was not touched by it. Of the city's 700 Jews, 111 were part of armed forces. After the war ended, an increasingly large number of Jewish young people went to university and became professionals. (*See also* **JEWISH RURAL SETTLEMENTS**, **SASKATCHEWAN INTERCULTURAL ASSOCIATION**) *Anna Feldman*

JEWISH RURAL SETTLEMENTS. Jews, who for many years were not allowed the privilege of farming in Europe, were among the first groups to establish agricultural settlements in western Canada. Their arrival coincided with a period of active immigration: Canada wanted to populate the west, and many of the Jewish newcomers, inspired by the "back to the land movement," wanted to farm. With land as the incentive as well as immigration propaganda and improved services, the Department of the Interior admitted people not only from the United States and Great Britain, the preferred countries, but from continental Europe as well. Jews, who at other times in Canadian history were subjected to many restrictions, were also welcomed then. However, unlike several groups including the Mennonites who were encouraged to settle blocs of land, the government ruled that the Jews could not do so: they had

to be interspersed with their non-Jewish neighbours.

The first attempt at Jewish farm colonization in Canada took place after a public outcry against the 1881 Russian pogroms. At that time, Sir Alexander T. Galt, Canadian High Commissioner in London, convinced Sir John A. Macdonald that assisting several hundred impoverished Jews to emigrate from Russia to Canada would be advantageous to both the refugees and to Canada. In May 1882, the future pioneers arrived in Montreal; 247 were sent to Winnipeg. When the government finally allocated land for them in 1884, only two-fifths of the original group remained. Twenty-six families formed the settlement of New Jerusalem, near the town of Moosomin. Ill fortune dogged the settlers, and the colony collapsed just five years later after a disastrous fire destroyed their crop of hay.

Between 1886 and 1907 two groups of Jews founded the Wapella settlement, north of Wapella: one group included John Heppner, from Russia, who was sponsored by Anglo-Jewish financier Herman Landau; and the other included Abraham Klenman and his son-in-law Solomon Barish. Klenman and Barish, who came from Bessarabia, financed themselves. In 1892 the Young Men's Hebrew Benevolent Society of Montreal, in an effort to cope with other Jewish refugees of the Russian pogroms, founded the Hirsch colony, about 25 km east of Estevan. The Jewish Colonization Association took over its supervision six years later. The Lipton colony was first settled by Jews from Romania in 1901, and later joined by Jews from Russia; it was Canada's only attempt to delegate to government officials the founding and administration of a Jewish agricultural settlement. The Jewish Colonization Association assisted the government in this operation. The

Samuel and Hanna Schwartz (on right) with daughter Simma and her husband, Jewish settlers (from Romania), Lipton district, ca. 1903.

Edenbridge colony near Gronlid, northeast of Melfort, grew naturally, the result of chain migration as emigrants followed the footsteps of their friends and relatives. Two separate groups, one from South Africa but originally from Lithuania, and the other from London, England, founded Edenbridge in 1906. Later, Jews from New York State joined them.

Also in 1906, three Galician Jewish teenagers, Philip Berger, Israel Hoffer and Majer Feldman, graduates of the Baron de Hirsch Agricultural College of Slobodka Lesna, helped to establish the Jewish farm settlement of Sonnenfeld, originally known as New Herman, approximately 80 km west of Estevan. Until the end of **WORLD WAR II**, many Jewish farmers were scattered throughout Saskatchewan. Some farmed individually while the remainder farmed in small settlements or in the larger colonies. For example, Jacob Pierce paid his $10 entry fee for the southeast quarter of 34-2-2 west of the second meridian on September 26, 1892, and received his patent on October 23, 1901; he and his sons, the first Jews to pioneer in the Oxbow area, were soon followed by others. Alsask, also known as Eyre, on the border of Alberta and Saskatchewan, was founded in 1910; nearby was Montefiore, another Jewish colony on the Alberta side of the border. Although some of the settlers both in Alsask and Montefiore first farmed in the United States, most originally came from Russia. For example, Max Feinberg's application for an Alsask homestead states that his previous occupation was farmer, his last place of residence was Denver, Colorado, and his place of birth was Russia.

The very gradual demise of the Jewish farm settlements was caused by many factors including drought, the "Dirty Thirties," economic depression, and World War II; this was followed by the mechanization of farm equipment, the need for ever-larger tracts of land, unfavourable weather conditions, plagues of insects and crop diseases, more children acquiring higher education and moving away from home, and the desire to live in larger Jewish centres. In spite of all these adverse conditions, there are a few descendants of the original settlers who still either farm or own the original homestead and rent out the land. Their ties to farming remain strong. (*See also* **ETHNIC BLOC SETTLEMENTS**, **JEWISH COMMUNITY, SASKATOON**)

Anna Feldman

FURTHER READING: Gutkin, H. 1980. *Journey into Our Heritage: The Story of Jewish People in the Canadian West.* Toronto: Lester and Orpen Dennys; Leonoff, C.E. 1975. *The Architecture of Jewish Settlements in the Prairies: A Pictorial History.* Saskatoon: Jewish Historical Society of Western Canada.

JEWITT-FILTEAU, NANCY (1962–). An outstanding female judoist, Nancy Jewitt-Filteau was born in Swift Current on August 3, 1962. Raised in Webb, Saskatchewan, she moved to Saskatoon and was a member of the **UNIVERSITY OF SASKATCHEWAN** Judo Club. Jewitt-Filteau competed at her first national senior judo championship in 1978 and won her first Canadian title in 1980. In total, she won three gold and four silver medals at national competitions. She was also a gold medalist at the 1987 Western Canada Summer Games held in Regina. In international events, Jewitt-Filteau earned a silver medal at the 1983 Pan-American Games in Venezuela, and a gold at the 1986 Commonwealth Games in Scotland. After failing to qualify for the 1988 Seoul Olympics, she retired and operated her own judo club at the University of Saskatchewan. Jewitt-Filteau was inducted into the **SASKATCHEWAN SPORTS HALL OF FAME** in 1992, but later decided to return to competition. She won a silver medal at the US Open in Colorado, and a bronze at the 1995 Pan-American Games in Argentina. She earned a spot on the Canadian Olympic judo team and participated in the 1996 Atlanta Olympic Games. She was eliminated from competition with a record of one win and two loses. Shortly after, she retired once again.

Holden Stoffel and Karen Zemlak

JOHN HOWARD SOCIETY. The John Howard Society of Saskatchewan is an independent voluntary advocacy group concerned with identifying and resolving issues related to crime, crime prevention, and the criminal justice system. Its roots began with John Howard, an English prison reformer in the late 18th century. His book, *The State of Prisons in England and Wales*, led to massive reforms in the 19th century, bringing prisons under government control and regulation, and introducing health and welfare measures for prisoners. The first John Howard Society, concerned with rehabilitation and aftercare of prisoners, began in British Columbia in 1931; all Canadian provinces now have local chapters. Their individual programs have expanded to include public education, community development, the evaluation and reform of the criminal justice process, research and resource development, and early crime intervention. The Society's mission statement is: "Effective, just and humane responses to the causes and consequences of crime." The Saskatchewan branches focus on creative, humane, and progressive responses to the problems of crime, and offer advocacy, direct service, and public education. The provincial society's two main programs, Primary Crime Prevention and Stop-Lift, focus on early intervention, and teach social responsibility and accountability to children and teens.

Merle Massie

JOHNS, HAROLD ELFORD (1915–). Born in Chengdu, West China on July 4, 1915, Harold Johns returned to Canada with his missionary parents in 1927. After taking MA and PhD degrees in physics from the University of Toronto, he was a lecturer at

Harold Johns, addressing a meeting of the Canadian Cancer Society, Saskatchewan Division, November 19, 1951.

the University of Alberta, where he made radiographic images of aircraft castings.

In 1945 he received a joint appointment in the Department of Physics at the **UNIVERSITY OF SASKATCHEWAN** as assistant professor and as physicist for the Saskatchewan Cancer Commission. There he created, almost single-handedly, a Canadian field of Medical Physics, and in 1948 was instrumental in securing Canada's first betatron. In 1951, he was the key figure in the development of the world's first Cobalt-60 unit for the treatment of cancer. Under his direction, radiation therapists and physicists at the University of Saskatchewan led the world in the development of high-technology cancer treatment.

In 1956 he was appointed head of the Physics Division of the Ontario Cancer Institute, and in 1958 professor and head of the Department of Medical Biophysics at the University of Toronto, where he continued to maintain an active research and teaching program until his mandatory retirement in 1980.

Johns published over 200 peer-reviewed papers; trained over 100 graduate and postdoctoral fellows, many of whom hold or have held key medical physics positions in Canada and around the world; and wrote the foremost textbook in medical radiation physics.

Sylvia O. Fedoruk

FURTHER READING: Houston, C. Stuart, and Sylvia O. Fedoruk. 1985. "Saskatchewan's Role in Radiotherapy Research," *Canadian Medical Association Journal* 132: 854–64.

JOHNSON, ALBERT WESLEY (1923–). Born on October 18, 1923, at Insinger, Saskatchewan, Johnson enjoyed a stellar career in the public service of Saskatchewan for nineteen years before going on to the public service of Canada, to the presidency of the CBC, to university teaching and research, and to the development of the South Africa/Canada Program on Governance. Johnson studied at the universities of Saskatchewan and Toronto, where

Albert Wesley Johnson, 1977.

he received degrees in political economy. It was from Toronto that Johnson was recruited to the public service of Saskatchewan by the Adult Education Division (1945). Twelve months later he was appointed to the newly created Budget Bureau. In 1949, Johnson was made responsible for advising on machinery of government and management processes. In 1952, at the age of 28, he was appointed Deputy Provincial Treasurer; in this position for the next twelve years, he was responsible for recruiting and developing a generation of some of the most dynamic public servants to serve in Saskatchewan and Canada. Originally based on a PhD dissertation he wrote while on educational leave at Harvard, Johnson's book *Dream No Little Dreams* describes in detail the workings of the T.C. DOUGLAS government.

In 1964, Johnson left Saskatchewan for the government of Canada, where he was appointed Assistant Deputy Minister of Finance responsible for federal-provincial fiscal relations. In this capacity he played a pivotal role in the introduction of national medicare; in the development of a new system for the equalization by the federal government of provincial government revenues; and in the design of a new and greatly expanded system of federal grants to the provinces for the financing of Canada's rapidly expanding universities and colleges. In 1968 he was appointed as Prime Minister Trudeau's economic adviser on the Constitution, and helped generate a series of national working papers on constitutional issues confronting Canada's governments. In 1970, Johnson was appointed Secretary of the Treasury Board. In 1973 he became the Deputy Minister of National Welfare, from which position he conducted with his provincial colleagues, directed by Canada's ministers of welfare, a major review of Canada's social security system. In 1975 Prime

Minister Trudeau appointed Johnson to the presidency of the Canadian Broadcasting Corporation, from which position he strove to increase the quality, quantity and exposure of Canadian programming. After his retirement in 1982, Johnson was appointed professor of Political Science at the University of Toronto and to short-term research chairs at Queens and at the Canadian Centre for Research and Development. During the 1990s, he oversaw a major governance program to assist in the establishment of a multi-racial democracy in South Africa.

Gregory P. Marchildon

Frederick W. and Joyce Johnson.

JOHNSON, F.W. (1917–93). Born in England on February 13, 1917, Frederick William Johnson was a distinguished representative of the Crown, the province, and its people. He began his education at the Regina NORMAL SCHOOL and later served with the Canadian Army in WORLD WAR II. In 1949, he received his law degree from the University of Saskatchewan. Johnson was appointed Queen's Counsel in 1963 and to the Court of Queen's Bench in 1965, serving as its Chief Justice from 1977 to 1983. He continued to represent the Crown as the sixteenth LIEUTENANT-GOVERNOR of Saskatchewan from 1983 to 1988, making him the first chancellor of the Saskatchewan Order of Merit. An honorary colonel of the 10th Field Regiment, Royal Canadian Artillery, Johnson was made an Officer of the Order of Canada in 1990 and received the Saskatchewan Order of Merit one year later. He died on June 20, 1993.

JOHNSON, WILBERT EARL (1917–2003). Born in Grey County, Ontario, on January 2, 1917, Earl Johnson took his primary and secondary education at Flesherton, Ontario. Following service overseas with the Canadian Army, he obtained a BSc in Agriculture in 1949, majoring in chemistry at the Ontario Agricultural College, Guelph. After graduating from the University of Saskatchewan with an MSc in Agriculture in 1951, specializing in soils, he was appointed soils specialist with the Saskatchewan Department of Agriculture. He travelled the province discussing tillage methods, wind and water erosion, and control of soil organic matter, and providing fertilizer recommendations from the Saskatchewan Advisory Fertilizer Council. Following retirement in 1978, he continued providing advice on soils as a part-time consultant; the general level of farm practice in Saskatchewan was raised significantly as a result of his studies and extension work.

Earl Johnson served as president of the Saskatchewan Institute of Agrologists (1963–64) and vice-president of the Agricultural Institute of Canada (1965–66). He participated in sessions of the International Soil Science Congress in Australia, New Zealand, the United States, and Scotland. In 1973 he was elected Fellow of the Canadian Society of Soil Science. In 1975 he received the Agronomy Merit Award presented by Western Co-operative Fertilizers. In 1977 the Saskatchewan Institute of Agrologists conferred on him its Distinguished Agrologist award. In 1978 he was made an honorary life member of the Agricultural Institute of Canada, and he was inducted into the Saskatchewan Agricultural Hall of Fame in 1989. He died in Regina on April 14, 2003.

Wilbert Earl Johnson, 1960.

JOHNSTON, JOHN FREDERICK (1876–1948).

Johnston was born on July 16, 1876, in Bogarttown, Ontario. He was well educated and came from a prosperous family that ran lumber and flour mills in Simcoe County. He came to Saskatchewan around 1905, first stopping near Yellow Grass before settling on a large farm near Bladworth. He became successful both as a farmer and as a businessman. He owned the lumberyard and hardware store in Bladworth, and a string of general stores as far away as Outlook and Kerrobert. In 1917 Johnston was elected to the House of Commons, representing Last Mountain, as a Unionist-Liberal supporting the Borden government. Johnston broke with the Liberals to join the new T.A. Crerar-led Progressive group within the House of Commons. In 1921, Johnston won the Progressive nomination and was re-elected in Last Mountain; he became the chief whip of the Progressives. He was a proponent of Progressive co-operation with the **WILLIAM LYON MACKENZIE KING** Liberal government. Johnston won the 1925 election as a Progressive but soon King convinced him to sit as a Liberal. He was re-elected as a Liberal in the 1926 election and in 1929 was appointed Deputy Speaker. In 1930, Johnston lost his seat as the Conservatives defeated the King government. Johnston returned to his farm, but made a political comeback in 1935 when he was elected to represent the riding of Lake Centre. Johnston finished his term and was again defeated in 1940, this time by Conservative **JOHN DIEFENBAKER**. Johnston received an appointment to the Senate in 1943 where he served until his death on May 9, 1948.

Brett Quiring

FURTHER READING: Morton, W.L. 1950. *The Progressive Party in Canada*. Toronto: University of Toronto Press.

JOHNSTON, TOM (1881–1969).

Born in Birmingham, England, on June 19, 1881, Johnston left school at the age of 13 and worked at a variety of jobs. He emigrated to Canada in 1901, and spent a couple of years in Manitoba, before coming to Saskatchewan in 1903 and establishing a successful farm near Cymric. Johnston was involved in the formation of United Farmers of Canada (Saskatchewan Section), and advocated for the organization's entry into electoral politics. In the 1934 provincial election, Johnston finished third in Lumsden for the Farmer-Labor Party (the predecessor of the CCF). In 1935 he challenged Liberal leader **MACKENZIE KING**

SASKATCHEWAN ARCHIVES BOARD R-B4071
Tom Johnston.

in the federal riding of Prince Albert, but was defeated. Johnston ran for the CCF in the 1938 provincial election in Touchwood and was one of ten CCF MLAs elected that year. Re-elected in the CCF sweep of 1944, Johnston served as Speaker. Re-elected twice, he spent a record twelve years in the Speaker's chair. On one occasion, Johnston took the extraordinary step to leave the Speaker's chair to enter into debate, a right rarely exercised by Speakers. Johnston retired in 1956, but remained politically active. At the age of 80 he sailed around the world on an ocean freighter to get a better understanding of the problems of the developing world. Returning to Saskatchewan, he called for the developed world to face the problems of abject poverty in developing nations. Johnston died in Regina on September 11, 1969.

Brett Quiring

JOHNSTONE, ANNIE (1899–1994).

Annie Johnstone was born at Souris River near La Ronge

SASKATCHEWAN ARCHIVES BOARD R-A22852
Annie Johnstone, ca. 1978.

on December 25, 1899. A northern Saskatchewan **MÉTIS**, she lived most of her life in Pinehouse Lake, where her husband farmed and managed a Hudson's Bay Company store. Mrs. Johnstone was a skilled practitioner of traditional Native medicine, tied closely to First Nations spirituality. She had an extensive knowledge of plants and herbs which she first acquired from her grandparents as a young girl, and later passed on to others. She was known to cure patients who had not been helped by modern medicine.

At the age of 15, Annie learned how to be a midwife from local women through first-hand experience, supplemented with information from a medical textbook. For sixty-five years she was nurse-midwife for the Pinehouse area. Despite her lack of formal training she successfully handled all kinds of births, including the most complicated, in an area where there were no doctors and transport was by canoe or dogsled. She delivered over 500 babies without the loss of a child or a mother. She received the Saskatchewan Order of Merit in 1991, and died at La Ronge hospital on July 24, 1994.

Michael Jackson

JONES KONIHOWSKI, DIANE (1951–).

Diane Jones Konihowski established herself as an outstanding pentathlete in the 1970s. Born in Vancouver on March 7, 1951, she spent the formative period of her life in Saskatoon. In 1967, Jones Konihowski competed internationally for Canada for the first time, and she quickly built an impressive record in world-class competition. She represented Canada at the 1972 Munich Olympics and was a gold medalist in the pentathlon at the 1975 Pan American Games in Mexico City. Although she placed sixth in the event at the 1976 Montreal Olympics, Jones Konihowski won a gold medal at the 1978 Commonwealth Games in Edmonton, and her second Pan American Games gold medal in 1979. She was a member of the Canadian Olympic team in 1980, but did not compete in the Moscow Olympiad as a result of Canada's decision to boycott the games. Jones Konihowski remains closely associated with amateur athletics in Canada. She has worked as a coach and sports administrator as well as a volunteer director for several national athletic boards. She received the Order of Canada in 1979, and is a member of the Canadian Olympic and **SASKATCHEWAN SPORTS HALL OF FAME**.

Daria Coneghan and Holden Stoffel

K

KAHKEWISTAHAW BAND. Chief Kahkewistahaw, a prominent leader, signed **TREATY 4** on September 15, 1874. His band was Rabbit Skin Cree and Saulteaux, and they hunted in the Wood Mountain and **CYPRESS HILLS** regions. They returned to the Qu'Appelle Valley once a year to receive annuity payments until a reserve was surveyed for them in 1881. Although drought, frost, and hail damaged crops in the 1880s and 1890s, wheat became their staple crop until January 1907, when 33,281 acres of their most fertile land were surrendered. The surrender forced most of the band's farmers to relocate and left only 11% of their arable land. On March 2, 1989, the Kahkewistahaw First Nation submitted a claim under the Specific Claims Policy, and on June 25, 2003, they signed a land claim agreement with the federal government addressing the injustice and providing funds to invest in economic development

DAVID MCLENNAN PHOTO

Treaty 4 monument, Fort Qu'Appelle, Saskatchewan.

and job creation. Currently run programs include social development, justice, a Head Start Program, Indian Child and Family Services, and drug and alcohol treatment programs. Kahkewistahaw is located 13 km north of Broadview; 426 of the 1,482 registered band members live on their 8,365.1-ha reserve. *Christian Thompson*

KALDOR, CONNIE (1953–). Connie (*née* Isabelle) Kaldor is a singer-songwriter known for her passionate and entertaining performances, wildly funny one moment and deeply personal the next. Kaldor's entire family was musically active. She was born in Regina and sang in the Lutheran church where her father conducted the choir. She initially earned a theatre degree from the University of Alberta in 1976, and joined alternative theatre groups including Toronto's Theatre Passe Muraille; but by 1979 she realized that she missed making music, and set out on the folk music circuit, accompanying herself on guitar and piano. She formed her own independent record label, now known as Coyote Entertainment, in 1981, and soon became a recognized part of the Canadian folk scene. Her ten albums stretch from *One of These Days* (1981) to *Vinyl Songbook* (2003). The title track from *Wood River* (1992) is considered by many to be the quintessential Saskatchewan song. Other notable prairie-themed recordings include *Saskatoon Moon*, *Hymn for Pincher Creek*, *Harsh and Unforgiving*, and *Maria's Place/Batoche*. A versatile performer, Kaldor was nominated for a Juno Award as Most Promising Female Vocalist in 1984, and won the Juno for Best Children's Album in 1989 for *Lullaby Berceuse*, a collaboration with children's entertainer Carmen Campagne. Her 2000 album *Love Is A Truck* was also nominated. She has written music for both dance and theatre productions, and created

the prairie musical *Dust and Dreams*, which premiered in Rosthern in 1996. Kaldor co-wrote and performed the theme song for the animated television show based on Lynn Johnston's popular comic strip, *For Better or for Worse*, for the Teletoon network in 2000. She wrote the story and songs for *A Duck in New York City* (2003), a storybook-CD which received a Juno Award. This was followed in 2005 by another Juno for *A Poodle in Paris*.

In 2004, Kaldor was joined by some of her musical friends in *Connie Kaldor @ Wood River Hall*, a thirteen-part television series on Vision TV. Her wicked humour and trained theatrical performer's sense have delighted her many loyal fans in small and large communities and in the major folk festivals all across Canada and the United States, as well as in India, China, and Europe. She is married to musician Paul Campagne; they live in Montreal with their two sons. *Richard Belford*

KALIUM CHEMICALS. Kalium Chemicals first began production and sale of potash in Saskatchewan in 1964 at Belle Plaine, west of Regina. Using the solution method, Kalium Chemicals retrieved salt deposits up to a mile below the surface by injecting water into the deposits and pumping the dissolved potash to a surface refinery and cooling pond. Still in operation today, the Belle Plaine mine is considered the world's lowest-cost potash mine, producing high-purity white potash for use in industrial products such as water softeners, alkaline batteries, and food sweeteners and additives. Although large deposits of potash were discovered in Saskatchewan in 1943, it was not until the 1950s and 1960s that serious exploration was undertaken. International Minerals and Chemicals (IMC) of Chicago became the first company to mine potash in Saskatchewan, opening its first of two underground

mines at Esterhazy in 1963. Production at Kalium Chemicals' solution mine in Belle Plaine and at Noranda Mines' potash operation at Colonsay, southeast of Saskatoon, also commenced in the early 1960s. By 1996, following a series of acquisitions and mergers, all four Saskatchewan mines had come under one operator, IMC Kalium, the potash unit of the American fertilizer giant IMC Global. In 1999, IMC Kalium was renamed IMC Potash. Today, IMC Potash is the world's largest producer and seller of potash for industrial and agricultural uses. (*See also* POTASH INDUSTRY) *Iain Stewart*

FURTHER READING: Johnstone, B. 2001. "IMC's Sask. Potash Mines Bright Spot," *Regina Leader-Post* (July 27): B7.

KAMSACK, town, pop 2,009, located approximately 80 km NE of Yorkton at the confluence of the Whitesand and Assiniboine Rivers and the junction of Hwys 5 and 8. The region was traversed by fur traders as far back as the late 1700s; in the late 1800s, the name *Kamsack* was derived from that of a well-known First Nations man in the area. In the mid-to-late 1880s the first settlers arrived, and Doukhobors came to the district in large numbers in 1899. During the first years of the 20th century, with the approach of the railway, settlers poured into the area from eastern Canada, the United States, and Europe. The Canadian Northern Railway was at Kamsack in 1904, and the first businesses were springing up on the townsite. In 1905 Kamsack was incorporated as a village; it became one of the province's fastest growing and most progressive communities. Kamsack attained town status in 1911, and in 1914 construction began on an electric light plant, the waterworks, and a sewage system. By the early 1920s, the population was over

Connie Kaldor.

Kalium Chemical Plant, May 1964.

2,000. The community suffered somewhat of a setback during the 1930s, but the establishment of a petroleum company in the town in 1936 proved somewhat of a boon. In 1937, Kamsack became one of only three communities in Saskatchewan with their own natural gas system, prior to SaskPower being given the authority in the 1950s to begin establishing a province-wide utility (Lloydminster had natural gas in 1934, and Unity's system was in place in 1944). On August 9, 1944, a tornado tore through the town. Locally referred to as the "Kamsack Cyclone," it damaged or destroyed 400 homes and 100 businesses, leaving three people dead and scores injured. The military was despatched to clean up the debris and help restore services. With the help of veterans returning from overseas, the biggest building boom in the community's history ensued; with the provincial trend toward urbanization, Kamsack's population was nudging 3,000 by the early 1960s. In 1962, however, it faced another setback. The CNR had employed approximately 200 people in its roundhouse and shops at Kamsack, but that year the railway abandoned the town as a divisional point; many railway company employees had to leave the community to find work, while those who remained had to seek new occupations. From that point on, the community's population has slowly declined. Today, Kamsack serves primarily as an agricultural service centre for the surrounding district. The Kamsack Historical Museum is located in the town's 1914 power plant, now a heritage property; the Kamsack Playhouse (also a heritage property) provides a venue for cinema, live theatre, and concerts. Kamsack has a 2,500-foot paved and lighted airstrip, and is one of a few communities on the prairies that still has passenger rail service. The original 1915 water tower has been designated a heritage property and is one of only a handful of its kind in existence in Saskatchewan. *David McLennan*

KANE, PAUL (1810–71). Irish-born painter Paul Kane immigrated with his family to York (Toronto), Upper Canada before he was 12. His return trip with Hudson's Bay Company brigades across the continent to Vancouver Island in 1846–48 made him famous. Before it, he worked as a portrait painter in the United States, ventured to Europe and studied sketching and painting in Italy, and made a trip to lakes Huron, Michigan, and Winnebago in 1845 to sketch landscapes and portraits of people and places on the North American frontier. In the autumn of 1846, he traveled up the **SASKATCHEWAN RIVER**, traversing Cumberland Lake on August 27 and reaching Carlton House on September 7. From there, he journeyed west by horse, visited a buffalo pound—constructed, according to his inimitably written field notes, "of they bouns of the Buffalo"—and stayed at **FORT PITT**.

Riding on to Fort Edmonton, which he reached on September 28, he found the buffalo "so numeras [*sic*] that they impeded [his] progress." After journeying to the Pacific Ocean and back, he made a return trip from Edmonton to Fort Pitt by cariole and dogs during the second week of January 1848, staying three weeks at Fort Pitt. In the late spring, he left the West, proceeding downriver with the annual HBC brigade in twenty-three boats to The Pas, leaving Edmonton on May 25 and arriving on June 12. He weathered a spring snowstorm en route, and met a "ware partey of Blackfeete, Blood Indians, Sursees, Grovants, Paganes, to the amount of 500."

The subjects of Kane's Saskatchewan portraits were **CREE** and **ASSINIBOINE**, as well as one Chipewyan. Fur trade posts, buffalo, and parkland landscapes captured his interest too. Not the first European to paint in what is now Saskatchewan (midshipmen George Back and Robert Hood of **FRANKLIN**'s first Arctic land expedition [1819–22] preceded him), Kane is seen as the first Canadian painter of the West. *Wanderings of an Artist* (London, 1859), based on his travels but written with the help of others, enjoyed Danish, French, and German translations long before the first Canadian edition appeared in 1925. Most of his over 500 sketches and paintings are held by the Stark Museum of Art, Orange, Texas, and by the Royal Ontario Museum in Toronto. *I.S. MacLaren*

KAPLAN, DAVID L. (1923–). David L. Kaplan was born on December 12, 1923, in Chicago, Illinois. He studied piano from an early age and began learning to play the clarinet in high school. During **WORLD WAR II**, he served as an army bandsman and then attended Roosevelt University in Chicago, graduating with a Bachelor of Music in 1948. He subsequently obtained a master's degree in music from Oberlin College in Ohio in 1950, and a PhD from Indiana University in 1978. From 1950 to 1955, Dr. Kaplan served as Director of Music at the Reynolds Community School District in Illinois, and from 1955 to 1960 he was Assistant Professor of Woodwinds at West Texas State University in Canyon, Texas.

In 1960, he developed a music education program within the College of Education at the **UNIVERSITY OF SASKATCHEWAN** and later established an independent Department of Music, where he served as department head from 1964 to 1982. As department head, Dr. Kaplan introduced a number of new programs, including bachelors' degrees in music and music education, masters' degrees in education (music) and arts (music), and a special-case PhD.

David Kaplan served full-time at the University of Saskatchewan from 1960 to 1991, teaching music theory, music education, world music, and music history. He has also held teaching positions at the

SASKATCHEWAN ARCHIVES BOARD R-A8470
David Kaplan.

Chicago Conservatory of Music, the University of New Mexico, the National Music Camp in Interlochen, Michigan, and the World Youth Orchestra of Jeunesses Musicales in Spain. His articles have appeared in the *Encyclopedia of Music in Canada*, the *School Musician*, the *Canadian Music Education Journal*, the *Illinois Music Educator*, and *The Clarinet*. He retired in 1991, but continues to serve as professor emeritus and as a sessional lecturer.

In addition to his academic career, Dr. Kaplan served as the Conductor and Music Director of the Saskatoon Symphony from 1962 to 1972; and in 1985 he established the Saskatoon Klezmer Band, for which he has written more than 200 arrangements and compositions. As a clarinetist, Dr. Kaplan has performed with the Cassenti Players of Vancouver, as well as the Amarillo (Texas) and Tri-City (Iowa) symphonies.

In November 2002, David Kaplan received the Order of Canada and the Queen's Golden Jubilee medal. In the summer of 2003, his extensive collection of instruments was put on display at the Diefenbaker Canada Centre at the University of Saskatchewan. *Damian Coneghan*

KARTUSCH, MICHAEL P. (1907–96). Born on September 20, 1907, for decades Michael P. Kartusch was involved in education and the promotion of community sports in Regina. His tenure with the Regina Catholic School Board lasted for forty-three years. A fixture on the Regina sports scene, Kartusch joined the Regina Pats junior hockey club in 1948 and served in various capacities until his retirement in 1979. He was also involved in softball, baseball, basketball, and football. For his lifetime devotion to teaching, amateur sport, and working with young people, Kartusch was inducted into the **SASKATCHEWAN SPORTS HALL OF FAME** and named to the Order of Canada in 1974. He died on July 12, 1996.

KARWACKI, DAVID (1965–). David Karwacki grew up in Saskatoon and attended the University of Saskatchewan, graduating from the College of Commerce in 1989. He currently continues his education through enrolment in the Birthing of Giants program at MIT in Boston. Karwacki is married to Laurie, an educator, and has four children. In 1990, Karwacki and three partners founded Star Produce Ltd., an international fresh produce distribution company. Karwacki has served as chief operating officer of the company, and is currently CEO. In the community, Karwacki served as the president of the Huskie Basketball Alumni Association, acted as the founding board member of the University of Saskatchewan Athletic Endowment Fund, and participated as a member of the St. Anne's faith community. Although he had no formal political experience, Karwacki won a decisive victory over opponent Jack Hillson at the October 2001 Liberal leadership convention. He inherited a troubled party with declining membership. Karwacki attempted to end the Liberal-NDP coalition but **JIM MELENCHUK** and Ron Osika remained in the coalition Cabinet as independents. Karwacki led the Liberals into the 2003 election. He went down to personal defeat in Saskatoon Meewasin and the party failed to elect any of its candidates, its worst electoral defeat since 1982.   *Winter Fedyk*

KATEPWA BEACH, located in the **QU'APPELLE VALLEY**, on the NE side of Katepwa Lake, on Hwy 56. Settlers arrived in the area in the 1880s and the first cottages were built in the early 1900s. The most significant development, however, has occurred more recently, with year-round populations rising from 45 to 225 over the past several decades. There are 550 cottages and homes at Katepwa Beach, and during the summer months the population can reach 1,000. The community encompasses Katepwa Point Provincial Park.   *David McLennan*

KATZ, LEON (1909–2004). Born in Poland in on August 9, 1909, Leon Katz immigrated to Ontario, Canada with his parents. He completed his BSc and MSc degrees at Queen's University, and received a PhD from the California Institute of Technology. He worked at the Westinghouse Electric Company, Pittsburgh, before moving to the **UNIVERSITY OF SASKATCHEWAN** in 1946. He collaborated with Drs. Haslam and Jones in bringing a 25 MeV betatron to Saskatchewan in 1948. This machine served as the first radiation therapy facility in the province to treat cancer patients, and also as a nuclear physics tool. Katz was a multidisciplinarian–engineer, nuclear and accelerator physicist, as well as radar and chaos theory specialist. He was instrumental in building the Linear Accelerator Laboratory, the predecessor of the **CANADIAN LIGHT SOURCE** (CLS), and served as its founding director from 1961 to 1975.

Katz also served on several national organizations. He was a member of the Science Council of Canada (1966–72), President of the Canadian Association of Physicists (1973–74), and member of the Council of Trustees of the Institute for Research on Public Policy (1974–86). After his retirement from the University of Saskatchewan, he served as director of the science secretariat of the government of Saskatchewan (1975-80), and as a member of several councils. He was elected Fellow of the Royal Society of Canada (1952) and Fellow of the American Physical Society (1966); awarded an honorary Doctor of Science degree by the University of Saskatchewan (1990); and appointed Officer of the Order of Canada (1974). Finally, Katz received the Prime of Life Achievement Award, University of Saskatchewan Retirees Association, and the Rotary Golden Wheel Award for Excellence (2000). He died on March 1, 2004.   *Chary Rangacharyulu*

KAWACATOOSE FIRST NATION. Chief Kawacatoose signed **TREATY 4** September 15, 1874, and two years later received a reserve in the Big Touchwood Hills. The reserve was originally named the Poor Man Reserve, as Kawacatoose is also referred to as Poor Man, although the correct translation is Lean Man or Skinny Man. When Kawacatoose died, his second eldest son Tawequasequape became chief. Band members began to farm with the implements, seed, and livestock provided through treaty, adding to their income by selling wood to the Agency and selling fence pickets and hay to local farmers. A band farm was started in 1949, adding revenue to a general band account; some farmers, however, remained independent. In 1981, the educational administration and control of the band's day school was transferred from the Department of Indian Affairs, and the building of Phase One of the Kawacatoose Education Complex began. Phase Two was completed in 1983, joined to Phase One by the Kawacatoose Recreation Centre (1980). The Kawacatoose First Nation is located 10 km north of Quinton, with facilities that include a band office, the Education Complex, a health clinic, water treatment plant, and private housing. Of the 2,559 band members, 1,092 live on the 9,672-ha reserve.   *Christian Thompson*

KEESEEKOOSE FIRST NATION. Chief Keeseekoose signed **TREATY 4** on September 15, 1874, and settled on the Swan River Reserve, Manitoba. Because of flooding, the band was relocated to their present reserve near the towns of Pelly and Kamsack, between the Cote and Key Reserves. Of the 1,951 Keeseekoose Band members, 626 live on the 8,475-ha reserve. The band-controlled St. Phillip's School sits on the same grounds as the old residential school, while their strip mall houses a gas station and convenience store, as well as the Yorkton Tribal Council Child and Family Services, Fort Pelly RCMP Detachment, and Treaty Land Entitlement Office (also serving the Key and Cote Reserves).

Christian Thompson

KELSEY, HENRY (1667–1724). Henry Kelsey was the first European to describe the northern plains. In 1690, the Hudson's Bay Company (HBC) sent him inland to persuade the "remoter Indians to a Trade with us." He was already well experienced, having made two overland trips along the coast of Hudson Bay. Little is known of the two years Kelsey stayed inland. The first year is only vaguely referred to in a long introductory poem. His actual journal

UNIVERSITY OF SASKATCHEWAN ARCHIVES A-10419

Leon Katz, with plans for the Linear Accelerator Building, 1961.

covers the short period from July 15 to September 12, 1691, when he was taken to meet the Naywatame. Kelsey left Deering's Point, near The Pas, Manitoba, and journeyed south across the Pasquia Hills and the upper Assiniboine River, apparently to the Touchwood Hills. After meeting the Naywatame, probably a Hidatsa band from the Missouri River, he ended his account; nothing else is known of his activities until he returned to York Factory in the summer of 1692. He never again referred to these inland experiences. Later, Kelsey advanced through the HBC ranks to become governor of York Factory. In 1722 he was recalled to England for reasons that remain unclear. Although his diary was published in 1749, doubts surrounded his accomplishments until his papers were found in Ireland in 1926; these included other journals written at the Bay, as well as descriptions of the **CREE** and Nakota. Kesley was the first to mention the bison and grizzly bear, and the only one to describe cremations and the "surround" bison-hunting technique. A printed copy of his Cree dictionary, in the British Museum, remains unpublished. *Dale Russell*

FURTHER READING: Epp, H. (ed.). 1993. *Three Hundred Prairie Years: Henry Kelsey's "Inland country of good report."* Regina: Canadian Plains Research Center/ Saskatchewan Archaeological Society; Kelsey, H. 1994. *The Kelsey Papers* (with an introduction by John Warkentin and including the introduction to the 1929 edition by Arthur G. Doughty and Chester Martin). Regina: Canadian Plains Research Center.

KELVINGTON, town, pop 1,007, located S of Greenwater Provincial Park, on Hwy 38 just N of its junction with Hwy 49. The town's economy is large-ly based on agriculture, with area farms producing grain, cattle, and exotic livestock. The first settlers arrived in the district around 1900. The community's location at the end of the CN line greatly contributed to its development, as Kelvington became an important grain-handling point and distribution centre. The former CN station, built in 1922, is now a heritage property. Today, the town has several dozen businesses and services, a number of which cater to the agricultural sector. Kelvington dubs itself "Canada's Hockey Factory," having had six players achieve success in the NHL; a large mural on the south edge of town depicts the players' hockey cards. The town also hosts an annual summer hockey tournament and hockey school in July, and a fair and sports day in August. Parks and lakes in the region offer recreational opportunities and attract tourists. Hunting and fishing are popular area activities, as are cross-country skiing and snowmobiling. *David McLennan*

KENDEL, DENNIS (1946–). Dennis Kendel, born on May 24, 1946, in Russell, Manitoba, earned his MD with Distinction from the **UNIVERSITY OF SASKATCHEWAN** in 1971 and was awarded a fellowship in the College of Family Physicians of Canada in 1993. He has served as president of the **SASKATCHEWAN MEDICAL ASSOCIATION**, the Medical Council of Canada, and the Federation of Medical Licensing Authorities of Canada; he has been board chair of Saskatchewan Blue Cross, and a board member of the Saskatchewan Health Information Network and of the Saskatchewan Health Quality Council. Dr. Kendel helped to raise the standard of medical care across Canada. He was instrumental in developing the policy that all Canadian physicians

Dennis Kendel.

be required to complete a minimum of two years' accredited postgraduate medical education, as well as passing a Medical Council of Canada Qualifying Examination evaluating clinical and communication skills, before being eligible for medical licensure in Canada. He has worked to improve patient safety by reducing systemic medical errors. His collaborative philosophy led to the successful implementation of the Triplicate Prescription Program, designed to eliminate the abuse and diversion of prescription drugs. He continues to lead interdisciplinary enhancements to collect drug data electronically. *Dan Dattani*

KENDERDINE, AUGUSTUS (1870–1947). Augustus Frederick Lafosse Kenderdine, a painter of landscapes and portraits, was an energetic organizer who participated in building post-secondary fine arts education in both Saskatoon and Regina. His sweeping romantic depictions of the Saskatchewan landscape, particularly the northern areas around Emma Lake, were indelibly marked by his training in England and France. His imagery recast the province's topography in the comforting image of Europe. As a teacher he influenced generations of landscape painters, among them **WYNONA MULCASTER** and **RETA COWLEY**. Kenderdine's passion for the "wilderness" of northern Saskatchewan, and his enthusiasm for attracting people to his summer art camps, corresponded with the beginnings of a tourist industry. Born in Charlton-upon-Medlock, England, Kenderdine first studied art with his godfather, Chevalier de la Fosse, a Belgian-born painter and photographer; then he apprenticed to local artists before establishing the business "Gus Kenderdine: Photographer and Art Dealer" in 1890. From 1890 to 1891, he studied with Jules Lefèvre at the Academie Julien in Paris. A turning point in his career occurred when his work was included in the Paris Salon and the Royal Academy's Annual Summer Exhibition in 1901. By this time,

Five of the six Kelvington sons who have played in the National Hockey League stand in front of their respective hockey cards, erected as a tribute to them at the entrance of the community. Left to right: Barry Melrose, Joey Kocur, Wendel Clark, Kerry Clark, and Kory Kocur. (Missing from the photo is Lloyd Gronsdahl whose hockey card is at the far left.)

Augustus Kenderdine, "The Buffalo Hunt," 1915, oil on canvas, 59.7 x 90.2 cm, MacKenzie Art Gallery, University of Regina Collection, gift of Estate of Dr. John B. Ritchie.

Kenderdine had married Jane Ormerod and had four children. The family immigrated to Canada in 1908 and homesteaded near Lashburn, Saskatchewan. Kenderdine was preoccupied by the rigours of farming and ranching until 1918, when he turned his farming operation over to his son. He started painting again, and during this period secured several portrait commissions.

In 1920 Kenderdine met the **UNIVERSITY OF SASKATCHEWAN**'s first president, **WALTER MURRAY**, who planned to build an art program. He provided studio space in the Physics Building, where Kenderdine could work and teach. In the 1926–27 term, Kenderdine began to teach non-credit classes which, by 1933, had become credit classes. In 1936 he established the University Art Camp at Emma Lake (the forerunner of the Emma Lake Artists' Workshops). In the same year, a School of Fine Art was established at Regina College by Norman MacKenzie who, as part of his bequest, appointed Kenderdine as the School's first head and curator of the gallery. Until his death, Kenderdine lived in Regina, returning each summer to Emma Lake. Kenderdine exhibited his work across Canada, but was best known in Saskatchewan. In 1991, the Kenderdine Art Gallery, located at the University of Saskatchewan, was named in his honour, thanks to a bequest by his daughter, Mae Beamish. His works can be seen in many public collections, notably: the Glenbow Museum, Calgary; the University of Saskatchewan permanent art collection; the **MACKENZIE ART GALLERY**; the **MENDEL ART GALLERY**; and the National Gallery of Canada. *Helen Marzolf*

FURTHER READING: Bell, K. 1991. *Augustus Kenderdine 1870–1947.* Saskatoon: University of Saskatchewan.

KENROC. Kenroc Building Materials Ltd. has supplied over one billion square feet of drywall since owner Ken Sexton founded the Regina company in 1967. Kenroc is the original member in a group of associated companies under common ownership, all of whom have their registered head offices in Regina. These include Kenroc Building Materials Co. Ltd., the Sexton Buying Group Ltd., Builders Choice Products Ltd., Pan-Brick Inc. and Sexton Investments Ltd. Combined sales of the Kenroc-associated companies would place it among the 100 largest in Saskatchewan.

Kenroc began in 1967 by supplying contractors with drywall—also known as gypsum board or gyprock—and quickly became the major supplier in

Augustus Kenderdine.

the province. As the business became more established, Sexton added other products necessary for the completion of any construction project from insulation to ceiling titles. The first major expansion came in 1976 when Kenroc opened a second location in Saskatoon. Since then, the company has expanded into rural areas working in concert with local lumber companies and eventually opened stores in Winnipeg, Edmonton, Calgary, Prince George, Vancouver and Minneapolis. The next step was to open a buying group to get the best possible prices by buying in large volumes. Sexton Building Materials was created in 1985 and now has hundreds of members stretching from British Columbia to Quebec. The company was renamed The Sexton Group. Builders Choice Products Ltd., which became part of Sexton's growing group of companies in 1986, is the only producer of light steel framing in Saskatchewan. The affiliate also sells tools across Canada. *Joe Ralko*

KERR, DONALD (1936–). Don Kerr, born in Saskatoon in 1936, received a BA Honours degree in English from the **UNIVERSITY OF SASKATCHEWAN**, and an MA from the University of Toronto. He studied in London, England, and returned to Saskatoon, where he has taught for both the English and the Drama departments at the University of Saskatchewan. Kerr began his writing career as a poet, and has published five volumes. He began writing plays in the 1980s, all of which have been of a political or historical nature. He has also written five short pieces that were broadcast on CBC Radio and covered topics such as a celebration of the city of Saskatoon, jazz, and the dismantling of VIA Rail. Kerr published his first collection of short fiction stories in 2000, his first teen fiction novel in 2001 (and has since con-

Donald Kerr.

tinued writing teen fiction using Candy as the main character), and co-wrote and published a history entitled *Saskatoon: The First Half Century* (1982). He has edited two collections of poetry with **ANNE SZUMIGALSKI** (1986, 1990), two collections of plays with Diane Bessai (1983, 1987), and several other works that reflect his political involvements. He has been an editor with *Next Year Country* (1973–77), Grain (1973–83), *NeWest Review* (which he was influential in bringing to Saskatchewan from Alberta in 1981, and then edited until 1985), *Our Schools/Our Selves*, and he is press editor for more than fifteen books.

Kerr was the first chair of the Saskatoon Municipal Heritage Advisory Committee (1981–86 and 1997–2000), and served on the committee for an additional five years. He was also the Saskatchewan governor for the Heritage Canada Foundation. Kerr has been involved in a number of cultural and arts organizations including the World University Service of Canada (1968–71), the Saskatoon Public Library Board (1971–82; chair from 1977 to 1982), the **MEEWASIN VALLEY AUTHORITY** (1979–83), and the **SASKATCHEWAN ARTS BOARD** (1991–96). He also belonged to SaskFilm (1997–2000). He has been on the boards of two regional publishers: Coteau Books of Regina (1983–95, and 1997 to present) and NeWest Press (1983 to present). *Christian Thompson*

KERR, ILLINGWORTH (1905–89).

The life and art of Illingworth Kerr, born in Lumsden, Saskatchewan on August 20, 1905, imitated the geography of his birthplace. Angular fields, rolling skies, and the simple structures of the prairie town dominated his early work and infused his later abstract experiments with the distinct spaces of the prairie. Trained in the landscape tradition of the "Group of Seven" at the Ontario College of Art, Kerr returned to the prairies to struggle with the subject matter of his birthplace.

He vividly described his life in his autobiography, *Paint and Circumstance*, completed in 1987. The writing is a reflection of his character, a pragmatic view of prairie life combined with romantic descriptions of his artistic practice. This romance with his craft was appropriate considering the many obstacles he overcame on his artistic journey. Although isolated in a small community, Kerr's talents were recognized and eastern relatives paid his way to art school in Toronto in 1923; there he was influenced by the prominent painters, J.E.H. MacDonald and F.H. Varley.

In the 1930s, Kerr returned to Saskatchewan. Working on harvest and railway crews as a sign painter, trapper, writer and illustrator, he still found time to create work in his tiny Lumsden studio located above the local pool hall. He eventually left to visit Britain and the continent, and

Illingworth Kerr, "Ravenscrag, Ross's Ranch," 1930, oil on canvas, 76.8 x 92.1 cm, MacKenzie Art Gallery, University of Regina Collection, gift of Mr. Norman MacKenzie.

he received instruction at London's Westminster School of Art. In 1938 he married Mary Spice, and they returned to Saskatchewan for the winter of 1939–40. Kerr completed commissions for Charlie Wong, a Lumsden restaurant owner, and exhibited his work at the Regina Art College. In the 1940s, after a series of art-related positions, he became the head of the Alberta College of Art. After retirement in 1967, he began the most productive period of his artistic life and exhibited widely the painted landscapes as well as the drawings and prints that demonstrated his fascination with the animal world. In 1973 Kerr was awarded an honorary doctorate from the University of Calgary. He received the Order of Canada in 1983. His work can be found in various prominent collections including the National Gallery of Canada, Ottawa, as well as many corporate and private collections across Canada. This recognition did not diminish his interest in the small community of his birth: Kerr was a founding member of the Lumsden Historical Society, and some of his drawings and prints can be found on display at the Lumsden Museum. Kerr died January 6, 1989. *Heather Cline*

FURTHER READING: Kerr, Illingworth. 1963. *Fifty Years a Painter*. Edmonton: Edmonton Art Gallery; —. 1992. *The Drawings of Illingworth Kerr*. Lethbridge: University of Lethbridge Art Gallery.

KERR, WILLIAM L. (1902–83).

William Les Kerr received many awards celebrating his achievements as a plant breeder, ecologist, naturalist, and sportsman, as well as his contribution to prairie horticulture. Born in Renfrew, Ontario in 1902, he graduated in 1926 from the Ontario Agricultural College at Guelph with a BSc in Agriculture and later earned an MSc from the University of Maryland. After spending one year at the Rosthern Experimental Farm involved with apple breeding, Kerr transferred to the Morden Research Station in Manitoba to assist with the fruit breeding program; there the "Kerr" apple-crab was named in his honour and has since been widely propagated and planted. He also was responsible for the development of the "Almey" ornamental crab and the "Toba" hawthorn, the only pink-flowering hawthorn hardy enough for the southern prairies. In 1942, after spending ten years at Morden, Kerr became superintendent of the **PRAIRIE FARM REHABILITATION ADMINISTRATION** (PFRA) Forest Nursery Station at Sutherland, which was responsible for the propagation and distribution of millions of tree seedlings to farmers for shelterbelt plantings. There he was involved in the breeding and selection of a large number of ornamental and fruit plants, a work that he continued well after retirement. The "Royalty" ornamental crabapple has been one of his most prominent introductions, being widely planted across North America and selected as one of Canada's Centennial trees in 1967.

In 1945 Kerr selected and introduced the Sutherland caragana, a very upright-growing form; the Sutherland larch; Fangstadt, Polar Bear, and Blue Fox willows; and the Wheeler poplar. Another outstanding success was the introduction of the "Sutherland Gold" golden elder in 1964, for which he received an Award of Merit in the Netherlands; this elder is still widely propagated. He later introduced a dwarf elder called Goldenlocks. Kerr also worked on flowering almonds, hazelnuts and cherries, and introduced several hardy chrysanthemums such as Sutherland Pink, Cree, Early Autumn, and Popeye. Kerr received honorary life memberships in the Saskatchewan Horticultural Association, the Western Canadian Society of Horticulture (of which he was a founding member), the Canadian Society for Horticulture, and the Saskatchewan Fish and Game League. He encouraged nurserymen in Saskatchewan to form an association, which became known as the Saskatchewan Nursery Trade Association, and in 1977 he received an honorary life membership from that organization. He received the Kiwanis International Distinguished Service Award for contributions to the city of Saskatoon, the Stevenson Gold Medal from the Manitoba Horticultural Association, and several Awards of Merit from the Western Canadian Society for Horticulture for individual plant introductions. In 1978 he received the D.R. Robinson Award from the Saskatchewan Horticultural Association in recognition of his plant breeding work. He was also involved with the Saskatoon Fair Board and the Canadian National Institute for the Blind.

Kerr was instrumental in the landscaping at the Forest Nursery Station in Saskatoon, which became the Saskatoon Forestry Farm Park and Zoo after its closure; he was equally responsible for the development of the Zoo. His love of wildlife inspired the formation of the Saskatchewan Wildlife Federation. Kerr was particularly interested in pheasants and was a technical advisor for a pheasant breeding, raising, and releasing program for twenty years. As a final tribute, the Les Kerr Foundation was established to provide funding for researchers and individuals with projects specializing in the breeding and development of new plants suited to prairie growing conditions. In 1982 the **UNIVERSITY OF SASKATCHEWAN** granted him an honorary Doctor of Laws degree. *Brian J. Porter*

KERROBERT, town, pop 1,111, located in the west-central region of the province, N of Kindersley at the junction of Hwys 21, 31, and 51. Beginning in 1907, a great land rush was on as word spread that the CPR would be constructing a line through the district. People largely of British and German origins came to the area, and in early September 1910, the townsite was surveyed and the hillside lots put up for sale. The auctioneer was Tobias C. Norris, who

The grocery department of Sample Bros. store, the first store in Kerrobert, ca. 1912-13.

would become the premier of Manitoba in 1915. Named for Robert Kerr, a CPR traffic manager based in Montreal who had retired in 1910, Kerrobert was a CPR divisional point and a trading centre for a large district. Additional land around the town was purchased for future development, and infrastructure and institutions were established in anticipation of a substantial boom which did not materialize. The development of the **OIL AND GAS** industry in the 1950s diversified the area economy. Five pipelines run through the district, and there is a major pumping station at Kerrobert. Grain and livestock production, however, remains vital to the economy today. A landmark in the business district is the Hanbidge Building, which once housed the law offices of Robert and Jack Hanbidge. **ROBERT LEITH HANBIDGE** served on Kerrobert's town council before becoming mayor; he went on to become the province's **LIEUTENANT-GOVERNOR** from 1963 to 1970. Heritage properties in Kerrobert include: the former 1911 CPR station; the library, housed in a Bank of Commerce building dating to 1911; the 1914 water tower, one of only a few of its kind left in Saskatchewan; and the 1920 court house, designed by provincial architect **MAURICE SHARON**. *David McLennan*

KETTLES, JAMES G. (1912–83). Born in Ramsayville, Ontario in 1912, James G. Kettles devoted a lifetime of service to police work in Canada. He assumed the office of Saskatoon Chief of Police in February 1954 and initiated a complete reorganiza-

tion of the force and restructuring of police headquarters. A respected writer and speaker on police matters, Kettles served as president of the Canadian Police Chief's Association. He was an active member of the Masonic Order, Saskatoon Rotary Club, and Saskatoon Board of Trade. For more than thirty-five years of police service, James Kettles was made a Member of the Order of Canada in 1972. He died on December 11, 1983.

KIDNEY RE-TRANSPLANT. A team of Saskatoon physicians performed Canada's first successful kidney re-transplant at **ROYAL UNIVERSITY HOSPITAL** in 1964. Stella Mossing was 19 years old and had been married for five months at the time of the operation. She received a kidney donated by her mother. Unfortunately it failed within hours of the operation, but a second kidney from an accident victim was successfully transplanted. A total of forty-nine physicians participated in assessment and evaluation; no less than fourteen surgical procedures were required. Dr. Neville J. Jackson, a vascular surgeon, led the re-transplant surgical team using techniques that had been in existence for less than a year. At the time, only five kidney transplants of any kind had been performed in Canada. Dialysis was also in its infancy, offering only a brief window of time for doctors to find a suitable kidney and save the patient's life. The Saskatoon team, a pioneer in the field, performed ten of the first 100 kidney transplants in Canada. *Joe Ralko*

KINDERSLEY, town, pop 4,548, located in the province's west-central region, between Rosetown and the Saskatchewan-Alberta border at the junction of Hwys 7 and 21. The first settlers began arriving in the district in 1907. The townsite was surveyed in September 1909 and on January 10, 1910, the village of Kindersley was incorporated; it was named after Sir Robert Kindersley, a major shareholder in the Canadian Northern Railway. Ten months later, Kindersley attained town status. The community, whose fortunes depended on grain farming, had a population of just over 1,000 by the early 1920s. In the early 1950s, major discoveries of oil and gas in the region ushered in an era of rapid development and a surge in Kindersley's population, which soared from 990 in 1941 to 1,755 in 1951, then to 2,990 in 1961. Today, agriculture and the oil and gas industry continue to form the basis of the economy. Kindersley is the main shopping, service, and administrative centre for a trading area population of approximately 40,000 people; strategically located on the main highway between Saskatoon and Calgary, it has an annual traffic count of over 5 million vehicles. Area attractions include the Addison Sod House and the Great Wall of Saskatchewan. Built between 1909 and 1911, the Addison house is the oldest continuously inhabited sod building in the province; and the "Great Wall"–a kilometre long, three metres wide, two metres high–was built over 30 years by Albert "Stonewall" Johnson entirely of stones and without the use of cement or mortar, for purely aesthetic purposes. *David McLennan*

KINDRACHUK, MICHAEL JOHN (1920–91). Born in St. Julien, Saskatchewan in 1920, Michael Kindrachuk made significant contributions to education, particularly in its multicultural facets. He earned his BA, BEd, and MEd from the UNIVERSITY OF SASKATCHEWAN and received his PhD from the Ukrainian Free University in Munich, Germany. In 1949, he joined the Saskatoon Public Schools and served as vice-principal, principal, director of guidance and special education, and area superintendent of elementary schools. Active in the Kinsmen and Rotary Clubs and the Saskatoon Multicultural Council, Kindrachuk's many honours and awards include the Queen Elizabeth II Silver Jubilee medal and membership in the Order of Canada. He died on May 20, 1991.

KING, ANDREW (1885–1981). During the heyday of travelling entertainment circuits, Andrew King's colourful promotional posters or show prints announced the coming of theatrical companies, circuses, and carnivals to communities across North America. Born in Winnipeg on October 23, 1885, King moved to Rouleau, Saskatchewan in 1909 where he established the *Rouleau Enterprise*. In 1912, he developed a show print business as a sideline and quickly became a major producer of posters for circuits that criss-crossed the continent. King's mastery of wood block printing and his willingness to experiment with the process gave his posters a simple yet dynamic and colourful design.

King named his concern Enterprise Show Print

Wood-block printed poster by Andrew King.

and its customers included several of the era's most recognizable entertainment companies: Conklin and Garrett, Odyson Circus, Royal Canadian Shows, and Terrell Jacobs Circus. The company also designed and printed posters for rodeos, sports days, thrill shows, agricultural fairs, and travelling theatrical companies. In addition to producing the standard 24-inch by 42-inch one-sheet print, King combined several sheets into billboards that were pasted onto barns or empty buildings. Using vibrant colours and larger-than-life shapes, they could be easily identified from street distances.

In 1944, King relocated his business to Estevan, purchased the town's newspaper, *The Estevan Mercury*, and renamed the poster business King Show Print. The latter concern continued to thrive as King experimented with printing processes other than wood block. In 1958, *The Estevan Mercury* was purchased by interests in Liverpool, England who continued to publish the newspaper but disbanded King Show Print. In recognition of his contributions to Canadian printing history, King was honoured with a permanent display of his work in Massey College Library at the University of Toronto. Andrew King died in Wilber, Nebraska on November 13, 1981. *Holden Stoffel*

FURTHER READING: Dunlop Art Gallery. 1987. *The Big Show!: Andrew King's Show Prints, 1919–1958.* Regina, SK: Dunlop Art Gallery; King, Andrew. 1970. *Pen, Paper & Printing Ink.* Saskatoon, SK: Western Producer Prairie Book; 1981. "Pioneer Newspaperman Dies at 96." *Regina Leader-Post* (November 16); Stacey, Robert H. 1979. *The Canadian Poster Book: 100 Years of the Poster in Canada.* Toronto: Methuen.

Kindersley in 1909 was a tent town. This photograph was taken at about the time the Canadian Northern Railway established the location for the town.

UNIVERSITY OF REGINA ARCHIVES AND SPECIAL COLLECTIONS
87-32-45

Carlyle King addressing University of Regina convocation, 1984.

KING, CARLYLE (1907–88). Carlyle King was born in Cooksville, Ontario, on November 25, 1907. He came to Saskatchewan in 1912, and since his father was a railway telegrapher and station agent, the family moved around the province. He received a BA (1926) from the UNIVERSITY OF SASKATCHEWAN, with honours in English and History, and an MA (1927) and PhD (1931) from the University of Toronto. He taught in the English Department at the University of Saskatchewan from 1929 until 1977. He was one of the first proponents of Canadian literature. He was head of the English Department (1949–64), dean of Academic Services (1967–71), then acting vice-president and in 1975 assistant to the president for Academic Services. He celebrated the University in three publications and wrote a history of research and scholarship at the University.

King's second life was politics. He was elected to the provincial executive of the CCF in 1939. He ran against GEORGE WILLIAMS for leadership of the party at the 1940 convention and lost, but gained about a third of the vote. He was elected president of the party in 1945 and remained until 1960, meeting every second Sunday with T.C. DOUGLAS. He ran a number of election campaigns and wrote CCF pamphlets including "What is Democratic Socialism?" King was also chair of the major pacifist organization in Canada, the Fellowship of Reconciliation.

Carlyle King was also a force in the arts and in libraries. He was a member of the SASKATCHEWAN ARTS BOARD from its first year, 1947, until 1964. He was on the board of the Saskatoon Art Centre, and president from 1957 to 1959. In 1957, as part of the province's GOLDEN JUBILEE, King edited an early collection of Saskatchewan writing, *Saskatchewan Harvest*. He was also active in music organizations but it was in libraries that he had his greatest influence. He was chair of the Library Advisory Council, set up by the Douglas government, for twenty years (1947–67). He was president of the

SASKATCHEWAN LIBRARY ASSOCIATION in 1955 and was chair for many years of the Library Legislation Committee of the Canadian Library Association. He was chair of the Saskatoon Public Library from 1958 to 1972. He received a Merit Award from the Canadian Library Trustees Association and in 1977 a branch Library in Saskatoon was named to honour his long service. King received an honorary degree from the UNIVERSITY OF REGINA in 1984. He died on March 18, 1988. *Don Kerr*

FURTHER READING: Kerr, Donald C., and Stan Hanson. 1998. "Pacifism and the CCF at the Outbreak of World War II," *Prairie Forum* (Fall): 211–43; King, Carlyle. 1981. "Recollections, the CCF in Saskatchewan." Pp. 31–41 in Donald C. Kerr (ed.), *Western Canadian Politics: The Radical Tradition*. NeWest Institute; —. n.d. "A Beginning in Politics: Saskatoon CCF, 1938–43," *Saskatchewan History* 36: 102–14.

KING, ROSS (1962–). Born July 16, 1962, and raised in North Portal, Saskatchewan, Ross King is a best-selling author of both fiction and non-fiction. The second of seven children, King attended school in Bienfait and Estevan, before moving on to the UNIVERSITY OF REGINA to study English literature. Completing an MA in 1986, King moved to Toronto to pursue a PhD at York University. He completed it in 1992, and moved to England to take on a research fellowship at London's University College.

In 1993, as his research fellowship was drawing near its end, King decided to write a novel based on his post-doctoral research into the 18th century. He sent the first few chapters of the manuscript of *Domino* to several publishers, and was offered a contract by London-based editor Christopher Sinclair-Stevenson under his imprint at Reed Books. *Domino* was published in the United Kingdom in 1995, appearing in Canada shortly thereafter.

King's second novel, *Ex-Libris*, was published in the UK in 1998. The non-fictional *Brunelleschi's Dome*, published in both the UK and the United States in 2000, was chosen the Book Sense Best Non-Fiction Book of the Year, spending several weeks on the *New York Times* best-seller list. King's second popular history, the best-selling *Michelangelo and the Pope's Ceiling*, was published in 2002 in both the UK and North America. It was nominated for the Governor General's Literary Award for Non-Fiction in 2003. *Justin Messner*

FURTHER READING: Macpherson, Margaret. 1998. "Sask. Author Wins Literary Sweepstakes Abroad," *NeWest Review* 24 (1): 6; Martin, Sandra. 2003. "Renaissance Man of the 21st Century." *Globe and Mail* (March 8), R4.

KING, WILLIAM LYON MACKENZIE (1874–1950). William Lyon Mackenzie King was Canada's longest-serving prime minister (1921–26; 1926–30;

1935–48). When Mackenzie King succeeded Sir Wilfrid Laurier as leader of the LIBERAL PARTY in 1919, the most significant threat to national unity came from the prairie west. King set off to rebuild Liberal support in the frustrated region by supporting the prairie position on such critical issues as tariffs, freight rates, natural resources, railways, and immigration. He lured former Liberal–Progressives back into party ranks, made sure to offer federal Cabinet posts to influential leaders, and sought to form strong relationships with the provincial governments of Alberta, Manitoba, and most specifically the ardently Liberal province of Saskatchewan under Premiers CHARLES DUNNING and JIMMY GARDINER. Both Premiers ended up as influential Ministers in King's federal Cabinets. Part of King's strategy in rebuilding Liberal fortunes in the west included representing a Saskatchewan constituency. After being defeated in the 1925 general election in the Ontario riding of North York, King was elected to represent the federal constituency of Prince Albert in a by-election on February 15, 1926. King held the Saskatchewan constituency for the majority of his career and was instrumental in the creation of the PRINCE ALBERT NATIONAL PARK in 1926. He was defeated in the riding in the general election of June 11, 1945, and held the seat of Glengarry, Ontario, for the remaining three years of his career. *Robert Wardhaugh*

FURTHER READING: Wardhaugh, Robert. 2000. *Mackenzie King and the Prairie West.* Toronto: University of Toronto Press.

KINGLETS. Kinglets (family Regulidae) are tiny, active insectivorous songbirds with boldly patterned wings. They have weak fluttering flight and hover at the tips of branches to glean insects from the vegetation and tree bark. They drink tree sap made available by sapsuckers. Nests are small cups placed high in coniferous trees. Their voice is a series of high-pitched *tse* notes, followed by a trill of *tse* notes or *liberty-liberty-liberty*.

Limited to the Northern Hemisphere, there are six species of kinglets; two of them occur in North America, including Saskatchewan. The drab looking, migratory ruby-crowned kinglet (*Regulus calendula*) breeds in coniferous and mixedwood stands in the boreal forest, and is a transient in southern Saskatchewan. Only adult male ruby-crowned kinglets have the red-coloured crown. The smaller golden-crowned kinglet has a boldly striped face and crown; adults of both sexes have a yellow to orange crown. This kinglet breeds in mature coniferous and mixedwood stands in the boreal forest and CYPRESS HILLS, and can overwinter in southern Saskatchewan. *Robert Warnock*

FURTHER READING: Alsop, Fred J., III. 2002. *Birds of Canada.* New York: Dorling Kindersley.

KING'S OWN RIFLES OF CANADA, THE. On May 15, 1924, the South Saskatchewan Regiment was divided into five regional battalions, the Moose Jaw Battalion continuing with the name "South Saskatchewan Regiment." A further reorganization of the militia on September 15 of that year saw the battalion re-designated The King's Own Rifles of Canada (KORC). The KORC was re-designated The King's Own Rifles of Canada (MG) on December 15, 1936 when it absorbed B Company, 12th Machine Gun Battalion, Canadian Machine Gun Corps. The outbreak of **WORLD WAR II** found the King's Own Rifles of Canada (MG) critically short of equipment, to the point where the influx of volunteers practiced drill and performed sentry duty carrying wooden cutouts in the shape of rifles.

For the first 29 months of World War II, the KORC continued as a reserve unit while it waited to be mobilized. As the possibility of mobilization seemed more and more remote, many of its members transferred to other units that had already been mobilized for war. Units such as Moose Jaw's 77th Field Battery, Royal Canadian Artillery (RCA), which was mobilized in 1939 for service as part of the 3rd Field Regiment, RCA, recruited large numbers of soldiers from the KORC. The first battalion KORC was eventually mobilized on January 29, 1942, for service with the 8th Canadian Division, 14th Infantry Brigade. Upon mobilization the name reverted to The King's Own Rifles of Canada. The 1st Battalion was assigned to coastal defense duties in British Columbia until it was demobilized on March 30, 1946. The battalion trained in Nanaimo; two companies were later deployed to serve with the Prince Rupert defense force.

Tradition has it that elements of the 1st Battalion also served in the Aleutian Islands, off Alaska's coast: as two of the Aleutian Islands had been temporarily occupied by the Japanese prior to the Battle of Midway, a combined Canadian and American force was deployed to remove them from these islands. A 2nd (Reserve) Battalion, KORC, served in the Reserve Army throughout the war. The King's Own Rifles of Canada became an armoured unit on April 1, 1946, when it was redesignated The 20th (Saskatchewan) Armoured Regiment. The 1st

Battalion, KORC, perpetuated the 46th Battalion, CEF; and the 2nd (Reserve) Battalion, KORC, perpetuated the 128th Battalion, CEF. *Gerry Carline*

KINISTINO, town, pop 702, located 30 km NW of Melfort on Hwy 3. The **SASKATCHEWAN RIVER** Forks are 30 km north of the community. In the 1870s, what was known as the Carrot River Settlement developed just to the south of today's community. In 1883, a post office was established and given the name Kinistino in honour of the **SAULTEAUX** chief, Kinistin. The settlement developed slowly for the first 25 years, until the construction of the Canadian Northern Railway through the area in 1905. Settlers to the area included people of Scottish, English, and Norwegian origins–as well as a Black man, Alfred Schmitz Shadd, who would become one the district's most-respected citizens. Having come to the Kinistino area from Ontario in 1896 to teach school, he was likely the only Black educator out of approximately 400 employed in the territories at the time. Shadd, seeing the great need for doctors in the area, returned to Ontario and completed his medical degree in 1898. He returned to Kinistino and set up a medical practice. He later moved his practice to Melfort, where he set up a drug store, became the editor of the newspaper, and served on the town's council. He ran unsuccessfully in the territorial election in 1901, and in 1905 came within 52 votes of becoming the first Black ever elected to a provincial legislature. Kinistino grew steadily over the decades, attaining town status in 1952 and reaching a peak population of 861 in 1966. For the past 10 years, the population has remained stable at close to 700. Kinistino is the main trading centre in the district; agriculture, a combination of both grain and livestock production, is the major industry.

David McLennan

KINISTINO FIRST NATION. The Kinistin and Yellow Quill Saulteaux people moved to the Qu'Appelle Valley from their ancestral territory

north of the Great Lakes, signing an adhesion to **TREATY 4** on August 24, 1876, at Fort Pelly. Attempting to maintain his traditional way of life, Kinistin broke from Yellow Quill and camped in the parkland of the Barrier River district. Uprooting his people again in 1885 to avoid the Resistance, he moved north into the caribou country of the Dene. Following **RIEL**'s defeat, Kinistin returned to Barrier River to choose a reserve. In February 1890 he sent for Reginald Beatty, extracting a promise to aid him in securing a reserve along the Barrier River. Beatty honoured his promise, and helped persuade the Department of Indian Affairs to create the Kinistin Reserve in 1900 (a clerical error changed the name to Kinistino). Of the two reserves (4,020.2 ha) held by the Kinistino Band, the main community is located 40 km southeast of Melfort, at the west end of Kipabiskau Lake; 306 of the 803 band members live there. *Christian Thompson*

KIPLING, town, pop 1,037, located SW of Whitewood on Hwy 48. The community was named in honour of Rudyard Kipling, the renowned British poet and author. Although the district was settled well before railways arrived, the present community developed as the Canadian Northern Railway came through in 1907–08. Although Kipling experienced substantial decline in the 1930s, **WORLD WAR II** saw it return to prosperity. In the decades since, it has been one of the limited number of communities in rural Saskatchewan to experience continuous growth. On January 1, 1954, Kipling attained town status. As the largest community in the region, centrally situated amidst a half a dozen rural municipalities, Kipling serves a substantial trading area. The economy is largely based upon a combination of grain and livestock production. The livestock industry has been significantly bolstered by the development of several large hog operations in recent years, and Kipling has become the headquarters for one of the world's leading companies conducting research on swine genetics. Heritage properties in the com-

Jack Keith's threshing outfit at the Elias Cumming farm in the Kipling area in 1896. Elias Cumming is driving the wagon in the foreground.

munity include Kipling's former CN station, built in 1908–09, and the rural municipality office, built in 1919. Additionally, the Kipling and District Historical Society Museum occupies a large site featuring some of the region's earliest buildings. To the south of Kipling stands the Bekevar Church, which was constructed by the district's Hungarian settlers in 1911–12.   *David McLennan*

KIRK, LAWRENCE E. (1886–1969). A distinguished agrologist whose selfless dedication improved farming and farm living, Lawrence E. Kirk was born on May 27, 1886, near Bracebridge, Ontario. Having settled with his family in Saskatchewan in 1902, Kirk was educated at the **UNIVERSITY OF SASKATCHEWAN** where he received his BA, BSc, and MSc between 1916 and 1922. Granted his Doctor of Philosophy from the University of Minnesota in 1927, he later held various teaching positions until 1931 when he became Dominion Agrologist in Ottawa. In 1937, Kirk returned to the University of Saskatchewan as Dean of the College of Agriculture. A decade later, he accepted the position of head of the Plant Industry Branch of the Agricultural Division, United Nations, and moved to Rome where he remained until his retirement in 1955. Lawrence Kirk's numerous honours include Fellowships in the Royal Society of Canada and the Agricultural Institute of Canada, an honorary Doctor of Laws from the University of Saskatchewan, and the Medal of Service of the Order of Canada in 1968. He died on November 28, 1969.

KITAGAWA, GENZO (1897–1976). A leader of the province's Japanese Canadian community, Genzo Kitagawa was born in Shiga-ken, Japan on April 28, 1897. In April 1911, he joined his father in Canada. He came to Regina in 1929 and opened Nippon Silk, a store that sold imported Japanese goods with branches in Vancouver and Calgary. When the Pacific War began in 1941, the name of Kitagawa's business changed to Silk-O-Lina in order to avoid unnecessary public harassment. The business grew substantially throughout the postwar era and three more stores were opened in Regina between 1964 and 1975. In recognition of his entrepreneurial spirit and his contributions to others, Genzo Kitagawa was the first Japanese Canadian invested into the Order of Canada in 1973. He died on March 22, 1976.

FURTHER READING: Gordon, G. *Issei: Stories of Japanese Canadian Pioneers.* Toronto: NC Press Limited, 1984.

KIYOOKA, ROY (1926–94). Roy Kiyooka, who was both a poet and artist, was born the son of immigrant Japanese parents in Moose Jaw, Saskatchewan, and died in Vancouver, British

GIBSON PHOTO/UNIVERSITY OF SASKATCHEWAN ARCHIVES A-303
Roy Kiyooka teaching at Emma Lake Art Camp, 1961.

Columbia. Kiyooka spent most of his adolescence in a multi-ethnic neighbourhood in east Calgary, where he soon felt its Anglo-Canadian discourse. Despite the influence of the traumatizing years during **WORLD WAR II** and the infamous evacuation of people of Japanese origin in British Columbia, his interest in art was strong. He managed to study at the Institute of Technology and at the Alberta College of Art from 1946 to 1949, and later (1955–56) made his way to the Instituto San Miguel de Allende in Mexico. His newfound artistic fame helped him achieve a position at the Regina College School of Art, where he was the third instructor to be appointed, following **KENNETH LOCHHEAD** and **ARTHUR MCKAY.** Also involved at the college were **DOUGLAS MORTON, TED GODWIN, RONALD BLOORE,** and **CLIFFORD WIENS.** These artists gravitated towards each other, and shared the feeling of Regina's physical isolation from any artistic centre. Their awareness led to the expansion of the Emma Lake Workshop by inviting major artists as instructors. Kiyooka was one of the leading figures of this workshop and had great influence over decision making. The very successful 1959 workshop, which introduced Abstract Expressionist painting to Saskatchewan, was a crucial decision made by Kiyooka in conjunction with his colleagues. In 1960, Kiyooka's new position at the Vancouver School of Art (Emily Carr College of Art and Design) required him to leave Regina, and he was not included in the *May Show.* Later, the work of the five painters (Lochhead, McKay, Morton, Godwin and Bloore) from this show traveled nationally, and they became known as the **REGINA FIVE.** Kiyooka's name does not appear as a member of the Regina Five, nor is his role in the Emma Lake Workshop mentioned; how-

ever, his contribution in the Regina art community was substantial.

In the late 1960s, he moved away from his familiar medium of painting and became involved in poetry, photography, video, film, and music. His experience in Vancouver in the mid-1970s influenced his interest in the Japanese Redress movement, as well as in issues of Asian-Canadian identity, which is evident from his art productions of this period. In 1978, Kiyooka was awarded the Order of Canada for his achievements as a painter as well as for his success as a teacher. Although he had great influence in the art community in Saskatchewan, he always felt that he was never given the recognition he deserved.   *Machiko Oya and Gail Chin*

KNIGHT, DORIS. Founder of Opera Saskatchewan, Doris Knight has introduced this multimedia art form to the entire province. Working full-time and on a voluntary basis, Knight has served as president of Opera Saskatchewan since its inception in 1992. Her efforts as a fundraiser and promoter of community involvement in the productions have given local performers, musicians, and technicians an opportunity to display their talents. Knight has also devoted her time to community organizations such as the United Appeal and the Canadian Diabetes Association. She was made a Member of the Order of Canada in 1996.

KNIGHT, LEITH (1924–). Leith Knight (*née* Docherty) is credited with preserving and popularizing Moose Jaw's history. Her weekly column has appeared in the local newspaper since 1969, and she was the city's first archivist at the Moose Jaw Public Library. Born in Moose Jaw in 1924 and educated there, she personally knew some of the city's old-timers. Her mother, the night telephone operator for local calls during Prohibition, also told her daughter some colourful tales. Knight's interest in history became more official in the early 1950s. Working at City Hall, she took minutes for the museum committee. A few years later, the Moose Jaw Public Library hired her; in 1968 she initiated a local history collection; and in 1969 she began her weekly column for the *Moose Jaw Times-Herald*. Knight retired from the Moose Jaw Public Library in 1983, but she still writes newspaper columns, and remains an active local historian. Knight is also an accomplished musician, and has served as organist and bell-ringer at several Moose Jaw churches. Her publications include *Birds of the Moose Jaw Area* (1967) and *All the Moose, All the Jaw* (1982), a local history.

Martha Tracey

KNIGHTS OF COLUMBUS. The Knights of Columbus is an international Catholic men's fraternal benefit society founded in 1882 by Father Michael J. McGivney of New Haven, Connecticut to render mutual aid and financial assistance to members and their families in times of need. As the organization grew and developed, the Knights began in addition to promote social and intellectual fellowship for members and their families, and also to reach out to the larger community through sponsorship of educational, charitable, religious, social welfare, war relief and public relief works. The first Knights of Columbus council in Saskatchewan was formed in Regina in 1907, followed by Saskatoon and Prince Albert (1910), Moose Jaw (1911), Weyburn (1914), Humboldt (1917), Yorkton and Gravelbourg (1919), and North Battleford (1920). Now Saskatchewan has over 10,000 Knights in more than 150 councils, including several French, Ukrainian and Filipino councils.

Over the years, the Knights have participated in many worthwhile projects and activities, both within the Catholic Church and in the larger Saskatchewan community. They support community projects in the areas of sports, education, health care, family life, youth, and children with special needs. In 2003 the Knights of Saskatchewan contributed over $1.8 million and 850,000 hours of volunteer service to charitable causes. *Bob Barkman*

FURTHER READING: Argan, W.P. 1982. *Knights of Columbus in Saskatchewan 1907–1982: A History of Achievement.*

KNOTT, DOUGLAS RONALD (1927–). Douglas Knott, born on November 27, 1927, in New Westminster, British Columbia, obtained a Bachelor of Science in Agriculture from the University of British Columbia in 1948, followed by a Master's and a PhD from the University of Wisconsin in 1952,

UNIVERSITY OF SASKATCHEWAN ARCHIVES A-2645

Douglas Knott, University of Saskatchewan Crop Science Department, inspecting a field crop inside a laboratory, 1970s.

specializing in plant genetics. That same year, Knott joined the UNIVERSITY OF SASKATCHEWAN Department of Field Husbandry. From 1965 to 1975 he was Head of the Crop Sciences Department; he served as Acting Dean of Agriculture in 1979 and again in 1989; and he was Associate Dean of Research from 1988 to 1993. In 1986 he was named as the first holder of the W.J. White Chair in Crop Science. He was instrumental in developing the Crop Development Centre at the University of Saskatchewan. Knott became an internationally recognized expert in wheat stem and leaf rust resistance. He developed methods for identifying genes that can be used in breeding rust resistant wheats, and an innovative way to transfer genes from wild wheats to domesticated varieties. His book, *The Wheat Rusts–Breeding for Resistance*, is highly regarded by specialists.

Knott has also developed several varieties of durum: Stewart 63 durum in 1963; Arcola in 1983;

Sceptre in 1985; and Plenty in 1990. Knott is a Fellow of the American Society of Agronomy, the Crop Science Society of America, and the Agricultural Institute of Canada; he has received an honorary life membership in the Canadian Seed Growers Association. His skills are in demand internationally: he was wheat research director for the Zambia-Canada Project from 1983 to 1988, and has been a research consultant and lecturer in Brazil, China, and Kenya. Knott served as president of the Saskatchewan Institute of Agrologists from 1958 to 1959, and as honorary secretary of the SIA from 1970 to 1974. In 1995 he was inducted into the Saskatchewan Agricultural Hall of Fame, and in 1999 was appointed a Member of the Order of Canada for his contributions to agricultural science.

KNOWLES, DOROTHY (1927–). Bringing images of prairie landscapes to the forefront of the Canadian and international art scenes, Dorothy Knowles has had exhibitions in cities such as Montreal, Toronto and New York, and her work is represented in numerous galleries and private collections. Born on April 6, 1927, in Unity, Saskatchewan, she grew up on a farm where she spent much time exploring the natural prairie surroundings. In 1944 she moved to Saskatoon. Originally interested in biology and intending to become a laboratory technician, she completed her BA from the UNIVERSITY OF SASKATCHEWAN in 1948. Though she was always interested in art and nature as a child, her artistic talent was formally discovered that summer, when she attended a six-week art course at Emma Lake, which was led by RETA COWLEY and James Frederick Finley. She took night classes in art in Saskatoon for the next four years and a summer class at the Banff School of Fine Arts, before enrolling at the Goldsmith School of Art in London, England. She is often mentioned in tandem with her husband, abstract painter WILLIAM PEREHUDOFF, who followed her to Europe; after touring Europe's art galleries together until they ran out of money, they

COURTESY OF THE MACKENZIE ART GALLERY 2000-028

Dorothy Knowles, "Anemones and Poppies," 1990, oil on canvas, 76.8 x 178 cm, Collection of the MacKenzie Art Gallery, gift of the artist.

returned to Saskatoon to establish their careers as artists and raise three daughters.

Knowles continued to attend the summer workshops at Emma Lake, where she encountered other artists and critics such as Will Barnet, Herman Cherry, and Clement Greenberg. It was Greenberg who encouraged her to move from experiments with abstract painting to realistic depictions of landscapes directly from nature; this would become her signature style. Often inviting comparisons to Impressionism, Knowles typically uses watercolour, acrylic, charcoal, and oil media for her paintings. Her work has been described as "lush and evocative," combining the traditional values of landscape painting with the innovation of Post-Painterly Abstraction. Her first one-person art show was held in 1954 at the Saskatoon Art Centre. At that time, she was still exploring mainly abstract styles, but as she spent more time either painting directly outdoors or from photographs, her transition to realism occurred. She is noted for capturing the richness and instability of prairie landscape.

Dorothy Knowles received the Saskatchewan Order of Merit in 1987 and was named a Member of the Order of Canada in 2004. She has also been recognized with the Century Saskatoon Award of Appreciation in the Arts (1982), and an honorary degree from the **UNIVERSITY OF REGINA** (1994). Her art has been commemorated on the Saskatchewan stamp of the Canada Day series of postage stamps, *Canada Through the Eyes of its Artists*. Her distinctive technique and style have inspired many other artists, and she is considered unmatched in her ability to represent images of the Canadian west. The government of Saskatchewan chose one of her pieces to present as a gift to the Governor General in 1965.

Lauren Black

KOREAN WAR. The Korean War commenced on June 25, 1950, when North Korean troops crossed the 38th parallel and attacked South Korea. Initially, Canada contributed three destroyers and a Royal Canadian Air Force transport squadron to the United Nations-led operation. By August, however, strong pressure from the United States resulted in the St. Laurent government announcing plans for a Canadian Army Special Force (CASF). The first Canadian unit to land in Korea was the 2nd Battalion, Princess Patricia's Canadian Light Infantry (PPCLI) in December 1950; the CASF, now called the 25th Canadian Infantry Brigade, followed in May. The PPCLI distinguished itself in a significant engagement at Kap'yong in April 1951. Thereafter, UN forces established a front near the 38th parallel where most of the fighting took place until the war ended on July 27, 1953.

In all, 26,791 Canadians served in Korea between 1950 and 1953. Twenty-nine of the 516 killed were from Saskatchewan. Efforts to recog-

nized veterans of the conflict have resulted in the creation of the Korean War Volunteer Service Medal and the dedication of a Korean War monument in Ottawa in 2003.

Holden Stoffel

FURTHER READING: Directorate of History and Heritage, Department of National Defence. 2002. *Canada and the Korean War*. Montreal: Art Global; Wood, James. 2003. "50th Anniversary of End of Korean War Marked." *Regina Leader-Post* (July 28): B2.

KOZIAK, METHODIUS (1904–81). Born in 1904, Brother Methodius Koziak, a noted Ukrainian Catholic educator at St. Joseph's College in Yorkton, organized a community lobby that successfully introduced Ukrainian-language legislation into the curriculum of the Saskatchewan Department of Education. He subsequently taught Ukrainian language fundamentals at the Sheptytsky Institute in Saskatoon for two years and authored *Ukrainian in Saskatchewan Schools: A Brief History*. For a lifetime of service to education and Ukrainian Canadians, Brother Koziak was invested as a Member of the Order of Canada in 1974. He died on April 4, 1981.

KRAMER, EILING (1914–99). Kramer was born July 14, 1914, in Highworth where he completed school. He worked a variety of jobs before purchasing a ranch in the area and began raising cattle. In 1949, he formed a successful auctioneering

DON HEALY/REGINA LEADER-POST

Eiling Kramer, October 1980.

business. During the 1930s, Kramer became active in the United Farmers of Canada and in the Farmer–Labor Party/CCF from its inception. He was CCF organizer of northwestern Saskatchewan in 1946 and helped organize the **SASKATCHEWAN FARMERS UNION** in 1950. He was elected SFU vice-president in 1951 and served until his election to the Legislature in 1952. Kramer was elected to represent the Battlefords where he would be re-elected seven times. **WOODROW LLOYD** appointed him Minister of Natural Resources in 1962. After the CCF defeat in 1964, Kramer was the Opposition critic of the government's highway policy. In 1971, Kramer was again appointed to Cabinet and served as one of **ALLAN BLAKENEY**'s key advisors on rural Saskatchewan. He assumed the portfolio of Natural Resources until he was moved to Highways and Transportation in 1972, in which position he remained until his retirement in 1980. During his term, the department undertook some of the greatest capital expenditures in its history, nearly completing the paving of the provincial highway system. Kramer retired from politics in 1980, settling in North Battleford. He relocated to Regina shortly before his death on May 5, 1999.

Brett Quiring

KRAMER LTD. Kramer Ltd., as it is now known, is a privately owned company which can trace its roots back to the 1920s in Alberta, at a time when most of the earth-moving work was done with teams of horses. The founder, Bob Kramer, went into business with his father-in-law, F.S. Mannix, buying sixty tractors in 1925 to pull elevating graders, which were among the first gasoline-powered crawlers in western Canada. Three years later, Caterpillar introduced the first crawler powered by diesel engines, giving the company a market lead it has never lost in the earth moving business.

By 1944, contractors involved in building roads, airports, pipelines and railway grades during **WORLD WAR II** were finding machines in short supply. Looking for equipment, Bob Kramer visited the Albert Olson Company in Regina; he discovered there were no machines available but the dealership was for sale. Kramer seized the opportunity, released his shares in the Mannix and Kramer partnership, and set up Kramer Tractor Ltd.

Since 1944, the business has grown with Saskatchewan's resource-based economy. In addition to road building, it serves customers in agriculture, forestry, mining, oil and natural gas and power generation industries. Kramer currently operates complete parts, sales and service facilities in Estevan, Kindersley, Regina, Saskatoon, Swift Current and Tisdale.

The company changed its name to Kramer Ltd. in 1990 because the core business had expanded from tractors to on-highway trucks, lift trucks, electrical power generation, industrial engines and agri-

Leo Kristjanson with College of Agriculture Building plans, January 1985.

cultural products. The company currently has approximately 200 employees. The president, Timothy Kramer, is the grandson of the company's founder. *Joe Ralko*

KRISTJANSON, LEO F. (1932–). Leo Kristjanson was born on February 28, 1932, the youngest of eight children. As a child, he worked at his parents' general store in Gimli, Manitoba in addition to working on the family farm. He attended the University of Winnipeg, earning a BA and MA in history. In 1957 he began studies in Agricultural Economics at the University of Wisconsin. Upon finishing his course work in 1959, he accepted a position with the Centre for Community Studies at the **UNIVERSITY OF SASKATCHEWAN**. The Centre had been established to undertake a program of applied social research related to the development of Saskatchewan communities. In 1960 he began lecturing in the Department of Economics and Political Science, and completed his PhD in 1963. In 1965, Kristjanson joined the Department of Economics and Political Science. He was vice-president (Planning) of the University from 1975 to 1980, and in 1980 he became president. Illness prevented him from completing his second term, and he retired in 1989. The atrium in the Agriculture building at the University of Saskatchewan is named in honour of his contribution to the University.

As president, Kristjanson sought funding for agricultural research and a new College of Agriculture building. He formed a "Sodbuster's Club" to raise planning funds and undertook a leadership role in raising over $12,000,000 from private sources for the construction of the building. He was also instrumental in improving the Soil Testing Laboratory, the Poultry Centre, the Kernan Crop Research Laboratory, the Horticulture Field Service Building, the Saskatchewan Institute of Pedology's Field Facilities, and the Large Animal Research Facility. He was also instrumental in having an art gallery become part of the new College of Agriculture building, named in honour of the first resident artist at the university, **AUGUST KENDERDINE**. Also during his term as president, the Centre for the Study of Co-operatives, the Toxicology Research Centre and the Centre for Agricultural Medicine were established.

Kristjanson made major contributions to rural Saskatchewan as a consultant to farm organizations, co-operatives, credit unions, and governments. He served on boards and participated in projects designed to improve living conditions for farmers and their communities. He was chairman of the Saskatchewan Natural Products Marketing Council from 1973 to 1979; a member of a committee to recommend restructuring of the Department of Co-operation; and chairman of the Board of Public Inquiry into the Poplar River Power Project, a provincial study of the environment. He also wrote extensively and has given many public speeches on co-operatives, population and rural development, marketing boards, and commissions. Leo Kristjanson was inducted into the Saskatchewan Agricultural Hall of Fame in 1990. *Blaine A. Holmlund*

KU KLUX KLAN. The Knights of the Ku Klux Klan, originated in Tennessee in the early years of the Reconstruction Era following the American Civil War, soon became synonymous with all the most sinister elements of life in the South, and faded from the scene until its resurrection at the time of **WORLD WAR I**. In the early 1920s it spread across the United States into Canada, and in late 1926 Klan organizers came to Saskatchewan to preach its message of racial and religious hatred and to sell expensive memberships to fund its activities. The first American Klansmen absconded with the treasury late in 1927, but by this time sufficient local people had taken out memberships to take over the leader-

ship of the organization. By the fall of 1928 local Klans had been established in over 100 Saskatchewan towns, usually signalling themselves by a ritual burning of crosses; their leaders claimed an overall membership of some 40,000, who had been attracted by the Klan's attacks on the "unassimilable" immigrants from central and southeastern Europe and on the Roman Catholic church for its "subversion" of the public school system. These attacks revived ancient prejudices dormant for years, spread animosity and suspicion across the province, and threatened groups friendly to the **LIBERAL PARTY**. Thus, Premier **J.G. GARDINER** led a counterattack on the Klan from the summer of 1928 onward, accusing it not only of disrupting social harmony in Saskatchewan but also of being a tool of the **CONSERVATIVE PARTY**. Both the Klan and **J.T.M. ANDERSON**, the Conservative leader, denied the charge, pointing out that the Klan membership contained known Liberals and Progressives as well as Conservatives, and that no proof existed of an alliance between the Klan and any political party. Nevertheless, both the Conservative and Progressive parties raised issues during the 1929 election campaign which drew upon the emotions aroused by the Klan and captured enough votes from the Anglo-Saxon and Protestant sector of the electorate to defeat the Liberals. The Klan convention in 1930 applauded the Anderson government's amendments to the School Act and its new immigration policy,

This postcard of a cross-burning in Regina, May 24, 1928, was addressed to "Hon. Geo. Spence, Parliament Bldgs, Regina Sask." Spence was a member of the provincial Cabinet at the time.

and some local Klans remained active until the worst of the Depression struck the province. In these circumstances, the Knights of the Invisible Empire became truly invisible throughout Saskatchewan and did not reappear for another fifty years.

Patrick Kyba

FURTHER READING: Robin, M. 1992. *Shades of Right: Nativist and Fascist Politics in Canada, 1920–1940.* Toronto: University of Toronto Press.

KUMAR, KRISHNA (1931–). Krishna Kumar was born in Indore, India on January 12, 1931. He did medical studies in India, including general surgery, then studied neurosurgery in Canada, becoming a Fellow of the Royal College of Surgeons of Canada (neurosurgery) in 1961. He was one of two neurosurgeons in Canada who first performed complex neurosurgical procedures for the treatment of Parkinson's disease and chronic pain, and he became an internationally-known expert and speaker in pain management. His neurosurgical procedures were televised on national networks. As a clinical professor at the **UNIVERSITY OF SASKATCHEWAN**, Dr. Kumar published scientific papers and encouraged students and residents to enter the field of neurosurgery.

Dr. Kumar was responsible for bringing the first magnetic imaging resonance unit to the Regina Health District and acquired a Stealth Navigational System for computer-directed surgery, the most sophisticated of its kind in Canada. He served as chair of the medical board of the Workers' Compensation Board of Saskatchewan for 20 years. He received a Quality Improvement Award from the **SASKATCHEWAN MEDICAL ASSOCIATION** and the Saskatchewan College of Physicians & Surgeons, a Community Appreciation Award in 1996, and an Excellence in Teaching Award in 1997. He received the Saskatchewan Order of Merit in 2000.

Michael Jackson

KUPSCH, WALTER O. (1919–2003). For more than fifty years, Walter Oscar Kupsch led a distinguished career in Saskatchewan as a geological research scientist and public servant. Kupsch was born in 1919 in Amsterdam, Netherlands and completed an undergraduate degree in Geology at the University of Amsterdam in 1943. He went on to graduate studies (MSc, PhD) at the University of Michigan, and in 1950 embarked on a long and exceptional career in Saskatoon as a government consultant and a professor of Geological Sciences at the **UNIVERSITY OF SASKATCHEWAN**. As a specialist in historical and glacial geology, Kupsch acquired a passion and fascination for the Canadian north–its

geology and its people. In 1965–66, he served as executive director of the Advisory Commission on the Development of Government in the Northwest Territories, and in the 1970s he was instrumental in forming a Territorial Legislative Assembly. In 1973 the government of Canada appointed him as director of the Churchill River Study. He also served on many other environmental assessment boards. Kupsch's commitment to academic life was equally commendable: he was a gifted and respected teacher, researcher, and historian. Kupsch was elected to fellowships in several professional societies, including the Royal Canadian Geographical Society (1957), the Royal Society of Canada (1963), and the Arctic Institute of North America (1973). He served as Director of the Institute for Northern Studies at the University of Saskatchewan from 1965 to 1973. Kupsch was appointed to the Order of Canada in 1996 for his lifetime devotion to research and public service. He died in Saskatoon in June 2003.

Iain Stewart

FURTHER READING: Warick, Jason. 1996. "Exceptional Effort Honoured by Award." *Saskatoon StarPhoenix* (July 13): A10.

KUZIAK, ALEX GORDON (1908–). Born October 15, 1908, in Canora, Alex Kuziak was educated in Canora, Yorkton, and Saskatoon. After spending a couple of years employed in odd jobs in Canada and the United States, he returned to Saskatchewan in 1930 to attend normal school in Regina. Kuziak returned to Canora to teach, although he left teaching five years later to become secretary-treasurer of the rural municipality of Keys.

© M.WEST, REGINA, WEST'S STUDIO
COLLECTION/SASKATCHEWAN ARCHIVES BOARD R-A7977

Alex Kuziak.

He also operated a real estate and insurance office in Canora and was the senior partner of Canora Electric and Heating. He served on the Canora School Board, Canora Union Hospital Board and on local cooperatives. Active in the CCF from its formation, Kuziak was elected in Canora in 1948. Re-elected in 1952, he was appointed to Cabinet as Minister of Telephones and Minister in charge of the Government Finance Office, the holding company for most of Saskatchewan's **CROWN CORPORATIONS**. After re-election in 1956, Kuziak was moved to the Mineral Resources portfolio where he remained until his defeat in 1964. The provincial parks system expanded significantly under his stewardship. Kuziak was also instrumental in the creation of the Saskatchewan Fisheries Co-operative that helped to expand Saskatchewan's northern fishing industry. In 1965, Kuziak ran for office again as the NDP candidate in the federal riding of Yorkton but was defeated. He was elected as an alderman for the city of Yorkton in 1971 and served one term. An excellent orator, Alex Kuziak was the first person of Ukrainian origin to serve in a Canadian Cabinet. A provincial government building in Yorkton, where he lives, is named after him.   *Brett Quiring*

KYLE, town, pop 478, located approximately 69 km NW of Swift Current, N of the **SOUTH SASKATCHEWAN RIVER** and Saskatchewan Landing Provincial Park. Ranchers operated in the district as early as 1883, and in 1923 the townsite of Kyle was established. The community grew steadily until the 1950s, at which point the population stabilized around 500. The Kyle area economy has traditionally been based upon agriculture, but in recent years oil and gas production has also become important. In 1964, the remains of a woolly mammoth were found by road workers 5 km west of the town. The bones were estimated to be about 12,000 years old; to commemorate the find, a concrete replica of the mammoth, approximately three metres high, was erected in the community.   *David McLennan*

KYLE, ELVA. A tireless volunteer in the areas of health care, the environment, and the arts, Elva Kyle has worked with the United Way both locally and nationally. She served as association president of the **MACKENZIE ART GALLERY** and chair of the Wascana Rehabilitation Centre during its regeneration in 1989. She has also occupied the post of national chairperson for Nature Conservancy, a conservation organization dedicated to protecting endangered and threatened habitats. Past president of the Regina YWCA and an active member of the Regina Symphony Orchestra, Elva Kyle was made a Member of the Order of Canada in 1999.

L

LA LOCHE, northern village, pop 2,136, located in NW Saskatchewan near the Saskatchewan-Alberta border, NW of Buffalo Narrows and just S of Clearwater River Provincial Park on Hwy 155. The community sits on the east side of Lac La Loche and immediately to the north is the main reserve of the Clearwater River Dene Nation. Although aboriginal peoples had traversed the area for generations, the origins of today's community began with the arrival of fur traders and, later, missionaries. Lac La Loche is one of the headwaters of the Churchill River and in 1778 Indian guides led Peter Pond over **PORTAGE LA LOCHE**, or Methy Portage, to the **CLEARWATER RIVER**. The 20-km portage bridged the height of land between the Hudson Bay and Arctic Ocean drainage basins and opened up the vast Athabasca region. *La loche* is French for the burbot, a variety of freshwater cod, and the word "methy" is derived from the Cree term for the same fish. Rival fur trading posts operated on Lac La Loche over the decades following Pond's "discovery" and from the mid-1800s a community began to develop on the west side of the lake. About the same time Catholic missionaries from Ile-à-la-Crosse began working in the area. In 1895 a mission was established at the site of the present community. In 1943, the Grey Nuns arrived at La Loche bringing Western education and nursing to the community. In 1962-63 a road from the south was built to the village, but it was not until

DOUG CHISHOLM PHOTO

The community of La Loche, 1999.

1974 that dial telephone services were available. In 1976, the community received television. Sewer, water, and electrical systems were developed in the 1970s and, in 1983, La Loche was incorporated as a northern village. The population is largely Métis and non-treaty Dene and is very young compared to the rest of the province. Over half of the population are children. Since the demise of the fur trade, La Loche has struggled with high unemployment (close to 50% today). La Loche Community School has an enrolment of close to 1,000; with 50 full-time teachers and a support staff of an additional 50 people, it is the largest employer in the community.

David McLennan

LA RONGE, northern town, pop 2,727, located near the geographical centre of the province, 237 km N of Prince Albert on Hwy 2 at the southern edge of the Canadian Shield. La Ronge is located on the west shore of scenic Lac La Ronge, Saskatchewan's fourth largest lake, which encompasses over 1,300 islands. La Ronge is the largest community in northern Saskatchewan, and along with the neighbouring northern village of Air Ronge and the First Nations communities of the Lac La Ronge Indian Band, the total area population numbers several thousand. La Ronge is a major service and transportation centre for the northern part of the province. Originally inhabited by Cree, the area began to see the incursions of fur traders in the latter 1700s. Numerous competing posts were operated intermittently on the lake throughout the 1800s. In the 1850s some activity began to be centred at what is now known as Stanley Mission as Reverend Robert Hunt oversaw the construction of Holy Trinity Anglican Church and the Hudson's Bay Company established a post at the site. The church at Stanley Mission is now Saskatchewan's oldest standing building. In the early 1900s, trading posts, an Anglican church and an associated residential school were built where the community of La Ronge now sits. Parents usually spent the winters working traplines and returned to the settlement in summer where they grew gardens and fished. In 1911, postal service was established. In the 1930s, La Ronge began to develop as a fly-in fishing resort and after the road was built from Prince Albert in 1947-48 tourism expanded. About the same time the provincial government introduced resource management and conservation officers to the area. Local government came to the community in 1955 when La Ronge gained village status with a population of around 400. Over the following decades the community grew rapidly, reaching a population of 933 by 1966 and almost doubling that a decade later, in 1976, with a population of 1,714. In 1983, La Ronge was proclaimed a northern town. La Ronge today is a base of governmental, institutional, industrial, and commercial activity and its business sector provides a wide range of goods and services. The economy is based on tourism, forestry, mining, commercial fishing, trapping, fur trading, dried meat products, mushroom and berry picking, and the wild rice industry. Lac La Ronge Provincial Park has an international reputation as a wilderness paradise; the park encompasses the lake, Precambrian Shield, boreal forest, and muskeg, and there are more than 30 documented canoe routes in the area.

David McLennan

LABOUR: *see essay on page 515.*

LABOUR AND CIVIC POLITICS. Organized labour has participated in civic politics in different ways and with varying levels of organization over the years. In some instances labour ran its own candidates, but normally worked with broader coalitions and citizen organizations. Sometimes labour organizations or their leaders formed and led the coalitions, but often labour supported other civic voter blocs. Some progressive candidates, **M.J. COLDWELL** in Regina for example, avoided running on labour slates and were successful. **LOUIS "SCOOP" LEWRY**, mayor of Moose Jaw, and **HENRY BAKER**, mayor of Regina, were examples of politicians whose initial success was due to organized labour campaigns. Labour organizations also ran or supported candidates for separate and public school boards. When local labour campaigns were effective, an opposing business-oriented political organization was usually set up to counteract them.

At one time there were restrictions on who was eligible to vote and to run for office. The financial deposit required for candidates often acted as a deterrent for working class candidates, and the local newspapers often provided slanted coverage. However, in many cases representatives of labour were appointed to serve on civic committees and agencies, and representatives of labour organizations presented briefs to city council on issues of concern to their members. One successful campaign was for a public streetcar service in Regina. Union locals organized Trades and Labour Councils (TLCs) in Moose Jaw, Regina, Saskatoon, and Prince Albert in 1906–07. The Moose Jaw TLC ran three candidates in the 1906 civic election and elected George Glassford, the first labour alderman in Saskatchewan.

After the settlement boom in 1913–14, a recession set in and over 4,000 were unemployed in Saskatchewan cities. The cities laid off workers and stopped public works projects. The Prince Albert TLC helped elect Robert Heggie, a boilermaker, to city council in an interim election in 1913. The TLCs in Regina, Moose Jaw, Saskatoon, and Prince Albert ran official Labour candidates in the 1914 municipal elections. They were concerned about the work-for-relief program and the unsanitary conditions for unemployed single men. H.D. Bailie was elected as the first Labour alderman in Saskatoon in 1914, and Moose Jaw elected R.H. Chadwick in 1916 and Alex McAndrew in 1917. The Regina TLC organized the Labour Representative League and elected the first labour alderman, Harry Perry, a bookbinder, in 1915. James Habkirk followed him in 1916, and in 1918 the Regina TLC ran five candidates. All were defeated as their patriotism was questioned when they were supported by *Der Courrier*, the German language newspaper. Between 1913 and 1919, the TLCs in Saskatchewan ran twenty-nine candidates for city council in these four cities, and elected ten aldermen.

During the 1930s there were labour campaigns in the cities. In the 1935 civic election in Regina, the Civic Labour League held candidate selection meetings at the ward level. A.C. Ellison, the labour candidate for mayor, was elected along with six labour aldermen out of ten on council. **BILL DAVIES** helped organize the Civic Reform Association in Moose Jaw, which developed a program, skillfully used the radio, and successfully ran candidates in the late 1940s and early 1950s. There were attempts to establish municipal sections of the CCF and NDP, and some labour support was given to various civic political organizations started by the Communist Party. Progressive candidates were sometimes elected to councils, and over the years drew financial and organizational support from unions and labour organizations. In later years, labour has focused on provincial and federal politics.   *Bob Ivanochko*

FURTHER READING: Cherwinski, W.J.C. 1972. "Organized Labour in Saskatchewan: The TLC years, 1905–1945." PhD dissertation, University of Alberta; Warren, J. 1985. "From Pluralism to Pluralism: The Political Experience of Organized Labour in Saskatchewan from 1900 to 1938." MA thesis, University of Regina.

© M.WEST, REGINA, WEST'S STUDIO COLLECTION/ SASKATCHEWAN ARCHIVES BOARD R-B8376

Bill Davies, as Executive Secretary of the Saskatchewan Federation of Labour and Moose Jaw alderman, was a key spokesperson for the successful Civic Reform Association in Moose Jaw.

LINDA HOLOBOFF PHOTO/SASKATCHEWAN ARCHIVES BOARD S-SP-A11063-2, SASKATOON STARPHOENIX FONDS

The legal character of activities such as picketing has been debated through the decades following the passage of the Trade Union Act in the 1940s.

LABOUR AND THE COURTS. As employment relationships changed in response to industrialization in 18th- and 19th-century Britain, workers chose to form organizations known as trade unions which could represent their collective interests as a counterweight to the power of their employers. Participation in trade unions was initially characterized as criminal activity because of the capacity of these organizations to influence the contractual relationship between an employer and an individual employee. By the early 20th century, statutory enactments in Britain and Canada had removed the stigma of criminality from trade unions. The courts continued, however, to impose civil consequences for many forms of union activity through legal actions designed to protect individuals and corporations from unlawful interference with their commercial undertakings.

In the context of criminal and civil law principles which placed severe restrictions on trade unions, it is perhaps not surprising that unions saw their experience with the courts as largely negative. When collective bargaining statutes similar to the Saskatchewan TRADE UNION ACT were passed in Canada in the 1940s, union disaffection with the courts was one of the reasons the administration of the new legislative system was put in the hands of independent labour relations boards on which the unions were explicitly represented. With emergence of the new collective bargaining statutes, it fell to labour relations boards to determine many of the issues associated with the employment relationship in unionized workplaces. In Saskatchewan as elsewhere, the courts nonetheless continued to play a significant role in certain aspects of industrial relations, notably in the case of industrial conflict. The Trade Union Act made strikes and other industrial action lawful under certain circumstances; but it did not, from the point of view of the courts, answer all questions about the legal character of activities associated with strikes, such as picketing.

It was clear that activity which was in itself criminal or legally wrongful, such as assault, destruction of property, or menacing behaviour, was not protected simply because it was associated with a strike. More complex questions arose, however, about whether picketing or other kinds of industrial action could still be the basis for traditional legal actions based on interference with the economic activity of employers, notwithstanding that a strike itself might be legal under the Trade Union Act. Labour disputes typically unfold and evolve rapidly, and remedies which require awaiting the outcome of a complete civil trial were not considered useful by employers. What employers often sought from the courts was immediate assistance in the form of an injunction, a remedy which drew on the power of the courts to ameliorate the situation of an employer who claimed to face drastic consequences if the activity initiated by the union was not brought to a halt in short order. On an application for an injunction, applicants are not required to prove the case fully on its merits, but only to make a plausible case that, before the case can be heard in its entirety by the court, they will suffer harm which cannot be reversed later.

The way in which the courts have approached the determination of applications for labour injunctions has changed significantly over time in Saskatchewan. In the first couple of decades following the passage of the Trade Union Act, the courts continued to place fairly serious limits on the activities which unions could carry out without incurring an injunctive order. In one case in 1964, for example, the Saskatchewan Court of Appeal upheld an injunction issued by a Queen's Bench judge which was partly based on a finding that, although the members of the union had been picketing peacefully, their picket signs were designed not simply to provide information, but to persuade others not to cross the picket line—which could be construed as interfering with the business interests of the employer.

Although the courts in Saskatchewan continued to entertain injunction applications in industrial disputes, they began to give trade unions more latitude with respect to activities which would be considered acceptable. In the 1980s, the Court of Appeal acknowledged that picketing by its nature is designed to persuade—not simply to inform—and decided that picketing was an acceptable part of strike action so long as it was conducted peacefully. More recently still, in 1998, the Saskatchewan Court of Appeal recognized that picketing as such is a form of expression protected by the Canadian Charter of Rights and Freedoms, and that the objective of inflicting economic harm on an employer is not an aberration, but an inherent component of picketing activity. The Court further recognized that the Trade Union Act gave rise to a new legal regime for trade unions, one in which industrial conflict, though subject to regulation, is regarded as a natural part of the collective bargaining relationship; the statute represented a conscious departure on the part of the legislature from a traditional system which stressed the property and commercial interests of employers.

Although trade unions still express concern that the courts are not a hospitable environment from their point of view, judicial decisions of the kind described above show that the courts are reinterpreting their role in labour relations in the light of legislative and constitutional developments.

Beth Bilson

FURTHER READING: Fudge, J. and E. Tucker. 2001. *Labour Before the Law: The Regulation of Workers' Collective Action in Canada, 1900–1948.* Toronto: Oxford University Press; Weiler, P. 1980. *Reconcilable Differences: New Directions in Canadian Labour Law.* Toronto: Carswell Methuen.

LABOUR COUNCILS AND THE CANADIAN LABOUR CONGRESS. The Canadian Labour Congress (CLC) was formed in 1956 when the Trades and Labour Congress of Canada (TLC), representing the skilled trades, amalgamated with the Canadian Congress of Labour (CCL), representing industrial workers. The CLC represents three million workers in Canada affiliated through their unions. The CLC prairie regional office in Regina delivers national political and educational programs, and assists the provincial federations of labour and the local district labour councils with their activities in Alberta, Saskatchewan, Manitoba, the Northwest Territories, and Nunavut. Saskatchewan currently has seven chartered labour councils: Regina and District Labour Council (chartered 1907), Saskatoon DLC (1912), Moose Jaw DLC (1906), North Battleford DLC, Prince Albert DLC, Weyburn DLC, and Humboldt DLC. There are as well two active labour committees: Yorkton and District Labour Committee, and Estevan Labour Committee. Once a committee has approximately 2,000 members from five different affiliates unions, the CLC can charter it. These labour councils and committees play an important role in the community. Besides having an interest in municipal politics, these organizations enlighten their respective communities on issues that affect working people; some issues are of a national nature, such as Employment Insurance and national childcare programs, while others are more regional in nature, such as closure of a plant and loss of local jobs. Many councils are very active in the community by holding Labour Day picnics, May Day events, seniors suppers and other events, which often include the less fortunate and the underemployed members of the community.

Rick Byrne and Bob Ivanochko

LABOUR AND EQUITY-SEEKING GROUPS.

The Saskatchewan labour movement has a long history of struggle for equality of all workers. In the late 1970s and early 1980s the **SASKATCHEWAN FEDERATION OF LABOUR** (SFL) and some affiliates established women's committees; through their local and provincial activism, demands for equality of women in the workplace and in the union movement intensified. Saskatchewan women have always played an active role in strikes and strike support. By the Saskatchewan Government Employees Association general strike in the public service in 1979 and in the Canadian Union of Public Employees hospital workers strike in 1982, women's presence was very evident on the picket lines and at the bargaining table. Women were also active in creating change in the labour movement through progressive organizations such as Saskatchewan Working Women. By the early 1990s the SFL structure was amended to ensure women's representation from unions with more than one representative on the SFL Executive Council. Women's presence in union conventions has increased over the years, and their influence in the policy direction of the labour movement is evident with resolutions to the conventions on issues such as equality rights, pay equity, childcare, and harassment protection.

The struggle of women workers to claim their place in the labour movement opened doors for other equality seeking groups. The labour movement has long supported the rights of Aboriginal peoples and their demands for self-government. In 1994 the SFL created a vice-president position for Aboriginal workers, and an Aboriginal Committee was created at the same time. This led to similar actions by unions belonging to the SFL. "Unionism on Turtle Island" was developed by the SFL as a popular education workshop to increase awareness of Aboriginal issues in the non-Aboriginal membership. Saskatchewan unions have led the way for changes

to collective agreements which recognize leaves for traditional hunting, hiring of Aboriginal peoples (particularly in the north), and other measures to remove barriers and increase participation of Aboriginal workers in their workplace and in their unions.

In the late 1990s the SFL created a committee to address the concerns of Gay, Lesbian, Bisexual and Transgendered (GLBT) workers; this was followed by the creation of a vice-president position to represent GLBT members. These actions were built upon many years of working with the GLBT community and of raising these issues at conventions of unions, labour councils, and the SFL. The labour movement provided support over many years by lobbying for changes to benefit and pension plans to include same-sex partners; they have also taken strong positions in support of same-sex marriage.

Equality rights for workers of colour and differently abled workers have also been critical issues in the labour movement's struggle for equality rights. Although vice-president positions have not been established for these two equality-seeking groups, there has been an emphasis over the years on issues which have significant impact on these workers. The labour movement has demanded that employers and unions provide anti-racism training and that collective agreements have clauses prohibiting discrimination. Unions have bargained to ensure that collective agreements have provisions removing barriers to hiring, training, and retention. Unions have worked with community groups of the disabled to ensure that these workers have opportunities in Saskatchewan workplaces, and that their collective agreements provide protections and special measures to ensure access to the workplace.

Young workers are another group regarded as "equality seeking" by the labour movement. The SFL and affiliated unions and labour councils have established Youth Committees and Youth vice-president positions, and have established and supported programs such as the SFL/CLC Summer Camp for 13- to 16-year-old sons and daughters of union members. The labour movement has supported the SolidarityWORKS! Program of the Canadian Labour Congress, which provides placement with a union or community group as well as education about the labour movement and global issues. Working with the Department of Labour, the union movement has delivered in high schools the Ready For Work program, which addresses the workplace health and safety issues of young workers. Youth issues have had a prominent place in the labour movement, particularly over the past fifteen years. *Barbara Byers*

LABOUR AND POLITICS.
For the first few decades of the 20th century, workers had not yet become a majority in Canada and only a small percentage of mainly skilled tradesmen were organized

into trade unions. Nevertheless, organized labour was growing as an interest group which exerted some influence over the political complexion of the broader society. They had achieved legal recognition and made some progress in struggles to abolish child labour and improve hours of work and working conditions. Unions had also played a role in achieving free public education and political reforms such as the secret ballot and a broadened franchise.

If unions were not yet a large part of the body politic in Canada, this was doubly true of Saskatchewan, which remained an overwhelmingly agrarian province for the first half century of its existence. But while trade unionists were not a significant percentage of the population, political and social ideas associated with labour exerted an indirect influence within agrarian and political organizations. Most immigrants to the province became farmers, but many were from urban working class backgrounds. Several of the leaders of the early farm organizations had previous experience in trade unions and labour and socialist parties. Indeed the Farmer's Union of Canada, a forerunner of the United Farmers of Canada, was founded in 1921 by former members of the One Big Union, a radical industrial union founded in 1919.

The 1930s would see tendencies associated with labour involved in both social democratic politics and extra-parliamentary struggles. In 1931, the small Independent Labour Party (ILP) joined with the United Farmers of Canada (UFC) to form the Farmer-Labour Group; the latter would become the provincial section of the **CO-OPERATIVE COMMONWEALTH FEDERATION** (CCF), which was founded as Canada's national social democratic party in 1932. The CCF in Saskatchewan would be mainly an agrarian party, but with an urban labour component. It had established itself as the main parliamentary opposition in Saskatchewan by the end of the 1930s.

On the extra-parliamentary scene, the **WORKER'S UNITY LEAGUE** (WUL) was a Communist-led union federation which headed many of the struggles of the urban unemployed and attempted to organize the coal miners in the Estevan-Bienfait district in 1931. The unemployed struggles in Saskatchewan and elsewhere were a factor leading to the establishment of unemployment insurance by the federal government in 1941. Organized labour became a significant influence in achieving legislative gains for both themselves and others after the CCF formed the provincial government in 1944; these gains included a new **TRADE UNION ACT**, which was one of the most advanced in Canada for that period. Provincial government employees were the first in the country to be given collective bargaining rights. Saskatchewan enacted the first provincial Bill of Rights. The province also pioneered hospital insurance and enacted in 1962 Canada's first universal medical care plan, which would soon become a federal-provincial program throughout Canada. Trade union activists played a role in all of these achievements.

In the 1960s, Canada and Saskatchewan saw an acceleration of transformations which had been evident for some time in the political economy and demographics of the country. Canada was urbanizing rapidly, and the public sector was becoming larger and more sophisticated. Trade unions were growing as a percentage of the work force and becoming more diversified, with public and service workers soon outnumbering industrial and craft workers. Women were also becoming a much higher percentage of the trade union movement.

Changes were underway in labour politics as the trade unions adapted to the evolving political economy. In 1961 the CCF and the Canadian Labour Congress (CLC) collaborated to found the **NEW DEMOCRATIC PARTY** (NDP) in an attempt to make a broader electoral appeal to urban working people; it was led by longtime Saskatchewan premier **T.C. DOUGLAS**. The new strategy enjoyed some limited success, and eventually the NDP governed four different provinces, whereas the old CCF had never won an election outside of Saskatchewan. There, the NDP became and has remained a predominantly urban party, but this has had more to do with changing demographics than with the transformation from CCF to NDP: farms became larger, and farmers became fewer and more conservative in Saskatchewan as in much of Canada. Paradoxically, the influence of organized labour within the NDP appears to have declined at the same time as the NDP became a more urban party. The old farmer-labour alliance dating back to the latter days of the CCF was gradually replaced by a leadership of urban professionals—middle-level civil servants and managers, lawyers, teachers, co-op and credit union bureaucrats, and other professionals. There has also often been conflict between public sector unions and the government, public institutions, and Crown corporations; this conflict has become a persistent source of tension between the NDP and the trade unions. Generally, the trade unions tend to support the NDP during provincial elections, and a majority of trade unionists vote for them; but the close connections of previous decades have declined. During the recent years of neo-liberal assault on the welfare state and trade union rights, the politics of organized labour has largely revolved around defending the gains of the past.

Lorne Brown

FURTHER READING: Brown, Lorne A., J.K. Roberts and J.W. Warnock. 1999. *Saskatchewan Politics from Left to Right*. Regina: Hinterland Publications; Warnock, J.W. 2004. *Saskatchewan: The Roots of Discontent and Protest*. Montreal: Black Rose Books.

Labour

Three Centuries of Working for Wages in Saskatchewan

J.W. Warren

Masters and Servants: Employment in the Fur Trade

From the early 1700s until the 1840s, a job with one of the fur trading companies like the Hudson's Bay Company (HBC) and the North West Company (NWC) provided virtually all the paid employment opportunities available in the northwestern interior of present-day Canada. It was a small workforce: in 1820, at the peak of fur trade activity, there were fewer than 2,000 wage workers employed by the fur companies. These workers accounted for a scant minority of the population of the fur country, which had a First Nations population that probably numbered in the hundreds of thousands. Paid employees in the fur trade were almost exclusively male; there is only one known example of a woman who went to work for the HBC–disguised as a man, her cover eventually blown by a pregnancy. In the parlance of the time, HBC employees were referred to as *servants*; the Montreal-based NWC preferred the French term *engagés* for its workers. Fur trade managers in the English-owned HBC were known as *officers*; in the NWC they were often referred to as *bourgeois* or *partners*. European society during the heyday of the fur trade was rigidly hierarchical; its class divisions were reflected in the way working relationships in the North American fur trade were structured.

Employees signed contracts, generally from three to seven years in length. Over the duration of their contracts, they were required to provide loyal and obedient service to their employers. There were stiff penalties for employees who quit their jobs, disobeyed orders, or were disrespectful to officers; these penalties could range from fines and forfeiture of wages to imprisonment and even flogging. Upward mobility was rare. There are only a handful of examples of servants who managed to earn positions in the ranks of the HBC officer class. The NWC was somewhat more liberal about advancement, but even within that company, movement from the lower to upper ranks was rare. The relationships between employers and employees were governed by master and servant laws, which included prohibitions on workers engaging in collective actions such as strikes to win improvements in wages and working conditions. It would not be until 1872, when the government of Sir John A. Macdonald passed The Trade Union Act, that Canadian workers could legally belong to an organization that tried to engage in collective bargaining. Nevertheless, fur trade workers did launch a number of strikes in support of improved wages and working conditions. The first strike known to have occurred in the territory that would become Saskatchewan took place in 1777 at Cumberland House: that first labour dispute, led by Orkney Islanders James Batt and William Taylor, resulted in an increase in wages for employees who worked at the HBC's inland posts, as opposed to those assigned to less arduous work at posts located on Hudson's Bay. While striking workers occasionally won improvements, they were more often fined, fired with their wages forfeited, or imprisoned for defying their masters.

The fur trade companies developed schedules to govern the wage rates for their servants and *engagés*. For example, there were three general classes of workers within the HBC. First the apprentice clerks, who could eventually hope to move into the officer ranks upon completion of their three-year apprenticeship period. Then there were two other *servant* classes for whom movement into the officer class was by and large out of the question: one included the voyageurs, canoemen, hunters and interpreters, who were generally First Nations, Métis or French Canadian; the other consisted of skilled tradesmen and labourers. The HBC relied heavily on recruits from Britain, especially men who hailed from the Orkney Islands, to fill the ranks of the latter group. In the NWC, workers in this category were a mixture of British, French Canadian and people of Aboriginal ancestry. Wage rates in this group were determined by craft: highest paid were skilled trades such as joiners (carpenters), stone masons, coopers (keg makers), and boat builders; sail makers and net menders made less; and labourers earned the least. Regardless of craft, wages in the fur trade tended to be higher than those available for similar work on the Orkney Islands or in Lower Canada.

The voyageurs of the northwest developed a distinct and colourful culture. Their endless miles of canoe paddling were accompanied by a repertoire of traditional songs, many of which were too ribald to have been recorded by the literati of the time. They valued humour and told tall tales; and they took great pride in feats of bravery and strength, paying special tribute to those who could carry the greatest number of ninety- pound packs over portages the furthest or the fastest. When competition between the NWC and HBC was at its highest, in the early 1800s, fur trade workers were able to earn higher wages and improved working conditions simply because they had the option of threatening to quit and go to work for the opposition. While this sort of action ran contrary to master-and-servant law, the rivalry between the two companies was so intense that masters did little to discourage deserters from their competitor's ranks. The Napoleonic Wars and the War of 1812 reduced the numbers of workers available for the fur trade, as able-bodied men were scooped up by naval press gangs in Britain or by the militias of Canada. The shortage of new workers, combined with inter-company rivalry, further strengthened the bargaining position of fur trade employees.

The fur trade made considerable use of the unpaid labour of Aboriginal women, who married *à la façon du pays* (what we now call a common-law relationship) or otherwise cohabited with fur trade officers and employees. These women performed important functions: they prepared food and hides; they made moccasins and snowshoes; and they acted as interpreters and diplomats, helping to build alliances with Indian bands, native trappers, and traders. Children from these unions became the founders of the Métis Nation; they were often employed by the fur companies as hunters, interpreters and voyageurs. The fur companies avoided hiring First Nations people for wage labour in districts where furs were plentiful, preferring to have Indians trapping for them out in the bush. There were significant exceptions, however, such as the Iroquois voyageurs from the Great Lakes region, who became famous for their skill at traveling by canoe.

Following the merger of the NWC into the HBC in 1821, wage rates fell and nearly a third of the workforce was laid off because of downsizing (many trading posts closed, and use of the trade route to Montreal was reduced). In the wake of post-HBC-NWC merger lay-offs, many Métis and First Nations people in the northwest earned their livings from self-employment, supplying buffalo meat and pemmican to the HBC and the region's early agricultural settlers. Many former fur trade employees became independent traders themselves; some started businesses as freight haulers, while others took up farming. This trend continued as the fur trade waned in importance over the mid-decades of the 19th century.

The Railroad Workers

The construction of the CANADIAN PACIFIC RAILWAY (CPR), which began in the early 1880s, saw a new wave of wage earners appear on the Canadian prairies. A small army of men and hundreds of horses and mules were required to build the roadbed and lay the tracks for the new railroad. Approximately 7,600 men were employed in the construction

of the CPR from central Canada to the Pacific coast; about of third of that number worked on the construction of the prairie section. Many of the men who came to work on the construction of the CPR had been employed on other railway projects. They often referred to themselves as *boomers* who traveled from one railway construction boom to another; their employers called them *navvies*. They were of mixed ethnicity, many just recent immigrants to Canada or the USA: the legendary "giant Swedes," who handled railway ties as though they were toothpicks, as well as Italians, Irishmen, Germans, British and Canadians; and the Chinese "coolies," who worked on the Pacific section of the project but did not participate in the work on the prairie portion of the line.

This work was physically demanding: ten-hour days were the norm, but twelve and even fourteen-hour days were not unheard of. Accommodations were Spartan: the men slept in crowded, airless, three-storey dormitory cars or tents. The quality of meals varied depending on the sub-contractor providing them; it was understood, however, that boomers simply would not work if they were not adequately fed. Wages compared well with those paid in the settled regions of the North America: the pay rates ranged from $1.25 to $2.50 per day, putting a higher-paid navvy in the same income range as a skilled carpenter in the east. The biggest cause for dissent among the boomers was the Company's frequent inability to pay wages on time.

Like the voyageurs before them, the navvies developed their own unique working culture; they were proud of their physical prowess and skill at laying tracks. Sub- contractors facing completion deadlines no doubt appreciated the boomers' penchant for wanting to set construction records. Men working on the CPR took pride in laying four or five miles of track in a single day, surpassing the efforts of boomers on other projects; the work was done with both strength and finesse, often in time with traditional working songs such as *"drill ye terriers drill."* Labour disputes erupted during construction of the railroads when wages were late or pay cuts were threatened. A strike by construction crews occurred near Maple Creek in 1883; the boomers' picket lines were broken by a contingent of North-West Mounted Police. In most of the strikes involving late wages, the boomers refused to return to work until their wages had been paid.

The men who operated the trains on the completed railway belonged to the running trades: skilled engineers, firemen, brakemen and conductors. The running trade's workers on the prairies went on strike in 1883 over a wage cut. After losing in that first attempt, they

SASKATCHEWAN ARCHIVES BOARD R-A18810

CPR employees, Broadview, 1907.

Digging a trench for a sewer on Central Avenue in Prince Albert, ca. 1910.

Construction of a building in Prince Albert, 1909. The mayor is laying the cornerstone.

increased their bargaining power by establishing locals of the US-based international railway unions: the Brotherhood of Locomotive Engineers, the Brotherhood of Locomotive Firemen, the Order of Railway Conductors, and the Brotherhood of Railroad Trainmen. The railway running trades brotherhoods were the first unions to appear in the territory that would become Saskatchewan. The unionized railroaders were in a much stronger position in 1892, when the CPR again attempted to implement a wage cut for workers on the prairie section of the line: the conductors and brakemen were able to defeat the company in a groundbreaking strike which saw the company recognize and bargain with their unions and provide raises as opposed to wage cuts.

The Settlement Boom

The completion of the CPR provided the transportation required for thousands of agricultural settlers to come west and take up homesteads: the population of the region that became Saskatchewan jumped from 91,279 in 1901 to 647,835 in 1916. Not everyone who came west had homesteading in mind: the region's new agricultural economy would require an infrastructure of railway branch lines, grain elevators, and towns and cities with repair shops, retail stores, warehouses, schools, hospitals and offices for clerks, realtors, insurance agents and lawyers. Skilled trades people and labourers working for wages were required to meet these needs. During the settlement boom, which lasted roughly from 1900 to 1913, many workers came west to take advantage of plentiful job opportunities and of wages that were typically higher than what could be earned in central Canada. For example, a carpenter in Regina in 1911 could earn up to 63.75¢ an hour while his counterpart in Toronto could expect to earn 52.5¢ an hour. However, the cost of living in the growing west was higher than it was in the settled parts of the country, and at times cancelled out any real advantage.

Skilled workers and labourers were in high demand during the settlement boom. Workers in this sector included carpenters, masons, bricklayers, plasterers, painters, plumbers, and electricians as well as

ordinary labourers. The ranks of the skilled trades were made up primarily of recent British immigrants or Canadians of British ancestry; labourers were a mixed group of British, Germans, and Eastern Europeans. The building trades workers, like the railway running trades before, brought their union organizations with them to the west. Most were members of craft unions, which promoted united worker efforts to encourage employers to bargain collectively with their employees, maintained apprenticeship systems for training new entrants to the various trades, and provided their members with a variety of benefit schemes and insurance plans, covering for instance funerals and emergency loans.

The province's new cities soon had labour temples, later called union halls, which hosted union meetings, libraries, lectures, and social events. The boom time unions held picnics, sporting events, and Labour

Labour Day parade, Regina, ca. 1913.

Highway bridge over the South Saskatchewan River, under construction, Saskatoon, 1907.

the seasonal nature of construction work on the prairies: they could expect four to five months a year when weather conditions did not permit outdoor construction. At the time, an average family could aspire to owning a home and living comfortably on an annual income of $1,200. In 1912, a skilled bricklayer making around $143 per month would have been in reasonable financial shape if it were not for the winter months, when there was little if any work.

The province's new unions received a warm welcome from Saskatchewan's first Premier, **WALTER SCOTT**. Prior to entering politics, Scott had been a unionized printer in Winnipeg; while owner of the *Regina Leader* and the *Moose Jaw Times*, Scott became one of the first employers in the province to engage in collective bargaining with his workers, who were members of the International Typographical Union. He was probably the first employer in Saskatchewan to recognize the eight-hour day, which was put in place at his newspapers by 1906. Scott won the support of organized labour when he insisted that the province's new Legislative Building be constructed under the provisions of a Fair Wage Clause included in the builder's contract. This clause ensured that local union wage rates would apply to work on the provincial government's first mega-project; he appointed one of the province's early labour leaders, Tom Molloy, as Fair Wage Commissioner, to ensure that the contractor met the conditions of the clause. Scott also introduced the province's first occupational health and safety rules, and established a modest workmen's compensation program.

Day parades complete with floats, bands and uniformed marching workers. Trades and Labour Councils, made up of representatives from the cities' various unions, were established in the larger centres; along with their union affiliates, they belonged to the Trades and Labour Congress of Canada, which had been established in Toronto in 1883 as a national voice for labour. Moose Jaw became home to the province's first labour council in 1906, and was soon followed by other centres. The unionized building trades had the practice of collective bargaining well established in the province's urban centres prior to the outbreak of World War I. Contract disputes with the employers' organizations, known as "Builder's Exchanges," occasionally resulted in strikes, but for the most part labour relations were fairly amicable. The construction sector was booming, with profit levels that allowed for steady increases in wages. Despite seemingly good wage rates, workers in the building trades were subject to lengthy periods of lay-off and down-time due to

The Hard Life of a Labourer

Construction labourers and workers in the province's small but growing mining industry fared much worse than skilled workers, even in the

Lumbermen eat a meal in the forest near Prince Albert (1903 or before).

Coal miners.

midst of boom time conditions. Workers on projects such as sewer and waterline construction in Regina and Saskatoon earned as little as 17.5¢ per hour while working under hazardous conditions; a regular work day was ten hours, and Sundays were the only days off. Miners in the coal fields of southeastern Saskatchewan generally earned higher wages than construction labourers, but working conditions underground were no better than those in a sewer line trench: during peak seasons, miners would be required to work 14-hour days, six days a week; they had the rent for small uninsulated company-owned shanties deducted from their pay, and were forced to shop at company stores with inflated prices. Urban day labourers gravitated to what housing they could afford. Regina's working class ghetto at the time was known as German Town—even though the majority of residents in the area were Eastern European, not German. Houses in the slum area were typically three-room shacks; they were all jammed together on 25-foot lots; very few of them had either sewer or water service; and there was no regular garbage pickup. Not surprisingly, the residents of German Town experienced a far higher rate of communicable diseases than people in more affluent parts of the city.

Out-of-town work usually required contractors to supply bunkhouse accommodation. Bunkhouses were generally overcrowded and poorly ventilated; the straw-filled mattresses and blankets were often ridden with bed bugs; and there was frequently nowhere to bathe or shower. On some jobs, room and board came "*found*," meaning free and on top of wages; in other instances, room and board were deducted from a worker's pay. Workers were typically paid in cash every Saturday, which proved a weekly bonanza for bar owners in the province. The forces of temperance including the Women's Christian Temperance Union campaigned for prohibition, deploring the fact that some families went hungry because Saturday's pay packet was squandered at the bar before the worker made it home. The battle for the prohibition of the sale of alcohol in the province was won in 1917, following the awarding of the electoral franchise to women in 1916; the taps would stay turned off until 1925.

The Bust

The settlement boom and the frenzied business speculation that accompanied it sputtered out by the time World War I began in 1914. With most of the good land taken up by homesteaders and further immigration stalled by the disruptions produced by the war, the Saskatchewan boom was over. Work dried up for the construction trades, and railway branch line construction came to a virtual halt. Unemployment rates initially soared, even though thousands of working-age men from the province had signed up for military service. The British-dominated building trades unions had a tough time sustaining even skeleton organizations during the war, as some lost over 75% of their membership to service in the military. Saskatchewan lacked the heavy industries that produced jobs through war-related production in other regions of Canada. Once it became clear that the war would be a long one, more workers left the province to seek jobs elsewhere, reducing the need for municipalities to provide relief work to the unemployed. Coal production in the province increased during the war; however, wartime labour laws stood in the way of miners who tried to organize unions to improve their wages and working conditions. Agriculture fared well during and immediately after the War: grain prices rose steadily, reaching record levels by 1919. Hired men were hard to come by during the war, and at peak times farm workers could earn wages that compared favourably with those of urban labourers.

Women in the Workforce

Women formed a low-paid minority of the labour force during the early decades of the 20th century. The traditional values of the time viewed motherhood and homemaking as the appropriate roles of women: indeed, when women had to take jobs it was seen as a sign of societal failure, or a dire necessity in the case of widows or women whose husbands were unemployed. Young women were considered eligible to perform wage labour in order to support a poor family or to earn pin money until such time as they found a husband and left both their parents' homes and the workforce. With limited knowledge or means of birth control, larger families were the norm, and working-class women of childbearing age typically had enough on their hands to make paid work something they sought only out of serious economic necessity. The reality was that many women needed to work. Many young women of limited means left the Dickensian poverty of the industrialized cities of Canada, Britain, and Europe to take low-paid work as domestic servants on the prairies. Affluent rural and urban families paid very little for the services of girls who worked unlimited hours with few days off. The province's first Minimum Wage Act, passed in 1919, applied only to female workers: it excluded domestic servants, even though these accounted for most of the women working at the time.

Secretarial work, retail store clerking, waitressing, teaching, nursing, and the new trade of telephone operator followed domestic service as the job categories containing the most women. The established craft unions of the day were somewhat slow to respond to the plight of female workers: they offered little more than a few words of encouragement when waitresses at Regina's Balmoral Café staged the first women's strike in Saskatchewan in 1918 to increase their wages of $5 a week, to reduce their work day from fifteen hours to ten, and to have at least one day off per week. While the Regina labour council did put the waitresses in touch with the appropriate craft union to assist them, it failed to employ the sort of boycott and picketing support the waitresses needed to succeed. When the province's mostly female telephone operators went on strike in 1918, they did so under the leadership of an organizer from the International Brotherhood of Electrical Workers. The strike was poorly managed: staged in the midst of the Spanish Influenza epidemic, it lacked public support and ended in a defeat for the workers. With Walter Scott now retired, the new leadership of the Liberal government was less sympathetic to labour and not prepared to grant concessions to workers in the government-owned telephone exchanges.

Teaching was another occupational category with a significant level of female participation. The numbers of women in the profession grew during World War I as male teachers left their jobs for military service. Many of the province's 5,000-plus teachers were members of the teachers' alliance by the end of the war. Wages for teachers were low compared to those for skilled tradesmen at the time, but there were other important issues facing teachers as well: these included the right to bargain collectively with their school boards, and the frustrations of a highly decentralized school system that placed teachers under the control of trustees who had little background in education.

During the first four decades of the 20th century, nurses in the province worked within a system that combined the virtues of selfless service of a Florence Nightingale with British military discipline. It was not until World War II produced a nursing shortage that nurses were allowed to continue working after they were married. Student nurses were among the most exploited workers in the province: they lived in hospital dormitories and worked countless hours for a meager allowance, under the direction of matrons who governed virtually every aspect of their lives. It took until the early 1970s, when nurses finally organized themselves into an effective union, that the last vestiges of the old authoritarian hospital workplace were overcome.

The Radicalism of 1919

At the end of World War I, Canadian workers were anxious to catch up after four years of stagnant wartime wages. Working people across Canada believed they had paid a higher price during the war than the business community: working men, farmers, and their sons made up the largest proportion of the volunteers who actually fought the war. Working people believed their sons bled while many of the country's business owners made windfall profits from war-related contracts. Workers' wages had been held down by wartime controls and laws which prevented strikes in war-related industries. Adding further to workers' concerns, returning service men and the shutdown of war-related industries produced a surge in unemployment. Many non-British immigrant workers and farmers suffered the indignity of losing the right to vote during the war. Immigrants of German ancestry were prevented from joining the Canadian military; union activists of foreign birth could find themselves deported or thrown into internment camps where alleged "enemy aliens" were held during the war. The government seemed confused about the geography of Europe: somehow determining that thousands of Ukrainians were a potentially dangerous alien force, they had them interned—even though the Ukraine was part of Russia and the Russians were among Canada's allies for most of the war. Non-British immigrant workers, who formed about half the workforce in the coalfields of western Canada, had plenty of reasons to call for major changes in the way the country was run in the post-war period.

Post-war tensions erupted in Winnipeg, Manitoba in the spring of 1919. On May 15, workers in the building trades and industrial plants began a general strike in which thousands of workers from most occupations walked out in support of wage and other contract demands. The Winnipeg General Strike occurred in conjunction with the rise of a small but vigorous labour movement in western Canada, known as syndicalism. The syndicalists argued that labour should be organized on a broader industry-wide basis than the system of individual craft unions that constituted the mainstream of the labour movement: for example, an industrial union for a railway shop should include all workers regardless of their craft. This ran contrary to the craft union model, which saw workers in a railway shop belonging to a variety of different unions—possibly one for the mechanics, one for the machinists, and another union for the maintenance staff. The syndicalists thus promoted the idea of One Big Union (OBU) that would someday be able to counter the power of business and government to advance the cause of labour. Supporters of the OBU were a small but vigorous minority among the strikers in Winnipeg; the majority of strikers were more concerned with traditional bread-and-butter craft union issues, such as improved wages and working conditions, than they were with starting a revolutionary union movement.

Events in Manitoba had implications in neighbouring Saskatchewan. This province's labour movement contained a small but vocal minority of OBU supporters. It also had a lot of trade unionists who were anxious to see improvements in wages and working conditions after all the sacrifices made during the war. Brief strikes in sympathy with the Winnipeg General Strike occurred throughout the province. The largest walkout occurred in Saskatoon and lasted over a week. In Regina, the labour council was divided over whether to stage a sympathy strike; the divisions over the issue became severe and resulted in the resignation of most of the Regina labour council's executive (those who supported the OBU). The Moose Jaw Labour Council sent a delegation to Winnipeg to investigate prior to launching its own general strike; the delegation returned convinced that OBU supporters were playing too large and too troubling a role in the Winnipeg strike, and the Labour Council chose not to stage a general sympathy strike in Moose Jaw, leaving the decision to each separate local.

The Winnipeg General Strike was put down violently by mounted police on June 21, 1919; two citizens were killed and a number were injured on what some would call Bloody Saturday. In the wake of Bloody Saturday, union leaders including Methodist preacher and future leader of the CCF, J.S. Woodsworth, as well as some supporters of the OBU were arrested. In Saskatchewan the houses of OBU activists were raided by the RCMP and some literature was seized. OBU organizer Phillip Christophers was kidnapped by a gang of vigilantes that included a Saskatchewan Provincial Police officer, and driven out of the country to Noonan, North Dakota during an organizing drive in the Saskatchewan coal fields. But other than that bizarre incident, no OBU organizers are known to have been officially arrested in Saskatchewan. The One Big Union experienced a phase of rapid growth in 1919, but suffered from an equally rapid decline. Organized labour in Saskatchewan would rely almost exclusively on traditional craft unionism for the coming decade of the 1920s.

The Stagnant 1920s

There was little for working people to roar about during the 1920s. Saskatchewan's business community and the province's labour movement eagerly anticipated a return to pre-war prosperity, but wishing didn't make it so: the provincial economy never matched the settlement boom growth for the next two decades. The building of new railway branch lines to service new farming communities had become an enterprise of the past. New building construction also lagged well behind pre-war levels for most of the decade: with the exception of a few flurries of construction activity like the one in 1928, the hopes of the building trades workers and contractors were never fully realized in the 1920s.

In the agricultural sector the high grain prices obtained during the war disappeared following the dismantling of the wartime orderly marketing system. However, crops were generally good, and despite the labour-saving new machinery coming onto the market, farmers still required a lot of hired labour, especially at harvest time. Railway-sponsored "Harvest Excursion Trains" annually hauled thousands of eastern and central Canadian men west during the 1920s to ensure that the harvest came off. The last major harvest excursions ran in 1928, when 24,000 workers came west to help with the crop; but by 1929 drought and low grain prices were taking their toll on the prairie economy, and fewer than 5,000 workers were required from the east.

There was some expansion in the kinds of employment available in Saskatchewan during the 1920s. Both wage earners and employers benefited from the growth in the added value manufacturing of agricultural products and natural resources that occurred during the decade. The province now had flour milling, meat packing, and oil refining industries. The service and manufacturing sectors were also expanding. The distributive systems required to supply and sustain agriculture continued to grow: the decade saw the expansion of businesses devoted to warehousing and to farm equipment sales and repair. Hopes for increased industrial production rose with a few new ventures like the General Motors assembly plant that was set up in Regina in 1927.

The Depression

The stock market crash of October 1929 signaled an economic depression that affected the entire western industrialized world. The impacts of the Depression were deeply felt in Saskatchewan, where low agricultural commodity prices combined with drought to ruin the farm economy. Thousands of people were thrown out of work across North America with the collapse of markets and the slow-down in commercial activity.

Conditions in the drought-stricken rural areas of the province were desperate. Teachers in rural areas shared the hardships of the Depression along with their pupils: local school boards were often unable to collect the taxes required to pay teachers' salaries. Many dedicated teachers, however, worked months on end without pay; by the late 1930s, the province's teachers were owed over $2 million in back pay.

For those in Saskatchewan lucky enough to have work during the Depression, things could still be tough: the constant fear of job loss through lay-off or arbitrary dismissal weighed heavily on the employed. In the unionized building trades sector, formerly agreed-to schedules were often ignored by employers; those who complained would be made aware of the thousands of people who would be happy to take their jobs.

This was the situation in the coal fields of southeastern Saskatchewan at the outset of the Depression. Miners in the region had been subjected to harsh conditions for the past two decades, and were determined by 1931 to establish a union that could bargain for better terms with the coal mine operators. The miners voted overwhelmingly to join the Mine Workers Union of Canada (MWUC); the union was known to have Communist leaders, but miners supported it nonetheless. People like T.C. DOUGLAS, an ordained minister from the nearby community of Weyburn, reasoned: "People shouldn't give up on a good cause just because a few Communists support it." The mine operators refused to negotiate with the new union local. On September 29, 1931, the miners and their families staged a car cavalcade in Estevan to publicize their demands. The car parade turned into a riot; many people were injured, and police bullets killed three of the protesters: Julian Gryshko, Nick Nargan, and Peter Markunas. The MWUC effort was defeated and a number of strike leaders were arrested, deported, or blacklisted. It would take until 1944 for the miners to win recognition by the mine bosses for their union.

Emergency relief for unemployed workers and poverty-stricken farmers in Saskatchewan was supposed to be provided by the municipalities, but local governments lacked the resources to cope with the magnitude of the crisis in the 1930s. The province was also cash-strapped, and appealed to the federal government for assistance. Ottawa's half-hearted response did little to solve the problem: modest relief measures were put in place for families, but single young males were denied relief and expected to find work even though there was seldom any to be found. Thousands of unemployed single young men became transient job seekers, hitching rides on freight trains and traveling across the country looking for jobs that did not exist. Alarmed by these thousands of potentially angry young men, the federal government established a system of relief work camps for single men; these camps, located in remote regions of the country, were operated by the Department of National Defense. To enforce attendance at the camps, municipal authorities were encouraged to deny even the assistance of soup kitchens to young men in the cities: if they wanted to stay warm and fed, the camps became about their only option. Conditions in the camps were bleak, and wages for working on government relief projects were only 20¢ a day. When inmates attempted to organize themselves and present their complaints to authorities, their leaders would be kicked out and blacklisted at other camps.

The government's unwillingness to improve these conditions led to a mass walkout of camp inmates in British Columbia in the spring of 1935. Under the leadership of the Relief Camp Workers Union the striking camp workers traveled to Vancouver, where they came up with the idea of taking their concerns to Prime Minister R.B. Bennett in person; they would hitch rides on freight trains and stage an On-to-Ottawa Trek. When the ranks of the Trekkers swelled to over 1,500, the Prime Minister decided to put an end to it long before it reached Ottawa; Regina was selected as the place to stop the protest and force the men to return to the camps. The efforts of police to arrest Trek leaders as a first step in stamping out the protest resulted in the Regina Riot of July 1, 1935. Following the riot, the government softened its stance somewhat, allowing the men to return to camps of their own choosing as opposed to a specially built internment camp at Lumsden, Saskatchewan. Within a year Prime Minister Bennett was out of office, and the new Liberal government abolished the relief camp system. (*See also* ON-TO-OTTAWA TREK AND THE REGINA RIOT.)

SASKATCHEWAN ARCHIVES BOARD R-A27560-1

Demonstration on Market Square prior to the Regina Riot.

By the late 1930s economic conditions were improving in many parts of Canada—but not in Saskatchewan, where agriculture remained plagued by drought and low prices. Nationally, though, the unemployment crisis was letting up a little prior to the start of World War II. The impacts of the Depression and of unforgettable events like the bloody strike in the coal fields and the Regina Riot convinced many Saskatchewan people that their society needed changing. This attitude was reflected by the CO-OPERATIVE COMMONWEALTH FEDERATION (CCF), a social democratic party that advocated a major restructuring of society in support of the interests of farmers and working people. The CCF comprised strong proponents of social measures long advocated by the nation's labour movement, including unemployment insurance, old age pensions, state-funded health insurance, and legislation guaranteeing trade union rights. By the close of the Depression the CCF was the official opposition in Saskatchewan.

War and Recovery

Canada's entry into World War II solved the country's unemployment problem as thousands of young men and women signed up for service overseas and industry began hiring to meet the demand for war-related production. Grain prices did not return to World War I levels during this

HILLYARD PHOTO/SASKATCHEWAN ARCHIVES BOARD R-B7253-5

6th Convention of the Saskatchewan Federation of Labour, 1949.

VIC BULL PHOTO/SASKATCHEWAN ARCHIVES BOARD R-A11354

Signing of a new civil service agreement, 1951.

war, but demand for dairy and meat products increased: the province's meat and dairy processing industries expanded, producing hundreds of new jobs in what would become thoroughly unionized sectors of the economy. As had been the case in World War I, Saskatchewan continued to lack the manufacturing industries that were producing record levels of new jobs in other parts of Canada. There were exceptions, though, such as the former General Motors Assembly plant in Regina, which was turned over entirely to armament production. The war effort had virtually eliminated the pool of unemployed men in the province, so the Regina plant did what other manufacturers across Canada were doing at the time and hired hundreds of female workers in addition to males to operate the plant. Wartime propaganda praised the role of women working in industrial plants, proclaiming the virtues of "Rosie the riveter."

In 1944, the year before the war ended, the CCF led by T.C. Douglas formed the government in Saskatchewan. One of the first actions of the new government was to enact some of the most progressive labour legislation in North America. The union movement; especially the aggressive new industrial unionists who belonged to the Canadian Congress of Labour, took full advantage of the new Trade Union Act to increase union membership in the province by over 100% between 1944 and 1956.

Women had entered the workforce in growing numbers during

the war. More women were employed in government offices and as teachers, as well as in a host of other occupations, filling places left by men who went overseas. The nursing profession relaxed rules on married women working as nurses, in part because so many nurses had gone overseas in support of the troops.

At the end of the war many feared there would be a severe recession and a return to high unemployment. But this was not the case. In Saskatchewan the economy grew, and so did new job opportunities. The war effort had demonstrated that well-considered government spending could act as an economic stimulant that would not throw the financial system into complete disorder. The CCF government invested public money in the expansion of the province's electrical grid into rural areas, in the construction of new roads and highways, and in new Crown-owned enterprises such as the Saskatchewan Government Insurance Office (SGIO), creating hundreds of new jobs in the process. The expansion of government services into new areas of health care and social welfare also contributed to the expansion of the public sector workforce. New government employees enjoyed the benefit of unions since the Douglas government was the first in Canada to allow its employees to unionize. The post-war period was one of steady improvement in the lives of most of the province's working people. Jobs were now relatively easy to come by; by the early 1960s most working families could plan to own their own home and car; and virtually everyone had a television set. The CCF's new minimum wage and minimum standards of work legislation, combined with the advances won by unionized workers through bargaining, made work life better and living standards higher for most working families. Minimum labour standards now provided every worker in the province with annual paid vacations; the standard legal work week was reduced from 48 to 44 hours, allowing virtually all employees to have two days off per week.

The crowning achievement of the CCF government was the introduction of universal free medical care in 1962; this measure constituted one of the greatest advances made by a government in the interests of ordinary people anywhere in North America. The effort to create MEDICARE provoked deep political divisions in the province. The labour movement became the CCF government's most stalwart ally through the demonstrations and the doctor's strike that accompanied the creation of medicare. Walter Smishek, a prominent Saskatchewan union official, represented labour on the committee that designed the basic framework of medicare and co-coordinated union support during the turbulent months of debate and protest. BILL DAVIES, long-time executive xecretary of the SASKATCHEWAN FEDERATION OF LABOUR, was the CCF Minister of Health who implemented the medicare plan. Working people, like other groups in society, benefited greatly from free access to health care: they were understandably relieved to be free from onerous health insurance premiums and the threat of financial ruin in the event of serious illness.

Changing Unions

The union movement experienced growth on many fronts during the post-war period. By the early 1970s Saskatchewan's workforce was one of the most unionized in the country, with over 20% of workers belonging to unions. Greater labour unity was achieved in 1956 when the unions from the craft-based Trades and Labour Congress merged with the industrial unions of the Canadian Congress of Labour to form the Canadian Labour Congress (CLC), which would play a leading role in 1961 in the formation of the New Democratic Party. Mergers between unions would become a trend during the 1970s and beyond. In many cases unions merged to counter the growing power of the multi-national corporations they bargained with. Mergers also occurred because the unions involved appreciated the cost advantages and other organizational efficiencies that are available through greater economies of scale. For example, as the meat packing industry consolidated during the 1960s and 1970, unions in that sector consolidated as well. The United Food and Commercial Workers (UFCW) union was created through the merging of a number of food industry unions over the course of the 1960s and 1970s; the UFCW now represents workers in meat-packing plants as well as in many of the retail stores that sell the meat.

Technological change became a growing threat to workers' jobs and the survival of their unions following World War II. For example, the Brotherhood of Locomotive Firemen was wiped out by the adoption of the diesel locomotive by the railways. Saskatchewan's clay sewer pipe and brick plant workers saw the ranks of their union shrink as fiberglass pipe came onto the market in the 1960s; to ensure strong union representation, the clay brick and pipe makers folded their original union into the larger and more powerful United Steel Workers of America. Unions have bargained incessantly to protect workers from job loss due to technological change; these efforts have won for many workers the right to be advised well in advance of any planned technological changes that might threaten jobs, as well as opportunities for displaced workers to retrain for other work in their bargaining unit.

Growing Canadian nationalism in the 1970s was an important force behind the creation of many new independent unions. The Saskatchewan section of the Retail Wholesale and Department Store Union (RWDSU) was one of the first unions in Canada to break away from its US-based international union—although this decision had as much to do with the indifference of the American head office to the wishes of its affiliates as it had to do with nationalism. What had been a radical move by the RWDSU in the 1970s became acceptable practice in the 1980s when Bob White led the Canadian Auto Workers out of their US-affiliated international union.

The Best of Times

Saskatchewan's working people enjoyed their highest levels of disposable income and greatest access to employment opportunities during the 1970s. The foundations for this period of relative prosperity had been laid by CCF governments from 1944 to 1964 through the creation of a number of Crown agencies in the utilities, resource and insurance sectors, and through the development of the province's infrastructure of highways, power and telephone grids. In combination with the private sector, the government had encouraged the construction of the province's first steel mill and a number of forest product processing companies. The Liberal government of ROSS THATCHER added to the province's economic potential by encouraging the development of its potash industry. The NDP government of ALLAN BLAKENEY, first elected in 1971, made a number of important reforms to the province's labour legislation; this was required since much of the labour-friendly legislation enacted by the Douglas government in the 1940s and 1950s had been dismantled by the Thatcher government. Thatcher's actions were reversed by the NDP within months of their taking office; the NDP also made improvements to the workers compensation system.

In its first term, the Blakeney government enacted some of the most advanced Occupational Health and Safety legislation in North America. Saskatchewan had a long and disturbing record as one of the Canadian provinces with the greatest proportion of workplace injuries and deaths. The new legislation was developed to reverse this trend. The right of workers to refuse unsafe work without fear of employer reprisals was one of the key features of the new Act, which had been developed in consultation with the province's federation of labour. The NDP also embarked on a series of initiatives that saw it take ownership control of major parts of the potash, uranium, and oil and gas industries. These moves were intended to increase resource revenues to the province, to ensure that head office jobs remained in Saskatchewan, and also to create a better work environment in the resource industries. Unions were encouraged to participate in management decisions that affected worker welfare and safety, and nominees from the labour movement were placed on the boards of Crown corporations.

Progress in improving wages and working conditions was made across a wide front of occupational categories. Non-nursing staff in the province's hospitals had been among the province's lowest paid workers until the 1970s, with wage rates barely above minimum wage. The unions for these workers succeeded in convincing the government to implement province-wide bargaining for health care employees. Under province-wide bargaining the health care unions were able to bargain huge wage increases for rural hospital workers, whose wages had lagged far behind their urban counterparts for decades.

Inflation and Wage Controls

By the mid-1970s double-digit inflation was viewed by governments and most other observers as the most critical problem facing Canadians. Government and the business lobby laid much of the blame for inflation on high wage settlements won by unionized workers. Labour argued that interest rates, corporate profit taking, and runaway energy costs were as much to blame for inflation as unions. In addition, with most organized workers locked into two- and three-year collective agreements, by the time negotiations on a new contract came around, workers' purchasing power had been substantially eroded by increases in the cost of living. Workers demanding 10-20% wage increases were often only trying to catch up for losses over the term of their previous agreement and to protect themselves against future inflation. Many collective agreements at the time had COLA (Cost of Living Adjustment) clauses built into them as another way to safeguard workers' purchasing power over the course of their collective agreements.

Federal politicians debated the wisdom of implementing nationwide wage and price controls during the 1974 federal election campaign. The Conservatives argued in favour of controls; Pierre Trudeau argued against them, claiming that prices could never be held down and only wages could be controlled. Trudeau won the election, then changed his mind and implemented wage and price controls in October 1975. In Saskatchewan, the NDP took advantage of a provision in the federal controls program that allowed provinces to set up their own wage and price control system; the provincial program would apply primarily to public sector workers. The NDP government argued that it would run its program with a lighter rein than the federal government. Saskatchewan's labour movement, especially the civil servants, opposed the measure; major labour demonstrations, including the nationwide Day of Protest of October 14, 1976 (Canada's largest strike), were held to protest controls and the policies of the NDP provincial government.

Wage controls, combined with the NDP government's imposition of back-to-work legislation on striking SaskPower workers, dairy workers, and hospital employees, created rifts between the government and sections of the labour movement. While the NDP lacked some of its usual labour support going into the 1982 provincial election, its defeat at the hands of the Conservatives had more to do with high mortgage interest rates and gas prices than with labour issues.

Tough Times in the 1980s

The Progressive Conservative government led by GRANT DEVINE dismantled much of the pro-worker legacy put in place by previous administrations. Labour legislation that was not changed often was not enforced, or was ignored. Building trades workers lost their ability to win and hold union certifications with contractors; the latter were allowed to "double breast," that is to create a new non-union spin-off company to avoid collective agreements. Public sector workers lost jobs when the government privatized many government services and sold off its highway equipment. Occupational health and safety regulations were not enforced, and the minimum wage was rarely increased over the course of Devine's nine years in office. Workers compensation benefits became more difficult for injured workers to collect. A whole range of other social programs that working people had come to rely on as part of Canada's traditional social safety net were reduced by government cutbacks.

Working families lost ground during the Devine years. Federal and provincial government restraint programs that put caps on public sector wage increases became a pattern followed elsewhere in the economy. The unions, weakened by the erosion of labour legislation and pattern bargaining, became less capable of winning significant wage increases. While inflation was down from its double-digit heights in the 1970s, it was still around and producing small but steady increases in the cost of living; the purchasing power of workers' incomes shrank in the 1980s and the 1990s, and is still shrinking today. By the 1980s, most families had two incomes. Women, who had entered the work force in growing numbers over the past four decades, would soon constitute 44% of the paid workforce. Many women worked to earn a greater degree of independence; some worked for the satisfaction that comes with employment; but most worked because families needed two incomes to make ends meet. Women in the labour movement encouraged their unions to support the principles of pay equity intended to eliminate the discrepancy between pay rates for men and women. Access to quality affordable daycare became another important cause for working women in the labour movement.

By 1986 the Conservatives had put the province heavily in debt with a series of consecutive deficit budgets. Not even the sale of income-generating Crown assets in potash mining, uranium mining, and forestry product manufacturing could pull the province out of deficit and debt.

Current Issues

The labour movement was hopeful that the defeat of the Devine government by the NDP in 1991 would mark a return to better times for working people and their unions. This, however, has not proven to be the case. The NDP of the 1990s did not echo the Blakeney government's eagerness to reverse the regressive labour legislation of its predecessor, and it moved very slowly to reverse even those elements of Devine legislation that were most irritating to labour. It was not until 1994 that the Trade Union Act was revised, and even then not everything was returned to pre-Devine status. The NDP blamed the fiscal mess left by the Conservatives for its own inability to make more substantial improvements in the lives of working families. Also at play was the NDP's new interest in having the business community on its side, assuming that any revised labour legislation had to be part of a broad consensus supported by employers.

The snail's pace of labour law reform since 1991 has rekindled debates within the labour movement over whether the Saskatchewan Federation of Labour and its affiliates should reconsider their automatic support of the NDP in provincial elections. The labour movement continues to await significant changes to labour laws in support of pay equity for women. Another early 21st century demand is the implementation of anti-scab legislation: already in place in Ontario and Quebec, anti-scab laws prevent employers from hiring professional strike breakers during labour disputes. Another current demand, referred to as "most available hours," would provide existing part-time employees in workplaces like big box retail stores with the opportunity to take on any new hours of work that come available, so that they might turn their part-time jobs into full-time employment.

The province's workforce is getting older: by the close of the 1990s the average Saskatchewan worker was 39.7 years old—the oldest average in Canada. The workforce is getting older because young people have been steadily leaving the province since the 1970s to seek job opportunities elsewhere. Most young people who enter the Saskatchewan workforce take low-paying part-time "Mcjobs" in fast food outlets and big box retail stores: this is because these are generally the only jobs available, and also because part-time work fits in well with an on-going post-secondary education. Unfortunately, once studies have been completed many graduates leave the province for brighter job markets. Employees in many of these workplaces lack the protection offered by a union. Unions are attempting to meet the challenge of bringing more young people into the ranks of labour by organizing workplaces like Wal-Mart and the fast food chains, where so many young people are working. Ongoing efforts by the labour movement in support of increases to the minimum wage and "most available hours" legislation are also intended to assist younger workers. The idea seems to be that if better jobs were available, more young people would remain in the province.

Another great challenge facing Saskatchewan is the need to make meaningful job opportunities available for the province's young and growing Aboriginal population. The province's labour movement has been supportive of employment equity legislation and of programs designed to provide a leg-up for Aboriginal people seeking employment. Unions like the United Steel Workers of America have been leaders in this regard: beginning in the 1970s, the Steel Workers included provisions in their collective agreements with uranium mining companies in Saskatchewan's north that allocate a proportion of the jobs available to Aboriginal northerners.

Saskatchewan's paid labour force has fluctuated in size between 400,000 and 450,000 workers over the past two decades. It is clearly the largest occupational sector in the province, far larger than the self-employment and farming sectors. Saskatchewan's wage earners, by far, pay most of the taxes in the province. Women now make up around 45% of the paid work force, and their role in institutions like the labour movement is becoming increasingly influential. Approximately 20% of the people currently working for wages in the province belong to unions and are generally the highest paid workers with the best benefits in the workforce. Questions are currently being asked as to whether growth in union membership has stalled, and whether the unions' past level of influence on public policy will re-emerge in the near future. Whether unions experience a surge in growth or not, the aspirations of working people and their families will clearly play a leading role in the future direction of Saskatchewan society in the 21st century.

LABOUR LEGISLATION. When social and economic problems increased in the early 20th century as more workers found jobs off the farm, Saskatchewan government officials offered few protections other than periodic inspections of factories, shops, mines, and other sites. In spite of growing trade unionism, with membership of the Dominion Trades and Labour Congress more than doubling between 1910 and 1918, the government of Saskatchewan into the 1920s apologetically enforced minimum regulation of hours of work and working conditions: laws for adult males—especially wage laws—were seen as an unconstitutional deprivation of liberty, with the exception of a few fair-wage schedules. As in many provinces, union leaders met with the executive branch of government about improving the lives of working people. In Saskatchewan, annual labour reports documented labour's suggestions and government's tepid responses from 1911 until the early 1940s.

A distinction is often made between "labour laws" that govern collective bargaining relations between employers and unions, and "employment laws" that affect individual employment relationships. In Saskatchewan, as in most provinces, separate statutes cover these matters. The Department of Labour has traditionally administered the Trade Union and the Construction Industry Labour Relations Acts dealing with organized labour. The Department of Labour also administers an Occupational Health and Safety Act and a Radiation Health and Safety Act dealing with both organized and unorganized labour. Another important piece of legislation is the Labour Standards Act, mainly addressing minimum standards for all workers such as hours of work, overtime, holidays, layoffs, and dismissals. There is also a Canada Labour Code for residents who work under federal laws.

Other legislation that is referred to as employment law includes matters such as federal Employment Insurance Legislation, and Workers Compensation and Pension Benefits legislation, found at both levels of government. Other examples of legislation are sometimes industry-specific, such as the early Fire Departments Platoon Act, or of a more general nature, such as the Victims of Workplace Injuries Day of Mourning Act. The Department of Labour has also administered from time to time legislation dealing with employment, such as the Employment Agencies Act, and legislation dealing with Women's Affairs. Many of the laws affecting working people were proposed by the labour movement at that time: talks between the Saskatchewan executive of the Trades and Labour Congress of Canada (TLC) and the government of the day were visionary and far-reaching even before 1920, when the Labour Division of the Department of Agriculture became an independent commission.

The TLC Saskatchewan executive would meet annually with government until the 1930s, with a broad set of proposals—some of them consistent with today's definition of labour and employment laws. As early as 1911 and into the 1920s they proposed improvements to the Factories Act, pleading for child protection laws for children less than 14, then 15 and finally 16 years of age. In 1920 they proposed an insured workers compensation scheme, including by 1921 details on its administration.

The Saskatchewan executive of the TLC requested a system of inspections for grain elevators and other establishments. They proposed licensing and reliable training for electrical, construction, plumbing and other journeymen throughout the 1920s. The Congress made presentations on minimum wage, first for women, then repeatedly for men and others who were exempt under the legislation. They proposed one day of rest in seven, a half-day holiday, improvements to the Masters Servants Act and implementation of other International Labour Organization's proposals; yet they never abandoned the quest for an eight-hour day. They proposed the first independent provincial **TRADE UNION ACT** as well as improvements to basic Labour Standards, Occupational Health and Safety provisions, and asked for insured compensation for workplace accidents and for a public pension plan.

An important gain dating back to 1919 was the establishment of a Minimum Wage Act that permitted investigators to determine the earnings required for "a girl dependent on her own earning ... to live in reasonable comfort." At that time, this was determined to be $15 a week, and minimum wage for experienced female workers in shops was set at that level. Unfortunately, lower wages were proposed for mail-order houses, factories, and laundries. This established an early precedent of divorcing minimum wage from the actual cost of living and from the original intent of the law. Minimum wages were reduced in the early 1930s, although gradually the Minimum Wage Act was amended to extend coverage to others. Yet, even today, domestic and agricultural workers remain outside the full coverage of the Act. In 1944 the Douglas government actually took the cumulative list of workers' suggestions—many contained in annual reports going back over thirty years—and began to implement them.

The list of accomplishments of the CCF government in its first term alone is impressive: it took over one of Canada's poorest and least industrialized provinces, yet promptly gave provincial employees free collective bargaining, made it easier for unions to organize, and presided over an series of reforms that made Saskatchewan the leader of social reform in Canada for twenty years. This involved far-reaching proposals to introduce and pass advanced trade union legislation that included public sector bargaining (1944). It involved provision for equalization and enrichment of education through a reorganized school system and increasing financial support by 300% (1945–46), as well as developing a universal hospital services plan (1947). The province established a compulsory no-fault automobile insurance plan (1946), and introduced Canada's first Bill of Rights (1947). Seniors and the mentally ill received free health care, full medicare being introduced in 1962. Despite many precedents being set in Saskatchewan, progress remains a struggle and patterns have varied with the government of the day. Organized labour has been very disappointed, for example, that the province has yet to develop "equal pay for work of equal value" legislation, relying instead on weakly enforced "equal pay for similar value" legislation passed in the 1970s.

Despite setbacks, however, Saskatchewan continues to pioneer innovations in labour legislation, introducing working people to the three-week vacation under Labour Standard by 1958, and passing in 1972 the first Occupational Health and Safety Act in Canada, which included sexual and other harassment as an occupational health issue by 1993–94. When other provinces were retrenching and reducing worker benefits in the 1990s, Saskatchewan continued to make improvements to pieces of legislation including the Trade Union Act, Occupational Health and Safety, Pension Benefits, Workers Compensation, and the Construction Industry Labour Relations Act. Labour Standards now provide for those who become disabled on the job. A very significant piece is the "most available hour's" legislation, which will allow part-time workers to claim additional available hours as they become available in their workplace. This was passed in 1995 but is yet to be proclaimed. *Merran Proctor*

LABOUR-MANAGEMENT DISPUTE (TEMPORARY PROVISIONS) ACT: *see* **LEGISLATION IN SASKATCHEWAN**

LABOUR RELATIONS BOARD. The Saskatchewan Labour Relations Board is an independent, quasi-judicial tribunal charged with the responsibility of administering the **TRADE UNION ACT**. It came into existence with the passage of the Trade Union Act, S.S. 1944. While there have been amendments to the Act, the concept of the Board has remained unchanged. The composition of the Board, as dictated by the Act, is one chairperson and two vice-chairpersons who are full-time members, and an unspecified number (currently eighteen) of members who are paid on a per-diem basis. Board members, with the exception of the chairperson and vice-chairpersons, are representatives of employees or employers. All members of the Board are appointed by the Lieutenant Governor in Council.

The basic function of the Labour Relations Board is to certify unions to represent groups of employees, and to guarantee the rights conferred by the Act on trade unions and individual employees. Part of this responsibility includes identifying the parties that will participate in the collective bargaining process, and to monitor and settle disputes. Three-person panels including the chairperson or a vice-chairperson, plus equal representation from employers and unions, conduct hearings. A decision, usually written, is rendered following the hearing. The Board attempts to conduct the hearings so as to identify the issues which are genuinely in dispute and to make the procedures accessible to those representatives of the parties who may have no legal training.

Donna Ottenson

LABOUR STANDARDS ACT: *see* LEGISLATION IN SASKATCHEWAN

LAC LA RONGE (55°15' 104°45'; Map sheet 73 P/2).

Lac la Ronge covers 1,414 sq. km and lies at an elevation of 364 m. It is located on the southern margin of the Shield, served by Hwy 2 and, north of the town of La Ronge, by Hwy 102. Most of the rugged shoreline and numerous islands that lie within the Shield form part of Lac la Ronge Provincial Park. The southern shore, south of the Shield margin, is much less rugged. Lac la Ronge probably derived its name from the French verb *ronger* "to gnaw." Certainly, the lake was a centre for a fur trade based largely on beaver pelts. In the winter of 1781–82 there were two trade posts on the lake, one established by **PETER POND** and the other by Jean-Étienne Wadin. The two quarrelled, and Wadin was fatally shot. In spite of this, the fur trade continued, a tradition maintained into the latter half of the 20th century by Robertson's Trading Post in La Ronge. A number of small First Nation reserves are located around the shore, while the main service centre for the region is the town of La Ronge

(pop. 2,727). Tourism based on camping, fishing, hunting and boating provides a significant source of income for the town.

Marilyn Lewry

LAC LA RONGE INDIAN BAND. Between 1897 and 1973, approximately twenty surveys were completed to define reserve boundaries for the Lac la Ronge Indian Band. Most of the reserves are located near Lac la Ronge, but parcels extend as far as Emma Lake and Prince Albert. Band members descend from the James Roberts Wood Cree Band, who adhered to **TREATY 6** on February 11, 1889, at Montreal Lake. They hunted, fished, and trapped around Lac la Ronge, living in camps near the lake and maintaining small gardens. Two distinct communities developed, one near Lac la Ronge and the other at Stanley Mission. In 1910, the Department of Indian Affairs attempted to establish these settlements as two distinct communities, recognizing one as the James Roberts Band (Lac la Ronge), and the other as the Amos Charles Band (Stanley Mission). Separate trust funds and annuity pay lists were established, but the reserve lands were not formally divided. On March 27, 1950, James Roberts and Amos Charles Bands were amalgamated as the Lac la Ronge Band. In 1983 the Kitsaki Management Limited Partnership originated with Kitsaki Meats; its varied and expanding economic development programs represent the diversity of the band. Of the 7,835 band members, 4,680 people live in communities at Grandmother's Bay, Sucker River, Little Red River, La Ronge, Stanley Mission, and Kitsaki. In total, this band controls 43,302 ha of land.

Christian Thompson

LAFLECHE, town, pop 446, located S of Gravelbourg at the junction of Hwys 13 and 58. Lafleche is named after Louis-François Richer

Laflèche (1818–98), a Roman Catholic missionary to Rupert's Land from 1844 to 1856, and the bishop of Trois-Rivières, Quebec from 1867 to 1898. The district began to be settled in 1905–06, and the townsite was established in 1913 when the CPR came through. People of British and German origins settled the district, and a large number of French settlers took up land in a vast area extending from west of **OLD WIVES LAKE**, south through Gravelbourg to Lafleche, and west toward Ponteix and down to Val Marie. In 1922, Ste. Radegonde Roman Catholic Church was built in Lafleche; its exterior was faced with brick from the **CLAYBANK BRICK PLANT**, and today it is both a heritage property and the oldest existing church in the community. In 1961, Lafleche had a peak population of 749. Generally, grain production is the major activity to the north of the community, while mixed farms and ranching operations are dominant to the south.

David McLennan

LAFOND, ALPHONSINE (1926–2000). Born at the Muskeg Lake First Nation on March 7, 1926, Lafond attended St. Michael's Indian Residential School in Duck Lake from 1933 to 1942. In 1958 she was elected councilor at her reserve, and lobbied to give First Nations people the right to vote. In 1960 Lafond was elected the first woman chief in Saskatchewan, and the first female tribal representative for the Shellbrook Agency. In 1975 she became the first First Nations woman appointed as justice of the peace, and in 1992 the first woman appointed as senator in the **FEDERATION OF SASKATCHEWAN INDIAN NATIONS**; in 1999 she became Chair of the Senate. Lafond was Saskatchewan Indian Women's Association Mother of the Year in 1986; she was awarded the Saskatchewan Order of Merit in 1988 and the Canada 125 Medal in 1992. She was living at Muskeg Lake First Nation at the time of her death on August 17, 2000.

Daria Coneghan

LAHRMAN, FREDERICK WILLIAM (1921–2003). Fred Lahrman worked for fifty-five years at the Royal Saskatchewan Museum in Regina as a wildlife artist and conservationist. Lahrman was born on September 4, 1921, at Mortlach, Saskatchewan and grew up south of the town in the Missouri Coteau. He developed an interest and appreciation of nature and began sketching birds and animals at an early age.

In 1946, Lahrman moved to Regina to pursue his art career. He was hired to do wildlife paintings at the Natural History Museum in 1947. For the next 55 years, Lahrman painted dozens of world-class background display dioramas for the exhibits at the Saskatchewan Museum of Natural History, later renamed the **ROYAL SASKATCHEWAN MUSEUM**. Lahrman's career included taxidermy, bird banding, wildlife photography, writing articles, doing illustrations for museum booklets and special publications

DOUG CHISHOLM PHOTO

Lac La Ronge.

DON HEALY/REGINA LEADER-POST

Museum of Natural History artist Frederick Lahrman holds a model of a golden eagle chick, June 1982.

of the Saskatchewan Natural History Society, and setting up the first interpretive displays in provincial parks.

Lahrman worked with longtime museum director, the late **FRED G. BARD**, in establishing the Wascana Canada Goose Flock in the early 1950s. They were also leaders in conserving the endangered whooping crane through public education and by working with other jurisdictions along the migration flyway, bringing North America's tallest bird back from the brink of extinction. Recognized nationally and internationally for his artistic ability and conservation work, Lahrman left a legacy of lifelike dioramas at the Royal Saskatchewan Museum for future generations to observe and appreciate. He died in Regina on June 29, 2003.

Lorne Scott

LAIRD, DAVID (1833–1914). Laird was born on March 12, 1833, in New Glasgow, PEI, and was educated at the Presbyterian Theological Seminary at Tutor, NS. In 1859 he founded, edited, and published the leading Liberal journal of the island. Laird was elected to the Charlottetown city council in 1860. He became a Liberal member of the House of Assembly in 1871. In 1873 he took part in the negotiations to incorporate Prince Edward Island into Confederation and won a seat in the House of Commons in Ottawa. Laird was made Minister of the Interior in 1873, and assisted in the expansion of the railway west. He obtained 75,000 square miles of territory in the **QU'APPELLE VALLEY** region. In 1876 his department created the Indian Act. That year he became the **LIEUTENANT-GOVERNOR** of the North-West Territories as well as superintendent of Indian Affairs. In 1877 he negotiated Treaty 7 with the Blackfoot and other tribes in southern Alberta. He remained Lieutenant-Governor after the Liberal

defeat in 1878, but left office in 1881. Due to the difficulties of transportation at this time, the Territorial Council was forced to relinquish most of its powers of administration to Laird. He used his position as Lieutenant-Governor to secure funding to develop local schools and pay for public works. He had little interest in territorial government, making little effort to discuss constitutional problems with the federal government. In 1882 he ran for federal office but failed to win his riding. In 1898 he was appointed Indian Commissioner for Manitoba and the NWT, and he presided over three more treaties, **TREATY 8** in 1900, Treaty 9 in 1905, and **TREATY 10** in 1906. He resigned his position as Commissioner in 1909 and became an advisor to the federal government on Aboriginal issues. He died January 12, 1914.

Jeremy Mohr

FURTHER READING: Robb, Andrew. 1965. "Laird, David." *Dictionary of Canadian Biography*. Toronto: University of Toronto Press; Thomas, Lewis H. 1978. *The Struggle for Responsible Government in the North-West Territories 1870–97*. Toronto: University of Toronto Press; Weeks, Blair (ed.). 2002. *Minding the House: A Biographical Guide to Prince Edward Island MLAs 1873–1993*. Charlottetown: Acorn Press.

SASKATCHEWAN ARCHIVES BOARD R-A1

David Laird.

LAIRD, ELMER (1924–). Elmer Laird has played an important role in Saskatchewan organic agriculture and environmental issues since the early 1970s. Born in the Swift Current area in 1924, Laird grew up on a family farm and endured the 1930s **DUST-BOWL** and **DEPRESSION** era. After serving in the RCAF in **WORLD WAR II**, he purchased land near Davidson in 1947 and began to farm. From 1952 to 1964, Laird was director of the Saskatchewan Farm Union District 10. In 1964, through External Aid, a federal government agency, Laird participated in an agricultural study in Ghana and Nigeria. Throughout the

1960s, he chaired the Provincial Policy Organization for the South Saskatchewan Irrigation Project. Low grain prices in 1969 prompted him to give up chemical use on his farm in order to save on input costs: this marked his conversion to organic agriculture. That same year, Laird married Gladys McKay, originally from Strasbourg. To encourage organic farming, study legal policies and exchange information, Elmer, Gladys and other National Farmers Union members in 1973 established the Back to the Farm Research Foundation. Gladys, a research librarian, environmentalist and advocate of organic farming, made major contributions to the Foundation's projects and worked with her husband until her death on November 15, 1999.

In 1983, Laird and his wife were instrumental in founding the Canadian Organic Producers' Marketing Co-op Ltd. in Girvin—the first certified organic producers co-operative that milled flour, and sold grain, oil seeds and legumes in Canada, the USA and Europe. In 2001, Laird retired from farming and leased his land to the Back to the Farm Research Foundation, which established an organic research and demonstration farm, the first of its kind in Canada, with Laird as manager. Laird continues to work with fellow activists to prevent transnational corporations from taking over the family farm, expose government policies which support chemical-intensive agriculture, and eliminate the use of GMO seed. Laird was a pioneer in his support of environmental protection and chemical-free agriculture, and his untiring efforts have helped establish many people in organic farming. *Raymond P. Ambrosi*

LAKE, SIR RICHARD STUART (1860–1950). Lake was born in Preston, Lancashire, on July 10, 1860. He worked for the British Admiralty in Cyprus for three years until 1883. He came to Saskatchewan that year to homestead near Grenfell with his younger brother Richard and their parents. He was vice-president of the Territorial Grain Growers Association, and a Justice of the Peace for the region. Lake was elected to the North-West Territories Assembly as a Conservative in 1898 and remained in that assembly for seven years. He failed to win a seat in Ottawa in 1900 but won in 1904 and helped the Conservatives in the House of Commons until defeated in 1911. Lake served on the Public Service Commission until 1915 when he was appointed **LIEUTENANT-GOVERNOR** of Saskatchewan. Lake was appointed to increase the commitment to the war effort on the home front. His father was a British war hero and his older brother Percy was serving with great distinction in the military, and later would be knighted. Lake was the first president of the Regina Recruiting League and the provincial president of the Red Cross. He improved the prominence of the latter organization to the point that Saskatchewan became the world leader in per-capita

SASKATCHEWAN ARCHIVES BOARD R-B450
Richard Lake.

donations to the Red Cross in 1918. Lake declined in 1921 to serve a second term as Lieutenant-Governor and moved to Victoria. He continued to play an active role in the Red Cross and the Canadian military effort in **WORLD WAR II**. He had a brush with death on the *Athenia*, a passenger liner which was torpedoed by the Germans on September 3, 1939. He died in Victoria on April 23, 1950. *Jeremy Mohr*

LAKE ATHABASCA (55°22' N 108°00' W; Map sheet 74 N/8). Lake Athabasca is the largest lake in Saskatchewan with a surface area of 7,935 km². It has the lowest elevation in the province at 213 m. Located in the northwest corner of the province and extending into Alberta, the rugged north shore comprises crystalline Archean rocks while the southern shore has extensive beaches and sand dunes derived from the Athabasca Basin. It is fed by the Peace, Athabasca and Fond du Lac rivers, and drains northward into Great Slave Lake via the Slave River. The name is of **CREE** origin; one possible meaning is "meeting place of many waters," which aptly describes its location and emphasizes a characteristic that contributed to its prominent role in the fur trade. **SAMUEL HEARNE** was the first European to see the lake in 1771. By 1788 a trade post was established at Fort Chipewyan (now in Alberta) and, somewhat later, to the east at Fond du Lac. From Lake Athabasca fur traders could access the Arctic, the Pacific and Hudson Bay. In the 20th century, the northern shores of the lake saw the development of gold and uranium mining. The clean-up of former mine sites and the preservation of the sand-dune ecosystem along the south shore are contemporary

issues of concern. Much of the latter ecosystem is now part of the **ATHABASCA SAND DUNES** Provincial Wilderness Park. *Marilyn Lewry*

LAKE DIEFENBAKER (50°43'N 107°30'W; Map sheet 72 J/11). Lake Diefenbaker is a T-shaped, artificial lake created along the valley of the **SOUTH SASKATCHEWAN RIVER** by the construction of the **GARDINER DAM** and Qu'Appelle River Dam, begun in 1959. It extends westward as far as Saskatchewan Landing. The reservoir, named after former prime minister **JOHN DIEFENBAKER**, is part of the South Saskatchewan River Project. When full, it is 225 km long and 556 metres deep, making this the largest lake in southern Saskatchewan. Because of the long stretches of open water and poorly consolidated shore materials, the banks of Lake Diefenbaker are vulnerable to erosion. Between 1968 and 1992, bank recession rates have commonly ranged up to three m/yr, with even higher rates in exposed areas. Unlike the creation of the more recent Rafferty and Alameda reservoirs, the formation of multi-purpose Diefenbaker Lake received widespread support in the 1950s. Recent economic analysis of the project concludes that it has made a significant economic and social contribution to the province, although irrigation benefits have been less than predicted. *Marilyn Lewry*

LAKOTA: *see* **DAKOTA/LAKOTA**

DAVID MCLENNAN PHOTO
Resorts along Lake Diefenbaker, such as that at Mistusinne, just southeast of Elbow, provide recreation and economic benefits.

DOUG CHISHOLM PHOTO
Lake Athabasca.

John Lamont.

LAMONT, JOHN HENDERSON (1865–1936).

John Lamont was born on November 12, 1865, and grew up in Dufferin County, Ontario. He graduated from the University of Toronto with a BA in 1892 and a LLB from Osgoode Hall a year later. He was called to the Ontario Bar in 1893. He practiced law in Toronto for six years before moving to Prince Albert, where he founded a law practice with W.F.A. TURGEON. In 1902, he became a Crown Prosecutor. In 1904, Lamont was elected to the House of Commons and formed a friendship with fellow Liberal member WALTER SCOTT. Lamont resigned his seat in 1905 to run for the new Legislative Assembly of Saskatchewan. He was the province's first Attorney General in a small Cabinet of four (with Walter Scott, J.H. MOTHERWELL and J.A. CALDER). Lamont resigned from Saskatchewan politics after two years to receive an appointment to the Saskatchewan Court of Appeal. Lamont served on the Court of Appeal for nearly twenty years before being appointed to the Supreme Court on April 2, 1927, where he served for eight years. Lamont was appointed to the Royal Commission to investigate charges of corruption by the Scott government. FREDERICK HAULTAIN chaired the commission, with Judge Newlands and Lamont as members. The Haultain Commission was one of three commissions established to investigate the Scott government. Even though Scott and his Cabinet were cleared of these accusations, several public servants and MLAs were found guilty of corruption and punished. Lamont died on March 10, 1936. *Gordon Barnhart*

LAMPMAN, town, pop 650, located approximately 50 km NE of Estevan on Hwy 361. Lampman was named for Canadian poet Archibald Lampman and is one of a number of locales in the area named for poets. The first settlers arrived in the district in about 1890, and after 1900 there was a substantial influx of German-speaking people into the region. In 1913, Lampman became the junction of two rail lines as the track linking Regina to the Port of Northgate on the Canada-US border was completed. The community grew slowly but steadily (except for a slight downturn during the 1930s) until the 1950s, when development of the area's oil industry began. A gas processing plant built at nearby Steelman in the late 1950s became a large area employer, and drilling rigs dotted the countryside. Lampman's population peaked at 830 in 1971, and thereafter stabilized at its current level. Lampman has a full range of businesses and services, many of which cater to the oilfield and agricultural industries which form the basis of the regional economy. (*See also* OIL AND GAS INDUSTRY) *David McLennan*

LANCASTER, RON (1938–). Recognized as the Saskatchewan Roughriders' most outstanding quarterback, Ron Lancaster continues to make important contributions to the Canadian Football League. Born in Fairchance, Pennsylvania on October 14, 1938, Lancaster played college football at Wittenburg University in Ohio and was signed by the Ottawa Rough Riders in 1960. He alternated at quarterback with Russ Jackson before being traded to the SASKATCHEWAN ROUGHRIDERS in 1963. Ron Lancaster spent the next sixteen years playing for the western Riders. Known as the "Little General" because of his determined, analytic play, he guided the franchise to five first-place finishes in the Western Conference, five Grey Cup appearances, and the team's first-ever Grey Cup championship in 1966. A two-time Schenley Award winner for most outstanding player, Lancaster established thirty CFL

Ron Lancaster, No. 23.

records during his nineteen-year career. Lancaster then coached the Roughriders for the 1978–79 seasons, but failed to generate the same success as he did at quarterback. During the 1980s he worked as a colour commentator on CFL broadcasts. In 1991, he returned to the field as head coach of the Edmonton Eskimos, leading the team to a Grey Cup victory in 1993. Four years later, he assumed command of the Hamilton Tiger-Cats, with whom he won the 1999 Grey Cup; he is currently the team's General Manager of Football Operations. Lancaster is a member of the SASKATCHEWAN SPORTS HALL OF FAME (1981), the Canadian Football Hall of Fame (1982), and the Canadian Sports Hall of Fame (1985). *Daria Coneghan and Holden Stoffel*

LAND USE. From cattle ranching on the southern prairies to uranium mining on the northern Shield, land use in Saskatchewan is as varied as the landscape itself. Land-use patterns reflect the balance between the lay of the province's natural resources and the wants and needs of its people. Indigenous peoples used the resources of the natural environment for survival, but since Euro-Canadian settlement began in Saskatchewan in the late 19th century that natural landscape has been drastically modified through human action, and land use has evolved with the changing needs of the population. Traditional land uses based on animal and plant habitat have had to compete with increasing demands for urban lands, recreation areas, transportation routes, and extractive industries such as agriculture and mining. Today, farming and ranching are the most common land use, with roughly 46% of the province's 651,930^2 km devoted to agricultural uses. Agricultural land in Saskatchewan is restricted to the Prairie and Boreal Plain Ecozones; in 2001, 58.5% of it was used for crops and 41.5% for pasture (mainly natural) and summerfallow. Slightly more than half of Saskatchewan's land area is covered by forest, mostly in the north. The Boreal Plain Ecozone (i.e., the central third of Saskatchewan) is dominated by commercial forestry in the north and by farming in the south. About half of the timber in Saskatchewan's northern forest has commercial value, but limited road access restricts commercial forestry land uses to its southern reaches. Approximately 8% of Saskatchewan's total land falls within protected areas, such as National Parks, Provincial Parks, recreation sites, and Protected Wildlife Habitat Lands. First Nations reserves currently occupy about 1% of the provincial land base, but could double over the next twelve years, as Treaty Land Entitlement claims are satisfied. Transportation uses, including rural roads, provincial and national highways, rail lines, and ground facilities for air transport, occupy approximately 2% of the total land area. Urban land uses (cities, towns, and villages) comprise less than 0.5% of the total.

Although important economically, lands used for mining and oil and gas exploration and production take up much less than 1% of the province's land base.

In southern Saskatchewan, 20% of the land is Crown or public land, while the remainder is privately owned. In the north, only 5% of the land is under private ownership. Land-use allocation on all Crown resource and parkland in the province is authorized by Saskatchewan Environment; land use for agriculture Crown land is authorized by Saskatchewan Agriculture and Food. *Iain Stewart*

FURTHER READING: Fung. K.I. 1999. *Atlas of Saskatchewan.* Saskatoon: University of Saskatchewan; Saskatchewan Environment and Resource Management. 1998. *The Ecoregions of Saskatchewan.* Regina: Canadian Plains Research Center.

LANDA, SAM (1912–). Sam Landa was born in Saskatoon on December 31, 1912, to the first Jewish family to settle in the city. He attended the UNIVERSITY OF SASKATCHEWAN and earned his medical degree from the University of Manitoba in 1938. Following his football career with the U of S Huskies, he was the original team doctor for the Saskatoon Hilltops, 1947–86, and continued doing surgery until the age of 80. He was the first president of the Canadian Association of Sport Sciences, inaugurated at the Pan American Games in Winnipeg in 1967, led the medical staff for the Canada Winter Games in Saskatoon in 1971, and was a member of the medical team at the Munich Olympics in 1972. That year he chaired ParticipACTION Saskatoon, the forerunning test community for the brilliant marketing agency behind the wildly successful ParticipACTION movement in Canada. For his 60-plus years of volunteer service to sports and medicine, he received the Kinsman Sportsman of the Year award and the CFQC-TV Citizen of the Year award, and was inducted into both the Saskatoon and Saskatchewan Sports Halls of Fame. He received the Order of Canada in 1977. *Donald A. Bailey*

LANDSLIDES. Slopes affected by landslides are common in southern Saskatchewan. Landsliding, the downslope movement of soil and rock under the force of gravity, is an important geological process and natural hazard in the valleys of the interior plains of western Canada. The region is characterized by poorly consolidated bedrock and Quaternary deposits which are especially susceptible to landsliding. The original low strength of the sedimentary bedrock, particularly Cretaceous shales, was further reduced as the rocks expanded following unloading. This occurred first as overlying sediments were removed by erosion in the late Tertiary, and then with the wasting of the Pleistocene ice sheets. While

this earth history predisposed the bedrock to landsliding, the failure of a slope nearly always requires a triggering event. The undercutting of a valley side by stream erosion is a common trigger, although most landslides are caused by heavy rain or snowmelt. Soil and weathered rock, especially those containing clay (shale, for example) have much lower shear strength when the pore spaces between minerals are saturated with water. Most of the landslides in Saskatchewan occur in Cretaceous shales such as the Bearpaw Formation. Slope stability in the shale bedrock is understood largely from geotechnical studies, notably those associated with the constructions of the Gardiner and Qu'Appelle dams, which impound LAKE DIEFENBAKER as part of the South Saskatchewan River Project.

Landsliding is the dominant process of valley widening. Individual landslides can extend for several kilometres along a valley side and cover tens of square kilometres. Geotechnical studies in the FRENCHMAN RIVER Valley north of Climax revealed that the valley is about 80 m less deep and almost three times wider than the original glacial meltwater channel; the valley fill is composed largely of landslide deposits. Nearly all the landslides in Saskatchewan are inactive and appear very old, suggesting that there must have been widespread slope failure associated with the initial downcutting of the valleys following retreat of the continental ice sheet. Recent landslides usually have reactivated old slides or are part of the process of scarp retreat. In 1956 a landslide along Echo Creek Valley near the town of Fort Qu'Appelle severed Highway 35 in a "rapid flow" movement that is rare in Saskatchewan. Many apparently inactive landslides may be moving at rates too slow to detect without careful monitoring (e.g., the Lebret slide in the QU'APPELLE VALLEY); they are easily reactivated when disturbed, typically by excavation or the shifting of streams. Landslides expose poorly consolidated materials to runoff erosion for years or even decades. Sediment-laden runoff from landslides affects the geometry and water quality of nearby streams, producing downstream impacts that often represent more significant hazards than the direct effects of landslides. Where landslides extend onto the valley floor, streams are impounded or diverted. *David Sauchyn*

FURTHER READING: Eckel, B.F., E.K. Sauer, and E.A. Christiansen. 1987. "The Petrofka Landslide, Saskatchewan," *Canadian Geotechnical Journal* 24 (1): 81–99; Sauer, E.K. and E.A. Christiansen. 1987. "The Denholm Landslide, Saskatchewan, Canada: An Update," *Canadian Geotechnical Journal* 24 (1): 163–68.

LANE, JOHN GARY (1942–). Gary Lane was born in Saskatoon on May 2, 1942. He received a BA in history in 1963 and a Bachelor of Laws in 1966, articling in Saskatoon before joining the

Gary Lane, in the Saskatchewan Legislature, November 1984.

Department of the Attorney General as a Crown Solicitor and executive assistant to the Attorney General. In 1971 he founded the firm Lane and Whitmore. Lane was elected as a Liberal to the Legislative Assembly for Qu'Appelle-Lumsden in 1971 and re-elected in 1975. Though considered a successor to Liberal leader DAVID STEUART, Lane, along with COLIN THATCHER, switched parties. After the Progressive Conservatives swept into power in 1982, Lane became Minister of Justice and Attorney General. In 1984 he was given the additional responsibility of the Employment Development Agency. In 1985 Lane became the Minister of Finance. He was also given responsibility for the Potash Corporation of Saskatchewan (PCS). Lane was appointed to the Cabinet Planning and Priorities Committee as well as to the board of the Crown Investments Corporation. Lane oversaw the privatization of PCS in 1989. Its sale prompted the NEW DEMOCRATIC PARTY to filibuster in the Legislature. It was the longest debate over legislation in Saskatchewan's history, and ultimately the government forced closure on the issue, a first for Saskatchewan. Lane was instrumental in establishing the Saskatchewan Pension Plan, the first of its kind in North America. Lane was also appointed as the Minister responsible for Saskatchewan Telecommunications and oversaw the establishment of individual line telephones to rural Saskatchewan. In 1989, Lane was returned to the positions of Minister of Justice and Attorney General. In 1991, he was appointed to the Saskatchewan Court of Appeal. *Dana Turgeon*

FURTHER READING: Saskatchewan Archives Board. J. Gary Lane Fonds. GR 634, Regina.

LANG, OTTO EMIL (1932–). Born on May 14, 1932, in Handel, Otto Lang was raised and educated in the Humboldt area. He earned degrees in arts and law from the UNIVERSITY OF SASKATCHEWAN. In

1953, Lang was selected Rhodes Scholar and spent two years at Oxford. He was appointed professor of law at the University of Saskatchewan and became dean of the College of Law before his thirtieth birthday. Prime Minster Lester Pearson appointed Lang as the Saskatchewan campaign manager for the 1963 federal election campaign. Although the Liberals failed to elect a single MP in Saskatchewan, it solidified Lang's position as the Liberals' main federal organizer in the province and brought him into conflict with ROSS THATCHER. Lang was the lone Liberal elected in 1968 and Trudeau appointed him to Cabinet without portfolio. Lang took over responsibility for the CANADIAN WHEAT BOARD in 1969, a position he held until his political defeat. The LIFT (Lower Inventories for Tomorrow) program that provided incentives for farmers to grow crops other than wheat or take land out of production was unpopular. Lang took on several other Cabinet posts beginning with the Manpower and Immigration portfolio in 1970 and Justice in 1972 after he was re-elected. Elected again in 1974, Lang was appointed Minister of Transportation in 1975. As Minister, he faced a bitter strike by airline pilots and air traffic controllers over bilingualism legislation that would have allowed French to be used in air traffic control. Facing the intense unpopularity of the Trudeau government in the west, Lang was defeated in 1979. He moved to Winnipeg in 1979 and was appointed vice-president of Pioneer Grain Company. He left in 1988 and has had corporate jobs since. He has served on several Boards of Directors.   *Brett Quiring*

FURTHER READING: Smith, David E. 1981. *The Regional Decline of a National Party: Liberals on the Prairies.* Toronto: University of Toronto Press; Wilson, Barry. 1980. *Politics of Defeat: The Decline of the Liberal Party in Saskatchewan.* Saskatoon: Western Producer Books.

Otto Lang.

LANGAN, HENRY J., SR. (1912–90). A distinguished WORLD WAR II Aboriginal veteran, Henry Langan was born on June 12, 1912 and grew up on the Cote Reserve. He joined the Canadian Armed Forces, earning numerous military decorations between 1941 and 1946. After his release from the army, he farmed on the reserve and served on the band council. In 1966, Langan became involved in Indian politics through his work with the FEDERATION OF SASKATCHEWAN INDIAN NATIONS and the National Assembly of First Nations. For his promotion of education and continued spirituality for Indians, he was appointed a Member of the Order of Canada in 1984. Langan died on February 9, 1990.

FURTHER READING: 2004. *Saskatchewan First Nations: Lives Past and Present.* Regina: Canadian Plains Research Centre, University of Regina.

LANGENBURG, town, pop 1,107, located 15 km inside the Saskatchewan-Manitoba border at the junction of Hwys 8 and 16. Yorkton, 70 km northwest, is the nearest city. The Langenburg area began to be settled in the mid-1880s by people who were predominantly of German origin and was named after Prince Hohenlohe-Langenburg, who had visited southeast Saskatchewan in 1883 and recommended the area for German settlement. In 1888 the Manitoba and Northwestern Railway was running trains into the fledgling hamlet, and by the turn of the century Langenburg had developed into a thriving agricultural community. The discovery of potash south of the community in the late 1950s brought about a period of unprecedented growth and prosperity, and Langenburg's population doubled between 1966 and 1976, growing from 668 to 1,269. Today, the community has a comprehensive array of businesses and services: health care and recreational facilities; fire, ambulatory, and police services; and two schools, which provide K–12 education to approximately 330 students.
David McLennan

LANGHAM, town, pop 1,145, located about 30 km NW of Saskatoon on the Yellowhead Highway. The NORTH SASKATCHEWAN RIVER lies a few kilometres to the north and west. Doukhobor families began settling in the region in 1899, followed by Mennonite settlers emigrating from the United States as well as people from eastern Canada and Great Britain. With the construction of the Canadian Northern Railway through the area toward Edmonton in 1904–05, the townsite began to develop. In 1905 the post office was established, and in 1906 Langham was incorporated as a village. It attained town status the next year. By the 1920s, the community's population was over 400; however, after the initial rush of settlement it began to decline, slipping to 305 by 1951. This trend was

reversed a decade later, when in the 1960s the Yellowhead Highway was routed from Saskatoon directly to Langham, reducing the driving time between the communities to about 20 minutes. Young professionals and businesspeople began locating their families to Langham and commuting to work in the city. What was once a service centre for the surrounding agricultural district mushroomed into a bedroom community for a number of people.   *David McLennan*

George Langley.

LANGLEY, GEORGE (1852–1933). Langley was born November 10, 1852, in Essex, England. He came to Canada in 1893 and homesteaded near Rosthern, later establishing a large farm in the Maymont district. He was elected as a Liberal to the first Saskatchewan Legislature in 1905, representing Redberry. While in the Legislature, Langley was also elected to the executive of the Saskatchewan Grain Growers Association (1910–17). Premier WALTER SCOTT had him negotiate with the Interprovincial Council of Grain Growers about grain storage facilities throughout the province. Langley was appointed to the Saskatchewan Commission of Inquiry to investigate the elevator system that recommended the province provide financial backing for the SASKATCHEWAN CO-OPERATIVE ELEVATOR COMPANY that was incorporated by an act of the Legislature in 1911. Langley was elected to the co-operative's board of directors at its first general meeting, and in 1914 was elected vice-president. In 1921 he assumed the presidency that he held until 1924. Scott appointed Langley to Cabinet in 1912 as Minister of Municipal Affairs, a position he held until 1921. He revamped the hail insurance system. Langley was a strong proponent of the CANADIAN WHEAT BOARD. He advocated the pooling of Saskatchewan grain and the amalgamation of existing farmers' co-operatives. Langley was defeated in 1921 in Redberry but successfully contested a deferred election in Cumberland. Shortly after, Premier **WILLIAM MARTIN** asked Langley for his resignation because Langley had attempted to exert pressure on a provincial magistrate. Langley resigned from Cabinet and a year later resigned from the Legislature. His relationship with the **LIBERAL PARTY** deteriorated after this point. In 1925 he returned to the SGGA executive as vice-president and advocated that the organization field candidates in the provincial election, a position he had steadfastly opposed while in the Liberal Party. Langley attempted a political comeback in 1929 when he contested the Redberry constituency as an independent Liberal but lost to the official Liberal candidate. He died on August 26, 1933.

Brett Quiring

LANGUAGE INSTITUTE. The Language Institute of the **UNIVERSITY OF REGINA** was created by both the federal and provincial governments in 1988 as a result of the Supreme Court of Canada's verdict in the Father André Mercure case. The Court agreed with Father Mercure that Saskatchewan was officially bilingual, but it allowed that the province could pass a new law making English the official language, which was done in March 1988. Fearing that the law voted by the Saskatchewan government would undermine the Meech Lake Accord, the Mulroney government offered more than $50 million to the Fransaskois, about $17.5 million of which was used for a new building and an academic program to serve the educational needs of the French community, as well as give others the opportunity to perfect their knowledge of French and to learn foreign languages.

The Language Institute changed over the years because of a drastic decline in funds provided by the federal government. Various strategies were adopted by the University to keep the Institute afloat, such as transferring the English as a Second Language program and Saskatchewan Centre for International Languages to the Institute. In 2002 the University opted, for economic and internal organizational reasons, to eliminate the Language Institute, transfer ESL programming to the Centre for Continuing Education and International Languages to the Faculty of Arts, and replace the Language Institute with a more modest version, l'Institut Français.

André Lalonde

LANIGAN, town, pop 1,289, located W of Big Quill Lake, and S of Humboldt, on Hwys 16 and 20. Lanigan developed with the arrival of the CPR in 1907. The small cluster of shacks which sprang up on the townsite quickly gave way to more substantial structures, and Lanigan was incorporated as a village on August 21, 1907. On April 15, 1908, the community attained town status, and by the end of the decade rail lines connected it to Saskatoon to the west and Wynyard to the east. By the end of the 1920s, rail lines were spreading in five directions as tracks had been completed to the northeast through Watson to Melfort, and north through Humboldt to Prince Albert. As a service and distribution centre for the surrounding agricultural district, Lanigan's population had grown to just over 500 by the early 1960s. In the mid-1960s, it received a substantial boost as the Alwinsal Corporation established a potash mine 11 km west of the community. The potash mine, which was purchased by the Potash Corporation of Saskatchewan in 1977, today employs approximately 325 people. Agriculture remains the other component in the area economy, and an integrated feedlot and ethanol plant is located 8 km east of the town. The feedlot has the capacity to hold close to 30,000 head of cattle, and the ethanol plant produces over 10 million litres of ethanol each year; the operation has about 50 full-time employees. Lanigan's museum is situated in the town's 1908 CPR station, one of only a handful of its type left standing in Saskatchewan. *David McLennan*

LAROCQUE, JOSEPH Z. (1881–1964). MÉTIS leader Joseph LaRocque was born on November 26, 1881, at Lebret, Saskatchewan. A founding member of the Métis Society of Saskatchewan (MSS), LaRocque was one of Saskatchewan's foremost Métis leaders of the early 20th century. In the 1930s he worked tirelessly alongside Joe Ross and Joe McKenzie to organize Saskatchewan's Métis, creating a provincial political organization to lobby government in order to address Métis grievances and raise awareness of Métis issues. In 1937, LaRocque was elected MSS president and quickly took government to task regarding the failure of the **SCRIP** system to provide the Métis with a land base. He also toiled to eliminate the Métis' extreme poverty and their lack of educational opportunities. In 1938–39, he lobbied the province to grant the Métis a land base, similar to the Alberta Métis Colonies established under the Metis Betterment Act. In 1939 LaRocque and the MSS eventually received $10,000 from the **W.J. PATTERSON** government to pursue their land claim against the federal government. Unfortunately, the claim was never pursued, as the lawyers hired by the MSS felt that the Métis land entitlement had been extinguished by the scrip system. In 1939, LaRocque was named honorary president of the MSS for his tireless efforts—only to see the organization disband during **WORLD WAR II**, when most MSS members enlisted. Following the war, the MSS quickly rebuilt itself. LaRocque was politically active as late as 1954, when he was still corresponding with Métis community leaders, addressing such issues as the government-sponsored experimental farms and the Métis relocation to Green Lake. J.Z. LaRocque married Mary Salamon of Lebret in 1914. He died in Lebret on January 2, 1964.

Cheryl Troupe

FURTHER READING: Barron, F.L. 1997. *Walking in Indian Moccasins: The Native Policies of Tommy Douglas and the CCF.* Vancouver: University of British Columbia Press; Dobbin, M. 1978. "Métis Struggles of the Twentieth Century: Saskatchewan Metis Society 1935-1950. Part One: Early Beginnings," *New Breed* (August): 16–19.

LARRE, LUCIEN (1933–). Born in St. Walburg in 1933, Father Lucien Larre was stricken by polio at the age of 5 and overcame great obstacles to help himself and others. In 1958, he was ordained into the priesthood. Having earned five degrees from the Universities of Ottawa and Alberta, Father Larre taught in Medicine Hat, Red Deer, and Regina. His experience in helping people with serious emotional problems led to the establishment of Bosco Homes in 1971. Larre also founded the Big Valley Jamboree in Craven, an annual country music festival with all proceeds going towards Bosco Homes. Father Larre was made a Member of the Order of Canada in 1983.

LASHBURN, town, pop 783, located 32 km SE of Lloydminster on Hwy 16. Settlement of the Lashburn area began in the spring of 1903 when a number of the Barr Colonists (*see* **BARR COLONY**) took up land. Additional settlers from eastern Canada arrived in 1904; in 1905, when the Canadian Northern Railway came through, the location for the townsite of Lashburn was chosen. The name is a combination of the word "Lash" (honouring a railway company solicitor, Z.A. Lash) and "burn," a Scottish word for a small stream. Lashburn grew steadily as additional settlers continued to pour into the region; they included a significant number of Mennonite families and, in the 1930s, people from the dried-out regions of southern Saskatchewan. By the mid-1960s, the community's population passed the 500 mark, and in 1979 Lashburn attained town status. The major industries in the area are oil and agriculture: more than 1,600 oil wells dot the district's rich agricultural lands. Today, Lashburn residents benefit greatly from the community's proximity to Lloydminster, a city of 21,000 people which provides Lashburn residents with employment opportunities, amenities, and services not locally available. The Lashburn Bluebirds dominated women's softball at both the provincial and national levels in the late 1970s. One exceptional player to come out of Lashburn was Brenda Staniforth. An inductee into the **SASKATCHEWAN SPORTS HALL OF FAME** and Softball Canada's Hall of Fame, Staniforth has played and coached Canadian women's softball at the international level.

Another Lashburn resident was **AUGUSTUS KENDERDINE**, who arrived there to farm in 1907 and went on to become perhaps the most significant painter in Saskatchewan before 1950.

David McLennan

LAST MOUNTAIN BIRD OBSERVATORY. Last Mountain Bird Observatory (LMBO) is located in the southeast corner of Last Mountain Regional Park, near the north end of **LAST MOUNTAIN LAKE** in south-central Saskatchewan. LMBO was established in 1989 as a charter member of the Canadian Migration Monitoring Network. Its purpose, and that of the approximately twenty other members of the network, is to monitor the numbers of forest-dwelling songbirds in Canada. Due to the lack of roads in most of Canada's northern forests, this group of birds is not easily monitored by a census on their breeding grounds, so the network was established to monitor the numbers, chronology, and migration ecology of birds as they migrate between their breeding and wintering grounds.

The monitoring method used at LMBO and other network stations is a combination of birds captured during systematic mist netting and birds seen during a daily census. Mist nets, made of fine mesh nylon, are strung between poles; a standard mist net is 2.5m high and 12m long, with a fine 30mm-mesh that is nearly invisible to birds. At LMBO, thirteen mist nets are operated in the same locations each year, and are opened from 7:00 a.m. To 1:00 p.m. each day of the spring and fall banding seasons. Spring banding is conducted from May 9 to May 31; fall banding is from August 3 to October 7.

Birds are quickly and safely removed from the nets and brought to the banding station for processing. For each bird captured, the species, age, sex, and a number of measurements are recorded. Before release, birds are banded with a uniquely numbered aluminum band; the band number and related information are forwarded to a central repository at the Canadian Wildlife Service in Ottawa. Since its establishment, almost 40,000 specimens of 114 species of birds have been captured and banded at LMBO. Although the major purpose of the establishment of the Observatory is the monitoring of songbird migration, public education is also an important component of its program. The public is welcome at the facility between 9:00 a.m. and 1:00 p.m. during the spring and fall banding seasons.

Alan R. Smith

LAST MOUNTAIN LAKE (51°05'N, 105°14'W; Map sheet 72 P/30.) Just 3 km wide, 93 km long and covering 2,312 km., Last Mountain Lake (LML), also called Long Lake, is located 48 km northwest of Regina. Its name commemorates a **CREE** legend describing how the Great Spirit made the last hills (east of Duval) from soil scooped from the valley now occupied by LML. Scientists say it formed c. 11,000 years ago from meltwaters of the continental ice sheet draining south into the Qu'Appelle glacial spillway.

In 1869, the Hudson's Bay Company (HBC) built Last Mountain House at the southern end of the lake; Isaac Cowie, clerk for the HBC, described one of the last great herds of buffalo in the region. Settlers arrived by 1885. In 1886 the Qu'Appelle, Long Lake and Saskatchewan Railway and Steamboat Co. built a branch line as far as Craven, intending to run a steam ship service along LML, but the rail link to Saskatoon was completed in 1890, bypassing the lake.

Canada's first federal bird sanctuary was designated on the lake in 1887. Initially covering 1,000 ha, Last Mountain Lake National Wildlife Area now covers 15,600 ha, protecting nesting and migratory birds. Proximity to Regina makes Last Mountain Lake an important recreation area. It provides some of the best fishing in southern Saskatchewan, as well as bird watching, sailing, boating, and camping from two provincial parks and other recreation areas.

Marilyn Lewry

LATIMER, ROBERT (1953–). Robert Latimer, a farmer from Wilkie, Saskatchewan, was born on March 13, 1953. In 1993 he was convicted of second-degree murder in the death of his 12-year-old daughter, Tracy Lynn Latimer. On October 24 of that year, Latimer chose carbon monoxide poisoning to end the twelve years of suffering Tracy had experienced as a result of the severely debilitating form of cerebral palsy with which she was afflicted. Robert Latimer argued that his love for Tracy and his desire to put an end to her pain had driven him to this extreme action, and that it had been a compassionate and merciful solution to Tracy's illness. The circumstances of Tracy Lynn Latimer's death, and her father's trial, garnered worldwide interest. Proponents of euthanasia lobbied the judicial system for a ruling called "compassionate homicide," recommending no prison time for Latimer. People with disabilities abhorred Latimer's actions, fearing the precedent that would be set if Latimer were not punished to the full extent of the law.

On November 16, 1994, a jury found Latimer guilty of second-degree murder; but the Saskatchewan Court of Appeal ordered a new trial after finding that the Royal Canadian Mounted Police might have tainted the case by improperly questioning prospective jurors. In December 1997, Latimer was again found guilty of second-degree murder. The minimum sentence for second-degree murder was twenty-five years in jail with no chance of parole for ten years, but Judge Ted Noble gave Latimer a "constitutional exemption," stating that Latimer acted out of love and compassion. He felt that based on section 12 of the Charter of Rights and Freedoms the mandatory minimum sentencing would be cruel and unusual punishment, and recommended that Latimer be eligible for parole after one year. However, in November 1998 the Saskatchewan Court of Appeal set aside Noble's sentence and imposed the mandatory sentence of at least ten years before becoming eligible for parole. After another appeal, in June 2000 the Supreme Court of Canada upheld the life sentence for Latimer, with no chance of parole for ten years. They suggested, however, that Latimer should consider asking for clemency through the rarely used "Royal Prerogative of Mercy." He refused to do so, maintaining that he had done the right thing by ending his daughter's suffering.

Elizabeth Mooney

LATTICE QUANTUM CHROMODYNAMICS. The **UNIVERSITY OF REGINA** installed Canada's largest Lattice Quantum ChromoDynamics (LQCD) computer facility in 2004 to study the fundamental aspects of the universe and the nature of matter. Randy Lewis, who joined the university's physics department in 1997, was named a Canada Research Chair in 2003 and received financial assistance from the federal and provincial governments to conduct the research. LQCD is the large-scale computing technique used by physicists around the world to develop a theoretical understanding of nature in terms of subatomic particles. The Regina computer, about the size of a five-drawer filing cabinet, is built from 260 Pentium-4 processors with more than 13,000 Gigabytes of disk space. Within a few months of being installed, the Regina facility had already attracted scientists from the TRIUMF Lab in Vancouver, the **UNIVERSITY OF SASKATCHEWAN**, and the University College of the Fraser Valley to discuss research opportunities. The computer is also being used by teams of scientists from York University and Simon Fraser University; special access is granted through an encrypted on-line connection to allow remote computers to talk to Regina's LQCD computer.

Joe Ralko

LAUBACH, FRANK (1857–1923). Franklin Ludwig Laubach was born in Edinburgh, Scotland. His father was a bandmaster, and at an early age he was put to work copying out band music, since printing was rarely done. At 17, playing in the orchestra of Sir Charles Halle at such fashionable places as Harrogate and Cheltenham, he became acquainted with many notable musicians. Later he played in various English and Scottish orchestras, and was bandmaster of the King's Bodyguard for Scotland. In 1904, Laubach came to Canada to join his son on a homestead, but almost immediately moved his family to Regina and organized the Regina Philharmonic Society that same year. He became choir director at St. Paul's Anglican Pro-Cathedral in 1905, and soon the group earned an

Frank Laubach.

enviable reputation. The inaugural concert of the Regina Orchestral Society (forerunner of the REGINA SYMPHONY ORCHESTRA) was held in 1908, with Laubach, its founder, as conductor; reserved seats were $1, while general admission was 50¢.

Laubach was one of the organizers of the first competitive provincial music festival in 1909. In 1911 he became part of the newly established music department at Regina College, where he taught violin and orchestral instruments. Laubach's interest was not restricted to classical works: he also conducted a dance orchestra, and early in WORLD WAR I a 600-voice children's choir at a fund-raising performance. He composed marches, church music and a light opera, and wrote *The Saskatchewan* (a march and two-step) to celebrate the province's inauguration in 1905. From 1915 to 1917, he was bandmaster of the 68th battalion of the Canadian Expeditionary Forces playing on troopships crossing the Atlantic. An acknowledged leader of Regina's musical life, he retired in 1922 and died in Vancouver. *Margaret A. Hammond*

FURTHER READING: Pitsula, J.M. 1988. *An Act of Faith: The Early Years of Regina College*. Regina: Canadian Plains Research Center.

LAURIE, PATRICK GAMMIE (1833–1903).

On August 25, 1878, Patrick Laurie launched the *Saskatchewan Herald*, the first newspaper in the Battleford region. Patrick Laurie was the son of Anglican minister William Laurie and Mary Ann Gammie; as a youth, he apprenticed in Toronto as a printer, beginning a long career in the newspaper business. After working in eastern Canada and briefly with the *Nor'Wester* newspaper in Red River, Laurie embarked on a 650-mile trip westward from Winnipeg to the Battleford region, walking the entire way beside an ox-cart that carried his printing press. His local stories were front-page news and he

was a strong supporter of the North-West Mounted Police.

Laurie's political interests were evident in his coverage of CONSERVATIVE PARTY rhetoric: he was an advocate for British imperialism, and praised the traditions and "character" brought west by the Anglo-Saxon governing bodies. However, Laurie did not agree with the settlement schemes of the Conservative government of 1881, whereby land was made available at low prices to encourage speedy settlement: he argued that immigrants should come west at their own expense, so that only the hardiest would undertake the challenge. Laurie insisted that the success of the west depended upon English farmers, Germans from the fatherland, and Anglo-Saxons born on Canadian soil; he described the Aboriginal peoples as obstacles to White settlement.

During the NORTH-WEST RESISTANCE of 1885, Laurie's editorials distorted the issues and ignored the plight of the MÉTIS people in the area. He also incorrectly reported that Indians were on the warpath and that the CREE and the Nakota of the area shared the views of Riel and his followers. From the late 1880s to the turn of the century, the

Patrick Gammie Laurie.

Saskatchewan Herald strongly criticized Clifford Sifton's agenda to populate the west with settlers from Europe. His influence on the Battleford community helped ensure that only White Anglo-Saxon settlers were welcome in the surrounding area.

Elizabeth Mooney

LAVALLÉE, MARY ANN (1920–99).

Born on the Cowessess Reserve on June 2, 1920, Mary Ann Lavallée received her early education at the Qu'Appelle Indian Residential School (Lebret), and later qualified as a registered nurse at St. Boniface Hospital. The course of her life changed when she married Sam Lavallée and they established a farm on the Cowessess Reserve. They encountered difficulty from two fronts: first in their attempt to modernize their farm and become economically competitive; and second in the lack of adequate educational opportunities for their children. They

began to work for change. Mary Ann was a firm believer in equal educational opportunities and in First Nations parents making the right decisions for their children. She became the instigator and active supporter (1950 to 1967) of establishing a home and school association on her reserve, and was instrumental in forming school committees on reserves across Saskatchewan and in encouraging kindergarten programs for the children.

Mary Ann Lavallée became interested in economic reform in 1960 when the specter of bankruptcy hung over their farm and Section 89 of the Indian Act prevented them, as First Nations farmers on reserve, from using land title as collateral for a loan; Section 89 made it almost impossible for them to operate a modern farm. Forced to plunge into the political arena, they struggled through nearly ten years and three successive federal governments until the Honorable ALVIN HAMILTON (then federal Minister of Agriculture) brought the issue into parliamentary debate. In 1969, Lavallée was invited to Ottawa to receive the personal signature of Jean Chrétien (then Minister of Indian Affairs and Northern Development) on documents that acted as loan guarantees from the Department of Indian Affairs. This saved the Lavallée farm and opened the door for other First Nations farmers. For twelve years Mary Ann Lavallée traveled across Canada as an unofficial spokesperson for First Nations people seeking social justice and social reform, also traveling to Australia to speak to Aboriginal people there. In 1974 she was chosen by the Saskatchewan Indian Women's Conference as Mother of the Year; and in 1978 she was appointed to the Science Council of Saskatchewan. In recognition of her work, Mary Ann Lavallée was honoured by the women's division of the Saskatchewan Department of Labour as one of the province's notable women (1980). She received a medal for outstanding service from the government of Canada, and was nominated to the Saskatchewan Agricultural Hall of Fame by both the

Mary Ann Lavallée.

Cowessess Band and the Saskatchewan Indian Agricultural Program (1986).

Christian Thompson and Carol Lavallée

LAW AND JUSTICE: *see essay on this page.*

LAW FOUNDATION OF SASKATCHEWAN.

The Law Foundation of Saskatchewan is a non-profit organization established in 1971 (The Legal Profession Act, 1990, Sec. 74–79). Its purposes are legal education, legal research, legal aid, law libraries and law reform. Funds are derived from interest on lawyers' mixed trust accounts. This monetary procedure for dealing with funds held in trust was made law in 1971, and is presently governed by the Legal Profession Act, 1990. The Law Foundation membership consists of the Minister of Justice or his/her designate, two people appointed by the Minister (at least one of whom must not be a Law Society member), and four members of the Law Society appointed by the benchers. Originating in Australia in 1967, the concept of Law Foundations was next initiated in British Columbia in 1969, and in Saskatchewan in 1971. *Raymond Ambrosi*

LAW SOCIETY OF SASKATCHEWAN. The

Law Society of Saskatchewan exists to self-govern the legal profession in the best interests of the public. The fundamental principle of judiciary independence from state government, private citizens, and administrative bodies is a cornerstone of Canadian society. A Law Society was originally created under an Ordinance of the North-West Territories in 1898. At that time its membership included lawyers throughout the region which in 1905 became Saskatchewan and Alberta. There were those who wished to see the Society continue to operate in both provinces, but in 1907 the province of Saskatchewan passed The Legal Profession Act, which established a separate provincial bar. The Society has been modified several times since then to reflect changes to the legal profession, including such things as the first admission of women law students in 1913.

The Law Society is governed by a group of elected lawyers and laymen known as Benchers, who manage and conduct all aspects of the Society. It seeks to regulate and uphold high standards of competence and integrity in its members, including: admission standards and education through the Saskatchewan Legal Education Society; the *Code of Professional Conduct*; and the discipline of errant law society members. The Society defends the independence of the legal profession, and works to improve the administration of justice and rules of law. It has an administrative liaison, maintains extensive libraries and a mentor program for lawyers, and offers a referral service for the public.

Merle Massie

Law and Justice

Louis A. Knafla

Introduction

Our knowledge of law and justice in the Saskatchewan region dates from European contact in the mid-18th century. First, fur traders of Britain's Hudson's Bay Company (HBC), and then later the French North West Company (NWC), made their way from Hudson Bay and Lake Winnipeg up the Churchill, North and South Saskatchewan, and the Assiniboine and Qu'Appelle rivers into the heartland of the Canadian prairies. A commingling of British common law, martial law, and master-servant relations governed the official criminal justice system of the HBC, while French civil and British criminal law comprised that of the NWC. Both of these systems were foreign to the indigenous customary law that governed relations between and within tribal societies, as well as to the habits of the immigrant peoples who settled the prairies. The history of law and justice is the story of how those disparate elements were eventually moulded into a criminal justice system.

The roots of crime and violence lay in local families, their communities and working relationships. Such roots underlay all European as well as North American societies. The customary law of the "blood feud" was the original justice system that governed violent actions in these societies: from the ancient Lombards and Visigoths to the Frankish and Anglo-Saxon kingdoms of the 6th century, to the Norman and English societies of the 12th century, to Scottish society of the late 17th, and North American Native societies for a long time. Since many fur traders were Scottish, they would have been familiar with the blood feud they encountered among Aboriginal peoples. The basic tenet of blood feud justice was compensation: all crimes, and even accidental deaths, were to be settled by compensation to the victim. The "blood feud" was a last resort, to be exercised by the kin of the victim against the kin of the perpetrator when the payment of compensation failed (i.e., could not be agreed upon). This blood feud justice was probably more successful than our modern criminal justice system in ameliorating the losses suffered by victims of crime and in restoring peace to the community: in the vast majority of all crimes, both kin groups were forced to come to an accommodation on the terms of compensation in a situation where individuals, families, and communities had to bring closure to violent acts.

From the outset, the HBC had complete jurisdiction of all criminal offences in Rupert's Land. The Board of Governors in London made the laws; its post "chief factors" were *ex officio* Justices of the Peace (JPs), and the post "councils" its grand jury. Its chief concerns were to regulate the behaviour of its employees, to prevent them from consorting with "country wives," and to prosecute sexual liaisons, whether male or female. Punishment was by the lash, imprisonment, or transportation to a foreign island. Thus the HBC used a mixture of common law, martial law (of the British navy), and master-servant law in handling crimes where both parties were British. Where there was a criminal trial, it was held aboard an anchored ship on Hudson Bay that flew the "King's Jack," where for employees the company logo stood for "Here Before Christ." They expected rough justice, British style: solitary confinement and brutal, multiple whippings with the cat o'nine tails for minor offences; and hangings for capital ones. The HBC, however, recognized Native peoples as First Nations, and in what they termed Indian Territories exercised discretion according to "local custom."

This was the custom that the HBC, and later the NWC, brought into the Saskatchewan area when traders paddled up the rivers flowing into Hudson Bay in the 1740s–what Chief Factor Peter Ogden later called "the custom of the country." Justice, according to the blood feud, allowed company men, middlemen, and Natives to interact with one another on a relatively level playing field when it came to handling a matter of crime; it was also surprisingly effective in maintaining law and order in a vast and lightly settled landscape of differing peoples and nationalities.

The Fur Trade Era, 1750-1869

The French established fur trading posts at Fort Paskoyac on the Saskatchewan River about 1750, at Fort St Louis (Nipawin) in 1753, and at Fort à la Corne in 1754; this resulted in a booming trade that was rife with alcohol and conflict. Later posts at Lake Athabasca in 1778, Lac la Ronge by 1779, and Fort Espérance in 1783 had more peaceful relations. The criminal justice policy of the NWC was to adopt Native customary law. The British HBC founded posts at Fairford House in 1795 and at Bedford House, on Reindeer Lake, in 1796. Carleton and Cumberland House, both established on the SASKATCHEWAN RIVER in 1793, and Fort Pitt later in 1829, became their major trading posts and were still vigorous by 1878. Surviving post journals reveal an administration of justice for company employees that was based on naval discipline and martial law. Chief factors brought order to disorderly posts with what one might call the law of necessity, beating employees with fists or clapping them in irons as discretion required. Official British law was seldom used. Thus, in a sense, the trading companies used their own informal system of justice when dealing with their own people.

In the first reported use of the blood feud, in 1754, Aboriginals who killed five HBC employees were sent for trial to Albany House and hanged as an example; there were no retributions. In 1778, when a Cree at Pangman Post on the NORTH SASKATCHEWAN RIVER was poisoned by John Cole and a group of HBC traders, the latter were killed by the Cree in blood feud; HBC officers reported that justice had been done. But when PETER POND, an interloper, killed a British man in a duel near Lake Athabasca in 1775, and another at Lac La Ronge in 1781, he was sent to Montreal for a criminal trial. What is surprising is how few crimes were reported in either company records or personal journals, which exist in large numbers.

The justice system changed with the Canada Jurisdiction Act of 1803, caused by an incident on the North Saskatchewan River at Fort de l'Isle. An employee of the XY Company (USA) killed an NWC trader in a theft dispute in 1802, and was sent for trial to Lower Canada. The resulting Act held that all crimes committed in Rupert's Land were to be tried in the superior courts of Lower or Upper Canada; it also allowed for local posses to search for suspects. In reality, the Act only applied to the Manitoba area; and with the new Canada Criminal and Civil Jurisdiction Act of 1821, the "private law" system of the HBC (which had amalgamated with the NWC), based on the custom of the country, was upheld and confirmed. While the Recorder of Rupert's Land, Adam Thom, appointed to the General Quarterly Court of the Red River colony of Assiniboia in 1839, claimed criminal jurisdiction throughout Rupert's Land, he seldom exercised it west of the colony; he charged the grand jury that any crimes committed beyond the colony should be handled by local custom—"the law of the land."

According to John Rowand, chief trader of the Athabasca district, the blood feud remained the customary practice for criminal offences throughout the region in the first half of the 19th century. Rowand himself was shot by an associate in 1854. His son, John Jr., failed to avenge his father for the family, but a Métis friend tracked down the associate three days later and shot him; there was no retribution

from the killer's family. This practice was confirmed by Governor Sir George Simpson before a British parliamentary Select Committee in 1857. It was also later confirmed as settled custom by the Supreme Court in *Regina v Haatq als Aht* (1884). Criminal activity, however, remained slight: only nine cases of homicide were reported for Rupert's Land between 1821 and 1857, of which eight charged were found not guilty.

The Territorial Era, 1870-1905

The era of the HBC came to an end in 1868, when the British Parliament granted Rupert's Land to the Dominion of Canada. In the following year, Parliament created the province of Manitoba; the area west to British Columbia, converted into the North-West Territories (NWT), continued the laws that had been observed until then. The Territories became part of Canada in 1870, and officers of the HBC became its JPs for the administration of criminal law in 1871. A legal system emerged in 1873 when the new Lieutenant-Governor was authorized to appoint coroners, JPs and Stipendiary Magistrates (SMs), as well as to construct jails and prisons, and the Governor in Council was authorized to enact ordinances and statutes for the regulation of public offences.

The immediate problem for law and justice in the Saskatchewan district in 1870 was that JPs who were former HBC officials had no knowledge of English or Canadian criminal law. They also had no personnel for law enforcement, and were required to prepare and implement all the paper work for the execution of legal process. Thus the Administration of Justice Act in 1873 provided not only for professional justices (SMs), but also for a professional police force: the North-West Mounted Police (NWMP). While SMs were empowered to hear non-capital criminal cases, capital ones were reserved to the courts in Manitoba; and while the NWMP were agents of the Dominion, in actual fact they were local officers who served the same local interests as the JPs of Assiniboia.

The creation of the NWMP coincided with the CYPRESS HILLS MASSACRE of May 1873. The event was both fact and myth: "depraved savages" who stole horses, local police who would not hunt them down, and drunken American ruffians who slaughtered the offending Natives.

SASKATCHEWAN ARCHIVES BOARD R-B368

First provincial jail and courthouse, Prince Albert, built in 1886, but not opened until 1888. Photo taken ca. 1907.

Lacking reliable accounts, the violence boiled down to three costly rounds of gunfire; the Natives eventually lost, and had their heads cut off and mounted on poles for display. The Americans involved went back across the border, and two years later Colonel J.F. Macleod resolved an international incident by traveling to Helena, Montana, to gain their extradition to Canada. The offenders were tried and released, and the last indictments were dismissed in March 1882.

The NWMP was an imperial, paramilitary force modeled after the Irish Constabulary and the French *gendarmes*. Their original legal duties were to enforce judicial writs and notices, act as jailers, and deliver prisoners to NWMP guardhouses for trial before their police courts. Each patrol covered 170,000 miles a year. The first court was held by Inspector L.N.F. Crozier at Fort Carleton in 1875; the second by Superintendent W.M. Herchmer at Fort Pitt in 1876; and the third by Commissioner Macleod at Fort Walsh in the same year. Non-commissioned officers acted as prosecutors, and constables as jail-keepers. The early prosecutions were primarily for Natives, Métis and traders charged with assault, theft, or liquor violations. Most charges came from informers, who received half of the fines levied.

Commissioner Macleod insisted on hard evidence for all convictions, no hearsay testimony, and release with warnings for most first offenders; otherwise he insisted on stiff penalties, which included fines of up to $200 plus costs. His purpose was to develop a society where such offences would not be committed. These magistrates, including Lieutenant Colonel Hugh Richardson at Battleford and Regina, and Commissioner A.G. Irvine at Fort Walsh, had extensive powers. The accused in major criminal cases could choose trial by jury, with six jurors forming the panel. Judges could sentence up to five years with hard labour; in general, however, the caseload was minimal, suggesting that the early frontier was not as violent as some historians have suggested.

Police courts in the Saskatchewan area prosecuted nearly 5,600 cases between 1874 and 1898, of which approximately 60% were by NWMP magistrates and 40% by civilian magistrates. Thus these lower courts heard about 224 cases yearly. Most of the cases involved the whisky trade, cattle and horse theft, prostitution, fighting, and gun battles. Where reports have survived, each case was heavily documented. Natives and Métis received leniency as the courts wished to accommodate them as Aboriginal peoples. If there was a bias at all, it was in handling local officials: when for example an HBC wagon train from Fort Garry was stopped outside of Fort Walsh for inspection and twenty-four gallons of illegal alcohol were found, no prosecution ensued.

The largest number of prosecutions in the early years occurred in the southwest, where Fort Walsh had 65% of the criminal cases; but the area's average was only 36 annually. The major change came in 1880, when charges in Commissioner Irvine's era (1880-86) increased by 500%. The focus was on new settlers, who occupied 87% of the criminal calendar; the magistrates wanted immigrants to learn quickly what would not be tolerated. The heavy calendars were now at Regina, Battleford and Prince Albert, and the conviction rate 73%. By the 1890s, liquor offences were most prevalent, civilian magistrates now carried the load (over 70% of the prosecutions), and the severity of punishments declined. Saskatchewan was looking more like a settled country.

When the Supreme Court of the North-West Territories was created by the Dominion Parliament in 1886, SMs became its judges. Judicial districts for the Saskatchewan area were established for East Assiniboia, Moosomin-Regina, and Battleford. The court system for criminal law was now in the hands of local JPs, SMs, police magistrates of the NWMP, five judges of the Supreme Court who sat in the headquarters of their judicial districts, and the judges who sat *en banc* to hear appeals from lower courts. Supreme Court judges rode in pairs for the assize circuits for each district. According to the Act of 1886, the law of the Territories was now the law of England as of 1870. But in practice little changed, as magistrates and judges were already following English criminal law and treatises where local circumstances were favourable. The Supreme Court heard few criminal cases for the Saskatchewan area, perhaps a dozen a year, and most of those on appeal. As before, magistrates worked to settle disputes; when they could not settle, they prosecuted and sentenced with vigilance.

The major figure was Justice Edward Ludlow Wetmore, who rode the Eastern Assiniboia judicial circuit from Moosomin between 1887 and 1897, the Saskatchewan circuit from Battleford between 1897 and 1907, and was the new province's first chief justice from 1907 to 1912. A prominent lawyer, mayor, and MLA from Fredericton, New Brunswick, Wetmore became an outstanding jurist: an expert in criminal procedure, he brought modern rules of legal process into the courtroom, with clear and cogent written judgments that became legal precedent for the region. He assisted in drafting territorial ordinances, and upheld Native customs and the rights of minorities. Court calendars were punctual, legal chicanery was not tolerated, and his jurisprudence was seldom

SASKATCHEWAN ARCHIVES BOARD R-B3813

Members of the first Supreme Court of the North West Territories, old courthouse, 1893. On the bench, left to right: Hon. E.L. Wetmore; Hon. LCol. McLeod; Hon. LCol. Richardson (Senior Justice); Hon. Justice Rouleau; Hon. Justice McGuire. Officers of the Courts, standing: left, Sheriff Benson; right, Dixie Watson, Clerk of the Court.

SASKATCHEWAN ARCHIVES BOARD R-A624

Edward Ludlow Wetmore, Chief Justice of Saskatchewan.

537

Detectives, lawyers, and judges in front of old courthouse in Regina, ca. late 1890s.

challenged. Only 4% of his verdicts were appealed, and only 20% of those were reversed.

Criminal activity was intermittent in the first two decades of the territorial era, and more than a quarter of the prosecutions involved Native peoples. The most frequent crime was horse stealing, and the second was violation of the liquor laws, which included drunkenness; both crimes had a heavy Aboriginal involvement. Such prosecutions involved a clash of two legal systems, as according to Native custom horse theft was on one hand a form of war, and on the other a display of male virility—an act to be praised. This changed by the 1890s when the NWMP clamped down on Natives through the influence of the Department of Indian Affairs (DIA), which wanted to show the United States that Canada could control its people. Montana businessmen were encouraged to inform on Natives who sold them stolen horses and purchased liquor to bring back across the border. When thirty-three horses were stolen from T.G. Baker of Montana and brought across the border, the NWMP sentenced eleven Natives to two-year sentences in Stony Mountain Penitentiary. The result was that increased NWMP manpower, patrols, and co-operation with the DIA and US army, coupled with stiff punishments, brought a decline in horse theft and Native trials by the 1890s.

Other crimes, however, went almost unnoticed by the NWMP. Apart from violent crimes against the peace, most assaults, property crimes, and moral offences were often ignored and not included in annual reports. While some assaults were prosecuted and given small fines, gambling, prostitution, narcotics, sports on the Sabbath, and white-collar crime went unnoticed—as did abortion and infanticide. The two exceptions, which they attempted to enforce at the turn of the century but soon lost interest in, were vagrancy, which JPs prosecuted as a socio-economic crime, and bawdy houses. Perhaps a major reason for this paradigm is that the NWMP established posts in immigrant villages and colonies as soon as they were established, using their influence to assist families in meeting the challenges of prairie life as well as instructing them on what activities would or would not be condoned.

Changes did occur after the introduction of the Criminal Code of Canada in 1892. Native customs became secondary to the exercise of a federal criminal law; confessions obtained by agents of the DIA were less likely to be admissible; the burden of proof in theft of horses and cattle was onerous; husband-wife testimony was circumscribed in domestic disputes; and an "unchaste character" could bring failure to convict in sexual offences. In addition, a new English definition of *mens rea* meant that the accused had to "know" exactly the consequences of his/her actions: just shooting or taking something was not "intent" in itself. Thus there was less judicial discretion in the criminal justice system than before, and fewer prosecutions per capita. People were less reluctant to make complaints to JPs, and prosecutors were less willing to indict.

There were, however, exceptions as the judges still adhered to a principle of old English law that the "black letter" did not apply when local customs were deemed more relevant. For example, when the Territorial Legislature enacted the "Prairie Fire Ordinance" in 1898, the Canadian Pacific and other railways became liable for the prairie fires caused by their locomotives, even though they were beyond local jurisdiction; Justice Wetmore saw to that. Local circumstances also circumvented the law when it was unwarranted. For example in 1879, as Prince Albert wanted a telegraph station, the HBC said that it could be erected only at its post two miles away, but the federal government said it would provide the services if the town would supply the poles. When HBC strung the poles to its post, over 100 citizens dug them out and piled them in the town. Ten of the leaders were arrested, and the HBC-appointed JP found them guilty. As the eight town policemen could not control the crowd which stormed the courtroom in protest and forced the JP out the window, the HBC relented and the station was placed in the town.

Local unrest was highlighted in the Riel Rebellion of spring 1885, a war that pitted Métis and Natives led by LOUIS RIEL, GABRIEL DUMONT, and POUNDMAKER against mounted police and militia near the banks of the SOUTH SASKATCHEWAN RIVER. Riel was defending a new provisional government for his people at BATOCHE, and attempting to settle land claims with the Dominion. The Rebellion was triggered by the "Frog Lake Massacre," where an HBC post was demolished with the loss of ten lives. The Rebellion itself was a tragedy of wasted human life and demolished farms and communities. At the ensuing trials, James Prendergast, later Chief Justice of Manitoba, was called upon by Archbishop Taché to serve as defense counsel for forty-two Natives and Métis who were charged at Regina with treason in the Rebellion. He persuaded them to plead guilty as a group to petty treason; after much wrangling they agreed, and forty received short prison terms while two were released. A study of all the trials has concluded that no irregularities occurred. Riel's treason trial was a major event in the history of the town as thousands of Natives and Métis came to witness the proceedings. While considered by some a political trial, the charge and venue were legitimate, the jury was scrupulously selected, and 107 days were allowed for appeals. The insanity issue for Riel, who was hanged, will however never be successfully resolved. But in spite of great fear, no further violence ensued. Reparations were given, the territorial budget was doubled, and settlements rebuilt.

Law and justice was often dispensed with equality. In July 1889, Motow, a Cree man, was tried before Judge Richardson in Battleford for attempted rape and indecent assault against a 15-year-old White girl at Qu'Appelle. Richardson, known as an impartial judge, had a jury of eight instead of six, and appointed a Métis JP to sit as an associate. The jurors convicted Motow, who had pleaded drunkenness, of indecent assault; he was sentenced to three months hard labour (maximum two years) and twelve lashes because the evidence against him was slim. But in the following year, when a White man was accused of raping a respectable mixed-blood woman, Richardson instructed the jurors to view the evidence regardless of race. When they found him guilty and he was sentenced to three years at Stony Mountain, the Regina *Leader* praised the judge's sentence.

In 1892, a 13-year-old girl in Qu'Appelle claimed she was raped by a "half-breed" on her way from church. Richardson, summoning a jury of twelve in Regina, allowed the testimony in Cree with translation for the jury. The accused pleaded not guilty with the claim that Native women were promiscuous. After Richardson explained the law of "unlawful carnal knowledge" to the jurors, they found the man guilty but recommended mercy because he was unfamiliar with the law: Richardson sentenced him to five years and twenty lashes. Four years later the Supreme Court made this a precedent by holding that the common law applied universally, but that the "ignorance of law" defense by Native peoples could bring a reduced sentence.

Co-operation with American authorities and local immigrant communities was always at the top of mounted police policy. In 1888, three Frenchmen stole some horses at Wolsley and, after shooting dead the farmer and the constable who had tracked them down, escaped to the US. Two of them were discovered and arrested, and Justice Wetmore had them extradited to the NWT, where he had them tried, convicted, and hanged: Macleod's previous efforts to work with the US authorities was thus reciprocated. At the turn of the century, the new Barr colony had conflicts with people in Battleford. The NWMP went in, were boarded in local homes, dispensed rations, and avoided further violence. Likewise, Mormons who practiced polygamy were normally not prosecuted. As for Doukhobors in the Battleford and Yorkton areas who did not believe in government regulations, they were sometimes arrested and tried, sometimes not; sometimes jailed as vagrants, and sometimes sent to asylums. In any case, the patience of the police was always tested.

The US boundary had contributed to considerable violence since the 1870s. Cattle rustling, horse theft and liquor running were frequent crimes, and finding witnesses and evidence was difficult. Informers helped, but sometimes they informed simply for their own financial benefit. The NWMP controlled the border by issuing passes, and also served as customs and quarantine agents. The 630-mile border over open range and badlands was porous, and the gangs of Butch Henry, Nelson and the Jones Boys, and Fred McBeth were often caught, tried, and released on technicalities. Charlie Parmer, an associate of Jesse James, crossed the border in 1905 to retire with his son Earl and a daughter on a homestead at Dundurn. Living in a log and sod shack, and sleeping with his revolver under his pillow, he left a legion of stories with his death in 1935.

The late 19th century was, in one sense, an era of male criminality. The gender issue can be seen in

the number of criminal indictments for juvenile offenders (under the age of 21) in the 1890s: 98% were males. The first prison in the area was constructed at Regina in 1885-86, and it was accompanied with an asylum. A similar institution soon followed at Prince Albert. The guiding principle of these institutions was punishment: the prisons were managed in a military manner, with strict discipline. They were also to be self-sufficient, and turned their inmates into farm work crews. The search for justice, however, required more effort in a rapidly growing immigrant population with a more complex market economy. Thus it is no surprise that indictable offences doubled in the years 1893-96, and that the conviction rate rose to 85%. Increased use of informers by the NWMP ensured that major crimes would be prosecuted and sufficient evidence gained for conviction.

The Agrarian Era, 1905–49

In its first decade the province, through Crown prosecutors, jurors, JPs and judges, took a tough approach on criminal offenders with a conviction rate of over 80%. This was complemented by the NWMP, who worked closely with immigrants to draw the line between acceptable and unacceptable behaviour. Ukrainians, for example, considered simple assaults, drunkenness, incest, and domestic violence as personal and family matters rather than affairs of the public state; thus the NWMP usually tried to mediate such acts rather than prosecute. But no such favours were shown to French immigrants at Duck Lake, or to Jewish ones at Qu'Appelle, whom the NWMP considered as lazy and not deserving of judicial discretion. Police leniency with labour may account for the fact that there was locally little violent labour unrest in the upheaval of 1919-24, compared to the rest of western Canada.

This approach to law and justice was enforced with penalty. A jail was built at Moosomin in 1908, the Regina jail opened in 1915, and Prince Albert's in 1921; they were used not only for violent offenders, but also for those who bore the brunt of class, racial and religious discrimination. These included, especially by the 1930s, workers on strike, Doubhobors, Jehovah's Witnesses, Orientals, and Communists. For example PETER VEREGIN, leader of the Doukhobor colonies in Saskatchewan and organizer of the Sons of Freedom breakaway group, was in and out of jail for assault, disturbing the peace, and riot from the day of his arrival from Siberia in 1903 until his deportation from Prince Albert jail in February 1933.

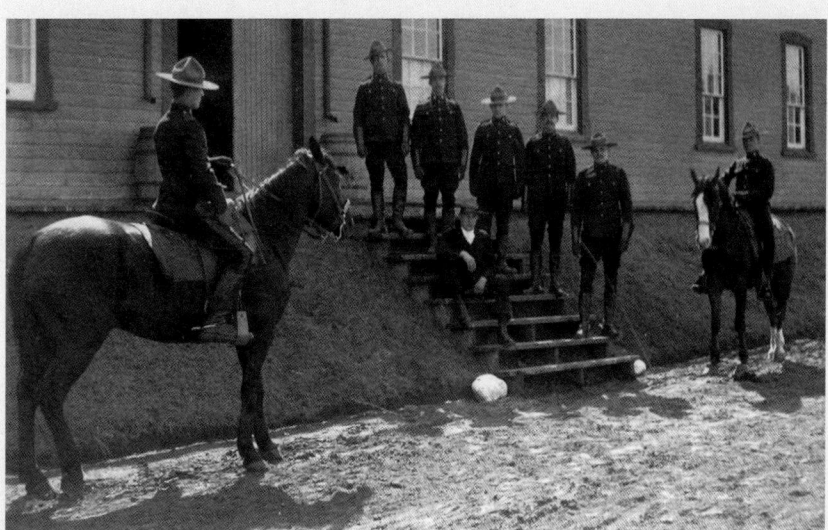

SASKATCHEWAN ARCHIVES BOARD R-B1682

RCMP detachment at Prince Albert, ca. 1915.

The territorial court system did not change immediately with the creation of the province. Once the provincial government was formed, the Legislature under the direction of Wetmore and FREDERICK HAULTAIN created a new court system: a Supreme Court of King's Bench with six judges, and a Court of Appeal with four. The goal was public access for complaints, diligent prosecution and evidence-gathering, and more jurors for the primarily rural population. Thus the districts were increased to eight in 1907, fifteen in 1915, and twenty in 1920. The same goal governed appeals: there were three districts for the appeal of criminal trials, centred in Regina, Moose Jaw, and Saskatoon.

Perhaps the most outstanding justice in the history of the province was Chief Justice Frederick Haultain. English-born, he was raised in Peterborough, Ontario and admitted to the Ontario bar in 1882. He established a law practice in Fort Macleod in 1884, and was Premier of the North-West Territories in Regina from 1891 to 1905. He was the opposition leader of the Provincial Rights Party between 1905 and 1912, became Chief Justice of the Saskatchewan King's Bench in 1912, and was Chief Justice of the Court of Appeal from 1917 to 1938. Haultain kept his ear to the ground, and was responsible for adapting the criminal justice system to the socio-economic reality of his era.

Magistrate Joseph Emile Lussier, the "Flying Magistrate of the North" from 1927 to 1957, lost only 11 of 362 jury cases as a defense counsel in Prince Albert between 1913 and 1927. This placed him in a unique role as an itinerant judge in a region of Native peoples, where he relied on discretion in administering law and justice. His imperative was not to impose common law on the Natives, but to improve human relations by adapting the law to local circumstances. A progressive reformer, he often sat in court without gown, and relied on fines and community service instead of prison.

Perhaps the best test of law and justice is how it processes capital crimes. Murder was not taken lightly by the courts, especially where the victim was the wife of the accused. When John Ireland, an invalid farmer, was tried for his wife's murder in Noseby before the Supreme Court in 1914, witnesses testified that he had often beaten her and threatened to kill her. After shooting her in the back of the head as she was washing dishes, he pleaded clemency for the hard life that had caused their domestic problems. The same plea was made by Harvey Clare, who locked his wife, her in-laws and children in their Manor farmstead in 1934, and set fire to it. Both men were found guilty, to be hanged, but Clare was reprieved to life imprisonment.

A wife's murder of her husband, however, could be more problematic. Catherine Tratch, a Ukrainian mother of eight, poisoned her husband with strychnine at Fish Creek in 1924; she claimed that a neighbour encouraged her to do so. Tried before the King's Bench at Prince Albert, her only defense was motherhood, and the judge found her guilty, to be hanged. While the judge warned the Minister of Justice that her defense was "based on ignorance," a public campaign for clemency that included Catholic and Anglican churches brought a commutation to life imprisonment; she was released in 1938. The murder of adults or children by women was seldom prosecuted. Only nineteen women were charged with the crime of murder or shooting with intent to kill between 1889 and 1940, and they were either acquitted or found guilty of manslaughter. Likewise, twenty-four were charged with infanticide but none was convicted.

Annie Rubletz's conviction for smothering her child in 1940 brought a clemency campaign and retrial that made national headlines, resulting in the Criminal Code being amended to make infanticide a female category of murder. In the trial at Yorkton, the jury attempted several times to ask the judge for ways to avoid a murder conviction. A reluctant guilty verdict by the jury caused a popular uproar. The girl was deemed to be of low mentality, weak character, and low morality (she had borne her brother's child the year before), living in poor conditions, and from a dysfunctional family. Petitions from churches and the businesswomen's association blamed her seducer, suggesting she needed guidance rather than death. The Appeal Court repealed her conviction, and she served one year at Battleford Prison.

The five women charged with murder in the Regina district were all acquitted. The most famous case occurred in the Supreme Court at Regina in 1913. A 22-year-old English farm wife was charged with conspiracy in murdering her aged husband in Pense with the help of her young lover, who committed suicide afterwards. She confessed, but it was ruled inadmissible. Newspapers published evidence of her complicity, including her own letters, but a compassionate jury found her not guilty. In another case, when in 1928 a Romanian housewife shot her husband in the back of the head with a revolver while he was eating pastries, his record of drunkenness and woman-beating brought her a suspended sentence.

In 1917, a Hungarian wife and mother charged her husband's former hired hand with raping her in the barn after locking the children in the house. Tried before the King's Bench at Regina, the accused claimed that he habitually slept and ate in the farmhouse, and that they had frequent consensual sex wherever her husband was away. As the jurors were all Hungarian, they acquitted him. Class and ethnicity also entered into the prosecution of a German farm labourer for raping four girls under the age of 14 in Regina between 1918 and 1922: as cross-examination revealed that the accused was one of several participants, all German, the jurors regarded the acts as consensual and acquitted him.

Cases such as these shaped popular understandings of sexual violence by holding that the criminal law did not discriminate on the basis of race or gender, but they did not reflect the same understandings regarding class or ethnicity. For example, in a study of sexual offences on the prairies between 1886 and 1940 by agricultural labourers as well as farmers and farmers' sons, of the cases that proceeded to trial 70% of the former were convicted and only 39% of the latter. The former, moreover, faced sentences of six months to ten years, while the latter seldom received more than a few months in jail. When a farmer of Strasbourg was sentenced to fifteen months in a solid case of attempted rape, the *Morning Leader* explained that the light sentence was necessary because he was married with seven children. Thus patriarchy and paternalism were of no protection to women who had been violated. But when a 15-year-old servant girl charged a labourer with rape at a farmhouse outside of Regina, his admission of drinking and use of foul language in court brought him a conviction and sentence of ten years in the Prince Alberta Penitentiary, even though she had managed to preserve her virginity.

In most of these cases the victim or accused were recent immigrants from non-English-speaking countries. When communities such as the Ukrainians had strong convictions against hired hands violating their daughters, the courts often acquiesced. Thus when a Ukrainian farmer near Regina accused his hired hand of abducting his daughter, the Supreme Court held that the daughter's consent was irrelevant. The fact that they had slept together on numerous occasions and that she had slept with a previous farmhand was also irrelevant: the accused, arrested with his "fiancée" in Southey while obtaining a marriage license, was convicted and sentenced to three months with hard labour.

In Regina, the Supreme Court tried two men in 1926 of having unlawful carnal knowledge of, or sexually assaulting, immigrant working-class young women. The common meeting place was the Palace Café. The verdicts were not guilty, with warnings to the men (one was married) to refrain from entertaining young "flappers." A similar case, involving the rape of a young Austro-French woman in Moose Jaw by two men, failed because the accused attacked successfully the moral reputation of the victim. Young women who worked in the cities had little hope of successful prosecutions for seduction, and such cases rarely made it to trial. When a 17-year-old woman of Regina was seduced and impregnated by an engaged man in 1923, the King's Bench trial turned on her going to cafés, skating rinks, and picture shows: this enabled the defense to claim that she was a sexually deviant girl who tried to force a respectable engaged man to marry her. The charges were withdrawn from the jury. When a 22-year-old graduate nurse was raped on a drive home to Moose Jaw in 1928, the defense argued that no grown woman could possibly be raped; the jury convicted on attempted rape, and the judge gave the accused only five months in prison with hard labour.

The problems of immigrants and the law were even more precarious with the Chinese. Mostly male, living in small communities, working in unskilled jobs, and speaking a language that was incomprehensible to non-Orientals, they were denied the vote in 1907. A Regina public health bylaw in that same year also discriminated against them in "stagnant water" cases involving their laundries. In a case of alleged arsenic poisoning in Regina's Capital Restaurant the same year, a neighbouring Chinese restaurateur was accused of supplying the poisoned porridge. Scared, he escaped, and every Chinese male in the town was rounded up. When fourteen of those arrested filed a suit of unlawful arrest against the mayor, chief of police, two town policemen, and an NWMP officer, they all won considerable damages. In the end, there was no evidence against the one man charged, and he was acquitted; the real perpetrator was never found.

Cases such as these demonstrate that the mounted police had always been hesitant to enforce municipal and provincial laws, especially when they bordered on social practice. In 1906 the province created a "secret service" of special constables to enforce its liquor legislation. Called "whisky spotters," they had offices in Regina, Weyburn, Saskatoon and Prince Albert. Thus when the province enacted the prohibition law in 1916 and the mounted police would not enforce it, the province formed the Saskatchewan Provincial Police (SPP) in the next year to enforce prohibition along with game and fire acts, school attendance, and public entertainment. The SPP, however, became involved in improper political influence, made few prosecutions, and did nothing on the crime front: thus their abolition in 1928, after prohibition ended in 1924, was not unexpected.

Another problem occurred during World War I: prosecuting the war effort on the home front. Stephen Malezewski, a Canora lawyer of Polish birth, collected stories of immigrant farmers who were the victims of extortion because of their German

or Ukrainian background from the Austro-Hungarian Empire. They were called "Galicans" or "Ruthenians," and he along with others was charged with bribery and threatened with deportation. In the end, there was only one conviction, in 1920; Malezewski was simply one of many who were called "enemy aliens" because of their birth or heritage. What is significant is that the mounted police were thwarted by their own witnesses, who were also immigrants. Policing of an even less savoury kind emerged in World War II. A group calling itself the Saskatchewan Veterans Civil Security Corps organized men deferred from military service to patrol the "Home Front." Drawn along military lines and headquartered at Regina, they grew to 6,500, spread over 216 primarily rural locations, drilled as a paramilitary police, and organized cavalcades and shooting competitions. Seeing themselves as "nativist" (in particular, anti-German, Russian, and Oriental), their goal was to fight pacifists and those disaffected by the war. They made false charges and false arrests, and at times terrorized some of the population; but a lack of funds and public support brought about their demise.

The inter-war years were not prosperous for the prairies, but violence on the labour front was relatively muted given the DEPRESSION of the 1920s and 1930s, especially as so much of the labour consisted of foreign immigrants. In the Estevan miners' strike of autumn 1931, the police refused them access to the business district; a battle ensued, in which three rioters were shot and killed. This was a forerunner of the REGINA RIOT of July 1935 during the "On-to-Ottawa Trek," when 500 strikers rioted on Dominion Day, and six were shot and one killed. But there was no aftermath. When farmers called a strike in 1939 over an inadequate government wheat price agreement, they struck and demonstrated, but no violence took place.

Discrimination against workers representing ethnic minorities was replicated with Oriental businesses. A provincial act of 1912 barred White women from working for Oriental establishments. In 1924 YEE CLUN applied to the Regina city council for a permit to employ White women who were more than willing to work for him. While he eventually won his permit, a group promoting "White Women's Labour Law" continued to influence the council until the Act's eventual repeal in 1969. Thus, in the absence of equality and human rights legislation, law and justice were impeded by local circumstances.

It was often the local police, and not the heirs of the NWMP, who were unwilling to accord the full letter of the law to minority people. This problem was finally put to rest by Chief Justice James T. Brown in 1933. In *R v Bohun* (SCS 1933), he heard a brutal murder case where a young, immature man, speaking limited English, was caught and accused of murder after a manhunt. Police asked him to do and say certain things, including making a confession, that were not voluntary. Brown not only dismissed the charge, but also wrote a memorandum to the commissioner of provincial police, setting down guidelines for handling accused people. This was considered a prime example of judicial legislation where authorities failed to heed common law principles of judicial process.

SASKATCHEWAN ARCHIVES BOARD R-A7536

Cpl. R.S. Pyne and Cpl. M.F.A. Lindsay, Carlyle RCMP, with seized still, 1938. Lindsay went on to serve as Commissioner of the Force (1967-1969).

The courts, however, were much less willing to interfere in family matters in spite of pressures from local prosecutors. Abortion became much more heavily prosecuted in the inter-war years: studies show that the conviction rate on the prairies was 36% from 1874 to 1916, and 61% from 1919 to 1939. A series of five cases in the King's Bench in 1920-21 centred on the activities of Jeanette Swift, a married woman and nurse, and William Bundy, an advertising manager who served as a procurer. While several of the women who underwent the procedures were given suspended sentences, Bundy pleaded guilty and was sentenced to eight months and fined $10; Swift pleaded the same and was sentenced to six months; another male procurer received four months. The court was cautious in these cases, even though Swift produced a catalogue of abortions she had performed on married women in rural areas, and on young single women in Regina. Such sentences suggest that judges were hesitant to interfere in intimate aspects of patriarchal life.

Indictments against women in the province were still low (5%) in that era; but indictments against juveniles increased 50% between 1922 and 1945, following the Canadian average. While the conviction rate remained high in the province, a major shift had occurred in recorded criminality: personal crimes dropped from 17% to 11%; non-violent property crime dropped from 50% to 44%; but violent crime against property rose from 11% to 13%. These figures were not changed by the impact of World War II, and they were similar in the late 1940s. By 1939 the conviction rate had returned to its earlier 85%. The main culprit, however, was "social crime": drunkenness, vagrancy, and prostitution—the remnants of the Great Depression.

Crime per capita was always lower in early Saskatchewan than in the rest of the country from the time in which criminal statistics were kept in 1891: the average rate of prosecutions per capita in the province was .07 in 1891 and 2.0 in 1911. The change came in the 1920s and 1930s, when the province doubled the per capita numbers in the rest of the country to 4.0. In these decades, the province tied its prairie neighbours with the highest rate of executions for capital crimes (65%), but had the lowest rate of pardons. Indictable offences in Regina, Moose Jaw, and Moosomin were among the highest in the country.

The first sign of reforming law and justice along more progressive lines came with prisons. The 1946 Penal Commission was a landmark in the history of the province's corrections; this was due in part to the effort of the CCF to humanize the criminal justice system. Punishment would now give way to rehabilitation. Crime prevention, probation, and the scientific treatment of offenders would be crucial to reduce the alarming growth of recidivism and the rising numbers of Natives who were being incarcerated. The ratio of Natives to non-Natives reached two to one per capita by 1946. Work camps and community service were seen as more helpful for vagrants, petty thieves, and drunks than jail time.

The Penal Commission was followed by the Saskatchewan Bill of Rights Act in 1947. One of the first in Canada, it brought freedom of conscience, opinion and religion, freedom of assembly and association, and freedom against arbitrary arrest and detention to be respected by private persons. Consolidated into the Saskatchewan Human Rights Code of 1979, it is called the "Bill of Rights." With enforcement in the Queen's Bench, it brought equality rights to immigrants, organized labour, Natives, women, and the poor. An outcome of the progressive legislation of the 1930s spurred by immigrant farming communities, it shifted the location of power for law and justice from the Legislature to the judiciary.

The Era of Industrial Capitalism, 1950–2000

Crime in the second half of the century remained active as the province coped with the socio-economic problems of farming communities, of deserted towns, and of growing cities that lacked strong economies. While the northern parts of the province were still largely undeveloped, the appearance of mining communities at places like Uranium City brought problems of their own: high wages were all too often accompanied by drunkenness, gambling, prostitution, and theft. A major change in criminal trials in the 1950s and 1960s was the significant rise in summary trials by police magistrates (PMs): an average of 960 indictable offences, and 30,000 summary offences, with the PM hearing 92% of all indictable offences. Of the latter, only 4% were acquitted, compared to 17% in the 1920s. There were examples of people pleading guilty with no criminal offence committed. The great growth of summary convictions suggests that too many important criminal cases were tried by PMs rather than by superior court judges.

The problem in the Cold War era was that the Criminal Code, which was growing by accretion, was piecemeal, often redundant, too discretionary, and lacking consistency in sentencing policies. More alternatives to imprisonment were needed, and different places for juvenile offenders. Thus in Saskatchewan too much "criminal activity" was being designed by social legislation. *Mens rea* (intent) had been brought full circle from the act itself, so that the act and not the intent was being prosecuted; finally, "attempted" acts were bringing more severe punishment than the real thing.

The Corrections Act of 1967 moved forward the idea of rehabilitation: from the prison, work training, probation and parole were directed to the community. Continually increasing numbers of juvenile, Aboriginal and Métis offenders, as well as females, caused social workers and social scientists who were moving into the corrections field to adopt new strategies. The trends were discouraging: by the 1970s Aboriginal and Métis males formed 65% of those admitted into prisons, while their female cohort represented 90%. The magnitude of rehabilitation had reached critical proportions.

The major figure in the criminal justice system of the late 20th century was E.M. "TED" CULLITON, Chief Justice of Saskatchewan from 1962 to 1981. Culliton made a reputation for allowing appeals against criminal convictions, a practice that few appeal courts made regular. A compassionate man, he encouraged personal appeals to his court, never increased a sentence, and often took account of good behaviour in sentencing—especially with Aboriginal people. A champion of criminal law reform, his goal was to rehabilitate offenders, not to inflict retributive punishment.

In the 1980s, with the passage of the Charter of Rights and Freedoms, the weaknesses of the criminal justice system in the province became apparent. Of ninety-two Charter cases before the Saskatchewan Court of Appeal, 80% were brought by the accused. A quarter of those cases found Charter violations, and over half of the lower court verdicts were reversed, although since the Supreme Court of Canada reversed some of those afterwards, the state of law and justice remained cloudy. Nonetheless, the Appeal Court was by the 1990s one of the most active per capita in Canada, and one of the most efficient. Criminal appeals by accused outnumbered those by the Crown ten to one, but the success rate was only 32% for the accused, and 80% for the Crown.

One of the remaining problems of the criminal law was the murky area of "social crime," of which prostitution was a prime example. In an effort to curtail such activity in downtown areas and core neighbourhoods, the province was elated when Parliament enacted Bill C-49 in 1985. The bill was part of a larger problem: sexual offences. It made street solicitation in public for sexual services a criminal offence. While criminal offences in the province increased 45% from 1977 to 1985, sexual crimes increased by more than 300%; crimes by young offenders alone increased by 100%. Thus, in some small measure, policing prostitution was seen as a cutting edge of policing sexual offences in general.

The activity was astounding. The police increased their manpower in Regina and Saskatoon, manned elaborate sting operations, and developed dossiers on the ladies of the street. In the following year there were 421 arrests under the bill (303 in Regina alone). The numbers for Regina were 2.5 times those of Winnipeg, and five times those of Calgary. The results, however, were sobering: fines were $50-$200 for women who made an average of $55,000 yearly. Other sexual offences increased, including gang rapes and pimp fire-bomb wars. Thus while a measure of control was achieved, there was no reduction in "official crime."

In January 1997, Regina became centre stage in Canada when Justice Ted Malone sentenced two university students to 6.5-year prison terms for killing a prostitute. The young men were cruising the streets of Regina looking for a prostitute when they encountered Pamela George of the Sakimay Reserve, who repeatedly rejected them. After one of them finally enticed her into his car with the other hiding in the trunk, "something went wrong" and she was found severely beaten in a ditch near the airport. The prosecution sought first-degree murder, but the jury found for manslaughter because their intent had been mitigated by drunkenness. Aboriginal communities, women's groups, and the public saw in action a biased judge who charged the jury with the comment that she was "a prostitute." Three years later, two Saskatoon police officers faced trial for assault and abandonment of three Aboriginals outside the city, two of whom froze to death. The result was that many saw two justice systems at work in Saskatchewan: one for Whites, and another for Aboriginals—symbolic of the racial discrimination that besets western Canadian society.

The century closed with the Saskatchewan Court of Appeal focused on the divisive subject of sentencing; divided on traditional versus alternative forms of punishment, the debate entered the public arena. The court had also responded to public debate in other areas of law and justice, such as: out-of-court statements are not inferior to statements given in court; no fresh evidence can be admitted where it is not weighty; juvenile court judges can transfer juveniles aged 15 to adult court for murder trials; sobriety tests do not trigger the right to legal counsel; and indecency laws can be enforced outside of equality rights against females swimming bare-breasted in public pools.

Conclusion

The major issues concerning law and justice heading into the 21st century are civil rights, marginalized and minority groups, and the criminal justice system. For Aboriginals, cases are heard where legal aid lawyers have little time to research them, interpreters may not know the terminology, and alternative punishments are few. For many ethnic minority groups, offenders should be seen as part of a web of interrelationships, not as individuals. Anti-social acts should be separated from historic crimes (the Ten Commandments), and treated within the complex behaviours that caused them.

One of the major problems confronting law and justice in Saskatchewan concerns Aboriginal people. The population of northern Saskatchewan is nearly 60% Aboriginal (much higher than in neighbouring prairie provinces, although with a similar percentage under the age of 16). Nearly 70% are on welfare, compared to less than 6% for non-Aboriginals; and their alcohol-related offences are nearly twenty times more frequent than for the rest of the population. Aboriginal women are charged with offences ten times more than non-Aboriginal women, and there are eight times as many Aboriginals in jail as non-Aboriginals. Clearly, this is a problem in law and justice—and in society—that has to be confronted. In a colloquium on "Empty Promises," referring to the Crown's promises to First Nations in the Proclamation of 1763, it was agreed that the over-representation of Aboriginals in prisons was not a result of discriminatory sentencing practices, but of complex factors that were beyond statutory remedy; one needed more relaxed standards of admissibility in the hands of judges for them to act upon the relevant information.

Evidence provided by Matthias Leonardy, writing at the end of the 20th century, suggests that the vicious circle of crime can only be ended when First Nations see the restoration of peace and harmony through mediation and reconciliation in their communities. It can be suggested that their Aboriginal rights are embedded in English and Canadian law, and that those rights are inherent ones—not contingent upon acts of government. Thus some form of delegated jurisdiction, such as the Peacemaker Court of Navajo customary law in the United States, might curtail that vicious circle where other efforts have failed. It may also provide the local discretion that lay behind the origins of law and justice in Saskatchewan. According to Judge Arnot, the successors of Britain's last 19th century colonial war (the Riel Rebellion) must now rebuild the country that Poundmaker dreamed of.

FURTHER READING:

Backhouse, C. 1999. *Color-Coded. A Legal History of Racism in Canada, 1900-1950.* Toronto: Osgoode Society.

Baker, W.M. (ed.). 1998. *The Mounted Police and Prairie Society, 1873-1919.* Regina: Canadian Plains Research.

Driedger, O., B. Grainger and S. Skinner. 1981. *Corrections: An Historical Perspective of the Saskatchewan Experience.* Regina: Canadian Plains Research Center.

Flanagan, T. and N. Watson. 1981. "The Riel Trial Revisited: Criminal Procedure and the Law in 1885," *Saskatchewan History* 34 (2): 57-73.

Hepworth, D. (ed.). 1979. *Explorations in Prairie Justice Research.* Regina: Canadian Plains Research Center.

Knafla, L.A. (ed.). 1986. *Law & Justice in a New Land: Essays in Western Canadian Legal History.* Toronto: Carswell.

LaPrairie, C. 1996. *Understanding the Context for Crime and Criminal Justice Processing of Aboriginal People in Saskatchewan.* Ottawa: Department of Justice.

Leyton-Brown, K. 1992. "The 'Poison Porridge' Case: Chinese and the Administration of Justice in Early Saskatchewan," *Great Plains Quarterly* 12 (2): 99-106.

Leonardy, M.R.J. 1998. *First Nations Criminal Jurisdiction in Canada.* Saskatoon: Native Law Centre.

McConnell, W.H. 1980. *Prairie Justice.* Calgary: Burroughs & Co.

LAWRENCE, THOMAS (1927–94). A respected agrologist and one of Canada's foremost forage variety breeders, Thomas Lawrence was born at Colonsay in 1927. He earned two degrees at the **UNIVERSITY OF SASKATCHEWAN** and his PhD at the University of Alberta in 1955. For thirty-four years, Lawrence worked at the Agriculture Canada Research Station in Swift Current, first as a grass breeder, then as principal research scientist, and finally as head of the forage production and utilization section. His work on grass cultivars has had an enormous impact on western Canada's perennial forage use. For his distinguished contributions to agronomy, Lawrence was made a Fellow of the Agricultural Institute of Canada and a Member of the Order of Canada in 1991. He died on December 8, 1994.

LAWSON, PATRICIA (1929–). Patricia Lawson has competed as a successful amateur athlete in several sports. Born in Saskatoon on November 18, 1929, she won an under-10 swimming competition, then every single track and field event she entered while attending Bedford Road Collegiate in Saskatoon. Lawson won provincial titles in six different sports and five Canadian titles in three sports. She broke records for the 220- and 440-yard events in speed skating, and became Canadian intermediate ladies champion in 1947 and Canadian senior ladies champion in 1949 and 1954. While attending the 1947 Canadian track and field championships, she won gold in shot put, the first time she had competed in the event. She won two Canadian basketball championships with the Vancouver Eilers in 1956 and the Saskatoon Adilman Aces in 1959. She was one of five Aces to represent Canada at the 1959 Pan

Am Games in Chicago. Lawson had similar success as a golfer: she was a five-time winner of the Saskatchewan Senior Women's championship, and a two-time winner of the Canadian Senior Women's title as a member of Team Saskatchewan with Joanne Goulet, Barb Danaher and Vivian Holizki.

Lawson graduated from the **UNIVERSITY OF SASKATCHEWAN** with a BA (1950) and a BEd (1953). She completed a Masters degree in physical education at the University of Oregon (1959) and a PhD at the University of Southern California (1967). From 1956 to 1990 she was a member of the faculty of the College of Physical Education at the University of Saskatchewan, and retired as a professor emeritus. In 1984, Lawson was president of the Canadian Association for Health, Physical Education and Recreation (CAHPER). She was also president of the Canadian Women's Intercollegiate Athletic Union, which improved opportunities for women in intercollegiate athletics, and served a term as chairperson for the National Advisory Council on Fitness and Amateur Sport. As a student at the University of Saskatchewan, Lawson received a major athletic award for her participation on a record thirteen intercollegiate teams, and was inducted into the University's Wall of Fame. She delivered the R. Tait Mackenzie Memorial Address and received a CAPHER award, the highest honour given for Canadian physical education. In 2000, Dr. Lawson was named a charter fellow of the North American Society of Health, Physical Education, Sport and Dance Professionals. She has been installed as both an individual and a team member in the **SASKATCHEWAN SPORTS HALL OF FAME.**

Bob Ivanochko and Holden Stoffel

LE COLLÈGE MATHIEU DE GRAVELBOURG: *see* **COLLÈGE MATHIEU DE GRAVELBOURG**

LEADER, town, pop 914, located 30 km E of the Saskatchewan-Alberta border at the junction of Hwys 21 and 32. Only a few ranchers were in the area when it was opened up to homesteaders, who began arriving in large numbers in 1907. Most were Germans from southern Russia. The German population was so significant that at least until the mid-1930s one of the qualifications for working in the local RM office was the ability to speak the language. In 1913 the railway arrived, and in September that year the village of Prussia (Leader's original name) was incorporated, another in the string of communities that grew up along the "Empress Line" as it progressed northwestward toward Alberta from west of Swift Current. **WORLD WAR I** prompted some in the community to suggest that such a strong German name for the town was inappropriate. Deliberations took place, and on November 1, 1917, the name Prussia was changed to Leader. At the same time, the town's original German street and avenue names were changed to numbers. After **WORLD WAR II** Leader's population skyrocketed, reaching a high of 1,236 in 1966. Today, Leader's several dozen business establishments provide a wide range of goods and services for a trading area which includes at least three rural municipalities. Many of the town's businesses operate in support of the region's grain and cattle industries; the Great Sandhills Terminal just east of town is a major grain handling facility. The Leader region is dotted with numerous points of interest. Leader has Saskatchewan's first and only reptile zoo. The nearby Estuary Hutterite Colony offers tours of varied local ecosystems, ranging from the riparian woodlands of the South Saskatchewan River Valley to the **GREAT SAND HILLS.** The region supports an abundance of wildlife, including mule and white-tailed deer, pronghorn antelope, and over 200 species of birds during spring and fall migrations. As a tribute to the regions' fauna, the community has erected a number of larger-than-life wildlife sculptures throughout the town. *David McLennan*

LEAGUE OF EDUCATION ADMINISTRATORS, DIRECTORS AND SUPERINTENDENTS (LEADS). In existence since 1969 as an organization for senior educational administrators in Saskatchewan, LEADS was formally recognized through legislation in June 1984, when the Saskatchewan Legislature adopted the LEADS Act. That act determined that all educators employed by boards of education working in supervisory, administrative, or similar capacities or who are regional directors of education must be members of LEADS. In 1991, LEADS was granted legislative authority, and it remains the only Canadian organization of its

Pat Lawson (11) with the 1947-48 University of Saskatchewan Huskiettes varsity basketball team. Teammates include Sylvia Fedoruk (5).

type to register its members prior to their employment with a provincial school division. LEADS maintains full disciplinary powers over its membership, and is governed by an elected executive chaired by a president. A government-appointed public representative sits with the executive. LEADS emphasizes the value of an active and collaborative membership working with other key stakeholder education groups in Saskatchewan.

Membership requirements include successful graduate studies, professional teaching certificate, success as a teacher, and evidence of good character. Associate membership is available to individuals who are employed in supervisory or consultative positions by Saskatchewan Learning, members of faculties of education, professional staff of the SASKATCHEWAN TEACHERS' FEDERATION or the SASKATCHEWAN SCHOOL BOARDS ASSOCIATION, and others approved by the executive. Offices are located in Saskatoon and staffed by the executive director and a full-time secretary. *Richard Nieman*

LEAVER, ERIC WILLIAM (1915–). Born in Langham, England on August 11, 1915, Leaver immigrated with his family to Saskatchewan, where he received his schooling. In the 1930s he invented and developed an automatic landing system for aircraft. During WORLD WAR II, he worked in the radar industry. After the end of the war, he formed Electronic Associates Ltd. with colleagues from the radar factory and in government. The company developed a robotic machine tools system, patented as AMCRO (Automatic Machine Control by Recorded Operation) in 1947. They specialized in developing electronic instruments such as field Geiger counters and other survey and automatic industrial process controls. The firm was eventually taken over and became Sentrol Systems. *Diane Secoy*

LEBANESE COMMUNITY. People of Lebanese/Syrian origin began immigrating to Saskatchewan in the early 1900s (some immigrants were born in what was western Syria prior to the border between Lebanon and Syria being redrawn after WORLD WAR I–those towns are now part of Lebanon–whereas the designation "Lebanese" is typically used by current families when referring to their heritage). A number of families settled in the southeast, in or near communities such as Radville, Ceylon, Lampman, and North Portal. Over forty individuals and families homesteaded or started businesses in small towns in the Swift Current district. Some only remained for a year or two before moving to larger centres, but many stayed and became part of the mosaic of life in rural Saskatchewan.

As with many other immigrants, Lebanese were facing social and economic hardships in their homeland and were looking for a better life for themselves and their families. However, some govern-

ment officials wished to restrict immigration to Canada of people from southeastern Europe and the Near East, including Syria/Lebanon. In a 1914 letter, W.D. Scott, Superintendent of Immigration, wrote: "None of the races belong to those likely to assimilate with the Canadian people; none of them are of a class whose presence could reasonably be expected to improve the status of the Canadian race, whether considered from a political, social, moral, mental, physical or economic standpoint."

Despite the fact that Lebanese were classified as Asians under the Immigration Act and therefore were required to pay $200 rather than $25 as a condition of landing in Canada, this was not a deterrent to everyone. The first to come were young men. Typically, they spent a year or two in the United States before coming to Canada. There was an established Arab community in the Detroit area and several members had relatives living in western states. These contacts provided an opportunity to earn some money, learn a little English, and become familiar with prairie farming practices. After taking out homesteads in Saskatchewan, some returned to Lebanon to get married or bring their existing families back with them; others married young women of Lebanese families in the United States.

Many of the families that came to the Swift Current district were from three small towns: Ain Arab, Bire, and Qaraoun in eastern Lebanon. Some were Muslim and others were Christian Orthodox. Both groups had difficulties maintaining their religious traditions. The Christians relied on infrequent visits from itinerant Greek Orthodox priests or traveled to the United States for religious rites. Most of them eventually turned to the Anglican Church, which came closest to the ceremonies and traditions to which they were accustomed.

Following a visit to Mecca in 1922, Alex Himour organized the parish of Jamah, with himself as sheik. A "cleansed" room in his house at Rush Lake became an improvised mosque, serving families in the immediate area and others in the Pambrun and Gouverneur districts; it never became the centre for Islam in western Canada as proclaimed in a *Leader-Post* article in 1922. However, Himour did travel throughout the west to perform religious rites.

Peddling was a common occupation in Lebanon and several Lebanese men used it as a way to supplement their incomes in early years. Saleh "Charlie" Gader started out by carrying wares on his back, frequenting farms in the McMahon district. He later traveled by horse and buggy and even learned to speak some Low German to better serve his Mennonite customers. Businesses were also established in small towns. The Haddad family operated general stores in Meyronne, McCord, Hazenmore, Eastend, and Morse. Several members of the Salloum family had stores, a bakery, café, and pool hall in Aneroid, Neville, Vanguard, and other com-

munities. The Kouri family owned a grocery store and meat market in Ponteix from the 1920s until 2000.

Perhaps the most well-known member of a Lebanese-Saskatchewan family was Ameen "King" Ganam, born at Swift Current in 1914. He learned to play the fiddle at an early age and was entertaining at dances by the age of 9. He formed a band in Edmonton in the 1940s, which regularly performed on radio. Ganam moved to Toronto in 1952. He had his own radio program and was also a regular performer on television country and western shows during the 1950s. The "King Ganam Show" aired in 1961. Ganam became one of the inaugural inductees into the Canadian Country Music Hall of Fame in 1989.

Several Lebanese immigrated to Swift Current and district in the 1950s. Most were related to established families, who assisted them in getting settled and finding employment. A few also came in the 1970s, including young women who were to become brides.

In 1982, several families in Swift Current and district organized classes to teach their children Arabic. An Islamic Centre was opened the same year. Since that time, it has provided a setting for Muslims of various cultures to worship together. The city of Swift Current recently opened a new cemetery. A section of it is reserved for Muslim burials, with plots oriented to face Mecca. It is a respectful acknowledgement of the ongoing presence of Lebanese heritage in the community and district. (*See also* VISIBLE MINORITIES) *Hugh Henry*

FURTHER READING: Abu-Laban, Baha. 1980. *An Olive Branch on the Family Tree: The Arabs in Canada*. Toronto: McClelland and Stewart; Salloum, Habeeb. 1989. "The Urbanization of an Arab Homesteading Family," *Saskatchewan History* 42 (2): 79-83; Waugh, E.H., B. Abu-Laban and R.B. Qureshi (eds.). 1983. *The Moslem Community of North America*. Edmonton: University of Alberta Press.

LEBRET, village, pop 207, located in the Qu'Appelle Valley on the NE shore of Mission lake, 6 km E of Fort Qu'Appelle on Hwy 56. In 1864, Bishop Alexandre Taché of St. Boniface passed through the QU'APPELLE VALLEY on his way home from Ile-à-la-Crosse. Seeing the opportunity for a Catholic presence, he returned to the area in 1865, and selected the site of present-day Lebret for a Catholic mission. In 1866 Abbé Ritchot arrived to open the mission, one of the earlier Roman Catholic missions established in what would become the province of Saskatchewan. It became the main centre of Catholicism for the Métis and First Nations people in the region and a base for OBLATE priests who travelled the southern plains to points such as Wood Mountain and the Cypress Hills. In 1884, a residen-

DAVID MCLENNAN PHOTO

Lebret.

tial school financed by the federal government was started, with Father Hugonard as the principal. In 1886, the parish priest, Father Louis Lebret, became the first postmaster of the community and, although he only held the position for a little more than six months, the office was named Lebret and the name became that of the community. Also in 1886, a rectory was built, which stands to this day. In 1899, the **SISTERS OF OUR LADY OF THE MISSIONS** arrived and began work in the community. In 1906, they founded Saint Gabriel's Convent. The Village of Lebret was incorporated on October 14, 1912. In 1925 the impressive fieldstone Sacred Heart Church was built and in 1929, the landmark stations of the cross and the small chapel shrine on the hill overlooking Lebret were erected. Until the latter half of the 20th

century Lebret was an important religious and educational centre. In addition to the residential school and the convent, there was a public school, and the Oblates established a theological training centre, Sacred Heart Scholasticate, on the south side of Mission Lake. The public school closed to Fort Qu'Appelle in 1980, the scholasticate in the 1960s, and the convent in the 1970s. The residential school was signed over to a First Nations school board in October 1973, at a ceremony presided over by the then Minister of Indian Affairs, Jean Chrétien. The school, which eventually became known as White Calf Collegiate, closed in 1998. Today, Lebret remains a picturesque, yet very quiet, community.

David McLennan

LEDINGHAM, GEORGE FILSON (1911–).
George Ledingham was born on January 31, 1911, in Moose Jaw. As a child he became very interested in birds and plants; that interest has continued throughout his lifetime, as shown by his choice of

career and his interest in all living organisms.

He attended **NORMAL SCHOOL** and taught for one year at a rural school near Keeler. He received his BSc in 1934 and his MSc in 1936 from the **UNIVERSITY OF SASKATCHEWAN**. He earned his PhD from the University of Wisconsin in 1939 with research on the phylogenetics of alfalfa. He remained on the farm during the war while teaching at Regina College and the Junior College in Moose Jaw. In 1945, he and his wife Marjorie and son Beatty moved to Regina, where he became a faculty member at Regina College. As Regina College became a campus of the University of Saskatchewan and then the **UNIVERSITY OF REGINA**, he was promoted through the ranks, becoming department chairman from 1969 to 1971. He taught classes in introductory biology, botany and genetics, even after retirement. He collected specimens of vascular plants, mosses and lichens, which formed the basis of the university herbarium. In 1990 the University recognized his contributions by officially naming the herbarium the George F. Ledingham Herbarium, which now contains more than 50,000 specimens of vascular plants, mosses and lichens. He is currently collaborating with John Hudson and Vern Harms on a *Flora of Saskatchewan*.

Ledingham has inspired thousands of students, some of whom have continued their studies and received graduate degrees in botanical topics. In 1965–66 he traveled the world in search of specimens of *Astragalus*, and on this trip found in Iran a new species, which bears the name *Astragalus ledinghamii*.

In 1945 he became a very active member of **NATURE SASKATCHEWAN** and the Regina Natural History Society. He held a number of executive positions with both societies and served for seventeen years as the editor of the *Blue Jay* magazine. He also contributed to many other studies such as the

COURTESY OF BRIAN MLAZGAR

Father Hugonard.

UNIVERSITY OF REGINA ARCHIVES AND SPECIAL COLLECTIONS 87-54-646

George Ledingham (right) with University of Regina President Lloyd Barber.

Coronach Power Project and the Lake Louise Project. In 1960 in the *Canadian Audubon* he called for a protected area to preserve some of the remaining grasslands from agricultural development, and was the driving force behind the preservation of a part of the short grass ecosystem. After twenty years of lobbying, the **GRASSLANDS NATIONAL PARK** in southern Saskatchewan was formally announced in 1981. He was instrumental in preserving three natural areas: an area in the Strawberry Lakes region south of Indian Head; a quarter section of land in the West Block, **CYPRESS HILLS** (now the Biology Field Station); and a short grass prairie near Moose Jaw.

Ledingham has been the recipient of many awards, including: the J.B. Harkin Award, given by National Parks in 1981; a special Environment Award from Environment Canada in 1985; the Pimlott Award from Canadian Nature Federation in 1985; an Honorary Degree from the University of Regina in 1986; and the Heritage Award by Canadian Parks Service in 1992. The George F. Ledingham Book Prize, which is awarded to a graduating student in biology at the May Convocation at the University of Regina, has been set up in his honour.

Gwen Jones

LEE, DOUGLAS A. (1926–). Born on May 29, 1926, Douglas Lee combined a long career in broadcasting with years of community involvement in fraternal, civic, and veterans' organizations. In 1959, he began working as production manager of Regina's CKCK-TV. He was promoted to operations manager in 1968 and administration and community relations director in 1971. In addition to his service to broadcasting, Lee's work for the community included chair of the Regina United Way and president of both the Regina Chamber of Commerce and the Ranch Ehrlo Society. He has also been active in the Red Cross, Boy Scouts, and the Royal Canadian Legion. He was appointed a Member of the Order of Canada in 1985.

LEGAL LAND SURVEY. The Dominion Land Survey System laid out nearly uniform land parcels that can be precisely described and located in the settled areas of the four western provinces.

This system was designed to describe essentially agricultural land areas in an understandable and detailed manner down to ten acres (4 ha) in size. Cities, First Nations reserves, federal parks, the older river lots, and lands that were Hudson's Bay Company posts were excluded from the survey. The system was based on a model used in the mid-western United States. Both plans used a one square mile land unit. The Canadian system was modified from the US system to exclude road allowances from the land to be used for agriculture. In Canada there were five variations in the system, largely related to

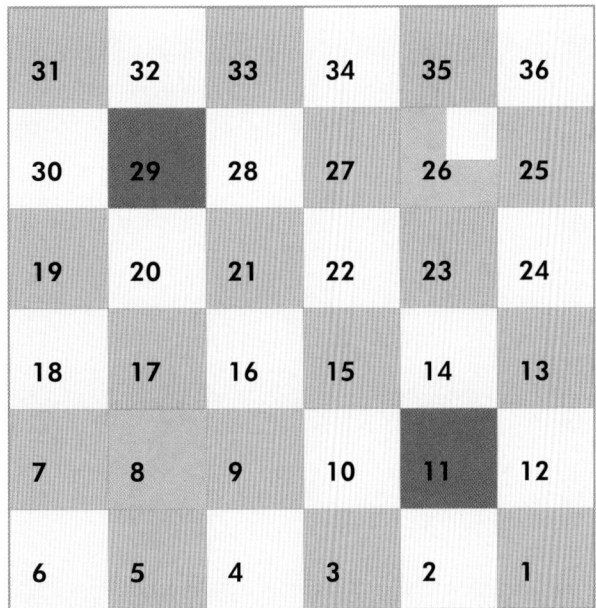

ADAPTED FROM *UNDERSTANDING WESTERN CANADA'S DOMINION LAND SURVEY SYSTEM.*

Figure LLS-1: Township Land Appropriations. In most townships, only 16 full sections were normally available to be homesteaded. The remaining sections were set aside as land appropriations as follows: sections 11 and 29 were reserved as school lands. All other odd-numbered sections were reserved for selection as railway grants. The Hudson's Bay Company retained section 8 and all of section 26 but the northeast quarter; in every fifth township the Company got all of section 26.

roadway accommodation and how the convergence of the lines of longitude was handled.

Difficulties in mountainous terrain and the overlapping of a flat grid system meant that only small portions of British Columbia were surveyed under the system. Almost all the settled areas of Manitoba, Saskatchewan, and Alberta were, however, surveyed and remain under the original land description system, except for the local areas already mentioned as being outside this system. When urban areas were being created, a new plan was laid over the original survey; and where this occurs, the city or town type of survey using blocks and lots prevails.

The basic system was a grid. The major grid boundaries comprised of township lines paralleling the lines of latitude, and of a system of range lines largely paralleling the lines of longitude. Within these east-west and north-south grid lines, which occur about every six miles (six miles plus road allowances) are divisions creating blocks of land called sections, as near as possible to one mile by one mile square, i.e., 640 acres or close to 259 ha. Figure LLS-1 and its legend show how the sections are numbered as well as the original land appropriations.

These sections are subdivided into quarters, and on occasion the sections may have been subdivided into legal subdivisions and quarters of legal subdivisions. The quarters contained more or less 160 acres (about 65 ha), and the legal subdivisions were sixteen per section or forty acres (16 ha) each. The townships, ranges, sections and legal subdivisions are numbered, while the quarter sections and quarters of legal subdivisions are identified by their com-

pass location, i.e., the southwest, southeast, northwest and northeast quarters within a section. Townships are numbered consecutively from the United States border northward, and ranges are numbered westward from each meridian. There are range lines at the prime meridian just west of Winnipeg, and thereafter at each meridian. The second range line is at 102° west longitude, and then every four degrees of longitude to the west. This allows identification of land parcels when the legal land description is known and understood.

The legal description of land follows a set sequence of quarter section, township, range, and meridian: the designation NW27-9-25W2, for instance, means the northwest quarter of section 27 in township 9 range 25 west of the second meridian, i.e., near Assiniboia. In the original survey marker pegs were set out on the quarter sections, and these survey stakes contained the land identification cut into them in Roman numerals.

The system was implemented on July 10, 1871, in Manitoba and continues to be used in more isolated areas. The survey was carried out in advance of the western movement of settlement. For instance, the Saskatchewan area survey began in 1877, Alberta in 1881, and a small area near New Westminster, British Columbia in 1874.

R.B. McKercher

FURTHER READING: Fung, K.I. 1999. *Atlas of Saskatchewan.* Saskatoon: University of Saskatchewan; MacGregor, James G. 1981. *Vision of an Ordered Land.* Saskatoon: Prairie Books; McKercher, R.B., and B. Wolfe.

1997. *Understanding Western Canada's Dominion Land Survey System*. Saskatoon: University Extension Press.

LEGAL RIGHTS OF WOMEN. The Saskatchewan Legislature early demonstrated a degree of commitment to women's equality. The University Act of 1907, for example, explicitly stated that women should have equal access to a university education, and in 1916 Saskatchewan became the second province to grant women the vote. The initiative for many changes came from women's organizations such as the Local Council of Women (founded in Regina in 1895), the WOMEN'S CHRISTIAN TEMPERANCE UNION, and the Women's Grain Growers Association. Such organizations promoted legislative change with respect to a number of issues that concerned many women, including restrictions on the sale of alcohol, participation by women in the professions and in civic life, and the protection of women and children from sexual exploitation.

Despite these signs that women's rights were gaining ground, it took many decades to put women on an equal footing with men with respect to their legal status within families and their claims to ownership of property. By the time the province was founded in 1905, the law recognized that not only single but also married women could own and manage their own property and could enter into contracts in their own right. These legal principles were of limited relevance to most married women, however, as they devoted their adult lives to raising children and homemaking rather than to paid work that would permit them to accumulate property. These wives and mothers could inherit property, or dispose of property they brought with them into the marriage, and in some cases they had joint title to property. The contributions they made through homemaking and child-rearing were not, however, reflected in any kind of property right.

Early legislation recognized the vulnerability of women and children, and was designed to ensure that they were protected from destitution and homelessness. Statutes were passed (initially in 1911) requiring men to provide financial support for dependent wives and children in the event of family breakdown or estrangement, and permitting unmarried women to seek financial support from the father of a child born outside of wedlock. Legislation passed in 1918 provided that widows and children would receive a share of the estate of a man who died without making a will; later legislation provided similar protection in cases where a man made a will that did not adequately provide for his dependents.

The Homesteads Act of 1915 provided that a husband could not dispose of the homestead–defined as the matrimonial home or, in rural settings, the "home quarter" (the 160 acres on which the matrimonial home was located)–without the

written consent of his wife. It also required that the wife receive her own independent legal advice prior to giving consent. This legislation, a version of which is still in force, did not give the wife a property right in the homestead, or any means of preventing a sale–only protection from having the homestead sold without her knowledge.

No legislation conferred on women any property rights with respect to property accrued during a marriage, unless inherited, earned outside the home, or formally held in joint title. In 1978 a Supreme Court of Canada decision denied Helen Rathwell of Tompkins, Saskatchewan, her claim to a share of half of the farm that she and her husband had worked on during their twenty-four-year marriage. The criticism generated by this case, along with others like Irene Murdoch's claim (Alberta), decided by the Supreme Court of Canada in 1975, triggered a re-examination of the law. In 1980, a Matrimonial Property Act permitted a judge to assess the value of the contribution made by women's unpaid labour to the accumulation of family assets, and to allocate a share of the property to the wife. This legislation was later amended to include a presumption that the wife would be entitled to a share of half the property acquired during marriage; this may be altered if it is demonstrated that the wife agreed to a different arrangement or that circumstances justify a different allocation. In interpreting such legislation, courts have held that women are entitled to a share in pensions, the value of a spouse's professional education, and the assets of family businesses. The most recent version of Saskatchewan's matrimonial property legislation, passed in 2001, is called the Family Property Act.

Current legislation also recognizes the rights of women who are partners to common law relationships; and the Family Property Act has extended these rights to partners in same-sex relationships. Changes in the last quarter century have also created a uniform national system of enforcement: this has eliminated many of the difficulties which once faced women attempting to obtain financial support when they or their spouses moved from one province or territory to another.   *Beth Bilson*

FURTHER READING: 1980. *Saskatchewan Women 1905–1980*. Regina: Saskatchewan Labour, Women's Division; 2004. *A Guide to the Law for Saskatchewan Women*. Saskatoon: Public Legal Education Association of Saskatchewan.

LÉGARÉ, JEAN-LOUIS (1841–1918). Jean-Louis Légaré was born in St. Jacques, Montcalm County, Quebec on October 25, 1841, the son of François-Xavier Légaré and Julie Melançon. Early in his life, he left for adventure and to find employment in the USA. By 1869, he became involved with the fur trade as a clerk at Fort Totton, North Dakota;

SASKATCHEWAN ARCHIVES BOARD R-A47
Jean-Louis Légaré.

this led to many subsequent independent business ventures and community development efforts. His MÉTIS employer, Antoine Ouellette, hired Jean-Louis to establish a business in the Wood Mountain area of southern Saskatchewan. In 1870–71, he organized his first camp at Little Woody, 15 miles south of Willow Bunch. In the spring of 1871, while on a trading expedition to sell furs, he collaborated with George Fisher, from St. François-Xavier, in establishing a store east of Wood Mountain. On April 15, 1873, Jean-Louis married Marie Ouellette, the daughter of François Ouellette and Josephte Bottineau. On October 5, 1875, Marie gave birth to their only child Albert Joseph. Tragedy struck this new family on December 4, 1876, when Marie Ouellette passed away after falling off a horse while she was visiting her father at Fort Walsh. Jean-Louis took her remains to Lebret, where she was buried. He never remarried.

In the spring of 1877, SITTING BULL and his tribe of Sioux numbering 4,000 came to the Wood Mountain area after the Battle of the Little Big Horn. Initially, Sitting Bull and his people traded with Jean-Louis. However, with the severe depletion of the buffalo, the Sioux were soon facing starvation. Jean-Louis, being a generous and compassionate man, provided money and supplies for the destitute group. By 1881, the Canadian and American governments wanted Sitting Bull and his tribe to return to their native land and establish a reserve, but the Sioux chief commented that he would only trust the word of his friend, Jean-Louis. As a result, both federal governments entered into an agreement with Légaré to enlist his help. In July, Sitting Bull and his people returned to Fort Buford, where he surrendered to US authorities. A bill for compensation of goods and services was sent to the Canadian and American governments, but Légaré was never fully repaid.

In 1882, he moved to Willow Bunch and constructed the first wooden house in the area with a private water line; this led to the establishment of the Willow Bunch waterworks. In 1884, he switched to trading horses for cattle in Manitoba; this began the establishment of a cattle industry in Willow Bunch. By 1886 the first school opened in Willow Bunch, of which Légaré was a trustee. In 1888 he traded more horses, this time for dairy cattle, and then began a cheese factory. This business enterprise failed by 1894 due to economic distress in the area. Being a devout Roman Catholic, in 1899 he donated 80 acres of land to the Saint-Ignace-des-Saules parish, and a church, rectory, convent and cemetery were built. From 1898 to 1918, Légaré held the position of first postmaster in Willow Bunch, as well as the offices of Justice of the Peace and census enumerator. He died On February 1, 1918, at 76 years of age and was buried in Willow Bunch. The Jean-Louis Légaré Regional Park was established in 1960, and in 1970 the Historic Sites and Monuments Board of Canada erected a plaque commemorating his life and achievements.

Louise-Marie Légaré

LEGISLATION: *see essay on this page.*

LEGISLATIVE BUILDING: *see* **SASKATCHEWAN LEGISLATIVE BUILDING**

LE MAY DOAN, CATRIONA (1970–). Saskatoon's Catriona Le May Doan holds the Olympic and World records in the 500-metre speed skating event. Born on December 23, 1970, she competed for the Saskatoon Lions Speed Skating Club, and became a member of the Canadian national team in 1988. Le May Doan dominated the World Cup speed skating circuit from 1998 to 2002, winning over forty medals in several events. Le May Doan's greatest accomplishments have perhaps come as an Olympic speed skater. A four-time Olympian, she earned gold and bronze medals at the 1998 Nagano Winter Games. Four years later at the Salt Lake City Games, she defended her Olympic title with a gold medal performance in the 500-metre event, becoming the first Canadian individual to defend a gold medal at any Olympic Games. Although she retired from competitive speed skating in May 2003, Le May Doan remains involved in the sport and also works as a motivational speaker. In addition to her many speed skating medals, she is a three-time recipient of the Canadian Female Athlete of the Year award, and the 2002 Lou Marsh Award as Canada's Athlete of the Year. *Daria Coneghan and Holden Stoffel*

FURTHER READING: Rediger, P. 1999. *Blades of Glory: The History of Speed Skating in Saskatchewan.* Regina: Saskatchewan Amateur Speed Skating Association.

Legislation in Saskatchewan

The entries in this section are arranged according to the following:

Family Law

Adoption Act, 1998
Child and Family Services Act
Children's Law Act, 1997
Family Maintenance Act, 1997
Family Property Act

Labour Law

Apprenticeship and Trade Certification Act, 1999
Construction Industry Labour Relations Act, 1992
Education Act, ss. 234-269
Essential Services Emergency Act
Health Labour Relations Reorganization Act
Labour Standards Act
Labour-Management Dispute (Temporary Provisions) Act
Occupational Health and Safety Act
Trade Union Act
Workers' Compensation Act

(*See also* LAW AND JUSTICE)

Family Law

Adoption Act, 1998
Formerly part of the Family Services Act, the Adoption Act has since 1990 governed the process of adoption within the province. The legislation sets out the consents required on the part of the birth mother, birth father and the child him/herself where the child to be adopted is 12 years of age or more. It also establishes the conditions for giving consent to an adoption, for revoking consent, and for dispensing with consent by court order. An order of adoption is granted only if a Queen's Bench judge believes that adoption is in the best interests of the child, and its general effect is to confer all the rights and obligations of parenthood upon the adoptive parents as if the child had been born to them. The Act also contains provisions governing step-parent adoptions, adoptions of children permanently committed to the Minister, adoptions of adults, international adoptions, and interprovincial placements. All documents and proceedings related to the adoption must ordinarily be kept confidential, but an adoption registry is maintained where information related to adoptions is recorded. The regulations provide for the release of non-identifying and identifying information from the registry.

Wanda Wiegers

Child and Family Services Act
The purpose of the Child and Family Services Act is to promote the well-being of children under 16 who are in need of protection by offering "services that are designed to maintain, support and preserve the family in the least disruptive manner." The Act establishes threshold criteria for interference with parental care and control of children. A "child in need of protection" is defined as a child who has suffered or is likely to suffer physical harm, a serious impairment of mental or emotional functioning, or has been exposed to sexual abuse, domestic violence, or "severe domestic disharmony" that is likely to cause physical or emotional harm. A failure to remedy a condition that will likely seriously impair the child's development, or a failure to provide essential medical, surgical or remedial care will also trigger state intervention. The Act establishes a duty to report where there

are reasonable grounds to believe that a child is in need of protection, and creates provincial offenses for the abuse, neglect and abandonment of children.

Where a child is in need of protection, the Act sets out a process for the provision of services to the family and, where a child is at risk of serious harm, for the apprehension and removal of the child from the parents' care. Depending upon an assessment of the child's best interests, a court may order that parental care be supervised for a specified period, that the child remain in foster care for a temporary period, or that the child be permanently committed to the Minister. Over the last decade, the Act has incorporated a greater emphasis on cultural heritage and continuity, particularly with respect to Aboriginal children. Band officials can now participate in hearings related to Status children, and kinship care or care by extended family members or those having a sufficient interest in the well-being of the child may be ordered. The Act also allows for delegation of powers to Indian Child and Family Service agencies which now provide child welfare services on reserves throughout the province.

Wanda Wiegers

Children's Law Act, 1997

The Children's Law Act, 1997 allows for applications regarding the custody of and access to children, the determination of parentage, and the guardianship of a child's property. The Act was significant when first passed in 1990 because it eliminated all distinctions related to the status of illegitimacy, securing equal treatment for children born inside and outside of marriage in accordance with section 15 of the Charter of Rights and Freedoms. As with the previous Infants Act, the Children's Law Act sets out the basic principles governing custody of and access to children. In making custody and access orders in contested cases, courts are to take only the child's best interests into account. Unless otherwise ordered, the parents of a child are the joint guardians of the child's property, but the Act also makes provision for guardianship upon the death of one or both parents. In addition, the Act allows for applications to determine parentage, establishes presumptions of paternity in certain circumstances, and sets out the conditions for jurisdiction in custody and access matters and for the enforcement of extra-provincial orders related to children.

Wanda Wiegers

Family Maintenance Act, 1997

The Family Maintenance Act, 1997 establishes a legal right to spousal and child maintenance. The Act, when first passed in 1990 by the Conservative government, significantly changed the parameters and grounds for spousal support obligations. Consistent with changes to the federal Divorce Act, enactment of the provincial legislation marked a shift away from a focus on fault as the basis for support to a focus on need, on compensation for economic advantages and disadvantages arising from the spousal relationship or its breakdown, and to a promotion of economic self-sufficiency where practicable. Under previous legislation, the Deserted Spouses' and Children's Act (and before that the Deserted Wives' and Children's Maintenance Act), an entitlement to support was contingent on proof of adultery, cruelty or a failure without sufficient cause to supply necessaries by the respondent spouse. Until 1985, a claim to support was lost if the claimant spouse was found guilty of adultery. The new Act not only moved away from fault-based claims, but also provided a critical source of support for unmarried cohabitants for whom relief was not available under the Divorce Act. Eligible spouses under the Act now include parents in a relationship of some permanence, or persons who have cohabited continuously as spouses for two years. The Act also provides a right to support for children regardless of whether the parents have married or cohabited. Where neither marriage nor cohabitation has occurred, a mother may claim prenatal expenses and maintenance for up to nine months.

Wanda Wiegers

Family Property Act

The NDP government of Allan Blakeney introduced The Matrimonial Property Act in 1979 in the aftermath of the Supreme Court of Canada's judgment in Murdoch v. Murdoch. In this 1973 case, a farm wife who had laboured for twenty-five years on the family ranch was denied a property interest when she separated from her husband because title was held in his name. Although the position at common law subsequently changed to recognize a spousal claim based on unjust enrichment, The Matrimonial Property Act went further to establish a presumption of an equal split of all property acquired during a marriage regardless of who held title to the property. The primary objectives of the Act were to recognize that domestic labour and financial provision were joint and mutual responsibilities of spouses,

and that this inherently joint contribution presumptively entitled each to an equal distribution of family property. By setting out specific exemptions and equitable considerations that would justify an unequal division, the Act structured judicial discretion and generated more predictable outcomes. In 2001, the name of the Act was changed to Family Property Act, and the right to claim possession and division of property was extended to unmarried couples who had cohabited as spouses for two years, both same-sex and heterosexual, provided the claim was made within two years after cohabitation ended.

Wanda Wiegers

Labour Law

Apprenticeship and Trade Certification Act, 1999

The Apprenticeship and Trade Certification Act, 1999 establishes an Apprenticeship and Trade Certification Commission, whose mandate is to identify trades which require the development of a workforce with particular skills, and to oversee the apprenticeship of new entrants to that trade. The Commission has members who represent employers and members of particular trades, as well as educational institutions, the government, and groups which are underrepresented in the skilled labour force. For each trade designated by them, the Commission develops an apprenticeship plan which includes a definition of the training objectives, a curriculum, and a progressive sequence of wages. The apprenticeship plan is designed to ensure that an apprentice can proceed to obtain the skills necessary to qualify as a journeyperson in the trade. The Act also permits the Commission to designate a sector in which employers have related labour market needs, and to encourage employers in the sector to work towards common training and skill requirements for employees.

Beth Bilson

Construction Industry Labour Relations Act, 1992

The Construction Industry Labour Relations Act was enacted in response to unique features of the construction industry, notably the emphasis in the building trades unions on representation of workers possessing particular skills (such as plumbing, carpentry, or sheet metal work), the mobility of the construction workforce as they move from project to project, and the ease with which construction companies can be given a new identity. The idea of a fixed bargaining unit tied to a particular geographic location, which is the basis of bargaining under the Trade Union Act, was not suitable to the construction industry from the point of view of the building trades. The first Construction Industry Labour Relations Act was passed in the late 1970s and repealed in 1982. A new version of the statute was passed in 1992. The Act sets out a scheme for bargaining between a building trade union representing employees in a particular craft, usually on a province-wide basis, and an organization representing the group of contractors who are named in certification orders for that craft. The province-wide agreement which results covers any construction project where one of the signatory employers is using employees from that craft group.

Beth Bilson

Education Act, ss. 234-269

Teachers are the only employees in Saskatchewan who are not eligible to support a union for certification under the Trade Union Act. A separate statute, the Teachers' Federation Act, established a body which is responsible for the interests and professional standing of teachers; and the Education Act provides, in sections 234-269, that the Saskatchewan Teachers' Federation (STF) is responsible for bargaining with respect to the salaries and working conditions of teachers. A bargaining committee of the STF bargains a province-wide agreement with representatives of the Saskatchewan School Trustees' Association. This agreement covers the major issues of compensation and conditions affecting teachers, but the Education Act also provides that school division boards (or the conseil scolaire in the case of the French-language school division) can bargain with committees representing local teachers concerning a limited range of issues such as teacher sabbaticals, pay for substitute teachers, and pay periods. This part of the Education Act sets out a process for conciliation of disputes designed to minimize the possibility of strike activity by teachers, and also an arbitration procedure for teacher grievances. These processes are overseen by an independent Educational Relations Board.

Beth Bilson

Essential Services Emergency Act

Unlike other jurisdictions, the Government of Saskatchewan, in passing the Trade Union Act

in 1944, chose not to exclude groups of workers from access to collective bargaining on the grounds that they performed an essential service. Thus, from that time, groups such as firefighters, police officers and health care workers were legally entitled to join unions and to go on strike. Furthermore, successive governments have generally not opted to enact legislation of the kind seen in other provinces which addresses industrial disputes in essential services, choosing instead to legislate workers back to work on an ad hoc basis when it is considered necessary. The exception to this was the Essential Services Emergency Act, enacted by the Liberal government of Ross Thatcher in 1966, which permitted the Cabinet to end any strike involving the delivery of water, heat, electricity, gas or health care, and to impose binding arbitration. This legislation was repealed when the Blakeney government was elected in 1971.

Beth Bilson

Health Labour Relations Reorganization Act

The Health Labour Relations Reorganization Act was passed in 1996 in response to the administrative restructuring of the Saskatchewan health care system. In the course of this restructuring, over 500 individual unionized employers in the health sector, including hospital and nursing home boards, home care districts and ambulance services, were replaced by 31 district health boards which assumed the responsibility for health care employees. The government appointed a commissioner, Mr. Jim Dorsey, an arbitrator and consultant from British Columbia, to consult with health care employers and trade unions with respect to the design of a new configuration of union representation and collective bargaining responsibilities. The commissioner recommended the creation of a single province-wide bargaining unit for paraprofessional employees and nurses, as well as district-based multi-employer units for support workers; and the Act and its accompanying regulations put this system in place, to be administered by the Saskatchewan Labour Relations Board. The legislation was amended in 2000 and 2002 to reflect a further consolidation of the health districts into a smaller number of units now called health regions.

Beth Bilson

Labour Standards Act

Labour standards legislation is designed to maintain a minimal level of terms and conditions of employment for all employees,

whether or not they are represented by unions. It typically deals with such issues as minimum wages, restrictions on hours of work, the provision of notice when employees are laid off, and the length of vacation leave. Employees can complain about violations of the standards, and their employers can be ordered to observe the standards if the complaint is found to be valid. Early in the history of the province, a 1906 Railway Act established fair wages for railway workers, and a Factories Act passed in 1909 restricted child labour and set limits on working hours for women. In 1919, a Minimum Wage Act, which incorporated several statutes, set standards with respect to wages and hours of work for all workers. Later entitled the Labour Standards Act, this legislation has been amended many times, most recently in 1994. In addition to the issues alluded to above, the statute includes provisions requiring that male and female employees be paid equal wages for equal or similar work; prohibiting the discharge of pregnant, disabled or injured employees; and setting out requirements for the payment of wages.

Beth Bilson

Labour-Management Dispute (Temporary Provisions) Act

This controversial statute was passed during the 1981-82 session of the Saskatchewan legislature to order striking workers at cancer clinics to return to work. The statute is generic in form, permitting the government to issue an order requiring any group of striking employees to return to work, and extending the provisions of existing collective agreements, during an election campaign. Particular provisions and schedules of the statute dealt with the situation of the health care workers which had resulted in the decision to pass the legislation. The labour movement expressed outrage at the legislation, and vowed to withdraw support from the New Democratic Party (NDP) government of Allan Blakeney. Although it is not clear how much influence the rift with labour had in the subsequent defeat of the government by the Conservatives under Grant Devine, there were constituencies where labour candidates were nominated to oppose NDP candidates. The generic portions of the legislation remain in force, though they have not been invoked on any later occasion.

Ken Leyton-Brown

Occupational Health and Safety Act

Even before the establishment of the province of Saskatchewan, the territorial government had passed legislation providing standards for safety in mines and putting in place a system of inspection to maintain those standards. Subsequent legislation imposed similar standards on railways and in factories, and this legislation was ultimately consolidated into a comprehensive Occupational Health and Safety Act. Legislative amendments in the 1970s completed the set of distinguishing features which are still at the heart of this statute: a statement that both employers and employees have responsibility for workplace safety; that employers and employees—both unionized and non-unionized—must jointly address health and safety issues through workplace committees; that employees have a right to refuse to work in conditions which are unsafe; and that the government will back up the requirements for health and safety by inspections and enforcement. The regulations which accompany the legislation lay out specific standards which must be met concerning a wide range of issues, including such things as air quality, exposure to noxious substances, protection from the risks created by machinery, first aid facilities, and emergency procedures. In 1994, Saskatchewan became the first province to add workplace harassment to the legislation as an issue of health and safety.

Beth Bilson

Trade Union Act

From the earliest days of European settlement in the west, some workers chose to be represented by trade unions in settling their wages and working conditions with their employers, a process which came to be known as collective bargaining. Till the end of the 19th century, trade unions were regarded as illegal organizations because they interfered with the commercial activities of employers; by the time Saskatchewan became a province, however, Canadian legislation had been passed declaring trade unions to be legitimate organizations. In the first decades after 1905, the legal status of trade unions and of their collective bargaining activities was somewhat unclear, though a number of employers engaged in bargaining with trade unions representing their employees. In 1938, the Saskatchewan legislature enacted the Freedom of Trade Union Association Act, which recognized the right of employees to form and join trade unions for the purpose of bargaining collectively with their employers. It did not, however, place a legal obligation on an employer to recognize or bargain with a trade union. When the

Douglas government came to power in 1944, it acceded to calls from the labour movement and from supporters of social democracy in eastern Canada, to pass new legislation. The Trade Union Act not only included a renewed statement of the right of employees to be represented by trade unions, but also gave the trade unions selected by groups of employees the exclusive legal right to represent those employees in matters concerning their terms and conditions of employment, and placed an obligation on employers in unionized workplaces to bargain in good faith. The statute also defined certain conducts by employers or trade unions as unacceptable and constituting an unfair labour practice. The administration of this new collective bargaining system was placed in the hands of an independent Labour Relations Board consisting of members representing employers and employees, as well as a neutral chair. Though there have been some amendments to the Trade Union Act, the basic framework has remained the same.

Beth Bilson

Workers' Compensation Act

Worker's compensation legislation represents an effort to provide financial protection for the loss of income through injuries which occur in the workplace, and was first conceived by Otto von Bismarck in Germany in the 1880s. Though legal doctrines with respect to contributory negligence and assumption of risk retarded the development of such legislation in Canada, Saskatchewan was one of the earlier provinces to enact a Workmen's Compensation Act in the 1910-11 session of the legislature. Under this statute, workers could prosecute an employer in court and seek compensation for injuries. Representatives of labour criticized this system as too cumbersome and as placing too great a burden on injured workers. The legislation was amended in 1929 to introduce the system we are familiar with today, in which compensation is paid out of a pool to which all employers are legally required to contribute. Claims under the Workers' Compensation Act (the name was changed in the amendments of 1979) are assessed and the administration of the fund supervised by an independent Workers' Compensation Board. The administration of the claims process now includes the oversight of an extensive system aimed at the rehabilitation and return to work of injured employees.

Beth Bilson

LEMBERG, town, pop 306, located SW of Melville on Hwy 22 between the villages of Abernethy and Neudorf. There was some settlement in the district in the early 1880s; many of these settlers, however, would leave within a number of years owing to the promised railroad not arriving and difficulties encountered in farming. Intensive settlement of the Lemberg area occurred in the 1890s as both Protestant and Roman Catholic Germans arrived. Ukrainians followed in 1902. Two years later, trains were running through the area and the townsite was developing rapidly. Lemberg was incorporated as a village on July 12, 1904, its name the German form of L'viv (today, an industrial centre in western Ukraine). By 1906 the population was 365, and in 1907 Lemberg attained town status. In 1911, **JAMES GARFIELD GARDINER**, future Premier of Saskatchewan and federal Minister of Agriculture, became the principal of Lemberg School, a position he retained until 1914, the year he first became an MLA. Gardiner bought a farm outside Lemberg and served as the community's mayor in 1919–20; he retired to his farm at Lemberg in 1958, passing away in 1962. His son, J.W. Gardiner, was the town's secretary-treasurer in the 1950s, at which point the town had reached a peak population of over 500. Lemberg continues to be a trading centre for the surrounding agricultural district, where grain and livestock production and a number of seed farms form the basis of the area economy. Community landmarks include: Trinity Lutheran Church, built in 1926 using an estimated 83,000 bricks; St. Michael's Roman Catholic Church, dating to 1901; and the former Weissenberg School, a fieldstone structure built in 1900. *David McLennan*

LENHARDT, MOLLY (C. 1914–95). Molly Lenhardt, born Stefanka Molly Bassaraba near Lake Winnipegosis, Manitoba, was a self-taught painter who was nationally acclaimed for her emblematic paintings of Ukrainian-Canadian culture. An only child whose parents were community leaders, she saw it as her calling to document Ukrainian costume, symbols, and paintings. Her figures, typically at the centre of the painting, stare confidently out at the viewer, surrounded by bright colours and the geometrical detailing of costume. Lenhardt's paintings were the subject of a retrospective organized by the Dunlop Art Gallery of Regina in 1990. Her work is included in the collections of the **SASKATCHEWAN ARTS BOARD**, the Canadian Museum of Civilization, the **MENDEL ART GALLERY**, the **UNIVERSITY OF SASKATCHEWAN**, and the **MACKENZIE ART GALLERY**. Lenhardt and her husband, Joseph, were married in 1940. In 1950, they purchased the Fairway Confectionary in Melville, which Molly continued to operate, after her husband's death in 1979, for the rest of her life. She served on Melville City Council from 1977 to 1979. The Fairway, which served as her studio and home, has since been designated a heritage property. *Helen Marzolf*

FURTHER READING: Marzolf, H. 1990. *Molly Lenhardt Retrospective*. Regina: Dunlop Art Gallery.

SASKATCHEWAN ARCHIVES BOARD R-A11260-3
Bill Leonard.

LEONARD, WILLIAM (1909–89). Bill Leonard, first executive secretary of the **SASKATCHEWAN GOVERNMENT AND GENERAL EMPLOYEES' UNION** (SGEU), was born in Collingwood, Ontario. Leonard was hired from Alberta in 1944 to be the first staff person employed by the Saskatchewan Civil Service Association as it moved to being the first organization of government employees in North America that was allowed to certify as a trade union, to bargain with its employer, and to have the right to strike. These new rights were contained in the Trade Union Act of 1944, passed by the newly elected **CO-OPERATIVE COMMONWEALTH FEDERATION** (CCF) government of Premier **T.C. DOUGLAS**. Bill Leonard was instrumental in establishing the first government employee collective agreement in 1945 and in administering what was to become Saskatchewan's largest union; he was a persuasive proponent of free collective bargaining for public employees across Canada. It would be another twenty years before other public employees won the right to free collective bargaining. Leonard retired in 1973 after nearly thirty years of service to the SGEU. *Doug Taylor*

FURTHER READING: Taylor, D. 1984. *For Dignity, Equality and Justice: A History of the Saskatchewan Government Employees' Union*. Regina: SGEU.

LEOPOLD, JOHN (1890–1958). John Leopold was born in Bohemia, now the Czech Republic, in 1890, and took out a homestead in Alberta in 1914. He tried to enlist in the North-West Mounted Police Expeditionary Force to fight the Bolsheviks in Siberia; but he was too small to meet the requirements for the NWMP, and the force was then dis-

criminatory towards most ethnic nationalities. They did recruit him, though, as he spoke five languages, and appointed him to the security intelligence service to spy on labour, socialist, and immigrant organizations. He led a secret life in Regina as Jack Esselwein, a painter, and became active in the Painters' Union, in which he served as secretary from 1922 to 1927. He regularly attended the Regina Trades and Labour Council, and after their formation Esselwein became the secretary of the Communist Party's Regina branch. He also took up work as an insurance agent and a real estate salesman, which allowed him flexibility to travel to and infiltrate organizations in other cities.

In 1927 he was transferred to Toronto, where the stress of his double life led to heavy drinking. The Communist Party exposed him in 1928, and he was transferred to Whitehorse. Leopold resurfaced as a regular member of the RCMP when he stood witness in the trial of the eight jailed leaders of the Communist Party in 1931. He returned to Regina on July 1, 1935, with files that convinced the police to arrest the leaders of the **ON-TO-OTTAWA TREK** which initiated the **REGINA RIOT**. Later he was involved in the early Cold War defection of Igor Gouzenko. Leopold was ultimately promoted to the rank of Inspector in the Research Section of the Intelligence Service. He retired one year later in 1952, and died in Ottawa in 1958. *Bob Ivanochko*

FURTHER READING: Hewitt, S. 2000. "Royal Canadian Mounted Spy: The Secret Life of John Leopold/Jack Esselwein," *Intelligence and National Security* 15 (1): 144–68; Parnaby, A., and G. Kealey. 1997. "How the 'Reds' Got Their Man: The Communist Party Unmasks an RCMP Spy." *Labour/Le Travail* 40: 253–67.

LEROY, town, pop 413, located SW of Watson, 13 km W of Hwy 6. The area economy is based on agriculture. Settlers to the district were largely of English, Scottish, Irish, Scandinavian, and German origins. In 1907 the first school, named Bogend, and in 1909 a post office, named Bog End (the variations of the spelling are correct), were established within 1.5 km of the present townsite. With the construction of the CPR line in 1920–21, the townsite was established and the name Leroy was adopted for the community; it was chosen to honour John Leroy, the son of one of the first families to settle in the district, who lost his life during **WORLD WAR I**. During **WORLD WAR II**, airmen from all over the British Commonwealth made Leroy a bustling place as they prepared and trained for the war effort at No. 5 Bombing and Gunnery School just west of Big Quill Lake. The years following World War II were prosperous times; Leroy's population more than doubled within ten years, growing from 213 in 1946 to 514 in 1956. Leroy attained town status in 1963. Beginning in the late 1960s, however, the commu-

nity entered a period of continuous decline. Between 1980 and 1990, the population of the town fell by 17% and that of the surrounding rural municipality by 25%. As the retail and service sector of the community was declining, some began to wonder if the community would completely disappear; what followed, however, has been a small-town success story. Proactive community leaders in Leroy vigorously pursued initiatives, innovations, partnerships, and new co-operative ventures, and have realized a significant degree of success in building a sustainable future. Volunteerism and fund-raising events led to the revitalization of social, cultural, and recreational facilities. Community-rooted business ventures, such as the Leroy Watson Co-op's establishment of an integrated farm supply service for fertilizers, crop protection, and seed, as well as the significant furthering of the area's hog industry, have led directly to the creation of over a hundred new jobs since 1990. The Saskatchewan government's Action Committee on the Rural Economy (ACRE) named Leroy a model community in terms of contemporary economic development strategies for rural Saskatchewan. *David McLennan*

LESLIE, E.C. (1893–1978). Born in River Hebert, Nova Scotia, on July 14, 1893, E.C. Leslie contributed to the profession of Law and post-secondary education in his adopted province of Saskatchewan. He served with the 85th Battalion, Nova Scotia Highlanders during **WORLD WAR I** and was commissioned as an officer in the field. Following his return from Europe, he earned a BA from Acadia University and an LLB from the **UNIVERSITY OF SASKATCHEWAN**. In addition to carrying on a general law practice, he served as a member of the Board of Governors of the University of Saskatchewan and was installed as the first Chancellor of the **UNIVERSITY OF REGINA** in October 1974. Awarded honorary degrees from Acadia and Queen's Universities and the University of Saskatchewan, Leslie was appointed an Officer of the Order of Canada in 1969. He passed away on December 7, 1978.

LEVEE, ROY (1935–). Born on August 7, 1935, to Glenn and Ella Levee, Roy grew up on the family farm near Radville, Saskatchewan. He graduated from the **UNIVERSITY OF SASKATCHEWAN** in 1957 with a BSc in agriculture, and was honoured with a Distinguished Agrologist Award in 1984. Levee (pronounced *lee-vee*) joined the family farming business in 1955. His wintertime off-farm employment over the years included urban assessment work with the Provincial Assessment Branch, and instructing farm business management for the provincial Department of Agriculture. His most notable achievement was his commitment to the **WEYBURN INLAND TERMINAL** (WIT), Canada's first inland grain terminal owned and operated by farmers.

Levee became a shareholder in the WIT in 1977, less than a year after the large grain facility opened on the outskirts of Weyburn. He was a WIT board member from 1977 to 1986, 1988 to 1995, and from December 1998 to April 1999. Except for 1977, Levee was an executive member of the board during all those years. In 1999, he was appointed to a non-voting position on the board as vice-president of corporate affairs. In 2003, he began his semi-retirement, leaving the farming to his son Kim, his son-in-law Lorne and his daughter Pam. Levee is credited for using his business and corporate sensibility as well as his interpersonal skills to save the terminal from bankruptcy in its early stages and help it grow through other tumultuous times. Walter Nelson, a Moose Jaw area farmer and businessman who is also a long-time WIT supporter, said Levee helped put the mark of "personal attention" on the terminal to make it appeal to farmer clients. *Deana Driver*

LEVINE, MARILYN (1935–2005). Marilyn Levine was a renowned Canadian-born ceramic artist who studied art and taught sculpture at the UNIVERSITY OF REGINA in the 1960s and early 1970s. She is widely recognized across North America for her realistic ceramic renderings of leather objects, such as handbags, satchels, garments, and briefcases. Her sculptures can be found in all major ceramic collections across the United States and Canada. Exhibitions featuring Levine's realist works have garnered international exposure for the award-winning ceramist. Her works have appeared in galleries throughout North America, from the MACKENZIE ART GALLERY in Regina to the Institute of Contemporary Art in Boston, and overseas from Paris to Tokyo. Levine was born on December 22, 1935, in Medicine Hat, Alberta. She moved to Edmonton in the 1950s to attend the University of Alberta, where she graduated with a master's degree in chemistry. Influenced by her parents' interest in art and design, Levine had a budding interest in painting. In 1961, she moved to Regina with her husband, Sidney. Unable to find employment in her field of chemistry, Levine enrolled in drawing, painting, art history, and pottery courses at the University of Saskatchewan's Regina Campus. She studied art as a non-credit student for several years while periodically teaching chemistry at Campion College. In spite of her strong background in science, Levine continued to drift toward a career in art. In 1964, she resigned from teaching chemistry altogether and enrolled in the School of Art at the Regina Campus. Levine opened her first solo show in 1966 at a small craft shop in Regina; through the next five years she held many more solo shows in Saskatchewan and across Canada, while continuing to teach ceramics classes in Regina. In 1969 she moved to the United States to enter the Graduate Sculpture Program at the

University of California (Berkeley). In her second year at Berkeley, she became intrigued with inanimate objects–particularly leather goods–as records of human experience and activity. Levine soon developed a remarkable talent for creating highly realistic ceramic representations of leather objects, paying meticulous attention to the aging, wearing, and shaping of the leather through time and use. In 1971 Levine again returned to Regina to teach ceramics and pottery at the university, but in 1973 she accepted an offer as assistant professor of sculpture at the University of Utah and moved back to the United States, this time permanently. She later resided in Oakland, California, where she died on March 29, 2005. *Iain Stewart*

FURTHER READING: Bismanis, M. and T. Long. 1998. *Marilyn Levine: A Retrospective*. Regina: MacKenzie Art Gallery.

LEWRY, LOUIS H. (1919–92). Born in Moose Jaw on April 16, 1919, Louis H. "Scoop" Lewry's career as a public servant included alderman and mayor of Moose Jaw and member of Parliament. Before entering politics, he worked as a reporter for Moose Jaw's CHAB radio, the *Regina Leader-Post*, and the now-defunct *Winnipeg Tribune*. First elected to Moose Jaw city council in 1948, Lewry served as mayor of Moose Jaw from 1949–56, 1964–70, and 1982–88. He was also elected CCF member of Parliament for Moose Jaw-Lake Centre in 1957. In addition to his four decades in public life, Scoop Lewry was a passionate coin collector and served as president of the Canadian Numismatic Association from 1987 to 1989. He was made a Member of the Order of Canada in 1980. Lewry died on February 24, 1992.

LEYTON-BROWN, HOWARD (1918–). Howard Leyton-Brown was born in Melbourne, Australia on December 19, 1918. He studied music in Australia, Germany, and Belgium, as well as in England with Carl Lesch and Max Rostal, before pursuing a career as a violinist and orchestral player. When WORLD WAR II broke out in 1939, Leyton-Brown joined the ROYAL AIR FORCE, where he served as a pilot for six years, including two years as a flying instructor at the training air base in Estevan, Saskatchewan. In 1944 he was sent to England, where he was awarded the Distinguished Flying Cross for his service as a bomber pilot. Following the war, he attended the Guildhall School of Music and Drama before joining the London Philharmonic Orchestra in 1948, initially as deputy concertmaster and later as concertmaster in 1951. He received his doctorate in musical arts from the University of Michigan in 1971.

Leyton-Brown immigrated to Canada in 1952, with his wife Myrl and two sons, to become head of

the string department of the Regina Conservatory of Music, a position he held until his retirement in 1987. Leyton-Brown also served as the conductor of the REGINA SYMPHONY ORCHESTRA from 1960 to 1971, and as its concertmaster from 1978 to 1989. He has appeared as a soloist with the symphony orchestras of Calgary, Lethbridge, Regina, and Saskatoon, the CBC orchestras of Winnipeg, Vancouver and Toronto, and several American orchestras. Leyton-Brown also served on the SASKATCHEWAN ARTS BOARD from 1967 to 1971, and on the Canada Council from 1971 to 1974.

Leyton-Brown has guest conducted various ensembles in Saskatchewan and elsewhere in Canada and the United States, and taught at the American Congress of Strings in Cincinnati in 1984 and Dallas in 1985. He conducted the South Saskatchewan Youth Orchestra during its tour of China and Japan in 1986, and has been broadcast as a soloist with orchestra and in recital on CBC radio as well as in Australia, England, Iceland and Switzerland. He has appeared on numerous TV programs, including two years of weekly chamber-music programs for CKCK TV in Regina. He has composed cadenzas to several violin concertos, has arranged works for string orchestra, and in 1980 completed Ernest Bloch's unfinished *Suite for Solo Viola*. He edited Violet Archer's *Twelve Miniatures* for violin and piano as well as violin works by Hallgrimur Helgason. He was named a Member of the Order of Canada in 1986, received the Lifetime Award for Excellence in the Arts in 1991, the Saskatchewan Order of Merit in 1996, and the Queen's Golden Jubilee Medal in 2002.

Damian Coneghan

LEYTON-BROWN, MYRL (1921–). Born on December 18, 1921, Estevan native Myrl Leyton-Brown has been a proponent of Canadian unity for several decades. Having earned a BA and MA from the University of Regina, Leyton-Brown was president of the Regina and Saskatchewan Canada Week committees and director of the Council for Canadian Unity. She helped launch the successful Encounters With Canada program in 1982, serving as provincial chair until 1990. Myrl Leyton-Brown's numerous honours and awards include the Queen's Silver and Golden Jubilee Medals, the Canada 125 Medal, and the Order of Canada in 1985.

LIBERAL PARTY. For the first thirty-nine years of its history, the Liberal Party dominated Saskatchewan politics. After 1944 and the coming to power of the CO-OPERATIVE COMMONWEALTH FEDERATION (CCF), the Liberal Party entered a slow electoral decline, reversed only between 1964 and 1971, when it returned to power under ROSS THATCHER, a former Moose Jaw CCF member of Parliament turned free-enterprise convert. In the era of its greatest victories—between 1905 and 1944 it won 74% of all constituency contests—Saskatchewan's Liberal Party presented itself as a friend of the farmer and the "non-English" settler. As opposed to the conservative Liberals of central Canada, and especially Quebec, or the "statist" provincial governments of Alberta and Manitoba, the Saskatchewan Liberals promoted co-operative, self-help policies, most famously in the government's financial support for the **SASKATCHEWAN CO-OPERATIVE ELEVATOR COMPANY**: by **WORLD WAR I**, the elevator company had become the world's largest grain handling facility, a success for which the province's Liberals took credit, but for whose operation they refused direct responsibility.

By 1921 the sweep of Saskatchewan's settlement and its burgeoning population had made the province the third largest in Canada and thus a political prize in national politics. Through its mastery of organizational detail, the Liberal Party delivered crucial seats to federal Liberals, who might count on Quebec loyalists to repeatedly win that province's seats but who faced a divided electorate in Ontario. The Saskatchewan Liberal organization became well known for its machine-like operation—patronage-based and leadership-focused. Saskatchewan's first two Premiers, **WALTER SCOTT** and **WILLIAM MARTIN**, sat in Parliament before entering provincial politics; the next Premiers, **CHARLES DUNNING** and **J.T. GARDINER**, reversed the process, leaving Regina for Ottawa and senior Cabinet portfolios. In these decades Saskatchewan offered the best illustration of the textbook theory that national parties through their provincial wings helped unify Canada.

The world changed for the Saskatchewan Liberals when they were removed from power in 1929 by a coalition of political forces helped by the newly arrived **KU KLUX KLAN**, which attacked the governing party for policies it termed insufficiently patriotic. While the Liberals were in opposition, economic **DEPRESSION** undermined world grain prices and drought destroyed the assumptions that sustained the original settler society. These calamities eventually passed; more ominous for the Liberals was the entrenchment of the CCF, which had arisen (initially under the name Farmer-Labour) as a protest against the injustices of capitalism and the existing party system. Unlike the Liberals, who had no other doctrine than economic prosperity and their own political perpetuity, the CCF assumed office with an economic and social program that guided their actions (and those of their successor, the NDP) for the rest of the century. They also believed in planning, and to this end transformed the largely patronage-based public service into Canada's first provincial professional service.

In this new commonwealth, the Liberals found themselves cast as conservatives. As if conforming to the role thrust upon them, they distrusted the new, expert bureaucracy and advocated less government and more private enterprise. While opinion was never monolithic in caucus or among supporters, its direction became clear by the late 1940s and never altered. Ross Thatcher's government reinforced the hostility to CCF policies, and at the same time distanced the provincial from the federal Liberals, who were themselves promoting national medicare.

Disillusionment with federal agricultural policy under Pierre Trudeau and loss of public confidence in the provincial party's ability to replace the governing NDP directed voter discontent toward a new alternative governing party: the Progressive Conservatives (PC). The return of the NDP to power in 1991 and the collapse of the PCs in scandal provided a momentary revival for the Liberals; but subsequent internal discord split the caucus, with disaffected Liberals joining a rump of Tories to form the **SASKATCHEWAN PARTY**. Following the 1999 election, the legislative remnant of Liberals coalesced for a time with the NDP; in the 2003 election, no Liberal candidates won a seat. From being the party that dominated government and then the opposition, the Liberal Party of Saskatchewan entered the province's second century excluded from the Legislature.

David E. Smith

FURTHER READING: Smith, D.E. 1981. *The Regional Decline of a National Party: Liberals on the Prairies.* Toronto: University of Toronto Press.

LIBRARIES, FIRST NATIONS AND MÉTIS.

The history of libraries for many First Nations and **MÉTIS** people comprises their oral culture: "Knowledge was inherent in all things. The world was a library" said Chief Luther Standing Bear. Elders are often compared to libraries: "their knowledge, their skills, attitudes and their experience constitute the record of the knowledge and the wisdom of the people. Their memories serve as collective knowledge and wisdom. Education is the process of communicating this knowledge and wisdom, through oral language, actions and behavior" (Blondin 1988: 3). Education and libraries were reinforced with the 1972 document *Indian Control of Indian Education*, which indicated that First Nations had the right to control their education systems by training Indian people to be teachers, and that education facilities had to be provided that would meet the needs of local populations. With this document, First Nations and Métis educational institutions became a reality.

The **FIRST NATIONS UNIVERSITY OF CANADA** (formerly Saskatchewan Indian Federated College) has libraries in three locations: Regina (1977); Saskatoon (1985); and Prince Albert (1992). These libraries support the classes offered with acquisitions written by, for, and about Indigenous peoples of the world. The mission of the **SASKATCHEWAN INDIAN CULTURAL CENTRE** (SICC) in 1973 was to assemble, organize, preserve, and make available print and non-print material relating to the history, language, and culture of First Nations peoples (with emphasis on Canada and Saskatchewan), and to serve all peoples as a source of reliable information on First Nations. The mission of the Pahkisimon Nuyeȥáh Library System is to provide library services that constitute educational and cultural resources to the peoples of Northern Saskatchewan.

In 1980 the **GABRIEL DUMONT INSTITUTE** of Native Studies and Applied Research (GDI) incorporated the **SASKATCHEWAN URBAN NATIVE TEACHER EDUCATION PROGRAM** (SUNTEP) along with its library system. The GDI Library functions to support information and research that meet the needs of GDI and its technical institute. This library has three branches, whose collections focus on Métis history and culture, as well as on issues of concern to Métis and First Nations Peoples. The Albert Branch Public Library, built in 1913 and situated in inner-city Regina, provides a glimpse into Aboriginal history. Through its collections and programs, it meets the needs of an inner-city community that is 40% Aboriginal.

Phyllis Lerat

FURTHER READING: 1996. *Gathering Strength: Report of the Royal Commission on Aboriginal Peoples*, Volume 3. Ottawa: Royal Commission on Aboriginal Peoples; Blondin, G. 1988. "A Case Study of Successful Innovation." Master's thesis, University of British Columbia.

LIBRARY CO-OPERATION.

Co-operation assisted the growth of library services in Saskatchewan, and continues to be a mechanism for library advancements today. A zeal for libraries and an ethic of co-operation motivated early library leaders to work together to expand library services province-wide. They shared resources and advocated for governments to fund and develop libraries. Over time, as more and different types of libraries developed, co-operation remained necessary for libraries to overcome perennial challenges: limited funds; serving a sparse population dispersed over a vast geographic area; and the reality that no library alone has the capacity to provide access to all information sources.

Co-operative practices were used in all aspects of library operations to produce efficiencies. Libraries exchanged bibliographic information, shared resources and technologies, and co-operated to build information tools such as bibliographies and indexes.

Libraries also sought to give Saskatchewan residents access to the total library materials in the province by arranging co-operative service policies. Reciprocal borrowing enabled residents to directly borrow material from any public library in the province. Interlibrary loans provided for the loaning of materials from one library to another. Public access to many specialized and academic collections was also arranged.

Most significantly, co-operative principles became the foundation for library organizational structures. The Library Inquiry Committee of 1967 recommended the development of regional and public library systems based on co-operative structures. It also recommended increased co-operation among all types of libraries. The Pahkisimon Nuye?áh Library System in northern Saskatchewan was established in 1990 as a federation of all types of libraries—the first organization of many types of libraries into a formal library system in Saskatchewan. In 1988, the Echo Valley Library Forum articulated a vision for formalized province-wide co-operation among all types of libraries. The Saskatchewan Library Association, the Saskatchewan Library Trustees' Association and, later, a Multitype Library Development Advisory Committee advanced the idea. In 1996, the Legislature passed The Libraries Co-operation Act establishing the Multitype Library Board to facilitate the development of the Saskatchewan Multitype Library System —a network of working relationships between any combination of autonomous libraries and information providers, established to share services and resources for mutual benefit. The Act mandated the Provincial Library to provide coordination support to the Board and the multitype system.

Rapid advances in technology, coupled with the establishment of the Multitype Library Board, increased collaborative opportunities, producing a period in which libraries achieved several co-operative innovations of note including: the Multitype Database Licensing Program (joint acquisition of large collections of electronic reading materials); Saskatchewan Libraries: Ask Us (the first province-wide public library collaborative online reference service in Canada); seamless online searching of many different library catalogues; and Saskatchewan Libraries website (www.lib.sk.ca), showcasing the collective resources and services of all types of libraries.

Library co-operation continues to grow and is expanding to include collaboration with other partners such as archives, educational institutions, and other types of information providers. *Melissa Bennett*

FURTHER READING: Minister's Multitype Library Advisory Committee. 1996. *Think Globally ... Search Locally: A Strategic Plan for the Implementation of a Multitype Library System in Saskatchewan.* Regina: Saskatchewan Provincial Library; 1992. *Saskatchewan Libraries, Independent But Together: A Vision for a Province-wide Multitype Library System.* Regina: Saskatchewan Library Association and Saskatchewan Library Trustees' Association.

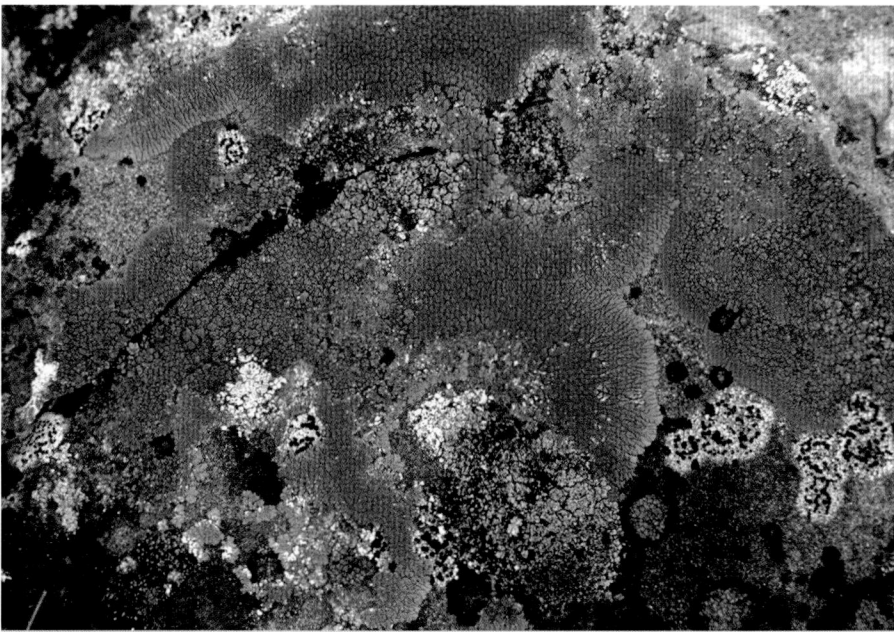

COURTNEY MILNE PHOTO
Rock lichen community.

LICHENS. Lichens are stable and self-supporting composites of a fungus and photosynthetic algae. Because of this dualism, they are difficult to put into a specific kingdom. The algae are either a green alga or a blue-green alga (Cyanobacterium), both of which contain chlorophyll. The lichen's body (*thallus*) benefits from the interaction between the fungal and algal components. The fungus gives structural support and protection to the algal cells, which by photosynthesis produce sugars and carbohydrates; the fungus utilizes some of these to obtain energy for growth and reproduction. This relationship enables both components to live in extreme environments normally hostile to their survival, so that lichens have a cosmopolitan distribution. The scientific name given to lichen refers to the fungal component; the algal component has its own name.

Lichens differ from what we normally understand as fungi. The greater part of the thallus is usually above ground; it varies in structure and remains visible throughout the year, bearing small fruiting bodies (*ascomata*). Some lichens are leaf-like (*foliose*), with upper and lower cortical fungal cells. The algal cells are between these surface cells and loosely arranged central fungal cells (*medulla*). The lower layer often has tiny structures (*rhizinae*) or a central holdfast (*umbilicum*) for attachment to the substratum. Other forms are upright and bushy, or pendant from trees (*fruticose*), or appearing as a crust (*crustose*) on trees or racks; they are often conspicuously coloured. These lichens differ slightly in their internal structure from foliose lichens.

Lichens have no protective cuticle and dessicate rapidly, becoming metabolically inactive for long periods of drought but regaining their physiological functions by re-moistening of the lichen body.

Moisture is therefore essential for lichen growth, and lichens obtain moisture from the atmosphere in the form of dew, fog or rain. However, beside beneficial nutrients such moisture can contain pollutants such as sulfur dioxide, sulfuric acid, nitric acid, and metals, especially in cities and industrialized areas. Because lichens are very sensitive to these toxins, which can seriously affect the delicate balance between the fungus and the algae, they are known worldwide as sensitive bio-indicators for assessing atmospheric pollution and health.

Lichens can reproduce in various ways: sexually by fruiting bodies containing spores, which upon germination need to join compatible algal cells to form a new lichen (*lichenization*); or vegetatively, whereby the lichen produces on the thallus small structures which contain algal cells surrounded by fungal strands, forming complete miniature lichen bodies. These are easily dispersed and able to form a new lichen upon a suitable substratum. A more successful form of vegetative reproduction is by fragmentation of the lichen body.

There are over 400 species of lichen known from Saskatchewan, with additional species to be discovered. Lichens are used as biochemical indicators for the dating of surfaces (*lichenometry*), and can be valuable indicators of climate change. They have economic uses as dyes, base ingredients for perfumes, cosmetics, medicines, and food for indigenous peoples. Because of their sheer mass, certain lichens in northern regions are a vital winter nutrient for barren-ground and woodland caribou. *Bernard de Vries*

FURTHER READING: Brodo, Irwin M., S. Duran Sharnoff and S. Sharnoff. 2001. *Lichens of North America.* New Haven: Yale University Press.

LIEUTENANT COLONEL D.V. CURRIE, VC, ARMOURY. Located in Moose Jaw, the Lieutenant Colonel D.V. Currie, VC, Armoury was constructed during the building boom of 1912–13 at a cost of $150,000. It was officially opened on July 3, 1913, on a ten-acre site fronting Main Street on the north end of Moose Jaw. The site was donated by the city, after some considerable discussion and prodding from the Minister of Militia, Sir Sam Hughes. The initial impetus for building the armoury came from several prominent local businessmen, including Walter E. Seaborn (insurance and property broker and later Lieutenant Colonel Commanding, 210th Battalion, CEF), **HERBERT SNELL** (City Counselor and Major, later Lieutenant Colonel Commanding, 46th Battalion, CEF) and Richard Loney (real estate developer and Captain, 95th Saskatchewan Rifles). Walter Seaborn had stated that no self-respecting city could call itself a city without having an armoury. Originally conceived as an armoury building with an outdoor drill square, the final design included space for several military and Cadet units as well as the Boy Scouts, and an enclosed drill hall 30 x 60 metres (100 x 200 feet). The design of the armoury was developed by one of the staff architects in the Department of Public Works under the direction of Chief Architect David Ewart, and was intended to suggest a medieval castle in its use of buttressing along the walls and a crenellated roofline on the main entrance. The castellated style had been applied to armoury designs in Canada since the 1880s.

During its 92-year history, the armoury has had many uses. It has been the home of the 95th Saskatchewan Rifles, the 60th Rifles, the King's Own Rifles of Canada, the 77th Battery, Royal Canadian Artillery, the 19th Medical Company, Royal Canadian Army Medical Corps, and the 142nd Transport Company, Royal Canadian Army Service Corps. It is currently the home of the Saskatchewan Dragoons. The armoury has been pressed into service as an isolation hospital during the influenza outbreak in 1919, a command centre during several major floods, and a morgue during the Trans-Canada Airline crash in 1954. The north end of the armoury was completely destroyed by fire on February 17, 1937. On June 13, 1988, the armoury was named the Lieutenant Colonel D.V. Currie, VC, Armoury in honour of David Vivian Currie, of Moose Jaw, who had won the Victoria Cross at Saint Lambert-sur-Dives, France during the Battle of the Falaise Gap in August 1944. (*See also* **VICTORIA CROSS SASKATCHEWAN RECIPIENTS.**) *Gerry Carline*

LIEUTENANT-GOVERNOR. The Lieutenant-Governor is the nominal chief executive officer of the province, an integral part of the Legislature, a formal link through the Crown with the federal government, and the provincial representative of the Sovereign. The Crown's representative, however, exercises executive power in name only, almost always doing so "on advice" of his or her Ministers. The prime functions of the Lieutenant-Governor are to symbolize provincial jurisdiction and to ensure continuity and legitimacy of the elected governments. The Lieutenant-Governor summons, prorogues and dissolves the Legislature; swears in Premiers and Cabinets; reads the Speech from the Throne; gives royal assent to legislation; and signs writs, Orders-in-Council, and proclamations. The Lieutenant-Governor also travels widely to promote civic values and national unity in the province, and confers Saskatchewan honours.

There are eleven Crowns in Canada: that for the country as a whole and those for each of the ten provinces. The Queen is Canadian head of state: the Governor General carries out most of her functions for federal jurisdiction and the Lieutenant-Governors do the same for provincial jurisdiction, reflecting the co-sovereign status of the provinces in Confederation. The provincial Crown was not as autonomous in 1867, the year of Confederation: the Lieutenant-Governors succeeded the Governors of the former individual colonies as chief executive officers of the new provinces, but were intended as agents of Ottawa, appointed, paid, and liable to dismissal by the central government. Furthermore, Lieutenant-Governors possessed major constitutional powers to subordinate the provinces to the will of Ottawa. However, the provinces realized, exercised and defended their co-sovereign status as Canada evolved into a more authentic federal state. Some major court decisions confirmed the autonomous status of the provincial Crown; the best known of these is the judgement by the Judicial Committee of the Privy Council in 1892 in the *Maritime Bank* case.

The constitutional powers of the Sovereign and her representatives fall into two categories: *statutory* and *prerogative*, both exercised "on advice" of the Cabinet. Statutory powers are those conferred by acts of Parliament or the Legislatures. Prerogative powers are the authority vested in the Crown through custom, tradition and precedent. The only use of the royal prerogative in which some discretion still exists for the Crown's representative is the exercise of the "reserve powers"–the right to summon and dissolve the Legislature and to name the First Minister (Premier). Some reserve powers of the Canadian Crown are statutory. Under sections 55–57 and 90 of the Constitution Act, 1867, the Lieutenant-Governor may withhold royal assent to legislation or, through the power of "reservation," may reserve assent for the pleasure of the Governor General (i.e., the federal government). A statutory power granted to the Lieutenant-Governor of Saskatchewan by provincial legislation is that of approving and signing special warrants concerning expenditure from the Consolidated Revenue Fund in specifically defined circumstances outside the normal parliamentary appropriation process.

During much of the 20th century the profile of the provincial vice-regal office steadily declined, together with the role of the Lieutenant-Governor as federal agent and his discretion in exercising prerogative powers. The CCF government of **T.C. DOUGLAS** closed **GOVERNMENT HOUSE**, the vice-regal residence built in 1891, as an economy measure. The last "reservation" of royal assent in Canada was by Lieutenant-Governor **FRANK BASTEDO** in Saskatchewan in 1963, which resulted in considerable friction with the CCF government of **WOODROW LLOYD**. However, starting with **STEPHEN WOROBETZ** in 1970, appointments by the federal government to the office of Lieutenant-Governor became much less overtly partisan, and the prestige of the office gradually recovered; **IRWIN MCINTOSH** (1978–83) contributed to this process. In 1983, **FREDERICK JOHNSON** was sworn in as sixteenth Lieutenant-Governor in the first publicly televised ceremony, and in 1984 the vice-regal office returned to Government House. Johnson was the first chancellor of the Saskatchewan Order of Merit, instituted in 1985. He and his successor **SYLVIA FEDORUK** faced the issue of the misuse of special warrants by the Progressive Conservative government of **GRANT DEVINE**, but declined to intervene. Premier **ROY ROMANOW** enhanced the status of the vice-regal position, in particular by holding regular meetings with Lieutenant-Governors Fedoruk, **JACK WIEBE**, and **LYNDA HAVERSTOCK**, a practice continued by his successor **LORNE CALVERT**. *Michael Jackson*

Lieutenant-Governors of Saskatchewan	
1905-1910	The Hon. Amédée E. Forget
1910-1915	The Hon. George W. Brown
1915-1921	The Hon. Sir Richard Lake
1921-1931	The Hon. Henry W. Newlands
1931-1936	The Hon. Hugh E. Munroe
1936-1945	The Hon. Archibald P. McNab
1945	The Hon. Thomas Miller
1945-1948	The Hon. Reginald J. M. Parker
1948-1951	The Hon. John M. Uhrich
1951-1958	The Hon. William J. Patterson
1958-1963	The Hon. Frank L. Bastedo
1963-1970	The Hon. Robert L. Hanbidge
1970-1976	The Hon. Dr. Stephen Worobetz
1976-1977	The Hon. George Porteous
1978-1983	The Hon. C. Irwin McIntosh
1983-1988	The Hon. Frederick W. Johnson
1988-1994	The Hon. Sylvia O. Fedoruk
1994-2000	The Hon. J.E.N. (Jack) Wiebe
2000-	The Hon. Lynda M. Haverstock

FURTHER READING: Eager, E. 1980. *Saskatchewan Government: Politics and Pragmatism.* Saskatoon: Western Producer Prairie Books; Leeson, H.A. (ed.). 2001. *Saskatchewan Politics: Into the Twenty-First Century.* Regina: Canadian Plains Research Center.

LILBURN, TIM (1950–). One of Saskatchewan's most honoured poets, Lilburn was born on June 27, 1950. He was raised in Regina, and educated at Campion College, **UNIVERSITY OF REGINA**, where he received a BA in English in 1973. Influenced by Catholic spirituality, Lilburn joined the Jesuit order in 1978, and in 1986 he published a book of religious poetry called *Names of God.* Lilburn, however, left the order in 1987, eventually resettling as an English and Philosophy professor at **ST. PETER'S COLLEGE, MUENSTER**, Saskatchewan. *Moosewood Sandhills* (1994) and *To the River* (1999) turned Lilburn's poetry towards nature, while *Kill-site* (2003) included more social conflicts and won the Governor-General's Award for Poetry. Lilburn has also published essays on the relationship of poetry to philosophy, most notably *Living In The World As If It Were Home* (1999) and *Thinking and Singing: Poetry and the Practice of Philosophy* (2002). Although Lilburn's literary journey has been shaped by Christian spirituality, he currently describes his own religious practice as "undetermined" and, as his philosophical essays make clear, he identifies most closely with the *via negativa*, the way to God that rejects clear theological images or doctrines in favour of dark, unspeakable intimations of divinity.

Gregory Maillet

LINDNER, ERNST FRIEDRICH (1897–1988). Nationally respected as a landscape artist, and influential in Saskatchewan as a teacher of art, Ernst Lindner was born in Vienna, Austria, and immigrated to Saskatoon with his parents in 1926. He became a self-taught freelance commercial artist and illustrator and, despite having no formal art education, eventually became Head of the Art Department at the Saskatoon Technical Collegiate (1936–62). Lindner's fame is largely derived from a substantial body of watercolour paintings examining the arboreal landscape near his Emma Lake summer home. Unique in that he abandons the horizon line traditional in the landscape genre, Lindner focuses instead on detailing the forest floor close up; here he depicts a highly textured glittering scatter of patterns resulting from the surface details of fallen branches and decomposing tree trunk stumps, all overgrown with fresh mosses and lichen. His microscopic fidelity has prompted some critics to label him a "magic realist." More than this, though, his interests in patterning, in undifferentiated compositions, and in the painterly question of surface versus illusory depth situate him more broadly as a late Modernist.

Indeed, Lindner was influenced by several of the great New York modern painters of the late 1950s and early 1960s, with whom he came into contact when they were invited to be occasional guest artists at the Emma Lake Workshops. Of particular note, when examining Lindner's work, is formalist Jules Olitski, famous for his ethereal colour-field abstractions. Like the early American transcendentalist writers Walt Whitman, Ralph Waldo Emerson and Henry David Thoreau, Lindner revels in an almost mystical nature, revealing the big within the small by locating the specific within the whole: his visual meditations on nature's decay and renewal at the microcosmic level metaphorically encode macrocosmic issues related to universal notions of generation and regeneration. Lindner himself has spoken elsewhere of "my belief in a continuity of life, death being only another form of life... Life revealed in the smallest growth is, to me, most meaningful. Forms change, life goes on."

Lindner was exhibited extensively throughout Canada during his lifetime. His work is held in over twenty-five major public and private collections across the country, including the National Gallery of Canada. The subject of numerous books, monographs and exhibition catalogues as well as the recipient of many awards, he received an Honorary Doctor of Laws degree from the **UNIVERSITY OF SASKATCHEWAN** in 1972, was elected a member of the Royal Canadian Academy of the Arts in 1977, was made a Member of the Order of Canada in 1979, and was awarded the **SASKATCHEWAN ARTS BOARD**'s Lifetime Award for Excellence in the Arts in 1988.

Jack Anderson

FURTHER READING: Heath, T. 1983. *Uprooted: The Life and Art of Ernest Lindner.* Saskatoon: Fifth House.

PATRICK PETTIT/REGINA LEADER-POST

Dwain Lingenfelter, January 1997.

LINGENFELTER, DWAIN MATTHEW (1949–). Lingenfelter was born on February 27, 1949, in Shaunavon. He studied at the **UNIVERSITY OF SASKATCHEWAN**, where he earned a political science degree. He operated his own farm near Shaunavon and briefly worked for Canada Customs. Lingenfelter was elected MLA for Shaunavon in 1978, and re-elected in 1982. He served as Minister of Social Services in the **ALLAN BLAKENEY** government from 1980 to 1982. He survived the Progressive Conservative landslide in 1982, and from 1982 to 1986 was Opposition House Leader, but was defeated in 1986. He was elected president of the Saskatchewan **NEW DEMOCRATIC PARTY** in 1987 and won the Regina Elphinstone seat vacated by Allan Blakeney in 1988. Lingenfelter became Opposition House Leader and Opposition critic for Privatization and Saskatchewan Government Insurance. In 1991, Lingenfelter was re-elected. He was appointed Minister of Economic Diversification

GIBSON PHOTO/ UNIVERSITY OF SASKATCHEWAN ARCHIVES A 5169

Ernst Lindner (left) and Russell Yuristy at the University of Saskatchewan's Emma Lake Campus, August 1973.

and Trade in the eleven-member "war Cabinet" of the newly formed NDP government. He also became government House Leader. He felt that economic growth required a collaborative effort between the public and private sectors of the economy. In 1995, Lingenfelter became Deputy Premier, and was appointed Minister of the Crown Investments Corporation in 1997. The 1999 provincial election cost the NDP nearly all of its rural seats. Due to his farming background, Lingenfelter was appointed Minister of Agriculture and Food in 1999 but resigned in 2000. He moved to Calgary as vice-president of government relations for Nexen, an international oil and gas company.　　*Jason Nystrom*

LITERATURE. The first written accounts produced in what became Saskatchewan were the diaries, letters, and reports of explorers, fur traders, government employees, and missionaries. The late 19th century saw the production of well-meaning but hopelessly derivative poetry and prose, in part through the encouragement of local literary societies (Regina and North Battleford, for example, had thriving clubs by 1885). Saskatchewan also sometimes provided the setting for Westerns on the American model of formulaic action and violence. In 1885, the **NORTH-WEST RESISTANCE** was still in progress when Torontonian Edmund Collins published *The Story of Louis Riel*, followed by a sequel, *Annette, the Métis Spy*. Ralph Connor's *The Foreigner: A Tale of Saskatchewan* (1909) typifies the many popular romances that followed: they feature forward-looking, optimistic celebrations of muscular outdoor life on the prairie. Production that can more narrowly be called "literature"—writing with an achieved aesthetic component—did not begin, however, until the 20th century.

Saskatchewan literature comes of age with the publication of **SINCLAIR ROSS**'s *As for Me and My House* (1941), a grim evocation of physical and psychological hardship in a small town, and **W.O. MITCHELL**'s *Who Has Seen the Wind* (1947), an at once realistic and idealized evocation of the small-town imaginative and spiritual resources available to an impressionable boy. Both writers grew up in Saskatchewan but eventually left the province; their famous novels were written while they lived elsewhere in Canada. Many others followed the familiar Saskatchewan story of out-migration while remaining powerful influences for aspiring Saskatchewan writers; they include **ELI MANDEL, JOHN NEWLOVE**, Fred Wah, **LORNA CROZIER**, and Dennis Cooley.

Institutions have been crucial in the development of literature in this province. The **SASKATCHEWAN ARTS BOARD**, the first of its kind in the English-speaking world outside Great Britain, was founded in 1948. It provides financial assistance to individual writers, and from 1967 to 1991 it ran the **SASKATCHEWAN SUMMER SCHOOL OF THE ARTS** at Fort

San in the **QU'APPELLE VALLEY**. Its successor for writing, the **SAGE HILL EXPERIENCE**, began in 1990. The 1970s witnessed an explosion of institutional literary activity. The province's professional theatres came into being in those years: Regina's **GLOBE THEATRE** in 1966, Saskatoon's **PERSEPHONE THEATRE** in 1974, while the **25TH STREET THEATRE** became professional in 1975. The founding of the **SASKATCHEWAN WRITERS GUILD** in 1969, and the 1975 establishment of Coteau Books and Thistledown Press, primarily to publish Saskatchewan writers, signaled an explosion of literary activity. Scores of writing groups nurture the ambitions of local writers throughout the province.

KEN MITCHELL must head the list of writers who have participated in and benefited from this support. Other Saskatchewan-born writers who did not have to leave the province in order to publish and make a living include **GUY VANDERHAEGHE, SHARON BUTALA, JOHN HICKS, GARY HYLAND, ROBERT CURRIE, GLEN SORESTAD, ANDREW SUKNASKI, BYRNA BARCLAY**, Connie Gault, Dianne Warren, Marlis Wessler, **BRENDA BAKER, GEOFFREY URSELL, BARBARA SAPERGIA**, and **DON KERR**. Others were born elsewhere but have flourished in the supportive provincial literary community: **ANNE SZUMIGALSKI**, Bonnie Burnard (at the beginning of her writing career), **ELIZABETH BREWSTER, DAVE MARGOSHES, VEN BEGAMUDRE, DAVID CARPENTER, STEVEN MICHAEL BERZENSKY**, Steven Ross Smith, and Sean Virgo.

Given the overwhelming surround of the land and the cycling seasons, it was once predictable that most Saskatchewan writing would be centrally concerned with the environment. Canadian literature in general used to be preoccupied with the effect of landscape on its inhabitants, and Saskatchewan is one of the prairie provinces that produced a large part of the Canadian fiction canon (Ross, Mitchell, Vanderhaeghe, Newlove, Rudy Wiebe, Robert Kroetsch, Margaret Laurence, Martha Ostenso, Gabrielle Roy). Although the natural world remains an important theme in Saskatchewan literature, it is by no means the only one: in fact, the writing is now so diverse that no useful thematic generalizations can be drawn. The recent appearance of creative non-fiction and First Nations writing is contributing to the diversity. The most influential Saskatchewan First Nations writer was **MARIA CAMPBELL**; the emerging generation includes Randy Lundy and **LOUISE BERNICE HALFE** (Sky Dancer). Formally, Saskatchewan literature remains rather traditional. Realism is still the dominant mode in prose, and the poetry tends toward an anecdote-based lyric, often featuring a distinctive vernacular voice. Finally, postmodernism has not been a strong feature of the province's literature.　*Ken Probert*

FURTHER READING: Dyck, E.F. (ed.). 1986. *Essays on Saskatchewan Writing*. Regina: Saskatchewan Writers

Guild; McCourt, E.A. 1970. *The Canadian West in Fiction*. Toronto: Ryerson; Probert, K.G. (ed.). 1989. *Writing Saskatchewan: 20 Critical Essays*. Regina: Canadian Plains Research Center.

LITTLE BLACK BEAR FIRST NATION. Cree Chief Kees kee hew mus-coo muskwa (Little Black Bear) signed **TREATY 4** on September 15, 1874, and settled on the reserve surveyed for his band in the File Hills (4 km south and 4 km west of Goodeve) in 1880. During the early 1800s, members of this Cree-Assiniboine band were nomadic, hunting and camping within in the **CYPRESS HILLS** area. Like most treaty bands in the province, members of Little Black Bear began farming once settled on reserve, progressing at the rate that technology, climatic conditions, and government policy allowed. This band has its own Band Membership Code, and band by-laws that govern all areas of its administration. Band-owned land in Balcarres holds their Lands Holding Company and Trust Office, while land in Ft. Qu'Appelle remains open for future development. Community infrastructure includes a band office, band hall, and swimming pool. Currently there are a total of 452 band members, 158 of whom live on their 17,006-acre reserve.　*Christian Thompson*

LITTLE MANITOU LAKE (51°44', 105°30'W: Map sheet 72/P 12). Located in central Saskatchewan just north of Watrous, Little Manitou Lake is named for the Algonquian word meaning "mysterious being." It covers 13.3 sq. km, with an average depth of 3.8 m, and is renowned for the purported healing properties of its saline waters. Lying within a former glacial spillway and fed by underground springs, the lake has mineral salt (sodium, magnesium and potassium) concentrations of 180,000 milligrams per litre; this high salinity gives it a specific gravity of 1.06, making the water exceedingly buoyant. People have visited the lake since at least the early 19th century, when some Assiniboine, suffering from smallpox, were reputedly cured by its waters. Recreational facilities were developed in the early 20th century, including dance halls, stores and hotels. A provincial park was designated there in the early 1930s, when construction of a luxury hotel was funded as a relief project. However, during the Depression tourism declined. In the 1950s the 290-acre park was divided, with part going to the Saskatchewan Society for Crippled Children (for Camp Easter Seal) and the remainder forming Manitou Lake Regional Park. During the 1980s a new spa was developed, and the old 1928 Danceland building restored, reviving Little Manitou Lake as a tourism and convention destination.　*Marilyn Lewry*

FURTHER READING: Schellenberg, R.M. 2001. *Lake of the Healing Waters: Manitou Beach, Saskatchewan, Canada*. Watrous, SK: Star Books.

LITTLE PINE FIRST NATION. Cree Chief Minahikosis (Little Pine) signed an adhesion to **TREATY 6** in 1879 near Fort Walsh, and though the band traditionally resided in the **CYPRESS HILLS** region they were moved and settled at the foot of Bluehill along the Battle River. In the winter of 1883–84 Little Pine and Lucky Man camped near **POUNDMAKER**'s reserve; although **BIG BEAR**, Little Pine, Lucky Man and Poundmaker wished for adjoining reserves, they were refused. Little Pine died in 1885 and his people were scattered. As part of the government's policy to keep all Indians on their respective reserves, a reserve was surveyed for the remnants of the Little Pine and Lucky Man bands in 1887. Their allotted acres did not correspond to what was entitled through treaty: this led to the May 29, 1997, settlement of a century's injustice. Through the settlement, the band has been able to purchase land and initiate other economic endeavours. The Little Pine First Nation continues to define its inherent right to self-government through its Government Act (Constitution, 2001), which allows for basic structure within the band and offers provisions for the Lands and Resources Management Act and the Election Act. Developmental projects include the Little Pine First Nation Racetrack, the Little Pine First Nation Cattle Venture, and a gas and convenience store. The band's facilities include the Little Pine Health Clinic and Medical Taxis, the Elders' Hall, the Chief Little Pine School, a band office, the Royal Canadian Mounted Police detachment (two constables working and residing on the reserve), and the Little Pine Daycare. The 17,567-ha reserve is located 53 km northwest of North Battleford; it has a population of 1,578, with 702 people living on reserve. *Christian Thompson*

LIVESTOCK FEED INDUSTRY. Saskatchewan's feed ingredient industry is estimated to be valued at $1.6 billion or 36% of total value of the crops produced. The feed industry has several components: feed ingredient producers (farmers and producers of byproducts), specialty feed ingredient producers, commercial feed processors and on-farm feed processors. Each segment has a distinct role that changes and responds to trends within the crop and livestock sectors.

The largest segment by value is that of feed ingredient producers who produce the crops and byproducts for processing into animal feed. The principal crops used for feed are **BARLEY, WHEAT, OATS,** field peas and **CANOLA** meal, arising from the processing of canola seed. Barley is used as a portion of the grain provided in swine and other monogastric diets, but can constitute the total grain portion for beef cattle and dairy cows. Hull-less barley, which was bred to have a loose hull and is removed in threshing, has greater utility in swine and poultry diets because of increased digestibility. Wheat can be used for all species of livestock, but is used primarily for higher digestibility and energy as a feed for poultry and added energy in swine diets. Oat grain has seen a resurgence partly due to the demand for oats for the food milling trade. Production levels for feed barley are affected by the demand and price for malt, where 80% of barley varieties grown are for malting, with malting acceptance being only 18–22% of malting barley produced; 75–80% of feed pea production is used for feed purposes. Canola seed is processed for its oil and the resultant 60% of the original seed is canola meal, the principal protein source produced in western Canada.

A number of other feed crops such as rye, triticale, and flaxseed produce specialized food products such as omega-3 enhanced eggs from flax. Other feed products arise from crop processing byproducts such as grain screening pellets. The processing of grain screenings arising from cleaning the exported grains prior to transport has resulted in savings to crop producers and allows value adding from increased livestock feeding enterprise. Changes in the crop and crop processing industries along with feed and food safety will increase the importance of this rapidly growing byproduct processing sector.

Crop production in Saskatchewan exceeds the capability of livestock to consume the feed crops grown. The majority of field peas and canola meal produced must be exported beyond Saskatchewan's borders. Barley is in considerable excess, being exported to Alberta where it must compete against imported corn from the United States. It is important that feed sources are competitive to sustain efficient animal production. Much research and concerted effort is being placed on creating new feeds and forms that give increased competitiveness.

Forages are often forgotten in a province so dominated by cereal crop production. Forages constitute over 50% of the diet for dairy, beef and other ruminants. Alfalfa, brome, crested wheat grass, cereal hays (mainly oats), cereal silages (mainly barley) and native hays form the bulk of forages stored for feeding. Pasture grazing usually involves grasses such as crested wheat, brome, Russian wild rye grass and native grasses. Grazing seasons vary in length (approximately four months) with a recent trend to extend the season by techniques such as "swath grazing." Production of alfalfa and timothy as forages for the export markets to Japan, Korea and Taiwan provides economic opportunities. Alfalfa dehydration plants for the manufacture of pellets and cubes have long been a mainstay of this industry segment, representing some of the larger feed manufacturing plants in Saskatchewan. The trend in market demand for longer fibre forage products is giving rise to double compressed hay bales (primarily timothy).

The commercial feed processors and on-farm processing facilities provide to the livestock industry a critical and important step. Feed compounders obtain feed ingredients, analyse nutrient content, formulate diets and process them by grinding or rolling, mixing and pelleting to service an industry and its animals demanding high quality performance feeds. As an example, rations are formulated to 0.1% of protein and are nutritionally balanced for over forty nutrients employing the most recent feed technology. Both complete feeds and supplements (protein, vitamin, mineral sources) are manufactured. Trends within the industry have seen a decline in complete feeds with supplement production growing. With this change the providing of nutritional expertise and management as a service is commonplace and forms the basis of a good marketing program of most commercial feed manufacturers.

The drive to specialization and increased unit size has shifted patterns of feed use in the industry. The poultry industries have relied on mainly on-farm processing (65%), and in the beef industry only supplements are typically purchased.

The livestock feed industry is rapidly changing not only responding to create new feeds with increased competitiveness but to capture opportunities. Because feed production is between crop production and livestock production, it is key to the health of both industries. *Vernon J. Racz*

FURTHER READING: Animal Nutrition Association of Canada (ANAC). 2001. *Statistical Handbook.* Winnipeg: Canada Grains Council.

LIZÉE, YVONNE (1899–1974). Yvonne Lizée (Sister Marie-Éphrem), a gifted artist and musician, was the first Canadian novice and the first Canadian-born convent Superior of the Soeurs de Notre-Dame d'Auvergne, one of many congregations of women seeking refuge in western Canada from France's anti-clerical legislation. She was born near

COURTESY OF SOEURS DE NOTRE-DAME D'AUVERGNE (PONTEIX)

Sister Yvonne Lizée.

Sherbrooke, Quebec, on December 2, 1899. In 1909 her family moved to a homestead west of Gravelbourg. She attended a country school, then completed her studies at the convent recently opened by the Soeurs de Notre-Dame d'Auvergne in nearby Ponteix. She left in 1916 for the congregation's training convent in France and returned three years later. While attending Normal School in Regina, she took piano, violin, painting and sculpting classes. After Normal School she taught at the Ponteix convent; in 1932, she became Superior of the convent, and in 1936 she officially launched a commercial course. From 1938 to 1942 she taught at Lac Pelletier, then came back to Ponteix. In 1945, she became Superior at Val Marie, where the congregation ran the local hospital. She was then sent to open a new hospital in Zenon Park. She returned to Ponteix in 1962, where she directed the *Foyer Saint-Joseph* nursing home. After becoming totally blind as a result of diabetes, she died on June 16, 1974.

Richard Lapointe

FURTHER READING: Lapointe, Richard. 1988. "Yvonne Lizée (soeur Marie-Éphrem, N.-D.d.C.)." Pp. 253–54 in *100 noms: Petit dictionnaire biographique des Franco-Canadiens de la Saskatchewan*. Regina: Société historique.

LLOYD, WOODROW STANLEY (1913–72).

Woodrow Lloyd was born in Webb on July 16, 1913. He was the youngest of twelve children born to Welsh settlers. He enrolled at the School of Engineering, UNIVERSITY OF SASKATCHEWAN in 1929. Due to the DEPRESSION, he was unable to return after the first year. In 1931, after a year spent working on the family farm, he trained as a teacher, hoping to finance his eventual return to university by teaching.

A fundamental part of Lloyd's education came from his family's passionate interest in politics. When the SASKATCHEWAN TEACHERS' FEDERATION (STF) was formed in 1933, Lloyd became involved and the following year became a councillor. At a local STF meeting he met Victoria Leinan. They married in 1936 and had two daughters and two sons. They settled in Vanguard where Lloyd became principal of the four-room school. He continued his studies and in 1940 was awarded a BA; the following year he received his Permanent Certificate for high school teaching. He enrolled in the RCAF during the war, but poor eyesight meant he was restricted to the drilling of cadets.

Elected to the presidency of the STF in 1940, he held the position for four years. In 1941, he became vice-principal of the high school in Biggar. He made contact with the local CCF and joined T.C. DOUGLAS' task force on the future of provincial education. Lloyd was elected in 1944. His appointment as Minister of Education made him Canada's youngest Cabinet Minister to date. As the MLA for Biggar, he

EVERETT BAKER PHOTO/COURTESY OF THE SASKATCHEWAN HISTORY AND FOLKLORE SOCIETY

Woodrow S. Lloyd (then Minister of Education) and Mrs. Lloyd, Regina, August 1947.

won the six subsequent elections, until he stepped down in 1971.

Lloyd established the controversial Larger School Units that brought changes to rural communities and a new system of taxation for education. A scheme of loans and bursaries to students, the first of its kind in Canada, also became a vital part of his program, and was soon copied by other provincial governments. Lloyd was a member of Treasury Board and, in 1954, represented the province at the Commonwealth Parliamentary Association Convention in Africa.

Following the 1960 election, Lloyd became provincial Treasurer and, in his first and only budget, demonstrated his belief that tax dollars were good dollars. In 1961 Tommy Douglas was elected national leader of the NDP and Lloyd became leader of the provincial CCF, and Premier. MEDICARE was introduced in 1962 followed by a DOCTORS' STRIKE that started on July 1. The government imported doctors to staff hastily established COMMUNITY CLINICS. An agreement was finally reached on July 23. In the 1964 provincial election, after twenty years in power, the CCF lost to the Liberals. As leader of the Opposition, Lloyd began to rebuild the party and reassess party philosophy but lost again in 1967. Lloyd supported the "Waffle Manifesto" that concerned itself with the ownership of Canadian resources. Discontented party members attacked his leadership and he resigned in 1970 but continued as an MLA until an election was called the following year.

He became resident representative for the United Nations Development Program in South Korea but died within two months on April 7, 1972.

Dianne Lloyd Norton

FURTHER READING: Koester, C.B. 1976. *The Measure of the Man: Selected Speeches of Woodrow Stanley Lloyd.* Saskatoon: Western Producer Prairie Books; Lloyd, Dianne. 1979. *Woodrow: A Biography of W.S. Lloyd.* Regina: Woodrow Lloyd Memorial Fund.

LLOYDMINSTER.

Lloydminster, pop 20,988 (7,840 in Saskatchewan), is known as the "Border City" as it is located on the Saskatchewan-Alberta border, 251 km east of Edmonton, Alberta and 275 km west of Saskatoon, Saskatchewan. The Lloydminster area was first settled in April 1903 with the arrival of about 2,600 Barr Colonists (*see* BARR COLONY) from England. The "Britannia Settlement," as it was known then, changed its name to Lloydminster to honour colony leader Reverend Lloyd for his efforts in leading the colonists, "minster" meaning "mother church." The newly founded hamlet of Lloydminster was located astride the 4th Meridian in the North-West Territories. When the provinces of Alberta and Saskatchewan were created in 1905, the 4th Meridian was selected as the interprovincial boundary, and Lloydminster was split in two: the Alberta portion of the divided community was incorporated as a village in Alberta on July 6, 1906, while the Saskatchewan portion was incorporated as a town in Saskatchewan in April 1907.

This unique situation resulted in the duplication of all municipal functions: two separate municipal councils, two municipal offices, two fire departments, etc. The two communities were amalgamated into a single municipality, the town of Lloydminster, by an Order-in-Council of both provinces on May 20, 1930. On January 1, 1958, Lloydminster received its charter as the city of Lloydminster, thus becoming the tenth city in both provinces. Lloydminster's rich agricultural soil allows for a variety of crops to be grown in addition to ranching. With the discovery of oil a rapid growth started, and the industry continues to dominate Lloydminster's economic landscape. In 1992 the Bi-Provincial Upgrader petrochemical facility was opened. Industry related to petroleum and manufactured homes, and established bases in the technology and services fields, as well as the growing commercial and industrial sectors, are also important to Lloydminster's economy.

Daria Coneghan

LOCAL HISTORY.

In Saskatchewan ordinary citizens, rather than professional writers or historians, have been collecting, researching, writing and publishing their own local history books about churches, clubs, businesses, rural areas, and towns. An estimated 2,000 local history books have been written and published in the province in the last fifty years. The earliest books and local memoirs were handwritten or typed, with a limited number of copies printed. As printing services grew more sophisticated, so did the histories. Today, a typical book filled with photo reproductions and stories is professionally printed and bound; the high costs involved mean books are actively marketed and sold as fundraising ventures for the organizing bodies. Many book projects started in response to provincial and federal anniversaries, such as the **GOLDEN JUBILEE** of 1955, the national Centennial in 1967, and Celebrate Saskatchewan 1980. Throughout the 1980s, in particular, it was fashionable for a town, village, municipality or ad hoc group of school districts to put together a history book; this tradition has continued, as communities prepare to celebrate Saskatchewan's centennial in 2005.

The style of history books has changed as the province has grown. The earliest histories celebrated the pioneer past. Later, themes such as ethnic and cultural history, Euro-First Nations contact, and regional history have become the norm. Families often contribute their stories, so the books tie local history to genealogy. As communities mature, sequels or updates to past history books are written to include new information or change historical perspectives. Filled with pictures, documents and pertinent artwork, local history books quickly become the community photo album: prized and rare photos of buildings, people, transportation, agriculture, and the natural world are brought together for everyone to own and enjoy, creating a reference archive of the community's visual memory. Perhaps the most interesting aspect of history book publication is the response of the communities, which includes an outpouring of oral history that picks up where the written history leaves off. For this reason, mundane details and controversial or disturbing stories can be left out of the written history, knowing that the oral memory will fill in the details. Communities can then collect this oral regeneration in newspapers, oral history projects, or in sequel histories, continuing the story as time goes by. These books are valuable resources, chronicling the rise (and in some cases, the decline and demise) of communities, families, churches, and businesses large and small across the province. *Merle Massie*

LOCHHEAD, KEN (1926–).

Kenneth Campbell Lochhead was born in Ottawa on May 22, 1926. His major art training was undertaken at the Pennsylvania Academy of Fine Arts in Philadelphia and at the Barnes Foundation in Merion, Pennsylvania. Scholarships allowed him to study in Europe and western Canada. After several short assignments, he was hired by Regina College (forerunner to the **UNIVERSITY OF REGINA**) in 1950 to direct its School of Art. He was also charged with developing what became the Norman **MACKENZIE ART GALLERY**.

Under Lochhead's guidance, both the School and the Gallery flourished, attracting energetic personalities and generating excitement. It was his significant role in the development of the Emma Lake

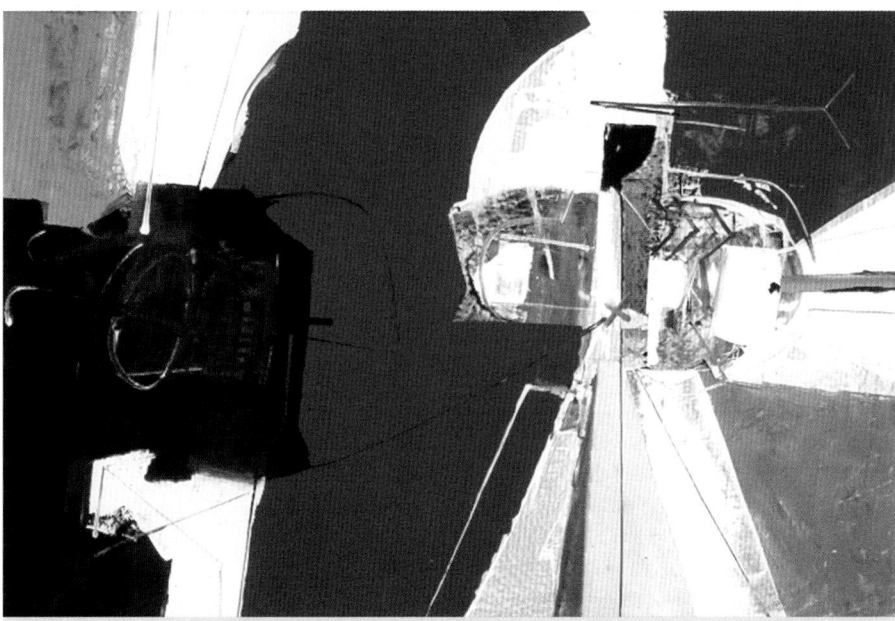

COURTESY OF THE MACKENZIE ART GALLERY 1962-001

Kenneth Lochhead, "Chevron Blue," 1962, enamel on masonite, 121.9 x 182.9 cm, MacKenzie Art Gallery, University of Regina Collection, gift of the MacKenzie Art Gallery Society.

Artists' Workshops, however, that attracted the most attention to the prairie region. While the Emma Lake camp dates from the 1930s, the workshops established a modernist direction. Visitors included such artists as Will Barnett (1957), Barnett Newman (1959), John Ferren (1960), Clement Greenberg (1962), and Jules Olitski (1964). These artists attracted international attention to Regina.

In his own work Lochhead developed a distinctive style, producing such notable works as "The Kite" (1952), "The Dignitary" and "The Bonspiel" (1954). His work was exhibited in numerous solo and group exhibitions in both public and private galleries in Canada and abroad. He began to win major commissions, completing an enormous wall mural at Gander Airport in Newfoundland in 1957–58. Other commissions included art for the Canadian Chancery Building in Warsaw, Poland; the Confederation Centre in Prince Edward Island; and the Centennial Concert Hall in Winnipeg. Then in 1961, with other Regina artists **ART MCKAY**, **RON BLOORE**, **TED GODWIN**, and **DOUG MORTON**, Lochhead displayed his paintings at the National Gallery of Canada. This show, "Five Painters from Regina," placed the Regina arts scene on the national map. In 1964, however, he was the first of the five to leave Regina, accepting a teaching position with the University of Manitoba. In 1973, he went on to York University in Toronto, and finally to the University of Ottawa.

Lochhead has served on many public boards, committees, and organizations throughout his career, including the **WASCANA CENTRE AUTHORITY** in Regina, the Art Gallery of Ontario in Toronto, and the National Capital Commission in Ottawa. He was awarded the Order of Canada in 1971 and an honorary degree from the University of Regina in 2001.
Mark Vajcner

FURTHER READING: MacDonald, C.S. 1991. *A Dictionary of Canadian Artists*. Ottawa: Canadian Paperbacks; Marzolf, H. 1988. *Kenneth Lochhead: Abstract Paintings, 1962–1967*. Regina: Dunlop Art Gallery.

LOHANS, ALISON (1949–).

Alison Lohans was born on July 13, 1949, in Reedley, California. She was first published when she was 12. She attended university at California State until 1971, receiving her BA in Music Education, and then immigrated to Canada. She attended the University of Victoria, where she received her postgraduate diploma in Elementary Education. She moved to Regina in 1976 and taught beginning band for three years, then left

PHOTO COURTESY OF ALISON LOHANS

Alison Lohans.

teaching to concentrate on writing. She has been a writing instructor for University of Regina Extension and for the **SASKATCHEWAN WRITERS GUILD**; she also has a number of private students. She received her MEd from the **UNIVERSITY OF REGINA** in 2002. Her first picture book was *Nathaniel's Violin*, for which she also wrote a musical score for young string players. She has published thirteen books for children and young adults, as well as numerous short pieces for adults and children, consisting of fiction, non-fiction articles, poetry, book reviews, and academic works. She has received many awards for her writing, including the Saskatchewan Young Readers' Choice Award, and she was short-listed for Book of the Year at the **SASKATCHEWAN BOOK AWARDS**.

Daralyne Fauser

LONGMAN, MARY (1964–). Mary Longman (Aski-piyesiwishwew), a Saulteaux, was born in Fort Qu'Appelle in 1964. She studied at the Emily Carr Institute of Art and Design, Concordia University, and at the Nova Scotia College of Art and Design, where she graduated with an MFA in 1993. Longman then pursued doctoral studies at the University of British Columbia, where she specialized in contemporary First Nations art in Canada. Her two- and three-dimensional work explores issues concerning suicide, adoption, the AIDS crisis, and land claims. Longman has shown her art in a number of group and solo shows including *Reservation X* at the Canadian Museum of Civilization in 1998, and *Saskdiaspora* at the Dunlop Gallery in 1999. She is the recipient of several awards, including a Canada Council award and a Canadian Native Arts Foundation Award.

Carmen Robertson

LONGMORE, ROSALEE (1952–). Rosalee Longmore was born on August 5, 1952 and grew up on a family farm at a time when many communities had their own hospitals, which provided a wide range of services. Her father being chronically ill, the family had to relocate to Saskatoon, where he died waiting for a kidney transplant. It was this experience that caused Longmore to pursue a career in nursing. After graduating from high school in Weyburn, she attended nursing school in Regina and in 1976 graduated as a registered nurse. She became an active member of the **SASKATCHEWAN UNION OF NURSES** (SUN) Local 66, where she served as vice-president, president, and member of the negotiating committee.

In 1984, Longmore held her first position on the SUN Board of Directors as the representative for long-term care nurses. She has been on the SUN Board ever since, and became president in May 1998. As SUN president she also serves as vice-president of the **SASKATCHEWAN FEDERATION OF LABOUR** and on the Executive Board of the Canadian

Federation of Nurses. Longmore is also chairperson of the Board of Directors of the Canadian Centre for Policy Alternatives, Saskatchewan Office, a left-wing research and policy think tank; a member of the campaign cabinet of the United Way of Regina; an active member of nursing regulatory agencies and government committees; and an executive member of the Regina Figure Skating Club and the Queen City Soccer Association.

One of the highlights of her career was in 1999, when she led 8,400 registered nurses and psychiatric nurses on strike. They were seeking pay equity with federal nurses, and protesting against increased workloads and overtime. Six hours after they hit the picket lines, the provincial government pushed through legislation ordering nurses back to work. Soon after Bill 23 was passed, thousands of SUN members from around the province held a rally in Regina. Nurses regarded the legislation as a direct attack on all organized workers because it restricted the right to free collective bargaining and the right to strike. SUN members unanimously defied the legislation, calling it an unjust law. A few days later the employers applied for and received a court injunction requiring SUN leaders to order their members back to work. SUN refused to obey the injunction. On April 19, the provincial government, the employers and SUN signed a Memorandum of Understanding outlining a framework for agreement, and nurses went back to work. However, the union remained changed forever by the events of 1999. (*See also* **SASKATCHEWAN UNION OF NURSES STRIKE**)

George Manz

LOONS. Loons (Family Gaviidae) are medium to large fish-eating birds with straight dagger-like bills that capture prey by underwater pursuit. Their long bodies, with legs set far back, make locomotion on land difficult. Immature and non-breeding plumages are similar in all loon species; identification thus requires careful attention to the exact pattern of head and neck. Loons nest on the banks of lakes and ponds, and overwinter on open water.

Globally, there are five species of loons; four have been recorded in Saskatchewan. The common loon (*Gavia immer*) is the one most commonly seen and heard in Saskatchewan. It is known for "loon's laughter," and is a common summer resident in lakes of northern Saskatchewan and the Aspen Parkland. It has a glossy black head and throat, a broken white neck collar, a stout, straight black bill, red-brown eyes, and a checkered black and white back. It requires disturbance-free conditions for successful nesting, and 18 m of water surface for flight take-off. The smaller red-throated loon (*G. stellata*) is a summer resident of the subarctic and northern boreal ecoregions in Saskatchewan, and a rare spring and fall transient in southern Saskatchewan. It has a gray head and neck, a dark

COURTESY OF TOURISM SASKATCHEWAN
Northern or common loon.

and slender upturned bill, a dull red patch on the foreneck and thin black stripes on the hindneck, and a medium-gray back with small spots. The Pacific loon (*G. pacifica*), an uncommon summer visitant to **LAKE ATHABASCA**, is a very rare spring transient and an uncommon fall transient in southern Saskatchewan. It has a dark slender bill, and pale gray nape, head and hindneck; the sides of its neck are black with white stripes; and the back is black, with rows of large white spots. The yellow-billed loon (*G. adamsii*) is a rare straggler species in Saskatchewan; it is very similar to the common loon, but is slightly larger and has a yellow-to-ivory bill.

Robert Warnock

FURTHER READING: Alsop, Fred J., III. 2002. *Birds of Canada*. New York: Dorling Kindersley.

LORCH SNOWPLANE. Named after its creator, the Lorch Snowplane changed winter transportation in Saskatchewan. Karl Lorch, when growing up in rural Saskatchewan in the 1920s, realized roads were virtually impassable during the winter months. His first experiments involved a makeshift snow machine with skis on the front and chained wheels on the back. After several more experiments, he developed a design that included a propeller-driven body consisting of the lightweight tubular steel frame, covered with cloth (linen) sheathing, favoured by aircraft manufacturers of the time.This creation involved all members of Lorch's family. The men welded the frame in the family-owned Ford garage, and Lorch's mother and sister installed the hand-sewn linen over the frame. They then sewed a flannelette lining to cover the snowplane's interior. The propellers were made of birch and walnut, and

SASKATCHEWAN ARCHIVES BOARD R-A20714-1
Lorch Snowplane, 1934 and 1935 models.

were pressed in an old book-press in the family home. The runners were constructed of white oak, and the curved fronts were made by soaking the boards in hot water on the kitchen stove, bending them in a specially-made press and drying them over the living-room register.

In later years, Lorch began full-scale production of the snowplanes in a heated building behind his father's garage. Eventually his production staff grew to twenty, as the demand for snowplanes increased throughout the Canadian prairies. A branch plant to build snowplanes for the United States mail carrier market was also established at Wolford, North Dakota. Production of Lorch snowplanes ceased in 1955 after the introduction of rotary snowploughs made roads more passable. By then, Lorch had manufactured more than 600 Lorch snowplanes. The contributions made by the Lorch Snowplane to the lives of hundreds of North Americans are impressive: doctors were able to visit their patients quickly; mail was delivered faster; school teachers could get to their country schools; and the Royal Canadian Mounted Police, armed forces, geologists, and many other important contributors to the social and economic well-being of Saskatchewan were able to provide their services in a timely and efficient manner.

Wayne Lorch

LUCAS, LOUISE (1885–1945). Louise Lucas (*née* Nachweih), known as the Mother of the CCF (CO-OPERATIVE COMMONWEALTH FEDERATION), worked to advance Saskatchewan farmers, especially farm women. Born in Chicago in 1885, the daughter of German immigrants, Louise Lucas and husband Henry immigrated to Milestone in 1911. They settled at Mazenod in 1920. Considering herself an equal partner on the farm, she became interested in the co-operative ideas of the farm movement and joined the local women's lodge of the United Farmers of Canada (UFC), Saskatchewan

Section. Elected a director in 1930, she became president of the UFC Women's Section from 1931 to 1933. In summer 1932, Lucas helped form the Saskatchewan Farmer-Labour Group and participated in the Calgary conference where the CCF was born. In 1933, at its first national convention, she introduced the health services section of the REGINA MANIFESTO. Lucas was a popular speaker in German as well as English. Despite her duties as a farmer and mother of six, she constantly toured Saskatchewan, spreading her message of co-operation, women's rights, and social justice. She served on CCF national and provincial councils, and ran—unsuccessfully—in the federal elections of 1935 (Battlefords constituency) and 1940 (Melville). She continued organizing in Melville until 1943, when she was nominated again; illness then forced her to withdraw. She died on October 17, 1945. Louise Lucas was inducted into the Saskatchewan Agricultural Hall of Fame in 1973.

Fay Hutchinson

FURTHER READING: Wright, J.F.C. 1965. *The Louise Lucas Story: This Time Tomorrow*. Montreal: Harvest House.

LUCKY MAN CREE FIRST NATION. The River People (included Chief BIG BEAR and Chief Little Pine) remained outside of treaty until Lucky Man (Papaway), as a headman in Chief Big Bear's Band, and Chief Minahikosis (Little Pine) adhered to TREATY 6 at Fort Walsh in 1879. Lucky Man requested to locate near Battleford, and was escorted there in 1883. In 1884 the chief requested a reserve adjacent to POUNDMAKER, Little Pine and BIG BEAR; but the federal government refused, fearing complications from the joint association of the bands. The 1885 Resistance scattered most of the Lucky Man and Little Pine people; those who remained settled on Little Pine's Reserve. By 1919 the Lucky Man Band had been reduced to nine persons. Research by

Rod King in 1972 initiated a claim that culminated in the selection of twelve sections of land in the Thickwood Hills by the band (1989). In 1994 the band opened the possibility of a claim for additional land, compensation for loss of land use, and failure to deliver treaty benefits; but this has not been settled. The band's chief and council have investigated numerous business ventures including bison and elk farming, investments in condominium projects, and gas and oil ventures; they currently have plans for a year-round eco-tourism facility that would employ most of their 86 band members, two of whom currently live on the 3,078.6- ha reserve, located 60 km east of North Battleford.

Christian Thompson

LUMSDEN, town, pop 1,581, located in the Qu'Appelle Valley, 25 km NW of Regina at the junction of Hwys 11 and 20. The first settlers arrived in 1881 and the area came to be colloquially known as Happy Hollow. In 1889, the Qu'Appelle, Long Lake, and Saskatchewan Railway came through the site of today's community en route to Saskatoon and Prince Albert, and the name Happy Hollow was changed to honour Hugh Lumsden, a senior engineer with the railroad. Thomas Hill opened a general store and had a post office at Lumsden in 1892, and a blacksmith shop and an implement agency were soon established. Other businesses followed. Grain elevators were erected—the first run by horse-power—and, in 1897, Lumsden had its first doctor. The first newspaper began publishing in 1900 and, in 1904, a flour mill was opened, which did a thriving business until it burned down in the 1920s. Lumsden attained town status on March 15, 1905. After the boom period prior to WORLD WAR I, Lumsden's population settled at around 500 and the community functioned primarily as a thriving farm service centre until the mid-1960s. With the construction of the four-lane divided highway through the valley early in the decade, people who worked in Regina began to establish homes in the community. Artists were attracted to Lumsden's quiet country lifestyle and picturesque setting, and city dwellers came to frequent the area's developing market gardens. The community, however, was beset regularly by floodwaters (major floods occurred in 1892, 1904, 1916, 1948, and 1969) and, in 1974, the highest water levels in the town's history were recorded. Schoolchildren from Regina came to help with the sandbagging. The town subsequently undertook the development of a major flood protection project, straightening the river's channel and building substantial dikes. This marked the beginning of a period of major population growth. Today, although town businesses, schools, administrative positions, and health care facilities provide a base of local employment, Lumsden is increasingly becoming a bedroom community for commuters to Regina.

David McLennan

LUSELAND, town, pop 602, located in the west-central region of the province, between the town of Kerrobert and the Saskatchewan-Alberta border on Hwy 31. Settlers began arriving in the district in the spring of 1906, with more coming the subsequent year. It was in the following years, however, that the district came to be substantially settled. The Luse Land and Development Co. of St. Paul, Minnesota, acquired 100,000 acres of land in the area and successfully attracted large numbers of German settlers from the mid-western United States. The CPR was building its line through the district in 1910 and, on December 10 that year, Luseland (name derivation apparent) was incorporated as a village. Developing as a service centre for the surrounding farming district, Luseland grew steadily, attaining town status on January 1, 1954. Through the 1950s and the 1960s the community grew substantially as rural populations shifted to urban centres and the development of the **OIL AND GAS** industry in the area boosted and diversified the economy. By 1966, Luseland had a population of 826. From 1953 to 1965 the number of homes in the community rose from 160 to 300 and, during the same period, the town was modernized with streets paved and sewer and water systems installed. Today, Luseland has a variety of businesses and services, recreational facilities and groups involved with sport, artistic and cultural activities. The Luseland Social Community Hall and Theatre, built in 1920, has been designated a heritage property, and for 85 years the dual-function facility has been a centre of community activity. One of Canada's most successful businessmen, billionaire Jimmy Pattison, originally hails from Luseland. When the community needed financial assistance to construct a motel, Pattison contributed $100,000 to the project and returned to Luseland for the official ribbon-cutting ceremony. Agriculture continues to dominate the area economy and consists of both crop and cattle production. The first modern concrete grain terminal built in the province by the **SASKATCHEWAN WHEAT POOL** was constructed in Luseland in the late 1980s and, at the time, it was the largest facility of its kind in western Canada. The oil and gas industry continues to gain in importance in the region, and five pipelines now run through the district. *David McLennan*

LUTHER COLLEGE, UNIVERSITY OF REGINA. Luther College's university campus in Regina teaches courses for degrees in Arts, Fine Arts, and Science. The College also offers a residence for 225 students, an active extra-curricular program including chaplaincy, and special events for the wider community. Founded in 1913 as Luther Academy in Melville, the school was sponsored by German Lutherans who brought teachers from the United States, offering an academic oasis for the children of prairie settlers. The educational philosophy was from Lutheran schools in the United States, which blended the German models of universities and "folk schools." Luther College thus emphasizes high-quality classroom teaching, the cultivation of leadership through extra-curricular involvement, and participation in a supportive community. In 1926 Luther College moved to Regina, offering the full high school curriculum plus the first year of university and attracting students from a broad religious and ethnic spectrum. Although the student body is no longer predominantly Lutheran, the College defines itself as a contribution from the Lutheran church to the wider community; it maintains a Lutheran and Christian identity while welcoming and supporting students from all faith backgrounds.

In the 1930s Luther initiated co-operation with Regina College, whereby its faculty provided courses at Regina College while Regina College faculty came to Luther to offer their subjects. When plans were made for Regina College to become the **UNIVERSITY OF REGINA**, Luther was invited to join this venture as a federated college. It opened its new school on the university campus in 1971 while continuing to operate its high school on Royal Street. Federation allows the College to retain its administrative, financial, and philosophical independence from the University while its students enjoy full academic integration with the University and the other federated colleges. Luther has a seat on the University of Regina Senate, which gives it a voice in shaping the overall curriculum at the University of Regina. Luther College believes that intellectual growth needs to be accompanied by spiritual, moral, and ethical growth. The University's mandate to the federated colleges is to assist it in reflecting on values. The colleges bring a diversity of students, faculty, and educational philosophies to the University community, as well as history, tradition, and heritage. A Luther graduate, **HENRY TAUBE**, is the only Saskatchewan-educated recipient of a Nobel Prize, and several alumni have been winners of the Rhodes Scholarship. Luther College today has about 11,000 alumni in 24 countries all over the world. *Richard Holdern*

LUTHERAN CHURCH-CANADA, CENTRAL DISTRICT. Lutheran Church-Canada, otherwise known as the LC-C, is a national Lutheran Church autonomously organized in 1988. Rev. Edwin Lehman was elected as the first national president, and Winnipeg was selected as the site for the national office. The Church body is divided into three "Districts": the Alberta-British Columbia District, which includes a few congregations bordering the western edge of Saskatchewan; the East District, which includes Ontario (with the exception of northwestern Ontario), Quebec, and the Atlantic provinces; and the Central District, formerly named Manitoba-Saskatchewan District, which is comprised of Saskatchewan, Manitoba, and northwestern Ontario to the Manitouwadge/Marathon area on the north shore of Lake Superior. The Central District office is located in Regina. Rev. Roy K. Holm was first elected district president. It was at this time of autonomy that the pastors and congregations in northwestern Ontario, who belonged to the Minnesota North District of the Missouri Synod, took the opportunity to join LC-C and became part of the Central District.

Following the American Revolution, United Empire Loyalists relocated to Upper Canada, Lower Canada, and the Maritimes. There was a second Lutheran emigration from New York State to Ontario in 1793. As changes occurred in early 19th-century Europe in the Prussian Union, and later in Russia and the Austro-Hungarian Empire, the privileges initially granted to the Germans were being eroded and the large German families were pressed into seeking land elsewhere. The transfer of Rupert's Land to the newly confederated nation of Canada paved the way for settlers to begin to flow into western Canada. To this end, the Canadian government conducted advertising campaigns in Europe, and many Germans sold their belongings and moved to the New World. Later, after each of the two World Wars, large numbers of Lutherans immigrated to Canada.

Lutheran Church-Canada remains in partnership with the Lutheran Church-Missouri Synod (LCMS) and is a member of the International Lutheran Council (ILC). Until the establishment of Canadian seminaries pastors were trained in the United States–either at Concordia Seminary in St. Louis, Missouri, or at Concordia Lutheran Theological Seminary in Fort Wayne, Indiana–and assigned to congregations in Canada. Lutheran Church-Canada has two seminaries: Concordia Lutheran Theological Seminary, St. Catharines, Ontario; and Concordia Lutheran Seminary, Edmonton, Alberta. Concordia University College of Alberta, established in Edmonton in 1921, is an accredited post-secondary institution. As early as 1879, the Lutherans at Town Berlin (Ossowo), Manitoba, not far from Portage la Prairie, were served intermittently by visiting pastors from Minnesota. The first resident missionary of the Lutheran Church-Missouri Synod, Rev. Herman Buegel, was sent to Winnipeg in 1891. By 1900, congregations were planted in Winnipeg, in the settlements north of Langenburg (Landestreu, Hoffenthal, Beresina), in Arat (Frankslake), and in Neudorf. As homesteaders continued settling the west, Lutheran congregations were established. When the Manitoba-Saskatchewan District was formed in 1922, there were seventy-five congregations and sixty-nine preaching stations. Rev. Paul E. Wiegner was elected as its first president.

The depression of the 1930s and the war years

of the 1940s had a pronounced effect on the congregations and ultimately the District. In the 1950s the massive shift of population from country to city accelerated, and new missions were opened to reflect the movement of the rural population into neighbouring small towns and urban cities. Throughout the decades the District carried through the various programs being produced by the Missouri Synod. Christian education, Sunday schools, vacation Bible schools, Bible classes, and in some areas parochial schools played a large role in these programs. Canadian Lutheran World Relief (CLWR), a co-operative Lutheran service organization, was established in 1946 to provide used goods for overseas shipment. CLWR continues to provide services and programs overseas, and is supported by the members of Lutheran congregations. A number of individuals from the District have entered the foreign mission field over the years–some as missionaries, others as educators, still others in their particular capacity in the mission field. In 2004 LC-C was working in three countries and also supporting projects in sister churches. At the close of 2003 the District had 102 congregations; membership in these congregations was 22,473 baptized and 16,105 communicant members. *Maxine Holm*

LUTHERAN THEOLOGICAL SEMINARY. The Lutheran Theological Seminary (LTS) was established in 1965. It came into being by the amalgamation of two prior seminaries, the Lutheran College and Seminary and Luther Seminary. When founded, it became an affiliated college of the UNIVERSITY OF SASKATCHEWAN and moved to the University campus in 1969. At the time it was established, it was the official seminary of the Lutheran Church of America and the Evangelical Lutheran Church of Canada. In 1986 these two churches were amalgamated into the EVANGELICAL LUTHERAN CHURCH IN CANADA. At that time LTS came under the control of the four

Western synods of that Church. From 1973 to 1984 the Lutheran Church Missouri Synod co-operated with LTS, providing a professor for the faculty and ordaining graduates. This was the only seminary in North America in which all three of the major Lutheran churches did co-operate. During those years there were hopeful negotiations aimed at merging the three Lutheran churches. When these negotiations broke down, the Missouri Synod withdrew from LTS.

In 1977, LTS became fully accredited by the Association of Theological Schools in the United States and Canada. At that time it was one of two seminaries in western Canada that had full accreditation. From its beginning, LTS co-operated with the other seminaries in Saskatoon; an arrangement was made with Central Pentecostal College, whereby the students who qualified could earn the MDiv degree from LTS. The co-operation with St. Andrew's College and Emmanuel St. Chad developed into the Saskatoon Theological Union. This union shares classes, has a common computerized catalogue of all three libraries, and publishes a common catalogue. *William Hordern*

LUTHI, ERNEST (1906–83). A very popular painter of agrarian Saskatchewan scenes, Ernest Luthi was born in Zeebach, Switzerland. His family immigrated to a homestead near Punnichy, Saskatchewan in 1914. After completing grade school in 1921, he worked on the railroad, later simultaneously taking correspondence classes in illustration from the Washington School of Art. Luthi then spent two years taking night classes at the Art Institute of Pittsburgh, Pennsylvania, receiving his diploma in 1928. Returning to Saskatchewan, he worked as a sign painter, a house painter, and a carpenter to support his art practice; and in 1951 he began painting full-time because of ill health.

Employing the typical prairie landscape paradigm that he in part helped popularize, Luthi's landscapes most often depict a vast uninterrupted expanse of land beneath an equally vast expanse of open sky. Rarely referring to a nature that is wild or distant, but rather one present, shaped and "shared" by mankind–from quaint homesteads tucked into the corner of an image behind a snowy clump of bush, to a line of monumental red and green grain elevators tracing the edge of the distant horizon just beyond freshly tilled fields, to a tiny church bathed in clear light and nestled in a valley–his work implies a calm sympathy between farmers and the bountiful nature they occupy. Depicting a peaceful rural world at various times of the year, Luthi links human processes to nature's seasonal cycles, constructing thus an arcadian vision in which man and nature are in absolute harmony.

While Luthi's subjects and simple compositions are often associated with nostalgic Folk Art, his formal art education precludes this categorization. Employing a sophisticated knowledge of light, perspective and colour, his watercolours and oil paintings are more rightly labeled naturalistic–representing the world as it is seen. Indeed, he utilized descriptive resource materials from which to make his paintings, including magazine images as well as his own photographs and pencil or pastel sketchbook drawings.

With neither cynicism nor disruptive worldly affairs disturbing the calm surface of his work, Luthi's paintings have been broadly collected. His work is included in Saskatchewan's major public and corporate collections as well as in numerous private collections. In recognition of his contribution to the visual arts in the province, he was awarded an Honorary Doctor of Laws degree from the University of Regina in 1975. *Jack Anderson*

LYONS, CLARENCE (1916–2004). Clarence Lyons, born on February 22, 1916, began work in 1939 at Burns Foods in Regina, where he spent about twelve years. During that time, he became active in the union later known as the United Packing Workers of America (UPWA), Local 226. He served as president of the local for several years before becoming a full-time union staff representative. In 1951, Lyons was hired as a full-time international representative for the UPWA International Union, a position he held until his retirement in 1984. He served the labour movement as an officer of the SASKATCHEWAN FEDERATION OF LABOUR, in the provincial CCF/NDP, in various Canadian Labour Congress committees, and as a member of the Saskatchewan Labour Relations Board. He was also the first president of the Saskatoon Community Clinic Board. Lyons and his wife Mabel were married for 64 years. He died in April 2004. *Clare Powell*

UNIVERSITY OF SASKATCHEWAN ARCHIVES A-508

Lutheran Theological Seminary, Saskatoon.

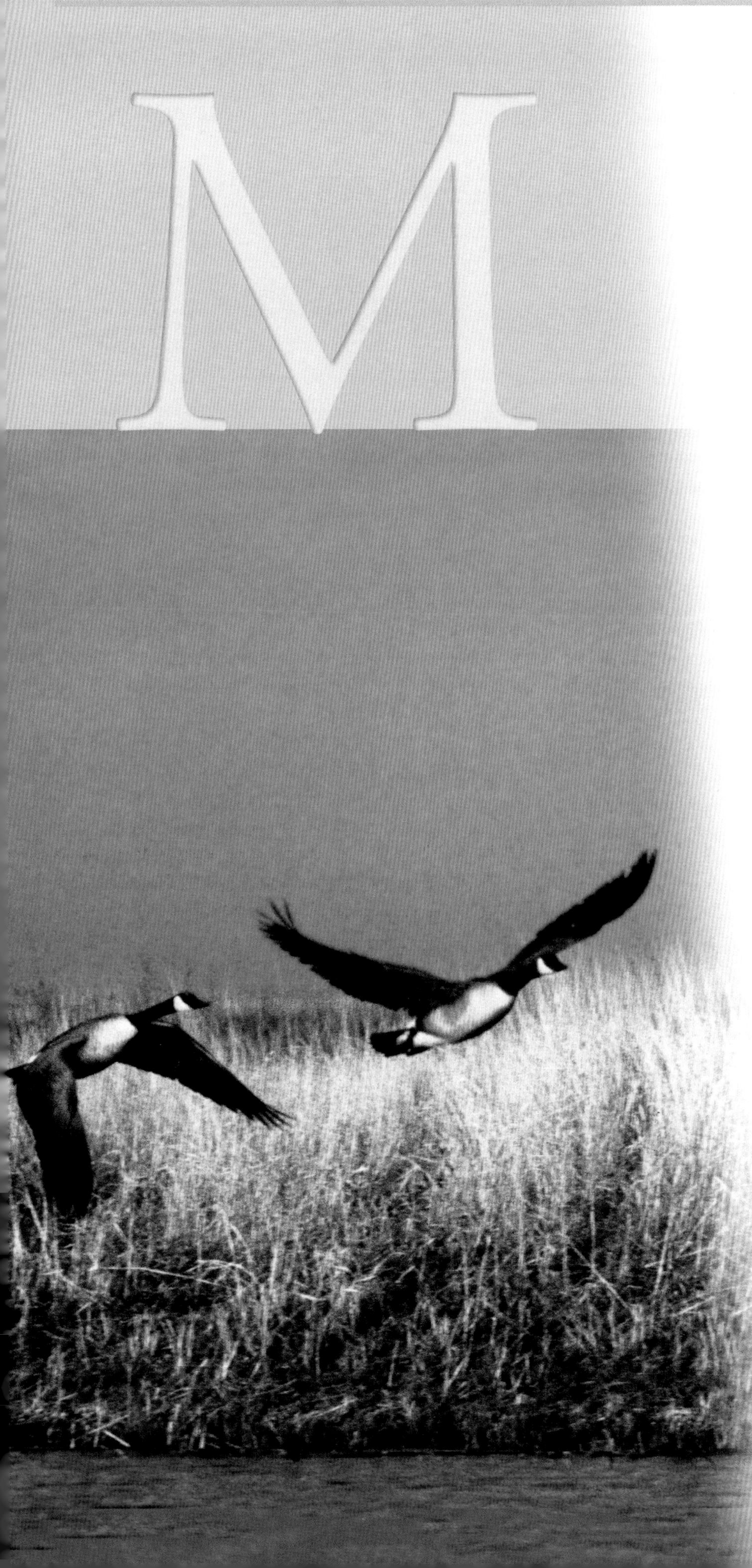

M

MACEWAN, GRANT (1902–2000). Popular historian, teacher, and highly regarded counsellor to prairie farmers, J.W. (John Walter) Grant MacEwan was born on a farm near Brandon, Manitoba on August 12, 1902. The MacEwan family moved to the Melfort district in Saskatchewan in 1915. MacEwan obtained a BSc in Agriculture at the Ontario Agricultural College in Guelph, and in 1928 obtained his Master's in Animal Science from the University of Iowa. That same year he began teaching at the **UNIVERSITY OF SASKATCHEWAN** in Animal Science, and soon became a popular livestock judge at shows and fairs across Saskatchewan. He was also in demand as a speaker and demonstrator of farming techniques, particularly in livestock: it is estimated that he talked to 40,000 people in one five-week period on the Better Farming Train that criss-crossed the province. During the 1930s his research showed it was possible to feed cattle on Russian thistle when all other forms of forage had died due to drought.

MacEwan also began writing books with fellow professor A.H. Ewen on animal husbandry, on general agriculture, and on breeds of farm animals. These became texts for universities and for farmers. Later, he launched out on his own writing history: his colourful prose made him a best-selling author with over fifty-five titles to his credit. In 1948

Grant MacEwen, ca. 1935.

MacEwan moved to Manitoba to become Dean of Agriculture and Home Economics at the University of Manitoba. He returned to Saskatchewan for a few months in 1952 to serve as agricultural editor of the *Western Producer*. Throughout his career in Winnipeg, Calgary and Edmonton, he maintained contact with agriculture in Saskatchewan. He was a popular choice as a livestock judge, for demonstrations, and for speaking engagements. In Alberta he worked first with the Canadian Council of Beef Producers, later as alderman and mayor of Calgary, as member of the Alberta Legislature, and as Lieutenant-Governor of Alberta. MacEwan was awarded honorary doctorate degrees from six universities, including the University of Saskatchewan. He died on June 16, 2000, in Calgary.

FURTHER READING: Macdonald, R.H. 1997. *Grant MacEwan: No Ordinary Man*. Saskatoon: Western Producer Prairie Books; MacEwan, G. 1990. *Grant MacEwan's West: Sketches from the Past*. Saskatoon: Western Producer Prairie Books.

MACKAY, ANGUS (1840–1931).

Angus MacKay was the first superintendent of the Indian Head Experimental Farm. Born January 3, 1840 in Pickering Township, Upper Canada, he received his education at a grammar school in Whitby. He married Elizabeth Gunn and they raised four children. In 1866 he was a lieutenant in the 34th Regiment of Fort Erie at the time of the Fenian raid. The son of a farmer, and a farmer himself, MacKay moved west in 1882 with three companions. Arriving at Indian Head, the four men took up homesteads which they farmed co-operatively. In December 1886 and October 1887, he accompanied Dr. William Saunders, the first director of the Experimental Farms Service, on his two western visits and assisted in choosing the land for the first Dominion experimental farm in the North-West Territories. During 1887, MacKay spent some time at the newly established Central Experimental Farm in Ottawa to become aware of the aims and expectations of the future experimental farm. His appointment as superintendent was made in late 1887.

To meet the needs of new settlers for accurate information on the best crop varieties to grow and animal breeds to raise under the harsh prairie conditions, he initiated long-term studies with field crops, animal husbandry and horticulture. In this capacity, he had a profound influence on the development of agriculture in the west. He also stressed summer fallowing as a means of raising crops successfully in drought years. A major facet of Angus MacKay's extension work was his cherished correspondence. In 1894 he listed 1,770 letters received and 2,448 dispatched; by 1905 the respective figures had increased to 7,820 and 7,874.

Angus MacKay was a member of the advisory

SASKATCHEWAN ARCHIVES BOARD R-A6805
Angus MacKay.

council in agriculture of the UNIVERSITY OF SASKATCHEWAN and in 1922, in recognition for his work in agriculture, the university conferred upon him the degree of Doctor of Laws. Upon his retirement in 1913, the government retained his services in an advisory capacity as Inspector of Western Farms, a position he held until his death at Indian Head on June 10, 1931. *Allan Smith*

FURTHER READING: Johnson, W.E. and A.E. Smith. 1986. *Indian Head Experimental Farm 1886–1986*. Research Branch Agriculture Canada Historical Series No. 23; Rossie, D.E. 1984. *Indian Head: History of Indian Head and District*. Regina: Brigdens Photo Graphics.

MACKAY, HAROLD (1940–).

An expert in the country's legal, business, and financial sectors, Harold MacKay was born in Regina on August 1, 1940, and received his early education at Weyburn Collegiate Institute. He earned his BA from the UNIVERSITY OF SASKATCHEWAN in 1960 and his LLB from Dalhousie University three years later. In addition to practicing as a lawyer, MacKay chaired the Federal Business Development Bank from 1981 to 1985 and the Task Force on the Future of the Canadian Financial Services Sector in 1998. Provincially, he served as special representative to Saskatchewan's Minister of Post-Secondary Education and as chair of the SASKATCHEWAN INSTITUTE OF PUBLIC POLICY. Recognized as an astute and unwavering leader, Harold MacKay was made an Officer of the Order of Canada in 2002.

MACKENZIE, CHALMERS JACK (1888–1984).

Born at St. Stephen, New Brunswick on July 10, 1888, Mackenzie was educated as a civil engineer at Dalhousie and Harvard. After service in WORLD WAR I, he came to the UNIVERSITY OF SASKATCHEWAN as Dean of Engineering in 1921, and

REGINA LEADER-POST
Chalmers Jack Mackenzie.

continued in this post until 1939. His research concentrated on the protection of concrete from erosion by the alkaline soils of southern Saskatchewan. This was a significant contribution to the building of the province because it had been discovered that the concrete then used was subject to rapid deterioration in the prairie soils. His research led to his being commissioned to design and build, with his students, major central bridges in Saskatoon. He joined the National Research Council in 1935, becoming acting president in 1939 thorough 1944, then president from 1944 to 1952. At the same time he served on the Atomic Energy Control Board, of which he was president from 1948 to 1961.

Mackenzie was a senior scientific administrator and government advisor at the national level at a time—the end of WORLD WAR II, the beginning of the atomic age, and the Sputnik era—when science policy and research activities became increasingly important for the country. His promotion of university and industrial research in a wide range of fields changed the face of Canadian research and the nature of the Canadian universities. His efforts were recognized by many awards, including membership in the Royal Society of London, the Royal Society of Canada, and the Order of Canada. He died in Ottawa on February 26, 1984. *Diane Secoy*

MACKENZIE ART GALLERY.

Located in Regina's Wascana Centre, the MacKenzie Art Gallery (formerly the Norman Mackenzie Art Gallery) is Saskatchewan's largest public art gallery with a collection of more than 3,500 art works and over 2,000 m² of exhibition space. The gallery owes its existence to the vision of Norman MacKenzie, KC, a notable Regina lawyer who built a substantial collection of Old Master drawings and paintings, contemporary Saskatchewan and Canadian art, and antiquities during the three decades before his death in 1936.

MacKenzie Art Gallery.

In his will, MacKenzie left much of his collection along with a portion of his estate to the **UNIVERSITY OF SASKATCHEWAN**, with the intention that a gallery be established in Regina. In 1953, under the direction of Dr. **WILLIAM A. RIDDELL**, Dean of **REGINA COLLEGE**, the first phase of the gallery was built on the college grounds. This facility soon proved inadequate, and a Massey Medal-nominated addition was constructed in 1957 to house an expanded gallery and the college's School of Art. In 1985, the MacKenzie made the transition from a university to a public art gallery by incorporating as a public, non-profit corporation governed by a board with

Augustus Kenderdine, "Portrait of Norman MacKenzie, K.C.," no date, oil on canvas, 61 x 50.5 cm, MacKenzie Art Gallery, University of Regina Collection, gift of Mr. Norman MacKenzie.

representation from the city, the **UNIVERSITY OF REGINA**, and the membership of the gallery. In 1990, after a vigorous public debate about the future of the gallery, including a city plebiscite which rejected plans for a new building adjoining the **ROYAL SASKATCHEWAN MUSEUM**, the gallery moved into its current home in the west wing of the provincial government's T.C. Douglas building. Through the years, the MacKenzie Art Gallery has developed a strong relationship to the artists and public of Saskatchewan, as well as a solid reputation among Canadian art galleries.

The gallery's first director, Richard Simmins (1953–57), raised the institution's profile locally through public programs and media exposure, and by supplementing borrowed exhibitions with shows of local and regional artists. Simmins' successor, **RONALD BLOORE** (1958–66), followed this pattern, but in addition brought the gallery to national attention through a series of notable, and sometimes notorious, exhibitions, including a 1960 hoax featuring the fictitious artist Win Hedore and the first exhibition of the **REGINA FIVE** (Ronald Bloore, **TED GODWIN**, **KENNETH LOCHHEAD**, **ARTHUR MCKAY**, **DOUGLAS MORTON**). A growing professionalism and an expansion of staff and resources have marked the tenure of Bloore's successors: Nancy Dillow (1967–78), Carol Phillips (1979–85), Andrew Oko (1986–95), and Kate Davis (1997–). The exhibition program has been developed on a balanced model with a mix of regional, national, and international art from historical and contemporary periods. Among the achievements have been major exhibitions of European and American artists, such as the critically acclaimed survey of international sculp-

ture, *Space Invaders* (1985). Other exhibitions have focussed on contemporary developments in Canadian art, including early solo shows of artists who have gone on to international success (e.g., Guido Molinari, **MARILYN LEVINE**, Jana Sterbak). Exhibitions of Saskatchewan artists have been central to the program, whether introducing emerging artists or offering retrospective views of artists with a national profile (e.g., Arthur McKay, **VICTOR CICANSKY**, **ALLEN SAPP**). Similarly, the collection includes a representative survey of contemporary and historical Canadian art, with a focus on the art of Saskatchewan and western Canada. Special collections include a survey of early modern European works on paper, Saskatchewan folk art, contemporary Canadian photography, and contemporary First Nations art.

Unique among the achievements of the gallery has been its leadership in presenting Aboriginal art and artists. In 1975, the MacKenzie was the first public art gallery in Canada to present traditional First Nations objects as fine art in the exhibition *100 Years of Saskatchewan Indian Art 1830–1930*, curated by Saskatchewan Métis artist **BOB BOYER**. In 1982, the MacKenzie presented the first major exhibition of contemporary First Nations art in Canada, *New Work by a New Generation*, curated by Aboriginal artist Robert Houle. In 1998, the MacKenzie hired Lee-Ann Martin, the first Aboriginal curator to serve as the Head Curator of a mainstream Canadian art institution. While critical relevance and usefulness as a teaching resource have been ongoing goals, the directors and staff have been careful to counteract the prevalent assumption that art galleries are elitist institutions. Consequently, exhibitions with serious art/historical significance or addressing difficult contemporary issues have been complemented by events with broad public appeal, such as the annual craft festival, Bazaart. Furthermore, since the 1960s, art education has been an important component of the gallery's activity. Programs such as the Travelling Art Program, school tours involving a multi-disciplinary approach, and MacKenzie Outreach, an extension program through which a gallery educator takes art exhibitions into smaller communities across the province, have served as models for other Canadian galleries. In the 1990s, the MacKenzie initiated Urban Outreach, an innovative program which extends art education to inner city schools and local First Nations Reserves. As a result of its commitment to the community, the gallery has seen its attendance rise to 100,000 visitors per year and its position established as one of Saskatchewan's most significant cultural institutions. *Timothy Long*

FURTHER READING: Riddell, W.A. 1990. *The Mackenzie Art Gallery: Norman Mackenzie's Legacy.* Regina: Mackenzie Art Gallery.

TUAN NGUYEN/REGINA LEADER-POST

Pat Totten, then director of the MacKenzie Infant Care Centre, June 1991.

SASKATCHEWAN NEW DEMOCRATIC PARTY ARCHIVES

Janice MacKinnon.

MACKENZIE INFANT CARE CENTRE. The Mackenzie Infant Care Centre (MICC) commenced operation in Regina in September 1986. MICC was established to meet the needs of young single mothers who attend classes at the Special Tutorial Class of Balfour Collegiate in Regina. The concept of MICC set the protocol for subsequent daycares throughout Saskatchewan and Canada.

Special Tutorial was founded in 1972 to assist young pregnant women to complete their education in a setting where they would have the opportunity to receive not only academic instruction, but also pre-natal classes as well as caring and esteem building. Special Tutorial at Balfour Collegiate was the second such class formed in Canada, and remains the longest-serving tutorial of its kind in the country.

It became evident that being a young mother and pursuing an education was a very onerous task: looking after a newborn, finding a babysitter, traveling to a babysitter and getting to school on time proved to be almost impossible for most young mothers.

For a number of years the staff at Special Tutorial recognized the need for safe, affordable daycare to meet the needs of the young mothers who attended the school. Shirley Schneider, who headed the Special Tutorial Class along with other dedicated staff members, encouraged the Regina community to support the concept of an infant care centre being an adjunct to the Special Tutorial Class. Thanks to the work of the Junior Service League of Regina and the Gannett Foundation, funding was procured to purchase a house across the street from the school, which was renovated to meet the criteria for a daycare. The Regina volunteer, service club and business community, as well as many individuals, continued to support the MICC with gifts of money and goods in kind.

The Mackenzie Infant Care Centre was named to recognize the contribution of Alex Mackenzie, who as an administrator of the Regina Board of Education had the vision to promote the establishment of the Special Tutorial Class at Balfour Collegiate.

In 2004 MICC served twelve infants under the age of one at the house site, and twelve toddlers up to the age of 18 months housed in the school. The young mothers continue to be encouraged to breast-feed their infants, and receive comprehensive parenting instruction as well as a wide array of information on how to be the best possible parent to their child. In addition to the specially trained care givers, many other professionals are on site to provide instruction, guidance and counseling to enhance the quality of life for these young women and their children. *Shirley Schneider*

MACKINNON, JANICE (1947–). Janice Christine Potter was born in Kitchener, Ontario, on January 1, 1947. Her academic background (BA Western Ontario, MA and PhD Queen's) brought her to teach at the **UNIVERSITY OF SASKATCHEWAN**. She is married to Peter MacKinnon, president of the university. They have two sons. Prior to entering politics, she served as president of the Saskatoon Co-Operative Association. In 1991 she won the provincial riding of Saskatoon-Westmount and was named Minister of Social Services. She was elevated to Finance Minister in 1993 when **ED TCHORZEWSKI** resigned. Mackinnon's first budget in 1993 set a precedent of long-term targets for deficit reduction. Re-elected in 1995 MacKinnon held the post of Finance Minister until 1997. She remained in Cabinet as Minister for Economic and Co-operative Development (1997–2001), Minister for the Information Highway (1998–2001), and Minister for Crown Investments Corporation (2001), and

also held the post of government House Leader. Considered one of the favourites to succeed **ROMANOW** as Premier, MacKinnon did not pursue the leadership in 2001. She gave up her seat later that year out of concern with the fiscal direction of the NDP. MacKinnon did not return to politics, despite interest from both **LORNE CALVERT**'s Saskatchewan NDP and Paul Martin's federal **LIBERAL PARTY**. MacKinnon's political philosophy, both in office and in private life, often ran contrary to traditional NDP positions and to those of her own party leaders. After leaving politics, MacKinnon continued as a professor at the University of Saskatchewan. She is the author of *Minding the Public Purse* and two other books, and is a political commentator in various media. She is a board member for **INTERNATIONAL ROAD DYNAMICS** and for the Institute for Research on Public Policy. *Greg Fingas*

FURTHER READING: MacKinnon, Janice. 2003. *Minding the Public Purse: The Fiscal Crisis, Political Trade-Offs, and Canada's Future*. Montreal: McGill-Queen's University Press.

MACKLIN, town, pop 1,330, located just inside the Saskatchewan-Alberta border, approximately 110 km S of Lloydminster. The community is served by Hwys 14, 17, and 31. Settlers first began arriving in the district in 1906–07. The name of the community honours E.H. Macklin, a chief business manager with the *Winnipeg Free Press*, whose paper chronicled the development of the railway. Developing a theme, the community's streets were named after famous newspapers: Times, Herald, and Tribune among others. By 1911, the population of Macklin was well over 300 and, on November 1, 1912, the community attained town status. Many who came to the area were German Catholics from southern Russia and the United States; they brought with them the unique game of bunnock which has become enthusiastically embraced by the community over the years. The game, a cross between bowling and horseshoes played with 52 horse ankle bones, is thought to have been developed by Russian soldiers posted in northern Siberia more than 200 years ago. Today, Macklin hosts the World Championship Bunnock Tournament, which draws as many as 250 teams. To commemorate Macklin's sport of choice, a 10-metre high bunnock (an exact replica of a horse's ankle bone enlarged 98 times) stands at the entrance to the town. Macklin has experienced continuous growth since its beginnings as a trade and service centre for the surrounding agricultural district. The agricultural industry remains important today, with mixed farming operations producing traditional crops such as wheat, as well as peas and sunflowers. The livestock industry has become increasingly diversified as animals such as bison and ostriches are raised in addition to cattle. Increasing exploration and development in the area's gas and oil fields has meant substantial growth in recent years. The town's population has been steadily rising and close to 70% are under the age of 45. Macklin and District Museum, housed in the stately 1919 home of the town's first bank manager, features artifacts and displays pertaining to Macklin's early development. *David McLennan*

MACLACHLAN, ETHEL (1875–1963). Ethel MacLachlan was a key player in the development of Saskatchewan's child welfare system. Born in Lunenburg, Nova Scotia, on April 15, 1875, of Scottish parentage, she received her education at the provincial Normal School in Truro, Nova Scotia, and taught for fifteen years at the Lunenburg Academy. In September 1909 she moved to Regina to take a business course. In 1910, Saskatchewan's Department of Neglected Children hired her for clerical work; but within a year she was inspecting the homes of adopted children, and eventually became the Superintendent's assistant. In October 1916, MacLachlan became the first woman in Canada to hold the position of Superintendent of Neglected and Dependent Children. MacLachlan believed that all children had the right to a "happy" life, and in her work as Superintendent she did all she could to ensure that more children had secure home environments.

In 1917 the Saskatchewan Legislature passed the Juvenile Courts Act, 1917 and established a process to hear and determine complaints against juvenile offenders. Recognizing her exceptional work in the matter of child welfare, her sympathetic nature, and the respect she received from children, the government appointed Ethel MacLachlan as the first Juvenile Court Judge in the province, where she was also the first woman to become a judge. The Juvenile Court aimed to treat young offenders differently than criminals, and in her capacity MacLachlan believed in the fair treatment of all children regardless of religion, race, ethnicity, culture, class or gender. Throughout her career she advanced the development of child welfare policies through her participation in provincial, national and international discussions regarding children in need of protection. Ethel MacLachlan died in Vancouver on April 14, 1963. *Kim Marschall*

MACLEAN, DONALD (1877–1947). Donald Maclean, leader of the **CONSERVATIVE PARTY** and His Majesty's Loyal Opposition from 1918 to 1921, was born in 1877. A lawyer by profession, he first won election to the Legislature in the war-time election of 1917, one of only seven successful Conservatives at a time when his party expected to do much better, given a Conservative government in power in Ottawa and the reports of two royal commissions the previous year which had confirmed the charges

of corruption levelled at the **SCOTT** administration by the Conservative Member for Prince Albert, **J.E. BRADSHAW**. A year later, when **W.B. WILLOUGHBY** resigned his seat to accept an appointment to the Senate, the remaining Conservative MLAs chose Maclean as leader. The major issue Maclean raised in the Legislature concerned language, in particular the need to make English the paramount language of instruction in the schools of the province, and Premier **MARTIN** did amend the School Act to limit severely the use of other languages in the province's schools. Nevertheless, this issue alone was not sufficient to bring down the government or even turn the Conservative party into a viable contender for power. In fact, events had overtaken Maclean and his tiny band of followers by the early 1920s: by this time activists in the farm movement had decided to enter provincial politics directly, and public opinion shifted to their political arm, the Progressives, as the more likely group to defeat the Liberals. Maclean saw the writing on the wall, and in April 1921, two months before the upcoming election, he resigned his seat and the leadership of his party to accept an appointment to the bench, where he remained until his death in 1947. *Patrick Kyba*

MACLEAN, HUGH (1878–1958). Born in Glasgow (Scotland) on July 30, 1878, MacLean emigrated with his family to Ontario in 1887 and graduated in medicine at the University of Toronto in 1906. He practised in Lang, Saskatchewan, then trained in surgery in Chicago and New York in 1912–13 before returning to Regina. He was unsuccessful in the Regina federal constituency for the Progressives in 1921 and for the CCF in 1935. He retired to California because of ill health in 1938, but remained an "eminence grise" to the CCF party. His speech on "Medical Health Service" to the CCF provincial convention in Regina on July 13, 1944, was a precursor to the **SIGERIST** report; MacLean sup-

Hugh MacLean.

ported Sigerist's appointment. He was later described by **T.C. DOUGLAS** as the "spiritual godfather" of both the **UNIVERSITY OF SASKATCHEWAN** Medical School and the University Hospital. MacLean died in La Jolla, California on January 1, 1958. *C. Stuart Houston*

John MacLeod, November 1987.

MACLEOD, JOHN (1940–). John MacLeod was born in Regina on April 18, 1940. He attended school in Regina and started work as an apprentice electrician on the **IPSCO** construction project in 1958. MacLeod became an officer of Local 2038 of the **INTERNATIONAL BROTHERHOOD OF ELECTRICAL WORKERS** (IBEW) in the mid-1960s. He served in a number of union positions over the next thirty years, and was elected full-time business manager for IBEW for a number of three-year terms. In 1970 he was elected vice-president of the **SASKATCHEWAN FEDERATION OF LABOUR** (SFL) and served on the executive for twenty years, including a two-year term as president.

For twenty years MacLeod was the president of the Saskatchewan Building and Construction Trades Council; he retired from this position in 2002. During his career he was appointed to the **LABOUR RELATIONS BOARD** and the Provincial Apprenticeship Board, as well as to other labour and government boards. Through his union positions he was involved in lobbying the premiers and officials during the **THATCHER**, **BLAKENEY**, **DEVINE**, **ROMANOW**, and **CALVERT** governments for labour legislation and regulations, particularly regarding the construction industry, with which he negotiated contracts in the province during a period of controversial legislative changes. *Bob Ivanochko*

MACLEOD, WENDELL (1905–2001). J. Wendell Macleod was born in Kingsbury, Ontario, on March 2, 1905, and spent his formative years in

SASKATCHEWAN ARCHIVES BOARD R-A5724

J. Wendell MacLeod (right) and Tommy Douglas, June 1961.

that general area. In 1929, he graduated from McGill, winning the Holmes gold medal, the first of many awards. After specialty training in gastro-enterology, he practised in Montreal.

The war years were spent as a naval officer in Halifax. From 1945 to 1952, he practised internal medicine in Winnipeg. But change was imminent, in both his career and his profession. During the post-war years, a new perspective on patient care was emerging, one that emphasized social and cultural factors. To Macleod and others, these changes necessitated a major revision in medical education.

In 1952, his appointment as first Dean of Medicine in the UNIVERSITY OF SASKATCHEWAN's newly established medical school provided the opportunity he sought. He recruited Canada's first full-time clinical faculty, and together they established an innovative curriculum. These innovations drew a mixed response from the medical establishment, but for Macleod and his supporters the challenges were exhilarating and profoundly satisfying.

Over the ensuing ten years, frustration overtook the initial euphoria. By 1961, several crises had converged, not least of which the looming medicare dispute. In 1962, having completed his second term as Dean of Medicine, Macleod accepted a position as secretary of the Association of Canadian Medical Colleges. There, his advocacy of progressive medical education continued.

He died in North Hero, Vermont, on June 10, 2001. But, for Macleod, the Saskatchewan years remained the richest experience of his life.

Anne McDonald

MACMILLAN BLOEDEL. In April 1965, MacMillan Bloedel and Powell River (Saskatchewan) Ltd., which later became MacMillan Bloedel, purchased Canada's first waferboard plant, which had been started by Wizewood Products Ltd. in September 1961. The wood used was aspen, then an under-utilized species. A $4 million expansion in 1968–69 added a second line, more than doubling the output and making it the largest particle board complex in Canada. A further investment of $14.8 million took place in 1983. In 1995, Macmillan Bloedel partnered with Saskatchewan Forest Products Corporation (SFPC) to form SaskFor, which provided one coordinated organization for planning, harvest and delivery to its major mills in the area. When SaskFor built a new mill in Hudson Bay to produce Oriented Strand Board for use in engineered beams, joists and flooring, the old waferboard mill was closed. In 1999, MacMillan Bloedel purchased SFPC's 50% ownership in SaskFor; this made it one of Canada's largest forest products companies. Later in 1999, MacMillan Bloedel was itself acquired by WEYERHAEUSER. *Jamie Benson and Murray Little*

MACMURCHY, GORDON (1926–2005). Gordon MacMurchy was born in Semans on July 4, 1926. In 1962 he was elected trustee of the Govan school unit and served until 1971 including two years as chairman. MacMurchy ran as the NDP candidate in Last Mountain in 1967, but lost. He was appointed provincial director of organization for the Saskatchewan NDP in 1969. The party became internally divided over the WAFFLE. MacMurchy ran for party president at the 1970 leadership convention, unseating incumbent president and Waffle sympathizer, Bev Currie. MacMurchy won Last Mountain for the NDP in 1971 and was appointed to ALLAN BLAKENEY's first Cabinet as Minister of Education, where he institutionalized the salary aspects of the collective bargaining process between teachers and school districts as the direct responsibility of the provincial government. In 1975 he was appointed Minister of Municipal Affairs. MacMurchy was appointed to the Political Committee of Cabinet and, along with ELWOOD COWLEY and Bill Knight, increasingly took control of party matters, including running the party's election campaigns. In 1979 MacMurchy was appointed Minister of Agriculture as the government focused on agriculture and transportation issues. He fought for the retention of the Crow Rate, the country elevator system, and an end to rail line abandonment. The government helped purchase a fleet of grain hopper cars. After his defeat in 1982, MacMurchy returned to Semans and became active in the community. He helped establish the Family Farm Foundation. He was elected mayor of Semans in 1982 and held that position until 1997. In 1986, he made one more attempt at provincial political office but was defeated. Gordon MacMurchy died on April 20, 2005. *Brett Quiring*

MACOUN, village, pop 170, located 27 km NW of Estevan on Hwy 39. The village was named after JOHN MACOUN (1831–1920), the Canadian botanist and explorer. The first homesteads in the Macoun district were filed around 1901, and over the following few years an influx of settlers arrived, many of Norwegian and Swedish origin. By October 1903, the community had grown large enough to be incorporated as a village, and the following two decades were to be Macoun's most active. By 1916, the population of the village was approaching 300. The community suffered a number of fires, the most tragic of which occurred on April 20, 1914, when a gas explosion in the hotel triggered an instant inferno that left 13 dead and many injured. One residence and three other businesses were also lost in the blaze. The 1930s also took a toll on the community, so that by 1941 the population had fallen to 129. The discovery of oil in the region in the early 1950s brought a return to prosperity, and offered diversification to an economy that had previously been solely based on agriculture. Today, Macoun is essentially a residential community, although its K–8 school remains a long-standing community institution. Farmer and businessman Leonard J. Gustafson, appointed to the Senate of Canada in 1993, was born and raised in Macoun.

David McLennan

MACOUN, JOHN (1831–1920). Born in Ireland on April 17, 1831, John Macoun was Canada's most important field naturalist in the mid and late 19th century. He was the naturalist on Sir Sandford Fleming's survey of the prairies in 1872. This survey prospected possible routes for a transcontinental railroad, and gathered information on the biological resources of the area. Following the completion of the survey, Macoun lectured on the agricultural possibilities of the region. He was appointed Dominion Botanist in 1882, and established the dominion herbarium. These and other collections which he organized became the base for the National Museum of Natural Sciences in Ottawa. His interest in natural history was general, not limited to plants. In 1909, he and his son James wrote *The Catalogue of Canadian Birds*, the first major work on the bird fauna of Canada since that of Sir JOHN RICHARDSON in 1851. Macoun died in Sidney, British Columbia on July 18, 1920. *Diane Secoy*

MACPHERSON, MURDOCH ALEXANDER (1891–1966). MacPherson was born at Grande Anse on Cape Breton Island on April 16, 1891. He was raised on his parents' farm and was sent to be educated in Richmond and Pictou. After graduation, he taught school for a brief period until he raised enough money to attend law school at Dalhousie University. In 1913 he established a law practice in Swift Current. MacPherson enlisted in the Canadian Expeditionary Force in 1916, and was wounded in 1917. After the war, he was appointed solicitor to the Soldier Settlement Board, which helped demobilized soldiers homestead. MacPherson established a law practice in Regina. In 1921 he challenged Liberal **WILLIAM MOTHERWELL** in the riding of Regina but lost. MacPherson was successful as a Conservative in the 1925 provincial election. Upon re-election in 1929, MacPherson became Attorney General in the **ANDERSON** government. He negotiated the transfer of natural resource rights from the federal government to the province. As the Depression began to take hold, MacPherson took on responsibility for the increasingly difficult portfolio of Provincial Treasurer. In 1934, MacPherson was defeated, along with all other members of the Anderson government. After a brief federal appointment, MacPherson returned to his law practice in Regina. He ran for the leadership of the federal **CONSERVATIVE PARTY** in 1940 and 1942, finishing second on both occasions. After **WORLD WAR II**, he represented the Saskatchewan's CCF government as legal counsel in its attempts to stop the railways from circumventing the **CROW'S NEST PASS AGREEMENT**. In 1959, Prime Minister **JOHN DIEFENBAKER** appointed MacPherson to the Royal Commission that examined railway and freight rate problems in the country. MacPherson lost again in the 1960 provincial election. In 1961 he was named a bencher of the **LAW SOCIETY OF SASKATCHEWAN** and received an honorary doctorate from the **UNIVERSITY OF SASKATCHEWAN**. He continued to practice law until his death on June 11, 1966. *Brett Quiring*

MAH, JEANNIE (1952–). Regina-born Jeannie Mah is an internationally recognized artist, who reinvents functional ceramics as thought-provoking sculpture. Mah's sophisticated vessels, hand-built in eggshell-thin porcelain, resemble oversized, idiosyncratic vases or cups, so fragile that a quick touch could demolish them. Her work has other uses: they eloquently carry the weight of historical and personal meaning. She inscribes images and texts on the delicate surfaces of her porcelain, reinterpreting everything from the decorative flourishes of great European commercial china to family photos. Other preoccupations are apparent in Mah's ceramic sculpture; she is an ardent cineaste, a committed francophile, and an accomplished video artist. Major works are installed in the Regina City Hall and the Regina Public Library. Other public collections with her works include the Gardiner Museum of Ceramic Art (Toronto), the Museum of Civilization (Hull, Quebec), the Municipalité de Nyon, Switzerland, and the **MACKENZIE ART GALLERY**. Mah studied at the **UNIVERSITY OF REGINA** (BEd, 1976, BFA, 1993), Emily Carr College of Art (Advanced Diploma, 1979), and Université de Perpignan (Certificat Pratique de Langue Française, 1er degré, 1988). Her work has been the subject of numerous articles and review catalogues, as well as solo and group exhibitions in Canada, the United States and Europe. *Helen Marzolf*

FURTHER READING: Laviolette, M.-B. 2001. *Cineramics*. Calgary: The Art Gallery of Calgary.

MAHARG, JOHN ARCHIBALD (1872–1944). Maharg was born at Orangeville, Ontario, in 1872. He settled near Moose Jaw in 1890, taking up grain farming and the breeding of registered cattle. He was one of the organizers of the Saskatchewan Grain Growers Association (SGGA) and was elected its first president, a post he held from 1910 to 1923. The SGGA obtained Saskatchewan government loans to build farmer-owned grain elevators. The **SASKATCHEWAN CO-OPERATIVE ELEVATOR COMPANY** was formed to operate these elevators and Maharg again was first president. Within fifteen years the company had 450 country elevators, two terminals, and it ran a grain-exporting business. Maharg also served as president of the Canadian Council of Agriculture from 1915 to 1917. In 1917 he was elected member of Parliament for Maple Creek as an independent supporting the wartime Unionist government. A year later he crossed to the Opposition with a group that was to help found the Progressive Party. In 1921 he left federal politics to become Minister of Agriculture for Saskatchewan. He ran and was elected provincially as an independent member for Morse constituency. He continued in the Cabinet until fall, when he resigned in a confrontation that resulted in the resignation of Premier **WILLIAM MARTIN**. Maharg served as leader of the Opposition until he left politics in 1924. Returning to his farming and off-farm interests, he represented the Co-operative Elevator Company on the provisional board of the newly formed **SASKATCHEWAN WHEAT POOL**. Maharg remained active with the Co-operative Elevator Company until its assets were sold in 1928 to the Pool. He died in November 1944. *Lisa Dale-Burnett*

FURTHER READING: 1995. *Salute to Saskatchewan Farm Leaders*. Saskatoon: Saskatchewan Agricultural Hall of Fame.

MAIDSTONE, town, pop 995, located between the Battlefords and Lloydminster at the junction of Hwys 16 and 21. Many of the first settlers in the Maidstone area were Barr Colonists, who arrived in the spring of 1903. With the construction of the Canadian Northern Railway through the region in 1905, the townsite was established and settlement of the area increased dramatically. The community was named after Maidstone, Kent, England. In the coming years, Blacks from Oklahoma settled just north of Maidstone, and a significant number of Mennonites would eventually come to take up land in the district. Among the district's early homesteaders was **JOHN HENRY "JACK" WESSON**, who took up land in 1907. Wesson went on to become one of the province's foremost farm leaders; among other accomplishments, he became the first president of the Canadian Federation of Agriculture in 1936 and

Gordon MacMurchy.

John Macoun.

Murdoch MacPherson.

John Maharg.

the president of the **SASKATCHEWAN WHEAT POOL** in 1937. As a trading centre for the surrounding agricultural district, the village of Maidstone grew steadily over the decades and attained town status in 1955. In the 1970s, the developing oil industry came to have a tremendous influence on the economy of the community, causing the town's population to grow from less than 700 at the beginning of the decade to over 1,000 by 1981. Today, with an expanding gas industry, close to 2,000 wells dot the surrounding countryside, while canola, grains, and purebred cattle dominate the district's agricultural output. The Shiloh Baptist Church, built by the district's Black community in 1911, was abandoned after 1940, but rediscovered in the early 1970s and restored. In 1991 the church and adjacent cemetery were designated a heritage property. (*See* **BARR COLONY**; **BLACK, EARLY SETTLEMENTS**).   *David McLennan*

MAKAHONUK, GLEN (1951–97). A senior library assistant at the **UNIVERSITY OF SASKATCHEWAN**, Glen Makahonuk served as president of the Saskatchewan division of the **CANADIAN UNION OF PUBLIC EMPLOYEES** from 1992 until his untimely death in 1997. During the same period, he served as president of CUPE Local 1975 (representing University of Saskatchewan support workers), regional and general vice-president on CUPE's National Executive Board, and vice-president with the **SASKATCHEWAN FEDERATION OF LABOUR**. Despite his many union offices, Makahonuk took pride in being part of the "rank and file." He continued his work at the university and found time to chair his Local's grievance committee for almost twenty years, handling over 1,200 grievances.

Makahonuk was a strong proponent of "social unionism." He believed that unions should not be focused solely on collective bargaining and grievance handling, but rather should strive to advance the broad interests of the working class and the

unemployed, forge strong ties with social justice coalitions, and organize workers. He was a constant fixture at picket lines. Indeed, he is fondly remembered as one of the best picketers during Saskatoon's Common Front municipal strike of 1994. It was also a common sight to see Makahonuk at the microphone speaking to resolutions at union conventions, which he saw as an opportunity for workers to educate each other about the issues facing the labour movement.

In letters to politicians and "letters to the editor," he called for measures to improve the lives of working people and the unemployed, such as anti-scab legislation, pay equity, a higher minimum wage, and well-funded social programs. While Makahonuk won widespread respect as a tireless labour activist, he was also a keen student of labour history, which helped shape his deep sense of social justice. He completed his Master's thesis on the Estevan coal miners' strike of 1931, and was a frequent contributor to *Briarpatch* and *Saskatchewan History*. Just prior to his death on December 10, 1997, Makahonuk authored the booklet *Class, State and Power: The Struggle for Trade Union Rights in Saskatchewan, 1905–1997*.   *Guy Marsden*

MAKI, DAVID MICHAEL (1944–). Born at Whitewood, Saskatchewan, on August 16, 1944, David Maki attended elementary school in a one-room log building. He studied at Regina Teachers College in 1964–65, and at the **UNIVERSITY OF REGINA** in 1965–66, majoring in Arts. His paid employment included farming, weather observer, fisherman, pipe fitter's helper, miner, electrician, union organizer, union representative (OPEIU Local 397) from 1975 to 1995, and traffic safety court justice from 1995 to 2002. Maki was actively involved in organizing the IMC Esterhazy potash mine, serving as the recording secretary on the provisional executive of the Oil, Chemical and Atomic Workers International, and

later as vice-president and president of the local. He was a bargaining committee member in 1974, when the mine was completely shut down by wildcat strikes on April Fools' Day and Hallowe'en. Both strikes were satisfactorily settled after 32 hours.

Maki became a full-time representative with the **OFFICE AND PROFESSIONAL EMPLOYEES INTERNATIONAL UNION** (OPEIU) in 1975. He played a key role in stopping the **DEVINE** government's plans to privatize **SASKATCHEWAN GOVERNMENT INSURANCE**, and was on the interim planning group of the **SASKATCHEWAN COALITION FOR SOCIAL JUSTICE** which organized two of the largest demonstrations in Saskatchewan history, on April 18, 1987 and June 5, 1989, against the Devine government's cut backs, lay-offs, concession bargaining, forced transfers, and privatization. As treasurer of the **SASKATCHEWAN FEDERATION OF LABOUR** (SFL) from 1978 to 1995, Maki was instrumental in restructuring the SFL and making it a more inclusive organization.   *Judy Boehmer*

MAKWA SAHGAIEHCAN FIRST NATION. From the time the members of the Makwa Lake Cree Band (Loon Lake) signed **TREATY 6** on September 9, 1876, until they were successful in receiving the Makwa Lake Reserve (Numbers 129 and 129A) in 1916, they continued to live much as they had prior to treaty. After acquiring their own reserve they began to develop agriculturally through raising cattle and farming. The band's infrastructure consists of a band office, warehouse, kindergarten, school, fire hall, band hall, and arena. The primary economic base is agriculture. Of the 1,196 registered band members, 753 live on reserve. The band controls a total of 5,881.7 ha of reserve land, the largest parcel of which is just west of the town of Loon Lake.

Christian Thompson

MALHOTRA, LALITA (1941–). Lalita Malhotra was born in Delhi, India, on November 2, 1941.

W. EYRE/UNIVERSITY OF SASKATCHEWAN ARCHIVES A-8776-3

Glen Makahonuk, speaking at a University of Saskatchewan CUPE/student rally, 1996.

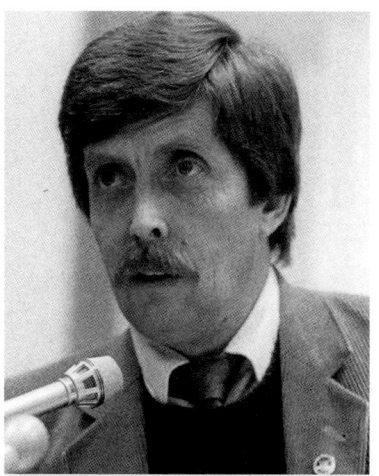

REGINA LEADER-POST

Dave Maki, Saskatchewan Federation of Labour, January 1985.

SASKATCHEWAN ARCHIVES BOARD
R-PS76-155-77

Ted Malone.

Following medical studies in India and post-graduate work in the United Kingdom, she emigrated to Canada in 1975. Her medical practice in Prince Albert has had a major impact throughout northern Saskatchewan. Her focus has been on women's health, with a special interest in teenage and high-risk pregnancies due to poor health, nutrition problems, and socio-economic status. The majority of her patients are northern Aboriginal people, for whom she has been an inspiration and a role model. Dr. Malhotra has delivered more babies, up to 300 per year, than anyone else in Saskatchewan.

Dr. Malhotra started the Women's Wellness Clinic in Prince Albert. She has served as president of the **GIRL GUIDES** in Prince Albert, patron of the city's music festival, and member of the India-Canada Association, as well as an elected member of the Prince Albert Health District and a member of its executive. She received both the YWCA Woman of Distinction Award and the Saskatchewan Order of Merit in 2001. *Michael Jackson*

MALONE, EDWARD CYRIL (TED) (1937–). Malone was born in Regina on July 17, 1937. His father had been involved in the **LIBERAL PARTY**, and his maternal grandfather was **JAMES GRASSICK**, one-time Regina MLA and mayor. Malone graduated in law from the **UNIVERSITY OF SASKATCHEWAN** in 1962. He helped a group of young lawyers organize the federal Liberal Party in Saskatchewan for **OTTO LANG**. Malone served as the Liberal campaign manager in Regina Lakeview during the 1967 and 1971 election campaigns. He was elected in the 1973 by-election and re-elected in the 1975 election. When **DAVE STEUART** was called to the Senate, Malone ran for party leadership in 1976 against fellow lawyer and Regina MLA Tony Merchant. The election bitterly divided the party. Malone won the leadership, but the party lost two seats in by-elections and two Liberals, **COLIN THATCHER** and **GARY LANE**, abandoned the party in favour of the Progressive Conservatives. Their switch resulted in Malone having to share Official Opposition status with the Conservatives. The 1978 campaign was a disaster for Malone and the Liberals. Facing responsibility for unpopular federal Liberal positions and beset by internal strife, the Liberals failed to elect a single member to the Legislature for the first time in the party's history. Although personally defeated, Malone remained leader until 1981 when he was appointed to the Court of Queen's Bench in Regina. *Brett Quiring*

MALTING INDUSTRY. Malt is the main ingredient for brewing beer. The malting process requires plump and clean **BARLEY** with high germinative energy and adequate levels of protein. The cleaned barley is first steeped under controlled conditions, and kernels are activated for growth. The grain is then transferred to the germination compartments, where attemperated air is supplied continuously with frequent turning of the germinating barley. The barley's enzyme package is developed during this period, and the cell wall materials and protein in the endosperm are degraded to required degrees. As a result, the starch granules are also exposed for further enzymatic attack that will occur later in the brewhouse. At the end of germination, the barley is kilned with large airflow at elevated temperatures to arrest the growth and generate the required malty flavour and colour. Rootlets are cleaned off before malt is transferred to storage silos for aging. The whole process of malting takes about eight days to complete, and the maturation in silos can take up to three weeks. Various specialty malt with particular colour or flavour intensities can be produced by selecting barley types and by varying the process conditions employed.

The high-quality malting barley from Saskatchewan produces malt with a strong competitive edge in the world market. The average annual revenue of sales for malt from the province is over $70 million; this success is supported significantly by the barley breeding program at the **CROP DEVELOPMENT CENTRE** at the **UNIVERSITY OF SASKATCHEWAN**. There, a number of malting varieties such as Harrington, Manley, Kendall, and Copeland were developed for both superior enzymatic potential and high starch content. These characteristics made it ideal for brewers to produce dry beers and low-carbohydrate beers. Although a large portion of the selected malting barley from Saskatchewan goes to export directly as barley, the cream of the crop (less than 10% of the average four million tonnes of barley produced annually) is retained in the province for malting at Prairie Malt Limited; Saskatchewan's only malting plant, it boasts an annual production of 230,000 tonnes of malt, requiring up to 300,000 tonnes of barley as raw material. Future market demand is expected to

Malting barley in its finished state.

emphasize the importance of barley supply chain management, traceability, and more formalized farming practices, as high-quality barley becomes one of the critical factors in the continued success of the malting industry in Saskatchewan. *Xiang S. Yin*

MAMMALS. Mammals are one of the group of animals with backbones, known as vertebrates. The members of the class Mammalia are distinguished from the other vertebrate classes by feeding their young by milk from skin glands, breathing with the aid of a muscular diaphragm, having only one bone in the lower jaw, having seven neck vertebra, and possessing three sound-conducting bones in the middle ear. They usually have hair. All of the mammals now found in Saskatchewan are placental mammals, which carry their developing young within the female's body until they are ready for birth, rather than keeping the developing young in a pouch (marsupials) or laying eggs (monotremes). Mammals have the largest and most complex brains of any group of animals, and their complex behaviours reflect this. Mammals gradually evolved from the synapsid reptiles, beginning in the Triassic (225–195 million years ago).

Mammals have a high body temperature which requires considerable food resources to maintain. Mammals living in areas where there are reductions in food sources due to dry or cold seasons may either migrate and leave the area, or go underground and hibernate. In Saskatchewan, for example, most **BATS** migrate south during the winter; caribou migrate through the boreal area looking for patches of **LICHENS** and vegetation; several types of

Malting Barley.

COURTESY OF SASKATCHEWAN ENVIRONMENT

The raccoon (*Procyon lotor*) is one of the seventy-two species of wild mammals found in Saskatchewan.

rodents hibernate; and the black bear goes into a deep sleep.

Mammals are found over the whole earth, missing only from the centres of ice sheets and the depths of the oceans. Their places in the ecosystems depend on their diets. Some, such as humans and bears, are generalists which can take advantage of a broad variety of foods. Others are more specialized in feeding, such as nectar-feeding bats or blood-feeding vampire bats. There are large numbers of herbivores that take advantage of plant communities. The **CARNIVORES** feed on the herbivorous mammals and other plant-feeders. The highest diversity of mammals is found in the wet tropics.

There are seventy-two species of wild mammals presently found in the province, out of approximately 4,400 known in the world. There are representatives of six of the twenty living orders of mammals: Insectivora (**SHREWS**), Chiroptera (bats), Lagomorpha (**HARES AND RABBITS**), Rodentia (**RODENTS**), Carnivora (carnivores) and Artiodactyla (**DEER, BISON**, and **PRONGHORN**). There are no species of mammals unique to Saskatchewan. The largest mammal in Saskatchewan is the male American bison, at one ton; the smallest is the pigmy shrew at 2 gr. The affinities of the fauna are mainly with Eurasia (deer, hares, bats, shrews, squirrels, wolves, etc), but some are with South America (raccoon, porcupine). The pronghorn is found only in the prairies of North America and has no living close relatives. A number of species have come in with settlement; these include, besides domesticated species such as cattle, the horse and the domestic cat, species considered vermin: the house mouse, brown rat, and black rat. Others from eastern Canada, such as the fox squirrel, have taken advantage of habitat changes by humans to travel into the province.

Several species have recently been lost from the fauna, such as the black-footed ferret and the Plains grizzly. A number of other species, particularly the larger carnivores, have been reduced by a combination of hunting for food, furs or sport, and habitat

loss due to agricultural development. Some, such as the swift fox and the American bison, have been the focus of successful conservation efforts to increase their depleted numbers. All wild mammals are protected by the provincial Wildlife Act, which controls their killing: for a number of species of fur-bearers and ungulates there are specified seasons and limits.

Diane Secoy

FURTHER READING: Banfield, A.W.F. 1974. *The Mammals of Canada*. Toronto: University of Toronto Press; Burt, W. and R.P. Grossenheider. 1976. *A Field Guide to Mammals*. New York: Houghton Mifflin; Macdonald, D. (ed.). 1984. *The Encyclopedia of Mammals*. New York: Facts on File.

MANDATORY MEDIATION. Mandatory mediation in Saskatchewan has its legislative roots in the farm debt crisis. The Farm Land Security Act, S.S. 1984–85–86, c.F-8.01 introduced a formal mediation process to resolve disputes between farmers and lenders in 1985. Mediation has been called "the most significant component of Saskatchewan's legislative attempt to deal with farm debt" and it is Saskatchewan's success with the farm program that supported other progressive mandatory mediation programs.

The idea of facilitating settlements in agricultural disputes had existed long before 1995. The Provincial Mediation Board Act, S.S. 1943, c. 15, which evolved out of The Debt Adjustment Act, S.S. 1934–35, c.88, established a board with the mandate to "endeavour to bring about an amicable arrangement for payment of the debtor's indebtedness" (s.5(1)). However, the board's role included broader tasks, such as advising the debtor or creditor, and inquiring into the validity of claims (s.5(1)).

It was in 1988 that mediation–by an independent trained mediator–was entrenched as a formal step in farm debt collection actions. The **SASKATCHEWAN FARM SECURITY ACT**, S.S. 1988–89, c.S-17.1 separated the functions of the board and mediators, made mediation a mandatory step, and delegated the responsibility for providing mediation to the Mediation Services branch of Saskatchewan Justice (now called the Dispute Resolution Office).

Saskatchewan's success with the farm debt mediation program (which has reached settlement rates of 70–80%) paved the way for broader legislative advancements. In 1994, the government introduced a program of mandatory mediation in the Court of Queen's Bench, which applied to all civil actions outside of family law cases (with some other exceptions). First established as a pilot project in Regina and Swift Current in 1994, the mandatory mediation program has since been expanded to Saskatoon and Prince Albert, and applies to 80% of all (non-family) civil cases in that court (The

Queen's Bench Act, 1998, S.S. 1998, c.Q-1.01, s.42). In all cases not exempted, a mediation must be held at the close of pleadings and before any other step can be taken in the action.

There has also been a long history of mediation in the labour sector. The parties to a grievance always have the option of referring the dispute to mediation (an option preserved by s.26.4 of The **TRADE UNION ACT**, regardless of the absence of such a term in a collective agreement). However, aside from the Minister's ability to appoint a "special mediator" to deal with a dispute, under s.23.1 of that Act, there is no mandatory element to the mediation addressed by this legislation.

Finally, there is a history of mediation in the family area as well. In 1994, the Saskatchewan government experimented with mandatory mediation "orientation" sessions for parties in family disputes (The Queen's Bench (Mediation) Amendment Act, S.S. 1994, c.20). Under these provisions, the parties had to attend for separate sessions with a mediator, to discuss the option of mediation. These legislative provisions were later repealed, and mediation in this area remains voluntary.

Michaela Keet

FURTHER READING: Benson, Marjorie L. 1996. *Agricultural Law in Canada 1867–1995: With Particular Reference to Saskatchewan*. Calgary: Canadian Institute of Resources Law; Keet, Michaela, and Teresa B. Salamone. 2001. "From Litigation to Mediation: Using Advocacy Skills for Success in Mandatory or Court-Connected Mediation," *Saskatchewan Law Review* 64 (1): 57; Layh, Donald H. 1992. "Legislative Options to Manage the Farm Debt Crisis." Donald E. Buckingham and Ken Norman (eds.). 1992. *Law Agriculture and the Farm Crisis*. Saskatoon: Purich Publishing.

MANDEL, ELI (1922–92). Elias Wolf Mandel was born on December 3, 1922, in Estevan. Growing up in the area provided him with a strong sense of Russian-Jewish culture and the prairie west, both featuring prominently in his poems. In 1935 Mandel's family moved to Regina, and in 1942 he began attending Regina College to study pharmacy. One year later, he joined the army and served overseas as a medical corpsman. After the end of the war, he returned to Saskatchewan and received his BA (1949) and MA (1950) from the **UNIVERSITY OF SASKATCHEWAN**. In 1949, Mandel married Miriam Minovitch and in 1950, they went to Toronto, where he worked on his PhD at the University of Toronto and began publishing poems in literary journals. From 1953 to 1957, he worked on his dissertation on Christopher Smart, wrote poetry, and taught at the Collège Militaire Royal de Saint-Jean. He completed his doctorate in 1957 and moved to the University of Alberta, where he stayed until 1967. He then divorced Miriam, married Ann Hardy, and returned to Toronto.

COURTESY OF ANN MANDEL

Eli Mandel, 1979.

That year also brought a major accomplishment for Mandel: he published the collection *An Idiot Joy* and received the Governor General's Award for Poetry in English. In 1970, he was included in the Oxford anthology, *15 Canadian Poets*. In the 1970s, Mandel moved to a new territory in his work, inspired by his memories of the prairies. He also became more involved in the Canadian literary community and less in the structures of the university. In 1978–79, he became the first writer-in-residence at the Regina Public Library, and in 1982 he was made a fellow of the Royal Society of Canada. Throughout his lifetime, Mandel wrote ten volumes of poetry and two essay collections; and he published articles and reviews on cultural politics, literature, literary theory, and art. He also edited several anthologies of Canadian, British, and American poets, such as *Five Modern Canadian Poets* in 1969 and *Eight More Canadian Poets* in 1972. Mandel served as professor at York University until his retirement. He won various awards, including a Centennial Medal in 1967 and a Silver Jubilee medal in 1977. He died in Toronto on September 3, 1992.

Dagmar Skamlová

FURTHER READING: Stubbs, A., and J. Chapman (eds.). 2000. *The Other Harmony: The Collected Poetry of Eli Mandel.* Regina: Canadian Plains Research Center.

MANITOU BEACH, resort village, pop 212, located 5 km N of Watrous on Hwy 365. The resort developed early in the 20th century when settlers discovered the mineral waters of Little Manitou Lake, long known to the region's indigenous population. The resort village was incorporated in 1919, and excursion trains brought vacationers and health-seekers from across the prairies to the lake and the spas that

developed. Danceland, built in 1928, became famous for its 5,000-square-foot maple dance floor, cushioned by a thick layer of horse hair. In the 1930s, as a relief project, the provincial government began the development of a provincial park at the lake and constructed the fieldstone buildings which were later taken over by the Saskatchewan Abilities Council, becoming Camp Easter Seal. The wheelchair-accessible resort now provides summer vacation opportunities for special children. Manitou Beach declined during the DEPRESSION and subsequent years, but entered a period of substantial growth in the 1980s and 1990s due to a renewed interest in the putative healing powers of its mineral waters. With a multi-million dollar investment infusion, Manitou Beach has again become a major centre for spa tourism. *David McLennan*

MAPLE CREEK, town, pop 2,270, located 40 km E of the Saskatchewan-Alberta border on Hwy 21, 8 km S of the Trans-Canada Hwy. Maple Creek serves as a gateway for an estimated 250,000 tourists each year heading to the Cypress Hills Interprovincial Park, FORT WALSH, and the historic site of the CYPRESS HILLS MASSACRE. The town got its name and its beginning in the fall of 1882, when construction of the trans-continental railway was halted and workmen spent the winter on the banks of a small creek lined with Manitoba maples—the creek which flows northward along the west side of the present town. In 1875, prior to significant settlement in the North-West Territories, the NWMP established Fort Walsh in the CYPRESS HILLS approximately 50 km southwest of the location. But with the coming of the railroad in 1883, Fort Walsh was abandoned and the NWMP detachment, "A" Division, relocated to new barracks near what was called Maple Creek. The Maple Creek post office was established that year. Within a few years, community institutions such as a school and churches were established. Ranching developed into the main industry in the area, and on April 28, 1896, Maple Creek was incorporated as a village. By April 30, 1903, the community had grown sufficiently to attain town status. However, as more settlers arrived, the vast ranching empires began to give way to fences, homesteads, and crop production. Maple Creek would become a community of firsts: in 1907, a gravity-fed water system was established, with water piped into the community from springs several kilometres to the southeast; a few years later, a sewage system was installed and an electric light system was established; and Maple Creek became one of the first communities of its size in the province to have most of its streets paved. While today agriculture remains the substantial contributor to the town's economy (generally speaking, crop production to the north and ranching to the south), gas exploration and production, tourism, various small manufacturing enterprises,

and service industries provide a significant degree of economic diversity. Maple Creek has two museums: the Oldtimer's Museum, established in 1926, houses artifacts and an extensive collection of photographs documenting the 1870–1910 frontier period of the region; and the Jasper Cultural and Historic Centre features theme exhibits depicting different aspects of pioneer life. Maple Creek, living up to its long-established moniker "The Old Cowtown," hosts five or six rodeos over the course of the year, as well as the Cowboy Poetry Gathering and Western Art and Cowboy Gear Show in September, and the Stock Dog Trials in October. Additionally, the Cowtown Livestock Exchange is one of the most important livestock auction rings in the country. Maple Creek also enjoys the warmest annual average temperature in the province and, subsequently, the largest number of frost-free days. *David McLennan*

MARCHILDON, ARTHUR (1920–96). Born March 10, 1920, Père Arthur Marchildon was committed to strengthening francophone communities in the province. Marchildon worked for L'ASSOCIATION CULTURELLE FRANCO-CANADIENNE de la Saskatchewan from 1952 to 1962. With Reverend Roger Ducharme, he created the province's first advanced French curriculum for secondary schools. In 1962, Marchildon founded the Roman Catholic francophone parish of St. André in North Battleford. He later established a French-speaking school and nursing home in connection with the parish. In addition to his responsibilities as a priest, Marchildon helped open ten *caisse populaires* or francophone credit unions across the province. He was made a Member of the Order of Canada in 1986. Père Marchildon died on April 6, 1996. (*See also* FRANCOPHONES; FRENCH EDUCATION IN SASKATCHEWAN)

MARGOSHES, DAVE (1941–). Dave Margoshes is a full-time writer and poet living in Regina. He was born in the United States, and attended school in New York City and rural New Jersey. He received a BA from the University of Iowa and later returned to its well-known Writers' Workshop for a MFA. Margoshes worked for various newspapers in the USA before moving to Canada in the early 1970s. Here he worked for newspapers in Vancouver and Calgary, and taught journalism at Mount Royal College and the Southern Alberta Institute of Technology. In 1986, he moved to Saskatchewan and began freelance writing. His work has been published in Canadian and American magazines, broadcast on CBC, and included five times in *Best Canadian Stories*. He was the writer-in-residence in Winnipeg in 1995–96, and Saskatoon in 2001–02. He still works occasionally as a freelance journalist, a teacher of journalism, an editor, and a leader at creative writing workshops, including the SAGE HILL WRITING EXPERIENCE.

DON HEALY/REGINA LEADER-POST

Dave Margoshes.

Margoshes is the author of novels: *Drowning Man* and *I'm Frankie Sterne*; and of collections of poetry: *Purity of Absence*, *Northwest Passages*, and *Walking at Brighton*. Other books include the story collections *Fables of Creation*, *Long Distance Calls*, *Nine Lives*, and *Small Regrets*. He is also the author of *Tommy Douglas: Building the New Society*, a biography of the Saskatchewan socialist Premier, and of a junior high school resource book, *Discover Canada: Saskatchewan*, which is used in schools in Canada and the USA.

Margoshes' work in fiction, poetry and nonfiction has been recognized with numerous awards and honours including: John V. Hicks Award (SASKATCHEWAN WRITERS GUILD), 2001; Stephen Leacock Poetry Award, 1996; co-winner, Prairie Fire Short Story Contest, 1996; Saskatchewan Writers Guild Literary Award for Fiction, 1994; Saskatchewan Writers Guild Literary Award for Fiction Manuscript, 1990; Saskatchewan Writers Guild Literary Award for Non-fiction, 1990. He helped to organize the SASKATCHEWAN BOOK AWARDS and served as their first chairman; for this, he received the Saskatchewan Writers Guild Volunteer Award in 2000.
Daria Coneghan

MARTENSVILLE, town, pop 4,365, located about 8 km N of Saskatoon on Hwy 12. The community developed on land which had been owned by area farmer Isaac Martens and his son, Dave Martens, who saw an opportunity to subdivide their property for residential development. Substantial growth occurred in the 1960s as Saskatoon was undergoing a period of significant expansion and suburbanites were looking for lower land prices and new homes. In 1966 Martensville was incorporated as a village; it attained town status in 1969. After water and sewer systems were completed in 1976, Martensville began to grow rapidly: between 1976 and 1981, the population grew from 960 to 1,966; ten years later, in 1981, the community had over 3,300 residents. Largely a bedroom community, the town thrives on the economic base provided by Saskatoon; Martensville residents benefit from easy access to the amenities and services that the city has to offer, without having to pay Saskatoon city taxes. Further, according to the 2001 Census, the median income for Martensville households was $58,683, while Saskatoon's was $41,991. Martensville made national headlines in 1992 as the result of an infamous sex abuse scandal.
David McLennan

MARTIN, AGNES (1912–2004). Internationally acclaimed artist Agnes Martin was born in Macklin, Saskatchewan. When her father died in 1914, the family went to live with her grandfather, devout Presbyterian Robert Kinnon, before moving to Calgary and Vancouver, where Martin grew up. She moved to the United States in 1931, and became a US citizen in 1950. Martin pursued a teaching profession, majoring in fine arts and education, with graduate work at the University of New Mexico. In 1957 she moved to New York, where her art was shown in the Betty Parsons Gallery, the centre of the Abstract Expressionist movement. Her work, reflecting the Taoist rejection of ego, evolved into characteristic "grid" and "line" paintings, using a geometric vocabulary to express concepts of space, nature, beauty, order, and perfection. Returning to the mesas of New Mexico in 1967, Martin stopped painting for a time, but resumed work in 1974. In her long career, Martin has garnered international acclaim and influenced scores of artists. Her work, exhibited worldwide, was welcomed in Saskatchewan at the MACKENZIE ART GALLERY in 1995. The sparse geometry of her art reminded many of the beauty of the Saskatchewan plains. In November 2003, her painting "Leaves" (1966) sold at an auction in New York for US$2.5 million–an artist record. She continued to work in Taos, New Mexico until her death on December 16, 2004.
Merle Massie

FURTHER READING: Haskell, B. 1992. *Agnes Martin*. New York: Whitney Museum of American Art; MacKenzie Art Gallery. 1995. *Agnes Martin*. Regina: MacKenzie Art Gallery.

MARTIN, WILLIAM MELVILLE (1876–1970). Martin was born August 23, 1876, in Norwich, Ontario, and died June 22, 1970, in Regina. He was a member of Parliament from 1908 until 1916 and served as Premier of Saskatchewan from 1916 until 1922, when he was appointed to the Saskatchewan Court of Appeal, serving from 1922 until 1961. He married Violette Florence Thompson of Mitchell, Ontario, in 1905. They had three sons.

Martin received his education in the Exeter public school and Clinton Collegiate in Huron County. In 1894 he entered the University of Toronto where he distinguished himself, both as a scholar and as an athlete. He graduated in 1898 with an honours degree in classics, and then attended the Ontario School of Pedagogy in Hamilton where he obtained a teacher's certificate. He taught for two years in Wellington County before returning to study law at Osgoode Hall. In 1903 he joined the law firm of his cousin, James Balfour, in Regina. Both the Martin and Balfour families had been active in Reform/Liberal politics in Ontario, and the Balfour law firm was also active in Liberal politics. In 1905 WALTER SCOTT, the federal member of Parliament for Assiniboia West, resigned his seat to become the first Premier of Saskatchewan. In the 1908 federal election William Martin won the newly created Regina constituency.

Martin became an effective spokesman for western interests, including the need for more railways, reduced freight rates, the incorporation of grain growers' organizations, and other economic, legal and farm related issues. He also addressed law reforms and the North-West Mounted Police, which had its western headquarters in Regina. He won re-election in 1911, strongly supporting the Liberal Unrestricted Reciprocity policy. He also advocated federal assistance for the construction of a proposed railway to Hudson Bay.

In 1916 the Saskatchewan provincial government became embroiled in charges of patronage, political corruption, and a bitter school policy dispute with some Protestant church leaders. Premier Scott suffered ill health and resigned in October 1916. JAMES CALDER, the logical successor, was taint-

SASKATCHEWAN ARCHIVES BOARD R-B2904

William Melville Martin, as Chief Justice, ca. 1960.

ed by the scandal and declined to lead the government. The party turned to William Martin who, as a devout Presbyterian, was expected to heal the rift that developed between Premier Scott and prominent Presbyterians.

The Martin government established several Royal Commissions and dealt decisively with those found guilty of inappropriate behaviour. Martin established and maintained a scandal-free administration. The most notable policies of the new government included granting women the right to vote in provincial elections, reforms of the educational system which required all children between the ages of 7 and 14 to attend an approved school, establishment of a government mortgage-lending organization for farmers, reform of the provincial courts, and passage of a **SASKATCHEWAN BILL OF RIGHTS** which demanded federal tariff reductions and the transfer to the province of Crown lands and resources.

In his first election as Premier in 1917, Martin and his **LIBERAL PARTY** won 50 of the 59 seats in the Legislature. Later that year, Martin endorsed a decision by some federal Liberals to join with the governing Conservatives to form a Union government which was committed to a more aggressive war effort and to the introduction of a policy of military conscription. The Union government also followed tariff and other domestic policies that were not popular in Saskatchewan. That led to the organization of a new western protest party—the **PROGRESSIVE PARTY** of Canada—to represent the interests of farmers. Provincially the Progressives (known as the United Farmers) were elected as minority governments in Ontario and Manitoba, and to a strong majority government in Alberta. Martin and the Saskatchewan Liberals blunted the Progressive appeal by bringing prominent farm leaders into the government, introducing legislation advocated by the Progressives, and calling a provincial election in June 1921 before the provincial Progressives were well organized.

The Liberals won the 1921 provincial election with a large majority, but faced a crisis in the federal election held later in 1921. The federal contest in Saskatchewan pitted Progressives against Liberals in many constituencies. Premier Martin made several speeches in support of Liberal candidates in which he also declared his personal opposition to many of the policies of the Progressives. That led to the resignation of **J.A. MAHARG**, the provincial Minister of Agriculture and a strong supporter of Progressives. The tensions in the Cabinet and caucus culminated in Martin's resignation as Premier at the age of 46. His successor, **CHARLES DUNNING**, was a former farm leader and enjoyed the support of members who supported the Progressives federally.

William Martin was appointed as a judge in the Saskatchewan Court of Appeal shortly after his resignation as Premier. There he joined Chief Justice Sir

FREDERICK HAULTAIN, the Territorial Premier before 1905. Martin succeeded Haultain as Chief Justice in 1941 and served in that capacity until his retirement in 1961 at the age of 84. During the war, Martin also served as custodian of Enemy Alien Property in Canada, and in 1949 he was chairman of a commission assigned the task of revising the Canadian Criminal Code.   *Ted Regehr*

FURTHER READING: Barnhart, Gordon L. (ed.). 2004. *Saskatchewan Premiers of the Twentieth Century.* Regina: Canadian Plains Research Center.

MATADOR FARMING POOL AND THE CO-OPERATIVE FARM MOVEMENT. Matador is the most successful of the co-operative farms established under the auspices of Saskatchewan's CCF government following **WORLD WAR II**. Set southwestern Saskatchewan, it is one of the original settlements of the province's postwar co-operative community movement and its last survivor. The co-operative tradition arose in western Canada at the end of the 19th century and became an integral part of the agrarian settlement of the west. This tradition of rural co-operation was overwhelmingly Rochdalian or *liberal democratic*, that is, a form of co-operative organization that accepted the existence of the capitalist market-place, respected the family ownership of farms as private property, and advocated the pooling of purchasing and marketing functions through farmer-owned co-operatives. A liberal democratic co-op tended to deal with a single aspect of a person's life: that concerned with credit, farm production marketing, retail supplies, and so on. In contrast, the co-op farms were *intentional co-operative communities*, which created a co-operative lifestyle for their members and linked a variety of co-operative institutions under one organizational roof. Co-operative community lifestyles tended towards the communal, and land and assets were owned and worked co-operatively.

The impulse for co-op farms grew out of the democratic socialist vision of the CCF government, first elected in 1944. Taking a bold leap forward in co-operative ideology, the CCF fostered the establishment of co-operative farm communities, which were to be harbingers of a new socialist lifestyle. In some cases, established farmlands were pooled by farmers attracted by the idea, while in others virgin land was given to returning war veterans, who built new communities where none had existed. The co-op farm concept rejected private property and the single-family farming unit in favour of co-operative ownership and lifestyle. Beginning in 1945, the new CCF government offered assistance in the form of free Crown lands, operational loans, and technical advice to those who were willing to farm co-operatively. Among the target groups were Saskatchewan war veterans, for whom it was hoped the co-op

farms would provide resettlement opportunities. Founding members of the Matador Co-operative Farm first came together in April 1946; all were demobilized veterans, mainly young, single men. As a group they were granted 10,000 acres of grass prairie, a 33-year lease on the property with an option to purchase after ten years, and rent payable at one-seventh the value of the crop. With about $40,000 in capital and the goodwill and support of the provincial government, the seventeen Matador veterans began their pioneering work, creating a community and turning dry southwestern Saskatchewan into productive farmland.

Despite a couple of crop failures in the early years due to hail and drought, Matador was soon producing large quantities of high-quality grain—so much, in fact, that the farm was unable to either market it or store it when the quota system was introduced in 1950. As a result, the Matador diversified into livestock, a move made easier by the large pool of labour available on a co-operatively run farm. For a number of years Matador was a thriving community, with its own school and co-operative store.

Conditions continued to improve until 1956, when the right-to-purchase clause in the leases kicked in and the farm faced its first major internal crisis. Three members left the co-op, taking their houses and families to the neighbouring village of Kyle. Although this loss was partially made up for by new members, the general trend of decline in co-op farms apparent in the wider community was firmly established. At the same time the number of production co-ops—a limited form of machinery pooling or pasture sharing—increased dramatically from 52 in 1949 to 313 in 1964. This form of co-op maintained the family farm unit and private ownership.

By the 1960s, the acculturation of the generation born at Matador was well underway. The on-site school closed in 1966 because of declining enrolment, and the remaining children were bussed to outside schools. Reaching maturity in the late 1960s, the majority of the children left the farm. For those who remained, the issue of land was resolved in 1974 when the NDP government established the Saskatchewan Land Bank. Under this program, the younger generation incorporated an entity called the Matador Farm Pool, leasing the original 10,000 acres of Matador land from the Land Bank, which had purchased it from the retiring co-op farmers, allowing them to take their equity out of the organization without burdening the next generation with an unmanageable debt. At the time, only about twenty-five people were left at Matador, but the transfer brought in another twenty. Together, they carried the co-operative farming tradition into the 21st century. In 1999, the group amalgamated with a Saskatchewan numbered corporation to become the Matador Farming Pool Limited. By 2004,

EVERETT BAKER PHOTO/COURTESY OF THE SASKATCHEWAN HISTORY AND FOLKLORE SOCIETY
Veterans planting trees at the Matador Co-op Farm, May 1948.

Matador had eight members; their families were still living on the original site, and engaged in the same general activities that have occupied Matador since its inception in 1946. Today the co-op farm concentrates on grain and cattle production, and also owns two seed-cleaning plants. In addition to the eight members and their families, the farm supports eight full-time and three part-time employees.

Matador played a notable part in the proliferation of co-op farms between 1945 and 1952. There were five co-op farms incorporated in 1946, twenty by 1950, and thirty-two during the peak year of 1952; about 1,000 people lived on these farms at that point. With Saskatchewan's total farm population at the time standing at 400,000, this represented a tiny fraction of active farm residents in spite of eight years of government support and encouragement. Matador itself had sixty-three residents, considerably higher than the average thirty to fifty on the other co-op farms. As time progressed, the co-op farm idea of 1944 no longer had much relevance or interest, and the number of registered co-op farms began a steady decline, with membership dropping by 50% over the next twenty years. It is important here to distinguish membership in the co-op from residency on the farms: with only one person per family being a member, there were consequently many more residents than actual co-op members, although everyone contributed to farm livelihood.

The co-op farms that remained in the 1970s were primarily extended family operations: related members of a family had chosen to incorporate as a co-operative in which each member held an equal interest. The once-great experiment in co-operative living had been reduced to a pragmatic solution to the need for ever larger amounts of land to sustain profitable farm operations. The new bond was traditional kinship—not the founders' dream of a socialist society. The reasons for the quick rise and gradual demise of the co-op farm movement are many. Initially, the input of the CCF government gave the movement credibility and support, but this waned after 1952 when the movement came to be viewed as one of narrow appeal and unimportant to CCF re-election. Second, the experiment did not achieve the critical mass of a powerful subculture that would have allowed it to survive in the dominant society and develop into a successful movement like HUTTERITE communal farms. With a relatively small membership and limited appeal to the wider Saskatchewan farm community that was itself on the path of depopulation, the co-op farm movement never matured beyond its initial utopian stage. In addition, the experience of military camaraderie that had underpinned the early years at Matador was changed in later years by marriage and loyalty to family and children: these traditional responsibilities and commitments modified the focus of the members' lives. The slow disintegration of other co-op farms had a demoralizing effect on those who remained in the movement. Matador, clinging to the original vision, became more and more an island in a sea of single-family farms that were themselves being amalgamated into ever larger units through the demands of the market and the capacity of new technology.

Inevitably, this trend affected Matador. Its land base did not grow, so the community shrank to fit the limited land base, which could support fewer and fewer families. The decline in the membership at Matador, in fact, reflected the general decline in numbers participating in farming in the province, which dropped by approximately 50% between the mid-1940s and mid-1980s. Nevertheless, the fact that an economically successful co-operative farm like Matador did not expand during its prime is somewhat puzzling. There are several possible explanations. The continuing uncertainty over land tenure and the unclear legal basis for co-op farm landholding was one cause. Likewise, the ideological commitment of the individual members varied, making it difficult for all its members to view Matador as a vanguard of social change. Because the co-op farm movement had deteriorated by the 1970s, Matador ended up dealing with the economic interests of its members rather than sustaining a radical vision for Saskatchewan agriculture. There was also the issue of leadership: the co-op farm movement was initially led by politicians and ideologically motivated bureaucrats, who inspired people to join and offered free land as an enticement, but were not co-operative farmers themselves. Unlike the Rochdale or liberal democratic co-ops of Saskatchewan such as the wheat pools and credit unions, which were initiated outside of government and led from within, the co-op farm movement never developed its own indigenous cadre of leaders.

Initial adherents to the concept came for a variety of reasons. Some were high-minded while others were opportunistic; some were revolutionaries while others were simply interested in government aid. And the commitment to co-operative living varied from person to person. As a consequence, there was no coherent, unified body of thought to guide the experiment and build loyalty. In addition, there was no indigenous secular utopian tradition to relate to, so participants were isolated in their pioneering activities. While the co-op farms had the advantage of external support, this support meant a certain level of dependence, which would later help undermine the experiment. The initial government activity on behalf of co-op farms did not allow a substantial self-help attitude to develop, which would have promoted mutual aid and interdependence among participants. Unlike Hutterite communal farms, which have flourished in the same time period using self-help and the ideology of growth, co-op farms turned more to government than to each other. As a result, the internal strength necessary to build a successful movement did not materialize. Despite the failure of the movement as a whole, Matador remains, after half a century, a symbol of a socialist experiment unique to Canada and has entered the mythology of Saskatchewan's democratic socialist identity.

George Melnyk

MATERNITY HOMES. Maternity homes, specializing in the care of parturient women from their surrounding areas, appeared in Saskatchewan as early as 1895. They reached peak numbers toward the end of the **DEPRESSION** and into the early years of **WORLD WAR II**. The homes were located mainly in rural towns and villages. Committed to avoiding the anxiety associated with home births and the assistance of the by-then-unfashionable midwife, these homes offered Saskatchewan women inexpensive maternity care in their own communities.They were most often run by a married or widowed woman who had only practical experience instead of formal training; by 1940, just over a third of maternity home matrons were graduate nurses. Such a home-based business was practical for a woman who was in need of an income and had some knowledge of childbirth. Though there was not a great deal of profit to be made, these nurses usually enjoyed long-term careers as health care providers.

The widespread use of these private maternity services represented a mid-phase in the transition from home to hospital births prior to the CCF building boom that radically increased the number of available **HOSPITALS** in the late 1940s. This post-war social policy also changed what was deemed adequate and efficient health care, and it soon became clear that maternity homes did not meet these modern standards. A small number did, however, operate until the early 1960s in more northerly and isolated areas.   *Laurel Halladay*

FURTHER READING: Halladay, L. 1996. "'We'll See You Next Year:' Maternity Homes in Southern Saskatchewan in the First Half of the Twentieth Century." MA thesis, Carleton University.

MATHESON, ELIZABETH (1866–1958). Elizabeth Beckett Scott was born near Campbellford, Ontario, on January 6, 1866. When she was 12, her family moved to Morris, Manitoba. Later she taught for three years, then registered at the Women's Medical College, Queen's University, Kingston in 1887. After a year of training, she went to Bombay, India, as a missionary. After contracting malaria, she moved back to Canada and married John "Grace" Matheson. The following year, the couple was posted to Onion Lake, Saskatchewan. Elizabeth returned to Toronto in 1896 to complete her medical training and receive an MD degree from the University of Trinity College, Toronto. The NWT College of Physicians and Surgeons refused to register her, so she went to Winnipeg to repeat fourth year medicine and received a second MD degree in 1904. In 1908, the three-storey hospital at Onion Lake, with four wards and an operating room, was completed. When her husband died in 1916, Elizabeth became principal of the Onion Lake school. She completed her career as Assistant

SASKATCHEWAN ARCHIVES BOARD R-A17686-1

Elizabeth Matheson.

Medical Supervisor of Public Schools in Winnipeg from 1918 to 1948. Elizabeth died in San Antonio, Texas, on January 15, 1958, at the age of 92. Her daughter, Ruth Matheson Buck, wrote her biography, *The Doctor Rode Side-Saddle* (1974, reprinted 2003 by the Canadian Plains Research Center).

C. Stuart Houston

MATTHEWS, VINCENT LEON (1922–88). Vince Matthews was born at Kincaid, Saskatchewan, on February 6, 1922. He began university in Saskatoon, and graduated from Medicine at the University of Toronto in 1945. By 1947 he was assistant to the director of Regional Health Services in Saskatchewan. He served as the Swift Current region's Medical Health Officer from 1948 to 1957. His principled yet practical approach, bolstered by certification as a specialist in public health in 1953

COURTESY OF A. PATRICIA MATTHEWS

Vincent Matthews.

and experience as a general practitioner in Maple Creek for two years, enabled him to help the region's administrator, board, and local physicians to make the medical, hospital, dental and public health programs function effectively. In 1957 he headed the Medical and Hospital Services Branch of Saskatchewan Health, and accepted an appointment as Acting Deputy Minister of Health a few days before the doctors' strike in 1962; he then became Associate Deputy Minister of Health. Matthews was head of the Department of Social and Preventive Medicine in the College of Medicine at the **UNIVERSITY OF SASKATCHEWAN** from 1964 until 1987. He was a celebrated national and international leader in public health, as well as a key player in Saskatchewan's evolving health system. He died suddenly in Saskatoon on July 7, 1988.   *Joan Feather*

REGINA LEADER-POST

Peter McCann, 1993.

MCCANN, PETER. Originally from Bolton, England, Peter McCann attended University in Edinburgh, Scotland, graduating with majors in biochemistry and microbiology. He worked in a variety of management positions in the food and beverage processing industries in England, Scotland, Sweden, and Malta. He continued his efforts in Newfoundland, Ontario, Alberta and Saskatchewan after he arrived in Canada in 1971. In Saskatchewan, McCann served as president of Prairie Malt Ltd. in Biggar, and was the founder and first president of the **GREAT WESTERN BREWING COMPANY** in Saskatoon. In 1994, he founded and became the first president of the BioProducts Centre, based at Innovation Place Research Park, and in 1995 he led the formation of the Canadian Value Added Cereals Consortium and then the Saskatchewan Nutraceuticals Network. In January 1997, he was appointed president of **AG-WEST BIOTECH INC.** During his tenure he was involved in the start-up of eight life sciences companies, was instrumental in assisting several multinational life sciences companies to establish in

Saskatchewan, and was frequently called upon to provide input to federal and provincial life sciences policy development and in regulatory affairs. While in Saskatoon, Peter McCann sat on the Boards of numerous Canadian ag-biotech organizations, including several private companies as well as National Research Council Plant Biotechnology Institute, Genome Prairie, Bioproducts Canada, BioCap Foundation, Biotechnology Human Resources Canada, and Canadian Agri-Food Marketing Council (CAMC). He was also active in the local community, serving as an elected alderman on Saskatoon City Council from 1982 to 2003. McCann semi-retired in 2003 and moved to Belleville, Ontario, but continues to act as a consultant for industry and government.   *Camille D. Ryan*

MCCARGAR, WILLIAM (1906–80). William C. McCargar was born on December 28, 1906, in Newcastle, Ontario and grew up in Moose Jaw, Saskatchewan. A self-taught folk artist, he worked for many years for the CANADIAN PACIFIC RAILWAY in Balgonie. He started painting as a hobby in 1958, and had his first exhibit, entitled *Windmills, Wagons and Railroads*, at the Dunlop Art Gallery in 1973. McCargar exhibited regularly with the SASKATCHEWAN ARTS BOARD annual exhibition, as well as in other local Regina shows. His work was featured prominently in *Grassroots Saskatchewan* at the MACKENZIE ART GALLERY in 1976 and in the magazine *Artscanada* in 1979. He also had a solo show at the Rosemont Art Gallery in Regina in 1975. McCargar died on February 18, 1980.

In April 1987, the Dunlop Art Gallery held a major exhibition of his works entitled *McCargar: Retrospective Exhibition*. He often painted images of rural Saskatchewan, capturing the all-familiar prairie manmade elements: grain elevators, trains, and telephone poles. His work is found in a number of private and public collections, including the Canadian Museum of Civilization in Hull (Quebec), the MENDEL ART GALLERY (Saskatoon), THE SASKATCHEWAN ARTS BOARD, and the UNIVERSITY OF SASKATCHEWAN.   *Daralyn Fauser*

FURTHER READING: Newman, M. 1990. "Cargar, William Coulsen." In *Biographical Dictionary of Saskatchewan Artists: Men Artists*. Saskatoon: Fifth House.

MCCONNELL, HOWARD (1886–1957). McConnell was born in Springbrook, Ontario, on January 27, 1886. He worked briefly as a teacher after high school and then moved in 1907 to Saskatoon to join his parents. He became the first president of the Student Representative Council at the UNIVERSITY OF SASKATCHEWAN in 1911. After graduating, he completed a law degree at Osgoode Hall in Toronto and was called to the Saskatchewan Bar in 1916. He operated a legal practice in

Saskatoon from 1916 until after WORLD WAR II and was appointed King's Council in 1929. McConnell served three terms on Saskatoon City Council between 1919 and 1922 and two terms as mayor in 1922 and 1923. In 1927 he ran successfully for the Conservatives in a provincial by-election in Saskatoon. The 1929 provincial election replaced the Liberals with a Conservative-Progressive coalition led by J.T.M. ANDERSON at the onset of the GREAT DEPRESSION. McConnell was first named Provincial Treasurer and later Minister of Municipal Affairs. In the former capacity he struggled with plummeting revenues to maintain even basic services, and in the latter he attempted through the SASKATCHEWAN RELIEF COMMISSION to coordinate relief programs. In the 1934 election every single government supporter was defeated. McConnell returned to his law practice and remained active in community organizations for the remainder of his life. He was a member of the University of Saskatchewan senate for twenty-three years, active in the UNITED CHURCH, and a Mason. McConnell died in Saskatoon on October 9, 1957.   *Michael Cottrell*

MCCONNELL, RICHARD GEORGE (1857–1942). Richard George McConnell was born in Chatham, Ontario, on March 26, 1857. He studied at McGill University and joined the Geological Survey of Canada in 1879. Much of his early survey work was done as assistant to GEORGE MERCER DAWSON in British Columbia and on the prairies, although he also participated in mapping in Quebec. Dawson and McConnell surveyed the coalfields of southern Alberta, but McConnell also mapped the area further east (now Saskatchewan) between the MISSOURI COTEAU and the CYPRESS HILLS, again taking particular note of coal deposits preserved on the Tertiary uplands. However, he is probably best known for his work in the Yukon and Mackenzie Valley: he studied the Klondike gold fields and in 1903 investigated the cause of the Frank slide in the Crowsnest Pass. After many years of work in the field, McConnell was promoted to the position of Deputy Minister of Mines in 1914 but, in the face of difficulties in finding adequate staff to fill the poorly paid positions in the Survey, he applied for superannuation and retired on May 7, 1921. He died in Ottawa on April 1, 1942.   *Marilyn Lewry*

FURTHER READING: McConnell, R.G. 1885. *Report on the Cypress Hills, Wood Mountain and Adjacent Country*. Geology and Natural History Survey of Canada Annual Report (New Series), Vol. 1, pt. C: 1–78; Zaslow, M.1975. *Reading the Rocks: the Story of the Geological Survey of Canada 1842–1972*. Ottawa: Macmillan.

MCCOURT, EDWARD (1907–72). Edward McCourt is often identified as a regional author for his ability to incorporate in his work the effect of the

prairie environment on individuals. His assessment of Saskatchewan, its landscape, history, and inhabitants was no less affectionate for being blunt and clear-sighted. Born in Mullingar, Ireland, on October 10, 1907, McCourt was two years old when his family emigrated to Canada, homesteading near Kitscoty, Alberta. His high school education was by correspondence, and he made his first trip to a city when he began studies at the University of Alberta. An exceptional athlete as well as a scholar, McCourt earned a BA from the University of Alberta and was its Rhodes Scholar in 1932. He earned both a BA (1934) and an MA (1937) while at Oxford. He worked briefly at Upper Canada College, Queen's University, and the University of New Brunswick prior to joining the faculty of the UNIVERSITY OF SASKATCHEWAN in 1944.

A prolific author, his literary output was notable for its range. Author of numerous academic articles, McCourt also published several short stories and began more extensive works with the publication of a novel, *Music at the Close*, in 1947, for which he received the All Canada Fiction Award. He authored six novels, including *Home is the Stranger* (1950), *The Wooden Sword* (1958), and *Fasting Friar* (1963). He is equally known for his works of non-fiction, particularly *Revolt in the West* (1958), about the NORTH-WEST RESISTANCE, and *Remembering Butler* (1967), an exceptional biography of Sir William Butler. His travelogues concerning Saskatchewan, the north, and Canada endure, owing to his astute and often humorous observations. One of the first discussions of prairie regional literature, *The Canadian West in Fiction* (1949) remains an important work of literary criticism. McCourt died on January 6, 1972.   *Cheryl Avery*

MCCUSKER, EMMET ANDREW (1890–1973). Emmet McCusker was born in Alfred, Ontario on February 9, 1890. His family moved west and homesteaded just north of the budding city of Regina in 1903. After his father died in 1908, Emmet helped run the farm, and then entered medicine at McGill University in 1911. In 1914 he joined the Canadian Expeditionary Force as a private in the Royal Canadian Army Medical Corps, serving in France and Belgium. In 1915 he was sent back to McGill to finish his medical course, graduating in 1916. Following re-enlistment, he was awarded the Military Cross at Hill 70 in 1917. McCusker took further training in diseases of eye, ear, nose and throat in Montreal, New York and Vienna before entering private practice in Regina in 1923. He became president of the Saskatchewan COLLEGE OF PHYSICIANS AND SURGEONS, the Saskatchewan Division of the CMA, the SASKATCHEWAN ROUGHRIDER Football Club, the Canadian Football Union and, as one of the Regina Flying Club's first graduating pilots, president of the Canadian Flying Clubs Association.

SASKATCHEWAN ARCHIVES BOARD R-A628

Howard McConnell.

SASKATCHEWAN ARCHIVES BOARD R-A17459

Emmet Andrew McCusker, at Regina Airport.

SASKATCHEWAN ARCHIVES BOARD PS64-201-07

Alexander Hamilton McDonald.

With the onset of **WORLD WAR II**, he was promoted to Lt. Colonel and was sent overseas as assistant director of Medical Services, First Canadian Division. Following promotions to Colonel and then Brigadier, he became deputy director of Medical Services, serving in England, Sicily and Italy. He was awarded the Efficiency Decoration, was made Commander of the Order of British Empire, and received the Greek Distinguished Service Medal. After World War II, McCusker was the first board chairman of the Medical Arts Clinic. In 1949 he was elected as member of Parliament for Regina City and became Parliamentary Assistant to the Minister of Health, Paul Martin, Sr. His efforts resulted, among other things, in bringing water to Regina from the South Saskatchewan River, in the building of a new post office, and in the extending of the main runway at Regina Airport.

McCusker was a co-owner of radio station CKRM, and a director of Ducks Unlimited. The Wascana Golf and Country, the Assiniboia, the Antipoh and the New Comemen clubs, the **KNIGHTS OF COLUMBUS**, and Notre Dame College each benefited from his wisdom. He died in Regina on January 20, 1973. *Murray M. Fraser*

MCDONALD, ALEXANDER HAMILTON (1919–80).

"Hammy" McDonald was born on March 16, 1919, and grew up in Fleming. In **WORLD WAR II**, he served as a flight lieutenant for the RCAF from 1940 to 1945. He married Madeline Anne Casey and they had three children. McDonald worked as a farmer and later became a businessman in Moosomin and Regina. He was active locally in the Canadian Legion, the Caterpillar Club, and the United Church. McDonald won the Moosomin constituency for the Liberals in the 1948 provincial election. He held this seat for five consecutive elections from 1948 to 1963 and resigned on May 25, 1965. McDonald was leader of the **LIBERAL PARTY**

from 1954 to 1959. Following his role as Opposition leader in the Saskatchewan Legislature, McDonald was provincial Agriculture Minister and Deputy Premier in Premier **ROSS THATCHER**'s Cabinet. Before finishing the term, McDonald resigned his seat. Less than three months later, Pierre Trudeau summoned McDonald to the Senate. He served on a number of committees and represented Canada as a member of the Commonwealth Parliamentary Association. In 1968 McDonald participated on the National Capital Commission. In the fall of 1968, McDonald was appointed deputy government leader in the Senate, making him responsible for steering all legislation through the Senate. By 1969 McDonald added chief whip to his list of responsibilities. McDonald died on March 31, 1980, shortly after delivering a speech in the Senate. *Erika Dyck*

MCDOUGALL, MEDERIC ZEPHIRIN (1903–89).

Born on December 29, 1903, Mederic McDougall was a long-serving member of the Métis and Francophone communities in St-Louis, Saskatchewan. He began his employment with the rural municipality of St-Louis in 1944 and served as a school trustee for eighteen years and a town councillor for three years. McDougall was a founding member and delegate of the Métis Association and president of the **ASSOCIATION CULTURELLE FRANCO-CANADIENNE** in his village. He received his appointment as a Member of the Order of Canada in 1985. He died on June 20, 1989.

MCDOWELL, STIRLING (1931–2002).

Born in Nipawin in 1931, Stirling McDowell attended the Saskatoon Normal School and earned Bachelor of Arts and Education degrees as well as a Master's of Education degree from the **UNIVERSITY OF SASKATCHEWAN**. He completed a PhD in Education at the University of Alberta. After teaching in Outlook and Rosetown, he joined the staff of the **SASKATCHEWAN**

TEACHERS' FEDERATION (STF) in 1957. He served as STF general secretary from 1967 to 1982, and then became secretary general of the Canadian Teachers' Federation in Ottawa until 1993. He retired to Saskatoon, where he continued to work on a contract and volunteer basis until his death in 2002. McDowell was the first chair of the Saskatchewan Universities Commission. His reputation for taking a co-operative approach to negotiations contributed to the **EDUCATION ACT** of 1978 and the development of a bi-level system of collective bargaining for teachers in 1973. In 1994–95, he chaired an independent committee on compensation for members of the Legislative Assembly, which resulted in Saskatchewan becoming the second province to make MLA salaries fully taxable. He was a delegate to many international conferences, including the founding convention of Education International in Stockholm in 1993. He was president of both the provincial and national associations for retired teachers, as well as an honorary life member of the Saskatchewan Teachers' Federation and the Canadian Educational Association. He received the Canadian Teachers' Federation Special Recognition Award in 1993, and in 1997 was awarded the Saskatchewan Order of Merit.

In 1991 the Saskatchewan Teachers' Federation established in his name a foundation for research into teaching. The Stirling McDowell Foundation is a charitable organization that funds research aimed at the improvement of teaching and learning in publicly funded elementary and secondary schools. Grants are given annually to teachers and others who submit research proposals to the Foundation. It encourages teachers to develop projects involving collaborative action research as a means of improving instruction and stimulating professional growth. The results of all McDowell projects are published by the Foundation and highlighted at an annual conference. *Verna Gallen and Bill Quine*

MCEWEN, CLIFFORD MACKAY (1896–1967). Air Vice-Marshal Clifford McEwen was born at Griswold, Manitoba on July 2, 1896, and raised in Moose Jaw. After receiving his education at the **UNIVERSITY OF SASKATCHEWAN**, he enlisted in the 196th Battalion of the Canadian Expeditionary Force in 1916. Becoming an officer shortly after arriving in England, McEwen was assigned to Britain's Royal Flying Corps, where he learned to fly. As a member of No. 28 Squadron, RFC, in Italy during 1918, he was credited with shooting down 22 enemy aircraft, making him an "Ace." For his wartime service, McEwen was awarded the Military Cross, the Distinguished Flying Cross with Bar, and the Italian Bronze Medal for Valour. During the interwar years, McEwen was a flying instructor; in 1930 he attended the Royal Air Force Staff College at Cranwell, Lincolnshire. At the outbreak of **WORLD WAR II** in 1939, he was a Group Captain stationed at Trenton, Ontario. In 1941, McEwen was promoted to Air Commodore and given command of the Royal Canadian Air Force's No. 1 Group at St. John's, Newfoundland, which was then waging a vital war against German U-boats in the North Atlantic. Promoted to Air Vice-Marshal, he was appointed Air Officer Commanding No. 6 (Bomber) Group in Yorkshire, England on February 28, 1944. This was a critical point in the strategic air offensive against Germany, and McEwen quickly established a rigorous training program, resulting in increased combat efficiency and reduced casualty rates. When the European war ended, he was designated commander of the Canadian bomber group to be sent to the Pacific Theatre to fight against the Japanese, but with the collapse of Japan in August 1945 the plan was scrapped. McEwen retired from the Royal Canadian Air Force in 1946 and became a private consultant to aircraft manufacturers. For two years he was a director of Trans-Canada Air Lines, the predecessor of Air Canada. McEwen died on August 6, 1967, aged 71; he is buried in Fund's Field of Honour, Pointe Claire, Quebec. On June 17, 2003, 15 Wing Moose Jaw was renamed Air Vice-Marshal C.M. McEwen Airfield, the first Canadian Forces airfield to be named in honour of a Canadian military aviation legend. *Jeff R. Noel*

MCFARLANE, DOUGLAS (1918–99). McFarlane was born in Wolseley on January 4, 1918. Educated in Summerberry, McFarlane worked on the family farm until 1940 when he joined the RCAF, attaining the rank of sergeant. He returned to farm in the Peebles district, married Frances Davidson, and they had four sons. McFarlane first ran for the Saskatchewan Legislature as a Liberal for Qu'Appelle-Wolseley in 1952, but was defeated. He was elected in 1956 and was re-elected in 1960, 1964, and 1967. He served in **ROSS THATCHER**'s Cabinet as Minister of Municipal Affairs from 1964

© M.WEST, REGINA, WEST'S STUDIO
COLLECTION/SASKATCHEWAN ARCHIVES BOARD R-A8391
Douglas McFarlane.

to 1965, when he was appointed Minister of Agriculture, a position he held until his defeat in 1971. During his tenure as Minister of Agriculture, the Liberals advocated a policy of diversification of Saskatchewan agriculture. In order to counteract decreasing wheat exports, the government passed legislation promoting the expansion of the livestock industry in the province. In 1971, after a failed attempt at re-election, McFarlane was appointed to the War Veterans Appeal Board in Ottawa and later moved to Charlottetown. He retired to Winnipeg in 1983 where he died on May 6, 1999. *Roberta Lexier*

FURTHER READING: Saskatchewan Archives Board. Douglas McFarlane Papers. GR 424. Regina.

MCGILL, FRANCES (1882–1959). Frances McGill was among the first Canadian women to become a pathologist, and for four decades enjoyed a reputation as a leading criminologist. Born in rural Manitoba on November 18, 1882, she completed her education in Winnipeg, including Normal School. She taught school during the summers to help finance studies at Manitoba Medical College, where she was one of the earliest women to graduate (1915). She then took a post-graduate course that included a stint in the Provincial Laboratory and work in forensic medicine. In 1918 McGill came to Regina when she was appointed Provincial Bacteriologist in Saskatchewan. In 1920 she was named Provincial Pathologist, and in 1922 was appointed director of the Saskatchewan Laboratories, positions she held until her retirement in 1942. McGill's duties came to include forensic pathology work for the **ROYAL CANADIAN MOUNTED POLICE** (RCMP). It took several criminal cases before the RCMP acknowledged that her expertise could save them from conflicting medical advice, and ordered that she be called immediately if a sudden

death exhibited the slightest signs of foul play. She also helped establish the first RCMP Crime Detection Laboratory, and taught Forensic Medicine at their Regina Training Barracks. On January 16, 1946, Frances McGill became the first woman appointed by the Canadian Minister of Justice as Honorary Surgeon to the RCMP. She died in Winnipeg on January 21,1959. Saskatchewan honoured McGill by naming a lake after her. *Myrna Petersen*

FURTHER READING: Hacker, C. 1974. *The Indomitable Lady Doctors.* Toronto and Vancouver: Clarke, Irwin & Company.

MCGILL, RUTH SWITZER (1909–74). Ruth Switzer McGill was a prominent barrister and solicitor in Regina, as well as an influential community leader. She was born on December 31, 1909, in Ontario; her family soon moved to Regina, where she attended school before going to the **UNIVERSITY OF SASKATCHEWAN**. After receiving a BA (English), she studied law, becoming the seventh woman to graduate from the University of Saskatchewan Law School (1932). She was admitted to the Saskatchewan Bar in 1933. Her father, Arthur McGill, had founded the Debenture Company of Canada, which specialized in the administration of insolvent farms, and served as its president until 1955; Ruth McGill then took over until her death. In 1965 she established with James Robb the law firm of McGill and Robb. McGill was active in community affairs from 1933 to 1964. She had numerous leadership roles in women's organizations, including the Provincial Council of Women, the League of Women Voters, and the Women's Canadian Club. Long involved with the Canadian Federation of Business and Professional Women's Club, she served as national president from 1948 to1950, and in 1962 she held the position of second vice-president of the International Federation. In 1946, she became the third woman elected to the Regina City Council. She served in this position for four years while simultaneously holding a position on the Regina Hospital Board. In 1948 she was also the chairperson of the Board of Health. Until her death on May 26, 1974, McGill continued to play a significant role in numerous women's organizations, while at the same time maintaining control of the Debenture Company of Canada and running a successful law firm. *Tracy Tomlinson*

MCINTOSH, C. IRWIN (1926–88). Cameron Irwin McIntosh was born in North Battleford on July 1, 1926, and educated at the **UNIVERSITY OF SASKATCHEWAN**. His father, Cameron Ross McIntosh, was a Liberal MP from 1925 to 1940. In 1952 Irwin McIntosh took over from his father as president of McIntosh Publishing in North Battleford. In 1978, when Lieutenant-Governor **GEORGE PORTEOUS** died

Cameron Irwin McIntosh, Lieutenant-Governor, November 1979.

in office, Pierre Trudeau appointed Irwin McIntosh as fifteenth Lieutenant-Governor of Saskatchewan. His tenure began in controversy when he expressed a public opinion in favour of capital punishment and was criticized by the Premier for doing so. He gradually restored positive relations between the vice-regal office and the NDP administration of **ALLAN BLAKENEY**, which had been cool since the time of **FRANK BASTEDO**. This was accomplished mainly through his support of the national unity campaign, following the election in 1977 of the first Parti Québécois government in Quebec, and his active participation in the provincial 75th anniversary program, "Celebrate Saskatchewan," in 1980. In 1981 Irwin McIntosh inaugurated the provincial vice-regal flag, based on a national pattern. Although he presided at the opening of the restored Government House in 1980, the office of the Lieutenant-Governor remained at the Hotel Saskatchewan. At the end of his tenure Mr. McIntosh publicly appealed for better accommodation for his successor. He died September 24, 1988.   *Michael Jackson*

FURTHER READING: Hryniuk, Margaret and Garth Pugh. 1991. *"A Tower of Attraction": An Illustrated History of Government House, Regina, Saskatchewan.* Regina: Government House Historical Society/Canadian Plains Research Center; Leeson, Howard A. (ed.). 2001. *Saskatchewan Politics: Into the Twenty-first Century.* Regina: Canadian Plains Research Center.

MCINTOSH, LACHLAN FRASER (1897– 1962). Born in Bottineau, North Dakota, on July 30, 1897, McIntosh moved in 1906 with his family

to the Qu'Appelle district where he was educated and began farming. Moving to Prince Albert, he became involved in the co-operative movement. In 1923 he helped organize the Saskatchewan Wheat Pool and was the first delegate from the Prince Albert region in 1924. McIntosh was involved in many Prince Albert organizations such as the Board of Trade and the Agricultural Society. In 1944, McIntosh was elected as the CCF member representing Prince Albert. He was appointed to **T.C. DOUGLAS'** first Cabinet initially as Minister of Public Works, but soon was asked to establish the new department of Co-operation. During his five years as Minister, the number of co-operatives and credit unions in Saskatchewan increased significantly, as did their membership. McIntosh served for a period as Minister of Agriculture. After re-election in 1948, he became Minister of Municipal Affairs where he implemented a program whereby the province paid half of the cost of upgrading 12,000 miles of the municipal grid road for all-weather travel. After **WOODROW LLOYD** became Premier in 1961, McIntosh was moved back into the Co-operation portfolio. He was still in office when he died on March 17, 1962.
Brett Quiring

Lachlan McIntosh.

MCINTYRE, DAVID L. (1950–). Composer, pianist and teacher David Leroy McIntyre was born on September 11, 1950, in Edmonton, Alberta. In 1969, having completed his associate diploma from the Royal Conservatory of Music of Toronto, he went on to study piano and composition at the University of Calgary, where he graduated with distinction in 1973. He continued his education at the University of Southern Mississippi, earning a master's degree in music composition in 1975. During this time, he spent his summers studying at the Banff Centre. From 1976 until 1995, McIntyre taught music at the **CANADIAN BIBLE COLLEGE** in Regina, as well as at the **UNIVERSITY OF REGINA** for a number of years. He became an Associate Composer of the Canadian Music Centre in 1989, and in 1993 helped to found

the Prairie New Music Festival. From 2000 to 2003, he served as Composer-in-Residence with the **REGINA SYMPHONY ORCHESTRA**, creating a number of new orchestral works. Since 1998, McIntyre has been conductor of the Prairie Pride Chorus. Over the years, he has published a variety of works for piano, flute, organ, brass, voice, and choir; and many singers, instrumentalists and organizations have commissioned works from him. *Butterflies & Bobcats* for piano was the commissioned work for the 2004 Eckhardt-Gramatté National Music Competition. McIntyre performs as pianist with the trio Contrasts, and can often be heard on CBC radio.
Erin Legg

MCKAY, ART (1926–2000). One of the **REGINA FIVE** artists whose 1961 National Gallery of Canada exhibition brought attention to art in western Canada, Arthur Fortescue McKay was born on September 11, 1926, in Nipawin, Saskatchewan. His father, Joseph Fortescue McKay, was the son of the last in a line of Hudson's Bay Company men which began in the 1700s; his mother, Georgina Agnes Newnham, was the daughter of the Bishop of Saskatchewan. The McKays moved to Winnipeg in 1930, to Prince Albert in 1935, and to Regina in 1940. McKay trained in the Canadian Army from 1943 to 1945 and studied at the Provincial Institute of Technology and Art in Calgary from 1946 to 1948. In 1947, he travelled to England and France to study at the Académie de la Grande Chaumière in Paris. He returned to Regina in 1951. McKay was hired at the School of Art, Regina College in 1952 and initiated the Emma Lake Artists' Workshops with director **KEN LOCHHEAD** in 1955. In 1956–57, he studied at the School of Painting and Sculpture at Columbia University, New York, and at the Barnes

Art McKay.

Foundation, Merion, Pennsylvania. As acting director of the School of Art in 1959, McKay, with **ROY KIYOOKA**, coordinated the Emma Lake Artists' Workshop. He acknowledged visiting artist Barnett Newman as an important influence.

In 1961, after an exhibition at the Norman **MACKENZIE ART GALLERY**, Richard Simmins mounted a National Gallery of Canada exhibition, *Five Painters from Regina*, which included McKay, **RON BLOORE**, **TED GODWIN**, **DOUG MORTON** and Ken Lochhead. By the 1997 MacKenzie Art Gallery retrospective, McKay's work had been shown in over forty-five exhibitions, and his mandalas had become synonymous with Canadian painting. With typical candour, though visibly unwell, he said at the opening: "If I'd known I was this good, I'd have painted more." Art McKay retired in 1987 and moved to Vancouver in 1994. Students and colleagues alike remember him as an unusual but gifted teacher, and in particular as a remarkably honest human being. He died on August 3, 2000. *Anne Campbell*

MCKAY, JAMES (1828–79). James McKay was an influential Métis guide, interpreter, trader and politician in western Canada in the second half of the 19th century. The son of a Scottish trader and an Aboriginal mother, he was noted for his facility with **ABORIGINAL LANGUAGES** and for his thorough knowledge of the prairies. These skills enabled him to play a key role in cross-cultural encounters in the west. He was also well educated and advanced rapidly in the employ of the Hudson's Bay Company between 1853 and 1860. He left the Company to engage on his own account in trading, freighting, mail transportation, and farming. In 1859 he married Margaret Rowand, a **MÉTIS** woman, and established an impressive home at Deer Lodge. McKay was appointed to the Council of Assiniboia in 1868, and as president of the Whitehorse Plains District Court.

When disturbances broke out in the Red River settlement in 1869–70 he was prepared to accept the Canadian government's plans for the administration of the west; but he refused to differ with his Métis friends, who opposed Canada's annexation, and served on the Métis Provisional Government with them. McKay became a prominent figure in the politics of the new province of Manitoba: he was president of the Executive Council from 1871 to 1874; a member of the Manitoba Legislative Council from 1871 to 1876; and speaker from 1871 to 1874. From 1874 to 1878, McKay served as Minister of Agriculture in the provincial government of Robert Davis.

Because of his linguistic skills and cross-cultural adroitness, McKay was involved in negotiations for Treaties 1 (1871), 2 (1872) and 3 (1873), and served as a government commissioner for **TREATY 5** (1875) and **TREATY 6** (1876). In these last two sets

of deliberations he acted both as an interpreter and negotiator, and on occasion crossed swords with those Aboriginal leaders who were opposed to signing the treaties. However, he must also be given credit for including some of the exceptional provisions in Treaty 6, such as the medicine chest clause and the promise of assistance in time of need. McKay typified the role played by the Métis as brokers between the original Native people and the European newcomers during this period of rapid change in western Canada. *Michael Cottrell*

MCKERCHER, MARGARET L. (1929–). Born on April 17, 1929, much of Peggy McKercher's career has revolved around community leadership in Saskatoon. A graduate of the **UNIVERSITY OF SASKATCHEWAN**, McKercher was the first woman to be elected to Corman Park municipality. She played an important role in establishing the **MEEWASIN VALLEY AUTHORITY**, an organization designed to preserve the **SASKATCHEWAN RIVER** Valley environment. One result of her work as the Authority's first chairperson was the creation of the **WANUSKEWIN HERITAGE PARK** in 1982 to its official opening a decade later. McKercher was invested as a Member of the Order of Canada in 1995, the same year she accepted the chancellorship of the University of Saskatchewan. She received the Saskatchewan Order of Merit in 2001.

MCKERRACHER, DONALD GRIFFITH (1909–70). Griff McKerracher, a leader in Canadian psychiatry, was a kindly and sensitive man with a keen analytical mind and an ability to bring out the best in others. He was born in Chatham, Ontario on February 18, 1909. He graduated from the University of Toronto as MD in 1935, and served in the Canadian Army in **WORLD WAR II**. In 1946 Premier **T.C. DOUGLAS** appointed him director of Psychiatric Services for Saskatchewan. He introduced a comprehensive training program for psychiatric nursing—a milestone event that expanded con-

UNIVERSITY OF SASKATCHEWAN ARCHIVES A-10576

Donald McKerracher, ca. 1970.

siderably on the earlier 1930 attendants' program of Dr. James W. MacNeill.

In 1954 McKerracher became founding professor and chairman of Psychiatry at the new medical school in Saskatoon. He had a major interest in psychiatric education and in improving both hospital and community care for psychiatric patients. He published many papers in social psychiatry with Dr. Colin Smith, introducing the concept of the comprehensive psychiatric unit in the general hospital, and emphasized the skillful use of community resources. He taught family doctors to become more effective in handling persons with mental and emotional disorders—"my one song," as he liked to call it. His programs became the nucleus of the later developments in the Saskatchewan Plan for small centres to provide complete psychiatric care in their regions. *Colin M. Smith*

MCKINNON, ELEANOR (1912–2004). Eleanor McKinnon was born in Weyburn on October 22, 1912, the daughter of Norman McKinnon, the owner of "Saskatchewan's foremost store." Norman was the founder and deacon of the Calvary (Baptist) Church in Weyburn; he preached the sermon when the minister (**T.C. DOUGLAS** after 1930) was away, and played the organ when the organist was away. Eleanor McKinnon attended Brandon College, then for nine years was secretary to Dr. Campbell at the Weyburn Mental Hospital. A day or two after T.C. Douglas was elected premier, he phoned Eleanor to offer her a job as his private secretary. She accepted—at $70 per month—but did not learn for years that she had been investigated by a CCF caucus committee as a possibly inappropriate appointment, since she came from a staunch capitalist and Liberal family. Her family remained Liberal, but Eleanor was an immediate convert to the CCF.

Eleanor McKinnon adapted quickly to being gatekeeper for the "open door" policy of her new boss, who attempted to see everyone who came. She was described as the centre of calm in near-chaos: the telephone rang every five minutes; and there was an avalanche of mail, particularly after each Sunday evening "Fireside Chat" on the radio, when she would put in hours of overtime, evening after evening, without extra pay. Every letter was answered: McKinnon composed most of the responses, but Douglas read every word and signed each reply, often writing in additional comments. When the time came for Douglas to consider a move to Ottawa as leader of the new party, the NDP, he asked Eleanor: "If I should let my name stand, would you accompany me?" Without hesitation she answered in the affirmative, and he took the job. Her salary of $315 a month did not go far in Ottawa when her rent was $100 a month, and she found it humiliating to have to sign in and out at the Parliament Buildings. Yet she spent twenty-seven years in Ottawa as T.C. Douglas' secretary until she retired in 1983. She died in Regina on January 4, 2004.

C. Stuart Houston

MCKNIGHT, WILLIAM HUNTER (1940–).

Born July 12, 1940, in Elrose, Bill McKnight was a farmer and a Progressive Conservative Party activist who played a leading role as party president in the 1970s revival of the provincial party. McKnight married Beverly Rae in 1961 and they have two children. He served in the House of Commons as MP for the Kindersley–Lloydminster riding from 1979 to 1993, and was in the Cabinet of Prime Minister Brian Mulroney for nine years, serving variously as Minister of Labour, Indian Affairs and Northern Development, Housing, Western Diversification, National Defence, Agriculture, and Energy, Mines and Resources. McKnight was branded a "hatchet man" for the Progressive Conservative government. As Defence Minister he closed armed forces bases, cut billions of dollars from planned defence spending and cancelled equipment contracts. Then came a standoff with Native warriors at Oka, Quebec in 1990 and the deployment of Canadian forces to the Gulf War in 1991. Land claims dominated his tenure at Indian Affairs and Northern Development (1986–88). In the Agriculture portfolio (1991–93), he was involved in the redesign of farm income safety nets while the industry was buffeted by several years of drought and low grain prices brought on by an international export subsidy war. While McKnight was Agriculture Minister, his son Robert decided he could not make a living from the family farm at Wartime and auctioned off the equipment. McKnight retired from politics in 1993 to operate consulting and business ventures from his base in Saskatoon.

Barry Wilson

MCLAREN, LORNE AUBREY (1928–).

Born in Saltcoats on August 17, 1928, and raised on the family farm, Lorne McLaren was employed with Morris Rod Weeder Co. in 1951. Rising through the ranks of the Yorkton-based farm implement manufacturing company, McLaren entered management and became company president in 1979. He also served as chairman of the Prairie Implement Manufacturers Association. McLaren won the Yorkton constituency for the Progressive Conservatives in the 1982 election and was appointed to the new government's first Cabinet as Minister of Labour. A strong opponent of trade unions, McLaren was charged with introducing the government's new labour legislation that sought to undo much of Saskatchewan's existing labour laws. McLaren was dropped from his position in 1985. Re-elected in 1986, McLaren was appointed government caucus chair between 1986 and his political retirement in 1991. After McLaren left politics, an RCMP investigation into the financial dealings of the

REGINA LEADER-POST
Lorne McLaren, April 1983.

PC caucus office uncovered his central role in a fraud scandal of filing false expense accounts. He eventually pled guilty to charges of fraud, theft and breach of trust. He was sentenced to three-and-a-half years in prison, the most serious sentence of all nineteen people convicted in the scandal.

Brett Quiring

MCLEAN, GRANT (1921–2002).

Grant McLean was an adventurer, documentary cameraman, director, producer, and film executive whose career spanned 26 years at the National Film Board of Canada. With Don Wilder, he established his own distribution company, McLean Wilder Associates (later renamed the Visual Education Centre), in Toronto in 1967. He was dedicated to the NFB's mission of creating socially conscious and educational but artistic documentaries, and was at the centre of many award-winning works. In 2002, he was named a Member of the Order of Canada for his contributions to Canadian film culture. Born in Yorkton, McLean came from a family of devoted public servants. His father, Allan Grant McLean, was grain commissioner for Saskatchewan and chairman of the federal **LIBERAL PARTY**; his uncle, Ross McLean, was commissioner of the NFB. Grant McLean studied at the University of Toronto before joining the RCAF and the NFB. During **WORLD WAR II**, he established his reputation as a man of action, making *Target Berlin* for the *Canada Carries On* series, filming the building of the first Lancaster bomber in Canada, and flying in one of its missions over Berlin to capture live footage of the war in action.

Always politically engaged, he took a United Nations commission in 1947 to document the Chinese civil war. The first Western cameraman to

film Mao Ze Dong, he also interviewed renowned Canadian surgeon Dr. Norman Bethune. The film that resulted from these encounters was highly controversial: *The People Between* (1947) was banned by the Canadian government, largely under pressure from the United States; critics believe that the film rankled because it showed the Communists under a balanced light and portrayed the Chinese as pawns exploited by nationalist ideologies, both Eastern and Western. The film *Bethune* (1964), made by Donald Brittain during McLean's ten years as director of production at the NFB, raised similar questions. In addition to producing *Bethune*, McLean had many notable achievements throughout the 1960s, including making groundbreaking issue-oriented documentaries in the field for the CBC TV *Perspectives* series, establishing the NFB's regional offices, and participating in the emergence of the influential *cinéma-vérité* style and the burgeoning of Quebec cinema. Under his brief fifteen-month tenure as acting commissioner, the NFB produced the internationally celebrated *Labyrinth* for Montreal's Expo '67. While Grant McLean was never appointed commissioner of the NFB–probably owing to his direct leadership style and his irreverent approach to bureaucracy–his vision and legacy are unchallenged and he is remembered in documentary circles as a man of great intelligence, conviction, and loyalty.

Christine Ramsay

FURTHER READING: Carol Cooper. 2003. "Obituaries: Grant McLean 1921–2002." *The Globe and Mail* (January 11), F8.

MCLEOD, HENRY WALLACE (1917–44).

Henry Wallace ("Wally") McLeod, the top-scoring fighter pilot of the Royal Canadian Air Force in **WORLD WAR II**, was born in Regina on December 17, 1917. He enlisted in the wartime RCAF in September 1940, and trained as a pilot at Prince Albert and Camp Borden, Ontario before being posted to Britain in the spring of 1941. Going on active operations on July 30, 1941, he served with several RAF and RCAF Spitfire squadrons. In May 1942, he was posted to the island of Malta, which sat astride German and Italian supply routes to their armies in North Africa. He claimed his first victory on June 8, 1942. His score climbed rapidly and he received a Distinguished Flying Cross in September, then a bar to his DFC–in effect, a second medal–in October of that year. Having destroyed twelve enemy aircraft and damaging several others, he returned to Britain late in that year. Malta had survived, contributing to the defeat of the Axis forces in North Africa. The cost to McLeod was high: in four months in Malta, he lost 25 pounds and had constant nightmares about crashing. Returned to Canada, he eventually took over the RCAF's No. 127 (Fighter) Squadron at Bagotville. In February 1944, he took this unit (renumbered No. 443 Squadron, RCAF) back to Britain in preparation for the Allied invasion of Europe, and led it into battle. Awarded a Distinguished Service Order for his courage and leadership during this period, he was reported missing after combat with German fighters over western Germany on September 27, 1944. He is buried in a cemetery at Rheinberg, northwest of Duisberg. McLeod's logbook claimed twenty aerial victories and four "probables." RCAF records credit him with 19 kills, one probable, and 9.5 damaged, the difference reflecting the scantiness of records in Malta. Although no member of the RCAF scored more "kills" than McLeod, his record was overshadowed by that of George "Buzz" Buerling, a Canadian who enlisted in Britain's RAF, transferring to the RCAF in 1944. September 2002 saw the naming of a major building at 15 Wing, the military air training base south of Moose Jaw, for Henry Wallace McLeod. A street in Regina's industrial district is jointly named for him and for broadcaster Jim McLeod (no relation).

Will Chabun

MCLEOD, IDA (1920–82). Ida McLeod, one of thirteen children, was born in 1920 and grew up on the Sandy Lake Reserve. Her father, a successful farmer, afforded her opportunities for higher education seldom experienced in that period: she began her university training in the 1940s, at a time when it was almost unheard of for a treaty Indian, and indeed a woman, to pursue a post-secondary education. Throughout the 1950s and 1960s she taught in many schools, and in the late 1960s she was principal of the James Smith School. Ida McLeod completed her Bachelor of Education Degree in 1971. She and her husband, **JOHN R. MCLEOD**, were instrumental in the development of the Cree Retention Committee, organized in the early 1970s; and in 1973 Ida established the Indian Language Program at the Saskatchewan Indian Cultural College (now **SASKATCHEWAN INDIAN CULTURAL CENTRE**). Working at the Centre, she developed curriculum, contributed to standardizing the Cree language, and developed reading materials in the Cree language. *Neal McLeod*

MCLEOD, JOHN. Born in Blackburn, England, Dr. John McLeod's efforts as a teacher and researcher have made significant advances in the field of education. He worked in England and Australia prior to coming to Canada in 1968 where he was the first director of the Institute of Child Guidance and Development at the University of Saskatchewan. There he helped create a clinic that provided diagnosis and remedial treatment for children with learning disabilities. A former Scholar-in-Residence at Harvard University, Dr. McLeod has received numerous honours and awards including the Canadian Education Association Whitworth Award for Educational Research in 1986 and a life-time achievement award from the Saskatchewan chapter of the Canadian Council for Exceptional Children in 2003. He was awarded the Saskatchewan Order of Merit in 2004.

MCLEOD, JOHN R. (1922–80). John R. McLeod was born in 1922 and raised on the James Smith Reserve. He is best known for his work with the **SASKATCHEWAN INDIAN CULTURAL COLLEGE** between 1970 and his death in 1980. Prior to this work, John was a driving force behind many of the school committees formed on reserves in the 1960s; and in 1970 he was appointed co-chair of the Task Force on Indian Education. Throughout his life, John R. McLeod was committed to Indian control of Indian education, the first arena from which elements of self-government have emerged. While some were devastated by the residential school experience, it solidified McLeod's resolve to survive as an Indian. In 1975 McLeod was asked to be the Chair of the **TREATY 6** Centennial Commemorations, and from that point he became an earnest student of Cree traditions. He spent a great deal of time with the Old Ones, including the late Jim Kâ-Nîpitêhtêw, who adopted McLeod as his son. *Neal McLeod*

MCLEOD, THOMAS H. (1918–). Thomas McLeod, born on August 11, 1918, in Weyburn, associated there with **T.C. DOUGLAS** as a teenager during the early 1930s. After taking a graduate degree in economics from Indiana University, he returned to Saskatchewan in the spring of 1944 to become Douglas' city organizer for the election campaign and a senior official in the new government. Together with Dr. Mindel Sheps in the **HEALTH SERVICE PLANNING COMMISSION**, McLeod helped plan the introduction of hospitalization in 1947. As the first secretary of the Economic Advisory and Planning Board, he was instrumental in hiring a

SASKATCHEWAN ARCHIVES BOARD R-A5335

Thomas McLeod.

dedicated group of economic advisors and policy planners. He was also key in creating the Budget Bureau, and would himself act as Deputy Provincial Treasurer for two years. Having obtained his PhD from Harvard University during a leave of absence from the public service, McLeod became Dean of Commerce at the **UNIVERSITY OF SASKATCHEWAN** in 1952. Following his academic career in Saskatchewan, McLeod went on to do extensive international development work in the Third World—in Turkey with the Ford Foundation, in Iran with the Harvard Advisory Group, and in Nigeria with the World Bank. He was also a senior official with the Canadian International Development Agency (CIDA), where he became advisor to the president on higher education and public administration. McLeod received the Order of Canada and the Vanier Medal in public administration, as well as a number of honorary doctorates from Canadian universities. He is the co-author (with his son Ian McLeod) of *Tommy Douglas: The Road to Jerusalem*, a major study of Douglas and his government. *Gregory P. Marchildon*

MCMASTER, GERALD (1953–). Gerald R. McMaster, a Plains **CREE**, was born on the Red Pheasant Reserve in 1953. He is a significant figure in contemporary Indigenous art in Canada because of his work as an artist, writer, curator, and prominent scholar. As an artist he works in both two-dimensional and installation media, using humour and irony to convey his comments on colonialism and stereotypes of plains First Nations. In 1981 McMaster was appointed Curator of Contemporary Indian Art and subsequently became Curator-in-Charge of the First Peoples Hall, at the Canadian Museum of Civilization. He created such important exhibitions as *In the Shadow of the Sun* (1988), *INDIGENA* (1992), and *Reservation X* (1999). Since 2000 he has worked for the Smithsonian Institute's National Museum of the American Indian in Washington, DC. McMaster began his education at the Institute of American Indian Arts, and recently received a PhD from the Amsterdam School of Cultural Analysis. From 1977 to 1981 he was coordinator of the Indian Art Program at the Saskatchewan Indian Federated College (now **FIRST NATIONS UNIVERSITY OF CANADA**). (*See* photo on facing page.) *Carmen Robertson*

MCMILLAN, IVAN (1911–2002). Ivan McMillan, a prominent figure in the prairie grain industry, was born on the family farm near Craik, Saskatchewan in 1911. He had hoped to join his father in his prosperous grain farming and horse breeding operation, but this was prevented by the advent of the **GREAT DEPRESSION**. After a year at the **UNIVERSITY OF SASKATCHEWAN**, he taught school and worked as a dairy inspector until he was able to

ROBERT WATSON/REGINA LEADER-POST
Gerald McMaster, November 1985.

resume farming in 1937. McMillan first gained recognition in agricultural circles for his efforts in improving grain production practices. In 1937, the family farm was selected as the site of an Experimental Substation of the Indian Head Experimental Farm. There, in co-operation with the Experimental Farm and the regional Agricultural Representative, McMillan experimented with seed varieties and implemented methods of cultivation, crop rotation, and fertilizer use that would ensure that the devastation of the 1930s would not be repeated. The annual field days attracted large crowds of interested farmers during the 1940s and 1950s.

As president, secretary, and committee chairman of the Craik Agricultural Society, McMillan spearheaded the organization of the annual agricultural fair, summerfallowing competitions, seed fairs, and field demonstrations. McMillan served as chairman of the District 15 Agricultural Board, and on the Royal Commission on Rural Development in the late 1940s. In 1954 and 1955 he was elected as president of the Agricultural Societies Association of Saskatchewan. He was honoured with a life membership in the provincial organization in 1962, and in the local Agricultural Society in 1975. In the 1970s McMillan became a spokesperson for the Palliser Wheat Growers Association. He was elected president of the Wheat Growers in 1975 and 1976, at the height of the controversial Crow's Nest negotiations, and appeared before the Snavely and Hall Commissions on Grain Transportation in that capacity.

McMillan earned numerous appointments to boards and commissions. He served as a director of the Canada Grains Council, a member of the Canadian Wheat Board advisory board, an advisor to the Canadian Grains Commission, and as a director on the board of governors of the Winnipeg Commodity Exchange. In 1978 and 1979 he was part of the Canadian negotiating team at the Geneva Wheat Conference. McMillan also played a major role in community development in Craik: he was a chairman of the building committees for both the Craik Memorial Rink and the Craik Hospital, a town councillor for many years, and first chairman of the amalgamated Davidson School Unit board. McMillan was inducted into the Saskatchewan Agricultural Hall of Fame in 1996. He also excelled in curling, and in 1968 was part of the Wilson rink from Saskatoon that won the Seagram Stone, the national seniors championship, with an unprecedented ten straight wins; he was inducted into the Saskatoon Sports Hall of Fame in 1989. Ivan McMillan passed away on February 25, 2002. *Joan Sandormirsky*

MCNAB, ARCHIBALD PETER (1864–1945).
Saskatchewan's most affable LIEUTENANT-GOVERNOR, Archibald Peter McNab preferred the name "Archie" to more formal vice-regal titles. Born May 29, 1864, in Glengarry, Ontario, McNab and his twin brother Neil moved west to Winnipeg in 1882 before homesteading at Virden, Manitoba. Successive years of drought forced Archie McNab to give up farming by 1887, after which he became a grain buyer for Ogilvie Flour Mills. In 1902, he was transferred to Rosthern where he invested in two grain elevators. McNab later sold his interest and moved to Saskatoon with his wife and three children. There he established the Dominion Elevator Company and

helped found the Saskatchewan Central Railway Company and the Saskatchewan Power Company.

McNab's political career began in 1908 with his election as Liberal MLA for Saskatoon City. Shortly after, he was named commissioner of Municipal Affairs and, in 1912, minister of Public Works. In addition to overseeing the construction of some of the province's most notable public buildings, McNab played an instrumental role in acquiring the UNIVERSITY OF SASKATCHEWAN for Saskatoon. In 1926, he secured a position on the local government board until accusations of impropriety forced his resignation four years later. Although he had been comfortably retired for six years, McNab accepted the vice-regal appointment on September 10, 1936.

During McNab's two terms as Lieutenant-Governor, the frugal character of GOVERNMENT HOUSE reflected the prevailing mood of a province suffering through DROUGHT and war. Nevertheless, an appropriate welcome was extended to King George VI and Queen Elizabeth during their visit to Government House in 1939. McNab also welcomed children to play on the grounds of the vice-regal residence before the CCF government announced the home's closure in September 1944. The last Lieutenant-Governor to live in Government House, Archibald McNab resigned on February 26, 1945, due to failing health. He died of pneumonia on April 29 of that year. *Holden Stoffel*

FURTHER READING: Cotcher, Maryanne. 2004. "McNab, Archibald Peter." P. 163 in *Saskatchewan Politicians: Lives Past and Present*. Regina: Canadian Plains Research Center; Hryniuk, Margaret and Garth Pugh. 1991. *"A Tower of Attraction": An Illustrated History of Government House, Regina, Saskatchewan*. Regina: Government House Historical Society/Canadian Plains Research Center.

SASKATCHEWAN ARCHIVES BOARD R-B3697
Archibald Peter McNab.

MCNAB, HILLIARD (1916–90).

Born on March 5, 1916, a respected chief of the Gordon Reserve, Hilliard McNab helped advance the cause of First Nations across the province. After an attempt at farming on the Reserve, McNab began a long political career on the Gordon Council in the 1950s, eventually becoming chief in 1968 until his voluntary resignation in 1982. He was a founding member of the Federation of Saskatchewan Indians and the SASKATCHEWAN INDIAN INSTITUTE OF TECHNOLOGIES. McNab served on the Saskatchewan Human Rights Commission from its inception to 1982 and was subsequently involved in the initial development of WANUSKEWIN HERITAGE PARK. In recognition of his invaluable counsel both on and off the Gordon Reserve, Chief Hilliard McNab was invested with the Order of Canada in 1984. He died on August 28, 1990.

FURTHER READING: 2004. *Saskatchewan First Nations: Lives Past and Present*. Regina: Canadian Plains Research Center.

MCNAUGHTON, ANDREW GEORGE LATTA (1887–1966).

Andrew George Latta McNaughton was born on February 25, 1887, in Moosomin, North-West Territories. He earned his BSc (1910) and MSc (1912) degrees at McGill University. At the outbreak of WORLD WAR I in 1914, McNaughton was given command of 4th Battery, Royal Canadian Artillery, Canadian Expeditionary Force. He distinguished himself with his scientific approach to gunnery, and by the end of the war, commanded the entire Canadian Corps artillery. After the war, he was appointed deputy chief of staff (1922–29), then chief of the general staff (1929–35), where he initiated the modernization of the Canadian militia. McNaughton then retired to civilian life. At the outbreak of WORLD WAR II, McNaughton left his civilian job as president of the National Research Council (1935–39) to command the 1st Canadian Infantry Division, taking it overseas to Britain in 1939. By 1942, he had been promoted to command 1st Canadian Army. While overseas, he was responsible for instituting many scientific innovations to the army, including better aircraft ranging methods and antitank ammunition. McNaughton had endorsed the disastrous Dieppe operation of 1942; that, and other political difficulties including poor relationships with other Canadian and British politicians, brought on his resignation in December 1943. Returning to Canada, he served as Minister of National Defence (1944–45) in the Mackenzie King government. After the war, McNaughton was variously appointed president of the Atomic Energy Control Board of Canada (1946–48), Canada's Representative to the United Nations' Atomic Energy Commission and Permanent Representative to the United Nations (1948–49), and president of the

SASKATCHEWAN ARCHIVES BOARD R-B9335

General A.G.L. McNaughton and James Gardiner (then federal minister of Agriculture) in England during World War II.

Canadian Section of the International Joint Commission (1950–62). He died on July 11, 1966.

John Chaput

MCNAUGHTON, VIOLET CLARA (1879–1968).

Violet McNaughton (*née* Jackson) was a leader in the Canadian farm, women's, peace, and co-operative movements. She became the most influential farm woman in Canada and in Saskatchewan during the first half of the 20th century. Born on November 11, 1879, and raised in radical north Kent in southeastern England, she worked as a schoolteacher. Immigrating in 1909, she joined her father and brother, homesteaders near Harris; in May 1910 she married John McNaughton, a neighbouring homesteader. A feminist sympathizer, she became an active agrarian feminist by 1914, when she began to organize farm women. Her ardour arose out of the dire living and working conditions on the rural prairies during the newcomer settlement period. As well, she had had a serious gynecological operation in 1911 while living in these conditions. Unable to have children as a result, she resolved during her lengthy recovery to work to make the world a better place for all children.

She organized the Women Grain Growers (WGG) in Saskatchewan, a group whose class and gender analyses made it one of the most radical in Canada, and was elected its first president in 1914. A leader of the Saskatchewan women's suffrage move-

ment, she also led the WGG's campaign for trained midwives as well as more nurses, doctors, and hospitals; the WGG wanted these services be to affordable and in close proximity to all farm families. As a result of their campaign, legislation in 1916 allowed for the establishment of union hospitals, municipal nurses, and municipal doctors. This was the first step on the long road to medicare in Saskatchewan and, later, Canada. McNaughton also helped to organize Euro-Canadian farm women's groups in several other provinces, and was president of the Inter-provincial Council of Farm Women and the Women's Section of the Canadian Council of Agriculture from 1919 to 1923.

By the early 1920s McNaughton was one of the three most influential people in the Saskatchewan Grain Growers' Association. As well, she was active in the Progressives, and helped to organize and maintain the Wheat Pools, the Saskatchewan Egg and Poultry Pool, and the *Western Producer*, the liveliest farm paper in Canada. She became the *Producer*'s women's editor in 1925. The "Mainly for Women" pages and the "Young Co-operators," edited by McNaughton and her staff, were read by tens of thousands of western farm women and their families. She strongly supported the WGG and its successors, as well as United Farm women in Alberta, Manitoba, and Ontario. She also promoted Homemakers' Clubs and Women's Institutes, and other farm women's groups. She retired as women's editor in 1950, but wrote a *Western Producer* column for nine more years. She died in Saskatoon on February 2, 1968.

Georgina M. Taylor

FURTHER READING: Taylor, G.M. 2000. "Let Us Co-operate': Violet McNaughton and the Co-operative Ideal." Pp. 57–78 in B. Fairbairn and I. MacPherson (eds.), *Co-operatives in the Year 2000: Memory, Mutual Aid, and the Millennium*. Saskatoon: Centre for the Study of Co-operatives, University of Saskatchewan.

SASKATCHEWAN ARCHIVES BOARD S-B2042

Violet McNaughton, ca. 1920.

SASKATCHEWAN ARCHIVES BOARD R-A3586

Alexander James McPhail.

MCPHAIL, ALEXANDER JAMES (1883–1931).

Alexander McPhail, born in Ontario on December 23, 1883, found himself at the head of a family of eight when his parents passed away. Undaunted, he and his family homesteaded in the Bankend district of Saskatchewan in 1906. McPhail became involved in several early farm and political movements, including the Saskatchewan Department of Agriculture, the **PROGRESSIVE PARTY**, and the Saskatchewan Grain Growers Association (SGGA), where he served as secretary. McPhail was a proponent of the wheat pool concept, where farmers could co-operatively market their wheat, negotiating better prices through volume selling. In 1923, he encouraged the SGGA to meet with the United Farmers associations of Alberta and Manitoba to discuss developing wheat pools in the three provinces, with a Central Selling Agency designed to market wheat internationally. McPhail was elected first president of the Saskatchewan Co-operative Wheat Producers Limited in 1924. Similar organizations were established in Alberta and Manitoba. The three Pools formed the Central Selling Agency in 1926 to market jointly the grain that farmers assigned to them under five-year contracts. The Saskatchewan Co-operative Wheat Producers, which would later become the **SASKATCHEWAN WHEAT POOL**, struggled with controversial issues in its formative years. McPhail was reluctant to purchase elevators, and campaigned against the idea of compulsory marketing, preferring the wheat pool to be voluntary. The stock market crash of 1929 hit the wheat pools hard, and the Central Selling Agency was taken over by the federal government. The elevator part of the operation, which formed in 1926 with the purchase of the **SASKATCHEWAN CO-OPERATIVE ELEVATOR COMPANY**, survived. Alexander McPhail died unexpectedly on October 21, 1931.   *Merle Massie*

FURTHER READING: Fowke, V. 1957. *The National Policy and the Wheat Economy.* Toronto: University of Toronto Press.

MCVICAR, IVY (1907–).

Ivy McVicar (*née* Bassett) has worked to better the community and the lives of rural women, locally, nationally, and internationally. Born in Brighton, England on March 6, 1907, she came to Canada that year with her parents. In 1920 they moved to Prairie River with the Soldier Settlers. After attending Normal School in Saskatoon, she taught near Prairie River. She married Archie McVicar on June 30, 1935; they had three daughters. Returning to teaching after her children were in school, she retired in 1970. Active in the Saskatchewan Homemakers Club and its successor, Saskatchewan Women's Institutes, McVicar became a Life Member. She served on the Federated Women's Institutes' board from 1977 to 1983, and was a voting delegate at several international conferences. She is also a Life Member of the Associated Country Women of the World.

As a director of the Saskatchewan Action Committee for the Status of Women, McVicar in 1975 sent a resolution (adopted 1979–80) urging the federal government to continue the spouse's allowance after the husband's death. Appointed to the Advisory Council to the Status of Women in 1983, she conducted a project in northeastern Saskatchewan (funded by the Secretary of State) that dealt with issues such as wife battering and child abuse, day care, equal pay, minimum wage, pension plans for housewives, and matrimonial property rights. Involved among others in the Red Cross, **CANADIAN GIRLS IN TRAINING**, and seniors' organizations, McVicar has also written stories and a play.   *Lorraine Waskowic*

M-DNA.

Biochemist Jeremy Lee and his former post-doctoral fellow Palok Aich at the **UNIVERSITY OF SASKATCHEWAN** discovered a new DNA molecule, M-DNA, which conducts electricity. The first patent on the discovery was filed in 1997, and five years later Adnavance was formed with the help of University Medical Discoveries Inc. (UMDI), a Toronto-based technology development company focusing on early-stage medical and life science research, to market the new technology. The letter "M" in M-DNA stands for "metal-containing." M-DNA is a marriage of molecular biology and electronics: conducting metal ions such as zinc, cobalt or nickel are inserted into the centre of the DNA helix, creating an effective semi-conductor that is only one molecule–roughly two nanometres–thick. Since DNA has the natural ability to self-assemble, M-DNA is in effect a self-assembling molecular wire that could become the building block for nanometre-scale bio-electric circuits; these tiny, speedier circuits could replace the smallest of silicon microchips that drive the world's information technology. M-DNA could also pave the way for highly sensitive new biosensors that help reduce adverse drug reactions, improve diagnosis of disease, predict the outcome of disease, and reduce the cost of drug development. In addition to medicine, M-DNA has possible applications in areas such as environmental monitoring, security, and national defense.   *Joe Ralko*

MEADOW LAKE,

town, pop 4,582, located 160 km N of North Battleford on Hwys 4 and 55. The history of Meadow Lake dates from the **FUR TRADE**. In 1799, **PETER FIDLER**, working for the Hudson's Bay Company, travelled south along the Beaver River from Ile-à-la-Crosse, then entered the Meadow River and followed it to its source, a lake that would become known as *Lac des Prairies*, or "Meadow Lake." He and his companions constructed a log building as a company post, naming it Bolsover House, after Fidler's birthplace in England. Although the post did not flourish and shortly closed, Fidler was a master surveyor and Meadow Lake was now on the map. As the fur trade increased dramatically along the western Churchill River during the 1880s, a route was established from Ile-à-la-Crosse south through Green Lake and then southeast toward Fort Carlton. Small settlements sprang up along the way. Eventually, people migrated westward to the Meadow Lake area, and around 1879 Cyprien and Mary Morin from Ile-à-la-Crosse became the first to settle permanently at the site of the future community. Other Métis families followed in the coming years. Preliminary surveys were made in the district and soon reports of the agricultural possibilities of the area surfaced. In 1888, the area directly west of the lake was surveyed for a future townsite, and in 1889 Cree signatories to **TREATY 6** assumed title to a reserve just north of the lake. They are now known as the Flying Dust First Nation. Cyprien Morin established a Hudson's Bay Company Post at Meadow Lake, traded in furs, and raised horses and cattle. The first Roman Catholic Church was built on the Morin's land. Although the Métis families who settled at Meadow Lake prospered, it was not until 1907–08 that subsequent settlers began to slowly arrive in the area. In 1919, a massive forest fire swept through the region and the waning fur trade in the Meadow Lake region was decimated. From Green Lake to Big River the earth was blackened, the lumber industry devastated. Land was, however, further opened up for homesteads and agriculture. The pace of settlement quickened and, by the end of the 1920s, most of the prime agricultural land was taken. The remaining marginal lands were taken up in the 1930s by **DUST BOWL** refugees from southern Saskatchewan. As the railroad approached at the beginning of the decade, an economic boom began, and Meadow Lake was incorporated as a village on August 24, 1931. By 1936, the population of the community was 800, and on February 1 that year, Meadow Lake attained town status. Ten years later, in 1946, the population was 1,456 and, in another decade, approaching twice that. Forestry, fishing, and farming dominated the economy, with the area's agricultural output ever increasing. By the mid-1950s, more grain was shipped out of Meadow Lake than from any other point in rural Canada. Meadow Lake continues to grow; the 2001 Census population figure cited above is no longer accurate, as the town now estimates its population at over 6,000. As well, the community serves an additional trading area population of 15,000 people. The primary industries in the region continue to be forestry and agriculture and, increasingly, tourism.

David McLennan

MEDIA: NEWSPAPERS, TELEVISION AND RADIO. The First Nations of the North American west fulfilled the social communicition function through powwows and the oral story-telling tradition. The first newspaper in what was to become Saskatchewan was the weekly *Saskatchewan Herald*, started at Battleford in 1878.

The *Saskatchewan Herald* was typical of early publications–published on a weekly (or less-frequent basis) and dealing heavily in local and territorial news, with occasional national, European or Imperial news if the mail provided it. A biographer of its founder described the territorial press as being "almost exclusively Conservative" in its politics. "Discovery, Civilization and Progress were the watchwords, along with Christian morality, were to provide the ingredients for a united and prosperous nation... There was an almost irrepressible optimism in the future through the development of the West."

Many publications of this sort began in the North-West Territories and pioneer-era Saskatchewan, though few survived. Exceptions were *The Moosomin World-Spectator* (founded as *The Courier* in 1884) and *The Leader*, founded in March 1883 by iconoclastic businessman-politician-writer-lawyer NICHOLAS FLOOD DAVIN of Regina. It evolved into the daily *Leader-Post*.

Publications in larger Saskatchewan centres began evolving as their communities grew. *The Leader*, for example, went daily in 1905. Becoming dailies in 1906 were the *Moose Jaw Times*, the *Saskatoon Phoenix* and the *Saskatoon Capital* (later *Star*). In Prince Albert, the *Herald* began publishing as a daily in 1911.

A Historical Directory of Saskatchewan Newspapers 1878–1983 lists hundreds of newspapers and magazines that have been published in Saskatchewan, ranging from *The Banish the Bar Crusader* (1914–17) to *The Klansman* (1929–30) to the leftist Regina weekly newspaper *The Prairie Fire* (1969–71). Significant for its longevity and influence is the Saskatoon-based *Western Producer*, founded after WORLD WAR I as *The Progressive*, which sought a pool for the selling of Saskatchewan farmers' grain. It was renamed in 1924 as *The Western Producer* and was taken over by the

SASKATCHEWAN WHEAT POOL in 1931. It was sold to a BC firm in late 2001.

In 1922, the Regina *Leader* began CKCK Radio, the first commercial radio station in the province. On February 11, 1923, CKCK became the first radio station in the British Empire to carry a live church broadcast. It carried the first play-by-play broadcast of a hockey game on March 14, 1923–a full week before famed broadcaster Foster Hewitt made his radio debut in Toronto. CKCK's creation was followed by that of CFQC in Saskatoon (1923), 10AB (predecessor of Moose Jaw's CHAB) in 1923, 10BI (forerunner of CKBI in Prince Albert) in 1925 and Moose Jaw's CJRM (forerunner of CKRM in Regina) in 1926.

In 1928, federal Conservative leader R.B. Bennett, no stranger to Saskatchewan through his membership in the Territorial Council of the North-West Territories, was an investor in a Conservative-oriented daily, the Regina *Daily Star*. Plans for a sister paper in Saskatoon were scuttled by the onset of the GREAT DEPRESSION. The colourful competition between the *Leader-Post* and the *Daily Star* ended in February 1940 when the *Star* closed, fatally injured by a modest advertising pool and federal government rationing of newsprint during WORLD WAR II.

In July 1939, the CBC began broadcasting to the prairies from a powerful transmitter at Watrous, selected for its central location and favourable transmission properties. CBC did not have a radio newsroom in Saskatchewan until 1954 and did not have its own TV station in the province. However, the CBC-TV signal was available in Saskatchewan through privately owned TV stations like CKCK (Regina), CFQC (Saskatoon), CKBI (Prince Albert), CJFB (Swift Current) and CKOS (Yorkton). This characteristically Canadian private-public partnership began eroding in 1969, when CBC acquired the TV arm of CHAB Radio. Overnight, CBC-TV went on the air with its own station, while CKCK-TV changed affiliation to the private CTV network. A similar situation occurred in Saskatoon in 1970, when a CBC TV station went on the air and CFQC-TV became a CTV affiliate.

Notable commercial media groups in Saskatchewan have been the SIFTON FAMILY (which by the 1970s owned the *Leader-Post* and *StarPhoenix*, CKCK-Radio and TV, and several media properties outside of the province) and the Rawlinson radio group (which started in Prince Albert, and acquired stations in North Battleford, Regina, and Saskatoon). By 2004, commercial TV stations were owned by either Winnipeg-based Global TV or Toronto-based Baton Broadcasting. The Sifton newspapers in Regina and Saskatoon were acquired in 1996 by Conrad Black's Hollinger Corp., which immediately terminated a quarter of their personnel, setting off a national political furor. By 2000,

the newspapers had been acquired by Global TV's corporate parent, Canwest Global.

Cable television service began in Estevan in 1961 and Weyburn the next year. Service to the remainder of Saskatchewan was delayed while the federal and provincial governments fought a long battle over the nature of cable TV providers and the telecommunications system linking them. A 1978 compromise saw cable outlets in Regina and North Battleford structured as locally controlled co-operatives; those in other centres were conventional private firms eventually acquired by the large regional Shaw cable firm.

An important development was the creation in 1979 of the School of Journalism at the UNIVERSITY OF REGINA. The 1990s saw innovations in the creation of Saskatchewan-based Internet web sites, either independent or allied with media outlets, a provincial educational broadcaster (the Saskatchewan Communications Network), and several First Nations media outlets. *Will Chabun*

MEDICARE. The ROMANOW report observed, "Canadians embrace medicare as a public good, a national symbol and a defining aspect of their citizenship." Medicare, as the national single-payer health care system is called, began in Saskatchewan on July 1, 1962, but operated without federal funding until July 1, 1968. Other provinces and territories joined over the following four years. The steps leading up to the adoption of medicare go back a long way: the idea of national health insurance was discussed as long ago as 1919, when it was a plank in the LIBERAL PARTY platform of that year. Because the Canadian Constitution assigns responsibility for health to the provinces, negotiations with the provinces about some kind of joint funding were unsuccessful until 1957, when the Hospital Insurance and Diagnostic Services Act was passed in Ottawa. This brought substantial federal funding to help pay for the hospitalization program in Saskatchewan, which had come into effect on January 1, 1947.

The seeds were sown for publicly funded hospital and medical care in the province with the Union Hospital Act of 1916, which was broadened in 1917 to enable municipalities to come together to build a union hospital and to levy taxes to finance its operation. About the same time, the Rural Municipalities Act was amended to give rural municipal councils authority to levy taxes to finance the municipal doctor system, enabling them to offer doctors an annual retainer fee in order to encourage them to practice in a given community. With the onset of the DEPRESSION in 1929, accompanied on the prairies by a devastating drought, money was extremely scarce, and little progress was made. However, in 1939, at the instigation of MATT ANDERSON of RM McKillop, the Municipal and Medical Hospital Services Act was passed, permitting municipalities to levy either a land tax or a personal tax to finance hospital and medical services. When the CCF government came to power in 1944, their platform called for comprehensive health insurance. The Hospital Insurance Act came into effect on January 1, 1947, guaranteeing every citizen of the province hospital care without a fee. No other jurisdiction on the continent could boast such a sweeping reform. **T.C. DOUGLAS** insisted on a small annual premium to help finance this insurance. The introduction of hospital insurance in Saskatchewan, and its wide acceptance by the physicians of the province, paved the way for the introduction of medical insurance.

The Saskatchewan Medical Care Insurance Act was passed on November 17, 1961, and after two delays became effective on July 1, 1962. Meanwhile, Douglas resigned as Premier to head up the newly created federal NDP, leaving **WOODROW LLOYD**, who had become Premier, to oversee the introduction of medical insurance. On July 1, 1962, almost all Saskatchewan doctors went on a three-week strike. Only those who lived through those fear-ridden days, when doctors abandoned their offices, can appreciate the pressure that Lloyd came under to capitulate and withdraw the insurance scheme. The Regina *Leader-Post* was vicious in its attacks; while doctors, with the moral support of the American Medical Association, were merciless, warning their patients that most doctors would be leaving the province if "socialized" medicine were introduced. Patients in turn appealed to their elected members. The Opposition Liberal Party promised to bring in their own scheme, which if it had seen the light of day would have left patients in much the same situation as patients in the USA find themselves today. If Woodrow Lloyd had withdrawn the legislation, the story of national medicare might never have been written. Through the mediation of Lord Taylor, a physician whom the government had brought from England, the strike came to an end after twenty-three days, and things returned more or less to normal.

In 1964 the Royal Commission on Health Services, chaired by Justice **EMMETT HALL** of Saskatoon, recommended that Canada should adopt national medical insurance; Hall stated later that the demonstrable success of Saskatchewan's medical insurance system played a role in this decision. When the federal Medical Care Act of 1966 came into effect on July 1, 1968, with the four principles of public administration, universality, portability and comprehensiveness, Saskatchewan began immediately to enjoy joint funding. The formula in effect meant that the costs of medicare would be split approximately 50–50 between the federal and provincial governments. Eventually, however, the federal government became disillusioned with a scheme that continually cost more, while they had nothing to say about how the money was spent. The provinces also found that constraints in the formula prevented them from bringing in needed reforms. In 1977 a new system was agreed upon, called Established Program Financing (EPF). The effect was that the federal government provided support on a block-funding basis, enabling the provinces to use the federal money to finance health initiatives, in addition to hospital and medical services. Unfortunately, annual increases to the federal contribution were tied to the rate of growth in Gross National Product (GNP); since health costs tended to grow faster than the GNP, the result was a gradual decrease in federal support. Later on this system was revised, enabling the federal government to cut support even more drastically. Thus, in the 1990s, as Ottawa cut back in an attempt to eliminate the deficit, the provinces came under severe fiscal strain and the Saskatchewan government in turn began cutting its support for health, introducing the concept of wellness as its rationale.

In 1984, the federal legislation enabling joint federal-provincial funding for hospital and medical services was consolidated under the Canada Health Act. This added a fifth criterion to the Medical Care Act of 1966: services had to be accessible to be eligible for federal funding, and providers would not be allowed to make additional charges (extra billing). By the end of the 20th century, questions were being raised about the need to amend the Canada Health Act, which dealt mainly with hospital and physician services, in order to produce a more seamless health care system, from the nursing home and Home Care to the Intensive Care Unit. Meanwhile, the right-wing press harped on the question of the sustainability of medicare. Because of these two factors, plus the phenomenon of ever-increasing waiting lists, Prime Minister Chrétien appointed Roy G. Romanow, QC, on April 3, 2001, to head up a Royal Commission. It was "to recommend policies and measures respectful of the jurisdictions and powers in Canada required to ensure over the long term the sustainability of a universally accessible, publicly funded health system that offers quality services to Canadians and strikes an appropriate balance between investments in prevention and health maintenance and those directed to care and treatment."

The Romanow Report, published in November 2002, contained forty-seven recommendations which, taken together, presented a roadmap "for a collective journey by Canadians to reform and renew their health care system." Three of these recommendations, in particular, held out revolutionary possibilities for the sustainability of a reformed system. The first put forward something new, a Canadian Health Covenant establishing governments' commitment "to a universally accessible, publicly funded health care system." The second recommended "a Health Council of Canada ... to facilitate co-operation and provide national leadership in achieving the best health outcomes in the world." This one was accepted immediately by the federal government and several provinces; but when the Council was established it was virtually a toothless old lion—a far cry from what was intended—due to differences of opinion among some provinces, particularly Alberta, BC, and Quebec. The third recommendation concerned the dire need to institute Primary Health Care; this idea was also strongly recommended by the Senate findings, known as the Kirby Report, which was published in the fall of 2002. The Kirby Report suggested that properly established Primary Care units could form the foundation required to make the whole system much better organized, bringing seamless health care within reach.

The advent of medicare represents perhaps the

Medicare Timeline

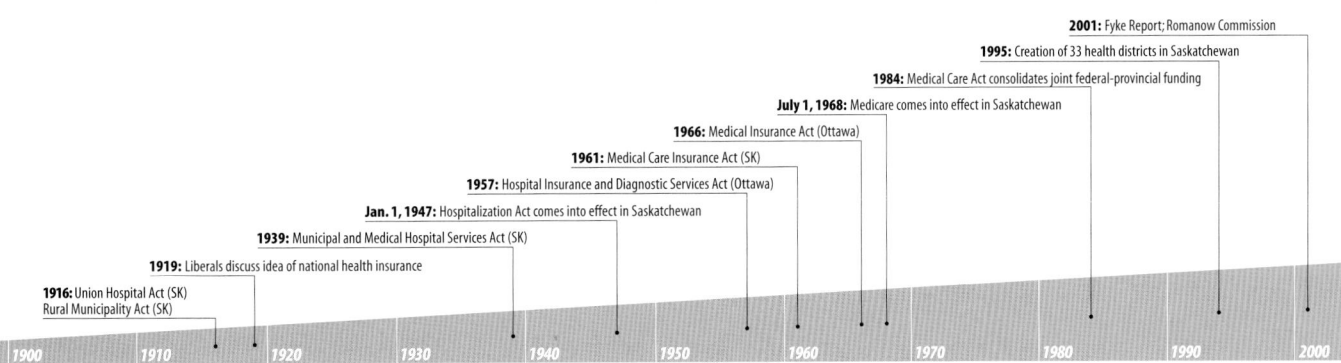

2001: Fyke Report; Romanow Commission
1995: Creation of 33 health districts in Saskatchewan
1984: Medical Care Act consolidates joint federal-provincial funding
July 1, 1968: Medicare comes into effect in Saskatchewan
1966: Medical Insurance Act (Ottawa)
1961: Medical Care Insurance Act (SK)
1957: Hospital Insurance and Diagnostic Services Act (Ottawa)
Jan. 1, 1947: Hospitalization Act comes into effect in Saskatchewan
1939: Municipal and Medical Hospital Services Act (SK)
1919: Liberals discuss idea of national health insurance
1916: Union Hospital Act (SK) / Rural Municipality Act (SK)

1900 1910 1920 1930 1940 1950 1960 1970 1980 1990 2000

greatest test of participatory democracy Canada has ever known. In 1962, community clinics sprang up in many districts—the Swift Current Health Region, which began functioning on July 1, 1946, showing the way. Regina, Saskatoon and Prince Albert still have successful functioning community health clinics. Within such organizations, grassroots decision-making results from community ownership of the system, giving individuals a feeling of empowerment that makes for volunteering services and explains why these agencies work effectively. Primary Health Care is a movement to generalize that kind of decentralized decision-making. At the outset of Saskatchewan medicare in 1962, there were those who believed that centralized control was necessary to guarantee the success of the innovation; whatever the reason, grass-roots community clinics were not encouraged, which set participatory democracy back for more than a generation. The advent of Primary Health Care may well solve the dilemma of how to achieve systematic central control, yet gain the dynamism inherent in local decision-making.

In 1995 a district health board structure was put into place, with the hope of making the administration more democratic and, one suspects, to deflect criticism away from the Department of Health. Thirty-two health districts were created, plus the Athabasca Health Authority in the far north. Two-thirds of the members of the boards were elected, and the rest were appointed to ensure a better balance concerning gender and minorities. Preliminary results suggest that the devolution increased local control; however, the Fyke Report (2001) recommended that the health districts be reduced in number, with appointed, instead of elected, boards. How to organize the administration of health services remains worrisome. Also worrisome is the increasing share of the provincial budget being taken up with public health, including medicare. The fear is that health costs will continue to rise faster than the growth of the economy, and that other services will be crowded out. One solution is to have the federal government accept a growing responsibility for financing medicare, and the other is for provinces to increase revenues; but a combination of both would seem the most likely outcome. The problem is that the federal government and the provinces suffer from insufficient revenue because of the pressure to cut taxes: under these circumstances it remains exceedingly difficult to increase revenues sufficiently to meet the demands of health care and leave enough funding for other essential services such as education, roads, and the environment. With drug costs increasing (cancer drug costs in Saskatchewan go up 22% each year), all governments are faced with some tough decisions. It has been suggested that one way around the dilemma is to raise taxes without appearing to do so, by means

of an increase in the provincial income tax devoted to health.

Medicare has come a long way. The steps often have been faltering and there have been stubbed toes, but a system of health services has taken shape that is the envy of many. As it continues to evolve to meet emerging needs, how the system will change or should change in the future will depend on the studies that are continuously commissioned and on the adoption of their key recommendations.

John A. Boan

MEEWASIN VALLEY AUTHORITY.

Meewasin—the Cree word for beautiful—is the valley of the **SOUTH SASKATCHEWAN RIVER** as it flows through Saskatoon. After years of virtual neglect, extensive studies on the environmental and cultural resources of the valley commissioned during the 1970s led to the creation of an autonomous agency dedicated to planning and developing the 80 km of river valley that extend through Saskatoon and the RM of Corman Park. Architectural planner Raymond Moriyama of Toronto prepared the *Meewasin Valley Project: 100 Year Conceptual Plan*; and in 1979 the four major stakeholders (city of Saskatoon, RM of Corman Park, **UNIVERSITY OF SASKATCHEWAN**, and province of Saskatchewan) created the Meewasin Valley Authority. Although the authority has little real power other than development review, it wields major influence over river policy. Through its work, the river has become a major part of Saskatoon's recreational and cultural landscape, with a 17-km trail system used by cyclists, joggers, walkers, and cross-country skiers. The Beaver Creek Conservation area and the Meewasin Valley Centre showcase extensive educational programs, whose highlight has been the development of **WANUSKEWIN HERITAGE PARK**, an 8,000-year-old northern plains Indian spiritual and cultural centre.

Merle Massie

MELENCHUK, JAMES WILLIAMS (1953–).

Born June 24, 1953, in Regina, Jim Melenchuk was educated at the Universities of Regina and Saskatchewan. Following graduation from medical school in 1980, he established a private practice in Saskatoon and was active in the province's medical community. Melenchuk also served the Saskatchewan **LIBERAL PARTY** in various capacities before contesting public office in the 1995 provincial election. Narrowly defeated in the constituency of Saskatoon Northwest, Melenchuk was one of several Liberals critical of **LYNDA HAVERSTOCK**'s leadership, and he helped remove her as party head.

Melenchuk contested and won the party leadership in 1996, but he was unable to prevent the disintegration of the deeply divided party. A year later, the Liberals lost their place as Official Opposition following the defection of four MLAs to the **SASKATCHEWAN PARTY**, one to the NDP, and one who

chose to sit as an independent. Despite losing a 1998 by-election in Saskatoon Eastview, Melenchuk contested the 1999 general election and narrowly won the constituency of Saskatoon Northwest. He decided to form a coalition with **ROY ROMANOW**'s NDP minority government and was rewarded with the Minister of Education portfolio. Although the Liberal Party endorsed the coalition at first, party members became opposed to the deal and Melenchuk was removed as leader in 2001.

Melenchuk sat in the house as an independent and remained in Cabinet as **LORNE CALVERT** became Premier. In 2003, Melenchuk became Minister of Finance and later joined the NDP. However, he was defeated in Saskatoon Northwest in the election later that year. In March 2005, Melenchuk was appointed as academic health sciences liaison between the government and the **UNIVERSITY OF SASKATCHEWAN**.

Holden Stoffel

FURTHER READING: French, Janet. 2005. "Melenchuk Lands Role as Gov't, U of S Go-Between." *Saskatoon StarPhoenix* (March 10), A3; Quiring, Brett. 2004. "Melenchuk, James Williams." Pp. 164–65 in Brett Quiring (ed.), *Saskatchewan Politicians: Lives Past and Present*. Regina: Canadian Plains Research Center.

MELFORT.

Melfort, pop 5,559, located 90 km east of Prince Albert and 178 km northeast of Saskatoon, in east-central Saskatchewan's parkland belt, is surrounded by the black loam of the fertile Carrot River Valley. Melfort is known as the "City of Northern Lights" because of the spectacular *aurorae* seen in the night skies for much of the year.

The first settlers came to the area in 1892 and established a settlement called Stoney Creek. In 1902 the Canadian Northern Railway surveyed the area, and in 1904 the railway was built about 2.4 km (1.5 miles) south of Stony Creek. As the railroad did not come near the settlement, the people moved the entire community to the railroad, buildings and all. The General Manager of the Canadian Northern Railway, Malcolm Hugh McLeod, asked Mrs. Reginald Beatty, the first White woman settler, to name the new settlement; she named it Melfort after her parents' estate in Argyllshire, Scotland.

The Farmers' Railway opened in July 1909, the first railroad built between Melfort and Regina. The settlement of Melfort grew quickly: it was incorporated as a village in 1903, achieved town status on July 1, 1907, and became Saskatchewan's twelfth city on September 2, 1980.

Melfort is located in one of the most productive farmland areas in Canada, the Carrot River Valley, a territory that has never known drought or severe crop failure.

The city is an agricultural service centre: most industries are agriculturally related and include meat processing, feed mills, seed cleaning plants, the manufacture of farm chemicals, and the largest grain storage capacity in northeast Saskatchewan. The sale and service of agricultural equipment and supplies represent a key component of the retail sales in the city. As the hub of northeast Saskatchewan, Melfort serves a trading area population of 60,000; tourism is also a major industry, with an estimated $9 million spent annually in the area by travelers. Melfort is served by four public elementary schools, Melfort and Unit Comprehensive Collegiate, and a Community College which provides a variety of educational opportunities for adults in the area. Cumberland Community College also offers a full range of first- and second-year Arts and Science classes from the **UNIVERSITY OF SASKATCHEWAN.** *Daria Coneghan*

MELVILLE. Melville, pop 4,453, is located 150 km northeast of Regina. It began its life in 1906 when the Grand Trunk Railway purchased a parcel of land for development. In 1907 J.W. Redgwick built the Pioneer Store, and soon a lumberyard and hardware store were also established in the area. Thirty blocks were surveyed and sold to settlers for between $60 and $400. In 1908 the railway was completed and the community was named Melville after the president of the railway, Charles Melville Hays, who died aboard the Titanic. The community's growth can largely be attributed to its designation as the second divisional point on the railway west of Winnipeg: in just two years the population grew from 66 in 1907 to over 1,000 in 1909, when Melville reached town status. The years between 1910 and 1914 were important to the community, and saw the construction of the first power plant, the hospital, the Melville Milling Company, the Coal Docks, and Luther College. The Melville Millionaires hockey team, also established at that time, won the Allan Cup (national championship) just three years into its existence.

Melville officially became a city on August 1, 1960. Since that time it has grown to become a service centre for poultry, livestock and grain farmers in the area; there is also a small manufacturing sector. Melville is home to the provincial government's Saskatchewan Crop Insurance head office, and to industrial leaders such as Babcock and Wilcox, and Century Glass. The community now has many organizations, service clubs, and sport, cultural and recreational activities. Melville has hosted a number of events such as the 1990 Saskatchewan Winter Games, the Southern Men's curling playdowns in 1996, and the Tankard Men's provincial curling championships in 1998. There is also a successful minor ball and hockey system, as well as figure skating, speed skating, batting cages, a swimming pool, two museums, and several parks. Melville has a daily newspaper, *The Melville Advance*, and the Parkland Regional Library. St. Peter's Hospital, controlled by

the Catholic Health Council, and St. Paul Lutheran Home provide health care to residents. There are three elementary schools, one junior high school, one high school, and one post-secondary college.

Daria Coneghan

MENDEL, FRED S. (1888–1976). Fred S. Mendel, a Saskatchewan-based meat packer who actively built markets for Saskatchewan's livestock as meat products, was born on December 18, 1888, in Recklinghausen, in the Ruhr Valley of Germany. He expanded his father's meat-wholesaling business into a meat-packing empire with branches in Poland, Hungary, Yugoslavia, Rumania, and Bulgaria. Mendel and his family were forced to leave Germany when the Nazis began their persecution of Jews in the 1930s. He came to Saskatoon and acquired a building in 1940, where he launched Intercontinental Packers; he also built a packing enterprise in Australia, hence the name Intercontinental. Initially Mendel's company specialized in canned hams for the United States market (*Time* called him "The Ham Man"), but a trade embargo ended that business, and for the next five years the firm focused on providing bacon for Britain—one of Canada's contributions to the war effort. Saskatchewan farmers entered the hog business, and the Mendel plant prepared the Wiltshire sides for transport to Britain.

After the war Mendel built plants in Regina, Red Deer, and Vancouver to compete for the Canadian market. He was a major contributor to his community and province, providing assistance for extension projects for Saskatchewan farmers and prizes for their livestock exhibits at fairs and exhibitions. He was an avid collector of art and made a major financial contribution for the creation of the gallery that bears his name, the **MENDEL ART GALLERY** of Saskatoon. In 1965, in recognition of his contributions to the province, Mendel received an honorary

Doctor of Laws degree from the **UNIVERSITY OF SASKATCHEWAN.** In 1971 he received the Canadian Industrial Development Award, given to the citizen who made the most significant contribution to Canada's industrial development; he was the only Saskatchewan resident and the only meat packer to receive the award. In 1974 he was installed into the Order of Canada. Mendel died in 1976 at the age of 87, still active in his last year as chairman of the board of Intercontinental Packers (today Mitchell's Gourmet Foods). At the time of his passing in 1976, Intercontinental Packers was one of Canada's "big five" meat packers. In 1990 Fred Mendel was posthumously inducted into the Saskatchewan Agricultural Hall of Fame.

MENDEL ART GALLERY. During the 1940s and 1950s, the focus of visual art in Saskatoon was the Saskatoon Art Centre, established in 1944 and located in the Standard Trust Building before moving to the King George Hotel in 1949. This organization hosted touring exhibitions of art and arranged shows of local artists. In 1960, Saskatoon businessman and art collector **FRED MENDEL** approached Mayor **SIDNEY L. BUCKWOLD** to initiate discussions for the creation of a new civic art gallery which would provide a permanent home for the Saskatoon Art Centre. Subsequently, Mendel donated $175,000 to build such a gallery, and the amount was matched by the provincial government and augmented by assistance from the municipal government. The Mendel Art Gallery & Civic Conservatory opened officially on October 16, 1964, with an exhibition of works from Mendel's personal collection. In 1967, the Saskatoon Gallery and Conservatory Corporation was established by the city. The Mendel Art Gallery is an autonomous freestanding organization, registered as a Canadian charity and certified under the non-profit Corporations Act of Saskatchewan. It is one of two public art museums designat-

COURTESY MENDEL ART GALLERY

Fred Mendel in front of the conservatory, ca. 1964: "I would like the resulting building to be of such character and personality, even if a controversial one, that we could all take pride in."

595

TROY MAMER PHOTO/COURTESY MENDEL ART GALLERY

Mendal Art Gallery, Saskatoon.

ed by the government of Saskatchewan as having provincial programming responsibilities. Two members of the Board of Trustees are elected by the membership, the remainder by civic appointment; the Board appoints the director and approves policies and budgets. In a 1999 survey, the Mendel was ranked as the sixteenth largest public art gallery in Canada by budget size, with the sixth highest overall attendance in the country. It maintains four primary exhibition galleries (8,000 square feet), a Gallery Shop, a public programs studio, and an auditorium. Regular staff is assisted by an active volunteer group to provide services for openings, special events, and membership and fund-raising campaigns.

The mandate of the Mendel Art Gallery is realized through its collection, exhibitions, publications, public and professional programs, extension services, and research. The Mendel is one of the major collecting art galleries in Saskatchewan. In 1965, Fred Mendel donated thirteen paintings to the Gallery, including paintings by the Group of Seven which became the nucleus of the Gallery's collection. Over the years, by donation and acquisition, the collection has grown to over 5,000 works by Saskatchewan, Canadian and international artists in a variety of media and styles. Works from the collection are exhibited regularly in the gallery, lent to other museums for display, and are available for research. Highlights of the collection include work by major Canadian contemporary artists, the Group of Seven, historical Saskatchewan artists, and Inuit and folk artists.

The Mendel is committed to situating the production of artists from this region in a national and international context, and to supporting Saskatchewan artists through solo and group exhibitions which explore trends in both historical and contemporary art production. Staff members conduct research and produce publications that both docu-

ment exhibitions and are used as critical tools to engage artists and their communities. Highlights include: *The Mendel Collection; Ernest Lindner: A Retrospective; Antoni Tapies; Eric Fischl: Paintings; Western Sunlight: C.W. Jefferys on the Canadian Prairies; The Photographs of David Octavius Hill and Robert Adamson; Paterson Ewen: The Montreal Years; Twenty-Five Years of Collecting; The Flat Side of the Landscape: the Emma Lake Artists' Workshops; Edward Poitras: Indian Territory; Corpus; The Post-Colonial Landscape; The Urban Prairie; Dorothy Knowles; William Perehudoff; Eli Bornstein; David Alexander; Women & Paint; Reviewing the Mosaic: Canadian Video Artists Speaking through Race; Plain Truth; Paul Fenniak; Voices: the Work of Joni Mitchell; Qu'Appelle: Tales of Two Valleys; Billy's Vision*; and *Indivisuals*.

Public and professional programs are developed in conjunction with a strategy that links the production of art to the society in which it is produced. As a consequence, the Mendel has made a strong commitment to presenting and interpreting difficult and challenging artwork in its community. Major initiatives over recent years include *Something on Sundays, Open Studio, The Reading Room*, and the School Tour Program. In 2000 the Curatorial Consortium, consisting of program staff, adjunct, independent and guest curators, was initiated to broaden the base of curatorial and public programs and to research regional, national and international interdependencies. The Mendel Art Gallery organizes touring exhibitions to provide increased access on a provincial, national and international level and to foster audience development, collaboration, and cross-cultural exchange. *Dan Ring*

FURTHER READING: Teitelbaum, M. 1989. *Twenty-Five Years of Collecting*. Saskatoon: Mendel Art Gallery.

MENNONITE CENTRAL COMMITTEE SASKATCHEWAN (MCCS). The Mennonite Central Committee Saskatchewan (MCCS) is the provincial arm of the larger Mennonite Central Committee Canada, which in turn is the national partner of the international Mennonite Central Committee with headquarters in Akron, Pennsylvania. The motto of all these organizations is to provide assistance to those in need "In the Name of Christ." MCCS does not officially represent or speak for any church or denomination. Though initially formed to assist needy Mennonites, it has developed a vision for worldwide assistance. Volunteers, funds and material are delivered by MCCS to any individual or group of peoples who have experienced violence, war, famine or natural disaster. MCCS works in the areas of service, relief, peace, justice and development, and has placed 1,400 workers in 58 countries.

The international MCC was organized in North America in 1920 to centralize the efforts of a number of local relief organizations formed to respond to an appeal for help from the Mennonite communities in Russia, which were devastated by war, famine and Communist persecution. In 1922, in Canada the principle relief organization was the Mennonite Board of Colonization headquartered in Rosthern. By 1930 this organization assisted the immigration of 20,000 Russian Mennonites to settle in Canada, mostly in the prairies. The Mennonite Central Relief Committee for Western Canada was formed in 1940 with a number of responsibilities, including collecting the *Reiseschuld* (immigrant's travel debt), taking care of the mentally ill and weak, providing relief in the province and abroad, and providing assistance for funerals. In 1947 this office moved from Rosthern to Saskatoon. These two organizations amalgamated in 1961 under the name Canadian Mennonite Relief and Immigration Committee (CMRIC). MCCS was finally created in October 1964 when the churches belonging to CMRIC and Mennonite Disaster Service joined together.

MCCS is supported by individuals, congregations and conferences of many different Mennonite and Brethren in Christ churches in Saskatchewan. All participation is voluntary and fundraising is done through general donations, special projects, thrift stores and an annual relief auction. Christian service volunteers come mostly from Mennonite and Brethren in Christ churches but may be from any church. *Leonard Doell*

MENNONITE CHURCH SASKATCHEWAN. The Mennonite Church Saskatchewan (MCS), also known as the General Conference, is one of many Mennonite groups. The MCS had its start in the Saskatchewan Valley north of Saskatoon when GERHARD ENS arrived with his family from the Ukraine in 1891, settling in Rosthern. As an agent of

Clifford Sifton, federal Minister of the Interior, and later an elected member of the first Saskatchewan legislature, Ens promoted Mennonite settlement. The first Mennonite church building in the North-West Territories was constructed of logs in the Eigenheim community west of Rosthern in 1896, under the leadership of Peter Regier. In 1902 Regier met with other Saskatchewan Mennonite ministers and leaders from Manitoba to seek co-operation in matters of common concern. That meeting is seen as the beginning of the Conference of Mennonites in Central Canada, forerunner of the Conference of Mennonites in Canada. A provincial organization of this Conference was formed in Saskatchewan.

Annual meetings of the ministers and deacons were replaced in 1959 by a delegate conference which drew more lay members into the work of the Church. The new body was named the Conference of Mennonites of Saskatchewan (CoMoS); in 2001 the name was changed to Mennonite Church Saskatchewan. Accompanying this organizational change were many others: worship services switched from German to English; the *Aeltester* system, where one bishop was in charge of many of congregations, was replaced by a system in which each congregation functioned separately under the auspices of the provincial Conference; the membership became more urban, with one-quarter of the forty congregations and one-third of the adult membership being urban by 2000; and unpaid, often untrained, lay leaders were replaced by trained, salaried ministers.

The MCS has promoted and coordinated many projects: starting and maintaining new congregations, including helping to build churches; promoting mission and relief work, with congregational women's organizations producing many bundles and kits distributed abroad through Mennonite Central Committee; setting up private schools, Bible Schools, Sunday Schools, Summer Bible Schools, and Children's Camps; and organizing chaplaincy ministries in hospitals and jails.

A unique project of MCS began with the initiative of the Youth Organization, formed in 1940. When the federal government closed the Dominion Experimental Farm in Rosthern in 1940, the Youth Organization bought the Farm, which included 640 acres of treed landscape with buildings, for $20,000. The renamed Mennonite Youth Farm was the venue for a number of institutions including an invalid home, a children's home, a handicapped children's home, and two homes for the mentally challenged. The products of the farm and livestock operations provided the institutions with food, and profits from the sale of milk in Rosthern were shared with various mission agencies. Though these institutions no longer exist, the campus still contains a modern 68-bed nursing home as well as seniors housing.

Verner Friesen

MENNONITE SETTLEMENTS. The Mennonites date their origin back to the spread of Anabaptism from Switzerland during the 16th century. A then fairly radical group of Anabaptists appeared in The Netherlands under the leadership of Menno Simons (1492–1559). Faced with persecution not only by Catholics but also by less communal-minded Protestants there, these people, who became known as Mennonites, began to move into northern Germany after 1525, particularly into West and East Prussia, where they were invited to occupy undeveloped territories as part of a German eastern colonization scheme that promised them exemption from military service. But by the 1780s, facing numerous problems from the Prussian government, the Mennonites began to leave Prussia to establish colonies in Poland and South Russia (present-day Ukraine). Invited by Catherine II and lured by military and tax exemptions and permission to found their own schools and local governments, they first established the large Chortitza (1789) and Molotschna (1803) colonies, then numerous other smaller colonies during the 19th century.

However, in 1874 Russian nationalism caught up with the German colonists of South Russia. Their military and taxation exemptions were revoked; their political autonomy was disrupted when their colonies were incorporated into larger Russian administrative units; records and schools had to use the Russian language; and "unqualified" Mennonite school teachers were replaced by Russian ones. That year Mennonites, Hutterites and other Russian-German Protestants emigrated to South Dakota. Other conservative Mennonites from the Chortitza colony moved to the East Reserve in the Steinbach area of Manitoba (southeast of Winnipeg). The following year, the conservative Mennonites of the Furstenland and Bergthal colonies moved to the West Reserve in the Morden and Winkler area (southwest of Winnipeg). By 1893 the overpopulation of these Manitoba "reserves" led to the emigration of some of the Mennonites who had settled in Manitoba to the Rosthern and Swift Current areas, respectively in 1893 and 1902.

The Saskatchewan Valley Settlement developed rapidly into a major bloc settlement, similar in many ways to its forerunners in South Russia, which developed in several stages between 1891 and 1918. The initial nucleus of this settlement came into existence in 1891–94 with the settling of the immediate area around Rosthern by immigrants of the *Rosenort Gemeinde* (later General Conference Mennonites) from West Prussia, Russia, and Manitoba. Furstenlanders migrated from the West Reserve in Manitoba to settle around Hague in 1895. A compact reserve consisting of as many as twenty villages was then established south of Rosthern, between Hague and Osler, by Old Colony Mennonites from Manitoba in 1895–1905. The

social organization of the conservative colonies in South Russia was systematically duplicated in north-central Saskatchewan: wide streets (a custom developed in Russia due to the possibility of thatched roofs catching fire), a *Schult* (village overseer), and German language schools and churches. These adjoining Mennonite settlements then expanded into a single vast settlement with the establishment of additional communities and congregations by Mennonite Brethren from the American Midwest (particularly Minnesota, Nebraska, Kansas, and Oklahoma), directly from Russia, or via Manitoba, in 1898–1918; by Krimmer Mennonite Brethren from Kansas and Nebraska in 1899–1901; by Sommerfelder or Bergthaler Mennonites from Manitoba in 1902; by General Conference Mennonites largely from the Midwest (Kansas, Oklahoma, Minnesota), but also directly from Russia or via Manitoba, in 1910–12; and by Bruderthaler or Evangelical Mennonite Brethren from Minnesota in 1912.

Most of the conservative Mennonites in the settlement arrived immediately from the West Reserve in Manitoba; they or their predecessors had formerly come to Manitoba largely from the Chortitza Colony and some from the Bergthal Colony in South Russia, but later arrivals from Russia as well as from Mennonite colonies in the United States included immigrants from the Molotschna Colony. The exodus of several thousand conservative Sommerfelder, Bergthaler, and Chortitza Mennonites from Saskatchewan and Manitoba to Mexico and Paraguay in 1922–28 was offset by a renewed mass influx of Mennonites, as well as German Lutherans, from Russia. The Canadian Mennonite Colonization Board was organized in 1922, and the Lutheran Immigration Board the following year, to assist the remaining Mennonites and Lutherans in Russia and in postwar refugee camps to escape famine and the new Communist regime. By the time the Soviet government forbade further emigration in 1930, 19,891 Mennonites and 12,310 Lutherans had been brought into Canada. 7,828 of the Mennonites, joined by small groups of Lutherans, settled in Saskatchewan (close to 3,000 in the Rosthern colony in 1923 alone). The Canada Colonization Association (CCA), the boards, and the ministers co-operated in settling the immigrants on tracts of land recently placed on the market. Commissions of 1.25% were paid by the CCA to a board or vice-versa for finding land and subsidizing settlement.

The influx of "Russlander" (Russian Mennonites arriving in the 1920s, as distinguished from the "Kanadier," who had arrived earlier) was met with some opposition. In 1919 the Canadian government had passed Orders-in-Council prohibiting Mennonites as well as Hutterites and Doukhobors from entering Canada. When the orders were repealed in 1922 by the new Liberal government, English Canadians continued their outcry against the Russian Mennonite "flood," which "flock to church while our boys fight," "don't conform to Canadian school laws," and bring "unsanitary habits and Asiatic diseases" (Archives of Saskatchewan). Today the Rosthern and Saskatchewan Valley settlement, originally covering at least forty-two townships, includes over 10,000 people of German origin in or near five towns (Rosthern, Warman, Langham, Waldheim, and Martensville), six incorporated villages, and at least seven unincorporated villages or hamlets. The population claiming German origin in these towns and villages typically ranged from about half to over 90% in 1971.

A second, even more extensive Mennonite Settlement developed around Swift Current and Herbert, then spread northeastward to include the Vermillion Hills region. This vast settlement had its origins in two rather different Mennonite colonies established immediately east and south of Swift Current. First to arrive were Sommerfelder Mennonites from Manitoba, who settled in the Main Centre-Gouldtown area north of Herbert in 1900. They were soon joined by General Conference Mennonites and Mennonite Brethren, settling around Herbert in 1903–05; within a couple of years at least 100 Mennonite families had settled there, most from Russian-German Mennonite colonies in the United States. Meanwhile, another Mennonite colony was developing south of Swift Current. In 1904, Old Colony Mennonites from the Manitoba reserves petitioned the Dominion government for a reserve of six townships. Within a year at least twenty villages had been founded in this colony, named after Old Colony villages in Manitoba and Russia. By 1911 there were already approximately 4,600 Mennonites in these colonies.

From these two nuclei settlements, Mennonite settlement expanded rapidly throughout the general region. General Conference Mennonites established churches within the Old Colony area at Wymark, Schoenfeld, Rheinland, and McMahon, while Mennonite Brethren built a church at McMahon and the Evangelical Mennonite Mission Conference churches at Wymark and Blumenhof. To the southeast, Mennonite Brethren established churches at Kelstern (1907), Flowing Well (Gnadenau congregation, 1907), and Woodrow (1909); and General Conference Mennonites at Neville (1914). To the northeast, Mennonite Brethren congregations included Bruderfeld (1901), Main Centre (1904), Herbert (1905), Greenfarm (1912), Turnhill (1913), Beechy (Friedensheim congregation, 1925), and Lucky Lake (1943); while General Conference Mennonites were found around Herbert (1904), Morse (1920s), Gouldtown (1926), Eyebrow (1929), Tugaske, Central Butte, Lawson, Gilroy, and Elbow (all during the 1920s). To the west, small Mennonite Brethren and General Conference Mennonite congregations were established in many communities.

Given the expansion and widespread distribution of Mennonite settlement in this region of Saskatchewan, it is difficult to estimate with any real accuracy the total Mennonite population; yet people claiming German origin number in excess of 10,000– close to 5,000 in Swift Current alone. But aside from the strongly Mennonite villages immediately south of Swift Current, only three towns or villages retained majority German proportions in 1971: Herbert, Morse, and Waldeck.

While the Rosthern-Saskatchewan Valley and Swift Current-Vermillion Hills settlements are the only really extensive Mennonite settlements in Saskatchewan, there are many smaller Mennonite concentrations widely scattered throughout the prairie portion of the province, mostly dating from the *Russlander* migration–the last substantial emigration from the Mennonite colonies in Russia–during the 1920s. The migration of *Russlander* resulted not only in the expansion of existing Mennonite colonies in Saskatchewan, but also in the foundation of new settlements as large farms were broken up in the Dundurn-Hanley, Herschel, and other areas.

Some ninety families settled marginal lands to form the Meeting Lake settlement, situated in the Thickwood Hills northeast of North Battleford, in 1926-30. By 1947 more Mennonites immigrated to the Meeting Lake settlement and other settlements from Eastern Europe in the wake of **WORLD WAR II**. Today the Meeting Lake and Thickwood Hills settlement includes about 1,500 people of German origin in and near two incorporated villages (Medstead and Rabbit Lake), three unincorporated villages or hamlets (Fairholme, Mayfair, and Glenbush), and at least twenty named localities. Mennonites and other Germans formed about a third (34.3%) of the population of Medstead in 1971 and over a quarter (26%) at Rabbit Lake, but probably predominated in the smaller communities. Bruderthaler established a congregation at Fairholme in 1927; the Mennonite Brethren church at Glenbush dates from 1928, the General Conference one from 1934; and other General Conference congregations were established at Rabbit Lake in 1926, and at Mayfair in 1928 and 1936. South of this settlement, some Mennonite families settled in the Lorenzo, Fielding, and Speers areas.

At an early date a Mennonite concentration had developed closer to the main Rosthern settlement, in neighbouring rural districts north of the village of Borden. Mennonite Brethren had settled at Hoffnungsfeld as early as 1904, General Conference Mennonites at Great Deer in 1912, as well as in the Clear Spring and Concordia districts. Other General Conference Mennonite congregations established in the northwestern region included Meadow Lake (1935), Pierceland (1931), Compass (1933), Daisy Meadow, Dorintosh and Capasin (1931); while

Mennonite Brethren churches were also established at Meadow Lake (1935), Pierceland (1939), and Compass (1938). In the west-central region an early Mennonite congregation was established by Mennonite Brethren in Christ at Alsask in 1910. During the 1920s *Russlander* Mennonites affiliated with the General Conference settled in the Herschel-Fiske area, as well as around Springwater, Harris, Ardath, Superb, Major, and Glidden. During the 1920s and 1930s a Mennonite Brethren concentration developed in the Lashburn-Waseca-Maidstone area.

Mennonites from a variety of different backgrounds settled in compact pockets in central Saskatchewan from an early date. Some Old Mennonite families from Ontario established a small congregation at Guernsey in 1905. Nearby, General Conference Mennonites from Kansas and Oklahoma formed the Nordstern (North Star) congregation at Drake in 1906–13. As Mennonite settlement spread, other General Conference churches were established at Watrous (1930) and Lampard, a Mennonite Brethren church at Watrous, and Mennonites also settled around Colonsay, Nokomis, and Lanigan. The Nordheim Congregation, affiliated with the General Conference, was founded in 1924 by *Russlander* at Sheldon Farms, west of Hanley, and at Pleasant Point, east of Dundurn.

In the east-central region, a congregation at Wynyard was established by the Evangelical Mennonite Mission Conference, one at Foam Lake by the Mennonite Brethren, and Mennonites also settled around Parkview, Wishart and Sheho. To the northeast, a Sommerfelder Mennonite reserve was founded in the Carrot River area as early as 1908; later, General Conference congregations served Carrot River (1926), Lost River (1916), and Petaigan (1931), with a Mennonite Brethren one at Carrot River (1926) as well. Similarly, an isolated Old Colony Mennonite settlement in the Swan Plain region, a marginal, heavily treed area near the Manitoba border, was later served by a General Conference mission. In south-central and southeastern Saskatchewan, Mennonites settled in the Truax-Dummer-Parry-Brooking area during the 1930s, as well as around Carnduff and Fleming. (*See also* **ETHNIC BLOC SETTLEMENTS, GERMAN SETTLEMENTS**)

Alan Anderson

FURTHER READING: Epp, F.H. 1974. *Mennonites in Canada 1786–1920*. Toronto: Macmillan; —. 1982. *Mennonites in Canada 1920–1940*. Toronto: Macmillan; Regehr, T.D. 1996. *Mennonites in Canada 1939–1970*. Toronto: University of Toronto Press.

MENNONITES. Mennonites are members of a small Protestant religious-cultural group which traces its origins to European Anabaptists of the early 16th century. The Anabaptists emphasized a radical theology of Christian discipleship, which demanded that true followers of Jesus apply all that he taught his disciples to all aspects of life. That meant, among other things, that they rejected participation in any secular, civil, military or official church affairs which they believed did not conform with that high standard of discipleship. They also insisted that all governments were ordained by God and should be obeyed and respected in all matters not inconsistent with the higher standards set by Jesus. Their antinomian theology, particularly their rejection of military service in time of war and of established religious authority, resulted in severe persecution by both secular and established church authorities. Many found refuge on scattered and remote agricultural lands, where a hard-working, abstemious, peaceable and, in most matters, law-abiding lifestyle earned Mennonites religious concessions and privileges.

Saskatchewan was an agricultural frontier to which Mennonites first came in the early 1890s. Most of those early Mennonite migrants, however, came in search of land rather than to escape religious persecution. In the 1870s the federal government had set aside two large tracts of land as Mennonite reserves. New limited-time reserves, to accommodate Manitoba Mennonites seeking additional land, were established in Saskatchewan—two in the early 1890s at Hague-Osler and near Swift Current, and a third in the Quill Lakes district in 1905. In the Hague-Osler and Swift Current reserves, the settlers established villages, communities and churches similar to those in Russia and the Manitoba reserves. Those early Mennonite migrants were joined in Saskatchewan by others coming directly from Russia, Prussia, Ontario, and the United States. Most of the later arrivals, including those in the Quill Lakes reserve, settled on traditional western homesteads or purchased railway lands; but they tried, in spite of different settlement patterns, to retain salient aspects of their religious and cultural heritage. Many more Mennonites arrived in the 1920s, following the disruptions of war and revolution in Russia, and after **WORLD WAR II**.

Flourishing communities were established in which Mennonites enjoyed a substantial measure of local administrative and educational control. But they came under very considerable pressure during **WORLD WAR I** because of their failure to integrate quickly into Canadian society. That resulted in the passage of legislation by the provincial governments of Manitoba and Saskatchewan requiring the organization of assimilationist English-language schools in all immigrant districts, and compulsory attendance at these schools by all school-age children. Those who refused to send their children to approved schools were subject to heavy fines and possible imprisonment. That led, in the early 1920s, to a migration of approximately 7,000 Manitoba and Saskatchewan Mennonites to Mexico and Paraguay.

The arrival of Mennonite migrants from the Soviet Union, however, more than offset the out-migration. The Mennonites who stayed, and those arriving in the 1920s, sought to influence the education of their children through elected local school boards, and by training future Mennonite teachers in denominational high schools at Rosthern, Saskatchewan, and Gretna, Manitoba.

Most Saskatchewan Mennonites lived in rural areas where they engaged in farming and farm-related ventures before World War II. Many of their young men, however, were conscripted for alternative wartime service during World War II. That experience, increased mechanization, and attractive educational, economic and cultural opportunities drew a rapidly increasing number to towns and cities. Wartime alternative service and post-war voluntary service in relief and rehabilitation work further enlarged Mennonite awareness of worldwide needs and of Christian opportunities to address those needs. Generously funded Mennonite relief agencies —most notably the **MENNONITE CENTRAL COMMITTEE**, which was first established in North America to assist distressed Mennonites in the Soviet Union, and the more recently organized Mennonite Economic Development Agency—initiated worldwide relief, aid and peace-making programs.

The basic unit of Mennonite institutional life is the congregation. In the early days leadership was provided by lay ministers and elders who were sometimes called bishops. More recently most congregations are served by salaried pastors and governed by democratically elected lay leaders. Beyond the congregation there are a number of provincial and national conferences. The various conferences reflect in part the date at which various groups arrived in Canada, and in part doctrinal differences and personality clashes. Today Saskatchewan Mennonites can be found in all walks of life. Their rural communities, like most others in Saskatchewan, have suffered considerable decline, and the largest churches are now in the cities, most notably in Saskatoon. Their membership, as reported in the decennial Canadian census returns, peaked in 1941, but declined slightly in the next five decades and more dramatically in the last ten years.

Theodore Regehr

MENTAL HEALTH SERVICES. Prior to 1905, Saskatchewan patients requiring mental hospital care were sent to Manitoba. In 1907, however, a young provincial health officer, Dr. David Low (1869–1941), was sent by Premier **WALTER SCOTT** to visit mental hospitals in eastern Canada and the United States in order to prepare recommendations for such care in the province. Low favoured the cottage system, but Dr. C.K. Clarke, a well-known Toronto psychiatrist, demurred; he felt its use would be questionable "for both economic and climatic rea-

sons," though he admitted that the cottage system "gives ideal conditions for the patients themselves." Low's plan, which included removing "all evidence of restraint in the management of the insane," was abandoned: the Saskatchewan Hospital North Battleford, a large pavilion-style mental institution, was built between 1911 and 1913.

Low's opinions were shared by Dr. James Walter MacNeill (1873–1945), who was born in Prince Edward Island and graduated with an MD degree from McGill University in 1901. After practicing in New Brunswick he moved to Hanley, Saskatchewan, in 1906 and served as a family doctor there until 1912. In 1908 he was elected to the provincial legislature and remained as a Liberal member until 1913. He was interested in social issues, and played a significant part in initiating the Homesteads Act that ended the right of a settler to sell the homestead without the consent of his wife.

In 1913 MacNeill spent eight months in England and the United States, studying psychiatry and familiarizing himself with mental hospital organization in order to prepare for his new role as the first medical superintendent of the Saskatchewan Hospital North Battleford. He remained there until 1945, periodically visiting other centres to keep himself up to date. In 1943, because of his concerns over the housing of the mentally handicapped at the Weyburn Hospital, he undertook a survey of eight institutions in eastern Canada and the United States, and made recommendations to the government that ultimately led to the building of the Moose Jaw Training School.

When MacNeill arrived at the North Battleford hospital in 1914, Cecilia Wetton reported, "The atmosphere was that of a prison, with cage beds, straitjackets, bars on the windows and a high walled airing court in which patients milled." She stated that MacNeill ordered the demolition of the airing court, removed the bars from the windows, forbade the use of mechanical restraints, and banished the use of the term "asylum," for which he substituted the word "hospital." Patients were treated as human beings with illnesses and in need of help. MacNeill was particularly interested in the therapeutic value of work as a source of meaning in a person's life. It was in this spirit (not in a commercial one) that he launched the farm and irrigation projects at the hospital and made the grounds a beauty spot. He was also receptive to new therapies such as metrazol and insulin, but was appropriately cautious in his assessment of them. He launched a two-year ward attendant training program at North Battleford in 1930, and at Weyburn (where a second mental hospital had been built in 1921) in 1931. He did much to ensure that persons charged with serious crimes had the opportunity of an examination by a psychiatrist in order to rule out mental illness.

As admissions to mental hospitals increased,

EVERETT BAKER PHOTO/COURTESY OF THE SASKATCHEWAN HISTORY AND FOLKLORE SOCIETY

Saskatchewan Hospital, Weyburn, August 1960.

MacNeill struggled with the constant problem of overcrowding: in 1913 provincial magistrates committed patients to the mental hospital, and in 1936 provision was made for voluntary admission in addition to magistrates' certificates. The patient population of the two hospitals soared from 2,000 in 1930 to over 4,000 in 1946, creating severe difficulties. Staff shortages resulted during WORLD WAR II, and the mingling of mentally ill patients with the mentally handicapped was much criticized by surveyors and made management more difficult.

Surveyors were encouraged by MacNeill to visit and assess the two hospitals. They came mainly from the Canadian National Committee on Mental Hygiene (now the Canadian Mental Health Association), but there were also inspections from other professional groups such as the American Psychiatric Association. They all had high praise for Dr. MacNeill and the hospital at North Battleford; since they often meted out censure on their visits to other facilities, there is no reason to doubt their objectivity. MacNeill retired on May 31, 1945, expressing satisfaction at seeing the hospital develop "into one of the finest institutions of its kind in the North American continent." A month later he died unexpectedly following a surgical procedure. MacNeill had been a beacon of light in a pessimistic era. He was a firm disciplinarian with staff, but his gentleness and dedication with patients was legendary. Since 1931 he had been in charge of all the mental services in Saskatchewan as its Commissioner of Mental Services, and he was justly proud of the honorary degree awarded to him by the UNIVERSITY OF SASKATCHEWAN in 1941 for his outstanding services to the mentally ill.

At the end of WORLD WAR II the advent of the government of Premier T.C. DOUGLAS created a halcyon period for mental health services. Dr. D.G. MCKERRACHER (1909–70) became commissioner of Psychiatric Services on November 1, 1946. The

"new" era emphasized community rather than institutional care. In 1950 a revised Mental Health Act was passed, with admission becoming almost entirely a medical function. Then in 1951 two important appointments were made: Dr. Abram Hoffer became director of the provincial psychiatric research program; and Dr. Humphrey Osmond (1917–2004) was appointed first as clinical director and later as medical superintendent of the Saskatchewan Hospital, Weyburn. Dr. Hoffer's contribution has been underestimated, perhaps because some of his concepts have not been widely accepted by the medical profession. However, he launched many research programs and stimulated adventurous, questioning, experimental and optimistic attitudes at a time when these had been lacking. He encouraged younger researchers, and boosted morale in the mental services generally. His interests were wide: two major ones were the biochemical basis of schizophrenia, and orthomolecular medicine (using vitamins including nicotinic acid). He published many books and papers that have generated and will continue to generate lively interest and discussion. He was acclaimed by patients and colleagues alike as an outstanding physician and researcher.

Dr. Osmond was associated with the Saskatchewan Hospital Weyburn from 1951 to 1961, during which time he transformed the hospital by attracting distinguished researchers from both academic and service disciplines to an institution that had been regarded by some as a backwater. He, too, published extensively. He was particularly interested in the possible therapeutic effects of hallucinogens and first coined the term "psychedelic." He also appeared in Aldous Huxley's book, *The Doors of Perception*, which describes Huxley's experience with mescaline. Hoffer and Osmond worked closely together. The departures of Osmond in 1961 and Hoffer in 1967 left major gaps in the provincial mental health research program.

The 1950s saw the development of the Saskatchewan Plan. This was a comprehensive proposal for all phases of emotional or mental treatment to be given within a health region, without recourse to a remote large mental hospital in which it was all too easy to forget about the patient. A team would provide continuity of care. Dr. F.S. (Sam) Lawson (1903–70), the Director of Psychiatric Services in Saskatchewan from 1955 to 1966, concurred strongly that the plan should be built around new, smaller mental hospitals. Kioshi Izumi (1921–96), a Regina architect, drew designs in conjunction with Osmond for such units in order to facilitate a therapeutic environment; the first was built at Yorkton in 1964. Dr. McKerracher, following his work in Saskatoon with Colin Smith, favoured general hospital units. In the end a compromise resulted, with the actual units having some of the characteristics of both. The decline in the actual numbers of patients in psychiatric institutions began about 1963; predictions of the total number of beds required under the Saskatchewan Plan turned out to be considerable over-estimates. Meanwhile the Mental Health Act had been rewritten in 1961, with admission to a mental hospital becoming discretionary and detention more difficult. Between 1960 and 1963 it was shown at University Hospital, Saskatoon, that a small open psychiatric ward in a general hospital could cope with all types of mentally ill patients. It became clear, however, that better support and after-care were necessary if results were to be sustained; psychiatric home care programs were thus launched in Saskatoon and spread across the province. Then in the Saskatchewan Hospital Weyburn, with Drs. F. Grunberg and H.G. Lafave providing leadership in finding alternatives to admission and developing improved after-care planning, the numbers of in-patients began to fall sharply: between 1963 and 1966 the population there dropped from roughly 1,500 to 500 patients. The causes of this tremendous decline can be debated, but major factors were certainly the effects of newer treatments on symptomatology, in conjunction with improved social programs. By 1971 the in-patient population had dropped so markedly that the Saskatchewan Hospital Weyburn was "phased over" into a 63-bed psychiatric centre and a 300-bed extended care facility. In North Battleford a similar process soon followed. New Centres or psychiatric wards were opened in hospitals in Saskatoon in 1955, Moose Jaw in 1956, Yorkton in 1964, Prince Albert in 1968, Regina in 1975 and 1978, and Swift Current in 1978. Out-patient and after-care services increased greatly. Between 1963 and 1980 the patient population in the two mental hospitals had decreased from 3,100 to 270—one of the largest reductions in the world—through careful pre-discharge planning.

In the 1960s the Ad Hoc Committee (1966), the

Frazier Report (1967–68), the Prefontaine Report (1968), and the paper "Crisis and Aftermath" pleaded for improved community services, which were needed as a result of de-institutionalization, and these demands were largely met. However, problems of funding and organization of the programs now dominate the agenda and need to be thoroughly evaluated. *Colin M. Smith*

FURTHER READING: Kahan F.H. 1965. *Brains and Bricks: The History of the Yorkton Psychiatric Centre*. Regina: Canadian Mental Health Association; Kildaw, Delores. 1990. *A History of the Saskatchewan Hospital North Battleford*. Saskatoon: University of Saskatchewan; Smith , Colin M. 1971. "Crisis and Aftermath: Community Psychiatry in Saskatchewan, 1963–69," *Journal of the Canadian Psychiatric Association* 16: 65–76.

MESSER, JOHN RISSLER (1941–). Born May 26, 1941, Jack Messer was raised in the Tisdale area. After completing his education, he moved to British Columbia and established a successful real estate business. He returned to school, attending both the University of British Columbia and the UNIVERSITY OF SASKATCHEWAN before establishing a farm near Tisdale. In 1967, Messer won the constituency of Kelsey for the CCF-NDP and was appointed the party's Agriculture critic. Messer was appointed to ALLAN BLAKENEY's first Cabinet as Minister of Agriculture in 1971. He introduced the controversial Land Bank program. After re-election in 1975, Messer was moved into Industry for a year, then was appointed Minister of Mineral Resources. Messer was supportive of the expansion of uranium mining and the exploitation of uranium reserves at Cluff Lake and Key Lake. Messer was also instrumental in the establishment of the Potash Corporation of Saskatchewan, serving on the corporation's first board and also serving on the Cabinet committee that nationalized a large portion of the province's potash sector. Re-elected in 1978, Messer resigned from the Legislature in 1980 to return to business. Messer returned to politics in 1990 as the NDP provincial secretary, the party's highest administrative position. He ran the NDP's 1991 election cam-

ROY ANTAL/REGINA LEADER-POST

Jack Messer, November 1991.

Table MD-1. Saskatchewan Meteorite Find Locations[1]

Location	Find date	Identified	Type[a]	Mass (kg)
Annaheim	1916	1916	Iron	11.8
Blaine Lake	1974	1974	Stone	1.9
Bruno	1931	1931	Iron	13
Burstall	1992	1992	Iron	0.4
Cartherwood	1965	1965	Stone	3.9
Delaine Lake	2000	2000[b]	Stone	3
Fillmore	1916	1968	Iron	0.1
Garden Head	1944	1964	Iron	1.3
Hodgeville	1970	1996	Stone	7
Kinley	1965	1968	Stone	2
Kyle	1980	2000[b]	Stone	7
Red Deer Hill	1975	1975	Stone	~30[c]
Springwater	1931	1931	Stony-iron	67.7[d]
Wynyard	1968	1982	Stone	3.5

[1] All of the Saskatchewan meteorite finds have been made serendipitously, and no unambiguous date exists on their actual fall dates. In many cases the meteorites were collected by farmers clearing their fields of rocks. Columns two and three distinguish between the year in which a meteorite was physically found and the year in which it was first identified as a meteorite.

Key:
[a] A detailed description of the various meteorite types can be found at the webpage of the Meteorite and Impact Advisory Committee to the Canadian Space Agency (MIAC)—http://miac.uquac.ca/MIAC/MIAC.html.
[b] Identified by the Prairie Meteorite Search—http://www.geo.ucalgary.ca/PMSearch.
[c] Numerous fragments from the Red Deer Hill meteorite have been found since 1975, and it is the estimated total recovered mass that is given in column five.
[d] Three meteorite fragments were actually found in Springwater, and the combined mass is given in column five. The Springwater meteorite was the very first example of a stony-iron meteorite (or pallasite) to be found in Canada.

paign, which resulted in ROY ROMANOW's election as Premier. In 1991, he was appointed president of SaskPower. He remained as president until he resigned in 1998 amid controversy around the sale of one of SaskPower's subsidiaries, Channel Lake Petroleum. Messer continued to maintain his farm in Tisdale and in 2003 was elected president of Ducks Unlimited Canada. *Brett Quiring*

METEORITE DISCOVERIES. A meteorite is a solid object of extraterrestrial origin that has survived its passage through the Earth's atmosphere and fallen to the ground. Derived from the main belt asteroid region in the solar system (with a rare few from the Moon and Mars), meteorites are broadly classified as stones (94% of falls), irons (5% of falls) and stony-irons (1% of falls). Saskatchewan's first recognized meteorite find was made on July 30, 1916, by William Huiras in the Annaheim area. The meteorite was an 11.84 kg iron. The two most recent meteorite finds in Saskatchewan were made during the summer of 2000 in the Delaine Lake and Kyle areas. The most numerously populated strewn field of meteorites to be discovered in Saskatchewan (and indeed all of Canada) is that in the Red Deer Hill area south of Prince Albert. John Hrynuik found the first fragment from this strewn field in May 1975. Since then more than thirty additional mete-

orite fragments have been recovered for a total known mass of 22.5 kg. All told, fragments from some fourteen distinct meteorite falls have been found in Saskatchewan since 1916, constituting eight stones, five irons, and one stony-iron (*see* Table MD-1).

None of the meteorites found in Saskatchewan was large enough to produce substantial impact structures on the ground. However, astroblemes (eroded remnants of craters created by the impact of larger objects such as small asteroids) do exist in Saskatchewan: the Viewfield crater is an example of an impact structure now buried by overlying soils, while the Gow crater in northern Saskatchewan subsequently filled with water to become a lake. (*See also* ASTROBLEMES.) *Martin Beech*

METEOROLOGY. Meteorology is the study of the earth's atmosphere, especially as it relates to weather forecasting. The weather at a particular time and place is normally described in terms of air temperature, precipitation, wind speed and direction, air pressure, and humidity (climate describes these same characteristics, but averaged across a period of many years). Saskatchewan's official instrumental weather records began in 1883 at the North-West Mounted Police barracks in Regina, where daily maximum and minimum temperatures and precipitation were recorded until 1932. The instrumentation was then relocated to the Regina airport, where it has remained. In Saskatoon, the Royal North-West Mounted Police began daily weather observation at Clark's Crossing on the SOUTH SASKATCHEWAN RIVER in 1889. The station operated until 1942, when Environment Canada opened a climate station with a full observation program at Saskatoon airport.

The Meteorological Service of Canada (MSC) has issued weather forecasts and warnings to Canadians since 1871. Until 1963, forecasts for eastern Saskatchewan were issued from Winnipeg and those for western Saskatchewan came from Edmonton. In 1963, Winnipeg's Prairie Weather Center became the forecasting office for the entire prairie region. However, three years later, Environment Canada established a provincial weather office in Regina to provide weather forecasting services for Saskatchewan. In 1978, forecasting responsibilities for the prairies were again centralized in Winnipeg, where they remained until 1993. Saskatoon's weather office then assumed forecasting duties for several years, but by 1997 Environment Canada had closed its Regina and Prince Albert weather offices and once again moved the forecasting section in Saskatoon back to Winnipeg. Today, the MSC administers its services through five regional offices. Edmonton is the regional forecasting and research headquarters for the Prairie and Northern Region, encompassing Saskatchewan, Manitoba, Alberta, the Northwest Territories, and Nunavut. Severe weather warnings for Saskatchewan are issued out of Winnipeg's Prairie Storm Prediction Center.

The MSC currently operates more than forty active climate stations across Saskatchewan. Principal stations, like those at the Regina and Saskatoon airports, provide automated and detailed records of hourly weather information, including air temperature, precipitation amount, wind direction, wind speed, sunshine hours, and atmospheric pressure. In sparsely populated areas, secondary climate stations only record daily temperatures and/or precipitation amount. Saskatchewan Environment also operates a provincial network of automated weather stations. Forty-eight remote stations are positioned throughout the province (primarily in the north) to collect hourly measurements of temperature, wind, and rainfall. The data gathered from this network are used in forecasting and fighting forest fires.

In addition to its network of automated weather stations, the MSC oversees a nationwide team of volunteer weather watchers. In the prairie provinces there are 5,000 volunteers in Environment Canada's weather watcher programs. These include CAN-WARN (Canadian Weather Amateur Radio Network), ALTAWatch (based in central Alberta), and the Severe Weather Watchers Program. Originally serving only southern Ontario, the CAN-WARN program has expanded westward to include

some 400 volunteers in Saskatchewan. Volunteers are weather enthusiasts and ham radio operators trained in spotting and reporting signs of ominous weather (such as hailstorms, thunderstorms, and tornadoes). Because many weather events are too localized to be detected by radar or satellite imagery, these volunteers provide a crucial link in Environment Canada's public warning and forecasting systems.

In compiling weather forecasts, the MSC supplements its data from the network of meteorological stations with an array of sophisticated computers models, weather radars, and satellite technology. The most advanced weather radar systems employ Doppler technology. Doppler radars allow meteorologists to quickly and accurately track severe storms and to monitor their formation, movement, and intensity. Environment Canada's National Doppler Radar Network has two radars in Saskatchewan: one installed in 1998 at Bethune (50 km northwest of Regina) and the other at Radisson (60 km northwest of Saskatoon) in 1999. These radars have a diametrical range of 250 km, and together cover most of Saskatchewan.

For purposes of generating and delivering weather forecasts, the MSC has divided Saskatchewan into thirty-one forecast regions: nine in northern Saskatchewan and twenty-two in the south. This allows forecasters to account for regional variations in land cover, terrain, and population distribution. The names and boundaries of the forecast regions roughly correspond with those of Saskatchewan's rural municipalities, geographic areas, and communities.

In more than 120 years of official meteorological observation, Saskatchewan has captured some remarkable weather records. The highest temperature ever recorded in Saskatchewan—indeed in all of Canada—was observed at Yellow Grass and Midale on July 5, 1937, when the temperature hit 45.0°C. The lowest temperature ever recorded in the province is -56.7°C, observed at Prince Albert on February 1, 1893. The windiest day was October 4, 1976, when maximum hourly wind speeds reached 142 km/hr in Melfort. And on July 3, 2000, 375 mm of rain fell on Vanguard in an eight-hour period, making it the most intensive storm ever recorded on the Canadian prairies.

Iain Stewart

FURTHER READING: Environment Canada. 1981. *Principal Station Data: Regina A.* Downsview: Atmospheric Environment Service; —. 1981. *Principal Station Data: Saskatoon A.* Downsview: Atmospheric Environment Service; Kyle, A. 2002. "Amateur Radio Operators do Their Part in Helping Environment Canada." *Moose Jaw Times Herald* (July 8), 2; Thomas, Don. 2003. "New Regional Weather Centre in the Forecast: Services Being Consolidated Across Canada." *Edmonton Journal* (January 10), B3.

MÉTIS AND NON-STATUS INDIAN LEGAL ISSUES. Until the mid-1980s, Saskatchewan's MÉTIS and NON-STATUS INDIANS did not possess Aboriginal status. With similar claims to disentitlement, the two groups formed in 1975 the Association of Métis and Non-Status Indians of Saskatchewan (AMNSIS). In the 1980s, this alliance ended after the Constitution Act, 1982 (s.35.2) declared the Métis to be one of three distinct Aboriginal peoples, thus rekindling Métis nationalism, and also after thousands of Non-Status Indians regained their "Indian" status under Bill C-31 (1985). As a result, AMNSIS dissolved in 1988 and the Métis Society of Saskatchewan (MN-S) reconstituted itself, leaving the Congress of Aboriginal Peoples to represent the province's Non-Status Indians. Since the mid-1990s, Saskatchewan's Métis have followed a rights-based agenda. In 1994, Métis Elders and the MN-S filed a (still pending) land claim for the province's northwestern corner, arguing that the Métis' Aboriginal title to the land was never extinguished by the 1889 and 1906 Half-breed Scrip Commissions.

The Métis also tried to obtain their Aboriginal animal harvesting rights through litigation. *R. v. Morin and Daigneault* (1996) granted Saskatchewan Métis with "Indian" fishing rights, while *R. v. Grumbo* (1996) briefly provided Métis hunting rights before being overturned. The Supreme Court of Canada's precedent-setting ruling in *R. v. Powley* (2003), which ruled that the Métis of the Sault Ste. Marie (Ontario) area have an Aboriginal right to hunt for food, provided they could prove their long-term occupancy, may impact upon Métis hunting rights in Saskatchewan, where such rights do not currently exist. Non-Status Indians have no litigation to affirm their rights and generally face a lack of co-operation from Status Indian bands, which do not want their band lists increased, lest their limited resources be further subdivided. Despite their diverging paths, both groups want their Aboriginal status reaffirmed, government to claim responsibility for them (as it does for Status Indians), and a restorative justice system that focuses on community and individual healing/empowerment rather than incarceration. In the future, the province's Métis and Non-Status Indian populations will try to expand their Aboriginal rights—which may prove difficult, particularly as their numbers are projected to rise significantly through the birth rate, as the number of self-identifying Métis increases (especially if Métis receive Aboriginal hunting rights), and as female unions outside of the Status community continue to disqualify their descendants. For the Métis, a proper enumeration is necessary before their Aboriginal rights are fully implemented.

Darren R. Préfontaine

FURTHER READING: Chartrand, P. (ed.). 2002. *Who Are Canada's Aboriginal Peoples?* Saskatoon: Purich

Publishing; Nichols, R. 2003. "Prospects For Justice: Resolving the Paradoxes of Métis Constitutional Rights," *Canadian Journal of Native Studies* 22 (1): 91–111; Sawchuck, J. 2000. "Negotiating an Identity: Métis Political Organizations, the Canadian Government, and Competing Concepts of Aboriginality," *American Indian Quarterly* 24 (3): 73–81.

MÉTIS COMMUNITIES. The Métis are one of Saskatchewan's founding people and have contributed to Saskatchewan's social, cultural, economic and political fabric. Métis settlement in what is now Saskatchewan predated the development of an agrarian society by over 100 years. In the later 18th and early 19th centuries, the Métis plied their various skills in the fur trade. After 1821 and the consolidation of the Canadian fur trade, and until the age of the railway, Métis traders criss-crossed what is now Saskatchewan in vast caravans of **RED RIVER CARTS**. The Métis also helped missionaries bring Christianity to the prairie west and the region's First Nations. They were also bison hunters and plainsmen *par excellence*. **MÉTIS WOMEN** became renowned for their skill in beadwork and embroidery, particularly through the flower beadwork motif. During the 1870s, with the consolidation of the prairie west into the new Dominion of Canada, the Métis patrolled the Canada-USA border to prevent a Fenian invasion; they also helped survey the region and paved the way for agrarian settlement, serving as guides and scouts; and during the Numbered Treaty (Treaties 1–7) process, they acted as interpreters.

In the settlement period (1896–1929), many Saskatchewan Métis persisted as squatters on Crown land and were known as "Road Allowance People." In the early years of agrarian settlement, Métis women delivered many of the pioneers' babies, while others tended the sick through the use of traditional medicines and remedies. Despite being a marginalized and dispersed population, Saskatchewan's Métis served in the Boer War (1899–1902), **WORLD WAR I** (1914–18), **WORLD WAR II** (1939–45), and in the **KOREAN WAR** (1950–53) in proportions much larger than the general population. They also began to move to the cities after World War II, contributing to the province's gradual urbanization; some were forced onto **MÉTIS FARMS** by the CCF government in the late 1940s and early 1950s. During the modern era, Saskatchewan's Métis laboured to build strong self-determining communities through education and training.

This is the documented history of Saskatchewan's Métis; their past can also be elucidated through both oral history and the archaeological record. In the oral tradition, as told by Elders, the Métis were a proud and independent people who "owned themselves," hunted bison, spoke their own Michif language, were stewards of the land, danced and jigged to spirited fiddle rhythms, told stories, had reverence for the elderly and the young, and were deeply religious. The archaeological record also provides insights to the Métis' past inhabitation of what is now Saskatchewan: fur-trade post sites such as Cumberland House, Métis wintering or *hivernant* sites such as Petite Ville (an hour northeast of Saskatoon) or Chimney Coulee in the **CYPRESS HILLS**, or remnants of Métis Road Allowance communities such as those at Crescent Lake (near Yorkton) or Katepwa (near Lebret) provide glimpses of how previous generations of Métis interacted with their environment, what they ate, and how their material culture progressed.

The spatial distribution of Saskatchewan's Métis is diverse. They live throughout the province, particularly in four urban centres: Regina, Saskatoon, Prince Albert, and North Battleford; recent statistics indicate that the Métis are overwhelmingly an urban population. However, they also live in the following towns and villages: Beauval, Buffalo Narrows, Cole Bay, Green Lake, Ile-à-la-Crosse, Jan's Bay and Turnor Lake in the northwest; Cumberland House and La Ronge in the northeast; Archerwill, Batoche, Big River, Cochin, Debden, Duck Lake, Leoville, Meadow Lake, Nipawin, Pine House, St. Louis, Spiritwood and Yorkton in the centre-parkland; and in the southern plains, Lebret, Lestock, Fort Qu'Appelle and St. Victor-Willow Bunch. The Métis have also lived in the province's urban centres since the fur trade. In fact, the two oldest continuously inhabited communities in Saskatchewan—Cumberland House (1774) and Ile-à-la-Crosse (1778)—are Métis communities. In addition it was a Métis, James Isbister, who founded Prince Albert, the province's third largest centre, in 1866.

There has not been, despite attempts in the late 1990s, a thorough enumeration of Saskatchewan's Métis. The 2001 Statistics Canada Census indicates that there are approximately 40,000 Métis in Saskatchewan, but the **MÉTIS NATION–SASKATCHEWAN** (MN–S) maintains that their number is closer to 80,000. An accurate enumeration for the province's Métis community is vital, however, as both the federal and provincial governments provide program funding based on population to the MN–S and its affiliates. Between the 1991 and 2001 census, there was a significant increase in the province's Métis population, owing to both a high birthrate and a large increase in the number of people self-identifying as Métis—as a result of increased awareness of Métis issues and of the perception that holding Métis status bestows specific benefits not available to the non-Aboriginal population.

Families, both nuclear and extended, are the main structure of Métis society. Métis family genealogies are traced through patrilineal descent. However, both matrilineal and patrilineal kinship ties have been important, especially since family clans were usually composed of sisters and their families, who often lived in close proximity. Even today, it is not uncommon in Métis families for maternal cousins who are raised together to consider themselves brothers or sisters. Saskatchewan's Métis are a mixture of Red River fur-trade and bison-hunting families who emigrated to the region from Manitoba after the Red River Resistance (1869–70), of fur-trade families that emerged in what is now Saskatchewan, and of First Nations, European and Euro-Canadian intermarriage into these Métis families. The ancestry of Saskatchewan's Métis is primarily Cree, Saulteaux, French Canadian and Scots-Orcadian; however, many Métis have English, Dene, Dakota, Iroquois, Lakota, Nakota and Dakota roots. Most traditional Métis family names are either of French-Canadian or Celtic-Orcadian origin; however, many Métis now have First Nations, Ukrainian, Scandinavian or German surnames. While the term "*métis*" means mixed, the Métis see themselves as a distinct Indigenous people, one of three constitutionally recognized Aboriginal peoples in Canada under the Constitution Act, 1982, s.35.2, and not merely as an amalgam of different parts.

The social, cultural and economic dynamics facing the Métis vary and are dependent on locale. This socio-economic landscape ranges from remote northern communities, which focus on traditional lifestyles, to timber-producing, ranching and farming communities, and finally to urban centres. Despite such variation within the province's Métis community, there are some consistent socio-economic trends. For instance, the Métis have a younger population, lower levels of educational attainment, higher levels of poverty, poorer health, and often suffer from a greater number of pathologies and face greater social displacement than the non-Aboriginal population. Therefore, the sociological landscape of Saskatchewan's Métis is markedly different from that of the non-Aboriginal population. Despite such discrepancies, Métis agencies have been working to address these problems, and since the 1980s have made great inroads towards ameliorating the social conditions. For instance, largely through Métis educational and training programs, a developing Métis middle class consisting of educators, administrators, entrepreneurs, government workers and skilled trades people has emerged and is primarily concentrated in the province's three largest centres.

The Métis' contribution to Saskatchewan's cultural life has been profound. Some of the more prominent Métis cultural events in Saskatchewan include Back to Batoche Days, the Prince Albert Métis Fall Festival, Lebret Métis Days, the John Arcand Fiddle Fest, and Palmbere Days (Palmbere Lake). Some of the Saskatchewan Métis cultural ambassadors include Janice Acoose (author), John Arcand (fiddle player), Rita Bouvier (poet), **BOB**

PHOTO BY ROBERT TINKER

Métis author, Warren Cariou.

BOYER (artist), **MARIA CAMPBELL** (author/playwright), Warren Cariou (author), Don Freed (singer/songwriter), and Andrea Menard (actor/singer). Traditional storytellers such as MN–S Senator Gilbert Pelletier and medicine person/activist Rose Richardson are also ensuring that traditional Métis stories are being preserved.

There are significant cultural areas within the province's Métis community. In the province's north, for instance, the cultural orientation of the Métis closely mirrors that of the local First Nations: Dene in the northwest, and Cree in the northeast. In central and southern Saskatchewan, the cultural makeup of the Métis is largely different from those living in the north in that they do not generally engage in traditional lifestyles and are less likely to speak an Aboriginal language. There are also linguistic variations among the province's Métis. In the northwest, a form of Michif with a significantly higher Cree content than the southern variety is spoken in Ile-à-la-Crosse, Beauval, Buffalo Narrows and Pinehouse. In Cumberland House, Swampy Cree is the first language of many Métis. In the centre-parkland (Cochin, North Battleford, Meadow Lake, Debden, Big River, Prince Albert, Archerwill, and Yorkton) and along the southern plains (Lebret, Fort Qu'Appelle, and Willow Bunch), Michif-Cree, which is a mixture of French nouns and Cree verbs, was the first language of many Métis prior to the 1950s and the advent of urbanization. Finally, in Batoche, Bellevue, Duck Lake and St. Louis, Michif-French, a dialect of Canadian French, was traditionally spoken. Métis community groups and institutions such as the **GABRIEL DUMONT INSTITUTE** are working to revitalize Métis languages.

The Métis have traditionally been a deeply religious people, with their own patron saint, St. Joseph. Religious adherence among contemporary Métis is difficult to discern; however, they generally practice Christianity, traditional Aboriginal spiritual-

ity, or a mixture of these two systems. Pilgrimages such as those to St. Laurent, near Duck Lake, continue to attract many Métis, particularly the elderly. Marian devotion is particularly strong in Ile-à-la-Crosse. Many Métis also exclusively practice Aboriginal spirituality through the burning of sweetgrass/sage, attending cleansing sweats, and giving thanks through the offering of tobacco.

The Métis have always had a tradition of political activism. In fact, as early as the 1870s the Métis had a governing council at St. Laurent (near Batoche), with **GABRIEL DUMONT** serving as its president. After the 1885 Resistance, most Métis disengaged from public life; however, in the 1940s they began to organize collectively through various political lobbies—the predecessors of the modern MN–S. Today, the MN–S is a parallel government that represents the political, social justice, cultural and economic interests of the province's Metis. Since the 1990s, the MN–S and its affiliates have worked towards self-government for the province's Métis community. This is primarily done through strategic partnerships with government, such as the tripartite process with the federal and provincial governments, and through the Métis Act, which strengthens the bilateral process between the province and the MN–S. At present, the MN–S is seeking to establish a Métis land base, with full resource extraction rights, in the province's northwest corner in order to implement full Métis hunting rights across the province (these currently exist only in the north) and to ensure the proper stewardship of Métis heritage—as in the agreement with Parks Canada to manage Batoche National Historic Park.

In mainstream politics, the province's Métis generally support the New Democratic or Liberal parties; as part of the larger Aboriginal vote, they will play an increasingly large role in Saskatchewan's political life in the decades ahead. Future challenges for the province's Métis include reforming the criminal justice system, preserving their languages and culture, maintaining and increasing access to education and employment, improving their standard of living, building self-governing communities, and establishing effective political leadership. *Darren R. Préfontaine*

FURTHER READING: Barkwell, L.J., L. Dorion and D.R. Préfontaine (eds.). 2001. *Métis Legacy*. Winnipeg and Saskatoon: Louis Riel Institute and the Gabriel Dumont Institute; Dorion, L., T. Paquin and D.R. Préfontaine. 2000. *The Métis: Our People, Our Story*. Edmonton and Saskatoon: Arnold Multimedia and Gabriel Dumont Institute.

MÉTIS CULTURE AND LANGUAGE. Canada has a founding people who once traversed North America's interior in **RED RIVER CARTS**, hunted **BISON** with military precision, danced and jigged to spirit-

ed fiddle rhythms, wore brightly adorned embroidered clothing as well as sashes or shawls, spoke their own unique language, prayed to the *Bon Dieu/Kitchi-Manitou* and to their patron saint, St. Joseph, and even had their own werewolf. These people were the Métis. "Métis" or *méstis*, as the word was known at the time of contact, means mixed in French. From *méstis* evolved *méchif* and *mitchif* or *Michif*, the name of a language, a culture and a people within the Métis nation. The epistemological roots of the word "Métis" are very important because the word presently denotes a distinct Indigenous nation with a talent for adopting other cultural traditions and making them their own. Indeed, the Métis have always practiced a culture which has fused First Nations (Cree, Saulteaux, Dene and Dakota), Euro-Canadian (*Canadien*), and European (Scots/Orkney) parent cultures into a unique synthesis.

Language is perhaps the most notable example of this talent for cultural transformation. The Métis were undoubtedly the most multilingual people in the history of Canada. Besides being well versed in a wide range of First Nations and European languages, they also invented Michif-Cree, a mixed-language based on Cree (and Saulteaux) verb structures and French nouns/noun phrases; Michif-French, a dialect of Canadian French which uses Algonquian syntax; and Bunjee, a Cree/Scots-Gaelic Creole. However, the Métis are best known for speaking Michif-Cree, which has long been studied by linguists since it has woven two unrelated languages into a coherent whole with a standardized syntax, verb structure, and noun phrases. Michif-Cree is currently spoken around Lebret, Yorkton, Debden, the Battlefords and Ile-à-la-Crosse.

Métis Elders or "Old People" have always transmitted cultural knowledge to younger generations through oral tradition. From this oral tradition emerged a rich storytelling culture that blended various First Nations motifs, such as the tricksters *Wisahkecahk* and *Nanbush*, with French-Canadian ones, such as *Chi-Jean* (from *Ti-Jean*), *le diable* (the Devil as a dog or handsome stranger), and *le rou garou* (from *loup garou*, a werewolf), a person who fell out of the Creator's favour. However, *le rou garou* was not just a werewolf since it had the attributes of the Cree trickster and could change into a variety of forms; rou garou stories were told to ensure that youth behaved themselves, particularly during Lent. From this storytelling tradition emerged a talent for creating nicknames, many of which often began with *chi* or "little," from a dialectal pronunciation of French *petit*.

Traditionally, the Métis were very spiritual: most practiced a folk Catholicism that was rooted in veneration of the Virgin and based on pilgrimages such as those to St. Laurent de Grandin (near present-day Duck Lake). It involved holding wakes for departed loved ones, sprinkling holy water during menacing thunderstorms, providing thanks to the Creator by offering tobacco, and ensuring that Christmas and Lent were strictly periods of spiritual reflection devoid of celebration or materialism.

Métis culture has always been festive and celebrated with great *joie de vivre*. The Métis style of dancing to fiddle tunes was very similar to their Celtic and French-Canadian antecedents, but seamlessly weaved in faster-paced First Nations footwork and rhythms such as in traditional drumming. These traditions vary among families and communities: for instance, the "Red River Jig," the signature fiddle tune and dance of the Métis, has many different versions and step patterns. House parties, focusing on jigging, dancing and fiddle playing, were a constant feature throughout Métis history, the climax of revelry being the *réveillon* (New Years' Eve). During such times of celebration, Métis women prepared a feast that included *les beignes* (fried bread), *la galette* (bannock), *les boulettes* (meatballs), *le rababou* (stew), and molasses cakes.

The Métis are also heirs of a vibrant material culture which emphasized the floral motif in bead, quill work and embroidery. After adapting the design from the Grey Nuns in the 1810s, generations of **MÉTIS WOMEN** produced countless *objets d'art* for their loved ones, for decoration, and for sale to non-Aboriginal collectors. Unfortunately, much of the legacy of the "Flower Beadwork People," as the Métis were once known, has been lost due to institutional mislabeling that called many of these pieces "Plains Cree" or "Ojibwa." Finding the proper provenance and restoring the voice of their Métis creators has been a concern for academics and the Métis community.

Darren R. Préfontaine

FURTHER READING: Bakker, P. 1997. *A Language of Our Own: The Genesis of Michif, the Mixed Cree-French Language of the Canadian Métis*. Oxford: Oxford University Press; Barkwell, L.J., L. Dorion and D.R. Préfontaine (eds.). 2001. *Métis Legacy*. Winnipeg and Saskatoon: Louis Riel Institute and Gabriel Dumont Institute; Troupe, C. 2002. *Expressing Our Heritage: Métis Artistic Designs*. Saskatoon: Gabriel Dumont Institute.

MÉTIS EDUCATION. Education in historic Saskatchewan Métis communities focused on skills related to hunting, trapping, and trade economies. The male children of buffalo hunters learned to ride horses at a very young age and were encouraged to be brave. Men initiated their sons and nephews into their areas of expertise, while girls were instructed in sewing, beadwork, quillwork, healing, and other skills essential to the mothers of large families. Parents who wanted their children to acquire literacy and increase their employment opportunities sent them away to be educated, usually to the Red River Settlement. Literate individuals often provided basic

instruction to family and community members. Families with adequate financial resources, particularly those with Euro-Canadian or British fathers, developed the practice of sending at least one son to be educated in Canada, Britain, or occasionally the United States. Among the Saskatchewan-born sons to benefit from this practice were Cuthbert Grant and Alexander Kennedy Isbister, who made significant contributions to Métis history.

The first schools in Saskatchewan were the result of missionary activity. **HENRY BUDD**, an ordained minister of Cree descent, established an Anglican mission and school at Cumberland House in 1840. In 1847, a Catholic mission and school were established at Ile-à-la-Crosse. In 1860 three members of the Order of the Grey Nuns were sent from Montreal to assist in education and health care; **SARA RIEL** (Sister Marguerite-Marie) worked at the mission school from 1871 until her death in 1883. Other early mission schools that served Métis communities were the Qu'Appelle mission, established in 1866 on Lake Katepwa, and Bishop Ovide Charlebois's small Catholic school built at Cumberland House in 1890. In 1879, **NICHOLAS FLOOD DAVIN**'s "Report on Industrial Schools for Indians and Half-breeds" advocated the inclusion of the Métis in federal schools. Parents negotiated school fees with residential school administrators, and some schools took Métis children as day students. However, by 1910 the federal government excluded Métis and **NON-STATUS INDIAN** children from their schools, limiting their responsibility to the education of treaty or status Indians. The provincial government also refused to accept responsibility for their education. With few exceptions, Saskatchewan education in the early 20th century excluded the Métis.

In 1938, it was estimated that approximately 3,500 children of Native ancestry were unable to access basic schooling. The Reid report on education in northern Saskatchewan in 1939 and the Piercy report that followed in 1944 painted a grim picture of Métis education, particularly in the north. However, it was not until the election of the CCF in 1944 that the Saskatchewan government accepted responsibility for the education of Métis children. Schools were constructed in many communities, and within a decade virtually all Métis children had access to an elementary education. Unfortunately, decades of poverty and neglect were difficult to overcome: very few Métis graduated from high school, attended university, or participated in other post-secondary training.

By 1974, only two schools in northern Saskatchewan offered Grade 12. In 1976, after a painful struggle, Ile-à-la-Crosse gained control of its school system. The same year, the Northern School Board became an elected school board with nine members representing different regions; today it is

known as the Northern Lights School Division. While northern Métis have seen an increase in educational autonomy, Métis living in central and southern Saskatchewan participate in the provincial system with slowly increasing success. The **GABRIEL DUMONT INSTITUTE** of Métis Studies and Applied Research, established in 1980, is the educational arm of the Métis Nation of Saskatchewan and the only Métis-controlled educational institution in Canada. (*See also* **DUMONT TECHNICAL INSTITUTE**)

Sherry Farrell Racette

MÉTIS FARMS. Rehabilitating Saskatchewan's dispossessed Métis was a primary concern for government from the 1930s to the 1950s. In 1939, the province's Liberal government and the Roman Catholic Church created a Métis farming or "rehabilitation" colony in Green Lake, which removed Métis from their southern road allowance communities and put them into a segregated northern community. In 1944, the new CCF government wanted to ameliorate the Métis' destitution by establishing a series of segregated Métis rehabilitation "farms" in the province's south, where eventually, after learning to farm, they could better integrate into the larger society. In 1945, the government purchased the Oblate-run Lebret Métis Farm; using it as a model, in the late 1940s it created other farms such as those in Baljennie, Crescent Lake, Crooked Lake, Duck Lake, Glen Mary, Lestock, and Willow Bunch. The Métis farms were plagued by administrative tension between the government and the Church, misunderstandings among the Métis regarding private versus communal ownership (Lebret and Willow Bunch were co-operatives), and blatant paternalism. The Métis had no input into the farms' governance, and officials, through the Department of Social Welfare and Rehabilitation (or, for Green Lake, the Department of Municipal Affairs) were often unhelpful or racist. More importantly, the government did not understand that the Métis preferred wage labour employment to farming. By the late 1950s, it was clear that the farms were a failure: southern Métis were moving to the cities in search of wage labour opportunities, while those living on the farms often subsisted on government relief. *Darren R. Préfontaine*

FURTHER READING: Barron, F.L. 1997. *Walking in Indian Moccasins: The Native Policies of Tommy Douglas and the CCF*. Vancouver: University of British Columbia Press; Quiring, D.M. 2003. "'The Ultimate Solution': CCF Programs of Assimilation and the Indians and Metis of Northern Saskatchewan," *Prairie Forum* 28 (2): 145–60.

MÉTIS HISTORY. The beginning of Métis history is hard to determine. However, Métis ethnogenesis, or self-identity, emerged in the mid-1750s in the Great Lakes region, as *Canadien*-Algonquian mixed-bloods recognized their distinctness and sought each other for marriage/trading alliances. Later, this self-awareness crystallized in the Red River when the Métis challenged the Hudson's Bay Company's (HBC) attempts to curb their lifestyle as fur trade provisioners and free traders. It was there, on June 19, 1816, that the Métis or *Bois-Brûlés* led by Cuthbert Grant defeated a party of HBC men and Selkirk Settlers at Seven Oaks. This self-identity further blossomed after the 1821 North West Company-HBC merger, when hundreds of Métis or *gens de libre* circumvented the HBC's fur trade monopoly in the 1830s–40s, fought the Dakota for access to the rich bison-hunting grounds of the Dakotas in the 1840s–50s, and resisted the Canadian state from 1869 to 1885.

In 1869, the Métis were not consulted about the transfer of Rupert's Land to the new Dominion of Canada. Angered, they formed a provisional government that was eventually led by **LOUIS RIEL**. From these negotiations emerged the Manitoba Act, which the Métis viewed as a treaty between the Métis nation and Canada. For the Métis, the Act's most important provisions included bilingual denominational schools, judicial and parliamentary systems (Section 22) and perhaps most importantly, through Sections 31–32, the extinguishment of their "Indian" title to the land, through the granting of 1.4 million acres of land to "the children of half-breed heads of families." For those Métis living in what is now Saskatchewan, the **DOMINION LANDS ACT** of 1879 (Section 125) also included provisions to extinguish the Métis' Indian title. This was done through the scrip system, whereby scrip commissioners gave the Métis land or money scrip in exchange for their Indian title; the system, however, was fraudulent and most Métis did not receive or hold title to any land.

After 1870, increasingly discriminatory attitudes within Manitoba forced hundreds of Métis to move to present-day Saskatchewan. They founded settlements such as Wood Mountain-Willow Bunch, St. Laurent, St. Isadore de Belleville, and **BATOCHE**, which augmented preexisting Métis communities such as Cumberland House and Ile-à-la-Crosse. Despite moving west, the Métis' many grievances—such as not having their Indian title properly extinguished, lack of proper political representation, and poor economic conditions—led them to send dozens of petitions to the federal government. Their reasoned pleas for redress were greeted with silence. In 1884, the Métis brought Louis Riel from the USA back to Canada in order to negotiate their grievances with Ottawa. Alliance building occurred throughout the fall and winter of 1884; but as 1885 approached, it became apparent that the French Métis' coalition with the English-speaking Métis, First Nations and Euro-Canadians had shallow roots. The **NORTH-WEST RESISTANCE** broke out in late March

1885. After having the upper hand early on at Duck Lake (March 26) and Fish Creek (April 24), thanks to **GABRIEL DUMONT**'s leadership and their superior marksmanship, the Métis succumbed to the larger, better equipped Canadian volunteer force at Batoche on May 12, 1885.

After 1885, the Saskatchewan Métis were marginalized. Many dispersed to parkland and forested regions, while others squatted on land along the approaches to road allowances. Hence, the Métis began to be called the "Road Allowance People," and settled in dozens of makeshift communities such as Crescent Lake and Little Chicago. In most instances, they did not own title to the land and thus paid no taxes, which precluded their children from obtaining an education. With this marginal existence emerged a myriad of social problems including poor health and self-esteem, as well as a lack of viable employment opportunities. Yet the Métis lived in their own communities, spoke their language, *Michif*, and served their country with great distinction in 1914–18 and 1939–45.

After 1945, the Métis slowly entered the province's mainstream. In order to rehabilitate the Métis, the CCF government in the late 1940s created **MÉTIS FARMS** such as those in Lebret and Green Lake—a move which unfortunately proved paternalistic and ultimately failed. In the 1950s, **JAMES BRADY** and **MALCOLM NORRIS** were addressing the Métis' economic, social and political marginalization. In the 1960s–70s, Métis societies advocated Métis empowerment, while increasing numbers of Métis began moving to the province's larger cities. Out of these efforts emerged the socio-cultural and educational apparatus of the **MÉTIS NATION–SASKATCH-EWAN**. Since the mid-1990s, the province's Métis have worked towards the building of self-governing institutions; they have obtained a land base in northwestern Saskatchewan and have had their Aboriginal rights, such as access to full hunting, restored.

Darren R. Préfontaine

FURTHER READING: Barkwell, L.J., L. Dorion and D.R. Préfontaine (eds.). 2001. *Métis Legacy*. Winnipeg and Saskatoon: Louis Riel Institute and Gabriel Dumont Institute; Peterson, J. and J.S.H. Brown (eds.). 1993. *The New Peoples: Being and Becoming Métis in North America*. Winnipeg: University of Manitoba Press; Sprague, D.N. 1988. *Canada and the Métis, 1869–1885*. Waterloo, Ontario: Wilfrid Laurier University Press.

MÉTIS NATION–SASKATCHEWAN. The Métis Nation-Saskatchewan (MN-S) represents the political, socioeconomic, cultural and educational interests of the province's Métis through a representative system based on twelve regions and approximately 130 locals (see Map). The governance structure includes a constitution, an Elders' advisory council, the MN-S Senate, and a cabinet—the Provincial Métis

Council—which is composed of a four-member executive, as well as of elected officials from the twelve regions and appointees for women and youth. Nine affiliated institutions deliver educational, training, business, and social justice programming.

The MN-S had its origins in the 1930s and 1940s. After 1885, some Métis entered mainstream politics to address the socio-economic ills plaguing Métis society. Others, such as Joe Ross, **J.Z. LAROCQUE** and Fred DeLaronde, organized Saskatchewan's Métis through "locals," a representative structure taken from organized labour. The first Métis political organization in the province was the Saskatchewan Métis Society (SMS), which represented Métis living in southern and central Saskatchewan. In 1941, it received a provincial grant of $10,000, which was used to hire a law firm to demonstrate that the Métis possessed an outstanding "Indian" title to the land. In 1946, the CCF government funded an SMS "reorganization" conference in which it tried to advance its own agenda, only to be stymied by geographical cleavages between northern and southern Métis.

From 1946 to 1967, Métis activists worked for the recognition of the Métis' "Indian" title to the land, control over the Métis Rehabilitation Farms, and better access to health care and education. However, lack of funding and divisions within the community made it difficult to address these issues. In the 1960s, Métis political organizations existed in both the province's north and south. The Métis Society of Saskatchewan (MSS), which was founded in 1964 and led by Joe Amyotte, represented Métis living in southern and central Saskatchewan; and the Métis Association of Saskatchewan (MAS), led by **MALCOLM NORRIS** and supported by **JAMES BRADY**, represented northern Métis and **NON-STATUS INDIANS**. In 1967, the two organizations merged, keeping MSS as its name.

The 1970s and 1980s were key decades in the development of the MN-S. For most of this period, **JIM SINCLAIR** led the province's Métis and Non-Status Indian political movement. There was a great deal of solidarity between the Métis and the Non-Status Indians at the time, which led to the founding in 1975 of the MN-S's predecessor, the Association of Métis and Non-Status Indians of Saskatchewan (AMNSIS). Despite radical rhetoric and group action by much of its rank-and-file, who were influenced by the American Indian Movement, the federal and provincial governments began providing AMNSIS with regular funding for program and service delivery. This created a shift in AMNSIS, as it began to focus less on community organization to achieve social justice and more towards executive meetings with government ministers in order to maintain program funding. In 1982, the Constitution Act (S. 35) recognized the Métis as one of three Aboriginal peoples in Canada, along with Indians and Inuit.

This recognition reinvigorated Métis nationalism, just as Bill C31 later allowed many Non-Status Indians to re-obtain their "status." As a result, AMN-SIS folded in August 1988, when a divisive referendum by its membership created a Métis-only political body, the new MSS, which in 1993 became the Métis Nation of Saskatchewan (MNS).

Since the early 1990s the MNS/MN-S, under the leadership of presidents **GERALD MORIN**, Jim Durocher and **CLÉMENT CHARTIER**, has worked towards implementing Métis self-government through litigation and strategic partnerships with government. For instance, in 1993 the province and the MNS initiated a bilateral process to deal with Métis issues, which eventually became a tripartite partnership with the federal government. In 1994, the MNS filed a land claim for the northwestern corner of Saskatchewan, centering on a number of Métis communities (which will likely be determined through a tripartite negotiation). Following that, in 1996 the Queen's Bench, in *R. v. Grumbo*, granted the province's Métis "Indian" hunting rights before being overturned a few years later by the Saskatchewan Court of Appeal. In 1997, however, Métis in northern Saskatchewan, through *R. v. Morin and Daigneault*, were granted full "Indian" hunting rights—a right which they still possess. The status of Métis hunting rights awaits the province's final interpretation of the recent Supreme Court decisions, *R. v. Powley* and *R.v. Blais* (2003), which argued that the Métis possess "Indian" hunting rights. Finally, in 2001 the province and the MN-S signed the Métis Act, which recognizes the Métis contribution to Confederation and strengthens the bilateral process through continued negotiations.

Darren R. Préfontaine

FURTHER READING: Chartrand, P. (ed.). 2002. *Who are Canada's Aboriginal Peoples? Recognition, Definition and Jurisdiction*. Saskatoon: Purich Publishing.

MÉTIS WOMEN. The first generation of Métis women in Saskatchewan were either born to European fur-traders and Indigenous women at posts such as Cumberland House (1775) and Carleton House (1790), or had accompanied their fathers or husbands into the region. Daughters had a variety of experiences depending on the duration of their parent's relationship, the commitment of a father to his family, his social class and affluence, and the cultural traditions that met and mixed in the home. Over time, as the population grew, children of mixed heritage tended to marry each other, blurring and mixing their diverse cultural heritages and creating a new people. Métis girls were expected to be active and helpful, running errands and caring for younger children. Sewing doll dresses and making moccasins from leaves gave way to learning

from mothers, aunts and grandmothers in the critical skills of sewing, quillwork, beadwork and embroidery. Women were involved in trapping, harvested wild plants and medicines, fished, hunted birds and small game, tanned hides, processed meat, and made all the clothing and footwear for their families. Their daughters worked beside them.

Mentored learning involved an older, experienced woman performing an action, with the young learner observing, copying the action and doing it independently under careful scrutiny. The process could be quite strict, and young girls were often required to repeat their tasks until successful. At other times, girls were allowed to use their mother's supplies with little direct instruction. Mistakes were met with teasing and laughter, success with praise and compliments. This combination ensured that certain standards were maintained, while creativity and innovation were encouraged. As they grew older, their learning continued as they joined circles of working women who engaged in collaborative projects or worked individually while chatting and telling stories. In this way, women learned to work together and were introduced to the collective values of their community.

Girls tended to marry young, often by their mid-teens, and marriages were usually arranged. If a young man accepted a pair of moccasins made by his future bride, a marriage contract existed. He might also be required to pay a bride's price of trade goods or horses. Winter was the wedding season, and weddings were community celebrations that could last several days. On the prairies, women were wrapped in buffalo robes and carried to elaborately decorated dog sleds, which transported them to a mission where a marriage ceremony could be conducted and later took them on a "wedding trip" to their new home. Motherhood quickly followed marriage. As Christian, particularly Catholic, influences grew, women were pressured to discontinue extended breast-feeding and other forms of traditional birth control. As a result, they had very large families and often died of complications related to childbirth.

Married couples and families were essential socio-economic units. Men and women had complimentary skill sets, and played equally important roles in supporting and sustaining community economies. Men obtained raw materials through the hunt, bringing home meat and hides, which women's skill and labour transformed into pemmican, dry meat, tanned hide and garments for family use or sale. During the fur trade, pemmican, which was often the only food available to workers and travelers, sustained an industry. From 1850 to 1870 there was a considerable market for Métis-style coats, jackets, saddles, and smaller items such as quirts, fire bags, watch pockets, and pouches. Red River cart trains loaded with these goods traveled to

SASKATCHEWAN ARCHIVES BOARD R-A8823

Three generations of the Desjarlais family, Lebret, late 1890s. Left to right: Magdeleine Klyne; Marie Justine and Rosine Desjarlais; Magdeleine Desjarlais.

consumers, and male traders often moved beyond their family circle for suppliers. Women's production continued to be critical to Métis economies, particularly as men found it increasingly difficult to make a living. In the first half of the 20th century, Métis women in Saskatchewan produced a huge volume of hooked and braided rugs, marketing them from door to door with berries, fish, or garden produce.

While Métis women had little direct political power, they exerted significant influence on husbands, brothers, and particularly sons—by refusing to work, making verbal appeals, and publicly admonishing or encouraging men. Many had engaged in battle, loading and repairing guns, making bullets, often standing just behind the men. Women could also be passionate advocates for peace, speaking as mothers and on behalf of the children. Their spiritual lives blended elements of traditional beliefs with Christianity: many worked tirelessly to support mission work, and devotion intensified after the 1885 resistance and collapse of traditional economies. Older women took particular comfort in religion during a time of profound loss and change. Large crosses became an important part of women's dress, and colours became darker and almost nun-like. Contemporary Métis women are becoming more visible in the political arena, but continue to work primarily at the community level. In the last twenty years, their participation in post-secondary education has dramatically increased, and Saskatchewan Métis women, as writers and artists, stand among the best in Canada.

Sherry Farrell Racette

FURTHER READING: Poelzer, Irene. 1986. *In Our Own Words: Northern Saskatchewan Métis Women Speak Out*. Saskatoon: Lindenblatt and Harmonic; Welsh, Christine. 1991. "Voices of the Grandmothers: Reclaiming a Métis Heritage," *Canadian Literature* 131 (Winter): 15–24.

MICHALENKO, JOHANNA (1910–).

Johanna Michalenko was a home economist, and a leader in both Ukrainian and mainstream organizations. Born in Edmonton in 1910 to Ukrainian immigrant parents, she graduated from normal school in 1929 and taught for several years. She obtained a BSc in Home Economics from the University of Alberta (1936), and studied at the University of Washington. Michalenko became a lecturer in the Faculty of Home Economics at the University of Alberta (among the first Ukrainian Canadian women to lecture at a university). In 1940 she moved to Saskatoon when her husband, Andrew, was appointed to the Engineering Faculty, **UNIVERSITY OF SASKATCHEWAN**. She became an adult education instructor in interior design. During the 1970s she was a member of the Standards Council of Canada (to facilitate standards in domestic and international trade). Active in several organizations, Michalenko held leadership positions in the Ukrainian Women's Association of Canada, the Consumers' Association of Canada, and the Saskatoon Council of Women. Especially active in the **CANADIAN FEDERATION OF UNIVERSITY WOMEN**, she was a delegate to two International Federation of University Women's triennial conferences, and attended two others. In 1972, she attended the United Nations Commission on Status of Women and Human Rights in Geneva. Johanna Michalenko, who now lives in Edmonton, has a son and daughter. *Natalie Ostryzniuk*

FURTHER READING: Saskatoon Business and Professional Women's Club. 1976. *Some Outstanding Women: They Made Saskatoon a Better Community*.

MICROBIO RHIZOGEN CORPORATION.

MicroBio RhizoGen is a Saskatoon-based, world-leading **BIOTECHNOLOGY** company specializing in the development and production of legume inoculants. MicroBio RhizoGen was launched in 1987 by Saskatoon agricultural scientist Steve Stephens and local businessman Murray Trapp. It has developed the technology behind using a naturally occurring bacterium, or inoculant, called rhizobium to increase yields of legumes and forage crops. When applied to crops such as alfalfa, chickpeas, dry beans, lentils, and peas, the bacteria enhance the plant's natural ability to absorb nitrogen from the air into its root system. These inoculants provide farmers with an organic, low-cost, environmentally friendly alternative to synthetic fertilizers. In 1995, a British investment firm took sole ownership of MicroBio RhizoGen; five years later the company was bought by the American firm Becker Underwood. MicroBio RhizoGen has research and manufacturing facilities in Saskatoon, and a staff of about fifty full-time employees. MicroBio RhizoGen has experienced growth in annual sales from $30,000 in its inception year to over $3.5 million in 2003. During the same period its market area expanded from western Canada to the United States and overseas. *Iain Stewart*

FURTHER READING: 2001. "MBR, Philom Start Talks," *Saskatoon StarPhoenix* (May 17): C6; Lyons, M. 2003. "Sask. Biotech Pioneer Hangs Up His Lab Coat," *Saskatoon StarPhoenix* (May 27): D7.

MIDALE, town, pop 496, located roughly midway between Weyburn and Estevan on Hwy 39. Many who first settled the Midale district were of Norwegian and Swedish origin and came from the states of Minnesota and Iowa. In 1907, Midale was incorporated as a village. With the opening of the Canadian Northern Railway line between Lampman and Radville in 1911, Midale became a junction for passengers and goods transferred between the railroads. Abandonment of the east-west line in the early 1950s was hastened by flood waters of the Souris River, which had undermined the integrity of much of the track. The discovery of oil in the Midale area in 1953 not only diversified the economy, which had been solely based upon agriculture, but also led to a doubling of the village population. Although the population subsequently levelled off, the oil industry has come to be the predominant contributor to the economy; today, pumpjacks dot the landscape. Agriculture continues to include grain and cattle production. Midale shares the distinction with the town of Yellow Grass as having had the highest temperature–45°C (113°F) on July 5, 1937–ever recorded in Canada. Notable personalities from the Midale area are Ken and Brad Johner. The multi-award winning performers were voted "Entertainers of the Decade" by the Saskatchewan Country Music Association in the 1990s. *See also* **OIL AND GAS INDUSTRY, SCANDINAVIAN SETTLEMENTS**. *David McLennan*

MIDDLETON, FREDERICK DOBSON (1825–98).

Sir Frederick Dobson Middleton was born on November 4, 1825, in Belfast, Ireland. He was educated in England at Maidstone Grammar School and the Royal Military College, Sandhurst. Upon passing out from Sandhurst, Middleton was granted a commission without purchase in the British army on December 30, 1842.

After being stationed with his regiment at the penal colony of Norfolk Island, New South Wales, he was sent to New Zealand, where he took part in the Maori Wars of 1845. Middleton was mentioned in dispatches for his part in that campaign. In 1848 Middleton went to India, where he served in various staff appointments during the Indian Mutiny of 1857. He was recommended for the **VICTORIA CROSS** and was gazetted a brevet major in recognition of his service during the Mutiny. Because he could not afford to obtain higher rank through purchase, Middleton turned to professionalism as a means to promotion, passing into the Staff College at Camberley in December 1866.

Middleton joined his regiment in Canada in 1868, accepting a series of staff appointments there before returning to England in 1870. In 1874, he took a staff position at the Royal Military College, Sandhurst, at a time when the college was undergoing profound changes brought on by the abolition of purchase and the introduction of competitive examinations for entrance into the British army. Middleton was rewarded for his work at Sandhurst with a promotion to the rank of colonel and an appointment, in 1879, as commandant of the college; he was also named a Commander of the Order of the Bath in 1881. In 1884, Middleton returned to Ottawa as major general, officer commanding the Canadian militia. On March 23, 1885, the Dominion faced a major crisis when **MÉTIS** and Aboriginal unrest in the North-West Territories grew into an armed uprising that began with the defeat of a government force of North-West Mounted Police and militia at Duck Lake by the Métis. The Canadian government responded by launching a military campaign, sending Middleton to Winnipeg to raise a North-West Field Force of 5,000 militia to quell the uprising. Middleton proceeded westward by rail, where he divided his force into three columns, each to march northward from various starting points on the **CANADIAN PACIFIC RAILWAY**. Middleton sent one column, under Colonel W.D. Otter from Swift

Sir Frederick Middleton.

Current, to relieve Battleford, which had come under siege by Chief **POUNDMAKER**'s band of **CREE** warriors. A second column set out from Calgary under Major General Thomas Bland Strange to overcome the Cree band led by **BIG BEAR**, which had carried out the killings at Frog Lake.

On April 6, Middleton personally led the main column from Qu'Appelle towards the Métis community of **BATOCHE**, where **LOUIS RIEL** had established a provisional government and taken hostages. On April 24, Middleton's forces met the Métis at Fish Creek where, after an inconclusive engagement lasting 6.5 hours, both sides withdrew. When reinforcements arrived two weeks later, Middleton led his force of 900 men to Batoche, where a battle between the militia and Riel's forces ensued. Middleton claimed victory at Batoche when Riel surrendered on May 15, ending the resistance. On June 22, the Cree uprising ended when the last of their captives were recovered, and the troops went home. For his efforts, Middleton received the thanks of the Parliament of Canada, a gift of $20,000 from the Canadian government, a knighthood on August 25, 1885, confirmation of his local rank of major-general, and a British pension of £100 a year for distinguished service. Middleton was forced to resign his appointment with the Canadian militia in 1890, after an investigation held him responsible for the seizure of stolen furs owned by a Métis named Charles Bremner. He was censured by the Canadian government, which characterized his actions as "unwarrantable and illegal." In his own defence, Middleton published a *Parting Address to the People of Canada*, refuting the Bremner charges.

Middleton and his family returned to England, where British official opinion agreed that he had been the victim of a political conspiracy in Canada. In 1896, he was appointed keeper of the Crown jewels. He spent his last years writing on various subjects, including his final account of the 1885 campaign, which was published in 1893–94. Major General Sir Frederick Middleton died suddenly in his quarters at the Tower of London on January 25, 1898.

Daria Coneghan

FURTHER READING: Brown, W. 2001. *Steele's Scouts.* Surrey, BC: Heritage House; Stanley, G. 1992. *The Birth of Western Canada: A History of the Riel Rebellions.* Toronto: University of Toronto Press.

MIDHA, KAMAL KISHORE (1941–). Kamal Kishore Midha was born at Kamalia, India, on October 26, 1941. He received his PhD from the University of Alberta in 1969 and his DSc from the **UNIVERSITY OF SASKATCHEWAN** in 1985. An internationally recognized authority on issues of bioavailability, bioequivalence, bioanalysis, pharmacokinetics and pharmacodynamics, he is best known for his groundbreaking research into the drug treatment

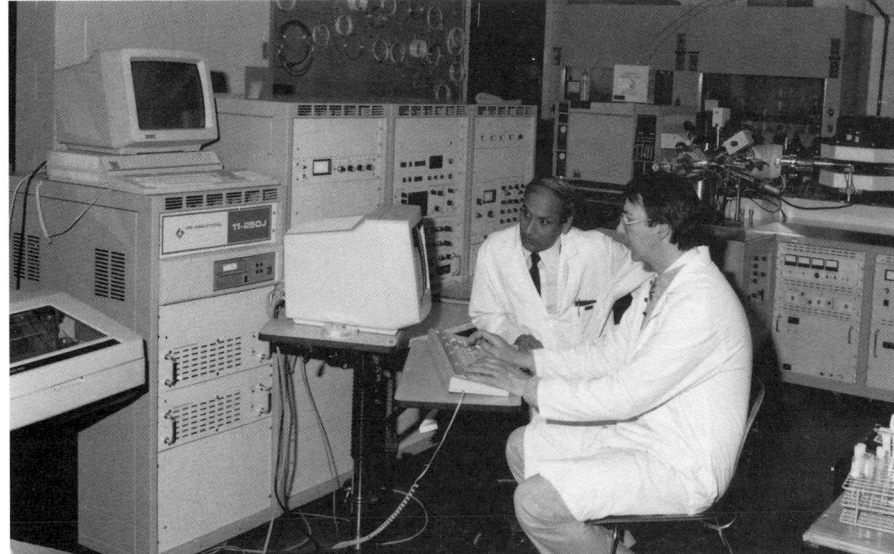

DIVISION OF AUDIO VISUAL SERVICES (U OF S) PHOTO/UNIVERSITY OF SASKATCHEWAN ARCHIVES A-10600

Dr. Kamal Midha and Dr. Gordon McKay operate a new hybrid mass spectrometer in March 1988.

strategies for psychotic and schizophrenic patients. As coordinator of an MRC Program Grant, his group attracted more than $6 million from granting agencies and industry. In May 2000 the group formed a not-for profit-research institute, Pharmalytics Inc., now located in Innovation Place, Saskatoon.

Midha holds Adjunct Professor positions in the Department of Academic Family Medicine and in the College of Pharmacy and Nutrition, University of Saskatchewan. As a Full Professor in the College of Pharmacy and Nutrition from 1979 to 1995, he and his colleagues founded the Drug Metabolism Drug Disposition research group. He has authored or co-authored 300 scientific articles and book chapters. Dr. Midha has received eight major awards, including the Kolthoff Gold Medal Award from the American Pharmaceutical Association in 1989. In 1994 he received the Distinguished Researcher Award from the University of Saskatchewan, and in 1995 was named a Member of the Order of Canada.

Gordon McKay

MILESTONE, town, pop 542, located between Regina and Weyburn on Hwy 39. Agriculture is the major industry in the region and consists of a combination of grain, specialty crop, and livestock production. Seed cleaning, pulse crop processing, and small manufacturers add diversity to Milestone's economy. The origins of Milestone date to 1893, when the CPR constructed the **SOO LINE** connecting Moose Jaw to Minneapolis. Significant settlement began around 1900 with settlers primarily hailing from eastern Canada, the British Isles, continental Europe, and the USA. By 1903, a substantial community had developed, and in 1906 the population was 244. In the subsequent decades, the community experienced steady growth; unlike many Saskatchewan communities, Milestone has had a

relatively stable population since the mid-1950s. Today, it has an array of amenities and services. Milestone's St. Aloysius Roman Catholic Church, completed in 1920, has been designated a heritage property. Until the town got its own resident priest in 1928, it was a mission of the Wilcox parish. In 1927, Father **ATHOL MURRAY** of Wilcox looked after the Milestone congregation; later, he compiled a record of all baptisms, marriages, and deaths from 1913 to 1931.

David McLennan

MILGAARD, DAVID (1952–). In a notorious miscarriage of justice, teenager David Milgaard was wrongfully convicted of the 1969 murder of Saskatoon nursing student Gail Miller. Throughout the twenty-three years he spent in prison, David Milgaard and his mother, Joyce, maintained his innocence and fought for his release. In 1991, federal Justice Minister Kim Campbell ordered the

ROY ANTAL/REGINA LEADER-POST

David Milgaard, June 1992.

Supreme Court to review Milgaard's case. Its report forced the Saskatchewan government to free Milgaard, though no acquittal was issued. In 1997, DNA evidence exonerated Milgaard, and led the **ROYAL CANADIAN MOUNTED POLICE** to arrest Larry Fisher, a serial rapist convicted of committing several Saskatoon crimes at the time of Gail Miller's death. Saskatoon police and prosecutors missed evidence connecting Fisher with Miller's murder at the time of Milgaard's trial. After Fisher's conviction in 1999, the Saskatchewan government issued an apology and a $10 million compensation package, the largest in Canadian history, to David Milgaard and his family. Through this terrible experience, Joyce Milgaard became a leading activist in overturning wrongful conviction cases across Canada. In 2004, the Saskatchewan government launched an inquiry to look into the way Milgaard's case was investigated and prosecuted.

Merle Massie

FURTHER READING: Edwards, P. and T. Tyler. 2004. "Joyce Milgaard Knocks Inquiry." *Toronto Star* (February 21); Eisler, D. and L. Perreaux. 1997. "Fisher Charged in Milgaard Case." *Maclean's* (August 4).

MILITARY HISTORY OF SASKATCHEWAN:
see essay on facing page.

MILITIA. During the 1950s, the militia in Saskatchewan was formed into two Groups: 20th Militia Group was located in the south of the province, and 21st Militia Group was headquartered in the north. 20th Militia Group consisted of two artillery regiments: one in Regina (10th Medium Regiment) and the other in Yorkton (53rd Field Regiment). The Yorkton regiment had batteries in

Moosomin and Indian Head. There was also an armoured regiment in Moose Jaw (Royal Canadian Dragoons) and reconnaissance regiments in Swift Current and Maple Creek (14th Canadian Hussars). The two infantry regiments of the Militia Group were the **SOUTH SASKATCHEWAN REGIMENT** and the Regina Rifle Regiment. There was a medical unit, a recruiting unit, an engineer company, a provost corps unit, an ordinance corps unit, and a service corps unit. At summer concentrations in Dundurn Military Camp, 20th Militia Group fielded up to 1,500 to 2,000 soldiers of all ranks; some units came from as far 300 miles away to train for the two weeks. In the years that followed, military budgets were greatly reduced and the militia group system was abandoned.

Orris Keehr

FURTHER READING: Brennan, J.W. (ed.). 1978. *Regina Before Yesterday: A Visual History, 1882–1945.* Regina: City of Regina; Mein, S.A.G. 1992. *Up the Johns! The Story of the Royal Regina Rifles.* North Battleford: Senate of the RRR.

MILK CONTROL BOARD. The development of a viable dairy industry represented an integral part of national and provincial agricultural policy during the early settlement years. Assisted by various loan and grant programs, milk production and processing expanded rapidly throughout rural areas and made a significant contribution to agricultural diversification–an important objective of government settlement policy. However, the unrestricted and haphazard nature of the expansion activity soon led to market instability, cutthroat competition, and bankruptcies, as well as volatile prices for producers, processors and consumers. The first attempt to bring

stability and order to the milk and dairy sector was to empower the Local Government Board in 1934. The amendment to the Local Government Board Act vested the Board with the power to inquire into any matter relating to the production, supply, distribution, or sale of milk; prescribe the area or areas within which Board orders had effect, and to require all persons who distributed, processed, sold or kept milk for sale to obtain authorization from the Board; classify milk producers and distributors and prescribe appropriate prices; and inspect records of milk producers and processors, imposing fines of $100 per day for each day the offender was in violation of Board orders.

The first efforts to establish orderly production and marketing came into effect on June 1, 1934. B.A. Cooke, of the Department of Agriculture, was transferred to the Board as Milk Administrator and charged with the onerous task of establishing within the Saskatchewan dairy industry a stable economic climate, conducive to future growth on a sustainable basis. The first steps taken by the Local Government Board consisted of licencing all distributors and setting milk prices at the producer and retail levels; in addition, distributors were required to pay producers twice monthly. During its first year of operations, the Local Government Board recognized that the task of stabilizing and bringing order to the chaotic milk industry would require more resources and specialized attention than was available to the Board, given the breadth of its overall regulatory responsibilities. The provincial government understood the difficulty the Local Government Board was experiencing in administering milk industry regulations: as a result, the Milk Control Act was passed in February 1935 and responsibility for administering the new Act was transferred from the Local Government Board to a newly formed Milk Control Board.

The new Milk Control Board, with B.A. Cooke as chairman and administrator, set as its objective the elimination of waste and duplication in the matter of milk distribution in the fluid markets. After a few years of operation, the Milk Control Board introduced in 1938 a production quota system as a necessary feature to ensure that the orderly marketing system established a stable balance between supply and demand for milk and milk products throughout the province. In the following decades production quotas and formula pricing became lasting features of the Milk Control Board's operating policies.

These continued to evolve over the post-war years, in keeping with changing market circumstances and technology. In 1972, Saskatchewan joined with other provinces and the federal government to develop and implement the National Milk Marketing Plan. This agreement recognized the national character of markets for industrial dairy

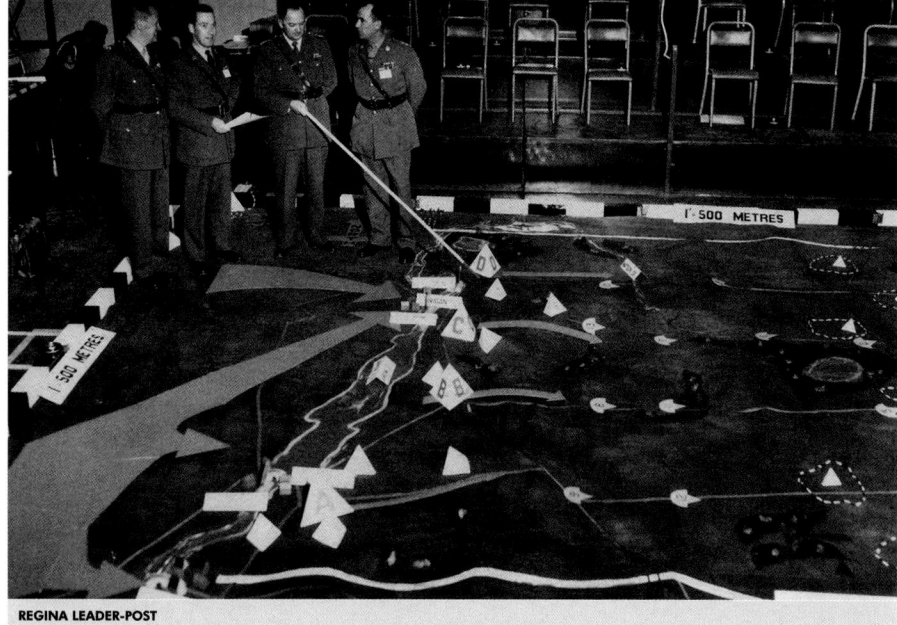

Two-day cloth-model battle exercise at HMCS Queen, May 1965.

products, and set out to establish national prices and a revenue pool for products such as cheese and butter. The Milk Control Board became the agency for administering policies within the province for fluid products, and the province's representative for managing the national system for industrial milk products. During this period of transition, S.H. Barber chaired and managed the operations of the Milk Control Board from 1973 to 2000—the longest period of service. Other Chairmen of note during this period were J.E. Ridley (1955–62), S. Swanson (1962–66), and W.B. Motion (1966–73).

In 1997 the four western provinces joined to form the Western Milk Pool, in which the revenues from all milk sales are pooled and distributed on an equitable basis among western milk producers. This shift from provincial milk pools to a regional pool was necessitated by processor rationalization and consolidation, which in turn created opportunities for the interprovincial marketing of fluid products. The Milk Control Board continues to manage the production, distribution and marketing of milk on behalf of the Saskatchewan dairy industry by administering orderly marketing policies that ensure production and marketing stability within the dairy sector. *Gerry Gartner*

FURTHER READING: Church, G.C. 1985. *An Unfailing Faith: A History of the Saskatchewan Dairy Industry.* Regina: Canadian Plains Research Center.

MILLAR WESTERN. Millar Western is a family-owned, western Canadian group of companies that traces its roots to 1906, when founder J.W. Millar opened a blacksmith shop in North Battleford. Millar's operations grew over the following decades to include sawmilling, construction, and chemicals processing in Alberta and Saskatchewan. In the 1980s, Millar Western expanded into the pulp sector, launching its first bleached chemi-thermo-mechanical pulp (BCTMP) mill in Whitecourt, Alberta. In 1992, Millar Western opened a second BCTMP mill in Meadow Lake, Saskatchewan. As the world's first successful zero-liquid-effluent-discharge market pulp mill, the facility earned international renown: rather than discharging treated mill waste water, or effluent, to the environment, it cleans and reuses this effluent, eliminating pollution concerns and significantly reducing fresh water intake requirements. Operating as Millar Western Pulp (Meadow Lake) Ltd., the mill is jointly owned by Millar Western and the government of Saskatchewan, and had 175 full-time employees in 2004. The Millar Western group sells products to markets around the world. Its chlorine-free pulp is sold to international papermakers for use in printing, writing and specialty papers, paperboard, tissues and towelling. Its lumber is sold in North America and Asia for use in residential and commercial construction. *Murray Little*

Military History of Saskatchewan

Stewart Mein

Introduction

The military history of Saskatchewan had its beginnings in the days before European contact when the warrior societies of the Aboriginal peoples formed the first military organizations in the region. The Plains CREE, ASSINIBOINE, Plains OJIBWA and the Wood Cree were all allied in a great confederacy; their enemies were the nations of the Blackfoot Confederacy to the west. As warfare was considered a highly prestigious occupation, most military operations took the form of lightning raids on enemy camps, the primary purpose of which was to obtain horses. These war parties were led by skilled warriors who, having taken part in many military expeditions in which they had shown great personal bravery, had established their places as leaders. The martial spirit of Saskatchewan's First Nations has continuously expressed itself to this day through those who served in the armed forces of Canada in two world wars and in the Korean conflict. That their courage and fighting ability remain is evidenced in those Aboriginal people of the plains and woodlands who continue to join the ranks of the Canadian Forces today.

Early Military History

The Europeans who first penetrated into the West came as explorers and fur traders. The French came from Canada and the English from Hudson Bay. In 1670, under its charter, the Hudson's Bay Company (HBC) was given the exclusive right to trade in all lands drained by rivers emptying into Hudson Bay. This vast uncharted region was given the name Rupert's Land, after Prince Rupert, the first governor of the Company. In 1690, the Hudson's Bay Company sent one of its employees, HENRY KELSEY, into the western interior to open trade with the native inhabitants of the region. Cumberland House, the first inland trading post of the Hudson's Bay Company, was built in 1774 on the SASKATCHEWAN RIVER, just inside the present eastern boundary of the province of Saskatchewan.

The intermingling of French, Scottish and English traders with the First Nations of the plains and woodlands sired a new nation of people, the MÉTIS, who soon became important intermediaries in the fur trade, between their European and First Nations relatives. Equipped with rifles and horses, they became efficient buffalo hunters, often becoming the main suppliers of meat and other bison products to the forts and trading posts in the region. To facilitate the annual quest for buffalo on the plains, the Métis established hunting parties that evolved into an impressive military organization, based on a ten-man unit with a captain at its head. With the westward expansion of trading companies, conflict over the control of the fur trade intensified until 1821, when the North West Company was absorbed into the Hudson's Bay Company. As a result of the merger the new company, which retained the name of the old HBC, consolidated its posts along the NORTH SASKATCHEWAN RIVER, keeping CUMBERLAND HOUSE, Fort Edmonton and FORT CARLTON, as well as other posts on the southern plains. The HBC enjoyed a lucrative monopoly of the fur trade until Rupert's Land was sold to the newly formed nation of Canada (*see* RUPERT'S LAND PURCHASE).

In 1868, Canada had entered into negotiations with the HBC to acquire Rupert's Land. The Canadian government looked to the sparsely populated lands of the West as territory into which the new country could expand. In 1870 Rupert's Land was formally annexed into the Dominion of Canada and became the North-West Territories. When the region became part of Canada, one of the first acts of the new nation was to establish its sovereignty over the vast sprawling land it had acquired. Unfortunately, the 15,000 or so native inhabitants of the North-West Territories had not been consulted about the transfer of the land to Canada. The first attempt to provide law and order in the newly acquired Territories occurred when the

M government of Sir John A. Macdonald created the North-West Mounted Police in 1873. The establishment of posts throughout the Territories occurred in 1874 after the Great March West. The first military activity in what is now Saskatchewan happened as an extension of Military District 10, which had been established in Winnipeg in 1870. A series of units, most notably the Battleford Rifles and a Prince Albert Infantry company, were initially set up in 1874. They existed fitfully until they came into their own at the outbreak of the NORTH-WEST RESISTANCE of 1885.

1885 North West Resistance

The 1885 Resistance consisted of two phases: the Métis Resistance around BATOCHE in the centre of the District of Saskatchewan, and the uprising of the Plains and Wood Cree of the TREATY 6 area which occurred in the western part of the District. The first incident of active resistance occurred when Métis forces under LOUIS RIEL and GABRIEL DUMONT decisively defeated a force of NWMP and Prince Albert Volunteers at DUCK LAKE. There followed a mobilization of Canadian militia led by Major General FREDERICK MIDDLETON; they set out from eastern Canada with the purpose of putting down the armed resistance in the West. Middleton's forces left Fort Qu'Appelle in the District of Assiniboia in March of 1885, and proceeded northward towards Riel's provisional capital at Batoche. The column was checked in its first engagement with the Métis at Fish Creek, but after linking with the steamer *Northcote*, Middleton continued his advance. In a four-day battle, from May 9 to 12, he put down all armed resistance by the Métis. Gabriel Dumont escaped to the United States; Riel was captured, taken to Regina, tried, and hanged.

The Cree uprising began in April of 1885 when a band of Plains Cree led by BIG BEAR and his war chiefs killed a number of people in the small community of FROG LAKE on the morning of April 2, 1885. The Cree had been goaded into this action as a response to government inaction and indifference to their plight. The uprising spread southward, forcing the abandonment by the NWMP of Fort Pitt and spreading panic among the inhabitants of Battleford. Other columns of Canadian militia were dispatched to Swift Current and Calgary to deal with this rapidly developing threat. The Cree under their chief POUNDMAKER soundly defeated the column, commanded by Lieutenant Colonel WILLIAM OTTER, sent to relieve Battleford. The defeat of the Canadians force was prevented from being a rout by the intervention of Poundmaker. The third column of Canadian militia, the Alberta Field force, led by Major General THOMAS BLAND STRANGE, pursued Big Bear's Cree warriors northward, fighting indecisive engagements at Frenchman's Butte and Steele Narrows. When eventually the uprising was put down, Big Bear and Poundmaker were captured and sentenced to imprisonment. Eight Aboriginals who had been identified as having taken part in the killings were tried and hanged at Battleford. With the Resistance defeated and the region pacified, settlers from all over the world flooded into the West, brought there by the newly completed CANADIAN PACIFIC RAILWAY. Land was opened to farming, and the First Nations were forced into a long period of obscurity.

Little remained of military organization in the West after the 1885 Resistance. The next time soldiers from Saskatchewan were called upon to fight for Canada was when another rebellion broke out thousands of miles away in South Africa. It was there that western units such as the 2nd Canadian Mounted Rifles and the Lord Strathcona Horse were sent to provide cavalry for the British forces. Women also played their part in the conflict as nurses. It was in South Africa that three of

Saskatchewan's 27th Light Horse Regiment, 1914.

Saskatchewan's soldiers were to win the VICTORIA CROSS, the British Empire's highest award for bravery. As Saskatchewan approached its entrance into the Canadian Confederation in 1905, a separate military district was created for the new province. Militia cavalry units such as the 20th Mounted Rifles, the 16th Canadian light Horse and the 27th Light Horse were then formed in the District. Infantry units such as the 95th Rifles of Regina, the 60th Rifles from Moose Jaw, the 105th Fusiliers of Saskatoon and the 52nd Regiment from Prince Albert were also formed. These units all provided men for the Canadian army in WORLD WAR I.

World War I

On the outbreak of World War I in August of 1914, the Canadian government began recruiting units to go overseas to fight alongside the armies of Great Britain and the other members of its Empire. The first contingent of the Canadian Expeditionary Force was assembled at Camp Valcartier in September of that year. Saskatchewan's soldiers were found in many units including the 5th (Western Cavalry) Battalion., which was raised from the cavalry units of the province and fought as infantry in the 1st Canadian Division. The 28th (Northwest) Battalion of the 2nd Canadian Division, initially recruited throughout Saskatchewan and the West, became primarily a Regina infantry regiment. The 46th Battalion was recruited from southern Saskatchewan. These units all saw service in the Canadian Corps and took part in its famous battles. Soldiers from the province were present at VIMY RIDGE and at the breaking of the German lines by the Canadians in the final hundred days of the war. Saskatchewan suffered many casualties in the Great War: in proportion, western Canada endured more losses than any other region of the country. One of its units, the 46th Battalion, became known as the "Suicide Battalion" because of its extraordinarily high numbers of dead and wounded. It was in response to the sacrifice of its citizens that the Canadian and provincial governments set up a system of benefits, which included land grants, for their returned servicemen. Veterans' organizations were also formed to aid in the process of rehabilitation and reintegration into civilian life. Again, in this war, Saskatchewan soldiers showed their bravery by winning eleven Victoria Crosses.

After the "war to end all wars," military activity around the world stagnated as most people tried to put behind them the horrors of that bloodiest of conflicts. The Canadian militia was reorganized, and in Military District 12 the infantry formed two units: the NORTH SASKATCHEWAN REGIMENT and the SOUTH SASKATCHEWAN REGIMENT. In later reorganizations, the SASKATOON LIGHT INFANTRY, the Prince Albert Volunteers, the Regina Rifles (see ROYAL REGINA RIFLES), and the KING'S OWN RIFLES OF CANADA in Moose Jaw would come into being. It was at this time that the Navy came to Saskatchewan in the form of two Naval Reserve half companies: one in Regina, which was to become HMCS Queen; and the other in Saskatoon, which was to become HMCS Unicorn. Canada's fledgling air force also was represented in Saskatoon.

The militia in Saskatchewan was given a new camp at Dundurn for its summer training. In October of 1929, the world suffered the GREAT DEPRESSION; the stock market came crashing down, and on the prairies the bottom fell out of the WHEAT market. The new camp at Dundurn was used to house hundreds of the now unemployed single men desperate for work. Work would come for them soon enough. Throughout Europe the aftermath of World War I and the onset of the Great Depression were to bring upheavals in the social structure; with the rise of ideologies such as fascism and communism, social unrest led to warfare. In Spain in 1936, volunteers from all over the world, including Saskatchewan, arrived to fight in the civil war involving Franco's fascists and their opponents. Germany, smarting from her humiliation after the Great War, found a new leader in Adolf Hitler; his Nazi party rearmed and began its expansion into the Rhineland and the surrounding countries of Europe. In the Pacific, Japan had also become a rising power, expanding into Manchuria and China. Meanwhile in Canada, the political changes brought about by the Statute of Westminster in 1933 meant a new relationship with Great Britain: Canada was now an autonomous dominion and the master of her own national policies.

SASKATCHEWAN ARCHIVES BOARD R-B7117

Major Pyman from the 5th Canadian Battalion interrogates a prisoner. Members of the Red Saskatchewans look on. Date and location unknown.

World War II

In Saskatchewan, in the summer of 1939 people turned out in the thousands to welcome the new monarch, King George VI, and his wife Queen Elizabeth. This show of unity with the people of Great Britain was to express itself in a more tangible way when WORLD WAR II broke out in September of that fateful year. Canada was to declare war on Germany ten days after Britain did so. The coming of war meant the mobilization of the naval, air, and militia units of the province. A number of Saskatchewan units including the Saskatoon Light Infantry went overseas with the First Canadian Division to begin the task of defending Britain from invasion. The prairies were also to provide for the war effort a service made possible by their unique geography: the open skies and vast prairie lands were an ideal place to train the air forces of the Commonwealth. The BRITISH COMMONWEALTH AIR TRAINING PLAN saw thousands of airmen from Canada, Great Britain, Australia, South Africa, and other Allied countries training to become the air forces that would have such a major part to play in winning the war. The Royal Canadian Air Force provided many squadrons of bombers and fighter aircraft that served in many theatres around the world, from the defense of Canada and Great Britain to campaigns in North Africa and the Far East.

It was in the Far East that the Canadian army was to suffer its first great tragedy of the war, in the British colony of Hong Kong. Although the colony was indefensible, two battalions of Canadian infantry had been sent there to reinforce its British garrison. One of the battalions, the Winnipeg Grenadiers, had many men from Saskatchewan serving in its ranks. When Japanese forces invaded Hong Kong in December 1941, the garrison, after a fierce resistance, was overwhelmed and many of the Canadians were killed in the action; one of the defenders, Sergeant Major John Osborn of Wapella, was awarded the Victoria Cross. The Japanese held many other Saskatchewan men as prisoners of war, including a future LIEUTENANT GOVERNOR of the province, GEORGE PORTEOUS. Meanwhile in Britain, the Canadian Army had not yet been committed to battle. Other Canadian divisions had been formed for service overseas, which contained many Saskatchewan units. The South Saskatchewan Regiment was mobilized into the Second Canadian Division, and the Regina Rifles into the Third Canadian Division. The Royal Canadian Air Force was providing squadrons for the defense of Britain and for bombing raids over Germany, while ships of the Royal Canadian Navy patrolled the English Channel and carried out escort duties for the convoys of merchant ships that crossed the Atlantic Ocean.

The Battle of the Atlantic against the U-boat menace lasted until the surrender of Germany in May of 1945. The small corvettes of the Royal Canadian Navy and the larger fighting ships, including those of the 10th Destroyer Flotilla such as the "Tribal Class" Destroyers, HMCS Athabaska and HMCS Haida, were manned by a high percentage of "prairie sailors," many of whom were from Saskatchewan. Many ships of the Royal Canadian Navy proudly carried the names of Saskatchewan communities; some, such as HMCS Regina and HMCS Weyburn, paid the ultimate price. In August 1942, Canada suffered another tragedy when some 6,000 Allied troops carried out an assault on the town of Dieppe on the west coast of France. The Second Canadian Division, which included the South Saskatchewan Regiment, made up the largest part of the assault force. In the battle, almost 4,000 were killed, wounded or taken prisoner. Among them were the men of the South Saskatchewan, including their commanding officer, Lieutenant Colonel Cecil Merritt, who was taken prisoner and later awarded the Victoria Cross. (See also DIEPPE RAID.)

In July of 1943, the First Canadian Division, which included the Saskatoon Light Infantry (SLI), had moved from guarding the coast of Britain to join the British 8th Army for the invasion of Sicily. As it was a machine-gun battalion, sub-units of the SLI were distributed throughout the Division to provide firepower for other infantry units. Fighting

SASKATCHEWAN ARCHIVES BOARD R-B12672
King George VI and Queen Elizabeth review the Regina Rifle Regiment, 1940s.

through Sicily and on to the mainland of Italy, the SLI fought in all the battles of the Italian Campaign until they were moved to northwest Europe in 1945. When the Allied armies finally opened the second front on the mainland of Europe on D-Day (June 6, 1944), the Regina Rifles were chosen to lead the Third Division's assault on Juno Beach. The Regina Rifles fought their way through Normandy, taking part in operations to capture Caen and Falaise, and up the western coast of France in the battles for the channel ports. They fought through Holland and into Germany until the latter's surrender in May of 1945. Major David Currie, fighting with the South Alberta Regiment, was awarded the Victoria Cross for his actions during the Falaise operation in capturing the town of St. Lambert, thereby slowing down the withdrawal of German forces in their retreat to safer defensive positions. Currie was the only Saskatchewan-born recipient of the Victoria Cross. During the last months of the war, Canadian units in Italy were reunited with those in northwest Europe for the final assault on Germany.

While Saskatchewan's soldiers were fighting overseas, the war had operated great changes to the province itself. Supporting the war effort had brought a return of prosperity. Many of Saskatchewan's citizens had been enrolled in the reserve army to train for home defense. A number of training centres had been set up in the province at Regina, Maple Creek, and Prince Albert for the army, and a number of others for the RCAF. By far the largest military establishment in Saskatchewan was CAMP DUNDURN. After its role housing homeless men in the Depression, it had been turned back to the army to be used to train troops for overseas. The camp facilities had been expanded to include a large hospital facility and a CANADIAN WOMENS' ARMY CORPS barracks. Because of its largely sandy terrain, Camp Dundurn became a major armoured corps training centre. It was also where the men of the reserve army took their compulsory military training; one of these men was Lieutenant T.C. DOUGLAS of the South Saskatchewan Regiment, who was also Premier of the province at the time. Other Saskatchewan units,

such as the King's Own Rifles from Moose Jaw and the Prince Albert Volunteers, served as part of the defense force on the west coast of Canada. Many other citizens of Saskatchewan worked in the civilian war effort, making guns and munitions in Regina as well as harvesting the bumper crops that now grew in the fields. The servicemen who returned to Saskatchewan after the war came home to a province much different from the one they had left five years earlier. In the post-war years land was set aside for returned veterans under the Returned Veteran's Act, and servicemen took advantage of educational and retraining schemes, filling classrooms at the UNIVERSITY OF SASKATCHEWAN and other provincial educational institutions. As housing was at a premium, new subdivisions sprang up in the cities in an attempt to cope with the increased demands.

The Cold War

While the world was turning its thoughts to peace, a new threat was looming on the horizon. The Soviet Union, which had been an ally through World War II, was now involved in spreading communism throughout the world; Saskatchewan would play a role in the fight for its containment. The Canadian Army had been reduced after World War II, and special units had to be raised to fight a new war in Korea from 1950 to 1953. Troops were also raised to become part of the newly formed North Atlantic Treaty Organization in Europe. At home, the militia took on the new role of national survival. To meet the threat of an attack on North America from Soviet long-range bombers carrying nuclear weapons, the RCAF was given the role of maintaining a series of radar lines across the country. A series of radar stations were set up across the province at Yorkton, Dana and Alsask as part of the Pinetree Radar Line (*see* AIR DEFENCE STATIONS). As in World War II, the prairies were again chosen to provide an air training plan for pilots of NATO countries: RCAF Station Moose Jaw was reactivated as a NATO flying training school, as was the RCAF station at Saskatoon.

Present Day

Saskatchewan continues to make a significant contribution to the Canadian armed forces of today. The distinctive services of Canada's

REGINA LEADER-POST
Snowbirds.

navy, army, and air force were lost in 1967 when they were replaced by a single unified service, the Canadian Armed Forces. In Saskatchewan, the only remaining component of the regular force is Canadian Forces Base Moose Jaw. The reserve force, however, maintains its presence through the army reserve units of 38 Brigade Group and the naval reserve units of HMCS *Queen* and HMCS *Unicorn*. Canadian Forces Base Moose Jaw, now designated at 15 Wing, is the home of a new NATO flying training program and of the famous air demonstration squadron, the SNOWBIRDS. Prairie sailors from Saskatchewan can now serve aboard ships of the Canadian navy that carry the names of the province's cities, HMCS *Regina* and HMCS *Saskatoon*. Although the South Saskatchewan Regiment was lost in one of the many reorganizations of the reserve force, the army reserve still carries on the proud traditions of Saskatchewan's regiments. 10TH FIELD REGIMENT, Royal Canadian Artillery, the now Royal Regina Rifles, the North Saskatchewan Regiment, and the SASKATCHEWAN DRAGOONS maintain their presence in the cities of Regina, Yorkton, Saskatoon, Prince Albert and Moose Jaw. These units of 38 Brigade Group are supported by 16 SERVICE BATTALION, 16 MEDICAL COMPANY, and 734 (REGINA) AND 737 (SASKATOON) SQUADRONS of the Communications Reserve. A number of cadet corps for all three elements of the Canadian Armed forces also exist in the province. Veterans from Saskatchewan who have served Canada are represented by various organizations including the Saskatchewan branch of the Royal Canadian Legion and the Army, Navy, and Air Force Veterans' Association.

Conclusion

Throughout the province's history, those from Saskatchewan who have served in the armed forces have made many sacrifices: the numerous memorials and cemeteries across the province bear testament to this, as do the many lakes and geographic features of northern Saskatchewan that have been named for those who gave their lives in the service of their country. As we have honoured the citizens of Saskatchewan who have served this province in the past, their tradition of service is continued by those who serve in the armed forces of Canada today and who will continue this tradition of service in the future.

FURTHER READING:

Beal, B., and R. Macleod. 1984. *Prairie Fire: The 1885 North-West Rebellion*. Edmonton: Hurtig.

Brown, G., and T. Copp. 2001. *Look to Your Front, Regina Rifles: A Regiment at War 1944-45*. Waterloo: Wilfrid Laurier University, Laurier Centre for Military Strategic & Disarmament Studies.

Brown, W.F. 2001. *Steele's Scouts: Samuel Benfield Steele and the North-West Rebellion*. Surrey, BC: Heritage House.

Buchanan, G.B. 1958. *The March of the Prairie Men: A Story of the South Saskatchewan Regiment*. Weyburn, SK: South Saskatchewan Regiment Association.

Dunn, J. 1994. *The Alberta Field Force of 1885*. Winnipeg: Hignell.

Flanagan, T. 1999. *Riel and the Rebellion: 1885 Reconsidered*. Toronto: University of Toronto Press.

Hildebrandt, W. 1985. *The Battle of Batoche: British Small Arms Fire and the Entrenched Métis*. Ottawa: Parks Canada.

Klancher, D.J. 1999. *The North-West Mounted Police and the North-West Rebellion*. Kamloops, BC: Goss Publications.

Light, D.W. 1987. *Footprints in the Dust*. North Battleford, SK: Turner-Warwick Publications.

McWilliams, J.L., and R.J. Steel. 1978. *The Suicide Battalion*. Edmonton: Hurtig.

Mein, S.A.G. 1992. *Up the Johns! The Story of the Royal Regina Rifles*. North Battleford: Senate of the RRR.

Morton, D. 1972. *The Last War Drum: The North West Campaign of 1885*. Toronto: Hakkert.

Stanley, G. 1992. *The Birth of Western Canada: A History of the Riel Rebellions*. Toronto: University of Toronto Press.

Stonechild, B., and B. Waiser. 1997. *Loyal Till Death: Indians and the North West Rebellion*. Calgary: Fifth House.

Winton, M.V. 1980. *Saskatchewan's Prairie Soldiers 1885-1980: A Pictorial History of Saskatchewan's Military Badges and Medals*. Regina: the author.

Canadian Military Organization and Terminology

Formations	
Corps	A subdivision of an army usually consisting of two or more divisions and commanded by a Lieutenant General.
Division	A self-contained organizational structure commanded by a Major General.
Brigade	Led by a Brigadier and comprised of three to four infantry battalions.
Units	
Battalion	An infantry unit of approximately 600-1,000 soldiers commanded by a Lieutenant Colonel.
Company	A subdivision of a battalion consisting of 80-200 soldiers led by a Captain or Major.
Platoon	A subdivision of a company comprised of 20-40 troops commanded by a Lieutenant.
Section	A small tactical unit within a platoon led by a Non-Commissioned Officer.

Sources: Bercuson, David D. and J.L. Granatstein. *Dictionary of Canadian Military History*. Toronto: Oxford University Press, 1992. *Canada and the Great War, 1914–1918: A Nation Born*. Ottawa: Veterans Affairs Canada, 1998.

Canadian Military — Comparative Ranks

Canadian Army	Royal Canadian Air Force	Royal Canadian Navy
Commissioned Officers		
General	Air Chief Marshal	Admiral
Lieutenant General	Air Marshal	Vice Admiral
Major General	Air Vice Marshal	Rear Admiral
Brigadier	Air Commodore	Commodore
Colonel	Group Captain	Captain
Lieutenant Colonel	Wing Commander	Commander
Major	Squadron Leader	Lieutenant Commander
Captain	Flight Lieutenant	Lieutenant
Lieutenant	Flying Officer	Sub-Lieutenant
Second Lieutenant	Pilot Officer	Midshipman
Non-Commissioned Officers		
Regimental Sergeant-Major	Warrant Officer I	Chief Petty Officer I
Company Sergeant-Major	Warrant Officer II	Chief Petty Officer II
Staff Sergeant	Flight Sergeant	Petty Officer I
Sergeant	Sergeant	Petty Officer
Other Ranks		
Corporal	Corporal	Leading Seaman
Lance Corporal	Leading Aircraftsman	Able Seaman
Private	Aircraftsman I	Ordinary Seaman

Source: Morton, Desmond. *A Military History of Canada: From Champlain to Kosovo*. 4th ed. Toronto: McClelland & Stewart, 1999.

MILLARD, PETER (1932–2001). Peter Tudor Millard, a professor of English at the **UNIVERSITY OF SASKATCHEWAN**, played important roles in the development of the visual arts in Saskatoon and in the struggle for more equitable treatment and acceptance of gays and lesbians in Saskatchewan. Born on July 21, 1932, to working-class parents in South Wales, Millard moved to Canada to study at McGill University and graduated in 1959 with the highest average, winning the Shakespeare Medal for English. He returned to England as a Canadian student and earned his doctorate from Linacre College, Oxford. He began lecturing at the University of Saskatchewan in 1963 and became a tenured professor in 1970. His academic specialization was the literature and culture of the 18th century. In 1988, as chair of the University of Saskatchewan Faculty Association, he led the faculty union in a lengthy strike which was ended by provincial back-to-work legislation.

Millard had a love for all of the arts, and in Saskatoon quickly engaged himself with many local painters and collectors. As a collector and part-time dealer, art writer and critic, and artist's mentor, he became one of the province's most active and effective promoters of the visual arts. He served as trustee and president of the **MENDEL ART GALLERY**, and through his chairmanship of the University of Saskatchewan Art Committee oversaw acquisitions to the University's extensive art collections. In 1975 he encountered the work of the idiosyncratic Saskatoon folk painter, **DMYTRO STRYJEK**, and became his dedicated champion, helping to organize several Stryjek exhibitions and authoring a critical appreciation titled *Stryjek, Trying the Colors*. Millard made numerous donations of artworks to prairie galleries, including the Winnipeg Art Gallery, which received his fine collection of early Inuit sculpture, and Regina's **MACKENZIE ART GALLERY**, which acquired the bulk of his Stryjek collection in 2000.

In the early 1970s, Millard embraced Saskatoon's emerging gay community and helped to establish the Saskatoon Gay Community Centre in 1972. He was a leader and spokesperson in most of the early battles to advance equal rights for lesbians and gays in Saskatchewan. In 1975 he led the Committee to defend **DOUG WILSON**, an openly gay graduate student who had been prohibited by the University of Saskatchewan College of Education, because of his sexual orientation, from supervising practice teachers. The support committee's work made Wilson's case one of the most publicized early gay rights struggles in Canada. Millard subsequently helped form a gay academic union at the University, and in 1998 taught the University's first course in gay and lesbian literature.

Millard worked tirelessly during the 1970s and 1980s to promote the inclusion of sexual orientation in Saskatchewan's human rights law. His influence was publicly credited by government members when **ROY ROMANOW**'s NDP government amended the Saskatchewan Human Rights Code to protect lesbians and gays in 1993. In 1995 the University of Saskatchewan established the Peter Millard Scholarship, Canada's first university-administered scholarship in support of gay/lesbian studies, to honour Millard's gay activism and his mentorship of gay and lesbian students on campus. Millard retired early to Gibsons, BC in 1992; but in 1998 he returned to Saskatoon, where he resumed most of his earlier activities. He died there on December 8, 2001.

Neil Richards

FURTHER READING: Millard, P. 1988. *Stryjek, Trying the Colors*. Saskatoon: Fifth House; —. 1991. "Human Rights and the P.C. Government." Pp. 33–48 in L. Biggs and M. Stobbe (eds.), *Devine Rule in Saskatchewan*. Saskatoon: Fifth House.

MILLER, THOMAS (1876–1945). Saskatchewan's shortest-serving **LIEUTENANT-GOVERNOR**, Thomas Miller was born July 21, 1876, near Grand Valley, Ontario. Miller was a young boy when his family settled in Regina, and it was there that he completed his entire education. In 1892, he began a two-year apprenticeship at the *Regina Standard*, a newspaper owned by J.K. McInnis and **WALTER SCOTT**. When Scott purchased the *Moose Jaw Times* in June 1894, he placed Miller in charge of the printing plant. Two years later, Miller was president and managing editor of the *Times*. His association with the Times and later the *Times-Herald* in Moose Jaw lasted more than fifty years.

Prime Minister **MACKENZIE KING** appointed Miller to the vice-regal office on February 27, 1945. Since **GOVERNMENT HOUSE** had been closed following Archibald McNab's tenure, Miller took up official residence in the Hotel Saskatchewan. His first official duties as Lieutenant-Governor involved numerous Victory Day celebrations following the end of World War II as well as hosting the Governor General, the Earl of Athlone, during his visit to the province. Miller was in poor health for some time when he died of a heart attack on June 20, 1945, a mere fifteen weeks after he had been sworn into office.

Holden Stoffel

FURTHER READING: Hryniuk, Margaret and Garth Pugh. 1991. *"A Tower of Attraction": An Illustrated History of Government House, Regina, Saskatchewan*. Regina: Government House Historical Society/Canadian Plains Research Center; 1945. "Lt.-Gov. Miller Dies Suddenly," *Regina Leader-Post* (June 20): 1.

MILLING. Grain milling is the process of grinding and separating wheat and other cereal grains into flour, animal feed, and other products such as rolled, flaked or dehulled grain products. In Saskatchewan's crop-based agriculture sector, wheat milling has historically been and remains the most important milling activity. Since the 1990s, milling of oats and other cereal grains and special crops has also become an important sub-sector. In the 1800s, wheat was ground using millstones; but by the early 1900s a new technology used a series of rollers to reduce the grain into varying sizes of flour particles, which were then separated into various product streams using machines called sifters and purifiers. The evolution from stone mills to roller mills enabled hard spring wheat to be ground into the high-quality, whiter flour with less bran content favoured for some food uses.

Flour mills were vital industries, especially for the early settlers, and played an important role in the development of agriculture in Saskatchewan. As evidenced in the literature of the early 1900s that promoted settlement in Saskatchewan, flour mills were seen as cornerstone industries fit to attract

GIBSON PHOTOGRAPHY/UNIVERSITY OF SASKATCHEWAN ARCHIVES A-8610

Bruce Schnell, Rita Cowley, and Peter Millard examine one of the works at a University of Saskatchewan art exhibition, 1982.

new settlers, additional business, and economic development. Hauling their wheat to the nearest mill, farmers obtained flour which was not only a staple food but also served as barter for other commodities. A portion of their crop was also sold to the mill for cash and exported from the prairie region.

In small communities, flour and grist mills were often the only industries to provide off-farm employment to rural people. Because of the services they offered, access to a mill was crucial to the settlement of the prairies, and difficulties in transportation necessitated a dense network of mills throughout the countryside. In 1915, at least thirty-seven flour mills were located in the towns of Annaheim, Asquith, Balgonie, Battleford, Blaine Lake, Canora, Cupar, Duck Lake, Esterhazy, Foam Lake, Grenfell, Hague, Herbert, Humboldt, Indian Head, Jasmin, Lanigan, Leney, Lloydminster, Lumsden, Maple Creek, Melville, Moose Jaw, North Battleford, Outlook, Prince Albert, Radisson, Regina, Rosthern, Saltcoats, Saskatoon, Shellbrook, Swift Current, Verigin, Weyburn, and Wilkie. Thrashing mills were found in an additional twenty-three towns.

Flour milling companies based in eastern Canada and the United States constructed grain elevators in the prairies to ensure a supply of grain. The Lake of the Woods Milling Company (est. 1887) owned thirty-two elevators in Saskatchewan by 1911; by 1927, the Ogilvie Flour Mills Company (est. 1881) was operating thirty-one elevators. The prairie milling trade was dominated by these two companies until Western Canada Flour Mills and Maple Leaf Mills (both est. 1907) also entered the grain trade. By 1911, Western Canada Flour Mills operated fifty-one elevators in Saskatchewan, which it later sold to PARRISH & HEIMBECKER in 1940. Maple Leaf Mills operated thirty-one elevators which were later sold to the FEDERAL GRAIN CO. (est. 1912) in 1929. These companies transported grain to their milling operations, and did not mill grain in Saskatchewan.

The Leslie and Wilson Milling Company in Saskatoon, which started operation in 1902, was equipped with electric motors which could process 100 barrels of flour per day; as the town's largest building, it was a proud symbol of modernity. Saskatoon's role as a supply centre was strengthened in 1912 when the Quaker Oats Company opened a mill on the site of the A.P. McNab mill. Expanded in 1936, the mill had an important role in the economic and cultural life of the city until the company withdrew from Saskatoon in 1972. For many years, the local hockey team was called the "Saskatoon Quakers." Built in 1904 in Moosomin, the Sutcliffe-Muir Mill, which had a capacity of 250 barrels per day, was seen as a key industry capable of attracting business, investment and settlement to the region. Yorkton's flour mill, built in 1898, was by 1912 considered a pioneer industry whose prod-

ucts had become household words in eastern Saskatchewan.

The Moose Jaw Milling Company, founded in 1900 by miller Donald Mclean, was purchased in 1908 by the New Prague Flouring Mill (Minnesota), which by 1970 was renamed International Multifoods; a state-of-the-art oat mill was added in 1911. Six months later the oat and flour mill burned down but was immediately rebuilt in 1912. The company marketed the Radium, Keynote, Saskana and Robin Hood brand of flours, the latter of which remains popular today. Through the 1930s, a company newsletter, *The Grist*, informed residents of local news including the activities of the Robin Hood bowling league. The company's logo, an image of Robin Hood, was first painted on the mill elevator in 1922 and was a Moose Jaw landmark for over fifty years. At its peak, the mill employed 200 people and could produce 4,000 barrels of flour and 1,200 barrels of rolled oats per day. The mill had tremendous influence on economic and social life in Moose Jaw, which came to be known as the "Mill City." Owing to milling overcapacity in Saskatchewan, decreasing export markets, as well as its location far from major markets, the mill closed in 1966.

The Esterhazy Flour Mill, constructed by James Saunders in 1906-07, operated until its closure in 1981. The plant was built with an elevator section powered by a kerosene engine and with a mill powered by a steam engine, which was replaced by a diesel engine in 1947. Designated as a seventy-five barrel mill, the operation was capable of producing 600 pounds of flour per hour. At one time, mills such as this were common across the prairies, but succumbed to fire or were closed down and razed. The Esterhazy mill, which operated until 1981, was designated a Provincial Heritage Property in 2004 and is the only remaining example of a flour mill of wood-frame construction in the province.

In Radisson, a 200-barrel mill and 16,000-bushel wheat elevator was built in 1908 by J. McLaren; serving the surrounding district, it was central to Radisson's role as a trading centre until it was destroyed by fire in 1942. In Humboldt, a 100-barrel mill, the McNab Flour Mill, was established in 1913 when A.P. MCNAB moved a mill from Saskatoon to the town. Destroyed by fire in 1956, the mill was rebuilt and now mills primarily mustard but continues to produce flour, albeit on a smaller scale than in the 1960s.

By 1929 there were forty-five flour and grist mills in the province, with a combined daily capacity of 7,000 barrels; but half the mills were inactive. During the GREAT DEPRESSION, low wheat prices and poor wheat crops encouraged the growth of small mills, which offered cheaper products to cash-strapped farmers. By 1935, the number of small milling operations had increased to fifty-five, with a combined daily capacity of 7,860 barrels.

Throughout the 1930s small mills, challenged by inadequate supply and restricted by limited markets, sold their own brands of cereal breakfast foods. In 1941, Saskatchewan had at least fifty-seven flour mills, with a combined daily capacity of 12,592 barrels. The majority (96%) were small operations with a capacity of less than 300 barrels per day. However, the most common mills had a maximum capacity of 100 barrels per day and comprised 75% of all mills. These local businesses served as grist mills, supplying local farmers with flour as well as selling flour commercially. Few of the small mills were able to survive in an increasingly competitive market, and most had closed by the mid-1900s. Some mills found local niches and continued operation into the 1980s and 1990s. Expansion of farms, rural depopulation, and inability to compete with large companies eventually ended the era of the small mills.

The Viscount Flour Mill, which closed in 2001, was the last of the small fifty-barrel mills that were once so crucial to Saskatchewan's rural society. Built in 1929 by Harry Carnation in Viscount, it was equipped with an Ontario-built roller mill and a European-built stone mill manufactured in the late 1800s. First powered by a diesel engine, the mill was converted to electric power in 1969 and could produce one ton of flour per day. Bought by Aloise Koller in 1964, approximately 60% of milling work involved providing grist for farmers, the remainder being devoted to commercial sale of flours to FEDERATED CO-OP, the SASKATCHEWAN WHEAT POOL, and health food stores. By the early 1990s, the mill no longer supplied grist for farmers and depended entirely on commercial sales. The Viscount mill, its building and equipment unchanged since 1929, is one of the few small flour mills that still exist in western Canada.

The Saskatchewan Wheat Pool built its first mill in 1949 as a way to add to the co-op's economic control, ensure fair treatment of farmers, and provide value-added manufacturing for prairie grain. In 1975, the Saskatchewan Wheat Pool and Manitoba Pool Elevators invested in CSP Foods, a major milling operation as well as manufacturer and distributor of baking products, as a value-added business for prairie grain. This partnership bought Can-Oat Milling in 1997.

After WORLD WAR II, and until the early 1970s, Canada sold wheat to many food-deprived countries and was the world's largest exporter of wheat flour, holding 20% of the world trade. As war-torn nations rebuilt, export demand for Canadian flour decreased. In the 1970s, export subsidies introduced by the European Union and the United States caused the international market for wheat flour become extremely competitive. Canadian federal and provincial governments chose not to compete, and by 1989 Canada's share of world trade in flour diminished to 4%. The loss of off-shore markets, a limited domestic market, and over-capacity led to plant closures.

Following the elimination of Canada-USA tariffs in 1991, exports of wheat flour to the United States increased gradually throughout the 1990s, resulting in the US becoming the most important export market for wheat flour and other milled grain products. At the same time, American milling companies, facing the high costs of refitting outdated mills, began purchasing Canadian mills to meet increasing demand for grain products. Since 1990, milling companies based in the US and Japan have invested substantially in the Canadian milling industry. Currently, 70% of Canada's milling capacity is owned and operated by large US interests. In Saskatchewan, Grain Millers (Minnesota) acquired Popowich Milling in Yorkton in 2001; and in 2002, Michigan-based Dawn Food Products bought CPS Foods from the Wheat Pool, as well as Humboldt Flour Mills Ltd. However, most of the smaller cereal grain and special crop milling companies operating in Canada are still owned and operated by Canadian interests.

Canadian grain-milling capacity increased significantly from 1994 to 2004, and two new mills—the first in thirty years—were built in Manitoba and Saskatchewan, close to the source of prairie grains. Mills located in prairie provinces account for 32% of Canada's milling. Export profits from milling in Saskatchewan increased 22%, from $25 million in 1997 to $32 million in 2001. Currently there are three large flour mills in Saskatchewan: J.M. Smucker (Canada) Inc. in Saskatoon, and the Dawn Food Products mills in Saskatoon and Humboldt. Oats are milled by Popowich Milling (Yorkton) and CanOat Milling (Martensville). Peas and flax are milled by Parrheim Foods (Saskatoon), and Randolph and James Flax Milling (Prince Albert). Nutrasun Foods, the largest dedicated organic flour mill in North America, began operation in 2000. Smaller processors of organic flour, oat flour and wheat flour are also found in the province. Future areas of growth are likely to involve organic flours, higher-value foods, and nutraceutical ingredients made from a growing range of cereal grains and special crops. *Raymond Ambrosi*

MILNE, COURTNEY (1943–).

Courtney Milne was born in Saskatoon in 1943. Since 1975, he has been a freelance photographer, exploring spiritualism in landscape and nature. He has taken formal training in photography and has completed two Masters degrees—in psychology, and in journalism and mass communications.

Milne has taken almost half a million photos on all seven continents for a series of books called The Sacred Earth Collection. Milne's works, which include several bestsellers, highlight the splendour of the prairie landscape and sacred locations around the world. Milne has presented slide shows of his

JOHN KENNEY/SASKATCHEWAN ARCHIVES BOARD
S-SP-A25654-2, SASKATOON STARPHOENIX FONDS
Courtney Milne, 1986.

works in international multimedia events including UNESCO's World Heritage Committee (1990), and the United Nations "Earth Summit" in Rio de Janiero in 1992. The presentations are often accompanied by music composed and performed by Saskatchewan and prairie artists. In 1997, *Love Songs From Planet Earth*, a live collaboration of Milne's images was premiered onstage with flutist Bettine Clemen and the SASKATOON SYMPHONY ORCHESTRA. His prints are in major museums and galleries in Canada and have been displayed at the Royal Ontario Museum, the UN Metropolitan Museum of Photography in Tokyo, and in many Canadian embassies.

Funds raised from his 1991 Canadian tour of The Sacred Earth Concert were donated to local environmental projects and endangered species programs. Milne has also donated more than 25 sets of Limited Edition prints to galleries and museums across Canada. Milne was awarded the Gold Medal for Distinction in Canadian Photography by the National Association for Photographic Art (1993), was selected to the 1995 jury for the International Photography Competition sponsored by the United Nations Environment Program, in Tokyo, Japan, where he presented The Sacred Earth Concert at the Metropolitan Museum of Photography, and was nominated for the 2004 prestigious Governor General's Awards in Visual and Media Arts. Milne was granted an honorary doctor of laws from the University of Regina in 2005.

Courtney Milne lives in Grandora, near Saskatoon, with his partner, Sherrill Miller, who works with him on projects. *Bob Ivanochko*

FURTHER READING: Milne, Courtney. 1995. *Prairie Light*. Saskatoon: Western Producer Prairie Books; —. 1991. *The Sacred Earth*. Saskatoon: Western Producer Prairie Books, 1991; —. 1999. *W.O. Mitchell Country* (portrayed by Courtney Milne; text by W.O. Mitchell; selected by Orm and Barbara Mitchell). Toronto: McClelland & Stewart.

MINERAL DETECTION.

Robert Kerrich and Derek Syman at the UNIVERSITY OF SASKATCHEWAN became pioneers in applying new detection methods for base-precious metals, with the potential for giving Canadian mining companies a decided advantage in evaluating new finds. The two researchers used mass spectrometry to analyse chemicals in rock samples, with detection levels as low as one part per billion. In 1999, Kerrich was awarded the Willet G. Miller Medal by the Royal Society of Canada for exceptional contributions to Canadian geoscience: he had provided the first clear evidence that the Earth's ancient oceanic and continental crust avalanched 3,000 km towards the Earth's core and returned to the surface as volcanoes. He also developed the standard model of how gold deposits are formed by fluids circulating through ancient mountain belts in areas where plates of the Earth's crust once collided. Recently, Kerrich led a $1 million research project for a consortium of fourteen Canadian mining companies. The four-year project used high-tech equipment to detect trace elements in rocks; results may help pinpoint ancient volcanic belts in the Canadian Shield likely to contain precious mineral resources such as gold. *Joe Ralko*

MINERAL RESOURCES.

Saskatchewan has a wealth of mineral resources and ranks fourth in Canada in terms of the value of mineral production. Saskatchewan's MINING history dates back to the mid-19th century, the same era when the homesteaders were arriving.

In 1857 the PALLISER EXPEDITION documented the presence of COAL seams in the Estevan area, and in 1859 GOLD was discovered in the NORTH SASKATCHEWAN RIVER by prospectors *en route* to the Cariboo gold rush in central British Columbia. Placer gold was extracted from the North Saskatchewan River between 1861 and 1918 using dredges and sluice boxes. Commercial coal production from underground operations in the Estevan area began in 1880. Other key events in Saskatchewan's mining history include: the first oil well, drilled at Fort Pelly in 1874; the first producing gas well, drilled at Belle Plaine in 1883; the earliest recorded clay production in 1886; the first significant gold discovery, made in 1913 at Amisk Lake—the staking rush that followed led to the discovery in 1915 of massive copper/zinc deposits straddling the border in the Flin Flon area, which are still being mined; the first attempts to recover SODIUM SULPHATE, made at Muskiki Lake in

1918; the first salt produced, near Senlac in 1920; a nickel, platinum, palladium deposit, discovered at Rottenstone Lake in 1928; gold and also pitchblende (**URANIUM** mineralization), discovered on the north shore of **LAKE ATHABASCA** and leading to the establishment of Goldfields in 1934; potash, discovered in an oil and gaswell near Radville in the early 1940s; uranium deposits, discovered in the Beaverlodge area in 1945 and leading to the development of the Uranium City area; a 1948 report of **DIAMONDS** found in an area between Prince Albert and Flin Flon (the discovery was never verified); the first underground potash mine, developed in 1958 just east of Saskatoon; high grade uranium deposits, first discovered in the Athabasca Basin in 1968; the first gold production from the La Ronge belt, in 1987 at Star Lake; and the first documented discovery of kimberlite (host rock for diamonds) at Sturgeon Lake in 1988.

Saskatchewan produces about one-third of the world's supply of both potash and uranium, and extensive reserves for future production have been identified. With the discovery of one of the largest clusters of kimberlite bodies in the world, the province could also become a significant diamond producer. With the broad diversity of mineral commodities identified to date (Figure MR-1), Saskatchewan will continue to be a significant mining jurisdiction.

Philip Reeves

FURTHER READING: Saskatchewan Industry & Resources. 2003. *Geology, and Mineral and Petroleum Resources of Saskatchewan*. Regina: Saskatchewan Geological Survey Misc. Rept. 2003–7.

MINERS, VICTORIA "TORY" (1888–1956).

In 1913, a young schoolteacher from Ontario moved to Saskatchewan. Victoria, or "Tory," Miners played a vital role in changing the working conditions of female teachers in the province. She did this by starting a movement to improve compensation for women teachers; the initial goal was to advocate not only for equal pay, but also for sufficient pay. The formation of the Saskatoon Women Teachers' Association (SWTA) took place in 1915; by 1918, with Miners as president, the SWTA became the largest teachers' local in the province. In 1919 she was a delegate at the founding meeting of the Canadian Teachers' Federation; in 1924 she achieved another important milestone for educators by becoming the first female public school principal in Saskatoon. As well as working to acquire better pay for teachers, Miners also influenced teachers to advance their own education. Following her own encouragement to others, she completed a BEd in 1936 and an MEd in 1937. Victoria Miners retired from public school teaching in 1948, but continued to instruct at the College of Education in Saskatoon. She died in a car accident in Ontario in 1956. *Karen Zemlak*

MINIFIE, JAMES MACDONALD (1900–74).

James M. Minifie, one of Canada's most illustrious journalists, was born in Burton-on-Trent, England on 08 June 1900. After emigrating to Canada in 1909, the Minifie family homesteaded at Vanguard, near Swift Current. At the age of 16, Minifie joined the Canadian Army and served in Europe during **WORLD WAR I**. On his return, he attended Regina College and the **UNIVERSITY OF SASKATCHEWAN**, graduating in 1923. He then studied at Oxford as a Rhodes scholar, and at the Sorbonne in Paris.

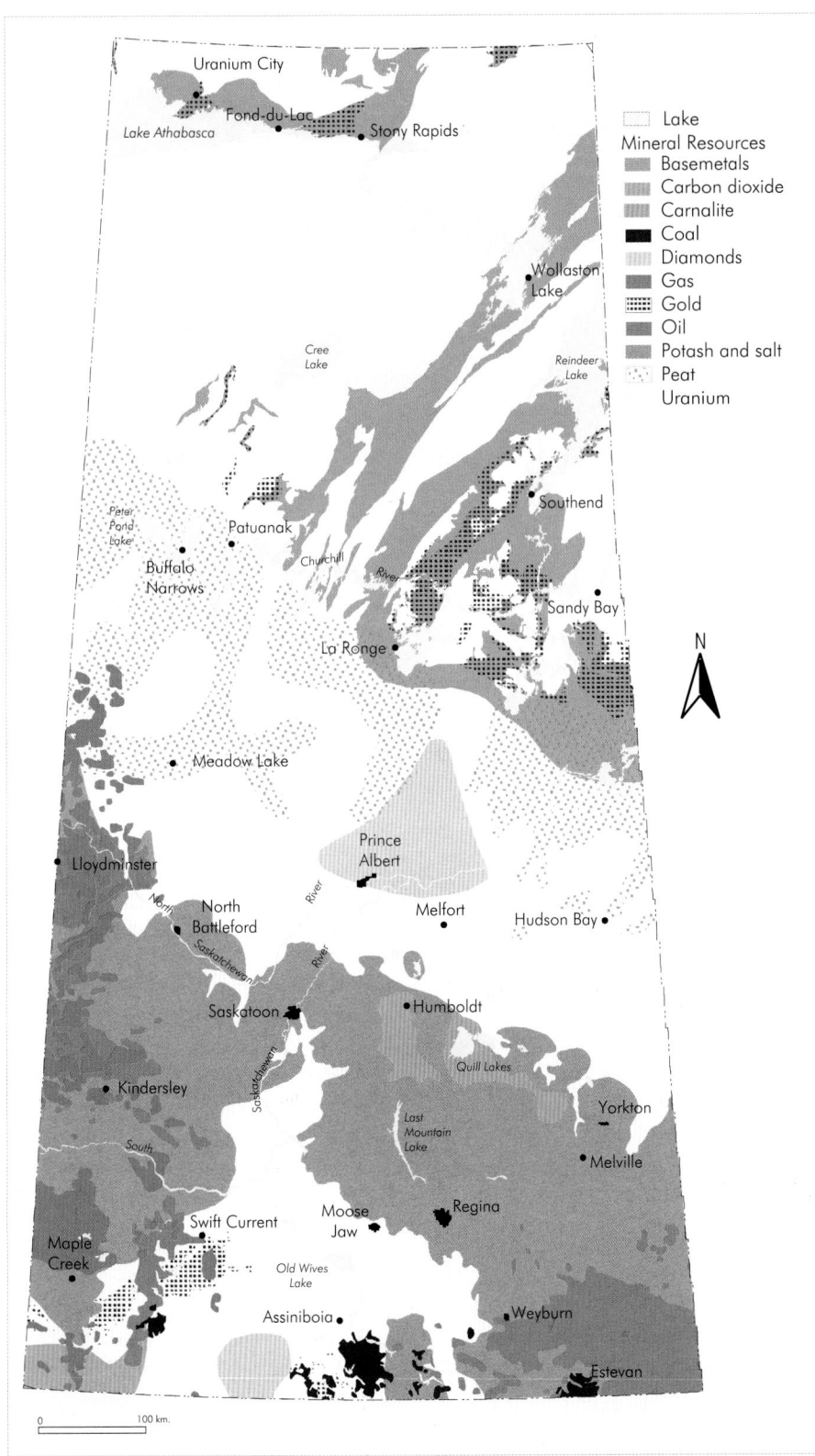

Lake
Mineral Resources
Basemetals
Carbon dioxide
Carnalite
Coal
Diamonds
Gas
Gold
Oil
Potash and salt
Peat
Uranium

Figure MR-1. Mineral resource map of Saskatchewan.

In 1929, Minifie joined the *New York Herald Tribune*, subsequently becoming its Paris correspondent. During **WORLD WAR II**, Minifie reported from London. While watching an air raid, an explosion cost him an eye. He was transferred to Washington, where he joined the Office of Strategic Services. After the war, Minifie joined the CBC as its Washington correspondent. First on radio, then on television, he built up a devoted following of listeners and viewers. He wrote several highly regarded books before being overtaken by illness in 1968. He later moved to Victoria, BC where he died June 13, 1974.

Mark Vajcner

FURTHER READING: James M. Minifie. 1964. *Open at the Top: Reflections on US-Canada Relations.* Toronto: McClelland and Stewart; —. 1976. *Expatriate.* Toronto: Macmillan.

MINING. Mining is the third largest industry in Saskatchewan. Many of the earliest instances of mining date back to the late 1800s. Since that time the province has made tremendous advances in mineral exploration, making Saskatchewan the third largest, non-fuel, mineral and **COAL** producing province in the country. With the total value of mineral sales in 2002 in excess of $2.4 billion, mining accounts for approximately 11% of Saskatchewan's gross domestic product. On an international scale, Saskatchewan is the largest potash and **URANIUM** producer in the world, supplying approximately 30% of the world's potash and 34% of the production of uranium. Reserves of potash are found across the southern plains of the province, and large deposits of uranium have been located in McArthur River, Cigar Lake, Rabbit Lake, McClean Lake, Cluff Lake and Key Lake.

Minerals mined in the province include copper, zinc, **GOLD**, lead, cadmium, platinum group metals, rare earths, nickel, silver and selenium. Saskatchewan is also home to many exploratory **DIAMOND** projects. On an industrial level, **SODIUM SULPHATE**, silica sand, clay, peat and salt are all being mined for various uses. Saskatchewan receives extensive economic benefits from the mining industry. In 2003, approximately 5,000 jobs in the industry and an additional 11,000 indirect jobs were dependent on mining in the province, and the industry pays in excess of $250 million in royalties and taxes. From 1987 to 1998 there was more than $10 billion invested into the Saskatchewan industry.

Julie L. Parchewski

MISSOURI COTEAU. The Missouri Coteau, hereafter called "the Coteau," is a narrow band of prairie upland that stretches from southern Saskatchewan to South Dakota. In Saskatchewan, the Coteau is a hummocky, pothole-dotted grassland underlain by thick glacial sediments. Approximately 15 to 40 km

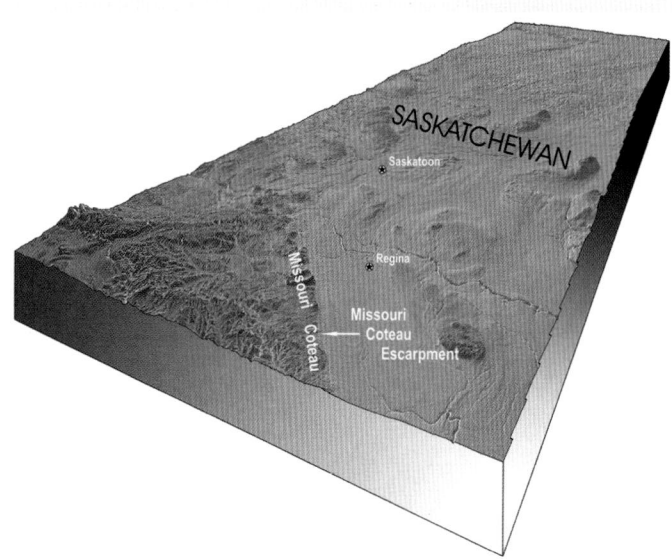

Three-dimensional colour shaded-relief digital elevation model showing the approximate location of the Missouri Coteau.

in width, it is bordered on the east by a prominent linear escarpment, and on the west by undulating topography and thinner glacial sediments. Throughout history, vistas of the Coteau's shimmering blue eastern slope have caught the attention of Aboriginal hunters, cattle ranchers and sightseers. Located in Saskatchewan's driest ecosystem, the Coteau is home to a diverse community of well-adapted wildlife and vegetation. Each spring, snowmelt fills innumerable ponds that become home and habitat to great numbers of incoming ducks, shore and wading birds, whose April and May arrivals are followed by flocks of grassland songbirds.

The origin of the Coteau lies deep below its grassy surface. Geophysical studies reveal linear structures in 2-billion-year-old crystalline rocks that underlie the Coteau at depths of 3 km. Above these ancient basement rocks, steep faults associated with basement structures penetrate hundreds of metres of sedimentary rock that began forming 550 million years ago—long and linear faults leaving their stamp on the Coteau's origin, location and appearance. During the Mesozoic era, the earth beneath the Coteau heaved and subsided in response to deep crustal forces. Nearly a kilometre of alternating up and down movement occurred during this 200-million-year period. The most recent upward crustal motions, beginning approximately 30 million years ago, created a regional highland that extends from the Coteau to the **CYPRESS HILLS** in southwest Saskatchewan. It was during this time that surface erosion formed the Missouri Coteau escarpment, which gradually eroded westward to its present position.

The Coteau we see today has been shaped by several glaciations. During the last glacial maximum, beginning about 25,000 years ago, the advancing ice eroded clay-rich sediment from older glacial deposits and bedrock. Flowing southward, the ice front encountered the pre-glacial Missouri Coteau escarpment, which deflected ice flow toward the southeast. At the same time, the glacier's momentum thrust huge slabs of sediment-laden ice onto high ground south of the escarpment. As glacier ice melted from the highlands, more than 60 m of sediments were deposited as hills and ridges, typifying the Coteau topography. The ensuing postglacial climate dictated the type of soil, vegetation, water resources, wildlife and land use we see today.

Lynden Penner

MISTAWASIS FIRST NATION. The **CREE** ancestors of the Mistawasis Band migrated from the woodlands of eastern Manitoba and the Great Lakes of Ontario. Chief Mistawasis, leader of a group of Cree known as the "House People," spoke strongly in favour of **TREATY 6**, signing it on August 23, 1876. In 1878 a well-wooded area, with hay meadows, rich farmland and good water was surveyed at Snake Plains. The Green Lake Trail (used for freighting from Fort Carlton to Green Lake) ran through the middle of the reserve, providing easy access to outside markets. This trail was used until the 1950s, and was then replaced by graded roads. The first school was built in 1878; the band also requested that a Presbyterian mission be established on their reserve, in part a result of their friendship with Reverend Mackay. In 2001 the band successfully settled a claim concerning land that had been surrendered in 1911, 1917, and 1919; and in addition to purchasing more land they were able to initiate new venues of economic development. The 12,544.3-ha reserve is situated 68 km north of Prince Albert, and operates an administration center, a health station, a school and a daycare. Currently 1,029 of the 2,119 band members live on reserve.   *Christian Thompson*

MITCHELL, CHARLES STUART (1909–86). An authority in rural municipal affairs, Charles Mitchell was born in Preeceville on April 5, 1909. He became interested in community activities at an early age and was first elected to the Rural Municipality of Preeceville in 1957. Three years later, he joined the executive of the **SASKATCHEWAN ASSOCIATION OF RURAL MUNICIPALITIES** (SARM) and subsequently served as vice-president and president. Mitchell's leadership role in SARM led to several other commitments on rural executives, councils, and boards such as the provincial Advisory Council on Transportation. In addition, he was an active member of the **SASKATCHEWAN WHEAT POOL** for over four decades and was instrumental in establishing the Sturgis Cooperative Farm in 1944. Charles Mitchell received the Order of Canada in 1979. He died on January 9, 1986.

MITCHELL, JOHN (1897–1955). John Mitchell, born in 1897 in Bradwardine, Manitoba, moved to Saskatchewan as a youngster. His family farmed in a small rural community 30 km from the railway at Marsden. He enrolled in the College of Agriculture at the **UNIVERSITY OF SASKATCHEWAN** in 1915, interrupting his studies to serve in the Canadian Expeditionary Forces from 1916 until 1918. He saw action in France as an officer in the artillery division and, wounded in 1917, he returned home. Mitchell completed his Bachelor of Science in Agriculture in 1924 and joined the **SASKATCHEWAN SOIL SURVEY** that same year. While a student, he had worked summers with the Soldiers' Settlement Board, assisting returning veterans to become farmers. In 1925, he became an instructor in the College of Agriculture and continued his work mapping **SOILS** and measuring their chemical and physical properties. He did graduate work at the University of Wisconsin, then one of the leading universities in soil science, completing an MSc in 1929 and a PhD in 1931 before returning to the University of Saskatchewan. He was appointed professor and Head of the Department of Soils in 1935, positions that he held for the rest of his career.

Mitchell was regarded internationally as a distinguished scientist. His papers dealt with topics as diverse as comparative ratings of Saskatchewan soils or the use of radioactive forms of phosphorus to determine the proportion of phosphorus taken up by plants. Soil Survey Report No. 12, covering most of southern Saskatchewan and written with Harold Moss and J.S. Clayton, is not only a highly readable description of the soils and how they formed, but gives ratings of their productivity. John Mitchell gave presentations on the themes of soil, scientifically based agriculture, stewardship of the land, and

good citizenship; for many years he gave radio addresses on the CFQC farm broadcast. He was the first president of the Saskatchewan Agricultural Graduates Association, and figures in the Saskatchewan Agricultural Hall of Fame. The John Mitchell Building, once the Soils and Dairy Building and presently the home of the Department of Drama, recognizes his contribution to the University of Saskatchewan. John Mitchell died in 1955.

Darwin Anderson

MITCHELL, JONI (1943–). Joni Mitchell (*née* Roberta Joan Anderson) is one of the foremost singer/songwriters of the post-Beatles generation. In a career of over thirty years, she has produced fifteen original albums, a collaborative project with jazz great Charles Mingus, two concert albums, two compilations, a collection of standards, and a retrospective collection of songs in orchestral arrangements. Her song writing, in its originality, adventurousness, and technical polish, has had great influence on musicians from many different backgrounds, including country, jazz, and r&b. Mitchell and her music have acquired iconic resonance within North American popular culture as the voice of a sensitive, self-exploratory intellectual bohemianism, associated with the visionary ideals of the 1960s youth movement.

Roberta Joan Anderson was born on November 7, 1943, in Fort Macleod, Alberta, where her father was stationed at an Air Force base. At the end of the war, the family moved to her mother's home province of Saskatchewan. Joan's early childhood was spent in Maidstone and North Battleford. Formal piano lessons were a disappointment, discouraging creativity and enforcing discipline through knuckle rapping. She contracted polio in 1953; the disease left her with a weak left hand. Months of convalescence encouraged her to develop an active imagination. When she was 11, the family settled in Saskatoon. In school, she showed special

JAY BLAKESBERG PHOTO
Joni Mitchell.

talent in visual art and in poetry, respelling her name Joni for its visual effect as a signature. A job at the Louis Riel coffee house led to contacts with folk musicians and her first singing engagements. In 1963, Joni entered the Alberta College of Art in Calgary, earning money by playing on the folk club circuit in the western provinces. After a year she left for Toronto, where she struggled to make a living as a folksinger and was compelled to give up a daughter, born in 1965, for adoption. Soon after, she married Chuck Mitchell and moved to his native Detroit, where the two performed and toured as a folk duo, while Joni began to gain attention as a songwriter. In 1967 she left her failing marriage and moved to New York, where she built up a following as a solo artist, touring Canada and the United States and making connections with established figures such as Judy Collins and Leonard Cohen. Through a contact with David Crosby, she moved to southern California late in 1967 and secured a recording contract with Warner Brothers.

From 1968 to 1979, Mitchell released one studio album almost every year. She enjoyed enormous commercial success in the early 1970s (peaking with *Court and Spark*, 1974); but her serious and independent artistic temperament set her increasingly at odds with the economic pressures and mass audience of the music industry. Some of her best known songs ("Both Sides, Now," "Woodstock") were made famous by other artists. Her musical style has evolved dynamically over time, incorporating a range of influences from folk, jazz, and rock'n'roll to African drumming and synthesized sampling. Her persona has also changed from album to album: flower child, confessional soul-searcher, social critic, seasoned raconteur. From the beginning, Mitchell produced her own albums, performing on guitar, dulcimer, and keyboards, and adding instrumental highlights like careful brushstrokes. In writing for the guitar, she has experimented with alternate tunings perhaps more than any other artist. Through highly sophisticated harmony and accompanimental figuration, as well as profound, intricately patterned lyrics, she elevated the pop song genre to the level of art song. Recurring themes include the conflict between love and independence, social nonconformity, and the journey quest. Mitchell has speculated in interviews on the possible influence of the plains landscape on her song writing aesthetic. She has referred to her Canadian childhood in many songs.

The *Mingus* album (1979) was simultaneously a high point in her progressive artistic evolution and a risky genre-crossing move that took its toll in lost fans and airplay. In 1983, Mitchell married bassist Larry Klein, who has co-produced her albums since that time. After a decade of obscurity, she returned to critical and popular success with *Night Ride Home* (1991). She began a new relationship in

1994 with Donald Freed, a songwriter from Saskatchewan. In 1997, Mitchell's family expanded when she was reunited with her birth-daughter, Kilauren Gibb. Throughout her career, Mitchell has also been active as a painter, creating the cover art for most of her albums; a retrospective exhibition was mounted in 2000 at the **MENDEL ART GALLERY** in Saskatoon. Since the 1990s, Mitchell has received numerous prestigious awards for artistic achievement–among them the *Billboard* Century Award, Sweden's Polar Music Prize, the ASCAP Founders Award, and the Governor-General's Performing Arts Award. *Lloyd Whitesell*

FURTHER READING: O'Brien, K. 2001. *Shadows and Light: Joni Mitchell*. London: Virgin Books.

MITCHELL, KEN (1940–). Kenneth Ronald Mitchell, one of Saskatchewan's best-known writers and playwrights, was born in Moose Jaw on December 13, 1940. He attended the Ryerson Polytechnical Institute and is a graduate of the **UNIVERSITY OF SASKATCHEWAN**, Regina Campus (precursor to the **UNIVERSITY OF REGINA**). During his university years, Mitchell wrote for the *Regina Leader-Post* and served as editor of the university newspaper, *The Carillon*.

The prairies and their people make up a continual topic of Mitchell's work. His first novel, *Wandering Rafferty* (1972), was set in Regina's beer parlour circuit. Successive novels and plays have told stories of foreign spies, confidence men, **TOMMY DOUGLAS**, and Norman Bethune. Mitchell's first stage play, *Heroes*, was first presented in England in 1972. Since then, it has been produced over fifty times in Canada, the United States, Europe, New Zealand, and Turkey. In total, Mitchell's body of work includes over twenty books and a score of stage plays. He has written for television and film, and his poems, stories and articles have been published in a variety of anthologies and collections.

For one of his better known works, *Cruel Tears* (1975), Mitchell took inspiration from William Shakespeare, writing a script based on *Othello*. This was set to music, creating a Canadian opera using contemporary country and western music. It became one of the first plays from the prairies to receive critical praise on the national level. His work in film includes *The Hounds of Notre Dame* (1981); the screenplay for this story of a small hockey town was nominated for a Genie award.

Mitchell has taught English at the University of Regina since 1967. He has held numerous visiting professorships in Canada, the United Kingdom, and China. From 1970 to 1975, he was director of creative writing at the Saskatchewan Summer School of the Arts.

Mitchell has played an active role on the Canadian literary scene. In 1969, he helped establish the **SASKATCHEWAN WRITERS' GUILD** and served as its first chairman. He was the founding editor of the prairie literary magazine, *Grain*, and helped establish the Saskatchewan Playwrights Centre in 1982. In recognition of his work in the literary arts, Mitchell was appointed a member of the Order of Canada in 1999 and received the Saskatchewan Order of Merit in 2001. *Mark Vajcner*

FURTHER READING: Currie, Robert (ed.). 1984. *Ken Mitchell Country*. Regina: Coteau Books; Kerr, Don and Diane Bessai (eds.). 1992. *Rebels in Time: Three Plays by Ken Mitchell*. Edmonton: NeWest Press; Mitchell, Ken. 1972. *Wandering Rafferty*. Toronto: Macmillan.

MITCHELL, MARJORIE (1948–83). Born on August 27, 1948, in Oxbow, Marjorie Mitchell skipped the Canadian women's curling team to its first Ladies' World Curling Championship in 1980. The Mitchell rink included Nancy Kerr, Shirley McKendry, and Wendy Leach from the Caledonian Curling Club in Regina. Having won the Saskatchewan play downs, the foursome went on to capture the Canadian title and later represented Canada in the world championship in Perth, Scotland. The Mitchell rink was inducted into the **SASKATCHEWAN SPORTS HALL OF FAME** in 1981. Mitchell served as chairperson of the first Scott Tournament of Hearts held in Regina in 1983. Shortly after the event she learned she had cancer, and died on October 18, 1983. The Marj Mitchell Award, established in 1998, is presented each year to the curler who best embodies the spirit of the game at the Scott Tournament of Hearts. The Marj

REGINA LEADER-POST

Marj Mitchell.

Mitchell Foundation was also created in her honour to promote curling at the junior high and high school levels. *Bob Ivanochko and Holden Stoffel*

MITCHELL, W.O. (1914–98). William Ormond Mitchell is best remembered for *Who Has Seen the Wind* and the *Jake and the Kid* stories which grew out of and defined the Saskatchewan prairie. He was born on March 13, 1914, in Weyburn. Two events in his early life indelibly marked him and, he claimed, made him a writer. When he was seven his father died, and his memory of this event was the genesis for his first novel, *Who Has Seen the Wind*, a lyrical work knit together by recurring motifs of birth and death. The second pivotal event occurred in 1926 when he contracted bovine tuberculosis of the wrist and was withdrawn from school. Forced in upon himself, he often wandered alone on the prairies, becoming acutely attuned to the "poetry of earth and sky." Out of this grew his remarkable ability to describe the prairie in all its moods. As one of the first Canadian writers to valorize his own region, he paved the way for others to write about their own place and people. The prairie landscape and what he called "the energy of death" are central to his exploration of loneliness and, most importantly, the bridging of one human to another. To cure his tubercular wrist, he and his family spent the winters from 1927 to 1931 in California and Florida; however, each summer they returned to Saskatchewan to spend time at their cottage at White Bear Lake. There he met Sheepskin, the Assiniboine chief of the reserve, and developed a sympathy for Native peoples which later led to his concern for the Stoneys of the Alberta foothills and inspired his novel *The Vanishing Point* (1973).

From 1931 to 1934, he studied philosophy at the University of Manitoba. After two years taking courses in journalism and play writing at the University of Washington, he landed in Alberta in the middle of the **DEPRESSION**. For the next four years he survived by selling magazine subscriptions, encyclopedias, insurance and radio advertisements, even doing a high-dive clown act for a carnival. He completed his BA at the University of Alberta, obtained a teaching certificate, and began writing seriously. His first two published short stories in *Maclean's* and *Queen's Quarterly* (1942) showed his talent for both the humorous and the more philosophically serious. That same year, he married Merna Hirtle.

In 1945, after two years of teaching, Mitchell moved to High River in the foothills of Alberta, where he turned to freelancing and completed *Who Has Seen the Wind* (published simultaneously in Canada and the United States in 1947), reviewed as one of the best Canadian novels ever written. From 1948 to 1951, Mitchell lived in Toronto where he was fiction editor for Maclean's. There he began to

SASKATCHEWAN ARCHIVES BOARD R-B6144

W.O. Mitchell conducting a class in short story writing at the "Writer and Drama Workshop" held at the Valley Center, Fort Qu'Appelle, in August 1956. Mitchell is reviewing a composition submitted by one of the students.

write the *Jake and the Kid* radio series for CBC (1950–56). Drawing on the oral narrative tradition of the prairies, he produced over 200 episodes about a hired man, a fatherless boy and his mother who live on a farm near the fictional town of Crocus, Saskatchewan. His humorous portrayal of Crocus and its eighty citizens entered the imaginations of Canadians across the country, and at the height of its success the series was described as Canadian culture in the making. Mitchell adapted the stories for a CBC television series (1961), but his most successful television plays were *The Devil's Instrument* (CBC, 1962) and *Back to Beulah* (CBC, 1974), which won the ACTRA award for best script. Similarly Mitchell exploited his *Jake and the Kid* material for the stage. His first play was a one-act adaptation of *The Day Jake Made Her Rain* for the drama workshop at Fort Qu'Appelle (1953). *Royalty is Royalty*, premiered by the Greystone Players of Saskatoon in 1959, was his first full-length play; based on *Jake and the Kid* stories about the visit of the Queen to Crocus, it was later adapted as the musical, *Wild Rose* (1967). The most popular of his nine plays, *The Black Bonspiel of Wullie MacCrimmon*, was first performed by Regina's Stoneboat Theatre in 1976.

Mitchell thought of himself as a teacher as well as a writer, and devoted much of his time to working with developing writers. In his first writing workshop in 1952 at Fort Qu'Appelle for the SASKATCHEWAN ARTS BOARD, he began teaching his "freefall" process, a spontaneous gathering of sensory and autobiographical fragments which go into the making of stories. He later established the creative writing program at the Banff Centre, which he headed from 1974 to 1986; and from 1968 to 1986, he held five writer-in-residencies at universities

across Canada. In 1968, the Mitchells moved to Calgary. By this time he had become one of the most publicly recognized authors in Canada, and was sought after to perform readings from his novels and from semi-autobiographical tales such as "Melvin Arbuckle's First Course in Shock Therapy" and "Take a Giant Step." These pieces became the genesis for the highly successful *How I Spent My Summer Holidays* (1981), a dark sequel to *Who Has Seen the Wind*, in which Mitchell returned to his prairie and Weyburn community roots. These two books, along with *The Vanishing Point*, established him as one of Canada's most accomplished novelists.

Mitchell was honoured by his home province, receiving his first honorary degree from the UNIVERSITY OF SASKATCHEWAN, Regina Campus (1972) and the Lifetime Award for Excellence in the Arts from the Saskatchewan Arts Board (1989). He received two Stephen Leacock Awards for humour and a further eight honorary degrees; he was also made an Officer of the Order of Canada in 1973, and named to the Queen's Privy Council in 1993. Mitchell died in Calgary on February 25, 1998. He will be remembered as the writer who put the Saskatchewan prairie on the literary map of Canada; but, recalling his Weyburn roots and the words inscribed on his father's gravestone, he expressed a wish that he too would be remembered as a caring, honourable man, "Loved by all who knew him."

Barbara and Ormond Mitchell

FURTHER READING: Latham, S. and D. Latham (eds.). 1997. *Magic Lies: The Art of W.O. Mitchell*. Toronto: University of Toronto Press; Mitchell, B. and O. Mitchell. 1999. *W.O.: The Life of W.O. Mitchell, Beginnings to Who Has Seen the Wind*. Toronto: McClelland and Stewart.

MITCHELL FAMILY. The Mitchell family of Saskatoon has a longtime association with the meat processing industry in Saskatchewan. The founding of the family company, Mitchell's Gourmet Foods Inc. (formerly Intercontinental Packers Ltd.), can be traced to the early 1800s, when the Mendel family of Westphalia, Germany, opened a successful meat-packing business. Decades later, Robert Mendel started an international canned ham business, packing and selling his product across Europe and the United States. In 1940, Robert's son FRED MENDEL left the family's European operations and imported the canned ham business to Saskatoon, where it later became Intercontinental Packers. Fred's daughter, Johanna Mitchell, was appointed director, and later president, of the new company. In 1976, Fred Mendel's grandson, Fred Mitchell, became the fifth generation to preside over the family company. Under his leadership Intercontinental Packers grew into one of the largest value-added pork processors in Canada. In 1986, Fred Mitchell launched the Mitchell's Gourmet Foods line of products; in 1998, Intercontinental Packers was renamed Mitchell's Gourmet Foods. That same year, Fred Mitchell passed away unexpectedly, leaving the company to his widow, LuAn Mitchell. LuAn led Mitchell's Gourmet Foods through a remarkable growth period, earning herself recognition as one of Canada's top female entrepreneurs. In 2002, LuAn sold her interest in the company to the Schneider Corporation. *Iain Stewart*

FURTHER READING: Block, Sheri. 2004. "Mitchell-Halter Aims to pass on Secrets of Success," *Regina Leader-Post* (March 8): B3.

MOCK SUNS: *see* SUN-DOGS

MOLLARD, J.D. (1924–). Born on a farm near Watrous, Saskatchewan, in 1924, Jack Mollard is an internationally honoured engineer, geoscientist, teacher, author, and consultant. A graduate of the UNIVERSITY OF SASKATCHEWAN, he began in 1947 a lifelong passion for interpreting the earth's physical geography, its natural resources and its geo-environment from 3-D air photos and, later, satellite images. Since opening a Regina-based consulting office in 1956, Mollard has led a small group of interdisciplinary specialists on some 5,000 projects on six continents and Mars. He takes delight in searching for hidden gravel and groundwater sources, spotting and avoiding terrain hazards, locating dams to store runoff waters, discovering northern transportation routes, and prospecting for oil, gas and economic minerals, including DIAMONDS and GOLD.

Jack Mollard has published over 100 technical and scientific papers and two textbooks, and has presented over 100 short courses in Canada and the United States. A gifted and generous speaker, he rarely declines an invitation, whether from interna-

Jack Mollard, February 1989.

tional universities, technical conferences, the United Nations, First Nations, or boyscout troops. He has long been a mentor to fellow engineers and geoscientists, and is well known for his infectious enthusiasm and warm personality. *Lynden Penner*

MOLLOY, TOM (1883–1959). Thomas Mullen Molloy was born in Sydney, Nova Scotia on September 13, 1883. His father worked as a telegrapher at Clarke's Crossing on the SOUTH SASKATCHEWAN RIVER, near Batoche, and relocated to Brandon, Manitoba, where Thomas finished high school. He entered the printing trade and became active in the Typographer's Union. He worked as reporter as well as a typesetter in Brandon and Winnipeg. He reported on the street railway strike in Winnipeg in 1906, and was chosen by the workers

Tom Molloy at a Credit Union convention, June 1947.

to arbitrate the settlement. Molloy moved to Regina to work on Premier SCOTT's *Leader*. In 1907, as president of the Typographers' Union, he helped establish the Regina Trades and Labour Council and served as its president. Scott, also a former union typesetter, appointed Molloy as the fair wage officer to supervise the construction of the SASKATCHEWAN LEGISLATIVE BUILDING in 1909.

Molloy was appointed in 1911 as Commissioner of Labour in a new branch of the Agriculture department responsible for labour legislation. He became Deputy Minister of Railways, Labour and Industries in 1927. In this position he was involved behind the scenes in major incidents like the 1931 Bienfait Coal Miners' Strike and the 1935 ON-TO-OTTAWA TREK, and he administered unemployment relief during the DEPRESSION. He retired in 1940. Molloy assisted with the development of credit unions in Saskatchewan by developing legislation in 1937. With Harry Fowler, he helped organize the Regina Co-operative Savings and Credit Union, of which he was president from 1937 to 1940. He was elected president of the newly created Credit Union Federation of Saskatchewan from 1938 to 1952. He served on other local, national and international credit union organizations, and is recognized as the father of credit unions in Saskatchewan. Molloy died in Regina on April 6, 1959. *Bob Ivanochko*

FURTHER READING: Purden, C. 1980. *Agents for Change: Credit Unions in Saskatchewan*. Saskatoon: Credit Union Central.

MONTREAL LAKE CREE NATION. Following their move from Grand Rapids at the northwestern end of Lake Winnipeg to the Montreal Lake region in the mid-1800s, the band signed an adhesion to TREATY 6 on February 11, 1889, under Chief William Charles, and its reserve was surveyed at the southern end of Montreal Lake in 1890. The Little Red River Reserve, surveyed in 1897 for the joint agricultural use of the Montreal Lake and Lac La Ronge Bands, was divided between the two in 1948. Little Red River Reserve (106B) is situated 39 km north of Prince Albert and currently hosts a sub-office with a band hall, health centre, day care, group home, and confectionery/gas outlet. The first Hudson's Bay Company post, constructed at Montreal Lake in 1891 in response to the establishment of the reserve, became the freighting depot for goods coming in and going out of the region. Until the late 1920s band members found ready employment as labourers and suppliers. Horses gave way to caterpillars, and airplanes and trucks started arriving by the end of the 1920s. An all-weather road was completed in 1937; whereas it significantly reduced labour employment, it also created a niche in early tourism as summer tourists began flowing into Montreal Lake in significant numbers. Forestry, recreation,

and tourism remain important to the economy of the band. The Montreal Lake Development Corporation (1985) has four subsidiary band-owned companies, and shares with the Lac La Ronge and Peter Ballantyne bands in three others. The Montreal Lake, Little Red River, Timber Bay, and Weyakwin communities form the Montreal Lake Reserve (8,288.8 ha), on which 1,773 of the 3,108 band members live. *Christian Thompson*

Geraldine Moodie self-portrait.

MOODIE, GERALDINE (1854–1945). Geraldine Moodie (*née* Fitzgibbon) was a pioneering woman photographer in the North-West Territories, best known for her work with Aboriginal peoples. Born in Toronto on October 31, 1854, to Agnes and Charles Fitzgibbon, she married John Douglas Moodie in England in 1878. Later returning to Canada, the Moodies briefly farmed in Manitoba, then moved to Ottawa, and in 1885 her husband received a commission with the North-West Mounted Police. They had six children.

Initially a watercolourist, Moodie soon focused upon photography. She established studios in Battleford (1891–96), Maple Creek (1897–1900), and Medicine Hat (1897). Subjects were diverse: portraiture, the North-West Mounted Police, First Nations, ranching, and wildflowers. In 1895, the Prime Minister commissioned her to photograph sites related to the NORTH-WEST RESISTANCE. In 1904–05 and 1906–09 she joined her husband in the eastern Arctic and adjacent Hudson's Bay District, and photographed the Inuit and First Nations, as well as the flora. Many images are preserved in the collections of the British Museum and National Archives of Canada.

Moodie continued her work during her husband's subsequent postings, which included Regina

(1910–11). Upon his retirement in 1917, they settled at their ranch in the CYPRESS HILLS, later going to Maple Creek and then British Columbia (1936). She died on October 4, 1945, in Alberta, and is buried in Calgary. *Donny White*

FURTHER READING: White, D. 1998. *In Search of Geraldine Moodie*. Regina: Canadian Plains Research Center.

MOOSE JAW. Moose Jaw, pop 32,131, is the province's fourth largest city. It is located 175 km north of the US border, nestled in a picturesque valley where the Moose Jaw River and Thunder Creek River meet. Moose Jaw is connected to three major highways, the CANADIAN PACIFIC RAILWAY mainline and a branch line of the CANADIAN NATIONAL RAILWAY, and is served by two bus lines. It is governed by a mayor and six aldermen elected at large. Moose Jaw was originally settled as a traditional Indian fur traders' camp at the "Turn" (known as Kingsway Park today) for both CREE and ASSINIBOINE nations, and there are burial grounds in the vicinity. It is thought that Moose Jaw derives its name from a Cree word meaning "warm breeze"; another explanation is that is was named after the local creek, which resembled the outline of a moose's jawbone. In July 1881, JAMES ROSS and Hector Sutherland registered the town site with the Dominion government and organized a permanent settlement, which began in 1882 when James Ross and his party of four arrived from Winnipeg on January 2. The Canadian Pacific Railway chose the juncture of Moose Jaw and Thunder Creek for a divisional point, and by the spring of 1883 the population had increased rapidly.

By 1885, Moose Jaw was a major settlement. In addition to the homesteading population and railway workers, Sioux who had retreated with SITTING BULL after the battle of the Little Big Horn settled in an adjacent village located in Kingsway Park, now known as Connor's Park. In the summer of 1885, the Dominion government sent 390 soldiers from Halifax to Moose Jaw to guard supplies and communication routes; they aided in suppressing the NORTH-WEST RESISTANCE led by LOUIS RIEL and GABRIEL DUMONT. A major fire in 1891 wiped out seventeen businesses and a church on Main Street; this incident, coupled with earlier fires, caused the town to make brick or stone construction mandatory: this is part of the reason why there are so many early red brick heritage properties today in downtown Moose Jaw. In 1903 Moose Jaw gained city status; it became the wholesale distribution centre for a large trading area and began the processing of agricultural products. The city's growth was closely related to the expansion of cereal agriculture. Today, Moose Jaw is an agricultural service centre whose industries include agriculture, manufacturing, serv-

ice and retail. CFB Moose Jaw (15 Wing), first established as a training facility in 1941, is the largest jet training base in Canada and the city's largest employer.

The public library, art museum, a swimming pool and other recreational facilities are located in the heart of the city in Crescent Park. The SASKATCHEWAN INSTITUTE OF APPLIED SCIENCE AND TECHNOLOGY provides education to post-secondary students. The city is serviced by two cable companies, four radio stations, a daily newspaper (the *Moose Jaw Times Herald*), and a weekly newspaper (*Moose Jaw This Week*). The city has two main tourist attractions: the TEMPLE GARDENS Mineral Spa, which uses hot mineral water from an underground aquifer; and the Tunnels of Moose Jaw, where notorious gangster Al Capone supposedly ran his bootleg operation and Chinese immigrants hid and ran their laundry operations. *Daria Coneghan*

MOOSE JAW POLICE SERVICE. Moose Jaw hired its first police constable shortly after the town's incorporation, in 1884. In the early days, the position combined the duties of town constable with those of license inspector, and in 1899, the constable also served as the chief of the volunteer fire brigade. The rapid growth of Moose Jaw in the early years of the 20th century changed policing, however, as it did in all the urban centres of western Canada, and in 1905 Chief Johnson was hired to meet these new challenges: he both expanded and reorganized the police department.

The first motorized vehicle was purchased in 1911 and a second police vehicle was purchased in 1920. During the 1950s, police cars were equipped with two-way radios and in the early 1960s, a Traffic Unit was established complete with a "state of the art" radar system. In the late 1970s, a Crime Prevention Unit was established to be more community-friendly and proactive in recognition of newly embraced contemporary policing methods, and the

first female officer was hired in 1981. The intent of these changes was to have the community take greater ownership of its problems. The 1998 community survey conducted by the current chief of police, Terry Coleman, clearly indicated the residents of Moose Jaw needed a closer relationship with the police service. This endorsed the concept of "community policing," which is now the strategy for conducting business. The Police Service presently has fifty-two police officers and twenty FTE support staff. *Terence Coleman*

MOOSE MOUNTAIN (49°47' 102°35'; Map sheet E/15). Moose Mountain is located in southeast Saskatchewan on Highway 9, about 15 km north of Carlyle. It forms a plateau covering approximately 13,000 km². Its maximum elevation is 830 metres, roughly 200 metres higher than the surrounding plains. Before the last continental GLACIATION, the upland was capped by Tertiary-age gravels. The advancing ice covered Moose Mountain, but once melting began the plateau was exposed as a drift-covered *nunatak* rising above the surrounding ice sheet. A short-lived PRO-GLACIAL LAKE (Lake Arcola) was formed along its southern edge by meltwaters trapped between the plateau and the encircling ice. Most of Moose Mountain is wooded with aspen, white birch, balsam poplar and green ash. Designated as a forest reserve under the Forest Reserves Act of 1906, its woods were exploited under the principles of "scientific forestry" and today it is one of only two Provincial Forests south of the Qu'Appelle River. As a wooded island in a prairie ecosystem, Moose Mountain hosts many bird and animal species more commonly found in the eastern deciduous forest or northern mixed-wood forests. It also has a number of rare plant species. The same environment that attracted woodland fauna also appealed to First Nations people, who built a large medicine wheel on the plateau. The White Bear Reserve was established in the southeast corner of

Moose Jaw Police Service, ca. 1930.

Moose Mountain under **TREATY 4**. Euro-Canadian settlers from the surrounding plains also utilized its natural resources for fuel, construction materials, hay and pasture.

Much of the area is now part of Moose Mountain Provincial Park, one of five original **PROVINCIAL PARKS** designated by the province in 1931. However, as far back as the 1880s settlers from the surrounding areas would come to Moose Mountain for recreation. Kenosee Lake, on the eastern side of the park, is the core area for recreational activities that include fishing, water sports, and hiking. This shallow lake, fed mainly by groundwater, fluctuates considerably in depth. South of the park boundary the area around White Bear Lake, in the White Bear Indian Reserve, has also been developed for more profit-oriented recreational ventures including a resort village, casino and golf course. Its proximity to Regina makes the park a favourite destination, and it is one of the most heavily used of all provincial parks. Named for wildlife sometimes found in the area, the "mountain" designation is clearly an exaggeration for this area of low hills rising above the Saskatchewan Plain. *Marilyn Lewry*

FURTHER READING: Sauchyn, D. 1988. "Field Trip Guide to the Moose Mountain Area." In A. Paul and R.W. Widdis (eds.), *Regina Geographical Paper. No. 5: The Moose Mountain Papers.* Regina: Department of Geography, University of Regina.

MOOSOMIN, town, pop 2,361, located 16 km W of the Saskatchewan-Manitoba border at the junction of Hwys 1 and 8. Settlers, mostly of English and Scottish origin, began arriving in the Moosomin area around 1881 in advance of the **CPR**'s push westward across the plains. The Moosomin post office was established in the fall of 1882, the name being derived from the **CREE** word for the "mooseberry," or high bush cranberry. By 1884, the community boasted five hotels, five general stores, two blacksmiths, two livery stables, nine implement dealers, a doctor, a lawyer, and a butcher. Additionally, a newspaper was established that year, which evolved into the *World-Spectator*, still publishing. Prior to the development of railroad branch lines, Moosomin served an area reaching from the **QU'APPELLE VALLEY** to the **SOURIS RIVER** district. With far-flung points throughout the North-West, stagecoaches provided communications as well as freight and passenger transit; Bertram Tennyson, the Poet Laureate's nephew, was one of the drivers. It may be that no other town in the eastern North-West Territories sent so many homesteaders and businessmen out onto the plains. In 1905, when the province of Saskatchewan came into being, Moosomin's population was already around 1,000 and growing. Moosomin's economy is largely tied to the region's agricultural industry, which has long consisted of

mixed farming. Other significant area employers are: the PCS Rocanville mine; TransCanada Pipelines, which has a pumping station northeast of Moosomin; the Government of Saskatchewan, which has several regional offices in the community; and the **OIL AND GAS INDUSTRY**, which has been making incursions into the region. In recent years, the Moosomin Moose, a recreational hockey team, raised over $500,000 toward the construction of a new $20 million integrated health care facility that is scheduled to open in early 2007. The team played three marathon hockey games, each temporarily a world record—the last being 130 hours long. Gordon Thiessen, formerly Canada's chief banker and monetary policy maker as the governor of the Bank of Canada, is a Moosomin high school graduate. Another of the community's notable citizens was General **ANDREW GEORGE LATTA MCNAUGHTON**. An army officer, scientist, and diplomat, he was born in Moosomin in 1887 and went on to become the president of the National Research Council of Canada, the senior Canadian officer in the United Kingdom during **WORLD WAR II**, and the Canadian Minister of National Defence; he was also the Canadian representative on the United Nations Atomic Energy Commission, and president of the Atomic Energy Control Board of Canada. *David McLennan*

MOOSOMIN FIRST NATION. In 1876, representatives of the federal government and the **CREE** of central Saskatchewan entered into **TREATY 6**. Yellow Sky and his band were not present for the negotiations, but in the spring of 1881 Yellow Sky's headman, Moosomin, signed an adhesion to the treaty. Yellow Sky was recognized as chief of Moosomin's band until 1884, when Indian Commissioner **DEWDNEY** appointed the latter as chief. A reserve was surveyed near Battleford in the spring of 1881. In 1903 the Canadian Northern Railway main line was constructed through the reserve, providing employment for band members and access to markets for their produce. Unfortunately it also attracted the interest of local settlers and politicians, and in June 1909 the reserve was surrendered and the band members relocated near Cochin. Disheartened by the poor quality of the new reserve, the band never recovered its economic stability. In 1986 it submitted a claim arguing that the surrender was invalid, and after years of negotiation the claim was ratified in 2003. The 1,343 band members now hold a total of 74,450.2 ha; of the 915 people on reserve, the majority live approximately 32 km north of North Battleford. The money received as part of the settlement has enabled the band to develop an educational trust and invest for the future. *Christian Thompson*

MORAN, PATRICK JOSEPH (1925–). Born in Calgary on July 22, 1925, Patrick Moran left an indelible mark on Regina's Wascana Centre, a 930-

ha parkland development. A graduate of the University of Alberta, Moran was hired as horticultural director of Wascana Centre in 1962 and promoted to executive director four years later. Until his retirement in 1987, Moran helped Wascana Centre acquire its reputation as one of North America's most beautiful landscaped parks. He has also been involved in numerous cultural societies and has volunteered his time to local organizations and missions in the developing world. Moran was made a Member of the Order of Canada in 1993.

REGINA LEADER-POST

Gerry Morin.

MORIN, GERALD (1961–). Gerald Morin, born in 1961 in Green Lake, Saskatchewan, is a **MÉTIS** politician and lawyer, former president of the **MÉTIS NATION–SASKATCHEWAN** (MNS) and the Métis National Council (MNC). Raised in Green Lake, a traditional Métis community, and heavily influenced by his grandfather Leon Morin, he decided in grade school to dedicate his life to advancing Métis rights. While attending Law School at the **UNIVERSITY OF SASKATCHEWAN**, he was president of the Native Law Students Association of Canada. Having received his LLB in 1987, he was called to the Saskatchewan Bar in 1988. In 1989, after articling for a year, Morin entered politics and was first elected MNS provincial secretary and then, from 1992 to 1995, president. In this capacity he strengthened the bilateral process with the provincial government, and advanced a Métis rights agenda that included restoring the Métis' Aboriginal hunting and fishing rights and creating a permanent Métis land base in the province. In 1994, he was the main plaintiff for the northwest corner of Saskatchewan in the MNS's land claim filed against the federal and provincial governments. In 1993, Morin was elected MNC president, a position that he held until 2003. In this capacity he initiated the

"Métis Nation Agenda," which through strategic partnerships with government and, if necessary, litigation, attempted to provide the Métis with "Aboriginal" animal harvesting rights, properly honour LOUIS RIEL and the Métis' place in Confederation, establish a national Métis definition, enumeration and registry, and strengthen Métis self-government.

Darren R. Préfontaine

FURTHER READING: Teillet, J. 2004. *Métis Law Summary, 2004.* Vancouver: Pape & Salter.

MORRIS, GEORGE H. (1904–89). An innovative agriculturist, George Morris contributed to the development of efficient tillage equipment on the Canadian prairies. Born in Llewellyn, North-west Territories on July 1, 1904, Morris established his first farm implement business in Bangor and a few years later introduced his renowned rod-weeder. In 1960, the Morris Rod-Weeder factory was opened in Yorkton, and has since grown to be one of the largest manufacturers of specialized farm equipment in western Canada. Recognized for his contributions to industrial development, farming, and his community, Morris received an honorary doctorate from the UNIVERSITY OF SASKATCHEWAN. He was made an Officer of the Order of Canada in 1980 and was awarded the Saskatchewan Order of Merit in 1988. Morris died on July 21, 1989.

MORRIS INDUSTRIES. Morris Industries, established in 1929, manufactures and markets advanced air-seeding, tillage and hay-hauling equipment to agricultural producers around the world. The company was founded by GEORGE MORRIS in Yorkton after he had invented the world's first automatic trip, a device that "trips" over stones then lowers back into the ground to continue working.

The automatic trip allowed farmers working stony land to greatly increase the life of their tillage equipment. This breakthrough in engineering became an industry standard that is still used throughout the world.

Morris Industries now has over 260 independent dealers and distributors in Canada, the United States and Australia. The company also provides product and services to China, France, Germany, Jordan, New Zealand, Saudi Arabia, Tanzania and the Ukraine.

Morris offices are located in Yorkton, Saskatoon, Minnedosa, Manitoba, Minot, North Dakota, Belgrade, Montana and Toowoomba, Australia.

Morris has led the industry in recognizing the importance of soil conservation and machinery efficiency. The revolutionary Morris Seed-Rite hoe drill combines the functions of a cultivator, seed drill and rod weeder in a single implement. This dramatically reduced costs for farmers and helped prevent soil erosion and moisture loss.

Wendy Morris, daughter of the founder, became president in 1992 and continues to serve as chair of the company's board of directors. (See also AGRICULTURAL IMPLEMENT INDUSTRY)

Joe Ralko

MORRIS RODWEEDER STRIKE. One of the most significant working-class struggles in Saskatchewan history occurred in Yorkton. While the workers—members of the RETAIL, WHOLESALE AND DEPARTMENT STORE UNION (RWDSU)—finally prevailed, the struggle to organize and sign a collective agreement between the company and more than 300 employees at Morris Rodweeder was an epic one. Dozens of workers were fired; the company was charged with several unfair labour practices; and the workers faced almost unprecedented hostility from the company, other businesses, the media, politicians, and much of the general public. Working conditions, poor pay and indiscriminate firings were among the reasons the workers wanted a union. Talking was not allowed during working hours. There were no showers, no washrooms and no sick benefits. If a worker became ill and stayed home, he simply lost his pay. There was no job security, and employee turnover was extremely high.

RWDSU began a full-scale organizing drive in mid-September 1972, led by organizers Ken Engel and Chris Banting, under the direction of secretary-treasurer LEN WALLACE. Morris management countered by laying off fifty workers and firing two key union supporters. When the union filed an application for certification with the LABOUR RELATIONS BOARD, the Board ordered that a vote be held on February 1, 1973. The union lost by two votes. Right after the vote, RWDSU began a new organizing drive. Within forty-eight hours, a majority of workers signed new cards, but Morris management refused to recognize or bargain with the union. The union's actions also caused increased hostility within the community of Yorkton. A "Concerned Citizens Committee" was formed to exert pressure on the public and politicians. The owner of the plant, GEORGE MORRIS, was considered by many to be a model citizen because of his charitable donations to the community. On August 22, the Court of Appeals threw out a second bid by the company to decertify the union, but the company still refused to bargain.

Employee frustration finally erupted at 2 a.m. on August 27, 1973. Twenty-five welders staged a sit-down strike. Supervisors ordered forklift operators to drive their vehicles into the welding area, spewing black smoke and almost running over some workers. The welders responded by building ten-foot-high barricades. When the day shift arrived at 6 a.m., no one knew if they would join the strike. They unanimously did so.

As more shifts arrived, more workers became strikers and refused to work, despite threats by management and the RCMP. A request was made to

Attorney-General ROY ROMANOW that the Mounties be allowed to forcibly evict the strikers. He turned down the request. Police and management departed from the plant, leaving ten workers inside. During the night, management tried twice to get in through a skylight, but retreated when they were met with a hail of metal parts. After ten days, management finally agreed to bargain and the workers ended their occupation. This first contract was far from ideal, and it would take another week-long strike in January 1977 before the workers received somewhat better wages and working conditions. *Clare Powell*

MORRISON, FRANCES (1918–). Born on September 28, 1918, in Saskatoon, Morrison received a Bachelor of Home Economics, UNIVERSITY OF SASKATCHEWAN (1939) and a Bachelor of Library Sciences, University of Toronto (1947). In 1943 she began her library career as Children's Department assistant, Saskatoon Public Library. She was chief librarian from 1961 to 1980; during her tenure she had charge of the construction of the new library (built 1966) and of the expansion of services in what became the Frances Morrison branch. She also supported establishment of the regional library system. She was president of the Saskatoon and SASKATCHEWAN LIBRARY ASSOCIATIONS, and vice-president of the Canadian Library Association (CLA). She chaired several important CLA committees, including its largest one, the public library section. Other involvements included the Saskatoon Business and Professional Women's Club, the Heart and Stroke Foundation, and the SASKATCHEWAN ARTS BOARD (chair). Upon her retirement in 1980, the Saskatoon Public Library Board named its main library in her honour. Her awards include the Queen's Silver Jubilee Medal (1977), the Outstanding Service to Librarianship Award of the Canadian Library Association (1981), and the Saskatchewan Order of Merit (1999). *Daria Coneghan*

Frances Morrison, February 1981.

MORSE, town, pop 248, located approximately 60 km E of Swift Current on Hwy No. 1 and the CPR main line. The first settler at Morse was a railway company employee, responsible for the maintenance of the track in the area. In 1896, he moved his family into the section foreman's house, one of only two buildings then at the townsite; a 14-foot-square wooden station, a water tank and a windmill were the only other structures. The townsite was surveyed in 1902, and between 1906 and 1908 carloads of Mennonite, English and Scottish settlers, their household effects, and livestock were unloaded from the rails. In 1906, the post office was established, followed by the construction of the school in 1908. Named for Samuel Morse, the inventor of the electric telegraph and the originator of Morse code, Morse was incorporated as a village in 1910. The population of the village was 298 in 1911; in 1912, the community attained town status. That same year, Morse was reportedly the third-largest grain marketing point in the province; in 1915, a record-setting 2.25 million bushels of **WHEAT** were shipped out of the community. In 1921, Morse reached a peak population of 559 people. However, as other towns and villages developed in the surrounding region, Morse's population slowly declined. Agriculture remains the main industry in the area today, the focus being on grain, oilseed, and beef production. The Morse Museum and Cultural Centre is housed in a large red brick schoolhouse built in 1912, which was saved from demolition by being declared a heritage property. *David McLennan*

MORTON, ARTHUR SILVER (1870–1945). Arthur Silver Morton is regarded as one of the most significant Canadian historians to emerge from the prairies. Born in Trinidad in the British West Indies on May 16, 1870, Morton was the son of Presbyterian missionaries who had left Nova Scotia for the warmer climate of the Caribbean. He studied at the University of Edinburgh, where he received a Bachelor of Divinity and an MA. In 1896, after a summer of study at the University of Berlin, Morton arrived in Canada, where he was ordained. He served as a minister until 1904, when he started his career as a lecturer in church history, first at the Presbyterian College in Halifax, and later at Knox College in Toronto. In 1914, Morton arrived at the **UNIVERSITY OF SASKATCHEWAN** and turned to the study of western Canada. The shift was both one of necessity, as **WORLD WAR I** cut him off from the source materials for the study of ecclesiastical history, and one of belief, as he felt an obligation to the history of his newly adopted home. Morton applied the stern historical discipline of the study of church history and the Middle Ages to his new field.

Among the books that he wrote on western Canadian history, *A History of the Canadian West to 1870–71* (1939) is possibly his most significant

SASKATCHEWAN ARCHIVES BOARD S-B858

Arthur Silver Morton, 1942.

contribution. His other works concentrated on prairie settlement, the **FUR TRADE**, and the history of the University of Saskatchewan. Morton was also instrumental in the decision of the University of Saskatchewan to offer archival facilities to the provincial government in 1936. The following year,

he was appointed Keeper of the provincial records of Saskatchewan. After his retirement from teaching in 1940, he devoted most of his time to cataloguing the public records of the North-West Territories up to 1905. He had laid plans for the preservation and indexing of all provincial records subsequent to that date when he suddenly died in January 1945. With the election of the CCF government, the arrangement between the University and the provincial government was formalized with the passing of the Archives Act (1945), which established the Saskatchewan Archives Board. *Mark Vajner*

MORTON, DOUG (1926–2004). Douglas Gibb Morton was one of the **REGINA FIVE** group of artists whose exhibition at the National Gallery in 1961 was proclaimed as a watershed for the development of abstract art in Canada. Born on November 26, 1926, and raised in Winnipeg, he studied with LeMoine Fitzgerald, of the Group of Seven, and continued his studies in Los Angeles, London and Paris. Morton returned to Canada in 1954 to manage the family business, MacKay-Morton Ltd., an industrial pipe distributor in Regina. A typical weekday for the next decade would allow for two painting sessions

COURTESY OF THE MACKENZIE ART GALLERY 1966-007

Douglas Morton, "2 Plus 2," 1966, acrylic on canvas, 215.1 x 215.3 cm, MacKenzie Art Gallery, University of Regina Collection.

of two hours each, one beginning at 6 a.m. and the other at 10 p.m.

His practical business sense was in sharp contrast to his adventurous and experimental approach to painting. Morton was keen on using bold colour and large canvasses; he was also a pioneer in the technique of attaching objects—a piece of Styrofoam or wood, for example—to the work in order to extend the image. Morton's inventiveness was especially appreciated at the Emma Lake workshops, where every summer twenty-five artists from across Canada and the United States would converge on the quiet Saskatchewan locale. He would arrive with his car jammed full of industrial paints and unconventional tools of application, which he would use energetically and spontaneously.

Morton's work was not as popularly received as those of fellow exhibitors RON BLOORE, TED GODWIN, KEN LOCHHEAD and ART MCKAY after their 1961 breakthrough in Ottawa. Other artists, who were aware of his exceptional eye for detail, did appreciate his painting and considered his reputation to be underrated. In addition to the rest of the Regina Five, Morton enjoyed a professional relationship with the American artist Barnett Newman, another proponent of bold colour and size. His noteworthy paintings include "Brownscape" (1961), "Fractured Black" (1964), "Green Centre" (1967) and "Token" (1970). Lochhead associated Morton's work with "wholeness of colour, full-bodied shapes of colour within the tradition of Matisse and Butler, Fauves and post-Fauves painters of Paris. He was pushing the frontiers of colour more than any other painter I knew."

After leaving MacKay-Morton in 1967, Morton spent two years as director of Visual Arts and associate professor of Art at the UNIVERSITY OF SASKATCHEWAN, Regina Campus. He was also a teacher and administrator at York University (1969–80), the University of Victoria (1980–85), and the Alberta College of Art (1985–87). He received an honorary degree from the UNIVERSITY OF REGINA in 2001. Morton died on January 4, 2004. *John Chaput*

MOSQUITO, GRIZZLY BEAR'S HEAD, LEAN MAN FIRST NATIONS. Until the Treaty Land Entitlement Act was enforced, the Mosquito Reserve included three bands: Mosquito Band #109, Lean Man Band #111, and Grizzly Bear's Head Band #110. The Mosquito Band is a Nakota/Cree band located in the Eagle Hills south of North Battleford. Their land was acquired after Misketo became leader of the band previously under Little Chief, and signed an adhesion to TREATY 6 on August 29, 1878. The band settled on the reserve in 1879–80. Grizzly Bear's Head originally signed TREATY 4 under Tepee Hoska at CYPRESS HILLS in 1877, but migrated to the Battleford area after Tepee Hoska died in 1882. The bands merged in 1951. After signing an adhesion to

Treaty 4, Lean Man settled in the Treaty 6 area south of Battleford in May 1882. The band's population continuously declined, and by 1931 only one member remained; this person joined the Mosquito Grizzly Bear's Head band. The Mosquito Reserve is approximately 9,297 ha in size and is situated 27 km south of North Battleford; while the Grizzly Bear's Head and Lean Man Reserve covers 3,476 ha and is located 24 km south of North Battleford. The bands also share ownership of 3.3 ha in the city of North Battleford, home to the Gold Eagle Casino (1996). All three bands have one order of governance for their combined population of 1,165 members, 610 members of whom reside on reserve land. Community infrastructure includes a band office, band hall and resource centre, school, health clinic, utility building, gas station and convenience store, and an RCMP detachment office. *Christian Thompson*

MOSS, GWENNA (1937–). Born on June 11, 1937, in Saskatoon, Moss received a BSc in Home Economics from the UNIVERSITY OF SASKATCHEWAN in 1959. She obtained Masters (1968) and PhD (1970) degrees in Extension and Adult Education at the University of Wisconsin. In 1971 Moss began to teach in the Extension Division, and has always maintained a commitment to adult education, extension, and instructional development. In 1975–77 she taught rural women at the University of Ghana, then returned to the University of Saskatchewan, where she became a professor of Continuing Education in the College of Education. She was Dean of Home Economics (1982–86), Associate Vice-President, Academic (1986–90), and Acting Vice-President, Academic (1990–91); she was the first woman appointed to a senior academic administrative post at the University of Saskatchewan. In 1992 she returned to the Extension Division and was responsible for the Instructional Development Program. In 2000 reorganization led to the establishment of the Gwenna Moss Teaching and Learning Centre. Awards given Moss for her academic and community contributions include the Saskatchewan Association for Lifelong Learning Roby Kidd Award (1996), the University Alumni Association Award of Achievement (1998), and an award as Outstanding United Way Volunteer (1999). She retired in 2004. *Karen Zemlak*

MOSSBANK, town, pop 379, located S of OLD WIVES LAKE, approximately 70 km SW of Moose Jaw and 35 km N of Assiniboia, off Hwy 2. The Mossbank area was first settled around 1907 as people of British, Scandinavian, and German origins took up land in the district. In 1915, Mossbank was incorporated as a village. The name was coined by Robert Jolly, a homesteader from Scotland, who had used the same name for a post office established on his farm in 1909. As a growing service centre for the

developing mixed farming district, Mossbank's population almost doubled in the five years between 1916 and 1921, jumping from 164 to 303. During World War II, the village population soared (from 358 in 1936 to 606 in 1941) as a BRITISH COMMONWEALTH AIR TRAINING PLAN base was established just east of the community. Work began on the site in 1939, but the facility closed in 1944. In 1946, one of the aircraft hangars was moved into the community to become what was known locally as "the longest school in Saskatchewan." On May 20, 1957, Mossbank became the scene of one of Saskatchewan's most famous political debates as Premier T.C. DOUGLAS and Liberal candidate ROSS THATCHER squared off over the issue of the province's CROWN CORPORATIONS. The popular consensus was that Thatcher equalled, and perhaps bested, his eloquent rival. Through to the mid-1960s, Mossbank prospered. Then began a period of decline, with which the community continues to struggle. Today, it retains a small core of local businesses and services, including a K–12 school with students from the town and the surrounding area. *David McLennan*

MOSSING, ROBERT LYNN (1936–). A dedicated proponent of the musical arts, Robert Lynn Mossing of Bengough was born on February 7, 1936, and educated at the Vandercook College of Music in Chicago and the University of Michigan. For over forty years, he has instructed the world-renowned Regina Lions Band, first as its assistant director from 1959 to 1970 and then as its executive director until 1999. Since then, Mossing has served as Director Emeritus and has accumulated numerous honours and awards for his work. A member of the Canadian and Saskatchewan Band Associations, Robert Mossing received the Order of Canada in 1995.

MOTHERWELL, CATHERINE GILLESPIE (1866–1952). Kate (Catherine) Gillespie Motherwell gained prominence not merely as wife and partner of the Honourable W.R. MOTHERWELL, but for involvement with First Nations people. Born in Ontario in 1866, she was a teacher when the Gillespie family moved to the Balcarres area (1889). Becoming interested in the First Nations, she accepted a position at Crowstand Mission school in 1894. In 1897 she took a nursing course and went to the Mistawasis Mission, where she was in charge of the day school, assisted by her father and sister. In 1901 she was appointed principal of File Hills boarding school in face of opposition from government officials because of her gender. She was later judged to have done excellent work by the standards of the day, working (with her sister, the matron) to prepare Indian youths to become farmers and farm wives, and doing missionary work. In 1908 she left

629

Catherine Motherwell.

her position to marry W.R. Motherwell, a widower with two children and provincial Minister of Agriculture (later federal Minister of Agriculture). In the Abernathy District, where the Motherwell farm, Lanark Place, was located, her involvements included Presbyterian missionary work. In 1940, the Motherwells retired there. After her husband's death in 1943, she remained in Saskatchewan, where she died on July 6, 1952. *Ann Leger-Anderson*

FURTHER READING: Dobbin, L.L. 1961. "Mrs. Catherine Gillespie Motherwell, Pioneer Teacher and Missionary," *Saskatchewan History* 14: 17–26.

MOTHERWELL, WILLIAM RICHARD (1860–1943).
William Motherwell was born in Ontario on January 6, 1860. He attended the country school in the winter and worked on the farm in Lanark County near Perth during the summer. When the Ontario Agricultural College was founded at Guelph in 1879, Motherwell received a scholarship and graduated in 1881. He worked that summer at Portage La Prairie, Manitoba. After returning home to Ontario for one last winter, Motherwell, then 21, headed west to stay. From the end of the rail line at Brandon, Manitoba, he joined a caravan of **RED RIVER CARTS** and wagons west.

In 1882, Motherwell was one of the first to select land in the Abernethy district. With a pair of oxen and a plough he broke the land and began to farm. A year later, he completed construction of a three-room log house. In 1884 Motherwell married Adeline Rogers (1861–1905). Two of their four children died at an early age. In 1897 they built the stone house that is the centre of the **MOTHERWELL HOMESTEAD** National Historic Site. He collected every stone that went into building his house and barn.

Motherwell was a co-founder and first president

of the Territorial Grain Growers Association in 1901. Adeline died in the spring of 1905 at the age of 44, in the midst of Motherwell's successful campaign to enter provincial politics. Motherwell took on his duties in the Saskatchewan Legislature and resided in Regina for three years with the 15- and 13-year-old children. He was appointed Saskatchewan's first Minister of Agriculture in 1906.

The homestead in Abernethy, referred to as "Lanark Place," again became the Motherwell family's centre in 1908 when Motherwell married Catherine Gillespie (1866–1952). Born and raised in Ontario, Catherine had moved west in her 20s to be a teacher and missionary to First Nations people. She was principal of the File Hills Boarding School, north of Abernethy, for seven years.

Motherwell set up Saskatchewan's Department of Agriculture on the track of "scientific agriculture." which was largely built around preserving soil moisture by summerfallowing and elaborate systems of soil tillage. Motherwell's educational efforts were initiated on a multitude of fronts through lectures, agricultural societies, institutes, bulletins, and the Saskatchewan College of Agriculture that he co-founded in 1908. He even advocated that nature study and school gardening be introduced in the public schools. Often in multiple languages, the bulletins were "how-to" manuals on such topics as summerfallowing, crop rotation, tree planting, farm diversification, co-operative associations, and dairying. A system of experimental farms, demonstration plots, and local fairs was established in Saskatchewan. The network of rail lines was also capitalized on as a vehicle for reaching farmers with demonstrations, lectures and exhibits inside special train cars known as the "Travelling Dairy," the "Special Seed Train," and the hugely successful "Better Farming Train." Motherwell's own home-

William Motherwell.

stead was arranged and run in a way that he consciously saw as a model for others to follow.

Motherwell resigned from his Saskatchewan Cabinet post in 1917, and his seat in 1918, to protest the provincial Liberals' pro-conscription stand, as well as their policy to curtail French language rights in the Saskatchewan public schools. He was nearly 62 years old in 1921 when he ran for federal politics and was elected in the Regina constituency. **MACKENZIE KING** invited him to serve as Canada's Minister of Agriculture, which he did from 1922 to 1930. After August 1930, Motherwell sat on the Opposition side of the House until King's Liberals returned to office in 1935.

In Ottawa Motherwell worked to improve the quality and continuity of exportable and home-consumed products. He also worked to achieve rust-resistant varieties of wheat, and established the Dominion Rust Research Lab in Winnipeg in 1926. He is credited with helping Canada become the first country in the British Empire to adopt policies to curtail tuberculosis, by setting up "Restricted T.B. areas" and an Accredited Herd System. Motherwell championed the cause of the prairie farmer through endorsing government regulation and financial aid to prairie farmers, as well as participation in co-operative enterprises.

The 1935 federal election was Motherwell's last. He retired from politics in 1939, just before he reached the age of 80. He died May 24, 1943. His homestead was designated a national historic site in 1966 because of its architectural interest and its historic associations with his career, and as an illustration of a prairie homestead of western Canada's settlement period. *Frieda Esau Klippenstein*

FURTHER READING: Dick, Lyle. 1989. "Farmers 'Making Good': The Development of Abernethy District, Saskatchewan, 1880–1920." In *Studies in Archaeology, Architecture and History.* Ottawa: Parks Canada; Shepard, R. Bruce. 1997. "W.R. Motherwell and the Dry Farming Congress in Canada," *Saskatchewan History* 49 (2): 18–27; Turner, Allan R. 1958. "W.R. Motherwell: The Emergence of a Farm Leader," *Saskatchewan History* 11 (3): 94–103; —. 1959. "W.R. Motherwell and Agricultural Education, 1905–1918," *Saskatchewan History* 12 (1): 81–96.

MOTHERWELL HOMESTEAD.
The Motherwell Homestead near Abernethy, property of **W.R. MOTHERWELL**, was named Lanark Place after his Ontario home and modeled after the idealized farmstead of 19th-century Ontarian emigrants. The homestead manifested conventional wisdom on manipulating the prairie environment for beauty and efficiency.

The property, replacing an earlier homestead (1882), is divided by function and dominated by the two-storey, Italianate fieldstone house (1887)–itself

COURTESY OF TOURISM SASKATCHEWAN

Motherwell Homestead.

divided, by Victorian conventions, into family, work, and public spaces (the Territorial Grain Growers Association was founded in the front room). It is surrounded by decorative landscaping, including flower gardens and a tennis lawn. The large, L-shaped red barn (1907), on the site of an earlier stone stable, is also of Ontario design. A dugout collected water while shelter belts gave protection from the elements, separated sections of the farm, and provided psychological security from the exposed prairie. This private microclimate was costly to maintain, requiring substantial support from Motherwell's political salary even as the farmstead proclaimed his social standing.

The farmstead fell into disrepair in the 1920s but was designated a National Historic Site in 1966 to commemorate scientific agriculture, western agrarian unrest, Ontarian settlement, and Motherwell's political career. Parks Canada undertook rehabilitation, replanting the shelterbelts and interpreting the site to the farm's heyday (1910–14). *Claire Campbell*

FURTHER READING: Clarke, I., L. Dick and S. Carter. 1983. *Motherwell Historic Park*. Ottawa: Parks Canada, National Historic Parks and Sites Branch; Parks Canada. 2003. *Motherwell Homestead National Historic Site of Canada Management Plan*; Thomas, G. and I. Clarke. 1979. "The Garrison Mentality and the Canadian West: The British-Canadian Response to Two Landscapes: The Fur-Trade Post and the Ontarian Prairie Homestead," *Prairie Forum* 4 (1): 83–104.

MOTHS: *see* **BUTTERFLIES AND MOTHS**

MOTT, FREDERICK DODGE (1904–81). Frederick Mott was born at Wooster, Ohio on August 3, 1904, the son of pioneer YMCA missionary leader and 1946 Nobel Peace Prize co-winner John Raleigh Mott. In a family dedicated to human welfare, Fred spent many months of his teens in Europe and the Far East as secretary to his father. He married a Winnipeg girl, Marjorie Heeney, on August 5, 1930, and graduated in medicine at McGill University, Montreal, in 1932. When illness forced him to forego his ambition to be a family doctor, his idealism took him to the wider field of rural health and medical care, which had gained great significance in the **DEPRESSION**. Under federal authorities he con-

RAY HUME/SASKATCHEWAN ARCHIVES BOARD R-A7994

Frederick Dodge Mott.

ducted medical care and public health activities among low-income farmers and migratory workers throughout the United States.

Henry Sigerist had recommended Mott to **T.C. DOUGLAS** as "the ablest man on the continent" to implement the hospitalization plan. The CCF government then hired Mott as chairman of the Saskatchewan Health Services Planning Commission from 1946 to 1951. He was also chair of the **SASKATCHEWAN HEALTH SURVEY** from 1949 to 1951. Against all odds, his administrative skills led to the almost flawless introduction of universal hospitalization in 1947. British Columbia encountered numerous problems when it next introduced hospitalization, so subsequently all other provinces sent their people to Saskatchewan to observe how it had wrestled with administrative problems which had no precedents in North America. In 1951 Mott acted also as Deputy Minister of Public Health and was Canada's representative to the World Health Organization. A man of integrity, he maintained good relations with Saskatchewan doctors.

Later, Mott set up a network of ten regional hospitals for the United Mine Workers of America, intended to serve half a million people; and at the end of his career he went to the University of Toronto to be a professor of medical care administration, from 1968 to 1972. He retired to Pittsford, New York, where he died on May 31, 1981.
C. Stuart Houston

MUELLER, MARGARET (1942–). Born on June 17, 1942, Margaret Mueller (*née* Robb) was the first of many Saskatoon speed skaters to achieve national and international success. Winner of four Saskatchewan and five Alberta provincial speed skating titles, Mueller was also a seven-time national champion. She represented Canada at the 1960 Winter Olympic Games in Squaw Valley, California, where she competed in the 500, 1,000, 1,500, and 3,000-metre events. As a student at the **UNIVERSITY OF SASKATCHEWAN**, Mueller continued to skate but also branched off into basketball and diving, winning three provincial diving championships. She was a member of six intervarsity teams, and received the 1964 Spirit of Youth award for leadership, academic achievement, and sportsmanship. Mueller attended graduate school in Madison, Wisconsin, where she coached state championship teams in track and field, basketball, and volleyball. In recognition of her contributions to amateur athletics, she was inducted to the **SASKATCHEWAN SPORTS HALL OF FAME** in 1995.
Bob Ivanochko and Holden Stoffel

MULCASTER, WYNONA (1915–). Wynona (Nonie) Croft Mulcaster was born on April 10, 1915, in Prince Albert, Saskatchewan, daughter of Richard and Valerie Rhona Mulcaster. She is renowned as an

JOHN KENNEY PHOTO/SASKATCHEWAN ARCHIVES BOARD S-SP-A26170-4, SASKATOON STARPHOENIX FONDS

Wynona Mulcaster, September 1986.

educator and artist. Her landscape paintings are associated with her contemporaries **RETA COWLEY**, **ERNEST LINDNER** and **DOROTHY KNOWLES**. Mulcaster's teaching career spans the period 1943–77. She served as Director of Art Education for the Saskatchewan Teachers' College, Saskatoon and as an Associate Professor in the Department of Visual Art, **UNIVERSITY OF SASKATCHEWAN**. Students included **ROBERT MURRAY**, **ALLEN SAPP** and **OTTO ROGERS**. She was inducted into the Sportsman Hall of Fame in 1994 for her contributions to children in the Saskatoon Pony Club, founded by her in 1945. Prior to landscape painting, her subject matter was horses.

Wynona studied art with Ernest Lindner from 1935 to 1945, and received her BA (Art and English) from the University of Saskatchewan in 1942. She attended the Banff School of Fine Arts, studying under H.G. Glyde and A.Y. Jackson, the School of Art and Design in Montreal, studying under Arthur Lismer, and numerous Emma Lake Artists' Workshops with Joseph Plaskett, Will Barnett and Kenneth Noland. She received a grant from the Canada Council for the Arts which enabled her to study art and art education by visiting major art galleries in Europe in 1958–59. She received an MFA at the Allende Institute, Mexico in 1976. Mulcaster creates a total sense of energy and space within her painting, as the relationship between land and sky represents an immediate perception of landscape or an ambiguous memory with close affinities to Emily Carr. Her painting technique of creating marks on paper is reminiscent of Hans Hoffman, theorist of the New York School, and his observation that pictorial depth is achieved by random placement of objects rather than arranging them to a vanishing point. Working primarily in acrylics on canvas or

paper, Mulcaster maintains a solid comprehension of modernist aesthetics. Her admiration for the European Impressionists and inspiration of new colour relationships and energy found within the Mexican landscape inform her print-making process.

In 1993, Mulcaster was presented the **SASKATCHEWAN ARTS BOARD** Lifetime Achievement Award for Excellence in the Arts. Her work is exhibited across Canada and collected in numerous private and permanent collections including the Saskatchewan Arts Board, Regina, the Canada Council Art Bank, Ottawa, the **MACKENZIE ART GALLERY**, Regina, the **MENDEL ART GALLERY**, Saskatoon, and the Glenbow Museum, Calgary. Mulcaster currently lives in San Miguel de Allende, Mexico but continues to visit and paint the prairies.   *Patricia Deadman*

MULTICULTURAL COUNCIL OF SASKATCH-EWAN.

Founded in 1975 by representatives of six regional multicultural councils, the Multicultural Council of Saskatchewan (MCoS) has become a leader in cross-cultural education. The Council is governed by an elected board of volunteer directors representing member organizations. These MCoS members include regional councils, unicultural organizations, specialized organizations, and affiliates representing thousands of volunteers committed to culture. MCoS supports its members by providing funding, administrative assistance, and training opportunities. The work of MCoS is supported by sponsors and partners, including Saskatchewan Lotteries, SaskCulture, Canadian Heritage, and the government of Saskatchewan.

The Multicultural Council of Saskatchewan provides diverse programs and services in the areas of

anti-racism, cross-cultural education, complementary health initiatives, youth development, and member services. The Council publishes the magazines *Multiculturalism Matters* and *Faces*; it develops partnerships with businesses, governments, and educational and community organizations to advance common goals. The Council represents ethnocultural communities by campaigning for cultural creativity and voicing cross-cultural concerns to government, businesses, and the general public. With a staff of four and an office in Regina, it is the secretariat for the Multicultural Council of Canada, a national organization dedicated to promoting cross-cultural understanding in the country.

Heather Robison

MULTICULTURAL EDUCATION.

Broadly speaking, multicultural education encompasses the policies, programs, and practices which evolved in response to our multicultural reality. Before the 1960s, Saskatchewan's education system sought, with few exceptions, to absorb immigrant and Aboriginal children into the culture of the English-speaking population. Since that time, the monocultural focus of the past has been replaced by a formal acceptance of ethnocultural diversity as a desirable characteristic of schools and society in general. The Canadian population was heterogeneous even before European contact, as the First Nations were culturally and linguistically diverse. With the arrival of increasing numbers of immigrants of various ethnic backgrounds, many of whom spoke neither French nor English, Canada's post-Confederation approach to nation-building was to stress assimilation, and the public school was seen as the means of creating a unified country. Many ethnocultural groups viewed this approach as an erosion of their identity, and created organizations and institutions to counter this pressure. Some even managed to affect legislation. The 1901 Act allowed for the hiring of teachers to teach in languages other than English, albeit only in the last hour of the school day. To ensure qualified teachers, the Training School for Teachers of Foreign Speaking Communities was established in Regina in 1909. Strong anti-French, anti-Catholic, and anti-foreigner sentiments, particularly following **WORLD WAR I**, however, resulted in legislation in 1919 banning all but English as a language of instruction in schools.

During the following fifty years, there was little or no acknowledgement of the increasing ethnocultural and linguistic diversity of Saskatchewan's population in the day-to-day teaching in schools. In some cases, students were even harassed and punished for using their home language. As a result, a significant number of students from minority ethnic and cultural groups experienced learning problems, and had lower academic achievement and higher dropout rates than children from the dominant group. Aboriginal students historically have been the least well served by educational institutions. As the keystone in a systematic attempt to assimilate Canada's Aboriginal people, the **RESIDENTIAL SCHOOLS** made a concerted effort to eradicate Aboriginal languages, cultural traditions, and beliefs. There were pockets of resistance: for example, in some schools in francophone communities, instruction continued to take place in French—except when the school inspector arrived, at which time French books were quickly replaced by English ones.

The post-**WORLD WAR II** era saw a gradual shift in Canadian attitudes from an assimilationist to a pluralist viewpoint. The terms of reference of the Royal Commission on Bilingualism and Biculturalism, established in 1963, included "contributions made by other ethnic groups." Eight years later, Prime Minister Pierre E. Trudeau announced an official Multiculturalism Policy for Canada. Initially, the prairie provinces emphasized a more linguistic view of multicultural education. In 1968, Saskatchewan amended The School Act to allow French to be used in schools designated for the francophone minority. In 1974, a second amendment broadened this to permit other languages to be taught or used as the language of instruction for part of the school day; an example is the Ukrainian-English Bilingual Program established in Saskatoon in 1979.

During the 1980s, the Minister of Education established the Indian and Métis Curriculum Advisory Committee and the Advisory Committee on Heritage Languages; and the Minister of Parks, Recreation and Culture set up the Task Force on Multiculturalism to make recommendations on how Saskatchewan's education system could better meet the needs of students from different cultural groups. In 1994, the Department adopted the *Multicultural Education and Heritage Language Education Policies*, which set out goals, principles, policy statements, and a plan for implementation. Other initiatives that were implemented during the 1990s as a result of directions also aimed to foster understanding, acceptance, and harmonious relations among people of different cultures. Outside the regular school system, groups of parents were also working hard to maintain their language and culture. A number of community ethnocultural associations organized heritage language schools—programs where in the evening or on weekends (hence the term "Saturday schools") volunteer teachers taught young people their heritage language and culture. These community groups have continued to grow both in number and size. They are currently supported financially and organizationally by a number of umbrella organizations (**SASKATCHEWAN ORGANIZATION FOR HERITAGE LANGUAGES, SASKATCHEWAN INTERCULTURAL ASSOCIATION,** and the **MULTILINGUAL ASSOCIATION OF REGINA**), which receive

funding from Saskatchewan Lotteries. Additional funding is also provided by Saskatchewan Learning and other government departments.

Despite these efforts, a number of cultural groups feel that the provincial school system does not meet the needs of their children, and have opted to run their own programs, schools or school systems. First Nations are increasingly educating their children in band schools. The francophone community has established its own education system, which operates parallel to the regular system. Schools on Hutterite colonies, although they operate within the provincial education system, offer a program that is modified to reflect the beliefs, values, traditions, and customs of the Hutterians. Some ethnocultural communities, such as Mennonites and Muslims, have established private schools with programs that include language and cultural components in addition to the regular subjects. For the majority of Saskatchewan children and youth, the education system will continue to pursue the goal of enabling them to interact and feel comfortable with others who are different, and to work towards greater social justice.

Joan Boyer

FURTHER READING: Fleuras, A., and J.L. Elliott. 1992. "Multicultural Education: Schooling with a Cultural Difference." Pp. 183–215 in *Multiculturalism in Canada: The Challenge of Diversity*. Scarborough: Nelson Canada; Wieler, E.E. 1987. M*ulticultural Education Theory, Policy, Practice, and Issues: A Literature Review*. Regina: Saskatchewan Instructional Development and Research Unit.

MULTI-FAITH FORUM, REGINA. At the time of the Gulf War in 1991, on the invitation of the **REGINA COUNCIL OF CHURCHES** several individuals from a variety of faith traditions came together to make a public protest about the War: this group formed the Regina Inter-Faith Peace Committee. Out of this experience, the group extended an invitation to other faith communities interested in a broader and ongoing dialogue to come together in a more formal way; as a result of these initiatives, the Multi-Faith Forum became a reality. The initial membership of the Forum was drawn from the Christian, Muslim, Hindu, and Unitarian communities. The Baha'i community, the Jewish community (Traditional and Reform), and the Saskatchewan Inter-Faith Spiritual Care Committee soon became members. Muslims for Peace became members in 2003.

Individuals and organizations who support the objectives of the Forum may become fully active members in addition to the official representatives of religious communities. Forum members meet monthly to discuss and act upon matters of mutual interest. Officers are elected annually. Meetings are held in facilities of the member religious communities on a rotational basis. The Forum is a place

where all, regardless of faith or cultural heritage, can come together with people of other faiths to promote among society at large the understanding, appreciation, and acceptance of the diverse religious communities. The Forum has been a resource to the Regina Public Schools values program; it also has given advice to hospital dieticians with respect to the dietary requirements of certain faith communities. The Forum organizes an interfaith service each year to mark World Religion Day, and in 2002 organized a service to mark the first anniversary of September 11, 2001. In June 2003, the Forum organized the official Thanksgiving Celebration at City Hall to mark the City of Regina Centennial.

Each year the Forum gives awards to those individuals and organizations which have shown exceptional merit in promoting its aims. Over the years it has organized Multi-Faith Fairs which have given the public at large the opportunity to learn more about the faiths represented in the Regina community.

Terry Marner

MULTILINGUAL ASSOCIATION OF REGINA. The Multilingual Association of Regina (MLAR), the first multilingual association in Canada, is a nonprofit coordinating agency established in 1978 with a volunteer board of directors. Since its inception, the organization has grown from three language schools with 200 students to more than twenty schools with 1,100 students and eighty-two volunteer teachers. MLAR has been working with teachers, students, parents, volunteers, school boards, and cultural organizations to promote the teaching of heritage languages in Regina and surrounding areas. It supports heritage language schools by offering facilities, providing in-service training for teachers, and promoting the benefits of learning heritage languages through workshops and seminars. MLAR organizes and prepares resource material and teaching aids for its teachers, conducts public speaking and writing contests, publishes a quarterly newsletter, commissions surveys and studies to determine the needs of groups teaching heritage languages, and hosts an annual open house to celebrate cultural diversity and foster social cohesion, mutual respect, and a shared sense of Canadian identity.

In 1992, MLAR worked with the **UNIVERSITY OF REGINA** to have a Certificate Program for heritage language teachers established through the university to provide more in-depth training. MLAR provided resources to establish the **SASKATCHEWAN ORGANIZATION FOR HERITAGE LANGUAGES** (SOHL), a provincial organization which now provides leadership and funding to heritage language schools across the province. In 2003, MLAR produced a video entitled " Heritage Languages: A Link to the Past, our Bridge to the Future" to develop awareness of heritage language learning among the general public.

Ved Arora

MUNICIPAL DOCTOR SYSTEM. The municipal doctor system was an important form of both pre-paid medical care and health services delivery in rural Saskatchewan before the implementation of **MEDICARE** in 1962. Under this scheme, rural municipalities, villages and towns hired local doctors, financed from local taxation, to provide medical services to their residents. The origins of Saskatchewan's municipal doctor system can be traced to the province's Public Health Act of 1909, which required every municipal council to appoint a medical health officer for the provision of public health services. From salaries for public health work emerged the idea of paying doctors an annual grant as an inducement to reside and practice in a community, as well as full salaries for the provision of medical services to the residents of the municipality. The rural municipality of Sarnia at Holdfast was the locus of this transition.

Concerned that Dr. H.J. Schmitt, their local physician and medical health officer, would leave the area because of difficulty collecting fees during a year of crop failures, in 1915 the rural municipality of Sarnia, without legislative authority, offered a grant of $1,500 as an inducement to stay. The following year the doctor accepted a contract at $2,500 per year to provide general practitioner services to all resident tax-payers. This was the first full-time municipal doctor contract in Canada. The provincial legislature subsequently amended the Rural Municipality Act in 1916 and 1919 in order to legalise the arrangements pioneered in Sarnia, thereby creating the first municipal doctor legislation. Subsequent amendments and further legislation between 1919 and 1941 permitted municipalities, towns and villages to offer a doctor a salary or fee-for-service payments for general medical care, surgery, maternity care, and public health work. To oversee and regulate the municipal doctor system, the Health Services Board was set up with equal representation of the province, the rural municipalities, and the medical profession.

During the 1930s, the municipal doctor scheme was adopted in areas where private practice was still viable, including some of the most densely populated and prosperous farm regions of the province. It also spread to Manitoba and Alberta and attracted the interest of the United States Committee on the Costs of Medical Care. The Committee sent the esteemed economist C. Rufus Rorem to study the scheme in 1929–30, and in its main report recommended the adoption of the system in similar areas of the United States. The program's fusion of preventive and curative services was celebrated in several high profile national health plans devised by government, labour, and agricultural organizations in the 1930s and 1940s, such as the federal Heagerty Health Insurance Committee.

Organized medicine was less than enamoured with the system, owing to lay control and salary remuneration, and maintained that it should be employed only in areas where private practice was no longer viable. Many municipal doctors favoured the scheme because it offered both guaranteed payment as well as opportunities for private practice among patients from the towns and villages within, and patients from outside, the boundaries of the municipality. These municipal doctors were strongly attached to their private practice privileges and their substantive private income. They objected to the development of the scheme into provincewide salaried general practitioner service in rural Saskatchewan, with no private practice permitted, as proposed by the **STATE HOSPITAL AND MEDICAL LEAGUE** from 1941 onwards, and by the CCF government's Health Services Planning Commission in 1945.

The CCF sought to extend the municipal doctor plans throughout rural Saskatchewan with the introduction of a grant-in-aid scheme in 1945. The system grew incrementally until 1947, its peak year, when it covered 210,000 people—nearly one-quarter of the population. By that year, the better rural practices had all been taken. In order to prevent the spread of these lay-controlled salaried medical care plans, from 1955 Saskatoon's doctor-controlled Medical Services Incorporated (MSI) expanded into rural Saskatchewan. Some communities switched to the MSI schemes because they offered free choice of physician anywhere in Saskatchewan, as well as access to specialist services in the cities and larger towns. With better transportation and rising incomes, many residents in rural Saskatchewan were no longer content with the services of the country doctor and demanded the skills of the specialist. By the mid-1950s a growing number of rural residents who paid taxes to maintain a municipal doctor received their medical care elsewhere. Other communities were forced to discontinue their municipal doctor schemes and obtain contracts with MSI when their resident physicians refused to resign salaried agreements. The Health Services Planning Commission sought to prevent municipal councils from opting out of the municipal doctor system by withholding and increasing the value of their municipal medical care grants. When the Douglas government announced its plans to introduce a provincewide medical services scheme in 1959, the municipal doctor system provided medical coverage to 103,750 persons. The scheme was discontinued with the introduction of medicare in 1962.

Gordon S. Lawson

MUNICIPAL ROAD NETWORK. Saskatchewan has the largest municipal (grid) road network in Canada, totaling 165,000 km. In combination with the province's highway network, the province boasts over 190,000 km of rural roads—the most roads per capita of any jurisdiction in the world. The provincial municipal road system is based on the late 19th century Dominion Lands Survey of the prairies provinces. This rigid survey system divided the southern half of Saskatchewan into square-mile sections and included allowances for north-south roads at one-mile intervals and east-west roads at two-mile intervals. Following **WORLD WAR II**, the rising popularity of automobiles and a growing rural population gave need for a safe, reliable transportation network linking farmsteads and trading centres across the province—a seemingly over-ambitious plan, given Saskatchewan's vast land area and dispersed population. However, a municipal road network would be extremely important to Saskatchewan's economy, particularly to the agriculture industry. By the 1950s the existing municipal road network had become inadequate and a financial burden for Saskatchewan's municipalities. In response, the **SASKATCHEWAN ASSOCIATION OF RURAL MUNICIPALITIES** initiated the Grid Road Program in 1952 and passed a resolution requesting the provincial government to address the rural road problem. The government formed the Municipal Advisory Commission, and in 1955, after a three-year study of Saskatchewan's rural transportation network, proposed a new 19,000-km system of municipal roads for the province. Offering technical and financial assistance to the municipalities during the expected 10-year construction period, the government backed the proposal and construction began in earnest in 1956. The new municipal road system would cover all settled parts of the province and be built to all-weather, all-season standards for motorized traffic. At an estimated cost of $50 million, the government and the municipalities each agreed to put in half.

Today, municipal roads are classified according to their function and traffic volumes, which in turn determine construction and maintenance standards. The six road classes and their percentages of the total 165,000-km municipal road network are as follows: primary municipal (5%), municipal (8%), main farm access (18%), special (2%), local access (25%), and land access (42%). Primary municipal roads link municipalities, highways and other primary municipal roads, and carry a minimum of 100 vehicles per day. Municipal roads provide major routes through municipalities and carry more than 60 vehicles per day. Main farm access roads carry a minimum of 30 vehicles per day, and access at least one permanent farm resident for every 1.6 km of road. Special roads lead directly into regional parks, resorts, industries, oil fields, and Indian reserves. Land access roads give access to land only. Local roads provide access to more than just land, but do not meet the standards of a higher classification. Of Saskatchewan's entire municipal road network, roughly 52,000 km are classified as gravel municipal roads and 111,000 km as gravel or earth access roads to farms, homes, fields, parks, industries, etc. Only 1,500 km (less than 1%) of municipal roads are paved, and roughly 3,500 km (2%) are surfaced with a dust-free membrane. Although the provincial government does provide some assistance for road upkeep, Saskatchewan's municipalities are largely responsible for the 165,000 km of municipal road in the province.

A second categorization system groups all rural roads (highways and municipal roads) in the province into seven classes based on their social, economic, and connective function. Classes 1 and 2 carry the highest traffic volumes and connect major cities and regional service centres with populations greater than 1,000. Classes 3, 4, and 5 link communities with populations of less than 1,000, and give access to large parks and industrial sites. Classes 6 and 7 carry the lowest traffic volumes and provide access only to individual residences, small industrial sites and parks, farmland, and other properties. Approximately 81% of Saskatchewan's municipal roads are designated as class 6 or 7; 18% as class 4 or 5; and less than 1% as class 2 or 3. In only 50 years Saskatchewan's municipal road program has evolved to its present-day form. Planning, constructing, and maintaining this extensive road system across a huge land area of few urban centres is a remarkable achievement. However, railway branchline abandonment, grain terminal consolidation, and rural depopulation are changing traffic patterns in rural Saskatchewan. Travel distances to educational, health, commercial, and recreational facilities are getting longer; rural people are becoming increasingly dependent on automobiles to reach facilities and activities away from their homes; and farmers are hauling agricultural commodities over longer distances by truck. Saskatchewan's municipal road network is experiencing increased traffic flow (especially intensive grain trucking) in some areas and reduced flow in others, and consequently the needs and functions of the network continue to change. *Iain Stewart*

MUNICIPAL SYSTEM IN SASKATCHEWAN.

Origins. Saskatchewan's municipal system has evolved over the past 100 years, but its foundations remain relatively the same. Its roots are traceable to 1883, when a few fledgling municipal entities, including fire and local improvement districts, were established through ordinances of the territorial governor which provided guidelines regarding geographic boundaries as well as governance matters such as elections, functions, and finances. Ultimately, however, the key foundations for the existing municipal system were laid in 1908 in the report of a commission appointed in 1906, which recommended that the province establish a municipal system consisting of cities, towns, villages, and

Table MS-1. Saskatchewan Municipalities

Type of Municipality	# of Municipalities	Minimum Population Criteria
Cities	13	5,000
Towns	145	500
Villages	289	100
Resort Villages	39	None
Rural Municipalities	296	None
Organized Hamlets	169	45 Voters
Northern Towns	2	500
Northern Villages	13	100
Northern Hamlets	9	50

rural municipalities. In 1908 a department to deal with municipal affairs was established, and in 1909 the Legislature enacted separate legislation to govern cities, towns, villages, and rural municipalities. To this day those remain the major categories of municipalities throughout most of the province–save for the Northern Administrative District, where there are no cities or rural municipalities. The rural municipal system was established by sub-dividing the southern region between the American border and the Northern Administrative District into municipalities. The original rural municipalities are approximately 1,000 square kilometres, but the handful of those established in 1977 from the conversion of improvement districts to rural municipalities are up to twelve times larger than the original ones.

Structure. The structure of the municipal system was established during the first few decades following the creation of the province. Over time neither the types nor the number of municipalities have changed very much. Unlike other provinces where there has been a reduction in the number of municipalities, largely through amalgamations, in Saskatchewan there has not been any such reduction. The number of municipalities has remained relatively high for most of the past century. As of June 2005 the types and number of municipalities are as listed in Table MS-1.

Municipal Legislation. Traditionally, Saskatchewan has had a fragmented statutory framework for municipal governance. Separate statutes have existed for the major categories of municipalities from the inception of the municipal system. During the past quarter century the original statutory framework has been reformed in order to modernize and rationalize the statutory framework. The major reforms have been the enactment of the following statutes: the Northern Municipalities Act, 1983, for municipalities in the northern half of the province; the Urban Municipality Act, 1984, for cities, towns, and villages in the southern half of the province; the Rural Municipality Act, 1989, for rural municipalities in the southern half of the province; and the Cities

Act, 2002, for the thirteen cities. The latter is a novel statute that provides cities with a greater degree of authority and autonomy to govern their respective municipalities, based on the principles of "natural person powers" and "areas of jurisdiction." When the Cities Act came into force in January 2003, all cities were granted the option to operate either under the Cities Act or under the Urban Municipalities Act. Subsequently, all cities opted to operate under the former rather than the latter. The towns and villages, in collaboration with provincial officials, have produced draft legislation for a new act, which has some of the same principles and features of the Cities Act and which they hope the provincial government will enact in 2005. In addition to the major municipal acts, municipalities are governed by dozens of other pieces of legislation related to an array of governance matters ranging from elections, municipal financing and public health to policing, pest control and cemeteries.

Municipal Functions. The functions of Saskatchewan municipalities have become more multifaceted over time. During the early developmental period of the system, the focus was primarily on the construction of roads and bridges, the development of sewer and water systems, public health care, and agricultural support for farmers. In general, local governments are responsible for an array of services within their boundaries, such as police and fire services, water and sewage treatment services, transportation services, land use planning and development services, library services, recreation, and cultural services.

Municipal Finances. Municipalities are funded through two major categories of revenue sources: first, revenues from own sources, such as property taxes, service user fees, and license fees; and second, revenues from transfers by the provincial and federal governments, such as grants in lieu of taxes and other types of conditional and unconditional grants. In Saskatchewan, municipalities do not have direct access to other major revenue sources such as income taxes, sales tax, or fuel taxes; the property tax base is the major source of revenue for all municipalities. Traditionally, municipalities have shared this tax base with school boards and continue to do so today. In recent years, representatives of the provincial government, municipalities, and school boards have been debating the merits of and modes for reducing the reliance of education on the property tax base. For most municipalities, the property value assessment is conducted by the Saskatchewan Assessment Management Agency (SAMA), an independent agency managed by a board of directors consisting of representatives from the municipal and educational sector, and of stakeholders.

Municipal Councils and Elections. Every fully incorporated municipality has a council headed either by a mayor in the case of cities, urban municipalities and northern municipalities, or by a reeve in the case of rural municipalities. Whereas in rural municipalities officials are elected for two-year terms with half of the representatives in each municipality elected each year, in all other types of municipalities they are elected for three-year terms, and all are elected at the same time. Northern settlements have an elected advisory committee comprised of a chairperson and either two or four other members, as determined by the electors at a public meeting. All municipalities in Saskatchewan have elected council members. The only exception to this are quasi-municipalities in northern Saskatchewan, known as settlements, for which the provincial Minister responsible for municipal government is the de-facto mayor and the local advisory committees serve as advisors to the Minister regarding local services, revenues and expenditures.

Provincial Municipal Oversight. Constitutionally, municipalities are creatures of the provincial government, which has a corresponding responsibility to oversee their operations. This function is performed primarily by the department responsible for municipal affairs and the Saskatchewan Municipal Board. The latter is a quasi-judicial body responsible primarily for ensuring sound financial borrowing practices of all municipalities; hearing and deciding on appeals regarding planning, assessment, fire prevention, municipal boundary, and development matters; and reviewing challenges to applications for alteration of municipal boundaries or amalgamation of municipalities. *Joseph Garcea*

FURTHER READING: Colligan-Yano, F. and M. Norton. 1996. *The Urban Age: Building a Place for Urban Government in Saskatchewan.* Regina: Century Archive Publishing; Morton, J. 1995. *The Building of a Province: The Saskatchewan Association of Rural Municipalities.* Regina: PrintWest.

MUNROE, HUGH EDWIN (1878–1947). Although the GREAT DEPRESSION of the 1930s hit Saskatchewan particularly hard, British parliamentary tradition ostensibly justified the appointment of Hugh E. Munroe to the office of LIEUTENANT-GOVERNOR on March 31, 1931. Munroe was born June 16, 1878, in Glengarry, Ontario. He received his medical degree from McGill University and pursued post-graduate training in Edinburgh. He later moved to Saskatoon where he established a practice and entered municipal and provincial politics. Munroe earned the rank of lieutenant colonel and was awarded the Most Excellent Order of the British Empire for distinguished service during WORLD WAR I. He resumed his medical practice and political activity upon returning to Saskatoon.

Despite the conspicuous contrast between the vice-regal lifestyle and that of most Saskatchewanians, Munroe and his wife Myrtle did not ignore the hardships outside of GOVERNMENT HOUSE. He supported functions and raised money for relief projects and veterans while she served as an honorary president and patroness of numerous charitable organizations. Understandably, the official functions at the vice-regal residence seemed frivolous when 66% of Saskatchewan's rural population was on relief by 1932. However, the provincial Legislature overwhelmingly defeated a motion to suspend the Office of the Lieutenant-Governor in 1934. With the public's support, Munroe carried out his duties as King's representative in Saskatchewan until September 9, 1936. He died in Florida on March 12, 1947. *Holden Stoffel*

FURTHER READING: Hryniuk, Margaret and Garth Pugh. 1991. *"A Tower of Attraction": An Illustrated History of Government House, Regina, Saskatchewan.* Regina: Government House Historical Society/Canadian Plains Research Center.

MURRAY, ATHOL (1892–1975). Born in Toronto on January 9, 1892, Père Murray was ordained in 1918 and sent to Regina. In 1923, he established a sports club later known as the Regina Argos Athletic Club for disillusioned youth. Four years later he was assigned to Wilcox, where he joined the SISTERS OF CHARITY OF ST. LOUIS at Notre Dame of the Prairies. Murray officially founded Notre Dame in 1933 as a liberal arts college affiliated with the University of Ottawa. Rooted in the Catholic tradition, the college places special emphasis on athletics, particularly hockey. Père Murray's dedication earned Notre Dame international recognition as Canada's largest co-educational residential high school. The college's hockey team, the Hounds, have won forty-eight provincial and four national championships while over 100 former players have been drafted by NHL teams. Père Murray is a member of the SASKATCHEWAN SPORTS HALL OF FAME (1967), the Canadian Sports Hall of Fame (1972), and the Hockey Hall of Fame (1998). He was invested as an Officer of the Order of Canada in 1968. He

died on December 15, 1975. Notre Dame College was officially renamed the ATHOL MURRAY COLLEGE OF NOTRE DAME in 1981.

Daria Coneghan and Holden Stoffel

FURTHER READING: Gorman, J. 1977. *Père Murray and the Hounds: The Story of Saskatchewan's Notre Dame College.* Sidney, BC: Gray's Publishing.

© M.WEST, REGINA, WEST'S STUDIO COLLECTION/SASKATCHEWAN ARCHIVES BOARD R-A8006

Athol Murray.

MURRAY, CHRISTINA (1866–1947). Born in Fredericton, NB, in August 1866, Christina Murray (Cameron) graduated from the University of New Brunswick in 1894. She married WALTER C. MURRAY in 1895; they had three daughters. In 1909 the family moved to Saskatoon, where her husband had begun his presidency of the new UNIVERSITY OF SASKATCHEWAN. Murray had numerous duties as university president's wife—assisting him, students, and staff—and both were awarded honorary doctorates in 1938, a year after his retirement. Becoming active soon after arrival, she increased her involvement during WORLD WAR I, and in 1919 housed nurses who were assisting flu victims. She had also become involved in women's organizations. In 1916 she founded, and became first president of, the Local COUNCIL OF WOMEN. She became Saskatchewan vice-president of the National Council, and worked to found the Provincial Council (becoming president in 1918.) She was one of four Saskatchewan women to attend the Women's War Conference in Ottawa in February 1918. A charter member of the University Women's Club, founded in 1918, she remained active until her death. She also served as president

Christina Murray and her daughters: from left to right, Christina, Lucy, Jean, and Mrs. Christina Murray.

of the **YOUNG WOMEN'S CHRISTIAN ASSOCIATION**. Later involvements included membership on the executive of the Saskatoon Arts and Crafts Society. Christina Murray died in Saskatoon on July 4, 1947.

Bob Ivanochko

FURTHER READING: Saskatoon Business and Professional Women's Club. 1976. *Some Outstanding Women: They Made Saskatoon a Better Community.*

MURRAY, GERTRUDE (1912–). Gertrude Murray was a leader in Canada in the field of school broadcasts and telecasts: the extensive co-operative plan she and others established made possible a high standard of school broadcasting across Canada. Murray was born on September 9, 1912, in Weyburn. As a child, she enjoyed writing stories for the *Torch Bearer*, a pamphlet distributed by the *Leader-Post*; this love of writing served her well later in her career with the provincial Department of Education. Following Normal School in Moose Jaw, Gertrude Murray taught school in Saskatchewan for thirteen years and then joined the Department of Education in the Audiovisual Branch. In 1950 she became Supervisor of School Broadcasts, and then was appointed Chief of Instructional Resources that included radio, television, film services and school libraries.

Murray prepared radio programs for every weekday from October to May each year; she wrote scripts for school broadcasts, and **RJ STAPLES** wrote the musical scores. To celebrate Saskatchewan's Diamond Jubilee in 1965, she collaborated with Staples on "Saskatchewan at Work" and "Saskatchewan Song." In 1966–67, she worked with the Canadian International Development Agency (CIDA) and traveled to West Africa with a team of five other Canadians, working with Ghana's Ministry of

Education and promoting the use of media along with curriculum research and development. UNESCO awarded Gertrude Murray a medal in 1965 for her report on the Year of the Child; and in 1977 she was awarded an AMTEC (Association for Media and Technology in Education in Canada) Leadership Award. Upon her retirement she continued to live in Regina.

Naomi Kral

MURRAY, ROBERT (1936–). Robert Murray was born in Vancouver on March 2, 1936 and grew up in Saskatoon, though he has resided in the United States since 1960. Although he is best known for his monumental metal sculptures painted in bright blues, yellows or maroons, he began his artistic career as a painter and print-maker. In 1956–58, he attended the Regina College School of Art (now the Department of Visual Arts of the **UNIVERSITY OF REGINA**), where he studied with painters **KEN LOCHHEAD**, **ARTHUR MCKAY** and **ROY KIYOOKA**. During that time Murray also participated in the Emma Lake Artists' Workshops, where he became acquainted with Jack Shadbolt, Barnett Newman and Clement Greenberg.

Murray's first three-dimensional work, *Rainmaker* (1959–60, steel painted black-green, 244 centimetres high), was commissioned for the fountain situated in front of Saskatoon's new City Hall. It signifies a break with the representational and cubist traditions in sculpture and is an effort to explore, through simple forms, the effect of colour on perception and the relationship between work and environment. The monumental sculpture consists of two steel plates shaped into arcs and placed on top of two vertical plates perforated with cut-out patterns, forming the base of the installation. With this work, Murray discovered the means to explore concerns similar to those of Modernist painting, but

freed from the limitations of the canvas or the gallery. The commission of Rainmaker prompted public outcry in Saskatoon. It raised questions and awareness about the role and nature of **PUBLIC ART**, and about the relationship between sculpture, architecture and audience. Initially, much of the criticism directed at the work suggested that a sheaf of wheat or a historical figure would have better represented the city than the abstract forms deployed in *Rainmaker*. Opponents also accused Murray of unethical behaviour for not "making" the work himself. Indeed, *Rainmaker*, one of the first Canadian attempts to explore the possibilities inherent in making large-scale abstract sculptural work from malleable metal, was executed at John East Iron Works, a local firm specializing in the manufacture of agricultural equipment. Although it is now common practice for artists to work with metal fabricating plants, this was a rare event in 1959.

Murray's contribution to the field of monumental sculpture marked a turning point in the tradition of public art in Saskatchewan, and played an important role in the development and popular acceptance of formalist trends in public sculpture. His large-scale works are now displayed in prestigious public and private collections across North America. *Annie Gerin*

MURRAY, ROBERT G. (1917–2003). Robert Gordon Murray was born in Saskatoon on June 10, 1917, and died there on October 16, 2003. He received his BA at the **UNIVERSITY OF SASKATCHEWAN** in 1938 and his MD at the University of Toronto in 1941. After service in the Royal Navy, he practised in Saskatoon until 1950, leaving to specialize in ophthalmology in Toronto and in neuro-ophthalmology at the Johns Hopkins University Hospital. He was the founder and head of the ophthalmology department at the University of Saskatchewan in 1955, until he became dean of Medicine in 1973. Between 1963 and 1973, he also spent one or two days each week in Regina as head of the Medical Care Insurance Commission. Although the medical profession and

Robert Murray, left, presents the Lindsay Gold Medal in Medicine to Harold Baldwin, May 1975.

government regarded each other with suspicion after the 23-day "doctor's strike" in 1962, he achieved a degree of co-operation and efficiency that no full-time bureaucrat could have aspired to in that climate and time, and was able to keep in check those doctors who were seen as attempting to "milk" the system. He was called out of retirement to serve as chair of the Saskatchewan Commission on Directions in Health Care, which reported in April 1990 after twenty-one months of study. *C. Stuart Houston*

MURRAY, WALTER CHARLES (1866–1945).

Walter Murray was born on May 12, 1866, in King's County, New Brunswick. He received his BA from the University of New Brunswick in 1866; later, as the Canadian Gilchrist scholar, he attended the University of Edinburgh, where he received his MA in philosophy in 1891. He then went on to teach philosophy at Dalhousie until he was appointed the first president of the UNIVERSITY OF SASKATCHEWAN in 1908. He remained there until his retirement in 1937. Murray is remembered for his vision of a "people's university" dedicated to serving the agricultural needs of Saskatchewan, but also to benefiting from relationships to other disciplines. He insisted, therefore, that despite some criticism the College of Agriculture be integrated with the other colleges on campus rather than be separated, as was the norm elsewhere.

Murray also served in numerous other public offices: he was on the board of trustees for the Carnegie Foundation, was the chair of the board of governors for the Saskatoon Hospital, and was very active in his own church. He was the recipient of honorary degrees from universities all over Canada as well as the United States. His commitment to building the "people's university" as well as his community service, deep faith, and renowned generosity to those in need have given him the title of "Prairie Builder." *Tina Beaudry-Mellor*

FURTHER READING: Murray, D.R. and R.A. Murray. 1984. *The Prairie Builder: Walter Murray of Saskatchewan*. Edmonton: NeWest Press.

MURRAY COMMISSION REPORT, 1988–90.

A well-written, logical and internally consistent report, compiled by the Saskatchewan Commission on Directions in Health Care, was released in April 1990 after twenty-one months of study and an expenditure of $1.6 million. The Commission was chaired by Dr. R.G. MURRAY, former dean of Medicine (1973–82). WALTER PODILUK, former director of the Saskatoon Separate School System, stepped down from his position as provincial Deputy Minister of Health to become deputy chair and executive director. The other five commissioners were: Morris A. Anderson, former president of Luther College, Regina; Berva Farr, RN and executive director of a senior citizens home in Regina; Maureen L. Kurtz, a former public health nurse, Tisdale; Bishop Blaise Morand, a Roman Catholic leader from Prince Albert; and Ernie Moen, a Cabri farmer. Dr. SYLVIA FEDORUK, a former physicist for the Saskatchewan Cancer Clinics, resigned from the committee when she was appointed Saskatchewan's LIEUTENANT-GOVERNOR.

This report, the first attempt to make a comprehensive plan for Saskatchewan health services since the Sigerist Report of 1944, described the Saskatchewan health care system as "open-ended, constantly expanding and lacking sufficient controls," with insufficient emphasis on health promotion and preventive medicine.

The report recommended an increased effort to achieve a more unique Saskatchewan character, with a sense of ownership, a focus on health, professional teamwork, effectiveness, adaptability, affordability, and consultation. Among the 262 recommendations was a suggestion to divide the province into fifteen comprehensive health services divisions, with fifteen councils to replace the 127 hospital boards, 133 nursing home boards, 108 ambulance boards, and forty-five home care boards. It was proposed that fifty-seven one-doctor hospitals in villages and towns be turned into medical services centres, some staffed by a registered nurse, and that medical doctors be clustered into groups of at least three. A provincial health promotion fund of $10 million per year, as well as a health analysis and development commission targeting 1% of the health budget for research, were also mooted. To balance these new expenditures, the commission proposed tighter controls on medical practice, more home care, and fewer hospital admissions. Nurses should be given greater responsibility and paid more. Pediatrics and obstetrics would be moved to University Hospital.

In 1993, NDP Health Minister LOUISE SIMARD announced the closure of fifty-two rural hospitals; but this resulted in thirty health regions until 2003, when their number was reduced to ten. The amalgamation of pediatrics and obstetrics at Royal University Hospital, with closure of those units at the other two Saskatoon hospitals, took place in 1995; the last childbirth in the St. Paul's Hospital obstetric unit was on June 25, 1995.

C. Stuart Houston

MUSCOWPETUNG FIRST NATION. This

Ojibway and CREE band signed an adhesion to TREATY 4 on September 8, 1875, under Chief Muscowpetung, but continued to live a nomadic life, residing in the borderland CYPRESS HILLS in hopes that the buffalo would return. A reserve was surveyed for them in 1881 adjoining that of PASQUA, and they began to settle there that autumn. From that time on, their agricultural development was noted as advancing in a most favourable manner. In 1882, at the request of the chief, the reserve was extended four miles (2.5 km) west along the Qu'Appelle to allow access to a better supply of wood; but two miles (1.2 km) along the south end of the reserve were removed as part of this compensation. The main economic base has remained agricultural, and the community infrastructure includes a school, band hall, band office, machine shop, gymnasium, medical clinic, and maintenance buildings. The reserve is located 11 km north of Edenwold. In addition to the band's 9,357.2 ha of land, its members share in the 37.1 ha of the Treaty 4 Reserve Grounds at Fort Qu'Appelle. The band has 1,108 registered members, 271 of whom live on reserve.

Christian Thompson

MUSIC. The origins of the province's musical tradition lie in military and police bands, church choirs, immigrant teachers, enthusiastic residents, and the example of the many travelling groups of instrumentalists and singers who came by rail across the continent from the earliest days of settlement. Within the first fifteen years, the NWMP Barracks and the Town Hall in Regina had rung to dozens of musical performances while Saskatoon, with a population of but a few hundred, had three music halls, a choral society and a small orchestra by 1903. A Philharmonic Society, formed in Regina in 1904, performed Haydn's Creation (1906) and Mendelssohn's Elijah (1908), and had already toured opera to Saskatoon (1905). In the late 1880s Ontario piano and organ businesses were advertising vigorously, and keyboards were an essential accompaniment for almost any social gathering in town and country. Church, school and community choirs were at the core of the Saskatchewan music festivals from 1909. Many church choirs exceeded fifty members, and in

Walter C. Murray.

the 1950s the Bishop's School for Choristers in the Diocese of Qu'Appelle had over 100 boys annually each summer. Choirs travelled several hundred miles to attend the provincial festivals.

Between 1907 and 1920, musical education had been placed on a sound footing by the development of the Conservatory of Music, first as a private school in 1907 and then at Regina College, and by such organizations as the Bell Conservatoire, the Palmer School of Music and LYELL GUSTIN's Studio in Saskatoon. The teachers were active choir and orchestral conductors, instrumentalists and recitalists. Gustin sent his best pupils to teach in communities adjacent to the city. He also inspired music appreciation for thousands of schoolchildren in twenty concerts annually presented in Saskatoon by over fifty local artists in the 1930s. This was the decade when music entered the school curriculum at all levels. While the Associated Board of the Royal Schools of Music and the McGill and Toronto Conservatories conducted province-wide examinations, the Western Board of Music, organized by the three prairie universities and the Departments of Education, sprang to life in 1936 as a result of the vision of ARTHUR COLLINGWOOD, whose Chair of Music owed its existence to UNIVERSITY OF SASKATCH-EWAN President MURRAY and the generosity of the Carnegie Corporation. The practical and financial support both men gave to the music festival movement through the university over many years was especially crucial during the DEPRESSION. From this period too came the Music Teachers' Association, whose national arm was established in 1936 by the western provinces.

Claims that Saskatchewan was isolated from the mainstream are hard to sustain. Many of its most distinguished practitioners were trained in Scotland, England, the United States or Australia, and were well known there. Some travelled annually to Europe, most to American cultural centres. Until the 1960s, the Music Festival Association brought excellent musicians from England to adjudicate. From the 1920s, radio broadcasts allowed residents in most larger places in the province to hear at least five leading orchestras weekly, and from 1931 the Metropolitan Opera as well as a wealth of professional chamber concerts, live and on record. Outstanding international stars—Emma Albani, Nellie Melba, John McCormack, Jan Kubelik, Fritz Kreisler, Marcel Dupré, Percy Grainger (honorary vice-president of Gustin's Musical Art Club), Gracie Fields and Artur Rubinstein among them—came across the prairie. The Women's Musical Clubs from the earliest days, and later the Celebrity Concert Series, the Young Artist Series and many other groups, often sponsored by service clubs, added to the range of visiting artists and gave valuable experience to local artists preparing for professional careers.

During the last half-century, a majority of young people have entered the festivals formerly dominated by adults, the range of instrumentalists competing has widened, and the number of local festivals has grown from one in 1926 to thirteen in 1939 to fifty-one in 2004. Adult and school choirs have become rarer; but youth choirs of a high standard have appeared in several places, and some have won national prizes. Several competitions have been created for solo performance and for composition. The emphasis on composition can probably be traced to MURRAY ADASKIN's enthusiastic endorsement of the art for his students in the 1950s. The province now has at work several nationally recognized composers. The symphony orchestras in Saskatoon and Regina have employed at least a dozen full-time professional musicians each for the last thirty years, and these people have expanded the opportunity for live chamber music. Both provincial universities grant undergraduate and graduate degrees in music, first begun in Saskatoon in the 1930s, abandoned in 1947 and revived again in the 1960s. All these developments are sustaining the standards which have been aimed at since the earliest pioneering days of the late 19th century.

Robin Swales

MUSKEG LAKE CREE NATION. Muskeg Lake Cree Nation signed TREATY 6 on August 23, 1876, under Chief Peteynakey (Petequakay, Petequacay). They continued to live as they had done prior to treaty, and except for planting small plots of potatoes, they are noted for the great number of furs they sold to the Hudson's Bay Company post in 1880. A 26,880-acre reserve was surveyed in 1881, with its southern boundary adjoining the Mistowasis Reserve. The reserve had hay lands, fertile soil, an abundance of water, and a good supply of spruce and poplar wood. In 1888 the Indian Agent documented that a number of band members were working for local settlers. Currently, their economic base includes agriculture, gaming, and many commercial developments (e.g., on urban reserve land in Saskatoon) under Creek Investments Limited (1993) and Aspen Development Incorporated. In 2004 this First Nation teamed with Canadian Magnetic Imaging to purchase and run an MRI clinic in Saskatoon. Community infrastructure includes a school, band office, fire hall, church, sports grounds, mechanic shop, resource centre, recreation centre, seniors' centre, kitchen shelter, community health centre, and community maintenance outbuildings. The band currently has 9,722 ha of land; the largest and most settled portion is located 93 km north of Saskatoon.

Christian Thompson

MUSKODAY FIRST NATION. Ancestors of the Muskoday or Muscotayo (meaning "No trees" or "Bald prairie") were from St. Peters Reserve near Selkirk, Manitoba, and included six Smith brothers. The brothers separated, and John Smith (Mis-ti-koo-na-pac) and his followers signed TREATY 6 at Fort Carlton on August 23, 1876. Their reserve was surveyed 19 km southeast of Prince Albert that September. Most families settled along the river in "river lots"; the remainder of the reserve was subdivided in standard sections in 1949 and 1950. Farming was the primary occupation during the early reserve period, and band members were noted for their excellent herds of Shorthorn and Holstein cattle. As technology and better seed evolved, however, grain farming increased and the Muskoday Band Farm was developed in 1963. The reserve employs several members as school bus drivers, teacher's aides, band office staff, manager and employees of the Muskoday Band Farm, road and equipment maintenance, and librarian of the North Central Saskatchewan Regional Library branch. The first school was established in 1878 under the C.M. Society. In 1998 Muskoday became the first band in Saskatchewan to use its own land code, allowing them control over leasing and land development on their 9,686.8-ha reserve. Of the band's 1,430 members, 463 live on reserve. *Christian Thompson*

MUSKOWEKWAN FIRST NATION. Chief Ka-nee-na-wup (One Who Sits Like an Eagle) and his Ojibway people lived along the Upper Qu'Appelle Lakes prior to signing TREATY 4 on September 15, 1874. When Ka-nee-na-wup died, his son Muscowequan (Hard Quill, Muskowekwan) became chief. A reserve was surveyed in 1883, incorporating the settlement where they had already started farming (just south of the Touchwood Post). In 1886 a school was opened on the reserve, including swings for the children; it received second place for the best school in the Territories in 1888 and 1889. The band's agricultural development progressed apace, possibly aided by the model farm attached to the school in 1903. It had a windmill that made flour from the wheat, supplied power for cutting firewood and building lumber, crushed grain, and pumped water to the main building. In 1993 Muskowekwan's Treaty Land Entitlement Claim was ratified, enabling the band to increase its land holdings to a total of 12,517.3 ha. The reserve is home to 365 members, from a total membership of 1,388 people. The Muskowekwan Reserve is located 64 km northwest of Fort Qu'Appelle; its infrastructure includes a band office and medical clinic, band hall, workshop, maintenance office, water treatment plant and pump house, school and teacherage, and an outdoor rink. *Christian Thompson*

MUSLIMS. Muslims arrived in Saskatchewan at the end of the 19th century. Most of them came from Lebanon and settled as farmers in southwestern Saskatchewan, around Swift Current. A significant number of Muslims also arrived in Saskatchewan in the 1960s; they came from Asia and the Middle East, mainly from countries with a large Muslim population. Since then, conflicts in Africa and Eastern Europe have resulted in a large number of Muslim refugees, and the Muslim population of Saskatchewan has continued to grow. According to Statistics Canada, in 2001 there were 2,230 people in Saskatchewan who identified themselves as Muslims, compared with 1,200 in 1991. At present, the majority of Saskatchewan Muslims reside in Saskatoon and Regina. However, there are smaller numbers of Muslims in other towns such as Prince Albert, Swift Current and Moose Jaw. Muslims who came to Saskatchewan in the 1960s were mainly associated with the universities as teachers, researchers and students; others were physicians. Many became involved in business and other occupations.

In 1978, the Saskatoon Islamic Center (Mosque) was established in a former church building; in the early 1980s, the Regina Islamic Centre and the Islamic Centre of Swift Current were also established in older church buildings. An Islamic Centre is a place where Muslims gather for prayers as well as for social and educational activities such as evening and weekend classes in Islamic studies, and Arabic language classes both for children and adults. In 2000, a full-time private elementary school (Saskatoon Misbah School) was established, providing classes that are based on the Saskatchewan curriculum; a similar school (Huda School) has been operating in Regina since 1999. At these schools students also receive religious instructions within provincial guidelines.

Apart from beliefs common to the other two monotheistic world religions, Muslims represent a diversity of cultures and languages: the origins of many Canadian Muslims can be traced to a wide range of countries in the Middle East, Asia, Africa, and Europe.

Muslims believe that there is only one God (Allah) and that Muhammad is the last prophet to whom God has revealed the Holy Quran, his final message for the guidance of mankind. Islam, which means "peace" in Arabic, is not a new religion: it simply reaffirms the message revealed by God to all the prophets from Adam to Jesus Christ. The five essential elements of Muslim faith include: belief in one God and Muhammad as the last prophet; five daily prayers; fasting in the month of Ramadan; Zakaat (giving a proportion of annual savings to help the less fortunate); and a pilgrimage to Mecca at least once in a lifetime for all capable individuals.

Shakeel Akhtar

MUSTARD. Mustard is an important crop grown by nearly 3,000 Saskatchewan farmers on approximately 240,000 ha annually. Saskatchewan is the world's largest exporter of mustard seed, and production is focussed on three types derived from two different species: yellow mustard (*Sinapis alba*), and brown and oriental mustard (*Brassica juncea*). Canada's first mustard cultivation occurred in Alberta in 1936; however, production has since moved to Saskatchewan, with almost 90% of the country's annual 227,000 metric tonnes grown in the province. All mustard types are members of the Cruciferous family and have yellow flowers with four petals. Individual plants can have over 200 flowers during their life cycle, and each plant can produce thousands of seeds. Mustard seeds contain oil, protein, fibre, and glucosinolates; the latter break down in the presence of water to impart the hot and pungent tastes associated with mustard. As well, yellow mustard seed contains mucilage, which is an important food industry ingredient.

Mustard is mostly used as a condiment. Yellow varieties give rise to traditional North American hot dog mustard, which has a mild sweetish taste. Aromatic and spicy Dijon mustard is derived from brown mustard; and English mustard is a mixture of brown and yellow, making it both hot and pungent. Japanese cuisine employs oriental mustard in the making of *wasabi*, and some Asian countries use oriental mustard oil for cooking. Yellow mustard has many other uses, most of which are associated with its mucilage. The mucilage acts as an emulsifier which helps suspend oils in water and prevents the separation of these ingredients in salad dressings and mayonnaise; it also has the ability to absorb liquid in food, helping keep prepared meats firm and moist during cooking. Mustard can also act as a preservative because the breakdown products of the glucosinolates inhibit the growth of certain yeasts, moulds and bacteria. Certain compounds found in mustard have been reported to decrease both blood cholesterol and blood glucose levels.

Saskatoon is home to the only mustard breeding program in North America. The Saskatchewan Research Centre, with Agriculture and Agri-Food Canada, breeds all three types of mustard for the condiment market, and is working on developing mustard varieties suited to non-food applications such as biodiesel and other industrial products.

The Saskatchewan Mustard Development Commission was formed on January 1, 2004, and collects a refundable levy of 0.05% on gross sales of mustard seed in Saskatchewan. This check-off will be used for research and development of the mustard industry; as a result, mustard seed production and processing should increase in Saskatchewan over the next ten to fifteen years. *William Greuel*

MYLES, MARGARET FRASER (1892–1988). *Née* Margaret ("Maggie") Fraser Findlay, Myles was the sole member of the fifth graduating class (in 1917) from the Queen Victoria Hospital nursing training program in Yorkton, Saskatchewan, and went on to achieve world prominence in nursing education. Born in Aberdeen, Scotland, on December 30, 1892, she emigrated to Saskatchewan just prior to **WORLD WAR I**, trained as a nurse in Yorkton and there met her future husband, Charles James Myles; they married on June 30, 1920. When Charles died on July 30, 1921, Maggie returned to Scotland and took a year of midwifery training. After her three-year-old son died in 1924, she studied nursing for three additional years at Edinburgh Royal Infirmary.

In 1927, Maggie returned to her alma mater in Yorkton to be matron of nurses. For three years she did most of the teaching of the student nurses, upgraded the curriculum, graduated five to seven registered nurses per year, and realized that her interests lay in education. She studied education at McGill University; this was followed by posts as director of Nursing Education at Philadelphia and Detroit, and then as the sole midwife tutor when the Simpson Maternity Pavilion opened in Edinburgh in 1937.

Myles' *Textbook for Midwives* appeared in 1953, and was constantly updated through the tenth edition in 1985 (when she was 92). Over half a million copies were sold, making it one of the most successful medical texts in world history. "Maggie" died in Kincardineshire, Scotland, on February 15, 1988. *C. Stuart Houston*

NAHKAWININIWAK: *see* **SAULTEAUX**

NAICAM, town, pop 761, located between Watson and Melfort at the junction of Hwys 6 and 349. The community is situated in an area of rich farmlands dotted with numerous small lakes and patches of wetland wilderness. The first settlers began taking up land in the district in 1904. Many were of Norwegian and Swedish origin, but additionally there were people of English and German origins among others. By 1910, a post office and a school had been established in the vicinity of the present community. In late 1918, the CPR purchased land for a townsite from Mrs. Ingeborg Knutson and, in 1919, the first businesses appeared. In December 1920, the first work train arrived in Naicam and Ingeborg Knutson had the honour of driving a ceremonial spike. On April 28, 1921, Naicam was incorporated as a village, its name derived from the first three letters of the names of two railway contractors, Naismith and Cameron. The population that year was 119. By the 1950s the population was over 500 and, on September 1, 1954, Naicam attained town status. Today, Naicam serves a trading area population of approximately 4,600 people within about a 30 km radius and a number of the community's businesses operate in support of the district's agricultural industry. Community attractions

Naicam, 1922.

include the Naicam Museum, located in the 1923 Pioneer School, and the town's original CPR station, which now houses a licenced dining room. During the summer months, the town's floral displays are an added attraction and, for two years running, Naicam was the provincial winner in its category in the nationally acclaimed "Communities in Bloom" competition. Saskatchewan singer-songwriter Stan Garchinski's musical career began with a family dance band called "The Cavaliers" in Naicam, and it was Garchinski's song that was chosen as the official song for Saskatchewan's Centennial.

David McLennan

NAINAAR, MARGE (1936–). Marge Nainaar was born in Durban, South Africa on July 27, 1936, and came to Canada with her husband and three preschool children in 1969. Interacting in the cultural diversity of Canada became her career and source of lifelong learning. Nainaar organized a Multicultural Society within the Saskatchewan Penitentiary, and founded an immigrant and refugee settlement agency in Prince Albert. Nainaar served as president of the Canadian Multicultural Federation (CMF), the Saskatchewan Association for Immigrant Serving Agencies (SAISIA), the Western Canada Association of Immigrant Serving Agencies (WCAISA), the Saskatchewan Council for Educators of Non-English Speakers (SCENES), the **SASKATCHEWAN ASSOCIATION OF MULTICULTURAL EDUCATION** (SAME), and the **MULTICULTURAL COUNCIL OF SASKATCHEWAN** (MCoS). Her experience led to her appointment to the Saskatchewan Multicultural Advisory Committee, the Canadian Multicultural Advisory Committee, and the Minister's Advisory Committee for Multicultural Legislation.

Nainaar served on numerous boards, committees and councils, including the Prince Albert Race Relations and Social Issues Committee, the Prince Albert Council of Women, the Citizens Advisory Committee to the Saskatchewan Penitentiary and Parole Board, the Regional Economic Development Authority, the National Organization of Immigrant and Visible Minority Women of Canada, and the Saskatchewan Council **GIRL GUIDES** of Canada. She has been recognized through many awards: Saskatchewan Volunteer Medal (2001); National Citizenship Citation Award (2001); Prince Albert Citizen of the Year (2001); Saskatchewan Tourism Volunteer of the Year Award (2001); Canada's 125th Birthday Commemorative Medal; Taylor Award for Outstanding Volunteer Work for the Correctional Services of Canada (2002); Saskatchewan Council for Educators of Non-English Speakers Award of Merit (2002); Queen's Jubilee Award (2002); Citizenship Award–Secretary of State (for promoting Canadian Citizenship throughout Saskatchewan); Canada 125 Provincial Award; Betty Szuchewycz Multicultural Award; Wolf Project

Award (for outstanding endeavour in race relations); Cultural Award–Saskatchewan Parks, Recreation and Culture; Valuable Contribution Award–Prince Albert Chamber of Commerce; Service to the Community Award–Prince Albert and District; City of Prince Albert Award of Merit; and YWCA 1994 Woman of Distinction Award.

Harlan Weidenhammer

NAKOTA (ASSINIBOINE). The Assiniboine are a Siouan-speaking people closely related linguistically to the Sioux and Stoney. Folk tradition suggesting a separation from the Yanktonai Sioux is not supported linguistically or historically. Linguistically, Nakota is on a continuum with the other Sioux dialects, no closer to one than the other, suggesting that the Assiniboine diverged from the Sioux at the same time the other Sioux dialects were differentiating from one another. The name Assiniboine derives from Ojibwa *assini?- pwa? n*, "stone enemy," meaning "stone Sioux"–often with the *-ak* plural suffix, later a final *-t*, and by the 19th century the final *-n* or *-ne*. Nakota is their name for themselves and the language that they speak.

Assiniboines were first encountered by Europeans in the woodlands and parklands, already adept canoe users in their role as trade middlemen. In 1737 La Vérendrye distinguished the Woodland Assiniboines, who knew how to take fur-bearing animals, from the Plains Assiniboines, who had to be taught. Communal buffalo hunting utilized dogs until horses were acquired. Assiniboines utilized the buffalo pound to entrap and process much larger quantities than could be taken by single hunters. In the 17th century Assiniboine territory extended westward from Lake Winnipeg and the Forks of the Red and Assiniboine rivers into much of central and southern Saskatchewan. From the earliest descriptions, the Assiniboines allied with Algonquian-speaking **CREES**, and later, in the early to mid-19th century, with **SAULTEAUX** or western Ojibwas. Historical sources suggest a westward expansion of Assiniboine territory during the 18th century through the parklands of the central **SASKATCHEWAN RIVER** and into eastern Alberta; but these farthest reaches represented interaction spheres, and not a migration of fully articulated social groups reflecting the fur traders' knowledge of the western prairies. **ALEXANDER HENRY THE YOUNGER** listed in 1808 only one of eight Assiniboine bands occupying territory within the boundaries of the United States, along the **SOURIS RIVER** in North Dakota. Population movements during the early 19th century shifted Assiniboine territory southward, and by 1840 three-quarters of the nation lived along the Missouri in the area of northwestern North Dakota and northeastern Montana. By the mid-19th century Assiniboine territory extended east from the Moose and Wood mountains to the **CYPRESS HILLS**, and north to south

from the **NORTH SASKATCHEWAN RIVER** to the Milk and Missouri rivers. Assiniboines first learned of the jurisdiction of the United States with the visit of Lewis and Clark, which marked the beginning of their incorporation.

The population history of the Assiniboines remains incomplete until well into the 19th century. A number of major disease episodes proved to be quite intrusive. The population was estimated at 10,000 before one-half to two-thirds were wiped out in the smallpox epidemic of 1780–81; the 1819–20 epidemic of measles and whooping cough again reduced the population by one-half. After the steamboats brought smallpox to the upper Missouri in the late 1830s the population began to recover, but as much as 60% of the population had been lost. After a slow recovery, two more smallpox epidemics struck the Assiniboine in 1856–57 and in 1869 before the population began another recovery.

By the last decades of the 19th century Assiniboine reservations and reserves were located in Montana and Saskatchewan within the larger region they had occupied during the previous century. In Montana, the Upper Assiniboines were located with the Atsina Gros Ventre on the Fort Belknap Reservation, and the Lower Assiniboines with Yanktonai, Sisseton/Wahpeton Dakota and a small number of Hunkpapa and other Teton stragglers of Sitting Bull's followers on the Fort Peck Reservation. In Saskatchewan, Assiniboines within **TREATY 4** were the reserve bands of Pheasant's Rump, Ocean Man, Carry the Kettle and Long Lodge, and **PIAPOT**'s Cree-speaking Assiniboines; and Assiniboines within **TREATY 6** were the bands of Grizzly Bear's Head and Lean Man, which often were known as the Battleford Stoneys.

Assiniboine population figures in the initial reservation/reserve period were complicated by tribally undifferentiated figures for the shared reservations in Montana, and similarly for some of the reserves in Canada. Contemporary population figures reflect the mixed heritage of many inter-marriages: Carry the Kettle 2,009; Ocean Man 346; Pheasant Rump Nakota 316; White Bear 1,898; Mosquito, Grizzley Bear's Head 1,049; Fort Belknap 2,245; and Fort Peck 4,197. Reservations in Montana and reserves in Saskatchewan remain homes for these respective tribes and First Nations. In every case a large proportion of their populations reside off-reserve, mostly in cities, encouraged to do so both by increased economic opportunities and by various government policy initiatives in the decades following **WORLD WAR II**. Since the 1970s, Nakota reserves in Saskatchewan have been leaders in the successful pursuit of land claims known as "specific claims," and this has resulted in resources for a wide range of economic development initiatives. A florescence of religious practice has occurred in the last three decades, as communities support one another in their search for health and well-being.   *David Reed Miller*

FURTHER READING: DeMallie, R.J. and D.R. Miller. 2001. "Assiniboine." Pp. 572–95 in R.J. DeMallie (ed.), *The Handbook of North American Indians*, Vol. 13, Part 1. Washington, DC: Smithsonian Institute.

NATIONAL GRAIN COMPANY. The story of National Grain is the story of the Peavey family in Canada. When western Canada was being settled, Frank Peavey had already established an empire of grain elevators across the American West, as well as lake shipping, rail cars and terminals on the Great Lakes and the West Coast. After completing the Canadian Northern Railway between Edmonton and Port Arthur, **WILLIAM MACKENZIE** and Donald Mann made a rail car available to American grain interests to view the west and select sites for new elevators; Frank Peavey's sons-in-law Frank Heffelfinger and Frederick Wells, along with Augustus Searle and Peavey executives E. Kneeland and Robert Evans, made the tour. After the Winnipeg Grain Exchange had introduced a wheat futures contract, allowing for hedging grain purchases, Heffelfinger and Wells proceeded to form the British America Elevator Company in 1906, with Mackenzie and Mann holding 40% of the capital stock. The agreement was to construct fifty new elevators on northern lines. By 1911, under Kneeland's leadership British America had 100 elevators–most of them in Saskatchewan.

A second company, the Security Elevator Company Ltd. was formed to build elevators on the newly constructed **GRAND TRUNK PACIFIC RAILWAY** (today part of **CANADIAN NATIONAL RAILWAY**). A third company, the National Grain Elevator Company, was formed in 1909 to operate elevators on both Canadian Pacific and Northern lines; in the same year Peavey purchased the Northern Elevator Company, the first line company to be established in the west (in 1893). In 1929 the close association between the Peavey interests and Augustus Searle was ended when the two parties agreed through an exchange of shares to divest their joint interests; Searle merged his grain interests into the new **SEARLE GRAIN COMPANY**. In 1940 the Peavey companies (British America, Northern, National, and Grand Trunk Pacific Elevator) were merged to form National Grain Company Limited, with George Heffelfinger, son of Frank Heffelfinger, as president. The new company had close to 400 elevators.

National Grain did not participate in direct overseas selling. An opportunity arose in the late 1960s, when the McCabe Grain Company was dispersed, to acquire the expertise needed to trade internationally. In 1967 **UNITED GRAIN GROWERS** purchased the McCabe elevators; Peavey interests purchased the feed and seed components. The McCabe company still existed with its experienced merchandizing staff, but had no physical facilities. In 1971 Heffelfinger and McCabe merged their interests to form National Grain Ltd., George Heffelfinger remaining president. Shortly after this merger the Peavey interests decided to reduce their dependence on commodities and began to seek a buyer for their Canadian grain and feed operations. Cargill Grain, already a massive diversified grain company located primarily in the United States, became the buyer: National Grain Ltd. was amalgamated with a Cargill Canadian subsidiary on January 1, 1975, to become Cargill Grain Company Ltd. National Feed and Livestock Ltd. became Cargill Nutrena Feeds Ltd.

Gary Storey

FURTHER READING: Anderson, C.W. 1991. *Grain: The Entrepreneurs*. Winnipeg: Watson and Dwyer Publishing; Wilson, C.F. 1978. *A Century of Canadian Grain*. Saskatoon: Western Producer Prairie Books.

NATIONAL POLICY. The National Policy is the collective term used to describe the series of initiatives developed by the Canadian government after Confederation to transform Rupert's Land into a political and economic unit. The ultimate goal of these policies was to forge a self-sufficient national Canadian economy. Central to this goal was the adoption of a land policy aimed at inducing immigrants to settle in the West, the construction of a trans-continental railway system, the creation of a federal police force, and the implementation of a protective tariff on manufactured goods.

Aspects of the National Policy were extremely controversial at the time and continue to provoke debate among historians. The federal government at the time was closely allied to the business community of central Canada, which saw the West as a hinterland to be exploited for its own benefit. There is little doubt that the regional interests of the West were subordinated to a definition of national interest that primarily benefited the central Canadian economic and political elite.

Westerners at the time developed a variety of practical grievances. These included a land policy which left some of the best land in the hands of the Hudson's Bay Company and the railways; a two-tier freight rate which discriminated against western customers and ensured a monopoly for the **CANADIAN PACIFIC RAILWAY**; and a tariff structure which inflated the cost of household goods and agricultural equipment, thereby undermining the profitability of western farmers. These grievances formed the basis of an enduring sense of **WESTERN ALIENATION**, which has periodically given rise to protest movements or regionally based third parties such as the **PROGRESSIVE PARTY**, the **CO-OPERATIVE COMMONWEALTH FEDERATION** and the Reform Party (*see* **CONSERVATIVE PARTY OF CANADA**). Although these parties differed in structure and ideology, all were dedicated to ensuring that all regions of the country shared the benefits of Confederation equally.

Carmen Howell

FURTHER READING: Bercuson, D.J. (ed). 1977. *Canada and the Burden of Unity*. Toronto: MacMillan of Canada; Friesen, Gerald. 1984. *The Canadian Prairies: A History*. Toronto: University of Toronto Press.

NATIVE PLANT SOCIETY OF SASKATCH-EWAN. The Native Plant Society of Saskatchewan (NPSS) is a provincial non-profit organization incorporated in 1995. In the early 1990s, as interest in native plants gained momentum, professionals, along with some native plant enthusiasts, recognized the need for an organization specializing in Saskatchewan's native plants. A working group was formed in 1994, which led to the development of the NPSS. The vision of the NPSS was expanded knowledge and appreciation of Saskatchewan's native plants. This vision was to be met by the society's mission to promote understanding and conservation of native plants and their ecosystems by facilitating research, communication and education.

The Native Plant Society started off small, but in just ten years the organization has grown rapidly. The NPSS now averages 200 members annually, offers a full slate of field tours and workshops, and its annual general meeting includes a major conference. Its core programs include: a website with a searchable database for native plant materials; a display booth; and *Native Plant News*, the society's quarterly newsletter, which is distributed across western Canada and the northern United States. Through the support of its partners the NPSS has completed many projects, such as six extension/educational publications, posters, youth and adult education programs, and research and restoration projects. The NPSS is an active organization and is represented in the Saskatchewan Prairie Conservation Action Plan, Saskatchewan Advisory Committee on Forage Crops, Saskatchewan Endangered Species Advisory Committee, Saskatchewan Agriculture Food and Rural Revitalization Stakeholders Group, and a Lakeland College program advisory committee

Garth Wruck

NATO AIR TRAINING PLAN. The NATO Air Training Plan was the natural extension of Canada's **WORLD WAR II** air training experience, where 131,553 Allied airmen graduated from the **BRITISH COMMONWEALTH AIR TRAINING PLAN** (BCATP). In response to the Soviet Union's creation of Communist satellite states, Western nations formed their own alliance: the North Atlantic Treaty Organization (NATO). NATO signatories desired a build-up of air power, and as early as the spring of 1949 Canada was approached to provide training of aircrews for other treaty members. Canada was seen as a suitable place in which to carry out air training since it was far from any potential European battlefront. On December 17, 1950, Brooke Claxton, Canada's Minister of National Defence, announced that the **ROYAL CANADIAN AIR FORCE** (RCAF) would initially train aircrew from the air forces of the United Kingdom, France, Belgium, Norway, Luxembourg, Denmark, Italy, Portugal and the Netherlands. The NATO Air Training Plan was to be extended numerous times throughout the 1950s. As in **WORLD WAR II**, much of the flying training for NATO was located in the prairie provinces: the topography is flat, and flying could be conducted away from the congested population centres of Ontario. Two pre-existing BCATP bases were used in Saskatchewan for NATO air training: Moose Jaw became No. 2 Flying Training School, while Saskatoon hosted No. 1 Advanced Flying School.

The program began with a five-week Pre-Flight Orientation Course at RCAF Station London, Ontario for foreign students, in which they became familiar with RCAF aircraft and flight terminology. Pilot recruits then proceeded to a Flying Training School (FTS) for thirty weeks of instruction on North American Harvard aircraft. Advanced Flying School (AFS) followed, where four to five months were spent on single-engine T-33 Silver Star jets, multi-engine Beechcraft Expeditors, or North American Mitchells. The curriculum at FTS changed somewhat in 1956 when the Primary Flying Training School was opened at Centralia, Ontario. After being given twenty-five hours' practice on the DeHavilland Chipmunk at Centralia, students proceeded to one of the three Flying Training Schools for 155 hours of instruction on Harvards. Pilots selected for multi-engine training continued their AFS training on Expeditors or Mitchells at Saskatoon. Single-engine pilot trainees flew 125 hours on T-33 Silver Stars at one of the other two Advanced Flying Schools. After 75 weeks of training, in which they had completed 305 flying hours, RCAF graduates were posted to an Operational Training Unit; NATO recruits returned to their home country.

Between 1950 and 1958, eleven NATO nations participated in the NATO Air Training Plan. The first class of trainees arrived in Canada in July 1950 and graduated in May 1951; the final class to graduate in the summer of 1958 had commenced training in July 1957. By the end of the NATO Air Training Plan in the 1950s, 3,218 Canadian aircrew had been trained, as well as 5,299 from other NATO signatory countries. Despite the formal termination of the plan in 1957, Canada continued to sign bilateral agreements with countries, both NATO and non-NATO, which were unable to train their own aircrew recruits. Denmark, Norway, the Netherlands, Turkey, West Germany, Malaysia, Jamaica, and Tanzania were some of the countries involved. The NATO Air Training Plan of the 1950s, built on the

experience Canada had garnered in air training during World War II, laid the foundation for the air training program Canada currently provides to NATO nations.   *Rachel Lea Heide*

NATURE SASKATCHEWAN. ISABEL PRIESTLY founded the Saskatchewan Natural History Society or Nature Saskatchewan (the Society) in 1949. Its vision is one of "Humanity in Harmony with Nature," and its mission is to promote appreciation and understanding of our natural environment through education, **CONSERVATION** and research, and to protect and preserve natural ecosystems and their **BIODIVERSITY**. During the early years, the Society focused on education about natural history through meeting programs and conservation advocacy; it has published the regional natural history journal *Blue Jay* since 1949. Since 1958, 23 special publications have been produced, including the Society history, *The Isabel Priestly Legacy*, in 1996. The Society also publishes a regular newsletter, *Nature Views*, and holds general membership meetings in late spring and early fall at various locations around the province; activities include local tours, resolutions, slide and award presentations, banquets and elections. Until the early 1980s, the Society was entirely run by volunteers; currently, a staff of 11 full time-equivalent positions based in Regina and elsewhere in the province conducts externally funded projects. Since 1981, the Society has received lottery monies to help fund its provincial office in Regina.

Nature Saskatchewan is represented on over 50 advisory committees and stakeholder groups, and actively lobbies governments for a better environment. In recent years, major externally funded programs have included voluntary habitat stewardship programs for species at risk (burrowing **OWLS**, loggerhead **SHRIKES**, piping plovers, and rare plants), shoreline conservation (Living by Water), the educational NatureQuest program for the schools (under development), Important Bird Areas in Saskatchewan, and Voluntary Sector Initiative pilot projects in habitat conservation and land management. The Society manages and inventories six nature sanctuaries: Turtle Lake, Rendek Elm Forest, Crooked Lake Fen, Van Brienen Land, Maurice G. Street Wildlife, and Brandon Land. With about 1,000 members in and outside Saskatchewan, it is the largest conservation organization in the province. It is affiliated with the Canadian Nature Federation, and with local natural history societies in Regina, Saskatoon, Moose Jaw, Prince Albert, Swift Current, Weyburn, Yorkton, Fort Qu'Appelle, Indian Head, Preeceville, and Luseland.   *Robert G. Warnock*

NEATBY, HILDA (1904–75). Hilda Neatby was among the first women to become a professional historian, and was the sole woman member of the

Massey Commission. She was born in Sutton, Surrey, England in 1904, to Andrew Neatby and Ada Neatby (Fisher). In 1906 Hilda, her parents, and eight siblings emigrated to Saskatchewan, settling in Earl Grey. After Andrew Neatby's medical practice failed, the family turned to farming. Conditions were initially desperate, and never became comfortable. The children were formed by the need to survive, their mother's determination, their father's religious training, and his constant reading to them. In 1924 Neatby received a BA Honours in history from the **UNIVERSITY OF SASKATCHEWAN**. She then spent ten years in study and university teaching. In 1934 the University of Minnesota granted her a PhD in history. She taught history and French at Regina College until 1946, when she began to teach history at the University of Saskatchewan. In 1958 she became head of the History Department, until 1969. She then spent several years at Queen's University, researching and writing its history.

Hilda Neatby played an important role on the Massey Commission (1949–51), was the first woman president of the Canadian Historical Association (1962), and became a Companion of the Order of Canada in 1967. She is best known for her 1953 book, *So Little for the Mind*, a stinging attack on Canadian education that triggered a national debate. Among her other publications were a history of Quebec and two collections of speeches on education. She died on May 14, 1975.   *Michael Hayden*

FURTHER READING: Hayden, M. (ed.). 1983. *So Much to Do, So Little Time: The Writings of Hilda Neatby*. Vancouver: UBC Press.

Hilda Neatby.

NÊHIYAWAK: *see* **CREE**

NEKANEET CREE FIRST NATION. The Nekaneet First Nation signed **TREATY 4** on September 15, 1874, under the leadership of Foremost Man (Front Man), who refused to relocate when other bands were forced out of the **CYPRESS HILLS** in 1882. From 1882 to 1913 they were denied a reserve, and between 1882 and 1975 did not receive annuity payments. On August 2, 1913, a reserve of 1,440 acres near Maple Creek was created, and in 1914 funds were authorized to fence it. Very little was done to aid the survival of this community, and it was not until 1955 that the band's children were permitted to attend local schools. On January 10, 1958, an Order-in-Council increased the reserve's acreage, but the poor quality of the land continued to prohibit any type of agriculture except small-scale cattle ranching. It was finally concluded that the band's members were indeed Treaty Indians, and they began receiving annuity payments in 1968. In 1987, Nekaneet band members sought compensation for outstanding lawful obligations, but it was not until 1998 that Canada accepted the band's claim for benefits. To this day, the band faces enormous economic problems, and band members are forced to seek employment off reserve. In order to improve their economic situation they must either obtain more agriculturally viable land or be financially aided in other enterprises. Currently 167 of the 407 band members reside on the 5,602-ha reserve, 121 km southwest of Swift Current.   *Christian Thompson*

NEW DANCE HORIZONS. New Dance Horizons is Saskatchewan's only professional dance company. Founded in 1986 by Robin Poitras and Dianne Fraser, its mandate is to support the creation, development, production and presentation of contemporary dance and related performing arts in the province. This is achieved through three main strands: NDH INTEMPCO, Performing Series, and Learning and Teaching series. NDH INTEMPCO is a project-based company dedicated to the celebration of original work by artistic director Robin Poitras. A foundation for creation, production and touring, it also supports co-productions with local and national dance artists. At least one new original work has been produced each season, including the Pelican Project, a series of processional performances by youth as well as established and emerging artists. The Performing Series features the works of guest choreographers and dancers such as Édouard Locke, Marie Chouinard, Davida Monk, Benoit Lachambre, Jocelyne Montpetit, and Daniel Leveille. This strand was expanded in 2001 to include the biannual Stream of Dance Festival, featuring contemporary prairie dance in a national and international context. The Learning and Teaching Series provides the community with workshops, lectures and residencies involving guest instructors. Guided by an advisory committee composed of local dance professionals, its many initiatives have included visiting artist programs with elementary and high school arts educators, and creative and technical training workshops offered in collaboration with local dance schools. Poitras has been the sole artistic director since 1991. In its inaugural year, the company had a budget of just $5,150; currently it tops $300,000.

Barb Cameron

FURTHER READING: Cameron, B. 1998. *A History of the Professional Dance Companies That Have Existed in Saskatchewan Since 1905.* Saskatoon: Dance Saskatchewan.

NEW DEMOCRATIC PARTY (NDP). The New Democratic Party (NDP) and its predecessor the **CO-OPERATIVE COMMONWEALTH FEDERATION** (CCF) have been the province's most successful provincial parties, winning twelve of the sixteen elections between 1944 and 2003. The national NDP was formed in 1961 and initially led by former Saskatchewan Premier, **T.C. DOUGLAS**. The Saskatchewan CCF was reluctant to officially adopt the NDP name, which was finally adopted only after election losses in 1964 and 1967. The NDP, led by **WOODROW LLOYD**, remained in opposition to the Liberal government of **ROSS THATCHER** from 1964 to 1971. While in opposition, the party criticized the government's privatization of various **CROWN CORPORATIONS**, the austerity measures after the 1967 election, and the introduction of deterrent fees on health care. The period was also a turbulent time for the party as the growing radicalism of the baby boom generation gave life to the **WAFFLE** Movement. The party tried to accommodate the group into its structure, but the Waffle's confrontational style made this ultimately impossible. The movement helped stimulate substantial debate over party policy: this, in part, contributed to programs later instituted by the Blakeney government, such as the Land Bank and the nationalization of part of the province's natural resource sector. Amid controversy, Woodrow Lloyd resigned as party leader in 1970; **ALLAN BLAKENEY** won the leadership contest over **ROY ROMANOW**, Waffler Don Mitchell, and George Taylor in one of most heated leadership contests in Saskatchewan history.

Benefiting from the unpopularity of the Thatcher government, the NDP swept to power in 1971, winning the highest percentage of vote in its history. Allan Blakeney became Premier, a position he held for the next eleven years. His government pursued a policy of interventionism in the province's resource sector. Royalty rates for natural resources were increased, and a number of Crown corporations were established in the sector—most notably **SASKOIL** and the Saskatchewan Potash Corporation. The policy was highly controversial, especially the nationalization of a large percentage of the province's **POTASH INDUSTRY**. The government also pursued development of the **URANIUM** industry, a move that upset large sections of the NDP's own membership. The government played a leading role in the constitutional negotiations that resulted in the patriation of the Canadian Constitution in 1982.

The Blakeley government was re-elected in 1975 and 1978, but defeated in 1982. The long-dormant provincial Progressive Conservatives, led by **GRANT DEVINE**, swept the province and left the NDP with only nine MLAs, the party's worst result since its inception. The party was forced into opposition, but quickly rebounded in the polls, regaining its urban base and winning the popular vote in 1986; but it still had significantly fewer seats than the Conservatives owing to the overrepresentation of rural Saskatchewan in the Legislature. Roy Romanow replaced Blakeney as leader in 1987. The NDP challenged the increasingly unpopular government on its reliance on deficit budgets and over the sale of Crown corporations such as **SASKENERGY**. In 1991, the NDP returned to power as the Devine government was soundly defeated.

Inheriting a substantial debt, the NDP government attempted to improve the province's fiscal position by implementing a variety of unpopular cost-cutting measures and increased taxation; the most controversial measure was the conversion of many local **HOSPITALS** into healthcare facilities. Succeeding in balancing the budget, the government was re-elected in 1995. It was again re-elected in 1999, but by the slightest of margins: the newly formed **SASKATCHEWAN PARTY** had won the popular vote, although the NDP won more seats. The government was forced to enter into a coalition with the **LIBERAL PARTY** to stay in power. The party lost nearly all of its rural seats as it was increasingly representing urban Saskatchewan. Romanow stepped down as party leader in 2001 and was succeeded by **LORNE CALVERT**. With the Saskatchewan Party seemingly gaining momentum, the Calvert government was widely expected to lose; however, in November 2003 Calvert pulled off an upset, winning a fourth consecutive term in government and re-establishing a majority in the Legislature.   *Brett Quiring*

FURTHER READING: Gruending, D. 1990. *Promises to Keep: A Political Biography of Allan Blakeney.* Saskatoon: Western Producer Books; Praud, J. and S. McQuarrie. 2001. "The Saskatchewan CCF-NDP from the Regina Manifesto to the Romanow Years." Pp. 143–67 in Howard Leeson (ed.), *Saskatchewan Politics: Into the Twenty-First Century.* Regina: Canadian Plains Research Center.

NEW GENERATION CO-OPERATIVE MODEL. The New Generation Co-operative (NGC) model is a business structure that allows farmers to increase their incomes and to offset some of the negative impacts of recent changes in agriculture. Saskatchewan's NGC Act makes it possible to achieve all the benefits of the NGC model.

Agriculture has been affected by changes in technology, institutional structures, regulations, integration of value chains, and the globalization of agricultural markets. Consumers today are demanding food products that offer choice, quality, consistency, and value. Saskatchewan farmers have also been impacted by the loss of the WGTA, or "Crow" subsidy. If agriculture is to survive in this province, it will require new strategies, different organizational structures, and creative attitudes.

The New Generation Co-operative model fulfils all of these requirements, providing opportunities for farmers to invest in ventures that add value to their raw commodities. The model is based on the many successful NGCs in the United States that process commodities including **BISON**, durum, organic grains, soybeans, eggs, and edible beans.

New Generation Co-operatives adhere to the basic principles of co-operation set out by England's Rochdale Society of Equitable Pioneers in 1844: democratic control and one member, one vote. The NGC share structure is characterized by three classes of shares: membership, equity, and preferred. The membership share gives the holder the right to vote and the right to purchase equity shares, which are attached to delivery rights. Only producers of the commodity can hold membership shares, thereby ensuring that control of the venture remains in the hands of the producers. Voting rights are tied to membership, independent of the level of investment. This ensures that no one member can exercise control over the group.

Each equity share gives the member the right and the obligation to deliver one unit (e.g., one bison or one bushel of durum) of product to the co-operative for processing. It is a two-way contract; the member is committed to deliver and the co-operative is committed to take delivery. The contract sets out the standards for quality, and delivery is regulated to keep the plant running at capacity. In the event that a member is unable or unwilling to make delivery, the co-operative will purchase the amount of the product covered by the contract and charge the cost towards the member's equity account. This strategy ensures that the co-op will have a consistent quality and quantity of product, and can focus on developing markets.

The purchase of equity shares represents both a significant investment on behalf of producer-members and a critical infusion of equity for the co-operative. The sale of delivery rights, in fact, is a mechanism for securing start-up capital, with member equity investment typically representing 35–50% of the start-up costs. This structure provides the obvious benefit to the co-operative of low debt, which is further augmented by member commitment. The loyalty of members is locked in through the contract and the investment; the member has made a large investment and will act to ensure the success of the venture. Equity shares are tradable and transferable; they have value and can be sold to other producers with the approval of the board of directors, as well as being passed on to the next generation.

The preferred share allows the co-operative to invite investment from non-producers, who cannot vote except in certain circumstances described in the legislation. The preferred share offers a limited, fixed rate of return. Communities and non-producers choose to purchase preferred shares because they want to support development in their communities and encourage job and wealth creation close to home.

NGCs are select- or closed-membership co-operatives. The feasibility study determines the most efficient plant size, which, in turn, determines the amount of product the plant can accept. Equity shares are issued to members based on the capacity of the plant. Once the allotment of shares is sold, the membership is closed. New members will be accepted and additional equity shares issued if the plant expands. Comprehensive feasibility studies and business plans are critical to the success of these ventures. NGCs often operate in niche markets, where it is important to understand the type, quality, and quantity of product demanded. A clear understanding of markets and consumers has enabled these ventures to serve markets that large corporations cannot.

Brenda Stefanson

FURTHER READING: Stefanson, Brenda. 2001. "New Generation Co-operatives: An Introduction." In *New Generation Co-operatives: Resource Materials for Business Development Professionals and Agricultural Producers.* Saskatoon: Centre for the Study of Co-operatives, University of Saskatchewan.

NEWLANDS, HENRY WILLIAM (1862–1954).

A respected lawyer and administrator of justice, Henry William Newlands served two successive terms as **LIEUTENANT-GOVERNOR** of Saskatchewan from 1921 to 1931. Born March 19, 1862, in Dartmouth, Nova Scotia, Newlands travelled west to Winnipeg in 1882 and, two years later, settled in Prince Albert where he practiced law. In 1897, he relocated to Regina where he served as inspector of the Land Titles Offices for the North-West Territories. He was appointed to the Territorial Supreme Court in 1904, the Saskatchewan Supreme Court in 1907, and the Saskatchewan Court of Appeal in 1920.

Post-war reconstruction and **DROUGHT** were two major concerns in Saskatchewan when Newlands was named Lieutenant-Governor on February 18, 1921. Accordingly, he attended official ceremonies and delivered speeches in support of soldier resettlement, a continued military presence in the province, and a rejuvenated agricultural economy. **GOVERNMENT HOUSE** functions were coordinated with the help of Newlands's unmarried daughter Edina, as his wife Mary lived in the United States for health reasons.

The start of Newlands's second term as Lieutenant-Governor in 1926 coincided with an improvement in Saskatchewan's economic fortunes. However, the stock market crash of October 1929 and the onset of the **GREAT DEPRESSION** ended all hope of continued prosperity. Newlands's failing health forced him to resign the vice-regal post in October 1930 even though his second term did not officially end until March 30, 1931. Henry Newlands and his daughter settled on a farm near St. Thomas, Ontario in 1936. He died there on August 9, 1954, at age 92.

Holden Stoffel

FURTHER READING: Hryniuk, Margaret and Garth Pugh. 1991. *"A Tower of Attraction": An Illustrated History of Government House, Regina, Saskatchewan.* Regina: Government House Historical Society/Canadian Plains Research Center; 1954. "Newlands' Funeral is Held in Ontario," Regina Leader-Post (August 10): 3.

NEWLOVE, JOHN (1938–2003).

Poet John Newlove was born on June 13, 1938 in Regina. His parents were Thomas Harold, a lawyer, and Mary Constant (Monteith) Newlove, a teacher. Newlove lived with his mother in several eastern Saskatchewan communities, particularly Verigin and Kamsack, where he attended school. He later studied at the **UNIVERSITY OF SASKATCHEWAN** for one year, but then left to hitchhike around the country. Newlove worked briefly at several jobs: he taught

ROY ANTAL/REGINA LEADER-POST

John Newlove, May 1984.

school in Birtle, Manitoba; was a social worker in Yorkton; and worked in radio in Weyburn, Regina and Swift Current. He also worked as a labourer in Saskatchewan and British Columbia.

Newlove spent several years in Vancouver reading about mythology and the history of exploration in Canada while learning the craft of poetry from artists and poets, among them Brian Fisher and **ROY KIYOOKA**, also from Saskatchewan. In 1962, he published a chapbook, *Grave Sirs*, and featured in poetry and literary magazines. Newlove was most prolific in the 1960s and early 1970s, publishing five more books of poetry by small presses by 1967 and three books by McClelland & Stewart by 1972. His last book, *Lies*, won the Governor General's Literary Award in 1972. Newlove received four Canada Council Grants between 1965 and 1981, and gave readings across the country. From 1970 to 1974 he lived in Toronto, working as a senior editor at McClelland & Stewart. He moved frequently over the next years to be writer in residence at universities in Montreal, London, and Toronto as well as at the Regina Public Library in 1979–80, and to teach in the writing program at David Thompson University in Nelson, BC, until its closure. He freelanced as an editor for *Canadian Poetry: The Modern Era* in 1977, and edited works by **GLEN SORESTAD** and other Canadian poets. In 1986 he became editor for the Commissioner of Official Languages. John Newlove has written some of the finest poems in Canadian literature, often incorporating Saskatchewan scenes and memories of his early life in his work. His book *The Fatman: Selected Poems, 1962–1972* has been praised as one of the most impressive in contemporary English language poetry. Newlove died on December 23, 2003.   *Bob Ivanochko*

FURTHER READING: Barbour, D. 1992. "John Newlove and His Works." Pp. 281–336 in R. Lecker, J. David and E. Quigley (eds.), *Canadian Writers and Their Works: Poetry Series*, vol 10. Toronto: ECW Press.

NEWSPAPERS. Although Canada's first newspaper, the *Halifax Gazette*, was founded in 1752, newspapers did not arrive in Saskatchewan until the mid-19th century after decades of evolution elsewhere. *The Nor'Wester*, the first newspaper in western Canada, began publication at Red River in 1860. The first newspaper in Saskatchewan (then the North-West Territories) was the *Saskatchewan Herald*, first published at Battleford in August 1878. **PATRICK GAMMIE LAURIE**, who previously worked for *The Nor'Wester*, was that newspaper's founder and editor. *The Saskatchewan Herald* predated any railway in Saskatchewan, and consequently Laurie transported his first printing press by ox cart on a 72-day trek from Fort Garry. In 1885, however, the railway arrived and other newspapers started up in the province: the *Prince Albert Times* and

SASKATCHEWAN ARCHIVES BOARD R-A12,656
P.G. Laurie in front of the Saskatchewan Herald building in which the paper was printed from 1878 to 1884.

Saskatchewan Review, the *Regina Leader*, the *Moose Jaw News*, the *Moosomin Courier*, the *Fort Qu'Appelle Progress*, and the *Qu'Appelle Vidette*. When Saskatchewan became a province in 1905, it had fifty-two different newspapers in print.

For the first decades, newspapers had a near-monopoly on advertising and news dissemination in their communities. Consequently, there was a vast variety of published material in each edition. Not all of Saskatchewan's early newspapers, however, were traditional city-focused publications. In 1912 the Students' Representative Council of the **UNIVERSITY OF SASKATCHEWAN** founded *The Sheaf*, which was dedicated to university news. One of Saskatchewan' largest weekly newspapers, the *Western Producer*, started in 1918 under the name of *Turner's Weekly* and concentrated on agriculture and farming issues. Other special-interest newspapers included the *Prairie Messenger*, the *Canadian Magyar Farmer*, and the *Banish the Bar Crusader*. From the earliest settlement days to the present, small-town newspapers have flourished and found an eager readership across the province. In 1919, these solitary newspapers formed the Saskatchewan Weekly Newspaper Association, which now comprises eighty-five members.

Saskatchewan newspapers, like all others, have adapted to technological changes. For example, linotype slowly replaced letterpress printing in the decades after 1886; offset printing was embraced across the industry after 1950; and since about 1990, digital pagination has replaced cut-and-paste boards. In recent years, most small-town newspapers farm out their printing to facilities in larger centres. The speed and ease of the Internet and computer software usually bring about a quicker, cheaper, and sharper newspaper product. During the **GREAT DEPRESSION**, the media monopoly of newspapers was assailed by radio, forcing the industry to consolidate. In 1928, the *Saskatoon Phoenix* merged with the *Saskatoon Daily Star* to become

the *Saskatoon StarPhoenix*. In 1930, the *Regina Morning Leader* and *Daily Post* merged to become the *Leader-Post*. In 1935, the *Moose Jaw Times Morning Herald* merged with the *Evening Herald* to become the *Moose Jaw Times-Herald*. As well, many newspapers such as the *Loreburn Herald*, the *Dundurn Enterprise*, and the *Alsask News* had ceased operation by 1929. Television in 1950 and the Internet in 1990 challenged newspapers both for the public's news attention and for advertising revenue. Commencing in 1980, local ownership of Saskatchewan's daily newspapers disappeared as the *Leader-Post*, *StarPhoenix*, and others were acquired by national media chains such as Thomson Newspapers, Hollinger and, more recently, CanWest Global. During 2000, national media chains such as Transcontinental and Glacier Ventures International also began purchasing small-town weeklies.

Gerald Heinrichs

FURTHER READING: Kesterton, W.H. 1984. *A History of Journalism in Canada*. Ottawa: Carleton University Press

NEXEN CANADA: *see* **SASK OIL**

NIELSEN, DORISE WINIFRED (1902–80). Dorise Winifred Webber was born on July 30, 1902, in London, England. After attending college and teaching in England, she emigrated to Saskatchewan in January 1927 to take up a teaching post near the present town of Spiritwood. She soon married a homesteader, Peter Nielsen, and gave birth to four children, one of whom died in infancy. By 1935 both Peter and Dorise were staunch supporters of the new CCF Party although Dorise's politics moved further left. She became a member of the Meadow Lake CCF executive and the Provincial Council of the CCF. The Meadow Lake CCF executive joined with Social Credit and Communist Party supporters to form the United Progressives. Nielsen as their candidate defeated the federal Liberal incumbent in 1940. She was the third woman to hold a seat in the Parliament of Canada. Considered one of the best speakers in the House, she worked conscientiously to bring attention to the plight of the west. While the Communist Party was outlawed (1940–42), she was spokesperson for its policies in Parliament, and active in the crusade to have its members released from prison. She also protested the internment of Japanese Canadians, advocated equal pay for women in the armed services, and proposed, successfully, that the new family allowance be payable to the mother. Following her defeat in 1945, she moved to Toronto and worked for the Labour Progressive (Communist) Party in various capacities. As the party dwindled, she sought other employment but could find very little that suited her abilities. Finally, in 1957 she moved to China, where she worked until her death on December 8, 1980, as an English teacher and polisher of English texts for the Foreign Languages Press in Beijing.   *Faith Johnston*

FURTHER READING: Johnston, Faith. 1989. "Dorise Nielsen, the Life and Times of a Canadian Woman in Politics." MA thesis, Carleton University.

NIGHTJARS. Nightjars are rather mysterious **BIRDS**, heard at night far more commonly than they are seen. Their closest relatives are **OWLS**. Many produce repetitive "nightjarring" calls, which have given the bird some of its names (e.g., poorwill and whippoorwill). In Ontario, an individual "whip" was counted to call over 16,000 times in a single night. Many calls are very familiar to those who live near them, such as the "good-lord-deliver-us" of the fiery-necked nightjar from southern Africa.

Nightjars' nocturnal nature has in part contributed to superstitions about them which are captured in their scientific name (*Caprimulgus*, from Latin *capra* "goat," and *mulgere* "to milk"). This results from the baseless belief that they suckle domestic animals at night. In fact, like **BATS**, most nightjars catch flying insects; but unlike bats, they detect prey visually, not using echolocation.

Currently there are eighty-nine species (family Caprimulgidae) known from around the world except Antarctica and some larger oceanic islands. Three species occur in Saskatchewan: common nighthawk, common poorwill, and whippoorwill. Most species occur in tropical woodlands, with temperate ones typically being migratory. Nighthawks nesting in Saskatchewan probably winter in northern Argentina.

Nightjars are large-eyed, nocturnal birds with tiny bills but a huge gape, and rather short necks and legs. They lack strong claws on the toes and do not use the feet to catch or hold prey. They are strong fliers. Some feed during sustained flight like swifts or swallows, but most sally in short flights

MARK BRIGHAM PHOTO
Poorwill on rock, Okanagan, BC

from a perch or the ground. Virtually all are cryptically coloured, usually in shades of brown or grey. They seem to have few predators. Most are small, ranging in size from 30 to 100 g, but appear larger due to their long soft plumage. Most have well-developed facial bristles around the mouth, the function of which is not clear.

Typically, nightjars remain motionless at daytime roosts or on the "nest." They do not build nests but lay two eggs in a shallow depression on the ground. Nesting is often synchronized with the lunar cycle, with chicks hatching so that when they need the greatest quantity of food the moon is full. Foraging occurs principally in low light: during the weak light around dawn and dusk, the dark parts of the night when the moon provides illumination, or around artificial lights. Nightjars' eyes are adapted to low light levels thanks to the presence of a *tapetum lucidum*, which reflects light and enhances the light-catching power of visual cells thus accounting for "eyeshine."

All three species found in Saskatchewan are capable of using torpor, an energy-saving strategy whereby metabolism and body temperature are reduced. The poorwill is perhaps most adept: its body temperature can fall to less than 5°C. In southern parts of the range (e.g., Arizona), it remains motionless for weeks at a time during the winter, in a manner akin to mammalian hibernation. This is the only bird in the world thus far known to do this.   *Mark Brigham*

FURTHER READING: Alsop, Fred J., III. 2002. *The Birds of Canada*. New York: Dorling Kindersley.

19TH INFANTRY BRIGADE. A military unit initially composed of five Saskatchewan-based regiments, the 19th Infantry Brigade was organized on December 15, 1936, with headquarters in Regina. It included the Regina Rifle Regiment, Prince Albert and Battleford Volunteers, **SOUTH SASKATCHEWAN REGIMENT**, **KING'S OWN RIFLES OF CANADA** (MG), and **SASKATOON LIGHT INFANTRY** (MG).

Following Japan's entry into **WORLD WAR II** in December 1941, the Canadian Army raised several formations and units for home defence. Stationed at Vernon, BC, the 19th Infantry Brigade formed part of the reorganized 6th Canadian Infantry Division beginning in July 1942. Of the Saskatchewan regiments, only the Prince Albert Volunteers remained with the 19th, along with the 3rd Battalion, Irish Fusiliers of Canada and the Winnipeg Light Infantry. The 19th Infantry Brigade was disbanded in October 1943.

FURTHER READING: Winton, Maurice V. *Saskatchewan's Prairie Soldiers 1885-1980*. The Author, 1980.

95TH REGIMENT. In 1904 the Canadian government implemented a new Militia Act, which reorganized the command structure of the **MILITIA** into five districts, one of which extended across western Canada. As part of the restructuring, authority was given to create a militia unit for the Assiniboia and Saskatchewan districts of the North-West Territories. The new unit, the 95th Regiment, was brought into being on July 3, 1905. The regiment took two years to organize. Initially, eight companies (A–H) were raised. Lieutenant Colonel Frank Ford was appointed the first commanding officer of the regiment on October 7, 1908; he was at the time Deputy Attorney General for the province of Saskatchewan. The first medical officer was Captain E.E. Meek, the city health inspector for Regina; and the first chaplain was Canon G.C. Hill, of St. Paul's Church, Regina– the regiment's spiritual home. On August 1, 1911, the regimental headquarters were moved to Saskatoon. On April 1, 1912, the regiment was again reorganized, this time into two regiments: all the companies in the south of the province remained in the 95th Regiment, while all the northern companies were organized into a new unit, the 105th Regiment (later 105th Fusiliers).

On June 30, 1912, the regiment was called to active duty under the provisions of the Militia Act, in aid of the civil power. On that day, part of Regina was devastated by a cyclone; the regiment was recalled from its summer training at Camp Sewell in Manitoba to patrol the streets of the city in order to guard against looting and the outbreak of fires. The 95th Regiment was redesignated the 95th Saskatchewan Rifles in September 1913. On the outbreak of **WORLD WAR I** in 1914, the 95th Saskatchewan Rifles were mobilized for home service. Drafts from the regiment were sent to units of the First Canadian Contingent, Canadian Expeditionary Force, then mobilizing at Camp Valcartier in Quebec. The Rifles also contributed to units of the second contingent, principally the 28th (Northwest) Battalion, CEF; this unit is perpetuated by the Royal Regina Rifles, the current successor to the 95th Rifles. With the general reorganization of the Canadian militia that took place in 1920, the 95th Rifles amalgamated with the 60th Rifles of Moose Jaw to become the **SOUTH SASKATCHEWAN REGIMENT**.

Daria Coneghan

NIPAWIN, town, pop 4,275, located NE of Melfort on Hwys 35 and 55. The **SASKATCHEWAN RIVER** passes to the west of the community. The first settlers began making incursions into the area around 1906, and by 1910 Nipawin's original townsite was developing about 6 km south of the present community. In 1924, the CPR announced its intention to establish a village at the community's present location. Within weeks, everything from the old townsite was relocated to the rail line. In 1928, a bridge to facilitate rail and road traffic west across the river was begun, which would bring an end to the ferry service and the cable car operation that was used to cross the river. A diverse economy based on forestry, trapping, agriculture, and business allowed the community to develop rapidly. In 1936 the population was 892, and in 1937 Nipawin acquired town status. By 1951, the population was over 3,000. In the early 1960s, the Squaw Rapids (now E.B. Campbell) Dam was completed, forming the large body of water now known as Tobin Lake northeast of the community. In 1986, the François-Finlay Dam was completed, creating Codette Lake to the town's southwest. Tourism—especially sports fishing—has become an important part of Nipawin's economy. On January 4, 2005, a world record was set when Father Mariusz Zajac of Carrot River landed, at 8.3 kgs or 18.3 lbs, the largest walleye ever caught ice fishing. Agricultural-based industries are significant employers, and Nipawin is one of the country's leading producers of honey. A 200-acre nursery produces trees and shrubs which are sold across western Canada, and innovative businesses such as fish farming and manufacturing fishing tackle have developed in recent years. Forestry remains an important component of the area economy. Nipawin is the birthplace of author **SHARON BUTALA** and painter **ARTHUR (ART) FORTESCUE MCKAY**, of **REGINA FIVE** fame.

David McLennan

NIXON, HOWARD R. (1928–). Born in 1951, a strong advocate of fitness and physical education, Howard Nixon of Saskatoon excelled as an athlete at the University of British Columbia where he earned his BPE in 1951. He continued to promote athletics at the varsity level as a coach and educator at the **UNIVERSITY OF SASKATCHEWAN**. In 1965, Nixon established the Provincial Youth Agency, known today as the Saskatchewan Department of Youth, Culture & Recreation. He also helped create *Katimavik*, a national youth program that has encouraged personal, social, and professional development of over 20,000 young people. Nixon has sat on numerous boards and councils regarding sports and physical

activity. Inducted into the **SASKATCHEWAN SPORTS HALL OF FAME** as a Builder in 1987, Howard Nixon was made an Officer of the Order of Canada in 2000.

N.M. PATERSON AND SONS GRAIN COMPANY. This has been a family-owned and operated company from its inception in 1908 until the present, when the third generation is managing the company. Norman Paterson was born at Portage La Prairie, Manitoba in 1883. He worked at various jobs connected with the grain business; in 1908 he moved to Fort William (today Thunder Bay), where he purchased screenings from the terminals and shipped them east as feed. In 1912 he started his own company, N.M. Paterson and Company, and in the same year built a small 50,000 bushel mixing house. In 1914 he constructed a 100,000 bushel cleaning and drying elevator. Needing to source grain for his terminal business he started the Royal Elevator Company, and purchased a line of fourteen elevators in south-central Saskatchewan. He formed the Interior Elevator Company to operate the Royal Elevator facilities. In 1920, now with seventy-six country elevators, he put all elevators under N.M. Paterson and Company, discarding the "Interior" name. While expanding his country elevator business, which peaked at 108 elevators in the 1940s, he was expanding his terminal capacity and going into lake shipping. By 1923 he had terminal capacity of 1,350,000 bushels. In 1915 he had purchased and operated three small lake vessels to move grain between terminal elevators; after adding four steel lake vessels, he formed Paterson Steamships Ltd. in 1926 and acquired thirteen more vessels. By 1930 the company operated a fleet of thirty-two vessels and had terminal capacity of four million bushels.

In 1940 Norman Paterson was named a Senator by Prime Minister **MACKENZIE KING**. During **WORLD WAR II** many of the company's vessels were loaned to the government for the war effort; seventeen were lost. By the 1950s the fleet was restored to thirty-five. Paterson's two sons, Donald and John, who had served in the **ROYAL CANADIAN AIR FORCE**, joined the company; John concentrated on shipping, and Donald on the grain business. In 1950 the grain and shipping companies became N.M. Paterson and Sons Ltd. In the 1960s the company began to consolidate its country elevators through trades with other companies, sales, and closures on abandoned rail lines. The company built its first high throughput elevator at Orkney, Saskatchewan in 1976. In 1978, facing high costs for new equipment for air pollution control as well as the need to refurbish a deteriorating facility, it closed its terminal in Thunder Bay.

In 1981 John Paterson died, and Norman relinquished the presidency to Donald. The company's head office was moved from Thunder Bay to Winnipeg. In 1983 Norman Paterson died, one

week after his 100th birthday. Donald and John each had two sons, who are now involved in the company. In 2004 the company had forty-six licenced primary elevators, of which twenty-three were in Saskatchewan, with storage capacity of 117,490 tonnes. The company owns NutraSun Foods, a pneumatic flour milling operation located in Regina; it produces a line of organic (NutraBake) and conventional (SunnyBake) Hard Red Spring and Hard White **WHEAT** flours.

Gary Storey

FURTHER READING: Anderson, C.W. 1991. *Grain: The Entrepreneurs*. Winnipeg: Watson and Dwyer Publishing Ltd.; Wilson, C.F. 1978. *A Century of Canadian Grain*. Saskatoon: Western Producer Prairie Books.

NO. 1 ADVANCED FLYING SCHOOL. By the Organization Order of June 13, 1951, the RCAF station at Saskatoon became No. 1 Advanced Flying School (AFS), part of the air force's expanded training program to accommodate NATO commitments. The reactivation of Saskatoon's former Service Flying Training School necessitated the relocation of a 142-bed Department of Veterans' Affairs hospital that had been using a number of buildings which the new No. 1 AFS would need. The veterans' hospital had been planning to move to Saskatoon's General Hospital once construction of a new wing there was finished. Since it was clear in April 1951 that construction might not be completed for at least another year, the Department of National Defence proposed that a temporary joint-occupancy plan for the veterans' hospital and the training station be devised. The presence of NATO trainees at **RCAF STATION SASKATOON** brought visits from dignitaries to No. 1 AFS. Canada's Minister of National Defence, Brooke Claxton, visited on April 27, 1954, and Lieutenant-General Finn Lambrechts, Commander-in-Chief of the Royal Norwegian Air Force, spoke with NATO students on November 11, 1954. On November 26, 1954, Colonel André Deperrois, France's Military Air and Naval Attaché for Canada, visited NATO trainees from France, and presented wings to the graduating class. (*See* **NATO AIR TRAINING PLAN**)

Rachel Lea Heide

NO. 2 FLYING TRAINING SCHOOL. On March 13, 1952, an Organization Order was issued, reactivating the air force base at Moose Jaw (effective June 1, 1952) as part of the RCAF's training expansion. The station became No. 2 Flying Training School (FTS) when that unit was relocated from Gimli, Manitoba, from May 4 to June 22, 1953; a single-engine Advanced Flying School was opened at Gimli in its place. RCAF personnel and their families were to become an integral part of the Moose Jaw community. For the first year of the station's existence, children living on the station attended local public and high schools. However, as early as

October 1952 the Moose Jaw school board realized that the city's schools would not be able to accommodate all the children from No. 2 FTS. The local school board and the commanding officer of Training Group Headquarters, which was responsible for No. 2 FTS, began serious discussions in February 1953 about building a Department of National Defence school on the Station.

On April 8, 1954, the most tragic flying accident in the station's history occurred when a NATO trainee in a Harvard collided with a Trans-Canada Airlines (TCA) North Star passenger liner over the city. All 35 TCA passengers and crew and the NATO pilot perished. Miraculously, only one person on the ground was killed when the North Star wreckage crashed into a house. The civil air route was moved twenty miles north, and No. 2 FTS training routes were moved south of the city.

The first class to graduate from No. 2 FTS was composed of eleven students from Great Britain, seven from France, five from Holland, and two from Canada. An increased number of NATO countries were represented in the graduating classes of the last months of the **NATO AIR TRAINING PLAN**. Between December 1, 1957, and May 31, 1958, 139 pilots from seven NATO nations graduated: 53 Canadian, 43 Turkish, 21 British, 12 Dutch, 5 Danish, 3 French, and 2 Norwegian. **RCAF STATION MOOSE JAW** continued to receive NATO students after 1958 because of post-Training Plan bilateral agreements. The Souvenir Program of Moose Jaw's Air Force Day reported on June 16, 1962: "Since June of 1953, Moose Jaw has graduated over 1,800 students from nine NATO countries and Canada." *Rachel Lea Heide*

NOKOMIS, town, pop 436, located to the NE of the N end of Last Mountain Lake on Hwys 15 and 20. The first homesteads were established in the Nokomis area around 1904, and the community developed a few years later at the junction of two competing railways as they came through the area. The north-south CPR line reached Nokomis in 1907, followed shortly thereafter by the east-west Grand Trunk Pacific (now CN). Nokomis developed rapidly at the intersection of the tracks, and was incorporated as a village on March 5, 1908. Five months later, on August 15, the community attained town status. The name *Nokomis* (Hiawatha's grandmother in Longfellow's epic poem) had been chosen in 1906 by Florence Mary Halstead for a post office she started southeast of the present townsite. By 1916, the town had a population of 508 and had developed into a substantial service centre for the surrounding agricultural district. Agriculture remains the basis of the area's economy today. Canadian author Max Braithwaite was born in Nokomis in 1911. The town has a museum that features the community's former CN train station, as well as a re-creation of a 1907 business district and wild life dioramas. The commu-

nity's Bank of Commerce building, built in 1907–08, has been designated a heritage property and now houses a bed and breakfast. Area attractions include the Last Mountain Lake National Wildlife Area; established in 1887, it was the first federal bird sanctuary in North America and is regarded as a wetland of international importance. *David McLennan*

NOLLET, ISIDORE CHARLES (1898–1988). "Toby" Nollet was born November 18, 1898, at Sentinel Butte, North Dakota. Nollet was educated at St. Benedict's Academy and St. Thomas Military College in Minnesota. During **WORLD WAR I** he served overseas with the American Expeditionary Force. He came with his father to settle at Freemont, Saskatchewan, establishing a ranching operation stocked with Aberdeen Angus cattle. In 1957, the ranch was sold to a group of neighbours, who formed the Neilburg Co-operative Grazing Association. For three terms Nollet was reeve of the rural municipality of Hillsdale and an active member of the United Farmers of Canada. He was a member of various co-operatives, including the **SASKATCHEWAN WHEAT POOL**, and helped to organize Canadian Co-operative Implements Limited in the area. He was elected a member of the provincial Legislature in 1944 and represented Cut Knife constituency for the CCF until he retired in 1967. He was Deputy Speaker of the Legislative Assembly from 1944 to 1946, when he became the Minister of Agriculture, a post he held until 1964 when the CCF was defeated; Nollet was the longest-serving Minister of Agriculture in Saskatchewan's history. Under his guidance, the Lands Branch and the Conservation and Development Branch were established, the latter pro-

SASKATCHEWAN ARCHIVES BOARD R-A8371

Isidore Nollet.

viding an engineering service to deal with soil and water problems, flood control, irrigation, and reclamation. Provincial community pastures were developed. Nollet supported development of the **SOUTH SASKATCHEWAN RIVER** project. Nollet was inducted into the Saskatchewan Agricultural Hall of Fame. He died on April 29, 1988, in Kelowna, BC.

Lisa Dale-Burnett

FURTHER READING: *Salute to Saskatchewan Farm Leaders.* 1995. Saskatoon: Saskatchewan Agricultural Hall of Fame.

NON-STATUS INDIANS. People who are identified as Non-Status Indians in Canada are individuals who are not considered as Registered Indians because either they or their ancestors were refused or lost their Indian status through the mechanisms of the Indian Act, and who do not identify as being Métis. The mechanism by which people lost their status was "enfranchisement." The most common method of enfranchisement was through intermarriage, whereby a Status Indian woman marrying a non-Indian man lost her Indian status–as did her children; this law existed until the Indian Act was amended in 1985. Other ways in which individuals could be enfranchised was by obtaining the federal right to vote (until 1960), feeing simple title to land, or receiving a university degree (until 1951). Prior to 1976 there was little political representation at the provincial level for Non-Status Indians in Saskatchewan. Beginning in 1976, the Métis Society of Saskatchewan partnered with Non-Status Indians in the province and formed the Association of Métis and Non-Status Indians of Saskatchewan. In 1988 the organization returned to a Métis-only political institution as a result of the recognition of the Métis in the Canadian Constitution. Nationally, Non-Status Indians were first represented in 1971 by the Native Council of Canada, now known as the Congress of Aboriginal Peoples; there is currently no territorial affiliate in Saskatchewan. (*See also* **MÉTIS AND NON-STATUS INDIAN LEGAL ISSUES**) *Rob Nestor*

FURTHER READING: Frideres, J. S. and R. Gagacz. 2004. *Aboriginal Peoples in Canada.* Toronto: Prentice Hall.

NORHEIM, WES (1940–). Wes Norheim was born on October 5, 1940, in Tubroise, Saskatchewan and raised in the hamlet White Bear. At the age of 18, he began working as a kiln operator, with Western Clay in Regina and became involved in his union local of the United Glass and Ceramic Workers of America, holding the offices of vice-president and president. In 1964, at the age of 23, Norheim was hired by the Canadian Labour Congress (CLC), as a general representative and in the 1970s became CLC regional director for the prairies and the Northwest Territories. Norheim served as a labour representative on two Workers' Compensation Board committees of review and was a labour representative on the minimum wage board. In 1993, he was appointed the labour representative on the Workers' Compensation Board, retiring from this position in 1998. He was the first labour member to sit on the SaskPower board of directors, as the Saskatchewan Federation of Labour nominee. Norheim was a long-time activist in the peace movement and has served as an executive member of the Regina Community Clinic. In retirement, Norheim worked to build a senior's organization for union retirees. In 2002 he became the first president of the Saskatchewan Federation of Union Retirees.

George Rosenau

NORMAL SCHOOL. The Saskatchewan Normal School was a publicly funded provincial postsecondary institution for the training of teachers. Such training began in Regina as early as 1890 with short courses for men and women who had completed Grade 8 and who sought certification to teach elementary school subjects, often in **ONE-ROOM SCHOOLS** in rural Saskatchewan. The term "normal school" is derived from the French *École Normale*, an institution that provided instruction in the "norms" of school instruction. The term was first adopted by training institutions in eastern Canada in the mid-19th century. The first permanent home for teacher training in the province was built in 1913 at the corner of Broad Street and College Avenue (originally 16th Avenue). Designed in the collegiate-Gothic style, the first classes were held there in January 1914 and the building was fully completed in 1915. To meet the growing demand for teachers as the population of Saskatchewan grew dramatically after **WORLD WAR I**, normal schools were also opened in Saskatoon and Moose Jaw in the 1920s. These three normal schools trained thousands of teachers until 1940, when the Regina and Saskatoon buildings were taken over by the **ROYAL CANADIAN AIR FORCE** to accommodate military training.

After **WORLD WAR II** teacher training resumed in Saskatoon and Moose Jaw, but was discontinued in Regina because of declining enrolment. The building in Regina housed various government departments until 1959, when teacher training moved again, this time from Moose Jaw to Regina. Regina College, the Normal School's neighbour on College Avenue, became a part of the **UNIVERSITY OF SASKATCHEWAN** in 1961. In 1964, the Regina and Saskatoon Teachers Colleges, as the normal schools were then called, were transferred to the University of Saskatchewan. The Regina Teachers College became the nucleus of the Faculty of Education for what became the University of Regina. With the completion of the Education Building on the University of Regina campus in 1969, the Normal School Building became the home of the Faculty of

Fine Arts and served as such until the mid-1990s, when that faculty moved on campus to what is now the Dr. William Riddell Centre. The Normal School building was internally gutted and, with its historical façade intact, officially opened in 2002 as the Canada-Saskatchewan Production Studios, a state-of-the art sound stage for the emerging Saskatchewan Film Industry. The Normal School represents what has been referred to as the "golden age" of schools in Regina; it remains a symbol of the optimism at the beginning of the 20th century, when Regina became the commercial and educational centre of "the bread basket of the world."

James McNinch and Mark Vajcner

NORQUAY, town, pop 485, located NW of Kamsack, approximately 35 km from the Saskatchewan-Manitoba border, on Hwys 8 and 49. The community is situated between the Assiniboine and Swan Rivers in a parkland setting, and cultivated land gives way to forest, lakes, and streams north of the town. During the first half of the 20th century, logging was a key part of the area economy. Today, the district surrounding Norquay sustains grain and livestock operations. Settlement of the area began in the late 1800s and increased in the early 1900s as railroads began to approach the region. Ranchers, homesteaders, lumbermen, and farmers were followed by store keepers, blacksmiths, teachers, and doctors. Settlers in the Norquay district were of diverse origins: at first, from eastern Canada, particularly Ontario, and from the British Isles; then, from the U.S. and continental Europe. Doukhobors disembarked the train at Yorkton and headed north; and many Scandinavians from both the U.S. and northern Europe arrived around 1906–08. Large numbers of Ukrainians arrived prior to **World War I** and again in the 1920s. In the 1930s, people from the dried out regions of southern Saskatchewan came to settle the forest fringes north of Norquay. With the arrival of the railway in 1911, the townsite developed and Norquay was incorporated as a village in 1913. The name of the community honours John Norquay, premier of Manitoba from 1878 to 1887. The village grew to have a population of just over 300 by the early 1940s; following **WORLD WAR II**, however, Norquay developed significantly. By the early 1960s, the population was over 500 and, in 1963, Norquay attained town status. The community had a peak population of 575 in 1986. Today, the town has a range of businesses and services, a number of which are involved with the district's agricultural industry. Hunting for bear, moose, elk, and white-tailed deer is popular in the area, as is fishing for pike, perch, walleye, and trout in both summer and winter months. A unique business in the town of Norquay is an award-winning magazine publishing company. *Prairies North* magazine, founded in 1998 as *Saskatchewan Naturally* magazine by

Michelle and Lionel Hughes, has been nationally and internationally recognized for its journalistic and photographic portrayals of life in Saskatchewan.

David McLennan

Malcolm Norris (centre) with J.C. Paulsen (left) and Saskatchewan Government Airways pilot Al Hartley at MacIntosh Bay, Lake Athabasca, July 1948.

NORRIS, MALCOLM (1900–67). A Métis leader and political activist, Malcolm Norris was born on May 26, 1900, in Edmonton, Alberta. The son of John Norris, a wealthy Scottish settler, and Euphrosine Plante, a **MÉTIS** from St. Albert, Alberta, Norris grew up proud of his Métis heritage. One of the most influential Métis leaders of the 20th century, he began working for the Hudson's Bay Company in 1919, but soon quit because of its discriminating trading methods. An avid socialist, Norris began in the 1920s to address the racism faced by Aboriginal people, and in the 1930s worked with other Métis leaders in organizing L'Association des Métis de l'Alberta. In 1944, Norris was hired by the CCF in Saskatchewan to support their northern reform programs. Norris had high hopes for this newly elected democratic-socialist government, and brought his long-time friend **JIM BRADY** to the province when the CCF gained power. During this time, Norris continued to be an outspoken defender of Aboriginal rights and traveled throughout northern Saskatchewan, educating and politicizing the Métis while working toward the complete economic independence of northern Aboriginal people. In 1964, the Saskatchewan CCF was defeated and Norris lost his position. He then became director of the Prince Albert Indian and Métis Friendship Centre, and in 1964 started with Jim Brady the Métis Association of Saskatchewan, which was based only in the province's north. In 1966, Norris suffered a stroke but continued his political career, confined to a wheelchair. In 1967, he returned to Alberta, where he suffered another stroke and passed away on December 5, 1967, in St. Albert.

Cheryl Troupe

651

FURTHER READING: Dobbin, M. 1987. *The One-And-a-Half Men: The Story of Jim Brady & Malcolm Norris, Métis Patriots of the 20th Century*. Regina: Gabriel Dumont Institute.

NORTH AMERICAN BAPTISTS.

German Baptist congregations began in North America in 1843, partly with the help of American Baptists. In 1851 a convention of eight churches, including one in Ontario, was organized; by 1880, there were five regional conferences in North America. In 1885, the Northwestern Conference (Dakota, Minnesota, Wisconsin, Iowa) agreed to send workers among the Germans pouring into the British North-West; Canadian Baptists promised ongoing financial grants to support workers and build chapels. Using Winnipeg as his base, F.A. Petereit came from Minneapolis, organizing a congregation at Edenwold in 1886. A second church was founded at Ebenezer in 1888, a third at Wolseley in 1894 (soon relocated to Neudorf), and a fourth at Josephsburg in 1899. These four, with congregations in Manitoba and Alberta and organized independently of the regional German Baptist body that had served them, became the Northern Conference (NC) of German Baptist churches in 1902. By 1930, there were seventeen German Baptist congregations in the province.

The BAPTIST UNION OF WESTERN CANADA, successor to the Manitoba Baptist Convention, continued its annual grants to the NC for many years, feeling an ownership for "its German work." The NC regarded the "English brethren" mainly as the source of fraternal encouragement and of funds "for our work," but the personnel, labour, and responsibility belonged to the Germans; this relationship ended in 1919 when the NC decided that outside assistance was no longer necessary.

The church letters which reported local activities and statistics to the annual conference reflect the upheavals of the prairies settlement era. Drought, hail, grasshoppers, and poor soil drove homesteaders away, leaving churches too poor to pay a preacher's salary or build a chapel. Some congregations survived for years on the occasional visits of the conference missionary or colporteur, or with the temporary help of seminary students sent by the mission committee for the summer; but town and country churches diminished and even disappeared amidst the economic crisis of the 1930s. Nonetheless, however poor, the churches had their men's and mixed choirs, their orchestras and brass bands, their Sunday schools, and youth ministries. As the 1930s and 1940s passed, the mood of uncertainty diminished: churches reported successful vacation Bible schools, fall and spring evangelistic meetings, and the advantages of the Saskatchewan Association and NC sessions they hosted. These association meetings included seminars for youth workers, Sunday school workers, and choir members.

In the post-WORLD WAR II years, buildings and parsonages were constructed or improved. Many of the churches had become anglicized, even as the German surnames and customs of the members persisted. By 1946, the German Baptist General Conference of North America had adopted the name "North American Baptist Conference" (NAB). With the last wave of German immigration from Eastern Europe and Germany in the 1950s, the NAB Conference turned away from its ethnic roots. It began a church extension program aimed at gathering believers in the growing areas of the post-war boom. There was no ethnic identification in these new churches, although young married couples raised in country or small town NAB churches often formed the nucleus and driving force for the new works. Two Regina churches and others in growing towns have been added to the pre-war sites. Today these are just as likely to include East Indian and Asian members as members of German, Scandinavian, Ukrainian, or English ancestry. The older small-town congregations are ethnically German, but new Canadians and intermarriage are diluting the "German" out of the NAB even there. Sixteen churches exist today, comprising just under 1,300 members.   *David Priestley*

FURTHER READING: Priestley, D.T. 1995. "North American Baptist Conference." Pp. 380–82 in A.W. Wardin (ed.), *Baptists around the World: A Comprehensive Handbook*. Nashville, TN: Broadman Press; Woyke, F.H. 1979. *Heritage and Ministry of the North American Baptist Conference*. Oakbrook Terrace, IL: North American Baptist Conference.

NORTH BATTLEFORD.

North Battleford, population 13,692, is located on the north bank of the NORTH SASKATCHEWAN RIVER at its junction with the Battleford River, 140 km northwest of Saskatoon, and 386 km from both Edmonton, Alberta and Regina, Saskatchewan. The city, situated on the YELLOWHEAD, serves as the hub for five major highways. When in 1905 the CANADIAN NATIONAL RAILWAY completed its work north of the river, rather than through the existing town of Battleford, the "new" community of North Battleford took shape; it grew rapidly, as many businesses and residents relocated from Battleford to the new rail site and the community began to attract entrepreneurs. In 1905 too, nineteen businesses were constructed; two churches, a post office, two doctors and a dentist were added to the community; and the North Battleford Public School District was organized.

The village of North Battleford was incorporated in 1906; a dispute with its Battleford neighbour on the use of the name resulted in the final documents being held up until March of that year. On August 15, 1906 North Battleford became a town, and in May 1913 the city of North Battleford was incorporated. The city started to grow after WORLD WAR II, and over the next decade the population doubled; it is now a key distribution centre for northwestern Saskatchewan's lumbering, farming and fishing areas.   *Daria Coneghan*

COURTESY OF GERRY CARLINE

NORTH SASKATCHEWAN REGIMENT.

The North Saskatchewan Regiment, a reserve infantry unit of 38 Canadian Brigade Group, is headquartered in Saskatoon, with a company in Prince Albert. The Regiment has a history going back to the earliest militia unit in the North-West Territories: No. 1 Company, Prince Albert Mounted Rifles, which was formed in 1879. On January 16, 1880, this unit was granted official status with an establishment of three officers and 42 non-commissioned officers and men. It disbanded in November 1884 but was reactivated in March 1885 as the Prince Albert Volunteers in response to the increasing hostilities exhibited by Métis forces, led by LOUIS RIEL and GABRIEL DUMONT. The Prince Albert Volunteers fought alongside the North-West Mounted Police in the first engagement of the NORTH-WEST RESISTANCE at Duck Lake. The Battleford Rifle Company, also mobilized in 1885 as a response to Aboriginal unrest in the area, fought under Lieutenant Colonel Otter at the Battle of Cut Knife Creek. With the conclusion of the 1885 Resistance, both these units were demobilized. As a result of its service during the Resistance, the North Saskatchewan Regiment today bears the battle honour "North-Canada 1885" on its regimental colour.

In the period after the BOER WAR, the MILITIA in Saskatchewan was reorganized; the first militia infantry unit, the 95TH REGIMENT, was formed in April 1905. The regiment formed companies throughout the province, including G Company in Saskatoon and H Company in Prince Albert. The 16TH MOUNTED RIFLES were also formed in 1905 and authorized to perpetuate the Battleford Rifle Company of the 1885 Resistance. With the further expansion of the militia in April 1912, the northern companies of the 95th Regiment were expanded to form a separate unit, the 105th Regiment (Fusiliers). In the following year, the militia in Saskatchewan again went through reorganization, and the Saskatoon area companies of the 105th Regiment (Fusiliers) became the 105th Regiment (Saskatoon Fusiliers), while the companies in the Prince Albert area became the 52nd Regiment (Prince Albert Volunteers). It was also at this time that the 105th established its alliance with the King's Own Yorkshire Light Infantry in England. This alliance continues to exist today between the North Saskatchewan Regiment and the 2nd Battalion, Light Infantry.

At the outbreak of **WORLD WAR I**, the 52nd Regiment (Prince Albert Volunteers), the 105th Regiment (Saskatoon Fusiliers) and the 16th Light Horse from Battleford provided troops for the **5TH (WESTERN CAVALRY) BATTALION**, CEF. The North Saskatchewan Regiment perpetuates the 5th (Western Cavalry) Battalion. A member of the 5th Battalion, Sgt. Raphael L. Zengel, MM, won the Victoria Cross on August 9, 1918. With the end of World War I, the militia in Canada was reorganized. From 1920 to 1924, all infantry units in northern Saskatchewan were organized into the North Saskatchewan Regiment. In 1924 the North Saskatchewan Regiment was broken up into four city-based infantry units: the **SASKATOON LIGHT INFANTRY**; the Prince Albert Volunteers; the **BATTLEFORD LIGHT INFANTRY**; and the Yorkton Regiment. The Saskatoon Light Infantry was to be later designated a machine gun battalion in 1936, when the Canadian Machine Gun Corps was disbanded.

The 1st Battalion Saskatoon Light Infantry (MG) was mobilized for active service on September 1, 1939, and embarked for the United Kingdom on December 8, 1939. It was designated 1st Division Support Battalion (Saskatoon Light Infantry) on May 1, 1943. The Battalion landed in Sicily on July 13, 1943, as part of the 1st Canadian Division. On September 3, 1943, the Battalion landed in Italy, where members of the Saskatoon Light Infantry (MG) fought throughout the remainder of the Italian campaign. The Saskatoon Light Infantry (MG) moved to northwestern Europe on March 4, 1945. Upon return to Canada in October 1945 the 1st Battalion was disbanded. The 1st Battalion, Saskatoon Light Infantry (MG) was the only infantry unit from northern Saskatchewan to have seen active service overseas. The 2nd Battalion, Saskatoon Light Infantry (MG) served in the Reserve Army in Canada. The Prince Albert and Battleford Volunteers had also been placed on active service on September 1, 1939, for local protective duty. The Regiment mobilized the Prince Albert Volunteers on March 5, 1942; this Unit served in Canada until it was disbanded on November 30, 1945.

After **WORLD WAR II**, the militia was again reorganized. In 1958, the Prince Albert and Battleford Volunteers and the Saskatoon Light Infantry amalgamated to become the 1st and 2nd Battalions of the North Saskatchewan Regiment. In 1972 the two Battalions amalgamated to form the North Saskatchewan Regiment, with Headquarters and A Company located in Saskatoon, and B Company in Prince Albert. Currently, members of the Regiment have worked with the Regular Force in Germany, Norway, and northern Canada. Personnel from the Regiment have also been called upon to serve in a number of United Nations peacekeeping operations in the Golan Heights, Egypt, Cyprus, Bosnia, and Croatia. The regimental motto is *Cede Nullis*, "Yield to None."　　*John Chaput*

NORTH SASKATCHEWAN RIVER (53°15' N, 105°05'W; map sheet 73 H/3). The North Saskatchewan River originates in the eastern slopes of the Rocky Mountains west of Red Deer in Alberta, and flows eastward to its confluence with the **SOUTH SASKATCHEWAN RIVER** 45 km east of Prince Albert, Saskatchewan. The North Saskatchewan River watershed encompasses a total area of 156,400 km^2, including the area tributary to Manitou Lake south of Lloydminster. About 41% of the total watershed area lies in Saskatchewan (63,600 km^2). Most of the flow in the river is derived from the mountain and foothill region of the watershed upstream of Edmonton, Alberta. At Edmonton, the mean annual flow is 213 m^3/s, whereas the mean annual flow at Prince Albert is 235 m^3/s (1912–2000). Peak flows typically occur in June or July, in conjunction with snowmelt at the higher elevations. Relatively little flow is generated from the prairie region of the watershed. The Battle River is the largest tributary entirely in the prairie region and has a mean annual flow of 14.1 m^3/s. The mean annual recorded flow volume for the North Saskatchewan River at Prince Albert is 7,508,000 dam^3 (cubic decametres).

The Saskatchewan portion of the watershed includes a portion of the Battle River watershed and Eagle Creek, which join the North Saskatchewan from the west and south. A number of rivers join the North Saskatchewan from the north, including the Monnery, Englishman, Turtlelake, Jackfish, Sturgeon, Spruce and Garden rivers. After the junction of the North and South Saskatchewan rivers, the **SASKATCHEWAN RIVER** flows eastward through the communities of Nipawin and Cumberland House. Major tributaries of the Saskatchewan River in the province include the Sturgeon-Weir and Torch rivers. The mean annual flow volume of the Saskatchewan River at the Manitoba-Saskatchewan boundary is 19,910,000 dam^3. (*See also* **HYDROLOGY**)
　　Bart Oegema

NORTHERN CREE COURT INITIATIVE. In northern Saskatchewan, a large number of community members are of Aboriginal descent (e.g., 90% of legal aid clients are Aboriginal) and speak an **ABORIGINAL LANGUAGE** as their first language. It has been suggested that the lack of effective communication between the court and Aboriginal clients has contributed to the alienation of members of northern Aboriginal communities from the administration of justice. In 1996, Judge Claude Fafard conceptualized the idea of a "Cree Court" in which Aboriginal residents of northern communities would be provided an alternative that addressed the considerable language barriers between the Court and its participants. In 1999 this idea was formally proposed, and the Northern Cree Court Initiative was developed. Its purpose is to provide legal services to **CREE**-speaking clients in northern Saskatchewan in a culturally sensitive manner. A Cree-speaking Circuit

North Saskatchewan River, near Fielding.

Court Party was established in three locations (Sandy Bay, Big River and Pelican Narrows) in October 2001. This Party consists of a Cree-speaking judge, a Cree-speaking Crown prosecutor, a legal aid lawyer who is currently taking Cree language training, and two court clerks, one of whom is Cree-speaking. This Circuit Court Party travels to the three court points at scheduled intervals throughout each month to hold court. Recently, the Circuit Court Party was awarded the Premier's Award of Excellence in the Public Service for its work in developing and operating a Cree-speaking provincial court. Over time, it is anticipated that the Northern Cree Circuit Court Initiative will serve to transform the delivery of justice services for northern Aboriginal communities through the increased application of alternative measures.

Kimberly Skakun

NORTHERN SETTLERS RE-ESTABLISHMENT BRANCH.

The DEPRESSION and DROUGHT of the early 1930s forced many farmers from the southern areas of the province to move to northern Saskatchewan's forest fringe areas, which were being opened for farming. Municipalities and provincial programs responsible for relief payments also encouraged urban dwellers to move north to establish farms. The peak years of migration were in 1931 and 1932, when more than 25,000 people settled on undeveloped land controlled by the Department of Natural Resources. Being unfamiliar with northern farming conditions, most settlers were not able to survive without assistance. The Northern Settlers Re-Establishment Branch was initiated under the provincial Department of Municipal Affairs in 1935 to consolidate assistance programs administered by several departments. The objective of the branch was to establish self-supporting agricultural communities by controlling and aiding land settlement. The program extended credit for breaking land, building farms, and buying livestock; direct relief was provided to permit recipients to improve

their land for subsistence farming. Some relief projects to develop community infrastructure, such as group building of schools and homes, roads and drainage systems, were organized. The Branch purchased caterpillar tractors and other equipment for breaking land and building roads, and organized agricultural education programs. Gideon Matte served as commissioner of this branch. Field staff duties included administering the Local Improvement Districts in the north, thereby providing similar functions to those of municipalities in the south. The branch was renamed the Northern Areas Branch in 1940, and became the Local Improvement Districts Branch of the Department of Municipal Affairs in 1942.

Bob Ivanochko

NORTH-SOUTH RELATIONS, 1905 TO THE 1980S.

For the first twenty-five years after Saskatchewan became a province, Ottawa retained control over many matters in northern Saskatchewan. The federal government retained control over Crown lands and natural resources, and as the years passed, cries for provincial control over lands and resources increased. While Ottawa appeared willing to relinquish that authority, not until 1930 did the Natural Resources Transfer Agreement (NRTA) give Saskatchewan control over many aspects of its northern region. During its extended period of control, Ottawa did little to develop the region's natural and human resources; while not opposing development, the federal government spent virtually nothing on infrastructure development. Some private industrial development did take place, most notably related to the mining operation of Hudson Bay Mining and Smelting at Flin Flon, Manitoba. In the 1920s, the company obtained permission to construct a hydro-electric dam within Saskatchewan at Island Falls on the CHURCHILL RIVER; and the ore body that supplied the Flin Flon mill lay partially in Saskatchewan. Ottawa did bring long-term change to one area of the near north with

the establishment of PRINCE ALBERT NATIONAL PARK (PANP) in 1927; while the park provided visible evidence that WILLIAM LYON MACKENZIE KING appreciated area voters electing him to the House of Commons, CREE in the area found themselves relocated outside the park boundaries.

Northern Saskatchewan remained isolated in the 1930s, with no highways or railways penetrating the region beyond the popular tourist destination of Waskesiu in PANP. Waterways and winter roads carried goods and people to and from the north; increasingly, aircraft played a role in opening up the north. As a result of the lack of adequate transportation systems, exploitation of the forests remained confined to the forest fringe area. Non-Aboriginals joined Aboriginals in trapping the fur-bearing animals of the region; and newcomers took the lead in developing a winter commercial FISHING industry. During the 1930s, concern increased about depletion of fur, fish, and game stocks. Newcomers to the region received much of the blame for this situation, leading to the federal and provincial governments making plans to protect the resources primarily for the use of the region's Aboriginal population; those plans were not implemented until the mid-1940s.

During the 1930s, the Box Mine and its community of Goldfields appeared on the north shore of LAKE ATHABASCA. A disappointingly low grade of ore and the onset of WORLD WAR II brought an end to that mining operation, and during the war years many newcomers left the region. Northern Aboriginals also participated in the war effort at home and abroad. The history of federal government control until 1930, the difficult financial situation faced by Saskatchewan during the 1930s, and the war ensured that the governmental presence in the north remained small until the 1940s. During the two decades following 1944, northern Saskatchewan underwent rapid change under the firm direction of the CO-OPERATIVE COMMONWEALTH FEDERATION (CCF) provincial government. A desire to reclaim northern resource wealth for the benefit of the entire province, concern for the welfare of northern Aboriginals, and a belief that socialist solutions held the answer to northern problems motivated CCF intervention. Visualizing a new prosperity based on traditional resources, innovative regulations reserved most game and fur resources for Indians and Métis. At the same time, a non-Aboriginal economy developed in the region: mining activity reached new heights with the development of URANIUM resources in the Uranium City area; driven by sport angling, tourism became an important part of the northern economy; and the forest industry slowly expanded. Aided by the DIEFENBAKER Conservatives' *Roads to Resources* program, the CCF built roads to some remote communities. But in spite of major changes, at the time of the CCF defeat

SASKATCHEWAN ARCHIVES BOARD R-A4287

On the move from Morse to Carrot River. Photo taken south of Star City, July 1934.

twenty years later, northern economic and social problems appeared overwhelming.

From 1964 to 1971, ROSS THATCHER and his Liberal government increased incentives for private enterprise to assume the primary role in developing the northern economy. Considerable success followed in developing the pulp industry; although the new Prince Albert Pulp Company mill sat outside the north, the pulp cutting operations provided some employment for northerners. Thatcher also brought a new approach to governmental relations with Aboriginals: through the newly created Indian and Métis Department, the Liberals sought to train northern Aboriginals and place them in private and public sector jobs. A new vision for the north arrived with the election of ALLAN BLAKENEY and his NEW DEMOCRATIC PARTY (NDP) government in 1971, and the role of government in the region expanded greatly. Establishment of the Department of Northern Saskatchewan (DNS) brought a much larger provincial governmental structure to the north. Although DNS was centralized at La Ronge, many other communities received enhanced government services, and newcomers to the region filled many new government positions. The NDP also sought to expand opportunities within the north and to involve northerners in determining the future of their region; but the lack of an adequate number of non-governmental jobs meant that unemployment and poverty continued to plague the region. Controversially, the NDP cancelled plans to build a pulp mill in the northwestern region, and added the Prince Albert pulp mill to the fold of CROWN CORPORATIONS.

Following their election victory in 1982, GRANT DEVINE and his Conservatives moved away from the NDP's emphasis on government initiatives and towards an expanded role for private enterprise. DNS's functions reverted to various other departments. Uranium mining remained important to the north, although the closing of Uranium City's mines meant that most of that community's population was forced to leave. The development of extremely rich uranium deposits in the region south of Lake Athabasca meant that mining remained one of the primary northern industries. The re-election of the NDP in 1991, this time led by ROY ROMANOW, brought some changes to the north's relationship with the south. Creation of a new agency, the Department of Northern Affairs, did suggest an increased role for the provincial government in the north. Both the province and Ottawa, which held responsibility for status Indians, continued to expand services in the region. Government infrastructure programs and various transfer payments did ease the plight of communities plagued by chronically high unemployment rates. Northern Saskatchewan remains a beautiful region blessed with abundant natural resources; but while govern-

ment and industry continue to remove northern wealth, many northerners participate little in that process.

David Quiring

FURTHER READING: Barron, F.L. 1997. *Walking in Indian Moccasins: The Native Policies of Tommy Douglas and the CCF*. Vancouver: University of British Colombia Press; Quiring, D. 2004. *CCF Colonialism in Northern Saskatchewan: Battling Parish Priests, Bootleggers, and Fur Sharks*. Vancouver: UBC Press.

NORTHUP, ANNA (1889-1977). Anna Northup, born in Granville, New York on June 17, 1889, graduated from the American School of Osteopathy in Kirksville, Missouri in 1915, and began her practice in Moose Jaw the following year. In 1922 she married Alfred Little, a widower with two sons, and from then on was known as Northup-Little. They had a son born in 1923, and later they adopted a daughter. In 1953 she moved her practice to Regina, joining Dr. Doris Tanner. Anna Northup-Little worked energetically to erase gender differences; in recognition of this work, she was named Quota Woman of the Year for Regina in 1961. She was the founder of the Saskatchewan Society of Osteopathic Physicians, and one of the organizers of the Canadian Osteopathic Association. She worked tirelessly although unsuccessfully towards establishing a professional relationship with the physicians of Saskatchewan, something that was taken for granted in the United States. She found it greatly disappointing that Canadian physicians could not be persuaded that a person with a degree in Osteopathy was as much a doctor as they were. She retired in 1962 and died in Regina on December 17, 1977.

Frederick W. Anderson

NORTH-WEST MOUNTED POLICE: *see* **ROYAL CANADIAN MOUNTED POLICE**

NORTH-WEST REBELLION: *see* **NORTH-WEST RESISTANCE**

NORTH-WEST RESISTANCE. The CREE uprisings of 1884 and 1885, and the MÉTIS Resistance of 1885, plunged the Saskatchewan District of the North-West Territories into turmoil, ending in armed conflict and open rebellion against the Dominion government. These two separate events have been combined in the history of Canada, where they have come to be known as the North-West Resistance of 1885 (also referred to as the North-West Rebellion, the 1885 Rebellion, and the Riel Rebellion). This clash of cultures was a significant milestone in the development of the West, having a profound impact on each of the three major ethnic groups living in central Saskatchewan at that time. For the Métis, whose resistance against the government culminated in the Battle of Batoche, it marked the end of their

independence as a nation. It also has become, in recent times, a symbol of their struggle to be recognized as a distinct people. For the aboriginal First Nations, principally the Cree of the TREATY 6 region, the uprising of 1885 was the outcome of frustrations over the breaking of treaty agreements made in good faith with the Canadian government. With their defeat, the bands of the Cree First Nation in the Saskatchewan District were relegated to reserves and their nomadic way of life ended, never again to be revived. For the European community, primarily Canadian and British, the North-West Rebellion marked the end of any significant settlement in the Saskatchewan District for well over a decade. Henceforth, immigration into the Territories was to occur primarily along the railway line in the districts of Assiniboia and Alberta, to the south.

Of those significant military engagements of the Rebellion which took place between Canadian forces and the Métis, led by LOUIS RIEL and GABRIEL DUMONT, only the initial skirmish at DUCK LAKE involved the North-West Mounted Police. This encounter became the only clear Métis victory. Elements of the North-West Field Force of the Canadian MILITIA, led by General FREDERICK MIDDLETON, took part in the other two battles, FISH CREEK and BATOCHE. The only decisive victory for government forces was at the Battle of Batoche. Of the engagements in which bands of the Cree First Nation took part, the FROG LAKE "MASSACRE" did not involve opposing forces. At FORT PITT, a victory for the Cree, the North-West Mounted Police were involved. The Canadian militia of Lieutenant Colonel W.D. Otter's Battleford Column was defeated at CUT KNIFE HILL, while the troops of the Alberta Field Force, including Steele's Scouts, took part in the skirmishes at FRENCHMAN'S BUTTE and STEELE NARROWS. The outcome of both these engagements was inconclusive.

The Métis Resistance. After migrating from Manitoba to new communities along the banks of the SOUTH SASKATCHEWAN RIVER, following the Red River Uprising of 1870, the Métis found that once again they faced the same problems as they had in the old Red River settlement. Among other things, they feared the loss of their land as they watched surveyors imposing upon their long narrow river lots the Canadian township system which divided the land into squares. In June 1884 a delegation of Métis, led by Gabriel Dumont, traveled to Montana to persuade their former leader, Louis Riel, to return to the Saskatchewan District to help them present their grievances to the Canadian government. During the summer of 1884 and the spring of the following year, angry meetings were held throughout the District, both in Métis and White communities, where the settlers also voiced their grievances against the Canadian government. The unrest in Saskatchewan culminated in the creation by Riel on

March 18, 1885, of a provisional government, centred in the community of Batoche.

The first shots of the resistance were fired on March 26, 1885, in a field near the small community of Duck Lake, when a force of about 100 North-West Mounted Police and volunteers from Prince Albert, under the command of Inspector **LIEF CROZIER**, clashed with a Métis force led by Gabriel Dumont. When the smoke cleared, twelve policemen and volunteers as well as five Métis, including Isidore Dumont, Gabriel's brother, lay dead, and the Métis in the District of Saskatchewan were in open rebellion. In response to the clash at Duck Lake, a column of Mounted Police was hastily dispatched northward from Regina to garrison the town of Prince Albert.

The Métis army was structured as it had been since the days of the buffalo hunt: the captains of the hunt were in charge of ten soldiers each, and the most important of the captains assumed command of the whole force; the army was governed by rules laid down for each man to follow. As the first shots of the uprising were being fired, the commander of the Canadian militia, British general Sir Frederick Middleton, was on his way to the West to take com-

mand of the North-West Field Force, which was hurriedly being assembled in Manitoba and in eastern Canada. Military District 10, which was headquartered in Winnipeg, had responsibility for all military activity in Manitoba and the North-West Territories. The first of its units to be mobilized for the field force was the 90th Rifles of Winnipeg. On March 23, 1885, General Middleton and the advance party of 100 riflemen of the 90th left Winnipeg by train, bound for Qu'Appelle Station (then called Troy) in the District of Assiniboia, North-West Territories. It was there that Middleton first heard news of the Duck Lake encounter.

On April 6, Middleton and his small force of westerners, now augmented by more infantry, artillery and cavalry from Winnipeg, and by **BOULTON'S SCOUTS** from Russell, Manitoba, set out from the small town of Fort Qu'Appelle on a 200-mile journey northward to Batoche. The troops covered 20 miles a day, reaching the Humboldt telegraph station in a five-day march. On April 17 the column stopped at Clarke's Crossing, on the South Saskatchewan River, to wait for the troops that had been sent from eastern Canada to catch up with them. There, Middleton split his force, now some

900 strong, into two groups and continued his advance northward along both banks of the river. On April 24, his troops experienced their first taste of battle: at Fish Creek, the Canadian militia suffered a severe setback at the hands of Gabriel Dumont's sharpshooters. After the check at Fish Creek, an even more cautious General Middleton continued his advance to the Métis headquarters of Batoche. There, he began a four-day siege in which the Hudson's Bay Company paddle wheeler *Northcote*, complete with one of his two Gatling guns and a seven-pound cannon, was employed against the Métis defenders. On May 12, 1885, the badly outnumbered Métis were finally overcome by Middleton's troops after a short, sharp battle. A few days later, Louis Riel surrendered and Gabriel Dumont escaped to Montana. Louis Riel was brought to Regina, where he was tried for treason before Judge Hugh Richardson. He was found guilty on August 1, 1885, and on November 16 he was hanged at the Mounted Police barracks in Regina. His body was then taken to Winnipeg for burial.

The Cree Uprising. A few days before General Middleton entrained for the North-West Territories from Winnipeg, the Cree band at Frog Lake, in the

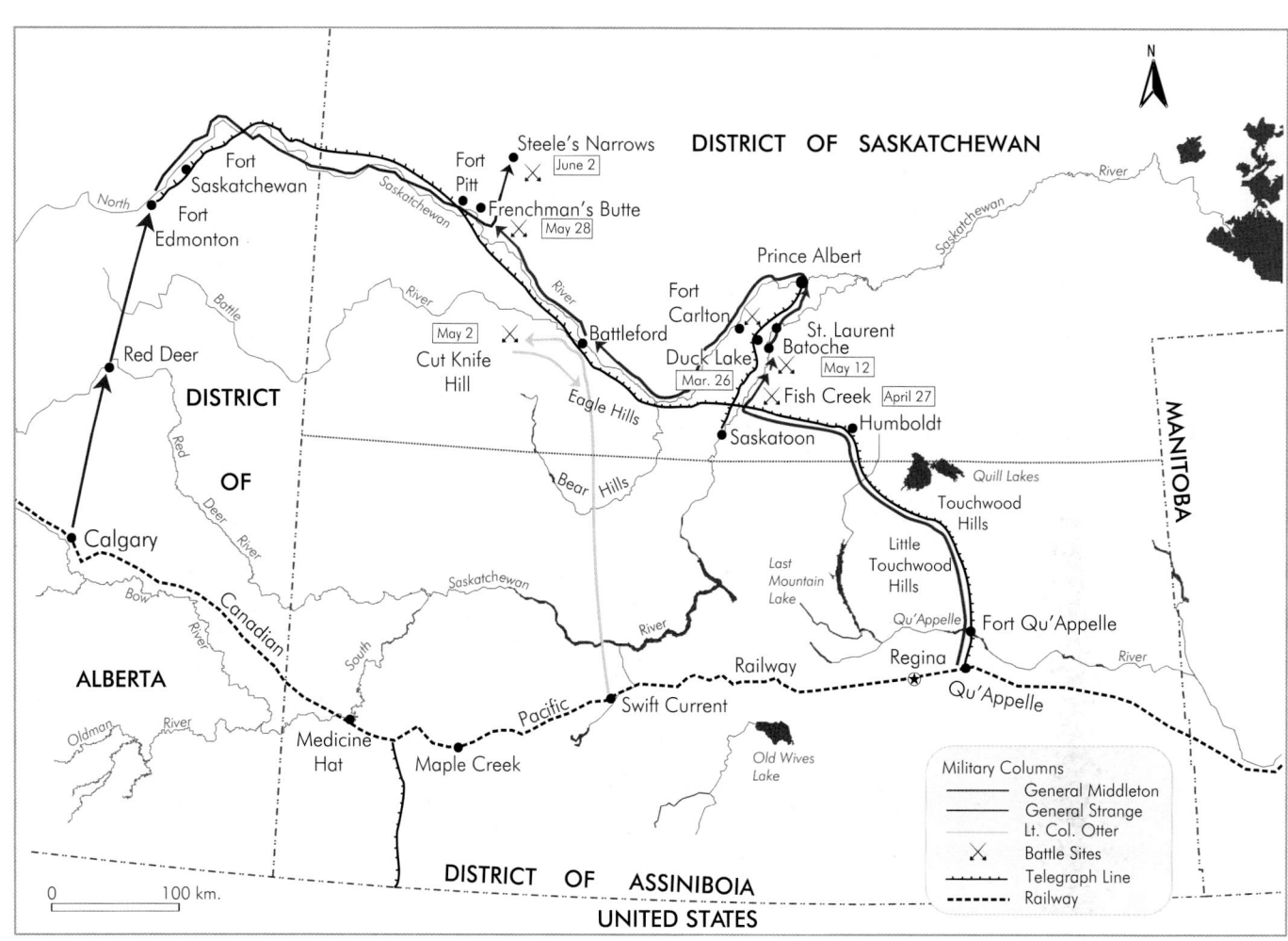

Troop movement and battles, 1885 Resistance.

Transport train en route from Swift Current to Saskatchewan Landing with supplies for General Middleton and Lt. Col. Otter. Photo donated by Reg. No. 4072, ex-S/Sargeant White.

FURTHER READING: Beal, B., and R. Macleod. 1984. *Prairie Fire: The 1885 North-West Rebellion.* Edmonton: Hurtig.

NORTH-WEST RESISTANCE AND FIRST NATIONS. There exists a common perception that First Nations were followers of **LOUIS RIEL** during the North-West Resistance of 1885. This notion is bolstered by the fact that thirty-three First Nations individuals were convicted of rebellion-related offenses, compared to nineteen Metis. Included were two of the principal leaders of the **CREE** (*Nêhiyawak*), **BIG BEAR** and **POUNDMAKER**, both convicted of treason-felony and in addition, eight First Nations men were hanged at Battleford in what came to be Canada's largest mass execution. In retrospect, the trials of the First Nations defendants were strongly biased by the prejudices of the day: the *Saskatchewan Herald* editorial of April 23, 1885, for example, concluded that "the only good Indians are the dead ones." The testimony of the few sympathetic observers of First Nations participation was dismissed. Chief Big Bear was convicted simply on the basis that he did not desert his band and was therefore guilty by association. His efforts to avoid violence at Frog Lake and **FORT PITT** were ignored. Chief Poundmaker was accused mainly on the basis of a letter found in the possession of Riel implying that the chief supported the Resistance, despite witnesses testifying that the chief's name had been put on the letter against his will. Poundmaker's attempts to forestall violence at the "Siege of Battleford" and the Battle of **CUT KNIFE HILL** were ignored. Big Bear and Poundmaker were actually *peace* as opposed to *war* chiefs; however, White juries failed to appreciate such subtleties.

Most of the First Nations individuals who were hanged were found guilty in connection with the Massacre of Frog Lake. The defendants did not have a lawyer, and to avoid difficulties in pronouncing names they were simply referred to by number. The fatal blow was dealt when Prime Minister Macdonald ordered that the defendants be tried on charges of murder, rather than treason, a change that resulted in death penalties. No evidence was presented against one of the hanged other than that he had been present at the event. Judge Rouleau, who had been stung by the burning of his house at Battleford, wasted little time in sentencing the defendants to death. Mitigating factors such as the suggestion that the initial intent of the Indians was simply to hold the Whites as hostages, and that it was only after the starving captors got access to the Hudson's Bay Company store's cache of liquor that events turned violent, were not taken into account. Local bands were brought in to witness the event, in the belief that this would discourage further trouble.

The federal government declared that twenty-eight First Nations bands had participated in the Resistance. This conclusion was questionable when

eastern part of the District of Saskatchewan (now part of the province of Alberta), under their chief **BIG BEAR**, rose in revolt to protest against the Canadian government's withholding of provisions. On April 1, 1885, the band killed nine people, and others were taken captive. The band then moved on to threaten Fort Pitt. The small, outnumbered garrison of Mounted Police under the command of Inspector Francis Dickens, son of the novelist Charles Dickens, was forced to abandon the post, leaving the civilians to be taken hostage. The police withdrew down the **NORTH SASKATCHEWAN RIVER** to the town of Battleford. The revolt of Big Bear's band raised fears of a larger Indian uprising among Canadian settlers in the western Saskatchewan and Alberta districts of the Territories. Battleford itself had come under siege from another Cree band under Chief **POUNDMAKER**, whose followers began to loot and burn some of the houses, including that of Hugh Richardson, the judge who later tried Louis Riel.

To counter the threat of a general Indian uprising, two more columns of the North-West Field Force were dispatched northward from the **CANADIAN PACIFIC RAILWAY**. One of the columns, under the command of Lieutenant Colonel Otter, an officer of the Queen's Own Rifles, set out from Swift Current to relieve Battleford. The Battleford Column reached the town on April 23, 1885, after a hard five-day march of 160 miles. Otter, having augmented his column with men from the Battleford Infantry Company, decided to set out after Poundmaker's Cree, who had withdrawn from the town. The two forces met at Cut Knife Hill on May 2; after an inconclusive seven-hour battle in which the Cree outmaneuvered the Canadians, Otter withdrew from the field. The battle could have easily ended in a rout for the Canadians if the troops had not retired in good order and if Poundmaker had

not refrained from seriously pursuing them. Otter marched back to Battleford; there he was joined by Middleton's forces, who had pushed on to the town after their victory at Batoche. Poundmaker surrendered to Middleton in Battleford on May 25.

The third column of Canadian militia, the Alberta Field Force, set out from Calgary, District of Alberta, under the command of Major General Thomas Bland Strange, a retired British artillery officer who had moved to the West. Strange's column included among others Steele's Scouts, a unit composed of North-West Mounted Police. The column marched north to Edmonton, then eastward along the North Saskatchewan River to Fort Pitt, in pursuit of Big Bear's band. Big Bear had remained in the Frog Lake area and had intended to join Poundmaker. On May 28, the forces of Strange and Big Bear clashed at Frenchman's Butte, where the Cree again gained the upper hand over the Canadians. However, Middleton had joined Strange from Battleford, thereby strengthening his force. Big Bear retreated northward across the Beaver River and into the forest wilderness, followed by the militia led by Steele's Scouts. After a brief encounter at Rat Foot Creek, now Steele Narrows, near Loon Lake, Big Bear's followers began to slip away from him. As he was making for Lac des Iles, on the Waterhen River, Big Bear's hostages were set free near the present-day community of Goodsoil. Finally, he was forced to surrender to the police at Fort Carlton, 100 miles away. With Big Bear's surrender on July 2, 1885, armed resistance ceased in the District of Saskatchewan, thereby ending the last military conflict on Canadian soil. In the aftermath of the Cree uprisings, both Big Bear and Poundmaker were given prison sentences, and eight of their followers were hanged at Battleford. (*See also* ABORIGINALS AND THE NORTH-WEST RESISTANCE.)

Stewart Mein

it became clear that either these First Nations had been coerced into participating and become involved by circumstance rather than intent, or that their absence from their reserve had been misconstrued. In the end, not a single chief supported the Resistance, all opting instead to live up to what they perceived as sacred treaty commitments; further proof of adherence to the treaties lies in the many statements of loyalty made by chiefs. Today, the sentences against First Nations leaders made during the Resistance still stand despite ample evidence that they were wrongly convicted. *Blair Stonechild*

FURTHER READING: Stonechild, B. and B. Waiser. 1997. *Loyal Till Death: Indians and the North West Rebellion.* Calgary: Fifth House.

NORTH-WEST TERRITORIES ACT. In 1869, Canada's federal government purchased Rupert's Land (*see* RUPERT'S LAND PURCHASE), providing for the "temporary Government of Rupert's Land and the North-Western Territory"; the corresponding Act placed local decision-making in the hands of a LIEUTENANT-GOVERNOR who could appoint a council of seven to fifteen persons. In 1875 the Act was consolidated and amended. It described in more detail the powers of the government and also reduced the council to five members. The territorial government had the authority to pass ordinances relating to regional matters such as roads, inheritance, public health, and alcohol control; ultimately, though, any ordinance passed by the territorial government could be amended or even vacated by the federal government. The 1875 Act also paved the way for a future Legislative Assembly of twenty-one members; electoral constituencies could be established when regions not exceeding an area of 1,000 square miles contained sufficient population.

In 1888, the Act was amended to provide for an advisory council of four elected members as a form of Cabinet alongside the Lieutenant-Governor; in 1891 this advisory council was replaced by an executive committee. Sir FREDERICK HAULTAIN, who became the first president of that committee, is often called the first Premier of the region. By 1897, a Cabinet replaced the executive committee and the elected Legislature also secured control of revenue spending. As a result, the North-West Territories then had a responsible government nearly equivalent to that of any province. From 1869 until 1905, however, the paramount issues for the region were regulated wholly by the federal government. These issues included Indian treaty negotiations, railway construction, immigration, and deeding land to settlers. Regarding the territorial government's share of power, historian L.H. THOMAS described it as "a system in which the territorial government would not be permitted to obstruct federal authority and policy." The North-West Territories Act ceased to apply to Saskatchewan after the federal Saskatchewan Act of 1905, but it remained in force thereafter for the Territories north of the 60th parallel.
Gerald Heinrichs

FURTHER READING: Herbert, T.L. 1956. *The Struggle for Responsible Government in the Northwest Territories, 1870–1897.* Toronto: University of Toronto Press; Lingard, C.C. 1946. *Territorial Government in Canada.* Toronto: University of Toronto Press.

NORWEGIAN SETTLEMENTS. The Birch Hills settlement was probably the earliest Norwegian settlement in what is now Saskatchewan, as it began to develop as early as 1894. The first Norwegian Lutheran congregation was established at Hanley in 1903, followed almost immediately by congregations near Langham and Birch Hills—so that virtually all of Saskatchewan's Norwegian settlements had come into existence by 1910. Around the turn of the century, large numbers of Norwegians had migrated northwards across the international frontier from earlier settlements they had established in Minnesota, the Dakotas, and Montana. Many settled in areas just north of the border. Today, Norwegian-Canadians form a substantial proportion in most of the rural municipalities along the border as well as in a corridor extending northwest from Estevan through Weyburn. They constitute between half and a quarter of the population of eight communities and a substantial proportion in another eight; in certain rural districts and unincorporated hamlets, Norwegians predominate. Altogether there are at least 4,000 people of Scandinavian (mostly Norwegian) origin in these communities today. Further west along the frontier, many Norwegian-Americans spread northward across the border from neighbouring settlements in Montana into the south-central frontier region, extending from the border northwards, through the Big Muddy Badlands and WOOD MOUNTAIN into the Cactus Hills. At least four early Norwegian Lutheran congregations were founded. Today, as many as 1,400 people of Scandinavian origin are scattered through eight rural municipalities and a dozen incorporated communities in this region. However, they form a majority only in two of the smallest communities; in the other communities and in the rural municipalities, they never form more than 15–20% of the population. While there are fewer people of Norwegian origin (perhaps about 800) in the southwest frontier region, south of CYPRESS HILLS they formed a well-defined settlement in this region in 1909–10. Immigrating from North Dakota, they settled in and around Climax, Frontier and Robsart, and established Norwegian Lutheran congregations in these villages as well as in Shaunavon. A continuous area of Norwegian concentration extends south into the adjacent Norheim and Hogeland districts in Montana.

A small concentration of Norwegians from North Dakota settled in the Simmie-Illerbrun area some 60 km to the north in 1906, establishing a Norwegian Lutheran congregation at Simmie. Today their descendants in the area number about 700, inclusive of a small minority in the nearby town of Gull Lake. A considerable number of Norwegians concentrated quite heavily in the region immediately to the northwest and north of Swift Current around 1906-08; six early Norwegian Lutheran congregations were established. Today, they do not form a majority in any incorporated community or rural municipality in this region; in smaller, unincorporated hamlets and rural districts, however, they predominate.

One of the largest primarily Norwegian settlements in Saskatchewan had begun to develop in the central region around Outlook and Hanley by 1903-06. Many of the original settlers came from largely Norwegian communities in the United States, such as Veblen and Langford (South Dakota), Northwood (North Dakota), and Hanley Falls (Minnesota); yet many had been born in Norway, and some had even arrived directly from there. The first Norwegian Lutheran congregation in Saskatchewan was founded at Hanley in 1903; several other early congregations "in town" were soon established. But most Norwegian Lutheran churches tended to become focal points for compact, solidly Norwegian districts out in the country. In fact, Scandinavian people do not comprise a majority in any community in the general region; yet as almost 3,000 people of Scandinavian origin live there, it is one of the largest concentrations of Norwegian people in Saskatchewan. Outlook has the largest number of people of Scandinavian descent for any rural community, with the possible exception of Melfort, and is the home of a Lutheran college with a strong Norwegian tradition.

A very small concentration of Norwegians developed in the area between Langham, Vanscoy and Delisle, about 60 km north of Outlook and immediately west of Saskatoon. The Norwegian Lutheran congregation founded near Langham in 1903 is one of the oldest in the province. Today, only about 300 people of Scandinavian origin remain in the area. A string of five primarily Norwegian settlements (but with substantial Swedish proportions in some communities and districts) wove its way across the north and east-central Saskatchewan prairies, from the Prince Albert region all the way to the Manitoba border. Today almost 10,000 people of Scandinavian origin live in these five settlements.

A large Scandinavian settlement around Shellbrook, west of Prince Albert, began to develop by 1904. The Parkside area southwest of Shellbrook was settled by people of both Swedish and

COURTESY OF THE BIRCH HILLS MUSEUM

Birch Hills, shown here in its early years, was one of Saskatchewan's earliest Norwegian settlements.

Norwegian origin who had immigrated via the midwestern states, as well as by immigrants directly from Sweden and Norway. Canwood, northwest of Shellbrook, became the focal point of a large area settled by people of diverse Scandinavian origins: chiefly Swedish and Norwegian, but also some Danish. The Ordale area, between Parkside and Canwood, due west of Shellbrook, was settled primarily by people of Norwegian origin related to those at Hagen in the Birch Hills settlement. Early Norwegian Lutheran congregations were established at Parkside, Shell Lake, and Shellbrook. In 1971 there were at least 1,500 people of Scandinavian origin within the settlement.

Some 30 km southeast of Prince Albert, the Birch Hills settlement was probably the earliest and remained the best defined, primarily Norwegian settlement in Saskatchewan. The Glen Mary district near the town of Birch Hills was first settled by Norwegian immigrants as early as 1894. In 1903 Rev. H.O. Holm, Home Mission Superintendent of the United Norwegian Lutheran Church, traveled through the region to determine the need for home mission work among the Norwegian settlers. Four days after he had organized the first Norwegian congregation in the province at Hanley (in the Outlook settlement), he founded the "Norden Skandianviske Lutherske Kirke" at Glen Mary. Later that same year, Pastor S.H. Njaa was sent from Hanley Falls, Minnesota to Hanley by a church board which had met at Canton, South Dakota; then he was posted to the Birch Hills settlement. Fairly close contact seems to have been maintained between the various settlements within the province, between them and similar ones in the midwestern states, and between them and certain areas of Scandinavia. It was largely through these contacts that the settlement around Birch Hills grew, as more and more people of Scandinavian origin migrated there from other

Scandinavia areas in the province, from the American settlements, and from Scandinavia itself. The Birch Hills settlement, together with an adjacent Swedish settlement north of Melfort, included over 3,000 people of Scandinavian origin. While Scandinavian people do not predominate in any town or incorporated village in the settlement region, they do form a very high proportion (over 90%) in many smaller communities and rural districts. The Hagen area west of Birch Hills, for example, is almost completely Norwegian, as are the districts of Queen Maud, Prestfoss, Viking, Norden, etc., north of Weldon.

About 50 km south of Melfort, another Norwegian settlement developed around Naicam. Immanuel Norwegian Lutheran Congregation, founded at Naicam in 1910, held all of its services exclusively in Norwegian during the early years (as did most, if not all, Norwegian Lutheran congregations), and has long held a Norwegian Christmas service. Virtually all pastors who served this congregation, as well as the Dovre Congregation, founded near Spalding in 1919, were Norwegian. A bilingual sign in Norwegian and English welcomes visitors to Naicam. The Scandinavian proportion is less than one-third in Naicam, and a quarter in Spalding; yet surrounding rural districts tend to be quite heavily Norwegian, as early placenames suggested. Today, an estimated 1,000 Scandinavians live in this settlement.

It is often difficult to determine when one Norwegian settlement dwindles and the next begins. To the east of Naicam and Spalding, Scandinavian settlement continues eastward 50 km into the Rose Valley area. However, Ukrainians outnumber Scandinavians in the village of Rose Valley, where people of Scandinavian origin comprise slightly over a quarter of the community population. To the south, only one in five residents in Fosston is Scandinavian, as many Poles settled in

this community. But the next village, Hendon, is largely Swedish and Norwegian; and Swedes, Norwegians and Icelanders comprise a substantial proportion of the town of Wadena. To the north of Rose Valley, Scandinavian people concentrated around Nora and Archerwill; the Dahlton district is largely Scandinavian. Further to the north, Scandinavians settled around Chagoness, Bjorkdale, and Stenen. Early Norwegian Lutheran congregations were founded at Nora, Rose Valley, Hendon and Wadena.

Norwegian settlement continued eastward past Kelvington into the areas around Margo, Ketchen, Preeceville, Sturgis, and Norquay. Early Norwegian Lutheran congregations included Margo, Poplar Grove at Ketchen (1918), and North Prairie at Preeceville (1908); again, virtually all pastors for decades have been Norwegian. An estimated 2,400 people of Scandinavian descent live in this region. While they constitute relatively low proportions in the principal communities, they form higher proportions in the surrounding rural areas. According to recent census data (2001), of 60,510 Saskatchewan residents claiming Norwegian ethnic origin, 15% (9,135) claim no other ethnic origin, whereas the vast majority, 84.9% (51,370) claim other origins besides Norwegian. (*See also* ETHNIC BLOC SETTLEMENTS, SCANDINAVIAN SETTLEMENTS, SWEDISH SETTLEMENTS, AMERICAN IMMIGRATION)   *Alan Anderson*

FURTHER READING: Loken, G. 1980. *From Fjord to Frontier: A History of Norwegians in Canada.* Toronto: McClelland and Stewart.

NUGENT, JOHN CULLEN (1921–). John Nugent was born on January 5, 1921, in Montreal and studied at St. John's University (Collegeville, Minnesota), where he was exposed to liberal ideals and the post-war renewal in the arts that was sweeping the Catholic Church. In 1948, he moved to Lumsden, Saskatchewan and executed liturgical commissions in silver and bronze, while supporting his family as a chandler. The simplified, yet expressive forms of his chalices and crucifixes demonstrate an interest in modern interpretations of early Christian and Romanesque models. Resistance from the Church hierarchy and from parishioners caused him to cease his liturgical work in the 1960s. After his candle works in Lumsden burned down in 1960, Nugent commissioned CLIFFORD WIENS to design a studio with a novel curved, conical design that earned the Regina architect a Massey silver medal award. In 1961, while on a trip to New York to study bronze casting, Nugent visited the studio of American sculptor David Smith; this encounter was to influence his move to welded steel abstraction. The awkward grace of Nugent's steel sculpture, for which he is best known, results from a constructivist collage of prefabricated elements. While often incor-

SASKATCHEWAN ARCHIVES BOARD R-B8560

John Nugent, Lumsden, making final inspection of a chalice, 1959. On the bench is one of his wood carvings, entitled "Mother and Child."

porating identifiable parts, such as wheels, his sculpture eludes easy metaphorical readings, instead creating meaning through unexpected combinations of forms and materials. Nugent's work represents an independent strain within Canadian abstract steel sculpture without direct ties to the Emma Lake Artists' Workshops or other western Canadian sculptors. Nugent's welded steel sculpture has met with controversy at times. His proposal for a soaring abstract monument to LOUIS RIEL was rejected by Premier ROSS THATCHER, who demanded in its place a representational figure. Unveiled in 1968, Nugent's heroic nude statue, to which the premier had forced him to add clothing, was removed from the Saskatchewan Legislature grounds in 1991 after protests from the Métis community. Nugent's *#1*

Northern (1976) was also removed from its site in front of Winnipeg's Canadian Grain Commission building in 1978, but was later restored in 1997. Nugent, who taught at the UNIVERSITY OF REGINA from 1970 to 1985, has also executed public commissions for the Banff Centre, the National Capital Commission (Ottawa), and the CBC Broadcast Centre (Regina). In 1983, his work was the subject of a major retrospective, *John Nugent: Modernism in Isolation*, organized by the MACKENZIE ART GALLERY in Regina. In the 1990s, Nugent shifted his attention from sculpture to photography. His work can be found in the collections of the MacKenzie Art Gallery, the Robert McLaughlin Gallery (Oshawa), the SASKATCHEWAN ARTS BOARD, the University of Regina, and the Winnipeg Art Gallery. *Timothy Long*

NUTHATCH. This small songbird is found in wooded regions, where it feeds by climbing through the branches and around the trunks of trees in search of insects under the bark. Nuthatches resemble WOODPECKERS in their habitat but are short-tailed perching birds (order Passeriformes) which walk up and down the trunks and branches of trees. They pry insects from under bark with their long, pointed bills. Their song consists of a series of nasal notes, which has been compared to that of a toy trumpet. There are approximately twenty-five species of the Family Sittidae, found in North America, Europe and Asia. Two species of nuthatches are resident in the province: the red-breasted nuthatch and the white-breasted nuthatch. The smaller (11 cm) red-breasted nuthatch (*Sitta canadensis*) breeds in the boreal forests and winters in the Aspen Parkland and townsites. The slightly larger (13–15 cm) white-breasted nuthatch (*S. carolinensis*) is a bird of the deciduous woods which has been expanding its range in the province from the east since it was first reported in 1914. *Diane Secoy*

FURTHER READING: Alsop, Fred J., III. 2002. *Birds of Canada*. New York: Dorling Kindersley; Godfrey, W. Earl.1986. *Birds of Canada*. Ottawa: National Museum of Natural Sciences.

SASKATCHEWAN NEW DEMOCRATIC PARTY ARCHIVES

Lorne Nystrom.

NYSTROM, LORNE EDMUND (1946–). Nystrom was born April 26, 1946, on the family farm near Wynyard. Trained to be a teacher, he graduated from the UNIVERSITY OF SASKATCHEWAN in 1970. He was active in the youth wing of the NDP, serving as leader of the Regina Campus NDP, president of the Saskatchewan New Democrat Youth, and as a vice-president of the federal NDP (1967–68). In 1968, while still a university student, he won the federal riding of Yorkton Melville at the age of 33. He won six more elections in a row. In 1993 Nystrom was defeated and the NDP lost official party status in the House of Commons. During his term out of Parliament, Nystrom operated a political consulting firm often involving projects overseas. He won the Qu'Appelle constituency in 1997, was re-elected in 2000, but was defeated in 2004. Nystrom served as the NDP's parliamentary critic in a number of areas: most notably youth, agriculture and food, the constitution, finance, banking, justice, and democratic reform. He has also served as NDP caucus whip and deputy House Leader. Nystrom ran three times for the leadership of the federal NDP (1975, 1995 and 2003) and came in third on each occasion. In 1992, he was appointed a co-chair of the Charlottetown Referendum Committee and was appointed to the Privy Council by Brian Mulroney. Nystrom edited a book on economics, *Just Making Change*. He is a partner in Regina businesses, is vice-president of a soybean enterprise, and continues his involvement in electoral reform. *Alan Whitehorn*

COURTESY OF TOURISM SASKATCHEWAN

Red-breasted Nuthatch.

OAT. Oat (*Avena sativa* L.) is the third most widely grown cereal crop in Canada, behind **WHEAT** and **BARLEY**. Cultivated oat is an annual plant with a spring growth habit. It is easily distinguished from wheat and barley by its panicle rather than spike inflorescence. The panicle has extended branching from the main stem, creating an open type of inflorescence, as opposed to a spike where the seeds are closer to the central rachis. Although oat has wide adaptation and can be grown across Canada, it is best adapted to moist fertile environments and is not widely grown in the drier regions of the prairies. Oat and other small-grain cereals were brought to Canada in the early 17th century by European colonists. Cereal crops were introduced to the prairies in the mid-1700s as trading posts became established in western Canada. Oat was an important feed crop for the early settlers on the prairies, who used horses as the main source of power for farming and transportation. Over the years, several factors have contributed to the relative importance of oat compared to other grain crops: size and makeup of the livestock industry, popularity and value of pulse and oilseed crops, and an increased interest in oat in the human food market.

Although oat production varies from year to

EVERETT BAKER PHOTO/COURTESY OF THE SASKATCHEWAN HISTORY AND FOLKLORE SOCIETY

Harvesting oat crop near Bright Sand, Saskatchewan, September 1944.

year, Saskatchewan statistics show a slight upward trend in harvested acres in the most recent twenty-year period. This trend is attributable to increased demand from the United States food market, and to an increasing demand in the livestock market, including the recreation horse feed market. The 1998–2002 five-year averages of harvested acres and production in Saskatchewan were 1.5 million acres and 1.3 million tonnes, respectively (SAFRR).

Cultivar development has played and integral role in sustainability and advancement of the oat industry. Canadian efforts in cultivar development date to the late 1800s. At that time, the majority of efforts consisted of observation and evaluation of American or European cultivars brought with settlers arriving in Canada or received from other research institutions. These varieties were generally susceptible to serious diseases such as smut and rust, and varied in adaptation to the diverse conditions of the prairies. These evaluation efforts allowed producers the opportunity to grow the most adaptable cultivar for a particular region. Varieties with the best general adaptation became predominant for extended periods of time.

In Saskatchewan, evaluation of oat cultivars was initiated at the Indian Head Experimental Farm in 1888 and at the UNIVERSITY OF SASKATCHEWAN in 1909. Currently, the University of Saskatchewan CROP DEVELOPMENT CENTRE (CDC) oat-breeding program is the only one in the province. Other breeding programs contributing to prairie oat production include the AAFC research centres at Winnipeg, Manitoba and Lacombe, Alberta. Although efforts continue to emphasize traits such as yield, maturity and disease- and lodging-resistance, since 1975 greater emphasis at the CDC has been placed on food and feed quality traits such as plumpness, test weight, colour, milling yield, hull content, as well as protein, oil and beta-glucan content. These traits have implications in both human and animal feed markets.

While the majority of oat is used as feed, either on-farm or through commercial trade, there has been increasing interest in oat as a functional food (a food product which provides specific nutritional/health benefits). The beta-glucan in oat, which is a form of soluble dietary fibre, is reported to lower blood cholesterol and possess anti-oxidant attributes. In addition to the conventional markets for oat and the increasing interest in its functional food properties, niche markets are developing for the hog and cattle industries. In western Canada, the marketing of oat was placed under the authority of the CANADIAN WHEAT BOARD in 1949. In 1974, as part of a new domestic feed grain policy, the federal government removed feed oat for the domestic market from the sole authority of the Board. In 1989, the remainder of oat marketing was removed from the authority of the Board. *Blaine Recksiedler*

FURTHER READING: MacKay, A. 1888. "Experimental Farm for the North-West Territories." Pp. 101–02 in W. Saunders (ed.), *Appendix to the Report of the Minister of Agriculture on Experimental Farms*. Ottawa: MacLean, Roger & Co; McKenzie, R.I.H. and D.E. Harder. 1995. "Oat." Pp. 98–112 in A.E. Slinkard and D.R. Knott (eds.), *Harvest of Gold*. Saskatoon: University of Saskatchewan Extension Press.

COURTESY OF BRIAN MLAZGAR

Father George Salamon, OMI, in Lebret, 1922. When Father Salamon died in 2000 at the age of 103, he was the world's oldest Oblate.

OBLATES OF MARY IMMACULATE (OMI): ASSUMPTION PROVINCE.

The Missionary Oblates of Mary Immaculate (OMI) are a Roman Catholic religious congregation of priests and brothers founded by Eugene de Mazenod in France in 1826. The first Oblates to come to Canada arrived from France in 1841. Non-French Oblates came to Canada during the settlement period in the West to tend to the needs of immigrants from Eastern Europe. In 1898, the first Polish Oblate, Fr. Albert (Wojciech) Kulawy came to Canada. Fr. Anthony Sylla, arrived in 1909, was appointed pastor of Rama, Saskatchewan in 1933; in 1939, he established a shrine and pilgrimage site there in honour of Our Lady of Lourdes. The Polish Oblates all belonged to Manitoba Province until 1926, when St. Mary's Province was formed for the German and Polish Oblates. In 1956, the Oblate Council established a separate Polish Oblate province in Canada: all the parishes served by Polish Oblates, as well as most of the Oblate priests, brothers and seminarians of Polish descent, became part of Assumption Province. In Saskatchewan, Assumption Province Oblates currently serve in the parishes of St. Henry's, Melville; St. Patrick's, Sturgis; and Mary Queen of All Hearts, Lestock–plus thirteen First Nations reserves. *Wojciech Wojtkowiak*

OBLATES OF MARY IMMACULATE (OMI): ST. MARY'S PROVINCE.

The establishment of St. Mary's Province on March 15, 1926, as a distinct religious Oblate community paralleled the immigration of the Russian-German, Polish and Ukrainian immigrants into western Canada. The Catholic bishops of western Canada had invited the Oblate Province in Germany to send priests to minister to the immigrant parishes and missions which had begun to be formed in the newly settled farm districts and among the railway and industrial workers of the cities. More than 80 brothers and priests were sent from the German Oblate Province to Canada up to 1939. Over the years, in addition to parish work in both rural and urban areas, St. Mary's Province Oblates have taught in St. Charles Scholasticate and ST. THOMAS COLLEGE; operated Marian Press, published *Our Family* magazine, and run Batschol Farm (all in the Battlefords); operated Queen's House of Retreats in Saskatoon; participated in missions in Brazil and Africa; and continued their ministry to and with the Aboriginal people of Saskatchewan. In response to changes within the congregation and the desire for collaboration in new ways, in December 2003 St. Mary's Province and four other English-speaking Oblate provinces regrouped to form "Lacombe Canada Province." *Nestor Gregoire*

OBNOVA CLUB.

Obnova, the Ukrainian Catholic student organization equivalent to the National Federation of Newman Clubs, was formed in L'viv, Ukraine in 1929. In 1934 Obnova, which means "renewal," was incorporated into the International Movement of Catholic Students, Pax Romana. Obnova aimed to provide Ukrainian Catholic students a forum where they could acquire formation in Catholic principles of faith, ethics and morals. The first organizational meeting of Ukrainian Catholic students at the UNIVERSITY OF SASKATCHEWAN was held on January 21, 1953, at the Newman Club. A temporary constitution was drawn up and a slate of officers appointed. The club selected the name "Sheptytsky Club," and established its centre of operations at the SHEPTYTSKY INSTITUTE. Members were mainly students enrolled at the University of Saskatchewan; but students attending SIAST (Kelsey Campus), Saskatoon Business College, and other institutions of learning were also welcomed. Several of the members were in the work force or professions, but enjoyed associating with the students; some members were not Ukrainian or even Catholic, but were accepted if they chose to accept Obnova's principles and to participate in its activities. The Obnova Club organized retreats, discussion groups, caroling, and communion breakfasts to promote the spiritual growth and development of the members. Cultural activities such as Ukrainian dancing, choir, and drama flourished. Social activities included dances, sporting events, tournaments, the annual formal graduation, and public speaking competitions. The Obnova Club ceased to exist some time in the mid-1980s. *William Gulka*

O'BRIEN, ANN GORDON (1895–1986). Born Ann Gordon on November 18, 1895 in Verdun, Montreal, Quebec, she married Montréal businessman William O'Brien and led an active social life combined with volunteer work at the Sisters of Service Hostel for Immigrant Women in Montréal. In 1941, after her husband's death, she entered the Sisters of Service in Toronto. In 1946 she was asked to be executive director of the newly formed Catholic Welfare Bureau, later called Catholic Family Services, in Saskatoon. Sister O'Brien remained executive director until her retirement in 1976. During her thirty years of service in Saskatoon, her work was officially recognized by many agencies and organizations; she was named Saskatoon's Citizen of the Year in 1974. On her retirement in 1976, the Board of Catholic Family Services and other public-spirited citizens established "The Sister Ann O'Brien Scholarship Fund" to commemorate her service and dedication to family service work. In 1980 she was named among the "Notable Saskatchewan Women: 1905–1980" and in 1982 Sister O'Brien School and O'Brien Crescent, Terrace & Court in Saskatoon were named in recognition of her work.

Ann O'Brien's gifts and skill as a social worker and family counselor are legendary. Her openness to all people regardless of class or creed, her dedication, concern, wisdom, advocacy and witness to Christian values were acclaimed and esteemed by all who knew her. She died at the SOS Retirement Centre in St. Catharines, Ontario, on April 12, 1986.

Patricia Burke

OCCUPATIONAL HEALTH AND SAFETY ACT: *see* **LEGISLATION IN SASKATCHEWAN**

OCCUPATIONAL HEALTH AND SAFETY LEGISLATION. Saskatchewan was the first province to introduce broadly based occupational health and safety legislation. Canadian government investigations of workers' health and safety date back to the 1880s, including an 1889 Royal Commission that documented widespread unhealthy working conditions, rampant disease, exploitation of child labour, and a lack of compensation to workers injured in industrial and agricultural work. Yet by the turn of the century the federal government still offered little in the way of legislation, hiding behind Factory Acts and federal-provincial jurisdictional issues. By the 1940s, provincial health departments, including an occupational component in the Saskatchewan Department of Public Health, provided workplace safety information and encouraged the training of occupational health professionals. Other early Saskatchewan efforts included developing through the Workmen's Compensation Board guidelines on accident prevention that became enforceable through regulation in 1959.

As part of the 1971 "New Deal for People," the Saskatchewan **NEW DEMOCRATIC PARTY** promised health and safety as a fundamental right of workers as a logical extension of **MEDICARE**. Legislation established a Provincial Occupational Health Council and specified the establishment of joint labour-management Occupational Health Committees in workplaces with ten or more employees. In 1975, the Act was further strengthened, specifying duties of employers and workers, and ratifying important asbestos regulations. By 1977, earlier legislation including the Mines Regulations Act was repealed in favour of integrated legislation based on the experiences of the first five years. The department's regulatory powers were enhanced and codes of practice established, prohibiting discrimination against members of Occupational Health and Safety Committees and strengthening the right to refuse "unusually dangerous work." Workers could now receive medical examinations and be assigned temporary alternative work without loss of pay when exposed to harmful substances. A system of fines was established including up to two years in prison for conviction of a serious offense.

Of lasting significance was the gradual development of a system of rights under the leadership of Associate Deputy Minister **BOB SASS**. These rights have been identified as the "right to know," the "right to participate," and the "right to refuse." The legislation of the 1970s reflected a belief that workplace accidents and disease could be eliminated, and that workers were key to finding and implementing the solutions. The legislation encouraged a broadly based regulatory system, and subsequent regulations proclaimed between 1981 and 2004 covered a range of workplace issues, from notification regarding occupational diseases, dangerous working conditions and accidents to first aid and emergency arrangements and mining protocols.

Innovations related to workplace violence and harassment were introduced in 1993, including the designation of a worker representative in workplaces with between four and ten employees as well as legislation to clarify owner, contractor and supplier responsibility for work place safety. Legislation identified harassment as a health and safety issue. Saskatchewan is the only province in Canada that includes "harassment" in occupational health and safety legislation. Women's groups welcomed the legislation as an effective way of addressing sexual harassment, and generally appreciated its preventative components as a route preferable to the lengthy process under Human Rights Legislation.

Regulations now cover most workplaces from construction sites to forestry and mill operations, to health-care facilities. They prescribe use of video display terminals (under the Radiation Health and Safety Act). Recent regulations on smoke-free workplaces include amendments to the Tobacco Control Act in 2004. Despite comprehensive occupational health and safety legislation, true health and safety remains elusive in Saskatchewan. April 28 is a national day of mourning in Canada for workers killed and injured on the job. Of the 953 Canadians who lost their lives in 2003 through workplace accidents, 28 were in Saskatchewan. *Merran Proctor*

OCEAN MAN FIRST NATION. Chief Kitchi-Kah-Me-Win (Great Seaman or Ocean Man, Kicheekahmenin, Kickekamewin) signed an adhesion to **TREATY 4** on September 9, 1875. In 1882 a 23,680-acre reserve was surveyed for this **ASSINIBOINE**, **CREE**, and **SAULTEAUX** band, adjacent to Chief Pheasant Rump's reserve in the Moose Mountains north of Kisbey. The band's agricultural development was noted in many reports over the years; but in 1901, following several years of persuasion, the band surrendered its entire reserve and amalgamated with the White Bear Band. Once relocated on the White Bear Reserve they began to rebuild, using their agricultural experience. In the 1970s Ocean Man descendants were part of a land claim launched against the federal government that eventually saw the successful re-establishment of both the band (1988) and their reserve (1992). The re-established reserve is located 18 km north of Stoughton and has a current land base of 4,128.4 ha. The reserve is home to 51 of the 324 registered members. Their economy is based on agriculture, off-reserve employment, and some gas and oil revenue. Facilities available include a band office, pow-wow grounds, school, day care, health clinic, community well, and water plant. In 1997, the Ocean Man band was noted for being the only First Nation in Canada with an elected all-female council and chief. *Christian Thompson*

OCHAPOWACE FIRST NATION. This Plains Cree band under Kakisheway (Loud Voice) signed **TREATY 4** on September 15, 1874. A reserve was surveyed for them on the north side of Round Lake and the Qu'Appelle River in 1876 (reserves for Chacachas and Kahkewistahaw were surveyed on the south side). As Kakisheway had requested to be relocated, in 1881 Surveyor John Nelson and Agent McDonald decided to place both Kakisheway and Chacachas on the same reserve, enlarging it to include members of both bands. Many members were away hunting when this occurred, and were upset when they returned to Crooked Lakes in 1882 to find they no longer had their own lands but were now amalgamated on to the Chacachas Reserve (1884). Approximately 45 band members joined Kakisheway; the others, including Chacachas, remained stragglers. In 1884 Kakisheway's son Ochapowace succeeded him and became chief of the amalgamated bands. Much of the old Chacachas Reserve has been purchased and re-designated reserve land through Treaty Land Entitlement, and now the descendants of Chacachas wait on the federal government to decide whether they will be re-established as a separate reserve once again. The band currently holds 18,279.7 ha of land; most of its population is located 8 km northeast of Broadview, with 564 of the 1,382 band members currently living on reserve. In addition to their controlling interest in Consolidated Capital Corporation, a high-quality beef program, the band has several major economic investments, the newest being the Winn Bay Sand Limited Partnership (2004).   *Christian Thompson*

OFFICE OF THE TREATY COMMISSIONER.

The Office of the Treaty Commissioner (OTC) was first created in 1989 to assist in resolving issues surrounding Treaty Land Entitlement. In 1996, the FEDERATION OF SASKATCHEWAN INDIAN NATIONS and the government of Canada entered into a five-year agreement that expanded the Commissioner's role to provide a forum for treaty discussions. The OTC is an independent body that facilitates a bilateral process to discuss treaty and jurisdictional issues between Saskatchewan First Nations and the government of Canada, with the government of Saskatchewan present as an observer. Exploratory tables in various areas of jurisdiction such as education, health, and justice discover areas of common understanding and agreement that exist amongst the parties. The discussion process is based upon the assumption that the Numbered Treaties signed mainly in the 1870s form the basis of the relationships between First Nation, federal, and provincial governments, and that such treaties provide an effective framework for dealing with present and future issues. Such a relationship entails respect by all levels of government for the right of First Nations to self-governance. Judge David Arnot, a member of the Provincial Court of Saskatchewan, was appointed by the government of Canada to be Treaty Commissioner on January 1, 1997. One of the Commissioner's primary activities is to educate the general public about mainstream society's role and obligations with respect to treaties, something that is being accomplished by means of school educational materials, publications, and a Speaker's Bureau.
Blair Stonechild

OFFICE AND PROFESSIONAL EMPLOYEES INTERNATIONAL UNION (OPEIU/COPE).

Saskatchewan Insurance Employees' Union, Local 1, a direct charter of the Canadian Congress of Labour, was certified as a bargaining unit and chartered in 1946. The local was comprised of thirty-one members employed by Saskatchewan Government Insurance Office. The first president of the local was Doreen Christiaens. The longest-serving president was Bill Wittal, who served for ten years in the 1970s and the early 1980s. Seven of the union's twenty-one presidents have been women.

In 1948, with William (Bill) Turner as president, Local 1 went on strike. The strike lasted eighteen days, resulting in a 35% wage increase for the members; the local was the first union to strike a CROWN CORPORATION. The local affiliated with the newly created Canadian Labour Congress on May 1, 1956, and with the SASKATCHEWAN FEDERATION OF LABOUR on October 9, 1957. On February 1, 1962, the Saskatchewan local affiliated with the Office Employees' International Union as Saskatchewan Insurance, Office & Professional Employees' Union, Local 397. Joining the larger organization supplied the strength and stability needed to remain a strong local union.

Local 397 provided strong vice-presidential representation to OPEIUs' International Executive Board. Bill Wittal, who retired as an OPEIU Representative in 1988, remains as vice-president emeritus of the International Executive Board—a rare and important achievement for him and the local union. In 1983, under the Progressive Conservative government, SGI planned to close motor vehicle offices around the province; in order to protect its members, OPEIU Local 397 was successful in getting the first-ever injunction against the Crown to stop the closures.

OPEIU Local 397 also worked with the NDP during the late 1980s to stop the privatization of SGI. In addition to an advertising campaign, members spent weekends leafleting around the province; this combined effort put sufficient pressure on the Conservative government to stop the privatization. On June 20, 2004, the OPEIU locals across Canada took another major step by separating from the international union. The new union, Canadian Office and Professional Employees' Union (COPE), has fifty-one locals and 34,000 members across Canada. COPE Local 397 has approximately 1,500 members in nine bargaining units.   *Judy Boehmer*

OGEMA, town, pop 292, located approximately 110 km S of Regina, midway between Weyburn and Assiniboia on Hwy 13. The district began to be settled between 1906 and 1908. Settlers to the area came from eastern Canada, some regions of Europe, and the United States. The Ogema post office was opened in 1910, and in 1911 the railway came through. In January 1915, a fire destroyed the east side of Ogema's Main Street, and although firewalls were an uncommon and costly proposition at the time, town councillors decided that to ensure against future disasters they would construct across the west side of the street a wall that was 70 feet long, 28 feet high, and sunk 8 feet into the ground. On the east side, a fire hall was built with one of its walls constructed to act as the opposite firewall. This unique pair of structures remain features of Ogema's Main Street to this day; interestingly, the contractor who built them was Robert John Lecky,

who had been the construction superintendent during the erection of the SASKATCHEWAN LEGISLATIVE BUILDING. Ogema prospered through the 1920s, witnessed an exodus during the 1930s, and saw a return to prosperity and growth during the post-WORLD WAR II period. It was a typical Saskatchewan community with an economy based on mixed farming and ranching. By the 1980s, however, rationalization and consolidation led to a massive loss of infrastructure, and Ogema, which had developed as a hub for the surrounding communities in terms of providing basic services, was rapidly overshadowed by the larger centres of Weyburn, Assiniboia, and Regina. In response, community leaders in Ogema and other area communities sought initiatives and partnerships, and advanced the concept of a regional economy. In 1999, members of various communities completed negotiations to purchase the CPR branch line that ran from Pangman to Assiniboia, and RED COAT ROAD AND RAIL became the first community-owned short line in the province. Community leaders also enticed BIG SKY FARMS to establish a 5,000 sow farrow-to-finish hog operation in the Ogema area, the first of that size in Canada. The result has been a significant degree of success in building a sustainable future. In recent years, the Saskatchewan Government's Action Committee on the Rural Economy (ACRE) named Ogema a model community in terms of contemporary economic development strategies for rural Saskatchewan. The Deep South Pioneer Museum, situated on a 12-acre site, is one of the largest in the province and contains a complete townsite comprised of over 50 historic buildings; the site has been used for the production of films. Ogema also has a well-preserved British American service station, which is thought to date to the WORLD WAR I era, and a 1911 CPR train station situated at the end of Main Street.
David McLennan

OGLE, FATHER ROBERT (1928–98). Father Bob Ogle was a priest, foreign missionary, author and a member of Parliament. He was born on December 24, 1928 in Rosetown, Saskatchewan, and was raised on a poor farm in a devout Irish Catholic family during the GREAT DEPRESSION. He studied for the priesthood at St. Peter's Seminary in London, Ontario, and was ordained in May 1953. He then returned to Saskatoon, where he became a parish priest, founded the Catholic Centre, and became the rector of St. Pius X Seminary. He later completed a Doctorate in Canon Law at the University of Ottawa. Father Ogle was a man of great energy and drive who wanted to make a difference. In 1964 he volunteered as one of the founding members of a diocesan mission team sent to the poverty-stricken region of northeast Brazil. There he engaged in pastoral work and organized literacy activities, farming co-operatives, and medical

SASKATCHEWAN NEW DEMOCRATIC PARTY PHOTO ARCHIVES
Robert Ogle.

programs. In 1969 he coordinated a relief operation and house-building program following disastrous floods near the mission. He later said that he was profoundly influenced by what he saw in Brazil, and that it changed his llife.

He returned to Saskatoon in 1970 and was installed in one of the city's largest parishes. He was a good pastor, especially skilled at getting people involved in projects; but he was restless. In 1976 he took a sabbatical and traveled the world, visiting Canadian international development projects. When he returned home, he wrote about it in a book called *When the Snake Bites the Sun*. The very night that he delivered his manuscript in September 1977, he received a call from a member of the NDP constituency organization for Saskatoon East, asking him to consider becoming a candidate in the next federal election. He had never belonged to a political party, but was ready for something big. It was unusual for a priest to engage in partisan politics, so he consulted with his bishop, with other priests, parishioners, friends, and even **OTTO LANG**, the Liberal incumbent. Eventually he decided to do it, and the Ogle legend began to take shape. He was a creative campaigner, who placed brief handwritten advertisements in the local newspaper and mounted an Ogle sign on a moveable trailer which he parked in the street whenever he went knocking on doors.

While Otto Lang went busily about his task as Transport Minister, Father Ogle became a well-known figure, riding a bicycle around the city to do his canvassing. He knocked on every door in the riding, many of them more than once. He used a low-key, pastoral approach on the doorstep, asking peo-

ple about themselves and their problems rather than telling them what to think or how to vote. Father Bob, as he was known, defeated Lang in 1979, entering the NDP caucus during the minority government of Joe Clark; he won again in 1980. He served as the NDP critic for external affairs, for the Canadian International Development Agency, and as the critic for health, in which position he steadfastly refused to follow his party's position on abortion, Father Ogle loved being an MP, and he approached that work on a pastoral basis as well, generally keeping a promise never to make personal attacks on political opponents. But his career was causing controversy within the Church. By 1984 the Vatican had decided that Parliament was no place for a priest, and despite the fact that he had already won his party's nomination as a candidate, Father Ogle was instructed not to stand for election. He agonized over the order and considered leaving the priesthood, but in the end he decided to obey, and did not contest the 1984 election. He was quoted at the time as saying that he was a priest first and hoped to remain one for the rest of his life. During his last fifteen years, Father Ogle was almost constantly ill. He was suffering from serious headaches and developed a bleeding ulcer even before he left politics in 1984. About a year later he had a heart attack, and eventually he was diagnosed with a cancerous and inoperable brain tumour.

Those who knew him well said that his afflictions often left him near despair, but he was a tenacious man, who loved life and refused to give up. In these pain-filled years he wrote two more books, initiated a project called Broadcasting for International Understanding, and hosted a retreat series on television. Father Bob Ogle was installed as an Officer of the Order of Canada in 1989 and received the Saskatchewan Award of Merit in 1995. His projects kept him (and his friends) busy, and he never lost his sense of humour. His health continued to deteriorate, however, and he died in Saskatoon on April 1, 1998, at the age of 69. The former Pius X Seminary, now a student residence on the University of Saskatchewan campus, has been renamed Ogle Hall in his honour. *Dennis Gruending*

FURTHER READING: Ogle, B. 1977. *When the Snake Bites the Sun*. Saskatoon: Texchuk Enterprises; — 1987. *North/South Calling*. Saskatoon: Fifth House.

OHLSEN, DIETER (1938–). A conservationist and spokesperson for the disabled, Dieter ("Ted") Ohlsen was born in Germany in 1938 and immigrated to Canada in 1956. After losing his sight in a hunting accident in 1960, Ohlsen became the province's first blind outfitter and fishing camp operator when he and his wife opened the Northern Light Lodge on Deschambault Lake in 1964. After making the facility fully accessible to the disabled,

Ohlsen established the first campground in northern Saskatchewan that was completely wheelchair accessible. Mr. Ohlsen was awarded an Achievement Award from the Canadian Rehabilitation Council for the Disabled and the Saskatchewan Order of Merit in 1987.

OIL AND GAS INDUSTRY. Saskatchewan's oil production is second only to Alberta among Canadian provinces, and provides about 20% of all Canadian production. The province's daily production was 425,000 barrels/day in 2001; in comparison, the world's largest oil exporting country, Saudi Arabia, produced on average 8.5 million barrels/day in 2001. Saskatchewan produces significant petroleum volumes from four major regions: Lloydminster, Kindersley-Kerrobert, Swift Current, and Weyburn-Estevan. The province has an 80,000 barrel/day refinery owned by **FEDERATED CO-OP** at Regina, an asphalt refinery at Moose Jaw, as well as two upgrading operations for heavy oil: one in Lloydminster, owned by **HUSKY ENERGY**, and one in Regina, owned by Federated Co-op and the province. The upgraders process heavy oil into a light synthetic oil which is easier to transport and has a higher value.

Saskatchewan is less important as a producer of natural gas. Most of the production takes place in the Swift Current region. The natural gas is predominantly dry, which means that natural gas liquids such as ethane (used in plastics and petrochemical production) and propane (used for transportation and a portable heating fuel) are not present in large quantities. The earliest exploration in Saskatchewan can be traced back to an unsuccessful effort to drill for natural gas in the 1880s in the Belle Plaine area near Regina. Exploration continued intermittently until the first commercial oil well in Saskatchewan was finally discovered in Lloydminster in 1943, but it represented only a modest discovery at the time: the Lloydminster oil was of such heavy gravity and high viscosity that it was difficult to produce, transport, and process into petroleum products.

Comparisons have been made between Alberta and Saskatchewan in terms of the rate and level of development of the oil and gas industry. Both Alberta and Saskatchewan petroleum resources were relatively late developers compared to major oil-producing regions in the Middle East, Indonesia and Texas. Major oil finds in western Canada, despite significant exploration efforts, proved elusive. The discovery of oil in Saskatchewan faced additional difficulties as compared to Alberta because less information was available about the presence of oil and gas deposits. In the early 1940s, the government of Saskatchewan provided incentives through concessions of millions of acres of exploration land for a fixed period to Imperial Oil, in return for substantial investment in exploration.

EVERETT BAKER PHOTO/COURTESY OF THE SASKATCHEWAN HISTORY AND FOLKLORE SOCIETY

Oil-well drilling near Climax, Saskatchewan, October 1952.

Imperial Oil drilled a number of exploration wells in this period, but no commercial discoveries were made, so their concessions expired. The Alberta industry made very modest commercial discoveries in the 1920s and 1930s, but the major boom in the industry took place with the discovery of oil at Leduc in 1947.

Major commercial development of Saskatchewan oil began in the early 1950s, and by the end of the 1950s the province was a significant oil-producing region. Although Saskatchewan production has grown over the years, Alberta oil and gas production has grown even faster. Favourable geology for oil and natural gas production has been unevenly distributed in the western Canadian sedimentary basin, which includes areas in BC, Alberta, Saskatchewan and Manitoba. According to the most recent projections from the National Energy Board, Alberta has the overwhelming majority of ultimately recoverable conventional oil resources in the WESTERN CANADIAN SEDIMENTARY BASIN; these do not include the Alberta oilsands, where recoverable reserves about ten times as large have been discovered. In addition to oil, Alberta has an even higher proportion of ultimately recoverable natural gas resources in the Western Canada Sedimentary Basin. Saskatchewan has approximately a quarter of the ultimately recoverable conventional oil resources, and less than 5% of ultimately recoverable natural gas resources. Manitoba and BC have even more modest allocations of ultimately recoverable conventional oil resources in the Western Sedimentary Basin, with shares of 1% and 4% respectively; but BC has a more favourable allocation of natural gas (12%).

Early development of Saskatchewan oil was dominated by large integrated multi-national oil companies. In the last two decades of the 20th century, these older companies sold most of their oil wells and land rights positions, so that the majority of Saskatchewan production now comes from younger, large Canadian and American independent (non-integrated) companies. There is also considerable activity on the part of more than 100 small oil companies with operations ranging from one to a dozen wells. Oil production trends in the province have been uneven: a peak in oil production was reached in the mid-1960s, followed by a low in production in the early 1980s, and then growth towards a new peak yet to be reached. Oil production growth in the 1990s was substantial, doubling from 1990 to 2001. Output in the mid-1990s surpassed the previous peak from the 1960s. A major driver for expanded Saskatchewan oil production in the 1990s was horizontal well drilling, which dramatically increased well productivity. Widespread use of horizontal well drilling was pioneered in Saskatchewan, the SASKATCHEWAN RESEARCH COUNCIL playing a substantial role in the research and development of that innovative technology.

In the second half of the 20th century, oil and gas production became an increasingly important part of the provincial economy, by 2001 representing 9% of the economic value created in the province and gross sales of $5.1 billion. This makes the industry only slightly less important than agriculture. Most of Saskatchewan oil production is currently exported to Minnesota and to the mid-western region of the United States, but substantial amounts are also shipped to Ontario. Saskatchewan is only a

small net exporter of natural gas: relative consumption of natural gas within the province is quite high compared to the rest of Canada, as natural gas is a critical input to the province's energy-intensive MINING, iron and steel, fertilizer, refinery, and heavy oil upgrader operations. Oil and natural gas provide a major source of government revenue through taxes on the value of production and sale of land rights. Annual revenues fluctuate depending on the international price of oil and the North American price of natural gas: from 1995 to 2000, direct oil and gas revenues ranged from a low of $500 million to over $1 billion, equal to 10-25% of all tax revenue raised in Saskatchewan. *David Hanly*

OILSEED PROCESSING INDUSTRY. The story of oilseed processing in Saskatchewan is primarily that of rapeseed and its successor, CANOLA. Recent years have seen close to a million tonnes of Saskatchewan canola processed annually through oilseed extraction plants in Saskatchewan and its bordering provinces. This is equivalent to nearly two million acres of canola, making it by far the most important oilseed being produced and processed in the province. FLAX, high erucic acid rapeseed (HEAR), and borage are others of importance. J. Gordon Ross operated the province's first oilseed crushing/extraction plant in Moose Jaw from 1945. He processed rapeseed, used initially as a lubricant in military ships, and was later instrumental in developing other markets for both the seed and the oil. Another extraction plant was constructed by SASKATCHEWAN WHEAT POOL (SWP) in conjunction with a flour mill in Saskatoon. It was built to extract linseed oil from flax, and began operations in 1946. In 1949 it also began processing rapeseed. Following WORLD WAR II the Moose Jaw plant ceased operations, and the SWP plant went through difficult times until rapeseed oil started being accepted for food uses. In 1963 another extraction plant, built by Agra Industries, began operation in Nipawin. While the Saskatoon plant used only hexane extraction to remove oil (as is done with soybeans), the Nipawin plant followed the more common practice, for high oil content seeds, of including an expeller pressing step. This involves the removal of about two-thirds of the oil by mechanically squeezing it from the seed prior to the hexane extraction step.

The conversion of the rapeseed crop to the more nutritionally desirable canola (1974–78) did much to ensure the future of the oilseed growing and processing industries in Saskatchewan and the rest of Canada. Canola-processing plants were constructed near the Saskatchewan border in Lloydminster, Alberta (1975) and in Harrowby, Manitoba (1982); both of these plants draw more than half of their canola seed from Saskatchewan farms. Another Saskatchewan canola crushing plant, built by CARGILL near Clavet, started operations in 1996. It is one of the largest canola crushing plants in North America. The SWP plant in Saskatoon became part of CSP Foods in 1975 but was closed in 1983. The other plants continue to crush primarily canola, but also some flax, HEAR, and high-stability canola. The Nipawin plant added a refinery and packaging plant in the ten years after it began crushing operations; this allowed it to produce bottled vegetable oils as well as margarines and shortenings for direct food use. In 1974 CSP Foods (which later became CanAmera Foods) purchased the Nipawin plant, and in 1985 the packaging operation was moved to Edmonton. In 2002 CanAmera Foods was purchased by Bunge Inc.

Two smaller specialty processors also operate in Saskatchewan. BIORIGINAL FOOD AND SCIENCE CORPORATION, which operates out of Saskatoon, uses special extraction processes in its operation to produce oils, particularly those high in gamma-linolenic acid, for use in nutritional supplements and for other markets. Since 1994, cold-pressed oils (canola and others) have been produced from an expeller pressing operation (without solvent extraction) by Goldburn Valley Oil Mills in Tisdale. Oilseed processing is one of the most important value-added agribusinesses in Saskatchewan, and appears to be a well-established industry. *Jim Dyck*

FURTHER READING: National Research Council. 1992. *From Rapeseed to Canola: The Billion Dollar Success Story.* Ottawa: National Research Council Publications.

OKANESE RESERVE. Chief Okanis (Okanese) signed an adhesion to TREATY 4 on September 9, 1875, and settled in the File Hills, 16 km northeast of Fort Qu'Appelle. Okanese was chief at the onset of the 1885 Rebellion, but not wishing to get involved he returned to the United States, where he died. His brother-in-law, Moostooacoop, became headman and remained so until his death in 1895. Following treaty, the band lived much as they had always done; but as resources became more scarce, families began growing crops, tending gardens, and raising cattle. The arrival of the CANADIAN PACIFIC RAILWAY in 1904 and of the Canadian Northern Railway in 1908 in Balcarres provided ready markets for whatever surplus band members could sell, as well as an opportunity to work as carpenters, blacksmiths, and mechanics. In 1879 a residential school was built on the reserve by the Presbyterian Church (File Hills Residential School); it closed in 1950, and a day school (File Hills Day School) was built under the auspices of the United Church. Of the 552 band members, 250 live on reserve. A Treaty Land Entitlement Framework Agreement was reached in December 1999, enabling Okanese to increase its land base to 9,389.9 ha and to obtain funds to further their economic development. Two recent accomplishments are the Swan Plain Lodge and the

band-operated community radio station (the first in the province). *Christian Thompson*

OKIMÂSIS, JEAN (1938–). Jean Okimâsis, born Jean Lillian Littlechief (White Bear First Nation) on November 12, 1938, was hired in 1982 as a Cree language instructor and curriculum designer by the Saskatchewan Indian Federated College, now FIRST NATIONS UNIVERSITY OF CANADA. She became the guiding force in making "Indian Languages" a full Department, spearheading the creation of the only full-degree program in First Nations languages in Canada. Okimâsis produced and continually refined a textbook, workbook, and language tapes for introductory Cree classes and, with the aid of Solomon Ratt, developed these works into *Cree: Language of the Plains,* published by the Canadian Plains Research Center (1999). In 1993, she was seconded by Saskatchewan Education and became chief writer for the Saskatchewan Education K–12 Curriculum Guide for Teaching Aboriginal Languages (1993). In addition, she was technical editor of Western Canadian Protocol (1998–99), a First Nations Languages curriculum project, and has been active with the Saskatchewan Cree Language Retention Committee as co-editor of their newsletter. Recognized for her role in furthering ABORIGINAL LANGUAGE education, Okimâsis received in 2000 the YWCA Woman of Distinction Award (Arts and Culture). Okimâsis was awarded an honorary doctorate from the University of Regina at the 2005 spring convocation. Retired since 2002, she runs with her husband Arok a Cree language consulting business. *Arok Wolvengrey*

OLASKI, SUZANNE CLAIRE. A native of Hamilton, Ontario, Suzanne Claire Olaski established a soup kitchen in Saskatoon in 1995 that fed hundreds of people everyday. She also created Community Alive Inc., a non-profit organization whose mandate is to operate a sixty-room hotel and convention centre called Cedar Lodge. Overlooking Blackstrap Lake, Cedar Lodge was founded by Olaski in 1997 and provides hotel/convention services and treatment programs. In addition, Olaski has worked in street missions and the ghettos of Oakland, California. She was awarded the Saskatchewan Order of Merit in 2004.

OLD BONE TRAIL. The Old Bone Trail was a short but common route connecting smaller settlements southwest of Saskatoon to the city's bone market. Merchants and settlers began to collect and sell BISON bones until the animals became virtually extinct in the late 1880s. The bones were collected in Saskatoon and sold to buyers in the United States for use in fertilizer, or as a colouring agent in paint and ink; the average return for a tonne of bison bones was $8. Homesteaders replaced bone mer-

chants on the trail after 1900, particularly Barr colonists passing through Saskatoon en route to Lloydminster, Alberta. It is estimated that 10,000 settlers traveled the Bone Trail between 1904 and 1905. *James Winkel*

OLD COLONY MENNONITE CHURCH. Of the approximately 8,000 Mennonites who immigrated from Russia to Canada during the 1870s, about 3,200 came from the Chortiza and Fürstenland colonies in southern Russia to a land reserve by the Red River in Manitoba. Despite being registered as the *Reinlaender Mennoniten Gemeinde,* members of the group were commonly called "Old Colony" Mennonites because of their connection to the Chortiza Colony, the oldest Mennonite colony in Russia. Beginning in 1895, many Old Colony Mennonites moved westward in search of isolated tracts of land. The first group resettled on a land reserve in the North-West Territories located in the Hague-Osler area. After 1904, others settled on reserves south of Swift Current and east of Prince Albert. By 1910, services were held in numerous villages, with total church membership well over 1,500 in Saskatchewan—making them the largest Mennonite denomination in the province. Intensely concerned about safeguarding their village way of life, preserving intact their private schools, and minimizing contact with outside influences, Old Colony leaders occasionally used forms of church discipline such as the ban and avoidance.

Following a Royal Commission of Inquiry in 1908 over the matter of Mennonite private schools, the government, during WORLD WAR I, began to enforce a policy of compulsory attendance at provincially accredited schools in which English would be the sole language of instruction. The issue deeply divided the Mennonite community. After several petitions, fines and imprisonment of numerous church members, almost 3,000 Old Colony Mennonites from Saskatchewan (less than 40% of the Old Colony Mennonites in the province) and another 4,000 from Manitoba migrated to Mexico and Paraguay during the 1920s. This mass exodus included all but two ministers and forced those remaining to reorganize the church, which officially registered in 1936 as the Old Colony Mennonite Church. Subsequent migrations involving Saskatchewan Old Colony Mennonites who were searching for more isolated agricultural frontiers took place during the 1930s and 1940s to Fort Vermilion in northern Alberta, and during the 1960s to Prespatou in northern British Columbia. During the 1960s, the Old Colony Mennonites in Saskatchewan, in cooperation with Bergthaler Mennonite Church, built the Warman Mennonite Special Care Home, which remains in operation today. Although the Old Colony leaders in Saskatchewan were more open to cultural accommodation than their counterparts in

Latin America, and despite the large influx of Old Colony Mennonites from Mexico back to Canada during the last three decades of the 20th century (the majority to Ontario), the active membership in Saskatchewan has continued to decline, numbering less than 300. *Bruce Guenther*

FURTHER READING: Epp, F.H. 1974. *Mennonites in Canada, 1786–1920: The History of a Separate People.* Toronto: University of Toronto Press; Plett, D. (ed.). 2001. *Old Colony Mennonites in Canada, 1875–2000.* Steinbach, MB: Crossway Publications.

OLD WIVES LAKE (50°06′N, 106°00′W: Map sheet 72 I/4). Old Wives Lake, the largest natural lake in southern Saskatchewan, lies in an internal drainage basin, on mixed-grass prairie, some 35 km southwest of Moose Jaw. Spring runoff and seasonal rains, mostly channeled into the Wood River, feed this shallow, saline lake. Salinity is sufficiently high that **SODIUM SULFATE** has been harvested commercially, especially during the 1950s and 1960s when water was diverted into nearby Frederick Lake, which served as an evaporation pond. The lake's extent varies enormously, depending on available water supply. In 1949 and in the late 1980s it was completely dry. Low water levels expose mud flats that attract many shorebirds. Usually, a large island called the Isle of Bays is located 5 km off-shore; sometimes, a second island is exposed. Waterfowl and shorebirds use the lake as a migratory staging ground and breeding ground. Once named Johnstone Lake after big-game hunter Sir **FREDERICK JOHNSTONE** (who visited in 1861), the lake was renamed in the 1950s as Old Wives Lake to commemorate a **CREE** legend about a group of old women who sacrificed their lives to save other members of their community from Blackfoot warriors. The Cree word *Notekeu (nôtikwêw)* means "old woman" and survives in the name of a tributary of the Wood River. *Marilyn Lewry*

OLIVER, EDMUND H. (1882–1935). To provide ministers for new churches, Edmund H. Oliver established the Presbyterian Theological College that later became St. Andrew's College at the **UNIVERSITY OF SASKATCHEWAN**. Oliver was born in Eberts, Kent County, Ontario in 1882. He received his BA from the University of Toronto in 1902, his MA a year later, and a PhD in 1905. On invitation from Dr. **WALTER MURRAY**, first President of the University of Saskatchewan, Oliver moved to Saskatoon to help establish the new university. He saw a need to establish a theological college on campus to train men for the ministry, and returned to Toronto to earn a theological degree in 1910.

Oliver studied economics, history and theology. He believed he was working on the "last Frontier"—the last chance for society to "get it right": through education, the Church and government could improve society. He arrived in the west at a time of great optimism: immigrants were flooding the prairies, and schools, churches and a university were needed to educate these new citizens.

With the outbreak of **WORLD WAR I**, Oliver enlisted as a chaplain. On the battle fronts in France, he waged battle against "demon rum," visited the sick, wrote letters on behalf of wounded soldiers, and advised families when a soldier was killed in action. He established reading rooms for soldiers on leave, and rode his bicycle around muddy fields, offering classes to infantry and books for them to read. He believed soldiers who survived would return home and become leaders in society. He thus helped to establish the University of Vimy Ridge. After the war, Oliver continued his work with the theological college and worked for the union of Presbyterians, Methodists and Congregationalists that eventually became the United Church of Canada in 1925.

Oliver served on two Royal Commissions to establish a system of co-operative farm credit and a liquor control system. He wrote five books, a novel, and many articles. During the **GREAT DEPRESSION**, he served as Moderator of the United Church from 1930 to 1932, and traveled the country urging people to donate food and clothing to those in need on the prairies. His time as Moderator was the culmination of his life's philosophy of service and co-operation in the new frontier. He died at the early age of 53 while working with youth at a summer camp. *Gordon Barnhart*

OLSON, LOUISE (CA. 1903–98). Louise Olson (her maiden name was probably Downing) was born about 1903 in England and came to Moose Jaw as a child. She taught in rural schools, studied at Regina **NORMAL SCHOOL**, and taught in Moose Jaw in the early 1920s. She moved to Saskatoon after marrying Carl Olson, a businessman; they had two sons and a daughter. Interested in drama, she joined the Little Theatre Club (established 1922) in Saskatoon. She acted in about thirty plays and directed several while doing staging, casting and other work; she also served as president of the Club. The group disbanded by mid-century, however, and she then founded the Saskatoon Community Players in 1952; she served as president for four years and directed several plays until the group disbanded in 1959. Olson was an adjudicator for high school drama in Saskatoon and around the province from 1933 to 1957, and was the director and producer of Quota Club's Children's Theatre for two seasons after **WORLD WAR II**. Her other involvements included being drama chair for the **SASKATCHEWAN ARTS BOARD** (1949–56) and participating in various Saskatoon radio productions. In 1955 she took a business course, and then began teaching and counselling at Saskatoon Business College, where she became principal. She retired at 70 and died in Toronto on April 19, 1998. *Bob Ivanochko*

OMBUDSMAN. The concept of ombudsman (a Swedish word meaning "legal representative") was formally established in Sweden in 1809, adopted in Finland in 1919, and rapidly expanded to Europe, Asia, Australia, and North America over the last fifty years. This dramatic spread of the institution was related to the post-**WORLD WAR II** development of the welfare state and its increasing involvement in the lives of ordinary citizens, and to an increased need for neutral ways to limit arbitrary government decisions. In 1972, the newly elected **NEW DEMOCRATIC PARTY** government of **ALLAN BLAKENEY**, with the support of the Opposition **LIBERAL PARTY**, enacted legislation to establish a Saskatchewan Ombudsman. There have been four ombudsman appointments to date, and each appointment has been unanimously supported by all the political parties in the Legislature.

A statutory ombudsman must meet a number of internationally recognized tests. In addition to being an independent officer of the Legislature and not the government, the ombudsman must be accessible to the public, possess broad powers of investigation, and have when necessary the authority to criticize government in public ways. The ombudsman's role must also be that of independent assessor of facts, and not of automatic advocate for the citizen. This role is somewhat paradoxical in that it is both "powerless" and "powerful": "powerless" in the sense that the role is one of recommending rather than enforcement; "powerful" in the sense that recommendations are almost invariably acted upon by governments to avoid public debate about their failings.

The Saskatchewan Ombudsman has always been a very active office, and has a long list of individual and system successes involving among others child protection, **CORRECTIONS**, **SOCIAL ASSISTANCE**, and **WORKER'S COMPENSATION** issues. This office has also developed some innovative organizational approaches by incorporating a mediation function in its processes, and a variety of outreach activities to connect with Aboriginal and northern persons as well as others in more remote parts of the province. In 1994, the Office of the Children's Advocate was established by a legislation which combined this Office with that of the Ombudsman. *Brett Quiring*

ONE ARROW FIRST NATION. One Arrow Cree First Nation signed **TREATY 6** on September 6, 1878; while the One Arrow Reserve is located 53 km southwest of Prince Albert, the band has a total of 9,331.4 ha surrounding the **SOUTH SASKATCHEWAN RIVER**. This band settled on its reserve late in the autumn of 1880, in what was considered a fine location to begin agricultural development. As the chief was old, a headman by the name of Crowskin was in charge of the band in 1882, and contributed much to its development. Today, the community consists of 1,358 members, with 458 people living on reserve. Their infrastructure includes a general store, rodeo grounds, sports grounds, school, health clinic, band office, skating rink, fire hall, band hall, and community maintenance facilities such as pumping station and water treatment plant. Current development includes a modern campground and an amphitheatre near Fort Carlton Historical Park.

Christian Thompson

ONE BIG UNION. In mid-March 1919, trade unionists from many parts of western Canada met in Calgary at the Western Labour Conference to discuss alternatives to the international craft union model of organizing workers which was promoted by the Trades and Labour Congress of Canada (TLC). The delegates, including representatives from Saskatchewan, supported a much more radical political posture for the labour movement. The western labour activists wanted to provide union representation to workers beyond the skilled trades. They rejected the craft union model of organizing workers trade by trade, and championed the idea of industrial unionism, which enrolls all employees in a workplace in one union, regardless of their occupation or skill level. The Western Labour Conference decided to hold a referendum on establishing One Big Union (OBU), and when the votes were taken there was widespread support in the four western provinces, including Saskatchewan. This was occurring immediately after the Winnipeg General Strike, and working-class solidarity was widespread and intense.

Thousands of workers in the four western provinces joined the OBU, particularly railway, forestry, and mining employees. In 1920, when the OBU was at its peak, it had at least 50,000 members between Thunder Bay and Vancouver Island. The TLC unions, with the help of employers and governments, went on a very effective counteroffensive to recover the craft unions' members, and the OBU membership slumped to about 5,000. The One Big Union remained a small labour central organization until 1956, when it joined the other national federations that were merging to form the Canadian Labour Congress.

Garnet Dishaw

196TH (WESTERN UNIVERSITIES) BATTALION. The 196th (Western Universities) Battalion was formed during WORLD WAR I, primarily from students who were enrolled in the universities of western Canada. The idea for the unit began in February 1916, when students from the universities of Manitoba, Saskatchewan, Alberta and British Columbia, wanting to maintain their university identity, lobbied the Minister of Militia and convinced him to authorize the formation of a western university battalion. Each university was to raise a

UNIVERSITY OF SASKATCHEWAN ARCHIVES A-1127

196th (Western Universities) Battalion at mess, Camp Hughes, 1916.

company of about 250 men. Thirty-three-year-old Captain Reginald Bateman, the UNIVERSITY OF SASKATCHEWAN's first Professor of English, who was serving in France with the 28TH (NORTHWEST) BATTALION, CEF, was brought back to Canada to command the Saskatchewan Company. The men received their preliminary training at the then-new university residence, Qu'Appelle Hall, and the company joined the other university companies at Camp Hughes in Manitoba, where the battalion was being formed. The Western Universities Battalion expected to serve in France as a formed unit; however, when the battalion was sent to England it was broken up and dispersed as reinforcements to other units. Many of the Saskatchewan Company were sent to the 46TH BATTALION in France, including Bateman, who was killed there on September 3, 1918.

Recruitment of university students in Saskatchewan had begun almost immediately upon war being declared in 1914. Among the first to answer the call to arms were students who were preparing themselves for the Church of England ministry at the University of Saskatchewan's Emmanuel College. The next appeal for enlistment made to university faculty and students came in September 1914 from the 28th Battalion, then recruiting in Regina. A number of professors, including Professors Bateman and Brehaut, and a group of their students, left their classrooms to join the battalion on November 1, 1914. The next call to University of Saskatchewan students to enlist came from McGill University in Montreal, where platoons of university students were being organized as part of the 58th Battalion, CEF. The University of Saskatchewan's contribution was to be two platoons, each consisting of a non-commissioned officer and sixteen other ranks. These university platoons were later to become reinforcements for the Princess Patricia's

Canadian Light Infantry, then serving overseas in France as a unit of the British army. Ross MacPherson, the editor of the University newspaper, *The Sheaf*, who had previously protested when professors left their classrooms to go to war, was one of those who enlisted. He subsequently received the Distinguished Service Order (DSO), and was killed in action.

The final group of University of Saskatchewan students to be enlisted was the "Duval draft" of March 1917. Edward Duval, superintendent of the Civilian Personnel Regionalization's Saskatoon division, recruited about fifty men, including twelve undergraduates, to train in the Qu'Appelle Hall offices formally used by the Western Universities Battalion. They were sent to France in mid-summer 1917 to serve as reinforcements. When the Borden government instituted conscription in May 17, 1917, forty-six University of Saskatchewan students were accepted into the air force and several others were enrolled into the University of Saskatchewan company of the Canadian Officers' Training Corps. Of the 330 University of Saskatchewan students who served overseas during WORLD WAR I, seventeen were awarded the Military Cross, thirteen the Military Medal, three the Distinguished Service Order, and one the Croix de Guerre. The names of Professor Bateman and the sixty-six students who gave their lives are inscribed on the tablets of the memorial gates at the entrance to the university.

Daria Coneghan

ONE-ROOM SCHOOLS. The first one-room schools began when a community of Aboriginal people or early settlers had enough children to qualify for a grant for a school. After receiving the necessary government approvals, they selected a site. Regulations stipulated that such a school should be

EVERETT BAKER PHOTO/COURTESY OF THE SASKATCHEWAN HISTORY AND FOLKLORE SOCIETY

Heading home from school by horse and wagon, May 1951, near Rosefield, Saskatchewan.

far from a slough; it should also be built on ground high enough that it would not flood, but low enough that the grass would grow. It was to be centrally located and readily accessible by the whole community. Church-operated schools were organized before government funding for buildings became available: in Cumberland House, for example, Rev. **HENRY BUDD**, an ordained Indian minister, started a school in the Anglican Church Chapel in 1842. **TREATY 5** promised a school in 1876, but it was not completed until 1908.

Community members were generally responsible for building the school. Some schools were built of local stone, some of sod or mud, and others of logs or lumber; some were even assembled on site using prefabricated materials. Early plans were obtained from other provinces, the USA or Europe; but after 1912, volunteer workers used plans provided by the provincial government. These plans required about 15 square feet per student, an 11-foot ceiling, and windows to the left; there would also be a cloakroom with hooks for outdoor clothes, a stand for a washbasin, and shelves for the lunch buckets. The typical schoolroom consisted of a blackboard at the front, some shelves under the windows for textbooks, a teacher's desk and chair at the front of the room, a pot-bellied stove near the centre or at the back, and single or double desks for the students. The outbuildings generally consisted of two privies, a stable, sometimes a coal and wood shed, and later a teacherage. Heating the non-insulated school was always a challenge: on average, a school used about twelve tons of coal and half a cord of kindling per year. The teacher or students were responsible for building the fire in the morning and cleaning stovepipes regularly; many a morning was spent huddled around a stubborn fire, or cleaning the soot out of each section of pipe. Unless the school had a reliable source of water, drinking water in the early

schools was supplied in a galvanized pail and a dipper. Later, sanitation rules required a fountain or a crock with a tap; but the fountain wasted too much water, so the latter became more popular.

Schools were usually supplied with maps—either the roller type that had to be purchased, or the flat ones supplied by the Neilson Company, with pictures of chocolate bars in each corner. The arrival of a globe gave students a more realistic view of what the world looked like; unfortunately, the relatively soft surface sometimes gave way to prying fingers and, because mice seemed to like the taste of glue, students on occasion found a family of pink babies nestled inside the sphere. For many students, school was a welcome break from the hard work on the farm. In remembering their experiences in a one-room school, people recall the many pranks they played on one another and on the teacher—from hiding grasshoppers in a girl's pencil box to plugging the chimney on the roof of the school. The teachers in these schools were usually women, some with a background of teacher training, others with only a Grade 8 standing. Some were very young; others came out of retirement to fill advertised positions. In the early years, teachers boarded with families in the community, travelling to school with some of their students. Many of these women found partners in the community and stayed on as wives and mothers. When teacherages became more common, they allowed single teachers some privacy and school boards a more reasonable option to hire married men, whose families quickly became contributing members of the community. In the early days teachers were scarce, and school boards were lucky to receive more than one response to their advertisements. During the 1930s, however, when jobs were hard to come by, some school boards received hundreds of applications. The teachers did not have security of tenure, and wages were sporadic, espe-

cially during the **DEPRESSION**. Teachers could be and sometimes were terminated at the slightest provocation. Turnover was high, the average being a new teacher every year.

A typical school had fifteen students in six grades; but enrolment could go as high as fifty, with eight or even ten grades. In the early years the government supplied readers but no other textbooks for Grades 1 to 6. Many parents could not afford to buy books, so the teacher spent countless hours writing notes and assignments on the blackboard. It was a common practise for the teacher to bring groups to the front of the room to hear them read or to teach a lesson; others often hurried with their assignments so that they could listen to what the children at the front were being taught. Drill and memory work were common in all subjects. Although the teacher followed the Provincial Programme of Studies for all subjects, the emphasis was on reading, writing and arithmetic. Spelling bees were often held on Friday afternoons; in some areas, these became community events or even competitions between school districts. One of the most traumatic events of the school year was the visit of the inspector. Although some inspectors were compassionate, others entered the school with an officious air, quizzing the children in various subjects and observing classroom proceedings with a critical eye. The teacher faced these visits with trepidation, and the children, who often thought he was inspecting them, caught that same sense of fear.

Games at recess and lunch hour, as well as physical education classes, were an important part of the one-room school. In summer, there were games like softball, pom-pom-pullaway, kick the can, ante-ante-I-over, hide-and-seek, red-light, and prisoner's base. In the winter there was ice for sliding, skating or shinny, and hills for sleighing. On cold or stormy days there were indoor games such as checkers, snakes-and-ladders, and charades. Special occasions were observed in the one-room schools. On Hallowe'en night there was usually a party for children, involving costumes and contests. For weeks before Christmas the teacher and students practised plays, poems and songs in preparation for an elaborate concert that was performed for the whole community; at the end of the concert, Santa Claus appeared with bags of treats for all the school and pre-school children. On February 14 there was a St. Valentine's box. Arbor Day was a day for clean-up and planting trees. The school was also used for anniversary celebrations, political meetings, Friday night dances, and various community functions.

Following **WORLD WAR II**, the demise of the one-room school coincided with automation, improvements in transportation, changes in education philosophy, and the gradual disappearance of small farms. The fate of the school buildings was varied: some were bought by local farmers to be used as outbuildings, some were abandoned to the weather, and a very few became museums, immortalizing their central role in the communities they served. As centres of learning and of community development, one-room schools in Saskatchewan were as significant to the development of this province as the thousands of wooden grain elevators that have also been relegated to history. *Rosella Mitchell*

FURTHER READING: Archer, J. 1980. *Saskatchewan: A History*. Saskatoon: Western Producer Prairie Books; Charyk, J.C. 1973. *The Little White Schoolhouse*. Saskatoon: Western Producer Book Service.

ONION LAKE FIRST NATION. Chief Seekaskootch's band signed **TREATY 6** at Fort Pitt on September 9, 1876, while other River **CREE** signed an adhesion to Treaty 6 in 1878 as the Makaoo Band. The bands received adjacent reserves in 1879. In 1885 they were accused of participating in the **FROG LAKE MASSACRE** and listed as "rebel Indians." The federal government refused to recognize a chief for these two bands until 1914, when they were told to amalgamate as the Onion Lake Band. The Onion Lake First Nation has educational facilities, a modern health centre, and indoor/outdoor sports facilities. There are both band-owned and privately owned businesses on reserve, providing the community with essential services and employing both residents and non-residents. Currently, 2,408 of the band's 4,003 members live on the 57,737.5 ha of reserve land, situated 50 km north of Lloydminster. The Onion Lake Reserve straddles the Saskatchewan-Alberta border, making it Canada's only border Cree Nation. *Christian Thompson*

ON-TO-OTTAWA TREK AND THE REGINA RIOT. In October 1932, Ottawa finally accepted responsibility for the single, homeless unemployed roaming the country in search of work and established a national system of camps under the auspices of the Department of National Defense (DND). The men were fed, clothed, sheltered and paid 20¢ per day in exchange for their labour on various make-work projects. Although the scheme was universally applauded at the beginning, it did not take long for the camps to become the focus of disillusionment and discontent, especially since Conservative Prime Minister R.B. Bennett seemed to place greater importance on where the men were, as opposed to what they were doing. In April 1935, hundreds of disgruntled men walked out of DND relief camps throughout British Columbia and descended on Vancouver in a bold attempt to reverse their dead-end lives and secure some meaningful employment. But no level of government wanted to help the men—least of all the federal government, which believed that the Communist Party of Canada had orchestrated the protest. Eventually, the relief

camp strikers decided to go to Ottawa and present their grievances directly to the Prime Minister.

An estimated 1,000 On-to-Ottawa trekkers left Vancouver by freight train in early June 1935. No one expected the men to survive the trip through the mountains; but the same kind of organizing zeal that had kept the strike going in Vancouver gave the trek a seemingly unstoppable momentum as it headed across the prairies. After the trek had left Calgary, picking up more recruits, the federal Minister of Justice publicly branded the trek a Communist plot and announced that the RCMP would stop the unlawful movement in Regina. Saskatchewan Premier **J.T. GARDINER** was infuriated by the federal order to dump the men on the doorsteps of the provincial capital like unwanted waifs; he also predicted that the massing of the mounted police could only lead to riot. But Gardiner's ranting and hand-wringing were dismissed as partisan theatrics, and all the Saskatchewan government could do was prepare for the arrival of the trek, now numbering an estimated 2,000 men, in the early morning hours of June 14.

The much-anticipated Regina showdown turned into a prolonged stalemate between the trekkers and the police, lasting over two weeks. On June 17, two federal Cabinet ministers met with the trek leaders in Regina, and after failing to reach any kind of agreement invited them to send a delegation to Ottawa to deal directly with the Prime Minister. But instead of resolving the standoff, the Ottawa meeting degenerated into a shouting match between Bennett and trek leader **ARTHUR "SLIM" EVANS**. The trekkers refused to give up, however, and tried to send a group of men eastward by car and truck on June 27—only to have the convoy intercepted by the mounted police. With no way out of Regina, and with their own funds exhausted, the trekkers decided to end the trek and return to the West Coast. Ottawa insisted, however, that the men had to disband on federal terms, that is, go to a nearby holding facility at Lumsden where they would be processed.

Sensing the Lumsden camp was a trap, the trek leadership turned to the Gardiner government for assistance on the afternoon of July 1, the Dominion Day holiday. Later that evening, while the provincial Cabinet was meeting to discuss the trekkers' request, the RCMP, with the support of the Regina City Police, decided to execute arrest warrants for the trek leaders at a public rally at Market Square. The mounted police could easily have made the arrests at any time during the day, but with clubs and tear gas at the ready, they chose to pluck the men from a peaceful fund-raising meeting. Not unexpectedly, the raid quickly degenerated into a pitched battle between the police, trekkers and citizens, which spilled over into the streets of downtown Regina. Order was restored early the next day, but only after

the city police had fired directly into a crowd of rioters. The toll was two dead—not one, as usually reported—and hundreds injured, as well as tens of thousands of dollars of damage to downtown Regina. A provincial commission, which included former Premier **WILLIAM MARTIN**, later blamed the trekkers for the riot while completely exonerating the police. The new Liberal government in Ottawa, meanwhile, insisted that its hands were tied by the findings of the Saskatchewan commission and refused to do anything further. *Bill Waiser*

FURTHER READING: Waiser, W.A. 2003. *All Hell Can't Stop Us: The On-to-Ottawa Trek and Regina Riot*. Calgary: Fifth House; Howard, V. 1985. *We Were the Salt of the Earth*. Regina: Canadian Plains Research Center.

OPEKOKEW, DELIA. Delia Opekokew, a member of the Canoe Lake First Nation, attended the Beauval Indian Residential School for her elementary grades, and the Qu'Appelle Indian Residential School at Lebret for high school. After obtaining a Bachelor of Laws degree from Osgoode Hall Law School at York University in 1977, she was called to the Bar of the Province of Ontario in 1979 and to the Bar of the Province of Saskatchewan in 1983. She was the first Aboriginal to be admitted to those law societies. Opekokew practiced family, criminal and First Nations law in Toronto as a partner in the firm of Zlotkin & Opekokew from 1979 to 1980, and as an associate in the firm of Blaney, McMurty, and Stapells from 1985 to 1990. She was counsel to the **FEDERATION OF SASKATCHEWAN INDIAN NATIONS** from 1980 to 1985. Between 1990 and 1998 Opekokew practiced alone, with clients from the Maritimes to Alberta, specializing in Indian treaty rights and

PHOTO COURTESY OF DELIA OPEKOKEW

Delia Opekokew.

Aboriginal law. During this time she was appointed as one of three commissioners to inquire into the shooting death of Leo Lachance by white supremacist Nerland. Her proudest achievement was the successful resolution of the Canoe Lake Cree Nation land claim, regarding the termination of social and economic rights in the lands given under **TREATY 10** but occupied by the Primrose Lake Air Weapons Range. Opekokew was council in the wrongful death case of Anthony O'Brien "Dudley" George in Ontario, and is now partner in the law office of Opekokew, Johnstone-Clarke in Saskatoon.

Charlene Crevier

OPERA. From early settlement in the 1880s, opera was on the cultural agenda. Visiting companies and international singers entertained the population, while local amateur groups performed small-scale operas and musical theatre. The large number of overtures, opera choruses and arias performed in symphony and solo vocal concerts suggests a public appetite for the genre. A highlight of the World Grain Exhibition of 1933 was a spectacular rendering of the most dramatic moments of *Aida*, with professional and local groups participating before several thousand. In the early 1930s, one could hear the Metropolitan Opera weekly broadcasts as well as recitals by such as Richard Crooks. Churches took on the challenge too: in 1934, Knox United in Regina rang to the sounds of *Carmen* with ten local soloists and the church choir; and the Regina Amateur Operatic Society of the 1920s was founded by the rector of St. Matthews Anglican and performed small-scale works there. Ambitious plans for Town Hall/ Opera Houses in Hanley, Indian Head, Melville, Prince Albert, Wolseley and elsewhere had already come to fruition, although some, like that for Regina's "palatial opera house" in 1905 with a capacity of 1,500 (roughly half the city's population at the time), did not. There was an Operatic Society in Regina in 1909 and an Amateur Society in Saskatoon in 1913, the first of many groups which formed, failed and re-formed over the century. Early local performances of Gilbert and Sullivan operas were complemented by such visiting groups as the Puck Opera Company, which appeared in Regina in 1887, and the Metropolitan Opera Touring Company in 1899. In 1905, one year after his arrival from Scotland, **FRANK LAUBACH** took his small Regina Concert Group and Opera Company to Saskatoon. Before **WORLD WAR I** and into the 1920s, Saskatchewan enjoyed both light and grand opera with touring companies from eastern Canada, Britain, America and Australia. None was as ambitious as the San Carlo Grand Opera, whose repertoire included *Faust, Cavalleria Rusticana, Lucia* and *Il Trovatore* in 1918 alone. Audiences also heard concerts by such stars as Emma Albani, Nellie Melba, Clara Butt, Marian Anderson, John

PHOTO COURTESY THE MOUNTNEY FAMILY, MOOSOMIN.

Cast of "HMS *Pinafore*," Moosomin Opera Hall, 1919.

McCormack, and Amelita Galli-Curci, whose concert in the Regina Armouries in 1929 to a crowd of 3,000 was a triumph.

The most active period for the local performance of the classics, however, was the latter half of the 20th century. Through the 1960s, the Canadian Opera Touring Company brought its productions to as many as eight Saskatchewan cities in a single year. The appointments of Richard Watson (formerly of Covent Garden) as director of the Regina Conservatory in 1951 and of his successor **HOWARD LEYTON-BROWN** in 1955 were followed by almost twenty years of annual opera productions, performed by local musicians. The foundation of the Saskatoon Opera Association in 1978 began a similar practice in that city; and two other groups, Prairie Opera and Co-Opera, added new works by Saskatchewan composers, and travelled to schools and between cities to develop enthusiasm for the art form. The Regina Lyric Light Opera continued the older tradition of Savoy opera and musicals. None of these organizations was able to mount more than an occasional (and usually financially unsuccessful) fully professional production. The closest the province ever came to this aim was achieved by Opera Saskatchewan, with one production in 1979 in Regina, followed by annual performances from 1992 onwards. Several opera stars were Saskatchewan-born, most notably June Kowalchuk, Emile Belcourt, **JON VICKERS**, Edith Wiens, and Nathan Berg. Opera coaches and chorus masters from the province have included Stuart Hamilton, Sandra Horst and Peter Tiefenbach in Ontario; Rachel Andrist in Brussels, Paris and Glyndebourne; and Grant Wenaus in Chicago and New York. Among operas composed in the province are *The Mystic Light* (Frank Laubach), *The Qu'Appelle River Legend* (Frank Thorolfson), *Grant, Warden*

of the Plains (**MURRAY ADASKIN**), *The Lay of Thrym* (Jack Behrens), *The Final Bid and The Garden of Alice* (**ELIZABETH RAUM**), and *The Snow Queen* (Robert Ursan). *Robin Swales*

OPHEIM, ELOISE E. Concerned by the prominence of drug culture in Canadian society, Eloise Opheim co-founded the Parents Resource Institute for Drug Education or PRIDE Canada. She also helped establish the Saskatoon branch of PRIDE. The organization's purpose is to educate parents about alcohol and drug abuse and to prevent children from becoming addicts. PRIDE also assists parents of addicted children with finding appropriate professional help. Opheim served as executive director of PRIDE Canada and president of the Saskatoon chapter in addition to her involvement with the International Federation of Parents for Drug-Free Youth. In recognition of her efforts to bring discussions about drug abuse problems into the mainstream, Eloise Opheim was appointed to the Order of Canada in 1990.

ORANGE ORDER. The Orange Order was born in the charged sectarian climate of northern Ireland in the late 1700s to defend the interests of Protestant settlers against the native Irish Catholics. Taking its name and inspiration from Prince William of Orange, who secured Protestant ascendancy in Britain and Ireland, Orange principles involved an uncompromising defense of the British Crown, and Protestant hegemony in Ireland. When Protestants began to emigrate from Ireland in large numbers after 1815, Orangeism was part of the cultural baggage they brought to their new homes. The British North American provinces proved to be extremely fertile grounds for its expansion, and throughout the Maritimes and Ontario Orange Lodges became central to the social life of many communities. They frequently served as school, church and town hall, offered opportunities for socializing, and afforded numerous practical benefits for early settlers. Also, the Orange Order flourished in Canada because of its religious and ideological compatibility with the British Protestant ethos of the Loyalists and other English-speaking Canadians.

As Canadians migrated westwards after Confederation, Orangemen, with their longstanding tradition as Queen's Frontiersmen, were in the vanguard. The first lodge west of Ontario was established in Red River in 1870, and membership grew rapidly. By the early 1930s, when the Order reached the peak of its popularity in Saskatchewan, with a membership of approximately 68,000, belonging to 274 lodges. In its composition, the Order appealed primarily to Canadians of Irish and British origin and to Protestant immigrants from Scandinavia, Holland, and Germany. As had happened originally in Ireland and then in eastern Canada, the Orange Order in Saskatchewan evolved into a multifaceted institution which offered a variety of services to its members and to the larger society. It was a social and recreational club, a mutual assistance network, an educational and moral improvement society, a social welfare organization, a vehicle for the expression of religious and cultural values, and an ideological and political pressure group.

As was to be expected given its roots, the Orange Order in Saskatchewan evinced continuing interest in Irish affairs. Of more immediate importance, however, were local and national issues, and the question of education was of particular interest to Orangemen because of their desire to see a non-denominational public school system assert the primacy of the English language and assimilate all immigrants to Anglo-Canadian cultural norms. The Orange Order was thus often at loggerheads with Roman Catholics, French Canadians, and non-British immigrants who espoused a more pluralistic vision of Saskatchewan society.

The popularity and political influence of the Orange Order in Saskatchewan peaked in the early 1930s. Although it continued to be a presence in rural Saskatchewan until the 1960s, the years after 1932 witnessed a steady decline: rural depopulation and mass media drained its membership base; and as the pioneering generations passed on, the original need for the support that the Order provided ceased to exist. The cultural values which the Order espoused also diminished in appeal after WORLD WAR II, as notions of diversity and multiculturalism gained favour. Nevertheless, the fact that Saskatchewan today is a predominately English-speaking community with a relatively high degree of cultural homogeneity among its non-Aboriginal population is one of the enduring legacies of the Orange Order.

Michael Cottrell

FURTHER READING: Cottrell, M. 1999. "The Irish in Saskatchewan, 1850–1930: A Study of Intergenerational Ethnicity," *Prairie Forum* 24 (2): 185–209; Houston, C., and W.J. Smyth. 1980. *The Sash Canada Wore: A Historical Geography of the Orange Order in Canada.* Toronto: University of Toronto Press.

ORGANIC FARMING AND INDUSTRY.

Organic farming has been practiced in Saskatchewan since European settlers arrived in the late 1800s. In general terms, it is a holistic system of production designed to promote the health and diversity of biological communities within the agro-ecosystem. In practical terms, it involves the production of agricultural products without the use of synthetic pesticides and fertilizers, and prohibits the use of animal growth hormones and antibiotics. Organic agriculture has spent much of the past century on the fringe of the agricultural mainstream, as the use of synthetic pesticides and fertilizers have dominated farm production. In recent years, however, increased consumer demand, driven by serious food health scares and concerns for the environment, have allowed organic farming to re-emerge as a viable alternative to conventional farming.

Today, Saskatchewan is a world leader in organic production, with over 1,000 certified organic producers and approximately 226,600 ha of organic farmland, of which 156,000 is for grain production (as of 2003). The major organic crops grown in the province include WHEAT, BARLEY, OATS, FLAX, lentils, peas, clover, and WILD RICE. Although small, there is a growing organic livestock component. In addition to production, Saskatchewan is home to ninety-four certified enterprises, eighteen of which are processors, which produce a range of products including flour, oatmeal, oilseed products, bread, cereal mixtures, meat products, and neutraceuticals. Total sales of organic products originating in Saskatchewan are estimated to exceed $30 million. Despite the presence of a vigorous processing sector, most of Saskatchewan's organic grains and oilseeds are exported, primarily to the United States, Europe, and Japan.

To be labelled organic, all production must be inspected and certified by a recognized certification body. Unlike the European Union and the United States, which have mandatory standards, the Canadian organic industry currently operates under a voluntary set of standards. There are four major certification bodies operating in the province: Organic Crop Improvement Association (OCIA), Pro-cert Organic Systems (Pro-cert), the Canadian Organic Certification Co-operative (COCC), and the Saskatchewan Organic Certification Association (SOCA). As the largest producer of organic products in Canada, Saskatchewan is home to numerous industry associations, most notably the SASKATCHEWAN ORGANIC DIRECTORATE (SOD) and the Canadian Organic Livestock Association (COLA).

Simon Weseen

FURTHER READING: The Saskatchewan Organic Directorate (SOD). 2000. *Organic Farming on the Prairies.* Moose Jaw: Grand Valley Press.

ORGANIZATION OF SASKATCHEWAN ARTS COUNCILS (OSAC).

Since 1968, OSAC and its members have been instrumental in integrating culture into the lives of Saskatchewan residents. The group of volunteers who founded the organization represented arts councils from Weyburn, Yorkton, Estevan, Swift Current, the Battlefords, Prince Albert, Nipawin and Moose Jaw. The main purpose of the original arts councils was to sponsor the Festival of the Arts organized by the SASKATCHEWAN ARTS BOARD. Once this program was discontinued, the groups decided to remain in existence and to continue to sponsor cultural activities in their communities. OSAC is now a vital network of over fifty volunteer-run arts councils and seventy school centres, which extends throughout the province.

OSAC, a non-profit organization not directly funded by government, is unique in Canada. Financial support is received from the Saskatchewan Lotteries Trust Fund for Sport, Culture and Recreation, the SASKATCHEWAN ARTS BOARD and the Department of Canadian Heritage. It coordinates the touring of both visual and performing arts in the province; and its provincial conference, the Saskatchewan Showcase of the Arts, is held in the fall each year. OSAC provides the Saskatchewan Art on the Move Visual Arts Touring Program and Performing Arts Programs to its members. Programming includes the Stars for Saskatchewan series, first organized in 1975; early artists included Maureen Forrester and the Canadian Brass. The Koncerts for Kids program was introduced in 1986, and in 1994 the Saskatchewan Junior Concert Society merged with OSAC. These programs assist arts councils in organizing performing arts series for adult and family audiences. OSAC provides funding to its members to assist with visual arts programming and performing artist fees. On an annual basis, approximately 250 live performances and 100 visual art exhibitions are presented to over 100,000 people in Saskatchewan. OSAC members are dedicated volunteers, committed to making culture a vital part of community life. They develop and encourage local interest in the arts, and ensure a solid future for culture in the province.

Nancy Martin

ORGANIZED FARM WOMEN IN THE WGG, THE UFC, THE SFU, AND THE NFU.

The Woman Grain Growers (WGG) and women in the United Farmers of Canada Saskatchewan Section (UFC), the Saskatchewan Farmers' Union (SFU), and the National Farmers' Union (NFU) represent one of three important streams of the farm women's movement in Canada. A first stream, the HOME-

MAKERS' CLUBS AND THE WOMEN'S INSTITUTES, came into being in Saskatchewan in 1911; and the third stream, the Saskatchewan Women's Agricultural Network, was founded in 1985. The WGG, also known as the Women's Section of the Saskatchewan Grain Growers' Association (SGGA), evolved out of the local work of VIOLET MCNAUGTON, a Harris farm woman who was active in the Hillview Grain Growers. She and her husband John saw the SGGA as the best vehicle for accomplishing the reforms in rural Saskatchewan that they regarded as necessary to better the lives of hard-pressed farm families. (The SGGA had originally been the Territorial Grain Growers' Association, established in 1902.)

In co-operation with Frances Beynon of the *Grain Grower's Guide*, McNaughton organized a Women's Congress in conjunction with the annual provincial meeting of the SGGA in 1913. The women at the Congress established a committee to organize the 1914 founding convention of the WGG. McNaughton, who was the most active member of the organizational committee, became the first president of the WGG in 1914. The women were full members of the SGGA and also members of the WGG, then the most radical women's organization in Saskatchewan in terms of class and gender analyses.

The WGG, which pushed the SGGA to consider issues besides those directly concerning the farm economy, agitated for numerous reforms that improved the lives of farm families, led the fight for women's vote in Saskatchewan, and waged a campaign for trained midwives and more nurses, doctors, and hospitals that were affordable and in close proximity to all farm families. This campaign resulted in a 1916 legislation that enabled the establishment of union hospitals, municipal nurses, and municipal doctors—the precursor of MEDICARE in Canada.

McNaughton and other members of the WGG executive were an important part of the SGGA Ginger Group that pushed the Association to help organize the Wheat Pool in the early 1920s. As well, the WGG established the Saskatchewan Egg and Poultry Pool in 1926. The WGG and the SGGA Ginger Group also pushed the SGGA to amalgamate with the Farmers' Union to form the United Farmers of Canada (UFC) in 1926. McNaughton and ANNIE HOLLIS, who were on the Amalgamation Committee that negotiated the marriage of the two organizations, devised a plan to ensure women's participation in the new UFC: its constitution guaranteed their presence on the executive and board of directors. In theory the president could be a man or woman, but the constitution specifically provided for a woman president and two women directors. This arrangement, which was a form of affirmative action, continued when the UFC became the Saskatchewan Farmers' Union (SFU) in 1949 and when the SFU joined with other farm groups to become the National Farmers' Union

(NFU) in 1968. Among the women who held the office of woman president (later referred to as the women's president), were Annie Hollis, LOUISE LUCAS, SOPHIA DIXON, BEATRICE TREW, and NETTIE WIEBE.

Early efforts to ensure women's participation included provision for women's locals in the WGG and women's lodges in the UFC, which were phased out by 1930. Then from the late 1920s onward an annual Farm Women's Week was held on the campus of the UNIVERSITY OF SASKATCHEWAN. Participants were entertained and educated, attending sessions of interest to farm women, such as poultry-raising, politics, and the farm economy. As well, they attended an annual general meeting in which they debated resolutions contributed by women at the local level. Approved resolutions were sent to the annual meeting of the general UFC or SFU. For many farm women, this week was their only holiday. The activities of this stream of the farm women's movement were always given full coverage on the women's pages of the *Western Producer*.

Georgina M. Taylor

FURTHER READING: Marchildon, R.G. 1985. "Improving the Quality of Rural Life in Saskatchewan: Some Activities of the Women's Section of the Saskatchewan Grain Growers, 1913–1920." Pp. 89–109 in C. Jones and I. MacPherson (eds.), *Building Beyond the Homestead–Rural History of the Prairies*. Calgary: University of Calgary Press; Wiebe, N. 1987. *Weaving New Ways*. Saskatoon: National Farmers Union.

ORTHODOX CHURCHES. The Orthodox Church (also called Eastern, Greek and Byzantine) is a family of self-governing churches which includes four of the original five patriarchates of the early Christian era: Constantinople, Alexandria, Antioch and Jerusalem, and "national" churches. The fifth, the Patriarchate of Rome, had separated from the other four in 1054 over the issues of Trinitarian theology and nature of authority in the church. The "national" churches of Orthodoxy are the Churches of Albania, Bulgaria, Cyprus, Czech Lands and Slovakia, Georgia, Greece, Poland, Romania, Russia and Serbia, their daughter churches in Europe and North and South America, the Orthodox Church of America, and the autonomous churches of Finland, Japan, Sinai and Ukraine. Each patriarchate, while independent, is in full agreement with the rest on all matters of doctrine, and between them there is full sacramental communion. The Patriarch of Constantinople is accorded the status of first among equals by other Patriarchs and heads of other churches.

In Greek the word "Orthodoxy" has the double meaning of "right belief" and "right worship." Orthodox believers consider themselves as guardians of the true faith of the early fathers of

the Church. Unique attributes include: iconography, onion-domed architecture, emphasis on theosis, and distinctive spiritual disciplines. The Ukrainian Orthodox Church and the Serbian Orthodox Church follow the Julian Calendar in their congregational-liturgical life, whereas the Greek Orthodox Church, the Orthodox Church of America, and the Antiochian Church follow a modified Gregorian one. Each Orthodox community in Saskatchewan patterned itself after the churches of its country of origin in terms of church-building design, liturgical rubrics, and governance. The normal pattern was for a group of immigrants to get together to form a congregation and then send a request for the services of a priest to the bishop of their home diocese in their country of origin. There are currently 135 Orthodox congregations and missions in the province. The Ukrainian Orthodox Church, an independent jurisdiction in eucharistic union with the Ecumenical Patriarchate of Constantinople, includes 108 congregations and missions. The Canadian Diocese of the Orthodox Church of America includes twenty-one congregations and missions; of these, six belong to the Romanian Orthodox Episcopate of America. The Greek Orthodox Metropolis of Toronto (Canada), under the jurisdiction of the Ecumenical Patriarchate of Constantinople, includes four congregations and missions. The Serbian Orthodox Church and the Antiochian Orthodox Church each have one congregation.

Orthodoxy was brought to Saskatchewan by East and Central European immigrant farmers and workers. The first Orthodox arrived in Saskatchewan in 1890. Thirty Romanian Orthodox families were homesteading in the Regina district in 1891; over the next two decades their numbers would swell to nearly 40,000. These Orthodox communities were scattered throughout settlements from the Manitoba border east of Yorkton to the Alberta border northwest of North Battleford, and southwest of Regina. Later, Greek, and more recently Bosnian, Ethiopian and Eritrean immigrants joined them. Scattered communities of converts from Protestantism have also become Orthodox. In addition to providing liturgical services, sacraments and faith education, the Orthodox churches of Saskatchewan have developed cemeteries, parish halls and cultural centres, summer camps for youth, seniors' complexes for their members and the community at large, student university residences, and cultural and language programs. *Yaroslaw Lozowchuk and Gerald Luciuk*

OSER, JEAN (1908–2002). Jean Oser was an internationally known film editor, an Oscar-winning dramatic filmmaker, and a catalyst in the development of the Saskatchewan film community in the 1970s. A formative member of the Department of Media Production and Studies, he became Professor

Jean Oser.

Emeritus of the **UNIVERSITY OF REGINA** in 1990. In 1991, he received a Lifetime Award for Excellence in the Arts from the **SASKATCHEWAN ARTS BOARD**. Born in Strasbourg (Alsace), Jean Oser grew up in Berlin with a passion for the moving image that would eventually lead to his collaboration with many of the world's legendary filmmakers. Intending to become a director, he apprenticed with Hans Richter and Walter Ruttman. "If you want to make good films," he once said, "don't be such a damn good editor, because they'll never let you out of the cutting room." In demand for his pioneering cutting techniques, he built his reputation as an editor for Austrian director G.W. Pabst and his cinema of social consciousness, working on such films as *Westfront 1918* (1930), *The Threepenny Opera* (1931), and *Kameradeschaft* (1931). Leaving Germany in the early 1930s, Oser lived and worked in Paris, eventually immigrating to the United States after serving with the French army in Morocco. In the 1950s, he worked with such talents as Garson Kanin, Burgess Meredith, and Jean Renoir. His time spent at 20th Century Fox earned him an Oscar in the Dramatic Short Film category for *A Light in the Window* (1953), an innovative profile of 17th century Dutch painter Johannes Vermeer. For the next thirty years, he was based in New York City, making industrial films, television features and series, documentaries, and travel films.

In 1970, Oser came to Canada, having been invited to Regina to help establish a film school at the University. Throughout the 1970s and early 1980s, he taught film history and aesthetics and inspired a generation of Saskatchewan filmmakers. He was a key figure in the filming of Allan King's prairie classic, *Who Has Seen the Wind*, in Arcola in 1977. His later work includes the television documentary *A History of World Cinema: A Personal View by Jean Oser*, shot by Regina's Camera West Film Associates Ltd., which premiered at the Kino Arsenal, Berlin, in May 1993. In 2000, the University of Regina's Department of Media Production and Studies instituted the Jean Oser Prize for excellence in Film Studies in his honour; the prize-winning essay is published in *Splice*, the magazine of the Saskatchewan Filmpool Co-operative. Jean Oser died in Regina on February 20, 2002. *Christine Ramsay*

FURTHER READING: Saul, Gerald. 1997. "Jean Oser," *Splice* (Winter 1997–98): 6–11.

OSLER, town, pop 823, located a 15-minute drive N of Saskatoon on Hwy 11. Named for Sir Edmund Boyd Osler, a wealthy financier and railroad contractor, Osler had its beginnings in 1890 as the Qu'Appelle, Long Lake & Saskatchewan Railway was completed, linking Saskatoon and Prince Albert. The post office was established in 1891, the same year as advance members of what would become a substantial bloc settlement of Mennonites began to arrive in the region. In 1903, Osler had a number of stores, a lumber yard, and a grain elevator. By the 1920s, three grain elevators lining the railway tracks were, along with the railroad station, the centre of Osler's economic activity. In 1928, the Osler Mennonite Church was built. Osler remained a small agricultural trading centre until the late 1970s, which began a period of substantial change. The community became an attractive place for people who wanted to live outside of Saskatoon yet continue to work in the city. From a population of 225 in 1976, Osler grew to 594 by 1986. The community continues to grow and new residential subdivisions and business lots continue to be developed; however, town residents largely benefit from easy access to the employment opportunities, services, and amenities that Saskatoon has to offer. *David McLennan*

OUTLOOK, town, pop 2,129, located about 90 km SW of Saskatoon and 30 km downstream from the **GARDINER DAM** on the E side of the **SOUTH SASKATCHEWAN RIVER**. The community is served by Hwy 15. Settlers had begun entering the district in the early 1900s, a few years before the CPR announced it would be developing a townsite above the river. On August 26, 1908, in advance of the coming railroad, the townsite lots were put up for sale. The railway named the location Outlook for its spectacular vantage over the river valley. Within a month, a sizable community had come into existence. On November 23, the first train rolled into Outlook, and on December 19, 1908, the new community was legally established as a village; it attained town status on November 1, 1909. Within five months, however, on March 20, 1910, residents were standing in the streets staring at smouldering ruins: a fire had claimed a good portion of the business district. The community rebuilt, so that by 1911 the population had reached 685. In 1912, the railway bridge was completed across the river. The **DEPRESSION** took its toll on the area: Outlook's population fell by more than 200 over the decade. Subsequently, Outlook and area residents were at the forefront of the campaign for the construction of a dam across the South Saskatchewan River. Today, the district has a diversified agricultural base producing sunflowers, corn, potatoes, and vegetables, in addition to more traditional crops. The Canada-Saskatchewan Irrigation Diversification Centre, located on the outskirts of the town, is a major leading research facility that promotes crop diversification and sustainable irrigation practices. The community's main attraction is the Sky Trail, part of the Trans Canada Trail and Canada's longest pedestrian bridge; it spans the former 1912 CPR railway bridge, which had been closed for a number of years. Beginning in September, 2003, the 33rd Field Engineer Squadron from Calgary began work on the bridge's refurbishment; the work was done under a national "Bridges for Canada" program which celebrated the centennial of the military engineers. Crossing more than a kilometre of river at a height of close to 48 metres (156 feet), the bridge was officially re-opened to pedestrian traffic by the Honourable Dr. **LYNDA HAVERSTOCK, LIEUTENANT-GOVERNOR** of Saskatchewan, on May 15, 2004. *David McLennan*

OWLS. Owls are solitary predators with soft plumage, sharp hooked bills and sharp talons. Large forward-looking eyes and feathered facial disks are

COURTESY OF TOURISM SASKATCHEWAN

Great horned owl.

distinctive to this avian order. They communicate by hooting, screeching or whistling. Their main foraging strategy is to perch and wait, then pounce on prey. Unlike most other birds, females are usually larger than males. Smaller owl species are insectivorous, while larger species consume rodents and other small mammals and birds. Owls regurgitate pellets of indigestible parts of prey. Most owl species nest in cavities (natural or man-made) or usurp tree nests of species such as crows.

There are just over 200 owl species in the world, divided into two families (Tytonidae and Strigidae); nineteen owl species occur in North America, and twelve of these are resident in Saskatchewan. The only member of the Tytonidae, the cosmopolitan barn owl (*Tyto alba*), measures between 36 and 51 cm, and has a distinctive heart-shaped face; it is an irregular breeder in southeast Saskatchewan, nesting in abandoned buildings. The eastern screech owl (*Otus asio*) measures between 20 and 25 cm, and is uncommon in the riparian woodland of the river valleys of the southeast. The owl that most people will see is the great horned owl (*Bubo virginianus*), which measures between 46 and 64 cm. This large, powerful owl can take prey larger than itself and is found throughout the province in open areas with trees, abandoned buildings, or ledges. The Arctic-breeding, mostly white snowy owl (*Nyctea scandiaca*), which measures between 51 and 69 cm, can winter in the grasslands and farmlands of Saskatchewan. The diurnal northern hawk owl (*Surnia ulula*) measures

between 36 and 43 cm and is usually found in open areas in the boreal forest, nesting in large tree cavities or abandoned tree nests. The other owl commonly seen in daylight is the declining and endangered long-legged burrowing owl (*Athene cunicularia*); measuring between 23 and 28 cm, it nests in burrows of rodents and badgers, in grasslands and pastures. The dark-eyed barred owl (*Strix varia*), measuring between 43 and 61 cm, has expanded its range in the boreal forest: increased numbers have been found in old-growth forest since the 1950s, nesting in abandoned nests. The great grey owl (*Strix nebulosa*), from 61 to 84 cm tall, is the biggest owl, with huge facial disks of dark grey concentric circles. It nests in tree snags in old-growth forest and bogs. The slender long-eared owl (*Asio otus*) measures between 33 and 41 cm and has distinctive closely-set ear tufts; it nests in abandoned tree nests in aspen groves, wooded coulees, and abandoned farmsteads. The threatened short-eared owl (*Asio flammeus*), from 33 to 43 cm tall, nests on the ground in the grasslands, farmlands and marshes of southern Saskatchewan, where there are large vole populations. The flat-headed boreal owl (*Aegolius funerus*) measures between 20 and 30 cm; it nests in tree cavities, in mature coniferous and mixedwood stands of the boreal forest. The northern saw-whet owl (*Aegolius acadicus*) is the smallest owl in Saskatchewan (18–20 cm) and nests in tree cavities in the southern Boreal forest, Aspen Parkland and **CYPRESS HILLS**.

Robert Warnock

FURTHER READING: Alsop, Fred J., III. 2002. *Birds of Canada.* New York: Dorling Kindersley.

OXBOW, town, pop 1,132, located approximately 60 km E of Estevan on Hwy 18. The name of the town was derived from the oxbow bend in the **SOURIS RIVER**, which passes along the community's south side. Settlers, largely of English, Irish and Scottish origin, began homesteading in the district in 1882. The community grew very rapidly: by 1916, the population was 678, and that number remained relatively constant through several decades. In the mid-1950s, significant development began in the area's oilfields, and for several years the region experienced boom times as drilling rigs, industry-related services and personnel moved into the area. Today, **OIL AND GAS**, as well as agriculture, drive the regional economy. Highlights of the Oxbow area include the new Moose Creek Regional Park and Golf Club, the Alameda Dam, Bow Valley Park, and the Ralph Allen Memorial Museum, named after the locally raised and renowned Canadian journalist, war correspondent, and author. Another of the town's famous sons is hockey player Theoren Fleury, who was born in Oxbow in 1968 and was the first player in the history of the NHL to score three short-

handed goals in one game. Oxbow's weekly newspaper, the *Oxbow Herald*, has been published since 1903.

David McLennan

OXNER, BERTHA (1885–1960). Born in Nova Scotia in 1885, Oxner became a teacher and in 1908 moved to Saskatchewan, where she taught in Saskatoon, Brock and Saltcoats. She then attended the **UNIVERSITY OF SASKATCHEWAN**, where she obtained a BA, and Chicago University, where she earned an MA; she also did post-graduate work at Chicago in textiles and clothing. Oxner returned to Saskatchewan, and in 1925 became assistant professor in household science at the University. She and Ethel B. Rutter developed the School of Household Science and its bachelor of household science degree. In 1930 she was appointed director of women's work. She developed extensive educational programs for rural women and the **HOMEMAKERS' CLUBS**. As well, she wrote a column in the *Western Producer*. In 1936 she assisted development of girls' Homecraft Clubs. She also organized the first Homemakers' Club on a First Nations reserve, and initiated courses for Métis women. Oxner was active in many groups: the Canadian Association for Adult Education, National Vocational Training Advisory Council, Canadian Association of Consumers, Canadian Home Economics Association, Saskatchewan Technical Education Committee, and Saskatchewan Farm Housing Committee. Retiring in 1949, she returned to Chester, where she died on December 7, 1960. In 1978 Oxner was inducted into the Saskatchewan Agricultural Hall of Fame.

Dagmar Skamlová

UNIVERSITY OF SASKATCHEWAN ARCHIVES A-3211

Bertha Oxner, 1953.

P

PAINTERS' STRIKE OF 1912. The Painters' Strike of 1912 is historically important because it was one of the early labour-capital conflicts in Regina; the issues and the way they were handled would be typical of labour relations in the construction trades for decades to come. The demands of the union, Local 509 of the Brotherhood of Painters, Decorators and Paperhangers of America, revolved around wages, the cost of living, job security and working conditions, including safety on the job. The strike, which lasted from July 22–31, was settled with a compromise agreement. The broader politics of the painters and other construction trades also set a pattern. Their active members would eventually become involved in the Independent Labour Party and later the CCF. While most were moderate reformers, a few, like **WILLIAM E. COCKS**, were solid socialists influenced by classical Marxism.

Lorne Brown

FURTHER READING: Makahonuk, Glen. 1982. "The Regina Painters' Strike of 1912," *Saskatchewan History* 35, no. 3 (Autumn); —. 1985. "Painters, Decorators and Paperhangers: A Case Study In Saskatchewan Labourism, 1906–1919," *Prairie Forum* 10, no. 1.

PALLISER AND HIND EXPEDITIONS. John Palliser, an aristocrat who served in the British army, first explored the North American west in

SASKATCHEWAN ARCHIVES BOARD R-A4962-1

Captain John Palliser.

677

1847 and 1848 when he travelled from Louisiana to modern-day Montana. In 1856 he began securing sponsorship for a second expedition in what is today western Canada. His funding (and much of his instruction) came from the Royal Geographical Society, the British Colonial Office, and the Hudson's Bay Company. Palliser's expedition left Britain in 1857 and travelled first through the USA before entering Canada at Sault Ste. Marie. His company consisted of James Hector, a geologist and physician; Eugène Bourgeau, a botanist; and John Sullivan, an astronomer. **THOMAS BLAKISTON**, the magnetical observer, followed a different route via Hudson Bay and met up with the expedition at Fort Carleton, near present-day Saskatoon.

During 1857 and 1858, the party travelled over what is today Saskatchewan, cataloguing the local flora, fauna, and minerals. They also mapped three distinct regions: thick wood country with many lakes in the far north; arid plains in the south; and partially wooded country in between. Palliser speculated that the valleys and partially wooded areas would be suitable for settlements. However, he also identified a large region in present-day southwest Saskatchewan and southeast Alberta rendered unsuitable by lack of rainfall and timber. This region is now known as the **PALLISER TRIANGLE**. In 1858 and 1859, Palliser's expedition travelled in the Rocky Mountains seeking passes to the Pacific Ocean. He returned to England in June 1860, and his general report was delivered to the British Colonial Office in April 1862 at the height of the American Civil War. For this reason, some historians assert the report received only muted attention.

The Hind expedition was formally named the Canadian Red River, Assiniboine and Saskatchewan Exploring Expedition; it was directed and funded by the Province of Canada and led by Henry Youle Hind, an English-born geologist and instructor at Trinity College in Toronto. The expedition departed from Toronto in 1857 with Hind and three other principals: George Gladman, a former fur trader; Simon Dawson, a surveyor; and W.H.E. Napier, an engineer. Their mission was to find a reliable route from Lake Superior to the Red River Settlement, and then to inspect the potential of the land west of Red River for its fitness for future settlement. In 1857 the party journeyed from Lake Superior to Fort Garry and mapped the area; in June 1858 it left Fort Garry and spent three months exploring what is today southern Manitoba and Saskatchewan. One of the expedition members, Humphrey Lloyd Hime, took the first photographs in Saskatchewan. Hind's preliminary report to the Legislative Assembly of Upper Canada was published in 1859; his later narrative book with maps and artwork was published in 1860. Like Palliser, Hind identified the river valleys as the best place for future settlement. Not surprisingly, Hind's writings were relied upon in later years

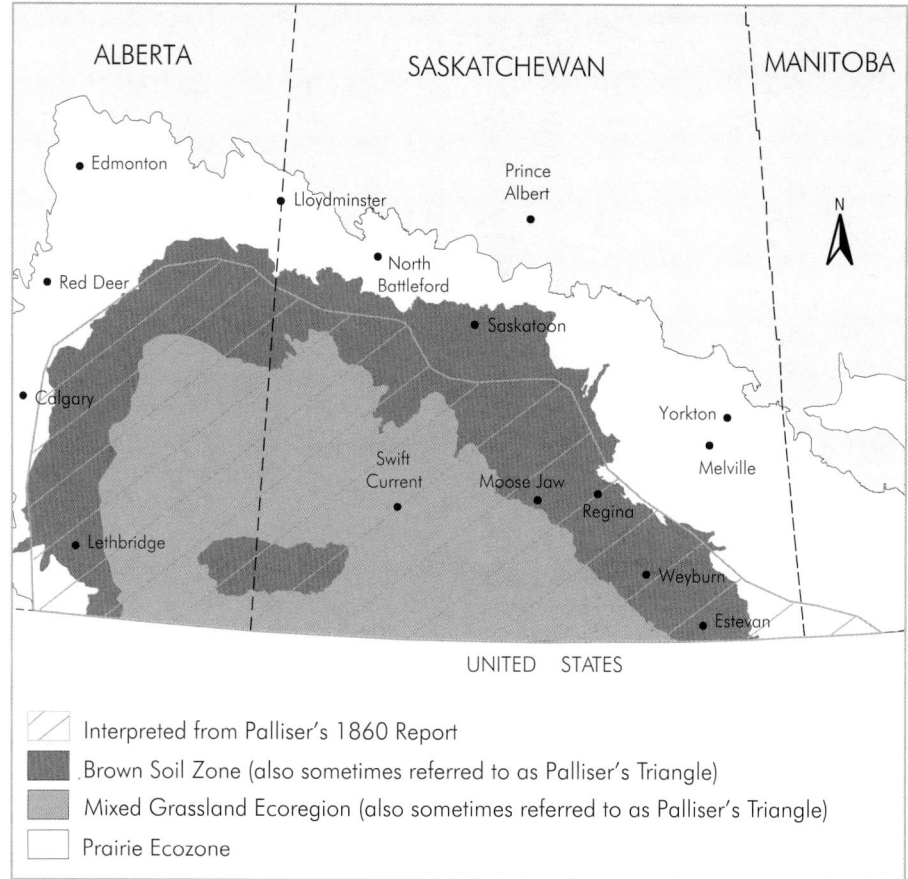

Interpreted from Palliser's 1860 Report

Brown Soil Zone (also sometimes referred to as Palliser's Triangle)

Mixed Grassland Ecoregion (also sometimes referred to as Palliser's Triangle)

Prairie Ecozone

CANADIAN PLAINS RESEARCH CENTER MAPPING DIVISION

Figure PT-1. Palliser Triangle (including various interpretations).

to bolster aspirations of expansion westward into Rupert's Land. Although Palliser and Hind were not the first Europeans to cross Saskatchewan, their expeditions were far more scientific and well-recorded than those of previous explorers. *Gerald Heinrichs*

FURTHER READING: Hind, H.Y. 1971 (1860). *Narrative of the Canadian Red River Exploring Expedition of 1857 and of the Assiniboine and Saskatchewan Exploring Expedition of 1858*. Edmonton: Hurtig; Huyda, R.J. 1975. *Camera in the Interior: 1858*. Toronto: Coach House Press; Spry, I.M. 1995. *The Palliser Expedition*. Calgary: Fifth House Publishers.

PALLISER TRIANGLE. The driest part of the Canadian prairies is often called the Palliser Triangle, after a 19th century explorer who first described a roughly triangular area that he felt to be poorly suited for farming.

In his final report to the British government Captain John Palliser suggested that a triangular portion of what is now the southern prairie provinces was a northern extension of the arid, central desert of the United States: "This central desert extends, however, but a short way into the British territory, forming a triangle, having for its base the 49th parallel from longitude 100° to 114° W, with its apex reaching to the 52nd parallel of latitude."

Palliser described this triangular area as "desert, or semi-desert in character, which can never be expected to become occupied by settlers." To this day Palliser's name is attached to the most arid region of the southern Canadian prairies.

The boundary of the Palliser Triangle is not fixed like a political boundary. Rather it fluctuates depending on climatic cycle, or the purpose of the person mentioning the region. Since Palliser's original pronouncement, the area that people generally call the Palliser Triangle has shrunk. Today boundaries of physio-graphic regions such as the brown soil zone or the mixed grassland prairie ecoregion are often used to indicate the Palliser Triangle (*see* Figure PT-1).

Characterized by its aridity, the mixed grassland ecoregion has an annual water deficit (the amount that the potential evapotranspiration exceeds the precipitation) of 524 mm. It is a natural grassland with few native trees or wetlands. Its landscape is diverse, from level, glacial lake plains to the rolling **MISSOURI COTEAU**. Climatic data for Leader, a town within this ecoregion, are typical of the area. In Leader the total annual precipitation is 352 mm and the annual snowfall is 101 cm. The mean July temperature is 18.9° C and the mean January temperature is -12.6° C.

Lisa Dale-Burnett

PHOTIQUE PHOTOGRAPHY BY KEPLER LTD./SASKATCHEWAN ARCHIVES BOARD R-A26809

Marie-Antoinette Papen.

PAPEN, MARIE-ANTOINETTE (1907–89).

Marie-Antoinette Papen played a key role during the first two decades of Saskatoon's CFNS French-language radio station. Born Marie-Antoinette de Margerie on June 9, 1907, in Sainte-Anne-des-Chênes, Manitoba, she taught in Hoey, Saskatchewan, from 1928 until her marriage to Belgian-born homesteader Charles Papen in 1934. Impoverished by the **DEPRESSION**, the Papens moved to Belgium in 1937. Stranded by the war, the family, including two sons and a daughter, came back to Saskatchewan in 1947. M.-A. Papen first taught school near Prud'homme; then, settling in Saskatoon in 1950, she became organizing secretary of the drive to fund French-language radio stations in Saskatchewan. After CFNS started broadcasting in November 1952, she hosted a daily program for women, *Au fil de l'heure*. In 1961, after the sudden passing of her husband, by then CFNS director, she became *pro tem* director and thereafter continued hosting *Au fil de l'heure* until her retirement in 1972. A woman of deep faith, she maintained a daily dialogue with farm and city women who belonged to a fundamentally conservative French catholic milieu during the era before and after Vatican II, when the role of women and the place of religion in society were hotly debated. She suffered a stroke in March 1977 and died on April 8, 1989.

Richard Lapointe

FURTHER READING: Lapointe, Richard. 1988. "Marie-Antoinette Papen." Pp. 312–15 in *100 noms: Petit dictionnaire biographique des Franco-Canadiens de la Saskatchewan*. Regina: Société historique.

PARHELIA: *see* SUN-DOGS

PARKER, REGINALD JOHN MARSDEN (1881–1948).

Reginald J. M. Parker was the eighth **LIEUTENANT-GOVERNOR** of Saskatchewan.

Born on February 7, 1881, at Liskeard, Cornwall, England, he emigrated to Canada in 1898 and worked as a farmhand before homesteading at Togo, North-West Territories. He served as a councilor in the rural municipality of Cote from 1904 to 1910 and as municipal reeve from 1906 to 1932. In June 1929, Parker was elected Liberal MLA for the Pelly constituency. He sat as a member of the Liberal opposition until the party regained power in 1934. Shortly after, he was appointed Minister of Municipal Affairs, a difficult portfolio to hold during the **DEPRESSION** but one he maintained until his party's defeat by the CCF in 1944. Parker accepted the vice-regal position from the Prime Minister and was sworn in as Lieutenant-Governor of Saskatchewan on June 25, 1945. From their official residence at the Hotel Saskatchewan, Parker and his wife welcomed a number of dignitaries to the province. Six days after hosting the High Commissioner of New Zealand, R.J.M. Parker died in office on March 23, 1948.

FURTHER READING: Wilson, Heather. 2004. "Parker, Reginald John Marsden." P. 188 in *Saskatchewan Politicians: Lives Past and Present*. Regina: Canadian Plains Research Center.

PARRISH AND HEIMBECKER GRAIN COMPANY.

The Parrish and Heimbecker Grain Company (P&H) is one of the first private Canadian grain companies still in existence; it was established in 1909 when William L. Parrish joined with Norman Heimbecker. Both founders had deep roots in the grain and **MILLING** business. William Parrish had been in the milling business with his father Samuel Parrish at Uxbridge, Ontario in the 1870s. He went west in 1881 before completion of the transcontinental railway and took up a homestead, which he farmed for three years. In 1886 father and son went into the grain business at Brandon, Manitoba. Norman Heimbecker's father and grandfather had both operated mills in Ontario for a long time.

In 1918 P&H purchased ten elevators from Calgary grain brokers. In 1922, when they had twenty country elevators, the two partners formed the Superior Elevator Company with the purpose of building a terminal at Fort William on Lake Superior. Unlike many other private companies, P&H expanded cautiously. They moved westward, and by 1975 had purchased the Ellison Milling and Elevator Company Ltd. at Lethbridge.

P&H has become a very diversified company: over the years it has acquired mills in Moose Jaw and Saskatoon, as well as steamships and feed mills. In 2004, P&H listed seven associated companies: New-Life Mills Ltd., P&H Foods, Golden Valley Farms, Cook's, Ellison Milling Company, Parrheim Foods, and Smith Brokerage Ltd. With seven elevators and

two processing facilities, Cook's is located in south-western Ontario and specializes in the marketing and procurement of edible beans, peas, lentils, coarse grains and oilseeds; New Life specializes in animal feeds, P&H Foods in poultry processing, and Ellison in flour milling. In 2004 P&H had nineteen licenced primary elevators, eight of which were in Saskatchewan.

Gary Storey

FURTHER READING: Anderson, C.W. 1991. *Grain: The Entrepreneurs*. Winnipeg: Watson and Dwyer Publishing; Fowke, V. 1957. *The National Policy and the Wheat Economy*. Toronto: University of Toronto Press; Wilson, C.F. 1978. *A Century of Canadian Grain*. Saskatoon: Western Producer Prairie Books.

SASKATCHEWAN ARCHIVES BOARD R-A15253

E.A. Partridge.

PARTRIDGE, EDWARD ALEXANDER (1861–1931).

Edward Alexander Partridge was born in Ontario in 1861. He homesteaded near Sintaluta, where he worked as a schoolteacher and served in the Yorkton Company during the 1885 **NORTH-WEST RESISTANCE**. In 1886 he married Mary Stephens, and they worked together building their farm and raising a family of five. Partridge, a widely read man, began to engage in an analysis of the difficulties western farmers were facing as a result of tariff-related high costs and low prices due to the actions of the private grain trade. In 1901, Partridge and other disgruntled farmers organized the Territorial Grain Growers Association. He soon concluded that the problem was the class nature of capitalism, and that more radical action was therefore needed. He helped organize the **GRAIN GROWERS' GRAIN COMPANY** and edited the farmers' news journal, the *Grain Growers' Guide*. He campaigned for public ownership of the elevator system, and the "Partridge Plan" resulted in government support for a co-operative elevator company.

In 1910 Partridge joined the "Siege of Ottawa" despite having lost a leg in an accident in 1908. Then great personal tragedy struck Partridge and his wife: in 1914 a daughter drowned, and their two sons were killed in **WORLD WAR I** service. Nevertheless Partridge would not rest: he joined the Progressive Party, and helped organize the Farmer's Union and the Saskatchewan Co-operative Wheat Producers Limited—later to become the Saskatchewan Wheat Pool. During the 1920s Partridge laid out his vision of a better world in his book, *War on Poverty*, whose message reflects the remarkable resilience of the human spirit. However, Partridge was not able to recover from one final loss: his wife's death. He left Saskatchewan, and ended his own life in Victoria in 1931.   *Murray Knuttila*

PASQUA (1828–89). Chief Joseph Pasqua was born in 1828 to the prominent Plains **CREE** Chief Mahkaysis, and came to lead his own band. From 1871 the government of Canada entered into the Numbered Treaties with various First Nations. In 1874 Pasqua and his band were living near present day Leech Lake, Saskatchewan, where they had survived predominantly on buffalo; but they had also planted gardens and were raising a small herd of cattle. In September of that year Pasqua attended the negotiation of **TREATY 4** in the **QU'APPELLE VALLEY**. According to the only written account of Pasqua's involvement in the negotiations, he pushed on the Canadian negotiators the fact that the Hudson's Bay Company had received £300,000 for the sale of Rupert's Land to the Dominion of Canada. This amount, he argued, should have been paid to Indians. Despite Canada's refusal to do so, Pasqua signed the Treaty.

Pasqua and his band took up a reserve of 57 square miles approximately five miles west of Fort Qu'Appelle; theirs was the only band to receive their cattle and oxen immediately, as they had already demonstrated to government officials that they could care for livestock, something it was commonly thought Indians did not have the skills to do. During the Resistance of 1885 Pasqua and his band did not become involved, and as a result were given assurances from Sir John A. Macdonald that they would be well treated. Pasqua succumbed to tuberculosis in March 1889, after fighting the disease for several years. After his passing Indian Affairs prevented the selection of a successor, as attempts were being made to eliminate the tribal system in Canada.   *Rob Nestor*

PASQUA FIRST NATION. Chief Joseph **PASQUA** signed **TREATY 4** in September 1874, and selected a reserve bordering Pasqua Lake for his **CREE**, **SAULTEAUX**, **ASSINIBOINE** and **SIOUX** people. This loca-

tion was to ensure that his people would have fish and waterfowl when other wild game was scarce. Pasqua had previously attempted to prevent the survey of reserve land and to instigate others to do likewise; as a result of his open defiance, treaty goods were withheld from his people. Pasqua traveled to see the **LIEUTENANT-GOVERNOR** of Manitoba to discuss the inadequacies of the treaties, explaining that First Nations people were starving. He died in 1889, and the band remained without a chief until the 1911 election of Ben Pasqua, Joseph's son. This election followed years of petitioning by the Pasqua band members, and once in office Ben pressed the department for an explanation as to why the band was kept without a chief for twenty-two years. He also requested that the chief's salary in arrears be paid to the band; the department refused. The early years of farming were difficult ones, and extra money was earned by cutting and selling wood. In June 1906 the band surrendered 16,077 acres for $8 an acre, which returned an average of $13.41 an acre to the government by public auction in Regina. In 1995 a claim was initiated by the Pasqua Band for restitution against the land taken in the 1906 surrender. Of the 1,630 band members, 531 live on the 9,468.5-ha reserve located 16 km west of Fort Qu'Appelle.

Christian Thompson

T. A. Patrick.

PATRICK, THOMAS ALFRED (1864–1943). Born at Ilderton, Ontario, on December 23, 1864, Patrick graduated in medicine from the University of Western Ontario in 1888. He practised medicine and surgery at Saltcoats until 1894 and in Yorkton until 1939.

Patrick was the first physician to seek office (1881) and the first to be elected (1897) to a

Legislature within the present boundaries of Saskatchewan. He sat in nine sessions of the Legislative Assembly of the North-West Territories, initially as an independent supporter of Premier **FREDERICK HAULTAIN**, but always as one of the strongest proponents in the fight for a more responsible form of territorial government. Patrick was the first to propose the present boundaries of Saskatchewan and Alberta. His election campaign of 1898 helped turn the tide against the idea of one large prairie province or of one southern ranching province and a northern mixed-farm province, or of making each of the four existing postal districts into provinces.

Patrick was an active promoter of Saskatchewan's third hospital, the Yorkton Queen Victoria Hospital. A few seconds after midnight on September 1, 1905, the day that Saskatchewan officially entered confederation, he delivered the province's first baby. Jennie was born to Trintie and Thomas Luke Gibney. On February 1, 1928, four hours after the bells had rung to celebrate the assumption of city status by Yorkton, Patrick delivered Muriel, born to Roslyn and Mayme Young—assisted in the delivery room by Jennie Gibney, RN. Patrick died September 6, 1943.   *C. Stuart Houston*

FURTHER READING: Houston, C.J. and C.S. Houston. 1980. *Pioneer of Vision: The Reminiscences of T.A. Patrick, M.D.* Saskatoon: Western Producer Prairie Books.

PATTERSON, CECIL FREDERICK (1892–1961). Born at Watford, Ontario, C.F. Patterson graduated from the Ontario Agricultural College with a BSc in Agriculture. He then took his Master's and Doctorate degrees at Urbana, Illinois. He came to the **UNIVERSITY OF SASKATCHEWAN** in 1921 as a lecturer in horticulture, under the late Dean **RUTHERFORD** of the College of Agriculture. In the following year, a Department of Horticulture was organized, and plans laid for a program of fruit variety testing and fruit breeding. In his thirty-nine years as head of the Department of Horticulture, Patterson was responsible for the introduction of more than thirty new varieties of hardy fruits, including apples, pears, plums, cherries, raspberries and strawberries. He was also responsible for an improved potato variety, well adapted to prairie growing conditions. In the realm of floriculture, his name became synonymous with a collection of lily varieties in pink, white, rose and other colours—the result of twenty years of patient crossing and selection. Other flower introductions included geraniums and gladioli. Patterson was a charter member of the Agricultural Institute of Canada, a Fellow of the American Society for the Advancement of Science, a charter member of the Western Canadian Society for Horticulture, and an honorary life member of the Saskatchewan Horticultural Societies Association. He was inducted into the Saskatchewan Agriculture Hall of Fame in 1973. Patterson Garden is an arboretum on the campus of the University of Saskatchewan, named in his honour.

PATTERSON, WILLIAM JOHN (1886–1976).

The response to two signal events in the history of Saskatchewan—the **GREAT DEPRESSION** of the 1930s and **WORLD WAR II**—fell largely to the Liberal government of Premier William Patterson, which was in power from 1935, when **JAMES GARDINER** departed to serve in the federal Cabinet, until the landslide victory of the **CO-OPERATIVE COMMONWEALTH FEDERATION** in the provincial election of 1944.

The sixth Premier of Saskatchewan, Patterson was the first Premier to be born in the province, the first to have seen military service, and the first to take office as a bachelor (he did not marry until 1937). Patterson himself was described as a popular, if lacklustre, leader. His government was successful in obtaining financial assistance from Ottawa to fight the Depression, made a forceful contribution to the reappraisal of federal-provincial relations at the time of the Rowell-Sirois Report, and passed important legislation in areas such as health care, taxation and labour standards which helped to establish the legislative framework familiar to citizens of Saskatchewan to this day.

Yet Patterson failed to make a strong or lasting impression as a public figure. Even at the time, he felt compelled to defend the record of what some called a "do-nothing government," and to point out that his government had managed to maintain public services and government credit in the face of adversity.

William Patterson was born at Grenfell, in what was then the Assiniboia District of the North-West Territories. His father, John Patterson, a railway section foreman, began work on the Grenfell section of the CPR in 1882. His mother, Catherine Fraser, had traveled out from Scotland. They built a small house at Grenfell with lumber brought overland from the end of the railway line at Broadview, and William, the first of their five children, was born there May 13, 1886.

After leaving school at the age of 15, Patterson worked in a bank, and then for the provincial Department of Telephones, before enlisting as a cavalry officer in 1916. He served in France, and was wounded in September 1918, in the same week that two of his brothers were also wounded in action. Returning to Saskatchewan, he studied law for a year with Grenfell lawyer G.C. Neff, and then moved to Windthorst where he opened an insurance and financial agency.

Patterson had displayed a precocious interest in politics, attending the first provincial leadership convention in 1905 before he was old enough to vote. In 1921, he was elected as the MLA for the Pipestone

© M.WEST, REGINA, WEST'S STUDIO
COLLECTION/SASKATCHEWAN ARCHIVES BOARD R-B4533
William Patterson, as Lieutenant-Governor, 1955.

constituency, and served in a number of Cabinet portfolios in the Gardiner governments. He became leader of the **LIBERAL PARTY** and Premier of Saskatchewan in 1935.

Facing the serious crisis of the Depression, the Patterson government sought to preserve and extend social programs that would relieve the financial difficulties of citizens and municipalities, while at the same time protecting the fiscal reputation of the province. The government instituted a sales tax to assist the beleaguered education system, extended pension and debt relief legislation, and expanded publicly funded care for tuberculosis, cancer and polio. The government also enacted legislation supporting the establishment of credit unions, permitting workers to form and join trade unions, and improving labour standards with respect to such issues as hours of work and days of rest.

Though Patterson believed strongly in encouraging the initiative of individuals, he also believed that government could play a vital role in society, particularly in assisting those who faced difficulties as a result of financial adversity or ill health. He saw the taxation revenue necessary to support well-administered government programs as a good investment, and placed great importance on careful management of public resources.

Though the Patterson government, and Patterson himself, were respected as conscientious and fiscally prudent stewards of provincial resources, the government faced growing competition from populist political parties based in western Canada, particularly the **SOCIAL CREDIT PARTY** and the Co-operative Commonwealth Federation. The CCF, under the leadership of **T.C. DOUGLAS**, swept the Liberals from power in 1944. Patterson stepped down as party leader in 1948, and resigned from the Legislature in the same year to take up a post with

the federal Board of Transport Commissioners. He was appointed as the first Saskatchewan-born **LIEUTENANT-GOVERNOR** in 1951, and served in that position until 1958.

Patterson faced straitened circumstances in his retirement, as there was no pension coverage for his years in the Legislature. In March 1958, Premier Douglas introduced a special bill that would provide a pension to Patterson at the maximum level provided under recently passed legislation. Patterson lived in quiet retirement until his death June 10, 1976.

Beth Bilson

FURTHER READING: Barnhart, Gordon L. (ed.). 2004. *Saskatchewan Premiers of the Twentieth Century.* Regina: Canadian Plains Research Center.

PAWSON, GEOFFREY (1938–). Born in Calgary on February 22, 1938, Geoffrey Pawson attended the Universities of Alberta and British Columbia. He earned his doctorate in social work at the University of Southern California at Los Angeles, and in 1966 founded Ranch Ehrlo Society in Regina. Since then, Pawson has headed the society, which provides residential treatment for youth battling drug addiction, alcoholism, and social problems. In addition to "The Ranch," Pawson created other community programs such as Ehrlo Community Services and the Child Welfare League of Canada. A recipient of distinguished service awards from the Canadian and Saskatchewan Associations of Social Workers, Pawson was invested as a Member of the Order of Canada in 2000 and awarded the Saskatchewan Order of Merit in 2001. In 2005, he was granted an honorary doctor of laws from the University of Regina.

PAWSON, RUTH (1908–94). A career educator and prolific landscape artist, Ruth Pawson was born in Ontario in 1908 and moved with her family to the prairies in 1912. Educated at the Regina **NORMAL SCHOOL**, Pawson taught primary school for four decades, including two years as a teacher for the Department of National Defence in Germany. She was also an accomplished artist who studied at Emma Lake and the Banff School of Fine Arts. In 1976, the Regina Public School Board named an elementary school in her honour. For her varied contributions to the province, Ruth Pawson received the Saskatchewan Order of Merit in 1993. She died on April 14, 1994.

PEACE ACTIVISM. Averting the ravages of war and creating the conditions for justice and peace have been goals of peace movements over Saskatchewan's first century. Before 1905 peace had been at risk owing to the failure of the Dominion to address the land claims of Indians and Métis; the aftermath of the armed rebellion of 1885 and the

681

hanging of Riel and several Indian leaders continue to challenge us to create peace through justice. Religious pacifism came along with some immigrants. In 1885 thousands of Russian **DOUKHOBORS** destroyed their weapons to protest Czarist militarism, and their persecution led to emigration to the Canadian prairies. Social gospel pacifism, in search of positive neutralism in foreign affairs, also influenced the early CCF under J.S. Woodsworth.

The Cold War transformed the peace movement: Peace Council groups wanting to avert war with the Soviet Union were widespread. American McCarthyism placed peace-oriented groups under suspicion, and underground RCMP officers infiltrated and tried to weaken them. The threat of nuclear war encouraged broad-based groups: by 1959 the University of Saskatchewan had one of the largest Canadian chapters of the student Campaign for Nuclear Disarmament (CUCND). In 1964 the Student Union for Peace Action (SUPA) was formed in Regina; this group linked anti-war objectives to community organizing for fundamental change, and was a precursor to the Canadian "New Left" and the anti-Vietnam war movement.

While Premier **T.C. DOUGLAS** spoke to disarmament rallies in the late 1950s, uranium was shipped from the north for NATO's nuclear arsenal. Antinuclear groups such as the Inter-Church Uranium Committee (ICUC) emerged in the 1970s. In 1980 the pacifist Mennonites helped stop a uranium refinery at Warman. In 1987 Saskatoon hosted the First International Congress on Uranium Mining, which brought peace and "green" activists together from several continents. Over Saskatchewan's first century, thousands of citizens have participated in rallies for nuclear disarmament and to end warfare. Peace coalitions and church-based groups like KAIROS continue to advocate peace through justice. The global challenges remain—as does the local need for peacemaking between Indigenous and settler peoples. *Jim Harding*

PEACOCK, ALBERT E. (1901–83). An innovative and progressive educator, Albert E. Peacock was born in Northport, Nova Scotia in 1901 and earned his Bachelor of Science degree from Mount Allison University in 1921. He completed his education at the Regina Normal School and the Universities of Chicago and Toronto before coming to Moose Jaw in 1922. Peacock taught at Ross Collegiate, Central Collegiate, and the technical high school that eventually bore his name. In 1937, he was appointed principal of the technical school and superintendent of schools in Moose Jaw. Following **WORLD WAR II**, he assumed the latter position until his retirement in 1966. Active in the Moose Jaw Rotary Club, YMCA, and the United Church, Albert Peacock received the Order of Canada in 1974 in recognition of his work in education. He died on February 16, 1983.

PEARSALL, VICTOR (1915–). Born in Luseland, Saskatchewan, on March 31, 1915, Victor Pearsall was a successful entrepreneur and aviator. At the age of 15, he was the youngest licensed pilot in Canada and later embarked on a decade-long career as a bush pilot in northern Saskatchewan. Pearsall also operated itinerant and permanent cinemas across rural Saskatchewan beginning in 1937. His additional business interests included a fish filleting and freezing plant, a fly-in fishing and tourist camp at Cree Lake, and a resort/tourist centre in Cochin. Pearsall also earned the distinction of being Canada's oldest licensed pilot after a record sixty-five years of flying. In 1986, the provincial government named Pearsall Lake in his honour and he was awarded the Saskatchewan Order of Merit in 1995.

PEDERSON, MARTIN PEDER (1921–2001). Martin Pederson was born on December 5, 1921, on his family's farm near Hawarden. He flew ninety-two missions with the **ROYAL AIR FORCE** during **WORLD WAR II** and after the war returned to Saskatchewan and farmed near Hawarden. Between 1950 and 1958 Pederson served terms as provincial president and national vice-president of the Young Conservative Association and president of the Saskatoon PC Association. These positions led to his selection as provincial PC leader in 1958. Pederson capitalized on the popularity of **JOHN DIEFENBAKER**, the federal PC leader, and the party's share of the popular vote rose from 2% in 1956. In 1964 Pederson was elected in Arm River and was the first Conservative in the Legislature since the 1934 provincial election. Diefenbaker provided little assistance to his provincial colleagues and tacitly supported Liberal leader **ROSS THATCHER** in his attempt to polarize anti-CCF/NDP sentiment behind the provincial Liberals. In 1967 Pederson lost his seat and resigned as party leader in 1968. Despite his

REGINA LEADER-POST

Martin Pederson, October 1958.

lack of electoral success, Pederson kept the PC Party viable during the 1960s, which contributed to the party's revival in the 1970s. In addition to politics and farming, Pederson operated trucking and insurance companies. From 1983 to 1987, under the PC government of **GRANT DEVINE**, Pederson served as chair of the Saskatchewan Liquor Board. Pederson died September 1, 2001. *Mike Fedyk*

FURTHER READING: Eisler, Dale. 1987. *Rumours of Glory: Saskatchewan and the Thatcher Years*. Edmonton: Hurtig Publishers; Wilson, Barry. 1980. *The Politics of Defeat: The Decline of the Liberal Party in Saskatchewan*. Saskatoon: Western Producer Prairie Books.

PEDIGREED SEED INDUSTRY. Pedigreed seed is genetically pure seed of a known variety, developed with unique characteristics such as disease resistance, or with special qualities for **MILLING** or malt markets. It is the role of the pedigreed seed industry and Saskatchewan Seed Growers to transfer that technology from the plant breeder to the commercial farmer. The term *pedigreed* means that the ancestry of the seed can be traced all the way back to the plant breeder who developed it. Pedigreed seed ensures specified germination for even emergence and productive stands. It contains uniform seed sizes, providing consistency in planting and crop performance. Optimum seed size encourages uniformity in the crop and promotes seedling vigour, high yields, and low disease levels to maintain crop health and minimal contamination from other crops or different varieties of the same crop. Freedom from other crop seeds, noxious weeds and other weed seeds is verified by federal regulations. This is accomplished by inspection of pedigreed seed crops by trained officers of the Canadian Food Inspection Agency (CFIA), administration of genetic crop purity standards by the Canadian Seed Growers Association (CSGA), and application of seed quality (germination and mechanical purity) standards of the Canada Seeds Act. The plant that processes the seed must meet accepted standards and practices monitored by the Canadian Seed Institute (CSI).

There are five classes of pedigreed seed: Breeder, Select, Foundation, Registered, and Certified. Breeder is the highest class, and is produced and maintained by the plant breeder; once this seed becomes available for multiplication, it is distributed to seed growers. Select, Foundation, and Registered are multiplication classes. Certified seed, the final pedigreed class, is the seed recommended for use by the commercial farmer. There are two stages in the production and identification of pedigreed seed. The first is the production of a pedigreed seed crop. If all the requirements for this are met, CSGA issues a Crop Certificate: this certifies that the crop meets the requirements for varietal purity and crop standards, and shows the pedigreed status. The second stage is the inspection of the seed by a licensed grader at a Registered Seed establishment to determine its eligibility for a grade under the Canada Seeds Act. Factors include germination, freedom from weed seeds and other crop kinds, and general quality. If the seed qualifies for an official grade, the licensed grader issues a label confirming the class of seed and the grade.

At each stage of pedigreed seed production, CSGA specifies the standards for isolation distances, land use history, maximum levels of off-types, and other crop kinds and weeds. CSGA maintains all the records of the seed crop, including where it was grown, who grew it, what other types of plants or seeds were found in the crop, its pedigreed status, and the destination of the seed. The Canadian Seed Growers Association, established in 1904, is recognized by the Canadian government as the sole seed pedigree issuing agency for all agricultural field crops in Canada (except potatoes). CSGA recognizes seven affiliated organizations in different regions of Canada.

The Saskatchewan Seed Growers Association (SSGA) is the affiliate recognized by the CSGA in this province. Formed in 1928, SSGA is incorporated as a non-profit organization, with the mandate to improve pedigreed seed production and usage within Saskatchewan. There are about 800 pedigreed seed growers in the province, producing an average of 425,000 acres of pedigreed seed annually. This represents more than a third of all the pedigreed seed acreage in Canada; nearly 40% of all the pedigreed **WHEAT** seed produced; more than half of all the lentil seed; half the pedigreed **FLAX** acres; a third of the **CANOLA** and **MUSTARD** seed; and nearly three-quarters of the pedigreed pulse seed production. The pedigreed seed industry is worth an estimated $390 million annually to the economy of the province.

Dave Akister

FURTHER READING: Smyth, S., P.W.B. Phillips and D. Spearin.2004. *Value of the Pedigreed Seed Industry to the Saskatchewan Economy*. Saskatoon: University of Saskatchewan, Department of Agriculture Economics.

PEEPEEKISIS FIRST NATION. Chief Can-ah-ha-cha-pew (Making Ready the Bow) signed **TREATY 4** on September 21, 1874. Upon his death his son Peepeekisis (Sparrow Hawk) became chief, and in 1884 the band moved from the **CYPRESS HILLS** to settle on a reserve in the File Hills, about 12 km east of Balcarres. When Indian Agent W.M. Graham arrived at the agency in 1896 the band was without a leader and was unable to prevent Graham's creation of the File Hills Colony (1898) on the reserve. The plan brought young male industrial school graduates (members of bands other than Peepeekisis) to live,

farm and eventually become members of the Peepeekisis Band. The original Peepeekisis Band members were displaced from their homes and deprived of the use of their communal lands. Their complaints led in 1945 to questions raised about the validity of the transfers into the band, but it was not until 1986 that they were able to submit a specific claim to the Department of Indian Affairs. In 2004, the Indian Claims Commission found Canada in breach of its lawful obligations to the band, and recommended that the claim be accepted for negotiation under Canada's Specific Claims Policy. It has yet to be settled. The reserve covers 11,258.7 ha, with an additional share in the 37.1 ha of the Treaty 4 Reserve Grounds (Fort Qu'Appelle). The band's infrastructure includes a band office, arena, gymnasium, school, health clinic, and other maintenance facilities; it has a membership of 2,215 people, 607 of whom live on reserve. *Christian Thompson*

PELICAN. The American white pelican (*Pelecanus erythrorhynchos*) is one of eight pelican species in the world and the only species found in Saskatchewan. It belongs to the family Pelecanidae of the order Pelecaniformes, characterized by fully webbed (totipalmate) feet and a large beak with a throat pouch. The white pelican is one of the largest birds in North America, with a wingspan of up to 3 m and weighing up to 7.75 kg. These graceful fliers nest on isolated islands which

protect them from mammalian predators and human disturbance. They are colonial nesters and usually lay two eggs (range one to four) in a nest that is not much more than a shallow depression in the ground. Their diet consists mainly of fish, which they capture individually or through a co-operative effort: a few birds will form a semicircle and slowly swim towards shore while beating their wings and herding their prey towards shallower water; in unison they dip their bill and catch any fish that swim into it. The bill of all pelicans, unique to the bird world, has a distensible throat pouch that can hold up to 13.5 litres. The pouch is not only used as a dip net to catch fish, but acts as a cooling device when this bare skin is fluttered.

Pelicans were reported nesting in Saskatchewan as early as 1879. In 1978, declining numbers resulted in the American white pelican being listed as a threatened species by the Committee on the Status of Endangered Wildlife in Canada (COSEWIC). Through protective legislation and public education pelican numbers increased, and in 1987 it became the first species to be "delisted" by COSEWIC. *Keith Roney*

FURTHER READING: Alsop, F.J., III. 2002. *Birds of Canada*. New York: Dorling Kindersley; Macoun, John. 1900. *Catalogue of Canadian Birds, Part I: Water Birds, Gallinaceous Birds, and Pigeons*. Ottawa: Geological Survey of Canada.

COURTESY OF TOURISM SASKATCHEWAN

American white pelican.

PELICAN LAKE FIRST NATION. This CREE band signed TREATY 6 in 1889 and continued to hunt and fish. In 1901 they were considered part of Kenemotayoo's band, but lived separately on the shores of Pelican Lake for many years before choosing a reserve on Chitek Lake. Mention of a reserve being surveyed for them in 1898 can be found in department records, and in 1902 it was noted that the Pelican Lake people were under the same chief and headmen as Kenemotayoo's Band, sharing in the ownership of the Big River Reserve. The first chief was Louis (later changed to Lewis) Chamakee. There were not many non-Indian people in the area until the early 1930s, when a settlement began to develop next to the reserve. Some band members began to farm, but found that money could be earned faster through trapping or selling wood. Their economic base today includes forestry, tourism, agriculture, fishing and trapping, the band has a social development office, band office, workshop, two schools, fire hall, health clinic, apartment complex, Treaty Land Entitlement office, and maintenance outbuildings. Businesses include the Chitek Lake Indian Development Company Ltd., Chamakese Summer Resort, Chitek Lake Houseboats Ltd., Pelican Lake Trucking Ltd., Junior Farms Ltd., Penn General Store Ltd., and Pelican Lake Mini-mall. Their reserve covers 9,076 ha, the most populated area of which is located 68 km southeast of Meadow Lake (Chitek Lake Number 191). Currently there are 1,205 band members, 784 of whom live on the reserve. *Christian Thompson*

PELICAN NARROWS, northern village, located 120 km NW of Creighton via the Hanson Lake Road and gravel Hwy 135. The community is situated near the narrows that join Mirond and Pelican Lakes which lie between the Sturgeon-Weir and Churchill River systems. Pelican Narrows is the administrative centre for the Peter Ballantyne Cree Nation and the majority of the townsite is reserve land. The Peter Ballantyne Cree Nation is the province's second largest First Nation and has a total population of about 6,700, with roughly 2,500 living in the Pelican Narrows area. Oral history places the Cree at the site around 1730. Summer camps where women and children stayed were established, while the men travelled to Hudson Bay to trade furs. Both the North West Company and the Hudson's Bay Company had trading posts established in the area in the late 1700s, but after the merger of the companies in 1821 there was not a post at Pelican Narrows for several decades. In 1874, the Hudson's Bay Company established a permanent post at Pelican Narrows, which became the Northern Store in 1987. Roman Catholic missionaries were traversing the area from the mid-1800s and established a permanent mission in 1878. Anglican missionaries arrived in the late 1890s and built a church in 1911.

Schoolchildren were sent away to RESIDENTIAL SCHOOLS for a number of years. In 1967, an all-weather road was built into the community and other services followed. *David McLennan*

PELLY, village, pop 303, located on Hwys 8 and 49, 32 km N of Kamsack, and 24 km W of the Saskatchewan-Manitoba border. The village is also located near the sites of two historic forts: Fort Pelly, from which the community takes its name, was a Hudson's Bay Company post from 1824 to 1912; and Fort Livingston, an early NWMP headquarters, was briefly the capital of the North-West Territories over the winter of 1876–77. In 1899, large numbers of Doukhobors arrived in the area; while many would move on to British Columbia, those remaining abandoned their communal villages to take up individual homesteads (*see* DOUKHOBOR SETTLEMENTS). After 1900, settlers of English, Ukrainian, German and Scandinavian origins took up homesteads. The community grew rapidly after the railroad arrived in 1909. During the 1950s and 1960s, the population hovered close to 500, and Pelly was an important service centre catering to the agricultural industry of the region. Today, it retains a core of businesses and services. During the winter of 1955–56, Pelly received 386 cm (12.7 ft.) of snow, an amount which stands as the highest snowfall ever recorded in Saskatchewan in a single season. *David McLennan*

PENTECOSTAL ASSEMBLIES OF CANADA. The origin of the modern Pentecostal moment goes back to Topeka, Kansas in 1901. In 1910 the movement came to Parkside, Saskatchewan. In 1919, Pentecostals in Saskatchewan joined the Assemblies of God (USA); 1920 saw the establishment of a national paper, *The Pentecostal Testimony*, in 1925 the Pentecostal Assemblies of Canada asked to be released from the Assemblies of God; and in 1926 W.E. McAlister became the first district superintendent of the Saskatchewan District of the Pentecostal Assemblies of Canada. In 1935, Pastor George Hawtin began the Bethel Bible Institute in Star City; in 1937 Bethel moved to Saskatoon; and in 1938 it was sanctioned by the Saskatchewan District. On May 1, 1962, Manitoba and northwestern Ontario joined in sponsorship of the Institute, which was renamed CENTRAL PENTECOSTAL COLLEGE.

Camp meetings and conventions have always played a role in the success of the Saskatchewan District. While camps were held each year in numerous places in Saskatchewan, the official camp for the Saskatchewan District was begun at Manitou Lake in 1942; Living Water Camp is now located on Adamson Lake near Prince Albert. In southern Saskatchewan, Plains Pentecostal Camp was established in 1973 and currently meets in Echo Valley. The Saskatchewan District began an official outreach to First Nations people in 1961 with the

appointment of Carson and Jean Latimer as full missionaries; in 1967 Pastor Sam Biro was appointed as full-time director for the First Nations work. Today the Saskatchewan District consists of a Bible College, camps, seventy churches, and missionaries both in Canada and overseas. *Wally Wildman*

PEREHUDOFF, WILLIAM (1919–). William Perehudoff was born in Langham, Saskatchewan and has maintained a connection to this area ever since. Currently dividing his time between Saskatoon and the family farm, which has been developed into an art compound encompassing studios and storage facilities for himself and his wife, DOROTHY KNOWLES, he continues his practice as a leading Canadian painter. In 1944, the Saskatoon Art Centre opened, and this provided Perehudoff with early and important access to art. Within a couple of years he was exhibiting regularly in group exhibitions such as the Saskatoon Exhibition and the Art Centre fall show. Throughout this phase of his development as an artist, he farmed in the summer and devoted himself to painting and his art education in the winter. In the late 1940s, Perehudoff worked as a labourer at FRED MENDEL's meat-packing plant, Intercontinental Packers, in Saskatoon. Like many artists of the time, Perehudoff had been influenced by the motivations and methodologies of social realist artists such as Diego Rivera. He was commissioned by Fred Mendel to paint murals for the meat-packing plant cafeteria walls. Except for brief periods, the murals remained in place until 2002, when they were acquired and donated to the MENDEL ART GALLERY in Saskatoon by Camille Mitchell, Mendel's granddaughter. The murals portray the entire meat-packing process from the delivery of live animals to the point at which the meat leaves the plant, destined for market.

Shortly after completing this commission, Perehudoff travelled to Colorado Springs to take instruction with influential French muralist Jean Charlot. A few years later, in New York, he studied with Amédé Ozenfant, the French Purist and associate of Le Corbusier. In 1962, Perehudoff met Clement Greenberg at an Emma Lake Workshop; Greenberg, a passionate advocate of abstraction, was perhaps the most prolific and influential New York art critic of the 20th century. The following year, Perehudoff worked with Kenneth Noland, a very important colourfield painter and a major influence.

Since the 1960s, Perehudoff has been a central figure in Canadian abstraction and perhaps its most celebrated colourfield painter. The effect of the flat plains and open skies that are so dramatically in evidence throughout Saskatchewan seem to some to be very present in his work. What seems certain is that over the years his subtle yet exacting command of colour and shapes, their resolution and correspondences, and their ability to communicate to the

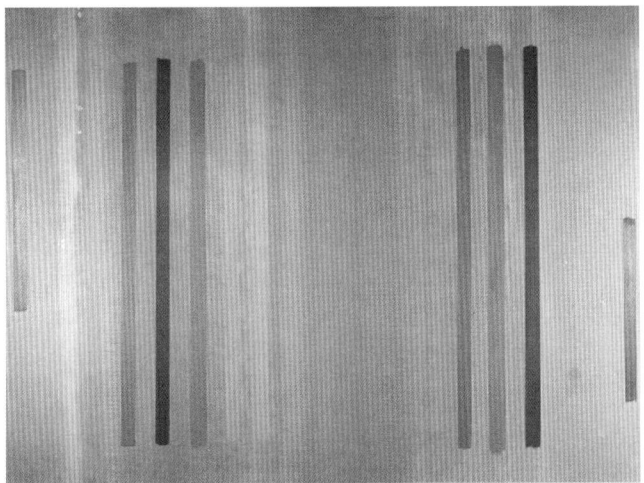

William Perehudoff, "La Loche #3," 1973, acrylic on canvas, 190.6 x 258.5 cm, Collection of the MacKenzie Art Gallery, gift of the artist.

Wilf Perreault, "Shady Lane," 1988, acrylic on canvas, 213 x 335.2 cm, MacKenzie Art Gallery, University of Regina Collection.

viewer, combine to form a kind of personal language. His international career is about his work, his mastery of form, and this very personal vocabulary. William Perehudoff received the Saskatchewan Order of Merit in 1994 and an honorary doctorate from the **UNIVERSITY OF REGINA** in 2003. He was named a Member of the Order of Canada in 1998.

Gilles Hebert

PERLEY, WILLIAM DELL (1838–1909).

Perley was born in Gladstone, NB, on February 6, 1838. He finished his education at Sackville Academy and the Baptist Seminary. His father, William Edward Perley, served over twenty years in the New Brunswick House of Assembly, seven of those years in Cabinet. In 1860, Perley moved to Maugerville, NB, to farm and served seven years on the county council. In 1878 and 1882, he ran federally for the Conservatives but lost. In 1883, Perley moved to Wolseley where he established a farm and later the local grain elevator. He took an active part in organizing the first municipal council to which he was elected chairman. In 1885 and 1886 he was elected to the Territorial Council. When the Territories were granted representation in the House of Commons in 1887, Perley was the first member elected in Assiniboia East as a Conservative. When the Minister of the Interior, Thomas White, suddenly died in 1888, Perley resigned his seat to create an opening for **EDGAR DEWDNEY**, whom John A. Macdonald wanted to fill the vacancy. Later that year Perley became the first senator from the future province of Saskatchewan. Perley remained active in the community, serving as the mayor of Wolseley during much of his time in the Senate and remained there until his death on July 15, 1909. *Brett Quiring*

FURTHER READING: Thomas, Lewis. 1978. *The Struggle for Responsible Government in the North-West Territories*. Toronto: University of Toronto Press.

PERREAULT, WILF (1947-). Wilf Perreault has been described as one of the most interesting of Canada's contemporary landscape painters. Born in Albertville, he took private art lessons as a child. His formal training began at the **UNIVERSITY OF SASKATCHEWAN**, where his concern for representational painting was at odds with the New York-style abstraction dominant at that time in Saskatchewan. He concentrated instead on abstract sculpture under the guidance of **OTTO ROGERS** and **BILL EPP**. He also encountered the landscape paintings of **RETA COWLEY** and **DOROTHY KNOWLES**, whose expressive play with light in the landscape would later serve as an influence. Perreault graduated with a BFA in 1970 and a BEd in 1971, and moved to Regina to teach art. There he returned to painting, and his explorations of his new city became linked with his search for a subject matter. Perreault eschewed the conventional views, becoming fascinated instead with the complex vistas to be found in the back lanes of the inner city. These hidden landscapes have sustained his interest throughout his career, providing an ongoing challenge to his skills in creating works that capture the play of light and reflection, evoking a human context that saturates his work with a sense of place. He developed an exacting method to capture the reflections in his often water- or snow-covered alleys. In layer after layer of thin washes, colour is used in precise brushstrokes to achieve paintings that are masterful renderings of texture and compositional elements and, above all, of light.

In 1978 Perreault earned his first solo exhibition at the **MACKENZIE ART GALLERY** and was then included in significant group exhibitions. When he

Wilf Perreault, in studio, October 1992.

received a Canada Council grant in 1981, he took a leave from teaching and concentrated on his art. Critical and commercial success followed, and he soon took a second leave, followed by working as an artist-in-residence with the Regina Catholic School Board. Since the 1980s Perreault has worked full-time as an artist, exploring various subject matters such as portraits, while never abandoning his fascination with back lanes. He has participated in solo and group exhibitions throughout Canada and the United States, and in 1989 was chosen to be one of five artists representing Canada in *Les Jeux de la Francophonie* in Morocco, where he won the Silver Medal. Perreault's work can be found in public, private and corporate collections throughout North America. He has received several public commissions and grant awards. In 1995, his charitable work was recognized with the Mayor's Award for Volunteer of the Year in Arts. That year he was also elected to the Royal Canadian Academy of the Arts, and in 2003 he received the Queen's Jubilee Medal.

Christine Sowiak

PERSEPHONE THEATRE. Saskatoon's main professional theatre was founded in 1974 by the Wright sisters, Janet and Susan, Saskatoon actresses who had already made a name for themselves in Canadian theatrical circles elsewhere, and by Janet's husband, Brian Richmond, who was to become the theatre's first artistic director. It was by design that its founders named this theatre in the heart of the Saskatchewan prairies "Persephone," for she was the daughter of Zeus and Demeter, the goddess of fertility and the fruitful earth, with a fondness for things agricultural. A theatre so named would be capable of growth and change, like the changing seasons of Saskatchewan, reproducing classic and new plays alike. To finance such a venture, the founders conceived a subsidized regional theatre, keeping the cost of tickets at a minimum to attract audiences, while maintaining a high standard of production. Funds have been raised from several sources: box office, Canada Council grants, **SASKATCHEWAN ARTS BOARD**, City of Saskatoon, local foundations, unions, companies, and private donations.

The choice of the three plays for the 1974–75 inaugural season was significant and defined the kind of company it was hoped Persephone would become—presenting excellent theatre, chosen from as wide a spectrum as possible. Accordingly, those plays were a recent American hit, *The Hot L Baltimore*, by Lawford Wilson; a classic, *A Doll's House*, by Henrik Ibsen; and a Canadian musical premiere, *Cruel Tears*, by Saskatchewan author **KEN MITCHELL**.

In its early years, Persephone faced many of the problems associated with establishing a first-rate theatre. In the first eight seasons, between 1974 and 1981, there were no fewer than six artistic directors,

until finally in 1982 the Hungarian-born Tibor Feheregyhazi was appointed to that position, where he has remained, giving the theatre remarkable stability for over twenty years. With his profound knowledge of theatre, his zest and enthusiasm for this difficult art, as well as an extraordinary gift of choosing playwrights and plays wisely for a Saskatchewan audience, Persephone has enjoyed a long succession of profitable seasons. The list of playwrights includes classic and contemporary, with plays ranging through tragedies and comedies of the standard repertoire, musicals, and contemporary Canadian productions. As a result, season ticket sales have grown from 1,250 in the early years to 2,851 recently.

Another early problem was that of finding a suitable venue for performance, rehearsal, construction of sets, properties and costumes. Its first season was at the **MENDEL ART GALLERY** and the second at the **UNIVERSITY OF SASKATCHEWAN**'s Greystone Theatre, before moving in 1976 to the St. Thomas Wesley Church Hall on 20th Street West. However, when the church hall could no longer be insured as a safe venue for theatre, a new space had to be found. Negotiations were thus started with members of Westgate Alliance Church to purchase their building in the Mount Royal district for $360,000, an additional $150,000 being needed for renovations. These amounts were realized from canvassed public donations as well as contributions by the federal, provincial and municipal governments.

Special projects have involved a national playwriting competition, to which seventy scripts were submitted, and the formation of a youth theatre program, with its own artistic director and a tour co-coordinator, which took plays and workshops to centres throughout Saskatchewan and provided classes for children and young people during the summer months. With a dedicated board and staff, Persephone has entered the 21st century with *élan*, and now has high hopes for a new theatre in the downtown heart of Saskatoon. *Robert Hinitt*

PERSONAL PROPERTY SECURITY ACT. The Personal Property Security Act (hereafter referred to as PPSA), first enacted as 1979–80, c. P-6.2 (proclaimed in force, May 1, 1981) and significantly modified in 1993 (see the Personal Property Security Act, 1993, R.S.S. 1978, c. 6.2), implemented in Saskatchewan one of the most modern regimes of secured financing law in the world. Secured financing law is that branch of the law regulating credit transactions under which a creditor takes security to guard against non-payment by the person to whom the credit was granted. It regulates relationships that arise where, for example, a bank or credit union loans money and takes a charge ("security interest") on the personal property (any type of tangible or intangible property other than

land) of the borrower (likely the property purchased with the loan), or when a seller agrees to sell personal property to a buyer on terms that the seller will remain the owner of the property until the purchase price is paid.

There are two principal aspects to this law. One is regulation of the rights and obligations of secured creditors and debtors. This part of the law focuses principally on ensuring that the debtor is treated fairly when he/she fails to repay the loan or purchase price and it is necessary for the creditor to seize the property taken as security. The second aspect of this law addresses situations where, for example, the person who has agreed to give a security interest in his/her car to a credit union or bank then sells the car to someone else without telling that person that the security interest exists. Simply stated, the law provides that a secured creditor will be entitled to seize the car from the buyer only if the security interest has been registered in a public registry. Buyers can protect themselves by searching the public registry before acquiring their interests. The PPSA also applies to certain types of leases of personal property, since the problem of third-person protection arises in the same way under leasing transactions.

The importance of the Personal Property Security Act can be appreciated only in a historical context. Until its enactment, personal property security law in Canadian common law provinces was a complex mixture of English law and laws influenced by legal and commercial developments in the eastern states of the USA. By the early 1920s Saskatchewan had developed a functionally adequate, but conceptually inconsistent, system of secured financing law. Each type of financing transaction was addressed in a separate statute, and each statute provided for the registration of the secured creditor's interest in a public registry. Little care had been taken to provide consistency of approach among these statutes; registration requirements were complex and often not met.

The first important move toward modernizing the secured financing law of Saskatchewan came in the 1950s when the decision was made to centralize registration of conditional sales contracts, chattel mortgages and assignment of book debtors rather than to have these transactions registered on a regional basis in court houses throughout the province. However, one of the major difficulties with the central registry for security interests was that registration involved the filing of paper copies of the financing transactions: this resulted in the need to store large volumes of paper and guard against the risk of loss through fire. Starting in the 1950s, the volume of registrations dramatically increased as a result of the expanded use of consumer and agricultural credit to acquire motor vehicles and agricultural equipment. Since registration of transactions and searches of the central registry had to be carried out manually, an ever-increasing number of registry clerks was required to provide the minimally acceptable level of service for persons using the system.

A study of the central registry by the Department of the Attorney General in the early 1970s led to the conclusion that the manual system of registration would soon break down or become prohibitively expensive to operate. By that time, it took several weeks to get confirmation of a registration or to obtain a search from the registry. Fortunately, computerization of records was becoming feasible, and attention was directed towards use of this technology to address the problem. Coincident with the study of the central registry, the Saskatchewan Law Reform Commission undertook a project designed to reform and modernize not only the registry, but also the entire legal infrastructure for secured financing law. The Commission prepared reports containing recommendations and draft legislation for a Personal Property Security Act that would provide a new law for all secured-financing transactions involving personal property, and a modern, computerized notice registry system. The proposals contained in the Law Reform Commission Act were inspired by legislation implemented in the 1970s in Ontario and Manitoba, which in turn was patterned on legislation in the United States. However, the Personal Property Security Act proposed by the Commission contained many novel features which at the time were viewed as radical. The draft law proposed by the Commission was enacted as the Personal Property Security Act, 1979–80, c. P-6.2.

The registry system that was established under the 1980 Act and modified under the 1993 Act employed the most up-to-date technology. All records are now kept in electronic form rather than as paper documents. Secured parties may register their security interests on-line and obtain electronic searches of the registry data base. The Information Services Corporation, the Crown corporation that now operates the Personal Property Security Registry, is currently planning further modernization of the system in light of technological developments that have occurred in recent years.

While the Saskatchewan Personal Property Security Act is not unique, the "novel" features contained in the 1980 Act and refined in the 1993 Act have influenced developments well beyond the borders of the province or of Canada. During the 1990s the Personal Property Security Act, 1993 provided a model for development of similar laws in all other common law jurisdiction in Canada except Ontario. The measures that were considered radical in 1980 became basic features of the Personal Property Security Acts of other provinces. Some of them were included in the Ontario Personal Property Security Act, 1989. The Saskatchewan Act was the basis for

the New Zealand Personal Property Securities Act enacted in 1999, and for recommendations put forward in 2004 by the Law Commission for modernizing the secured-financing law of England and Wales. *Ronald C.C. Cuming*

PETER BALLANTYNE CREE FIRST NATION. This band signed **TREATY 6** on February 11, 1889, under the Lac La Ronge Indian Band. It has a number of reserve sites, the most populated of which is Pelican Narrows (184B). The total land base consists of 27,920.4 ha, all of which is located within 100 km of Flin Flon, Manitoba—except for Southend/Reindeer Lake, 200 km northwest of Flin Flon, and property in the city of Prince Albert. The economic base consists of fishing, forestry, trapping, and commercial developments, and the infrastructure includes a band office, warehouse, schools, fire hall, senior citizens home, arena, gymnasium, greenhouse, administration building, health clinic, health staff residences, and other maintenance buildings. Of the 7,535 band members, 3,647 live on reserve. *Christian Thompson*

PETER CHAPMAN FIRST NATION. The Peter Chapman and James Smith Bands were amalgamated as the James Smith Band in 1902, and the boundaries of James Smith Reserve were adjusted to accommodate the increased band membership. In May 1990 the James Smith Cree Nation requested that the Indian Claims Commission conduct a claim by descendants of the Peter Chapman Band in relation to the taking of their reserve and its subsequent sale. The Peter Chapman claim was rejected in 1998, and a request to the Commission to conduct an inquiry into the validity of the 1902 surrender has not been completed. As with the Chakastapaysin Band, the Peter Chapman Band is recognized at some level by governmental offices, but has not been re-established as a band independent from James Smith. *Christian Thompson*

DOUG CHISHOLM PHOTO
Peter Pond Lake.

PETER POND LAKE (55°55'N; 108°44'W; Map sheet 73 N/15). Peter Pond Lake is located in west-central Saskatchewan, southwest of the Shield margin. Covering 778 sq. km. and elevated at 421 m, it is fed from the southwest by the Dillon River (known in Dene as *Ayjere Deszay*, "Buffalo River") and from the northwest by the Methy River. The lake is divided into two parts: Big Peter Pond and Little Peter Pond, separated by a narrows. Little Peter Pond Lake discharges into Churchill Lake and ultimately the Churchill River via the Kisis Channel. The village of Buffalo Narrows (pop. 1,137) is located on Highway 155 between the two lakes. Previously known as Big Buffalo and Little Buffalo Lakes, the lakes are described by **PETER POND** on his 1785 map of North America as "Beef Lake." Besides Buffalo Narrows, there are two hamlets on the lakeshore: Dillon, at the mouth of the Dillon River, and Michel on the west shore. The lakes were renamed in honour of Peter Pond, who in 1778 traveled from the **CHURCHILL RIVER** via "Beef Lake" and Methy Portage to the **CLEARWATER** and Athabasca Rivers. Old Fort Point on the west bank is a reminder of a North-West Company trader who over-wintered there in 1790–91. *Marilyn Lewry*

FURTHER READING: Kupsch, W.O. 1954. "Bituminous Sands in Till of the Peter Pond Lake Area." Department of Mineral Resources Report #12; Marchildon G. and S. Robinson. 2002. *Canoeing the Churchill.* Regina: Canadian Plains Research Center.

PETERS, EARL (1910–93). Earl Peters, who farmed in the Laird area north of Saskatoon, contributed his efforts towards the diversification of Saskatchewan agriculture. He worked closely with researchers at the **UNIVERSITY OF SASKATCHEWAN** and Agriculture Canada in crop development and new cropping methods to promote **SOIL CONSERVATION.** Using his own financial resources, he was among the first to experiment with winter **WHEAT, CANOLA**

and **PULSE CROPS** such as peas, lentils, faba beans, and broad beans. In 1976 he co-founded the Saskatchewan Pulse Crop Growers Association to promote production and marketing of edible legumes, and served as the association's first president. Earl Peters also served on the Laird council for thirteen years, ten of them as mayor. During his tenure, he was responsible for major improvements to the village; he was also a leader in the Carlton Branch Line Rail Retention committee and in the local Lutheran church.

PETIT, CLAUDE (1935–). A distinguished serviceman and athlete, Claude Petit has memorialized the contributions of **ABORIGINAL VETERANS** and is considered a role model for the Native community. Born in Duck Lake on October 1, 1935, Petit served as a paratrooper with the Canadian Armed Forces for sixteen years. He was instrumental in creating a monument to Aboriginal veterans in Ottawa as well as an Aboriginal Veterans Millennium Medal. Petit also founded the Western Canadian Native Minor Hockey Championship in Saskatoon and served as president of the Saskatchewan Boxing Association for nine years. For twenty-three years, he organized Back-to-Batoche, a Métis celebration that he also helped establish. Petit received the Order of Canada in 1998 and was awarded the Saskatchewan Order of Merit in 2002.

PETTERSON, IDA M. (1912–99). Ida M. Petterson (Strom) was an Estevan businesswoman and community leader who became the first woman to serve as mayor of a Saskatchewan city. Born near Lake Alma, March 30, 1912, she was educated in local schools. In 1929 she married Knute Petterson, a farmer; they had four children. After some difficult years on the farm, she started a grocery store in Estevan that was converted in 1963 to a self-serve laundry. In 1964, Ida Petterson became a life insurance underwriter; by 1967 she was the top salesperson in Saskatchewan for Family Life.

In 1960 Petterson became the first woman to be elected to the Estevan city council, remaining on it for six years. She sat on every council committee, and worked for a new city library building and the Estevan Regional Nursing Home. In 1968 she unsuccessfully ran for mayor. In 1970, she again ran, and was elected, thereby becoming the first Saskatchewan woman to serve as mayor. Re-elected for a second term, she was defeated in 1976. Improvements made during her mayoralty included a new city hall, water and sewer upgrades, more paved streets, new curling rink, and underground sprinkler systems in parks. Despite numerous infrastructural improvements, the city's debt load was reduced by about one-third by the end of her two terms. In 1992, she received the Saskatchewan Order of Merit. She died in Estevan, February 22, 1999. *Lisa Dale-Burnett*

PETTICK, JOSEPH (1924–). Joseph Pettick has been in practice as an architect in Saskatchewan for more than 50 years. The highlights of his career include the design of several of Regina's tall buildings: the Saskatchewan Power Corporation (1963), the Saskatchewan Government Insurance (1974), the Regina City Hall (1976), and the Bank of Montreal (1981). Born in Hungary, he immigrated to Canada as a child with his mother, joining his father on a farm in the Kipling area. The family relocated to Regina during the **DEPRESSION**, and when **WORLD WAR II** broke out Joseph joined the navy as a stoker first class, working on a frigate. On his discharge, he began an apprenticeship with the Regina architectural firm, Portnall and Stock, receiving professional accreditation in 1954. During this time, he achieved the position of associate and chief draftsman, but was unable to participate in design work, which was regularly given to architects with academic credentials. To rectify this situation, he spent a year studying at the University of Oklahoma in Norman with renowned American expressionist architect Bruce Goff, and with Mendel Glickman, engineer for several of Frank Lloyd Wright's major works. When Pettick returned to Regina in 1955, Portnall and Stock offered him a partnership and the prospect of heading a branch office in Saskatoon, which he declined in favour of starting his own firm. In 1956, after a chance meeting with David Cass-Beggs, general manager of the **SASKATCHEWAN POWER CORPORATION**, he was offered the job to start preliminary studies of the program, location and design of the company's new head office in Regina. Pettick was granted an honorary doctor of laws from the University of Regina in 2005. *Bernard Flaman*

PEZER, VERA (1939–). Vera Pezer is well known for her contributions in sports and her administrative career at the **UNIVERSITY OF SASKATCHEWAN**. Born on January 13, 1939, she was raised in Meskanaw. Her academic degrees are from the University of Saskatchewan: BA in English (1962); MA in Psychology (1964); and PhD in sports psychology (1977). In 2001 she retired from a 35-year career there that began in student counseling in 1966 and focused upon student relations. Numerous administrative positions included a ten-year stint as Associate Vice-President, Student Affairs and Services. Outstanding in sports, Pezer led the Saskatoon Imperials to national fastball championships in 1969 and 1970. She is also a golfer, but is primarily known in curling. Pezer skipped her rink to three consecutive Canadian Ladies Curling Championships, from 1971 to 1973, a record that still stands. Her team is in the Canadian Curling Hall of Fame, and provincial and Saskatoon Sports Halls of Fame. Pezer also coached the Canadian Junior Curling Championship rink in 1975, and has been

JEFF VINNICK PHOTO/SASKATCHEWAN ARCHIVES BOARD
S-SP-A19532-5, SASKATOON STARPHOENIX FONDS

Vera Pezer, December 1982.

the sports psychologist for the Canadian curling team at two Olympic Games. In 2003 she published *The Stone Age: A Social History of Curling on the Prairies*. She has served on a numerous (mainly sports-related) boards–local, provincial, and national. She has won many awards, and an award for student volunteers was named after her. Pezer lives in Saskatoon. *Bob Ivanochko*

FURTHER READING: Saskatoon Business and Professional Women's Club. 1976. *Some Outstanding Women: They Made Saskatoon a Better Community.*

PHEASANT'S RUMP NAKOTA FIRST NATION. The Pheasant's Rump Nakota Reserve is located 10 km northwest of Kisbey and incorporates 7,966.5 ha of farmland, rolling hills, ravines, bush, and ponds. An adhesion to **TREATY 4** was signed in 1876, and a reserve was granted in 1881. Agricultural development was hindered by a series of droughts and early frosts, but in 1887 samples of the band's produce won many prizes at the Cannington and Carlyle fairs. The Pheasant's Rump people entered the 1890s supplementing their income by freighting for settlers, cutting and selling cordwood, hauling timber, selling lime from their kiln, and making plough beams, sleds and collars. In 1898 Inspector Alex McGibbon was authorized to obtain a surrender of the Pheasant's Rump Reserve through Section 39 of the Indian Act, and in 1901 the band was amalgamated onto the White Bear Reserve. In 1986 a Land Settlement Agreement was signed between the federal government and the descendants of the original band, who in 1990 were again recognized as a band. In 1992 land purchased under the Agreement was granted reserve status. In 2004 there were 343 registered band members, 149 of whom lived on reserve. *Christian Thompson*

PHELPS, JOSEPH (1899–1983). Born in Ontario on August 12, 1899, Joseph Phelps accompanied his family to the Wilkie area of Saskatchewan in 1909. Phelps began farming at an early age, and at seventeen became a Saskatchewan Grain Growers Association district director. His interest in politics continued as he participated in the founding of the Saskatchewan Farm-Labour Party in 1932. He also joined the CO-OPERATIVE COMMONWEALTH FEDERATION (CCF) party, and successfully ran in the Saltcoats constituency in the 1938 provincial election. Phelps again won in Saltcoats in 1944, when the CCF came to power. Premier T.C. DOUGLAS appointed Phelps as his Minister of Natural Resources and Industrial Development; in that position, Phelps played a leading role in creating numerous new and controversial CROWN CORPORATIONS. He also oversaw reorganization of the SASKATCHEWAN POWER CORPORATION and early rural electrification. Northern Saskatchewan, where CCF interventions in fish, fur, forestry, and retailing created controversy, occupied much of Phelps' attention. Following electoral defeat in 1948, Phelps devoted energy to developing the WESTERN DEVELOPMENT MUSEUM; and from 1949 to 1954, he served as president of the SASKATCHEWAN FARMERS UNION, the successor to the United Farmers of Canada (Saskatchewan Section), which flourished under his leadership. During the 1950s, he also sat on the provincial Royal Commission on Agriculture and Rural Life, and issued a dissenting minority report when the commission reported. Phelps remained active until his death on March 15, 1983.   *David M. Quiring*

FURTHER READING: Archer, J.H. 1980. *Saskatchewan: A History*. Saskatoon: Western Producer Prairie Books; Quiring, D. 2004. *CCF Colonialism in Northern Saskatchewan. Battling Parish Priests, Bootleggers, and Fur Sharks*. Vancouver: UBC Press.

PHILLIPS, R.H.D. (BOB) (1921–). Bob Phillips, born on December 3, 1921, in Regina, started post-secondary education at Regina College and, after an interruption during WORLD WAR II, completed a BA in economics and political science at the UNIVERSITY OF SASKATCHEWAN. He gravitated to journalism almost immediately, working for Canadian Press, the *Leader-Post*, and for three years in the 1950s for United Press International in London, England. In 1960, he joined the SASKATCHEWAN WHEAT POOL as an economist and director of research, organizing a research staff and becoming embroiled in some of the major agricultural and economic issues of the day. For thirteen years, until his retirement in 1986, he was the publisher of the *Western Producer*, a weekly newspaper concerned with prairie agriculture. He also built Western Producer Prairie Books into a significant publishing company, and oversaw the expansion of Modern Press into Saskatchewan's second largest printer. Along the way, he wrote a weekly column and published two books: *Western People* and *People and Places*. Phillips has been involved in many community groups, including

active work in the Presbyterian Church and the universities in Saskatoon and Regina. Honours include: honorary Doctor of Laws from the UNIVERSITY OF REGINA (1988); Citizen of the Century award from the city of Saskatoon (1989); Fellow of the Agricultural Institute of Canada (1989); honorary life member, Saskatchewan Institute of Agrologists (1990); meritorious service award, Nutana Branch of the Royal Canadian Legion (2000); and Member of the Order of Canada (2002). Since 1986, he has been partner and principal, with his wife Tanyss (Bell) Phillips, of Bell Phillips Communications Inc. of Saskatoon, a family-owned publishing company.

Barry Wilson

PHILLIPS, ROGER (1939–). Born in Ottawa on December 17, 1939, and trained as a physicist, Roger Phillips' foresight and creativity transformed Saskatchewan-based IPSCO into an international leader in steel production. As chief executive officer beginning in 1982, Phillips initiated an ambitious modernization project of IPSCO's Regina facilities and subsequently opened two large steelworks in the United States. During his tenure as CEO, Phillips built IPSCO into one of North America's most efficient, safe, and environmentally conscious steel producers. Beside his business interests, Mr. Phillips was active in organizations like the Council of Canadian Unity, Saskatchewan Chamber of Commerce, and Economic Council of Canada. He was invested as an Officer of the Order of Canada in 1999 and received the Saskatchewan Order of Merit in 2002.

PHILOM BIOS INC. Incorporated in 1980, Philom Bios develops, manufactures and markets microbial products that improve crop productivity. Founders JOHN CROSS, George Khachatourians and John Schaw saw the opportunity to help farmers grow better crops and be more profitable as they faced increasing competition in the agricultural marketplace. An unsuccessful attempt to raise capital in 1982 left the company with considerable debt, but an investment through the Canadian Immigrant Investor Program enabled an active research program to begin. The first fermentation research initiative was at the National Research Council–then called the Division of Biological Sciences–in Ottawa; the research and development program was later expanded and relocated to the Plant Biotechnology Institute in Saskatoon, and to the Agriculture Canada Lethbridge Research Station. Today all corporate, research, manufacturing and marketing activities are centred in Saskatoon. Philom Bios has three main products. JumpStart, the world's first commercial PHOSPHATE INOCULANT, improves phosphate fertility efficiency in essentially all crops; the active ingredient, penicillium bilaii (a naturally occurring soil fungus), was discovered and patented by Agriculture and Agri-food Canada in Lethbridge,

Alberta and licensed for commercialising to the Plant Biotechnology Institute in Saskatoon in 1986. TagTeam, the world's first combination phosphate and nitrogen inoculant for pulse crops, won the 1998 Canadian Agricultural Marketing Association Award for the best direct marketing campaign as well as the 1998 ABEX Award for Saskatchewan New Product Award. N-Prove is a nitrogen inoculant for pulse crops. Philom Bios is the only Canadian-owned company supplying high value inoculants to prairie farmers. With a multidisciplinary staff of fifty-five, the company generated annual sales of approximately $10 million in 2003. In 2002, Philom Bios received three SABEX Awards: for Marketing, Growth and Expansion, and Business of the Year.

Tara L. Procyshyn

PHOSPHATE INOCULANT. The world's first phosphate inoculant, discovered by scientists working at the Agriculture and Agri-Food Canada research facility in Lethbridge, Alberta, was refined in a Saskatoon laboratory and marketed under the brand name of JumpStart. PHILOM BIOS was established in 1981 to collaborate with the federal agriculture research scientists and then commercialize the phosphate inoculant for use by farmers. An inoculant is a live micro-organism which, when added to the soil or applied to the seed, gives growing plants access to important nutrients like nitrogen and phosphate. Field tests by Philom Bios have shown an average yield increase of about $9.81 more profit per acre on cereal grains, oilseeds and pulses; in 2003, this translated into a $30 million increase in net profit for prairie farmers. JumpStart, a safe method of supplying phosphate to growing plants, reduces the need to place high rates of fertilizer phosphate near sensitive seeds such as CANOLA, peas, and lentils. The active ingredient in JumpStart is the naturally occurring soil fungus *Penicillium bilaii*, which grows on plant roots and makes less available forms of residual soil phosphate immediately available for crop use.   *Joe Ralko*

PIAPOT (1816–1908). Piapot (Payepot) was born to a CREE mother and an ASSINIBOINE father in 1816; shortly after his birth his parents died of smallpox. When he was a small boy, he and his grandmother were captured by a band of Sioux, with whom he lived for the next fourteen years until he was rescued by a Cree war party. In 1830 Piapot became chief. He would lead his people in the last major inter-tribal engagement between the Cree and the Blackfoot on the Oldman River in 1870. After this last battle Piapot made his home in the QU'APPELLE VALLEY. In 1874, when TREATY 4 was negotiated, Piapot was not present: he was away hunting, and as a result did not learn of the negotiation until after it had been signed. In 1875 he met with Treaty Commissioner William Christie, and

EDMUND MORRIS PAINTING/COURTESY OF THE LEGISLATIVE BUILDING ART COLLECTION

Chief Piapot.

after seeking guarantees that he would receive farm instructors, mills, more tools, and medical assistance, he signed an adhesion to Treaty 4. However many of the terms Piapot believed he had negotiated would not appear until **TREATY 6** in 1876.

Piapot was part of a group of chiefs who wanted a large reservation surveyed for them in the **CYPRESS HILLS** area. Canada, however, feared the concentration of a large Indian population in one area, and refused. As a result, Piapot was eventually forced to select a home in the Qu'Appelle Valley, where a reserve of fifty-four square miles was surveyed—well short of the 110 square miles his band was entitled to under the Treaty. Throughout the rest of his life Piapot continually challenged the Canadian government by holding ceremonies and by fighting to have Treaty rights recognized. He died on his reserve in 1908. *Rob Nestor*

PIAPOT CREE FIRST NATION. Chief **PIAPOT** (Payepot) signed an adhesion to **TREATY 4** on September 9, 1875, originally seeking a reserve in the **CYPRESS HILLS** region. After much persuasion he settled on a reserve bordering the Carry the Kettle Reserve in August 1883. Following a disastrous winter in which many of his people died, he abandoned that reserve and was permitted to select a new one 29 km north and 11 km east of Regina in September 1884. Officials deposed Piapot following an unlawfully held **SUN DANCE**; but on the day that the Order-in-Council was passed he died, after asserting his autonomy and demonstrating he would not be controlled. The band's main economic base is agriculture, and the community's infrastructure includes a band office, recreation centre, fire hall, arena, elementary and high schools, day care, medical clinic, outdoor rink, and a gas bar that includes a

restaurant, laundromat, pool hall/arcade and convenience store. Currently the band has 1,935 registered members, 550 of whom live on the reserve. The band controls 21,617.9 ha of land, with additional shares in the 37 hectares comprising the Treaty 4 Reserve Grounds adjacent to Fort Qu'Appelle. *Christian Thompson*

PIC INVESTMENT GROUP INC. A small chemical distribution company founded in 1976 with one supplier and four distribution lines, PIC Investment Group Inc. has grown into a $100-million business with divisions ranging from exporting alfalfa to Asia to operating resorts in northern Saskatchewan. The original corporation, Prairie Industrial Chemicals Ltd., was founded by Jim Yuel and increased its sales to $5 million within the first four years, establishing branch offices and warehouses throughout the prairies. By 1991, the company had diversified into chemical packaging, chemical manufacturing, transportation, import and export and property management with combined sales exceeding $26 million.

A major reorganization created several separate companies, each with a core business. Ownership of the new operating companies remained in the hands of Prairie Industrial Chemicals Inc.; a corporate name change took place creating PIC Investment Group Inc. to more realistically reflect the new mandate of the parent company. Since the restructuring, PIC Investment has facilitated many acquisitions, invested in several emerging businesses and financed internal growth within the original companies. ClearTech Industries, Caron Transportation Systems, Panther Industries, Hydor-Tech Limited, Round Table Management, PIC Flight Services and Adventure Destinations International (ADI), established in 2003, comprise the PIC Investment portfolio of companies. Adventure Destinations properties include Thompson's Camps and Twin Falls Lodge, formerly named Beyond La Ronge Lodge, which are located on the **CHURCHILL RIVER** system. Jim Yuel was recognized for his entrepreneurial efforts by being inducted in 2004 into the Saskatchewan Chamber of Commerce Hall of Fame. *Joe Ralko*

PILOT BUTTE, town, pop 1,850, located just E of Regina between Hwys 1 and 46. The community's name is derived from an area hill, which had long been used as a lookout point. With the construction of the railway through the region in 1882, the area's sand and gravel deposits were extensively utilized, and in the following years, as settlers began farming in the district, Pilot Butte developed. Brickyards became major local employers; within several years the community boasted a number of businesses and churches, and a school. The brickyards closed during **WORLD WAR I**, however, and with automobiles facilitating easy transportation into Regina, Pilot

Butte began to lose its population—a trend that would continue for years. In 1923, the village was disbanded owing to the loss of residents. After the new **TRANS-CANADA HIGHWAY** was completed in the late 1950s, living in Pilot Butte began to become a popular option for those who wanted to commute to work in the city. Pilot Butte re-acquired village status in 1963; in 1966 the population was 405; but between 1976 and 1981, the community's numbers jumped from 585 to 1,255. Although Pilot Butte is largely a bedroom community, its growth has spurred the development of recreational facilities and essential business services, particularly home-based enterprises. Other than a couple of houses, there are virtually no reminders of the community's formative years, as most early structures have been destroyed. In 1995, a severe storm struck the community, damaging most of the modern homes. *David McLennan*

PINDER, ROSS (1918–2004). Born on January 21, 1918, one of Saskatoon's most respected entrepreneurs, Ross Pinder received his license in pharmacy from the **UNIVERSITY OF SASKATCHEWAN** in 1939. Pinder's career in pharmacy was interrupted by **WORLD WAR II**, and after serving in the Royal Canadian Army Medical Corps, he rejoined Pinder's Drugs as its president. Until his retirement in 1990, Ross Pinder oversaw the expansion of the family business from three drugstores in Saskatoon to twenty-three, including branches in Regina and Calgary. Active in Saskatoon community affairs, Pinder was a founding member of the Canadian Corps of Commissionaires and the United Way, and served on the board of St. Paul's Hospital. He received the Saskatchewan Order of Merit in 1997. He died on July 10, 2004.

PINDER FAMILY. Through four generations, the Pinder family of Saskatoon has held a prominent place in Saskatchewan business. Abraham Pinder was the first generation of Pinders to arrive in Saskatoon. After emigrating from Yorkshire, England, Abraham spent thirty-five years in North Toronto before moving west in 1912 to Saskatoon, where he established himself as a successful contractor. His son, Robert Mitford Pinder (1891–1946), arrived in Saskatoon in 1914 after graduating from the Pharmacy College in Winnipeg. Robert found work with the Saskatoon Drug and Stationary Company and, through his entrepreneurial ambition, quickly climbed the company ranks from employee to store manager to part-owner. Although much of Robert's time was devoted to his business interests in retail pharmacy, he was actively involved in community affairs, serving Saskatoon as an alderman from 1928 to 1933 and as mayor from 1935 to 1938. Robert passed away in 1946, leaving to his family the foundation for what would become one of Saskatchewan's best-known family businesses, Pinder's Drugs. His two sons, Robert Ross and Herb Sr., took control of the three-store family business, and through several decades expanded it to a twenty-store retail chain in Saskatoon, Regina, and Calgary. Herb Sr. was an active member in the business community. He developed Saskatoon's first retail shopping centre and established Saskatchewan's first oil-drilling firm. In 1964, he became Minister of Industry and Commerce under ROSS THATCHER's Liberal government. The Pinder's Drugs chain was entrusted to a third generation of Pinders when Herb Sr.'s eldest son, Herb Jr., rose to the helm as company president. In 1992, the Pinders sold their family business to Shoppers Drug Mart, ending thus more than seventy-five years in the pharmacy business.   *Iain Stewart*

FURTHER READING: Moen, K. 2002. "Representation Above Board," *Saskatchewan Business* 23: 15–16.

PINE, GRACE DAVIS (1910–2002).

A selfless volunteer from Saskatoon, Grace Davis Pine's devotion to numerous worthy causes earned her the Order of Canada in 1997. Born on January 12, 1910, and a graduate of the UNIVERSITY OF SASKATCHEWAN, Pine worked at the Saskatoon Sanitarium laboratory until 1973. Meanwhile, she helped children in developing nations through her work with Save the Children. Pine founded the Saskatoon chapter of the organization in 1967 and occupied various posts at regional and national levels. She devoted her time to peace organizations, environmental groups and cultural associations including the SASKATOON SYMPHONY, MENDEL ART GALLERY, and WESTERN DEVELOPMENT MUSEUM. Grace Pine died on June 22, 2002.

PINELAND CO-OPERATIVE STRIKE.

The longest active strike in the history of Saskatchewan and among the top ten for Canada, this strike began on June 7, 1985, and carried on until December 13, 1993, when a new agreement was finally reached. The small retail store in Nipawin with approximately fifty workers became the focal point in the province for the many problems encountered by part-time workers in the retail and service sector. Health and welfare benefits and the assignment of hours on the basis of seniority were the main issues that held this unit together for such a long period of time. The Pineland Co-op was organized by the RETAIL, WHOLESALE AND DEPARTMENT STORE UNION (RWDSU) in the early 1970s, and this local had never engaged in a dispute before 1985. Retail co-operatives and their parent, FEDERATED CO-OPERATIVES, had once led the way in wages and benefits for employees, but by the 1980s that had changed: co-operatives succumbed to the corporate mentality of hiring part-time workers, who were primarily women with no benefits or guarantee of hours.

The RWDSU's Retail Co-operative Division levied a $5 per member assessment to assist picketers, and the SASKATCHEWAN FEDERATION OF LABOUR imposed a boycott on all RWDSU-certified Co-ops as well as on the many that were not unionized. Over the years, there were frequent busloads of supporters who made the long trip and spent a Saturday on the line in this northeastern community. During the course of the strike, many other bargaining units in the retail sector achieved some success in securing the same bargaining objectives for part-time workers. Nipawin Co-op employees were finally victorious, and secured what up to then was one of the best agreements ever reached, guaranteeing most available hours and part-time benefits. Only five picketers went back to work after the strike in positions they had requested; but they had to work alongside scabs who had been hired during the lengthy struggle. The union decertified a year and a half later in a close vote. In the mid-1990s the provincial government did pass legislation addressing some of the issues concerning part-time benefits; it also legislated a "most available hours" provision, but government members have thus far refused to proclaim it.   *Paul Guillet*

PINK, WILLIAM (FL. 1766–70).

Between 1754 and 1774, the Hudson's Bay Company sent men inland to winter with the CREE on the northern plains in order to persuade them to trade at York Factory. Most of these men being illiterate, their travels are unknown. Consequently, the four journals of William Pink, although poorly written, are valuable for our understanding of Cree life. Pink's 1766–67 journal is brief and vague. He was taken inland by Mou'sin'ni'ki'sick, a Cree leader, perhaps to the Eagle Hills. His next three journals are more detailed, though still poorly written. Each year the group returned from trading at Hudson Bay and left their canoes at the post ruins at Fort à la Corne. In 1767 and 1768 they walked overland north of the NORTH SASKATCHEWAN RIVER to eastern Alberta. In 1779 they went more directly west, through the Eagle Hills and onwards to Manitou Lake. After returning to York Factory in the summer of 1770, Pink left for England. Pink's life has not been studied, and his journals remain unpublished. He was the first to fully describe a BISON pound and how wolves were snared, and to identify the Blackfoot and Blood tribes whom he met west of Manitou Lake. He also first recorded the Cree names for Turtle Lake, Red Deer (modern Monnery) River, Frog Lake Creek, Beaver River, and Battle River.   *Dale Russell*

FURTHER READING: Russell, D. 1991. *Eighteenth-Century Western Cree and their Neighbours.* Archaeological Survey of Canada Mercury Series, Paper 143. Ottawa: Canadian Museum of Civilization.

PINSONNEAULT, ROLAND A. (1913–2002).

Born in St-Cyprien de Napierville, Quebec, on September 22, 1913, Roland Pinsonneault came to Saskatchewan at an early age and spent his lifetime promoting the French language and culture. Beginning in the 1930s, Pinsonneault farmed east of Gravelbourg and soon became involved in the SASKATCHEWAN WHEAT POOL, the ASSOCIATION CULTURELLE FRANCO-CANADIENNE, and COLLEGE MATHIEU. A founding member and president of *la Cooperative des publications fransaskoises*, he played an important role in the revival of *l'Eau Vive*, the only Francophone weekly newspaper in the province. Pinsonneault was awarded an honourary doctorate from the UNIVERSITY OF REGINA and was the first recipient of the *Ordre de la Fidelité Française du Conseil de la vie française*. He was invested in the Order of Canada in 2000. Pinsonneault died on March 2, 2002.

PIONEER GRAIN COMPANY.

The Richardson family has been synonymous with the grain industry in western Canada from the early days of settlement to the present. James Richardson came to Canada from Ireland in 1823. He started in Kingston, Ontario with a tailor shop, and when he took payment in grain, he was forced into the grain business. He gave up his tailor shop, and with his two sons formed James Richardson and Sons in 1857. He built his first elevator at Kingston in 1882, and another at Neepawa, Manitoba in 1890. James Richardson was to arrange the first shipment of wheat from western Canada through the lake system to Liverpool, England in 1883. In 1913 the Richardsons formed two subsidiaries, Pioneer Grain Company Ltd. and Eastern Terminals Ltd. By then the company had twenty-six licenced elevators, sixteen of which were in Saskatchewan. By 1921, Pioneer had expanded to over 100 country elevators. In 1931, forty-four elevators of the Saskatchewan and Western Elevator companies were amalgamated into Pioneer; these elevators had been operated by the Richardsons since the mid-1920s. In 1947 Pioneer acquired twenty-three elevators from the failed Reliance Grain Company. In 1952 it purchased 146 elevators when the Western Grain Elevator Company was sold; Federal Grain also took some of Western's elevators. In 1953, Pioneer acquired another twenty-two elevators of the Independent line. When Federal was sold in 1972, Pioneer became the largest private grain company.

The Richardsons always had strong interests in grain terminals. After leasing terminal space for several years, in 1917 they built a terminal at Port Arthur with a capacity of two million bushels; over the years they added capacity, until in 1974 this terminal had a capacity of 7.7 million bushels. The Richardsons partnered with Federal Grain to form Westland Elevator Ltd. in order to purchase the 7.5

million-bushel terminal at Fort William. It was sold to the Pools in 1972 along with the Federal sale. On the West Coast they became one-third owners with Federal and Searle of a 1.5 million-bushel terminal in North Vancouver; the Richardsons became sole owner of this terminal in 1972. This terminal suffered an explosion and fire in 1975, and was rebuilt and expanded to four million bushels; its name was changed from Burrard Terminal Ltd. to Pioneer Grain Terminals Ltd. In 1961, the Richardsons became part owner of a five million-bushel terminal on the St. Lawrence at Sorel, Quebec.

Pioneer is a diversified company: Pioneer Chemical Division, for example, was established in 1947. It was not directly involved in overseas selling until it acquired Whitson, Neilson and Francis of London as a wholly owned Richardson subsidiary. In 1927, James Richardson and Sons Limited created the largest privately owned investment and commodity dealer in the country, which became Richardson Greenshields of Canada Limited in 1982. The firm had seventy offices worldwide; it was purchased by a major Canadian bank in 1996. Today, Richardson Financial Group Ltd. is the financial arm of the company and invests in Canadian companies outside of Pioneer's main core business. The company is also involved in real estate, pipeline construction, shipping, fuel oil distribution and manufacturing, and air transportation: Tundra Oil and Gas Ltd. has wells and pipelines in the Williston Basin; Lombard Reality Limited is responsible for the company's real estate interests; and their feed and fertilizer division is represented by Topnotch Feeds Ltd. and Topnotch Nutri Ltd. In 1999 the company purchased Canbra Foods Limited, which is located at Lethbridge and processes canola to produce margarine and other vegetable oil products.

The company has always been headed by a Richardson. James Richardson, who died in 1892, was succeeded by his son George. When George died in 1906, his brother Henry became president; and when the latter died in 1918, George's son James became president. Upon George's death his wife Muriel served as president until 1966, when she was replaced by her son George. The latter's son, Hartley T. Richardson, became president in 1983—the seventh family president of James Richardson and Sons.

Gary Storey

FURTHER READING: Anderson, C.W. 1991. *Grain: The Entrepreneurs*. Winnipeg: Watson and Dwyer Publishing; Fowke, V. 1957. *The National Policy and the Wheat Economy*. Toronto: University of Toronto Press; Wilson, C.F. 1978. *A Century of Canadian Grain*. Saskatoon: Western Producer Prairie Books.

PIONEERS. The transition of the Canadian West from native prairie and parkland to a surveyed, fenced, and densely populated agricultural economy

PHOTO COURTESY OF THE UNITY AND DISTRICT HERITAGE MUSEUM

William Kutz's "sod house" homestead at or near Unity, Saskatchewan. The sod house was built in 1907.

occurred in a remarkably short period of time. The resulting clash of cultures, ideologies, languages, politics, and ways of life has reverberated through and defined much of the first century of Saskatchewan's history. Both the myth and the reality of pioneer life, including all its variations and its reckoning of winners and losers, come to shape a part of the provincial identity. Pioneering in Saskatchewan involves the essentially agricultural concept of breaking the land, growing crops and building farms—and by extension, concentric circles of settlement: communities (roads, schools, halls, clubs, health care facilities and other services), municipalities, and eventually a provincial identity. The physical, emotional, and social demands of this concept were different in each area of the province, depending on the environment (grassland, parkland, or forest fringe) and the ethnic makeup of each community. As a result, the pioneering stage of each area came earlier or later depending on immigration and **ETHNIC BLOC SETTLEMENT** patterns, railway, and homestead development. The earliest homesteads on the open grasslands of southeastern Saskatchewan were developed as much as fifty years ahead of the pioneering phase of the forest fringe and bush land north of the **NORTH SASKATCHEWAN RIVER** during the 1920s and 1930s. Changes in agricultural techniques and implements, transportation, political infrastructure and social arrangements combined with geographic issues to produce unique pioneering experiences across the province.

Deconstructing the pioneer experience is a complex undertaking. First and foremost is the need to recount the realities of pioneer life. Stories of isolation, loneliness, brutal climatic extremes, and unbearably hard work are commonplace. At the same time, stories about devastation and setbacks,

racism, starvation and death are intertwined with stories of co-operating and community building, community spirit, local culture, recreation, arts, music, dance, fairs and merriment. Taking the homestead bet and breaking land, sometimes hundreds of miles from established cities or railheads, meant that pioneers had to rely on their own resources. Everything from food, shelter, and clothing to medical and spiritual needs, economic interests, social and cultural activities had to be created using the tools at hand. However, common experiences were evident, despite differences of race, gender or ethnicity. These experiences necessitated a spirit of neighbourliness and community creation, as people worked together towards common goals or helped each other in times of stress and hardship. This dual narrative of the pioneer life—hard times, but good times—is instantly recognizable and has led to the creation of an archetypical pioneer figure in popular culture.

This pioneer myth is a universal figure with identifiable characteristics. Words such as rugged, stalwart, honest, hardworking, entrepreneurial, moral, hopeful, resourceful, and visionary are used to describe a pioneer. It is an inclusive and encompassing myth, as most people can find a pioneer within their genealogical heritage. Moreover, it has been popularly used to describe those who are the first to do a particular job: the first doctors, lawyers, storekeepers, livery barn owners, blacksmiths, nurses, or teachers are all considered pioneers. However, the myth includes only those who were victorious in their pioneer gamble. People who attempted the pioneer life and found it lacking or were defeated by it, are not part of the myth, although their tribulations provide much of the adverse situations required to create the symbolic heroism.

Pioneer symbolism can be successfully applied to persons regardless of gender or ethnicity, with the glaring exception of Aboriginal people. The pioneer narrative and myth assumes that Aboriginal people are either pre-pioneer historical figures or merely irrelevant. The decline of many rural Saskatchewan communities since **WORLD WAR II** has produced a flood of published histories that proudly tell about the pioneer era "before they are lost." The few pages devoted to Aboriginal history focus primarily on pre-contact, not current, Native life. Although there are variations, these history books are essentially tools used to identify and celebrate individual communities. The idea of home and community creation on the frontier, of building something from nothing, is an integral part of the pioneer story. It is also the main vehicle by which non-Aboriginal Saskatchewan residents legitimize their presence in this province. By telling and retelling the stories of the pioneers, local and academic historians along with writers, storytellers, artists, musicians, and politicians have used the pioneer narrative to explain and legitimize concepts of progress, prosperity, economic opportunity and community creation—all of which are contingent upon the absence of Aboriginal people.

Merle Massie

FURTHER READING: Francis, R.D. 1989. "In Search of a Prairie Myth: A Survey of the Intellectual and Cultural Historiography of Prairie Canada," *Journal of Canadian Studies* 24 (3): 44-69; Mycak, S. 1996. "A Different Story by Helen Potrebenko: The Prairie Pioneer Myth Revisited," *Canadian Ethnic Studies* 28 (1): 67–75.

PIONEERS, FEMALE. The term "pioneer" lends itself to images of men toiling in the fields, but ethnically and racially diverse female pioneers played an important role in the development of the province of Saskatchewan. Aboriginal women built farms and settlements alongside both Aboriginal and Euro-Canadian men in the early settlement period. As more Euro-Canadians immigrated from eastern and central Canada, the British Isles, the United States and Europe, "civilized" White women displaced Aboriginal women as preferred marriage partners for White men.

Although women were indispensable in building communities, they were often disadvantaged by their gender. Women were attracted to western Canada by the cheap land but government officials felt that women were not effective farmers. Unlike the United States, where single women and female heads of households could claim the 160-acre lots, the Canadian government, under the 1872 **DOMINION LANDS ACT**, barred women from holding the $10 homesteads offered to men. Only widows or deserted women with dependent children were accepted, and the clause was interpreted narrowly so as to limit the number of female homesteaders.

The majority of female immigrants thereby came to Saskatchewan not as landowners in their own right, but as the wives, daughters or sisters of male agriculturalists. Others came independently to take advantage of employment opportunities, generally in female-appropriate occupations as domestic servants, teachers, nurses, seamstresses and waitresses.

Immigrants to Saskatchewan often found themselves in unfamiliar circumstances. While life in Saskatchewan often offered women more freedom and opportunities than they had previously enjoyed, most were unprepared for the hardships they faced. Many came from developed areas, sometimes equipped with modern amenities, where they were in close contact with neighbours and friends. Such women were usually ill prepared for the isolation and daily toil of frontier life. Those who came from upper- or middle-class homes, or who had spent the majority of their working lives in factories, were frequently not equipped with the domestic skills necessary to manage their new homes. Many women, especially those on homesteads whose closest neighbours were miles away, found the lack of social contact unbearable.

Farm women, who "hauled the double-load" of both domestic and agricultural duties, faced unique challenges. They cared for children and home, tended chickens, cows and gardens, and worked in the fields when necessary. The cash that female pioneers earned from selling excess butter, eggs and produce was often essential to the family income, but, in spite of their contributions, they were unable to claim an equal share in the farm and its products. In Saskatchewan, this injustice resulted in a push for equal rights in the form of campaigns for suffrage, homesteads for women and parental rights, as well as lobbies for health care, education and other community programs. Saskatchewan women both broke the land and broke ground in other areas, and, in part, the traditions of equality and social services in our province are rooted in the female pioneer experience.

Erin Millions

FURTHER READING: De Brou, David and Aileen Moffat (eds.). 1995. *"Other" Voices: Historical Essays on Saskatchewan Women*. Regina: Canadian Plains Research Center; Prentice, Alison, et al. 1996. *Canadian Women: A History*. Toronto: Harcourt Brace & Company; Strong-Boag, Veronica. 1986. "Pulling in Double Harness or Hauling a Double Load: Women, Work, Feminism on the Canadian Prairies," *Journal of Canadian Studies* (Fall): 95–106.

PIPE CEREMONY. The pipe is very sacred to First Nations people. In the past, it was used to open negotiations between different nations as a way for good talk to take place. This ceremony was also regarded as the way by which participants would be truthful, respectful and abide by the decisions and agreements that were made during the meeting time. Tobacco that has been blessed through prayer is normally used for the ceremony. The pipe is usually kept in a sacred bundle that is owned by the pipe carrier, and only he (or a helper) is allowed to open the bundle to prepare for the ceremony. After all preparations are accomplished, the ceremony can start. When asked, the pipe carrier can do the ceremony in almost any location. The participants sit in a circle with the pipe carrier. Amongst some First Nations, the men sit in an inner circle and the women sit in an outer circle; in others, all sit in one circle. Women who are in their menstrual period are required to excuse themselves from participating in this ceremony because it is believed that they have great power and could do harm to the ceremony. The helper places the sacred tobacco into the pipe and lights it in front of the pipe carrier. The pipe carrier, who is the host of the ceremony, says prayers to seven cardinal points: the Four Directions; the Above or Spirit World; the Below or Mother Earth; and the Centre or all living things. The pipe is then passed to the participants for them to either touch or smoke it. The passing of the pipe can be repeated several times. The tobacco is then allowed to "die" and the pipe is disassembled to be returned to the bundle until the next ceremony. After this, the pipe carrier may speak a few words of gratitude about life and expectations; each participant is also invited to speak such words; and the ceremony is considered closed.

William Asikinack

PIPITS. Pipits are songbirds of open country, whose approximately sixty-five species occur on all continents except Antarctica. They belong to the family Motacillidae within the perching birds (order Passeriformes). Their hind toe is elongated and curved. Unlike most songbirds they walk rather than hop. They have slender bills and long tails with white outer tail feathers. Songs are given in flight while circling high above the earth. Food items are principally invertebrates. The other members of the family are called "wagtails" from their habit of moving their long tail up and down as they move along the ground; they are usually brightly coloured, in contrast to the cryptic brown plumages of the pipits.

Six species of pipits and wagtails are found in North America. The only breeding species in Saskatchewan is Sprague's pipit (*Anthus spragueii*), a denizen of native grasslands where little or no shrub is present. They tolerate light and moderate grazing. It is the only pipit endemic to North America, and because of cryptic plumage and behaviour this small (10–15 cm) bird is easily missed on the breeding grounds or in migration to the southern United States or central and northern Mexico. Sprague's pipit is most commonly observed as a speck in the sky while it circles and sings a high-pitched, slightly descending *tzsee-tzsee-tzsee-tzsee-tzsee*.

The slightly larger (15–17 cm) American pipit (*Anthus rubescens*) breeds in the alpine or arctic tundra of North America and Eurasia. North American birds winter south to El Salvador but may be seen during migration in Saskatchewan, where they use open habitats with little or no vegetation such as beaches, mud flats, or ploughed fields.

Brenda C. Dale

FURTHER READING: Alsop, Fred J., III. 2002. *Birds of Canada*. New York: Dorling Kindersley; Robbins, M.B. and B.C. Dale. 1999. "Sprague's Pipit (*Anthus spragueii*)." In A. Poole and F. Gill (eds.), *The Birds of North America*. Philadelphia: The Birds of North America, Inc.; Verbeek, N.A.M. and P. Hendricks. 1994. "American Pipit (*Anthus rubescens*)." In A. Poole and F. Gill (eds.), *The Birds of North America*. Philadelphia: The Birds of North America, Inc.

PLACE NAMES. Place names or toponyms are more than just labels: they often provide valuable information about the landscape and settlement history of an area, and about the way in which people perceived that land. The First Nations who roamed the plains and the wooded north assigned names to the landmarks they encountered, many of which survive today. The name of the province itself comes from *kisiskâciwani-sîpiy*, "swift flowing river," which was what the **CREE** called both branches of the **SASKATCHEWAN RIVER**. Waskesiu is a somewhat shortened version of *wâwâskêsiw-sâkahikan*, "red deer (or elk) lake." The Wathaman River, in the far north, comes from the Woods Cree *othaman*, meaning "vermilion," because the river's banks were a source of red dyes for the Indians.

Many more First Nations names exist in translation, including Gull Lake, Birch Hills, Meadow Lake, and Buffalo Narrows. Most famous among these is undoubtedly Qu'Appelle, which originated with a Cree legend about a spirit that travelled up and down the valley calling out people's names; their response was "*kâ-têpwêt?*" meaning "Who calls?" which was translated by early French-speaking travellers as "*Qui appelle?*" and is well known today in the abbreviated form of Qu'Appelle.

Whereas First Nations place names were inspired by the natural surroundings and their connections, the arrival of Europeans provided varied additions. The oldest European name still in use today in Saskatchewan is Fort à la Corne, which bears the name of Louis Chapt, Chevalier de la Corne, brother-in-law to the La Vérendrye brothers, who founded that trading post in the Saskatchewan valley in 1753. This practice of naming places after people, both the famous and the locally prominent, continues to the present. The Europeans also introduced the concept of commemorating their former homes (e.g., Bangor, Stockholm), with the result that the map of Saskatchewan is dotted with names

from virtually every country in northern Europe, as well as from eastern Canada and the United States.

Official responsibility for Saskatchewan place names rested with the Canada Permanent Committee on Geographical Names at Ottawa through the 1950s and beyond. Gradually, though, the province began to exert control. Abram Bereskin became Controller of Surveys for the Department of Natural Resources in 1946, and was given responsibility for the place names file. It was Bereskin who oversaw the bulk of the geo-memorial project of naming features for the almost 4,000 Saskatchewan servicemen who died during **WORLD WAR II**. In association with the province's Golden Jubilee in 1955, there was also a flurry of naming features after pioneer families. In all, it was a remarkable period with over 5,000 official names being added to the Saskatchewan map prior to Bereskin's retirement in 1968. At the same time, political interference was the order of the day and too many names were submitted, or vetoed, for partisan reasons. An unconscionable number of features were named for men (and they were invariably men) whose major contribution to the province was to have served the Department of Natural Resources (DNR) for twenty or more years. Bereskin also had a weakness for Dominion Land Surveyors (DLS), whether or not their work had any impact on Saskatchewan. The first legislation on the topic was the Geographic Names Board Act of 1974, and since 1976 the Board has taken responsibility for names in the province. Activity has slowed down dramatically, but is also more measured and consistent with national and international standards.

The first significant effort at recording the origins of the province's place names was *What's in a Name*, a project launched by E.T. (Pete) Russell, principal of Henry Kelsey school at Saskatoon. Under Russell's guidance, students corresponded with people in every corner of Saskatchewan and collected stories on the origins of place names; the resulting book went through three editions and many reprints, illustrating the enduring popularity of the topic. While *What's in a Name* helped to preserve an array of information that might otherwise have been lost, it was not supported by research and much of the information in the book can best be regarded as folklore. In the 1990s, Bill Barry began a more systematic look at the historical record. *People Places: Saskatchewan and Its Names* (1997) provided the first comprehensive look at the topic, and has prompted considerable further research. The historical background to these names is now much better understood, but huge gaps in our knowledge still remain.

Bill Barry

FURTHER READING: Barry, B. 1997. *People Places: Saskatchewan and Its Names*. Regina: Canadian Plains Research Center; —. 1998. *People Places: The Dictionary of Saskatchewan Place Names*. Regina: People Places Publishing; Russell, E.T. 1980. *What's in a Name: The Story Behind Saskatchewan Place Names*. Saskatoon: Western Producer Prairie Books.

PAT PETTIT/REGINA LEADER-POST
Plains Health Centre, April 1993.

PLAINS HEALTH CENTRE, REGINA. This eleven-storey structure, built for $9 million between 1970 and 1974, resulted from the Hartman-Argue Report in 1965, and served as a tertiary referral and university training hospital for southern and eastern Saskatchewan from 1974 to 1998. Initially all patient rooms were private, with a large "picture window" which gave the patients the benefit of healing light plus a prairie view. For those privileged to work in it, or to train in it, or especially to be patients in it, it was a magical place—both because of its architectural design and also because the co-operation of staff and students attained the best results for their patients.

For thirteen years this hospital fulfilled its functions in all the major branches of surgery and medicine, at the same time becoming a well-recognized training centre in those disciplines as well as in family medicine. In 1987, the **UNIVERSITY OF SASKATCHEWAN** discontinued most full-time professorships and their teaching programs, and decreased its support for surgery.

In 1992, the Atkinson Report suggested the Plains Health Centre be closed. In 1998 the building was decommissioned as a hospital at a cost of $21 million, and converted to a central educational institution for the **SASKATCHEWAN INSTITUTE OF APPLIED SCIENCE AND TECHNOLOGY**.

Murray M. Fraser

PLANT DISEASES. Plant diseases have accompanied humans throughout their evolution, affecting the quality and quantity of food available to them. Wet years often resulted in the destruction of most or all of the crops grown by early human farmers, and famines were common. Some plant diseases had a strong influence on the course of history of certain countries. Most famous in recent times is Ireland's late blight epidemic of potatoes in 1845, which contributed to a famine resulting in the death of an estimated one million people and the emigration of another 1.5 million, primarily to North America.

Plant diseases and the associated science of plant pathology that studies causes of plant diseases, gained attention in Saskatchewan at the beginning of the 20th century, when severe epidemics of the stem rust fungus caused serious losses in wheat. As a result of the rust epidemic of 1916, with an estimated loss of 100 million bushels of wheat, the Dominion Laboratory of Plant Pathology was established on the campus of the UNIVERSITY OF SASKATCHEWAN in 1919. This laboratory eventually became part of the Canada Department of Agriculture Research Station that evolved into the Agriculture and Agri-Food Canada Research Centre Saskatoon, where there is still a strong emphasis on the study of plant diseases. In the Department of Biology, where the laboratory was initially housed, courses on fungi and plant diseases were first offered in 1920 and a strong tradition in the study of plant diseases was established. Since then, several other private, federal and provincial organizations have been active in conducting research on diseases, developing disease management strategies or supporting farmers in Saskatchewan by offering diagnostic and advisory services.

Plant diseases are defined as plant disorders due to microoganisms or adverse environmental conditions. These eventually become visible in the form of symptoms such as spots, blights, rots, wilts, and galls. Depending on the disease, symptoms can be found on all plant parts such as roots, stems, flowers, and leaves. Microorganisms that cause diseases on plants are called pathogens and include viruses, phytoplasms, bacteria, fungi, and nematodes. Adverse environmental conditions that can result in plant disease include temperature, moisture, mineral nutrients, and pollutants at levels above or below the tolerance level of plants. Most plant diseases are, however, associated with microorganisms; and in Saskatchewan most of these are caused by fungi.

While in the early days research on plant diseases was focused on diseases of wheat such as stem rust, bunt and various root rots, further diversification of the cropping system brought new crops into Saskatchewan, and with them new diseases. Currently more than sixty arable and horticultural crops are grown in the province, and there are several hundred diseases that are causing more or less severe damage on those plant species. Damage can range anywhere from less than 1% to total crop failure. Because most fungi require moisture to be able to infect a plant, more damage is encountered in years with wet summers. A lot of research has concentrated on the breeding of resistant crop varieties as the most economical way of disease control, and on the development of strategies to reduce the impact of diseases by other means. Emphasis is placed on the development of so-called integrated disease management strategies that incorporate sound cropping practices, good crop rotations, healthy seed, the use of resistant cultivars, the use of fungicides only when required, and the use of biological control methods where available. Plant diseases also affect ornamental crops including trees, shrubs, and flowers in house gardens and parks. A well-known disease of a city tree species is Dutch Elm disease, which has migrated with beetles into Saskatchewan and is endangering elm trees in the province. Plant diseases are also common on forest trees and can cause serious economic damage in timber production. Rots and staining of wood due to fungi are the most common diseases found in forestry. Many fungi attacking trees belong to the commonly known mushrooms and bracket fungi, some of which are edible. Forest pathology is a special area in the large field of plant pathology, dealing specifically with those micro-organisms that infect forest trees. From 1947 until 1965 Saskatchewan had a forest pathology laboratory of the Forest Department, before research on forest pathology problems across the three prairie provinces was consolidated in Edmonton.

Sabine Banniza

FURTHER READING: Agrios, G.N. 1997. *Plant Pathology*. San Diego: Academic Press; Bailey, K.L., B.D. Gossen, R.K. Gugel, and R.A.A. Morrall. 2003. *Diseases of Field Crops in Canada*. Ottawa: Canadian Phytopathological Society; Conners, I.L. 1972. *Plant Pathology in Canada*. Ottawa: Canadian Phytopathological Society.

PLANT ROOT SIMULATOR. Jeff Schoenau, a University of Saskatchewan soil scientist, and the Saskatoon company that commercialized his technology, won a 2004 Synergy Award for Innovation from the National Science and Engineering Research Canada (NSERC). Schoenau developed the technology used by Western Ag Innovations Inc. to create the Plant Root Simulator (PRS), a simple soil testing probe and forecasting software that has benefited researchers and farmers in Canada and around the world. The PRS system has been used to improve yields on 3.4 million acres of farmland in western Canada, with an estimated economic impact of almost $60 million since 1998. It simulates the function of a plant's roots and helps researchers and farmers see the soil from a plant's perspective. The device simplifies the collection and analysis of soil samples, and vastly improves the ability to measure and predict fertilizer use and requirements.

Joe Ralko

PLAYWRIGHTS. Although there was some encouragement of Saskatchewan drama in the 1970s and 1980s, including GLOBE THEATRE productions of works by its playwright-in-residence Rex Deverell and others, a new era began in 1982 with the establishment of the Saskatchewan Playwrights Centre (SPC), based in Saskatoon. Before then, aspiring writers had to depend on some writing courses at the universities or in schools, and on others sponsored by the SASKATCHEWAN ARTS BOARD. Nonetheless, several successful dramatists, such as Len Peterson, Maureen Hunter and KEN MITCHELL, emerged. The SPC, however, was designed to serve both established and new dramatists in developing their scripts and promoting their works, within and outside the province. To that end, the Centre conducts regular workshops of members' works, and sponsors special events with Canadian dramatists throughout the province. Other services include script analysis, a newsletter, and a catalogue of plays by local writers which is distributed throughout the country. It also sponsors an annual Spring Festival of New Plays—a week-long presentation of public readings and workshops in Regina.

Largely under the aegis of the SPC, but also with the assistance of the universities and the Globe and PERSEPHONE THEATRE companies, the province has produced some outstanding dramatists and their works. As well as Ken Mitchell, whose popular *Cruel Tears* predated the formation of the SPC, notable dramatists include BARBARA SAPERGIA, Connie Gault, Dianne Warren, Marlis Wesseler, Eugene Stickland (later playwright-in-residence at Calgary's Alberta Theatre Projects), DON KERR, Mansell Robinson, and others. More recently, even community theatre groups such as REGINA LITTLE THEATRE have promoted Canadian playwrighting through competitions for original scripts. Such groups as Saskatoon's Off-Broadway Dinner Theatre, Rosthern's Station Arts Centre, and the Barn Playhouse, north of Saskatoon, have sponsored original productions linking popular music with dramatic scenarios. Large community theatrical productions have been staged in Fort Qu'Appelle and other centres. This burgeoning activity seems set to increase as time passes.

Richard Harvey

PODILUK, WALTER (1927–). Walter Podiluk has brought insight, expertise, and character to each of the positions he has occupied. Born in Blaine Lake on March 4, 1927, Podiluk earned his BEd and BA from the UNIVERSITY OF SASKATCHEWAN. His most prominent leadership roles include serving as Director of Education of the Saskatoon Catholic School Board, Deputy Minister of Social Services and Health, and Special Consultant to the Minster of Health. An astute administrator, Podiluk has given generously of his time to numerous councils, boards, and associations as well as community groups. Awarded an honorary doctorate from his alma mater in 1987, Podiluk was invested as a Member of the Order of Canada in 1996.

UNIVERSITY OF SASKATCHEWAN ARCHIVES A-10346

Zenon Pohorecky (left) and D'Arcy Hande, October 1989.

POHORECKY, ZENON S. (1928–98). Zenon

Stephen Pohorecky can be characterized as an artist, academic, activist, anthropologist, and archaeologist. His chief contribution to Saskatchewan's cultural development lies in his teaching, having taught thousands of students over his thirty-year career as a **UNIVERSITY OF SASKATCHEWAN** professor of anthropology and **ARCHAEOLOGY**. In this, and in his extensive volunteer service, Pohorecky fostered racial and ethnic tolerance, civil liberties and human rights, and encouraged an informed and deeper understanding of the ancient and contemporary cultures of the province.

Born in western Ukraine, he moved with his family to Edmonton when he was an infant, then to Saskatoon and Winnipeg. He obtained two MA degrees, from the University of Manitoba (fine arts and philosophy) and from the University of Toronto (anthropology and archaeology). His PhD was awarded by the University of California at Berkeley in 1964 for his dissertation, "Archaeology of the South Coast Ranges of California." He undertook three seasons of field work (1958–60) surveying for archaeological sites in the area to be affected by the South Saskatchewan reservoir, and took up his post as the first anthropologist/archaeologist employed by a Saskatchewan university in 1964.

Pohorecky served on many boards dedicated to cultural development and, in addition to academic papers on rock art and archaeological resource management, wrote a number of popular, encyclopedic publications: *Saskatchewan People* (1978), *Ethnic Organizations in Saskatchewan* (1977), *Saskatchewan Indian Heritage: The First 200 Centuries* (1970)—as well as a series of articles in the daily newspaper in 1970, intended to increase understanding about the history, culture and legal rights of Saskatchewan Aboriginal peoples. Much of this work was pioneering, and not necessarily pop-

ular at the time; as he taught in his introductory university classes, one of the duties of anthropology is to challenge existing assumptions and to confront our prejudices about why things are as they are.

Tim E.H. Jones

POITRAS, EDWARD (1953–). For more than

two decades, Aboriginal artists in Canada have challenged the master narrative of history. Edward Poitras continues to be in the forefront of this artistic investigation, and his works have been included in nearly all major exhibitions of contemporary Aboriginal art in Canada since 1980. Born in Regina, Poitras is a member of the Gordon First Nation. In 1974, he studied with Sarain Stump, who was instrumental in creating the Indian art program at the Saskatchewan Indian Cultural College in Saskatoon; Stump introduced Poitras to diverse artistic and philosophical approaches that continue to inform his art practice. In 1975–76, Poitras attended Manitou College in La Macaza, Quebec, where Mexican Aboriginal artist Domingo Cisneros imparted an approach that recognized mixed ancestry as a powerful source of energy, creativity and contradiction. Following this time in Quebec, Poitras taught at the Saskatchewan Indian Cultural College and at the University of Manitoba. During much of the 1980s, he taught at the Saskatchewan Indian Federated College, University of Regina (now **FIRST NATIONS UNIVERSITY OF CANADA**).

By the early 1980s, Poitras' artistic benchmark became his masterful ability to combine seemingly contradictory materials such as natural elements, circuit boards, plastic, and transistors. Early large-scale installations capture the drama of ritual and performance. Both *Day Break Sentinel* (1983) and *Big Iron Sky* (1984) reflect Poitras' preoccupation with the suspended figure. These installations reveal the artist's mastery in creating an elegant tension between formal concerns and conceptual contradictions. These works also inspired several performance-based works including *Das Cheval Dance* in 1984, with Robin Poitras. Edward Poitras perhaps pushed his investigation of the suspended figure to its zenith with the installation entitled *Internal Recall* (1986–88). Here, seven life-size figures kneel with their hands bound with rope that attaches to the ceiling; on the wall, words associated with the signing of treaties with First Nations on the prairies act as connecting links between the act of binding and the notion of binding contracts, as well as the legacy of broken promises. Contrasting sharply with *Internal Recall's* bound figures, *Coyote* (1986) frees Poitras from the limitations of history. For many Aboriginal peoples today, *Coyote* has become a symbol of defiant survival in the face of the tragic effects of colonial imperatives. Perhaps most noteworthy is Poitras' installation at the XLVI Venice Biennale in 1995: he was the first Aboriginal artist to represent

Canada at this prestigious international arts exhibition.

Poitras' work has also been featured in many solo exhibitions at institutions such as Western Front, Vancouver (1998), Articule, Montreal (1991), and The Power Plant, Toronto (1989). In 2002, the **MENDEL ART GALLERY** organized the traveling exhibition, *Qu'Appelle: Tales of Two Valleys*, which featured a significant body of his recent work.

Selected group exhibitions include: *A History Lesson*, Museum of Contemporary Canadian Art, Toronto (2004) and **MACKENZIE ART GALLERY**, Regina (2003); *Lost Homelands: Manuel Pina, Edward Poitras, Jorma Puranen, Jin-me Yoon*, Confederation Centre Art Gallery and Museum, Charlottetown and the Kamloops Art Gallery (traveling 1999–2000); *The Post-Colonial Landscape*, Mendel Art Gallery (1993); *INDIGENA: Perspectives of Indigenous Peoples on 500 Years*, Canadian Museum of Civilization, Hull, Quebec (traveling 1992–95); *IV Biennal of Havana, Cuba* (1991); *Biennial of Canadian Contemporary Art*, National Gallery of Canada (1989); *Star Dusters*, Thunder Bay Art Gallery, Thunder Bay, Ontario (1986); *New Work by a New Generation*, MacKenzie Art Gallery, Regina (1982). His work is included in numerous private collections and art institutions throughout Canada, notably the Canadian Museum of Civilization, Indian and Northern Affairs Canada, MacKenzie Art Gallery, Mendel Art Gallery, **SASKATCHEWAN ARTS BOARD**, and the Thunder Bay Art Gallery.

Despite national and international recognition, Poitras continues to be inspired by collaborations with communities in Saskatchewan. He frequently shares in the development of performance art, dance and theatre works with individuals from diverse artistic backgrounds. In August 2004, he participated in *Grasslands–Where Heaven Meets Earth*, a site-specific collaborative art performance in **GRASSLANDS NATIONAL PARK**, Val Marie, Saskatchewan. Other recent collaborative projects involve exhibitions designed to address critical issues related to land, including *In-X-Isle* (2000) and *I.R.80A* (1998), both at Neutral Ground in Regina, as well as *Nomadic Recall* (1999) and *Back Tracking the New Museum* (1997), at Sakewewak First Nations Artists' Collective in Regina. In 2002, Poitras received the Governor General's Award in Visual and Media Arts in recognition of his significant contribution to the arts in Canada.

Lee-Ann Martin

POLISH SETTLEMENTS. An overwhelming

majority of early Polish immigrants to Saskatchewan came from Galicia, a province of the Austro-Hungarian Empire also known as Austrian Poland. After **WORLD WAR I**, Galicia became part of the recreated Republic of Poland. Poles were deeply committed to their Roman Catholic faith, and in

Saskatchewan they built or significantly contributed to the founding and development of over fifty churches, missions and parishes during the settlement period; these serve as a beacon to identify the locations of Polish immigration. Polish immigrants first came to Otthon in 1894 to complement a larger number of Hungarian settlers in this area; St. Cunegunda church was founded in the late 1890s. The first Polish and Ukrainian immigrants arrived in Candiac in 1896. In 1908, Polish settlers requested the name "Sobieski" for a hamlet, but were unsuccessful as Candiac was approved. The establishment of St. Joseph church there soon followed; the community was led by a dynamic Silesian-born Polish priest, Rev. Franciszek Pander, who had been ordained in Montreal in 1908. Father Pander also served a number of other churches in the area with sizeable Polish contingents: St. Columbkille at Grenfell (1903); St. Anne at Kipling (1907); and St. Patrick at Glenavon (1909).

Poles first arrived at Lemberg in the mid-1890s, and they were the largest ethnic group involved in the establishment of St. Michael in 1901. They also contributed significantly to the founding of St. Mary at Grayson (1907) and St. Elizabeth at Killaly (1911). Large numbers of Ukrainians and Poles from the Borszczów district of Galicia began to arrive in the area of Alvena, Fish Creek, and Prud'homme in the late 1890s. Poles and Ukrainians from the Buczacz district of Eastern Galicia first settled at Tiny, Buchanan, and Rama around 1901. St. Mary church was established Kowalowka (1905) and Sts. Peter and Paul church at Dobrowody (1907). As more Polish settlers came, they were mostly responsible for the establishment of St. Anthony at Rama (1922), St. Anne at Buchanan (1929), and St. Andrew Babola near Invermay. A few immigrants arrived at Cedoux in 1902, followed by a contingent of thirty Polish families who arrived at Weyburn on the SOO LINE by train from Chicago in 1903.

Polish settlers first crossed the SOUTH SASKATCHEWAN RIVER at Petrofka north of Saskatoon in 1903, and led in the establishment of a number of communities and churches in the Redberry Lake area as settlement gradually moved westward toward North Battleford: Holy Trinity church at Orolow (1909), Holy Ghost at Albertown (1912), St. Michael the Archangel at Krydor (1913), St. Joseph at Alticane (1918), and St. Anthony at Redfield (1918). A small rectory was built in Krydor in 1926, which eventually evolved into a parish centre for all these churches; the Sokal district of Eastern Galicia was the source of many of these Polish immigrants. Polish immigrants from Wielkie Oczy began arriving in the Ituna-Goodeve-Hubbard area in 1904. They founded the original St. Stanislaus church in 1906 between Ituna and Hubbard. Other Polish churches were subsequently organized: Our Lady of Perpetual Help at Goodeve (1907), Little Church in the Bush

near Jedburgh (1909), and Sacred Heart at Beckenham (1915). Polish immigrants began arriving in the early 1900s in the Kamsack, Mikado, Sturgis and Norquay districts; however, they were scattered among much large numbers of Ukrainians throughout this entire area.

Poles founded Our Lady of Perpetual Help church in 1908 in the countryside north of Wishart. Smaller Polish churches were later established at Model Farm (Sacred Heart, 1915) and Krasne (Our Lady of Visitation, 1928). Our Lady of Perpetual Help was eventually relocated in Wishart and evolved into a parish centre. The first Polish immigrants came to the Melfort area in 1904. Polish immigration into the area east of Prince Albert and north of the NORTH SASKATCHEWAN RIVER started around 1906, and a number of small churches were formed: Sts. Peter and Paul at Claytonville (1910), Sacred Heart of Jesus at Janow Corners (1922), Mary of Perpetual Help at Honeymoon (1924), and St. Thaddeus at Henribourg (1928). Poles first came to Fosston in 1914, followed by a much larger influx in the 1920s. St. Mary Queen of Poland at Fosston was soon established, followed by the missions of St. Rose of Lima at Rose Valley and St. Felix at Archerwill. This new wave of immigration led to a sizeable Polish presence in a number to churches that had already been established: St. Mary at Wadena, St. Joseph at Kelvington, St. Theresa at Lintlaw, and St. Helen at Kuroki and High Tor. (*See also* ETHNIC BLOC SETTLEMENTS, UKRAINIAN SETTLEMENTS)

Lindy Kasperski

FURTHER READING: Renkiewicz, F. 1982. *The Polish Presence in Canada and the United States*. Toronto: Multicultural History Society of Ontario.

POLITICAL HISTORY OF SASKATCHEWAN: *see essay on page 699.*

POLITICAL SCIENCE. The discipline known since WORLD WAR II as political science was originally taught at the UNIVERSITY OF SASKATCHEWAN as political economy in the British tradition. After the mid-1960s, American influence on the discipline increasingly affected the teaching of political science in Saskatchewan and elsewhere in Canada. In 1966, the Regina campus of the University of Saskatchewan hired four new US-educated faculty members to staff a political science committee of instruction in the social science division. While the Regina faculty was initially organized around an interdisciplinary approach, at about the same time political scientists and economists at the University of Saskatchewan in Saskatoon dissolved their joint department into two separate disciplines. After the Regina campus became the UNIVERSITY OF REGINA in 1974, the social science division system was abandoned in favour of formal disciplinary departments including a political science department.

The political science curriculum at the two universities has been subject over time to changing political issues, faculty interests, and ideological predispositions. There have been some differences between the two departments in emphasis and political ideology in the past, but these differences are minimal today. Core offerings include Canadian governments and politics, the Canadian constitution, political parties and interest groups, the politics of women, Aboriginal and other minority groups, provincial government and politics, political theory, comparative government and politics, international relations, and institutions. Both universities offer a Bachelor of Arts program in political science. Since the 1980s these have been four-year degree programs. Both departments offer Masters degree programs in political science, but neither has a doctoral program; study at that level is available through the CANADIAN PLAINS RESEARCH CENTER at the University of Regina.

Although political science is considered a separate discipline, its study remains closely linked to the broad study of the social sciences and other disciplines. Cross-disciplinary and joint programs are available, and classes in other subject areas can be accepted as credit for students with a major in political science. Disciplines such as history, philosophy, religion, sociology, economics, administration, geography, and anthropology address subject matter that is relevant to political science. Political scientists work in government, political parties, trade unions, business, media, agriculture, the arts, law, and other occupations, as well as in academic settings.

Joseph Roberts

POND, PETER (1739–1807). Despite Peter Pond's questionable reputation, Buffalo Lake, in northwestern Saskatchewan, was renamed after him. He was associated with several killings, yet he opened the far North-West to the fur trade and, although untrained, made the first detailed maps of northwestern Canada. Indirectly, he helped establish the North West Company.

Pond's memoirs cover only his early years as a soldier and trader in his native United States. However, his maps show that from 1775 to 1788 he occupied posts near Dauphin (Manitoba), Prince Albert, Lac la Ronge, Ile-à-la-Crosse, and, most famously, LAKE ATHABASCA. By 1776, traders had moved up the CHURCHILL RIVER to Ile-à-la-Crosse. In 1778, a coalition of traders sent Pond to evaluate the rumoured wealth in furs further north in the Athabasca district. When Pond made his historic crossing of PORTAGE LA LOCHE, it was already a long-established route used by CREE and DENESULINE travelling to Hudson Bay. Pond believed a river from Athabasca led directly to the Pacific Ocean; his enthusiasm led a fellow trader, Alexander Mackenzie, to make his famous journey to the Arctic

Ocean in 1789. Pond, however, had left the west the previous year—his partners may have forced him out after the murder of John Ross in 1787. Pond had already been involved with the death of Jean-Etienne Waddens at Lac la Ronge in 1782. Impoverished, Pond died, back home in Connecticut, a puzzling and controversial man. *Dale Russell*

FURTHER READING: Duckworth, H.W. (ed.). 1990. *The English River Book: A North West Company Journal and Account Book of 1786.* Montreal: McGill-Queen's University Press; Gough, B.M. 1983. "Pond, Peter." Pp. 681–86 in F.G. Halpenny (ed.), *Dictionary of Canadian Biography*, Volume 5. Toronto: University of Toronto Press.

PONTEIX, town, pop 550, located SE of Swift Current off Hwy 13. After a 1907 scouting mission, the community was founded by Father Albert Royer, who came from the parish of Ponteix in the region of Auvergne, France. He established the French-speaking parish of Notre-Dame d'Auvergne, north of the present community, across the Notukeu Creek. In 1913–14, as the CPR was building its line toward Shaunavon along the south side of the Notukeu, the community shifted to the townsite on the rail line, retaining the name Ponteix in honour of Father Royer's former parish. Ponteix developed as a bilingual community over the decades. Community attractions include the Notukeu Heritage Museum at the Centre Culturel Royer, which features displays of archaeological and palaeontological artifacts. The Henri Liboiron collection consists of locally found arrowheads and other stone tools dating back several thousands of years, and the museum provides information on the 70–75 million-year-old ple-

siosaur found in the area in 1993. The Notre Dame d'Auvergne Church, built in 1929, is the largest column-free church in the province's southwest; it houses a 500-year-old oak sculpture of the Virgin Mary holding the dead body of Christ in her lap—a gift to Father Royer which came from France after reportedly surviving the French Revolution hidden in a haystack. Other Ponteix landmarks include the Convent of Notre Dame and the former Gabriel Hospital, both founded by the Sisters of Our Lady of Chambriac, who joined Father Royer in Ponteix in 1913. The hospital, completed in 1918, was largely financed by the Michelin family, whose tire-producing empire is headquartered in Auvergne, France; the contribution was made on the condition that the hospital be named Gabriel, after a family son who had been killed in **WORLD WAR I.** *David McLennan*

POOLE CONSTRUCTION. Saskatchewan was the birthplace of the PCL family of companies, one of the largest general contracting organizations in North America, with annual billings of more than $3 billion. PCL's founder, Ernest Poole, laid the groundwork for the organization in 1906 in the southeast community of Stoughton, where he established a reputation for the quality construction of farm houses, barns and stores.

In 1910, the headquarters for the company, then named Poole Construction Co. Ltd., moved to Rouleau, as Poole's crew of about thirty carpenters tackled larger, more demanding projects, such as town halls, schools, banks and rinks throughout Saskatchewan and into Manitoba. The company headquarters moved to Moose Jaw in 1913, and then to Regina in 1914. In 1932, after nearly ten years of working in the Edmonton market, Poole

moved its headquarters there. Edmonton remains the corporate hub of the international organization today. However, over the years, PCL has maintained its commitment to Saskatchewan through district offices in Regina and in Saskatoon.

PCL has helped shape the Saskatchewan skyline, having built many significant projects such as the McCallum Hill Twin Towers, Regina General Hospital, and Saskatchewan Indian Federated College, all in Regina; numerous buildings at the **UNIVERSITY OF SASKATCHEWAN** in Saskatoon, including the Chemical Engineering Building and the Geology Library; the Town 'N Country Mall in Moose Jaw; and the Northern Lights Casino in Prince Albert.

An important historical milestone occurred in 1977, when the employees purchased Poole Construction from Poole's sons, John and George. Two years later, the name of the company changed to PCL Construction Ltd. The sale, and accompanying transition to employee ownership, represented a huge cultural shift: the employees now had a vested interest in the success of the organization.

PCL now has offices in approximately twenty-five major centres in Canada, United States and the Bahamas, with each office operating in different construction sectors or geographic areas. *Joe Ralko*

POPULATION TRENDS: *see essay on page 705.*

POPULISM. Populism is associated with the political revolt of western prairie farmers in the United States in the latter part of the 19th century. Following the US Homestead Act of 1862, large tracts of land in the west were opened to European settlers. The first great world economic depression began in 1873 and lasted until 1896: prices for farm products fell, and farmers could not make the payments on their mortgages or their bank operating loans. A political movement arose, the Farmers' Alliances, which attacked the Republican and Democratic parties as representatives of finance capital and big business; with support from some labour organizations they met at Lincoln, Nebraska in 1890 and formed the People's Party, also known as the Populist Party. Populism has always been identified with independent family farmers operating within the capitalist system. It emerged first in France, and then became a major political force in Russia. Common to all the populist movements was support for private ownership of farmland; patriarchal values were dominant, as the father was head of the family and held title to the land, which was passed from father to son. There was strong opposition to the old feudal system of peasant farming, where a rent was paid to a landlord, as well as to the emerging socialist movement, which proposed public ownership of all natural resources including land.

The towers of Notre Dame d'Auvergne, Ponteix, are visible from miles away.

In Europe, the United States and Canada supporters of populism saw a fundamental conflict between "the people," identified as farmers, workers and small business owners, and "the plutocracy," the rich who lived off their labour. Populism in Canada is identified with the prairie farmers' movements in the early part of the 20th century, such as the Grain Growers Associations, and with the formation of the **PROGRESSIVE PARTY** in the early 1920s. While the Progressive Party collapsed in 1926, the populist tradition was revived with the formation in the 1930s of the Social Credit Party and the **CO-OPERATIVE COMMONWEALTH FEDERATION**. Like the earlier movements, the new parties were opposed to "monopoly capitalism" while defending the property rights of farmers and small businessmen. They had the support of the reformist trade union movement, which rejected Marxism and socialism. Populism on the Canadian prairies took several forms, reflecting the different histories and political cultures of the three provinces.   *John W. Warnock*

FURTHER READING: Laycock, D. 1990. *Populism and Democratic Thought in the Canadian Prairies 1910–1945.* Toronto: University of Toronto Press.

PORCUPINE PLAIN, town, pop 820, located in east-central Saskatchewan, just NE of Greenwater Lake Provincial Park on Hwy 23. The Porcupine Provincial Forest lies immediately southeast of the community and to the east loom the Porcupine Hills. During the first two decades of the 20th century, prior to intensive settlement, the primary activity in the region concerned logging interests. After **WORLD WAR I**, land was opened up for soldiers returning from overseas and by the mid-1920s civilian settlers were taking up land. In 1921, a **RED CROSS OUTPOST HOSPITAL**, the second in the province, was opened northeast of the present hamlet of Carragana; soon one-room schools and churches began to dot the countryside. With the arrival of the railway the Porcupine Plain post office was established (1929) and the townsite began to develop. As forestry was the primary basis of the economy, Porcupine Plain became known as the cordwood capital of Saskatchewan. It was incorporated as a village on April 9, 1942, and, on January 1, 1968, the community attained town status. Today, agriculture is the main industry in the region, forestry being second; cereal grains and oilseeds are the main crops grown. Over the past few years, intensive hog operations have been developed in the area. Porcupine Plain is the main service, supply, and business centre for a substantial trading area population. The region is very popular for hunting and fishing; there are a number of outfitters in the district, and nearby Greenwater and Marean Lakes are popular resort destinations.

David McLennan

Political History of Saskatchewan

Dan de Vlieger

Observers of political events generally agree that societies where populations periodically determine, by way of a free vote, which political parties get to form their governments usually exhibit political practices and ideas that are not far removed from the daily preoccupations and concerns of these populations. Saskatchewan's political history over the past 100 years appears to provide ample illustration of such an observation: some people indeed seem convinced that there is something different about the political sentiment of Saskatchewan's population as compared to that of its neighbours, because for 45 out of the 100 years of the province's existence the population voted for ostensibly social democratic administrations. One such observer, Seymour Martin Lipset,[1] writing in the 1950s, was evidently struck by the fact that in terms of such demographic dimensions as ethnicity, economic activities, social behaviour, religious sentiments, legal environment, and time of settlement, there was no significant difference between the populations of the three prairie provinces that explain the fact that Saskatchewan's political behaviour appeared, at least at first glance, to be divergent—especially when such a different voting pattern occurred in a place and at a time (North America in mid-20th century) that was generally antagonistic toward "socialist" or "leftist" politics. Other observers of this presumed radicalism of Saskatchewan voters have seen it very differently: Evelyn Eager, for instance, concluded that Saskatchewan "electors have not tended to radical behaviour in the sense either of favouring extreme change or of casting their votes mainly for basic principle."[2]

Saskatchewan politics during the past century has evidently not been quite in the same groove as that taking place in surrounding jurisdictions; it has at times taken directions that were both innovative and easily categorized as extremely radical by those opposing such measures. The introduction of **MEDICARE** in the early 1960s and the dramatic events following its implementation may be taken as the most obvious of such directions. While some observers may judge this innovative measure as purely inspired by ideological fervour, it can equally be viewed as a measure motivated by a concern for access to affordable healthcare by a population thinly spread out over a large geographic area and whose relatively low average income was subject to major fluctuations from one year to the next. The fact that the Saskatchewan government's initial introduction of this kind of public policy measure was shortly followed by the introduction of medicare as a countrywide program would indicate that the major intent behind the measure was less ideological than its original detractors believed.

In giving an overview of the politics of Saskatchewan during the 100 years since its inception, several important background elements must be kept in mind. Created as a province in 1905 by federal legislation (the Saskatchewan Act), carved out of a huge territory at the same time that the current boundaries of its two neighbouring provinces were settled, it was inhabited by a population overwhelmingly consisting of newcomers, the greater part of whom were engaged in agricultural pursuits. The 1901 census data of what was to become Saskatchewan give a population total of 91,279 (90.8% rural), while the 1906 census returns provide a figure of 257,763 (86.8% rural)—an increase of 182% in only five years.[3] This remarkable phenomenon of a rapidly increasing population, mostly originating from elsewhere, continued apace from 1905 until about the beginning of the **GREAT DEPRESSION**. By 1931, only a quarter of a century since its creation as a new political entity, Saskatchewan had a population of 921,785. Since then, for about the next 75 years, the province's population figures have been remarkably stable, fluctuating modestly between around 920,000 and 990,000. This pattern of population dynamics—an initial rapid expansion, mostly resulting from immigration, followed by a long period of practically zero growth—has had major implications for successive governments and makes it possible to divide the political history of the province into three time periods.

In the first period, from 1905 to 1929, provincial governments were preoccupied with building an infrastructure which, however modest in scope, attempted to provide to a widely dispersed population some minimal services such as roads, schools and health facilities, where none had existed before. These matters were all constitutionally regarded as being of a merely local or private nature, and thus exclusively under provincial jurisdiction. The province's financial resources were extremely limited and originated mostly from the federal government; there was no practical possibility, even if the province had desired to do so, of extracting a steady source of revenue from a newly settled population that had come in without wealth. In addition the one potential source of revenue for the province, control over Crown lands, had by the terms of the deed creating the province remained under federal jurisdiction: this created a degree of financial dependency on the federal government that was deeply resented by the population as a whole and remained a source of considerable friction between the provincial and federal levels of government. This situation, coupled with the federal government's long-standing policy of maintaining high tariffs on American manufactured goods, forced the population to pay higher prices for much-needed agricultural machinery and other implements: as a result there was a widespread feeling that the population in the western provinces was deliberately, unfairly, and unjustifiably kept in a state of colonial dependency by a federal government that was constituted on the basis of a party system dominated by central Canadian interests. From the very beginning of Saskatchewan's existence as a province there was thus a climate of resentment directed both against the federal government, whether Liberal or Conservative, and against the traditional party system that formed its base. This climate of distrust and resentment also meant that Saskatchewan voters very early on began to differentiate between provincial and federal politics, and became quite accustomed to supporting different political groupings in federal elections and in provincial elections.

From 1905 until the devastation visited upon the province's population in the late 1920s and early 1930s by the twin scourges of the Depression and successive years of severe drought, the general political situation in the province can best be described as one of gradual consolidation of provincial governmental institutions and of slow growth in governmental services under a succession of LIBERAL PARTY administrations. This long period of Liberal Party dominance came to an end in 1929; this end symbolizes the conclusion of the province's initial period of rapid demographic and economic expansion that had mainly been fuelled by the pioneering efforts and optimism of a newly arrived population.

Supported by electoral victories in six consecutive elections, Liberal administrations dominated the provincial political scene under the leadership of premiers WALTER SCOTT (1905–16), WILLIAM MARTIN (1916–22), CHARLES A. DUNNING (1922–26) and JAMES G. GARDINER (1926–29). This remarkable string of electoral successes was largely based on the close ties that existed then with the dominant organizational institution of the mainly agrarian electorate: the SASKATCHEWAN GRAIN GROWERS' ASSOCIATION (SGGA). The closeness of these ties is evident in the ready exchange of personnel between the leading figures in the Association and the provincial Liberal Cabinet: for example the province's first Minister of Agriculture, W.R. MOTHERWELL, who held this portfolio from 1905 to 1918, was one of the founders of the Association and its first president, while Charles Dunning, before he became Premier, had been a very influential member in the Association as a regional director and vice-president.[4]

While provincially the electorate repeatedly returned the Liberal Party to government in the period from 1905 to 1929, the same level of support for Liberal politicians contesting seats in federal general elections was not quite as evident: in the sixteen federal constituencies contested in the federal election of 1921, for instance, the province's voters elected fifteen Progressives and only one Liberal. This is significant for at least two reasons. In the first place, the candidates operating under the Progressive banner were supported and sponsored by a political association which, while officially separate from the SGGA, had been created by it and was widely recognized by the voters as being the arm of the Association for federal electoral purposes. Secondly, the results of this election provided clear evidence that Saskatchewan voters were already quite at ease with the practice of supporting and voting for a

Premiers of Saskatchewan...

SASKATCHEWAN ARCHIVES BOARD R-A245

Walter Scott
(1905-1916).

SASKATCHEWAN ARCHIVES BOARD R-B4621

William Martin
(1916-1922).

SASKATCHEWAN ARCHIVES BOARD R-A631-1

Charles A. Dunning
(1922-1926).

© M.WEST, REGINA, WEST'S STUDIO COLLECTION/SASKATCHEWAN ARCHIVES BOARD R-A632-2

James G. Gardiner
(1926-1929, 1934-1935).

particular political party at the provincial level while supporting a different political party in federal elections. This characteristic has been an enduring feature of the Saskatchewan voting public until the present; it underscores the fact that the Saskatchewan electorate is not tied firmly to any particular partisan or ideological perspective. The existence and importance of this pattern have not been lost on politically active people, and provincial political organizations have been disposed to differentiate themselves from federal political parties with which they share much of the same outlook, ideas, and members by adopting a different name. This phenomenon was already present at the very start of the province's existence when conservatives in the 1905 and 1908 Saskatchewan elections operated under the name of the Provincial Rights Party. This same kind of superficial distinctiveness can also be observed where separate legal entities are created, sporting different names and operating at the different levels of federal and provincial politics, but whose links with one another in terms of leadership and membership are much in evidence. Such a situation may be seen in the case of the SASKATCHEWAN PARTY, a provincial party that contested its first election in 1999 after the demise of the provincial Progressive Conservative Party, and whose ties to the federal CONSERVATIVE PARTY are clearly observable.

The rise of the PROGRESSIVE PARTY on the Saskatchewan political landscape in the 1920s was indicative of a growing restiveness in the population with respect to a number of social and economic issues. Many returning World War I veterans were disillusioned with federal government actions, and their return into the social fabric was not made any easier by the economic downturn of the early 1920s. Issues of long-standing irritation with federal policies, such as the continued federal control over public lands, the lack of action in eliminating protective tariff barriers, and evident reluctance on the part of the federal government to establish a wheat marketing board, contributed to a growing consensus that the existing traditional avenues of political action were not working in the interest of the Saskatchewan population. This evident dissatisfaction with federal policies and political parties in the aftermath of World War I prompted Premier Martin to distance his

Liberal administration from the federal Liberal Party. The postwar restiveness was exacerbated by increasingly prominent differences related to ethnic and religious concerns, especially regarding school policies. This ethnic and religious unrest grew more pronounced in the 1920s: it was the source of the sudden appearance of the KU KLUX KLAN on the provincial scene and contributed to the channeling of organized support to candidates in the 1929 election who, although campaigning under different labels, were seen as being in a likely position to defeat provincial Liberal candidates. The result was the defeat of the Liberal government.

The individual who became the new Premier, J.T.M. ANDERSON, was the leader of the provincial Conservative Party and formed a government with the support of MLAs who had been elected either as Independents or as Progressives. To underline the fact that his administration was buttressed by the support of legislative members of diverse political leanings, he dubbed his government the "Co-operative Government." The period from 1929 to 1944, inaugurated with the election of Premier Anderson's Co-operative Government and ending with the election of the CO-OPERATIVE COMMONWEALTH FEDERATION (CCF) under the leadership of Premier T.C. DOUGLAS, may be seen as the second period or phase in the evolution of Saskatchewan's politics. It was a period of transition between a long line of successive Liberal administrations and a situation of enduring division, involving governments popularly understood to be to the "left" alternating in office with administrations generally viewed as being to the "right."

Premier Anderson's government was beset by major problems right from the start. While the province in 1930 finally received jurisdiction over public lands, this long-awaited goal was initially of little benefit: with the Depression taking an increasingly heavy toll on the economic health of the province's population, there was no demand on the part of individuals to buy land or to pay for licenses to explore for natural resources. Additionally, severe drought conditions contributed to deepening the economic malaise, and the Premier had to face criticism from factions within his own party who felt that their leader had abandoned true conservative principles by forming an alliance with Progressives

SASKATCHEWAN ARCHIVES BOARD R-A629-1
J.T.M. Anderson (1929-1934).

SASKATCHEWAN ARCHIVES BOARD R-A2670
William J. Patterson (1935-1944).

© M.WEST, REGINA, WEST'S STUDIO COLLECTION/SASKATCHEWAN ARCHIVES BOARD R-WS15159-1
T.C. Douglas (1944-1961).

© M.WEST, REGINA, WEST'S STUDIO COLLECTION/SASKATCHEWAN ARCHIVES BOARD R-A245
Woodrow S. Lloyd (1961-1964).

P

and Independents. At the same time, the bitterness that was engendered during and after the 1931 ESTEVAN COAL STRIKE in southeastern Saskatchewan, which resulted in the death of three strikers at the hands of the police, also helped to undermine the support Anderson had originally received in the 1929 election.[5] In the election of 1934 the Anderson administration was therefore soundly defeated and replaced by a Liberal party administration still operating under the leadership of James G. Gardiner. The Conservative defeat was so devastating that between the elections of 1934 and 1975 the party only managed to elect one member, and that only for one term, to the provincial legislature. Premier Gardiner left office in 1935 in order to take up the position of Minister of Agriculture in the federal Liberal government formed by W.L. MACKENZIE KING after the defeat of the Conservatives under R.B. Bennett. The successor to Gardiner as Premier of the province and leader of the provincial Liberal Party was WILLIAM J. PATTERSON, who led his party to a repeat victory in 1938.

Judging only from the perspective of the legislative seats won by the Liberal Party in the 1934 and 1938 elections (in 1934 it won 50 of the 55 seats available, and in 1938 it won 38 out of 52), the government led by Premier Anderson may be seen as a mere hiatus in the normal pattern of Liberal administrations—perhaps due to a temporary disaffection with the provincial Liberal Party on the part of voters who were quite willing to return things to "normal" after a less than satisfying experience with a non-Liberal government. Such a conclusion does not, however, take into account the evident political volatility of a significant portion of the electorate. In both the elections of 1934 and 1938, large numbers of voters supported party organizations that were relatively new on the provincial scene, instead of distributing their votes between the two main traditional parties. In the 1934 election 24% of the votes went to a newly formed coalition grouping, the Farmer-Labour Party; in the 1938 election the successor to that party, the CCF, received 19% of the votes while another 16 % voted for the SOCIAL CREDIT PARTY. Both of these new political creations were seen by their supporters as more inclined to address the difficulties experienced by "ordinary" individuals than were the two traditional parties, which were seen as subordinate to the federal Liberal and Conservative parties. The same kind of disaffection for the two traditional parties during this period can be seen in the results of the 1940 federal election, when both the CCF and Social Credit parties succeeded in sending several of their members to the House of Commons.

This inclination on the part of a good portion of the Saskatchewan electorate to throw its support behind political movements, both provincially and federally, in opposition to the two traditionally dominant parties did not arrive unheralded. In a number of ways it was foreshadowed by fissures that had opened up in the agrarian population and by the rise within the urban population of organizations championing the particular concerns and interests of labour groups. In the agrarian sector the SGGA, which had for a very long time enjoyed a near-monopoly as the voice representing farming interests, experienced a dwindling of support and a decline in its membership. In part it was supplanted by a more vocal and impatient farmers' organization, organized in 1921 and styling itself the Farmers' Union of Canada, while in the same general period (1925) in the urban sector the Independent Labour Party was formed. The Liberal Party in the arena of politics and the SGGA in the arena of agrarian interests had jointly been the two preeminent organizations in the province from 1905 until the early 1920s, but both had seen their preeminence increasingly challenged during the decade of the 1920s. The election of 1929, when the Liberal Party's long period of political success ended, can therefore be regarded as constituting an obvious ending to the first period of the province's political story. The next period, stretching for about 15 years between the elections of 1929 and those of 1944, can then be seen as an interlude during which major changes in the province's social and economic arenas contributed greatly to a realignment of political forces which concluded with a new provincial administration being formed by the CCF under the leadership of Premier T.C. Douglas.

The election of 1944 initiated another long period, of about sixty years' duration, during which a stable pattern of political activity has become manifest. Political dominance now alternates between two political tendencies: the one side of this recurring contest is formed around

© M.WEST, REGINA, WEST'S STUDIO COLLECTION/SASKATCHEWAN ARCHIVES BOARD R-A245

W. Ross Thatcher (1964-1971).

SASKATCHEWAN ARCHIVES BOARD

Allan E. Blakeney (1971-1982).

SASKATCHEWAN ARCHIVES BOARD 82-773-754A

Grant Devine (1982-1991).

OKTOBER REVOLUTION PHOTOGRAPHY

Roy Romanow (1991-2001).

the CCF and its successor, the NEW DEMOCRATIC PARTY (NDP), while the other side can be viewed as coalescing behind the leader of whatever political organization seems at any particular time to have the best chance of defeating the CCF/NDP. Recurring contests between these political tendencies have led to an alternation in the holding of the political reins of governmental power. In the first twenty years of this period, from 1944 to 1964, the provincial government was formed by the CCF, first led by T.C. Douglas (1944–61) and then by Premier WOODROW S. LLOYD (1961–64). This long hold on power by the CCF ended with the 1964 election, in which the overriding issue of importance was the controversy surrounding the province's introduction of medicare. The Liberal party was successfully able to capitalize on this issue and won the election, forming a new government under the leadership of Premier W. ROSS THATCHER; this administration remained in office until the election of 1971, when it was defeated by a resurgent NDP under the leadership of ALLAN E. BLAKENEY. The government that was formed by Premier Blakeney remained in power for eleven years, being re-elected in 1975 and 1978. By the time that the next provincial election was scheduled to take place, in 1982, it was evident that the major organized political force opposing the Blakeney government was the Progressive Conservative Party. Led by D. GRANT DEVINE, the Progressive Conservatives won an overwhelming victory, capturing 55 of the 64 available seats and reducing the New Democrats to a rump group of only nine members, who were largely centred in the province's two major cities.

Premier Devine's administration was re-elected in 1986, but was confronted with increasing difficulties and scandals in the following years. In his last year in office, Devine failed to bring a provincial budget to a vote in the province's Legislature and resorted to financing the government's expenditures by the use of special warrants instead of a legislatively supported budget. This unusual and constitutionally questionable practice ended when the government's constitutionally mandated five-year time limit to hold office without an election began to run out and the Premier was forced to call an election. The 1991 election, which took place exactly five years plus one day after the 1986 election, resulted in an outcome that was almost the reverse of the election of 1982: the New Democrats, under the leadership of ROY J. ROMANOW, elected members to 55 out of the 66 available seats, and the Progressive Conservatives only ten. One of the dubious distinctions that can be attached to Saskatchewan's political history during this period came in the aftermath of the defeat of Premier Devine's government, when convictions for fraud were obtained against the majority of the members of his Cabinet—a feat unmatched in any other political jurisdiction in the Commonwealth.

Premier Romanow returned his party to power in

OFFICE OF THE PREMIER

Lorne Calvert (2001-).

the elections of 1995 and 1999. In 2001 he resigned as leader of the NDP and was succeeded as leader of that party and Premier of the province by LORNE A. CALVERT, who in turn succeeded in winning the 2003 general provincial election. This sixty-year period exhibits a pattern of fluctuation in holding political power between a political party, the NDP, popularly seen as being "to the left" of the political spectrum, and a variety of political parties generally viewed as being "to the right" of that spectrum. This pattern does not by itself reveal anything about the political concerns and actions of the various governments that have held office between 1944 and the present; those concerns and actions, however, are discernable in the social and economic framework that developed over that period.

The significant reality of Saskatchewan politics is that it is played out against the backdrop of an economy that mostly delivers meager returns on investments. The agricultural sector, which was for a long time the dominant engine of the provincial economy, has been notoriously subject to fluctuations in price for its products on the world's markets; moreover, it is frequently at risk from the vagaries of the climate. In addition, even though a growing proportion of the province's gross domestic product derives from such resources as POTASH, OIL AND GAS, URANIUM, and FORESTRY products, these products do not, taken together, provide financial returns on a scale that can compare with the level of abundance available in many other provinces. Saskatchewan's geographical location, coupled with a small domestic population, lies at too large a distance from major markets to make manufacturing on any large scale a likely profitable undertaking. Consequently provincial governments, faced with a narrow taxation base, have primarily relied on two sources for the financing of public programs: transfers from the federal government, and careful management of activities under immediate government control.

In societies whose governments are faced by periodic elections, demands for government services, as well as the actual needs of various population segments, do not readily permit governments the luxury of prudently "managing" programs and services under their jurisdiction within the available financial means. Opposing groups that aspire to power are apt to claim that those in power could do a lot more, and a lot better, with a lot less. This dilemma, which faces democratically elected governments in many jurisdictions, is not infrequently at play in Saskatchewan precisely because (a) it is difficult for governments to increase revenue and thus promise to expand services by taxing previously untapped areas of largesse, and (b) the population is so widely dispersed over a large area that the delivery of government services is often more expensive on a per capita basis than in other jurisdictions.

Demands for telephone services, for adequate road networks, for electricity, and for accessible and not financially ruinous hospital and medical services provided the challenge to the government elected in 1944 and to those subsequently elected under the same partisan banner. The avenue chosen by the Douglas administration and its successors was to try to deliver such an expansion of services through direct government involvement in providing them, thereby keeping control both over the services themselves and over their costs. The preferred administrative mechanism used for many of these innovations was to create CROWN CORPORATIONS. Major Crown corporations, such as SaskTel, SaskPower, and SaskEnergy, came to be familiar features of Saskatchewan's economic and political landscape. Other areas, such as automobile and hospital insurance, were also brought under governmental control, and in the early 1960s this extension of government programs through the creation of Crown corporations or by way of setting up provincial controls over the delivery of a variety of services culminated in the creation of the province's medicare program. The introduction of this program proved to be highly divisive, although it provided a model for what within a few years would come to be a nationwide set of programs. The crisis that was engendered by the introduction of this program led in the election of 1964 to the defeat of the CCF administration, which was by then headed by Premier Lloyd.

Over the last sixty years the main contention in the province's politics has largely been over the manner and extent to which the provincial government should be involved in delivering or controlling services and programs. In the electorate's view, the political party identified as being willing to initiate and execute the delivery of public programs is the CCF/NDP, while its opponents—whether in the form of the Liberal Party, the Progressive Conservative Party or, more recently, the Saskatchewan Party—have generally been seen as displaying a willingness to reduce, curtail, or eliminate what some voters and interested parties perceive as unnecessary or mismanaged public programs and services. The rhetoric that accompanies this long-standing contest between these two tendencies in Saskatchewan's politics is often couched in ideological language, especially among individuals who are deeply involved in partisan activities. The manner in which the support in voting swings between these two sides without any evidence of it being primarily motivated by such starkly opposite ideological perspectives points to a motivation that stems from concerns of a perhaps more mundane or practical, but perhaps not any less important, nature.

While this fluctuation in electoral support has been a constant pattern in provincial elections over a long period, important changes have taken place within the population over the course of the last sixty years that have had an impact on where the two parties involved draw their major electoral strength. Until about 1980 the New Democratic Party generally drew electoral support from voters in both urban and rural areas of the province. In the 1982 election it became evident that the major degree of support that it retained in that election was much more concentrated in urban than in rural areas. In the following elections this picture has remained similar, and in the elections of 1999 and 2003 the electoral outcomes clearly support this general observation: it is from the rural areas that the party—regardless of the name it employs—which represents the tendency opposed to the position generally identified with the NDP consistently receives its heaviest electoral support; and it is from the major urban areas that the NDP draws its heaviest electoral support. The political profile of the province's population has largely become a rural/urban divide, with the two main opposing political tendencies reflecting the social and political outlooks of those two publics. The demographic profile of the provincial population has undergone major changes in the last half century. Until the 1950s it was not only predominantly rural, but most of that rural population lived and worked on farms, while many urban dwellers tended to be aware of and sensitive to the needs and concerns of the agricultural population. This has changed: in 2001 approximately 65% of the province's inhabitants lived in urban centres, and the close family or economic ties that many urban dwellers at one time had with their rural counterparts have lessened. Increasingly, it is possible to speak of two solitudes in Saskatchewan—one urban and one rural. It is also possible to conclude that this division is clearly projected on the political scene.

NOTES

1. Seymour Lipset. *Agrarian Socialism* (Los Angeles: University of California Press, 1959).
2. Evelyn Eager. *The Conservatism of the Saskatchewan Electorate: Politics in Saskatchewan* (Don Mills, ON: Longmans Canada, 1968).
3. Census figures are quoted from John A. Archer, *Saskatchewan: A History* (Saskatoon: Western Producer Prairie Books, 1980), 355.
4. Evelyn Eager. *Saskatchewan Government* (Saskatoon: Western Producer Prairie Books, 1980).
5. Archer, *Saskatchewan*, 220.

DON HALL PHOTO

The Legislative Chamber, Saskatchewan Legislative Building.

Population Trends

P

Alan Anderson

GREG MARCHILDON PHOTO
Portage La Loche.

PORTAGE LA LOCHE. For over a century, traders and explorers travelling to the far North-West crossed Portage la Loche, linking the **CHURCHILL** and **ATHABASCA RIVER** drainage systems in northwestern Saskatchewan. The English called it Methy Portage, anglicized from the Cree *mathay* for "mariah fish." To the Denesuline it was *hoteth choghe*, the "big portage." The portage was already well established when **PETER POND** was taken across it in 1778, the first known European trader to reach the Athabasca. Traders, including **HENRY THE ELDER**, had learned of it from **DENESULINE** and **CREE** as they established posts along the upper Churchill River as far as Ile-à-la-Crosse. The 19 km-long level portage is easy walking until the spectacular, steep, 180-metre descent into the **CLEARWATER RIVER** valley. Because of the strenuous climb, brigades bringing furs from the north went only 2 km south along the portage to tiny Rendezvous Lake, where they exchanged their loads with brigades bringing goods from the south. Man-hauled carts were used by 1836, while in 1848 an unidentified "Indian" was hiring out horses. Later, by 1874, oxen were introduced which were wintered at Bull's House on Peter Pond Lake. Then, in 1883, the portage was abandoned when steamboats began operating on the Athabasca River, from Athabasca Landing, northeast of Edmonton. Local activity has maintained the portage, although the old cart ruts are disappearing with the use of all-terrain vehicles.   *Dale Russell*

FURTHER READING: Kupsch, W.O. 1977. "A Valley View in Verdant Prose: The Clearwater Valley from Portage La Loche," *The Musk Ox* 20: 28–49; Marchildon, G. and S. Robinson. 2002. *Canoeing the Churchill: A Practical Guide to the Historic Voyageur Highway.* Regina: Canadian Plains Research Center.

Prior to the 1870s, the lands which would become incorporated into the province of Saskatchewan were inhabited sparsely by First Nations, and during the early 19th century by **MÉTIS** and the fur traders of the North West Company and Hudson's Bay Company. However, by the mid-1870s the new Dominion of Canada sought both European and American immigrants to supplement the inadequate migration of eastern Canadians as farming settlers out west. Canadian politicians began to view western Canada as ideal for expanding Canadian agriculture, especially **WHEAT** farming. In 1870 the Dominion government purchased Rupert's Land from the Hudson's Bay Company, then enacted the **DOMINION LANDS ACT** in 1872; but although the Act opened this territory to free homesteading, it had a limited effect in attracting settlers. When the **CANADIAN PACIFIC RAILWAY** reached Regina in 1882, homesteaders began to arrive; but it was not until a more aggressive settlement policy was inaugurated in 1896 by Clifford Sifton, Minister of the Interior, that larger numbers of settlers came. Sifton sought to attract immigrants from Central and Eastern Europe as farmers, and opened alternate quarter-sections of railway lands in a first phase, creating a checkerboard settlement pattern. As **ETHNIC BLOC SETTLEMENTS** rapidly proliferated, there was a concomitant increase in ethnic diversity.

Population Growth

This settlement process was well underway when the province of Saskatchewan was created in 1905. Regina, the "Queen City," was the focal point of the new province, the seat of the provincial government. Saskatoon, emerging out of the Temperance Colony and destined to be the location of the larger university, had a population of only 4,500 when it officially became a city in 1906. That same year the first census of the new province revealed a population exceeding a quarter of a million, the vast majority (84.4%) being rural. The population continued to increase rapidly through the early 1930s, fed by the largest immigration flow in Canadian history, most of which headed west. World War I only temporarily interrupted this massive flow. By 1931 the Saskatchewan population already numbered close to a million and represented 8.9% of the total Canadian population; in fact Saskatchewan had the third largest population of any province in Canada, after Ontario and Quebec. The population peaked at 931,547 in 1936, then declined during the late 1930s and 1940s to 831,728 in 1951, owing to the **DEPRESSION** and recurrent drought (*see* Table 1).

The population then began to slowly increase again with the postwar "baby boom," but did not recover to the 1936 level until the early 1960s. By this time, however, Saskatchewan contained only about 5% of the Canadian population. As shown in the table, fluctuations have characterized overall population trends in Saskatchewan during the past several decades, and the net population gain between 1981 and 2001 came to only 1.1%. With the exception of Newfoundland, Saskatchewan has the slowest growing population of any province in Canada.

Population density in Saskatchewan averages only 1.7 people per square kilometre; among Canadian provinces, only Newfoundland has a lower density. Yet there are great differences between areas: density is as low as 0.1 in northern areas and less than 1.0 in 257 out of 297 rural municipalities, whereas in Saskatoon and Regina it exceeds 3,000 per square kilometre in some residential areas. **RURAL SASKATCHEWAN** has long experienced depopulation and decline, particularly during the Depression and dust storms of the "Dirty Thirties" when some areas—especially semi-arid areas—lost as much as three-quarters of their population and many smaller communities were turned into virtual ghost towns, in contrast to towns which survived as regional service centres.

There has been a marked shift in population from rural to urban (*see* Table 1 on the following page), so that by 1970 a majority of Saskatchewan's population was urban. Today almost two thirds (64.3%, 629,036 in 2001) of Saskatchewan residents live in urban places—mostly Saskatoon and Regina, which together contain 38.3% of the total population, or 375,036 residents within the city limits. The Saskatoon urban region (CMA) has experienced more rapid population growth than the Regina urban region since 1951, and Saskatoon had passed Regina as the largest city in Saskatchewan by the mid-1980s.

Typically, the urban region population tends to increase faster than the city proper: this has been the case in Regina since 1981, in Saskatoon since 1996. Saskatoon proper had a population of 196,811 in 2001, while there were 178,225 residents of Regina: this represented a slight increase of 1.6% in Saskatoon during the past five years, whereas Regina's population declined by 1.2%. The Saskatoon CMA had a population of 225,927 in 2001, an increase of 3.1% since 1996, whereas the Regina CMA had declined 0.4% to 192,800.

The urbanization of the Aboriginal population (*see* ABORIGINAL POPULATION TRENDS) has contributed to urban growth: in 2001, 36.2% (47,070) of the Aboriginal identity population was on reserve, compared to 46.7% (60,840) in urban places, including 26.8% (34,935) who lived in Saskatoon (where they constituted 9.8% of the city population) and Regina (8.7% of the city population). Yet despite this significant and continuing rural to urban shift, the Aboriginal population still remains less urbanized than the general population. Overall, the urban proportion of population in Saskatchewan is less than in the neighbouring prairie provinces (80.9% in Alberta and 71.9% in Manitoba) or than in Canada as a whole (79.7%).

Population Change

Population change is measured in terms of natural increase or decrease, based on offsetting fertility and mortality trends, as well as controlling for migration. According to demographic transition theory, if the gap between the birth rate and death rate narrows, the population trend becomes static (the usual case recently for the general Saskatchewan population); whereas if the birth rate remains high while the death rate starts to decline, the gap widens, making for rapid population growth (the case currently for the Aboriginal population). Conversely, if both the birth rate and death rate are high, population growth is limited (the historic case for Aboriginal population). In Saskatchewan the rate of natural increase has fluctuated since the 1940s, and a recent decreasing trend can be noted: for example from 10.3 per 1,000 in 1985 to 3.3 in 2001. Yet overall birth and death rates have remained relatively stable for more than half a century—therefore population growth in this province has been largely dependent upon positive net migration. While the Saskatchewan fertility rate is one of the highest in Canada, the absolute number of births is declining.

The "baby boom" of the 1950s through the early 1960s was followed by the "baby bust" period of reduced fertility, then the "echo boom" during the late 1970s through the early 1980s, when the many former "baby boom" babies had now grown up and were reproducing. The Saskatchewan birth rate peaked at 27.9 per 1,000 in 1947, declined slightly, then was high again during the "baby boom"; it declined markedly to 16.2 in 1973 (perhaps primarily due to increasing cost of living, together with improved, more reliable and accessible contraception), then began increasing again during the "echo boom." Couples with children are currently declining proportionately in Regina, whereas non-family households, lone-parent families, and couples without children are increasing.

Ethnocultural variations in fertility trends must be noted, however. Some VISIBLE MINORITIES, usually recent immigrants from high-fertility countries, tend to have higher birth rates. Aboriginals, MENNONITES, and HUTTERITES have exhibited larger average family size, although in all three cases fertility has been declining (among Aboriginals, fertility rates remain far higher on reserves than in cities, which thus reduces the rate of Aboriginal urbanization).

The Saskatchewan death rate, long in the 7.5–8.5/1,000 range, increased to 9.2 in 2001, perhaps to some extent due to the "baby boom" generation of the 1950s now reaching retirement age, but mostly due to a significant expansion of older-aged population. Each year, 62% of deaths occur among people aged 75 and older. During the past several decades, the Aboriginal mortality rate has been steadily decreasing, while still remaining much higher than for non-Aboriginal population for certain causes of death and illnesses.

Migration

Population change is not simply a matter of measuring the rate of natural increase/decrease, or fertility and mortality trends: migration serves as a crucial counterpoint to natural increase/decrease. Population

Table 1. Population Growth and Urbanization

Year	Population	Percent Population Change	Urban Population	Percent Urban
1901	91,279	-----	14,266	15.6
1906	257,763	182.4	48,462	18.8
1911	492,432	91.0	131,395	26.7
1916	647,835	31.6	176,297	27.2
1921	757,510	16.9	218,958	28.9
1926	820,738	8.3	242,532	29.6
1931	921,785	12.3	290,905	31.6
1936	931,547	1.1	280,273	30.1
1941	895,992	-3.8	295,146	32.9
1946	832,688	-7.1	316,760	38.0
1951	831,728	-0.1	251,018	30.2
1956	880,665	5.9	318,013	36.1
1961	925,181	5.1	395,868	42.8
1966	955,344	3.3	464,979	48.7
1971	926,242	-3.0	485,159	52.4
1976	921,323	-0.5	510,048	55.4
1981	968,313	5.1	563,166	58.2
1986	1,009,613	4.3	620,198	61.4
1991	988,928	-2.0	623,397	62.4
1996	990,237	0.1	627,178	63.3
2001	978,933	-1.1	629,036	64.3

Sources: Census data extrapolated from Canada Year Book; Dominion Bureau of Statistics; Statistics Canada

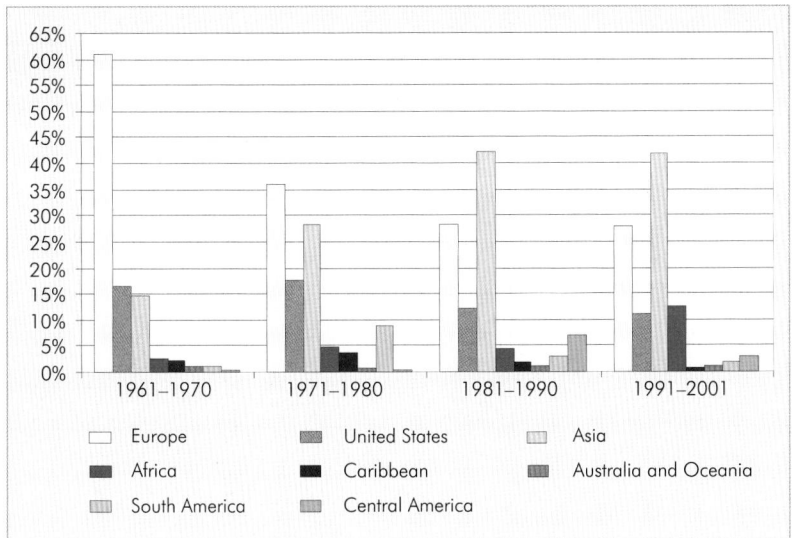

Figure 1. Country of origin for immigrants living in Saskatchewan, 1961-2001.

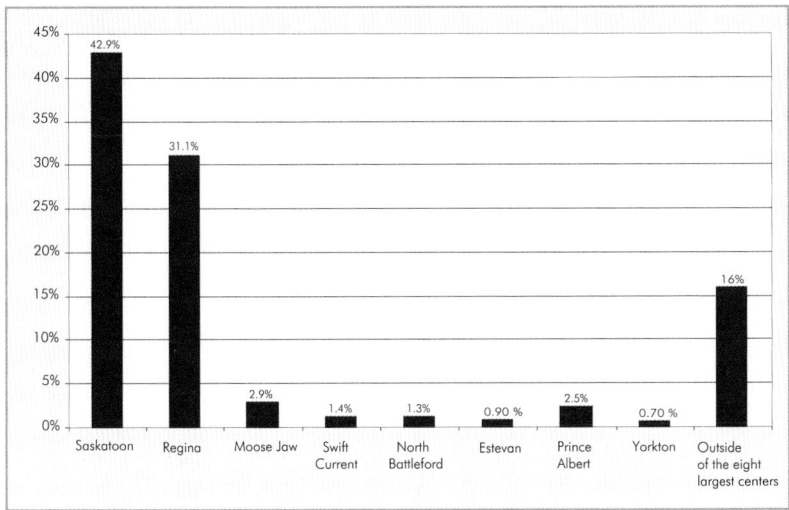

Figure 2. Residence for Recent Immigrants in Saskatchewan, 2001.

growth occurs when in-migration exceeds out-migration. Migration can be international (between other countries and Saskatchewan), inter-provincial (between Saskatchewan and other provinces), or intra-provincial (within Saskatchewan). Saskatchewan had one of the highest immigration rates in Canada during the first two decades of the 20th century. By 1931 immigrants made up more than a third (34.6%) of the province's population, the rest of which was seldom more than second- or third-generation. But then the immigration flow was greatly affected by the Depression, with low urban employment and recurrent drought making for persistent RURAL DEPOPULATION: Saskatchewan had become an unattractive destination for immigrants. Between 1931 and 1945, the province suffered from the lowest immigration rates to Canada in history. The Canadian immigration rate was increasing again by 1951, but Saskatchewan was no longer a prime destination. Moreover, in recent decades most immigrants into Canada have headed for Toronto, Montreal, and Vancouver—the country's three largest metropolises. Between 1981 and 2001, Saskatchewan experienced positive net international migration (i.e., more immigrants arriving than emigrants leav-

ing); however, the net gain in population was only 30,985. While 18% of Canadians are foreign-born, only 5% of Saskatchewan residents are. In terms of population growth, it has long been problematic that a substantial proportion of immigrants and refugees eventually leave the province: Saskatchewan now has one of the lowest immigrant retention rates in Canada (57%).

The foreign-born (immigrant) population of Saskatchewan has been aging, yet immigrants have also been arriving: for example, 30% of foreign-born people arrived before 1961, 23.8% during the 1990s. Visible minority populations in Saskatchewan, while increasing, remain minimal. Despite new immigration from Asia, Africa, and Latin America, fully half of the immigrants in Saskatchewan and 87.1% of immigrants who arrived before 1961 are of European origin. Increasing numbers of immigrants and refugees are arriving from Latin America, Tropical Africa, the Middle East, South Asia, East Asia, and Southeast Asia. Currently a third of government-assisted refugees arrive from Sudan and a quarter from Afghanistan; yet in recent years refugees have also come from Europe: Poland, the former Yugoslavia, and the former Soviet Union. Now 42% of immigrants into Saskatchewan have come from Asia, and a majority of them are members of visible minority groups (*see* Figure 1). Almost three quarters of recent immigrants live in Saskatoon and Regina (*see* Figure 2). Most recent immigrants are skilled workers, family class, or refugees. Their educational levels are far higher than non-immigrant residents: over a quarter of the adults possess a university degree.

As for inter-provincial migration, Saskatchewan has long had sustained net migration losses, primarily affected by changing economic conditions. The largest annual loss was in 1989–90 (19,928), and the largest over a five-year period in 1987–92 (69,721). The net loss of population over two decades from 1981 to 2001 was 120,000, of which 76,690 was to Alberta, 34,358 to British Columbia, and 13,594 to Ontario. There has been in recent decades a vast movement out of Saskatchewan (*see* Table 2): between 1981 and 2001, out-migrants totaled 482,676, compared with 357,615 in-migrants. Alberta has been both the major destination (60% of out-migrants) and the major source of inter-provincial migrants (half of all in-migrants).

Table 2. Inter-provincial Migration Into and Out of Saskatchewan, 1981–2001		
	Out-Migration	**In-Migration**
Total	482,676 (100%)	357,615 (100%)
Alberta	232,340 (48.1%)	155,650 (43.5%)
British Columbia	99,025 (20.5%)	64,667 (18.1%)
Ontario	63,183 (13.1%)	49,589 (13.9%)
Manitoba	59,940 (12.4%)	59,574 (16.7%)
Quebec	7,406 (1.5%)	7,691 (2.2%)

To some extent, leavers and arrivals could be the same people: someone might go to Alberta to work, then return to Saskatchewan. But this degree of major out-migration has not been equaled in other provinces. The exodus has been influenced by many factors, especially unemployment or limited employment opportunities, farm sales and closures, and leaving to retire in warmer climates. The greatest movement has been between Saskatchewan and its more affluent neighbour, Alberta: so distance can be a factor. Age of migrants is also an important consideration: younger members of the labour force seem most likely to leave; 51.5% of out-migrants in 1981–2001 were aged 15–29. In a sense, the two provincial universities often educate young people to leave. This large number of young adult out-migrants certainly has an effect on the most important reproductive cohorts, again affecting population growth.

The third basic type of migration, intra-provincial, largely assumes the form of urbanization (rural to urban migration), but could also refer to other types of movements including from rural farm to rural non-farm, changing residence within the city (intra-urban), or moving from one city to another (inter-urban). Analyzing these movements can become very complicated: there are distance and temporal factors, as well as socio-cultural factors. For example, while there has recently been substantial migration of non-Aboriginal people out of mining communities in the far north, the Aboriginal population up north has been growing: rural depopulation has to a considerable extent augmented urban populations. There has been continuous out-migration from reserves, especially of young adults, due to a lower standard of living, less health care, limited educational opportunities, unemployment and low income, harsh living conditions, and so on; yet as conditions improve in some reserves, return migrants may be attracted back.

Lower birth rates mean that the main source of population growth has to be migration. But in recent years the capital, Regina, has not been attracting either inter-provincial or intra-provincial migrants as well as other cities in the province: in fact, considering who moved into each city during the past five years (1996–2001), we can note that smaller cities (including Lloydminster, Melfort, Yorkton, Swift Current, North Battleford and Weyburn, but not Estevan) have attracted proportionately more migrants (typically in the 20–30% range) than Saskatoon, Regina, Moose Jaw, or Prince Albert (typically in the 14–18% range).

Population Composition

Saskatchewan had an exceptionally high male disproportion in the sex ratio until the 1940s, ranging between 118.1 in 1901, with a peak of 145.6 in 1906, to 113.2 in 1946. Since then the sex ratio has become more balanced: 109.4 in 1951, and 100.3 in 1986. It must be noted that during the past decade, partially owing to a higher age-specific mortality rate for males, the older the age cohorts, the more females outnumber males. The dependency ratio—the proportion of the total population aged 65 and older (elderly dependency) together with those aged 15 and younger (child dependency)—has been gradually declining since the 1960s: it was 56.8 in 2001. Child dependency has declined from 69.9 in 1901 to 60.0 in 1961, then to 33.2 in 2001, whereas old age dependency has increased from 4.4 in 1901 to 16.3 in 1961, then 23.6 in 2001. Compared with other provinces, Saskatchewan has a high proportion both of elderly and young: 29.2% of the provincial population is under the age of 20, 19% over the age of 60. The provincial age structure has been affected by significant out-migration of young adults as well as by rural decline: many smaller communities have an inverted age structure, with very few children and many middle-aged or elderly adults. There is a "youth bulge" among Aboriginal population, a disproportionate number of people in younger age cohorts; even in urban areas almost half of the Aboriginal population is under 20 years of age. In many Saskatoon and Regina inner-city schools, Aboriginal pupils now form a majority. The Aboriginal dependency ratio (74.9) is far higher than for the general population, and even higher (82.8) on reserve, but lower in Saskatoon and Regina (68.3). The median age on some reserves is under 20, and all northern reserves have child dependency ratios exceeding half the total population there.

The ethno-cultural composition of the Saskatchewan population has changed dramatically over the years. With the settlement process and high immigration between the 1880s and the 1920s, much of the prairie land area was rapidly converted into ethnic bloc settlements. Increasing intermarriage or exogamy over time has led to an increasing proportion of the population claiming multiple rather than single ethnic origins, although recent immigrants have tended to be more endogamous. Visible minorities now constitute 2.9% of the Saskatchewan population (compared to 13.4% nationally). Visible minorities are concentrated in the province's two largest centres; in 2001, visible minorities made up 5.6% of Saskatoon's population and 6.3% of Regina's population. Altogether, 80.8% (20,290) of the province's visible minority population lives in these two cities. (*See also* ETHNIC BLOC SETTLEMENTS, RURAL POPULATION, URBAN ETHNIC DIVERSITY, VISIBLE MINORITIES, INTER-PROVINCIAL MIGRATION, INTERNATIONAL IMMIGRATION, ABORIGINAL POPULATION TRENDS, URBAN ABORIGINAL POPULATION)

George Porteous, 1976.

PORTEOUS, GEORGE (1903–78). A selfless devotee to the service of others, the Honourable George Porteous was born in Douglas, Lanarkshire, Scotland on April 7, 1903. He attended secondary school in Saskatoon and earned his BA from the UNIVERSITY OF SASKATCHEWAN in 1927. His outstanding social service activities with the YMCA began in 1922 as boys' work secretary in Saskatoon. He held other positions with the "Y" in Victoria, Montreal, and Brantford before joining the war effort. In 1941, Porteous went to Hong Kong with the Winnipeg Grenadiers and following the colony's surrender was a prisoner of war for the remainder of the conflict. He was decorated as a Member of the Most Excellent Order of the British Empire for his efforts in maintaining prisoner morale during this period. He returned to Saskatoon after his release and was named executive director of the Saskatoon Community Chest and Council Inc. Porteous was invested with the Order of Canada in 1974 and was appointed LIEUTENANT-GOVERNOR of Saskatchewan on March 3, 1976. He died in office on February 6, 1978.

PORTNALL, FRANCIS HENRY (1886-1976). Francis Henry (Frank) Portnall was born on May 3, 1886, on the Isle of Wight, England. He began his architectural training at the age of 14 and then was hired as a draftsman with the London firm of Weir, Burrows and Weir. In 1906, he immigrated to Canada and worked on a farm in Manitoba. After harvest that year, Portnall was hired by the Toronto architectural firm, Darling and Pearson, and moved to Regina to supervise the construction of the Metropolitan Methodist Church, now the Knox-Metropolitan United Church (ironically, he collaborated on a revised design when this church was destroyed by a tornado six years later). Portnall returned to Winnipeg, but by 1909 was back in Regina as the junior partner of Frederick Chapman Clemesha. Clemesha and Portnall quickly became known for their residential designs; against strong international competition, their design for the Manitoba Legislative Building in Winnipeg placed second. Portnall served overseas during WORLD WAR I and rejoined the firm in 1919. He practised alone after Clemesha moved to California in 1922. Portnall is perhaps best remembered for his churches, schools, and many beautiful homes in the Old Lakeview area of Regina. He was also well-known in the arts as an accomplished portrait painter and vocalist. He died in Regina on September 13, 1976.

Ross Herrington

POS PILOT PLANT. POS Pilot Plant is a non-profit, confidential research organization that specializes in extraction, fractionation, purification, and modification of biologically derived materials. The company, which was founded in July 1977, is located in the Innovation Place Research Park on the UNIVERSITY OF SASKATCHEWAN campus. POS Pilot Plant, the largest pilot plant operation of its kind in North America, has grown from eighteen employees in 1977 to over ninety employees in 2003. The company employs people from a wide range of disciplines: scientists, engineers, technicians, operators, tradespeople, logistics and information researchers, and administrative personnel. POS Pilot Plant is dedicated to finding personalized solutions for clients' bioprocessing needs. Services provided include: process and product development, optimization and scale-up; hazard analysis and critical control points; protocols and good manufacturing practice plans; and ingredient sourcing, shelf-life testing and analytical development. There are also consulting services, and support services concerning materials management, maintenance, and information. POS Pilot Plant serves bioprocessing industries including nutraceuticals and functional foods; cosmetics and fragrances; fats, oils and lipids; food and ingredients; animal feeds; and BIOTECHNOLOGY and agricultural biotechnology.

Jessica Pothier

POST-SECONDARY EDUCATION LIBRARIES. The first post-secondary education library in Saskatchewan was established at the UNIVERSITY OF SASKATCHEWAN in 1909, developing from a handful of books to 51,013 books in 1933. Two special collections—the Shortt Collection of 5,170 volumes of Canadian and American History, and the Prairie Provinces Collection of 1,665 volumes—defined prairie history. Several affiliated theological colleges developed their own libraries, supplementing the main university library's general collection. By 2003, the University of Saskatchewan Library's collection consisted of more than five million items, and a growing collection of digital materials that served more than 20,000 faculty and students.

The UNIVERSITY OF REGINA library began in 1911 as a small, unorganized collection of books housed in the Regina College. By 1920, the collection consisted of 505 volumes kept in locked glass cases in a room that doubled as a public waiting room. By 1965, the collection had increased to approximately 121,000 volumes. With the establishment of the University of Regina in 1974, the library developed a union catalogue for itself and the libraries of three federated colleges (Campion, Luther, and Saskatchewan Indian Federated College—now the FIRST NATIONS UNIVERSITY OF CANADA). In 2003, the library's collection exceeded two million items.

Long before there were technical institutes, library services informally supported technical training. By 1941, vocational and academic training cen-

POS Pilot Plant.

tres were set up in Saskatchewan, and by the late 1950s Saskatchewan established technical institutes to provide credit training in a wide range of occupations. Since 1988, the **SASKATCHEWAN INSTITUTE OF APPLIED SCIENCE AND TECHNOLOGY** (SIAST) has been the pre-eminent organization providing such training. The four SIAST campus libraries have shown tremendous growth in resources and services since their inception. With campus libraries in Moose Jaw, Prince Albert, Regina, and Saskatoon, trained library staff now serve on- and off-campus patrons in every part of the province.

Expanding library services to meet the post-secondary education needs of First Nations and Métis peoples has been a unique Saskatchewan achievement. The Saskatchewan Indian Federated College, **SASKATCHEWAN INDIAN INSTITUTE OF TECHNOLOGY**, **SASKATCHEWAN INDIAN CULTURAL CENTRE**, and the **DUMONT TECHNICAL INSTITUTE** have provided services. The creation of the First Nations University of Canada in 2003 was a major development in the Aboriginal control of Aboriginal education.

Other specialized libraries providing targeted services for post-secondary education support are the libraries of the Centre for Co-operative Studies, and the Native Law Centre and Theological College libraries located at the University of Saskatchewan. Briercrest Family of Schools College Library, in Caronport, serves high school, college, seminary, and distance-learning students. Staff enthusiasm and a keen sense of co-operation have been key features of library services in Saskatchewan. The existence of local networks, and participation in the Council of Prairie and Pacific University Libraries (COPPUL), a consortium of twenty-two university libraries located in Manitoba, Saskatchewan, Alberta, and British Columbia, help member libraries to co-operate and collaborate in order to enhance information services through resource sharing, collective purchasing, document delivery, and many other library activities. *Tej Harrison*

POTTER CLUBB, SALLY (1917–92). Born on February 6, 1917, Sally Potter graduated from Saskatoon **NORMAL SCHOOL** and taught for four years in rural schools at Bounty, Pike Lake and Hoosier. She then returned to Saskatoon, where she married James E. Clubb on October 15, 1946; the couple had three children. Her seminal book, *Saskatoon's Historic Buildings and Sites* (1973), co-written with **W.A.S. SARJEANT**, helped spur provincial legislation to protect Saskatchewan's architectural legacy. Among her other published writings are: *Saskatoon: The Serenity and the Surge* (1966) and *Our Story: 75 Years of Caring: St. Paul's Hospital* (1982). She also wrote a series of articles on ethnic groups in the province. Potter Clubb later worked as a supply teacher in Saskatoon and Delisle, and as a library assistant at the **UNIVERSITY OF SASKATCHEWAN**

College of Medicine. She also served on a civic committee to identify and list historic buildings and sites. She died on February 9, 1992, in Saskatoon.
Ruth Wright Millar

FURTHER READING: Sarjeant, W.A.S. 1993. "A Saskatoon Historian: Sally Potter Clubb, 1917–1992," *Saskatoon History Review* 8: 1–4.

POTASH INDUSTRY. Potash production is a major Saskatchewan industry, which has played a significant role in the economy for over 40 years. The ten producing mines in the province are among the largest and most modern in the world. Underground potash deposits were laid down by evaporation in an ancient inland sea; three major layers of potash are separated by layers of salt. Potash deposits are located from the Alberta border west of Saskatoon, through much of the central portion of the province, to the southeast corner and beyond. Much of Saskatchewan's deposits are 3,000-3,500 feet underground; but they are deeper further south, beyond conventional shaft and mining techniques. Operations are located where potash-bearing ore is 7-11 feet thick. Most potash in Saskatchewan is in the form of potassium chloride (KCl). Recoverable reserves are well over 100 billion tons. Of the potash produced, 95% is used for fertilizer, and the remainder for industrial purposes. Potash was first found in Saskatchewan in 1942 during oil drilling. Further discoveries in the 1940s and early 1950s confirmed enormous deposits. However, three projects in the 1950s encountered formidable water

problems during shaft sinking, which hampered development.

Production commenced in 1962 when water problems were overcome at the International Minerals and Chemical (IMC) mine near Esterhazy; the Potash Company of America (PCA) then rehabilitated its flooded mine. A surge of development by other companies resulted in twelve companies opening ten mines by 1970. Industry expansion exceeded market growth, producing a crisis that threatened some mines with closure. Having earlier pressed for rapid development, the government was then forced to intervene and introduce a "rationing-pricing" plan, which saved the industry from disaster. As the industry recovered, a new NDP government pressed for increased provincial revenues and wanted to participate actively in plant expansions. Industry resistance grew, especially after a major taxation increase. Eventually, most companies stopped paying provincial levies, refused to expand capacity, launched court actions to thwart government initiatives, and stopped supplying standard production information. Federal actions further complicated matters. The government responded by announcing on November 12, 1975, that it would seek powers to acquire, by expropriation if necessary, ownership of part or all of the potash industry.

From 1975 until 1982 a **CROWN CORPORATION**, Potash Corporation of Saskatchewan (PCS), acquired through negotiation ownership of four mines and the producing property of another operation mined under contract. These acquisitions, together with plant expansions, resulted in PCS owning 40% of

RON GARNETT—AIRSCAPES

IMC Potash, Esterhazy.

Saskatchewan's productive capacity. PCS, a very profitable operation which was aided by good marketing conditions, played an active role in international industry affairs and contributed materially to a growing Saskatchewan economy. It also planned on further expansion and diversification. At the same time, negotiations resumed between the government and potash producers, including PCS, on royalties and other provincial payments. The agreement reached brought the government significantly higher revenues while ensuring potash producers a reasonable rate of return. Potash markets became more difficult when the government changed in 1982: PCS expansions continued without an accompanying marketing strategy; and incurred heavy losses. By 1988, PCS was privatized as part of a broader privatization program; the process was completed in 1991, just before another change in government. Studies concluded that the province had lost a significant amount of value in the process.

The privatized PCS Inc. has since acquired another mine and expanded into nitrogen and phosphorus production, becoming a diversified fertilizer producer. It is now a very profitable operation, potash still providing its main strength. International Minerals and Chemicals (IMC) has acquired two other mines, bringing its total ownership to four. **CARGILL** now has a major stake in IMC. Agrium, formerly Cominco, is the only other potash operator in the province. Thus, the industry has been effectively rationalized into three firms, each with diversified fertilizer operations. The ten mines completed by 1970 still constitute today's capacity. A small potassium sulphate (K_2SO_4) operation near Wynyard combines standard KC_1 with Mg_2SO_4 from Quill Lake to produce K_2SO_4, used for specialty fertilizers. Three mines are located near Esterhazy and Rocanville, one at Belle Plaine between Moose Jaw and Regina, while the other six are between Lanigan and the Saskatoon area. Production in the last twenty years totalled 230 million tonnes of KCl sold for $22.7 billion. Provincial direct revenues during this time were over $2 billion. Direct employment has been stable near 3,000, plus associated activities. Capital spending over the last twenty years totalled $1.6 billion. While potash has made an important contribution to the Saskatchewan economy, it is debatable whether it has achieved its full potential for the province. *John Burton*

FURTHER READING: Richards, J., and L. Pratt. 1979. *Prairie Capitalism: Power and Influence in the New West.* Toronto: McClelland and Stewart; Saskatchewan Department of Mineral Resources. 1976. *Potash: Challenge for Development.* Regina: Queen's Printer.

POULTRY BREEDS. The term "poultry" includes all bird species that reproduce freely under man's care. Saskatchewan has them all. Predominant are

UNIVERSITY OF SASKATCHEWAN ARCHIVES, R.D. CRAWFORD FONDS, MG 132, FILE C.26.9

Roosters of some heritage breeds that were popular on Saskatchewan farms until the 1950s. Left to right: White Wyandotte, Barred Plymouth Rock, Light Sussex, White Jersey Giant.

chickens and turkeys. There are hundreds of poultry breeds, such as Plymouth Rock and Leghorn, distinguished by outline or silhouette, and there are many hundreds of varieties within breeds, such as Barred Plymouth Rock and Single Comb White Leghorn, distinguished by feather colours and patterns and by head adornments. The leading academic reference book is *Crawford's Poultry Breeding and Genetics* (1990).

Poultry breeds in Saskatchewan can be divided into three categories. Fancy poultry, bred for perfection of feather and form, are kept and exhibited by hobbyists. Little attention is paid to production (eggs and meat) performance. A Canadian monthly publication, *Feather Fancier,* provides news and information, and sources of breeding stock, books, and equipment for hobbyists.

Heritage breeds were used in the past for food production but they have been discarded now by the commercial poultry industry. Light Sussex, Barred Plymouth Rock, and Brown Leghorn chickens, and Bronze turkeys are examples. A national organization, Rare Breeds Canada, provides communication and coordination of activity for conservationists who want to maintain these old breeds.

The commercial poultry industry provides eggs and meat for consumers. Only a few breeds and varieties are utilized–White Leghorns for eggs, White Plymouth Rocks and White Cornish for broiler chicken meat, and white turkeys for meat. They are bred by multinational corporations using sophisticated breeding and selection procedures. Their production stocks are distributed throughout the world. All of our eggs and poultry meat come from these production stocks although none of them are bred in Saskatchewan. *R.D. Crawford*

FURTHER READING: Crawford, R.D. (ed.). 1990. *Poultry Breeding and Genetics.* Amsterdam: Elsevier.

POULTRY FARMING AND INDUSTRY. The definition of poultry can be far-reaching if one accepts it as "avian species that readily reproduce

under human care (domesticated) and provide an economic return to caregivers." However, the major farming contribution of poultry is from chickens and turkeys; a small number of farms have ducks and geese. The poultry that arrived in Saskatchewan with European pioneers included chickens, turkeys, ducks and geese. Birds were reared extensively and were frequently scavengers in the farmyard; for most, reproduction was via brood females and natural incubation. These birds were an important source of meat and eggs for farmers; the extra product was marketed locally. As time passed, chicken and turkey production evolved into a more sophisticated industry, some farmers raising more birds to provide a larger component of farm income. Poultry extension demonstrated the potential to make money feeding poultry rather than exclusively marketing the grain. Poultry breeders developed "Record of Performance" testing to assist in selection of superior birds and prove the value of their stocks, which they marketed to other producers. In the case of chickens, early production focused to a large degree on dual-purposed strains that provided reasonable amounts of both meat and eggs.

Poultry farming has changed dramatically since then. The number of farms keeping poultry has decreased, but the number of birds has increased. Although many farmers still maintain small poultry flocks, farming has changed from a backyard source of food and minor income to a sophisticated and intensive business. Marketing has also shifted from an open market system to marketing boards that control production in Canada to increase bargaining power regarding the value of meat and eggs. There are four marketing boards in the poultry area in Saskatchewan: **CHICKEN FARMERS OF SASKATCHEWAN**, **SASKATCHEWAN BROILER HATCHING EGG PRODUCERS MARKETING BOARD**, Saskatchewan Commercial Egg Producers Marketing Board, and **SASKATCHEWAN TURKEY PRODUCERS MARKETING BOARD**. They were established in the 1970s to stabilize supply and to ensure profit. Saskatchewan poultry farming has also become specialized and can be divided into four major components: farms devoted to egg production for human consumption; farms that keep multiplier breeder flocks to provide broiler hatching eggs (broiler breeder farms) for local hatcheries; broiler producers (chicken meat); and turkey producers. The source of birds for meat and egg production has also changed: a small number of multinational companies have supplanted local breeders and supply the same genetically superior animals as found elsewhere in the world. Local breeders no longer exist because competition and the high cost of sophisticated breeding programs have resulted in extreme consolidation of the breeding industry.

Although feeding varies according to the class of poultry because of different nutrient requirements, key ingredients are similar for all types of production. Feeds are either manufactured on farm or, more frequently, purchased from commercial feed manufacturers. Nutrient-balanced diets are composed of cereal grains (primarily wheat), protein concentrates (soybean meal, canola meal), supplemental fat (vegetable oil, tallow), and vitamins and minerals. Mash diets (ingredients ground and mixed together) are fed to laying hens and breeding birds, but meat chickens and turkeys are usually fed crumbles and pellets (heat- and pressure- processed) to obtain maximum productivity.

In 2003 there were sixty-six egg producers in Saskatchewan, producing approximately 24 million dozen eggs from 832,000 laying hens. At the current price of $1.60 per dozen, the value of egg production approximates $32 million. After hatch, pullets are reared to nineteen weeks of age before starting the egg production cycle, which typically lasts one year. Both pullets and hens are primarily housed in cages located in environmentally controlled barns. Automated feeding, watering and egg collection are standard in most egg production barns. Day-old pullets are purchased from hatcheries that specialize in hatching egg-production pullets. The vast majority of hens lay white-shelled eggs that are derived from crosses of White Leghorn strains. Pullets can be raised by egg producers or by specialized farms until they are ready to lay. Egg production has increased dramatically as a result of genetic selection, from 175 to over 300 eggs per hen per year between 1925 and 2000. Most eggs are marketed to a commercial processor in Saskatoon, where they are graded and then distributed to customers in Saskatchewan and western Canada.

Chicken meat production involves two types of farms: broiler breeder farms, which produce hatching eggs; and broiler producers, which raise chickens to be marketed for meat production. In 2003, Saskatchewan had nineteen broiler breeder producers, with 200,000 breeders producing an income of approximately $8.5 million. Broiler breeder males and females are purchased from one of a small number of multinational primary breeding companies, each derived from specific two-way crosses. As a consequence, the commercial broiler that is raised for meat is a four-way cross. Each of the original pure-line strains used in the four-way cross is selected by the primary breeder for a wide range of production and health parameters. Breeders are raised on litter floors (e.g., straw) in environmentally controlled barns, and reach sexual maturity at about twenty-four weeks of age. During the breeding period males and females are primarily kept in barns with combination slat and litter floors. Again, feeding, watering, and usually egg collection are automated. Most modern barns have roll-away nests, where eggs roll to a collection belt after being laid. Generally ten males are kept per 100 females in natural mating flocks. Each hen is capable of laying 175 eggs in a forty-week egg production cycle; 85% of the eggs produce broiler chicks for a total of 148 chicks. Hatching eggs are picked up from breeder farms by the broiler hatchery in Wynyard (Lilydale Foods) on a biweekly or weekly basis. The eggs are placed in setters for eighteen days and then transferred to hatchers for the last three to four days of incubation. Broiler chicks are distributed from the hatchery to broiler producers in the province.

In 2003, ninety-eight Saskatchewan broiler chicken producers marketed 41.4 million kg of live chicken worth approximately $51 million. As with other classes of poultry, broiler production has become much more intensive, with barns holding 20,000 to 30,000 birds and farms often having multiple barns. Birds are housed on litter floors with automated equipment for feeding and watering. As with most types of poultry production, farms are run on an all-in all-out basis for disease control reasons. In this type of production, all chicks for the farm are placed together at hatch and marketed to the processor in Lilydale Foods on the same day. Between broiler production cycles, the barns are cleaned and disinfected prior to the arrival of the next flock of chicks. Male and female broilers are raised together; the market weights depend on specific markets: across Canada, broiler market weights vary from 1.7 to 3.0 kg; but the current Saskatchewan market is for birds in the 1.70 to 1.75 kg weight range. Broilers are usually marketed between thirty-two and thirty-nine days of age, and producers will place 6.7 broiler flocks per year. As with egg production, broiler productivity has increased markedly over the years: birds took 120 days to reach 1.8 kg in 1925, but take only thirty-three days to reach the same weight now. The Canadian industry has increased in size to support a growth in per capita consumption of chicken from 9.5 kg in 1960 to 30.5 kg in 2003. This represents a major change from previous times, when chicken was a meat for special occasions.

Saskatchewan has a small but well-managed turkey industry: twenty producers marketed 5.8 million kg of live turkey in 2003, valued at approximately $8.8 million. Although a specialized turkey hatchery was at one time present in Saskatchewan, day-old turkey poults are now purchased from hatcheries in neighbouring provinces. As with other classes of poultry, turkeys are the result of strain crosses derived from a small number of multinational primary breeders. Birds have white feathering, in contrast to the bronze turkey that was common in Saskatchewan years ago. Selection of turkeys has resulted in much improved growth rate and breast muscling: modern birds have far more breast meat compared to the "broad breasted" strains of yesteryear. Turkeys are reared sex-separate, and most of the current Saskatchewan production consists in hens marketed at relatively small body weights (5 to 7 kg) for the whole-bird market. Males (toms) are usually kept to larger weights and used for further processing into a wide range of meat products. Turkey production in Saskatchewan has shifted from seasonal to year-round, and at the same time the industry has changed from outdoor or range rearing to environmentally controlled barns with litter floors.

Henry L. Classen

POUNDMAKER (C. 1842–86). Chief Poundmaker (Pihtokahanapiwiyin) was born in the Battleford region around 1842 and raised by **CREE** relatives. As a young adult, he was adopted by Chief Crowfoot, a Blackfoot, thereby creating family ties between two nations. Poundmaker was proficient as

A view of the laying cages of the Zenith Poultry Farm, located four miles east of Regina, May 1957.

SASKATCHEWAN ARCHIVES BOARD R-B8775
Poundmaker.

a herbalist and a healer, an ability perhaps inherited from his father Sikakwayan, a well-known **ASSINIBOINE** medicine man. Poundmaker's mother was a mixed-blood Cree, sister of Chief Mistawasis. Poundmaker received his name because of his expertise in building and utilizing pounds for hunting buffalo. Shortly after signing **TREATY 6** he became chief of 182 people, who settled on a reserve about forty miles west of Battleford. He quickly established himself as a fine orator, speaking out against the failure of the federal government to live up to treaty commitments. Poundmaker was not against the concept of the treaties, but he wanted a treaty that would make sense to his people. He wanted respect shown to his people, and provisions that they would need in times of famine. In 1885 Poundmaker, members of his band, and members from nearby bands traveled to Battleford to ask for rations. When they arrived at the village they found the community deserted and helped themselves to some supplies. In response, Lieutenant-Colonel William Otter and 325 troops were sent to Cut Knife Creek, where Poundmaker and his Cree followers were encamped. On May 2 a battle occurred, and Otter was forced to withdraw, with Poundmaker stepping in to prevent further bloodshed. When Poundmaker heard of **RIEL**'s defeat at **BATOCHE**, he traveled there and surrendered his arms; he was

immediately imprisoned. Poundmaker was tried and convicted of treason in Regina, and sentenced to serve three years at Stony Mountain Penitentiary (Manitoba). To avoid angering his powerful father, Chief Crowfoot, Poundmaker's hair was not cut and he served only seven months of his sentence. Even though his prison time had been shortened, it destroyed his health, and while visiting Chief Crowfoot in 1886 (shortly after his release) he suffered a lung hemorrhage and died at the age of 44. On October 13, 1972, a plaque commemorating Poundmaker was unveiled by Jimmy Poundmaker, his grandson, at the Cut Knife battlefield site on the Poundmaker Reserve. (*See also* **CUT KNIFE HILL, BATTLE OF**) *Christian Thompson*

FURTHER READING: Estlin Bingaman, S. 1975. "The Trials of Poundmaker and Big Bear, 1885," *Saskatchewan History* 28 (3): 81–94.

POUNDMAKER AG-VENTURES. Poundmaker Ag-Ventures Ltd. near Lanigan is Canada's first integrated facility where ethanol, a clean-burning fuel that reduces harmful emissions, is made from grain, and cattle are fed the by-product of the brewing process.

Poundmaker Ag-Ventures was established in 1970s when area farmers were looking for an alternative market for their grain. The feedlot that originally could handle 4,500 cattle was expanded by the mid-1980s to 8,500. Poundmaker Ag-Ventures provided area farmers with an opportunity to diversify and market their grain locally.

In 1991, based on the recommendations of a series of feasibility studies, a 10,000-head feedlot and a 10-million-litre ethanol plant were constructed. Money was raised through a secondary share offering which expanded the local ownership base to 200 people from the original fifty. Shareholders also obtained the first right to deliver their grain to the new facility, assuming price and quality of their grain was equal to the grain being offered by farmers who were not shareholders. In 1998, another expansion resulted in a one-time feedlot capacity of 28,500 head and yearly marketing of 54,000 cattle.

More than 8,500 bushels of **BARLEY** and **RYE** each day is mixed with barley silage, green feed and hay and then combined with the wet distiller's grain, which is also called mash, to be fed to the cattle in the feedlot.

Grain is processed with enzymes and the mash is distilled to produce a high quality alcohol. Fuel grade ethanol is about 99% pure alcohol and has a number of important properties that make it an excellent fuel additive for automobiles. Ethanol is a clean burning fuel, containing 35% oxygen that encourages a more complete combustion of gasoline in automobiles and, as a result, reduces harmful emissions.

Poundmaker Ag-Ventures has fifty employees, generates annual sales of $47 million and uses 3,500 bushels of grain each day. With that grain, the company produces 35,000 litres of ethanol daily, and the by-product from the distilling process is added to the feed for the cattle. Ethanol has been embraced by consumers. More than five billion litres of ethanol now is mixed with gasoline in Canada and the United States each year. *Joe Ralko*

POUNDMAKER CREE FIRST NATION. Chief **POUNDMAKER** (Pitikwahanapiwiyin) signed an adhesion to **TREATY 6** on February 22, 1876, at Fort Carlton, and chose a reserve 40 km northwest of North Battleford in 1881. Once a member of Red Pheasant's band, Poundmaker broke away to create a band of his own. He was a good leader and orator, and is recognized for negotiating the inclusion of the "famine clause" in Treaty 6. He died at Blackfoot Crossing near Gleichen, Alberta, and the band remained without a chief until 1920. His remains were returned to the reserve in 1967 and laid to rest on Cutknife Hill. It was announced in 1998 that 904.4 ha were being purchased and set apart as reserve land for the band under the Saskatchewan Treaty Land Entitlement Framework Agreement, increasing the reserve's size to 13,181.1 ha. The band's economic base is agricultural, but also includes businesses such as the Kanatinak Store and Gas Bar. Their infrastructure includes a band office, medical clinic, band hall, school and teacherage. There currently are 1,299 registered band members, with 569 people living on reserve.

Christian Thompson

PRAIRIE CENTRE FOR ECUMENISM. Established in 1984 from an initiative of the Roman Catholic diocese of Saskatoon, the Centre for Ecumenism is sponsored by six local churches: Anglican, Evangelical Lutheran, Presbyterian, United, Ukrainian Greek Catholic, and Roman Catholic. In 2000 the name was changed to the Prairie Centre for Ecumenism to more accurately reflect its growing mission: "to be an instrument for Christian reconciliation and unity in obedience to the Spirit, serving the prairie provinces; to foster understanding among all religious communities, locally and regionally." Modern ecumenical activity is based on the belief and acknowledgement that spiritually, Christians are one, while maintaining and respecting the many differences. The motto of the Prairie Centre is "Gathering the Family of Jesus," but it is also supportive of multi-faith endeavours which foster understanding with and among non-Christian faith communities and traditions. The Centre carries out its educational work through workshops, summer institutes, bulletin inserts, and presentations to parishes and church groups. It has a resource centre with books, audio-visual materials, articles and periodicals and, in conjunction with the Canadian Centre for Ecumenism in Montreal, sponsors a website for information on ecumenical matters in Canada and throughout the world: www.ecumenism.net.   *Anne Keffer and Margaret Sanche*

PRAIRIE CONSERVATION ACTION PLAN.

Saskatchewan's Prairie Conservation Action Plan (PCAP) complements similar provincial prairie conservation efforts in Alberta and Manitoba. It builds upon the first PCAP put forward for the three prairie provinces by World Wildlife Fund Canada in 1989, and the first Saskatchewan PCAP that was launched in 1998. In 2003 PCAP Partners renewed and updated this Action Plan to conserve native prairie. The PCAP vision is that the native prairie be sustained in a healthy state in which natural and human values are respected. The five goals of the PCAP are: to sustain a healthy native prairie grazing resource; to conserve the remaining prairie resource; to maintain native prairie biological diversity; to promote complementary sustainable use of native prairie; and to increase awareness and understanding of native prairie and its values. Relative to these goals, the PCAP Partners developed twenty-five objectives and seventy-eight actions in the 2003–08 Action Plan. Progress is tracked annually though the production of partner updates. In 2004, the PCAP Partnership consisted of twenty-five groups representing industry, federal and provincial government agencies, several non-government organizations, and Saskatchewan's two universities. Chaired by the Saskatchewan Stock Growers Association, the partnership manages the PCAP though a consensual and co-operative approach.   *Robert Warnock*

FURTHER READING: PCAP Committee. 1998. *Saskatchewan Prairie Conservation Action Plan.* Regina: Canadian Plains Research Center; PCAP Partnership. 2003. *Saskatchewan Prairie Conservation Action Plan 2003–2008.* Regina: Canadian Plains Research Center.

PRAIRIE FARM REHABILITATION ADMINISTRATION (PFRA).

The Prairie Farm Rehabilitation Administration (PFRA), a branch of Agriculture and Agri-Food Canada (AAFC), was established by the federal government in 1935 to help mitigate the impacts of a prolonged and disastrous **DROUGHT** which forced thousands of people to leave the prairies between 1931 and 1941. PFRA's original mandate was to deal with the problems of soil erosion and lack of water resources required for agricultural development in the drought-affected areas of Manitoba, Saskatchewan and Alberta. Emergency programs included on-farm dugouts for the conservation of water, strip farming to prevent extensive soil drifting, seeding of abandoned land to curb erosion and create community pastures, and extensive tree-planting projects to protect the soil

from wind erosion. As a result of another drought in 1961, the federal government expanded PFRA's work area to include all agricultural areas of the prairie provinces—more than 80% of Canada's agricultural land base.

Today, AAFC-PFRA work with prairie people to help develop a viable agriculture industry and a sound rural economy in Manitoba, Saskatchewan, Alberta, and the Peace River region of British Columbia through the promotion of soil conservation activities and the development of local water resources. As part of AAFC's shift towards the development and delivery of various national programs, PFRA staff are now playing significant roles in environment-based AAFC initiatives across the country. These programs are targeted towards the development of sustainable national standards for the agriculture industry, and the promotion of environmental stewardship within the sector.

To address the inherent lack of water resources on the prairies, PFRA was for many years heavily involved in large-scale water development and conservation programs. One of those major enterprises was the South Saskatchewan River Project (SSRP). PFRA designed and supervised construction of the SSRP, a monumental undertaking that entailed the development of two dams (Gardiner and Qu'Appelle) and a massive reservoir in south-central Saskatchewan. The project, which began in 1959 and took eight years of round-the-clock work to complete, is epitomized today by 225-km long **LAKE DIEFENBAKER**, which supplies drinking water to approximately 50% of Saskatchewan's population.

PFRA operates thirty dams in southwestern and south-central Saskatchewan, along with twelve major diversion works. Twenty-three of these dams make up PFRA's Southwest Saskatchewan Water Supply System. Developed in the mid-1940s, the system is used to deliver water to 600 irrigators, 17,400 ha of land, and five communities—Swift Current, Gravelbourg, Lafleche, Eastend and Herbert.

With a growing emphasis on the merits of irrigation and the increasing likelihood of a dam and reservoir on the nearby **SOUTH SASKATCHEWAN RIVER** (what would later become the SSRP), PFRA established an irrigation farm at Outlook in 1949. What is now the Canada-Saskatchewan Irrigation Diversification Centre (CSIDC) was established to introduce irrigation technology, new cropping practices, and alternative crops to south-central Saskatchewan. CSIDC is an important part of an irrigation-based crop development and diversification program on the prairies that includes applied research and demonstration facilities at Carberry, Manitoba, and Lethbridge, Alberta. In 1963, PFRA gained a valuable tool for fighting soil erosion and improving living conditions for farm residents when all federal government shelterbelt activities were centralized at Indian Head, Saskatchewan, and

made the responsibility of PFRA.

Now known as the Agriculture and Agri-Food Canada **PFRA SHELTERBELT CENTRE**, the Indian Head facility celebrated 100 years of operation as a federal tree nursery in 2001. Today, the Shelterbelt Centre distributes five to seven million seedlings annually to some 10,000 applicants for field, farmyard, wildlife habitat and agroforestry plantings. Since 1901, the Centre has distributed more than 650 million seedlings to eligible prairie clients.

PFRA operates eighty **COMMUNITY PASTURES** across the Prairies, with sixty-two pastures in Saskatchewan covering 710,000 ha. Not only do these federal government pastures make up one of the largest ranching operations in North America, but by keeping these lands under permanent cover, a great deal of the prairies' diverse plant, insect, bird, reptile and mammal life is maintained. In Saskatchewan, forty-nine of the pastures—some of the last uncultivated land on the prairies—provide a home for "species at risk" as defined by the Committee on the Status of Endangered Wildlife in Canada. Over the past two decades, PFRA-led studies and demonstrations have promoted a better understanding and adoption of measures to address soil erosion, marginal land use, riparian zone management, water quality, and adaptation to climatic risk and change.

Through federal-provincial partnership agreements, PFRA delivers programs and services that help rural clients with activities that contribute to rural renewal, adaptation, and sustainable development. These programs are designed to integrate the economic, social and environmental aspects of agriculture and rural communities. PFRA offers technical and financial assistance in a wide range of areas including: soil and water conservation; water supply development and wastewater treatment; irrigation; rangeland management; community pastures; shelterbelts; engineering, surveying and drafting; project management; economic planning and rural development; integrated resource management; environmental analysis and sustainable agriculture; and wildlife and waterfowl habitat.

With its headquarters in Regina, PFRA has an extensive network of twenty-seven offices throughout the prairie provinces. Its twenty-two district offices (ten in Saskatchewan) are focal points for the delivery of federal agricultural services in the prairie region.   *Wayne Wark*

PRAIRIE FARM REHABILITATION ADMINISTRATION (PFRA) SHELTERBELT CENTRE.

When the early settlers arrived in the North-West Territories, they found a treeless region with an extreme climate that would not support many of the plants that they had brought with them. In 1901, under the Department of the Interior the government of Canada established at Indian Head, in what

AGRICULTURE AND AGRI-FOOD CANADA 91-08-079

Shelterbelt Centre, Indian Head.

is now Saskatchewan, the Forest Nursery Station, dedicated to researching, cultivating, and supplying hardy trees and shrubs to prairie farmers. Advice was provided as to where to plant the trees and how to care for them. The group plantings, known as shelterbelts, were planned to protect the settlers, their land and their livestock from the strong winds, as well as to provide relief during the cold winters and shade during the hot summers. Initially, broadleaf species such as American elm, caragana, green ash, Manitoba maple, poplar and willow were grown, as were evergreen varieties of larch, pine and spruce. The Colorado spruce, recognizable in most prairie farm shelterbelts, was not introduced until 1937. Seed from trees found in cold countries was collected and grown to assess survival under prairie conditions.

Orders for trees and shrubs grew at a rapid rate, and a second nursery was established in 1913 at Sutherland, near Saskatoon. Over the years, both stations tested and distributed many tree and shrub species; these plantings have done much to reduce soil erosion, trap snow for additional moisture, help increase farm water supply, and provide shelter for wild life. Both centres have also tested a range of fruit trees. Public information activities, such as fair displays, newspaper advertisements, pamphlets, and presentations to farm groups increased the profile of the nursery. In 1920, the CPR donated to the Forestry Associations of Western Canada a railway coach which traveled to stations with displays promoting the benefits of tree planting, forestry, and shelterbelts.

During the severe droughts of the 1930s the nurseries, in conjunction with the newly formed PFRA (**PRAIRIE FARM REHABILITATION ADMINISTRA-** **TION**), worked to plant over 2,000 km of shelterbelts and demonstrated their use for soil conservation across the prairies. In 1963, the shelterbelt program became part of the PFRA. Two years later, with improvements to the Indian Head facility that included a new water reservoir as well as irrigation and cold storage facilities for trees and shrubs, the Sutherland nursery was shut down.

The Indian Head nursery has grown from its original quarter-section (64 ha) to a full section (256 ha). Between 1901 and 2001, more than 570 million evergreen and deciduous tree and shrub seedlings were distributed by the Indian Head Nursery as a service to prairie farmers as well as to federal, provincial, municipal and other agencies.

Today the Nursery produces twenty-nine hardy tree and shrub species, and its sophisticated facilities allow stable and healthy seedling production for clients. The Centre has three distinct business units focused on research, technology development, and tree production and distribution. Conservation and ecological issues such as reduction of greenhouse gas emissions, soil and water conservation, and enhanced wildlife habitat combine with economic and social returns for rural residents. Each year, approximately five million seedlings are distributed, free of charge, to prairie farmers and rural landowners. The Indian Head Nursery is now known as the Agriculture and Agri-Food Canada PFRA Shelterbelt Centre. *Merle Massie and Allan E. Smith*

FURTHER READING: Kulshreshtha, S. and E. Knopf. 2003. *Benefits from Agriculture and Agri-Food Canada's Shelterbelt Program: Economic Valuation of Public and Private Goods.* Ottawa: Government of Canada.

PRAIRIE PIMPLES. "Prairie pimples" or "pimple mounds" are micro-topographic features found on the flat to gently undulating floors of some glacial spillways, meltwater channels, and floodplains in southern Saskatchewan. In uncultivated or partially uncultivated areas, intact mounds are generally quasi-circular in shape, less than 0.5 metres high and between 10 and 20 metres in diameter. Most mound soils are disturbed by rodents, especially near their centre, and composed mainly of sandy silt or silty clay mixed with an abundance of pebbles and cobbles. In cultivated areas most mounds have been leveled off for agricultural purposes, but they can be seen on aerial photographs as light-coloured patches against the surrounding darker soils. In some areas, these patches are so abundant that the fairly regular pattern seen on aerial photographs is referred to as an "outbreak of prairie pimples." Similar mound features across North America are known as pimple mounds, freckled land, earth mounds, or mima-like mounds. Although their origin has been debated by scientists for over a century, the process that formed these mounds still remains a mystery. Some popular theories include groundwater discharge, seismic activity, permafrost processes, and bioturbation by burrowing animals such as the pocket gopher.   *L. Lee-Ann Irvine*

FURTHER READING: Cox, G.W. 1984. "Mounds of Mystery," *Natural History* 93 (6): 36–45; Geiger, B. 1998. "Mounds (or Heaps?) of Confusion," *Earth* 7 (4): 34–37.

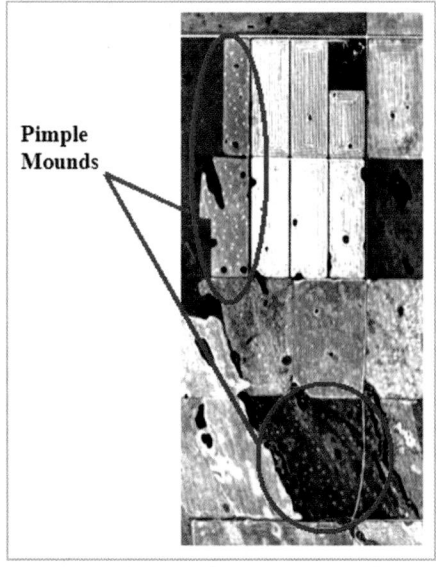

Pimple Mounds

COURTESY OF INFORMATION SERVICES CORPORATION, REGINA

Air photo. Location: T31-R23-W2, east of Watrous.

PRAIRIE RUBBER CORP. Prairie Rubber Corp. started in 1996 as a community-based, economic development idea involving local investors, the town of Assiniboia and Recovery Technologies. The first tires were shredded in 1999 and a new, $4.2 million processing facility opened in 2001. The company employs thirty-six people and generates $5 million in annual sales by recycling the rubber, steel and fibre from scrap tires. The rubber is ground into a wide variety of particle sizes for different markets from sports fields to roofing tiles. FieldTurf, a Montreal-based company that manufactures and installs sports fields, is Prairie Rubber's primary customer. FieldTurf can be found in 30 baseball parks around the world including Tampa Bay, Tokyo and Mexico City Dome, about two dozen soccer teams in England, Russia, Scotland and Spain, and fifty college and professional football stadiums teams in Canada and the United States, including Ottawa and Detroit. New uses for the recycled rubber have included asphalt for paving and moldings for products as diverse as mud flaps and buckets. Steel is sold to IPSCO in Regina while the fibre is used in the Alberta oil patch. *Joe Ralko*

PRAIRIE SWINE CENTRE. Prairie Swine Centre Inc. is a non-profit research and technology transfer corporation, affiliated with the UNIVERSITY OF SASKATCHEWAN, with expertise in three disciplines: nutrition, engineering, and behaviour. The mission of the Prairie Swine Centre is "to provide a centre of excellence in research, graduate education and technology transfer, all directed at efficient, sustainable pork production." Swine production efficiency, environmental sustainability, and animal welfare mark the major thrusts of the Centre. The research program seeks to improve the financial position of pork producers by defining feeding and management systems that maximize net income. In addition, the Centre carries out research to address issues and opportunities in environment, barn air quality, worker health and safety, odour reduction technologies, and animal well-being.

The Centre, established in 1991, has fifty employees and a research and development budget of $2.7 million; it operates both public and contract research programs to meet industry needs. The animal facilities include a 280-sow farrow-to-finish farm with a range of capabilities that allow for pigs to be housed individually through to commercial-scale group sizes. In addition, the facilities contain specialized features for intensive research including metabolism monitoring. A subsidiary, PSC Elstow Research Farm Inc., operates a 600-sow farrow-to-finish facility, as well as a feed mill to conduct near-market research under conditions reflective of typical commercial barns operating in western Canada. *Lee Whittington*

PRAIRIES. Grasslands occupy a vast area in North America, from the Rocky Mountains on the west to the deciduous forests on the east, and from the boreal forests in the north to the Gulf of Mexico. In Canada, mixed-grass and fescue prairie dominate these grasslands. The aspen parkland—a narrow band of grassland with scattered occurrences of aspen groves—separates these grasslands from the forests. The grasslands surround a small, geologically unique upland that has a lodgepole pine vegetation similar to that found in montane regions to the west. Thus grassland, aspen parkland, and montane forest regions constitute the Prairie Ecozone in Canada. This ecozone covers the southern one-third of Saskatchewan, approximately 24 million hectares, extending from the boundary with the United States to the Boreal Plain Ecozone.

Physiography. The Prairie Ecozone is essentially a level to gently rolling plain with numerous subdued uplands dispersed throughout most of its extent. Small but prominent uplands rise above this plain in its southern part. Elevations in the Prairie Ecozone are lowest in the northeastern part of the area. The MISSOURI COTEAU and then the WOOD MOUNTAIN and CYPRESS HILLS plateaus represent successive increases in elevation, from approximately 1,000 m in the northeast to 1,100 m in the southwest.

Geology. Glacial deposits, which represent the surficial sediment throughout the Prairie Ecozone, may be hundreds of metres thick. They are generally thinner in the Prairie Ecozone than in the Boreal Plain Ecozone, and parts of the Cypress Hills and Wood Mountains were not glaciated. As a consequence, the regional topography of today closely mirrors the shape of the bedrock surface that existed prior to glaciation. Also, the composition of the glacial deposits is strongly influenced by the nature of this underlying bedrock. Late Cretaceous and Tertiary age rocks cover older Phanerozoic rocks throughout the Prairie Ecozone. The Tertiary rocks formed mainly in river and lake environments, whereas the Cretaceous rocks are of marine origin.

The youngest rocks of Tertiary age contain appreciable amounts of gravels and quartzites, which have resisted millions of years of GEOLOGICAL EROSION. This has maintained the surface in the Cypress Hills far above the surrounding lands, where the softer and older sands and clays have been largely or entirely removed. Geologists believe that a thickness of about 1 km of Tertiary rocks has been eroded from Saskatchewan's landscape and that before erosion, the extent of the Tertiary deposits may have been much greater than presently known.

Glacial deposits, however, have a profound influence on the nature of the local landscape throughout the ecozone. Till plains and hummocky moraines, often with an abundance of glacial kettles, are a dominant feature of the area. Nearly level glaciolacustrine areas are also common, as are glaciofluvial areas that are often modified by wind to form dunes. Valleys and rivers cross this plain, flowing through the Beaver, North and South Saskatchewan, Red Deer, Assiniboine, Qu'Appelle and Souris rivers to the Churchill and Nelson rivers and into Hudson Bay, and through the Frenchman River to the Missouri River and the Gulf of Mexico.

A dominant regional feature is the Missouri Coteau, a major northeast-facing bedrock escarpment. Many large ice-pushed ridge complexes are located along this escarpment. The Dirt Hills, south and southwest of Regina, are among the largest and best developed ice-pushed ridges in the world. The

Glenn Flaten, (centre left) Chairman of the Saskatchewan Hog Marketing Commission, presented Vice-president Kristjanson (centre right) with a $90,000 cheque, the final instalment of the SHMC's initial commitment of $310,000 toward the capital cost of the Prairie Swine Centre, April 1980.

soft shale and mudstone bedrock was thrust upward by the force of the advancing glacier, so that in places bedrock overlies younger glacial deposits. Postglacial events have also impacted on Saskatchewan's landscape. Underfit streams, with their characteristic floodplains, are active in channels that originated as meltwater channels from the ice or spillways from glacial lakes. Lakes such as those in the QU'APPELLE VALLEY have formed between alluvial fans that blocked the glacial valley where present-day creeks enter it. Sand dunes have been active since glaciation.

Climate. The climate in the Prairie Ecozone ranges from semiarid to humid continental, with long and cold winters, short and very warm summers, and cyclonic storms. Temperatures are highest at lower elevations in the south, progressively decreasing with increasing altitude and latitude. Precipitation is generally low, but it increases slightly from south to north and more markedly from west to east. This precipitation trend, when combined with temperature gradients described above, has created a series of climatic zones from cool semiarid in the southwest to moderately cold subhumid in the northeast. Climatic zonation also occurs in response to altitude, as moderately cold semiarid to subhumid conditions prevail on uplands in what is otherwise the driest part of the ecozone.

Landforms and Soils. Most landforms in the Prairie Ecozone are of glacial origin. Nearly level ground moraine (till plains), glaciolacustrine and glaciofluvial plains are major contributors to the "flat prairie" landscape, although glacial kettles break this monotony in some areas. Gently rolling to hilly hummocky as well as ridged moraines and sand dunes add to the diversity of the landscape. Valleys and coulees, sometimes with enclosed lakes, are often the most striking landscape features.

Soils strongly reflect climate and natural vegetation and the associated landform. Soils formed in glacial till, the sediment that constitutes ground moraine and hummocky moraine, are usually loam textured, while those formed in glaciolacustrine deposits have higher proportions of silt and clay, and those formed in glaciofluvial deposits have more sand and gravel. Chernozemic soils are synonymous with a grassland vegetation, so the entire Prairie Ecozone is dominated by them. Brown Chernozemic soils are associated with mixed grasses in the sub- to semiarid region; Dark Brown Chernozemic soils with a more productive mixed-grass vegetation in the semiarid region; and Black Chernozemic soils with a fescue prairie-aspen grove parkland vegetation in the subhumid region. Dark Gray Chernozemic soils occur in areas transitional to the boreal forest. Solonetzic soils occur in all of the soil climatic zones in association with parent materials containing a high content of sodium salts; Regosolic soils prevail on recent deposits such as

alluvial flood plains and sand dunes; and Gleysolic soils prevail in wetland areas.

Groundwater. In the Prairie Ecozone, the basal aquitard of Precambrian and Paleozoic rocks is overlain by bedrock aquifers. These aquifers in turn are confined by an upper aquitard of Cretaceous shale. The Judith River and Ravenscrag aquifers are the most important of these bedrock aquifers in this ecozone. The Hatfield and Tyner valley and several other buried valleys lie on the bedrock surface and provide valuable sources of groundwater for the ecozone. Aquifers also occur within the glacial sediments, most notably within and at the surface of the Floral Formation. Surficial aquifers, representing sandy and gravelly glacial deposits, are scattered throughout the ecozone.

Vegetation. The Prairie Ecozone is a grassland region. A mixed-grass community dominates the southwestern, warmer, and more arid part of the ecozone, represented by the Mixed Grassland Ecoregion. A late summer moisture deficit, caused by low precipitation and high evapotranspiration, and periods of extensive droughts typify the climate of this area. The resulting mixed-grass vegetation includes what are often referred to as "short grasses" (blue grama grass and sedge) and "mid to tall grasses" (wheatgrasses, June grass, needle-and-thread, and porcupine grass), along with pasture sage and moss phlox.

Northward and eastward from the mixed grassland, moisture deficits are less severe and DROUGHTS are less prolonged. "Mid-grasses" dominate these areas, along with an increase in the extent of shrublands, aspen grove woodlands, and wetlands: this is the Moist Mixed Grassland Ecoregion. A belt, representing a transition from the grasslands to the south and the boreal forest to the north, extends diagonally from southeast to northwest across the southern part of the province. Summers are cooler in this region, winters are longer and colder, and snow cover is more continuous than in the regions to the south and west. Summer evaporation and precipitation rates in this area are almost equal, which minimizes the potential severity of the late summer moisture deficits. Here, a mosaic of trembling aspen surrounds numerous wetlands, forming groves in a sea of plains rough fescue grasslands: this is the Aspen Parkland Ecoregion.

The smooth climatic and vegetation zonation that extends from southwest to northeast across the southern part of the province is interrupted by a prominent upland. High elevations result in a climate that is cooler and more moist than the surrounding dry grasslands. Vestiges of a montane forest, dominated by lodgepole pine, that once extended all the way to the Rocky Mountains remain to this day: this is the Cypress upland.

Many small wetland areas, or sloughs, occur throughout the Prairie Ecozone. In the more humid

parts, these sloughs tend to be more permanent, the water is relatively fresh, and they are ringed by willows and trembling aspen. In drier parts of the ecozone, however, the sloughs are less permanent and more saline, and the transition from the wetland to the grassland is a sharp one. Most freshwater wetlands are characterized by emergent vegetation such as sedges, bulrushes, cattails, and reed grasses on their margins. In the open water, submerged growth of pondweeds, yellow watercrowfoot, and greater bladderwort may be present. Saline wetlands do not have a marginal ring of willows, but rather have shorelines heavily encrusted with white salts and usually bare of vegetation except for a few salt-tolerant plants like red samphire. Salt-tolerant grasses, such as seaside arrow-grass and alkali grass, grow at the margin of the salt crusts.

Wildlife. Historically, the prominent species on the prairie was the BISON. The PRONGHORN antelope, though an animal of the open plains, ranged well into the parkland. Elk grazed on the grassland around the edges of aspen groves. The wolf was the main predator of the ungulates. Settlement and widespread cultivation of the grasslands has caused some species to come near the brink of extinction (as in the case of bison) or to currently occupy a small portion of their former range. An abundance of assorted mice and voles inhabit the matted vegetation in unburned or ungrazed grassland. The thirteen-lined ground squirrel also prefers longer grasses. Richardson's ground squirrel forms extensive colonies on knolls, gravel ridges, and overgrazed areas. The northern pocket gopher spends most of its life underground, feeding on succulent roots in pastures and haylands; its mounds of soil become an annoyance during haying. Coyote, red fox, and the re-introduced swift fox feed chiefly on RODENTS, birds, and INSECTS. The badger feeds predominantly on ground squirrels, which it captures by digging (*see* CARNIVORES). The snowshoe hare inhabits aspen groves during the day, emerging to feed at night, while the white-tailed jack rabbit frequents pastures, cultivated fields, and open, arid prairie, seldom penetrating wooded areas except as shelter from blizzards (*see* HARES AND RABBITS). The striped skunk reaches its highest densities in agricultural areas, and the woodchuck has also prospered as a result of agricultural and forestry practices.

Characteristic grassland birds include western meadowlark, horned lark, upland sandpiper, and chestnut-collared longspur. The vesper sparrow, clay-colored sparrow, chipping sparrow, and sharp-tailed grouse are more abundant on prairie adjacent to woodland. The brown-headed cowbird followed the bison herds and fed on insects associated with them; its migratory nature led it to lay eggs in other birds' nests rather than build its own. The ferruginous hawk and Swainson's hawk will nest on the ground in open arid prairie, while the red-tailed hawk is common to parts of the prairie that supply trees for nesting. In the winter, large flocks of snow bunting and common redpoll frequent grasslands, fields, and road edges, feeding on seeds of forbs and grasses exposed above the snow.

The prairie has more fish species than the boreal plain, this being the result of additional warm water species being found in the Qu'Appelle, Assiniboine, and Souris river systems. Reptile species are most numerous in the prairie, preferring the warmth of a dry arid region. Fourteen species of reptiles occur here, 11 of which occur in the mixed grassland. An additional three species of amphibians occur in the prairie as compared to the boreal plain.

Human Activity. More than 80% of the economic activity of the province is generated in this ecozone, with agriculture as the dominant land use. Called the breadbasket of Canada, much of Canada's and Saskatchewan's cropland and rangeland and pasture are located in the Prairie Ecozone. The other major activities contributing to the economy are mining (**COAL, POTASH,** mineral, and aggregates) and **OIL AND GAS** production. Despite the dominance of agricultural activities on the landscape, the majority of the population is found in urban communities. The 1991 population of this ecozone was approximately 827,000 or 84% of the total population of Saskatchewan. Ten of Saskatchewan's 13 cities are located in this zone, and 81% of the population lives in urban centres. Also, this ecozone has a higher proportion of its labour force in secondary industries than the national average, reflecting the importance of its major urban centres in serving national and international markets.

Agriculture has diversified considerably in recent years in the Prairie Ecozone, from traditional grain crops to more oilseed crops, such as **CANOLA, FLAX,** and sunflowers. Producers have increasingly adopted more sustainable farming practices, including conservation tillage and reduced **SUMMERFALLOW,** reducing the risk of water and wind erosion. The Prairie Ecozone has also been experiencing a trend towards increased livestock production. Agriculture, and to a lesser degree urbanization, have transformed more than 80% of the native prairie landscape. Most of the rough fescue grassland has been ploughed, and much of the remainder has been significantly modified by livestock grazing and haying. Almost all of the tall-grass prairie is gone. Less than 20% of the once abundant mid-grass prairie remains in its native state, about one-quarter of the mixed-grass prairie and aspen parkland. Approximately 40% of the original 2 million hectares of wetlands have been converted to agricultural use. All landscape areas within this ecozone have been cultivated or grazed for at least 20% of their area, and many show 100% cultivation or grazing levels.

Over the past 100 years, the Prairie Ecozone has

undergone development by natural resource industries, largely agriculture and **FORESTRY,** but also oil and gas extraction and refining, hydroelectric power generation, fisheries, and **MINING.** Although these industries have fostered a thriving economy and high standard of living, they have also greatly modified the original ecosystems, diminishing wildlife and plant populations. The Prairie Ecozone has vast amounts of a wide range of non-renewable resources, including oil, natural gas, potash, coal, sodium sulphate, and clay products; it currently contains 14,000 active oil wells and 7,000 active gas wells.

Forested lands are scattered, occurring in gullies, ravines, and areas of higher elevation. Generally the use of such forests has been for recreation or as a source of fuel wood. There is relatively limited commercial fishing activity in this zone. Commercial aquaculture, gill netting and harvesting of brine shrimp, minnows, and leeches occur on selected prairie lakes. There are several private trout hatcheries. The Prairie Ecozone is a popular destination for anglers, providing almost half of all recreational fishing in the province. As well, 22% of the provincial trapping harvest occurs from this ecozone. Over half of the provincial total of hunting of big game and more than 80% of the hunting for bird species occurs in the Prairie Ecozone.

Just under 9% of this ecozone is in some form of park or protected area. Canada's only national park dedicated to the protection of grasslands, **GRASSLANDS NATIONAL PARK,** occurs in this zone. Saskatchewan's Watchable Wildlife Society has identified 90 "eco-sites" in the province that represent areas with a high degree of natural significance for ecotourism. The Prairie Ecozone contains 55 of those sites. (*See also* **ECOZONES AND ECOREGIONS; GLACIAL DEPOSITION**)

Donald F. Acton, Glenn A. Padbury and Colette T. Stushnoff

FURTHER READING: Acton, D.F., G.A. Padbury and C.T. Stushnoff. 1998. *The Ecoregions of Saskatchewan.* Regina: Canadian Plains Research Center and Saskatchewan Environment and Resource Management.

PRATT, CHARLES COWLEY (1816–88). Also known as Askenootow (Worker of the Earth), Pratt was born in 1816 among the Young Dogs band of **CREE/ASSINIBOINES,** *nêhiyaw-pwâtak,* at the fish weir between Mission and Echo Lakes in the Qu'Appelle Valley. His mother was Cree/Assiniboine and his father was a **MÉTIS** buffalo hunter, Zacharia Floremond. He is remembered as an Anglican lay reader/catechist and schoolteacher (1851–84), interpreter for **TREATY 4** at Fort Qu'Appelle (1874), and the first First Nations person from the Canadian plains to receive a western education. In 1822 his people sent him on the Hudson's Bay Company Swan River fur brigade to present-day Winnipeg to

be educated at the Anglican Church Missionary Society's (CMS) Red River Indian Mission School (est. 1820). The condition under which he was sent was that he be returned once he had learned how to read and write. Pratt rejoined his buffalo hunting people in 1832, and between 1835 and 1848 he worked for the Hudson's Bay Company as a boatsman and labourer in the Swan River district. In 1850 he returned to the CMS as an interpreter and schoolteacher.

Over the course of his career, Pratt established five inland missions (Fort Pelly, Qu'Appelle Lakes, Round Lake, and Little and Big Touchwood Hills), observing the devastating impact of European expansion on his people: once healthy, independent buffalo hunters, they were then reduced to small, starving bands, wrought by waves of disease epidemics and rounded up on reserves. As per CMS policy, Pratt and other Native church workers received half the salary and supplies received by their European counterparts. By choice and necessity he lived among and followed the traditional livelihood patterns of his people: buffalo hunting, fishing, gathering, and trapping. As a mediator between worlds, Askenootow did his best to help his people adjust to hard and changing times. His baptismal namesake was Josiah Pratt, secretary of the CMS at that time. Askenootow later adopted Cowley as his middle name after the Reverend Abraham Cowley, with whom he spent his earliest years as a CMS interpreter and schoolteacher. In 1841 he married Catherine Sinclair of Norway House, with whom he had twelve children. Widowed in 1869, he married

PHOTO COURTESY OF WINONA WHEELER

Charles Cowley Pratt.

Elizabeth Kashepuyas in 1874. Charles Pratt took treaty with his lifelong friend George Gordon in 1874, and remained in the service of his people until a paralytic stroke forced his retirement in 1884. He died in 1888.

Winona L. Wheeler

PRECAMBRIAN HISTORY. Precambrian (> 0.54 billion years or b.y. old) rocks underlie all of Saskatchewan, but in the southern two-thirds of the province they are covered by younger Phanerozoic rocks. The exposed Precambrian Shield rocks include several Archean (> 2.5 b.y. old) continental landmasses (cratons) and younger, Paleoproterozoic (2.5–1.6 b.y.) orogenic belts separating them. The cratons are thought to be the precursors of our modern continents and probably moved about the Earth's surface on tectonic plates, much as continents do today. The orogenic belts represent zones along which two or more tectonic plates were amalgamated. They are analogous to the Himalayas, where India collided with Asia, and would have been mountain belts for tens of millions of years following the collisions. However, over time such belts in Saskatchewan have been worn down by erosion. The most obvious example is the TRANS-HUDSON OROGEN, which occupies the southeastern part of the Precambrian Shield. It was a complex orogeny that resulted from the amalgamation of three Archean cratons between 1.9 and 1.8 b.y. ago. These were: the Rae-Hearne (Churchill) Craton, which occupies almost all of the remainder of Saskatchewan's exposed Shield; the Sask Craton, which is exposed only in very small areas west of La Ronge and in the Pelican Narrows area; and the Superior Craton, which is mainly exposed in Ontario and Quebec but may extend into the Kamsack-Carnduff area under Phanerozoic cover. The Thelon-Taltson Orogen affected only the northwestern corner of Saskatchewan; it resulted from 2.0–1.9 b.y.-old amalgamations of the Slave Craton, located in the northwest of the Northwest Territories, and from smaller cratonic slices extending into northern Alberta.

Each craton developed independently before amalgamation, but afterwards its geological history was shared with its new neighbour. This development likely included earlier cratonic amalgamations and breakups extending back to about 2.7 b.y. ago, before which the young, hot planet may have used other ways to cool. The Rae-Hearne Craton extends southward under Phanerozoic cover rocks almost to the American border, northeastward to the Arctic Islands and beyond, and is bounded by the Thelon-Taltson and Trans-Hudson orogens; granitoid rocks as old as 3.1 b.y. north of LAKE ATHABASCA record the earliest known phase of its history. Cycles of widespread volcanism, plutonism, and sedimentation at about 2.7 b.y. and 2.6 b.y. probably record early collisional events as the craton was being assembled. Granites and sedimentary rocks 2.3 b.y.

old concentrated in the extreme northwest may record the accretion of small cratonic slivers to the western margin of the Rae-Hearne Craton. 2.0–1.93 b.y.-old granitoid emplaced northwest of Lake Athabasca and northeast of La Loche resulted from consumption of an oceanic plate west of the craton. Closure of that ocean occurred when the Slave Craton and a number of smaller cratonic slivers that were also riding on the approaching ocean plate collided with the Rae-Hearne Craton. The resulting Taltson-Thelon Orogen involved major mountain building, associated metamorphism, and granite emplacement throughout the northwest between 1.93 and 1.90 b.y. ago.

The Sask Craton underlies virtually the entire Trans-Hudson Orogen and extends southward to the vicinity of the American border, but is poorly understood because of its limited exposure. The early history is recorded by sedimentary and 3.1 b.y.-old granitic gneisses, some of which carry hints of an otherwise unrecognized 2.7 b.y. ago tectonic event. A widespread 2.53–2.43 b.y.-old igneous suite may have resulted from the breaking off of the Sask Craton from a larger pre-existing cratonic body. Volcanic and granitoid rocks dominate the Reindeer Zone, and were derived as a result of ocean plate consumption between 1.92 and 1.83 b.y. ago. The eventual collisions and associated mountain building of the Trans-Hudson Orogen were underway by 1.86 b.y. ago or earlier. By 1.83 b.y. ago, all of the oceanic plates had been consumed and the three cratons amalgamated. The resulting metamorphism ended by 1.80 b.y. ago, after which subsidence following the orogenic activity created an extensive but shallow basin for deposition of the Athabasca Group. The Precambrian Shield was intruded by minor granite at 1.76 b.y. ago and subsequent diabase at 1.27 and 1.1 b.y. ago, but has otherwise formed a stable basement for the deposition of younger Phanerozoic sedimentary rocks. (*See also* GEOLOGY)

Janis Dale

PREECEVILLE, town, pop 1,074, located in the north-eastern parkland, about 105 km N of Yorkton at the junction of Hwys 9, 47, and 49. The vast area of the Porcupine Provincial Forest lies to the north, and Preeceville sits along the upper reaches of the ASSINIBOINE RIVER. Fur trading activity in the area dates to the latter 1700s. Ranching activities, which had begun in the late 1800s, gave way to homesteads after the township was surveyed in 1900. The Canadian Northern Railway arrived in 1912; on February 6 of that year the fledgling hamlet was incorporated as a village, its name honouring the Preece family upon whose land the community was built. With the arrival of the rails, settlement of the district increased, many settlers being of Scandinavian and Ukrainian origins. The community experienced a period of rapid growth during the

1940s, its population almost doubling over the decade. On November 30, 1946, Preeceville attained town status with a population of 540; it had a peak population of 1,272 in 1986. The area economy is based on agriculture, a combination of grain and livestock production. Preeceville is a supply and service centre for a trading area population of approximately 5,500. Major annual events include: the Preeceville Lions Trade Show each April; "Western Days," the summer fair held in July; and the Musher's Rendezvous, a major winter festival featuring sled dog races that attract competitors from as far away as Minnesota, the Yukon, and Alaska.

David McLennan

PREHISTORIC ART. Saskatchewan's inventory of the archaeological sites and artifacts that survive today is enriched by a wide variety of art, although the particular climatic and soil conditions of Saskatchewan are inimical to preservation of items other than the most durable. The art remaining is mostly composed of stone. Both parietal or *rock art* (rock paintings and carvings on immovable stone surfaces) and *portable art* objects have been found. Unfortunately, virtually all of the examples of artistic expression are without authorial or precise temporal context; they exist as surface artifact finds or enigmatic open-air carvings or paintings on rock walls or boulders. Some of the rock art can generally be assigned meanings or purpose, and can be approximately dated by comparing the Saskatchewan examples with those observed elsewhere. The 70-plus rock painting sites in the Canadian Shield in the north of the province are likely the work of the direct ancestors of today's Wood CREE residents, made by shamans or other individuals to assist in curing or divining practice, and may conceivably be as old as 2,000 years.

The St. Victor Petroglyphs south of St. Victor, and about a dozen or so petroglyph boulder sites probably date to 300 to 800 years before present, and may be the work of carvers with roots in the Eastern Woodlands, east of the Plains. Many such carvings were made with a pecking and grinding technique; however, a series of sites in the SOURIS RIVER valley contain figures made by drilling small holes in the soft sandstone. Several of the boulder petroglyphs feature a human-like head and face as the sole figure. The original context of the best known of these, the Weyburn Petroglyph (now in the ROYAL SASKATCHEWAN MUSEUM), and its similarity to shell mask figures from burial mounds in Manitoba and various midwestern states suggest that they served as mortuary art.

Figures of BISON, composite water creatures, turtles, human hands, grizzly bear paws, humans, four-pointed stars, crescents and geometrics appear incised on about a dozen red pipestone "tablets," which probably came into the province as valued trade items from the horticultural villages of the Dakotas. Future mineralogical analysis would be needed to determine if most or many are catlinite, quarried in southwestern Minnesota. They appear to date to just before the inception of the historic period, 300 to 500 years ago. Other stone portable and semi-portable art creations include a small number of hard stone tablets or discs bearing turtles, human hands and a few other motifs, as well as several small boulders bearing representations of the human foot. Many of these motifs also appear in the petroglyph sites of the south and in the pipestone tablets—but what these correlations and motifs mean, if anything, is uncertain. Some connection or influence from the Mississippi iconographic traditions of the Late Prehistoric seems likely.

Some of the figurative **BOULDER MONUMENTS** or boulder configurations in the grasslands of the south have what we today might (perhaps mistakenly) classify as art. These include representations of humans, a bison, a salamander, probably a number of snakes, and definitely a much larger number of turtles than the half-dozen or so recorded to date. Out of all this we see that turtles are among the most prominent art symbols, appearing in various media; historic northern Plains Indian groups regarded the turtle as a symbol of longevity or fertility, and it was used by the Mandan and Hidatsa of North Dakota in bison-hunting ceremonies. All the art forms discussed to this point are two-dimensional. However, two of the three petroglyph boulders near Herschel—especially the largest—are carved partially in the round. Both may be categorized as ribstones, esoteric representations of bison which were used to encourage hunting success.

Additionally, portable sculpted items made of various stone materials including limestone, granite, other hard stones (and even a bison of natural asphalt), have been found by collectors. These items are finely crafted, and at least some of them were probably kept in medicine bundles to be periodically used ceremonially. Some atlatl weights (if indeed they are that) represent animals such as weasels or otters. These examples do not exhaust the topic of the art of the prehistoric peoples of Saskatchewan. Most of the pottery vessels made by generations of Saskatchewan artisans is decorated in one manner or another, ranging from simple finger pinches to incisions, and even drawings (on some burial pots). Various utilitarian items such as a rib handle with a fish incised for holding stone scrapers, and a functional pestle with added features that identify it as a penis attest to the fact that humans here a long time ago, as elsewhere, followed the universal impulse to exercise their creative and even playful imaginations. *Tim Jones*

PREHISTORY, NORTHERN SASKATCHEWAN.
The archaeological record of the forests of northern

TIM JONES PHOTOS

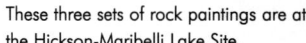
These three sets of rock paintings are at the Hickson-Maribelli Lake Site.

Left, a group of small paintings on a boulder in the water in Smith Narrows between Hickson and Maribelli Lakes. The crescent attachment on top of the anthropomorphic figure's head is unusual, but the very stylized depiction of the human form is not. Possibly this element indicates special powers possessed by this individual.

Centre, this striking figure appears to be a combined human and animal form, although the extremely stylized nature of the figure makes it impossible to say. Certainly such an interconnectedness between the human and natural worlds is documented ethnographically for the Northern Cree cultures of the region. The horns strongly suggest spiritual power.

Right, these three figures are very bright in colour, but are different from the majority of other rock paintings in northern Saskatchewan in that they are not a reddish-brown ochre colour, but a dark chocolate brown. The central figure is obviously human, but shown in the sparest possible fashion. The mark next to it is clearly a smoking pipe, based on other painted northern Saskatchewan examples, and the bird figure may well be the powerful thunderbird deity prominent in Subarctic Indian mythology.

Saskatchewan is not well known. This is in part because the amount of research in this area of the province has been limited, in part because the archaeological deposits are shallow and the preservation of materials poor. On the whole, the surface soils in the north have been remarkably stable since deglaciation, largely because of the anchoring effect of the heavy vegetation. As a result, there has been little erosion and deposition, and stratified deposits are therefore rare. Given this situation, it has been very difficult to discern the sequence of changing archaeological cultures over the millennia. Also, because the forest **SOILS** are acidic, all bone tends to decompose relatively quickly. Since most archaeological occupations do not contain bone, it is not possible to determine the animals that were relied upon for food, nor is it possible to learn during which season the occupations occurred. The latter is accomplished in other environmental settings (i.e., the grasslands) by examining such things as tooth eruption and wear patterns in order to determine the time of year in which an animal died. An equally critical problem is that this lack of bone reduces the archaeologist's opportunity to obtain radiocarbon dates. In short, the forested region of northern Saskatchewan presents archaeologists with some major research challenges. Therefore, it has been necessary to extrapolate some interpretations from neighbouring regions, such as the Barren Grounds, where there are some stratified deposits and where there is better preservation of the bones of food animals. In the southern edge of the forest, stratified deposits in the **SASKATCHEWAN RIVER** valley have also been very important.

By 10,500 years ago, the glacier front had receded to about the latitude of the present-day **CHURCHILL RIVER**; however, the newly exposed lands would have been a chaotic environment of buried ice blocks, raging meltwater rivers, and glacial lakes. In particular, ponded against the ice front was a huge northwestern arm of Glacial Lake Agassiz. It is not surprising, therefore, that human colonization of the north does not seem to have begun until after 9,000 years ago. The hunting weapon employed by these people appears to have been the atlatl, a throwing stick with a hook at one end which is used to propel small spears (darts). In the upper Churchill River basin, three Cody complex lanceolate, stemmed spear points have been found, which on the plains date to about 9,000-8,500 years ago. The people who produced the Cody complex were established plains bison hunters, so the presence of some of these people in the upper Churchill River region probably reflects continued warming in postglacial times, which allowed grasslands (and **BISON**) to expand well north of the historically known limits.

Shortly after 8,000 years ago, the glacial front retreated north, out of the province, and it is likely that the barren-ground caribou population had increased and was migrating seasonally. In any case, people making lanceolate spear points (Plano complex) had clearly become well established, with a subsistence economy focused on barren ground caribou. These people would have lived in small, mobile bands that followed the caribou in their movements between the tundra adjacent to the ice front in the summer and the forests to the south in the winter. This economic cycle has been referred to as "herd following," and was characteristic of the occupants of the northern transitional forest until historical times, when it was recorded in some detail for the **DENE** (Chipewyan) of northern Saskatchewan. It is therefore the oldest subsistence economy in the north, and during the summer took people out onto the open tundra of the Barren Grounds.

In the millennia that followed, a succession of archaeological cultures have been recognized in the forest-tundra transition zone and the neighbouring Barren Grounds—all produced by the herd followers. These, best known from the Barren Grounds to the north of the province, are: Shield Archaic, about 7,500-3,500 years ago; Arctic Small Tool, about 3,500-2,650 years ago; Taltheilei, about 2,650-1,400 years ago; and pre-contact Dene, about 1,200-250 years ago. The Shield Archaic is characterized by the introduction of large, side-notched points, and the continuing production of small numbers of leaf-shaped points suggests a development out of the preceding Plano culture. While this may have been the case, it is clear that the Arctic Small Tool culture was brought into northern Saskatchewan by some bands of Paleo-Eskimos from the Arctic coastal regions, probably because deteriorating (colder) climatic conditions had made life in the Arctic increasingly difficult. These Paleo-Eskimos crafted remarkable miniaturized stone tools, delicately flaked from fine-grained, flinty stones. As for Taltheilei, this culture appears to have been brought to the region by peoples from the northwest, the Mackenzie valley region. Taltheilei is recognized by the presence of stemmed dart points and chithos; the latter are disc-shaped hide-working tools that were chipped from coarse stone. A major volcanic eruption on the Alaska/Yukon border, about 1,250 years ago, may have forced pre-contact Dene (ancestral Chipewyan) to move into this region. These people made small side- and corner-notched projectile points, many of them arrowheads.

The second major subsistence economy of northern Saskatchewan was that present in the boreal forest proper, including the Churchill River basin. This economic system was more broadly based, being oriented to taking moose, woodland caribou, black bears, beavers, fish, and waterfowl. Plant foods such as cattail and bulrush roots, as well as berries would also have been important. In the boreal forest, the impact of milder and drier conditions during the Hypsithermal was particularly important. This climatic period reached its peak aridity and temperatures about 9,000-6,000 years ago, at which time the grasslands expanded northward and were bordered by a band of open deciduous forest (equivalent to the contemporary aspen parklands) that extended almost as far north as the Churchill River. This northern extension of the grasslands, along with the deciduous forest, appears to have been sparsely occupied by peoples who

made lanceolate (Plano Complex) points. This cultural group appears to have been followed, by at least 6,000 years ago, by some bands of Mummy Cave series peoples, best known from the more southerly grasslands. These peoples employed side-notched points to arm their atlatl darts. Following this, peoples related to those who produced the Oxbow and McKean cultures of the grasslands occupied this region. On the southern grasslands, these cultures date to about 5,000-4,000 years ago and 4,000-3,000 years ago respectively; they may have similar dates in this boreal forest region. These people occupied a forest environment much the same as that known historically, and were generalized hunters and gatherers. They probably relied heavily on fishing, and used some kind of watercraft.

Following 3,000 years ago, the archaeological record is unclear but, as has been noted, Taltheilei cultural materials appear in the north about 2,650 years ago. While some Taltheilei peoples remained in the far north as herd followers, others expanded south throughout the boreal forest. In this environment, they would have been generalized hunters and gatherers. About 1,500 years ago a new material culture, with ties to the Eastern Woodland cultures of the Great Lakes, made its appearance. Known as Laurel, it was characterized by pottery vessels made in a cone shape and often elaborately decorated with impressions made by notched tools. Peoples of this culture expanded eastward as far as Prince Albert and La Ronge, and as far north as Southend on **REINDEER LAKE**. Initially, these people appear to have used the atlatl; however, by the end of Laurel times, around 900 years ago, the bow and arrow had come into vogue and small stone arrowheads with side-notches were made.

The peoples of Laurel culture are believed to have maintained lifeways very similar to those of the historic occupants of the boreal forest. They would have made canoes in the spring, and travelled, fished and hunted from these watercraft throughout the open water seasons. They almost certainly made dip and seine nets, as well as fish weirs of poles and stones. In the winter they would have made toboggans and snowshoes in order to move efficiently over the deep snow pack within the forest. In late Laurel times, a small amount of Blackduck pottery appeared in the Saskatchewan forests. This pottery style is characterized by its globular shape and by elaborate impressed decoration on the rim and neck. It is best known from sites in southern Manitoba, adjacent Minnesota, and northwestern Ontario.

Although pre-contact Dene materials remained in place in the western and northwestern sections of the boreal forest during Laurel times, about 700 years ago a new and vigorous culture expanded throughout the boreal forest of northwestern Ontario, northern Manitoba and northern

Saskatchewan. Called Selkirk, the peoples who produced this material culture made globular pottery vessels inside fabric bags, decorating them quite simply with a line of punctates around the lower rim. Also characteristic of this culture are side-notched arrowheads, barbed harpoon points, and ground stone celts (axes). This culture, which ended with the introduction of fur trade goods about 300 years ago, is generally considered to have been produced by the ancestors of the Crees of northern Saskatchewan.

David Meyer

FURTHER READING: Brandzin, V. 1997. "The Spruce Rapids Site (GdMo-5): An East-Central Saskatchewan Laurel and Selkirk Occupation Site," *Saskatchewan Archaeology* 18: 1-102; Gibson, T.H. 2001. *Site Structure and Ceramic Behaviour of a Protohistoric Cree Aggregation Campsite*. Oxford: Archaeopress, BAR Inernational Series 947; Gordon, B.H.C. 1996. *People of Sunlight, People of Starlight: Barrenland Archaeology in the Northwest Territories of Canada*. Hull: Archaeological Survey of Canada, Mercury Series Paper 154; Meyer, D., and D. Russell. 1987. "The Selkirk Composite of Central Canada: A Reconsideration," *Arctic Anthropology* 24 (2): 1–31.

PREHISTORY, SOUTHERN SASKATCHEWAN.

Written history in Saskatchewan began in 1690 with **HENRY KELSEY**; the time before that is "prehistory." Theoretically, prehistory in the province extends back to about 12,000 years ago, but the earliest scientifically (radiocarbon) dated site is from about 10,000 years ago, near Ponteix. This entry provides information on the prehistoric human presence in southern Saskatchewan. The data become less precise as we go back further in time, due in part to the fewer numbers of people, the likelihood that their traces are more deeply buried, and the erosional forces that have affected their remains. The information itself is what archaeologists call "material culture": the physical remains of past human activities that are still present on or within the land.

The Environment. Material culture is found in a physical context: the environment. Over thousands of years, environments change. When humans first set foot in what is now Saskatchewan, the northern half was still covered by glacial ice. The land surface closest to the ice sheet was tundra; moving south, first was boreal or northern forest, and then the area from Regina south, which was open woodland and aspen parkland. But this changed relatively quickly: over the last 8,000 or so years, the two dominant ecosystems in Saskatchewan have been the boreal forest in approximately the northern half of the province, and the plains ecosystem (grassland and parkland) in the southern half, with the border between the two moving north or south a few kilometres with climatic fluctuation. The **BISON** was the dominant animal in the plains ecosystem. The large ice age **MAMMALS**, including mammoths, horses, camels, and sabre-toothed cats, were mostly gone by the time humans arrived.

Material Cultures and Their Sequence. The prehistoric material cultures of southern Saskatchewan have varied over time, with some aspects changing more than others. Some such materials are characteristic of times and places: these *artifacts* then become diagnostic of those times and places. Less diagnostic, but contextually important, aspects of material cultures are *features*, marks left on and within the earth by human activity, such as hearths. The most distinctive diagnostic materials from southern Saskatchewan's prehistory are stone *projectile* points and pottery or *ceramics*, the latter extending back to a maximum of about 2,000 years in time and the former back to the first humans. Based on such materials, archaeologists have identified three cultural periods in North America, all of which apply to southern Saskatchewan, predictably named the "Early" (12,000-8,000 years ago), "Middle" (8,000-2,200 years ago), and "Late" (2,200 years ago to A.D. 1690) periods. The first two of these are identifiable mostly by projectile points; the third is identified both by projectile points and ceramics in association with certain other tools that make up distinctive assemblages.

The oldest scientifically dated site in Saskatchewan is at Ponteix, where a hearth and associated stone tool-making debris dates to 10,000 years ago, in the middle of the Early period. The earliest peoples hunted mostly bison by various methods, including still-hunting, impounding or surrounding; they also took a wide variety of smaller mammals as well as fish. Vegetable materials were important resources too, but these have not been

well preserved. Spears were used to kill animals, so that the projectile points characteristic of this cultural period are spear points (*see* accompanying photo). In fact, the second-oldest radiocarbon-dated archaeological site, Heron Eden, contains 9,000-year-old spear points in direct association with the bones of about three dozen bison, of a variety larger than the modern one. Over the Saskatchewan prairies a number of spear points identical to types excavated and dated in sites elsewhere in North America, especially in the American Plains, have been found (Clovis, Folsom, Eden, Hell Gap, etc.); unfortunately, most are surface finds, and therefore not datable. However, the fact that many of these finds are made of Swan River Chert, a chippable stone type found primarily in eastern Saskatchewan and western Manitoba, suggests that local people were present at this early period. This interpretation is supported by the discovery of a spear point made of Swan River Chert at the St. Louis Site in 2002, dating to about 7,800 years ago. Over 4,500 years or so of occasional human occupancy, the environment of the St. Louis site changed from forest to parkland.

The Middle period is marked by an increase in specialized artifact types, such as pestles and grinding stones, associated with use of vegetable resources, and by a reduction in projectile point size as well as style changes. Notched dart points become common, the notches likely being used for attaching to short spears or darts that were launched with throwing sticks or *atlatls*. Bison remained the predominant resource, as during the Early period.

The Late period is marked by three important shifts identifiable in the archaeological record: a switch to much smaller notched stone projectile points, arrowheads, launched with bows; the introduction and rapid dispersal of use of ceramics to

carry and heat food and water (*see* accompanying photo); and a marked increase in use of mass bison kill techniques (drives and jumps) as a means of procuring this all-important animal.

The archaeological record in southern Saskatchewan, then, shows both a series of identifiable changes in technology and lifestyle, yet a continuity in the nature of the primary resource, bison. The record also shows an identifiable increase in efficiency of resource extraction and preparation practices, along with an increase in the use of vegetable materials.

The lifeways of prehistoric peoples in southern Saskatchewan reflect the hunting-gathering lifestyle, with heavy emphasis on the bison resource. Bison are non-territorial bovines capable of frequent movement, including regular migrations. Some populations were probably resident in relatively small home ranges the year round, but the majority—as much as 90% or more—migrated onto the grasslands for the summers and into lightly wooded areas for the winters. Environments favoured by both resident herds and winter migrants tended to be lightly wooded hills and stream valleys on the grasslands, while in the parkland they were distributed more widely. In the open grasslands, these places favoured by bison also contain human habitation site concentrations, usually near water, with an inferred linkage to resident bison herds and presence of winter migrants.

Population and Ethnicity. How many people may there have been in the plains ecosystem in Saskatchewan at any one time? Based on the use of bison as the dominant resource, and on historic records, an educated guess would be 10,000–15,000 persons during most years. What was the ethnicity of the prehistoric people occupying what is now

Clovis-type spear point made of yellow jasper found near Lake Diefenbaker.

Reconstructed pottery vessel from Cutbank, 27 cm tall.

southern Saskatchewan? There is sound evidence for projecting ethnicity back in time a short way via recognizable artifacts, especially pottery, so that a **CREE** presence in the northern edge, Blackfoot and Atsina in the southwest, and **ASSINIBOINE** in the south-centre and southeast can be inferred with a high level of likelihood. Beyond that, however, implying ethnicity to material cultures becomes very difficult largely because a generic stone toolkit, one well-adapted to the environment of the Plains region, was developed early and persisted because of its suitability. The ethnicity of the most ancient cultures is a matter of guesswork, and hence is avoided by archaeologists.

The prehistory of southern Saskatchewan is not unique in North America, but its archaeologists have contributed substantially to the development of material culture histories within the plains and boreal forest environmental contexts. Several projectile point and pottery types (Oxbow, Besant, Avonlea) have been identified and named here first. One of the earliest scientific excavations in North America that analysed geo-environmental information along with archaeological information was done at the Mortlach Site in 1954.

Concentrations of sites related to hilly and stream valley wooded environments and to related resource distribution have been identified in Saskatchewan as well, contributing to theoretical explanations of prehistoric human settlement and movement patterns. These and other works have contributed to the regional culture history of the continent.   *Henry Epp and Tim E.H. Jones*

FURTHER READING: Epp, H. (ed).1993. *Three Hundred Prairie Years: Henry Kelsey's "Inland Country of Good Report."* Regina: Canadian Plains Research Center; Epp, H.T. and I. Dyck (eds.). 1983. *Tracking Ancient Hunters: Prehistoric Archaeology in Saskatchewan.* Regina: Saskatchewan Archaeological Society; Epp, H. and I. Dyck. 2002. "Early Human-Bison Population Interdependence in the Plains Ecosystem," *Great Plains Research* 12: 323-37; Walde, D., D. Meyer and W. Unfreed. 1995. "The Late Period on the Canadian and Adjacent Plains," *Journal of American Archaeology* 9: 7-66; Wettlaufer, B. 1956. *The Mortlach Site in the Besant Valley of Saskatchewan.* Regina: Department of Natural Resources.

PREKINDERGARTEN PROGRAM.

Saskatchewan Learning's Prekindergarten Program was initiated to offer vulnerable 3- and 4-year-old children an early start in school and life success. The design of the program was based on research that demonstrated both the short- and long-term benefits of prevention and early intervention programs for children. Evidence of short-term benefits included improved intellectual performance, increased social skills, improved health, and higher self-esteem.

Long-term benefits included lower rates of juvenile crime, fewer teen pregnancies, and fewer failed grades and school drop-outs.

In 1997, Saskatchewan Learning along with eight urban school divisions introduced the Prekindergarten Program in twenty-six **COMMUNITY SCHOOLS** in North Battleford, Prince Albert, Regina, and Saskatoon. By 2003, more than 100 programs were established in approximately forty-five communities throughout the province.

Prekindergarten is an **EARLY CHILDHOOD EDUCATION** program that lays the foundation for school success and focuses on social development, self-esteem, educational growth, and language development. Programming is developmentally appropriate and based on learning through play. Qualified teachers and teacher associates work closely with families and community partners such as regional health authorities to address the needs of the children. Children attend Prekindergarten four to five half-days each week. Time is also dedicated for family activities such as reading programs, family recreation nights, visits to community sites, and supportive opportunities for parents. Families are invited to be active partners in this education program by supporting their child's learning at home, offering feedback to strengthen the Prekindergarten program, and becoming involved in multiple classroom and school initiatives.   *Kathy Abernethy*

PRESBYTERIANS.

The first Presbyterians in Saskatchewan were probably young men from the Orkney Islands working for the Hudson's Bay Company; the first Scottish settlers arrived as part of the Selkirk Colony in 1825. From there, the Kildonan congregation sent out Rev. James Nisbet, accompanied by two "catechists" serving as interpreters. On August 6, 1866, they camped on the banks of the **NORTH SASKATCHEWAN RIVER**, at a place later named Prince Albert, and established a mission there. On May 8, 1877, John Mackay was ordained by the Presbytery of Manitoba and came to the North-West. A church was built in Prince Albert in 1881, and Mackay became the first resident missionary at Mistawasis, formerly the Snake Plains Reserve. An important development occurred when the General Assembly, at the request of the Presbytery of Manitoba, appointed a Superintendent of Missions for the North-West: the Rev. James Robertson resigned from the pulpit of Knox Church, Winnipeg to accept this task, which he fulfilled until his death in 1901.

By 1883, the **CANADIAN PACIFIC RAILWAY** reached as far as Swift Current. There followed rapid expansion of mission work among the Ojibwa bands in the **QU'APPELLE VALLEY**. The Rev. Hugh Mackay was appointed in 1884 as missionary to that area, and his daughter Christina opened, at her own expense, a school at Mistawasis. The *Acts and Proceedings* of

the 1886 General Assembly listed the Presbytery of Regina for the first time, including congregations at Prince Albert and Edmonton. Regarding missions the Proceedings stated, "There are thirteen reserves under our care." The May 1888 issue of the *Proceedings* also stated that "32% of the [Caucasian] population of the North Territories is Presbyterian." By 1890, there were eleven missions under the care of seven missionaries on nineteen reserves, and six schools were built or under construction.

Other denominations were very active in the 1890s in the North-West. In 1899, the General Assembly appointed a committee "to meet and confer with other evangelical churches, having power to enter into an arrangement with them that will bring about a more satisfactory state of things in our Home Mission Fields." The Methodists named a committee for this purpose in 1902, and "Union" Sabbath Schools resulted from this co-operation. In 1912 a Presbyterian theological school was opened in Saskatoon. The Assembly Minutes of 1915 declared that there were 350 ministers and missionaries preaching the Gospel in 965 places in the province; and it was reported that "the hospitals at Wakaw and Canora continue to render the most efficient service."

In January 1917, meetings were held with Methodists regarding church union, and in 1918 the Presbyterian Church gave its support to any region demanding local union. As the move towards church union advanced, some Presbyterian members were reluctant to amalgamate with the Methodists for theological reasons. After the 1924 General Assembly, those attending a November 5 meeting agreed that "a Provisional Synod of the Presbyterian Church be formed for Saskatchewan." Votes were held in congregations, and in only seven were the negative votes sufficient to keep the property and manse with the Presbyterian Church. On June 10, 1925, the United Church of Canada came into being.

The Presbyterian Church never fully recovered from its near demise in 1925, although there was modest growth through the 1950s and 1960s. Some people, however, tried to encourage positive action. In the 1950s, **GEORGE PORTEOUS** urged the General Assembly to build seniors' homes, but the appeal fell on deaf ears. A decade later, Jack Wells and others were willing to contribute generously to the building of a Presbyterian residence on the campus at Saskatoon, but lay people in general felt unable to support these projects. Although many Presbyterians have viewed their mission as one of simply surviving as a denomination, there are many who continue to work for the well-being of their Church: they welcome the opportunity to share in the ecumenical movement and are active on the Board of the **PRAIRIE CENTRE FOR ECUMENISM**.

Walter Donovan

PRICE, GEORGE LAWRENCE (1892–1918). Private George Lawrence Price was the last soldier killed in battle during **WORLD WAR I**. Born on December 15, 1892, in Kings County, Nova Scotia, Price moved to Moose Jaw as a young man. In October 1917, he enlisted in the 210th Infantry Battalion (Frontiersmen), Canadian Expeditionary Force, and completed his basic training with the 1st Saskatchewan Depot battalion in December. Price was subsequently transferred to the 15th Canadian Reserve Battalion in England on February 6, 1918. He joined the **28TH CANADIAN INFANTRY BATTALION**, a Saskatchewan-based unit, on May 1. Price died at Mons, Belgium about two minutes before the signing of the Armistice on November 11. Originally buried in the Havre Old Communal Cemetery, his final resting place is the St. Symphorien Military Cemetery near Mons.   *Gordon Goddard*

PRIESTLY, ISABEL M. (1893–1946). Isabel M. (*née* Adnams) Priestly was born on July 25, 1893, near Newbury, Berkshire, England. An avid botanist, she gave up advanced studies, married a Canadian soldier, Robert J. Priestly, and came with him to Canada. Active in natural history groups in Calgary and Victoria, she developed an interest in **BIRDS** in Winnipeg. On moving to Yorkton, she led nature walks, reported sightings in a weekly nature column in the *Yorkton Enterprise*, and made botanical collections. She and her group of enthusiasts compiled a list of birds of the Yorkton area, which created interest provincewide. This led to formation of the Yorkton Natural History Society (of which she was president) and to the publication of the quarterly *Blue Jay* (of which she was editor). She encouraged reports from amateurs and professionals alike, with

Isabel Priestley.

a steady rise in membership and recognition across the continent. She died unexpectedly in Yorkton on April 23, 1946. Cliff Shaw edited the *Blue Jay* until 1948, when a provincewide society, the Saskatchewan Natural History Society, was formed to carry on the work she had begun.   *Mary I. Houston*

FURTHER READING: Belcher, M. 1996. *The Isabel Priestly Legacy: Saskatchewan Natural History Society, 1949–1990*. Regina: Saskatchewan Natural History Society.

PRINCE ALBERT. Prince Albert, population 34,291, is the third largest city in Saskatchewan. It is located on the south shore of the **NORTH SASKATCHEWAN RIVER** near the geographical centre of the province, 141 km north of Saskatoon. Referred to as the "Gateway to the North," Prince Albert is situated where the agricultural prairie of the south and the forest belt of the north meet. The site first gained recognition as a meeting place (*kistahpinanihk*) for First Nations people. In 1862, a group of English Métis and First Nations established the Isbister Settlement there. In 1866 the Reverend James Nisbet was invited to establish his Presbyterian mission next to the Isbister Settlement. Nisbet named his new settlement in honour of the Prince Consort to England's Queen Victoria; Prince Albert grew rapidly until the **CANADIAN PACIFIC RAILWAY** assumed a more southerly route. Prince Albert's municipal history began in 1885, with the election of the Honourable Thomas McKay as mayor; it was also the year that the community was incorporated as a town. One year later, in 1886, Prince Albert became the Saskatchewan headquarters of the North-West Mounted Police. The first train arrived in October 1890, and thus the town was opened to the newly emerging society of the late 19th and early 20th centuries. Some notable figures who lived in Prince Albert at the time include author Lucy Maud Montgomery as well as a young Boris Karloff, honing his skills with Prince Albert's Harry St. Clair Players before becoming one of the most somber characters in Hollywood history.

Prince Albert officially became a city on October 8, 1904, and by 1910 the new city was booming. In addition to having access to the wealth of the forest and agricultural industries, Prince Albert was a hub of steamboat and railway activity and a centre for commerce. By then the population had grown by over 65% and elaborate homes were built, many of which still stand today. Samuel Mcleod, who served as mayor both in 1886 and in 1919, built Keyhole Castle; this home, encompassing the individualism popular in early 1900s architecture and featuring keyhole-shaped windows and scrolled gables, has been named as a Canadian Historic Site—as has the original town hall, built in 1893. In the early 20th century, Prince Albert constructed the La Colle Falls

Dam in the hopes that inexpensive power would attract industry, but this dream was never realized, and the city was driven to the brink of bankruptcy: on July 29, 1913, construction was halted and the site abandoned. The dam can still be seen as it was left, at the 293-foot stage of development.

Since 1945, Prince Albert's economy has been revived by resource development and the growth of tourism. With the development of the pulp mill in 1968, forestry became the second most important industry after agriculture. Numerous gold and uranium discoveries in the 1970s and 1980s increased employment and stimulated the economy of northern Saskatchewan. Throughout the 1990s the city has seen tourism emerge as its third largest industry. Today it continues to expand, spurred on by growth in the commercial and industrial sectors and by diamond exploration in the area. Archibald Stansfield Belaney, the famous author and environmentalist known as **GREY OWL**, made his home in what is now the **PRINCE ALBERT NATIONAL PARK**. Three prime ministers have represented Prince Albert in the House of Commons: Sir Wilfrid Laurier, **WILLIAM LYON MACKENZIE KING** and **JOHN DIEFENBAKER**.   *Daria Coneghan*

PRINCE ALBERT NATIONAL PARK. Prince Albert National Park is situated 60 km north of Prince Albert near the geographic centre of Saskatchewan. Encompassing a region of 3,874 km², it is Saskatchewan's largest protected area and Canada's tenth largest national park. Archeological evidence in the park suggests that Aboriginal cultures first migrated into the area more than 6,000 years ago. The park was officially opened by Prime Minister **W.L. MACKENZIE KING** on August 28, 1928. Straddling the northern boreal forest and aspen parkland ecozones, Prince Albert National Park captures a distinctive segment of Canada's natural habitat. Patches of fescue prairie and aspen parkland in the southern reaches of the park give way to mixed-wood and boreal forests in the north. The undulating terrain of uplands and lowlands (ranging in elevation from 488 to 732 metres above sea level) is the result of the great continental glaciers of the last Ice Age. The park is noted for its glacial topography of eskers, kettle lakes, drumlins, and rolling moraines. Roughly 30% of the park's area is aquatic habitat, consisting of thousands of lakes, streams, creeks, bogs, fens, and marshes. This diversity in terrestrial and aquatic habitat attracts an abundance of wildlife, such as black bear, elk, caribou, **DEER**, moose, timber wolf, lynx, fox, coyote, **HARE**, beaver, badger, otter, and over 200 species of birds. Prince Albert National Park is home to Canada's only fully protected white **PELICAN** nesting colony and to one of the few remaining free-roaming herds of plains **BISON**. The park is also widely recognized as the former residence of the celebrated 1930s naturalist,

Archibald Belaney (better known as **GREY OWL**). Grey Owl's remote log cabin sits on the isolated shores of Ajawaan Lake, where he kept vigil on his beloved park from 1931 to 1938. Prince Albert National Park draws 200,000 visitors annually for its natural beauty and for its recreational offerings, which include swimming, boating, canoeing, fishing, golf, hiking, and backcountry camping. The village of Waskesiu, on the south shore of Waskesiu Lake, is the only community within the park boundaries. *Iain Stewart*

FURTHER READING: Environment Canada. 1986. *Prince Albert National Park Resource Description and Analysis*. Winnipeg: National Resource Conservation Section, Parks, Prairie and Northern Region; Waiser, W.A. 1989. *Saskatchewan's Playground: A History of Prince Albert National Park*. Saskatoon: Fifth House.

PRINCE ALBERT POLICE SERVICE. The Prince Albert Police Force has its origins dating from 1885, when William Dilworth was hired as the first constable. His appointment came after a town meeting agreed to hire police protection for the growing community. Due to the law enforcement jurisdiction of the North-West Mounted Police, Constable Dilworth was appointed with limited powers, which included general maintenance issues such as handling complaints of roaming wild dogs. The first chief of police, Robert J. Jones, was appointed in 1900. This hiring signified the shift away from limited police powers towards an independent and structured law enforcement agency.

The Saskatchewan Provincial Police assisted Prince Albert's six-officer police force in 1918 as the need for increased law and order grew. In the 1920s, as the community of Prince Albert was faced with a declining population and increasing financial concerns, the Provincial Police, and later the RCMP, temporarily managed policing functions. Despite this interruption, by 1929 the city's police force had been reorganized and it resumed its development into a comprehensive law enforcement agency.

Highlights of the evolution of the force include

the creation of a full-time Detective Branch (1956), the opening of the Identification Branch (1958), the formation of the Traffic Division (1970), the establishment of the Mobile Crisis Unit (1976), the purchase of the first police dogs (1976), and the hiring of the force's first female officer, Marilyn Lewis (1977). As of 2004, seventy-two police officers and twenty-eight civilians served the community of Prince Albert in areas such as crime, narcotics, traffic offences, domestic disturbances, and public safety. *Erin Legg*

FURTHER READING: Frith, Joan. 1986. *Prince Albert Police: 100 Years 1886–1986*. North Battleford: Turner-Warwick Printers.

PRINCE ALBERT-RED DEER FORKS TRAIL. The origin of the Prince Albert-Red Deer Forks Trail can be traced back to the early 1800s. It was primarily used by First Nations and Métis traders during the height of the fur trade. The trail connected Prince Albert, one of the province's earlier settlements on the **NORTH SASKATCHEWAN RIVER**, to the forks of the Red Deer and **SOUTH SASKATCHEWAN** rivers, more than 400 km to the southwest, near present-day Leader. Although the trail connected two very important waterways, it was eventually replaced by branch line railways and surveyed roads. *James Winkel*

PRIVATE VOCATIONAL SCHOOLS. Private vocational schools are privately owned institutions that deliver vocational training at the post-secondary level. Sometimes also referred to as career colleges, private vocational schools offer occupation-specific programs that provide an avenue for individuals to either enter the workforce or expediently update their current employment skills. The private vocational schools sector in Saskatchewan currently encompasses approximately fifty schools delivering a diverse array of almost 250 training programs to approximately 4,900 students in twelve communities across the province. Programs typically offered include career training in business and computer

technology, cosmetology, medical office assisting, and massage therapy; more unique offerings include guitar construction, culinary arts, and radio/television broadcasting. Enrollments at private vocational schools range from one or two to hundreds of students. The majority of schools are located in Saskatoon and Regina; but there is a strong rural presence, with schools operating in all regions of the province.

Private vocational schools play an important role in the province's post-secondary education sector. They have the ability to respond relatively quickly to labour market needs and to provide timely training to meet emergent workforce demands. Their programming array provides Saskatchewan residents with access to a broad spectrum of training opportunities, and enhances training accessibility not only from a geographic perspective but also in terms of having flexible program entrance options and minimal waiting times.

In Saskatchewan, private vocational schools had their beginnings in the early 1900s, and the sector grew slowly for several decades. By 1981, there were fifteen private vocational schools in the province, with a total enrollment of approximately 1,700 students. The 1980s marked a period of substantial growth for the private training sector, as federal funding through the Canadian Jobs Strategy program became available and enhancements to student financial assistance were introduced. By 1989, there were fifty-nine schools registered in the province, with an enrollment of approximately 5,200 students.

As is common across Canada, private vocational schools in Saskatchewan are regulated by the provincial government. Typically, regulatory requirements have a consumer protection orientation and address matters related to educational quality standards, governance, accountability, dispute resolution, and financial security. The first Saskatchewan legislation governing private vocational schools was the Trade Schools Regulation Act, which came into force in 1939. It was eventually replaced in 1980 by the Private Vocational Schools

Prince Albert Police Service, ca. 1920s.

Regulation Act. In turn, the 1980 legislation was replaced with the Private Vocational Schools Regulation Act, 1995, which remains in force in 2004.

The Saskatchewan Association of Career Colleges (SACC) is the industry association that represents many of the private vocational schools operating in the province. It serves as a voice for the private training sector, and works to strengthen the sector by facilitating communication amongst its membership, representing its membership on various provincial boards and committees, performing a liaison function with government, and acting as an advocate for its students. SACC members automatically become members of the National Association of Career Colleges (NACC), an umbrella organization that works to support the advancement of the private training sector at the national level.

Patrick Chopik

PRIVATIZATION. With the election of the Progressive Conservative government led by **GRANT DEVINE** in April 1982, the issue of selling the province's publicly owned **CROWN CORPORATIONS** became a priority of the new administration. A senior Cabinet minister, Graham Taylor, was put in charge of this initiative; some highly publicized conferences were held, with internationally known speakers, to promote the concept which had become known as privatization. Beginning in the early 1980s, a number of Crown corporations and major Crown assets were sold to private companies or individuals as private investors. Sask Oil and Gas Corporation, which had been established by the **BLAKENEY** NDP government in the 1970s, was privatized in 1986. This sale immediately became a political issue: in its last three years as a Crown corporation, **SASK OIL** made profits of $31 million, $44 million and $41 million respectively; these earnings resulted in substantial dividends for the provincial treasury. Privatization ended that flow of revenue to the provincial treasury and transferred it to the new private shareholders, 75% of whom were non-residents of Saskatchewan. Within 6 months of being privatized, Sask Oil laid off one-quarter of its workforce, and the company was transferring its exploration focus to Alberta.

In 1988, the provincial government sold off 510 billion cubic feet of natural gas reserves which had been owned by SaskPower; this was the equivalent of fifteen years' consumption by residential consumers in the province. This natural gas was sold to a private energy corporation for $325 million. Those sceptical of the wisdom of the sale pointed to the fact that at the time, the wholesale market price for that volume of gas entering the province at the Alberta border was $984 million.

In 1987, SED Systems, a high-tech firm in Saskatoon jointly owned by the province, the uni-

versity, and its employees, was privatized when the provincial government sold the sophisticated research company to Fleet Aerospace of Ontario. The loss of the head office to another province and the fact that seventy workers lost their jobs caused further controversy.

Privatization also involved government departments. In 1983, the Highways Minister terminated 157 workers from his Department, and the following year another 237—telling the former employees and the public, "I'm giving them an opportunity to work in the private sector." It was announced that in future, private contractors would build the province's highways. In May 1984, the Highways Department privatized more then 400 pieces of road-building equipment in a giant auction sale on the Exhibition Grounds in Saskatoon. This move drew adverse comments from the opponents of privatization because dumping that quantity of highway machinery on the market all at one time depressed the price and yielded only $6 million during the auction. Much of the road-building and earth-moving equipment was bought up by out-of-province contractors. The replacement value of the equipment was estimated to be $40 million.

In 1982, SaskPower's coal operations in southeastern Saskatchewan were privatized. A huge dragline was sold to Manalta Coal of Alberta, with the government of Saskatchewan guaranteeing the loan the company took out to buy it. Two years later, the province's $129 million investment in the Poplar River Coal Mine at Coronach was sold to Manalta for $102 million; furthermore, the provincial government lent Manalta $89 million to make the transaction, and guaranteed the private Alberta company a thirty-year coal supply agreement for the Coronach Power Station.

The privatization initiatives of the 1980s saw a wide range of assets in provincial parks—everything from ski hills to wild animal parks, boat rentals, food concessions, golf courses, and winterized cabins and condominiums—sold, leased or in some way transferred to private operators. Higher fees were charged for services, hours of operation were cut, jobs were lost and lower wages were paid to the workers.

In 1986, the Prince Albert Pulp Company and related assets were privatized. The giant forestry corporation **WEYERHAEUSER** of Tacoma, Washington bought the mill for no money down and thirty years to pay at a preferred interest rate, with no payments required in years when the company's profits were less than 12%. Also under the agreement, the province was obliged to build many miles of forest roads each year for Weyerhaeuser.

SaskMinerals was a small but quite successful Crown corporation that produced **SODIUM SULFATE** at Chaplin and Fox Valley, and peat moss at Carrot River. In its forty years of operation, it had made a

profit every year but one. The sale of SaskMinerals to two out-of-province companies again prompted a reaction by those opposing privatization. They pointed out that the sale realized $15.9 million–less than the earnings of SaskMinerals for three years when it was publicly owned.

Some privatization caused less public debate, such as the sale of the Sask Computer Utility; but most of the deals drew widespread media and public attention as well as stiff opposition from privatization opponents. With the defeat of the Conservative administration in 1991, the privatization program was discontinued, but not reversed, by the incoming **ROMANOW** NDP government.

Garnet Dishaw

PROGLACIAL LAKES. Proglacial lakes develop along the front of glaciers from meltwater released along the ice margin. The weight of the glacier depresses the underlying ground; this depressed area is exposed as the ice retreats, and meltwater becomes trapped in this lower area in front of the glacial margin to form a proglacial lake. With the loss of the overlying weight of the ice, the land gradually rebounds upwards, a phenomenon called isostatic uplift, permitting the lake to drain. Numerous proglacial lakes formed with the retreat of the Laurentide ice sheet during the Wisconsinan **GLACIATION**. Some proglacial lakes were long-lived, covering large areas, while others existed only for a short time or covered small areas. Glacial meltwater typically is full of fine-grained sediments consisting of sand, silt and clay-sized particles often produced by **GLACIAL EROSION** processes. When this meltwater reaches a lake basin, it slows and deposits its load of sediment onto the floor of the lake. Former proglacial lake basins are identified by flat, relatively featureless plains composed of fine sediments identified as glaciolacustrine deposits. On occasion, large blocks of ice can break off the glacial margin to form icebergs that drift around the lake, scraping plough marks in the lakebed or depositing drop stones as they melt.

Proglacial lakes covered thousands of square kilometres of Saskatchewan; many, such as the former Glacial Lake Regina, lasted less than 1,000 years. Today the silts and clays from this former lake support rich agricultural soil but pose considerable engineering difficulties: the clays, dominated by montmorillonite, have a tremendous ability to expand with the addition of water and to contract on its absence. This results in heaving and cracking of sidewalks, roads, and foundations. It is believed that when Glacial Lake Regina drained, it did so quickly and catastrophically, eroding a large channel now occupied by the much smaller contemporary **SOURIS RIVER**. Other sizable proglacial lakes include Glacial Lake Saskatchewan, whose basin area expanded and contracted following the retreat of the ice margin for almost 2,000 years. The lake was initiated southwest of Saskatoon, and gradually moved northeastwards with the retreating ice margin beyond what is now Prince Albert; eventually this lake joined Lake Agassiz to the east. Other proglacial lakes include Glacial Lake Melfort, Glacial Meadow Lake, Glacial Cree Lake, and Glacial Lake Athabasca. Along with the fine glaciolacustrine deposits, some former shorelines and deltas have been identified as associated with these former lakes. *Janis Dale*

FURTHER READING: Christiansen, E.A. 1979. "The Wisconsinan Deglaciation of Southern Saskatchewan and Adjacent Areas," *Canadian Journal of Earth Sciences* 16: 913–38.

PROGRESSIVE PARTY. In the late 19th and early 20th centuries, Canada underwent a period of social reform during which various groups offered their own sets of solutions to address the many problems that attended the rise of an increasingly urban and industrial society. Amongst these reform efforts was the so-called Progressive Movement, which sought to protect agrarian interests by challenging national economic policies which they believed supported the commercial and financial interests of central Canada at their expense. Although farmers had openly talked of creating a third party after the defeat of the Liberals and their policy of reciprocity in 1911, they remained loyal to the traditional parties as part of their support for the war effort on the understanding that conditions would improve for them. However, when the Union Government failed to implement legislation favourable to farmers, including removal of the national tariff, the movement took concrete political expression with the formation of the Progressive Party in 1920. Led by Thomas A. Crerar, who had earlier resigned from the federal Cabinet in 1919 as Minister of Agriculture, the Progressive Party united dissident Liberals in Ontario and prairie farmers to promote free trade, nationalization of the railways, and direct democracy. Under Crerar, the Progressives broke the two-party pattern of federal politics in the 1921 federal election by winning 65 seats and forming the second largest party in Parliament. Yet despite this initial success, the Progressives were unable to overcome deep internal divisions, and by 1930 they had all but disappeared as an effective national political force; remnants from the party joined the CO-OPERATIVE COMMONWEALTH FEDERATION in 1932, and others linked with the federal Conservatives to form the Progressive Conservative Party in 1942.

The Progressives' inability to remain viable at the national level mirrored developments in Saskatchewan. Since 1905, the Saskatchewan LIBERAL PARTY had cultivated farmers' support—thereby dampening farmers' demands for independ-

ent political action—by appointing prominent members from the Saskatchewan Grain Growers Association (SGGA) to the provincial Cabinet, and by consulting with the SGGA before implementing legislation affecting the province's farmers. Provincial Liberal efforts to mollify the farmers' political movement were further reinforced by Premier W.M. MARTIN'S decision to sever all ties with the federal Liberals in 1920, and by his appointment of J.A. MAHARG, a Progressive MP and prominent farm leader, to the provincial Cabinet in 1921 just months before the provincial election, which the Liberals won handily in June. Nevertheless, the Progressives managed to elect six members to the Legislature, a considerable achievement given the absence of a provincial organization. However, during the course of the 1921 federal election, held in December, Martin angered the SGGA when he supported a federal Liberal candidate rather than a Progressive candidate in the Regina riding. Charging Martin with bad faith, Maharg subsequently resigned, and the SGGA—which had long resisted direct political activity—soon authorized the creation of a committee to assist provincial constituencies in organizing for political action. But while Saskatchewan Progressives took 15 of 16 seats in the 1921 federal election, the Progressives were never able to build upon their initial success in 1921, electing just six members in the 1925 provincial election, and only five members in 1929.

The Progressives' failure to form a government in Saskatchewan can be attributed to a number of factors, including amongst other things the SGGA's decision to withdraw from active political participation in 1924, which undermined the Progressives' organizing capabilities, as well as the return of agricultural prosperity in the late 1920s, which in turn undercut the appeal to farmers of a third party protest movement. The Progressives' inability to take power in the province may also be attributed to the emergence of CHARLES AVERY DUNNING, who had the necessary credentials to remind Saskatchewan farmers that the provincial Liberal Party was in fact a farmers' party. Dunning, elected leader of the Liberal Party and Premier of Saskatchewan in 1922 following Martin's resignation, and himself a successful farmer, had earlier served as vice-president of the SGGA as well as general manager of the SASKATCHEWAN CO-OPERATIVE ELEVATOR COMPANY, which provided farmers with loans and grants to establish their own grain elevators. Given this background, Dunning could present himself as one of the Grain Grower's own, a declaration made all the more credible when, shortly after being elected, he asked the SGGA for copies of all resolutions passed at their annual conventions since 1918, presumably as a guide for future government policies and in order to buttress his argument that the welfare of the farmers rested not upon the creation of a third

party, but on their ability to influence existing political organizations. In effect, then, Dunning sought to discredit the farmers' political movement without seeming to discredit the SGGA itself, a strategy that appears to have worked given the SGGA's subsequent decision to withdraw from politics. With the SGGA now adopting a neutral political stance, and with the Progressives in disarray, Dunning's appeal to an agrarian electorate appeared unassailable as he led the Liberals to a series of successive by-election victories before winning the 1925 provincial election with a solid majority. However, Dunning soon accepted a portfolio in MACKENZIE KING's federal Cabinet, and J.G. GARDINER was subsequently sworn in as Premier.

In the 1929 provincial election that followed, the Liberals were relegated to minority government status, with the largest opposition party formed not by the Progressives, but by a newly revived CONSERVATIVE PARTY headed by J.T.M. ANDERSON. Given their failure to achieve electoral gains, the Progressives soon allied themselves with Anderson and forced the Liberals from office on September 6, 1929, leaving the government in the hands of the Conservatives and cementing a Progressive-Conservative alliance in the province that lasted until 1934. Yet the demise of the Saskatchewan Progressives was not sealed until February 1930, when the United Farmers of Canada, Saskatchewan Section—the result of an amalgamation of the SGGA and the Farmers Union of Canada in 1926 and from which the Progressives hoped to draw support—decided that a new political party should be created to represent the interests of farmers. In the wake of this decision, the Progressive Party in Saskatchewan ceased all activities, and the Co-operative Commonwealth Federation eventually came into being. *Damian Coneghan*

FURTHER READING: Archer, J. 1980. *Saskatchewan: A History.* Saskatoon: Western Producer Prairie Books; Barnhart, Gordon (ed.). 2004. *Saskatchewan Premiers of the Twentieth Century.* Regina: Canadian Plains Research Center; Brennan, J.W. 1969. "Charles Dunning and the Challenge of the Progressives: 1922–1925," *Saskatchewan History* 22 (1): 1–12; Calderwood, W. 1968. "The Decline of the Progressive Party in Saskatchewan, 1925–1930," *Saskatchewan History* 21 (3): 81–99.

PROHIBITION AND TEMPERANCE. In 1915, Premier WALTER SCOTT and the Liberal government halted the sale of liquor in Saskatchewan. In April 1915 all bars had to close by 7:00 pm, and the following July Scott decreed that all bar and club licenses were to be abolished; a public prosecutor was appointed to follow up and charge individuals and businesses for non-compliance. At the same time, the Saskatchewan government took over the wholesale aspects of the liquor industry. Saskatch-

COURTESY SOUTH-WESTERN SASKATCHEWAN OLDTIMERS' ASSOCIATION MUSEUM AND ARCHIVES

Saskatchewan Provincial Police seize alcohol in Maple Creek, Saskatchewan, September 7, 1920.

ewan thus became the first province in Canada to ban private sector sale of alcohol; by 1917 all the other provinces except for Quebec joined the prohibition movement.

With the country steeped in the Social Gospel message of morality, Saskatchewan prohibitionists demonized those who manufactured, sold, and consumed alcohol. Alcohol was seen as a threat to world peace during **WORLD WAR I**; it was blamed for violence in families and for high crime rates in the province. During the prohibition era the crime rates and arrests for drunkenness dropped. At the same time, fewer police were needed to patrol in urban centres, and rates of Monday morning absenteeism in the work force fell sharply. The **WOMEN'S CHRISTIAN TEMPERANCE UNION** and other proponents of an alcohol-free society likened the success of prohibition to a social revolution.

Bar and hotel owners and employees demanded some form of compensation for the loss of revenues and income, at least until they could generate alternative jobs or business ventures; but the government refused to compensate those involved in the sale of alcohol, arguing that the monies could not come from the provincial coffers given that public opinion was overwhelmingly in favour of prohibition. According to Scott, the citizens of Saskatchewan felt that alcohol was unpatriotic and more dangerous than German submarines. On April 1, 1918, the federal government prohibited the manufacture, importation, and transportation of beverages containing more than 2.5% alcohol. Provincial governments regulated the sale of alcohol within the province, while the federal government regulated trade in alcohol between provinces. Canada became a "dry" country, the only exceptions being the alcohol needed for medicinal and religious purposes.

Scott and the Liberal government promised the Saskatchewan people ongoing referenda regarding prohibition. The Canada Temperance Act of 1919 replaced prohibition as public opinion was shifting toward greater tolerance of alcohol consumption. The Saskatchewan government abandoned the prohibition and temperance movement in 1925, but continued to control wholesale outlets for selling and distributing alcohol.   *Elizabeth Mooney*

FURTHER READING: Finkel, A. and M. Conrad. 2001. *History of the Canadian Peoples: 1867 to the Present.* Toronto: Addison Wesley Longman; Heron, C. 2003. *Booze: A Distilled History.* Toronto: Between the Lines.

PRONGHORN. The indigenous pronghorn antelope (*Antilocapra americana*), evolving from ancestral forms originating in North America 25 million years ago, is the only surviving species of the Family Antilocapridae. It became a major ungulate on the Great Plains from central Mexico to southern Alberta and Saskatchewan. Estimates suggest that 30–40 million existed prior to European settlement. Pronghorns are smaller than most horned and antlered North American mammals; mature males and females can attain body weights of 70 kg and 56 kg respectively. The horns of males are bony extensions of the skull, covered by a blackish sheath that develops a forward-projecting prong; these sheaths are usually cast off in early November. Females are hornless. Large eyes set in protruding bone-rimmed sockets provide keen eyesight. This, and the pronghorn's ability to attain a running speed of 100 kilometres per hour, serves the animals well in open, treeless habitats. Their reddish-tan coat with white and dark coloration blends with the brown prairie vegetation. The long white erectile hairs of the rump patch, raised by muscles into an expanded rosette when a pronghorn is alarmed, trigger the rump glands to secrete pheromones, providing both a visual and olfactory communication between herd members. Canadian pronghorns inhabit and feed on mixed prairie regions supporting shrubs, forbs, and grasses. Rutting-season males gather and control female harems in September. A gestation period of approximately 250 days usually produces twin kids. Pronghorn mortality factors include predation by coyotes and bobcats, heavy snowfall increasing the difficulties of obtaining food, and accidental traffic deaths on highways and railroads.   *George Mitchell*

FURTHER READING: 2001. *Natural Neighbours: Selected Mammals of Saskatchewan.* Regina: Canadian Plains Research Center.

COURTNEY MILNE PHOTO

Pronghorn.

PROVINCIAL PARKS. In 1930 the federal government transferred control of natural resources to the government of Saskatchewan. This provided the provincial government with the opportunity to create a provincial parks system in 1931. The majority of the original provincial parks were previously dominion forest reserves established by the federal government in the late 1800s or early 1900s. **CYPRESS HILLS**, **DUCK MOUNTAIN**, Good Spirit Lake, **MOOSE MOUNTAIN**, Katepwa Point, and **LITTLE MANITOU** were the original provincial parks, and Greenwater Lake was added in 1932. Nipawin Provincial Park (now Narrow Hills) was established in 1934, and Lac la Ronge Provincial Park in 1939. No facilities, however, were developed at these latter two parks until the 1960s, and Little Manitou ceased to be a provincial park in 1956. Economic conditions were a major impetus for establishing the first provincial parks. During the early years of the **GREAT DEPRESSION**, the provincial government used provincial parks to generate employment and build a tourism industry. The government employed several thousand relief camp workers to build much of the early infrastructure of the provincial parks, including the two artificial lakes in Cypress Hills and stone chalets at Moose Mountain and Little Manitou. The government also promoted tourism by advertising provincial parks in the United States and elsewhere.

By 1933, as economic conditions worsened, the government stopped investing in provincial parks, and during **WORLD WAR II** the park system was largely ignored. The provincial government began rebuilding the provincial parks after the war and recognized that population trends would create an increased demand for outdoor recreation opportunities. In 1957, the government hired Bill Baker, a recreational consultant, to analyze Saskatchewan's future recreational needs. Baker's reports provided the blueprint for a massive expansion of the park system during the 1960s and early 1970s. He also made recommendations on the development of the recreation potential of **LAKE DIEFENBAKER**, which was created when **GARDINER DAM** was built on the **SOUTH SASKATCHEWAN RIVER**. On the basis of Baker's recommendations, Meadow Lake (1959), The Battlefords, Echo Valley, Pike Lake, Rowan's Ravine (1960), Buffalo Pound (1963), Danielson (1971), Douglas and Saskatchewan Landing (1973) provincial parks were established. Recreation and public access facilities were developed in **LAC LA RONGE** and Nipawin (now Narrow Hills) provincial parks. In addition, nearly 200 recreation sites were established, and a number of natural and archaeological protected areas were designated. Also, during this period provincial parks started to develop educational programs and interpretive trails.

The 1970s and 1980s were marked by increased emphasis on environmental management of resources. This culminated in the 1990s with the adoption in all provincial parks of the ecosystem-based management system, which requires park management decisions to take into consideration the inter-relationships among all elements of the environment. During this period, provincial parks also began to rely increasingly on user fees and private sector partnerships to address funding challenges. In 1986, eleven new provincial parks were established. Four existing recreation sites, Blackstrap, Candle Lake, Crooked Lake and Makwa Lake, were all designated provincial parks. Nine historic parks (Touchwood Hills Post, **CANNINGTON MANOR**, Last Mountain House, Steele Narrows, Wood Mountain Post, Fort Pitt, Fort Carlton, St. Victor Petroglyphs, and Cumberland House, which were established in the 1960s 1970s), were also designated as provincial parks. In 1986, **CLEARWATER RIVER** was designated as the first provincial wilderness park, and three others, **ATHABASCA SAND DUNES**, Wildcat Hill (1992) and Clarence-Steepbank Lakes (1994) were later designated. These parks are all in remote areas of northern Saskatchewan; their designation as provincial parks was indicative of an increased emphasis on nature-based tourism as well as ecosystem management. Visitors to these parks are encouraged to minimize their impact on the environment, and natural processes such as forest fires and tree diseases are not interfered with, unless they threaten people and resources outside of the park boundaries.

By 2004, Saskatchewan's provincial Parks covered over 1,148,287 square hectares, containing some of the most beautiful natural and cultural landscapes in the province. These lands include 34 provincial parks, 8 historic sites, 130 recreation sites, and 24 protected areas.

Mike Fedyk, Ken Lozinsky and Bob Herbison

PRUDHOMME TRUCKS LTD. Prudhomme Trucks Ltd., a truck carrier that offers expedited service utilizing Tridem vans, generates about $16 million in annual revenue. The company, which employs about 150 people, provides freight service to customers across Canada from its Regina headquarters. Founded in 1990 by Monique and Denis Prudhomme, the company has established trailer yards in all major western Canadian cities. Monique Prudhomme has been recognized as one of the Top 100 Women Business Owners in Canada by *Chatelaine* and *Profit* magazines. *Joe Ralko*

PSYCHIATRIC NURSING. At the Saskatchewan Hospital North Battleford from 1914, and at the Saskatchewan Hospital Weyburn from 1921, ward attendants cared for mentally ill patients. They were trained "on the job" and paid a salary while training. They provided custodial care to patients and performed their "occupational therapy" on the grounds and in the garden, kitchen and laundry. In 1930, formal on-the-job two-year ward attendant training programs were begun. After a study commissioned by the new CCF government in 1944, a three-year in-hospital psychiatric nursing training program commenced in September 1947, leading to a Diploma in Psychiatric Nursing. In 1948, an Act Respecting Psychiatric Nurses was passed, and the Saskatchewan Psychiatric Nurses' Association began registering psychiatric nurses.

In 1972, because of the use of psychotropic drugs, the reduction in patient numbers in the mental hospitals, the move away from large and expensive mental institutions, and the trend to relocate all nursing education away from the in-hospital model, the Psychiatric Nursing Training Program was reorganized and moved to the Wascana Institute of Applied Arts and Sciences (now the **SASKATCHEWAN INSTITUTE OF APPLIED SCIENCE AND TECHNOLOGY**). This operated until the mid-1990s, when the Registered Psychiatric Nurses' Association of Saskatchewan (RPNAS; the name was changed in 1993) was asked to consider a joint venture with the **UNIVERSITY OF SASKATCHEWAN**, the Saskatchewan Institute of Applied Arts and Sciences, and the College of Nursing at the University of Saskatchewan to develop a nursing work force across the province with baccalaureate degrees rather than with diplomas.

The Nursing Education Program (NEP) of Saskatchewan began in September 1996, but generated increasing concern that it was not adequately preparing students for psychiatric nursing. In 2001, after an external review, the RPNAS denied approval of the program, as well as registration to anyone who completed the NEP after 2002. *Angela Martin*

PSYCHOLOGY. Psychology is the scientific study of behaviour and mental processes of humans and other organisms. The term "psychology" (from Greek *psyche logos*, study of the soul) was coined in the 17th century and came into popular usage in the 19th century as the discipline emerged from the study of philosophy; 19th-century pioneers included German scholar Wilhelm Wundt, Francis Galton in England, Sigmund Freud in Vienna, and William James in America. Psychology was taught in Canada as a branch of philosophy until well into the 20th century. The first independent psychology departments appeared in eastern Canadian universities in the 1920s, and in the west by mid-century. However, psychology was among the first subjects taught when the **UNIVERSITY OF SASKATCHEWAN** began offering classes in 1909 in Saskatoon. The University's first president, **W.C. MURRAY**, himself a philosopher-psychologist, taught psychology classes in the Department of Philosophy.

The Department of Psychology at the University of Saskatchewan came into existence in 1946 and achieved a distinctive identity under the leadership of Gordon McMurray during the next two decades.

Its faculty was comprised of only two or three members until the 1960s, when the department went through a phase of modest growth as Canadian universities expanded and psychology became a highly popular subject across the country. The first professor appointed to teach psychology in Regina was Duncan Blewett, who was hired in 1961. The psychology department that was founded in Regina in 1965 had only three faculty members initially, but grew rapidly over the next decade. In 1974, when the **UNIVERSITY OF REGINA** became independent from the University of Saskatchewan, the period of rapid expansion of Canadian universities had come to an end. However, the popularity of psychology among students and the general public continues to the present day.

Psychologists study fundamental processes in perception, learning and memory, human development, social and interpersonal interactions, personality theory and measurement, the biological basis of behaviour, assessment and treatment of psychological disorders, history and theory of the discipline, cultural psychology, and more. Researchers at Saskatchewan universities have made significant contributions in each of these areas, and in new areas of applied research such as health and forensic psychology. The undergraduate psychology programs at the province's two universities cover all the core areas of the discipline and also include a number of specialized courses. Both universities offer masters and doctoral programs in a range of specialties including clinical psychology. The education faculties at the two universities also offer training in educational psychology, a field that has evolved somewhat independently from the rest of the discipline.

The majority of psychologists in Saskatchewan work as clinicians in health facilities or in private practice, providing services to people with psychological disorders or other problems of adjustment in life. A smaller number work as researchers and consultants in industry or the public sector, or teach in university settings. The profession of psychology is regulated under provincial law by the Saskatchewan College of Psychologists, and use of the title "psychologist" or "doctoral psychologist" is limited to qualified individuals who are members of the College. The Psychological Society of Saskatchewan, a fraternal organization, publishes a journal, *Saskatchewan Psychologist*, and sponsors professional and public events. Another fraternal organization, the Saskatchewan Educational Psychology Association, represents the interests of educational psychologists in the province. *William E. Smythe*

FURTHER READING: McMurray, G.A. 1982. "Psychology at Saskatchewan." Pp. 178–91 in M.J. Wright and C.R. Myers (eds.), *History of Academic Psychology in Canada*. Toronto: C.J. Hogrefe.

PUBLIC ART. Before Saskatchewan was constituted, First Nations people and settlers had already claimed the land with artworks they placed in shared spaces. Today, petroglyphs, religious effigies and monuments that predate the province are routinely encountered by diverse publics. Following this early history, public art in Saskatchewan is most often associated with the memorial: an artifact intended to honour or preserve the memory of a person, an event or an idea. For example, in Gravelbourg, Kamsack and Moosomin, war memorials safeguard the names of soldiers killed in service. They also provide mourners with sites where they can gather and commiserate. In Rama, Esterhazy and Kronau, field stone grottos host cycles of religious statuary. Since 1990, Moose Jaw has sponsored a number of murals celebrating moments from the city's history. In Saskatoon, bronzes of Sir Wilfrid Laurier (1972), of Métis leader **GABRIEL DUMONT** (1985), and of former Governor General **RAMON HNATYSHYN** (1992), all by **BILL EPP**, root into the land an institutional interpretation of Canada's political history. By sponsoring and facilitating the production of these artworks, governments and communities attempt to create a collective portrait showcasing personalities they admire, values they champion, and memories they treasure. Public art marks a site for remembrance and social ritual.

But public artworks can also be viewed as aesthetic landmarks or symbols of urban regeneration. Indeed, during the 20th century new tendencies in public art emerged. Artists such as **JOHN NUGENT**, **ROBERT MURRAY** and Edward Gibney, more interest-

COURTESY OF THE SASKATCHEWAN ARTS BOARD

Taras Polataiko, "Artist as Politician: In the Shadow of the Monument," 1995, cibachrome print documenting the 1992 performance by Taras Polataiko, 92.8 x 59.3 cm, Saskatchewan Arts Board Permanent Collection.

ed in contemporary art practices than in commemoration, installed large-scale abstract sculptures in public places. Alongside this trend appeared site-specific artworks that reflect on their physical and human surroundings. In Regina's Wascana Park, for example, considering the history of the location, Doug Hunter installed *Oskana* (1989), a collection of bronze bison skulls surrounded by carved stones. For *Antsee* (2002), Kim Morgan appropriated a decaying tree in the city's Victoria Park and brought it back to life by populating it with a colony of shimmering aluminum ants.

In 1992, Saskatoon-based artist Taras Polataiko presented a bracing critique of the tradition of public art in Saskatchewan. Transfigured into a breathing monument, completely bronzed and hoisted onto a pedestal, the artist installed himself facing the aforementioned monument to Hnatyshyn. Today, Polataiko's performance work only survives in photographs. Yet it still generates crucial questions: about the relationship public art cultivates with sponsors, viewers, and the spaces it inhabits; and about the role public art plays in the selective consolidation of community, the creation of public memory, and the consecration of taste in the public sphere. *Annie Gerin*

PUBLIC LIBRARIES. Public libraries have always played an essential role in the educational, recreational, cultural, and community development of

COURTESY OF KIM MORGAN

Kim Morgan, "Antsee," 2002.

Saskatchewan. Towards these ends, Saskatchewan libraries have provided excellent public services through their development of co-operative practices and through their willingness to utilize the latest technological advances to meet the needs of their patrons. Libraries were first established in Saskatchewan's two major cities, Regina and Saskatoon, in 1909 and 1913 respectively. In 1914, to meet the needs of its dispersed rural population, the Travelling Libraries were started by the province's Legislative Library. They consisted of large wooden boxes with sixty to eighty books that were loaned to a group or community for one year. These travelling libraries existed until 1961, and contained as many as 100,000 books in the 1930s. The Open Shelf Library, begun in 1912, was phased out as regional libraries were created.

In 1953, the Provincial Library was created to extend and improve library services in Saskatchewan. **MARY DONALDSON** was named the first Provincial Librarian, and it was her vision of library co-operation as a means of developing public library services in Saskatchewan that was the basis for the foundation of the present public library service in the province. The first regional library was established in north-central Saskatchewan in 1950. By 1967, seven regional libraries replaced the many random private libraries that existed across the province: Lakeland Library Region (North Battleford area); Wapiti Regional Library (Prince Albert area); Wheatland Regional Library (Saskatoon west area); Parkland Regional Library (Yorkton area); Chinook Regional Library (Swift Current area); Palliser Regional Library (Moose Jaw area); and Southeast Regional Library (Weyburn area). Each regional library covers a large geographical area with a substantial population, and represents a group of cities, towns, villages, and rural municipalities that have joined together to deliver public library services. The northern Pahkisimon Nuye?áh Library System is a federation of thirteen northern community libraries and fifty school libraries. It has a legislated mandate to act as the central library for northern Saskatchewan, and acts as the coordinating agency for all school, regional college, public, and special libraries in the region.

The Public Libraries Act of 1996 established a structure for the provincial public library system to ensure equitable access to basic library services for all residents of Saskatchewan. The purpose of the provincial public library system is to ensure the existence of a Saskatchewan union catalogue composed of the records of many libraries, interlibrary loans, reciprocal borrowing, and autonomous library boards. Also through the Act, the Provincial Library is entrusted to coordinate and support the province-wide library system. Historically, the Provincial Library's mission has been "to work co-operatively with all libraries and communities to secure equi-

table access to library resources, information, and services for Saskatchewan people." The Provincial Library also administers the Libraries Co-operation Act, which encourages co-operation and resource sharing among all types of libraries throughout the province to benefit Saskatchewan people, and also acts as a coordinator and facilitator with the boards in the provincial public library system.

The Regina Public Library and the Saskatoon Public Library serve as special resource centres, and provide large resource collections available to all residents throughout Saskatchewan via interlibrary loan and reciprocal borrowing. Both libraries have Local History Rooms that offer historical material on the entire province while focusing on the history of their own city. Both Regina and Saskatoon public libraries have contributed extensively to the culture, economy, and general well-being of their respective cities by offering expert information retrieval skills in an increasingly electronic age, by providing substantial employment in the library sector, by patronizing local businesses, and by generally improving the market worth of their communities. Both libraries provide assistance in the field of traditional literacy and also in the field of information literacy.

Public libraries in Saskatchewan circulate over eleven million books and other items from their collections annually. About 50% of the population are registered borrowers of one of the 320 public library branches or service points available in communities in every area of the province. In addition to circulating books and other library materials, public libraries provide answers to information questions, borrow books from other libraries on behalf of library patrons, and provide access to online, full-text information via library websites. A relatively new role for libraries is providing public access to the Internet.

The main challenges faced by public libraries in the 21st century are the emergence of library networks connecting libraries, patron access to catalogues and other library services, access to electronic books and journal articles, and the provision of digitized information. The democratic vision, however, of service to all with equitable, free-to-the-individual, and open access to Saskatchewan libraries will remain paramount.

Roger Bakes

FURTHER READING: Archer, J.H. 1980. *Saskatchewan: A History*. Saskatoon: Western Producer Prairie Books; Bocking, D.H.1979. *Saskatchewan: A Pictorial History*. Saskatoon: Western Producer Prairie Books; Smith, D.E. 1992. *Building a Province: A History of Saskatchewan in Documents*. Saskatoon: Fifth House.

PUBLIC SERVICE COMMISSION. The Public Service Commission (PSC) normally consists of a chairperson, who serves "at pleasure," and four other members appointed by the Premier for terms

of six years. The Commissioners are supported by 100 or so civil servants, mostly located in Regina. The PSC is the main body for all personnel administration or human resource concerns for the Civil Service, and is considered to be an arm of the executive branch of the government. This differentiates it from the federal PSC in Ottawa. There, the PSC is a watchdog for the Legislature and the Parliament, as the goal is to prevent civil servants being hired on the basis of patronage. In the case of Saskatchewan, having the PSC as part of the executive makes it more difficult, if not impossible, to prevent patronage appointments. On the other hand the Saskatchewan PSC, operating as an arm of the executive branch, is in a better position to satisfy the personnel administration needs of the Civil Service.

Robert McLaren

PUHL, TERRY (1956–). Born in Melville on July 8, 1956, Terry Puhl was a dependable outfielder for fourteen seasons with the Houston Astros. He played bantam and midget league baseball in Melville, and signed with Houston as a non-drafted free agent in 1973. Puhl spent four seasons in the team's farm system before being called up to the majors in 1977. He made an immediate impact with a seventeen-game hitting streak, earning a place in the Astro's everyday lineup. Known for his outstanding defensive abilities, Puhl is in the top three all-time for fielding percentage by an outfielder who has played 1,000 games or more. He committed a minuscule eighteen errors in 2,596 chances for a .993 percentage. A 1978 National League All-Star, Puhl and the Astros won the NL West Division pennant in 1980. Although the team later lost to the Philadelphia Phillies, Puhl batted an impressive .526 in the NL Championship Series. Granted free agency by the Astros in 1990, Puhl was signed and released by the New York Mets. He spent his final season with the Kansas City Royals in 1991. In fifteen major league seasons, he played in 1,531 games with a career batting average of .280. He is second in games played and stolen bases by Canadian-born players. Terry Puhl was inducted into the **SASKATCHEWAN SPORTS HALL OF FAME** in 1994, and in the Canadian Baseball Hall of Fame in 1995.

Daria Coneghan and Holden Stoffel

PULSE CROPS AND INDUSTRY. "Pulse crops" refers to a group of more than sixty different grain legume crops grown around the world. The seeds of pulse crops are important in human nutrition. They are typically made up of 20-25% protein and 40-50% starch; they are also rich in dietary fibre and usually have only small amounts of oil. The protein of pulse seeds is high in the amino acids lysine and methionine, making pulses nutritionally complementary to cereals, which are deficient in these two essential amino acids. Pulses are the main source of

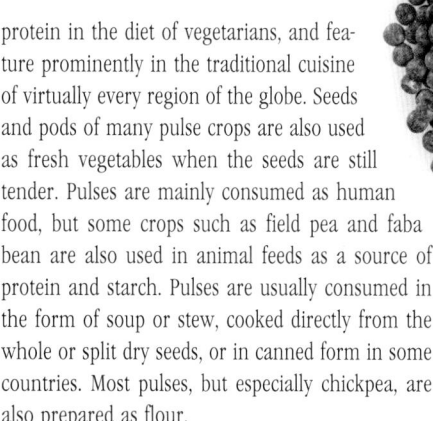

Pulse crops: left, red kidney beans; centre, French green lentils; right, peas in pod.

protein in the diet of vegetarians, and feature prominently in the traditional cuisine of virtually every region of the globe. Seeds and pods of many pulse crops are also used as fresh vegetables when the seeds are still tender. Pulses are mainly consumed as human food, but some crops such as field pea and faba bean are also used in animal feeds as a source of protein and starch. Pulses are usually consumed in the form of soup or stew, cooked directly from the whole or split dry seeds, or in canned form in some countries. Most pulses, but especially chickpea, are also prepared as flour.

The five most important global pulse crops are common bean, field pea, chickpea, lentil, and faba bean. All five are grown in Saskatchewan. Pulse crops are valuable as an annual legume in crop rotations because they provide breaks in disease cycles that affect the major cereal and oilseed crops. They also provide a diversified source of farm income. An important feature of pulse crops, as of other legumes, is their ability to fix nitrogen from the atmosphere in association with bacteria known as Rhizobia, thereby reducing the requirement for nitrogen fertilizer.

Historical records of farms and research stations in Saskatchewan from 1900 to 1950 show that some pioneering farmers produced beans and peas. The modern pulse industry started in the 1960s, when farmers began producing and exporting field peas and lentils. During the 1970s the industry grew slowly but steadily, building on progress in research and development in **AGRONOMY** and plant breeding, especially for lentil, field pea and faba bean. In the 1980s the industry began a dramatic expansion in response to international market demand from pulse importers in countries where cereal and oilseeds crops had begun to replace pulse crop production. In Saskatchewan, many small pulse processing companies were established to meet the demand for cleaning and exporting increasing amounts of bulk and container pulses, especially large green lentils, green peas and yellow peas. In the 1990s Saskatchewan added chickpea and dry bean to the list of pulse crop exports. By 2001, pulse crops were grown on about six million acres, representing over 11% of the cropland in the province.

Saskatchewan pulses are currently exported to more than 130 countries around the world. Over the past thirty years, the province's pulse industry has become one of the major global suppliers of lentil and field pea. Saskatchewan now has more than 100 pulse exporting companies dedicated to shipping bulk or containers to almost every pulse importing country worldwide; on a global scale, it is now the largest exporter of lentil and field pea. By 2003, at least ten companies were active in the business of dehulling and splitting peas, lentils and chickpeas for domestic and overseas markets. Other associated industries that have expanded, complementing the growth of the pulse crop industry, are specialized farm equipment manufacturing, the Rhizobium inoculant industry, agricultural chemicals, and the organic pulse crop industry.

Each crop sector within the pulse industry produces a diverse range of products that changes in response to market demand. The lentil crop originally consisted of green lentils of various sizes, but since 1996 the red lentil crop has been expanding. Shipments of French green lentils are exported to Europe each year. Most of the field pea crop is the yellow type, grown for either human food or animal feed. Green peas are grown for human consumption; and small amounts of other types such as marrowfat for snack foods, maple types for bird feed, and small-seeded forage types are also grown. Saskatchewan produces both kabuli (large white-seeded) and desi (small brown-seeded) chickpeas. The other pulse crops, such as common bean and faba bean, are grown in smaller quantities. Most dry bean production is pinto or black bean. Small amounts of medium-sized faba bean are grown each year for consumption in Mediterranean markets.

The pulse industry has become a significant part of the Saskatchewan agricultural economy, providing both full-time and seasonal employment in the farm input, grain processing, and transportation sectors. It is a vital and growing segment of Saskatchewan agriculture. *Albert Vandenberg*

QR

QUAALE, GORDON (1921–2004). Gordon Loyal Quaale was born on September 24, 1921, at Weldon, Saskatchewan, and died on June 20, 2004, in Nanaimo, BC. He was a trade union activist who carried the traditions of the 1940s' socially active unionism to a new generation in the 1970s. After being discharged from the Navy in 1945, Quaale went to work as a carpenter, an Industrial Standards Officer for the provincial government, and a union representative for the Canadian Congress of Labour and the National Union of Public Service Employees (NUPSE). In 1963, NUPSE merged with the National Union of Public Employees to form the **CANADIAN UNION OF PUBLIC EMPLOYEES** (CUPE). Quaale worked as a CUPE representative until 1973, when he became the acting director for Saskatchewan.

Much of Quaale's career was spent working with health care workers; he was the chief negotiator during the Estevan and Prince Albert hospital

GLEN BERGER PHOTO/SASKATCHEWAN ARCHIVES BOARD
S-SP-A17234-8, SASKATOON STARPHOENIX FONDS

Gordon Quaale, August 1981.

strikes in 1969–70. Quaale worked hard for the unity of health care workers, and in 1973 the first provincial hospital agreement was reached. When wage controls threatened the hard-won gains of public employees, he organized CUPE and lobbied the SASKATCHEWAN FEDERATION OF LABOUR for a massive demonstration, which was held on February 2, 1976. Quaale said that his work with the predominantly female heath care workers made him a convinced feminist, and he encouraged women activists and hired women staff representatives. He also supported CUPE's efforts to organize Aboriginal workers and train Aboriginal activists.

James Holmes

QUAKERS: *see* **RELIGIOUS SOCIETY OF FRIENDS**

QU'APPELLE, town, pop 648, located 50 km E of Regina just off Hwy 1 on Hwy 35. The Hudson's Bay Company had a trading post a short distance southwest of Qu'Appelle from 1854 to 1864; however, it was with the coming of the railway in 1881–82, that the community began to develop. The first post office established in 1882 was known as Troy, but the name was changed to Qu'Appelle Station in 1884. Qu'Appelle Station became the base for the telegraph line running north through Humboldt to Fort Battleford and Edmonton, as well as a major jumping off point for settlers. An immigration agent was stationed in the young community, and passengers and mail were carried by stagecoaches to Fort Qu'Appelle, Prince Albert, Fort Battleford and Edmonton. Freight was also transported northward by cart and wagon to the Saskatoon, Duck Lake, and Prince Albert areas. The community's prominence as a disembarkation and distribution centre led General MIDDLETON in 1885 to establish an initial staging point at Qu'Appelle, before heading north for his rendezvous with history. The years of the 1880s were boom times for the community and a number of structures dating to the era still stand in the town. Knox Presbyterian Church (United in 1925) was built in 1884 and, in 1885 St. Peter's Anglican Church was constructed, becoming the pro-Cathedral church of the Diocese of Qu'Appelle for sixty years. The stone rectory next door, built in 1894, is now a private residence. Another of the town's landmarks, the Queen's Hotel, which officially opened in 1884, was lost in an early morning blaze on April 16, 2003. The completion of the Qu'Appelle, Long Lake, and Saskatchewan Railway in 1890, linking Regina, Saskatoon, and Prince Albert, dealt a great blow to the town's economic fortunes, as Regina, and not Qu'Appelle, now delivered settlers and supplies to northern territories. Yet businessmen continued to attempt to establish industries in the community—a flour mill, a creamery, a felt and boot factory—and the great influx of

settlers into the District of Assiniboia in the early 1900s meant continued growth. The population of the community was 434 in 1901, but by the end of the first decade of the 20th century, it was near 1,000. In 1911, the Grand Trunk Pacific line was completed from Melville to Regina, and trade was again diverted from Qu'Appelle. Diminished somewhat in stature, the town, however, continued in its role as a service and supply centre for the surrounding agricultural district for many decades. By the 1960s, though, Qu'Appelle was entering a period of general decline. The newly-constructed TRANS-CANADA HWY was completed in the late 1950s; long-time businesspeople were also retiring, and fewer and fewer people were stepping in to fill the voids. Many businesses closed for good. In 1966–67, Highway 10, the direct link from Balgonie to Fort Qu'Appelle, was built, greatly reducing the traffic on Hwy 35 through Qu'Appelle to the valley. The hospital was closed and the CPR station was torn down by the end of the decade. However, over the course of the 1970s, the community's fortunes would begin to turn around as city-dwellers, young couples with families seeking affordable housing and lower taxes, and retired farmers moved into the town. Jobs in Regina became the major source of employment and commuting became a part of townspeople's routines. Today, about 80% to 90% of the town's workforce drive to and from the city each day. At present, only a small core of businesses remains in the community, including three rather unusual businesses for a small community. A print shop has operated for many years, and a tattoo parlour, which also accommodates those interested in body piercing, is thriving. Microbiologist Sheila Blachford and chemist John Blachford have operated an analytical laboratory in Qu'Appelle for close to 15 years and, accredited in both Canada and the United States, the company's services include microbial, toxin, biochemical, and chemical testing. Heritage properties in Qu'Appelle include the 1906 town hall/opera house and the former Royal Bank building (originally the Northern Bank) built the same year.

David McLennan

QU'APPELLE RIVER (50°29'N, 101°29'W; Map sheet 62 k/6). The east-flowing Qu'Appelle River, 430 km long and rising at the Qu'Appelle dam, 12 km southwest of Elbow, joins the ASSINIBOINE RIVER just east of the provincial boundary. Its tributaries include the Moose Jaw River and Wascana, Loon, Jumping Deer, Pheasant and Kaposvar creeks. The Qu'Appelle is a misfit stream, occupying a former glacial spillway once far larger than the present valley. Discharge of its tributaries is highly variable, greatest during spring run-off and dwindling to a trickle in late summer. Much of the flow in the Qu'Appelle itself is controlled. Water enters the river via the QU'APPELLE VALLEY dam, and about 100 kilo-

BRYAN SCHLOSSER/REGINA LEADER-POST
Qu'Appelle River, west of Lumsden, November 1987.

metres downstream flows through Buffalo Pound Lake, a major source of domestic water for Regina and district, where a dam and control structure govern downstream discharge.

The word *qu'appelle* is French for "who calls" and is derived from its Cree name, kah-tep-was ("river that calls"). There are several versions of the origin of this name, but the most popular suggests it refers to a Cree legend of two ill-fated lovers. The Cree name occurs at Katepwa Beach, Katepwa Lake and Katepwa Point Provincial Park, all in the Qu'Appelle Valley north of Indian Head.

Marilyn Lewry

QU'APPELLE VALLEY The Qu'Appelle Valley runs from west to east across southern Saskatchewan. Its westernmost origins now lie flooded under the Qu'Appelle arm of LAKE DIEFENBAKER. The valley ends a few kilometres across the Saskatchewan-Manitoba boundary at St. Lazare, where the QU'APPELLE RIVER joins the ASSINIBOINE. Ultimately, the river's waters flow to HUDSON BAY via Winnipeg, the Red River, Lake Winnipeg, and the Nelson River.

About 14,000 years ago the last continental ice sheet to sweep across Saskatchewan was in northward retreat as the climate warmed. When the ice sheet stalled at the site of the future Qu'Appelle Valley, vast quantities of meltwater flowed west to east across the ice sheet face, cutting deep into sediments laid down by previous GLACIATIONS and creating a valley some 180 metres deep and roughly 2 km across.

After the ice sheet retreated further north, the valley emptied of water, leaving a small remnant

COURTNEY MILNE PHOTO
Qu'Appelle Valley.

river that winds down the valley. Underground springs feed valley lakes. North and south of the valley coulees snake into the landscape. Most of the time these coulees are dry; but in spring, after the snowmelt, they funnel water and sediment from the surrounding plains down to the river. Over millennia this sediment has partially infilled the valley.

Moisture levels are the key determinant of valley vegetation. In coulees or hollows, or where valley slopes face north, moisture levels are higher, and trees and thick bush can be found. On the driest, south-facing slopes, there are cacti amongst the shortgrass. Bur oak trees grow on the easternmost valley slopes, the only native occurrence of oaks in Saskatchewan. Isolated patches of native prairie grass, protected from the plough by slope or bush, can still be found along valley's edge, a reminder of the original native grasslands that once stretched across the plains.

First Nations peoples have resided in the valley for millennia. Originally, they benefited from the abundant fish in the lakes and river. Deer and other game were plentiful in the valley coulees, and trees provided both shelter from the wind and fuel for fire. In the fur-trade days pemmican was shipped down valley on a Hudson's Bay Company cart trail to supply the paddlers of the fur trade in more forested regions. Today the valley is home to First Nations, small towns, farmers and ranchers, and cottagers clustered around the valley lakes.

Norm Henderson

FURTHER READING: Christiansen, E.A., D.F. Acton, R.J. Long, W.A. Meneley and E.K. Sauer. 1977. *Fort Qu'Appelle Geology: The Valleys, Past and Present*. Regina: Saskatchewan Museum of Natural History and Saskatchewan Culture and Youth; Henderson, Norman. 2001. *Rediscovering the Great Plains: Journeys by Dog, Canoe and Horse*. Baltimore: Johns Hopkins University Press; Herriot, Trevor. 2000. *River in a Dry Land: A Prairie Passage*. Toronto: Stoddart.

QUILL LAKES (51°55'N, 104°22'W (Big Quill Lake) Map sheet 72 P/16). Three lakes constitute Quill Lakes: Big, Little and Middle Quill (or Mud Lake). Elevated at 152 m, Big and Little Quill average 500 sq. km. Located north of Wynyard, they are in an internal drainage basin fed by numerous small streams. Big Quill's mean depth is only 1.5 m. Its extent varies with inflow and evaporation rates. The waters are saline, especially during times of drought. Mineral precipitates include sodium-magnesium sulphates and potassium sulphates. The lakes and surroundings wetlands are a stopover and breeding ground for migrating birds, particularly waterfowl and shorebirds. Designated as a Ramsar site (after the Ramsar Convention in Iran, aiming to protect wetlands of international importance) in 1987, this was the first Canadian implementation site for the North American Waterfowl Management Plan (NAWMP). Measures to protect wildlife include designation of the islands in Middle Quill Lake as a provincial wildlife refuge to preserve colonies of American white **PELICANS** (Pelecanus erythorhynchos), and the 1998 designation as an Important Bird Area (IBA). Big Quill has Saskatchewan's largest breeding population of piping plover (Charadrius melodus circumcintus). The lakes were named for the bird quills collected and shipped to England for use as writing pens. *Marilyn Lewry*

RABBITS: *see* **HARES AND RABBITS**

RADISSON, town, pop 401, located halfway between Saskatoon and North Battleford at the junction of Hwys 16 and 340. The **NORTH SASKATCHEWAN RIVER** lies 12 km to the south. Settlement in the area began in the early 1900s, and the first few businesses were built on the present townsite in 1904 in anticipation of the coming railway. The Canadian Northern Railway came through in 1905; that year, some 65 buildings were erected, among them the railway station, a hotel, and the first grain elevator. The Radisson school district was formed in 1905, with classes held in temporary quarters until a school building was completed the following year. Radisson was incorporated as a village in 1906 and attained town status in 1913. The community was named after Pierre-Esprit Radisson, the colourful explorer and fur trader whose exploits led to the founding of the Hudson's Bay Company. The Radisson district economy is based on the cattle industry and diversified grain farming. The community has a core of businesses, services, and recreational facilities. Radisson's school, after 100 years in operation, was closed in June 2004 after a controversial decision made by the Saskatoon (West) School Division. Two months later, on August 27, community members lined the streets as their students left on buses to travel the 25 km to the village of Maymont.

David McLennan

RADVILLE, town, pop 735, located approximately 50 km SW of Weyburn, on Long Creek, at the junction of Hwys 28 and 377. The region was settled in the early 1900s largely by British, French, and Scandinavian pioneers. By 1910, rail had been laid to the location of Radville. The townsite was surveyed, and construction began immediately: Radville, the railway company had decided, was to be an important centre. They were looking to construct a roundhouse and railway yards roughly midway between Winnipeg and Lethbridge, and Long Creek provided the reliable source of water that was needed. In 1911 it was incorporated as a village, construction of the roundhouse began, and a wide range of businesses were started. By the 1920s, the population was over 1,000. The town's importance as a railway hub diminished substantially when the roundhouse was shut down in the 1950s; yet today Radville remains an important commercial and cultural centre in the district. The town has over 100 businesses, a number of which cater to the district's agriculture and oil and gas industries. The town hosts several popular annual events including the Long Creek Rodeo and the Kinsmen Mud Fling and Demolition Derby. Three of Radville's earliest buildings have been designated heritage properties, including the Canadian Northern Railway Station, which was built in 1912 and now houses a museum.

David McLennan

735

RAIL LINE ABANDONMENT. The process of abandoning rail branch lines began in Saskatchewan almost as soon as the last line was completed. By the early 1960s, **CANADIAN NATIONAL** (CN) and **CANADIAN PACIFIC** (CP) railways were claiming that the operation of many grain-dependent branch lines was a money-losing proposition; under the transportation legislation of that time, the federal government would provide funding to subsidize these losses. Concerns over branch line abandonment caused the federal government to set up the **HALL COMMISSION** in 1975. The Commission recommended the closure of some branch lines and the inclusion of others in a permanent network. However, in the mid-1990s the railways were still unable to abandon all of the highest-cost branch lines. The federal government set up the Robson Committee, which gave permission to the railways to abandon all 525 miles (845 km) of high-cost branch lines. The Canada Transportation Act of 1996 streamlined the abandonment process, and branch line abandonment accelerated. In the next five years the railways abandoned over 1,450 (2,333 km) miles of prairie branch lines, half of this process taking place in Saskatchewan. Branch line abandonment was accompanied by closure of much of the vast network of country grain elevators. This brought an increase in hauling distances for farmers, with resulting negative effects on Saskatchewan's network of secondary highways.

Paul Beingessner

RAILS. Rails and coots are members of the family Rallidae (order Gruiformes), which are found in the wetlands of all the continents except Antarctica. There are approximately 143 species in the world. They are small to medium-sized omnivorous **BIRDS** with large feet, short tails, and small wings; many species have lost the ability to fly. Nine species occur in North America; four are known in Saskatchewan. All of these species are migratory.

COURTESY OF THE ROYAL SASKATCHEWAN MUSEUM

Sora rail.

The most familiar of these birds is the American coot (*Fulica americana*). This plump grey bird with a white shield on the forehead is very aggressive, and is frequently seen chasing any other water bird which approaches its nesting territory. Coots build their floating nest of vegetation on well-vegetated permanent sloughs and lakes of the south and centre of the province; there are some records from the north.

Rails are heard more often than seen. When disturbed, they are more likely to move off through the vegetation than to fly. Their body shape ("thin as a rail") helps them move through the bulrushes and cat-tails. The sora (*Porzana carolina*), a medium-sized rail with a barred body and back, grey face and chest, and black mask, is fairly widespread. Its whinnying call can come from a small slough or the edge of a lake. The Virginia rail (*Rallus limicola*), with a longer bill and cinnamon chest with barring on the side, is heard "grunting" around the larger marshes of the south and centre. The tiny yellow rail (*Coturnicops novaboracensis*) is seldom seen, but its clicking call can be heard in the larger marshes of the southern half of the province. *Diane Secoy*

FURTHER READING: Alsop, Fred J., III. 2002. *Birds of Canada*. New York: Dorling Kindersley.

RAILWAY UNIONS. Railways expanded quickly in North America in the mid-1800s and Railroad Brotherhoods were started in the 1860s to 1880s to represent the workers in the new trades. These were international craft unions with headquarters in the United States. The big four brotherhoods were Locomotive Engineers, Locomotive Firemen and Enginemen, Railroad Trainmen, and Railway Conductors.

As the railways came west, the construction of the CPR required about 7,600 workers. There were experienced railway workers who moved from one construction project to the next but most were tramp workers and recent immigrants. Living conditions and wages in these moving camps were poor and the pressure to meet progress deadlines was great. In June 1883, a strike of 130 railway workers coincided with the unrest of the First Nations near Maple Creek. The North-West Mounted Police arrested the foreman and took steps to support the railway construction. In December 1883, engineers and firemen without a union started a strike against pay cuts.

Shortly after the completion of the railway the workers in the running trades founded locals of the brotherhoods on the Western Division of the CPR. By 1892 the four brotherhoods had established locals in the prairies including divisional points in Saskatchewan. The CPR proposed a wage cut that year and demanded employees sign a loyalty oath. The union men struck and gained public support

against the CPR's union-busting methods of importing scabs and mercenaries. The settlement favoured the workers and their unions were recognized.

The brotherhoods led the development of trade unions in the railway communities on the prairies. These brotherhoods only represented the elite crafts of the railway workers. The majority of workers involved in maintenance of equipment and the trackbed, the clerks, freight handlers, and many other trades were not yet unionized. They were also less well paid, less skilled, and often seasonal workers.

A number of additional international brotherhoods were organized on a craft basis for telegraphers, machinists, boilermakers and maintenance of way employees. There were also attempts to create Canadian and industrial unions that included all the trades in one union. The largest union was the Canadian Brotherhood of Railway Employees and Other Transport Workers. It covered many classes of workers on the Grand Trunk and Canadian Northern Railways. An international union, the Brotherhood of Railway & Steamship Clerks, Freight-handlers, Express and Station Employees organized these workers on the CPR.

During the interwar period, railway centres in Saskatchewan such as Biggar, Melville, Moose Jaw, North Battleford, Prince Albert, Regina, Saskatoon and more than thirty-nine other Saskatchewan communities had locals of several railway unions.

The bargaining process was very complex, with multiple unions bargaining with different railways and with different contracts for different parts of the country. The unions tried various methods of co-operation to coordinate bargaining. The unions also coordinated lobbying efforts to initiate legislation to regulate the railways, improve working conditions, and increase safety. The strike by 130,000 railway workers against the CPR and CNR in 1950 was the largest strike in Canadian history. The federal government set a precedent by legislating them back to work.

Technological changes such as diesel locomotives, increasing competition by trucking, air and water transportation, and the abandonment of branch lines led to a rapidly decreasing work force on the railways and the railway unions were forced to consolidate. In 1968, four of the brotherhoods merged and became part of the United Transportation Union (UTU) with other transport workers. The Brotherhood of Locomotive Engineers (BLE) worked with the UTU in the Canadian Council of Railway Operating Unions and considered amalgamation with the UTU. Their members rejected the merger and merged with the Teamsters to form the Teamsters Canada Rail Conference. Railway conductors formerly with the UTU and Brotherhood of Maintenance of Way Employees have also joined with the Teamsters. In 1998 the BLE opened an

SASKATCHEWAN ARCHIVES BOARD S-SP-A19881-5, SASKATOON STARPHOENIX FONDS

Ali Hussain Rajput, March 1983.

UNIVERSITY OF REGINA ARCHIVES AND SPECIAL COLLECTIONS 80-2-93

William Ramsay.

SASKATCHEWAN ARCHIVES BOARD R-A7553

Sarah Ramsland.

Engineer Training Centre in Saskatoon to train railroad engineers using senior engineers and a locomotive simulator.

The dangerous work on the railways is recognized in a monument erected in Melville in 2000 that names nineteen workers killed on the job between 1914 and 1974. These are only the CN workers out of Melville who worked between Rivers, Manitoba and the Watrous area in Saskatchewan.

Bob Ivanochko

FURTHER READING: Greening, W.E. and M.M. MacLean. 1961. *It Never Was Easy, 1908–1958: A History of the Canadian Brotherhood of Railway, Transport and General Workers*. Ottawa: Mutual Press; Logan, H.A. 1948. *Trade Unions in Canada; Their Functioning and Development*. Toronto: Macmillan.

RAJPUT, ALI HUSSAIN (1934–). Born in a farming village with the number 30 but no name in Sind, Pakistan, on December 8, 1934, Ali was the gold medallist when he graduated in medicine from the University of Sind. After post-graduate training in Chicago, New York, Ann Arbor and Kingston, he joined the staff of the **UNIVERSITY OF SASKATCHEWAN** and University Hospital in 1967, and was head of the Division of Neurology from 1985 to 2001. A Professor Emeritus since 2002, he is director of the Saskatchewan Centre for Parkinson's Disease and Movement Disorders. Author or co-author of 166 scientific papers and twenty-four book chapters, Ali is a recognized international authority on the diagnosis and treatment of Parkinson's disease. He has followed personally for years, until autopsy, more patients with Parkinsonism and patients with Essential Tremors than any other doctor in the world, and is a leader in the analysis of dystonia. His honours include the Saskatchewan Order of Merit (1993), Tony Dagnone Spirit of Royal University Hospital Award (1996), Officer of the Order of Canada (the first Canadian of Pakistani origin and

first Muslim Canadian to be so honoured, 1997), Morton Shulman Award (2001), and Distinguished Canadian Award (2002). *C. Stuart Houston*

RAMSAY, WILLIAM (1876–1965). William Ramsay, born in Ontario in 1876, graduated from Queen's University, Kingston in 1902 with a BA and took graduate courses at the University of Chicago, where he completed his PhD in 1927. Ramsay taught at various public schools in Ontario before joining the staff of Regina's Central Collegiate in 1910. Six years later he joined the faculty of the **UNIVERSITY OF SASKATCHEWAN** as a professor of Classics. He was dean of Regina College from 1934 to 1940. A gifted educator and able administrator, Ramsay served as dean at a difficult period in the College's history: in 1934 Regina College was absorbed by the University of Saskatchewan and faced an uncertain future, as the economic depression had reduced enrolment and resulted in persistent financial shortfalls. Ramsay's guidance, however, ensured the survival of the college and its eventual growth into the **UNIVERSITY OF REGINA**. Retiring in 1940, Ramsay received an honorary doctor of laws degree in 1961. He died in Saskatchewan in 1965. *Mark Vajcner*

FURTHER READING: Pitsula, James M. 1988. *An Act of Faith: The Early Years of Regina College*. Regina: Canadian Plains Research Center.

RAMSLAND, SARAH KATHERINE (1882–1964). Sarah McEwen was born July 19, 1882, in Minnesota, the granddaughter of a Democratic member of the state legislature. She taught school before her marriage to Magnus O. (Max) Ramsland. The Ramslands moved to Buchanan after 1905, where Max brokered real estate. Max Ramsland was elected as a Liberal MLA for Pelly in 1917 but died in the influenza epidemic of November 1918. The Liberals felt obliged to support his widow and three

children. Following a precedent set the previous year in British Columbia, they invited Mrs. Ramsland to run in the by-election. Women's issues were not raised in the campaign. Neither her sex nor her widowhood made much difference to the voters, who elected her (as Saskatchewan's first woman MLA), although with a smaller majority than her husband had received. Ramsland's performance in the Legislature was clean but undistinguished. Ramsland was neither a feminist nor a social-reform activist. She was simply a loyal Liberal backbencher. Ramsland was re-elected in 1921 by a reduced margin, and was defeated by a Progressive candidate in 1925. Hours before her final legislative session ended, she introduced a resolution calling for an amendment to federal divorce laws that would permit women to apply for divorce on the grounds of a spouse's adultery, on equal terms with men. After her defeat, Ramsland worked for the provincial library. She was active in several women's organizations, later married Regina businessman W.C.F. Scythes, and died April 4, 1964. Not until the CCF victory in 1944 was another woman elected to the Saskatchewan Legislature.

Elizabeth Kalmakoff

FURTHER READINGS: Kalmakoff, Elizabeth. 1994. "Naturally Divided: Women in Saskatchewan Politics, 1916–1919," *Saskatchewan History* 46 (2): 3–18; —. 1993. "Woman Suffrage in Saskatchewan." MA thesis, University of Regina.

RANCHING. Saskatchewan reported nearly 3 million beef cattle in the 2001 Census of Canada. While the majority of these cattle were reared on mixed farms, ranching remains extremely important, especially in the southwest of the province, where 40% of the land is unimproved rangeland. Ranching involves the rearing of stock for commercial purposes; it is an extensive rather than an intensive form of land use. The need for access to large areas

R

EVERETT BAKER PHOTO/COURTESY OF THE SASKATCHEWAN HISTORY AND FOLKLORE SOCIETY

Gilchrist Brothers ranch house. At the time this photo was taken, ca. 1941, it was the largest ranch in Canada.

of grazing has meant that ranchers have always been dependent on public lands. These areas are usually found in hinterland regions far from markets, where other more intensive forms of commercial agriculture are unable to compete. During the first decades of settlement ranchers leased Crown land from the federal government. Today community pastures run by the **PRAIRIE FARM REHABILITATION ADMINISTRATION** and by the provincial government make grazing available to a wide spectrum of ranching enterprises. On these pastures, many of the traditions and methods of working cattle on "open range" have been maintained for more than a century. *Simon Evans*

RAO, KRIS (1932–2000). Kris Rao was born in Sina, Mysore, India, on August 2, 1932. He graduated from Stanley Medical College in Madras, where he married a fellow medical student, Leela Leelavathi. After completion of their internships they left India and obtained residency positions in Middletown, Connecticut–Kris in Radiology and Leela in Pathology. He did his final years of radiology in Saskatoon and spent his professional career with Associated Radiologists in that city. Kris was a tireless volunteer, giving of his time and expertise to local, national and international charities–including short stints with MEDICO-CARE in Afghanistan. He was a founder of the first Hindu temple in Saskatoon. Rao believed we all have a responsibility to give back to our community and country some of the benefits we have received; this he did in full measure. He received a number of honours, the greatest being the Order of Canada in 1992. He died during a visit to India on January 10, 2000. *Gordon Bray*

RAUM, ELIZABETH (1945–). Elizabeth Raum was born on January 13, 1945, in Berlin, New Hampshire and became a naturalized Canadian in 1985. A composer and oboist, she earned her BMus from the Eastman School of Music in 1966. Raum was principal oboist with the Atlantic Symphony Orchestra in Halifax, Nova Scotia prior to joining the **REGINA SYMPHONY ORCHESTRA** in 1975. Her renewed interest in composition led her to study with **THOMAS SCHUDEL** at the **UNIVERSITY OF REGINA** from 1980 to 1984. Here she received her MMus (Composition) with her opera *The Garden of Alice.* Considered one of Canada's most "accessible" composers, she writes prolifically in diverse styles and for a wide variety of genres including ballet, chamber, orchestra, and vocal. Raum won the award for Best Musical Score for *Sparkle* (director, Jeff Beesley), at the Saskatchewan Film and Video Showcase '98, profiling her 1993 work *A Prairie Alphabet Musical Parade.* Film collaborations have been broadcast nationally; her music has been heard in Europe, Russia, China, Japan, and throughout the Americas. The CBC and numerous groups within the province have commissioned Raum's works, and she has also written many works for children. She is an associate of the Canadian Music Centre. In 2004, the Regina Symphony Orchestra presented the premiere of her concerto *Persephone and Demeter*–written for, and featuring her daughter, virtuoso violinist Erika Raum. That year, she was awarded an honorary doctorate by Mount Saint Vincent University in Halifax. Elizabeth Raum lives in Regina. *Fiona Stevenson*

FURTHER READING: Kallmann, H. 1992. *Encyclopedia of Music in Canada,* 2nd ed.

RAWLCO COMMUNICATIONS LTD. Rawlco Communications Ltd. is a Calgary-based broadcaster with Saskatchewan roots. Established in 1946 by **ED RAWLINSON** (1912–92), a Saskatchewan resident born in Qu'Appelle, it became one of Canada's most successful broadcasting companies. Rawlinson had a fascination for radio broadcasting: in 1946 he purchased CKBI radio in Prince Albert, and soon after became chairman of his own company, Rawlco Communications Ltd. The company acquired prominent radio and television stations in Prince Albert, North Battleford, Meadow Lake, Saskatoon, Regina, Calgary, Ottawa, and Toronto. Rawlco Communications Ltd. also became a partner in the New Country Network, a Canadian-owned country music television station. In 1975, Rawlinson's two sons, Gordon and Doug, both from Prince Albert, entered the broadcasting business. The Rawlinson brothers formed Rawlco Radio Ltd., a Saskatchewan-based radio broadcasting company. During the next twenty years, Rawlco Radio Ltd. purchased and operated radio stations in Saskatchewan, Alberta, and

LINDA HOLOBOFF PHOTO/SASKATCHEWAN ARCHIVES BOARD S-SP-A7776-1, SASKATOON STARPHOENIX FONDS

Kris Rao, November 1977.

Ontario. In 1999, Ralwco Radio Ltd. consolidated its holdings to focus only on Saskatchewan radio; it currently operates eleven stations in the province. Ed Rawlinson died in 1992; his son Gordon is now president and CEO of Rawlco Communications Ltd.

Iain Stewart

FURTHER READING: Anonymous. 2001. "Rawlco Radio's $1 Million Will Assist First Nations' Business Education," *Saskbusiness* 22: 14.

RAWLINSON, EDWARD A. (1912–92).

Born on June 2, 1912, a pioneer in Saskatchewan broadcasting, Edward Rawlinson of Qu'Appelle became Canada's youngest chartered accountant in 1934. His keen business sense led to the purchase of numerous radio stations across Saskatchewan and Manitoba beginning with Prince Albert's CKBI in 1946. Eventually, Rawlinson organized his group of radio and television stations into RAWLCO COMMUNICATIONS Ltd., of which he was chairman. Ed Rawlinson figured prominently in many community, provincial, and national organizations such as the Western Association of Broadcasters, the Institute of Chartered Accountants, and the University of Saskatchewan Board of Governors. In 1989, he received the Saskatchewan Order of Merit. He died on August 8, 1992.

SASKATCHEWAN ARCHIVES BOARD S-F470
Donald Rawson.

RAWSON, DONALD STRATHEARN (1905–61).

Donald Rawson was born in Claremont, Ontario, on May 19, 1905. He entered the University of Toronto in 1922, specializing in limnology. He demonstrated outstanding ability as a student and was awarded a doctorate at age 24; his doctoral thesis investigated the bottom fauna of Lake Simcoe. He was influenced by able men such as E.M. Walker, A.G. Huntsman, W. Harkness and J.R. Dymond, who kindled in him a love of the outdoors and of biology. In 1928 he joined the staff of the Department of Biology, UNIVERSITY OF SASKATCHEWAN, where he became head of the Department in 1949.

Rawson married Hildred Patton in 1932; they had two sons, Eric and Bruce, and a daughter, Mary. His research in limnology covered two distinct periods. From 1928 to 1934 he concentrated on lakes of the newly established PRINCE ALBERT NATIONAL PARK. This work involved physico-chemical, biological, and fisheries studies, and included specific experiments in fisheries management. From 1935 to 1941 he carried out extensive research in the National Parks of the Canadian Rockies and in Riding Mountain National Park, Manitoba. The primary aim of these investigations was the collection of limnological information as applied to fisheries management, but contributions of fundamental significance also resulted, spanning the gap between theoretical and applied science. In the late 1930s Rawson surveyed saline lakes in southern Saskatchewan.

In 1942 Rawson began work on Canada's large northern lakes (including REINDEER, ATHABASCA and Great Slave Lakes) that brought him international fame. After 1947 he devoted most of his attention to investigations of LAC LA RONGE and Amisk Lake in the CHURCHILL RIVER drainage system. Subsequently, many other northern Saskatchewan lakes were studied. He had a profound influence on the many graduate students who were involved with him in these investigations. He was particularly interested in the practical applications of his limnological studies: for example, he was instrumental in setting up a sound fisheries research program in Saskatchewan, under the jurisdiction of the Department of Natural Resources. He also played a part in the founding of the Canadian Society of Wildlife and Fishery Biologists.

Rawson was an efficient administrator employing tolerance and understanding. The W.P. Thompson Biology Building and the strong department it houses were largely his creation. He was a champion wrestler at the University of Toronto, and for many years coached wrestling at the University of Saskatchewan. Although all his studies took place in Canada, his outlook was international. He traveled widely in the United States and Europe, familiarizing himself with leading limnological investigations abroad.

He received many honours during his lifetime. He was president of the Limnological Society of America and of the Canadian Conservation Association; director of the Fisheries Research Board of Canada; a member of the Royal Commission on Fisheries for Saskatchewan; and a Fellow of the Royal Society of Canada. Rawson's death on February 16, 1961, at the peak of his scientific and teaching career, was a monumental loss to science in Canada.

U. Theodore Hammer

FURTHER READING: Rawson, D.S. 1936. "Physical and Chemical Sudies of Lakes in Prince Albert National Park, Saskatchewan," *Journal of the Biological Board of Canada* 2 (3): 227–84.

RAYMORE, town, pop 625, located approximately 100 km N of Regina on Hwys 6 and 15. Four First Nations reserve lands lie a short distance to the northeast and the southeast of the community. The area was largely settled by people of German and British origins, and the community had its beginnings with the construction of the GRAND TRUNK PACIFIC RAILWAY through the area. In 1908, the first small wooden structures began to appear on the stretch of prairie that would become Main Street. Raymore was incorporated as a village in 1909. By 1912, the business district had substantially developed and the Bank of British North America had established a branch here. Raymore's numbers peaked at just under 700 in 1986; only in recent years has the number of residents somewhat declined. Mixed farming remains the basis of the area economy, and a number of farm equipment dealers are among Raymore's core of businesses. The Raymore Pioneer Museum houses a collection of the district's historical artifacts; the museum site has been designated a heritage property.

David McLennan

REAL PROPERTY.

Saskatchewan's land holding system, as with all of English Canada, grew out of English roots. The Norman monarchs from 1066 took the position that all land was owned by the king, with a fee simple estate the largest interest the Crown would grant while retaining to itself some rights to the land. This premise continues today and manifests itself in the Crown's right to expropriate as well as in escheat laws, whereby if there exist no will and no heirs, land reverts to the Crown. This is the source of the term "the Crown has underlying title" in all the land in Saskatchewan. In the colonial expansion of the 17th century, the British Crown asserted sovereignty over the land now comprising Saskatchewan as part of Rupert's Land, defined as the watershed of the rivers flowing into Hudson Bay. By Royal Charter of 1670, England's King Charles II granted Rupert's Land to the Hudson's Bay Company in fee simple, including governance rights (Charter of the Hudson's Bay Company, 1670 (U.K.), 22 Charles II, c.2). In the 1700s, both French and English fur traders moved inland.

Nearly a century later, the 1763 Treaty of Paris (Definitive Treaty of Peace between France, Great Britain and Spain, February 11, 1763, 42 Cons. T.S.320) allocated northwestern North America to the English. England issued the 1763 Royal Proclamation declaring that only the Crown could buy land from the Indians who inhabited the west. (Royal Proclamation of 1763, October 7, 1763, (U.K.), Privy Council Register, Geo.III, Vol.3 at 102). After the formation of the Dominion of Canada in 1867, Canada passed the Rupert's Land Act 1868 (31–32 Vict. c. 105.) to purchase Rupert's Land from the Hudson's Bay Company for £300,000 plus future land rights. The lands were formally conveyed to Canada by imperial order in 1870 (Order of Her Majesty in Council Admitting Rupert's Land and the North-Western Territory into the Union at the Court of Windsor, June 23, 1870, P.C.1879, S.C. 1872, p. lxiii).

In 1869–70, resistance to Ottawa's preemptory actions concerning western lands led to armed struggle, known as the "Red River Rebellion" or "Red River Resistance." The settlement of this conflict involved the creation of Manitoba as a province in 1870 (The Manitoba Act, S.C. 1870, c.3), with much smaller boundaries than at present. In 1871, the British North America Act, 1871 (34 & 35 Vict. 29 June 1871–now called the Constitution Act, 1871) authorized Canada to make provinces out of territories. Between 1871 and 1877, Canada negotiated seven major treaties with Aboriginal tribes in the North-West to open western lands for settlement. (Another numbered treaty, Number 10, covered land in the northern part of the province, but was not signed until 1906.) The English version of the treaties read that the Indians agreed to "cede, release, and surrender" the land, but differing interpretations of this phrase are the source of tensions that continue to the present. In 1992 the governments of Canada and Saskatchewan and the FEDERATION OF SASKATCHEWAN INDIAN NATIONS agreed on a "Treaty Land Entitlement Framework Agreement" to address unresolved land claims arising out of the numbered treaties.

The DOMINION LANDS ACT, 1872 (An Act respecting the Public Lands of the Dominion, S.C. 1872, c.23, s.10) established the present survey system, based on the American model of quadrilateral sections, ranges and townships (An Act Concerning the Mode of Surveying the Public Lands of the United States. (a), U.S.C. s.1, 1805). The township is the basic unit, six miles by six miles square, divided into 36 sections. Each section is one square mile, containing 640 acres and further subdivided into quarter-sections of 160 acres. The first meridian is just west of Winnipeg, marked by a monument on the TRANS-CANADA HIGHWAY; the second meridian is just west of the Manitoba border in Saskatchewan; and the third meridian is in western Saskatchewan. Homesteads were identified by "land location": e.g., NW1/4 25-15-10-W2 means northwest quarter of Section 25, Township 15, Range 10, West of the 2nd Meridian. The Hudson's Bay Company was granted Section 8 and three-quarters of Section 26 (and all of every fifth section 26) in surveyed townships as part of the 1870 purchase price. Sections 11 and 29 in each township were reserved as school lands to be sold as revenue to fund education. Canada offered free homesteads of 160 acres for anyone who would break the land and live on it for three successive "six-month years" (meaning six months within a calendar year) (Dominion Lands Act, 1872, s.33.) Later,

25 million acres were granted to the CANADIAN PACIFIC RAILWAY as part of government grants to build a transcontinental railway to join British Columbia, and thus to carry settlers and manufactured goods to western Canada and return grain for export.

The land-holding system consisted of a Crown grant of land and issuance of a patent for the grant. The patent was registered and a title created. In 1878 and subsequent years, the North-West Territories Council enacted ordinances requiring the registration of all instruments related to land (An Ordinance Respecting the Registration of Deeds and Other Instruments Relating to Lands in the North-West Territories, C.O. 1878, An Ordinance to Extend and Amend the Registration of Titles Ordinance, C.O. 1881, an Ordinance to Further Amend "The Registration of Titles Ordinance 1879". An Ordinance to Amend and Consolidate, as amended, the Registration of Titles Ordinance of 1879, and the Ordinance Amending it, C.O. 1884). In 1886, the North-West Territories Act, R.S.C. 1886, c.50 adopted British law as of July 15, 1870, in the Territories. English law continues to apply today, unless overruled by a Canadian or provincial statute. The Act also gave the Territories control over property and civil rights (s. 13(9)), except that control of "land" was retained by Canada for national policy settlement purposes. The Torrens system of land registration was introduced effective January 1, 1887, through the Territories Real Property Act, 1886 (An Act respecting Real Property in the Territories, S.C. 1886, c.26; R.S.C. 1886, c.51.). The Torrens system was developed by a customs officer in Australia, designed to simplify and expedite land transactions. The system was based on "indefeasibility" of title, meaning that the registered title is guaranteed by the state as being a valid record of the interests in the land, avoiding the need for verifying the contents of any land document that had characterized the British system. The details of the system were formalized in the Land Titles Act 1894, 57–58 Vict., c.28. Most landowners in Saskatchewan during the 20th century at one time or another visited the "Land Titles Office" in Humboldt, Regina, Moose Jaw, Saskatoon, Yorkton, North Battleford, Swift Current, or Prince Albert.

Beginning with an Order-in-Council in 1887, Ottawa reserved mines and minerals to the Crown. Titles issued before this policy were called "freehold," passing mineral rights to the landowners; after this policy, most titles reflected the words "minerals in the Crown." In 1898, Ottawa also vested all water in the Crown with the North West Irrigation Act 1898 61 V. c 35. In 1905, Ottawa divided the North-West Territories into the provinces of Alberta and Saskatchewan. Unlike the situation with respect to the first four provinces of Confederation, Ottawa retained jurisdiction over Crown land, providing the

provinces with subsidies "in lieu of public lands" (An Act to Establish and provide for the Government of the Province of Saskatchewan, 4–5 Edward VII, c.42. [The Saskatchewan Act, 1905] An Act to Establish and provide for the Government of the Province of Alberta, S.C. 1905, c.3). S.21 of the Saskatchewan Act reads: "All Crown lands, mine, minerals, and royalties, and interest in water under the North West Irrigation Act 1898 are vested in the Crown and administered by the federal government."

In 1930, the federal government released control of Crown lands to the provinces of Saskatchewan and Alberta in the Natural Resources Transfer Agreement (Constitution Act, 1930, R.S.C. 1970, App.II. No.25). The Provincial Lands Act S.S. 1931, c. 14 provided the framework for provincially held land, including leased land for mineral and forestry development, and ranch land. The federal government created the PRAIRIE FARM REHABILITATION ADMINISTRATION (PFRA) to assemble land that had proven unsuitable for cultivation during the DEPRESSION and create a network of community pastures (Prairie Farm Rehabiliation Act, S.C. 1935, c.23). In 1982, the Constitution of Canada enshrined provincial jurisdiction over specific aspects of non-renewable natural resources, forestry resources, and electrical energy (Constitution Act, 1982, s.92A). The Land registry system continued intact in all its major principles throughout the 20th century. In 2001, the Act received a major overhaul as the paper-based title system was transformed to a computer-based registry system, in the Land Titles Act, S.S., 2000 c.L-5.1. This new system integrated land survey and land titles registries, providing Internet-based land survey examination, title registration, and an integrated spatial database (GIS).

Marjorie L. Benson and Don Purich

RECREATIONAL CO-OPERATIVES. In addition to providing valuable services, community-based recreational facilities also play an essential role in fostering a sense of community spirit, which is a critical component of successful community development. Recreational co-operatives therefore provide indirect support for the community-development projects initiated by other types of co-operative organizations, such as Small Business Loans Associations and Rural Development Corporations.

Recreational co-operatives have been common in Saskatchewan since the early 1920s. Residents of the province are presently active in a wide variety of these organizations, including community halls, curling rinks, recreation centres (which provide gymnasiums, meeting halls, hockey arenas, swimming pools, concession stands, etc.), museums, golf courses, waterslides, television services, and community theatres. A number of community-based recreational facilities are owned and controlled on a co-operative basis, but are not registered as such, so statistics gathered by the Saskatchewan Department of Justice do not accurately reflect the number of these organizations currently active in the province. In addition, the financial data do not reflect the value of donated materials and volunteer labour that have been invested in establishing and maintaining these facilities.

Although the total number of recreational co-operatives declined (mainly as regards community halls) over the course of the 1990s, statistics show those still active to be in good financial health. Despite the fall in numbers, assets reported by this sector remained remarkably stable, and liabilities declined substantially during the decade. The slight increase in revenues produced over the same period a corresponding increase in surplus, which would be rolled back into the individual organizations for upgrades, improvements, or targeted projects. Member equity also increased.

There was a marked decline in the number of community halls operating as co-operatives during the 1990s, with numbers falling from 145 to 102. Curiously, there was only a 13% drop in active membership during the same period, as well as a 47% rise in the number of employees, although the wage bill decreased considerably, reflecting a large number of part-time workers.

CURLING and recreational facilities serve a wide variety of needs, providing gymnasiums, curling rinks, meeting halls, hockey arenas, swimming pools, concession stands, and many other services. Like the community halls, most of these organizations are relatively free of debt and tend to operate on a break-even basis. The number of co-operatively owned curling rinks and recreational centres and their corresponding memberships declined during the 1990s, although not as significantly as the community halls. In 1989 there were more than 100 of these facilities serving over 8,000 members. By the end of the next decade the number had fallen to fewer than ninety, with active membership declining by more than 40%. As might be expected, the number of people employed by this type of co-operative fell dramatically as well (from 117 to 49: a drop of 58%), and wages declined accordingly. Most notable was the 82% drop in capital investment, although this was matched by a 79% decline in liabilities. Assets remained relatively stable over the decade, and member equity increased from $8.3 to $9.3 million.

People also co-operate to provide themselves with cable television services. At the end of the 1990s there were only five TV co-operatives in the province, but despite their small number these organizations generate a surprising amount of economic activity. They employ more than 130 individuals, with a wage bill of $3 million. Revenues during the course of the decade rose from $11.8 million to $26.9 million; assets increased by 50%, from $20 million to $30 million; and member equity almost quadrupled, rising from $6.4 million to $23.2 million.

There are a few other types of recreational co-operatives, including golf, community theatre, museums, and waterslides. Although their revenues, assets, and member equity are significantly lower than the other types of recreational co-ops in the province, they nevertheless provide valuable services to the members of the communities in which they operate.   *Nora Russell*

FURTHER READING: Fulton, Murray, et al. 1991. *Economic Impact Analysis of the Co-operative Sector in Saskatchewan*, Research Report Prepared for Saskatchewan Department of Economic Diversification and Trade; Ketilson, Lou Hammond, et al. 1998. *The Social and Economic Importance of the Co-operative Sector in Saskatchewan*, Research Report Prepared for Saskatchewan Department of Economic and Co-operative Development; Herman, Roger, and Murray Fulton. 2001. *An Economic Impact Analysis of the Co-operative Sector in Saskatchewan: Update 1998*.

RED COAT ROAD & RAIL. When the **CANADIAN PACIFIC RAILWAY** (CPR) announced the abandonment of the 115-km section of rail line from Pangman (mileage 36.5) to Assiniboia, Saskatchewan (mileage 108.0), a group of four people (Kevin Klemenz from Bengough, Roger Dahl from Viceroy, Ed Howse from Pangman, and Lonny McKague from Ogema) decided to buy the rail line in 1999, for $1.1 million dollars. There were 170 shareholders, who raised $145,000; the fundraising, in addition to grants and loans from the federal and provincial governments, the Rural Municipalities of Lake of the Rivers #72, Bengough #40, Excel #71, Key West #70 and Norton #69, formed the short-line organization called Red Coat Road & Rail (RCRR). The seven elevators in the six towns along the RCRR were all formerly owned by the **SASKATCHEWAN WHEAT POOL** (SWP). None of the elevators along the rail line are owned by RCRR, but they do have individual marketing agreements with the short-line to use the rail line to load producer cars. RCRR has a contract with the **SOUTHERN RAILS CO-OPERATIVE** to maintain the rail line and pull the producer cars. The rail line interchanges with the CPR at Assiniboia. Red Coat Road and Rail is an organization consisting of representatives of the communities adjacent to the rail line, as well as of the town of Ogema and villages of Viceroy and Pangman.

Carol Peterson

RED COAT TRAIL. The Red Coat Trail is a historic land trail established by the North-West Mounted Police (NWMP), whose brightly coloured uniforms resulted in the naming of this trail. It entered Saskatchewan near Roche Percée and meandered west until it reached the Alberta border in the **CYPRESS HILLS**. In the summer of 1874 the NWMP embarked on a long and arduous trek across the trail through what was then the North-West Territories. The Dominion government, eager to survey and settle the west, dispatched the force to maintain law and order at a place called "Fort Whoop-Up," located near the junction of the Belly and Bow rivers in present-day Alberta. A force of 275 men, more than 300 horses, 140 oxen, 73 wagons, and over 100 **RED RIVER CARTS** left Dufferin, Manitoba on July 9. The force generally followed the **BOUNDARY SURVEY TRAIL**, careful enough not to veer too far south and cross onto American soil. Intense prairie

Planting the Red Coat Trail marker northwest of Orkney, June 1961.

heat, insects, lack of drinking water and feed for the animals created unbearable living conditions: the force thus broke into splinter divisions along the way in an attempt to increase its efficiency. On September 10, the main NWMP contingent reached the junction of the Belly and Bow rivers; however, Fort Whoop-Up was nowhere to be found. It was only several weeks later that the NWMP, with the assistance of Métis guide Jerry Potts, found the fort at the junction of the Belly and St. Mary's rivers. By the time the NWMP arrived there, much of the unrest had subsided. The arrival of the NWMP signaled the permanent establishment of the force, later to become the **ROYAL CANADIAN MOUNTED POLICE** (RCMP), in the Canadian west. *James Winkel*

RED CROSS OUTPOST HOSPITALS. In 1920, the first Red Cross Outpost Hospital in the British Empire was built at Paddockwood, Saskatchewan. This post-**WORLD WAR I** Red Cross program served small, remote communities (often soldier-settlement areas) unable to afford municipal hospitals. Built and maintained by the communities, these hospitals were staffed and supplied by the Red Cross. This successful partnership led to a total of twenty-four outposts in Saskatchewan, over 200 across Canada, and more around the world. A "Nurse-in-Charge," not a resident doctor, managed each hospital and lived in the community full-time. With the nearest doctor typically thirty or more miles away, Charge Nurses delivered babies, stitched wounds, administered medicine, set bones, treated fevers, gave vaccinations, and offered practical medical advice. Often forced by circumstance to make diagnoses and prescribe treatment in a doctor's stead, these nurses worked admirably outside the bounds of accepted nursing practice. The Red Cross name and flag gave instant recognition, and promoted trust for people of all nationalities. By 1946, over 37,000 inpatients and 27,000 outpatients had been treated in Saskatchewan outposts, with 8,800 births recorded. Over the years, as communities matured and transportation improved, each hospital was turned over to community management or closed. Saskatchewan's Red Cross Outpost Hospitals included, in order of establishment: Paddockwood, Carragana, Bengough, Eastend, Cutknife, Meadow Lake, Willow Bunch, Kelvington, Big River, Lucky Lake, Broderick, Wood Mountain, Bracken, Nipawin, Tuberose, Rabbit Lake, Rockglen, Loon Lake, Endeavour, Pierceland, Leoville, Hudson Bay Junction, Arborfield, and Buffalo Narrows. *Merle Massie*

RED EARTH FIRST NATION. The area of the Red Earth and Carrot River Reserves once included a trail that led from the parklands to the **SASKATCHEWAN RIVER** delta, and which was used until the 1930s. The region marked the territorial boundary between the Plains and Swampy **CREE**,

and Red Earth was the most northern Plains Cree community. By the late 1800s clusters of cabins under the leadership of Kiseyinis ("Little Old Man"), his son Mihkwanakeskam, his daughter Jessie and son-in-law Pahkwayis, as well as his daughter Harriet and son-in-law Newakeyas were established; a fifth site was occupied by Cecim, an unrelated Plains Cree. Kiseyinis and Cecim signed an adhesion to **TREATY 5** on September 7, 1876, and reserves were surveyed for them in 1884 (Red Earth) and 1894 (Carrot River). The Red Earth people were able to maintain their traditional way of life, supplementing it with gardens and livestock as the need arose. In the 1930s, however, drought caused a localized extinction of beaver and a drop in muskrat numbers, leading to the closure of the Hudson's Bay Company store on Red Earth. This, along with the infringement of farmers along the Carrot River into their hunting grounds, forced band members to rely more heavily on their gardens, livestock, and wage labour. The Red Earth First Nation is located 75 km east of Nipawin and has 1,189 band members, 1,032 of whom live on reserve. *Christian Thompson*

RED PHEASANT FIRST NATION. Prior to signing treaty Chief Wuttunee (Porcupine) and his **CREE** band hunted and fished along the Battle River, and as settlers moved into the Battleford region where they conducted trade. Though Wuttunee was chief at the signing of **TREATY 6** on September 9, 1876, he was not in favour of the treaty and appointed his brother Red Pheasant to sign for him. The department recognized Red Pheasant as the band's chief from that point. In 1878 the band settled on their

reserve in the Eagle Hills, where the land was good and there was enough forest to enable them to hunt. Red Pheasant day school opened in 1880, and St. Paul's Anglican Church was built in 1885 on land set aside for that purpose when the reserve was surveyed. The reserve is located 33 km south of North Battleford, with an infrastructure that includes a band office, band hall, school and teacherage, public works building, fire hall, and a treatment centre. The main economic base is agriculture, but the reserve hosts a band-owned grocery store, and in 1997 the band signed an oil and gas agreement with Wascana Energy Inc. The band's successful completion of a Treaty Land Entitlement Agreement has enabled them to increase their reserve's size to 29,345.7 ha, and invest in furthering economic development. The band has 1,893 registered members, 608 of whom live on the reserve.

Christian Thompson

RED RIVER CART. The Red River Cart played a prominent role in the development and settlement of the North-West Territories and Saskatchewan. The two-wheeled carts were used extensively in eastern Canada soon after European arrival in the early 1600s, but did not arrive on the prairies until the early 1800s. As fur traders and explorers pushed west into the settlement of Red River, Manitoba, it became apparent that not all of their travel could be conducted by York boat or canoe. By 1801 plans were undertaken to build an all-wooden, two-wheeled cart held together with green buffalo hide that tightened exceptionally well after drying. The two wooden wheels were approximately 1.5 metres

SASKATCHEWAN ARCHIVES BOARD R-A3278

Red River Cart.

in diameter, and the open box could hold loads of up to 450 kg. The entire cart had two long poles protruding from the axles, which were lashed to a mule, horse, or oxen. Because the carts were made entirely of wood they could easily be repaired along the trail, could float across shallow streams and be pulled through swamps or bogs, and were exceptionally sturdy. They were very easy to operate, and it was not uncommon to have one driver manage a brigade of carts at one time. At the peak of their existence it is estimated that as many as 2,500 Red River Carts traversed trails in a single year through what is now Saskatchewan. During that time the carts carried more than 600 tonnes of freight for the Hudson's Bay Company (HBC) alone. The resistance to use axle grease, for fear of dust collection, led to the wheels producing a high-pitched squeal that could be heard several kilometres away. One of the routes that experienced the majority of traffic from Red River Carts was the **CARLTON TRAIL**: throughout the 1860s the HBC reported on average 300 carts making one trip per season on this trail, carrying supplies, provisions, and furs. Over time, the carts were replaced by steamboats that traveled along navigable waterways such as the **NORTH** and **SOUTH SASKATCHEWAN RIVERS**, and by locomotives on the railways.

James Winkel

REDBERRY LAKE (52°42' N; 107°10' W: Map sheet 73 B/11). Redberry Lake is located in the boreal parkland ecoregion, 56 km northwest of Saskatoon and 13 km east of Hafford. Scientifically investigated by Rawson and Moore in 1938–40 and by Hammer and associates from 1971 to 1988, it is a closed, saline lake, with no outlet. Salinity measured 12g/L in 1926, and 24g/L in 1988; this increase was associated with declining lake depth during drought.

In 1974 the lake had an area of 53.4² km. and a maximum depth of 18 m. The water is very clear. It stratifies thermally every spring as the upper waters warm up while cold water persists below 9 m to 14 m; oxygen depletion occurs only slightly in this cold layer. The salt content of the lake is mainly magnesium, sodium and sulphate. The pH of the water in 1974 was 9.2. Plankton populations (microscopic free-floating organisms) are relatively low. Bottom populations are dominated by chironomids (fish fly larvae) in deep waters, and damsel fly nymphs and the amphipod *Hyallel azteca* in shallow marginal waters.

In 1940–41 **D.S. RAWSON** stocked the lake with whitefish (*Coregonus clupeaformis*). Its salinity was then15g/L. The fish grew so rapidly that a commercial fishery was initiated in 1946; but it ceased after 1981 as salinity increased to 20g/L and the fish could not survive. During this period 500,000 kilograms of whitefish were harvested. Redberry Lake was declared a Migratory Bird Sanctuary in 1925,

and became a Provincial Wildlife Refuge in 1986. Lake islands are the nesting grounds for white pelicans (*Pelicanus erythrorhynchos*). California and ring-billed **GULLS**, black and common terns, and double-crested **CORMORANTS** also nest there and feed in lake waters. The lake is an important spring and fall staging ground for ducks and other waterfowl. White-winged scoters (*Melanitta deglandi*) use the lake and are being studied by the Canadian Wildlife Service. In 2000 (after nomination by First Nations, local conservation groups, and local, provincial and federal government), UNESCO's Man and Biosphere Program designated Redberry Lake as the Redberry Lake Biosphere Reserve (*See* **CONSERVATION**).

Redberry Regional Park was established on the northwest portion of the lake in 1968. There is a beach area with waters suitable for wading and swimming. A service area was established and a golf course developed. The Saskatoon Sailing Club is based at the lake; recreational boating is important; and many cottages have been built. Proximity to Saskatoon has made this site a prime recreation area.

U. Theodore Hammer

REDEKOP, NANCY (1941–2001). Nancy Evelyn Redekop (*née* Goodmanson) was born on July 30, 1941, and grew up in Girvin, Saskatchewan. She graduated as a Registered Psychiatric Nurse from the Saskatchewan Training School (STS) in 1962. After a brief stay in Ontario she moved back to Moose Jaw, where she was employed at Valley View (formerly STS); she was a supervisor there for many years. Redekop was president of the Moose Jaw Branch of the Registered Psychiatric Nurses Association of Saskatchewan (RPNAS) from 1976 to 1979, and held positions on the national body. In the 1980s, she was among those responsible for establishing the Canadian Mental Health Association. She worked tirelessly for the organization at the provincial and national levels, and received an award from the provincial body in the summer of 2001 and a national award posthumously.

Redekop was a member of the **CANADIAN UNION OF PUBLIC EMPLOYEES**, Local 600 and served many years as president of this local. She was a health and safety advocate and often taught Occupational and Safety courses at union schools. She was also the first woman elected president of the moose Jaw and District Labour Council—a position she held for many years, stepping down in 1997 just prior to her retirement from Valley View. She became Recording Secretary of the **SASKATCHEWAN FEDERATION OF LABOUR** (SFL) in 1988, a post she held until 1996. She was appointed by the SFL to several boards, including the Minimum Wage Board and a special committee established in 1994 to create a "most available hours" system for part-time workers. She died on July 8, 2001, after a brief battle with cancer.

Barbara Byers

REDHEAD EQUIPMENT LIMITED. Redhead Equipment Ltd. is a diversified company which generates $130 million in annual revenue serving the trucking, construction, oil and gas, and agricultural industries in Saskatchewan. It has six state-of-the-art facilities employing over 240 people, with two locations in Regina, two in Saskatoon, one in Lloydminster and one location in Swift Current. Redhead provides 24-hour emergency parts and service.

Redhead Equipment was originally a Champion motor grader dealer, but expanded in 1971 to also become the John Deere construction equipment dealer. In 1990, operations diversified by adding Mack trucks. In 1991, Redhead Equipment resigned as the John Deere dealer and acquired the Case Equipment dealership, including both construction and agricultural equipment. In 1998, Champion was purchased by Volvo Construction Equipment and as a result, in 2001 Redhead Equipment added Volvo construction equipment to its product line.

Redhead Equipment got its start in 1948 under the name of W.F. Fuller Machinery Limited. Gordon Redhead worked there until 1968, at which time he purchased the business and changed the name to Redhead Equipment Ltd. In 1980, Gary Redhead, Gordon's son, bought out his father's interest in Redhead Equipment and became the president and chief executive officer.

Joe Ralko

REDVERS, town, pop 917, located in the SE corner of the province at the junction of Hwys 8 and 13. It is situated 19 km from the Saskatchewan-Manitoba border, and 67 km north of the international boundary. French and British homesteaders began settling in the district in the 1890s, and during the first decade of the twentieth century a significant number of Danish people came to the area (*see* **DANISH SETTLEMENTS**). The community was named for Sir Redvers Buller, a general and the commander of the British forces during the **BOER WAR**. The Redvers post office was established in 1902. By 1911, the population was 200 and it remained around that number until after World War II. Subsequently, Redvers experienced a period of exceptional growth: during the 1950s and the 1960s it was one of the fastest growing communities in the province. The population has been fairly stable since the mid-1980s, and Redvers continues to be an important commercial centre serving a large surrounding area, with a full range of businesses, services, professional and trades people, and an array of modern facilities. The town also has its own newspaper, the *Redvers New Optimist*, which is published weekly. The area's economy, predominantly based upon agriculture, is supplemented by oilfield operations and associated services.

David McLennan

© M.WEST, REGINA, WEST'S STUDIO COLLECTION/COURTESY
OF THE SASKATCHEWAN SPORTS HALL OF FAME AND MUSEUM
George Reed.

REED, GEORGE (1939–). Often considered the greatest fullback in the history of professional football, George Reed played for the Saskatchewan Roughriders for thirteen seasons. Reed was born in Vicksburg, Mississippi, on October 2, 1939, and attended Washington State University. After turning professional at age 21, he began his distinguished career with the Riders in 1963. George Reed carried the ball 3,243 times for 16,116 yards. He rushed for 1,000 yards or more in a season eleven times, and tallied 134 touchdowns on the ground and three more through the air. He was a ten-time Western Conference All-Star and an eleven-time Canadian All-Star. Reed participated in four Grey Cup championships, and helped the Riders to their first title in 1966. He won the Schenley Award in 1965 as the CFL's most outstanding player. In 1975, his final year in the league, George Reed was awarded the Tom Pate Memorial Trophy by the Canadian Football League Players' Association for his outstanding playing ability and community service. Following his retirement, Reed served on the Saskatchewan Special Olympics Committee and chaired the Easter Seals campaign. In October 1975, the George Reed Foundation for the Handicapped was established, including Reed's Club 34 to assist mentally and physically challenged youth. Reed served two terms as president of the league's Players' Association and was also a director of the **SASKATCHEWAN SPORTS HALL OF FAME**, of which he has been a member since 1979. He received the Order of Canada (1978) and was inducted into the Canadian Football Hall of Fame (1979) and the Canadian Sports Hall of Fame (1984). George

Reed's #34 jersey is permanently retired in the Canadian Football Hall of Fame.

Daria Coneghan and Holden Stoffel

FURTHER READING: Kelly, G. 2000. *Green Grit: The Story of the Saskatchewan Roughriders.* Toronto: HarperCollins.

REFORM PARTY (CANADIAN REFORM CONSERVATIVE ALLIANCE). A right-wing populist federal political party, the Reform Party and its successor, the Canadian Alliance, enjoyed great political success in Saskatchewan and replaced the Progressive Conservative party as the province's dominant federal party. The Reform Party was founded in 1986 by a group of Alberta conservatives led by future party leader Preston Manning. Brian Mulroney's Progressive Conservative government had alienated the Reform Party's original activists largely because of the government's unwillingness to severely curtail the welfare state and the government's fixation on constitutional issues. The new party tapped into the **WESTERN ALIENATION** sentiment that was prevalent throughout the region, dating back to the settlement period. Reformers were critical of the constitutional negotiations (Meech Lake) that the government was pursuing and which they believed sacrificed the needs of the west to the interests of central Canada, particularly Quebec. They argued that the government's priorities had to change and that the west must be given a larger role in Confederation. To this end, the party championed such issues as an elected, equal and effective Senate based on the United States model, as well as the increased use of referendums and plebiscites.

The Reform Party's first test was in the 1988 federal election, where it fielded candidates only in the four western provinces but failed to elect a single member. After the election, the party continued to rise in popularity, even winning an Alberta by-election. The party was buoyed by the unpopularity of the Mulroney government, and in the 1993 election it captured the Progressive Conservative's old western base, winning 53 seats—all but one of them coming from western Canada. In Saskatchewan, the Reform Party won the popular vote, but elected only four MPs. The party soon became a lightning rod for controversy, as it was charged with being inherently racist, bigoted and boorish. These accusations haunted the party throughout its history and were the major barrier to its success outside of the west. In the 1997 election, the party increased its representation in Saskatchewan to 8 seats as the national party won 60. In 2000, the party recast itself as the Canadian Alliance in a bid to woo Progressive Conservative voters. Under the leadership of Stockwell Day, it improved its results, including in Saskatchewan where ten seats were won, but still remained largely a western party. Leadership prob-

lems plagued the party, and Day was replaced by Stephen Harper. Under the latter's leadership, negotiations were initiated with the Progressive Conservatives, leading to the merger of the two parties into the new **CONSERVATIVE PARTY** in December 2003.

Brett Quiring

FURTHER READING: Laycock, D. 2002. *The New Right and Democracy in Canada: Understanding Reform and the Canadian Alliance.* Toronto: Oxford University Press; Manning, P. 2002. *Think Big: My Adventures in Life and Democracy.* Toronto: McClelland & Stewart.

REGINA. Regina, pop 178,225, Saskatchewan's capital, is situated 160 km north of the US border. Because of its location in the heart of the Canadian plains, it is sometimes referred to as the City on the Horizon. Regina is the commercial and financial centre of the province; it was named in honour of Queen Victoria, mother-in-law of then Governor General the Marquess of Lorne.

The site was originally an area where **CREE** and Métis came to hunt buffalo. The Indians piled buffalo bones together in a belief that the buffalo would not leave an area that contained the bones of their kind. The Cree name for this special place was *oskana kâ-asastêki* "where the bones are piled": the first settlement at the site was thus called "Pile O' Bones." Explorers, fur traders, surveyors and settlers passed through the area as it was one of a very few locations where there was water, wood, and shelter from winter blizzards and summer grass fires. In 1882 the **CANADIAN PACIFIC RAILWAY** was built across the plains, and Regina was founded near the Pile O' Bones (Wascana) Creek. Homesteaders were attracted to the area by the **DOMINION LANDS ACT**, which allowed them to claim 160 acres of land for $10.

As the influx of people required policing, the North-West Mounted Police (later called the **ROYAL CANADIAN MOUNTED POLICE**) were sent west and moved their headquarters to Regina. The headquarters later moved to Ottawa, but the RCMP Training Academy remains in Regina to this day. In 1883, Regina replaced the more northern site of Battleford as the capital of the North-West Territories. On December 1 of that year it became a town, and Dr. David L. Scott was elected as the town's first mayor on January 10, 1884. In 1903 Regina, with a population of 3,000, became a city; its first mayor was Jacob W. Smith. In 1905 Saskatchewan became a province, and in 1906 Regina was confirmed as its capital. Its population then grew rapidly, reaching over 30,000 inhabitants by 1911. In 1908, work began on the **LEGISLATIVE BUILDING**, situated on Wascana Lake, which took four years to complete; 300 men worked day and night for a year and a half just to prepare the stone front of the building.

In 1912 the **REGINA CYCLONE** tore through the

Regina, from the south, Saskatchewan Legislative Building in foreground.

an average of 4.1 metres. The Legislative Building, the Saskatchewan Centre of the Arts, the Royal Saskatchewan Museum, and the Saskatchewan Science Centre are all located in Wascana Centre. Regina's downtown has grown to include two enclosed shopping centres, the Scarth Street pedestrian mall, the twin McCallum Hill Towers, several bank buildings, hotels, office buildings, and the City Hall. A series of enclosed pedestrian walkways were also built to connect many downtown buildings.

Most citizens are native-born, and one-quarter are of British origin. Large groups of people of German, Ukrainian and Scandinavian ancestry have also made Regina their home. During the past two decades many First Nations people have moved to the city. The largest religious denominations are Roman Catholic, United Church, Lutheran, Anglican, and Greek Orthodox.

Regina is largely dependent on the surrounding agriculture and natural resources. The **SASKATCHEWAN WHEAT POOL**, the world's largest grain-handling co-operative, is headquartered in Regina. The city has diversified its economy, and telecommunications, manufacturing, data management, software development, and other technological industries are steadily growing. Regina accounts for approximately one-third of the total value of manufacturing activity in the province. **IPSCO** Inc. (steel and pipe manufacturer) and Consumers' Co-operative Refineries Ltd. (heavy oil upgrader) are the largest firms in this sector.

Regina is located on the **TRANSCANADA HIGHWAY**, on the main line of CP Rail, and on a branch line of the **CANADIAN NATIONAL RAILWAY**. It is served by six airlines and two bus lines.

Regina is governed by an elected mayor and ten councillors. Public and separate (Roman Catholic) school boards administer Regina's tax-supported elementary and high school systems.

The **UNIVERSITY OF REGINA** and the **SASKATCHEWAN INSTITUTE OF APPLIED SCIENCE AND TECHNOLOGY** provide education to post-secondary students. The **FIRST NATIONS UNIVERSITY OF CANADA** is the country's only university college run by and for First Nations people. The 97-year old **REGINA SYMPHONY ORCHESTRA** is one of the city's most distinguished cultural institutions. In addition to the Royal Saskatchewan Museum, the Regina RCMP training academy and its Centennial Museum host thousands of visitors each year. Regina has two art galleries, the **MACKENZIE ART GALLERY** and the Dunlop Art Gallery. The **GLOBE THEATRE** provides live theatre and has gained national recognition for its professional theatre production. The Agridome on the Exhibition Grounds hosts many concerts and exhibitions. Regina is served by one community cable channel, one French-language and three English-language TV stations, nine radio stations, and one daily newspaper, the *Leader-Post*. The city

city, killing 28 people, injuring hundreds, destroying more than 400 buildings, and leaving 2,500 people homeless; it took the city two years to repair the damage, evaluated at over $5 million. The city's growth was halted by an economic depression in 1913, and then by the outbreak of **WORLD WAR I**. But in the 1920s it started to prosper again. In 1920, Regina resident **ROLAND GROOME** became the first commercial pilot in Canada; with his partner Ed Clark he opened there the first licensed aerodrome in the country, and eight years later a permanent airport opened. By 1924, Regina was Canada's largest distribution centre for farm equipment and supplies; the population increased from 34,400 to 53,200 during the 1920s.

In 1929 the **DEPRESSION** hit, and the government started a number of projects to create work. Men were hired to drain Wascana Lake and deepen it, using only hand shovels and dump wagons to do the job; the dirt they removed was then used to build Willow Island in the lake. The Albert Street Memorial Bridge, known as "the longest bridge over the shortest span of water," was built. Workers also began creating a park around the lake and the Legislative Building; today, **WASCANA CENTRE** is one of the largest urban parks in North America.

In 1935, a group of unemployed men in British Columbia began a train trip to Ottawa to demand help from the federal government. The **ON-TO-OTTAWA TREK**, as it was known, stopped in Regina where police tried to enforce government-issued arrest warrants for seven of the trek leaders; violence broke out, resulting in the death of one

policeman and injuries for several officers and trekkers. This tragic incident is known as the "Regina Riot."

Conditions improved in the late 1930s. During **WORLD WAR II** Regina became home to three air training schools for soldiers, and the General Motors car assembly plant reopened to make equipment for the war. After the war Regina began to prosper again, and in the 1950s the population grew by 57%. An oil pipeline linked Regina with oil fields in Alberta and refineries in eastern Canada. The city built the Saskatchewan Museum of Natural History (later renamed the **ROYAL SASKATCHEWAN MUSEUM**), a new post office, and a geriatric centre; the latter became Wascana Hospital, and was later renamed the Wascana Rehabilitation Centre. By the early 1960s, Regina was growing at a rate of 4,500 new residents a year. Economic diversification and movement from farms to the city caused an increase in the population of nearly 10% between 1991 and 1996. Since that time, however, growth has been considerably slower. In 1992, Governor General **RAMON HNATYSHYN** visited Regina and signed a proclamation giving the city its new flag and Coat of Arms.

Regina has been transformed from a flat, treeless settlement into a city of parks, streets and buildings. Today, there are more than 300,000 hand-planted trees throughout Regina. On March 29, 2004, the city completed the "BIG DIG," a three-month, $18-million clean-up operation to salvage Wascana Lake, the city's historic body of water; crews worked around the clock to deepen the lake

is home to the **SASKATCHEWAN ROUGHRIDERS**, a Canadian Football League team. Regina has twice hosted the CFL's Grey Cup, in 1995 and in 2003.

Daria Coneghan

REGINA ARMOURY. Prior to **WORLD WAR I**, armouries had been built in many locations throughout Saskatchewan. In Regina, however, adequate facilities for military training were lacking: earlier attempts to build an armoury, dating back to 1906, had come to nothing, and the eight units of the Regina garrison had to train in various buildings scattered throughout the city. In 1926, a number of Regina businessmen who were also senior officers in the militia decided to form a corporation, the Regina Armoury Association, to raise funds through a bond issue to build an armoury in the city. The bond issue was to be retired by receiving the rent that was paid out by the Department of National Defence for the other buildings being used for military purposes throughout Regina. The armoury committee set about to convince **CHARLES DUNNING**, then Finance Minister in the federal government, that it would be in the best interests of the Department of National Defence to have a "Grade A" armoury built in the city. Dunning agreed, and a holding company was formed in 1927 to begin its construction.

In the fall of 1927, a suitable building site had been found on the Regina Exhibition Grounds, and construction began. **POOLE CONSTRUCTION** Company of Regina was the chief contractor. The armoury was completed in March 1929; the bond issue was retired in 1937, when the Armoury Association transferred the title to the building to the Department of National Defence for the sum of $1. Just inside the main door of the armoury is a bronze plaque that commemorates the names of the members of the Armoury Association who by their efforts made the building a part of the Regina heritage: Colonel J.S. Rankin, Colonel Alfred Styles, Lieutenant Colonel A.P. Linton, Lieutenant Colonel C.E. Gregory, and Lieutenant Colonel R.H. Matthews. Over the years, the Regina Armoury has been used for many purposes other than military training: political meetings, musical and athletic events, industrial shows, and various other civilian activities. Perhaps the most outstanding event that was held in the armoury for many years was the annual armistice service, which was started in order to supply funds for the upkeep of the Soldiers' Plot in the Regina cemetery. At the end of **WORLD WAR II**, the service was taken over by the Regina Branch of the Royal Canadian Legion; it is now held in the Exhibition building on the Regina Exhibition Grounds. Today, the Regina Armoury continues to be the home of the Regina units of **38TH BRIGADE GROUP: 10TH FIELD REGIMENT**, Royal Canadian Artillery, **ROYAL REGINA RIFLES**, **16TH SASKATCHEWAN SERVICE BATTALION**, and

16TH MEDICAL COMPANY. Other organizations that use the armoury include the cadet corps and the Military Museum of Saskatchewan. *Lillian Mein*

REGINA ANTI-POVERTY MINISTRY. The Regina Anti-Poverty Ministry (RAPM) is an outreach ministry of Wascana Presbytery of the United Church of Canada which does anti-poverty advocacy and education work with and for low-income. RAPM grew out of the Regina Downtown Chaplaincy, which helped serve the needs of Regina's low-income community from 1971 to 1995. In 1996, the International Year for the Eradication of Poverty, the ministry changed its name and constitution to better express its transformation into a strictly justice-and-advocacy model of ministry. RAPM's objectives are divided between exercises in individual advocacy, where the support is provided to low-income people whose needs conflict with the established system, and systemic advocacy, where deficiencies within the system are identified and addressed by educational campaigns and representations to governing bodies. These objectives are achieved by networking with other denominations, faith groups, and relevant organizations. The RAPM board is itself a mix of United Church members, ecumenical multi-faith partners, representatives of community organizations, and low-income volunteers. RAPM has played a prominent role in promoting anti-poverty policies such as adequate income security, affordable housing, childcare and transit, equity programs, and fair taxation. *Peter Gilmer*

REGINA AUTO THEFT STRATEGY. On November 30, 2001, a task group was brought together to develop a strategy that would be effective in reducing the incidence of motor vehicle theft in Regina. The task group consisted of service providers from Saskatchewan Justice, Saskatchewan Social Services, the **REGINA POLICE SERVICE**, and the Regina Intersectoral Committee who directly worked with auto theft offending youth. Through the communication, coordination and collaboration among these service providers the Regina Auto Theft Strategy was developed in January 2002. This strategy was founded upon evidence-based practice that suggested the application of risk management and risk-reduction strategies in the rehabilitation of young offenders. Specifically, the objective of the Regina Auto Theft Strategy was to substantially reduce auto theft through three guiding principles: strict supervision of youth who are at risk to reoffend; effective combination of enforcement and rehabilitation; and early intervention and education in crime and its consequences. The following four categories of youth (aged 12–17) were identified, and differential responses were developed for each: youth at risk, first-time offenders, repeat offenders, and chronic repeat offenders. Phase two of the

Regina Auto Theft Strategy was announced on May 29, 2003. Phase two is an expansion of phase one to adult offenders aged 18 to 22 who have become increasingly involved in auto thefts. The expansion includes targeting repeat offenders through the use of electronic monitoring devices, increasing the use of alternative measures for low-risk, first-time offenders, and providing education and prevention for at-risk youth. *Kimberly Skakun*

REGINA BEACH, town, pop 1,039, located 58 km NW of Regina near the SW end of Last Mountain Lake. Homesteaders were making incursions into the region in the 1880s and, by the early 1900s, the area that came to be known as Regina Beach was gaining popularity as a summer resort destination. With the CPR running through Regina Beach in 1912, the area was easily accessible to residents of Regina and, for many years, the railroad ran excursion trains to the developing lakeshore resort. The Regina Beach Yacht Club was established in 1913. In 1920, Regina Beach was incorporated as a village and recreational facilities and services including hotels, boathouses, dance pavilions, summer cottages, and boat excursions. Following **WORLD WAR II**, the importance of the railway declined and the car became the primary mode of transportation to the lake. The last excursion train made its trip to Regina Beach in 1949 and regular passenger service ended in the 1960s. For a number of decades, Regina Beach's population hovered around 300, but in the 1970s it began to increase and, in 1980, Regina Beach attained town status. Substantial construction occurred during the following decade and many new homes were built as commuting to work in Regina became increasingly popular. The year-round population grew from 488 in 1966 to 921 in 1991 and, today, the population of the community more than doubles when seasonal residents arrive at their summer cottages. The annual Canada Day fireworks display over the lake is one of the town's premier events. *David McLennan*

REGINA COUNCIL OF CHURCHES. The Christian church has always been part of the social fabric of the city of Regina. Anglican, Lutheran, Orthodox, Presbyterian, and Roman Catholic churches began as ethnic-based missions, primarily caring for their own people. The Methodists, Congregationalists, and some Presbyterians later merged to create the United Church, which some describe as the first "home grown" church to appear in Canada. As a result of interdenominational cooperation reflected in the Regina Ministerial Association, the Regina Conference of Churches was created in 1965 to enable clergy and lay people to come together. Initially, the Regina Conference of Churches was comprised of individual member congregations. In 1989 it changed its name to the

Regina Council of Churches, and today the Council is primarily made up of representatives of the various mainline and orthodox churches, with a representative from the Regina Evangelical Ministerial Association. Membership is open to all congregations and individuals who subscribe to the ecumenical aims and objectives of the Council. Christian member groups help refugees and other new immigrants in need, as well as the urban poor (*see* REGINA ANTI-POVERTY MINISTRY) and those who have been incarcerated.   *Terry Marner*

REGINA CYCLONE. Known as the Regina Cyclone, an enormous tornado hit Regina at approximately 5:00 p.m. on June 30, 1912, with a velocity of 800 km per hour. The tornado formed 18 km south of the city and was roughly 400 metres wide by the time it reached Regina. In just twenty minutes it completely levelled a number of houses, and caused other houses to explode as the pressure inside the structures rose when the tornado passed overhead. The storm damaged the Metropolitan Methodist Church, the library, the YWCA, and numerous other downtown buildings; in the warehouse district, it destroyed many of the storage buildings. The CPR Roundhouse was stripped to the rafters, and boxcars were pulled from the tracks and hurtled into the air. Future film star Boris Karloff, who had been travelling in the area during the tornado, later organized a benefit concert that helped raise some of the funds needed for the reparation of the damage. The cyclone claimed twenty-eight lives and was the worst in Canadian history in terms of deaths. It also rendered 2,500 persons temporarily homeless, and caused over $1,200,000 in property damage. It took the city two years to repair the damage and ten years to pay off its storm debt. (*See also* TORNADOES)   *Dagmar Skamlová*

REGINA DALES. The Regina Dales athletic club was formed in 1929, taking its name from the Dales Tea Room, whose owner, Mah Park, helped establish the club. The Dales provided an opportunity for young people living in one of the city's poorer areas to participate in a wide range of sports. From the outset, however, the greatest emphasis was placed on rugby football. The Dales formed two teams, and at first they simply played each other. They lacked proper equipment and a prepared field, but they made rapid progress, and within a year were challenging local high school teams. In 1931 the Regina Juvenile Rugby League was formed, and the Dales completed an undefeated season. In the absence of any other leagues in the province they claimed the provincial juvenile crown and challenged the Winnipeg Young Men's Hebrew Association for western Canadian honours, losing in the final in Winnipeg. In 1933 the Dales entered the junior ranks, and led by their quarterback **PAUL DOJACK** they defeated the Regina Pats to win the city junior championship. In 1934 they won the provincial junior crown. In 1937, with Paul Dojack as coach, they became junior champions of western Canada, and challenged for the national title, losing to Hamilton's Italo-Canadians in the final (27–2), played in Hamilton. In 1938 they played the Montreal Westmounts in Montreal and won the national junior championship (4–3) in a game referred to as the "ice bowl." By this time the Dales had become one of the dominant teams in Canadian junior rugby football. They owed their success to the strong organization that backed them, to the ambitious and able people who helped coach the team, and to their special relationship with Regina's senior team, the Roughriders, whose roster during the 1930s, 1940s and 1950s included dozens of former Dales. The Dales suspended operations during WORLD WAR II,

and attempts to revive the league that had been formed during the 1930s were unsuccessful. In 1954 the Dales joined together with the Regina Bombers to form the Regina Bomber-Dales, which the next season became the Regina Rams—the most successful junior football club in Canada.   *Ken Leyton-Brown*

REGINA FIVE. This name was given to a group of artists—RON BLOORE, TED GODWIN, KEN LOCHHEAD, ART MCKAY and DOUG MORTON—after an exhibition at the National Gallery of Canada in Ottawa in 1961 brought their work to national attention. (*See also* ARTS AND CULTURE)

REGINA LITTLE THEATRE. Regina Little Theatre (RLT) is the oldest continuously producing English-language theatre in western Canada. RLT was established in the spring of 1926 by Walter Read and Captain G.R. Chetwynd "to present the best plays for the entertainment of the members and to encourage new talent in all areas of the theatre." RLT's first productions were two one-act plays presented to members only on November 29, 1926, in the 600-seat Regina College Auditorium. This arrangement was typical in the first two seasons. The first public presentation was *Officer 666*, staged at the Grand Theatre in February 1927.

In 1928, Darke Hall was built on College Avenue. Described by Read as "an admirable theatre, one which few cities can rival," it was used for RLT performances for many years, initially for a token annual rent of $30. In the early 1930s, RLT helped found the Saskatchewan Branch of the Dominion Drama Festival, and encouraged Little Theatre Clubs throughout the province. In 1931, RLT's $2 annual membership fee provided admission to "club" performances, plus a half-price ticket for public performances. By 1933, there were 800 members; membership in 2002–03 was 882. Over the years, more than 7,000 community volunteers have participated in RLT productions, with nearly half a million tickets sold.

RLT ventured into competition in 1933 for the provincial playdowns of the Dominion Drama Festival. Until the Festival's demise in 1971, RLT won many national honours for its productions, directors, and performers. It continues to compete in the Saskatchewan Community Theatre Inc. provincial festival each spring. The Society's voice is the newsletter *Masks and Faces*, established in 1941.

In 1956, RLT bought a former puffed-wheat factory and paint shop on South Railway Avenue (now Saskatchewan Drive) for rehearsals, storage, social events, and small-scale performances. Productions continued in Darke Hall and local high schools until the Regina Performing Arts Centre opened at Angus Street and 4th Avenue in 1989. An executive, appointed annually by the members at a general meeting, manages the Society's affairs. For many

CPR yards in Regina after the 1912 cyclone.

years, the Regina Little Theatre season has consisted of four or five full-length plays. Since the 1950s, annual one-act play evenings have facilitated the development of directors, actors, and emerging playwrights. Scholarships are awarded to promising active members. Regina Little Theatre has encouraged community theatre development throughout Saskatchewan and fostered the growth of other Regina companies such as Theatre Regina, Regina Summer Stage, and Regina Lyric Light Opera.

Lyn Goldman

REGINA MANIFESTO. During the DEPRESSION of the 1930s, the League for Social Reconstruction (LSR), a left-wing intellectual think-tank, emerged in the east while a new political party, the CO-OPERATIVE COMMONWEALTH FEDERATION (CCF), was born in Calgary. The Regina Manifesto, initially penned by LSR academics, was approved by the delegates attending the first full national CCF convention in 1933. It suggested that social and economic equality could be achieved by a new workers' party—the CCF—a federation of farmer, labour and socialist organizations. The opening clauses noted that capitalism's class domination and exploitation produced "inherent injustice" and "glaring inequalities." Addressing human needs, not just making profits, should be society's goal, achieved through a planned and socialized economy. The Manifesto's fourteen-point program included planks on public ownership, socialization of finance, and increased funds and crop insurance for farmers. The Manifesto sought a national labour code, the right to unionize, and more social rights including insurance for accident, old age and unemployment. The CCF prophetically envisioned state-financed medicare available to all, and favoured increased public expenditure on housing, hospitals, and relief payments. In foreign affairs, the Manifesto reflected a distrust of military entanglements, and favoured disarmament and a revitalized League of Nations. While the CCF replaced the Regina Manifesto with the more moderate Winnipeg Declaration in 1956, the Manifesto anticipated many of the features of the modern Canadian welfare state.

Alan Whitehorn

REGINA POLICE SERVICE. From its humble beginnings as a one-man operation (with James Williams, a former North-West Mounted Police corporal, appointed as Town Constable in 1892), the Regina Police Service has grown to nearly 500 people, including both active officers and civilians. In the early years, police dealt with stray animals and transients, enforced sanitation laws, kept streets free from obstruction, dealt with bullies and fighting, served as fire fighters, provided an ambulance service, maintained an auto patrol, and even rang the town bell. As the city grew, many of these responsibilities devolved to other services.

Originally housed in City Hall, the police service and jail soon outgrew their welcome. A police station was built in 1931 as an unemployment relief project. New stations and communication centres at Halifax Street and Osler Street have been built as needed. The Regina Police Service has established many programs through the years, including the School Safety Patrol in 1949, the Canine (K–9) section in 1973, Block Parent and Neighborhood Watch in 1975–76, Special Weapons and Tactical Team (SWAT) in 1975, the Cultural Liaison Program in 1983, Crime Stoppers in 1984, the 9-1-1 service in 1985, Victim Services Unit in 1989, and Bike Patrols in 1990. The first woman officer was hired in 1957, and the first Aboriginal officer in 1964. *Merle Massie*

REGINA RIOT: *See* **ON-TO-OTTAWA TREK AND REGINA RIOT**

REGINA SYMPHONY ORCHESTRA. The Regina Symphony Orchestra (RSO) is Canada's oldest continuously performing orchestra. Its first concert, as the Regina Orchestral Society, was given on December 3, 1908, under the direction of its founder, L. FRANK LAUBACH. What was then an amateur group with musicians and singers from the community has developed into a professional orchestra with musicians who come from all over the world. Its musicians provide an important resource for Opera Saskatchewan, the Regina Philharmonic Choir, and performers visiting the city. They regularly perform for government functions; they are faculty members in the Music Department at the UNIVERSITY OF REGINA and they teach music lessons to countless young performers. The RSO's mandate is to promote and enhance the performance and enjoyment of live orchestral music in Regina and southern Saskatchewan. Consequently, one of its most deliberate undertakings is extensive outreach into the community through forty school concerts that reach 12,000 students; its annual outdoor concert; fifteen free concerts in churches, libraries, and a brew pub; its mentoring of the young musicians in the South Saskatchewan Youth Orchestra; and its four-day New Music Festival.

In its early incarnations as the Regina Philharmonic Society and the Philharmonic and Orchestral Society, the orchestra consistently performed works for orchestra and choir. Upon Laubach's retirement in 1922, there began an evolution that resulted in the separation of the Regina Symphony Orchestra and the Regina Choral Society. Laubach was succeeded first by George Coutts and then by W. Knight Wilson, who developed a disciplined but collegial relationship with the musicians that resulted in skilled performances and rapport with performing soloists. He remained with the orchestra until 1955. He was succeeded by John

Thornicroft, who conducted the orchestra for the next four years. The 1960s and early 1970s saw significant changes to the orchestra's situation. Grants from the Canada Council, the SASKATCHEWAN ARTS BOARD, and the City of Regina grew from $25,000 in the late 1960s to nearly $400,000 currently. The transformation of Regina Campus into the University of Regina in 1974 resulted in a larger music faculty, which in turn brought professional musicians to Regina and thus to the RSO.

Kathleen Wall

REGINA VINEYARD CHRISTIAN FELLOWSHIP. The Vineyard movement was born in southern California in 1977, and grew quickly under the leadership of John Wimber. This group caught the imagination of many spiritually hungry individuals with its emphasis on intimate worship and an openness to the experience of God's supernatural presence. The denomination has now grown to include 1,300 churches worldwide, including sixty congregations in Canada. Currently in Saskatchewan there is one Vineyard Church. Located in Regina, it was founded by Garth and Kathryn Johnson in January 1997. They led the church until October 1999, when Garry and Lily Ann Paul assumed the pastoral responsibilities. The Fellowship's membership has varied between fifty and 100 members over the years. A congregation was begun in Saskatoon but it no longer exists.

While the Vineyard is theologically conservative, holding to all of the tenets of Christian orthodoxy, the fellowship believes that their faith must be practiced in a way that communicates most effectively to contemporary generations. They place a high value on "keeping things simple," and aspire to a life that is "naturally supernatural." In practice, they believe that everyone should be involved—the purpose being "to extend, through acts of love and testimony of God's goodness, the loving kingdom of God."

Garry Paul

REGINA WARTIME INDUSTRIES LTD. Saskatchewan's largest wartime munitions plant, Regina Wartime Industries Ltd., was based in the former General Motors car assembly plant on Winnipeg St., in Regina. The factory was built in 1927, but closed in 1929 as a result of the poor economic conditions brought about by the GREAT DEPRESSION. During WORLD WAR II, the building was obtained by the Dominion Government and used to manufacture anti-tank gun carriages, Oerlikon gun parts, as well as two-pound anti-tank guns and the famed "six-pounder" anti-tank gun. At the height of the war, Regina Wartime Industries Ltd. employed over 1,000 people, some of whom were reportedly working on a secret weapons project, which was ultimately abandoned with the end of the war.

Lauren Black

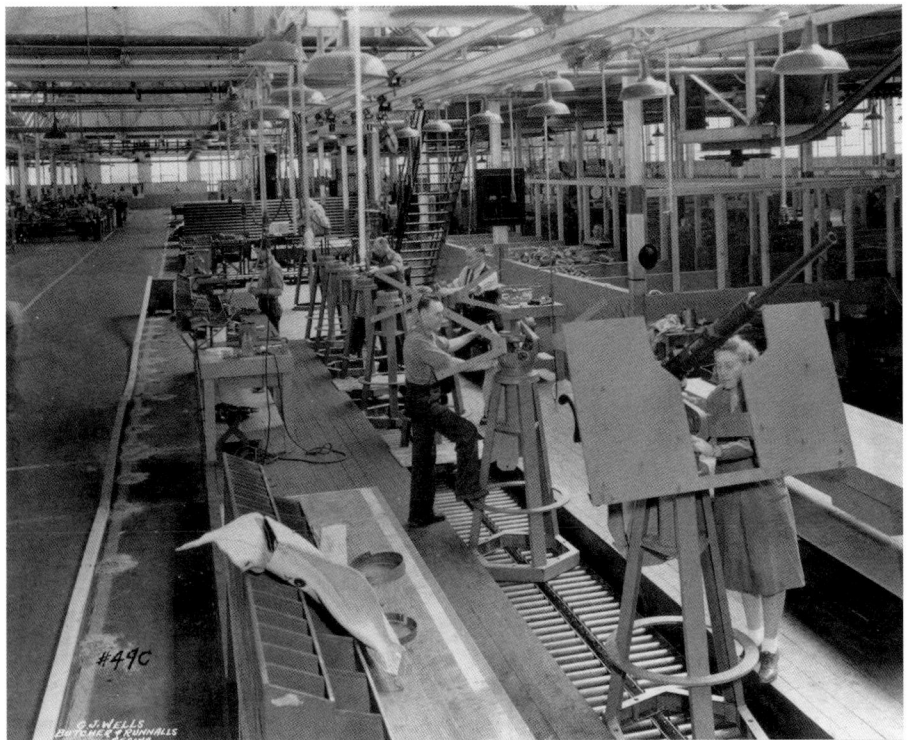

Interior of Regina Industries Limited, the largest munitions plant in Saskatchewan.

FURTHER READING: Drake, E.G. 1955. *Regina: The Queen City.* Toronto: McLelland and Stewart; Riddell, W.A. 1981. *Regina: From Pile O' Bones to Queen City of the Plains: An Illustrated History.* Burlington, ON: Windsor Publications.

REGIONAL AIRLINES. Great distances, low population densities, and economic cycles shaped the structure of commercial **AVIATION** in Saskatchewan. Barnstormers and flight training operations formed the early beginnings of aviation in the 1920s. A decade later, bush pilots established small operations at remote bases, transporting prospectors, trappers and goods to isolated regions. Commercial aviation began in full force when companies established whole plane charter operations that provided the revenue base to finance expansion into unit toll passenger scheduled routes. In 1932 a group of northern aviators established M & C Aviation, based in Prince Albert. In the southern tier Prairie Airways, established in 1938, transported passengers and mail between Regina, Moose Jaw, and Saskatoon. In a further development, the Saskatchewan government purchased M & C Aviation in 1947 to form the Crown corporation **SASKATCHEWAN GOVERNMENT AIRWAYS** (Saskair). The government developed an extensive network of routes and charter bases in the northern half of the province. Regional airlines based in Edmonton and Winnipeg dominated routes south of Prince Albert. Canadian Pacific Airlines (CPA) purchased Prairie Airways in 1941, continuing the service with newer aircraft for more than a decade.

Trans-Canada Airlines (TCA), the forerunner of Air Canada, arrived in 1946 on a system of short-haul east-west routes across the province under a federal mandate that gave the Crown carrier both a regional and national transport role. Pacific Western Airlines (PWA) took over CPA's loss-making operations in 1957 on a route system that included Regina, Moose Jaw, Saskatoon, Prince Albert, North Battleford, Lloydminster and Edmonton. After experiencing five years of losses, the privately owned company handed the entire route system back to Trans-Canada Airlines at a time when the latter was forming new strategies and acquiring larger aircraft

on its east-west trunk routes. Regional services did not fit TCA's operational plans, and the Crown airline withdrew in 1963 by contracting the prairie routes to Winnipeg-based Transair. The agreement included the transfer of several aircraft from TCA and payment of a federal subsidy. Despite efforts to increase revenues, Transair faced heavy financial losses on the north-south route after its three-year subsidy ended; it curtailed flight frequencies, and abandoned flights to Yorkton and Brandon.

In 1965 a private company, North Canada Air (NORCANAIR), purchased government-owned Saskair and began plans to integrate northern and southern tiers of the province into a single, unified system. Following a period of regulatory and financial negotiations, Transair withdrew from Saskatchewan and Norcanair acquired rights to add Saskatoon and Regina to its route system. The con-scc-tholidated routes now provided same-plan flights from Uranium City, Stony Rapids and La Ronge to Saskatoon and Regina, with no overnight stop in Prince Albert. The consolidation allowed passengers travelling to and from northern Saskatchewan to make connections in Saskatoon and Regina with Air Canada to domestic and international destinations. Norcanair extended its north-south routes into the United States–to Minot, North Dakota, and later Minneapolis, Minnesota.

Deregulation led to rapid consolidation of regional airlines. Alberta-based Time Air acquired NORCANAIR in 1987 and was itself incorporated into Canadian Regional Airlines, a division of Canadian Airlines International (CAI). A series of acquisitions, followed by financial reversals, led to the take-over of CAI by Air Canada in 2000 and the demise of Canadian Regional Airlines. Air Canada formed its own regional airline, Jazz Air, in a strategy to compete with a new concept in the industry: discount airlines.

M & C Aviation's "Lady Wildfire" on ice at Big River, winter 1931–32.

The thinly travelled north-south route system within the province, which relies mainly on local traffic, is served primarily by Transwest Air, a company formed by the merger of two northern charter operations.   *Merv Samborsky*

REGIONAL ECONOMIC DEVELOPMENT.

Regional economic development is a continuing process in which employment and income are increased in an area of the province. A variety of core functions and services are required to support development: co-ordination; organizational development and planning; education and training; information; research and development; promotion and marketing; and local project and initiative management assistance. Regional Economic Development Authorities (REDA) provide some or all of these necessary functions. They were created as part of the NDP government's "Partnership for Renewal" economic strategy in 1992. They have since become the prevalent government-sponsored regional organization, with 28 REDAs located throughout Saskatchewan. The mandate of a REDA is to improve a region's economic growth and diversification through co-operation and collaboration with its residents. This grassroots process encourages residents and communities to organize, plan, and achieve sustainable economic development by creating wealth and employment and by attracting new investment. A key component of regional economic development is to target sectors with the greatest potential for growth, and then to develop a long-term strategic plan. Typically, development takes between five to seven years to occur.   *Holden Stoffel*

FURTHER READING: Phillips, P.W.B. 1998. "Whither Saskatchewan? A Look at Economic Policies 1975–2000," *Canadian Business Economics* 6: 36–49; Stabler, J.C. and M.R. Olfert. 2002. *Saskatchewan's Communities in the 21st Century: From Places to Regions*. Regina: Canadian Plains Research Center.

REGIONAL PARKS.

The creation of Saskatchewan's regional parks reflects the co-operative spirit that is a hallmark of the province: a growing economy inspired communities to set aside land for recreation areas that enhanced their quality of life; localities that lacked sufficient money or resources joined together and built campgrounds, golf courses, and swimming pools. Today, regional park authorities operate the province's 101 regional parks. Beginning in the 1960s, local and regional communities partnered with the provincial government to establish a regional park system. The Regional Parks Act of 1960 granted funding to local governments, which established and operated grounds for recreational purposes. The initial Parks Assistance Program provided 60% of the necessary revenue for capital development; by 1965, a park maintenance

DOUG CHISHOLM PHOTO
Reindeer Lake.

program had been instituted. Officially organized in 1961, Thomson Lake Regional Park was the first to enter the new system; the most recent addition is Mainprize Regional Park, which joined in 1994.

In February 1962, the Saskatchewan Regional Parks Association (SRPA) was created to act as a uniform voice representing the growing number of regional parks. The Association adopted a constitution, and since then has provided an effective liaison between provincial government, rural municipalities, and member park authorities. The SRPA has campaigned to make regional parks an affordable alternative to provincial and national parks. This determined marketing approach resulted from changes in government funding and cutbacks that threatened the sustainability of the regional parks system throughout the 1990s. Since 1999, the provincial government has provided the SRPA with four consecutive capital grants of $500,000; this funding has helped cover the cost of improving infrastructure throughout the parks system, and renewed the partnership between government and regional parks.

The 101 regional parks are divided into four directional zones and occupy a unique place in Saskatchewan's **ECOREGION** classification system. The abundance of parks means that most are within a short distance of major cities and other notable tourist sites across the province. Destination parks are suitable for long visits because of their numerous campsites, facilities, and activities. Nature and hiking trails are available at most parks while all offer birding. Over half of all regional parks have golf courses ranging from nine sand-green holes to eighteen grass-green holes. Fishing is another popu-

lar activity at regional parks, most of which provide a boat launch. Several parks are adjacent to beaches, and over twenty have swimming pools. Three parks in the system operate ski hills.   *Holden Stoffel*

FURTHER READING: Clancy, M. and A. Clancy. 1999. *Discover Saskatchewan: A User's Guide to Regional Parks*. Regina: Canadian Plains Research Center.

REGIONALIZATION OF HEALTH.

In 1992, a major component of **NEW DEMOCRATIC PARTY** government health reforms was the creation of thirty regional authorities (a much higher number than the fifteen recommended by the **MURRAY COMMISSION** in 1990), to deliver health programs and services. These replaced over 400 health care boards, which had lacked a coordinated approach to planning and delivery of services. Two additional districts in Northern Saskatchewan were formed in 1998. This sweeping but contentious structural reform made Saskatchewan a leader in Canada. By the end of the 1990s all provinces except for Ontario had regionalized.

The regions were funded by the provincial government, and had no power of taxation. The regional focus was intended to create an integrated and responsive system, responsible for a wide range of health services, including mental health, community, long-term care, residential and acute care services, health promotion, and public health.

With the passage in 1993 of The Health Districts Act, the Union Hospital and the Ambulance Boards were disbanded and their assets transferred to the districts. There were also voluntary affiliations. The structure and composition of the health boards were designed to increase public participation. The district health boards had twelve members (fourteen each in Regina and Saskatoon), including eight elected members. At the time, Saskatchewan was the only province to elect board members by universal suffrage. The first board elections were held in 1995 and the second in 1997. However, the stress of change was exacerbated by an unprecedented era of restraint in health care funding in the mid-1990s, owing to federal policies as well as the continuing trend of rural depopulation.

The 2001 **FYKE COMMISSION** nevertheless concluded that regionalization had been positive overall. The thirty-two health districts were collapsed into twelve regional health authorities. Board members would no longer be elected, but appointed by the province.

Although regionalization continues to pose problems, there is far less fragmentation in the system. There is now an important group of senior managers attuned to the needs of the whole, not just its constituent parts. There is less duplication of services among agencies. Admission to long-term residential care is more streamlined and needs-based. There are improved partnerships with education, social services, and municipal governments. Health care has been enabled to become a system.

Denise Kouri

REINDEER LAKE (57°15'N, 102°15'W; Map sheet 64 E/1). Most of Reindeer Lake is located in northeastern Saskatchewan, although part of its eastern shore and northeastern tip are in Manitoba. Reindeer is Saskatchewan's second largest lake, covering 6,650 km² with a maximum length of 233 km. It is elevated at 337 m, and drains southward into the **CHURCHILL RIVER**. Reindeer Lake has a highly indented shoreline with numerous islands. Located near its southern end is the almost circular Deep Bay, covering an **ASTROBLEME** that probably formed about 100 million years ago. Although a number of explorers, including **DAVID THOMPSON**, traversed Reindeer Lake, it was not heavily used during the fur trade era. Several trading posts were established in the 1790s and early 1800s, but none lasted more than a year or so.

Southend Indian reserve (2001 population: 696), at the southern tip of the lake, lies at the terminus of Highway 102. This provides the lake's only Saskatchewan road access, although the tiny community of Kinoosao, near the Manitoba border, is served by Highway 394 from Lynn Lake. Most employment is related to the provision of services to local communities, but Reindeer Lake also supports a tourist industry; there are several fishing camps on the lake.

Marilyn Lewry

RELIGION: *see essay on this page.*

Religion

R

Leona Anderson, Bryan Hillis and Margaret Sanche

Religious and philosophical beliefs, affiliations and sensibilities of the people of Saskatchewan have intersected in important ways throughout their history, and in many respects are key components of their identity. The sacred ways of Aboriginal peoples prior to the colonial encounter most certainly had an impact on the way they envisioned the land and interacted with each other and with the land. Early settlers to the province brought with them a variety of their own religious beliefs and practices. The interaction between the belief systems of early European immigrants and First Nations peoples has played an important role in the development of Saskatchewan. More recently, new immigrants to Canada from Asia and the Middle East have altered the religious profile of the province. Immigration to Saskatchewan, in some respects similar to that of the rest of Canada, has influenced the multicultural make-up of the province and increased the effects of globalization. This essay seeks to trace in broad strokes some of the major events and issues in Saskatchewan's religious history, and to capture some of the diversity of its religious profile.

Like so many other cultural forms, the pattern of religious growth in Saskatchewan is dominated by the immigration of diverse people. As indicated in Table 1 on the following page, based on Statistics Canada material, Protestant immigrants greatly outnumbered all others in the twenty years of exponential growth between 1901 and 1921–representing over 70% of the population, with Catholics making up another 20% of the total. ANGLICANS, PRESBYTERIANS, ROMAN CATHOLICS, Methodists, Congregationalists, LUTHERANS, DOUKHOBORS, MENNONITES and HUTTERITES added to the existing religious landscape as settlers from other parts of Canada and immigrants from the United States, Britain and Western, Central and Eastern Europe came to this country in search of land as well as political and religious freedom. By the time the flood of immigration had subsided in the late 1920s and 1930s, most of the religious diversity of Saskatchewan had been established, with the addition in the census of UKRAINIAN CATHOLICS, BAPTISTS, PENTECOSTALS, ORTHODOX, JEWISH and others, although "others" are reflected in the 1931 census only as Buddhist and "other non-Christian" adherents. The formation of the UNITED CHURCH OF CANADA in 1925, through the union of Congregationalist, Methodist and the majority of Presbyterian churches, changed the religious statistics reported in subsequent censuses; "unionist" congregations account for the United Church numbers before 1925.

From the 1940s to the 1970s, Saskatchewan's religious diversity remained relatively stable. The larger denominations (Anglican, Presbyterian, Lutheran) experienced a slight decline as immigration from Europe to Canada decreased; only the percentage of Roman Catholics increased slightly. At the same time there was a noticeable influx of immigration from Asia, Southeast Asia and the Middle East as Hindus, Muslims and Sikhs were first counted in 1981. While we know that there were many people of Aboriginal traditions (*see* **FIRST NATIONS RELIGIOUS OVERVIEW**) living in Canada, they were not listed as a separate religious group until the 1981 census, probably in large part because their sacred ways were not acknowledged by census takers before that time.

By the time of the 2001 census, the most noticeable change in the religious landscape of the province was that one in six Saskatchewan residents reported no religious affiliation at all, an increase of 40% over the 1991 census. From 1991 to 2001, the number of Catholics (Roman and Ukrainian) had declined by almost 4%, and the Protestants had declined by over 12% over the same ten-year period. The Roman Catholic denomination remained the largest individual denomination, followed by the United, Lutheran, and Anglican Churches: these four denominations accounted for almost two thirds of Saskatchewan residents in 2001. Compared to the national averages, Saskatchewan, like the Atlantic provinces, had a higher number of Protestants (47%) compared with a national average of 29%.

Also reflecting the relatively small proportion of immigrants coming to this province, the proportion of non-Christians is smaller at 2%, compared to the national average of 6%. In part, this may be due to the fact that recent immigrants from various Asian countries are just as likely to report "no religion" as "non-Christian" in their census responses. Immigration patterns are reflected also in the location of the non-Christian population, with Regina and Saskatoon reporting a higher proportion of non-Christians than other parts of the province. While Statistics Canada did not report on the religious affiliation of the First Nations population, we do know that reserve residents who identify themselves as Christian are more likely to be Roman Catholic (39% vs. 32% for the province as a whole) or Anglican (27% vs. 7% for the province), and that the proportion of Protestants on reserves is lower than the provincial average (35% vs. 47%).

An important component of religious or spiritual life in the province is reflected in the philosophical beliefs and practices of First Nations peoples, who prefer not to describe their traditions as "religions" because this would encourage non-Aboriginal peoples to consider their sacred ways as being a separate aspect of their lives. While we cannot be sure of what the sacred ways of First Nations peoples were prior to the arrival of European and other immigrant groups, historians and indigenous studies scholars are striving to discover them by drawing upon the writings of missionaries and anthropologists, as well as upon the oral histories of First Nations Elders. CREE COSMOLOGY, CREE

Table 1. Religion Census Data 1901–2001											
Denomination (Detailed)	1901	1911	1921	1931	1941	1951	1961	1971	1981	1991	2001
Total Population	91,279	492,432	757,510	921,785	895,992	831,728	925,181	926,245	956,440	976,040	963,150
Catholic	17,828	91,351	147,517	234,242	244,051	236,643	277,716	292,805	310,005	316,935	305,380
Roman Catholic	17,828	91,351	147,517	189,925	201,173	199,424	242,888	258,630	279,840	296,725	286,810
Ukrainian (Greek) Catholic				44,317	42,878	37,219	34,828	34,175	30,090	20,155	17,615
Other Catholic									75	55	955
Protestant	66,566	358,166	538,121	630,114	589,308	542,260	594,235	558,285	556,680	515,884	452,210
Adventist	129	794	2,897	3,385	3,515	2,547	2,522	2,285	2,210	1,920	1,535
Anglican	16,155	76,402	116,355	126,984	117,827	95,476	94,593	87,210	77,725	69,930	65,745
Baptist	2,443	18,636	23,722	22,645	19,485	15,606	16,184	15,000	16,785	15,415	16,725
Doukhobor	8,773	8,580	7,175	7,965	7,662	4,536	3,202	1,675	1,065	720	465
Jehovah's Witnesses						5,077	7,564	9,880	9,815	8,130	6,565
Latter Day Saints	13	662	1,442	1,609	1,367	1,356	1,902	2,455	6,155	5,699	6,040
Lutheran	6,234	56,942	92,093	113,802	104,853	91,454	95,311	90,850	88,785	82,160	78,525
Mennonite and Hutterite	3,787	14,586	20,568	31,372	32,553	26,270	28,174	28,530	29,245	29,190	24,465
Pentecostal		5	1,076	4,976	8,305	8,044	9,150	12,375	16,435	17,710	14,605
Presbyterian	16,396	97,929	162,356	68,034	54,927	33,290	25,080	20,805	16,070	11,575	7,010
Salvation Army	134	565	1,554	2,017	1,969	2,011	2,418	3,295	3,050	2,185	1,650
United Church	12,354	81,631	106,422	243,686	230,795	247,345	296,253	274,285	263,375	222,120	187,450
Protestant, Other	148	1,434	2,461	3,639	6,050	9,248	11,882	9,640	25,965	49,850	41,895
Orthodox	2,588	25,117	47,237	31,160	37,748	34,506	32,166	26,675	22,495	19,505	14,280
Greek Orthodox	2,588	25,117	47,237	31,160	37,748	34,506	32,166	26,675	21,065	11,775	6,045
Ukrainian Orthodox									805	5,675	5,050
Other Orthodox									625	2,055	3,185
Non-Christian	314	2,580	6,554	6,367	5,596	3,377	3,097	2,125	5,765	7,885	9,010
Buddhist	18	125	97	88	70	72	86	140	985	1,885	3,050
Hindu									1,155	1,680	1,585
Islam / Muslim									1,125	1,185	2,230
Jewish	296	2,060	5,328	5,047	4,081	3,017	2,710	1,765	1,580	1,375	865
Sikh									220	565	500
Other Non-Christian	0	395	1,129	1,232	1,445	288	301	220	700	1,195	780
Para-Religious Groups	0	0	0	0	0	765	0	0	605	2,725	6,670
Aboriginal Spirituality (Native Indian or Inuit)									455	1,990	5,885
Other Para-religious Groups	0	0	0	0	0	765	0	0	150	735	785
No Religious Preference / Affiliation	0	0	0	0	0	4,652	0	34,090	59,995	107,225	150,275
No Religion						4,652		34,090	59,045	105,740	148,540
Agnostic									140	430	450
Atheist									130	320	435
Other, non-religious									680	735	850
Other Religions	3,983	15,218	18,081	19,902	19,289	9,525	17,967	12,265	895	5,881	25,325

Table prepared by Katherine McGovern.

RELIGIOUS ETHOS, DAKOTA-LAKOTA SPIRITUALITY, and DENESULINE WORLD-VIEW are representative of some of the current First Nations' sacred perspectives. In these worldviews, there is a sense of holism wherein establishing and maintaining a circle of right relationships between and among humans, as well as between the human and natural worlds, is absolutely critical. What Christian missionaries and others often dismissed as animism or polytheism was actually a way of seeing in the entire world a wondrous creation in which humanity has a special responsibility to uphold the circle. Christian missionaries often overlooked the sense of a single creating Spirit that permeates most First Nations' sacred systems. Animals such as the buffalo, which played a central function in the survival of the northern plains peoples, assumed a key role in the Aboriginal spirit world. First Nations peoples prayed to the spirits of these animals for help, even as these animals were killed for human use. Their use was not simply for consumption: they were regarded as an integral part of the kinship of all creation. Prayers of intercession and supplication were not made for the sake of one person alone, but for the entire community. Ceremonies and religious rites like the SUN DANCE, VISION QUEST, SMUDGE and PIPE CEREMONY reflected the communal nature of these sacred ways. Thus, the spirituality of the community was defined not only by humans, but also by the entire spectrum of nature and reality as it appeared to the indigenous peoples. Sacrifice was an important aspect of these worldviews; but it was sacrifice for the sake of the entire community, as demonstrated in the rigours of the Sun Dance and Vision Quest ceremonies. Through these sacrifices, the long-term well-being of the community was ensured among First Nations peoples of the Canadian plains.

There is no question that the spiritual life of First Nations peoples in the province was seriously undermined by the European settlers, and that many of their indigenous beliefs, customs and practices were lost while others were seriously jeopardized. Today, however, many of these traditional practices are being reclaimed. The impact of the Christian missionary period on the history of the area of Rupert's Land which is now Saskatchewan is important to our understanding of the development of religion in the province. Recent scholarship, for example, has focused on the nature of the missionary impulse which inspired and motivated Anglican, Roman Catholic, Methodist and other missionaries to brave the difficulties of mission life in order to spread the Christian faith. In addition, historians are exploring attitudes of the missionaries towards the First Nations communities, and the reactions of the latter towards missionary teaching and catechesis. Also central was the role of the Hudson's Bay Company in fostering and supporting, or in some cases discouraging, the work of the missionaries. Missionary strategies also changed from the early days when missionaries traveled with the migrating First Nations communities, to the later period when churches and schools were established and the missionaries worked to persuade First Nations peoples to give up their nomadic lifestyles and remain near the mission. Another significant aspect of the missionary period was the less than noble competition and rivalry between different church denominations, and the various strategies used by each to bring the First Nations peoples into their particular fold. It is important to note at this juncture that many First Nations Christians did not give up their sacred ways and were able to integrate both sets of beliefs. As James Treat (2004) notes: "Understanding the relationship between native people and Christianity is thus an important aspect of understanding the experience of native peoples. The many dimensions of this relationship are also among the most divisive issues within native communities today, a situation that calls for critical and engaged scholarship."

PHOTO COURTESY OF IRENE AND OVIDE DESJARLAIS

Bishop Lajeunesse arriving at Ile-à-la-Crosse in 1946.

Finally, it is important to place the missionary period within the context of the European cultural and social milieu from which the Christian missionaries came, and within the worldview or sense of providential mission they brought to their ministry. In the case of both Anglican and Roman Catholic missionaries, the catechizing work led to the establishment of educational institutions. When the Canadian government proposed that industrial and residential schools be established and operated by the churches, this seemed like a good idea–from the church and public perspective of that time. It must be pointed out, however, that some of the First Nations leaders were also in favour of the establishment of schools for their children because of the importance they accorded to education. Much historical, not to mention legal, work continues to be carried out on the origins and history of the RESIDENTIAL SCHOOLS, the policies of the federal government, and the overall impact on First Nations' communities–including the impact of separating children from their parents and extended families for long periods of time. Instances of sexual, physical and emotional abuse continue to be important subjects on the Saskatchewan agenda. The First Nations' traditions of language use, of relationship to the land, of spiritual ceremony, and of family relationships evidence the importance of sacred ways and are fundamental to the preservation of their cultures (see ABORIGINAL PEOPLES OF SASKATCHEWAN).

In the case of the Christian churches which were involved in missions to First Nations peoples in the early years of this province, the revisiting and reexamination of the residential school experience by both First Nations peoples and the churches, and the long drawn-out period of negotiations for settlements and healing have had a profound impact on all those involved. An expression of the new understanding regarding the relationship of the Catholic missionaries with the First Nations peoples in the past can be found in the apology given by the Missionary Oblates of Mary Immaculate to the First Nations peoples at Lac-Ste-Anne, Alberta in July 1991:

> We apologize for the part we played in the cultural, ethnic, linguistic, and religious imperialism that was part of the mentality with which the peoples of Europe first met the Aboriginal peoples and which consistently has lurked behind the way the Native peoples of Canada have been treated by civil governments and by the churches. We were, naively, part of this mentality and were, in fact, often a key player in its implementation. We recognize that

this mentality has, from the beginning, and ever since, continually threatened the cultural, linguistic, and religious traditions of the Native peoples.

Other church groups involved in operating residential schools have apologized to First Nations peoples as well and have endeavoured to make amends in various ways for instances of abuse or general cultural damage, and to assist with the healing process. The vilification of all the residential schools and their impact has been particularly painful for those men and women who as missionaries and teachers had dedicated their lives to a religious ideal which is now generally regarded as having been seriously flawed. This part of the story of the relationship of the Christian churches with First Nations peoples, many of whom are devout and active Christians themselves, will continue to unfold in the coming years. Certainly, much has been learned by everyone, and the approach of the Christian community in spreading its Gospel has changed, as respect for and solidarity with others of differing religious beliefs have become essential cornerstones of interfaith and intercultural relations.

When we turn to the composition of early immigration to the province, we note that its participants were diverse ethnically as well as in terms of the religions they practiced, although the majority was from the Christian tradition. In many cases during the settlement period, these immigrant groups for the first time encountered face-to-face peoples from other countries, who spoke different languages, followed different cultural practices, and lived their lives according to the principles of different religious traditions. In general, it would seem that every distinct group that migrated into Saskatchewan encountered a somewhat similar situation: they lived in close proximity to others who came from dissimilar religious backgrounds, yet they shared with these groups many of the same experiences, such as geographic and cultural isolation. Although responses to life in the province in the early settlement years varied, many similar trends can be identified. For example, language, culture and religion were closely intertwined in the identity of most of the non-English-speaking groups, and a fortress mentality often developed. Early settler communities tended to become "fragment cultures," and their sense of national and religious identity became tied increasingly to their "frozen-in-time" memories of what life had been like in their country of origin at the time of their emigration. As Peter Van de Veer notes in *Transnational Religion*:

> It is often argued and sometimes demonstrated that migrant communities tend to become conservative in religious and social matters. They would do so to retain an identity under the pressures of assimilation. Moreover, since they are often challenged in a multicultural environment to explain their beliefs and practices they tend to become more aware of them. This kind of conscious conservatism or reactionary traditionalism has been observed in a number of migrant groups.

Thus, in many cases, the beliefs and cultural practices of European settler communities in Saskatchewan became even stronger than they had been in their homeland.

As various ethnic communities became more established and more accustomed to life on the prairies, the ties of a common language, culture and religion in each respective group were loosened somewhat, and over time a tolerance of selected differences emerged. In many cases this occurred coincident with the advent of the first prairie-born generation. In some groups, threats from the outside become great enough that an element of the original triad (language, culture, religion) had to be abandoned or else taken underground. A case in point would be the German people, who were the focus of a great deal of animosity during and after World War I and World War II: they generally retained their religion, whether Catholic, Lutheran or Baptist, but were willing to forego their language in favour of facility in the English language and a degree of assimilation into the dominant culture, partially as a means of deflecting negative attention. In some ways, such forced adaptations had the effect of broadening opportunities. The German Catholic newspaper published by St. Peter's Abbey, for example, was compelled to publish in English after World War I: for a time *St. Peter's Bote* was published in both German and English (*St. Peter's Messenger*), and then in English only. As *The Prairie Messenger*, it reached a much larger readership than would have been possible had it remained a German-language newspaper; it continues to be a lively Catholic weekly newspaper, with subscribers from all parts of Canada and beyond.

European religious life on the prairies was reshaped in important ways with the Social Gospel movement that brought together various Christian groups in the cause of political and social betterment. As Richard Allen notes in *The Social Passion*, the SOCIAL GOSPEL was not a uniquely Canadian movement but "was part of a widespread attempt in Europe and North America to revive and develop Christian social insights and to apply them to the emerging forms of a collective society... Put in more dramatic terms, it was a call for men (and women!) to find the meaning of their lives in seeking to realize the Kingdom of God in the very fabric of society." The Anglican, Presbyterian, and Methodist denominations dominated the movement after 1890. As fighting social evil was more important than mere theological rhetoric, many of the devout from these denominations formed a wide array of social institutions in Canada to reform the existing order. The evils of liquor became one of the focal points of these social reformers, so that in 1907 the Anglican, Presbyterian, Methodist and Baptist Churches, together with the WOMEN'S CHRISTIAN TEMPERANCE UNION (WCTU), the Royal Templars of Temperance and the Trades and Labour Councils of Regina and Moose Jaw, met in Regina to form the Social and Moral Reform Council. Differences among the religious groups on the topic of liquor soon surfaced, however: Presbyterians, Methodists and Baptists were total abolitionists, while Anglicans, Lutherans and Roman Catholics had serious reservations about total abolition. Social Gospel people were also concerned about assisting the newly arrived immigrants: Presbyterians organized welcome committees in most congregations, while Methodists also tried to "Canadianize" downtrodden peasants. More influenced by the Social Encyclicals of the Catholic Church and less by Social Gospel theology, the Roman Catholics were also interested in welcoming new immigrants, partly out of a spirit of Christian hospitality, but also perhaps to prevent the loss of Catholic faithful to the Protestant fold.

One of the most visible leaders and spokesmen for the Social Gospellers was J.S. Woodsworth, MP for Winnipeg North, whose criticisms of capitalism found many supporters in the League for Social Reconstruction, formed in 1930, which together with a number of other groups eventually became the CO-OPERATIVE COMMONWEALTH FEDERATION (CCF) in 1933. As this occurred, many of the Protestant churches that had nurtured these ideas lost interest in social reform on the political level as they tried to keep themselves above the political fray. Still, there were many from the Social Gospel movement of the Protestant churches who distinguished themselves as leaders in the CCF, the best known of whom was T.C. DOUGLAS, a Baptist minister from Weyburn.

R

EVERETT BAKER PHOTO/COURTESY OF THE SASKATCHEWAN HISTORY AND FOLKLORE SOCIETY

Little stone church (Anglican), Deer Creek, June 1943.

Perhaps the most significant change in the religious life of Saskatchewan over the past forty years has been the new spirit of Christian ecumenism, which has impacted on every denomination to some extent. When we recall the general intolerance between various denominational families prior to Vatican II, and the climate of competition and antagonism which often characterized relations between leaders and members of different Christian churches, it is truly amazing to reflect on the changes which have occurred. The intolerance of one another's beliefs and practices was evident in large and small ways among church leaders and the members of congregations alike in the early half of the last century. In addition, there were strong antagonisms between particular groups: the English Protestants and Irish Catholics, for example, and many others. In one particularly ignominious period in the late 1920s and early 1930s, intolerance turned into religious hatred when a branch of the KU KLUX KLAN was established in Saskatchewan; the KKK recruited members, spearheaded attacks against Catholic and non-English immigrants (particularly the French), and are believed to have been involved in the adoption of anti-Catholic, anti-French policies by the provincial government. During the settlement years, when everyone was struggling to make a living, and later, during the World Wars and the DEPRESSION, religious intolerance was often inseparable from mutual ethnic hostility, mostly based on ignorance and fear. It would seem that religious divisions were very much a part of daily life in Saskatchewan, as elsewhere in Canada, for much of the first half of the 20th century.

There were signs of ecumenism, however, even in these early decades: some of the earliest forms of ecumenical co-operation had occurred at the grassroots level in various social reform movements spawned by the Social Gospel. Grassroots ecumenism was also an important factor in the years leading up to the formation of the United Church of Canada in 1925, when all the Methodist and Congregationalist groups as well as all but 22 of the 854 Presbyterian churches in the province joined the new denomination. Geography and climate made co-operation and this type of union an attractive option for struggling communities of faith, particularly in the rural areas. Ecumenism at other levels continued to thrive as formal discussions of the 1950s and 1960s involved Protestant theologians and church leaders who were concerned with difficult questions of authority and doctrine. As a result of some of these discussions, various Protestant denominational families dissolved their differences and formed larger denominations such as the Evangelical Lutheran Church in Canada, while others formed councils and committees to continue their work together, as the Regina and Saskatoon Council of Churches would demonstrate.

With the Second Vatican Council of 1962–65 and its focus on ecumenism, there began a long process of change in the relationships among the Christian churches which is still unfolding on many levels and in many ways. In July 2001, the Evangelical Lutheran Church in Canada and the Anglican Church of Canada signed the Waterloo Declaration establishing a relationship of full communion between them, so that it is not unusual for a Lutheran minister to be leading worship in an Anglican church on a Sunday morning or vice versa. In 2004, Lutherans and Catholics celebrated the fifth anniversary of the signing of their Joint Declaration on the Doctrine of Justification—an event that had represented the culmination of thirty years of dialogue and marked a profound change in the relationship of these two churches. Grassroots ecumenism continues to thrive in its contemporary manifestations: in Saskatoon, for example, a United Church congregation and a Roman Catholic parish have entered into a covenant relationship with one another, agreeing to shared elements of prayer, worship, study, social justice/outreach projects, concerts and social events each year, and breaking down barriers to genuine Christian friendship. Members of the many Saskatchewan Eastern Christian groups (Catholic, Orthodox, and others) have also begun to come together in recent years to explore their common heritage in events such as the Windows to the East lectures held each year at ST. THOMAS MORE COLLEGE in Saskatoon. During the annual Week of Prayer for Christian Unity, there are many interdenominational prayer gatherings, social activities and other ecumenical events throughout the province. In addition to the work of the PRAIRIE CENTRE FOR ECUMENISM, interdenominational groups have been formed to work for common concerns: some of these are the Interchurch Uranium Committee, Friends of Sophia (an ecumenical group of Christian feminists), local branches of KAIROS (Canadian Ecumenical Justice Initiatives), and interchurch groups in the Battlefords, Craik, Davidson, Melville, Prince Albert, and other communities as well as in Saskatoon and Regina. At the province's two universities, campus ministers and chaplains work together to provide ecumenical experiences for students, and the denominational theological and liberal arts colleges collaborate with one another in their academic course offerings. Throughout the province, church organizations have collaborated in caring for the poor and establishing soup kitchens and food banks, seniors' villages, and ministry for and with urban Aboriginal people, and for families and children in need—all in an effort to witness to the Gospel as Christians without borders.

There had been some early fears that to have unity, churches would have to become uniform in authority, doctrine and practice, thus losing their unique identity and expression of faith. Over the years, however, as people from different churches have begun to meet, as they have entered into one another's worship space, have shared meals, prayer and Bible studies together, and have experienced an increasing number of inter-church marriages, they have found that what is different can still be "of the Spirit" and, indeed, a source of new life for their faith communities. Unity in diversity can be difficult, but it is not impossible. The lessons learned by the immigrant communities as they moved through the various stages from intolerance and fear of strangers to acceptance, mutual respect and friendship are now being put to good use by church communities.

In addition to religious traditions that reflect the belief systems of the majority of residents (Christianity and Aboriginal traditions), Saskatchewan is home to many smaller communities holding various religious beliefs. Jewish, Sikh, and Muslim communities, for example, though small in numbers, have long histories in the province. The earliest Jewish immigrants settled in Saskatchewan in the late 1800s; the population of this community waxed and waned through the 20th century, with migration patterns significantly influenced by global economic and political events and conditions. SYNAGOGUES in Saskatchewan, historically and at the present time, function as community centres and as houses of study and prayer for the Jewish people, as evidenced by the BETH JACOB SYNAGOGUE and the TEMPLE BETH TIKVAH in Regina, as well as the AGUDAS ISRAEL SYNAGOGUE/JEWISH COMMUNITY CENTRE and the SHIR CHADASH SYNAGOGUE in Saskatoon. The SASKATOON JEWISH FOUNDATION, whose purpose is to maintain or enhance the religious, cultural, educational, welfare and other activities of the congregation, and HADASSAH-WIZO, a worldwide, non-political women's volunteer Zionist organization that supports education, career training, health care, as well as women, child and youth services, exemplify the commitment of the Jewish community to the maintenance of their religious beliefs and the betterment of life.

The first Sikhs arrived in the province in the late 1960s. SIKHISM in Saskatchewan is represented by the Sikh Temple in Saskatoon, which opened in 1985, and by the Sikh Temple of Regina, which opened in 1988. The arrival of MUSLIMS in Saskatchewan began with a small number of immigrants at the end of the 19th century. A wave of Muslim immigrants arrived in the 1960s, many of them seeking religious freedom and greater opportunities. Today, most Saskatchewan Muslims reside in Saskatoon and Regina, but they are a diverse community hailing from a variety of geographical locations including the Middle East, Africa, Asia, and Europe. There are Islamic centres (mosques) in Regina, Saskatoon, and Swift Current.

Significant numbers of immigrants from Asia began arriving in Saskatchewan in the 1960s; these are represented by the Hindu and Buddhist communities in the province. HINDU COMMUNITIES in Saskatchewan have been a part of the province's demography since the early 1960s. Most of the early Hindu immigrants practiced their faith through daily or weekly worship in their homes, or by regular reading of Hindu scripture. Hinduism is a diverse religious tradition, and although the majority of members of this community immigrated to Canada from India and Africa, they came from different regions and differed in the particulars of their practices. As their numbers grew, however, Hindus in Regina and Saskatoon began building temples. In Saskatoon, the SHRI LAKSHAMI NARAYANA TEMPLE, one of the earliest temples on the prairies to be built in accordance with Hindu architectural style, was formally inaugurated in 1985. In Regina there are presently two Hindu Temples: the SRI SRI RHADHA KRISHNA TEMPLE, which opened in 1978; and the HINDU TEMPLE, which opened in 1990. In all of these temples, cultural and spiritual activities that meet the needs of the diverse Hindu community are conducted.

Buddhists in the province belong to a variety of different traditions and come from many countries. In Regina, this community is represented by the HAI DUC BUDDHIST PAGODA, a Mahayana Buddhist temple established in 1990 to serve the needs of the Vietnamese Buddhist community, and by the WAT BUDDHADHAMMA, a Theravadin Buddhist temple founded in 1992 by immigrants from Laos and Thailand. There are Buddhist temples also in Saskatoon, for example the AVALOKITESVARA BUDDHIST TEMPLE SOCIETY INC., which was incorporated in 1997. In addition to these Buddhist communities, there are a number of organizations that draw heavily on Buddhist teachings and practices and have members from various backgrounds: for example Regina Insight

Table 2. Religious Membership and Membership Change in Regina and Saskatoon				
	Regina		Saskatoon	
Religion	2001	% change from 1991 to 2001	2001	% change from 1991 to 2001
Total Population	190,015	0.30%	222,630	6.60%
No religion	34,385	35.00%	41,590	44.30%
Roman Catholic	58,440	-3.30%	63,165	6.20%
Ukrainian Catholic	2,320	-21.10%	5,420	6.50%
Adventist	170	-40.40%	205	-43.80%
Anglican	9,595	-13.10%	12,195	-10.40%
Baptist	4,270	16.80%	4,350	0.20%
Brethren in Christ	80	-5.90%	110	-68.10%
Christian and Missionary Alliance	1,930	-34.00%	1,845	-42.20%
Christian Reformed Church	120	-17.20%	150	-33.30%
Evangelical Missionary Church	490	24.10%	970	41.60%
Hutterite	70	27.30%	175	12.90%
Jehovah's Witnesses	1,005	0.50%	1,465	-28.50%
Latter-day Saints (Mormons)	835	-4.60%	885	118.50%
Lutheran	20,340	3.80%	13,090	6.80%
Mennonite	865	-23.50%	8,610	-19.30%
Methodist (1)	105	200.00%	385	60.40%
Non-denominational (2)	585	53.90%	645	38.70%
Pentecostal	1,935	-26.00%	3,325	6.60%
Presbyterian	1,250	-48.50%	1,885	-22.60%
Salvation Army	310	-8.80%	270	-44.90%
United Church	32,645	-16.60%	38,595	-7.90%
Protestant not included elsewhere (3)	2,955	-3.00%	4,430	-8.30%
Greek Orthodox (4)	1,495	-22.90%	1,375	-42.90%
Serbian Orthodox	45	350.00%	20	xxx
Ukrainian Orthodox	710	-12.30%	1,405	7.30%
Orthodox not included elsewhere (5)	850	93.20%	640	70.70%
Christian not included elsewhere (6)	5,580	125.50%	6,460	95.20%
Aboriginal spirituality	755	96.10%	970	351.20%
Buddhist	1,140	79.50%	1,435	54.30%
Hindu	620	-14.50%	695	15.80%
Islam/Muslim	770	37.50%	1,145	151.60%
Jewish	375	-23.50%	325	-47.60%
Pagan (7)	215	975.00%	235	261.50%
Sikh	290	38.10%	180	-23.40%

Source: 2001 Census of Population - Statistics Canada
Note: Religions selected for this table represent counts of 20,000 or more for Canada.
(1) Includes persons who report "Methodist." Excludes Free Methodist and Evangelical Missionary Church.
(2) Includes persons who report only "non-denominational."
(3) Includes persons who report only "Protestant."
(4) In 1991, included counts for Greek Catholic.
(5) Includes persons who report "Orthodox." Also includes Armenian Apostolic, Bulgarian Orthodox, Ethiopian Orthodox and Macedonian Orthodox.
(6) Includes persons who report "Christian," as well as those who report "Apostolic," "Born-again Christian" and "Evangelical."
(7) Includes persons who report "Wicca."

Meditation Community, founded in 1993 to explore Buddhist teachings on dharma and practice Insight Meditation; among the many activities of this community are retreats, meditation classes, and discussion groups.

In addition to the religions described above, the Saskatchewan religious landscape includes a number of smaller and newer traditions. For example, the UNITARIAN FELLOWSHIP IN SASKATCHEWAN is represented by three Unitarian congregations in Regina, Saskatoon and Wynyard. An examination of the history of the BAHÁ'Í Faith indicates that members of this community were already present in Saskatchewan in the early 20th century; today, the Baha'i community has centres in the province's principal cities and towns. The SRI SATHYA SAI BABA ORGANIZATION in Saskatchewan reflects the religious commitment of the followers of Sri Sathya Sai Baba, a revered spiritual teacher who resides in India; the province has two Sai Baba Centres, in Regina and Saskatoon, both formed in the 1980s. (*See also* Table 2 for recent membership numbers for Regina and Saskatoon religious communities.)

This overview of the provincial religious landscape would not be complete without some reference to the proliferation of new religious movements that attract members from many different walks of life. Included here are proponents of various New Age religions including PAGANISM or neo-paganism, as well as other emerging movements including Scientology, Raelians, UFO groups, and many others. In the last few decades, globalization has had serious consequences for Saskatchewan's religious life: the impact of globalization is perhaps most visible in the manner in which new immigrants, for example Muslims, Buddhists, Hindus and Sikhs, negotiate their respective identities in the province. The religious identity of some of these immigrant communities has become increasingly tied to particular ethnicities: a study of immigrant religious congregations in Regina and Saskatoon shows that religious institutions often serve a dual purpose for immigrants—providing them with a place to practice their beliefs and also to receive ethnic, cultural, and linguistic reinforcement. Moreover, for some members of ethnic congregations, religious identity becomes a focal point: joining a mosque, temple or gurudwara, or "becoming religious" facilitates a sense of belonging within the Canadian multicultural society.

In the context of sustaining both a religious and an ethnic identity, tensions sometimes arise with regard to issues of authenticity (content of primary concepts, important historical and religious figures, etc.), of transmission of cultural identity to subsequent generations, of language fluency, and of inter-communal disagreements. There are important differences, however, between these new waves of migrant communities and earlier ones: religious identities, like ethnic identities, are becoming increasingly transnational, a term that refers to the sense of living between two or more kinds of national or ethnic identities which emerges when people travel between different countries. Today, immigrants are closer to those they left behind because of telephone, e-mail, air travel, and other contemporary means of communication and transportation. Many new immigrants retain citizenship with their home countries, and many operate businesses with close links to their countries of origin. The terrorist attacks in New York and Washington on September 11, 2001, had a profound impact on some immigrant communities, the members of which were called upon to explain their religious, ethnic, and political identities. They also had a profound impact on the Christian community in Saskatchewan: although the initial response of the general public may have been to blame all Muslims for what had happened, not unlike the blame heaped on innocent German Canadians in another era, at the same time a significant component of this response was the realization of the importance of understanding the ways of other religious and ethnic communities.

Closely related to the development of Christian ecumenism in Saskatchewan and to the impact of September 11 and the following "war on terror" are endeavours to bring about understanding between and among Christians and other faith traditions. Both Regina and Saskatoon have active multi-faith organizations such as the Regina Multi-Faith Forum, Multi-Faith Saskatoon, the Saskatoon and Regina Council of Churches, the Regina Anti-Poverty Ministry, and the Prairie Centre for Ecumenism. Organizations like these sponsor events such as an annual Festival of Faith and World Environment Day; they also provide communication links between different faith groups, encourage inter-faith dialogues, and support multi-faith presentations and programming in their communities. In *Unknown Gods*, Reginald Bibby tells us that people of the prairies tend to be more active in their religious communities, in part because of the rural nature of the area. His more recent research, *Restless Gods*, also indicates that people of the prairies are 2% above the national average in terms of "experiencing God" and 3% above the national average in terms of engaging in private prayer frequently. Given these tendencies and Saskatchewan's varied religious history, there is every reason to believe that the diversity which existed in this area from the beginning will continue to flourish with every new exploration that Saskatchewan residents make in their individual and corporate religious journeys.

FURTHER READING:

Allen, R. 1971. *The Social Passion: Religion and Social Reform in Canada, 1914–28*. Toronto: University of Toronto Press.

Appadurai, A. 1996. *Modernity at Large: Cultural Dimensions of Globalization*. Minneapolis: University of Minnesota Press.

Archer, J.H. 1980. *Saskatchewan: A History*. Saskatoon: Western Producers Prairie Books.

Asad, T. 1993. *Genealogies of Religion*. Baltimore: Johns Hopkins University Press.

Bibby, R. 1987. *Fragmented Gods: The Poverty and Potential of Religion in Canada*. Toronto: Irwin Publishing.

——. 1993. *Unknown Gods: The Story of Religion in Canada*. Toronto: Stoddart Publishing.

——. 2002. *Restless Gods: The Renaissance of Religion in Canada*. Toronto: Stoddart Publishing.

Biles, J. and H. Ibrahim. 2005. "Religion and Public Policy: Immigration, Citizenship, and Multiculturalism—Guess Who's Coming To Dinner?" Pp. 154–177 in P. Bramadat and D. Seljak (eds.), *Religion and Ethnicity in Canada*. Toronto: Pearson Educational Canada.

Butcher, D.L., C. Macdonald, M.E. McPherson, R.R. Smith and A. McKibbin Watts. 1985. *Prairie Spirit: Perspectives on the Heritage of the United Church of Canada in the West*. Winnipeg: University of Manitoba Press.

Carter, P.A. 1971. *The Decline and Revival of the Social Gospel: Social Political Liberalism in American Protestant Churches, 1920–1940*. Hamden, CT: Shoe String Press.

Fung, Ka-iu. 1999. *Atlas of Saskatchewan*. Saskatoon: University of Saskatchewan.

Grant, J.W. 1984. *Moon of Wintertime: Missionaries and the Indians of Canada in Encounter Since 1534*. Toronto: University of Toronto Press.

Huel, R. 1996. *Proclaiming the Gospel to the Indians and the Métis*. Edmonton: University of Alberta Press.

Irwin, L. 1994. *The Dream Seekers: Native American Visionary Traditions of the Great Plains*. Norman: University of Oklahoma Press.

Lane, G. 1980. *Saskatchewan's Sturdy Strands of Faith*. Regina: Saskatchewan Diamond Jubilee Corporation.

Miller, J.R. 1996. *Shingwauk's Vision: A History of Native Residential Schools*. Toronto: University of Toronto Press.

Rawlyk, G.A. 1990. *The Canadian Protestant Experience, 1760–1990*. Burlington, ON: Welch Publishing.

Smillie, B.G. 1983. *Visions of the New Jerusalem: Religious Settlement on the Prairie*. Edmonton: NeWest Press.

Treat, J. (ed.). 1996. *Native and Christian: Indigenous Voices on Religious Identity in the United States and Canada*. New York and London: Routledge.

RELIGION AND "NON-ABORIGINAL" WOMEN IN SASKATCHEWAN.

The story of women and religion in Saskatchewan is mainly that of women's involvement in variants of the Christian faith. Evangelical Protestants and Roman Catholics predominate, but other sorts of Protestant women as well as Christian Orthodox women have also been present. Non-Christian women have also been woven into the provincial religious fabric. Whatever the faith, women have often found solace, meaning, and community in religious institutions. For increasing numbers, however, religion has lost its influence and may be seen as oppressive. As for depth of conviction, it can be difficult to gauge because affiliation, especially in the past, has been essential to respectable standing in the community. Among the earliest newcomer arrivals were missionaries, dedicated women working as teachers and nurses among Aboriginals or settlers. Roman Catholic women were mainly affiliated with orders, the Grey Nuns, for example, but occasional laywomen like ONÉSIME DORVAL also came. If Protestant, women might be wives of the missionary minister, the unpaid half of a team, or a single woman like Presbyterian LUCY BAKER. Sometimes they engaged in challenging ventures, rare then for females but justified in terms of religious obligation. Ultimately, they, like other women, dwelled in a subordinate sphere.

During the early 20th century newcomer influx, Protestant women, usually affiliated with evangelical or partially evangelical denominations which included Methodists, Presbyterians, Anglicans and Baptists, increased in numbers and prominence. Mostly hidden are women's efforts to establish churches, but well recorded is the fact that women were the backbone of local churches: they often constituted a majority of the church-goers. Their ladies' aid and female missionary societies (domestic and foreign) greatly assisted church survival and expansion. Well established and nationally organized, they also provided a respectable women's sphere within the essentially patriarchal structure of the institutional church. As well, women taught Sunday school and engaged in other pastoral, educational, and charitable undertakings (sometimes as deaconesses). They had little voice in governance, however, and ordination in major denominations was unthinkable until well into the 20th century. Evangelical Protestant activism went beyond church confines, propelling women into major interdenominational efforts to uplift community life, such as the WOMEN'S CHRISTIAN TEMPERANCE UNION and the YOUNG WOMEN'S CHRISTIAN ASSOCIATION. Women's concern about youth was expressed in their support for CANADIAN GIRLS IN TRAINING: founded during WORLD WAR I, it became a popular organization for teenage girls in Saskatchewan and elsewhere.

Roman Catholic women also became more numerous, but were ethnically divided and often looked upon with disdain by the culturally dominant (and often evangelical Protestant) British Canadians. Emigrant Quebec women were in an especially difficult position, and the parish church in their settlements functioned as a bulwark of identity. Continental European women, too, found that involvement in their ethnic parishes served as a point of identity. Immigrant or not, few Roman Catholic women questioned their subordinate position within the Church, and some entered religious orders. Well into the century, these orders provided not only opportunities for women but also a cheap labour source for Roman Catholic health care institutions and educational facilities. For laywomen, bodies like altar guilds and the CATHOLIC WOMEN'S LEAGUE came to provide opportunities for service in a place of their own. Others also increased their numbers, including German and Finnish Lutherans as well as Orthodox Christian women. Their churches, too, might function as a familiar landmark in a strange, sometimes hostile, society, although they often perpetuated patriarchal structures.

Non-Christian women were most likely to be Jewish. They first arrived late in the territorial era when several Jewish agricultural settlements were established in the southeast. Rural or urban, they often faced discrimination, but continued to perpetuate Jewish traditions within the home. They also began to engage in auxiliary assistance to community and synagogue, and formed their own organizations. By mid-century women's long-familiar activities and interests were stagnating in many religious bodies. By the 1970s, resurgent FEMINISM led to controversies about women's place in religious institutions. Efforts to address feminist-oriented concerns were unsettling for many, while delivering too little for others. For many Protestants a touchstone was female ordination. Although the United Church had accepted it since 1936, few had followed the first to be ordained, Saskatchewan's LYDIA GRUCHY. By the mid-1970s more women were doing so, and denominations like Anglicans and Presbyterians opened their doors. In 2002 the Saskatchewan Synod of the Evangelical Lutheran Church in Canada elected the first female Lutheran bishop in the country. In the meantime, Jewish women worked also to lessen barriers. Religion, however, had lost much of its appeal and meaning to diverse women; today, women remain the backbone of many religious bodies, but those who remain are often more conservative.

Of the many women who have dropped out, some seek new directions—more spiritual than religious. Feminism has often had an impact, but also important are such factors as secularization, openness, emphasis upon individuality, and the presence of "new religions." For some, Buddhism in western dress—insight meditation, for example—is an answer. For others, New Age spiritualities offer female empowerment, affirm the individual, and answer the search for interconnectedness between humans and nature. Wicca (feminist witchcraft), Goddess worship (often linked to Wicca), and eco-feminism are among the possibilities. Celtic spirituality, with and without a Christian component, is also attractive. Also present is an upsurge of interest in Aboriginal spirituality on the part of Aboriginal and non-Aboriginal women. Especially difficult is the Aboriginal struggle to come to terms with the enforced imposition of Christianity: if some spurn it, others, Protestant and Catholic, often seek to blend the two traditions. And for others, a different answer such as the Baha'i faith has been found. The story of women and religion becomes more complex as today's immigration brings into the province Buddhism, Hinduism, and Islam, in which women are likely to adhere to supportive roles within masculine-dominated systems. *Ann Leger-Anderson*

FURTHER READING: De Brou, D. and A. Moffatt. 1995. *"Other Voices": Historical Essays on Saskatchewan Women*. Regina: Canadian Plains Research Center.

RELIGIOUS SOCIETY OF FRIENDS.

The Religious Society of Friends (Quakers) is a faith which began in Britain in the mid-17th century. Friends have a strong spiritual belief that God dwells within everyone, and strong social beliefs in peace, social justice and respect for creation.

The first Quakers in Saskatchewan were members of a conservative strand of Friends, (Halcyonia Meeting), who settled in the Borden area in the late 1890s, where their descendents continue to live and worship as a non-affiliated Quaker meeting. Later, a group of more liberal Quakers (Swarthmore Meeting) settled in the Unity area, but by the mid-20th century they had merged with the United Church. By the 1960s there were a number of liberal Friends in Saskatchewan, living mostly in Regina and Saskatoon. In 1966, these Quakers helped found Prairie Monthly Meeting, which affiliated with the national Quaker body, Canadian Yearly Meeting.

In the following decades, Prairie Monthly Meeting was eldered by such Friends as the late Mary Hinde and the late Martin Cohnstaedt, both of whom combined a deep spirituality with social activism. During the Vietnam War, Saskatchewan Friends assisted American draft-resisters in entering and remaining in Canada. Since the 1970s, several Friends in the province have been active in opposing uranium mining, and in 1995 Prairie Monthly Meeting endorsed the 1994 Christian leaders' statement opposing the nuclear industry in Saskatchewan—making the Quakers an endorsing denomination of the Inter-Church Uranium Committee, an inter-church group which opposes uranium mining on both peace and environmental grounds.

Friends have worked on global development issues through the Saskatchewan Council for International Cooperation, and on Aboriginal rights issues through the Canadian Friends Service Committee. Others have expressed their spirituality in such areas as medicine, professional writing, the humanities and social sciences, and in work involving renewable energy systems. In the 1990s, Prairie Monthly Meeting helped initiate an Alternatives to Violence Program in Saskatchewan, which helps people in prisons and in the wider community to learn non-violent ways of dealing with anger and personal pain.

After the events of September 11, 2001, Saskatchewan Friends joined in the work of local and national peace organizations, bearing witness–in a time of war, fear and oppression–to a vision of peace, love, hope and justice for all.

David Greenfield

REMAI FAMILY. Frank, Joe and John Remai are three brothers whose Saskatoon businesses have been responsible for building almost 10,000 residential units throughout the prairie provinces since 1962. The brothers' business interests were once intertwined, but eventually they separated their companies.

The Frank P. Remai Corporate Group, which includes P.R. Developments Ltd., employs more than 700 people, according to the annual rankings produced by *Saskatchewan Business* magazine, and has annual revenues of $120 million. Major recent Saskatoon P.R. Developments Ltd. projects include the Hong Kong Bank building, The Riverwalk and MacKenzie condominiums and The Franklin, a full-service, high-rise retirement home. The Ramada Renaissance, now called the Radisson, was a high-rise apartment and hotel complex built by the firm in 1984 in the city. In addition to its Saskatoon presence, P.R. Developments built and operated the West Harvest Inn, College Park Developments and Marian Gardens in Regina. It also owns the Executive Royal Inn Hotel chains in Saskatchewan and Alberta.

Remai Construction, a separate company owned by Joseph Remai, employs another eighty people, producing $26 million in revenue annual. The head office is Saskatoon; an office was opened in Edmonton in 2003.

The Remai Group is primarily an investor, developer and manager of multifamily and commercial rental real estate in Saskatchewan and Alberta. The company is also active in residential condominium development in Saskatchewan and Alberta and owns and manages the Colonial Square Motel in Saskatoon.

Joe Ralko

REMPEL, JACOB (1903–76). Born in a Mennonite community in Ukraine on June 26, 1903, Rempel and his brothers fled after the destruction of

L.G. SAUNDERS PHOTO/UNIVERSITY OF SASKATCHEWAN ARCHIVES A-10727

Jacob Rempel, 1956.

the community during the Russian Revolution in 1919. They came to Langham, Saskatchewan in 1923. Rempel completed high school in Prince Albert and entered the **UNIVERSITY OF SASKATCHEWAN** on a scholarship in 1928, where he earned High Honours in Biology in 1931 and an MSc in freshwater biology in 1933. In 1934 he was hired to teach at Regina College, taking leave to earn a PhD in entomology at Cornell University in 1936. He returned to the University of Saskatchewan in 1946. In 1961 he was appointed Rawson Professor, a position he held until his retirement in 1970.

Professor Rempel was an outstanding teacher. In addition to entomology classes he taught biological sciences to thousands of humanities and social sciences students. He also guided the research of many graduate students. He made lasting contributions to science in several research areas, beginning his career with the study of the midge *Chironomus hyperboreus* in **PRINCE ALBERT NATIONAL PARK**. This led to work on chironomid (fish fly) taxonomy. He then turned to biting flies: first to the ecology and control of blackflies, which adversely affected cattle populations; and then to mosquitoes, which were vectors of the virus causing the western equine sleeping sickness (encephalitis) which occurred as a pandemic in the late 1930s.

He closed off his distinguished research career with classic studies in insect embryology. He studied the development of the bertha army worm, two species of beetle, and the black widow spider. His last major contribution, *The Evolution of the Insect Head: The Endless Dispute*, was published a year before he died. It clarified an issue that had elicited twelve different theories. Overall, Rempel had contributed more than fifty publications.

He won many honours. He was elected a Fellow of the Royal Society in 1956, and received the Centennial Medal in 1967 "in recognition of valuable service to the Nation."

In 1971 he received the Gold Medal of the Entomological Society of Canada. He was president of the Entomological Society of Saskatchewan and of the International Conference on Diseases of Nature Communicable to Man. He also served for ten years as associate editor of the *Canadian Journal of Zoology*, and for a similar period on the Advisory Panel on Entomology of the Defence Research Board of Canada.

During his freshwater biology studies he married Greta Halliday, and they had three children. After his retirement, he moved to Victoria, but remained active in research until just before his death on May 30, 1976.
U. Theodore Hammer

FURTHER READING: Rempel, J. 1950. "A Guide to the Mosquito Larvae of Western Canada." *Canadian Journal of Research* 28: 207–48; — 1953. "The mosquitoes of Saskatchewan." *Canadian Journal of Zoology* 31: 433–509.

RENAUD, ANDRÉ (1919–88). Born in Montreal on January 25, 1919, André Renaud was ordained an Oblate priest in 1944 and served throughout the Yukon and Northwest Territories. Later, he earned his Masters and PhD from the University of Ottawa. Between 1954 and 1963, Renaud established the Indian Social Development Bureau for the Coordination of Educational Research, the Indian and Eskimo Association of Canada, and the Society for Indian and Northern Education. He taught at the **UNIVERSITY OF SASKATCHEWAN** from 1961 to 1974 and during that time created the Indian and Northern Education Program. Renaud was a tireless promoter of cultural education around the globe and was awarded the Canadian Centennial Medal for achievement in Native education. He was invested as an Officer of the Order of Canada in 1973. André Renaud passed away on January 15, 1988.

RENNIE, DONALD ANDREWS (1922–). Don Rennie was born at Medicine Hat, Alberta, and raised on a farm near Gull Lake, Saskatchewan. He received his Bachelor of Science degree in Agriculture from the **UNIVERSITY OF SASKATCHEWAN** in 1949 and his PhD in Soil Science from the University of Wisconsin in 1952. That year, Rennie joined the Soil Science Department at the University of Saskatchewan. He served as Dean of Agriculture between 1984 and 1989. From 1966 to 1970 he was headquartered in Vienna, Austria, as head of the **SOILS** section in an international project jointly conducted by the Food and Agriculture Organization and the International Atomic Energy Agency. Rennie is recognized around the world for his work on soils, and has acted as a consultant to governments and international organizations. He was instrumental in the establishment of the Saskatchewan Institute of Pedology, which integrated federal, provincial, and university programs and activities in soil science. His views on the danger of misuse of summerfallow have caused farmers to consider the merits of minimum tillage and continuous cropping. He has conducted research into soil deterioration, soil salinity, nitrogen transformation and movement in soils, and dust-fall accumulation in soils in the vicinity of potash refineries.

Rennie received the Canadian Centennial Medal Award in 1967 and the American Chemical Society Award in 1966 for his research on the phosphorous chemistry of soils and on fertilizer-phosphorous management practices for cereal grains. Additional awards received include: Fellow of the Canadian Society of Soil Science (1971); Fellow of the American Society of Agronomy (1972); Fellow of the Soil Science Society of America (1976); and Fellow of the Agricultural Institute of Canada (1976). He was winner of the Agronomy Merit Award in 1979, and in 1983 was inducted into the Saskatchewan Agricultural Hall of Fame. He became a Member of the Order of Canada in 1992.

REPTILES. Reptiles are animals with backbones, scaled skins, and lungs. Saskatchewan has examples of three of the five modern kinds of reptiles: two species of turtles, one lizard and nine snakes. All of these reptiles are active only in the warm spring and summer months, and spend the cold time of the year below the frost-line underground. In many species the females are considerably larger than the males, particularly in the older age groups; this larger size means that they can produce more eggs and, in live-bearing species, maintain a higher body temperature, which aids in the proper and more rapid development of the embryos. The province is at the meeting point of the eastern woodlands fauna (e.g., snapping turtle, red-bellied snake) and the western plains fauna (e.g., short-horned lizard, bullsnake, Western rattlesnake). All species are on the northern margins of their distributions. Twelve species are confirmed members of the provincial fauna (see Table REP-1).

The large snapping turtle and the smaller but more numerous painted turtle occur in the rivers of the Missouri drainage and in large permanent ponds in the southeast. The painted turtle occurs as far north as the **SASKATCHEWAN RIVER** and **DUCK MOUNTAIN**. Both are opportunistic feeders, taking fish and other live prey, plant material, and carrion. The greater or eastern short-horned lizard is a small, flattened, short-tailed lizard found in the **FRENCHMAN RIVER** valley, where it overwinters in the rock piles of the coulee slopes; it feeds on ants.

Table REP-1. Reptiles of Saskatchewan			
Common Name	Species	Family	Distribution
Snapping turtle	Chelydra serpetina	Chelydridae	southeast corner
Painted turtle	Chrsemys picta	Emydidae	southeast; north to Duck Mountain
Greater short-horned lizard	Phrynosoma hernandesi	Iguanidae	Frenchman River valley
Western hog-nosed snake	Heterodon nasicus	Colubridae	southern prairies
Yellow-bellied racer	Coluber constrictor	Colubridae	extreme southern prairies
Bullsnake	Pituophis catenifer	Colubridae	prairies
Red-bellied snake	Storeria occipitomaculata	Colubridae	lower Qu'Appelle Valley
Smooth green snake	Opheodrys vernalis	Colubridae	southeast corner
Red-sided garter snake	Thamnophis sirtalis	Colubridae	whole province, except southwest and northeast
Wandering garter snake	Thamnophis elegans	Colubridae	southwestern dry prairies
Plains garter snake	Thamnophis radix	Colubridae	prairies and aspen parklands
Western/prairie rattlesnake	Crotalus viridis	Viperidae	Frenchman and South Saskatchewan valleys of the southwestern corner

All of the snakes are **CARNIVORES**. The western hog-nosed is distinguished by the upturned tip of its snout, which it uses for digging in search of prey such as toads, and by its habit of playing "possum" by rolling on its back when threatened. It produces in its posterior salivary glands a weak venom which subdues its small prey but has no effect on larger organisms. The large bullsnake is an important predator on native rodents as well as domestic rats and house mice. The smaller and rare yellow-bellied racer preys on small **RODENTS**. The red-bellied snake and the smooth green snake are small insectivorous snakes from the eastern woodlands.

Saskatchewan has three species of the widespread genus of garter snakes, which all have a yellow or orange mid-dorsal stripe. They are often found around water, where they feed on frogs, fish, leeches and insects, as well as small rodents. The plains garter snake is the most common reptile species in the province, famous for setting up overwintering dens in rural house basements. The western rattlesnake of the southwest is the only snake potentially poisonous to humans.

Diane Secoy

FURTHER READING: Didiuk, Andrew B. "Amphibians and Reptiles." Pp. 143–44 in *Atlas of Saskatchewan.* Saskatoon: University of Saskatchewan; Stebbins, Robert C. 2003. *Peterson Field Guide to Western Reptiles and Amphibians.* New York: Houghton Mifflin.

COURTESY OF THE ROYAL SASKATCHEWAN MUSEUM

Plains garter snake.

Innovation Place, University of Saskatchewan, 2004.

RESEARCH PARKS. Saskatchewan has two university-related science and technology campuses: Innovation Place at the **UNIVERSITY OF SASKATCHEWAN**, and the Regina Research Park at the **UNIVERSITY OF REGINA**. The province's science parks had their beginning in the mid-1970s at the University of Saskatchewan. The government of Saskatchewan was approached in 1974 by a pharmaceutical company inquiring about the availability of land on the University of Saskatchewan (U of S) campus for an applied research and production facility. University officials and representatives from the federal and provincial governments began discussions in 1975 with the objective of developing university land north of the main campus to house research institutes and industrial science as well as technology activity that could be complementary to university activity. The federal Department of Regional Economic Expansion commissioned a study to investigate the feasibility of a science park to be located in Saskatoon. In 1976 the U of S approached the provincial **CROWN CORPORATION**, Saskatchewan Economic Development Corporation (**SEDCO**), with the suggestion that if such a park was developed it might assist in the relocation of the National Hydrology Research Institute from Ottawa to Saskatoon. SEDCO undertook further feasibility studies, and later in 1976 entered into discussions with the U of S with the objective of leasing university land for the purpose of such a park.

On June 20, 1977, a lease between the province of Saskatchewan, represented by SEDCO, and the University of Saskatchewan was executed, creating the Saskatoon Research Park. The land lease was for a term of eighty-four years expiring in 2061; the financial terms required SEDCO to pay the

University the appraised value of the land in annual payments including interest over the first twenty-one years of the lease. The University retained unrestricted approval rights over all physical development and all tenants of the park. The lease created a body, the Management Advisory Committee, to review and approve tenants. In 1978 the first building project, the SEDCO Centre (presently known as the Galleria), was approved and commenced construction. In 1979 a second building, the **SASKATCHEWAN RESEARCH COUNCIL**'s Resources Research Centre, was also approved. In 1980 the first tenants of the Saskatoon Research Park took occupancy within the Galleria; a year later the Park changed its name to Innovation Place. Growth was initially slow, with a third building added in 1982 and a fourth in 1984, but the latter half of the decade resulted in rapid growth: six major building projects were initiated, including the National Hydrology Research Centre.

By 1990 the park was home to forty-one tenants employing 750 people. This level of growth was largely a result of a focus on the strengths of the local technology sector rather than on marketing the park to organizations outside of Saskatchewan. A strong effort was undertaken by park management to create a package of service tenants that made occupancy in the park attractive to potential clients. During the early 1990s Innovation Place began to develop an internationally recognized cluster of plant **BIOTECHNOLOGY** companies, which had its beginnings in the strong industrial collaboration efforts of the National Research Council's Plant Biotechnology Institute. These efforts attracted scientists from international companies; the growth in plant science was aided by the development of a

state-of-the-art multi-tenant research greenhouse complex within the park. In 1995 SEDCO ceased operations as a Crown corporation; the assets and staff of Innovation Place were transferred to a new Crown corporation, the Saskatchewan Opportunities Corporation (SOCO). The growth of the biotechnology sector helped stimulate a major period of development in the late 1990s: new laboratory buildings and a major expansion to the greenhouse complex were completed, as was a new building to house clients within the information technology sector.

The same period saw the beginnings of the Regina Research Park. The Saskatchewan government began discussions with a group of Regina community leaders, with the intention of exploring the feasibility of duplicating the success of Innovation Place at the University of Regina (U of R). These discussions resulted in 1998 in a lease between SOCO and the U of R for land on its campus, which already housed two buildings with industrial technology occupants. Another two buildings, one for the petroleum research sector and one for the information services sector, were constructed and completed in 2000. By 2005, Innovation Place had celebrated its twenty-fifth anniversary of tenant occupancy and the Regina Research Park its fifth anniversary of operations. The parks were home to 120 organizations in Saskatoon and thirty organizations in Regina; all combined, these tenants employed 2,800 people.   *Doug Tastad*

RESERVES, URBAN. Urban satellite reserves are properties located either in whole or in part within or adjacent to existing urban municipalities; they are governed and managed by Indian Band Councils. Under the federal Indian Act, such urban satellite reserves have the same legal status as other Indian reserves found in other parts of the province; they differ from another type of urban reserves which exist in other provinces by virtue of urban municipalities expanding to the point where their boundaries are contiguous with those of the long-standing neighbouring reserve. They also differ from urban properties which are held by Band Councils as part of their land holdings but have not been granted official reserve status.

Properties acquired by Band Councils in urban areas are not automatically converted to reserve status. They acquire such status only after the federal Cabinet approves a formal request submitted to it by the Indian Band Councils that govern what might be termed "base reserves" or "home reserves" in other parts of the province. The conversion of any non-reserve properties to reserve properties requires conscious decisions both by the Band Council and federal Cabinet, based on a prescribed process. The process for converting such properties to reserves is defined in two documents. The first document is the Treaty Land Entitlement Framework Agreement

(TLEFA), which is a Saskatchewan-specific comprehensive land claims agreement signed in 1992 by the federal government, the province of Saskatchewan, and twenty-two entitlement bands in the province. The second is the Additions to Reserve Policy (ARP), which is the official policy of the federal government that applies to properties earmarked for reserve status, regardless of how they are acquired by Band Councils. Both policies stipulate parallel and similar processes aimed at ensuring, among other things, negotiations and agreements between the councils of the Band, the urban municipality, and the school divisions. Although negotiations and agreements related to provision and payment of services and bylaw compatibility are identified as a desirable goal, they are not a precondition to having properties converted to reserve status. In some cases such properties have been converted to urban satellite reserves in the absence of such negotiations or agreements.

During the past two decades, over twenty such satellite reserves have been created in municipalities of various sizes such as Prince Albert, Saskatoon, Regina, Yorkton, Fort Qu'Appelle, Lebret, Duck Lake, Meadow Lake, and North Battleford. Such reserves have been created and used for commercial and institutional purposes; to date, none has been created or used for residential purposes. Invariably, they have been created because the Band Councils are seeking to capitalize on the location of such reserves in urban areas which generally serve as regional service centres and in which they can establish and operate either profitable commercial ventures or various types of First Nation governance, educational, and service agencies. The two main advantages of urban satellite reserves over urban properties which do not have reserve status are: first, Band Councils who govern and manage them have extensive flexibility in the types of arrangements that they enter into with neighbouring municipal governments for services and service fees as well as for bylaw compatibility; second, bona fide First Nation members who work or operate businesses on such reserves are exempt from taxation.   *Joseph Garcea*

FURTHER READING: Barron, L.F. and J. Garcea. 1999. *Urban Indian Reserves: Forging New Relationship in Saskatchewan.* Saskatoon: Purich Publishing; —. 2000. "Reflections on Urban Satellite Reserves in Saskatchewan." Pp. 400–28 in R.F. Laliberté et al. (eds.), *Expressions on Canadian Native Studies,* Saskatoon: University of Saskatchewan Extension Press.

RESIDENTIAL SCHOOLS. The purpose of the residential schools was the education, integration and assimilation of Aboriginal children into mainstream Canadian society. The government removed Aboriginal children from their homes and home communities, and transported them to residential schools which were often long distances away. The residential school system predates Confederation and in part grew out of Canada's missionary experience with various religious organizations.

The federal government began to play a role in the development and administration of this school system as early as 1874, mainly to meet its obligation, under the Indian Act, to provide an education to Aboriginal peoples. Residential schools were established by the churches in 1820, and by the government in 1874.

The government controlled all aspects of the admission of Aboriginal peoples to the schools, including arrangements for the care of such persons over holiday periods as well as the methods of transporting children to and from residential schools. Aboriginal children were often taken from their families without the consent of their parents or guardians.

It is estimated that there were in excess of 100 residential schools in operation throughout Canadian history in every province and territory except New Brunswick and Prince Edward Island, with a peak of seventy-four schools in operation in 1920. There were twenty residential schools in Saskatchewan, operated under the authority of the Roman Catholic Church, the Anglican Church, and the Methodist and Presbyterian Churches (*see* Table RS-1 on facing page).

The federal government operated nearly every school in partnership with various religious organizations until April 1, 1969, when it assumed full responsibility for the school system. The last federally run residential school in Saskatchewan closed in 1983. Most residential schools ceased to operate by the mid-1970s, with only seven remaining open through the 1980s.

In recent years, individuals have come forward with personal and painful stories of the abuses that took place in the residential schools. The hearings of the Royal Commission on Aboriginal Peoples uncovered many of these personal accounts.

On January 7, 1998, the government of Canada announced Gathering Strength—Canada's Aboriginal Action Plan, which calls for: a renewed partnership with Aboriginal peoples, based on recognizing past mistakes and injustices; the advancement of reconciliation; healing and renewal; and the building of a joint plan for the future. The federal government offered a Statement of Reconciliation, which acknowledged its role in the development and administration of the residential schools and offered an apology to survivors of residential schools:

"Sadly, our history with respect to the treatment of Aboriginal people is not something in which we can take pride. Attitudes of racial and cultural superiority led to a suppression of Aboriginal culture and values. As a country, we are burdened by past actions that resulted in weakening the identity of Aboriginal peoples, suppressing their languages and cultures, and outlawing spiritual practices. We must recognize the impact of these actions on the once self-sustaining nations that were disaggregated, disrupted, limited or even destroyed by the dispossession of traditional territory, by the relocation of Aboriginal people, and by some provisions of the Indian Act. We must acknowledge that the result of these actions was the erosion of the political, economic and social systems of Aboriginal people and nations.

One aspect of our relationship with Aboriginal people over this period that requires particular attention is the Residential School system. This system separated many children from their families and communities and prevented them from speaking their own languages and from learning about their heritage and cultures. In the worst cases, it left legacies of personal pain and distress that continue to reverberate in Aboriginal communities to this day. Tragically, some children were the victims of physical and sexual abuse.

The Government of Canada acknowledges the role it played in the development and administration of these schools. Particularly to those individuals who experienced the tragedy of sexual and physical abuse at residential schools, and who have carried this burden believing that in some way they must be responsible, we wish to emphasize that what you experienced was not your fault and should never have happened. To those of you who suffered this tragedy at residential schools, we are deeply sorry."

Lorena Fontaine

RESTORATIVE JUSTICE. Saskatchewan was a pioneer and innovator in criminal justice. Perhaps the most significant change in the criminal justice system since European contact was the introduction of restorative justice, and Saskatchewan judges and communities were among the first in Canada to use the concept; they embraced it with more vigour than anywhere else outside of the Yukon.

The concept of restorative justice is both new and ancient. A form of restorative justice was at the core of many First Nations traditions, but it is very new to the British system of justice. To understand what restorative justice is today, and why it represents such a fundamental change, a quick look at the system brought to Canada by the British is necessary. Under British law, one who breaches the law of the land is considered to have offended against the King or Queen, and a central tenet is that the Crown has the right to punish such behaviour. In contrast, restorative justice gives the victim and the local community a much more central role. It ignores punishment, though not accountability, and seeks to "put things right" between the offender, the victim, and the community. The process tends to purge the anger that perhaps led to the offence and

Table RS-1. Saskatchewan Residential Schools					
Name	Location	Religion	Opened	Closed	Comments
All Saints Indian Residential School	Prince Albert	Church of England	1948	1951	The school amalgamated with St. Alban's Residential School to form the Prince Albert Indian Residential School.
Battleford Industrial Residential School	Battleford	Church of England	1883	1914	
Beauval Indian Residential School	Beauval	Roman Catholic	1895	1995	The Meadow Lake Tribal Council operated as the Beauval Indian Education Centre from 1985 to 1995.
Cowesses Indian Residential School (Marieval Indian Residential School)	Marieval	Roman Catholic	1898	1968	
Crowstand Indian Residential School	Kamsack	Presbyterian	1888	1915	
Emmanuel College	Prince Albert	Church of England	1889	1949	
File Hills Colony School (File Hills Indian Residential School)	Okanese Reserve	United Church	1889	1949	
Gordon Indian Residential School	Punnichy	Church of England	1889	1996	
Guy Indian Residential School	Sturgeon Landing	Roman Catholic	1926	1964	
Ile-à-la-Crosse Indian Residential School	Ile-à-la-Crosse	Roman Catholic	1897	unknown	
Lac La Ronge Indian Residential School (All Saints Indian Residential School)	Lac La Ronge	Church of England	1907	1947	The school was deliberately destroyed by fire in 1947 and relocated to Prince Albert.
Muscowequan Indian Residential School	Lestock	Roman Catholic	1895	1976	
Prince Albert Indian Residential School	Prince Albert	Church of England	1951	1969	
Qu'Appelle Industrial School (Qu'Appelle Indian Residential School)	Lebret	Roman Catholic	1883	1981	Destroyed by fire in 1904; rebuilt in 1905; destroyed by fire in 1932; rebuilt in 1936; Qu'Appelle Indian Residential School Council took complete control of the school in 1981.
Regina Industrial School	Regina	Presbyterian	1890	1910	
Round Lake Indian Residential School	Whitewood	United Church	1886	1950	
St. Alban's Indian Residential School	Prince Albert	Church of England	1944	1951	The school amalgamated with All Saints Indian Residential School to form the Prince Albert Indian Residential School.
St. Anthony Indian Residential School	Onion Lake	Roman Catholic	1894	1974	
St. Barnabas Indian Residential School (Onion Lake Indian Residential School)	Onion Lake	Church of England	1892	1943	The school was destroyed by fire in 1943 and relocated to St. Alban's in Prince Albert.
St. Michael's Indian Residential School	Duck Lake	Roman Catholic	1894	1972	
St. Phillip's Indian Residential School (Keeseekoose Day School)	Kamsack	Roman Catholic	1899	1969	
Thunderchild Indian Residential School (St. Henri of Thunderchild)	Delmas	Roman Catholic	1901	1948	It was speculated that students deliberately burned down the school in 1948.

Further reading: Miller, J.R. 1996. *Shingwauk's Vision: A History of Native Residential Schools.* Toronto: University of Toronto Press; Milloy, John Sheridan. 1999. *A National Crime: The Canadian Government and the Residential School System, 1879-1986.* Winnipeg: University of Manitoba Press; Royal Commission on Aboriginal Peoples. 1996. *Looking Forward, Looking Back.* Vol. 1 of the Royal Commission on Aboriginal Peoples. Ottawa: Canada Communications Group.

certainly resulted from it, and to begin a healing process.

Restorative justice can take many forms, but sentencing circles are its essence. The ancient process of circle consensus-seeking was first utilized by Judge Barry Stewart in the Yukon; shortly after, in 1992, Judge Claude Fafard was inspired by the success of that experiment and presided over Saskatchewan's first sentencing circle (the first in Canada outside of the Yukon), and Saskatchewan remained in the forefront of its use for many years after. Dean Martin Stewart had been charged in Sandy Bay with assault: as Judge Fafard knew local elders, a circle was organized when the regular

docket was finished, involving Stewart, family members, a representative of the police, the Crown Prosecutor, a legal aid defence lawyer, and the victim. Clockwise around the circle, as in every circle since, people discussed what Stewart could do to make amends, how the community could help him change, and what he could do to reconcile with the victim. The discussion progressed, and as in almost every such circle held since, a consensus emerged, which satisfied not just the community representatives, but also the diverse interests of the victim, the accused, the Crown, and the court. In contrast to the formal atmosphere of traditional court, emotions were given a free rein. Highly personal stories were

told by many, including elders, who like Stewart had suffered the impact of poverty, overcrowding, community and cultural dislocation, criminal behaviour, but most of all, alcoholism. Their example offered Stewart a way out of his unacceptable lifestyle.

Very quickly, communities all over northern Saskatchewan embraced the idea of sentencing circles. Circles became the norm in the Provincial Court in northern Saskatchewan, and what at first had been a very tentative experiment became a more formalized practice. Guidelines were eventually adopted by the two judges who serviced northern Saskatchewan from La Ronge, and these were ultimately enunciated by Judge Fafard in the

Joseyounen case. The Saskatchewan Court of Appeal in the case of *R. v. Taylor* upheld the notion that in order to have a circle the accused must show a willingness to reform and be part of an identifiable community; the victim (or a surrogate) must be willing to participate, as must traditional elders or respected non-political community leaders. This important decision achieved two things. It made part of Saskatchewan law a sentencing process that purges emotions such as anger, and that reconciles the accused with his own community and the victim. It also demonstrated how innovative the circle process can be: as part of his sentence, Taylor was banished to an uninhabited island.

These cases, and the hundreds of circles that were held in the Saskatchewan Provincial Court throughout Saskatchewan, had a great impact across Canada. They were influential in persuading the Parliament of Canada to enact provisions for the adoption by the Supreme Court of the principles of restorative justice. In no small part due to the work of those small Aboriginal communities throughout northern Saskatchewan, restorative justice came to benefit Canadians everywhere. *Ross Moxley*

RETAIL AND WHOLESALE CO-OPERATIVES.

Consumer co-operative activity first appeared on the prairies at the turn of the 20th century, when agricultural producers began joining together to form buying clubs in order to make bulk purchases of farm supplies and basic commodities. These initial forms of co-operative activity have grown into an extensive retailing system. Virtually all economic activity in this sector is carried out by FEDERATED CO-OPERATIVES LIMITED (FCL), its affiliated retail co-ops, and a number of retails that fall into the "other" category.

FCL provides wholesaling, manufacturing, and administrative services to more than 300 retail co-ops across western Canada and northwestern Ontario; about 170 of these are in Saskatchewan. According to *Saskatchewan Business* magazine, FCL is Saskatchewan's second-largest corporation in terms of gross sales. Divisions within FCL are representative of the types of services and products it provides to member retail co-ops. These divisions include retail operations, consumer products, building supplies, agricultural products, distribution services, forest products, refining, and environmental and technical services. The miscellaneous retails in the province are involved in such diverse enterprises as a bookstore, laundromat, restaurants, and buying clubs. Although FCL is a transprovincial co-operative, the figures in this entry reflect only that portion of the enterprise deemed to be owned or operating within Saskatchewan.

FCL and its affiliates have experienced a pattern of steady growth over the past ten years despite fluctuations in Saskatchewan's economic fortunes. The size of the organization enables the system as a whole to achieve economies of scale, while the concentration of affiliated retails in small rural centres enhances responsiveness to local needs.

At the end of the 1990s, FCL assets in Saskatchewan were estimated to be $486 million, which represents 50% of the organization's total assets across the prairies and into Ontario. At the same point, revenues and surpluses generated from sales to Saskatchewan retail co-operatives were $895 million and $74 million respectively. There was a slight rise in the number of employees over the decade, from 1,183 to 1,207 individuals; and the wage bill rose from $44.5 million to $50 million. Over the same period, capital investment increased from $14.5 million to more than $25 million, and member equity rose from $153 million to $275 million.

The approximately 170 retail co-operatives affiliated through FCL deliver a wide variety of goods and services throughout the province, with particular concentration in small rural communities. Merchandise provided by the retails includes groceries, general goods, petroleum products, feed, and crop supplies. More than one-third of the province's population are members of these organizations. Although the number of affiliated retails and active membership experienced a slight decline during the 1990s, assets held by the retails increased from $355 million to more than $519 million. Combined with a dramatic fall in liabilities over the same period—from $122 million to $64 million—this resulted in an increase in member equity of more than 95%, from $233 million to $455 million. Affiliated retails recorded revenues of just under $1 billion at the end of the 1990s, up by 20% from the beginning of the decade, while the surplus rose from $35 million to $61 million. These organizations provided employment for more than 5,000 people during the 1990s, and at the end of the decade, the wage bill amounted to well over $80 million.

Including such diverse enterprises as a bookstore, a laundromat, restaurants, and buying clubs, about a dozen miscellaneous co-operatives at the end of the 1990s held assets in excess of $123,000, and more than $93,000 in members' equity for their 1,100 members. Interestingly, although the number of these organizations increased over the decade, active membership fell by 20% and assets by 28%. Liabilities also fell considerably, however, which helped contribute to the rise in member equity. Revenues totalled $349,000 at the end of the 1990s, a slight decline from a decade earlier; and capital investment was practically nonexistent. Reflecting the small size of most of these co-ops, only thirteen employees were identified, with a total wage bill of $39,000. The increase in the number of employees and the fall in the wage bill suggests that salaries were relatively insignificant, averaging only $3,000 per year. *Nora Russell*

FURTHER READING: Fulton, Murray, et al. 1991. *Economic Impact Analysis of the Co-operative Sector in Saskatchewan*, Research Report Prepared for Saskatchewan Department of Economic Diversification and Trade; Ketilson, Lou Hammond, et al. 1998. *The Social and Economic Importance of the Co-operative Sector in Saskatchewan*, Research Report Prepared for Saskatchewan Department of Economic and Co-operative Development; Herman, Roger and Murray Fulton. 2001. *An Economic Impact Analysis of the Co-operative Sector in Saskatchewan: Update 1998*.

RETAIL, WHOLESALE AND DEPARTMENT STORE UNION (RWDSU).

Just prior to the end of WORLD WAR II, the United Retail, Wholesale and Department Store Union (headquartered in New York), in co-operation with the Canadian Congress of Labour (now the CLC), launched a drive to organize workers in Saskatchewan. The campaign got off to a good start, and in the first year more than half a dozen shops had been organized. By 1947, local unions had been established in most major centres of the province, including Regina, Saskatoon, Prince Albert, Weyburn, North Battleford, Swift Current, and Moose Jaw. At the international level the reaffiliation of three large locals had been completed, and the word "United" was deleted from the name of the union. Also in the late 1940s, RWDSU members in Saskatchewan established the Saskatchewan Joint Board to coordinate the affairs of local unions in the province. Locals paid a modest per-capita fee to the Joint Board, hired a provincial representative located in Regina, and eventually opened a second union office in Saskatoon. By the mid-1960s, membership numbered over 2,000.

As RWDSU grew larger, its influence in the affairs of the Saskatchewan labour movement increased and the Joint Board became a leader in many campaigns of the SASKATCHEWAN FEDERATION OF LABOUR (SFL), ranging from lobbying to improve labour and social legislation (including hours of work, minimum wage, occupational health and safety) to the first publicly administered medicare plan in Canada. Despite the effectiveness of RWDSU in Saskatchewan and its organizational success, a strong disagreement with the International over the autonomy of the Canadian area came to a head in 1970, when Saskatchewan members voted by secret ballot (1,601 to 16) to disaffiliate from the International. In spite of the fact that such a vote was permitted by the International Constitution, the CLC and the SFL expelled the Joint Board and denied it the right to participate in any activities sponsored by the central labour bodies. Except for a brief arrangement with the Canadian Food and Allied Workers, the Joint Board was on its own until 1983, when it affiliated with the Canadian Area of the International Longshore and Warehouseman's Union (ILWU), and was permitted to rejoin the CLC and the SFL. The Joint Board was nevertheless forced to fight off raiding attempts by Congress affiliates, and to a great extent was denied assistance from many affiliates in its battles with employers.

Concurrent with the growth of RWDSU's reputation as a strong and progressive union, opposition by employers at the bargaining table intensified, and strikes and lockouts became more common and longer than ever before. For instance, union members at **MORRIS RODWEEDER** in Yorkton barricaded themselves in the plant in a successful fight for a first agreement, and members at Pineland Co-op in Nipawin maintained a picket line for eight and a half years (possibly the longest strike in Canada). Laundry workers, packing house workers, Coca-Cola employees, warehouse workers, hotel staff, and co-op employees at both the retail and warehouse level used picket lines and/or plant occupation to win better working conditions and job security. As well, more employers began using the courts to counter the successful activities of the union. This attack fell short of what employers had hoped for, and the union won a number of cases that proved beneficial to all workers, including a Supreme Court of Canada decision upholding secondary picketing as a legitimate activity, the protection of working conditions during a period of collective bargaining, and confirmation of the right to picket a shop located in a shopping mall. Many employer-instigated injunctions to limit the size of picket lines were also defeated by the Joint Board.

Today the RWDSU Saskatchewan Joint Board represents approximately 6,000 members and employs a staff of six full-time representatives and three full-time clerical employees. It bargains close to 100 collective agreements, wins a majority of the hundreds of grievances filed by members, continues to organize new members, provides twenty-two annual scholarships for post-secondary education (open to members and their children), has established employer-funded but jointly administered pension and dental plans, publishes *The Defender* (a four-page newsletter) eleven times a year (and has done so for about thirty-five years); and has amassed a provincial strike fund in excess of $4 million. During the almost sixty years since the RWDSU Joint Board entered the Saskatchewan labour scene, even its critics admit that it has had a tremendous and beneficial impact on the lives of workers and their families. It has organized, bargained hard, and been in the forefront of the political battles for legislation designed to benefit all of Saskatchewan's citizens.

Chris Banting

REZANSOFF, PAUL J. (1942–). Paul Rezansoff was born on March 16, 1942. After teaching art for twenty-four years in Swift Current, he continues to promote arts and culture in his community. He is responsible for a number of artistic "firsts" in Swift Current, including a volunteer art gallery and a National Exhibition Centre gallery. Rezansoff has also facilitated the hosting of musical and artistic entertainment in the city. He served as president of the Swift Current Allied Arts Council and the Saskatchewan Society for Education through Art, and was vice-chair of the **SASKATCHEWAN ARTS BOARD**. He has received the Saskatchewan Volunteer Medal (1996), the Queen's Silver Jubilee Medal (1977), the Queen's Golden Jubilee Medal (2002), and in February 2001 was invested as a member of the Order of Canada.

RICHARDSON, ERNIE (1931–). Born in Stoughton, Saskatchewan on August 4, 1931, Ernie Richardson skipped one of the best-known rinks in Canadian curling history. The Richardson rink included Ernie, his brother Garnet (Sam), and cousins Arnold and Wes Richardson. Mel Perry replaced Wes Richardson beginning in the 1963 season. Known for their aggressive, take-out style of play, the Richardson rink dominated provincial, national, and international events between 1959 and 1963. They won five Saskatchewan Men's curling titles (1959–60, 1962–64) and competed in five Canadian championships. In 1959, they became the youngest team to win the Brier. The team repeated as Canadian champions in 1960, 1962, and 1963, becoming the only rink in Canadian curling history to have won four national championships. The Richardson team also won four Scotch Cup world championships in the same years as their Brier wins. The Richardson rink was inducted into the **SASKATCHEWAN SPORTS HALL OF FAME** and the Canadian Curling Hall of Fame in 1973. Ernie Richardson received the Order of Canada in 1978.

Daria Coneghan and Holden Stoffel

RICHARDSON, JOHN (1787–1865). Born in Dumfries, Scotland on November 5, 1787, Richardson studied medicine at Edinburgh. As surgeon to **JOHN FRANKLIN**'s first Land Arctic Expedition, he collected natural history specimens in present-day Saskatchewan from October 23, 1819 to July 10, 1820, and from June 12–20, 1822. During the second expedition, he passed through this area from June 15 to July 23, 1825. After mapping much of Great Bear Lake and the Arctic Ocean shore from the mouth of the Mackenzie to the mouth of the Coppermine, he walked to Carlton to be in time for the 1827 spring bird migration. He left Fort Resolution on Great Slave Lake on Christmas day 1826, entered Saskatchewan at Methye Portage in late January, and arrived at Carlton on February 12, 1827, where he stayed until May 21. He was at Cumberland House from May 24 to June 18. His assistant naturalist on the second expedition was **THOMAS DRUMMOND**. As surgeon with John Franklin's two Land Arctic expeditions, Richardson in 1819–22 and 1825–27 described many new species or subspecies of plants, **BIRDS** and **MAMMALS**, and one new species of **FISH** from the

PHOTO COURTESY OF TURNER CURLING MUSEUM

Ernie Richardson (left) was the first to skip four Brier champions. Ernie, his brother Sam and cousin Arnold (second and third from right) won the 1959, 1960, 1962 and 1963 Canadian and world titles. Another cousin, Wes (far right), played lead for the first three of those years and was replaced by Mel Perry in 1963.

SASKATCHEWAN RIVER. This inventory of local natural history, published in five volumes, was more complete than for any other "pre-settlement" area in North America, and led to Richardson's recognition as the greatest surgeon-naturalist in the history of the British Empire. In 1848, he came through Saskatchewan in the fastest canoe travel recorded, en route to the Arctic to search for his missing former chief, John Franklin. In later life he was physician in charge at Haslar Hospital (England), then the largest brick building in the empire and the largest hospital in the world. He retired to Grasmere, in the English lake country, where he died on June 5, 1865.

C. Stuart Houston

FURTHER READING: Houston, C.S. 1999. "List of New Species Added to North American Natural History, 1825–1827, by Surgeon-Naturalist John Richardson." Pp. 391–400 in R.C. Davis (ed.), *Sir John Franklin's Journals and Correspondence: The Second Arctic Land Expedition*. Toronto: Champlain Society.

RIDDELL, WILLIAM ANDREW (1905–2000).
W.A. Riddell was principal of Regina College and the Regina Campus of the UNIVERSITY OF SASKATCHEWAN from 1961 to 1969. Born in Hamiota, Manitoba on July 6, 1905, Riddell received a BA (1925) and BSc (1926) from the University of Manitoba, an MSc (1928) from the University of Saskatchewan, and completed his PhD (1931) in chemistry and biology at Stanford University. Riddell taught at Regina College during the 1930s before holding various research positions with the federal and provincial governments. In 1950 he returned to Regina College, serving as dean until his appointment as

SASKATCHEWAN ARCHIVES BOARD R-A3272

William Riddell.

principal. Riddell was instrumental in developing the College's School of Art and in the expansion of the Norman MACKENZIE ART GALLERY.

Perhaps his greatest contribution was his tireless effort to raise the College to full degree-granting status. In 1959 the University of Saskatchewan Board of Governors did just that and, within two years, design and construction of a new campus in Wascana Park began. The University of Saskatchewan Regina Campus, as the College was renamed, was the forerunner of the UNIVERSITY OF REGINA. Riddell was made an Officer of the Order of Canada in 1974. An annual lecture was established in his honour at the University of Regina, and later a new building housing the Faculty of Fine Arts and Student Services became the Riddell Centre, in recognition of his long-standing support of the fine arts in the province. Riddell died in Regina on May 27, 2000.

Mark Vajcner

FURTHER READING: Riddell, W.A. 1974. *The First Decade: A History of the University of Saskatchewan, Regina Campus, 1960–1970*. Regina: University of Regina.

RIEGERT, PAUL WILLIAM (1923–2002).
Paul Riegert, an entomologist, civil servant, professor and author, was born on December 5, 1923, in Laird, Saskatchewan. Educated at Hamburg School and Laird High School, he entered the UNIVERSITY OF SASKATCHEWAN in 1941, receiving a BA in Biology in 1944. He went on to post-graduate training at Montana State College, where he obtained an MSc in Entomology in 1948, and at the University of Illinois (1950–54), where he was awarded a PhD in Physiology and Entomology.

In 1944, Riegert started a twenty-four-year career in entomology with Canada Agriculture at the Dominion Entomological Laboratory in Saskatoon. His initial investigations involved the biology and control of red-backed cutworms and wheat stem sawflies. After 1948 he was involved in insect physiological/ecological research and population surveys, and studied the effects of weather on grasshopper abundance. Considerable emphasis was placed on population dynamics for grasshoppers, including annual surveys of population density and forecast of outbreaks. These surveys, attempting to control grasshopper damage to crops, were of considerable help to farmers.

After joining the UNIVERSITY OF REGINA in 1968, Riegert taught many courses in entomology as well as cell and animal physiology. His research focused on the bioenergetics and nutrition of insects. He published several books documenting the history of entomology and pest control in Canada as well as several local histories, and continued to do so after his retirement. He died on May 9, 2002, in Saskatoon.

Kathleen Gullacher

SASKATCHEWAN ARCHIVES BOARD R-A2305

Louis Riel.

RIEL, LOUIS "DAVID" (1844–85).
MÉTIS patriot and martyr, founder of Manitoba, Riel was born at St. Boniface, Red River, on October 22, 1844, to Louis Riel and Julie Lagimodière. The husband of Marguerite Monet (*dite* Bellehumeur) and father to Jean and Angélique, he was executed for high treason at Regina, North-west Territories, on November 16, 1885. Handsome, intelligent and religious, Louis Riel seemed, even as a child, destined for greatness; from his activist father he inherited a strong sense of duty and love of community, and from his mother he acquired an intense piety. In 1858, local priests hoped to make the young Riel one of their own by sending him to the reputed Collège de Montréal; however, after the trauma of his father's death in 1864, Riel left the college and went to work in a law firm. After a failed courtship, he returned to the Red River in 1868.

Louis Riel first came to prominence during the Red River Resistance (October 1869–May 1870): at the age of 24, educated and articulate, he arrived home in time to participate in the Métis resistance against Canada's annexation of Rupert's Land. Eventually, becoming president of the Métis-led Provisional Government, Riel formed partnerships with many French Métis, and used Métis boatmen and BISON hunters to enforce the governing council's will, particularly against the Canadian Party, a collection of Euro-Canadian annexationists and "loyal" French and English Métis. Riel eventually won the backing of most of the Provisional Government's delegates by advancing a Franco-phone-Catholic rights agenda—as opposed to others, such as William Dease, who championed the Métis' corporate Aboriginal rights. With the Manitoba Act, Riel and his followers provided Manitoba with bilingual public and educational institutions (Section 22); however, only Sections 31–32 dealt with the Métis' Aboriginal rights through the individual extinguishment of their "Indian" title to the land. As a result of these provisions and the execution of Thomas Scott, an Orangeman and francophobe, by a Métis tribunal on March 4, 1870, the Red River insurgency was viewed in Ontario as a "French" rebellion rather than an Aboriginal resistance.

From 1870 to 1884, Louis Riel led a restless existence. He defended Manitoba against a Fenian attack (1871); was exiled in the USA after a bounty was put on his head for Scott's execution (1871–76, 1878–82); was elected several times to Parliament for the riding of Provencher, despite never being able to take up his seat (1873–74); and was incarcerated in insane asylums in Québec (1876–78). In the USA, Riel worked with the Republican Party, serving as a special deputy; he also taught school, and became an American citizen in 1883. Then on June 5, 1884, Riel was invited to return to the Saskatchewan District of the North-West Territories to fight once again for his peoples' rights.

Louis Riel's role in the 1885 uprising would have profound consequences: the socio-economic and political marginalization of the Métis; the subjugation of the plains' First Nations; the preparation of the region for agrarian settlement; and English and French Canada's first rift in Confederation. Through the summer of 1884, Riel tried to build consensus among the English and French Métis, Euro-Canadian settlers, and First Nations in order to address their many grievances against the federal government, including Ottawa's failure to recognize the Métis' land tenure, to honour First Nations' treaties, to prevent starvation on the reserves, and to provide western Euro-Canadians with proper political representation, agricultural markets and transportation infrastructure. However, this nascent coalition dissolved due to the federal government's divide-and-conquer strategy and to the reluctance to take up arms on the part of First Nations, Euro-Canadians and English Métis. Thus Riel and his adjutant, **GABRIEL DUMONT**, could rely on less than 300 Métis in their struggle with the Canadian state. After two brief guerrilla skirmishes at **DUCK LAKE** (March 26) and **FISH CREEK** (April 24), and a final entrenched battle at **BATOCHE** (May 9–12), the Métis resistance ended. Riel was captured, and prepared to defend himself and the Métis cause. However, the trial was unfair: the jurors were all anglophone and Protestant, and the judge had close ties to the ruling Conservatives. Riel was sentenced to hanging despite the jury's plea for mercy. Lucid and articulate in the defence of his sanity, Louis Riel went to the gibbet knowing that posterity would rehabilitate him and his beloved *métis canadien.*

Louis Riel's legacy has been profound. No figure in Canadian history has been more analyzed, has had more differing interpretations or has been more controversial. For the Métis and for many others, Riel was a valiant leader who not only became a martyr for his people, but was also a visionary and humanitarian who saw the potential of the prairie west as a place where the world's oppressed could live in harmony. For others, now in the minority, Riel was a mad man, a deluded prophet, an apostate and a grafter, who inflamed passions and almost tore the country asunder. In addition, Riel's voice has been appropriated for various political ends by prairie regionalists, Québec nationalists and English Canadians, conscious of the culpability of their ancestors in his death. Recently, however, Riel has largely been viewed as a victim of English-Canadian intolerance. In 1998, for instance, an exoneration bill, Bill C-417, was introduced in Parliament before dying on the floor. The bill was a *cause célèbre*–a debate, which continued with the CBC's and the Dominion Institute's efforts to retry Riel in 2002, without Métis participation. Louis Riel will continue to haunt Canada as long as there are conflicting visions of our common past. *Darren R. Préfontaine*

FURTHER READING: Braz, A. 2003. *The False Traitor: Louis Riel in Canadian Culture*. Toronto: University of Toronto Press; Flanagan, T. (ed.). 1976. *The Diaries of Louis Riel*. Edmonton: Hurtig; Siggins, M. 1994. *Riel: A Life of Revolution*. Toronto: Harper Collins.

RIEL, SARA (1848–83). Sara Riel was one of the first Métis women in the Red River region to join the Grey Nuns (**SISTERS OF CHARITY**); she did missionary work for over a decade at Ile-à-la-Crosse in what is now Saskatchewan. Born on October 11, 1848, in St. Boniface, she was the daughter of Jean-Louis Riel and Julie Lagimodière, and the sister of Métis leader **LOUIS RIEL**; she and her brother were known to have a close relationship and to share religious beliefs. Sara Riel joined the Grey Nuns in the latter 1860s; she relocated in June 1871 to Ile-à-la-Crosse, her father's birthplace and the family's ancestral home, and the site of a major missionary effort. She served in the community's mission, including its school and hospital. Between 1876 and 1880 she became godmother to several of the community's children. Earlier, in 1872, Sara Riel had suffered from a severe case of pneumonia and was believed to be dying. After being given the Last Sacrament, she experienced a seemingly miraculous full recovery, and later obtained permission to change her name to Sister Marguerite-Marie, in honour of the saint who had been invoked in prayers. Throughout her life, Sara Riel and her brother corresponded; letters remain which speak of their relationship and of her time spent at Ile-à-la-Crosse. She died of tuberculosis on December 27, 1883. *Cheryl Troupe*

FURTHER READING: Jordan, M. 1974. *To Louis–From Your Sister Who Loves You–Sara Riel*. Toronto: Griffin House; Siggins, Maggie.1994. *Riel: A Life of Revolution*. Toronto: Harper Collins.

RIEL REBELLION: *see* **NORTH-WEST RESISTANCE; ABORIGINALS AND THE NORTH-WEST RESISTANCE**

RIGELHOF, TERRENCE FREDERICK (1944–). Terrence Frederick Rigelhof, born on April 24, 1944, in Regina, completed a BA at the **UNIVERSITY OF SASKATCHEWAN** and studied at St. Paul's Seminary in Ottawa, in training for the priesthood. He withdrew from this program but completed a theology degree at the University of Ottawa in 1967, and received an MA in Philosophy from McMaster University in 1968. Subsequently, he lectured at St. Mary's University in Halifax and at the University of Prince Edward Island. He has taught Humanities and Comparative Religion at Dawson College in Montreal since 1974. Rigelhof has published three novels and a collection of short stories; his novel *Badass on a Softail* and his collection of short stories *Je t'aime, Cow-boy* have been translated into French. He is best known for his artistic memoir *A Blue Boy in a Black Dress*, which was short-listed for the Governor General's Award in 1995. Rigelhof regularly writes book reviews for newspapers and journals, and published *This is Our Writing*, a critique of major Canadian literary figures, in 2000. He has written a biography of George Grant, his professor at McMaster, and following a stroke in early 2003, he published *Nothing Sacred: A Journey Beyond Belief* (2004), which expands on his 1995 memoir. *Bob Ivanochko*

RIPARIAN RIGHTS. Riparian rights establish ownership and use of streams and rivers. These rights include not only the stream and riverbeds, but also a usufructuary right to the water itself. Their importance extends to projects that range from underwater mining and resource rights to the construction of dams, docks and bridges. Riparian rights in Saskatchewan are vested in the Crown by virtue of the Northwest Irrigation Act of 1894, which was introduced in order to ensure central control and thereby prevent substantial legal conflicts over water rights, such as were taking place in the United States. Therefore, rights involving riverbeds as well as river water were appropriated by the federal government according to the 1894 legislation, and then transferred to the province by a 1938 amendment to the Constitution Act, 1930.

The province issues licenses through the Saskatchewan Water Corporation (1984), or SaskWater, for any large-scale commercial enterprises, while domestic use by households and farms does not require such licenses. These licenses are issued after an environmental assessment of the "instream" impact to ensure that the stream or river's ecosystem will not be jeopardized. In anticipation of increasing demand for Saskatchewan water and the importance of water law, the province passed the Saskatchewan Watershed Authority Act in 2002. *Brock Pitawanakwat*

Al Ritchie.

RITCHIE, ALVIN HORACE (1890–1966).

A hockey and football pioneer in western Canada, Al Ritchie was born in Cobden, Ontario in 1890. He moved to Regina with his family prior to **WORLD WAR I**, in which he served as an artilleryman. Ritchie returned to Regina after the war, and worked as a customs and excise appraiser for the federal Department of Customs until his retirement in 1956. Known as the "Silver Fox," Ritchie coached the Regina Pats junior hockey and football teams and is the only person in history to have won national championships in both sports. He guided the Pats hockey club to Memorial Cup championships in 1925 and 1930, and the football team to the 1928 Canadian title. As coach of the Regina Roughriders (later Saskatchewan Roughriders), Ritchie led his teams to win fifty-six consecutive games and nine western championships—but never the Grey Cup, despite four consecutive appearances in the final between 1929 and 1932. Ritchie worked as a scout for the NHL's New York Rangers from 1933 until the time of his death. He was inducted into the Canadian Football Hall of Fame (1963), the Canadian Sports Hall of Fame (1964) and posthumously to the **SASKATCHEWAN SPORTS HALL OF FAME** (1966). Al Ritchie died on February 21, 1966.

Daria Coneghan and Holden Stoffel

FURTHER READING: Calder, B. and G. Andrews. 1984. *Rider Pride: The Story of Canada's Best-Loved Football Team.* Saskatoon: Western Producer Prairie Books.

ROBINSON, MARGUERITE E. (CA. 1902–75).

Born in Minneapolis, USA in about 1902, Marguerite E. Robinson (née Armatage) came to Regina as a teenager, and in the early 1920s was a clerk at Simpson's mail order facility. She trained as a nurse at the Regina General Hospital, graduating in 1925, and worked mainly as a private duty nurse. In 1937 she married L. McK. Robinson, a widowed lawyer with five children, who served several terms on City Council. She became active in women's organizations such as the Local Council of Women and the League of Women Voters (established 1938), sat on the Victorian Order of Nurses board, and served on the Regina Natural History Society executive board.

Writing since the 1930s, she covered numerous subjects including nature, local history, and especially the history of public health and health care in Saskatchewan. Although her study of public health is in manuscript form, she was the published author of *The First Fifty Years* (1967), an authorized account of the **SASKATCHEWAN REGISTERED NURSES ASSOCIATION** done for its fiftieth anniversary. Robinson died on April 17, 1975, in Regina.

Ann Leger-Anderson

ROCAN, MARY (1913–2004).

Mary Rocan played a pioneering role in bringing women's issues to the attention of the provincial government. Born in Brownlee on August 19, 1913, she later moved to Regina; her schooling included high school and business school. She joined the provincial government as a stenographer in 1937. In 1945, Rocan became secretary to the Minimum Wage Board in the newly established Department of Labour. In 1952 she was promoted to Assistant Director of the Labour Standards Branch. Seven years later she became founding supervisor of Saskatchewan's first Women's Bureau, a one-person bureau. Her duties

Mary Rocan.

as executive secretary to the Minimum Wage Board continued as part of her job until retirement in 1975. Subsequently, she served as Chair of the Minimum Wage Board from 1979 to 1990.

As Women's Bureau supervisor, Rocan attended the Saskatchewan hearings of the Royal Commission on the Status of Women. In 1973 she was appointed to the Task Force that reviewed the Commission's recommendations as they applied to Saskatchewan; the resulting report, entitled *Saskatchewan Women, '73*, made it clear that the issues facing women nationally also faced Saskatchewan women. Rocan's community involvements included a leadership role in the Soroptimists and service on the boards of the YWCA, Family Service Bureau, and Pioneer Village. Her many awards included the Governor General's Award in Commemoration of the Person's Case for her efforts to secure women's equality in the workplace (1993). She died on April 19, 2004, in Regina.

Merran Proctor

ROCANVILLE,

town, pop 887, located 25 km N of Moosomin and 15 km S of the **QU'APPELLE VALLEY** on Hwy 8. Above the **QU'APPELLE RIVER** northeast of the town lies the Fort Esperance National Historic Site, the location of two North West Company fur trading posts dating to the late 18th century. The name Rocanville honours the first postmaster, A.H. Rocan Bastien; the community dates to 1884, when a post office was established within a few kilometres of the present townsite. The CPR station was built in 1904, and the community developed as a service and supply centre for the surrounding farming district, with grain and cattle production being the primary activities. In recent years, the area's agricultural industry has grown to include dairy, elk, and fallow deer producers, as well as several beekeepers. In 1924 a local entrepreneur, Ernie Symons, began mass-production in Rocanville of an oil can that he designed for use on farm and industrial machinery. Symons Oilers proved to be the best of their kind, and a small shop turned into a factory. During **WORLD WAR II**, the oil cans were greatly in demand for the maintenance of aircraft, tanks, and other military equipment; by the end of the war, over one million had been produced at the Rocanville plant. On July 1, 1973, the community honoured Ernie Symons for 50 continuous years in business: the day was proclaimed Symons Day, and a giant-scale model oiler was erected on a base at the east entrance to the town. After Symons' death, the factory was purchased by another company, which changed the oil can's design; however, it proved unsuccessful and the plant folded in the late 1980s. Recently, local residents have undertaken the restoration of the oil can factory, which was declared a heritage property in 1996. In the late 1960s, a **POTASH** mine was developed 16 km northeast of Rocanville; acquired by the Potash

Corporation of Saskatchewan in 1977, it continues to employ approximately 330 people. In recent years, the oil industry has been making considerable incursions into the area. The Rocanville and District Museum site has one of the province's most impressive assemblies of vintage tractors, as well as a collection of historic buildings. *David McLennan*

ROCHE PERCÉE (GEOGRAPHICAL FEATURE). Roche Percée or "pierced rock" is located along the **SOURIS RIVER**, and adjacent to the **SOO LINE** of the CPR, 17 km southeast of Estevan. It is a geological feature, a place of worship for the **ASSINIBOINE** people, and a village of 169 people in 2001. The material out of which the Roche Percée structure was formed was once sand on a river bottom; now soft sandstone, it erodes rapidly. The pierced rock which attracted attention over the centuries has broken in the 1900s and is now a simple outcropping.

Assiniboine Chief Dan Kennedy indicated that his people lived in Roche Percée in the late 1700s, returned there to worship up to 1955, and used to eat the wild plums of the area. Prior to European settlement this area was also a battleground. Petroglyphs have been found in the vicinity. *Gregory Salmers*

ROCHE PERCÉE, village, pop 162, located SE of Estevan in the Souris River Valley. It is situated just off Hwy 39, a short distance from the Canada US border. The name of the community is derived from a unique landform, long known to First Nations peoples who camped in the area. Their name for a large, hollowed sandstone outcropping was translated by Métis travelling through the region as la Roche Percée. James Hector of the Palliser Expedition (*see* **PALLISER AND HIND EXPEDITIONS**), who visited the area in 1857, was the first to note coal along the Souris. The North-West Mounted Police made their first major camp here, the Short Creek Camp, during their 1874 trek westward. The **COAL**-mining industry, which gave life to the community, had its beginnings in the 1880s, when individual entrepreneurs and small-time operators began digging the coal, then transporting it by barge down the **SOURIS RIVER**, into the Assiniboine, and then on to Winnipeg. The first viable coal mine in the area was established in 1891. The CPR's **SOO LINE** came through in 1893 and within a few years, dozens of mines were in operation and many lived at the mining camps in the district. Local farmers used coal mining income to help them establish their farming operations. It was a few years before the village proper developed and, on January 12, 1909, Roche Percée was incorporated. Although agriculture, consisting of grain and cattle production, was important in this sandy region, the community's fortunes have always been closely related

to the coal mining industry. Underground operations began to give way to surface "strip" mining by electric shovels in the 1930s and, by the mid-1950s, the era of underground coal mining in the region had come to an end. Today, there are only two companies mining coal in the Estevan-Bienfait area. Their huge dragline operations, however, produce an annual production of approximately 12 million tonnes. Today, Roche Percée is essentially a residential community as businesses, services, and the school have long given way to those in the nearby city of Estevan. *David McLennan*

ROCK ART: *see* **PREHISTORIC ART**

ROCKGLEN, town, pop 450, located on Hwys 2 and 18, 54 km S of Assiniboia and approximately 18 km N of the Canada-US border. Rockglen is situated amidst the Wood Mountain uplands (*see* **WOOD MOUNTAIN PLATEAU**). The higher elevations of the area, along with those in the **CYPRESS HILLS**, were left unglaciated during the Wisconsinan period (*see* **GLACIATION**); thus, remnants of the Tertiary landscape remain. Lacking significant depths of **GLACIAL DEPOSITION**, the Rockglen area hills have yielded many fossils of animals from the Paleozoic and Mesozoic eras. Imprints of tropical plants can be found between layers of sandstone and in the lignite **COAL** seams of the area. Petrified wood is common. Rockglen is located in a picturesque valley surrounded by hills topped with rock formations that have been given names such as Table Rock and the Queen's Chair. Cattle and sheep ranchers began operating in the district in the late 1800s; as the area was opened for homesteading, people of British, French, and Scandinavian origin took up land. The railroad came through in 1926, and amidst rapid construction at the new townsite, the descriptive name of Rockglen was adopted for the burgeoning community. The 1930s were extremely difficult times for the area. In the 1940s, however, a period of recovery and then prosperity began. Today, Rockglen provides the district with a range of businesses and services, as well as an array of facilities for social and recreational activities. Beyond Rockglen are located a number of historic sites and regional parks, as well as **GRASSLANDS NATIONAL PARK**, which is about a half-hour drive west. Native prairie grasses are still to be found in the region's vast tracts of uncultivated land. *David McLennan*

RODENTS. There are twenty-seven native rodent species in Saskatchewan (*see* Table RO-1 on the following page). At least two more species (the long-tailed vole, *Microtus ochrogaster*, and the Western harvest mouse, *Reithrodontomys megalotis*) may occur naturally because they are found nearby. Additional species associated with European settlement are the Eastern fox squirrel (*Sciurus niger*)

and Eastern gray squirrel (*Sciurus carolinensis*) of eastern North America, and the European house mouse (*Mus musculus*), the Norway rat (*Rattus norvegicus*), and occasionally the black rat (*Rattus rattus*). The squirrels occur widely in urban areas of southern Saskatchewan. The rats are commensal species in buildings and garbage dumps. Efforts at eliminating rats from many parts of the province have been successful. House mice are found mostly at building sites, but small numbers are found in the wild in the south.

Beavers are the largest Saskatchewan rodents; exceptional individuals exceed 39 kg and 1.2 m in length. The 12 g olive-backed pocket mouse is the smallest species. The shortest rodents in the province are the extremely short-tailed 120 mm sagebrush voles. The most common rodent in the province is the meadow vole; deer mice, although more abundant in the southwest, are rarely seen. The semi-aquatic beavers and muskrats have dense fur that traps an insulating layer of air that prevents the skin of the animals from contacting water. These pelts are highly desirable, and European exploration and early economic development of Saskatchewan were largely driven by the search for and the marketing of beaver pelts. Beavers remain the dominant fur-producing species: the 28,299 pelts sold in 2001–02 from the province were 32% of the total fur take, representing $688,000 (approximately 35%) of the value of furs produced in that year. Over-trapping virtually extirpated the species by the early 1900s. However, due to reintroduction, the animals are now found in virtually all suitable habitats across the province.

Beavers are known for their large flattened tail that is slapped on the water as a warning and serves as a site for storage of fat. The animals dam small streams; the impounded water is used for protection as well as transport and cache of branches and

DAVID KRUGHOFF PHOTO

Female porcupine, Buffalo Pound Park, February 2005.

Table RO-1. Saskatchewan's Native Rodents

Species	Scientific Name	Family	Length	Tail	Mass	Distribution
American beaver	Castor canadensis	Castoridae	1.25 m	330 mm	12-29 kg	Provincial
North American porcupine	Erethizon dorsatum	Erithizontidae	775 mm	225 mm	8-11 kg	Provincial
Northern pocket gopher	Thomomys talpoides	Geomyidae	195 mm	56 mm	90 g	Central and south
Ord's kangaroo rat	Dipodomys ordii	Heteromyidae	270 mm	145 mm	65 g	Southwest
Olive-backed pocket mouse	Perognathus fasciatus	Heteromyidae	120-145 mm	59 mm	10-13 g	Central and south
Southern red-backed vole	Clethrionomys gapperi	Muridae	135-145 mm	36 mm	15-18 g	North, Central, Cypress Hills
Sagebrush vole	Lemmiscus curtatus	Muridae	120 mm	18 mm	25 g	South, especially Southwest
Prairie vole	Microtus ochrogaster	Muridae	150 mm	28 mm	40 g	Central and Southeast
Meadow vole	Microtus pennsylvanicus	Muridae	145 mm	37 mm	25-60 g	Provincial
Taiga vole	Microtus xanthognathus	Muridae	178-207mm	39 mm	82-112 g	North
Western heather vole	Phenacomys intermedius	Muridae	140 mm	30 mm	26 g	North, north central
Common muskrat	Ondatra zibethicus	Muridae	450-550 mm	138 mm	900-1100 g	Provincial
Northern bog lemming	Synaptomys borealis	Muridae	127 mm	1524 mm	32 g	North, Central
Bushy-tailed woodrat	Neotoma cinerea	Muridae	350 mm	163 mm	300 g	Lower Frenchman River
Northern grasshopper mouse	Onychomys leucogaster	Muridae	130-140 mm	35 mm	30-40 g	South
White-footed mouse	Peromyscus leucopus	Muridae	170 mm	76 mm	16 g	Southeast
Deer mouse	Peromyscus maniculatus	Muridae	160 mm	75 mm	22 g	Provincial, except Northeast
Black-tailed prairie dog	Cynomys ludovicianus	Sciuridae	390 mm	86 mm	1 kg	Southwest- Val Marie region
Northern flying squirrel	Glaucomys sabinus	Sciuridae	320 mm	143 mm	150 g	North, Central
Red squirrel	Tamiasciurus hudsonicus	Sciuridae	320 mm	124 mm	240 g	North, Central, Cypress Hills
Richardson's ground squirrel	Spermophilus richardsonii	Sciuridae	205-320 mm	75 mm	330-410 g	Central, South
Franklin's ground squirrel	Spermophilus franklinii	Sciuridae	390 mm	135 mm	450 g	Central, Southeast
Thirteen-lined ground squirrel	Spermophilus tridecemlineatus	Sciuridae	270 mm	94 mm	160 g	Central, South
Least chipmunk	Neotamias minimus	Sciuridae	215 mm	95 mm	40-45 g	Central, Southeast
Woodchuck	Marmota monax	Sciuridae	530 mm	130 mm	1.1-2.3 kg	North, Central, and Southeast
Meadow jumping mouse	Zapus hudsonicus	Zapodidae	210 mm	130 mm	17 g	North, Central
Western jumping mouse	Zapus princeps	Zapodidae	230-250 mm	141 mm	25 g	Central, South

sections of tree trunks, from which the bark is eaten for winter food. The animals make well-defined trails and often canals that lead from the pond to treed areas. In ponds, the animals build large lodges with an entrance under the water. On rivers, beavers burrow deeply into the banks to make shelters. Beaver ponds provide habitat for waterfowl, frogs, and other aquatic organisms. Flooding often drowns trees that remain standing, providing habitat for swallows and other cavity-nesting birds. Over long periods, beaver dams gradually fill in with vegetation that, in northern areas, can eventually convert a small stream into a series of bogs.

The second-largest Saskatchewan rodent is the porcupine, which occurs throughout the province, including the sparsely treed plains. The animals eat a variety of vegetable foods during the summer, and subsist on the cambium layer of bark and sometimes needles of conifers during the winter. Pressed by a threat, they instinctively crouch and raise their quills. This is a habit that, while effective against most predators, accounts for the many porcupines

run over on roadways. Porcupines cannot throw their quills, but loose ones can fly off when the animal attempts to slap the attacker with its heavily quilled tail. Once imbedded, the barbed quills work their way into the flesh; cutting the ends of the hollow quills may cause them to relax and make them easier to pull out. Porcupines mate in the manner of other mammals, with the female flattening her quills.

Burrowing by rodents such as ground squirrels and northern pocket gophers turns over the soil. Soil mounds are locations for the establishment of new plants. Northern pocket gophers can become numerous in alfalfa plantings and gardens, and do considerable damage by eating the roots. The animals' mounds can make the ground rough, making haying difficult and occasionally resulting in damaged machinery. In addition to using their powerful front limbs, pocket gophers dig with their teeth. They also burrow under the snow and fill the snow tunnels with dirt from burrowing; when the snow melts in the spring, a pattern of dirt casts is left.

They regularly forage above ground during the night, and are a frequent prey of the great horned owl. Northern pocket gophers are sometimes called "moles" because of the mounds of earth they push to the surface; but moles are insectivorous animals whereas pocket gophers are vegetarian. "Pocket" applies to the external cheek pouches that are used for transporting food. While "gopher" is often used for ground squirrels, "ground squirrel" is preferred to avoid confusion with pocket gophers.

Richardson ground squirrels prefer grasslands with sparse vegetation, and often increase in numbers when grazing reduces vegetation. Control measures are most effective before the young are born in late April and early May, and before the females start to enter hibernation in August. Unlike Franklin's ground squirrels ("bush gophers"), which are frequently encountered in the parklands, and also the distinctive thirteen-lined ground squirrel ("striped gopher"), Richardson's ground squirrels do not have to drink water to survive.

Rodents are implicated in the spread of disease.

Hanta virus can cause serious infection in humans. The virus is highly contagious among deer mice and other small rodents, but it does not cause severe illness. Spread of the virus to humans is usually through dust from dried droppings or urine. Wearing dust masks and rubber gloves when cleaning up mouse nests or dusty areas frequented by mice, such as granaries, is recommended. Sylvatic plague, while rare, can be contracted during handling of Richardson's ground squirrels and prairie dogs.

Numbers of small rodents vary dramatically. In forested areas, meadow voles undergo a 3–5 year cycle. On the plains, where weather is less predictable, very large numbers of meadow voles and deer mice occur when favourable conditions prevail. Meadow voles are particularly likely to increase because of the short 3–4 week generation time and ability to breed year-round, especially if food such as unharvested crops is available under heavy snow cover. Many rodents hibernate in winter. Northern populations of black-tailed prairie dog undergo true hibernation, whereas more southern populations do not. Other hibernators include meadow and Western jumping mice, woodchucks, all the ground squirrels, and probably olive-backed pocket mice.

Tim Schowalter

FURTHER READING: Baker, R.J., et al. 2003. *Revised Checklist of North American Mammals North of Mexico.* Museum of Texas Technical University Occasional Papers, Number 229; Banfield, A.W.F. 1974. *The Mammals of Canada.* Toronto: University of Toronto Press; 2001. *Natural Neighbours: Selected Mammals of Saskatchewan.* Regina: Canadian Plains Research Center.

ROE, JEAN A. Originally from Newfoundland, Jean Roe is an active member of Saskatchewan's social community. During **WORLD WAR II**, she was director of the United Services Organization at Corner Brook, Newfoundland. After moving to Saskatchewan in 1966, she became involved with the Moose Jaw City Council, serving as alderwoman from 1979 to 1988. She has been director of the Canadian Arthritis Society and coordinator of the XYZ Society of Moose Jaw. On April 21, 1982, Roe was invested as a Member of the Order of Canada.

ROGERS, OTTO DONALD (1935–). Otto Rogers was born on December 19, 1935, and grew up on a farm near Kelfield, Saskatchewan. He went to high school in Kindersley, and then in 1952–53 to the Saskatoon Teachers' College, where **WYNONA MULCASTER** influenced him to study art. He completed a BSc in Art Education and an MSc in Fine Art from the University of Wisconsin, where he studied from 1954 to 1959. His work won prizes at state exhibitions, and he received several scholarships and awards. After a few months in New York, he

COURTESY OF THE MACKENZIE ART GALLERY 1977-022

Otto Rogers, "Pink Sky," 1975, acrylic on canvas, 182.7 x 182.7 cm, MacKenzie Art Gallery, University of Regina Collection, gift of the MacKenzie Art Gallery Society.

returned to teach in the Art Department at the **UNIVERSITY OF SASKATCHEWAN**; there he was a professor of art from 1960 to 1984, helped organize the Emma Lake Art Workshops, and was head of the department for twelve years. Rogers has worked in a number of media and has received numerous awards for his painting, sculpting and graphic arts. His work is available in major galleries and in private collections in many countries. His abstract work is greatly influenced by prairie space and by his religious beliefs.

Barbara Nelson, whom he married in 1959, introduced him to the Baha'i faith, and Rogers became a leader in local Baha'i activities. He accepted increasing responsibilities within the Baha'i Board in Canada and internationally. These responsibilities and his ongoing artwork led Rogers to move to Haifa (Israel) to work at the Baha'i headquarters' International Teaching Centre. Rogers returned to Canada in 1998 to Milford, Ontario, where he works out of his award-winning studio, designed by the architect Siamak Hariri, who is married to Rogers' daughter Sasha. Sasha Rogers, also a painter, is greatly influenced by her father's work.

Bob Ivanochko

ROMAN CATHOLIC CATHEDRALS. When the first Catholic missionaries and settlers came to Saskatchewan, one of the first community buildings to be constructed was the church. The first churches were necessarily humble affairs, but as time went on and the communities grew and prospered, more substantial structures were erected. When communities were able to do so, the churches were adorned with special works of liturgical art in the form of stained glass, statues and crucifixes, carved altars, stations of the cross, and specially constructed baptismal fonts, tabernacles and other liturgical items. The key church building in each diocese is its cathe-

dral, which will often surpass ordinary churches in architectural design and décor.

Holy Rosary Cathedral, the mother church of the Regina archdiocese, was built in 1912–13 under the aegis of Olivier Elzéar Mathieu, Regina's first archbishop. It is of cruciform/Romanesque design, with elegant twin spires that dominate the skyline of Regina's west-central area, now known as the Cathedral District. The cathedral contains a series of stained glass windows designed by French artist André Rault, a ceramic mural by artist Lorraine Malach, entitled "The Glorious Mysteries," and a Casavant organ which was rededicated in 1993 and named the McGuigan Casavant Organ in honour of Sister Marion McGuigan, educator and humanitarian. Holy Rosary Cathedral suffered a disastrous fire on April 12, 1976, in the south end of the church; the damage was repaired, the church redecorated, and a further redecoration took place in 1992.

Sacred Heart Cathedral was built on the site of the first Catholic mission in Prince Albert, near the banks of the **NORTH SASKATCHEWAN RIVER**. It was completed in 1914 at a cost of approximately $103,000. The cathedral's exterior was constructed of a dark red-brown contrasting with naturally light Manitoba Tyndall stone. The cathedral was built in the form of a cross, in keeping with the Romanesque style, and buttresses help to support the walls. In niches above the doors are statues of the Virgin and Saint Joseph, and another niche in the apex of the roof holds a bronze statue of the Sacred Heart. The interior of the cathedral contains paintings by Count **BERTHOLD IMHOFF** and Peter Haip, high-relief Stations of the Cross, statues of Mary, Joseph, Saint Patrick, Saint John, and a life-size statue of the Sacred Heart, and beautiful stained-glass windows, four of which are twenty-five feet tall. Dedication of the cathedral took place on May 2, 1915.

St. Paul's Cathedral. The cornerstone of the present St. Paul's was laid by Sir Wilfrid Laurier on July 25, 1910, and a year later the completed church was formally dedicated by Archbishop Langevin of St. Boniface. A chime of Packard bells and a Casavan organ were installed in 1912. Although St. Paul's was named a pro-cathedral in 1921, it was not until March 1934, with the establishment of the new Diocese of Saskatoon, that it was elevated to the rank of cathedral. In 1945 stained glass windows were installed in memory of those parishioners who had lost their lives in **WORLD WAR II**, and additional ones were installed following the fire of 1976. Because it was built as a parish church rather than as a cathedral, St. Paul's is simpler in style than the other Catholic cathedrals in Saskatchewan.

St. Peter's Cathedral. Benedictine monks arrived at Muenster, Saskatchewan on May 21, 1903. On June 29, the decision was reached by the monks and the first German-Catholic settlers to erect

Cathedrale Notre-Dame de L'Assomption (our Lady of the Assumption), Gravelbourg.

a 20' x 40' log church near the monastery. It was called St. Peter's Church in honour of Abbot Peter Engel, OSB, of St. John's Abbey, Minneapolis. In 1907 the foundations for the second, larger church (120' x 56') were laid. Financial difficulties delayed its construction until 1909, and the church with its two 60' towers was officially opened on July 10, 1910. When Count **BERTHOLD IMHOFF** visited the abbey in 1919, he offered to paint the entire sanctuary as a gift to Abbot Bruno Doerfler, his friend; this included eighty life-sized paintings of saints. Imhoff later painted the rest of the church for $3,000. He further honoured Abbot Bruno by painting the abbot's face on his depiction of St. Paul. On May 6, 1921, St. Peter's Colony became St. Peter's Abbey Nullius under the ecclesiastical jurisdiction of the abbot, with St. Peter's as the cathedral church. In 1998 the territory became part of the Saskatoon Diocese, and St. Peter's is no longer a cathedral.

Our Lady of the Assumption Cathedral. The patron of the church, when it was built in 1919 and later named cathedral church of the newly formed diocese of Gravelbourg in 1930, was St. Philomena. In 1963, the name of the cathedral was changed to Our Lady of the Assumption. The church building is considered to be a landmark in the Gravelbourg community. Of particular interest is the artwork of Fr. Charles Maillard, who between 1921 and 1931 embellished the church with scenes from the Old and New Testaments. The Bishop's Chair is a Louis XIV-style episcopal throne dated to 1780.

Gravelbourg ceased to be a separate diocese in 1998, and its cathedral is now a "co-cathedral."

Margaret Sanche

FURTHER READING: 1988. *Archdiocese of Regina: A History, 1910–1985.* Muenster, SK: Saint Peter's Press; Lavigne, S. 1990. *Kaleidoscope, Many Cultures–One Faith: A History of the Diocese of Prince Albert.* Muenster, SK: Saint Peter's Press; Robertson, D.F. 1982. *The Sword of St. Paul: A History of the Diocese of Saskatoon, 1933–1983.* Saskatoon: Episcopal Corporation of Saskatoon.

ROMAN CATHOLIC CONGREGATIONS OF MEN RELIGIOUS.

Although Jesuits and other Roman Catholic priests sometimes accompanied early explorers and fur traders in their travels though the western prairies, the first Roman Catholic religious order to establish missions in the Canadian North-West was the Congregation of the Missionary Oblates of Mary Immaculate (OMI), founded in 1822 by Eugène de Mazenod in France. Oblate priests had came from France to Red River in 1841; later, in 1846, Fathers **ALEXANDRE TACHÉ**, OMI and Louis-François Laflèche had established the first Roman Catholic mission in what is now Saskatchewan at Ile-à-la-Crosse. During the settlement period in the west in the latter part of the 19th century, with the coming of the railroad and the opening up of agricultural land for homesteads, other religious congregations of priests and brothers

arrived to serve the pastoral needs of the new communities. Members of religious orders engaged in parish work in rural areas and cities, and established educational institutions, both secondary and post-secondary. Later, other works were undertaken, including the publication of Catholic newspapers and catechetical materials, as well as the establishment of retreat houses and seminaries.

In addition to the French Oblates, who served primarily as missionaries to the Native peoples and as pastors to the French Catholics, other members of that order came to Saskatchewan to serve the Catholics of German and Polish descent; eventually, these Oblates were separated from the French and English Oblates into separate Oblate provinces. The Benedictines came to the Muenster area from Collegeville, Minnesota, and set up St. Peter's Abbey in 1903. They established parishes for the German people who had come to form St. Peter's Colony, and in 1904 began publication of *St. Peter's Bote*, the forerunner of the present-day Catholic newspaper, the *Prairie Messenger*. In 1927, they established **ST. PETER'S COLLEGE**.

The Franciscans (Order of Friars Minor, OFM), who had opened their first western Canadian friary in Edmonton in 1909, began to travel from there to the Sedley-Kendal area to preach retreats in 1926. In 1930, they were invited by Archbishop McGuigan to establish a friary in Regina, and in 1932 they founded Regina Cleri Seminary for the training of young men for the priesthood. Over the years, the Franciscans also engaged in parish work, established a Franciscan Third Order, and in 1963 founded St. Michael's Retreat House (Lumsden), a work which continues today.

The Basilians (Congregation of St. Basil, CSB) came to Saskatoon from Toronto in 1936 to found **ST. THOMAS MORE COLLEGE** as a federated Arts college on the campus of the university, and they continue to be involved in this work to the present time. Basilian priests also taught at St. Paul's High School and engaged in parish work in Saskatoon for many years.

The Jesuits (Society of Jesus, SJ) established Campion High School/College in Regina in 1917–18, and continue to serve on faculty at **CAMPION COLLEGE**, a federated college of the **UNIVERSITY OF REGINA**.

The Redemptorists (Congregation of the Most Holy Redeemer, CSsR) came to Yorkton in 1904, and later became involved in parish and mission work in Regina and Moose Jaw (1914), Prince Albert (1930), and Saskatoon (1934).Some Redemptorists transferred to the Ukrainian Catholic rite in order to better serve the pastoral needs of the Ukrainian Catholics of Saskatchewan.

A number of other religious congregations of men served in Saskatchewan over the years, including Missionaries of La Salette, the Premonstratension Fathers, Les Fils de Marie Immaculée, Brothers of Christian Schools (who founded the Ukrainian **ST. JOSEPH'S COLLEGE** in Yorkton), Prêtres de Sainte-Marie, Brothers of the Sacred Heart, the Canons of the Immaculate Conception, Prêtres de Ste-Marie de Tenchebray, the Dominicans, Prêtres des Missions Etrangères, Society of Christ, Frères St-Gabriel, and Missionaries of the Holy Family.

At the present time, men's religious congregations continue to serve in the province of Saskatchewan. In the Regina Archdiocese we find Franciscans, Jesuits, Missionaries of the Holy Family, Oblates of Mary Immaculate, and Society of Christ; in Prince Albert Diocese there are Missionaries of the Holy Family and Oblates of Mary Immaculate; in Saskatoon, Basilians, Benedictines, Missionaries of the Holy Family, Oblates of Mary Immaculate, and Redemptorists; and in the northern dioceses, the Oblates of Mary Immaculate.   *Margaret Sanche*

ROMAN CATHOLIC CONGREGATIONS OF WOMEN RELIGIOUS.

Catholic women religious ("sisters" or "nuns") played a significant role in laying the foundation of the province's education, health care, and social service systems. Hundreds of members of over 30 different religious orders established schools and **HOSPITALS** during the pioneer era, and today continue to serve in a wide variety of ministries. While most of the pioneering nuns came from Europe, their numbers quickly grew as prairie girls "entered the convent" taking vows of poverty, chastity and obedience—thereby dedicating their lives to the service of God through the education of youth and care of the sick, aged, needy and poor.

By the 1930s nearly forty boarding schools had been established in Saskatchewan by various teaching orders. The first nuns to come to this province were three **SISTERS OF CHARITY OF MONTREAL** ("Grey Nuns"), who opened a school in Ile-à-la-Crosse in 1860 and also ran an orphanage. They were followed by the Sisters of the Assumption, who came from Nicolet, Quebec in 1891 and taught in a **RESIDENTIAL SCHOOL** at Onion Lake until 1972. They also had boarding schools and taught in Battleford (1893–1962), Thunderchild (1901–48), Biggar (1927–68) and Val Marie (1939–82). Les Filles de la Providence came in 1897 from Brittany, France to Prince Albert, where they opened a boarding school for girls. Later, they built similar schools in Prud'homme, St. Louis and St. Brieux, and taught in almost twenty public schools in the area.

The Grey Nuns taught in Indian Residential Schools in Lebret (1884–1975), Lestock (1897–1932), and Beauval (1927–71). The **SISTERS OF THE PRESENTATION OF MARY** came from Quebec in 1903 to work with the Oblates in the Residential School for **CREE** First Nations in Duck Lake, and later expanded their educational work to twelve schools in Prince Albert and the surrounding region. In

1904 the **SISTERS OF OUR LADY OF SION** came from Paris to Prince Albert, where they ran a boarding and day school for girls until 1951, when it was turned over to the Presentation Sisters. The **SISTERS OF OUR LADY OF THE CROSS** came from Grenoble, France in 1905 to open a boarding school in Forget (1905–64), followed by others in Montmartre (1920–70), Wauchope (1917–64), Redvers (1964–80), and Cantal (1940–64). In 1905 the Sisters of the Cross came from LaPuye, France and ran boarding schools in Bellegarde (until 1964), Lafleche (1915–58), and Willow Bunch (1914–63). They taught in several public schools as well.

The next group of Sisters came just before **WORLD WAR I**. In 1913 the **SISTERS OF NOTRE DAME** came from Auvergne, France to Ponteix, where they ran a boarding school until 1952 and taught in six public schools (1940–76). The Sisters of Sion also ran boarding schools in Moose Jaw (1914–91) and Saskatoon (1919–66), operated a women's residence in Saskatoon (1917–76), and taught in several elementary schools in both cities. In 1913 the **SISTERS OF CHARITY OF ST. LOUIS** came from Quebec to open a school for boys in Moose Jaw, followed by schools in Radville (1915–73), Wilcox (1920), Swift Current (1920-61), and eight others in the southern region of the province. The **URSULINE** Sisters, a teaching order founded in Italy in 1535, came from Germany to this province in 1913 and opened boarding schools for girls in Bruno (1922–82), Vibank (1923–70), and Prelate (1919–). The Ursulines taught in over 100 locations throughout Saskatchewan. By the mid-1960s the Prelate Ursulines alone had ninety teachers in villages and towns, mainly in the western part of the province. In 1921 the Loretto Sisters came from Toronto to Sedley, where they operated a girls' boarding school for seventy years, with seventy Sisters serving there during that period. In addition, they taught in numerous schools in Regina, Weyburn, Estevan and Saskatoon.

Other teaching orders and their major schools included the **SISTERS OF OUR LADY OF THE MISSIONS** (Lebret 1899–74 and Regina 1926-69), the Sisters of the Child Jesus (Prince Albert 1915 and North Battleford (1925–82), **SCHOOL SISTERS OF NOTRE DAME** (Leipzig, 1926-69), Sisters of St. Joseph of Toronto (Rosetown 1935–70), Sisters of Jesus and Mary (Gravelbourg, 1915–70), Missionary Oblates (Gravelbourg 1918 and Lestock 1932–79), and the Ukrainian-rite **SISTERS SERVANTS OF MARY IMMACULATE** (Yorkton 1915). In most of the Sisters' schools, choral singing, piano, drama and art were given a major place in education, thus contributing to the rich cultural life characteristic of the province today.

The first Catholic hospitals were opened in 1907 by the Grey Nuns in Regina and Saskatoon (with schools of nursing attached), followed by others in

Biggar (1923-67), Rosthern (1927–35), Gravelbourg (1928–2000), Ile-à-la-Crosse (1927–2001), La Loche (1943–81), Zenon Park(1972–73), and Esterhazy (1987–89). In 1906 the **SISTERS OF CHARITY OF THE IMMACULATE CONCEPTION** came from Saint John, New Brunswick to Prince Albert, where they opened St. Patrick's Orphanage (1906–73) and Holy Family Hospital (1910–97). In Regina they also ran a school for girls from 1921 to 1968. In 1911 three **FRANCISCAN SISTERS OF ST. ELIZABETH** came from Austria to Humboldt, where they opened a hospital and a school of nursing (1923-69), as well as hospitals in Macklin (1922), Scott (1924–32), and Cudworth (1924); they later served in Seniors' Homes in Saskatoon and Humboldt. A hospital was opened in Moose Jaw by the **SISTERS OF PROVIDENCE OF ST. VINCENT DE PAUL** from Kingston in 1912, and in Estevan by the Sisters of St. Joseph of Peterborough in 1937. The Notre Dame Sisters ran hospitals in Ponteix (1918–69), Val Marie, and Zenon Park. Homes for the Aged were founded by the Sisters of Our Lady of the Cross in Whitewood (1920–68), Marcelin (1944–56), Prince Albert (1956–92), and Weyburn (1953–70).

Other religious orders engaged in social work. The Sisters of Service who came to Saskatoon from Toronto (1946–76) ministered among families in crisis. They did similar work in Regina and carried out an extensive Home Religion Program by correspondence from 1934 to about 1980. They also conducted workshops to train catechists in the rural areas of the province. The Sisters of Social Service of Hamilton came in 1923 to Stockholm to minister to the Hungarian Catholic community, and in 1949 to Regina where they engaged in parish work and teaching. In 1951, Father G.W. Kuckartz, OMI, of Battleford, founded the **SISTERS OF MISSION SERVICE** to serve in a wide variety of ministries.

The province owes much to these hundreds of nuns who devoted their lives to the education of youth and the care of the sick and needy, often in situations of extreme hardship and poverty. They served as apostles of Catholic faith as well as founding mothers of the province's education, health and social service systems, thereby helping to shape a more gentle Saskatchewan culture.   *Teresita Kambeitz*

ROMAN CATHOLIC DIOCESES AND BISHOPS.

The first Roman Catholic administrative and pastoral structures established during the missionary period in the prairie west of Canada were apostolic vicariates covering vast geographical territories. Parishes, dioceses and archdioceses were formed later, when the Catholic population increased with the arrival of settlers from other parts of North America and Europe. At the time of Saskatchewan's entry into Confederation in 1905, the province was part of one large vicariate which was administered as a mission of the Diocese of St.

Albert (Alberta). The Apostolic Vicariate of Saskatchewan had been erected in 1890, with Prince Albert as the see city, and Bishop Albert Pascal, OMI, had been consecrated as its first apostolic vicar in 1891. By 1905, Catholic priests, sisters and brothers were continuing to minister to First Nations and Métis, mainly in the north and central regions of Saskatchewan; by that time Catholic settlers from eastern Canada, the British Isles, western and eastern Europe, and the United States had begun the great migration to the Canadian prairie lands, bringing with them the need for Catholic parishes, schools and hospitals. As the Catholic population of the province increased, the diocesan territories were changed to meet the needs of the people.

The Vicariate of Saskatchewan became the Diocese of Prince Albert (suffragan of St. Boniface) in 1907; and a few years later the geographical territory of the diocese was reduced with the formation in 1910 of the Vicariate of Keewatin in the north, and the Diocese of Regina in the south. The Diocese of Prince Albert became a suffragan diocese of Regina in 1915 when the latter became an archdiocese; and in 1921, with the increase in the Catholic population of Saskatoon, its name was changed to Diocese of Prince Albert and Saskatoon. Also in 1921, the Benedictine Abbey of St. Peter and its surrounding parishes became the Diocese of Muenster (St. Peter's Abbacy or Abbey Nullius). The Diocese of Saskatoon was established as a separate diocese in 1933; at that time also the northern boundary of the Diocese of Prince Albert was moved to forty miles north of Green Lake to include a portion of the Diocese of Keewatin. In September 1998, diocesan boundaries were changed again, this time forming fewer dioceses with larger geographical territories. The former Diocese of Gravelbourg was amalgamated with other dioceses; most of its parishes became part of the Archdiocese of Regina, with the German-Catholic St. Joseph's Colony parishes added to the Diocese of Saskatoon. The parishes of the Abbey Nullius of Muenster were incorporated into the Diocese of Saskatoon, and a portion of the northern part of the Archdiocese of Regina was also transferred to the Saskatoon Diocese at that time.

Saskatchewan Roman Catholics are currently in the care of five dioceses: three full dioceses in southern Saskatchewan (Regina, Prince Albert and Saskatoon), with the Archdiocese of Regina as the metropolitan see; and two regions in northern Saskatchewan, which are part of dioceses in Manitoba and the Northwest Territories.

The Archdiocese of Regina has been served over the years by the following archbishops: Olivier-Elzéar Mathieu (bishop 1911–15/archbishop 1915–29); James McGuigan (1930–34); Peter Monahan (1935–47); Michael Cornelius O'Neill (1947–73); Charles Halpin (1973–94); and Peter Mallon (1995–).

The Diocese of Prince Albert has been in the care of bishops Albert Pascal, OMI (apostolic vicar 1891–1907; bishop 1907–20); Joseph-Henri Prud'homme (bishop of Prince Albert and Saskatoon 1921–33; bishop of Prince Albert 1933–37); Reginald Duprat (1938–52); Leo Blais (1952–59); Laurent Morin (1959–83); and Blaise Morand (1983–).

The Diocese of Saskatoon has had six bishops: Gerald Murray, CSsR (1934–44), Philip Pocock (1944–51), Francis Klein (1952-67), James Mahoney (1967–95), James Weisgerber (1996–2000), and Albert LeGatt (2001–).

The Diocese of Gravelbourg was served by seven bishops: Jean Villeneuve, OMI (1930–31), Louis Melanson (1932–36), Joseph Guy, OMI (1937–42), Joseph Lemieux, OP (1944–53), Aimé Décosse (1953–73), Noel Delaquis (1973–95); and Raymond Roussin, SM (1995–98).

During the period that St. Peter's Abbacy was an Abbey Nullius, it was served by the following abbots-ordinary: Michael Ott, OSB (1921–26), Severinus Gertken, OSB (1926–60), Jerome Weber, OSB (1960–90), and Peter Novecosky, OSB (1990–98).

The territories of two northern dioceses have portions of Saskatchewan under their jurisdiction: Keewatin-LePas Archdiocese (The Pas, MB) and Mackenzie-Fort Smith Diocese (Yellowknife, NT). The present bishop of Mackenzie-Fort Smith is Denis Croteau, OMI (1986–), and the archbishop of Keewatin-Le Pas is Peter Sutton, OMI (1986–).

Margaret Sanche

ROMAN CATHOLIC MISSIONS IN THE NORTH-WEST AND SASKATCHEWAN (19TH–20TH CENTURIES).

The establishment of Catholic missions among the First Nations of Saskatchewan, like those of Manitoba and Alberta, did not come about as a result of a preconceived plan or strategy on the part of the Missionary Oblates of Mary Immaculate. The establishment, as well as the location, of these missions was a pragmatic response to circumstances and needs. To begin with, the Oblates were always short of human and financial resources: missions could not be established where it was convenient for the missionaries, but where the chances of a successful venture were highest. When the **SAULTEAUX** in the immediate vicinity of St. Boniface demonstrated little interest in Oblate efforts, the latter turned their attention to the Chipewyan of Île-à-la-Crosse, who were reported to be more receptive to the Christian message. In addition to a receptive audience, Oblate missions tended to be established at or near a Hudson's Bay Company post, where First Nations were accustomed to come to trade at seasonal intervals.

ALEXANDRE-ANTONIN TACHÉ and *abbé* Louis-François Laflèche were responsible for the establishment of St. Jean–Baptiste Mission at Île-à-la-Crosse in 1846. In time, this mission served as a strategic central base for the expansion of the missionary frontier, as missionaries visited **LAC LA RONGE**, **REINDEER LAKE**, Cumberland, Pelican Lake, Portage La Loche, as well as Fort Chipewyan on **LAKE ATHABASCA**, which became the main base for the establishment of missions in the Mackenzie Basin. In this early period of the expansion of the missionary frontier in the northern and central regions of what is now Saskatchewan, other missions were established at Green Lake and Battleford (1875), Onion Lake and Cumberland House (1877), and Pelican Narrows (1878). In the meantime, with the exception of accompanying **MÉTIS** buffalo hunters, there was little missionary activity in the southern regions. In 1865, Bishop Taché visited the **QU'APPELLE VALLEY** and selected the site for St. Florent Mission for the purpose of facilitating the instruction of the large number of Métis resident in the region and the dispensing of sacraments to them. From Lebret, Joseph Lestanc, Jules Decorby and Joseph Hugonnard accompanied the hunters in their camps in Willow Bunch, **WOOD MOUNTAIN**, and the **CYPRESS HILLS**. After 1870 a large number of Métis left Manitoba and settled in the Duck Lake region, and permanent missions were founded at St. Laurent de Grandin (1871), Duck Lake (1877), and St. Louis de Langevin (1885).

The decline of buffalo and the signing of treaties with the Plains tribes necessitated a change in Oblate strategy and a consolidation of their missionary efforts. Since there was a definite advantage to being located on or near a reserve, some missions were relocated and new ones erected. Early schools built by the Oblates in their missions, and those established later by the federal government and confided to the jurisdiction of the Oblates, became extensions of their frontier "parish." Through practical education the Oblates hoped to continue and enhance their apostolic and missionary efforts, and simultaneously prepare the First Nations for the changes necessitated by the end of the old order based on the buffalo hunt. The advance of settlement created additional responsibilities for Oblate missions, which henceforth would have to minister to the needs of settlers until regular parishes were erected and staffed with a resident clergy. The first mass in Regina, for example, was celebrated in 1885 by Pierre Saint-Germain, an Oblate stationed in Willow Bunch. The settlement era imposed incredible linguistic demands on missionaries because of the polyglot nature of the newcomers, and increased the labours of the missionaries because the immigrants were spread out over large areas of the province. From Fort Ellice, near the Manitoba–Saskatchewan border, Jules Decorby initially ministered only to the Indians and Métis but, when settlers began to arrive in the region in the 1880s his ministry took him as far as Swift Current and, in these travels, he laid the foundations for future parishes in Lestock, Marieval, St. Philippe, Moose Jaw, and Swift Current. Itinerant missions among newly arrived settlers were gradually replaced by permanent parishes that served outlying or frontier areas. While the Oblates continued to assume responsibility for the First Nations missions, secular clergy were arriving in larger numbers to serve as pastors in the settled areas. The erection of the Diocese of Regina in 1910 was indicative of a maturing Catholic establishment in Saskatchewan.

Raymond Huel

ROMAN CATHOLICS. The history of Roman Catholicism in Saskatchewan goes back to the early French explorers and fur traders who brought their Catholic faith with them to the Canadian North-West. The first Roman Catholic mission to serve the Métis and Native peoples of the region was established by the French **OBLATES OF MARY IMMACULATE** at Ile-à-la-Crosse in 1846 (*see* **TACHÉ, ROMAN CATHOLIC MISSIONS IN THE NORTH-WEST AND SASKATCHEWAN**). In the following decades, Oblates and groups of women religious arrived to set up churches, schools and hospitals in the newly formed communities. Catholic schools established in the early years became the basis for Catholic education rights set out in the Saskatchewan Act of 1905 (*see* **SEPARATE SCHOOL DIVISIONS**). During the settlement period at the end of the 19th and in the early part of the 20th centuries, many Catholics were among homesteaders and other settlers who arrived in what is now Saskatchewan from Quebec, Ontario, the Maritimes, Britain, and continental Europe. Soon there was a pressing need for more dioceses and bishops, priests and sisters to serve the religious, educational and health-care needs of the Catholic communities. As more newcomers arrived, the ethnic make-up of the Catholic population shifted from mainly French- and English-speaking to include also German, Polish, Ukrainian and other groups.

Many of the Catholics who came to the Canadian west settled together in formal or informal bloc settlements or colonies, and their shared culture, language and religious faith helped to form strong communal identities during those difficult early years. For these groups, it was important to have priests and sisters who could speak the same language. In the case of German- and Polish-speaking people from eastern Europe, Oblate priests were recruited from Germany and Poland. The German Catholics who came from Minnesota and settled in St. Peter's Colony were served in their own language by the Benedictines of St. Peter's Abbey. As for the English-speaking Roman Catholics from eastern Canada and Britain, there were requests from them for English-speaking priests and bishops as well. Over the years, even as English became the common language of all Catholic immigrant groups, including those arriving more recently from other parts of the world, the Saskatchewan Catholic Church has taken on a distinctly western Canadian, multicultural flavour. Much of the early work of the Catholic Church in Saskatchewan involved establishing Catholic institutions such as schools, hospitals and orphanages, and these works were taken up by congregations of women and men religious. Catholic lay people became involved as well in various works within the Church and in the larger community (*see* **CATHOLIC WOMEN'S LEAGUE, KNIGHTS OF COLUMBUS**).

In the area of Catholic higher education, the first idea of the Saskatchewan French bishops had been to follow the model of Quebec and establish classical colleges in various regions of the province, with studies to be carried out in the mother tongue of the local community. These colleges would offer high school/secondary schooling as well as first- and second-year university-level courses; students would then go on to what western bishops eventually hoped to establish as one Catholic university for western Canada. In accordance with this plan, in the years following **WORLD WAR I**, Catholic classical colleges were established in Regina (English), Gravelbourg (French), St. Peter's Colony (German), and Yorkton (Ukrainian). Because of the perception that the attendance of Catholic students at the new non-denominational **UNIVERSITY OF SASKATCHEWAN** in Saskatoon would undermine the one-Catholic-university plan and might be a threat to the faith of the Catholic students, it took several years before there was a Catholic presence at the University (1926), and ten more years before a Catholic federated college was established (1936). At the present time, there are two federated Catholic colleges in Saskatchewan: **CAMPION COLLEGE** at the **UNIVERSITY OF REGINA**, and **ST. THOMAS MORE COLLEGE** at the University of Saskatchewan.

During the province's settlement years and following, a great many parish churches and shrines were constructed throughout the province. The Catholic people participated in devotions and pilgrimages which complemented their Sunday worship and other parish-based gatherings. A significant development for the Catholics of Saskatchewan, as for the rest of the Catholic world, was the Second Vatican Ecumenical Council of 1962–65. Vatican II heralded changes in the Catholic Church's understanding of itself and its relationship with the modern world and other faith traditions. In the forty years since then, the Council has had a profound impact on virtually every aspect of Catholic life: changes can be seen, for example, in the relationship between the Saskatchewan Catholic Church and First Nations peoples, in the relationship of Catholics with people of other Christian denominations and non-Christian faith traditions (*see* **PRAIRIE CENTRE FOR ECUMENISM**), and in the increased awareness of the need for Catholics to become involved in working for the common good of the larger community—not only through works of charity, but also through involvement in social justice concerns at home and in the developing world. According to the 2001 Canadian Census, there were at that time 286,815 Roman Catholics in Saskatchewan, representing 29.8% of the total population of the province. *Margaret Sanche*

FURTHER READING: Fay, T.J. 2002. *A History of Canadian Catholics: Gallicanism, Romanism and Canadianism.* Montreal and Kingston: McGill-Queen's University Press.

ROMANIAN SETTLEMENTS. Romanian settlements included immigrants of Romanian ethnic origin, and also people of other ethnic origins—Ukrainians, Germans, and Jews—who had emigrated from "Greater" Romania (historical Romania at its maximum extent). The complex ethnic settlement patterns of "Greater" Romania were duplicated in the Canadian prairies. After 1895, Transylvanian and Bukovinian Romanians and Hungarians settled near Dysart, while Bukovinian Romanians and Ukrainians settled around Yorkton as well as in the Boian-Ispas area in Alberta. Between 1901 and 1908 some 200 Jewish settlers from Bukovina established forty homesteads to the east of Dysart in the Lipton area, and Romanian Jews also settled in the Hirsch and Hoffer colonies. While Romanians were already in Regina by the turn of the century, they were largely a rural farm population. A Romanian settlement began to develop in the Dysart-Lupescu area during the 1890s, where St. George Romanian Orthodox parish was established in 1907. The Kayville-Dahinda area was also settled after 1905 where first Sts. Peter and Paul parish was founded in 1906, then St. Mary's by a dissident group in 1915. By 1906 a Romanian settlement straddling the Saskatchewan-Manitoba border had developed, comprising the parishes of St. John the Baptist at Shell Valley, St. Elias the Prophet at Lennard, and Holy Trinity at MacNutt, together with the parish of Sts. Peter and Paul founded at Canora in 1920. At Elm Springs, first settled in 1905, the Ascension of Our Lord parish was founded in 1926. Down south in the Assiniboia-Wood Mountain area, the parish of Sts. Peter and Paul at Flintoft was established in 1911, and the community of Wood Mountain, settled by Romanians by 1914, was served by Holy Transfiguration parish from 1929. Romanians had moved into the nearby town of Assiniboia by the 1930s; today one parish priest serves several parishes in surrounding districts.

St. Nicholas parish in Regina, founded in 1902, is the first Romanian Orthodox parish in North America. Regina is the seat of the Archimandrite administrator of the Western Canada Deanery of the Romanian Orthodox Episcopate of America

REGINA LEADER-POST

Built in 1902, St. Nicholas Romanian Orthodox Church is the second oldest building in Regina's downtown area and the oldest Romanian church in North America.

(Episcopia Orthodoxa Romana din America), whose presiding Bishop is based near Detroit; in turn this Episcopate is affiliated with the Orthodox Church in America (OCA), based in New York City. While there is no specifically Romanian Orthodox parish in Saskatoon, there is an OCA parish. The Romanian Orthodox parishes in Saskatchewan are all members of the Episcopate. A split occurred in the 1950s between the Romanian Orthodox Missionary Episcopate of America, based in Detroit but closely tied to the Patriarchate in Romania, and the anti-Communist Romanian Orthodox Episcopate of America: this division within Romanian Orthodox Christians continues today despite political changes in Romania. During the early years of Romanian settlement in Saskatchewan, priests were sent from Romania, but in more recent times they are more likely trained in seminaries in Winnipeg or Detroit. Some Romanians may be members of the eastern rite Greek Catholic Church in Transylvania (dating from 1697); however, their descendants in Canada have tended to participate in eastern rite Ukrainian Catholic or western rite Roman Catholic parishes rather than form their own parishes.

The early Romanian immigrants to Saskatchewan were mostly young men; by 1920 husbands and fathers had been joined by their families and supplemented by second-generation migration from the United States. Over 80% of the early settlers were homesteaders; an estimated 15% were manual labourers, who helped build the streets and sewer system in Regina; and about 5% were in small businesses (including grocery stores, bars, insurance companies, confectionaries, coffee shops and restaurants, hairdressers, shoeshine parlours) established between 1905 and 1920. Many urban women home-

makers earned extra income in cottage industries such as dressmaking. Romanian women shifted gradually from being farmwives to urban occupational diversity. Today, at least two-thirds of Romanian women in the prairie provinces work outside the home. Romanian voluntary associations in Saskatchewan have included a mutual aid society in Regina, linked to American counterparts based in Detroit. In 1928 the Bok-O-Ria Romanian restaurant and Social Club appeared in Regina (bok-o-ria is a phonetic spelling of *bucurie* or pleasure). Women's and youth organizations such as ARFORA (the Romanian Orthodox Women's Auxiliary) have been closely tied to the church; however, with a weakening of Romanian identity younger women have become less active in such organizations.

Progressive acculturation of Romanians in Saskatchewan has been reflected in the loss of ability to speak Romanian (by the 1970s only about 6% of people claiming Romanian origin in Saskatchewan were still speaking Romanian as the primary language at home). It has been caused by intermarriage, especially with Ukrainians, and high and increasing rates of exogamy since the second generation; changing family values among youth; involvement of women in the wider community after the first generation; a shift from the extended family to the nuclear family; and a continuous movement away from the Romanian Orthodox church. Yet there have been signs of continuing interest in Romanian culture as well: for example the second generation formed in 1965 the Eminescu Romanian Dance Group, which has performed widely in North America.

In 1914, most of the 8,000 Romanians living in Canada had settled in the prairie provinces; by 1921 this population had increased to over 29,000. Of all Romanian-speaking immigrants, some 85% were from Transylvania, Bukovina, and Banat; another 10% included Vlachs from throughout the Balkans (Thrace, Bulgaria, Greece, Macedonia, and Serbia), so perhaps only 5% were actually from the "Old Kingdom" of Romania. But with the arrival of a second wave of Romanian immigrants in central Canada after WORLD WAR II, the proportionate distribution of Romanians in Canada would change: in 1991, 28,665 Canadians claimed Romanian-only ethnicity, compared to 45,405 who claimed other ethnic identities as well. In 2001, 10,290 Saskatchewan residents claimed Romanian ethnicity—1,930 solely and 8,360 in combination with other ethnicities. (*See also* ETHNIC BLOC SETTLEMENTS, GERMAN SETTLEMENTS, HUNGARIAN SETTLEMENTS, JEWISH RURAL SETTLEMENTS, UKRAINIAN SETTLEMENTS) *Alan Anderson*

FURTHER READING: Patterson, G.J. 1999. "Romanians." In P.R. Magocsi (ed.), *Encyclopedia of Canada's Peoples*. Toronto: University of Toronto Press.

ROMANOW, ROY JOHN (1939–). Roy Romanow was born in Saskatoon on August 12, 1939. His parents were Ukrainian immigrants who had settled on the west side of Saskatoon. Despite English being his second language, Romanow performed well in school and entered the UNIVERSITY OF SASKATCHEWAN in the fall of 1957 to study political science. After completing his first degree, he entered the university's College of Law, graduating in the spring of 1964. While at university, Romanow was heavily involved in student politics, becoming president of the Students' Representative Council. He was also an outspoken advocate of the provincial CCF and its introduction of MEDICARE.

Romanow began practicing law but had his eye set on politics. In 1966, he secured the CCF's nomination for the Riversdale constituency in Saskatoon and was successful in the provincial election the next year. Recognized as a top debater in the Legislature, he was the natural leader of a new group of MLAs who encouraged him to run for leadership of the party when Premier WOODROW LLOYD resigned in 1970. The party establishment's surprise at his willingness to challenge the old guard turned into astonishment when Romanow forced the contest into a third ballot, almost beating former Lloyd Cabinet Minister ALLAN E. BLAKENEY. As a major asset in the NDP's election victory the following year, Romanow was appointed Deputy Premier, House Leader and Attorney General by Blakeney.

The 1970s were a time of innovation and expansion for the Saskatchewan government. Romanow initiated the province's first human rights code and accompanying commission, a new ombudsman office, the first provincial legal aid plan, the Indian constables program with the RCMP and the MEEWASIN VALLEY AUTHORITY to enhance Saskatoon's riverbank environment. By 1979, national unity had become a priority for the Blakeney government and Romanow became Minister of Intergovernmental Affairs and one of the chief negotiators of a new Constitution for Canada. The compromise "Kitchen Accord" bringing together all the provinces (except Quebec) and the federal government was handwritten by Romanow in an eleventh-hour set of negotiations involving federal Justice Minister Jean Chrétien and his provincial counterparts including Roy McMurtry of Ontario.

Many in Saskatchewan felt that the Blakeney government had been overly preoccupied with the Constitution, and the NDP was routed in the provincial election of 1982. Narrowly defeated in Riversdale, Romanow used his time out of office to reflect on his career and he co-authored *Canada Notwithstanding*, a book about the making of the Canadian Constitution. In 1986, Romanow re-entered political life, winning back the Riversdale constituency and taking over the leadership of the NDP after Blakeney resigned a year later. In

Roy Romanow (right) with Roy McMurtry and Jean Chrétien, the authors of the "Kitchen Accord", 1979.

from Saskatchewan, beginning an eighteen-month inquiry on the future of health care in Canada. Conducting multi-layered consultations that captured the attention of Canadians and the media, as well as initiating extensive research, he delivered his major report, *Building on Values*, in November 2002.   *Gregory P. Marchildon*

FURTHER READING: Barnhart, Gordon L. (ed.). 2004. *Saskatchewan Premiers of the Twentieth Century.* Regina: Canadian Plains Research Center.

ROMANOW COMMISSION, 2001–2002.

Just two months after he stepped down as Premier of Saskatchewan in 2001, ROY ROMANOW was appointed as chair and sole member of the Commission on the Future of Health Care in Canada. A Royal Commission set up under Part A of the Inquiries Act, the Romanow Commission was given eighteen months to complete a national study on public health care and recommendations as to its future.

The work of the Commission was conducted from Saskatchewan with the administrative office located in Saskatoon and the research office located in Regina, the only time a major federal Royal Commission was operated outside Ottawa. The location seemed logical because of Saskatchewan's heritage as the birthplace of both hospitalization and medicare in Canada.

During its tenure, the Commission conducted a multi-layered series of consultations including an innovative "Citizens' Dialogue" involving day-long deliberations of randomly selected Canadians as well as public hearings that were the focus of intense public and media attention. The Romanow Commission's final report *Building on Values: The Future of Health Care in Canada*, was delivered on time and within budget in November 2002.

The Romanow Commission's final report offered forty-seven distinct recommendations concerning the future of public health care in Canada. The more transformative recommendations linked governance and financial changes at the intergovernmental level with substantive health reform changes by federal, provincial and territorial governments. These included: a strengthening of the Canada Health Act; the creation of a national platform for home care services; a fundamental change in the federal transfer mechanism; the linking of medication management to improved prescription drug coverage, along with the establishment of a National Drug Agency; a basic revamping of Aboriginal health care programming; the creation of a national Health Council; and a national focus on primary care reform.   *Gregory Marchildon*

RONEY, KEITH (1948–).

Lawn bowling champion Keith Roney was born in Regina on February 11, 1948. He grew up in Bulyea, Saskatchewan, where

Opposition, he fought against the **PRIVATIZATION** initiatives of the Conservative government led by **GRANT DEVINE**. Then, on October 21, 1991, the NDP swept to a massive victory, setting the stage for a decade-long government headed by Romanow.

As Premier, Romanow inherited a government that was almost bankrupt after years of fiscal mismanagement and a struggling agricultural economy. Tackling the debt crisis with a speed and commitment that surprised almost everyone, Romanow insisted on restoring the public's confidence in the ability of government to manage its finances. At the same time, his government pioneered major reforms in health care, including regionalization. By the mid-1990s, Saskatchewan was beginning to register budget surpluses, leading a trend that was soon followed by other jurisdictions in Canada. Health reform had also achieved some success although the closing and conversion of dozens of rural **HOSPITALS** drew much criticism.

Romanow pursued an incremental economic strategy for the province that encouraged private sector initiative with only modest public investment in the 1990s, eschewing both the mega-development strategy pursued by Devine that had produced so much debt in the 1980s and the active expansion of the **CROWN CORPORATION** sector as had occurred under Blakeney in the 1970s. He initiated a major review of the future of the Crown sector that ultimately called for greater investment outside Saskatchewan and in a more competitive business and regulatory environment within the province. In agriculture, he favoured more market-sensitive safety nets that would encourage even greater diversification. He pushed through a forest strategy that required partnerships with new Aboriginal business-

es in the province. He also introduced welfare reforms aimed at encouraging independence through earned income supplements and training initiatives.

By his second term in government, Romanow was able to turn some of his attention to national issues. He was a leader in the social union negotiations that ultimately produced the National Child Benefit and the Social Union Framework Agreement (SUFA). He tirelessly fought against the threat of Quebec's secession in the federation, trying to forge a balance between Ottawa's centralism and the radical decentralism urged by Quebec and Alberta. He had Saskatchewan intervene in the Quebec secession reference before the Supreme Court of Canada to make it clear that decisions on the future of Canada triggered by Quebec's separation must involve provinces like his own, and he supported the federal government's Clarity Bill on the rules surrounding any future referendum on separation.

Romanow's government emerged with a minority in the provincial election of 1999. Years of budgetary constraint along with deteriorating relations with rural voters facing an increasingly uncertain future and organized labour following a bitter nurses' strike had taken their toll. Romanow initiated a coalition with the three sitting Liberal members to provide some stability for his government. A year later, Romanow decided to announce his resignation, making way for a leadership convention. After **LORNE CALVERT** was selected leader, Romanow left the Premier's office in February 2001.

After only three months in retirement, however, Romanow was asked by Prime Minister Chrétien to become the sole chair of a Royal Commission. He accepted on the condition that it would be directed

he played fastball, curling, and hockey. After graduating with a degree in biology from the **UNIVERSITY OF REGINA**, Roney began working at the **ROYAL SASKATCHEWAN MUSEUM** in 1971; today, he is the museum's curator of Life Sciences. Roney began his lawn bowling career in 1979 with the Regina Lawn Bowling Club. In 1985, he played one year with the Canadian team, and in 1987 won his first Canadian championship. He was invited again to join the Canadian team in 1988, and continues to play with them. Roney plays in the singles, pairs, triples, and fours divisions of both the national and the provincial teams. He has competed and won several times in the North American challenge and the US Open. Roney has played all over the world, including in two World Bowls, two Commonwealth Games, three tournaments in Hong Kong, and five Asia Pacific Bowls Championships. Roney's biggest success came when playing in the pairs division in the 2004 Men's World Bowls Championship in Ayr, Scotland: it was the first time Canada had won gold in that division.

Erin Legg

ROSE, GERALD F. (1920–99). Admired for a lifetime of volunteer service, Gerald Rose was born in Saskatoon on October 26, 1920. He graduated from the **UNIVERSITY OF SASKATCHEWAN** with a BA in 1940 and served with the Royal Canadian Corps of Signals until 1945. Rose returned to Saskatoon and joined his father's dry-cleaning and fur business, eventually becoming general manager and president. He lent his business expertise to numerous organizations and contributed to the financial success of the 1979 Western Canada Summer Games and the 1989 Jeux Canada Games in Saskatoon. Rose served on the Saskatoon Economic Development Board and the St. Paul's Hospital Board. Committed to his community, Gerald Rose was appointed as a Member of the Order of Canada in 1998. He died on March 25, 1999.

ROSE VALLEY, town, pop 395, located in the east-central parklands, SW of Greenwater Lake Provincial Park and 38 km N of Wadena on Hwy 35. Settlers began arriving in the district around 1904–05; most were of either Scandinavian or Ukrainian origins. The Rose Valley townsite was purchased by the CPR in 1923 and, in 1924, construction of the railway from Wadena through the townsite to Tisdale was completed. Businesses began to be established in 1924 and the new community was named after a rural post office which was moved to the townsite the same year. In 1940, Rose Valley was incorporated as a village, and by 1961 the community had a peak population of 627. In 1962, Rose Valley attained town status. Agriculture is the area's economic mainstay and is based upon grain and livestock production. Rose Valley serves the district with a core of businesses, as well as

health and recreational facilities. There are a number of service clubs and community-based organizations. Rose Valley School is a K–12 facility, which had 171 town and area students enrolled in the fall of 2004. Students from the village of Archerwill are bussed to Rose Valley to attend Grades 10 through 12. Scattered throughout the district are a number of pioneer churches which have been designated heritage properties.

David McLennan

ROSENAU, GEORGE (1941–). Norman George Rosenau, born in Regina on March 27, 1941, and raised in southwest Saskatchewan, became a well-known advocate of public services, public employees, and the rights of injured and disabled workers. Rosenau began his career as a psychiatric nurse at the old Moose Jaw Training School, now known as Valley View Centre, a facility for the mentally disabled. In 1974 he became a vocational rehabilitation counsellor for the **WORKERS' COMPENSATION** Board, where he became active on the union bargaining committee, a unit of the **SASKATCHEWAN GOVERNMENT EMPLOYEES' UNION** (SGEU). He was elected to SGEU's provincial executive and as a vice-president from Regina in 1986. He became the president of SGEU in 1988, replacing Barb Byers who had been elected president of the **SASKATCHEWAN FEDERATION OF LABOUR**.

Rosenau took on the leadership of SGEU at a time when its members were under attack by the policies of the provincial government, **GRANT DEVINE**'s Progressive Conservatives. **PRIVATIZATION** and cutbacks to public services, wage restraints and back-to-work legislation became the mantra of Devine's public policy. Rosenau became an eloquent and vigorous leader against these policies, and a prominent figure in the media and the labour movement. SGEU's battle with the provincial government came to a head when, in the dying days of his second term, Grant Devine announced "Fair Share Saskatchewan," a plan to dismantle government departments based in Regina and Saskatoon and transfer them to smaller communities across the province. Rosenau led SGEU in challenging Fair Share in the courts, and mobilized its members as well as public opinion. In 1991, Grant Devine was replaced in the provincial election by **ROY ROMANOW**'s NDP.

The large debt and deficit the NDP inherited from the Conservatives became the excuse for further government cutbacks and large-scale public sector layoffs in the early 1990s. Rosenau challenged these policies as forcefully as he did cutbacks by the previous government. After six years as president, he stepped down and returned to the Workers' Compensation Board. In 1998, he was offered the position of manager of the Office of the Worker's Advocate, a Department of Labour agency advocating and representing workers in disputes with the

Workers' Compensation Board. He retired from the agency in 2002, but has continued assisting injured and disabled workers, and has been active in the Saskatchewan Centennial Workers Celebration Committee.

Doug Taylor

ROSETOWN, town, pop 2,471, located 115 km SW of Saskatoon at the crossroads of two major Hwys: No. 4, following the historic north-south trail between Swift Current and the Battlefords; and east-west Hwy 7, linking Saskatoon, Kindersley, and Calgary. The first settlers arrived in the area in 1904–05, following what was known as the "Old Bone Trail" that ran southwest from Saskatoon and was known as such for the bison bones which were collected along it and shipped to eastern Canada to be made into lampblack and fertilizer. In 1907, a post office was established on an area farm and named Rosetown in honour of James and Ann Rose, from Lancashire, England, who had come to the district in 1905. With the arrival of the Canadian Northern Railway in the region in 1908–09, settlers began arriving in larger numbers, and in 1909 businessmen were establishing themselves at the townsite. Rosetown, which was incorporated as a village in August 1909, attained town status on November 1, 1911. In the early 1920s its population was approaching 1,000. On the night of June 16, 1923, the "Rosetown Cyclone" struck. Area farm buildings were tossed to the wind and Rosetown's business district was severely damaged, as was the community's hospital. However, the community quickly rebuilt and prospered as a transportation hub and distribution centre situated in productive crop lands. Today, the community's 200 businesses serve a trading area population of over 8,100 people. Area attractions include the petroglyphs and other archaeological sites near the village of Herschel, and the Twin Towers Ski Resort, located 3 km south of the hamlet of Stranraer.

David McLennan

ROSS, ALEXANDER (1880–1973). Born in 1880 in Forres, Harashire, Scotland, Alexander Ross emigrated to Regina in 1889. After passing his junior matriculation exam at the University of Manitoba in 1896, he obtained an interim teacher's certificate and began to teach at Kronau. In January 1898 Ross joined the James Balfour law firm as an articling student, and at the age of 21 he accepted a partnership in the Regina law firm of T.C. Johnstone. Ross joined the **95TH REGIMENT** in Regina in 1908 as a lieutenant. At the outbreak of **WORLD WAR I** in 1914, he joined the **28TH (NORTHWEST) BATTALION**, CEF and was given command of B Company as a major. In June 1915 the 28th Battalion arrived in England, where it joined the 6th Brigade, 2nd Division of the Canadian Corps. In September of that year the Battalion was sent to the front lines in France. At the Battle of the Somme

(1916), Lieutenant-Colonel **J.F. EMBURY**, the commanding officer, was wounded and Ross took command of the Battalion. Lieutenant-Colonel Alexander Ross led the 28th Battalion at the Battle of Vimy Ridge on April 9, 1917. Previous attempts to capture the German position had failed. However, after three days of fighting the Canadian Corps successfully took the ridge–but at a cost of 3,598 soldiers killed and 7,004 injured. Of the battle, Ross said that it was "Canada from the Atlantic to the Pacific on parade. I thought then ... that in those few minutes I witnessed the birth of a nation." Ross was awarded the Distinguished Service Order for his part in the battle. He received a bar to his Distinguished Service Order for his efforts in planning and directing operations that enabled the Battalion to seize a new section of the line during the May 1918 German offensive.

On his return to Regina in 1919, Ross assumed command of Military District 12. A year later he resumed his law practice, and in 1921 was appointed District Court Judge for the Yorkton District. At that time he joined the Great War Veterans Association and was named honorary treasurer when it became the Canadian Legion in 1926. That same year he organized the Yorkton Branch and became its first president. He served in that capacity until being elected provincial president in 1930. Ross was also the national chairman of the Canadian Legion War Services' Board of Directors from 1927 to 1934. As chairman, he developed a program of auxiliary services such as education and training for active soldiers, so that their transition into civilian life after the war was made easier. Ross was named Dominion president of the Canadian Legion in 1934, a position he held for four years. In 1955, the **UNIVERSITY OF SASKATCHEWAN** awarded Alexander Ross the degree of Doctor of Laws; he was also awarded the Centennial Medal for his distinguished service. General Ross died on October 19, 1973.

Daria Coneghan

ROSS, JAMES HAMILTON (1856–1932).

Ross was born in London, Canada West, on May 12, 1856, and moved with his family to Manitoba in the early 1870s. In 1882 he moved to what is now Saskatchewan and established the first mixed farming operation in the Moose Jaw district. He married Barbara Elizabeth McKay in 1886. He was elected to the North-West Council in 1883, then to the Legislative Assembly of the North-West Territories in 1888. His colleagues selected him as Speaker in 1891, the highest office available to an MLA at the time. Ross resigned the speakership in a budget controversy over responsible government. He joined the original Executive Council led by **FREDERICK HAULTAIN** and guided the Territories' first labour legislation through the Assembly. Although a Liberal, he was a supporter of Premier Haultain's plan to obtain provincial status for the Territories. When

responsible government was granted to the North-West Territories in 1897, Ross entered the first Cabinet as Commissioner (Minister) of Agriculture, Commissioner of Public Works, and Territorial Secretary. He relinquished these positions in 1899 to become Territorial Treasurer. He showed tremendous administrative and political skill in keeping the North-West Territories solvent. In 1899 Ross was appointed a treaty commissioner. Ross led the negotiations with the First Nation bands from Athabasca, in what is now Alberta. He assisted **DAVID LAIRD** in negotiating **TREATY 8** and traveled throughout the North-West. Appointed commissioner of the Yukon Territory in 1901, he was the first commissioner to reside in Government House in Dawson City. Despite suffering a paralytic stroke in 1902, he became the first member of Parliament to represent the Yukon Territory in a by-election in 1902. Summoned to the Senate of Canada in1904, he served there until his death in Victoria on December 14, 1932.

Michael Thome

FURTHER READING: Lingard, C. Cecil. 1946. *Territorial Government in Canada: The Autonomy Question in the Old North-West Territories*. Toronto: University of Toronto Press; Thomas, Lewis Herbert. 1956. *The Struggle for Responsible Government in the North-West Territories, 1870–97*. Toronto: University of Toronto Press.

ROSS, SINCLAIR (1908–96).

James Sinclair Ross is considered one of Canada's greatest literary artists–the first native-born Saskatchewanian to be so considered, with the possible exception of **W.O. MITCHELL**. Certainly his first novel, *As For Me and My House*, has become a standard text in Canadian studies here and abroad, and several of his stories have been adapted for film and television. Ross was born on January 22, 1908, on a farm near Shellbrook. He attended first grade at Wild Rose School before his parents, Peter and Catharine Ross, permanently separated; Catharine took young "Jimmy" with her to the Indian Head district, where she worked as a housekeeper for farm families. Jimmy Ross was remembered in Indian Head as a precocious student and reader. He left high school in Grade 11 to work at the Union Bank of Canada in Abbey, Saskatchewan. That bank was taken over by the Royal Bank of Canada, where Ross spent the rest of his working life. He transferred to branches in Lancer (1928) and Arcola (1929). In Arcola, he began writing short stories under the name of Sinclair Ross, and started work on *As For Me and My House*. (The fictional town of Horizon bears some resemblance to Arcola.) At that time, he also travelled to Regina for a term in the Conservatory of Music at Regina College, taking advanced music studies. He was an accomplished pianist and organist, playing in the churches of various communities.

In April 1933, Ross transferred to a bank posi-

tion in Winnipeg, and moved there with his mother. That year, he won third prize (worth £20) in a major literary competition in London, England, the Nash's Short Story competition, with a short story called "No Other Way"; it was published in the October 1934 issue of *Nash's Pall-Mall*. In 1935 his short story, "A Field of Wheat," was published in *Queen's Quarterly*, the first of a dozen Sinclair Ross stories to appear during the 1930s and early 1940s in *QQ*. This period marks his finest output as a creative writer, for it included the short stories "The Painted Door," "A Lamp at Noon," "Cornet at Night," and other tales which have become widely anthologized in Canada and translated abroad.

Ross sent his first novel, *As For Me and My House*, to Reyal and Hitchcock in New York, where it was published in 1941 to scant and unenthusiastic reviews. A psychological portrait of the wife of a small-town church minister, the novel also illustrated the relentless despair of life in a prairie community at the depth of the "Dirty Thirties." It takes the form of a diary written by Mrs. Bentley, the otherwise unnamed wife of Philip Bentley, a failed artist and church minister. The novel was ignored by a readership looking for wartime escapism, and Ross himself perceived the novel as a failed venture. Nevertheless, *As For Me and My House* was reprinted in paperback and eventually recognized as one of the finest novels of modern Canadian literature. Many writers, notably Margaret Laurence, **LORNA CROZIER**, and Robert Kroetsch, have cited its influence on their work.

Ross enlisted in the Canadian Army in 1942 and was sent overseas with the Ordnance Corps; he was stationed in London until 1946. He said in a later interview that he was grateful for the war, for he lived in cosmopolitan London for four years, taking in theatre, opera, music and art for the first time in his life. After the war, Ross returned to Winnipeg and the Royal Bank. Later that year he was transferred to the bank's Montreal office, where he worked in the public relations division. McClelland and Stewart republished *As For Me and My House* in 1957 in its New Canadian Library series, and the novel began appearing on university literature courses across the country. A second novel, *The Well*, was also published in 1957, and in 1968 the paperback *The Lamp at Noon and Other Stories*. This was the Canadian public's first encounter with Ross's stories, and the publication generated much critical interest in his work. A later novel, *Whir of Gold*, appeared in 1970, and his final literary effort, *Sawbones Memorial*, in 1974. The latter, a short novel of 138 pages, is a *tour de force* of narrative construction that examines the complex social relationships of a Saskatchewan town called Upward in 1948. The central character is Doctor "Sawbones" Hunter, a 75-year-old family doctor with a troubled history in the town; the entire book takes place during the evening of his retirement and birthday party. It has a sense of humour and warmth uncharacteristic of Ross's earlier work.

Upon retirement from the bank in 1968, Ross moved to Athens to finish his writing career as an expatriate. He had always been private, even reclusive, disheartened by the public response to his later work. He relocated to Málaga, Spain, in 1973, just before the appearance of *Sawbones Memorial*. He later returned to Canada in ill health to live in Vancouver, where he resided until his death on February 29, 1996. The following year, Saskatchewan artists and readers erected a monument to Sinclair Ross in Indian Head, featuring a bronze statue by Regina sculptor **JOE FAFARD**.

Ken Mitchell

FURTHER READING: McMullen, L. 1979. *Sinclair Ross*. Boston: Twayne Publishers; Mitchell, K. 1981. *A Reader's Guide to Sinclair Ross*. Regina: Coteau Books.

ROSTHERN, town, pop 1,504, located about equidistant between the cities of Saskatoon and Prince Albert at the junction of Hwys 11 and 312. Situated between the converging branches of the **NORTH** and **SOUTH SASKATCHEWAN RIVERS**, Rosthern lies within close proximity to a number of historic sites: **BATOCHE**, Fish Creek, Duck Lake, and Fort Carlton are all within a short drive; as well, the National Historic Site of the Seager Wheeler Farm is just a few kilometres to the east. Rosthern benefits from the tourism these sites generate, and the community retains its traditional position as a service centre for the surrounding farming population, a position it has maintained for more than a century. The Qu'Appelle, Long Lake & Saskatchewan Railway was running through to Prince Albert in 1890, and Mennonite settlers began taking up land in the Rosthern district shortly thereafter. The Rosthern post office was established in 1893, and by 1898 the community had developed sufficiently enough to be incorporated as a village. The population of Rosthern had grown to 413 by 1901, and in 1903 the community attained town status. By 1911, the town numbered well over 1,000 residents. In 1928, **WILLIAM LYON MACKENZIE KING** laid the cornerstone for Rosthern's post office. Today, Rosthern has a substantial business community providing virtually every type of good and service. The Station Arts Centre, located in the former 1902 railway station, houses a tea room and an art gallery, and hosts a number of musical performances and theatrical events throughout the year. The Rosthern Mennonite Heritage Museum is located in one of the most prominent structures in the community, and houses artifacts pertaining to the area's pioneer history. The museum is housed in one of the several heritage properties in the town, many of which are over a century old. An interesting archaeological discovery was made in the Rosthern area in recent years: an almost entirely intact **MÉTIS** *hivernant* village. Known as "Petite Ville," the site, which is believed to date to the 1860s (thus predating permanent settlement at Batoche), was declared a provincial heritage site by ministerial order in February 2005. It is the best preserved of only a few *hivernant* sites identified in the province.

David McLennan

ROULEAU, town, pop 434, located 50 km SE of Moose Jaw on Hwy 39 and the CPR **SOO LINE**. After the Soo Line was completed in 1893, the Rouleau post office opened in 1895, the name honouring Charles-Borromée Rouleau, a judge of the Supreme Court of the North-West Territories. Agriculture, particularly grain farming, has traditionally been the community's economic base, and Rouleau is reputed to be the province's first "million bushel town." During the first decade of the 20th century, Rouleau was booming as a trading centre for a large area; however, the construction in 1911–12 of rail lines to the east and west of the community drew some of the life blood out of the town's commerce, and the loss of business cut inroads into the town's population. From a peak of just under 700 in 1911, Rouleau's numbers fell to below 500 by 1916. Subsequently, however, the community has enjoyed a comparatively stable population; today, in addition to the traditional agricultural output of the area, crops such as lentils, canaryseed, peas, chickpeas, and sunflowers are grown. In 2003, Rouleau became the location for the filming of CTV's hit comedy series, *Corner Gas*, which stars Tisdale-born comedian **BRENT BUTT**. As the fictitious town of "Dog River," Rouleau now bustles each summer with film crews. Another star in Rouleau in recent years has been Christina Beck, a student at Rouleau School: from 2002 to 2004, Beck was the winner of five provincial championships in the track and field events of shot put and discus. *David McLennan*

ROWELL-SIROIS REPORT: *see* **ROYAL COMMISSION ON DOMINION PROVINCIAL RELATIONS**

ROYAL, JOSEPH (1837–1902). Joseph Royal was born May 7, 1837, in Repentigny, Lower Canada, the son of poor, illiterate parents. Following successful careers as a journalist, publisher and lawyer in Montreal, he became a well known spokesman for **MÉTIS** and **FRANCOPHONE** rights in Manitoba, and founded the first French-language newspaper in the west (*Le Métis*) in St. Boniface in 1871. During the 1870s, he served Manitobans as a provincial Cabinet minister and later as an MP. In 1888, he succeeded **EDGAR DEWDNEY** as **LIEUTENANT-GOVERNOR** of the North-West Territories, at a time when the Territories had just been granted an elect-

ed assembly and were agitating for complete responsible government. For the whole of his term, Royal sought to balance the reforming aspirations of westerners with Ottawa's firm resolve to resist them. In 1891, an amended North-West Territories Act saw many of the administrative and executive powers of the Lieutenant-Governor pass to a four-man Executive Committee headed by **F.W.G. HAULTAIN**, a leading proponent of Territorial autonomy. The social highlight of the term of Royal and his wife Agnes as the vice-regal couple in Regina undoubtedly was the opening of the new and much grander **GOVERNMENT HOUSE** in late 1891. Following the end of his term in 1893, Royal lobbied for a Senate appointment; when this did not occur, he returned to the east and resumed his journalistic career in Ottawa and Montreal. His last years were not affluent, and he died in Montreal in 1902 after a long illness. *Garth Pugh*

ROYAL AIR FORCE. The Royal Air Force has been active in Canada throughout the history of military aviation, though mainly in a supportive or advisory capacity initially. The Royal Flying Corps and the Royal Naval Air Service, forerunners of the Royal Air Force, made administrative and instructional personnel available at training establishments in Canada. Many young Canadians served in these units during **WORLD WAR I** and before the establishment of the Royal Canadian Air Force in 1924. As a result of this experience in organization and co-operation, it was logical to consider Canada as the training ground for the **BRITISH COMMONWEALTH AIR TRAINING PLAN** (BCATP) when it was established in 1939. This agreement was signed by Australia, Canada, the United Kingdom, and New Zealand, on December 17, 1939, and the first schools were opened April 29, 1940. Growth thereafter was rapid, and by the end of 1943 there were 97 schools and 187 ancillary units operating at 231 sites. This number includes 27 RAF schools, seven of which were located in Saskatchewan. The choice of sites for these facilities was often controversial and more often than not politically motivated. However, it was obviously of considerable interest to a local community to be included in the list of successful candidates. The immediate economic benefits breathed new life into sections of the country still suffering from a long period of drought and depression, and in many cases this boost to the local economy resulted in the growth of new industries and services which lasted far beyond the period of wartime activity.

The schools staffed and administered by the RAF were at Swift Current, Caron, Assiniboia, Moose Jaw, North Battleford, Estevan and Weyburn. Swift Current was home to two different schools: No. 32 Elementary Flying Training School (EFTS), which operated from July 1941 to November 26, 1941, when it moved to Bowden, Alberta, and thereafter to

Table RAF-1. Number of Pilots who Graduated from British Commonwealth Air Training Plan Schools in Saskatchewan					
Schools	Pilots Graduated	R.A.F	R.C.A.F.	R.N.Z.A.F.	R.A.A.F.
No. 39 S.F.T.S.	893	812	30	48	3
No. 33 E.F.T.S.	1837	833	3		1
No. 34/25 E.F.T.S.	2096	2070	21	4	1
No. 32 S.F.T.S.	1207	1178	26	2	1
No. 35 S.F.T.S.	941	930	11		
No. 38 S.F.T.S.	823	795	23	4	1
No. 41 S.F.T.S	1055	1011	35	2	7

No. 39 Service Flying Training School, (SFTS), which was active from December 15, 1941, until March 24, 1944. No. 33 EFTS at Caron was initially operated by the RAF (January 5 to May 25, 1942), and then was joined by a civilian-operated school from Boundary Bay, British Columbia, No. 18 EFTS. The school was disbanded on January 1, 1944. Assiniboia was the site of another of the joint RAF civilian-operated elementary schools. No. 34 EFTS (RAF) was formed on February 11, 1942, and was joined by No. 25 EFTS (RCAF), operated by Central Manitoba Flying Training School Ltd. on July 6, 1942. Training ceased on July 28, 1944. Originally numbered No. 10 SFTS at Tern Hill in Shropshire, England, this school was moved as a unit to Moose Jaw in November 1940 and renumbered No. 32 SFTS; it was finally disbanded on October 17, 1944. As is well known, this school continued under different direction, and is now the home of the SNOWBIRDS, Canada's famous aerobatic team, and of the NATO international flying training school. No. 35 SFTS North Battleford operated from October 4, 1941, to February 25, 1944–after which it continued as No 13 SFTS (RCAF), relocated from St. Hubert, Quebec. No. 38 SFTS was stationed at Estevan and was in service from April 27 until February 11, 1944. No. 41 SFTS Weyburn also operated during a similar period, January 1, 1942 to January 22, 1944.

The students trained at these schools were predominantly RAF; but as the following numbers indicate, some were from other partners in the plan (see Table RAF-1). Students from EFTS continued their training at SFTS so that these figures do not indicate the total number of pilots produced by the BCATP; nor do they indicate the total involvement of RAF personnel trained at RCAF schools, including Bombing and Gunnery as well as Air Observer schools. Such schools–at Regina, Saskatoon, Mossbank, Dafoe, Prince Albert, Yorkton, and Davidson–trained a total of 24,775 students, of which approximately 4,500 were RAF, 1,500 RNZAF, and 2,500 RAAF. In addition to the obvious importance and success of this program, the impact on society in general should not be overlooked. Cultural influences were noticeable, and the warmth and hospitality of the host communities resulted in lasting friendships and in many cases marriages, which in turn led to resettlement for one or the other of the partners. *Howard Leyton-Brown*

ROYAL CANADIAN AIR FORCE STATION, MOOSE JAW.

Royal Canadian Air Force Station Moose Jaw is located in the hamlet of Bushell Park, approximately 6 km south of the city of Moose Jaw. Following its closure as a Service Flying Training School for Great Britain's ROYAL AIR FORCE at the end of WORLD WAR II, the air base was used briefly as a municipal airport by the city of Moose Jaw, prior to its activation as a Canadian military air base in 1952. Following extensive renovation and new construction upon its activation, No. 2 Flying Training School (the "Big 2") commenced flight operations on May 4, 1953, using rebuilt war surplus North American Harvard single-engine trainers and new Canadian-built CT-133 Silver Star advanced jet training aircraft. On April 1, 1966, Royal Canadian Air Force Station Moose Jaw was renamed Canadian Forces Base Moose Jaw. *Jeff Noel*

ROYAL CANADIAN AIR FORCE STATION, SASKATOON.

In 1927, the Canadian Department of National Defence (DND) began to encourage the formation of civilian flying clubs to train Royal Canadian Air Force (RCAF) personnel. As an inducement the Department, on the basis of a long-term loan, offered clubs deHavilland Gipsy Moth airplanes. As a result, the Saskatoon Aero Club was formed in 1928. During this period the RCAF was also required to provide an airmail service across the prairies, so the city of Saskatoon was asked to build an airfield that could accommodate this service; to this end, the Saskatoon Airport was formally opened in 1929.

In January 1940, the airport was leased to the federal government to serve as the RCAF's No. 4 Service Flight Training School (SFTS) under the BRITISH COMMONWEALTH AIR TRAINING PLAN (BCATP), a program designed to train aircrew personnel during WORLD WAR II. Five large hangars, barracks, classrooms, workshops, a hospital and a control tower were built to accommodate the new RCAF station. In 1944 the Saskatoon Airport air radio was installed to provide navigational facilities, air-to-ground communication, and weather information. Radio operators manned the station 24 hours a day, 7 days a week. When the war ended in 1945, No. 4 SFTS was closed, and in November 1946 the airport was transferred to the Department of Transport.

The airport was expanded again in 1950 when the RCAF announced its decision to establish a training station there. Construction began on new barracks, married quarters, runways, offices, and a huge new hangar. On January 1, 1952, the RCAF's No. 1 Advanced Flying School (AFS) began to train RCAF, ROYAL AIR FORCE, and North Atlantic Treaty Organization (NATO) air crews on B-25 Mitchell light bombers and Beech C-45 Expeditors. Saskatoon's No. 1 AFS trained men in instrument flying from 1956 until 1962, when RCAF Station Saskatoon was transferred from Training Command to Air Transport Command and the training school was moved to RCAF Station Rivers (Manitoba). In the summer of 1964, RCAF Station Saskatoon closed and the four hangars were again turned over to the Department of Transport. *Daria Coneghan*

ROYAL CANADIAN AIR FORCE WOMEN'S DIVISION.

On July 2, 1941, the government of Canada granted permission for women to be enlisted into the Royal Canadian Air Force (RCAF). In February 1942, in response to the decision, the RCAF created the Royal Canadian Air Force Women's Division (RCAF WD). Initially, RCAF WD members served as cooks, clerks, assistants, drivers, telephone operators, and textile workers. However, as war demands increased, the duties of the RCAF WD expanded to include policing and technical trades. Members of the RCAFWD served in virtually all stations, schools and units of the RCAF throughout Saskatchewan. The motto of the Women's Division was "They Serve That Men May Fly." In 1945, the RCAF WD was demobilized; from 1951 onward, women were recruited directly into the RCAF. *Peter Borch*

FURTHER READING: Dombrowski, N.A. (ed.). 1999. *Women and War in the Twentieth Century: Enlisted With or Without Consent.* New York: Garland; Higonnet, M.R. (ed.). 1987. *Behind the Lines: Gender and the Two World Wars.* New Haven: Yale University Press; Klein, Y.M. (ed.). 1997. *Beyond the Home Front: Women's Autobiographical Writing of the Two World Wars.* London: Macmillan.

ROYAL CANADIAN ARMY SERVICE CORPS.

Formed on November 1, 1901, as a branch of the

Royal Canadian Army Service Corps

COURTESY OF GERRY CARLINE

COURTESY OF TOURISM SASKATCHEWAN

Royal Canadian Mounted Police.

Active Militia, the Canadian Army Service Corps (CASC) provided various support services to fighting troops. In Military District No. 10, the 7th Mounted Brigade No. 20 Company was raised in Regina on November 15, 1913. For its commendable efforts throughout **WORLD WAR I**, the Corps received the designation "Royal" on November 3, 1919.

During both world wars and the Korean War, Saskatchewan personnel provided reinforcements to the Royal Canadian Army Service Corps (RCASC), as complete units were not sent to the front lines. In 1954, 142 Transport Company RCASC (M) was formed in Regina and Moose Jaw from elements of 22 Transport Company. The Moose Jaw portion of this unit was disbanded in 1965 when 142 Transport Company became Transport Company of 16 (Regina) Service Battalion. Since 1998, the main transport section for all Saskatchewan units has been 17 Wing Winnipeg supported by Camp Dundurn.   *Gordon Goddard*

FURTHER READING: Warren, Arnold. 1961. *Wait for the Wagon: The Story of the Royal Canadian Army Service Corps.* Toronto: McClelland.

Royal Canadian Electrical & Mechanical Engineers

COURTESY OF GERRY CARLINE

ROYAL CANADIAN ELECTRICAL AND MECHANICAL ENGINEERS. On May 15, 1944, engineering units of the **ROYAL CANADIAN ORDNANCE CORPS**, **ROYAL CANADIAN ARMY SERVICE CORPS**, and Royal Canadian Engineers were organized into the Royal Canadian Electrical and Mechanical Engineers

(RCEME). Due to the growing complexity and power of guns, radios, radar, and vehicles, forming a separate engineering corps made the best use of technical skills in support of army equipment. Disbanded in 1968, the RCEME was reorganized in 1984 and is now known as the Electrical Mechanical Engineers. The Forward Logistics Group of 16 (Regina) Service Battalion was re-designated **16 (SASKATCHEWAN) SERVICE BATTALION** in 1987.   *Gordon Goddard*

ROYAL CANADIAN MOUNTED POLICE. The Mounted Police's connection to Saskatchewan predated the creation of the province by over thirty years. Sparked by the brutal massacre of a group of Indians in the **CYPRESS HILLS** by some American whiskey traders, Prime Minister John A. Macdonald created the North-West Mounted Police (NWMP), an institution modeled after the Royal Irish Constabulary, which he believed would ensure the orderly development of the Canadian prairies in contrast to the perceived lawlessness that seemed endemic in the American West. In 1874 the first Mounted Policemen came west, crossing the future provinces of Saskatchewan and Alberta in an event that would become known as the Great March West, but which in reality nearly ended in disaster because of poor planning and leadership. The Mounted Police that soon established itself across the prairies, eventually choosing Regina as its headquarters and the location for its training depot, was not a normal police force. On one hand, the NWMP did have a conventional side. For example, it dealt with a wide

range of crimes from murder to seduction and from abortion to libel. In performing this role it attempted to balance law and order with community policing needs. In some instances, as was the case with prostitution, the balance often involved the NWMP looking the other way. In other examples, such as when the Mounties elected to rigidly enforce liquor laws, as occurred in Prince Albert, a huge civilian furor forced the police to back down.

The force also performed a wide range of non-traditional duties that reflected the still basic structure of the Euro-Canadian society that was displacing First Nations people on the prairies. Some of this labour included reporting on the quality of crops and helping settlers establish themselves, enforcing a variety of federal and later provincial ordinances and statutes, particularly the Indian Act, arresting and transporting to asylums those deemed insane, and even delivering mail. It also served as a *de facto* prison branch in the years before 1914, as Mounted Police guardrooms held on average more than 1,000 prisoners a year, most of whom had been convicted of minor offences or were awaiting trial.

Because of its paramilitary nature, the government also attempted to use the Mounted Police to deal with the serious challenge to order posed by the North-West Resistance. The Mounted Police performed poorly on that occasion, however, especially in an encounter at **DUCK LAKE**, a fact that earned them the disdain of the commander of the Canadian military force, General **FREDERICK MIDDLETON**.

The Mounted Police survived the Duck Lake

debacle and a challenge to its existence posed by the 1896 election of the federal Liberals, a party that championed provincial rights and viewed the Mounted Police as intricately tied to the **CONSERVATIVE PARTY**. Through its actual work and popular works of fiction, the force eventually prospered–especially on the prairies, where it became an important institution and symbol. That significance was demonstrated in 1905 when the now Royal North-West Mounted Police (RNWMP) (the "Royal" was added in 1904 as a reward for the service of its members in the **BOER WAR**) became the police force of the new provinces of Saskatchewan and Alberta, despite the fact that under the British North America Act policing was a provincial and not a federal responsibility. The force's work continued as it had before.

With the beginning of **WORLD WAR I** in 1914, everything changed. Saskatchewan was home to thousands of immigrants, including many from Canada's new enemies, Germany and the Austro-Hungarian Empire. Overnight, with the onset of war, many of the newcomers became "enemy aliens." Fearing the presence of a fifth column across the prairies, the federal government increased RNWMP ranks by 505 non-commissioned officers and constables shortly after the war began. Almost of all of these new recruits were trained at Regina, home of the Mounted Police and also the location of a reserve unit capable of dealing with a major disturbance. Until the end of 1916 the Mounted Police mixed regular policing duties with new war work including the monitoring of enemy aliens in Alberta and Saskatchewan–the latter task mandated by an Order-in-Council passed by the federal government in October 1914. Then, wishing to devote more resources to the broader issue of national security and to a RNWMP unit to be sent overseas, the Mounted Police gave up its regular policing duties as Alberta and Saskatchewan created new provincial police forces that began operating on January 1, 1917.

Despite being replaced by the **SASKATCHEWAN PROVINCIAL POLICE** (SPP), the RNWMP, which became the Royal Canadian Mounted Police (RCMP) in 1919, never left Saskatchewan. It continued to enforce federal statutes like the Opium and Narcotic Drug Act; offered assistance to federal government departments by performing a wide range of duties such as conducting investigations of immigrants seeking to become naturalized citizens; and spied on radicals (including Communists from 1921 on) and others, including labour unions and ethnic communities, who it believed challenged the established order. Indeed, the most famous Mountie of the interwar period was **JOHN LEOPOLD**, who working undercover as a Regina house painter by the name of Jack Esselwein infiltrated the Communist Party of Canada, and later gave court testimony that helped

to send to jail several senior party leaders.

These varied roles represented the general pattern of the RCMP's work in Saskatchewan until 1928, when for financial reasons the provincial government elected to eliminate the SPP and replace it with the RCMP. The RCMP expanded its numbers in the province and returned to regular policing duties in addition to the other tasks it had been performing. With the arrival of the **GREAT DEPRESSION**, the RCMP in Saskatchewan found itself surrounded in controversy, as it was at the forefront of controlling the discontent of many citizens suffering from the economic breakdown. In September 1931, under suspicious circumstances, Mounted Policemen shot and killed three striking miners in a confrontation in downtown Estevan. Then in 1933 the RCMP leadership in Saskatchewan elected to storm a relief camp at the exhibition grounds in Saskatoon; the raid sparked a riot that resulted in a number of injuries and arrests, and in the death of a Mounted Policeman. Finally, and most famously of all, it was the RCMP in June 1935 that prevented unemployed protesters, travelling to Ottawa from Vancouver as part of the **ON-TO-OTTAWA TREK**, from leaving Regina. On July 1 the RCMP commander in Regina ordered the arrest of the Trek leaders at a large public gathering; this action sparked a massive riot in the centre of Saskatchewan's capital and resulted in the death of a city policeman, dozens of injuries and arrests, and considerable property damage. Once again, however, the RCMP escaped official blame (which the Trek leadership received) for what became known as the Regina Riot.

The RCMP's work on behalf of the provincial and federal governments in the Depression ended any challenges to its domination of policing in Saskatchewan, although the force still found itself at times embroiled in controversy, particularly when it came to dealing with Aboriginal Canadians. For citizens living outside of major cities, the RCMP continued to be the only police presence that they knew. In turn, the presence of the RCMP training depot and museum in Regina became an important tourist attraction for the city and the province. In 1998 and 1999 the RCMP celebrated the 125th anniversary of first its creation and then its deployment. Welcoming the celebrations, the citizens of Saskatchewan offered a warm welcome to the famous RCMP musical ride and a re-enactment of the original march west. *Steve Hewitt*

FURTHER READING: Macleod, R.C. 1976. *The NWMP and Law Enforcement, 1873–1905.* Toronto: University of Toronto Press; Baker, W. (ed.). 1998. *The Mounted Police and Prairie Society, 1873–1919.* Regina: Canadian Plains Research Center; Hewitt, S.R. 1997. "Old Myths Die Hard': The Mounted Police in Alberta and Saskatchewan, 1914–1939." PhD Dissertation, University of Saskatchewan.

Royal Canadian Ordnance Corps
COURTESY OF GERRY CARLINE

ROYAL CANADIAN ORDNANCE CORPS.
The Royal Canadian Ordnance Corps traces its roots back to 17th-century New France when supplies were needed to sustain men enlisted to repel an Iroquois raid. In 1871, an ordnance depot within the Canadian Stores Department was established as part of the Militia. It was responsible for all stores and equipment including the purchase, repair, and disposal of all items required by the military. The Ordnance Stores Corps was officially created in 1903, followed by the Canadian Ordnance Corps in 1907.

In addition to its military functions, the Corps supported the Allied Expeditionary Force to Siberia in 1919 and various organizations such as the Boy Scouts, Red Cross Disaster Relief Agency, and government relief camps in the 1930s. In 1936, No. 12 Detachment, Permanent Active Militia and No. 1 Army Field Park, Non-Permanent Active Militia were established in Regina. On September 11, 1939, 1st Ordnance Field Park was mobilized, arriving overseas in December. Personnel were recruited based on their civilian occupations and skills for individual units. Many volunteers were more senior in age than those selected for combat duty. Camp Dundurn remains the central Ammunition Depot for western Canada. *Gordon Goddard*

FURTHER READING: Rannie, William F. 1984. *To the Thunderer His Arms: The Royal Canadian Ordnance Corps.* Lincoln, ON: The Author.

ROYAL COMMISSION ON DOMINION PROVINCIAL RELATIONS (ROWELL-SIROIS REPORT).
The Liberal government of **MACKENZIE KING** created the Royal Commission on Dominion Provincial Relations in 1937, whose task was to assess the economic relationship between the federal government and the rest of Canada. Between 1937 and 1940, the Commission received reports and initiated studies from every province. It documented the Saskatchewan people's reaction to the regional disparity evident in their province after the **GREAT DEPRESSION**. Information in the Rowell-Sirois Report indicated that Saskatchewan experienced huge social and political upheaval in the decade following the Stock Market Crash of 1929, and that it

experienced more financial setbacks than most of the other provinces. Saskatchewan residents voiced concerns over the federal government's capacity to provide for them in times of economic instability. Ottawa exhibited limited success in helping the provinces recover from the fiscal damage after the Depression and other global financial crises. Saskatchewan, Quebec, Ontario, and Alberta introduced income tax, and taxes on gasoline increased by 50% across the country; Saskatchewan and Quebec introduced sales tax at this time to help deal with financial losses suffered during the 1930s.

The four western provinces opposed the federal government's policies of freight rates, control over natural resources, and tariffs on the sale of wheat, and protested the differences in the standard of living between central Canada and the prairies. In 1940, the Rowell-Sirois Report recommended that unemployment insurance and contributory pensions become federal responsibility and that each province collect 10% of the mining and petroleum revenues from the federal government. It advised that health care remain within provincial jurisdiction, but with guidance from the federal government, further suggesting that the federal government take over all provincial debt. Saskatchewan was to receive exceptional grant status based on needs defined by the nature of its farm economy.

The Report stated that provinces would surrender income taxes, corporation taxes, and succession duties to federal jurisdiction: in exchange, the federal government would provide a guaranteed income for all provinces. Saskatchewan, Manitoba, and the Maritimes saw the recommendations as a way of addressing the inequality between themselves and the more affluent provinces. The Rowell-Sirois Report was eventually deemed a failure and shelved. Some of the recommendations were in evidence in the policies of federal governments that followed the Liberals of the 1940s. The federal government established control over Employment Insurance, and the National Adjustment Grant proposal paved the way for present-day equalization principles. The Royal Commission on Dominion Provincial Relations (Rowell-Sirois Report), although shelved, is to this day the most complete investigation into the fiscal relationships between the federal and provincial governments. *Elizabeth Mooney*

ROYAL REGINA RIFLES. The Royal Regina Rifles, a Saskatchewan-based Reserve infantry unit of **38TH CANADIAN BRIGADE GROUP**, traces its origin to the **95TH REGIMENT**, formed in the Districts of Saskatchewan and Assiniboia, North-West Territories, in 1905. The 95th became a rifle regiment in 1908. During **WORLD WAR I** , it provided drafts to units of the Canadian Expeditionary Force, including the **28TH BATTALION**, which fought as part of the 6th Brigade, 2nd Division. After the war, the regiment

underwent several reorganizations and amalgamations until it became the **SOUTH SASKATCHEWAN REGIMENT** on March 15, 1920. The 1st Battalion of this regiment, located in Regina, was renamed the Regina Rifles on May 15, 1924. Between the wars, the regiment was hampered by a lack of proper training facilities until the **REGINA ARMOURY** was built in 1928, followed by a military training camp at Dundurn. On December 15, 1936, the Regina Rifles amalgamated with units of the 12th Machine Gun Battalion, retaining the Regina Rifles name.

In 1939, at the outbreak of **WORLD WAR II**, the Regina Rifles were mobilized for local protective duty. In June 1940, the regiment recruited men from Regina, North Battleford and Prince Albert to form the 1st Battalion for overseas duty. The Battalion mobilized at **CAMP DUNDURN**. As there were many farmers in the unit, they were given the nickname "The Farmer Johns," later shortened to "The Johns." As the regiment went on to win distinction in one engagement after another, their proud battle cry "Up the Johns!" became one of the most famous in the Canadian Army. The Battalion was moved to Debert, Nova Scotia to become part of the defence force for the east coast of Canada. On August 24,

1941, the Regina Rifles embarked for Britain as part of the 7th Brigade, 3rd Canadian Infantry Division. After guarding the shores of southeastern England against the threat of invasion, the Regina Rifles were selected to be one of the initial battalions of infantry to land on Juno Beach as part of the invasion of Normandy on D-Day.

On June 6, 1944, the Battalion landed at "Nan" sector on the western side of Juno Beach. The Reginas destroyed German gun positions on the beach and moved onward, successfully clearing the village of Courseulles-sur-Mer and pushing further inland. The Regina Rifles suffered 108 casualties on the first day of fighting in Normandy, and moved the furthest inland that day towards its objective. After the assault, the regiment reorganized in time to repulse a counterattack by the tanks of the 12th SS Division.

After taking part in the capture of Caen, the 1st Battalion continued along the west coast of France, taking part in the battles for the Channel ports. Fighting through Belgium and the Netherlands, the Battalion attacked across the Leopold Canal, taking part in the battle of the Scheldt. It pushed on through Germany, and at the end of the war in Europe, on May 5, 1945, provided a 4th Battalion from its ranks to become part of the occupation force. The 1st Battalion was disbanded on January 1, 1946; a 2nd Battalion served in the Reserve Army throughout the war; and a 3rd Battalion was raised as part of the defence force for the west coast of Canada. As testament to its role in war, the Regina Rifles Regiment earned twenty battle honours, ten of which are depicted on the current regimental badge.

Following the war, the reserve battalion carried on the regiment's name and traditions. In 1951, the

Royal Regina Rifles on an Internal Security exercise, Regina Armoury, May 1986.

DAVID MCLENNAN PHOTO

Royal Saskatchewan Museum.

COURTESY OF THE GRENFELL MUSEUM

King George VI and Queen Elizabeth, Broadview, 1939.

Rifles raised D Company of the 1st Canadian Rifle Battalion, 27th Brigade, for service with NATO forces in Germany. A second company was raised to became part of the Queen's Own Rifles of Canada, which served in the Commonwealth Division during the Korean War. In 1982, Queen Elizabeth II awarded the title "Royal" to the Regiment, and appointed the Princess Royal, Princess Anne, as its Colonel-in-Chief. Members of the Royal Regina Rifles have served in numerous peacekeeping operations in Cyprus, the Golan Heights, Croatia, Bosnia, and Afghanistan. The Royal Regina Rifles perpetuate the 28th (Northwest) Infantry Battalion, CEF.   *George Bell*

FURTHER READING: Brown, G. and T. Copp. 2001. *Look to Your Front–Regina Rifles: A Regiment at War, 1944-1945.* Waterloo, Ontario: Laurier Centre for Military, Strategic and Disarmament Studies; Mein, S.A.G. 1992. *Up the Johns: The Story of the Royal Regina Rifles.* Regina: Senate of the Royal Regina Rifles.

ROYAL SASKATCHEWAN MUSEUM. The Royal Saskatchewan Museum showcases the natural, geologic, and First Nations history of Saskatchewan. Drawing 140,000 visitors annually to its Regina location, the Royal Saskatchewan Museum offers a range of educational programs, exhibits, and research activities. The museum's history in Saskatchewan dates back to 1906, when the Provincial Museum of Natural History (as it was called then) first opened in the Regina Trading Company Ltd. building. The Provincial Museum moved to the **SASKATCHEWAN LEGISLATIVE BUILDING** in 1911, and then in 1916 to a more permanent home in Regina's Normal School building, where it remained for nearly forty years. On May 16, 1955, Governor General Vincent Massey officially opened

the museum's current location in Regina's **WASCANA CENTRE** and dedicated the new building to the pioneers of Saskatchewan. The facility was constructed as a Golden Jubilee project commemorating Saskatchewan's 50th anniversary in Confederation. Her Majesty Queen Elizabeth II and His Royal Highness the Duke of Edinburgh visited the museum's new location during their 1959 royal visit to the province. The Royal Saskatchewan Museum houses three main galleries: the Life Sciences Gallery highlights Saskatchewan's ecological regions and their native animals, birds, fish, and insects; the First Nations Gallery celebrates 12,000 years of Aboriginal history and culture in the province, and presents a unique selection of artworks and artifacts; and the Earth Sciences Gallery details the prehistoric and geologic history of Saskatchewan. Each gallery offers colourful dioramas, murals, displays, hands-on exhibits, and interactive-learning stations. The museum is also a storehouse for representative collections of floral, faunal, and fossil specimens from around the province. Since the 1950s, the Royal Saskatchewan Museum has been actively involved in the excavation of fossils in southwestern Saskatchewan. In 1995, the museum opened the Royal Saskatchewan Museum Fossil Research Centre in Eastend. The Fossil Centre relocated in 2000 to Eastend's T. Rex Discovery Centre, home of Saskatchewan's only *Tyrannosaurus rex* skeleton.
                                                Iain Stewart

ROYAL UNIVERSITY HOSPITAL. In 1944, a survey of the health needs of Saskatchewan (SIGERIST Report) recommended that a University Hospital of 500 beds be constructed for scientific teaching, clinical instruction, and research. Premier **T.C. DOUGLAS** dedicated the building on May 14, 1955. He said: "This hospital is a monument which

will draw comment when the province celebrates its 100th Anniversary, that the people of Saskatchewan, in 1955, built better than they knew."

By 1958 the hospital was fully occupied, and it became necessary to plan for expansion. The addition was opened by Queen Elizabeth II on July 31, 1978, with 333,000 square feet dedicated to outpatient facilities, emergency services, and operating suites. A second expansion project added three new floors on top of the addition. It was opened on May 23, 1990, by Governor General **RAMON HNATYSHYN**, who conveyed the title "Royal" bestowed on the hospital by the Queen.

In 1992 the hospital became part of a conglomerate Saskatoon District Health Board, but it continued as the principal teaching hospital of the College of Medicine. It provides special services (cardiovascular medicine/surgery, neurosciences, obstetrics, and pediatrics) to the Saskatoon Regional Health District and the entire province.   *Louis Horlick*

ROYAL VISITS. Royal visits began in 1882 with Princess Louise, daughter of Queen Victoria and wife of the Marquis of Lorne, Governor General of Canada. The future King George V and Queen Mary came in 1901. The Duke of Connaught, son of Queen Victoria, inaugurated the **SASKATCHEWAN LEGISLATIVE BUILDING** as Governor General in 1912. The Prince of Wales visited Saskatchewan in 1919 and 1927. The historic national tour of King George VI and Queen Elizabeth in 1939, the first by a reigning monarch, drew huge crowds across Saskatchewan. Princess Elizabeth and Prince Philip visited in 1951, returning in 1959 as Queen Elizabeth II and the Duke of Edinburgh. They came for the RCMP centennial in 1973 and for major provincial tours in 1978 and 1987. Princess Margaret attended Saskatchewan's 75th anniversary in 1980,

R

Table RV-1. Royal Visits to Saskatchewan 1882–2005

Visitor(s)	Location(s)	Date
Princess Louise and the Marquis of Lorne	Regina	August 1882
Duke and Duchess of Cornwall and York	Regina, Moose Jaw	September 1901
Duke and Duchess of Cornwall and York	Qu'Appelle, Regina	October 5, 1901
Prince Arthur, Duke of Connaught	Regina	April 1906
The Duke and Duchess of Connaught and Princess Patricia	Moose Jaw, Regina (opening of the Legislative Building)	October 1912
The Duke and Duchess of Connaught and Princess Patricia	Regina	July 1916
The Prince of Wales	Saskatoon, Maple Creek, Gull Lake, Swift Current (whistle stops), Regina, Qu'Appelle Valley	September–October 1919
The Prince of Wales and Prince George	Regina, Moose Jaw, E.P. Ranch	August 1927
King George VI and Queen Elizabeth	Broadview (passed through on train), Regina, Moose Jaw, Saskatoon. Brief pauses in a number of communities that their train passed through (large crowds in Melville and Watrous).	May–June, 1939
Princess Alice and the Earl of Athlone	Regina, small rural communities, Moose Jaw	April and August 1941
Princess Alice and the Earl of Athlone	Moose Jaw, small rural communities	June 1944
Princess Elizabeth and The Duke of Edinburgh	Regina, Moose Jaw, Swift Current, Saskatoon	October 1951
Princess Margaret	Prince Albert, cottage at Lake Waskesiu	July 1958
Queen Elizabeth II and The Duke of Edinburgh	Saskatoon, whistle stops at Hanley and Chamberlain enroute to Moose Jaw, Regina, whistle stops at Indian Head, Broadview, Moosomin	July 1959
Lord Louis Mountbatten	Regina	April 1966
Princess Alexandra and the Honourable Angus Ogilvy	Regina (Canadian Centennial)	June 1967
Queen Elizabeth II and The Duke of Edinburgh	Regina (RCMP Centennial)	July 1973
The Duke of Edinburgh	Regina	November 1977
Queen Elizabeth II, The Duke of Edinburgh and Prince Edward	Regina, Moose Jaw, Lloydminster, Yorkton, Melville, Fort Qu'Appelle, Balcarres, Saskatoon, Cory Potash Mine	July 1978
Princess Margaret	Saskatoon, Prince Albert, Muskoday First Nation, Zenon Park, Tisdale, the Battlefords (Saskatchewan's 75th Anniversary)	July 1980
Princess Anne (The Princess Royal)	Regina, Wilcox, Gravelbourg, Estevan, Alameda, Moosomin, Saskatoon, Qu'Appelle Valley	July 1982
The Queen Mother (Queen Elizabeth)	Regina	July 1985
The Duke of Edinburgh	Regina, Last Mountain Lake, a farm near Kroneau	June 1987
Queen Elizabeth II and The Duke of Edinburgh	Regina, Saskatoon, Wanuskewin Heritage Park, Canora, Veregin, Kamsack, Kindersley, a farm near Flaxcombe	October 1987
The Duke and Duchess of York	Regina, Stanley Mission, La Ronge, Saskatoon, Prince Albert, Arrowhead Island on Lac La Ronge, Nipawin, Meadow Lake, Swift Current	July 1989
Prince Edward (The Earl of Wessex)	Regina, Pasqua First Nation, Echo Lake, Fort Qu'Appelle	August 1994
Prince Charles (The Prince of Wales)	Regina, 15 Wing Moose Jaw, Assiniboia, Saskatoon, Wanuskewin Heritage Park	April 2001
Prince Edward (The Earl of Wessex)	Regina, Lloydminster, Prince Albert, Melfort, Moose Jaw	June 2003
Princess Anne (The Princess Royal)	Regina, Saskatoon, North Battleford	June 2004
Queen Elizabeth II and The Duke of Edinburgh	Regina, Lumsden, Saskatoon (Centennial celebrations)	May 2005

Princess Anne visited in 1982, the Queen Mother in 1985, and Prince Andrew, Duke of York, in 1989. The 1990s saw only one visit, that of Prince Edward, the Queen's youngest son, in 1994. Charles, Prince of Wales, paid his first visit in 2001 and Prince Edward, as the Earl of Wessex, came for his second visit in 2003. (*See* Table RV-1) *Michael Jackson*

FURTHER READING: Jackson, M. 1990. *The Canadian Monarchy in Saskatchewan.* Regina: Government of Saskatchewan.

RUNCIMAN, ALEXANDER MCINNES (1914–2000). "Mac" Runciman was born on October 8, 1914, in Invergordon, Scotland. His family emigrated to Canada and acquired a half-section of land near Balcarres, Saskatchewan in the spring of 1929. Runciman gradually took over the farming operation from his father; this phase of his life, however, ended with **WORLD WAR II**. In 1939 he joined the Ordnance Corps of the Canadian army. He rose from the rank of private to subconductor of ordnance, the

Alexander Runciman receiving his honorary degree from Chancellor John Diefenbaker, October 1977.

most senior non-commissioned officer rank in the army, equivalent to regimental sergeant major. After the war he returned to Saskatchewan; the family farm had been lost by then, but under the Veteran's Land Act Runciman acquired a piece of property about five miles southwest of Abernethy. In 1952, he joined what was then called the "Lemberg Local Board" of **UNITED GRAIN GROWERS** (UGG). In 1955 he became a UGG director, and then president in 1961; he served in that capacity until 1981.

Runciman was also appointed to the board of directors of the Great West Life Assurance Company in the early 1960s. He went on to serve on the boards of a number of major Canadian companies, including Canadian Pacific, the Royal Bank, and Massey Ferguson. In 1984, he became a founding director of Power Financial Corporation. He also served on many government and industry bodies, including terms as the founding president of both the Rapeseed Association of Canada (now the Canola Council of Canada) and the Canada Grains Council. Within a year of his retirement from UGG, he was invited to chair the board of governors of the University of Manitoba, one of the two universities from which he had received honorary PhDs (the other being the **UNIVERSITY OF SASKATCHEWAN**). Mac Runciman passed away on December 6, 2000. He is remembered as one of the great leaders of Canadian agriculture and one of Saskatchewan's most distinguished citizens.   *Paul D. Earl*

FURTHER READING: Earl, Paul D. 2000. *Mac Runciman: A Life in the Grain Trade*. Winnipeg: University of Manitoba Press.

RUPERT'S LAND PURCHASE. Before Saskatchewan became a province, it was part of the North-West Territories and its geographic and economic future was determined by the sale of Rupert's Land. Rupert's Land, the territory granted by the British Crown to the Hudson's Bay Company (HBC) in 1670, was purchased by the government of Canada in 1870: approximately 3 million hectares (or 7 million acres) were purchased for $1.5 million in Canadian currency (£300,000). The HBC was granted one-twentieth of the best farmland in the region, and the company held on to its most successful fur-trading operations. The Rupert's Land Purchase drastically altered the historic relationships that Saskatchewan **MÉTIS** and First Nations peoples had with the land, the Canadian government, and the social environment in the prairie region. Indian and Métis people, who were not consulted about the sale, were seen as a deterrent to successful settlement of the west. The Métis, led by **LOUIS RIEL**, successfully negotiated Manitoba's entry into Confederation in 1870: they were promised title to the lands they farmed and an additional 1.4 million acres for their children. However, the promises made by John A Macdonald and the Liberal government were not kept; the Manitoba Resistance of 1869–70 ended with the dispersal of the Métis people to northern Saskatchewan to rebuild their communities.

The Métis people settled on the land, establishing their traditional patterns of hunting, trapping, and farming; their customs, languages, beliefs, and community systems became part of Saskatchewan's social landscape. **MÉTIS WOMEN**, the largest segment of the population, encouraged settlement and the practice of Catholicism, and ensured the well-being of their extended kinship system. The relationships between the Métis and the federal government followed familiar patterns as the latter repeatedly ignored the Métis' bid for recognition as a distinct ethnic group. The Resistance of 1885 silenced the political voice of Métis people for the next several decades.

The Rupert's Land Purchase also adversely affected Indian populations in the North-West Territories after 1870. Looking to avoid the violence and bloodshed of the Métis resistances as well as the Indian Wars in the United States, seven treaties between the federal government and Indian people were signed between 1871 and 1887. The Canadian government, however, failed to live up to the agreements made in these treaties. Broken treaty promises, the Dominion Lands Act of 1872, the Indian Act of 1876, and the encroachment of White settlers indicated a disregard for the Indigenous people of the North-West Territories which has left a legacy of bitterness still being addressed in the 21st century.

Elizabeth Mooney

FURTHER READING: Finkel, A. and M. Conrad. 2001. *History of the Canadian Peoples: 1867 to the Present*. Toronto: Addison Wesley Longman.

RURAL ELECTRIFICATION. In 1949, the Saskatchewan government passed the Rural Electrification Act. The **SASKATCHEWAN POWER CORPORATION**, a publicly owned utility, purchased existing small-town generators and started to expand into rural areas. However, costs to place power poles, string power lines, and wire buildings for electricity were high. The Rural Electrification Act set out three ways in which rural residents could access power: as an individual, if the farm was close to existing power lines and could be tied in easily; as a power district, where at least seven farms applied for power and shared the costs of bringing it in; and as an electricity co-operative association, with 100 farms buying power wholesale from the Saskatchewan Power Corporation, then building and maintaining their own distribution system.

Rural residents, anxious to access a reliable power source, responded enthusiastically: using loans and volunteer labour, over the next fifteen years most Saskatchewan farms became electrified. Electric lights in halls, schools, rinks, and churches changed the social life of communities. Electric appliances such as refrigerators, stoves, washing machines, furnaces, water heaters, and indoor plumbing freed rural women from daily drudgery. Radio and television brought new forms of entertainment. The farming day was extended by safely lighting barns and shops, and new shop tools improved operations. Large-scale livestock production (such as dairy, chicken, and hog barns) was possible. New businesses, from appliance dealerships, repair shops, and meat lockers to processing plants and manufacturing businesses, revitalized rural Saskatchewan.   *Merle Massie*

FURTHER READING: White, C.O. 1976. *Power for a Province: A History of Saskatchewan Power*. Regina: Canadian Plains Research Center.

RURAL POPULATION. Since reaching a peak of 138,713 in 1941, the number of farms in Saskatchewan has steadily declined: there were 50,598 farms in 2001, which represented a 63.5% decline. The largest decrease in Saskatchewan (as shown in Figure RP-1) occurred between 1941 and 1951; the smallest declines of 12.5% and 9.6% occurred in the ten-year periods from 1971 to 1981 and 1981 to 1991 respectively. The slower rates of decline in these two decades are possibly the results of greater stability in **FARMING** operations and more favourable prices and farming conditions in comparison to the earlier and latter decades in the sixty-year period under consideration. The decline in farm numbers was largely the result of the incorporation of smaller farms into larger farm units—not the retirement or removal of land out of production. In 2001, the average size of farms in Saskatchewan was 519 ha, which was 2.96 times larger than the average 175-

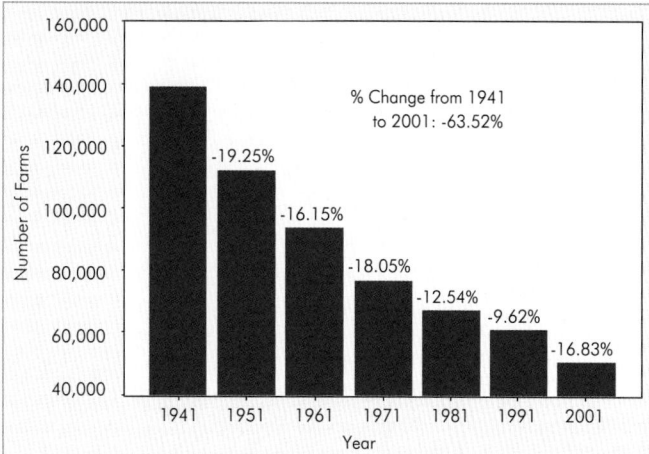

Source: Constructed by author from Statistics Canada, Census of Agriculture, various reports

Figure RP-1. Number and Percentage Change of Farms in Saskatchewan, 1941 to 2001.

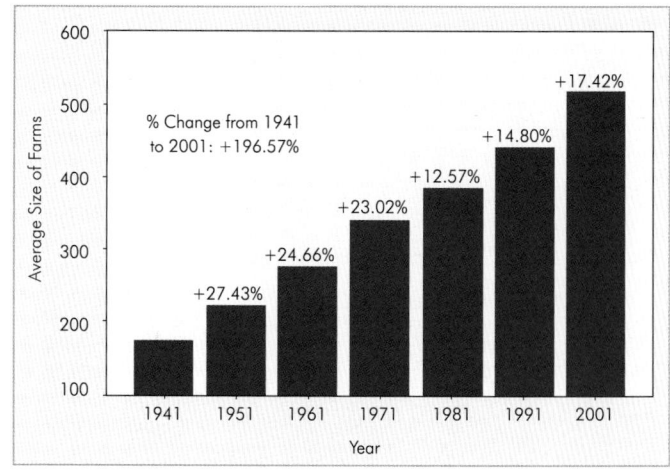

Source: Constructed by author from Statistics Canada, Census of Agriculture, various reports

Figure RP-2. Average Size (hectares*) and Percentage Change in Size of Saskatchewan Farms 1941 to 2001.

*1 hectare = 2.471 acres

ha farm in 1941 (as indicated in Figure RP-2). Saskatchewan has the biggest farms in Canada: this is the result of the large arable land base and of agro-climatic factors which require larger farm units for viable farms operations.

The relative increase in farm size for each of the ten-year periods under consideration generally followed a pattern similar to the reduction in farm numbers: the largest increase in farm size of 27.4% occurred between 1941 and 1951, with the smallest increases of 14.8% and 12.6% occurring respectively in the 1981 to 1991 and 1971 to 1981 periods. Concomitantly, the earlier time period was characterized by the largest decrease in farm numbers, and the latter two decades were those in which the smallest decreases in farm numbers occurred. Some of the main forces behind the increase in farm size and the reduction of farm numbers have been the mechanization of farming, the substitution of capital for labour, and the application of other technologies such as fertilizers, herbicides, and insecticides. As a result, the farm population is increasingly dependent on off-farm inputs, in comparison to previous time periods when the majority of farm inputs were produced on the farm. The increased dependence has created a cost-price squeeze which has also contributed to fewer but larger farms.

Farmers in Saskatchewan are more likely to rely on crop production, particularly **WHEAT**, in comparison to farmers in Manitoba and Alberta, who tend to have more diversified operations; however, they too are responding to changing marketing conditions and engaging in more diversified types of crop and livestock production. The relative size of the farm population has also declined, and is not immune to the demographic factors that affect the rest of the population: the general declining fertility rate since the "baby boom" is also apparent here. In comparison to previous periods when farm families of six or more were relatively common, the farm family of the 1980s, 1990s and the beginning of the 21st century are more likely to have only one or two children. In 2001, the total farm population in Saskatchewan was 123,385, which represented a 15.2% decline from 1996 and made up 12.6% of the provincial population.

Like the majority of modern industrialized nations, Canada has witnessed an increasing concentration of its population in larger urban centres. This urbanization, which possibly began at the time of the initial settlement or shortly thereafter, has transformed a basically rural country into an urbanized nation dominated by a relatively small number of large metropolitan centres. It has created an almost complete reversal of the rural urban population from shortly after Confederation in 1867 to the start of the new millennium in 2001: in 1871 less than one in five (19.6%) of the Canadian population was classified as an urban resident, whereas one in five (20.1%) was part of the rural population in 2001. There is considerable variability in the relative sizes of the rural and urban populations across the different regions and provinces of Canada. For much of its history Saskatchewan could be considered a rural agricultural province, although the majority of the provincial population is now urban. A larger proportion of the Saskatchewan population was classified as rural residents for all sixty years under consideration than was evident for the total Canadian population for those years: this is largely due to the greater involvement and dependence of the Saskatchewan labour force on farming, **MINING**, **FORESTRY**, and other extractive activities in comparison to the residents of other regions and provinces.

Urban Saskatchewan residents are largely distributed between two major centres (Saskatoon and Regina) and ten smaller regional centres. Of the 978,933 people living in Saskatchewan in 2001, 196,811 resided in Saskatoon and 178,225 lived in Regina. Saskatoon experienced a 1.6% increase in its population from 1996 to 2001, while Regina had a loss of 1.2% of its population during this same five-year span. Ten smaller regional centres accounted for 138,844 of Saskatchewan's residents in 2001; seven of these experienced a decline in their populations from 1996 to 2001. The three centres that increased their populations were Lloydminster, Humboldt and Estevan. Urbanization in Saskatchewan and other provinces is more than the increasing concentration of population in larger centres: it is also the increasing concentration of businesses, services (education, health) and opportunities, and the relative decline or closure of these services in the rural areas and trade centres. With the closure of grain elevators, businesses, schools, **HOSPITALS** and other services, the rural population is required to travel greater distances for these services.

The changing relative size of rural and urban populations is largely the result of migration of population from rural to urban areas for employment, educational and other opportunities, and of the displacement of people out of farming as a result of mechanization and other technological developments. As indicated earlier, the farm population is not isolated from the demographic trends which characterize the general population in Canada and other industrialized countries. The graying of the Canadian and other populations is also evident in the farm operator population in Saskatchewan: in 2001, the average age of the farm operators in Saskatchewan was 50.9 years, which was 1.5 years greater than in 1996; and the average age of farm operators is greater than that of other Canadians in the self-employed and general labour forces. As

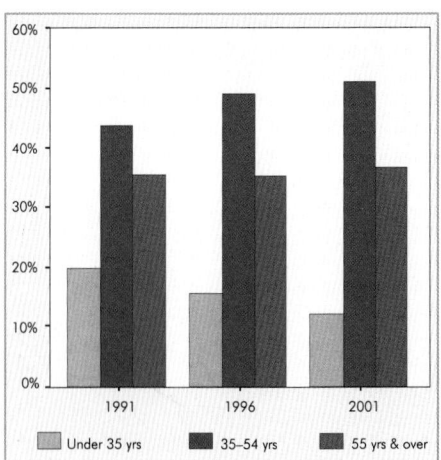

Source: Statistics Canada, 2001 Census of Agriculture, Profile of Saskatchewan Farm Operators, Who's Minding Saskatchewan's Farms?

Figure RP-3. Percentage Distribution of Saskatchewan Farm Operators by Age Group, 1991, 1996, 2001.

shown in Figure RP-3, the percentage of farm operators in the age group under 35 years of age decreased by 7.7% from 1991 to 2001, while the percentages in the two older age groups increased during that ten-year period. The relative increase or stability in the older age group is possibly the result of the operators continuing to farm beyond the normally accepted retirement age of 65, because few younger operators are willing or able to purchase farm operations. Other reasons that discourage younger people from entering farming are the attractions of higher and more regular incomes, regular hours, paid vacations, and other benefits associated with non-farm occupations most likely located in urban centres.

All age groups participate in non-farm work at varying rates as a means to supplement the variable and somewhat uncertain incomes derived from the farm operation. This participation has increased for all age groups: the largest increase occurred in the youngest age group, in which the proportion working at a non-farm job went up from 46% in 1991 to 56% in 2001. The decrease in the number of farmers in all age groups and the dramatic decline of those belonging to the younger age group introduce some serious questions about the farmers of the future and the future of farming. *David Hay*

RURAL SETTLEMENT PATTERNS. Rural settlement patterns describe the "distribution of farmsteads and dwellings" across the rural landscape. Most rural settlement in Saskatchewan is associated with agriculture, although northern communities and Indian reserves could also be included. A settlement can be considered rural where the greater part of the working population is employed in primary sector activities; rural homes may be isolated from one another (dispersed) or clustered together in small groups (hamlets) or larger villages. Rural

settlement patterns in Saskatchewan have been greatly influenced by the policies and practices implemented in the late 19th century to promote the spread of agriculture. Foremost was the Dominion land survey that divided the prairies into a grid of six-mile square townships, each subdivided into 36 square-mile sections. Land within each township was allocated for differing purposes; most even-numbered and some odd-numbered sections were available as homesteads. A homestead comprised one quarter-section of land; each homesteader had to build a home on that land. This resulted in a predominantly dispersed settlement pattern, comprised of isolated farmsteads. One way to lessen the resulting isolation was for neighbours to locate farmsteads on adjacent corners of land, creating a cluster of homes sometimes referred to as a "four-corner hamlet." (*See* **LEGAL LAND SURVEY**)

The density of rural settlements varies across the province. It is influenced by a number of factors including the characteristics of the physical environment and the economic orientation of farms. Fewer farmsteads were located in the semi-arid southwestern region, where early farms were typically one-half section or more in size (because many homesteaders purchased an additional quarter-section as a pre-emption). Density was greater in the park belt, where smaller and more numerous farms were the norm—especially on land reserved for the settlement of particular groups, on which both odd and even-numbered sections were made available for homesteading (*see* **ETHNIC BLOC SETTLEMENTS**). The density of rural settlement diminished, beginning in the late 1920s in the southwest and in the 1950s in all areas, as rural depopulation and farm enlargement took hold. The abandonment of farmsteads was particularly evident in areas that proved ill suited to crop production and reverted to pastureland. As farm size increases, the number of farmsteads continues to decline.

Not all rural settlement in the province is dispersed. Some **MÉTIS** and a few Euro-Canadian settlers had occupied land in advance of the survey. They tended to cluster along creeks and around trading posts and trails. Other clustered settlements were formed in the late 19th century, under special provisions of the **DOMINION LANDS ACT**. The "hamlet clause" of the Act permitted certain religious groups to establish farm villages. Both Mennonite and Doukhobor settlers took advantage of the clause to establish farm villages in Saskatchewan. Mennonites settled near Rosthern, northeast of Saskatoon, and near Swift Current, in the southwest. These settlements fell into three categories: organized villages with a communal administration; unorganized villages; and four-corner hamlets. Both village types initially adhered to the *Strassendorf* (street village) pattern, with houses aligned on either side of a central street. Some villages such as Blumenhof, south

of Swift Current, have survived in modified form; but Mennonite settlements were subject to the same economic forces felt elsewhere in Saskatchewan, and many farmsteads have been abandoned. Out-migration of more conservative Mennonites in the 1920s also diluted enthusiasm for the traditional ways. Doukhobor settlement patterns varied over time, but also included a number of street villages built on reserves located in five areas across the park belt.

Other clustered rural settlements were located on purchased land. The most prominent contemporary examples are the more than fifty Hutterite colonies, spread throughout agricultural Saskatchewan but concentrated particularly in the southwest. Colonies typically house between 80 and 120 individuals, living in a housing complex at the heart of the colony. Orientation of buildings is governed by tradition: housing and communal kitchen are typically arranged in a north-south direction, while secular buildings such as barns are oriented east-west. Rural settlement patterns today are greatly influenced by economic forces that have encouraged a steady increase in farm size and a reduction in the farm population. As more farmers depend on off-farm work for survival, many no longer reside on their land. At the same time, the attractions of rural living have encouraged the development of hobby-farms around larger urban centres. Rural settlement patterns, while still reflecting earlier influences, continue to respond to the shifting social and economic conditions of the 21st century. *Marilyn Lewry*

FURTHER READING: Friesen, R.J. 1977. "Saskatchewan Mennonite Settlements: Modification of an Old World Settlement Pattern," *Canadian Ethnic Studies* 9 (2): 72–89; Pacione, M. 1984. *Rural Geography*. London: Harper & Row; Tracie, C.J. 1996. *"Toil and Peaceful Life": Doukhobor Village Settlements in Saskatchewan, 1899–1918*. Regina: Canadian Plains Research Center.

RUTHERFORD, WILLIAM JOHN (1868–1930). William John Rutherford, known as "Saskatchewan's first agricultural scientist," was responsible for establishing the **UNIVERSITY OF SASKATCHEWAN**'s College of Agriculture, the first of its kind in Canada to be located on a university campus along with a College of Arts. Rutherford was born in Potsdam, New York in 1868. His family moved to Dundas County, Ontario, where he received his primary and secondary education. He earned a Bachelor of Science degree in Agriculture at the Ontario Agricultural College of Guelph, where he later taught animal science. He also taught at the University of Iowa at Ames, and at the University of Manitoba from 1906 to 1908. That year he was appointed Deputy Minister of Agriculture with the Saskatchewan government, and a year later became Dean of the College of Agriculture at the new cam-

UNIVERSITY OF SASKATCHEWAN ARCHIVES A-1335

William Rutherford (as Dean) addressing Agricultural Society Convention in the University of Saskatchewan Livestock Pavilion, ca. 1920s.

pus in Saskatoon, where he organized the Department of Animal Husbandry. Under his guidance, the college and the university farm adjacent to it became famous in the world of agricultural science: in a new area of settlement, with many problems in farming arising from a unique set of climatic conditions, Rutherford made a lasting contribution to Saskatchewan agriculture. Having died in 1930, he was posthumously inducted into the Canadian Agricultural Hall of Fame in 1966 and in the Saskatchewan Agricultural Hall of Fame in 1972.

RYE. Although it is not immediately obvious, upon close examination we see that rye (*Secale cereale*), like the other temperate cereal crops (WHEAT, BARLEY and OAT), is a grass that has been highly modified by the domestication process. All four crops are native to southeast Europe/southwest Asia, where their wild relatives still grow. Domestication of rye probably occurred in northern Europe over 5,000 years ago when, as a weed of the other cereals, it came to predominate in fields, was harvested, used, and hence became a crop in its own right. It is likely that during the Middle Ages in Europe rye was more important than wheat as a human food. In eastern Europe and Russia rye has traditionally been an important component of local breads, and these areas are now the major producers of rye. Compared to the other temperate cereals, rye is now a relatively minor crop in the rest of the world. Early settlers, particularly those from eastern Europe and Russia, introduced rye into Canada.

The rye plant resembles other grasses in its pattern of growth. Starting from a seed, leaves are produced above ground and then, depending on the environment, a number of tillers (stems) are produced from the base of the plant. Within each of these tillers a single ear is produced, which in the case of fall-seeded rye will usually emerge in May (later in the case of spring-seeded rye). Each ear will contain up to sixty flowers that produce a single grain after pollination. Unlike other cereal crops, rye is cross-pollinated, requiring pollen from another rye plant for fertilization. Because of this, rye is very susceptible to a fungal disease called ergot. If infected, individual grains are replaced by hard black ergot bodies, which contain a number of undesirable and even toxic components. Ergot poisoning was relatively common in Europe in areas of high rye consumption because rye heavily contaminated with ergot bodies was milled and used to make bread. Hallucinogenic compounds are present in the ergot body, and early cases of ergot poisoning were referred to as "St. Anthony's Fire."

As a crop, particularly as a prairie crop, rye has a number of positive attributes. Foremost among these, it is the most cold-hardy of the temperate cereals. Unlike fall-seeded wheat (the next cereal in terms of cold-hardiness), rye does not require the same care in terms of management practices in order to survive throughout the winter and regrow in the spring. A fall-seeded crop provides cover for the ground from late fall to early spring (reducing erosion), and allows the crop to take full advantage of spring moisture and escape disease. In addition, rye tends to be resistant to diseases other than ergot and to be drought-tolerant. As such, rye would appear to be the ideal grain crop for the prairies.

Rye grain is used for animal feed, milled to make bread, or used to make rye whiskey. Compared to wheat bread, rye bread is dark in colour and does not rise as much because of its lower level of gluten proteins. However, rye has high levels of soluble fibre, which is now recognized as a valuable component of the human diet; the same high levels of soluble fibre limit the value of rye as an animal feed: if used in an animal ration, the level of rye is usually limited to approximately 25% in order to avoid feeding problems. The inclusion in the ration of enzymes that break down the soluble fibre has been shown to help alleviate this problem. Recent research has also shown that the level of soluble fibre is under genetic control, and could be either increased or decreased through plant breeding.

A significant increase in the demand for rye (through increased use as an animal feed, increased human consumption, or use as a fuel stock for ethanol production) could possibly be stimulated by either appropriate breeding work or through the promotion of the beneficial effects of rye in the human diet. Until this occurs, rye is likely to remain a minor crop on the prairies. Despite its desirable attributes, with little incentive to carry out research because of the low demand, rye appears likely to remain a "Cinderella" crop of Canada and the prairies for the foreseeable future, compared to wheat, barley and oat.   *Graham Scoles*

FURTHER READING: Bushuk, W. (ed.). 2001. *Rye: Production, Chemistry and Technology*. St. Paul, MN: American Association of Cereal Chemists.

S

SAGE HILL WRITING EXPERIENCE. The Sage Hill Writing Experience is a summer residential writing workshop that draws students from across Canada and abroad. It runs for ten days each July/August near Lumsden, offering adult workshops in poetry, fiction, novel writing, playwriting, non-fiction, and children's writing—all led by esteemed Canadian writers. It also offers an annual fall Poetry Colloquium, and a summer Teen Writing Experience. Sage Hill evolved from the now-defunct Saskatchewan Summer School of the Arts. From 1966 to 1989, the School ran each summer and included programs in writing, **MUSIC**, **VISUAL ART**, **DANCE**, photography, and drama. In 1989, after funding cutbacks, the **SASKATCHEWAN ARTS BOARD** announced that the School was to be closed. The **SASKATCHEWAN WRITERS GUILD** initiated the Sage Hill program; after the closure of the School, the Guild set up a steering committee and obtained funds in order to maintain Sage Hill, which is the only ongoing professional-level residential program to have survived the closure.

From 1990 to 1993, the Sage Hill Writing Experience took place at a former radar base near Saskatoon, and in 1994 it moved to its current location at St. Michael's Retreat Centre. Sage Hill is facilitated by an executive director and a nine-member

KATE HILL PHOTO

Patrick Lane is one of the esteemed writers who have been members of the Sage Hill faculty.

board of directors. Faculty have included **SANDRA BIRDSELL**, Di Brandt, **LORNA CROZIER**, Patrick Lane, Robert Kroestch, **GUY VANDERHAEGHE**, Jane Urquhart, Don McKay, **ANNE SZUMIGALSKI**, and many others.

Holly Luhning

SAINTE-MARIE, BUFFY (BEVERLY) (1941–).

Singer-songwriter, visual artist, actor, and educator, Buffy Sainte-Marie was born on February 20, 1941, of **CREE** parents on the Piapot Reserve near Craven, Saskatchewan. She was orphaned as a baby and adopted by a part-Micmac family who raised her in Massachusetts and Maine. She was later adopted according to tribal customs on the Piapot Reserve by a Cree family related to her natural parents. Sainte-Marie started playing guitar at 17, and became an important artist in Greenwich Village (New York) folk music circles by the early 1960s. She toured North America's college, reservation, and concert hall circuits, known as a writer of love and protest songs. By age 24, she had appeared in the United States, Canada, Europe, Australia, and Asia. Among her earliest Canadian performances were the 1964 Mariposa Folk Festival and Expo '67.

Buffy Sainte-Marie recorded several albums, including her highly political first album *It's My Way* (1964), which won Billboard's Best New Artist award. This was followed by *Many a Mile* (1965), *Little Wheel Spin and Spin* (1966), and *I'm Gonna Be a Country Girl Again* (1968), which saw her move away from folk towards a country style. Her first all-electronic vocal album, *Illuminations* (1969), signalled her interest in technology. Sainte-Marie's rock breakthrough album, entitled *She Used To Wanna Be a Ballerina* (1971), followed. She continued to write and record throughout the 1970s. Some of her best-known songs were recorded by other artists, including "Until It's Time for You to Go," recorded by Elvis Presley, Cher, Neil Diamond, Ginette Reno, and Barbra Streisand. "The Universal Soldier," made popular by Donovan, became the anthem of the peace movement. She wrote several songs about First Nations people, including "Native North American," "Now That the Buffalo's Gone," "Soldier Blue," and "My Country 'Tis of Thy People You're Dying." As a songwriter, Sainte-Marie is best known for "Up Where We Belong," written with her husband, record producer Jack Nitzsche, and Will Jennings. This song was on the soundtrack for the American film *An Officer and a Gentleman*, and won an Academy Award in 1983 after being recorded as a duet with Joe Cocker and Jennifer Warnes.

In the late 1970s, Sainte-Marie began to study experimental music, employing computers and MIDI devices. She earned a PhD in Fine Art from the University of Massachusetts, and holds degrees in oriental philosophy and in education. She has also pursued acting and the visual arts. Her visual art

PHOTOGRAPHY DEPARTMENT, UNIVERSITY OF REGINA

Buffy Sainte-Marie, Convocation, University of Regina, 1998.

combines colours and light, using scanned-in photos, fabrics, feathers, or beads. Her work has been shown at the Glenbow Museum (Calgary), Emily Carr Gallery (Vancouver), **MACKENZIE ART GALLERY**, Institute for American Indian Art Museum (Santa Fe, USA), Isaacs Gallery (Toronto), and others. With her son, Sainte-Marie was a performer on the Canadian-aired American children's television show *Sesame Street* from 1975 to 1981. As well, she has appeared on CBC radio and TV, notably in *Superspecial* (1978), *Pascan: PowWow* (1982), and *The Many Moods of Buffy Sainte-Marie* (1983).

In 1992, Sainte-Marie released a comeback album, *Coincidence and Likely Stories*. In 1993, she helped found the Juno Award "Music of Aboriginal Canada," which she won in 1997 for her collection of old and new songs, *Up Where We Belong* (1996). She has won several awards and honours, including the Saskatchewan Recording Industry Association's Lifetime Achievement Award (1994); she is a member of the Juno Hall of Fame (1995) and of the Order of Canada (1998). In 1997, she performed with the **REGINA SYMPHONY ORCHESTRA** and a cast of powwow singers and dancers, donating funds from the concert to the Saskatchewan Indian Federated College. Always interested in education, Buffy Sainte-Marie founded the non-profit Nihewan Foundation for Native American Education in 1969. Its most recent endeavour is the Cradleboard Teaching Project, whose objectives are to provide core curriculum based on Native American cultural perspectives and to build computer networking relationships among partnered Native and non-Native schools. The first pairing of this type was between a mainstream Hawaiian class and a class of Native students in

Saskatchewan. Buffy Sainte-Marie has taught digital music at several colleges, and lectures regularly on a variety of topics. She has been an adjunct professor at York University in Toronto and at the Saskatchewan Indian Federated College in Regina. She holds an honorary Doctor of Laws (1996) from the **UNIVERSITY OF REGINA** and an honorary Doctor of Letters (2003) from the **UNIVERSITY OF SASKATCHEWAN**.

Colette P. Simonot

SAKIMAY FIRST NATION. Chief Sakimay (Sah-ka-ma, Sah-kee-may) and his **CREE** followers signed **TREATY 4** on September 15, 1874. When Sakimay passed away, the band was without a chief for many years; a young man (about 30 years old) by the name of Yellow Calf was their spokesman with the Indian Agent 1883. The reserve formed part of the western boundary of the Crooked Lake Reserves. Members of this band were the brothers and children of Chief Sah-kee-may with their families. The Sakimay Reserve is located 16 km northeast of Grenfell, and is the most populated portion of the land belonging to this band. The reserve area also includes the Shesheep, Little Bone and Minoahcuk reserves. The band's total land base is 11,295.2 ha; it has a population of 1,340 people, 238 of whom reside on the reserve. Band infrastructure includes a band office, band hall, clinic, machine shop, trade shop, training centre, and maintenance buildings. Primary economic endeavours involve agriculture and tourism; a gas station and convenience store are planned on their urban reserve land in west Regina.

Christian Thompson

SAKUNDIAK, PETER (1922–). Peter Sakundiak's contributions to the **AGRICULTURAL IMPLEMENT INDUSTRY**, particularly the grain auger produced by his company since 1948, have simplified the handling of grain for farmers across the country. Born in 1922 in Mikado, Saskatchewan, Peter Sakundiak grew up on his family farm. At the age of 18, he moved to Regina, and worked on his brother's farm for several years. In 1948, he formed Sakundiak Farm Equipment and in a small shop began manufacturing a disc harrow designed by his brother Alex; but owing to rising costs and space limitations, production was short-lived. In 1949, at a farmer's request, Sakundiak manufactured a grain auger, an invention which appeared in the 1940s but was not readily available. It proved a popular item, and Sakundiak's growing company moved to the family farm in 1955. Through the 1960s and 1970s Peter Sakundiak continued to improve the design of his augers, which enjoyed constant demand throughout the grain-producing prairies. Moving to a larger facility in Regina in 1974, the company also began manufacturing grain bins. Sakundiak, a member of Farm Equipment Manufacturer's Association since 1989 and Prairie Implement Manufacturers since

1975, is an implement manufacturer whose products have benefited prairie farmers for over half a century.   *Raymond Ambrosi*

SALEMKA, IRENE (1931–). Born on October 3, 1931, in Steinbach, Manitoba, the daughter of a Lutheran pastor, Irene Salemka studied voice in Regina, Montreal, Toronto, and in Germany. By the late 1940s she was winning scholarships in Saskatchewan festivals, and by 1953 she had received awards from the CBC's "Opportunity Knocks" and "Singing Stars of Tomorrow." Recognized for her performance as Juliette at the 1952 Montreal Festival, she made a spectacular debut as Cio Cio San at Toronto's Royal Alexandra Theatre in 1953 in the presence of an admiring Vincent Massey. Her first place among 200 singers at Carnegie Hall in 1955 launched her into the New Orleans Opera and appearances at Sadler's Wells, London, and in Basle. A leading soprano of the Frankfurt Opera, she also sang in Amsterdam, Barcelona, Berlin, Bremen, Cologne, Munich, Rome, Stuttgart and Vienna. A White Russian audience in Paris called her out for ten encores. Her versatility and popularity were evident in 1965 when she gave a concert in London, performed with eight European orchestras, made two television operas (*The Gypsy Prince* and *La Boheme*), and premiered a new opera in Bremen (*Roulette des Herzens*, by the Austrian Igo Hofstetter). Salemka returned to Canada that year to perform in Regina, Moose Jaw and Weyburn, and made recordings with the CBC in Montreal and Toronto. She supported Lutheran charities, on one occasion performing to an audience of over 1,000 in Regina. Her recordings include

UNIVERSITY OF REGINA ARCHIVES AND SPECIAL COLLECTIONS
84-11-395

Irene Salemka.

performances with Dietrich Fischer-Dieskau. In 1972, she received an honorary degree from the UNIVERSITY OF SASKATCHEWAN, Regina Campus. She now lives in Ontario.   *Robin Swales*

SALTCOATS, town, pop 494, located 27 km SE of Yorkton on the Yellowhead Hwy, No. 16. The town is situated in an attractive setting as a crescent-shaped lake forms the south and eastern boundaries of the community. Anderson Lake was named after William Anderson, a Scot, who settled in the immediate area in 1882 and the district was originally known as Stirling, after Stirling, Scotland. Though the first settlers were predominantly of Scottish and English origin, a walk through the historic Saltcoats cemetery reveals that Irish, Welsh, German, Hungarian, Ukrainian, Icelandic, Scandinavian, and Métis people also came to call the district home. Significant development began to occur in the area in the late 1880s as the railway was being built toward Yorkton. In 1887, the nucleus of a business community began to form with the first entrepreneurs conducting their affairs out of tents. Later, lumber was hauled in from Langenburg by ox team and shacks were erected. With the arrival of the Manitoba and Northwestern Railway in 1888 the name of the community was changed to Saltcoats, after Saltcoats, Scotland, the birthplace of one of the major shareholders in the railway. The Saltcoats post office was also established in 1888 and on April 4, 1894, Saltcoats was incorporated as a village, the first community established as such in what is now Saskatchewan. In 1910, Saltcoats attained town status. Today, agriculture, manufacturing, the Esterhazy area potash mines, and the city of Yorkton provided employment and Saltcoats has a small core of local businesses. A number of notable people have come from the town of Saltcoats. Thomas MacNutt served as a member of the Territorial Assembly from 1902 to 1905 and, after the formation of the province, became the first Speaker of the Legislative Assembly of Saskatchewan. He was also a member of the House of Commons in Ottawa from 1908 to 1921. Gordon Barnhart, University Secretary of the University of Saskatchewan, was Clerk of the Legislative Assembly of Saskatchewan from 1969 to 1989 and Clerk of the Senate of Canada from 1989 to 1994. Barnhart is also an author and editor of a number of books relating to Saskatchewan history. Saltcoats also celebrates being the hometown of Joan McCusker, who with the famed SANDRA SCHMIRLER rink, became a Canadian, World, and Olympic curling champion.   *David McLennan*

SALVATION ARMY. The Salvation Army was founded in 1865 by General William Booth and his wife Catherine in London, England. Booth's motto was "soup, soap, and salvation": he believed that no one would hear the gospel if they were hungry or

SASKATCHEWAN ARCHIVES BOARD R-A1673-2
Salvation Army citadel, Prince Albert (no date).

dirty. The work of the Salvation Army was born in an effort to meet the needs of the marginalized. The Army grew rapidly, and in 1886 the first Army Corps was opened in Canada. In the early 1890s, the work of the Army spread west with the first officers arriving in Moose Jaw. Today, the Salvation Army operates in thirteen cities in Saskatchewan, providing a variety of services including shelter, food, pro-bono services, homes for teenage girls, and other essential services to those who are less fortunate.   *Kristiana MacKenzie*

SAND DUNES: *see* **GREAT SAND HILLS**

SANDERSON, SOL. Sol Sanderson was Chief of the FEDERATION OF SASKATCHEWAN INDIAN NATIONS from 1979 to 1986. Beginning with Sanderson's term, the First Nations became much more active in asserting their political rights, and succeeded in having them included in the Canadian Constitution in 1982. Sanderson was instrumental in ensuring that the treaties were entrenched in the Constitution as well as recognized at the international level: he led a delegation to London that lobbied the British

RICHARD MARJAN PHOTO/SASKATCHEWAN ARCHIVES BOARD
S-SP-A22662-3, SASKATOON STARPHOENIX FONDS

Sol Sanderson, November 1984.

Parliament on behalf of Treaty Indians. Sanderson was a founding leader of the Assembly of First Nations, and a senior spokesperson at the First Ministers' Conferences pertaining to Aboriginal people. He also played an important role in the move towards Indian government, which involves control over First Nations schools as well as over three post-secondary institutions: the **SASKATCHEWAN INDIAN CULTURAL CENTRE**; the **SASKATCHEWAN INDIAN INSTITUTE OF TECHNOLOGIES**; and the Saskatchewan Indian Federated College (now **FIRST NATIONS UNIVERSITY OF CANADA**). Sanderson also was prominent in the Treaty Land Entitlement process in Saskatchewan.

Rob Nestor

SANDISON, JOHN EDGAR (1925–2004).

Born on November 22, 1925, "Johnny" Sandison was a television and radio broadcaster and community volunteer. After serving in the Royal Canadian Navy beginning in 1943, Sandison remained with the naval reserves until retiring in 1985. His broadcast career began in 1953 with CKRM, and in 1958 he joined CKCK radio and subsequently CKCK-TV, where he remained for thirty-four years, retiring in 1996. Sandison volunteered his time with organizations such as the Alzheimer's Association, the Hospitals of Regina Foundation, and the Canadian Diabetes Association. He was awarded the St. John Ambulance Officer Grade Medal, a long service medal from the Corps of Commissionaires, and was invested as a Member of the Order of Canada in 1997. Sandison died on August 17, 2004.

SAPERGIA, BARBARA (1943–).

A prominent Saskatchewan writer of poetry, stories, plays, and programs for television and radio, Barbara Sapergia was born in Moose Jaw, Saskatchewan in 1943. She studied English literature at the **UNIVERSITY OF SASKATCHEWAN**, where she received her BA in 1964, and at the University of Manitoba, where she earned her MA in 1966.

Sapergia, with **ROBERT CURRIE**, **GARY HYLAND**, and husband **GEOFFREY URSELL**, founded Coteau Books in 1975. She has remained heavily involved in its operation, acting as a member of the co-operative's board of directors and as editor of over 20 titles for young readers.

Sapergia's published works include the poetry collection *Dirt Hills Mirage* (1980), the novels *Foreigners* (1984) and *Secrets in Water* (1999), and a collection of short stories, *South Hill Girls* (1992). She is also known for her plays, which include the productions *Lokkinen* (1982), *The Great Orlando* (1985), *Matty and Rose* (1985), and *Roundup* (1990). In all, seven of her plays have been professionally produced, and two of them, *Lokkinen* and *Roundup*, have also been published. Most recently, Sapergia has focused her energies on writing for television. She is one of three partners in

Moose Jaw Light and Power Artistic Productions Ltd; and along with Geoffrey Ursell, she has created and written for the nationally televised preschool series *Prairie Berry Pie*. Sapergia lives with her husband in Saskatoon.

Justin Messner

FURTHER READING: Hillis, Doris. 1988. *Plainspeaking: Interviews with Saskatchewan Writers.* Regina: Coteau Books; 2004. *Saskatchewan Writers: Lives Past and Present.* Regina: Canadian Plains Research Center; Van Luven, Lynne. 1992. "South Hill Girls Are Memorable; Saskatchewan Writers' Stories Powerfully Recreate Small-town Life." *Edmonton Journal* (May 17), D8.

SAPP, ALLEN (1929–).

Allen Sapp, one of Canada's foremost artists, is renowned for his depiction of the day-to-day reserve life he experienced growing up in the 1930s. Sapp, a descendant of Chief **POUNDMAKER**, was born on January 2, 1929 on the Red Pheasant Reserve, south of North Battleford. His mother suffered from tuberculosis and eventually died during his adolescence. Sapp's father later married Martha Dressyman, and Sapp was raised by his maternal grandmother and grandfather, Albert and Maggie Soonias.

As a child, Sapp was often ill and spent long hours in bed. To pass away the time, and encouraged by his grandmother, Sapp took up drawing. When he grew older, Sapp in turn cared for his grandmother until she died in 1963. He then moved to North Battleford to try to make a living as an artist, selling his paintings on the streets for a few dollars. He struggled, selling door to door, until 1966 when he met Dr. Allan Gonor. Gonor recognized Sapp's talent and encouraged him to paint what he knew best—life on the reserve. A friendship and part-

nership grew, and by the 1970s Sapp's work was known throughout North America and as far away as London, England. Over the years, his work and life story have been the subject of numerous books and television documentaries such as the National Film Board of Canada's *Colours of Pride*, and the CBC's *On the Road Again* and *Allen Sapp, By Instinct a Painter*. Books include *A Cree Life*, by John Warner, and *Two Spirits Soar*, by W.P. Kinsella.

Sapp has received numerous awards and honours, including the Order of Canada, the Saskatchewan Order of Merit, membership in the Royal Canadian Academy of Arts, an honorary Doctorate from the **UNIVERSITY OF REGINA**, as well as the **SASKATCHEWAN ARTS BOARD** Lifetime Achievement Award and a National Aboriginal Lifetime Achievement Award. In 1989, North Battleford opened a public gallery to honour Allen Sapp and Dr. Allan Gonor. The Allen Sapp Gallery-Allan Gonor Collection, the only public gallery in Canada dedicated to the work of a living artist, houses comprehensive archives on Sapp and boasts the most extensive permanent collection of his art in Canada. In 2003, Sapp won the Governor General's Literary Award for his illustrations in the children's book *The Song Within My Heart*.

Dean Bauche

SARJEANT, WILLIAM ANTONY SWITHIN (1935–2002).

Bill Sarjeant received his BSc and PhD in Sheffield and his DSc in Nottingham, England. In 1972 he and his wife Margaret moved to Saskatoon, where he joined the Department of Geology. Sarjeant was a voracious reader, folksinger and harmonica player, collector, naturalist, author of historical fantasies and of more than fifty articles on Sherlock Holmes, as well as an influential

COURTESY OF THE ALLEN SAPP GALLERY (THE GONOR COLLECTION)

Allen Sapp's "Baby was Crying."

member of the Saskatoon and Saskatchewan heritage communities.

First and foremost he was a geologist and paleontologist who wrote the ten-volume bibliography, *Geologists and the History of Geology*, and had the world's largest private collection on the history of GEOLOGY–part of an 85,000-volume personal library. He co-authored *The Tracks of Triassic Vertebrates: Fossil Evidence from North-West England*, a coffee table book on fossil traces of dinosaur footprints, and wrote over 350 articles on geology topics. He was a member of the International Jurassic Sub-Commission of the International Union of Geological Sciences. He received the 1990 Sue Tyler Friedman Medal, given by the Geological Society of London, and the 1991 Founder's Medal of the Society for the History of Natural History of London. In 1998 he was elected a Fellow of the Royal Society of Canada.

At various times Sarjeant was chairman of the Special Committee on the Identification of Historic Buildings for Saskatoon City Council, a member of the Saskatchewan Heritage Advisory Board, a director of Saskatchewan Culture, president of the Saskatoon Environmental Society, and a member of the Preservation Committee of the Society for the Study of Architecture in Canada. He was also an executive member of the Saskatoon branch of the Community Planning Association of Canada, a member of the Saskatchewan Archives Board, and chairman of the Saskatchewan History Advisory Board.

He co-authored *Saskatoon's Historic Buildings and Sites* (1973) with Sally Club, as well as a version of Bill Delainey's MA thesis: "Saskatoon: The Growth of a City" (1974). With John Duerkop he wrote the official souvenir of Century Saskatoon, called *Saskatoon: A Century in Pictures* (1982). He edited the annual *Saskatoon History Review* for sixteen years. He was a major force behind drafting the Saskatchewan Heritage Act, led the fights to save the

CPR Station and the Capitol Theatre in Saskatoon, and helped create the Municipal Heritage Advisory Committee Award. Amongst the awards he received were a 1977 provincial award for contributions to the heritage community, a Century Saskatoon Medal in 1982, and Saskatoon City Council's 1990 Volunteer Heritage Public Service Award.

John Duerkop

SASKATCHEWAN. The name Saskatchewan is derived from CREE *kisiskâciwanisîpiy*, meaning "swift-flowing river." Saskatchewan became a province of Canada on September 1, 1905. Located between Alberta to the west and Manitoba to the east, its boundaries extend from the US border along the 49th parallel to the border with the Northwest Territories along the 60th parallel. Saskatchewan covers 6.5% of Canada, an area of 651,036 km². Of this, 591,670 km² are land and 59,366 km² are covered by water. The land is divided between the mostly crystalline rocks of the PRECAMBRIAN Shield in the northern third of the province and the sedimentary rocks of the WESTERN CANADIAN SEDIMENTARY BASIN in the south. Mineral resources include world-class deposits of URANIUM and POTASH. Four ecozones span the province: prairie, boreal plains, boreal shield, and taiga shield. The climate is continental, characterized by large seasonal temperature ranges and low precipitation.

Humans began to occupy the land as ice retreated at the end of the last GLACIATION. Distinctive cultures evolved, dependent on the natural resources available in the different ecozones. European contact with Aboriginal peoples occurred during the FUR TRADE era (ca. 1690–1820), and increased when agricultural settlement began in the late 19th century. In the early 20th century, that settlement history produced an ethnically mixed, largely agrarian population concentrated on farms and in communities across the prairie ecozone. A century later, agricul-

ture has declined in relative importance and more people live in urban areas (64.3%) than in the countryside. The 2001 census recorded Saskatchewan's population at 978,933, while provincial estimates for July 2004 were 995,391. The 2001 median age (36.7yrs) was slightly below the Canadian average. Saskatchewan had the highest proportion (15.1%) of inhabitants over 65 in Canada, but also relatively more people under 20 years of age (29.2% versus 25.9% for Canada). 13.5% of people identified themselves as Aboriginal, an increase of 17% since 1996. Although only 2.9% of the population were self-identified as visible minorities, a total of 94 different ethnic groups were recognized, ranging from 275,060 people claiming German ethnicity to just 10 people identified as Moroccan.

Saskatchewan typically has a lower unemployment rate than the Canadian average (6.3% versus 7.4% in 2001) and a higher proportion of people working (63.5% versus 61.5%); of the latter, 13.9% work in agriculture and 3.3% in other primary industries. A further 11.1% of workers are employed in manufacturing or construction, and 71.1% in service industries. Business and industry make the major contribution to Saskatchewan's economy, but 20% of workers are employed by the public sector, especially in health and education. In 2003 provincial GDP was $36.519 billion, of which 8.7% was derived from agriculture and 12.3% from other primary industries. 12% came from manufacturing or construction, and 67% from an ever-increasing range of service industries (Figure SK-1). Export trade is important to Saskatchewan; in 2003 the largest single export commodity was crude oil (Figure SK-2): Saskatchewan can no longer be described as the "wheat economy." *Marilyn Lewry*

SASKATCHEWAN ARTS BOARD. The establishment of the Saskatchewan Arts Board by Order-in-Council in 1948 and the Arts Board Act in 1949 signified a major development for the arts in

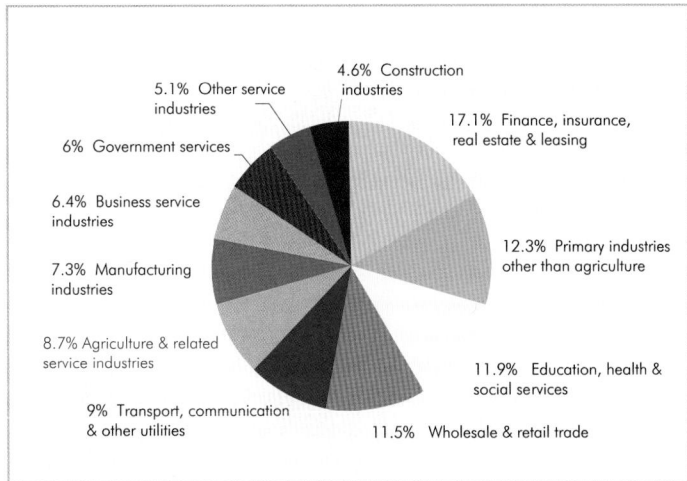

Figure SK-1. Provincial GDP, 2003.

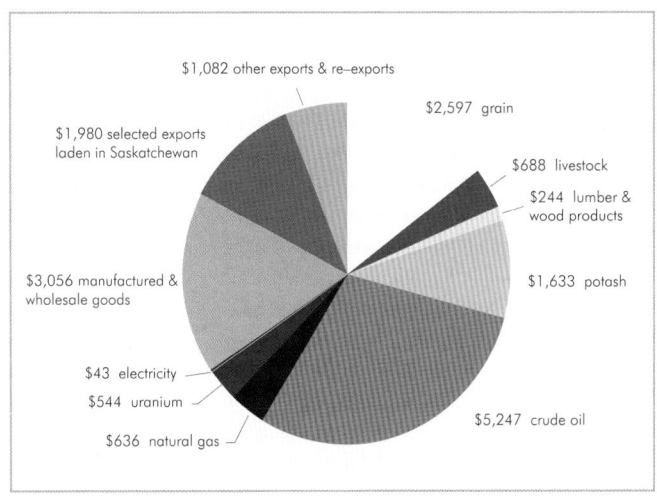

Figure SK-2. Exports, 2003 ($millions).

Saskatchewan and North America. Outside the United Kingdom, where the British Arts Council had just been established, the Arts Board was the first of many: a public arts agency operating and granting funds "at arm's length" from government. The creation of the Arts Board was one of several cultural initiatives undertaken by the government of **T.C. DOUGLAS**. As part of a larger program of building a public infrastructure to enable individual growth and self-realization, it was based on the Premier's belief that "the people of the Prairies are hungry ... for things of the mind and the spirit: good music, literature, paintings and folk songs. This was why the Arts Board was established."

In 1948 there was little professional arts activity in the province, and many organizations operated without staff. The Arts Board rapidly launched a number of programs to make the arts available to the people of Saskatchewan and to stimulate artistic growth. Several high-profile initiatives engaged the community and caught the attention of the media– particularly outreach programs and tours aimed at smaller towns and villages, workshops to improve artistic standards, and programs to raise public awareness. By 1968, the Arts Board had a unique Permanent Collection, the School of the Arts at Fort San, and consulting services and grant programs which became the agency's signature functions.

In the early 1970s, the government made two decisions which had a profound effect on the Board's future: first, the province created the Department of Culture and Youth in 1972; and then in 1974 it established the provincial lottery system, a portion of the profits from which were dedicated to culture. This system strengthened groups dedicated to community participation and arts education, as well as service organizations such as the **SASKATCHEWAN WRITERS GUILD**. However, it posed an ongoing challenge to the development of a unified policy and leadership for the arts in the province. It contributed to the ongoing and sometimes heated debate about "professional and amateur" in the arts; and, as lottery revenues increased rapidly, challenged the government to provide increased support to the Arts Board.

The cultural landscape has changed enormously since 1948, in no small measure due to the Arts Board. The Board's early decision to concentrate on raising artistic standards has resulted in an ever-expanding number of practicing artists and arts organizations worthy of public support. With the availability of lottery money for activity that had formerly been its responsibility, the Arts Board entered in the mid-1970s a phase characterized by much greater attention to the growing needs of practicing artists and arts organizations. This strategy responded to the shift in the arts in Saskatchewan, but it resulted in the Board loosening its ties to organizations and activities that had previously occupied a

COURTESY OF THE SASKATCHEWAN ARTS BOARD

This 1950 work by McGregor Hone, "By the Radio," was the first work of art collected by the Saskatchewan Arts Board for their permanent collection.

large portion of its time. It also fostered a perception that the Board had lost interest in its development and community-based mandate–a perception that the Board began to address as it went into its fifth decade. This shift and its impact substantially influenced the third phase of the Board's history, from 1990 to the present: the restoration of the Arts Board as the province's single arts agency, with a unified focus for provincial arts policy and funding. In 1990, this idea found full voice as the key recommendation of the provincial government's Arts Strategy Task Force; but it remains only a vision at present. The Task Force Report led to the proclamation of a new Act in 1998, which emphasized a broader application of its powers and responsibilities, particularly in the areas of arts and education, cultural industries, and Aboriginal arts. The latter area had been previously addressed by the Board, but it was not until the late 1990s that formal steps were taken to meet the needs and aspirations of

ABORIGINAL ARTISTS. The new Act also spoke to the concept of peer assessment and community input into the development of the Board's operating policies and programs.

In 2004, moving toward its 60th anniversary, the Board directed support to 99 artists, 45 organizations, and 47 projects for a total of over $5.3 million. Recipients of its grants constitute a who's who of Saskatchewan artists. The opportunities for the arts in Saskatchewan and for the Board are many: an ever-expanding community of artists; global markets for Saskatchewan artists; new technologies; and the changing demographics of Saskatchewan. Its mission statement, fashioned in 2000, commits the Board to cultivating an environment where the arts will thrive for the benefit of everyone in Saskatchewan, a task that allows it to respond to emerging needs and opportunities while keeping faith with those who brought the Board into existence and nurtured its early years.   *Jeremy Morgan*

FURTHER READING: Johnson, A.W. 2004. *Dream No Little Dreams: A Biography of the Douglas Government of Saskatchewan, 1944–1961.* Toronto: University of Toronto Press; Riddell, W.A. 1979. *Cornerstone For Culture: A History of the Saskatchewan Arts Board from 1948 to 1978.* Regina: Saskatchewan Arts Board.

SASKATCHEWAN ASSOCIATION FOR LIFE-LONG LEARNING (SALL).

The Saskatchewan Association for Lifelong Learning (SALL) was established in 1971. It drew its membership and structure from roots in the Canadian Association of Adult Education (CAAE) and the Association of Adult Education (AAE), Saskatchewan Division.

Prior to 1970, the AAE, Saskatchewan Division, provided a focus for people who were interested in the promotion of adult learning opportunities. Activities were limited to a one-day annual meeting organized by the Extension Division, **UNIVERSITY OF SASKATCHEWAN** and conducted by an executive which met several times a year. The meetings brought together a varied group of people: members of the Saskatchewan Women's Institute, field staff of the **SASKATCHEWAN WHEAT POOL**, school board members and a few school board staff, clergy (most from the United Church), Department of Education staff, agriculture extension workers and local committee members, and university extension staff.

A feeling emerged that the organization did not quite fit the needs of those interested in the promotion of adult education, and that it did not reflect Saskatchewan. The province had a rich background in adult education that had evolved out of developments in the 1940s connected to the evolving agricultural economy and infrastructure needs in rural Saskatchewan. In 1944, the CCF government headed by Premier **T.C. DOUGLAS** was the first government anywhere to establish an Adult Education

Division within the Department of Education. The Farm Radio Forums (1939–65) and the high profile 1957 Royal Commission on Agriculture and Rural Life had raised the level of awareness for the need for adult education. The large co-operative movement and school boards also played a significant role in supporting adult learning activities. The extension role in agriculture and rural life carried out by the College of Agriculture and later the Extension Division at the University of Saskatchewan was unique in Canada. In 1971, a small committee developed a proposal for a more appropriate organization to address the current needs. Drs. Brock Whale and **HAROLD BAKER** of the University of Saskatchewan Extension Division provided the major leadership. Herb Kindred from the **UNIVERSITY OF REGINA**, Lorne Sparling from the Community College in Prince Albert, and several other individuals met to draft a mandate and a constitution for the Saskatchewan Association of Lifelong Learning (SALL). The main goals of the new organization were to provide a network for those interested or involved in the promotion and/or offering of adult learning, and to advocate the cause of adult learning to decision makers and to the general public.

Those involved in adult education at that time were volunteers from various geographic locations who had many divergent aspirations. To have a means of communication was thus very significant. Annual conferences and regional learning events provided opportunities for members to network, learn about new initiatives in adult and post-secondary education, and engage in policy forums on adult education. SALL established several awards to honour adult education practitioners and programs: the Roby Kidd award in 1992, to mark SALL's twentieth anniversary; and the Adult Education Program of the Year Award as well as the Community Adult Educator of the Year Award, both in 1994.

For over two decades, SALL was the major vehicle through which many Saskatchewan adult educators and policy makers communicated and shared ideas. In the 1960s few resources, public or private, were devoted to adult education, and few decision makers were concerned that adults should have more learning opportunities. SALL brought renewed attention to issues in adult education in Saskatchewan at a time when post-secondary education was rapidly developing in the 1970s and 1980s. SALL's participation in forums and consultations on provincial and federal initiatives ensured that the provincial adult and post-secondary education sector had an opportunity to voice concerns and make recommendations. In 1998, the SALL Board of Directors dissolved the organization because its original mandate had been met. Today, adult education is relatively well resourced and has become a priority in Saskatchewan. Several vested-interest groups

including the Saskatchewan Literacy Network, the Saskatchewan Council on Educators of non-English Speakers, and the Saskatchewan Adult Basic Education Association continue to advocate for adult learners.   *Lorne Sparling and Donna Woloshyn*

SASKATCHEWAN ASSOCIATION FOR MULTICULTURAL EDUCATION.

The Saskatchewan Association for Multicultural Education (SAME) is a provincial non-profit organization committed to developing respect and understanding among Saskatchewan residents through multicultural and anti-racist education. SAME promotes the recognition, understanding, and acceptance of diversity and social justice issues leading to action in educational contexts, primarily K–12 schools. In 1981, the Saskatchewan Multicultural/Intercultural Education Ad Hoc Committee was created. This group hosted the first Provincial Conference on Multicultural Education in 1983, following which, SAME was incorporated in 1984. SAME has published two editions of *Saskatchewan Cultural Profiles* that include brief descriptions from a variety of ethnic groups of their cultural life, especially how it is lived in Saskatchewan. SAME has produced several other publications available through the resource centre. The most recent resource developed is the *Voices of Saskatchewan Story Kits*. These kits combine familiar children's books with recordings by Saskatchewan residents with a variety of accents; the kits are designed to familiarize young students with the diversity of sounds of spoken English and other languages. The organization loans these and other materials to educators in the province.

SAME also supports teachers and students with workshops, displays, presentations, and assistance with curriculum development and event planning. Currently, SAME offers interactive drama workshops to enable participants to explore issues such as racism, as well as DIVE (Discovering Identity Valuing Equality), a youth leadership program in which high school students design and deliver their own diversity projects. The Saskatchewan Association for Multicultural Education fosters projects, research, and publications that raise awareness about cultural identity, anti-racism, equity, and other social justice issues. It addresses social justice and community concerns by co-operating with other organizations, institutions, and agencies in furthering multicultural and intercultural education. SAME promotes awareness of the Canadian context and being responsive to changes in multicultural policies, demographics, and educational needs as appropriate.   *Rhonda Rosenberg*

SASKATCHEWAN ASSOCIATION OF AGRICULTURAL SOCIETIES AND EXHIBITIONS.

Agricultural societies were active in this area long before Saskatchewan entered Confederation. By the

1880s settlers were arriving in western Canada from regions that had well-established, active networks of agricultural societies–the Maritimes, for instance, since 1789. Many new settlers were aware of the way an organized society could help them exchange information on crop and animal husbandry; they saw the agricultural society as a way to display their crops, livestock and domestic arts and crafts. Perhaps more important, the societies provided an opportunity for the social gatherings so essential to the homesteaders. Fourteen exhibitions were held in 1885, and the growing value of agricultural societies was recognized.

Today, as in years past, this network of grassroots, non-political, volunteer-based organizations works to encourage agricultural production, support the agricultural industry, and enhance the quality of life. This they do by delivering programs and events, from business and industry specific trade shows to community celebrations; by providing facilities, from riding arenas to community halls; and by supporting other business and community groups. Seminars, workshops, field days, clinics and rallies happen year round in many communities through the efforts of the agricultural society. The fair provides an opportunity for rural-urban interface as well as a stage and marketplace for local artists and artisans; it also celebrates the local identity and character of the community. Youth groups and the 4-H movement in Saskatchewan are huge beneficiaries of agricultural society programming, and major users of their facilities. Many agricultural societies offer scholarships to deserving young members of their communities. Two programs–Boys and Girls Farm Camps and Ploughing Matches–are of particular interest in the history of agricultural societies.

No other activity of agricultural societies touched the lives of more farm boys and girls than the summer camps hosted at Class A and B fairs. From 1915 to 1978, more than 50,000 Saskatchewan youth demonstrated their skills in competition for the much coveted T. Eaton gold watch at Class B fairs, and for scholarship awards at Class A fair camps. The ploughing matches, designed to educate farmers in one of the most important farm practices in western Canada, became popular events because of the promotion they received from agricultural experts who saw good ploughing as the foundation of a good seedbed. After severe drought and hot dry winds caused serious soil erosion problems across much of central and southern Saskatchewan in the 1930s, new tillage practices were adopted and the plough fell out of favour. Amendments to the Agricultural Societies Act 1910 provided for the societies to be administered by the Extension Department, College of Agriculture, at the **UNIVERSITY OF SASKATCHEWAN**. The University and its new College were to become the focal point of agricultural education, research and teaching; agricultural and home-making technology could readily be made available to farm families through educational activities sponsored by agricultural societies.

The first province-wide annual convention of agricultural societies took place in 1911, and the 1920 convention created the Saskatchewan Agricultural Societies' Association (SASA). Convention resolutions usually concerned themselves with agricultural production and marketing, the welfare of the rural community, environmental and health issues, and farm safety issues. Societies and the Association were distant from the federal level of government, but often directed resolutions at Ottawa. SASA was instrumental in developing conferences, tours and educational events with the Extension Department, and in helping organize the annual Farm and Home Week of the University of Saskatchewan. In 1975, the Saskatchewan Association of Fairs and Exhibitions (SAFE) came on the scene, acting for provincial (Class A) and regional (Class B) fairs in matters specific to larger operations, midways and attractions. The Saskatchewan Association of Agricultural Societies and Exhibitions was created in 1987 through the merger of SASA and SAFE. The board of directors includes elected representation of the member societies, and ex-officio membership for Saskatchewan Agriculture (SAFRR), Agriculture Canada (AAFC) and the University of Saskatchewan Extension Division. The Association, while not active in political issues, is assertive in speaking for better living conditions in rural Saskatchewan, for both farm and non-farm families. More recently the Association has played a greater role in supporting agricultural awareness programming at Saskatchewan's agricultural fairs.

Judy Riemer

SASKATCHEWAN ASSOCIATION OF HEALTH ORGANIZATIONS. The Saskatchewan Association of Health Organizations (SAHO) is a non-profit, non-government association of health agencies in Saskatchewan. It provides leadership, support and services to more than 160 members, including Saskatchewan's regional health authorities, independent hospitals and special care homes, and various agencies and associations that provide health services, education and regulation.

While collective bargaining is its best-known service, members also use SAHO to provide high-quality, low-cost services in the areas of labour relations, payroll, workplace health and safety, education for board members and employees, advocacy and communications, employee benefit plans, and materials management. SAHO has the broadest membership and the widest range of services of any provincial health care association in Canada.

The association has consistently supported and advocated for a seamless system of client-centred health services, democratic participation in the health system, teamwork among health professionals, and sustainable, adequately funded health care.

SAHO was formed in 1993 through the amalgamation of the Saskatchewan Health-Care Association (est. 1918), the Saskatchewan Association of Special Care Homes (est. 1953), and the Saskatchewan Home Care Association (est. 1981). It merged with the Hospital Systems Study Group in 1995. SAHO has a head office located in Regina, and a branch office in Saskatoon.

Jill Forrester

SASKATCHEWAN ASSOCIATION OF RURAL MUNICIPALITIES. The Saskatchewan Association of Rural Municipalities (SARM) was founded in 1905. The association is governed by a ten-member board: eight are elected directly (president and vice-president elected for one year terms, and six directors elected for two year terms); and two are ex officio members—one the elected president of the Rural Municipal Administrators' Association (RMAA), and the other the appointed executive director. With its office in Regina, SARM serves its members in a variety of ways: reviewing and interpreting provincial and federal legislation; lobbying provincial and federal governments to change legislation; communicating important political developments to members; delivering a range of insurance plans and employee benefit plans to rural municipalities; operating a Trading Department that provides the benefit of volume purchasing of products for municipalities; delivering casual legal services to rural municipalities; publishing the **RURAL COUNCILLOR** magazine; and administering various funds for municipalities on behalf of the provincial and/or federal governments, including the Treaty Land Entitlement Tax Loss Compensation Fund and the Wildlife Habitat Trust Fund.

Dale Harvey

SASKATCHEWAN ASSOCIATION OF SCHOOL BUSINESS OFFICIALS. The Saskatchewan Association of School Business Officials (SASBO) became an official organization in 1945, created by provincial statute. The most recent Saskatchewan School Business Officials Act (1981) was revised in June 2004 to provide the Association with a clear mandate of self-governance over the membership. Membership includes all school business officials who are certified Secretary Treasurers and Superintendents of Administration actively employed by Boards of Education. Membership in SASBO is mandatory as a condition of employment as a School Business Official. The Saskatchewan Association of School Business Officials Act (2004) provides for certified Assistant School Business Officials to become associate members of the Association.

The School Business Official for a Board of Education is the general business administrator and serves as the chief financial officer, as well as being expected to serve both the financial and business administration of the school division. School Business Officials must have at least two years of post-secondary education in the administrative and financial field as well as two years of related work experience, or hold a Bachelor of Administration or Bachelor of Commerce degree from a recognized university, or a similar degree acceptable to the Board of Education. The Association identifies and responds to the changing needs of the profession and its members. It provides for the professional level of its members by initiating and sustaining an educational program of workshops, seminars, conferences, and meetings that is meaningful to all involved in school business management. The Association continues to update and change policies within the membership's manual and handbook as needed in the changing profession. The Association continues to participate in providing quality K–12 education, which is dependent upon the co-operative action of educators, school business officials, and other educational stakeholders.

G. Paul Baskey

SASKATCHEWAN BILL OF RIGHTS. In 1947, a year before the United Nations General Assembly adopted the *Universal Declaration of Human Rights*, Saskatchewan passed into law a bill of rights which was, and continues to be, unique. The Saskatchewan Bill of Rights covered both fundamental freedoms and equality rights. In the first category, section 3 protected freedom of conscience, opinion and religion. Section 4 protected freedom of expression. Section 5 protected peaceable assembly and association. Section 6 protected against arbitrary arrest and detention. The second category prohibited discrimination in employment (section 8), occupations and businesses (section 9), property (section 10), accommodation and services (section 11), and professional associations and unions (section 12).

The first category of the *Saskatchewan Bill of Rights* broke new ground in Canada as it protected civil libertarian values. And to this day it is the only legislation in Canada to extend this protection from abuse by powerful private institutions and persons. The explanation for these two important contributions to Canadian civil liberties law lies in the biography and ideology of Premier **T.C. DOUGLAS**. As a teenager Douglas moved with his family to Winnipeg in 1919. That same year, he witnessed the actions of the police in suppressing the Winnipeg General Strike: on June 21, 1919, from a rooftop vantage point on Main Street, Douglas witnessed Mounties charging the strikers with clubs and guns, a streetcar being overturned and set on fire, and a man being shot. In 1930, he moved to Weyburn following his ordination as a Baptist minister; a year later, he saw some workers, wounded by bullets shot by the police, brought to Weyburn from the coal workers riot in Estevan. On July 2, 1935, as a CO-OPERATIVE COMMOWEALTH FEDERATION (CCF) candidate in a federal by-election, Douglas came to Regina to deliver a radio broadcast and learned about what had occurred in the Regina Riot of the previous day. He went to see an old friend, Dr. HUGH MACLEAN, who told him that for hours he had been kept busy extracting RCMP bullets from wounded young ON-TO-OTTAWA Trekkers. For nine years prior to becoming Premier, Douglas served as a member of Parliament for the Weyburn constituency. This was the heyday of fascism in Germany and Italy. As a member of Parliament, Douglas paid special attention to the abuses of these police states. He kept an ear out, when no one else might notice, for rumours from these places of secret arrests and midnight trials. In sum, Douglas brought to the premiership in 1944 strong interests and credentials as a civil libertarian: this is the very personal story behind the governmental decision to protect fundamental freedoms in the *Saskatchewan Bill of Rights*.

Extending the reach of this protection from abuse at the hands of private institutions and persons flows from the CCF philosophy that the individual is vulnerable to abuse at the hands of corporations and other powerful private actors, not just at the hands of the state, as traditional liberalism would have it. The justification for such a bill of fundamental freedoms from abuse by private actors is that no one argues that equality rights ought not to be applied to private actors. All human rights codes in Canada have as their main purpose protecting individuals from such discrimination in employment, housing, services, professions, and unions. The argument from the left is, Why should fundamental freedoms be regarded any differently?

Ken Norman

FURTHER READING: McLeod, T.H. and I. McLeod. 1987. *Tommy Douglas: The Road to Jerusalem.* Edmonton: Hurtig; Remple, Ryan. 1991. "Fundamental Freedoms, Private Actors and the Saskatchewan Bill of Rights," *The Saskatchewan Law Review* 55 (2): 263, 264, 273, 276 and 279; Shackleton, D.F. 1975. *Tommy Douglas.* Toronto: McClelland and Stewart.

SASKATCHEWAN BOOK AWARDS. Begun in 1993 by the SASKATCHEWAN WRITERS' GUILD, the SASKATCHEWAN LIBRARY ASSOCIATION, and the Saskatchewan Publishers' Group, the Saskatchewan Book Awards (SBA) has gained national recognition as one of the best-run writers' events in Canada. Celebrating the achievements of both Saskatchewan authors and publishers, SBA offers cash awards of $1,500 plus invaluable publicity. There are thirteen categories, each of which is juried by two well-known, out-of-province authors.

The awards gala is held at the end of November to encourage giving Saskatchewan books as Christmas gifts. Prior to the gala, shortlist brunches in Saskatoon, Regina and other centres feature readings by nominated authors. All nominated books are available for sale and autographing at these functions.

The SBA mandate is to recognize excellence and diversity in Saskatchewan writing and publishing, and to promote greater awareness of Saskatchewan books and authors. A volunteer board and an executive director give direction. SBA receives support from the SASKATCHEWAN ARTS BOARD, Sask Culture, and the Regina Arts Commission. Corporate and private sponsorships are the major source of funding.

In 2000 the Saskatchewan Book Awards, working with other literary and arts organizations, achieved provincial government recognition of the position of Poet Laureate for the province. A search committee chose poet/publisher/teacher GLEN SORESTAD as the first recipient of the honour.

Joyce Wells

SASKATCHEWAN BOOK BUREAU. In 1936, the Book Bureau was organized to supply textbooks, reference books, and library books at a uniform and reasonable price throughout the province. In 1940, the Book Bureau opened a display of all reference and library books approved by the Department of Education. This display was open to teachers and students, and was a welcome opportunity to review the books prior to purchasing. It proved to be a valuable complement to the descriptive catalogue and supplementary lists of approved titles provided by the Department. Although the school library was deemed to be an integral part of the school program, the DEPRESSION years created great difficulty for school boards in maintaining their libraries; this was particularly noticeable in some rural areas. To address this challenge, the Department of Education provided in 1941–42 a special grant for rural districts with low assessments for the purchase of supplementary reading materials. These books were purchased through the Book Bureau and forwarded to the districts. This practice continued for several years.

In the late 1940s and into the 1950s, the Book Bureau worked closely with school libraries in many areas such as selecting books and editions, providing book displays for conventions, and offering better library service to the schools. The Book Bureau supplied the books for workshops and laboratories at the Summer School each year. In 1950–51, the Book Bureau began experimenting with a "special ordering" process for library books. Under this system, a list of suitable library titles was prepared by the supervisor of SCHOOL LIBRARIES. The Bureau did not stock the books, but rather would collect orders from schools and districts, then place a bulk order—thereby providing a better rate of discount from the publishers. In 1971, the Book Bureau experimented with stocking a number of textbooks, workbooks, and some auxiliary materials on a consignment basis. This was in addition to the regular practice of stocking authorized books and special-ordering other materials not regularly stocked.

In the early 1990s, the implementation of CORE CURRICULUM had a significant impact on the operation of the Book Bureau. The practice of "resource-based learning" saw dramatic increases in the number of books and in the type of materials recommended for use in schools. This resulted in a name change for the Book Bureau—to Saskatchewan Learning Resources Distribution Centre (LRDC). Over the ensuing years, the ever-growing lists of recommended learning resources proved to be incompatible with a bulk warehousing operation, and on March 31, 2003, the LRDC operation was discontinued. The Department continues to provide a retail service for the sale and distribution of documents and resources that it produces. *Leanne Miles*

SASKATCHEWAN BROILER HATCHING EGG PRODUCERS' MARKETING BOARD (BHE). This marketing board, founded on August 12, 1985, is responsible for the management of the province's supply of eggs used for hatching chicks to produce broilers, the most common type of chicken raised for human consumption. Duties of the BHE include negotiating prices with local processors and developing long-term strategies for the province's hatching egg industry. BHE membership is limited to Saskatchewan hatching egg producers with quota rights that are auctioned annually. In 2003 Saskatchewan had seventeen such producers for 176,000 hatching chickens. The BHE establishes overall quota after consultation with the CHICKEN FARMERS OF SASKATCHEWAN Board and local processors to determine the province's hatching egg requirements. In May of 2000 the Lieutenant-Governor-in-Council assigned the BHE's powers to the Minister of Agriculture; since then the Minister has appointed an administrator to oversee the board and to resolve any problems between the BHE and the CFSB stemming from a Memorandum of Understanding between the BHE and AgriFood Council to drive the Expansion Agreement of 1998.

John Chaput

SASKATCHEWAN CANCER AGENCY. The Saskatchewan Cancer Agency (or SCA; this name has been used since 1997) is guided by the mandate set out in the Cancer Foundation Act of 1979, which changed the 1930 founding name of Saskatchewan Cancer Commission to Saskatchewan Cancer Foundation. The SCA is committed to providing programs for the diagnosis, prevention and treatment of cancer to the residents of Saskatchewan. Its two outpatient treatment centres provide radiation and chemotherapy treatment, as well as supportive care services. The current Saskatoon Cancer Centre building, located adjacent to the ROYAL UNIVERSITY HOSPITAL, opened in 1988. The Allan Blair Cancer Centre, within the Pasqua Hospital (previously the Regina Grey Nuns) in Regina since 1939, underwent a major expansion in 1996.

The patient lodges in Saskatoon and Regina, built by the Canadian Cancer Society and operated by the SCA, opened in 1983 and 1985 respectively, to provide a "home away from home" for out-of-town cancer patients. Provincial treatment programs include the Community Oncology Program of Saskatchewan (COPS) and the Malignant Hematology/Stem Cell Transplant Program. Since 1997, the COPS program, partnering regional health authorities and the SCA, provides selective chemotherapy treatments and supportive care in sixteen certified COPS centres throughout the province. This allows cancer patients to be treated closer to home. Since 1998, the Malignant Hematology/Stem Cell Transplant Program in Saskatoon provides highly specialized services in acute and chronic leukemia, lymphoma and myeloma management, and autologous (patient's own) and allogenic (related and unrelated donor) stem cell and bone marrow transplantation.

The Screening Program for Breast Cancer provides screening mammography for Saskatchewan women aged 50–69 who are not on active follow-up for breast cancer. The Prevention Program for Cervical Cancer was implemented in August 2003. The SCA is actively involved in basic biomedical, translational, clinical trials, and epidemiologic research. The Saskatchewan Cancer Research Unit, with a grant from the Terry Fox Foundation, began operation in 1990. It currently houses 40-60 scientific research staff, who are employed by the SCA or the UNIVERSITY OF SASKATCHEWAN College of Medicine. The SCA employs a wide range of health professionals, including medical, radiation and pediatric oncologists, physicists, radiation therapists, nurses, social workers, and health records staff. It receives 96% of its annual funding in the form of an operating grant from the government of Saskatchewan, of which 79% goes to cancer treatment, 15% to prevention, education and screening, and 6% to research. *Robert Allan*

SASKATCHEWAN COALITION FOR SOCIAL JUSTICE (SCSJ).

The SCSJ is an umbrella organization encompassing numerous church, labour, anti-poverty, and other so-called "popular sector" organizations, founded for the purpose of opposing what it considered the right-wing agenda of the Progressive Conservative provincial government of GRANT DEVINE. The idea for forming the group was first discussed at Regina in April 1987, during a meeting that brought together representatives from

the Association of Métis and Non-Status Indians of Saskatchewan, the National Farmer's Union, the FEDERATION OF SASKATCHEWAN INDIAN NATIONS, the Catholic Church's Social Action Department, the Saskatchewan Action Committee on the Status of Women, the SASKATCHEWAN FEDERATION OF LABOUR, Seniors Action Now, and the Saskatchewan Conference of the United Church of Canada. In May of that year, a second meeting of eighty representatives from fifty organizations established an "interim planning group" in order to initiate the process of organizing the coalition and planning an event to protest the fiscally conservative provincial budget. The result brought out some 7,000 people to march on the Saskatchewan Legislature on June 20, 1987– the largest demonstration in the province's history. Shortly thereafter, the SCSJ was officially founded in October 1987 and held its first "Peoples Convention" at Saskatoon in April 1988. By that time it had also associated itself with the Pro-Canada Network, a national anti-free-trade coalition, and thus became involved in the effort to sway public opinion against the proposed Canada-United States Free Trade Agreement. Many members of the group campaigned against the Devine government in the provincial election of 1991 as well, in which the Progressive Conservatives were defeated by the New Democratic Party led by ROY ROMANOW.

Despite the early enthusiasm generated by the SCSJ, the organization had a turbulent history over the next years. A number of commentators have hinted that "coalition movements" such as the SCSJ were little more than an expedient association of leaders from various social and political organizations, which had neither significant input from the membership of its constituent groups, nor the ability to mobilize large numbers of people except for the occasional short-term event that might temporarily energize their membership. An even more serious problem, as might be expected in such a broad collection of groups, was that conflict and suspicion soon emerged, particularly between the more moderate members of the labour and farm groups, and other more left-leaning activists. Meetings became increasingly fractious, and by the mid-1990s growing numbers of activists lost interest. Some, who became frustrated by the constraints of operating within the SCSJ and by the group's hesitancy to speak out against what they saw as the right-wing policies of the Romanow government, later went on to help found what would become the New Green Alliance party. Others simply felt that with the election of the New Democratic Party in Saskatchewan, their work was done. The SCSJ is presently not nearly as active as it was in the late 1980s and the early 1990s, and exists largely on paper. Its significance lay not so much in its longevity, but rather in the way in which it represented–together with all of its attendant advantages and drawbacks–a contempo-

rary example of the attempt to construct a formal, broad-based social movement organization in the province. *Tim Krywulak*

SASKATCHEWAN COMMERCIAL FISHER-MAN'S CO-OPERATIVE FEDERATION LTD. (SCFCFL).

The SCFCFL is an umbrella organization serving and promoting the interests and concerns of the many individual member co-operatives of Saskatchewan's COMMERCIAL FISHING industry. Commercial fishing is a way of life and an important source of income for many families in northern Saskatchewan, where some 700 licensed commercial fishermen belong to local fishing co-operatives. In the 1950s and 1960s, Saskatchewan's commercial fishing industry experienced steady growth, and at its peak consisted of twenty-five fishermen's co-operatives operating under the central marketing agency, Co-operative Fisheries Ltd. But the following decades brought hard times to the industry, due in large part to uncertain market prices and demand, rising transportation costs, and poor weather conditions. Throughout the 1970s commercial fishing suffered as production levels dropped, returns diminished, fish processing plants closed, co-operatives became inactive, and ultimately, in 1980, CO-OPERATIVE FISHERIES LTD. dissolved. In spite of a decade of setbacks, Saskatchewan's fishermen and their co-operatives remained steadfast in their determination to improve the industry, and in 1982 a new central co-operative, the SCFCFL, was formed. Working with government departments, Aboriginal groups, member co-operatives, and other agencies, the SCFCFL has taken major initiatives to revitalize commercial fishing in Saskatchewan. Recent efforts include restoring inactive co-operatives, improving lakeside facilities, opening new holding facilities and packing plants, and promoting fishing as a traditional way of life. *Iain Stewart*

SASKATCHEWAN COMMUNITY SCHOOLS ASSOCIATION.

In 1981 an initial constitution and bylaws set out the objectives of the Saskatchewan Community Schools Association (SCSA), and members began to promote the community school principles: to communicate and disseminate information; to provide in-service opportunities; and to serve as a support network for members. During the early 1980s there were eleven COMMUNITY SCHOOLS in Regina, Saskatoon, and Prince Albert. The SCSA membership consisted primarily of community school coordinators, who would meet at their own expense in a central location, usually on a Saturday in the community of Davidson. Coordinators relied on their peer group for support, using the gathering to discuss common issues and concerns related to their line of work. Under the leadership of Fay Stupnikoff, a community school coordinator in Prince Albert, the SCSA began to evolve and grow stronger.

Executive and general meetings were held on a regular basis, and a newsletter was written and distributed in order to achieve SCSA's objectives. The newsletter, still circulating, provides information and shares success stories from community school programs across the province. Annual provincial conferences were organized, and the attendance at the SCSA conferences soon climbed to over 600 participants. The SCSA has also co-hosted the National Conference for the Canadian Association of Community Education in Saskatoon in 1993 and 2002. In l996 the provincial government expanded the community school program, and SCSA membership increased; general meetings and conferences were now attracting school staff as well as parents, youth, and other community education partners. In 2000, representatives from WEYERHAEUSER, an international pulp and paper company in Saskatchewan, approached the SCSA to form a partnership: the *Planting Dreams Program* was launched to help children in community schools, with an emphasis on supporting EARLY CHILDHOOD DEVELOPMENT opportunities with initiatives such as the "Readiness to Learn Backpack Project." Each community school pre-kindergarten program received backpacks filled with interactive educational material to lend to small children and their families. In 2001, existing community schools received further recognition for their ideas and approaches in education when the Role of the School Task Force Final Report recommended that all provincial schools adopt the community school philosophy.

Maureen Strawson and Fay Stupnikoff

SASKATCHEWAN COMPUTER UTILITY CORPORATION (SASKCOMP).

SaskCOMP was formed in May 1973. In its first annual report, general manager L.T. Holmes wrote that the consolidation and rationalization of computer services was a common activity, but that the combination of services for universities, government departments, and CROWN CORPORATIONS was unusual: SaskCOMP had therefore the unique opportunity to build a "special blend of innovative and production qualities" and establish a leadership position for Saskatchewan. By 1981, SaskCOMP was leasing IBM's largest system. After several major capacity increases, SaskCOMP became the eighth largest computer operation in Canada. Increased capacity was needed as emphasis on delivery of services shifted to online processing. At that time, SaskCOMP also began to focus on providing computing services to school boards across the province. It also participated in the Minnesota Educational Computing Consortium, a North American leader in educational computing, which permitted computer-equipped schools in Saskatchewan to access all materials available within the consortium. In 1986, SaskCOMP's services deployed the first disaster recovery service in western Canada; in 1987, its revenues reached a record $32 million. Despite SaskCOMP's profitability, it was sold by the DEVINE government to form Westbridge.

Daryl Hepting

SASKATCHEWAN CONFERENCE OF MENNONITE BRETHREN CHURCHES.

The Mennonite Brethren Church began in 1860 as the result of a schism within the Mennonite Church in the Molotschna Colony of southern Russia. The first Mennonite Brethren to arrive in North America—approximately 200 families who were part of the larger Mennonite migration during the 1870s—settled in the United States. Within a decade, they began commissioning itinerant evangelists to conduct meetings among Mennonites living in southern Manitoba. Through their persistence, a congregation was organized in 1888 near Winkler, which in turn was instrumental in starting several satellite congregations nearby, comprised largely of former Sommerfelder and Old Colony Mennonites. The Mennonite Brethren's insistence on baptism by immersion hampered the growth of these congregations.

This nondescript beginning was augmented by a steady trickle of Mennonite Brethren immigrants from the United States during the 1890s and the early decades of the 20th century. Some settled in Manitoba, but most were attracted by free homesteads and cheaper land in Saskatchewan. They settled in two main areas that became known as Rosthern *Kreis* (District) in the north and Herbert *Kreis* in the south. The first Mennonite Brethren church to be organized in Saskatchewan was located in Laird in 1898; within two decades six more congregations had been started in the area. The first congregation in the southern district was organized in 1904 in Main Centre; seven more were initiated during the next decade. In 1914, the Mennonite Brethren churches in Canada organized themselves as the Northern District Conference, one of four Mennonite Brethren districts in North America. By 1923, almost twenty Mennonite Brethren congregations had been formed in western Canada, with a membership totaling approximately 1,800, of which 80% were located in Saskatchewan.

The 1920s inaugurated a time of rapid expansion for the young denomination as a wave of more than 20,000 German-speaking Mennonites (dubbed *Russlaender*), who were fleeing the Bolshevik revolution and its aftermath, settled in western Canada. Between 4,000 and 5,000 were Mennonite Brethren; this influx dramatically changed the complexion and demographics of the denomination. By 1930, there were almost 4,000 Mennonite Brethren scattered across western Canada in over forty congregations (only 55% were in Saskatchewan, signaling a gradual shift in influence to places such as Winkler, Manitoba, Coaldale, Alberta, and Yarrow, BC). As Mennonite Brethren numbers in Canada increased, several provincial conferences were created and the Northern District Conference was reorganized as the Canadian Conference of Mennonite Brethren Churches in Canada in 1946.

The Mennonite Brethren have distinguished themselves by their aggressive involvement in Christian education. Despite difficult pioneering conditions, the Mennonite Brethren in Saskatchewan managed to start a Bible school in Herbert as early as 1913. Aided by the incoming Russlaender immigrants, this initiative was followed by more than twenty Bible schools (seven in Saskatchewan), five high schools, and a Bible college before the mid-1940s. The only one of these schools still in operation in Saskatchewan is BETHANY COLLEGE in Hepburn, which began in 1927.

The Mennonite Brethren's emphasis on personal conversion prompted the sending of numerous foreign missionaries and, more recently, an aggressive church-planting campaign in Canada. The Mennonite Brethren share a natural compatibility with other evangelical Protestant groups, which has led to a significant degree of contact, borrowing of resources, and involvement with numerous evangelical organizations. Attendance in the 250 Mennonite Brethren congregations numbers approximately 45,000, making it the largest Mennonite denomination in Canada; less than 10% of this number come from the thirty Mennonite Brethren congregations now in operation in Saskatchewan. *Bruce Guenther*

FURTHER READING: Regehr, T.D. 1996. *Mennonites in Canada, 1939–1970: A People Transformed*. Toronto: University of Toronto Press; Toews, P. and K. Enns-Rempel (eds.). 2002. *For Everything a Season: Mennonite Brethren in North America, 1874–2002*. Fresno: Historical Commission.

SASKATCHEWAN CONSERVATION DATA CENTRE (SKCDC).

Since 1992 the Saskatchewan Conservation Data Centre has served the public by gathering, interpreting and distributing standardized information on the ecological status of Saskatchewan wild species and communities. The SKCDC was formed as a co-operative venture between the province of Saskatchewan (Saskatchewan Environment), the Nature Conservancy (USA), and the Nature Conservancy of Canada. Currently, the SKCDC resides in the Resource Stewardship Branch of Saskatchewan Environment. The SKCDC is a member of NatureServe and its affiliate, NatureServe Canada. NatureServe is a non-profit conservation organization that provides the scientific information and tools needed to help guide effective conservation action. NatureServe and its network of natural heritage programs, of which SKCDC is a part, are the leading source for information about rare and endangered species as well as threatened ecosystems. The NatureServe network includes seventy-four independent Natural Heritage Programs and Conservation Data Centres throughout the Western Hemisphere, with some 800 dedicated scientists and a collective annual budget of more than $45 million. In 2004 the SKCDC had over 9,500 mapped occurrences for species of special concern in Saskatchewan, and continues to collect data. These occurrences are stored electronically in the SKCDC Biotics database. Biotics is a data management software which allows for spatial data management, tabular data management, data import/export and reconciliation, and reporting; it has a spatial component (GIS) that supports digital mapping, spatial analyses, and data visualization. The Biotics Application at SKCDC supports on-line initiatives like the Ecosystem Image Information System, the Bird Atlas, and the Project Review website.

Steve Porter

SASKATCHEWAN CO-OPERATIVE ASSO-CIATION (SCA).

The SCA is a provincial coalition that promotes the co-operative model for community and economic development. It was one of eight regional affiliates of the Canadian Co-operative Association when the national body was formed in 1987 through the amalgamation of the Saskatoon-based CO-OPERATIVE COLLEGE OF CANADA (which was dedicated to training and research) and the Co-operative Union of Canada (which focused on national organization and government relations). In 2003, the SCA became incorporated and autonomous but maintained a close working relationship with the national association. Services are concentrated in five areas: Youth Education and Involvement (including employment and training); Member Services and Communications (to promote general and individual members' needs to the public); Leadership and Co-operative Education (to develop individual potential); Co-operative Development (by lobbying government and supporting international initiatives); and Government Relations (on the provincial level). One of its most ambitious and successful endeavours has been the Saskatchewan Co-operative Youth Program, which the SCA and its predecessors have been conducting since 1928. The program engages between 300 and 400 youths, aged 14 to 18, in summer seminars to study co-operative principles and their relationships to various issues and conditions. *John Chaput*

SASKATCHEWAN CO-OPERATIVE ELEVA-TOR COMPANY (SCEC).

The SCEC, established in 1911, was an important farmer-owned enterprise in the early years of the province's agricultural development. It was a partnership between farmers and the provincial government: the province provided financing, and close connections were kept

between provincial politics and the leadership of the co-operative. The SCEC built a province-wide network of farmer-owned grain elevators that were later taken over by SASKATCHEWAN WHEAT POOL (SWP) and formed the nucleus of the Pool's elevator system. The province formed the SCEC in response to years of complaints and agitation by farmers about what they saw as unfairness and lack of genuine competition among the existing "line" elevator companies. Two important impulses in shaping the SCEC were Sintaluta farmer E.A. PARTRIDGE, a farmer activist, and WALTER SCOTT, Saskatchewan's first Premier.

Partridge had long advocated government ownership of elevators, a position he promoted in speeches and writings and which became known as the "Partridge Plan" of 1908. The idea of government ownership was too radical for government leaders: although the Manitoba government gave in to pressure and purchased elevators in 1910 (not successfully), in Saskatchewan Premier Scott engineered a Royal Commission on Elevators which in 1910 recommended co-operative ownership by farmers instead of government ownership. In line with Scott's intentions and the commission report, the SCEC was incorporated in 1911 by special legislation. Farmers had to pay only $7.50 for a $50 share in the new company. The balance—85% of the capital needed—was a government-guaranteed loan to be repaid out of earnings.

The Saskatchewan approach served as the model, in organizational and financial terms, for the Alberta Farmers' Co-operative Elevator Company, created in 1913.

In its first year the SCEC built forty elevators and leased six more; in 1912 it built ninety-three. By 1916 the SCEC had over 190 elevators in operation; by 1917, 230. With 318 licensed elevators in 1920, SCEC had edged out UNITED GRAIN GROWERS (UGG) to become the operator of the largest elevator system in the prairies. Its network grew to over 400 in the mid-1920s. The elevator co-op remained closely connected, ideologically and personally, to the governing LIBERAL PARTY and to the Saskatchewan Grain Growers' Association (SGGA). Three men, in particular, epitomized the intertwined elites of these bodies: for more than a decade, JOHN A. MAHARG was president of both the SGGA and the SCEC, in 1921 simultaneously serving as provincial Minister of Agriculture in the Liberal government; meanwhile, CHARLES A. DUNNING, first manager of the SCEC, went on to become Premier of Saskatchewan; and J.B. Musselman, autocratic secretary of the SGGA and another influential Liberal, found refuge in a post in the SCEC under Maharg when reformists drove him out of office in the SGGA. These close ties to the government drew criticism from farmers who were not Liberals, and from those who were purists regarding the co-operative principle of political neu-

trality. Activist farmers also saw the co-op as too conservative: too content to remain an elevator company, too timid in challenging the wider marketing system, and too aloof from members. Its directors were elected at a large central meeting instead of in country districts; it did not pay patronage refunds, which is considered a key co-operative principle; moreover, the company did not bring the returns that farmers had hoped for.

Discontent came to a head following the organization of Saskatchewan Wheat Pool in 1923–24: the pool (together with its counterparts in Manitoba and Alberta) represented a new vision of central selling and orderly marketing. But now the pool needed elevators through which to move its grain, and the SCEC was noticeably reluctant to aid it. The SCEC proved so difficult to win over that pool organizers decided to reach agreements with private elevator companies first; frictions continued, and in 1925 the pool began building its own elevators and submitted a proposal to buy those of the SCEC. At the annual meeting in December 1925 the SCEC board, led by Maharg, attacked the pool, while pro-pool delegates attacked the board. In the end SCEC delegates voted to force the SCEC to consider the pool's offer, repudiating the board. Finally, in April 1926 a special meeting of co-op members voted 366 to 77 to sell. SCEC investors did not lose. They had paid $7.50 for their shares originally (the balance being paid out of profits), but received $155.84 from the sale. Arbitrators valued SCEC's elevators at $11 million. In 1926, the SCEC came to an end as its elevator network was taken over by the pool, providing a huge boost to the growing network of SWP country elevators. The pool's elevator network, which totaled eighty-nine in 1925–26, grew at a stroke by 451 country elevators and three terminals.

Brett Fairbairn

FURTHER READING: Fairbairn, G. 1984. *From Prairie Roots: The Remarkable Story of Saskatchewan Wheat Pool.* Saskatoon: Western Producer Prairie Books; Irwin, R. 1993. "The Better Sense of the Farm Population': The Partridge Plan and Grain Marketing in Saskatchewan," *Prairie Forum* 18 (1): 35–52; MacPherson, I. 1979. *Each For All: A History of the Co-operative Movement in English Canada, 1900–1945.* Toronto.

SASKATCHEWAN DENTAL PLAN.

Established in 1974, the BLAKENEY government's Saskatchewan Dental Plan provided universal dental care for children between the ages of 4 and 13. Although children's dental plans were first introduced in Newfoundland in the 1950s and Prince Edward Island in 1971, Saskatchewan's program was unique in terms of its organization. In particular, salaried dental therapists were at the core of a program that reached out to approximately 120,000 children in the province and dramatically raised the standard of dental care and hygiene to one of the highest in North America.

The origins of the Saskatchewan Dental Plan lay in the SASKATCHEWAN HEALTH SURVEY Committee. In 1951, the Committee reported that dental disease was one of the province's most "extensive" medical problems. Some within the CCF wanted the government to follow in New Zealand's path by creating a school-based dental plan run by dental nurses; but opposition from dentists, combined with the then-prevalent belief that dental nurses were not qualified to provide dental care, blocked change. By the 1971 provincial election campaign, however, the NDP was promising an insured dental care service for children. After much internal discussion and dispute over the implementation details, the program was finally introduced in September 1974.

The Saskatchewan Dental Plan team that traveled out to the province's schools was made up of one dental therapist helped by a dental assistant performing preventative and corrective dentistry. Dentists working for the plan supervised from eight to ten teams each. While some concerns about the dental therapists were raised initially, an independent study of the Plan after its sixth year revealed that the quality of the work equaled or exceeded that performed by private practice dentists. In addition, the Plan resulted in Saskatchewan having the highest proportion of children receiving dental care in North America. Further, some of the treatment procedures adopted by the dental teams, including the wearing of masks and rubber gloves, eventually became the standard for dental care in Canada and the United States.

The Saskatchewan Dental Plan attracted international attention and was emulated in other jurisdictions–including Manitoba, which implemented a dental plan for its residents outside the city of Winnipeg in 1976. Despite its success, the Saskatchewan Plan was terminated by the DEVINE government in June 1987. School dental outreach was turned over to private dentists, and the Plan's 400 employees were laid off. *Gregory P. Marchildon*

SASKATCHEWAN DRAGOONS. The Saskatchewan Dragoons are a reconnaissance regiment of the Canadian Forces Primary Reserve, located in Moose Jaw. The unit, part of 38TH CANADIAN BRIGADE GROUP, Land Forces Western Area, traces its beginnings to the formation of the 95th Regiment of Canadian Militia on July 3, 1905, when Saskatchewan was part of the North-West Territories. The 95th Regiment consisted of eight companies, two of which, A and B, were located in Moose Jaw. On February 1, 1913, A and B Companies were expanded to form a new regiment designated the 60th Rifles of Canada. During WORLD WAR I, the 60th Rifles contributed drafts of more than 5,000 soldiers to many units of the Canadian

Saskatchewan Dragoons

COURTESY OF GERRY CARLINE

Expeditionary Force, including the 128th, 210th and the 46th (South Saskatchewan) Canadian Infantry Battalions from Moose Jaw. The 46TH CANADIAN INFANTRY BATTALION became known as the "Suicide Battalion" for its high casualty rate during the war.

The 60th Rifles of Canada amalgamated with the 95th Saskatchewan Rifles on March 15, 1920, to form the SOUTH SASKATCHEWAN REGIMENT, which in 1924 was re-designated the KING'S OWN RIFLES OF CANADA. On December 15, 1935, the Regiment was the King's Own Rifles of Canada (MG) on absorbing units of the 12th Machine Gun Battalion. On the outbreak of WORLD WAR II, the King's Own Rifles of Canada (MG) was mobilized for local protective duty. Many of its members transferred to 77 FIELD BATTERY, which was mobilized early in the war. A former KORC member, Major (later Lieutenant Colonel) D.V. Currie, won the VICTORIA CROSS while serving with the South Alberta Regiment. The Moose Jaw armoury, the present home of the Saskatchewan Dragoons, was named in his honour in 1988.

On January 29, 1942, with its name reverting to the King's Own Rifles of Canada, the Regiment mobilized the 1st Battalion for home defence. The 1st Battalion was assigned to coastal defence duties in British Columbia until it was demobilized on March 30, 1946. Some elements of the 1st Battalion served with the joint Canadian-American Aleutian Islands invasion force, formed to fight the Japanese, who had occupied that part of Alaska. A 2nd Battalion served in the Reserve Army throughout the war. The King's Own Rifles of Canada became an armoured unit on April 1, 1946, and was designated the 20th (Saskatchewan) Armoured Regiment. It was renamed the Saskatchewan Dragoons (20th Armoured Regiment) on July 31, 1954. It is from this numerical regimental designation that the unit bears the Roman numeral "XX" on its cap badge. On May 19, 1958, the unit was designated the Saskatchewan Dragoons.

In 1970, the unit was reduced to the status of an independent squadron, "A" Squadron, the Saskatchewan Dragoons, with the remaining squadrons and the Regimental Band reverting to nil

strength. A brief revival of the armoured role began in 1984 when the unit received an operational tasking and began to train with Cougars, a type of wheeled armoured vehicles. The Saskatchewan Dragoons currently operate a headquarters troop, an "A1" echelon (logistics support personnel) and reconnaissance troops in Moose Jaw, with another reconnaissance troop in Swift Current.

The Saskatchewan Dragoons have served in United Nations peacekeeping operations in Cyprus, the Golan Heights, Bosnia, and Croatia, and have provided emergency assistance during the Manitoba flood of 1997 and the battle against forest fires (Operation Peregrine) in British Columbia in 2003. Queen Elizabeth II approved the appointment of His Royal Highness the Earl of Wessex, KCVO, as Colonel-in-Chief of the Saskatchewan Dragoons on June 22, 2003. The Saskatchewan Dragoons perpetuate the 46th and 128th Battalions, CEF, and carry the sixteen battle honours won by the 46th Battalion in World War I. *John Chaput*

FURTHER READING: McWilliams, J.L. and R.J. Steel. 1978. *The Suicide Battalion.* Edmonton: Hurtig.

SASKATCHEWAN EGG PRODUCERS (SEP). The SEP is a supply management marketing board created pursuant to the Saskatchewan Agri-Food Act. The objective of the SEP, like other supply management boards, is to stabilize and support producer incomes, and to deliver a reliable supply of quality product to consumers at reasonable prices. Over the past three decades, supply management has proven itself to be a successful agricultural stabilization policy. The SEP was established in 1969. Together with similar egg boards in every other province, it participated in 1972 and 1976 in the establishment of Canada's national supply management system for eggs, operated by the Canadian Egg Marketing Agency (CEMA).

The SEP and the CEMA regulate three components of the egg market. First, imports of eggs and egg products are held to roughly historic levels. Second, prices paid to producers are stabilized and supported at minimum levels, reflecting a fair assessment of the producer's cost of production. Third, Canadian production is targeted to meet domestic market requirements. Saskatchewan generates approximately 4.5% of Canada's egg production. Within Saskatchewan, the SEP regulates the production and marketing of eggs by virtue of its mandate derived from the Agri-Food Act: this includes managing the disposal of egg surplus to table requirements by shipping these eggs to processing plants for breaking, pasteurization, and delivery to industrial markets. Approximately seventy producers in Saskatchewan generated 20.8 million dozen eggs (gradings) in 2003.

The SEP supports CEMA's on-farm food safety

and biosecurity program: known as the "Start Clean Stay Clean" program, it sets standards of production and management for every aspect of an egg operation in order to minimize the risks of food contamination. Every producer is scored on fulfillment of these standards. The SEP also supports CEMA's guidelines for appropriate handling of livestock, which are specified in its manual known as *Recommended Code of Practice for the Care and Handling of Pullets, Layers and Spent Fowl*. This manual is endorsed by the Canadian Agri-Food Research Council. *Michael Katz*

SASKATCHEWAN FARM SECURITY ACT.

On June 24, 1988, GRANT DEVINE's Conservative government responded to the dire circumstances of Saskatchewan's farm economy by enacting The Saskatchewan Farm Security Act (SFSA). The 1980s had seen several misfortunes visit Saskatchewan farms: low commodity prices, record high interest rates, persistent drought, grasshopper infestations, spiraling input costs, and plummeting land values. The SFSA was intended to staunch the economic dislocation of Saskatchewan's farmers by consolidating and modernizing Saskatchewan's historic farm legislative protection and by introducing innovative new legislation.

The Act co-opted historic legislation that had protected certain farm assets from creditors' seizure for over 100 years. Since 1888, when the North-West Territories passed an Exemption Ordinance, a farmer's machinery and livestock had been essentially exempt from seizure, unless the farmer was a corporation or had granted an interest in such assets to secure their purchase price. Exemption protection was retained under the SFSA to protect a non-corporate farmer's livestock, crops, machinery, tools, homestead, and one motor vehicle from seizure and sale by most creditors.

Legislation was also retained, as first enacted in the 1930s, mandating strict procedural requirements before a creditor could seize farm machinery—the breach of which provided severe penalties: return of the machinery, followed by payment to the farmer of 1.5 times the machinery's fair market value. The SFSA also retained legislation in which vendors selling articles to farmers were restricted to seizing the sold assets and were disallowed any action against the farmer for a shortfall after sale of the article. Similarly, mortgages securing the purchase price of farmland offered no remedies to mortgagee other than recovery of the mortgaged land, a restriction mortgagees first encountered in the 1930s. Borrowing the principle from predecessor legislation, the Farm Security Act enacted in 1944, the SFSA expanded the requirement that any mortgage on a farmer's homestead required the consent of the Farm Land Security Board. Failing to obtain this consent, called an Exclusionary Order, meant

that the mortgagee could not register a Final Order of Foreclosure so long as the farmer, farmer's spouse or children (under the age of 18) continued to reside on the homestead.

New protection was also introduced under the SFSA. Farmers who lost their land through an order for foreclosure or cancellation of agreement for sale, or who had voluntarily transferred their land to their creditor, were given a right of first refusal to repurchase their land at the price the mortgagee was able to negotiate for it on the market. Also new was Saskatchewan's first requirement that guarantors—individuals guaranteeing the debt of a farmer—had to receive independent legal advice before a guarantee was valid. New homestead protection was introduced, allowing any farmers who had defaulted on a mortgage executed before June 24, 1988, to have a three-year reprieve from any foreclosure action if they were making a sincere and reasonable effort to meet their mortgage obligations.

The Act also introduced regimented pre-foreclosure proceedings, requiring a newly created board, the Farm Land Security Board, to prepare a financial report concerning the farmer's operations. This report was provided to the farmer, the mortgagee and Mediation Services in contemplation of mandatory mediation sessions during which the farmer and the mortgagee were obligated to negotiate in good faith to explore settlement options. If negotiations were unsuccessful, the board was required to prepare a court report which formed the primary evidence before a presiding judge, who had to determine if farmers were making a sincere and reasonable effort to meet their obligations or had a reasonable possibility of meeting their obligations. Only upon a judge's order could a foreclosure action be initiated.

In 1992, when the NDP government of ROY ROMANOW was elected, the farm economy was still in crisis. The Romanow government created a Debt Advisory Committee to recommend amendments to the SFSA in order to ensure that farmers had an assurance of continued tenancy of their land. Based on the Committee's recommendations, the SFSA was amended to give farmers a right to lease back their farmland for six years after they had lost it, either by a Final Order of Foreclosure or by voluntary quit claim. The six-year leaseback rights were introduced on September 20, 1992, and applied to farmland subject to foreclosure or quit claim until June 1, 1997. The 1992 amendments to the SFSA also allowed creditors under provincial control, principally credit unions, to ask farmers to waive their exemption protection for crops, livestock and farm machinery to allow farmers more access to credit. A 1988 case, *LeBlanc v. Bank of Montreal*, held that chartered banks were not subject to Saskatchewan's exemption protection because the province could not pass legislation that conflicted with the federal

powers given to chartered banks under the Bank Act. To gain an equal footing with banks, provincial lenders successfully sought an amendment to the SFSA to allow farmers to seek independent legal advice and waive exemption protection for farm assets so long as the creditor was providing new financing to the farmer.

The SFSA is one of Saskatchewan's most significant pieces of legislation. Within a short time of its enactment, it was the most judicially interpreted legislation in provincial history—reflecting decades of Saskatchewan's legislative attempts to preserve the viability of its farm community. *Donald H. Layh*

SASKATCHEWAN FARMERS UNION.

Members attending the United Farmers of Canada (Saskatchewan Section) annual convention in November 1949 were faced with a serious decision. Membership numbers had declined and it was agreed that an effort must be made to revitalize the farm movement. JOSEPH L. PHELPS was elected as president, and the Saskatchewan Farmers Union (SFU) was born. A dynamic leader and inspirational orator, Phelps possessed the leadership qualities needed to draw attention to the grievances of the farm community. Grain exports and prices had become depressed after WORLD WAR II; government promises to compensate farmers under the British Wheat Agreement were unfilled; rail transportation service for grain was unreliable. Phelps aggressively tackled these and other problems with governments and government agencies. Numerous farm organizational meetings were held. SFU membership and locals expanded rapidly in response to this new militancy, which had been absent since the 1920s. The SFU, dedicated to preserving the family farm, quickly developed women's and youth programs. "Farm Women's Week" was a major annual event, and farm women became members of the Associated Country Women of the World (ACWW), an United Nations affiliate. Farm youth engaged in leadership workshops and promoted public speaking and art competitions. Annual "Prairie Queen" competitions sparked youth interest and served as successful fundraising projects.

The SFU succeeded the UFC on the Interprovincial Farm Union Council (IFUC), with Phelps becoming its chairman. Phelps acted to expand IFUC membership to include Manitoba, and shortly thereafter Ontario and British Columbia. He drew a sharp distinction between direct membership policy-making organizations and the composition of the Canadian Federation of Agriculture (CFA). While the CFA had a high profile in Ottawa, Phelps felt it was too compromising toward federal politicians, bureaucrats, and policies. The SFU had become a member of the Saskatchewan Federation of Agriculture (SFA) upon its transition from the UFC: early withdrawal from the SFA was inevitable.

Membership maintenance in a voluntary organization was quickly recognized as a chronic problem. Phelps petitioned the provincial government for implementation of a one-half mill per acre Rand Formula type of dues collection on all farm land. Premier T.C. DOUGLAS declined, but eventually offered a voluntary requisition method of dues collection through municipal offices.

Phelps was succeeded as president by Fred Woloshyn in December 1954. Following a constitutional dispute with the SFU executive, Woloshyn resigned in March 1955. This was disruptive for union membership, which was slow to recover. SFU vice-president Chris Hansen succeeded to the presidency, while Manitoba Farmers Union president Jake Schultz became IFUC chairman. Hansen spent considerable time in attempting to restore member confidence in SFU leadership, but funds were declining. Saskatchewan FEDERATED CO-OPERATIVES and UNITED GRAIN GROWERS provided some grants to assist the union; however, re-entry into a restructured Federation of Agriculture became a condition. Alfred P. Gleave was elected SFU president in 1957, at a convention which also narrowly voted to rejoin the Saskatchewan Federation of Agriculture. Gleave was elected IFUC chairman. Orderly marketing of farm products had been a consistent policy. Initiatives were taken to form a supply-managed producer-controlled egg marketing board. Saskatchewan producers eventually became part of a national supply-managed egg program.

Large grain surpluses and depressed prices in 1958 triggered a major campaign among prairie farm organizations for a deficiency payment program for WHEAT. Backed by a 1,000-person delegation, a petition of 300,000 signatures was presented to Prime Minister JOHN G. DIEFENBAKER and his Cabinet on March 10, 1959. On March 4, 1960, the Prime Minister announced a one-year acreage payment of $40 million. Other major issues affecting the future of farming were arising, in particular transportation. The federal government appointed a Royal Commission on Transportation, which was to review rail line configuration and the Crow Rate. In December 1960, the Canadian Wheat Board jurisdiction was removed in the sale of feed grains to feed mills. On December 16, 1960, the IFUC was renamed the National Farmers Union Council. ROY ATKINSON succeeded to the SFU presidency in December 1962 and was later installed as NFU chairman.

Interest was emerging in 1963 toward the formation of a direct-membership National Farmers Union. Because most major farm policy problems were centred with the federal government, stronger representation was needed. In 1965, a drought in eastern Ontario drew attention to the need for an eastern drought relief fund to finance the purchase and shipment of prairie feed grains to needy Ontario farmers. The fund was launched and assisted to strengthen interprovincial bonds between farm union members. In 1969, feed grain prices had plummeted as surpluses increased. A rally of 6,000 farmers took place in Saskatoon on April 10, 1969. On July 14, 1969, 2,500 tractors clogged Saskatchewan highways at fifty points in a four-day demonstration. Prime Minister Pierre Trudeau addressed demonstrators in Saskatoon and Regina, but did little to reassure farmers after an earlier statement in which he had asked the rhetorical question: "Why should I sell your wheat?" In the meantime, four provincial farm unions had agreed to "go national." The groundwork was set for the founding convention of the National Farmers Union in Winnipeg on July 30–31, 1969. The Farmers Union of Alberta (FUA) refrained from joining, but many FUA members did join. Roy Atkinson was elected NFU president, and Ontario Farmers Union president Walter Miller became vice-president. SFU women's president Evelyn Potter was elected NFU women's president. A new chapter in the history of the farm movement was about to begin. *Stuart A. Thiesson*

FURTHER READING: Gleave, A.P. 1991. *United We Stand: Prairie Farmers 1901–1975*. Toronto: Lugus Publications.

SASKATCHEWAN FEDERATION OF AGRICULTURE.

Beginning in 1907, prairie co-operatives and grain organizations played a leading role in the formation of regional and national farm organizations. In 1939 a primary objective of the Canadian Federation of Agriculture (CFA) was to have all provincial farm organizations (commercial and non-commercial) join a provincial federation. Prairie groups such as the Co-operative Conferences and the Western Agricultural Conference already existed and became part of the CFA structure. In Saskatchewan the Co-operative Council, formed in 1928, was renamed the Saskatchewan Federation of Agriculture (SFA) in 1944. The purpose of the Federation was to advance the well-being of Saskatchewan agriculture. It believed that farm organizations working together to develop and promote provincial, national and international farm policies could achieve more security and a better life for farm families. Not only was it important to present policy recommendations to governments: one also had to be persistent in protecting the interests of the membership in relation to both existing and proposed legislation.

Membership was open to farm organizations that established farm policies and had a membership structure accountable to farmers. SFA membership grew after 1966 to more than fifteen organizations, which included co-operatives, marketing boards, municipal associations, commodity and women's groups. They financed the SFA on an "ability to pay" basis and in relation to the size of their membership. Member organizations sent at least two delegates and a wide range of resolutions to semi-annual and annual meetings for debate and possible approval. Most farmers belonged to one or more of the SFA member organizations; this meant that most views on farm policy issues were expressed in the SFA forum. Policies of a provincial nature were presented to the Saskatchewan government; policies of a regional and national level were submitted to the Western Agricultural Conference and Canadian Federation of Agriculture general meetings; international policy issues were submitted to the International Federation of Agricultural Producers.

The Saskatchewan Federation of Agriculture was a strong supporter of the Canadian Wheat Board and International Grain Trade Agreements. From the beginning to the end the SASKATCHEWAN WHEAT POOL played a major role in developing farm policy and providing finances; several of its vice-presidents were SFA presidents. However, tension among members, particularly on marketing issues, existed in the federation-type structures from their inception a century ago and ultimately caused the demise of the Saskatchewan Federation of Agriculture in 1984. Saskatchewan is now represented at the Canadian Federation of Agriculture table by Saskatchewan Wheat Pool and the Agricultural Producers of Saskatchewan (APAS). *Gary Carlson*

SASKATCHEWAN FEDERATION OF LABOUR (SFL).

The Saskatchewan Federation of Labour is the central body for trade unionists and the largest labour organization in the province. The Federation represents over 90,000 workers from three dozen unions. Membership in the SFL is voluntary, and local unions decide to affiliate by democratic vote of the members. The SFL is itself affiliated with the Canadian Labour Congress, the national trade union central. SFL activities include lobbying governments for better labour laws, promoting a favourable image of unions and workers to the media and the public, and speaking on behalf of the half-million wage earners in Saskatchewan.

The first federation of labour was established by the old Canadian Congress of Labour (CCL) in 1944, and represented the industrial unions which had members in meat-packing plants, foundries and steel mills, the forestry industry, and several Crown corporations. The first Federation of Labour was headed by HUB ELKIN, a packinghouse worker from Moose Jaw. The early SFL was closely allied with the new CCF government, which passed labour legislation that was advantageous to workers wishing to organize. In 1953, the craft unions set up a second—and to some extent rival—Saskatchewan Federation of Labour to house the unions and membership of the skilled trades such as carpenters, electricians, plumbers, and organized employees in the printing

SASKATCHEWAN ARCHIVES BOARD R-B11003

First Constitutional Convention of the Saskatchewan Labour Federation, Regina, 1944.

trades and the craft unions on the railways. This second provincial labour central was chartered by and affiliated to the Trades and Labour Congress of Canada (TLC). The first president of the Saskatchewan Federation of Labour (TLC) was Andrew Tait.

In 1956, the TLC and CCL merged to form the Canadian Labour Congress (CLC), and the provincial federations amalgamated as well. In the fall of 1956 at the old Labour Temple on Osler Street, in Regina, the two groups joined to establish one Saskatchewan Federation of Labour. The first president of the new federation was Fred McClelland, a stationary steam engineer from Saskatoon. In 1978, the SFL made history by electing **NADINE HUNT** as its president, the first woman in Canada to head a provincial federation of labour. *Garnet Dishaw*

SASKATCHEWAN GOVERNMENT AIRWAYS. Saskatchewan Government Airways (SGA; Saskair), the province's first and only government-

owned commercial airline, was formed through Order-in-Council No. 1200/47 on August 15, 1947. It was created by the **CO-OPERATIVE COMMONWEALTH FEDERATION** government, elected in 1944, to operate a provincial air service to northern Saskatchewan—as a commercial airline and as an aid in the development of the region. The **CROWN CORPORATION** maintained operations until 1965, when the newly elected Liberal government sold it to a consortium of private investors to form North Canada Air Limited, more commonly known as NORCANAIR.

James Winkel

SASKATCHEWAN GOVERNMENT AND GENERAL EMPLOYEES' UNION (SGEU). The forerunner to the SGEU was founded on February 21, 1913; it was called the Saskatchewan Civil Service Association (SCSA). The object of the SCSA was "the promotion of social intercourse and sports among the civil servants in the Parliament Buildings." Harry Wilsmer was its first president,

and Premier **WALTER SCOTT** the honorary president. For most of the 1920s and 1930s the SCSA acted as a social club and lobby group. Membership was voluntary, and the SCSA tended to be dominated by senior management. One of the major achievements of the SCSA was the passage of the Public Service Superannuation Act in 1927.

A change in the character and role of the SCSA came with the election in 1944 of the **CO-OPERATIVE COMMONWEALTH FEDERATION** (CCF), led by **T.C. DOUGLAS**. The CCF had as part of its election platform the passage of a **TRADE UNION ACT** that for the first time anywhere in North America would give all workers, including government employees, the right to join trade unions, to bargain collectively with their employers, and to strike. The SCSA, encouraged by Douglas, decided to take advantage of the new legislation and became affiliated with the Trades and Labour Congress. In 1945, history was made when the first collective agreement was signed between the Government of Saskatchewan and the SCSA.

From 1945 to 1972, the SCSA never engaged in strike action, despite a change in government from CCF to Liberal in 1964, and then to the **NEW DEMOCRATIC PARTY** (NDP) in 1971. With changing times and high inflation, the first strike by the Association (renamed the Saskatchewan Government Employees' Association in 1962) was at the province's liquor board stores. Successful action on wages and benefits as well as challenges to legislated wage controls spread during the 1970s. A successful general walkout in 1979 by the Public Service bargaining unit, the largest in SGEA and the province, was declared illegal by the courts.

The Association shed its remaining social club inclinations and renamed itself the Saskatchewan Government Employees' Union (SGEU) in 1981. In

SASKATCHEWAN ARCHIVES BOARD R-A3046

Villagers meet Saskatchewan Government Airways plane at Stony Rapids, 1951.

ROBERT WATSON/REGINA LEADER-POST

SGEU members at the Regina Correctional Centre took job action, November 1992.

1982 the NDP was defeated in the provincial election, and the Progressive Conservatives led by **GRANT DEVINE** were elected. During the 1980s, the SGEU fought many battles over government cutbacks and privatization by the Devine government. Cutbacks continued under the newly elected NDP government led by **ROY ROMANOW** in 1991, as the government argued it had inherited a huge debt from the PC years. By 2004, SGEU represented over 18,000 workers in more than seventy different bargaining units.

Doug Taylor

FURTHER READING: Taylor, D. 1984. *For Dignity, Equality and Justice: A History of the Saskatchewan Government Employee's Union.* Regina: SGEU.

SASKATCHEWAN GOVERNMENT CORRESPONDENCE SCHOOL.

The first distance education school in Saskatchewan was established within the Department of Education in 1925 by **CATHERINE SHELDON-WILLIAMS**. The mandate of the school was to meet the educational needs of the children of settlers, trappers, and traders in remote and sparsely populated areas of the province where the formation of school districts was difficult. Until 1930, the school offered kindergarten to Grade 8. In 1931, the school expanded to include Grades 9 to 11, and in 1941 Grade 12 was added. Today, the Saskatchewan Government Correspondence School offers courses in Grades 9 to 12. While the Correspondence School began as "education by mail" for school-aged students, its modes of delivery and client base have evolved and continue to do so. In the early days, Sheldon-Williams served less than fifty students from her office in a small room of the West Wing of the Legislative Building. She prepared lesson sheets individually to suit the level of each of her

students, as well as doing her own typing and clerical work. Today, the Correspondence School supports each year more than 5,000 Saskatchewan school-aged and adult students by offering a wide range of educational programs to meet their individual needs. Curriculum-based courses, evaluation materials, and educational resources are designed and developed by teams of subject-specialist teachers, editors, and desktop publishers. These educational resources provide the basis of the distance teaching and learning program of the Correspondence School. The materials are also available to classroom teachers throughout Saskatchewan as references for planning and delivering their own educational programs.

Changes in technology have increased the flexibility of the school in meeting the needs of Saskatchewan learners with regard to registration, material distribution, and examination processes. For example, a custom-designed automated computer system provides the school with easy access to course, student, examination, financial, and management information. As well, advances in technology have transformed the distance learning process by strengthening opportunities and options for students, and by increasing student and teacher interactivity in distance learning. The school uses a multimodal approach in course design and delivery which includes print, kits, audio CDs, CD-ROMs, and on-line and televised learning resources. Today, many students submit their assignments through e-mail, and all have access to real-time teacher tutoring and student sharing via the Internet. The school will continue to reach out to the citizens of the province, demonstrating its motto: "No distance is too great."

Cathy Luciuk

Saskatchewan Correspondence School, December 1948.

SASKATCHEWAN GOVERNMENT EMPLOYEES' ASSOCIATION STRIKE OF 1979.

On November 16, 1979, Saskatchewan labour history was made when 12,000 public employees, members of the Saskatchewan Government Employees' Association (SGEA—now the **SASKATCHEWAN GOVERNMENT AND GENERAL EMPLOYEES' UNION**) started a general walkout that was to last four weeks. This was the province's largest and longest strike at the time; it would change SGEA from a social club/lobby group into a vital and modern trade union. Saskatchewan was the first province in Canada to allow public employees the right to join trade unions, to strike, and to obligate their employer to bargain with them in good faith. The left-wing government of **T.C. DOUGLAS** and the **CO-OPERATIVE COMMONWEALTH FEDERATION** (CCF), elected in 1944, passed ground-breaking legislation with the Trade Union Act that was declared that same year. The SGEA at the time was a cautious and conservative organization which reflected its social club origins and a "loyalty to the Crown" public-servant mentality.

Despite these new rights, provincial government employees did not exercise their right to strike until the mid-1970s, when sporadic strikes were taken to address long-standing issues on working conditions, hours of work, and low pay. These issues came to a head in 1979 when government intransigence on these issues resulted in a positive strike vote. New, younger members brought up in the turbulent 1960s were entering the growing public sector in Saskatchewan and were challenging the established leadership of the Association. Concerns that the leadership of the Association had regarding the strength of the membership were overcome when SGEA members overwhelmingly walked out and remained solid during a very long and cold four weeks. The strike appeared to be on the verge of great success through the solidarity of the membership, and it was hoped that the conciliator involved would recommend substantial movement on many of the outstanding issues, some of which had been of concern for decades.

However, the strike was brought to an unexpected halt when a small group of SGEA members successfully convinced a Provincial Court judge to declare the strike illegal and order the employees back to work. The rationale used was that while a majority of members who voted had supported strike action, the number who voted in favour of job action was less than 50% of the entire membership. A frustrated membership returned to work, aware that most sitting MLAs would not be in the legislature if this voting criterion had applied to them. Despite the court order, substantial gains such as the concept of earned days off were made as a result of the strike. The strike also forged a strong leadership and an active membership that would abandon its social club roots. SGEA changed its name in 1981 to become the Saskatchewan Government Employees' Union.

Doug Taylor

SASKATCHEWAN GOVERNMENT INSURANCE (SGI).

Saskatchewan Government Insurance (SGI) has been providing a variety of insurance products to Saskatchewan residents for more than 50 years. The former Saskatchewan Government Insurance Office (SGIO) was established in 1945 to ensure that affordable, good quality insurance would be available to Saskatchewan people. The move was prompted by poor provincial economic conditions which, driving many private insurers out of the market, made it difficult for some residents to obtain insurance. Over time, SGI has evolved into three distinct operations: SGI CANADA, SGI CANADA Insurance Services Ltd. (SCISL), and the Saskatchewan Auto Fund. SGI, under the trade name SGI CANADA, conducts a competitive property and casualty insurance business offering a comprehensive line of home, tenant, farm, automobile extension and commercial coverage. SCISL, a subsidiary of SGI CANADA, sells similar insurance products in Manitoba (except for automobile insurance), Ontario, Prince Edward Island, and New Brunswick. SGI also acts as the administrator of the Saskatchewan Auto Fund, the province's compulsory auto insurance program. The Auto Fund is a not-for-profit operation which does not receive money from, or pay dividends to, the province.

Karen Schmidt

SASKATCHEWAN GOVERNMENT INSURANCE OFFICE STRIKE OF 1948.

In 1944 the new CO-OPERATIVE COMMONWEALTH FEDERATION government of T.C. DOUGLAS introduced and passed the TRADE UNION ACT, which guaranteed for the first time anywhere in North America the right of government employees to organize into trade unions and to bargain collectively with their employer. Public employees in the civil service, mental hospitals and CROWN CORPORATIONS would quickly take advantage of the new legislation to organize themselves into the labour movement. One of the new Crown corporations established by the CCF government was the Saskatchewan Government Insurance Office (SGIO), which was given a monopoly on providing automobile insurance throughout the province. The workers had organized into the Saskatchewan Government Insurance Employees' Union (SGIOEU)–later to become part of the OFFICE AND PROFESSIONAL EMPLOYEES INTERNATIONAL UNION, a component of the Canadian Congress of Labour.

The low wages at the Office put the new CCF government's support of the labour movement to the test. When management at SGIO refused to deal with a new higher pay scale for their employees, the members of SGIOEU voted to strike and walked off the job in November 1948. After strong lobbying from the provincial labour movement and even the national CCF, the government intervened; a new pay scale was offered, and the strike was settled. This would be the last provincial government employees strike until the 1970s, and it foretold the rise of militancy among public sector unions thirty years later.

Doug Taylor

SASKATCHEWAN GRAIN GROWER'S ASSOCIATION (SGGA).

Grain growers' associations were formed on the Canadian prairies in the early 1900s in an attempt to reform the grain-marketing system so that it better served the needs and interests of farmers. Throughout the late 1800s, farmers were becoming increasingly agitated over the collusive and unfair trade practices of the railways and elevator agents. In particular, farmers were upset over the railways' refusal to allow farmers to load their grain directly onto railcars, which forced the farmer to sell his grain to the elevator operator at prices often determined by the operator. Concerned about the rise in social unrest, a Royal Commission was appointed on October 7, 1899. The Commission consisted of three Manitoba farmers and issued its report in March 1900, recommending amongst other things that railways be compelled to furnish farmers with cars for shipping their own grain, and that flat warehouses be provided to allow farmers to accumulate their grain for later shipment. The Manitoba Grain Act was subsequently enacted in July 1900 to regulate the grain trade, and farmers viewed its passing as a major victory. Yet the following year, the railways ignored farmers' requests for cars, prompting a group of farmers to gather in Indian Head on December 18, 1901, the outcome of which was the founding of the Territorial Grain Growers' Association. With WILLIAM MOTHERWELL as the Association's first president, the Association soon pushed for an amendment to the Manitoba Act which would allow farmers to bypass the local elevator and in effect reserve a railway car–taking precedence over later orders by local operators–provided that the farmer had enough grain to fill a rail car. Yet despite enactment of this amendment, the railways again failed to provide farmers with rail cars for direct loading. In response, the Grain Growers sued the CANADIAN PACIFIC RAILWAY's station agent at Sintaluta for ignoring farmers' orders for rail cars. The Association won the case, in the process energizing the agrarian movement and establishing itself as an important and influential farmers' organization. Over the years, the Territorial Grain Growers' Association underwent a series of transformations: in 1905 it was renamed the Saskatchewan Grain Growers' Association; in 1927 the SGGA joined the Farmer's Union of Canada to form the United

Farmers of Canada–Saskatchewan Section; in 1949 the UFC–SS was restructured and renamed the Saskatchewan Farmers Union; in 1969 the SASKATCHEWAN FARMERS UNION, Manitoba Farmers Union, Ontario Farmers Union, and British Columbia Farmers Union amalgamated to form the National Farmers Union, which received its charter from Parliament in 1970. The NFU's mandate is several-fold, and includes efforts to promote economic and social justice for farmers, to ensure that the family farm is the primary mode of food production in Canada, and to employ sustainable agricultural practices that protect the environment.

Damian Coneghan

SASKATCHEWAN HEALTH RESEARCH FOUNDATION (SHRF).

On January 31, 2003, The Saskatchewan Health Research Foundation Act created SHRF to organize, manage, and allocate most Saskatchewan government health research funding. SHRF's mandate is to encourage and facilitate health research, assist the Minister of Health with a provincial health research strategy, pursue additional resources for advancing health research, and inform the public and health professionals about research results and benefits. SHRF builds on the legacy of two previous organizations, the Saskatchewan Health Research Board (1979–92) and the Health Services Utilization and Research Commission (1992–2003). Located in Saskatoon, SHRF works closely with the province's universities, health sector, and community organizations to achieve its vision: *Building a Healthy Saskatchewan through Health Research*. Its board includes leading health researchers, government representatives, and private-sector individuals. Dr. Elizabeth Harrison is the first board chair, and June Bold is the first CEO. SHRF defines health research broadly to include basic "bench" science, clinical investigations, health services and policy research, and research into the determinants of population health. Research funding is allocated through grant competitions, with excellence and relevance as critical deciding factors.

June Bold

SASKATCHEWAN HEALTH SURVEY, 1949–51.

In July 1948, the government of Canada allotted Saskatchewan $43,506 to survey "present health services and facilities" in preparation for an eventual national health insurance program. A committee of twelve had one representative each from the following: registered nurses, dentists, urban municipalities, rural municipalities, labour, the hospital association, the farmers' union, and the Swift Current Health Region; there were also two medical doctors: G.G. Ferguson (registrar of the Saskatchewan College of Physicians and Surgeons) and C.J. HOUSTON. Dr. FRED MOTT was chair, and Dr. MALCOLM G. TAYLOR was research director and secretary. The diverse group met amicably; as each question came up, it was hammered out to the point of agreement. No minority report was submitted, nor were interim reports supplied to the organizations that each member represented. After more than two years' work and twenty-five meetings, the two-volume report contained a catalogue of Saskatchewan's health resources and an estimate of future needs. Saskatchewan's report was exemplary for both the co-operative spirit of the endeavour and the completeness and unanimity of the report. Of 115 recommendations, the first was that "a comprehensive health insurance program should be undertaken at the earliest possible date."

C. Stuart Houston

SASKATCHEWAN HERITAGE FUND.

The Saskatchewan Heritage Fund was an investment fund set up and administered by the provincial government between 1978 and 1992. It received and invested the province's natural resource (primarily OIL, POTASH, and URANIUM) revenues and attempted to save resource revenues for future generations. The Fund was established under the Heritage Fund (Saskatchewan) Act of the provincial Legislative Assembly on May 2, 1978, and was formed by the merger of the former Special Investments Account and the Energy and Resource Development Fund (which had been set up earlier to manage the increasing flow of revenues resulting from higher oil prices). The initial capital was about $465 million, but this grew over the years so that the balance of the Fund was frequently over $1 billion. The Fund received all non-renewable resource revenues, invested these, and paid a dividend of not more than 80% of the Fund's balance each year to the provincial Consolidated Fund (later the General Revenue Fund), from which all provincial expenditures take place. The Fund provided investment capital, usually in the form of loans, to provincial CROWN CORPORATIONS such as the Potash Corporation of Saskatchewan. Capital projects such as HOSPITALS, restoration of historic buildings, airports, and universities were also financed, and the Fund provided monetary incentives to the petroleum industry. The Fund was most active during the BLAKENEY government; during the DEVINE government it was less significant, and was finally wound down by a repeal of the Act in 1992, when it was seen as no longer necessary. During its existence, the Fund was an important mechanism for enabling the provincial government to assume greater control over resource management.

Michael Pretes

SASKATCHEWAN HISTORY AND FOLKLORE SOCIETY.

The Saskatchewan History and Folklore Society's (SHFS) mandate is to gather, preserve, and promote interest in Saskatchewan's past. It was formed in 1957, with EVERETT BAKER as its first president. In 1959, Baker initiated a project to mark the trail from WOOD MOUNTAIN to the CYPRESS HILLS: this path had first been used by the NAKOTA, Nehiyawak, Gros Ventre, Siksika, and later the MÉTIS fur traders; the same trail was used by the North-West Mounted Police from 1875 to 1912. The SHFS has grown to become a multi-faceted company that funds research projects for individuals interested in exploring Saskatchewan's past; it also provides a bursary for undergraduate students majoring in Canadian plains history at the UNIVERSITY OF REGINA. The SHFS assists local communities in recognizing the contributions of Saskatchewan people to their province and to the history of Canada; each year the Society presents its award to an individual who has contributed significantly to the understanding of the province's history. It also publishes the popular *Folklore* magazine.

Elizabeth Mooney

SASKATCHEWAN HOME BUILDERS' ASSOCIATION.

The Saskatchewan Home Builders' Association (SHBA), the voice of the Saskatchewan residential construction industry, has represented its members for over sixty years. The SHBA is the provincial level of the Canadian Home Builders' Association (CHBA), a national non-profit organization. The CHBA is organized at three levels–locally, provincially and nationally–and members of local Home Builders' Associations are also members at the provincial and national levels. All three levels of the CHBA work together to serve members by keeping them informed, involved and prepared for current business challenges. Members also work in the community with charitable organizations, and help build and rebuild communities. The SHBA represents 325 residential construction industry members, of which fifty-five are new home builders and eight are renovators. Other members represent various areas of the housing industry, such as land developers, trade contractors, product and material manufacturers, building product suppliers, lending institutions, insurance providers, and service professionals. On average, SHBA members build over 1,000 new homes each year, which represents over 72% of all new homes built in the Regina and Saskatoon regions. Since the mid-1950s, residential construction values have averaged 47% of the total construction value in the province, with the balance coming from commercial and institutional construction. Since its inception, the SHBA has worked to protect the affordability of new homes and to reduce the amount of legislation imposed on the industry. It has also worked closely with all levels of government on such topics as human resource development and taxation. SHBA is committed to developing a professional industry with builder members who are required to protect consumers through independent warranty programs and an Association code of ethics.

Alicia McGregor and Ken McKinlay

SASKATCHEWAN HOUSING INDUSTRY.

The housing construction industry encompasses new and renovation residential construction. Housing is important from both a social and an economic perspective: from a social perspective, it is the foundation for community development as it contributes directly to the health, social, and educational well-being of people and communities; and from an economic perspective, the construction and maintenance of housing creates businesses and jobs in a variety of sectors such as manufacturing, retail, construction, legal, and financial. Over the past thirty years, new residential construction activity has experienced wide fluctuations: new home construction reached its highest level in Saskatchewan in the mid-1970s; from 1971 to 1988, new housing starts totaled 131,367 units; and new starts peaked in 1976, when more than 13,000 new homes were constructed in the province. A prime determinant of the demand for new housing is the underlying pattern of demographics and household growth. The housing boom in the 1970s is mainly attributed to the maturing of large numbers of baby boomers. In the period following 1988, the aging of these baby boomers, together with lower fertility rates, reduced real income growth, volatile interest rates, and recessions, reduced the demand for new housing units.

New housing construction and land development are very conspicuous. However, the less noticeable renovation expenditures generally exceed new home construction expenditures; strength in the resale market, robust housing starts, and the effects of a strong job market typically drive renovation spending. Housing has a tremendous impact on the economy, and because of the multiplier effect of residential construction activity on the rest of the economy, there is a strong relationship between housing and employment. In addition to the direct employment generated in the actual design and building of housing units, there is indirect labour involved in the supply of goods to manufacturers of residential building products, and in the trading and transportation of materials to contractors and construction sites. Canada Mortgage and Housing Corporation (CMHC) estimates that for every $1 million spent directly on new housing construction, 5.4 person-years of direct employment are created and a further 18.2 person-years are indirectly created in other sectors of the economy. The share of Gross Domestic Product (GDP) accounted for by residential construction expenditures is an indication of the direct contribution that residential construction makes to the economy: since 1970, the share of total GDP accounted for by total residential construction expenditures in Saskatchewan has ranged between 1.7% and 6.6%, the highest shares being recorded in the years 1976 and 1977.

In Saskatchewan, the residential construction

industry is characterized by a large number of small- and medium-sized firms, and only a handful of large-sized firms. In a 1993 study, the Saskatchewan Home Builders' Association (SHBA) estimated that there were more than 700 residential contractors in the province. Based on the survey respondents, only 10% of residential contractors had six or more full-time employees. The existence of a large number of small firms reflects the fragmented nature of the residential construction industry as well as the ease of entry into the industry, since small firms may enter the industry when demand is buoyant and withdraw when demand is slack.

Saskatchewan Housing Corporation

FURTHER READING: Denhez, M. 1994. *The Canadian Home: From Cave to Electronic Cocoon.* Toronto: Dundurn Press.

SASKATCHEWAN INDIAN CULTURAL CENTRE. The Saskatchewan Indian Cultural Centre, located in Saskatoon, was created in 1972 as the "Saskatchewan Indian Cultural College," and funded under the federal government's Cultural Education Centres Program. The mission of the institution is to strengthen and support Indian education and cultural awareness of Indian people; it does so in close consultation with Elders. The Centre assists First Nations communities in various capacities, ranging from language and resource development to library and band training. The Centre also collaborates with other institutions and organizations to enhance developments in the education and tourism industries. The Centre is very active in the publication of materials in First Nations languages and holds language workshops on a regular basis. Recently the Centre has concentrated on the development of a keeping house/museum as well as of a store to market the institution's products.

The Centre has recently entered into a partnership with the **WESTERN DEVELOPMENT MUSEUM** as the major First Nations partner in the Museum's 2005 project called "Winning the Prairie Gamble: The Saskatchewan Story." The Centre's library has been active in the development of web sites, including the "Remembering Our Heroes" site that documents the role that First Nations veterans played in Canada's war efforts, as well as in updating the First Nations Periodical Index and the Aboriginal Arts Gallery.

Rob Nestor

SASKATCHEWAN INDIAN GAMING AUTHORITY. The Saskatchewan Indian Gaming Authority (SIGA) was incorporated on January 11, 1996, as a non-profit corporation with the goals of creating First Nations employment opportunities, developing First Nations Management expertise, utilizing First Nations capital assets, and providing positive cash flow for First Nations and Saskatchewan.

SIGA's first Casino Operating Agreement with the Saskatchewan Liquor and Gaming Authority (SLGA) expired in June 2002, and a new agreement was signed that remains in effect until 2027. The board of directors of SIGA is made up of seven members, with the **FEDERATION OF SASKATCHEWAN INDIAN NATIONS** and the Tribal Councils nominating four and the SLGA nominating three.

SIGA operates four Casinos: the Bear Claw Casino on the White Bear First Nation, the Gold Eagle Casino in North Battleford, the Northern Lights Casino in Prince Albert, and the Painted Hand Casino in Yorkton. SIGA employees well over 1,000 people, 70% of whom are First Nations. SIGA uses a portion of its profits to support education, culture, arts, sports and youth programs for First Nations peoples and communities; it has net incomes in the $25-$30 million range, of which more than 95% comes from gaming revenue. *Rob Nestor*

SASKATCHEWAN INDIAN INSTITUTE OF TECHNOLOGIES. Originally established as the Saskatchewan Indian Community College, its name was changed to the Saskatchewan Indian Institute of Technologies (SIIT) by the Legislative Assembly of the Federation of the Saskatchewan Indians in 1985. The SIIT became the first technical institute in Canada to be controlled by First Nations. Initially, it delivered adult academic upgrading courses, life skills courses, and basic management training to First Nations. The programming evolved to include certified technical and vocational training, as well as the delivery of specific technical and vocational training to First Nations communities.

On July 1, 2000, the Saskatchewan government recognized SIIT as a fully functioning provincial post-secondary institution, with the ability to award its own certificates and diplomas and to be recognized by both Indian and non-Indian communities. This certification allows students to transfer their credits to other institutions and have their certificates and diplomas recognized by all employers in the province. SIIT has campuses at nine different locations: Saskatoon, Regina, Fort Qu'Appelle, Yorkton, Prince Albert, North Battleford, Onion Lake, Meadow Lake and La Ronge. *Rob Nestor*

SASKATCHEWAN INSTITUTE OF APPLIED SCIENCE AND TECHNOLOGY (SIAST). SIAST was established by provincial legislation in 1988 within a policy framework outlined in *Preparing for the Year 2000: Adult Education in Saskatchewan*. It provides vocational and technical training that responds to provincial and national labour market needs. The merging of the province's four existing technical institutes and urban colleges (Saskatchewan Technical Institute and Coteau Range Community College in Moose Jaw; Wascana Institute of Applied Arts and Sciences and Regina

Plains Community College in Regina; Kelsey Institute of Applied Arts and Sciences, Advanced Technology Training Centre, and Saskatoon Region Community College in Saskatoon; and Northern Institute of Technology, Prince Albert Regional Community College, and Meadow Lake Vocational Centre) into one institution enabled it to respond quickly to changing technologies and shifts in employment demand.

The roots of the four technical institutes can be traced to vocational and academic training centres set up during **WORLD WAR II** to assist with rehabilitating and training war veterans. In Saskatoon, the Canadian Vocational Training School, established in 1941, was the forerunner to SIAST Kelsey Campus. It was named the Central Saskatchewan Technical Institute in 1963, and given an expanded mandate to provide credit training in a wide range of occupations. Renamed the Saskatchewan Technical Institute of Saskatoon in 1967, it continued to expand its course offerings and enrollment.

SIAST Wascana Campus began as centres offering adult education and wartime training. The Regina Vocational Centre provided training in what was originally the residence of the **LIEUTENANT-GOVERNOR** of Saskatchewan. In 1972, the Saskatchewan Institute of Applied Arts and Sciences (SIAAS) opened the School of Nursing at the Regina General Hospital, with Health Sciences as the first division. In 1973, it was renamed the Wascana Institute of Applied Arts and Sciences (WIAAS). New programs in agriculture, vocational education and extension led to many campus moves to accommodate program expansion. In 2000, all Wascana campus programs were consolidated in a single building, formerly the Regina Plains Health Centre.

SIAST Palliser Campus started in 1958 under the name of Saskatchewan Technical Institute (STI). It was to provide a central facility for continued education in various technical and trade occupations. Temporarily located in Regina until the new construction was completed in Moose Jaw, the new technical institute opened in 1961. In 1963 some programs were transferred from the Canadian Vocational Training School in Saskatoon. Through the 1960s the institute in Moose Jaw expanded rapidly; its name changed several times, reverting back to Saskatchewan Technical Institute (STI), from 1968 until 1987.

SIAST Woodland Campus originated in programs initially delivered by vocational training centres in northern Saskatchewan and Natonum Community College in Prince Albert. A community action committee in the mid-1970s led to a provincial announcement in 1981 to build a fourth provincial technical institute in Prince Albert. The Northern Institute of Technology, which opened in 1985, was designed to offer adult education and training programs in more than thirty areas, with special emphasis on programs that reflected the training needs of people living in northern Saskatchewan.

In 1988 the new institute, SIAST, operated as an autonomous organization, with a president and a board of directors. In 1997, SIAST moved toward becoming one provincial institute. This entailed a name change for each campus, the formation of SIAST-wide divisions with provincial deans (each responsible for programs at several campuses), and a campus director located at each campus. As the province's second largest public training institution, its mandate is to deliver technical education and trades training, as well as adult basic education, to certify training, and to facilitate brokerage and delivery of programs to other technical institutions, colleges, professional bodies, or industry. The institute offers a wide range of full-time and part-time, credit and non-credit opportunities through Extension Services. SIAST also provides customized training for overseas clients in trades and technology, and training to international students through its International Services.

SIAST works closely with industry through trade boards with the Saskatchewan Apprenticeship and Trade Certification Commission in order to provide training for apprentices in the majority of Saskatchewan's apprenticeable trades. Linkages between SIAST and the province's two universities occur primarily at the program level through credit recognition and transfer, and in the delivery of extension university courses at its Prince Albert and Moose Jaw campuses. SIAST is also working with private vocational schools and industry for credit transfer arrangements to enhance student mobility and employer recognition. In 2001 SIAST officially launched a fifth campus, the "Virtual Campus," a technology-enhanced learning (TEL) initiative that expanded its borders. SIAST is also involved in **CAMPUS SASKATCHEWAN**, through which it works with other post-secondary institutions to use TEL to increase opportunities for people in Saskatchewan to access high-quality education and training.

SIAST would not have become what it is today without influences that helped define the role of public training institutions in the development of the province. These include increased provincial and federal interest in building the nation's economy, new converging workforce needs in industry, and increasing federal involvement in technical and vocational education through federal provincial agreements for funding over nine decades.

Lorne Sparling

SASKATCHEWAN INSTITUTE OF PUBLIC POLICY.

The Saskatchewan Institute of Public Policy (SIPP) is a non-profit and non-partisan research institute based at the **UNIVERSITY OF REGINA**, which is devoted to policy research that is relevant to Saskatchewan. SIPP was created in 1998 as a partnership between the University of Regina, the government of Saskatchewan (both of which provide core funding), and the **UNIVERSITY OF SASKATCHEWAN**. As part of its mandate, SIPP has conducted and disseminated policy research on a broad range of issues including Aboriginal self-government and economic development, public finance and taxation, health care reform, agriculture and rural development, and public ownership and governance. SIPP has also sponsored conferences on issues of national concern including federalism, the social union, and urban Aboriginal issues.

In addition to conducting research, SIPP reaches out to the general policy community through public lectures and presentations, an armchair discussion series, and its regular briefing notes and public policy papers. For students, SIPP organizes and runs a President's Leadership Program as well as an annual competition for student public policy papers. In contrast to purely free standing, university-based or internal government-based policy think tanks, SIPP is a pioneering effort at creating a policy collaboration between university and government that preserves its independence in analysis and prescription.

Gregory P. Marchildon

SASKATCHEWAN INTERCULTURAL ASSOCIATION.

The forerunner of the Saskatchewan Intercultural Association (SIA) was the Saskatoon Folk Arts Council, formed in 1964 to represent locally the Canadian mosaic. The mission of the SIA is to recognize and support the right of every ethnocultural group to retain its distinctive cultural identity without political or social impediment and for the mutual benefit of all citizens. The Council's primary goal was the development and promotion of yearly events, which included fifteen to twenty affiliated performing groups. Ethnic histories were written as brief accounts of the Russians, Jews, Ukrainians, Norwegians, Scots, Hungarians, Germans, Greeks, and French, and afterwards other ethnic communities.

With each decade the organization adjusted its organization and structure: it became the Saskatoon Multicultural Council in 1981, and the following decade broadened again to become the Saskatchewan Intercultural Association. The Council was active in province-wide celebrations of Saskatchewan's 75th anniversary. For Saskatoon's centennial the Council commissioned an original work, *The Spirit of Saskatoon*, which was produced in April 1982. In the 1980s the Saskatoon Multicultural Council became involved with the city in the three-day festival known as "Folkfest"; it also expanded its participation in the Canada Day festivities with the Saskatoon Optimist Club, met the Public School Board's request for educational resources, and continued its awareness-raising essay and poster contests.

A major concern became the preservation of heritage languages. The Association established the Multilingual School: eleven Association member groups (Chinese Mandarin School, Escuela Hispánica, German Language School, Hellenic School Association, Japanese Language School for Children, Nehiyawan Parents Group, Norwegian Cultural Society, Pakistani Association, Punjabi School, Saskatoon Chilean Association, and Saskatoon Club Italia) began instructing at Holy Cross High School. Currently, there are some 800 students attending classes, and approximately ninety teachers from twenty-one different ethnocultural groups are involved in offering classes. Current innovative programs and activities of the SIA reflect the new multiculturalism by entrenching more substantive aspects that follow the national picture: among these programs are Performing Arts, the Saskatoon Multilingual School, and the Equity and Anti-Racism Committee. (*See also* **URBAN ETHNIC DIVERSITY, VISIBLE MINORITIES**) *Rodolfo Pino*

SASKATCHEWAN JAZZ FESTIVAL.

Founded in 1986 by the Saskatoon Jazz Society, the Saskatchewan Jazz Festival produces the largest cultural event in Saskatchewan and is the only festival that presents itself in multiple communities. Once a three-day event, it now covers ten days in late June and early July in the cities of Saskatoon, Regina, North Battleford, Prince Albert and Moose Jaw. The festival's heart lies in Saskatoon, where it originated, with just over 90% of its performances taking place on the city's streets, in parks, the Bessborough Hotel's gardens, the historic Broadway Theatre, and a variety of clubs and venues throughout downtown. Many performances are free to the public and promote the talents of local musicians. Touring acts from all over Canada and the world make up approximately 40% of the festival's performances. In 2004, Regina played host to fourteen concerts featuring twenty local and touring groups; and North Battleford, Prince Albert, and Moose Jaw each hosted one show.

With a mandate to promote jazz music in its diverse forms, to provide a forum for artists and music educators, and to support the development of musicians, the festival offers an eclectic program. Jazz is the core for concert programming and makes up over half of the performances each year. Related genres include styles with roots in jazz or improvisational influences: blues, gospel, funk, R & B, soul, and world music are all regulars in the eclectic lineup. The festival delivers jazz education to high school musicians and vocalists, bringing in educators from all over Canada to provide instruction and workshops. It also reaches out into the community by offering concerts in special care homes in Saskatoon, thus taking the festival to those who would otherwise be unable to participate. Individual and corporate communities embrace the festival in the roles of patron and financial supporters.

Patti Gera

SASKATCHEWAN LAND SURVEYORS' ASSOCIATION (SLSA).

The SLSA is an organization of Saskatchewan land surveyors and professional surveyors who are registered to practice in accordance with the provisions of the Land Surveyors and Professional Surveyors Act. This self-governing professional organization was originally established in 1910 and has been entrusted with the stewardship and standards of the survey profession, with responsibility for the establishment, re-establishment and maintenance of the network of survey monuments that serve as the basis for the system of land registration and ownership in the province. The objectives of the Association are to ensure the proficiency of its members; to regulate its members in the practices of professional land surveying and professional surveying; and to govern its members in accordance with the Act, the by-laws, and all other applicable acts or regulations. Professional land surveying is sometimes referred to as legal or boundary surveying, while professional surveying involves other types of surveying such as construction, topographic, photogrammetric, hydrographic and geodetic, as well as Geographic Information Systems (GIS). As of 2004, there were eighty-one fully licensed Saskatchewan land surveyors, of whom seven were life members and forty-six were also registered as professional surveyors.

Carl Shiels

SASKATCHEWAN LEGISLATIVE BUILDING.

Located in the capital city of Regina, the Legislative Building houses the Legislative Assembly of the province of Saskatchewan; it is the largest capital building in Canada, and a symbol of British parliamentary democracy and provincial pride. The creation and passage of laws and other legislative responsibilities are carried out in the building's Chamber and Executive Quarters. Less than a year after Saskatchewan became a province on September 1, 1905, planning for the proposed Legislative Building began with the selection of an appropriate site, followed by a competition for the building's design. The architectural plans of Edward and W.S. Maxwell of Montreal were chosen on December 20, 1907. The Maxwell brothers designed the building's floor plan in the shape of a Latin cross, with a monumental dome over the intersection of the major and minor axis. The façade and interior reflect the influence of the beaux-arts style, a popular architectural movement of that era.

Work on the Legislative Building's foundation began on August 31, 1908. Although the original plans specified red brick for the exterior, Premier **WALTER SCOTT** decided that Tyndall stone should be used instead; quarried from Manitoba, the cream-

SASKATCHEWAN ARCHIVES BOARD 90-600-09

The Saskatchewan Legislative Building and gardens.

coloured limestone remains one of the most distinguishing features of the Legislative Building. Governor General Earl Grey laid the cornerstone on October 4, 1909, and the first session of the Legislative Assembly was held in the Chamber on January 25, 1912. Built at a cost of roughly $1.75 million, more than double the original estimate, Saskatchewan's Legislative Building was officially opened by Governor General, the Duke of Connaught, on October 12, 1912. Since then, the grounds surrounding the building have developed into one of the largest urban parks in North America. A series of renovations were made to the building during the 1960s through to the 1980s. In 1997 a four-year restoration project repaired the Legislative Building's structural deficiencies, and improved safety and accessibility.

Holden Stoffel

FURTHER READING: Barnhart, G.L. 2002. *Building for the Future: A Photo Journal of Saskatchewan's Legislative Building*. Regina: Canadian Plains Research Center.

SASKATCHEWAN LIBRARY ASSOCIATION.

The Saskatchewan Library Association (SLA) is a provincial, volunteer, charitable organization designed to further the development of library service in Saskatchewan, and through libraries, the culture of the province. The Saskatchewan Library Association includes as members individuals, institutions, and organizations, who share a common interest in library service. The majority of the operational funds for SLA are provided through Saskatchewan Lotteries and membership fees, with program funding through corporate sponsorships, and government partnerships. Formed in 1914, the Saskatchewan Library Association consisted of a group of seventeen people from urban centres who pressed the government to provide rural communities with library facilities. After four years, the organization ceased to exist. SLA formed again in 1942, when the Canadian Library Council was developing and needed provincial representation. Since that time SLA has been actively involved in legislation changes, presenting briefs to the minister in charge of libraries, and in the evolution of the provision of library service in the province. SLA provides information, advocacy, awareness, education, membership benefits, and cultural opportunities for library workers and the public at large through its general operations and annual long-term programs, such as Saskatchewan Library Week, the Summer Reading Program, the *Forum* newsletter, and its web site: www.lib.sk.ca/sla/.

Established in 1976, Saskatchewan Library Week (SLW) is SLA's major advocacy campaign, occurring annually during the third week of October. The goal of the program is to raise awareness of libraries and their services. Various contests and promotional activities are held during the week in many libraries across the province. SLA provides SLW materials for all libraries in the province, including public, school, post-secondary, and special libraries. Since 1977, the annual Summer Reading Program (SRP) has motivated children and their families to visit their library and read during the summer. Children's performers are an important part of the festivities, touring the various library systems of the province during July and August. SLA convenes the Summer Reading Committee with library participants from around the province, and provides financial support and printed materials to all interested libraries. SLA provides SRP materials for all public libraries in the province.

The SLA administers and raises funds for the **MARY DONALDSON** Trust Fund, established in 1967 to finance an annual public lecture on a topic of interest on, or closely related to, the library field. In 1977, the Trust established an annual Mary Donaldson Award of Merit to recognize library support workers and the essential services that they perform in Saskatchewan libraries. The award is presented annually to a full-time or part-time Saskatchewan student who is attending the library technical program at the **SASKATCHEWAN INSTITUTE OF APPLIED SCIENCE AND TECHNOLOGY** (SIAST). The award and the lecture honour **MARY DONALDSON**, the first Provincial Librarian in Saskatchewan. SLA also presents the SLA **FRANCES MORRISON** Award to individuals for outstanding service to libraries, and administers the Saskatchewan Libraries Education Bursary in partnership with Saskatchewan Learning and the Saskatchewan Provincial Library.

SLA's continuing education offerings extend beyond those made available at the annual conference/spring seminar. Educational events are held throughout the year at various locations around the province to assist in furthering the education and information resources of its members, as well as any interested parties in the library community. SLA continues to provide leadership and coordination to programs that promote libraries. It fosters appreciation and development of Saskatchewan literary arts, forges partnerships between cultural agencies and libraries, and promotes expertise in the library field.

Judith Silverthorne

SASKATCHEWAN MAFIA. This is a term of respect used to describe members of the federal public service who had come to Ottawa from the Saskatchewan government. Over twenty relatively senior public servants and central agency policy analysts left Saskatchewan after the election victory of a right-leaning Liberal government under Premier **ROSS THATCHER** in 1964. Many were quickly hired by a federal Liberal government committed to an agenda of modernizing the welfare state under Prime Minister Pearson. Some members of the Saskatchewan Mafia proved to be instrumental in introducing equalization, extending post-secondary education, and implementing national **MEDICARE**. The most prominent members of the Saskatchewan Mafia included **A.W. JOHNSON**, who became Secretary to the Treasury Board, Deputy Minister of National Welfare and President of the Canadian Broadcasting Corporation; **TOMMY SHOYAMA**, who became Deputy Minister of Finance and Chairman of Atomic Energy

RON GARNETT—AIRSCAPES
Salt deposits, Chaplin.

Canada; and **DON TANSLEY**, who became Senior Vice-President of the Canadian International Development Agency (CIDA) and the first Deputy Minister of Fisheries and Oceans. While other former Saskatchewan civil servants would also go on to have stellar careers in Ottawa, the collective impact of the Saskatchewan Mafia would influence a generation of public servants in the government of Canada. *Gregory P. Marchildon*

SASKATCHEWAN MEDICAL ASSOCIATION (SMA). The SMA, a division of the Canadian Medical Association, was organized in August 1905. It dissolved in September 1936 because of the costs of running two professional organizations during the **DEPRESSION**. The functions of the SMA were then transferred to the **COLLEGE OF PHYSICIANS AND SURGEONS**.

To lighten the workload of the College, the SMA was reconstituted under it in 1967. In 1972, a legislative amendment stopped the College from collecting dues on behalf of the SMA because of the perception that licensing physicians, while also representing their economic interests, constituted a conflict of interest for the College. Consequently, the SMA legally incorporated as a separate entity.

Membership in the SMA has been voluntary, but in 1986 legislation was adopted to allow the SMA to check off dues for non-member fee-for-service physicians. In 1996 this concept was expanded further by allowing the collection of dues from non-members working under contract and salaried arrangements.

The mission of the SMA is to advance the educational, professional and economic welfare of Saskatchewan physicians; to advance the honour and integrity of the profession; and to promote quality health practices and services within a quality health care system. *E.H. Baergen*

SASKATCHEWAN MINERALS. Saskatchewan Minerals' inception as a **CROWN CORPORATION** dates back to 1948, when a low-grade **SODIUM SULPHATE** plant was officially opened at Chaplin, Saskatchewan, by Premier **T.C. DOUGLAS**. Saskatchewan Minerals flourished through the 1950s and 1960s as demand for sodium sulphate grew. It acquired a second plant near Mossback in 1954, and began construction on a third at Ingebrigt in 1966. In 1981, Saskatchewan Minerals purchased an additional operation at Gladmar. However, by that time market demand had shifted away from low-grade sodium sulphate toward a higher grade commonly used in detergents. In 1984, Saskatchewan Minerals closed its low-grade sodium sulphate plants at Mossbank and Gladmar, and introduced state-of-the-art equipment at its Chaplin plant, which enabled production of detergent-grade sodium sulphate. In 1988, Saskatchewan Minerals was privatized by Premier **GRANT DEVINE**'s Progressive Conservative government, and subsequently became a division of Goldcorp Inc., a profitable gold company headquartered in Toronto. Saskatchewan Minerals is now one of North America's leading producers of high-grade sodium sulphate. Sodium sulphate from the Chaplin mine is purchased by domestic and international blue-chip customers for use in laundry and dishwater detergents, pulp and paper, glass, textiles, starch, dyes, carpet and room deodorizers, and livestock mineral feed. *Iain Stewart*

SASKATCHEWAN MINING ASSOCIATION INC. The Saskatchewan Mining Association Inc. is a not-for-profit corporation owned by the **MINING** companies active in the province. Its roots date back to 1964, when the organization was known as the Saskatchewan Chamber of Mines, headquartered in Prince Albert. At this time its main focus was the exploration and development activity occurring in the Saskatchewan shield. In 1965, probably triggered by the growth of the potash industry, the organization adopted a more province-wide mandate, changing its name to the Saskatchewan Mining Association; its headquarters were moved to Regina. The Association's main objectives are to inform and advise members of existing laws, regulations and policies affecting the mining industry. It also makes representations to the various federal and provincial agencies involved in the regulatory and licensing processes that affect this industry. The Association aims to enhance the general welfare of the mining industry through the support and promotion of technical innovations in the fields of health and safety standards, waste disposal, environmental protection, and extractive metallurgy research and development. It promotes a co-operative approach within the industry to support socio-economic development, especially in areas of the province that are affected. This includes recruitment and training of workers, and promotion of Saskatchewan service industries in support of mineral development. In addition, the Association undertakes public education aimed at enhancing the well-being of the industry in the province. *Philip Reeves*

SASKATCHEWAN MUSIC FESTIVAL ASSOCIATION (SFMA).

The SMFA is one of the province's oldest organizations and has influenced all Saskatchewan music. Its structures and programs have been followed throughout Canada. Inspired by Governor General Earl Grey's vision of a dominion-wide festival, the SMFA was established in 1908 in Regina by Fred Chisholm and **FRANK LAUBACH**. All Saskatchewan musical groups were invited to the first provincial festival in 1909 in Regina. The annual festival moved to Saskatoon, Prince Albert and Moose Jaw, and then continued the rotation. Excellent railway service allowed participants, including large ensembles, to come from all parts of the province. To satisfy increasing demands, local festivals were added, beginning at Unity in 1926. Expansion continued until there were fifty-one in 2002, including one fully bilingual event at Gravelbourg. An early president, Chief Justice Brown, secured a government grant to be administered by the **UNIVERSITY OF SASKATCHEWAN** under its president, **WALTER MURRAY**. Murray, another early SMFA president, provided office space for the SMFA secretary and a car to facilitate festival fieldwork. He used the SMFA's success to secure a grant from the Carnegie Foundation to establish a University Chair of Music in 1931.

Adult vocal ensembles and solos were eligible for the first festival, with other categories added gradually: piano, strings, woodwinds, brass, speech arts (English and French), instrumental ensembles, percussion, special education, and First Nations

drum/song. Ages range from six years to "senior open," and festivals may add classes to suit local needs. Provincial awards kept increasing until several hundred performers competed through a system of district winners. This format has since been used by the Federation of Canadian Music Festivals in all provinces. The continued growth of large ensembles encouraged the formation of many provincial associations to accommodate various categories such as choral and band. The SMFA frequently commissions works for test pieces and special celebrations.

An annual concerto competition, established in 1979, provides cash prizes; the winner is a featured soloist with the Regina and Saskatoon Symphony Orchestras. A biennial opera competition (since 2000), provided by the late Gordon C. Wallis, is administered by the SMFA; the winner also appears with both symphonies. The University of Saskatchewan transferred its funding to the **SASKATCHEWAN ARTS BOARD** in 1966. The SMFA is now funded by the Saskatchewan Lotteries Trust Fund for Sport, Culture and Recreation, the Saskatchewan Arts Board, the Department of Culture, Youth and Recreation, and SaskCulture. Anticipating its 100th Anniversary in 2008, the SMFA and its festivals plan appropriate celebrations, including special centennial classes. *Mossie Hancock*

SASKATCHEWAN ORDER OF MERIT: *see* HONOURS AND AWARDS

SASKATCHEWAN ORGANIC DIRECTORATE (SOD).

The SOD, formed in 1998, exists primarily to represent certified organic producers in Saskatchewan; however, organic processors and traders are also eligible for membership. The main purposes of SOD are to assist in the development of the organic industry and initiate activities that provide professional development and technical assistance to producers, processors, and consumers. In addition, SOD attempts to form strategic alliances with government agencies and organizations, with the goal of furthering organic agriculture and promoting the expansion of markets. An example of this is the creation of the Organic Agriculture Protection Fund (OAPF), a subsidiary of SOD, which seeks to protect organic markets that may be eliminated as a result of the introduction of genetically modified (GM) crops.

Membership in SOD is often achieved through association with organic certification bodies in Saskatchewan. The main certifiers in Saskatchewan are: Pro-cert Organic Systems (Pro-cert); the Saskatchewan Organic Certification Association (SOCA); the Organic Crop Improvement Association (OCIA); and the Canadian Organic Certification Co-operative (COCC). However, at present not all of these bodies are strongly associated with SOD, and this is reflected in low producer membership num-

bers for these certifiers. In addition to producer memberships, SOD attempts to obtain representation from other industry stakeholders; typically, these include corporate groups, consumers, and membership-at-large.

As with many agricultural organizations, funding for SOD is obtained through membership fees. Although many organic producers currently pay a check-off on their production, none of this money goes to SOD because it do not have a development commission (or board) legislated under the Saskatchewan Agri-Food Act to support development programs such as research, the provision of information to producers, policy development, and promotion. *Gary Storey*

SASKATCHEWAN ORGANIZATION FOR HERITAGE LANGUAGES (SOHL).

The SOHL was founded in 1985 to act as a provincial umbrella organization for the promotion and development of heritage language education in Saskatchewan. The organization is funded primarily through SaskLotteries. The mission of the SOHL is accomplished by identifying and securing funding available at the provincial and national levels for the support of local heritage language schools, by providing organizational advice and assistance for the establishment of heritage language schools at the local level throughout the province, by providing skill-development opportunities for heritage language teachers, and by developing and identifying resource materials which will enhance the teaching of heritage languages. The SOHL, in its advocacy capacity and throughout its history, has presented numerous briefs to the federal and provincial governments on the benefits of supporting heritage language programs for both social and economic reasons. The organization has also developed a variety of promotional materials targeting students and the general public. The SOHL, with over fifty regular members, has a wide variety of programs for language teachers, school administrators, and language students. This includes celebration of Heritage Language Recognition Day, a bursary program for teachers, a provincial conference, resource materials and a resource centre, professional skills development workshops, support of immersion camps, a newsletter, funding for Heritage Language Schools, and Mini-language Learning Lessons in the regular school system. SOHL members offer language instruction in over twenty-five different languages. Regular membership is open to any organization interested in developing, teaching, and/or promoting the use of heritage languages. *Joanne Reilly*

SASKATCHEWAN PARTY.

The Saskatchewan Party has been an active right-wing political party in Saskatchewan since 1997. With the Progressive Conservative party beset with the legacy of fraud scandals while in government and the **LIBERAL PARTY** fraught with internal division, a group of four Conservative MLAs and four Liberal MLAs joined to form the Saskatchewan Party in August 1997. Ken Krawetz was named the interim leader, and the party surpassed the Liberal party in the Legislature to become the official opposition. After the formal founding and registration of the party, former Reform party MP **ELWIN HERMANSON** was elected as the party's first leader in April 1998. The party soon became embroiled in controversy as it endorsed policies such as the abolition of the Saskatchewan Human Rights Commission. Circumstances of its birth also became a contentious issue as opponents charged the party with being a recasting of the unpopular Progressive Conservative party, trying to avoid its record.

However the party struck a cord with some voters unhappy with **ROY ROMANOW**'s New Democratic government, and nearly swept rural Saskatchewan in the 1999 election. Although the Saskatchewan Party won the popular vote, it failed to carry enough seats to form government. With a large number of MLAs and momentum on its side, it seemed poised to defeat the government of **LORNE CALVERT** in 2003. However, a strong campaign by the NDP, and concerns about the ambiguity of several Saskatchewan Party promises regarding Saskatchewan **CROWN CORPORATIONS**, made the campaign much more difficult than expected. In spite of an increased number of seats in the Legislature, the party lost the popular vote and again failed to defeat the government. Party leader Hermanson stepped down shortly after the loss, and Swift Current MLA **BRAD WALL** assumed the leadership unchallenged. *Brett Quiring*

SASKATCHEWAN PENAL COMMISSION. On March 1, 1946, the government of Saskatchewan formally appointed a commission to investigate the province's penal system. The four-member body, known as the Saskatchewan Penal Commission, was mandated to scrutinize all components of the province's penal institutions, including the physical aspects and the established practices under which they operated. Heading the Commission was Dr. Samuel Laycock, as chairman, with Reverend Clarence Halliday and barrister William Holman forming the remainder of the investigative arm of the group; government employee Christian Smith received appointment as the Commission's secretary.

The Commission reviewed the work of the earlier, federally appointed Archambault Commission, visited the province's jails and other Canadian and American penal institutions, and finally compiled its findings into the *Report of the Saskatchewan Penal Commission*. In carrying out its mandate, the Commission faithfully adhered to the government's direction as to the progression and scope of its investigation.

The report, submitted to the provincial government on September 13, 1946, commented on virtually every aspect of the provincial penal system, from physical infrastructure to established practices and programs. In it, the Commissioners discussed the ideas of crime and punishment, and recommended sweeping changes throughout the administration and operation of Saskatchewan's jails, regarding future construction and new directives for the discipline, education, labour, and overall well-being of Saskatchewan inmates. The Commissioners roundly criticized the preponderance of what they believed to be an outdated, restrictive and ineffective penal orientation; they espoused a system founded on scientific knowledge and informed by modern methods and research. They urged that disciplines such as medicine, psychology, and sociology should form the basis for a more humanistic and effective system to deal with the problems of crime and rehabilitation.

Although relatively few of the Commission's recommendations were followed, its work did represent a significant shift in the overall direction of Saskatchewan penology. Probably the most important development to result from the Commission's *Report* was the establishment of a Corrections Branch within the Department of Social Welfare. Previously administered by the Department of Public Works, the new positioning of the penal system meant that the department dedicated to social programming and the well- being of Saskatchewan residents now held the responsibility for the operation and maintenance of the province's penal institutions. *Derek Donais*

FURTHER READING: Skinner, S., O. Driedger and B. Grainger. 1981. *Corrections: A Historical Perspective of the Saskatchewan Experience*. Regina: Canadian Plains Research Center.

SASKATCHEWAN POLICE COLLEGE. The Saskatchewan Police College, with its offices and classrooms located at the **UNIVERSITY OF REGINA**, has been training municipal police officers on this campus since 1975. Housing the Saskatchewan Police College at the University of Regina has provided a positive learning environment for police officers, and this successful working partnership has enhanced the experience of police training by offering recruits and senior officers the opportunity to access university facilities such as classroom space, residences, recreation facilities, and libraries. In addition to providing in-service ongoing developmental training to municipal police officers, the College also offers positions on its in-service training courses to other enforcement and regulatory agencies: Saskatchewan Environmental and Resource Management (SERM) officers, Department of Social Services staff, Fire Investigators and Fire Commissioner personnel, and members of other police services often access its courses.

The Saskatchewan Police College operates under the authority and control of the **SASKATCHEWAN POLICE COMMISSION** by virtue of the Saskatchewan Police Act (1990). The Saskatchewan Police College's mission is to collaborate with Saskatchewan Municipal Police agencies and their memberships in order to provide professional police services to the people of Saskatchewan through the training of recruits and senior police officers. Beginning in 1995, the University of Regina and the Saskatchewan Police College embarked on extensive discussions, meetings, and planning events that culminated in 1999 in a unique partnership and a

ROY ANTAL/REGINA LEADER-POST
Saskatchewan Police College trainee and supervisor during an exercise on traffic control.

new degree program offered by the University: the Bachelor of Arts in Police Studies, a four-year degree program which combines police training with liberal arts education.   *Patricia Joyce*

SASKATCHEWAN POLICE COMMISSION.

The Saskatchewan Police Commission is a body corporate created under statute. Part II of the Police Act, 1990, sets out the legislated framework for the commission and its staff. Staff members include a Director, the Director of the SASKATCHEWAN POLICE COLLEGE, training staff, and clerical support staff. The Saskatchewan Police Commission consists of five community persons who are each appointed for a three-year term by Order-in-Council. A commission member is only eligible to sit on the commission for two three-year terms. The current commission is comprised of five persons: the chair, the vice-chair, and three members. The Saskatchewan Police Commission holds regular meetings to deal with issues related to policing, and consults as regularly as necessary with the Saskatchewan Association of Chiefs of Police, the Saskatchewan Federation of Police Officers, Boards of Police Commissioners, and other community groups or individuals.

Section 19 of the Police Act, 1990, outlines the role and responsibilities of the commission,and provides it with its mandate: "to promote adequate and effective policing throughout Saskatchewan." In order to fulfill its mandate the commission has a series of responsibilities under section 19 that include audit, oversight of training, and the creation of a policy and procedures manual. In matters of discipline, the commission hears appeals or reviews from discipline, and makes the final decision on sanctions or dismissal of municipal police officers. Subject to the approval of the Lieutenant Governor in Council, the commission is responsible for regulations under the Municipal Police Discipline Regulations, 1991, the Municipal Police Clothing and Rank Regulations, 1991, the Municipal Police Equipment Regulations, 1991, the Municipal Police Recruiting Regulations, 1991, the Municipal Police Training Regulations, 1991, and the Municipal Police Report Forms and Filing Systems, 1991.

There are approximately 1,200 municipal police officers in Saskatchewan, providing policing to Regina, Saskatoon, Weyburn, Estevan, Moose Jaw, Prince Albert, Luseland, Dalmeny, Caronport, Vanscoy, Corman Park and Stoughton. The newly created File Hills First Nations Police Service was created under the authority of the Police Act, 1990; it started as three-year transitional model, going from ROYAL CANADIAN MOUNTED POLICE policing to a stand-alone First Nations police service, and provides policing for five First Nations in southeastern Saskatchewan—Little Black Bear, Okanese, Starblanket, Peepeekis, and Carry the Kettle.

The Commission also supervises the Saskatchewan Police College and approves course training content and changes to curriculum. The Saskatchewan Police College provides basis recruit and in-service training; however, it is not responsible for recruiting of prospective police officers: that responsibility rests with each individual police service.   *Murray Sawatsky*

SASKATCHEWAN POPULATION HEALTH AND EVALUATION RESEARCH UNIT (SPHERU).

Established in 1999, SPHERU's mission is to inform health, social and economic policy, influence the education of health professionals, and provide a resource for public debate. SPHERU is a multi-disciplinary partnership between the UNIVERSITY OF REGINA, the UNIVERSITY OF SASKATCHEWAN, the SASKATCHEWAN HEALTH RESEARCH FOUNDATION, Saskatchewan Health, and the SASKATCHEWAN ASSOCIATION OF HEALTH ORGANIZATIONS. SPHERU maintains offices at both provincial universities and in Prince Albert, and pursues funding from provincial and federal agencies.

Because the most important determinants of population health are embedded in economic, social, and political structures of inequality, research is conducted under two broad categories. The first deals primarily with health-determining conditions (e.g., socio-economic status, the environment, social roles, and early childhood development) and the relationships between these. The second concerns evaluation studies of interventions to make social and environmental conditions more health-promoting and more equitable in their allocation of health risks and opportunities across different population groups.

Research partners include community groups, policy workers, and researchers from other universities across Canada and internationally. SPHERU's unique contribution to Saskatchewan lies in its focusing not on health policy or health care, but in its insistence that all public policy be designed in a manner that reduces the inequalities that lead to ill health.   *Ann M. Bishop*

SASKATCHEWAN POWER CORPORATION.

Saskatchewan Power Corporation (SaskPower) was established as the Saskatchewan Power Commission in 1929 to provide safe, reliable, cost-effective power to Saskatchewan residents. In 1949 the Commission became a CROWN CORPORATION called Saskatchewan Power Corporation; the government also passed the RURAL ELECTRIFICATION ACT, an important piece of legislation that set the stage for electrical service to all farms in the province. Today SaskPower is the principal supplier of electricity in Saskatchewan. It generates, purchases, transmits, distributes, and sells electricity and related products and services to more than 436,000 residential, farm, industrial, and commercial customers. (*See* Table SP-1, right.)

                    Karen Schmidt

SASKATCHEWAN PROPERTY MANAGEMENT CORPORATION (SPMC).

SPMC was founded under the Crown Corporations Act in 1986 and continued under its own act in 1987. Its mandate is to provide commercial support services to government departments, CROWN CORPORATIONS, agencies, boards, and commissions of the government. The intent is to maximize value and gain economies of scale by serving the needs of one major client: the Saskatchewan government. SPMC has four main service lines: accommodation, commercial, information technology, and corporate support. Accommodation services own, lease, maintain, build, furnish and provide security for office space and buildings around the province, including Crown corporation buildings, service centres, and provincial parks. Commercial services provide vehicles, executive air travel, purchasing services (particularly office, medical, and janitorial supplies), sales and salvage, postal services, warehouse and distribution, records management, relocation services, and conference facilities at the Echo Valley Conference Centre. Corporate Support services offer communication, human resources, legal, investigative, risk management, and insurance services. The new Information Technology line maintains all government internal web-based information, e-mail, telecommunications, and computer support. To provide this support, SPMC works closely with the private sector to source supplies, negotiate contracts, provide maintenance, and present expertise in architecture, engineering and construction.   *Merle Massie*

SASKATCHEWAN PROTECTIVE SERVICES MEDAL: *see* HONOURS AND AWARDS

Table SP-1. Saskatchewan Power Corporation—Contribution to Saskatchewan's Economy, 2003*	
Assets	$3.6 billion
Capital spending	$267 million
Community donations	$1.4 million
Debt ratio	57%
Dividend to CIC	$168.5 million
Earnings	$187 million
Employees	2,376 across Saskatchewan
Local purchasing (includes employee earnings of $199 million)	$681 million
Local suppliers supported	1,100
Return on equity	14%
Revenue	$1.2 billion

*All numbers are for the fiscal year ending December 31, 2003.

SASKATCHEWAN PROVINCIAL BUILDING AND CONSTRUCTION TRADES COUNCIL.

The Saskatchewan Provincial Building and Construction Trades Council was created in 1989 as an umbrella organization for unions involved in Saskatchewan's construction industry. Prior to 1989, the construction trades had been represented since the 1940s by two councils, one in the northern and the other in the southern part of the province. The fifteen unions affiliated with the council are responsible for building much of the infrastructure and the places we work and live in; they represent a variety of trades, such as ironworkers, insulators, boilermakers, electricians, painters, millwrights, plumbers, pipefitters, sheet metal workers, plasterers, teamsters, operating engineers, and general construction workers. The affiliates are totally autonomous and negotiate their own collective agreements. The Building Trade Council represents all workers in the building, construction, fabrication, and maintenance industry, in order to foster safer working conditions and to improve the quality of life for those workers and their families.

The Building Trades Council assists in the selection process for labour representatives to many industry and government boards and commissions. They provide a forum for the unions in Saskatchewan's construction industry to develop a common front on issues affecting this sector, such as industry legislation, occupational health and safety, and trades apprenticeship. The council is affiliated nationally with the Canadian Building and Construction Trades Department in Ottawa, and internationally with the Building and Construction Trades Department, American Federation of Labor-Congress of Industrial Organizations (AFL-CIO) in Washington, DC. *George Rosenau*

SASKATCHEWAN PROVINCIAL POLICE.

On January 1, 1917 a new era of law enforcement began in Saskatchewan, when the Saskatchewan Provincial Police (SPP) took over day-to-day policing duties from the Royal North-West Mounted Police (RNWMP). Since the province's creation the Mounted Police had been the province's police force—except in the major urban centres, where municipal police services had been introduced. But with the outbreak of **WORLD WAR I** and the commitment of the RNWMP to both Canada's broader domestic security and the overseas war effort, the Mounted Police's leadership sought methods for transferring resources to these new priorities. Part of the solution was the creation of the SPP, and next door in Alberta of the Alberta Provincial Police. Under the leadership of Commissioner Charles Mahoney, who would serve in the position for the entire existence of the force, the Saskatchewan Provincial Police signed up recruits for a new policing adventure. Some of the new members joined

SASKATCHEWAN ARCHIVES BOARD R-B 7535-1

Members of the Saskatchewan Provincial Police (SPP) at Moose Jaw, c. 1926.

from the Mounted Police, either right away or after the war; others had no previous policing experience. Because of a wartime labour shortage, finding policemen proved difficult until the post-war period, so that in its initial years the force remained under strength. Eventually its ranks numbered as many as 175 members, and at its disbandment it had 140 members.

The SPP quickly carried out across the province the regular policing duties that had been surrendered by the RNWMP; the latter continued to have a presence in Saskatchewan through the enforcement of federal statutes such as the Opium and Narcotic Drugs Act, the offering of assistance to federal government departments, and the carrying out of secret intelligence operations against Communists and other radicals.

For SPP members, policing involved tracking down criminals ranging from common thieves to cattle rustlers to murderers. Members carried revolvers, handcuffs and nightsticks, and travelled the province using a wide variety of methods including horses, primitive motorcycles and automobiles, and, in the north at wintertime, dogsleds.

The lifespan of the force, however, was short. In 1928 the government of Saskatchewan replaced the SPP with the RCMP, with some SPP members joining (or rejoining) the Mounted Police, usually keeping the same rank. The demise of the SPP was not incompetence but cost. The Saskatchewan government, even before the arrival of the **GREAT DEPRESSION**, was increasingly worried about expenditures, and in the case of policing the math was simple: having its own police force cost $500,000 a year; while the RCMP could do the same job for $200,000. In following this path the Saskatchewan

government began a trend that in 1932 would see several other provinces accept the RCMP as their provincial police force out of financial necessity. Less of a concern in 1928 was the apparent loss of provincial autonomy to a police force with its headquarters in Ottawa instead of Regina. Ottawa and Regina issued assurances to the public at the time that the relationship between the senior Mountie in Saskatchewan and the provincial government, specifically the Attorney-General, would be exactly the same as that between Commissioner Mahoney and his boss in Regina. *Steve Hewitt*

FURTHER READING: Macleod, R.C. 1994. "The RCMP and the Evolution of Provincial Policing." Pp. 44–56 in R.C. Macleod and D. Schneiderman (eds.), *Police Powers in Canada: The Evolution and Practice of Authority*. Toronto: University of Toronto Press; Robertson, D.F. 1976. "The Saskatchewan Provincial Police, 1917–1928." MA thesis, University of Saskatchewan.

SASKATCHEWAN REGISTERED NURSES' ASSOCIATION (SRNA).

The Saskatchewan Registered Nurses' Association (SRNA) is the professional, self-regulatory body for the registered nurses of the province. The SRNA is governed by an elected council consisting of president, president-elect, and seven members-at-large. Two public representatives are appointed by the provincial government, and the SRNA executive director serves as an ex-officio member of council. The SRNA is the official voice of nursing in the province, speaking out on health care issues on behalf of registered nurses and the public.

The Saskatchewan Registered Nurses Act was passed on March 10, 1917. The Act of Incorporation declared **JEAN E. BROWNE**, Elizabeth Van Valkenburg,

Norah Armstrong, Jean Wilson, Effie Feeny, Ruth Hicks, **HELENA WALKER**, and Granger Campbell as members of its first council. They represented hospitals at Moose Jaw, Prince Albert, Weyburn, Yorkton, and Saskatoon.

The mandate, mission, and structure of the SRNA have evolved to keep pace with changes in the provision of health care and in the environment within which registered nurses practice. The current power and authority for the SRNA comes from The Registered Nurses Act, 1988, which describes the Association's mandate and role in setting standards of education and practice for the profession, in order to ensure competent nursing care for the public.

Sandra Bassendowski

SASKATCHEWAN RELIEF COMMISSION. In 1931, J.T.M. ANDERSON's Conservative government created the Saskatchewan Relief Commission to administer the provincial relief program. During its two-and-a-half year existence, the Commission managed the spending of $31.5 million. Henry Black of Regina was named to head the Commission; a relief officer, supported by a local voluntary committee of four, was appointed to manage the relief effort in each affected rural municipality. The process was straightforward as each applicant sat down with the relief officer and completed a four-page questionnaire. Before being forwarded to the Commission in Regina, each questionnaire had to be vouched for and approved by the local committee. In each and every case, an undertaking to repay was taken since the vast majority of those in need of relief were not bankrupt, nor were they paupers or indigents in the ordinary sense. In fact, many had substantial assets—their farms—but there was no market for farm property or assets. The Commission thought of itself as supplying short-term credit, thus allowing individuals to retain their self-respect. There were two repayment options, depending on the type of relief obtained: a straight promissory note was signed, or a lien was attached on a crop. No attempt was made to enforce collection of these notes. Up to May 31, 1934, $40,542 of direct relief notes had been repaid, and over $2.5 million had been repaid on the seeding advances; the Relief Commission also accepted wheat as repayment at 70¢ a bushel.

In 1931, three-quarters of Saskatchewan's population was wholly dependent on agriculture: when the crops failed, the result was disastrous, and in 1931–32 approximately one out of every three Saskatchewan residents received some form of relief. Whereas Saskatchewan had been self-sufficient in animal feed, by August 1933 almost $3 million worth of feed had been imported from Alberta and Manitoba. One hundred villages throughout the province lost their tax base completely. As a result, the Commission started to look after the needs of the single, homeless unemployed men of

SASKATCHEWAN ARCHIVES BOARD R-B2465-1
Saskatchewan Relief Commission Emergency Relief Order form.

Saskatchewan. It operated camps and dining halls in Regina, Moose Jaw and Saskatoon, using these as bases to place the men in jobs on farms. During 1932–33, 9,627 single homeless unemployed men were taken care of in the camps. The Department of Highways also put hundreds of men to work on road projects and bush-clearing. Married men were offered three days of work, single men one day; the salary was 25¢ an hour—about the price of two quarts of milk at the time. No cash was paid: rather, men received purchase orders for the necessities of life. The Relief Commission distributed two kinds of relief: direct relief which included food, fuel, clothing and shelter; and indirect relief (agricultural rehabilitation), which included feed, binder twines, harness, seed, or mechanical supplies.

During the second year of the Commission's existence, actual distribution of relief supplies was done by the rural municipalities. In all cases, the goods were purchased from local merchants. In total, the Commission provided approximately $6 million in direct food relief, $3.3 million in fuel, $2 million worth of clothing and shelter, $7 million worth of seed, and $8 million worth of gopher poison, grasshopper poison, harness, and garden seeds. Between 1931 and 1934, $50,000 worth of coal was purchased for various school divisions, and 28,000 packages of flower seeds were distributed through the parishes in affected areas. Many competent salesmen and executives, who had previously earned up to $500 per month, were walking the streets and more than willing to accept a relatively low-paying job at the Relief Commission. Having this caliber of employee on hand was in some measure responsible for the extremely low overall program administration cost of 3.18%. There were, however, allegations

of abuse. In response, in 1931 Commission chairman Henry Black placed advertisements in many Saskatchewan weekly newspapers, appealing to citizens' patriotism and asking for information on anyone suspected of taking advantage of relief distribution. In all, Black received about a dozen replies; typical of the responses was a letter from a woman who said that neighbours of hers were keeping a dog and that Black should force them to get rid of it. On August 15, 1934, a month after taking office, J.G. GARDINER's Liberal government disbanded the Saskatchewan Relief Commission and fired most of its 160 head office employees.

Don Black

SASKATCHEWAN RESEARCH COUNCIL (SRC). The SRC is the provincial organization dedicated to applying science and technology to Saskatchewan's economic development since 1947. Created to advance development of the province in the physical sciences, SRC has become a market-driven corporation, selling services and products to companies in Saskatchewan and throughout the world. SRC's services today range from testing for the presence of Bovine Spongiform Encephalopathy (BSE, known as Mad Cow disease) in cattle to developing more efficient ways of extracting thick heavy oil from the ground. Growth of the skill sets and problem-solving techniques at SRC parallels the needs of industry operating within the provincial economy.

Originally, when SRC had a staff of three people, research was conducted by providing grants-in-aid to specific applied research activities at the **UNIVERSITY OF SASKATCHEWAN**. SRC's first Director of Research was Dr. T.T. Thorvaldson, head of the Department of Chemistry at the University. Since then, SRC has become more self-sufficient, generat-

Saskatchewan Research Council-sponsored rock analysis experiment at the University of Saskatchewan, July 1961.

ing about $26 million in annual revenues from fee-for-service research and commercial services, while employing 240 staff in facilities in Regina and Saskatoon.

SRC has a track record of success collaborating with other research centres, private sector companies and academics to provide a coordinated approach to problem solving. Over the years SRC has published 2,600 reports that are in the public domain, while another 2,700 confidential project reports were completed for clients where privacy was required for commercial reasons.

Cores areas of competency for SRC reflect Saskatchewan's engines of economic growth: agriculture/biotechnology, energy, environment, manufacturing/value-added processing, and mining and minerals. Major projects completed by SRC include: a residential energy conservation research report that became part of the National Building Code; and mapping the groundwater resources of the province south of the **PRECAMBRIAN** Shield. SRC scientists have evaluated Saskatchewan's extensive lignite reserves as well as developed processes for the milling of uranium at pilot plant scale. In recent years, SRC has been investigating ways to transport slurries of coal, other minerals and oil sands by pipeline. SRC also helps maintain the quality of Canada's beef cattle industry through the operation of a bovine blood laboratory, where testing can be done for a variety of infections including the so-called Mad Cow disease. Internationally, SRC's efforts are focused on the direct support of Saskatchewan-based firms operating outside the province. *Judy Peters*

SASKATCHEWAN RIVER (53°54' N, 101°46' W; map sheet 63 F/13). The Saskatchewan River is formed by the confluence of its two major branches: the **NORTH SASKATCHEWAN** and **SOUTH SASKATCHEWAN** rivers. This occurs approximately 45 km east of Prince Albert in an area known as "the Forks." The river then flows for 550 km eastward into Manitoba, eventually draining into Lake Winnipeg. With its two branches included, the overall length of the Saskatchewan River is 4,618 km, crossing the prairies from the Rocky Mountains to Manitoba. Dams across the river downstream from Nipawin helped create Tobin Lake, a recreational area renowned for its walleye fishing. These dams are used by SaskPower to generate hydroelectricity. In the Cumberland Delta area close to the Manitoba border, the Saskatchewan River divides into numerous channels. The first **FUR TRADE POST** built in Saskatchewan was located here in 1774 by **SAMUEL HEARNE**. Cumberland House played a crucial role in the fur trade, strategically located for access not only along the Saskatchewan River and its tributaries, but also to the **CHURCHILL RIVER** and the northwest. The name of the river is derived from the **CREE** word *kisiskâciwani-sîpiy*, meaning "swift-flowing river."

Marilyn Lewry

SASKATCHEWAN ROUGHRIDERS. Canadian **FOOTBALL** evolved from English rugby football, a game that began at a soccer match in Rugby, England in 1823 when a player named William Webb Ellis suddenly picked up the ball, started to run with it and was tackled by an opponent. The game was introduced to North America by the

British Army garrison who played the game with McGill University. The first recorded game of football in Canada was played at the University of Toronto College on November 9, 1861. Associations were organized in each province and the Canadian Rugby Union (CRU) was established in 1884 as the governing body.

Regina's first organized rugby football team were members of Regina's North-West Mounted Police (NWMP) who traveled to Winnipeg to play two games against the Winnipeg Football Club in 1888. The first recorded game of football in Saskatchewan was played by the NWMP in 1890 and in 1907 the Saskatchewan Rugby Football League was formed. It was also in 1907 that the CRU standardized aspects of the game that brought it closer to what it is today.

On September 13, 1910, the Regina Rugby Club was formed and adopted the colours of old gold and purple. Nine days later, on September 22, the Saskatchewan Rugby Football Union (SRFU) was organized and adopted CRU rules. Teams from Regina, Moose Jaw, Saskatoon, Prince Albert and Weyburn were to compete in the league; however, only Regina and Moose Jaw were able to organize teams that first season. Regina and Moose Jaw played their first game in Moose Jaw on October 1, 1910 that saw the Moose Jaw Tigers claim a 16–6 victory.

On October 21, 1911, the Alberta, Manitoba and Saskatchewan Unions formed the Western Canada Rugby Football Union (WCRFU). Winnipeg realtor Hugo Ross donated the championship trophy bearing his name. He subsequently drowned in the sinking of the SS *Titanic* in April 1912. Only teams registered with the CRU were eligible to compete for the Grey Cup, a trophy donated by Governor General Earl Grey for the Rugby Football Championship of Canada. Since the WCRFU was not a full member of the CRU, the 1911 Western Champions, the Calgary Tigers, were not allowed to compete for the national championship.

The Regina Rugby Club changed its colours in 1911 to blue and white to match the Regina Amateur Athletic Association. The colours were changed again in 1912 to red and black, the infantry colours of the Canadian contingent which fought with Teddy Roosevelt in the Spanish-American War. The team kept these colours for 36 years. The Regina Rugby Club changed its name to the "Regina Roughriders" in 1924. One theory is that they were named after this Canadian contingent that had become known as the "Roughriders." The other theory is that the name came from the NWMP who were called Roughriders because they broke the wild horses that were used by the force.

The Grey Cup game was suspended from 1916–19 during **WORLD WAR I**. In 1921 the WCRFU joined the CRU and the Edmonton Eskimos became

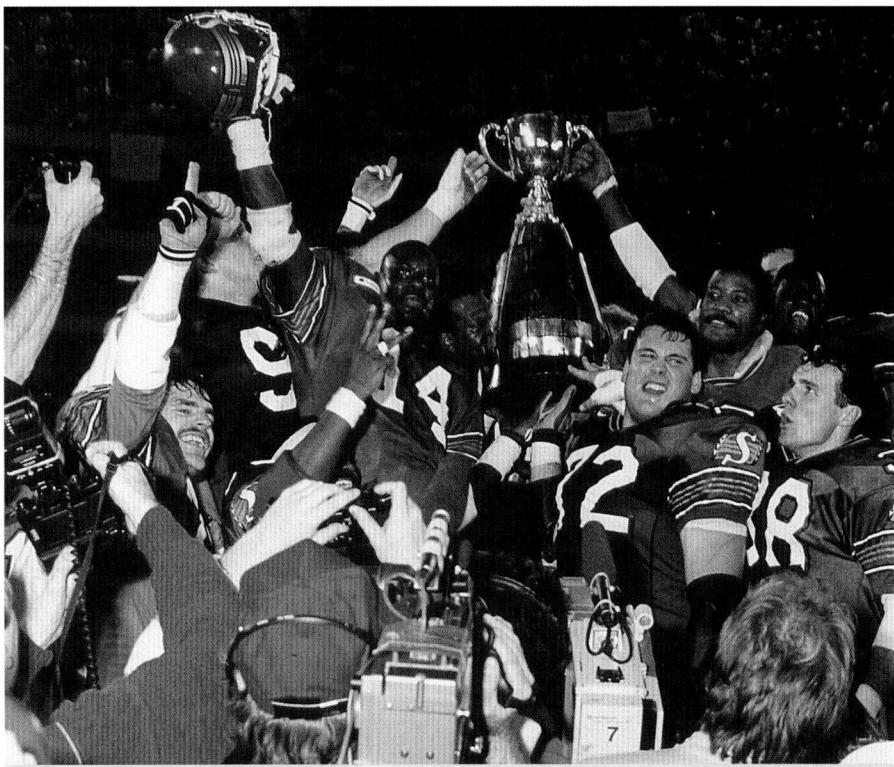

Saskatchewan Roughriders 1989 Grey Cup win.

the first Western team to play in a Grey Cup game. Although the Saskatchewan Roughriders won the Western Conference Championships seven times between 1928 and 1951, they were unsuccessful in obtaining a Grey Cup victory. The Regina team played its first Grey Cup in 1923, losing to Queen's University 54–0. The team played its second Grey Cup game on December 1, 1928, in the first Grey Cup game ever covered by radio broadcast. In 1929, Regina's "Jersey Jack" Campbell made the first-ever forward pass thrown in a Grey Cup game. On December 3, 1932, the Regina Roughriders became the first team to win five Division Championships and play in five consecutive Grey Cup games.

In 1936 the Western Interprovincial Football Union (WIFU) was formed with Winnipeg Blue Bombers, Calgary Bronks and Regina Roughriders. A white ball was used at games played under floodlights in western Canada to enhance its visibility for the spectators.

Regina's Taylor Field opened in 1946. The field was named after Neil J. "Piffles" Taylor, a prominent Regina rugby and football player who left the game in 1916 to serve as a pilot in **WORLD WAR I**. After spending a year as a prisoner-of-war he was released in 1918. Despite the loss of an eye, Taylor played as quarterback for the Regina Roughriders and claimed victory over Calgary, winning the 1919 Hugo Ross trophy. Taylor served as president of the Regina Roughriders, the CRU and the WIFU.

When the Moose Jaw and Saskatoon teams dissolved in 1948, the Regina Roughriders became a

provincially owned and operated club popularly known as the Saskatchewan Roughriders, a name they would officially adopt on April 1, 1950. Financial constraints prevented the team from replacing their worn out uniforms. In 1948 executive member Jack Fyffe found a set of green and white jerseys at a surplus store in Chicago and the legacy of "Green and White" was born. In 1989 the uniform was updated with the addition of silver and black to the "Green and White" along with a new logo.

Tragedy struck the Saskatchewan Roughriders on December 9, 1956, when Flight #810 flying from Vancouver to Regina crashed into the side of Mount Slesse in the Rockies: 62 passengers and crew were killed including Winnipeg Blue Bomber Calvin Jones and Roughriders Gordon Sturtridge, Mel Beckett, Ray Syrnyk and Mario DeMarco who were returning from the Shrine All Star Game in Vancouver. The families of Mel Beckett and Mario DeMarco donated the Beckett-DeMarco trophy to recognize the Most Outstanding Offensive Lineman in the West.

On November 26, 1966, the Saskatchewan Roughriders, led by coach Eagle Keys, won their first Grey Cup defeating the Ottawa Rough Riders 29–14 in Vancouver's Empire Stadium. The Saskatchewan Roughriders again represented the Western Division in the 1967, 1969, 1972 and 1976 Grey Cup games. On November 19, 1989, Head Coach John Gregory led The Saskatchewan Roughriders to their second Grey Cup victory on a last-second field goal by Dave Ridgeway, defeating the Hamilton Tiger-Cats 43–40

at Toronto's Skydome in the highest scoring game in Grey Cup history. In the 1997 Grey Cup, Saskatchewan was defeated 47–23 by Toronto, a team they had not faced since the 1930 game between Regina and Balmy Beach. Regina hosted the Grey Cup game on November 19, 1995, and on November 16, 2003. At the 1995 game, the Baltimore Stallions became the first and only American-based team to win the trophy, defeating the Calgary Stampeders 36–20.

Though they play in the CFL's smallest market, The Saskatchewan Roughriders have been referred to as the most loved team in the CFL. On October 14, 1995, 55,438 fans crammed into Regina's Taylor Field, whose capacity was 27,732, to watch Saskatchewan beat Calgary 25–23. Their fans are known for their loyalty, enthusiasm and "Rider Pride" and make every home game a province-wide celebration. *Daria Coneghan*

SASKATCHEWAN SCHOOL BOARDS ASSOCIATION.
The Saskatchewan School Boards Association, founded in 1915 under its former name of the Saskatchewan School Trustees Association, represents boards of education in the province. Boards of education, made up of elected trustees, are essential members of local government, ensuring the wishes of the community are reflected in its schools. A trustee works as part of a team; school boards make decisions that shape the education of the province's children, and the Association supports boards in this role. The Association and its members care about and fight for the needs of children, schools, and communities. Local, democratic control of education, combined with the Association's strong advocacy voice, ensures all students receive a quality education.

The Association is a non-profit organization dedicated to excellence in public education by providing leadership and services for all of the province's boards of education. The Association represents all school divisions–public, separate, and francophone–and reflects the rural, urban, and northern diversity of the province. Membership in the Association is voluntary and is open to school boards and First Nations education authorities. The Association is governed by a provincial executive that consists of: a president elected at an annual Convention; representatives elected from seven branches or regions of the province; a Catholic section representative; an urban public boards caucus representative; a rural representative; an Aboriginal representative; and a representative from the *Conseil scolaire fransaskois*.

Members of the executive act as advocates for education, addressing local and provincial issues; they also represent the Association on many working groups involved in education and local government. Association staff supports the Executive and boards in their roles as advocates, and helps to ensure effective two-way communication among member boards, the executive, the education community, and the community at large. Much time is spent working with government and opposition MLAs, senior officials, other local governments, partners in education, agencies, and other bodies that can or do have an impact on school boards and publicly funded education in Saskatchewan. A large portion of the work is representative in nature and reflects the desire of school boards to have the Association act as an advocate for school boards in the service of children.

The Association also provides many direct services to boards, such as trustee education and board development, administrator development, legal services, employee relations, education and research, communications, and an insurance plan and an employee benefits plan.   *Ardith Stephanson*

SASKATCHEWAN SCHOOL LIBRARY ASSOCIATION (SSLA).

The SSLA is the third school library organization affiliated as a Special Subject Council of the **SASKATCHEWAN TEACHERS' FEDERATION**. The first association for school librarians was formed at a meeting called by **LYLE EVANS** at the Saskatchewan Teachers' Federation building in Saskatoon on April 18, 1959. The aims of the new organization included: the promotion of the school library and school librarianship; the encouragement of the use of the school library within the curriculum and in the life of the school generally; and the encouragement of co-operation with all organizations concerned with strengthening educational programs.

The first annual conference was held at Valley Centre, on April 1–2, 1960. The conference theme was "What is good library service for Saskatchewan schools?" and the guest speaker was the Hon. W.S. Lloyd, Minister of Education. In 1964, *Interim Standards for School Library Service in Saskatchewan*, provincial guidelines to improve service, were well received.

In 1970, the association became the Saskatchewan Association of Educational Media Specialists (SAEMS). The reorganized association included the interests of the library and audiovisual specialists in the province. In 1988 the association changed its name again, to the Saskatchewan School Library Association (SSLA), with a priority on school libraries, their programs, and teacher-librarians. SSLA received international recognition in 1990 with a Commendation Award from the International Association of School Librarianship for the development of a leadership-training program to support resource-based learning.

SSLA was affiliated with the Canadian School Library Association (CSLA) and the Association of Teacher-Librarians in Canada (ATLC). In June 2004,

these two organizations merged to form the Canadian Association of School Libraries (CASL). Notable teacher-librarians and school library advocates are honoured annually by the following awards: the John G. Wright Distinguished Service Award, the Connie Acton Award of Merit, the Art Forgay Award, and the Alixe Hambleton Bursary. In 2003, the SSLA received the Angela Thacker Award from ATLC for establishing the Willow Awards–Young Readers' Choice Awards in Saskatchewan. The SSLA's first website, developed in 1998, was later moved to the Saskatchewan Teachers' Federation server.   *Judy Nicholson,*

SASKATCHEWAN SCHOOLS: EARLY HISTORY.

When we think of the one-room school, the countryside usually comes to mind: most towns and villages began with a one- or two-room schools that often had more rooms added as the population grew. A new school district was established when enough settlers with children had come to a district to warrant the construction of a school. A petition was circulated asking the Department of Education to allow the citizens to build a school and to hire a teacher; the petitioners usually had to outline the anticipated costs and to explain how they proposed to fund the school. In the original land survey, certain quarter sections of land had been designated as the school quarters; when the land was sold, the proceeds helped to fund a school (*see* **LEGAL LAND SURVEY**). There were no teacher training schools in the North-West Territories during the 1850s: all the teachers came from Ontario.

The first school classes were held in town halls or community centres. Soon the school trustees saw the need to build a regular wooden school building; these were usually two- and four-room schools in villages and towns. As the towns grew in size, there was a need for more permanent, larger schools. In 1890, Regina built its first brick five-room school, called the White School because it was made of white brick. Some of the larger schools were made of stones and brick; the latter came from the towns of Claybank or Estevan. In 1895, another brick school in Regina was built of red brick and naturally called the Red School. It had high school grades up to Grade 12; the first high school graduation class was in 1898–99. This school was later renamed the Alexander School; a section of it was used for teacher training and was called the **NORMAL SCHOOL**.

In 1905, when part of the Territories became the province of Saskatchewan, the Saskatchewan government set up its own Department of Education. At that time, both the provincial and federal governments wanted to develop the prairie provinces: the Homestead Act gave settlers a free one-quarter section of land (160 acres or 65 ha) on the condition that they develop the land for agricul-

ture. This notice was sent to all European countries, and also to the United States and Asia. In a matter of several years, the southern part of Saskatchewan was populated with families whose homesteads dotted the prairies nearly every half mile; most of the families had four to five children of school age. The province and the communities were faced with the urgent task of giving these children an education. Little one-room wooden schools were built nearly every seven to eight miles, as parents felt that the children should not walk more than four miles to a school. Most areas had as many as six to eight small, one-room country schools, in which teachers single-handedly taught all the subjects up to Grade 8. The Department of Education set up correspondence courses in these schools for the Grade 9 and 10 students. Each of these schools had enrolment of 35 to 40 students; in some, a teacherage was built for the teacher's lodging in exchange for doing the janitorial work for the school.

SASKATCHEWAN ARCHIVES BOARD R-A12518-2
Wood stove, Latham School, built in 1906.

The teacher had to start the fire in the school's wood stove at about 6:00 a.m. in order to get the school warm enough by 8:30 a.m. The teacher also had to keep the school clean and wash the floors every other week. The school also became the entertainment centre for the community: bingos and whist drives took place nearly every weekend during the winter season; and twice a year the school would put on special programs for the parents. The Christmas concert and track-and-field events were highlights that drew large crowds. Some of the schools had **4-H CLUBS**, which were organized by the Department of Agriculture and where students received training in showmanship as well as in the care of farm animals. Some of the one-room schools were closed during the months of January and February due to very cold weather and poor roads; to make up the required 200 teaching days a year, the school year would start in August.

The students used many different means of transportation to and from their schools. In summer, they would walk, ride horseback, or drive a horse

Ready to go to school by horse and buggy, ca. 1948.

and buggy or a two-wheel cart; during the winter months, they used a cutter or a box sled. The farming community often found it difficult to pay the teachers' salaries, and many of them would have to work for their board and room. Farmers would take turns boarding the teacher for a month. During the 1930s, since many rodents destroyed the farmers' crops, municipalities paid the students 1¢ for gopher tails and 2¢ for a pair of crow's legs; the teacher's job was to collect these tails and legs and pay the students the money on behalf of the municipalities.

The Department of Education then started to amalgamate many of the village and one-room schools into school units in order to reduce the cost and also to give the students a better education with more qualified teachers and better equipment. A drop in the enrolment of the one-room school had also caused problems in keeping them open. The school units built larger four- to six-room schools in the towns. The students now had to be transported to these schools. In summer, the school units used busses and wagons that held about ten students; during the winter most of the roads were blocked, so the students were transported by bombardiers and snow planes. High school students were transported to larger towns, which were about 20 miles (30 km) apart: changes in society had created changes in education that required more technical equipment, better science labs, and more qualified teachers.

Regina's first high school, Regina Collegiate Institute, was built in 1908 on College Avenue. It had five science labs, and a large auditorium for the fine arts and for school functions. When the school opened in 1908, it had 204 students and a teaching staff of five; by the 1920s there were over 1,000 students; and in 1935, it had 3,020 students and a staff of 75 teachers in its 32 classrooms. The school used a shift system to take care of the large enrolment.

Alex Youck and Jim Slough

SASKATCHEWAN SCIENCE CENTRE. The Saskatchewan Science Centre is a non-profit community organization dedicated to promoting better public understanding and appreciation of science. The Centre is an informal educational facility for the province of Saskatchewan. It creates opportunities for students, teachers and families to interact with science and learn from a hands-on perspective. The Science Centre does this through two facilities: the Powerhouse of Discovery and the Kramer IMAX Theatre. The Powerhouse of Discovery features hands-on exhibits that explore basic scientific principles, while the Kramer IMAX Theatre presents films, primarily science- or nature-oriented, in the giant-

A multi-storey display greets visitors to the Saskatchewan Science Centre in Regina.

screen IMAX format. Innovative programs for everyone from preschoolers to senior citizens enhance the effectiveness of both. The Powerhouse of Discovery is located inside the former city powerhouse, a landmark on the north shore of Wascana Lake since 1914. The red-brick exterior has been left essentially unchanged, while the interior features three floors of exhibit space, a laboratory, a roof-top observatory, a 100-seat theatre, a gift shop, a restaurant, and meeting rooms. *Scott Langen*

SASKATCHEWAN SOIL SURVEY. The Saskatchewan Soil Survey was established on recommendations of a Royal Commission appointed as a result of a Better Farming Conference held in Swift Current in 1920. In its report the Royal Commission specifically recommended that a reconnaissance soil survey be undertaken to outline the various soil areas and to classify them as to their suitability for grain growing and stock raising. It also recommended that the reconnaissance survey be followed by a more complete agricultural survey in order to render the investigational work of the College of Agriculture and the Experimental Farms more effective. Although the broad open prairie, parkland and forest regions were recognized as far back as the **PALLISER EXPEDITION** of the late 1850s, apart from sketchy notes of the Dominion Land Surveyors little information was available on the **SOILS**, landscape features, **CLIMATE**, native vegetation, and **GEOLOGY** of the province. The first soil survey, covering a block of four rural municipalities near Moose Jaw, was started in 1921 under the direction of Professor R. Hansen, head of the Soils Department at the **UNIVERSITY OF SASKATCHEWAN**. As noted in that report, the party worked from a car, examining the soils in the fields. When the field map was completed, several samples of each soil type were collected and subjected to physical and chemical analysis in the laboratory.

Over the next decade, under the direction of A.H. Joel and **F.H. EDMUNDS**, a geologist from Liverpool University, soil surveys were carried out throughout southern Saskatchewan. Work was halted early in the 1930s as financial support from both the federal and provincial governments was withdrawn, but in 1935 the soil survey was resumed under the Prairie Farm Rehabilitation Act. With the publication of Soil Survey Report No.12 in 1944 and Soil Survey Report No.13 in 1950, by **J. MITCHELL**, H.C. Moss and J.S. Clayton, the preliminary soil survey of the agricultural area of the province—covering some sixty-eight million acres or nearly half of the agricultural area in Canada—was complete.

In the late 1950s the soil survey, under the leadership of J.G. Ellis and D.F. Acton, embarked upon an ambitious project to remap the agricultural areas of the province in more detail, utilizing newly available aerial photographs and a new system of soil classification. It was a task that would become the focus of the survey for next forty years. Along the way the soil survey completed the South Saskatchewan Irrigation project, which documented the **IRRIGATION** potential of lands in the vicinity of **LAKE DIEFENBAKER**; conducted soil surveys for First Nation reserves; compiled a detailed biophysical inventory of the **PRINCE ALBERT NATIONAL PARK**; and extended soil inventories into the Northern Provincial Forest regions as part of the Agricultural Rehabilitation and Development Act (ARDA) program to evaluate the agricultural capability of Saskatchewan's land resources. Since the completion of the survey in 1998, the focus has been to transform the soil inventory information into digital form for use with modern Geographical Information Systems (GIS).

Glenn Padbury

FURTHER READING: Ellis, J.G. 1987. *History of Soil Science Department and Soil Survey 1949-1985.* Saskatoon: Saskatchewan Institute of Pedology; Moss, H.C. 1983. *History of the Saskatchewan Soil Survey 1921-1959.* Saskatoon: Saskatchewan Institute of Pedology.

SASKATCHEWAN SPORTS HALL OF FAME AND MUSEUM. The Saskatchewan Sports Hall of Fame and Museum (SSHFM) recognizes exceptional Saskatchewan athletes, championship teams, and sports builders whose contributions to athletics have been made at the provincial, national, and international levels. The SSHFM also preserves sport history and educates the public on sport in Saskatchewan life. Founded on October 31, 1966, the Hall was originally called the Molson's Sports Hall of Fame. In 1974, its name changed to the Saskatchewan Sports Hall of Fame, while "Museum" was added to its title in 1990. The Hall moved to two different venues before occupying the Land Titles Building in Regina as its permanent home in 1979. Since then, its collection of artifacts and sports memorabilia has grown substantially. As of the 2004 installation ceremony, 175 athletes, 122 builders, and 91 teams had been inducted into the SSHFM. *Elizabeth Mooney*

SASKATCHEWAN SUMMER SCHOOL OF THE ARTS. Staged in the beautiful Qu'Appelle Valley from 1967 to 1991, the Saskatchewan Summer School of the Arts offered students instruction in visual arts, crafts, drama, music, and writing. The **SASKATCHEWAN ARTS BOARD** recognized the need for a permanent school of the arts following the success of its popular summer workshops begun in 1950. Coinciding with this need was the availability of the Fort Qu'Appelle Sanatorium as an artistic retreat. Opened in October 1917, Fort San provided treatment for thousands of people who suffered from tuberculosis. By the mid-1960s, however, the sanatorium was only in partial use because of the successful drive carried out against the disease. With

the support of the provincial Liberal government, Fort San was extensively renovated for use as an arts school. Premier **ROSS THATCHER** officially opened the revived facility on July 29, 1967.

Over 1,200 children and adults attended the seven-week program at the School during the summer of 1968. Existing facilities were expanded and improved throughout the 1970s as the popularity of the School increased. Several well-known instructors taught at the Saskatchewan Summer School of the Arts, and many talented artists emerged from the Fort San experience. In 1991, however, the School closed due to a lack of funding. *Holden Stoffel*

FURTHER READING: O'Connor, Kevin. 2004. "Historic Centre Shutting Down." *Regina Leader-Post* (April 2), B2.

SASKATCHEWAN TEACHERS' FEDERATION. The Saskatchewan Teachers' Federation (STF) is the professional organization of teachers in Saskatchewan's publicly funded elementary and secondary schools. It is responsible for acting as the voice of teachers to government and the public, bargaining collectively on behalf of its members, regulating teacher conduct, promoting teacher professionalism, and advocating for teachers, children and public education.

The STF was created in 1933 when three earlier teacher groups disbanded to form a new organization that would represent all teachers in Saskatchewan. At the time, many teachers were struggling to cope with years of **DROUGHT**, economic **DEPRESSION**, geographic isolation, and dictatorial school boards. A growing sense of frustration led in 1919 to a teachers' strike in Moose Jaw, said to be the first recorded action of its kind by teachers in Canada. Against a backdrop of hardship and unrest, STF organizers were able to enroll over 90% of teachers as members of the new federation. In 1935, government passed an Act Respecting the Teaching Profession, the first legislation in Canada to require all teachers to be members of the provincial teachers' organization as a condition of their employment.

In the decades that followed, the STF was able to improve teachers' salaries and working conditions and to raise the status of the teaching profession. To establish a stable base from which to fund these improvements and to enhance the quality of education for students, it participated in a successful campaign to establish larger school units. It secured access for teachers to boards of reference, promoted a professional program of teacher education, and assumed a collaborative role in the development of curricula and educational policies. The STF also established plans that provided teachers with pensions, income protection, counselling services, health benefits, insurance coverage, professional development opportunities, and research grants.

The STF was the first teachers' organization in Canada to take responsibility for the administration of a pension plan for teachers.

The STF has helped to develop among educational organizations a unique tradition of co-operation that has resulted in a relatively conflict-free history of education in Saskatchewan. The STF is represented on the Board of Teacher Education and Certification, the Teacher Classification Board, the Teachers' Superannuation Commission, and the senates of the province's two universities. Educational partners also include the **LEAGUE OF EDUCATIONAL ADMINISTRATORS, DIRECTORS AND SUPERINTENDENTS** (LEADS), the **SASKATCHEWAN ASSOCIATION OF SCHOOL BUSINESS OFFICIALS** (SASBO), and the **SASKATCHEWAN SCHOOL BOARDS ASSOCIATION**.

As a founding member of the Canadian Teachers' Federation, STF has worked actively with teachers' organizations in other provinces and countries. Although the STF is politically non-partisan, many of its members have contributed significantly to the social, economic, and political life of the province. The organization itself has established numerous policies and programs to address social and economic issues of importance to teachers, such as racism, homophobia, and child poverty.

STF has approximately 12,000 members who work in almost 800 schools in Saskatchewan and who belong to geographically defined local STF associations. Policies are set by a Council of teachers elected annually by the associations, and are implemented by a provincial executive elected from and by the Council. Programs operate out of offices in Saskatoon and Regina in three areas: teacher welfare, professional services, and administration-communications.

In 1991 the STF established the Dr. **STIRLING MCDOWELL** Foundation for Research into Teaching. Supported by individual and corporate donations, the Foundation is a charitable organization that provides funding for teacher research into teaching and learning in the primary and secondary education systems. It was created to give teachers a greater role in developing educational knowledge.

Verna Gallen and Bill Quine

FURTHER READING: McConnell, G. 1983. *Arbos 1983: Memories 1933–1983.* Saskatoon: Saskatchewan Teachers' Federation; Tyre, R. 1968. *Tales out of School: A Story of the Saskatchewan Teachers' Federation.* Saskatoon: Saskatchewan Teachers' Federation.

SASKATCHEWAN TRANSPORTATION COMPANY (STC). STC is a common bus carrier that provides passenger transportation, parcel express, and freight services to communities across the province. In 1946, STC was established as a **CROWN CORPORATION** and has operated continuously ever since. STC travels more than five million kilo-

SASKATCHEWAN ARCHIVES BOARD R-PS 77-1840-166
STC buses at the Regina Bus Depot.

metres per year across twenty-eight bus routes, serving 275 communities in Saskatchewan. STC owns and operates main terminals in Regina, Saskatoon, and Prince Albert, and works with 206 private bus companies to provide passenger and freight services to rural communities throughout the province. STC maintains its head office in Regina and employs 234 people. Due to a steady, 20-year decline in bus ridership, STC has faced operating losses for many years; in 2003, the company lost more than $2.1 million.

Iain Stewart

SASKATCHEWAN TURKEY PRODUCERS' MARKETING BOARD (SASK TURKEY).

Sask Turkey was founded on January 14, 1974, to manage the province's supply of turkeys to meet consumer demand for this meat. Sask Turkey's duties include negotiating the province's overall quota with the Canadian Turkey Marketing Agency, negotiating prices with local processors, and developing long-term strategies for the province's turkey industry. Sask Turkey membership is limited to Saskatchewan turkey producers with quota production rights that are auctioned annually; no individual or corporation is permitted to hold more than 18% of the overall provincial quota. In 2003 Saskatchewan had seventeen such producers and yielded 5.87 million kg of (live) turkey for approximately $8.9 million in farm gate returns. The province's turkey production has been relatively stagnant since 1980. Most processing is done out-of-province since Lilydale, a major processor/distributor, decided in 2003 to reduce output at its plant in Wynyard, the only turkey processing facility in Saskatchewan. A board of directors elected from registered producers oversees Sask Turkey's duties.

John Chaput

SASKATCHEWAN UNION OF NURSES.

On January 19, 1974, nurses voted unanimously to "form a labour organization to represent nurses in Saskatchewan." By the end of its first year, the Saskatchewan Union of Nurses (SUN) was the official bargaining agent for nurses in seventy-six hospitals and five nursing homes. Membership totaled

approximately 2,500. In 1998, when the Dorsey Commission ruled that SUN should represent all registered nurses, registered psychiatric nurses, and graduated nurses employed by health districts and their affiliates in the province, SUN's numbers swelled to nearly 8,500. In 1982, SUN negotiated the first professional accountability clause that provided a formal mechanism for nurses to address issues of workload and patient safety. This resulted in nurses sending hundreds of work situation reports that documented unsafe staffing levels throughout the province during the 1980s.

There were labour disputes in 1974, 1976, 1988, and 1991, but none were as important as the strike of April 1999. Only hours after nurses began walking the picket line, the government of Saskatchewan pushed through legislation ordering nurses back to work. Bill 23's back-to-work legislation imposed a minor wage increase for nurses as well as fines for the union and any nurses who refused to return to work. In response, about 2,000 nurses held a rally where they voted to defy the legislation, calling it an unjust law. Days later, SUN refused to obey a court injunction obtained by the SASKATCHEWAN ASSOCIATION OF HEALTH ORGANIZATIONS (SAHO). The impasse finally ended on April 18, 1999, when the government, SAHO and SUN signed a memorandum of understanding and nurses went back to work.

SUN currently represents approximately 7,700 registered nurses and registered psychiatric nurses in acute care, long-term care, home care, public health, and community health.

George Manz

SASKATCHEWAN UNION OF NURSES STRIKE.

One of the most memorable labour disputes in Saskatchewan occurred in the spring and early summer of 1999: over 8,400 members of the SASKATCHEWAN UNION OF NURSES (SUN) began negotiations with the SASKATCHEWAN ASSOCIATION OF HEALTH ORGANIZATIONS (SAHO) in November 1998; no agreement having been reached on the issues of wages and heavy workloads caused by a shortage of nurses, SUN members on December 9 voted to strike if necessary, by a margin of 74%. Negotiations continued for almost four months without success. On April 5, the union served strike notice. A last-minute meeting between Premier ROY ROMANOW, SUN president ROSALEE LONGMOORE and SAHO board chairperson Brian Rourke failed to resolve the impasse, and SUN members began a province-wide walkout on April 8, 1999, promising to maintain essential services.

That same day, the government passed legislation ordering the nurses to return to work. They refused, staying on the picket lines for a further week despite a court injunction and threats of huge fines. On April 15, SUN president Longmoore offered to ask her members to go back to their jobs while

negotiations resumed, if the government would remove the back-to-work legislation and would agree to a memorandum of understanding addressing pay equity and patient safety issues. The Health Minister and SAHO agreed, the memorandum was signed on April 19, the striking nurses returned to work, and mediator Stephen Kelleher was appointed to try to reach a new collective agreement. Talks again broke down four days later, and Kelleher adjourned the proceedings.

On April 27, SUN complied with an April 11 ruling of the court that ordered the union not to call for further strike action by its members. On May 18, GEORGE SEMENIUK was appointed as a conciliator to get the talks going again; but it was not until July 2 that a tentative agreement was reached, and on July 27 SUN members voted by a 76.6% majority to ratify the new contract. Meanwhile, in response to a contempt-of-court ruling that would have levied a fine of $120,000 on the union, SUN offered to "purge its contempt" by donating the money to hospital foundations in Saskatoon and Regina.

During the strike, nurses held a series of information meetings, rallies and demonstrations around the province. At such a rally in March, SUN members placed hundreds of old duty shoes on the steps of the Legislature: calling this a "Shoe-in," Longmoore told the public and the media that it "symbolized the nurses who are leaving this profession because of forced overtime and working conditions that are unacceptable and unsafe." While SUN did not achieve the 22% increase in wages and benefits they wanted, the final package amounted to 13.7%, which was twice what was originally

TERRY CHEVALIER/REGINA LEADER-POST

Members of the Saskatchewan Union of Nurses brought their duty shoes to the steps of the Legislature, protesting the chronic shortage of nurses, March 12, 1999.

offered. Also, the government announced that it would fund 200 new nursing positions. *Clare Powell*

SASKATCHEWAN URBAN MUNICIPALITIES ASSOCIATION.

At the turn of the 20th century, the local city, town and village governments of the day believed it was necessary to have an organization through which they could, on a collective basis, express to the provincial government their needs and desires for legislative and financial services. In 1906 the Union of Saskatchewan Municipalities was formed, under the leadership of Regina mayor Peter McAra Jr. The name would later change to the Saskatchewan Urban Municipalities Association (SUMA).

Delegates to the founding convention identified the reason why working collectively would benefit individual municipalities. They felt individual municipalities were too small to lobby the provincial government alone. They also recognized that different municipalities wanted different things and would present a multiplicity of requests to the government, thereby effectively paralyzing the province. The inaugural convention boldly stated: "Municipal organization will be the mouthpiece of the province."

Today SUMA represents 13 cities, 145 towns, 252 villages, 31 resort villages, and 33 northern municipalities. SUMA remains the provincial voice of urban municipal governments; through strength in unity it advocates, negotiates and initiates improvements in local provincial and federal legislation, as well as providing programs and services to enhance urban life in Saskatchewan.

Andrew Rathwell

SASKATCHEWAN URBAN NATIVE TEACHER EDUCATION PROGRAM.

The Saskatchewan Urban Native Teacher Education Program (SUNTEP) is the GABRIEL DUMONT INSTITUTE's oldest program. Created in 1980 to address the chronic shortage of Aboriginal teachers in the province's education system, particularly in larger urban centres, SUNTEP has graduated approximately 700 students with BEd degrees. By employing cross-cultural educational techniques, SUNTEP excels at producing teachers who can integrate theory and practice. SUNTEP is located in Prince Albert, Saskatoon and Regina, and receives its accreditation through the UNIVERSITY OF SASKATCHEWAN and the UNIVERSITY OF REGINA. Each SUNTEP centre is unique and provides its students with a quality education, focusing on different cultural aspects. SUNTEP Prince Albert specializes in drama and has its own theatre troupe; Saskatoon emphasizes Métis history; and Regina excels at traditional Métis dancing. The Prince Albert centre, due to a large First Nations enrollment, weaves Métis and First Nations culture into its programming. Other Aboriginal educational institutions in Canada

First reunion of the Saskatchewan War Brides Association, Saskatoon, 1976. The woman in the centre of the front row was a World War I bride.

have emulated SUNTEP's successful example of personal empowerment. SUNTEP remains, however, the only Aboriginal Teacher Education Program (TEP) with a specifically Métis focus. Many of its graduates have become employed in a variety of fields other than teaching, including administration, consulting, curriculum development and Métis governance.

Darren R. Préfontaine

SASKATCHEWAN VETERINARY MEDICAL ASSOCIATION.

Veterinary medicine deals with health and disease in vertebrates at the level of individuals, populations, and ecosystems. At least six years of university education, four of them in a veterinary college, culminate in a Doctor of Veterinary Medicine (DVM) degree. All veterinarians who enter practice must successfully complete a national examination. Licenses to practice are granted by the Saskatchewan Veterinary Medical Association (SVMA). Some veterinarians undertake postgraduate education, as interns, residents or graduate students, to become specialists or research scientists in fields such as surgery, internal medicine, pathology, and public health, or in a particular species or class of animal like horses, dairy cattle, poultry, or wildlife. This usually leads to a graduate degree or diploma in a specialty society. Veterinarians work in private practice, involving small animals, food animals and horses; in government employment dealing with domestic animal, wildlife or public health; in the pharmaceutical and biologicals industry; or at university and research institutions. The SVMA, largely self-regulating, is "dedicated to the protection of the public by ensuring the proficiency, competency, and ethical behaviour of its members," and takes a strong interest in animal welfare. In 2004 the SVMA had approximately 550 members. *N.O. Nielson*

SASKATCHEWAN VOLUNTEER MEDAL: *see* HONOURS AND AWARDS

SASKATCHEWAN WAR BRIDES ASSOCIATION.

Established in 1975, the Saskatchewan War Brides Association (SWBA) has provided opportunities for war brides to meet and share their experiences. The first of the war brides associations to emerge in Canada, the SWBA received its charter on July 14, 1975. Any woman who had been married overseas to a Canadian serviceman serving abroad was eligible for membership. The first reunion was held on April 10, 1976, in Saskatoon; subsequent reunions have been held alternatively in Regina and Saskatoon. In 1991, Saskatchewan sponsored an international convention of war brides, which was attended by over 450 war brides. Out of it emerged Ben Wicks's *Promise You'll Take Care of My Daughter: The Remarkable War Brides of World War II*. In the meantime, SWBA membership had grown rapidly, reaching nearly 400 in the mid-1980s. Most war brides were British, and made up the last major influx of immigrants from the British Isles. Frequently of urban background, they often began their new lives in postwar Saskatchewan in relatively primitive conditions on farms or in small communities, faced with challenges unlike what they had known back home. Some went back; but most adjusted and settled into community life.

Kay Garside

SASKATCHEWAN WHEAT POOL.

Saskatchewan Wheat Pool was for many years the province's largest and most visible business corporation as well as the most important organization of farmers. Its grain elevators have served as landmarks for many farming communities across the province. Its head office is in Regina. Officially renamed the Saskatchewan Wheat Pool (SWP) in 1953, the Saskatchewan Co-operative Wheat Producers Ltd. was incorporated on August 25, 1923. The Pool has gone through peaks and troughs in its eighty years of existence on both its commercial and policy sides.

Wheat Pool flour mill and elevator, July 1956, Saskatoon, Saskatchewan.

It began as a grain-pooling co-operative, performing a marketing and price-equalizing function similar to the Canadian Wheat Board. Almost bankrupted in 1929–31, the SWP relinquished this function to become simply a handling or elevator co-operative. From the 1930s to the 1990s, it also played an active role in policy advocacy for farmers towards all levels of government. This activity resulted in the SWP's fall annual meeting, where delegates debated resolutions on agricultural issues in what was referred to as "the Farmer's Parliament." The Pool conducted educational campaigns for farmers and the general public.

On the commercial side, the SWP grew to become a dominant player in the western Canadian grain industry from the early 1970s until 1992, handling over 60% of the province's grain and generating net earnings as high as $72.7 million (1981). From 1993 onward the provincial market share eroded, declining to 22% by 2004. Multi-million-dollar losses from 1999 to 2003 forced a massive debt restructuring in early 2003, a further paring down of the SWP's grain-handling locations, and divestment from twenty-five subsidiaries during the period 1999 to 2004. These changes were the new CEO's attempt to bring the co-op's focus back to its core activity of grain handling. The plan appeared to work, as SWP posted its first net earnings ($5 million) in six years in 2004. SWP still bills itself as having "the most efficient and sophisticated grain handling, processing and marketing network in western Canada."

Saskatchewan Wheat Pool was not the first farmer-owned co-operative in the province: elevator co-operatives had been established in the early 1900s to provide competition for the "line" companies that were believed to collude on prices and grades. The GRAIN GROWERS' GRAIN COMPANY (which merged with Alberta Farmers' Co-operative Elevator Company in 1917 to form UNITED GRAIN GROWERS) and Saskatchewan Co-operative Elevator Company (formed in 1911) were successful in offering alternatives for farmers. However, farmers remained discontented because of a lack of patronage refunds from the co-operatives, and because they remained dependent for marketing on the Winnipeg Grain Exchange, which they believed was tainted with speculation and price-setting. After an August 1923 co-op formation sales pitch by Aaron Sapiro, a co-op aficionado from the United States, farm leaders in each of the prairie provinces began their campaign to contract farmers to deliver their grain to a provincial wheat "pool." The Alberta Wheat Pool began operations in 1923, followed that same year by the Saskatchewan Wheat Pool, and Manitoba Pool Elevators in 1924. In Saskatchewan's case, the 1923 pooling drive fell short of its target as too few farmers signed the intimidating pooling contracts that were required before the Pool could start. The second drive in 1924 was successful and became a kind of community mobilization. Newspapers backed the pooling movement, employees were given time off to help enroll farmers, and many town councils declared June 10, 1924, a civic holiday: Pool Sign-up Day. The Pool was declared a success on June 26, with 45,725 original contract signers.

In its early years, the SWP was integrated functionally with the Alberta and Manitoba pools. The grain would be marketed and the revenues pooled so that all farmers would receive the same price for each grade of grain, regardless of when they delivered. This helped farmers who often faced a seasonal price slump associated with delivering immediately after harvest. The prairie pools jointly owned and controlled a central selling agency, which provided direct selling into overseas markets in order to bypass the low prices achieved by hedging through the Winnipeg Grain Exchange. The central selling agency was successful for several years until a series of events caused financial burdens from which it could not recover: the 1929 stock market crash ("Black Tuesday"), multiple-crop-year carryovers, an overpayment on the 1929 crop, and a persistent inability to sell wheat overseas prompted the federal government to take control in the 1930–31 crop year. The federal government forced liquidation of the agency's stocks, and ended up paying $22 million in guarantees to the banks which had been financing the central selling agency's margin calls. Contracting through the prairie pools was abolished, and the SWP, along with the two other pools, essentially became an elevator company. The pooling concept for marketing was reincarnated in the 1935 Canadian Wheat Board.

Meanwhile, the Pool had been growing as a grain-handling or elevator company. The co-op pools were often denied handling agreements with elevator companies, so they began to construct and acquire elevators of their own. The SWP built its first elevator in Bulyea in 1924. Major gains in market share were made through the 1926 purchase of 451 elevators and three terminals from Saskatchewan Co-operative Elevator Company, and through the 1972 acquisition of Federal Grain Company (which allowed for monopoly in 217 locations). The SWP's elevator complement peaked in 1971 with 1,224 elevators, which enabled it to capture 67% of provincial grain handling (approximately 8.9 million tonnes). With the threat of branch line abandonment and the impending removal of the Crow Benefit (this rail freight subsidy was removed in 1995), consolidation of the Pool's grain handling system became necessary if the Pool was to remain competitive. The Pool began closing hundreds of its traditional wooden elevators (600 were closed between 1971 and 1982), which left many rural residents upset by the fact that a focal point in their community had been abandoned.

The Pool expanded into Manitoba and Alberta in 1990 under the subsidiary AgPro Grain Inc. The grain-handling system was further consolidated and upgraded through the 1997 announcement of Project Horizon, which called for $270 million to be spent on the construction of 22 inland terminals throughout Saskatchewan (14), Manitoba (2) and Alberta (6). The Pool attempted to gain international presence in grain handling through its 1997 investments in Mexico, Poland, and England (the Polish and English holdings were divested in 2000, and the project in Mexico in 2004). In 2003, the SWP operated 43 high-throughput grain handling and marketing terminals throughout Saskatchewan (35), Manitoba (3), and Alberta (4). The Pool also owned 11 seed-cleaning and specialty plants, two wholly owned export terminals located in Vancouver (built in 1968) and Thunder Bay (purchased in 1959), and part-interest in the export facility in Prince Rupert, British Columbia (built in 1982).

Grain handling and marketing has been the Pool's core business activity, but over the years the Pool has been very diversified. Its divisions once consisted of agri-products, agri-food processing, livestock production and marketing, and publishing. The livestock production and marketing division and the publishing division were fully divested between 2002 and 2004. Today, SWP has ownership interest remaining in Can-Oat Milling (the world's largest industrial oat miller), Prairie Malt Limited (one of North America's largest single site maltsters), Ag Pro Grain Inc., Western Co-operative Fertilizers Ltd. (one of western Canada's largest fertilizer wholesalers), and Interprovincial Co-operative Ltd. (ranked twenty-second on Saskatchewan's Top 100 Companies List in 2004). Numerous other subsidiary companies have included the *Western Producer* farm newspaper (1923–2002), CSP Foods (1975–2002), Robin's Donuts (1987–2000), Heartland Livestock Services (1994–2001), Poundmaker Ag-Ventures (1991–2002), InfraReady Products Ltd. (1994–99), PrintWest Communications (1992–98), and CanGro Aquaculture (1991–2004).

The Saskatchewan Wheat Pool became well known for operating as a dual purpose organization: returning millions of dollars to members in the form of patronage refunds, and acting as the farmers' voice on agriculture policies. The SWP undertook lobbying efforts and direct discussions with all levels of government on issues such as railway transportation costs, the Crow Rate Subsidy, taxation, and health services. These policy activities were supported by a widespread educational effort, focused particularly on members' participation in the Pool's multi-tier democratic structure. This structure included advisory committees at each handling point, district meetings and elections, a province-wide delegate body that discussed policy, and a board of directors, elected by the delegates, that took great interest in agricultural issues. Up to the 1990s, the Pool was widely perceived as the most powerful agricultural lobbying and interest group in the province.

An important principle of being a co-operative is that members build up equity in the co-op through patronage and are entitled to repayment of their equity upon exit or retirement from the co-operative. In the early 1990s SWP foresaw the mass retirement of over half of its membership within the next decade; this would have put the Pool in a capital shortage position and hindered any plans for diversification or grain handling system upgrades. The Pool delegates approved a proposal to convert

most equity into publicly traded shares that would be traded on the Toronto Stock Exchange (TSE). Two classes of shares were created. Only farmers are entitled to Class A shares: one share per farmer-member allows them to vote for farmer delegates in each of the districts; the elected delegates then vote for members of a board of directors, one elected director per district. The remainder of equity was converted to Class B shares, which began trading on the TSE under the stock symbol swp.b on April 2, 1996. They opened at $12, and rose as high as $24.40 in 1998; but accumulating debt levels, lost market share, and multi-million dollar net losses since 1999 dropped share values to as low as $0.20 in the last few years. The net losses forced a $470 million debt-restructuring plan to be implemented in early 2003. In October 2004, when SWP posted its first net earnings in six years, shares were trading at $0.37.

Compared to the 45,725 original contract signers, over 71,000 farmers (based on Class A shares in 2003) still hold membership in the SWP, which is the only prairie pool still remaining. After numerous failed talks to conduct a three-way merger between the pools, Alberta Wheat Pool merged with Manitoba Pool Elevators in 1998 to form Agricore; Agricore merged with United Grain Growers in 2001 to become Agricore United. SWP still operates with a farmer-elected board of directors. Nine Saskatchewan farmers have taken on the role of board president: ALEXANDER JAMES MCPHAIL (1924–31), Louis C. Brouillette (1931–37), JOHN HENRY WESSON (1937–60), CHARLES W. GIBBINGS (1960–69), E.K. (TED) TURNER (1969–88), Garf Stevenson (1988–93), Leroy Larsen (1993–2000), Marvin Wiens (2000–04), and Terry Baker (2004–).

Kathy Lang

FURTHER READING: Fairbairn, G. 1984. *From Prairie Roots: The Remarkable Story of Saskatchewan Wheat Pool.* Saskatoon: Western Producer Prairie Books; Fowke, V.C. 1973. *The National Policy and the Wheat Economy.* Toronto: University of Toronto Press.

SASKATCHEWAN WILDLIFE FEDERATION.
The Saskatchewan Wildlife Federation was formed in 1929 by a group of sportsmen concerned about game populations; their goal was to manage wildlife through seasons and bag limits. At the request of the Federation, the provincial government created the Fish and Wildlife Development Fund in 1970. A portion of each hunting and fishing license went into the fund for the purpose of habitat acquisition and enhancement; the fund has acquired some 200,000 acres of prime habitat over the years. The Saskatchewan Wildlife Federation also holds title to 60,000 acres of wildlife habitat land through its Habitat Trust program. Volunteer landowner stewardship programs, such as the Wildlife Tomorrow

program, have been in operation since 1974. Firearms safety and hunter education training for first-time hunters have been conducted by Federation members for over forty years. Conservation schools, youth camps and other outdoor education programs have also been a priority for the Federation for many years. The Saskatchewan Wildlife Federation participates on many government committees and task forces and works with other organizations to promote the wise use, management and conservation of Saskatchewan's natural resources. Sustainable forestry, fisheries enhancement, and fish and wildlife management are just a few of the areas to which the Federation directs its attention and expertise. The Saskatchewan Wildlife Federation membership has reached a high of 34,000 in 130 branches throughout the province. The Federation's mission is to ensure a wildlife legacy that surpasses that which has been inherited. *Lorne Scott*

SASKATCHEWAN WOMEN'S AGRICULTURAL NETWORK (SWAN).
SWAN was established in 1985 as an educational support group for farm women, and became part of the Canadian Farm Women's Network with opportunities to make contacts through national and international meetings and conferences. It soon assumed an advocacy role, seeking to blend agricultural concerns with women's issues and perspectives.

SWAN organized annual conferences and regional workshops to develop farm women's knowledge, skills, and assertiveness. It participated in research projects that examined the multiple roles and contributions of women on the farm, as well as their health and well-being. A critical SWAN project (1999) documented Agriculture Canada's erosion of support for farm women.

For over a decade SWAN had contacts with provincial governments, and after 1992, it was invited to participate in several provincial lobby treks to Ottawa and to present at House of Commons standing committee hearings. Also, the media, farm groups, and women's organizations asked SWAN to serve as the voice of farm women. Directors served on advisory boards, including the Prairie Women's Health Centre of Excellence, Farm Support Review Committee, Farm Stress Line Advisory Committee, and the Centre for Agricultural Medicine. In 1995, on its tenth anniversary, SWAN's request for designation of Saskatchewan Farm Women's Week was granted by the provincial Department of Agriculture. In 1999, SWAN spearheaded a Gold Ribbon Campaign to support struggling farm families.

In 2000, the original group of farm feminists was replaced by others who, due to family obligations and off-farm employment, were unable to sustain the meeting and lobby work. SWAN's voice is now silent. *Noreen Johns*

TAMMY TAMPALSKI PHOTO/SASKATCHEWAN ARCHIVES BOARD S-SP-A11283-1, SASKATOON STARPHOENIX FONDS

Saskatchewan Working Women at a Saskatoon City Council meeting, January 1979.

SASKATCHEWAN WORKING WOMEN (SWW).

The SWW was a grassroots, feminist organization of female wage earners which operated from 1978 to 1990. SWW was formed by an alliance of trade union women and community-based feminists. Members of SWW came from many different political backgrounds, including the **WAFFLE**, the **NEW DEMOCRATIC PARTY**, various Communist, Trotskyist and Marxist-Leninist parties, the women's movement on university campuses and women's centres, and the trade union movement. Some SWW women were also involved in the organizing drives of the Service, Office and Retail Workers' Union of Canada (SORWUC), a feminist trade union active in Saskatchewan and BC. SWW originated because an increasing number of women were joining the workplace and becoming both unionized and mobilized.

Increased labour movement mobilization in the mid to late 1970s around wage and price controls, as well as a series of public sector strikes, activated large numbers of women workers for the first time. More specifically, a group of women in the labour movement recognized that women needed to find their collective voice because unions were in large part not willing to tackle women's issues, nor would they provide a supportive environment to do so. For only $5 per year, any working woman, whether paid or unpaid, whether unionized or non-unionized, could become a member of SWW. Chapters were formed in Regina, Saskatoon, Prince Albert, Swift Current and Lanigan. SWW was headed by an elected provincial body and had a constitution; but individual chapters of the organization enjoyed a fair degree of independence to mobilize on issues in their own communities.

SWW took on a multitude of issues important to working women, including: right to strike, part-time work, daycare, technological change, workplace rights, organizing women workers, strike support, affirmative action, equal pay, sexual harassment,

violence against women, reproductive rights, effects of racism on Aboriginal communities, domestic workers' rights, and international solidarity. SWW produced a newsletter, *Working Women*, and popular pamphlets, as well as many policy papers and briefs to government. It also held annual conventions and conferences on such issues as rural women, **PRIVATIZATION**, and organizing in the service sector. While educating the public and lobbying the government on working women's issues was one focus, SWW also held study sessions on such issues as capitalism, socialism, feminism, racism and other issues, in order to hone a working-class analysis

SWW was known for working in dozens of left-wing coalitions, and was a founding member of the People's Budget Coalition, the organization that ultimately wrote the first alternative budget. SWW put women's issues on the bargaining table and into the public sphere. It can be credited for union policies on daycare and sexual harassment, as well as contract language in such areas as maternity leave and equal pay.

Cara Banks

SASKATCHEWAN WRITERS GUILD.

Saskatchewan writers have supported and used the programs and services of the Saskatchewan Writers Guild (SWG) since its inception in 1969. One of the first writers' organizations in Canada, the Guild is the pre-eminent writing organization in the province, serving writers at all levels of development. From the beginning, the Guild set itself a broad mandate: to improve the standard of writing in Saskatchewan by promoting professional attitudes toward the craft; to improve the status of writers by, among other things, encouraging publication, providing market and workshop information, sponsoring workshops and seminars, and speaking on behalf of both professional and non-professional writers; and to encourage liaison with other provincial and federal agencies concerned with writers and writing standards. Noted for its innovative edge, the SWG

has implemented unique programs that now have a national profile in the writing community. *Grain*, an award-winning literary magazine, offers a national and international stage for fresh, previously unpublished writing. The Saskatchewan Writers and Artists Colonies provide a place where writers and artists can work their craft, free from distractions and interruptions.

From workshops to print and electronic newsletters, mentorships to manuscript evaluations, awards and scholarships to author readings, or just getting together, the Guild has been central to the development of writers and of a writing community in Saskatchewan. The SWG acts as an advocate for writers, encourages the development of young writers, and strives to improve public access to writers and their work. This collaborative approach has been crucial to new initiatives such as the **SASKATCHEWAN BOOK AWARDS**, the Festival of Words, the Saskatchewan Playwrights Centre, and the Poet Laureate program. The SWG funds those local writing groups that form the backbone of Saskatchewan's writing community. It has evolved into a professional organization of nearly 600 members, with an annual budget of over $500,000. The Guild has a staff of eight, split between its office in Regina and the *Grain* office in Saskatoon. Membership is open to all writers and to those with an interest in Saskatchewan **LITERATURE**.

Susan Hogarth

SASKATOON.

Saskatoon, pop 196,811, is situated on the banks of the northward-flowing **SOUTH SASKATCHEWAN RIVER**, 235 km northwest of Regina, 348 km north of the US border, and 225 km east of the Alberta border. It serves as a regional centre for the northern prairies and for central and northern Saskatchewan.

Archaeological evidence shows that hunting tribes were here 6,000 years ago. Campsites, tipi rings, buffalo kills, and a medicine wheel uncovered at **WANUSKEWIN HERITAGE PARK**, north of the city, indicate regular winter habitation by Native peoples. The first European settlers arrived in 1882, when John Lake of the Temperance Colonization Society came to examine the land granted to the colony by the Dominion government and to choose a site for the colony's administrative centre. This settlement on the east riverbank was called Saskatoon, after the **CREE** name for the berry bushes native to the area. Isolation, poor crops, and the North-West Resistance inhibited the community's growth after the first Temperance Colony settlers arrived in 1883.

Colony leaders lobbied for a rail connection; in 1887 the government granted the request, allowing a rail line to be built from the main **CANADIAN PACIFIC RAILWAY** line, across the river at Saskatoon and towards Prince Albert. The railway located the station on the lower, flatter western bank to provide easier access to the water. The Temperance Society surveyed a new town site with the station as its centre, and in 1901, with a population of 113, the west-side settlement was incorporated as the village of Saskatoon while the original east-side settlement became Nutana. Saskatoon became a shipping centre exporting buffalo bones, cattle and grain.

The first burst of growth to the area came when the Saskatchewan Valley Land Company, a colonization company organized by midwestern capitalists, purchased over one million acres of land between Regina and Saskatoon. The settlement of land by the immigrants was vital to the community's growth. In 1903, over 1,500 Barr colonists (*see* **BARR COLONY**) arrived from England and purchased goods from local merchants before migrating to the Lloydminster area.

Barr colonists who remained in the area established a third settlement, Riverdale, on the west side of the railway. In 1906, the villages of Saskatoon, Nutana and Riverdale (now Riversdale) amalgamated to form the city of Saskatoon, with a population of 4,500. The population soared over the next decade, new railway lines were constructed, and Saskatoon became the major distribution centre for central-southern Saskatchewan as well as a hub of western Canada's railway network. At the height of the boom in 1912, Saskatoon was Canada's fastest growing city, with an estimated population of 28,000. Quaker Oats, Robin Hood Flour, and the Massey Harris and Rumely farming implement companies were among the first industries to establish themselves in the city. As Saskatoon's economy was dependent on the wheat economy, growth declined during **WORLD WAR I**, the global recessions of the 1920s, and the **DEPRESSION** of the 1930s. A lack of

waterpower, isolation from large markets, and the dearth of investments prevented diversification of the economy through industrialization.

Significant development resumed after **WORLD WAR II**. Saskatoon founded the expansion of its industrial base on the mining industry. In the 1940s five **POTASH** mines were in operation making Saskatoon the "Potash Capital of the World." Increasing exploitation of oil and minerals in the western and northern parts of the province diversified the local economy. Chemical, textile, fibre optics, steel fabrication, food processing, engineering, and machinery industries established themselves, so that by the 1960s manufacturing had become increasingly important. Since the 1990s, major businesses have located in the city and there has been a significant development of high technology as many research firms located in the University's Innovation Place **RESEARCH PARK**. As a result of its economic growth, the city has increased its population more than 300% between 1951 and the present.

Saskatoon is located on **GLACIAL DEPOSITS** within the belt of a large river, which gives the city a variable topography of rolling parkland and nearby oxbow lakes. The river is spanned by seven bridges, both rail and road, connecting Saskatoon, Riversdale and Nutana. A zoning plan for city development was established in 1929. During the two economic depressions the city acquired property through forfeiture of holdings, and in 1957 a "land bank" was developed through the purchase of available properties. The removal of the rail yards and their pedestrian overpass from the city centre in 1964–65 allowed for development of a downtown retail mall. Residential expansion is predominant in the north-

eastern sector, and country acreages in the Municipality of Corman Park are in increasing demand.

The initial settlers were from eastern Canada, the United Kingdom, and the United States. Then the city saw an increase in immigration from most parts of Europe, notably Ukraine and the Austro-Hungarian Empire, as well as from war brides and persecuted religious groups including Menonites, Hutterites and Doukhobors. Later decades saw an increase in immigration from India, Pakistan, Asia and Latin America, as well as a rapid growth in the Aboriginal population.

Saskatoon's public transport began with the operation of a ferry from 1884 until 1907, when the first bridge was built. In 1913 streetcars were introduced; they were eventually replaced by trolley buses, and then by buses. **CANADIAN NATIONAL** transcontinental main line and a secondary line of Canadian Pacific Railway serve Saskatoon commercially, while VIA Rail maintains a minimal transcontinental passenger service. The present John G. Diefenbaker airport handles national and US flights. **SASKATCHEWAN TRANSPORTATION COMPANY** provides provincial bus service and long distance service by Greyhound Bus Lines. Owing to its central location, Saskatoon is able to support over 90 local freight transport companies.

Saskatoon has seven radio stations, three TV stations, CBC studios, a daily newspaper, two community newspapers, and a weekly agricultural newspaper. Several outside telecommunications serve the area; however, **SASKTEL**, the province's telephone company, is the primary provider of telecommunications services and Internet access to the public and other service providers.

The city charter, first introduced in 1906, specified a commission government requiring the city's officers to be the mayor and at least one appointed commissioner. In early elections, men voted in wards where they owned property; in 1920, however, female suffrage was introduced and the ward system was abolished. The ward system was reintroduced in 1973, and again abolished in 1988; after citizen protest, it was re-introduced yet again in 1991. City council now consists of the mayor and ten councillors, one for each ward and elected for three years. The city has two standing committees and several advisory committees, boards, and commissions with citizen representation. The Urban Municipality Act (1984) and the Planning and Development Act (1983) govern the relationship between municipal and provincial governments. In 1979 the **MEEWASIN VALLEY AUTHORITY** was established to conserve the riverbank and oversee development along the river corridor.

The **UNIVERSITY OF SASKATCHEWAN**, its associated religious colleges, the SIAST-Kelsey Institute, the **FIRST NATIONS UNIVERSITY OF CANADA**, and the

RON GARNETT—AIRSCAPES

The City of Saskatoon, from the east.

Saskatoon Public Library are the city's key educational institutions. Saskatoon is home to two professional theatre companies, PERSEPHONE and 25TH STREET, several festivals, and a symphony orchestra. Cultural and recreational facilities include the WESTERN DEVELOPMENT MUSEUM, Ukrainian Museum of Canada, MENDEL ART GALLERY and Civic Conservatory, Saskatoon Zoo and Forestry Farm Park, Centennial Auditorium and Convention Centre, Credit Union Centre, Prairieland Park, and WANUSKEWIN HERITAGE PARK. Saskatoon hosts events year-round: the Children's Festival, Jazz Festival, Folkfest, the Exhibition, the Riverfest with the River Roar and Taste of Saskatchewan, the Fringe Festival, the Canada Remembers Airshow, the Enchanted Forest, and SHAKESPEARE ON THE SASKATCHEWAN.

Daria Coneghan

SASKATOON-BATTLEFORD TRAIL.

The Saskatoon-Battleford Trail was not used extensively until the 1890s, when the first railway reached Saskatoon. Prior to this date, much of the overland traffic into Battleford (the capital of the North-West Territories) came from the nearest railway line at Swift Current via the Battleford-Swift Current Trail. However, when the railway reached Saskatoon the Saskatoon-Battleford Trail, a much shorter route, was used by traders, settlers, and the North-West Mounted Police. Traffic peaked along the trail between 1903 and 1905, when Barr Colonists (*see* BARR COLONY) moved through the area en route to present-day Lloydminster.

James Winkel

SASKATOON CIVIC DISPUTE.

One of the longest and largest public sector strike/lockouts in Saskatchewan history began in mid-August 1994 in Saskatoon. After more than two years of bargaining, members of four locals of the CANADIAN UNION OF PUBLIC EMPLOYEES (CUPE), transit workers (ATU), electrical workers (IBEW) and the police union were unable to agree on a new contract. The police went on strike, some CUPE members walked out in sympathy, and the city began lockouts. The police reached a settlement, but it would be ten weeks before the 2,300 other workers agreed to a new contract.

The solidarity shown by members of the six unions was almost unprecedented: during the long dispute, not one person crossed the picket lines, even though many faced severe financial strains. Also unusual was the high degree of public support for the strikers, including over $100,000 in donations from across Canada. An agreement was finally reached on October 18. There was no wage increase for 1992 or 1993, but a total of 6% increase in wages and benefits for 1994, a dental plan, other health benefits, improved vacations, and assurances to transit workers that their jobs would not be contracted out.

Cheryl Stadnichuk

SASKATOON COUNCIL OF CHURCHES.

The Saskatoon Council of Churches has been actively promoting Christian unity, dialogue, and co-operation since the early 1960s. With a similar mandate and membership as the national Canadian Council of Churches, with which it has been affiliated, the Saskatoon Council brings one important distinction. Unlike many such councils in Canada and around the world that until recently were formed by the Protestant mainline churches, the Saskatoon Council has enjoyed active participation and membership by Roman Catholics since its inception. The Council's membership is comprised of both lay and ordained representatives of the member churches. The Saskatoon Council was incorporated as a charitable organization in 1974. Over its many years of service it has provided a forum for local churches to engage each other in reflection on social and theological issues of concern. The Council has organized local ecumenical education projects, social justice advocacy, and inter-religious encounters. Recognizing in 1984 that its major role is as a "thinking reflective body" and as a catalyst for other ecumenical endeavours, the Council has since relinquished its active programming to the Saskatoon Centre for Ecumenism (now PRAIRIE CENTRE FOR ECUMENISM), established by six of the Council's member churches. Since 1985, it has provided leadership in the Local Church Leaders' Group, a regular gathering of ecumenical and denominational leaders in Saskatoon.

Nicholas Jesson

SASKATOON GATEWAY PLAYERS.

Gateway Theatre had its first organizational meeting on April 20, 1965, continuing the tradition of little theatre begun by the Little Theatre Club of Saskatoon (1922–49), Saskatoon Community Players (1952–59, headed by Louise Olson), and Stage 8 (1962–63). Its initial mandate was to produce plays and to assist in establishing a professional theatre. With 1967 came incorporation (a board of eight, with Dennis Beerling as first president), a name change to Saskatoon Gateway Players, and a renewed production mandate. A parallel group, Saskatoon Theatre for Children, formed in 1963 to present an annual children's show, usually around Easter. In 1976, the group became amalgamated with Gateway and continues now as Gateway Theatre for Children. From 1963 to 2003, this theatre wing produced fifty plays, including première productions of four original scripts by local actor/playwright Larry Fitzgerald.

Gateway operates from rented studio space (three different locations over the years) shared with other amateur companies, principally Saskatoon Summer Players. Renovations at its current location have created two rehearsal studios, a set storage and construction bay, archives and office space, a green room, and an extensive costume

repository providing rentals to companies throughout the province. Gateway's performance venue is Castle Theatre, an apron-proscenium facility built by the Saskatoon Collegiate Board and opened in 1966.

Since 1968, Gateway has offered a five-play season, with a regular four-day run that was increased to five in 1982. Additional productions are occasionally mounted outside the regular season. Although Gateway rarely employs professional performers or directors, its actors and technicians are often employed in local professional productions or have gone on to professional careers. Many Saskatoon-raised performers actually began by taking weekly children's theatre classes conducted principally by Holly Knott (oral expression) and Rosemary Hunt (creative drama). Gateway's choice of plays favours world theatre classics, comedies for a general audience, and small-scale musicals, but it strives also to stretch and develop its artists and audiences in terms of subject matter and theatrical challenge. Long known for strong production values and spectacular sets (many created by ROBERT HINITT), Gateway has kept apace of professional companies in producing works of such playwrights as Edward Albee, Arthur Miller, Tennessee Williams, David French, Timothy Findley, Al Pittman, Sharon Pollock, and Michel Tremblay. A stalwart member of THEATRE SASKATCHEWAN, Gateway has frequently served as rotational host of its full-length festivals. From 1966 until 2003, it had thirty-two entries in these events, garnering ninety-six awards.

Ian C. Nelson

SASKATOON JEWISH FOUNDATION.

In the 1970s and 1980s Saskatoon's Jewish Community lost, through deaths and relocation, a number of long-time members who had been very active in the community. Also at that time, some Jewish congregations throughout Canada found their memberships had declined to the point where they could no longer finance their institutions. Some of the members of Congregation AGUDAS ISRAEL felt that a long-term solution to the financial problem would be collecting, retaining and investing money and using only the income to meet appropriate needs. Advice was sought from the board of directors of the Jewish Foundation of Manitoba, a foundation that had been formed many years before to assist the Jewish communities in Manitoba and that had been able to amass a significant capital base. As a result of the investigation, a motion was approved in the fall of 1986 to establish the Saskatoon Jewish Foundation. The motion stated that "the purpose of the foundation is to receive donations of money or property; and to invest the money or manage the property; to utilize the money from the investments and the property to maintain or enhance the religious, cultural, education, welfare and other activities of the congregation and the Saskatoon Jewish community." The Foundation has made grants to

Congregation Agudas Israel members, and children of members of Congregation Agudas Israel have been assisted with grants enabling them to attend a B'nai Brith Camp in Pine Lake, Alberta. Children of Congregation Agudas Israel and of the local Jewish community have also been helped to join in the biannual "March of the Living" to Poland and Israel, and also to participate in a program which includes Holocaust education and a tour of the Holocaust Museum in Washington DC, as well as to attend educational programs at the Hebrew University of Jerusalem and educational institutions on this continent and in Israel.   *Gladys Rose*

Saskatoon Light Infantry

COURTESY OF GERRY CARLINE

SASKATOON LIGHT INFANTRY. The Saskatoon Light Infantry (SLI) was an infantry unit of the Canadian army formed on May 15, 1924. It began as the Saskatoon company of the **95TH REGIMENT**, which was expanded into the 105th Regiment (Saskatoon Fusiliers) in 1912. Many members of the 105th Regiment fought in the **5TH (WESTERN CAVALRY) BATTALION** and the 28th Battalion, CEF, in **WORLD WAR I**. In the military reorganization of 1920, all infantry units in the northern part of the province were combined into the **NORTH SASKATCHEWAN REGIMENT**. In 1924, the North Saskatchewan Regiment was divided into four city-based infantry units located in Saskatoon, Prince Albert, Battleford and Yorkton. On December 15, 1936, the SLI was amalgamated with "C" Company, 12th Machine Gun Battalion, to form the Saskatoon Light Infantry (Machine Gun). The SLI (MG) was mobilized on September 1, 1939. The 1st Battalion of the regiment was sent to Britain on December 8, 1939, as part of the 1st Canadian Division. It was the only infantry unit from northern Saskatchewan to see active service overseas during **WORLD WAR II**. On July 13, 1943, the 1st Battalion, SLI (MG) landed in Sicily with the 1st Canadian Division and fought in the Italian campaign until March 1945, when it was transferred to Holland. 1st Battalion, SLI (MG), returned to Canada in November 1945. Its battle honours included: Sicily, Ortona, Liri Valley, Hitler Line, Gothic Line, Lamore Crossing, Rimini Line, and Apeldoorn. The 2nd Battalion SLI (MG) remained in Canada as part of the Reserve Army. In 1958, the Prince Albert and Battleford Volunteers amalgamated with the Saskatoon Light Infantry to become respectively the 1st and 2nd Battalions of the North Saskatchewan Regiment. In 1969, the 1st and 2nd Battalions merged to form the North Saskatchewan Regiment, with headquarters of "A" Company located in Saskatoon, and "B" Company in Prince Albert.   *Peter Borch*

UNIVERSITY OF SASKATCHEWAN ARCHIVES A-6390

Saskatoon Light Infantry return to Saskatoon, October 3, 1945.

FURTHER READING: Bercuson, D.J. 1994. *Maple Leaf Against the Axis: Canada's Second World War*. Don Mills, ON: Stoddart; Blackburn, G.G. 1996. *The Guns of Victory: A Soldier's Eye View: Belgium, Holland, and Germany, 1944-45*. Toronto: McClelland & Stewart; Zuehlke, Mark. 2003. *The Line: Canada's Month of Hell in World War II Italy*. New York: Douglas & McIntyre.

SASKATOON MULTILINGUAL SCHOOL. In the late 1970s there was very little government or public recognition of the importance of heritage language schools. Finally, in 1982 Saskatoon school board officials, the Department of Education, the **MULTICULTURAL COUNCIL OF SASKATCHEWAN** (McoS), and the Regina Multilingual Association (MLAR) met with **SASKATCHEWAN INTERCULTURAL ASSOCIATION** (SIA) (formerly Saskatoon Multicultural Council) members and appointed a committee to establish and promote a Multilingual School. Under the leadership of Avra Watson and the late Mile Kindrachuk, arrangements were made with the Catholic school system to house the Saskatoon Multilingual School (SMS). Eleven member associations joined together to form the new school, and classes officially began in September 1983 at Holy Cross High School. In 1986, the Saskatoon Public School Board approved offering classroom space for heritage language classes without rental fees. At this time, the creation of a part-time position for a heritage language coordinator provided for SMS teachers professional development opportunities such as in-service training, workshops, and class visits.

In 1989, Avra Watson worked with the College of Education at the **UNIVERSITY OF SASKATCHEWAN** to arrange for a certificate program to be offered in Methods of Teaching Heritage Languages for SMS instructors. This program has been crucial for developing a core of well-trained teachers and improving the quality of heritage language instruction available to Saskatchewan youth. In 2004, with the support of the Saskatchewan Intercultural Association (SIA), there are 28 heritage language schools united under the SMS title, offering 24 languages to approximately 940 students. Seventy-two of these students are enrolled in high school credit courses through the SMS. These students spend many hours of their personal time studying one or more heritage languages. There are about 130 heritage language instructors, and hundreds of volunteer parents who donate their time and energy to provide educational opportunities for children and to nurture a truly diverse and inclusive community.   *Eleanor Shia*

SASKATOON POLICE SERVICE. Police services in Saskatoon date back to 1882, when the North-West Mounted Police (NWMP) began to serve there. In 1889 Saskatoon hired its first full-time police officer; but the NWMP continued to serve the city as well until 1910, when the Saskatoon Police

Department was created. By this time the force had grown to include a chief, a deputy chief, two sergeants, five constables, and a detective; and by 1919, the police service in Saskatoon had grown to twenty-two members. The building of police headquarters in 1930 and the addition of a radio system to the Saskatoon Police Department in 1940 were significant milestones, and in 1970 the force consisted of 207 members. The first female officers were hired in 1973; and in 1979 community policing was introduced in order to facilitate a more positive relationship between the police service and the public by, among other things, assigning officers to a given district for at least a year—thereby allowing officers to become familiar with the people and the problems of the area. In 1992, the Saskatoon Police Department was renamed the Saskatoon Police Service. It has since then introduced a number of important programs to improve policing in the city, such as the Bicycle Detail and community mail-in reports; it has also instituted an Aboriginal Liaison and a Community School Liaison. In 2003, the force consisted of 355 members, with approximately 215 additional special constables, volunteers, and civilians. Sixteen ROYAL CANADIAN MOUNTED POLICE and a number of integrated units are also involved in the operations of the Saskatoon Police Service.

Melanie Neuhofer

SASKATOON SYMPHONY ORCHESTRA. The Saskatoon Symphony Orchestra (SSO) was established in 1931 and played its first concert under the direction of ARTHUR COLLINGWOOD, Professor of Music at the UNIVERSITY OF SASKATCHEWAN. It has maintained a close relationship with the university, with many of its conductors having part-time faculty appointments. The orchestra made particular gains during the 1970s and 1980s, when it entered into its first collective agreement with players and all orchestra players were for the first time paid for their service. The first full-time music director and general manager were hired during this period, and the orchestra began to attract celebrity guest artists.

The Saskatoon Symphony Orchestra has held its concert series in various locations, beginning in Convocation Hall at the university. In 1939 it moved to the Bessborough Hotel's ballroom, and in 1949 the Capitol Theatre became its home. Later, in 1955, the gymnasium of the university was the location, and finally in 1968 Saskatoon's Centennial Auditorium became the permanent home of the orchestra. More than 30,000 persons currently enjoy concerts each year from September to May. A well-rounded and active season is presented. Up to sixty-two musicians play (depending on the work being performed). Ten of the musicians are employed on an annual salary as core players, while the remainder are hired as "per-service" musicians. A typical performance season includes: eight Master Series

concerts held in the Centennial Auditorium; four chamber concerts held in Third Avenue United Church; four concerts featuring the core musicians, held in the Adam Ballroom of the Delta Bessborough; and numerous school concerts and performances for both private and public events. The Annual Festival of New Music has emerged in recent years, and in the 2003–04 season a family series, "Classics for Kids," debuted. CBC broadcasts the orchestra on at least an annual basis. Thanks to funding assistance from the Canada Council, a composer-in-residence has been hired twice to compose specific works for the orchestra to première.

The Saskatoon Symphony Orchestra is the only symphony in the northern part of the province. While there are other smaller orchestral groups and bands, no other organization has the resources to perform the major symphonic repertoire presented by the SSO on a monthly basis. Not only does it provide opportunities for the citizens of Saskatoon to hear this repertoire—its very existence serves as a magnet for orchestral performers. These musicians enrich the musical life of the community as soloists, as players in the wide range of other musical groups the city offers, and as music teachers. Support from corporate sponsors has enabled the Saskatoon Symphony to take concert performances to communities such as Swift Current, Lloydminster, Bruno, and Yorkton. It intends to build and maintain a presence in rural Saskatchewan.

Karen Conway

SASKATOON WOMEN'S CALENDAR COLLECTIVE (SWCC). A co-operative with a localized and evolving membership, the Saskatoon Women's Calendar Collective (SWCC) has made Canadian women's history an annual bestseller for over thirty years. In 1972, five UNIVERSITY OF SASKATCHEWAN students formed the SWCC with the aim of producing popular history focusing solely on the lives and achievements of Canadian women. Few secondary sources on women's history existed, and this largely undiscovered territory had yet to become mainstream in either academia or school curricula. None of the founding women had any prior experience of publishing, but the format they decided upon—a daybook calendar—was inspired: it enabled them to transform an extraordinary diversity of subjects into an accessible and practical format. With assistance from a federal grant, the 1974 first edition of *Herstory: The Canadian Women's Calendar*, was published.

That calendar was remarkably successful. Although the first members of the SWCC might not originally have looked further than a single year, it was clear they had struck a chord with a large reading audience. Producing the *Herstory* calendar became an annual event. Over fifty women have been members of the Collective, and by 2005 they had published a combined 1,680 pages of biogra-

phies, photographs, and organizational histories about Canadian women in *Herstory*. An anthology, *Inspiring Women*, was published in 2003.

Cheryl Avery

FURTHER READING: Holmlund, M. and G. Youngberg (eds.). 2003. *Inspiring Women: A Celebration of Herstory*. Regina: Coteau Books.

SASKENERGY. SaskEnergy provides natural gas transmission and distribution services across the province. It does not own natural gas reserves, but purchases supplies from independent producers. The corporation's roots are in SaskPower, which was designated as the provincial authority for natural gas distribution in 1951. SaskEnergy assumed that responsibility in 1988 when it was created as a separate CROWN CORPORATION to provide Saskatchewan people with a reliable, safe and economical source of energy. Today SaskEnergy provides natural gas service to more than 325,000 residential, farm, commercial and industrial customers in the province. Since 1992, it has invested $750 million in capital spending projects to extend natural gas service to more rural and remote communities, and to upgrade its infrastructure. SaskEnergy has seven wholly owned subsidiaries: TransGas collects natural gas from producers and transports it either to pipelines for export or to SaskEnergy for distribution to customers; Many Islands Pipe Lines transports natural gas interprovincially and internationally; Bayhurst Gas holds natural gas royalty interests; SaskEnergy International is involved in international consulting;

Table SE-1. SaskEnergy—Contribution to Saskatchewan's Economy, 2003*	
Assets	$1.2 billion
Capital spending	$77.6 million
Community donations	$1.4 million
Debt ratio	72%
Dividend to CIC	$26.7 million
Earnings	$41 million
Employees	805 across Saskatchewan
Local purchasing (includes employee earnings of $61.5 million)	$95 million
Local suppliers supported	3,878
Partners	137 independent plumbing and heating contractors in 59 communities
Return on equity	14%
Revenue	$692.2 million

*All numbers are for the fiscal year ending December 31, 2003.

Swan Valley Gas Corporation distributes natural gas in western Manitoba; Saskatchewan First Call Corporation operates a database of pipeline locations for use by landowners and others; and 6019021 Canada Inc. holds an interest in a natural gas distribution franchise in Nova Scotia. (*See* Table SE-1) *Karen Schmidt*

SASKFERCO PRODUCTS INC. SaskFerco Products Inc., which began production in 1992, is a commercial joint venture involving **CARGILL LTD.** (50%), Investment Saskatchewan (49%) and Citibank Canada (1%). Located near the village of Belle Plaine, west of Regina, SaskFerco is one of North America's largest producers of two types of nitrogen fertilizer: granular urea and anhydrous ammonia.

Built at a cost of $435 million, the facility now produces 2,850 tonnes of granular urea, the solid form of nitrogen fertilizer, per day; 1,860 tonnes of anhydrous ammonia, a liquid, per day; and 670 tonnes of urea ammonium nitrate, known as UAN solution, per day. Farmers in western Canada and the northern tier of the United States are the main customers of these products. Granular urea production was expanded in 1997 and the UAN solution facility was added in 2004.

SaskFerco is the largest natural gas customer in Saskatchewan, requiring 25 billion cubic feet (BCF) annually to make the nitrogen fertilizer. It is unique in the global fertilizer industry because no wastewater from the facility is dumped into any river, lake, or stream. All SaskFerco wastewater is disposed of in an evaporation pond located within the 80-acre production site.

SaskFerco employs 140 people full-time at its Belle Plaine manufacturing complex and corporate office in Regina. The company has a granular urea warehouse in Carmen, Manitoba. *Joe Ralko*

SaskFerco Products Ltd., Belle Plaine, January 1993.

SASKMEDIA. The Saskatchewan Educational Communications Corporation, known as SaskMedia Corporation, was established on July 23, 1974. Its goal was to expand provincial educational media resources (16 mm films, video programs, audio programs, media kits) through purchase, development, production, duplication and distribution activities; to provide public access to educational media materials; and to enhance rural educational opportunities through media technology. To this end, the corporation was involved in purchasing duplication rights to certain approved educational programs; developing and producing programs for a variety of government departments and agencies involved in public education such as Education, Health, Agriculture and others; providing duplication services of audio and video programs to enable schools to build their own media resource collections; and distributing the 16 mm film collection through its loan service to clients. Over the years, a number of SaskMedia productions were broadcast within Saskatchewan, in Ontario, as well as across western Canada in cooperation with the Saskatchewan school broadcasts. SaskMedia received a number of awards for its productions, such as the Award of Merit from the Association for Media and Technology in Education in Canada, and the Certificate of Honourable Mention for Distinguished Service to the Mentally Retarded Through Sports, from the Kennedy Foundation in the United States. Following a change in government, SaskMedia was closed on March 31, 1983. *Leanne Miles*

SASKOIL. SaskOil was established in 1973 by the government of Saskatchewan to facilitate direct government investment in exploration and development in Saskatchewan's **OIL AND GAS INDUSTRY**. The creation of SaskOil was partly encouraged by the rapid increases in the price of oil in 1973. The

Saskatchewan government also wanted a window on the industry to increase its knowledge of the oil and gas industry production economics. The company grew rapidly in the 1970s through significant government investment in acquisition of existing companies and exploration. By 1976, SaskOil was reported to be producing 6% of Saskatchewan oil production. As the company grew, it acquired production and land positions not just in Saskatchewan but in other parts of western Canada. Besides exploration and development of petroleum, SaskOil also established a research and development branch to develop petroleum technologies; in 1986, the research and development branch of SaskOil was transferred to the **SASKATCHEWAN RESEARCH COUNCIL**.

The majority of SaskOil was sold to private shareholders in 1986. In 1996, SaskOil was renamed Wascana Energy. The Saskatchewan government's remaining interest was sold when Canadian Occidental Petroleum acquired Wascana Energy in 1997. At the time of the sale, Wascana Energy was producing about 70,000 barrels of oil equivalent/day from holdings across western Canada. Canadian Occidental Petroleum merged its other Canadian oil and gas production assets with Wascana Energy to create a new Canadian division under the same corporate name, Wascana Energy. The new Wascana Energy had production of about 100,000 barrels of oil equivalent/day in 1997. In 2000, Canadian Occidental Petroleum was renamed Nexen following a buy-out of the interest of the U.S.-based Occidental Petroleum. In 2001, Wascana Energy, controlled by Nexen, was renamed Nexen Canada. *David Hanly*

SASKTEL. SaskTel (Saskatchewan Telecommunications) has been delivering **TELECOMMUNICATIONS** services to the people of Saskatchewan for more than 90 years. Recognized as one of the leading telecommunications companies in the world, it is the only remaining provincially owned telecommunications corporation in Canada. SaskTel's roots are in the Department of Railway, Telephones and Telegraphs, which was established in 1908. The department was given authority to establish and operate local and long-distance telephone lines; its goal was to provide cost-effective service to as many farms, homes and businesses as possible. In 1947, responsibility for telecommunications was transferred to a new **CROWN CORPORATION** called Saskatchewan Government Telephones, which was later renamed SaskTel. Today SaskTel provides 425,000 residential and business customers with competitive voice, data, dial and high-speed internet, wireless, digital television, and e-business solutions. The corporation also maintains investments in companies that provide directory publishing, remote security monitoring, system design, project management, engineering consulting, software sales, cable television, transaction clearinghouse, wireless point

Table ST-1. SaskTel—Contribution to Saskatchewan's Economy, 2003*	
Assets	$1.2 billion
Capital spending	$128 million
Community donations	$1.7 million
Debt ratio	38%
Dividend to CIC	$76.6 million
Earnings	$85.1 million
Employees	4,153 across Saskatchewan
Local purchasing (includes employee earnings of $272 million)	$489 million
Local suppliers supported	4,100
Partners	140 dealers in 50 locations
Return on equity	13%
Revenue	$899.4 million

*All numbers are for the fiscal year ending December 31, 2003.

of sale, broadband internet streaming, internet transaction tracking, and advertising services, as well as telecommunication services to business customers in British Columbia, Alberta, Ontario and Quebec. Before 2000, SaskTel was provincially regulated, allowing it to establish billing and service structures tailored to provincial priorities. It became regulated by the Canadian Radio-Television and Telecommunications Commission (CRTC) on June 30, 2000. (*See* Table ST-1) *Karen Schmidt*

SASKTEL FIBRE OPTICS. In 1984 SASKTEL completed construction of the world's longest commercial fibre optics network, which covered 3,268 km to link fifty-two communities at a time when the previous longest fibre optics network had been less than 10 km. This achievement propelled SaskTel towards building an all-digital communications network and

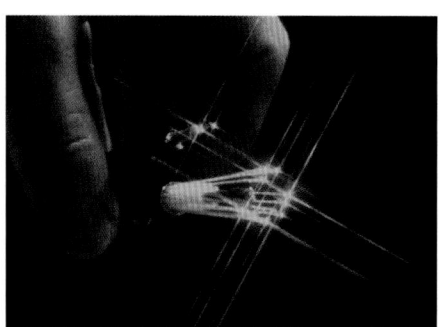

COURTESY OF SASKTEL

A fibre-optic cable containing 12 very thin glass fibres is compared with a conventional cable composed of copper wire. The fibres carry pulses of light instead of electronic signals, and about 670 conversations can be carried on just two fibres.

spawned a subsidiary to market SaskTel's TELECOM-MUNICATIONS expertise to global markets. SaskTel International was formed in 1986 to market the corporation's expertise in advanced telecommunications technologies, particularly fibre optic systems, to clients around the world; since then the company has done business in dozens of countries as a contract consultant or equity partner. Meanwhile, Saskatchewan residents continue to benefit from the fibre optic network. This technology converts all forms of messages to symbols of light and then transmits the messages on hair-thin strands of ultrapure glass. Each strand of fibre optic cable could originally hold 672 telephone conversations or one video channel or 45 megabits of data per second; over the years this has increased a hundredfold.

SaskTel engineers have also developed technology that requires a repeater only every 50 km rather than every 3 km for the coaxial cable. In 1986 SaskTel and Northern Telecom began testing the world's first fiber/coax hybrid (FCH), which was followed by field trials in 1987; this resulted in the world's first FCH network being introduced with pick-and-play Video-On-Demand (VOD) in 1988. This technology is now used by cable TV and telephone companies around the world. The service called MAX offers standard cable television pay service and VOD to SaskTel customers across the province. SaskTel has also launched a partnership with several schools: by using fibre optics and touch-tone phones, students have instant on-line access to almost 200 educational videos. The expertise gained through this program was used by the Hospitality Network Canada Inc. in 1995 to bring videos and video games to hospital and hotel guests throughout Canada and internationally. *Joe Ralko*

SASS, ROBERT (1937–). Bob Sass was born in 1937 in the Bronx, New York, and graduated from Cornell University in 1967 with a Masters degree in Science. He came to Saskatchewan in 1969 as an Associate Professor of Administration at the Regina campus of the UNIVERSITY OF SASKATCHEWAN. He joined the Saskatchewan Department of Labour as a Labour Consultant and Chief Conciliation Officer. This complemented his earlier experience as an organizer, international representative, and negotiator for municipal employees and as the education and research director for Local 91 of the International Ladies Garment Workers in New York. In Saskatchewan, Sass was quickly promoted to Assistant Deputy Minister, then in 1974 to Associate Deputy Minister of Labour, with responsibility for Occupational Health and Safety. He immediately helped bring in some of the first regulations to protect asbestos workers, and proceeded to overhaul the province's Health and Safety legislation. Sass pleaded for proper labeling of industrial products, noting that "chemicals are coming into the workforce by

the hundreds and thousands each year." He urged the federal government to take on the disclosure battle with big business—something provinces could not do alone.

Bob Sass's criticism of federal legislation did lead to improved labeling. In Saskatchewan, he helped draft 1981 regulations under the Occupational Health and Safety Act that instituted a process for obtaining information on hazardous chemicals. Employers were required to provide to employees a list with products clearly labeled and emergency procedures noted in the event of leaks or spills. By 1988, all of this contributed to a Canada-wide federal/provincial agreement establishing a uniform system of identifying and labeling hazardous substances under the Workplace Hazardous Material Information System (WHMIS). Today, Bob Sass continues to urge Canadians to go beyond the current boundaries of traditional bureaucracy and labour laws. He wants them to capture broader meaning and morality in connecting work to everyday life, and emphasizes the link between a healthy family life and a humane work place. He envisions establishing a Workers' Environment Board in workplaces such as he chaired for the potash mines in the late 1970s, when the mines were still under public ownership. Workers, being in the majority, would be able to address matters such as pace of work, how jobs are designed, and how work is organized. *Merran Proctor*

SAULTEAUX. The Saulteaux or Plains Ojibway (Nahkawininiwak in their language) speak a language belonging to the Algonquian language family; Algonquian people can be found from Newfoundland to the Rocky Mountains, and from Hudson Bay to the southeastern United States. Algonquian languages comprise Algonkin, Blackfoot, Cheyenne, Cree, Delaware, Menominee, Ojibwa, Ottawa, Potawatomi, Sauk/Fox, and Nahkawiwin (Saulteaux). The name *Saulteaux* is said to come from the French word *saulteurs*, meaning *People of the Rapids*; this name refers to the location around the St. Mary's River (Sault Ste. Marie), where French fur traders and the Ojibwa met to trade in the late 17th century. Amongst some storytellers there is a migration story that predates contact with the people of France and England. It relates the movement of the people to the west, where they began to settle and set up with their neighbours, the Lakota and Dakota, alliances which allowed for peaceful coexistence. It was during the fur-trade rivalry between the French and English that these alliances were broken.

With the fur trade in decline, the disappearance of the bison, and the increase of settlers of European origin, the *Nahkawininiwak*, along with other plains First Nations, began the treaty-making process with the newly developed government of

Canada. Nahkawininiwak leaders signed, on behalf of their various bands, Treaties 1 and 2. Later, in 1874 and 1876, *Nahkawininiwak* were signatories to Treaties 4 and 6. These four treaties ceded to the government of Canada much of the land of southern Manitoba and southern Saskatchewan, as well as portions of Alberta. In return, the First Nations were promised annuities ($3-$5 per person per year), reserves, education, as well as hunting, fishing and trapping rights.

In Saskatchewan, the following First Nations communities have *Nahkawininiwak* speakers: Cote, Cowessess, Fishing Lake, Gordons, Keeseekoose, Key, Muskowpetung, Nut Lake, Pasqua, Poorman, Sakimay, Saulteaux, and Yellowquill. In addition, the following communities have a mixture of *Nahkawininiwak*, *Nêhiyawêwin* and other languages: Cowessess, Gordons, White Bear, and Keeseekoose. There is some movement to adopt the original name of *Anishinabe*, which is the name that the Ojibway people used in earlier times to identify themselves. In the late 19th and early 20th centuries, many of the ceremonies and traditional beliefs of the *Nahkawininiwak* were banned by law. In the 21st century some of these ceremonies are being revived, belief systems such as the *Midewiwiwin* are being reintroduced, and some *Nahkawininiwak* have adopted Plains ceremonies such as the **SUN DANCE**. *William Asikinack*

FURTHER READING: Peers, L. 1994. *The Ojibwa of Western Canada: 1780 to 1870*. Winnipeg: University of Manitoba Press; Tanner, H.H. 1992. *The Ojibwa*. New York: Chelsea House; Ward, D. 1995. *The People: A Historic Guide to the First Nations of Alberta, Saskatchewan and Manitoba*. Saskatoon: Fifth House.

SAULTEAUX FIRST NATION. On April 7, 1993, the Saulteaux First Nation celebrated the ratification of its Treaty Land Entitlement Claim, enabling them to purchase 56,000 acres of land within Saskatchewan (farm land, Crown land, and land for tourism as well as commercial, urban and residential purposes). This ratification resolved the century-old Treaty Land Debt owed the band as signatories to **TREATY 6** on August 18, 1954. The Saulteaux band's largest populated area is located 35 km north of North Battleford. This Ojibway-speaking band owns 13,138.9 ha of land, and 540 of the 1,066 band members live on reserve. Infrastructure includes a band office, band hall, fire hall, school, clinic, arena, and various structures required for the band's maintenance. *Christian Thompson*

SAUNDERS, CHARLES (1867–1937). Sir Charles Edward Saunders was born in London, Ontario on February 2, 1867. He graduated from the University of Toronto, and received a PhD from Johns Hopkins University in 1891. In 1893 he and

SASKATCHEWAN ARCHIVES BOARD R-A350
Charles Saunders.

his wife, Mary Blackwell, ran a music school and wrote a music column in *The Week* magazine. Unable to earn a living, he moved to Ottawa in 1902 to accept an appointment from his father William at the Central Experimental Farm. It was under William Saunders' direction that experimental farms were established in Canada. In 1904 Charles Saunders discovered Marquis, a strain of **WHEAT** that matured seven to ten days earlier than other varieties—in particular Red Fife, which was the main variety at that time. Marquis had good **MILLING** qualities and became the standard for other wheat varieties. The Marquis wheat was tested in Saskatchewan and Manitoba from 1907 to 1909, and did extremely well.

By 1920 over 90% of the 17 million acres of wheat in western Canada were Marquis. The introduction of this hardy early-ripening wheat allowed farmers to grow the crops further north, doubling the amount of arable land on the prairies, and was responsible for the reputation Canada gained for producing the best hard spring wheat in the world. In 1921, Saunders was made Fellow of the Royal Society of Canada and received an honorary LLD degree from the University of Western Ontario. Due to ill health, he moved to France in 1922. In 1925 he was awarded the Flavelle Medal for Science from the Royal Society of Canada and an honorary doctorate from the University of Toronto. In gratitude to Saunders, Canadian farmers independently raised funds to increase his annual pension from $900 to $5,000 a year. In 1934 he was knighted by King George V. In recognition of his work with the French language as a writer and connoisseur, he was made Officier de l'instruction publique and Médaillé de l'Académie française by the French Government. Saunders died on July 25, 1937.

Daria Coneghan

SAVAGE, CANDACE (1949–). Candace Savage was born on December 2, 1949, in Grande Prairie, Alberta, and grew up with the love of books and reading. Both her parents were teachers, and according to them her first word was "book." In 1967, Savage entered the University of Alberta on a scholarship, and graduated with not only an Honours Degree in English, but also the Governor General's Gold Medal and the Rutherford Gold Medal. In 1970, she married Arthur Savage, a physics graduate, and they moved to Saskatoon, where she began to write. Her first books, *A Harvest Yet to Reap* (co-authored) and *Our Nell: A Scrapbook Biography of Nellie L. McClung*, explored the history of women in western Canada. Arthur decided he wished to write also, and together the couple produced a book of western Canadian **MAMMALS**. Wildlife, natural sciences, environmental issues, and women's history became the subject areas of the many works Candace Savage has published since 1979. She also produced a children's book, *An Amazing Journey Through the Last Great Age of Magic*, which examined the practice of magic and its transition to science in the 17th century. Candace Savage's books have been reprinted in several languages, and many of her publications are available in school libraries in Alberta, as gifts of the provincial government. She is a frequent guest speaker at schools, conferences and festivals.

Savage has been shortlisted for the Bill Duthie Award, BC Book Awards, for *Bird Brains* (1995), and the Science in Society Book Awards, Canadian Science Writers' Association for *Aurora* and *Bird Brains* (1994 and 1995). She received the Honour Roll, Rachel Carson Institute, Chatham College (1994), and the Honour Book Award, Children's Literature Roundtable, for *Trash Attack!* (1991). In 2004, she completed *Prairie: A Natural History*, which won two **SASKATCHEWAN BOOK AWARDS**.

The birth of her daughter in 1979, followed two years later by the death of her husband, Arthur, meant that Savage was on the move yet again, working in Edmonton and Yellowknife before returning to Saskatoon in 1990 for a term as writer-in-residence at the Public Library. Savage now shares her home with her daughter and her partner, Keith Bell. *Christian Thompson*

SAVAGE, ROBERT (1917–). "Doc" Savage spent only a brief time in Saskatchewan, but it was a very dramatic period. Born in England to a family living in desperate poverty, he was sent as a young boy to work on farms in Ontario. In the **GREAT DEPRESSION** of the 1930s, Savage was unemployed and rode the tops of freight trains to look for work with thousands of other jobless young men. He joined the Communist Party and was active in the party's trade union arm: the **WORKERS' UNITY LEAGUE**.

Doc Savage was prominent in the Relief Camp

Workers Union (RCWU), a League affiliate which organized the residents of work camps set up by the government of R.B. Bennett. The RCWU called a general strike of relief camp workers in the spring of 1935, and the camps emptied their inmates into Vancouver. Although he was only 18 at the time, Savage was put in charge of Division 3 of the RCWU, which included the union militants who had been blacklisted out of the government work camps. Division 3 undertook some of the most aggressive demonstrations and protests by the unemployed during the Depression.

Doc Savage was also one of the leaders of the 1935 ON-TO-OTTAWA TREK, which ended in Saskatchewan with the REGINA RIOT. After the riot, Savage avoided arrest, which was the fate of other Trek leaders, by traveling to the then remote northwestern part of Saskatchewan and then moving west. In the years that followed, he organized saw mills and lumber camps for the International Woodworkers of America, and was an active member of the Canadian Seaman's Union while working on merchant marine ships around the world.

Robert Savage got the name "Doc" after coming to the aid of a fellow worker who needed some medical attention. He is now retired and living in Quesnel, BC.   *Garnet Dishaw*

SCANDINAVIAN SETTLEMENTS. During the latter 19th century, large areas of Minnesota and the Dakotas became compact bloc settlements of Scandinavians, even more highly organized than their German counterparts for the preservation of ethnic identity; by 1890, close to 20,000 Norwegian immigrants had settled in South Dakota alone. Relatively few Scandinavians had immigrated as yet into Saskatchewan, but this situation changed markedly: despite little active encouragement of emigration in Scandinavia itself by the Canadian government, the number of people of Scandinavian origin resident in Saskatchewan increased from 1,452 in 1901 to 33,991 in 1911. During that decade large areas of the province were settled by people of Scandinavian origin, who thus added to the compact bloc settlements already established by Swedes in 1885 and 1889, by Icelanders in 1886–93, and by Finns in 1887.

By 1911, Scandinavian and Finnish immigrants and Scandinavian-Americans had founded a dozen primarily Norwegian settlements, half a dozen smaller Swedish settlements, three Icelandic, one Danish, and a couple of Finnish settlements. The most recent census data (2001) revealed that 109,560 Saskatchewan residents claimed Scandinavian (including Finnish) ethnic origins, of whom 14% (15,310) claimed only a single Scandinavian ethnic origin while the vast majority, 86% (94,260) claimed more than a single ethnic origin: 55.2% (60,510) were of Norwegian origin, 27.3% (29,900)

of Swedish origin, 8.6% (9,375) Danish, 5.6% (6,100) Icelandic, and 3.4% (3,675) Finnish.

While there is much evidence that the Scandinavian groups in Saskatchewan rapidly assimilated into general Canadian society, a tradition-oriented attitude often prevailed within Scandinavian and especially Finnish bloc settlements. In the earlier years of settlement, a high proportion of Scandinavians and Finns, like other ethnic groups, settled in fairly well-defined bloc settlements. Moreover, by 1926 a considerable proportion of them still had not adopted Canadian citizenship. While Scandinavian-Canadians were noted for their contribution during the World Wars, it must be remembered that they were neither from countries hostile to Britain and Canada (as was the case for immigrants from Germany or Austria-Hungary), nor were they pacifists (as were the Mennonites, Hutterites and Doukhobors): their contributions to the Canadian cause and the Scandinavian one were therefore not incompatible. Nor did the British-Canadian population in Saskatchewan tend to view Scandinavian immigrants as "unassimilable": in fact, even the KU KLUX KLAN, which drew some support from Scandinavian settlers, suggested that "trained" Scandinavian immigrants should be allowed to settle on the land.

Yet decades of de-emphasizing Scandinavian identity, in the school system but also in the local prairie community (where people of Scandinavian origin seldom predominated) and through intermarriage, brought about significant differences between generations in attitudes towards ethnic identity. Scandinavian-Canadians have tended to feel that it is possible to maintain a general interest in the "Scandinavian connection" without maintaining an ability to speak a Scandinavian language. The proportion of Scandinavian-origin population in Saskatchewan claiming an ability to speak a Scandinavian language declined from 59% in 1941 to 40% in 1951, 28% in 1961, and 20% in 1971; by 1971, hardly 1% actually used such a language as the primary language spoken in the home. Many, if not most of the original Scandinavian settlers in this province had formerly lived in the United States (for periods of time ranging from a few years to a couple of generations), so a considerable proportion probably already considered English to be their primary language before immigrating to Canada. If the 1950s represented a decisive decade of linguistic change among Scandinavian-origin people in Saskatchewan, it could be noted that ethnic language loss during that decade was actually occurring more rapidly among the Scandinavian-origin rural farm population (from 43% in 1951 to 30% in 1961) than among the rural non-farm (36% to 32%) or urban (29% to 24%). Yet in 1971 a higher proportion of Scandinavian-origin rural population (23% for rural farm population and 25% for rural

non-farm) than in urban areas (17%) could still speak a Scandinavian language. A far higher proportion of older people than younger retained this ability (67% of the 65+ group, compared to 38% of the 45-64 group, 16% of the 35–44 group, 6.5% of the 20–34 group, 3.9% of the 9–19 group, and 2.1% of the 1–9 group). Differences exist between the Scandinavian/Finnish groups in propensity to maintain fluency in the traditional ethnic language. There is little contrast between the four Scandinavian groups: out of 36,000 people of Norwegian descent living in Saskatchewan in 1971, 6,800 (18.9%) claimed that they spoke Norwegian as their mother tongue, compared to 3,400 out of 15,000 Swedes (23.5%) speaking Swedish, 1,300 out of about 5,000 Danes (24.6%) speaking Danish, and 840 out of some 3,000 Icelanders (27.1%) speaking Icelandic. A major contrast, however, can be drawn between these Scandinavian groups proper and the Finns: 745 (43.2%) of the 1,700 Finns could speak Finnish; this may be due to the fact that their language is totally unrelated to Scandinavian languages or to English.

While today many of the Lutheran parishes in rural Saskatchewan may be classified as ethnic parishes of a general denomination, for several decades they were all in ethnic sub-denominations patterned after national churches in Scandinavia and Germany. During this early period the ethnic nature of each sub-denomination was very evident: where Lutherans of various Scandinavian origins settled in one area, Norwegians, Swedes and Danes each organized their own congregations; and the Scandinavian Lutheran churches tended to support bloc settlement isolationism, ethnic traditionalism, and religious conservatism. These sub-denominations have been consolidated into more general Lutheran organizations since the 1940s; but at the individual congregation level, many Lutheran churches, especially those in rural areas, remain virtual ethnic parishes. Services in all parishes, however, are almost invariably conducted in the English language. An increasing proportion of people of Scandinavian origin are not Lutherans but converts to various evangelical sects. In fact, the proportion of Scandinavian/Finnish people in Saskatchewan who are Lutherans has steadily declined: from 67.1% in 1941 to 56.2% by 1951, 45.3% by 1961, and 40.4% by 1971.

Scandinavian-origin people in Saskatchewan tend to be familiar with a wide variety of Scandinavian folk traditions related to foods, performing arts, décor, and clothing. In the solidly Norwegian rural districts, many types of typically Norwegian baking are occasionally prepared, such as at Christmastime. Scandinavian folk dancing and music can be seen or heard at ethnic gatherings such as the annual *Islendingadagurinn* or Icelandic Day in Gimli, Manitoba, at a smaller version near Foam Lake, Saskatchewan, as well as in Saskatoon and Regina. Interior home décor cannot be underestimated. While some weaving may still be practiced, most of it is brought or imported directly from Scandinavia, as is traditional clothing or complete folk dress (such as the women's *bunad*). In Scandinavia, full folk costume is worn only on special occasions such as national days, baptisms, weddings, confirmations, or family gatherings (usually by older women, hardly ever by men); in Canada such full dress is restricted to ethnic gatherings, folk performances, and festivals. Finally, it should be stressed that visits "home" to Scandinavia seem to still be quite common, particularly for the older generation; families may return every two or three years, sometimes even every year, or exchange visits with relatives in Scandinavia.

When the **MARTIN** government outlawed foreign-language teaching during school hours in 1919, there were few schools in Scandinavian settlements in Saskatchewan to which the legislation could apply. Three reasons may be singled out as accounting for the relative lack of interest in teaching Scandinavian languages: first, because of a high standard of education in Scandinavia, the immigrants were already literate in their traditional languages and well prepared to adjust to English; second, many of the people of Scandinavian origin who settled in Saskatchewan had already settled in the United States long enough to have become familiar with the English language; and third, like other minorities, the Scandinavians were under considerable pressure to conform to the British group. Scandinavian settlers in Saskatchewan thus never really made much of an attempt to control the schools or to use their languages in the schools.

Scandinavian voluntary associations in Saskatchewan underwent a rapid transformation from an orientation toward the ethnic group to one toward the general society. They still are, for the most part, centred on Lutheran congregations: for example, among Norwegian Lutherans the *Kwende-Forening*, a ladies club, quickly became the Ladies Aid; and the Ungdoms Forening, a young peoples' association, became the Young People's Luther League. Other youth groups were directly descended from similar ones in Scandinavia, such as the Little Children of the Reformation, the Lutheran Daughters of the Reformation, and the Dorcas Girls' Society. The Norwegian Lutheran Outlook College of 1911 became the Saskatchewan Lutheran Bible Institute in 1938; the Saskatchewan Norwegian Lutheran Association on 1911 disappeared with church mergers; and the Norwegian Lutheran Church Seminary at Saskatoon of 1937 is now the Lutheran Theological Seminary of the **UNIVERSITY OF SASKATCHEWAN**. Moreover, the closure during the past couple of decades of the rural school houses, which were also focal points for Scandinavian activ-

ities in bloc settlements, went far in lessening the significance of Scandinavian ethnic identification. When people of Scandinavian origin had immigrated into Saskatchewan from their bloc settlements in the American midwestern states, they had brought with them their associations; although most of these organizations are no longer found in Saskatchewan, a large Scandinavian Club developed in Saskatoon, as well as a Norwegian Cultural Society and Sons of Norway Chapter.

Aside from some periodicals imported from Scandinavia itself, such as *Norske Ukeblad*, magazines and newspapers in Scandinavian languages or pertaining to Scandinavian culture have found their way into Saskatchewan from Ontario, Manitoba, and particularly Minnesota. The *Hyrden*, the bimonthly Norwegian-language paper of the former Norwegian Lutheran Church in Canada, became the *Shepherd*–the monthly English-language magazine of the Evangelical Lutheran Church of Canada–and is now the *Lutheran*. Also published in English was the *Lur*, the monthly magazine of the Alberta-based Scandinavian Historical Society, as well as the newsletter of the Saskatoon Scandinavian Club.

There can be little doubt that increasing intermarriage tends to affect profoundly the ability to maintain ethnic identity and ethno-cultural traditions. In 1961, 36.5% of married people claiming Scandinavian origin in Saskatchewan had married within their group; by 1971, 80.9% of the Canadian-born family heads claiming Scandinavian ethnicity were married to spouses of other ethnic origins. Opposition to marrying outside the Scandinavian Lutheran group declined sharply by the third generation. However, there has been relatively less intermarriage of Scandinavian-Canadians within the rural bloc settlement context in the prairies. Tens of thousands of descendants of the original Scandinavian and Finnish settlers in Saskatchewan remain concentrated in specific rural areas, where they have preserved some aspects of Scandinavian ethno-cultural identity. Yet while there are numerous rural pockets where people of Scandinavian origin predominate, they were seldom concentrated to the extent that they formed a majority of the population in a local town or village. Most Scandinavian immigrants in Saskatchewan (with the possible exception of Icelanders and Finns) did not actually settle within well-defined, compact, homogeneous ethnic settlements, but rather in dispersed patterns of rural settlement, or in cities or communities with mixed populations. This has doubtless facilitated their intermarriage and has served to lessen their emphasis on Scandinavian languages and traditions, and their link with Lutheranism. (*See also* **ETHNIC BLOC SETTLEMENTS, NORWEGIAN SETTLEMENTS, SWEDISH SETTLEMENTS, ICELANDIC SETTLEMENTS, FINNISH SETTLEMENTS, DANISH SETTLEMENTS, AMERICAN IMMIGRATION**)   *Alan Anderson*

SCARLETT, SAM (D. 1941). Sam Scarlett, a skilled machinist, a talented athlete and football player, and a superb public speaker, was one of the most interesting and colourful labour activists in Saskatchewan trade union history. Born in Scotland, he immigrated to Canada around the turn of the century, settling in Galt, Ontario. He went to the United States in 1908 or 1909, where he was soon involved in huge labour struggles such as the massive strikes by iron miners on the Mesabie Range in northern Minnesota. He was a trusted colleague of legendary figures such as "Big Bill" Haywood and Joe Hill of the Industrial Workers of the World (IWW or Wobblies). As part of the authorities' campaign to suppress syndicalists and labour agitators Scarlett was framed on a murder charge and accused of over a hundred separate crimes. He was imprisoned a number of times for several years. Sympathetic biographers estimate that he was arrested 160 times while fighting for workers' rights and defending picketers. After being released from one jail sentence in a general amnesty, he was deported back to Scotland.

Scarlett returned to Canada in the early 1920s as a harvest hand, and began organizing again for the IWW; he also joined the Communist Party. Sam Scarlett was one of the best platform speakers of his day. He could move listeners to laughter and tears in quick succession. He used to rent a theatre in Saskatoon on Sundays when movies were not permitted, and speak to large audiences about some radical or militant subject. He was a devoted syndicalist and an admirer of the Soviet Union. For a time in the late 1920s he lived in the Porcupine Plain district of northeast Saskatchewan. He was always available to go to the support of working people locked in battle with their bosses. Scarlett became a legendary figure in the labour movement for his self-sacrifice and devotion to the working class. After the IWW faded, he did a lot of work for the Communist-sponsored labour federation, the **WORKERS UNITY LEAGUE** (WUL).

In the late summer of 1931 Sam Scarlett and other organizers for the Mine Workers Union of Canada were sent to the Bienfait-Taylorton area to organize a union among the underground **COAL** miners. Scarlett was in poor health at the time, but his obvious commitment to the workers and his ever-present good humour brought many of the coal miners into Local 27 of the Mine Workers Union of Canada, a WUL affiliate. After the **ESTEVAN COAL STRIKE** ended with the murder of three strikers by police, Scarlett was arrested and charged with rioting and disturbing the peace. He was convicted, at least in part on perjured testimony by the coal operators, and sentenced to one year in jail and a $100 fine.

Sam Scarlett moved to New York City during **WORLD WAR II** to avoid incarceration, which was a fate encountered by other Communist Party members in Canada in the 1940s. He died there in 1941.

Garnet Dishaw

SCHERESKY, ALVIN (1930–). Alvin Scheresky, a pioneer of **ORGANIC** agriculture in Saskatchewan, was born on July 19, 1930, in North Dakota. While attending college in Tennessee, Scheresky was strongly influenced by a lecture about the **FARMING** methods advocated by J.I. Rodale (1898–1971), one of the first advocates of sustainable organic agriculture in the United States. After immigrating to Saskatchewan in 1959, Scheresky began farming in 1960 in the Glen Ewen-Oxbow area, using conventional farming methods. By 1964, Scheresky converted his operation to organic farming, bought a stone flour mill, and began selling a variety of organic grains, flours and cereals to a small base of customers. His business expanded dramatically during the 1970s, as he supplied both individual buyers and small distributors of organic produce in British Columbia. He was one of the first organic farmers in North America to have production facilities on the farm to process and add value to grains, and he operated the first organic flour mill in the province. Since 1975, Alvin's wife Cleadith has worked together with her husband in their family business.

In 1987 Scheresky, together with a half-dozen other local organic farmers, worked with Tom Harding, a co-founder of OCIA International from Pennsylvania, and with Eugene Hauser, an exporter from Quebec, to form the Saskatchewan chapter of the Organic Crop Improvement Association (OCIA), an organic farmer's organization which began in the USA; this became the first organization to confer organic certification in Canada. While they first sold grain primarily to the domestic market, by 1988 Oxbow area producers were among the first in Canada to export grains certified by OCIA to the European market. The OCIA in Saskatchewan became the largest certifier of organic farmers in Saskatchewan and devised many of the policies used by other similar organizations, which followed their pioneering efforts. Scheresky served as the president of Saskatchewan Chapter #1 from 1989 until 1990.

Scheresky actively promoted organic agriculture and assisted scores of aspiring organic farmers, who benefited from his extensive knowledge of polycultures, seeds, and methods for managing soil organic matter, moisture balance, and pest control. Scheresky's vision that organic production should protect soil fertility, produce high-quality food, and engage the farmer directly in value-added production served as a blueprint which influenced many others. He grew organic grains and operated A. Scheresky Milling, a precision grain cleaning and **MILLING** operation. Located in a 372 square metre (4,000 square foot) plant and warehouse, the operation produced at its peak approximately 90,719 kg

(200,000 lbs) of various whole grains, flours and cereals each month. Scheresky sold his operation and retired in 2001. He still has close ties with organic farmers and consultants, and maintains several test plots where he continues to refine techniques and methods for organic farming.

Raymond Ambrosi

SCHMEISER, PERCY (1931–). Percy Schmeiser, a farmer and implement agent from Bruno, Saskatchewan, has been a public figure most of his life, serving as mayor of the town of Bruno from 1966 to 1983 and as a member of the provincial Legislative Assembly for the Watrous constituency from 1967 to 1971. However, he gained world fame in 1998 over his legal battle with seed and chemical corporation Monsanto. Schmeiser was sued and eventually convicted of violating the patent on a genetic sequence contained in **CANOLA** plants developed and owned by Monsanto; he was charged with obtaining and using the seed without signing a contract and paying the required fees to Monsanto. While Schmeiser was not the only farmer in Canada sued by Monsanto for this patent infraction, his case was the most public, as he chose not to pay the fine and became the first farmer to challenge the charge through the Canadian court system. The case eventually went to the Supreme Court of Canada, which ruled in favour of Monsanto. The increased use of **BIOTECHNOLOGY** in plant breeding has led private firms such as Monsanto to become plant breeders and seed suppliers, and has therefore necessitated new ways to make a profit in an area where none was previously required. The case of Schmeiser and Monsanto publicized how these new means of profit protection—through patents and legal contracts with farmers—function and hold up legally when challenged.

Stephen Weiss

Percy Schmeiser.

Sandra Schmirler.

SCHMIRLER, SANDRA (1963–2000). Internationally renowned curler Sandra Marie Schmirler was born in Biggar, Saskatchewan on June 11, 1963. As a natural athlete, Schmirler's favourite sport was **CURLING**: she played on her high school team and won the provincial playoffs in her senior year. Schmirler continued curling while attending the **UNIVERSITY OF SASKATCHEWAN**. After graduating in 1985 with a BSc in Physical Education, she moved to Regina, where she was employed as a swimming instructor and lifeguard. In 1992, she was appointed supervisor of the South East Leisure Centre. In Regina, Schmirler curled as a member of Katy Fahlman's team, which won the 1987 provincial championships. By the 1990–91 season, Schmirler decided to become skip of her own team–Team Peterson (renamed Team Schmirler in 1996–along with Jan Betker, Joan McCusker, and Marcia Gudereit). In its premiere season, the team won the provincial championship; it competed in the 1991 Scott Tournament of Hearts, but did not make it to the playoffs.

During the 1992–93 season, Schmirler's team won both the provincial and national titles. Schmirler was awarded the all-star skip award that year at the Scott. The team then went on to compete in and win their first world championship, and was named Team of the Year by SaskSport. Team Peterson was once again the national champion after winning the 1993–94 Scott. They returned for their second world championship, won the title, and became the first Canadian team to win consecutive world titles; SaskSport named them Team of the Year for the second time in 1994. In the 1996–97 season, Team Schmirler won for the third time both the national and the world championships.

After competing successfully in the 1998 Nagano Winter Olympics, Team Schmirler won the first Olympic gold medal ever to be awarded for the sport of curling. In the 1998–99 season, it was unable to win the provincial championship but enjoyed other successes, including being named Team of the Year by the Canadian Press in 1998 and being inducted into the Canadian Curling Hall of Fame in March 1999. However, in mid-1999, two months after giving birth to her second daughter, Schmirler was diagnosed with cancer; she passed away on March 2, 2000, at the age of 36. Her memory continues to be honoured today: in January 2000, the Sandra Schmirler Foundation was established to provide assistance to children in families facing a life-threatening illness; later that year, Schmirler was awarded the Saskatchewan Order of Merit posthumously; and in the fall of 2000 she was inducted into the Canadian Sports Hall of Fame.

Daria Coneghan, Erin Legg and Holden Stoffel

FURTHER READING: Lefko, P. 2000. *Sandra Schmirler: The Queen of Curling*. Toronto: Stoddart.

SCHNEIDER, WILLIAM GEORGE (1915–). Born in Wolseley, Saskatchewan on June 1, 1915, Schneider received his BSc and MSc degrees from the UNIVERSITY OF SASKATCHEWAN, and graduated with a PhD from McGill University in 1941. He worked at the Woods Hole Oceanographic Institute, Massachusetts, from 1943 to 1946, and returned to Canada, hired by the National Research Council (NRC), in 1946. He continued his research in pure chemistry, on molecular forces and structure. From 1967 to 1980 Schneider was President of the NRC, where he continued the work of C.J. MACKENZIE and E.W.R. Steacie to make the NRC an important force in the international research community. For his efforts, he was made a member of the Royal Society of London, the Royal Society of Canada, and he received the Order of Canada. *Diane Secoy*

SCHOOL BROADCASTS AND TELECASTS. In 1931 the Government Correspondence School began experimenting with the use of radio to deliver evening lessons covering high school courses in English, history, science, Latin, and German; later on, geography was added to the list. The educational broadcasts, prepared by the teachers in the Correspondence School, were intended to supplement the work in the courses. They were discontinued in 1936, however, due to the prevailing economic conditions. The initial successful experiment with school radio broadcasts did convince the Department of Education of the potential of the medium to support learning, and in 1938 the government amended the School Grants Act and the Secondary Education Act to provide grants to schools to assist with the purchase of radios and film projectors.

Other provinces also became interested in the potential of radio to support education in the 1930s. The British Columbia Department of Education began broadcasting programs for schools on the Canadian Broadcasting Corporation network in 1936, and in the winter of 1940–41 the CBC carried some of these programs over its prairie transmitter. The programs were well received by teachers and students in schools, and in 1940 representatives from departments of education in the four western provinces met to discuss potential co-operation in the production and scheduling of school telecasts.

In 1941, the Saskatchewan Department of Education established the Audio-Visual Instruction Branch to assume responsibility for distribution of audio-visual aids, the development and sponsorship of school broadcasts, and the supervision of the rural circuits of the National Film Board. Morley P. Toombs, a superintendent of schools, was appointed as head of the branch. In the 1941–42 school year, the Saskatchewan Department of Education began offering school radio broadcasts on Tuesdays and Fridays. The first programs to be broadcast were a language arts series entitled "Highways to Adventure" for Grades 5 to 10, and a junior music series for Grades 1 to 4.

In 1942–43, national school broadcasts were added to the schedule, and a series called "Heroes of Canada" was produced with support from all departments of education across the country. The Canadian Teachers' Federation was also involved in supporting this endeavour. By 1944–45, school telecasts were offered four days per week; programming was provided through a combination of national, western regional and provincial programs by CBC, and a network of private stations that included CKRM Regina, CHAB Moose Jaw, CFQC Saskatoon, CKBI Prince Albert, and CJGX Yorkton. At the same time, the Department of Health and the Department of Education co-operated to produce a series of health education programs called "Health Highways."

In 1945, RJ STAPLES joined the Department of Education as supervisor of music and introduced a new kind of music programming, which served as a model for classroom instruction. Over the years, music programming became an important feature of the school broadcasts and became a mainstay in the music education of students throughout the province. In 1950 GERTRUDE MURRAY joined the Department as supervisor of school broadcasts, replacing J.W. Kent who had served in this capacity since 1945. From 1951 to 1953, music and other school programming was produced in a small studio in the Department of Learning offices until the production studio work was transferred to the CBC studio in 1954; there the provincial radio programming continued to be produced until 1982, when school radio broadcasts were discontinued.

Experiments with school telecast programming were started in the 1954–55 school year. The programs originated in Toronto and were prepared and presented by the School Broadcasts Branch of the CBC under the direction of the National Advisory Council of School Broadcasts, which had membership from Departments of Education across Canada. In Saskatchewan, CKCK-TV and local distributors assisted with the first experiment by helping to equip schools with television sets. These early experiments with educational television continued, and the amount of programming expanded. By the 1963-64 school year, a full schedule of school telecasts was offered on the CBC network with programs contributed through provincial, western regional, and national arrangements. This programming would be replaced when the Saskatchewan Communications Network (SCN) began broadcasting school telecasts on the SCN cable channel.

Over the years, CBC played a significant role in the production of programs for the school telecasts, in addition to serving an important role as broadcaster. However, many of the video programs were produced by independent film producers and by the Government Services Branch of the provincial government. In 1974, SASKMEDIA Corporation was established to provide support for educational programming. Many audiovisual productions in a variety of formats were prepared by the corporation during the years that it operated prior to its dissolution in 1974. Since that time, production work has been contracted to independent producers. Many of the school broadcast and telecast programs won awards over the years for their quality and instructional design. The programs have provided a major resource support for schools over the years.

As audio and video playback machines became available, the Department established an audio and later a video duplication service so that schools could obtain copies of educational programs; this technology allowed teachers to use programs at their convenience in accordance with their instructional plan. The service was operated at various times by the Government Services Branch of Executive Council, by SaskMedia, by Saskatchewan Education, and through a contracted service provider. The audio service was eventually discontinued, but the video duplication service continues to be provided with assistance of SCN, which clears video broadcast and duplication rights for programs on the recommendation of Saskatchewan Learning.

Delee Cameron and Leanne Miles

SCHOOL GOVERNANCE. Throughout Saskatchewan's history, the governance of public schools has been in the hands of local residents, through boards of education composed of elected school trustees. For school governance and electoral purposes, the province has been divided into geographic areas. In the early years, these areas were called school districts. The districts were five miles by four miles, and each had a school at its centre, governed by the local school board. Over the years, more than 5,000 school districts were formed. In 1944, the provincial government introduced legislation called the Larger School Units Act, whereby school districts could amalgamate into larger governance areas, with one elected board of education responsible for all schools within the boundaries of the school unit. Gradually, many of the school districts in rural areas joined to form larger school units, while districts in the larger urban centres (as well as in some towns and villages) continued to function as discrete governance areas.

In 1978, the provincial government introduced the **EDUCATION ACT**. This statute brought greater uniformity by renaming all school districts and larger school units as school divisions, and by giving each of the divisions a unique number. This arrangement was also extended to northern Saskatchewan, where schools had previously been controlled more directly by the provincial government. Each school division has a board of education with a minimum of five members and a maximum of ten, as prescribed by the Minister of Learning. In most urban school divisions, school trustees are elected on an at-large basis. In rural areas, the school divisions are divided into sub-divisions, each of which elects one member to the board of education. To participate in an election as either a candidate or a voter, a person must live within the boundaries of the school division. Eligibility is based on place of residence; ownership of property in the division is not necessary, nor does it confer eligibility on non-residents.

Canadian constitutional law includes provisions that have a direct impact on the governance of schools in Saskatchewan, based on faith in one case and on language in the other. As required by the constitution, Saskatchewan legislation enables the members of the minority faith in a particular area (either Protestant or Roman Catholic) to establish a **SEPARATE SCHOOL DIVISION** in the area, to elect a school board consisting exclusively of members of that faith, and to govern their own separate schools. As required by section 23 of Canada's Charter of Rights and Freedoms, Saskatchewan law also provides for a **FRANCOPHONE** school division under the governance of a francophone board of education elected by francophone residents. First Nations schools located on Indian reserves fall under federal and band jurisdiction, and are not part of the school governance framework set out in this entry.

As of January 1, 2004, Saskatchewan has eighty-two school divisions: sixty-six public, fifteen separate (fourteen Roman Catholic and one Protestant), and one francophone. This number is likely to be reduced in the future through further restructuring into larger governance areas. Apart from specific matters unique to the separate and francophone school boards, all boards of education have the same statutory powers and duties.

Although they are required to comply with all relevant Saskatchewan legislation, they are not agents of the provincial government but rather are a type of local government. By law, the boards are autonomous corporate bodies with broad authority to own property, employ staff, and enter into contracts. As democratically elected bodies, they are directly accountable to local residents for their policies, actions, and decisions. Board meetings are open to the public, and the minutes of board meetings are a public document. Boards of education are responsible for the delivery of school services within their school division. For this purpose, key powers and duties assigned to boards of education include the following: to own and operate schools and to determine the grades to be offered in each; to determine the attendance area for each school and to arrange student transportation services as the board considers necessary; to close schools; to determine (subject to provincial curriculum policy) the program of instruction in each school; and to employ teachers, administrators, and support personnel required for the delivery of programs.

Saskatchewan's publicly supported schools are funded through a combination of provincial grants and locally generated revenues. A key financial responsibility of school boards is to raise the required local share for their school division by establishing annual mill rates for the levying of property taxes. Boards of education are supported in a variety of ways in carrying out their governance responsibilities. Each board employs a director of education to serve as its chief executive officer. For each school, there is either a local board of trustees or a local school advisory committee. These bodies provide policy and program advice, and also carry out a range of administrative functions with respect to their school, as delegated by the board of education.   *Michael Littlewood*

SCHOOL LIBRARIES. School libraries have played an important role in teaching and learning in Saskatchewan for almost a century, and over the years the Department of Education (now called Saskatchewan Learning) has supported their development and growth. The earliest reference to school libraries was in the 1898 annual report of the Superintendent of Education for the North-West Territories, D.J. Goggin. He recognized the need and advocated for the establishment of libraries in all school districts. In 1901, funding was guaranteed to school libraries in the School Grants Ordinance, dedicated to the expansion of library collections. This had a positive impact in promoting school library development. By 1909, library inspectors recognized the need to encourage educators to understand the value of library resources and to use them in their teaching. Effective selection of learning resources was also identified as an issue. By 1928, school

inspectors recommended that school library consultative services be established at the provincial level.

During the **DEPRESSION**, school libraries suffered as a result of the economic conditions of the times. School libraries were in poor condition generally, and old worn-out books could not be replaced. However, school inspectors believed in the importance of a good reference collection to support the new curriculum's "assignment" approach to instruction, and continued to encourage school boards to support school libraries. In one area of the province, sixteen school boards co-operated in organizing a Library and Mechanics Institute, which provided boxes of books to schools in the area, as well as circulating adult books to encourage interest among the taxpayers. In the 1940s, as the province began to recover, the Department of Education provided a higher level of support for school libraries. Grant money was provided to purchase books and send them to the schools; and in the 1944–45 school year, **LYLE EVANS** was appointed as the first provincial supervisor of school libraries with the Department of Education. Throughout the 1950s and 1960s, the supervisor of school libraries worked with teachers to integrate reading and research into the instructional program, so that students would have a richer educational experience. In 1945–46, the Department created the School Libraries Division, and the supervisor assisted school divisions to develop unit- and school-level libraries, and also provided lists of suitable learning resources to support the curriculum.

The Department of Education provided other supports to schools in accessing suitable resources to support instruction in the early years as well, with the establishment of the **SASKATCHEWAN BOOK BUREAU** in 1936, the provision of school broadcasts (beginning originally in 1931), the establishment of the Audio Visual Branch of the Department in 1941, and the provision of grants to schools for the acquisition of radios, slides, films, and projectors in 1937. Over the years, school radio broadcasts—and later, school telecasts—provided support to teachers, as did the film loan service and video duplication services. The formation of larger school units following the passing of legislation in 1944 had the effect of allowing the larger units to provide stronger school library services. School libraries grew both in number and in size, and in 1964 the Saskatchewan Association of School Librarians published *Proposed Standards for School Libraries in Saskatchewan*. These standards helped to provide guidance to school divisions in building their school library programs. In that same year the Regina Campus of the **UNIVERSITY OF SASKATCHEWAN** introduced an undergraduate major in Library Science and the Department of Education established grants for the purchase of library resources. The following year, demonstration school library projects were initiated to provide examples of the contribution of school libraries to the educational program.

From the millions of resources published/produced each year, school librarians must select those most appropriate for the curriculum and their students. In the 1940s, the Department of Education began assisting schools with this task by creating a materials evaluation process that continues today. The Department gathers and screens potential materials, arranges for them to be evaluated by classroom teachers, and compiles annotated bibliographies of recommended learning resources. The first initiatives took the form of displays and lists of recommended books. In 2004, bibliographies of recommended materials are available on-line and in print form. Teacher-librarians who add these resources to their library collection can be sure the resources meet quality standards and are relevant to the subject areas. In addition, the Department of Education helps teacher-librarians select materials that are free of gender, ethnic, and cultural stereotyping by publishing guidelines such as *Selecting Fair and Equitable Materials*. In 1984, a full-scale curriculum review led to a new vision for education in Saskatchewan, as described in a document called *Directions*. Subsequently, **CORE CURRICULUM** was introduced. Resource-based learning is a key component of Core Curriculum, and enables students to use not just one textbook, but rather a wide variety of print and non-print resources. Resource-based learning means an expanded role for teacher-librarians, who work with teachers to plan units of study that integrate resources with classroom assignments, and teach students the processes needed to find, analyze, and present information. A school library stocked with relevant learning resources provides a foundation for learning success.

In 1987, the Department of Education released *Resource-Based Learning: Policy Guidelines and Responsibilities for Saskatchewan Learning Resource Centres*. In 1988, *Learning Resource Centres in Saskatchewan: A Guide for Development* was published. These documents became blueprints for school library development in Saskatchewan, and helped teachers and teacher-librarians make resource-based learning a reality. Electronic technology has added a whole new dimension to resource-based learning. An abundance of information is available on the World Wide Web. To help teacher-librarians select the best, the Department of Learning coordinates the evaluation of websites and recommends in an on-line database those suitable for school use. Electronic technology also makes it possible for the Department to deliver actual learning resources to schools as well as recommending materials. The full text of many journals and newspapers, and encyclopedias, dictionaries, atlases, and other reference materials is available on-line. The service gives teachers and teacher-librarians access to a wealth of resources.

Delee Cameron and Loraine Thompson

SCHOOLPLUS. The School^PLUS^ initiative in Saskatchewan is the result of public consultations undertaken by the Role of the School Task Force (1999–2001), which consulted with the public to identify expectations for the role of the school in meeting the emerging needs of children and youth in the 21st century. The findings of the Task Force were accepted by the government of Saskatchewan in 2002 and supported by seven human-service departments. The Task Force Report acknowledged that schools have two key functions to fulfill: they must continue to nurture the development of the whole child intellectually, socially, spiritually, emotionally and physically; but in the future they must also serve more coherently as centres at the community level for the delivery of appropriate and integrated education, social, health, recreation, culture, justice and other services for children and their families.

The School^PLUS^ initiative is based on the attainment of five goals: all Saskatchewan children and youth should have access to the supports they need for school and life success; the well-being and education of children and youth is a shared responsibility; a harmonious and shared future with Aboriginal peoples is envisioned; high-quality services and supports will be linked to schools at the community level; and there will be strengthened capacity for high-quality and integrated learning and support programs. School^PLUS^ development is being guided by three mutually supportive strategies: community engagement and action planning; integrating school-linked services; and strengthening educational capacity. School^PLUS^ is an ambitious plan to provide the opportunity for all children and youth to achieve excellence in learning and life; the opportunity for all communities to share in supporting children and youth as they learn and grow; and the opportunity for every citizen in our province to share in the promise of a prosperous future.

Don Hoium

SCHOOL SISTERS OF NOTRE DAME (SSND). The congregation of the School Sisters of Notre Dame was founded in Bavaria, Germany by Blessed Theresa of Jesus Gerhardinger in 1833. The purpose of the Congregation was the education of girls from poor families. Theresa believed that the transformation of society depended on the family unit and that women were instrumental in developing Christian values within the family. In 1847, five SSNDs came to the United States to educate German immigrant children. An invitation to administer the orphanage in St. Agatha, Ontario brought the SSNDs from Wisconsin to Canada in 1871.

The SSNDs came to Saskatchewan from Ontario in 1927 to establish a boarding school in Leipzig, Saskatchewan. The four pioneers were Sisters Cajetan Schneider, Petra Beyer, Agnes Busch and Miriam Walsh. In the following years, the congregation was invited to staff schools in Revenue, Handel, Salt Lake, Wilkie and Saskatoon. In the mid-1970s the Sisters' ministry was broadened to include parish ministry, religious education, chaplaincy, counseling, and diocesan marriage tribunal work. Over the years, forty-one Saskatchewan women joined the congregation and served in Canada, England, Italy, South America and Africa. There are currently eight School Sisters of Notre Dame in Saskatchewan, serving in a variety of ministries.

Joan Helm

SCHOOLS AND COMMUNITY DEVELOPMENT. The well-being of children and youth as they grow, learn, and develop is central to the connection between families, schools, and community development. From the earliest times among Aboriginal peoples, and then later with immigrant settlers, the entire community often shared in the responsibility of raising and teaching children and youth. During the period of the one-room school, the schoolhouse was often a central gathering place serving many purposes for people of all ages. "Work Bees" provide another example of people working together to address needs, strengthen local opportunities, and build community and community spirit. In addition to providing day-to-day instruction, schools have worked with members of the community to organize nutrition programs, community kitchens, clothing exchanges, parenting support groups, and locating social and health services such as immunization clinics and safety programs. A number of schools share resources and space to provide daycare programs in high schools, family and seniors' computer times, pre-kindergarten programs, first aid programs, dance classes, family literacy initiatives, and continuing and adult education programs.

Schools rely on the knowledge and expertise of members of the community to enhance learning: senior citizens are often invited to talk about the past; when schools engage with First Nations and Métis communities to honour traditional ways of knowing, they begin with the inclusion of Elders. Locally developed curriculum initiatives, in such areas as history and culture, as well as agriculture and forestry, enrich student learning and strengthen the relationship between the community and the schools. Parents contribute to leadership in schools by joining committees and governance bodies such as school boards, parent teaching associations, community school councils, and sharing circles. Through such groups, development can occur for the benefit of the entire community in conjunction with local town councils and other community groups. Recreation programs and the joint use of buildings and facilities are notable examples, common in Saskatchewan, where partnerships benefit the entire community. Many schools continue to be at the heart of community development initiatives in the province. (*See also* **COMMUNITY SCHOOLS**, **SCHOOL**^PLUS) *Ted Amendt, Sue Bland, and Faye Moen*

SCHOOLS, INCLUSION AND DIVERSITY. Within Saskatchewan schools, inclusive educational practice has evolved since the 1960s, particularly in the education of students with exceptional needs. The provincial motto *From Many Peoples, Strength* captures the understanding that the diverse background of Saskatchewan's people has always been one of the province's greatest assets. The classroom of today reflects the diversity in our communities (*see also* **SPECIAL EDUCATION**). The first major step away from the institutionalizing and segregating practices that typified the pre-1960s was the establishment of separate schools in the 1960s: as an option to institutionalizing, a student with intensive needs could live at home and be educated at a special school during the day. Although exclusive in nature, the fact that the special schools were located within regular communities set the stage for the vast changes to took place in the 1970s.

In the 1970s, a variety of instructional settings and options were developed, from segregated programs located in institutions and special schools to regular classroom placements in neighbourhood schools. The 1980s witnessed a further emphasis on the rights of persons with disabilities, and the gradual merger of regular education with special education. Increasingly, collaboration was emphasized between regular classroom teachers and special education teachers on behalf of students with special needs. Although not without debate and controversy, inclusive education, collaborative program delivery, and the rights of all students to attend their neighbourhood/community school became the dominant theme and direction of the 1990s. The benefits of inclusion for students with special needs, non-disabled peers, teachers, and society in general became well documented and endorsed by learning theory and "action-based" evidence. As the 1990s ended, two studies, the Saskatchewan Special Education Review and the Task Force and Public Dialogue on the Role of the School, took place. Both committees reported recommendations that further characterized and defined preferred educational direction. Central to their recommendations was that Saskatchewan schools should be community-oriented and inclusive, and established through collaborative partnerships and shared accountability.

In response, Saskatchewan Learning reaffirmed the philosophy of inclusive schools and committed to support their development. The *Minister's Response to the Report of the Special Education Review Committee: Directions for Diversity*

(*2000*) defined an inclusive school as a supportive, caring, and responsive learning community. Within this context, diversity is viewed not as an obstacle but as an opportunity to enrich school culture and provide increased opportunities for appreciation of differences. Diversity is expected, welcomed, and respected. In 2002 the *Children's Services Policy Framework* was distributed to all schools and divisions. In 2003, the Community Service Delivery Model was initiated to provide a mechanism and enhanced funding for service integration. Resources were produced in the areas of intellectual and multiple disabilities and inclusive education, reading difficulties and disabilities, and fetal alcohol spectrum disorders. Components of the *Caring and Respectful Schools Initiative* include a conceptual framework to strengthen schools as respectful learning communities, and to enhance curriculum resources to support the personal and social development of children and youth. It outlines prevention, early intervention, and crisis response strategies for dealing with issues related to harassment, bullying, aggression, and violence. The initiative builds on the successful practices and programs of schools and communities across the province, and is a central component of **SCHOOL**^PLUS.

Schools, as a social institution, have a critical role to play in ensuring that children and youth have the opportunity to achieve success in life. Saskatchewan Learning, school divisions, families, communities, and service providers work together to support all students. Through joint efforts, students are provided with a continuum of programs and services in the regular classroom, school, and home community.

Christine Boyczuk, Judy Cormier,
Larry McGuire, and Kevin Tunney

SCHUDEL, THOMAS (1937–). Thomas Schudel was born on September 8, 1937, in Defiance, Ohio. A composer, bassoonist and teacher, he completed his BSc in Music Education and Master's in Theory and Composition at Ohio State University and received his Doctor of Musical Arts degree at the University of Michigan in 1971. He joined the faculty at the **UNIVERSITY OF SASKATCHEWAN**, Regina Campus in 1964 and became Head of the Music Department in 1975, a post he held until 1978. Counterpoint, analysis, and woodwinds were among the classes he taught during his tenure. In 1972, Schudel's Symphony No. 1 garnered first prize in the City of Trieste International Competition for Orchestral Compositions. His works have been performed across Canada and internationally; many are published in Canada and the USA. Thanks to commissions from provincial groups such as the **SASKATCHEWAN MUSIC FESTIVAL ASSOCIATION** (SMFA), his music has been showcased throughout the province. The SMFA included his works in their

REGINA LEADER-POST
Thomas Schudel, 1992.

2004–05 syllabus, thus reaching children in many communities. Other works have been commissioned by the Saskatchewan Music Educators Association and the Saskatchewan Choral Federation, as well as by the Canada Council and the CBC.

The Contemporary Directions Ensemble, of which Schudel, along with fellow musician **ELIZABETH RAUM**, was a founding member, was incorporated in the late 1970s. This group of professional Regina musicians promoted contemporary music through performance into the late 1980s.

Fiona Stevenson

SCHULMAN, ANN L. (1941–2003). Ann Caspell was born on July 19, 1941, in Kindersley and graduated from the **UNIVERSITY OF SASKATCHEWAN** with a Bachelor's Degree in Nursing in 1965. She married Mayer Schulman in March 1965. A role model for nurses, she had an infectious laugh and a warm and caring presence. For many years she provided compassionate care to children and their families in the children's oncology program at the **ROYAL UNIVERSITY HOSPITAL** and was one of the founders of Camp Circle O'Friends, a camp for children with cancer and their siblings. She held many executive positions in Swim Canada, and accompanied the Canadian Swim Team to many international events and two Olympic games. She was inducted into the **SASKATCHEWAN SPORTS HALL OF FAME** in 2003.

As executive director of the Saskatchewan Institute for Prevention of Handicaps, she developed many primary prevention programs for children. Her years of volunteerism led to many awards: Canadian Progress Club Volunteer of the Year; President's Award from Swim Canada; University of Saskatchewan Alumni Association Award of Achievement; and Saskatchewan Sport Volunteer of the Year. She was inducted as an Officer to the Order of Canada in 2002, and died in Saskatoon on April 23, 2003.

Karen Wright

SCHWANN, PAUL (1933–74). Dr. Paul Schwann helped pioneer sports medicine in Saskatchewan. Born in Regina, he played junior football for the **REGINA DALES** and junior hockey for the Regina Pats. He graduated from the University of Alberta Faculty of Medicine in 1958, and later interned at the Regina General Hospital. Schwann served as team doctor for the Regina Pats, the Regina Rams, O'Neill and Miller high schools, various **UNIVERSITY OF REGINA** Cougar teams, and the **SASKATCHEWAN ROUGHRIDERS.** He was recognized by the Canadian Academy of Sports Medicine for his work in team sports in 1972. Dr. Schwann initiated fitness and athletic training programs, and developed the first testing for SaskTel employees; he believed that physical and mental fitness were crucial to healthy living in every workplace. Dr. Schwann died on October 4, 1974. In 1982, the Dr. Paul Schwann Applied Health and Research Centre at the University of Regina opened and became a nationally accredited human performance testing facility. The city of Regina named Schwann Place in University Park East in his honour. *Elizabeth Mooney*

SCIENCE AND TECHNOLOGY: *see essay on page 845.*

SCOTT, town, pop 110, located SW of Wilkie. The area was first settled around 1905; a significant number of those who came to the region were of German Catholic origin, and mostly from Russia. With the construction of the **GRAND TRUNK PACIFIC RAILWAY** through the area, the townsite developed. Scott was incorporated as a village in 1908 and attained town status in 1910. The community was named for Frank Scott, a railway company treasurer. The 1911 Census recorded a population of 420– the largest the community would ever have. Although the population hovered between 200 and 300 from the 1920s to the early 1970s, by the early 1950s the town's commercial sector had been reduced to a handful of establishments, superseded by the business communities in nearby Wilkie or Unity. Over the past few decades, the community's numbers have plummeted. Scott is notable for the experimental farm established in the early 1900s; the Agriculture and Agri-Food Canada operation focuses on research related to oilseeds and cereal crops in the northwestern region of Saskatchewan. *David McLennan*

SCOTT, THOMAS WALTER (1867–1938). Walter Scott was born on a farm near Ilderton, Ontario, on October 27, 1867. In 1885, he moved west to Portage La Prairie and worked as a journalist with C.J. Atkinson, owner and editor of the *Manitoba Liberal*. In 1886, Scott followed Atkinson to Regina where he worked for the *Regina Journal* before buying half of the *Regina Standard* and all

of the *Moose Jaw Times*. In 1895, he bought the *Regina Leader* from **NICHOLAS FLOOD DAVIN**. Scott supplemented his income with land speculation in and around Regina. Scott married Jessie Read and they adopted Dorothy, Jessie's niece. They had no children of their own.

Scott was first elected to the Canadian House of Commons in 1900 for the constituency of Assiniboia West, defeating the incumbent Nicholas Flood Davin. Scott represented his constituency in the North-West Territories as a backbencher in the Wilfrid Laurier government and was re-elected in the general election of 1904. Scott and the Minister of the Interior, Clifford Sifton, influenced the development of the autonomy bills which created the two new provinces of Alberta and Saskatchewan. Three controversial issues arose: one province or two; should the provinces have control of mineral rights; and should there be separate schools. Two provinces were created; the two provinces did not gain the right to control their own mineral rights until twenty-five years later; and separate schools were allowed but within one public school system. On September 4, 1905, Saskatchewan became a province.

Lieutenant-Governor **AMÉDÉE FORGET** chose Walter Scott as the first Premier. The first general election was on December 13, 1905. Under the campaign slogan "Peace, Progress and Prosperity," the Scott government won a majority. Scott and his government were re-elected in 1908 and 1912. As Premier, Minister of Public Works and, later, Minister of Education for eleven years in total, Scott led his government in building a public administration and infrastructure for the new province. He supervised the construction of the legislative building in Regina and opened the **UNIVERSITY OF SASKATCHEWAN** in Saskatoon. Agriculture was the cornerstone of the new government, and the University of Saskatchewan became the first university in Canada to have a College of Agriculture alongside the other professional colleges.

Walter Scott.

From 1905 to 1916, the Scott government used the co-operative model to assist farm families to build and maintain a rural telephone system and the Saskatchewan Co-operative Elevator Company. The government provided financial backing, but the farmers were required to invest some of their own money in the co-operative and thus had a voice in its operation. The Scott government set a bold social policy by banning the bar and establishing government-controlled liquor stores. This was a step toward full **PROHIBITION**, which came under the leadership of Scott's successor, **WILLIAM MARTIN**. In 1916, the Scott government passed legislation to provide the franchise to women.

Throughout his premiership, Scott suffered from manic depression and was absent from his office up to six months of each year. With extra effort during his days of good health and with loyal support from **JAMES CALDER**, his Deputy Premier, Scott was able to lead an active and progressive government. By 1916, two problem areas began to weigh heavily on Scott. Reverend Murdock MacKinnon, a Presbyterian minister in Regina, launched a public campaign against the Scott government for its legislative amendments to the School Act, which, according to MacKinnon, encouraged the Catholics to establish their own school system. At the same time, the Scott government was accused of graft in the letting of contracts for public projects. Several members of the Scott government were accused of accepting bribes in a vote concerning the distribution of liquor licenses. Full investigations cleared Scott and his Cabinet of any wrongdoing, but the charges and the battle with MacKinnon were enough to force Scott to resign in ill health on October 20, 1916.

The Scotts retired to Victoria, but his health never recovered to the point that he was able to return to his career in journalism. In 1935, Scott was committed to the Homewood Sanitarium in Guelph, Ontario, where he died on March 23, 1938.

Walter Scott's legacy was assisting in the creation of Saskatchewan by building its public administration and civil service, fostering a public infrastructure with a legislative building and a provincial university, and promoting an agricultural industry and a rural way of life for thousands of new settlers. To assist the **FARMING** population, under a co-operative model, the Scott government led the way in the establishment of an elevator system and rural telephone companies. Scott was a man of the people and won all five elections he contested with ever larger majorities. His social policies of closing the bars and granting the vote to women were progressive for the time. Under Scott's leadership, the provincial **LIBERAL PARTY** became a strong force that stayed in office continuously from 1905 to 1944, with one exception from 1929 to 1934. *Gordon L. Barnhart*

FURTHER READING: Barnhart, Gordon L. 2000. *"Peace, Progress and Prosperity": A Biography of Saskatchewan's First Premier, T. Walter Scott.* Regina: Canadian Plains Research Center; — (ed.). 2004. *Saskatchewan Premiers of the Twentieth Century.* Regina: Canadian Plains Research Center.

SCOTTISH SETTLEMENTS. The settlement of people of Scottish origin in Saskatchewan dates back more than two centuries to the **FUR TRADE**. Scots headed not only the North West Company, but also the rival McLeod and Co., and they played a prominent role in the Hudson's Bay Company, which recruited personnel from the Orkney Islands and from Lewis in the Outer Hebrides. Many Scots involved in the fur trade as managers, factors, traders, and explorers took Native wives, with the result that many **MÉTIS** were partly of Scottish origin and Scottish surnames became frequent among Native Indians and Métis. The Scottish influence on Native and Métis culture was further reflected in music (fiddle music and reels) and food (bannock). When Thomas Douglas, Earl of Selkirk, established a large settlement of Highland Scots north of Winnipeg in 1811, within five years these settlers were confronted by Métis led by Cuthbert Grant, who was partly of Scottish origin himself. Several decades later, it was William MacTavish who advised the Métis to form their own "provisional government" in Manitoba in 1869. Scots settled at Prince Albert as early as 1866; their settlement spread west and south into the MacDowall and Roddick areas. Métis partly of Scottish origin again played a role in the **NORTH-WEST RESISTANCE** in Saskatchewan in 1885; yet it was another Scottish-Canadian, Prime Minister Sir John A. Macdonald, who sent Canadian troops westward to quell this rebellion.

Gaelic-speaking crofters who had been considered "surplus population" in the Highlands and Outer Hebrides during the Highland Clearances were sent to the Saskatchewan prairies during the 1880s. In 1883–84, inspired by the philanthropic effects of Lady Cathcart, nearly 300 crofters settled the St. Andrew's and Benbecula Colonies near Moosomin and Wapella. Then in 1888 seventy-nine crofter families from Lewis settled forty-two homesteads around Dunrea, north of Killarney and west of Pelican Lake, in the District of Turtle Mountain, Manitoba, and from Harris twenty-seven homesteads around Hilton, north of Pelican Lake, in the District of Argyle. The following year another wave of forty-nine crofter families (252 persons) arrived under the auspices of the Imperial Colonization Board and settled fifty-six homesteads in the Lothian Colony around Dunleath, Stornoway, and Kessock, north of Saltcoats, as well as sixteen homesteads in the King Colony west of Saltcoats. While the Pelican Lake settlements succeeded, the Saltcoats colonies had essentially failed by 1900 due to adverse climatic conditions, and many of the settlers had scattered.

During the 1880s, Scottish settlers were also attracted to the **QU'APPELLE VALLEY**, settling around Abernethy in the Qu'Appelle Farming Colony, and at Indian Head, where the extensive Bell Farm was located. By 1890, Scottish-Canadians from Ontario homesteaded to the north of Regina around Lumsden, Craven, Condie, Tregarva, and Brora. They spread eastward, settling around Glenbrae, Markinch, Cupar, Dysart, Dalrymple, and the McDonald Hills. Further north, following the Arm River Valley; many communities along the Qu'Appelle, Long Lake, and Saskatchewan Railway between Regina and Saskatoon were given Scottish names (including Lumsden, Bethune, Findlater, Craik, Girvin, Davidson, and Dundurn). After 1902, Scottish-origin migrants from Ontario and Nova Scotia, as well as from Scotland itself, settled neighbouring districts to the east of this line (such as Lothian, the Allan Hills, and Burnmore). Meanwhile, between 1885 and 1907, Scottish settlement continued to spread in southeastern Saskatchewan, from Wolseley southeastward into the Moffat district, where a steady influx of Lowland Scottish immigrants from Ayrshire, Perthshire, Aberdeenshire, and the Lothians concentrated in four townships centred on the Presbyterian kirk in Moffat; to this day their fine stone houses bear testimony to their masonry skills. Scottish settlers also concentrated around Glenavon and Peebles, and in the Moose Mountain region (around Arcola, Carlyle, Douglaston, Inchkeith, Langbank, Kennedy, Kelso, Doonside). Orkney Islanders founded their own communities such as Orcadia in Orkney RM just west of Yorkton, and Orkney and Burnbrae in southwestern Saskatchewan.

The Scottish impact in Saskatchewan was pronounced: **PATRICK GAMMIE LAURIE** founded the *Saskatchewan Herald* at Battleford in 1878; Thomas MacNutt was the first Speaker of the Saskatchewan Legislature; **WALTER SCOTT** became the first Premier of Saskatchewan and editor of the *Regina Leader*; **ARCHIBALD PETER MCNAB** was Lieutenant-Governor from 1936 to 1944; and

Thomas MacNutt, a Scot, was the first Speaker of the Saskatchewan Legislature.

Premier **T.C. DOUGLAS** led the CCF and its transformation into the NDP.

By 1911 there were over a million Canadians of Scottish origin, 282,000 of them in western Canada and 70,000 in Saskatchewan. By 1941 the population of Scottish origin in Saskatchewan was over 108,000; people of Scottish origin were estimated to comprise 35% of the population of Avonlea, 29% of Lashburn and Wapella, 28% of Lumsden, and 23% of Saltcoats. By 2001, 172,300 Saskatchewan residents claimed to be of Scottish descent—16,600 (9.6%) solely and 155,700 (90.1%) partly. They comprised the third largest ethnic category in the province's population.

Lasting Scottish influence in Saskatchewan is reflected in pipe bands, Highland games, Presbyterian and United churches, and some Anglican and Catholic parishes (such as St. Andrew's, founded in 1888 as the focal point of St. Andrew's colony). Numerous Scottish place names are found throughout Saskatchewan, e.g., Stranraer, Buccleuch, McMichael, Macrorie, Bannock, Jedburgh, Glenburn, Glenbogie. Glenside even has Scottish street names (Arran, Kintyre, Islay). However, as many communities were named by enthusiastic railwaymen who happened largely to be of Scottish origin, not all community names were indicative of Scottish settlement: for example, McMahon, Glen Bain, McLeod, and Gilnockie were settled mainly by Germans; Glen Mary by Norwegians; Kylemore by Icelanders and Poles; Murraydale by Cree; Buchanan by Ukrainians and Doukhobors; and Glen McPerson by French, Germans and Norwegians. (*See also* **ETHNIC BLOC SETTLEMENTS**)   *Alan Anderson*

FURTHER READING: Norton, W. 1994. *Help Us to a Better Land: Crofter Colonies in the Prairie West.* Regina: Canadian Plains Research Center.

SCRIP. The Manitoba Act of 1870 provided a land grant of 1.4 million acres for distribution among the **MÉTIS** in exchange for extinguishing their indigenous title to the land. Dollar-valued land certificates known as scrip entitled the bearer to receive government-surveyed homestead lands at a later date. Although scrip allowed individual claimants to choose any western lands open for settlement, it initiated the widespread dispersal of the Métis from Manitoba. An estimated two-thirds of the province's 10,000 persons of mixed decent in 1870 departed over the next twenty years. Most Métis headed west and settled near the Catholic mission settlements around Fort Edmonton and the **SOUTH SASKATCHEWAN RIVER**.   *Holden Stoffel*

FURTHER READING: Flanagan, Thomas. 1991. *Métis Lands in Manitoba.* Calgary: University of Calgary Press; Sprague, D.N. 1988. *Canada and the Métis, 1869–1885.* Waterloo, ON: Wilfred Laurier University Press.

SEARLE GRAIN COMPANY. In 1921 Stewart A. Searle, newly graduated from Yale University, and his father Augustus Searle formed the Searle Grain Company Ltd; Stewart became vice-president and general manager. The headquarters were initially in Melfort, Saskatchewan. The company began operations in 1921-22 with twenty-five elevators, all located on Canadian Northern Lines in northeastern Saskatchewan. Starting as an inexperienced grain buyer, Augustus Searle had by 1895 become chief executive officer of several grain companies. When the Canadian Northern Railway owners looked for investors to build elevators on their newly constructed lines, they invited the Peaveys, then an established grain family in Minneapolis, to tour the west. The Peaveys took with them Augustus Searle, and the tour led to the formation of several individual companies, all on different rail lines.

Augustus Searle, along with Peavey associates, purchased two existing elevator companies. In 1914 Searle formed the Home Grain Company Ltd; starting with fifteen elevators, it grew to seventy-three by 1923–all of them were in Alberta. With H. Sellers and J.C. Gage, the Searles formed the Northland Elevator Company to lease and operate the 7.5 million-bushel terminal at Fort William; later they were involved in terminal ownership and operations on the West Coast. In 1929 the Searles moved to consolidate their operations, merging the Saskatchewan Elevator Company, the Liberty Elevator Company and the Home Elevator Company with the Searle Elevator Company. This made the Searle Grain Company, with 277 elevators, the third largest non-farmer-owned company.

Between 1929 and 1948, Searle acquired the Malden Elevator Company, the Standard Elevator Company, and the Quaker Oats Company; and in 1948 it purchased fifty-one elevators left over from the dispersal sale of the Reliance Elevator Company to the three Pools and **UNITED GRAIN GROWERS** a year earlier. With 417 elevators, this made Searle the largest of the private companies. In the 1960s, with the growing concern over duplication of facilities and competition, private companies began to consider mergers. In 1967 the Searle Grain Company amalgamated with the Federal Grain Company, Alberta Pacific being included in the merger. The new company, named Federal Grain Company Ltd, was sold to the Pools five years later, in 1972.

Gary Storey

FURTHER READING: Anderson, C.W. 1991. *Grain: The Entrepreneurs*. Winnipeg: Watson and Dwyer Publishing; Fowke, V. 1957. *The National Policy and the Wheat Economy*. Toronto: University of Toronto Press; Wilson, C.F. 1978. *A Century of Canadian Grain*. Saskatoon: Western Producer Prairie Books.

Science and Technology

Diane Secoy

Science (from Latin *scientia*) originally meant knowledge of any kind; we now use this word to mean the rational examination of the natural world without resort to supernatural explanations for conditions or events. *Technology* originally meant the study (Greek *logos*) of tools and activities or crafts (Greek *techne*) that transform the natural environment and make life easier. The word is now used to mean the tools and techniques themselves; increasingly, it also means the application of scientific knowledge to the solving of industrial problems. Humans are not the only species whose members make things to protect themselves or use tools to help them in acquiring food: some bird species build elaborate nests, sea otters use stones to crack open shells, and chimpanzees prepare sticks to prod anthills. But humans make a far greater range of immensely more complex tools.

Technology is considerably older than science. Humans, including our hominid ancestors, have been using tools for over three million years, as attested by stone axes and scrapers dating from that time in eastern Africa. Over the ages, all societies have developed technology to better their lives in providing food and shelter. Technology is therefore ancient and universal; science, on the other hand, is of much more recent origin and was limited to a handful of civilized societies until a few hundred years ago. The search for natural explanations of the world and the universe began in ancient Greece around 500 BCE, but did not really become widespread until after the 17th century in Europe and elsewhere. Worldwide, science and technology are now major influences on our lives and have created domains of increased specialization.

Following the clearance of the land by the melting of the most recent GLACIERS, starting certainly 25,000 years ago but possibly as early as 70,000 years ago, Palaeo-Indians moved from Siberia into the Americas, bringing with them their traditional technology. Life would not be possible in the climatic conditions of post-glacial Saskatchewan without the tools to hunt animals, dig out and prepare plants for food and medicines, build shelters and boats, prepare skins for clothing, and start and maintain fires. This technology thus involved materials such as stone, bone, antler, horn and wood, as well as animal hides, teeth and claws. Dyes were also prepared from natural pigments to add an aesthetic value to purely utilitarian functions.

The exploring and colonizing Europeans brought their own technologies with them, as well as their early science. PETER POND and other early 18th-century explorers brought steel tools, guns, powder and the compass to the region. The use of steel (rather than stone or copper) axes and knives as well as the introduction of guns for hunting and armament made a great impression on the indigenous inhabitants, as always happens with the advent of new technology. These objects quickly became prized trading items, which could be obtained in exchange for furs, hides, meat and other local products.

During the 19th century, work on Saskatchewan's natural environment and its population was carried out by people from outside the area. Early in the century, the nature of exploring changed from the individuals or small groups sent out by the fur companies to larger groups sent by the British government to map northwestern Canada and identify travel routes. Of great importance were the British naval expeditions of the 1820s led by Sir JOHN FRANKLIN: these expeditions, intended at first to find the hypothetical Northwest Passage to the Pacific Ocean, were broadened to map not only the coast but the interior drained by the rivers which emptied into the polar seas. The natural history notes and collections kept by Dr. JOHN RICHARDSON resulted in a number of informative writings–most notably the first scientific treatise on the birds of North America. Many North American bird species were first described from skins collected in the central and northern areas of what is now Saskatchewan.

The process of cataloguing the natural resources of the province continued with the formal establishment in 1842 of the Canadian Geological Survey, the oldest scientific agency in Canada. The Survey mapped the mineral deposits of the province, particularly in the northern Shield. In the 1860s and 1870s, the southern parts of the province were surveyed for possible transcontinental railway routes. By intent and interest the surveyors, who might be engineers, geologists or natural historians such as JOHN MACOUN, also catalogued the soils as well as the plant and animal species they encountered. Such surveys of the prairie soils led to the federal government encouraging farmers from eastern Canada and western Europe to settle on the prairies. The federal government also developed in 1881 the Indian Head Experimental Farm, a part of the network of AGRICULTURE CANADA RESEARCH STATIONS, to assist immigrant prairie farmers to adjust to the special practices needed to till cold prairie soils under dry climatic conditions.

Natural history surveys identified the Saskatchewan prairies as an important part of the mid-continental migration flyways, and led to the establishment of the Last Mountain Lake Bird Sanctuary in 1887—the first Canadian sanctuary for wild species, and the second in North America. This early protection of the migrating flocks of birds from their northern breeding grounds to their wintering ground further south was an important part of the growing recognition of the need for the CONSERVATION of the wild species which had been so abundant when the first European settlers came to North America.

The maturation of Canadian science and technology continued in the 20th century. In Saskatchewan, work in these areas began to be done by local people, and not only by outsiders.

A major factor was the development of the UNIVERSITY OF SASKATCHEWAN (U of S). Established in Saskatoon in 1909, it was intended from the outset that part of its mandate was to be applied research, particularly in agriculture, as well as general education in the arts and sciences. It was the first university in Canada to integrate agriculture with the traditional disciplines in a single institution. As it grew, it added various branches of engineering as well as the health sciences, which were becoming increasingly dependent on technology. The philosophy of sponsoring research applied to local problems is seen in the first grant bestowed by the Saskatchewan government to the university: in 1918 a sum of $25,000 was granted, of which $10,000 went to Professor R.D. McLaurin, a chemist, to investigate the production of methane from straw. In the 1930s, emphasis was placed on drought problems and on means of controlling grasshopper outbreaks, although the economic depression obviously reduced the ability of the government to fund the university. The addition of the chemist JOHN SPINKS to the faculty in the early 1930s illustrates the "coming of age" of the scientific capabilities of the province and the West as a whole, a process which was accelerated when Spinks succeeded in providing refuge for the German chemist GERHARD HERZBERG when he was forced to flee Nazi Germany. Herzberg, who received a Nobel prize in chemistry, is one of two Nobel-winning chemists associated with Saskatchewan; the other is HENRY TAUBE, born in Neudorf, who received his prize in 1983.

The expansion of the scientific and technological capabilities of Canada to meet the demands of World War II led to important changes in the structures of support for these activities. The National Research Council (NRC), formed originally in 1916 to conduct applied research for industrial concerns, expanded during the war under the direction of C.J. MACKENZIE. Following the war, Mackenzie strove to place Canada within the internationally recognized research countries by strengthening the support for pure or basic science as well as for project or targeted research; he also increased the level of extramural funding, particularly to the universities. This increase in scientific research necessitated expansion, and the NRC gave rise to a

Photos from top:

NEIL CRICHTON PHOTO/SASKATCHEWAN ARCHIVES BOARD 64-412-07

Saskatchewan Research Council Building, University of Saskatchewan, Saskatoon, 1964.

GIBSON PHOTO/UNIVERSITY OF SASKATCHEWAN ARCHIVES A-7563

Left to right, Dr. Leon Katz, Dr. V.V. Vladimirskii, President J. W. T. Spinks examining equipment in Linear Accelerator Lab, November 1964.

UNIVERSITY OF SASKATCHEWAN ARCHIVES A-7740

Robert Coupland, director of the Matador Project, taking a soil sample in a field of grass, 1969.

UNIVERSITY OF SASKATCHEWAN ARCHIVES A-5289

Gerhard Herzberg, at a dinner to honour him for his 1971 Nobel Prize in Chemistry, February 2, 1972 in Marquis Hall.

PETER WILSON PHOTO/ SASKATCHEWAN ARCHIVES BOARD S-SP-A 21886-16, SASKATOON STARPHOENIX FONDS

Henry Taube, winner of the 1983 Nobel Prize in Chemistry in 1983, giving a lecture, Saskatoon, May 1984.

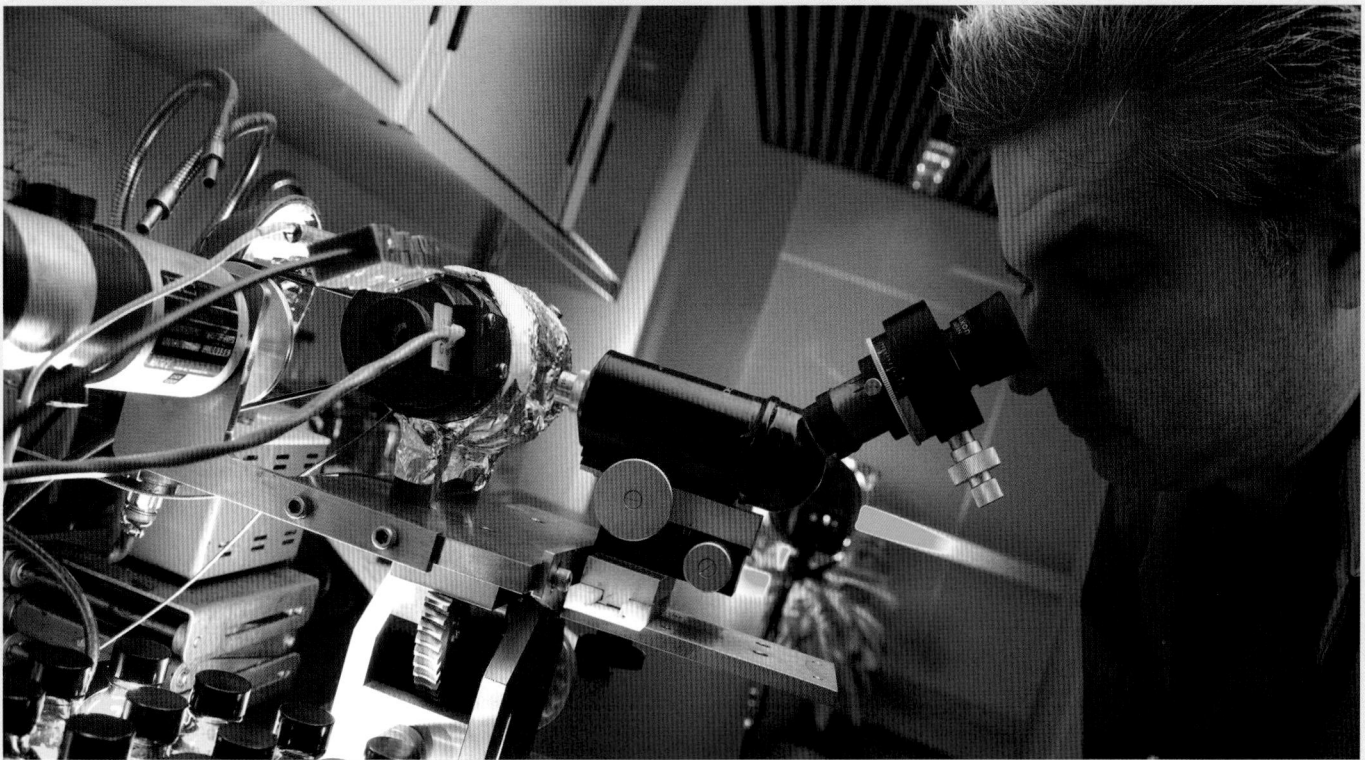

At the Petroleum Technology Research Centre, Regina Research Park, University of Regina, technologist Kevin Rispler uses the spinning drop tensiometer to screen chemicals for an optimal combination that can be used to enhance oil recovery.

number of other agencies to lead and support research in science and technology, defense, medicine, atomic energy, and space. This increased attention to high-level technology was further stimulated by the launching of the Sputnik satellite by the USSR in 1957. With expansion, NRC was able to fund large-scale projects involving great numbers of researchers and major pieces of equipment.

The first of these "Big Science" projects in 1962 was the Linear Accelerator at the University of Saskatchewan, under the direction of LEON KATZ. Another ambitious initiative in 1966 was the MATADOR Project, under ROBERT COUPLAND, aimed at the long-term study of a natural grasslands community. This project was also significant because it involved a new institution: the small church-run Regina College was linked to the University of Saskatchewan and became the Regina Campus of the university in 1961. Expansion of the institution followed, including the hiring of a number of faculty members in all of the basic sciences, and, shortly afterwards, the addition of faculty members in engineering. Following the development of the UNIVERSITY OF REGINA (U of R) as a separate institution in 1974, both universities have continued to expand their research capabilities in a wide range of scientific and technological areas, both in research units and as individuals.

This expansion has been enhanced by partnerships between the two universities, the government, agencies, and industrial partners. These partnerships can take the form of funding, but increasingly they result in the growth of research parks on or near university land. The SASKATCHEWAN RESEARCH COUNCIL, started by the provincial government to fund targeted university research, opened a laboratory on the U of S campus in 1958, in order to benefit from this close association. Agriculture Canada, a natural partner for the College of Agriculture, set up the Saskatoon Research Station at the university in 1957. The research parks at both institutions continue to grow while science-based technologies are becoming more and more important as determinants

of economic growth. The U of S has a number of agriculture-based units, particularly in biotechnology as well as in health and engineering; the CANADIAN LIGHT SOURCE is a scion of the early Linear Accelerator. The U of R, as a younger institution, has fewer such units so far; these are in petroleum engineering, as well as in information and environmental sciences. The addition of the third university, the FIRST NATIONS UNIVERSITY OF CANADA, has provided possibilities of greater participation by First Nations people in both research and industry. The presence of the SASKATCHEWAN INSTITUTE OF APPLIED SCIENCE AND TECHNOLOGY and of the SASKATCHEWAN INDIAN INSTITUTE OF TECHNOLOGIES allows for the provincial training of the workforce so important for the successful development of technology-based industry.

In addition to the universities, research and development take place in government agencies and in the industry. The POTASH industry has developed processes, such as the world's first solution mine at Kalium in 1964, which allow easier access to the type of mineral that would otherwise require excavation. The ROYAL SASKATCHEWAN MUSEUM in Regina undertakes significant studies into the ecology and paleontology of the province; the SUBSURFACE GEOLOGY LABORATORY continues to explore the mineral deposits of the province; and the Saskatchewan Science Centre ensures that simpler aspects of science and technology are popularized and made accessible to children and adults alike.

At the beginning of the 21st century, Saskatchewan's research and development activities are performed and funded by a network of university researchers, federal and provincial government agencies, international agencies, and industry. The conspicuous presence of these institutions within the province indicates the importance of their activities to all areas of society, as well as the "coming of age" of Saskatchewan: the bread basket of the world has become a region where increasing diversification reflects the more dynamic role played on the national and international stage. (*See* HISTORY OF SASKATCHEWAN)

SEBESTYEN, EDMUND ALEXANDER (1920-). Born on March 10, 1920, journalist Edmund Sebestyen has promoted the city of Saskatoon to its residents and the rest of the world. From 1948 to 1991, he worked as a journalist with the Saskatoon *StarPhoenix* newspaper in various positions from editorial cartoonist to executive vice-president. Sebestyen was vice-president of the 1971 Canada Winter Games and assisted with the construction of Mount Blackstrap as the ski venue. Mr. Sebestyen is also involved with organizations such as Tree Canada Foundation and the International Newspaper Marketing Association, of which he was president. He was named Saskatoon's CFQC-TV "Citizen of the Year" in 1986 and was invested as a Member of the Order of Canada in 1994.

SECONDARY PICKETING SUPREME COURT DECISION. In a far-reaching decision, the Supreme Court of Canada ruled that secondary picketing is legal. The court ruling occurred after a long labour dispute between RETAIL WHOLESALE AND DEPARTMENT STORE UNION (RWDSU) Local 558 in Saskatoon and Pepsi Cola, which started in 1997. RWDSU members began to picket several retail outlets and a hotel. Pepsi obtained an injunction to halt the secondary picketing, but the Supreme Court of Appeal overturned the injunction. The legal dispute finally ended up in the Supreme Court of Canada, which in a precedent-setting decision in 2002 unanimously ruled that secondary picketing is now legal in Canada. This means that workers can not only picket their employer, but can also engage in secondary picketing against their employer's customers.

George Manz

SEDCO/SOCO. The government of Saskatchewan has used a variety of corporate structures to attempt to stimulate the growth of small business in the province through direct investment or financing. The Saskatchewan Economic Development Corporation (SEDCO) was established as a Saskatchewan CROWN CORPORATION in 1963. Its purpose was to foster economic development in Saskatchewan primarily through commercial loans to provincial companies. From an asset base of $10 million in 1966, SEDCO grew to an asset base of over $250 million at its peak in 1990. In addition to lending money through mortgages and other secured debt instruments, at various times SEDCO provided equity investments in businesses, constructed industrial parks and buildings for companies, provided business advice to its clients, and developed the first science park in Saskatchewan, Innovation Place.

SEDCO began suffering substantial losses in the early 1980s as a result of the failures of businesses it had provided with financing. In 1982 the CONSERVATIVE PARTY formed government after over

a decade of New Democratic governments. SEDCO had suffered some high-profile business failures in advance of the 1982 election, and the new government was much more conservative in its approach to making annual expense reserves in anticipation of future failures. The losses resulting from these reserves immediately eroded the retained earnings built up over the nearly two decades of SEDCO's existence. Losses continued throughout the 1980s, resulting in an ever increasing deficit in retained earnings; the election of the NEW DEMOCRATIC PARTY in 1991 did nothing to reverse the trend. In the eyes of the government, these losses created a low level of confidence from the general public in the competence of SEDCO, and during 1994 it was announced that it was to cease operations; it did so in 1995, and all the assets of the company were transferred to its parent company, Crown Investments Corporation (CIC).

The Saskatchewan Opportunities Corporation (SOCO) was created in 1994 to provide a new investment option for small businesses within targeted industrial sectors, while also reacting to public concerns over the performance of SEDCO. SOCO was established with a much more restricted mandate than SEDCO, the focus being equity investment rather than mortgage financing. The size of transactions was to be generally limited to under $3 million, and retail business was excluded from SOCO's investment policy. The six strategic sectors identified were agriculture, forestry, tourism (cultural industries), mining, energy, and advanced technology. The mandate and objectives all dealt with supporting the growth of the economy through strategic investment in Saskatchewan businesses. Investment guidelines were established that stressed the importance of the viability of their clients and the need for co-investment with other financial institutions.

In August 1995 Innovation Place, the science and technology park developed by the province on UNIVERSITY OF SASKATCHEWAN land, was transferred to SOCO from CIC. Innovation Place had been initiated by SEDCO in 1977. The transfer of this major asset dramatically increased the scope of SOCO's operations. Innovation Place and later the development of the Regina Research Park were managed by a division of SOCO separate from the Investments Division. In 2002, as part of the provincial budget it was announced that the province's investment activity carried on by both SOCO and CIC would be consolidated within CIC's subsidiary, CIC Industrial Interests Inc. (CIC III). This subsidiary held the assets of investments CIC had made in private industrial projects; as a result, these investment assets of SOCO were transferred to CIC later that year. These assets, together with those of CIC III, were combined and used to form a new Crown corporation: Investment Saskatchewan. The assets and staff of Innovation Place and the Regina Research Park

remained with SOCO, which has since restricted its activity to the development and management of specialized real estate owned by the government for economic development purposes—primarily Innovation Place and the Regina Research Park.

Doug Tastad

SEDGWICK, RAYMOND (1914–97). Raymond Edward "Buff" Sedgwick was born at Elrose, Saskatchewan on March 16, 1914. He worked in the trucking industry prior to joining the army; after his discharge in 1946 he returned to Saskatchewan, working for the Intercontinental plant in Saskatoon. Sedgwick became shop steward and vice-president of his local, the United Packing House Workers. He served as president of the Saskatoon and District Labour Council, and as a vice-president on the SASKATCHEWAN FEDERATION OF LABOUR (SFL) executive council. Sedgwick was a political activist, deeply involved in provincial, federal and civic politics. He was a founding board member of the Saskatoon Community Clinic. He worked as a representative with the Canadian Labour Congress for more than twenty years, retiring in 1979. He died on November 3, 1997. In his memory the SFL established the Ray Sedgwick Scholarship of up to $6,000 for the successful applicant to the Labour College of Canada Residential Program.

George Rosenau

SEIFERT, LILLIAN (1911–98). Born in Montreal in 1911, Blanche Lillian Seifert moved to Saskatchewan in 1924. While her husband operated a grain elevator, Seifert began a career that focused on caring for people who suffered from illness or misfortune. Throughout rural Saskatchewan she responded to various medical emergencies, delivered many babies, and offered her assistance to doctors. Seifert's work also involved visiting senior citizens, consoling the bereaved, and comforting the terminally ill. She retired to Maple Creek in 1973 and despite personal illness, Lillian Seifert continued to show exemplary leadership in volunteering. She was awarded the Saskatchewan Order of Merit in 1987 for her selfless community work. Seifert died in 1998.

SEMENIUK, GEORGE (1938–). Born in 1938, George Semeniuk is one of the longest-serving labour leaders and most experienced trade union staff representatives in the province. Following his schooling, he went to work in 1956 for Burns Foods at a meat-packing plant in Prince Albert, and immediately joined the United Packinghouse Workers of America Local 234P. He became active in the union, and served as president of Local 234P for six years; he was also president of the union's provincial council for two years.

In 1969 Semeniuk was hired as a full-time

union staff representative with the RETAIL WHOLESALE AND DEPARTMENT STORE UNION. In 1970, he moved to the United Food and Commercial Workers (UFCW) as a union representative, becoming an International Representative with the union in 1988. In 1989, he was named Western Assistant to the Canadian Director of UFCW, a position he held until he retired from the union in May 1997. From 1997 to 2000 Semeniuk served as a senior labour relations officer with the provincial Department of Labour, conciliating, mediating and settling industrial disputes.

George Semeniuk was also president of the SASKATCHEWAN FEDERATION OF LABOUR for two years, serving on its executive for seventeen years. He was a Canadian Labour Congress vice-president for one term, and president of the Prince Albert Labour Council for two years. In his three decades of service to the labour movement, George Semeniuk bargained numerous collective agreements, settled countless grievances and arbitrations, and presented cases to the Labour Relations Board. He also advised the Minister of Labour on occupational health and safety issues, and was named to the board of directors of the Potash Corporation of Saskatchewan.

George Semeniuk is now retired and living in Saskatoon.   *Garnet Dishaw*

SEPARATE SCHOOL DIVISIONS. Separate school divisions in Saskatchewan are publicly funded school divisions whose mandate is to provide religious and general education to members of the Christian community of the province. Members of the faith concerned (either Protestant or Catholic) are constitutionally guaranteed a right to denominational schooling and are entitled to establish a separate school system centred on the teachings of their faith. In Saskatchewan, the separate school divisions are primarily Catholic, although Protestant separate school divisions do exist. There are currently fourteen Catholic separate school boards in the province. These school boards educate over 37,000 students from kindergarten to grade twelve. The distinctive mission of Catholic school boards and schools emanates a commitment to integrating the faith into all aspects of Catholic schooling.

The separate school concept was established in Ontario in the 1840s, when a compromise was reached that provided for the right to denominational schooling for the Ontario Catholic community. These rights were later to be enshrined in the British North America Act of 1867 (later called the Constitution Act); the guarantee of minority denominational schooling rights was one of the most contentious issues in Confederation.

Church-run schools in Saskatchewan were established shortly after the arrival of the first European settlers. In 1875, The Northwest Territories Act was passed, representing the first time that schools were established by law in the Territories. The Act provided for separate schools that were to be publicly funded through the property tax. Over the next few years, governors of the North-West Territories developed the policies that would lay the foundations for schools. The Ordinance Providing for the Organization of Schools in the North West Territories was passed in 1884; Section 29 of the Ordinance established that Protestant and Catholic public and separate schools were to be protected. The role of the separate schools became an issue in the negotiations with the federal government over provincial status; education, and particularly the status of denominational rights and schooling, was the main issue for discussion between the government of the North-West Territories and the federal government.

The Saskatchewan Act was passed in 1905, allowing for schools to remain essentially as they were before the province entered Confederation. This Act reaffirmed the status of separate schools and the right to denominational schooling as set out in the Constitution Act of 1867; it provided that Catholic elementary schools (grades one to eight) were to be funded in the same manner as public schools. Subsequently, in 1907, the Secondary School Act was passed; this legislation outlined the processes for establishing high schools, but there were no provisions in the Act for the establishment of separate high schools.

The period from 1910 up until WORLD WAR I saw the establishment of many Catholic separate school districts. Starting in 1918, however, there was considerable pressure applied to Premier SCOTT to eliminate separate schools in the province. Separate schools came under attack once again in the 1930s. The Conservatives, under Premier J.T.M. ANDERSON, enacted legislation that prohibited French as a language of instruction and prohibited the wearing of religious garments and the display of religious symbols in public schools (often referred to as the "garb and symbol" law). These pieces of legislation were thinly veiled attempts to control the expansion of Catholic education in Saskatchewan.

The period of 1950 to 1962 saw unprecedented growth of Catholic separate schools in Saskatchewan, with nine new Catholic separate school divisions being established. In 1951, the Catholic Section of the Saskatchewan School Trustees' Association was established. This group was charged with representing the interests of the Catholic school boards and schools in the province. Although there were six new Catholic separate school divisions established in the 1960s, three of them did not survive and were disestablished before the beginning of the 1970s. In 1964, the right to local taxation and government grants was extended to Catholic high schools, allowing many existing private denominational high schools to be absorbed into existing Catholic separate school divisions. No new separate school divisions were established in the 1970s or 1980s. In 1978 the Education Act was passed, affirming the provisions for denominational schooling and instituted procedures for the establishment of Protestant and Catholic separate school divisions and schools.   *Paul M. Newton*

FURTHER READING: McDonough, K. 2003. "Saskatchewan." Pp. 13–19 in J.J. Flynn (ed.), *Catholic Schools Across Canada: Into the New Millennium*. Toronto: Canadian Catholic School Trustees' Association.

SERGEANT BILL. Saskatchewan's most famous goat, Sergeant Bill left his hometown of Broadview to serve as the mascot of the Fifth Canadian Battalion in France during WORLD WAR I. Bill was gassed, wounded, and decorated (his medals included the 1914 Star, the General Service Medal, and the Victory Medal) before he safely returned to Canada, finishing his years out to pasture in his hometown. After his death, plans were to display him in the province's proposed War Memorial Museum. Instead, Bill resided briefly during the 1920s in the reading room of the SASKATCHEWAN LEGISLATIVE BUILDING, where the area where he stood became a designated meeting place, and then returned to Broadview, where he is now honoured in the Broadview Museum.   *David McLennan*

SASKATCHEWAN ARCHIVES BOARD R-A10210-1
Sergeant Bill.

SERVICE EMPLOYEES INTERNATIONAL UNION (SEIU). In 1945, employees of St. Paul's Hospital in Saskatoon formed the Building Service Employees International Union (BSEIU) Local 287 in 1945 with seventy-five charter members. A year later Saskatoon City Hospital became BSEIU Local 293. Moose Jaw Union Hospital was organized as Local 299 in 1946; Swift Current became Local 336 in the following year. These two locals worked together for several years, even jointly hiring business agents. Saskatchewan Joint Council, BSEIU #15 was also formed in 1946 and acted as a coordinating body for Saskatchewan locals. Later the three Saskatoon hospital locals amalgamated and became

BSEIU 333 and in 1964 the Local 333 University Hospital section became their own Local 333UH. In 1968 the union changed its name to Service Employees International Union (SEIU). In 1972, SEIU began bargaining hospital and nursing home contracts directly with the province. Provincial negotiations were established for nursing home workers with the two employer organizations–Saskatchewan Association of Special Care Homes and Saskatchewan Health-Care Association in 1983. In 1997, the provincial government established the Dorsey Commission which created three new bargaining units in the health sector that reflected the newly reformed health delivery system. The three units were nurses, health service providers and health support practitioners. SEIU represents some of the service providers. In 2000 SEIU Canada became the first Canadian union to receive its own charter, recognizing its independence from the international union. Today, Local 299 represents over 1,950 members in south-central Saskatchewan, Local 333 represents 7,000 workers in north-central Saskatchewan, and Local 336 represents 1,250 in the southwest part of the province. These members work in healthcare, municipalities, school boards, community-based organizations, light industrial, day cares, addictions and group homes, intermediate care homes, Canadian Blood Services and service industries.   *Barbara Cape and Tanya Sosulski*

SERVICE FRANSASKOIS D'ÉDUCATION DES ADULTES (FRANSASKOIS ADULT EDUCATION SERVICE).

The *Service fransaskois d'éducation des adultes*, first called the *Centre fransaskois d'éducation permanente* (Fransaskois Centre for Continuing Education), was established by COLLÈGE MATHIEU on January 7, 1986. With its headquarters located at Collège Mathieu in Gravelbourg, the *Service fransaskois d'éducation des adultes* provided communities who requested them with services similar to the adult education programs offered by the community colleges of the day. However, the *Service fransaskois d'éducation des adultes* was different from the regional colleges because it operated in French and it served the entire province. Three months after its inception, the *Service fransaskois d'éducation des adultes* offered its first course, computer science. Later, education officers were placed in various communities around the province, particularly those with a significant francophone population. In 1990, the *Service fransaskois d'éducation des adultes* introduced a training program for employees and volunteers from francophone groups and organizations in the province.

Although its primary focus was community education, the *Service fransaskois d'éducation des adultes* soon added professional training programs leading to diplomas and certificates. It has also acted

as an educational broker and has worked in partnership with various colleges and universities. In 2000, the *Service fransaskois d'éducation des adultes* changed its name to *Service fransaskois de formation aux adultes*. It is now involved in a number of literacy programs around the province, and is responsible for a distance-education program leading to a certificate in entrepreneurship and small business.   *Michelle Arsenault*

734 (REGINA) AND 737 (SASKATOON) COMMUNICATION SQUADRON, COMMUNICATIONS RESERVE.

The Communication Reserve is part of the Information Management Group of National Defence Headquarters of the Canadian Forces. Its mission is to provide combat-capable information technology and management services to the Canadian Forces, and links to the Canadian military and civilian communities across the country. The Communication Reserve uses modern equipment such as digital radios, ground satellite terminals, fibre optics and computers. Communication Reservists are trained as ground soldiers and wear the army uniform; however, they are often called upon to work and train with other elements (Army, Navy or Air Force) of the reserve and regular forces. Some units in the Communication Reserve also provide manning support to the Navy Transportable Tactical Command Centres. The history of the Communication Reserve goes back to the beginning of the 20th century; some units trace their formation back to the original Signals units created in 1903. Many units of the Communication Reserve began as militia field signals squadrons of the Royal Canadian Corps of Signals. In 1974, after a reorganization of the Canadian Forces, the Communication Reserve adopted its current structure.

734 (Regina) Communication Squadron specializes in tactical and strategic communication, employing voice, electronic and telecommunication systems. Its mandate is to provide individual and collective support to Canadian Forces operations, both domestic and international. Many of its members have served in various UN and NATO peacekeeping missions around the world. This unit also provides communication support to the Army Reserve. Training is a year-round activity, and soldiers are expected to attend Tuesday evening training and up to two weekend training activities per month. Once fully trained, they can apply for various full-time and part-time employment opportunities available throughout the year. 734 (Regina) Communication Squadron is located at the Queen Building in Regina.

737 (Saskatoon) Communication Squadron specializes in tactical and strategic communication, employing voice, electronic and telecommunication systems. Its mandate is to provide individual and collective support to Canadian Forces operations, both domestic and international. Many of its members

have served in various UN and NATO peacekeeping missions around the world. The unit also provides communication support to the Army Reserve. Training is a year-round activity, and soldiers are expected to attend Tuesday evening training and up to two weekend training activities per month. Once fully trained, they can apply for various full-time and part-time employment opportunities available throughout the year.   *Stewart Mein*

77 FIELD BATTERY. The 77 Field Battery was formed in Moose Jaw following the authorization of 10th Brigade, Canadian Field Artillery on February 2, 1920. The 10th Brigade was renamed several times over the next two decades, and its batteries were utilized on several fronts once World War broke II out. 77 Field Battery was mobilized with 3 Field Regiment.   *Holden Stoffel*

SEYMOUR, MAURICE MACDONALD (1857–1929). Born July 7, 1857, in Goderich, Ontario, Seymour obtained his medical degree from McGill University in 1879, then moved west. He was a member of the North-West Territories Medical Council from 1885 to 1905, served twice as president, and organized the SASKATCHEWAN MEDICAL ASSOCIATION in 1906. From 1905, he was in charge of public health in the new province, first as a branch within Department of Agriculture, then within Municipal Affairs, and finally as a separate department. He reacted quickly to local and provincial needs by drafting ground-breaking legislation for municipal doctors, municipal hospitals and free tuberculin testing of cattle. He organized the Saskatchewan Anti-tuberculosis League, hired its first physician and director, R.G. FERGUSON, and chose the site for the first sanatorium.

Under the "Seymour Plan," doctors immunized against diphtheria in September and October, small-

SASKATCHEWAN ARCHIVES BOARD R-A5569

Maurice MacDonald Seymour.

DEBORAH MARSHALL PHOTO/COURTESY OF SHAKESPEARE ON THE SASKATCHEWAN

Performance of *Macbeth*, directed by Mark von Eschen, Shakespeare on the Saskatchewan, 2004.

pox during November and December, and typhoid during January and February. He made public health simple and easy to understand, with such slogans as "Do not spit" and "Swat the fly." A great organizer, a man of varied gifts and charming personality, he died in Regina on January 6, 1929.

C. Stuart Houston

SHAKESPEARE ON THE SASKATCHEWAN.

Located in a striped tent on the banks of the **SASKATCHEWAN RIVER** in Saskatoon, the company was founded by Gordon McCall in 1985 as a summer theatre to develop "a multi-faceted Saskatchewan ensemble company that illuminates Shakespeare and other works for contemporary audiences." McCall (1985–90) specialized in strongly physical, imagistic productions of Shakespeare, often set in historical or contemporary Saskatchewan. Featuring a young ensemble of actors largely trained in improvisational theatre, the company developed a fast-paced, high-energy house style particularly well suited to Shakespeare's romances and comedies. Of note was the company's bilingual **ROMEO & JULIETTE** [*sic*], co-produced with Robert Lepage and members of Théâtre Repère, Québec; featuring English-Canadian Montagues battling French-Canadian Capulets in contemporary Saskatchewan, it toured nationally in 1990.

Alternating between striking contemporary and simpler classical interpretations, the theatre under Henry Woolf (1991–2001) settled into its current pattern of offering two plays by Shakespeare and his contemporaries in repertory, as well as a second stage of light operetta, cabaret, and shorter, more contemporary, experimental fare. Currently directed by Mark von Eschen (since 2002), the company continues to develop young Saskatchewan actors on its second and mainstage, alongside well-established company members. Featuring a seven-week season,

it remains Saskatchewan's oldest, largest and best-developed professional summer repertory company.

Moira Day

FURTHER READING: Day, Moira. 1996. "Shakespeare on the Saskatchewan 1985–1990: The Stratford of the West," *Essays in Theatre* 15 (1): 69–90.

SHARMA, RAJENDRA KUMAR (1942–).

Rajendra (Raj) K. Sharma was born on January 2, 1942, in Hathras, India, and came to Canada in 1976. At the universities of Manitoba and Calgary, he made several milestone discoveries in the area of signal transduction, particularly calmodulin-regulated systems in brain and cardiac muscles. In 1991, he joined the Department of Pathology in the College of Medicine, **UNIVERSITY OF SASKATCHEWAN**, and the Cancer Research Unit of the **SASKATCHEWAN CANCER AGENCY**. Dr. Sharma is a dedicated scientist with an

international reputation for conducting innovative research. He has discovered and purified more than a dozen new proteins, mostly related to the area of signal transduction, and characterized their properties. He demonstrated for the first time the role of the enzyme N-myristoyltransferase (NMT) in causing colorectal cancer. He has received over $2 million in grants and has trained numerous students and postdoctoral fellows. His extensive publication list includes 162 scientific papers, and he has arranged symposiums internationally. In recognition of his contribution to research and scholarly activities, he was awarded a Doctor of Science degree at the University of Saskatchewan in 2004.

Svein Carlsen

SHARON, MAURICE WILLIAM (1875–1940).

Many of Saskatchewan's most impressive public buildings were designed by its second Provincial Architect, Maurice William Sharon. Sharon was born in St. Thomas, Ontario on November 1, 1875. He graduated from the School of Practical Science (now the University of Toronto's Faculty of Applied Science and Engineering), and then apprenticed six years in architects' offices. Arriving in Regina in 1906, he was first employed by the province as a cartographer and has been credited with drawing the first official map of the new province. He subsequently went into an architectural partnership with a former employer, Neil R. Darrach. Sharon and Darrach's Regina works include Westminster United Church, the Donahue Block, and the Guaranty/Western Trust Building.

Sharon's tenure as Provincial Architect from 1916 to 1930 coincided with the province's boom years. Among his works are the Saskatchewan Hospital at Weyburn, the Provincial **NORMAL SCHOOL** at Saskatoon, and the 1928 ballroom addition to **GOVERNMENT HOUSE**, Regina. However, his most dis-

CALVIN FEHR PHOTO/GOVERNMENT OF SASKATCHEWAN, HERITAGE

Weyburn Court House, designed by Maurice Sharon, and now a Provincial Heritage property.

tinctive and prominent designs are several elegant court houses. Yorkton Court House, a Provincial Heritage Property, is an example of the Beaux Arts style; it was featured on the $1 stamp of Canada Post's Canadian Architectural Heritage series. Estevan Court House (also a Provincial Heritage Property) is considered Saskatchewan's finest example of the Colonial style, exhibiting a symmetric design and fine detailing in stone and brick. Sharon's other Colonial courthouse designs are Assiniboia and Weyburn (both Provincial Heritage Properties), Gravelbourg, Kerrobert, Melfort, Prince Albert, Shaunavon, and Wynyard.

Sharon was active in the formation of the Saskatchewan Association of Architects in 1912 and served two terms as its president. A Liberal supporter, Sharon lost his position as Provincial Architect following the election of the Conservative government in 1929. He spent his remaining years in BC, where his few subsequent works have all since been demolished. The excellence of his architectural capabilities is perhaps best attested to by the fact that many of Maurice Sharon's buildings are still standing almost a century later, and over a dozen of them have been formally designated as Municipal or Provincial Heritage Properties. Maurice Sharon died September 8, 1940.   *Margaret Sharon*

FURTHER READING: Saskatchewan Association of Architects. 1986. *Historic Architecture of Saskatchewan.* Regina: Saskatchewan Association of Architects & Focus Publishing.

SHARP, J.W. (BILL) (1914–98). Bill Sharp was born in Texas on August 13, 1914, but his major achievements took place in Saskatchewan through his work to establish a steel tubulars facility and a steel company in Regina, both of which were ultimately very successful.

After obtaining a degree in chemical engineering from the University of Washington, Sharp started working for the Kaiser group of companies in California, where he gained important experience under the tutelage of Henry J. Kaiser. In 1948 he moved to Vancouver, where he took a job working for an independent ready-mix company and developed various ideas about starting a new cement company on the West Coast, which however never came to fruition. In 1955 he went to Regina, where through the new Industrial Development Office of the government of Saskatchewan he obtained a copy of their study on the cement market in the prairie provinces; with their assistance, he put together a group of investors and a plan to build a cement plant.

At the same time, the provincial government had been trying to interest private businesses from both Germany and the United States in building a steel pipe manufacturing plant in Regina to serve a

new and growing market for gas distribution systems, particularly in Saskatchewan. Building on his success with the cement plant, Sharp put together a number of investors and a financing package for a new pipe mill, named Prairie Pipe Manufacturing Company Ltd., which ultimately became **IPSCO INC,** one of the most successful steel companies in North America today. In the early 1960s, Sharp began to spend less and less time in Regina, and in 1965 **JACK TURVEY** succeeded him as president of IPSCO. While Sharp remained as non-executive chairman of the board, he was less involved in the day-to-day business and eventually retired to Victoria, where he died on June 20, 1998.   *John Comrie and Roger Phillips*

SHAUNAVON, town, pop 1,775, located 53 km S of Gull Lake and 76 km N of the Canada-US border. On September 17, 1913, the CPR offered lots for sale on the Shaunavon town site. The railroad had decided that the barren piece of land would be a divisional point on its Weyburn-Lethbridge line. The very next day, the first issue of the *Shaunavon Standard* proclaimed that 370 business and residential lots had been purchased within eight hours; a flurry of construction (both buildings and rail line) followed. By late 1914, Shaunavon had a population of over 700, comprised of people of British, Scandinavian, French Canadian, and German origins. That same year, the first rodeo was held. Early settlers dug lignite **COAL** out of the hills around Shaunavon to heat their homes. Later, coal was mined for profit. Over the decades, grain farming became as important as **RANCHING,** and locally produced **WHEAT** won top awards at international agricultural shows. With the discovery of oil in the region in 1952, Shaunavon again experienced a substantial rise in its population, coupled with a housing boom. The **OIL INDUSTRY** remains important to this day. Shaunavon has now over 200 businesses and a wide range of services, as well as facilities for recreation and social and cultural events. Three buildings have been declared heritage properties: the Shaunavon Courthouse, completed in 1927, which since 1958 has also served as the town hall; the Grand Hotel, built in 1929; and the Shaunavon Hotel, built in 1915. The Shaunavon Pro Rodeo, held each July, continues the tradition begun in 1914. In February 2004, the town was the centre of national attention when visiting NHL personalities and the CBC produced a fifteen-hour live television broadcast "Hockey Day in Canada." **HAYLEY WICKENHEISER,** Olympic gold medallist and member of Canada's national women's hockey team since 1995, was born here.   *David McLennan*

SHAW, MATT (1910–97). Matt Shaw was born in 1910 at Pilot Butte, Saskatchewan, and raised in the Assiniboia area. As the Dust Bowl and **GREAT DEPRESSION** struck in the early 1930s, Shaw joined

the tens of thousands of young unemployed men who were "riding the rails," looking for increasingly scarce jobs. When the federal government of R.B. Bennett established a network of relief camps in remote areas to house jobless, homeless men, Shaw was one of the first and most effective opponents of what he called the "slave camps." He joined the Relief Camp Workers Union (RCWU), which was an affiliate of the Communist-led **WORKERS UNITY LEAGUE,** and became one of the union's most prominent and successful leaders and platform speakers. As was the case with many RCWU organizers, Shaw entered the relief camps under different names in order to avoid the blacklist with which the authorities kept out agitators. Shaw's original family name was Surdia, but it was while using the alias Shaw that he became widely known, and he continued to use that name after the Depression.

Matt Shaw was not only on the **ON-TO-OTTAWA TREK:** he and **BILL DAVIES** preceded the Trek by a day or two, and had the immense task of arranging food and lodging for 1,200 hungry young men involved in the Trek. Shaw was jailed for a time after the Regina Riot, despite the fact that at the time he was in Toronto doing fundraising for the Trek. During **WORLD WAR II,** Matt Shaw served with the RCAF. After his military service, he returned to Regina and worked as a skilled mechanic. In later years, he and his wife Marion operated a store in McLean, Saskatchewan, before retiring in Regina.

Matt Shaw was a lifelong radical and champion of the working class. He was also one of the great orators of the left-wing of the labour movement. Even in his later years, he could deliver persuasive and inspirational speeches without ever referring to written notes; trade union audiences marveled at his spellbinding oratory. He died in Regina in October 1997, at the age of 87.   *Garnet Dishaw*

SHEEP FARMING AND INDUSTRY. Sheep have been a part of Saskatchewan's economy for nearly 140 years, with the first sheep arriving on the Canadian prairies in the early 1800s. It has been noted that many of the large cattle ranches in southern Saskatchewan were actually established first as sheep operations. In 1889 the town of Maple Creek became a distribution point for 30,000 sheep that had been trailed across country from Idaho and Montana; these sheep comprised the fine wool range breeds. Ranchers felt they needed the hardiness, grazing habits and wool quality that they could obtain from the French Rambouillet and the Spanish Merino breeds, even though their conformation to produce meat left much to be desired. The largest flocks are still located in the southern part of the province; however, they only consist of 500–1,000 ewes and are now made up of the dual-purpose breeds: Targhee, Columbia, and other white-face crosses. The first sheep to arrive at the

SASKATCHEWAN ARCHIVES BOARD R-A13116-2

Ewes and lambs on the farm of Ed McCallum, east of Leinen, May 1956. Agricultural Representative Doug Grant of Swift Current is in the background.

UNIVERSITY OF SASKATCHEWAN sheep farm in 1911 were Shropshires. The sheep sector of the farm was quite dynamic during the first twenty years of its operation; various breeds were kept for judging and display purposes, but the Shropshire breed remained dominant for quite some time. Throughout the years many other sheep-breeding programs were undertaken and many research trials were conducted at the University of Saskatchewan.

The post-war period was not kind to the Saskatchewan sheep industry. Australia became the world supplier of fine wool; with synthetic fibres replacing wool in many types of clothing, the price of Canadian wool dropped; and the development of New Zealand as a major exporter of low-priced lamb affected the Canadian lamb market. Saskatchewan's sheep population has shifted with the changing times: its numbers peaked in 1934 at 381,000, and declined to below 100,000 head in 1974; an all-time low of 53,000 occurred in 1986. Since then sheep numbers have steadily risen, and the provincial ewe flock now stands at 70,000; this makes Saskatchewan the fourth-largest sheep producing province in the country.

Sheep production in this province consists of farm flocks, range flocks, and finishing operations; there is also some interest in dairy operations. There is a wide variety of breeds: Suffolk, Hampshire, Dorset, Columbia, Targhee, Rambouillet, North Country Cheviots, Canadian Arcotts, Rideau Arcotts, Texels, Katahdin and Dorper are the most common. Farm flocks range in size from sixty to 250 ewes, and generally market lambs that are fed to a finished weight of 110 pounds, the usual target weight for slaughter lamb in Canada. Range flocks are much larger and tend to be found grazing on short-grass prairie in the southwestern part of the province. These lambs are usually weaned off grass and sold as feeder lambs through the big fall sales, or direct to feedlots. There are several feedlot operations in the province, the largest being located north of Regina. Lamb makes its way to Canadian and American markets via order buyers, feedlots, and public auctions. Many lambs are sold through the assembly service of the Saskatchewan Sheep Development Board.

Sheep are often overlooked as an opportunity in agriculture, a factor that has been slowly addressed in recent years. Sheep production remains a viable alternative within sustainable agriculture: a relatively low cost of entry, a higher biological efficiency (more than one offspring), and additional opportunity areas such as wool and dairy make sheep production attractive. In addition, sheep provide a positive ecological grazing control where they are used to manage weeds such as leafy spurge and others found in emerging reseeded forests. With the advent of round bale feeders, portable electric fencing and many other labour-saving devices, more and more women are becoming the flock caretakers and managers. However, there are many challenges in producing sheep, including predator problems (coyotes) and the need to reach economies of size in order to supply markets on a continual basis.

The provincial industry is comprised of three associations which represent various subsectors, the largest of which is the Saskatchewan Sheep Development Board (SSDB). With its office in Saskatoon, it has the provincial mandate for industry development and is considered the voice of the industry; it also publishes the sheep industry's quarterly newsletter *Sheep Shape*. The Southern Saskatchewan Wool Growers Association was established in 1914, which makes it the oldest association still in existence. It was instrumental in the gathering and organizing of large shipments of wool. Currently there are five wool collection depots in the province, where the wool is transported to either the Canadian Co-operative Wool Growers in Carleton Place, Ontario, or to the wool depot in Lethbridge, Alberta. There are about twelve active shearers in Saskatchewan.

Purebred sheep production is represented by the Saskatchewan Sheep Breeders Association, which manages the purebred shows and sales in the province. Some of the other organizations that oversee the business of their breeds are the Saskatchewan Katahdin Association and the Western Katahdin Sheep Co-operative Ltd. The latest organization to be formed in the province is Canadian Prairie Lamb (CPL); incorporated in 2003, this group took the initiative to develop some value-added lamb products. Today CPL has a product line that includes raw and cooked marinated lamb kebabs, two varieties of cooked appetizer lamb meatballs, lamb sausage, and a product called "cooked lamb in Moroccan orange sauce." CPL is leading the way in Canada when it comes to the processing and marketing of value-added lamb products.

Colleen Sawyer

SHELDON-WILLIAMS, CATHERINE (1869–1949). Born in Hampshire, England in May 1869, Sheldon-Williams was educated in private schools. After her father died, her mother brought the family to Canada in 1889 to farm in the Cannington Manor area. She began to teach in Wolseley, then in 1920 moved to Regina, where she began to work for the Department of Education. In 1925 she started

SASKATCHEWAN ARCHIVES BOARD R-A6505

Catherine Sheldon-Williams (left) and her sister, Dorothea.

the Outpost Correspondence School, which developed into the **SASKATCHEWAN GOVERNMENT CORRESPONDENCE SCHOOL**. Her interests in education were many. In 1922–24 she was convenor of the Local Council of Women (LCW) Education Committee. She served on the Collegiate Board for two decades (first elected in the early 1920s as the LCW candidate). She was also elected to the Public School Board in 1935, where she served four years, and led a campaign for the construction of a technical school in Regina. Briefly engaged in politics, she announced her candidacy as an Independent in the 1938 provincial election; this was a quixotic venture: she never campaigned, merely stating that she stood for non-partisanship, and dropped out before the election. Sheldon-Williams received a life membership in the Local Council of Women in 1949. She died in April of the same year.   *Ann Leger-Anderson*

SHELDON-WILLIAMS, INGLIS (1870–1940).

Inglis Sheldon-Williams is recognized as one of Saskatchewan's major early artists. Born in Hampshire, England on December 25, 1870, he was the son of a landscape painter. Sheldon-Williams first came to Canada in 1887, homesteading at Cannington Manor in southeastern Saskatchewan. He returned to England in 1891 and began his art studies. In 1894, he came back to Canada to complete his homesteading duties; from 1896 until 1898 he studied at the Slade School of Art in London.

Between 1899 and 1904, Sheldon-Williams travelled extensively in South Africa, India and Europe, producing drawings and watercolour illustrations that were published in periodicals in London.

Following his marriage in 1904, he lived in Gloucestershire, England, exhibiting regularly at the Royal Academy in London, the Paris Salon, and a variety of other exhibitions in both London and Europe.

In 1913, Sheldon-Williams returned to Saskatchewan as a well-trained, mature artist. His work had developed from the 19th-century English tradition of Romanticism, with the emphasis placed on the story or subject of a painting. He captured the feelings of vastness and loneliness of the prairies, and his best work was produced in Regina during the next five years.

By 1914 he had met Norman MacKenzie, a prominent lawyer and art collector, who became a great supporter. In Regina he found an atmosphere conducive to painting, a receptive public, and the financial support that enabled him to depict the events and scenes of a growing city. He worked in both watercolour and oil paint, and with his reputation being quickly established, he was regularly commissioned to undertake portraits of prominent members of city and provincial governments. These included Sir **FREDERICK HAULTAIN**, Premier of the North-West Territories, the Hon. **A.E. FORGET**, Lieutenant-Governor of Saskatchewan, and the Hon. **WALTER SCOTT**, Premier of Saskatchewan.

In 1916, Sheldon-Williams was asked to organize the School of Art at Regina College and to provide classes for the students. In October 1918, he went to the front in Europe as an official Canadian war artist. He made an attempt to return to Canada in 1924, but was unable to find work. Following a nervous breakdown in 1925, he travelled in Europe,

and between 1927 and 1934 he settled in Italy. During that time he exhibited intermittently in England and Canada, and continued to send work to Canada to be sold. From 1934 until his death on November 20, 1940 he lived in Hampstead, London.

Paul Fudge

FURTHER READING: Ainslie, Patricia. 1982. *Inglis Sheldon-Williams: Exhibition Catalogue.* Calgary: Glenbow Museum; Christie, Robert. 1980. *Watercolour Painting in Saskatchewan 1905–1980.* Saskatoon: Mendel Art Gallery.

SHELLBROOK, town, pop 1,276, located 44 km W of Prince Albert and served by Hwys 3, 40, and 55. Settlers began arriving in the area in the late 1800s and, in 1894, a post office named after the Shell Brook was established. The Shell Brook (more of a river) passes just to the north of the present community, flowing east to the Sturgeon River, which in turn flows into the **NORTH SASKATCHEWAN** west of Prince Albert. The community is situated near the northern edge of agricultural settlement in the province and as the early settlers arrived the land had to be cleared of the jack pine forests before crops could be planted. The trees, however, provided an early cash crop and logs were rafted into Prince Albert where many were converted into railway ties. Larger numbers of settlers began to arrive in the district in the early 1900s, with significant representation from people of British and Scandinavian origins. In 1910, the Canadian Northern Railway reached Shellbrook from Prince Albert and the community developed as a service centre for the surrounding agricultural region. Today, approximately 50 businesses provide a wide range of goods, services, and professional expertise. The town has a library, and a museum located in the former Canadian Northern Railway station built in 1909. The town's golf course is rated as one of the finest in the province. Additionally, **PRINCE ALBERT NATIONAL PARK** is just a short drive north of the community and there are seven regional parks and numerous lakes in the district, accommodating fishing, swimming, boating and camping. One of Canada's most respected writers, **JAMES SINCLAIR ROSS**, was born in the Wild Rose school district just northeast of Shellbrook in 1908.   *David McLennan*

SHEPTYTSKY INSTITUTE. The history of the Sheptytsky Institute begins with the formation of the **UKRAINIAN CATHOLIC BROTHERHOOD** in Saskatchewan in 1932. In 1934, the Brotherhood established a *bursa*, a residence and cultural/spiritual centre for young Ukrainian Catholic men from rural Saskatchewan who came to Saskatoon to further their education. The Markian Shashkevych Bursa was established in 1935. Due to increased need, in 1944 the Brotherhood replaced the Bursa

Inglis Sheldon-Williams, "The Fire Guard," 1923, oil on canvas, 66 x 88.9 cm, MacKenzie Art Gallery, University of Regina Collection, gift of Mr. Norman MacKenzie.

with a larger residence. Construction of the Metropolitan Sheptytsky Institute began in 1950 on six lots on College Drive purchased for $1,650. On October 5, 1952, the cornerstone was laid and blessed by the newly appointed Exarch of Saskatoon, Andrew Roborecki. On August 16, 1953, the Sheptytsky Institute opened, administered by the Episcopal Corporation of Saskatchewan. Fr. Peter Kryworuchka was the first rector. The Markian Shashkevych Bursa was closed on October 6, 1953.

The Sheptytsky Institute continued as a "male only" residence, providing spiritual, cultural and social activities. Ukrainian classes for students on campus and in the city of Saskatoon were taught for a number of years. In addition to the classes, many teachers attending Summer School availed themselves of the lectures on Ukrainian history, culture and traditions offered by Fr. Kryworuchka and others. From August 28, 1955, until 1966, Musée Ukraina Museum was officially housed in the Institute. In March 1975, the Metropolitan Sheptytsky Society was formed and incorporated. On December 1, 1975, the Society assumed control of the management of the Institute on behalf of the Episcopal Corporation.

In 1979–80, the Institute and residence officially became co-ed. The kitchen was modernized, and the Ukrainian Catholic Religious Education Center added. In 1984, a library was opened and operated out of the Institute for a short time. In 1998, the Society entered into a management agreement with ST. THOMAS MORE COLLEGE. At this time, Sister Gloria, SSMI, was appointed Ukrainian Catholic Campus Pastoral Minister. Laurie Friesen assumed this position in 2002, and in 2004 she was appointed to the dual role of Campus Pastoral Minister and Eparchial Youth Coordinator. In 2000, major renovations to the Institute were completed. In 2003, the management agreement ended, with management responsibilities reverting to the Society. *William Gulka*

SHERMAN, MARION (CA. 1909–98). Born about 1909 in Ontario, Sherman was a home economics graduate of the Macdonald Institute and the University of Toronto. Moving to Saskatchewan in 1930, she became a dietician in Saskatoon. In 1938 she married Pete Sherman; they moved to Regina, then settled in Prince Albert in 1942. In 1946 Sherman worked with the Regional Libraries supervisor to establish the North Central Saskatchewan Regional Library, the first regional library on the prairies. She became board chair when the library opened in Prince Albert (1950), and served until 1984. In 1962 Premier **W.S. LLOYD** and Sherman opened new regional headquarters. She also served as a city councillor from 1949 to 1982, helped organize the Prince Albert Health Region, and worked for senior citizens' facilities, subsidized housing, and the establishment of a community

service centre. After retirement, the Marion Sherman Bursary for Children's Librarians was created in her honour. Awards included Prince Albert Citizen of the Year (1960), Saskatchewan Library Trustees' Association Honorary Life Membership (1975), and membership in the Order of Canada (1978). Marion Sherman died on April 23, 1998, in Prince Albert. *Daria Coneghan*

SHILLINGTON, EDWARD BLAIN (1944–). Born August 28, 1944, in Moose Jaw, Ned Shillington was raised on a farm south of the city. He graduated in law from the **UNIVERSITY OF SASKATCHEWAN** in 1968 and articled in Regina before joining a practice in Moosomin. In 1968 Shillington helped Regina NDP MLA Ed Whelan research changes to the insurance act brought forward by the **THATCHER** government that forced the repeal of the proposed legislation. He ran for the NDP in Moosomin in 1971, but narrowly lost. Shortly after the election he became an assistant to Attorney-General **ROY ROMANOW**, a position he held until winning the NDP nomination in Regina Centre. Shillington was elected in 1975 and appointed Minister of Consumer Affairs where he introduced rent control legislation. He served as deputy government House Leader and chair of the legislative review committee. Leaving Cabinet in 1980, Shillington returned to practicing law. In 1982, he was one of only eight New Democrats to survive the Conservative sweep and took on significant critic duties. Shillington was re-elected in 1986 and 1991. In 1992 he was re-appointed to Cabinet as Associate Minister of Finance, assisting Finance Minister **ED TCHORZEWSKI** to deal with the debt crisis and was vice-chair of treasury board. He resumed the chair of the legislative review committee. Re-elected in 1995, Shillington left Cabinet in 1998 and resigned his seat before the 1999 election to become a consult-

SASKATCHEWAN NEW DEMOCRATIC PARTY ARCHIVES

Edward (Ned) Shillington.

ant. He later moved to Calgary to establish a consultancy firm. *Brett Quiring*

SHILOH ASSEMBLY CHURCH. Shiloh Assembly Church (Apostolic) is an affiliated group of the Pentecostal denomination. The Church started meeting in home Bible classes in 1979, with five founding members. After two years, the group purchased a small building in Regina, where public worship began on a weekly basis. The group works with other denominations: Bethlehem Apostolic Church (Edmonton), Showers of Blessing (Calgary), Bethlehem Apostolic (Toronto), and United Church of Jesus Christ Apostolic (Fort Lauderdale, Florida). Shiloh works with people of many cultures; it has supported missionaries in Indonesia, Mexico, Jamaica, and sent Bibles to Russia. It also sponsors children through World Vision, and provides support to local evangelists in other parts of the world as needed. Shiloh Assembly believes in the traditional formulation of the Nicene Creed.

Zechariah S. Taylor

SHIR CHADASH SYNAGOGUE. Congregation Shir Chadash ("New Song") is a conservative and egalitarian synagogue, established in Saskatoon in March 2000. The Congregation, although small, quickly became a close-knit, congregational family dedicated to *kavanah* (spiritual feeling) under the leadership of Rabbi Steven J. Kaplan. The cantor for Shir Chadash is Dr. Allan Dolovich.

Approximately fifty families founded Congregation Shir Chadash. It has a cemetery within Saskatoon's Woodlawn Cemetery. Hebrew School and conversational Hebrew language classes are available for children, youths and adults. Congregation Shir Chadash has active Hadassah-WIZO and Sisterhood organizations, as well as a newsletter called *Kol Echad* ("One Voice"). The annual community kosher Passover Seder has been celebrated since Shir Chadash began, and has become one of its signature events. Congregants break the Yom Kippur fast together, and observe Sukkot (Festival of Tabernacles) with meals served in the community sukkah. *Linda Epstein*

SHOAL LAKE FIRST NATION. The Shoal Lake First Nation consists of 1,479 ha of land, 92 km east of Nipawin and 20 km downstream from the Red Earth Reserve. The community's single village is referred to as Pakwaw Lake, and is situated on the western edge of the reserve. The Shoal Lake Band originated with three individuals—Okakeek, Osawask, and Kis-moswakapaw—the last two being brothers. Living on the western edge of the **SASKATCHEWAN RIVER** delta in the 1850s these Swampy **CREE** were familiar with both the rich resources of the delta's lakes and rivers, and with White agricultural practices. An adhesion to **TREATY**

5 was signed in 1876, and a reserve surveyed in 1882. By the turn of the century people subsisted on gardening, ranching, hunting and fishing, and new arrivals of farmers in the Carrot River area following WORLD WAR II offered both off-reserve employment and a market for their agricultural products. An all-weather road was built to Shoal Lake in 1960-61, expanding options of band members to utilize increased training and employment opportunities. There are 747 registered band members, with 632 people living on reserve. *Christian Thompson*

SHOKEIR, MOHAMMED H.K. (1938–).

Mo Shokeir was born in Mansoura, Egypt on July 2, 1938. He graduated in medicine from Cairo University in 1960 and then attained diplomas in general and orthopedic surgery. As a Fulbright Scholar from 1964 to 1969, he studied medical genetics at the University of Michigan, where he obtained his Masters and Doctoral degrees. In 1969 he was recruited as a Queen Elizabeth II Scientist to the UNIVERSITY OF SASKATCHEWAN's Department of Pediatrics. Apart from a three-year tenure at the University of Manitoba (1972–75), Dr. Shokeir remained a University of Saskatchewan faculty member throughout his career.

Dr. Shokeir blended exemplary medical genetic service with outstanding research as well as wise and productive administrative leadership. In recognition of his distinguished career as an educator, Dr. Shokeir was awarded in 1998 the Excellence in Teaching Award from the College of Medicine, University of Saskatchewan. During his 17-year tenure as pediatric department head (1979–96), Dr. Shokeir militated with uncompromising vigour for the well-being of Saskatchewan children.

Dr. Shokeir's research included contributions to the understanding of Wilson's Disease and Huntington's Disease, as well as the description of

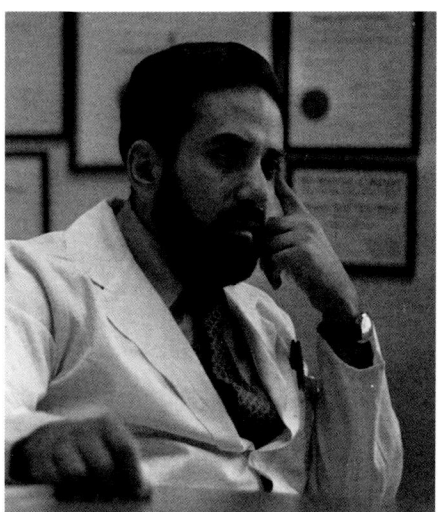

SASKATCHEWAN ARCHIVES BOARD S-SP-A7688-1, SASKATOON STARPHOENIX FONDS

Mohammed Shokeir, September 1977.

two new genetic syndromes, the Pena-Shokeir I and Pena-Shokeir II Syndromes, which bear his and his co-investigator's names. *Alan Rosenberg*

SHORE, EDWARD WILLIAM (1902–85).

One of the most intimidating and talented defensemen to play in the NHL, Eddie Shore was born in Fort Qu'Appelle on November 25, 1902. He played two seasons with the Melville Millionaires before joining the Regina Caps in 1924–25 and the Edmonton Eskimos the following season. When the Western Canada Hockey League folded at the end of the 1925–26 season, Shore was traded to the Boston Bruins, where he established a new record of 130 penalty minutes in his first NHL campaign. Shore anchored the Bruins to their first-ever Stanley Cup championship in the 1928–29 season. Known for his crushing body checks, Shore collided with Toronto's Ace Bailey in a December 1933 game, ending the latter's playing career. Despite this, Bailey shook Shore's hand at centre ice prior to the start of the Ace Bailey Benefit Game between the Toronto Maple Leafs and a team of All-Stars in February 1934. Shore himself suffered numerous serious injuries as a result of his violent style of play.

Shore was once again a pivotal factor in the Bruins' second Stanley Cup title in 1938–39, but he knew his NHL days were numbered. The following season, he purchased the Springfield Indians of the American Hockey League and became player-owner. Shore ended his NHL career with the New York Americans, and devoted himself to the Springfield franchise until he sold it in 1976. In fourteen NHL seasons, Eddie Shore registered 284 points and 1,047 penalty minutes in 550 regular season games. A seven-time First All-Star, he is the only defenseman to win the Hart Memorial Trophy on four occasions. Shore was inducted to the Hockey Hall of Fame in 1945 and the SASKATCHEWAN SPORTS HALL OF FAME in 1990. He died in Springfield, Massachusetts on March 16, 1985.

Daria Coneghan and Holden Stoffel

FURTHER READING: Podnieks, A. et al. 2002. *Kings of the Ice: A History of World Hockey.* Richmond Hill, Ontario: NDE Publishing.

SHOREBIRDS.

Shorebirds (order Charadriiformes) are primarily small to medium-sized wading birds. There are approximately 216 species of shorebirds in the world, with about thirty-two species commonly occurring in Saskatchewan. Saskatchewan species are members of three families: Recurvirostridae (stilts, avocets), Charadriidae (plovers) and Scolopacidae (sandpipers, snipe, curlews, phalaropes, godwits, willets, yellowlegs). In Saskatchewan, most species frequent shallow wetlands and beaches of lakes, ponds or streams. Most shorebirds feed on terrestrial or aquatic inverte-

brates, often insects; some eat seeds or plant material. All shorebirds in Canada and the United States are migratory. Some breed in Saskatchewan, mostly around alkali or other shallow prairie wetlands, e.g., American avocet (*Recurvirostra americana*), Wilson's phalarope (*Phalaropus tricolor*), and piping plover (*Charadrius melodus*), or in upland prairie habitat, e.g., willet (*Catoptrophorus semipalmatus*), long-billed curlew (*Numenius americanus*), marbled godwit (*Limosa fedoa*), and upland sandpiper (*Bartramia longicauda*). Some, such as lesser yellowlegs (*Tringa flavipes*), solitary sandpipers (*Tringa solitaria*), and short-billed dowitchers (*Limnodromus griseus*), breed in boreal areas of Saskatchewan. Many other species of shorebirds migrate from South America to breed in the arctic, and stop-over (stage) in Saskatchewan during spring (late April through May) and/or fall (mid July to September). Tens to hundreds of thousands of sanderling (*Calidris alba*), red-necked phalaropes (*Phalaropus lobatus*), stilt sandpipers (*C. himantopus*), and white-rumped sandpipers (*C. fuscicollis*) stage in Saskatchewan each spring. The area of Chaplin/Old Wives/Reed lakes has been listed as a site of hemispheric importance in the Western Hemisphere Shorebird Reserve Network, and the QUILL LAKES area as a site of international importance owing to the large numbers of shorebirds that often use these areas for rest and foraging during the migration period. Shorebirds are known for their variable mating systems, from monogamy and polygyny to polyandry. In most monogamous species, both parents incubate and care for the young. Only female Wilson's snipe (*Gallinago delicta*) incubate, but males often return at hatch to help care for chicks. After laying a clutch of eggs, female Wilson's phalaropes try to obtain a new mate, since only males care for eggs and young. All Canadian shorebirds except solitary sandpipers lay their eggs in a small depression, or "scrape," on the ground. The nest is not lined with feathers, but some dead leaves, grass, or pebbles may be tossed into it. The clutch (almost always four eggs) is incubated by one or both parents. Eggs hatch in 3–4 weeks, depending on the species. The young, extremely precocial, are covered in down and have their eyes open at hatch. Chicks are able to walk and feed themselves within hours, and need only be brooded and guarded by their parent(s). Adults normally migrate south in July and August, with young-of-the-year following several weeks later. Around the turn of the century, numbers of many of the larger shorebirds declined due to unregulated hunting, and later as a result of the loss of native habitat to agriculture. Today, only Wilson's snipe can be legally hunted in Saskatchewan. There is still concern about habitat loss, since most species are dependent upon shallow, temporary wetlands as feeding sites, and these sites quickly dry out during droughts. Of

COURTESY OF THE ROYAL SASKATCHEWAN MUSEUM

Spotted sandpiper.

the species of shorebirds breeding in Saskatchewan, piping plovers and mountain plovers (*Charadrius montanus*) are listed nationally as "endangered," and long-billed curlews as a "species of special concern." *Cheri L. Gratto-Trevor.*

FURTHER READING: Alsop, Fred J., III. 2002. *Birds of Canada*. New York: Dorling Kindersley; Gratto-Trevor, C.L. et al. 2001. P*rairie Shorebird Conservation Plan*. Edmonton: Canadian Wildlife Service, Prairie Habitat Joint Venture; Hayman, P., J. Marchant and T. Prater. 1986. *Shorebirds: An Identification Guide to the Waders of the World*. Boston: Houghton Mifflin.

SHORT LINE RAILWAYS. The term "short line railways" is used to describe small railways that may vary from a few kilometres to several hundred kilometres in length. The larger short lines are sometimes called regional railways. Many small railway companies built the railway network in Saskatchewan in the early part of the 20th century; gradually, these amalgamated into the two national carriers, **CANADIAN NATIONAL RAILWAY** and **CANADIAN PACIFIC RAILWAY**. The rail network in Saskatchewan remained in the hands of these two companies until the late 1980s. In 1987, the federal government passed a new National Transportation Act (NTA), which allowed for monies to be taken from the Crow Benefit transportation subsidy for the purpose of funding grain transportation on branch lines abandoned by the federal railways. The Act also required the federal railways to offer for sale any lines that they wished to discontinue. The offer was to be made first to the general public, and then to the three levels of government; if the sale was to a federal, provincial or municipal government, the price was to be set at net salvage value.

In 1989, the government of Saskatchewan passed the Saskatchewan Railway Act, which paved the way for the creation of common carrier short line railways in the province. The first such short line appeared that same year: **SOUTHERN RAILS CO-OPERATIVE** (SRC) was a farmer-owned short line comprised of two branch lines in southern Saskatchewan. Initially, SRC received funding from the Crow Benefit under an agreement negotiated with the federal government. Following the successful creation of SRC, the federal railways ceased abandoning branch lines in the province until 1995. At that time, the federal government initiated the Robson Committee to decide the fate of 535 miles (860 km) of high-cost branch lines. The committee having recommended the abandonment of each of these lines, the federal government exempted the railways from the provision to offer these lines for sale to the public and to governments.

Several other short lines sprang up in Saskatchewan in the following years, taking in much of the grain-dependent branch line network. In addition to common carrier short lines—those that offer transportation services to the general public—the province has a number of private short line railways that serve specific industries. These are found at coal mines, forest products facilities, and large grain elevators; they too are regulated under the Saskatchewan Railway Act. *Paul Beingessner*

SHOYAMA, THOMAS KUNITO (1916–). Thomas K. Shoyama was born in Kamloops, and graduated from the University of British Columbia with BA and BComm degrees in 1938. From 1939–45, "Tommy" served as editor of the New Canadian, a weekly civil rights newspaper, which he continued to publish from an internment camp in

Kaslo, BC. In 1946, after a brief stint in the Canadian Army Intelligence Corps, he was encouraged to join the government of Saskatchewan by George Tamaki, an old university friend and fellow Japanese-Canadian. Working for **GEORGE CADBURY** and **T.H. MCLEOD**, Shoyama was hired as a research economist within the newly established Economic and Planning Board (EAPB) His first tasks included working on a new system of public hospital insurance, developing a system for administering diverse **CROWN CORPORATIONS**, and working out an economic development plan based on the province's undeveloped natural resources. In 1950, he became Cabinet's chief economic advisor, secretary to the EAPB, and **T.C. DOUGLAS**' closest policy advisor. Shortly after the election of 1964, Shoyama became a senior research economist with the newly established Economic Council of Canada. In 1968, he became Assistant Deputy Minister of Finance, and by 1975, after a brief term as Deputy Minister of Energy, Mines and Resources, he was appointed Deputy Minister of Finance.

During these years in Ottawa, Shoyama was recognized as one of the most senior members of the "**SASKATCHEWAN MAFIA**." Retiring in 1979, Shoyama moved to Victoria, where he joined the public administration faculty at the University of Victoria.

Shoyama's profound and abiding commitment to public service has been recognized through several national awards, including Officer of the Order of Canada (1978), the Outstanding Achievement Award in the Public Service of Canada (1978) and the Vanier Medal in Public Administration (1982). In 1992, the government of Japan awarded Mr. Shoyama the Order of the Sacred Treasure in recognition of his many contributions to the Japanese-Canadian community. *Gregory Marchildon*

REGINA LEADER-POST

Tommy Shoyama, November 1981.

SHREWS. The order Insectivora, which includes the shrews (family Soricidae), is the oldest living order of placental **MAMMALS**. Shrews (about 290 species) are found worldwide, except for Australia, southern South America and the polar regions. Shrews are very small, with none being longer that 5 cm and 180 g; the lightest mammal in the world, at about 2 g (mass of a penny), is a shrew. Their small size leads to one of their chief problems, that of heat conservation and high metabolic rates. They need a continual source of energy (namely food) to keep warm and alive. They do not hibernate, and how they procure food during the cold parts of the winter is mostly a mystery. The seven species found in Saskatchewan are **CARNIVORES** feeding chiefly on arthropods, but they will sometimes kill and eat other small mammals.

Several of the shrew species (the common shrew *Sorex cinereus* and the pygmy shrew *Microsorex hoyi*) are found in a variety of habitats throughout the province. The American water shrew (*S. palustris*) and the Arctic shrew (*S. arcticus*) live in boreal waterside habitats. The prairie shrew (*S. haydeni*) and dusky shrew (*S. obscurus*) live in marshy areas in the grasslands, while the short-tailed shrew (*Blarina brevicauda*) is limited to the streams of the aspen parkland in the southeast corner.

Shrews are both diurnal and nocturnal; yet they are rarely seen, even though in many places they are the most common species of terrestrial mammal. Because of this, their biology is not as well understood as that of larger species. Many patrol for insects and other arthropods beneath logs or fallen leaves, and in cavities beneath rocks. Rodent surface runways and burrows may also be followed. Shrews are most commonly associated with moist conditions; but some inhabit arid areas, and aquatic adaptations in the water shrews enable them to dive and swim to feed on aquatic arthropods.

They typically have long pointed noses, with small but functional eyes and visible external ears. Their teeth have high ridges, which break the chitinous exoskeletons of their prey. They are short-haired and dark- furred, often with a lighter belly. They usually have a long scaly tail covered in very short hairs. The feet are five-toed and generally unspecialized. Their litters range from two to ten young, with usually one litter per year; since they usually live only one season, this gives them only one chance to reproduce. They are preyed upon by weasels, snakes, small **OWLS**, and other shrews.

Except for the duck-billed platypus, shrews are the only mammals known to be venomous. The short-tailed shrew is an example of a species with venomous saliva. The neurotoxic venom is delivered into the wound along a channel in the first lower incisor teeth from specialized salivary glands located near the base of these teeth, and incapacitates prey.

Short-tailed shrews can thus kill mice considerably larger than themselves. *Mark Brigham*

FURTHER READING: Banfield, A.W.F. 1974. *Mammals of Canada*. Toronto: University of Toronto Press.

SHRI LAKSHAMI NARAYANA TEMPLE. Shri Lakshami Narayana Temple in Saskatoon was formally inaugurated on March 31, 1985. At the time it was the first and only Hindu temple west of Toronto and east of Vancouver that was built in accordance with the Hindu architectural style.

It was in the early 1960s that a few members of the Hindu community made Saskatoon their home. Soon the need for a Temple was felt. In 1974, a Hindu Temple Fund was established. The somewhat loose organizational structure of the early Hindu community was given a formal shape with the incorporation of Vedanta Society of Saskatchewan on June 20, 1977. In the year 1981 an old church was acquired to house the first self-standing Hindu temple in Saskatoon. Subsequently, the modern temple was built in accordance with authentic Hindu architectural principle; to meet the needs of a growing community, it was expanded during 2002–03. In addition to providing a place of worship, marriages have been performed and special prayer meetings have been organized at times of sorrow. Music and Yoga classes as well as language classes in Hindi and Gujarati have been organized for both children and adults. Many special religious festivals are celebrated regularly. The temple also plays an important role in meeting diverse needs of the community by organizing spiritual discourses, meditation sessions, workshops and seminars, and events for youth groups, and regularly invites holy men and well-known scholars to impart their wisdom and knowledge to benefit the community at large. It has been actively involved in organizing and sponsoring many multi-faith and charitable activities for which the Saskatoon Hindu community is well recognized. At the Annual Vegetarian Banquet of the Temple held on March 7, 2002, the trustees of the Temple announced a donation to the **UNIVERSITY OF SASKATCHEWAN** for the establishment of the Vedanta Endowment Lecture Fund. (*See also* **HINDU COMMUNITIES**) *Braj Sinha*

SHRIKES. Shrikes are predatory songbirds (order Passeriformes, family Laniidae) with hooked beaks. Their plumage is usually a combination of gray, black and white. This family of about twenty-nine species of thrush-sized birds occurs in the Northern Hemisphere and Africa. Many of them cache their prey (small rodents, birds and insects) on thorns or twigs, rather than eating it immediately. Both North American species are known from Saskatchewan. The loggerhead shrike (*Lanius ludovicianus*) is a fairly common summer resident of the grasslands

and aspen parklands which nests in shelterbelts and shrubby areas. It sits on an exposed perch watching for prey; its black wings with a white central patch are visible when flying. The Northern shrike (*L. excubitor*) is an uncommon winter resident in the southern two-thirds province; there are a few reports of summer residence and nesting in the northwest corner. It is very similar to the loggerhead shrike in appearance, with a gray back and black mask and tail, but the underside is grayish due to fine barring. *Diane Secoy*

FURTHER READING: Alsop, F.J., III. 2002. *The Birds of Canada*. New York: Dorling Kindersley.

SHUMIATCHER, JACQUI (1923–). Jacqui Shumiatcher is a woman whose passion for the fine arts is matched only by her generous support of them as a benefactor. Born Jacqueline Fanchette Clotilde Clay in Vendin-le-Vieil, Pas de Calais, France, in April 1923, she moved with her family to Regina in 1927. Her first job was instructor of typing and shorthand at Sacred Heart Academy. Subsequent jobs involved Simpson's audit department, the Regina Airport meteorology department, a mortgage company, Scott Collegiate, and the Saskatchewan government. In 1955 she married **MORRIS SHUMIATCHER**, whom she met when he was counsel to **T.C. DOUGLAS**; she later established Managerial Services Ltd. in support of her husband's law office.

Her financial assistance, along with her husband's, has been a great help to organizations such as the Regina **GLOBE THEATRE**, the **REGINA SYMPHONY ORCHESTRA**, and the **MACKENZIE ART GALLERY**. As well, she has been a prominent patron of the **UNIVERSITY OF REGINA**, the Saskatchewan Federated

PHOTO COURTESY OF JACQUI SHUMIATCHER
Jacqui Shumiatcher.

Indian College (now the **FIRST NATIONS UNIVERSITY OF CANADA**), and a diversity of groups that include **REGINA LITTLE THEATRE**, Lyric Light Opera, Juventus Choirs, the Youth Ballet Company of Saskatchewan, and **NEW DANCE HORIZONS**. Other major involvements have included the National Conference of Canadian Clubs, the Dominion Drama Festival, the Regina Council of Women, and the Women's Business and Professional Club.

Jacqui Shumiatcher has received numerous awards, including the Saskatchewan Order of Merit (2001) and an honorary Doctor of Laws degree from the University of Regina (2002). *Nick Miliokas*

REGINA LEADER-POST

Morris Shumiatcher, December 1984.

SHUMIATCHER, MORRIS CYRIL (1917–2004).

Morris Cyril Shumiatcher was born in Calgary, Alberta on September 20, 1917. He graduated from the University of Alberta in 1940 with a BA and in 1941 with an LLB, and from the University of Toronto in 1942 with an LLM. He received his Doctorate of Jurisprudence after serving with the Royal Canadian Air Force from 1943 to 1945. In 1946, he moved to Saskatchewan to accept the position of Law Officer of the Attorney General and became personal assistant to Premier **T.C. DOUGLAS**. He drafted numerous innovative statutes including the Farm Security Act and the **TRADE UNION ACT**. In 1948 he was appointed the youngest King's Counsel in the Commonwealth at the age of 31. He authored the Saskatchewan Bill of Rights, which was the first Bill of Rights in Canada and preceded the United Nations Declaration of Human Rights by one year. He convened the first meeting of Treaty Indians and published a text of their treaties in 1946. He entered

private practice in 1949 and defended cases across western Canada, appearing in the Supreme Court of Canada numerous times. In 1979, he published *Man of Law: A Model*, in which he outlined the characteristics that make up the ideal lawyer.

Shumiatcher was president of the Norman **MACKENZIE ART GALLERY**; president of the **REGINA SYMPHONY ORCHESTRA**; honorary president of the Monarchist League of Regina; president of the Duke of Edinburgh Award Committee for Saskatchewan; president of the Royal Commonwealth Society; member of the Board of Directors for the Saskatchewan Centre of the Arts; member of the Board of Directors of Beth Jacob Synagogue; honorary solicitor of the Regina Press Club; and member of the National Council of the Canadian Bar Association. He served for fourteen years as the Honorary Consul General for Japan and Dean of the Consular Corps for Saskatchewan. He endowed the annual lecture series "Law and Literature" at the College of Law, **UNIVERSITY OF SASKATCHEWAN**; the Robert E. Bamford Memorial Award; and the Morris and Jacqui Shumiatcher Scholarship in Law. In recognition of his numerous contributions he was made Officer of the Order of Canada (1981), he also received the Schneider Communication Award (1982), the B'nai Brith Citizen of the Year (1991), the Canada 125 medal (1992), the Canadian Bar Association Distinguished Service Award (1995), a Life Membership in the Regina Bar Association (1997), and the Saskatchewan Order of Merit (1997). Morris Shumiatcher died on September 23, 2004. *Daria Coneghan*

SIEMENS TRANSPORTATION.

Erwin Siemens started Kindersley Transport with a single truck in 1962, and has expanded this enterprise into one of the largest, most modern transportation companies in western Canada employing 1,600 people in ten different divisions—Siemens Transportation Group Inc.

The Siemens Transportation Group Inc. now generates more than $203 million in annual revenue from truckload and less-than-truckload services through a network of strategically located service centres in Canada and the United States. Divisions include International Truckload, Less Than truckload service, International Flat Deck service, Ground Courier service, and Warehouse Distribution and third party transportation service.

Kindersley Transport Ltd. remains the most well-known company within the Siemens Transportation Group. Other members of the Siemens Group include: PMK Logistics, Edge Transportation, HWT, Quill Transport Ltd., Triangle Freight Services, Mid-Sask Ag Services Ltd., Creekbank Transport of Toronto based and Hi-Tech Express Inc. of Minneapolis, and Tiger Courier.

Tiger Courier, launched in 1984 as a regional

courier providing ground service between nine points in the prairie provinces, has become one of the most aggressive ventures for Siemens. Tiger provides service to over 10,000 locations across Canada from terminals in Toronto, Winnipeg, Regina, Saskatoon, Edmonton, Kelowna, Calgary and Vancouver. *Joe Ralko*

SIFTON FAMILY.

The Sifton family has a long association with Saskatchewan's newspaper industry. Sir Clifford Sifton (1861–1929), a publisher and distinguished statesman who served as a federal Cabinet minister under Prime Minister Sir Wilfrid Laurier, founded the Sifton newspaper dynasty in 1899 with his purchase of the *Manitoba Free Press*; he later purchased Saskatchewan's two daily papers, the *Morning Leader* in Regina and the *StarPhoenix* in Saskatoon, in 1928. As the owner of three daily newspapers (among other business enterprises), Sir Clifford established Toronto-based Armadale Corporation to manage his family's holdings. In 1953, ownership of the Sifton papers was divided between two of Sir Clifford's five sons, Victor (1897–1961) and Clifford Jr. (1893–1976). Victor ran the Winnipeg paper, and the two Saskatchewan papers fell to Clifford Jr.'s control. While presiding over Armadale Corporation, Clifford Jr. and his son Michael C. (1931–95) diversified the family holdings through the acquisition of television and radio interests in the west, including Regina's CKCK radio in 1922 and CKCK-TV (western Canada's first privately owned TV station) in 1954. In 1960, Clifford Jr. formed Armadale Communications to operate Sifton's broadcasting properties. Between 1928 and 1995, three generations of Siftons—Sir Clifford's son (Clifford Jr.), grandson (Michael C.), and great-grandson (Michael G.)—were directly involved in running the Saskatchewan papers and made frequent visits to the province to oversee their operations. From 1992 to 1995, Michael G. resided in Saskatoon while serving as publisher of the *StarPhoenix* and *Leader-Post*. By the mid-1990s, Armadale Communications had dissolved all of its radio and TV interests, including CKCK-TV, which was sold in 1977 to Harvard Communications (owned by the **HILL FAMILY** of Regina). The Sifton newspaper dynasty in Saskatchewan ended in 1995, when Armadale Corp. sold its two Saskatchewan papers to Hollinger Inc. Following the sale, Michael G. remained in the newspaper business as a senior executive with Hollinger Inc. He is now president and CEO of Osprey Media Group, which owns 22 daily papers in Ontario. *Iain Stewart*

FURTHER READING: Hall, D.J. 1981. *Clifford Sifton.* Vancouver: UBC Press; Powell, C. 2001. "Sifton Family Back in Papers," *Marketing Magazine* 106: 4; Powers, N. 2002. "Sifton Family has a Storied Past in Paper's History," *Saskatoon StarPhoenix* (October 17): E17.

SIGERIST COMMISSION. One of Premier T.C. DOUGLAS's priorities, within two days of his election on June 15, 1944, was to contact Dr. Henry Sigerist, professor of the history of medicine at Johns Hopkins University, and author of *Socialized Medicine in the Soviet Union* to head a health study commission. Sigerist began work on September 6, 1944; completed visits and hearings on September 23; finished the report at five minutes after midnight on October 1; and presented his formal report on October 4. He served without pay.

Sigerist accomplished a great deal during his three-plus weeks in Saskatchewan. He recommended establishment of district health regions for preventive medicine, each centred on a district hospital equipped with an x-ray machine, a medical laboratory, and an ambulance. He advocated rural health centres of eight to ten maternity beds, staffed by a registered nurse and one or more municipal doctors. He proposed that the municipal doctor plans should be maintained and developed. He noted that the public must be educated to seek medical advice at the centre, so that doctors would no longer spend a large part of their time driving around the country. The downside was that Saskatchewan was saddled with too many small, one-doctor HOSPITALS: Sigerist did not foresee the rapidity of technological changes in FARMING and road transportation that were already on the horizon, nor could he have been expected to predict the advent of "the pill," with its corresponding drop in birth rates. Sigerist proposed "free hospitalization," which he estimated would cost $3.60 per person per annum and would require another 1,000 to 1,500 hospital beds in Saskatchewan, including a 500-bed university hospital attached to a new medical college in Saskatoon.

Professor Milton Roemer of the University of California, Los Angeles, correctly described the Sigerist report as "one of the most advanced health services reports of its time." It provided the blueprint for medical care in Saskatchewan for half a century.

C. Stuart Houston

SIGGINS, MAGGIE (1942–). Author, journalist, broadcaster and filmmaker, Maggie Siggins is a native of Toronto, Ontario. Born on May 28, 1942, she studied journalism and received a Bachelor of Applied Arts from the Ryerson Polytechnical Institute in 1965. Siggins began her career as a reporter for the *Toronto Telegram* and, during the 1970s, worked as a political reporter, commentator, interviewer, and producer for both CBC and CITY-TV in Toronto, as well as contributing to various national magazines. Siggins moved to Regina in 1983. Her book on the Thatcher murder case, *A Canadian Tragedy: JoAnn and Colin Thatcher*, was published in 1985. It was the basis of the CBC miniseries *Love and Hate* which was broadcast on CBC in Canada, NBC in the United States, and in over

SASKATCHEWAN ARCHIVES BOARD S-SP-A22920-15, SASKATOON STARPHOENIX FONDS

Maggie Siggins, December 1984.

forty different countries. *A Canadian Tragedy* won the Arthur Ellis Crime Writers of Canada Award.

Some of Siggins' other works include: *Brian and the Boys: A Story of Gang Rape*; *Riel, A Life of Revolution*; and *In Her Own Time: A Cultural History of Women*. Her *Revenge of the Land* won the Governor-General's Award for Literary Non-Fiction in 1992, and was adapted in 1998 as a television mini-series for broadcast on CBC and CBS.

Siggins has also written several documentaries, including *Mr. and Mrs. Mark Go to Yorkton*, *Twin Stars*, and *Scarred by History*. Her second episode of the *Scarred by History* series, "Nanjing Nightmares," was nominated for two awards at the YORKTON SHORT FILM & VIDEO FESTIVAL. Siggins has also been active in studying and teaching journalism. She spent 1985 and 1986 in China, where she worked at the New China News Agency and taught at the Beijing Broadcast Institute. Before that, she held the Max Bell Chair in Journalism at the UNIVERSITY OF REGINA (1983–84). She continues to lecture, write, and work as a documentary filmmaker.

Mark Vajcner

SIKHISM. The Sikh faith, founded in 1499 by Guru Nanak, originated in the northwestern province of Punjab in India. After the partition of India in 1947, many Sikhs immigrated to Britain, the United States, and Canada. Although there were Sikhs in British Columbia as early as 1900, the first Sikhs arrived in Saskatchewan in the late 1960s. The first few families settled in Saskatoon, and in 1969 the first family settled in Regina. Owing to the small numbers of Sikhs in the province at that time, there was no official Gurdwara (Sikh temple): the worship ceremonies were held in the homes of various Sikh fam-

ilies until 1977, when the Odd Fellows Hall in Regina was rented. During the 1980s, members of the Sikh communities from both Saskatoon and Regina traveled to many Gurdwaras across the country in an effort to raise funds for the purchase of temples in their respective cities. With the opening of the Sikh Temple of Saskatoon in 1985 and the Sikh Temple of Regina in 1988, their goal was realized. In the late 1980s and early 1990s the Sikh population in Saskatchewan had climbed to almost 200 families. However, like many Saskatchewanians drawn by greater opportunities in other Canadian provinces, many Sikhs have left the province, and their number has now dwindled to about 100 families. The main concentration of Sikhs remains in Saskatoon and Regina, but there is still a Sikh presence in many rural communities in Saskatchewan.

Harvey Basi and Melanie Neuhofer

SIMARD, ROSE MARIE LOUISE (1947–). Simard was born April 17, 1947, in Val d'Or, Quebec, and raised in Meadow Lake. She received a BA in philosophy and a degree in law from the UNIVERSITY OF SASKATCHEWAN. Simard articled in Regina and was admitted to the Bar in 1971. She worked as assistant to Legislative Council from 1973 to 1974. Simard was the first woman to hold the position of Legislative Council and Law Clerk for Saskatchewan (1974–78). She left that position to found her own law firm. Simard was a member of the Attorney General's committee on the consolidation of the Queen's Bench and District Courts in 1979. She was also a board member of the Medical Council of Canada and the Canadian Nurses Association, vice-chairperson of the Saskatchewan Human Rights Commission, and a consumer representative on the Council of the COLLEGE OF PHYSICIANS AND SURGEONS. Simard was elected as MLA for Regina

SASKATCHEWAN NEW DEMOCRATIC PARTY ARCHIVES

Louise Simard.

Lakeview in 1986, a position she held until 1991. She was the Opposition health critic, critic for women's issues, and for other portfolios. In 1991 she was elected in Regina Hillsdale when the NDP formed the government. Simard became the Minister of Health and Minister responsible for the Status of Women, positions she held until her resignation in 1995. Simard orchestrated the "wellness" approach to health care that included hospital closures in rural Saskatchewan and the establishment of health districts and boards. She joined the law firm of McPherson, Leslie and Tyerman in April 1995. In 2000, she was hired as the CEO of the **SASKATCHEWAN ASSOCIATION OF HEALTH ORGANIZATIONS** (SAHO) and is the employer representative for provincial health care employee contract negotiations.   *Dana Turgeon*

SIMMIE, LOIS (1932–). Lois Simmie, an author who has specialized in children's literature and short fiction, was born on June 11, 1932, in Edam, Saskatchewan. She spent her youth in small towns, where her father was a grain elevator agent, and this background is reflected in many of her stories. She taught writing classes for many years, including numerous workshops at the Saskatchewan Summer School of the Arts and sessions at the Canadian Authors Association conferences. She was writer-in-residence at the Saskatoon Public Library in 1987–88. Her work includes *They Shouldn't Make You Promise That, An Armadillo is Not a Pillow, Betty Lee Bonner Lives There, Auntie's Knitting A Baby, Oliver's Chickens, What Holds Up the Moon? Who Greased the Shoelaces?* and *Secret Lives of Sargent John Wilson.* Her short story *Red Shoes* was adapted as a feature film in 1986, and the play *Auntie's Knitting a Baby*, based on her book, was presented by **25TH STREET THEATRE** in 1991. Her work is included in several anthologies and has been broadcast on CBC. Lois Simmie has won several awards recognizing her achievements: the **SASKATCHEWAN WRITERS GUILD**'s Literary Award for Fiction (1983), the **SASKATCHEWAN BOOK AWARD** for Children's Literature (1995), and the Crime Writers of Canada's Arthur Ellis Award (1995).

Daria Coneghan

FURTHER READING: Hillis, D. 1988. *Plainspeaking: Interviews with Saskatchewan Writers.* Regina: Coteau Books.

SIMPSON, EDITH CHILD ROWLES (1905–97). Edith Child Rowles Simpson, a leader in the fields of home economics and rural education, was born in Manchester, England on April 9, 1905. Her family moved to Canada in 1910, homesteading near Empress, Alberta. Simpson took her public and high school education at Empress and her teacher training at Saskatoon. She taught in a number of

Edith Child Rowles Simpson, ca. 1949.

rural schools in Saskatchewan and studied household science at the **UNIVERSITY OF SASKATCHEWAN**, winning the Rutter prize as the most distinguished graduate of 1932. In later years she obtained an MSc from the University of Wisconsin and a PhD in Education from Columbia University. She joined the University of Saskatchewan in 1932, where she held a number of university positions: Assistant Professor in the College of Agriculture from 1941 to 1944; Dean of Women from 1944 to 1950; Assistant Professor in Home Economics from 1950 to 1954; and from 1965 to her retirement in 1972 she was Professor and Dean of Home Economics. Simpson provided guidance to **HOMEMAKERS' CLUBS** and **4-H CLUBS**. She did research on the preservation and use of cultivated and native fruits of Saskatchewan, and on the freezing of vegetables most suitable for prairie gardens. She received honorary awards from the Canadian Home Economics Association, the Canadian Dietetic Association, the 4-H Council and the College of Home Economics, and was named a Fellow of the Saskatchewan Home Economics Association. In 1981 she was inducted into the Saskatchewan Agricultural Hall of Fame, and in 1987 became a Member of the Order of Canada. Edith Rowles Simpson died on December 29, 1997, in Saskatoon.

SIMPSON, GEORGE (1787–1860). Sir George Simpson was born in 1787 in Scotland. After finishing his education in the local parish school Simpson went to London, where he worked for his uncle at a London sugar brokerage in 1810. Through brokerage business, Simpson met a board member of the Hudson's Bay Company (HBC). He was appointed governor-in-chief *locum tenens* of the HBC in 1820. Although Simpson knew little about Rupert's Land and the fur trading business, he seized the opportunity for adventure. He sailed for New York in March

1820 and traveled to Montreal, the capital of the **FUR TRADE**. One of Simpson's first tasks was to address the trade wars between the North West Company (NWC) and the HBC. He brought discipline and order to the Company, and took advantage of the turmoil within the ranks of the NWC to promote a merger between the two fur trading companies. In 1821, the HBC and the NWC amalgamated under the HBC name. Simpson was described as affable in temperament, but his officers and other employees understood that he would not allow any insubordination in the ranks of the newly formed company. He won the loyalty of the commissioned officers in the HBC by introducing profit shares in the company, but did not extend this privilege to those in the lower ranks.

Simpson was also reputed to take a hard line with the Indian people he relied upon for the success of the fur trade. In 1822, he stated that their character and nature meant that they had to be ruled with an iron hand to keep them in a "proper state of subordination" which would require them becoming dependent on the Hudson's Bay Company. He went on to say that no credit or ammunition would be given to the Indians dealing with the HBC trading posts unless they proved to company officials that they were working harder and exhibiting more civilized behaviour.

George Simpson's epic journeys across the hinterland were well documented in his journals. He traveled thousands of miles at record-breaking speeds, outdistancing the most seasoned guides and traders. Between 1824 and 1829 he traveled across the West following the main trading routes, and inspected first-hand the operations at the inland posts. In 1826, he was named governor of all the HBC territories in Canada. He developed the expertise that would ensure that the HBC controlled the fur trade for the next 40 years. His word was law, and for this reason he acquired the nickname "Little Emperor."

Sir George Simpson.

Simpson developed relations with mixed-blood women, in a manner known as marriage *à la façon du pays*. He had several Native "wives," whom he regarded as little more than sexual partners, and assigned them new mates when he tired of them. Paradoxically, he opposed marriages between other fur traders and Indian or mixed-blood women. After his marriage to his British cousin Frances Simpson, non-White wives were not welcome in the Simpson household. George Simpson fathered several illegitimate children, but although he made provision for all of them, they were kept at a distance from himself and his English wife. Frances was not able to make a smooth transition from her London home to the Canadian West, and owing to failing health she moved back to London in 1834. That same year George Simpson moved to Montreal, where he became a prominent member of the Anglo-Scottish business elite. While he was governor, Simpson used his contacts to secure the interests of the HBC from friendly government leaders. His business interests expanded to include buying land to sell to settlers; he invested and managed two banks; and he held part ownership in the new railway and shipping projects. Simpson traveled North America and further afield to increase the HBC's and his own vast holdings. By the late 1850s, the new mode of trade and travel, the railroad, profoundly affected trade practices and the HBC. The sale of Rupert's Land to Canada was already being discussed when Simpson's health began to fail, forcing him to contemplate retirement. He died on September 7, 1860.

Elizabeth Mooney

FURTHER READING: Newman, P.C. 1998. *Empire of the Bay: The Company of Adventurers That Seized a Continent.* Toronto: Penguin Books.

SIMPSON, GEORGE WILFRED (1893–1969).

George Wilfred Simpson was a descendant of Loyalists who resettled in Canada after the American Revolution. He received his primary and secondary education in Ontario. After a brief stint as a schoolteacher and homesteader in Saskatchewan, he enrolled in the College of Arts at the **UNIVERSITY OF SASKATCHEWAN** and graduated with a BA in 1919. He earned an MA in History from the University of Toronto in 1930. Simpson taught at the University of Saskatchewan from 1922 to 1957, eventually becoming Head of the History Department and Assistant Dean of the College of Arts and Science. During **WORLD WAR II**, he was Chair of the Advisory Committee on Co-operation in the Canadian Citizenship Branch of the Department of National War Services. He helped initiate the formation of the Saskatchewan **ARCHIVES**, and was the first provincial archivist from 1945 to 1948. In addition, he was instrumental in establishing *Saskatchewan History*, a publication of the Saskatchewan Archives, in 1948.

EVERETT BAKER PHOTO/COURTESY OF THE SASKATCHEWAN HISTORY AND FOLKLORE SOCIETY

Professor George and Muriel Simpson, October 1953.

There was a large Slavic population in Saskatchewan, and Simpson befriended many members of the Slavic community. As a non-Slav he helped them considerably to raise their image *vis-à-vis* the predominant Anglo-Saxon population. Simpson was instrumental in introducing Slavic Studies at the University of Saskatchewan, and helped establish similar programs in other Canadian universities. He was an editor of the first comprehensive history of Ukraine to be published in English, and wrote many articles on Ukrainian and Slavic history. In 1947, the Free Ukrainian University awarded Simpson an honorary Doctorate—following which, his colleagues in the department gave him the appellation "Ukrainian Scholar." He was further honoured by the Royal Society of Canada, the Shevchenko Scientific Society, the Ukrainian Free Academy of Sciences, the Canadian Historical Association, the Canadian Association of Slavists, the American Historical Association, the Canadian and American Geographical Society, the Canadian Political Science Association, and many other scholarly societies and institutions. Simpson was also active in the United Nations Association and World Refugee Committee of Saskatchewan. In the 1960s, he served on the Board of Governors at the University of Saskatchewan. After his retirement in 1958, the University bestowed upon him an honorary Doctorate for being a "teacher of rare quality, inspiring, sympathetic, and greatly beloved."

Victor O. Buyniak

FURTHER READING: Buyniak, V. 2000. "Professor George Simpson–A Friend of Ukrainians." Pp. 230-44 in *Collected Papers on Ukrainian Settlers in Western Canada, Part Four.* Edmonton: Shevchenko Scientific Society in Canada, vol. 38 (in Ukrainian); Prymak, M.

1988. "George Simpson, the Ukrainian Canadians and the 'Pre-History' of Slavic Studies in Canada," *Saskatchewan History* 41 (2): 52-66.

SINCLAIR, JIM (1933–).

Jim Sinclair, born on June 3, 1933, in Punnichy, Saskatchewan, is a **NON-STATUS INDIAN** political leader, and former president of the Métis Society of Saskatchewan (MSS) and the Association of Métis and Non-Status Indians of Saskatchewan (AMNSIS). Growing up poor in an Aboriginal squatter community in the Qu'Appelle Valley, Sinclair had a strong sense of social justice, eventually becoming an MSS fieldworker in 1964. Through charisma and political skill, he was elected to the MSS board in 1967, and in 1971 became MSS (later AMNSIS) president. During his eighteen-year tenure as MSS/AMNSIS president, he challenged institutional racism, fought for the **MÉTIS'** and Non-Status Indians' Aboriginal rights, and tried to obtain for them adequate housing, more alcohol treatment centres, and increased educational and employment opportunities. In the 1970s he established the Native Council of Canada (now the Congress of Aboriginal Peoples), which included both Métis and Non-Status Indians in its membership, and served as its first interim president. Throughout his political career, Sinclair tried to entrench the rights of Métis into Canada's Constitution. This occurred in 1982, when along with other Métis leaders such as **HARRY DANIELS** he successfully lobbied to have the Métis put into the Constitution Act, 1982 (s.35.2). With the dissolution of AMNSIS in 1988 and the creation of the newly formulated MSS, a Métis-only political body, Sinclair left Métis politics. From 1994 to 1996, he led the Congress of Aboriginal Peoples, which represents non-Status, off-reserve Aboriginal people, and in 1996 was elected president of its Saskatchewan branch.

Darren R. Préfontaine

SINGER, STACY (1977–). One of the world's most accomplished baton twirlers, Stacy Singer was born in Regina on April 12, 1977. At age 8, Singer won a gold medal in the junior division at the 1985 World Baton Twirling Championships in Germany and became the youngest Canadian baton twirler to compete at a world event. She went on to place first at every provincial and national freestyle twirling championship from 1985 until her retirement in 1993. During those years, Singer won seven individual gold medals at World Baton Twirling Championships. She also collected the 1991 world team baton twirling championship medal as a member of the Regina Buffalo Gals. The only competitor to have ever won two gold medals at a world event, Singer was a three-time grand national champion. Her many honours include being named Canadian Sports Federation Junior Athlete of the Year in 1985, 1989 and 1990, as well as 1992 SaskSport Female Athlete of the Year. Singer was inducted into the SASKATCHEWAN SPORTS HALL OF FAME in 1998.

Daria Coneghan and Holden Stoffel

REGINA LEADER-POST

Stacey Singer, April 1991.

SINTALUTA, town, pop 145, located 16 km SE of Indian Head on Hwy 1. Sintaluta had its beginnings in the early 1880s as the first settlers began arriving in advance of the railroad. They were mainly of British origin, from Ontario. The name Sintaluta is derived from a LAKOTA Sioux term referring to a fox tail, which in turn referred to the nearby headwaters of the Redfox Creek, flowing north to the QU'APPELLE RIVER. Sintaluta developed as a service centre for the surrounding agricultural district. By 1911, the population was approaching 400, seven grain elevators lined the tracks, and the town had a large school and a substantial commercial sector. As well, Sintaluta had become well known as a centre of farmer's agitation for economic and political rights. In 1902, Sintaluta farmers took the CPR to court for failing to provide enough grain cars, as had been stipulated under the Manitoba Grain Act; when the farmers won, EDWARD ALEXANDER PARTRIDGE, who played an important role in the case, emerged as a leader for western grain producers. Sintaluta remained an important trading centre until the 1960s, but by the 1970s both the population of the community and the number of local businesses began to decline. School children are now bussed to Indian Head, and the town's two remaining grain elevators are now privately owned. Sintaluta has a number of fine brick and stone structures, many of them over a century old.

David McLennan

SINTALUTA CASE, THE. The 1902 Sintaluta Case was an important manifestation of the western Canadian agrarian movement. The CANADIAN PACIFIC RAILWAY (CPR), along with elevator companies, dominated the grain-marketing system in the west, making it difficult for prairie farmers to sell and transport their grain. In the fall of 1901, a severe boxcar shortage led to a devastating grain blockage. Neither the CPR nor the elevators were capable of handling the unexpectedly large harvest, and farmers lost nearly one-half of the record wheat crop because of spoilage. Frustrated by the inability to unload their grain effectively, farmers from the QU'APPELLE VALLEY convened on December 18, 1901, at Indian Head, where they organized the Territorial Grain Growers' Association (TGGA), a collective organization designed to act on their behalf.

In 1902, the TGGA requested amendments to the Manitoba Grain Act of 1900, which Parliament passed before the session ended. Under the new clauses, every railway agent was to maintain an order book that allocated boxcars on a first-come, first-served basis. Despite these amendments, the CPR continued to allot all of its boxcars to the elevator companies, and another record crop was at risk of being spoiled. The violation of the car-distribution clauses prompted the TGGA to take legal action against the CPR agent at Sintaluta. In December 1902, magistrates ruled in favour of farmers represented by the TGGA, and the decision was later sustained in an appeal before the Supreme Court. The Sintaluta Case not only compelled the CPR to assign boxcars according to the amended Manitoba Grain Act, it also justified the organization of the TGGA.

Holden Stoffel

FURTHER READING: Knuttila, M. 1994. *"That Man Partridge:" E.A. Partridge, His Thoughts and Times.* Regina: Canadian Plains Research Center; Patton, H.S. 1928. *Grain Growers' Co-operation in Western Canada.* Cambridge, MA: Harvard University Press.

SISTERS OF CHARITY OF MONTREAL (GREY NUNS). The congregation of the Sisters of Charity of Montreal (the Grey Nuns) was founded by St. Marguerite d'Youville in Montreal in 1737, in response to the needs of the poor in the area. The Grey Nuns came west and served at Ile-à-la-Crosse from 1860 to 1905 and from 1917 to 2001, teaching, operating an orphanage, and establishing a Catholic hospital. They also served in Lebret (1884–1975), Lestock (1897–1932), Regina (1907–78), Saskatoon (1907–), Beauval (1910–71), Biggar (1923–2000), Rosthern (1927–35), Gravelbourg (1928–), Portage La Loche (1943–81), Prince Albert (1955–60), Lisieux (1958–68), Albertville (1960–63), Buffalo Narrows (1968–82), Zenon Park (1972–73), and Esterhazy (1987–).

In Saskatchewan, the Grey Nuns are known for their work in health care administration and nursing: St. Joseph's Hospital, Ile-à-la-Crosse (1927–2001); Grey Nuns' Hospital, Regina (1907–74); St. Paul's Hospital, Saskatoon (1907–99); St. Marguerite Hospital, Biggar (1923–67); St. John's Hospital, Rosthern (1927–35); St. Joseph's Hospital (1928–2000) and Foyer d'Youville (1961–2000), Gravelbourg; St. Martin's Hospital, La Loche (1943–81); and St. Anthony's Hospital, Esterhazy (1987–). In addition, the Grey Nuns were involved in teaching, pastoral care, parish ministry, nursing education, and in the Elmwood Residences in Saskatoon. At the present time, the Grey Nuns continue to serve in a variety of ministries in Saskatoon, Gravelbourg and Esterhazy.

Margaret Sanche

SISTERS OF CHARITY OF ST. LOUIS (SCSL). The Sisters of Charity of St. Louis, a teaching congregation, was founded in France in 1803 in the aftermath of the French Revolution. Settling in Quebec in 1902, they established schools and acquired Canadian members to staff them. From these foundations, they sent Sisters to the newly founded dioceses of western Canada. In 1913 the Sisters of Charity of St. Louis came to Moose Jaw, where they established St. Louis College, a school for boys. They taught in Moose Jaw's separate schools for many years, and left the city in 2001.

Radville welcomed the Sisters in 1915 when St. Louis Academy was built, followed in 1922 by St. Olivier Elementary School. Declining numbers caused the Sisters' withdrawal from Radville in 1973. At Wilcox, the Sisters established Notre Dame of the Prairies Academy in 1920. When Père ATHOL MURRAY asked the Sisters to accept "his boys" into

863

their school, Notre Dame College of Canada was born.

Over the years, other centres in Saskatchewan benefited from the work of the Sisters, including Swift Current, Willow Bunch, Shaunavon, Melville, Marquis, Saskatoon, Weyburn, Wolseley, and Claybank. At present, the Sisters of Charity of St. Louis continue to maintain residences in Regina (since 1924) and Wilcox. *Maria L. Gerritsen*

SISTERS OF CHARITY OF THE IMMACULATE CONCEPTION (SCIC).

In 1854, Honoria Conway, a native of Ireland, founded the Sisters of Charity of the Immaculate Conception, the first English-speaking congregation of sisters to be founded in Canada. Saint John, New Brunswick, had been overwhelmed by an influx of impoverished Irish immigrants, a cholera epidemic, and many orphaned children needing care and education; the religious congregation was formed in response to these needs. The SCIC first came to Saskatchewan in 1906, when three sisters arrived in Prince Albert to care for and teach the children at St. Patrick's Orphanage. Holy Family Hospital was constructed in 1910, and the first patient arrived on Christmas Day that same year. The sisters were involved in the work of the hospital until it was closed in 1997. Over the years, the sisters also responded to other needs in Saskatchewan: in Regina they operated Rosary Hall, a residence for young women, from 1921 to 1968; in Holdfast, they taught from 1924 to 1976; and in Saskatoon, sisters have provided leadership in the Catholic Health Association of Saskatchewan since 1988, as well as involvement in parental and pastoral care from 1988 to 1998, and journalism and university chaplaincy from 1993 to 2002. *Rose Ketchum*

SISTERS OF LORETTO: INSTITUTE OF THE BLESSED VIRGIN MARY (IBVM).

The Institute of the Blessed Virgin Mary (Sisters of Loretto, IBVM), whose special work is education, was founded in the early 1600s by an Englishwoman, Mary Ward. Five Loretto sisters came to the diocese of Toronto from Ireland in 1847 at the request of Bishop Michael Power to establish Catholic educational institutions for girls. Many years later, members of the congregation came west from Toronto to Saskatchewan, to the Archdiocese of Regina in 1921 and to the Diocese of Prince Albert in 1922. In Saskatchewan, the Loretto sisters established girls' boarding schools and taught in Catholic elementary and high schools in Sedley (from 1921), Regina (1932), Weyburn (1950), Estevan (1945) and Saskatoon (1922–32; 1960–). Besides teaching in the schools, the sisters offered music lessons and organized choirs; for many years they taught summer catechism classes in the rural areas of the province. Over the years, a number of young women who were educated by the

Lorettos in Saskatchewan became members of the religious congregation. Most of the Lorettos who served in Saskatchewan have returned to Toronto for retirement; the few remaining are involved in a variety of ministries, including high school and hospital chaplaincy, parish ministry, and art education. *Margaret Sanche*

SISTERS OF MISSION SERVICE (SMS).

The congregation of the Sisters of Mission Service was founded July 16, 1951, at Battleford, Saskatchewan by Rev. Godfrey W. Kuckartz, OMI; Mary Catherine Cannon was the co-foundress. Both were born and received their early education in Saskatchewan. Kuckartz was Superior of St. Charles Scholasticate in Battleford when he founded the Community, and it was there that the first Sisters, all from Saskatchewan, began their training and ministry. Kuckartz envisioned a modern religious congregation of women whose garb, manner and lifestyle would make them readily available to people in missions at home and abroad. He stressed the importance of "contact with the people": this contact would take place through the service the Sisters provided as domestic workers, professional teachers, nurses, and social workers.

The Sisters have served in numerous locations in Saskatchewan over the years. Presently they work in the areas of lay formation, spiritual direction, parish ministry, the healing ministry of reiki, and pastoral care in homes and hospitals. The Congregation now serves in British Columbia, Alberta, Saskatchewan, Manitoba, and Brazil. *Joan Kuffner and Leona Meier*

SISTERS OF NOTRE DAME D'AUVERGNE (SND).

The congregation of Sisters of Notre Dame d'Auvergne (the name used in Canada) had its beginnings in Usson-en Forez, France in 1730. Their first Rule was approved in 1745 and they were given the name still used in France: Soeurs de Notre Dame de Chambriac. In 1913, at the request of Fr. Albert Royer, the founder of the town of Ponteix, six Sisters came from France to Saskatchewan to establish and staff a school and a hospital. Today the Sisters continue to minister in Ponteix and Saskatoon. Their apostolate continues to focus primarily on youth, the sick and the poor. *Rose-Alma Dumont*

SISTERS OF OUR LADY OF SION (NDS).

The Congregation of Our Lady of Sion (Notre-Dame de Sion) was founded in 1843 in France. In 1904, twenty-four members of the congregation came to Prince Albert from Lewiston, Maine. In 1905, they established their first girls' school, the Academy of Our Lady of Sion, which they operated until 1951. Sion Sisters came to Moose Jaw in 1914 and to Saskatoon in 1917, establishing girls' high schools and teaching in the Catholic schools. In Saskatoon, they oper-

ated Rosary Hall from 1934 to 1974, taught summer catechism classes to rural children, and instructed adults in the Catholic faith. Currently, all the Saskatchewan members live in Saskatoon, in retirement or engaged in various ministries in the areas of multifaith and ecumenism, social justice and poverty concerns, parish pastoral care, and service to and with Native people. *Margaret Sanche*

SISTERS OF OUR LADY OF THE CROSS.

The congregation of the Sisters of Our Lady of the Cross (Notre Dame de la Croix) was founded in 1832 in Murinais, France for the education of young girls, and the care of the sick and elderly in their homes. On invitation from the La Salette priests, Sisters M. Alype, M. Ludovic and five others came to Forget, Saskatchewan from France in 1905. They established a bilingual school, which opened on March 1, 1906, as St. Joseph Academy for boys and girls, both boarders and day-scholars. Other schools where the Sisters taught were St. Hubert via Whitewood (1907–68); St. Anne Convent, Wauchope (1917–64); Sacred Heart Convent, with three public school classrooms; Montmartre (1920–70); and the School for Mentally Challenged Children and Adults, Redvers (1964–80). The congregation also founded and owned Joan of Arc Home; St. Hubert Mission via Whitewood (1920–68); St. Joseph Home, Marcelin (1944–56); Mount St. Mary Home, Weyburn (1953–77); and Mount St. Joseph, Prince Albert (1956–92). At present, Sisters of Our Lady of the Cross are in Saskatoon and Prince Albert, where they assist in teaching, nursing, social services, and parish work. *Marie Raiwet*

SISTERS OF OUR LADY OF THE MISSIONS (RNDM).

The congregation of the Sisters of Our Lady of the Missions (RNDM) was founded by Euphrasie Barbier in Lyon, France in 1861. In 1898 Sisters came to Marieval, North-West Territories (now Saskatchewan) and in 1899 to Lebret, where the congregation served for 100 years. In 1904 Sisters went to Wolseley, and then to Regina in 1905. In Regina they began a private school, Sacred Heart Academy, taught in the separate schools, opened Sacred Heart College (affiliated with the Universities of Saskatchewan and Ottawa), and later established Marian High School. They served at St. Andrew's near Wapella in the 1940s, and in Saskatoon since 1950. Wherever the Sisters taught, they offered their students opportunities in music, drama, public speaking, art and sports, home economics, and secretarial training. Missionary work in Canada also meant teaching catechism in small towns during summer holidays, participating in the Summer School of Liturgical Music in Lebret and the Lay Ministry Program in Regina, and operating homes for mentally challenged adults. Sisters have also served in missions in India, Vietnam, the

Philippines, and Peru. There are currently thirty-five Sisters of Our Lady of the Missions in Saskatchewan, some in active ministry and others in retirement.

Winifred Brown

SISTERS OF PROVIDENCE OF ST. VINCENT DE PAUL (SP).

The congregation of the Sisters of Providence of St. Vincent de Paul was founded in Kingston, Ontario, in 1861 to care for the poor. Catherine McKinley was the first member and Superior of the congregation, which eventually spread across Canada. The Sisters' history in Saskatchewan began in 1912, when typhoid raged through Moose Jaw and local clergy appealed to the Congregation, which had come west four years earlier to Daysland, Alberta. Sisters Mary Angel Guardian Mangan and Mary Camillus Bradley arrived in Moose Jaw on November 14, purchased a building that day, and welcomed their first patient two weeks later. Providence Hospital grew with the new city, becoming respected for its nursing and training programs.

By 1939, Saskatchewan's settlers were ageing and the Depression had left many poor. The Sisters took on the care of the indigent elderly, purchasing the former Presbyterian College in Moose Jaw and renovating it to become St. Anthony's Home. The hospital and home operated independently until 1983, when the administrations merged. In 1995 both institutions closed, and the new Providence Place for Holistic Health opened to care for the aged, and the Sisters' duties shifted from administration and medical services to pastoral care duties.

Gayle Desarmia

SISTERS OF SERVICE (SOS).

Founded by Catherine Donnelly in Toronto in 1922 as the first English-speaking Canadian Catholic religious order, the Institute of Sisters of Service was formed to minister to the immigrants of rural western Canada. The Sisters' garb was a simple grey dress, cloak and hat rather than the long religious habit and veil worn by women religious at that time. The SOS opened their first Saskatchewan mission in 1934 in Regina, where they operated a Correspondence School for Religious Instruction in the winter, and traveled to rural areas to teach catechism in the summer. SOS also taught in public schools in Marquis (1936–43), the Bergfield area (1938–48), and the Sinnett area (1940–68); served in Saskatoon as social workers for the Catholic Welfare Council and its successor, Catholic Family Services (1942–76); and operated a residence for Catholic women students attending St. THOMAS MORE COLLEGE at the UNIVERSITY OF SASKATCHEWAN (1946–68). The Sisters were involved in education and social work in La Loche, (1975–79), Green Lake (1979–83) and La Ronge (1983–94), and in pastoral ministries in Regina at Campion College (1976–80) and Holy Rosary

Cathedral, as well as in parishes at Milestone (1991–94) and Radville (1997–2002). The community left Saskatchewan in 2003.

Patricia Burke

SISTERS OF THE CHILD JESUS.

In 1667, Anne Marie Martel, under the direction of a Sulpician priest, began instructing poor uneducated women in the region of Le Puy, France. In 1896 Bishop Paul Durieu of New Westminster, BC, requested Sisters of the Child Jesus to come and teach the Native children in his territory. Four Sisters traveled from France to Canada and began their work at St. Joseph's Mission, near William's Lake.

In 1915, the congregation, based then in North Vancouver, agreed to send Sisters to Saskatchewan to carry out domestic work for Bishop Pascal and the many priests who lived in the clergy residence in Prince Albert. In the following years, Sisters also came to St. Hippolyte, North Battleford, Albertville, Saskatoon and Jackfish Lake. They taught in both public and separate schools, nursed, and did pastoral works in parishes, homes and hospitals. At the present time there are Sisters of the Child Jesus in North Battleford and Saskatoon, where they continue to be involved in pastoral ministry.

Marianne Flory

SISTERS OF THE PRESENTATION OF MARY (PM).

The congregation of the Sisters of the Presentation of Mary was founded in the Ardèche, southern France in 1796 by Anne-Marie Rivier to educate young people in academics and in the Catholic faith. In 1853, six Sisters from France came to teach in Marieville, Quebec. Fifty years later, in 1903, twelve Sisters journeyed from Quebec to Saskatchewan to work with the Oblates at St. Michael's School in the Duck Lake area. Shortly thereafter, Stobart Public School Board in Duck Lake hired Sister Marie-de-la-Trinité to teach in their two-room school. So began the Presentation Sisters' participation in French-English education and culture on the prairies of Saskatchewan. In subsequent years, the Sisters taught in Saskatoon, Marcelin, Prince Albert, Wakaw, Zenon Park, Green Lake, Debden, Spiritwood, Bellevue, Vawn, Makwa, Albertville, North Battleford, Melfort and Regina. Parish work and ministry to Native peoples have also been a part of the Sisters' work for the last twenty years.

Emma Rousseau

SISTERS SERVANTS OF MARY IMMACULATE.

Upon invitation from Father Achille Delaere of the Redemptorists, the first Sisters Servants of Mary Immaculate arrived in Yorkton in 1915. In 1916 they started teaching religion and providing home nursing care. With money borrowed from the Sulpicians of Montreal, the Sisters moved into their new convent in December 1916.

In Yorkton, the Sisters cared for Sacred Heart

Institute (1917–45), Sacred Heart Academy (1945–73) and Sacred Heart High School (1974–2000). They also conducted a music school at these institutions, specializing in piano and musical theory. They were involved in every Catholic elementary school in Yorkton until the 1980s and taught in St. Joseph's Junior High School (*see* ST. JOSEPH'S COLLEGE). The Sisters' tradition of music as an important part of education has been maintained by Yorkton's Catholic schools.

From Yorkton, the Sisters established convents in other parts of the province. In Saskatoon they administered a women's hostel (1928–93), taught in Catholic schools (1942–76), and have been managing the Ukrainian Catholic Religious Education Centre since 1980. In Regina they cared for a women's hostel (1939–60s), managed the Ukrainian Catholic Religious Education Centre (1974–80), and taught at St. Joseph's School (1939–74). In Prince Albert they taught at St. John's (1956–71) and at St. Michael's and St. Paul's schools (1971–76), and provided a principal and teacher at St. Ann's School (1959–71); they also worked with female inmates at the federal penitentiary. In the summers, the Sisters provided Ukrainian Catholic parishes with catechetical programs and teachers. Over a hundred women born in Saskatchewan became Sisters Servants, mainly due to the encouragement of the Redemptorists in the Ituna and Yorkton areas. Although vocations have declined, the Sisters Servants of Mary Immaculate have been closely identified with the Ukrainian Catholic Church of Saskatchewan and continue to contribute to its life and work.

Victoria Hunchak

SIOUX: *see* DAKOTA/LAKOTA

SITTING BULL (1836–90).

Sitting Bull, Chief of the Hunkpapa Sioux, was born in 1836 in Dakota Territory. Under Chief Red Cloud, Sitting Bull was one of the leaders who fought against American movement into Sioux territory in the 1860s. In the early 1860s the Sioux were granted the Black Hills of South Dakota under Treaty; however, the early 1870s saw reports of gold and the area was flooded with white prospectors. The conflict reached a climax on June 25, 1876, with the Battle of the Little Big Horn, in which the Sioux led by Sitting Bull defeated George Custer and the 7th U. S. Calvary. In November 1876 Sitting Bull crossed the international boundary into Canada and sought refuge in the CYPRESS HILLS near WOOD MOUNTAIN. There he was met by James Walsh of the North-West Mounted Police, who assured the chief that he would be protected from attack by the US Cavalry as long as he obeyed the laws of Canada and did not make raids into the US–terms that Sitting Bull agreed to.

Between 1877 and 1881 numerous attempts were made by both American and Canadian officials

Sitting Bull.

to have Sitting Bull return to the US. He had hoped to remain in Canada, but Canadian officials were not willing to grant him a reserve or provide rations. As a result, in July 1881 Sitting Bull, accompanied by the Wood Mountain fur trader JEAN-LOUIS LÉGARÉ, surrendered to American officials at Fort Buford, North Dakota. Sitting Bull took up residence on the Standing Rock Agency and for a time toured with Buffalo Bill's Wild West Show. In December 1890 he was shot and killed by a group of Indian police who were attempting to issue a warrant for his participation in the Ghost Dance. *Rob Nestor*

16TH MEDICAL COMPANY. 16th Medical Company, a Reserve unit that provides medical support to the other units of **38TH CANADIAN BRIGADE GROUP**, traces its lineage to 21st Field Ambulance of **WORLD WAR I** and 10th Field Ambulance of **WORLD WAR II**. The latter unit moved from Ontario to Saskatchewan prior to 1939 and trained at Camp Dundurn in 1940–41. Once deployed overseas, 10th Field Ambulance provided medical support to the 6th Infantry Brigade. In the late 1970s, 19th Medical Company, located in Regina and with sub-units in Saskatoon and Moose Jaw, was absorbed into **16TH (SASKATCHEWAN) SERVICE BATTALION** and re-designated 16th Medical Company. In later years, medical companies were removed from service battalions and 16th Medical Company again became an independent unit, having detachments located in Regina and Saskatoon. *Holden Stoffel*

16TH MOUNTED RIFLES/16TH LIGHT HORSE. Raised on July 3, 1905, the 16th Mounted Rifles was Saskatchewan's first **MILITIA** regiment. It was originally formed in 1885 as the Battleford Rifle Company and fought at the Battle of **CUT KNIFE HILL**. Demobilized after the **NORTH-WEST RESISTANCE**, the Battleford Rifles were perpetuated by the 16th in the aftermath of the **BOER WAR**. The regiment was re-designated the 16th Light Horse in 1908.

Details of the 16th were placed on active service upon the outbreak of **WORLD WAR I**. It was one of eight former militia units to be amalgamated into the **5TH BATTALION, WESTERN CAVALRY**, that came to be known as the "Red Saskatchewan" for the preponderance of men from the province. Switched to infantry duty because of a lack of horses, the 16th saw its first action in Flanders in February 1915 and remained in the battlefield for the duration of the war. Battles in which it participated included Ypres (1915), the Somme (1916) and Cambrai (1918).

Postwar reorganization led to a change in name (16th Canadian Light Horse) in 1920 and amalgamation with the Saskatchewan Mounted Rifles (22nd Light Horse) in 1936. Renamed the **BATTLEFORD LIGHT INFANTRY** in **WORLD WAR II**, reconnaissance and tank companies were dispatched to the United Kingdom but did not go into battle. The rest of the regiment was placed on local protective duty.

Following World War II, another reorganization merged the Battleford Light Infantry with the Prince Albert Volunteers under the name "Prince Albert and Battleford Volunteers"—formerly the name of the Prince Albert Volunteers and a continuation of the 105th Regiment (Saskatoon Fusilliers). In absorbing the Saskatoon Light Infantry in 1955, the combination became the second incarnation of the North Saskatchewan Regiment. *John Chaput*

16TH (SASKATCHEWAN) SERVICE BATTALION. 16th (Saskatchewan) Service Battalion, a reserve unit that provides combat service support to the other units of **38TH CANADIAN BRIGADE GROUP**, was organized in 1965 as a training unit with headquarters in Regina. In 1973 the Battalion was reorganized with 142nd Transport Company, Royal Canadian Army Service Corp (RCASC), and 5th Ordinance Company, Royal Canadian Ordnance Corps (RCOC), in Regina, becoming their supply and transport component; the maintenance personnel from Increment A, 2nd North Saskatchewan Regiment—formerly 37th Technical Squadron, **ROYAL CANADIAN ELECTRICAL AND MECHANICAL ENGINEERS** (RCEME)—in Saskatoon, became its maintenance company. A military police platoon was also established. The Battalion was designated 16th (Regina) Service Battalion in 1976, and re-designated 16th (Saskatchewan) Service Battalion in 1987.

In order to carry out the various functions required to keep troops operational, the Battalion has a wide variety of trades available. Unit members can be trained as maintenance, transport, supply, intelligence, food services, administration and military police personnel. Technicians are trained in the maintenance and repair of vehicles and weapons. Transport specialists learn to drive various types of military vehicles safely in all types of weather and terrain, and under varied conditions. Supply personnel learn to take responsibility for stores and equipment distribution and accounting in order to facilitate smooth training operations for the unit. Food services personnel are instructed in the preparation and provision of meals for all circumstances and under varying conditions. Administration staff

A reservist with the 16th (Saskatchewan) Service Battalion prepares to assist with flood relief in Winnipeg, 1997.

duties include maintenance of unit files and records, keeping of pay records and files, and typing. Military police personnel provide services in crime detection, traffic and crowd control, route marking, investigations, and other police duties.

16th (Saskatchewan) Service Battalion is located in Regina and Saskatoon. Members of the Battalion continue to augment the Regular Force on various peacekeeping missions. The Battalion perpetuates Saskatchewan units of the former RCASC, RCOC and RCEME. *Stewart Mein*

FURTHER READING: Warren, A. 1961. *Wait for the Wagon: The Story of the Royal Canadian Army Service Corps.* Toronto: McClelland; Rannie, W.F. 1984. *To the Thunderer His Arms: The Royal Canadian Ordnance Corps.* Lincoln, ON: W.F. Rannie.

60 BATTERY (ANEROID, SASKATCHEWAN).

Captain Gordon S. Howard organized the first MILITIA unit in Aneroid, Saskatchewan in 1925. Called the 10th Field Brigade Ammunition Column, it was part of the Non-Permanent Active Militia. In 1927, 60 Battery Canadian Field Artillery (CFA) was formed with Major Howard, Captain A.W. Boulter, and Lieutenant E.C. Jacobs as officers. The battery included men from the immediate Aneroid district as well as nearby Kincaid, Vanguard, Neville, and Ponteix. The Department of National Defence converted Aneroid's Beaver Lumber Company buildings into an armoury in 1927, giving 60 Battery a home.

A 24-hour guard was immediately posted around the armoury following the outbreak of WORLD WAR II in September 1939. On July 24, 1940, 60 Battery mobilized for active duty and was soon up to strength. Captain Jacobs and senior Non-Commissioned Officers from the battery conducted training at a camp located on the town's exhibition grounds. On February 1, 1941, 60 Battery, 76 Battery from Indian Head, and 37 Battery from Portage la Prairie were designated 17th Field Regiment, Royal Canadian Artillery. Commanded by Lieutenant-Colonel W.C. Thackerey, the regiment served in England, Wales, Italy, and Northwest Europe. It was disbanded at the end of the war. *Holden Stoffel*

64 FIELD BATTERY. 64 Field Battery in Yorkton traces its lineage to the Yorkton Regiment, one of four regiments created when the NORTH SASKATCHEWAN REGIMENT was reorganized on May 15, 1924. The Yorkton Regiment was converted to artillery on December 15, 1936, and designated the 64 Field Battery. It constituted one of four batteries of the 17th Field Brigade Royal Canadian Artillery (RCA) that served in WORLD WAR II. Following the war, the batteries of the 10th, 17th, and 22nd Field Brigades RCA were reorganized into the 10th Medium Artillery Regiment RCA. The early 1960s saw the

Regiment converted to the 10th Field Artillery Regiment RCA. Today, the 10TH FIELD REGIMENT has two batteries: 18 Field Battery in Regina and 64 Field Battery in Yorkton. *Holden Stoffel*

COURTESY OF ARTHUR SLADE

Arthur Slade.

SLADE, ARTHUR GREGORY (1967–). Arthur Slade, an award-winning author, was born in Moose Jaw on July 9, 1967. He grew up on the CYPRESS HILLS ranch of his parents, Robert and Anne (Shea), herself a writer. After completing high school in Gull Lake, he went to the UNIVERSITY OF SASKATCHEWAN, where he received an honours degree in English in 1989. Arthur married BRENDA BAKER, a Saskatchewan singer, writer and entertainer in 1997; their daughter, Tori Lorranne, was born in 2003.

Arthur Slade began writing novels in high school. Following university, he worked in Saskatoon, writing radio advertising. After five years, he decided to focus on writing for young people. His seventh novel, *Draugr*, was the first to be published and was nominated for a SASKATCHEWAN BOOK AWARD and a Small Press Book Award. Slade's novel, *Dust*, received the 2001 Governor-General's Literary Award for Children's Literature, the 2001 Saskatchewan Book Award for Children's Literature, and the 2002 Mr. Christie's Book Award. In 2003, *Return of the Grudstone Ghosts* received the Saskatchewan Young Readers' Choice Diamond Willow Award. In addition to his novels, Arthur Slade has written articles, a biography of John Diefenbaker, and comics. *Marion Perry*

FURTHER READING: Ferguson, Collene. 2003. "Few Authors can Match Arthur Slade's Versatility." *Regina Leader Post* (November 29).

SLINKARD, ALFRED EUGENE (1931–). Alfred Slinkard, a key builder of Canada's half-billion-dollar PULSE CROP INDUSTRY, was born in Rockford, Washington, on April 5, 1931. He obtained his Bachelor and Master of Science degrees at Washington State University and his PhD at the University of Minnesota. He was recruited from the

University of Idaho to the newly created CROP DEVELOPMENT CENTRE of the UNIVERSITY OF SASKATCHEWAN in 1972. As plant breeder of new lentil crops, he developed the varieties Laird in 1978 and Eston in 1980. By 1990, Canada had overtaken both Turkey and the United States as a major supplier of green lentils to Latin America and the Mediterranean. Over the past twenty-eight years, Slinkard has advised pulse growers in virtually every municipality in Saskatchewan and has authored over 300 books, journals, and extension publications. Since 1984 he has been advisor to the Saskatchewan Pulse Growers Board, and from 1986 to 1992 he was chairman of the board of Newfield Seeds. During the 1990s he developed improved varieties of chickpeas and field beans suitable to prairie conditions. In 2000, there were 128 pulse crop processors in Saskatchewan processing Slinkard's lentil and pea varieties.

Since retiring in 1998, Slinkard has been active in developing spice crops for Saskatchewan. During his career he obtained numerous recognition awards, including fellowships in the American Association for the Advancement of Science, the American Society of Agronomy, and the Agricultural Institute of Canada. He received the Canadian Seed Trade Association Scientific Achievement Award, the Canadian Society of Agronomy Outstanding Researcher Award, the Western Co-operative Fertilizers Agronomy Merit Award, and honorary life memberships in the Saskatchewan and Canadian Seed Growers Associations and the Saskatchewan Pulse Crop Growers Association. In 2000 Slinkard was inducted into the Saskatchewan Agricultural Hall of Fame, and in 2004 into the Canadian Agricultural Hall of Fame.

SLOVAKS: *see* CZECH AND SLOVAK SETTLEMENTS

SMALL, WILLIAM (1927–). Bill Small was born in Craven in November 18, 1927, and devoted much of his time to agricultural endeavours. He was a founding director and chairman of the Canadian Western Agribition and Western Canadian Farm Progress Show respectively. Small's name is included on the Honour Roll of the Canadian Association of Exhibitions and Fairs. He was made an Honorary Director of the Saskatchewan Agricultural Graduates of the UNIVERSITY OF SASKATCHEWAN and received a Distinguished Graduate in Agriculture award. Inducted into the Saskatchewan Agriculture Hall of Fame in 2000, Small was awarded the Saskatchewan Order of Merit in 2002.

SMISHEK, WALTER EDMUND (1925–). Walter Smishek was born in Poland on July 21, 1925. He attended Teachers' College in Saskatoon for six weeks but left to work for Western Grocers.

© M.WEST, REGINA, WEST'S STUDIO
COLLECTION/SASKATCHEWAN ARCHIVES BOARD R-A8382
Walter Smishek.

Smishek became active in the trade union movement and served as a representative for the **RETAIL WHOLESALE AND DEPARTMENT STORE WORKERS UNION**. He became Executive Secretary of the **SASKATCHEWAN FEDERATION OF LABOUR** in 1960, and further served on the political action committee of the Canadian Labour Congress and as a vice-president of the SFL. He represented labour on the **UNIVERSITY OF SASKATCHEWAN** senate for six years and on the senate executive committee for three years. In 1961, as a member of the Advisory Planning Committee on Medicare, he wrote a dissenting report which opposed user/deterrent fees, the overemphasis on fee-for-service as the means of physician remuneration, and other issues.

Smishek was elected to the Saskatchewan Legislature as the member for Regina East in 1964 and represented this area of the city through five elections until 1982. Following the election of the NDP government in 1971, Smishek served as Minister of Health (1971–75), Finance (1975–79), and Urban Affairs (1979–82). He served as a member of Treasury Board, and as its chairperson from 1975 to 1979. From 1978 to 1982 Smishek served as chair of a Cabinet Committee on Social Policy and was the Minister-in-charge of the Social Policy Secretariat. Smishek was best known for his leadership in health programming including the introduction of School Dental Program and the Prescription Drug Plan. After Smishek was defeated in the 1982 election, he worked for the federal department of Indian and Northern Affairs. *Alex Taylor*

SMITH, DAVID LAWRENCE (1914–83). Larry Smith was born in Regina on April 18, 1914, where

his father was Livestock Commissioner for Saskatchewan before he died on the battlefield in Passchendaele in 1917. Smith received his DVM from the Ontario Veterinary College (OVC) in 1943 and his PhD from Cornell University in 1955. He was professor and head, Department of Pathology and Bacteriology at OVC before becoming the founding dean of the Western College of Veterinary Medicine (WCVM) at the **UNIVERSITY OF SASKATCHEWAN**, from 1964 to 1974. Through his leadership and integrity the WCVM quickly became a strong institution. He secured a cost-sharing agreement among the western provinces served by WCVM, the first example of interprovincial cost sharing of post-secondary education in Canada. He was a strong proponent of research and of formal postgraduate education in veterinary medicine. He helped implement CIDA programs in university education in Uganda (1969–70), Malaysia (1974–76), and Somalia (1981–83). He was elected to both the Canadian and Saskatchewan Agricultural Halls of Fame, and received the St. Eloi medal from the College of Veterinary Surgeons of Quebec. *N.O. Nielson*

SMITH, GEORGE (1926–). George Smith was born on August 23, 1926, in London, England, into a working class family of seven children. He married Jean Mary Boyes in 1957. Later, the Smiths were advised to move to either western Canada or Arizona because of their daughter's asthma: they chose Saskatchewan. A strong union supporter prior to his move to Canada, Smith had organized a local of the Transport Workers Union after a stint in the British army, which he had joined in March 1943 at the age of 16. In 1958, he started working at SaskPower and became a member of the Oil, Chemical and Atomic Workers Union Local 9-649. He was particularly active around occupational health and safety issues. As a gas instrument technician, part of his responsibilities included repairing and calibrating gas meters. This involved replacing mercury in the meters. After discussions in the shop, the workers found out that they all had similar health problems, which were later associated with mercury poisoning.

As shop steward for the technicians, Smith was active in the struggle to clean up the work place. He was also active in the Regina and District Labour Council, first as treasurer in 1959-60 and later as president during the struggle against wage controls in Saskatchewan. He became famous for carrying a black coffin across Wascana Lake in the winter, signifying the end of free collective bargaining. Because of health problems Smith retired at the age of 53 to British Columbia, where he and his wife did relief work in lighthouses in the Queen Charlotte Islands, and later in Ucluet and Prince Rupert. *Patricia Gallagher*

SMITH, JOSEPH (FL. 1753–65). Joseph Smith's three journals, although poorly written, provide us with one of the earliest glimpses of **CREE** life and of the French traders on the northern plains. In 1756 Washcabitt, a Sturgeon Cree leader from the **ASSINIBOINE RIVER**, asked the Hudson's Bay Company (HBC) at York Factory to send men to oppose the newly arriving French traders. Smith and Joseph Wagonner, a **MÉTIS**, went with him in 1756–57 and again in 1757–58. The group traveled out to the plains near Good Spirit Lake by way of Red Deer River and returned down Swan River. Smith casually mentions **BISON** pounds, the earliest such reference, but does not describe them. Apparently, neither Smith nor **ANTHONY HENDAY** kept a journal of their 1759–60 inland journey, probably to central Alberta. Smith's third journal is from 1763-64, when he wintered with Cree leader Meesinkeeshick, apparently near the Eagle Hills. Smith returned inland in 1764-65, but died on his return to York Factory. The HBC gave his furs, which he had traded illegally, to "the Woman who was his Cannoe Mate & Tent Mate ... & his Child." *Dale Russell*

FURTHER READING: Russell, D. 1991. *Eighteenth-Century Western Cree and their Neighbours.* Archaeological Survey of Canada Mercury Series, Paper 143. Ottawa: Canadian Museum of Civilization.

SMUDGING. Smudging is a sacred ceremony of most First Nations. Depending on the geographic location, sweetgrass, sage and/or cedar can be burned to purify the body, mind, heart and spirit of all persons who enter the ceremonial area. This allows the people to participate fully in whatever event is happening later; smudging can also be done as a separate sacred ceremony. Many First Nations people understand that there are negative forces which can cause harm: smudging is a method to protect oneself from these. Smudging should be done starting the burn at the tip of the plant. The plant should be used until about 5 cm, including the roots, are left; this part is to be returned to Mother Earth to assist in replenishing her. During the smudging, people through motions of their hands cover their body with the smoke; completion is indicated by turning the palms of the hands down. After each person has carefully smudged, the smoke is allowed to stop burning. *William Asikinack*

SNELL, HERBERT (1880–1932). Lieutenant-Colonel Herbert Snell was born in Stockbridge, Yorkshire, England on August 20, 1880. His family emigrated to Port Hope, Ontario. Snell entered the merchant trade at a young age, working in various locations throughout western Canada. In 1905 he settled in Moose Jaw, where he established his own retail store four years later. He was elected an alderman for Moose Jaw in 1911. Given command of the newly raised 60th Rifles of Canada in 1913, Snell was instrumental in the construction of the Moose Jaw Armoury and the mobilization of troops at the outbreak of **WORLD WAR I**. He was appointed commanding officer of the 46th (South Saskatchewan) Infantry Battalion, CEF, after its authorization on February 1, 1915. Although seriously wounded in a training accident in England later that year, Snell left hospital to become commanding officer of the 9th Reserve Brigade. He went to France in April 1917, and temporarily commanded the 46th Battalion before taking over 4th Divisional Wing, Canadian Corps Reinforcement Camp and Divisional School. Snell returned briefly to Moose Jaw in 1919, even though his business had been closed during the war. In 1922 he joined the Robert Simpson Department Store of Montreal, in which he later became vice-president and general manager. Herbert Snell died of complications from wounds on November 12, 1932.

Gerry Carline

FURTHER READING: McWilliams, J.L. and R.J. Steel. 1978. *The Suicide Battalion*. Edmonton: Hurtig.

SNOW ROLLER. A rare winter phenomenon, a snow roller is formed when the wind blows wet snow into a roll. Three weather conditions must occur simultaneously and in the proper order for snow rollers to take shape. First, there has to be sufficient accumulation of light, fluffy snow. Secondly, once the snow has stopped falling, the temperature has to rise above the freezing mark, making the snow sticky. Finally, a strong wind is required to roll the snow up in layers. If the wind is strong enough, the moving ball of snow becomes cylindrical, often with a hole through it lengthwise. Snow rollers range in size from that of eggs to small barrels. Their tracks are sometimes several metres long and less than one centimetre deep. Recorded snow roller sightings have occurred in Regina on December 25, 1993, and near Willow Bunch in February 2001.

Holden Stoffel

FURTHER READING: Blevins, Kevin. 1993. "Nature's Snowballs Graced Regina." *Regina Leader-Post*, A3 (December 27); 2001. "Snow Rollers: A Rare Sight." *Moose Jaw Times Herald*, 8 (February 3).

SNOWBIRDS 431 (AIR DEMONSTRATION) SQUADRON. The Snowbirds are the Canadian air force's aerobatics team, based at **15 WING MOOSE JAW**. One of only three military aerobatics teams in the world to fly nine-plane formations, the Snowbirds consist of eleven pilots, ten aircraft technicians, one logistics officer, and one supply technician. All squadron members are Canadian Forces personnel with years of military experience. Initially an unofficial demonstration flying team, the Snowbirds were

COURTESY OF GERRY CARLINE

established at Canadian Forces Base Moose Jaw in 1971. The squadron's name was determined through a contest held at the base's elementary school. The Snowbirds became a permanent unit in September 1977 and received squadron status on April 1, 1978, as 431 (Air Demonstration) Squadron. The team flies the Canadair CT-114 Tutor, a Canadian-designed and produced subsonic jet-trainer with a unique red, white, and blue colour scheme. The goal of the Snowbirds is to demonstrate the skill, professionalism, and teamwork of the Canadian Forces, and to achieve perfection in formation flight. Each year, the team performs at approximately seventy air shows at fifty different locations across North America.

Peter Borch

FURTHER READING: Baraton, J.-P. 1990. *Snowbirds 1971–1990: A 20-Year History*. Calgary: J.P.B. Publications; Oberle, L.P. 2001. *The Canadian Forces*

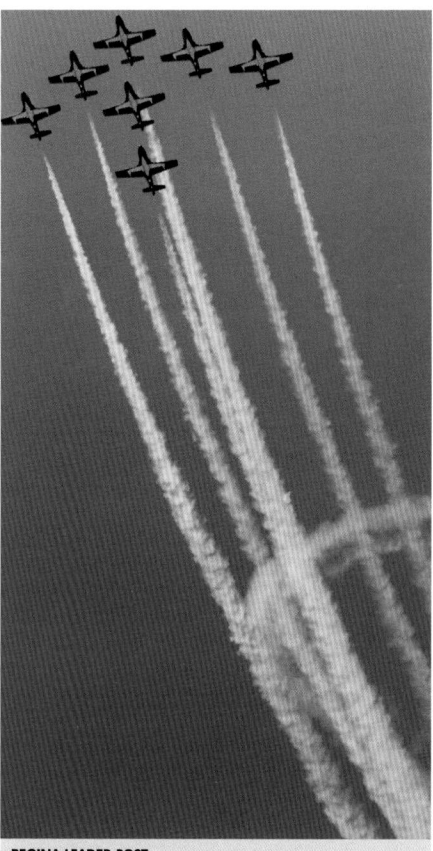

REGINA LEADER-POST
Snowbirds in formation.

Snowbirds: 431 Air Demonstration Squadron. Mankato, MS: Capstone High-Interest Books; Philp, O.B. 1990. *Snowbirds from the Beginning*. Sydney, BC: Porthole Press.

ROY ANTAL PHOTO/REGINA LEADER-POST
Snowbird pilots climb out of their jets after launching their 27th season in 1997.

SASKATCHEWAN ARCHIVES BOARD R-A8366
Gordon Snyder.

SNYDER, GORDON TAYLOR (1924–). Born September 17, 1924, in Moose Jaw, Snyder was educated at the Moose Jaw Technical School. Snyder enlisted in the RCAF in 1942, serving in Canada. After discharge, he worked for the CPR as a fireman and was promoted to engineer in 1956. Active in the railroad unions, he served in a variety of posts in the Brotherhoods of Firemen and Locomotive Engineers. Snyder was involved in youth wing of the CCF. In 1960 he was elected to the Saskatchewan Legislature, replacing long-time CCF MLA and railroader Dempster Heming of Moose Jaw. Snyder was re-elected in 1964 and in 1967, when he was appointed critic of Health. Following the NDP victory in 1971, Snyder was appointed Minister of Labour, a post he held for eleven years until the government's defeat. Snyder reversed much of the **THATCHER** government's legislation, repealing the Emergency Services Act and removing barriers for the creation of trade unions. The province overhauled the scope of labour legislation; the first forty-hour work week was established in Canada; the Occupational Health and Safety board was strengthened; more stringent safely legislation was introduced; and the **WORKERS' COMPENSATION** Board was expanded. The Minimum Wage Board was re-established to develop a process of constant review of the minimum wage, tying it to a percentage of the average industrial wage. The minimum wage was the highest in Canada. The role of the Women's Bureau, the forerunner of the Women's Secretariat, was greatly expanded. In 1972 the province was the first in Canada to introduce legislation insuring equal pay for similar work. Snyder was defeated in 1982 and retired from public life. *Brett Quiring*

FURTHER READING: Shaak, L. 2002. *Without Regrets: Gordon Snyder's Reflections.* Moose Jaw: On Stage Consulting; Snyder, Gordon. 1997. "Social Justice for Workers." In Eleanor Glor (ed.), *Policy Innovation in the Saskatchewan Public Sector, 1971–1982.* North York: Captus Press.

SOCCER. Soccer is commonly called "football" outside Canada and the United States, and was generally known as such in Saskatchewan until after **WORLD WAR I**, when rugby evolved into what is now known as football in Canada. Members of the North-West Mounted Police introduced soccer to the Canadian west as early as 1874. Saskatchewan's first recorded team was Regina Fairmede in September 1888, and the first recorded result a 3-0 victory for St. Catherines over Lindsay, published in the *Saskatchewan Review* of June 28, 1889. Grenfell, Battleford, Saltcoats and Moosomin also were active in the 19th century. Further growth led to the formation in 1906 of the Saskatchewan Soccer Association (SSA), which divided the province into eighteen districts and offered the Challenge Shield for the Saskatchewan men's championship. Soccer maintained a steady following throughout the 20th century, and has seen a dramatic rise in youth participation since the 1980s. More than 30,000 players are registered with the SSA. Outstanding players have included Norman Sheldon, who played in Prince Albert from 1906 to 29, **DAVID GREYEYES** of Muskeg Lake Reserve (1937–49), and Kevin Holness of Regina, who enjoyed a rare two-goal game for Canada against Honduras in 1996.

John Chaput

SOCIAL ASSISTANCE. In Canada, adult citizens are expected to be as economically independent as possible. Whether a person can be self-sufficient depends on the individual's capacity to work, on opportunities for employment or self-employment, and sometimes on other circumstances. Often as a result of a combination of factors, there are occasions where people find themselves in financial need and without a personal resource to turn to. Social assistance (sometimes also referred to as "welfare") is a form of public benefit that is designed to help people in financial need. Its purpose is not to address poverty as such, but rather to prevent extreme economic hardship or destitution.

When Saskatchewan was created in 1905, people in need were expected to rely on family, friends, or charitable organizations. As the provincial economy and social relationships became more complex, governments gradually assumed more responsibility for helping individuals in need. While the first social assistance programs in Saskatchewan were organized by municipal governments, this service is now provided by the province, with partial and indirect financial support from the federal government. The

way most people in Saskatchewan get income for their personal or family needs is through employment or self-employment. Like most developed countries, Canada has a series of social security measures that protect economically vulnerable people such as children or the elderly, or reduce the negative impacts of misfortunes such as illness, injury, or unemployment. Social assistance is intended to provide last-resort income support in the absence of other sources of income from employment or social insurance.

Because it is a last-resort source of income support, social assistance uses a "budget deficit" system for determining eligibility for benefits. An estimate of the individual or family's basic needs is constructed, based on family size and composition. The household's income resources are then compared to the budget, and if a deficit exists, this amount is the benefit. This approach to benefit eligibility is also sometimes called "needs-testing." Some other qualification rules may also apply. Applicants are expected to explore all alternatives to social assistance, particularly work ("employment-testing"). Those with more than a modest level of cash, real estate, vehicles, or other possessions may be considered ineligible because the asset may be deemed a resource available for current needs ("asset testing").

The budget-deficit system means that the applicant's other income sources generally result in benefits being reduced dollar for dollar. There are some exceptions, such as partial exemption of employment income, a policy that is intended to encourage employment activities. There is considerable debate in social policy circles about the effectiveness of earnings exemptions compared to other approaches to encouraging employment and self-sufficiency. Social assistance has tended to be a controversial program. The availability of an unearned cash benefit from government is seen by some as a work disincentive; in fact, there is practical evidence that long-term reliance on social assistance may erode peoples' capacity and will to be self-sufficient. While social assistance ensures everyone's basic needs are met in the short term, some believe it is also a factor in reinforcing poverty and economic exclusion. It is therefore important that social assistance be closely connected to employment services and other supports that help people restore their capacity to support themselves.

As the last line of defense against financial need, demand for social assistance tends to be affected by major trends in social and family arrangements, and by cycles in the labour market and the economy. A long-term upward trend in caseloads occurred between the 1970s and the early 1990s, with generally declining demand from that time forward as the Saskatchewan and federal governments adjusted cash benefit and other programs to encourage employment. As controversial as such programs may be at times, basic income support programs like social assistance are an important component of our social security system. They are one of the means by which we enforce an implicit social contract among citizens of Saskatchewan: that we do not allow members of our community to suffer extreme deprivation for reasons beyond their control. Carefully designed and managed, social assistance and other basic income support programs can prevent destitution and help economically marginalized people move back into the mainstream of the community.

Rick August

SOCIAL ASSISTANCE HEALTH SERVICES PLAN.

This plan, implemented on January 1, 1945, was the first comprehensive, provincial social assistance health services scheme established in Canada. It provided pensioners and other welfare recipients with both medical and hospital services free of charge, and was the **DOUGLAS** government's first step towards the establishment of universal hospital and medical care programs in Saskatchewan. The basic principles of the medical component were devised during a single amicable evening in Regina by Premier Douglas and representatives of the medical profession on August 23, 1944. The plan was administered by the Department of Health–unlike the scheme introduced in Ontario in 1935, and later in Alberta, British Columbia, and Nova Scotia, each of which was administered by the appropriate provincial medical association. The Douglas administration insisted that the management of public funds must remain the responsibility of a government accountable to the people. The program provided valuable administrative experience for the province's universal hospital and medical services plans.

Gordon Lawson

SOCIAL CREDIT PARTY.

The Social Credit Party of Saskatchewan was first formed in the wake of the party's sweep to power in Alberta. Originally a progressive-reform party, it tried to form an alliance with the CCF. Although making inroads into the CCF's organization and its membership, the party leadership was steadfastly opposed to an alliance. The party's presence caused considerable concern among the politically dominant **LIBERAL PARTY**, which worried that it would sweep Saskatchewan as it had Alberta. The 1935 federal election and 1938 provincial election proved the party to be a hollow force after it only managed to elect two members in each election. After 1938 the party disintegrated, but was later revived in 1955 by "Socred" organizers from Alberta and British Columbia. Even though they failed to convince Progressive Conservative leader **ALVIN HAMILTON** to join them in their "anti-socialist" crusade, they did manage to field a full slate of candidates in 1956, electing three candidates to the Legislature. Social Credit retained a respectable

result in the 1960 election, but all its MLAs were defeated and the party returned to obscurity and ceased running candidates after the 1967 election.

Brett Quiring

SOCIAL GOSPEL.

Saskatchewan residents embraced the Social Gospel message sweeping across Canada in the late 19th and early 20th centuries. Its proponents argued that a society reflecting and striving for the "common good" would be a healthy and economically equitable society. People in the west tried to cope first with a huge influx of immigrants, then with the aftermath of **WORLD WAR I**, and finally with the financial and social devastation experienced during the **GREAT DEPRESSION**. Worries over growing numbers of non-British immigrants, the widespread use of alcohol, and the rise of liberalism prompted an evangelical zeal amongst the Protestant elite in Canada. Concerned politicians, clergy, and others equated "social problems" like poverty, the threat of communism, and rising unemployment rates with a lack of religious morals. Proponents of the Social Gospel promised eternal salvation to those who were patriotic, followed the Bible, attended Church, and worked to eliminate drunkenness, poverty and greed. During the early 1900s, Saskatchewan women enthusiastically supported this doctrine, and actively participated in the Suffrage Movement and the **WOMAN'S CHRISTIAN TEMPERANCE UNION**. Having political influence as new voters, they combined religious dogma with social activism to push for social change, lobbying the federal and provincial governments to legislate abstinence from alcohol, observation of the Sabbath, and an end to prostitution.

Traveling across the prairies in the 1930s, politician William Aberhart likened federal politicians to thieves and sinners, and offered salvation to the "common workers" if they voted for the **SOCIAL CREDIT PARTY**. Methodist minister J.S. Woodsworth used the tenets of the Social Gospel to foster strong social consciousness through political activism in Saskatchewan. He was one of the driving forces behind the formation of the **CO-OPERATIVE COMMONWEALTH FEDERATION** (CCF), which united labour groups, socialists, and farmers in pursuit of a better society. The name Co-operative Commonwealth Federation reflected the Social Gospel philosophy and practice of co-operating for the common good. Eschewing capitalism and favouring social programs, Woodsworth traded his earlier religious affiliation for a broader-based political platform dedicated to social reform. Baptist minister **T.C. DOUGLAS** was another activist who used Social Gospel beliefs to further a socially conscious political agenda. His career paralleled Woodsworth's, first as a Christian minister and then as leader of the CCF. Douglas was elected as Premier of Saskatchewan in 1944 and led the first socialist

government in North America. Well known for his oratory skills, honesty, and religious fervour, Douglas and the CCF dramatically altered Saskatchewan and federal politics. Universal **MEDICARE**, old-age pensions, unemployment insurance, and the family allowance programs originated with T.C. Douglas and the CCF in Saskatchewan.

Elizabeth Mooney

FURTHER READING: Kerr, D. 1992. *Talking Back: The Birth of the CCF*. Regina: Coteau Books; Whelan, Ed and P. Whelan. 1990. *Touched by Tommy: Stories of Hope and Humour in the Words of Men and Women Whose Lives Tommy Douglas Touched*. Regina: Whelan Publications.

SOCIAL POLICY: *see essay on page 873.*

SOCIAL WORK.

The social work profession promotes social change, problem solving in human relationships, and the empowerment and liberation of people to enhance well-being and prevent dysfunction. Utilizing theories of human behaviour and social systems, social work intervenes at the points where people interact with their environments. Principles of human rights and social justice are fundamental to social work.

Social workers are employed in child welfare and family service settings, health organizations, mental health clinics, business and industry, schools, correctional systems, welfare administration agencies, community organizations, and in private practice. Client populations served by social workers include children and youth at risk, people with disabilities, low-income people, those with chemical dependencies, the homeless, offenders, the elderly, employees, neighbourhoods, and families. Social work roles range from direct practice to community development to policy-making. Since 1995, the Social Workers Act has required that a person using the title "social worker" be registered with the Saskatchewan Association of Social Workers (SASW). Registration indicates that social workers have met the professional standards to practice social work. As the regulatory body, SASW carries a central responsibility for the protection of the public: it establishes, maintains, and develops standards of ethical practice, and supports development of skills and competency among its members.

Since 1973 social work education and training in Saskatchewan has been offered by the Faculty of Social Work, **UNIVERSITY OF REGINA**. Both undergraduate and graduate studies programs are available through the faculty. Social work classes are available in Regina and Saskatoon as well as in other urban, rural, and northern communitites using face to face, audio, video, and internet teaching methodologies. The Faculty of Social Work also works with a wide variety of government and community agencies to help social work students obtain practical experience to integrate with their academic training. Also, unique in Canada is the School of Indian Social Work of the FIRST NATIONS UNIVERSITY OF CANADA, the aim of which is to develop social work knowledge and skills based on the culture, values, and philosophy of First Nations. *Richard Hazel*

SOCIOLOGY AND SASKATCHEWAN DEVELOPMENT.
Sociology is a discipline concerned with the study of institutions, organizations, communities and other social structures, and their relationship to everyday life. English-Canadian sociology in the first half of the 20th century was strongly influenced by the Chicago School via McGill University, by political economy at the University of Toronto, as well as by American functionalism and the London School of Economics. While individual sociology courses were offered much earlier, a sociology department was not established until the late 1950s at the UNIVERSITY OF SASKATCHEWAN, and the early 1960s at the UNIVERSITY OF REGINA. The two departments now offer study opportunities in many subdisciplines including class, race and gender relations, socialization and social organization, criminology, and social research methods.

In the years following WORLD WAR II, sociologists played a significant role in "reconstruction" programs in Canada. In Saskatchewan, sociologists played a role in the Royal Commission on Agriculture and Rural Life and in studies of local government, adult education, and other areas. More recently, sociologists have been involved in policy initiatives concerning health reform, justice, labour policy, social security, intergovernmental relations, and the operation of CROWN CORPORATIONS, among others. There are approximately 1,800 practising sociologists in Saskatchewan. Principal occupations include management and finance, sales and service, and public administration, with smaller proportions in the health, resource, and manufacturing sectors. Over the past three decades, sociology as a discipline has become less focused and more diverse; and the discipline's influence on social policy has become less direct. Sociology graduates commonly go on to other post-secondary programs such as law, education, police services and social work, where their sociological training adds perspective to their professional development. *Robert Stirling*

SODIUM SULPHATE. Natural sodium sulphate deposits are found in several alkaline lakes with constrained drainage in the southern part of Saskatchewan. In its natural form it is commonly called Glauber's salt or mirabilite. Sodium sulphate can also be produced artificially through several chemical processes. Currently about 50% of sodium sulphate is artificially produced in the world. Saskatchewan is a world leader in naturally produced sodium sulphate, currently producing 6% of the total world supply. The four major companies extracting sodium sulphate in the province are Goldcorp Inc., MILLAR WESTERN INDUSTRIES, Ormiston Mining and Smelting Co. Ltd., and SOTEC Products Ltd. All production of sodium sulphate in Saskatchewan is in the natural form thanks to the abundance of alkaline lakes. There are presently 21 major sodium sulphate deposits, with more than 500,000 tonnes of sodium sulphate mineral deposits in each. During the production stage several techniques may be used to extract the product, depending on the nature of the deposit. Common practices include dredging and solution mining or pumping brine into evaporation ponds, where natural evaporation concentrates the minerals and crystallization occurs. The sodium sulphate crystals are then extracted from the mixture.

In Saskatchewan there are two grades of sodium sulphate: the first is a salt cake grade, which is primarily used for wood digestion in the pulp and paper industry; the second is a detergent grade product that is used in detergents, glass, dyes, textiles, tanning, and in the chemical industry. Saskatchewan has five operating sodium sulphate facilities where the annual productive capacity is 530,000 tonnes. The consumption rate of sodium sulphate is falling owing to environmental concerns, especially in North America. The industry, however, is attempting to be proactive with these concerns by creating an alternate use for sodium sulphate. There has been research done to use the product as a pollution control agent at coal-fired plants; the sodium sulphate would be added to the COAL to improve its efficiency and reduce the waste released into the environment. The decline of its use in North America is being offset by the expanding markets in Asia and Eastern Europe: both regions are developing in the areas of textiles, glass and detergents, and therefore represent a high demand for sodium sulphate. In Saskatchewan, research and development work is being carried out to create value-added products with sodium sulphate, which can now be used in the manufacturing process of certain fertilizers, soda ash, sodium bicarbonate, and caustic soda.

Julie L. Parchewski

SOIL CONSERVATION. The SOILS of Saskatchewan are fragile, and tillage operations have contributed largely to some of the environmental problems facing agriculture. For a century, Saskatchewan farmers used summerfallow as a means to control weeds and conserve moisture; this practice, however, led to soil erosion and the loss of soil nutrients. Producers have changed the manner in which they manage soil resources and moved to a lesser disturbance of soil: conservation tillage. In 1980 there were 7 million ha of fallow land, but this had declined to only 3.4 million ha by 2000; it now represents only 13% of Saskatchewan's agricultural land base. Summerfallowing is more frequent in the Brown Soil Zone and less in the Black Soil Zone, where soil moisture is more plentiful.

Increasingly farmers have adopted conservation tillage practices: this means less tillage that tends to leave more of the previous crop residue on the soil surface after planting. Tillage systems can be classified into three types: conventional tillage, minimum tillage, and zero tillage. The latter two systems are generally referred to as "conservation tillage," incorporating most of the crop residue into the soil, thus making the soil less susceptible to wind and water erosion. With zero tillage there is no tillage done prior to seeding. Many farmers who tend to follow

EVERETT BAKER PHOTO/COURTESY OF THE SASKATCHEWAN HISTORY AND FOLKLORE SOCIETY

Sodium Sulphate reservoir and plant, Chaplin, May 1948.

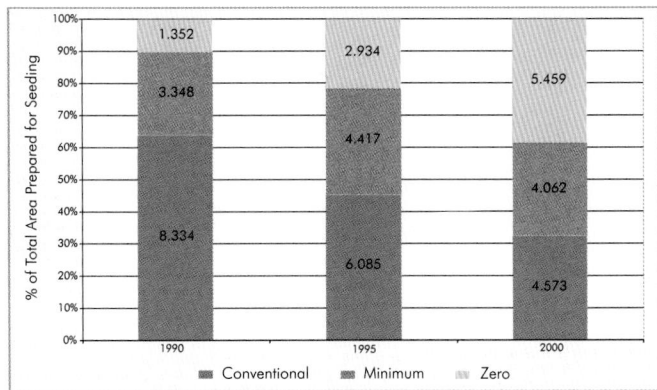

Figure SC-1. Trends in tillage practices, Saskatchewan, 1990–2000. (Figures provided are in millions of hectares.)

conservation tillage by including summerfallow in their rotation no longer till the soil, but instead apply chemicals to kill weed growth; this practice is referred to as chem-fallow. Zero tillage or direct seeding has gained popularity. Because of the higher incidence of weeds, higher application of herbicides is required. In the census year 2001, 13,248 farms reported some use of zero till and/or direct seeding. These farmers constituted 30% of the total producers in the province in that year. Also, 5.46 million ha were under zero tillage, representing 38.7% of the total area prepared for seeding during that year. Much of this area tended to be concentrated in the Dark Brown and Black Soil zones.

Interest in conservation tillage methods is thus increasing for economic and environmental motives. Progress made during the last decade is shown in Figure SC-1. In 1990, almost two-thirds of the total area prepared for seeding was done using conventional tillage systems; only 10% of the total was under zero tillage. By 2000, this had increased over threefold to 5.46 million ha.

Conservation tillage methods require fewer field operations, resulting in less labour and energy use by farmers. The reduced use of fossil fuels reduces emissions of carbon dioxide. The correspondingly higher use of herbicides for weed control leads to higher incidence of pathogens and insects. More fertilizer is required, which means higher energy use to manufacture the fertilizer.

Through direct seeding and minimum and zero till, as well as seeding permanent cover crops and maintaining native grasslands, carbon sinks are created by plants which remove carbon from the air and store it in the soil. On account of adoption of zero tillage, which increases soil organic matter, Saskatchewan producers have been able to decrease emissions of carbon dioxide into the atmosphere by 3.83 million tonnes. These carbon stocks in the soils are known as "carbon offsets," and have been recognized as a means for Canada to meet its targets for reduction of greenhouse gas emissions. Saskatchewan farmers are becoming more environmentally conscious, having reduced summerfallow in their crop rotations and having adopted reduced tillage practices. This has led to a more sustainable agriculture. In 1987 the Saskatchewan Soil Conservation Association (SCCA) was formed "to promote conservation production systems to improve land for future generations." The organization promotes the use of minimum and zero tillage operations; it also serves to represent farmers' interests at the governmental level on issues relating to soil conservation and the Kyoto Agreement.

Gary Storey and Suren Kulshreshtha

FURTHER READING: Kulshreshtha, S.N., and G. Storey. 1999. "Soil Conservation Practices." In *Atlas of Saskatchewan*. Saskatoon: University of Saskatchewan.

Social Policy

Rick August

Overview

Social policy refers to the aspects of public policy that affect the distribution of income and wealth within a community, the relationships between people in communities, the well-being of individuals and family units, and the relative security or risk that individual citizens experience in their relationship to the economy. Social policy is generally considered to include policy and programs dealing with income security and income redistribution, as well as health, education, and social services that support individuals' quality of life in communities. Saskatchewan, in the past half-century, has frequently been an innovator in this aspect of public policy development.

It is common to make a distinction between social and economic policy, the latter being broadly concerned with wealth creation; but the two are very closely linked. Economic activity provides the material means to support social programs, while social policy helps ensure the human resource base and stability of social relations that are preconditions to a healthy economy. The most effective social policy is developed with strong reference to economic issues and relations, and vice versa. Social policy can have a number of purposes: it can redistribute resources among individuals or family units to ensure that "social minimum" standards of living are maintained; it can influence or modify relationships among citizens to make a community more cohesive and secure; it can also shape peoples' social or economic behaviours, or mediate the impacts of market forces and social trends on individuals and families.

In simpler societies of the past, social matters were resolved within families, through informal responses from communities, or through voluntary charitable actions. In Saskatchewan, as in other maturing communities, economic and social relations became more complex as the economy developed, and people became more mobile than they were at the time of the province's formation. Families or communities gradually lost the capacity to deal with the range of social risks their members encountered. To bridge this gap, citizens have asked their governments to organize social policy solutions in order to provide protections that families and communities cannot adequately provide. At the time of Saskatchewan's formation, government's social responsibilities were relatively limited; but citizens' expectations have increased significantly over time: in the current budgets of both Saskatchewan and Canada, social programs now represent over half of public expenditures.

Some social programs and policies have been in place so long that people tend to take them for granted, but social programs reflect collective choices and priorities that may change over time. The local "relief" programs and labour camps that were considered adequate unemployment protection in the early 1930s, for example, were eventually replaced by unemployment insurance and social assistance. Views on these programs in turn have evolved as public values change and as governments acquire experience of income security issues. The expansion of social policy is one of the factors that have increased the relative size of the public sector relative to the private sector of the economy, but social policy is not necessarily intended to replace or compete with the market economy. People who live in market economies like Saskatchewan's enjoy freedom of choice and personal economic opportunities that may not be available in more structured economic environments. By reducing social risks, social policy can stabilize the economy, reduce social conflicts, and help secure a stable, healthy and motivated population that is able to participate in, and benefit from, a market economy. (*See* Figure 1.)

Every society makes choices, through its social policies, about the balance between individual and social responsibility. Some believe that Saskatchewan people rely more than most on government to provide collective responses to social issues. It can be argued that there are

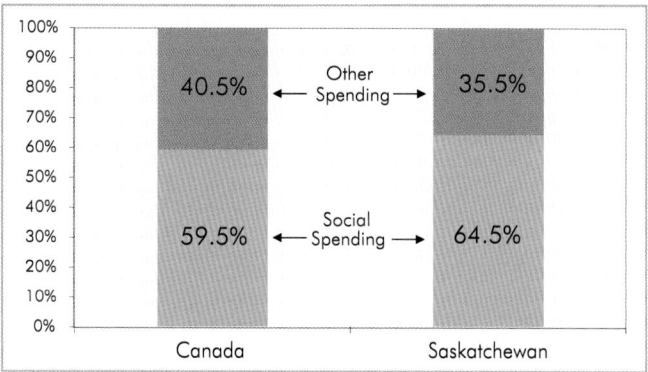

Source: Statistics Canada, CANSIM Table 385-0001.

Figure 1. Social spending by Canada and Saskatchewan, 2003/04 (includes general purpose transfers to other governments as social spending).

circumstances specific to Saskatchewan that may have served to increase expectations on government: the land area is large, the population sparse, and the climate extreme; the province's former strong reliance on commodity production also made it more vulnerable than most to economic forces.

The province is also, in historical terms, a new and still developing entity. Descendants of European settlers and more recent arrivals from around the world still struggle to forge with the Aboriginal population the sense of being "one people," with a shared vision for the future. Social policy has historically been influenced very strongly by ideology, with the result that there are varying degrees of support among the public for particular social programs. Over time, social policy practitioners have struggled to replace ideological assumptions with more scientific, evidence-based approaches appropriate to an emerging behavioural science. To the extent that social policy development becomes more scientific, its outcomes will be more predictable, so that better choices can be made about public investment. A critical analysis of current social policies would reveal many flaws, some of them quite serious. Given the scale of government spending on social programs and their importance to the lives of Saskatchewan people, better social policy is an important goal for the future.

Mechanisms for Social Policy

Governments at the federal, provincial or local level formulate most social policy. While they have the principal role in establishing social policy and often in funding social programs, the actual implementation of social policy may occur in a number of ways, often involving non-government stakeholders. Some social policies and programs are implemented directly by government through programs and services delivered by public servants. In Saskatchewan certain social services such as child protection functions are organized this way. Government may also pay a private business or individual to deliver a social program directly to citizens. Some residential services for adults requiring special care, for example, are operated by private individuals or corporations, while private businesses are active in areas such as disability supports.

Other services may be delivered by agencies or institutions outside of government, but subject to varying degrees of government control or influence exercised through funding relationships. These so-called "third party" social policy agents can range from small local community social service organizations to large, complex and long-standing institutions

like school boards or regional health authorities. Often the delivery agents have mixed sources of funding from levels of government and non-government sources. The role of non-government and quasi-government organizations in the delivery of social policy has increased over the last three decades, while government's direct role has narrowed. Some social policies are implemented by regulating markets or relations between citizens, rather than by providing social benefits or services. An example of this type of policy would be labour laws and regulations that set minimum standards for wages and employment conditions. By influencing the behaviour of employers towards their employees, these public policy measures help society maintain minimum work and living standards among the significant proportion of the population that makes a living through paid employment.

Governments may also transfer funds directly to citizens to help them buy the supports or services they need from existing private or public markets. A significant proportion of tax revenue is spent on such transfers to individuals. Federal public pensions that help ensure that citizens are not destitute in old age are paid to millions of older Canadians; federal and provincial child benefits are paid to over 80% of all families with children. There are also provincial programs that transfer funds to individuals: social assistance, for example, provides last-resort income support to individuals and families, while the Saskatchewan Employment Supplement helps low-income parents offset child-related costs of working. (See Figures 2 and 3.)

Jurisdiction in Social Policy

When Canada's first constitution, the British North America Act, was adopted by the British Parliament in 1867—with Saskatchewan's formation nearly four decades in the future—governments had limited involvement in the social affairs of citizens. The constitution reflected a division of responsibilities between the federal and provincial levels of government, including social policy responsibilities. The Act assigned provinces jurisdiction over the "Establishment, Maintenance, and Management of Hospitals, Asylums, Charities, and Eleemosynary Institutions in and for the Province, other than Marine Hospitals"—roughly the extent of social policy in the middle of the 19th century. Courts have interpreted this clause in modern terms to mean that provinces have jurisdiction over social policy, except where powers are specifically granted to the federal government. The same division of powers was preserved when the constitution was made an act of Canadian rather than British law in 1982. The constitution does not necessarily preclude the federal government acting within provincial jurisdiction, but it must do so with the consent of the province or provinces concerned.

There have been circumstances in Canada's history that have resulted in an expansion of federal social powers through constitutional amendments. Federal unemployment insurance and pensions, for example, both came about by virtue of amendments to the constitution, in 1940 and 1951 respectively, with unanimous consent of the provinces. The boundaries between federal and provincial social responsibilities, clear enough in theory, are somewhat unclear in practice. The federal government has responsibility for the management of the national economy, and therefore has substantial control over the conditions that affect demand for social programs. Provinces also claim that the powers of taxation set out in the constitution have not expanded along with the wider responsibilities of provincial governments for social policy. The federal government has developed mechanisms to pro-

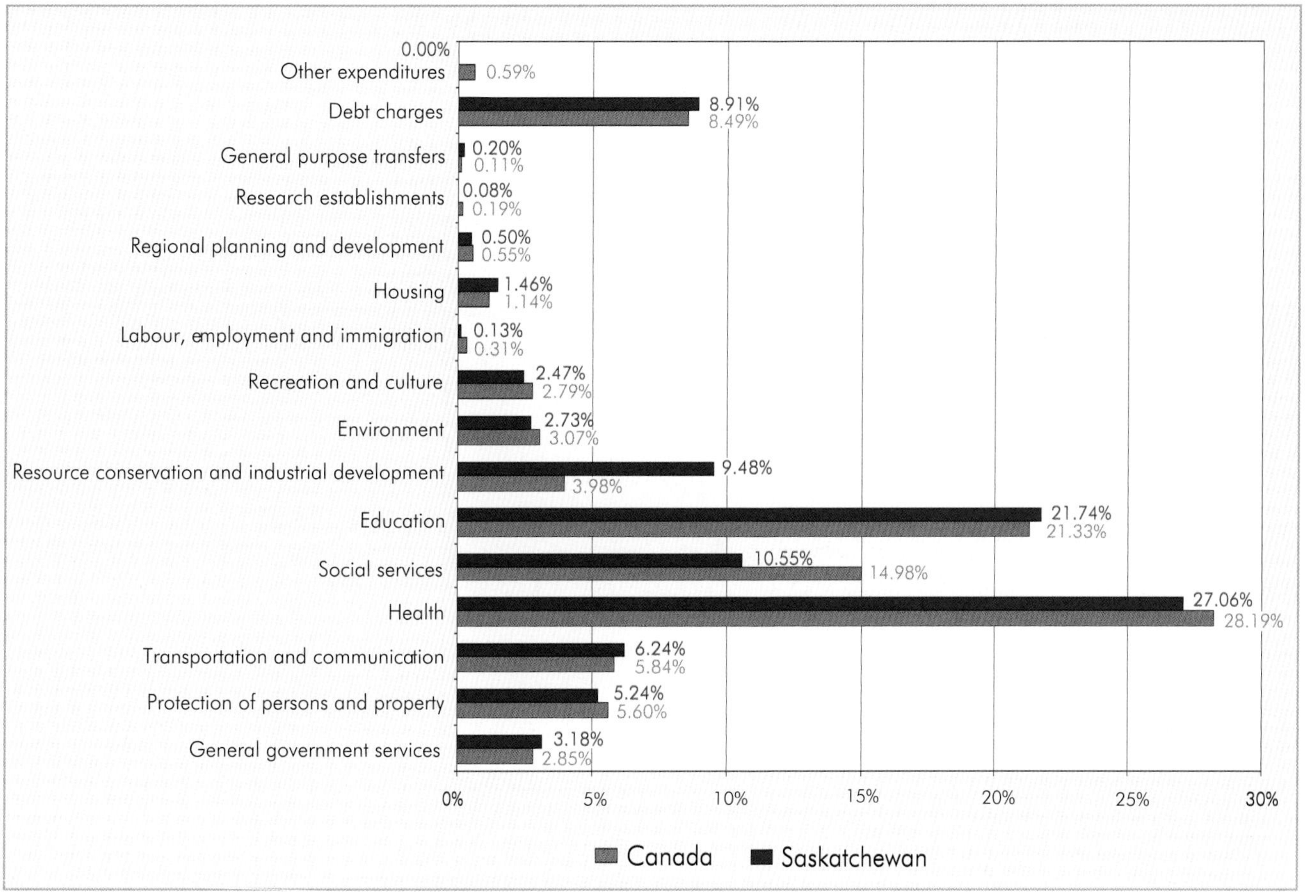

S

Figure 2. Consolidated Federal Government and Provincial Government Expenditures, 2004.

Figure 2 bar chart data:

Category	Canada	Saskatchewan
Other expenditures		0.59%
Debt charges	8.49%	8.91%
General purpose transfers	0.11%	0.20%
Research establishments	0.19%	0.08%
Regional planning and development	0.55%	0.50%
Housing	1.14%	1.46%
Labour, employment and immigration	0.31%	0.13%
Recreation and culture	2.79%	2.47%
Environment	3.07%	2.73%
Resource conservation and industrial development	3.98%	9.48%
Education	21.33%	21.74%
Social services	14.98%	10.55%
Health	28.19%	27.06%
Transportation and communication	5.84%	6.24%
Protection of persons and property	5.60%	5.24%
General government services	2.85%	3.18%

vide funding to provincial and territorial social programs—but at the expense of tensions, and occasionally conflicts, over the social policy independence of provincial jurisdictions.

A number of models have emerged for federal involvement in provincial and territorial social programs. When Saskatchewan municipalities and the provincial government were under severe financial pressure from unemployment relief costs during the DEPRESSION, the federal government provided ad hoc financial support for about three years. There have been mechanisms for cost-sharing programs between governments, such as the Canada Assistance Plan that existed from 1966 to 1995. More recently the federal government has opted for less open-ended block grants to provinces for health and social services, with varying degrees of conditions attached. These federal transfers are significant revenue sources for the provinces and territories, totaling $21.8 billion in 2003–04 to support health, post-secondary education, social assistance, and social services. One further model of social policy development is implemented through strategic co-operation among governments. This has been employed only once to date, in the development of the National Child Benefit, Canada's first major new national social program since the 1960s. In this case, the federal government and all provinces and territories except Québec agreed to work together to reduce child and family poverty, and also agreed on a strategy of providing both child benefits and employment support to parents.

Under the National Child Benefit, the federal government created a new benefit that was intended to replace basic benefits for children in

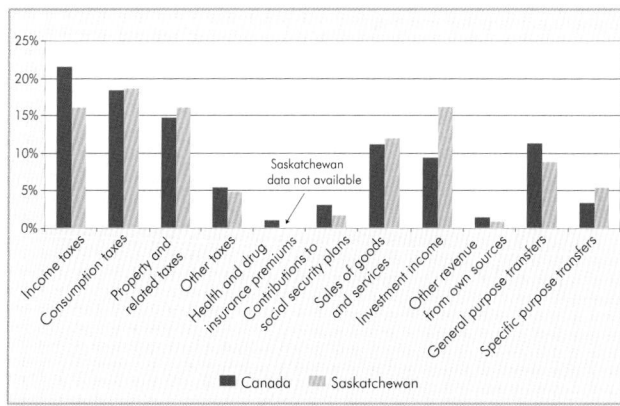

Figure 3. Consolidated Federal Government and Provincial Revenue, 2004.

provincial social assistance. The new child benefit was intended to improve work incentives by equalizing child benefits between welfare and working poor families. Where the new federal benefit created costs savings for provinces, these are reinvested in further supports for low-income families. Saskatchewan has an employment-oriented policy agenda for fighting family poverty which is very consistent with the National Child Benefit strategy, and the province was therefore a strong advocate for the initiative, which came about as a result of direction from provincial Premiers and the Prime Minister. The province's National Child Benefit reinvestments include a suite of programs called

Building Independence that encourage parents to increase their earnings and improve their families' living standards. The National Child Benefit served as the model for a more permanent protocol for co-operation between the federal government and the provinces and territories in social policy. In 1999 all Canadian jurisdictions except Québec entered into the Social Union Framework Agreement (SUFA); the longer-term effect of SUFA on federal-provincial relations, if any, is still unknown.

Municipal governments in Saskatchewan currently have a somewhat more limited role in social policy and programs, although that was not the case in years past. As social policy developed away from a base in family and charity, the first public social programs were municipal or governed by local bodies. At the onset of the Depression of the 1930s, local governments in Saskatchewan were responsible for both income support and health programming. While education remains, in part, locally governed and financed, responsibility for health, income security and social services has migrated, in stages, to the provincial government, which in some cases delegates implementation responsibility back to local or regional bodies. One area of social programming where municipalities continue to play a role, direct and indirect, is housing: some municipalities are active with other partners in development of public, private and non-profit housing assets, particularly for low-income people. Municipal governments have powers to regulate land assembly and land use, which in turn affect the supply, quality, and cost of housing. Local governments also have a strong influence over neighbourhood and community issues that are important to peoples' everyday lives.

Social outcomes are also influenced by non-government organizations operating at various levels and with a range of mandates. National policy institutes like the Caledon Institute or Canadian Policy Research Networks are primarily focused on social policy analysis, while other organizations such as the Fraser Institute or the C.D. Howe Institute address a range of public policy issues. The SASKATCHEWAN INSTITUTE FOR PUBLIC POLICY, a co-operative endeavour of the universities and the provincial government, offers Saskatchewan perspectives on social and other public policy issues. Professional organizations also influence social policy outcomes, based both on their interests as professions and their ethical frameworks. Various medical professions are very influential in the form and content of health services. Organizations like the Saskatchewan Association of Social Workers include advocacy around social issues as an element of ethical conduct in the profession. There are also a large number of community-based organizations that influence social outcomes, either by providing services or by helping finance aspects of social programs. The activities and policies of community-based organizations represent, in one sense, a local response to community needs, and a local aspect to social policy development. In 2003 there were over 1,400 voluntary and non-profit organizations in Saskatchewan—active in education, health or social services.

Aboriginal communities and organizations are also increasingly active in social policy and programs. In Saskatchewan, both First Nations and Métis organizations provide or fund a variety of social services, and have expressed interest in greater involvement in social policy development. Some of these organizations, like the First Nations child and family service agencies, operate under provincial legal authority, while others are independent non-profit organizations that receive funding or fees for service from a variety of sources. There is also an international dimension to social policy, whose standards can be an issue in international relations; governments and international organizations sometimes attempt to influence social policy in other countries by trade policy, aid, or even sanctions. Social standards can also be an issue in trade pacts like the North American Free Trade Agreement, in part because firms operating in different social environments will incur different costs that will affect competitiveness. Social standards can also be influenced by international bodies like the United Nations, the World Trade Organization, or the International Monetary Fund. The world continues to move towards a greater reliance on international trade, greater movement of capital and labour between countries, and more open national economies. The international organizations that now exist, most of which were created after World War II, face new challenges, not only to mediate national interests, but also to create inclusive debate on policy issues.

Methods of Social Policy Interventions

There are three basic approaches that governments use to achieve social policy outcomes: they can establish and operate public services, either directly or through arm's-length organizations; they may provide funding to non-governmental organizations to offer services to citizens; they may also establish a direct relationship with citizens, not mediated by service providers, to resource a particular outcome. In Saskatchewan, social assistance and child welfare systems are examples of direct government services. Health services and primary and secondary education services are provided by service sectors closely aligned with and funded by governments. In recent years there has been a trend for government to reduce its direct role in service provision, and for allied service systems to assume greater autonomy and accountability for effectiveness of their services.

Since the 1970s, private and non-profit service organizations have increased their role in delivery of social policy outcomes. Delivery agents can range from private enterprises such as personal care homes, private preschools and family child care providers, to a wide range of services provided by non-profit organizations. Local providers, private or non-profit, can usually claim the advantage of responsiveness to community needs. Because the locally based service delivery system has expanded so quickly, however, concerns are emerging about coordination and effectiveness of public investment in this sector.

Governments also sometimes rely on programs that provide financial resources directly to citizens, who in turn use these resources to help them buy goods or services in local markets. Examples are the development of the federal Canada Child Tax Benefit, which provides a cash benefit each month to all lower-income parents in Canada for their children's needs, and the Saskatchewan Employment Supplement, which helps low-income working parents in Saskatchewan with child care and other employment-related costs.

Historical Development

In the view of many analysts, the depth and breadth of social policy is a function of the level of economic development and organization of a society. In the 19th century, when present-day Saskatchewan was part of the North-West Territories, Canada was primarily an agricultural and resource-based nation, with most economic activity associated with producing crops and primary products for export. In the last half of the 19th century, as Canada's economy and society became more complex, charitable institutions such as hospitals and asylums expanded, and public funding of such institutions became more common. Social programs emerged to address problems and issues that individuals and families were poorly equipped to handle on their own. One of the first examples of broad-based social programming was the organization of schools, with its policies of compulsory schooling. This reflected a recognition that children would need more education than their parents had, and that families could not provide the level of education that coming generations of citizens would need to prosper in a developing society.

The growth of population centres and labour markets led as well to other public policy responses such as public health laws and greater regulation of employment conditions. On a national level, one of the first modern social programs that emerged—around the time of World War I in most of the country, but later in Saskatchewan—was workers' compensation. If social policy reflects the complexity of society, it is also often shaped by great events. World War I, for example, and the recession and social unrest that followed it, set in motion forces that resulted in several new, if rudimentary, social programs. Saskatchewan introduced mothers' allowances in 1916, and modest pensions for the elderly and infirm in the 1920s. The Depression, which was particularly severe and prolonged in Saskatchewan, ushered in a more interventionist period in income security, which would lead to programs such as unemployment insurance and social assistance.

World War II ended the Depression and raised the general level of attention to and interest in greater social justice as a goal for modern democratic governments. Two decades of economic expansion after the war were capped by a very rapid period of expansion of social programs in the 1960s and early 1970s. Saskatchewan pioneered a publicly funded health care program that became a national model in 1966. In the same year the federal government launched the Canada Pension Plan, and the Guaranteed Income Supplement for seniors. The Canada Assistance Plan and the Saskatchewan Assistance Plan of 1966 improved income support and social services. National unemployment insurance was expanded and enriched significantly in 1971.

Events since the early 1970s, however, have checked the headlong growth of social programs. Economic events like the oil crises of the mid-1970s at first were viewed in Keynesian terms, as down-cycles to be buffered by counter-cyclical government spending. In fact, these events were part of a long-term trend, eventually known as "globalization," which would result in significant structural changes to economies and labour markets, and increased demand pressure for the major social supports that are sensitive to economic conditions. Early instincts to spend or borrow their way out of recessions set governments on a course of deficit financing and debt that placed even greater pressure on social programs than external events did. Provincial governments, including Saskatchewan's, implemented rigorous deficit and debt reduction measures in the early 1990s; the federal government did the same, culminating with major social program funding cuts in the 1995 federal budget. Since that time, most governments have established reasonably stable finances, and social policy development is moving forward once again, albeit rather cautiously.

Analytical Perspectives

As a young behavioural science, social policy still generates a good deal of debate and discussion. To a great extent, public authorities are still experimenting and learning how to address social issues constructively and to shape human behaviour in ways that serve the interests of the individuals affected and of communities as a whole. Social policy debates play out along a number of dimensions, depending on the opinion or belief system of the observer, or the evidence available to inform judgments. A non-exhaustive review of these dimensions might include some of the following, many of which are conceptually linked or related.

Public Versus Private Responsibility

In the period of initial European settlement and the more agriculturally dominated era of Saskatchewan's history, governments were active in enforcing boundaries on individual citizens' behaviour relative to others, but took less responsibility for assuring the well-being of private citizens. The assumption was that such welfare issues were private matters for individuals, families, churches and charities to address. The situation today is quite different. Measures to protect the well-being of citizens take up the majority of the budgets of modern governments, which are themselves much larger in scope than in the 19th century. Most citizens have come to expect that the state will enforce a minimum living standard, provide basic education, and ensure that health care needs are met. Some view government as having a responsibility to repair any major deficiency in citizens' lives, be it lack of housing, low income, or other problem.

The historic peak of the era of public responsibility was the early 1970s, the last period of significant social program expansion. Since that time, the public has lost a degree of confidence in government's ability to solve problems for citizens. The cost of social protection was one of the factors which generated government debt and deficits that necessitated cutbacks in the early 1990s. Evidence has also emerged of negative outcomes associated with very high degrees of social protection, particularly dependency and loss of personal capacity for independence, when programs are not oriented toward active roles in the economy. At the root of the "public versus private" debate is the concept of citizenship: those who support a more interventionist state see government as the means to redress inequities and provide personal security; those who lean towards a less active state see citizens as having more personal responsibility for managing their own lives and solving their own problems.

Government as Provider or Facilitator

Another aspect of the debate over the role of the state in social policy has to do with how government is expected to achieve social outcomes. Perspectives on the means for achieving social policy outcomes are changing over time.

In much of the post-war period of social program expansion, government was seen as directly acting to provide goods and services to citizens to produce social outcomes. This is still the basis of much social policy. However, an alternative view has emerged in some areas, particularly in income security, where cash entitlements to citizens by the state have been criticized as contributing to dependency. An example of this debate concerns social assistance (commonly called "welfare"), which has always been a controversial program with the public. Designed to be a "last-resort" income source for people with no other means, modern social assistance programs evolved out of ad hoc government assistance to people in economic distress. Over time, some analysts came to view welfare as a solution to poverty, based on a simple premise: if citizens lack money, government will provide it, regardless of the reason for the need. The preamble to the 1966 Canada Assistance Plan actually envisioned a society without poverty as a result of such welfare measures.

As history proves, social assistance has not eliminated poverty. In fact, some would argue that welfare actually reinforces poverty by drawing low-income people out of the labour market. Critics have argued that the premise of welfare should change, from benefits as a source of income security to cash or service supports that should explicitly encourage employment and self-sufficiency outcomes. In this example, the proposed shift would be from government providing a citizen with income, to government facilitating citizens to meet their own needs through paid employment. A recent study by the Canadian research firm Pollara Inc. indicates that a shift in public opinion is taking place about the role of government. In 1989, 51% of Canadians thought that government's role was to "solve problems and protect people from adversity," and 28% thought it was to "help people equip themselves to solve their own problems." A follow-up survey in 2001 indicated that by that time only 31% thought government should solve problems, and 48% saw government in a facilitative role (*see* Figure 4). The notion of facilitative policies places a burden on governments to develop more sophisticated and evidence-based approaches, since facilitation requires the policy to influence behaviours—which is more complex than simply meeting needs.

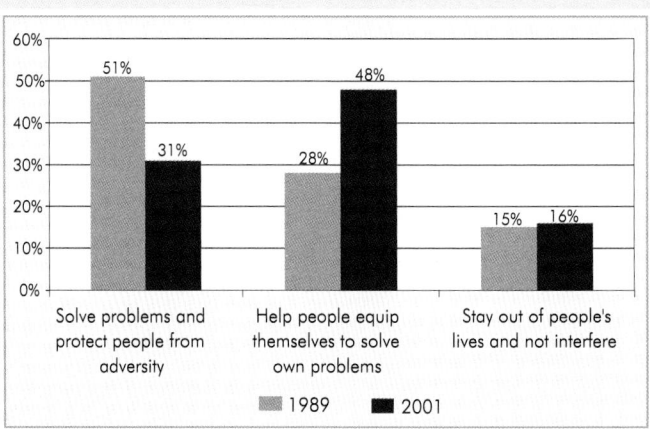

Source: Pollara, Inc., 2001.

Figure 4. Canadian public opinion on the role of government.

accurately predict the measures that will achieve desired outcomes in advance. Prescription also reduces consumer choice, sometimes without a strong evidence base to justify such restriction. Enabling policies, on the other hand, entail more risk for public authorities because they rely on an appropriate response from citizens, and in some cases markets. Sometimes more time is required to effect a change, since the policy depends on a behavioural response of citizens. Governments are also sometimes reluctant to surrender direct control of outcomes. Proponents argue, on the other hand, that the outcomes are more consistent with the intent of policy because citizens' resources and motivations are contributed to shaping outcomes.

Security or Self-sufficiency

There is considerable debate between those who think social policy's goal should be to ensure that a person's unmet needs are satisfied, regardless of circumstances or behaviour, and those who focus on supports that promote self-sufficiency. Those who favour a security focus argue that social policy's principal role is to redistribute resources (goods, services, income) within society to ensure that all citizens have a more equal standard of living. Those who favour self-sufficiency argue that unconditional entitlements become unaffordable because demand grows over time, and that entitlements can undermine incentives for people to manage their own lives and solve their own problems. The long-term best interests of citizens, proponents would argue, are served by their capacity for independence. While a self-sufficiency framework does not preclude public support of individuals, it suggests that support should be conditional and framed so as to encourage self-sufficient behaviours.

Prescriptive or Enabling Social Policy

Closely related to the "provider or facilitator" debate is the issue of the tactics used by social policy to achieve the desired outcomes. Prescriptive interventions by government use relatively direct means to ensure a given outcome: provision of goods or services meeting certain standards, or regulations that govern the behaviour of individuals, businesses or institutions. Enabling tactics use government authority and resources more indirectly to create conditions that encourage desirable outcomes; Shlomo Angel (2000) describes enabling social policy as setting boundaries, providing support, and relinquishing control of the detailed process of implementation. An example of prescriptive social policy in Saskatchewan is licensed child care: the government prescribes the model through funding rules and regulations, funds a variety of agencies to deliver the service, and subsidizes lower-income parents if they use that form of child care service. A more enabling approach might allow for parent choice among approved child care options, and the use of subsidies to increase parents' economic leverage to increase care quality.

As in other aspects of social policy, public opinion has shifted over time. In the post-war growth period the public had a relatively strong faith in the capacity of governments to shape outcomes by regulation and other prescriptive intervention. The principal failings of prescriptive policies arise from the inexactness of social policy—in effect, the unlikelihood that government planners or elected representatives can

Active or Passive Policies

One critique that has emerged of post-war "welfare state" programs is that these, by providing unconditionally for citizens' needs, have encouraged and expanded dependence on government. In the long run, since government is financed by the economic activity of citizens, policies that discourage employment, enterprise and self-support, it is argued, are unsustainable and unhealthy, both for society and its members. Trends in social assistance are often cited to support this critique. In Saskatchewan, for example, social assistance was consolidated under new federal and provincial legislation in 1966, putting into place a new and more unconditional welfare regime. Although applicants were expected to explore work or other options for self-support, financial assistance was basically a right for those who could establish need, regardless of the circumstances. Citizens in need were given resources that addressed their immediate income situation, but very little was done to support economic rehabilitation.

In the quarter-century following implementation of this approach, social assistance use increased by about 180%; whereas a welfare caseload in the 1960s consisted of people unable to work, by the early 1990s a typical welfare recipient was a working-age single mother. While most would acknowledge other factors than program design in this trend, it is also generally agreed that economic dependency, particularly of working-age adults, is undesirable for both the dependent person and society as a whole. The Organization for Economic Co-operation and Development (OECD), a policy body whose membership consists of industrialized countries with developed social security systems, has been a forceful critic of passive social policies and their negative long-term impacts on the lives of lower-income peoples (OECD, 1988, 1994). The OECD promotes what it calls "active" social policies in their place. The active/passive program critique formed part of the basis for unemployment insurance reforms in Canada in the 1990s; it has informed, to some degree, initiatives like Saskatchewan's Building Independence programs, designed to fight poverty by helping low-income people to remain in the work force.

Residual or Structural Social Policies

Few would argue, in principle, with the maxim that prevention is better than cure—in social policy as in everything else. Since people have different views on the role of government, however, there are also differing views on the degree to which social policy should proactively shape behaviours, or simply react to problems that emerge. This debate, for example, would oppose social assistance as a last-resort response to income need, on the one hand, to income redistribution programs or an employment policy, on the other hand. Similarly, investment in acute medical treatment models in health care is sometimes contrasted to "population health" approaches intended to reduce demand for treatment services. In practice, governments still gravitate to a surprising degree towards short-term, residual responses—despite evidence that more structural, long-term policies provide better value for taxpayers' money. Residual responses may provide more limited benefits, but they are immediate, relatively easy to identify, and outcomes can be more readily attributed to specific actions than some longer-term structural solutions.

Structural, institutional or preventive strategies, on the other hand, can often demonstrate their benefit in theory, but are quite hard to achieve in practice. Their rather abstract promise of benefits must compete with immediate priorities for service responses to existing demand: while research may support, for example, a population health strategy, headlines still stress surgical waiting lists. There is much greater benefit, to citizens and society, from an employment strategy to prevent economic marginalization; but most social advocacy in this area is still directed towards issues concerning short-term welfare. Another factor creating resistance to structural change is the vested interest that inevitably develops in existing program models. Service providers' interest in the status quo is often very strong, and much more focussed in opposition to change than are the more diffuse forces in favour of change. Service consumers also tend to defend the status quo as preferable to the uncertainties of change. In a province and country with four- to five-year electoral cycles, it can be difficult to convince elected representatives to choose long-term change over short-term benefit. History suggests that the pressures of crisis situations are sometimes needed to force consensus on structural change. Examples of structural change in social programs are in fact relatively rare. On a national level, the most recent major example would be the National Child Benefit: in its simplest terms, it is a re-engineering of the structure of benefits for children in order to make employment more attractive for parents; it has also facilitated major changes to Saskatchewan income support and employment programs to support employment outcomes for low-income parents.

Equality or Equity

Differences of opinion exist as to whether the fundamental goal of social policy should be equality or equity among citizens. The distinction is a subtle but important one: equality arguments favour policies that try to assure more equivalent life outcomes, while equity policies do not attempt to modify outcomes directly, but rather seek to increase fairness in conditions that facilitate social outcomes. To some extent the debate is a false one, as neither perspective is really achievable in absolute terms. Those who favour greater equality might for example set an ideal of complete income equality across a society, or equal health outcomes; these goals, however, are not practically achievable, even in extremely regulated and regimented societies. Equity arguments are more concerned with opportunity: social policy operates through real people who are remarkably variable in their outlook, personal capacities, motivations and adaptabilities. Some believe that, because no public intervention can guarantee outcomes, the best approach is to focus on conditions that support the desired outcomes, thus increasing the likelihood that positive life outcomes such as good health, or secure and rewarding employment, will result.

Outcomes-based Social Policy

An important development in recent years, in all public policy, but particularly in social policy, has been the emergence of a critical perspective on political or ideological approaches, and a bias towards outcomes-based analysis, in both the evaluation of existing measures and the development of business cases for new initiatives. An outcomes orientation is also intended to replace program performance measurement by throughputs—dollars spent, consumers served, etc.—rather than the actual effect of the program relative to its original intent. If only throughputs are considered, a program can appear to perform adequately, but may not actually achieve its goals. Outcomes orientation encourages organizations to engage to a greater extent in strategic planning, a process by which an organization articulates a vision that expresses the most basic intent of its activities. Using the vision as a reference point, the strategic plan lays out values the organization wants to adhere to, principles to be applied in finding solutions to problems, goals that orient the organization's work, and measurable objectives around which an action plan can be developed to move towards achieving the vision.

The strategic plan makes the purpose and plan of an organization much more explicit. It therefore acts as a guide to management and governance. A strategic plan also provides the basis for more rigorous performance management, since the indicators of success or failure have been identified for comparison over time with actual outcomes. Almost all public authorities now engage in strategic planning and performance management. One positive outcome has been a renewed emphasis on developing a knowledge base in social policy, and more rigorous approaches to program evaluation. Improving the knowledge base for social policy will be a gradual, long-term process reflecting the complexity, and sometimes unpredictability, of human behaviour.

Organization and Financing of Social Programs

It is sometimes assumed that the funding, financing or resourcing of social policy measures is a matter for governments. In reality, almost all social policy relies at least in part on mixed resources of individuals, governments, labour markets, voluntary organizations and the consumers of service themselves. Governments involve themselves in social programs in a number of ways. The approach in which government provides services and funds them through tax revenue has sometimes been called the "social utility" model; the closest example to this in present-day Saskatchewan would be the fully publicly insured portions of the health care system, which are financed almost entirely by federal and provincial government contributions. However, even this system represents a mixed approach, as evidenced by the various charitable organizations that raise funds for health services, a growing corporate role in capital facilities development, and an increasing range of user charges. The elementary and secondary education systems are largely funded by the provincial government and local property taxpayers, but families are still expected to contribute school supplies, and some school-related activities levy fees on parents for participation.

Another form of social program organization and finance is referred to as "social insurance": "insurance" because it involves premiums or contributions by individuals to buy protection against risks, and "social" because the insurance program is managed by government. The role of government is to force pooling of risks in a way that private insurance would not. For example, Canada's Employment Insurance program relies on cross-subsidies to those at greater risk of unemployment, with premiums from those at lesser risk; such mandatory programs also ensure that high-risk people can be insured, which may not be the case in private insurance. Another form of social insurance program is the Canada Pension Plan. By levying a payroll tax on earnings, the Canada Pension Plan forces citizens to save for retirement during their working years. The funds that people contribute are managed and invested under rules and procedures that provide more security than most private investments. The Canada Pension Plan, along with the universal Old Age Security pension, private pensions, and the income-tested Guaranteed Income Supplement, form a system that has sharply reduced seniors' poverty since the 1960s.

Some social programs and services are organized on a community basis, with mixed funding from governments, service consumers and charitable sources. Sometimes these are services that operate with local autonomy within a philosophical or religious framework provided by a provincial or national organization. Other community-based services are united by ideology or focused social goal; still others are simply responses to specific priorities of local communities, or developments in areas that are not priorities for government funding. Other social provision is market-based, sometimes with targeted public subsidies to help equalize the purchasing power or consumer capacity of citizens buying services. For example, the Saskatchewan and Canada income security systems for families, rather than providing goods or services, provide parents with a cash benefit for children's needs. Almost without exception, parents purchase goods and services for children in private markets, without

governments getting involved in supply issues.

Some social needs are simply defined as outside the boundaries of social programs, for reasons of policy, cost to government, or priority. Major sub-sectors of health care, for example, such as prescription drugs or dental needs, are either beyond the scope of public health care or insured under more restrictive or exclusionary rules. In health care many people purchase private supplementary health insurance or receive coverage as a benefit of employment; Saskatchewan also has a system of supplementary or extended health coverage that the provincial government makes available to various categories of low-income people. The choice of program organization or costing model is one that happens in the context of a given time or place, and should not be considered beyond change or reconsideration. Different choices at periods in our social policy history could have resulted in quite different configurations of social programs. For example, national legislation was drafted in 1943 for a contributory, social-insurance style health program, more than two decades before Canada adopted Saskatchewan's model of a health social utility. It is quite conceivable that some of today's social programs like unemployment insurance or public health care could change their form or financing arrangements as their economic and social context changes, or as more is learned about effective and sustainable program approaches.

The possibility of change—even quite fundamental change—to social policies and programs should be welcome, despite the inevitable concerns of those involved in the status quo. Social policy is not a new discipline, but that social measures should so effectively dominate the fiscal affairs of government is certainly new. Most of the major instruments of social policy are in their first or second iterations. The emergence of evidence-based and outcomes-oriented approaches to social policy, and the application of concepts such as comparative advantage to social decision-making, promise changes in the coming century at least as profound as in the last.

FURTHER READING:

Angel, S. 2000. *Housing Policy Matters: A Global Analysis.* New York: Oxford University Press.

Beveridge, W. 1942. *Social Insurance and Allied Services.* New York: MacMillan.

Canada, Department of Finance. 2005. *Total Federal Support for Health, Post-Secondary Education and Social Assistance and Social Services (2004–05).* Ottawa: Minister of Finance.

Grauer, A.E. 1939. *Public Assistance and Social Insurance: A Study Prepared for the Royal Commission on Dominion-Provincial Relations.* Ottawa: The King's Printer.

Guest, D. 1997. *The Emergence of Social Security in Canada.* Vancouver: University of British Columbia Press.

Inge, P., P. Conceição, K. Le Goulven and R.U. Mendoza (eds.). 2003. *Providing Global Public Goods: Managing Globalization.* New York: Oxford University Press.

Lightman, E. 2003. *Social Policy in Canada.* Don Mills, ON: Oxford University Press.

Organization for Economic Co-operation and Development. 1988. *Social Policy Studies No. 6: The Future of Social Protection.* Paris: OECD.

———. 1994. *Social Policy Studies No. 12: New Orientations for Social Policy.* Paris: OECD.

Statistics Canada. 2004. *Cornerstones of the Community: Highlights of the National Survey of Nonprofit and Voluntary Organizations.* Ottawa: Minister of Industry.

Westhues, A. 2003. "An Overview of Social Policy." Pp. 46–72 in A. Westhues (ed.), *Canadian Social Policy: Issues and Perspective.* Waterloo: Wilfrid Laurier University Press.

SOILS. Soils are natural bodies formed by the cumulative effects of climate, vegetation, geological material, topography, and drainage. These effects are expressed by the development of a series of layers or "horizons" extending from the surface downward into the unaltered geologic or parent material (*see* Figure S-1, inset). This whole succession of horizons is referred to as the "soil profile." In describing soils, three main horizons are recognized from the surface downwards and are indicated by the letters A, B and C respectively. The A horizon, the uppermost layer, usually contains most of the organic matter (the source of most plant nutrients) and is thus darker in colour than the rest of the profile; soil in the A horizon typically constitutes the plough layer in cultivated soils. The B horizon, typically brownish in colour, is often slightly finer in texture (more clayey) than the A horizon. The C horizon represents the largely unaltered geologic deposit and is commonly referred to as the soil parent material, or the material from which the soil was developed; in most Saskatchewan soils the C horizon occurs between 50 and 100 centimetres. Most Saskatchewan soils have developed in **GLACIAL DEPOSITS**, laid down either by ice or by water from the melting ice. Glacial till, the material carried and deposited by ice, is the most common type of parent material; soils developed in glacial till are commonly loamy in texture. Sandy and gravelly soils are typically developed on glaciofluvial deposits laid down by moving meltwater, while silty and clayey soils are found mainly in former glacial lakes.

Over broad regions and long periods of time, differences in climate and in the related natural vegetation have a pronounced effect on soil formation. Thus, in Saskatchewan over the past 10,000 years, forces of climate acting upon the landscape and geologic materials left by the retreating glaciers have created broad distinctive zones of vegetation and soil; in fact, in no other part of the country are these zonal relationships so clearly displayed (*see* Figure S-2, left). In the southwest, a dry climate yielded short-grass prairie vegetation and Brown or Dark Brown soils having a thin surface layer low in organic matter. These dry conditions give way northward and eastward to parkland vegetation, characterized by a mix of aspen groves and fescue grasslands reflecting slightly cooler and moister conditions compared to the prairie region. There the soils have high levels of organic matter at the surface, and are thus dark or black in colour. Further north, under an even cooler and more humid climate, forest vegetation prevails and the soils have little or no organic matter, which gives them a distinctive grey appearance. In Saskatchewan, soils are classified or named according to the Canadian System of Soil Classification, which is based on a concept first developed by early (1870s) Russian soil scientists: soil is a natural body with "horizons" and "profiles" that reflect influences of climate and vegetation acting on the surficial material. Thus, classification of Saskatchewan soils is based mainly on the kinds, degree of development, and sequence of soil

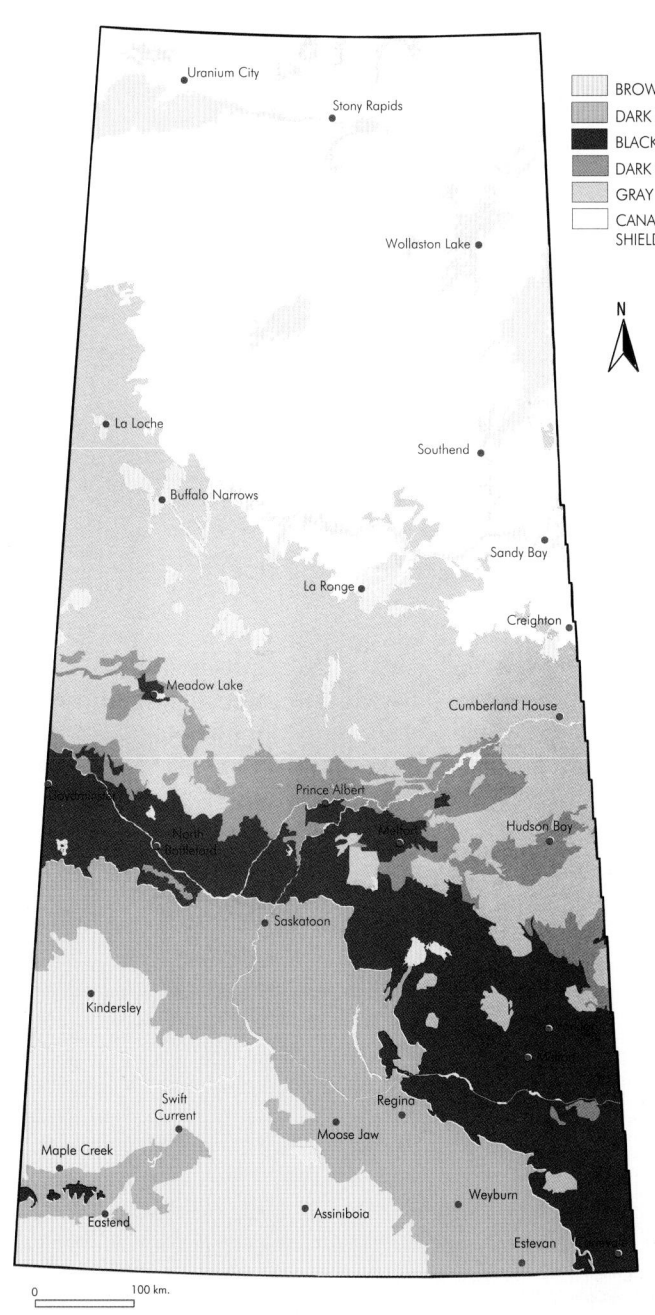

	BROWN
	DARK BROWN
	BLACK
	DARK GRAY
	GRAY
	CANADIAN SHIELD

Figure S-2. Soil Zones of Saskatchewan.

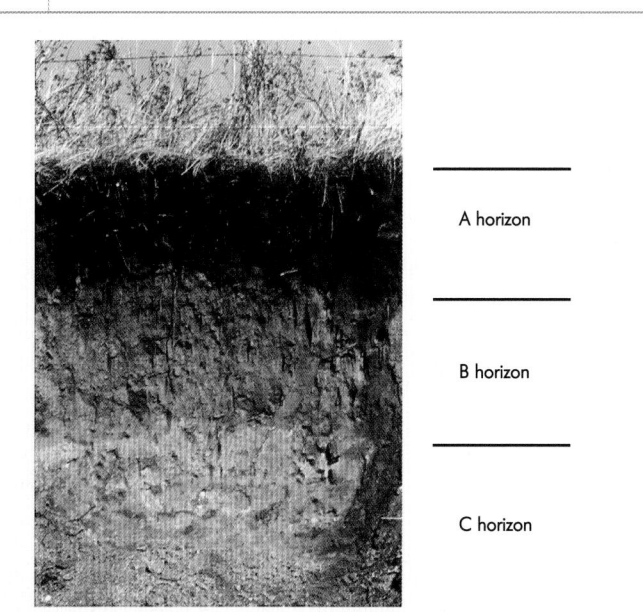

Figure S-1. Soil Profile of Chenozemic Soil.

horizons. All but one of the major soil orders in Canada occur in Saskatchewan.

Chernozemic soils, which dominate the southern prairie region of the province, are characterized by dark-coloured A horizons, brownish-coloured B horizons, and light-coloured C horizons with lime carbonate accumulation. Within the prairie region several major soil zones have been mapped: commonly referred to as the Brown, Dark Brown, and Black soil zones, they are based on the increasing soil organic matter content and darker colour of the surface soil horizons, and generally reflect the climatic gradient from the southwest to the northeast. The Dark Gray Chernozemic soils have somewhat lighter-coloured surface horizons than those of the Black Chernozemic soils, and are characteristic of soils developed in a transitional environment between grassland and forest. Solonetzic soils, found exclusively in the prairie region, are typically associated with salty (saline) deposits having high amounts of sodium. The profiles are characterized by a hard compact B horizon, which can commonly interfere with water penetration and root development. Vertisolic soils develop in fine (heavy) textured clayey deposits where continuous churning within the soil (due to the clay's unique shrink-swell characteristics) results in little or no profile development.

Grey Luvisolic and Brunisolic soils are typical forest soils. The Grey Luvisolic profile has a thick, light greyish-coloured leached A horizon, and a clay-enriched B horizon, whereas the Brunisolic profiles are typically found on sandy or gravelly deposits and have a light grey to whitish-coloured A horizon underlain by a bright reddish-brown coloured B horizon. Organic soils are typically found in a water-saturated environment in the forest regions, where thick (>50cm) deposits of peat have developed. Cryosolic or permanently frozen soils, found sporadically in peatlands, have the unique combination of a thick surface layer of undecomposed Sphagnum peat supporting a dense coniferous forest. Gleysolic soils are poorly drained mineral soils typically found in the depressional areas (sloughs) within the prairie region. Regosolic soils have little or no profile development, usually because of more or less continuous erosion.

Glenn Padbury

SOLDIER SETTLEMENT ACT.

The Soldier Settlement Act (August 29, 1917) provided WORLD WAR I veterans with free quarter-sections of land and $2,500 interest-free loans. R.L. Borden's Conservatives envisioned soldiers homesteading on Crown lands in four areas: Manitoba's Interlake region, Saskatchewan's PALLISER TRIANGLE, Alberta's Peace River, and in the forest fringe north of the prairie region. Opponents noted, however, that lands provided by the Act had already deterred homesteaders due to poor productivity or distance from rail shipping. Why should soldiers scratch a living on land

far from civilization, when corporations such as the CANADIAN PACIFIC RAILWAY and the Hudson's Bay Company held an estimated 300,000 acres idle for speculative purposes? "Conscript wealth as well as labour!" cried prairie populists.

William Morris Graham drafted a face-saving plan for the Borden government. A former Indian Commissioner at Regina who spent World War I appropriating Indian lands in the name of unrealized "greater production," Graham advised Borden's new Unity Government to open reserve lands for soldier settlement. The 1919 revision of the Act diverted attention from idle corporate lands and created, in Graham's words, "open season for Indian reserves." By 1922, the Board had loaned $16,363,585 to 4,095 veterans in Saskatchewan; it had also approved another 6,000 loans, but only 3,251 men had settled on land: 500 had occupied parts of the Porcupine Forest Reserve; 10,000 acres in the Kamsack area had been made available by migrating Doukobours; 27,000 acres were purchased by the Board from the HBC; and eight reserves surrendered 163,000 acres. The bulk of this land was purchased by the Soldier Settlement Board at set prices. The 1992 Treaty Land Entitlement Framework Agreement was designed in part to address this expropriation.

Scott Broad

FURTHER READING: Carter, S. 1999. "Infamous Proposal: Prairie Indians and Soldier Settlement After World War I," *Manitoba History* 37: 9-21.

SOLOMON, GEORGE C. (1913–94).

George C. Solomon, born in 1913 in Regina, was instrumental in developing a variety of diverse enterprises, including Western Tractor, Western Equipment, IPSCO, Steelco, Sask Steel Fabricators, Construction Equipment Ltd, Industrial Sales Ltd, Sterling Rentals, Tobin Tractor, Poli Twine, and Central Canada Distilleries. In addition to these business accomplish-

SASKATCHEWAN ARCHIVES BOARD R-A16764

George Solomon.

ments he served as a corporate director of banks, breweries and other corporations. He also sat on the boards of directors of the SASKATCHEWAN ROUGHRIDERS, the YMCA, the SALVATION ARMY, the Boy Scouts of Canada, the Canada Council of Christians and Jews, the Regina Exhibition Board, and the Duke of Edinburgh Awards. He was also instrumental in raising funds for the UNIVERSITY OF SASKATCHEWAN, for CAMPION and LUTHER COLLEGES at the UNIVERSITY OF REGINA, and for Notre Dame at Wilcox. Solomon made a significant contribution to Canada's effort in WORLD WAR II by organizing the fuel distribution system for the BRITISH COMMONWEALTH AIR TRAINING PLAN in Saskatchewan. He also played a major role in acquiring and providing much of the heavy construction equipment and other material, which was rushed north to complete the Alaska Highway. He was recognized by the government of Canada for his efforts when he was appointed to be the Honorary Colonel of the ROYAL REGINA RIFLES.

Solomon was the recipient of the 1973 Human Relations Award by the Canada Council for Christians and Jews, the Duke of Edinburgh's Award in 1978, an honorary doctorate by the University of Regina in 1980, and the Citizen of the Year award by the B'nai B'rith in 1981. He was inducted into the Saskatchewan Order of Merit in 1985, was awarded the Jubilee Medal in 1977 and the Canada 125 Medal in 1993, and was appointed as a Member of the Order of Canada in 1993. George C. Solomon died in 1994.

Cliff Walker

SOO LINE RAILWAY.

Founded in 1883 by Minneapolis millers, and known originally as the Minneapolis and then the Saint Paul & Sault Ste. Marie, the Soo Line railway derived its name from the pronunciation of "Sault." The Soo Line was built to provide a shorter, cheaper route for western grain to the eastern seaboard; it was later expanded to Emerson, Manitoba. By 1894 the line was completed to North Portal, Estevan, Weyburn, and Moose Jaw. The Soo Line accelerated growth in southeast Saskatchewan and brought American settlers to the area. In 1961, it absorbed the Wisconsin Central and the Duluth, South Shore & Atlantic, creating the "new" Soo Line, with 8,000 miles (12,875 km) of track and 7,600 employees. The railway was restructured, so that by 2001 it had 3,200 miles (5,150 km) of track, about 3,000 employees, and was a wholly owned subsidiary of the CPR. The Soo Line has been known as the "little jewel" because of its profitability.

Gregory Salmers

SORESTAD, GLEN (1937–).

Born in Vancouver on May 21, 1937, Glen Sorestad and his parents moved back to Saskatchewan in 1947. There he attended a rural school near Buchanan and graduated from Sturgis Composite High School. He began

Glen Sorestad.

his teaching career in Yorkton in 1957.

Sorestad joined the staff of Evan Hardy Collegiate in 1969. As English Program Coordinator he established the Creative Writing program there, and was a key figure in organizing the groundbreaking Prairie Writers' Conference.

In 1975 Sorestad and his wife, Sonia, co-founded the literary publishing house, Thistledown Press, in Saskatoon. Over the years Thistledown became known as one of the finest literary publishers in Canada. After twenty-five years as publisher, Sorestad retired in January 2000 with the publication of over 200 literary titles to his credit. Many of them have been translated and published in various foreign countries.

He continues to live and work in Saskatoon. His career has taken him all over North America and to various countries in Europe. He is the author of a dozen books of poetry, of many short stories, and is the co-editor of many well-known anthologies. Sorestad has given over 300 public readings of his poetry, visiting every province in Canada as well as many parts of the United States and Europe. He was the guest at a reception held in his honour at the residence of the Canadian Ambassador in Oslo, and his readings have been broadcast on Norway's public radio network.

An active member of the **SASKATCHEWAN WRITERS' GUILD** since its formation in 1970, Sorestad was given a Founders' Award by the Guild in 1990. He is also an active member of the Writers' Union of Canada, and was recently honoured as a Life Member in the League of Canadian Poets.

In November 2000, Sorestad was appointed the first Poet Laureate of Saskatchewan at the **SASKATCHEWAN BOOK AWARDS**. In November 2001, he received the Saskatoon Book Award for his poetry collection, *Leaving Holds Me Here.*   *Joyce Wells*

SOURIS RIVER (49°00'N, 101°59'W: Map sheet 62/F4). With headwaters at Cedoux, Saskatchewan, the Souris River flows past Estevan, south into North Dakota before turning north to join the **ASSINIBOINE RIVER** near Brandon, Manitoba. Water from the Souris ultimately drains to the Arctic Ocean, via the Nelson River. In the 1890s it was used to barge coal from **ROCHE PERCÉE** to Winnnipeg. While the upper reaches of the Souris register no flow in some drought years, in other years flooding has been a problem. In the 1990s the Rafferty and Alameda Dam Project was undertaken in part to protect Minot, North Dakota, from flooding. Under an agreement with the United States, Saskatchewan can retain about 50% of the water flowing in the Souris Basin.

An older dam, Boundary Dam (1957), was built on Long Creek, a tributary of the Souris, to provide cooling water for Boundary Dam Generating Station. A channel links Boundary Dam and Rafferty Dam, allowing water to flow between the two reservoirs. The reservoirs provide water for the newer Shand Power Station. Fishing and boating are enjoyed in the reservoirs, and hunting and trapping have been traditional activities in the river valley. Water from the Souris is also used for irrigation. The name of the river comes from the French word for "mouse." In the United States it is often called the Mouse River.   *Gregory Salmers*

SOUTH, GORDON A. (1912–). Born on April 20, 1912, Gordon A. South farmed near Whittome, Saskatchewan, and was actively involved in seed growing. He was director of the Saskatchewan Computer Corporation and served on provincial and national boards of the Canadian Seed Growers Association between 1948 and 1967. He was named CSGA's Robertson Associate in 1955, their highest honour. Additionally, Gordon South was involved with the Canadian Grain Commission Standards Committee, the Whittome Wheat Pool Committee, the Saskatchewan Co-operative Credit Society, as well as numerous advisory boards. He was named honorary life member of the Agricultural Institute of Canada (1977), received the Queen's Silver Jubilee Medal (1978), and was awarded an honorary doctor of laws degree from the **UNIVERSITY OF SASKATCHEWAN** (1981). On April 8, 1981, he was invested as a Member of the Order of Canada.

SOUTH SASKATCHEWAN REGIMENT. Authorized in the districts of Assiniboia and Saskatchewan on July 3, 1905, the South Saskatchewan Regiment originated as the 95th Regiment. Headquartered in Regina, the 95th had eight companies consisting of approximately 80 to 200 men in each. A Company and B Company of the 95th were formed into a new regiment, designated the 60th Rifles of Canada. Beginning on August 6, 1914, troops from the 95th Saskatchewan Rifles and the 60th Rifles of Canada were placed on active service. Both regiments contributed dozens of officers and hundreds of other ranks to the 46th Battalion, Canadian Expeditionary Force (CEF), throughout **WORLD WAR I**. After the war, on March 15, 1920, the 95th Saskatchewan Rifles amalgamated with the 60th Rifles of Canada and was renamed the South Saskatchewan Regiment. It was reorganized into five regiments in May 1924: the Regina Rifles Regiment, the Assiniboia Regiment, the Weyburn Regiment, the Saskatchewan Border Regiment, and the South Saskatchewan Regiment. The South Saskatchewan Regiment was once again reorganized on December 15, 1936, with the amalgamation of the Weyburn Regiment and the Saskatchewan Border Regiment.

South Saskatchewan Regiment

Mobilized for active duty on September 1, 1939, as the South Saskatchewan Regiment, CASF, the regiment embarked for Europe on December 16, 1940. Once there, the South Saskatchewans performed valiantly, especially during the Dieppe Raid on August 19, 1942. On that day, the regiment landed on the beach at Dieppe in the dim light of the early morning and entered the small village of Pourville, believing that surprise had been achieved. However, the Germans had detected the raid and the South Saskatchewan Regiment was met with heavy gun fire. It suffered 84 casualties, and many of the survivors spent the rest of the hostilities as prisoners of war. The commanding officer, Lieutenant-Colonel Charles Cecil Ingersoll Merritt, won the **VICTORIA CROSS** for his inspiring leadership during the raid. Following Dieppe, the reconstituted South Saskatchewan Regiment landed in Normandy on July 8, 1944, as a unit of the 6th Infantry Brigade, 2nd Canadian Infantry Division. Stationed there until the end of the war, the regiment disbanded on December 15, 1945. The South Saskatchewan Regiment was placed on the Supplementary Order of Battle List in September 1968.

Cec Law, Peter Maulé,
Gregory Salmers, and William Sutherland

FURTHER READING: Buchanan, G.B. 1958. *The March of the Prairie Men: A Story of the South Saskatchewan Regiment.* Weyburn, Saskatchewan: South Saskatchewan Regiment Association.

RON GARNETT—AIRSCAPES

South Saskatchewan River.

SOUTH SASKATCHEWAN RIVER (53°15'N, 105°05'W; map sheet 73 H/3). Originating in the Rocky Mountains, the South Saskatchewan River is a combination of the Oldman, Bow and Red Deer rivers and begins where the Oldman and Bow join, west of the city of Medicine Hat in Alberta. It flows in an easterly direction. After winding its way across the southern Alberta prairie grasslands, the Red Deer River adds its water a few kilometres east of the Alberta-Saskatchewan provincial boundary. The river continues flowing in an easterly direction into **LAKE DIEFENBAKER**, where it changes its course to follow the northward slope of the land from Elbow to **GARDINER DAM**. The flows downstream of Lake Diefenbaker are controlled by Gardiner Dam, which has significantly changed the natural regime in the river, resulting in lower flows in the spring and early summer, and higher flows in the late fall and winter. After Gardiner Dam the river continues to flow in a northeasterly direction, past the city of Saskatoon, into the parkland region to join the **NORTH SASKATCHEWAN RIVER**, east of Prince Albert, and become the **SASKATCHEWAN RIVER**.

The South Saskatchewan River watershed encompasses a total area of 172,900 km², about 30% of the total watershed area being in Saskatchewan (51,800 km²). In a typical year more than 80% of the flow in the river is derived from the mountain and foothill region runoff. Peak flows typically occur in late May or June, in conjunction with mountain snowmelt runoff from the eastern slopes of the Rocky Mountains. The mean annual inflow into Saskatchewan is approximately 7.2 million dam³; the majority of this flow (93%) is passed through Lake Diefenbaker. The Swift Current Creek basin, which flows into Lake Diefenbaker just north of the city of Swift Current, is the only major watershed in Saskatchewan which contributes its waters into the South Saskatchewan River. (*See also* **HYDROLOGY, IRRIGATION, MEEWASIN VALLEY AUTHORITY**)

Bart Oegema

SOUTHERN RAILS CO-OPERATIVE. In 1989, Southern Rails Co-operative (SRC) became the first common carrier short line of the modern era. SRC was created and owned by farmers along two Saskatchewan branch lines. These were the Colony subdivision: a former CP line running from Rockglen to Killdeer, and the portion of the CN Avonlea subdivision from Parry to Avonlea. Both of these lines were slated for abandonment by the major railways; SRC was seen by Saskatchewan Highways and Transportation as a prototype that could serve as a model for similar branch lines. SRC operated these two separate branch lines with an innovative power unit: the Brandt Road Rail Vehicle was built on the chassis of a Kenworth highway tractor, and could operate on both road and rail; in this way, it was able to move between the two branch lines, which were 160 km apart. SRC was organized as a traditional co-operative, with ownership held by farmers able to utilize the railway. It served **SASKATCHEWAN WHEAT POOL** elevators at Truax and Parry and producer car loading sites at Killdeer, Canopus and Rockglen. By 2004, much of the original track operated by SRC was no longer in service, but the company had expanded along the Avonlea subdivision into Moose Jaw.

Paul Beingessner

SOUTHEY, town, pop 693, located 55 km N of Regina at the junction of Hwys 6 and 22. Settlers began arriving in the area around 1902–03, and by the time the **CANADIAN PACIFIC RAILWAY** arrived in 1905 most of the available land in the area was taken up. With the arrival of the railway the townsite was established and one of the original settlers suggested the name Southey in honour of a favourite English poet, Robert Southey (1774–1843). Subsequently, many of the community's streets were given the names of writers and poets, such as Coleridge, Burns, Browning, Kipling, and Keats. Homesteaders in the district were predominantly of German and Scandinavian origins, with lesser numbers of Romanians, Hungarians, and people hailing from the British Isles. The community developed rapidly in the years from 1905 to 1912, and experienced steady growth in the ensuing years. Southey was incorporated as a town in 1980. Situated on rich agricultural lands with a mixture of dark brown and black sandy loam and silty clay soils suitable for growing a variety of crops, Southey serves an area of about 1,500 people involved in mixed farming, the production of grain, specialty crops, and oilseeds. The town's original school, built in 1906, has been designated a heritage property and is now located on the town's museum grounds. Some Southey residents commute to work in Regina.

David McLennan

SPACE ENGINEERING DIVISION (SED). A company that originated within the **UNIVERSITY OF SASKATCHEWAN**'s Institute of Space and Atmospheric Studies in 1965 has grown to become a world leader in satellite technology systems. Called the Space Engineering Division (SED), its mandate is to design and build rocket instrumentation for upper atmospheric studies. Today, SED Systems employs 250 people, has annual sales of $50 million, and is a division of Calian Ltd., a company wholly owned by Calian Technology Ltd. SED Systems was awarded the largest contract ever to a Canadian company by the European Space Agency in 1998 when it was selected to build a 35-metre, deep-space antenna in

COURTESY OF SED SYSTEMS

European Space Agency 35 Meter Deep Space Antenna, New Norcia, Australia.

Australia; five years later, SED won another contract to build a similar antenna in Spain. Over the years the growth and expertise of the SED Systems has matched the need of its clients, and the company has developed and installed satellite tracking systems in areas as diverse as the Canadian Arctic and Guam, an island in the Pacific Ocean. Customers have included industry giants such as Boeing Satellite Systems and government space or telecommunications organizations in Brazil, India, and Japan. WorldSpace Corporation contracted SED to provide feeder link stations for the first-ever digital radio service via satellite. SED then earned a contract in 2000 to design, manufacture and install the Uplink Delivery System, which encodes and relays radio programming from XM Radio's programming centre in Washington, DC, to XM Radio's two high-powered Hughes 702 geo-stationary satellites for broadcast to XM-Ready receivers anywhere in the continental United States.   *Joe Ralko*

SPACE SHUTTLE EXPERIMENT. Growing a protein crystal in space was the first Canadian experiment conducted on board a space shuttle. The experiment, developed by UNIVERSITY OF SASKATCHEWAN biochemist Louis Delbaere, was selected for NASA's *Discovery* shuttle in 1990; two years later another of his experiments was conducted on *Mir*, the Russian space station.

The results showed that protein crystals grown in space are of better quality than when grown on earth. The protein crystal grown in 1992 on the *Mir* space station provided information on antibody-antigen interaction, a fundamental process of the immune system whereby antibodies recognize and bind to foreign particles called antigens, which are subsequently removed from the body.   *Joe Ralko*

SPANISH INFLUENZA EPIDEMIC. The "Spanish Flu" was named in May 1918, since the Spanish media was the first to document this epidemic during a period in WORLD WAR I when most countries had strict censorship. The Spanish Flu was an extreme strain of the influenza virus, which was transmitted by inhaling infected air. Scientists have hypothesized that this virus originated in China as a strain of avian influenza, which mutated and infected herds of swine. This virus was contracted by humans, and was dispersed throughout society as people and goods moved along Asian-European trade routes. In the trenches of World War I, the Spanish Flu quickly spread. Infected soldiers began returning to their homelands, thus carrying the virus throughout the world.

Symptoms, such as chills, fever, headaches, pains, weakness, coughing up blood, and delirium, appeared suddenly. It was not uncommon for a person to be healthy in the morning, yet die from the virus by the evening. Two effects of the Spanish Flu

COURTESY OF NINITA HAUTZ

Ida Hautz (born 1896) on her wedding day, December 8, 1918. Shortly after their marriage, she and her husband traveled to the Saskatoon area to visit Ida's sister, Maria Walter. While there, she contracted Spanish influenza and died on March 10, 1919. At 23 years of age, she was in the demographic which had the lowest survival rate. Although transporting of dead bodies was restricted, her body was, in fact, sent by train to her home community in the Landestreu district, arriving on a bitterly cold day, this according to her younger brother, whose sad task it was to travel by horse and wagon to the train station and bring his sister's body home for burial.

were the increased risks of contracting a respiratory infection such as pneumonia, or becoming inflicted with cyanosis, a bluish skin discoloration that resulted from severely diminished amounts of haemoglobin in the blood. The Spanish Flu was difficult to treat because medical understanding of viral infections did not occur until the 1930s. Just as with today's influenza, there was no cure for the Spanish Flu. The most popular remedies were bed rest or drinking alcohol. Because of PROHIBITION in Saskatchewan, alcohol could only be obtained with a doctor's prescription from one of two distributing pharmacies in the province. Other preventative measures to which people resorted were folk remedies or wearing of masks.

The infection rate of the virus in Saskatchewan was about one in every four families. This virus was most detrimental to the 20 to 40 years age group, where the survival rate was 50%. As the epidemic spread through out the province, a shortage of doctors was apparent. Approximately 10% of doctors were on military service, while many others became sick or died themselves due to the virus. Furthermore, 87% of the population lived in rural areas, yet had access to only a third of the province's hospital beds. Most deaths from this epidemic occurred at home. Often, bodies were stacked upon

one another while undertakers waited for coffins. Once coffins were available, burial permits were often overlooked in order for the bodies to be quickly laid to rest. The transportation of dead bodies was not permitted, in order to control the spread of the virus. Communities were quarantined, schools were closed, church services cancelled, and public meetings were banned. Because of the impact of the virus on the 20 to 40 years age group, many children were left orphaned by this epidemic.

The Spanish Flu gradually weakened in 1919, and by 1920 had run its course. It has been estimated that the total deaths worldwide from this epidemic reached 50 to 100 million. In Canada, 50,000 people died, including 5,000 in Saskatchewan. As a result of this epidemic, there were demands for an increase in the number of HOSPITALS throughout the province, an increase in doctor's salaries, and more training on caring for the sick at home.   *Erin Legg*

FURTHER READING: Lux, Maureen. 1997. "The Bitter Flats: The 1918 Influenza Epidemic in Saskatchewan," *Saskatchewan History* 29 (1).

SPARRO. More than 100 nuclear physicists and graduate students from thirty research institutions in seven countries including the UNIVERSITY OF REGINA began working on a research project in 1998 into the fundamental building blocks of nature. Subatomic Physics at Regina with Research Offshore, or SPARRO, is the name of the research group working on this major international project known as Hall-D GlueX. The purpose of GlueX is to try to create particles that do not exist in nature and determine what holds or glues the particles together.   *Joe Ralko*

UNIVERSITY OF REGINA, PHOTOGRAPHY DEPARTMENT

SPARRO, University of Regina physics project.

SPARROWS, NATIVE. Native sparrows belong to the family Emberizidae. This family contains about 320 species; most of these are New World, but there are also species in Africa and Eurasia. Their conical bills aid in removing the husks of the hard grass and forb seeds that make up their winter diet. During the breeding season they add insects to their diet and that of their young. Their plumage tends to browns, although some are more colourful. Thirty-

COURTESY OF THE ROYAL SASKATCHEWAN MUSEUM

White-throated sparrow.

one species have been confirmed for the province, making it the second largest family after the ducks. They are migratory.

Many native sparrows are common in Saskatchewan, but some species are hard to identify unless they produce their distinctive songs. There are provincial records for twenty-one of the thirty-two species that occur in North America, with the notable absence of *Aimophila*, which has five species on the continent. *Amphispiza* is also absent, except for one recorded visit by the black-throated sparrow (*A. bilineata*) in 1991. Most of the native sparrows in Saskatchewan nest in small trees or shrubs, either on low branches or on the ground. Species that prefer open, grassland habitats build well-concealed nests in existing or scraped-out depressions. During the nesting period, adult birds eat mostly spiders, insects, and grass and forb seeds; but many species feed their young a diet consisting entirely of insects. After breeding, some species migrate only as far as the central or southern USA, while others spend the winter in northern or central Mexico.

All but one of the small (13–14 cm in length) native sparrows in Saskatchewan are members of the genus *Ammodramus*. The grasshopper sparrow (*A. savannarum*) and Baird's sparrow (*A. bairdii*) have similar breeding ranges, preferring to nest in lightly grazed parts of the Grasslands and Aspen Parkland. Le Conte's sparrow (*A. leconteii*) and the sharp-tailed sparrow (*A. caudacutus*) both breed in wet meadows and bog edges in boreal and parkland areas; but Le Conte's prefers drier conditions and is more widespread. The species with the widest range in this group is the savannah sparrow (*Passerculus sandwichensis*), which nests in pastures, wet meadows, and open, forested habitats.

Most of the mid-sized (14–16 cm) native sparrows that have been observed in Saskatchewan belong to *Spizella* or *Melospiza*. Species with restricted breeding ranges include the American tree sparrow (*S. arborea*), which breeds in the extreme northeast corner, and Brewer's sparrow (*S. breweri*), which nests in shrubby habitats in the southwest. Lincoln's sparrow (*M. lincolnii*) and the

swamp sparrow (*M. georgiana*) can be found nesting in shrubby marshes across subarctic and boreal areas, while the clay-coloured sparrow (*S. pallida*) and the Vesper sparrow (*Pooecetes gramineus*) are common throughout the Grasslands and Aspen Parkland. Widespread species include the chipping sparrow (*S. passerina*), which breeds in urban areas, farmsteads, and forests, and the song sparrow (*M. melodia*), which prefers to nest in wooded habitats close to water. The last mid-sized species on record is the field sparrow (*S. pusilla*), considered a regular non-breeder that probably nests in the southeast.

The largest native sparrows that have been observed in Saskatchewan are 17–19 cm in length; most are members of *Zonotrichia*. Three species are regular breeders in boreal areas and include the white-throated sparrow (*Z. albicollis*), the white-crowned sparrow (*Z. leucophrys*), and the fox sparrow (*Passerella iliaca*). This group also includes Harris' sparrow (*Z. querula*), which breeds in the extreme northeast corner of the province, the lark sparrow (*Chondestes grammacus*), which prefers dry grassland with scattered trees and shrubs, and the golden-crowned sparrow (*Z. atricapilla*), a rare visitor associated with montane thickets and shrubs.

Other members of the family which occur in the province are the towhees, junco, and longspurs. The black, white and chestnut-coloured spotted towhee (*Pipilo maculatus*) is the common towhee of the province, nesting in shrubby habitats in the grasslands and parklands. It and the Eastern towhee (*P. erythrophthalmus*), which nests in the lower Qu'Appelle Valley, used to be considered a single species, the rufous-sided towhee. The green-tailed towhee (*P. chlorurus*) is a rare visitor. The little dark-eyed junco (*Junco hyemalis*) is a common migrant through the province and a summer resident of the forests, either in the north or in the **CYPRESS HILLS**. Juncos have several plumages, but all have the distinctive white outer-tail feathers seen in flight.

The longspurs and snow buntings are birds of open habitats. These small birds are hard to see as they move through the dead grasses, camouflaged except for the strongly marked head and chests of the breeding males. The chestnut-collared longspur (*Calcarius ornatus*) is a common nester in the grasslands and grassed areas of the parklands. McCown's longspur (*C. mccownii*) is more localized to the shortgrass prairies of the southwest, but does occur in other grasslands to the east. The Lapland longspur (*C. lapponicus*) is a common transient on its way to its breeding ground in the Arctic, and occurs in large flocks which may contain thousands of birds. Smith's longspur (*C. pictus*), which is also seen as a transient, is much less common. The snow bunting (*Plectrophenax nivalis*), another Arctic nester, is seen only as a winter visitant throughout

the province and may occur in large flocks of white-bellied, brown-backed birds.   *Glenn Sutter*

FURTHER READING: Alsop, F.J., III. 2002. *Birds of Canada*. New York: Dorling Kindersley.

SPECIAL EDUCATION. The era from 1905 to 1945 was one of slow development in recognizing exceptional pupils and providing special classes and separate schools for their education. Students who were blind were sent out of province to special schools in Montreal or Brantford. Students who were deaf were sent to Winnipeg until 1929, when Saskatchewan built the School for the Deaf in Saskatoon. Special classes, with an emphasis on vocational preparation, were established in larger urban centres for youth with difficulties in academic programs. Beginning in the late 1920s, students who were gifted were provided special classes in Saskatoon. Samuel Laycock of the **UNIVERSITY OF SASKATCHEWAN** promoted special classes for gifted learners; to this day, the Samuel Laycock Memorial Lecture is a legacy of his influence.

The era from the 1950s to the 1970s reflected growing consciousness among both parents and professionals about the educational benefits for students with disabilities. Parents of children with disabilities organized into effective advocacy groups and worked to develop services to improve the education of these children. Special schools for children with multiple disabilities and intellectual or cognitive disabilities were developed in larger centres, operated primarily by parents' associations. In the 1970s there was a growing awareness that students with special needs could benefit from access to a broader range of educational programs. The development of the *cascade model* advocated the creation of an array of instructional locations from the regular classroom to special settings. Although children had to qualify for placement based on their abilities, the model was considered a major advancement; at the same time, remedial reading teachers' roles also began evolving into that of learning resource teachers.

The era from the 1970s to the 1990s was one of much change in services and programs for children and youth with exceptional learning needs. Extensive debate focused on innovative ways to better educate students with exceptionalities in regular school programs and settings. These changes were facilitated by increasing the range of services and supports provided to neighbourhood schools and classrooms (*see* **SCHOOLS AND INCLUSION**). Reflecting changing attitudes and values, Saskatchewan amended the School Act in 1971, making mandatory the education of all students, including those with disabilities. It was the first province to do so. The funding formula for the provision of government grants to school boards was changed to a per student rate, no longer providing grants for special-education classrooms and thus encouraging schools to consider a wider range of locations where exceptional students could be served. At the school level, the educational program plan designed for each child became the critical organizer for identifying needs of students and the planned provision of services and supports.

Teacher training at the University of Saskatchewan provided a focal point in the preparation of school-based resource teachers. The expanded role of these teachers, no longer tied to the special-class model of service delivery, became a natural support to classroom teachers who were working with an increasingly diverse student body. The Shared Service model, adopted by Saskatchewan Education in 1982, reshaped support services across all provincial schools. Initially, educational psychologists and speech language pathologists were employed, but Shared Service soon expanded to include special education consultants, social workers, and counselors. The Department of Education shifted from employing provincial consultants in disability areas to drawing on personnel from school boards and deploying them to those teachers requesting consultative support. Two innovations further supported parents in seeking neighbourhood school experiences for children with disabilities. First, home-based early childhood development programs were provided for at-risk and developmentally delayed pre-school children. Second, the education regulations were changed so that school boards could provide centre-based programs for developmentally delayed children, beginning at age 3.

The period from the 1990s to the present has focused on reform efforts. Building inclusive schools was highlighted in the special education review, *Directions for Diversity: Enhancing Supports for Children and Youth with Diverse Needs* (2000). Strengthening schools has involved linking with professionals from other agencies. There has been a rapid expansion in the employment of educational assistants and in the use of new technologies, and an increased emphasis on accountability for better preparing students for life in the community. In an effort to make special-education teacher training more accessible, both provincial universities have reviewed their programs and introduced innovations such as technology-enhanced learning and on-line courses. *Harry Dahl and Leonard Haines*

FURTHER READING: Saskatchewan Education. 2000. *Directions for Diversity: Final Report of the Special Education Review Committee*. Regina: Saskatchewan Education.

SPECIAL LIBRARIES. During the 19th century, specialized libraries began to be developed throughout the world to support the unique information needs of a wide variety of public and private institutions. The chief characteristic distinguishing these from other libraries was the specialized focus on practical client needs in support of the work of the host organization, rather than on recreation or education as in the case of public and academic libraries. The establishment in 1876 of the headquarters of the Territorial Government in the geographic area representing present-day Saskatchewan provided the impetus for special library development. Among the earliest special libraries were the North-West Government Library, subsequently the Saskatchewan Legislative Library (first recorded expenditure for books and subscriptions in the fiscal year 1876–77); the North-West Mounted Police Library (recreational collection in some barracks as early as 1875; founding of a central circulation library at the Regina Barracks in 1893); the North-West Territories Department of Agriculture Library (1898); and the Law Society of the North-West Territories Library (1898). After 1905, as services and agencies developed in the province, the variety and scope of special libraries increased to include libraries supporting the court system and private law firms, police agencies and prisons, newspapers and business corporations, museums and art galleries, professional and voluntary societies, medical and health institutions, ethnic associations and religious institutions, agricultural research facilities, and government departments.

Some of the most recent and important changes in special libraries have been driven by the introduction and expansion of electronic information sources available in commercial databases and on the Internet. In this world of diverse and continually evolving information media, special libraries continue to address client needs by building relevant resource collections, by providing sophisticated access to those collections, and in particular by adding value to factual data by compiling, tabulating, or synthesizing retrieved information and delivering it to the client in whatever print or electronic form is required. *Marian J. Powell*

SPECIALIZED LIVESTOCK. Specialized livestock raised for economic livelihood by Saskatchewan farmers and ranchers includes prominent species such as elk (wapiti), white-tailed **DEER**, **BISON**, and wild boar. Other species raised in Sasatchewan that are also included under the definition of specialized livestock are: ostriches, emus, llamas, alpacas, reindeer and fallow deer.

Prior to 1987, specialized livestock species were managed by the provincial Department of the Environment, recognizing the owners with zoo licenses. In 1987, the government transferred the management of licensing producers to the Department of Agriculture. Today, the Departments of Agriculture and Environment work together in regulating and managing the specialized livestock industry. It should be recognized that some of the species, such as white-tailed deer, mule deer, elk, and reindeer are indigenous wild species in the province. Hence, this results in the need for regulation by both departments as these animals fall under their respective regulations.

In 1995, the Crow Rate transportation subsidy was eliminated in Canada, resulting in agriculture diversification in Saskatchewan. From 1995 to 2000, both the number of specialized livestock producers and the number of animals in western Canada grew by approximately 26%–30% per year. In 2000, chronic wasting disease was discovered in Saskatchewan farm-raised elk and in free-ranging wild mule deer. This discovery forced the closure of export markets for the elk and deer industries, which halted the rapid expansion the industry had experienced.

Saskatchewan is currently home to approximately 25% of the Canadian deer herd, 36% of the Canadian elk herd, and 24% of the Canadian bison herd. According to Saskatchewan Agriculture and Food 2001 statistics, over 580 deer and elk operations are raising an estimated 7,250 mule deer, white-tailed deer and reindeer, and 38,000 elk. Approximately 560 bison producers are raising 41,500 bison. The wild boar population of Saskatchewan is estimated between 15,000 and 20,000 head (including approximately 2,700 sows), raised by an estimated 150 producers.

With the rapid expansion of the specialized livestock industries in the 1990s, infrastructure and support expanded as well. The white-tailed deer, elk, wild boar and bison industries each have provincial producer associations, with both the elk and bison associations having developed national associations to address such issues as animal health, marketing, and relations with other countries. As well, governments and university research and support groups in western Canada exist to assist the specialized livestock industries. For example, at the **UNIVERSITY OF SASKATCHEWAN** individuals were assigned to examine marketing, nutrition, meat science and veterinary medicine for specialized livestock species. For all species the single most prominent challenge is developing and expanding new and current markets.

Elk. The primary market for the elk industry is in breeding stock and export sales of antler velvet to countries such as Korea, while competing against other countries such as the United States, New Zealand, China and Russia. When the price for velvet antler products dropped in the late 1990s, owing to the Asian economic downturn, interest was spurred in the marketing of elk for venison and bulls for trophy hunt ranches. Since the legalization of elk farming in Saskatchewan in 1987, the elk industry has demonstrated innovation in the areas of handling, nutrition, and artificial insemination. Current issues challenging the elk industry include the investigation and live animal diagnosis of chronic wasting disease, the determination of specific nutrient requirements that match digestive physiology and optimize production, disease issues such as better tuberculosis testing methods, developing diagnostic tests for parasites such as *Parelaphostrongylus tenuis* and *Elaphostrongylus cervi* to facilitate live animal trade, factors affecting antler growth, velvet antler efficacy trials, velvet antler quality assurance standards, venison production, and marketing and product development.

White-tailed Deer. The primary market for white-tailed deer is the sale of adult male bucks to trophy hunt ranches and breeding stock. In the early 1990's white-tailed deer operations were few, as most of the "specialized livestock" interest was being directed toward the elk and bison industries. However, as the value of elk and bison breeding stock increased, more interest was being generated in the white-tailed deer industry. Much like the elk industry, the white-tailed deer industry has shown innovation and expertise in the development of feeding programs, handling systems, and artificial insemination methods. Challenges for the white-tailed deer industry include better testing/investigation of chronic wasting disease, how antler growth can be enhanced through nutrition and genetics, control/eradication of necrobacillosis, developing diagnostic tests for parasites such as *Parelaphostrongylus tenuis* and *Elaphostrongylus cervi* to facilitate live animal trade, better testing/investigation of tuberculosis, marketing structures for trophy ranches and venison markets, venison quality and product development, as well as several aspects revolving around nutrition as related to digestive physiology and production requirements.

Bison. The commercial production of bison is also relatively new to western Canada, with rapid increases in animal and producer numbers throughout the 1990s. However, what sets bison apart from the deer and elk industries is that in Saskatchewan, bison are classified as a domestic species and require fewer regulations. In federal jurisdiction, however, bison are regulated as a captive ungulate. The main product of the bison industry is a red meat that is low in fat and cholesterol and high in protein. Other products of the bison industry include sales of breeding stock, hides, bleached skulls for art work, trophy ranching, and tourism. The main advantage of bison is that no other continent outside of North America commercially farms a significant number of bison. Thus, North America is the only major supplier of bison products to the world. The bison industry has also made strong advancements in the areas of handling and nutrition throughout the 1990s. However, much like the deer and elk industries, the bison industry is going through a series of growing pains. Bison meat production is at a disadvantage in Saskatchewan because there is no federally licensed or European-licensed bison slaughter facility located within the province. Without this licensing, bison meat products cannot be exported beyond provincial borders to importing countries such as the United States and Europe. As such, the Saskatchewan industry is currently transporting live animals to licensed slaughter plants in Alberta or the United States. Another primary challenge to the industry is the marketing of its red meat while competing with high-volume meat protein sources such as beef, chicken, and pork. Other obstacles that need to be addressed include bull fertility between and within age groups, growth characteristics and differences between "plains" and "wood" bison, and if dif-

ferences exist, how to optimize bull feeding and production through the wintering period, and investigation into diseases such as malignant catarrhal fever, Johnes disease and testing of tuberculosis.

Wild Boar. The main product of the wild boar industry is domestic red meat sales and export to Europe and Asian countries. Other saleable products include breeding stock, animals sold to trophy hunt ranch operations as well as animals sold into ethnic markets. Both full-blooded wild boar and commercial standard-bred (hybrid cross with domestic swine) are being raised. The main challenge for the wild boar industry is the marketing of the red meat and structures/infrastructure involved. Federal and European-licensed slaughter plant availability for wild boar also needs to be developed. Issues involving animal handling and containment, meat consistency and quality, marketing and product development are challenges to the wild boar industry.

Other Species. Other species that are termed "specialized livestock" include mule deer, reindeer, fallow deer, ostrich and emu. Challenges to these industries are specific to each species. However, as with the elk, white-tailed deer, bison and wild boar, most of the emphasis is placed on market development and access, market identification, product development and supply, development of production targets, optimization of production, and enhanced knowledge of nutrition and health as it relates to each species. *Murray S. Feist*

FURTHER READING: Haigh, J.C. and R.J. Hudson. 1993. *Farming Wapiti and Red Deer.* Missouri: Mosby-Year Book; Martin, J., R.J. Hudson and B.A. Young. 1993. *Animal Production in Canada.* Edmonton: University of Alberta Press.

SPECIES AT RISK. In 1999, fifteen species were formally identified in The Wildlife Act as being at risk of extinction in Saskatchewan (*see* Table SAR-1). This formal designation protects six **BIRDS**, three **MAMMALS**, and six plant species from being disturbed, collected, harvested, captured, killed and exported. Formal listing is pending for another thirty-two species. Species listed under Saskatchewan's Wildlife Act undergo an extensive scientific and public review process; they are prioritized using the ranks provided by the **SASKATCHEWAN CONSERVATION DATA CENTRE**. Through standardized methods, CDCs throughout North America assign conservation ranks to species. Once a species is identified as a candidate for formal listing, a detailed status report is written based on the species' biology, changes in population size, distribution, and potential threats to the species or its habitat. An independent committee of Saskatchewan scientists, the Scientific Working Group (SWG), reviews the status report and recommends a status designation. Public concerns are addressed in the review process through consultation

COURTESY OF TOURISM SASKATCHEWAN

White-tailed deer.

COURTESY OF TOURISM SASKATCHEWAN
Burrowing Owl.

with the Endangered Species Advisory Committee (ESAC). ESAC is comprised of twelve stakeholder groups that provide feedback and advice to the government regarding status designation, conservation, and recovery of species at risk. To ensure continuity with other jurisdictions, Saskatchewan uses the same ranking criteria and definitions as the Committee on the Status of Endangered Wildlife in Canada (COSEWIC), which assesses the national status of Canadian species. Species identified as at risk by COSEWIC are put forth to the federal government and may be listed under the federal Species at Risk Act (SARA).

Jeanette Pepper

Table SAR-1. Saskatchewan Species at Risk

	Extirpated	Endangered	Threatened
Birds	Eskimo curlew (*Numenius borealis*) Greater prairie chicken (*Tympanuchus cupido*)	Burrowing owl (*Athene cunicularia*) Piping plover (*Charadrius melodus*) Sage grouse (*Centrocercus urophasianus*) Whooping crane (*Grus americana*)	
Mammals	Black-footed ferret (*Mustela nigripes*) Grizzly bear (*Ursus arctos arctos*)	Swift fox (*Vulpes velox*)	
Plants	Small white lady's slipper (*Cypripedium candidum*)	Hairy prairie clover (*Dalea villosa*) Sand verbena (*Tripterocalyx micranthus*) Tiny cryptanthe (*Cryptantha minima*) Western spiderwort (*Tradescantia occidentalis*)	Slender mouse-ear-cress (*Halimolobos virgata*)

Definitions:
Extirpated: Any native wild species of plant or animal that no longer exists in the wild in Saskatchewan.
Endangered: Any native wild species of plant or animal that is threatened with imminent extirpation or extinction.
Threatened: Any native wild species of plant or animal that is likely to become endangered if the factors leading to its endangerment are not reversed.

SPENCE, AHAB (1911–2001). Ahab Spence was born at Split Lake, Manitoba, on July 1, 1911. He attended Emanuel College in Saskatoon, studying theology, and completed a Bachelor of Arts degree from the UNIVERSITY OF SASKATCHEWAN (1952). Spence worked as an Anglican priest in the Diocese of Saskatoon (1937–65), with the Department of Indian Affairs and Northern Development (1965–70), and with the Manitoba Indian Brotherhood, serving as the organization's president from 1974 to 1976. He taught at the Saskatchewan Indian Federated College from 1980 to 1998 in the Indian Languages Department, and was recognized as professor emeritus. Dr. Spence received an honorary law degree from the University of Saskatchewan (1964), the national Aboriginal achievement award for education (1985), and was invested as a Member of the Order of Canada in 1982. He died on April 5, 2001.

SPENCE, GEORGE (1880–1975). Spence was born in the Orkney Islands on October 25, 1880. He received his public school education in England, and attended the Leith Academy Technical College in Scotland, where he studied electrical engineering. In 1900, he spent three years in the gold fields of the Klondike. He then farmed in Manitoba, and sometimes worked on survey parties with the CPR. In 1912, he settled on a homestead at Monchy, south of Swift Current, on the United States border in one of the driest parts of the Canadian prairies.

Spence was elected to the Saskatchewan Legislature in 1917, then re-elected in 1921 and 1925. He resigned in 1925, and was elected a member of Parliament. Two years later he returned to provincial politics, and in succession was appointed Minister of Labour and Industries, Minister of Highways, and Minister of Public Works. During the period 1927 to 1938 he was influential in the building of ten branch railway lines in southwestern Saskatchewan, and the beginnings of the present-day numbered highway system.

He was acting chairman of the Better Farming Commission in 1920 that led to the establishment of the Swift Current Research Station, where dryland farming problems have been studied since 1921. Spence was appointed director of the PRAIRIE FARM REHABILITATION ADMINISTRATION in 1938. The engineering and financing of joint federal, provincial and local conservation projects were concluded. He was responsible for much of the planning of the SOUTH SASKATCHEWAN RIVER project. Following his retirement from PFRA in 1947, Spence served for ten years on the International Joint Commission, dealing with the allocation of water from sources shared by Canada and the United States.

He was made a Commander of the British Empire in 1946 and in 1948 received an honorary degree from the UNIVERSITY OF SASKATCHEWAN. He

SASKATCHEWAN ARCHIVES BOARD R-B434
George Spence.

wrote a book, *Survival of a Vision*, and a treatise on the growing of tender roses. George Spence died in Regina on March 4, 1975.

Adapted from Saskatchewan Agricultural Hall of Fame

FURTHER READING: MacEwan, Grant. 1958. *Fifty Mighty Men*. Saskatoon: Western Producer Prairie Books.

SPENCER, MARGUERITA (RITA) (1892–1993). Born into the large musical McQuarrie family of Glace Bay, Nova Scotia on December 28, 1892, Spencer studied piano, organ and cello at Halifax Ladies' College and at McGill University. She also studied nursing at the Toronto General Hospital. In 1922 she wed Roy Aubrey Spencer; they moved to Saskatoon, where he taught engineering at the UNIVERSITY OF SASKATCHEWAN. During WORLD WAR I she accompanied silent movies; she also played

GLEN BERGER PHOTO/SASKATCHEWAN ARCHIVES BOARD
S-SP-A7669-1, SASKATOON STARPHOENIX FONDS

Marguerita Spencer, September 1977, at the age of 84, rehearsing for one of her two yearly concert recitals.

troop concerts then and during WORLD WAR II. In Saskatoon, Spencer continued her studies under Helen Davies Sherry, LYELL GUSTIN, and others. She performed on a weekly CBC program and with the SASKATOON SYMPHONY ORCHESTRA, and headed the Saskatoon Women's Musical Club and the Musical Arts Club. She also composed: of her nearly forty compositions, she is best known for *Prairie Suite No. 1* and *24 Preludes*; but many of them appeared on music festival programs and conservatory exams throughout Canada. Partly blind in old age, Spencer used a tape recorder and transcriber. She received the Queen's Silver Jubilee Medal and recognition in international music sources. Spencer died on May 5, 1993, in Saskatoon.

Ruth Wright Millar

SPICES AND INDUSTRY. Emerging spice crops in Saskatchewan include coriander (*Coriandrum sativum* L.), caraway (*Carum carvi* L.), dill (*Anethum graveolens* L.), anise (*Pimpinella anisum* L.), and fenugreek (*Trigonella foenum-graecum* L.). All of these are members of the carrot family (Apiaceae), except fenugreek, which is a member of the legume family (Fabaceae). All of these spice crops are summer annuals in Saskatchewan, except caraway, which is a biennial. More than 8,000 ha each of coriander and caraway seed are harvested annually, and most of it is exported as whole seed. Dill and anise are grown on only a few hundred hectares each year, and most of the seed is exported to the United States as whole seed. Fenugreek is grown on only a few hundred hectares each year, and has been exported to the United States as whole seed or as fenugreek flour. One company in Saskatchewan constructed a processing facility in 2004 that uses a patented process to produce an odourless fenugreek powder with up to 80% fibre. The demand for sources of high fibre for use in foods and nutraceuticals is steadily increasing, and is expected to continue to increase with the concern over the high rate of obesity in North America.

MUSTARD seed (family Brassicaceae), brown and oriental, is the most important spice crop in Saskatchewan. Canada is the second largest producer in the world with over 200,000 tonnes per year, and the largest exporter with 160,000 tonnes per year. Saskatchewan produces 80–90% of the Canadian mustard seed, primarily in the Brown and Dark Brown soil zones. Seed yields range from 700 to 800 kg per hectare, depending upon type, yellow mustard seed being the lowest yielding. The protein content of mustard seed ranges from 25–36%, whereas the oil content ranges from 28–39% depending upon the type. Mustard seed is exported as whole seed. Most of the brown mustard seed is exported to Europe; most of the oriental mustard seed (hotter) is exported to Asia; and most of the yellow mustard seed is exported to the United States. Yellow mustard seed is low in oil: this facilitates its

use in dry milling for flour and wet milling for mustard pastes, and as a binder and protein extender in processed meats. The seed coat of yellow mustard contains mucilage, which absorbs water and keeps processed meat dry.

Al Slinkard and Ray McVicar

FURTHER READING: Kehler, C. (ed.). 1999. *Herb and Spice Production Manual*. Regina: Saskatchewan Herb and Spice Association.

SPIDERS. Spiders belong to the phylum Arthropoda, class Arachnida, order Araneae. There are approximately 32,000 described spider species in the world, with thousands more yet to be discovered. Saskatchewan has recorded about 455 species, and just over 600 species are estimated for the province. Major challenges in spider taxonomy include revising a number of the family groups and the identification of immatures.

There are twenty spider families in the province, including eleven families that are specialized web-builders. The major web-building families include the Araneidae (orb-web weavers), Agelenidae (funnel-web weavers), Theridiidae (cob-web weavers), and the Dictynidae. The other web-building families are the Linyphiidae, Amaurobiidae, Hahniidae, Uloboridae, Tetragnathidae (long-jawed orb weavers), Mimetidae (pirate spiders), and the Pholcidae (daddy-long-legs spiders). The nine remaining families are hunting spiders, including the Philodromidae and Thomisidae (crab spiders), Lycosidae (wolf spiders), Anyphaenidae and Clubionidae (sac spiders), Salticidae (jumping spiders), Gnaphosidae (ground spiders), Pisauridae (nurseryweb spiders), and the Oxyopidae (lynx spiders).

The eyesight of the hunting spiders tends to be more acute than that of the web-builders. The salticids (jumping spiders) use their keen vision to stalk their prey, much like a cat, before pouncing on resting insects. The crab spiders often lie in wait on flower heads for their prey, which includes flies,

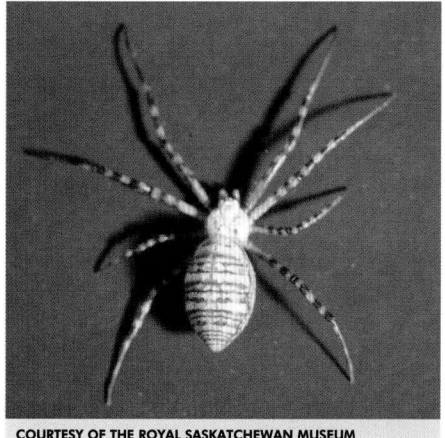

COURTESY OF THE ROYAL SASKATCHEWAN MUSEUM

Banded Garden Spider (*Argiope trifasciata*).

COURTNEY MILNE PHOTO

Web of an orbweaver spider of the genus *Araneus* spp.

butterflies and even bumble-bees. One species of crab spider, *Misumena vatia* (goldenrod spider), has the ability to change its colour from white to yellow and back, which helps to camouflage it against the flower head.

Spiders can readily be distinguished from insects as they have two body segments, eight legs, eight eyes (occasionally six), and no antennae. Almost all spiders have a pair of poison glands which aid them in subduing their prey. The strength and toxicity of the poison varies from species to species. Except for allergic reactions, bites from Saskatchewan spiders are not harmful to humans. However, the bite of Saskatchewan's most venomous spider, the black widow spider (*Latrodectus hesperus*), can produce a severe reaction.

A major attribute of spiders is their ability to spin silk. Spiders may use their silk to construct webs that aid in capturing prey, to wrap their eggs in, and to set down a dragline that may serve as a safety line or as a way to retrace their path. Adults and immatures also use silk to "balloon" from one area to another. A ballooning spider will climb up on vegetation, a fence post or another higher vantage point, lift its abdomen into the air and release some silk threads. As the wind catches this thread, it will lift the spider up and transport it from a few metres to even thousands of kilometres as it is completely at the mercy of the prevailing air currents.

Spiders can be found in almost every part of the world. In Saskatchewan, they range from the grassy prairies of the south to the forests and lakes of the north. On a wet morning, the ground may be covered with hundreds of dew-covered webs. These webs often belong to the funnel-web weaving spiders, the Agelenidae. Their web has a funnel built

into the web that allows the spider to retreat and lie in wait for unsuspecting prey. Another common type of web is constructed by the orb-weaving spiders. Their webs are circular and can be found almost anywhere. One of the more common orb-weaving spiders is the Plains orb-weaver, *Araneus gemmoides*. Its webs can be found attached to buildings and among vegetation. Later in the summer and early fall, the female becomes quite large as she fills up with eggs. Soon after she lays her eggs in a silken case, she dies. The females of the wolf spiders, the Lycosidae, have the unique characteristic of carrying their egg sacs attached to their spinnerets. Once the spiderlings hatch, the female carries them on her back for several days before they disperse. The females of the nurseryweb spiders, the Pisauridae, also carry their egg sacs, but in this case they use their chelicerae or front pair of jaw-like organs. The nurseryweb spiders are also unique in being almost semiaquatic. *Dolomedes triton* will dive beneath the water's surface in search of prey among aquatic vegetation; these spiders are also called "fishing spiders" as they are capable of catching small fish.

While many people have an aversion to spiders, most spiders are extremely beneficial. They are carnivorous and feed on numerous arthropods including insects. They probably consume more insects than all the other insectivorous animals combined, helping to maintain the balance of nature. Silk strands have also been used for the cross hairs in certain optical instruments. *Keith Roney*

FURTHER READING: Gertsch, W.J. 1979. *American Spiders*. New York: Van Nostrand Reinhold; Levi, H.W. 1968. *Spiders and Their Kin*. New York: Golden Press;

Preston-Mafham, R. and K. Preston-Mafham. 1984. *Spiders of the World*. New York: Facts on File Publications.

SPINKS, JOHN WILLIAM TRANTER (1908–97). Born in Norfolk, England on January 1, 1908, Spinks was educated in England and then immigrated to Canada in 1930 to work at the UNIVERSITY OF SASKATCHEWAN. In the hard economic times of the early 1930s, the university offered him and other young academics the choice of a $500 stipend for the academic year, or resignation. He took his stipend to Darmstadt, Germany and the laboratory of Dr. GERHARD HERZBERG. In 1935, Dr. Spinks returned to Canada and arranged the invitation for Dr. Herzberg to join the staff at the University of Saskatchewan. Herzberg thus joined the exodus of Jewish scientists to other Western countries after the establishment of the Nazi government in Germany. Spinks continued his research on atomic energy, including the effects of radiation from radioactive isotopes on organisms. He was the president of the university from 1959 to 1975, during which time (the post-*Sputnik* period) it greatly increased its scientific research activities. He also presided over the growth of the Regina campus of the university and its evolution to a separate institution. He was honoured as an excellent teacher, as well as an imaginative researcher and concerned administrator. He received numerous honours, including Companion of the Order of Canada in 1970. Spinks died in Saskatoon on March 27, 1997. *Diane Secoy*

SASKATCHEWAN ARCHIVES BOARD R-B5723

John Spinks.

SPIRITWOOD, town, pop 907, located 125 km W of Prince Albert and about 110 km NE of North Battleford at the junction of Hwys 3, 24, and 378. The district began to be settled around 1911–12; however, growth in the area was slow until the coming of the railway in the late 1920s. The first settlers primarily engaged in ranching. The

Spiritwood post office, which had been established in 1923, was named after Spiritwood, North Dakota, the hometown of the first postmaster, Rupert J. Dumond. After the railway arrived, settlers of diverse origins poured into the district and many businesses were established. On October 1, 1935, Spiritwood was incorporated as a village and, by September 1, 1965, the community had grown large enough to attain town status. Today, as the largest community in the region, the community functions as the major supply, service, and administrative centre for a trading area population of several thousand including four First Nations communities. Mixed farming predominates and consists primarily of grain production. A Spiritwood company that focuses on pig genetics, producing breeding stock and commercial swine, has roughly 50 employees. There is some forestry in the region north of Spiritwood. The town has a complete range of recreational facilities and, additionally, there are six golf courses in the district, six regional parks, and about 35 lakes within an hour's drive.

David McLennan

SPORTS AND RECREATION IN SASKATCHEWAN—HISTORY: *see essay on facing page.*

SPORTS MEDICINE.

Sports Medicine in Saskatchewan began with team physicians, including: Grant McFetridge with the Roughriders in the early 1940s, followed by Beattie Martin, Sr., Jim Froggott, David Rolston, Ian Thom and Ed Jones; Sam Landa with the Saskatoon Hilltops, 1947–86; and TAL HUNT with the UNIVERSITY OF SASKATCHEWAN Huskies, 1959-64, followed by Walter Hader, 1964–96. Dr. Bill Orban, the first Canadian PhD in Exercise Physiology and Director of Physical Education at the University of Saskatchewan, developed the widely used 5BX and10BX exercise programs, and established the first fitness assessment unit. The first Sports Injuries Clinic was started in1970 in the Department of Rehabilitation. Dr. PAUL SCHWANN came to Regina in 1958, focusing his medical practice on sports medicine; in recognition, the Paul Schwann Applied Health and Research Centre, University of Regina, was opened in 1982. Dr. JOHN F. ALEXANDER began a sports medicine practice in Regina in 1967, and was a team physician for the Roughriders from 1969.

The 1970s saw the development of sports medicine organizations, each with lectures and conferences. The Saskatchewan Athletic Trainers Association was formed in 1971, and the Saskatchewan Academy of Sports Medicine Inc. (SASM) in 1975; Dr. Marlys Misfeldt was the first female sports physician in the Academy. The Saskatchewan Summer Games in Regina in 1975 included a sports injuries conference. Symposia were held coincident with the Grey Cup in 1995 and

2003. In 1974, Sports Physiotherapy Saskatchewan was formed under the guidance of Charles Armstrong, Arlis McQuarrie, Diane Crosby, and Liz Harrison. In 1988 the Sports Medicine and Science Council of Saskatchewan was formed, which included the Saskatchewan Academy of Sports Medicine, the Saskatchewan section of Sports Physiotherapy, Sask. Sport Inc., the University of Saskatchewan College of Kinesiology, and the UNIVERSITY OF REGINA Faculty of Kinesiology and Health Sciences. The Council's budget in 2004 was over half a million dollars, providing numerous programs and services to all sports activities including medical coverage of events, medical equipment loans, first aid courses, sports nutrition, drug lectures, and other educational resources.

In recognition for their services as builders of sports medicine in Saskatchewan, Dr. Sam Landa (1986), Dr. John F. (Jack) Alexander (1988), Dr. Walt Hader (1997), Dr. Paul Schwann (2001), and Dr. Bill Orban (2003) were inducted into the SASKATCHEWAN SPORTS HALL OF FAME AND MUSEUM.

Walter J. Hader

SPRINGSIDE, town, pop 525, located 25 km NW of the city of Yorkton at the junction of the Yellowhead Hwy and Hwy 47. The region began to be settled in the 1880s by Scottish, English, German and, later, Ukrainian homesteaders. Those that settled in the immediate vicinity of Springside were largely of British extraction, either from other regions of Canada or from overseas. The name of the village was derived from nearby freshwater springs, which long were a watering stop on the old prairie trails system. Springside grew steadily, and by the 1950s the population was over 300. The town has a small but varied business community, modern recreation facilities, seniors' housing, a library, churches, and a volunteer fire department. Springside Elementary School provides K–8 education to approximately 70 students; high school students attend classes in Yorkton. Good Spirit Lake Provincial Park and Whitesand Regional Park, both located a short distance north of the town, provide Springside residents with additional recreational opportunities.

David McLennan

SRI SATHYA SAI BABA ORGANIZATION.

The Sri Sathya Sai Baba Organization is named after one of the most revered contemporary spiritual teachers. Sathya Sai Baba currently lives in Puttaparti in South India. Respecting all faiths is the creed of all members of the Sai Movement, so the Sri Sathya Sai Baba Organization is not an evangelical or proselytizing organization. Its fundamental objective is to awaken the divinity in all men and women: this is achieved by propagating, through practice and examples, the basic principles of the five eternal values of Truth, Right Conduct, Peace, Love and

Non-violence. There are over 1,200 Sathya Sai Baba Centres in over 145 countries worldwide. Saskatchewan has had two Centres, in Regina and Saskatoon, since the 1980s. They jointly hosted a retreat in 1999 with an attendance of about 400 spiritual seekers. Their service activities include involvement with the home care and hospital patients; seniors' homes; the Food Bank; Habitat for Humanity; tree planting, and so on. Sai Baba Centres conduct a nine-year program of Sathya Sai Spiritual Education known as EDUCARE for Children aged five to fifteen, free of cost; the curriculum includes study of the major religions of the world and Education in Human Values. The Sai Organization in Saskatchewan is working under the guidance of Sri Sathya Sai Baba towards individual and societal transformation using the four principles that he laid down: "There is only one religion, the religion of love; there is only one language, the language of the heart; there is only one caste, the caste of humanity; there is only one God, he is omnipresent."

M.V. Kanchana

SRI SRI RHADHA KRISHNA TEMPLE. The *Sri Sri Rhadha Krishna* Temple was opened in the fall of 1978. This marked the inception of the first *Vaisnava* (devotees of the Hindu God Krishna) Hindu temple in Saskatchewan. Prior to this time the Regina Hindu community gathered in each others' homes and in civic halls to worship. The philosophic foundation of the *Sri Sri Rhadha Krishna* Temple is firmly grounded in the teaching of Lord Chaitanya, a 15th-century Hindu saint; this tradition identifies Krishna as the Supreme Godhead. Devotees seek spiritual enlightenment through the path of *Bhakti Yoga* or the selfless devotion to Krishna. Methods of worship include the singing of hymns, chanting of the holy *mahamantra* (a powerful Vedic sound), and discourses related to the *Bhagavad-Gita*.

The temple is open for worship every Sunday. All devotees remove their shoes before entering the temple, and women may cover their heads as an indication of respect. The weekly service begins with *Vaisnava Puja* or worship of Krishna, followed by Bhajans or hymns. A short class is given in English, which relates the contents of the *Bhagavad-Gita* and associated scriptures; open discussion is always encouraged. There is then a period of meditation and chanting of the mahamantra, and the service concludes with the main *puja*. Following this, a vegetarian meal is provided. In addition to weekly services the temple is open during many of the major *Vaisnava* festivals; other ceremonies and spiritual activities include marriages, funeral prayers, as well as the celebration of birthdays, anniversaries and other special occasions. (*See also* HINDU COMMUNITIES)

Jai Ram and Kavita Ram

ST. JOSEPH'S COLLEGE.

ST. JOSEPH'S COLLEGE. From 1919 to 1973, Brothers of the Christian Schools with their Provincial Offices in Toronto provided Catholic high school education to young men in Yorkton. Completing the complex of buildings–an eastern-rite Redemptorist monastery, St. Mary's Ukrainian Catholic Church, and Sacred Heart Academy for elementary children and high school girls under the SISTERS SERVANTS OF MARY IMMACULATE–St. Joseph's College was intended for Ukrainian Catholic boys. While laymen were sometimes employed as teachers beginning in 1920, they were the exception until 1963, when the College offered university-level courses in affiliation with the UNIVERSITY OF SASKATCHEWAN. Sisters had taken care of the kitchens beginning in 1929, and began teaching regularly in 1968. Laywomen teachers entered the school in 1972. With declining enrolments for a private Catholic boarding school, the school became a co-educational junior high school jointly operated by the Catholic and the public school systems in 1973, but closed in 1979. The buildings were demolished in 2004.

Paul Laverdure

ST. PETER'S COLLEGE, MUENSTER. The foundation of St. Peter's College was laid in the 1904 "Act of Incorporation of the Order of St. Benedict," which provided for the establishment of a school able to grant matriculation, certificates, and diplomas. The Benedictine founders envisioned a high school/ college to prepare the young men of the region for active lay or religious life. Abbot Michael Ott launched a fundraising drive in 1919, and in 1921 Michael Hall was opened. In 1926, an agreement was reached with the UNIVERSITY OF SASKATCHEWAN for affiliation to allow Arts and Sciences credit courses to be offered at St. Peter's. The student population was drawn from across western Canada, but the college mainly served the young men of St. Peter's Colony.

In 1959 the university-level classes were opened to women, and attendance increased. Although the high school portion was closed in 1972, demand for university classes continued to grow; with the need for a broader range of course offerings, lay faculty were added. In 1997, the College established the Centre for Rural Studies and Enrichment to serve the needs of rural communities. Now a fully affiliated College of the University of Saskatchewan, St Peter's offers courses in Fine Arts, Sciences, Humanities, Social Sciences, Agriculture and Business, and hosts retreats for artists and writers. *Colleen Fitzgerald*

FURTHER READING: Fitzgerald, C. 2003. *Begin a Good Work: A History of St. Peter's Abbey, 1903–2003.* Muenster, SK: St. Peter's Press.

Sports and Recreation in Saskatchewan—History

Pat Rediger

From 1905 until the 1940s, sports and recreational activities were primarily a personal responsibility for families. As the years passed, sport and recreation have become regional, provincial, national and international concerns with new programs and events being organized every year. This has led to larger sporting events, such as the Olympics, but families and children still organize their own activities for fun and enjoyment. Sport and recreation remains an important facet in Saskatchewan residents' lives.

1880–1919

Sports and recreation were simple in Saskatchewan's early years: transportation limited individuals to participating on local teams and clubs, with few inter-community competitions. Much of the settlers' recreation and leisure activities originated in the home: hospitality was a main concern, and visits were encouraged among neighbours. At these spontaneous and prearranged visits, baseball games and dances often occurred. When schools were built, they became the home for recreational activities. Annual picnics held at the schools were the biggest event at that time, and sports days–where baseball, wrestling, horseshoes, horse racing, soccer, boxing and foot races occurred–became a staple later in the period. The YOUNG MEN'S CHRISTIAN ASSOCIATION (YMCA) and YOUNG WOMEN'S CHRISTIAN ASSOCIATION's (YWCA) played important roles in providing recreational and sporting activities for citizens. The first YMCAs came into existence in Moose Jaw (1905), Regina (1907) and Saskatoon (1913), while the first YWCAs formed in Moose Jaw (1907), Regina (1910) and Saskatoon (1911).

SASKATCHEWAN ARCHIVES BOARD R-B5

Old Crossing picnic, near Regina, May 24, 1896.

Lacrosse was the first sport in Saskatchewan and Canada, thanks to the Aboriginal peoples, who introduced settlers to the game. CURLING was also a part of Saskatchewan life in the late 1880s. From 1880 to 1904, the Royal Caledonian Curling Club of Scotland's North-West Territories branch controlled Saskatchewan curling. By 1889 Regina featured its first curling club, and soon afterwards Qu'Appelle and Indian Head built their own clubs. It was not until 1904 that a provincial association was formed to managed the various clubs across

S

Curling, Battleford, 1911.

The law students lacrosse team, Regina, were Champions in 1914. Seated second from the left is Neil J. ("Piffles") Taylor. Taylor served in the Royal Flying Corps in World War I and was a prisoner of war for a year. Upon his return to Regina after the war, he played and coached rugby, in addition to practicing law and serving as a city alderman. In recognition of the important role he played in the development of football in Western Canada, Regina's Taylor Field was named for him.

Saskatchewan. After World War I, curling became a staple for residents, and almost every community held bonspiels throughout the winter. Moose Jaw's Aquatic Club, located on the Moose Jaw River, was a key recreational and sporting site: SWIMMING, diving, CANOEING, DANCES, and regattas occurred periodically at this location. The Saskatchewan Football Association formed in 1906, with the Wapella Club taking home the first league championship trophy.

Favourite summer activities in this period included BASEBALL, FOOTBALL, kites, hide-and-go-seek, horseshoes, and marbles for boys; and hopscotch, skipping rope, and tag for girls. Meanwhile, winter pastimes included skating, sleighing, skiing, and fox-and-hound games. With the onset of WORLD WAR I in 1914, recreational and sporting activities decreased significantly as residents and communities focused on the war

effort. Communities provided recreational activities such as dances for local army training camps, while park construction and other recreational activities, such as sports days, ceased during the period. One sport organization to stem from the war was the Junior Provincial Hockey League, which was formed by the Saskatchewan Amateur Hockey Association in 1917 to fill in the gap left by senior players who had enlisted as soldiers.

Physical Training Class, Yorkton, 1914. The man standing at center is the school inspector, J.T.M. Anderson, who would be elected premier in 1929.

SASKATCHEWAN ARCHIVES BOARD R-B8607

Water Sports Day, Swift Current.

1920–1938

Automobiles, trains, new roads, and buses provided Saskatchewan residents with the opportunity to travel to neighbouring communities for sport and recreation events, including dances and sports competitions. The 1920s featured competent boxing and a professional hockey team, the Regina Capitals. In their first year, the Capitals came within one game of playing in the Stanley Cup finals; unfortunately this success was not long lived, and professional hockey only lasted for a few years. The franchise was sold to Portland, Oregon in 1926. Boxing was popular and successful in Saskatoon, Moose Jaw and Regina throughout the 1920s. Moose Jaw's Jack Reddick went on to become the Canadian light-heavyweight champion, while Regina's Jackie Lewis was Saskatchewan Boxing Champion and Western Boxing Champion in the same year.

On July 15, 1925, Saskatoon's first pool, the Victoria Park Swimming Pool, opened its doors to local residents. As well, tennis, softball, lawn bowling, baseball, soccer, and golf provided Saskatoon's citizens with plenty of entertainment. In the 1920s, tennis thrived in several communities along the CANADIAN NATIONAL RAILWAY (CNR) thanks to O.J. Rowe, the assistant superintendent of the CNR in Biggar, and later superintendent for western Canada; his passion for the game drove him to request the CNR to fund various tennis courts in the communities. George Ward was hired as the first Saskatoon Playgrounds Association's director in May 1930. Ward was responsible for the sports arena in Westfield Park, a football field, the Avenue H Swimming Pool, four knockdown rinks, a cricket pitch, and two softball backstops. His hard work and dedication had a tremendous impact on the recreation field for over thirty-five years.

The 1930s were a difficult period for Saskatchewan and Canadian citizens. The GREAT DEPRESSION limited recreation and sporting programs in many ways, but Regina's rowing and canoeing athletes continued to capture several awards at the Canadian Henley and Northwestern United States regattas, thanks to Harry Duckett's instruction and the athletes' devotion and skill. Drought and hard times did not stop Moose Jaw from constructing Saskatchewan's first municipal indoor pool in 1932. The Moose Jaw Natatorium featured the latest technology, but it faced problems because the hot mineral water that was used for the pool corroded the pipes on a regular basis, and the water remained cloudy despite the filter system; despite the problems, the pool was a tremendous success and a popular tourist attraction.

At that time the majority of Saskatchewan's residents spent their leisure time on inexpensive modes of recreation such as picnics and dances, and travel between neighbouring communities for sport and recreational activities decreased. Sport and recreation budgets greatly diminished or evaporated from schools and communities, which forced youth to return to games such as kick-the-can, red-light, and shinny, in which the puck was improvised from any available material in the area, including frozen horse manure.

1939–1949

WORLD WAR II began in 1939, and once again sport and recreational activities were hampered by dedication to the war effort. Saskatchewan communities continued to provide entertainment in the form of dances for nearby training camps. Owing to lack of funding, the Moose Jaw Natatorium ceased its aquatic activities and placed flooring over the pool area to provide less expensive activities. Cadet Corps programs were initiated to attract youth to the war movement; all other sports and non-war-related activities were discouraged by the school boards. Elementary school children transformed Halloween into a fundraiser for the "Milk-for-Britain" program, and Junior Red Cross Programs appeared in the schools. The UNIVERSITY OF SASKATCHEWAN in Saskatoon also introduced a Canadian Officers' Training Corps program to its curriculum.

Government officials felt that physical training was an important component to the war movement, which eventually led to the development of the National Physical Fitness Act of Canada on July 24, 1943. On April 1, 1944, Saskatchewan followed suit by introducing the Saskatchewan Physical Fitness Act. At that time, the Saskatchewan Council on Physical Fitness made suggestions to the Minister of Health and Welfare on the best programs for physical fitness. Sports and recreation were not entirely removed from people's lives, however: in 1940 the Regina Boxing Club was established, and rugby remained a popular, though not well funded, activity for school children. To commemorate soldier's efforts at the end of the war, several communities constructed parks, rinks, sports fields, libraries, and swimming pools rather than the traditional, unusable monuments.

On March 31, 1948, the Saskatchewan Division of Physical Fitness, created in October 1944, was no longer under the control of the Department of Public Health; instead, it came under the control of the Department of Education because the majority of the division's participants were school age children. In 1948, the Saskatchewan High School Athletics Association (SHSAA) was established; it worked with the Division of Fitness and Recreation to fund high school football, basketball, curling, tennis, and track and field activities. The Division for

Fitness and Recreation was in charge of supplying some sports equipment to communities, especially in rural areas; in 1945 it also published *Saskatchewan Recreation* magazine to inform the public of various sports topics and events. More importantly, the division focused on promoting sport and recreation leadership skills to Saskatchewan's citizens through the University of Saskatchewan's Summer School and other organizations.

1950–1959

The 1950s provided further growth in the sport and recreation fields. Prince Albert was home to the first regional library in 1950; Regina's recreational facilities included swimming pools, seventeen playgrounds, sixteen rinks for skating and recreational hockey, three community centres, and more. Saskatoon hosted the 1951 Canadian Olympic Speed Skating Trials in February, which was a first for Canada. Changes to the National Physical Fitness Act occurred in the early 1950s: in 1952, the Minister in charge of administering the Act was transferred from the Health and Welfare Division to the Education Division; then, in 1954 the Act was repealed by the federal government, which eliminated Saskatchewan's recreational funding from the federal level. As high school students became more involved in professional athletics, individuals became concerned that the students would neglect their educational responsibilities to focus on these activities: efforts were therefore taken to reduce any aspects of the students' activities that would interfere with their schoolwork.

Saskatchewan developed some strong Olympic competitors during this period, such as George Genereaux, a 17-year-old from Saskatoon, who won the gold medal in clay pigeon trapshooting; this was the first Olympic gold medal for Canada since 1936.

The 1955 Saskatchewan GOLDEN JUBILEE, celebrating Saskatchewan's 50th anniversary, dramatically increased the level of sports and recreation in Saskatchewan. Grants were distributed by the Saskatchewan Golden Jubilee Committee, which were used to build community halls and recreational facilities. The committee was also successful in attracting major sporting events to the province: the Macdonald Brier Dominion Curling Championships, the Western Canadian Volleyball Championships, and the North American Figure Skating Championships. Not everyone was excited about the explosion of sports and recreation in Saskatchewan. In 1955 the Regina City Council passed controversial legislation that permitted the Regina Braves baseball club to play three games every Sunday. Delegates from the United Church, the Northside and Central Women's Christian Temperance Union, and the Regina Presbytery of the United Church protested against the legislation because Sundays were the Christian sabbath day and should not include professional sporting events. However, council retained its decision and Sunday games became a reality.

A new health and physical education curriculum was introduced into schools in September 1956. The modification was in response to the Kraus-Weber Fitness Test, which demonstrated that Saskatchewan's youth became less physically active once they entered the school system. This led to new gymnasiums being built in elementary schools, and to more educators skilled in the new program. One focus of the Fitness and Recreation Branch of the Department of Education was the creation of a recreation leadership course that would educate participants in various recreational activities such as administration, crafts, sports and athletics, and program planning. The program consisted of two-week courses for three years, which led to a Certificate in Recreation Leadership. Saskatchewan's recreational leaders also modeled their programs on successful Alberta and Manitoba recreation projects; delegates from the three provinces began to meet once a year, starting in 1958, to discuss recreation issues.

1960–1969

As gymnasiums were built in Saskatchewan schools, physical educators were hired to replace volunteers. In rural areas, the gymnasiums were tremendous assets because they provided year-round entertainment and activities for youth. *Saskatchewan Recreation* magazine ceased publication in the fall of 1960; during that year, the government passed the Regional Parks Act, and Thomson Lake was the first park formed under the legislation. Recreation delegates established the Saskatchewan Recreation Association (SRA) in October 1961 after several years of discussion; the SRA was responsible for coordinating and promoting all levels of recreation.

Several organizations began to merge in order to form more efficient and focused establishments. In 1962, Saskatoon's Parks Board and Playgrounds Association formed the city's Parks and Recreation Board.

RALPH VAWTER PHOTO/SASKATCHEWAN ARCHIVES BOARD 60-570-01

Rythmic playtime for a Grade 2 class at Lakeview School in Regina, 1960.

VERN KENT PHOTO/SASKATCHEWAN ARCHIVES BOARD 3527

Recreational activity of a more spontaneous sort: a "Jam-can" bonspiel on a clearing in a snow-covered back yard.

ALAN HILL PHOTO/SASKATCHEWAN ARCHIVES BOARD 62-381-22

Ralph Punter, Prince Albert, competes in the Senior Men's Slalom event at the Provincial Ski Meet, March 1963.

The University of Saskatchewan, the city of Regina and the Saskatchewan government formed the WASCANA CENTRE AUTHORITY, which maintained Wascana Park and the Legislature. Wascana Park became an excellent spot for sports and some aquatic activities. At the provincial level, the Continuing Education Branch formed in 1963, when the Adult Education Branch joined with the Fitness and Recreation Division. Throughout the 1960s, the provincial government focussed on Saskatchewan's youth. The Saskatchewan Youth Act was passed in 1965, which led in 1966 to the establishment of the Provincial Youth Agency, responsible for improving youths' lives by encouraging skill development, primarily through sport, cultural and recreational activities.

The Provincial Youth Agency immediately divided Saskatchewan into eleven regions, based on population sizes. It also encouraged the development of Regional Recreation Agencies to manage each region's recreational programs. Another significant contribution by the Youth Agency was its assistance in creating, in November 1969, Saskatchewan Sports and Recreation Unlimited, a unified sports administration centre that worked closely with the provincial government to provide administrative assistance to sports and recreation organizations. Local recreation boards increased dramatically in the 1960s, from 73 in 1966 to 415 in 1969. The SASKATCHEWAN ROUGHRIDERS defeated the Ottawa Rough Riders 29–14 in the Grey Cup final in 1966; this was the ninth time that Saskatchewan competed in the final, the previous time being in 1951.

Gordie Howe Day took place in Saskatoon on July 22, 1966, to honour the Saskatoon native for his remarkable hockey achievements: nicknamed "Mr. Hockey," he completed 32 professional hockey seasons, won four Stanley Cups, was the National Hockey League's Most Valuable Player six times, and scored 801 goals and 1,049 assists in his career. To commemorate his achievements, the city changed the name of the Holiday Park Sports Complex to the Gordie Howe Park. The Molson Sports Hall of Fame in Regina was officially opened on October 31, 1966; the facility was a joint venture between Molson Ltd. in Regina and the Saskatchewan Branch of the Amateur Athletic Union. The Saskatchewan Recreation Association became the Saskatchewan Parks and Recreation Association in mid-October 1967 to acknowledge the important role that parks play in the recreation field.

1970–1979

The Saskatchewan Recreation Society, now known as the Saskatchewan Association of Recreation Professionals (SARP), officially opened in 1970 to represent the growing number of recreation professionals in the province. The mission of this non-profit organization is to improve parks and recreation services throughout Saskatchewan. In 1973, the society became independent from the Saskatchewan Parks and Recreation Association. Funding for the society's programs and projects came from Saskatchewan Lotteries, which began in 1974. At the beginning of the 21st century, the organization supports approximately 291 recreation professionals, compared to its initial membership of seventeen members. Throughout the 1970s, various government departments became increasingly involved in sport and recreation programs; the Department of Tourism and Renewable Resources and the Department of Municipal Affairs provided funding for several recreation and sport facilities.

Dairy Producers played an important role in hosting an annual awards banquet, financially assisting annual meetings through its Fitness Foundation. After long deliberations, Sask Sport Inc., the provincial sport federation, was established on September 29, 1972, thanks to volunteers and supporters from the Provincial Youth Agency. Sask Sport Inc. strives to ensure that people of all ages and abilities are able to participate in sport. In 1973, Sask Sport introduced the Saskatchewan Sweepstakes Lottery; due in part to the success of the lottery, Sask Sport Inc. received its license to manage Saskatchewan's major lotteries from the provincial government the following year. Sask Sport Inc. also joined other western provincial organizations to form the Western Canada Lottery Foundation. Sask Sport Inc. created the Saskatchewan Lotteries Trust Fund to handle the distribution of the lottery funds in the early 1970s. In its first year, the Trust designated $341,405 to 44 Saskatchewan groups; in 2004 they distributed approximately $29 million, which is estimated to benefit up to 12,000 sport, culture, and recreation groups.

In 1972 another recreation publication, *Recreation Saskatchewan,* emerged thanks to the Saskatchewan Parks and Recreation Association. As well, on April 1 the provincial government passed the motion for the Department of Culture and Youth Act, which amalgamated with the Youth Agency to form the new department. The Department of Culture and Youth was the first sport and recreation agency to have a high stature within the provincial government. Sport and recreation programs experienced tremendous growth throughout the 1970s: by 1972, 505 municipal recreation boards were formed, and in 1978 that number had risen to 700. The Sport and Recreation Branch of the provincial government was established in 1973; its mission was to promote and encourage all sport, recreation and physical activities, to work with provincial sports and recreation agencies to improve their programs, to provide the best competitive situations for those interested in higher levels of sport, to respond to special needs of citizens, to act as consultants for sports and recreation projects, and to encourage non-competitive programs.

The Saskatchewan Sports Hall of Fame first received financial assistance from the provincial government in 1974. Since then, the provincial government and Saskatchewan Lotteries have funded the Hall, whose mission is to promote and safeguard Saskatchewan's sports history. In the late 1970s, Saskatchewan Sports and Recreation Unlimited and the Saskatchewan Sports Hall of Fame moved into the Land Titles Building in Regina, thanks to funding from the Saskatchewan government and the Saskatchewan Lotteries Trust Fund for Sport, Culture and Recreation. In 1974, Saskatchewan became a member of the National Coaching Certification Program, designed to develop provincial coaches; a similar program was initiated for officials in 1974–75.

As 1974 wore on, sport research became a priority to Sask Sport Inc. and the Department of Culture and Youth, which assigned a Research Committee to approve grants for appropriate research projects that were important to sport development in Saskatchewan. An Evaluation and Forward Planning Committee was formed in 1976 to discuss the past and future programs of Sask Sport Inc., as well as how efficiently those programs were being conducted. In 1977, Saskatchewan Sports and Recreation Unlimited and Sask Sport Inc. decided to incorporate sport, recreation and cultural organizations into one building, known as the Administrative Centre for Provincial Sport, Culture and Recreation Associations. Sask Sport requested funding in December of that year to cover the costs of renovating the historic Land Titles Building for the project, and the administration center opened in September 1979.

1980–1989

The Saskatchewan Recreation Facilities Association was established in October 1982 to act as an organizational and support outlet for all Saskatchewan recreation facility staff members. Its goal was to provide better services for all communities. The association was needed because an overwhelming number of facilities were being built across the province, and volunteers were organizing most of these facilities. Experienced and knowledgeable personnel were required to run them properly. A Fitness Leadership Instruction Program for Seniors was introduced in 1982 by the Saskatchewan Parks and Recreation Association; its success led officials to found the Saskatchewan Seniors Fitness Association, which would oversee senior's physical activity development in Saskatchewan. Volunteers remained an invaluable commodity for sport and recreation organizations; however, as programs expanded more time and devotion was required from these volunteers. So in the 1970s and 1980s, the Saskatchewan Parks and Recreation Association took over the responsibility of organizing and assisting volunteers and professionals in recreation. The association listened to its volunteers' and employees' concerns over facilities, funding and work responsibilities, and strove to meet those needs in order to ensure that recreation activities continued to succeed.

1990–1999

During the 1990s, more individuals were spending more time at work, which left them with less time for leisure activities. However, sport and recreation remained an important part of people's lives, which led to large economic benefits for Saskatchewan: a study by the consulting firm KPMG declared that in 1991 sport, culture and recreation created over $1 billion in economic revenue, as well as 23,000 jobs for citizens.

Recreation and sports officials worked hard to promote their fields, especially to youth. The goal of the various youth initiatives was

COURTESY OF TOURISM SASKATCHEWAN

TED GRANT PHOTO/COURTESY OF TOURISM SASKATCHEWAN

COURTESY OF TOURISM SASKATCHEWAN

This page and facing page: Today, Saskatchewan citizens can watch or participate in a wide variety of sport and recreation activities year-round. From top to bottom, left to right: Thoroughbred racing at Marquis Downs, Saskatoon; baseball; Waskimo Winter Festival, Regina; curling; canoeing; golfing at Elbow Harbour.

COURTESY OF TOURISM SASKATCHEWAN

COURTESY OF TOURISM SASKATCHEWAN

ALAN MILLS PHOTO/COURTESY OF TOURISM SASKATCHEWAN

to promote healthy lifestyles and to keep youth from getting involved in dangerous behaviours such as drugs, alcohol, and delinquent activities. Statistics showed that girls who were active in recreation and sports had higher levels of self-esteem and self-worth than non-active girls; as well, there was far less risk of youths following an unhealthy lifestyle if they participated in sports or recreational activities.

Various organizations including Sask Sport Inc., Saskatchewan Parks and Recreation Association, Saskatchewan Council of Cultural Organizations, and the Department of Municipal Government worked to ensure that youths at risk of following dangerous lifestyles had the opportunity to get active in sports and recreation. KidSport, a children's charity, developed in the 1990s to increase participation in sport and recreation. The program targets disadvantaged children, so that they will have the opportunity to get involved in recreational activities; the goal is for children to learn the principles of teamwork, responsibility and dedication, and to acquire mental, physical, personal and social wellness by getting involved in a physical activity. In 1992, the Rural Sports Hall of Fame opened in Indian Head; notable inductees have included CKRM's Willie Cole and Barry Trapp of Hockey Canada. Sports Halls of Fame are also located in Saskatoon, Yorkton, North Battleford, and Regina.

The 21st Century

The Sport Medicine and Science Council of Saskatchewan was established on January 1, 2000, to provide information on nutrition, sport first aid, drug education, and mental training for athletes. It was created through the amalgamation of the Sport Medicine Council of Saskatchewan and the Saskatchewan Sport Science Program. During the spring of 2001, the Saskatchewan Department of Culture, Youth and Recreation was established, with the mission to strengthen the social, cultural, recreational and artistic activities in Saskatchewan centres. The department also played a role in determining how lottery and casino funds were allocated and used. Concern has grown over the inactivity and obesity of Saskatchewan's residents: studies indicate that 52% of all adults and 68% of youth aged 13 to 19 can be considered inactive; women are more likely to be inactive than men; and 32% of children are obese. As a result, several programs and initiatives have been introduced to reverse this problem.

In August 2001 the Department of Culture, Youth and Recreation introduced a strategy to increase Saskatchewan's physical activity rate 10% by 2005. The Saskatchewan Physical Activity Council was established in September 2003 for this purpose; it is assisted by the Saskatchewan Parks and Recreation Association, SaskCulture Inc., and Sask Sport Inc. Saskatchewan is not alone in promoting physical activity: the Canadian government has also supplied funds for various initiatives across the country. On October 19, 2001, the Canadian Professional Coaches Association founded the "Let's Get Moving" campaign, which has spread to Saskatchewan communities. Its mission is to keep youth and children from entering into dangerous lifestyles by offering various sport and recreation programs, and by improving physical education in schools.

Sport and recreation events contribute large economic rewards to Saskatchewan communities: in 2000, the total economic impact was over $1.1 billion. Visitors spend significant revenue on accommodation, food and drink, souvenirs, travel, entertainment and recreational activities during their stay, which translates into financial contributions to the community and the province's economy. These events also result in job creation: in 2000 over 4,100 jobs were created through sport, and over

6,300 jobs maintained by recreational activities. RespectEd is a Sask Sport Inc., Saskatchewan Parks and Recreation Association, Canadian Red Cross and SaskCulture Inc. initiative to create sport, culture and recreation environments that are free from harassment and abuse. Sask Sport Inc. has worked to promote the benefits of amateur sport and physical activities through the media with its "SPORT. It's More Than A Game" campaign; the campaign was introduced in 1994.

The SASKATCHEWAN SPORTS HALL OF FAME AND MUSEUM continues to prosper: a new attendance record of 30,660 was set in 2003, which surpassed the 2002 record by nearly 7,500 individuals. The Regina Sports Hall of Fame was established on October 9, 2003. The goal of the Hall is to recognize individuals who have made a difference in amateur sport in Regina. The first inductees were Laurie Artiss, Al Ford, Ken MacLeod, Charles Leibel, Lorne Davis, and Fred England. On May 28, 2004, the Saskatchewan Parks and Recreation Association lost one of its cherished members when George Garfield Rathwell passed away: he had become the Director of Regional Parks in 1962, and remained an important contributor to Saskatchewan recreation for more than twenty years. The Saskatchewan Regional Park system, which includes over 100 parks, exists thanks in part to Rathwell's hard work and years of dedication. Sport and Recreation continues to thrive and alter over the years: new programs and initiatives are constantly being added and revised to better represent and suit Saskatchewan's residents. Only one thing seems to remain constant: the province's willingness to provide and participate in sport and recreational activities.

Aboriginal Involvement in Sport and Recreation

From 1948 to 1963, the Physical Fitness and Recreation Division supplied funding and consulting services for northern communities, but unfortunately the organization had a negligible impact upon the area. Due to provincial organizations' failure to promote sport and recreation in northern communities, the government formed the Department of Culture and Youth and the Department of Northern Saskatchewan in 1972 to concentrate on the region. The first Northern Saskatchewan Games and Cultural Festival was held in 1980 in La Ronge. This remains an important and popular competition for northern Saskatchewan residents: it draws, on average, over 800 participants and numerous fans to the event. Northern Saskatchewan culture is unique compared to the south, but it also costs more to fund programs in the north—which is why the same level of sport and recreation programs was not provided. In 1983, northern communities achieved autonomous local governments, and began to demand recreation activities and facilities. The provincial government responded by hiring recreation directors to oversee the developments.

The Northern Recreation Technology Training Program began in 1984 to train recreation directors. The Community Services Division was the department in charge of the northern governments' initiatives to develop volunteers for the various sport and recreation events and programs. In 1982, the Department of Northern Saskatchewan ceased to exist, and the responsibilities of the Community Services Division were transferred to the Saskatchewan Culture and Recreation office.

COURTESY OF THE SASKATCHEWAN SPORTS HALL OF FAME AND MUSEUM

Paul Acoose, one of the first inductees into the Saskatchewan Sports Hall of Fame.

Throughout the 20th and the beginning of the 21st centuries, Aboriginal sport and recreation has expanded and met with provincial, national and international success. At the North American Indigenous Games, a competition that includes teams from across North America, Saskatchewan won the overall title for four consecutive championships.

The Saskatchewan Indian Summer Games began in 1974. Since then, the games have been a popular aspect of Aboriginal communities: in 1997, approximately 3,000 athletes attended the event. The Saskatchewan Indian Winter Games, introduced in 1980, continue to be a successful annual event for Aboriginal youth. The Aboriginal community was home to several star boxers, including Don Laliberté, who was the Canadian Heavyweight Champion; Weslie Sunshine; Jessie Laframboise, a strong bantam-weight fighter; and Dana Laframboise, a successful lightweight boxer. The Saskatchewan First Nations Sports Hall of Fame officially opened on July 14, 1994, in Saskatoon. The first inductees were Alex Wuttunee Decoteau, who captured sixth place in the 5,600 metre event at the 1912 Olympic Games; Paul Acoose, an accomplished runner who set a world record in the 15-mile race event; David Greyeyes Steele, an exceptional soccer player; Arthur Obey, a pioneer of the Saskatchewan Indian Recreation Movement; and Frederick George Sasakamoose, who was the first Treaty Aboriginal to play in the National Hockey League.

Northern communities recognize volunteers for their dedication to Aboriginal sport in Saskatchewan: awards are presented in the Youth, Elder/Senior and Open Age categories for the five northern regions. The Aboriginal Participation Initiative was a program established in 2003 by the provincial government to develop sport, recreation and culture services for First Nations and Métis school children. In 2004, the FEDERATION OF SASKATCHEWAN INDIAN NATIONS (FSIN) introduced a new set of championships for various Aboriginal sports, including softball, soccer, hockey, volleyball and basketball. At the 2003 National Aboriginal Hockey Championships, Team Saskatchewan brought home the gold medal in the Bantam Men's Division, and placed fifth in the Bantam Women's Division. FSIN, along with Sask Sport Inc., SaskCulture Inc., and the Saskatchewan Parks and Recreation Association, is working towards creating a sporting and recreation environment that is free from racism. These organizations believe that physical activities should be held in a safe environment and be available to everyone who is interested in participating.

Sport and Recreation for Women

Women have not participated in sports as often as men throughout Saskatchewan's history for several reasons: lack of encouragement, negative stereotypes about women being "unfeminine" if they are athletic, and prohibition from competing in sports. However, some early women did participate in competitive activities. In 1891, approximately sixty women participated in the Regina and Saskatoon rifle-shooting contest; and in 1913, the University of Saskatchewan initiated its first women's ice hockey program. The University of Saskatchewan was a major contributor to women's sports. It hired Clare Hamilton and Ethel Mary Cartwright to be women's physical education instructors;

Cartwright established the university's first course in physical education specialists in 1933, women being the only participants in the program until 1938. The University also introduced in 1916 a stellar swim team, led by Harry Bailey, that won eleven straight intervarsity championships.

ETHEL CATHERWOOD broke the world record in the ladies' running high jump with a 5 foot 3 inch jump at the 1928 Amsterdam Olympic Games. This was the first year that women had their own program in the Olympics: until then, women were either unable to participate or were forced to compete in the men's events. PHYLLIS DEWAR captured four gold medals at the British Empire Games in 1934; her teammates, Phyllis Haslam and Margaret Hutton, also distinguished themselves by their performances at the Games. Women were officially allowed to participate at the provincial level in curling in 1948. In 1974, the Saskatchewan Recreation Branch of the provincial government funded a conference to discuss how sport and recreation affected women, as there were several concerns over why women were not participating in sport and other recreational activities. Although there were several successful female athletes in Saskatchewan's early years, only a small percentage of women became involved in sport or recreation activities in that period. Studies also indicated that females were less likely to be physically fit than men. However, by 1975 a large number of women had joined either athletics or recreational programs; at the same time, though, women's activities received less funding, coaching, and opportunities for competition compared to men's activities.

During the 1990s and early 2000s, several women attracted provincial, national and international attention. SANDRA SCHMIRLER and her teammates, Jan Betker, Marcia Gudereit and Joan McCusker, became national household names by capturing six provincial championships, three Canadian championships, three world championships, and gold at the first women's Olympic curling event in 1998. As well, CATRIONA LE

UNIVERSITY OF SASKATCHEWAN ARCHIVES A-926

University of Saskatchewan Basketball Team, 1921-1922.

MAY DOAN remains a Saskatchewan idol for her twenty-three years of speed skating and three Olympic medals—gold and bronze at the 1998 Nagano Games, and gold at the 2002 Salt Lake City Games.

Special Needs Sport and Recreational Activities

Camp Easter Seal opened in 1954 to adults and students with special needs; in 1956 it moved to a permanent location at Manitou Beach in Watrous. The camp provides boating, swimming, arts and crafts, camping experiences, and more; today, it is managed by the Saskatchewan Abilities Council. In the early 1960s, provincial organizations such as the Coordinating Council on Rehabilitation began to take an interest in providing recreational activities for physically and developmentally challenged individuals.

Camp Tamarack, located 25 km from Prince Albert, was founded in 1977 and continues to provide education, recreation, and sporting activities for learning-disabled youth and children. Teenagers and children 7–13 years old are able to keep up with their education during the summer while canoeing, swimming, learning lifesaving skills, and working on arts and crafts. Throughout the 1970s, the Provincial Youth Agency took part in providing and scheduling recreational opportunities for individuals with special needs.

Unfortunately, the ability to participate in sports and recreation activities is often dictated by the willingness of parents, caregivers, and rehabilitation centres to allow the special-needs person to participate. Fear that either non-disabled persons will tease the individual or that the activity may be too dangerous to the individual are reasons to inhibit recreation and sport involvement. Community staff may also prevent those with special needs from joining their sport and recreation programs because they may not understand the physical and social limitations and skills of those with special needs. Another inhibitor for special needs persons remains the availability of activities in their community, and how close the activities are to the individuals because they often do

SASKATCHEWAN ARCHIVES BOARD R-A13537-4

Swimming lessons at Camp Easter Seal, August 1957.

SASKATCHEWAN ARCHIVES BOARD R-A13538-2

Practicing archery at Camp Easter Seal, August 1957.

not have their own form of transportation. Fortunately, more programs are being developed for those with special needs. For example, the Special Olympics, established in 1975, have opened doors for many such individuals; there they strive for success, while learning various skills and gaining confidence in their abilities.

Attempts have been made to integrate people with special needs into regular programs. The Saskatchewan Games have had success with both groups competing at the same time, rather than having the non-disabled group participate one week and then the special needs athletes compete a few weeks or months later. At the 2002 North American Indigenous Games in Winnipeg, a large number of Special Olympic athletes attended the competition. The first Provincial Special Olympics Curling Bonspiel occurred in Melfort, and the first Provincial Special Olympic Golf Tournament was hosted by Nipawin in 2002. The 2004 Special Olympics National Winter Games in Prince Edward Island were a tremendous success for Saskatchewan's athletes: overall 17 medals—three gold, nine silver, and five bronze—were collected.

Grants, Lotteries and Casino Funds

The 1943 National Physical Fitness Act brought federal funding to Saskatchewan to develop sports and recreation for ten years. Starting on September 1, 1959, the Provincial Fitness and Recreation Division offered grants to communities that established municipal recreation boards, commissions, and other sport and recreation agencies. The division also awarded grants to develop recreation leadership courses and for other community fitness projects. The Provincial Youth Agency provided grants for initiating regional recreation organizations and projects in 1966; one of the grants provided, the Lighted School House Grant, was instigated to increase the usage of school facilities for community sport and recreation activities.

In 1975–76, the provincial government initiated the Social and Recreation Opportunities for Handicapped Grant Program to develop programs and make them more accessible for those with physical and learning disabilities. Throughout the 1970s, the Provincial Youth Agency was responsible for various grants including the Community Recreation Leadership Initiating Grants, Special Grants (for several events and sport and recreation programs), and Regional Grants. Saskatchewan Lotteries was introduced in 1974 after the provincial government passed legislation in 1973 to allow Sask Sport Inc. to administer major lotteries in the province. Sask Sport Inc. is a non-profit sport federation that is governed by volunteers; Saskatchewan is the only jurisdiction in North America that allows volunteers to operate its major lotteries.

Lottery profits are allocated by the Saskatchewan Lotteries Trust Fund for Sport, Culture and Recreation. One payment is directed to all contractual obligations of the lottery, and other payments are made to the lottery ticket distributors, licensing fees, and the exhibition associations. The remaining lottery profits are divided so that 50% of the proceeds benefits sport, 35% benefits culture, and 15% benefits recreation activities and programs. In the 1970s, Sask Sport Inc. became involved in the Western Canada Lottery Corporation with the Alberta and Manitoba governments. Sask Sport Inc., along with other provinces and territories, coordinates on-line games such as Lotto 6/49 and Super 7 through the Interprovincial Lottery Corporation. In 2004, Saskatchewan Lotteries benefited over 12,000 sport, recreation and culture organizations. The funds are used for programs such as summer camps, youth at risk, and sport for all.

In 1994, the Saskatchewan government introduced the Associated Entities Fund (AEF) to disperse part of the province's casino profits to various community groups: Métis organizations, non-profit community programs for children, youth and families, and exhibition associations, as well as other sport, recreation and cultural activities and facilities benefit from the funds. AEF was renamed the Communities Initiatives Fund in 2002.

Provincial and National Games

The first Canada Games, held in 1967 in Quebec City, had a major impact upon Saskatchewan because each sport had to be registered as a provincial association to compete in the games; this rule prompted various provincial organizations throughout the province. When the Provincial Youth Agency came into existence in 1966, one of its initiatives was to sponsor the first Saskatchewan Summer Games in 1968; their popularity triggered the formation of four more provincial associations and encouraged other provincial organizations to improve for the next event. The next games were not held until 1972, when Moose Jaw hosted the event.

The agency was also involved in the organization of the 1971 Canada Winter Games that were hosted by Saskatoon through $100,000 in federal financial support. The Department of Natural Resources also provided funding, which was mainly used to build Mount Blackstrap for the skiing events. The Western Canada Games, the Canada Games, and the Saskatchewan Games all encouraged sport development and participation in the 1970s. The Western Canada Games, established in 1971, featured athletes, managers, officials and coaches from British Columbia, Alberta, Saskatchewan, Manitoba, the Northwest Territories and the Yukon. In the 21st century, Nunavut was added to the games as an entity separate from the Northwest Territories. In 1988, the first Saskatchewan Senior 55+ Summer Games were held in Melville; held every two years, they involve about 800 participants.

Sask Sport Inc. remains a member of the Saskatchewan Games Council, an organization that manages the administrative duties of the Summer and Winter Games. It assists in bids for the games, handles liaison with provincial sports governing organizations, is a consultant on games protocol, and performs other crucial duties. Sask Sport Inc. was also involved in the formation of the Saskatchewan Games Program, an initiative to assist in the development of the Summer and Winter Games in 1972. North Battleford hosted the first Saskatchewan Winter Games in 1974. In that same year, the Sport and Recreation Branch sponsored a five-day training camp to assist Saskatchewan officials in selecting athletes for the 1975 Canada Winter Games. The branch held similar duties in 1977 when it organized a camp to prepare athletes and officials for the Canada Games in St. John's, Newfoundland.

The Saskatchewan Games are held every two years, the summer and winter games occurring one year after another. The games, coordinated by Saskatchewan Culture, Youth and Recreation and by the Saskatchewan Games Council, are funded by Saskatchewan Lotteries, souvenir sales, the Saskatchewan Games Council, and the host community. The events provide athletes with the opportunity to participate at a higher level of competition. Once the games are over, the host community continues to receive benefits from the event, in the form of state-of-the-art facilities and equipment for the area's athletes. Weyburn hosted the 2004 Saskatchewan Summer Games, and the event attracted a large number of athletes, coaches, officials, volunteers and spectators. (*See also* COMPETITIVE GAMES)

Entrance of St. Thomas More College, Saskatoon.

ST. THOMAS COLLEGE, NORTH BATTLE-FORD. The OBLATES OF ST. MARY'S PROVINCE founded the Oblate House of Studies in Battleford in 1932. As the junior complement to the education of their seminarians, they also established a boys' classical college named St. Thomas College. In the fall of 1932 the college opened with twenty-two students and offered Grades 9 to 12, plus the first two years of a BA program (in affiliation with the University of Ottawa). In 1946 the Oblates decided to build new college facilities in North Battleford, and the city offered them a site overlooking the NORTH SASKATCHEWAN RIVER valley. In October 1950, the new St. Thomas College opened with 120 students. In 1966 St. Thomas College became part of the North Battleford Separate School system, and a shift in the student population occurred: most were now day students. Enrolment peaked in 1975 with 425 students, of whom 90 were boarders. The change in direction in education and the decline in demand for boarding schools for boys led to the closure of St. Thomas College in the summer of 1984, and to the transfer of the student body and teaching staff to the new John Paul II Collegiate. The former college facilities are now part of North Battleford's Don Ross Community Centre. *Nestor Gregoire*

ST. THOMAS MORE COLLEGE. St. Thomas More College (STM) is a federated Catholic liberal arts college on the campus of the UNIVERSITY OF SASKATCHEWAN in Saskatoon. In 1913, Saskatoon Catholics had asked for a Catholic college at the university; in 1926 the first step was taken when Fr. Basil Markle arrived to teach scholastic philosophy and serve as Catholic chaplain. St. Thomas More

College was eventually founded in 1936 by the Congregation of St. Basil of Toronto (Basilians). Under the federation agreement negotiated by Superior-General Fr. Henry Carr of the Basilians and President **WALTER MURRAY** of the University, STM is financially and legally independent, but academically merged with the university. STM faculty members offer courses to eligible students for credit towards University of Saskatchewan degrees. In 1936, the college opened with three faculty and 39 students, and STM classes were taught in university classrooms. At the present time, the college is housed in a large stone building and includes a chapel, library, art gallery, auditorium, cafeteria, student lounge, campus ministry area, classrooms, and administration and faculty offices. In 2004–05, faculty numbered 54, with over 2,100 STM-registered students. The college chapel houses works by artists Lionel Thomas and William Kurelek. *Margaret Sanche*

FURTHER READING: Sanche, M. 1986. *Heartwood: A History of St. Thomas More College and Newman Centre at the University of Saskatchewan.* Muenster, SK: St. Peter's Press.

ST. WALBURG, town, pop 672, located in NW Saskatchewan, approximately 90 km NE of Lloydminster and 130 km NW of North Battleford on Hwy 26 just NE of the crossroads of Hwys 3 and 21. To the north lies the Bronson Provincial Forest and to the east lie the popular resort and vacation destinations of Brightsand and Turtle Lakes. Settlement of the area began in the early 1900s. The community is named for the wife of the first postmaster, but also to honour St. Walburga, an 8th-cen-

tury English nun educated by the Benedictines, who was canonized for a life dedicated to evangelical work among the German people. In 1921, the rail line to St. Walburg was completed and in 1922 the community was incorporated as a village. By this time, St. Walburg had a substantial population of people of German origin among English, Scottish, Irish, French, and Scandinavian homesteaders. In 1939 a number of Sudeten Germans who had been vocally opposed to Adolph Hitler came to the area, having fled Czechoslovakia. St. Walburg's early economy was fairly diverse. While farming and ranching were developing to become the main industries, fish, fur, and railroad ties were exported from the area in addition to agricultural products. For two decades district sawmills supplied ties for the province's expanding railways. Additionally, local history illuminates that a significant underground industry in the manufacture of home brew augmented many a farmer's income. On February 1, 1953, St. Walburg attained town status and, in the early 1980s, the community had a peak population of just over 800. Today, the area economy is based upon cattle and grain production, as well as an OIL AND GAS sector that has been continually expanding over the past couple of decades. Tourism continues to be a factor as regional resort areas develop. St. Walburg is the main centre in the region and has in excess of 65 businesses providing a range of goods and services. A key area attraction is the former studio and home of Count **BERTHOLD VON IMHOFF**, located a short distance from the town. In 1998, the town honoured this famous artist with the installation of a life-sized bronze statue created by another renowned local artist, Susan Velder. Other works by Velder include a bust of **T.C. DOUGLAS** at Saskatchewan's Legislative Building and a statue of Queen Elizabeth II riding her favourite horse, Burmese, which was commissioned in honour of the Queen's Golden Jubilee. *David McLennan*

STAINED GLASS. Colour, glass and fire are the essential elements of stained glass, but it requires the alchemy of light to become truly visible. It is possibly the most widespread "public art" in Saskatchewan, yet thousands of windows in hundreds of churches remain largely unseen: only from inside are the colours set aglow by the prairie light. The first stained glass was probably in the Anglican church at Stanley Mission: after a first shipment was lost on the tortuous river journey from Hudson Bay, parchment was substituted until a new set of windows arrived safely in 1860. As churches sprang up in the wake of the railways, many were enlivened with glass from studios in England, Ontario and Quebec. Pioneer priests sometimes brought windows from ancient English churches, like the *Ascension* in All Saints, Watrous (1912).

The "traditional" style popularized by England's

FRANK KORVEMAKER PHOTO/GOVERNMENT OF
SASKATCHEWAN, HERITAGE

Stained glass, All Saints Anglican Church, Watrous.

William Morris continued well into the 20th century. After the two world wars the dead were often memorialized, as in *Christ in the Ruins* and *The Four Freedoms*, now at the **REGINA ARMOURY**. In addition to the expected Christian scenes, historic figures (including Inuit and Plains peoples) often appeared, such as the sombre Mounties in the Regina RCMP chapel (1943); the Canadian service men and women in the Cornwall Street Legion in Regina; and Gandhi and Mother Theresa in St. Andrew's United, Moose Jaw (1967). Many of these were made by the Robert McCausland studio of Toronto, as was a large *Nativity* in St. John's Cathedral, Saskatoon. There are fine windows in St. Aidan, Moose Jaw; in St. Paul's Cathedral, First Presbyterian and Knox-Metropolitan United (in the Tiffany manner), all in Regina; and there is a huge *Last Supper* in Third Avenue United, Saskatoon.

When costly art became unaffordable during the 1930s, the priest-artist Charles Maillard simply painted his designs onto the windows of the Assumption Cathedral in Gravelbourg. Nearly fifty years later, those peeling windows were replaced with authentic fired glass by the Rault studios of Rennes, France. Beginning in 1949, French *Maître Verrier* André Rault carried out some thirty installations in Saskatchewan, among many in North America. Departing from the heavily detailed English style, Rault's work has a modern directness, often incorporating the gem-like element of *dalle de verre*, a unique thick glass. In the *Our Lady* suite of 34 windows at Holy Rosary Cathedral, Regina (1953-

55), *dalle* bejewels Mary's various halos. A small masterpiece in *dalle*, *Corpus Christi*, is at Notre Dame College, Wilcox—near another artist's vision of Hitler and Mussolini drowning in a Jewish sea. Other interesting Rault windows are at Blessed Sacrament (1956), St. Anthony, and Little Flower, all in Regina, and in other communities such as Lafleche, Estevan, Humboldt, and Tisdale. Contemporary Saskatchewan artists such as David Johnson and Lee Brady continue to create in this luminous medium.   *Patrick Burns*

FURTHER READING: Delahaye, X.G. 2004. *Atelier Rault: Maîtres Verriers Bretons, Rennes.* Paris; Raguin, V. 2003. *The History of Stained Glass.* London: Thames and Hudson.

STANDING BUFFALO DAKOTA FIRST NATION. Chief Standing Buffalo (Tatankanaje) became the heredity leader of his **DAKOTA** band following the death of his father in 1871. In 1877 he was given permission to begin farming on the north side of the Qu'Appelle lakes, and in 1881 a reserve was issued in that location. Band members were successful agriculturalists and wage labourers, and by 1901 all households were self-sufficient (the band had even purchased two binders from their own funds). In 1903 a request for additional acreage was refused, even though it was acknowledged that their acreage was insufficient: they had received 80 rather than the usual 640 acres allocated per family of five. In 1907 the loss of government-owned hay land created a major setback and forced band members to rely on wage labour, which also dissolved with the collapse of the national economy prior to **WORLD WAR I**. In 1920 Standing Buffalo and his son Julius Standing Buffalo went to Ottawa to seek an increase to the reserve's acreage. This was not granted until 1956, long after Standing Buffalo's death in 1921. Although agriculture remains an element in the economy of the community, employment continues to centre on wage labour. The Standing Buffalo First Nation Reserve (2,246.1 ha) is located 8 km northwest of Fort Qu'Appelle; 411 of the 1,062 band members live on the reserve.   *Christian Thompson*

STANLEY MISSION is located 80 km NE of La Ronge on the **CHURCHILL RIVER**. Although in an area long-frequented by the region's indigenous people, the settlement of Stanley Mission began with the arrival of the Anglican Church. The Missionary Society of the church had already established a presence in Africa and South America when it started building missions in Rupert's Land in 1822. The primary goal was to convert aboriginal people to Christianity, but the Society also wanted to develop small, self-sufficient agricultural communities that would use hunting and fishing to supplement the food produced. In 1845, the Hudson's Bay Company

granted permission to the Anglican Church to establish a mission in what was then known as the English River (now Churchill) district. Reverend Robert Hunt arrived at **LAC LA RONGE** in 1850 and in 1851 chose a site on the north side of the Churchill River for the mission. The first buildings erected were the parsonage and a schoolhouse, followed by a warehouse, a storeroom, barn, icehouse, and a carpenter's shop. Between 1854 and 1860 Reverend Hunt oversaw the construction of the magnificent Holy Trinity Anglican Church, now the oldest building standing in Saskatchewan. The lumber was cut locally; however, the locks, hinges, and the thousands of pieces of coloured glass which would comprise the stained glass windows came from England. The name Stanley Mission honours Reverend Hunt's ancestral home, Stanley Park, Gloucestershire, England. Although the Hudson's Bay Company opened a trading post on the south side of the river in 1853, it was on the north side of the river, around the mission, that a thriving community developed. Through the 1860s and 1870s the farm land under cultivation was increased and a grist mill for grinding local wheat into flour was constructed. By the early 20th century, though, the situation at the mission was changing. The mission and residential school at La Ronge were gaining greater importance at the expense of Stanley Mission and by 1905 had

COURTESY OF TOURISM SASKATCHEWAN

Holy Trinity Church, Stanley Mission

DOUG CHISHOLM PHOTO

This aerial photo shows the location of the community of Stanley Mission today relative to the site of Holy Trinity Church, where the community was originally established.

replaced Stanley Mission as the Church headquarters in the district. Around 1919–20, an epidemic, perhaps influenza, perhaps smallpox, claimed, according to one source, about 30 lives. Then, in the 1920s, rival trading posts competing with the Hudson's Bay Company on the south side of the river created additional activity in that area, and with the creation of First Nations reserves and the subsequent construction of houses, also on the south side, the population of Stanley Mission began to dwindle. By the early 1960s virtually all of the buildings were situated across the river from Holy Trinity Church. In 1978 an all-weather road was built from La Ronge and with it came all of the trappings of the modern age. Today, approximately 1,500 people live in the community: a small number on the point of land across the river from the church, which is technically the Northern Settlement of Stanley Mission; and the remainder, and bulk of the population, members of the Lac La Ronge Indian Band who live on the adjacent reserve. Holy Trinity Anglican Church is a Provincial Heritage Property, a National Historic Site, and is incorporated into Lac La Ronge Provincial Park. It is accessible only by water.   *David McLennan*

STAPLEFORD, ERNEST W. (1874–1959).
Educator and president of Regina College, Ernest Stapleford was born in St. Catharines, Ontario in 1874. He graduated from Victoria College at the University of Toronto in 1905, and spent two years abroad studying at Oxford and travelling across Europe and the Middle East. Upon his return to Canada he entered the Methodist ministry. After a period of time in Vancouver, Stapleford came to Regina to serve as president of Regina College from

1915 to 1934, and as principal from 1934 to 1937. He guided the college through the financial difficulties caused by WORLD WAR I, the rapid growth of the 1920s, and the severe economic downturn of the 1930s. In 1934 Regina College was taken over by the UNIVERSITY OF SASKATCHEWAN. Three years later, Stapleford resigned stating that his work, as far as the college was concerned, had ended when the university took over the college. He later served in an administrative capacity with Victoria College in Toronto. Stapleford was a charter member of the Canadian Institute of International Affairs. The annual Stapleford Lecture at the UNIVERSITY OF

REGINA is named after him and his wife MAUDE. He died in Toronto in February 1959.   *Mark Vajcner*

FURTHER READING: Pitsula, J.M. 1988. *An Act of Faith: The Early Years of Regina College.* Regina: Canadian Plains Research Center.

STAPLEFORD, MAUDE (1884–1962).
Maude Stapleford (*née* Bunting) was a Regina community leader who promoted the arts, the welfare of children, and justice for women. Born on September 19, 1884, in St. Catharines, Ontario, she received a BA from Victoria College in 1907. That same year she married ERNEST STAPLEFORD, a Methodist minister; they had four children. They came to Regina when he became president of Regina College in 1915. Active in college life, Stapleford gathered around her local artists, distinguished visitors, and women involved in community betterment. She participated in many women's organizations. As president of the Regina WOMEN'S CHRISTIAN TEMPERANCE UNION (WCTU) in 1915, she addressed the Saskatchewan legislature on WOMAN SUFFRAGE. She was president of the Regina Council of Women (RCW) from 1921 to 1926 and convened several RCW committees, including the Arts and Letters Committee and the Babies Welfare Committee. As convenor of the Committee on Laws, she campaigned for legislative reforms benefiting women and children. She assisted the development of a fund providing free care for tubercular mothers and children, and was a founder of the Regina University Women's Club and of the Regina branch of the Victorian Order of Nurses. Other activities included the YOUNG WOMEN'S CHRISTIAN ASSOCIATION, the Imperial Order Daughters of the Empire, and the General Hospital

SASKATCHEWAN ARCHIVES BOARD R-A3589

Ernest William Stapleford.

SASKATCHEWAN ARCHIVES BOARD R-A17103

Maude Stapleford.

Women's Auxiliary. She and her husband supported the **LIBERAL PARTY**; at its 1917 convention, Maude Stapleford seconded **WILLIAM MARTIN**'s nomination as leader, and was one of two women convention officers elected from the floor. The Staplefords left Regina in 1937. She died on September 12, 1962, in Toronto.

Elizabeth Kalmakoff

STAPLES, RJ (1904–72). Rj Staples is regarded as one of Canada's outstanding music educators. Born in Grenfell, Saskatchewan in 1904, he went on to graduate from the University of Manitoba and the Winnipeg Teachers' College. He continued studies at the **UNIVERSITY OF SASKATCHEWAN**, Columbia University, and Florida State University. He studied under Ernest von Dohnányi (considered one of the top ten of the older school of musicians living at that time), Robert Shaw, Irvin Cooper, Marion Atkinson, and Harvey Brooks, a trumpet teacher and pupil of one of the world's greatest trumpet players, Herbert L. Clarke. After teaching at several elementary schools throughout Saskatchewan and Manitoba between the years 1924 and 1932, Staples was appointed director of Music at Central Collegiate in Regina. He was also the advisor on School Music Courses to the provincial Department of Education from 1935 to 1940, and served as provincial supervisor of Music from 1945 until 1969. He felt it was important for children to respond to music through free physical movement and through making and playing their own instruments. He created for broadcast *Making Music Together* (1945), and with **GERTRUDE MURRAY** worked closely to produce for the primary levels the series *Rhythmic Patterns* (1950) and *Sounds and Songs*, for which he worked as script writer, arranger, and commentator (1948–66).

Staples' extensive involvement in music throughout his lifetime did much to promote music

SASKATCHEWAN ARCHIVES BOARD R-A10937

Rj Staples.

education in Canada. He directed choirs, bands and orchestras, and authored forty-two works in the field of school music, published in Canada and the United States. He was a pioneer in the use of the recorder in schools on this continent, and the inventor of the "Record Indicator" and "Chord Indicator" devices. He also conducted workshops in school music methods in several provinces and in seven different states.

As an alternative to competitive music festivals, Staples organized a series of Saskatchewan "music meets" that would involve both classroom performance and massed singing. A guest commentator would offer advice for improvement, and sometimes hold workshops for classroom teachers. Staples often prepared the students for the massed singing through a series of records prepared for school broadcasts that he wrote, narrated, and produced. His long association with summer school courses through the University of Saskatchewan, which were started in 1946 and featured total involvement in all aspects of classroom music, were extremely popular; and when they were established at Fort Qu'Appelle, his dream of an arts centre was partially realized.

Staples was also a scriptwriter and commentator for CBC Music Broadcasts from 1948 until his retirement in 1969. He passed away in British Columbia on November 15, 1972. *Gail Saunders*

STAR CITY, town, pop 482, located equidistant from the communities of Melfort and Tisdale off Hwy 3. The first few settlers arrived in the area in 1898–99 and, in 1902, one of the first couples in the area, Mr. and Mrs. Walter Starkey (homestead entry May 1, 1899) opened a post office in addition to the small store they operated out of their log home. The name Star City was chosen, honouring the Starkeys and reflecting the early pioneers' hopes for development in the area. The first settlers came via the railway to Prince Albert and then travelled with horses or oxen and wagon from there. As the railroad progressed westward, many would find work involved with its construction. In 1904, the Star City townsite was surveyed and lots were put up for sale. The Starkeys moved in from their homestead and built a substantial general store. In 1905, many businesses were started. A hotel was built. On April 6, 1906, with a population of 109, Star City was incorporated as a village. Lumbering was big business as the parklands were cleared for agriculture. The community grew steadily and with a population of just under 600 in 1921, Star City attained town status. The population remained fairly stable until the mid-1960s. Today, Melfort and Tisdale provide Star City residents with many sources of employment, goods, services, recreation, and culture. Star City retains a small core of essential businesses and services and has paved, tree-lined streets throughout its well-kept

residential neighbourhoods. Fourth Street features fine examples of pre-**DEPRESSION** era architecture.

David McLennan

STARBLANKET, NOEL (1946–). Noel Starblanket, born in 1946, is a member of the Starblanket Reserve. In 1971 he was elected chief of his reserve at the age of 24, thus becoming the youngest chief in Canada at that time. Starblanket was elected Third Vice-Chief of the Executive of the **FEDERATION OF SASKATCHEWAN INDIAN NATIONS** (FSIN), and held the position of president of the National Indian Brotherhood or NIB (now the Assembly of First Nations) for two terms between 1976 and 1980. While president of the NIB, Starblanket enhanced public awareness of First Nations issues and needs, and contributed to building the Brotherhood into a strong political lobby group. He also served as Director of Treaty Rights and Research for FSIN, and attended law school at the **UNIVERSITY OF SASKATCHEWAN**. Starblanket, along with Morley Watson and Vern Bellegarde, formally initiated the idea to form a competitive Native hockey team. This became a reality in 1992 when a small group of people decided to take their application to the Saskatchewan Junior Hockey Leagues board of governors. Lebret was subsequently granted an expansion franchise, and the Lebret Eagles was formed. Starblanket, who is now involved with **TREATY 4** government, remains a strong and independent thinker; he is well known for his hard-driving leadership and for securing a place for the discussion of First Nation's rights. *Christian Thompson*

STARBLANKET FIRST NATION. The Starblanket band adhered to **TREATY 4** in 1874 under Chief Wah-pi-moos-toosis (White Calf), a leader of the Calling River Cree whose territory extended from the File Hills to **WOOD MOUNTAIN** and the **CYPRESS HILLS.** A reserve was surveyed in 1876 near Crooked Lake, but the band did not settle there, moving instead to the File Hills, where they received a reserve in 1880. In 1983 the successful completion of a land claim filed by the band was fulfilled in part through the transfer of the Lebret student residence; it was followed in 1994 by the transfer of Crown-owned lots in the town of Fort Qu'Appelle to reserve land. The new centre constructed on this urban reserve land has provided economic growth to both the town and the First Nation. The main 5,611.9-ha reserve is located 18 km northeast of Fort Qu'Appelle, with an additional 1,715.3 ha of reserve land purchased through the claim agreement. Of the 535 band members, 233 live on reserve.

Christian Thompson

STARLINGS. There are 114 species of starlings and mynas in the songbird family Sturnidae in the Old World. The chunky European starling (*Sturnus* *vulgaris*) was introduced from Europe to New York City in 1890 and spread quickly across North America south of the Arctic. It arrived in Saskatchewan in 1938 and is now in almost all human-modified and open habitats in Saskatchewan. It has a short, square tail, pointed triangular wings, and straight pointed bill. All adults have black overall plumage with an iridescent sheen of green and purple, and yellow bills. In winter the new adult plumage shows white specks at feather tips, and the bill becomes gray in colour. Their song consists of groups of trilling melodies, clear whistles and twitters, and imitations of songs of other species. They use their bill to pry open grass and eat insects, grains and fruits. They are considered a pest species because they are aggressive competitors of bluebirds, woodpeckers and others for nest holes and they form huge foraging and roosting flocks. As a non-native species, it has no legal protection in Canada. Three species of mynas have also been released in North America but they have not been as successful.   *Robert Warnock*

FURTHER READING: Alsop, Fred J., III. 2002. *Birds of Canada*. New York: Dorling Kindersley.

STASESON, GORDON (1926–).

Born in Regina on May 9, 1926, Gordon Staseson has shown dedicated leadership in support of several sporting, economic, and civic organizations and initiatives. An avid sportsman, Staseson was a talented junior hockey player and minor league coach, but his most notable contributions to athletics came as an administrator. He served as president of the **SASKATCHEWAN ROUGHRIDERS** from 1979 to 1982 and chairman of the CFL Board of Governors in 1983 and the Canadian Figure Skating Championships in 1984. Committed to the advancement of his community, Staseson played an instrumental role in the building of the Regina Agridome, the Canada Centre, and the Queensbury Centre. For his tireless promotion of Regina and the province, he received an honorary doctorate from the **UNIVERSITY OF REGINA** in 1989 along with many other awards. Gordon Staseson was awarded the Saskatchewan Order of Merit in 2004.

STATE HOSPITAL AND MEDICAL LEAGUE.

Founded in Prince Albert in 1936, the State Hospital and Medical League was a well-organized lobby group dedicated to the establishment of a universal medical and hospital services plan in Saskatchewan. A large number of voluntary and governmental organizations became affiliated with the League, including **HOMEMAKERS CLUBS**, fraternal societies, agricultural organizations, the **SASKATCHEWAN TEACHERS FEDERATION**, co-operative groups, and municipal governments. In 1941 the League unveiled its *Eight-Point* Plan of State Medicine for

Saskatchewan, which envisaged a medical care system based on group practice clinics staffed by salaried doctors. Vigorous promotion of this *Eight-Point Plan* led to conflict with organized medicine, which insisted that doctors be paid on a fee-for-service basis. After the CCF came to power in 1944, the League assisted the Douglas government in implementing its health care agenda by sponsoring public meetings for the organization of health regions. Yet in its self-proclaimed role as the "watch-dog of the people," the League was a vocal critic of government health policy, such as the acceptance of fee-for-service remuneration. The resulting friction alienated the government's supporters in the League and contributed to its declining membership. The League disbanded during the 1950s.   *Gordon S. Lawson*

STATUS OF WOMEN OFFICE. In November 1964, a Women's Division was established as part of the Labour Standards Branch within the Saskatchewan Department of Labour. The Division Supervisor was **MARY ROCAN**, who was head of the unit for the next twelve years. It was one of the first provincial government units in Canada dedicated to the advancement of women. Labour Standards administered employment-related Acts including the Female Employment Act. The Women's Division investigated, examined and evaluated information, legislation and conditions relevant to the employment of women. Renamed the Women's Bureau in 1966, it took on the roles of researching Saskatchewan women's participation in the labour force and providing career information to women. During the 1970s the Bureau's role shifted to the promotion of equal opportunity, prevention of employment discrimination against women through intensive education, and monitoring of suspected discrimination. In 1974, a group of private citizens called the Saskatchewan Advisory Council on the Status of Women was established to provide advice and recommendations to the government on women's issues.

On January 1, 1984, the Women's Secretariat Act established the Women's Secretariat as a separate government agency reporting directly to the first Saskatchewan Minister Responsible for the Status of Women, Pat Smith. The Secretariat provided research, policy analysis, and administrative support to the government on matters related to the status of women. During the late 1980s and throughout the 1990s, the Women's Secretariat was responsible for ensuring that women's concerns were integrated into the mainstream of government planning and policy development. The social and economic well-being of women, the elimination of violence, and the promotion of the value of women's paid and unpaid work were priorities for the Secretariat.

Effective April 1, 2002, the Women's Secretariat was merged with the Department of Labour, and the

Status of Women Office was created. The office provides strategic direction and leadership to government on policy direction affecting the status of women, and is a single window into government for women's organizations. This new structure includes advisors on Women's Policy in all government departments and major Crowns, whose roles are to facilitate a gender perspective in the development of programs, policies and legislation, and to identify and provide analysis on issues impacting women. In October 2003, the *Action Plan for Saskatchewan Women* was released along with a companion piece, *Government Initiatives Responding to Women's Issues*. Annual forums are held to provide an opportunity for women's groups to talk about issues and provide feedback on *Action Plan* progress reports.

Donna Braun and Gail Quinney

STEAMBOATS. A reliable form of transportation was required to haul supplies and trade goods into the **FUR TRADE** regions and return with large quantities of furs. The beginning of prairie settlement also required an efficient transportation system: one trip of a steamboat in a few days could eliminate a four-month trip for 400 **RED RIVER CARTS** and their crews; the cost of shipping could be reduced by 50%. The Hudson's Bay Company (HBC) explored the navigational potential of the **SASKATCHEWAN RIVER** by sending the *International*, a Red River steamboat, as far upstream as Carlton House in 1865. The company's goal was to use steamboats to reorganize its transportation system along the 940-mile waterway from Fort Edmonton to the mouth of the Saskatchewan River at Grand Rapids, near Lake Winnipeg. Steamboats were being used to connect Winnipeg with the American railroads to the south, and through Lake Winnipeg to the Saskatchewan River in the north.

The first steamboat for the Saskatchewan River route was built above Grand Rapids in 1873; it was rushed into service, but wrecked on its first trip. The *Northcote*, built in 1874 to specifications similar to boats on the upper Mississippi and Missouri Rivers, made a successful voyage to Fort Carlton in late summer. It was the first of several steamboats that would navigate the treacherous Saskatchewan river waters that presented a number of natural obstacles to regular shipping by steamboat. These challenges included the low water levels, particularly in late summer; rocks and rapids; and shifting river channels. In 1877 the *Lily* started operations. By 1882 the new steamboats *North West* and *Marquis* were brought into service; that same year the Saskatchewan River broke its channel near Cumberland Lake, creating a marsh that lowered the river level and reduced the effective shipping season.

The *Northcote* and other steamers were used to carry troops and tow barges of supplies to **BATOCHE** during the **NORTH-WEST RESISTANCE** in 1885. The

COURTESY OF THE NIPAWIN AND DISTRICT LIVING FORESTRY MUSEUM

Steamboat, pre-1910.

Northcote was seriously damaged when the **MÉTIS** lowered a ferry cable that tore off the wheelhouse. After the battle the repaired *Northcote* was used to ferry the wounded to hospital in Saskatoon. As a prisoner, **LOUIS RIEL** was transferred part of the way to trial in Regina by steamship. At first the HBC used the ships for their own transport, but later they established shipping companies that provided general freight and passenger services. There were a number of accidents and shipwrecks, but the main problem was the uncertainty of schedules and the high costs of transporting shipments stranded by low water. The last of the steamers, the *North West*, stopped service in 1896.

A number of companies used steamboats along parts of the Saskatchewan River where water conditions allowed more regular service. Local ferries were used for freight and passenger service. The Pas Lumber Company used steamboats to pull logs up the Carrot River to sawmills until 1954. William Pearson used two smaller steamboats on Last Mountain Lake from 1905 until 1913 for passenger and excursion service–but mainly as a method to encourage Americans to purchase land from his extensive holdings in the area. Finally the extension of rail service made the steamboat obsolete.

Bob Ivanochko

FURTHER READING: Barris, T. 1977. *Fire Canoe: Prairie Steamboat Days Revisited*. Toronto: McClelland and Stewart; Peel, B. 1972. *Steamboats on the Saskatchewan*. Saskatoon: Western Producer Prairie Books.

STECHISHIN, SAVELLA (1903–2002). Savella Stechishin (*née* Wawryniuk) worked to secure the integration of Ukrainian Canadian women into Canadian society while maintaining their Ukrainian heritage. Born on August 19, 1903, in Western Ukraine, she immigrated to Canada with her family in 1913, settling in Krydor, Saskatchewan. She

moved to Saskatoon to attend high school, and then completed **NORMAL SCHOOL**. In 1921 she married Julian Stechishin, and they had three children. In 1930 she became the first Ukrainian woman to graduate from the **UNIVERSITY OF SASKATCHEWAN** and the first Ukrainian Canadian to major in Home Economics. In 1926 Stechishin co-founded the Ukrainian Women's Association of Canada, serving as its president for ten years; in 1936 she helped found the Ukrainian Museum of Canada in Saskatoon. For twenty-five years she was a columnist and women's page editor of the Ukrainian-language *Ukrainian Voice*, writing about nutrition and health. In 1957 she wrote the first extensive cookbook on Ukrainian cuisine in English, *Traditional Ukrainian Cookery*. She was also the author or co-author of several books and articles on Ukrainian culture. Stechishin was a Member of the Order of Canada, a recipient of the Saskatchewan Order of Merit, and was given an award by the president of Ukraine. She died in Saskatoon on April 22, 2002.

Natalie Ostryzniuk

FURTHER READING: Ostryzniuk, Natalie. 1999. "Savella Stechishin, an Ethnocultural Feminist, and Ukrainian Culture in Saskatchewan," *Saskatchewan History* 51 (2): 12–28.

STEELE, PHYLLIS LENORE (1909–88). Phyllis Steele was born in Entwistle, Alberta on May 22, 1909. She undertook medical studies when women were a rarity in medical schools, graduating from the University of Alberta in 1934. She began at Marquis, Saskatchewan, and then bought a practice in Balcarres in 1939. She was sympathetic and helpful to her many patients of First Nations ancestry. She first opened a thirteen-bed hospital in a house, and in 1951 was instrumental in the building of a modern 28-bed hospital. Dr. Steele also led a successful campaign for construction of Parkland Lodge in

1959 and of a Senior Citizens' Enriched Housing Unit in 1985. She served several terms as a town councillor and was Citizen of the Year in 1973. By her retirement in 1980 she had delivered over 5,000 babies. In 1986 she celebrated a record fifty years as coroner. Her autobiography, *The Woman Doctor of Balcarres* (1984), pulled no punches. She received the Saskatchewan Order of Merit in 1985 and became a Member of the Order of Canada in 1987. She died in Regina on March 26, 1988.

Michael Jackson

STEELE, SAMUEL BENFIELD (1849–1919). Sir Samuel Benfield Steele's association with Saskatchewan was as a North-West Mounted Police (NWMP) and military officer. Steele was born in Medonte Township, Upper Canada on January 5, 1849. He joined the militia and participated in the campaigns against the Fenian incursions of 1866 and the Red River Rebellion of 1870. Upon hearing that the government intended to form a mounted police force for the North-West Territories, Steele applied to join and was accepted into the NWMP with the rank of staff-constable in 1873. This was the beginning of a distinguished thirty-year career with the NWMP, in which he participated in the March West, served during the construction of the **CANADIAN PACIFIC RAILWAY** (CPR), and fought in the **NORTH-WEST RESISTANCE**. Steele's initial duties with the force involved patrolling the frontier, breaking horses, training recruits, carrying out reconnaissance patrols, and policing whiskey traders. In August 1875, Steele was promoted to chief constable and assigned to Swan River Barracks (Fort Livingstone, Saskatchewan). He was part of the NWMP contingent stationed at Fort Walsh in October 1877, when the **SIOUX** led by **SITTING BULL** sought refuge there from the United States government.

In 1880, Steele was promoted to inspector and given his first independent command at Fort Qu'Appelle. Up to this point, his responsibilities had mainly been dealing with Aboriginals; but with the coming of the transcontinental railway, he was charged with negotiating settlement and construction disputes, and with policing the rail line. Steele also laid out the NWMP post at Regina. When the railway reached Fort Calgary in 1883, he was sent there as commanding officer. The North-West Resistance prompted Steele to return to Saskatchewan. Given a leave of absence from the NWMP, Steel joined the Alberta Field Force and, as a major, commanded a paramilitary unit which had been organized at Fort Calgary in April. Known as Steele's Scouts, the unit was composed of twenty members of the NWMP, twenty civilian scouts, and twenty-two members of the Alberta Mounted Rifles. They departed northward from Calgary on April 20, and pursued **CREE** chief **BIG BEAR** until his surrender in July. The Scouts were disbanded in August and Steele,

Savella Stechishin.

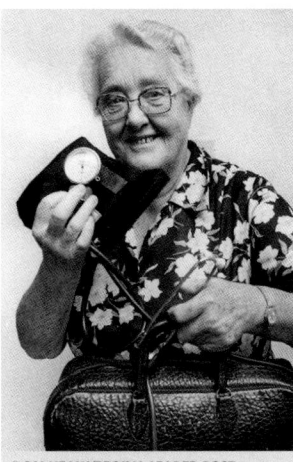

Dr. Phyllis Steele, August 1981.

Major Samuel Steele.

David Steuart.

returning to the NWMP, was promoted to superintendent. Steele returned to patrolling construction camps adjacent to the CPR and was present at the driving of the last spike. He was then posted to Battleford where he spent most of his time training recruits. Later in his career, Steele presided over the policing of the Klondike gold rush.

Steele was given command of Lord Strathcona's Horse in the South African War, and was instrumental in creating the South African Constabulary. In **WORLD WAR I** he commanded the second Canadian contingent of the Canadian Expeditionary Force which was sent overseas in 1915. In 1916 he was appointed general officer commanding the Shorncliffe area in England. Sam Steele died in London, England on January 30, 1919. He was buried in St. John's cemetery in Winnipeg.   *Peter Borch*

FURTHER READING: Brown, W.F. 2001. *Steele's Scouts: Samuel Benfield Steele and the North-West Rebellion.* Surrey, BC: Heritage House; Steele, S.B. 1972. *Forty Years in Canada: Reminiscences of the Great North-West with Some Account of His Service in South Africa.* Toronto: McGraw-Hill Ryerson; Stewart, R. 1979. *Sam Steele: Lion of the Frontier.* Regina: Centax Books.

STEELE NARROWS, BATTLE OF. The battle of Steele Narrows took place on June 3, 1885, and was the last engagement of the **NORTH-WEST RESISTANCE**. Often called the Battle of Loon Lake, it was an encounter between Steele's Scouts, led by **SAM STEELE**, and the Woods and Plains **CREE** warriors led by **BIG BEAR**. Steele's advance party and the Cree were both surprised when they came upon each other at the Narrows. The Cree withdrew to an entrenched position on a hill overlooking the Narrows and, low in ammunition, Steele's troops withdrew also. A peace delegation from the Cree camp approached Steele's Scouts but was fired upon. A battle followed, where several Scouts were wound-

ed and at least five Cree were killed. Today, Steele Narrows is a provincial historical site located approximately 10 km west of Loon Lake.

Lauren Black

STEGNER, WALLACE (1909–93). Most people assume that the American novelist and historian Wallace Earle Stegner was born in Saskatchewan, because of its significance in his book *Wolf Willow*, "a history, a story, and a memory of the last plains frontier," published in the United States in 1962. It is a collection of short stories, reminiscences, and historical accounts about the **CYPRESS HILLS** region around Eastend (called Whitemud in the book). Stegner's parents homesteaded there during the period 1914 to 1920, and his childhood experiences clearly had a great impact on his life. *Wolf Willow* became one of his most popular books, and a standard reference text for history of the region. Stegner was actually born in Lake Mills, Iowa on February 18, 1909, and after studying at the University of Utah became a professor of English at Stanford University in 1945. He published over a dozen works of fiction, history, and criticism, mostly set in the American West. Award-winning novels included *The Big Rock Candy Mountain*, *Fire and Ice*, and *On a Darkling Plain*. His novel *Angle of Repose* won the Pulitzer Prize in 1971. In 1973 he was awarded an honorary degree by the **UNIVERSITY OF REGINA** for his contribution to literature. Wallace Stegner died on April 13, 1993.   *Ken Mitchell*

STENSRUD, HOWARD J. (1927–). Born in Meacham, Saskatchewan on December 22, 1927, Howard Stensrud has been a leader in providing educational opportunities, residential employment programs, and improved living conditions for handicapped Saskatonians. He was a member of the Saskatoon Association from the Mentally Retarded from 1965 until 1993 and its president from 1967 to

1969. He helped found Cosmopolitan Industries and Cosmo Golf Ltd., which provide work programs for hundreds of handicapped people. The Saskatchewan Association of Rehabilitation Centres has also benefited from his expertise and counsel. Howard Stensrud was invested as a Member of the Order of Canada in 1994.

STEUART, DAVID GORDON (1916–). "Davey" Steuart was born in Moose Jaw on January 26, 1916 but his family eventually moved to Prince Albert. In 1951 he was elected to city council in Prince Albert and served for almost a decade. He served two terms as mayor of Prince Albert and was elected president of the **SASKATCHEWAN URBAN MUNICIPALITIES ASSOCIATION**. In 1958 Steuart, as a member of the **LIBERAL PARTY** executive, was instrumental in **ROSS THATCHER**'s successful bid for leadership. Steuart was elected party president at the same convention in 1959. He ran unsuccessfully for the Saskatchewan Legislature in 1960, but was elected two years later in a by-election in Prince Albert. Steuart was re-elected and the Liberal Party formed the government in 1964. He was appointed Minister of Health with responsibility for implementing the government's user fees program. He went on to be Minister of Natural Resources, and was appointed Deputy Premier in 1965. In 1967 Thatcher gave up the Finance ministry to his deputy. His budgets have been blamed for the Liberals' defeat in 1971. Steuart was re-elected and sat in opposition. Shortly after the election Ross Thatcher died of a heart attack. Steuart became interim leader and won the leadership in December 1971. After four years as opposition leader, the Liberals did poorly in the 1975 election and Steuart resigned two days later. **TED MALONE** was elected leader at the 1976 leadership convention. Steuart was appointed to the Senate that December and served for fifteen years until his retirement in 1991.   *Steven Lloyd*

Terry Stevens, August 1985.

STEVENS, TERRY (1936–).

Terrence Hugh Edwin Stevens was born in Winnipeg, Manitoba on July 4, 1936. He initially worked in construction, retail sales, and credit work, and as an organizer for the **NEW DEMOCRATIC PARTY**. In 1967 he became an organizer with the **UNITED STEEL WORKERS OF AMERICA** (USWA). Between 1968 and 1971, Stevens played a major role in organizing the Duval Corporation, Cominco, Allan Potash and the Central Canada Potash mines. In 1972 the United Stone and Allied Product Workers at the Potash Company of America mine of Patience Lake merged with the USWA: the USWA then represented the workers at all five Saskatoon area potash mines. Stevens also assisted with the organization by the USWA of workers at the **URANIUM** mines at Key Lake, El Dorado, and Uranium City. He served on the Saskatoon Development Board and was a union representative on the **CROWN CORPORATION** SMDC board of directors. He also served as a vice-president on the **SASKATCHEWAN FEDERATION OF LABOUR** executive council. In 1992 Stevens joined the Department of Labour as executive director of the Occupational Health and Safety Division. In 1995 he headed the department's Labour Relations and Mediation Division, until his retirement in 2001.

George Rosenau

STEVENSON, LAWRENCE H. (1915–98).

Lawrence Stevenson was born on August 3, 1915. A former chief of the Pasqua First Nation, he was responsible for establishing the first credit union on a Saskatchewan Indian reserve. Additionally, he was involved in organizations such as the **FEDERATION OF SASKATCHEWAN INDIAN NATIONS**, the Lebret School Board, the Fort Qu'Appelle hospital, Kinookimaw Resort, and the **SASKATCHEWAN POWER CORPORATION**. He was invested as a Member of the Order of Canada in 1985. Stevenson died on November 8, 1998.

STEVENSON, THERESA (1926–).

Born on the Cowessess First Nation on June 26, 1926, Stevenson was taken to the residential school at Marieval at age 6 and remained there until age 15. In 1950 she married Robert Stevenson; they had three children. In 1955 they moved to Montana, and lived there until their return to Regina in 1970. In the late 1970s Stevenson founded Regina Indian Community Awareness, Inc. (RICA) and served as executive director. RICA provided urban First Nations people with housing, food, clothing, and social services. She was instrumental in developing and maintaining Silver Sage Housing, which provides low-income housing to First Nations people. In the mid-1980s she developed Chili for Children, a program that continues to provide hot lunches for Aboriginal school children in low-income Regina neighbourhoods. She served as senator in the **FEDERATION OF SASKATCHEWAN INDIANS** (FSIN) from 2001 to 2003. Present community involvements include membership in the Saskatchewan First Nations Women's Council. Stevenson's many awards include FSIN Citizen of the Year (1988), Member of the Order of Canada (1994), Saskatchewan Order of Merit (1995), National Aboriginal Achievement Award for Community Development (1999), and an honorary degree from the **UNIVERSITY OF REGINA** (1999).

Daria Coneghan

STEWART, ALAN CARL (1893–1958).

Alan Carl Stewart, soldier, lawyer and politician was, as **T.C. DOUGLAS** said, a "political stormy petrel, a doughty fighter who feared no foe." Born at Moosomin on September 27, 1893, he was invalided home from **WORLD WAR I**: near-fatal injuries at Passchendaele left him with a life-long scar above his left eye. A brilliant criminal lawyer, he served as Yorkton's city solicitor as well as president of the Yorkton Branch of the Canadian Legion and of the Yorkton Board of Trade, and recruited new commercial firms. Serving as town councillor and then as Yorkton's first mayor, Stewart fought every election in a rough-and-tumble manner, speaking without notes. Narrowly defeated in the provincial election of 1925 and in the federal election of 1926, he won election to the Saskatchewan Legislature in 1929. As Minister of Highways, he launched an unprecedented $20 million construction program, laying out a system of numbered highways that criss-crossed Saskatchewan. Defeated in 1934, he was elected as a Unity candidate in 1938. In federal politics, he was defeated as an Independent Liberal in 1945 but elected in 1949. Following four years in Ottawa, war-related ill health forced his retirement; he died in Long Beach, California, on July 26, 1958.

C. Stuart Houston

STEWART, JOHN W.B. (1936–).

John Stewart was a soil scientist at the **UNIVERSITY OF SASKATCHEWAN**. He was born in Northern Ireland on January 18, 1936. He received his BSc, BAgr, and PhD at Queen's University, Belfast, and was later awarded a DSc from that university in 1988. Stewart came to the University of Saskatchewan in 1964 as a post-

Theresa Stevenson and Ovide Mercredi (then national chief of the Assembly of First Nations) at a fundraising dinner for Chili for Children, May 1996.

Alan Carl Stewart.

John Stewart.

doctoral fellow in the Department of Soil Sciences. After joining the Department in 1966 he moved up through the academic ranks to become Head of Soil Sciences from 1981 to 1989, and then Dean of Agriculture from 1989 to 1999. He was recognized internationally for his research in soil science. His early research focused on phosphorus and sulfur cycling in geo-ecosystems; this led to the development of conceptual and predictive simulation models for phosphorus and sulfur in soil-plant systems, and to predicting the effects of climate change and land-use changes on ecosystems. His publications were wide-ranging, and his work extended to the United States, Brazil, the Philippines, Ghana, Nigeria, and the United Kingdom. Stewart has served on numerous national and international boards and committees, including the Scientific Committee on Problems of the Environment. His numerous awards include: fellowships from the Canadian Society of Soil Science (1987), *Wissenschaftskolleg zu Berlin* (the Berlin Institute of Advanced Study, 1989), and membership in the American Society of Agronomy (1990) and the Soil Science Society of America (1990). *Gary Storey*

STOMP PORK FARM LTD. Founded in 1985, Stomp Pork Farm Ltd., a privately owned company, now markets 600,000 hogs annually worth $90 million. Ivan and Sharon Stomp own and operate the business from their head office located about 40 km southeast of Humboldt. In 2001, Stomp Pork Farm Ltd. was devastated by a fire in which 14,000 pigs were killed and several wooden barns were destroyed. Instead of giving up, however, the company teamed up with the Leroy Agra-Pork Co-op Ltd., a new generation co-operative formed in the area, to establish a $40-million production system. Stomp built a 5,500 sow farrow-to-early-wean operation as well as a 20,000 head nursery project. Leroy Agra-Pork erected four 10,000 head finisher sites. In addition to the hog expansion, Stomp also constructed a world-class feed manufacturing facility that will add value to an estimated three million bushels of locally grown grain each year. The hog facility, the first new generation pork production co-op in western Canada, ships product throughout the prairie provinces and the northern tier of the United States. In 2004, Sterling Pork Farm Ltd., an affiliate of Stomp Pork Farm Ltd., bought all of the assets owned by the SASKATCHEWAN WHEAT POOL and its subsidiary operation, Heartland Pork, for the production of hogs. The transaction completed the Saskatchewan Wheat Pool's exit from the hog industry, expanded Stomp's facilities to sixteen locations in the province and strengthened its market share. *Joe Ralko*

STONECHILD, NEIL. On November 29, 1990, Neil Stonechild, age 17, was found frozen to death in a remote field on the outskirts of Saskatoon. Partially clothed and wearing only one shoe, Saskatoon police ruled Stonechild's death accidental, sparking outrage amongst Aboriginal groups who believed that Stonechild's death was the result of a routine practice by police of abandoning Aboriginal men at the edge of the city in the middle of winter. However, it was not until February 2003, following the deaths of Lloyd Dustyhorn, Rodney Naistus, and Lawrence Wegner in January and February 2000, and in the wake of allegations by Darrell Night that he was forced out of a police cruiser at the edge of the city on the night of January 28, 2000, that the provincial government finally agreed to demands for an inquiry into Stonechild's death. On October 26, 2004, the provincial government released its report, noting there was clear evidence that Stonechild had been in police custody on the night of his death, and criticizing senior levels of the Saskatoon police force for conducting a superficial and defensive investigation of Stonechild's death. The report made eight recommendations, including increasing the number of Aboriginal police officers, providing better training in race relations and anger management for police officers, and improving the public's ability to file complaints against the police. During the course of the investigation, two officers were charged with unlawful confinement, and the city's deputy police chief was charged with disreputable conduct under the Police Act. On November 12, 2004, Saskatoon's police chief fired two officers at the centre of the Stonechild case, though both officers maintained they had had no contact with Stonechild. *Damian Coneghan*

STORER, EFFIE LAURIE (1867–1948). Effie Laurie Storer was the first female journalist in the North-West Territories. She was born in 1867 in Windsor, Ontario, to Patrick and Mary Eliza Laurie. Her father started the first territorial newspaper, the *Saskatchewan Herald*, in Battleford in 1878 (Saskatchewan being the district name); her newspaper career began there in 1882, probably because her father lacked the money for male apprentices. In 1885, during the NORTH-WEST RESISTANCE, she met Constable John Henry "Harry" Storer, whom she married in 1889; they had no children. They farmed near Stinking Lake until Harry's death at Vimy Ridge in 1917.

Storer then returned to work as a professional journalist, presumably out of financial necessity. She worked for the *Saskatchewan Herald*, the *Moose Jaw Times*, and the *Regina Leader*, serving as women's page editor for both the *Herald* and the *Times*. In 1936 she returned to Battleford to help care for her ill brother, Richard, and to help run the family newspaper. After Richard's death the *Saskatchewan Herald* folded, and Storer retired from journalism. She moved to British Columbia,

Effie Laurie Storer.

and in her remaining years she worked on her memoirs, which were never published. She died in 1948. *Dana Turgeon*

STOREY AND VAN EGMOND. The Regina architectural firm of Storey and Van Egmond, formed in 1907, became over the next forty years one of Saskatchewan's most prolific architectural offices (around 1924 the name changed to Van Egmond and Storey). The firm designed many buildings in Regina such as the Ackerman Building, H.G. Smith Warehouse, Assiniboia Club, Regina Telephone Exchange (now SaskSport), Balfour Collegiate, and more than fifty homes and twenty apartment blocks (such as the Madrid and Balfour). They also designed the Land Titles Building and Nutana Collegiate in Saskatoon, the Bank of Montreal in Estevan, North Battleford's Mental Hospital, and Melville's Town Hall/Opera House.

Edgar M. Storey was born on September 16, 1863, in Cherry Valley, Ontario. He worked in the New York branch architectural office of R.P. White from 1880 until 1893, and then moved to Kingston, Ontario to start his own practice. In 1905, he established his practice in Regina. He died in Regina on August 24, 1913, and is buried in the Regina Cemetery. William Gysbert Van Egmond was born on September 16, 1883, in Egmondville, Ontario. He attended the Beaux Arts School in Toronto and was hired as a draftsman by Gowinlock and Baker. He then worked in New York before coming to Regina in the summer of 1906, where Edgar Storey hired him as a draftsman. In early 1907 the two men collaborated in winning a competition for a new public school in the north end of Regina (Albert School), and the partnership of Storey and Van Egmond was established. Van Egmond continued with the firm for over forty years. He suffered a

BERNARD FLAMAN PHOTO/PHP 267 GOVERNMENT OF SASKATCHEWAN, HERITAGE

Melville Town Hall Opera House.

heart attack on October 9, 1949, on a trip to Stoughton; he is buried near Edgar Storey.

Storey's son, Stanley Edgar, was born at Kingston on August 3, 1888, and came to Regina with his father in 1905. After working in his father's firm, he studied architecture at Queen's University in Kingston and at the Massachusetts Institute of Technology. He then returned to Regina prior to the death of his father. Like many of his contemporaries, Stan joined the army in 1915 and transferred to the Royal Flying Corps in 1918. He was invalided home shortly before the armistice, and soon rejoined Van Egmond. After Van Egmond's death, Stan carried on the practice with Wen C. Marvin. Stan Storey died in Regina on November 5, 1959. All three architects became charter members of the Saskatchewan Association of Architects upon its formation in 1911. William Van Egmond and Stan Storey were elected Fellows of the Royal Architectural Institute of Canada. *Ross Herrington*

FURTHER READING: Gilbert, E.J. 1969. *Up the Years with the S.A.A.: A Brief History of the Organization of the Saskatchewan Association of Architects.* Saskatoon: Saskatchewan Association of Architects; Norman MacKenzie Art Gallery. 1982. *Early Domestic Architecture in Regina: Presentation Drawings and Plans.*

STORY, GERTRUDE (1929–). Author of poetry, fiction for adults and children, radio plays and commentaries, Gertrude Story was born on September 19, 1929, near Sutherland, Saskatchewan. Her experiences growing up in a German-Canadian farming community provided a background for her later writing. After completing high school, she worked

for a time as a bank clerk before marrying Joseph LeRoy Story, a country schoolteacher, and living with him in a rural teacherage, where they raised two children. She began to write amusing stories and commentaries based on their rural life, which were broadcast on CBC Radio. In 1988, some of these stories were reworked for the book *The Last House on Main Street.* After being widowed, she started taking classes at the UNIVERSITY OF SASKATCHEWAN in 1976. She received her BA in 1981, convocating as the most distinguished graduate and receiving the university's Arts Prize and the President's Medal. Her first book, a collection of poems, *The Book of Thirteen*, was published in 1981 and followed by several others, as well as con-

tributions to anthologies and periodicals. She received the Saskatchewan Culture & Youth Poetry Prize in 1978, a CBC Radio Literary Award in 1980, and the SASKATCHEWAN WRITERS' GUILD Children's Literature Award in 1982. An active member of the Saskatchewan Writers Guild, she spent much time teaching the craft of writing at Guild-sponsored workshops and at writer-in-residence programs at the Prince Albert, Saskatoon and Moose Jaw public libraries, as well as at the University of Winnipeg.

Margaret A. Hammond

FURTHER READING: Hillis, D. 1985. *Voices & Visions: Interviews with Saskatchewan Writers.* Regina: Coteau Books; 2004. *Saskatchewan Writers: Lives Past and Present.* Regina: Canadian Plains Research Center.

STOUGHTON, town, pop 720, located 60 km E of Weyburn and 60 km N of Estevan at the junction of Hwys 13, 33, and 47. About three years prior to the CPR arriving in the district in 1904, a small settlement by the name of New Hope had begun to develop a short distance from today's community. When the railway surveyed and named the present townsite Stoughton, New Hope disappeared as people relocated to be on the rail line. Stoughton was incorporated in 1904, with tracks running northwest to Regina and east into Manitoba. The line from Regina still remains the longest straight stretch of track in North America, and is the second longest in the world (the longest is in Australia). The community faced a significant downturn during the 1930s, but in the years following WORLD WAR II growth was steady. The area economy is mainly based upon agriculture (grains, oilseeds, and pulse crops), OIL AND GAS production, and related oilfield support services. One of the best-known rinks in Canadian curling history, the Richardson rink, came from Stoughton. The Richardson rink was inducted into

COURTESY OF STOUGHTON AND DISTRICT MUSEUM

Stoughton, Dominion Day celebrations, 1927.

the Canadian Sports Hall of Fame, and skip **ERNIE RICHARDSON** was honoured with the Order of Canada in 1978.   *David McLennan*

STRASBOURG, town, pop 760, located E of Last Mountain Lake 80 km N of Regina on Hwy 20. The history of Strasbourg dates to 1885 with the arrival of the first German settlers. Immigration literature circulated in Germany called the area *Neu Elsass*, with the hope a German name would attract settlers, and the colony that developed in the Last Mountain area came to be known as the Neu Elsass Colony. In 1886, a post office was established in the district which was named Strassburg, after the European community which had been occupied by Germany since 1870. The immigration literature had shown that a railway was to be built from Regina along the east side of Last Mountain Lake and north to Prince Albert and the first settlers had expected the development within a few years. When the railway did not come, discouraged settlers left for less isolated locations. Those who remained faced a period of slow development and prairie fires and bad weather which claimed many crops. Finally in the early 1900s the CPR was progressing toward the district and a townsite was established followed by building boom. The railway arrived in 1905 and, on April 19, 1906, the village of Strassburg was incorporated. On July 1, 1907, the community attained town status. The railway brought an influx of settlers of various origins and the area began to develop a multi-cultural flavour. Rapid development occurred in the period prior to **WORLD WAR I**. Following the war, Strassburg, Germany, again became Strasbourg, in Alsace, France; amidst some considerable controversy, the spelling of the name of the Saskatchewan town was changed to its present form in 1919. In 1921, the population of the town was 514 and it hovered around the 500 mark until the post-**WORLD WAR II** period when, again, the community experienced significant growth. Today, the town continues as a market, service, and cultural centre for a mixed farming district of roughly 2,500 square km (1,000 square miles). Strasbourg also benefits from tourist traffic to Rowan's Ravine Provincial Park, the migratory bird sanctuary on the lake's north end, and the resort communities situated on the lake's east side. The Strasbourg and District Museum housed in the 1906 CPR station, now a heritage property, displays pioneer and First Nations artifacts. The building was purchased by the community in 1971 after the station had closed the previous year.   *David McLennan*

STRUM, GLADYS (1906–). Gladys Strum (*née* Lamb) was a prominent activist in the **CO-OPERATIVE COMMONWEALTH FEDERATION** (CCF). Born on February 4, 1906, on a Manitoba farm, she moved to Saskatchewan in 1922. She taught school and secured **NORMAL SCHOOL** training. In 1926 she mar-

RALPH VAWTER PHOTO/SASKATCHEWAN ARCHIVES BOARD
60-800-01

Gladys Strum, January 1961.

ried Warner Strum, a farmer near Windthorst; they had one daughter. Her CCF involvement began in 1935, under the tutelage of **LOUISE LUCAS** (whom she met as a result of participation in **HOMEMAKERS' CLUBS**). In 1944 Strum was elected president of the Saskatchewan CCF, the first woman in Canada to head a political party. In 1945 she won a close federal race in the Qu'Appelle constituency, becoming the fifth woman member of Parliament; the following year she was defeated. In the 1960 provincial election she successfully ran in the constituency of Saskatoon City, but lost her seat in the 1964 Liberal sweep. Strum, who now held BA and BEd degrees from the **UNIVERSITY OF SASKATCHEWAN**, returned to teaching and caring for the farm.

Strum balanced the often-competing roles of wife, mother, farm woman, teacher, and politician. Personal experiences, including her husband's recurring battle with tuberculosis as well as the marketing difficulties of farmers, had led her to embrace CCF policies, but she disliked CCF unwillingness to affirm women's equality. She denounced women's inferior place in politics, and lobbied Premier **T.C. DOUGLAS** for appointment of a female Cabinet minister. She retired to Penticton, British Columbia, in 1968.   *Tina Beaudry-Mellor*

FURTHER READING: Taylor, G. 1986. "Gladys Strum: Farm Woman, Teacher and Politician," *Canadian Women's Studies* 7 (4): 89–93.

STRYJEK, DMYTRO (1899–1991). Dmytro Stryjek was born on November 5, 1899, in the village of Lanivtsi, Ukraine. In 1923 he immigrated to Canada, settling in Hafford, Saskatchewan. In 1926 he joined the **CANADIAN NATIONAL RAILWAY**, retiring 38 years later. During his working life he gardened

and kept bees, but there is little reference to making art. The outdoor life had its effect, however: Stryjek stored up observations of nature that later informed the vitality of his artwork. He once stated that he "worked 38 years on the railroad and every five minutes the sky is changing." He was also influenced artistically by the Hafford Ukrainian Catholic church and its rich decoration. When he did start painting, he was misunderstood and sometimes referred to as "Durny Stryjek" (Crazy Stryjek). A local acquaintance explained that it was very strange for an old man to use crayons and pencils as if he were a child.

Stryjek moved to Saskatoon in the late 1960s and began to show his artwork. From 1975 to 1979, he was in the Saskachimo Exposition, an annual exhibition of cattle, agricultural industry, and homemade goods. One room was set aside for the display of art: it was here that his work began to gain attention, and he was awarded a red ribbon in 1978. In 1975, Stryjek was included in "Saskatchewan Primitives" at the **MENDEL ART GALLERY**. In 1979, he was featured in "Ukrainian Themes: Four Folk Artists" at the Shoestring Gallery. From that time, Stryjek began to receive support and encouragement. Today, his work is found in the collections of the Canada Council Art Bank, Dunlop Art Gallery, Glenbow Museum, Mendel Art Gallery, **MACKENZIE ART GALLERY**, **SASKATCHEWAN ARTS BOARD**, Ukrainian Museum of Canada, Canadian Museum of Civilization, and Winnipeg Art Gallery.

In 1988, *Stryjek: Trying the Colours* was presented at the Thunder Bay Art Gallery, Ukrainian Canadian Art Foundation, MacKenzie Art Gallery, Edmonton Art Gallery, Ukrainian Museum of Canada, and Glenbow Museum. In 2001, *Dmytro Stryjek: Poetic Vision* was shown at the MacKenzie Art Gallery. Stryjek is known for his exquisite colour and sophisticated compositions. The work combines a wealth of observation about prairie space with an expressive visual freedom, often verging on the abstract. His portraits of religious figures, political heroes and pop star idols were influenced by icon painting—small format, elaborate borders, and stylized poses. Stryjek was a prolific worker until his death on March 5, 1991.   *Kate Davis*

FURTHER READING: Millard, P. 1988. *Stryjek: Trying the Colours*. Saskatoon: Fifth House Press.

STUDENT ACTIVISM. The 1960s were a time of upheaval and rebellion worldwide, with much of the political activism localized on university campuses. Saskatchewan universities felt the impact of this era acutely, and students were active participants in many of the movements that emerged. The **UNIVERSITY OF SASKATCHEWAN** had opened in 1909 in Saskatoon and expanded to include a Regina Campus in 1961; although both campuses experienced some upheaval during the 1960s, students at the Regina Campus became much more involved in the movements, and this activism came to define the culture of the young campus. The Saskatoon Campus remained relatively staid throughout the period.

The first major event to mobilize the university campuses in Saskatchewan was the attempt by Premier ROSS THATCHER in November 1967 to assume control over the large university budget. On both campuses, the students, faculty members, and employees joined together in a battle against what was seen as a threat to the academic freedom of the university. The campaign was successful, and Thatcher backed away from his demands. This event caused the university community, especially in Regina, to mobilize and began an era of rebellion and resistance that would characterize the period.

Two other major events rocked the Regina Campus. The first was the so-called *Carillon* Crisis in 1968, and the second was the occupation of the offices of the Dean of Arts and Science in 1972. These two events pitted the students against the university administration over such issues as autonomous student government and student representation on administrative boards. The Saskatoon Campus only experienced one other major upheaval: the occupation of the Arts Building in 1971. This action was taken to protest the firing of a popular faculty member and to demand student representation on university committees. As with protest movements worldwide, the turmoil of the 1960s had faded on the University of Saskatchewan Campuses by the mid-1970s. The UNIVERSITY OF REGINA was established in 1974, providing for two independent universities in the province. A new tradition began to be developed, and the activism of the 1960s was left behind. *Brett Quiring*

FURTHER READING: Hayden, Michael. 1983. *Seeking a Balance: The University of Saskatchewan, 1907–1982.* Vancouver: University of British Columbia Press; Lexier, Roberta. 2002. "Economic Control Versus Academic Freedom: Ross Thatcher and the University of Saskatchewan, Regina Campus," *Saskatchewan History* 54 (2): 18–30; —. 2003. "Student Activism at the University of Saskatchewan, Regina Campus, 1961–1974." Master's thesis, University of Regina.

STURDY, JOHN HENRY (1893–1966). Born on January 27, 1893, in Goderich, Ontario, Sturdy came to Saskatoon in 1912. He was educated at the UNIVERSITY OF SASKATCHEWAN and the Saskatoon NORMAL SCHOOL. He began a teaching career but enlisted in the Canadian Expeditionary Force and saw action in France at the Battle of Somme. He farmed for a short period before accepting a position as principal in Fort Qu'Appelle. He was defeated as a Farmer-Labour Party candidate in the 1934 election

SASKATCHEWAN ARCHIVES BOARD R-B5445-18
John Sturdy.

in Qu'Appelle-Wolseley. In 1935 he was elected to the executive of the SASKATCHEWAN TEACHERS' FEDERATION and later that year was appointed general secretary, the organization's top administrative position. In 1940 he left the STF to take a position as the overseas assistant director of educational services for the Canadian Legion. He returned to Saskatoon for the 1944 election and was elected for the CCF in Saskatoon City. Sturdy was included in T.C. DOUGLAS' first Cabinet as Minister of Reconstruction and Rehabilitation. The government took more responsibility for welfare and social justice programs. The province's jails began to practice a restorative model of justice. After re-election in 1948, 1952 and finally in 1956, he was appointed as Minister without portfolio acting as special advisor to the Premier on minority groups. In 1956, Sturdy chaired the Committee on Indian Affairs, which recommended that the provincial franchise be extended to First Nations people, that they no longer be restricted to reserves, and that they be allowed to purchase liquor. Sturdy retired from politics in 1960 and moved to Victoria, BC, where he died September 20, 1966. *Brett Quiring*

STURGEON LAKE FIRST NATION. CREE Chief Ah-yah-tus-kum-ik-im-am (William Twatt) and four headmen signed TREATY 6 near Fort Carlton on August 23, 1876, and received a reserve at Sturgeon Lake in 1878, about 29 km northwest of Prince Albert. The band was commonly known as the William Twatt Band, but it changed its name in 1963 to the Sturgeon Lake Band, and later to the Sturgeon Lake First Nation. Farming progressed quickly, and by 1955 there were eight tractors, five of which were owned by individual farmers. Cattle were the main industry, but as grain farming expanded the herds decreased in size. In the 1970s, most cultivated land on the reserve was utilized as a band-operated farm; when the band farm was phased out in 1981, land was leased to off-reserve farmers, but this practice was discontinued because of problems in collecting lease payments. During the early reserve period, people supplemented their income by trapping muskrat on the Sturgeon, Shell and Red rivers, cutting cordwood, working in lumber camps, and working as housekeepers in Prince Albert. In 1989 the discovery of kimberlite on the reserve began a hunt for DIAMONDS, as companies staked their claims on land surrounding the reserve. The 2001 settling of a grievance between the band and the federal government concerning a loss of timber revenue that dated back to 1906 has enabled the community to expand its economic opportunities. The community's infrastructure includes a band office, school, gymnasium, fire hall, band hall, community health clinic, and a healing lodge. Currently 1,578 of the 2,188 band members live on their 9,209.5-ha reserve. *Christian Thompson*

STURGIS, town, pop 627, located in a rolling parkland topography 10 km E of Preeceville on Hwys 9 and 49. The town is nestled between hills to the north and south and a regional park, through which the ASSINIBOINE RIVER flows, forms the southern boundary of the town, greatly adding to the community's aesthetic appearance. In 1902 area townships were surveyed and opened up to home-

COURTESY OF THE STURGIS STATION HOUSE MUSEUM
Sturgis Composite High School Junior Baseball Club, 1951.

steaders and land purchasers, and over the following few years increasing numbers of settlers came to the district from the United States, eastern Canada, England, the Scandinavian countries, Poland and Ukraine. The district was originally known as Stanhope, but when an area post office established in 1908 was given the name Sturgis, the name stuck and became that of the community. The railway arrived in 1911 and by September 3, 1912, the fledgling community had grown large enough to be incorporated as a village. Sturgis eventually became the junction of important east-west and north-south rail lines and by the 1950s the community had become the largest cattle shipping centre in the eastern area of the province. The community had population of roughly 350 at the outset of WORLD WAR II, but in the post-war period, Sturgis experienced rapid growth, attaining town status in 1951. By the early 1980s, the population of the town was just shy of 800. Today, approximately 5,500 people live in the community and the surrounding region, including Preeceville. Agriculture is the major industry in the area and consists of grain production, cattle ranching, and an intensive hog operation that produces 70,000 hogs annually. Timber and logging are an important secondary industry. The Sturgis Station House Museum is located in the former 1912 Canadian Northern Railway Station. The community's junior men's and junior women's lacrosse teams have won numerous medals and championships over the years. The town's premier event is a long-running sports day and rodeo, billed as "Saskatchewan's Largest," which takes place on July 1 each year in a natural amphitheatre.

David McLennan

SUBSURFACE GEOLOGICAL LABORATORY.

The Saskatchewan Subsurface Geological Laboratory in Regina is a centralized provincial repository of drill hole cores and cuttings from wells drilled for the exploration and development of petroleum and natural gas, industrial minerals, and sedimentary uranium deposits. A precursor facility was established in the 1940s under the sponsorship of the UNIVERSITY OF SASKATCHEWAN in order to preserve subsurface geological data for research by the geo-scientific community. Storage was expensive and collection depended on the vagaries of an industry new to the province. Petroleum exploration and development in the province expanded rapidly in the 1950s and there was widespread recognition that subsurface data were expensive and unique to a particular well location. These factors rationalized the requirement for centralized data storage in Regina under the Petroleum and Natural Gas Act and Regulations 1952.

The present laboratory building was constructed in 1958 under the administration of the Saskatchewan Department of Mineral Resources

(now Saskatchewan Industry and Resources) as a mechanized warehouse and library that is open, with certain restrictions, to the public and department staff. It had an area of 5,262 m^2 and was designed to hold 150,000 boxes (approximately 230,000 linear metres) of core, stacked in steel racks to a height of 3.5 m, as well as two million vials of drill cuttings. Subsequently the building was expanded and by 2004 had an area of 7,312 m^2 and contained 350,000 boxes of core taken from 20,000 wells, as well as 3.3 million vials of drill cuttings. Geophysical well geoscientists and engineers use these materials in order to evaluate projects for exploration of undeveloped land and expansion of known pools and deposits, to reduce operational risks, and—more generally—to pursue research into the origin and geological environments of petroleum and mineral resources in the province.

Laurence W. Vigrass

SUDOM, ANNA MAYE (1923–).

An advocate for people with physical and mental disabilities, Ann Sudom was born in Avonlea on April 12, 1923, and moved to Regina with her family in 1960. As a mother to three physically and mentally challenged children, Sudom devoted herself to working with the disabled through such organizations as the Saskatchewan and Regina Associations for the Mentally Retarded, Voice of the Handicapped, and Cosmopolitan Activity Centre. She also served as president of the Regina and provincial Councils of Women and as a representative for the National Council of Women. In 1982, Sudom was awarded a YWCA Women's Award for outstanding achievement in health and the Saskatchewan Order of Merit in 1990.

SUKNASKI, ANDREW (1942–).

Poet and visual artist Andrew Suknaski was born on July 30, 1942, on a homestead near Wood Mountain, Saskatchewan. To develop his interest in visual arts, he studied at the Kootenay School of Art in Nelson, BC. and at the Montreal Museum of Fine Arts' School of Art and Design, receiving a diploma of Fine Arts from the Kootenay School in 1967. He also attended the University of Victoria, Notre Dame University in Nelson, the University of British Columbia, and Simon Fraser University. For a time he was a migrant worker across Canada, and wrote as he travelled. He was, among others, editor for Anak Press and Deodar Shadow Press. In 1969, he founded the underground magazine *Elfin Plot* in Vancouver and created concrete poems, exhibiting at the Expo in Buenos Aires in 1971. From 1977 to 1978, Suknaski was writer-in-residence at St. John's College, University of Manitoba. Among his early works published in chapbooks, pamphlets, and Al Purdy's anthology *Storm Warning* (1971), was the notable *On First Looking Down From Lions Gate*

Bridge (1976). His first collection was *Wood Mountain Poems* (1976), edited by Al Purdy, followed by *The Ghosts Call You Poor* (1978) and *In The Name of Narid* (1981). *Ghosts* won Suknaski the Canadian Authors' Association Poetry Award in 1979. *Octomi* (1976) and *East of Myloona* (1979) were published as small chapbooks. *Montage for an Interstellar Cry* (1982) and *Silk Trail* (1985) were the first and third parts respectively of a larger work that was to be called "Celestial Mechanics."

Suknaski's poems have appeared in such anthologies as *Number One Northern* (1977) and *Studio One: Stories Made for Radio* (1990). For a time, Suknaski worked as a researcher for the National Film Board, contributing to such films as *Grain Elevator* (1981), by Charles Konowal, and *The Disinherited* (1985), by Harvey Spak. In 1978, Spak had made a documentary of Suknaski entitled *Wood Mountain Poems*, considered by Steven Scobie in *The Land They Gave Away* to be "the best critical statement we have on the poet's life and work." Suknaski's Polish and Ukrainian heritage, as well as his concern for First Nations and the people and place of Wood Mountain, feature strongly in his realist poetry. Although poor health in more recent years has prevented him from writing, his work continues to be studied across Canada. *Shelley Sweeney*

SUMMERFALLOW.

Summerfallow or fallow is the practice of allowing land to lie idle during the growing season. Traditionally farmers use summerfallow one year as a risk-management strategy to improve the chances of growing a crop the following year; during the fallow year, farmers control weeds by either tilling the land or spraying herbicides. In the dry prairie climate, the success of agriculture is largely dependent on farmers' ability to manage water. The value of summerfallow in Saskatchewan was discovered by accident in 1885 when the Qu'Appelle Valley Farming Company of Indian Head provided horses and wagons to transport military supplies for the NORTH-WEST RESISTANCE: the land that was allowed to lie fallow that summer had more moisture and hence a larger crop in 1886. By 1889, the Indian Head Experimental Farm reported that "fallowing the land is the best preparation to ensure a crop." Up until the 1960s, summerfallow was widely promoted as sound agriculture practice on the prairies.

The main objective of summerfallow is to increase soil water reserves; during the fallow year, it is necessary to control weeds by either tilling or spraying herbicides. While only 30% or less of the precipitation from the fallow period is conserved, this additional moisture helps ensure there is adequate moisture to grow a crop the next growing season. A secondary benefit is the release of plant nutrients from the soil organic matter, which reduces the need for fertilizer applications in the subsequent

SASKATCHEWAN ARCHIVES BOARD R-A12328

Jack F. Case summerfallowing with twelve horses on a one-way, 1932.

crop. Additional rotational benefits include providing breaks in insect and disease cycles. Since the fallow year has no production, farmers must recoup their costs and make up for the lost production in subsequent years. In the drier areas of the prairies, land traditionally lay fallow every second year. In areas with better moisture conditions, the economics of summerfallow production are less attractive: land is either continuously cropped or left fallow every third or fourth year.

Summerfallow also has several major disadvantages. While many people have long believed that resting the land with summerfallow was good for the soil, scientists concluded that long-term use of summerfallow degrades soil quality and is not sustainable. The main soil degradation issues associated with summerfallow are soil erosion, soil organic matter depletion, and soil salinity. Since the soil on fallow land is left bare for long periods of time, the exposed soil is vulnerable to wind and/or water erosion. While wind erosion occurs every year, severe dust storms are more common in drought years like those experienced in the 1930s and late 1980s. On sloped topography, exposed soil is easily washed away during intense rain storms or spring snowmelt. Conservation practices developed to address these problems include strip-cropping, field shelterbelts, and conservation tillage. Recently, the use of non-selective herbicides like Glyphosate (Roundup™) to control weeds in fallow has become more common; this practice, known as chemfallow, leaves the previous year's crop residue on the soil surface to protect it. During a summerfallow year, soil microorganisms mineralize soil organic matter, releasing soil nutrients; this provides the short-term benefit of providing nutrients for the following crop. Since few fertilizer inputs are used on summerfallow land, over the long term the soil's natural fertility is

slowly mined from the soil organic matter in the form of harvested grain. Currently, scientists estimate that 30% of the soil organic matter has been lost since cultivation began.

Soil salinity is a state where the soil contains enough dissolved salts to hinder plant growth. Summerfallow is considered a major cause of increasing salinization of soils. It does this by raising the soil water table in sensitive areas: salts move with the rising groundwater, and accumulate in the root zone and on the soil surface. Current estimates show that 38% of prairie farmland is affected by salinity to some degree. Over the past forty years, agrologists have worked with farmers to develop farming systems that make better use of limited soil water resources while reducing the need for summerfallow. The key to these systems is better snow trapping: this is achieved with conservation tillage practices such as direct seeding, which leave the crop residue standing to trap snow and improve water conservation by reducing evaporation losses associated with tillage. Pest cycles are broken by using more diverse crop rotations. As a result, there has been a steady decrease in the use of summerfallow since the mid-1970s: the percentage of cultivated land in Saskatchewan in summerfallow dropped from 38% in 1976 to 16% in 2001. *Blair McClinton*

FURTHER READING: Gray, J.H. 1996 (1967). *Men Against the Desert.* Saskatoon: Western Producer Prairie Books; MacEwan, G. 1980. *Illustrated History of Western Canadian Agriculture.* Saskatoon: Western Producer Prairie Books.

SUN DANCE. The Sun Dance, also called Rain or Thirst Dance, is a sacred ceremony of First Nations peoples who live in the grasslands of Saskatchewan. The host can use any one of the three names,

depending upon the reason for doing the ceremony. This ceremony, which lasts from four to eight days, can take place from early spring to mid-summer. The participants usually begin with the SWEAT-LODGE CEREMONY, and gather to celebrate the renewal of life, good growing seasons, a safe community, good health, and so on. The Sun Dance lodge is built in a circle with the entry facing east, signifying the coming of light. Prior to this, the host will have chosen the centre pole, and a selected group of males will bring the pole to the site where the ceremony is to be held. The pole is not allowed to touch the ground until it is placed standing in the centre of the lodge. At the top of it sits the Thunderbird nest, for it is the Sacred Thunderbird as represented by the mighty Eagle who is the messenger for prayers sent to the Great Mystery. The host and the participant dancers continue to dance in shifts for several days, while stepping to the beat of the drum and saying prayers which are carried to the Creator. This sacred ceremony is one method for traditional Plains Indians to reaffirm their belief in their sacred ways. The BISON is honoured during this ceremony by the placing of specific parts of its body at the base of the centre pole; in some ceremonies, a bison robe may be placed inside the lodge to indicate the host's honoured spot. During the actual dance, the participating dancers will always face the centre pole with their eyes on the Thunderbird nest; they will continue until dusk of the final day, dancing and saying prayers for the good of family, community, and Mother Earth. At the end of this ceremony, people may pledge to host another Sun Dance some other time. Once the ceremony is over, the participants will leave the site and have a traditional feast.

William Asikinack

SUN-DOGS (PARHELIA, MOCK SUNS). Sun-dogs or parhelia (from the Greek "beside the sun") are the two bright patches of light that are occasionally seen to flank the rising or setting sun. Parhelia are characteristically located 22° either side of and at the same elevation as the sun. They are produced by the refraction of sunlight through hexagonal-shaped ice crystals. Such ice crystals typically form in cirrus clouds at heights of between 5 and 10 km or, in very cold weather, they can form in ice clouds situated close to the ground. The hexagonal ice crystals that produce parhelia are typically a few tenths of a millimetre across, and are either plate or column-like in profile. Sun-dogs are formed when plate ice crystals are orientated with their hexagonal faces parallel to the ground. Randomly orientated column ice crystals will produce a circular halo with a radius of 22° about the sun. Reflection of sunlight from the upper and lower faces of near-horizontally orientated plate ice crystals can produce sun pillars (vertical columns of light extending above and below the sun). Sun-dogs are often seen in Saskatchewan skies

ROY ANTAL/REGINA LEADER-POST

Sun-dogs, February 1989.

on bright cold days. Moon-dogs (paraselenae) can also be produced by the refraction of moonlight through hexagonal plate ice crystals. *Martin Beech*

SURES, JACK (1934–). Jack Sures is one of Canada's premier ceramicists and art educators. His work includes everything from small vessels to large architectural commissions to graphic works on paper. His attention to surface detail is organic, rich, and mesmerizing. Sures was born in Brandon, Manitoba in 1934. He received a BFA from the University of Manitoba (1957) and an MA in painting and printmaking from Michigan State University (1959). It was during his graduate studies that he attended his only ceramic class. In 1960, he travelled to London, where he worked part-time at the Chelsea Pottery and at a ceramic cat factory. He travelled through Europe and the Middle East in 1961–62.

In 1962, Sures set up his own pottery studio in Winnipeg. Faced with no equipment, his "true ceramic education" began and his ingenuity enabled him to create a wheel out of a milk separator. It was at this studio that the first gas kiln in Manitoba was built. In 1965, he accepted the opportunity to set up the ceramics and printmaking programs at the **UNIVERSITY OF SASKATCHEWAN**, Regina Campus. He came to Regina and built a gas kiln at the university as well as one in Moose Jaw. In the same year, he received a Canada Council Grant to work and study in Japan, which he did in 1966.

Sures became Chair of the Department of Visual Arts at the university in 1969, and switched his teaching focus to printmaking. During this time he continued to create ceramic pieces that included murals, and to exhibit across Canada and the United States. In 1972, he received a Senior Canada Council

Grant to work in France. He lived and worked in Paris until 1973, when he was appointed by the United Nations Handcraft Development Program to set up a ceramics program in Grenada. His ingenuity once again came through when he engineered a kiln that would use nutmeg shells as its fuel. He returned to Regina in 1974.

In 1979, Sures completed a 2,900 square foot mural for the Sturdy-Stone Centre in Saskatoon. Later, he did a terrazzo floor for the Wascana Rehabilitation Centre in Regina, and a mural for the Canadian Museum of Civilization's Group Visitors Entrance in Ottawa. In 1989, he was awarded the Grand Prize in design at "Mino '89," an international ceramics competition held in Japan. Sures retired from teaching in 1998. He has been honoured for his teaching and contributions to society at large. In 1991 and 1992, he received Alumni Association

R.W. CHRISTENSEN PHOTO/SASKATCHEWAN ARCHIVES BOARD
68-1137-06

Jack Sures, March 1969.

Awards for Excellence in Undergraduate Teaching and for Research. In 1991, he received the Order of Canada. He was elected to the International Academy of Ceramics, received the Canada 125 medal, and in 2003 he was awarded the Saskatchewan Order of Merit. Sures has also travelled widely, giving lectures, demonstrations, and workshops. He has served as a consultant to the Canada Council, **WASCANA CENTRE AUTHORITY** (Regina), and the Banff Centre. His work is included in various collections such as the Pecs National Museum, Hungary, the **MACKENZIE ART GALLERY**, and the **SASKATCHEWAN ARTS BOARD**. *Julia Krueger*

SUTHERLAND, GEORGE (FL. 1744–99). George Sutherland, probably born in Wick, Scotland, was one of many residents of the Orkney Islands off northern Scotland to serve with the Hudson's Bay Company (HBC) in the Canadian **FUR TRADE**. Accustomed to isolation and a harsh environment, the Orcadians were also noted for their boat-building skills and their capacity for hard work. George Sutherland arrived in Fort Albany in 1793, and in 1800 he was appointed inland officer at Carlton House. On his arrival, he was accompanied by his first Cree-Métis wife, Papamikewis (Jenny), a remarkably well-educated woman who was fluent in English, **CREE** and Nahkwewin. Sutherland fathered four children with Papamikewis and subsequently established a liaison with a second Cree woman named Pasikus (Anising). He had nine children with her, and another ten with his third wife, Neototosim (Four-Breasted).

According to family history, George Sutherland spent the latter part of his life living a traditional Aboriginal lifestyle with his Cree children and grandchildren. Fluent in the Cree language, he taught his family how to hunt **DEER** by constructing pounds, a traditional buffalo-hunting technique he improvised for hunting smaller game. He also continued to trade at Fort Carlton, occasionally supplying pemmican to the HBC. Sutherland died suddenly while hunting near present-day Hague, and his family buried him with all his possessions, which reportedly weighed close to 1,000 pounds. Over the next two generations, Sutherland's descendants constituted themselves into a distinct group of *nip-isihkopawiyiniw* (Willow Cree). Two of the prominent leaders of this community, Kapeyakwaskunam (One Arrow) and Kahmeeyestoowaegs (Beardy), were signatories of **TREATY 6** in 1876, and both took reserves in the Duck Lake area. The Sutherland name is still common in the area today.

Michael Cottrell

SUTTER, CHRISTIAN T. (1919–). Recognized for his contributions to Canadian agriculture, Christian Sutter was born in Redvers, Saskatchewan on December 1, 1919. After serving in the Royal

Canadian Air Force, Sutter returned to farming where he helped develop the Hereford breed of cattle. Later, as president of the Hereford Cattle Association, he played an important role in promoting beef exports to the Japanese market. Sutter was also involved in the creation of the Canadian Western Agribition in Regina, and served as its first president from 1971 to 1974. He received the Saskatchewan Order of Merit in 1986 and the Order of Canada in 1990.

SWALLOWS. Swallows (family Hirundinidae) have pointed wings and forked tails; their heavy flight muscles give them a characteristic "broad-shouldered" appearance. Their flight is rapid, smooth and flowing. Most species eat exclusively insects caught in flight. Nesting habits vary within the family: some species make mud nests; many species are gregarious nesters.

Globally there are ninety swallow species, distributed among all of the continents except Antarctica. There are nine species of swallows in North America; seven of these breed in Saskatchewan. Purple martins (*Progne subis*) nest colonially in nest boxes or cavities of dead trees in southern Saskatchewan, but face stiff competition from the introduced European starlings for nest sites. Purple martins are the largest swallow, with unmistakable bluish-black plumage. Tree swallows (*Tachycineta bicolor*) are stocky and broad-winged; adult males have distinctive blue-green backs, gray brown tails and wings, and white underparts. They nest in nest boxes and treed areas of Saskatchewan. Violet-green swallows (*T. thalassina*) are found in the badlands of southern Saskatchewan and in the CYPRESS HILLS (Ft. Walsh); they are distinguished from the tree swallow by their brilliant green to purple plumage with white sides. Northern rough-winged swallows (*Stelgidopteryx serripennis*) are found in banks of watercourses and gravel pits in the grasslands and parklands of Saskatchewan. They are larger and stockier, with shorter tail and wings than bank swallows (*Riparia riparia*), which are often found close by, and have a short bill and brown plumage. Bank swallows are small-headed and slender with thin wings, white underparts, and a long notched tail. They are found in cutbanks of watercourses, roads and railways, and gravel pits. Cliff swallows (*Hirundo pyrrhonota*) nest in mud cups in cliffs, and on bridges and buildings in southern Saskatchewan and around LAKE ATHABASCA. They have a short, square tail, dark throat, buffy rump, and chestnut-coloured face and nape. In contrast, the cosmopolitan barn swallow (*H. rustica*) has a rusty forehead and neck, long, deeply forked tail, dark iridescent blue-black upperparts, and buffy to cinnamon underparts. It nests in buildings and on bridges (even in machinery) throughout Saskatchewan.

Robert Warnock

FURTHER READING: Alsop, Fred J., III. 2002. *Birds of Canada*. New York: Dorling Kindersley.

SWEAT-LODGE CEREMONY. The sweat-lodge ceremony is practiced by many First Nations people in Saskatchewan and across North America. A purification ceremony, it can be performed by itself or as a prelude to other ceremonies such as the SUN DANCE. The site of the lodge is usually chosen with great care. A fire-pit is dug, where specially chosen rocks are heated. These rocks range in size from 25 cm to 50cm and can hold heat for a long time. A pit, which will hold the hot rocks during the ceremony, is then dug in the centre of the spot where the lodge will be built. The builder then gathers supple saplings, which are bent to form a dome; amongst many First Nations this dome represents the womb of Mother Earth. The saplings are covered with layers of blankets, and sometimes canvas tarpaulins are placed over the blankets (in earlier times furs and bark were used). The opening of the lodge usually faces east. Once the ceremony is ready to begin, one person will remain on the outside to look after the heated rocks and put them in the central pit during the ceremony.

The ceremony usually takes place in the late afternoon, and sometimes lasts until dawn of the next day. There are two styles: one where only heated rocks are used, and another where water is poured on the rocks. Either will produce the desired effect of sweat. When the rocks are heated to the point where they are considered ready, the participants strip naked or to light undergarments. The host then enters the lodge on hands and knees; the others follow in the same manner and sit in a circle around the centre pit. Once all the participants are

inside the lodge, the fire-tender begins to pass in the heated rocks, which are placed in the pit. The number of rocks used vary from as few as sixteen to as many as sixty-four. The number and placement of the rocks are as important as the overall ceremony; each First Nation will focus of different aspects as they relate to different needs. Once a number of heated rocks are passed into the Lodge, the entry is closed and the host begins to pray. Participants can say prayers in their own way during this time. After some time, everybody leaves the lodge and then comes back in so as to prevent any health hazard. This process can be repeated as many as four times, depending on the needs of the participants. At the end of the ceremony, everyone wishes everyone else a good life. After the ceremony is over, a traditional feast is often held by the family of the host.

William Asikinack

SWEDISH SETTLEMENTS. The first Swedish settlement in Saskatchewan was the New Stockholm Colony, developed between 1885 and 1887 to the west of Esterhazy in southeastern Saskatchewan. In the village of Stockholm, Swedes form only 10% of the population and are outnumbered four to one by Hungarians; the neighbouring smaller village of Dubuc (to the west) actually has twice as high a Swedish proportion. The Swedish Lutheran congregation at Stockholm was the earliest Scandinavian Lutheran Church in Saskatchewan. Later, a Norwegian Lutheran congregation was established at Atwater, the closest village to the north. Approximately 400 people of Scandinavian origin still live in this settlement, if we include those who moved into the town of Esterhazy. Another Swedish colony was soon founded in 1889 at Percival, just

COURTNEY MILNE PHOTO

Rocks and saplings of a sweat lodge.

east of Broadview and 35 km south of Stockholm; not more than 500 people of Scandinavian origin are found today in the Percival-Broadview area. About 80 km to the east is the small village of Kirkella, Manitoba; some 200 people of Swedish origin reside in the Kirkella area, extending across the provincial boundary to Fleming and the Rotave district in Saskatchewan.

Perhaps the largest primarily Swedish settlement in Saskatchewan is the Admiral area, east of Shaunavon in the southwestern region. People of Scandinavian (mostly Swedish) origin comprise half of the population in the village of Admiral. Swedish settlement extended westward to the town of Shaunavon (which also had a substantial Norwegian element and a Norwegian Lutheran congregation), southward into the Sordahl district, and northward towards Simmie (where Norwegians concentrated). Some 600 Scandinavian people live in this settlement today. A number of small Swedish concentrations could be noted, such as the Lunnar Swedish Lutheran congregation (closed in 1968) in the Fairy Hill district near Earl Grey, northeast of Regina, and around Kindersley. Many Swedes settled within or adjacent to several predominantly Norwegian settlements, such as at Canwood and Parkside, Melfort and the Fairy Glen district, Wadena and Hendon, or in the Outlook settlement. According to recent census data (2001), 29,900 Saskatchewan residents claim Swedish ethnic origin, of whom 88.6% (26,500) also claim other ethnic origins, compared to just 11.4% (3,400) claiming only Swedish origin. (*See also* ETHNIC BLOC SETTLEMENTS, NORWEGIAN SETTLEMENTS) *Alan Anderson*

SWEEPRITE MANUFACTURING. Sweeprite Manufacturing Inc., a Regina-based company founded in 1985 by Les Hulicsko, is in the business of manufacturing and selling industrial equipment. While the company's primary focus has been on power road sweeping equipment, Sweeprite now also manufactures a pothole patching machine.

The company's street sweepers are manufactured to different configurations for a variety of applications. Throughout its history, Sweeprite has been known for products with low operating costs, simple operation, reliabilyt, and easy maintenance.

This has been especially important to the contract-sweeping market because the majority of contractors have limited resources to spend for maintaining equipment. The company has paid special attention to the needs of these customers, and has continuously designed and improved its equipment accordingly.

Gateway Capital Corp., a capital pool corporation with shares that trade on the TSX Venture Exchange, bought Sweeprite from Huliscko in 2003 and has operated as Sweeprite Mfg. Inc. since the purchase. Annual sales are approximately $10 million. Depending on business seasonality, Sweeprite employs 25 to 50 people. *Joe Ralko*

SWEET GRASS FIRST NATION. Chief Sweet Grass (Weekaskookwasayin) signed TREATY 6 on September 9, 1876, with the Fort Pitt Indians, but was killed about six months later. He was succeeded by his son, Apseenes (Young Sweet Grass); he was unable to hold the band together, which began to splinter. In 1882, Young Sweet Grass and seventeen followers joined Wah-wee-kah-oo-tah-mah-hote (Strikes him on the back), who had signed Treaty 6 at Fort Carlton on August 28, 1876. Wah-wee-kah-oo-tah-mah-hote was chief from 1876 to 1883; but he was deposed in 1884, and Young Sweet Grass became chief. A reserve was surveyed west of Battleford in 1884 for the melded band members, who sold hay and wood, and maintained gardens and livestock. Currently the band controls 20,354.6

ha of land, the largest block of which is located 26 km west of North Battleford. There are 1,577 registered members, 537 of whom live on reserve.

Christian Thompson

SWIFT CURRENT. Swift Current, pop 14,821, is situated in southwestern Saskatchewan, midway between Regina and Medicine Hat on the TRANS-CANADA HIGHWAY. The city took its name from a creek that flows through it and empties into the SOUTH SASKATCHEWAN RIVER. The region features the CYPRESS HILLS, which boast the site of Fort Walsh and a colourful history. The Cypress Hills, a sacred area where peaceful meetings took place among Aboriginal peoples, was known as "Whoop-Up" country in the 1860s. This was essentially a Blackfoot area, infiltrated by the American traders of Fort Whoop-Up, Fort Slideout, Fort Standoff, Fort Robber's Roost, and Fort Whiskey Gap. CREE, ASSINIBOINE, and Mountain Stoneys were affected by the trade of whisky and rapid-fire weapons, and "wolfers" (hunters and trappers) as well as American traders met in this area. In 1873, wolfers from Fort Hamilton followed up on horse thieves and killed sixteen Nakota or Assiniboine men (*see* CYPRESS HILLS MASSACRE). By 1876, the only BISON left to sustain the First Nations' traditional lifestyle were to be found in this area. Following the battle of Little Big Horn, SITTING BULL and 4,000 Hunkpapa Sioux found refuge in the Cypress Hills. Fort Walsh, built in 1875, became a base for the North-West Mounted Police in 1878.

In 1882, the CANADIAN PACIFIC RAILWAY bridged the local creek and decided to build a depot. For some time, Swift Current was the freight terminus for goods hauled north and south on overland trails; the BATTLEFORD TRAIL that ran from the settlement cut deep wagon ruts which are still visible today. The settlement of Swift Current began the following spring. In 1898 a Local Improvement District was established; on September 21, 1903, the hamlet of Swift Current became a village under the Village Ordinance Act; and on March 15, 1907, it became a town, following a census which indicated a population of 550. At the turn of the century, settlers began arriving from the United States, Europe, and eastern Canada. With an economy founded on ranching and farming, Swift Current was incorporated as a city on January 15, 1914. In later years, oil and natural gas discoveries in the area helped to diversify the economy. Today, with one of the highest non-local traffic counts along the Trans-Canada No. 1 Highway, the city has prioritized tourism in terms of local development. *Daria Coneghan*

SWIFT CURRENT HEALTH REGION. The "Dirty Thirties" did not come to an end in southwestern Saskatchewan until after WORLD WAR II. From 1929 to 1945, drought and poverty conspired with

Technicians prepare to put an engine into a street sweeper at Sweeprite Manufacturing, March 1997.

few medical facilities and remoteness to create a medical backwater. In a study of the health status of the region conducted in 1945–46, Dr. ORVILLE HJERTAAS reported instances of children dying or lying bedridden because their parents could not afford medicines or simple surgical procedures, and that there was a shamefully high infant mortality rate. He found that doctors were almost as poor as everyone else, making do with payments in chickens and VEGETABLES, and had an average cash income of $27 and a relief payment of $75 per month.

In 1944, the first CCF government led by Premier T.C. DOUGLAS was elected on a platform which included the gradual establishment of publicly insured medical care. Some towns and municipalities in the province already had local health plans, but distribution was patchy.

The CCF government hired a number of internationally prominent health experts. Henry Sigerist proposed the long-term plan; but it was people such as Dr. FRED MOTT, Drs. Cecil and Mindel Sheps, Dr. Len Rosenfeld, and MALCOLM TAYLOR who developed a working operational plan and saw to its implementation. They quickly got legislation in place for a first regional public health demonstration area. Community leaders in the southwest corner of Saskatchewan, led by the secretary of the Rural Municipality (RM) of Pittville, BILL BURAK, were ready to try the experiment. RMs like Pittville and Webb had some experience running co-operative medical and hospital service plans along the lines of that designed by MATT ANDERSON of RM McKillop in 1939. Although the government had in mind a gradual approach, the committee which set up Swift Current Health Region #1 decided to provide a full range of services from the start. For under $20 a person ($15 per person plus 2.2 mills on the property tax), they organized a program that included doctor services, hospitalization, childrens' dental care, and a professional public health service including nurses, immunization programs, and health inspectors. The district was run by the secretary-treasurer of RM Webb, Stewart Robertson. The doctors' representative to the board was a young practitioner, Dr. Cas Wolan, who later became a renowned kidney transplant surgeon. The board was chaired by Carl Kjorven, a farmer from Pennant.

The Swift Current health plan began on July 1, 1946. The first medical officer of health was Dr. Arthur Peart. He was briefly succeeded by Dr. Lloyd Davey, and then in July 1948 Dr. VINCENT MATTHEWS became the third medical officer of health, staying on for nearly ten years. He was also the accounts assessor, and kept statistical records which ultimately proved the success of the experiment and later provided a great deal of evidence to the HALL COMMISSION set up by the Canadian government to make recommendations about a national MEDICARE program in 1961.

During those early years, there were many crises, but the number of doctors practising rose from nineteen in 1946 to thirty-six in 1948. The polio epidemic of 1947 nearly bankrupted the region, but it was saved by the timely establishment of provincial funding for hospitalization. There were also floods and outbreaks of food poisoning, and debates over whether the actions of two doctors who purchased X-ray equipment and prescribed its use constituted a conflict of interest (the decision was yes: thereafter, all diagnostic equipment was owned and operated by the hospitals). Robertson, Wolan and Matthews met informally for morning coffee to sort out problems as they appeared, and the board and doctors worked together to make improvements.

The Swift Current Health Region began the first universal hospital and medical care program in North America—two years ahead of the British Health Service. It probably also had the first regional childrens' dental program in North America. As a result of the preventive and educational work of the nurses and improved access to doctors, the infant mortality rate dropped to the lowest in Saskatchewan. The Swift Current Health Region provided a functioning model to the Saskatchewan government while it was designing the provincial medicare system, introduced in 1962.

Those who remember the early days of the Swift Current Health Region credit a sound board and their positive collaboration with the doctors of the region for succeeding with Canada's first and most ambitious experiment in medicare.

Maureen Mathews

SWIMMING. Competitive swimming was slow to evolve in Saskatchewan. Swimming was confined to natural bodies of water until pools were built in Regina in 1909, Moose Jaw in 1910, and Saskatoon in 1913. The province's first accomplished swimmers were those of the UNIVERSITY OF SASKATCHEWAN team of the 1920s and 1930s. PHYLLIS DEWAR of Moose Jaw achieved national renown in 1934 when she won four gold medals at the British Empire Games in London, England. Organization withered during WORLD WAR II, but was fully re-established by the early 1950s and augmented by the addition of synchronized swimming through the leadership and instruction of Betty Lou Dean of Regina. An important milestone was a clinic conducted in 1963 by James "Doc" Counsilman, head swimming coach at Indiana University and for the United States Olympic team. Most of Saskatchewan's coaches attended the clinic and imparted new training techniques to their swimmers. Provincial records tumbled in every discipline and age group, and Saskatchewan became genuinely competitive at the national level; several swimmers have represented Canada at Olympic Games in

each decade since the 1970s. Swim Saskatchewan is the regulatory body for the sport in the province. There are ten "winter" clubs that compete year-round: Battlefords Kinsmen, Manta Ray (Meadow Lake), Moose Jaw Kinsmen Flying Fins, Prince Albert Sharks, Regina Optimist Dolphins, Regina's Y's Men's Marlins, Saskatoon Goldfins, Saskatoon Lasers, Swift Current Monarchs, and Yorkton Optimist. Summer clubs are maintained in Assiniboia, Biggar, Estevan, Humboldt, Kindersley, Melfort, Melville, Moosomin, Nipawin, Oxbow, Regina, Rosetown, Swift Current, Watrous, and Weyburn.

John Chaput

FURTHER READING: Conrad, P.C. 1990. *In the Winning Lane*. Regina: Swim Saskatchewan.

SWINE INDUSTRY. The swine industry is a value-added industry in Saskatchewan, converting approximately 680,000 tonnes or 27 million bushels of feed grains with an approximate value of $90 million into two million market hogs with an approximate farm gate value of $240 million. There are three major meat processors manufacturing for the domestic Canadian and export markets: Mitchell's Gourmet Foods (Saskatoon), World Wide Pork (Moose Jaw), and Harvest Meats (Yorkton). Saskatchewan is also home to a number of significant swine genetics companies, producing high value breeding stock for the North American commercial swine industry.

The swine industry is a valued industry in Saskatchewan, employing an estimated 4,000 people directly in production and production-related jobs, with an additional 4,200 positions in pork processing and value adding. This equates to approximately thirteen jobs created for every Saskatchewan pork producer. The industry provides a full range of employment from part-time casual to professional.

In 2003, Canadian production exceeded 28 million market hogs, or 2.2% of world pork production, of which Saskatchewan produced approximately 7% of the national total. The industry is composed of two basic types of production units, farrow-to-finish and multi-site. Farrow-to-finish implies all aspects of production from breeding, to farrowing (birthing) and growing the animals to market weight are all conducted on one farm site and usually within one barn. This barn will have defined areas for each activity (breeding, farrowing, nursery, grow-finish), with the barn typically housing from 150 to 1,200 sows, and producing 3,300 to 26,000 market pigs per year. Beginning in the early 1990s a new structure known as multi-site production was adopted in North America as a popular method when increasing production unit size. The initial motivation for developing a multi-site farm was the desire to maintain excellent health status of younger animals by removing them from the shared airspace of older animals. A combination of weaning (removal from the sow) and transport to a clean nursery site was demonstrated to increase growth performance, and to offer a risk management strategy by allowing any disease cycle to be broken, thus ensuring animal health and well-being. The developing system also allowed specialization of production facilities and personnel skills since each production unit was focused on one aspect of production and large enough to employ several people. Approximately half of the production in Saskatchewan takes place in farrow-to-finish farms, with the other half on multi-site farms.

A significant aspect of the western Canadian pork industry in general, and reflected in Saskatchewan's production in particular, is the role of the Hutterian Brethren. Accounting for approximately one-third of the pigs marketed in the province, **HUTTERITE COLONIES** utilize the farrow-to-finish production system. They typically have 300 to 600 sows and produce 6,600 to 13,000 pigs annually.

With over 40% of Canada's arable farmland, Saskatchewan is considered an ideal location to raise hogs. Wide open spaces allow for competitive local grain production, manure produced by pigs is a local crop nutrient source, and distance between barns helps to reduce pathogen movement, aiding in maintaining healthy, productive herds. Hog density per square kilometre of arable farmland has been cited as a measure of industry potential when compared to the swine industry in other regions and countries. In this regard Saskatchewan has significant potential with seven hogs produced per square kilometre versus Alberta at seventeen, Manitoba at seventy-six, Ontario at 126, and Quebec at 208. Internationally by comparison, densities in Canada are low compared to Iowa at 212, North Carolina at 484 and the Netherlands at 1,350 pigs per square kilometre of arable farmland.

Saskatchewan hog production displaces approximately 11,000 tonnes of urea fertilizer (46-0-0) and about 7,000 tonnes of phosphate fertilizer (11-15-0) each year worth an estimated $7 million.

To put pig production into perspective on a local level, a typical 1,200 sow barn farrow-to-finish uses 8,600 acres of feed grains annually, provides employment for ten full-time and five indirect personnel, has annual sales revenues of $5 million, and provides nutrients in the form of manure to 3,600 acres over a three-year nutrient management program. The economic benefits from pork production provide benefit to the local community through employment and expenditures. *Lee Whittington*

SYMONS, ROBERT DAVID (1898–1973). Born on April 7, 1898, in Sussex, England, Robert David Symons was the son of a painter and of a musician. He came to Canada as a teenager to work on a ranch in Maple Creek. Following active service

UNIVERSITY OF REGINA ARCHIVES AND SPECIAL COLLECTIONS
84-11-383

Robert David Symons.

in **WORLD WAR I**, Symons returned to western Canada, where he became a rancher, and then a game warden in 1927. In 1945, Symons returned to ranching northwest of Fort St. John, BC, retiring in 1961 to his home and studio in Silton, Saskatchewan, on the shores of **LAST MOUNTAIN LAKE**. Throughout his life he sketched, painted, and took notes on the world around him.

Starting in 1951, Symons worked periodically as a commissioned artist for the Saskatchewan Museum of Natural History (now the **ROYAL SASKATCHEWAN MUSEUM**) in Regina, painting many of the famous dioramas and habitat displays. He also taught art classes, wrote, and gave lectures on natural history, **ART**, and **LITERATURE**. Upon retirement, Symons worked to bring his experiences to life through painting, drawing, and writing. He wrote and illustrated many well-known books, including *Many Trails* in 1963, *The Broken Snare* in 1970, and *Where the Wagon Led* in 1973. His artwork is prized by collectors, and has been exhibited in the National Gallery of Canada. In 1970, he was awarded an honorary degree by the **UNIVERSITY OF REGINA**. He died in Silton on February 1, 1973. *Merle Massie*

SYNAGOGUES. Following the destruction of the Second Temple in 70 AD, the synagogue was and still continues to be the community centre, the house of study, and the house of prayer for the Jewish people. However, a synagogue building is not necessary for prayer. Services may be conducted provided there is a knowledgeable leader and, for the orthodox, a minyan, that is a quorum of ten Jewish men over the age of 13. On the other hand, the Conservative and Reform movements accept a *minyan* of ten Jewish men and women. Another important part of a religious service is a Torah scroll on which the Five Books of Moses are inscribed; some early settlers brought Torah scrolls with them to their Saskatchewan homes.

Sparsely settled Saskatchewan necessitated ingenious solutions when no *minyan* was available. A Lipton colony pioneer, for example, on learning that one of his parents had died, went into the forest to say *kaddish*, the prayer for the dead; the forest became both his *minyan* and his congregation. When possible, a *minyan* met in people's homes: for the high holidays, Jews from scattered small towns and villages would gather in a home or in a Jewish farm colony to celebrate and pray. When it was not possible to attend a synagogue, some would choose a central location to meet for services in a rented hall, a theatre and, later, even a curling rink. For example, during **WORLD WAR II**, the Jewish people from Neville, Admiral, Vanguard, Cadillac, Tompkins and Herbert joined the Jews of Swift Current who had rented the Masonic Lodge hall; occasionally they hired a religious leader from Regina to lead the services.

Sometime before 1885 the Jewish farm colonists of "New Jerusalem" constructed the earliest known synagogue in Saskatchewan. Eventually synagogues were built in Canora, Edenbridge, Estevan, Hirsch, Yorkton, Kamsack, Lipton, Melfort, Melville, Moose Jaw, North Battleford, Prince Albert, Regina, Rosthern, Saskatoon, and Sonnenfeld. The Kamsack synagogue was completely destroyed by a cyclone and rebuilt 1944. Synagogue buildings in Saskatchewan tended to be small, modest wooden structures. Because Saskatchewan Jews in earlier days were orthodox, the women sat at the back of the building while the men sat in the front; or a curtain separated the male and female members of the congregation. In a few of the buildings there was an upstairs women's gallery.

The Jewish population in Saskatchewan's rural areas as well as its smaller centres has dwindled considerably over the years. Once-active communities no longer exist, and their synagogues have either been destroyed over time or stand unused. One exception is the Edenbridge farm colony's synagogue: in 1976, through the efforts of descendants and relatives of original Jewish settlers, the provincial government declared the restored building, the cemetery, and the forty acres of forested land on which they stand a Regional Historic Site; the **SASKATCHEWAN WILDLIFE FEDERATION** maintains the site.

In 1919, one of the province's more attractive synagogues was built in Saskatoon at the cost of approximately $12,000. The structure, of Greek design and approximately forty by sixty feet, had the finest plumbing available. A newspaper reported that the upstairs consisted of a large auditorium with a semicircular gallery above; the seats and furnishings were made of oak. This synagogue is no longer in use by Saskatoon's Jewish community.

At the present time there are two synagogues in Saskatchewan: **BETH JACOB** in Regina, and Congregation **AGUDAS ISRAEL** in Saskatoon. Beth Jacob is an unaffiliated member of the conservative movement. A group belonging to the Reform movement also meets at Beth Jacob from time to time. Congregation Agudas Israel is affiliated with the United Synagogues of Conservative Judaism. **SHIR HADASH**, which seceded from Congregation Agudas Israel, is an unaffiliated conservative congregation in Saskatoon.   *Anne Feldman*

SYNCHROTRON: *see* **CANADIAN LIGHT SOURCE**

SYNTHETIC SUGAR. Raymond Lemieux and George Huber were the first in the world to synthetically produce sucrose or common table sugar in 1953. This groundbreaking work was accomplished at the National Research Council's Prairie Regional Laboratory in Saskatoon, a facility on the **UNIVERSITY OF SASKATCHEWAN** campus now known as the Plant Biotechnology Institute (PBI). This sucrose synthesis was a foundation event in stereochemistry. Sugars are found virtually everywhere in living systems, and their shape determines what they do: sugars on the surface of cells, for example, determine blood type, and act as receptors for cell signaling. These receptors are often "hijacked" by viruses and bacteria to invade our bodies and cause disease. Likewise, some antibiotics are based on complex sugars of just the right shape to block the receptors on the surfaces of bacteria and viruses. Practical applications of this synthesis range from tests for blood typing to antibody tests, vaccine development, and design of new medicines.   *Joe Ralko*

COURTESY OF THE ESTATE OF ANNE SZUMIGALSKI

Anne Szumilgalski.

SZUMIGALSKI, ANNE (1922–99). Governor General's Award winning Saskatchewan poet Anne Howard Szumigalski was born on January 3, 1922 in London, England but spent almost fifty years of her life in Saskatchewan. During **WORLD WAR II** she worked as a medical auxiliary, interpreter, and welfare officer with the British Red Cross throughout Europe. There she met her husband, Jan Waclaw Szumigalski. In 1951, the Szumigalskis and their two young daughters moved from Wales to Saskatoon. In 1956, they purchased a home in the Mayfair area where Anne lived for the rest of her life. *Woman Reading in Bath*, Anne's first solo book of poetry, was published in 1974. Throughout her life, she published twelve books of poetry, one

book of memoirs and essays (*The Word, The Voice, The Text*), and one play (*Z: A Dramatic Meditation on Oppression, Desire and Freedom*). *Z* has been produced for the stage twice, won the Saskatchewan Book of the Year award in 1995, and a new edition was published posthumously. Anne Szumigalski enjoyed performing and did so often, providing voice, acting, and dancing for various performances. She wrote radio dramas, words for dance, and a liturgy.

Szumigalski was especially well known in the Saskatchewan writing community for her long and involved service to it and its members. She was a founding member of the **SASKATCHEWAN WRITERS' GUILD**, the Saskatchewan Writers' and Artists' Colonies, the literary journal *Grain* (for which she also worked on the editing staff for nine years), the Saskatchewan Moving Collective (a dance group), and the AKA artist-run centre in Saskatoon. She taught for ten years at the Saskatchewan Summer School of the Arts, and was the first writer-in-residence at the Saskatoon Public Library as well as a writer-in-residence at the Winnipeg Public Library. Among her many awards were two nominations for the Governor General's Award for Poetry, and one winning nomination (for *Voice*, 1995), a Founder's Award from the Saskatchewan Writers' Guild, Woman of the Year for 1988 (YWCA), and the Saskatchewan Order of Merit. She died in Saskatoon from complications due to cancer on April 22, 1999.   *Frances Bitney*

FURTHER READING: Clark, J.L. 1997. "Anne Szumigalski: Biography in Outline," *Prairie Fire* 18: 14–16.

TACHÉ, ALEXANDRE-ANTONIN (1823–94).

Alexandre-Antonin Taché, a Missionary Oblate of Mary Immaculate, was born on July 23, 1823, in Rivière-du-Loup, Quebec. Sent to the Red River missions in 1845, Taché became the first French-Canadian Oblate to serve in the North-West. In 1850, he was named coadjutor to Bishop Joseph-Norbert Provencher and, upon the latter's death in 1853, became Bishop and, later in 1871, Archbishop of the Ecclesiastical Province of St. Boniface. As a missionary bishop, Taché was responsible for sustaining and expanding missions to the First Nations and the **MÉTIS**. With the arrival of settlers in the west, his responsibilities increased because of the need for traditional Catholic parishes and institutions such as schools and hospitals. Taché wanted to settle large numbers of French-speaking Catholics in the west and, to this end, he became involved in promoting immigration from Quebec and repatriating the Franco-Americans. His vision of a bilingual and bicultural west never materialized, and French

BENNETTO & CO. PHOTO/SOURCE: PROVINCIAL ARCHIVES OF MANITOBA N2959

Alexandre-Antonin Taché, ca. 1890

and Catholic rights in Manitoba and the North-West Territories were severely restricted by an Anglo-Protestant majority that was suspicious of bilingualism and confessional schools. Taché played a key role in the establishment of the Roman Catholic Church in western Canada and left an indelible imprint on the character of the French community in that region. He died in St. Boniface, Manitoba, on June 22, 1894.

Raymond Huel

FURTHER READING: Huel, Raymond. 2003. *Archbishop A.-A. Taché of St. Boniface: The "Good Fight" and the Illusive Vision.* Edmonton: University of Alberta Press.

TAGGART, JAMES GORDON (1892–1974).
Born September 28, 1892, Taggart grew up on a farm near Truro, NS. He Studied at the Provincial Agricultural College in Truro and the Ontario Agricultural College in Guelph. After working as a district representative for the Guelph agricultural college, he moved to Alberta where he taught and was later principal of the Vermilion School of Agriculture. In 1921 Taggart moved to Regina where he demonstrated tractors for the Ford Motor Company. Later that year he became the first superintendent of the Dominion Experimental Farm in Swift Current. He won the Swift Current seat for the Liberals in 1934 provincial election. Taggart served as Saskatchewan's Minister of Agriculture from 1934 to 1944, first under **GARDINER**, and then **PATTERSON**. Starting in 1939, Taggart held a number of appointments related to the war effort, including food administrator with the federal Wartime Prices and Trade Board and chairman of the Meat Board. When the Patterson Liberals were defeated in 1944, Taggart moved to Ottawa where he continued to work on various boards, and later provided post-war guidance to the Agricultural Prices Support Board.

SASKATCHEWAN ARCHIVES BOARD R-A2823

James Taggart.

In 1949 Taggart had a second chance to work under Jimmy Gardiner when he was appointed federal Deputy Minister of Agriculture, which he held until 1959. He focused the attention of federal authorities on the importance of prairie agriculture to the nation's economy. He was made a Commander of the British Empire, his professional colleagues elected him a Fellow of the Agricultural Institute of Canada, and several universities gave him honorary degrees. He died June 11, 1974.

FURTHER READING: 1995. *Salute to Saskatchewan Farm Leaders.* Saskatchewan Agricultural Hall of Fame.

TANAGERS.
Tanagers are brightly coloured insect- and fruit-eating tropical songbirds related to warblers. They have stout, pointed bills. The males are commonly more brightly coloured than the females.

There are over 254 species of tanagers in the Western Hemisphere, mostly in South America. In North America there are six species; three tanager species are found in Saskatchewan. The Western tanager (*Piranga ludoviciana*) regularly breeds in mixedwood stands in the southern boreal forest and **CYPRESS HILLS**. It has wingbars, a short tail, a small bill and pointed wings. Adult males during the breeding season have reddish-orange heads and black and yellow bodies. The scarlet tanager (*Piranga olivacea*) is a rare, irregular summer resident of the southern boreal forest and deciduous woods of the **QU'APPELLE VALLEY** and **MOOSE MOUNTAIN**. The adult male goes from yellow-green to a brilliant red with black wings during the breeding season. Summer tanagers (*Piranga rubra*) have been reported a few times in southern Saskatchewan as summer transients. They are larger, with longer heavy bills, and may appear to be crested. Males are bright red during the breeding season.

Robert Warnock

FURTHER READING: Alsop, Fred J., III. 2002. *Birds of Canada.* New York: Dorling Kindersley.

TANSLEY, DONALD D. (1925–).
Born in Regina on May 19, 1925, Tansley served overseas with the Regina Rifle Regiment. He joined the provincial government's Budget Bureau in 1950 after graduating in arts and commerce from the University of Saskatchewan. He worked in the Treasury until 1960, and was then appointed executive director of the Government Finance Office. Two years later, he became Chair of the Saskatchewan Medical Care Insurance Commission, the body charged with implementing medicare. In 1964, Tansley was hired by Premier Louis Robichaud of New Brunswick to become his Deputy Minister of Finance and Industry and to advise on the modernization of his government. In 1968, he

SASKATCHEWAN ARCHIVES BOARD R-A10698

Donald Tansley.

accepted the position of Vice-President of the Canadian International Development Agency (CIDA) in Ottawa. From 1973 to 1975 he studied the International Red Cross, producing a far-sighted and prescient report on its future role in the world. Tansley was later appointed Administrator of the Anti-Inflation Act and Deputy Minister of Fisheries and Oceans. Tansley was notable for his great organizational skills and his ability to work in highly difficult circumstances. In 1999, he received the Order of Canada as well as the Henry Dunant Medal, the highest award conferred by the International Red Cross and Red Crescent. He was also made a Companion of the Order of the Canadian Red Cross.

Gregory P. Marchildon

TAUBE, HENRY (1915–).
Henry Taube was born at Neudorf on November 30, 1915. He was the youngest of four brothers born to German farming immigrants who had come to Saskatchewan from the Ukraine in 1911. At the age of 13, Taube attended Luther College in Regina. After completing grade twelve, he remained at Luther College as a laboratory assistant thanks to his chemistry teacher, Paul Liefeld, and was able to take first-year university classes. His appreciation of Liefeld was expressed in 2004 in the form of a substantial donation to Luther College.

Henry Taube attended the **UNIVERSITY OF SASKATCHEWAN**, successfully completing a BSc in chemistry in 1935 and an MSc in 1937. In 1940 he received a PhD from the University of California (Berkeley). Since positions at Canadian universities were scarce he remained at Berkeley as an instructor, becoming a US citizen in 1942. He also taught and conducted research at: Cornell University

UNIVERSITY OF SASKATCHEWAN ARCHIVES A-8702

Henry Taube.

(1941–46); the University of Chicago (1946–62), where he was Chair of the Department of Chemistry from 1956 to 1959; and Stanford University (1962–86), where he was Chair of the Department of Chemistry from 1972 to 1974 and from 1978 to 1979. He became a Professor Emeritus in 1986. Taube married Mary Alice Wesche in 1952; they have two daughters and two sons.

Universally recognized as the founder of the modern study of inorganic mechanisms, Taube is the author of more than 300 scientific papers and articles on such subjects as the electronic mechanisms involved in the composition and reactivity of inorganic coordination compounds. He developed new techniques to study aspects of chemical reactivity. He has been the recipient of numerous awards, including the National Medal of Science in 1977, and the Nobel Prize in Chemistry in 1983 for his work on the mechanism of an electron transfer reaction. He also received a Doctor of Laws degree in 1973 from the University of Saskatchewan.

Alan Smith

FURTHER READING: Olsen, Richard (ed.). 1998. *Biographical Encyclopedia of Scientists*, Vol. 5. New York: Marshall Cavendish Corporation.

TAXATION. The taxation authority of the federal and provincial governments is prescribed in the Constitution Act, 1867, with federal authority including both direct and indirect modes of taxation and provincial authority limited to direct taxation. At the time Saskatchewan became a province, there was already a broad range of municipal levies that included a personal income tax, a business tax, a property tax, succession duties and a poll tax of $2 per person to finance education. Upon becoming a province, Saskatchewan introduced its own revenue measures, including a supplementary revenue tax on land in support of education, user fees, and a general corporations tax on most businesses including financial institutions, telegraph and railways. It also received an annual subsidy from the federal government in lieu of natural resource levies. Once **WORLD WAR I** began, Saskatchewan and other provinces introduced a Patriotic Revenues Tax on both urban and rural properties. This was raised throughout the war and was renamed the Public Revenue Tax in 1917, the same year the federal government introduced a personal income tax as a temporary war measure.

After World War I, the province continued to rely on a combination of property-based levies, corporation taxes, and user fees. However, in 1928 it began moving toward the modern-day tax regime by introducing a gasoline tax. In 1930, a constitutional amendment provided Saskatchewan with the authority to tax natural resources. The province introduced a personal income tax in 1932, while at the same time abolishing municipal governments' right to levy income taxes. Finally, in 1937 Saskatchewan introduced a broad-based sales tax at a rate of 2% to finance education. A rapid increase in provincial tax rates occurred as Canada entered the **GREAT DEPRESSION**, a period of lower incomes, high unemployment, and increasing demands for public services. This was especially true in western Canada, which was confronted with drought and crop failures throughout the 1930s.

Owing to the difficult financial positions of provinces during that period, the federal government appointed a **ROYAL COMMISSION ON DOMINION PROVINCIAL RELATIONS** in 1937, referred to as the Rowell-Sirois Commission, to examine the economic and fiscal basis for Confederation and the distribution of legislative powers. It recommended a shift in taxing powers, as well as the national government's assuming full control over personal and corporate income taxation in Canada in exchange for provincial compensation. This led in 1942 to the federal Wartime Tax Agreement Act, which provided the federal government with unrestricted access to personal and corporate income taxation to finance the war effort and manage the wartime economy. The federal government also introduced federal succession duties, a gasoline tax, and user fees. In exchange, provinces received financial compensation from the federal government. For Saskatchewan, compensation came in the form of the federal government assuming the province's net debt charges less any revenue collected from succession duties. Once assuming full control over income tax, the federal government rapidly increased tax rates and expanded the income tax base by lowering personal exemptions.

Following **WORLD WAR II**, the federal government retained exclusive control over income taxation and lowered income taxation levels. In 1947, Saskatchewan entered with the federal government into a five-year Tax Rental Agreement that extended federal control over the application of income taxes, in exchange for a guaranteed annual payment based on a per capita amount. That year also witnessed the federal government withdrawing from the taxation of gasoline (introduced as a war measure), permitting provinces to increase their reliance on this revenue source as a means of financing highway development. The Tax Rental Agreements formed the basis for the administration of the personal and corporate income taxation until 1962, when the federal government entered with all provinces except Quebec into Tax Collection Agreements that permitted provincial flexibility to levy income taxes based on a percentage of the federal tax assessed.

During the years following World War II the tax system was relatively stable, but provincial tax rates increased to keep pace with the public's demand for provincial services, including an increase in the province's sales tax to 3% in 1950 (this tax was also renamed the Education and Hospitalization Tax). During this period, Saskatchewan also witnessed strong growth in provincial revenues resulting from the development of its natural resources, although international market forces created considerable revenue volatility for the province. The introduction of Saskatchewan's **MEDICARE** reform in 1962 required a significant increase in provincial revenues. The provincial sales tax was increased to 5% (also renamed the Education and Health Tax), although additional exemptions were introduced, bearing on reading materials, medical supplies, and farm-based exemptions. As part of this initiative, the province also increased personal and corporate income taxes and introduced annual health premiums (later abolished in 1974).

Strong revenue growth during the period 1965 to 1971 permitted a reduction in provincial taxes. The Education and Health Tax was reduced 4% in 1965 (the tax rate returned to 5% in 1968), while the following year saw the personal income tax surtax reduced, "nuisance" levies eliminated, tax-free marked gasoline permitted for farm trucks, and Home Owner Grants (later renamed Property Improvement Grants) introduced. The province also introduced the Tobacco Tax in 1965 (the tax would increase rapidly in the late 1970s and 1980s). During the late 1970s, an important consideration was the significant rise in the price of energy: provincial royalties and taxes began to increase significantly, and in response the federal government introduced the National Energy Program. It signed controversial five-year agreements with the energy-producing provinces with respect to energy pricing, taxation and incentives to protect Canadian energy consumers and redistribute the net proceeds from high international prices to the benefit of all Canadians.

The 1970s also saw a shift in tax distribution toward income-based levies for individuals, and higher corporate taxes. Provincial personal income tax rates increased from about one-third of federal tax to over one-half by 1980, although part of that increase was linked to a shift in tax room from the federal government to the provinces as a means to fund health care and social spending. Property Improvement Grants were increased significantly for homeowners, businesses and farmers to reduce the effect of local property taxes. The general Corporation Income Tax rate was increased, while the Corporation Capital Tax was introduced in 1980. Provincial tax rates increased in the 1980s to address budgetary deficits. The Corporation Income Tax rate was increased to its current rate of 17% by 1986, although lower tax rates were applied to small businesses and the value-added sector. The Corporation Capital Tax was also increased and expanded to apply to resource production. Personal taxes also increased during that time, with the exception of the Fuel Tax, which was eliminated for a brief period between 1982 and 1987. Of particular note was Saskatchewan's introduction in 1985 of Canada's first provincial Flat Tax, which resulted in a significant revenue increase. Property Improvement Grants were also eliminated in 1985. The Education and Health Tax was increased to 7% in 1987. These changes reversed the impact of the earlier shift to greater reliance on progressive taxation, and created very high personal and business taxation levels.

Tax levels became even higher in the early 1990s to address large provincial budgetary deficits. Revenue increases occurred in the Corporation Capital Tax, the Fuel Tax, and the Education and Health Tax (the tax rate went as high as 9%). A new Deficit Reduction Surtax was introduced, which effectively increased personal income tax levels by 10% in 1992. Balancing the provincial budget in 1994–95 permitted a return to more competitive tax levels, beginning with the introduction of targeted personal and business tax reductions. General tax reductions began in 1997 with reductions in the Education and Health Tax, the personal income tax rate, and the small business income tax rate.

In 1999, the province's Personal Income Tax Review Committee examined the fairness and competitiveness of the personal tax system. It recommended significant reforms that lowered personal taxation levels by eliminating the Flat Tax, Deficit Reduction Surtax and High Income Surtax; and it shifted reliance from income to consumption taxation by broadening the sales tax base to achieve lower marginal income tax rates. As part of its reforms, Saskatchewan increased family-based tax credits to improve tax fairness, and introduced a

universal child tax credit that is unique in Canada. These reforms were fully implemented by 2003. The challenge of raising adequate revenue to support key public services, including health and education, continues as Saskatchewan approaches its centenary: this is illustrated by an increase in the provincial sales tax rate to 7% in 2004. *Kirk McGregor*

TAYLOR, MALCOLM GORDON (1915–94).

Malcolm Taylor was born on August 31, 1915, at Arrowhead, Alberta. He began teaching in the depths of the **GREAT DEPRESSION**, but saved enough money to go to Berkeley, where he graduated with a BA (Cum Laude) in 1942, an MA (1943), and a PhD in Political Science in 1949. His doctoral dissertation was entitled "The Saskatchewan Hospital Services Plan." Returning to Canada, he became a member and research director of the Saskatchewan Health Services Planning Commission (1948–51), and later was research consultant to the Hall Commission. He wrote several books, numerous articles, and made over 300 public addresses while at the Universities of Calgary and Victoria, where he was respectively first principal and first president. Probably his most influential book was *Health Insurance and Canadian Public Policy* (1978, 1988). He also wrote *The Administration of Health Insurance in Canada* (1956), *The Financial Aspects of Health Insurance* (1958), and *Insuring National Health Care: The Canadian Experience* (1990). Throughout his life he played a fundamental role in assuring full and complete health care for every Canadian. He died in Victoria on September 10, 1994. *John A. Boan*

TAYLOR, TILLIE (1922–).
Tillie Taylor (*née* Goldenberg), lawyer and magistrate, has had a lifelong commitment to social justice. Born on November 11, 1922, she was the eldest of the four children of J.M. Goldenberg, a Saskatoon lawyer, and Sarah Goldenberg. In her youth, she was active in the Youth Congress Movement, an international organization aimed at finding solutions to poverty and conflict. In 1941 she received a BA degree from the **UNIVERSITY OF SASKATCHEWAN** and married George Taylor, later a prominent labour lawyer. Returning to university after the birth of two daughters, she received her LLB degree in 1956. She worked as a deputy registrar in the Land Titles Office in the Saskatoon law school. In 1960, she became the first woman to be appointed to the ranks of magistrates who later became judges of the Provincial Court of Saskatchewan. She continued to demonstrate a commitment to social justice through work with the Canadian Research Institute for the Advancement of Justice, the Canadian Council for Social Development, and the **JOHN HOWARD SOCIETY**. In 1972, she became the first chairperson of the Saskatchewan Human Rights Commission; in this

position, she helped to develop the mandate of the Commission and to set its direction. On retirement from the bench, she continued to participate in community organizations. In 1996, she received the Saskatchewan Order of Merit. *Beth Bilson*

TCHORZEWSKI, EDWIN LAURENCE (1943–).
Born April 22, 1943, in Alvena, Ed Tchorzewski completed his secondary schooling in Hudson Bay. He completed a BA in political science at the **UNIVERSITY OF SASKATCHEWAN** and taught in Humboldt with the separate school system.

Tchorzewski was elected for the NDP in Humboldt in the 1971 general election. He was appointed to Cabinet in 1972 as Minister of Culture and Youth and for Consumer Affairs. Tchorzewski moved into Education in 1975, Health in 1977 and Finance in 1979. In 1982, Tchorzewski lost in Humboldt as the Blakeney government was defeated. He was elected in Regina North East in a 1985 by-election. Re-elected in 1986, Tchorzewski was appointed deputy leader.

In 1991, the NDP was returned to power and Tchorzewski was re-elected in the new constituency of Regina Dewdney. He was appointed to Romanow's first Cabinet as Minister of Finance. In the 1992 budget, Tchorzewski introduced increases in taxation and cut government spending that ultimately balanced the provincial books in 1993. Tchorzewski left the Finance portfolio shortly before

REGINA LEADER-POST

Ed Tchorzewski, October 1985.

the 1993 budget to take the less demanding position of Provincial Secretary. Later in 1993, he took on responsibility for Education for several months and in 1995 took over as Minister of Municipal Government. Re-elected in 1995, Tchorzewski served his last term as a government backbencher. Tchorzewski was elected president of the federal NDP in 1997, and in 1999 he resigned from the Legislature to become chief of staff to federal NDP leader Alexa McDonough. Tchorzewski returned to Saskatchewan to be the NDP's campaign manager in 1999. In 2002, Tchorzewski was hired as special advisor to newly elected Premier **LORNE CALVERT**. In 2004 he was hired as provincial secretary of the NDP. *Brett Quiring*

TEACHER EDUCATION: *see* **NORMAL SCHOOL**

TELECOMMUNICATIONS. The telephone came early to Saskatchewan: considered to be one of the most compelling and practical "modern conveniences" in the late 19th century, it was introduced at Regina in autumn 1882 by the Bell Telephone Company, a subsidiary of the Boston-based National Bell Telephone Company (est. 1877). The North-West Mounted Police (NWMP) also operated a rudimentary network in the prairie city to connect their barracks with various government buildings. At Indian Head, east of Regina, Major William R. Bell similarly installed a telephone system on his 53,000-acre farm, using barbed wire for the lines. It was **LOUIS RIEL**'s **NORTH-WEST RESISTANCE** in 1885, however, that largely stimulated telephone development in Saskatchewan's portion of the then North-West Territories, because of the instrument's capacity for swift and direct verbal communication by which an emergency could be explained to any listener without the need for a specially trained telegrapher to relay or receive messages at either end of the line. Consequenlty, with Riel's defeat the Bell company began to expand its operations in the Territories. It absorbed the NWMP's system into its Regina plant, and subsequently established its first exchange in the growing city in 1887. A second exchange was built at Moose Jaw in 1893, though this was later sold to a private investor in 1899–only to change ownership again in 1905 when purchased by the newly incorporated Saskatchewan Telephone Company.

Other towns in the region also began to develop telephone service independently of the Bell system at that time. A common feature among several of them was the extension of rural lines to connect local farmers, an expensive and unprofitable part of the early telephone business. Prince Albert (1890), Moosomin (1892), Yorkton (1900), and Saskatoon (1903) all had privately owned plants of their own, although the Bell company eventually acquired the first three. In the meantime, the corporation extended long-distance circuits to Indian Head, Lumsden, Moose Jaw and Moosomin near the Manitoba border, with connections to Winnipeg and intermediate points.

At the formation of Saskatchewan as a new province within Confederation in 1905, the Liberal administration of Premier **WALTER SCOTT** undertook to create the basic apparatus of state necessary to provide essential social services for the growing community. A priority was the construction of a government-owned telephone network in response to public demand. Hence, in 1908 the Liberals established a Department of Telephones to oversee the development of a provincial telecommunications system that could unite all Saskatchewan residents into a single community, at low cost to subscribers and taxpayers alike. The plant would include government-owned trunk lines for long distance, municipal exchanges and, most importantly, rural systems built, owned and operated by small joint-stock companies organized by local farmers with aid and regulation from Regina. Because private corporations like the Bell company invested only in profitable urban, not unprofitable rural systems, responsibility for providing telephone service in a province where most of the population lived on scattered homesteads fell by default upon government assistance and the principle of public ownership as a social service organized through the state.

For the next ninety years, the history of telecommunications development in Saskatchewan paralleled the history of the Department of Telephones and its several incarnations. Construction of several long-distance trunk lines commenced in spring 1909 under the direction of **JAMES A. CALDER**, the first Commissioner (later Minister) of Telephones. Additional routes were planned for the 1910 building season from late April to late October or the first snow fall. Within the next three years, the provincial system jumped from twenty exchanges and 100 toll offices serving 3,412 subscribers over 1,132 pole-miles of long-distance circuits in 1910, to ninety-three exchanges and 284 toll offices serving 14,826 subscribers over 3,172 pole-miles of long distance by 1913. These figures did not include the incorporation of 327 farmers' mutual companies or the construction of 7,554 pole-miles of rural lines to serve an additional 8,024 subscribers. Part of this rapid growth was also due to the government's purchase of the Bell plant (1909) and other independent systems that had operated formerly in Saskatchewan. This gave the Department of Telephones a monopoly of long-distance service which was retained until 1997.

With the onset of an economic recession in 1913 and the outbreak of **WORLD WAR I** a year later, work slowed on the provincial network, owing to higher costs, shortage of materials, and insufficient manpower (now needed for Canada's military effort overseas). When peace returned in 1918, however, building resumed on long-distance and rural lines, until by 1924 the department announced that "telephone service has pretty well saturated the province." In fact, more than 97,000 residents subscribed at an average annual rate of $24 to the provincial system, which had grown to 64,744 pole-miles of long-distance and rural lines. Pace was also maintained with the latest advances in telephone technology. Beginning in 1908, the old magneto sets with their weak local battery and bell cranks were replaced by the "central energy" system, by which the electric current needed to transmit messages was generated from the central exchange rather than the individual telephone. This permitted changes in set design from the familiar wooden magneto wall box to the slender candlestick desk model and more compact wall set. The transition also increased switchboard capacity to accommodate many more manual connections by fewer operators, whose role was further reduced by the concurrent development of automatic "machine switching" and dial technology, first installed at Saskatoon (1907) and Regina (1908), which allowed subscribers to complete local calls without operator assistance. This was available only in urban centres until 1974, when the province completed the conversion of the entire network to automatic switching; until then, rural subscribers relied on the older central energy system over party lines.

Following World War I and during the period from 1925 to 1930, telephone development in Saskatchewan was extensive as the economy improved and public demand accelerated. Although the provincial system expanded only modestly in terms of pole-mileage, the Department of Telephones invested heavily in replacement of aging circuits, enhancement of carrying capacity over existing lines, and improvement in quality of long-distance transmission. Exchange offices were expanded, new technology was adapted, and additional wire was strung. Rural construction was also so extensive at the time that by 1929 over 50% of Saskatchewan farmers–the largest ratio in North America–had telephone service. With 13.2 telephones per 100 residents, Saskatchewan fell just short of the national average of 13.8.

When the stock market crashed later that year, followed by the **GREAT DEPRESSION** and **WORLD WAR II**, expansion of long-distance facilities and rural lines was curtailed for nearly twenty years. The number of subscribers to the provincial system plunged, capital expenditure was slashed, many farmers' mutual companies defaulted on loans and collapsed, while work on rural telephones halted almost completely. The only high point of the 1930s was the inauguration of the Trans-Canada Telephone System (TCTS) in 1932, to which Saskatchewan contributed a large share. Slightly improved economic conditions brought some relief in the late 1930s, when the Department of Telephones returned to modernization and limited extension of the provincial plant. World War II interrupted any further progress, however, owing to the dearth of labour and construction materials, which were needed overseas. At home, meanwhile, the Department of Telephones struggled between 1940 and 1945 to meet the demands of Canada's domestic war effort, by providing connections to the many training camps established in the province.

With the return of peace and a strong economy in 1945, telephone development grew tremendously. Although still hampered by post-war shortages of equipment and supplies, the construction, extension and renewal of the provincial system moved at a vibrant pace. The old department was also reorganized in 1947 as a Crown corporation under a new name, Saskatchewan Government Telephones (SGT), by the recently elected (1944) CCF administration of Premier **T.C. DOUGLAS**. This positioned the province for the unprecedented growth of the public plant during the 1950s, when more telephones were added to the system than in all previous years combined. The period also witnessed an aggressive program of dial conversion in every urban and rural exchange, which, when completed in 1974, made Saskatchewan the first province in Canada to achieve that goal. Between 1955 and 1958, meanwhile, SGT completed construction of its portion of the transcontinental radio-relay microwave network, sponsored by the TCTS. These advances in both service and technology made possible the inauguration of Direct Distance Dialing, whereby subscribers could make their own long-distance calls across North America without operator assistance. This included residents of Saskatchewan's undeveloped far north, where automatic dial exchange for local and limited long-distance calls was available by 1963. Finally, the period from 1945 to 1963 saw the steady renewal and improvement of rural telephones, which now provided service to over 63% of Saskatchewan farmers.

Further development of the provincial telecommunications network increased over the next two decades. Various projects begun in the 1950s, such as the dial-conversion program, construction of additional microwave systems and the burial of circuits underground, continued at a regular pace. Expanding upon available technology, closed-circuit television transmission was inaugurated in 1965 and 1966 on the campuses of both provincial universities for distance learning. Push-button, touch-tone telephones were also introduced in 1967. SGT participated at the same time in the expansion of telecommunications via satellite (1972) and trans-Canada computer connections for digital transmission (1973). Work similarly continued on SGT's Unserved Area Program, begun in 1966, to connect

all farmers to the government-owned network; this program and the buried cable project were both completed in 1976. These achievements paved the way for a new Rural Service Improvement initiative, by which all farmers' systems were assimilated into the provincial plant by 1990.

The two most significant developments of this twenty-year period were, however, the transformation in SGT's status as a central player in the Canadian telecommunications industry under a new trade-mark and name, **SASKTEL**, in 1969; and the Crown corporation's pioneering work in fibre-optic technology. Using high-speed streams of laser-generated light impulses to carry computer-coded voice, image and data information through strands of glass no thicker than a human hair, a fibre-optics telecommunications system has far greater information-handling capacity than any transmission method of the past. SaskTel engineers began to explore the possibilities of the new technology in the late 1970s, and in 1980 the corporation commenced construction of a fibre-optics network which, when completed in 1984, was the world's longest. A year later, the TCTS followed Saskatchewan's lead by building a coast-to-coast fibre-optics network to serve the country as a whole.

In the 1980s and early 1990s, SaskTel's telecommunications monopoly in Saskatchewan was challenged by the federal government and the Ottawa-based Canadian Radio-television & Telecommunications Commission (CRTC) to permit competition along with federal regulation. After strong resistance and much discussion, in 1992 NDP Premier **ROY ROMANOW** reached a compromise with the Conservative administration of Prime Minister Brian Mulroney. SaskTel was granted a five-year moratorium, which the Crown corporation used to streamline its organization, personnel, rates and services, in advance of external competition and CRTC regulation. The moratorium was extended in 1997 for another two years, after which SaskTel came fully under federal regulation.

In the meantime, a variety of long-term projects initiated prior to 1980 were brought to fruition, such as touch-tone dialing, the Rural Service Improvement program, Individual Line Service (to remove the last rural party-lines), and air-to-ground radio-telecommunications. The completion of the province's fibre-optics network in 1984 permitted the adaptation of further services, such as Direct Overseas and zero-plus dialing for the unassisted placement of international calls by individual subscribers. Advanced digital technology was also made available for Saskatchewan businesses, as SaskTel adopted a "Total Telecommunications" concept to become a full-service provider to every customer. In fact, in 1987 a digital switching modernization program was announced to convert the province to an all-digital network over the next decade. The same

year, SaskTel International was incorporated as a wholly owned subsidiary of the Crown corporation to undertake contract work around the world. Among its many achievements was the design, system and management audit, as well as the installation and commissioning of telecommunications and control systems, for the English Channel Tunnel project in 1990–94. Later developments included the introduction of high-speed internet, cellular and personal communications services, starting in 1998.

Since 1908, when the Liberal government of Premier Walter Scott established a Department of Telephones with a simple mandate to connect all settled portions of the new province by means of a publicly owned and operated telephone network, telecommunications in Saskatchewan has grown by leaps and bounds. In just over nine decades, the provincial plant developed from a rudimentary system spliced together from local systems acquired and subsequently linked by government-built trunk lines into one of Canada's most sophisticated and successful networks. Throughout that long process, Saskatchewan helped to pioneer Canadian telephony and communications as a major participant and occasional leader, adapting much of the technological innovation upon which the growing industry depended and still depends. Over the years, consequently, the old Department of Telephones and its successors, SGT and SaskTel, scored an impressive number of firsts nationwide, culminating with the complete conversion of the provincial plant to advanced all-digital technology in 1995–a year ahead of schedule–making Saskatchewan the first province in the country to achieve that goal.

Ronald S. Love

FURTHER READING: Love, R.S. 2003. *Dreaming Big: A History of SaskTel.* Regina: SaskTel.

TEMPLE BETH TIKVAH. Temple Beth Tikvah is Regina's Reform Jewish congregation. It was formed in 1990 by a group of people who wanted a liberal alternative to the existing traditional Jewish congregation in Regina. Reform Judaism strives to make traditional Jewish writings and doctrines meaningful to modern Jews. To Reform Jews, personal choice is important as is the equality of men and women. Since the Temple's inception, women and men have had equal opportunities and responsibilities to participate in worship and take on leadership roles in defining the policies and managing the affairs of the Temple. Reform services are observed in a mixture of English and Hebrew. The Hebrew language connects participants to history, culture, and to other Jews all over the world while prayer in English provides access to worship for those who are unable to read Hebrew.

Temple Beth Tikvah is a member of the Union of American Hebrew Congregations (UAHC) and the

Canadian Council of Reform Jews (CCRJ). Through its membership to the Reform movement in North America, Temple Beth Tikvah has hosted a number of visiting rabbis from places as diverse as Texas, New York, Toronto, Edmonton, Winnipeg, and Calgary. The Temple has hosted educational and cultural events for the Jewish community and the community at large. While the size of the Temple could sustain it, religious education for children under 13 years of age was offered. The Religious School curriculum included Jewish history, knowledge of Jewish customs and holidays, religious observance, Hebrew language education and Bar and Bat Mitzvah preparation. The Temple has prepared eight students for their Bar or Bat Mitzvah.

Adult education was also a primary activity for the Temple. The Temple has hosted both formal and informal educational opportunities for adults, including book clubs, Hebrew language education, Torah study, and topical presentations. The Temple received a grant to provide a "Taste of Judaism" class for unaffiliated Jews, and also facilitated several conversions. Temple Beth Tikvah used the facilities of several organizations in Regina including the Rotary Senior Citizen's Centre, the Cathedral and Al Ritchie Neighborhood Centres, the Cornwall Alternative School, the Unitarian Centre and Beth Jacob Synagogue.

In recent years the membership of the Temple has declined. Currently the Temple operates as a *chaverah*, the Hebrew word for a group of friends. Observance of holidays and the Sabbath are now held for a smaller group of people in homes. The Temple is still an incorporated charity and maintains its affiliation with the Reform Jewish movement in North America. *Elyse Fisher*

TEMPLE GARDENS. People have been enjoying the rejuvenating, soothing and mineral-rich geothermal waters, drawn from ancient sea beds 1,350 metres below the surface, at Temple Gardens Mineral Spa in downtown Moose Jaw since 1993.

The mineral-rich water was discovered accidentally in 1910 by a crew drilling for oil. The water, heated from a much deeper molten mass within the earth's core, travels under its own pressure to the spa from the well located about 400 metres away. The mineral water is similar to the waters from the Upper Hot Springs in Banff, Alberta, the Radium Hot Springs in British Columbia and the famous mineral pools in Bath, England.

About 1,000 local investors bought shares to finance construction of the hotel that features indoor and outdoor pools open year-round. The pools contain 100,000 gallons of mineral water and are linked by a channel through which guests can swim even during the coldest winter months because the water temperature is constant at 40°C (104°F).

Business has been brisk since the day the spa, located in the heart of downtown Moose Jaw, opened. Annual reviews are approaching $11 million for the facility that provides 220 full time jobs. *Joe Ralko*

TENNIS. Shortly after their founding in the 1880s and 1890s, many Saskatchewan towns laid out clay tennis courts on vacant lots. These attracted both men and women players, who competed locally and regionally. In 1912, tennis enthusiasts organized the Saskatchewan Lawn Tennis Association, which from 1913 held provincial championships in men's and women's singles, doubles, and mixed doubles. Tennis was extremely popular in the 1920s. Regina, for example, had nineteen different clubs that competed regularly in leagues. The province's best player was Walter Martin, son of former premier **W.M. MARTIN**, who placed second in the national junior championships from 1925 to 1927, won three national intercollegiate championships, and was a member of Canada's international Davis Cup team from 1931 to 1934. The **DEPRESSION** of the 1930s and **WORLD WAR II** reduced the number of players and competitions.

In the 1950s and 1960s, tennis changed because the largest clubs constructed courts with hard surfaces. Smaller clubs, both rural and urban, disbanded because they could not afford these improvements. Competitive tennis became centred at two urban clubs, the Riverside in Saskatoon, and the Civil Service, later renamed the Lakeshore, in Regina. In the 1970s tennis experienced a boom, with the number of players increasing dramatically. Hard-surfaced tennis courts were built at schools and in smaller communities; and competition at the Saskatchewan Summer Games, beginning in 1972, sparked new interest. Also, from 1974 until 1976 Saskatoon hosted a professional tournament that attracted the country's top players. Tennis became a year-round sport with the opening of indoor clubs in Regina in 1977 and Saskatoon in 1978.

In the 1980s and 1990s, the number of people playing tennis declined, but the sport also experienced successes. In the early 1980s, the Saskatoon

Members of the Prince Albert Tennis Club gather for an afternoon of tennis, July 11, 1891.

club started a wheelchair tennis program, and in the 1990s it hosted three national tournaments. Four men have made major contributions to tennis in Saskatchewan. Dr. J.B. Kirkpatrick of the **UNIVERSITY OF SASKATCHEWAN** organized clinics and tournaments for decades, and also recorded the history of the game. His colleague Dr. John Leiceister was both a top player and organizer. Bill Ebbels of Regina won seven provincial singles titles—more than any other player—and served often on provincial and club executives. Don Axtell, who arrived in Regina in 1968 after playing US intercollegiate tennis, raised the level of play by example, and helped organize the game at the club, provincial, and national levels. *Sandra Bingaman*

FURTHER READING: Bingaman, S. 2004. *For the Love of the Game: Tennis in Saskatchewan, 1883–2001.* Regina: Tennis Saskatchewan and Saskatchewan Sports Hall of Fame and Museum.

10th Field Regiment

10TH FIELD REGIMENT. Saskatchewan's artillery unit, 10th Field Regiment, Royal Canadian Artillery (RCA), is a unit of 38th Canadian Brigade Group, Land Forces Western Area. The Regiment can trace its roots back to 1910, when the 26th Field Battery in Regina was formed. During **WORLD WAR I** the Regina battery of the Regiment acted as a recruiting depot for overseas service. The formation of the 5th Brigade, Canadian Field Artillery, occurred in 1914. One of the 5th Brigade's batteries was reorganized into the 10th Field Brigade, with the 18th Field Battery remaining in Regina. In 1920, the unit was reorganized as 10th Brigade, Canadian Field Artillery, having as sub-units 77th Field Battery in Moose Jaw, and 18th Field Battery in Regina. Batteries from other cities in the province were added over the next two decades. During **WORLD WAR II**, 10th Field Brigade was broken up and its batteries utilized in different areas. 18th Battery was sent to England, where it retrained as an anti-tank battery, joining the Canadian Anti-Tank Regiment in the 2nd Canadian Division in 1940; from 1942 to 1945, 18th Battery became part of the 2nd Anti-Tank Regiment which was part of the 5th Division. 77th Battery was mobilized with 3rd Field Regiment; 113th Battery (Regina) was mobilized with 4th Field Regiment; and 60th Battery (Aneroid) joined with

76th Battery (Indian Head) to form part of 17th Field Regiment.

Following the war, the batteries returned home and were reorganized into the 10th Medium Regiment, RCA. When 113rd Battery disbanded in 1956, 10th Medium Regiment comprised 18th Battery (Regina), 21st Battery (Saskatoon), and 44th Battery (Prince Albert). In the reorganization of the militia in 1961, the Regiment again converted to a Field Regiment, consisting of 18th Battery (Regina), 65th Battery (Grenfell), and a revived 76th Battery in Indian Head. Yorkton's 64th Battery, formerly part of the 53rd Field Regiment, joined 10th Field Regiment in 1968, after 53rd Field Regiment and its batteries in Melville, Kamsack and Canora were disbanded. About the same time, 22nd Field Regiment, along No. 1 Hwy, was reduced to nil strength, and some of its batteries in Indian Head, Grenfell and Broadview were transferred to 10th Field Regiment. The current 10th Field Artillery Regiment consists of a regimental headquarters, as well as 18th Battery in Regina and 64th Battery in Yorkton. The unit also maintains a training affiliation with 26th Field Regiment in Manitoba and with 116th Independent Field Battery in Kenora, Ontario.

John Chaput

FURTHER READING: Nicholson, G.W.L. 1972. *The Gunners of Canada: The History of the Royal Regiment of Canadian Artillery.* Toronto: McClelland and Stewart.

TERRITORIAL ASSEMBLY. In 1905, Saskatchewan and Alberta were recognized as separate provinces under the Dominion of Canada. Full provincial status for Saskatchewan came about after a lengthy stretch of political wrangling over a geographic region known as the North-West Territories. When the Canadian government purchased Rupert's Land and the North-West Territories from the Hudson's Bay Company in 1870 (*see* **RUPERT'S LAND PURCHASE**), the Territories consisted of the District of Keewatin, which was north and east of Manitoba, and later to be divided into Assiniboine, Saskatchewan, Alberta, and Athabasca. The area was marked for settlement, and the population began to expand as homesteaders moved into the region.

The federal government appointed a provisional government in 1869, with a **LIEUTENANT-GOVERNOR** and Council who settled in Winnipeg. After the **NORTH-WEST TERRITORIES ACT** passed in 1875, the appointed Council governed from the territorial capitals: first from Battleford, and then from Regina. Three stipendiary magistrates were also appointed. The federal government's agenda was to see to it that the prairie regions were developed according to national interests and needs. Electoral districts were defined on the basis of a population of 1,000 adults in an area not exceeding 1,000 square

SASKATCHEWAN ARCHIVES BOARD R-B490

North-West Council in session, 1884. At the head of the table is Lieutenant-Governor Dewdney.

miles. If these conditions were met, municipal organizations could then tax the inhabitants. Schools districts grew from the tax base, with religious minorities setting up separate school systems.

In 1888, an amendment to the Act allowed for an elected Territorial Assembly consisting of twenty-five members. Four members were appointed to oversee matters of finance, with jurisdiction held by the new governor, **JOSEPH ROYAL**. **F.W.G. HAULTAIN**, one of the four appointees, was later to lead the Territories into becoming provinces; he found himself in opposition to government agents like Minister of the Interior **EDGAR DEWDNEY**, who opposed the Assembly's demands for autonomy. Although the Territorial Assembly had some power, the Territories remained under the control of the federal government. Ottawa negotiated Indian treaties, controlled all lands and resources, and controlled all expenditures through a grant system. Although the Territories were now equally represented, the amendment did not allow for an executive body that might negotiate on their behalf with the federal government. The Territorial Assembly counseled the federal government to implement the amendment of 1891; with this amendment, the Assembly would be able to use the French language during its proceedings, have say over property law, determine electoral boundaries, and control the use of intoxicants in the Territories. The Lieutenant-Governor, for the first time, could now appropriate funding from Parliament on the advice of the Territorial Assembly. The Assembly felt that this latest amendment was a huge step towards autonomy.

Western farmers constantly petitioned the federal government to address high tariffs, rising freight rates, and meager grants that did not meet the needs for better roads, schools, bridges, and other infrastructure. The districts were divided between the reformers who wanted local control and the loy-

alists who wanted to remain under federal jurisdiction. In 1897, the Territorial Assembly was granted "responsible government" with another amendment to the North-West Territories Act. F.W.G. Haultain, who was asked to remain with the new government, let the federal government know that local taxation would not solve their fiscal woes: he felt that the immigrants needed for the region would go elsewhere if the taxation system was too demanding. The Territorial Assembly lobbied the federal government for the same subsidies the provinces were receiving.

On May 2, 1900, the Territorial Assembly formally approached the federal government to ask for provincial status. Meanwhile, the geographic boundaries between the Territories and Manitoba were changing. Premier Roblin of Manitoba and Premier Haultain of the Territories offered inducements for settlers to remain in each area; promises of railroad and debt-free farming were made to entice settlement. There were also arguments about separate schools for Catholic students, which became an issue within the argument for autonomy. While Manitoba had been granted a separate school system in 1870, the provision was disallowed in 1890. The Territories, however, still retained the dual separate/public system granted to them under the North-West Territories Act of 1875. The sentiment of the day indicated that support for a dual school system was situated in the Territories, while Manitoba was against public taxes supporting a religious agenda. Wilfrid Laurier was himself a Catholic, and it appeared that Ottawa would be in the middle of a serious rift in western politics. By 1904, Laurier decreed that separate schools must be a guaranteed right in any new provinces. The Territorial Assembly, led by Premier Haultain, continued its fight for autonomy until Saskatchewan and Alberta became provinces in 1905.

Elizabeth Mooney

FURTHER READING: Thomas, L.H. 1970. "The North-West Territories, 1870–1905," *Canadian Historical Association Booklets* 26: 10–17.

TERRY, GEORGE (1923–). Saskatchewan's most decorated Aboriginal war veteran, George Terry has dedicated much of his life to the service of his country and community. Born on May 30, 1923, he served in **WORLD WAR II** and the **KOREAN WAR** as a medic, supply officer, and parachutist. After retiring from the Canadian Armed Forces, Terry volunteered with Senior Citizens Action Now in Moose Jaw, the Moose Jaw Aboriginal Association, the Moose Jaw Royal Canadian Legion, and the Moose Jaw City Council Race Relations Committee. He also spends his time as a counsellor with various organizations. In addition to the Order of Canada, Terry has received thirteen armed forces medals.

RON VOLDEN PHOTO/COURTESY OF THERESE LEFEBVRE PRINCE
Texas gate, south of Fort Walsh.

TEXAS GATE. A "Texas Gate" refers to a grid which prevents cattle and horses from entry while allowing the driver of a vehicle to pass through without having to open gates. The term is not to be found in many dictionaries or encyclopedias; it appears to have originated with the northern migration of cattle—the great cattle drives from Texas in the late 1870s—and is in common usage in the northern American western states and the Canadian west. In Texas, these gates are called "cattle guards." In the SARM 1997 Resolution No. 15, both terms are used and "Texas" is spelled with a lower case "t": "Whereas, many individuals and oil companies install cattle guards, commonly known as texas gates, on road allowances without approval from council." *Therese Lefebvre Prince*

THATCHER, COLIN (1938–). Colin Thatcher was born in Toronto, Ontario on August 25, 1938. The only son of Saskatchewan Liberal premier **ROSS THATCHER**, Colin was a rancher and politician, and the only former government Minister to be convicted of murder. On August 12, 1962, Thatcher married JoAnn Geiger; they were divorced in 1980; in the settlement JoAnn was awarded nearly $1 million, and the two engaged in a custody battle over the

youngest child. In the meantime, Thatcher had entered politics in 1975 as Liberal MLA for Thunder Creek. In 1977 he joined the Conservative Party, and in 1982 became Minister of Energy and Mines. Disputes between Premier **GRANT DEVINE** and Thatcher resulted in the latter's resignation on January 17, 1983. On January 21, 1983, JoAnn's body was found in the garage of her Regina home. In November 1984, Thatcher was convicted of first-degree murder and sentenced to life in prison with no chance of parole for 25 years. He served his sentence at an Edmonton maximum security prison until 1998, when he moved to the Ferndale minimum-security facility near Mission, BC. He is scheduled to be released in May 2009. *Daria Coneghan*

THATCHER, WILBERT ROSS (1917–71). Ross Thatcher was born on May 24, 1917, in Neville. Thatcher's father, Wilbert, went into the hardware business in the Moose Jaw area during the 1920s. He was successful and his chain of stores expanded even during the depth of the **DEPRESSION**. While attending school Ross Thatcher helped in his father's stores and established his business skills. Thatcher graduated from high school at the age of 15. He attended Queen's University, graduating with a Bachelor of Commerce at the age of 18. Thatcher landed a job as the executive assistant to the vice-president of Canadian Packers in Toronto. By the late 1930s his father called him home to work in the family business. Thatcher's father fell ill and the running of the businesses fell on Ross.

He was attracted to the CCF's activism and its interest in economic development. Thatcher believed that private business was not spurring the type of economic development that Saskatchewan needed, so the government had to step in. In 1942, he was elected to Moose Jaw city council on a labour-reformist slate and served a two-year term. Thatcher won the federal riding of Moose Jaw for the CCF in 1945.

Thatcher was not a natural fit with the CCF. As an MP, Thatcher was clearly on the right wing of the CCF caucus. His interest in business and the importance of the profit motive were so dominant that his relationship with the party was uncomfortable. In 1955 he broke from the CCF over its policy on corporate tax rates. After initially sitting as an independent, Thatcher contested the 1957 election campaign as a Liberal in the riding of Assiniboia. During the campaign Thatcher attacked the Saskatchewan CCF's record in creating **CROWN CORPORATIONS**. The attack upset Premier **T.C. DOUGLAS**, who challenged Thatcher to a debate. Thatcher accepted, and the debate took place in May 1957 in Mossbank and was broadcast across Saskatchewan. The debate itself was largely regarded as a draw; however, the mere fact that Thatcher stood toe-to-toe with Douglas was a victory. It gave Liberals a

hope that they had found someone who could finally challenge Douglas.

Thatcher lost to CCF candidate **HAZEN ARGUE** in the 1957 election and again in 1958, but he was viewed as the possible saviour of the Saskatchewan **LIBERAL PARTY**. After leader **HAMMY MCDONALD** was forced out of his position in the summer of 1959, Thatcher contested the party leadership and won on the first ballot. Thatcher brought to the party the zeal of a convert in attacking his former party. Thatcher led the party into the 1960 election where he fought Douglas over the issue of **MEDICARE**. Although he increased support for his party, he failed to defeat the CCF.

The Liberals were gaining momentum, and the opposition and protest against medicare helped to solidify anti-CCF opposition. Thatcher also worked to incorporate many Conservatives and Socreds into his party in order to defeat the CCF. The Liberals won three by-elections from the CCF during the term. In 1964, Thatcher's work paid off as he defeated the CCF for the first time in twenty years.

Thatcher believed that government needed to control spending by reducing what he saw as waste and inefficiency. He reduced taxes and sold several of Saskatchewan's Crown corporations. He further set out to promote that Saskatchewan was "open for business" to outside investors who, he believed, had been scared away by twenty years of socialism. He attracted investment that resulted in the rapid expansion of the potash industry and provided subsidies for the development of pulp mills in the north.

Thatcher's relationship with the federal Liberals was a stormy one. He demanded complete control over the party in Saskatchewan and resented both Pearson's and Trudeau's attempts to establish a separate federal organization in the province. Further exacerbating the difficulties were disagreements over federal agriculture policy, which upset many

SASKATCHEWAN ARCHIVES BOARD R-A8359
Ross Thatcher.

farmers and hurt provincial Liberal fortunes.

Thatcher was re-elected in 1967, but shortly afterward his government began an unannounced austerity program that caught even senior Ministers off guard. In the 1968 budget, Thatcher cut government programs, raised taxes, and introduced widely unpopular utilization fees on medical procedures. The cuts were accompanied by a downturn in the agricultural and potash industries. Thatcher became increasingly combative with friends and foes alike. His government became isolated and increasingly vulnerable and was defeated by **ALLAN BLAKENEY** and the NDP in 1971.

On July 22, 1971, three weeks after the election, Thatcher died of a heart attack at his Regina home.

Brett Quiring

FURTHER READING: Eisler, Dale. 1987. *Rumours of Glory*. Edmonton: Hurtig Publishers; Smith, David. 1975. *Prairie Liberalism: The Liberal Party in Saskatchewan 1905–1971*. Toronto: University of Toronto Press.

THAUBERGER, DAVID (1948–). David Thauberger is renowned for his paintings of the vernacular architecture and cultural icons of Saskatchewan. Together with his paintings of popular culture and postcard images of tourist meccas far and wide, his images of Saskatchewan are clever debates involving art, culture, and how we view our world, presenting a hyper-real picture of our context that transcends regionalism while capturing the heart of what it means to be from Saskatchewan. His trademark geometric shapes, bright colours, flat surfaces and "special effects" contribute to paintings that are ironic and humourous, but also genuine and heartfelt. Thauberger experiments with the surfaces of his paintings, blending application techniques such as toothbrush "spatter" with flocking, glitter, rhinestones, and nails to create works that nevertheless present a unified if highly tactile surface.

David Thauberger was born in Holdfast. He studied ceramics at the **UNIVERSITY OF SASKATCHEWAN**, Regina Campus, where "funk" artist David Gilhooly served as an early mentor, inspiring Thauberger and others to create art that was rooted in their own geographical region. He earned his BFA in 1971 and his MA in 1972 from California State University (Sacramento). He then studied with Rudy Autio at the University of Montana in Missoula, earning his MFA in 1973. In his ceramic work, Thauberger created complex and quirky tableaux that made use of a wide range of non-traditional materials—enamels, acrylics, crayons and wax—to create surface effects.

Back in Regina, he became increasingly engaged with surface effects and the formal aspects of flatness and frontality that painting offered and, with no formal training in the medium, turned to painting around 1974. Thauberger worked as a con-

David Thauberger, "Dream Home (Ethnic Version)," 1980, acrylic on canvas, 115 x 172.7 cm, MacKenzie Art Gallery, University of Regina Collection, gift of Mr. Douglas Rawlinson.

sultant for the **SASKATCHEWAN ARTS BOARD** (1974–78, 1983–85) where he became aware of the work of many so-called "folk" artists in the province. At first, the work of **WILLIAM MCCARGAR**—followed by Wesley Dennis, Harvey McInnes, **MOLLY LENHARDT**, Sam Spencer and **JAN WYERS**—repulsed him, but he soon came to value their grassroots approach to making art and dealing with the prairies. He researched, purchased, and championed their work, curating exhibitions and contributing to documentaries, and in return learned important lessons about making art within a specific place. Having been included in a number of significant ceramic exhibitions in the early and mid-1970s, Thauberger began showing his paintings, most notably in *David Thauberger: Prairie Pictures* (Dunlop Art Gallery, 1979) and is the only painter included in the prestigious *Pluralities 1980* (National Gallery of Canada, 1980). Since then, his work has been seen in numerous public exhibitions throughout Canada, has received national commercial success, and is included in collections across North America. Thauberger is a member of the Royal Canadian Academy of the Arts, and is the recipient of many awards and grants. He has been a visiting artist across the country and has served on the board of the Canada Council for the Arts. *Christine Sowiak*

FURTHER READING: 1988. *David Thauberger: Paintings 1978–1988*. Regina: MacKenzie Art Gallery; 1989. *Saskatoon Imagined: Art and Architecture in the Wonder City*. Saskatoon: Mendel Art Gallery; Tousley, Nancy. 1981. "David Thauberger: Paintings, Drawings and Prints." *Parachute* 22 (Spring).

THAUBERGER, JOSEPH (1909–98). Joseph Thauberger was born August 26, 1909 in Bessarabia (now Moldova) and came to Saskatchewan at the age of 2. He farmed at Vibank, where he joined the provincial **SOCIAL CREDIT PARTY** in 1935. He ran in the 1938 provincial election in the Qu'Appelle–Wolseley constituency. Despite coming in third in that election and the next four elections in Humboldt constituency, Thauberger's conviction in his beliefs was not diminished. He was elected the first president of the Social Credit Party in 1949 and acclaimed as the president of the Social Credit League in 1952. These positions gave Thauberger a political platform for speaking out against the control of the economy by the government and the banks. After 1956 Thauberger did not run in any more provincial elections, but continued to teach Social Credit policy. He was elected president of the Catholic section of the Saskatchewan School Trustees Association for 1964–65. In 1972 he wrote a book that explained his economic ideas in layman's terms. During the 1980s Thauberger parted ways with the Social Credit Party, believing that it had become too radical. He founded the Canada Party, a federal party that embodied many of the same ideals as Social Credit at the height of its popularity. Thauberger ran in the 1993 federal election as its leader at the age of 84. He announced his retirement from politics following the election. Thauberger died in Regina on April 21, 1998.

Stephane Bonneville

FURTHER READING: Thauberger, J.A. 1972. *Will Inflation Ruin Us?* Regina: New World Publishing Co.

THE KEY FIRST NATION. Followers of Chief Owtah-pee-ka-kaw ("He Who Unlocks" or "The Key") were residing along the Shoal River in southwestern Manitoba in the mid-1800s. The band included

Saulteaux, Saulteaux-Cree, and Saulteaux-Orkney individuals when The Key signed adhesion to **TREATY 4** September 24, 1875, and was told his people would be relocated further west. A reserve was surveyed 145 km northeast of Fort Pelly in 1878; but when the agent visited it in 1880 the land was badly flooded, and he relocated the band nearer to Fort Pelly. From their part in the fur trade, most adult male members were experienced carpenters, blacksmiths, boat builders, and salt or lime makers—the solidity of their houses and shelters attested to this. Their initial years of re-establishment were hard, but improved through their agricultural endeavours. In 1905 and 1909, portions of their land were lost through surrenders, curbing further agricultural expansion. In 1954 Gwen O'Soup was elected chief—the first Aboriginal woman in Canada to hold this position. In 2004, 289 of the 1,030 band members lived on their 6,404.8-ha reserve, located 15 km south of Norquay.

Christian Thompson

THEATRE. Although there were itinerant entertainers such as singers or magicians in the North-West before the 1880s, serious theatre production coincides with the advent of the railways and the immigrants they brought to provide eager audiences. After the CPR established Regina in 1883, its first theatre was on the second floor of the town hall (over the jail), built in 1886. Despite its increasing inadequacy, this served for local and touring productions of melodrama, vaudeville and even operetta until replaced by the fine "electrical" Regina Theatre in 1910. This pattern was repeated in Saskatoon a little later, where the Empire Theatre became the principal house. Both housed the frequent tours of British rep and American stock companies, the San Carlo or Beecham Opera companies, vaudeville, and local productions. Visitors included such names as Sarah Bernhardt, Mrs. Patrick Campbell, Ethel Barrymore, and the Marx Brothers—all touring "the breadbasket circuit." Costs reduced large-scaling touring, but smaller companies from Winnipeg, Calgary and Moose Jaw helped fill the void and visited smaller centres, which often had an "Opera House." Another important source of drama and education, especially in rural Saskatchewan, was **CHAUTAUQUA**, which flourished between the wars.

With the decline of touring, however, local community theatre began to increase. In Regina, the Operatic Society operated from 1910 to 1950, and the Community Players, formed in 1924, led to the formation of **REGINA LITTLE THEATRE** in 1926. This group continues as the oldest continuously producing amateur company in Canada. Saskatoon Little Theatre existed from 1922 to1949, and was succeeded by Saskatoon Community Players (1952–59) and eventually **SASKATOON GATEWAY PLAYERS** (1965–), spearheaded by Emrys Jones and Tom Kerr of the **UNIVERSITY OF SASKATCHEWAN**. Promoted by the

COURTESY OF BIGGAR MUSEUM AND GALLERY

Performance at the Majestic Theatre in Biggar, Saskatchewan, 1919. The theatre opened in 1911.

Saskatchewan Drama League (formed in 1933) and later by the **SASKATCHEWAN ARTS BOARD** and the Department of Education, community and school theatre survived the **DEPRESSION** and war years, even in some quite small places, and increasingly flourished in the second half of the century, encouraged by dedicated people such as **MARY ELLEN BURGESS**, **HILDA ALLEN**, **CAL ABRAHAMSON**, Kay Nouch and her husband, **FLORENCE JAMES**, **ROBERT HINITT**, Margaret and Harold Woodward, Donna and Roy Challis, Betty and Keith Woods, and many others. At present, **THEATRE SASKATCHEWAN** has some eighty-six affiliated groups, many in small towns and villages all over the province.

Many similar groups, dedicated to various forms of theatre, have been established over the years: the Saskatchewan Drama Association (1978–) to promote child and youth drama; Regina Lyric Light Opera; Regina Summer Stage (founded by Sylvia Oancia); Saskatoon Summer Players; and Prairie Opera, among the most notable. Earlier, university drama club productions provided opportunities for students at the University of Saskatchewan and Regina College during the 1930s and early 1940s, but the universities were to become even more important later. Not only did the senior university nourish the fledgling Saskatchewan Drama League in the 1930s and 1940s, but it was the first Canadian university to establish a drama department, led by Emrys Jones from 1946. His teaching there, at the Banff School and elsewhere, enormously influenced all aspects of theatre in the province, as did the efforts of colleagues Walter Mills, Tom Kerr, and Henry Woolf. Establishment of a drama (later theatre) department at the University of Saskatchewan, Regina Campus in the 1960s did much the same, especially under the leadership of Eric Salmon (who started a short-lived professional company, which encouraged the Kramers to pursue that goal) and such influential teachers as Gabriel Prendergast.

Finally, the province was prepared and anxious for permanent professional theatre in its principal cities. Starting with a touring school company, Sue and Ken Kramer founded the **GLOBE THEATRE** in 1966, and began adult productions of challenging repertoire in 1969. These were also performed in Saskatoon for several years. A permanent theatre in 1981 gave the Globe the home base and stability it needed, and touring eventually ceased. Saskatoon's two professional theatre companies developed later. **25TH STREET THEATRE**, under the aegis of Andras Tahn from 1972, produced such memorable Canadian dramas as *Paper Wheat* before it eventually disbanded; but **PERSEPHONE THEATRE** (1974–) has managed more longevity under the direction of Tibor Feheregyhazi. A more recent success has been the annual **SHAKESPEARE ON THE SASKATCHEWAN** summer productions of the Bard's works in accessible form.

Richard Harvey

THEATRE SASKATCHEWAN. In the early 1930s an amateur theatre festival for groups in the province was established; at the 1933 competition, participants formed the Saskatchewan Drama League to "promote a right relationship between drama and the life of the community" through adjudicated festivals and other services, in alliance with the national Dominion Drama Festival (DDF). Annual regional competitions of the DDF consisted of several categories, including one for adult groups in rural areas. Senior winners were normally invited to a national play-off each year. The League disbanded in 1954, and its functions were transferred to the **SASKATCHEWAN ARTS BOARD**, which continued the yearly festivals. The last cross-Canada competition occurred in 1969, and although many other regional organizations disbanded as a result, Saskatchewan kept the tradition of a regional festival under the title DDF/Theatre Saskatchewan. The name changed to Theatre Saskatchewan in 1982.

After years of voluntary direction, a new era began in 1983 when increased funding, largely from lotteries, made a part-time office and executive director possible; these became full-time in 1986. Services were also improved: grants for equipment, a much-expanded lending library, more local and international festivals, new-play and other workshops, apprenticeships, and formation of the Margaret Woodward Hall of Fame to recognize significant contributions to theatre in the province. As a result, and despite fluctuations over the years, the organization presently includes eighty-six active community clubs and over 4,500 members, who entertain tens of thousands of theatre-goers in every part of the province. *Richard Harvey*

ROY ANTAL/REGINA LEADER-POST

Gordon Thiessen addressing the Regina Chamber of Commerce, September 1999.

THIESSEN, GORDON (1938–). Gordon Thiessen was born in 1938 in Ontario, but grew up in several small towns across Saskatchewan. Studying economics at the UNIVERSITY OF SASKATCHEWAN, he completed his BA in 1960 and MA in 1961, and took his PhD from the London School of Economics in 1972. Thiessen began working for the Bank of Canada in 1963 in research and analysis. From 1973 to 1975 he served as visiting economist at the Reserve Bank of Australia. Returning to the Bank of Canada, he was appointed Advisor to the Governor in 1979, Deputy Governor in 1984, Senior Deputy Governor in 1987, and finally Governor for a seven-year period between 1994 and 2001. His leadership was marked by transparency and accountability, as he presided over an era of economic boom, setting bank rates and promoting anti-inflation while distancing Canadian monetary policy from American practices. As a result, the Canadian dollar weakened against the world market, which drew criticism from business leaders. Since his resignation in 2001, Thiessen has been awarded the Order of Canada. He is a member of the University of Saskatchewan Board of Governors, the founding chair of the Canadian Public Accountability Board, a member of the Institute for Public Policy, and a director of both IPSCO and Manulife Financial. *Merle Massie*

38 Canadian Brigade Group

COURTESY OF GERRY CARLINE

38 CANADIAN BRIGADE GROUP. One of three reserve army brigade groups within Land Force Western Area, 38 Canadian Brigade Group (38 CBG) was created on April 1, 1997. Headquartered in Winnipeg, the brigade consists of thirteen army reserve units and geographically extends from Thunder Bay, Ontario to Saskatchewan. Citizen soldiers from 38 CBG have served in domestic operations such as the 1997 Manitoba floods, 2002 G7 Summit, and 2003 British Columbia forest fire emergency. Members have also served in international peacekeeping missions in Bosnia-Herzegovina, Congo, and Southwest Asia. The 38 CBG includes five Saskatchewan-based units: Saskatchewan Dragoons, North Saskatchewan Regiment, Royal Regina Rifles, 16th (Saskatchewan) Service Battalion, and 16th Medical Company. *Holden Stoffel*

THODE, HENRY GEORGE (1910–97). Born in Dundurn, Saskatchewan on September 10, 1910, Thode studied at the UNIVERSITY OF SASKATCHEWAN for his BSc and received his PhD in Physics from the University of Chicago in 1934. He joined the faculty at McMaster University, where during his term as vice-president (1957–61) he built Canada's first research nuclear reactor. He served as president of the university from 1961 to 1972. The building of

UNIVERSITY OF REGINA ARCHIVES AND SPECIAL COLLECTIONS
84-11-426

Henry Thode.

the reactor at McMaster gave an impetus to the development of research and graduate student training, not only at that university but throughout the Canadian university system. As a scientist Thode worked on the structure and isotopic abundance in terrestrial and meteoric materials. Following the lunar landings, he obtained rocks from the moon and studied their composition and theorized on the age and composition of the moon.

He served as president of the Royal Society of Canada, was a member of the Royal Society of London, and was the first scientist to be made a Companion of the Order of Canada. Thode died on March 22, 1997. *Diane Secoy*

THOMAS, LEWIS H. (1917–83). Born on April 13, 1917, prairie history expert Lewis H. Thomas was noted for his contributions to research, writing, and teaching in both Saskatchewan and Alberta. He was Provincial Archivist of Saskatchewan, Associate Professor of History at the University of Regina, and Professor of History at the University of Alberta. Awards recognizing his work include an honorary doctorate of laws from the University of Saskatchewan (1972), the American Association for State and Local History's Award of Merit, and life membership in the Canadian Historical Association. On October 5, 1983, Thomas was invested as a Member of the Order of Canada. He died on November 22, 1983.

THOMPSON COMMITTEE (1960–62). The Advisory Planning Committee on Medical Care consisted of twelve members: its Chair, Dr. W.P. THOMPSON, recently retired as president of the UNIVERSITY OF SASKATCHEWAN; BEATRICE TREW and Cliff Whiting (representing the people of the province); Drs. J.F.C. Anderson, E.W. BAROOTES, and C.J. HOUSTON (COLLEGE OF PHYSICIANS AND SURGEONS OF SASKATCHEWAN); Dr. I.M. Hilliard (College of Medicine); Donald McPherson (Saskatchewan Chamber of Commerce); W.E. SMISHEK (SASKATCHEWAN FEDERATION OF LABOUR); and Dr. V.L. MATTHEWS, former Health Minister T.J. Bentley, and Deputy Minister of Public Health Dr. F.B. Roth (the last three representing the government of Saskatchewan). John E. Sparks served as the non-voting secretary. Six of the twelve members were medical doctors.

The committee received its instructions on April 26, 1960, and deliberations began on May 9. The committee held 23 meetings for a total of 43 days; it conducted 33 public and 7 private hearings, analysed 50 study documents, and received 1,226 pages of documentation in 49 briefs. Teams of committee members visited health care programs in Australia, New Zealand, Great Britain, Holland, Norway, Sweden and Denmark. The committee was instructed to report to Walter Erb, Minister of Public Health, on "the extent of public need in the various fields of health care as related to a medical care program," following the broadest possible interpretation. They studied in detail the doctor-sponsored plans (GMS and MSI), municipal doctor plans, the plan for public assistance recipients, as well as existing mental health, cancer and tuberculosis programs.

The interim report, issued on September 25, 1961, recommended that health services be developed in a coordinated way, that physicians be paid on a fee-for-service basis, with use of modest "utilization fees" of $1 for a first office visit and $2 for a home visit, and that the program be administered by an independent commission who reported to the Minister of Public Health. Such a plan was estimated to cost close to $20 million per year. Walter Smishek appended a 17-page minority report, in which he argued the case for a system with salaried physicians and for making the Minister of Public Health directly responsible for its administration. The three representatives of the College of Physicians and Surgeons appended a 3.5 page minority report, signed also by Donald McPherson, recommending a less ambitious and less expensive plan which included a selective aid program for those not covered by existing plans, at an estimated cost of $3.6 million per year. They added that mental health services and rehabilitation facilities required attention before an all-inclusive plan was introduced.

Between this interim report and the final report, momentous events took place. The CCF government passed the Saskatchewan Medical Care Insurance Act on November 17, 1961, and four days later appointed WILLIAM GWYNNE DAVIES, former executive-secretary of the Saskatchewan Federation of Labour, as Minister of Public Health. This appointment, from the doctors' viewpoint, was the equivalent of raising a red flag in front of a bull. The health plan was slated to begin on April 1, then was postponed to July 1. The doctors began the "23-day doctor's strike," which they termed a work stoppage, on July 1. Lord Stephen Taylor persuaded both sides to moderate their positions, and the Saskatoon Agreement was signed on July 23; this agreement was adopted into law at a special session of the Legislature on August 2. Meanwhile the department operated with Dr. Vince Matthews as acting Deputy Minister from June 30, 1962 to September 1, 1963–at which time J.G. Clarkson was appointed Deputy Minister. One week later, ALLAN BLAKENEY, a man whose integrity was recognized by most doctors, took over the ministry. It was an anti-climax when the final report of the Thompson Committee was submitted on September 26, 1962: it added useful data and details, but was now, after the fact, an interesting document for historians to ponder.

C. Stuart Houston

THOMPSON, DAVID (1770–1857). David Thompson was one of North America's greatest

explorers and mapmakers. His expertise reached from Lake Superior west to the Pacific Ocean, and from LAKE ATHABASCA south to the Missouri. Several years after joining the Hudson's Bay Company (HBC) at age14, he was sent inland to posts on the Saskatchewan River. In 1787–88, he wintered with the Peigan in southern Alberta, where Saukamappee, an adopted CREE, taught him the history of the northern plains: tribal battles, the first horses, the introduction of guns, and the devastating 1781–82 smallpox epidemic. In 1789, while recuperating from a broken leg at Cumberland House, both he and PETER FIDLER were taught mapping skills by Philip Turnor. Over the years both men separately surveyed almost identical river systems. Suddenly, while at REINDEER LAKE in 1797, Thompson left the HBC to join the North West Company. Much of his fifteen-year career with the NWC was spent outside of Saskatchewan, mostly in the far west where he explored routes through the Rockies and to the Pacific. After retiring to the east in 1812, Thompson drew his famous map of the North-West. He also formally married his MÉTIS wife, Charlotte Small, whom he had met in 1799 at Ile-à-la-Crosse. By 1840, through poor business ventures, Thompson was reduced to poverty. Infirm and growing blind, he tried unsuccessfully to earn money from writing an account of the west. In 1916, the sprawling manuscript was edited for publication. His complete manuscript, a final 1843 map, and almost all his many field books remain unpublished. *Dale Russell*

FURTHER READING: Thompson, D. 1962. *David Thompson's Narrative, 1784–1812*. Toronto: Champlain Society.

THOMPSON, DOUGLAS (1913–2003). Born on March 10, 1913, Douglas Thompson was active in many aspects of rural life. He served as a board member with the Saskatchewan Municipal Hail Association for thirty-one years, and was the organization's president from 1964 to 1993. He was also involved with the Assiniboia Agricultural Society and the 4-H CLUB, for which he received medals from Queen Elizabeth. In addition to maintaining his own farm near Vantage, Saskatchewan, he spent time volunteering with youth and the elderly in his community. Thompson was named an honorary life member of the Saskatchewan Agricultural Societies Association in 1976 and was invested as a Member of the Order of Canada in 1994. He died on August 15, 2003.

THOMPSON, WALTER PALMER (1889–1970). Born on April 3, 1889, a biologist, professor, and administrator, Walter Palmer Thompson was known for his contributions to science and scholarship at the UNIVERSITY OF SASKATCHEWAN. Educated at Harvard University, Thompson's field of research

involved plant genetics. His expertise led to appointments as Professor and Head of the Department of Biology, Dean of Arts and Science, and President Emeritus of the University of Saskatchewan. The University's W.P. Thompson Biology Building is named in his honour. Thompson received numerous awards including the Flavelle Medal presented by the Royal Society of Canada in 1950 and was invested as a Companion of the Order of Canada in 1968. He died on March 30, 1970.

THOMSON, WATSON (1910–69). Watson Thomson's appointment as Saskatchewan's director of Adult Education by Premier T.C. DOUGLAS on June 15, 1944, was the zenith of his career. Here was Thomson's chance to implement a province-wide program of community-based learning according to his communitarian socialist commitments. His mandate was to develop the "biggest adult education program in the country."

Born in Glasgow, Scotland, in 1910, Thomson came to Saskatchewan following experience as an adult educator in Alberta and Manitoba. He was co-founder of the Prairie School for Social Advance (PSSA) for which Douglas promised support. In his first radio address entitled "Power to the People," delivered just six weeks after he arrived in Saskatchewan, Thomson had this to say: "The knowledge we want to convey is not knowledge for its own sake but for the sake of changing and recreating our human world nearer to the heart's desire of ordinary, decent people everywhere."

The new director moved quickly to put his action-oriented community-based adult education program into effect throughout Saskatchewan. His pedagogical emphasis was "not [on] study alone, but [on] study that leads to action." Against "solitary education for private ends," Thomson advocated "public education for social ends, for building, co-operatively, a new and more truly *human* society."

Thomson's agenda to organize adult education for social change by creating study-action groups in every rural community and town was well under way when he was dismissed in January 1946. False allegations had spread within the CCF and elsewhere that Thomson was affiliated with the Communist Party. He became politically suspect in an era when "red-baiting" was gaining momentum. He would go on to become a professor at the University of British Columbia.

Thomson died in Vancouver on November 25, 1969. His Saskatchewan legacy of learning in community remains a touchstone for opponents of tendencies to commercialize education as a private rather than public good. *Michael Collins*

THRASHERS. Thrashers or mimids (family Mimidae) are solitary medium-sized, long-tailed songbirds that forage mainly on the ground, using

J. PEPPER PHOTO/© SASKATCHEWAN ENVIRONMENT/SKCDC, 2001. ECOSYSTEM IMAGE INFORMATION SYSTEM

Brown thrasher *(Toxostoma rufum)*.

their long sturdy bills to toss leaves and twigs in their search for food. They eat insects, fruits and grains. Most species run on the ground instead of flying in order to escape from predators. They nest in bulky stick cups in shrubs. Their flight is low and rapid. The name *mimid* or *mimic thrush* is based on the ability of many species to imitate sounds, particularly bird songs, in their environment.

There are thirty-four mimid species globally; eleven of those occur in North America. Four have been recorded in Saskatchewan. Brown thrashers (*Toxostoma rufum*) are reddish-brown overall, and buffy-coloured and heavily streaked underneath; they have long decurved bills, and are long-tailed. This is the most commonly encountered species. They breed in thick tangled riparian and aspen thickets in southern Saskatchewan, and in cleared areas of the southern boreal forest. The gray catbird (*Dumetella carolinensis*) is found in similar habitats as the brown thrasher, but is less frequent in shelterbelts. Gray catbirds are slaty-gray overall, with rufus undertail coverts, a black cap, and a long black tail. The other two species are more rarely encountered. The northern mockingbird (*Mimus polyglottus*) is an irregular breeder in thickets in southern Saskatchewan. It has long legs, and conspicuous white patches on broad black wings. As its name suggests, the northern mockingbird imitates the sounds of dozens of birds, insects, other animals, and machinery. Sage thrashers (*Oreoscoptes montanus*) are erratic breeders limited to sagebrush flats in the extreme southwest. The sage thrasher is brownish gray overall; its whitish underparts have heavy brownish streaks; and is smaller and longer-winged (with crisp white wingbars) than other thrashers.

Robert Warnock

FURTHER READING: Alsop, Fred J., III. 2002. *Birds of Canada*. New York: Dorling Kindersley.

THRUSHES AND BLUEBIRDS. The thrushes are a family of small to medium-sized songbirds with unspecialized bills which walk or hop when feeding on the ground. They are classified either in

the Family Turdidae, with about 330 species worldwide, or merged with the Old World flycatchers in the Family Muscicapidae, with about 450 species. Their plumage tends to be browns, although some, such as the bluebirds, have blues or rusty reds in their plumage. The males are more brightly coloured than the females and the young have spotted breasts. They are birds of wooded areas, particularly along the edges. Many have complex songs and are part of the "dawn chorus." Saskatchewan has ten of the twenty-eight species which occur in North America. They are all migratory.

The most familiar member of the family is the American Robin (*Turdus migratorius*) which breeds throughout the province. This chestnut-red breasted bird has benefited from settlement and the planting of deciduous trees in either the grasslands or the boreal forest regions. Four members of the genus *Catharus* are regularly found in the province. The cinnamon-brown Veery (*C. fuscescens*), with its deep flutelike call, is a fairly common breeding bird in the aspen parklands and wooded areas of the grasslands settlements. Swainson's Thrush (*C. ustulatus*) breeds in the aspen parklands and into the boreal regions; it is a common transient further south. The very similar Gray-cheeked Thrush (*C. minimus*) is a less common transient in the south and a rare summer resident in the boreal region; its main breeding grounds are further north. The Hermit Thrush (*C. guttatus*), another small brown thrush with light breast spotting is most recognized by the male's distinctive territorial song. It is a fairly common breeding bird in the boreal region and an uncommon transient further south. The Wood Thrush (*Hylocichla mustelina*), with bright brown spots on the white chest and belly, is a rare transient species from its breeding grounds in the eastern forest region.

Two hole-nesting bluebirds (genus *Sialia*) occur in the province. The Eastern Bluebird (*S. sialis*), with its blue head and back and chestnut belly, breeds in the eastern parklands region. Once more widely spread, it declined after the aggressive hole-nesting European Starling came into the province in the 1940s. The Mountain Bluebird (*S. currucoides*), in which the male is a uniform aqua-

COURTESY OF THE ROYAL SASKATCHEWAN MUSEUM

Male Mountain Bluebird.

marine, nests sporadically throughout the grasslands and into the southern boreal forest. Both species nest in nature in holes in dead trees or snags. The provision of nestboxes for bluebirds is a common sight along many roads in the grasslands as attempts are made to increase these native species. The nest boxes also provide space for Tree Swallows, another species which has suffered from competition from the invading starlings and **HOUSE SPARROWS**.

Two western species are transient. Townsend's Solitaire (*Myadestes townsendi*) is an uncommon winter resident in a few regions of the south, with one breeding record in the **CYPRESS HILLS**. The Varied Thrush (*Ixoreus naevius*) occurs sporadically in the south, usually in the fall.

Lorne Scott and Diane Secoy

FURTHER READING: Alsop, Fred J. III. 2002. *The Birds of Canada*. Toronto: Dorling Kindersley.

THUNDERCHILD FIRST NATION. Chief Peyasiw-awasis' (Thunderchild) headmen signed an adhesion to **TREATY 6** in August 1879 at Sounding Lake, Alberta. A reserve was surveyed for the band, 85 km northwest of North Battleford and adjoining the Moosomin Reserve. The Indian Commissioner initially thought it preferable to settle Thunderchild on the Moosomin reserve, but this arrangement was not satisfactory and Thunderchild's people moved to the reserve already set aside for them. After Chief Moosomin died (in or around 1902), his son (Josie Moosomin) was elected chief by the band on May 3, 1904; his election, however, was not recognized by the Department of Indian Affairs until June 21, 1909, just days after the surrender was secured. As the only federally recognized chief of the Thunderchild and Moosomin Bands, Thunderchild spoke in relation to the surrender of prime land, which had been first sought following complaints about the agricultural success of the bands in the late 1880s, and which continued to grow after the construction of the Canadian Northern Railway through the reserves in 1903 enhanced the land's value and benefited band members by providing work as well as a market for their produce. On October 2, 2003, the Thunderchild First Nation successfully settled a land claim against the 1909 surrender of their reserve land. Currently, 780 of the 2,227 Cree band members live on reserve, with an infrastructure that includes a band office, fire hall, school, teacherages, gymnasium, hall, and resource centre. The band currently holds 11,875.6 ha of reserve land.

Christian Thompson

THUNDERSTORMS. Thunderstorms, while highly variable from year to year, are generally experienced from late April to the end of September in southern Saskatchewan, and from late May to the end of August in the north. During late fall and winter the weather situations conducive to the formation of thunderstorms occur only rarely in the province, and even then only in the south. The core of a thunderstorm is a convection current of relatively warm, moist air ascending rapidly and forming cumulus clouds of great vertical extent. In these clouds, rain drops and ice crystals are often mixed. Electrical gradients are produced between different parts of the cloud dominated by positive and negative charges respectively, and within-cloud lightning strokes result. The earth's surface having a positive charge and the bottom of the cloud being negatively charged, cloud-to-ground lightning strikes ensue.

Rain from thunderstorms is usually short-lived but intense. Occasional thunderstorms give rise to localized flash flooding, as near Parry, Saskatchewan, on June 19, 1999, when 92 mm of rain in four hours washed out the railway line and caused Long Creek to flood for three days through Dunnet Regional Park near Avonlea. Besides lightning and heavy rain, the tall cumulonimbus clouds of well-developed thunderstorms often produce hail and strong gusty winds; the most severe cases very occasionally generate a tornado. Strong wind gusts accompanying the arrival of a thunderstorm are known as downbursts or microbursts, and can do substantial damage. In the Oxbow area on the night of July 29, 1995, downburst winds exceeded 100 km/hr and created havoc, scattering lightly constructed buildings like chaff. *Alec Paul*

TIMLIN, MABEL (1891–1976). Mabel Timlin, a professor of economics at the UNIVERSITY OF SASKATCHEWAN, made major contributions to the fields of economic theory and immigration policy. This Norwegian American was born in Forest Junction, Wisconsin, on December 6, 1891. She taught school in Wisconsin, then in 1916 came to Saskatchewan, teaching in Bounty and Wilkie. In 1918 she moved to Saskatoon, where she attended Business College, and taught night school. During the 1920s and 1930s she studied part time, obtaining degrees in English (BA, 1929) and economics (PhD, University of Washington, 1940).

Her lifelong employment at the University of Saskatchewan began in 1921. She worked as a secretary, part-time reader in economics, and after 1940 as a full-time member of the Department of Economics, from which she retired as Professor Emeritus (1959). She became well known for her work on Keynesian economics, monetary and fiscal controls in Canada, welfare economics, the relations between theory and practice in public policy, and Canada's immigration policy. Timlin was the first woman social scientist to become a Fellow of the Royal Society of Canada (1951) and President of the Canadian Political Science Association (1959-60). She received Canada's Centennial medal (1967), an

Honorary Doctor of Laws degree from the University of Saskatchewan (1969), and the Order of Canada (Member, 1976). *Marianne Gosztonyi Ainley*

FURTHER READING: Ainley, Marianne Gosztonyi. 1999. "Mabel F. Timlin, 1891–1976: A Woman Economist in the World of Men," *Atlantis: A Women's Studies Journal* 23 (2): 28–38; Neill, Robin. 1991. *A History of Canadian Economic Thought.* New York: Routledge.

TINNEY, PHYLLIS (1942–). Born in Bassano, Alberta in 1942, Phyllis Tinney moved to Saskatchewan in 1965, settling near Tompkins. She developed a unique program for teaching swimming to people inhibited by fear, handicap, or disability. Indeed, her greatest achievements were made when instructing disabled swimmers. A tireless volunteer, Tinney served as president of the local branch of the Canadian Red Cross and examiner for the Royal Life Saving Society. She also founded Wheelchair Sports in North Battleford. In 1986, Tinney received the Saskatchewan Order of Merit.

TISDALE, town, pop 3,063, located 40 km E of Melfort on Hwys 3 and 35. People began settling the area around 1902 and before the railway arrived, the locality was known as Doghide after the Doghide River, which flows along the town's east side. With the construction of the Canadian Northern Railway from Hudson Bay to Melfort in 1904 the townsite was named Tisdale in honour of Frederick W. Tisdale, a civil engineer with the railroad. The first wave of settlers largely came from eastern Canada, Great Britain, and the United States. Through the 1920s people from continental Europe came to the area and in the 1930s, people from the dried-out southern plains migrated to the region. Tisdale attained town status on November 1, 1920. The community grew gradually at first, but with the advent of modern machinery the heavy bush in the region was cleared and its agricultural potential came to be realized. Tisdale, already established as the major supply and service centre for a sizable surrounding territory, developed rapidly from the WORLD WAR II era through to the mid-1970s and came to be known as "the Land of Rape and Honey." Today, approximately one-third of the farmland in the region is cropped with canola and the area has long been known for its honey production. The honey industry began to develop significantly in the 1940s. Today, more than 4 million kg of honey– 10% of that produced in Canada–comes from the district. The largest pulse crop processing facility in Canada is also located in the area, as is the largest alfalfa dehydrator in Saskatchewan. When, in the 1970s, the population began to shrink, Tisdale's community leaders were determined not to accept the decline that was so common throughout Saskatchewan's rural communities: a collectivist

spirit enabled the development of creative counter-active and aggressive initiatives. Success bred success and local investment attracted outside capital. Among the initiatives are a city-sized shopping mall that is 100% locally owned; the Tisdale REXplex which houses health care services, educational facilities for all ages, a library, a multi-purpose auditorium, a performing arts theatre, an aquatic centre, a regulation-size arena, a curling rink, a rifle, hand gun, and archery range, several meeting rooms, and a kitchen with the capacity to serve more than 500 meals; the Doghide River Trail system, which is a scenic route for walking, cycling, and cross-country skiing; and five inland grain terminals, which today make Tisdale the largest grain handling centre in Saskatchewan. Tisdale is the hometown of comedian/actor/writer BRENT BUTT, the star of the hit TV series *Corner Gas*. *David McLennan*

TITANIC RUSTICLES. Microbiologist Roy Cullimore used his experience gained as part of the 1996 research team that studied the *Titanic* shipwreck to develop treatment systems for bacteria-contaminated water on the prairies. The former UNIVERSITY OF REGINA professor has applied his practical and theoretical knowledge to help people deal with water contamination through his consulting company, Droycon Bioconcepts Inc. Cullimore's role in the 1996 research project, supported in part by the Discovery Channel, was to determine the nature of the growths that were developing on the bow section of *Titanic*, which sank on April 15, 1912, after being struck by an iceberg. The wreck was discovered in 1985 about 500 km off the coast of Newfoundland, 3.5 km below the surface of the Atlantic Ocean. The Cullimore team called the growths on the *Titanic* "rusticles," and concluded that they were not a single species of a plant or animal but rather a complex of microbial communities living within an iron-rich, calcium-deficient and porous concrete-like home. Rusticles were found to

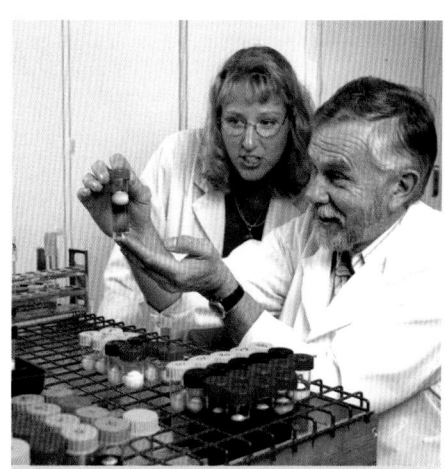

PHOTOGRAPHY DEPARTMENT, UNIVERSITY OF REGINA

Roy Cullimore and assistant at the University of Regina conducting research on the *Titanic*.

937

be extracting iron from the steel of the *Titanic* and then exporting that iron into the oceanic environment as red dust and yellow slimes. Cullimore was subsequently able to "grow" rusticles in a laboratory environment and apply this knowledge to develop patented technology to test for bacteria contaminating prairie water supplies; in partnership with the Prairie Farm Rehabilitation Administration, he has also developed treatment systems for bacteria-contaminated water. *Joe Ralko*

PHOTO COURTESY OF LARISSA LOZOWCHUK

Mary Tkachuk.

TKACHUK, MARY (1912–2003). Mary Tkachuk (*née* Janishewski) was a mentor, businessperson, and leader in the Ukrainian community in Saskatoon, with a special interest in music. Born in Mundare, Alberta on March 6, 1912, she was educated in Edmonton and attended Teachers' College. In 1935 she moved to Saskatoon with her husband, Paul. They established a music store that became known for its extensive stock of music, ethnic handicrafts, literature and, later, videos. She soon became active in the Ukrainian Women's Association of Canada, and in 1936 was a founding member of the Ukrainian Museum of Canada. In 1964 she helped to found the Saskatoon Folk Arts Council, and later became Saskatchewan's director on the National Folk Arts Council. She served as first woman president of the national Ukrainian Self-Reliance League (1990–96). As well, she was committed to encouraging the appreciation of, and participation in, the world of music: she conducted adult and children's choirs for over sixty-five years in both Ukrainian and mainstream communities, and produced three publications featuring Ukrainian music. Tkachuk received awards such as the Saskatoon Century Award, the Ukrainian Canadian Congress Centennial Medal, and the American Association for State and Local History Award of Merit. She died in Saskatoon on April 28, 2003. *Natalie Ostryzniuk*

TOOTOOSIS, GORDON. Gordon Tootoosis was born and resides on the Poundmaker First Nation

near Battleford. He has served as chief of his band as well as vice-chief of the **FEDERATION OF SASKATCHEWAN INDIAN NATIONS**. Tootoosis has been involved in rodeos as a champion calf roper and team roper, and has also been involved in powwow dancing, making tours of Europe and South America in the 1960s and 1970s. However, Tootoosis is best known for his acting abilities: he made his film debut in 1972 acting alongside Chief Dan George and Donald Sutherland in the movie *Alien Thunder.* Tootoosis has appeared in over 25 programs; he is best known for his roles as Albert Golo in the television series *North of 60*, and as Big Bear in the movie of that name. In 2005 Tootoosis was named to the order of Canada. *Rob Nestor*

TOOTOOSIS, JOHN BAPTISTE (1899– 1989). A central figure in the development of modern Indian political organizations, Tootoosis was a tireless promoter and defender of treaty rights, and deserves some of the credit for the entrenchment of Aboriginal rights in the 1982 Constitution Act. Tootoosis was born on Poundmaker Reserve on July 18, 1899, of **CREE**, Assiniboine and **MÉTIS** ancestry. His grandfather was Yellow Mud Blanket, brother of the legendary Cree Chief **POUNDMAKER**. He enjoyed a sheltered childhood in a close-knit family until the age of 13, when his father sent him to Delmas Residential School to receive a Euro-Canadian education. It was an extremely traumatic experience, which resulted in his lifelong criticism of the residential school system and of the control the Roman Catholic Church exercised over Aboriginal people. Tootoosis returned to the reserve when he was 17, and his father gradually introduced him to the community's political system, where he developed a solid grasp of his people's history and treaty rights. When the Poundmaker band council decided to

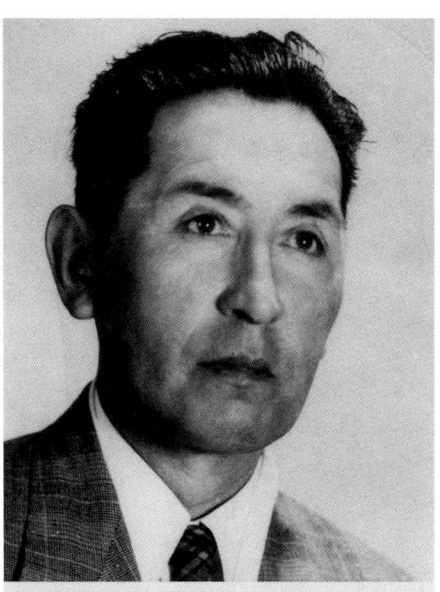

SASKATCHEWAN ARCHIVES BOARD R-A7662

John Tootoosis.

select a new chief in 1920, the young Tootoosis was their first choice; however, the Indian Act's regulations stipulated that chiefs had to be at least 25 years old, and Tootoosis was replaced with another candidate. He began to assert a leadership role in the community anyway, resisting the efforts of government officials to alienate part of the Poundmaker Reserve land base. His entry into the political arena coincided with the appearance of a new assertiveness among Aboriginal peoples across Canada following **WORLD WAR I**. When Tootoosis' father passed away in 1932, he was chosen to represent the Battleford bands in the League of Indians of Western Canada. Throughout the 1930s and 1940s he travelled across Canada, receiving no salary and relying on small donations from individuals. His efforts finally bore fruit in the years after **WORLD WAR II**. In 1946, Tootoosis was instrumental in the amalgamation of the various Aboriginal organizations in Saskatchewan into the Union of Saskatchewan Indians. In 1959, the original Union was transformed into the Federation of Saskatchewan Indians, and Tootoosis was elected its first president. He made the promotion and defense of treaty rights his main priority.

In 1970 Tootoosis was appointed to the Senate of the Federation of Saskatchewan Indians, and served as an active elder statesman for the remainder of his life; he also served as Ambassador to the World Council of Indigenous People conferences held in Canada, the USA, South America, Australia and Sweden. Tootoosis was married in 1929 to Louisa Angus from Thunderchild Reserve and together they had thirteen children; their children and grandchildren continue his example of service to First Nations peoples. *Michael Cottrell*

FURTHER READING: Tootoosis, T. 1998. "The Value of Oral History in First Nations Education, Part II: John B. Tootoosis 1899–1989," *Eagle Feather News* (November): 5.

TOPONYMS: *see* **PLACE NAMES**

TORNADOES. Tornadoes are occasionally produced by severe thunderstorms in Saskatchewan. The province averages about fifteen tornadoes reported annually, although there is a large annual variation. About one strong tornado (F2 or greater on the six-point Fujita scale), capable of inflicting major damage, can be expected each year; some years there are none, while in others several may be experienced. Tornado season runs from May to August. Saskatchewan's most damaging tornado, rated F4, hit Regina on the afternoon of June 30, 1912, causing twenty-eight deaths in the city, hundreds of injuries, and huge property losses (*see* **REGINA CYCLONE**). The only other F4-rated case was at Kamsack on August 9, 1944; it resulted in three dead, forty-four injured, and many buildings in the town destroyed. Fortunately, such events have been

COURTESY OF THE KAMSACK POWERHOUSE MUSEUM

Above, damage suffered in Kamsack from an F4 tornado, August 1944.

Fujita Wind Damage Scale (modified for the Canadian prairies)

F0 Gale tornado (40-72 mph)
Light damage, damage to chimneys, tree branches broken, small trees pushed over, empty granaries moved, phone lines knocked down, damage to sign boards.

F1 Moderate tornado (73-112 mph)
Surface of roofs peeled off, quonsets blown over, curling rinks destroyed, farm machinery and implements destroyed, windows blown out, full granaries lifted and destroyed, fair buildings (grandstands) destroyed, small farm buildings destroyed, mobile homes moved over, moving cars pushed off roads.

F2 Significant tornado (113-157 mph)
Weak structures destroyed, roofs torn off, boxcars knocked over, large trees uprooted, small objects become missiles (grass, straw), plucked chickens, structures picked up and thrown, livestock picked up and thrown, houses explode, farm machinery scattered and destroyed, mobile homes demolished.

F3 Severe tornado (158-206 mph)
Heavy cars lifted and thrown, combines picked up and thrown hundreds of yards, farm houses lifted and dropped 60 feet away, roofs thrown hundreds of yards, roofs torn from well-constructed houses.

F4 Devastating tornado (207-260 mph)
General destruction (e.g. Kamsack tornado, 1944, and Regina cyclone, 1912), well-constructed houses destroyed, large flying objects become missiles.

F5 Incredible tornado (>260 mph)
Incredible phenomena will occur.

F3 and F4 Tornadoes in Saskatchewan

Date	Latitude*	Longitude*	Location	Time (CST)	Direction**	Length (km)	Width (m)	Dead	Injured
F3 Tornadoes									
July 22, 1908	49 16	102 33	Frobisher	1610	280	13	400	3	12
July 16, 1909	53 08	109 57	Golden Valley			16			4
July 22, 1920	49 22	102 57	Cullen	1600	280	20	100	1	8
August 15, 1922	49 31	108 48	Eastend					2	4
June 18, 1927	51 46	103 59	Elfros	1200	290	12	200	1	6
July 6, 1935	51 37	109 29	Smiley	1830	250	10		2	
June 29, 1963	50 37	101 34	Spy Hill	1930	190	22	800	1	1
July 8, 1989	50 10	103 17	Peebles	1600	260	16	150		
F4 Tornadoes									
June 30, 1912	50 20	104 42	Regina	1650	200	20	150	28	300
August 9, 1944	51 30	101 59	Kamsack	2300	225	35	400	3	44

Source: Alexander H. Paul (Geography, University of Regina), The Saskatchewan Tornado Project. Report to SGI, May 1995, Regina, Saskatchewan.
* Latitude and Longitude indicate the location of the first touch down.
** Direction indicates the direction from which the tornado approached in degrees clockwise from due North (e.g. 225 indicates a tornado travelling SW to NE).

rare. Most of the province's reported tornadoes are weak (F0 or F1) and do only limited damage; many touch down only on fields or woodland. In recent years, forecasting and public awareness have improved, and since 1945 only three tornado fatalities have occurred in the province. This is no cause for complacency, however: an area of Narrow Hills Provincial Park, northwest of Nipawin, was visited by a tornado on July 2, 2003, which destroyed several residential trailers, turned over a tractor-trailer unit, and caused a number of injuries; the storm also dropped baseball-sized hail that is typical of tornado-producing thunderstorms. This event occurred at latitude 54°N–a reminder that tornadoes have been reported from the province's forested northlands as well as from the prairie. *Alec Paul*

TOURISM: *see* TRAVEL AND TOURISM

TRACE ANALYSIS FACILITY. A UNIVERSITY OF REGINA research team led by Renata Bailey, an analytical and environmental chemist, is trying to identify and analyze micro-organic contaminants such as pesticides and pharmaceuticals, which enter the environment from various sources including agriculture, forestry, petroleum production, and urbanization. Utilizing the university's $1.9-million Trace Analysis Facility (TAF), the research will initially focus on the over 200 registered active ingredients of pesticide formulations and their subsequent breakdown products. The TAF is used to identify and analyze these contaminants, to study how they move through the environment, and to examine how they break down in air, water and soil. It will also help investigate the impacts of these substances, for example the declining fertility of some aquatic species and the spread of antibiotic-resistant bacteria. Saskatchewan has the greatest area of cultivated land in Canada, and more agricultural pesticides are applied in the province than anywhere else in the country. The location in Regina–which itself produces measurable industrial, urban and horticultural emissions–will allow for the study of a model "urban environment" that can be applied to other population centres. Proximity of the TAF research team to the aquatic system of the Qu'Appelle Valley and to the Environment Canada air monitoring field station at Bratt's Lake will be similarly advantageous: Bratt's Lake is only 30 km outside of Regina, and less than 150 km from the United States. *Joe Ralko*

TRACK AND FIELD. Saskatchewan has enjoyed widespread grassroots participation and international success in track and field (also called "athletics") since the 1920s. Earl Thomson, born in Birch Hills but a California resident from the age of 8, insisted on representing Canada at the 1920 Summer Olympics in Antwerp and won the gold medal in the

COURTESY OF THE SASKATCHEWAN SPORTS HALL OF FAME AND MUSEUM

Earl Thomson (centre, in shorts) won an Olympic gold medal for Canada in the 110-metre men's hurdles at the 1920 Summer Games in Antwerp. The source of the photo is unknown but is probably from a Canadian military track meet in Ontario during the final months of World War I.

110-metre men's hurdles in world-record time. American-born ETHEL CATHERWOOD, who moved to Scott as a toddler and then Saskatoon to finish high school, was a sensation at the 1928 Olympics in Amsterdam: already dubbed "The Saskatoon Lily" by Canadian reporters, she became a national heroine by winning the women's high jump. Stan Glover of Saskatoon was a bronze medallist on the men's 4x400-metre relay team in the same Olympics. School meets at both elementary and high school level became commonplace by the 1920s and, along with adult participation in the YMCA and other urban athletic clubs, established track and field's popularity. Saskatoon took pre-eminence and maintained it, in great part through the influence of a succession of three outstanding coaches: Joe Griffiths, who discovered and assisted Catherwood early in a career that would extend to the 1950s; Bob Adams, a former national decathlon champion who guided athletes from 1955 to 1983; and Lyle Sanderson, who led the University of Saskatchewan team from 1968 to his retirement in 2004. Griffiths, Adams or Sanderson played some role in the development of the majority of the province's elite athletes.

Aspiring runners, leapers and throwers have long been able to compete as early as grade school, while the Saskatchewan High Schools Athletic Association has maintained well-organized competition and adequate coaching standards since its inception in 1948. The UNIVERSITY OF SASKATCHEWAN has long been a popular destination for athletes; the University of Regina's track and field program achieved more modest but tangible success by 2000. Many promising athletes have proceeded from secondary school to more competitive universities outside the province, especially in the United States where warmer climates and tougher competition

are the norm. Saskatoon was also a leader in promoting athletics. It was Griffiths who organized the first provincial high school championships in 1922. The city has been a frequent venue for major events such as national championships and Olympic trials, and in 1965 began an annual indoor meet (soon to become the Knights of Columbus Games) that featured a blend of world-class stars and regional standouts. Vancouver sprinter HARRY JEROME, born in Prince Albert, tied the world record for 100 metres (10.0 seconds) at the Olympic trials in Saskatoon on July 15, 1960; and American pole vaulter Bob Seagren set an indoor world record at the Knights of Columbus Games on December 29, 1966.

Pentathlete/heptathlete DIANE JONES KONIHOWSKI of Saskatoon and middle-distance runner LYNN KANUKA WILLIAMS of Regina earned international acclaim in the 1970s and 1980s respectively: Jones Konihowski's pentathlon gold medal at the 1978 Commonwealth Games in Edmonton highlighted a decade of achievement; Kanuka earned the bronze medal in the women's 3,000 metres at the 1984 Olympics in Los Angeles, and was among the world's finest road and cross-country racers. In addition to a long string of participants in Olympics and other international competitions, Saskatchewan has also produced exceptional Paralympians. ARNOLD BOLDT of Osler, who lost his right leg in a childhood farm accident, astonished the world with his high-jumping prowess, clearing as high as 2.08 metres in a career that included five Paralympic high jump gold medals (1976–92). Colette Bourgonje of Saskatoon, rendered a quadriplegic by a car accident at 18, became a world-class wheelchair racer and cross-country skier. CLAYTON GEREIN of Pilot Butte has won twelve Paralympic medals, five of them gold, since 1988; and fellow wheelchair racer Lisa

Franks of Moose Jaw was a double gold medallist at the 2004 Paralympics in Athens.   *John Chaput*

TRADE UNION ACT: *see* **LEGISLATION IN SASKATCHEWAN**

TRADITIONAL ECOLOGICAL KNOW-LEDGE. Although the concept has existed in diverse Indigenous cultures for centuries, the term "Traditional Ecological Knowledge" (TEK) came into widespread use in scholarly circles during the 1980s. However, there is no universally agreed-upon definition. Indigenous knowledge is defined by the Royal Commission on Aboriginal Peoples (1996) as a "cumulative body of knowledge and beliefs, handed down through generations by cultural transmission, about the relationship of living beings (including humans) with one another and their environment." TEK is a subset of this wider body of Indigenous knowledge that interprets how the world works from a particular cultural perspective. Research on TEK reveals that Indigenous people have made many contributions in disciplines that include health, pharmacology, environment, ecology, conservation, education, land and resource development, agriculture, and even architecture, engineering and astronomy. Today, most people do not realize the benefits from all these discoveries every time they dress, dine, travel, and visit their physicians and pharmacies. In one estimate, at least 75% of plant-based prescription drugs in the Western world are derived from medicinal plants first discovered by Indigenous people. Food plants from tribal lands also feed 60% of humanity.

Common characteristics of TEK are often described as holistic, experiential, personal, and transmitted through Indigenous languages: it is holistic in the sense that the world is viewed as an interconnected whole; it is experiential insofar as it is connected to a certain lifestyle and environment; it is personal because it is rooted in experience and lays no claim to universality; and it is properly examined and interpreted through Indigenous languages and Elders. There are aspects of Indigenous knowledge that cannot be properly shared or explained using Western scientific frameworks and languages. TEK is not considered fixed and static: it evolves, and is validated through collective analysis, consensus, and community processes. TEK is transmitted in many different symbolic and coded forms which include practical teachings, oral stories, metaphor, songs, dances, art, ceremonies, and daily cultural activities that encapsulate abstract and practical principles of the natural world. Many people, regardless of their cultural background, are turning to TEK in order to understand how to maintain balance in their lives, how to relate to other humans, and how to practice respect for the earth.

Compared with Traditional Ecological Knowl-edge, Western scientific knowledge is often described as linear, reductionist, and causal: it relies on logical empiricism, the five physical senses, mathematics, observation, and experimentation in coming to know natural reality. Although major differences exist between the two types of knowledge, TEK, which involves rational observation of natural events, classification, and problem solving, is also a part of the process of science.   *Herman Michell*

FURTHER READING: Battiste, M. and J. Henderson. 2000. *Protecting Indigenous Knowledge and Heritage: A Global Challenge*. Saskatoon: Purich Publishing; Cajete, G. 2000. *Native Science: Natural Laws of Interdependence*. Sante Fe, NM: Clear Light Publications; Inglish, J.T. (ed.). 1993. *Traditional Ecological Knowledge: Concepts and Cases*. Ottawa: International Development Research Centre, International Program on Traditional Ecological Knowledge.

TRANS-CANADA HIGHWAY. In July 1962, after more than fifty years of debate, controversy, and federal-provincial negotiations, the last official link in the Trans-Canada Highway opened between Revelstoke and Golden, BC, making the $1.4 billion, 7,821-km highway the longest national highway in the world. In 1894 businessmen and farmers formed the Ontario Good Roads Association to promote the economic benefits of roads and lobby for highway improvements. In 1912 Conservative Prime Minister Robert Borden passed a bill promoting road building, and by 1919 a Canada Highways Act was passed allocating money to each province for road improvement. A federal-provincial partnership agreement was struck to encourage motorists to use Canadian routes, rather than spend their money along American highways, and also to meet the needs of the expansion of inter-provincial trucking. In 1948 the notion of building a Trans-Canada highway was discussed. In December 1949, the Trans-Canada Highway Act became law, calling for a two-lane highway, 22–24 feet wide to be built following the shortest practical east-west route to be selected by the province. The federal government paid for half of the costs; however, if the highway cut through national parks, Ottawa would pay the entire cost. In 1957, Saskatchewan became the first province to finish its section of the Trans-Canada Highway; the 654 km-long road is the major east-west highway across Saskatchewan; it extends from Fleming through Regina, Moose Jaw, Caronport, Chaplin, Swift Current, and Maple Creek.   *Daria Coneghan*

TRANS-HUDSON OROGEN. The Trans-Hudson Orogen (THO) (*see* Figure THO-1) is the highly eroded remains of an ancient mountain belt in northern Canada, which originally (about 1.8 billion years ago) would have rivalled the Himalayas in grandeur. It is part of the Precambrian Canadian Shield, and its geological history marks an important stage in the forging of the North American continent. The THO extends from its main outcropping region in northern Saskatchewan and Manitoba, northeasterly to underlie the Phanerozoic rocks of the Hudson Bay Lowlands, under Hudson Bay, across Baffin Island, and possibly across Greenland under the glaciers, with a branch into northeastern Quebec and Labrador. To the south, it has been traced in subsurface under the Phanerozoic strata of the Great Plains into northern Montana and the Dakotas.

Like all orogens (tectonic mountain belts), regardless of their time of formation, the THO formed as a result of the collision of tectonic plates, which in this case (Figure THO-2) were three Archean microcontinents: the Superior Province (SP

Laying blacktop west of Swift Current on the Trans-Canada Highway, August 1954.

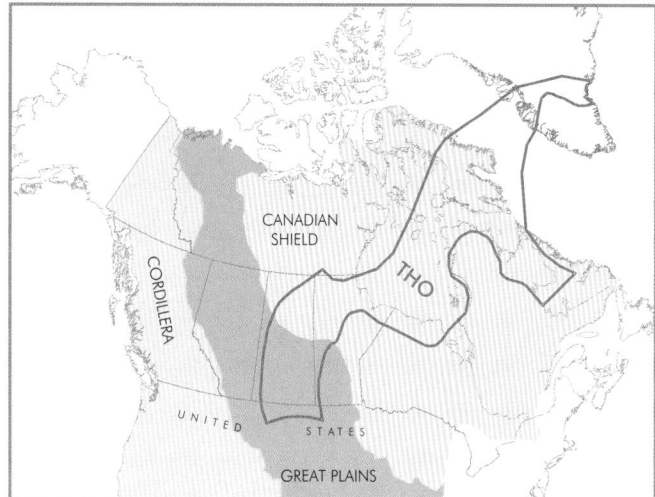

Figure THO-1. Location of the Trans-Hudson Orogen.

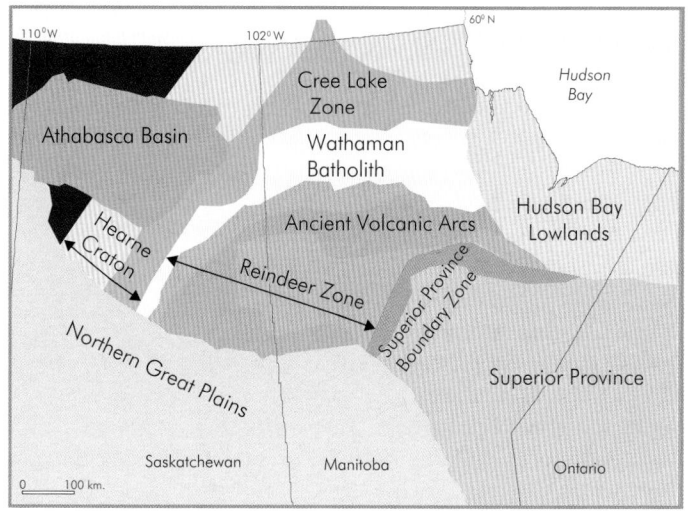

Figure THO-3. Metamorphosed ancient volcanic arc rock in northern Saskatchewan and northern Manitoba.

on Figure THO-2), the Churchill Craton (CC on Figure THO-2), and the now mostly buried Sask Craton (SC on Figure THO-2). These were once scattered several thousand kilometres apart in the early Proterozoic Manikewan Ocean.

The exact borders of these microcontinents are speculative because of their considerable modification (deformation) during collision. The present-day outline of North America is shown on Figure THO-2 for location purposes only.

The Manikewan Ocean contained at least two long chains, or arcs, of largely submarine volcanoes (Figure THO-2), the result of ancient plate-subduction-related volcanism, not unlike several similar chains of volcanic islands in the modern-day south Pacific. Erosion of these volcanoes, along with erosion of the various microcontinents, produced thick piles of sedimentary rock which, along with the volcanic rock, make up much of the rock material in the present THO. In Saskatchewan alone, irregular patchwork piles of metamorphosed ancient volcanic arc (AVA, see Figure THO-3) rock, locally greater than 10 km thick, underlie more than 10,000 square km of terrain. Volcanoes were active mainly between about 1.9 and 1.8 billion years ago, although we can no longer identify individual volcanoes because of deformation and erosion.

All orogens, including the THO, are identified by the folding and faulting that has affected the rocks, and by the metamorphism that has transformed various rocks into their metamorphic equivalents such as schists and gneisses. This plate tectonic closure of the Manikewan Ocean not only produced the THO, but also formed the proto-continent or core of North America (Figure THO-2).

Also like all orogens, the THO contains hundreds of huge bodies of intruded granitoid rocks, such as the gigantic Wathaman batholith (WB, see Figure THO-3) in Saskatchewan and Manitoba. The WB was injected about 1.855 billion years ago into

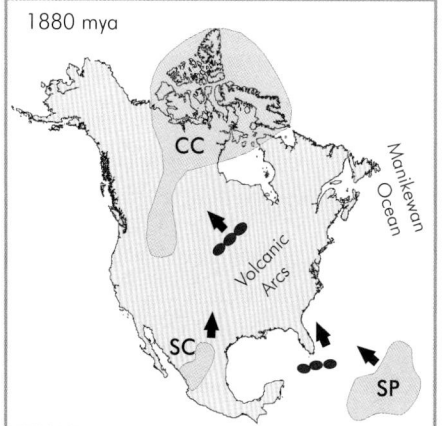

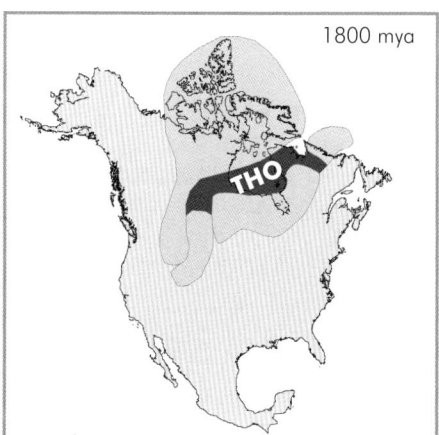

Figure THO-2. Plate movement which formed the Trans-Hudson Orogen. Heavy arrows in the left map indicate the relative movement directions of the various cratons and the closure direction of the Manikewan Ocean. The map at right shows the collision and the resulting mountain belt.

older, mainly marine, volcanic and sedimentary rocks, most of which had been deposited between about 1.9 and 1.855 billion years ago. Although most of these rocks were deposited on the Manikewan seabed, underlain by oceanic crust (Reindeer Zone, RZ on Figure THO-3), some were deposited on ancient continental shelves formed by "under-the-sea" extensions of older continental crust: the Hearne Craton in the west (part of the CC) is overlapped by the Cree Lake Zone (CLZ on Figure THO-3); and the Superior Craton in the southeast is overlapped by the Superior Province Boundary Zone (SPBZ, see Figure THO-3). The Sask Craton (SC) has been buried as rocks of the THO were thrust over it during collision. *M. Stauffer*

TRANSPORTATION: *see essay on facing page.*

TRAVEL AND TOURISM. The tourism industry in Saskatchewan, which includes over 5,500 individual tourism operators and organizations providing

services to the tourist, is comprised of eight major sectors: passenger transportation (scheduled and charter air, rail, boat, bus, taxicab and limousine services); travel services and travel trade (travel agencies, tour operators, other travel arrangements and reservations services); arts, entertainment and recreation (theatre companies and dinner theatres, spectator sports); heritage institutions (museums, historic sites, zoos and botanical gardens); amusement, gambling and recreation (amusement and theme parks, casinos, golf courses, marinas, skiing facilities); accommodation services (hotels, motels, resorts, bed and breakfast establishments/vacation farms, RV parks and campgrounds, hunting and fishing camps, recreational vacation camps); restaurants (including drinking places); and select retail operations (liquor stores, gasoline stations, and gift, novelty and souvenir stores).

In Saskatchewan, the tourism industry includes: 128 regional, provincial and national parks; 250 golf courses; 95 outdoor adventure operators; 600

heritage and cultural attractions; 225 museums; 52 art galleries; 6 casinos; 2 spas; 130 handicraft, antique and tea shops; 532 hotels and motels; 142 bed and breakfast/vacation farm establishments; 141 lakeside resorts; and 328 fishing or hunting outfitter camps. There are seven organized tourism regions in the province: north, west-central, Saskatoon, east-central, southwest, Regina, and southeast. There are also six major travel corridors: the Northern Woods and Water Route (Highways 9 and 55), the Trans-Canada Yellowhead (Highway 16), the TRANS-CANADA HIGHWAY (Highway 1), the Red Coat Trail (Highway 13), the CANAM International (Highways 35, 39, 6, 3 and 2/102), and the Saskota Flyway (Highway 9). In 2001, these businesses, organizations and regions supported almost 8 million annual trips to and within the province and over $1.3 billion in traveller expenditures. Annually, 3.5 million trips of less than twenty-four hours are made in the province; another 4.3 million trips of one or more nights are also made each year. These overnight or longer trips are made for a variety of purposes: 42% to visit friends or relatives; 34% for pleasure; 10% for business or convention purposes; and 14% for personal or other reasons.

Saskatchewan residents account for 93% of trips for less than twenty-four hours, while other Canadians account for 4% and United States visitors for 3%. For tourism purposes, the trips of one or more nights are the most important; Saskatchewan residents account for 65% of these longer trips, other Canadians for 29%, United States visitors for 5%, and visitors from other countries account for 1%. However, Saskatchewan residents account for only 45% of expenditures by those making trips of one or more nights in Saskatchewan, while other Canadians account for 35%, United States visitors for 17%, and those from overseas for 3%. Visitors come to Saskatchewan for outdoor experiences (over 1.6 million annual overnight or longer trips) and for cultural and heritage attractions (almost 800,000 trips). Key attractions include: northern fishing, canoeing and winter experiences; attractions such as WANUSKEWIN HERITAGE PARK, the Eastend T-Rex Discovery Centre, the Saskatchewan Science Centre, and the four WESTERN DEVELOPMENT MUSEUMS in Moose Jaw, Yorkton, North Battleford and Saskatoon; six full-service casinos in Regina, Moose Jaw, North Battleford, Yorkton, Prince Albert, and White Bear Reserve; Temple Gardens Mineral Spa in Moose Jaw and Manitou Springs Resort and Mineral Spa at Manitou Lake; Prince Albert National Park, Cypress Hills Interprovincial Park, Meadow Lake Provincial Park, and Nipawin Regional Park; and golf courses such as Elk Ridge near Prince Albert National Park, Deer Valley near Regina, Evergreen at Nipawin, and the Willows and Moon Lake in Saskatoon. *Bonnie Baird*

Transportation

Brian Cousins

Introduction

The vastness of Saskatchewan's land-locked prairie, woodlands and Precambrian Shield has always created transportation challenges. Transportation has been a critical social, economic and political issue for the region—demanding innovation and fueling controversy. Well before European settlement in what became Saskatchewan, the region's indigenous peoples witnessed particular changes that dramatically affected the nature and quality of their life. Spain's introduction of horses to the Americas in the 16th century had extended to the Saskatchewan plains by the mid-18th century, probably achieved through contact and trade with indigenous peoples to the south and possibly aided by the emergence of bands of feral horses that spread through many areas of North America. Horses came to replace dogs in helping to meet the transport requirements of the prairies' nomadic First Nations, who met subsistence requirements by pursuing buffalo and other game.

The introduction of the FUR TRADE, particularly in the northern half of Saskatchewan, introduced a new concept of commerce among First Nation peoples and created new transportation requirements for harvesting fur and delivering it to markets via distant trading posts. The arrival of railroads led to the single greatest transformation of the southern half of the province by facilitating an era of mass immigration and agricultural cultivation. When RED RIVER CARTS gave way to trains, waves of immigration brought settlers from Europe to create farms and communities across the prairie. In the process, much of the traditional lifestyle of the region's indigenous peoples was compromised.

The combination of a widely dispersed agricultural economy and the introduction of assembly-line production and lower costs for automobiles and trucks made Saskatchewan an instant market for the new horseless carriages. They were put to use on what would become Canada's largest network of highways and roads, building on the trails of indigenous peoples and early settlers. By 1957, Saskatchewan had one registered vehicle for every 2.7 residents, well above the national ratio of one to 3.7.

After the advent of commercial aviation, aircraft soon appeared in Saskatchewan. A Saskatchewan-based plane was the first licensed commercial aircraft in Canada, and Regina resident ROLAND GROOME became the nation's first licensed commercial pilot.

Aerial photography surveys were initiated by the Royal Canadian Air Force (RCAF) in 1924, the year it was formally created. The surveys and new accessibility (made possible by aircraft) sparked increased mineral exploration and development in northern Saskatchewan. During the years of World War II, Saskatchewan was home to more than twenty aviation training schools under the BRITISH COMMONWEALTH AIR TRAINING PLAN (BCATP). In 1946, the first air ambulance service in the Commonwealth and North America was established in Saskatchewan. The following year, the service had three aircraft: a Norseman, a Stinson and a Fairchild Husky, the latter being Canada's first commercially operated aircraft licensed and fitted to use jet propulsion. Aircraft also added an important dimension to forest fire detection and suppression: in 1947 Saskatchewan pioneered the use of "smokejumpers," firefighters who were parachuted into newly discovered fires to stop them from spreading.

The province's reliance on railroads increased as potash resources were developed across the central grain belt of Saskatchewan from the 1950s through to the 1970s. Potash production, virtually all of which is transported by railcars, grew to more than 8 million tons each year—still well short of the annual grain haul (which averages more than 22 million tons), but a major growth factor for railway transportation in Saskatchewan and for the province's mineral sector.

However, railway economics and policies were not all expansionary. In the last half of the 20th century passenger services were severely reduced—a result of less demand but also a reflection of the railroads' primary interest in profiting from freight hauling. Then, in search of lower-cost, higher-efficiency grain transportation, new words were introduced to the prairie lexicon: "inland grain terminals" (dramatically reducing reliance on community-based elevators) and "rail line abandonment" (shifting grain transport increasingly to trucks and the road system), creating a new era of agricultural transportation demands and issues. For many decades, grain transportation has been a topic of heated debate—in the provincial Legislature, in the national Parliament, and in the coffee shops and kitchens in hundreds of Saskatchewan communities. The "Crow Rate" agreement, the use of the Hudson Bay Port of Churchill, the demise of community elevators (and sometimes of the communities themselves), and the role of independent short-line rail services remain common topics of discussion in family and community forums across the plains.

Even when rail passenger service was at its zenith in Saskatchewan, it did not fully meet the needs for inter-community passenger and freight services in the province. As a result, the SASKATCHEWAN TRANSPORTATION COMPANY (STC) was created as a provincial bus service in 1946; in 2004, the provincially subsidized Crown corporation continued to serve 275 Saskatchewan communities with a fleet of 41 buses.

Beyond the CANOES and YORK BOATS of the fur trade, Saskatchewan's use of water transport briefly included participation in the era of steam-powered riverboats. But riverboats, together with most passenger train services and the streetcars and electric trolley coaches of Saskatchewan's larger cities, are no more. Today's transportation priorities are largely focused on coping with the growing number of automobiles and trucks (there were more than 750,000 vehicles registered in Saskatchewan in 2004), ensuring adequate air services, and developing alternative rail facilities to transport rural grain production. The federal government has largely divested its operation of transportation services in Saskatchewan. The only rail passenger service is Via Rail's national route, which passes through Saskatchewan via Melville and Saskatoon. Navigational aids and docks have been discontinued on northern waterways. Airports are now a municipal, provincial, or private responsibility; however, air traffic continues to increase with major expansions made to air terminal facilities by municipal airport authorities in both Saskatoon (2003) and Regina (2005).

No single account can fully document the transportation challenges that confronted Saskatchewan people as they developed an economy and population dispersed over vast distances. However, the following summaries and individual entries provide a brief but colourful overview of transportation in the province.

Water

Canoes and York Boats

The canoes of indigenous First Nations were common in many regions of Canada including northern Saskatchewan, where the CREE and DENE used them for travel along a vast network of waterways. Canoes were the region's primary means of seasonal transport when lakes and rivers were free from ice. The early European explorers, fur traders and settlers soon took to using canoes, the speed and agility of which had been acknowledged by Samuel de Champlain as early as 1603, upstream on the St. Lawrence River. The larger birch-bark canoes typically used by voyageurs throughout Canada measured almost eight metres in length and at least a metre in beam, held cargo of up to 1,400 kg, and required five to seven paddlers.

The use of canoes by the voyageurs of the fur trade gave the merchants of Montreal and the fledgling North West Company (NWC) an advantage over the Hudson's Bay Company (HBC): it allowed them to go inland to meet trappers instead of expecting them to travel great distances to their posts. The HBC soon responded by developing inland posts, including Cumberland House in 1774 and Ile-à-la-Crosse in 1776—the first non-indigenous settlements within the borders of what was to become Saskatchewan.

Early in the 1800s, the HBC also designed and manufactured York Boats. Though more cumbersome on portages than canoes, the 12-metre boats, first made at the company's York Factory post, had definite advantages: they could carry twice the cargo of a large canoe, and they could use a sail when crossing lakes if wind conditions were right. They became particularly common on the SASKATCHEWAN RIVER system and were used until the early 1900s, complementing the more agile service of canoes.

The major fur trade routes of Saskatchewan were the CHURCHILL, Athabasca and NORTH SASKATCHEWAN RIVER systems. Two of the most widely known and well-used portages that linked together all three of these watersheds are located in northern Saskatchewan: on the west side of the province the Methy Portage connects Lac La Loche to the CLEARWATER RIVER and the Churchill and Athabasca watersheds; on the east side of the province the Frog Portage connects the Sturgeon Weir and North Saskatchewan River systems to the Churchill watershed. Combined, these two portages form an integrated system of overland linkages that enabled travelers to follow water routes from the prairies all the way to the Arctic Ocean. The fur trade and European exploration went hand in hand. People such as HENRY KELSEY, SAMUEL HEARNE and DAVID THOMPSON—among the first Europeans to journey through Saskatchewan and make contact with the area's Aboriginal peoples—are now better remembered for their exploration and early mapping than for their service to the companies of the fur trade.

Canoes were *not* commonly used by First Nations people inhabiting the plains for obvious reasons. A land without birch or pitch, essential to build and maintain a traditional canoe, would not support the development and use of such a craft. As well, the waterways of the plains were generally slower-moving and unbearably long because of the many twists and turns carved out of the land by this slow-moving water. This usually meant that for the more southerly plains, ground transport was much faster than traveling by water. Plains Indians, however, *did* use temporary "bull boats" for crossing rivers and for downstream travel on fast-flowing rivers. A bull boat could be created in a few hours by sewing buffalo skins onto a frame of bent willow branches. However, flat-bottomed boats have won their place in Saskatchewan's transportation history: scows and skiffs, usually hand-made, became common in many areas of the province—particularly in the north, where they have long been a mainstay of commercial fishing operations.

HBC records describe a particular attempt in 1869 to revive river transport (as an alternative to using cart trails) as part of the fur trade on the Saskatchewan plains. A fleet of flat-bottomed boats was built at Fort Qu'Appelle out of poplar planks, using spruce gum and buffalo grease as a seal. A difficult six-week journey to Fort Ellice (on the Assiniboine River just across the contemporary border with Manitoba) left the crews disheartened and much of the cargo damaged: the experimental voyage was over and not attempted again.

Steamboats

In August 1874, the newly constructed Hudson's Bay Company SS *Northcote* completed its maiden voyage from Grand Rapids, near Lake Winnipeg, to Carlton House on the North Saskatchewan River: a total distance of 790 km (490 miles) upriver via Cumberland House and Prince Albert. It was the beginning of an ambitious but troubled new era in western Canadian transportation. The following year, service was extended to Edmonton; after 1877 the *Northcote* was modified to include passenger cabins, eventually accommodating as many as fifty people. The largest riverboat to ply the Saskatchewan River waters was the *Marquis* (built for the Hudson's Bay Company in 1882), with a length of 67 metres (207 feet).

A particularly dramatic use of steamboats occurred during the NORTH-WEST RESISTANCE of 1885. Several of the paddle wheel boats were commandeered by the military to transport troops in the campaign against Chiefs POUNDMAKER and BIG BEAR. The HBC's *Northcote* was used as a gunboat in the battle of BATOCHE, but was disabled in its first day of combat when Métis forces critically damaged the smokestacks and wheelhouse by lowering a ferry cable across the river. The *Northcote*'s military career included transportation of wounded militia from the battlefield at Batoche to a field hospital at Saskatoon. The steamboat was also used to transport LOUIS RIEL to Saskatoon before he was taken by land to Regina, where the Métis leader was imprisoned until his trial and subsequent execution.

Other companies followed the HBC lead and used steamboats on both the North and South Saskatchewan rivers. However, the development of rail transport and the continuing problems of shifting sandbars and shallow waters would limit the lifespan of steamboat transport in Saskatchewan. The HBC ended its use of steamboats in 1896. Ten years earlier, the *Northcote* had been beached at Cumberland House; it never sailed again but disintegrated over the years, remnants of its boilers now serving as an historic site in the community. The last steamboat service to Saskatoon was in 1908, when the *City of Medicine Hat* hit a traffic bridge and capsized. Smaller vessels continued to ply the waters of Last Mountain Lake until 1913, and on the Carrot River steamboats pulled logs to sawmills as recently as 1954.

Two other forms of non-recreational use of water transport continue in Saskatchewan, though to a much lesser extent than in earlier years: river crossing ferries and barge shipping on northern waterways. As of 2004, twelve seasonal river ferries were operated by the Saskatchewan Department of Highways and Transportation. Each can hold up to six ordinary-sized vehicles, except for a larger ferry near Riverhurst that can take fifteen cars in a single crossing. At its peak in

the early 1950s, Saskatchewan's ferry fleet totalled 36; many were manufactured in the province by the Highways department.

New bridge construction steadily reduced reliance on ferry service. One of the longest running ferry sites, located on the BATTLEFORD TRAIL, was established at The Landing (north of Swift Current) on the SOUTH SASKATCHEWAN RIVER in 1883. It continued until 1951, when construction of a major new bridge was completed. In contrast, the latest ferry service was introduced at Buffalo Narrows in 1957 when the first all-weather road to the northwest Saskatchewan community was completed. Northern ferry services at Buffalo Narrows and Cumberland House were among those that were discontinued when bridges were constructed. However, further north, commercial water transport continues. Under contract with the provincial Highways department, the Hatchet Lake First Nation provides seasonal barge transportation service to the community of Wollaston Lake in northeastern Saskatchewan. Commercial barge services based near Fort McMurray in Alberta used to be the primary means of shipping heavy goods to communities on Lake Athabasca; construction of a seasonal road to the lake in 1999–2000 changed the pattern of shipping to Saskatchewan's most northerly region. Nevertheless, limited barge service continues to be provided on LAKE ATHABASCA by private firms. A number of "ice roads" are also constructed each year across northern lakes; they are particularly important for shipping supplies to the communities of Wollaston Lake and Fond du Lac.

Land

Dogs and Horses

As with canoes and York boats, the use of dog teams was an essential means of transport in support of the northern Saskatchewan fur trade. Some studies suggest that the use of dog teams originated in Siberia 4,000 years ago and spread to the Inuit peoples of North America and then to other northern First Nations. In addition to pulling winter sleds, dogs would also carry packs on their backs. The use of dogs for transportation predates the fur trade, but new breeds were introduced after European contact. The earliest "royal mail" services, initiated in what was then the North-West Territories, included use of dog teams for winter transport. Long distances covered by "dog trains" included the trek from Fort Garry to Fort Pelly, Fort Carlton, and on to Edmonton.

The use of dog teams for trapping and for travel between northern Saskatchewan camps and communities was a primary means of northern winter transportation; but it faced sudden decline during the 1960s and 1970s. Though large track-driven snowmobiles had been introduced in the 1940s, their use was largely confined to industry and government. It was the introduction of smaller "snow machines," gasoline-powered with skis and tracks (first manufactured by companies such as Polaris and Bombardier in the late 1950s), that won quick acceptance as an alternative to dog teams in meeting the transportation needs of northern trappers. Snowmobiles continue to be a primary transportation vehicle for trapping and commercial ice fishing in northern areas. They also became immensely popular for recreation purposes across the province. Dog teams remain part of the northern Saskatchewan culture; however, today the teams are raised primarily for racing or as a hobby.

Dogs were also a primary means of transportation for the Plains Indians. An A-frame shaped TRAVOIS (usually measuring about 2.5 metres in length and one metre at the base) was harnessed to the dog's back; the natural spring of the tree trunks, used for the frame, allowed the travois to slide over mud, grass, stones or snow. Dogs also helped

DAVID MCLENNAN PHOTO

The Riverhurst ferry on Lake Diefenbaker (shown here preparing to load vehicle traffic) is Saskatchewan's largest ferry. It is 35.6 metres (117 ft.) long, 14 metres (46 ft.) wide, and weighs 90.7 tonnes (100 tons). During winter months an ice road across the lake is laid out and maintained by the Saskatchewan Department of Highways and Transportation.

hunting parties by driving deer and buffalo towards waiting hunters and by forcing buffalo over cliffs or into pounds. Although the arrival of horses by the mid-1700s reduced dependence on dogs, travois continued to be used extensively into the mid-1800s. The concept of the dog travois was also adapted to fit horses prior to the introduction of wagons.

The advent of horses significantly enhanced the mobility of the migratory Plains people in pursuing buffalo and other game: horses could more readily carry lodge poles and heavier loads of food, clothing and supplies. The first European to describe horses on the Canadian plains was ANTHONY HENDAY, believed to the first White man to cross the prairies: in 1754 he described the Indian horses as "fine tractable animals, about 14 hands high; lively and clean made." As the accepted definition of a horse required it to be over 15 hands high, the original Indian horses of the plains must be considered ponies.

Prairie Trails

A number of routes had been established by First Nations in relation to inter-tribal contact between the Missouri and Saskatchewan river systems. However, formal trails associated with horse-driven carts and wagons emerged more clearly during the introduction of the fur trade and European settlement. Many trails were created to connect major trading posts, forts or stations of the North-West Mounted Police as well as a number of church missions. Some trails involved payment of tolls—typically 25¢—to private land owners, who provided short cuts around bogs or mud holes, or who had constructed wooden bridges. It was the location of rail lines in the late 1800s and early 1900s that would define transportation patterns and the location of hundreds of grain elevators and communities across the southern half of Saskatchewan. But before the railways could carry new settlers to their homesteads, the network of trails which had been created in the province served as the main transportation routes that would lead to the transformation of the natural prairie to farmland.

Many of the early settlers who used those trails during the 19th century traveled to Saskatchewan in Red River carts—made popular by the Red River colonists who had established what was, at the time, the most westerly "settlement" in Canada in southern Manitoba. Before the arrival of steamboats and the railways, as many as 2,500 of the carts,

with their large wooden wheels and wooden axles lashed to a horse, mule or ox, would bring newcomers to the plains of Saskatchewan each year. In the 1870s, a Red River cart could be purchased in Winnipeg for between $10 and $15; pulled by oxen, it would average about 15 miles per day while horse drawn carts could travel 15 to 25 miles.

Roads and Highways

Another key influence in determining the eventual road structure of the southern half of the province was the "grid" system of surveying the land. After the Rupert's Land Act of 1870 was passed by the federal government, transferring land from the Hudson's Bay Company to Canada, surveyors began their work on the plains west of Manitoba in 1873. The survey system and grid structure were patterned after similar work in the western United States, ensuring provisions for road access to the thousands of family farms that were created on the prairies. Over time, the provincial and rural municipality road system would expand to over 190,000 km of highways, grid roads and farm access roads—the largest road network of any province in Canada. Initially, all roads in Saskatchewan were considered a municipal responsibility. It was not until 1912 that the provincial government appointed a Board of Highways Commissioners to plan a provincial highway system; the first Department of Highways followed in 1917.

Provincial legislation initiated licensing of Saskatchewan vehicles in 1906 when just 22 vehicles were registered in the province. The legislation also set speed limits: 10 miles per hour in cities, and 20 miles per hour elsewhere. By 1911, there were 821 registered vehicles located in 136 different communities. That year, a Ford Model T Touring Car sold for $1,025; only six years later, mass production of the vehicles reduced the price to $545, causing a surge in demand. The demand for vehicles in Saskatchewan, as well as anticipated population growth, led to the establishment of a General Motors assembly plant in Regina in 1928.

There were two eras when the expansion of vehicle use was briefly stalled: the GREAT DEPRESSION saw the number of vehicles registered in Saskatchewan decline from 128,000 in 1929 to 91,000 in 1934; during WORLD WAR II production of new automobiles, trucks and tires for domestic use was restricted, and fuel rationing was implemented. During the Depression years, "BENNETT BUGGIES" became common in Saskatchewan and elsewhere. Derisively named after Prime Minister R.B. Bennett, automobiles pulled by horses were used by farmers too impoverished to purchase gasoline. "Black top" and "pavement" were added to the vocabulary in the 1930s when hard surfaced roads were first introduced. But for most areas, the attainment of adequately graded and graveled roads was the more important objective: by 1931, fewer than 3% of farms had gravel road access, and in 1944 Saskatchewan had only 222 km of hard surfaced roads. It was not until the 1950s that the provincial government would support municipalities in undertaking a massive upgrade of Saskatchewan's grid road system and begin a more significant introduction of pavement across the province.

The largest stretch of black top built in Saskatchewan was the TRANS-CANADA HIGHWAY, begun in 1950 and completed seven years later. Saskatchewan became the first province to complete its section of the national highway, originally cost-shared with the federal government and constructed to agreed standards nationwide. The original Saskatchewan portion of the highway was 653 km in length; it reduced the border-to-border driving distance by 89 km and eliminated 23 level railway crossings. The first "four-lane" highways in Saskatchewan were completed in 1961 from Regina to Lumsden and Regina to Balgonie. The

Wood Mountain Trail.

Saskatoon cloverleaf.

first highway "cloverleaf" interchanges were opened in 1967: one in Regina at the junction of Highways 1 and 6; the second in Saskatoon at the intersection of Highways 11 and 14. Roads north of Meadow Lake, Prince Albert and Nipawin developed much later than in southern Saskatchewan; many were initially constructed as "resource access" roads by the provincial Department of Natural Resources during the 1940s and 1950s.

Before the advent of northern highways, horse and tractor-drawn "trains" were used to haul supplies by sleds to many northern communities during winter. In addition to its southern bus service, for a period of several years the Saskatchewan Transportation Company was also responsible for organizing northern tractor trains to haul supplies to communities such as Montreal Lake, Lac La Ronge and beyond. From 1947 to 2000, three northern road spines (central, west, and east) were developed. A fourth northern highway to the province's first settlement of Cumberland House was completed in 1967. The central highway to La Ronge was completed in 1948, pushing further north in stages to Missinipi, then to Southend and Points North, on the western shore of Wollaston Lake. In 2000, a seasonal (primarily winter use) road was constructed to Stony Rapids on the southeast shore of Lake Athabasca. Road access to the northwest reached Buffalo Narrows in 1956 and La Loche by 1963. The "Semchuk Trail" was completed in 1979 to serve the then new uranium mine site at Cluff Lake; the road was named after Martin Semchuk, who used to build winter ICE ROADS through the area and across Lake Athabasca to Uranium City.

In the northeast, the Hanson Lake Road between Smeaton and Creighton (on the border with Flin Flon, Manitoba) gained highway status in 1964. Spurs were built to the Churchill River communities of Pelican Narrows in 1967 and Sandy Bay in 1972; road access to Deschambault Lake was added in 1974. Today, the northern highways network remains a work in progress, with new roads continuing to be planned and developed. As of 2004, the provincial highway network extended more than 26,000 km, with 20,500 km surfaced and 1,100 km of divided, four-lane highways. By 2004, the Trans-Canada Highway had been "twinned" from Grenfell in the east to the Alberta border; the easternmost end of the highway's twinning will be completed by 2007.

Saskatchewan's highways (*see* HIGHWAY NETWORK) serve many purposes. Providing access to communities, industry and farms is more demanding than elsewhere in Canada because Saskatchewan residents are more widely dispersed: more than half of the population lives in communities under 20,000 (as per the national census of 2001). Key east-west and north-south trade corridors are necessary to support economic diversification and expansion, and to permit Saskatchewan's export-driven economy to maintain efficient access to markets. Throughout the grain belt, massive increases have occurred in the volume of grain hauled by truck to inland terminals, permitting producers to take advantage of the lower grain-loading charges assessed by the railroads because of the efficiencies offered by such terminals. Another demand placed on Saskatchewan's road network is the sheer volume of traffic: the number of motor vehicles registered (to say nothing of out-of-province trucking and tourism traffic) more than doubled from the 1960s to the 1990s. As of 2004, there were more than 750,000 licensed vehicles and 115,000 licensed trailers registered in the province.

Rail

The CANADIAN PACIFIC RAILWAY (CPR) was Canada's first national rail service and the first company to construct a railway across the prairies. Through the contentious Canadian Pacific Railway Act of 1881, the government of Sir John A. Macdonald provided the company with an initial subsidy of $25 million and title to 25 million acres of prime Canadian land. CPR trains arrived in what was to become Saskatchewan in 1882. The company received additional federal assistance after dramatically demonstrating the value of its service in 1885 when the new railway was used to transport troops to the North-West Territories to suppress the North-West Resistance. Federal land grants to the CPR and other smaller rail companies continued until 1894, usually involving 6,400 acres per mile of construction. By 1914, through additional branch line construction and acquisition of other rail companies, the CPR's western Crown land grant totaled 29 million acres. To place the magnitude of this acquisition of land resources in context, the land set aside for First Nation reserves to meet Indian Treaty obligations in all of Canada now totals 7.7 million acres—just over one-quarter the amount acquired by the CPR in western Canada a century ago.

The company was not required to accept lands which "consist in a material degree of land not fairly fit for settlement"; this charter provision permitted the CPR to look afar in making its land selections. As well, the company often delayed making these selections in order to avoid paying taxes and to benefit from rising values of the lands it eventually chose. The railway actively promoted immigration: not so much for the immediate benefit of increasing its passenger business, but to encourage agricultural production that would create long-term freight transport business for the new railway. Of equal importance to the CPR's shareholders, promoting immigration helped attract buyers for some of the company's acquired lands. By 1914, the CPR had sold about half of its original western land grant for $84 million. Countless millions more were realized over future years from the prime lands the company kept and developed with hotels and other commercial enterprises, many of which are still operated today by the company's subsidiaries and partnerships.

Through the influence of its land holdings, CPR decisions would also affect the development of many western Canadian communities. For example, in Regina, the railway located its station east of the original townsite, creating its own subdivision and selling individual lots. The discord which that decision created with local and federal authorities contributed to the CPR's choice of Moose Jaw, instead of Regina, as its Saskatchewan operational headquarters. However, the single most

Railway construction.

important action by the CPR that affected early Saskatchewan communities was a decision to change the route of the first rail line across the plains.

Sandford Fleming (whose many achievements included devising the concept of "standard time" and the division of the world into 24 time zones) did the initial survey for the CPR. His preferred route to the Pacific Ocean was via the Yellowhead Pass, through Humboldt and Battleford. The route was written into the CPR's charter of incorporation approved by Parliament in early 1881. But those who feared that American railways might extend into southern Canada prevailed, and in 1882 Parliament passed the necessary legislation to authorize the first rail line to be much further south, en route to the Rocky Mountain's Kicking Horse Pass, very close to the United States border. The change in route meant that established towns from Prince Albert to Edmonton had to wait another decade before the arrival of rail service; it also meant that the CPR had the power to influence town site development along the more southerly route. As well, the new route led to the government's decision in 1883 to the move the North-West Territories capital from Battleford to Regina.

The CPR would receive further federal government subsidies in 1897 to build a second route through the Crow's Nest Pass of the Rocky Mountains. The "Crow Agreement" subsidies, in exchange for fixed rates on grain traffic, would be a major influence on the long-term economics of agriculture in Saskatchewan. Canadian Pacific has proven the most venerable railway company in Canada and continues to have a major presence in Saskatchewan. In 2004, the company continued to operate about 22,500 km (14,000 miles) of rail line service in Canada and the United States. However, many other railroad companies have been, and continue to be, players in responding to the province's evolving transportation requirements. CANADIAN NATIONAL RAILWAYS (CNR) was created in 1918 and consolidated several companies across the nation, including Canadian Northern and Grand Trunk Pacific, which were both active in Saskatchewan. Canadian National became the largest rail company in Canada and was an aggressive competitor with Canadian Pacific: occasionally the two companies would race each other to extend service to the same areas.

Meanwhile, between 1889 and 1894, the St. Paul and Sault Ste. Marie Railway became an important service in southern Saskatchewan, following a line from the United States through Portal, Estevan and Weyburn to its terminus in Moose Jaw. Known as the SOO LINE, this railway became an important route for Americans who came to Canada not as struggling homesteaders, but as well-to-do land buyers: most had already become well established in the Midwest, later moving to the Canadian prairies in the "ultra-modern heated coaches" of the Soo Line. Indeed, 400,000 acres of the land sold along the Soo Line had been purchased by the Luse Land Co. from the CPR for the purpose of resale to American buyers. The Soo Line would eventually become a subsidiary of the CPR.

Although railroads in Saskatchewan have become important for the transport of potash, lumber and other goods produced in the province, their history has been tied to the transport of grain—primarily to grain ships docked at the "Lakehead" of Lake Superior (Thunder Bay) or to the Pacific ports of Vancouver and Prince Rupert. The creation of port facilities at Churchill on the Hudson Bay was accompanied by construction of the "Hudson Bay Route," providing a shorter rail line and lower shipping costs to Atlantic markets; however, the short shipping season from the port of Churchill prevented this alternate route from fully meeting the volume expectations of its promoters.

Even while debates continued over many years as to the ability of the railroads and governments to maintain the "Crow Rate" subsidy, rail line abandonment plans were put forward by the railways and became the subject of national commissions of inquiry. Federal approval for such abandonment and the advent of large inland grain terminals increased the use of grain hauling by truck via provincial roads; it also led to the emergence of "short line" railways, primarily for hauling grain but also used for coal and northern wood products. These purpose-specific rail services, which must negotiate interchange agreements with the larger railways, have been developed both as co-operatives and private companies in several regions of the province.

Urban railways were also part of Saskatchewan's rail transportation history. Electric railways began service in Regina and Moose Jaw in 1911, and in Saskatoon in 1913. Motor buses replaced the Moose Jaw railway in 1932, but streetcars continued to provide service in the province's two largest cities until 1950–51. In the late 1940s, Regina and Saskatoon introduced electrical trolley buses before converting to strictly motor buses by 1974. One of the most destructive fires in

Saskatchewan's history created a setback for the Regina Transit Service in 1949: fire destroyed the car barns, 17 trolley coaches, nine gasoline buses, five steel streetcars, and nine wooden cars. Two years later, the rail-driven streetcars were no more.

Air

The invention of aircraft and their use during World War I would bring a new transportation era to Saskatchewan immediately after the war years. American "barnstormers" had performed in some Saskatchewan locations before the war. Commercial air services were seriously introduced to the province in post-war years by Saskatchewan pilots and engineers who had been trained for military flying. However, the history of air transport in the province was not without its problems and setbacks.

The first commercial AVIATION service in Saskatoon was set up by Stan McClelland, following his World War I military service. After his Curtis "Jenny" biplane had been successfully tested on April 21, 1919, a lottery was held to determine who would have the opportunity to be his first passengers a week later. On the biplane's first official flight, a vehicle appeared on the airstrip and caused the pilot to attempt a premature lift off; although the aircraft was ruined, there were no serious injuries. Undeterred, McClelland had another Jenny in place the very next month, and he piloted the first long-distance, cross-country flight in Saskatchewan from Saskatoon to Regina. A leaking gas tank meant unscheduled stops in Davidson and Disley, but the potential of flight had been established in the province. That same year saw McClelland undertake his own barnstorming flights at fairs across the province; a fifteen-minute flight for $15 was the thrill of a lifetime for those who dared to be his passengers.

"Bush" planes and "bush" pilots quickly became part of the Canadian north, including northern Saskatchewan. Planes soon used skis and floats, bringing great versatility to their use there, particularly in support of northern mineral exploration. Colourful pilots and legendary aircraft have formed part of modern northern history since the Vickers Viking flying boat first appeared over northern Saskatchewan communities as part of RCAF aerial photography surveys undertaken in the 1920s. Aircraft names became as common in the north as Fords and Chevrolets in the south: Fairchilds, Stinsons, Ansons, Norsemans, Beavers and Otters—and the bush pilots who flew them—ended the isolation that northern Saskatchewan had felt since the economic focus of the province had shifted from north to south at the end of the 19th century.

The initial novelty of air transport largely waned in southern Saskatchewan until World War II. Then, as part of the Allied war effort, the province became a primary training centre for British Commonwealth pilots through the BRITISH COMMONWEALTH AIR TRAINING PLAN. Following the war, in 1947, one of Canada's most sophisticated northern air services was established when the province created Saskatchewan Government Airways, which was privatized as Norcanair (North Canada Air) less than two decades later. The first of over 1,600 single-engine Beaver aircraft (the first all-metal Canadian bush plane) was produced by the Quebec-based DeHavilland company in 1947. This Beaver (CF-FHB) was used in the interior of British Columbia before being acquired by Norcanair in 1969 and used at its Uranium City base until 1980; it was then acquired by the Canada Aviation Museum in Ottawa, where it remains on display still sporting its blue and white Norcanair colours.

A series of airline mergers involving companies such as Canadian Pacific Airlines, Pacific Western Airlines, Transair, Canadian Airlines, Norcanair, and Air Canada led to an economic rationalization of air services within the province which, for some areas, meant service reductions. By the 1970s, attempts to provide regularly scheduled service to cities such as Yorkton and North Battleford could not be economically sustained. Athabasca Airways and La Ronge Aviation replaced Norcanair in providing scheduled air services from the far north to La Ronge, Prince Albert, Saskatoon, and Regina. In 2000, the two airlines merged their scheduled service under the banner of Transwest Air.

Since 2000, air traffic in centres such as Regina, Saskatoon, Prince Albert and La Ronge has been growing, supported by expanded charter and air freight services and by a new era of low-cost passenger flight competition. That competition saw West Jet Airlines lead the challenge of Air Canada's near-monopoly on inter-provincial flights from Saskatchewan. In 2004, more than 2,500 Saskatchewan residents held over 2,800 licences as pilots of aircraft, helicopters, gliders, ultra light aircraft, and balloons. 2,151 were private pilot licences; another 673 concerned commercial and airline personnel. There were 1,705 aircraft of various types registered in the province: 1,373 private, 306 commercial, and 26 government-owned.

Conclusion

As Saskatchewan marks its centennial as a province, transportation remains a critical public policy topic. The provincial government and rural municipalities face enormous costs for maintaining Saskatchewan's massive road network, particularly when rural populations continue to decline owing to mechanization and the increasing size of most modern farms. Meanwhile, expanding urban centres must cope with increased traffic flows and related demands for new roads, overpasses and thoroughfares. Key north-south and east-west road and rail trade corridors are considered essential to support future economic growth. Twinning of key highways (two lanes in each direction) is a public expectation to accommodate continued growth in highway traffic and to address related safety concerns. To fully participate in a modern global economy, including tourism development, Saskatchewan requires convenient airline connections to the rest of the world. Maintaining and increasing the use of public transportation services in larger urban centres, school bussing in rural settings, and transportation services for persons with disabilities are also topics on the public agenda. These varied issues ensure that transportation will continue to be a primary interest for Saskatchewan during its second century as a province.

FURTHER READING:

Berton, P. 1970. *The Last Spike: The Great Railway, 1881–1885.* Toronto: McClelland and Stewart.

Dempsey, H.A. 1984. *The CPR West—The Iron Road and the Making of a Nation.* Vancouver: Douglas and McIntyre.

Eagle, J.A. 1989. *The Canadian Pacific Railway and the Development of Western Canada.* Montreal: McGill-Queen's University Press.

First Nations and Northern Statistics Section. 2003. *Basic Departmental Data—2002.* Ottawa: Department of Indian Affairs and Northern Development.

Henderson, N. 2001. *Rediscovering the Great Plains: Journeys by Dog, Canoe, and Horse.* Baltimore: Johns Hopkins University Press.

Marchildon, G. and S. Robinson. 1998. *Canoeing the Churchill: A Practical Guide to the Historic Voyageur Highway.* Regina: Canadian Plains Research Center.

Peel, B. 1972. *Steamboats on the Saskatchewan.* Saskatoon: The Western Producer.

Rossiter, S. 1996. *The Immortal Beaver.* Vancouver: Douglas & McIntyre.

Saskatchewan Education. 1992. *Wings Beyond Road's End.* La Ronge: Pahkisimon Nuye-ah Library System.

Thompson, J. Herd. 1998. *Forging the Prairie West.* Toronto: Oxford University Press.

MEG MILLAR PHOTO/COURTESY OF NORM HENDERSON/PUBLISHED IN *PLAINS ANTHROPOLOGIST* (VOL. 39, 1994)

Husky and travois.

TRAVOIS. The travois (from a French word akin to *travail*, to work) is a wooden load-bearing frame fastened by a leather harness to a dog or horse. The basic dog travois consists of two aspen or cottonwood poles notched and lashed together at one end with buffalo sinew; the other ends rest splayed apart. Cross-bars are lashed between the poles near the splayed ends, and the finished frame looks like a large letter A with extra cross-bars. The apex of the A, wrapped in buffalo skin to prevent friction burns, rests on a dog's shoulders, while the splayed ends drag over the ground. Travois, used by all Plains Indian nations, were once commonplace throughout the Plains area of what is now Saskatchewan. They are unique to North America: they are not known to have existed in other grassland realms such as the steppes of Europe or the pampas of South America. Travois are ideally suited to their environment: over native grassland the dragging ends move silently and almost without friction; but outside of grasslands the contraption is not very useful, for bush or gullies are impassable.

First Nations women both built the travois and managed the dogs, sometimes using toy travois to train the puppies. Buffalo meat and firewood were typical travois loads. Dogs can tack up and down grassy hill slopes and ford shallow rivers with a travois; but temperature is a serious constraint on travois work, for on warm days dogs overheat easily. Sadly, the original Plains Indian dogs that once pulled travois can no longer be found, as they have mixed with European dogs. In historic times Plains Aboriginal peoples constructed much larger versions of the dog travois and hitched them to horses. Horse travois allowed the transport of the increased material wealth accumulated by some First Nations skilled in the mounted buffalo hunt; children or ill adults could ride on the horse travois load rack as well. The

rack ride is smooth, but riding a horse pulling a travois has a few disadvantages: the rider's legs hang uncomfortably over the travois poles alongside the horse's flanks, and control over the horse is diminished by the loss of thigh-to-horse contact.

Norm Henderson

FURTHER READING: Ewers, J. 1955. *The Horse in Blackfoot Indian Culture.* Washington, DC: Smithsonian Institution, Bureau of American Ethnology Bulletin 159; Henderson, N. 2001. *Rediscovering the Great Plains.* Baltimore: Johns Hopkins University Press.

TREATY RIGHTS: *see* **ABORIGINAL TREATY RIGHTS**

TREATY 4. While negotiators for the British Crown struggled to contain First Nations' demands, the strategy of the Cree and Saulteaux was to gain full compensation for their lands. Agricultural assistance, medical aid and other promises had been verbally made at earlier negotiations of the Numbered Treaties; however, these terms did not appear in the written text of Treaties 1 and 2. Records of the discussions proved that the Crown had indeed made promises beyond what the federal government initially planned: these omissions upset the First Nations, who responded by obstructing the surveying of land and the movements of settlers. While the issue of the "outside promises" was eventually resolved in 1875 through a revision of Treaties 1 and 2, the dissatisfaction over the Canadian government's failure to recognize its treaty commitments set the backdrop for the negotiation of Treaty 4. The treaty ceded 195,000 square km of territory ranging from the southeast corner of present-day Alberta through most of southern Saskatchewan to west-central Manitoba. Canada sent the Hon. Alexander

Morris, Lieutenant-Governor of the North-West Territory, David Laird, Minister of the Interior, and William Christie, retired HBC factor, with an escort of 105 militia to Fort Qu'Appelle on September 8, 1874, to conduct negotiations on behalf of the British Crown.

The Saulteaux, aware of the dissatisfaction of their tribal kin with Treaties 1, 2 and 3, were hesitant to enter into negotiations. On the other hand the Plains Cree, led by Loud Voice (Kakiishiway), had indicated their willingness to listen to the Commissioners. **CHARLES PRATT**, a Cree catechist, served as official translator. While approximately 2,000 had gathered, this represented less than half of the First Nations of the area, and the Assiniboine, who were in the midst of hunting buffalo, were not present at all. With Treaty 4 being the first major treaty to be negotiated in the North-West Territories, the First Nations elected to confront the Crown over the large settlement of money and land that had been made with the Hudson's Bay Company (HBC). On September 8, 1874, the first day of talks, the First Nations indicated that they were not yet sufficiently prepared to meet with the Commissioners. On the second day, Saulteaux spokesman "The Gambler" expressed disappointment that the Commissioners were not camped with the First Nations, and questioned why they chose to stay at the HBC post.

The First Nations requested more time to meet amongst themselves. On the third day the Saulteaux sent a request to have the meeting moved to the Indian camp, but this idea was rejected. The Saulteaux, who were the most numerous, tried to prevent the Cree from attending meetings, at one point making the threatening move of cutting down the tent of one of the chiefs. Tensions were high as the First Nations debated how to approach the issues that would have such momentous consequences for their future. Lead Commissioner Alexander Morris decided to proceed with an address to the Cree, during which he outlined the Queen's promises of a "bounty and benevolence" which included reserves, agricultural provisions, schools, and annuities. Morris frequently mentioned concern about the well-being of children and the yet unborn; and the treaty, he promised, would last "as long as the sun shines and water flows." The Commissioner increased the pressure by claiming that he could not stay long. On the fourth day, the Commissioners agreed to move the meeting tent away from the HBC post, as the First Nations did not feel free to speak out on the Company's property. Grievances about the HBC were again raised by The Gambler, who claimed: "The Company has stolen our land."

Morris countered that the Crown had paid compensation to end the Company's trading monopoly. This explanation was still not satisfactory, prompting influential Chief **PASQUA** to say, "We want that money." On the fifth day, the Saulteaux continued to demand that the activities of the Hudson's Bay Company be restricted, something that Morris replied he did not have the power to do. As the talks began to fall apart, Loud Voice called for the unity of the Cree and Saulteaux as the leader of the Saulteaux, Chief Cote, threatened to leave. After Morris cautioned that it would be a long time before another treaty offer was made, Cote agreed to stay another day. On the following and final day, Cree leader Loud Voice offered the opinion that a treaty would be a good thing. Another spokesman, Kamooses, sought reassurances that the Queen's intentions were good and that "my child will not be troubled for what you are bringing him." After receiving this assurance Kamooses, speaking on behalf of the assembly, stated that they were willing to accept the same terms as Treaty 3. That afternoon, thirteen chiefs placed their "x" on the treaty.

The written terms of Treaty 4 included: reserves of one square mile for every five persons; annuities of $25 for a chief, plus coat and medal, a $15 annuity per headman, and a $5 annuity for each individual; a suit of clothing every three years per chief; blankets, calicoes and British flag (given once); $750 worth of powder, shot and twine annually; two hoes, a spade, scythe, axe and seed per family; a plough and two harrows per ten families; oxen, a bull, four cows, carpenter's tools, five hand saws, five augers, a crosscut saw, a pit saw and a grindstone per chief; there was to be a school on the reserve; no liquor was to be allowed; and hunting, fishing and trapping rights would be respected.

A year after the treaty was signed, confusion reigned as to whether it was valid. Chief **PIAPOT** pressed to expand treaty terms to include clauses concerning farm instruction, machinery, gristmill, medicines, stores, and blacksmiths; and the Indians delayed taking annuities for four days in a futile attempt to further these demands. Implementation of the treaty was very slow. Ottawa believed that the First Nations would continue to survive by hunting the buffalo for another decade, while the chiefs expected agricultural help immediately and were disappointed when told that the treaty stated they had to be settled on their reserves first. In 1876, surveyor Wagner began laying out reserves for Gordon, Pasqua, Kawacatoose, Day Star, and Sakimay.

In 1874, when Treaty 4 was negotiated, the First Nations had insisted on having a Treaty Ground set aside to conduct treaty business. When settlers began to occupy the area, the First Nations applied to the government for assurance that the site would be safeguarded. As Indian Agent Allan Macdonald advised the Deputy Superintendent General of Indian Affairs, "this site ... represents the place on which the Treaty was signed, also where the Indians have assembled to receive their annuities ever since, and they feel a strong attachment to it." In the summer of 1879 the Deputy Minister of

the Department of the Interior concurred: a 1,300-acre site was formally surveyed. Government officials, however, began to doubt the wisdom of having large congregations of Indians in one place—a reflection of the tensions arising from starvation and dissatisfaction with the implementation of treaty terms. In 1882, **EDGAR DEWDNEY** instructed the Indians to take payment of their annuities on their reserves rather than at the Treaty Ground. This plan was met with resistance. Piapot, for example, planted a flag at the Treaty Ground and told Dewdney: "Where I have the flag, that is the land promised for the treaty and that is where I want to get my money." Dewdney confirmed to Ottawa that "the Indians have been told that the Treaty Ground was to be kept for them, it was promised, and the agreement should be carried out as sacred as if the land was an Indian Reserve." The outbreak of the **NORTHWEST RESISTANCE** in 1885 brought about the imposition of the pass system that forbade First Nations to leave their reserves without permission; treaty payments were then moved to reserves, leaving the Treaty Ground in disuse. In 1894, after seeking clearance from the Department of Justice, Indian Affairs informed the Department of the Interior that the Treaty Ground was "no longer required for the purpose for which it was set apart ... it is handed over to your department."

In 1995, after extensive negotiations, the federal government agreed to a settlement just over a century after the Treaty Ground had been abolished. The settlement has made possible the purchasing of much of the original site and enabled the construction of the Treaty 4 Governance Centre, which includes the Chiefs' Legislative Assembly for the 35-member First Nations, a Keeping House and Archives for the preservation of Treaty 4 culture and heritage, and offices for government agencies and other organizations.   *Blair Stonechild*

TREATY 5. Treaty 5, signed in 1875, included three Saskatchewan First Nations: Cumberland House, Shoal River, and Red Earth. Treaty 5 dealt mainly with the Manitoba area, and was unique in the fact that the Treaty Commissioner dealt individually with regional bands rather than with a large treaty area. Water was an important issue because the geographic region covered Lake Winnipeg as well as portions of several important rivers. During the negotiations of Treaty 5, Treaty Commissioner Morris used the strategy of separating the general idea of treaty from the issues of establishing specific reserves. In exchange for access to an area of approximately 100,000 square miles, the Indians of Treaty 5 were to receive reserves of 160 acres per family of five, annuities of $5 per year, clothing and medals, articles for cultivation, education, and the right to hunt, fish and trap; they were to ban alcohol and to keep peace and order.   *Rob Nestor*

FURTHER READING: Ray, A., J. Miller and F. Tough. 2000. *Bounty and Benevolence.* Montreal: McGill-Queen's University Press.

TREATY 6. Treaty 6, between the Queen and bands of Cree and Stoney First Nations, was negotiated and signed at Fort Carlton and Duck Lake in August, and at Fort Pitt in September, 1876. There were many subsequent adhesions to the treaty by individual bands, well into the 20th century. Treaty 6 covers 121,000 miles^2 (309,760 km^2): in what is now Alberta, the Treaty 6 area situated between the Athabasca and South Saskatchewan Rivers, east of the mountains; in what is now Saskatchewan, it extends roughly from a northern limit between 55° and 54° latitude to the South Saskatchewan, then Qu'Appelle rivers. The treaty contained, with some variations, the standard written clauses of the earlier numbered treaties signed with First Nations: surrender of Indian land rights; provision of assistance in the transition to an agricultural economy; provision of reserves (in Treaty 6 the equivalent of one square mile per family of five); establishing schools on reserves; and annuities of $5 per person (more to chiefs and headmen).

However, Treaty 6 was unique in several respects as a result of bargaining between Lieutenant-Governor Alexander Morris and Chiefs Mistawasis and **AHTAHKAKOOP**, who led the First Nations negotiators at Fort Carlton. Treaty 6 contained significantly increased agricultural assistance, in the form of animals and supplies, than other treaties did or would. In negotiating these increased agricultural provisions, the First Nations probably had considerable assistance from the expert translator they hired, English-Métis farmer **PETER ERASMUS**. The treaty contained a unique clause stipulating that a "medicine chest" be kept for the benefit of each band. That clause remains controversial, but it probably signifies what we now call "medicare." The most substantial change contained in Treaty 6 was an entirely new clause written at Fort Carlton, guaranteeing that if the First Nations in the treaty were "overtaken by any pestilence, or by a general famine," then relief would be provided; that "famine clause" was demanded by Red Pheasant headman (and later chief) **POUNDMAKER**.

The Cree and Stoney at Fort Carlton probably understood well the amounts of agricultural supplies and some other treaty provisions they actually negotiated. However, although they had in Peter Erasmus probably the best translator available, it is doubtful that they understood such terms as "cede, release, surrender and yield up ... all rights, titles and privileges" to their land. In the record of the treaty negotiations that Alexander Morris submitted to Ottawa, there was no indication that land rights surrender was even discussed or explained. Erasmus read the written treaty, including the legally worded surrender clause, to the assembled First Nations; but the semantic differences between the languages and cultures may well have been too vast for even the best translator to bridge. It also appears likely that a key part of the surrender clause, that defining the limits of the territory actually surrendered, was absent from the written document when Erasmus read it and the chiefs signed it at Fort Carlton and Duck Lake. Because of a small change he made in the territorial limits from the instructions he had received from Ottawa, it is possible Alexander Morris added the boundaries description at or after the subsequent talks at Fort Pitt. During 1877 and 1878, several bands that had not been present at the initial negotiations signed adhesions to Treaty 6.

Soon after the treaty was first signed, some bands chose reserves, moved to them, and began receiving treaty agricultural supplies. Others refused to choose reserves, and tried to hold out for better terms. But in 1879 the last of the great buffalo herds vanished, and the holdout bands had to adhere to the treaty to survive. Chief **BIG BEAR** was the most determined, but he finally signed in 1882; by that time, he had negotiated promises of additional treaty supplies, promises that continued to be sweetened as he delayed taking a reserve. Treaty 6, as well as the other numbered treaties, contained no provision compelling the First Nations to take reserves: these and other treaty provisions were meant to be in addition to the First Nations' usual way of life, Morris said at the negotiations at Forts Carlton and Pitt. The right to hunt and fish, with some restrictions, was contained in the written treaty text.

However, after 1879 the Canadian government used increasing hunger among the First Nations to force them on to reserves: only First Nations who were actually settled and working for rations would receive food. The government believed that keeping First Nations in a state of near-starvation would bend them to its will; it also realized that this policy was likely to cause death and illness–as it did. The First Nations interpreted the loss of the buffalo to be the "general famine" covered under the famine clause of Treaty 6, and many observers in the North-West agreed. But the Canadian government insisted that its grudging distribution of rations was a matter of favour, not a treaty obligation. As for the provision of treaty agricultural supplies, it was done in a disorganized, parsimonious and careless manner, with the result that many bands did not receive anything like the quantity or quality they were entitled to under the treaty. The lack of implementation, or at best the very poor implementation, of the provisions of Treaty 6 was the major reason some First Nations individuals participated in the **NORTH-WEST RESISTANCE** of 1885.   *Bob Beal*

TREATY 8. Treaty 8, signed in 1899, covers portions of the boreal forest area in northern Saskatchewan. Unlike Treaties 1 through 7, which were signed between 1871 and 1877, it was not agricultural development or transcontinental transportation, but mining that spurred the treaty signing process in the north. Under Treaty 8, Indians would have the right to hunt, fish and trap throughout the surrendered tract except in those areas that were taken up from time to time for settlement, mining, lumbering, trading or other purposes. Treaty 8 also made provisions for reserves and allowed Indians to hold their land collectively as bands, or individually in severalty. The other provisions of the Treaty were similar to those of the 1870s treaties and included annuities, ammunition and twine, education, rights to hunt, fish and trap, clothing, and medals and articles for cultivation. Treaty 8 provided the federal government with terms for peaceable economic development, at a time when neither federal nor provincial government had the means to deal with any kind of Indian resistance to development in the northern parts of the province.   *Rob Nestor*

FURTHER READING: Ray, A., J. Miller and F. Tough. 2000. *Bounty and Benevolence*. Montreal: McGill-Queen's University Press.

TREATY 10. Treaty 10, signed in 1906–07, covered the northern portions of the province which were not included by Treaties 6 or 8. The area of Treaty 10 also encompassed regions that were not surrendered by those groups who adhered to **TREATY 6** but had traditionally occupied lands within the Treaty 10 region. This Treaty was largely modeled on **TREATY 8**. In exchange for access to the surrendered territory and similarly to the promises made under Treaty 8, it was agreed that Canada would provide reserves, annuities, clothing and medals, articles for cultivation, education, and the rights to hunt, fish and trap. As in the case of Treaty 8, it was access to mining and timber resources that most interested the government and spurred its desire to conclude a treaty in the northern portions of the province. For the Indians who took part in these negotiations, it was the maintenance of traditional livelihoods, access to lands, and the provision of health and education that were most important.   *Rob Nestor*

FURTHER READING: Ray, A., J. Miller and F. Tough. 2000. *Bounty and Benevolence*. Montreal: McGill-Queen's University Press.

TREES. All of the broad-leaved trees of Saskatchewan are flowering plants (angiosperms) and dicots (i.e., where seedlings have two seed leaves or cotyledons). They are deciduous, shedding their leaves at the end of summer. Broad-leaved trees are also called hardwoods because of the high density of their wood (compared to softwoods such as conifers). The eight species which regularly exceed 10 m in height at maturity, or large trees, are the subject of this entry. Eleven other native woody dicots can be small trees: speckled alder, water birch, mountain ash, two or three willows, saskatoon, chokecherry, pincherry, wild plum, mountain maple, and nannyberry. The diversity of broad-leaved trees mirrors their nationally and globally higher diversity as compared to coniferous trees.

Five of these trees (Manitoba maple, green ash, American elm, bur oak, eastern cottonwood) belong to the western elements of the eastern deciduous temperate forest of North America, and commonly occur together. The other three species (trembling aspen, balsam poplar, white birch) are associated with both the boreal forest and the eastern deciduous forest but are usually thought of as boreal species.

Manitoba maple (*Acer negundo*: family Aceraceae) is most prevalent along the river valleys and coulees of south-central and southeastern Saskatchewan, with an extension westward along the **SOUTH SASKATCHEWAN RIVER**. It is associated with green ash and with American elm, trembling aspen, white birch, and balsam poplar in the north-central and northeastern part of its range. The mature tree is usually 10–15 m in height, with diameters up to 50 cm; it has ridged, light grey bark, and the opposite leaves are normally divided into several parts. The winged seeds spin like helicopters when released from the tree.

The distribution of green ash (*Fraxinus pensylvanica*: family Oleaceae) is almost identical to that of Manitoba maple, excluding the South Saskatchewan. Green ash is a denizen of alluvial floodplains, lake shores, and coulees. It may be confused with Manitoba maple, but its opposite leaves are divided into five or seven leaflets. The 3 cm- long winged seed spins when released from the tree. Mature trees may be over 20 m tall, with diameters over 50 cm; the trunk is straight and tapers a little, with ridged brownish-grey bark. It is an important landscaping tree.

American or white elm (*Ulmus americana*: family Ulmaceae) is often planted for shade. The most extensive natural stands, with the largest trees, are found on the rich alluvial soils of the floodplains of the Carrot and Saskatchewan rivers near the Manitoba border. The species also occurs in the Dirt Hills and in the wooded coulees of the **MISSOURI COUTEAU**, but is much smaller in these prairie environments. The tree reaches heights of 25 m and diameters of over 50 cm, with entire, sharply toothed, opposite leaves up to 10 cm long and dark, ridged and furrowed bark. The species has been ravaged by beetle-borne Dutch elm disease, and most natural populations are in serious decline.

Bur oak (*Quercus macrocarpa*: family Fagaceae) is found in the southeast of the province, mainly along the valleys of the **QU'APPELLE** and **SOURIS RIVERS**, with a small population along the **ASSINIBOINE RIVER**. The alternate leaves are deeply lobed, and the bark is rough and deeply furrowed. This tree is relatively small in Saskatchewan, reaching heights of 15 m and diameters of 30 cm.

The eastern cottonwood (*Populus deltoides*: family Salicaceae) is a large poplar found along the flood plains of the North and South Saskatchewan rivers, and sporadically along the Qu'Appelle and Souris river valleys. It also inhabits moist, sandy depressions in the **GREAT SAND HILLS**. The tree reproduces by seed and by suckering from roots and branches carried downstream by water. The leaves, triangular and with rounded teeth, have a length of 5–10 cm. The cottony seeds are borne in capsules called catkins. Cottonwood can be a large tree over 25 m in height and 100 cm in diameter, with corky, deeply furrowed bark. These trees are used in shelterbelts and for landscaping (often as hybrids). The alluvial ecosystems dominated by cottonwood are considered endangered because of changes produced by hydroelectric dams that prevent the spring floods which have for ages created the alluvial seed beds required for the perpetuation of this species.

Trembling aspen (*P. tremuloides*) is perhaps the best known of our native broad-leaved trees. It is found from coulees in the south to the groves of the Aspen Parkland to the boreal forest. It makes up the bulk of pure hardwood stands in the Boreal Plain and is a major component of mixedwood forests (associated with white spruce or jack pine). It becomes less common northward across the Boreal Shield, and is rare in the Taiga Shield. This is a slender, graceful tree having smooth bark (made whitish-green by a powdery bloom) and a rounded crown. The leaves, with fine teeth, are nearly circular with a short tip. The leaf stalk is flattened, which enables the leaves to tremble in the slightest breeze, giving the tree its name. The downy seed is found in capsules on the long catkins, but the tree usually reproduces vegetatively by suckering. The trembling aspen, which may attain heights of over 30 m and diameters of over 40 cm, is a source of commercial pulp and wood products.

Balsam poplar (*P. balsamifera*) is a tree of moist depressions, lake shores, and river valleys. It ranges from the Qu'Appelle and Saskatchewan valleys to the boreal forest to the Northwest Territories (NWT) border. This species has a bullet-shaped crown occupying the upper half of the trunk. The bark is dark and furrowed on the bottom of the trunk, but smoother and olive-green higher up the bole. The cottony seeds are in capsules on long catkins. The finely toothed leaves are egg-shaped, with a gradually tapering, pointed tip. The resinous buds give off an exquisite scent on moist spring evenings. The name of the tree derives from this scent, which resembles the perfume of the balm of

Gilead (*P. candicans*), itself deriving its name from a resemblance to that of the Old World balm of Gilead (*Commiphora gileadensis*). Balsam poplar can be a very large tree, with heights of over 30 m and diameters of over 100 cm.

White birch, Saskatchewan arboreal emblem.

White birch (*Betula papyrifera*: family Betulaceae) is the arboreal emblem of the province of Saskatchewan. This tree is found from **MOOSE MOUNTAIN** and the **CYPRESS HILLS** north through the boreal forest to the NWT border. Birch seldom forms pure stands of any extent, being almost always associated with other broad-leaved or coniferous trees. It flourishes in dry sandy sites and on rock outcrops as well as in moist, rich riparian areas such as river valleys and lake shores. The leaves are egg-shaped, with large, pointed teeth and a length of up to eight cm. The winged seeds are dropped from the catkins in fall and winter, and it is common to see the scales and seeds scattered over snow surfaces beneath birch trees. The outer papery bark peels away from the trunk over time.

The shapely coniferous trees of Saskatchewan's boreal forest and Cypress Hills are all naked-seeded plants (gymnosperms) in the family Pinaceae. Their seeds are borne on scales arranged into cones (hence the name coniferous). They all have needle-like leaves and fragrant, resinous wood of considerable commercial value in some species. Mature trees have short branches, straight trunks, and conical to columnar crowns. All are evergreen (their needles live for two or more years), with the exception of tamarack, our only deciduous conifer. All of our species are shade-intolerant, and most of the canopy of an old stand must be removed in order for these species to be successfully regenerated by fire or logging (balsam fir is the exception to this rule). The

low diversity of this group (six species) is typical of the boreal forest, an unproductive biome with harsh winters and short, dry summers. The native conifers are widespread across the rest of the Canadian boreal forest.

The native pines are tough trees adapted to growth on dry sands or rocky sites. Lodgepole pine (*Pinus contorta*) and jack pine (*P. banksiana*) are sister species thought to have arisen from an ancestral pine whose population was split by the last continental ice sheet. Jack pine is found from the prairie-forest ecotone to the NWT border, while lodgepole pine is restricted to the Cypress Hills. Both species have 2–4 cm-long needles, grouped in pairs. Both attain heights of 20–25 m and diameters of over 40 cm. The cones are serotinous, i.e., their scales stay firmly closed until heated in a forest fire or by sun-warmed ground. The cone scales of lodgepole pine are armoured with prickles. These pines grow in pure stands, but associations with trembling aspen, white birch or black spruce (for jack pine only) are fairly common. Jack pine is an important lumber species.

White spruce (*P. glauca*) and black spruce (*P. mariana*) are trees of moist to wet sites. White spruce is the signature tree of the southern boreal mixedwood zone (the Mid-boreal Upland). It is also a conspicuous tree of moist, nutrient-rich riparian zones bordering waters across the Boreal Plain. Its prominence in the forest declines on the Shield, and it is virtually absent north of Lake Athabasca. Black spruce is the characteristic boreal conifer of poorly drained fens and bogs (peatlands) with cold and nutrient-poor organic (peaty) soils. On the Shield it also occurs on rocky upland sites. White spruce has longer needles (2 cm) than black spruce (1.25 cm), and its cones are up to 5 cm long and narrowly cylindrical, while black spruce cones are egg-shaped and up to 2.5 cm long. Black spruce cones are serotinous. The presence of minute white hairs on the young twigs of black spruce conclusively differentiate it from white spruce. White spruce is the largest provincial tree, reaching heights of over 30 m and diameters well over 50 cm. Black spruce is a smaller tree, with a narrower crown and down-sweeping branches; it has a height of over 20 m and a diameter of over 30 cm. White spruce is the most valuable lumber tree in Saskatchewan.

Tamarack or larch (*Larix laricina*) is a deciduous conifer found in swamps with groundwater flow or in very acid black spruce sphagnum peat bogs with little groundwater influence. The species occurs throughout the provincial boreal forest. Tamarack is the most shade-intolerant of the native conifers and always grows in open stands. Its soft, light-green needles (up to 2.5 cm long) appear in clusters of 10–20 on dwarf twigs. In autumn, it lights up the wetlands with a gorgeous golden-yellow display as its needles turn colour and fall. Larch cones are about 1.5 cm long and open to shed seed in the fall. The tree may attain a height of over 25 m and diameters of over 40 cm.

Balsam fir (*Abies balsamea*) seedlings are able to grow in the shade of other trees and, in the absence of fire, may become the canopy dominants. Because fir sheds its cone scales and seeds each fall, it has no canopy seed bank and if fire sweeps through a stand the species is likely to be extirpated, with no seed bank available for reestablishment. Balsam fir is of sporadic occurrence in Saskatchewan (largely restricted to the southern half of the boreal forest), most often appearing on moist, rich sites in riparian areas in the lee of lakes or rivers, where the trees have the greatest chance of escaping periodic forest fires. Fir needles are flat; the bark is smooth and grey, with resin-filled blisters that pop when pressed, exuding the aromatic resin characteristic of this fragrant tree. The crown is narrow, pyramidal, and spire-like at its apex. The tree may attain a height of over 25 m and a diameter of over 40 cm. *Robert A. Wright*

FURTHER READING: Farrar, J.L. 1995. *Trees in Canada*. Ottawa: Natural Resources Canada, Canadian Forest Service; Hosie, R.C. 1969. *Native Trees of Canada*, 7th edition. Ottawa: Canadian Forest Service, Department of the Environment; Johnson, D., L. Kershaw, A. MacKinnon and J. Pojar. 1995. *Plants of the Western Boreal Forest and Aspen Parkland*. Edmonton: Lone Pine Publishing.

TREW, BEATRICE JANET (1897–1976). Beatrice Trew (*née* Coates) was born on December 4, 1897, in Coates Mills, New Brunswick. She

Beatrice Trew.

received teacher training in Fredericton and moved to a school at Manor, Saskatchewan in 1917. The following year she taught at Lemsford, where she met and married J. Albert Trew, a district farmer. When the Lemsford **HOMEMAKERS CLUB** was formed in 1920, she was elected first secretary-treasurer. She later became president of the Swift Current district Homemakers. In 1944 she was elected MLA for Maple Creek. Defeated in 1948, she returned to her active role in Homemakers and in the local church; she received a life membership in the Lemsford Homemakers Club. Trew was a member of the national council of the CCF for eleven years, and vice-president of the Saskatchewan section of the party for eight years. When the **SASKATCHEWAN FARMERS UNION** was organized in 1950, she and her husband joined; she became women's district director in 1953, and was elected women's president of the provincial farm union in 1958, a post she held for five years. She represented farm union women at three meetings of the Associated Country Women. Trew was a member of the Thompson Advisory Planning Committee on Medical Care, which in 1961 laid the groundwork for Canada's first universal medical care plan. The committee study took her to England, Holland, Norway, Sweden, and Denmark. She died in a traffic accident on June 4, 1976. *Bob Ivanochko*

TROTCHIE, CLARENCE (1923–87). MÉTIS activist and leader Clarence Trotchie was born on October 14, 1923, in Round Prairie, Saskatchewan. He came from a large family, and grew up on the outskirts of Saskatoon. His early years were spent like other Métis of his generation, working low-paying seasonal jobs. At the age of 17 he enlisted in the army, only to be discharged when his age was discovered; a year later he re-enlisted, returning home in 1945. His **WORLD WAR II** experience had a great impact on him and drove him to become socially and politically active upon returning to his community. In the late 1960s, he worked with other Métis to form Métis Local 11, a local division of the provincial Métis Society of Saskatchewan (MSS), serving as local president for a number of years. In 1971–72 he served as MSS area director and was instrumental in organizing the Native Alcohol Centre. In 1973, the Native Alcohol Centre–the precursor to the Métis Nation-Saskatchewan affiliate, Métis Addictions Council of Saskatchewan–became the responsibility of the MSS, with Trotchie as its director from 1973 to 1978. He was also involved in organizing housing initiatives for Métis families, forming SaskNative Rentals in 1978, and establishing in 1979 the Touchwood Training School at a farm purchased by Trotchie, with the intent of addressing the issues of employment and education and of creating skills training programs for Métis youth. Trotchie was also instrumental in having the Round Prairie

Clarence Trotchie, December 1983.

Cemetery designated as a historic site in 1973. He died on April 10, 1987, in Saskatoon. *Cheryl Troupe*

TROTTIER, BRYAN (1956–). A talented all-round player through eighteen NHL seasons, Bryan Trottier was born in Val Marie, Saskatchewan on July 17, 1956. He played junior hockey with the Swift Current Broncos (later Lethbridge) of the Western Canada Junior Hockey League before joining the New York Islanders for the 1975–76 season. Trottier made an immediate impact in his second NHL game with a hat trick and two assists. He finished the year with ninety-five points and won the Calder Trophy as top rookie. Centered between Mike Bossy and Moose Jaw native **CLARK GILLIES**, Trottier won the Art Ross Trophy as top scorer and Hart Trophy as most valuable player in the 1978–79 season. The following year, the Islanders won the first of four consecutive Stanley Cup championships while Trottier earned the Conn Smythe Trophy as playoff MVP. Although his point production diminished along with the Islanders dynasty, Trottier's post-season experience earned him a spot with the Pittsburg Penguins. Two more Stanley Cup wins followed in 1990–91 and 1991–92 before Trottier retired at the end of the season. After a short stint in the Islanders' front office, Trottier played forty-one games for the Penguins during the 1993–94 season. He retired a second time, and remained with the club as an assistant coach until 1997. Trottier coached the American Hockey League's Portland Pirates for one season and returned to the NHL as an assistant coach with the Colorado Avalanche, helping the team to their second Stanley Cup title in 2001. He coached the New York Rangers for fifty-four games during the 2002–03 season. Bryan

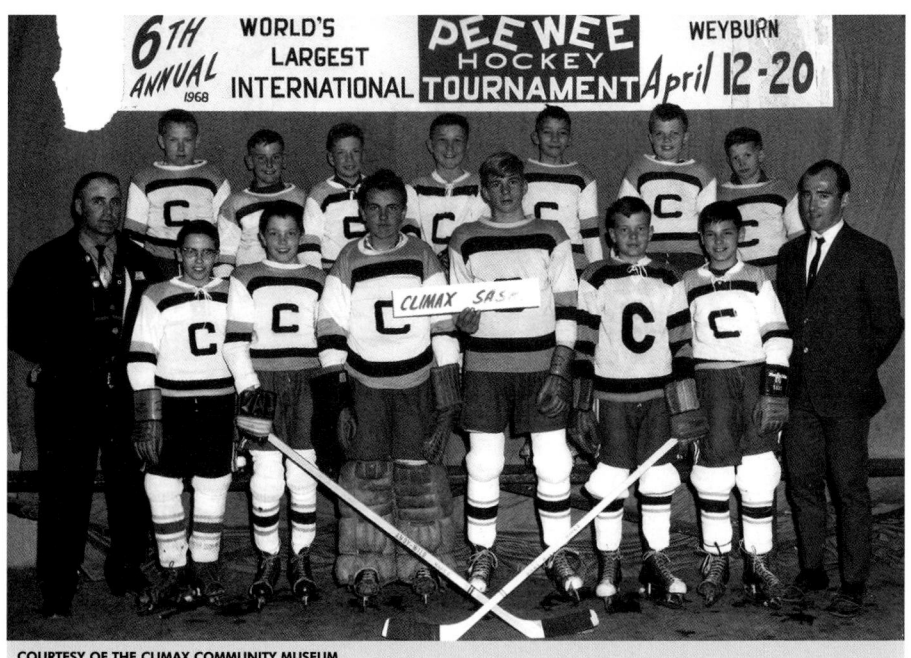

Bryan Trottier (back row, centre) with the Climax Hockey Team, 1968.

Trottier scored 524 goals and added 901 assists for 1,425 points in eighteen NHL regular seasons. The league's sixth-highest all-time scorer when he retired, he was inducted into the Hockey Hall of Fame and SASKATCHEWAN SPORTS HALL OF FAME in 1997.   *Daria Coneghan and Holden Stoffel*

FURTHER READING: Podnieks, A. et al. 2002. *Kings of the Ice: A History of World Hockey.* Richmond Hill, Ontario: NDE Publishing.

TROUPE DU JOUR, LA. *La Troupe du jour* is the only francophone professional theatre company in Saskatchewan. It was founded in 1985 in Saskatoon by a group of young people led by Alphonse Gaudet, the first artistic director, who has continued to have close connections with the company. This group had been doing amateur theatre in French in the city and at the UNIVERSITY OF SASKATCHEWAN; they were determined to offer opportunities to a diverse francophone community to see and participate in plays of high artistic quality. Under current artistic director Denis Rouleau, who joined the company in 1989, the high ideals of the original players have been maintained and expanded. Others who have made important contributions to the company are Ian Nelson, Laurier Gareau, Adrienne Sawchuk, Frédérique Baudemont, and Raoul Granger. The quality of *La Troupe*'s work has been recognized on several occasions by prestigious awards.

La Troupe has offered a full and varied season every year since 1986: plays, shows, and dramatic readings for adults, adolescents and children; festivals and workshops for the formation of actors, directors, technicians, and playwrights; touring shows to schools and community halls throughout Saskatchewan and to other provinces and countries; and collaborative productions and creative projects with other professional companies, both local and across Canada. *La Troupe*'s unique situation in a region where the minority francophone public is scattered and diverse in origin has created particular challenges for survival. These have been artistic, linguistic, and financial. Under Rouleau's direction, the company has risen admirably to these challenges, offering a wide range of choices in its programming, experimenting boldly with fresh new approaches to theatre, encouraging creativity in the community, collaborating with other theatre companies, providing a chance to see good theatre for French and immersion school students, and playing with bilingualism in highly original ways.

La Troupe du jour had its own theatre space, Le Bas-Côté, between 1990 and 1996. During that time, it was able to offer subscription series, build a loyal public, expand its touring initiatives, and advance many of its artistic objectives. Since 1996, it has been obliged to share space, usually a church hall, with other groups and companies, and to move frequently. The lack of permanent theatre space and the reduced presence of the company on the local cultural scene due to this lack of recognizable premises continue to be major problems. At the same time, the energy and vision of Denis Rouleau and all the members of the company, along with their determination to serve artistically the francophone and francophile community throughout Saskatchewan, remain exemplary.   *Louise H. Forsyth*

FURTHER READING: Forsyth, L.H. 2001. "La Troupe du jour de Saskatoon: une compagnie-laboratoire." Pp. 135–50 in H. Beauchamp and J. Beddows (eds.), *Les théâtres professionnels du Canada francophone: Entre mémoire et rupture.* Ottawa: Le Nordir.

TRUCK TRANSPORT. Tremendous advances in trucking transportation have been made since 1898, when the first commercial truck, bought by the Robert Simpson Company of Toronto, was used in Canada. Originally, the cabs of the trucks had no doors, heaters, or automatic–if any–windshield wipers; thirty miles was considered a long run and would take all day to complete. The shift from horse to truck in 1914 was one of the greatest developments of World War I. However, the trucking industry almost came to a halt in the late 1920s because the roads needed for long-distance commuting were non-existent. By the early 1930s, an excess of cheap manpower was available owing to the GREAT DEPRESSION, and the highway systems project was well underway.

In the late 1930s, Saskatchewan had only 132 miles of paved road and 2,402 miles of gravel. At this time, a group of ambitious truckers formed the Saskatchewan Motor Transport Association; by the 1950s, the name was changed to the Saskatchewan Trucking Association (STA). The STA represented the industry in government discussions regarding issues such as deregulation, weights and measures. During WORLD WAR II, trucks were essential for carrying supplies, soldiers, and other materials. By 1940, there were 278,777 commercial vehicles registered in Canada, and fierce competition grew between the railway and trucking industries. The golden age for many long-haul truckers was the mid-1950s to 1970: there was no traffic congestion, new training methods were implemented, and two-way radios emerged. The Trans-Canada Highway opened at Roger's Pass in BC in the early 1960s; in 1970, the $1 billion highway was completely paved and spanned 7,821 km.

Today, Saskatchewan has over 185,000 km of rural public highways, one of the most developed road systems in Canada. Since the 1970s both the amount and type of truck traffic have changed, with truck traffic volumes tripling. Saskatchewan's truck grain hauling is seventeen times higher than in the early 1970s; in 1997, Census Canada listed trucking as the number-one employer of Canadian men. The removal of the Crow Rate subsidy on railway grain hauling forced railway companies to abandon some Saskatchewan rail lines. The trucking industry responded by expanding its fleet of trucks and employees so that grain would reach the market in large quantities and at a reasonable rate.

In the early 1990s the trucking industry was deregulated. Safety, engine emissions, employee welfare, tracking technology, and customer satisfaction are now the STA's main concerns. One initiative is to follow the National Safety Code Standards which

955

will benefit and protect all drivers. In Saskatchewan, trucks transport 95% of goods moved within the province, and over 28,000 people are employed by the transportation industry. Approximately 2,400 registered trucking companies import hundreds of millions of dollars into Saskatchewan every year.

Pat Rediger

TUBERCULOSIS CONTROL. The Saskatchewan Anti-Tuberculosis League was founded in 1911, at the instigation of provincial health commissioner Dr. **MAURICE SEYMOUR**, with the appointment of Dr. W.M. Hart of Duluth, Minnesota, as the first medical superintendent. TB was then an epidemic raging out

of control in Saskatchewan, with nearly 1,000 new cases every year, and one or two deaths each day.

Dr. Hart joined the medical corps during **WORLD WAR I** and chose not to return to Saskatchewan. The first TB sanatorium was built at Fort Qu'Appelle ("Fort San"), with Dr. **R.G. FERGUSON** in charge. Dr. H.C. Boughton headed the follow-up department until 1925, when the Saskatoon San was opened under his direction; he retired in 1959. Dr. R.W. Kirkby directed treatment of veterans and children at Fort San until he took charge of the Prince Albert San when it opened in 1930. Dr. Ferguson then became director of medical services and general superintendent of all three sanatoria, with the

appointment of Dr. T.W. Hamilton as medical superintendent at Fort San from 1930 until his death sixteen years later.

Dr. Ferguson was a leader, an educator and a researcher of international importance. Under his leadership, Saskatchewan had the lowest tuberculosis death rate in Canada from 1921 to 1940. In January 1929 Saskatchewan became the first jurisdiction in North America to provide TB treatment at no cost to the patient. In the 1930s, Dr. Ferguson and Dr. A.B. Symes, from the Indian Hospital in Fort Qu'Appelle, established the value of BCG (Bacillus Calmette-Guérin) vaccination among newborn Aboriginal infants and student nurses; the vaccination was about 80% effective in preventing tuberculosis among high-risk subjects. The first mass x-ray surveys in North America were made possible by Bob Connell, who ingeniously modified a 35 mm camera to photograph the fluoroscopic image of the chest that was projected on a fluorescent screen. The first mass x-ray survey was conducted in Melville in 1941, and the first provincewide survey was completed by August 1947. The fifth and final provincewide survey was completed in 1962.

When Dr. Ferguson retired in September 1948, he was succeeded by Dr. John Orr as director of medical services for all three sanatoria. Dr. Orr introduced the prophylactic use of antibiotics in the treatment of children under 5 with a positive tuberculin reaction, and the vaccination of negative tuberculin reactors among newborn First Nations children. In the latter program, from 1953 to 1964, Ms Josie Walz traveled throughout northern Saskatchewan by canoe, dog team and airplane, in an effort to reach those in remote areas. In 1957, Dr. G. Dudley Barnett succeeded Dr. Orr as director of tuberculosis for the province, and began centralizing all patient records on readily sorted IBM punch cards. This database attracted international attention. By 1955 early detection, segregation and treatment with adequate antibiotics resulted in early discharge and the creation of vacant beds. The Prince Albert San was closed in 1961; the final use of beds at Fort San was in 1972; and Saskatoon San discharged its last patient on June 26, 1978.

In June 1973 the League established the Dr. George Ferguson Professorship, and began funding which initiated and developed the Division of Respiratory Medicine at the **UNIVERSITY OF SASKATCHEWAN**. Dr. V.H. Hoeppner was the League's final director of TB Control. He continued in that post for Saskatchewan Health when the responsibility for TB was transferred back to the provincial government in 1987 and the League formally became the Lung Association. In the early 21st century, TB remains a problem in the Aboriginal population, with about sixty-five new cases per 100,000 population; but cases are quickly identified and treated, so that deaths from TB are rare. Directly Observed

SASKATCHEWAN FILM BOARD PHOTO/SASKATCHEWAN ARCHIVES BOARD R-B2413

Saskatchewan Sanatorium, Fort Qu'Appelle.

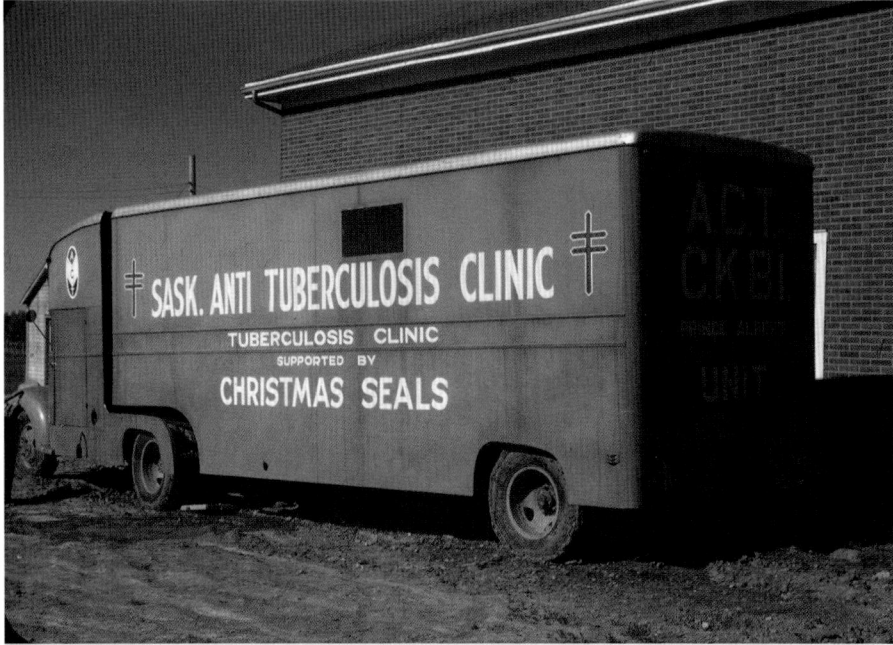

EVERETT BAKER PHOTO/COURTESY OF THE SASKATCHEWAN HISTORY AND FOLKLORE SOCIETY

Mobile anti-tuberculosis clinic in Gravelbourg, Saskatchewan, June 1947.

Therapy (DOT) now helps prevent development of resistant bacteria. In the non-Aboriginal, Canadian-born segment of Saskatchewan's population, there is each year less than one new case of TB per 100,000 people–a remarkable achievement. Dr. Brian Graham, as the CEO of the Lung Association of Saskatchewan, is presently involved in the Ecuador Tuberculosis Project, using lessons learned in Saskatchewan to establish an effective TB control program in a Third World country.

For seventy-six years, the Saskatchewan Anti-Tuberculosis League was in charge of the tuberculosis program throughout the province. Typically, less than half the money was provided by the provincial government, while an equal amount was contributed by the two municipal organizations, the **SASKATCHEWAN ASSOCIATION OF RURAL MUNICIPALITIES** and the Saskatchewan Association of Urban Municipalities. Some municipalities thus expended more money on one disease, tuberculosis, than they did on roads. Additional support came from the Christmas Seals Campaign and radio amateur hours sponsored by Associated Canadian Travellers, from the Imperial Order of the Daughters of the Empire, and from the general public. The League had outstanding lay presidents, including Peter McAra, A.B. Cook, E.G. Hingley, and Ken More. It provided 10.5 million days of patient care over sixty-one years, and was one of the most efficient, successful and best-supported voluntary grassroots organizations that any government ever funded.   *G. Dudley Barnett*

FURTHER READING: Houston, C.S. 1991. *R.G. Ferguson, Crusader Against Tuberculosis.* Toronto: Dundurn Press; Larmour, J.B.D. 1987. *A Matter of Life and Breath: The 75-year History of the Saskatchewan Anti-tuberculosis League and the Saskatchewan Lung Association.* Saskatoon: Saskatchewan Lung Association.

TUCKER, WALTER ADAM (1899–1990). Tucker was born in Portage la Prairie, Manitoba, on March 11, 1899. At the age of 18 he graduated with a BA from the University of Manitoba. In 1923 he attended the College of Law at the **UNIVERSITY OF SASKATCHEWAN** and graduated with high academic standing. In 1925 Tucker began practicing law in Rosthern.

Tucker was elected to the House of Commons from Rosthern in 1935. From 1945 to 1948 Tucker was parliamentary assistant to the Minister of Veterans Affairs. He resigned from Parliament to lead the Saskatchewan Liberals in the 1948 election campaign. As leader, he attempted to rebuild the party after its disastrous defeat in 1944, and promoted the party's new identity as the defender of capitalism. The CCF was firmly entrenched in the political landscape of the province, however, and although Tucker was elected to represent Rosthern provincially in 1948 and 1952, the party was defeat-

© M.WEST, REGINA, WEST'S STUDIO
COLLECTION/SASKATCHEWAN ARCHIVES BOARD R-A8051-1
Walter Tucker.

ed twice and he resigned as leader.

In 1953 Tucker resigned his seat in the Saskatchewan Legislature and was again elected to the House of Commons for the constituency of Rosthern. Tucker, a veteran of both world wars, led the federal committee that introduced bills that provided for the rehabilitation of veterans of **WORLD WAR II**. He retired from politics in 1958. During the years 1958 to 1963 Tucker practiced law in Saskatoon. In 1963 he was appointed to the Court of Queen's Bench where he served until 1974. He died on September 19, 1990.   *Dwayne Yasinowski*

FURTHER READING: Kritzwiser, H.H. 1946. "The Liberals Choose a Proven Leader," *Western Business and Industry* 20 (8); Smith, David E. 1975. *Prairie Liberalism: The Liberal Party in Saskatchewan 1906–71.* Toronto: University of Toronto Press.

TURGEON, WILLIAM FERDINAND-ALPHONSE (1877–1969). Turgeon was born on June 3, 1877, in Petit-Rocher, NB, and raised in New York. His father, Onésiphore, was a member of Parliament and a senator. In 1893 he attended the Collège de Lévis in Quebec, and then Laval, where he received a BA in 1900. He apprenticed at a law firm in St. John, NB, and moved to Prince Albert in 1903, as it was the judicial centre for the North-West Territories. He founded a law practice and soon was invited to become a Crown prosecutor.

Turgeon connected with the "Liberal Machine" and with Monsignor Albert Pascal, bishop of Prince Albert. He was elected to the provincial Legislature and appointed Attorney General in 1907, a position he held until 1921. He spearheaded the development of a provincial telephone system, the University of

Saskatchewan, and co-operative elevators. His most notable achievement, however, came in the field of Francophone rights.

In 1921, Turgeon accepted a seat on the Saskatchewan Court of Appeals. He rose to the position of Chief Justice before his retirement from the bench in 1941. He set a benchmark no one else has yet surpassed: the most Royal Commissions served on by one person (twelve). Instead of retiring, Turgeon began his diplomatic career. By the time he retired in 1956, he had served as the ambassador to Argentina, Mexico, Belgium, Ireland and Portugal, and was the first Canadian ambassador to Chile. He retired to Prince Albert, where he died on January 11, 1969.

Turgeon received many honours, including the Order of Canada, and had a street in Regina and a school in Prince Albert named for him. His former residence in Regina was moved in 1983 to its present location. Now known as the Turgeon International Hostel, it is a provincial heritage site.   *Dana Turgeon*

FURTHER READING: Morrissette, Pierre. 1976. "La carriere politique de W.F.A. Turgeon, 1907–1921." MA thesis, University of Regina.

SASKATCHEWAN ARCHIVES BOARD R-A251
William Turgeon.

TURKEY VULTURE. The turkey vulture (*Cathartes aura*) is one of the seven members of the family Cathartidae or New World vultures. These carrion-feeding birds, with their naked heads, weak, tearing beaks and long soaring wings, resemble the Old World vultures, which are carrion-feeding hawks. However, DNA analysis shows the New World vultures to be closely related to the storks.

The turkey vulture is found throughout Central and southern North America. In Saskatchewan, it is

R.J. LONG/© SASKATCHEWAN ENVIRONMENT/SKCDC, 2001.
ECOSYSTEM IMAGE INFORMATION SYSTEM

Turkey vulture (*Cathartes aura*).

an uncommon nester in river valleys and coulees of the southeast. It can be seen soaring in the thermals of summer days, with its distinctive rectangular black wings and small head.   *Diane Secoy*

FURTHER READING: Alsop, Fred J., III. 2002. *Birds of Canada*. New York: Dorling Kindersley.

TURNER, EDWARD KERR (1927–). Ted Turner was born on April 6, 1927, near Maymont, Saskatchewan. After graduating from the University of Saskatchewan School of Agriculture in 1948, he became active in the Maymont Agricultural Society and the Young Farmers Club. In 1951 he was elected to the SASKATCHEWAN WHEAT POOL committee and became a district delegate in 1957; he was elected director in 1960, first vice-president in 1966, and president in 1969, a position he held until 1987. During his presidency, Turner fought tenaciously for farm programs more relevant to the needs of farmers. He voiced the concerns of farmers to governments and to other farm groups provincially, nationally, and internationally, and was consulted by key officials in Ottawa on agricultural policy.

Turner served on the Conference Board of Canada and as chairman of Canada's International Trade Advisory Committee (ITAC) Task Force on Agriculture. He was advisor to the Canadian government delegation at International Wheat Agreement negotiations in Geneva in 1971 and 1978. Turner represented Canadian farmers at conferences of the International Federation of Agricultural Producers on six occasions. He served on the advisory committees to the CANADIAN WHEAT BOARD (1969–82) and to the Economic Council of Canada. Turner headed the Pool at a time when there was a dramatic reduction in rail lines, and therefore a parallel reduction in country elevators: large centralized elevators were built, and the Pool launched into value-added manufacture of agricultural products. Sometimes unpopular decisions had to be made as a result of the changing scope of prairie agriculture; but Turner fought to maintain a basic structure of rail lines to serve prairie grain farmers and to preserve the powers of the Canadian Wheat Board.

When he retired as president of the Pool, Turner served two years as executive director of Prairie Pools Inc. In 1989 he was elected Chancellor of the UNIVERSITY OF SASKATCHEWAN. He was named a Member of the Order of Canada in 1990, and was awarded an honorary Doctor of Laws degree from the University of Saskatchewan, an honorary life membership in the Agricultural Institute of Canada, and the Saskatchewan Co-operative Order of Merit. In 1995 Turner was inducted into the Saskatchewan Agricultural Hall of Fame.

TURPEL-LAFOND, MARY ELLEN (1963–). On March 5, 1998, Mary Ellen Turpel-Lafond became the first Treaty Indian to be appointed Provincial Court Judge in Saskatchewan. Born Mary Ellen Turpel at Norway House, Manitoba, her academic background includes a BA (Carlton University), LLB (Osgoode Hall Law School), LLM (Cambridge University), SJD (Harvard), and a Certificate of International and Comparative Law of Human Rights (University of Strasbourg). Turpel-Lafond has taught at several universities, including Dalhousie University, where she became the first Aboriginal person to receive tenure at a Canadian law school. In 1995–96 she was Aboriginal Scholar at the UNIVERSITY OF SASKATCHEWAN. She has also worked with the FEDERATION OF SASKATCHEWAN INDIAN NATIONS, and prior to her appointment practiced law on the Asimakaniseekan Askiy reserve in Saskatoon. Turpel-Lafond has been involved with such issues as self-governance, restorative justice, human rights, Fetal Alcohol Syndrome, and the relationship of Aboriginal and non-Aboriginal communities. *Time* magazine has recognized her as one of the 100 Global Leaders (1994) and as one of the top twenty Canadian leaders for the 21st century (1999). She has received an Honorary Doctorate of Laws from the UNIVERSITY OF REGINA (2003).   *Erin Legg*

TURTLEFORD, town, pop 465, located approximately 90 km NW of North Battleford at the junction of Hwys 3, 26, and 303. The first settlers began entering the district in 1907–08. The community is situated in proximity to what was once a ford of the Turtlelake River and the name Turtleford was coined by the community's first postmaster, John Bloom. The post office opened in 1913 and train service into Turtleford began in 1914. By the spring of 1915, dozens of places of business had been established including four general stores, a drug store, two livery and feed stables, and two lumber yards. The railroad brought an increasing number of settlers to the district and, over the following decades, the once heavily forested area was cleared and the agricultural production of the region steadily increased. Turtleford became the main supply and service centre for the surrounding farming population. The agricultural output of the district largely

consists of cattle and grain. Somewhat ironically, as the land was cleared of the forest, the Turtleford town council of 1931 saw the need to beautify the community and handed out to residents maple, Russian poplar, and elm trees to plant, many of which are still standing today. Some logging activity continues in the region to the north of Turtleford. In the 1960s, resort communities began developing at the nearby Brightsand and Turtle Lakes and the town continues to benefit from a growing seasonal tourist industry. Today, the summer population in the area is estimated to reach between 4,000 and 5,000. In 1983, Turtleford attained town status and, to commemorate the event, an enormous turtle sculpture was constructed at the town's tourist information centre, and now "Ernie" is billed as Canada's largest turtle. Over the past 20 years, the development of the OIL AND GAS INDUSTRY has come to be significantly important to the Turtleford economy. Several businesses providing oilfield services have developed and the industry provides much off-farm employment. The Turtleford town office is situated in the former 1920 Bank of Commerce building, now a heritage property. The community's premier annual event is the Turtleford Agricultural Fair held at the beginning of August. The event is considered one of the best country fairs in Canada, and in 2005 the 89th annual fair was held.   *David McLennan*

TURVEY, JACK NELLIS (1911–98). Jack Nellis Turvey was born in Harris, Saskatchewan, on February 12, 1911, but moved to Vancouver after the death of his father. As a smallish child unwilling to give any quarter, he grew up as something of a fighter, a trait he carried with him throughout his business career. He frequently scrapped with business and union leaders and politicians in later life, usually trying to preserve or grow one of the many business interests he developed in western Canada.

He graduated from the University of British Columbia in 1934 with a BA in economics, and spent most of his early business career working as an accountant, although he never obtained formal training or certification in this area. After working at a number of west coast businesses through the 1930s and early 1940s, he joined Marwell Construction in 1949, where in 1955 he acquired many of the contacts and expertise he would draw on for much of his career.

While working for Marwell, he met BILL SHARP, and with Sharp's help he became the first Secretary-Treasurer of IPSCO in 1956 and stayed with that company for much of the rest of his career, retiring as chairman of the corporation in 1981. As IPSCO's leader, he made a major contribution to the eventual success of that company and is best known in Canadian business history in this regard.

However, in addition to his career at IPSCO, Turvey also contributed greatly to the development

Jack Turvey.

of industry in western Canada through his ownership of such enterprises as Western Construction, Estevan Brick, and Pe Ben Industries Ltd. He eventually retired to Vancouver, where he died on June 20, 1998. *John Comrie and Roger Phillips*

TUXFORD, GEORGE STUART (1870–1943).

Born in Wales in February 1870, George Tuxford emigrated to Moose Jaw with his wife in the 1890s; they settled on a farm and maintained a large herd of livestock. In the summer of 1898, at the height of the Klondike gold rush, Tuxford led a herd of cattle from Moose Jaw across the Canadian Rockies to Dawson City, in what became the longest cattle drive in Canadian history. He then joined the 16th Mounted Rifles and was given command of the newly organized D Squadron in Moose Jaw. He was promoted to Lieutenant Colonel when the squadron was expanded to regimental size and was renamed the 27th Light Horse. At the outbreak of WORLD WAR I in August 1914, Tuxford organized mounted units from the west to serve as dismounted troops in the 5th (Western Cavalry) Battalion of the Canadian Expeditionary Force (CEF), then mobilizing at Camp Valcartier, Quebec. He was named the Battalion's first commanding officer.

On April 22, 1915, Tuxford became one of twelve Canadian infantry battalion commanders to be assigned to the front line in the Second Battle of Ypres; he was one of nine commanding officers to survive. On March 10, 1916, Tuxford released an After Action Report on Second Ypres that provided an account and assessment of the decisions and actions that had taken place during the battle; the report was an important document in the development of Canadian combat leadership and command. Tuxford went on to lead his battalion in the Battle

of Festubert (May 19–26, 1915) until he was invalided out of the line with a severe illness on May 22. On March 16, 1916, he returned to duty and was promoted to Brigadier-General. He was given command of the 3rd Canadian Infantry Brigade of the 1st Division; he held this position for over three years, becoming the longest serving brigade commander in the Canadian Corps. While Tuxford commanded the 3rd Brigade, the 1st Division fought in the Battle of Mount Sorrel (June 1916), the Somme (September-November 1916), Arras (April-August 1917), Ypres (October-November 1917), the Second Battle of Arras (August-September 1918), and the Battle of the Hindenburg line (September-October 1918). Brigadier-General George Stuart Tuxford died in 1943. *Daria Coneghan*

FURTHER READING: Dancocks, D.G. 1988. *Welcome to Flanders Fields–The First Canadian Battle of the Great War: Ypres, 1915*. Toronto: McClelland and Stewart.

25TH STREET THEATRE. 25th Street Theatre was founded in 1971 by UNIVERSITY OF SASKATCH-EWAN graduates as an experimental centre for the arts. While its first season (1972–73) featured a mix of music, cabaret, dance and new plays (KEN MITCHELL's *Pleasant Street*, Andras Tahn's *Covent Garden*), 25th soon became a professional theatre (1975) committed to developing and producing new work, especially that of Saskatchewan artists. Under Andras Tahn (1975–83), 25th specialized in collective creations exploring Saskatchewan's story, feelings and values. They collaborated with Theatre Passe Muraille's Paul Thompson to produce their first collective, *If You're So Good, Why are You in Saskatoon?* (1975), and worked with other theatre collectives, most notably Theatre Network (Edmonton). However, 25th was best known for *Paper Wheat* (1977), a celebratory history of Saskatchewan's co-operative movement. First created and toured through Saskatchewan by Andras Tahn and the company (1977), it was substantially revised by Guy Sprung and then toured both provincially and nationally (1979). 25th also premiered early works by such nationally known playwrights as Brad Fraser, Linda Griffiths, and Jim Garrard.

The early 1980s were marked by crises in space and funding and changing leadership: Layne Coleman (1980–81), Tahn, Coleman and Griffiths (1981–83), and Gordon McCall (1983–84). Under Tom Bentley-Fisher (1985–97), 25th concentrated on developing Saskatchewan playwrights through mentorship programs, production, and festivals. It produced over thirty original Saskatchewan plays in its 144-seat warehouse theatre on Duchess Street, Saskatoon (1985–97). Highlights included work by Rod McIntyre, DON KERR, Scott Douglas, Greg Nelson, Mansel Robinson, Archie Crail, ANNE SZUMIGALSKI, SHARON BUTALA, BARBARA SAPERGIA, Pam Bustin and

Kit Brennan, as well as the Canadian premiere of Saskatoon-born Joanna McClelland Glass's *Play Memory* (1986), Dianne Warren's *Serpent in the Night Sky* (1991)–Saskatchewan's first play nominated for a Governor General's Award–and work by Ken Mitchell and Connie Gault, two of Saskatchewan's most successful continuing playwrights. 25th also founded the Saskatoon Fringe Festival (1989), one of the oldest, largest fringes in western Canada. Building on earlier cross-cultural experiments (*Jessica*, 1981), 25th also launched a "Festival of New Indian and Métis Plays" (1995) and premiered work by MARIA CAMPBELL, HARRY W. DANIELS, Joe Welsh, and Greg Daniels. Despite renewed crises in space and funding, 25th continues to run the Saskatoon Fringe and the eleven-day Hericane Festival of Women's Art (1999). Under Glen Cairns (1998–99) and Sharon Bakker (1999–), it has remained a centre where Saskatchewan artists are "provided exposure, facilities and training" to help them explore and develop creativity in the arts. *Moira Day*

FURTHER READING: Benson, E. and L.W. Conolly. 1989. *Oxford Companion to Canadian Theatre*. Toronto: Oxford University Press; Twenty-fifth Street House Theatre. 1982. *Paper Wheat: The Book*. Saskatoon: Western Producer Prairie Books.

27TH LIGHT HORSE: *see* 14TH CANADIAN HUSSARS

28th Battalion

28TH (NORTHWEST) CANADIAN INFAN-TRY BATTALION. The 28th (Northwest) Canadian Infantry Battalion was a unit of the 6th Canadian Infantry Brigade, 2nd Canadian Division, Canadian Expeditionary Force. The 28th Battalion was recruited in 1914 from Saskatchewan as well as Fort William and Port Arthur (now Thunder Bay) in Ontario, and sent to Britain as part of the second Canadian contingent in June 1915. In September 1915, the 28th Battalion was sent to the front lines in France. In 1917, it participated in the allied victories at VIMY RIDGE and the Third Battle of Passchendaele. A member of the 28th Battalion,

Private **G. PRICE**, was the last solider to be killed on the Western Front. Following the armistice, the battalion was involved in the occupation of Germany and then repatriated to Canada in May 1919. The 28th (Northwest) Infantry Battalion, CEF, is perpetuated by the **ROYAL REGINA RIFLES**.   *Peter Borch*

FURTHER READING: Christie, N.M. 1998. *Winning the Ridge: The Canadians at Vimy, 1917.* Nepean, ON: CEF Books; Dancocks, D.G. 1987. *Spearhead to Victory: Canada and the Great War.* Edmonton: Hurtig; MacDonald, L. 1978. *They Called it Passchendaele.* London: Joseph.

TYRRELL, JOSEPH BURR (1858–1957). Born on November 1, 1858, in Weston, Joseph Burr Tyrrell was one of several pioneer geo-scientists responsible for surveying the west in the late 19th century. Graduating from the University of Toronto in 1881, he was hired by the Geological Survey of Canada and worked there until his resignation in January 1899. After a period as assistant geologist he conducted numerous geological surveys, making important mineralogical and paleontological discoveries. His work in what is now Saskatchewan began during reconnaissance surveys of Manitoba (1887–91) that included a strip of land extending west of Yorkton between the **QU'APPELLE VALLEY** and the **CHURCHILL RIVER**. In the 1888 field season, Tyrrell contracted typhoid and almost died.

In 1892 Tyrrell surveyed the lands between **LAKE ATHABASCA** and the Churchill River, assisted by **D.B. DOWLING**. Dowling started from Edmonton, traveling to Fond du Lac via Lake Athabasca. Tyrrell began at Prince Albert, traveling via Green Lake to Ile-à-la-Crosse and then by way of Cree Lake to Black Lake. They met at Fond du Lac and explored the

J.B. Tyrrell, 1886.

region between Lake Athabasca and **WOLLASTON LAKE** before separating again. Dowling's party then surveyed the route from Wollaston to **REINDEER LAKE** before traveling up the Churchill River to Ile-à-la-Crosse. Tyrrell aimed for the same destination, but through uncharted territory along the Geikie River. In his report on the region, Tyrrell describes the terrain, and maps observed rock types and glacial features.

The routes through Lake Athabasca and Reindeer Lake were used again during epic journeys made by Tyrrell into the Barren lands in 1893 and 1894. In the first of these he was accompanied by his younger brother; his goal was to follow a route north of Black Lake that had been observed the previous summer. The second journey into the Barrens began on Lake Winnipeg and proceeded via Reindeer Lake to Hudson Bay.

After his resignation from the Survey, Tyrrell worked successfully as a mining consultant. Although he specialized as a geologist, he was also trained as a botanist and zoologist. His interest in exploration led him to edit the diaries of **SAMUEL HEARNE** and **DAVID THOMPSON**. He received many honours in his life including the Flavelle Gold medal from the Royal Society of Canada. Tyrrell died in Toronto on August 26, 1957.   *Marilyn Lewry*

FURTHER READING: Inglis, A. 1978. *Northern Vagabond: The Life and Career of J.B. Tyrrell.* Toronto: McClelland & Stewart; Tyrrell, J.B. and D.B. Dowling. 1896. Report on the Country Between Athabasca Lake and Churchill River. *Geological Survey of Canada Annual Report* (new series), Vol. 8, 1D–120D; Zaslow, M. 1975. *Reading the Rocks: The Story of the Geological Survey of Canada, 1842–1972.* Toronto: Macmillan.

U

UHRICH, JOHN MICHAEL (1877–1951).

Uhrich was born on June 7, 1877, in Formosa, Ontario. He completed school in Walkerton, Ontario, and briefly taught school there. While completing a medical degree at Northwestern University in Chicago, Uhrich came to Saskatchewan to teach school during his summer breaks. He graduated in 1907 and in 1909 established a medical practice in Hague.

Uhrich won the Rosthern constituency for the Liberals in the 1921 election. He was appointed to Cabinet as Provincial Secretary after **CHARLES DUNNING** became Premier in 1922. In 1923 Uhrich was given the added responsibility of Minister of Public Health upon the department's creation. The provincial government's role in the municipal hospital system increased and the number of hospitals across the province expanded. Uhrich's greatest contribution was in the field of preventive medicine. Public inspection of water and milk supplies began, as well as immunization programs for smallpox and diphtheria. In 1929 he enacted legislation for the

SASKATCHEWAN ARCHIVES BOARD R-B4070

John Uhrich.

provincial government to assume the cost of treatment for tuberculosis in the province.

Uhrich was re-elected in the 1925 and 1929 elections. The defeat of the **GARDINER** government in 1929 relegated Uhrich to the Opposition. When the Liberals returned to power in 1934, Uhrich assumed his former role as Minister of Public Health and in 1938 he also took on Public Works. In 1940 the Canadian Public Health Association granted Uhrich a lifetime membership. Due to ill health, he retired from politics in 1944. When **LIEUTENANT-GOVERNOR** Reginald Parker died in office in 1948, Uhrich filled the position until his own death on June 15, 1951.

Brett Quiring

UKRAINIAN CATHOLIC BROTHERHOOD OF CANADA.

The Ukrainian Catholic Brotherhood of Canada came into existence on July 14, 1932, in Regina, Saskatchewan in response to the 1929 decision of the **J.T.M. ANDERSON** government which forbade the teaching of religion in schools and the banning of visitations to schools by Catholic priests and nuns. Catholic trustees, including Ukrainian Catholic trustees, gathered in Regina to create the Catholic School Trustees. The Ukrainian Catholic Brotherhood of Canada followed. The Brotherhood was concerned with the teaching of religion in schools, organizing Ukrainian teachers in Saskatchewan, and creating an umbrella organization to which all **UKRAINIAN CATHOLICS** and their organizations could belong and be represented. The first Convention was held at the Prosvita Hall adjacent to St. George's Cathedral in Saskatoon on December 28–29, 1932. The first constitution was adopted at this time. It identified the four aims that guide the Brotherhood's endeavours: Catholic faith, Ukrainian culture, Canadian citizenship, and social development.

The years 1932–35 saw an explosion in the number of branches created. The majority of these were in Saskatchewan. Since 1932, Brotherhood members have contributed to their communities locally, nationally and internationally by protecting the rights of individuals, safeguarding the Ukrainian Catholic Church from political interference, and promoting the use of the Ukrainian language. The Brotherhood is active in each eparchy in Canada and operates at three levels: branch, eparchial, and national.

In addition, the Brotherhood was instrumental in the organization of the Markian Shashkevych Bursa (1935–53) and the construction of the Metropolitan **SHEPTYTSKY INSTITUTE**, a co-ed student residence in Saskatoon. Quarterly Eparchial meeting are held, with Eparchial and National Conventions held every three years on a staggered rotation. The four aims that inspired and guided the Brotherhood at its inception continue to give the movement purpose and direction. In 2005 there were five branches in Saskatchewan: Saskatoon, Regina (two), Yorkton and Canora. *William Gulka*

UKRAINIAN CATHOLIC WOMEN'S LEAGUE OF CANADA.

The Ukrainian Catholic Women's League of Canada (UCWLC) provides resources to allow members to contribute to the Church and society. Fundamental aims include the promotion of Catholic faith, Ukrainian culture, Canadian citizenship, and charitable activities. The League is a national organization of over 6,000 members, many of whom live in Saskatchewan. It maintains offices in Canada's five eparchies (Byzantine dioceses): Toronto, Winnipeg, Saskatoon, Edmonton and New Westminster. The UCWLC was organized nationally in 1944 and granted federal charter in 1980; it is organized with a national executive, eparchial executive, and local branch executive. In 1951, when Saskatchewan was declared a separate exarchate

(missionary diocese) under Bishop Andrew Roborecki, the first provincial president was Micheline Malko of Saskatoon. *Alice Derow*

UKRAINIAN CATHOLICS.

From 1901 to 1911, the Ukrainian Catholic population on the territory that became Saskatchewan increased rapidly as the province was settled by eastern European immigrants. Most Eastern Catholics were Ruthenians, belonged to the Byzantine (Greek) rite and began to call themselves Ukrainians as Ukrainian national self-consciousness grew and displaced the older ethnic Ruthenian identity. Just as it is difficult to say who was Ukrainian prior to 1931 because civil jurisdictions such as Austrian, Hungarian, Polish, and Russian rather than language or ethnic origin were used for passport and self-identification purposes, most Ukrainian Catholic settlers in Saskatchewan were sometimes erroneously counted in Roman Catholic or Orthodox statistics until the 1931 Canadian Census made a separate category for them. Most came from Galicia and, to a lesser extent, Bukovyna, both provinces of the Austro-Hungarian Empire. While most used Ukrainian as a vernacular, some used Romanian, and others Polish or Russian; but all used Old Church Slavonic as a liturgical language, as well as the liturgy of St. John Chrysostom, common to both Orthodox and Greek Catholics. The canon law organizing the life of the Church contains significant differences from Roman canon law, since it grows out of Greek Orthodox canons, yet acknowledges the Pope of Rome as the head of the Church.

Many of the immigrants' faith and loyalty to Rome were shaken by the efforts of those who sought to assimilate them into English Protestant organizations or into Roman Catholic parishes. It is estimated that in the early part of the 20th century about one-half to two-thirds of all recent Ukrainian

ROY ANTAL/REGINA LEADER-POST

Members of the St. Athanasius Ukrainian Catholic Women's League, March 1989.

PATRICK PETTIT/REGINA LEADER-POST

Descent of the Holy Ghost Ukrainian Orthodox church, Ukrainian Christmas Eve, January 1992.

Catholic immigrants eventually joined other religious denominations. In Saskatchewan, in descending order of numbers involved, Ukrainian Catholics joined Ukrainian Orthodox, Roman Catholic, Russian Orthodox, Romanian Orthodox, Presbyterian and Methodist (both going into the United Church of Canada in 1925), and Baptist churches. By 1931 the large-scale move to other churches had ended, and over 30,000 people claimed adherence to the Ukrainian Catholic Church within Saskatchewan, somewhat more than those who claimed adherence to Orthodox churches.

Nicetas Budka, a diocesan priest from the Eparchy of Lviv, was named the first bishop for all Eastern Catholics of Canada in 1912. While he chose Winnipeg as his see, he and his successor, Basil Ladyka, worked extensively in Saskatchewan, where a third of Canada's Eastern-rite Catholics lived. Saskatchewan's demographic importance to the Eastern Catholic Church was made evident when Rome established the Saskatoon Apostolic Exarchy (missionary diocese) on April 7, 1951. It was raised to the status of an Eparchy (or diocese) on November 3, 1956, as a suffragan of the Byzantine Archeparchy (archdiocese) of Winnipeg. The number of Eastern Catholics, almost all of them Ukrainians, in Saskatchewan between 1941 and 1951 was nearing 40,000; and geographical dispersal of the faithful required immense travel for Winnipeg's bishop. Saskatchewan's first bishop (1951–82) was Andrew Roborecki, who chose St. George's parish in Saskatoon as his cathedral. He was followed by Basil Filevich (1984–95), Cornelius Pasichny (1995–98), and Michael Wiwchar (2000–).

While the 2001 Canadian Census reported about 17,000 Ukrainian Catholics in Saskatchewan, the Eparchy released figures in 2003 showing that something less than 13,000 Ukrainian and other Eastern Catholics were officially members, placing them at 1.3% of Saskatchewan's population, and dropping. They were organized in over 100 parishes and missions, cared for by twenty diocesan and religious priests (Congregation of the Most Holy Redeemer, Redemptorists), as well as eighteen religious sisters (Ukrainian Catholic Sisters of St. Joseph, Ukrainian Catholic Sisters Servants of Mary Immaculate, and Ukrainian Catholic Sisters of the Holy Family) and two brothers (Redemptorists), caring for missions, schools, and hospitals.

The Eparchy heads the Ukrainian Catholic Council of Saskatchewan, the Ukrainian Catholic Brotherhood of Canada, the Ukrainian Catholic Eparchy Youth Ministry, the Ukrainian Catholic Women's League of Canada-Saskatchewan, the Right Reverend Mitrat John Olynyk Bursary Fund for Seminary and Seminarians, the Andrew Roborecki Foundation, the Eparchial Vision for Renewal Commission, the **SHEPTYTSKY INSTITUTE** (a co-educational institution for post-secondary students at the

UNIVERSITY OF SASKATCHEWAN), St. George's Ukrainian Senior Citizen's Residence, St. Volodymyr Villa Corporation (condominiums), Musée Ukraina Museum, St. Volodymyr Ukrainian Park and Summer Camp, St. Michael's Camp at Madge Lake, and Fides Club (Business and Professional Ukrainian Catholic Men's Club). The Eparchy is supported by the Ukrainian Councils of the Knights of Columbus in Saskatchewan.

Although Ukrainian Catholics are well organized and comprise the seventh-largest religious group in Saskatchewan, the depopulation of rural Saskatchewan where most Ukrainian immigrants had originally established themselves, and continued assimilation into the Roman Catholic Church have raised the question whether the Eparchy would be suppressed or reintegrated into the Archeparchy. The question became acute during the interregnum of 1998–2000, when the Eparchy relied on the Metropolitan Archeparch (Archbishop) of Winnipeg for episcopal services. Rome's transfer of Bishop Wiwchar from Chicago to Saskatoon allayed these questions, however, and the Eparchy of Saskatoon continues to organize and provide local religious leadership to Saskatchewan's Eastern-rite Catholics.

National, linguistic, and ritual differences continue to divide Eastern Catholics in Canada's larger urban centres; but Saskatchewan's stable population and relative lack of new immigration that would strengthen Old World differences have created a new ecclesiastical situation. Since 1991, the close identification of the Eparchy with Ukrainian Catholics is gradually waning because a majority of Ukrainian Catholics living in Saskatchewan now speak English as a first language. This breakdown of the Ukrainian language is creating a more broadly based Byzantine Catholic population using English as a vernacular and, increasingly, as a liturgical language that is more welcoming to a younger English-speaking generation who would have previously left to attend English services elsewhere. While Ukrainian became the official liturgical language when the Second Vatican Council allowed vernacular languages to be used in liturgical worship, the younger generation's pressure to use English and to adopt the Gregorian calendar in place of the older Julian calendar is slowly creating a neutral meeting place for all Eastern Catholics, even those from a background other than Ukrainian. However, Roman Catholicism, other denominations, and even a lack of religious affiliation continue to attract individuals; and the number of Eastern Catholic Christians, once a distinctive mark of Saskatchewan, is steadily declining. *Paul Laverdure*

UKRAINIAN LABOUR FARMER TEMPLE
ASSOCIATION. The Ukrainian Labour Farmer Temple Association (ULFTA) grew out of the Ukrainian Social Democratic Party (USDP) in May

SASKATCHEWAN ARCHIVES BOARD R-B8842

The Ukrainian Labour Temple, Regina. This building was used from 1918 to 1927. The Association moved into a new facility in 1928.

1918 in Winnipeg, in response to a growing conservative reaction to the left-wing political activities in Canada that followed the Russian Revolution. The USDP leadership wanted to attract more members by broadening its activities into cultural, educational and humanitarian activities. They built a Labour Temple in Winnipeg with donations from members across the country, initiated a variety of cultural programs, and printed a national weekly, *Ukrainian Labour News*, to replace their banned paper, *Working People*.

The ULFTA quickly grew to have branches in many Ukrainian immigrant communities in Canada. It was the largest secular Ukrainian organization in the country until **WORLD WAR II**. John Alexiewich traveled to the Ukrainian settlements in the province, building the organization. In Saskatchewan there were labour temples or branches in twenty-five communities. The organization was particularly attractive as it provided social and cultural activities to the isolated and lonely. It fought against discrimination and defended the rights of workers. Educational programs included literacy in the English and Ukrainian languages, as well as class politics. Orchestras as well as drama and dance groups kept old-country traditions alive. The Labour Temples were used for organizing labour actions such as the Winnipeg General Strike and the Bienfait "red" hall for the Miners' Strike in 1931, and in Regina participated in the **ON-TO-OTTAWA TREK**. The ULFTA, which had maintained contacts with the Soviet Union, was shut down by the RCMP in January 1940. Many of their leaders and journalists were imprisoned along with the Communist leadership, and their Labour Temples were confiscated on the basis of new sections to the Defense of Canada

Regulations under the War Measures Act. The Labour Temples in Bienfait, North Battleford, Saskatoon, and Swift Current were sold by Custodian of Enemy Property between 1940 and 1943. In 1942 the Association of United Ukrainian Canadians (AUUC) was created to replace the ULFTA. Urbanization, old age, assimilation and repression due to Cold War politics led to a shrinking membership. In Saskatchewan only the Regina branch remains and organizes the Poltava Ensemble of Song, Music, and Dance.   *Bob Ivanochko*

FURTHER READING: Hunchuk, S.H. 2001. "A House Like No Other: An Architectural and Social History of the Ukrainian Labour Temple, 523 Arlington Avenue, Ottawa, 1923–1967." MA thesis, Carleton University; Krawchuk, P. 1996. *Our History: The Ukrainian Labour-Farmer Movement in Canada, 1907–1991.* Toronto: Lugus.

UKRAINIAN LANGUAGE TEACHING.

The Laurier-Greenway agreement of 1887 allowed a bilingual system of public education in Manitoba. On the basis of this agreement, Ukrainians and other ethnic groups in Saskatchewan convinced their government to authorize, in 1909, establishing the "School for Foreigners" in Regina. The various Ukrainian educational organizations then submitted resolutions asking that Ukrainian be introduced into the curriculum of their respective provincial universities in view of the number of Ukrainian settlers in the west. Unfortunately, opposition to the bilingual system in the prairies became very vocal, especially during WORLD WAR I, and the Regina School was closed. An era had come to an end: the Ukrainians, among others, had to rely again on their own resources. To allow their children to learn about their ancestral heritage some student-resident institutions were founded. In Saskatchewan, the first such institute was established in 1916; it eventually evolved into the Mohyla and subsequently the Sheptytsky Institutes in Saskatoon, devoted to the learning and dissemination of the Ukrainian culture in the province. These endeavours were supported by GEORGE W. SIMPSON, a professor of history at the UNIVERSITY OF SASKATCHEWAN, who during the 1930s began introducing some material about Ukraine in his history courses.

WORLD WAR II was a powerful stimulant in the development of Slavic studies. With the help of George Simpson and Brother Methodius of St. Joseph's College in Yorkton, Ukrainian was gradually introduced into the programs of the University of Saskatchewan and the provincial high schools. A non-credit course in elementary Ukrainian was offered in 1943 at the University of Saskatchewan. Two years later, CONSTANTINE H. ANDRUSYSHEN came to the newly established Department of Slavic Studies, and the Ukrainian language was added to the credited subjects at the University. In 1952 it was

recognized as a high school subject by the Department of Education; simultaneously it was introduced into the Summer School at the University, and in 1958 into the School of Correspondence's curriculum. The University of Saskatchewan was the first institution in North America to offer such courses.

From there on, the teaching of Ukrainian in Saskatchewan began to spread; very soon it became evident that an association of teachers of Ukrainian had to be organized. Some previous attempts had been made is 1916 and 1958, but had proved to be premature. Eventually such an association, Saskatchewan Teachers of Ukrainian, was founded in the fall of 1966 as a special chapter of the SASKATCHEWAN TEACHERS' FEDERATION. The association started publishing a newsletter, *Tema*, which encompasses information and professional material; annual conferences took place as well. Subsequently the STU was instrumental in initiating co-operation in the development of Ukrainian programs between the prairies provinces; the newly established UNIVERSITY OF REGINA also introduced programs in Ukrainian. In 1976 the society "Ukraina" donated to the University of Saskatchewan a monument to the Ukrainian poet, writer and feminist, Lesya Ukrainka; this led to the initiation of an academic exchange agreement between the University of Saskatchewan and the Chernivtsi State University in southwestern Ukraine, again the first such attempt among universities in North America. Over 100 scholars and students have availed themselves in this exchange opportunity. The educational contacts with Ukraine grew and spread to other institutions as well. By 1979 a bilingual English-Ukrainian program was introduced in St. Goretti School in Saskatoon; the same academic year saw the highest number of centres, over fifty at all levels, offering Ukrainian with an enrollment of over 2,600 students. To accommodate the demand, several university and secondary school specialists started co-operating in the preparation of numerous manuals and materials, and introduced innovative language, literature and culture teaching methods. The Department of Education established a special position of Language Consultant and Facilitator for Ukrainian.

With the dissolution of the Soviet Union, more contacts were established with the independent Ukraine and an agreement for co-operation in education with Ukraine was signed in 1990, which made provisions for annual exchanges of high school and university students and educators between Saskatchewan and Ukraine. Subsequently two Canada-Ukraine Education Conferences were held in Ukraine, in 1991 and 1994; delegations from education ministries of Ukraine and Saskatchewan exchanged visits; and in 1996 a Ukrainian and Canadian team of specialists co-operated in the preparation of educational materials for secondary

schools in Ukraine and Canada. In 1998 an academic unit, the Prairie Centre for the Study of Ukrainian Heritage, was initiated at ST. THOMAS MORE COLLEGE, University of Saskatchewan; and in 1999 a Lesya Ukrainka Chair in Ukrainian Studies was founded. In 2002 a consortium for the study of Ukrainian at secondary and higher level was established, and contacts were made with other centres on this continent and in Ukraine. In the summer of 2003 the first successful session for students from Saskatchewan took place at the newly founded Ukrainian Catholic University in Lviv. (*See also* UKRAINIAN SETTLEMENTS, ASSOCIATION OF UNITED UKRAINIAN CANADIANS)   *Victor Buyniak*

UKRAINIAN SETTLEMENTS.

Initial Ukrainian immigration to Saskatchewan coincided with the great European migrations of the late 19th and early 20th centuries. Over 170,000 individuals of Ukrainian origin set out for Canada during the period 1891–1914 as part of the Canadian government's effort to recruit agriculturalists from east, central and south Europe. Originating primarily from western Ukraine (the former Austro-Hungarian lands of Galicia and Bukowina), Ukrainians were attracted to Canada by the promise of free land: homesteads of 160 acres. The majority eventually concentrated in bloc settlements located across the prairie-parkland of western Canada. As traditional cultural and social practices were recreated by the new arrivals and new forms of community and social life emerged, the cultural landscape of the region–extending southeastward from Edmonton across Saskatchewan to Stuartburn, Manitoba–assumed a distinctive character, identified as it was with the Ukrainian inhabitants. In Saskatchewan, the first Ukrainian settlements were established in the Montmartre-Candiac area by 1895–96, and in 1897 around Yorkton, notably in the districts of Beaver Hills, Crooked Lake, and Wroxton. Subsequently, other early settlements appeared in the districts of Fish Creek-Rosthern (1898) and Redberry Lake (1903), as well as in the Samburg district northeast of Prince Albert in 1906. By 1911 the population of Ukrainian origin in the province had reached 22,276; this represented 29.5% of the total number of Ukrainian residents of Canada, but only 4.5% of the total population of Saskatchewan. Nevertheless, by 1921 a number of provincial districts emerged as distinct areas of concentrated Ukrainian settlement: Insinger (2,408), Redberry (2,086), Ituna-Bon Accord (1,453), Goodlake (1,424), Sliding Hills (1,149), Preeceville (1,102), and Clayton (1,101).

Only 1,291 individuals of Ukrainian origin resided in urban areas in 1911; although this number had doubled in 1921 to 2,807, Ukrainians still accounted for only 1.3% of the total urban population of Saskatchewan. After WORLD WAR I the Ukrainian community of Saskatchewan benefited

DAVID MCLENNAN PHOTO

Krydor Orthodox Church. This Ukrainian settlement near Hafford was named for Peter Krysak and Teodor Lucyk, early Ukrainian pioneers in the area. Krydor is the birthplace of Stephen Worobetz, the province's first Lieutenant-Governor of Ukrainian ancestry.

from renewed European immigration, growing from 28,907 to 50,700 between the years 1921–31. This tapered off, however, because of the difficult economic circumstances associated with the **GREAT DEPRESSION** and consequent provincial out-migration, and the Ukrainian population declined to 50,530 in 1941. At this time, Ukrainians began to move to urban centres in greater numbers: in 1921, there were 179 residents of Ukrainian origin in Regina, but by 1941 there were 1,619, constituting 2.3% of the city's population. Saskatoon, too, had a small number of Ukrainian residents in 1921: 352; but this reached 2,499 in 1941, comprising 5.7% of the population. This urbanizing trend resulted in a shift in the socio-economic character of the community. In 1941, signaling a departure from agricultural work, some 28.2% of gainfully employed Ukrainians were engaged in other industries or professions, including 5.6% employed in trade, finance, and the professional and public services.

By 1941, Ukrainians in Saskatchewan constituted 8.9% of the provincial population and 26.1% of the total number of Ukrainians in Canada. This percentage increased only marginally despite the influx of postwar Ukrainian immigrants to Canada: during the period 1947–54, for example, only 2,025 (or 6.2%) chose Saskatchewan as their destination. Subsequent restrictions on immigration from the Soviet Union had bearing on Ukrainian population growth in the province, so that the community in Saskatchewan would become overwhelmingly Canadian-born: whereas in 1941 there were 55,036 Canadian-born individuals of Ukrainian origin, representing 69% of the total Ukrainian population in

the province, by 1961 this increased to 80% and in 1971 to 87%. The indigenized or Canadian-born nature of the Ukrainian-origin population has had an impact on the cultural character of the community. In 1971, there were over 55,385 persons in Saskatchewan who claimed Ukrainian as their mother tongue; this number declined to 44,175 in 1981, and to 27,610 in 1991. Moreover, with the disappearance of the postwar immigration from the demographic map over time, home language use has declined: only 2,835 individuals in 1991 claimed Ukrainian as the language used in the home. As for Ukrainian adherence to the two traditional faiths—Ukrainian Orthodox and Ukrainian Catholic—the numbers have diminished as well: Ukrainians gravitate toward the Roman Catholic, United, and Anglican faiths, or increasingly declare no religious affiliation at all. In 1991, those of Ukrainian origin in the province who identified with Eastern Orthodoxy (and Ukrainian Orthodoxy in particular) numbered 15,095, while there were 18,700 adherents of the Ukrainian Catholic faith.

Perhaps the most important development resulting from the indigenization of the Ukrainian population is the high rate of intermarriage with members of other ethnic groups. Consequently, not only were there 76,810 individuals in Saskatchewan in 1981 who identified Ukrainian as their single origin: there were also an additional 23,280 individuals who reported Ukrainian as part of their roots—in effect, multiple origins. In 1996 the total number of single- and multiple-origin Ukrainians was 125,395, representing 12.7% of the provincial population; after Manitoba, this is the second highest percentage

among provinces. In 2001, Saskatoon, Regina, Yorkton, Prince Albert, Canora, North Battleford registered the greatest number of Ukrainian residents, although a number of towns and villages continue to have large concentrations of Ukrainian inhabitants, notably Kamsack, Ituna, Wynyard, Hafford, and Wakaw. As for single- and multiple-origin Ukrainians, the total number decreased slightly in 2001 to 121,740 individuals. Currently, the Ukrainian community is the sixth largest in the province.

The steady out-migration by Ukrainian origin people from Saskatchewan has been significant, the vast majority leaving for British Columbia, Alberta, and Ontario. Nevertheless, a long history and the continuing presence of relatively large numbers in the province have provided a foundation for a strong and thriving organized community. For example, the Saskatchewan Provincial Council of the Ukrainian Canadian Congress, an umbrella organization that promotes the interests of the community, represented in 2004 some 209 active Ukrainian organizations. Meanwhile, the community boasts forty-four Ukrainian dance groups, four choral groups, and three museums. Since 1973, the Ukrainian community in Saskatoon has organized the popular *Vesna* festival, an annual event showcasing Ukrainian Canadian arts and culture. Other significant developments include a publicly funded bilingual program at both elementary and secondary levels, which has been in existence since 1979. The University of Saskatchewan continues to serve as an important centre of higher learning in the field of Ukrainian Studies with the creation in 1998 of the Prairie Centre for the Study of Ukrainian Heritage. The New Community Credit Union was created in 1939 as the first Ukrainian credit union in Canada and remains active; and the Mohyla and Sheptytsky institutes were established in 1916 and 1953 respectively, providing an enriched cultural environment for Ukrainian university graduates. (*See also* **ETHNIC BLOC SETTLEMENTS**, **UKRAINIAN LANGUAGE TEACHING**, **ASSOCIATION OF UNITED UKRAINIAN CANADIANS**) *Bohdan Kordan*

FURTHER READING: Luciuk, L.Y. and B. Korda. 1989. *Creating a Landscape: A Geography of Ukrainians in Canada.* Toronto: University of Toronto Press; Kordan, B. 2000. *Ukrainian Canadians and the Canada Census, 1981–1996.* Saskatoon: Heritage Press.

UKRAINIAN SISTERS OF ST. JOSEPH OF SASKATOON.

This Eastern Rite order of nuns was founded in 1896 in the Village of Tsebliv, Ukraine by Rev. Father Prelate Cyril Siletzky (1835–1918). Its primary apostolate was to perform works of Christian charity organizing schools, caring for orphans, the sick and the aged, teaching catechism, and supporting the priests in their work.

The first two Sisters of St. Joseph arrived in Saskatoon in March 1961, and immediately began preparing themselves for the task of operating the Eparchy's new nursing home, which was well into its planning stage. Other Sisters soon joined them, and collectively they earned the legal rights of ownership to St. Joseph's Home. The 85-bed home has been under the consistent and uninterrupted administration and spiritual care of the Sisters for its entire 40-year history. In 1969 one of the Sisters left Saskatoon to establish the community in Brazil; within three years two young Brazilian Sisters of Ukrainian ancestry came to Canada to assist in the operation of St. Joseph's Home. Sisters from Brazil continued to augment the community's numbers, which had only received two lasting vocations from Canada, until December 1992, when the first of several Sisters from a free Ukraine started to arrive. In addition to their 24-hour service at the Home, the Sisters pray and teach catechism, operate a *Sadochok* (Ukrainian preschool), participate in parish activities, serve on various boards and committees, deliver retreats and lectures, make and decorate vestments, write icons and articles, work in and support the missions, and comfort and counsel the faithful. *Theodosia Papirnik*

UKRAINIAN-ENGLISH BILINGUAL EDUCATION.

Since the late 1940s, the province of Saskatchewan has been a leader in the area of Ukrainian curriculum development for secondary and post-secondary education. In the mid-1970s, the province embarked on a new initiative which focused attention on the development of Ukrainian bilingual programming for the elementary level. Initial discussion about the possibility of a Ukrainian-English bilingual program in Saskatchewan began in 1975, one year after the implementation of a similar program in Alberta. In the spring of 1979, after concerted lobby efforts by parents and community members, the Board of Education for Saskatoon Catholic Schools agreed to pilot a partial immersion (bilingual) Ukrainian language program, enriched with cultural elements and religious education.

The first Ukrainian-English bilingual kindergarten was introduced at St. Goretti School in Saskatoon in September 1979. The close proximity of this school to Ukrainian churches, halls, and a museum provided students with linguistic and cultural support, while a Catholic high school nearby allowed for growth and expansion to the upper grades. Shortly after the program's inception, the school division requested curricular support for program development from the provincial education ministry. In 1981, the Department of Education agreed to provide funding for bilingual curriculum development. In subsequent years, the department also provided the support of a Ukrainian language consultant.

The goals of the Ukrainian-English Bilingual Program are threefold: to provide children with the opportunity to learn to communicate in two languages; to develop an understanding and appreciation of the Ukrainian cultural and religious heritage in Canada; and to develop positive attitudes about other languages, cultures, and traditions. The program follows the regular provincial curriculum in all subject areas, with half of each instructional day conducted in Ukrainian and the other half in English. Various cultural projects and special events enhance the curriculum, giving parents and community members the opportunity to visit the school as presenters, volunteers, or guests. Enrolment in the Ukrainian-English bilingual program in Saskatoon remains constant. In 2001 the K–8 elementary program was relocated to Holy Family School, while the high school program has remained at E.D. Feehan High School. A highlight for students in the senior grades is the opportunity to participate in a three-week exchange program with Ukraine.

Nadia Prokopchuk

UNEMPLOYMENT DURING THE GREAT DEPRESSION.

Unemployment among Canadians in the GREAT DEPRESSION reached an estimated 30% of the work force by January 1933–a proportion never seen before or since. Saskatchewan was particularly hard hit because of the collapse of agriculture and the construction industry–the two main employers in the province at the time. Before WORLD WAR II there was no unemployment insurance or "safety net" provided by the state, so that being unemployed was the worst catastrophe that could befall working people. The single unemployed had to rely on private charity, and the married unemployed on a mixture of charity and very sporadic municipal relief. Pressure from the organized unemployed and the public compelled all levels of government to begin programs to deal with the situation. In Saskatchewan, these would include "work for relief" projects in the cities, a program to place the unemployed on farms for $5 a month, provincial relief camps of which there were at one time twenty-three in the province, and government-subsidized soup kitchens and hostels. The inadequacy of such arrangements led to protests on a continuous basis.

Before 1930 the unemployed had never been organized in significant numbers or for any length of time: they had no bargaining power and often moved from one locality to another in search of work, which made it difficult to develop organizational loyalty and stable leadership. This time, the massive numbers and horrendous conditions necessitated organization, and within a couple of years there existed organizations of the unemployed in most cities and in many of the larger towns in Canada, including Saskatchewan. Some of the unemployed organizations developed locally and

almost spontaneously, but many of the most effective were organized by the National Unemployed Workers' Association (NUWA), which grew rapidly after its formation in 1930. The NUWA was in turn affiliated to the WORKERS' UNITY LEAGUE (WUL), a radical labour federation which led many of the trade union and working class struggles of the first half of the 1930s. The NUWA organized associations of the married and single unemployed, unemployed war veterans, as well as the wives and families of the unemployed, and often formed district associations and even block committees in some localities. By 1932, the city of Saskatoon alone had six such organizations.

By the very nature of their situation, the unemployed had to be unorthodox and often disruptive in making their demands upon governments. They took up petitions and sent delegations to confront politicians and government officials. They also participated in street demonstrations, mass outdoor rallies, and strikes on relief projects and in relief camps. These led inevitably to clashes with the police, which in turn stimulated more unrest. Events in Regina and Saskatoon over an eight-month period in 1932 illustrated the extent of the unrest and growing disorder. A May Day parade in Regina involved an estimated 10,000 participants and spectators, and resulted in scattered violence and nine arrests. In October, several hundred workers involved in a Regina relief project went on strike. On November 7, about eighty RCMP and city police dispersed a rally of unemployed in Saskatoon, which resulted in what the Canadian press called "the bloodiest riot ever seen in this city": dozens of unemployed and policemen were injured, and several people arrested. Similar, though usually less spectacular, occurrences became frequent in Regina and Saskatoon and several smaller cities in the province.

Disturbances became a major phenomenon throughout Canada, and would become more pronounced in 1933. May Day parades were banned that year in Regina, Saskatoon and Moose Jaw. There were police raids on labour halls and the offices of alleged radicals. On May 8, a demonstration of unemployed was broken up by RCMP and city police at a relief camp on the outskirts of Saskatoon. Many people were injured, and RCMP Inspector L.I. Sampson was killed after being struck by a rock and dragged by his horse. Twenty-two people were later convicted of charges ranging from rioting to unlawful assembly, to assaulting police. Government authorities were alarmed that disorder might become general and continuous. They feared the single homeless unemployed most of all because they were the most difficult to intimidate. It was for this reason that the federal government established relief camps under the auspices of the Department of National Defence (DND) and forced thousands of single homeless men to go to these camps or face arrest for vagrancy. The Dundurn camp in Saskatchewan became the largest in the province: it could accommodate 2,000 people when full. This DND program may have calmed matters slightly in the cities, but merely transferred the trouble to the camps, which were very unpopular from the beginning. Many camps were soon organized clandestinely by the Relief Camp Workers' Union (RCWU), and were plagued by strikes and disturbances throughout their existence.

Matters came to a head in the early summer of 1935 when the unemployed walked out of their BC relief camp and into Vancouver, where they would soon commence the On-to-Ottawa Trek to take their grievances to the Bennett government. Bennett ordered the Trek stopped in Regina, and the result was the so-called Regina Riot on July 1, which occurred when police attacked a crowd of trekkers and Regina citizens. Scores were injured, and one policeman and one trekker were killed. Many people were arrested and the Trek was disbanded, but they had driven the nails into the coffin of the Bennett government, which was overwhelmingly defeated in the federal election of October 1935. (*See* ON-TO-OTTAWA TREK AND THE REGINA RIOT.)

The organized unemployed did win some improved conditions for relief recipients, and they left some immediate and long-term legacies. The hated federal relief camps were abolished by the new MACKENZIE KING government in 1936. A federal unemployment insurance system, always one of the main demands of the organized unemployed, was implemented in 1941. The organized unemployed of the Great Depression were in many ways pioneers of the socially positive state developed in Canada from the 1940s.

Lorne A. Brown

FURTHER READING: Brown, L. 1987. *When Freedom Was Lost: The Unemployed, the Agitator, and the State.* Montreal/Buffalo: Black Rose Book.

UNION HOSPITAL AND MUNICIPAL HOSPITAL CARE PLANS.

Saskatchewan pioneered two distinct and innovative programs for financing the construction, maintenance, and administration of hospital facilities and the services they provided: Union Hospital Districts (UHDs) and municipal hospital care plans. In 1916 legislation was introduced to permit the formation of UHDs. These arrangements empowered rural municipalities, villages and towns to form local authorities and pool their limited resources to establish and maintain hospitals. Although UHDs were formed in Alberta and Manitoba, it was in Saskatchewan that municipal hospitals grew to provide the bulk of hospital accommodation. Municipal hospitals were a response to local needs, and seem to have been the first in North America. Saskatchewan lacked the wealthy philanthropists who financed and con-trolled many of the hospitals elsewhere in Canada. Municipal hospital care plans provided payment for the hospital services obtained by residents of a municipality from general revenues and, later, personal taxes. Both UHDs and municipal hospital plans appear to have originated in the town of Lloydminster along the Saskatchewan-Alberta border. In 1913 the local hospital in Lloydminster, which had closed in 1912 for financial reasons, was reopened as a union hospital and provided hospital care to all residents. In 1916 both Saskatchewan and Alberta passed legislation to legalize this experiment in both the maintenance and administration of hospital facilities and pre-paid hospital care financed from general revenues. In 1917 Saskatchewan passed a more general Union Hospital Act to facilitate the establishment of similar pre-paid hospital service plans. By 1942, 100 municipalities provided their residents with hospital services. Municipal hospital care plans were superseded by the introduction of a provincewide hospital service plan in 1947. The provision of hospital grants by the T.C. DOUGLAS government facilitated the continued growth of UHDs. When national hospital insurance was introduced in 1957, Saskatchewan had 119 municipal hospitals with 64% of the province's hospital beds.

Gordon S. Lawson

UNITARIAN FELLOWSHIP IN SASKATCHEWAN.

The Regina Unitarian Fellowship was founded in 1956 in Regina. It is a member of the worldwide Unitarian Universalist Association, headquartered in Boston, and of the Canadian Unitarian Council, headquartered in Toronto. The Wynyard Unitarian Church was founded by Icelandic immigrants who were members of the Icelandic Free Church movement. The Saskatoon Unitarian Church began as a Fellowship after WORLD WAR II and is now the largest Unitarian Church in Saskatchewan, with full-time ministry since the 1970s. The Regina Unitarian Fellowship is the only non-creedal, non-dogmatic and non-hierarchical organization in Regina's religious community; there are no formal religious days, but Unitarians join Christian and other faiths in celebrating Holy Days of various kinds. The roots of Unitarianism go back to freethinking Greek philosophers such as Socrates; religious leaders are democratically elected, and are free to hold individual views on the major religious issues of our time. All members are encouraged to further develop their personal spirituality and to examine other viewpoints. There are currently two lay chaplains who officiate at rites of passage. Unitarians have had women ministers and ministers of different sexual orientations for over a hundred years. All individuals in the congregation share the pulpit and have the right to express their views.

The original Unitarians long ago rejected the concepts of Trinity and Original Sin. All religious thought should be critically examined with the goal to improve one's religious consciousness. Unitarians celebrate the achievements of people like Socrates, Jon Hus (theologian), Michael Servetus (Spanish theologian), Walt Whitman (poet and sexual liberationist), William Blake (poet), Mark Twain, Thomas Jefferson, John Adams, John Quincy Adams, William Taft, Albert Schweitzer (humanitarian), Clara Barton (founder of the American Red Cross), Charles Dickens, Benjamin Franklin, Samuel Morse, Frank Lloyd Wright (architect), and many more. Outstanding Canadian Unitarians include Lotta Hitchmanova (Unitarian Service Committee), Alexander Graham Bell, JOHN BROCKELBANK (politician), Howard Pawley (politician), Stan Calder (gay rights activist), and Philip Hewett (author of numerous books on Unitarianism in Canada).

Richard D. Jack

UNITED CHURCH OF CANADA.

The United Church of Canada is Saskatchewan's second largest religious denomination (after Roman Catholic), with 19.5% of the population claiming United Church affiliation. Saskatchewan Conference, which is subdivided regionally into seven presbyteries with a total of 343 congregations, is one of thirteen conferences of the national United Church. The Saskatchewan United Church maintains two hospital chaplaincies, three urban outreach ministries, and several church camps. It shares with Manitoba and Alberta a theological school campus (St. Andrew's College, Saskatoon) and a training centre (Calling Lakes Centre, Fort Qu'Appelle). The national All-Native Circle Conference has oversight of six Saskatchewan Aboriginal congregations. The theology of the Saskatchewan United Church is generally liberal Protestant in tone, and its polity is conciliar: authority and oversight rest not with individuals, but with elected bodies comprising both lay and clergy members.

The history and development of the Saskatchewan United Church are closely related to the European colonization of the region. Officially formed in 1925 in a national union that brought together the Canadian Methodist Church, the Congregational Union of Canada, and two-thirds of Canadian Presbyterians, the Saskatchewan United Church traces its roots to the prairie missionary activity of Methodists and Presbyterians in the late 1800s. (The Congregational church was much smaller and did not participate heavily in mission.) Initial interest by these two large denominations in Canada's prairie west centred on "Indian work": Methodist encounters with Aboriginal communities in Saskatchewan were few, but the Presbyterians established missions in the south, first at Round Lake and File Hills, both of which eventually became the sites of the United Church's only Saskatchewan Indian RESIDENTIAL SCHOOLS (in 1886 and 1889 respectively).

When the federal government began aggressively seeking settlers for the prairie west in the 1880s, Anglo-Protestants were the immigrants of choice, due to the assumption of their loyalty to British-Canadian authority, their language, and their customs. As these potential parishioners began arriving in numbers to set up their prairie homesteads, the Methodists and Presbyterians raced to provide ministry personnel to the territories. Both denominations found their mission resources stretched to the limit. They also discovered that many new prairie communities were finding their way, economically and socially, through structures of co-operation, and had little taste for religious competition among Protestant denominations. The two denominations had begun formal union talks at a national level, and they signed a policy of "Co-operation on the Frontier" in 1899. Rural communities, especially in Saskatchewan, went further and began forming local union churches, the first being at Melville in 1908. Such unions spread rapidly, and by the time of the national church union in 1925, over 400 congregations in Saskatchewan claimed some sort of union status–more than in any other province in Canada.

The Saskatchewan United Church inherited a mixed theological legacy, one that was at once progressive–rooted in the Social Gospel of the early 20th century–and colonialist, equating Protestant Christianity with British-Canadian cultural norms. On the progressive side, **LYDIA GRUCHY** became the first female ordained minister in any mainline denomination in Canada at a service in Moose Jaw in 1936; and **EDMUND H. OLIVER**, who served as founding Principal of St. Andrew's College (1912–35) and Moderator of the national United Church (1930–32), championed social issues and the cause of women's ordination. Many Saskatchewan United Church laity and clergy have been active in progressive political and agrarian movements and social causes. Since 1966 a "Brief Committee" has made an annual presentation of the social and economic concerns of the Saskatchewan United Church to members of the provincial Cabinet. The United Church has played an active role in ecumenical justice groups, and has strongly supported, at the Conference (provincial) level, national United Church decisions to promote inclusive language, feminist theologies, and the full rights and privileges of all members regardless of sexual orientation. On the colonialist side, however, the United Church for many years assumed the superiority of its own Anglo-Saxon culture; it worked for the assimilation of immigrants, and continued to operate Indian Residential Schools in Saskatchewan until 1950.

The contemporary Saskatchewan United Church faces, along with other mainstream churches, the aging of its membership, the closing of congregations due to the depopulation of rural communities, and a shortage of both funds and ministry personnel, especially in rural areas. It also confronts the task of building bridges between Aboriginal and non-Aboriginal communities, both within and beyond the Church. Increasing co-operation with other denominations has led to participation in the Saskatoon Theological Union, the Prairie Centre for Ecumenism, and in ecumenical "shared ministry" congregations, particularly with Lutheran and Anglican partners. As in the early 20th century, it is through collaboration that the Saskatchewan United Church may again find its life renewed.

Sandra Beardsall

UNITED GRAIN GROWERS (AGRICORE UNITED).

United Grain Growers (UGG) was a prairie-wide agricultural marketing, handling, and supply company from 1917 to 2001. The UGG name, like that of its successor Agricore United, was a familiar sight on grain elevators and other facilities across the prairies. Today Agricore United remains (in its own words) "Canada's leading farmer-directed agri-business." The company's head office is in Winnipeg. UGG was formed in 1917 by the merger of two earlier farm co-operatives, the **GRAIN GROWERS' GRAIN COMPANY** (GGGC) of 1906 and the Alberta Farmers' Co-operative Elevator Company of 1913. Combining the businesses of its predecessors, it both marketed farmers' grain and operated a growing network of country and terminal elevators through which that grain was handled. It also inherited small farm-supply and livestock-marketing businesses. Additional services were added and expanded as the company grew.

At first UGG faced criticism from farmers who were advocates of farmer co-operation. Like its predecessors, it did not pay patronage refunds, which was considered a co-operative principle. Its extensive farm-supply activities also undercut local co-operative associations that were spreading and organizing themselves in the 1920s and 1930s. Activists charged that UGG was not a true co-operative. Criticism abated in the 1930s, largely because UGG joined with other co-operatives, particularly the three prairie wheat pools, to make common cause in educational programs and agricultural lobbying. Meanwhile the company continued to expand: at the end of 1917 it operated 332 country elevators, 184 coal sheds, and over 200 warehouses. UGG continued to build and purchase elevators through the 1920s, reaching 468 in total by 1932. This number declined during the **DEPRESSION**, but the company expanded again in the 1940s to 1960s. UGG made major purchases from the Gillespie (1943), Reliance (1947), Midland and Pacific (1954), Canadian Consolidated (1959), and McCabe (1968) grain and elevator companies. The system peaked in size in the 1960s with over 800 elevators. A period of consolidation followed, and by 1990 the company operated country elevators and annexes at 276 points.

UGG had begun with terminal elevators at Fort William and Port Arthur. In 1925 it bought a controlling interest in a terminal in Vancouver, and in 1927 it constructed a new terminal at Port Arthur. As the company grew and purchased facilities from other companies, it acquired additional terminals, expanded their capacity, and undertook a series of modernizations from the 1950s until the 1980s. Livestock was a growing business over the years. The farm-supply business evolved: machinery, lumber, fruit, and vegetables disappeared, while feeds and especially fertilizers and crop-protection chemicals increased in importance. The company also took over and continued the publication of the *Grain Growers' Guide*, renamed *Country Guide* in 1928. The Public Press, a UGG subsidiary responsible for the *Guide*, also purchased a number of other farm publications over the years, notably *Canadian Cattlemen* (1953).

UGG's feed operations were consolidated into a new company, United Feeds Ltd., in the 1960s and 1970s. Other operations were consolidated and centralized in Winnipeg in the 1970s. The company became increasingly involved in the marketing of various agricultural crops, including non-**CANADIAN WHEAT BOARD** grains, export grain, and domestic feed grain (1974), as well as specialty crops such as corn, sunflowers, and lentils (1978). In the 1980s the company continued to expand in the livestock business and to create selective new enterprises such as Farm Decision Resources, a research and consulting agency. Meanwhile it restructured, streamlined, and downsized less profitable activities. Field services were reduced; oilseed and pet-food interests were shut down or sold; the printing division and Public Press were sold in 1991 (although Agricore United retained the company's most popular titles until 2003).

UGG had a number of well-known presidents and managers, who were important figures in the agriculture industry. These included T.A. Crerar and John Brownlee; one of the best known in later years was **A.M. (MAC) RUNCIMAN**, a farmer from Abernethy. Runciman was president of UGG from 1961 to 1981, a key period in the company's transformation. While UGG was governed by farmer-investors from across the prairies, it emphasized business more and philosophy less than did the other farmer-controlled co-operatives of the same era. Under Runciman's leadership, UGG became known as a critic of centralization and government regulation, and an advocate of more flexible, market-oriented policies in grain marketing and transportation.

At first UGG continued to participate in joint ventures with other farmer co-operatives. In 1970 it joined with the three prairie wheat pools to form XCAN Grain Ltd., although UGG's participation lasted only until 1974. Over time the company converted more to an investor-driven model, and it was restructured legally and financially a number of times. In 1965 its charter was amended to provide for greater capitalization and for more shares to be held by any one shareholder. The company was reorganized in 1992–93 in preparation for a public share offering: its shares are now publicly traded on the Toronto Stock Exchange. After this conversion, UGG was no longer generally recognized as a co-operative.

In 1997 UGG concluded a strategic alliance with US-based Archer Daniels Midland (ADM), which grew to the point where ADM was reported to own more than 20% of Agricore United in 2004. Further change came as the company strove to expand in the face of changing conditions in the agribusiness sector. Competitors Alberta Wheat Pool (1923) and Manitoba Pool Elevators (1925) merged in 1998 under the name Agricore. In 2001 UGG acquired Agricore from its shareholders in exchange for 20 million shares in UGG; Agricore became a wholly owned subsidiary, absorbed in 2003. Agricore United retained a substantial element of control by farmer-members. As of 2004, twelve of fifteen directors of the company were elected by farmer-members who did business with the firm; the other three were elected by shareholders, including strategic partner ADM. A minimum of two of the twelve elected directors must be from Saskatchewan.

In 2004 Agricore United had 87 licensed primary elevators (1.2 million tones storage capacity), of which thirty elevators with 356,000 tonnes capacity were in Saskatchewan.   *Brett Fairbairn*

FURTHER READING: Colquette, R.D. 1957. *The First Fifty Years: A History of United Grain Growers Limited.* Winnipeg: Public Press; Earl, P. 2000. *Mac Runciman: A Life in the Grain Trade.* Winnipeg: University of Manitoba Press.

UNITED STEEL WORKERS OF AMERICA (USWA).

The USWA started to organize in Saskatchewan in the 1950s. The membership was mainly located in Regina at IPSCO, Dominion Bridge, Westeel, Westank Willock, and Federal Pioneer Electric. In 1968, a fierce competition occurred amongst Oil, Chemical and Atomic Workers (OCAW), Tunnel and Rock Workers Union, Local 168, United Stone and Allied Product Workers, and USWA to represent the miners at the Duval potash mine near Saskatoon. The Steelworkers, spearheaded by Terry Stevens, a steelworker organizer from Winnipeg, were successful in organizing Duval Corp. (PCS Cory Local 7458), Cominco (Agrium Local 7552), Allan Potash (PCS Allan Local 7689), and Central Canada Potash (IMC, Local 7656) between 1968 and 1971. Workers at Potash Company of America (PCS Patience Lake Local 189) became Steelworkers in 1972 when their former

union, United Stone and Allied Product Workers Local 189, merged with USWA.

Collective bargaining in the industry was very difficult; lengthy strikes took place at Cominco in 1972, 1979 and 1995, at Duval in 1973 and 1975, and at PCA in 1975. The Steelworkers supported the public ownership of the potash industry and the formation of the Potash Company of Saskatchewan brought in by the **ALLAN BLAKENEY** government. Bargaining at the new publicly owned mines of PCS Cory (Duval) and PCS Allan (Allan Potash Mines) greatly improved union members' benefits. These included paid sick days, long-term disability, life insurance, pensions, vision and dental coverage for the employees and their family members, as well as a new job evaluation program–known as Co-operative Wage Study (CWS)–an employee and family assistance program, and double time for overtime. Steelworkers were also successful in obtaining these benefits for their members in the non-publicly owned PCS mines.

Steelworkers were the first to organize a branch of the Toronto Dominion Bank; Develcon, a high-tech electronics firm; the office staff of the Saskatoon law firm, Mitchell, Taylor, Romanow and Ching; and the office employees of Saskatchewan Mutual Insurance.

The membership of the union has fluctuated over the years owing to mine and plant closures at Dominion Bridge, Great West Steel, Eldorado Nuclear, Westeel, Westank Willock and Federal Pioneer.

In September 2004, a merger between the International Woodworkers of Canada and USWA created the largest industrial union in western Canada, with a Saskatchewan membership of 4,500. The merged union has members in the manufacturing of steel, pipe, agricultural equipment, wood and allied products, among office and technical employees, as well as in uranium and potash mining and milling.   *Terry Stevens*

UNITY, town, pop 2,243, located approximately 90 km SW of the Battlefords at the junction of Hwys 14 and 21. Settlement of the area began in 1904 and Unity began to develop with the arrival of the **GRAND TRUNK PACIFIC RAILWAY** in 1908. By the early 1920s, Unity's population was over 600 and growing. The community experienced somewhat of a decline during the 1930s, but subsequently recovered, particularly after **WORLD WAR II**. Much of the community's return to prosperity and future growth was due to oilfield exploration and resultant developments. After natural gas was discovered near Unity, local furnaces and coal stoves were converted to burn the gas and, in 1944, Unity became one of only three communities in Saskatchewan with their own domestic natural gas system, prior to SaskPower being given the authority in the 1950s to establish the provincial utility. (Lloydminster had natural gas in 1934, and Kamsack's system was in place in 1937.) Drilling for oil in the Unity area also revealed a substantial deposit of sodium chloride (common salt) laid down when much of Saskatchewan was covered by inland seas. In the late 1940s, a salt mine was developed and, today, the mine, operated by Sifto Canada, is the community's largest employer with 60 employees. Further, exploratory drilling also revealed extensive deposits of potash, and the first attempt at potash mining in Saskatchewan, indeed, in Canada, was made near Unity in the early 1950s. The industrial activity in the area, combined with modified and more successful agricultural practices after the dry years of the 1930s, caused the town's population to skyrocket. The community's numbers rose from 682 in 1941, to 1,248 in 1951, and, between 1955 to 1965, approximately 100 new homes were built in the town. By 1966, the population was 2,154. Despite industrial development, agriculture remains the major concern in the region. Unity has three large modern inland terminals, as well as substantial farm machinery dealerships. Unity has been participating in the nationally

COURTESY OF THE UNITY AND DISTRICT HERITAGE MUSEUM
Unity townsite, 1920s.

acclaimed "Communities in Bloom" competition since 1999, winning first place in their population category that year and again the next. In 2003, the town's floral displays and attractive appearance earned Unity a national "Communities in Bloom" championship. *David McLennan*

UNIVERSITY EXTENSION, UNIVERSITY OF SASKATCHEWAN.

The extension and outreach function of the **UNIVERSITY OF SASKATCHEWAN** began in 1910 through the College of Agriculture: its primary purpose was to provide information on improved farming practices to rural families. In 1913, a Department of Women's Work was established to extend information relating to the home; in 1949, this program became known as "Women's Service" and was carried on in collaboration with the numerous **HOMEMAKERS CLUBS** throughout the province. In 1916, the University became responsible for Boys and Girls Club Work; in 1945, the newly formed provincial Department of Agriculture became a partner in administering this youth program; later, District 4-H Councils were formed and local leaders were trained to support the program. In 1967, there were over 3,000 voluntary leaders and almost 13,500 4-H members, a number that declined as the rural population of the province declined. For many years, the Extension Department worked closely with the agricultural societies (seventy-two member societies in 1967) and horticultural societies (thirty-nine member societies in 1967) in the province, and for a period provided their headquarters, with a staff person assigned to their administration.

In the early years, almost all instruction was on a face-to-face basis, with extension and faculty specialists traveling by train to the rural communities. A "Better Farming Train" was sponsored from 1914 to 1922; box cars were used as a moving headquarters for lectures, exhibits, and demonstrations on home and farm improvement; afterwards, an agriculture lecture car was attached to various trains until the early 1930s.

During the 1940s the federal and provincial departments of Agriculture collaborated with the University of Saskatchewan in the "Co-operative Extension Program." Every third year saw the publication of a "Saskatchewan Guide to Farm Practice" designed to help take confusion out of good farm practice recommendations for farmers and homemakers. After **WORLD WAR II**, the need for broader adult education was recognized as important to rural citizens, and University Extension provided a new program, Adult Education Services. For the first time a staff member was employed to offer programming through evening classes, lecture series, conferences, and seminars. A Public Affairs program was also established in collaboration with the Saskatchewan Council of Public Affairs. Increasing

SASKATCHEWAN ARCHIVES BOARD S-B6206

The University of Saskatchewan, Extension Division, sponsored the 'Better Farming Train' to tour across Saskatchewan and showcase agricultural innovations developed at the University.

demands for programs of continuing education encouraged some colleges to initiate extension-type programs, and work began in 1963 to create a meaningful multi-college extension program. In 1965, a Department of Extension Program was also established at the University's Regina Campus.

During the 1960s a number of faculty of the Extension Division completed graduate studies in adult education and related disciplines, and taught courses in the new interdisciplinary Master of Continuing Education degree program offered by the College of Graduate Studies. This program fostered improved professional competence to many mature students working in adult and continuing education in the province, as well as nationally and internationally. During the latter half of the 20th century, an increasing number of adult education programs and services were transferred from other parts of the campus to the Extension Division. The off-campus academic programs, including Summer School and Inter-session Programs, were among the first. As the Community Colleges and later Regional Colleges were established, the Extension Division administered off-campus courses, primarily first- and second-year university courses, through the provincial college system. At the same time, in response to the increasing demand for off-campus

instruction, Extension Division employed instructional designers to work with faculty in a variety of subjects to increase the effectiveness of distance teaching. A later phase was to make courses available on-line to all areas of the province (*see* **CAMPUS SASKATCHEWAN**). By the 1990s, the Division included extension credit studies, an instructional design group, a prior learning assessment office, and a second-language instruction unit. An extension press was established, and an office for marketing extension publications was instituted under the name of "U-Learn." At the beginning of the 21st century, new Extension programs include: Business and Leadership, Humanities and Social Sciences, Agriculture, Food and Horticulture, Community Arts, Environment, Science and Technology, Women's Studies, Community Development, Music in Early Childhood, Career Development, Indigenous Peoples, and Seniors programs. *Harold R. Baker*

UNIVERSITY OF REGINA.

The University of Regina traces its origins to 1911, when the Methodist Church established Regina College to offer high school education to the young people of the city and surrounding area. The school was located on College Avenue at the south edge of the downtown district and across Wascana Lake from the

Regina College, 1928.

SASKATCHEWAN LEGISLATIVE BUILDING. In 1925 the college affiliated with the **UNIVERSITY OF SASKATCHEWAN** and began to offer the first year of the Bachelor of Arts degree. **ERNEST STAPLEFORD**, President of the College (1915–37), hoped to expand the academic program to a full degree course, but President **WALTER MURRAY** of the University of Saskatchewan firmly and successfully opposed the plan: he did not want to relinquish Saskatoon's monopoly on university education in the province.

The **DEPRESSION** of the 1930s brought Regina College to the brink of bankruptcy. With considerable reluctance, the college agreed in 1934 to a takeover by the University of Saskatchewan. While the arrangement provided financial security, it postponed for a generation the dream of attaining university status. In March 1954 a group of citizens gathered at City Hall to form the Regina College Citizens' Committee. Led by lawyer George H. Barr and including individuals from a variety of community organizations, the group lobbied for a full degree program in Regina. In 1959 their efforts were finally rewarded: the University of Saskatchewan, under heavy pressure from increasing baby boom enrolments, decided to allow the expansion to proceed. The second year of the BA program was introduced in the fall of 1961, and the third year in the fall of 1964. On July 1, 1961, Regina College officially became the University of Saskatchewan, Regina Campus. The university hired architect Minoru Yamasaki to draw up a master plan for the development of a new campus on a 300-acre site on the southeast edge of the city. The Classroom and Laboratory Buildings were completed in the summer of 1965, followed rapidly by the Physical Education Centre in 1966, the Library in 1967, the Education Building in 1969, a temporary Student Services' Building in 1969, College West in 1972, and the Administration/Humanities Building in 1973. In addition, there were two federated colleges, the Roman Catholic **CAMPION COLLEGE** and **LUTHER COLLEGE**, whose buildings opened respectively in 1968 and 1971.

As the planning and construction of the campus proceeded, new professional programs were added to the Arts and Science core. The Board of Governors approved the establishment of a Faculty of Education in 1964. This was followed a year later by the School of Public and Business Administration, which evolved in 1968 into the Faculty of Administration. The Faculty of Engineering was established in 1965, the Faculty of Graduate Studies in 1968, and the School of Social Work began offering courses in 1973. The number of full-time faculty members increased from 23 in 1959 to 308 in 1972; full-time student enrolment soared from 327 to 4,009 over the same period. Despite numerous attempts to devise an organizational structure that met the needs of both the Regina Campus and the Saskatoon Campus, it soon became apparent that the one-university model was not working. The provincial government in 1973 appointed a Royal Commission on University Organization and Structure, chaired by former Supreme Court Justice **EMMETT HALL**. The Commission reported that it had found "two campus groups warring within the bosom of a single university" and recommended the establishment of two separate institutions. This became reality on July 1, 1974, when the University of Regina came into existence.

After a lull in enrolment in the 1970s, the number of full-time (or full-time equivalent) students began to increase, rising from 4,762 in 1982 to 7,615 in 1992 to 12,447 (9,428 full-time and 3,019 part-time) in 2003. In 1976 the University of Regina entered into an agreement with the **FEDERATION OF SASKATCHEWAN INDIAN NATIONS** to recognize and

Aerial view of the University of Regina campus.

support the Saskatchewan Indian Federated College, which has since evolved into the **FIRST NATIONS UNIVERSITY OF CANADA**. New programs have been added over the years, such as Journalism, Film and Video, Human Justice, and Kinesiology and Health Studies. The Language Institute Building went up in 1991, and the W.A. Riddell Centre, housing the Faculty of Fine Arts, Student Services, and the Students' Union, in 1997. New construction since then includes two storeys added to the Education Building, expansion of the Research Park adjacent to the campus, a residence complex, and a Centre for Kinesiology, Health and Sport. The University of Regina has developed from its modest roots as a junior college into a well-rounded university that provides a full range of academic programs, professional training, scholarly research, and public service, all in keeping with its motto: "As One Who Serves."

James M. Pitsula

UNIVERSITY OF SASKATCHEWAN. Two years after the province of Saskatchewan was created, the Legislative Assembly passed the University of Saskatchewan Act in 1907. The government of **WALTER SCOTT** had the vision to create a full University and not just a college when the population of Saskatchewan at that time was merely 250,000. The Premier and the first president of the University, **WALTER MURRAY**, knew that the province's population would increase and that this was to be an institution to serve on a large scale. The Act specifically mentioned that the University would be open to women as well as men, and there were two women out of eight in the first graduating class. The board of governors maintained its policy of being a non-denominational University, but remained sensitive to religious interests: theology colleges were therefore welcomed and closely allied to the University. Emmanuel College, under the auspices of the Anglican Church, moved from Prince Albert and became affiliated in 1909; built in 1912–13, Emmanuel College, now known as the College of Emmanuel and St. Chad, was one of the first buildings constructed on the site. In 1912, the Presbyterians formed a college that became known as St. Andrew's College in 1924; it was taken over by the United Church in 1925. The Lutheran College and Seminary, now known as the **LUTHERAN THEOLOGICAL SEMINARY**, was established in 1920. After a lengthy period of development, the Catholic presence at the University of Saskatchewan became **ST. THOMAS MORE COLLEGE** in 1936; it was made into a federated college in 1953. The most recent affiliation with the University of Saskatchewan was Central Pentecostal College, in 1983.

E.H. OLIVER delivered the first class at the University of Saskatchewan in the Drinkle Building in downtown Saskatoon on Wednesday, September 29, 1909. In spring of 1910 construction started on

University of Saskatchewan, Saskatoon.

the new campus, and on July 29 of that year Prime Minister Sir Wilfrid Laurier laid the cornerstone for the Administration Building. At the laying of the cornerstone, Premier Scott said: "Saskatchewan is essentially an agricultural province... It is in keeping with the character of our province that the main part of the highest institution of learning in the province shall be an agricultural college." This was actually the first Canadian University to have a College of Agriculture. Based on the principle of "service to the community," many community-based programs developed out of the extension department of the College of Agriculture, including **4-H CLUBS**, Farm and Home Week, the **HOMEMAKER'S CLUB** (Women's Institute), the Farm Train, the National Farm Radio Forum, and a variety of short courses. Many associate the development of the cooperative movement as an outgrowth of the extension department. As Walter Murray said, "All are greatly benefited by the intercourse and better prepared for service in the state, where the farmer, the doctor, the lawyer, the teacher and the engineer must work together for the public good." These professions did work together on one campus as the University expanded its offerings and established new colleges.

Over the years, several new colleges were added to the University of Saskatchewan: Arts and Science, 1909; Agriculture, 1912; Engineering, 1912; Law, 1913; Pharmacy, 1914; Commerce, 1917; Medicine, 1926; Education, 1927; Home Economics, 1928 (closed in 1990); Nursing, 1938; Graduate Studies, 1946; Physical Education, 1958; Western College of

Veterinary Medicine, 1964; Dentistry, 1965; and Physical Therapy, 1976. Today, the University has thirteen colleges with the largest cross-section of health sciences colleges in the country, and is well known for its scientific discoveries. Scientists at the University have developed new varieties of wheat to combat the early frosts and rust, which are now grown all over the world. A new formula for concrete was developed to increase its strength and resistance to chemical reactions in the soil. A linear accelerator, the forerunner to the **CANADIAN LIGHT SOURCE** Syncrotron, was installed at the University to lead the way in nuclear physics research; this is Canada's only syncrotron, and one of the largest research projects ever undertaken in the country. In 1951, the world's first non-commercial Cobalt 60 therapy unit, developed at the University for cancer treatment, was opened. Finally, two Nobel Prize winners were affiliated with the scientific community at the University of Saskatchewan: **GERHARD HERZBERG** (1971) and **HENRY TAUBE** (1981). These are just some examples of the world-recognized achievements of this comparatively young academic institution.

The University of Saskatchewan also has a broad offering in the humanities and fine arts. In 1959 it acquired four Amati instruments (two violins, one cello, and one viola), and in 2003, the president established the University of Saskatchewan Amati Quartet in residence. This is one of only three Amati quartets in the world (the Amati family in Italy made these fine instruments between 1607, for the viola, and 1690, for the cello). The University of Saskatchewan is also home to some of the best athletic teams in Canada and has earned national championships in various sports. The Huskie Athletic program promotes good sportsmanship, athletic excellence, and team spirit on campus. The University is the product of a bold new vision inspired by Walter Scott and Walter Murray. The fieldstone and Tyndall stone buildings are all built in the same architectural style: the look of permanence, tradition and beauty has combined to produce a campus that is reputed to be one of the most attractive in Canada. As the University approaches its 100th anniversary, the present campus and academic offerings adequately reflect the original vision.

Gordon L. Barnhart

UNIVERSITY SPORTS. University sports in Saskatchewan reflect the spirit and tenacity of the province's residents. Expectations of strong academic ability and physical prowess went hand in hand in 1912, according to the **UNIVERSITY OF SASKATCHEWAN** yearbook, the *Greystone*. Athletes competed in soccer, rugby, track and field, tennis, fencing, and hockey. Women and men played in inter-varsity, city and provincial sports leagues. The Huskies represented teams at the University of Saskatchewan, while intramural sports encouraged the average athlete to enjoy recreational team play. Known as rugby until 1948, football in Saskatchewan was first played at the University of Saskatchewan campus in 1911. Individual campuses had their own teams until 1914–15, when the first official varsity team formed. In 1927 University of Saskatchewan professor Evan Hardy, known as the "father of inter-collegiate football," formed the Western Intercollegiate Rugby Union League. Prior to the 1960s, the Huskies team played against the Saskatoon Hilltops and the **SASKATCHEWAN ROUGHRIDERS**; today's Saskatchewan Huskies are ranked as one of Canada's best university football teams. Sports on campus continued to play a huge role in university life. The early years of hockey at the University of Saskatchewan included women's and men's teams competing on outdoor rinks; Rutherford Rink, built in 1929, remains home to the Saskatchewan Huskies hockey team. Basketball took hold in 1914, when the gym was in the basement of the College building and caused consternation for teams who played there: the building was known for its low ceilings, which made outside shots rather difficult.

The province is also home to the **UNIVERSITY OF REGINA** Cougars sports programs, which originated in the early 1960s; the Cougars joined the Canadian Interuniversity Athletic Union in 1968. In particular, the Cougettes and later the Lady Cougars gained prominence in women's basketball between 1977 and 1979, finishing with an impressive second-place standing in the country and an 11–5 record. The winning continued through the 1980s and 90s with the Lady Cougars continuing to place in the top ten

nationally; in 2001, the team won a national title. The men's Cougars also did well in basketball by becoming one of the top four teams at the nationals in recent years. Success in Saskatchewan university sports is also attributed to the efforts of the Canadian Interuniversity Athletic Union Central (CIAUC), which was founded in Ontario and Quebec in 1906 and by 1919 expanded into Saskatchewan and further west. The CIAUC provided universal rules and coaching practices, guided the standards for building sports facilities, and established professional coaching and management positions and strategies. In 1961, the Canadian Interuniversity Athletic Union (CIAU) integrated the latest scientific coaching methods, state of the art communication systems, and the coordination of national and international competitions. Saskatchewan university sports teams benefited further as the CIAU expanded under the supervision the federal government. The CIAU provided Saskatchewan teams with opportunities to train, engage in sports research and testing, identify and recruit talented athletes, and have access to international competitions through government funding. In 2001, CIAU changed its name to Canadian Interuniversity Sport (CIS).

Elizabeth Mooney

UPSON, GEORGE C. George C. Upson was an early Canadian aviator who served in the Royal Flying Corps (renamed the **ROYAL AIR FORCE**) during **WORLD WAR I**. Afterwards he joined the peacetime Royal Canadian Air Force (RCAF), serving at its flying boat base at Ladder Lake, northwest of Prince

Albert. Because the federal government controlled Saskatchewan's natural resources until 1930, the RCAF was used for firefighting, forestry protection, and survey work in the province's northern areas. A sub-base was located at Ile-à-la-Crosse, but later moved to La Ronge. When Saskatchewan acquired control of its natural resources in 1930, the federal government turned five Canadian-built Vickers Vedette flying boats over to the province for use in this work. "Uppy" Upson, by now a civilian, was flying one of these aircraft northwest of Big River on May 27, 1936, when his aircraft encountered a storm; he parachuted to safety, although his passenger, firefighter Philip Clement, was killed. Previously, only six Canadian aviators had saved their lives through the emergency use of parachutes; Upson was the first to do so in Saskatchewan. He later flew for Canadian Airways, and during **WORLD WAR II** commanded the RCAF's No. 6 (Bomber Reconnaissance) Squadron at Alliford Bay, BC, from August to December 1942, at which time he was posted to a staff position at 4 Group headquarters in Prince Rupert. A lake and a river in northern Saskatchewan bear Upson's name.

Will Chabun

URANIUM. Uranium is one of the most abundant elements in the earth's crust: it is 500 times more common than gold. Traces of uranium can be found in human tissue and some foods, while larger amounts can be found in rivers, oceans, rock and soil. Most of the uranium that is mined is used as fuel to generate power in nuclear reactors, and ultimately provides 17% of all electricity used in the

Eldorado mine, 1954.

world today. Other uses include medical diagnosis, food preservation, agricultural production, and manufacturing purposes. Canada is the world's top producer of uranium, with 33% of the world's total yield in 2002. Mining companies sell Saskatchewan uranium to electric power utilities in Canada, the United States, Europe, and the Far East. The earliest records of uranium discovery date back to the mid 1930s. In 1943, the federal government established Eldorado Mining and Refining Limited, which was later named Eldorado Nuclear Limited. The company was responsible for all Canadian uranium interests. In 1949, a uranium mine was developed in the Beaverlodge area, and three years later Uranium City was established as the hub for uranium mining. The late 1960s saw a large increase in exploitation due to the Rabbit Lake discovery and the following projections of high demands for uranium.

In 1974, the provincial government created the Saskatchewan Mining Development Corporation, a Crown corporation that would govern all mining in the province. It was during the 1970s that extensive uranium reserves were located in the Athabasca Basin and, following this find, several more mines were established in the 1980s in Cluff Lake, Key Lake, Cigar Lake and Rabbit Lake. In 1988, the Saskatchewan Mining Development Corporation merged with Eldorado Nuclear Ltd. to form the **CAMECO CORPORATION**. About 88% of the uranium shipped from Saskatchewan goes to global markets. The value of mineral sales for uranium in 2001 was $562 million; the uranium industry created approximately 5,000 jobs in the province (1,334 direct jobs, 364 contractor jobs, and an additional 3,400 spin-off jobs). **COGEMA RESOURCES INC.** is one of the largest uranium producers, with headquarters in Saskatoon. JCU (Canada) was established in late 2000 as a subsidiary of Japan-Canada Uranium Co. Ltd. Canada is a signatory of the International Non-proliferation Treaty, which is safeguarded by the International Atomic Energy Agency. *Crystal Wallin*

URANIUM CITY. Uranium City is located on the northern shore of **LAKE ATHABASCA**, 724 km northwest of Prince Albert and 48 km south of the Saskatchewan–Northwest Territories border. Uranium ore was first discovered in northern Saskatchewan in the late 1930s. However, with the onset of **WORLD WAR II**, the Canadian government imposed a ban on private exploration for the mineral, and created Eldorado Mining and Refining Ltd. to control all uranium-related exploration activities. The lifting of the ban after the war sparked a staking rush in the Athabasca region, and the need for a convenient service centre to serve the growing number of mines in the region quickly became apparent. As a result, the provincial government created the remote community of Uranium City with input from Eldorado Nuclear, specifically to support uranium mining

activities in the region. Construction of the community began in 1952 with plans to accommodate and provide the necessary infrastructure for 5,000 people. Between 1953 and 1955 Uranium City developed rapidly, and by 1956 it was the fastest growing community in Saskatchewan.

Uranium City's history follows the same trajectory as that of other single-industry towns in Canada. The community boomed in the 1950s, nearly died in the early 1960s, and experienced a brief upswing in 1967 and 1968 when demand for uranium increased. However, the upsurge was not strong enough to absorb the area's capacity to produce uranium, and in 1969 Eldorado Mining and Refining Ltd. announced cutbacks. In 1971 Eldorado came close to shutting down as there was no market for uranium because of stockpiling. Gunnar Mines Ltd. and Lorado Uranium Mines Ltd. began operations in 1955 and 1957 respectively, but by the mid-1960s these operations had ceased. The uranium market recovered somewhat in 1974. New finds were discovered, and Eldorado announced a major expansion program, including plans to overhaul its operations in northern Saskatchewan. Eldorado also committed large capital expenditures to accelerate the development of new assets and refurbish existing facilities at the Beaverlodge operation. Nevertheless, in June 1982 Eldorado permanently closed its Beaverlodge operation, citing increased operating costs, falling ore grades, and a "soft" uranium market as reasons for the shutdown. Although as a single-industry community the residents of Uranium City were familiar with boom/bust cycles, the announcement of the mine closure came as a shock

to the townspeople and had profound effects. Businesses folded, and the population declined dramatically from almost 2,500 residents on the eve of the announcement in December 1981 to 200 in 1986. Between 1982 and 1985, water and sewer utilities were shut off to outlying residential areas; services were provided to the remaining population, who moved into the Core and Hospital Hill area of the community.

While closure of the mines marked the beginning of the end for Uranium City, it was not the end of uranium mining as new, richer deposits were discovered in other areas of northern Saskatchewan. However, rather than constructing new resource-based communities, the labour force commuted to the mines on a seven-day-in, seven-day-out basis, a system which enabled some Uranium City residents to maintain generally well-paying mining jobs. The prime employer in Uranium City, however, became the hospital, which served the entire Athabasca region. Regardless of the hospital jobs, nearly all the people of Uranium City left and most of the businesses closed. Many of the unoccupied buildings in the community collapsed, presenting safety concerns for some residents. The struggling community suffered a further setback in 2003 with the opening of a new hospital at Stony Rapids. Many businesses relied heavily on the hospital for their operations, and the shift of regional health care services to Stony Rapids meant a considerable reduction in business for those in Uranium City. The remaining residents of Uranium City and the community itself were once again faced with a very uncertain future.

Lesley McBain

DOUG CHISHOLM PHOTO

Uranium City core area in 2003, some twenty years after the closing of the Beaverlodge operation.

URBAN ABORIGINAL POPULATION. Of 130,190 Saskatchewan residents self-identifying, in whole or part, as Aboriginal in the 2001 Census, a third—43,695 (33.6%)—were First Nations population on reserve, another 22,275 (17.1%) rural Aboriginal population off reserve, and almost half—60,840 (46.7%)—were Aboriginal people in urban areas, including 34,935 in the two Census Metropolitan Areas (CMAs) of Saskatoon and Regina and another 25,905 in other urban centres. In Saskatoon, 20,275 Aboriginal people were counted (9.1% of the total city population), of which 11,290 were First Nations (including 11,025 Registered Indians), 8,305 MÉTIS, and 680 mixed Aboriginal or other Aboriginal identifications. Regina had an Aboriginal-identity population of 15,685 (8.3% of the total city population), of which 9,200 were First Nations, 5,990 Métis, and 495 other Aboriginal. Prince Albert had an Aboriginal-identity population numbering 11,640 (29.1% of the total city population), including 5,375 First Nations, 5,950 Métis, and 315 other Aboriginal. In North Battleford, residents identifying as Aboriginal numbered 3,180 (18.5% of the city population), of whom 1,875 were First Nations, 1,285 Métis, and 25 other. Other significant urban Aboriginal concentrations were in Lloydminster (2,000), Yorkton (1,825) and Moose Jaw (1,405). In absolute numbers, Saskatoon and Regina rank respectively fifth and seventh among CMAs by size of Aboriginal-identity population, yet have among the highest proportionate number of Aboriginal residents; while among smaller cities Prince Albert stands out as having a relatively high Aboriginal population, now approaching a third of the city's total population.

A rapid urbanization of the "Native Indian" population in Saskatchewan occurred during the 1960s. The urban proportion within this population increased from just 5.5% in 1961 to 21.7% in 1971. Much of this change was in the two largest cities. In Regina the "Native Indian" population increased from 539 to 2,860, and in Saskatoon from 207 to 1,070. Since 1971 the urban Aboriginal population has continued to increase, although at a slower rate each decade. By 1991, in both Regina and Saskatoon, 5.7% of the total city population identified as Aboriginal. However, a greater number of residents claimed some Aboriginal ancestry than identified as Aboriginal (entirely or partially): in Regina, respectively 12,765 compared to 11,020, and in Saskatoon 14,225 compared to 11,920. This discrepancy remained in 2001: in Regina 17,575 claimed to be solely or partially of "North American Indian" or Métis ethnic origin (11,950 Indian, 5,625 Métis), compared to 15,685 identifying as Aboriginal; and in Saskatoon 22,850 claimed to be of "North American Indian" (14,970) or Métis (7,880) ethnic origin compared to 20,275 identifying as Aboriginal. Using the identity rather than ethnic origin data, one may

note that the Aboriginal-identity population has increased in absolute numbers and proportionately during the past decade: for example, in Saskatoon from 11,920 (5.7% of the city population) in 1991 to 15,550 (7.5%) in 1996 and 20,275 (9.1%) in 2001; today, approximately one in every ten residents is Aboriginal. The Aboriginal populations of Saskatoon and Regina have gradually become more dispersed throughout these cities, while still remaining largely concentrated in poorer neighbourhoods. Today in Saskatoon, for example, out of sixty neighbourhoods only two still lack any Aboriginal residents. In two inner-city neighbourhoods, which are the poorest in the city, close to half the population is now Aboriginal; in another two neighbourhoods (also poor), over a third of the residents are Aboriginal; in another four, 20–29%; in eleven 10–19%; and the remaining thirty-eight neighbourhoods contain less than 10% Aboriginal residents—many as few as 1–3%.

Examination of recent five-year gross migration rates of Aboriginal population in Saskatoon and Regina reveals that in-migration into these cities has usually been matched, more or less, by out-migration; yet this may now be changing in favour of in-migration. Recent research reveals that an increasing proportion of urban Aboriginal population consists of long-term or "permanent" residents. In Saskatoon, the 2001 Census revealed that for the urban Aboriginal-identity population aged 1 year and over (19,690), 61.1% had lived in the same residence last year, 27.6% in the same city but at a different address, 8.8% in Saskatchewan but had changed residence, and 2.5% outside the province. Whereas for the Aboriginal-identity population aged 5 years and over (17,560), 26.3% lived at the same city address five years ago, 46.3% had changed address within the city, 20.1% outside the city but within the province, and 7.3% outside the province. In Regina, for the Aboriginal-identity population aged 1 year and over (15,265), 63.9% had not moved in the past year, 26.9% had moved within the city, 6.3% outside the city but within the province, and 2.9% outside the province. And for the Regina Aboriginal-identity population aged 5 years and over (13,360), 32.1% had not moved during the past five years, 49.2% had moved within the city, 13.2% within the province but outside the city, and 6.1% beyond the province. Thus these findings seem to be quite comparable for both Saskatoon and Regina, revealing a very substantial pattern of mobility within the city every few years, yet less movement between urban and rural (e.g., reserve) areas. The urban Aboriginal population is young: in both Regina and Saskatoon half of the Aboriginal identity population is under 20 years of age (in Regina, respectively 50.4% and 48.7% in 1996 and 2001; in Saskatoon 49.8% and 47.9%). This means that an increasing number of young Aboriginal people are

born and raised in the city, with little or no familiarity with reserve or rural life.

The cities provide more opportunities for education, and urban Aboriginal youth are becoming better educated. Several thousand Aboriginal students are enrolled at the UNIVERSITY OF SASKATCHEWAN, FIRST NATIONS UNIVERSITY OF CANADA, and SASKATCHEWAN INDIAN INSTITUTE OF TECHNOLOGIES in Saskatoon; and at the UNIVERSITY OF REGINA, First Nations University of Canada, and GABRIEL DUMONT INSTITUTE in Regina. While the increasing urban Aboriginal presence is felt at virtually every level of education, it is especially dominant at the elementary level. In fact, several inner-city schools in Saskatoon and Regina now have a majority of pupils who are Aboriginal. There are also high schools pursuing an Aboriginal curriculum, such as Joe Duquette School in Saskatoon. (*See* Table UAP-1.)

Clearly, with urbanization Aboriginal people have been diversifying within the labour force and earning higher incomes. Now almost one-third of urban Aboriginals within the experienced labour force are in sales and service occupations; they are becoming relatively prominent in trades, business and finance, and education occupations; but fewer (although increasing numbers) are found in management, health, and science occupations. The unemployment rate, as well as dependence upon government transfer payments, while slightly better for urban Aboriginals, is still excessive compared to the provincial rates for non-Aboriginal population (4.8% unemployment). (*See* Table UAP-2.)

There is wide variation in average family income in neighbourhoods having the largest Aboriginal concentrations. In 1996 in Saskatoon, for example, average income for Aboriginal families ($20,800 rounded) was less than half that of Saskatoon families in general ($48,900), and ranged from a low of approximately $7,000 in one neighbourhood to a high of $39,900 in another. In the neighbourhood having the highest Aboriginal proportion, average family income was $13,500.

Saskatoon and Regina currently have the highest proportion of Aboriginal population living below the statistical poverty line (the Low Income Cut-off or LICO) of any CMA in Canada—almost two-thirds of the Aboriginal population in each of these cities: in 1996 in Saskatoon 64% of the Aboriginal population was below the LICO, compared to only 18% of the non-Aboriginal population; in Regina 63% of Aboriginals were below the LICO, compared to 14% of non-Aboriginals. Aboriginal unemployment rates and the LICO rate in all census tracts having the highest Aboriginal concentrations far exceeded non-Aboriginal rates. Moreover, average income for Aboriginal-identity population lagged far behind the non-Aboriginal populations in Saskatoon and Regina (by approximately $9,000 and $12,000 respectively). One the whole, then, despite indica-

Table UAP-1. Highest level of education attained, Aboriginal population aged 25 years and over

	Saskatoon	Regina	Saskatchewan
Population	8,590	6,665	54,695
Less than high school graduation	32.8%	35.1%	44.9%
High school graduation	8.3%	8.3%	7.2%
Some post-secondary	17.2%	20.1%	13.9%
University/Trade/college certificate	29.5%	27.5%	27.8%
University degree	12.2%	9.0%	6.1%

Table UAP-2. Selected Employment data, Aboriginal-identity population, 2001

	Saskatoon	Regina	Saskatchewan
Average income	$20,267	$20,469	$18,693
Average income if full time for one year	$30,949	$32,661	$30,140
Participation rate in labour force	58.4%	58.4%	54.5%
Population in experienced labour force	6,655	5,055	39,100
Employment rate	45.4%	46.3%	42.0%
Unemployment rate	22.3%	20.7%	23.0%
Government transfer payments as % of income	24.4%	25.2%	27.7%

Table UAP-3. Housing conditions, Aboriginal-identity population in Saskatoon and Regina, 2001

	Saskatoon	Regina	Saskatchewan
Number of dwellings	8,105	6,425	43,650
Ownership	2,730 (33.7%)	2,055 (32.0%)	15,300 (35.1%)
Minor repairs needed	2,830 (34.9%)	2,020 (31.4%)	15,050 (34.5%)
Major repairs needed	965 (11.9%)	1,040 (16.2%)	9,780 (22.4%)
More than one person per room	3.8%	3.0%	8.7%
Median household income	$26,700	$26,531	$27,166

tions of increasing occupational diversity among urban Aboriginal population in Saskatchewan, this population remains disproportionately poor. There is contemporary concern among urban Aboriginal residents over increasing crime rates in poorer inner-city neighbourhoods. These neighbourhoods, which have the highest Aboriginal concentrations, have the greatest prevalence of Aboriginal youth gangs, as well as of violent sexual assaults, armed robbery, both residential and business break and entry, vehicle theft, petty theft, and prostitution.

Housing conditions for urban Aboriginal population are improving. Much research and many policy recommendations have been reflected in increasing collaboration between Aboriginal organizations such as the Saskatoon Tribal Council (STC) and Central Urban Métis Federation Inc. (CUMFI) and universities, civic government (particularly City Planning), housing consortia, and community organizations—all recently linked in the comprehensive Bridges and Foundations Project on Urban Aboriginal Housing in Saskatoon. Among the urban

Aboriginal population home ownership is increasing and overcrowding lessening; however, many families are still struggling with relatively limited incomes and poor housing conditions, and demand for affordable housing far exceeds availability. (*See* Table UAP-3.)

In Saskatoon, in all neighbourhoods where Aboriginal residents form significant proportions (over 10%), the proportion of Aboriginal families headed by lone parents far exceeds the proportion in non-Aboriginal families: for example, in the city as a whole in 1996, 11% of Aboriginal families were headed by single parents, compared to 4% of non-Aboriginal families; the proportion in Aboriginal families ranged from a minimum of 23.8% to a maximum of 68.8% for particular neighbourhoods. The rate of lone-parent families as well as common-law relationships among Aboriginals continues to be relatively higher than among non-Aboriginals: in Saskatoon in 2001, among 20,220 Aboriginal census families, 12.3% were headed by lone parents and 8.9% were common-law relationships; in Regina, of

15,650 families, 10% were lone parent and 12.6% common law; and in Saskatchewan, of 130,020 Aboriginal families, 9.9% were headed by lone parents and 10% were common law.

Aboriginal businesses and institutions (such as the FEDERATION OF SASKATCHEWAN INDIAN NATIONS, Saskatoon Tribal Council, SASKATCHEWAN INDIAN GAMING AUTHORITY, MÉTIS NATION–SASKATCHEWAN administrative offices, FIRST NATIONS BANK OF CANADA, White Buffalo Youth Lodge, Career Village in Saskatoon, and institutions of higher education in Regina and Saskatoon) are becoming a common part of the urban scene, some located on URBAN RESERVES. These not only meet the needs of the urban Aboriginal population, they also serve to reinforce First Nations and Métis identities within an urban context. For example, attrition of Aboriginal language use has tended to be most pronounced in urban areas: of 20,275 Saskatoon residents who identified themselves as Aboriginal in 2001, 11.8% recognized an Aboriginal language that they first learned and still understood, compared to only 4.4% of the 15,685 Aboriginal residents in Regina and 25.5% of the 130,190 Aboriginals in Saskatchewan; 8.2% in Saskatoon still spoke that language at home, compared to only 2.0% in Regina and 22.4% in the province; and 15.5% in Saskatoon claimed at least some knowledge of an Aboriginal language, compared to 7.2% in Regina and 29.4% in Saskatchewan.   *Alan Anderson*

URBAN ETHNIC DIVERSITY. Saskatchewan's immigration record provides a key to understanding the ethnic diversity of its urban areas. In the late 19th century most migrants originated from Central Canada, the United States and the British Isles. These were joined by groups from Central and Eastern Europe in the boom years between the mid-1890s and WORLD WAR I. However, until after World War II most of the population resided in rural areas. Although some distinctive ethnic neighbourhoods emerged in urban areas, such as Germantown in Regina, ethnic diversity was more closely associated with the geography of ETHNIC BLOC SETTLEMENTS in rural Saskatchewan. This situation has changed in the last fifty years. Liberalization of Canada's Immigration Act in the 1960s has resulted in greater immigration from non-traditional sources such as East and South Asia. Most such immigrants have settled in urban areas, and particularly in Regina and Saskatoon. In addition, substantial rural-urban migration has led to increase in the number and mixing of ethnic groups in urban areas. Again, Regina and Saskatoon have been the major beneficiaries of this process. Consequently, although both cities lack the extremely diverse ethnic structures of Montreal, Toronto and Vancouver, their populations are more cosmopolitan than those of other cities in Saskatchewan. In 2001, the census identified 93 ethnic groups in Canada with populations exceeding 15,000. All but three of these groups were identified in Regina and Saskatoon; many smaller ethnic groups were recorded in Saskatchewan's other cities.

Despite the above, most post-1960s immigration has bypassed Saskatchewan. Consequently, its cities have relatively few immigrants compared with Canada as a whole, and in most cases recent immigrants (1991–2001) account for less than 1% of their populations. Low levels of immigration largely explain the small size of visible minority populations. Only in Regina and Saskatoon do visible minorities exceed 5% of the population. Because of this, ethnic diversity is more associated with the presence of large Aboriginal-identity and multiple-ethnic populations. Among provinces and territories Saskatchewan has the fifth largest Aboriginal-identity population, and approximately half resides in urban areas. This is a lower rate of urbanization than in the population as a whole (64%), but one that is slowly increasing. The size and concentration of the Aboriginal population varies considerably between cities. Largest totals are found in Saskatoon and Regina, where Aboriginal peoples account for 9.8% and 8.7% of the respective populations. Proportionately larger Aboriginal populations are found in Prince Albert, North Battleford, Lloydminster, and Yorkton. These concentrations reflect proximity to and migration from First Nations reserves in central and northern Saskatchewan. In contrast, the small sizes of Aboriginal populations in cities in southern Saskatchewan reflect the comparative absence of nearby reserves.

In 2001, half of Saskatchewan's population reported multiple-ethnic origins; this proportion exceeded levels in all other provinces and territories. Rates in excess of 50% were recorded in most cities, those of Saskatoon (53.7%) and Regina (53.5%) being virtually identical. High rates of multiple ethnicity reflect inter-ethnic marriage and other forms of social union among descendents of former immigrant populations. The vast majority of ethnic mixing involves European ethnic origin groups. In Regina and Saskatoon the most common multiple-ethnic associations involve British, German, French, and Ukrainian ethnic groups. Other prominent associations involve Aboriginal groups. The relative absence of multiple ethnic origins involving visible minority groups reflects the dominance of non-immigrants and long-established immigrants in the populations of both cities, and the tendency of new immigrants to report single rather than multiple ethnic origins. Over time, immigration and rural-urban migration have interacted with intra-urban mobility to produce distinctive ethnic geographies in Saskatchewan's cities. These are best observed in Regina and Saskatoon. Whereas immigrant "reception areas" are not readily identified in either city, data for 2001 show limited localization of recent

immigrants, seldom exceeding 5–10%. In both cities a strong association exists between the distribution of recent immigrants and areas with low to middle incomes and high densities of rental housing.

Visible minorities are found in all neighbourhoods in both cities. Their distributions correspond closely to those of recent immigrants, but show evidence of greater concentration. Again, concentration is more pronounced in Saskatoon, where visible minorities form 28% of Greystone Heights and 15% of Riversdale. In Regina, greatest concentrations are found in Gladmer Park (14%), Core (12%) and Downtown (11%). These distributions reflect relative ease of entry into neighbourhood housing markets, plus access to services in downtown areas and along high-access corridors such as 8th Street in Saskatoon. The Aboriginal identity populations in both cities exhibit pronounced concentration. In Saskatoon, most (74.1%) of the Aboriginal population resides west of the South Saskatchewan River, with concentrations exceeding 30% in the inner-city neighbourhoods of Riversdale and Pleasant Hill. To the east of the river, most neighbourhoods have Aboriginal concentrations of less than 7.5%. A similar contrast is observed in Regina. Almost two-thirds (64.4%) of the Aboriginal population reside north of the CPR mainline. Concentrations exceeding 30% are found in Washington Park, to the northwest of the city centre, and in Core, immediately to the east. Most suburban neighbourhoods, and all those in the city's southern suburbs, have Aboriginal concentrations of less than 5%. In both cities the concentration of Aboriginal peoples is closely associated with the distribution of low-income households and with areas of significant social and economic disadvantage.

Generally, highest multiple-ethnic concentrations are found in suburban neighbourhoods such as Westhill Park in Regina and Silverwood Heights in Saskatoon. Concentrations also tend to be higher south of the CPR mainline in Regina and east of the SOUTH SASKATCHEWAN RIVER in Saskatoon. The high concentrations in suburban neighbourhoods reflect upward social mobility and greater integration of Canadian-born and long-established immigrant communities. Inner-city neighbourhoods in both cities display relatively low multiple-ethnic concentrations. (*See also* VISIBLE MINORITIES, URBAN ABORIGINAL POPULATION) *Bernard D. Thraves*

URBAN GEOGRAPHY. Saskatchewan's urban geography is defined by the size, location and function of its urban areas and by their interaction with each other as an urban system. In 2001, this system comprised thirteen cities, fifty-one towns, two villages, two First Nations reserves, plus the urbanized parts of six rural municipalities. These settlements account for less than 0.2% of the province's surface area, but house 63.4% (629,036) of its population.

Two first-order cities, Saskatoon (196,811) and Regina (178,225), dominate the urban system. Together they account for almost 60% of the urban population and form the cores of two census metropolitan areas that rank 17th and 18th in size within the national urban system. The absence of second-order cities with populations of 50,000 to 150,000, together with numerous towns with fewer than 2,500 persons, indicates a relatively narrowly based urban-industrial economy.

Saskatchewan's urban system initially developed rapidly. From 1883 to 1904, seventeen communities incorporated as towns, with fifty-seven more by 1913. While forty-four of these are now classified as urban settlements, most Saskatchewan towns (96 of 147) are classified as non-urban settlements—all but two of these (94) having populations of less than 1,000, the threshold by which most urban areas are recognized. Generally, those communities that were first to incorporate as towns now rank among the province's largest urban centres: for example, Regina, Moose Jaw and Prince Albert incorporated as towns between 1883 and 1885, and as cities between 1903 and 1904. During the 1920s and 1930s the growth of Saskatchewan's urban population slowed considerably. By the end of **WORLD WAR II** less than one-third of the population was urbanized (30.2% in 1951), and although the urbanization rate has now increased to almost two-thirds, it remains lower than in Manitoba (71.9%) and Alberta (80.9%), and in Canada as a whole (79.7%). In the early 1980s Saskatoon eclipsed Regina as Saskatchewan's largest city, and it continues to grow at a faster rate.

Recently (1996–2001), urbanization has continued with only small rates of population change for all classes of urban area, and with no consistent relationship between class size and growth rate. Nevertheless, data for individual communities show considerable variation. Between 1996 and 2001, only three of thirteen cities and sixteen of fifty-one towns experienced population growth. The most rapidly growing communities are within commuting distance of Saskatoon (Martensville +25.5%, Warman +22.6%, Dalmeny +9.5%) and Regina (Pilot Butte +25.9%, White City +11.7%, Balgonie +9.5%). These communities provide evidence of strong but highly localized counter-urbanization within the urban system. Population decline is most evident in towns with traditional links to agriculture (Kamsack −11.3%, Foam Lake −6.5%, Assiniboia −6.4%, Eston −6.3%, Gull lake −5.8%), or mining (Esterhazy −9.8%, Lanigan −5.8%) and forestry (Hudson Bay −5.3%, Meadow Lake −4.8%). The community of La Ronge (−8.0%) in northern Saskatchewan has also experienced significant population loss.

Most (98.7%) of Saskatchewan's urban population is found in settlements located south of 54°N. Many of these were established in the late 19th and early 20th centuries at regular intervals along rail lines, and were designed to serve as collection and distribution points for their surrounding agricultural hinterlands. Numerous examples exist of towns that competed to attract investment by railway companies. Saskatoon, for example, owes part of its success to it being linked to three transcontinental railways by 1908. Similarly, Moose Jaw and Melville prospered from their selection respectively as divisional points for the **CANADIAN PACIFIC RAILWAY** and **GRAND TRUNK PACIFIC RAILWAY** (later **CANADIAN NATIONAL RAILWAY**). The railways helped establish the business districts of the cities and towns along their routes, and sometimes spurred the development of special purpose zones such as Regina's Warehouse District. They also contributed to the more general sorting of land uses. Not all of this was beneficial. In Regina and Saskatoon the railways formed physical barriers that helped reinforce class divisions based on ethnic neighbourhoods. As urban development progressed, railway lands often impeded the expansion of central business districts and the circulation of road traffic. In Saskatoon, these problems were partly resolved in the 1960s by the removal of the CNR railyards from the city centre. Today, the railways have much less influence on urban growth and development, but linkage to the provincial and national transportation network is still important. In 2001, 78.7% of Saskatchewan's urban population resided in cities and towns connected to each other along Highways 1 (38.4%) and 16 (40.3%).

The only parts of the urban system found north of 54°N are the forestry resource town of Meadow Lake (2001: 4,582), the service and administration centre of La Ronge (2,727) and its adjacent First Nations community of Kitsakie (560), plus a small part of the city of Flin Flon (267) which extends across the provincial boundary from Manitoba. All other settlements are classified as non-urban. These include the town of Creighton (1,556) and several First Nations reserves that have populations exceeding 1,000 persons.

All urban areas in Saskatchewan contribute to its industrial space economy. The most diversified economies are found in Regina and Saskatoon. These cities also provide specialized functions that are recognized nationally. Aside from its role as provincial capital, Regina has important functions in financial and insurance services, and in information and cultural industries. In Saskatoon, functional specialization is based on educational services at the **UNIVERSITY OF SASKATCHEWAN** and on provision of services to the mining sector. Although neither city has a large secondary industrial sector, manufacturing is relatively more important in Saskatoon. In contrast, Saskatchewan's small urban areas generally perform a narrow range of services for their immediate hinterlands. Nevertheless, some have

developed specialized functions based on one or more industrial sectors. These include manufacturing at Wynyard and Hudson Bay, mining at Esterhazy, oil extraction at Oxbow, transportation services at Kelvington, and educational services at Gravelbourg and La Ronge. A cluster of towns around Regina and Saskatoon, including Pilot Butte, Martensville and Warman, serve largely as dormitory communities for people employed in the two cities. In contrast, the increasing tendency for farm families to live off-farm is reflected in agriculture forming the dominant livelihood of residents in communities such as Eston, Outlook, and Gull Lake.

Bernard Thraves

FURTHER READING: Artibise, A.F. 1979. "The Urban West: The Evolution of Prairie Towns and Cities to 1930," *Prairie Forum* 4 (2): 237–62; Nader, G.A. 1976. *Cities of Canada*, Vol. 2. Toronto: Macmillan.

URBAN HEAT ISLANDS. It is well known that the air in urban areas is often warmer than that in the surrounding countryside. The region of warmth created by a city is known as an urban heat island. In cities worldwide–and indeed in Saskatchewan's two largest cities, Saskatoon and Regina–the intensity and form of the heat island effect is strongly

influenced by regional climate, topography, land use, and city size.

The urban heat island effect is most pronounced on calm, cloudless evenings, when natural rural surfaces cool more rapidly than city surfaces. Heat in cities is generated by heat-retaining construction materials such as concrete, masonry and asphalt, which alter the radiative, thermal, moisture, and aerodynamic properties of the natural surface cover. Air pollution from domestic, industrial, and automobile combustion processes also contributes to urban heat. In the temperate climates of Saskatoon and Regina, urban heat island intensities are greater during the cold autumn and winter months due to heat release from anthropogenic sources such as space heating, transportation, manufacturing, and lighting.

Regina is an ideal site for urban heat island formation: its built-up area is flat, compact, and surrounded by a vast plain so that topoclimatic effects are minimal (*see* Figure UHI-1). In Saskatoon, cold air drainage along the South Saskatchewan River valley causes some interference in heat island genesis. However, in both cities the built environment exerts a warming influence on daily temperatures. Nocturnal air temperatures in the city centres of Regina and Saskatoon are, on average, 3–4°C warmer than in the surrounding countryside; and

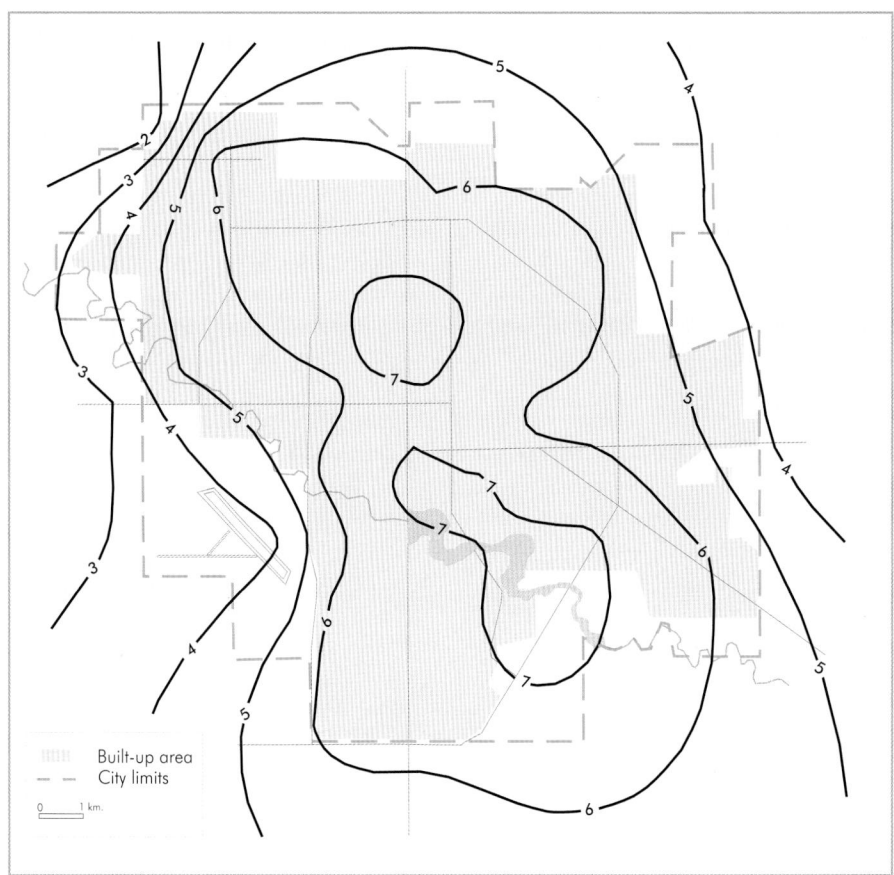

Built-up area
City limits
0   1 km.

IAIN STEWART, 2000

Figure UHI-1. The Regina heat island shown by isotherms (numbers indicate °C) on October 8, 1996, at 2200 hrs. The surrounding countryside is 3-5°C cooler than the city centre at 7°C.

under ideal nocturnal heat island conditions, urban-rural temperature contrasts, measured at the same time, can reach 6–8°C. In spite of the abundance of parks and open spaces in Regina and Saskatoon, both cities exhibit a discernible heat island influence. It is expected that heat islands of lesser intensity may be detectable in smaller cities and towns throughout Saskatchewan.

The urban heat island effect has many implications for Saskatchewan's cities. Warm urban temperatures may reduce energy requirements for space heating during winter months and increase demands for air conditioning in the summer. The heat island effect may lead to fewer frosts and a longer growing season for urban horticulturists. The survival of exotic trees, plants, animals and birds in the city may also be influenced by urban heat. The heat island effect will assume greater significance in Saskatoon and Regina with continued population growth and urban expansion.   *Iain Stewart*

FURTHER READING: Landsberg, H.E. 1981. *The Urban Climate*. New York: Academic Press; Ripley, E.A., O.W. Archibold and D.L. Bretell. 1996. "Temporal and Spatial Temperature Patterns in Saskatoon," *Weather* 51: 398–405; Stewart, Iain D. 2000. "Influence of Meteorological Conditions on the Intensity and Form of the Urban Heat Island Effect in Regina," *The Canadian Geographer* 44: 271–85.

URBAN RESERVES. Urban satellite reserves are properties located either in whole or in part within or adjacent to existing urban municipalities. They are governed and managed by Indian Band Councils. Under the federal Indian Act, such urban satellite reserves have exactly the same legal status as Indian reserves found in other parts of the province. Urban satellite reserves differ from another type of urban reserves which exist in other provinces by virtue of urban municipalities expanding to the point where their boundaries are contiguous with those of the longstanding neighbouring reserve. They also differ from urban properties which are held by Band Councils as part of their land holdings, but have not been granted official reserve status.

Properties acquired by Band Councils in urban areas are not automatically converted to reserve status. They acquire such status only after the federal Cabinet approves a formal request submitted to it by the Indian Band Councils that govern what might be termed "base reserves" or "home reserves" in other parts of the province. The conversion of any non-reserve properties to reserve properties requires conscious decisions both by the Band Council and federal Cabinet, on the basis of a prescribed process which is defined in two documents. The first document is the Treaty Land Entitlement Framework Agreement (TLEFA), which is a Saskatchewan-specific, comprehensive land claims agreement signed in 1992 by the federal government, the province of Saskatchewan, and twenty-six entitlement bands in the province. The second is the Additions to Reserve Policy (ARP), which is the official policy of the federal government that applies to properties earmarked for reserve status, regardless of how they are acquired by Band Councils. Both policies stipulate parallel and similar processes aimed at ensuring, among other things, negotiations and agreements between the councils of the Band, the urban municipality, and the school divisions. Although negotiations and agreements related to the provisions and payment of services and bylaw compatibility are identified as a desirable goal, they are not a precondition to having properties converted to reserve status. In some cases such properties have been converted to urban satellite reserves in the absence of such negotiations or agreements. During the past two decades, over twenty such satellite reserves have been created in municipalities of various sizes such as Prince Albert, Saskatoon, Regina, Yorkton, Fort Qu'Appelle, Lebret, Duck Lake, Meadow Lake, and North Battleford.

Such reserves have been created and used for commercial and institutional purposes; to date, none has been created or used for residential purposes. Invariably, they have been created because the Band Councils are seeking to capitalize on their location in urban areas which generally serve as regional service centres, in which they can establish and operate either profitable commercial ventures, or various types of First Nation governance, educational, and service agencies. The two main advantages of urban satellite reserves over urban properties which do not have reserve status are as follows: first, Band Councils who govern and manage them have extensive flexibility in the types of arrangements that they enter into with neighbouring municipal governments both for services and service fees, and also for bylaw compatibility; second, bona fide First Nation members who work or operate businesses on such reserves are exempt from taxation.

Joseph Garcea

FURTHER READING: Barron, F.L. and J. Garcea. 1999. *Urban Indian Reserves: Forging New Relationships in Saskatchewan*. Saskatoon: Purich Publishing; ——. 2000. "Reflections on Urban Satellite Reserves in Saskatchewan." Pp. 400–28 in Ron F. Laliberté et al. (eds.), *Expressions on Canadian Native Studies*. Saskatoon: University of Saskatchewan Extension Press.

URSELL, GEOFFREY (1943–). Geoffrey Ursell is a writer, editor, film and video producer, and music composer. Born in Moose Jaw on March 14, 1943, Ursell spent most of his youth in Saskatoon. After finishing his MA at the University of Manitoba and his PhD at the University of London, England, he

A.K. PHOTOS
Geoffrey Ursell.

returned to Saskatchewan in 1973. In 1975, he and three local writers from Moose Jaw founded the Thunder Creek Publishing Co-operative. As a small literary publishing house, the Thunder Creek Co-op published under the name Coteau Books, which has since become a well-known Regina-based literary press. Ursell now serves as its president and publisher while residing in Saskatoon with his wife, **BARBARA SAPERGIA**. As a playwright, he has received prestigious awards for two of his most acclaimed works: *The Running of the Deer* won the Clifford E. Lee National Playwriting Award in 1997, and the popular *Saskatoon Pie!* earned a **PERSEPHONE THEATRE** National Playwriting Award in 1991. Ursell's play, *Gold On Ice* (2003), celebrates the accomplishments of the **SANDRA SCHMIRLER** Olympic curling team. Ursell boasts an impressive list of publications in poetry and fiction. His first book, *Perdue: Or How the West Was Lost*, won the Books in Canada First Novel Award in 1984. Other notable books of poetry and short stories include *Jumbo Gumbo: Songs, Poems, and Stories for Children* (1989), *Way Out West* (1989), *The Look-Out Tower* (1989), and *Trap Lines* (1982).

Ursell's collections of short stories, poems, and songs have appeared in numerous anthologies and periodicals. As a songwriter and composer, he has prepared music for other playwrights, and many of his compositions are featured on two record albums: *Prairie Grass, Prairie Sky* and *Songs From No. 1 Hard*. He has also written drama for television and radio. He is best known for his ten-part mystery-comedy series for CBC Radio Saskatchewan, *The Rum-Runners of Rainbow Ravine*, as well as for *Distant Battles*, a CBC television drama based on the 1885 **MÉTIS** resistance. Over and above his long-standing commitment to Coteau Books, Ursell has served as president of the **SASKATCHEWAN WRITERS' GUILD**, president (and founder) of the Saskatchewan Playwrights' Centre, writer-in-residence for the Saskatoon and Winnipeg public libraries, and instructor of Canadian literature and creative writing at the **UNIVERSITY OF REGINA**.   *Iain Stewart*

FURTHER READING: Geoffrey Ursell Papers 89-1. University of Regina Archives, 1993; Higgins, M. 2003. "Musical Tells Story of Sandra Schmirler Curling Team." *Moose Jaw Times Herald* (July 18): 11; Smith, S.R. 2003. "Tenacity Fed by Passion for Literature." *Saskatoon StarPhoenix* (March 8): E12.

URSULINES (ORDER OF ST. URSULA, OSU).

St. Angela Merici founded the Company of St. Ursula in Italy in 1535. As an alternative to marriage or cloistered religious life, membership offered women an opportunity for ministry to other women. Originally the members lived in their own homes, but from 1585 on they were required to live together in community. In August 1912, a group of Ursulines came to Winnipeg from Germany. They began teaching, but the pre-war anti-German atmosphere made life difficult for them. In 1913 they came to Saskatchewan, where they eventually established three independent congregations with motherhouses in Bruno, Prelate and Vibank. In 1922 the Bruno Ursulines opened St. Ursula Academy, a boarding school for girls, which served the area for sixty years. At one time they numbered more than 100 sisters in Saskatchewan and taught in twelve locations in the former Muenster Abbacy area. Currently, most of the twenty-eight members live in the Humboldt area, with four serving in Brazil. The Sisters are involved in various ministries, with a view to faith education and the promotion of healthy family life.

In 1919 the Prelate Ursulines founded St. Angela's Convent and boarding school, which was renamed St. Angela's Academy and continues to thrive today. Offering Grades 9–12, the school attracts girls who wish to take their high school within the context of a residential Christian community. In its 85-year history, more than 230 Ursulines of Prelate have served in educational ministry in eighty-six different locations, mainly in the western half of the province. Today the congregation has seventy members in Saskatchewan and Alberta. In 1969, the General Administration moved to Saskatoon, which since then has been the centre of the congregation's ministries.

In 1919, a group of Ursulines opened a convent in Vibank; over the years more than eighty sisters have served in twenty locations, mainly in the Regina area. The Vibank Ursulines amalgamated with the Ursulines of Chatham, Ontario in 1953 and gradually reduced their Saskatchewan missions until today five Sisters remain in pastoral ministry in Regina.

Marian Noll, Magdalen Stengler and Teresita Kambeitz

FURTHER READING: Stengler, M. 2004. *Where to Now? The Story of the Ursuline Sisters of Prelate 1919–2003.* Battleford, SK: Marian Press.

UTOPIANISM.

In scholarly literature the word *utopia* refers to two distinct phenomena, which are often related: one of these is the intentional community—a group of persons who establish a community to enact some social purpose, for example to create a more religious or a more co-operative society; the other sense denotes a literary and cultural expression rather than a physical community. In Saskatchewan there have been many intentional communities, some with a clearly utopian flavour, and there have been various expressions of the idea of utopia in political history, books, and painting.

Before White settlement on the plains, the Aboriginal peoples are said to have lived in harmony with the natural world. When settlers began to arrive in the 1880s, many colonies were founded which could be considered intentional communities; in some cases the intention was to preserve an ethnic and/or religious identity, such as the German Catholic colony at St. Joseph's near Regina or the Hungarian colony at Esterhazy. Many of the Hungarian colonists contributed accounts to a pamphlet which extolled the North-West as a beautiful land of opportunity in order to attract more of their compatriots to immigrate. British settlers founded the "aristocratopia" of **CANNINGTON MANOR**, while a number of young French aristocrats participated in a similar experiment at St. Hubert (Whitewood). Members of the Temperance Colonization Society travelled from Toronto to select the site of what was to become Saskatoon, a community dedicated to the idea of total abstinence from alcohol. A more secular experiment was the **HARMONY INDUSTRIAL ASSOCIATION** co-operative colony in the Qu'Appelle Valley near Tantallon. Jewish settlers established nine colonies in Saskatchewan, and at the turn of the century the Doukhobors arrived to settle in some sixty communal villages in the eastern parkland. Nearly 2,000 British settlers arrived in 1903 to found the **BARR COLONY** around Lloydminster. A small number of settlers from Boston came in 1906 to establish Bostonia, near Glidden.

Since the settlement period there have been various kinds of intentional community. Undoubtedly the most prominent are the nearly sixty Hutterite colonies located primarily on the western side of the province. After **WORLD WAR II** a number of co-operative farms were established, the best known being what is now the **MATADOR FARMING POOL**, near Kyle. In addition there are part-time intentional communities such as the writers' and artists' summer colonies at St. Peter's, Muenster, and at Emma Lake, and the naturist colony of Green Haven east of Regina. The most familiar form of utopianism is utopian literature. Both the Paynter brothers who established the Harmony Industrial Association went on to write utopian books. Agrarian activist **E.A. PARTRIDGE**'s *War on Poverty* of 1926 contained a lengthy description of the western Canadian republic of Coalsamao, a co-operative state with a military organization. Another imagined utopia was set out in the so-called **REGINA MANIFESTO** of 1933, which marked the founding of the CCF Party in Regina. This party dedicated itself to the establishment of a co-operative commonwealth and laid down a framework for a social democratic state which the CCF began to put in place after it was elected in 1944. But utopian ideas can also be expressed in other arts: Saskatoon painter Betty Meyers suggests a co-operative utopia in her 1993 series of paintings called "People pulling Together"; there was a clear utopian theme in Thomas Mawson's plan for Regina as a garden city; and the architecture of the "Tower of God" at Athol Murray College of Wilcox is meant to represent the ideal of religious tolerance. In some cases utopianism is no more than a name (the Utopia School District, or the town of Edenwold). Many of the intentional communities had aims of self-preservation and prosperity, which is a limited kind of utopianism. However, some looked beyond this to the possible transformation of society, and the most persistent utopian idea is that of co-operation: it inspired the constitution of the Harmony Industrial Association, and fifty years later the *Regina Manifesto*; it was the philosophy of the Barr Colony as expressed in Isaac Barr's pamphlets; and it was also the basis of the Matador co-operative farm.   *Alex MacDonald*

FURTHER READING: Partridge, EA. 1926. *A War on Poverty: The One War That Can End War.* Winnipeg: Wallingford Press.

V

VACCINE AND INFECTIOUS DISEASE ORGANIZATION (VIDO). Originally known as the Veterinary Infectious Disease Organization, VIDO was established at the **UNIVERSITY OF SASKATCHEWAN** in 1975 to carry out practical research on the common Canadian infectious diseases of livestock. It was established with a grant provided by the Devonian Group of Charitable Foundations of Calgary, and with supplementary funding from the provincial governments of Alberta and Saskatchewan, the University, and subsequently a great many livestock and poultry organizations. VIDO represented a new and unique model for funding practical goal-oriented research, and established an international reputation by developing several new vaccines to prevent neonatal diarrhea, or scours, in newborn calves (Vicogen, Ecostar, Ecostar 2RC); *Haemophilus somnus* infection of cattle

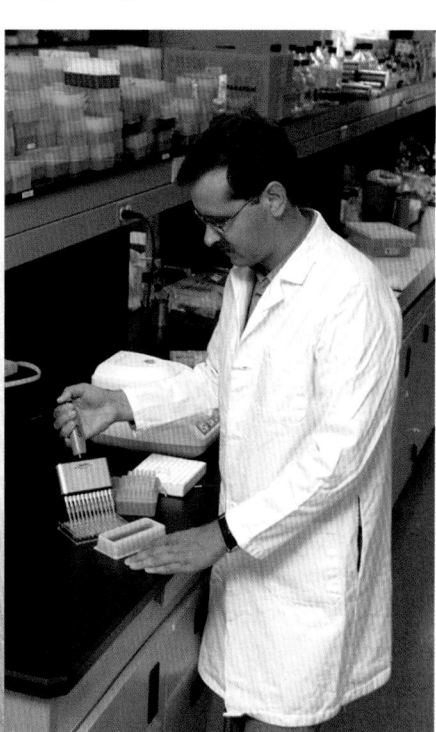

Alexander Zakhartchouk, VIDO scientist.

UNIVERSITY OF REGINA ARCHIVES AND SPECIAL COLLECTIONS 77-2-1

A.B. Van Cleave.

SASKATCHEWAN ARCHIVES BOARD R-A2940

Hadley Van Vliet.

MARGARET VANDERHAEGHE PHOTO/COURTESY OF MCCLELLAND AND STEWART

Guy Vanderhaeghe.

(Somnu-Star and Somu-Star Ph); shipping fever pneumonia in cattle (Pneumo-Star); pneumonia in pigs (Pleuro-Star); and adenovirus infection in turkeys (Hevlan-TC). It also developed new management and disease prevention programs for cattle and swine. In 2003, VIDO changed its name and opened an expansion to its building that now provides 80,000 square feet of ultramodern laboratory space for a staff of 145 researchers. It uses the most modern research tools of genomics and bioinformatics to develop new vaccines and vaccine delivery technology. *Stephen Acres*

VALENS, JOHN ALEXANDER (1873–1955).

Born near Lucknow, Ontario, on September 4, 1873, Valens came west in 1895, attended Brandon Collegiate and normal school in Winnipeg, taught in Estevan, and then graduated from Manitoba Medical College in 1905. He practised medicine in Saskatoon, delivered over 5,000 babies–most of them at home– and was director of the cancer clinic from 1936 to 1944. He was narrowly defeated as one of two Liberal candidates for the two-member Saskatoon City constituency in the provincial election of 1921, though his running mate, **ARCHIBALD MCNAB**, was elected at that time.

Valens was president of the Saskatchewan division of the Canadian Medical Association from 1919 to 1920. He was on the council of the **COLLEGE OF PHYSICIANS AND SURGEONS OF SASKATCHEWAN** from 1933 to 1944, as well as its registrar in 1945. He was also a member of the **UNIVERSITY OF SASKATCHEWAN** senate from 1922 to 1946, of the Saskatoon Collegiate board from 1915 to 1924, and a member of the board of Saskatoon City Hospital for many years. His chief legacy is his collection of biographies of early Saskatchewan medical doctors, summarized in a series of articles in *Saskatchewan Medical Quarterly* (1942–51), and now available in the Saskatchewan Archives. He died in Saskatoon on June 28, 1955. *C. Stuart Houston*

VAN CLEAVE, ALLAN BISHOP (1910–92).

A.B. Van Cleave, known as "Van" to countless students and colleagues, was born on August 19, 1910, in Medicine Hat. He obtained BSc (1931) and MSc (1933) degrees in chemistry from the **UNIVERSITY OF SASKATCHEWAN**. During his university years, he married Dorothy Yeo. Their family consisted of Galen, Elaine, Dalton and Carol. After PhD degrees from McGill and Cambridge, in 1937 he joined the Department of Chemistry and Chemical Engineering at the University of Saskatchewan, where he built a reputation as an educator and researcher in surface chemistry. In 1962 he became chairman of the Division of Natural Sciences of the Regina Campus of the University of Saskatchewan. He was appointed director of the School of Graduate Studies in 1965 and then Dean in 1969, when that School became a Faculty. For five years he also was Dean of the University College of Graduate Studies, which oversaw graduate education on both campuses of the University. From 1974 until his retirement in 1980, he continued as Dean of Graduate Studies at the **UNIVERSITY OF REGINA**.

He is best known for his work in designing the new high school chemistry curriculum in the 1960s. Dr. Van Cleave was a Fellow of the Royal Society of Canada, a Fellow of the Chemical Institute of Canada, and a member of many organizations such as the Defence Research Board, the Faraday Society, the Saskatchewan Research Council, and the Canadian Institute of Mining and Metallurgy. He also served as chair of the Canadian Services College Advisory Board (1965) and as president of the University of Saskatchewan Alumni Association (1949–51). He received the Centennial Medal (1967), the Order of Canada (1976), and an Honorary Doctorate from the University of Regina (1980). He died on 27 April 1992. *W. David Chandler*

VAN VLIET, HADLEY (1914–68). Hadley Van Vliet was born in 1914 of immigrant Dutch parents

on a farm near Quinton, Saskatchewan. He received a Bachelor of Science degree in Agriculture at the **UNIVERSITY OF SASKATCHEWAN**, and a PhD at the University of Wisconsin. Van Vliet started his teaching career in 1938 as instructor in agricultural economics at the University of Saskatchewan. Students held him in high regard, and his influence on them was a profound. He served a term as president of the Saskatchewan Agricultural Graduates Association, and another as president of the Saskatchewan Agricultural Economics Society. In 1968 he was named a Fellow of the Agricultural Institute of Canada. He died suddenly in December 1968, two days after he had given the principal paper at a meeting of the Saskatchewan branch of the Canadian Agricultural Economics Society. Van Vliet was posthumously inducted into the Saskatchewan Agricultural Hall of Fame in 1973.

VANDERHAEGHE, GUY (1951–).

Guy Clarence Vanderhaeghe was born on April 5, 1951 in Esterhazy, the only child of Clarence Earl and Alma Beth Vanderhaeghe. The family lived on the edge of town and Clarence worked in the local potash mine's mill until Guy was 13, when they moved to a farm nearby. Vanderhaeghe attended school in Esterhazy until age 17, when he went to Saskatoon to attend the **UNIVERSITY OF SASKATCHEWAN**. Inspired by a professor, he began what would be a lifelong passion: the study of history. He earned an Honours degree in that subject in 1971, and then an MA (1975); he also earned a BEd at the **UNIVERSITY OF REGINA** (1978). He has worked as a teacher, archivist, researcher, editor, and writer in residence. He lives in Saskatoon, often working as Visiting Professor at **ST. THOMAS MORE COLLEGE**.

Man Descending: Selected Stories (1982) made him famous overnight; it won the Governor General's Award for Fiction and Britain's Faber Prize. Although this was his first book publication, his earlier stories appeared in *The Trouble With*

Heroes and Other Stories (1983). More obviously an uneven, eclectic young writer's book, the collection ranges from realistic contemporary tales to two curious philosophically self-conscious stories set in biblical times. In *Man Descending*, Vanderhaeghe settled into writing realistic fiction set in modern times. Echoing the title in several ways, the stories are never pessimistic; but there is a sense that the possibilities of life for most people are distinctly limited, and that disappointment is what most men can look forward to. The distinctive flavour of Vanderhaeghe's early writing is often created by first-person narrators who exhibit a curious mix of hope and self-loathing, careful watchfulness and self-delusion. Humour, violence, irony, philosophical, religious, mythological allusion, and a serious dose of cynicism frequently appear in this fiction.

Ed, the protagonist in the last two stories of *Man Descending*, is the central character and narrator of Vanderhaeghe's first novel, a black comedy, *My Present Age* (1984). Ed is trying to find his wife, who has left him; but his search is doomed by the bad choices he has made in the past and by hilariously awful people who compound his problems.

Homesick, winner of the City of Toronto Book Award in 1989, is set in 1959 in a southeastern Saskatchewan town much like Esterhazy. It is the story of the uneasy relationship that develops between 73-year-old Alec Monkman, his widowed daughter Vera who left home at 19, and her troubled 12-year-old son, for whose sake she has left the city and returned.

The short stories collected in *Things as They Are?* (1992) range widely in character and subject matter; they have in common the conviction of the writer protagonist of the last story that one must in fact accept things as they are. Vanderhaeghe's two plays, *I Had a Job I Liked. Once* (1991) and *Dancock's Dance* (1995), neatly echo a major shift in his writing. The former, which won the Canadian Authors' Association Award for Drama, is a contemporary story about a boy striking out at the privileged teens who despise and torment him; a principled Mountie wants to help him, but cannot. *Dancock's Dance* marks Vanderhaeghe's move into historical subjects. It is based on the true story of inmates of the Saskatchewan Hospital for the Insane running the institution when the great **SPANISH INFLUENZA EPIDEMIC** of 1918 took the regular staff out of action.

Vanderhaeghe has said that he resisted historical subjects because he was afraid that his training as a historian would interfere with the imagination required to write fiction. That he was right to overcome his reluctance was clear with the appearance of *The Englishman's Boy* (1996), which won two **SASKATCHEWAN BOOK AWARDS** and the Governor General's Award for Fiction. An ambitious novel about the dangers and the inevitability of myth making, it alternates between two narratives: the 1873

CYPRESS HILLS MASSACRE perpetrated by American wolfers is the source of one; the other concerns the compromised efforts of an idealistic Canadian screenwriter working in 1920s Hollywood to tell the authentic story of the massacre, which would cast the wolfers as villains and the Indians as victims.

The Last Crossing (2002), winner of three Saskatchewan Book Awards and the 2004 CBC's Canada Reads contest, is also set in the 19th-century North American West. Two Englishmen set out to find their brother, who has disappeared; they are aided by Jerry Potts, a **MÉTIS** (who in real life did guide Mounties). Once more, Vanderhaeghe has written a realistic western, filled with elements typical in that genre (challenging physical environment, violence, First Nations, crime, bravery, idealism, villains, woman in distress) and crafted them into a unique story. Much of the novel is narrated in turn by three of the major characters.

In 2004, Vanderhaeghe was made an Officer of the Order of Canada, won the Writers' Trust of Canada Timothy Findley Award, and was awarded the Saskatchewan Order of Merit.   *Ken Probert*

FURTHER READING: Calder, A. 2000. "Unsettling the West: Nation and Genre in Guy Vanderhaeghe's *The Englishman's Boy*," *Studies in Canadian Literature* 25 (2): 96–107; Horava, T. 1996. "Guy Vanderhaeghe: A Bibliography," *Essays on Canadian Writing* 58: 241–66.

VEGETABLES. Vegetable crop production on the Canadian prairies began with home gardens: home-grown vegetables represented an important source of nutrition and variety in the pioneer diet; they were consumed fresh in the summer and preserved in root cellars or as pickles for the long prairie winter. Each wave of settlers introduced vegetables popular in their homelands. While potatoes, cabbage, peas, beets, carrots and beans thrived in the brief, drought-prone prairie summers, others like tomatoes and cucumbers were less well adapted. The search for better production methods and for vegetable crops and varieties suited to the prairie climate began with the settlers and continues today. The area devoted to vegetable crop production in Saskatchewan grew with the population: by 1910, the province had over 16,000 ha of potatoes. Until the 1940s, the vast majority of this production was for household use or local sale. However, the shift towards urbanization following **WORLD WAR II** created a demand for vegetables amongst town dwellers who no longer had the yard space or time to tend a garden. This demand allowed some growers to expand their farms and to focus their production on the crops that provided the greatest returns in the city markets. Development of superior rail and later road networks allowed better access to more distant markets, but also brought locally grown produce into competition with imports from the rest of the

continent. Today, over 90% of the vegetables consumed in Saskatchewan are grown on specialized vegetable farms and purchased through supermarket chains. Presently, less than 10% of the vegetables consumed in Saskatchewan are grown within the province; the adjacent provinces of Manitoba and Alberta provide 20% of Saskatchewan's vegetable needs, while imports from the southern United States, Mexico, and other warm regions represent the remainder. The value of the fresh vegetables annually imported into Saskatchewan exceeds $20 million. Over 50% of the vegetables consumed have been processed in some way (frozen, canned, pickled), but Saskatchewan has few commercial-scale processors.

In 2002, there were over 150 market gardens producing vegetables in Saskatchewan, and this number is slowly increasing. The market gardens, scattered throughout the province, are usually close enough to population centres to allow quick delivery of fresh product. The number of commercial-scale vegetable and table potato operations in Saskatchewan had declined to less than twenty by 2002, as local growers were unable to compete against imported produce. The commercial farms tend to be in the warmer areas of the province and are usually on irrigated land. The number of seed potato growers has expanded from just six in 1990 to more than thirty in 2002; although seed potatoes can be grown without irrigation, the majority are grown on land irrigated from **LAKE DIEFENBAKER**. In 2002, the 2,600 ha of seed potatoes and 1,500 ha of table potatoes produced in Saskatchewan had a combined estimated farm gate value of $38 million. The estimated farm gate value of all other vegetable crops grown in the province, based on 277 ha of production, was $1.2 million in 2002. Potatoes have always been the most important vegetable crop grown in Saskatchewan: they represent an excellent source of energy, vitamins and protein, and are popular in the cuisine of many cultures; they are also relatively easy to grow, store well, and can be used in many forms. Today, local growers produce most of the potatoes consumed fresh in the province, but virtually all processed potato products (chips and fries) are imported. Today, seed potatoes represent the single most valuable vegetable crop in Saskatchewan. The warm days and cool nights characteristic of prairie summers give local seed potatoes excellent vigour and yield potential, while the cold winters and great distances between seed farms help keep the seed disease-free. Saskatchewan-grown seed potatoes are exported throughout Canada, the Pacific northwestern United States, and Mexico.

The development of earlier maturing super-sweet types of corn in the 1980 s increased demand to the point where today corn is the second most widely grown vegetable crop in Saskatchewan; the locally grown corn crop is destined for sale within days of harvest. Cabbage is still the third most popular vegetable crop in the province; however, the area planted to this crop has declined due to decreasing popularity with consumers and to increasing production costs; some of the cabbage crop is kept in cold storage for up to six months. Saskatchewan vegetable growers plant smaller quantities of over thirty other vegetable crops, with new crops introduced each year in response to changing market demand. Growers are always looking for new crops or varieties with higher yields, better or different flavour, and superior nutritional characteristics. *Doug Waterer*

FURTHER READING: Waterer, D., R. St. Pierre, K. Tanino, B. Bors, B. Vladicka, and L. Gilmore. 2002. "Horticulture in Canada: Spotlight on the Prairies," *Chronica Horticultura* 42: 20–23.

VERIGIN, PETER (1859–1924). Peter Vasilevich Verigin (also recorded as Veregin) was born in Slavyanka, Russia on June 29, 1859; he became leader of the pacifist Russian sect of Doukhobors in 1886. In 1882 he was moved into Lukeria Klamakova's home, where he was taught all the religious and administrative aspects of this large sect of communally living peasants. The Doukhobors rejected secular government, the Bible, and the divinity of Jesus Christ; they were pacifists who resisted military service and did not consume meat or alcohol. For these reasons, they were persecuted and exiled to inhumane conditions in Georgia, Russia. In 1887 Verigin was exiled to Siberia.

In 1898–99 over 7,400 Doukhobors were admitted to Canada, where they established a communal lifestyle in what was later to become Saskatchewan; Verigin arrived in Yorkton in 1902. In 1905, Frank Oliver became Minister of the Interior and, interpreting the Dominion Act more strictly than his predecessor Clifford Sifton, began to pressure immigrants to register their communal

SASKATCHEWAN ARCHIVES BOARD R-B2194

Peter Verigin.

lands under individual ownership and swear an Oath of Allegiance, a requirement for being granted homestead titles. When Doukhobors refused to swear this oath, their homesteads were cancelled. By 1907 their communal land system had ended, and in 1908 Verigin led 6,000 Doukhobors to British Columbia. Peter Vasilevich Verigin was killed in a train explosion on October 29, 1924; the cause of the explosion was not determined. *Daria Coneghan*

UNIVERSITY OF REGINA ARCHIVES AND SPECIAL COLLECTIONS 79-7-8

John Vernon.

VERNON, JOHN (1932–2005). Actor John Vernon was born Adolphus Raymundus Vernon Agopsowicz in Regina on February 24, 1932. From 1935 to 1953 he attended St. Joseph's School and Campion College, where his acting career began under the direction of Rev. Arthur Nelson, S.J. and MARY ELLEN BURGESS at REGINA LITTLE THEATRE. He studied at the Banff School of Fine Arts, the Royal Academy of Dramatic Arts (RADA) in London, England, and with the Hornchurch Repertory Company near London. Returning to Canada, he worked at the Stratford Festival and in Toronto in theatre, radio and television. He left *Royal Hunt of the Sun* on Broadway in 1966 to return to Canada for *Wojeck*, his most popular television series.

Vernon's many major roles in Hollywood movies included: *Point Blank*, starring Lee Marvin; Alfred Hitchcock's *Topaz*; *Dirty Harry*, with Clint Eastwood; and *Animal House*. He was guest star on numerous television series such as *The FBI*, *Bonanza*, *Gunsmoke*, *Mission Impossible*, and *In the Heat of the Night*. His resumé listed more than 85 film roles since his debut as the voice of Big Brother in *1984* in 1956. Vernon was married to Nancy West, with whom he had four children, including actress Kate Vernon. He was awarded an Honorary Doctorate of Laws by the UNIVERSITY OF REGINA in 1976. Vernon died at his home in Los Angeles on February 1, 2005. *Lyn Goldman*

VETERANS' LANDS ACT: *see* **SOLDIER SETTLEMENT ACT**

VETERINARY MEDICINE. Horses were an essential element in the early development of what was to become Saskatchewan. The first veterinarian, W.G. Boswell, was a member of the Boundary Commission that mapped the Canada-USA boundary in 1872–76; the second was J.L. Poett, with the North-West Mounted Police on its "march west" in 1874. Subsequently NWMP veterinarians not only cared for horses but acted as "game guardians" and assisted in domestic animal disease control. John G. Rutherford served in the NORTH-WEST RESISTANCE of 1885, and went on to become Canada's first Veterinary Director General in the Canada Department of Agriculture.

When the SASKATCHEWAN VETERINARY MEDICAL ASSOCIATION was established in 1909, fifty-six veterinarians signed the register. The health of Saskatchewan's livestock has been well served by its veterinary profession. The prompt detection in 1950–51 of foot-and-mouth disease in cattle near Regina by Harold Hunter contained a potentially catastrophic situation with a minimum of cost and disruption.

The provincial Department of Agriculture has played an active role in maintaining livestock health by instituting disease control programs, providing veterinary diagnostic laboratory services, supporting local veterinary practices, and developing policies and regulations for disease control. *N.O. Nielson*

VICKERS, JONATHAN STEWART (1926–). From the late 1950s to the late 1980s, Jon Vickers was Canada's pre-eminent operatic tenor. Known for the heroic roles he played, Vickers performed in most of the major opera houses of the world, enjoying particularly close relationships with Covent Garden in London and the Metropolitan Opera in New York. Vickers was born on October 29, 1926 in Prince Albert to Myrle and William Vickers, a school principal and a lay preacher in the Presbyterian and Methodist churches. His early life in Saskatchewan decisively shaped his personality and worldview: strong faith, hard work, a sense of duty, and tremendous loyalty were inculcated in him by his family and formed the basis for his subsequent career. In 1946, Vickers left Saskatchewan for good, working first for the F.W. Woolworth Company in small-town Manitoba and northern Ontario, and subsequently for the Hudson's Bay Company in Winnipeg. Coincidentally, his wife, Henrietta (Hetti), whom he married in 1953, had lived in Moose Jaw for six years in the 1940s, when her father was the minister of Metropolitan United Church in Regina.

In 1950, after several years singing and performing in churches and amateur productions, Vickers received a scholarship to attend the Royal Conservatory of Music in Toronto, where he studied

Chancellor Edward (Ted) Culliton bestows Jon Vickers with an honorary degree from the University of Saskatchewan at Fall convocation, November 23, 1963.

with George Lambert. Although he obtained increasing numbers of engagements with the Toronto Opera Festival and the Canadian Broadcasting Corporation, by the mid-1950s he was at the point of quitting singing in order to better provide for his growing family when he came to the attention of David Webster, the general administrator of the Royal Opera House, Covent Garden. Vickers auditioned for him in Toronto in November 1955, and by the following summer had agreed to an eighteen-month contract. Vickers made his Covent Garden debut on tour in Cardiff as Gustavus III in Verdi's *Un ballo in maschera* on March 4, 1957; his first London performance followed on April 24 (Don José in *Carmen*). His immense success with the London public was confirmed by his performance of the demanding role of Enée in Berlioz's *Les Troyens* in June of that year. Other important debuts soon followed: Bayreuth (Siegmund, 1958); Vienna (Siegmund, 1959); San Francisco (Radames, 1959); and the Metropolitan Opera in New York (Canio, 1960), where he was to appear regularly for the next twenty-seven years.

Vickers was a highly individual singer who essentially created his own vocal category (*Fach*) to suit the characteristics of his unique voice and personality: a big sound, carefully controlled but capable of immense power and passion; dramatic stage presence; and a preference for passionate, tragic roles over the empty, romantic ones characteristic of much of the traditional tenor repertory. Vickers' distinctive timbre is unmistakeable, as is his highly expressive delivery of the text. In later years, some critics grew uncomfortable with what they saw as mannerisms in his singing: a frequent alternation between full-voiced singing and almost crooning (also on long-held syllables), distorted vowel sounds, and rhythmic freedoms. No other tenor of his time performed such a variety of demanding, dramatic roles. In his prime, Vickers owned the roles of Siegmund (*Die Walküre*), Florestan

(*Fidelio*), Otello, Tristan, and Enée, and also enjoyed particular success as Parsifal, Hermann (*Queen of Spades*), Canio (*Pagliacci*), and Don José. He also appeared at the Metropolitan as Laca (*Jenúfa*), Alvaro (*La forza del destino*), and Samson (both Handel's and Saint-Saëns'); in Boston as Benvenuto Cellini; and in Paris as Monteverdi's Nero (*L'incoronazione di Poppea*). His Peter Grimes, although apparently disliked by the composer, is regarded by many as definitive, and survives in a 1981 BBC video production from Covent Garden. Among his many recordings, those of Grimes (Davis, 1978), Otello (Karajan, 1974), Tristan (Karajan, 1972), Enée (Davis, 1970), Siegmund (Karajan, 1967), and Florestan (Klemperer, 1962) are particularly noteworthy.

Like Callas, Vickers believed firmly that his place was to serve the composer, not himself. Paradoxically, this deference to the composer often expressed itself in violent arguments with conductors and directors that gave him the reputation of being difficult and egotistical. Yet Vickers demanded no less of himself than he did of others, always searching for the moral and dramatic truth of a character. For Vickers, opera was not entertainment and, in later years, he attacked what he saw as the increasing commercialism of the business. Like many Canadians who attain international fame, Vickers had an ambivalent relationship with his native land. For many years, he owned and operated a farm near Orangeville, Ontario, but moved to the Bahamas in 1973 for tax reasons. Although his honours included the Order of Canada (Companion, 1969) and a Governor General's Performing Arts Award (1998), he often felt unappreciated by Canadians, and on occasion publicly attacked Canada for its lack of culture and lack of public support for the performing arts. Yet he chose to make two concert performances of *Parsifal*, Act II, in Kitchener-Waterloo in 1988–his final performances.

Stephen McClatchie

FURTHER READING: Williams, J. 1999. *Jon Vickers: A Hero's Life*. Boston: Northeastern University Press.

VICTORIA CROSS: SASKATCHEWAN RECIPIENTS.

The Victoria Cross (VC) is the highest recognition of military valour in the British Commonwealth and is awarded without regard to rank, service or length of service. The Victoria Cross was established in 1856 by Queen Victoria, who was inspired by the bravery of returning veterans of the Crimean War. The VC takes precedence over all other decorations and is worn nearest the buttons of the tunic. Prince Albert, the Queen's Consort, contributed to the design of the medal made from bronze Russian guns captured during the Crimean War. The medals were originally to have been inscribed "For the Brave"; however, the Queen felt that all who went

into battle were brave, therefore "For Valour" was more appropriate. The Queen presented the first Victoria Cross medals at a ceremony in Hyde Park on June 26, 1857, to sixty-two veterans of the Crimean War including one Canadian, Lieutenant Alexander Dunn of the 11th Hussars. Lieutenant Dunn was awarded the medal for saving the life of two of his men in the Charge of the Light Brigade at Balaclava. Ninety-three other Canadians have since received the award.

A total of seventeen Victoria Crosses have been awarded to men from Saskatchewan or associated with Saskatchewan. The first of these, Surgeon Lieutenant Dr. Campbell Mellis Douglas, had been awarded the Victoria Cross on May 7, 1867, for rescuing seventeen stranded servicemen from an island in the Indian Ocean. Douglas was later to volunteer to serve in Saskatchewan during the **NORTH-WEST RESISTANCE** of 1885; after arriving in Swift Current he went to Saskatoon, where he treated the wounded from the battles of **FISH CREEK** and **BATOCHE**. For his efforts Douglas was awarded the North-West Canada Medal; following the Resistance he returned to England, where he died on December 31, 1909.

Three Victoria Crosses were awarded to residents of Saskatchewan during the South African or **BOER WAR** (1899–1902). Ten more were awarded in **WORLD WAR I**, and three in **WORLD WAR II**. In World War I (1914–18), Saskatchewan's VC recipients fought in Belgium and northeast France as members of the Canadian Corps. During World War II (1939–45), the first Saskatchewanian to receive the VC was stationed in Hong Kong when Japanese forces overran that colony in 1940. Saskatchewan VC recipients also fought at Dieppe and in northwest Europe. Only one VC winner, Major David Currie, was born in Saskatchewan.

The Saskatchewan Victoria Cross recipients are: *Beet, Harry Churchill (1873–1946).* Corporal Harry Beet, 27 years old, was presented with the Victoria Cross in 1901 for his actions at Wakkerstroom, South Africa, while serving with the British army. Beet rescued a wounded comrade, tending to his injuries and providing protection for their position until they were both rescued. Beet was

Victoria Cross.

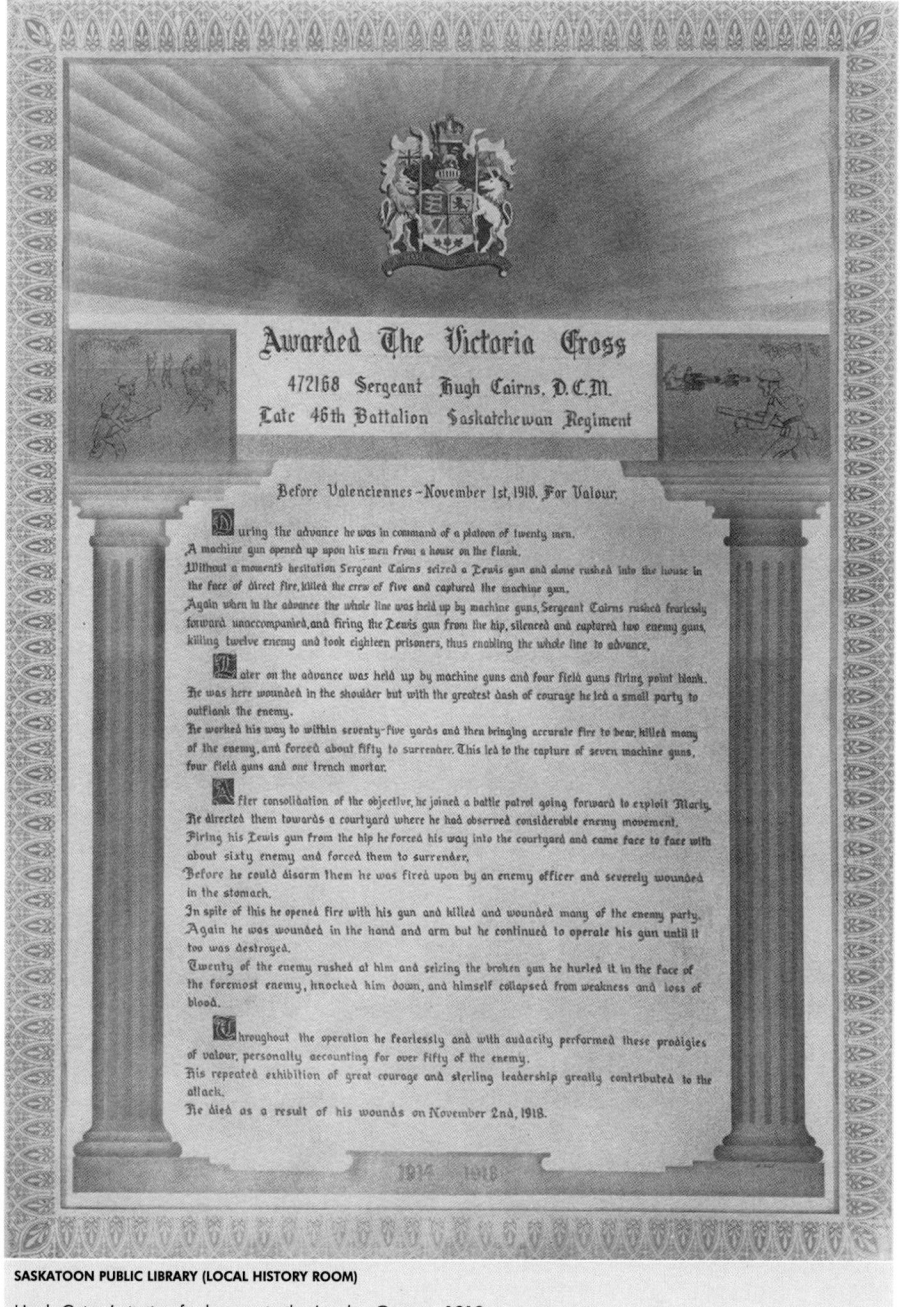

Awarded The Victoria Cross

472168 Sergeant Hugh Cairns, D.C.M.
Late 46th Battalion Saskatchewan Regiment

Before Valenciennes–November 1st, 1918. For Valour.

During the advance he was in command of a platoon of twenty men.
A machine gun opened up upon his men from a house on the flank.
Without a moment's hesitation Sergeant Cairns seized a Lewis gun and alone rushed into the house in the face of direct fire, killed the crew of five and captured the machine gun.
Again when in the advance the whole line was held up by machine guns, Sergeant Cairns rushed fearlessly forward unaccompanied, and firing the Lewis gun from the hip, silenced and captured two enemy guns, killing twelve enemy and took eighteen prisoners, thus enabling the whole line to advance.

Later on the advance was held up by machine guns and four field guns firing point blank.
He was here wounded in the shoulder but with the greatest dash of courage he led a small party to outflank the enemy.
He worked his way to within seventy-five yards and then bringing accurate fire to bear, killed many of the enemy, and forced about fifty to surrender. This led to the capture of seven machine guns, four field guns and one trench mortar.

After consolidation of the objective, he joined a battle patrol going forward to exploit Marly.
He directed them towards a courtyard where he had observed considerable enemy movement.
Firing his Lewis gun from the hip he forced his way into the courtyard and came face to face with about sixty enemy and forced them to surrender.
Before he could disarm them he was fired upon by an enemy officer and severely wounded in the stomach.
In spite of this he opened fire with his gun and killed and wounded many of the enemy party.
Again he was wounded in the hand and arm but he continued to operate his gun until it too was destroyed.
Twenty of the enemy rushed at him and seizing the broken gun he hurled it in the face of the foremost enemy, knocked him down, and himself collapsed from weakness and loss of blood.

Throughout the operation he fearlessly and with audacity performed these prodigies of valour, personally accounting for over fifty of the enemy.
His repeated exhibition of great courage and sterling leadership greatly contributed to the attack.
He died as a result of his wounds on November 2nd, 1918.

1914   1918

SASKATOON PUBLIC LIBRARY (LOCAL HISTORY ROOM)

Hugh Cairns' citation for bravery in the *London Gazette*, 1919.

born in Nottinghamshire, England, in 1873. In 1906, he and his wife emigrated to Saskatchewan. He served with the Canadian Army during World War I, and by 1918 had risen to the rank of Captain. In 1937 Beet moved to British Columbia, where he died in 1946.

Cairns, Hugh (1896–1918). Sergeant Hugh Cairns joined the army in 1915 and was awarded the Distinguished Conduct Medal for his bravery at Vimy Ridge in 1917. Cairns received the Victoria Cross posthumously for his actions at Valenciennes, France on November 1, 1918. When during the advance a machine-gun opened fire on his platoon, 21-year-old Sergeant Cairns seized a Lewis gun and single-handedly, in the face of direct fire, rushed the post, killed the crew of five and captured the gun. He led three other rushes against machine gun emplacements, killing twelve enemy soldiers, and capturing many others as well as the guns. After the position was consolidated, Cairns went with a battle patrol to exploit the village of Marly; he forced 60 enemy soldiers to surrender, but was severely wounded and collapsed from weakness and loss of blood. Throughout the operation he showed the highest degree of valour, and his leadership greatly contributed to the success of the attack. He died the next day, November 2, 1918. Hugh Cairns was born in England in 1896. His family emigrated to Saskatoon in 1911. In 1936 the town of Valenciennes renamed a street in his honour, and he was awarded the Legion of Honour by the French government. In Saskatoon, a street, a school, a baseball field and the armoury are named after him. A memorial to Cairns, who was also an active football player, was erected near Saskatoon's University Bridge in 1921. The statue is of Hugh Cairns, and around the base are the names of seventy-five Saskatoon football players who did not return from the war.

Cockburn, Hampden Zane Churchill (1867–1913). Lieutenant Hampden Zane Churchill Cockburn of the Royal Canadian Dragoons (RCD) was presented with the Victoria Cross on October 11, 1901, for his actions on November 7, 1900, at Komati River, South Africa. During the Battle of Liliefontein, 32-year-old Lieutenant Cockburn and his men, while acting as the rearguard for a column of troops, found themselves under fire from an overwhelming number of Boers. During a hectic running battle over many hours, the Dragoons twice prevented the capture of artillery pieces under their protection. Cockburn was wounded, and all his men were killed, wounded, or taken prisoner. Cockburn was born on November 19, 1867, in Toronto, Ontario. At the outbreak of the South African War, he gave up his law practice to enlist. During the war he took part in forty-five engagements and earned the Queen's South African medal with clasps for Cape Colony, Diamond Hill, Johannesburg, and Orange Free State. At the same time that he was presented with his VC, he received a sword of honour voted to him by the Toronto city council. In recognition of his services, he was appointed a major in the Governor General's Bodyguard. Cockburn later moved to western Canada, where on July 13, 1913, he was killed in a riding accident on his ranch at Maple Creek.

Combe, Robert Grierson (1880–1917). Thirty-six-year-old Lieutenant Robert Grierson Combe was awarded his Victoria Cross posthumously. On May 3, 1917, Combe's battalion was ordered to occupy the German trenches near the town of Acheville, France. The Germans had anticipated an attack, and by the time the Canadians reached a point 500 yards from the German lines, Combe was the only officer in his company still alive. Combe and the other survivors found themselves caught in an artillery crossfire between the Germans and a barrage from their own guns. Leading six of his surviving comrades, he attacked the enemy position, capturing 250 yards of trench and eighty prisoners. Combe was fatally wounded by a sniper's bullet in the final charge. Born in Aberdeen, Scotland in 1880, he emigrated to Canada around 1906. After living in Moosomin for two years, he opened a drug store in Melville and then in Dubic. In 1914, Combe enlisted and was accepted for a commission. He went overseas to England with the 53rd Battalion as a major, but accepted a reduction in rank to lieutenant so that he could be assigned to the front line in France, where he joined the 27th (City of Winnipeg) Battalion. In

1919, the Prince of Wales presented Lieutenant Combe's Victoria Cross to his widow, Jean Combe, at the Legislative Building in Regina. His portrait hangs in the Peace Tower in Ottawa as well as in the museum in Melville. A lake in northern Saskatchewan and the Melville Branch of the Royal Canadian Legion are named in his honour.

Currie, David Vivian (1912–86). David Vivian Currie was born in Sutherland, Saskatchewan, on July 8, 1912. In 1939 he joined the militia, and enlisted in the regular army in January 1940. He was promoted to captain in 1941 and to major in 1944. Currie was awarded the Victoria Cross for his heroism on August 18, 1944, at St. Lambert-sur-Dives, France. Major Currie was in command of a small mixed force of Canadian tanks, self-propelled anti-tank guns and infantry which was ordered to cut one of the main escape routes from the Falaise pocket. His force was held up by strong enemy resistance in the village of St. Lambert-sur-Dives, and two tanks were knocked out by 88mm guns. Major Currie immediately entered the village alone on foot at last light through the enemy outposts in order to rescue the crews of the disabled tanks—which he succeeded in doing in spite of heavy mortar fire. The following morning, Currie's 115 troops attacked the village of 3,000 enemy soldiers, and by noon they had captured half the village. All of Major Currie's junior officers were killed or wounded, leaving Currie to direct all aspects of the assault until his force was relieved over thirty-six hours later. After the war he spent eight years in Baie Comeau, Quebec, and in 1953 he moved to Montréal. In 1960 Currie was appointed Sergeant-at-Arms of the Canadian House of Commons. David Currie, the only Saskatchewan-born Victoria Cross recipient, died in Ottawa on June 20, 1986. The Moose Jaw armoury is named in his honour.

De Wind, Edmund (1883–1918). Lieutenant Edmund De Wind was awarded his Victoria Cross posthumously. On March 21, 1918, at Racecourse Redoubt near Grougies, France, he held this important position with only two NCOs for seven hours, though twice wounded, until another section could be sent to help him. On two occasions he got out on top of his trench, under heavy machine gun and rifle fire, and cleared the enemy from the position, killing many of them. He continued to repel enemy attacks until he was mortally wounded and collapsed. De Wind, born in County Down, Ireland in 1883, emigrated to Canada in 1910. He joined the 31st Battalion, CEF, as a private in 1914 and arrived in France in September 1915. He saw action on the Somme and at **VIMY RIDGE**. He was commissioned a lieutenant in the British army in September 1917. Mount De Wind in Alberta was named in his memory.

Flowerdew, Gordon Muriel (1885–1918). Lieutenant Gordon Muriel Flowerdew was awarded his Victoria Cross posthumously. On March 30, 1918, in the Bois de Moreuil, France, Lieutenant (acting Captain) Flowerdew, 33 years old, was commanding C Squadron of the Lord Strathcona's Horse, a unit of the Canadian Cavalry Brigade. His squadron was ordered to charge two entrenched lines of enemy, each about sixty strong, having machine guns at their centre and flanks. One line was about 200 yards behind the other. Flowerdew ordered one troop, under Lieut. Harvey, VC, to dismount and provide covering fire while Flowerdew, leading the remainder of the squadron, charged, passing over both lines and killing many of the enemy. Although the squadron had about 70% casualties, including Lieutenant Flowerdew who was fatally wounded, the enemy broke and fled, and the position was captured. Gordon Flowerdew, born in Billingford, England in 1885, emigrated to Canada in 1903, homesteading north of Duck Lake. He moved to British Columbia sometime after 1910, and in 1914 he enlisted as a private in the Lord Strathcona Horse. He was commissioned an officer in 1916 and given command of C Squadron in 1918.

Knight, Arthur George (1886–1918). Sergeant Arthur Knight received his Victoria Cross posthumously for his actions on September 2, 1918, at Villers-les-Cagnicourt, France. When a bombing section which he was leading was held up, Sergeant Knight went forward alone, bayoneting several enemy machine-gunners and trench mortar crews, and forcing the rest to retire. Then bringing forward a Lewis gun he directed fire on the retreating enemy. His platoon went in pursuit and Knight, seeing about 30 of the enemy going into a tunnel leading off the trench, again went forward alone, killing an officer and two NCOs and taking 20 prisoners. He was killed in action a few days later. Knight, born in Sussex, England in 1886, came to Regina in 1911; there he worked as a carpenter. Knight was awarded the Croix de Guerre by the Belgian government in 1917. Knight and Sussex Crescents in Regina are named in his honour.

Merritt, Charles Cecil Ingersoll (1908–2000). Lieutenant Colonel Merritt received his Victoria Cross for acts of gallantry and leadership at Dieppe, France while commanding his battalion, the South Saskatchewan Regiment, during the Dieppe Raid. From the point of landing at Pourville, his unit's advance had to be made across a bridge which was swept by very heavy machine-gun, mortar and artillery fire. The first landing parties were mostly destroyed, and the bridge was thickly covered with their bodies. A daring lead was required; waving his helmet, Lieutenant-Colonel Merritt rushed forward shouting, "Come on over! There's nothing to worry about here!" He personally led the survivors of at least four parties in turn across the bridge. Quickly organizing these, he led them forward, and when held up by enemy pillboxes he again led rushes which succeeded in clearing them. Although twice wounded, Merritt continued to direct the unit's operations, and while organizing the withdrawal he stalked a sniper with a Bren gun and silenced him. He then coolly gave orders for the departure and announced his intention to hold off the enemy. When last seen, he was collecting Bren and Tommy guns to prepare a defensive position from which he successfully covered the withdrawal from the beach. The success of the unit's operations and the safe re-embarkation of a large portion of it were chiefly due to his personal daring. Merritt, however, was captured and became a prisoner of war until he was liberated in 1945. Merritt was born in Vancouver, British Columbia in 1908. He was educated at Lord Roberts School, Vancouver, University School, Victoria, and Royal Military College in Kingston, Ontario. Since 1929, he had been an officer in a Vancouver regiment, the Seaforth Highlanders of Canada. In 1942, he was transferred to the South Saskatchewan Regiment. Upon his release as a POW at the end of the war, he returned to Vancouver. Merritt, a lawyer, served as a member of Parliament from 1945 to 1949. In 1951 he was appointed commanding officer of the Seaforth Highlanders. He died on July 12, 2000.

Milne, William Johnstone (1892–1917). Private William Johnstone Milne was awarded his Victoria Cross posthumously on April 9, 1917, for his actions at Vimy, France. During the attack, 24-year-old Private Milne observed an enemy machine gun firing on the advancing troops. Crawling on hands and knees, he succeeded in reaching the gun, killing the crew, and capturing the gun. When the line resumed the attack, he located a second machine gun and succeeded in capturing it and putting the crew out of action. Milne, a member of the 16th (Canadian Scottish) Battalion, CEF, was born near Glasgow, Scotland in 1892. He emigrated to Canada in 1910, and worked for four years on a farm near Caron until he enlisted at Moose Jaw. Milne Channel in northeast Saskatchewan is named after him. Using public donations, the Canadian War Museum purchased his Victoria Cross at an auction in London, England.

Mullin, George Harry (1892–1963). In January 1918, Sergeant Mullin was informed that he had been awarded the Victoria Cross for his actions on October 30, 1917, in Passchendaele, Belgium. 25-year-old Sergeant Mullin single-handedly captured a German pillbox that had withstood heavy bombardment and was causing heavy casualties, holding up the attack. Mullin rushed a snipers' post in front, destroying it with grenades, shot two gunners and forced the remaining ten to surrender. His clothes were riddled with bullets, but he never faltered; his actions helped to save many lives. Mullin was born in Portland, Oregon in 1892. His family moved to Moosomin when he was 2 years old. He enlisted for military service in 1914 and was awarded the Military Medal in 1917. After the war, he returned to Moosomin and served with the militia in the Assiniboia Regiment, attaining the rank of major. He was appointed Sergeant-at-Arms for the Saskatchewan Legislature in 1934. During World War II, he volunteered for service in the Veterans' Guard in 1940. In 1947 he returned to Regina and resumed his duties as Sergeant-at-Arms. The government of Saskatchewan named a northern lake in his honour. Mullin lived in Regina until his death in 1963.

O'Leary, Michael (1890–1961). Lance-Corporal Michael O'Leary was serving in the British army when he was awarded the Victoria Cross for his actions at Cuinchy, France in 1915. O'Leary, 25 years old, was one of a storming party that was advancing on the enemy lines when he rushed to the opposing front, killing five Germans who were holding the first barricade. He then attacked a second barricade 60 yards further on, capturing it after killing three of the enemy and taking two of them prisoner. He thus practically took the position by himself and prevented the rest of the attacking party from being fired upon. O'Leary was born in Ireland in 1890, and trained in Regina with the North-West Mounted Police in 1913. He rejoined the British Army in 1914, but returned to Canada in 1921 to join the Ontario Police Department. In 1923 he took a job with the Michigan Central Railroad Company's Ontario operations. He returned to England in the early 1930s and served as a Captain with the British Army's Royal Pioneer Corps during World War II. He died in London, England in 1961.

Osborn, John Robert (1899–1941). Sergeant-Major John Robert Osborn was awarded his Victoria Cross posthumously for sacrificing his life to save the lives of his comrades. On December 19, 1941, in the British colony of Hong Kong, the company of the Winnipeg Grenadiers to which he belonged had become divided during an attack on a steep rising hill, Mount Butler. A part of the company, led by Company Sergeant-Major Osborn, captured the hill at the point of the bayonet and held it for three hours until they were forced to withdraw under heavy fire. Osborn and a small group covered the withdrawal, and when their turn came to fall back he single-handedly engaged the enemy while the remainder of the group successfully rejoined the company. During the afternoon, the company was cut off from the battalion and completely surrounded by the enemy, who were able to approach to within grenade-throwing distance of the slight depression that the company was holding. Several enemy grenades were thrown, which Osborn picked up and threw back. The enemy threw a grenade which landed in a position where it was impossible to pick it up and return it in time. Shouting a warning to the others, Sergeant-Major Osborn threw himself on the live grenade, which exploded, killing him

instantly. John Osborn was born in Norfolk, England on January 2, 1899. In World War I, he joined the Royal Naval Volunteer Reserve and served as a seaman, seeing action at the Battle of Jutland in May 1916. At the end of the war he moved to Wapella, Saskatchewan where he farmed for two years before moving to Manitoba. In 1933 he joined the Winnipeg Grenadiers and was called to active duty on September 3, 1939.

Pearkes, George Randolph (1888–1984). Major George Randolph Pearkes of the 5th Canadian Mounted Rifles Battalion was awarded the Victoria Cross for his actions in October 1917 at Passchendaele, Belgium. Although wounded in the right thigh, Pearkes continued to lead his men against repeated enemy counter-attacks and was able to capture an enemy strongpoint. Pearkes was born in Watford, England in 1888 and emigrated to Alberta to study farming in 1906. He began training with the Royal North-West Mounted Police at the Regina Depot in 1911, and in 1915 he joined the Canadian Army. By the end of the war he had been promoted to Lieutenant Colonel, and in addition to receiving the Victoria Cross he was awarded the Military Cross, Distinguished Service Order, and French Croix de Guerre. He rose to the rank of Major General after the war, and was made commander of the 1st Canadian Infantry Division in Britain at the start of World War II. He returned to Canada to take over as officer commanding, Pacific Command. He was made a Commander of the Order of the Bath and received the United States Order of Merit. Pearkes was elected to Parliament and became Minister of Defence in 1957. He was appointed Lieutenant-Governor of British Columbia from 1960 to 1968. He died in 1984.

Richardson, Arthur Herbert Lindsey (1872–1932). Sergeant Arthur Richardson received the Victoria Cross in 1900 for his actions at Wolve Point (Wolwespruit), South Africa, where a party of 38 Lord Strathcona's Horse came into contact and was engaged at close quarters by a force of 80 of the enemy. When the order was given to retire, Sergeant Richardson rode back under very heavy crossfire to save a comrade who had been shot from his horse and wounded. Seeing that the man was in danger of being taken prisoner, he retrieved him and rode off under a hail of Boer fire. Richardson was born in England in 1872 and emigrated to Canada in 1892. He joined the North-West Mounted Police in Regina in 1894. After the war, Richardson returned to Saskatchewan, and in 1908 moved back to Liverpool, England where he died in 1932.

Zengel, Raphael Louis (1894–1977). Sergeant Raphael Zengel, a Military Medal holder, was awarded the Victoria Cross for outstanding bravery during the Battle of Amiens, France in World War I. On August 9, 1918, east of Warvillers, 23-year-old Sergeant Zengel was leading his platoon forward to

the attack when he realized that an enemy machine-gun was firing into the advancing line. He rushed forward ahead of the platoon to the gun emplacement, killed the officer and operator of the gun, and dispersed the crew. Later that day he was rendered temporarily unconscious by an enemy shell. Upon recovery, he continued to direct harassing fire at the enemy. Zengal was born in Fairbault, Minnesota, in 1894. He and his widowed mother emigrated to Burr, a small town south of Humboldt, in 1906. In 1914 he moved to Manitoba, where he joined the Canadian Army. After the war, Zengel moved to Alberta and then to British Columbia, where he died in 1977. In 1951 the National Geographic Board of Canada named Mount Zengel, in the Jasper, Alberta region, in his honour.

Daria Coneghan and David G. Marshall

VIETNAMESE COMMUNITY. As in other Canadian provinces, thousands of Vietnamese refugees came to settle in Saskatchewan during the late 1970s and early 1980s. The "Boat People," as they came to be known, fled their homeland to find a safe haven in Canada after the Vietnam War ended with the collapse of South Vietnam in April 1975. A large majority of them now live in Regina and Saskatoon. The 2001 Census recorded a total of 1,870 Saskatchewan residents with country of origin as Vietnam, among whom 915 resided in Regina and 770 in Saskatoon. Over the years, Vietnamese-Canadians have rebuilt their lives and have created community organizations and built places of worship that reflect their cultural origins. Today, many residents are attracted to the Vietnamese cuisine offered at an increasing number of Vietnamese restaurants in Saskatoon and Regina. Having established themselves as residents of Saskatchewan, members of the Vietnamese-Canadian community continue to preserve their heritage through many socio-cultural activities: both Regina and Saskatoon have their own Buddhist tem-

TUAN NGUYEN/REGINA LEADER-POST

Regina's Vietnamese community marked the mid-Autumn festival with handmade lanterns, dragon dances and lively music, September 25, 1988.

ples, Vietnamese-Canadian Associations, Vietnamese-Canadian Senior Citizens Associations, Vietnamese Buddhist Associations, Vietnamese Roman Catholic Associations, and Vietnamese Heritage Language Schools. The Vietnamese community in Saskatoon has recently begun its weekly Vietnamese language radio program on Community Radio Station (CFCR FM 90.5). The once "Boat People" and their children, the second-generation Vietnamese-Canadians of Saskatchewan, are now making significant contributions to the province's workforce as business people, educators, engineers, doctors, nurses, and pharmacists. (*See also* **VISIBLE MINORITIES**, **URBAN ETHNIC DIVERSITY**) *Vinh-The Lam*

FURTHER READING: Adelman, H. 1982. *Canada and the Indochinese Refugees*. Regina: Weigl Educational Associates.

VIEWFIELD IMPACT STRUCTURE (49°35'N; 103°34'W).

Viewfield Impact Structure is one of five verified meteorite impact structures in Saskatchewan, and an example of one of the 150 known sites in the world. Other confirmed meteor impact structures in Saskatchewan are Carswell, Gow Lake, Deep Bay, and Maple Creek. Viewfield Impact Structure is located south of the town of Stoughton. It was discovered in 1972 during oilfield drilling activity. It is 2.4 km in diameter, and 100 m deep from the top of the rim to the bottom of the structure. The impact event occurred in the Early Jurassic period, about 190 million years ago. None of the features of the structure is visible on the surface, as the crater is buried under 1,000 m of overburden.

Another name for meteor crater is **ASTROBLEME**, derived from the Greek words for star (*astron*) and wound (*blema*). Astroblemes can be important sources of minerals: the Viewfield Structure forms a trap for hydrocarbons, and is an important source of oil. With over fifty active wells in its rim and a reserve of 27 million barrels, it accumulates 400 barrels per day. *Gregory Salmers*

VIMY RIDGE.

Located in northern France between the cities of Lens and Arras, Vimy Ridge is 8 km in length and rises 61 m above the Douai Plain. The German Army occupied the strategically important ridge in September 1914 and fortified it with barbed wire, concrete bunkers, artillery, trenches, underground medical facilities, and living quarters. French and British forces tried to gain control of Vimy Ridge throughout 1915 and 1916 but were unsuccessful.

Commanded by British Lieutenant-General Sir Julian Byng, Canadian troops took over the front line at Vimy Ridge during the winter of 1916. After careful training and rehearsal, the Canadians began to heavily bombard the ridge on March 20, 1917. The artillery fire continued for days before the four

GERRY CARLINE PHOTO

Vimy Ridge Monument.

Canadian infantry divisions attacked the ridge at dawn on Easter Monday, April 9. This marked the first time that Canadians fought together and they gained control of Vimy Ridge three days later. Of the forty-nine battalions engaged at Vimy, four were recruited in Saskatchewan: the 5th, the 28th, the 46th, and the 1st Canadian Mounted Rifles. *Peter Borch*

FURTHER READING: Berton, Pierre. 1986. *Vimy*. Toronto: McClelland & Stewart; Christie, N.M. 1998. *Winning The Ridge: The Canadians at Vimy, 1917*. Nepean ON: CEF Books; McWilliams, James. 1978. *The Suicide Battalion*. Edmonton: Hurtig.

VIP (MEGA GROUP).

Mega Group began as Volume Independent Purchasers (VIP Stores Inc.), a buying group for five independent retail and appliance stores in western Canada. In 1992, VIP Stores partnered with a Montreal buying group called Magasins D'Ambeulement BV Inc. In 2000, the two groups merged to form Mega Group. The company maintains its corporate head office in Saskatoon where it also handles finance and credit, information technology, data processing, human resources and sales. Mega Group has also developed a franchise program with Countrywide and Sleep Experience brands. The group in Montreal now is responsible for retail systems, advertising and design while a Toronto office takes care of merchandising and buying.

Mega is the largest member-owned group in Canada, with more than 450 member retailers in furniture, appliances, and consumer electronics. Mega negotiates with suppliers and uses its size to leverage better deals. Mega also functions as a co-operative, with profits reinvested back to the retailers. In furniture, Mega Group trails only Sears, The Brick and some regional players in buying power in

most Canadian markets. In electronics, Mega is fourth in Canada.

Mega Group was ranked among Canada's 50 Best Managed Companies in 2000 and 2003, and now does $420 million in business each year. *Joe Ralko*

VIREOS.

Small birds, plain olive or gray above, white to yellow below, vireos are often confused with warblers but are actually more closely related to shrikes. Feeding high up in deciduous trees, vireos are best recognized in breeding season by their distinctive songs. They are distinguished from warblers by their relatively stouter bills and slower movements as they forage in trees for berries, insects and larvae. This family of approximately fifty species of songbirds is limited to the Western Hemisphere. Of the fifteen species found in North America, five extend their range to Saskatchewan. Red-eyed (*Vireo olivaceus*) and warbling vireos (*V. gilvus*) are widely distributed. Blue-headed (*V. solitarius*) and Philadelphia vireos (*V. philadelphicus*) are largely restricted to the boreal forest except during migration; the yellow-throated vireo (*V. flavifrons*) breeds only in the extreme southeast corner, in **MOOSE MOUNTAIN** and the lower Souris Valley.

The red-eyed vireo occurs in wooded areas throughout the province; it is scarce and local in the grasslands. More clearly marked than most vireos, it is distinguished by a black-bordered white eyebrow line and a gray cap. Its oft-repeated song, a series of separate phrases, is a frequently heard woodland sound, even at the height of summer. The warbling vireo, one of the plainest of vireos, olive-backed with a pale white eyebrow line, can be found in treed areas in the southern half of the province. Its song is a continuous warble, unlike the broken phrases of other vireos. The Philadelphia vireo is an uncommon summer resident of the boreal forest, occasionally noted in the parklands. Its song is similar to that of the red-eyed vireo, but higher and slightly slower. Philadelphias show more yellow below than other vireos except the yellow-throated vireo. The blue-headed vireo, fairly common in the northern mixed forests, can be identified by distinctive white eye rings, a gray head, white throat, and barred wings. The rarest of our vireos, the yellow-throated, has a bright yellow throat, yellow eye rings, and barred wings. It is most likely to be seen in Moose Mountain Provincial Park.   *J. Frank Roy*

FURTHER READING: Alsop, J.F., III. 2002. *The Birds of Canada*. New York: Dorling Kindersley.

VISIBLE MINORITIES. The term "visible minorities" has long been used in Canada to distinguish ethnic groups of non-European (i.e., non-White) origin from the European-origin ethnic groups which predominate in this country, as well as from Aboriginal Canadians. The implication is that "visible minorities" are "visible" in so far as they are racially distinct from "White" (and Aboriginal) ethnic groups.

People of non-European immigrant origins in Saskatchewan have settled mainly in larger cities (Saskatoon and Regina), especially in recent decades; yet there are examples of longstanding non-European immigration into rural Saskatchewan: as café owners Chinese have long been widely dispersed in rural communities, and an early Black settlement was established at Eldon near Maidstone in 1909. According to the 2001 Census, visible minorities comprised only 2.9% of the total population of Saskatchewan (compared to 13.4% of the total population of Canada); Saskatchewan residents of non-European origin (excluding Aboriginals) numbered 27,580. This visible minority population is extremely diverse.

The largest visible minority population is of East Asian origin or ethnicity, with a total of 9,155 residents, most of whom were Chinese. Another 635 residents claimed Korean ethnic origin, and 435 Japanese (many likely being descendants of Japanese deported from British Columbia during **WORLD WAR II**).

People of Southeast Asian origin numbered 5,630. Most (3,030) were Filipino, with people of Vietnamese, Cambodian, Malay and Singaporean origin accounting for the remainder.

The Black population of Saskatchewan numbered at least 4,165 in 2001. Extremely diverse, it represents people from many cultures. Blacks have come to Saskatchewan from the United States, the Caribbean, and directly from Africa. In fact, the largest increase currently consists of new arrivals from Sudan.

There were at least 4,090 residents of South Asian origins, reflecting wide ethno-cultural diversity —they include Sikhs, Indian Hindus, Pakistani and Bangladeshi Moslems, Sri Lankan Tamils (Hindus) and Sinhalese (Buddhists), as well as Christians from throughout the region.

In 2001, 2,005 residents of Saskatchewan were of Latin American origins. Part of the larger Hispanic community, they have come from diverse countries of origin, mostly from Chile but with increasing immigration from Central America.

Saskatchewan residents of Middle Eastern origins totaled 1,475 in 2001, according to census data. Most are Arab and Muslim, and have arrived recently, although some Syrians and Lebanese have long lived in Saskatchewan. Other groups from this region include Iranians, Afghans, Turks, Armenians and Palestinians. Some are Chaldean and Artiochean Christians.

Apart from these specific ethnic origins, 420 residents have listed other "visible minority" origins, and 640 residents were either of mixed or undifferentiated "visible minority" origins.   *Alan Anderson*

VOICE OF WOMEN. Founded in Toronto on June 10, 1960, the national Voice of Women (VOW) began as the response of women trying to find a peaceful solution to the growing worldwide nuclear threat. VOW's first Saskatchewan branch was established in Regina on February 1961: as the first VOW chapter in the province, it would play an important role in founding other chapters and a provincial umbrella organization. The Regina Voice of Women was formed through the efforts of women like Mary E.P. (Betty) Henderson, chief librarian at Regina College. Early members included prominent names from the political left wing: Irma Douglas, wife of **T.C. DOUGLAS**; Victoria Lloyd, wife of **WOODROW S. LLOYD**; and Ann Blakeney, wife of **ALLAN BLAKENEY**.

The escalation of the Cold War and the advent of the women's movement brought a sharper focus to VOW's activities. It was vocal during the 1963 debate over bringing nuclear weapons into Canada; as well, in 1964 the Regina Voice of Women held its first vigil at the Suffield, Alberta, Experimental Station, opposing research into chemical weapons. Anti-Vietnam activities became a focal point, and the Saskatchewan VOW's efforts included writing letters and taking part in protests; it also campaigned against sale of war-related toys. Reflecting VOW's involvement in the women's movement; the Saskatchewan VOW presented a brief to the Royal Commission on the Status of Women.

The Saskatchewan VOW's membership (like that of the national VOW) decreased during the late 1960s. In 1971, national reorganization occurred and VOW became less broadly based, focusing upon campaigning for specific issues related to women and children. Although VOW still exists, the Saskatchewan VOW disbanded in the late 1980s.   *Maryanne Cotcher*

FURTHER READING: Ball, C. 1994. "The History of the Voice of Women/La Voix des Femmes: The Early Years." PhD dissertation, University of Toronto; Macpherson, K. 1987. "Persistent Voices: Twenty-Five Years with Voice of Women," *Atlantis* 12 (2): 60–71.

VOLUNTARY SECTOR. The voluntary sector is as old as Saskatchewan itself: its roots can be traced back to the beginning of the 1900s. The voluntary sector is made up of what are commonly known in Saskatchewan as community-based organizations (CBOs). Today there are at least 8,000 such organizations in the province. They include a diversity of organizations such as historical and heritage associations, day care centres, sports and recreation clubs, art and culture organizations, social clubs, universities, hospitals, food banks and hot meal programs, environmental groups, trade associations, places of worship, advocates for social justice, and groups that raise funds to cure diseases (*see* Figure VS-1). Some would include co-operatives and community economic development organizations in their work on the voluntary sector, but these are not included here.

In provinces and territories across Canada and internationally, there are many different labels for the voluntary sector, such as: charitable or philanthropic organizations, nonprofit organizations, non-government organizations (NGOs), solidarity organizations, social economy, third sector, and civil society organizations. The voluntary sector is viewed as one of four sectors that provide services or programs to people; the others include the government sector, the private sector, and the informal sector, which includes family and friends. For example, a recreation program like a teen basketball program may be organized through a municipal government recreation department, a voluntary sector neighbourhood association, an exclusive private club for the elite, or it may take place when friends and family meet during certain nights of the week at a local school to play a game.

Through their voluntary sector initiatives, both the federal and Saskatchewan governments define this sector. It "consists of organizations that exist to serve a public benefit, are self governing, do not distribute profits to members, and depend to a meaningful degree on volunteers. Membership or involvement in these organizations is not compulsory, and they are independent of, and institutionally distinct from, the formal structures of government and the private sector. Although many voluntary sector organizations rely on paid staff to carry out their work, all depend on volunteers, at least on their boards of directors." It is generally acknowledged that the voluntary sector is not a unified sector with clearly defined boundaries; there appear to be five generally accepted key characteristics which set it apart from the government, private, and informal sectors. First, the voluntary sector is characterized

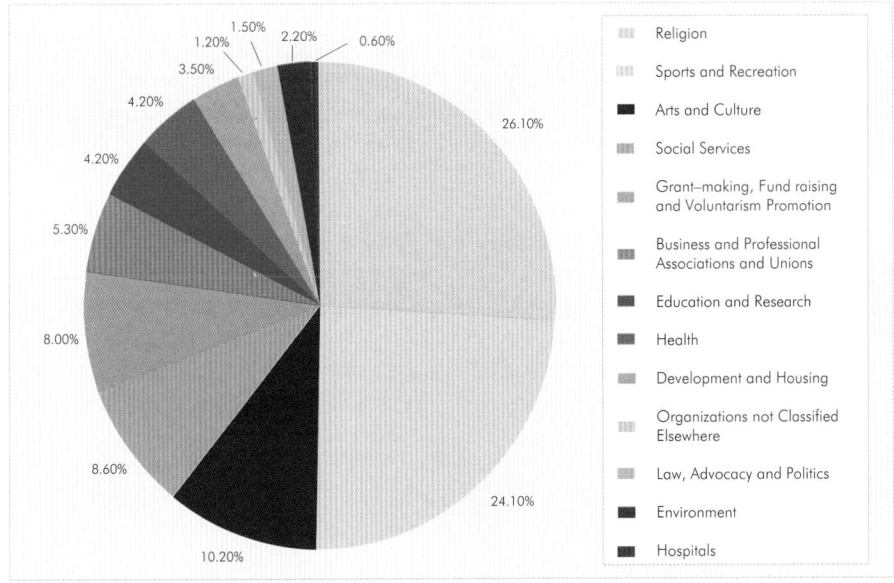

Legend:
- Religion
- Sports and Recreation
- Arts and Culture
- Social Services
- Grant–making, Fund raising and Voluntarism Promotion
- Business and Professional Associations and Unions
- Education and Research
- Health
- Development and Housing
- Organizations not Classified Elsewhere
- Law, Advocacy and Politics
- Environment
- Hospitals

Pie chart values: 1.50%, 2.20%, 0.60%, 1.20%, 3.50%, 4.20%, 4.20%, 5.30%, 8.00%, 8.60%, 10.20%, 24.10%, 26.10%

Source: *Cornerstones of Community: Highlights of the National Survey of Nonprofit and Voluntary Organizations*

Figure VS-1. Primary activity areas of nonprofit and voluntary organizations, Saskatchewan, 2003.

by independence and autonomy from governments; however, there may be a funding relationship and corresponding expectations. Second, there is a central role for volunteers to donate their time and talents; volunteers receive no remuneration for the work they do at CBOs. Third, these organizations are non-profit-distributing in that their financial resources and assets are not owned by anyone (e.g., there are no shareholders). Fourth, voluntary sector organizations are self-governing, with their own internal structures and degree of organizational permanence, in order that they may regulate their own activities through internal democratic processes involving one vote per person. Fifth, many of these organizations are formally incorporated or registered under specific legislation with provincial, territorial or federal governments.

Saskatchewan persists in having one of the highest per capita CBO rates when compared with other provinces and territories across Canada. In 2004, a national study revealed that it had an estimated 8,000 voluntary organizations; this is about 800 organizations per 100,000 people. This places Saskatchewan in second place when compared to other provinces: it is surpassed only by the territories, with 825 organizations per 100,000 people. The national average is about 500 organizations per 100,000 people. Some of these organizations are formally registered as charities with the federal government, and governed by the Income Tax Act as well as the regulations of the Canada Revenue Agency. Others are registered as nonprofits with the province of Saskatchewan, Corporations Branch, and are governed by the Nonprofit Corporations Act. Some may register as nonprofits with the federal government. It is worth noting that some organiza-

tions register as charities as well as nonprofits. The number of community-based organizations formally registered with the provincial government as nonprofits and/or with the federal government as charities has increased steadily over the past forty years in both Saskatchewan and across Canada.

There is another group of organizations in Saskatchewan which are not registered as either a charity or a nonprofit. Some of these are new organizations which are just organizing themselves, while others have been around for many years and have made a conscious decision to not register their organizations. It appears that no one knows for sure how many of these types of organizations exist in Saskatchewan—or across Canada. Voluntary sector organizations exist in rural and urban communities as well as southern and northern areas of Saskatchewan. Recent studies show that volunteer participation rates are higher in rural areas of the province; one study showed that Saskatchewan's rural volunteer rate was 42%, yet the national volunteer rate for the same year was only 33%. This tendency for Saskatchewan's rural and small communities to have more volunteers and CBOs than their urban counterparts has been noted by a number of rural researchers.

To better understand the impact these 8,000 CBOs have on our society, it is useful to group them by the nature of their work. The following categories were adopted for a nationwide Canadian study in 2004: arts and culture, sports and recreation, education and research, universities and colleges, health, hospitals, social services, environment, development and housing, law and advocacy, grant-making and fund raising including voluntarism promotion, international, religion, and finally, business

and professional associations, and unions. In Saskatchewan in 2003, 26% of all CBOs fell into the religion category; 24% fell into the sports and recreation category; and 10% were in the arts and culture category. In each of these instances, Saskatchewan was above the national average. Within each of these categories, CBOs may adopt a variety of functions. They may provide services or programs (e.g., offer a sports program for children who live in poverty, or provide counseling for people with a mental health problem); they may engage in research or fund-raising activities; they may have a focus on regulating practitioners active in the field (e.g., social workers); they may engage in advocacy work to change government policies and gain better access to services for people they serve; and finally, they may be involved in community-building activities including citizen engagement and social networking, so that no one is excluded from activities in their communities. Some voluntary sector organizations do a number of these functions simultaneously.

Volunteers form the backbone of voluntary organizations. Since 1997, Saskatchewan has placed first among all provinces and territories for its high voluntarism rate. In a national study in the year 2000, 42% of Saskatchewan residents over the age of 15 volunteered their time; this was the highest percentage across Canada. The national average volunteerism rate for that same year was 27%. Voluntary organizations receive funding from a number of sources in order to provide programs and services to their members or the general public. Each organization has a different blend of funding from governments, fund raising, fee for service, and donations from corporations and individuals. Financial donations to charities constitute a critical element of survival for some organizations. Since 1995, Saskatchewan has placed in the top three provinces/territories for the rate of tax-filers who donated money to charities; in 2001 the tax-filer donor rate was 27%, with an average donation of $270.

A historical glimpse of Saskatchewan CBOs affords one an interesting picture. A century ago, volunteers played a significant role in many organizations because many CBOs did not have any paid staff; in particular, there was a heavy reliance on women as volunteers. Organizations formed to respond to the needs and issues of the day. Some of the earliest community-based organizations to emerge were inspired by the active involvement of people who were members of churches or ethnic groups; men's and women's church auxiliaries were especially prolific. Other early CBOs in Saskatchewan included: the YWCA Travellers' Aid Department, which helped immigrants; the Victorian Order of Nurses, which delivered home-based nursing services; the Midwives at Little Pine Reserve, who regularly helped deliver babies; the

Saskatchewan Anti-Tuberculosis League; the Women's Grain Growers' Association; the HOMEMAKERS' CLUBS of Saskatchewan, which worked to increase awareness of the need for social reforms; the Canadian Red Cross; the Bureau of Public Welfare; the older First Nations women, who volunteered to teach young girls to bead; and the North Gate Junior Red Cross Society, with eleven children as members.

In the 1930s and 1940s, the face of the voluntary sector changed because of the devastating economic climate and the drought on the prairies. A number of voluntary sector organizations began working with governments to serve the needs of people who found themselves without any source of income—for example the United Hebrew Relief, SALVATION ARMY, UKRAINIAN LABOUR-FARMER TEMPLE ASSOCIATION, War Veterans Associations, and Children's Aid Society. Other groups were not restricted to income assistance, for example the GIRL GUIDES and CANADIAN GIRLS IN TRAINING, Boy Scouts, YMCA, Community Chest (now known as the United Way), Kiwanis Clubs, Society for Crippled Children, and 4H CLUBS for children and teens.

In the 1950s and 1960s, nursing homes for seniors as well as homes for the developmentally disabled adult population emerged. The National Committee on Mental Hygiene became the Canadian Mental Health Association in Saskatchewan. The Lac la Ronge Workshop was administered by a volunteer board of directors, and focused on training and employment for First Nations and MÉTIS peoples. Fraternal groups such as Freemasons and Shriners existed in many communities.

During the 1970s and 1980s many of these voluntary sector organizations continued to exist; some shifted their foci; and a few others closed their doors. In the early 1970s the Saskatchewan Native Women's Association was formally established. Emergency shelters for women and children fleeing abusive homes increased in numbers. There was an increase in the number of food banks and meal programs provided by "soup kitchens"; many of these began in places of worship or in community centres. There were also multicultural centres, child care programs, community reintegration programs offered by the ELIZABETH FRY SOCIETY and JOHN HOWARD SOCIETY, community mental health clinics, employment supports programs, legal aid, sports groups including those for disabled athletes and Special Olympics, leisure clubs, craft clubs (e.g., quilting), animal protection agencies, and parent-teacher associations.

With the major restructuring of government social and health programs in the 1980s and 1990s, including shifts in funding, the voluntary sector struggled. In 2000, the federal government's Voluntary Sector Initiative, a multi-year/multi-million dollar/multi-partner initiative, began to explore a number of critical issues facing the voluntary sector. These included accountability, funding, advocacy and liability issues for volunteers. In 2002, the office of the Premier of Saskatchewan released a document which spoke specifically to the value of community-based organizations and the need to create healthy relationships between the provincial government and CBOs.

The United Nations proclaimed 2001 as International Year of the Volunteer (IYV). This proclamation pointed to the growing awareness of the importance of volunteers in society. First, their primary role has always been as volunteer members of boards of directors: the boards of directors of CBOs are responsible for developing and overseeing the fiscal, human resource, administrative, management, and policy directions of their organizations. Second, volunteers are involved in service and program delivery: for example volunteers run sports programs, deliver meals on wheels to isolated elderly people, and engage in historical research on cultural phenomena. In Saskatchewan, during IYV, the province developed the Saskatchewan Volunteer Pin program and enhanced the Saskatchewan Volunteer Medal program. In general, over the past twenty years we have seen the evolution of a number of new groups that once again reflect the issues of our current times. Some examples are: First Nations arts groups; the Saskatchewan AIDS Network; the Saskatchewan Intercultural Association, which focuses on equity and anti-racism; Immigrant Women of Saskatchewan; Gay and Lesbian Health Services; Good Food Box Programs; and the Saskatchewan Eco-Network. Once again, voluntary sector organizations arise to deal with current social, economic, and political issues of the day.

The voluntary sector in Saskatchewan has been influenced by a myriad of conditions. In the late 1800s and early 1900s, when Saskatchewan was first being settled, organizations grew and became more formalized to deal with the lack of health and educational services. By the 1940s, the voluntary sector and governments had to shift into crisis response mode because of the high unemployment rate and the subsequent stress this placed on families and individuals. Over the past fifty years, Canadians have witnessed government restructuring and downloading of responsibilities to other governments and the voluntary sector; a shift in government philosophy regarding who deserves services and who does not; a shift in public policies toward deinstitutionalization; privatization of many public services; the medicalization and then de-medicalization of certain illnesses; cuts to funding of certain programs in the name of debt reduction; and rural depopulation, with a corresponding increase in urbanization. Finally, longer-term trend analysis done in other countries points to possible decreases in volunteer participation in Saskatchewan CBOs because of people's changing lifestyles, involving an increase in two-earner families, in farm families seeking off-farm employment to survive, in single-parent families, and in commuting time to jobs.

The voluntary sector has had and continues to have a major presence in Saskatchewan communities: it works to meet people's unmet needs, engage people in community events, inspire healthy living, and advocate for changes in government policies. The voluntary sector has a significant economic presence too: in 2004 it received approximately $3.5 billion in revenues and employed approximately 71,000 staff—a disproportionately large share of these staff were women when compared to other sectors.

Gloria DeSantis

FURTHER READING: Brock, K. and K. Banting (eds.). 2001. *The Nonprofit Sector and Government in a New Century.* Montreal and Kingston: McGill-Queen's University Press; Hall, M. et al. 2004. *Cornerstones of Community: Highlights of the National Survey of Nonprofit and Voluntary Organizations.* Ottawa: Ministry of Industry, Statistics Canada, catalogue no. 61-533-XIE.

VONDA, town, pop 322, located approximately 45 km NE of Saskatoon on Hwy 27. People were settling the district in the 1890s, and with the construction of the Canadian Northern Railway through the area (in 1904–05) the community developed: Vonda was incorporated as a village in 1905 and became a town in 1907. Although the district was multicultural (the region included Mennonite, Ukrainian, Polish, Hungarian, and British settlers), Vonda, along with the communities of Prud'homme and St. Denis, reflected a significant French presence. While English language education was transferred to the town of Aberdeen in the mid-1960s, Vonda retains the École Providence, a K–10 French language institution. Developing as a service centre for the surrounding agricultural district, Vonda's population grew to over 400 by the early 1930s. Over the following decades, however, the community declined, its numbers falling to close to 200 by the early 1960s. Subsequently, the town experienced renewed growth, partly owing to commuters working in Saskatoon who took up residence in the town. As well, an agricultural equipment manufacturer brought many much-needed jobs to the community. Two structures have been designated heritage properties: the former Bank of Commerce, dating to 1906; and the Vonda Rink, housed in an aircraft hangar that was built in the early 1940s at the BRITISH COMMONWEALTH AIR TRAINING PLAN base in Davidson. (*See also* FRENCH SETTLEMENTS.)

David McLennan

W

WADENA, town, pop 1,412, located NE of Little Quill Lake at the junction of Hwys 5 and 35. The first settlers in the region were the Irish Milligan family, who arrived in the early summer of 1882 and for the next ten years lived a very isolated life; before 1900 there were very few people in the Wadena district, and ranching was the major activity. It was not until the early 1900s that substantial tracts of land were broken for the purpose of crop production. Some of the first buildings began to appear on the Wadena townsite in 1904, and by 1905 business was booming and the community developed rapidly as settlers of diverse origins arrived in the district. In 1906, with a population of 141, the townsite was incorporated as a village and named after Wadena, Minnesota, the home of one of the first families to settle here in the spring of 1904. In 1912 the community, which had become a thriving agricultural service centre, attained town status. By the early 1920s, the population of Wadena was well over 500; it soared from 595 in 1936 to 1,081 in 1951. At this point, Wadena was also substantially rebuilding and modernizing its business sector, as a fire in 1949 had claimed all but three enterprises in the commercial district. Today, it is one of the region's most important distribution and service centres, with a trading area population estimated to be approximately 21,000. Agriculture is the main industry and the town's retail sector and

COURTESY OF WADENA AND DISTRICT MUSEUM

Wadena Station, spring 1908.

professional community provide a wide range of goods and services. The Wadena Wildlife Wetlands are recognized as important staging grounds for a wide variety of birds including many endangered species. The Quill Lakes attract over 1 million birds annually (Big Quill Lake is Canada's largest saline lake), and a network of boardwalks, nature trails, and viewing towers have been developed throughout the area. Every spring the community hosts the Shorebirds and Friends Festival, which highlights the ecological importance of the region. Wadena is the hometown of broadcaster and journalist **PAMELA WALLIN**, who in 2002 was appointed Canada's Consul General to New York City; in 1994, a main street in the community was renamed Pamela Wallin Drive.   *David McLennan*

WAFFLE. "Waffle" designates an organization of New Left political activists who sought to transform the **NEW DEMOCRATIC PARTY** (NDP) during the late 1960s and early 1970s. The group originated out of a collection of Ontario academics who were concerned about the growing Americanization of Canada and the lack of a strong left-wing party to incorporate the growing youth movements of the 1960s. Believing the NDP provided the best vehicle for their reforms, the Waffle released its platform "For a Strong Socialist Independent Canada" (Waffle Manifesto) at the 1969 federal NDP convention in Winnipeg. The document was highly controversial and was defeated by convention. However, the Waffle received support from some within the Saskatchewan NDP, particularly winning over some in the old populist wing of the party. A loose group of Waffle supporters contested the provincial party executive election at the 1969 provincial NDP convention and won a majority; but the Waffle became embroiled in a variety of conflicts with the party, and they gradually lost influence. The group had difficulty winning party nominations, but managed to nominate and then elect John Richards as an NDP MLA from Saskatoon-University. The Waffle left the NDP in 1973; divided by internal ideological strife, the organization withered slowly until its dissolution in the early 1980s.   *Brett Quiring*

FURTHER READING: Gruending, D. 1990. *Promises to Keep: A Political Biography of Allan Blakeney.* Saskatoon: Western Producer Prairie Books.

WAGE CONTROLS. On October 13, 1975, the federal Liberal government of Pierre Trudeau introduced a program which it described as an attack on inflation. A key section of the Anti-Inflation Act dealt with a prices-and-incomes policy, and established guidelines for what was described as "responsible social behaviour in determining prices and incomes of groups, together with machinery for administering the guidelines." The legislation applied to both

RICHARD GUSTIN/SASKATCHEWAN ARCHIVES BOARD R-B11501
Anti-wage control demonstration in the rotunda of the Saskatchewan Legislative Building, October 14, 1976.

the public sector and private companies with 500 or more employees, and was administered by the Anti-Inflation Board (AIB), chaired by Jean-Luc Pépin. Farmers, fishermen and regulated industries were exempt from the price controls.

Ostensibly, the legislation was supposed to control both spiraling prices as well as wages, but the prices of all necessities of life except clothing were excluded from the price control side and subject only to price control guidelines. Under the guidelines, price increases were to reflect only increases in the cost of production; the core of the program was thus reduced to wage controls. Workers were to be restricted to maximum wage increases of 10% in the first year of the anti-inflation program, 8% in the second year, and 6% in the third year—regardless of increases in the cost of living. Wage settlements had to be submitted to the AIB, which had the power to roll back increases in accordance with the guidelines established by the legislation. Understandably, trade union leaders saw the legislation as the end of free collective bargaining, with unions bargaining, not with their employers (be they private or public), but with the AIB in Ottawa. They insisted that free collective bargaining could not exist with a legislated ceiling imposed on wage gains, and vowed to both defy and fight controls in any way possible.

Provincially, the NDP government of **ALLAN BLAKENEY** stated in the Throne Speech of 1976 that "in seeking contract settlements with employees in the public sector, the government will be guided by the federal proposals subject to appropriate adjustments designed to maintain fair rates of pay for various classes of employees in relation to their counterparts in other prairie provinces." On March 2, 1976, the NDP government introduced its own version of the federal wage control program, the

Saskatchewan Public Sector Prices and Compensation Board. However, the provincial government did not pass legislation or even an Order-in-Council making the program law. It simply issued a document couched in legal language, printed by the Queen's Printer, in a format that looked like legislation but was called "Terms of Reference." The Terms of Reference stated clearly that rulings on prices and wages made by the Saskatchewan Board "shall be made in accordance with the national guidelines." The Board was composed of three individuals: Everett Wood, retired NDP MLA; Jim Maher, businessman and former Liberal MLA; and Ernie Boychuk, Chief Judge of the Provincial Magistrate's Court. The Board had no power to roll back prices, fees, or wages—only to make recommendations to the Minister of Finance.

The imposition of wage controls federally and provincially provoked an immediate and militant response from organized labour. Unions in Saskatchewan and across Canada rallied to a call by the Canadian Labour Congress and staged a mammoth work stoppage on October 14, 1976. It was estimated that over one million workers walked off the job that day to demonstrate their opposition to wage controls. Rallies were held in every major city, and in Saskatchewan almost 28,000 people participated in the voluntary work stoppage. While many groups were affected by controls, the federal government itself states that "some 4.2 million working Canadians had their wage increases limited. Unions were severely restricted in their ability to bargain for higher pay." Wage and price controls were phased out in 1978, and the AIB was dissolved the following year. Saskatchewan withdrew from the program on September 30, 1977.   *Patricia Gallagher*

WAGMAN, FRED (1937–). Born on February 6, 1937, Fred Wagman's broadcasting career began in 1957, and helped prepare him for an innovative role in cable television and local television production. In 1975, Wagman was appointed president and chief executive officer of Cable Regina, a television co-operative known today as Access Communications. Part of Wagman's vision is his focus on community, either through cable television programming or his involvement in such organizations as the Saskatchewan Roughriders Football Club and the Regina Chamber of Commerce. He received the Saskatchewan Order of Merit in 2001 in recognition of his service to the community.

WAHPETON DAKOTA RESERVE. Ancestors of the Wahpeton Dakota Band hunted the borderland between the United States and Canada before moving into the Prince Albert area in 1878 under Chief Hupa-yaktao. Without treaty, an Order-in-Council reserved 80 acres for every five people in 1894, with additional acreage added in 1917 and 1930. Over time the original four encampments of Dakota blended their memberships, and political boundaries diminished. By the late 1970s the band neared commercial-scale beef and grain production, but insufficient land and operating capital limited further growth. The entrepreneurial spirit of the band translates into the management and administration of modern programs in education, health, and social development, as well as a number of business investments. They own shares in the **FIRST NATIONS BANK OF CANADA** (Saskatoon), a walk-in Health Clinic (Prince Albert), and are part of a joint venture with the Prince Albert Development Corporation. In partnership with the Meadow Lake Tribal Council and the Peter Ballantyne Cree Nation, the band also owns three Super 8 Motels. The 1,547 ha of the Wahpeton Dakota Reserve lie in two holdings approximately 50 km northwest of Prince Albert; of the 428 registered band members, 270 live on the reserve.
Christian Thompson

WAKABAYASHI, ARTHUR TSUNEO (1932–). Born on May 12, 1932, Arthur Wakabayashi's career with the federal and provincial public service spanned more than thirty-five years. Provincially, he has served as Deputy Finance Minister, vice-chair of the Saskatchewan Securities Commission, and as Regina's honorary consul-general of Japan. Federally, he has held the positions of Assistant Deputy Minister to the Solicitor General, economic development coordinator, and Saskatchewan's representative in the Canada-US Free Trade negotiations. In 2004, he was elected to his second term as chancellor of the **UNIVERSITY OF REGINA**. Wakabayashi received the Lieutenant-Governor's medal of the Institute of Public Administration of

Canada in 1988, and was invested as a Member of the Order of Canada in 2001.

WAKAW, town, pop 884, located approximately 65 km S of Prince Albert at the junction of Hwys 2, 41, and 312. Beginning in the 1880s a few people took up ranching in the area; significant settlement, however, began in the late 1890s. The Wakaw district would come to be settled by people of Ukrainian, Hungarian, French, and German origins. In 1903, a Presbyterian mission was founded on a point at the west end of Wakaw Lake, followed in 1906 by the construction of a small hospital. The Wakaw post office was established at the location in 1905 and stores and a gristmill were also built at the site. Thus, Wakaw had its beginnings on the lakeshore. When the rail line was surveyed, a new townsite was established somewhat less than a kilometre west of the lake. Wakaw is the Cree word for "crooked" and refers to the shape of the lake. After the trains were running through the young community, Wakaw quickly developed into a sizable service and shopping centre for the surrounding agricultural district. In 1919, a young lawyer who had just been called to the Saskatchewan Bar came to the village looking to establish his first practice. Over the next five years, **JOHN GEORGE DIEFENBAKER** honed skills that would take him far in life. By the 1930s, Wakaw had several hundred residents and, on August 1, 1953, the community attained town status. Today, Wakaw has a wide range of businesses and services. Wakaw Lake has one of the province's busiest regional parks, as well as a number of resort communities. There are approximately 1,000 cottages in the area. A resident doctor, Dr. **FRED CENAIKO**, has been practicing in Wakaw for 41 years.
David McLennan

WALDHEIM, town, pop 889, located approximately 50 km N of Saskatoon on Hwy 312. The town of Rosthern lies to the northeast, and the Petrofka Bridge across the **NORTH SASKATCHEWAN RIVER** lies to the northwest. The origins of the community date to the early 1890s with the settlement of large numbers of Mennonites in the area, a presence which remains strong in Waldheim to this day. The name Waldheim means "forest home" in German, and was chosen as the district was well treed. The Waldheim post office was established in 1900, and with the arrival of the Canadian Northern Railway and the construction of the station in 1909 Waldheim became a railway centre for the developing agricultural community in the rich farmlands of the surrounding area. In 1912, Waldheim was incorporated as a village. From a population of 230 in 1916, it has grown steadily over the decades, reaching over 500 by the early 1960s. In Canada's centennial year, 1967, Waldheim attained town status. Today, although the town's residents benefit from the

amenities that nearby Saskatoon has to offer, Waldheim itself has a strong business community providing a wide variety of goods and services, as well as a number of recreational facilities. An attractive feature of the town is the centrally located Sam Wendland Heritage Park. The site includes the former Canadian Northern station. Now a heritage property, the building serves as the Waldheim library.
David McLennan

WALKER, ERNEST (1948–). Ernest Gordon Walker, an archeologist and anthropologist, was instrumental in the establishment of **WANUSKEWIN HERITAGE PARK**. Born in Saskatoon and educated at the Universities of Saskatchewan and Texas, he has pursued a two-pronged career in prehistoric research and forensic science. Walker's research has focused on North American prehistory in the northern plains and American southwest. His archeological work in Saskatchewan is characterized by co-operation with First Nations Elders and authorities, who have named him Miyo Peyasew (Red Thunderbird) and Honorary Chief. Walker began excavations at Wanuskewin, 5 km north of Saskatoon, in 1982 and was a major force behind the establishment of the area as a park in 1992. He is also noted specifically for his knowledge of Aboriginal prehistoric burial grounds, and of human reaction to climate change over the millennia. Walker is frequently consulted by police agencies for forensic investigation of human skeletal remains involved in homicides or suspicious deaths. He is a Supernumerary Special Constable with the RCMP, and a Saskatchewan coroner. A professor at the University of Saskatchewan since 1984, Walker is a Member of the Order of Canada and a recipient of the Saskatchewan Order of Merit.
John Chaput

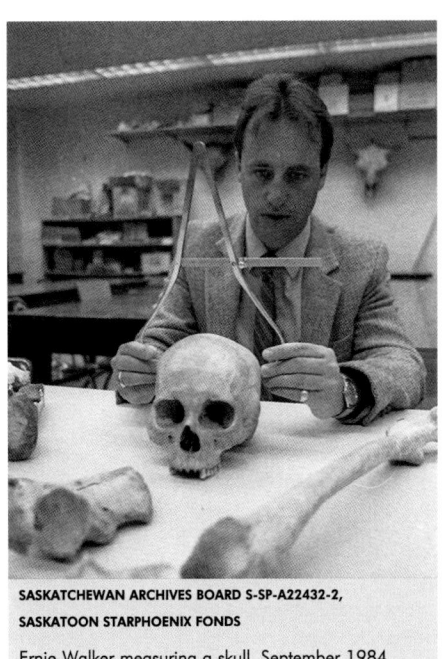

SASKATCHEWAN ARCHIVES BOARD S-SP-A22432-2, SASKATOON STARPHOENIX FONDS

Ernie Walker measuring a skull, September 1984.

995

SASKATCHEWAN ARCHIVES BOARD R-A8065

Helena Walker.

WALKER, HELENA B. (BEATRICE) (1887–1963).

Born on February 26, 1887, in Nova Scotia, Helena Walker attended school there, and received an MA in 1909 from Nova Scotia University (Acadia). In 1912 she came west and taught first at Pense and then at the Collegiate Institute in Regina, where she also attended NORMAL SCHOOL. In 1920 she married Ashley Walker; they had two children. First elected to the public school board in 1925 as the Local COUNCIL OF WOMEN (LCW) candidate, she resigned when she became the LCW candidate for city council in 1932. The new Civic Government Association also endorsed her; she became the first woman councillor, and was re-elected. She did not run in 1936, but returned to council in 1939–40 and subsequently served two terms. She served in numerous organizations, and chaired a committee that instituted a pension plan for the police; other efforts included a proposal to hire a policewoman. A leader in women's organizations (Women's Canadian Club, University Women's Club, and Local Council of Women), Walker was also a central figure in directing women's war efforts, becoming president of the Women's Voluntary Services established in 1943. She died on April 6, 1963, in Regina.
Ann Leger-Anderson

WALKER, MARJORIE (C. 1902–76).

Marjorie Walker (maiden name unknown), teacher and participant in women's organizations, was born in Liverpool about 1902 and came to Saskatoon with her parents in 1913. After attending Saskatoon NORMAL SCHOOL, she taught in several rural schools and the Saskatoon Public School System. She married William Walker; they had two daughters and two sons. In the civic election of 1947 she became the first woman elected to Saskatoon City Council, where she served for eight years; re-elected three times, she led the polls by a wide margin. She served

on several municipal bodies as well as being city representative to a number of groups. During her first year on council she was also a member of the Saskatoon Public School Board, having first been elected in 1944. She was a leader in home and school organizations, as well as vice-president of the Canadian Trustees Association. Walker also played a leadership role in the community, her involvements including the Saskatoon COUNCIL OF WOMEN and St. Mark's Anglican Church. She returned to education in 1953, soon becoming a teacher at the new North Park School. She retired in 1965, and died in Saskatoon on February 11, 1976.
Bob Ivanochko

FURTHER READING: Saskatoon Business and Professional Women's Club. 1976. *Some Outstanding Women: They Made Saskatoon a Better Community.*

WALL, BRAD (1965–).

Brad Wall, Leader of the Official Opposition Saskatchewan Party, was born November 24, 1965, in Swift Current. He earned a degree from the UNIVERSITY OF SASKATCHEWAN and later moved to Ottawa where he worked for a back-bench MP in Brian Mulroney's Progressive Conservative government. Wall returned to Saskatchewan and served as a ministerial assistant in the final years of Grant Devine's Tory government. In 1991 he ran for the Conservative nomination in Swift Current and was defeated.

Wall was Director of Business Development for the city of Swift Current when the SASKATCHEWAN PARTY formed in 1997. Capitalizing on this new political opportunity, he contested the 1999 provincial election and handily won the Swift Current riding. During his first term as an MLA, Wall served as the Saskatchewan Party's Justice critic and was later appointed critic for the Crown Investments Corporation. Re-elected in 2003, he was acclaimed Leader of the Saskatchewan Party Opposition on March 15, 2004. Since then, Wall has sought to expand the party from its rural base into the cities.
Holden Stoffel

FURTHER READING: Wood, James. 2004. "Wall Has Smooth Ride to Leadership." *Regina Leader-Post* (March 15): B1.

WALLACE, LEN (1925–).

Leonard Robert Wallace, born in Saskatoon on August 31, 1925, was an active member of the RETAIL, WHOLESALE AND DEPARTMENT STORE UNION (RWDSU) for forty-two years before his retirement in 1989. For thirty-eight of those years Wallace was a full-time employee of the union. Wallace's formal education was at Buena Vista elementary school in Saskatoon, followed by a brief stint in high school. He served in the Navy during WORLD WAR II, and afterwards started a job at Shelley Brothers warehouse in Saskatoon. His commitment to trade unions began in earnest in 1946

when he was fired from the warehouse for trying to organize a union. He was eventually reinstated, but moved on to FEDERATED CO-OPERATIVES in Saskatoon, which was already organized by the RWDSU International, based in New York. He quickly got active in the union and was hired as a full-time union representative in 1951. He went on to be elected president of the Saskatchewan Division of the union and then secretary-treasurer, a position he held until his retirement in 1989.

Wallace's career as the international representative came to an end in 1970 when he was fired for being one of the leaders of Saskatchewan members in their successful drive to disaffiliate from the American-based organization. Out of this campaign the current structure of the Saskatchewan Joint Board, RWDSU was formed. Throughout the 1970s and 1980s, the independent RWDSU Saskatchewan more than doubled its membership, to the point where it became the province's largest private sector union of the day. Like all other committed trade unionists, Wallace was a social activist who realized there was work to be done outside the bounds of his own organization. He served as vice-president of the SASKATCHEWAN FEDERATION OF LABOUR during the 1960s and again in the mid-1980s; he was also vice-president of the Canadian Labour Congress during the 1960s. He was a leader in the fight for universal health care, and after medicare came in he sat as a member of the medical care insurance commission. He was a founding member of the Regina COMMUNITY CLINIC.

In the 1960s Wallace was the recipient of the Nuffield Foundation Scholarship which provided him with a six-month education leave to Oxford University in England. In the 1970s he was an important figure and organizer in the fight against wage and price controls at both the federal and provincial levels. In his 80th year, he is still an activist, frequently sitting on arbitration boards and continuing to submit reports and prepare briefs.
Paul Guillet

SASKATCHEWAN ARCHIVES BOARD R-PS72-1747-06

Len Wallace.

Pamela Wallin, University of Regina convocation, 2002.

WALLIN, PAMELA (1953–). One of Canada's most accomplished and respected broadcast journalists, Pamela Wallin was born in Moose Jaw and raised in Wadena. She attended the UNIVERSITY OF SASKATCHEWAN, Regina Campus (predecessor of the UNIVERSITY OF REGINA), where she graduated with a Bachelor of Arts in psychology and political science. Beginning her career as a social worker, Wallin changed course after co-hosting a noon-hour openline show on CBC Radio. From 1975 to 1978, she held numerous positions with CBC Radio in Regina, Toronto, and Ottawa; in 1978 she joined the *Toronto Star*, working in the Ottawa bureau.

Wallin's long association with CTV began in 1981, when she joined the network to co-host its morning show, *Canada AM*, with Norm Perry. She reported from Buenos Aires in 1982, covering the Falklands War and the subsequent collapse of the Argentine government. In 1984, on the eve of the visit to Canada of the Chinese premier, Wallin and Perry hosted *Canada AM* from Beijing. Then in 1985, Wallin was appointed Ottawa bureau chief—the first woman in Canadian television history appointed to head a bureau. As bureau chief, she produced and hosted *Question Period* and regularly anchored CTV's weekend *National News* program. Wallin left CTV in 1992, and for the next three years co-anchored CBC's *Prime Time News* with Peter Mansbridge. In 1995 she established her own production company, based in Toronto, which produced such shows as *Pamela Wallin Live*. In 2000, she hosted the Canadian version of the hit game show, *Who Wants To Be A Millionaire?*

In late 2001, Wallin hosted *Canada Loves New York*, a demonstration of Canadian solidarity after the September 11 terrorist attacks. Shortly after, she was appointed Canadian consul general to New York, a position she assumed in June 2002. Wallin has written several books, among which her 1998 best-selling memoir *Since You Asked, and Speaking of Success: Collecting Wisdom, Insights and Reflections*, a collection of the perspectives of the many celebrated people she has interviewed over the years. She is a recipient of the Saskatchewan Order of Merit (1999), and has received nine honorary doctorate degrees, including a degree from her alma mater, the University of Regina, in 2002.
Mark Vajcner

FURTHER READING: Wallin, Pamela. 2001. *Speaking of Success: Collected Wisdom, Insights and Reflections.* Toronto: Key Porter Books.

WALLMAN, ARTHUR L. (1928–). Born with spastic paralysis on July 12, 1928, a determined Arthur Wallman of Kelvington overcame his disability and worked as a successful musician, singer, and broadcaster. From 1952 to 1957, Wallman played with Regina band "Johnny Manz Radio Rangers." In 1960, he began his broadcasting career at CKSW in Swift Current, and for the next thirty-six years was known as "the voice of Swift Current." Wallman also led the dance band "Art Wallman and the Ambassadors." He produced a record in 1982 and published his autobiography three years later. In 1989, Wallman received the Saskatchewan Order of Merit and a Heritage Award for his contributions to country music.

WALTON, DOROTHY (1909–81). Dorothy Walton (*née* McKenzie) was an outstanding all-round female athlete. She was born in Swift Current on August 7, 1909, and educated at the University of Saskatchewan. While earning her BA and MA, Walton played on fourteen university athletic teams and was the first female awarded the oak shield as the university's outstanding athlete. Walton moved to Toronto in 1932 and won the Ontario badminton championship three years later. As 1938 Ladies' Singles event winner, she became the first and only Canadian to date to win an event at the All-England Championships.

Walton was also a talented tennis player. She won fifty-four tennis titles in western Canada between 1924 and 1931, and was one of Canada's top-ranking tennis players in the late 1930s. She was awarded the 1940 Rose Bowl as Canada's Outstanding Female Athlete and was named one of the country's top female athletes for the first half of the 20th century in 1950. Inducted to the Canadian Sports Hall of Fame in 1961 and the Saskatchewan Sports Hall of Fame in 1966, Walton was invested as a member of the Order of Canada in 1973. Dorothy Walton died in Toronto on October 17, 1981.
Bob Ivanochko and Holden Stoffel

FURTHER READING: Ransom, Diane. 1985. *Pioneers and Performers: University of Saskatchewan Sport, 1909-1984.* Saskatoon: University of Saskatchewan; Saskatchewan Sports Hall of Fame. 1980. Regina: The Board of Directors, Saskatchewan Sports Hall of Fame.

WANUSKEWIN HERITAGE PARK. The Wanuskewin Heritage Park is located northeast of the city of Saskatoon. It opened in June 1992, after three years of planning for a park that would not only preserve centuries of cultural heritage, but also help build a bridge between First Nations and non-First Nations people of the province. The mission of Wanuskewin is to operate, on a sustainable basis and under the leadership and guidance of First Nations people, a heritage park that contributes to increasing public awareness, understanding and appreciation of the cultural legacy of the northern plains people. Wanuskewin provides linkages between First Nations and non-First nations peoples, business, government, and academic organizations by creating partnerships, developing curricula for educational programming, and providing a First Nations cultural and heritage development model. Wanuskewin has become an important educational resource in Saskatchewan, with an average of 14,000 school children participating in educational programs on a yearly basis.
Rob Nestor

WAPELLA, town, pop 354, located 24 km NW of Moosomin on Hwy 1. The townsite was developed in 1882 when the CPR was being built through the area. In the following couple of years, a substantial settlement of former Scottish crofters developed over a broad district to the south. The Scots would be joined by English neighbours in 1884, and between 1886 and 1907 about 50 Jewish families, largely from southern Russia, settled on homesteads to the north. Canada's famous BRONFMAN FAMILY got its start on a homestead in the Wapella area in 1889. By 1911, Wapella's population was nearing 500. Mixed farming has long been the area's major industry; today's agricultural production consists of livestock and grain, along with some specialty crops. However, the discovery of oil in the region in 1952 has slowly but steadily added diversity and stability to the district economy. Wapella has a small core of local businesses, services, and recreational facilities. A museum is located in the community's former Anglican Church, and the town has several service clubs and community organizations.
David McLennan

WAR MEMORIALS. Complementing the local war memorials built by communities across the province, the Albert Memorial Bridge in Regina was Saskatchewan's first war memorial erected on behalf of the public. It was constructed as a make-work project at the start of the DEPRESSION, and many of the 1,302 men who built it were unemployed veterans of WORLD WAR I. Dedicated on November 10, 1930, the bridge cost $250,000 to build and was nearly two and a half times over budget; despite this expense, the bridge remains incomplete as a memorial to fallen soldiers who served in World War I. The Honourable JAMES F.

BRYANT, then provincial Minister of Works and the person largely responsible for the bridge's construction, intended for the government or some organization to raise funds for commemorative plaques inscribed with the names of the province's war dead. Once struck, the bronze tablets were to be installed on the inner face of the large pylons located at each end of the structure. Yet this never happened, even though the Albert Memorial Bridge was re-dedicated on October 2, 1988, after a $1.4 million restoration. The recesses in the pylons remain empty today.

However, Bryant's promise of honouring Saskatchewan's veterans was finally realized sixty-five years later. On November 10, 1995, the Saskatchewan First World War Memorial, located west of the SASKATCHEWAN LEGISLATIVE BUILDING in Regina, was officially dedicated. Prominently displayed on several bronze plaques are the names of the 5,348 men and women from Saskatchewan killed during the war. Designed by Regina architect Bill Henderson, the monument stands on the former site of a memorial statue honouring the 28th (North-West) Battalion, Canadian Expeditionary Force. This statue now forms the left corner of the First World War Memorial. In 2000, the committee of the Saskatchewan War Memorial Project began planning a second provincial war monument. Similar in design to the First World War Memorial, it will feature the names of almost 5,000 Saskatchewanians killed in WORLD WAR II, the KOREAN WAR, and postwar peacekeeping and military operations. It will be built immediately south of the existing memorial, and is slated for completion and dedication during the province's centennial year.   *Lloyd Jones and Holden Stoffel*

FURTHER READING: Argan, W., P. Cowa and G.W. Staseson. 2002. *Regina–The First 100 Years: Regina's Cornerstones: The History of Regina Told Through Its Buildings and Monuments*. Regina: Leader-Post Carrier Foundation.

WARBLERS. Known as "feathered gems" or "butterflies of the bird world," the 115 species of wood warblers are all found in the Western Hemisphere. The males in spring are easily identified as they are distinctively garbed mainly in yellows, olives or blue-grays. Most species also have black (or more rarely chestnut red) patches or stripes on the head or breast. Fall birds, especially the young, are much more difficult to identify. The territorial songs of the males are also distinctive: some are staccato, others are high pitched and sibilant, while a few are loud and ringing. The call notes which are made by all birds are mostly simple chips. Saskatchewan has records of thirty-two species.

The group is found in the greatest variety in southeastern Canada and the northeastern United States, where over thirty species may be found. Numbers decline to the north, south and west, but almost twenty-five species may be found in the band of mixedwood forest that crosses central Saskatchewan. Species drop out one by one to the north and east, so that the only species that reach the extreme northeastern corner are the Tennessee, yellow, yellow-rumped, blackpoll and Wilson's warblers, the northern waterthrush, and the common yellowthroat. Similarly, the number of species declines as one travels to the south and west: in many areas south of the aspen parkland the only breeding species are the ubiquitous yellow warbler and the common yellowthroat.

The appearance of the most aberrant of warblers, the yellow-breasted chat, compensates to some extent the loss of species richness in southern Saskatchewan. Huge by warbler standards, the chat is a denizen of the brush tangles and thickets of the province's southern watercourses, and is particularly abundant along the South Saskatchewan and

Yellow warbler (*Dendroica petechia*).

Souris rivers. The high altitude lodgepole pine, aspen and spruce forest of the CYPRESS HILLS attracts birds that would otherwise be found much further north: the Tennessee and orange-crowned warblers, the American redstart, and the ovenbird. The Cypress Hills is the only area where one may expect to see mountain species such as MacGillivray's warbler and Audubon's warbler (the mountain race of the yellow-rumped warbler).

Warblers vary tremendously in the habitats they select. Yellow warblers may be found in almost any type of shrubbery and forest edge, and are the only species that regularly nests in farmsteads, towns and cities; and yellow-rumped warblers nest in almost any type of forest. It is no surprise that these two species are the most abundant in Saskatchewan. Other species are much more particular. Stands of mature mixedwood forest are favoured by so many species that the trees themselves are partitioned amongst them. Many species favour thickets along watercourses, but the only species to nest in marshes is the common yellowthroat.

Warblers are almost exclusively insect-eaters. Most are gleaners, capturing insects off the leaves and twigs or, in the case of the black-and-white warbler, tree limbs and trunks. The Wilson's and Canada warblers, as well as the American Redstart, capture most of their food on the wing. The most specific food requirements belong to the Tennessee, Cape May, and bay-breasted warblers, which are so closely tied to the spruce budworm that their numbers explode in response to budworm outbreaks and decline sharply thereafter. Warblers lay four to seven whitish eggs, usually with dark markings; nests are placed in a tree, a shrub, or more rarely on the ground.

During migration many species of warblers, especially those in breeding in mature mixedwood forests, migrate in a northwest-southeast direction and thus are rare at that time in the southwestern corner of the province. Most other species are frequently seen as migrants throughout the southern part of the province. Almost every species of warbler winters in tropical areas from extreme southern

First World War Memorial on the grounds of the Saskatchewan Legislative Building.

United States to Bolivia in South America; the only species that regularly winters in Canada (but not in Saskatchewan) is the yellow-rumped warbler.

Alan R. Smith

FURTHER READING: Curson, J., D. Quinn and D. Beadle. 1994. *Warblers of the Americas.* Boston: Houghton Mifflin; Dunn, J.L., K.R. Garrett and R.T. Peterson. 1997. *A Field Guide to Warblers of North America.* Boston: Houghton Mifflin.

WARD, NORMAN MCQUEEN (1918–90). Born in 1918 in Hamilton, Ontario, Norman Ward joined the Department of Economics and Political Science at the UNIVERSITY OF SASKATCHEWAN in 1944, and remained there until his retirement in 1985. Through a series of important books, articles and reports on representation, bilingualism, procedure in the House of Commons, election expenses, and government information, he established himself as an authoritative interpreter of national politics and institutions. The politics of his adopted province also won his attention, as evidenced by *Politics in Saskatchewan*, which he co-edited in 1968, articles in *Saskatchewan History*, and long membership on the Saskatchewan Archives Board and chairmanship of the province's Public Administration Foundation. His scholarship did not cease on retirement: his biography of *Jimmy Gardiner: Relentless Liberal*, was published in 1990. Norman Ward's literary achievements were not confined to academic scholarship. His humorous essays were published in three volumes: *Mice and the Beer* (1960), for which he won the Leacock Medal for Humour; *The Fully-*

RICHARD MARJAN PHOTO/SASKATCHEWAN ARCHIVES BOARD
S-SP-A21258-4, SASKATOON STARPHOENIX FONDS

Norman Ward and his wife, Betty, January 1984.

Processed Cheese (1964); and *Her Majesty's Mice* (1977). Elected a Fellow of the Royal Society of Canada in 1962, he was named an Officer of the Order of Canada in 1976. Ward died in Saskatoon in 1990.

David E. Smith

WARMAN, town, pop 3,481, located 15 minutes N of Saskatoon. Like nearby Martensville, Dalmeny and Osler, Warman has in the past 30 years developed essentially into a "bedroom community" for people working in Saskatoon. The townsite of Warman grew up at the junction of the east-west running Canadian Northern Railway and the north-south running QLLS railway. It was named after Cy Warman, an American journalist who followed and reported on the construction of the Canadian Northern. Warman remained a small community until the 1950s. Since then, the burgeoning population has led to the development of a large range of local businesses, services and recreational facilities: there is a local RCMP detachment, a fire department, an ambulance service, a medical clinic, and a special care home. Warman's elementary and high schools provide K–12 education to close to 900 students. The major annual event in the community is the Warman Diamond Rodeo and Family Days.

David McLennan

WARSHIPS WITH SASKATCHEWAN NAMES. Beginning in WORLD WAR II, the Canadian navy has frequently honoured a variety of Saskatchewan communities in the naming of its warships. There have been several warships with Saskatchewan names, ranging in size from destroyers, frigates and corvettes, down to the small but vital harbour tankers (oilers) such as HMCS *Dundurn*. Two ships with Saskatchewan names, HMCS *Regina* and HMCS *Weyburn*, were sunk during World War II. Currently HMC ships *Regina* and *Saskatoon* represent the province in Canada's naval fleet. (*See* Table WSN-1 on the following page.)

Malcolm French

WASACASE, IDA (1937–93). Ida Wasacase was an activist, renowned lecturer, and advocate of First Nations bilingual and bicultural education, who played a key role in establishing a working relationship between the Saskatchewan Indian Federated College, the UNIVERSITY OF REGINA, and both federal and provincial governments. Ida Wasacase was born on November 27, 1937, on the Ochapowace First Nation reserve. She graduated from the Round Lake Residential School in 1954 with a Governor General's Award in French, and a year later received her "Permanent Teachers Certificate A" from Tuxedo Teachers' College in Manitoba. She gained over fifteen years of teaching experience across Canada in primary and secondary schools, and three years in Germany with the Department of National Defence. She then taught at the universities of Brandon,

UNIVERSITY OF REGINA ARCHIVES AND SPECIAL COLLECTIONS
85-18-6

Ida Wasacase.

Laurentian, and Saskatchewan. Wasacase worked as a consultant in the areas of language and cross-cultural development for the Manitoba Department of Education, the Department of Indian and Northern Affairs, and the Saskatchewan Indian Cultural College. She was appointed Associate Director of the Saskatchewan Indian Federated College in 1976. She was promoted to Director of the College one year later, and remained in that position until 1982, in which year she received the Order of Canada. Ida Wasacase died on May 13, 1993, and despite her short life is remembered as a key figure in Indian control of Indian education in Saskatchewan.

Rob Nestor

WASCANA CENTRE AUTHORITY. In 1962, the Saskatchewan Legislature passed the Wascana Centre Act, creating an eleven-member board from participating parties—the government of Saskatchewan, the city of Regina, and the UNIVERSITY OF REGINA—as the Wascana Centre Authority. The Authority is responsible for reviewing and coordinating all the use, development, conservation, maintenance, and improvement of land, water, and buildings within the 930-ha domain of Wascana Centre in Regina. What began as a simple dam on Wascana Creek in the 1880s (creating the original Wascana Lake) has been improved and extended through the years. The provincial Legislature was built on the south shore; the reservoir has been drained and re-excavated twice, once as a DEPRESSION relief project, then again in 2004; and many trees and shrubs have been planted. In 1960, the expansion of the UNIVERSITY OF SASKATCHEWAN to create a full Regina campus prompted a unified development plan for the lake, Legislature, campus, and nearby areas. Soon after, the Wascana Centre Authority came into being. The Wascana Centre includes walking and

Table WSN-1. Warships Bearing Saskatchewan Names

Name	Class	Commissioned	Disposition	Comments
HMCS *Battleford*	Flower Class Corvette	July 31, 1941	Paid off July 18, 1945	
HMCS *Eastview*	River Class Frigate	June 3, 1944	Paid off January 17, 1946	
HMCS *Kamsack*	Flower Class Corvette	October 4, 1941	Paid off July 22, 1945	
HMCS *Melville*	BANGOR Class Minesweeper	December 4, 1941	Paid off August 18, 1945	
HMCS *Moose Jaw*	Flower Class Corvette	June 19, 1941	Paid off July 8, 1945	
HMCS *Orkney*	River Class Frigate	April 18, 1944	Paid off January 22, 1946	Named to honour Yorkton, but to avoid confusion with HMS *York* & USS *Yorktown*
HMCS *Poundmaker*	River Class Frigate	September 17, 1944	Paid off November 25, 1945	Named to honour North Battleford, but to avoid confusion with HMCS *Battleford*
HMCS *Qu'Appelle* (I)	River Class Destroyer	February 8, 1944	Paid off May 27, 1946	Ex HMS *Foxhound* named for the River rather than the Town
HMCS *Qu'Appelle* (II)	MACKENZIE Class Destroyer Escort	September 14, 1963	Paid off March 28, 1994	Named for the River rather than the Town
HMCS *Regina* (I)	Flower Class Corvette	January 22, 1942	Torpedoed & sunk off Trevose Head, Cornwall August 8 , 1944 with loss of thirty lives	
HMCS *Regina* (II)	HALIFAX Class Frigate	September 3, 1994	In service	
HMCS *Rosthern*	Flower Class Corvette	June 17, 1941	Paid off July 19, 1945	
HMCS *Saskatchewan* (I)	River Class Destroyer	May 31, 1943	Paid off January 28, 1946	Ex HMS *Fortune* named for the River rather than the Province.
HMCS *Saskatchewan* (II)	MACKENZIE Class Destroyer Escort	February 16, 1963	Paid off December 3, 1993	Named for the River rather than the Province
HMCS *Saskatoon* (I)	Flower Class Corvette	June 9, 1941	Paid off June 25, 1945	
HMCS *Saskatoon* (II)	KINGSTON Class Maritime coastal Defense Vessel	December 5, 1998	In service	Ship's sponsor is the Hon. Sylvia Fedoruk former Lieutenant Governor of Saskatchewan
HMCS *Swift Current*	BANGOR Class Minesweeper	November 11, 1941	Paid off October 23, 1945	
HMCS *Waskesiu*	River Class Frigate	June 16, 1943	Paid off January 26, 1946	Named to honour Prince Albert but to avoid confusion with HMS *Prince Albert*
HMCS *Weyburn*	Flower Class Corvette	November 26, 1941	Mined and sunk off Gibraltar February 22, 1943 with loss of seven lives.	

bicycle paths, marina, bandstand, pool and picnic areas, and art galleries. Besides the provincial Legislative Building there are several important edifices: ROYAL SASKATCHEWAN MUSEUM, CBC, SASKATCHEWAN SCIENCE CENTRE, University of Regina, and SIAST. (*See also* "BIG DIG") *Merle Massie*

WASKESIU UPLAND. The Waskesiu upland includes the upper elevations of Prince Albert National Park as well as the upland area north of the park known as the Thunder Hills. Elevations range from 550 m at the base of the upland to over 750 m. The system of external drainage consists mainly of streams that originate in the upland and, controlled by its relief, drain downslope to the adjacent lowlands. The upland in the southern part drains to the south via the Sturgeon and Spruce rivers, which empty into the NORTH SASKATCHEWAN RIVER near Prince Albert. The remainder of the upland drains eastward into Montreal Lake and then northward into the CHURCHILL RIVER system via the Montreal River.

Like most major uplands in the province, the landscape is primarily a plain composed of unstratified clay and stones (till) deposited by glaciers. At the upper elevations the landscapes are gently undulating to moderately rolling, although those in the northern part are generally rougher and have steeper slopes than those in the south. Surficial sediments are comprised mainly of loamy textured glacial till, although clayey sediments, derived from erosion of the surrounding uplands during deglaciation, occur sporadically in the southern regions. In most instances, the small, rounded hills (knolls) and upper slopes are comprised of glacial till, with the clayey stratified sediments overlying the till on the lower slopes. Sediments derived from glacial lakes (glaciolacustrine) are rare in the northern part of the upland, but shallow sandy materials are commonly found overlying the till on the lower slopes. As usual in these types of landscapes, the depressional areas are filled with organic materials. Steeply sloping cliffs or escarpments dissected by numerous large, deep-set valleys occur in the southern part of the upland. Many have relatively small streams, called "misfit streams," indicating the valleys were likely former channels formed by the passage of water melting from glaciers. Areas of sandy and gravelly sediment are often found at the base of the escarpment. The steeply sloping escarpments, in contrast to the upper plateau-like tops of the uplands, are almost devoid of wetlands except along the small creeks themselves.

Mixed stands of trembling aspen and white spruce are dominant on the well-drained sites in the southern part of the upland. In the northern part of PRINCE ALBERT NATIONAL PARK and to the south in the Thunder Hills, coniferous stands of jack pine and black spruce are by far the most prevalent. Black spruce and tamarack are, as expected, the dominant tree species on the poorly drained peatlands.

FURTHER READING: Acton, D.F., G.A. Padbury and C.T. Stushnoff. 1998. *The Ecoregions of Saskatchewan.* Regina: Canadian Plains Research Center.

WASKEWITCH, GUS (1917–96). Born on January 11, 1917, Gus Waskewitch of Onion Lake dedicated over three decades of his life to mentorship and development in his community. He established the Onion Lake School and the Eskweskeet Rehabilitation Centre. Waskewitch also spoke to youth about alcohol and drug addictions, and developed a counselling program. Additionally, he served as a Senator with the **FEDERATION OF SASKATCHEWAN INDIAN NATIONS** and as a member of the Onion Lake Council of Elders. He was appointed to the Order of Canada in 1988. He died on November 7, 1996.

WASPS: *see* **HYMENOPTERA**

WAT BUDDHADHAMMA. Wat Buddhadhamma is a Theravadin (Thai and Laotian) temple that has served the Theravadin Buddhist community of Regina for twelve years. The primary language for religious services is Laotian; prayers and chants are recited in Pali. There is a small library with some Buddhist texts that are mainly in Pali; the comments on the texts by Buddhist masters are in Laotian, with some in English. The temple is the main religious centre of the community, and the Buddha's image and the resident monk are the focus of the worship. Followers show their respect by holding their hands joined over their heads, at their chests, and on the floor three times; the same procedure is used to salute the monk who sits at the side of the altar. Homemade food is offered in a basket placed on the altar. The service involves communal prayer and chanting, and lasts about an hour. During the major ceremony, lunch is served: homemade food is offered first to the Buddha and the monk, then to the congregation. Theravadin Buddhists are not vegetarians, but they do not involve themselves in the slaughter of animals. They are always careful to offer some food to the spirits of the temple in order to obtain protection from them.   *Yuan Ren*

WATER QUALITY. Water quality in Saskatchewan is affected by a variety of human activities. Uses that consume large quantities of water while degrading its quality include agriculture, mining and milling, oil and gas production, and municipal and domestic uses (*see* Table WQ-1). In Saskatchewan, most water pollution originates from non-point (i.e., unconfined) sources such as agricultural runoff. Point sources of pollution, which originate from a specific

Table WQ-1. Water Use in Saskatchewan

Type of use	Amount (million m³)	Percentage of use
Agriculture	557.4	67.0
Municipal & domestic	171.2	20.6
Industry & commerce	52.8	6.3
Mining	25.8	3.1
Thermal power generation	17.1	2.1
Oil & gas	6.7	0.8
Total	831.5	100.0

Source: *2003 State of the Environment Report,* p. 45

localized origin such as an effluent pipe, are carefully monitored and for the most part have been cleaned up. Agriculture is Saskatchewan's leading industry and its biggest consumer of provincial water resources. Irrigation, which alone accounts for two-thirds of all provincial water consumption, is a chief contributor to water contamination. Surface runoff and return flow from irrigated fields may contain dissolved salts and other pollutants such as chemical fertilizers and pesticides, which wash into nearby watercourses or leach through the soil into underlying groundwater. Similarly, waste and by-products from intensive livestock operations can potentially contaminate water systems though leakage and percolation.

Domestic and municipal activities also impact water quality. Urban centres sometimes discharge large amounts of industrial waste and underground leachates. Although the larger cities use tertiary sewage treatment to remove pathogens and solid wastes, the risk for accidental waterway contamination still exists. Smaller centres are not as thorough in their treatment of sewage, and run a greater risk of surface and groundwater contamination. Leaching of wastes from landfill sites can also contaminate groundwater; and storm-water runoff from the urban watershed picks up contaminants, washing them into drainage basins and ultimately into natural waterways and aquatic ecosystems. Mining and milling operations are a potential source of water pollution if their tailings and residual wastes are not properly contained and treated. Until reclaimed, decommissioned mine sites are especially dangerous sources of groundwater contamination. Effluents from wood processing mills are carefully monitored and controlled in Saskatchewan. The pulp mill at Meadow Lake, for example, has successfully eliminated the discharge of polluted effluent through its zero-effluent treatment system. Wastewater from the mill is collected, decontaminated, evaporated (to produce a clean distillate), and then recycled back into the milling process.

Oil and gas production, through accidental oil spills and improperly disposed drilling wastes, may release toxins into surface and groundwater sources. Dams and water control structures also directly

impact water quality in Saskatchewan's waterways. Changes in the water's temperature (thermal pollution) and chemistry are often observed downstream from dams and reservoirs. In addition, dams trap sediment, contaminants, and nutrients in their upstream reservoirs. The accumulation of nutrients (such as nitrates and phosphates from agricultural runoff) in a water body will stimulate the growth of algae and deplete the water oxygen. This can lead to the death of fish, and produce visual and odour problems that reduce the water's aesthetic and recreational appeal. Poor water quality threatens the survival of sensitive aquatic ecosystems both upstream and downstream of a water control structure.

Surface and groundwater quality in Saskatchewan is assessed through the Water Quality Index (WQI), a composite measure of the chemical and organic makeup of the water in a particular drainage basin. Depending on the specified use (e.g., recreation, irrigation, livestock watering, protection of aquatic life) of the water in that basin, its quality is rated from "poor" to "excellent." Drinking water for human and livestock consumption is a high-priority use in Saskatchewan, and is therefore subject to stringent testing and treatment measures. Source water must be tested to ensure safe levels of biological, chemical, and physical contaminants that make it suitable for drinking. The most common method for removing harmful bacteria and viruses from drinking water is through the addition of chlorine. In Saskatchewan's rural areas, surface and groundwater quality and the provision of clean water for domestic consumption are major concerns. Groundwater forms the most abundant and most widely distributed of Saskatchewan's water reserves, and provides 30% of the province's population with its domestic water; however, the quality, yield, and reliability of Saskatchewan's groundwater vary significantly. Groundwater in deep wells is difficult to treat, and water quality in dugouts and small reservoirs is generally quite poor.

Agencies such as SaskWater, Saskatchewan Environment, and the Saskatchewan Watershed Authority are directly involved in the management of the province's water resources. Saskatchewan Environment's Drinking Water Quality section ensures safe drinking water for the province. The Saskatchewan Watershed Authority, a Crown corporation, was established through the consolidation of water management divisions at SaskWater, Saskatchewan Environment, and the Saskatchewan Wetland Conservation Corporation. The Saskatchewan Watershed Authority has a broad mandate to manage and protect water quality in Saskatchewan.

Iain Stewart

WATER TRANSPORTATION. The history of water transportation in Saskatchewan begins with the small birchbark canoes used by generations of the original inhabitants of the province before European contact. This mode of travel would have been ideal for many of the rivers as well as the smaller to medium-sized lakes in the province. After European contact, larger birchbark canoes were designed and built to carry the heavier payloads of the fur trade. The main fur trade water routes in the province included the **CHURCHILL RIVER** system in the north (*see* Figure WT-1), the **QU'APPELLE RIVER** and lakes in the south, and the **SASKATCHEWAN RIVER** between the two. By the first part of the 18th century, French fur traders had penetrated west into Saskatchewan by canoe, building two posts a short distance east of the forks of the North and South Saskatchewan rivers in the early 1750s. They were followed by English, Scot and American fur traders from Montreal. One small but famous group included Thomas and Joseph Frobisher, **ALEXANDER HENRY**, and their chief guide Louis Primeau, who were the first non-Aboriginals to canoe north from the Saskatchewan River to the Churchill system. By the second half of the 1770s, **PETER POND** had crossed the height of land separating the Hudson Bay watershed from the Arctic watershed at the Methye Portage just north of present-day La Loche. It was only a matter of time before this canoe route through Saskatchewan became part of a larger trans-Canada water route to the Arctic and Pacific oceans.

During the course of the 19th century, **YORK BOATS** would replace canoes as the principal means of water transportation in the province. York boats were wooden rowboats about twelve metres long, with a pointed bow and stern. Although more difficult to portage, York boats had several advantages: they could carry and deliver twice the payload, with only slightly larger crews. Uniformly built with standardized ribs and hull planks, York boats lasted two seasons in place of the one-season life span of a fragile birchbark canoe. They could also handle rougher water on the large lakes, and had large sails. Finally, lower-paid and lower-skilled York boat rowers could replace more expensive and higher-skilled voyageurs. By the early 1820s, the Hudson's Bay Company was regularly using York boats on the Churchill and Saskatchewan river routes. As the link

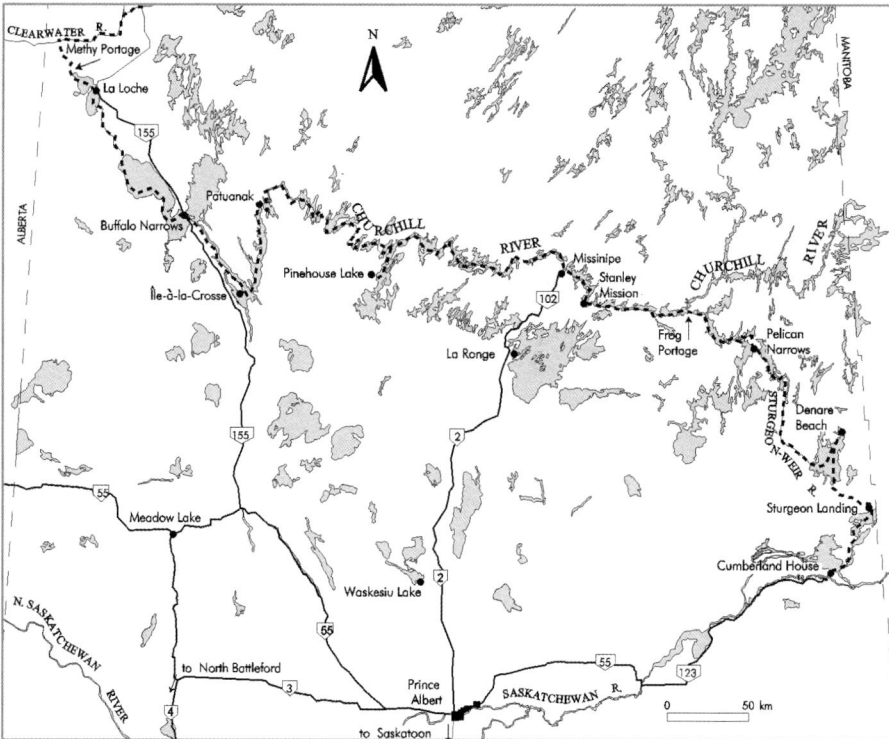

Figure WT-1. Saskatchewan's "Voyageur Highway" from Cumberland House to Methy Portage.

from the Churchill to the Athabasca and the Mackenzie River, the 19-km long Methy Portage posed a major challenge to York boats. The problem was solved by having two York boat brigades, one traveling west and north of the portage (the Mackenzie Brigade) and one traveling south and east of the portage (the La Loche Brigade), with trade goods and furs exchanged annually on the portage without the need to haul the clumsy boats across. Water transportation on the rivers and lakes of the **QU'APPELLE VALLEY** during the fur trade was less important than the critical logistics involved in the Saskatchewan and Churchill river routes. The area was used to collect pemmican from Aboriginal traders, most of which was transported north in **RED RIVER CARTS**. From Fort Qu'Appelle for example, trails led to Chesterfield House on the **SOUTH SASKATCHEWAN RIVER** and to Fort Carlton on the **NORTH SASKATCHEWAN RIVER**.

By the 1850s, Lieutenant **THOMAS BLAKISTON** of the Palliser Expedition (*see* **PALLISER AND HIND EXPEDITIONS**) was assessing the feasibility of **STEAMBOAT** travel on the Saskatchewan River. The Hudson's Bay Company first put a steamboat called the *Lily*—touted as the successor to the York boat—on the Saskatchewan River in 1873; this was followed one year later by the famous *Northcote*. From the beginning, seasonal variations in the water level along with shifting sandbars sabotaged steamboat travel on the South Saskatchewan River. The *Northcote* was used as a troop carrier to reinforce General **MIDDLETON**'s forces at **BATOCHE** on the South Saskatchewan River in the 1885 Resistance.

Although steamboat travel on the North Saskatchewan River was less treacherous, the steamboat era was short lived, in part because of the precipitous decline of the fur trade by the late 19th century, the rising importance of land travel, the beginnings of air travel, and the introduction of boats driven by internal combustion engines. By the early 20th century, rail travel was the primary means of transportation in the province, with road construction and travel rapidly growing during the rest of the century. Today, water transportation is mainly recreational in nature; motorboats are responsible for the bulk of the remaining commercial water transportation.

Gregory P. Marchildon

WATERHEN LAKE FIRST NATION. According to Department of Indian Affairs reports, the Waterhen Lake First Nation signed an adhesion to **TREATY 6** in January 1913 under Chief Running Around, and in 1916 a reserve was surveyed for them. The Indian Agent noted that the chief wanted assurance that their traditional way of life would be protected. The Waterhen Lake First Nation hunted and trapped in the area around Lost Lake, and would go as far as Primrose Lake. In 1946 their traditional hunting and trapping areas fell within the regulations of the Fur Act, dividing northern Alberta and Saskatchewan into Fur Conservation Areas and restricting trapping privileges to local residents (primarily First Nations and **MÉTIS**). In 1954 many of these Fur Conservation Areas became part of the Primrose Lake Air Weapons Range, and therefore subject to a claim launched by several bands in 1975 for compensation for the loss of traditional hunting, trapping and fishing lands. In the case of the Waterhen Lake band, their claim was rejected. The Waterhen Lake (Sîkîp Sâkahikan) Cree Nation is the largest band in the Meadow Lake Tribal Council; 729 of its 1,631 registered members live on the 7,972.2-ha reserve, located 39 km north of Meadow Lake. The economy includes trapping, lumber industry, and tourism; there are a multipurpose office, warehouse, school, teacherage, fire hall, lift station, arena, drop-in centre, and other community maintenance structures. *Christian Thompson*

WATROUS, town, pop 1,808, located 110 km SE of Saskatoon at the junction of Hwys 2 and 365. There were only a few settlers in the district in 1903, but between 1904 and 1906 homesteaders' sod houses and shacks began to dot the country for miles around. When the **GRAND TRUNK PACIFIC RAILWAY** came through in 1906, the townsite was surveyed and named after Frank Watrous Morse, the general manager of the railway. In the period leading up to **WORLD WAR I**, there was a great influx of settlers into the area and most of the available homestead land was occupied. Very early on, area residents discovered the mineral waters of Little Manitou Lake, about 5 km north of Watrous, which had long been known to local First Nations populations. Manitou Beach became a popular resort destination, and the town of Watrous greatly benefited over the years as throngs of tourists passed through the community en route to the lake. In 1939, Watrous became the location for the Canadian Broadcasting Company's only broadcasting outlet between Winnipeg and Vancouver—so chosen because the minerals in the area make the soil highly conductive. Radiating from the base of the 465 foot (142 metre) tower, 120 wires each 500 feet (152 metres) long are buried under the earth grounding the system. CBK Radio station's 50,000-watt transmitter far exceeded the expectations of providing coverage for the prairie provinces: engineers estimate that to equal the coverage of CBK, an eastern radio station would have to have four times the power. Reception has been reported from as far away as Australia. Once a popular tourist attraction with a full-time staff of 14, the CBK transmitter is now operated from Regina. Watrous remains an important service centre for the district and a major shopping centre for area farm families. It also benefits from its proximity to three potash mines, which are major employers of town residents. Agriculture, a substantial part of the area economy, includes a diverse array of crops as well as livestock production. Cattle are raised in the area's pastures and marginal lands, and there are intensive hog and dairy operations in the district. Tourism generated by Manitou Beach adds to a diversified economy. All Saints Anglican Church in Watrous may also have the oldest stained glass window in Canada. The window,

brought to Watrous in 2,000 pieces from England by the first vicar of the church, dates back to pre-Reformation times. *David McLennan*

WATSON, town, pop 794, located NW of Big Quill Lake at the junction of Hwys 5 and 6. Settlement of the area began in the early 1900s; a substantial number of immigrants were German-American Catholics who began arriving in 1902. They settled in a broad arc ranging from the Watson district northwestward through to the Humboldt, Bruno, and Cudworth areas. With the Canadian Northern Railway progressing westward from Winnipeg toward Edmonton in 1905, the townsite developed and was given the name Watson in honour of Senator Robert Watson of Manitoba, who had owned the land upon which the community sits. Incorporated as a village in 1906 and a town in 1908, Watson grew steadily and experienced significant growth in the decades following **WORLD WAR II**. Today, its economic base is agriculture, complemented by a number of industrial and manufacturing firms. The Watson and District Heritage Museum is located in the town's 1906 Canadian Bank of Commerce building. Another Watson landmark is a 25-foot (7.62 metre) high fibreglass Santa Claus statue, which commemorates the community's Santa Claus Day, held on the first Saturday of December. (*See also* **GERMAN SETTLEMENTS**) *David McLennan*

WAVECOM ELECTRONICS. WaveCom Electronics (now known as VCom) is a Saskatoon-based designer and manufacturer of state-of-the-art cable television (CATV) and wireless telecom products. WaveCom was established in 1988 by current chairman and chief executive officer Dr. Surinder Kumar, a former professor of electrical engineering at the **UNIVERSITY OF SASKATCHEWAN**. Innovative research and development has kept WaveCom on the cutting edge of four key areas in the technology sector: digital video, broadband wireless, advanced analog, and data-over-cable. WaveCom has a manufacturing plant and a high-volume production facility in Saskatoon, as well as research facilities in both Saskatoon and Victoria, BC. Since its inception in 1988, WaveCom has seen remarkable growth, currently employing 290 people in its Saskatoon and Victoria facilities, and generating annual revenues of roughly $30 million from customers worldwide. *Iain Stewart*

FURTHER READING: Martin, P. 2003. "Saskatchewan's Top 100," *Saskatchewan Business* 24: 17–26.

WAWOTA, town, pop 538, located just NE of Moose Mountain Provincial Park and Kenosee Lake on Hwy 48, 46 km W of the Saskatchewan-Manitoba border. Settlers began entering the district around 1882 as the transcontinental railway was being built

through the Moosomin area to the north. The townsite of Wawota was established by the CPR in 1905 as the railway proceeded westward with the construction of its line from Reston, Manitoba, to Wolseley. The track became operational in 1906, and the little mixed train that ran back and forth on the line became affectionately known to local residents as the "Peanut." With the railway came a construction boom, and Wawota was incorporated as a village in 1907—the name being derived from a First Nations word meaning "deep snow." In 1961, the CPR line was abandoned and the "Peanut" made its last run that August. Wawota lost its two grain elevators, and eight families whose livelihoods were tied to the elevators and the railway left the village. While many believed this was the death knell for the community, Wawota continued to grow, reaching a peak population of 676 in 1986 and attaining town status in 1975. Today, agriculture continues to dominate the area economy. The community's 1919 Union Bank of Canada building has been designated a heritage property, and on the Wawota and District Museum site are a 1905 schoolhouse and a fire hall dating to 1909. *David McLennan*

WAXWINGS. The two waxwings found in Saskatchewan are widespread members of a small family (Bombycillidae) of three species found in the Northern Hemisphere. These small (15–20 cm) fruit-eating songbirds have distinctive elegant gray and brown plumage, with a small crest and black mask.

Both the cedar waxwing (*Bombycilla cedrorum*) and the Bohemian waxwing (*B. garrulus*) are noticeable as they gather in large noisy flocks. The cedar waxwing nests throughout the southern half of the province, and some overwinter. The main winter waxwing is the wandering Bohemian, seen in mobile flocks which move from one fruit tree to another as they strip the fruit. They are particularly attracted to mountain ash, found as ornamentals in the townsites. In the summer the species migrates further north to nest, including in the northern boreal forest of Saskatchewan. *Diane Secoy*

FURTHER READING: Alsop, Fred J., III. 2002. *Birds of Canada*. New York: Dorling Kindersley.

WAYGOOD, KATHRYN B. (1944–). Kate Waygood (*née* Lofft) is committed to community involvement in urban planning issues and to preservation of Canada's built heritage at municipal, provincial, and federal levels. Born on August 20, 1944, in Winnipeg, she earned a BA at the University of Toronto (1972), and taught high school geography in Toronto. On July 14, 1973, she married Bruce Waygood; they moved to Saskatoon in 1977. In 1978 Waygood became involved in a widespread citizen protest related to zoning issues in older neighbourhoods, which caused a fundamental shift in planning practices for Saskatoon. Elected to City Council in 1979 on this issue, she served for twenty-four years (1979–2003), Saskatoon's longest serving woman councilor to date. Waygood was Saskatchewan Governor to Heritage Canada from 1987 to 1994, and Chair from 1992 to 1994. She received the Saskatoon YWCA Rosalee Early Award for her contribution to Community Heritage in 1984, the Distinguished Contribution Planning Award from the Association of Community Planners of Saskatchewan in 1995, and the Saskatoon YWCA Women of Distinction Award in the area of Heritage and Culture in 1997. Since 2000, Waygood has been co-director of the Community-University Institute for Social Research (CUISR) in Saskatoon.

A. Margaret Sarjeant

WEBSTER, DAVID (1885–1952). Born in 1885, David Webster was one of Saskatoon's first architects, opening his practice in 1906. He was responsible for the design of the castle-style Saskatoon schools built between 1910 and 1914: Caswell, Albert, King Edward, Westmount, King George, and Sutherland. Other well-known projects from this period include the King George Hotel, City Hospital Nurses' Residence on King Street, and Hopkins House on Saskatchewan Crescent West. From 1915 to 1918 Webster served in wartime Europe; he resumed his practice in 1919. Post-war projects included the Modern Press Building, Royal Canadian Legion on 19th Street, the Capital Theatre (associate architect), the Saskatchewan **NORMAL SCHOOL**, Saskatoon Police Station, and the Post Office Building. In 1930 he formed a partnership with Edward Gilbert. During the lean years of the 1930s their major projects included Saskatoon Armouries, Davis Dairies, Saskatoon City Hall and Civic Centre, and the Ukrainian National Federation Hall.

SASKATCHEWAN ARCHIVES BOARD R-A6420
David Webster.

In 1939 his son John became a partner in the firm, and Webster left to become Deputy Minister of Public Works for Saskatchewan until 1948, leaving to supervise the construction of University Hospital until 1950. Webster was elected a Fellow of the Royal Architectectural Institute of Canada in 1930. He held membership card Number One from the Saskatchewan Association of Architects, and served as Association president for six terms between 1918 and 1936. David Webster died on January 01, 1952.

Ann March

FURTHER READING: E.J. Gilbert. 1969. *Up the Years with the S.A.A.* The Saskatchewan Association of Architects.

WEDGE, JAMES BALFOUR (1922–76). Born in Saskatoon on June 25, 1922, James Wedge attained his Bachelor of Science degree in accounting in 1944, and his law degree in 1948. He was named Queen's Counsel in 1960 and was employed with the firm Maguire, Wedge, McKercher & McKercher (now McKercher McKercher & Whitmore, LLP). Wedge served with the Canadian Infantry Corps and was a member of the naval reserves. He was active in the Saskatoon City Council, the Saskatchewan and Canadian Bar Associations, and was vice-president of the Saskatchewan Heart Foundation. James Balfour Wedge was invested as a Member of the Order of Canada in 1973. He died on April 2, 1976.

WEEDS. We commonly think of weeds as particular plant species such as wild oats, Canada thistle, or dandelions. A more general definition of a weed is a plant that is growing where someone does not want it to grow; a more optimistic definition of a weed is that it is a plant whose virtues have yet to be discovered. There are about 120 weed species infesting major field crops throughout the province, the vast majority of which are not native. Most originated in Europe and Eurasia, and were introduced into Saskatchewan by explorers and early settlers. Some arrived as contaminants in livestock feed, in packing material, or in grain to be used for planting the first crops. Others were introduced as ornamentals and have escaped cultivation to become serious weed problems. Of the forty-one weed species that have been declared noxious under the province's Noxious Weeds Act, thirty-nine are not native to the province.

Weeds are one of the major constraints to profitable crop production. It is commonly accepted that more time, energy and resources go into fighting weeds than in any other agricultural activity. Weeds cause major economic losses because they compete with crop plants for water, nutrients and light, and thus reduce crop yields. Crop yield reductions vary depending on a number of factors including: the weed species present (some are more competitive than others); the crop the weeds are growing in

(some crops are more competitive than others); the relative time of emergence of the weeds and the crop (weeds that emerge before the crop cause much greater losses than weeds that emerge after the crop is up); the weather conditions (some weeds do best in hot, dry conditions, others thrive in cooler, wetter conditions); and crop management practices such as seeding dates and rates, seeding depth, fertilizer amounts and placement, crop plant density and crop row spacing. Farmers can minimize crop losses due to weeds by adopting appropriate crop management practices and crop rotations. However, in spite of farmers' best efforts and the fact that they spend several hundred millions of dollars on herbicides each year, it is estimated that crop yield losses in Saskatchewan still amount to more than a half billion dollars annually.

While reductions in crop yield represent the major economic loss due to weeds, they can cause losses in other ways, interfere with human activities, and pose a danger to health. Some weed species can affect the grade, and thus the value, of crop and livestock products (absinthe in wheat, stinkweed-tainted milk). Some weeds are toxic to livestock and may result in death or reduced productivity. Sharp awns and burs can cause physical injury and discomfort to livestock, and can also lead to reduced production or product quality. The presence of green weeds in a mature crop can delay crop harvest, and this may result in losses from weathering or sprouting. Green weed material that contaminates grain can lead to heating and spoilage of the grain in storage. Weeds also cause problems by reducing water flows in irrigation canals and drainage ditches, and by increasing snow-plowing costs on highways and secondary roads. Some weeds contribute to the discomfort endured by hay-fever sufferers and asthmatics; others such as poison ivy and stinging nettles are severe skin irritants; and some such as poison hemlock are extremely toxic to humans.

A wide variety of control measures which have been developed to aid in the battle against weeds can be categorized as follows: prevention aims to avoid the introduction of new weed species into an area or to prevent the spread of existing species to uninfested areas; cultural controls include crop rotations and crop management practices that aim to maximize the competitiveness of crops against weeds. Examples include the use of high-quality seed, optimum seeding rate, date and depth, optimum fertilizer rates, and placement and appropriate row spacing. Mechanical (physical) controls include the use of mulches, timely mowing, tillage, and burning to prevent or destroy weed growth. Chemical control involves the use of non-selective and selective herbicides to control weed growth. After the introduction of 2,4-D to Saskatchewan in 1946, selective herbicides quickly became the preferred means of weed control on most farms, and they still hold that position. The recent, widespread adoption of zero-tillage/direct-seeding crop production systems is largely due to the availability and relatively low price of the non-selective herbicide, glyphosate, and a wide variety of selective herbicides that control a broad spectrum of weeds in crops. Biological control utilizes a living organism (insects, diseases, and grazing animals) to control weeds. Successful control of some weeds in Saskatchewan has been achieved with insects, but development of biological controls is a slow, difficult process. Integrated weed management refers to the practice of integrating several control measures.

It is unlikely that weeds can be entirely eliminated. Weedy plant species have evolved along with agriculture for the past 10,000 years and have repeatedly demonstrated their resilience and ability to adapt to all of the management practices, and to control the measures farmers and weed scientists have been able to devise. Some species have adapted well enough to survive in highly disturbed areas and so thrive where soils are intensively tilled. Others are best adapted to undisturbed sites, and become more problematical in fields that are under zero-till or direct-seeding management systems. Many weedy species are capable of producing large quantities of seed, and have evolved very effective seed dispersal mechanisms that involve wind, water, animals, birds, and humans. Many have developed varying degrees of seed dormancy that constitute a very effective survival mechanism. Some weeds, especially perennial species, can propagate and spread by both seed dispersal and vegetative means. More recently, some weed species have evolved resistance to herbicides: this continues to be an increasing problem in Saskatchewan and throughout the world, wherever crop production involves the intensive use of herbicides. As a result, more attention is being paid to the development and adoption of integrated weed management strategies that aim to reduce our reliance on chemical herbicides. However, weeds are extremely adaptable and have shown that they can survive in virtually every agricultural situation. Thus the farmer's goal is not to eradicate weeds, but to adopt economical and environmentally sustainable weed management practices that minimize their impact and spread.

F.A. (Rick) Holm

WEIGH-IN-MOTION SCALE. International Road Dynamics (IRD) is a Saskatoon-based company that has refined and marketed around the world a weigh-in-motion (WIM) scale designed in the 1970s by a group of transportation engineers at the **UNIVERSITY OF SASKATCHEWAN**. The automatic scale, developed under the direction of Professor Art Bergan, could capture key information about vehicles passing over computer-assisted scales without requiring the vehicle to stop. In fact, the technology

COURTESY OF INTERNATIONAL ROAD DYNAMICS

Installation of a weigh-in-motion scale.

was accurate at obtaining weights for vehicles traveling at speeds up to 112 km/hour with axle weights of up to 50,000 pounds each. Bergan went on to establish IRD, a Saskatoon firm of which his son Terry is now president and which specializes in supplying products and systems to the global Intelligent Transportation Systems (ITS) industry. Private corporations, transportation agencies, and highway authorities around the world use IRD's products and advanced systems to manage and protect their highway infrastructures. Integrated with a number of other communications and data collection technologies, IRD's WIM systems help to reduce costs significantly for commercial vehicle operators, while extending the life of highways and improving roadway efficiency and safety.

Joe Ralko

WEIR, ROBERT (1882–1939). Weir was born in Wigham in Huron County, Ontario, on December 5, 1882. He worked his way through normal school and completed a physics degree from the University of Toronto in his spare time. Weir taught mathematics at Regina Collegiate before **WORLD WAR I**, when he enlisted in the Canadian Army and quickly rose to the rank of major. Wounded during the battle of Passchendaele, Weir finished the war in a military hospital in London. He was a school inspector when he returned to Saskatchewan in 1919, but quit on doctor's advice and began farming in an attempt to improve his health. He acquired a mixed farming operation near Melfort and established a breeding program for purebred horses, cattle, sheep and swine.

Weir won the Melfort riding for the Conservatives in the 1930 federal election and was appointed Minister of Agriculture in the new R.B. Bennett government. When the prairie wheat pools could not make payments for wheat contracts, the federal government took control over wheat sales,

which led to the re-establishment of the **CANADIAN WHEAT BOARD** in 1935. He provided the foundation for the Prairie Farm Rehabilitation Act in 1935 that sought to promote agricultural land improvement to help alleviate the effects of the Depression and to provide work for unemployed labourers. As the federal Minister from Saskatchewan, Weir, along with Railway Minister R.J. Manion, was appointed to negotiate for the federal government with the On-to-Ottawa trekkers. Weir was defeated in the 1935 election. He returned to his farm but was killed in a farm accident on March 7, 1939.

Brett Quiring

FURTHER READING: Abel, P.M. 1930. "Saskatchewan's Cincinnatus," *Country Guide* (September); Howard, Victor. 1985. *"We Were the Salt of the Earth!": The On-To-Ottawa Trek and the Regina Riot.* Regina: Canadian Plains Research Center.

SASKATCHEWAN ARCHIVES BOARD R-B11272

Robert Weir.

WELSH SETTLEMENT. The Welsh are one of the smallest ethnic groups in the Saskatchewan population. One of the principal reasons for their relative paucity was that the mines and metalworks of Wales were attracting large numbers of migrants during Saskatchewan's pioneering period, so the Welsh rural surplus had a closer and more convenient destination. By 1921, only 1,587 Welsh immigrants were recorded in Saskatchewan, a mere 0.21% of the provincial population, although this is an underestimate as many emigrants from Wales were often labelled as British. Subsequently, small numbers of Welsh continued to arrive in the province and raise families; by the 2001 census, 13,935 people claimed Welsh ancestry, of whom 965 (6.9%) claimed Welsh-only ethnicity, compared to 12,965 (93.0%) who claimed to be partly of Welsh origin. Together they comprised just 1.45 % of the total provincial population.

Most early Welsh immigrants scattered throughout the region, although by 1921 52 % were in census divisions 5, 6, 7 and 11, and within these areas 19.5% were in the three cities of Saskatoon, Regina and Moose Jaw. The major exception to this dispersion lies in the distinctive Welsh settlement area around Bangor, in southeastern Saskatchewan. However, the 250 Welsh settlers who arrived in 1902-03 were actually immigrants from the Welsh colony in Patagonia, southern Argentina: they were attracted by the prospect of homestead land as well as the imposition of the Spanish language and Argentine military conscription on the formerly Welsh school system in the Chubut settlement. Welsh members of Parliament helped raise money for the charter of a vessel to bring them to Canada. Soon after they arrived, they established three school districts: Llewellyn in 1903, and Glendwyr and St. David's in 1904. In addition, their religiosity led them to create four mainly Welsh congregation churches in the area: St. Asaph's Anglican (1902), St. David's Anglican (1907), Llewelyn Bethel United (1910), and Seion United (1911, dissolved in the 1960s). As with most small ethnic groups that do not have a constant replenishment from the homeland, they have largely lost their language and culture. However the concentration of Welsh names in the area still survives, together with a pride in the Welsh heritage that led to a major centennial celebration in the summer of 2002 and to a book of family histories.

But the Welsh cannot only be considered in relation to the settlement of the province. One of the most influential figures in the early 19th century mapping of western Canada was **DAVID THOMPSON**, born in London of Welsh-speaking parents. In addition, many major figures in Saskatchewan life were of Welsh heritage. Prominent among these were two Premiers (**WOODROW LLOYD** and **ALLAN BLAKENEY**), Lewis H. Thomas, a pioneering archivist of the

province in 1948–57, Howard Richards and Adrian Seabourne, both graduates of the University of Wales who became professors of geography at the two universities (the latter was also instrumental in the development of rugby in the province), and George Taylor, from Blackwood in Wales, who was one of the province's prominent labour lawyers in the 1970s. These provide a few examples of how the Welsh, despite their small numbers, have helped the development of the province. (*See also* **ETHNIC BLOC SETTLEMENTS, ENGLISH SETTLEMENTS**)   *Wayne Davies*

WESSON, JOHN HENRY (1887–1965). John Henry Wesson was born near Sheffield, England in August 1887. In 1907 the family immigrated to Canada, settling on a homestead near Maidstone, Saskatchewan. Upon arrival, "Jack" Wesson joined the Saskatchewan Grain Growers Association, serving as a board member from 1917 to 1924. He was a persuasive exponent of the principle of co-operation, and was active in the organization of the **SASKATCHEWAN CO-OPERATIVE ELEVATOR COMPANY**. In 1924, Wesson was elected to the board of directors of Saskatchewan Co-operative Wheat Producers Limited, later to be known as the **SASKATCHEWAN WHEAT POOL**. He became Pool president in 1937 and continued in that role until his retirement in 1960. He was active in bringing most of the major farm organizations of Canada together in the Canadian Federation of Agriculture in 1937, and became first president of that organization. Following **WORLD WAR II**, Wesson worked with leaders of farm movements in other countries to bring about the establishment of the International Federation of Agricultural Producers. In recognition of his contribution in helping to mobilize the full resources of agriculture in the support of Canada's war effort, Wesson was made a Commander of the British Empire in 1946. The **UNIVERSITY OF SASKATCHEWAN** in 1961 conferred upon Jack Wesson the honorary degree of Doctor of Laws. The citation presenting him to convocation contained these words: "His

SASKATCHEWAN ARCHIVES BOARD R-A15276-2

John Henry Wesson.

voice became the voice of Prairie wheat farmers and upon occasions, the voice of the whole of Canadian agriculture. With purpose and dignity he spoke, and was listened to, in provincial, national and international councils. Wherever the welfare of the Canadian farmer was discussed, John Wesson was to be found, and the weight of his judgment and influence was to be felt." He was posthumously inducted into the Saskatchewan Agricultural Hall of Fame in 1973.

WESTERN ALIENATION. Western alienation refers to the longstanding regional discontent in British Columbia, Alberta, Saskatchewan and Manitoba. Since the early settlement of the prairies, western Canadians have expressed dissatisfaction with the geographic distribution of power and influence across Canada. Western Canadians feel that their provinces are not given their fair share of federal transfer dollars, and that western interests are poorly represented in the federal government. These feelings have been relatively consistent over time, despite considerable changes in the western Canadian demography, economy, political landscape and global environment.

Western alienation's roots lie in the quasi-colonial nature of the region's development. The west was in many ways the creation of the federal government and its policies. It was a debtor region, with debt largely held by central Canadian financial institutions; and western Canadians confronted a national government that was geographically and psychologically distant from their own region and concerns.

Numerous policy decisions inflamed western alienation over the 20th century, as western Canadians viewed national policies as corrosive to western interests and aspirations. For example, from 1879 to the end of **WORLD WAR II**, a large source of regional discontent was the National Policy, a tariff policy that was seen to benefit central Canada alone, while increasing costs for goods across Canada. In 1980, the National Energy Program was seen to have damaged the Alberta and Saskatchewan economies for the benefit of central Canada. However, specific policy grievances are matched by an equally large grievance that western Canada is not treated equitably: many western Canadians feel that western interests are seen as "regional" rather than "national," and that people outside the west are not concerned with the interests of western Canada.

Over the decades, western Canadian efforts to improve the representation of western interests in the federal government have included protest parties, populism, as well as calls for decentralization and for electoral and Senate reform. To date, none of these efforts has been successful at creating systematic change in the distribution of power in Canada, and western alienation remains high after more than a century.

Overall, western alienation is deeply rooted in the west and is an integral part of the west's political culture. While residents in all four western provinces express regional discontent, Saskatchewan and British Columbia residents are found to be the most aggrieved, while Manitoba residents are the least dissatisfied. Albertans, despite their long-standing outspokenness on regional issues, tend to fall between their highly discontented (Saskatchewan and British Columbia) and less discontented (Manitoba) neighbours.   *Loleen Berdahl*

WESTERN CANADA SEDIMENTARY BASIN.

A sedimentary basin such as the Western Canada Sedimentary Basin is a large geological feature comprised of thick sedimentary deposits. It is a repository for sedimentary rocks, many of which were deposited above sea level or in shallow seas but are now found at considerable depth as a result of subsidence of the crust that accompanied sedimentation. The Western Canada Sedimentary Basin forms the northern portion of a much larger basinal feature that extends from the Gulf of Mexico to the mouth of the Mackenzie River. Geographically, it underlies the interior plains physiographic province and extends from the eastern edge of the Canadian Rocky Mountain system to the southwestern margin of the Canadian Shield. In simplest terms, the Western Canada Basin may be regarded as a wedge of sub-horizontal sedimentary strata above Precambrian crystalline basement. This wedge has a maximum thickness of about 5,500 m along the

edge of the Rocky Mountain Foothills, and generally thins northeastward to a zero-edge along the margin with the Canadian Shield (*see* Figure WCSB-1). This simple wedge is modified by a thickening to about 3,300 m in the **WILLISTON BASIN** in southern Saskatchewan. There is marked thinning over a major structure in southern Alberta (Sweet Grass Arch).

Consolidated rocks that comprise the sedimentary wedge range in geological age from Cambrian to late Tertiary. The Cambrian strata were formed about 550 million years ago and rest on older deformed crystalline rocks of Precambrian age. The youngest consolidated rocks were deposited about five million years ago. Much of the upper surface of the sedimentary wedge is masked by unconsolidated glacial drift laid down by continental ice sheets during the Pleistocene Epoch (about two million to 11,000 years before present). Western Canada Sedimentary Basin strata can be referred to two broad divisions that reflect contrasting geological conditions: the lower succession of Cambrian to Jurassic age (to about 350 million years before present) is composed largely of carbonate rocks, with an important component of evaporite minerals (anhydrite, halite and potash), and was formed before the major uplift of the Canadian Cordillera; the upper succession of mid-Jurassic to Tertiary age, which consists mainly of shale and sandstone, was deposited following major mountain building and uplift in the Cordillera. (*see also* **GEOLOGY**, **MINERAL RESOURCES**, **ELK POINT SEA**)   *Laurence Vigrass*

WESTERN COLLEGE OF VETERINARY MEDICINE.

In the first University of Saskatchewan's *President's Report* (1908–09), President **WALTER MURRAY** recommended that the University make a provision for a "College of Veterinary Science" in the building plans for the University.

Although a College was not established until 1963, classes in veterinary sciences were taught through the College of Agriculture in 1913 and an animal diseases laboratory was established in 1924. Eminent research parasitologist Seymour Hadwen served as a research professor at the University of Saskatchewan from 1923 to 1929, during which time he became the first Canadian veterinarian elected to fellowship in the Royal Society of Canada (1926). In 1930 Dr. J.S. Fulton was named head of the Veterinary Sciences Department, where he gained national and international fame by developing vaccines used to prevent Western Equine Encephalitis (WEE) in horses in the late 1930s. The University began selling the vaccine in 1939 for 75¢, undercutting the cost of a similar vaccine sold in the United States for $1.80 per dosage. Revenues from the sale of the vaccine financed the construction of the Virus Laboratory Building (renamed the J.S. Fulton Laboratory in 1964) from 1947 to 1948. Dr. Fulton also discovered that the same virus caused a human disease previously diagnosed as non-paralytic poliomyelitis and produced a vaccine for humans. From 1947 until 1972, one of the first women veterinary scientists in Canada, Dr. Althea Burton, worked on WEE.

The **DEPRESSION** of the 1930s and the higher priorities of a medical school, an arts building and an adequate library postponed the construction of a Western College of Veterinary Medicine. In 1957 Professor V.E. Graham's survey of current and anticipated needs found the average values of livestock in the western provinces over the previous seven years amounted to $679.5 million. He determined that 350 veterinarians were needed in the western provinces but at the time there were only 50 veterinarians in private practice in Saskatchewan. Clearly the veterinary colleges in Ontario and Quebec were not supplying enough veterinarians to the western provinces and something had to be done. Finally, in 1963 an agreement was reached and the federal government provided capital funding support of 25%; the province of Saskatchewan committed $1 million and the four western provinces agreed to share the operating costs. The University was authorized to begin recruiting staff for the Western College of Veterinary Medicine on August 29, 1963. The first classes were held in 1965 in an interim-housing unit built to satisfy the federal government's insistence that classes begin immediately. Construction on the main building began in 1966, and occupancy and official dedication occurred in 1969. A major expansion of these facilities was

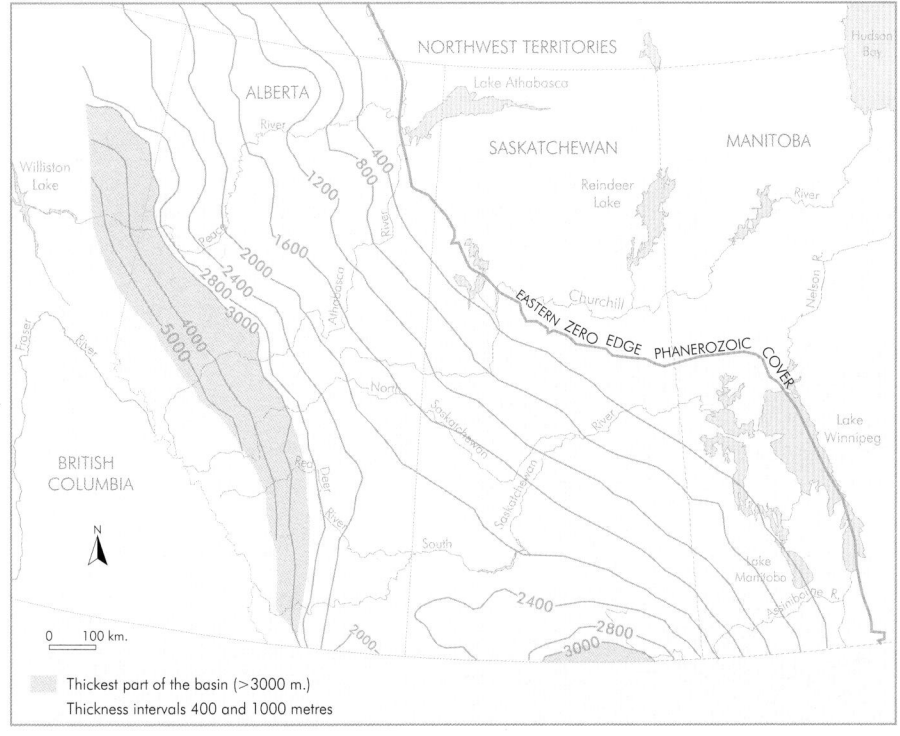

Figure WCSB-1. Western Canada Sedimentary Basin showing thickness of sedimentary strata above Precambrian basement.

completed in 1981 and in 1988.

The University of Saskatchewan is now a major veterinary medical centre in Canada. The Western College of Veterinary Medicine focuses on teaching, research and services and is the only veterinary teaching hospital in Canada with an MRI dedicated to pets and the only facility in western Canada able to provide radiation therapy for animal cancer patients. The presence of the College led to the establishment on campus of a federal Animal Pathology Laboratory; VIDO (a self-reliant veterinary research institution); the Toxicology Centre; the Canadian Co-operative Wildlife Health Centre and the Prairie Diagnostic Services.   *N. Ole Nielsen*

WESTERN DEVELOPMENT MUSEUM. The Western Development Museum (WDM) began as a grassroots movement to preserve prairie agricultural history: responding to the need to rescue artifacts from a fast-disappearing heritage, the Saskatchewan government passed the Western Development Museum Act in 1949.

The first formal WDM location to admit visitors in 1949 was a refurbished hangar building in North Battleford, followed during the same year by a similar structure in Saskatoon. A third hangar was procured in Yorkton and opened to the public in 1951. It was not until 1976 that the fourth WDM exhibit branch opened in Moose Jaw. This was the first branch to open in a building specifically constructed for the Museum; but by then new facilities had been erected in both Saskatoon and Yorkton, and the North Battleford branch had relocated to another, improved hangar building. This was upgraded in the mid-1980s with the addition of a new, all-season exhibit wing. In 1984, with an ever-growing collection of artifacts and with new exhibits continually being developed, the WDM acquired and renovated a large warehouse in Saskatoon to accommodate centralized services including collections, conservation, research, exhibits, education and public programs, and marketing and administration. The WDM Curatorial Centre, as this facility eventually was renamed, includes a large area of environmentally controlled storage to house the portion of the WDM collection currently not on display in any of the four exhibit branches. The entire collection is comprised of approximately 80,000 artifacts.

Although the WDM mandate, as prescribed in the WDM Act, applies to all locations, each branch has developed its own particular focus. By 1989, the nature of this growth had evolved sufficiently to inspire adoption of individual theme names. The Moose Jaw branch is now referred to as the History of Transportation; the North Battleford branch as the Heritage Farm & Village; Saskatoon as 1910 Boomtown; and Yorkton as the Story of People. Core funding for operation is received from the province of Saskatchewan, and the communities within which the four branches reside offer varying levels of local assistance. The WDM operation is served by permanent and temporary staff as well as a large volunteer contingent. Annual visitation to exhibits and a wide range of public and education programs has exceeded 200,000 for all locations. The Western Development Museum promises to evolve and grow as a major custodian of Saskatchewan's history.

David Klatt

WETTLAUFER, BOYD N. (1914–). Boyd Wettlaufer was born in 1914 at Asquith, Saskatchewan and raised in Bracebridge, Ontario. He became interested in archaeology as a youngster. While serving with the RCAF during WORLD WAR II, he visited the National Museum of Canada in Ottawa and, learning that professional archaeology was poorly developed throughout the country and virtually non-existent in the west, was encouraged to get the proper training in the discipline. Following the war he enrolled at the University of New Mexico, where he majored in archaeology and minored in geology before returning to Canada for fieldwork. His important 1951 report for the National Museum described the location and contents of 202 sites, listed the names of 324 collectors, and assessed the general state and potential for archaeology in southern Saskatchewan. During the early 1950s he directed a landmark excavation at the Mortlach site, generating several firsts for Canadian archaeology: first use of the radiocarbon dating method (seven cultures dated between 1445 BC and AD 1780); first use of the multidisciplinary approach; and first naming of archaeological cultures on the prairies. His subsequent excavations at the Long Creek site in 1957 extended the northern plains archaeological record by another 1,500 years, to 3000 BC.

Boyd Wettlaufer's pioneering contributions to prairie archaeology have remained of fundamental importance for more than fifty years. In 2004, he was invested as a Member of the Order of Canada, and was awarded an honorary life membership by the Saskatchewan Archaeological Society. In 1983 the Society dedicated to him its book, *Tracking Ancient Hunters*, with the recognition that he "lifted Saskatchewan archaeology out of the realm of speculation and placed it on a firm foundation."

Ian Dyck

WEYBURN. Weyburn, population 9,534, is located on the Souris River in southeastern Saskatchewan, about 75 km from the American border and 116 km southeast of Regina at the juncture of three major highways including the east-west TransCanada and of major routes into Canada's north and Alaska. Some claim that Weyburn was named after the brother-in-law of a railway construction contractor; others, however, believe that the city got its name when, on a hot summer's afternoon, an exploring Scot came across the SOURIS RIVER and exclaimed "Wee Burn!" Original buffalo trails, buffalo rubbing stones, effigies of a medicine wheel, and a medicine snake have been found in the area south of the T.C. Douglas Centre, indicating that First Nations settlement in the area dates back to the late 1800s. This area is located on the highest point for miles around, and is named Signal Hill because smoke signals originating there could be seen a great distance.

The community of Weyburn was founded in 1899, and a settlement started to take shape around

EVERETT BAKER PHOTO/COURTESY OF THE SASKATCHEWAN HISTORY AND FOLKLORE SOCIETY

Boyd Wettlaufer with 13 cultural strata marked at the Mortlach site, September 11, 1954.

a station house and freight shed. In 1902, an influx of Americans brought in a number of new business enterprises from across the border, and Weyburn was incorporated as a village. On August 5, 1903, Weyburn was incorporated as a town, and it achieved city status on September 1, 1913. Weyburn City Hall was constructed in 1914. The **SOO LINE RAILWAY** runs through Weyburn, connecting western Canada's main rail lines at Moose Jaw with the American rail centres in Minneapolis and Chicago. Weyburn is also on the rim of the **WILLISTON BASIN**, one of the richest oil sources on the North American prairies. As one of the largest Saskatchewan cities near the Williston Basin's vast oil deposits, Weyburn has become an oilfield service centre: more than 600 wells operate in the immediate area.

From the first days of settlement, Weyburn's rich prairie soils have produced a substantial share of western Canada's exportable wheat, making this city the country's highest-volume inland grain-handling centre. From this have grown a major farm service and supply sector, as well as the site of Canada's largest privately owned inland grain terminal, the **WEYBURN INLAND TERMINAL**. Oil and agricultural production continue to dominate Weyburn's economy. *Daria Coneghan*

WEYBURN INLAND TERMINAL. Weyburn Inland Terminal (WIT) is the first inland grain terminal in Canada to be completely owned and operated by farmers. The $5.5 million grain-handling facility, located on Highway 39 about 3.5 km southeast of Weyburn, opened November 2, 1976, with a 540,000 tonne annual throughput capacity for wheat, barley and other grains.

The terminal was built after 1,300 southern Saskatchewan farmers, who wanted to add more responsiveness and fairness to Canada's grain-handling system, raised the $1.6 million needed to begin construction. The terminal was built despite opposition from the provincial government, **SASKATCHEWAN WHEAT POOL**, National Farmers Union and various churches. Many of the concerns were that the terminal would contribute further to the decline in small towns and the depopulation of rural Saskatchewan as well as increase the traffic of grain trucks on Saskatchewan highways.

The early years were difficult and, due to inexperience and an unchanging grain-handling industry, the company lost money. An ingenious refinancing scheme saved WIT in 1980 and the company has had steady profits since 1990. The company is now one of the most profitable grain-handling facilities in Canada with the latest expansion in 2001 bringing WIT's total capacity to 112,000 tonnes, four times its original size. The company offers cleaning and drying of grain, storage grain condominium facilities, a pelleting plant, fertilizer and chemicals sales. WIT can dry sixty tonnes of grain per hour

and clean 200 tonnes of wheat per hour. About 600 tonnes can be shipped per hour. WIT also owns Vigro Seed and Supply in Sedley, a specialty seed cleaning business, and the grain elevator at Lake Alma, Saskatchewan.

Weyburn Inland Terminal Ltd. has amassed an impressive list of fourteen "firsts" since its creation, including being the first in Canada to do protein testing, cleaning and drying of grain on the prairies, as well as the first in Canada to build grain condominium storage units. WIT was the first to pay farmers for the refuse in their grain and the first to win the **CANADIAN WHEAT BOARD** "Quality First" award for excellence in handling shipments to American mills. *Deanna Driver*

WEYERHAEUSER. Weyerhaeuser came to Saskatchewan in 1986 with the purchase of Prince Albert Pulp Company, including the Prince Albert Pulp Mill and Saskatoon Chemicals, from the Saskatchewan government. Through the transaction, Weyerhaeuser also acquired from the province a sawmill near Big River. As part of the acquisition agreement, Weyerhaeuser committed to construct an uncoated free sheet fine paper mill in Prince Albert. This was completed in August 1988; two sheeting machines to supply the customer-size sheet market were added in 1990 and 1991. Since 1986, Weyerhaeuser has upgraded its pre-existing Saskatchewan facilities. The largest investment was an economic and environmental enhancement project at Prince Albert Pulp & Paper, which was completed in 2000; this $315-million project reduced the amount of electricity and natural gas Weyerhaeuser purchases to operate the pulp and paper mill. In May 1999, the Wapawekka Lumber Ltd. sawmill was opened near Prince Albert, a $22.5-million joint venture between Weyerhaeuser and the Lac la Ronge Indian Band, Montreal Lake Cree Nation, and Peter Ballantyne Cree Nation. An extensive upgrade of Weyerhaeuser's Big River sawmill was completed in March 2001, which increased the sawmill's annual capacity from 90 million to 210 million board feet of dimensional softwood lumber.

On November 1, 1999, Weyerhaeuser acquired **MACMILLAN BLOEDEL**, adding two oriented strand board mills in Hudson Bay to its holdings in Saskatchewan: the **CARROT RIVER** sawmill and the Hudson Bay plywood mill. The newer oriented strand board mill in Hudson Bay (OSB 2000) was officially opened in June 2001; this $200-million mill has annual production capacity of 600 million square feet of OSB. The Carrot River sawmill has capacity to produce 80 million board feet of stud-length lumber annually. The Hudson Bay plywood mill has an annual capacity of 112 million square feet of softwood plywood. In 2004, Weyerhaeuser directly employed more than 1,600 Saskatchewan residents at its manufacturing facilities, and was

licensed to operate on 4.94 million hectares of forest in Saskatchewan. *Wayne Roznowsky*

WHEAT. Wheat production in Canada dates back to the early 17th century. It spread westward from present-day Quebec, reaching Manitoba in the early 19th century with the Selkirk settlers. The first recorded attempt at growing wheat in present-day Saskatchewan took place in the **CARROT RIVER** Valley some time between 1753 and 1756, and is ascribed to the Frenchman Chevalier de La Corne. Commercial production of spring wheat likely started in the 1880s with the introduction of the cultivar Red Fife. Wheat rapidly became the most important crop grown in Saskatchewan, reaching four million hectares by 1919.

Wheat is currently grown from the US-Canadian border north to the fringes of the cultivated land base, across all Saskatchewan soil types–which reflects the crop's wide adaptation. The majority (>99%) of the wheat produced in Saskatchewan is grown under dryland conditions. Wheat is grown twelve months of the year when one takes into account spring and fall-sown types. Saskatchewan currently accounts for roughly 60% of the wheat grown in western Canada; in the province, wheat accounts for 44% of the area sown to crops (excluding tame/seeded pasture).

Currently there are seven market types and two species of wheat grown in Saskatchewan. Common wheat (*Triticum aestivum* L.) is grown on 4,136,302 ha, based on the five-year (1998–2002) average (SAFRR, 2003), and accounts for five of the market types. Of the common wheat grown in Saskatchewan, 98.8% has a spring growth habit. The Canada Western Red Winter class is currently the sole market class with a winter growth habit. Of the spring wheats, the Canada Western Red Spring (CWRS) wheat class represents approximately 85.5% of the spring-sown common wheat production in Saskatchewan. The remaining area is divided between Canada Prairie Spring Red (CPSR), Canada Prairie Spring White (CPSW), Canada Western Extra Spring (CWES), and Canada Western Soft White (CSWS). The CPS class accounts for approximately 12% of the area–the split between red-grained and white-grained varieties fluctuating in recent years, with a shift to red-grained types. The CWES class accounted for 3% of the spring wheat area in 1997, but has since dropped to about 1% as a result of reduced market opportunities. The CSWS class is limited to production under irrigation, and is grown in trace amounts (0.05% of the seeded spring wheat acreage).

The CWRS wheat class is considered a high-protein premium bread wheat. However, this type of wheat has proven to be quite versatile in its end-uses, ranging from noodles to bread. Grain protein levels typically range between 13% and 15%. The

COURTESY OF TOURISM SASKATCHEWAN

Wheat.

Marquis variety, released in 1909, was the benchmark for what eventually became known as CWRS wheat. Current varieties of CWRS wheat tend to have higher protein levels and stronger gluten characteristics than Marquis and its early progeny. The CPS class was created in 1985 with the registration of the variety HY320. This class was designed to address markets that do not require a premium high-protein product. Typically, CPS wheats are 15%–20% higher yielding than CWRS wheats, with a protein level that is 1% to 1.5% units lower. CPSR wheat varieties are meant to be used in the production of flat and French-type breads. In recent years, however, high-yielding CPSR varieties have been used as livestock feed and a starch source for ethanol production. The CPSW class is meant to address market needs in the Pacific Rim. The primary end-use being targeted by CPSW wheat is the production of oriental noodles; to date, this has largely been a market-development effort. CWES wheat has very strong gluten properties, and was initially developed as a blending wheat to "carry" low-protein, weak-gluten European wheat flours. With the advent of gluten extraction factories and the imposition of crippling import tariffs into the EU, the CWES class lost its intended primary markets. A secondary market was developed in the USA, but this was in turn lost once the USA developed its own extra-strong gluten wheat varieties. The CWSW class has been grown on a limited scale in Saskatchewan since the early 1970s. CWSW wheat is a low-protein wheat used to make pastry and cookie flours. The low-protein (< 11.0%) requirement necessitates irrigation to maximize grain yield and to control the crop's nitrogen status. Winter wheat tends to be higher yielding (by 12% to 25%) than CWRS wheat if early season moisture is adequate. Red winter wheat traditionally has had excellent milling quality. The protein level of winter wheat

tends to be similar to that of CPS wheat. As is the case with CPSR wheat, a significant portion of current winter wheat production is being used as livestock feed. In order for winter wheat to survive the winters in Saskatchewan, it is seeded into standing crop stubble which traps snow; the latter in turn provides insulation to the winter wheat seedling crown as it over-winters.

The second species of wheat (*Triticum durum*) grown in Saskatchewan is represented by one market type, the Canada Western Amber Durum (CWAD) class. Durum wheat production in Saskatchewan was initiated in the 1920s and has grown to be the second most widely produced wheat in Canada. The area seeded to CWAD wheat in Saskatchewan averaged 1,879,892 ha between 1998 and 2002. Saskatchewan accounts for roughly 83% of Canadian durum wheat production, which is concentrated in the traditionally lower-rainfall portions of the province, the brown and dark brown soil zones. Durum wheat typically has a protein level similar to that of CWRS wheat; it is used in the manufacture of pasta, bulgur, couscous, and bread. Within the last five years a subtype of CWAD durum has been introduced: the Extra Strong CWAD subclass addresses a preference for very strong gluten durum types in the Italian market. It is anticipated that up to 15% of CWAD production in Saskatchewan could shift to this ES type once more varieties are in place.

Over the last twenty years, common wheat production in Saskatchewan has declined by 37% while the durum wheat area has increased by 13%. This change in production reflects higher returns for durum and continuing low prices for bread wheat, as a result of hefty subsidies for wheat production and export enhancement in the EU and the USA, relative to Canada.
Pierre Hucl

FURTHER READING: Slinkard, A.E. and D.B. Fowler (eds). 1986. *Wheat Production in Canada–A Review*. Saskatoon: University of Saskatchewan Extension Press; Slinkard, A.E. and D.R. Knott. 1995. *Harvest of Gold. The History of Field Crop Breeding in Canada*. Saskatoon: University of Saskatchewan Extension Press.

WHEELER, BERNELDA WINONA (1937–). Bernelda Wheeler was born on April 8, 1937, at Muskopetung. She lived on the Gordon First Nation Reserve until 1946, when her family moved to Manitoba. She attended Birtle and Brandon residential schools and graduated in 1955 from Churchill Public High School. She first worked in radio as an announcer for CBC Northern Service, and later returned to CBC radio, gaining recognition for her work on "Our Native Land" as a host, producer, and investigative documentary journalist. Referred to as the First Lady of Native Broadcasting, she received a special award for Native Broadcasting in Canada

(1982). In the late 1960s she had also turned to journalism, writing for newspaper columns in western Canada; today she writes three regular columns for *EagleFeather News*. She has also published many short stories and poetry, and is best known for her children's books. In 1983 Wheeler began theatre acting, and is a member of the Sage Ensemble theatre group.
Daria Coneghan

WHEELER, SEAGER (1868–1961). A native of the Isle of Wight, Seager Wheeler immigrated to Saskatchewan in 1885. After working for a few years on his uncle's farm near Clark's Crossing, he took up a homestead in the Rosthern district, specializing in seed production. In 1911 he won the world championship for **WHEAT** at the New York Land Show; in the seven years following he won four more world championships with wheat produced on his farm.

He originated several varieties of wheat, two of which, Kitchener and Red Bobs, made a significant contribution to the agricultural economy of western Canada. Although his name is usually associated with wheat, Wheeler also played an active role in the improvement of oats, barley, and potatoes. Wheeler joined the Canadian Seed Growers' Association in 1908 and took a leading part in its affairs throughout his lifetime. In 1919 his book, *Profitable Grain Growing*, was published by the *Grain Growers' Guide*. In recognition of his outstanding contribution to agriculture, an honorary Doctor of Laws degree was conferred upon him by Queen's University in 1919.

FURTHER READING: Friesen, V.C. 2001. *Where the River Runs: Stories of the Saskatchewan and the People Drawn to Its Shores*. Calgary: Fifth House.

SASKATCHEWAN ARCHIVES BOARD R-A8496-1

Seager Wheeler.

White's studies of coumarin in sweet clover formed the basis for later successful production of coumarin-free sweet clover, which helped to eliminate the problem of bloating in cattle. He developed the first sunflower hybrid, and contributed to the production of that crop in Canada and the United States. He crossed wheat with wheat grasses: this pioneering work later enabled plant breeders to transfer wheat stem rust resistance to wheat from a wheat grass. In recognition of his outstanding work, White became an honorary life member of the Canadian Seed Growers Association in 1961, Fellow of the Agricultural Institute of Canada in 1963, and recipient of the University of Minnesota outstanding achievement award in 1986. The Senate of the University of Saskatchewan established a William J. White Chair in the Crop Science (today Plant Sciences) Department, to which distinguished faculty members are named. He was inducted into the Saskatchewan Agricultural Hall of Fame in 1991. White died on February 28, 1993. *Daria Coneghan*

WHITE BEAR FIRST NATION. Chief Wahpemakwa (White Bear) signed TREATY 4 in 1875 and accepted a reserve on the east side of Moose Mountain in 1877. While his Cree and Saulteaux members explored some agriculture, they preferred to follow their traditional lifestyle. In 1901 the Ocean Man and Pheasant Rump Bands were amalgamated onto the reserve, with the promise that its boundaries would be extended; but it was two years before this occurred, and only after the band agreed to pay $1.23 an acre for the land. Descendants of the amalgamated communities became involved in a claim against the federal government to regain the surrendered reserves. This claim enabled the White Bear Band to invest funds received as part of the settlement for their own economic development. In recent years the band has assumed control of the White Bear Lake resort (1978–79), and built the White Bear Golf Course (1987, 1992), White Bear Oil and Gas, Ltd. (1993), and the White Bear Casino and Lodge (1996). Reserve facilities include the band office, an arena, powwow grounds, a health clinic, and a school gymnasium. Currently, 785 of the 2,118 band members live on the 12,038.4-ha reserve. *Christian Thompson*

WHITE CITY, town, pop 1,013, located 12 km E of Regina on Hwy 1. It is a bedroom community largely populated by urban professionals escaping the high property taxes of Regina. The community's origins date to the late 1950s, when farmland east of Regina was expropriated for the construction of the TRANS-CANADA HIGHWAY. The landowner chose to subdivide the rest, and White City had its beginnings. The population was 80 in 1966, 340 in 1976, 783 in 1986, and 907 in 1996. The community is known for its large homes situated on sizeable lots,

which, on average, measure 140 x 200 ft. Although many residents work in Regina, White City has a large manufacturer of steel products, a number of home-based businesses, and a K–8 school. White City and an adjacent residential development, Emerald Park, share golf courses and an array of other recreational facilities. *David McLennan*

WHITECAP DAKOTA FIRST NATION. Historically referred to as the Moose Woods Sioux Reserve, the 1,677.4-ha Whitecap Dakota Reserve is located 26 km south of Saskatoon. Chief Wapahaska (White Cap) and his band settled along the South Saskatchewan River, and though not having signed treaty they received a reserve in June 1881. Band members farmed and worked as wage labourers in Prince Albert and the surrounding area. White Cap was unwillingly swept into the 1885 Resistance, and following RIEL's surrender was tried for treason but was acquitted. Band members trickled back to the reserve to begin rebuilding, and in the process switched to raising cattle. Over the years they developed one of the largest, top-quality slaughter and breeding-stock herds in the district, and expanded to include dairy cattle and draught horses. When cattle prices fell in 1905, they opened what was probably the first commercial feedlot in Canada, wintering cattle on consignment for settlers, and finishing slaughter animals for meat buyers and packers. However, they were unable to remain competitive in the cattle market after WORLD WAR II, and while their economic ventures diversified, most band members turned to off-reserve employment. There are 456 registered band members, 222 of whom live on the reserve. *Christian Thompson*

WHITEWOOD, town, pop 947, located 21 km E of Broadview at the junction of Hwys 1 and 9. The CPR main line was built through the area in 1882; immediately Whitewood, its name derived from the white poplar trees in the area, became an important supply centre and point of disembarkation for multitudes of settlers of diverse origins. John Hawkes was the editor of the *Whitewood Herald* from 1897 to 1900, and later the first Saskatchewan Legislative Librarian and author of *The Story of Saskatchewan and Its People*. He described Whitewood in the 1880s as the most cosmopolitan place in the North-West, and added that to conduct business in the town at the time one ought to have known eleven languages. Finns, Swedes, Hungarians, Czechs, English, Scottish, and Irish settlers, among others, took up land in the region. One of the more interesting settlements to develop in the Whitewood district in the mid-1880s was that of a group of titled French and Belgian nobility. Much like the British gentry to the south at CANNINGTON MANOR, the "French Counts," as they were locally known, tried to build on the prairies a life similar to the aristocratic style

COURTESY OF WINONA WHEELER

Winona Wheeler.

WHEELER, WINONA L. (1958–). Born on April 25, 1958, in Victoria, British Columbia, Wheeler attended high school in Port Albeni before moving to Manitoba and graduating there. Upon her marriage in 1975 to her first husband, she became a member of the Fisher River First Nation. She earned a BA in History at the University of Manitoba (1986), an MA in History at the University of British Columbia (1988), and a PhD in Ethnic/Native American Studies, at the University of California, Berkeley (2000). In 1988 Wheeler became an assistant professor in the Department of Native Studies, UNIVERSITY OF SASKATCHEWAN; in 1996 she moved to what is now the FIRST NATIONS UNIVERSITY OF CANADA, Saskatoon Campus, where she is Dean.

Daria Coneghan

WHITE, WILLIAM JAMES (1908–93). William (Bill) White was born on December 18, 1908, on a farm at Ruddell, Saskatchewan. He obtained his bachelor's and master's degrees in Agriculture from the UNIVERSITY OF SASKATCHEWAN, and a doctorate degree from the University of Minnesota, specializing in plant breeding and genetics. White started with the Saskatchewan Department of Agriculture in 1934 as an agricultural promoter. In 1935 he moved to the federal service with the Dominion Forage Crops Laboratory in Saskatoon, serving seventeen years as Head. He was appointed Head of the Crop Science Department, University of Saskatchewan, in 1958. In 1965 he became Dean of Agriculture, a post he held until retirement in 1974. White's early research concerned alfalfa breeding and the role of tripping and cross-pollination in seed setting. White was the first rapeseed breeder in North America; he produced the varieties Golden and Nugget. Changes in breeding resulted in the crop which is today known as CANOLA.

to which they had been accustomed in Europe. They brought a retinue of servants along with all the accoutrements of a sophisticated society, built beautiful residences, and initiated a number of optimistic but ultimately unsuccessful business ventures–among them sheep ranching, a sugar beet plantation, a brush manufacturing company, and a cheese factory. For a variety of reasons, all of the business ventures failed, and by the early 1900s all of the "French Counts" had left, most returning to France. They did leave behind, however, the well-endowed parish of St. Hubert, southwest of Whitewood; the descendants of their servants and workers would contribute a French-speaking presence in the area. In April 1892, the first issue of the *Whitewood Herald* rolled off the press. It is now Saskatchewan's oldest continually published weekly newspaper and its editor, Chris Ashfield, is the fourth consecutive generation of his family involved with the province's weekly newspaper industry. By 1906, the population of Whitewood was over 500 and the town was a well-established trading centre for the surrounding agricultural district. Today, the area industry consists of mixed farms and livestock operations, with cereal grains and oilseeds being the main crops grown. Whitewood's St. Joseph's Church, built in 1959, was the first important work of notable Saskatchewan architect, **CLIFFORD WIENS**. Whitewood also has a number of heritage properties ranging from residences and commercial buildings to churches, many dating to the 1890s.

David McLennan

WICKENHEISER, HAYLEY (1978–). One of Canada's best women's ice hockey players, Hayley Wickenheiser was born in Shaunavon on August 12, 1978. She first played hockey on boys' teams and

PHOTO BY GARY M. HOUSTON, CYPRESS PARK

Hayley Wickenheiser, February 2004, at "Hockey Day in Canada" in Shaunavon, Saskatchewan.

later joined a girls' peewee league after the Wickenheiser family moved to Calgary in 1990. At age 15, she joined the Canadian women's national hockey team that won four gold medals at the 1994, 1997, 1999, and 2000 World Championships. The team also collected the silver medal at the 1998 Nagano Winter Olympics before winning gold at the 2002 Winter Games in Salt Lake City. Wickenheiser is also a talented softball player and was a member of the Canadian women's softball team that participated in the 2000 Summer Games in Sydney. She became the second Canadian woman to compete in both a summer and winter Olympiad. Wickenheiser is an advocate for women and girls in sport and speaks on the subject around the country.

Daria Coneghan and Holden Stoffel

FURTHER READING: Proctor, Steve, Dahlia Reich and Beverley Ware. 2002. *Heroes with Heart: Canadian Athletes You Can Look Up To.* Toronto: Winding Stair Press.

COURTESY OF THE OFFICE OF THE LIEUTENANT GOVERNOR

John "Jack" Wiebe.

WIEBE, JOHN E.N. (1936–). Farmer, former Liberal MLA, former **LIEUTENANT-GOVERNOR** of Saskatchewan, and former Senator, The Honourable Jack Wiebe was born in Herbert, Saskatchewan on May 31, 1936. Wiebe graduated from the University of Saskatchewan and built a successful farming operation in the Main Center district of the province. He was owner and president of L&W Feeders Ltd. from 1970 to 1985. A long-time Liberal strategist and fundraiser, he represented the constituency of Morse in the Saskatchewan Legislative Assembly from 1971 to 1978. Prime Minister Chretien appointed Wiebe the province's eighteenth Lieutenant-Governor on May 31, 1994, marking the first time a farmer held the vice-regal post since Reginald Parker (1945–48). Wiebe's term as the Queen's representative in Saskatchewan ended on February 16, 2000. Shortly thereafter, on April 6, he received a second government appointment, this time to the Canadian

Senate. Jack Wiebe retired from the Upper Chamber on January 31, 2004, citing family reasons for leaving seven years before the mandatory retirement age of 75.

Holden Stoffel

FURTHER READING: Cowan, Pamela. 1999. "A 'Royal' Couple." *Regina Sun* (December 26); Knisley, Jim. 1995. "Pomp, Pageantry & Power." *Regina Leader-Post*, D1 (March 25).

WIEBE, NETTIE (1949–). Nettie Wiebe, born on January 22, 1949, at Warman, Saskatchewan, graduated from the **UNIVERSITY OF SASKATCHEWAN** and received a PhD in Philosophy from the University of Calgary in 1983. A farmer and activist, she served as women's president of the National Farmers Union (NFU) from 1988 to 1994, and was president and CEO of the NFU from 1995 to 1998. She was also vice-chair of the Farmer Railcar Coalition from 1998 to 2004, and Via Campesina coordinator for North America/Mexico from 1996 to 2004. She is the author of several publications including: *Farm Women: Cultivating Hope and Sowing Change* (1995), *Weaving New Ways: Farm Women Organizing* (1987), and *Quest for Land* (1991). She is a speaker at local, national and international forums such as the GATT rally (Geneva, December 1993), IATP (Minneapolis, 1993), as well as a panelist in local and national forums. In 2001, she ran for the leadership of the provincial NDP, losing to **LORNE CALVERT**.

Daria Coneghan

WIENS, CLIFFORD (1926–). Clifford Wiens is one of the most influential architects ever to call Saskatchewan home. In a forty-year career starting in 1956, his Regina office produced a bold range of buildings–large and small–that combine the pragmatism and romanticism that co-exist at the heart of prairie culture. Such buildings as the John Nugent Studio (St. Mark's Shop) in Lumsden (1960), the **UNIVERSITY OF REGINA** Heating and Cooling Plant (1968), the Silton Summer Chapel (1967) and the Regina CBC Broadcast Centre (1983) all possess his trademark: innovative structural problem-solving, along with deft artistic composition of powerful, simple tectonic forms set against broad plains landscapes. He is the winner of three Massey Medals, Canada's top award for architecture–more than any other Saskatchewan architect. Wiens grew to prominence after EXPO 67, when a wave of nationalism led Canadians to demand more original and expressive architectural forms. His dialogue of built with natural form is comparable to the work of fellow westerners Arthur Erickson of Vancouver, Douglas Cardinal and Peter Hemingway of Edmonton, and Etienne Gaboury of Winnipeg. But Wiens stands out even among this distinguished company for the rigour and originality of his construction details, some of them born of his training and parallel

John Nugent studio in Lumsden, Saskatchewan, ca. 1960.

Wild rice harvesting, Mercer Lake, 1997.

career as an industrial designer.

Wiens was born on April 27, 1926, on his family farm near Glen Kerr, in the grain belt west of Regina. His Mennonite family put a strong emphasis on self-reliance, and while growing up he developed the wide range of wood frame construction, metalworking and mechanical skills needed for the operation of their farm. After several years of farming and studies in art at Banff and in agriculture at Saskatoon, he was accepted into the Rhode Island School of Design in 1949. He arrived on full scholarship, intending a career as an industrial designer–in particular, of farm equipment. He soon switched to the architecture program, which was then steeped in the high Modernism of the Bauhaus. Upon graduation, Wiens worked with Regina architects, notably **JOSEPH PETTICK**, modestly contributing to the design of the breakthrough **SASKATCHEWAN POWER CORPORATION** building. At the same time, he developed close intellectual, artistic and friendship links with the **REGINA FIVE**, some of Canada's most acclaimed and advanced abstract painters of the period.

His Regina practice was unusual for its extremely wide range of clients and building types. Bold detailing and elegant spaces characterize even the most modest of his works, notably a trio of churches: Roman Catholic St. Joseph's in Whitewood (1959); Mennonite Brethren in Regina (1961); and Roman Catholic Our Lady in Moose Jaw (1966). Some of his more prominent later works include Nakusp Hot Springs Spa in BC (1974), Prince Albert City Hall (1984), and Camrose Lutheran College (1986). In the mid-1990s, Wiens wound down his Regina practice and moved to Vancouver, where he continues to design and consult. He has also served as visiting professor at the University of Arizona and Arizona State University. Wiens is the first Saskatchewan architect to be given a career retro-

spective, in a major exhibition planned for the **MENDEL ART GALLERY** in October 2005. *Trevor Boddy*

WILD RICE INDUSTRY. Wild rice (*Zinzania palustris*) is a native North American aquatic cereal grain that historically grew in Canada in lakes and riverbeds, in southeast Manitoba and west and north of the Great Lakes. This nutritious grain was utilized for centuries by Aboriginal people; it was considered as a sacred grain in their diet. Early French explorers referred to the grain as *riz sauvage* (wild rice) and adopted the nutritious grain as a food source in their travels. In the 1930s, wild rice was first introduced into northern Saskatchewan as a food supplement for fur-bearing animals and waterfowl. In the 1980s, development agencies in pursuit of a northern agricultural economic strategy supported the rapid expansion of commercial production for human consumption. Eventually an area encompassing the western headwaters of the **CHURCHILL RIVER** basin, across the Precambrian Shield and to the Cumberland Delta in the east was growing wild rice.

Wild rice is an annual plant that grows from seed each spring in the shallow waters (maximum depth of 1.75 m) of slow-moving rivers and lake bays. In order to preserve the sensitive aquatic environment, provincial law forbids the usage of commercial fertilizers, herbicides or insecticides to enhance production. This naturally grown product qualifies for organic certification, and is often designated as such to gain market access and recognition. Harvesting is done by airboats that skim on the water at a speed of 15–20 km per hour with specially designed collection trays to gather the ripened kernels of grain. Since seeds do not ripen uniformly, this harvesting process must be repeated up to four times per site. The grain is very prone to shattering, and the fallen grain becomes the seed source

for ensuing crops. The harvested wild rice is matured during a curing process of ten to fourteen days, during which time the kernels harden and darken to their characteristic dark brown and black coloration. After curing, the wild rice is parched at high temperatures to gelatinize the starch and reduce the moisture content to less than 10%. Dehulling and grading as to kernel size are the final stages in processing. No additives, flavourings or colourants are used in the processing of this natural food product.

Wild rice, a nutritious grain high in protein and fibre, is an excellent source of B vitamins and is low in fat content. It is a very versatile food item which can be consumed in soups, salads, main entrees and desserts. The annual production of wild rice can be quite variable; however, Saskatchewan is the major producer of wild rice in Canada with an annual production of approximately 0.9 million kg, as compared with a total Canadian production of 1.36 million kg. In the United States, mainly in Minnesota and California, paddy wild rice is grown under commercial farming conditions where approximately 9 million kg are grown each year; in Minnesota there is a small-lake wild rice harvest of approximately 0.227 million kg each year. Saskatchewan's naturally grown lake wild rice is marketed across North America and Europe, and is recognized as a premium product owing to its large kernel size, dark coloration, and nutty flavour. *John Hemstad*

WILKIE, town, pop 1,282, located approximately 55 km SW of North Battleford at the junction of Hwys 14 and 29. Settlers began arriving in the fall of 1905, and building at the townsite began in 1907. In 1910 Wilkie became a town, and the first history of the community was published by the Wilkie Press that year. Wilkie grew through to the end of the 1950s, becoming a centre of over 1,600. After 1960 it declined, as did many rural communities in the province. Wilkie's community leaders, however, did not accept decline as inevitable: when the hospital was closed in 1996, they responded with proactive and imaginative initiatives to foster economic development. Partnerships were formed with the town of Unity and other neighbouring communities. A number of new agriculture-based businesses were started, creating close to 100 new jobs and revitalizing not only the local economy, but also community spirit. Residents made conscious efforts to shop locally and use as many local services as possible. Today, the town has a diverse array of businesses, a range of medical services, an RCMP detachment, and a number of churches, recreational facilities and cultural organizations. The adjacent Wilkie Regional Park has facilities for camping, swimming, baseball, and golf.   *David McLennan*

WILLIAMS, CHARLES CROMWELL (1896–1975).
Charlie Williams was born in Moosomin on February 9, 1896, and went to school in Wapella. He took one year of arts education at Brandon College before accepting a job as a telegraph operator with the CPR in Manitoba. He joined the Order of Railroad Telegraphers and became active in the labour movement.

He enlisted in the Canadian Army in 1915 and served on the front lines before being wounded by a grenade at the Battle of Amiens in August 1918. On returning to Canada he worked for the Grand Trunk Railway as a station agent at numerous places across the prairie provinces. He was stationed in Regina in 1931 and became active in the Regina labour community, serving as his local's president for six years, as secretary of the provincial Committee of Railway Brotherhoods and in the Trade and Labour Congress (TLC).

In 1937 Williams won a spot on the Labour-dominated Regina City Council. He ran for the CCF in the Regina by-election in 1938, but was defeated.

Williams and the entire Labour slate were defeated in the 1939 city council election. He ran for mayor in 1940 but was defeated. Williams was successful on his second try for mayor in 1941 and was re-elected twice before being elected to the Saskatchewan Legislature in 1944.

Williams was Minister of Labour in **T.C. DOUGLAS**' first Cabinet in 1944 and piloted a series of major reforms in labour legislation in the province. He introduced mandatory two-week holidays, expanded the number of statutory holidays, and introduced workers' compensation. Under his leadership, Saskatchewan became the first province to guarantee the right to collective bargaining. Williams spent twenty years as Minister of Labour, the longest any Saskatchewan Minister has served in one portfolio.

He retired from provincial politics in 1964, but contested the 1965 Regina municipal election and served on council until his final retirement from politics in 1973. He died while on vacation in Vancouver on January 31, 1975.   *Brett Quiring*

WILLIAMS, CHARLES MELVILLE (1925–).
"Red" Williams taught diploma, degree, and postgraduate students in Agriculture and Veterinary Medicine from 1954 to 1992 as a professor of Animal Sciences and an Extension Specialist. He was nominated "Teacher of the Year" in 1981. In addition to being an inspiring and award-winning teacher for over fifty years and serving on many university and provincial committees and boards, Williams produced over 300 newspaper columns, and handled over 1,500 rural and agriculture-related speaking events and over 4,000 radio editorials. He earned his BSA Masters of Science in Agriculture from the University of British Columbia, and obtained his PhD at Oregon State University in 1955. He joined the Department of Animal Science at the **UNIVERSITY OF SASKATCHEWAN** in 1954. For over thirty years, he assisted First Nations and **MÉTIS** people

to develop viable farm enterprises; more recently, he was responsible for the Agricultural Sector of the Royal Commission on Aboriginal People (1993). At the same time, he has been active in developing country (Third World) issues, ranging from extended service in some countries, to CUSO (Canadian University Students Overseas), to board member of the North/South Institute, to consultant on development projects in nineteen countries.

Williams' concerns about the problems facing agriculture and farming led him to enter the political arena and, while unsuccessful in being elected, he took the time to prepare several important briefs and position papers to address his concerns. His early involvement in animal welfare issues led to the development of a Code of Ethics for Livestock and Poultry Production in Canada. In addition, he has been active in his professional organizations, often holding executive positions in the Canadian Society of Animal Science, the Saskatchewan Institute of Agrologists, and the Agricultural Institute of Canada. The results of his research on the types and effects of windbreaks, overhead shelter, and straw bedding on feedlot cattle have been widely used in western Canada. He was also involved in an intensive study of the performance and metabolic responses of lactating dairy cows accommodated in a loose-housing barn and subjected to variable temperature, humidity and wind conditions. Subsequently, he directed a study of the effects of breed and environmental factors on hair coat density in cattle. For his outstanding professional service and accomplishments, Williams became a Member of the Order of Canada (1989), a Fellow of the Agricultural Institute of Canada (1972), and an Honorary Life Member of the Canadian Extension Society (1970). He also received the Confederation Medal (1992), the Queen's Jubilee Medal (1979), and Century Saskatoon–City of Saskatoon Scroll (1982).

Philip Thacker

Charles Cromwell Williams, June 1963.

George Hara Williams.

Lynn Williams.

Wellington Willoughby.

WILLIAMS, GEORGE (1894–1945). George Hara Williams was born November 17, 1894, at Binscarth, Manitoba. After service in **WORLD WAR I** he attended the Manitoba Agricultural College and in 1920 was appointed director of livestock and equipment for Saskatchewan with the Soldier Settlement Board.

In 1921 Williams began farming at Semans. He joined the farmers union in 1923 and was president of the United Farmers of Canada from 1929 to 1931. Williams also served briefly as secretary of the Marxist Farmers' Educational League and was founder and secretary of the short-lived Farmers' Political Association formed in 1924.

Williams and **M.J. COLDWELL** co-chaired the 1932 convention that brought delegates from the United Farmers of Canada together with members of the Independent Labour Party to form a new party, the Farmer-Labour Group. In 1934 this group was renamed the **CO-OPERATIVE COMMONWEALTH FEDERATION** (CCF). Williams, elected in the Wadena constituency, was one of five successful CCF candidates in the 1934 provincial election. M.J. Coldwell, CCF party leader, was not elected. Williams remained floor leader of the CCF group in the Legislature, and leader of the Opposition. When Coldwell was elected in a federal election in 1935, Williams became leader of the provincial CCF. He served as secretary, office manager and party organizer during 1935, and as party president, organizer and leader from 1936 to 1941.

In 1941 Williams took up active military duty. At the CCF annual convention in 1941 **T.C. DOUGLAS** was elected leader. Just before the 1944 election, Williams was discharged from the army and returned from overseas service. He was instrumental in rallying rural support for the CCF. Tommy Douglas appointed Williams Minister of Agriculture, a post he filled until February 1945 when failing health forced him to resign. He died on September 12, 1945 in Vancouver. *Lisa Dale-Burnett*

FURTHER READING: Steininger, Friedrich. 1976. "George H. Williams: Agrarian Socialist." MA thesis. University of Regina.

WILLIAMS, LYNN (1960–). Lynn Williams (*née* Kanuka) was a dominant track and field athlete in the 1970s and 1980s. Born in Regina on July 11, 1960, she placed in the top three of every middle distance track event and cross-country distance event she entered between 1973 and 1981. Williams studied and trained at the **UNIVERSITY OF SASKATCHEWAN** and San Diego State University before relocating to British Columbia in 1982. She established eleven Canadian running records between 1983 and 1989.

Williams won the bronze medal in the 3,000-metre event at the 1984 Los Angeles Olympics. She finished fifth in the 1,500 metres and eighth in the 3,000 metres at the 1988 Seoul Olympics. Her other international wins include bronze in the 3,000-metre event at the 1983 World Student Games, gold in the 3,000 metres and bronze in the 1,500 metres at the 1986 Commonwealth Games, and bronze at the 1989 World Cross Country Championships.

Lynn Williams was awarded the Dr. Phil Edwards Trophy as Canada's top track athlete in 1988 and 1989. She was inducted into the **SASKATCHEWAN SPORTS HALL OF FAME** in 1994. Williams is an advocate for stay-in-school, anti-drug, and physical fitness campaigns across Canada and has served as a track and field analyst for television networks. *Bob Ivanochko and Holden Stoffel*

WILLIAMSON, ROBERT G. (1931–). Born in Oxley, England on November 2, 1931, Robert Williamson is recognized for his work promoting social justice and economic development with circumpolar and Arctic nations. He received his degree in anthropology from Carleton University and his doctorate from the Royal University of Uppsala in Sweden. His career began at the **UNIVERSITY OF SASKATCHEWAN**, where he helped pioneer the Institute of Northern Studies and the Arctic Research and Training Centre. Williamson is credited with founding the Eskimology Section at the Department of Northern Affairs, and *Inuttitut*, an Inuit magazine. He has received numerous awards and honours including the Order of Canada in 1986.

WILLISTON BASIN. The Williston Basin is a sedimentary basin centred near Williston, North Dakota, which underlies some 250,000 km² in North Dakota, Manitoba, Saskatchewan, Montana and South Dakota (*see* Figure WB-1). This major geological feature is essentially a near-circular sub-basin within the Western Interior Basin of the United States and the adjoining **WESTERN CANADA SEDIMEN-**

TARY BASIN. The thickness of sedimentary strata at the centre of the basin is about 5,000 m. The sedimentary succession thins outward, and is just over 3,300 m on the International Boundary south of Regina. The outer limit of the basin is commonly set where the basin fill thins to 2,400 m. The oldest strata in the Williston Basin were laid down in Cambrian time approximately 550 million years ago. These beds rest upon more ancient Precambrian crystalline rocks, the "Basement" of petroleum geologists. The youngest beds are late Tertiary in age, deposited about five million years ago. Important reserves of petroleum have been developed in the Williston Basin; many of the producing oil pools are located in southeastern Saskatchewan. Lignite coal in the near-surface Tertiary rocks is mined in Saskatchewan and North Dakota; deeply buried potash beds may be exploited in the future. (*See also* **MINERAL RESOURCES**) *Laurence Vigrass*

WILLOUGHBY, WELLINGTON BARTLEY (1859–1932). Willoughby was born on July 10, 1859, in Charlton, Peel County, Ontario. After completing high school in Hamilton he attended the University of Toronto and graduated with a BA and a degree in law. He was called to the Ontario Bar in 1886 and practiced in Toronto for more than ten years. He ran unsuccessfully for the Conservatives in the 1896 federal election. In 1897 he moved to Moose Jaw to establish his own legal practice, specializing in real estate, and developed other business interests. In 1908 he was appointed city solicitor for Moose Jaw.

In 1908 he was elected as a Conservative MLA for Moose Jaw and he was re-elected twice. Willoughby worked to unite members of the federal **CONSERVATIVE PARTY** and supporters of the Provincial Rights grouping to form the beginnings of a provincial Conservative Party under the leadership of **F.W.G. HAULTAIN** in 1911. When the party did not improve its standing in the 1912 election Haultain stepped down and Willoughby became the Opposition leader. Willoughby was an effective leader in the Legislature, maintaining a clear ideological alternative to the Liberals, especially on the controversial issue of education. Willoughby insisted that schools should serve as vehicles of Canadianization. Liberal support increased to 51 seats and the Conservatives lost one seat in the 1917 election.

Although Willoughby held his seat in Moose Jaw, he was persuaded by Prime Minister Borden to accept a seat in the Senate to make way for Donald McLean from Saskatoon as the new Conservative Party leader. Willoughby served briefly as Conservative leader in the Senate but retired shortly before his death on August 1, 1932. *Michael Cottrell*

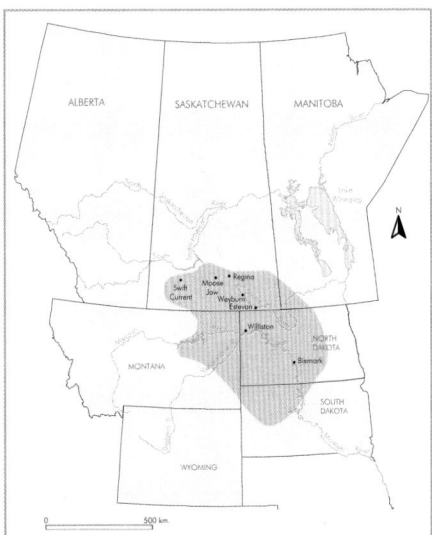

CANADIAN PLAINS RESEARCH CENTER MAPPING DIVISION

Figure WB-1. Areal extent of the Williston Basin.

WILLOW BUNCH, town, pop 395, located SE of Assiniboia on Hwy 36. One of the oldest settled communities in the province, Willow Bunch is situated amidst a picturesque landscape of alkaline lakes, rolling hills, and wooded coulees. By the 1860s, Red River **MÉTIS**, pursuing the bison as they retreated southwest, began establishing winter camps, and became *hivernants* in the area. In early 1870, as tensions at Red River reached a peak, about thirty families, uncertain of their future in the new province of Manitoba, relocated somewhat west of the present town. Later that year, **JEAN LOUIS LÉGARÉ**, who would become recognized as the founder of Willow Bunch arrived, and today Jean Louis Légaré Regional Park, just south of the community, is named in his honour. The first settlement, however, would only be temporary: as the bison began to disappear, many of the Métis moved on–many permanently–while others returned to the district to adopt a more sedentary life. Prior to the turn of the century, more Métis families arrived, and a life of herding and ranching replaced the great buffalo hunts. From around the time of the province's inauguration in 1905 until the end of **WORLD WAR I**, a wave of French-Canadian settlers arrived, and crop production became increasingly combined with ranching. In 1926 the long-anticipated and much-delayed **CANADIAN NATIONAL RAILWAY** line finally arrived, and the community's future prospects changed. By the mid-1950s the population was approaching 800; in 1970 the community celebrated its centennial. Today Willow Bunch retains its heritage through institutions such as the museum, the school (with its intensive French language program), and the Métis and francophone cultural organizations. Agriculture remains the major industry in the area; however, the Poplar River Power Plant, located southeast of Coronach, provides an important source of employment. The community's most famous resident was **ÉDOUARD BEAUPRÉ**, known as the Willow Bunch Giant; other notable residents of the town include pioneering aviator Charles Skinner and the musical Campagne family of Hart Rouge fame. All of these are now honoured in the town's museum, formerly a convent and boarding school and now a heritage property. (*See also* **FRENCH SETTLEMENTS, FRENCH AND METIS SETTLEMENTS**) *David McLennan*

WILLOW BUNCH GIANT: *see* BEAUPRÉ, ÉDOUARD

WILSON, DOUGLAS (1950–93). Doug Wilson, a gay educator, activist, writer, human rights advocate and politician was born in Meadow Lake. In 1975, while an Education student at the **UNIVERSITY OF SASKATCHEWAN**, Wilson placed an ad in the student paper advertising the Gay Academic Union. The Dean of Education took swift action, prohibiting an "avowed homosexual" from supervising student teachers in the city's high schools. A Committee to Defend Doug Wilson was formed by local gay

activists, professors, and students, in order to protest Wilson's treatment and demand his reinstatement. Wilson's case attracted significant local and national media coverage, and resulted in a Saskatchewan Human Rights Commission investigation. The University countered by applying for an injunction, claiming that the Commission had acted improperly because sexual orientation was not a specified category in the provincial human rights code. The University successfully obtained the injunction and the investigation was prohibited. However, public opinion favoured Wilson.

Wilson's case was historic because it exposed Saskatchewan residents to **GAY AND LESBIAN ACTIVISM**, which ultimately paved the way for policy changes on campus and throughout the province. Subsequently, Wilson was a key member and leader of local gay activist groups. He was appointed to the position of Executive Director of the Saskatchewan Association on Human Rights from 1978–83. Subsequently he held the position of race relations consultant for the Toronto school board. Wilson became the first openly gay candidate to run in a federal election, when he ran as the NDP candidate for Rosedale in the 1988 election. Wilson died of AIDS-related pneumonia in 1993. *Valerie J. Korinek*

WILSON, JAMES ROBERT (1866–1941). Born September 16, 1866, near Almonte, Ontario, James Wilson moved west with his parents in 1883, being among the first to settle in the Dundurn district. Wilson served in the medical corps during the 1885 Resistance. He tried various enterprises from farming to railroad contracting before starting a successful general store in Saskatoon in 1899. In 1902 he opened a flour mill in Saskatoon and later expanded into a grain company, both of which he eventually sold to Quaker Oats.

James Robert Wilson.

Elected overseer for the village of Saskatoon in 1903, Wilson guided the community through the growth that would lead to the community's incorporation as a city in 1907. Saskatoon's first mayor from 1907 to 1908, Wilson used his personal wealth to guarantee loans for the city to build its basic sewer infrastructure. He unsuccessfully contested the provincial election for the Conservatives in Saskatoon in 1908. Wilson was elected to Saskatoon city council in 1914 and remained there until 1919.

Wilson was elected in the riding of Saskatoon as a Unionist in 1917. Upon the appointment of **JAMES CALDER** to the Senate, Wilson was brought into the Cabinet in 1921 as Minister without portfolio. A few months later he was defeated in the Progressive sweep of the province. He remained involved in many community causes, including being a proponent of the Hudson Bay railroad. Wilson served as chair of the Dominion Farm Loans Board before his death on April 3, 1941. *Brett Quiring*

WITCHEKAN LAKE FIRST NATION. Witchekan Lake Cree First Nation signed **TREATY 6** on November 21, 1950. Reserve land for the band had been surveyed about 90 km northeast of North Battleford many years before; today it constitutes 6,520.1 ha of land. Economic endeavours include agriculture, forestry, trapping, and fishing; with its successful acquisition of the Bapaume Community Pasture in 1997, this band was the first in Saskatchewan to acquire a Crown community pasture through a Treaty Land Entitlement Agreement. The community infrastructure includes a band office, school, fire hall, band hall, community health clinic, and assorted community maintenance facilities. The band currently has 578 members, of whom 380 live on reserve. *Christian Thompson*

WOLFE, SAM (1923–93). Wolfe was born in Toronto on June 6, 1923, and received his MD there in 1950. For six years he was an exemplary family doctor at Porcupine Plain, Saskatchewan. A Rockefeller scholarship led to his Doctorate in Public Health from Columbia University in 1961. A longtime supporter of universal, public medicare, he was appointed as one of the first members of the Medical Care Insurance Commission. When in 1962 the doctors went on strike, he helped organize the airlift of ninety doctors from Britain. He resigned his professorship, under protest, from the Department of Social and Preventative Medicine and joined the Saskatoon Community Clinic as its first Medical Director. He promoted a community-based, team practice of primary health care. He encouraged the establishment of a Drug Formulary which became the model for the Saskatchewan Prescription Drug Plan. He presided over and enjoyed the defence against the harassment of the Clinic by the medical establishment. As Professor of Family and

Community Medicine at Meharry University, Nashville (USA), he established in 1968 a Community Health Centre in the Black ghetto; he then had a distinguished career as Chair of Health Administration and Public Health at Columbia University. He published extensively, and wrote two books with Robin Badgley: *Doctors' Strike* and *The Family Doctor*. He died in New York City on December 10, 1993.   *John Bury*

WOLFE GROUP OF COMPANIES. John Wolfe began his career as a housing contractor in 1969 and built a group of companies with a portfolio that touches virtually every aspect of society from homes and hotels to service stations and warehouses. The Wolfe Group of Companies is a multi-disciplined team of professionals who work together with clients, architects and consultants. Wolfe Group offers full construction services with extensive experience in general contracting, construction, project management, design-build and fast tracking.

The Saskatoon-based, privately owned company is capable of handling a wide range of projects: light and heavy industrial; commercial (service and retail); multi-storey; multi-family; retrofit and renovations; tenant improvements; turnkey ventures; and pre-engineered building systems.

A glimpse at the company's project portfolio reveals the diversity of its skills ranging from construction of three McDonald's franchises in Regina to construction of senior and social housing facilities in Saskatoon. In addition, Wolfe was responsible for the $12-million expansion of the **VACCINE AND INFECTIOUS DISEASE ORGANIZATION** (VIDO) building on the **UNIVERSITY OF SASKATCHEWAN** campus and $2.5 million addition to the Parktown Hotel, both in Saskatoon, construction of the $9.7-million, four-floor, Petroleum Technology Research Centre (PTRC) on the **UNIVERSITY OF REGINA** campus, and the $6.6-million renovation to Calgary City Hall. Wolfe also was responsible for construction of health care facilities in Fort Qu'Appelle, La Loche, Saskatoon, Shaunavon and Tisdale. In the financial services industry, Wolfe has completed projects for the Royal Bank of Canada, Alberta Treasury Branch and credit unions. Leisure and cultural centres in Lanigan, Lloydminster and Saskatoon were Wolfe projects as well. In 2004, the company has constructed healing lodges, RCMP detachments, light industrial warehouses and religious buildings.
Joe Ralko

WOLLASTON LAKE (58°15'N, 103°15'W; Map sheet 64 L/3). Wollaston Lake is located in northeastern Saskatchewan, approximately 550 km north of Prince Albert. Elevated at 398 m, covering 2,681 sq. km, and in places more than 50 m deep, Wollaston straddles the watershed between the Churchill and Athabasca Drainage Basins, with out-

DOUG CHISHOLM PHOTO
Wollaston Lake (community and lake), 2003.

flow to the Arctic through both the Mackenzie River and Hudson Bay. This unusual drainage pattern was described by **DAVID THOMPSON** in 1796 as "perhaps without parallel in the world."

SAMUEL HEARNE learned of the lake in 1770 from guides who described a route through Wollaston to the Mackenzie River. Although well known to fur traders by the mid-1800s, difficult portages limited its use to small parties. Wollaston has been known by several names. Hearne's guides named it Manito Lake (meaning supernatural or mysterious lake). In 1883 Émile Petitot mapped it as Great Hatchet Lake or Wollaston Lake, the latter name given by **JOHN FRANKLIN** in 1821 to honour the English chemist William Hyde Wollaston.

The western shore of Wollaston Lake is accessible via Highway 906. There is scheduled air service to the village of Wollaston Lake and to Points North Landing, a service centre for nearby **URANIUM** mines. Although this industry provides jobs for northerners, it has also raised concerns over possible contamination of Wollaston Lake. This is significant as the lake not only provides domestic water for the local inhabitants, but also supports a commercial and recreational fishery.   *Marilyn Lewry*

FURTHER READING: Sebert, L.M. 2004. "Mysterious Wollaston Lake (Northern Saskatchewan)," *Association of Canadian Map Libraries and Archives* 119: 15–18.

WOLSELEY, town, pop 766, located on the Trans-Canada Hwy and the CP main line, approximately 100 km E of Regina. Wolseley is one of Saskatchewan's oldest towns and was listed as one of Canada's ten prettiest by Harrowsmith magazine in

2000. The town, incorporated in 1898, was named after the illustrious Colonel Garnet Joseph Wolseley. The age of the community is reflected in its streetscapes and architecture. Many of the town's stately homes and public buildings were built with brick that was produced locally. A number of buildings have been designated either municipal or provincial heritage properties; one of them, the Wolseley Court House, was constructed during the Territorial period and is the oldest existing court building in the province. Wolseley grew quickly in the early 20th century, and many of its businessmen were successful entrepreneurs. The Beaver Lumber Company, which became one of the largest lumber supply companies in Canada, had its beginnings in the town. The original Beaver Lumber office building is now at the town's museum. By 1916, the population of Wolseley was over 1,000 and it had become a substantial centre for trade, social and cultural activities. In 1954, Wolseley had Saskatchewan's first drive-in theatre: built for 225 cars, it was still in operation fifty years later. Although the population has dropped over the past few decades, Wolseley remains an active community. Agriculture and its subsidiary activities dominate the economy.
David McLennan

WOMAN SUFFRAGE. The prairie provinces were the first to grant the vote to women: Manitoba did so in January 1916, closely followed by Saskatchewan and Alberta. In Saskatchewan, there was little opposition to woman suffrage—and little campaigning in its favour. The Alberta-Saskatchewan division of the **WOMEN'S CHRISTIAN TEMPERANCE UNION** (WCTU) had endorsed the idea since 1904, and the wife of Premier **WALTER SCOTT** signed a WCTU suffrage petition in 1909. But despite the quiet support of many women, the Saskatchewan government did not discuss the issue until 1912. British suffragist Barbara Wylie, on a Christmas-time visit to her brother, David Wylie, the Conservative MLA for Maple Creek, addressed public meetings in Regina, Moose Jaw and Maple Creek. MLA **J.E. BRADSHAW** (Conservative–Prince Albert) subsequently proposed in the legislature that it approve women's enfranchisement in principle; with one exception, and with some jocularity, the members who spoke to the resolution supported it. The Premier later stated that although the government favoured woman suffrage in principle, it would not act without proof that women themselves wanted the vote. The challenge was taken up by Francis Marion Beynon, women's editor of the *Grain Growers' Guide*, and her sister Lillian Beynon Thomas, of the *Winnipeg Free Press*, who urged their readers to write to Premier Scott to register their desire to vote. Over the next four months, Scott received more than 200 letters, mainly from rural women, arguing on both egalitarian and pragmatic grounds for votes for women.

In February 1913, a women's meeting held in conjunction with the annual meeting of the **SASKATCHEWAN GRAIN GROWERS' ASSOCIATION** (SGGA) circulated a petition for woman suffrage. Between May and December 1913, a petition campaign organized by **VIOLET MCNAUGHTON** and sponsored by the SGGA produced more than 100 petitions from almost as many rural locations. These petitions were not placed before the Legislature because they were addressed to the Premier. In December, Bradshaw again proposed a resolution supporting woman suffrage, which passed unanimously. The government acknowledged that it had heard from more than 2,000 women during 1913, but said it could not grant the vote to women because the issue had not been discussed during the 1912 election campaign. In early 1914, Political Equality Leagues were established in Moosomin, Battleford and Prince Albert, and the Women's Grain Growers' Association (WGGA) was founded, with Violet McNaughton as president. McNaughton recognized that an effective suffrage campaign would need to unite the farm women's movement with urban women's organizations. She met with WCTU leaders, including Nellie Andrews and Margaret Armstrong, and agreed to organize a coalition of rural (WGGA) women and urban (WCTU) women to campaign for the vote. The founding meeting of the Provincial Equal Franchise Board (PEFB) in February 1915 resolved that there would be no active campaign during the war; but it decided to raise funds, compile a list of speakers, and reactivate the WCTU petition campaign.

On May 27, a delegation of women formally presented new petitions to the Legislature. In response, Premier Scott did not undertake to introduce legislation, but acknowledged that although he did not have an electoral mandate, public opinion could become strong enough to require action; he urged the women to gather more signatures. Premier Scott met with the Regina leadership of the WCTU and asked them to submit petitions from parts of the province that had not yet been heard from. During the first six weeks of 1916, another thirty-seven villages submitted petitions, and Regina increased its total. In the throne speech of January 1916, the government announced that it would enact woman suffrage; on Valentine's Day, when another large delegation attended at the legislature to present petitions totalling 10,000 names, the Premier reiterated this commitment. The bill granting Saskatchewan women the right to vote in provincial elections on equal terms with men received royal assent on March 14, 1916.

The Saskatchewan government had reacted to events in Manitoba. There the issue of votes for women had been controversial: Rodmond Roblin's Conservative government had stood firm against it; the Liberal opposition of T.C. Norris had championed it. The Manitoba Political Equality League was founded in 1912 by leading Manitoba suffragists including Nellie McClung and the Beynon sisters; but success came only after the Roblin government was defeated in August 1915. By September, not only Manitoba but also the Alberta government had indicated their intention to grant woman suffrage during the upcoming legislative session; when Scott saw that woman suffrage was inevitable, he took steps to ensure that Saskatchewan would not be left behind.

Elizabeth Kalmakoff

FURTHER READING: Kalmakoff, E.A. 1993. "Woman Suffrage in Saskatchewan." MA Thesis, Department of History, University of Regina; MacDonald, C. 1948. "How Saskatchewan Women Got the Vote," *Saskatchewan History* 1 (3): 1–8.

WOMEN AND AGRICULTURE. Women have been important to the success of agricultural operations in Saskatchewan. In the homesteading era, for example, women often worked alongside men to bring land into production, raised poultry and sheep, and kept gardens to provide for their families and earn household money. Women also sold eggs, butter, and cream to augment family income–activities that became even more crucial during the **DEPRESSION**. All too often, however, these activities were not considered farming. Today, Saskatchewan farm women are working on the farm, in the farm household and at off-farm jobs, and continue to do volunteer work in their communities. It is only recently that married women have been able to designate themselves as farm operators. A female farmer was not previously unheard of; but those who were counted as such would have been widows (usually) or single women (occasionally). As currently defined, a farm operator is a person responsible for the day-to-day management decisions made in operating an agricultural operation. Since 1991, Statistics Canada has allowed farm operations to report more than one operator on each farm in the Census of Agriculture.

Because of this reporting change, farm women are more likely to be recognized for their involvement in agricultural production. As well, the number of women farm operators in Saskatchewan increased from 20% in 1996 to 22% in 2001; this figure is lower than the Canadian average, and reflects the predominance of grain and oilseed farms in which men have traditionally been the sole operators. Women as sole operators are still rare, and are

Katie Threinen feeding poultry on her family farm in east-central Saskatchewan, 1957.

found in only 3% of Saskatchewan farms. Over half of them are more than 55 years old: this reflects the traditional practice whereby women have become sole operators only when their husbands are no longer farming. However, the number of younger women who are categorized as sole operators is slowly increasing: more women are choosing to enter agriculture, and farm families are beginning to consider not only their sons but also their daughters as possible successors on the farm. As well, women do have higher than average representation in some of the newer types of farm operations in the province, such as greenhouses and nurseries, sheep and goat production, and fruit tree production. The farms women manage as sole operators tend to be smaller and have lower total farm capital. Saskatchewan farm women as a whole are also working off the farm in ever-increasing numbers, with 49.4% holding off farm jobs in 2001.

Information from Statistics Canada only includes women who indicate they are farm operators. Many farm women do not consider themselves so, although they considerably assist the viability of the farm. This is gradually changing, however, and farm women's contributions to farm success are becoming more visible. A recent study of farm work, for example, showed that Saskatchewan farm women are much more involved in farm work than the data on women farm operators suggest: while only 22% indicated they were farm operators, many more are operating farm machinery, caring for farm animals, driving farm trucks, running errands, managing the farm books, dealing with sales people and buyers, and supervising farm work. Saskatchewan farm women, in fact, are more involved in farm work than women elsewhere in Canada, and more than they were twenty years ago. They are, however, still responsible not only for child rearing but for the majority of household work as well as gardening, canning and freezing. As well, farm women are being increasingly called on to care for chronically ill family members in face of the aging rural population and decline of rural health care services. Some 86% of farm women also do unpaid community and volunteer work on a regular basis. Saskatchewan farm women are thus heavily involved in farming operations, and over the past twenty years their contributions have increased. Many factors are driving these changes: changes in attitudes, easier farm machinery operation, increase in non-farm employment, and need for family labour to make ends meet. *Diane Martz*

WOMEN AND EDUCATION. By the early 20th century, an era of massive newcomer arrival to Saskatchewan, formal barriers to female education had largely disappeared. Still operating, however, were social expectations and assumptions, shaped by ethno-cultural and class considerations: percep-

tions differed as to the value of female education and its proper nature. Most Saskatchewan youth at the time secured only a basic education, a few years at best—perhaps only intermittent sessions determined by family farm obligations. What is now called secondary education was also available to female students, but only in larger communities or in schools run by religious orders; among the latter were female-only institutions. Only a minority of females (as well as males) went to these institutions, let alone graduated, until well into the 20th century. As for university education, the University of Saskatchewan, which officially opened in 1913, always admitted women (though until 1915 for the College of Agriculture); but few enrolled, forming a far smaller percentage of the student body than in the secondary institutions. Initially, even though it was above the national average, only about 17% of the university student body was female. Increases did occur, and starting in the 1950s female participation began to rise significantly. Now the two universities in Saskatoon and Regina have slightly more female than male undergraduate students. Gendered expectations still operate: women tend to concentrate in certain areas like education, social work and the humanities, although law and engineering also have significantly more female students today.

The curriculum female students have been taught has been affected by gender considerations. Historically, female education in Saskatchewan was largely linked to the presumed proper destiny of women: marriage, with its associated roles of mother, wife, and homemaker. An undercurrent was the acquisition of income-earning skills, so that a women could, if necessary, support herself. At the elementary level, the three "Rs" were taught to all, but disagreements arose about subsequent curriculum. By the early 20th century, domestic (or household) science appeared to be the answer to the vexed question of what to teach females: courses were instituted in the existing educational system, particularly in the larger urban schools; the UNIVERSITY OF SASKATCHEWAN offered the first classes in domestic science in 1917; and the School of Household Science was established in 1928. This new "science" was also made available to rural and farm women through University Extension and the Homemakers Clubs. Opportunities also developed for the female minority requiring educational qualifications for work deemed suitable for women. Especially favoured was elementary teaching, and many women attended the short courses as well as lengthier programs offered through the NORMAL SCHOOLS (which continued into the mid-20th century). Young women might also train as nurses, a respectable female occupation by the 20th century, learning their craft at nursing schools that the newly established hospitals set up and maintained until training was taken over in the late 20th centu-

ry by technical institutes and universities. As the need for office workers grew, many secondary institutions offered business and commercial courses for women. New social demands also led to the emergence of proprietary schools, some run by women, which provided for example beauty parlour training as well as secretarial and stenography courses. By the late 20th century, training for women for what were called "non-traditional" trades, such as carpentry and motor mechanics, was possible.

Women's involvement in education has been heavily gendered. Since the latter 19th century, women had been viewed as natural teachers of young children (and were expected to accept half the pay of a male teacher). Working as a "schoolmarm" was deemed a suitable job for a young single woman with some education who sought to earn a living and enjoy some degree of financial independence. Such women became rural elementary schoolteachers in one-room schools. The work, if sometimes rewarding, was also difficult: working and living conditions were often primitive, and the morals of single female teachers were constantly scrutinized by local school boards and members of the community. Few stayed in such inhospitable environments, many choosing to leave to marry a local farmer or to seek another job, perhaps in a better- equipped school in a more established community. City teachers sometimes attempted to upgrade their profession, as with the Saskatoon Women Teachers' Association, formed in 1918. Improvements in working conditions came slowly; also, teacher shortages and changing attitudes ended single women's dominance during the postwar decades. Now the majority of female school teachers are married and have families—something not allowed before WORLD WAR II.

Before 1939, the female secondary school teacher was a rare phenomenon: men dominated instruction at this level and received higher salaries than female teachers. Unusually well-educated women, like E. Don Cathro and Helena B. Marsters (later Walker—*see* HELENA WALKER) in Regina, filled a few positions in the collegiate institutes that were established before WORLD WAR I. Better paid than their elementary school counterparts until 1973, when wage parity was attained, their pay was still below that of male teachers; women, often with families, have now become the norm at the secondary level. Although men dominated secondary teacher training after the war and into the 1970s, they are now once again very much the minority in both elementary and secondary school training in Saskatchewan. At the University of Saskatchewan, only a handful taught: the University was a man's world; until 1947 women were allowed in the Faculty Club only once a year. Even so, the Saskatchewan record in this regard was better than the national average for the years between 1920 and 1974, when it began to lag. Among the faculty were women like **MABEL TIMLIN** and **HILDA NEATBY**, who established national reputations. Even now, women still constitute a minority in higher education and tend to be over-represented in part-time or inferior positions at the University of Saskatchewan and the **UNIVERSITY OF REGINA**.

Outside the classroom, women until recently have had few opportunities. Historically, female principals have been few, and likely in charge only at the elementary level. In the past, the occasional woman doing pioneering work found a place: **CATHERINE SHELDON-WILLIAMS**, for example, while working for the Department of Education started the Outpost Correspondence School in 1925; this was the beginning of the provincial Correspondence School designed to provide educational opportunities to those in sparsely settled or remote areas. As the educational bureaucracy has expanded, more women now occupy positions of responsibility in high schools, as directors or superintendents of education, and as managers and directors in the provincial department of education. Despite the significant changes of recent decades, the result in part of the impact of feminism, the world of women and education is in many respects still a gendered one.

Ann Leger-Anderson

FURTHER READING: Corman, J. 2002. "Returning to the Classroom: Married Women Fill the Void for Teachers in Saskatchewan," *Atlantis* 27: 81–90; Hallman, D.M. 1997. "Telling Tales in and out of School: Twentieth Century Women Teachers in Saskatchewan" *Saskatchewan History* 49: 3–17; Poelzer, I. 1990. *Saskatchewan Women Teachers, 1905–1920: Their Contributions*. Saskatoon: Lindenblatt and Hamonic.

WOMEN AND POLITICS: POST-SUFFRAGE TO THE 1970S. The success of the 1916 suffrage movement gave women in Saskatchewan the right to vote and to hold public office. **SARAH RAMSLAND** became the first Saskatchewan woman MLA in 1919 and was Liberal member for the Pelly riding until 1925. It was two decades before another woman won a seat in the Legislative Assembly. Between 1919 and 1967 six women in total were elected to the provincial legislature: three Liberals (Ramsland, **MARY BATTEN**, and Sally Merchant), and three from the **CO-OPERATIVE COMMONWEALTH FEDERATION** (CCF)/**NEW DEMOCRATIC PARTY** (NDP) (**BEATRICE TREW, GLADYS STRUM, MARJORIE COOPER**). Two women became members of Parliament: Dorise Nielson (1940–45), who won on the Unity ticket in North Battleford; and Gladys Strum, who held office from 1945 to 1949 (Qu'Appelle Constituency) for the CCF. Several women sat on municipal councils or, more likely, on school boards.

As elsewhere, Saskatchewan women were most active in supportive auxiliary roles. Soon after enfranchisement Liberal women in Regina formed an association. As Liberal women's associations proliferated, Conservative women also organized. Provincial associations emerged as well. Both parties depended on women as canvassers, constituency organizers, fundraisers, hostesses, publicists, clerical workers, and recruiters. Although women were rarely involved in policy formation, the contributions they made to the parent party organizations were extremely valuable.

Saskatchewan women had been actively engaged in the populist movements characteristic of the prairies, and when the CCF emerged during the 1930s from the agrarian movement of the previous decade, many women were attracted by its pledge to end the economic upheaval brought on by the **DEPRESSION**. The egalitarian ideology of the CCF, combined with the activism of farm women in the agrarian movement, led some Saskatchewan women to anticipate a prominent role in its development. The majority, however, worked at the grassroots level, carrying out tasks similar to those of Liberal and Conservative women.

Some CCF women were more deeply involved in the workings of party, usually able to do so because of the support, or at least acquiescence, of husband and family. They served on the provincial executive and local committees, acted as campaign managers for local candidates, and (rarely) ran as candidates themselves. As well, some functioned as political educators in the province. Through small farm gatherings, community meetings, and summer camps, CCF women educators played an important role in spreading the party's principles and in recruiting support. The contributions made by women were essential to the development of the CCF as well as to its success in the 1944 provincial election.

By the end of the 1940s women's primary responsibilities in all political parties continued to focus on the recruitment of volunteers, fundraising, media coverage, supervision of voters' lists, organization of social events, and getting out the vote at election time. Although the CCF had promised women equality within the party, only one woman, Beatrice Trew, was elected to the Legislative Assembly during that decade (1944–48). The two old-line parties elected no women during the same time. However, those women who worked endlessly for their political beliefs displayed remarkable energy and determination. As previously, they adhered to the social norm that prioritized women's responsibility for the household and family, and sought to balance it with their work in public life. As well, women continued to face opposition to female participation in the political arena, especially when they desired to participate in policy formulation or run for office.

Between 1948 and 1952 no women sat in the Legislative Assembly. Four women were elected between 1952 and 1970; but women's involvement in policy-making continued to be negligible, regardless of party affiliation. The defeat of the CCF in 1964 contributed to the renewal of interest in women's issues in the party and a re-evaluation of the role women played; in 1965 the Provincial Women's Committee was formed. Also important to this development was the resurgence of feminism in North America, which awakened many women and men in Saskatchewan to the secondary role women had played in political organizations.

At the national level the Report of the Royal Commission on the Status of Women (1970) included a recommendation that called for amalgamation of partisan women's associations with the party itself–a sharp departure from the decades-old auxiliary groups. In accordance with the report, Saskatchewan parties instituted changes to their constitutions. Women's committees and associations were either amalgamated into the provincial party organizations, as with the NDP, or they remained intact while women's representation on the party's provincial council increased, as with the Liberal Party. Such changes were part of a movement that aimed to secure greater equality for women in all

SASKATCHEWAN ARCHIVES BOARD R-A26907

Women's Liberal Club executive at Saskatchewan Beach, June 1939.

aspects of society. Both men and women then began to recognize the importance of women's equal representation in Saskatchewan's governing bodies.

Joanna Leach

FURTHER READING: Kalmakoff, E. 1994. "Naturally Divided: Women in Saskatchewan Politics, 1916–1919," *Saskatchewan History* 46: 3–18; Taylor, G.M. 1984. "'The Women ... Shall Help to Lead the Way': Saskatchewan CCF-NDP Women Candidates in Provincial and Federal Elections, 1934–1965." Pp. 141–60 in J.W. Brennan (ed.), *Building the Co-operative Commonwealth: Essays on the Democratic Socialist Tradition in Canada*. Regina: Canadian Plains Research Center.

WOMEN AND POLITICS SINCE THE 1970S.

Women's participation in politics from the time of their enfranchisement (1916) to 1970 usually involved casting ballots and participating in auxiliary party organizations: they were rarely acceptable as policy-makers or as candidates. Although resurgent feminism (and other factors) has had an impact since 1970, Saskatchewan women have made only moderate advances in politics; in fact, on the federal level, no Saskatchewan woman has served in the House of Commons since the 1940s. Women are still most likely to hold elective office on the municipal level—on city councils, school boards, and the like. In the 1970s two women did become mayors: in 1970 IDA M. PETTERSON became mayor of Estevan and served until her 1976 defeat; that same year, M. ISABELLE BUTTERS was elected mayor of Weyburn and served until 1982. A few others ran, but lost.

As for the Legislative Assembly, only six women were elected up to 1967; between then and 1975, no female MLAs served. Before 1982, no more than three served at one time; numbers increased slightly during the 1980s, and in 1991 twelve were elected—eleven NDP and one Liberal. Since then the number of female MLAs has hovered around ten (in 2004 there were six NDP and four Saskatchewan Party). The first women were appointed to Cabinet in the 1980s, JOAN DUNCAN and Patricia Smith being named in 1982 by the newly elected Progressive Conservative government. Thirteen have served up to the present time. Although organizations like the Women's Liberal Association have folded, women continue auxiliary work. They also have a voice, albeit small, in party governance, and in 1989 LYNDA HAVERSTOCK became head of the (faltering) LIBERAL PARTY. During the 1970s criticism of women's subordinate and limited place increased in all parties; most pronounced among New Democrats, the party's response to that criticism (and to women's issues) led some women to dismiss conventional politics.

Since 1970 women's involvements have been affected by complex changes including feminism,

structural transformations in politics and parties, and the near demise of leftist policies and parties. However, women are not always welcomed as equals, and many women also lack interest. Women have become acceptable in the symbolically important ceremonial post of LIEUTENANT-GOVERNOR: SYLVIA O. FEDORUK was the first, appointed in 1988 and serving until 1994; Lynda M. Haverstock was appointed in 2000.

Ann Leger-Anderson

WOMEN ENTREPRENEURS OF SASKATCHEWAN INC. (WE).

Women Entrepreneurs of Saskatchewan (WE) was established as a non-profit membership organization in 1995 to help women in businesses. Although one-third of provincial businesses are owned and operated by women, the large membership of WE–650 members–suggests the importance of assistance. WE is funded by Western Economic Diversification Canada and is part of the Women's Enterprise Initiative network, which assists women across western Canada. WE's head office is in Saskatoon, with a branch in Regina.

Since its inception, WE has sought to eliminate the barriers that confront women entrepreneurs. It seeks to help women (urban and rural) who want to start or purchase a business, or expand an existing business. Crucial financial assistance is provided through a loan program to businesses that are majority-owned and operated by women. Business advisors provide essential information. Training workshops are offered in a variety of formats, including face-to-face training and distance learning. WE also provides opportunities for women to network and assist other women, through mentoring programs, member events, and an annual Business

Symposium. Besides providing assistance to women, WE offers youth programs, whose target is elementary and high school students, with an aim to increase youth's awareness of entrepreneurship as a career option.

Laura Small

WOMEN IN SPORTS.

Organized sports began for both men and women in the 1880s as soon as there were permanent newcomer settlements. As towns were established, their citizens began skating, curling, and playing a variety of ball games, and were soon competing with neighbouring towns. Later, facilities such as golf courses and gymnasiums gave residents additional athletic opportunities. The 1920s were a golden age for both men's and women's sports in Saskatchewan. In larger centres, leagues in baseball, basketball, and tennis attracted hundreds of participants. In sports like golf, bowling, and curling, women competed in daytime events and evening mixed competitions. At the UNIVERSITY OF SASKATCHEWAN, athletic director Joe Griffith began actively recruiting and coaching talented athletes of both genders, particularly in swimming and track and field. His star competitor was ETHEL CATHERWOOD, a high jumper who captured the gold medal at the 1928 Olympics. In 1929, the University established an independent women's sports program.

WORLD WAR II (1939–45) and its aftermath brought new opportunities for women athletes. Twenty-six softball players from Saskatchewan took part in the All American Girls Professional Baseball League from 1943 until 1954. Synchronized swimming, a sport in which only females participate, began in 1941 at the Regina YOUNG WOMEN'S

SASKATCHEWAN ARCHIVES BOARD R-B1615

Prince Albert Tumblers hockey team, 1907.

CHRISTIAN ASSOCIATION (YWCA). Immediately after the war, the Saskatchewan High School Athletic Association was formed to encourage interschool athletic competition for both boys and girls. Also, many sports began offering clinics to attract the large number of children born shortly after the war. Figure skating, for example, attracted many young girls who were often taught by more senior skaters, some of whom later skated professionally in traveling ice shows.

As the baby boom continued in the 1950s, more girls participated successfully in recreational and competitive athletics. The first women's gymnastics club in Saskatoon produced three national champions, Gail Daley and sisters Glenna and Patti Sebastyen, within ten years of its founding. Women track and field athletes from the University of Saskatchewan also had success at the national level and obtained places on Canada's international teams; and a Saskatoon women's basketball team won the national championship in 1959.

Opportunities for women in sport increased in the 1960s as governments began to encourage this type of healthy activity. In 1967, the Canadian government initiated the Canada Winter Games, followed by the Summer Games two years later. These games brought together the best athletes in many sports from each province, with women competing in about two-thirds of the events. The 1970s brought even more growth. In 1972, the Saskatchewan government began sponsoring the Saskatchewan Summer and Winter Games. Aside from the benefits of additional competition, these games provided needed facilities in the province's smaller cities. Also, the provincial government began channeling lottery profits into sports through an organization called SaskSport. This money allowed sports organizations to set up permanent offices and hire administrators and coaches, many of them women, to do work previously done by volunteers.

With this new interest and funding, more girls and women became involved in sports. Schools, including the newly independent UNIVERSITY OF REGINA, fielded women's teams and also provided both recreational and competitive opportunities in individual sports. Women took up sports such as rowing, SOCCER and HOCKEY, which had previously attracted men only, and they also participated in new sports such as ringette, an almost exclusively female ice sport started in the mid-1970s. At first, it was difficult for these teams to get access to facilities such as rinks, but the athletes and their parents pushed hard for equal ice time.

Saskatchewan women athletes achieved national and international prominence during the 1970s. Local women curlers captured seven national titles during the decade, and also took four junior titles. In track and field, Saskatoon's Diane Jones (now JONES KONIHOWSKI) gained a reputation as a world-class

pentathlete, competing in three Olympic Games and winning gold in this event at the 1978 Commonwealth Games.

The 1980s and 1990s saw a continuation of the expansion of women's athletics in Saskatchewan, with women continuing to move into traditionally male sports such as cycling and wrestling. The province also continued to produce national and international champions. Some of the most successful of these were Regina's SANDRA SCHMIRLER's curling foursome, who won the world championship in 1993, 1994 and 1997, and captured the Olympic gold medal in 1998. Saskatoon speedskater CATRIONA LE MAY DOAN also won several world titles and repeated as Olympic gold medallist in 1998 and 2002. HALEY WICKENHEISER, of Shauvanon, and three other Saskatchewan women played on the 2002 gold medal Olympic hockey team. *Sandra Bingaman*

WOMEN IN THE LABOUR FORCE. Traditionally, reference to women in the labour force has focused on women in the paid labour force. Yet in Saskatchewan's agricultural-based economy, as in many other Canadian communities, economic development relied greatly on women's unpaid labour. The 1871 Order-in-Council that became the Dominion Lands Act of 1872 allowed for a basic 160-acre grant to any family head or male of 21 years of age, subject to a $10 fee. However, it was the proof of cultivation and residence in the homestead, usually for at least three years, that allowed for the acquisition of more land and access to more and better acreage. Farming relied on rudimentary tools, backbreaking work, and a short and demanding climate cycle. By law it was male farmers who owned the means of production, organized the work, sold the produce, and managed the proceeds. Wives, sis-

ters, and daughters were the unpaid help. For women on Saskatchewan farms it was not until 1907 that a law concerning married women's property rights allowed them to hold, administer, and dispose of property. Yet when the first Bureau of Labour was added to the Department of Agriculture in 1911, provisions for employment services still targeted "farm labourers" and "domestics" as distinct gender categories for subsidized passage to Saskatchewan from Great Britain, reflecting the stereotypes of the day.

The earliest laws related to women who worked outside the farm gate were found in federal legislation of the 1880s and 1890s. These included child labour laws and provisions under the Factories Act, pieces of legislation that an 1889 Royal Commission on Labour identified as poorly drafted and poorly enforced. While the legislation restricted hours of work to a maximum forty-eight hours a week and disallowed night work between the hours of 11 p.m. and 6 a.m., with one meal break for a full day's work, most small shops were excluded from the legislation. Workplaces included were almost never monitored. Related legislation called "Masters and Servants Acts" helped insure that employers retained an upper hand with employees such as clerks, apprentices, service workers and others, often hired or contracted for little pay other than room and board. Stiff fines or imprisonment could result from broken contracts or absences without leave, or for failing to obey the employer or perform specific duties.

The notion of women as domestic helpers not entitled to equal property rights, salaries, or decision making to support independence provided the backdrop to the struggle of Saskatchewan women for equality in the labour market—a goal yet to be

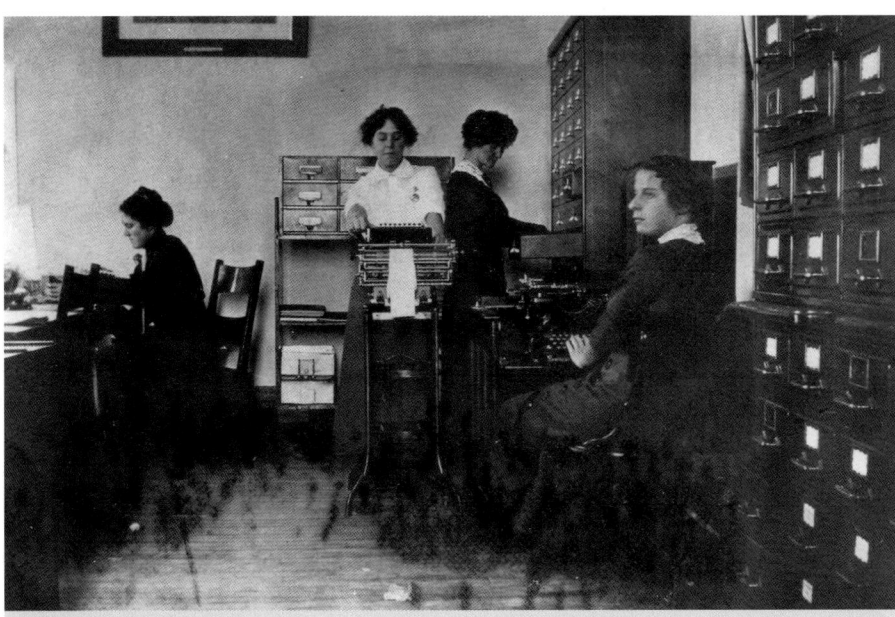

SASKATCHEWAN ARCHIVES BOARD R-A21768

Women office workers, Land Titles Office, Regina, ca. 1913–1914.

achieved across Canada. While Saskatchewan was one of the first provinces after Manitoba to receive the vote in 1916, working conditions for women improved little during the first part of the 20th century. The years prior to **WORLD WAR I**, particularly from 1906 to 1912, saw growth in the cities that led to the development of an urban working class including building tradesmen, painters, typographical workers, and city and railway workers. Union activity for better wages and working conditions targeted these traditionally male-dominated jobs. Many union contracts distinguished between skilled and unskilled workers, offering more favourable provisions for skilled workers, again usually male.

With World War II, women replaced men on the farm, in ammunitions plants, railways, shops and banks, earning 50% to 80% of the wages men earned. Hours of work increased while working conditions deteriorated in the name of patriotism. With the end of the war, minimum wage laws were introduced in Saskatchewan in 1920 but would continue to follow a two-tiered approach. At first, minimum wages only applied to shops and factories in the cities, and as they were expanded reflected a system that valued men's work more highly than women's. Minimum wage orders continued to reflect this two-tiered system into the 1970s, favouring construction, well-drilling, truck driving, logging and lumbering work over female-dominated care giving and retail sales. Union contracts in many establishments also reflected gender biases, with clerical professions slotted at the bottom of wage-and-benefit scales even though unionized workers fared better than did those who were not organized.

Women's work in Saskatchewan leading up to and following **WORLD WAR II** continued to be treated as secondary. Women were forced to leave jobs because they married, and certainly because of pregnancy. They were required to leave jobs when men returned from war. Seats in professional schools such as law, engineering and medicine were reserved for men while women were not expected to apply. With the rare exception, managers, professors, school principals, and trade union leaders were men. Skilled trades and politics were the purview of men.

In Saskatchewan the struggle for stronger labour laws and property rights including pensions, maternity leave, equal pay, and non-discriminatory treatment in the workplace regardless of gender or marital status, was taken up by women in both the public and private sectors. Early initiatives were supported by the creation of a one- person Women's Bureau in 1964, followed by an expanded Women's Secretariat and the Women's Division of the 1970s. An activist Human Rights Commission, along with enhanced funding for women's groups following the 1971 Royal Commission on the Status of Women, also helped move the agenda forward in

the 1970s. Unions, especially the **SASKATCHEWAN FEDERATION OF LABOUR** and women's groups such as Saskatchewan Working Women, which had active chapters in most corners of Saskatchewan, addressed workplace issues such as sexual harassment, affirmative action, technological change, daycare, pay equity, and the role of women in unions.

Maternity leave, included under the Unemployment Insurance Act in 1971, became a workable reality for Saskatchewan women by 1973, when the province introduced its first Maternity Leave provisions under the **LABOUR STANDARDS ACT**. The legislation was enforced vigorously for a period of time by the Woman's Division, and made more flexible in 1976 to ensure the right of women to return to their jobs. Waiting periods and the length of benefit period gradually increased through the 1990s, currently coinciding with the federal employment legislation which permits a year's leave. "Equal pay for comparable work" legislation was introduced in 1965, later amended to permit referrals of an equal-pay dispute to the Human Rights Commission, with penalties for non-compliance. Saskatchewan's legislation was seen to be a little stronger than the standard "equal pay for equal work" legislation that was starting to be implemented across the country, and "comparable work" set the stage for "equal pay for similar work" legislation in 1973. Under this provision similar work in the same establishment, requiring similar skill, effort and responsibilities as well as working conditions, paved the way for future debate about equal pay for work of equal value, a concept not yet enacted in Saskatchewan. By 1976 legislation adopted the Saskatchewan Federation of Labour's suggestion that wages of other employees not be reduced to accommodate an equal-pay ruling. Paternity, adoption and bereavement leave, and graduated notice of termination linked to technological change also helped women gain more equal footing in the workplace by the early 1980s.

Other changes to legislation included the enforcement of Maintenance Orders in 1986, and the introduction of a Saskatchewan Family Income Plan (FIP) in the early 1970s. FIP, when first introduced in the mid-1970s, was designed to ensure that children would not fall below the poverty line if their family income was no higher than minimum wage. Governments allowed it to be eroded by not building in an inflation factor, but later it helped establish a model on which to build the National Child Tax Benefit. The Saskatchewan Women's Division, unions, and community women's groups also played a significant role in mobilizing women to support the inclusion of the equality provision in the Constitutional amendments of 1983, including a Charter of Rights that led to the gradual elimination of discriminatory clauses in many pieces of legislation. Noteworthy were changes to widow's benefits under the Workers' Compensation Act (benefits

were eliminated on remarriage), and pension benefit legislation (pensions died with the contributor– usually the husband).

Despite improvements, Saskatchewan women still face inequality in the working world whether the work is paid or unpaid. In terms of work in the home, studies consistently show women doing more unpaid work than men. Working women still earn less than 70% of men's wages, and their participation in the paid work force is still lower than men's (60% versus 72%).

Merran Proctor

WOMEN OF SASKATCHEWAN: *see essay on page 1025.*

WOMEN'S CHRISTIAN TEMPERANCE UNION (WCTU).

The WCTU, already well established in the Dominion, came to the North-West Territories in the mid-1880s when unions (groups) were formed at Regina and other town sites along the new **CANADIAN PACIFIC RAILWAY** route. Despite slow initial growth, by 1917 the WCTU was flourishing with over 1,600 members in seventy-three local unions organized into six districts. Members were usually middle-aged, middle-class, married, evangelical Protestant, English-speaking townswomen. Leaders were prominent, well-educated women, active in other women's organizations, and likely married to men of substance in the community.

The WCTU sought to organize women for temperance work, protect the home from evil influences, work for national progress, conserve moral values, and build God's kingdom on Earth. Members pledged themselves to total abstinence, to educate others (especially children) to follow suit, to pressure churches to use grape juice in place of wine, and to boycott stores selling liquor. They also expressed growing concern for women's rights, worked to help the poor, provided night accommodations for weary travelers, and assisted people in trouble, notably young women. In 1910, for example, a Saskatoon Union established a Rescue Home for Unwed Mothers, which they operated until the **SALVATION ARMY** acquired it in 1935.

Between 1910 and 1930, the WCTU was a prominent women's organization in Saskatchewan, closely allied with progressive reform and the Social Gospel. It actively worked for objectives such as prohibition and women's suffrage–reforms obtained during **WORLD WAR I**. However, by the 1920s the WCTU had become so single-mindedly attached to prohibition that its membership polarized. Many moderates left, while remaining members, along with new "dry" supporters, became increasingly conservative, moralistic, coercive and xenophobic in rhetoric, goals and activities. During the 1920s members feared the impact of Canada's relaxed immigration laws, the failure of prohibition, and the "Roaring Twenties" culture that was perceived as morally depraved. After 1930, the WCTU in Saskatchewan continuously declined in membership and influence. By 1970 it had disappeared altogether.

Marcia McGovern

FURTHER READING: McGovern, M.A. 1977. "The Woman's Christian Temperance Union Movement in Saskatchewan, 1886–1930: A Regional Perspective of the International White Ribbon Movement." MA Thesis, University of Regina.

WOMEN'S HEALTH. Historically, women's health in Saskatchewan and elsewhere was not a separate area of practice or research. When women's health was considered, it was generally in the context of healthcare as a whole, or narrowly focused on maternal, reproductive, and babies' health. The social and women's movements of the late 1960s and early 1970s precipitated changes in women's consciousness regarding health care; it was out of these movements that the importance of addressing women's specific health care needs emerged. Beginning in the 1970s, gender differences between men's and women's health were recognized and researched as an important determinant of health. Today, many local health districts and regions in Saskatchewan do provide specific women's health programs and services.

In the late 19th and early 20th centuries, isolation, cultural practices, financial problems, and a lack of doctors often meant that midwives and experienced older women were called upon to deliver babies and provide care for women in their homes. During the 1920s and 1930s, efforts to improve care for women continued to focus largely upon women as mothers. Concern about high maternal—and infant—mortality rates led to efforts to reduce them; improvements included assistance grants to women in need, pre-natal education and care, and increased medical competency. As well, most women (unless they lived in very isolated regions) gave birth in hospitals by the 1950s.

During the 1960s focus shifted, and birth control became a central issue. Prior to 1969, women in Canada could not legally obtain information on, or prescriptions for, artificial birth control. The public distribution of birth control information and sale of contraceptives was legalized in 1969; abortion, however, was still left in the Criminal Code. In 1970 a large-scale Abortion Caravan travelled from Vancouver to Ottawa to demand the decriminalization of abortion; a contingent from Saskatchewan, members of Women's Action Community Health Care (WACH) participated. In 1988 the Supreme Court ruled that the federal abortion law, which had seriously restricted women's access to abortion services, was unconstitutional, and struck down the provisions of the criminal code pertaining to abortion. In July 1992 the Women's

Health Centre, an outpatient clinic at the Regina General Hospital, began providing a variety of services about reproductive choices to women. Already in existence, Planned Parenthood (incorporated in Regina in 1986 and later in Saskatoon) was providing education, birth control, and information about sexually transmitted diseases as well as unplanned pregnancy options.

Specific health needs of women, other than reproduction, began to receive attention from Saskatchewan's Regional Health Authorities and non-profit women's groups. Separate mental health services for women were offered, as well as information presentations on a wide array of issues affecting women (e.g., menopause, eating disorders, breast-feeding, sexually transmitted diseases). A province-wide mammography screening program for breast cancer funded by the provincial government through the **SASKATCHEWAN CANCER AGENCY** began in 1990. In 2002 the Prevention Program for Cervical Cancer was started, followed later by bone density testing programs for women. In 1972, the Canadian Cancer Society established "Reach for Recovery" programs across Canada. Breast Cancer Action Saskatchewan, a provincially based, non-profit group was established in 1994 to make the lives of those affected by breast cancer more manageable through advocacy, education, support, and networking.

In 1996, as part of a national strategy to address women's health, the federal government established five research centres across Canada. The Prairie Women's Health Centre of Excellence (PWHCE) was established in 1997 to focus on community-based research, policy advice, and social factors to promote women's and girls' health and well-being in Saskatchewan and Manitoba. Concern about not only the physical but also the mental health of women was expressed in attention to abuse-related issues. The Provincial Association of Transition Houses of Saskatchewan (PATHS), a non-profit organization providing services to abused women and their children, was formed in 1984. PATHS brought together Transition and Interval Houses, temporary emergency shelters, and second-stage housing under a provincial umbrella.

Since the 1970s women's groups from across Saskatchewan have provided specialized information and services on many areas of women's health. The DisABLED Women's Network of Saskatchewan promotes self-help for disabled women. Immigrant Women of Saskatchewan, located in Regina and Saskatoon, provides resources to newly arrived women from other countries. Lesbian health information is provided by Gay and Lesbian Services located across the province. Aboriginal and Métis women's groups focus on a wide range of counseling, family and health services for women. There are also groups that specifically offer information

and services for young women, sex-trade workers, women living in poverty, those affected with HIV/AIDS, and rural women across the province of Saskatchewan.

Wendee Kubik

WOMEN'S MOVEMENT, 1970–2004. The women's movement in Saskatchewan in the 1970s resulted from the radicalization of women's issues in the 1960s. Its relationship to the political realm has often been problematical. Major concerns included childcare, technological change, unionization, pay equity, abortion rights, protection against violence, and women's health. A critical strategy was the development of organizational coalitions for the purpose of advocacy and pressure; they have dealt with violence, abortion rights, health, international solidarity, and racism. In some cases coalitions were based on national initiatives, particularly regarding abortion rights. Also, the Saskatchewan Action Committee on the Status of Women, an attempt to unite women under a representative umbrella organization, emerged in the mid-1970s.

Several issues were related to the workplace, where women's participation was on the increase: by 2000, they accounted for 46% of the paid workforce in the province (compared with 37% in 1980). The income gap between men and women, though narrowing, is still present: in 1999 it was 66% of men's income, compared to 45% in 1980. As well, women have traditionally been confined to ghettoized workplaces: service work, health, food and accommodation sectors, education, and sales—much of it part-time. Aboriginal women faced additional hurdles: lower-end jobs, inequality in employment and income, and racism.

In the 1970s new organizations developed, partly mirroring developments elsewhere in Canada, as radicalization occurred. They focused on working and poor women's rights and needs, as opposed to more traditional women's organizations, which were grounded in middle-class perspectives. Significant among these in terms of unionization and working women's rights was Saskatchewan Working Women (SWW), which developed in the latter 1970s as a response of radicalized women to the need for an organization with a working-class position that focused on women's issues in the workplace. The 1970s also saw the emergence of community-based organizations focusing on health issues, including abortion, reproductive rights, and protection from violence. They developed from university women's centres and self-help groups, and included women's centres and crisis centres in Regina and Saskatoon. Regina's Transition House and Saskatoon's Interval House, which focus upon providing shelter against violence, were among the first such initiatives in Canada. Women's health was, and is, also an important issue: early organizations were Regina Coalition for Reproductive Choice,

Healthsharing and, later (1995), the Prairie Women's Health Centre of Excellence.

Rights of Aboriginal and immigrant women became an important concern, and Aboriginal women's services, organizations, and support groups developed; women are now playing a more formal role in Aboriginal government. Immigrant women developed self-help organizations, such as Immigrant Women of Saskatchewan and the Congress of Black Women. A recurring concern, equal pay for equal work, came to the fore in 1991 when the SASKATCHEWAN FEDERATION OF LABOUR sponsored a pay equity coalition to pressure the new NDP government. Advocacy has achieved a policy framework for pay equity which has had limited success: it applies to government sector women (1997) and health workers (1998), but not to poor women in ghettoized workplaces or to non-union private sector women. Government's response to women's pressure did lead to the development of structures devoted to women's policy, research and service that date back to the 1960s. Shifts have occurred, from the Women's Bureau, Division, Secretariat, and now the Status of Women's Office. Although the 2002 move to totally eradicate this function failed in the face of protest, the attempt illustrated waning governmental support of a wide range of women-centred initiatives.

In the 1970s, expanded government financial and program support for social assistance initiatives had meant growth of women's organizations. Many, however, became dependent upon government financing; governments chose to shift responsibility to these organizations for provision of services in order to meet rising demand with less expenditure on their part. This policy led to difficulties when governments (provincial and federal) reduced support. By the late 1980s, a time when the women's movement was no longer front-page news, federal and provincial Conservative governments slashed funding. Such cuts severely handicapped organizations—Aboriginal, White, and immigrant—and resulted in a significant drop in advocacy and service. The 1991 provincial election lessened financial constraints, but the strategy of leaving service delivery to women's organizations remained. Many organizations, unable to engage in social action, were forced to scramble for funding and to focus upon delivery of services.

The progressive anticipations of the women's movement, born in the 1970s, have been eroded by neo-liberal policies; in addition, new demands and issues need attention. At present, significant organizations maintain critical services and research; sporadic joint actions emerge; new initiatives are developing around Aboriginal feminism; and the Prairie School for Union Women, begun in 1997, is evidence that working women's initiatives are continuing. *Sheila M. Roberts*

Women of Saskatchewan

Historical Overview

Ann Leger-Anderson

When John Hawkes noted in 1924 that women had made immeasurable contributions to the making of the province, he implicitly privileged the newcomers of favoured ethnicity, namely British Canadians.[1] Writing from the vantage point of 2004, the story is far more complex: many newcomers then looked upon as inferior are now a part of the provincial story; Aboriginals, long marginalized, are now claiming their rightful place; and new immigrants are present. This essay primarily discusses the dominant newcomer women of the 20th century.[2]

SASKATCHEWAN ARCHIVES BOARD R-A19719

Métis family in the Auvergne district, ca. 1908.

In 1870, when the future Saskatchewan became part of the newly established North-West Territories, its women were Aboriginal. Some were MÉTIS—women of mixed blood who were part of FUR-TRADE history. Others soon arrived, such as Red River Métis no longer comfortable in the new province of Manitoba. The vast majority, however, were full-blooded Indians, often Cree, who followed traditional ways. By the early 20th century, newcomers—who had originally been a mere trickle—overshadowed Aboriginals. Perhaps the first was a missionary wife, Mrs. Robert Hunt, who accompanied her husband to a new Anglican outpost, Stanley Mission, in the mid-1850s. In 1860 three Grey Nuns (SISTERS OF CHARITY) arrived at Ile-à-la-Crosse to assist the work of the OBLATE priests. Other women with missionary objectives followed, teaching and providing medical care. If Roman Catholic, they were usually members of religious orders; but some came as laywomen—ONÉSIME DORVAL, for example. If Protestant, women likely came, as had Mrs. Hunt, as half a missionary team led by a minister husband. Some were single women, however, like Presbyterian LUCY BAKER, who spent her life in the Prince Albert area. Among others was perhaps the first female medical doctor in what was to become Saskatchewan: ELIZABETH MATHESON. She arrived in Onion Lake in 1892 with her Anglican missionary priest husband, who demanded she finish her medical training to better minister to the needs of Aboriginals. Women also served as staff members of the schools that sought to teach White ways, an effort then regarded as worthy. They were usually in a subordinate role, the school being under direct male authority; a rare exception was Presbyterian CATHERINE GILLESPIE (later MOTHERWELL), who was principal of the File Hills boarding school from 1901 to 1908, in spite of opposition from some government officials.

W Not all late-19th-century newcomers had missionary intentions. Some undertook commonly expected—and demanding—auxiliary roles as paid helpmates of men, often doing laundry work or providing food and board. They might serve as domestic servants in early newcomer homes. Some followed other occupations. Prostitutes, for example, were a mixed lot that included Aboriginals; the ones partially visible in the pages of history tended to be newcomers, and in the territorial decades were likely to be tolerated, so long as they remained in special areas. There were other sorts, too, like the notorious Mrs. Habourg (there are variant spellings), whose Moose Jaw restaurant was a front for peddling the whisky that she ingeniously smuggled in.

Other Victorians who arrived are suggestive of the female diversity in the territorial era, and sometimes of the opportunities occasionally present. Maritimer CATHERINE SIMPSON HAYES, for example, was a woman of many talents who led a double life. In 1879 she arrived in the Prince Albert area; after a failed marriage, she surfaced in Regina with two children and apparently portrayed herself as a widow, although her husband was actually farming in Ontario. Living in the territorial capital until 1900, she was soon a prominent figure in its cultural life, working as a journalist and author. She became the lover of NICHOLAS FLOOD DAVIN, owner and editor of the *Regina Leader* and the local printer; hidden behind her façade of Victorian respectability and her glorification of women's sphere of domesticity (so strong that she never became a suffragist) were her two children by him. Another was GERALDINE MOODIE, a pioneering woman photographer who set up studios in Battleford, then Maple Creek, during the 1890s, undeterred by her growing family and the demands made upon the wife of a North-West Mounted Police officer. In early Saskatoon, Grace Fletcher became storekeeper, seller of buffalo bones, and owner of much real estate; her career as a successful businesswoman was perhaps impelled by an alcoholic husband.[3]

Occasionally girls left traces of their lives. May Clarke, for example, had come to early Regina with her English immigrant family. In 1887, when she was 13, her father sent her to work for Nicholas Davin; as a printer, the latter was in need of able workers and willing to stretch gender boundaries, and he taught her tasks usually reserved for males. Typical, though, was her being forced to quit when family obligations—her mother's illness—demanded it. Many came and went, as for example, the bookish and impish Lucy Maud Montgomery. In summer 1890 she arrived in Prince Albert, a 16-year-old girl intending to live with her long-absent father and her stepmother; the latter, however, turned out to be jealous and demanding, and Lucy was glad to leave a year later. Her journal provides rare glimpses of the past: insights into the Prince Albert school life (including her teacher's unwanted affections), and into the interests and outlook of a relatively privileged girl.

Most women and girls who came in the late 19th century (and somewhat later) have been lost to history.[4] Sometimes they came alone, although they often had relatives nearby. Most often they came as members of family units, usually homesteader families, perhaps associated with a colonization project or bloc settlement. Besides British Canadians, females of many ethnicities settled: Hungarians, Scottish crofters, Swedes, Norwegians, Finns, Danish, Romanians, Icelanders, and German-speaking peoples, including Mennonites. Different in religion were the women who were part of several Jewish agricultural settlements. At century's end came Doukhobor women and girls, whose understanding of the Christian faith, including views of marriage and divorce, was at odds with the host society; British Canadians, misperceiving their labours, viewed them as victims of terrible male-imposed drudgery. Female Britishers came too, perhaps connected with distinctive settlements like CANNINGTON MANOR. Some came as part of emigration schemes undertaken to reduce the surplus female population. Present also were the French; Quebecois women in particular had a difficult time and found their immediate environs strange, primitive, and isolated.[5]

As the new century opened, female diversity increased. Among recently arrived newcomers were the wives and children of the men in the sheepskin coats, the people later called Ukrainians. Female and male alike were often seen in British Canadian eyes as inferior, with alien religion, customs, and lifestyles, including marriage of young girls, female field labour, and male violence (which worsened with heavy drinking). Ukrainian wives and mothers (as was usually the case with non-Anglo immigrant groups) were likely to feel caught between old and new worlds, bound to home and old country language, expected to uphold ethno-cultural traditions, yet perhaps derided by their own children adapting to new ways. After the 1905 replacement of Clifford Sifton with Frank Oliver as Minister of the Interior, American farmers and their families became favoured—when White. Blacks were deemed undesirable; yet some arrived, mainly from Oklahoma. Among those who came in early 1910 and subsequently developed a farming community in Eldon district was the Mayes family, whose matriarch, Hattie Mayes, became the backbone of her community and church, her influence illustrating the informal power women of diverse sorts could wield.

In the late 19th or early 20th century, newcomer females were seen, when noticed at all, as wives, mothers and homemakers, their triform role central to the agricultural economy that Ottawa deemed the prairie destiny. Women were helpmates, essential to the agrarian enterprise: such was suggested by promotional literature, travel accounts, eulogies, editorials, even women themselves. Only marriage could end the plight of the bachelor homesteader: the woman could then share the burden of work, give birth to the children who would soon become contributing, productive family members, and make the house a home. Wife, mother, homemaker, then, gave the male a stake in making his enterprise successful. Men themselves sometimes sought wives in newspaper letters or ads. "Getting a mate" was a theme in appeals directed towards women: Come west, fill a badly needed job like teacher or domestic servant, then find a marriage partner, thereby making an even greater contribution to development. Finding mates (or jobs, or both) was also a leitmotif of British women who sought a solution to the surplus female population at home. By the eve of World War I, however, Saskatchewan's gender imbalance had ceased to be a major problem.[6]

SASKATCHEWAN ARCHIVES BOARD R-A20815

Sandy Trebick with chickens, mid-1920s.

Only rarely acceptable was woman as farmer; women's field work was itself problematic, and British Canadians frowned upon its presence among some newcomers.[7] "Woman as farmer" was culturally deviant, acceptable only in exceptional circumstances: in fact, the 1911 census listed only 12% of women in Saskatchewan's paid labour force as general farmers; mainly 25- to 64-year-olds, they were most often widows who had taken over the farm after the husband's death and were likely assisted by their children. Hardly any women were *bona fide* homesteaders. Married women, of course, could not claim homesteads, and the 1872 DOMINION LANDS ACT prohibited acquisition by single women. Only under stringent conditions were women, usually widows with dependents who presumably would handle heavy outside farm work, allowed to file for a homestead. This law came under attack, and an English immigrant-turned-farmer who had settled in the Qu'Appelle Valley, GEORGINA BINNIE-CLARK, became the major spokeswoman advocating its amendment. Ineligible herself, she had been forced to buy land, and struggled under what she condemned as undue financial burdens. She carried her case to the media and to Ottawa, and homesteads for women turned into a petition-signing crusade: there were over 11,000 signatures when presented to the government in 1913.[8]

For the vast majority of women and girls, owning a farm was doubtless inconceivable under any circumstances: their lives were lived as daughters, then as wives, mothers, and homemakers on farms and homesteads (*see also* PIONEERS, FEMALE). Their conditions were often hard, their plight sometimes noted. Initial settlement was of course difficult because of primitive isolated conditions; it was especially so for the newcomer minority from urban backgrounds, unaccustomed to the unrelenting hard work that was the lot of farm women and girls. Subsequently, farms often remained remote from services, with health care being perhaps the female's greatest concern, given her responsibility for family well-being and her frequent pregnancies. As well, farm homes were likely small, poorly constructed places with few, if any, amenities. Making the house a home was the woman's domain—a difficult task, especially when available cash generally went into the farm operation. Even if the image of drudge may sometimes be overdrawn, hard work never let up. In fact, women's unpaid labour, so often overlooked, was crucial because it was their responsibility to keep husband and children fed, clothed, sheltered, and healthy. Farmwomen's work usually included such tasks as upkeep of a garden, caring for poultry, and processing of foodstuffs. The stereotypical image of a food-laden farmhouse table, however, hides a not uncommon reality on the prairies: poor limited diets. The woman might also keep the farm accounts, and bring in supplementary income to help keep the farm afloat by selling surplus eggs, milk, or butter. Typically, farm women made do and provided what they could of necessities and amenities.

This picture is a general one, and factors such as ethnicity, class, location, immediate circumstances, family expectations, individual traits, and luck affected actualities. The similarities in women's responsibilities, the commonality of women's tasks, the usual conviction that women's proper role was wife, mother and homemaker are striking, however, and sometimes raise questions about the existence of a female frontier, or more generally a female culture. To answer them is difficult given that the above-listed factors—especially class, ethnicity, and location—might divide women. Yet another consideration was the pervasive conviction that woman's place was subordinate, that the male had certain obligations to protect and to be the breadwinner, that the female was incapable of assuming certain obligations of the man's world. There were, though, many variations on these basic themes, and some were informed by a far more denigrating view of women than others. Even so, the sense of male dominance was pervasive, and the double standard with its apotheosis of female sexual purity and acceptance of male waywardness held sway.

Such views were, of course, also pervasive in urban centres where a small minority of newcomer females lived.[9] Nevertheless, the rapidly growing cities and larger towns, in contrast to the rural areas, provided more options: lives there were often easier, more exciting, and more varied. Young, old, middle-aged, of favoured ethnicity or not, class-privileged or not, females often felt the pull of the towns and cities. Important for many were employment opportunities, circumscribed as they were.[10] The typical female wage earner was a young single woman: a newly wedded female normally left the work force, likely to return only if required by economic necessity, perhaps widowhood or an incapacitated husband. Perceived as temporary workers and paid less than men, females were also regarded as fit workers only in certain jobs.

SASKATCHEWAN ARCHIVES BOARD R-A7583

Domestic servants, Government House, 1898.

SASKATCHEWAN ARCHIVES BOARD R-B2604-1

Young English women brought over for household service, 1920.

Other factors also determined what jobs were open to females: class, ethnicity, and demand. Rare in agrarian Saskatchewan were factory jobs, then the preferred employment among unskilled women. Present was the still common opposition to female workers in industrial jobs; available, however, was domestic service, the traditional mainstay. Only a few were elite positions, like those held by English/British Canadians at Regina's GOVERNMENT HOUSE. Far more likely were jobs in urban homes, from middling to stately; and such positions were greatly preferable to employment in rural homes, where actual need was greatest. Recruitment schemes, targeting English domestic help, brought few: the "servant problem," urban and rural, was a concern well into the 20th century.

The rapidly developing economy of early 20th-century urban Saskatchewan provided a range of female jobs. Among them were telephone operators, women having been deemed more polite and less critical of low wages than males. Office jobs multiplied in government agencies, insurance and real estate operations, and mail order operations (like Regina's two huge ones, Simpson's and Eaton's): unlikely to demand high pay or authority, females were welcome in white-collar jobs of varying skill levels. Salesclerks were readily employed, often in department stores or the new dime stores. Urban centres, large and small, needed hotel and restaurant workers.[11] A few women were self-employed, even entrepreneurial, most likely running a small confectionery store or a boarding house; but there were others too, such as "Lady Brokers" and Saskatoon Nursery proprietor Mrs. E. Marriott.[12] Expanding government functions also might create positions, as in the case of ETHEL MACLACHLAN, appointed Superintendent of Neglected and Dependent Children, and soon thereafter becoming the first Juvenile Court Judge in Saskatchewan, in 1917.

Some moved into the "female professions," which compared to the male professions were less prestigious, lower in pay, and characterized by little control or authority. Newest was nursing, most likely private duty work after training (and working) in the nursing schools affiliated with the new hospitals. The premier female profession, however, remained teaching, rural and urban. Present even in early territorial days, working perhaps in makeshift private schools, female teachers became ubiquitous, especially the elementary school teacher. Most school marms were rural, but women were likely to prefer an urban school because working and living conditions were better (even though the pay was about what the school janitor received). The new urban collegiates provided occasional jobs in prewar Saskatchewan, and some dedicated spinster teachers remained there for decades. E. Don Cathro, for example, a Queen's graduate, was already teaching in Regina when the new collegiate opened; she moved there in 1909, and taught English until her retirement in 1935.[13] Women religious, of course, were the backbone of nursing and basic teaching for the Roman Catholic population.

Whether in these or other jobs, who did what was affected by class and ethnicity, as well as by a closely associated factor: education. Most newcomers did regard basic schooling as appropriate for girls; it was, nevertheless, usually subordinate to family needs and obligations. Some females, most often affluent English-speaking girls, secured secondary education, perhaps in a same-sex religiously affiliated school[14] or small tax-supported facilities, or, by the eve of World War I, collegiate institutes that provided traditional academic instruction, complete with Latin as well as business and commercial subjects. A few females went to the new University of Saskatchewan, where classes were first held in 1909. By then, regardless of level, household science was frequently lauded as the best education for girls and young women—a posture indicative of the ongoing fear that education, especially advanced education, undermined home and family. At the new university, only in 1928 did a School of Household Science open (*see also* WOMEN AND EDUCATION).

What females could or could not do, what they could or could not study, was partially governed by custom, practice, and expectations. All, however, stood equal (or rather unequal) before the law. Married women's position, especially, was inferior, although the traditional principle of coverture had been modified. In the territorial era, for example, married women had limited property and contractual rights, which were carried over after 1905 but were significant mainly for a few urban women. Of especial importance to farmwomen, the newcomer majority, was the absence of any traditional dower right, a loss dating back to the Territories Real Property Act of 1886 (subsequent legislation did not fully redress difficulties). Rural or urban, husbands were legally dominant. Although some modification occurred, women had limited legal rights, even over the children; the concept of marital rape was nonexistent; legal divorce was rare and costly—and stigmatized the woman; and deserted wives had little recourse. Single women had more rights, and property-owning single women (including widows) acquired the right

SASKATCHEWAN ARCHIVES BOARD R-A6514

Miss Emily Johnson (in doorway), telegrapher at Fort Qu'Appelle, ca. 1900

SASKATCHEWAN ARCHIVES BOARD R-A14580

Teacher Myrtle Cross with her students, Butterton, 1918.

to vote locally before married women did. Single or married, women could not vote in provincial or federal elections[15] (*see* LEGAL RIGHTS OF WOMEN).

Limited rights and subordinate position notwithstanding, women were essential to the newcomer settlement process in what became Saskatchewan. Crucial were their roles not only as wives, mothers and homemakers, but also as participants in the paid labour force. They made other contributions to newcomer development, usually as a result of seeking to replicate the world they had left behind or to ameliorate conditions. These varied roles and contributions interacted in complex ways, and sometimes led to tensions among different sorts of women. To re-establish religious institutions, and to influence society through them, was important for many newcomer women.[16] Although Jews and other non-Christians were among the newcomers, Christians (of many denominations) predominated, and the female Christian was often seen as having a special religious propensity; in any case, she was more likely to be a church member. Women might also look upon a local church as a focus of identity in an otherwise strange or isolated world, as a place for socializing, or as a pleasant change of pace for special occasions. The religious community or personal devotions might provide crucial sources of solace and comfort in a world beset by danger and death. What contributions a woman was able to make towards furtherance of her religion in the larger community depended upon a denomination's assessment of woman's nature and duties.

Within Roman Catholicism women religious were subordinate to male priests but carried out important traditional functions, staffing hospitals, charitable institutions, and schools. Among the major Protestant denominations that formed the culturally dominant group—Presbyterian, Methodist, Anglican, Baptist—and were evangelical or had evangelical wings, women carved out a different sort of separate subordinate sphere of auxiliary work: besides Sunday School teaching, they were active in ladies' aids and female missionary societies; found in urban and rural areas, they were major expressions of women's religiosity, and the initial major women's organizations. Although women's work merely replicated what was already well established, the demands of a new, sparsely populated land sometimes led to tasks not usually seen as fit for women's hands.[17] Woman as preacher, however, was an unbreachable barrier, and Protestant women had no direct say in the general governance of their denominations. Another practice also signalled women's subordinate status: until the late 20th century, a woman would likely join her husband's denomination if different from hers.[18]

Women also had been moving beyond denominational confines, establishing a wide range of organizations, largely urban-based. Through them women contributed to community development, assisted others, enlarged their own rights, pursued interests, and sometimes influenced policy formulation. Members tended to be British Canadian, more affluent, better educated, married women. They joined for many reasons: some serious, like contributing to the community, pursuing interests, or developing leadership skills; and some less so, like looking for a rationale for leaving the house, an opportunity to socialize, or a means of social climbing. For a select group, organizational work was a substitute career, welcome at a time when well-to-do married women rarely worked outside the home.

The first major organizations that breached denominational confines represented voices of evangelical Protestant womanhood, and had among their objectives improvement of the female lot: WOMEN'S CHRISTIAN TEMPERANCE UNION (WCTU) and YOUNG WOMEN'S CHRISTIAN ASSOCIATION (YWCA). Both dated back to the 1870s in Canada, the former having American roots, the latter English. The WCTU spread rapidly in prewar Saskatchewan, becoming the largest of women's organizations; its reformist enthusiasms were many, and it was frequently critical of the impact of the status quo upon women and families. The YWCA emerged as women sought to provide protected environments for young women pouring into the burgeoning cities to work or study; the first branch was established in Moose Jaw in 1907. Earlier, in 1895, a Local COUNCIL OF WOMEN was founded in Regina. Initially it was little more than an umbrella group of women's religious auxiliaries, but its objective was the establishment of a local hospital, and it later dealt with numerous issues, including women-related ones. Several additional councils emerged during World War I, and a provincial body was formed.

Other organizations developed, among which were professionally oriented ones like the Saskatchewan Registered Nurses Association (1917) and the Saskatoon Women Teachers' Association (1918). Cultural interests found expression in the WOMEN'S MUSICAL CLUBS of Regina (1907) and Saskatoon (1912), or the Women's Educational Society associated with Regina College. University graduates formed the University Women's Clubs of Regina (1915) and Saskatoon (1918), soon affiliated with the CANADIAN FEDERATION OF UNIVERSITY WOMEN. Women who sought to promote Canadian and imperial identity joined the IMPERIAL ORDER OF DAUGHTERS OF THE EMPIRE, present from 1909; women of other national identities also formed organizations; still other associations provided important auxiliary assistance to institutions like the new hospitals. These—and other—women's organizations were largely based in cities and towns. The new province, however, was primarily agricultural: of great importance, therefore, were two women's organizations that sought to ameliorate the harsh conditions of life on farms and homesteads, and in rural communities. Largely attracting English-speaking newcomers, they rapidly developed throughout the province and numerous women belonged to both. In 1911 the Homemakers' Clubs of Saskatchewan were founded, patterned after the Women's Institutes that first emerged in mid-1890s Ontario (*see* HOMEMAKERS' CLUBS AND THE WOMEN'S INSTITUTES); and in 1914 came a uniquely Saskatchewan contribution, the more radically oriented Women Grain Growers, which was open only to bona fide farm women (*see* ORGANIZED FARM WOMEN IN THE WGG, THE UFC, THE SFU, AND THE NFU).

Rural or urban, women's organizations in Saskatchewan rapidly grew during the 1910s; many of them had a feminist cast, at least of a maternal sort that saw in the efforts to secure an enlarged sphere for women an expression of woman's mothering instinct. Some women also began to focus upon the organizational needs of youth, especially girls, and embraced two new organizations that quickly spread to Saskatchewan: GIRL GUIDES (1910) and CANADIAN GIRLS IN TRAINING, present by 1918. Specifically for rural youth were the Girls and Boys Clubs, established in 1918 (later, 4-H CLUBS).

By the eve of World War I, the lives of more affluent urban girls and women followed familiar Edwardian patterns. Whether they were significantly freer than "back east" is difficult to ascertain, living as they did within the social setting that had developed and that many found enjoyable. Annie Brown, for example, a Lieutenant-Governor's wife, apparently quite liked the social whirl of Government House and her many organizational involvements; as well, her life demonstrated how the new land provided opportunities for social mobility. Most urban females were not so comfortably off, and some lived difficult lives. For example, the girls and women of East End Regina, filled with continental European immigrants living in cramped unsanitary conditions, had limited options; and yet, some among them had comparatively unheard-of opportunities. The vast female majority lived on farms and home-steads, and few had the advantages of a Catherine Gillespie Motherwell, able to shift back and forth from a comfortable farm home to affluent circles of the capital city. Their lives were sharply different—even more so for the many girls and women who differed in language, expecta-tions, and lifestyle from the host society. Even the comfortably off (in relative terms) had few amenities, and neither they nor most urban dwellers were likely to engage in a recently expanded sphere of female activity—sports: tennis, golf, women's hockey, and basketball were enjoyed only by the few[19] (*see* WOMEN IN SPORTS).

An increasing number, though a minority, were dissatisfied with their position in Saskatchewan. Already organizationally active, they were concluding that their participation allowed at best limited opportu-nity to enhance communities, shape development, or influence policies and practices: women, therefore, needed a direct voice in the body politic; they needed the vote. A short-lived campaign, mainly a massive petition-signing effort that galvanized many heretofore passive women, resulted in victory, and Saskatchewan became the second province to grant the vote, in March 1916 (*see* WOMAN SUFFRAGE). As befitted an overwhelmingly agricultural province, the movement was primarily agrarian; the WGG provided crucial leadership and worked in conjunc-tion with the WCTU, with its base in urban centres; of especial impor-tance in this movement was VIOLET MCNAUGHTON. More and more women endorsed suffrage, doing so for many reasons. Perhaps above all, it was seen as a tool for reform, especially prohibition, but also for other reforms that would uplift community and province. It was a way for women to advance their own interests, to redress their loss of dower law rights and secure homestead rights. As well, making females full cit-izens was a timely democratic reform. Males, however, were the voters and legislators, the power holders. After several years of stonewalling, the Liberal government decided the time had come: women, they con-cluded, had shown they wanted the vote. Enfranchisement had become a sign of progress: Saskatchewan now stood for progress.[20]

By March 1916, women were busily engaged in supporting the war effort, their activities perhaps a factor making female enfranchise-ment more palatable. Their contributions were usually made through urban and rural organizations, the IODE playing a significant leadership role.[21] In fact, the growth of women's organizations during the war years is partially attributable to women's determination to participate in the war effort. Their many activities included raising funds for diverse projects such as ambulances, hospitals, and relief efforts; they also knit, made bandages, assembled soldiers' comforts, collected reading materi-als, and conserved food and clothing. Aboriginal women on reserves also contributed, their efforts soon forgotten. Although occasional women served as military nurses, the average English-speaking woman worked on the home front, her patriotic fervour sometimes reaching fever pitch, and contributed to increased Canadianizing efforts, suspi-cions about enemy aliens, and the drive for English-only schools. The war's end was marked by another catastrophe: the flu pandemic; throughout the province women worked to alleviate suffering however they could. Then came the 1920s, a decade of building upon the forma-tive years that had brought into being the third most populous province in the Dominion.

The more fervent suffrage supporters, who foresaw a new era of women's activism, were soon disappointed. Women interested in politics tended to do little more than undertake auxiliary work in the extensive network of women's Liberal and Conservative associations that

emerged. The experiences of the first woman MLA, SARAH RAMSLAND (Pelly constituency) are instructive, given the hostile opposition to her candidacy. In 1919 she won a widow's seat in a by-election, then won again in the 1921 election, but only by a plurality of votes cast by a badly divided electorate choosing among four candidates; and in 1925 she lost a two-way race to the candidate who had come in last in 1921. Locally, a few women were elected to school boards, more often public than high school, and some were appointed to library boards. How significant were the women's efforts to encourage their sisters to run, like those of Regina's Local Council of Women, is difficult to determine. As for the hope—and fear—of women voting as an influential bloc, that turned out to be a myth. Perhaps related, little redress occurred of still unequal legal rights; and many of the most active former suffragists, who also wore a WCTU hat, were appalled when Prohibition ended. As for the Persons' Case decision of 1929, the result of the work of the Alberta Five, Saskatchewan women displayed moderate interest at best; some, in fact, saw the Senate as an undemocratic, unelected body that should be abolished.

The (still small) urban spearhead did continue to provide more options and opportunities for women than did rural Saskatchewan, especially during the boom years of the late 1920s. As before, a range of jobs existed, and well-educated single women still occasionally found career niches in a male-dominated world. Dr. FRANCIS MCGILL, for exam-ple, had recently launched what was to be a lengthy career in patholo-gy, including forensic pathology. Dr. LILLIAN CHASE, a student of Banting's, began to practice in Regina in 1925, becoming head of the Regina General Hospital medical staff in 1932. EDITH ROWLES SIMPSON headed the School of Household Science, finally established in 1928 at the University of Saskatchewan. Occasional women engaged in pioneer-ing work, as did CATHERINE SHELDON–WILLIAMS when she single-handedly began the Outpost Correspondence School in 1926.

Still typical was the young single female worker who left the work force after marriage: wife, mother, homemaker—these roles were still privileged. Job paths were familiar, including white-collar positions, nursing, sales jobs, restaurant and hotel work, domestic service, and teaching (still more rural than urban). The plight of women workers did receive some attention, but little improvement.[22] In 1919 a Minimum Wage Board had been established, its aim to determine wages, hours, and conditions of labour. Unfortunately it did not cover most employed

SASKATCHEWAN ARCHIVES BOARD R-A21545

Staff, Royal Hotel, Strasbourg.

SASKATCHEWAN ARCHIVES BOARD R-B9197

Hay Creek Homemakers, 1918 or 1919.

became more plentiful; automobile ownership rapidly increased; and battery radio sets became popular. How "gendered" was the use of autos and radios is an interesting question: Who decided where to drive, and when? Who drove? Who listened to what programs? Whatever the answers, women themselves might prefer links to the outside world over spending limited funds on home improvements. Even when money was available, however, women might do without. The end result was a rural Saskatchewan dotted with cramped, poorly constructed homes without plumbing, running water, electricity, or central heating. Another facet of some farm women's lives, market-oriented production outside the WHEAT economy, received attention with the WGG's promotion of the Egg and Poultry Pool in 1926. A Saskatchewan farm woman, the widowed Isabelle Bryce, of Arcola, became the first woman to win a prize at the 1924 International Livestock Exposition at Chicago, for her Clydesdales.

females, and its authority was limited. Little could be done, for example, to raise wages that at the beginning of the decade generally fell below a living wage, calculated at $15. By the mid-1920s Employed Girls Councils were found in Regina and Moose Jaw, their aim to discuss problems and help the workers learn about existing legislation. In Regina, the Local Council of Women was involved, its committee convenor, MABEL HANWAY, dedicated to improving conditions of women workers and also active with the Employed Girls' Councils. The Women's Labour League was also present, its concerns partially focused upon female workers.

Organizations remained active, and additional ones were established. Among them was the professionally oriented Canadian Women's Press Club (Saskatoon and Regina). Culturally focused ones included the Women Artists' Association that spread provincially by the late 1920s, and the Canadian Daughters' League in Regina (1927) and Moose Jaw (1930); as well, the important Arts and Letters Committee of Regina's Local Council of Women was founded. Women were also involved in fledgling cultural groups promoting drama, for example LOUISE OLSON in Saskatoon. The decade saw organizational efforts among women of non-dominant ethno-cultural roots. Some local affiliates of national bodies were established: for example, a Regina branch of the CATHOLIC WOMEN'S LEAGUE (1919) and a Saskatoon branch of the National Council of Jewish Women (mid-1920s). In Saskatoon there emerged in 1926 what was to become a national organization with its origins in the province: the Ukrainian Women's Association of Canada. In agrarian Saskatchewan the Homemakers' Clubs and WGG (as well as its post-1926 successor, the women's section of the United Farmers of Canada) remained active and sought extensive betterment of conditions for women, their families, and local communities.

As for females in rural and farm areas, improvements were relative.[23] Life was, of course, extremely primitive in remote places still being settled; but in already established districts, it eased for some women—at least in certain respects. Mechanization began to ease harvest time burdens because where combines were used, women no longer had to feed large threshing crews. Links with the outside world often increased, English-speaking females benefiting most; telephones in rural homes

For most women, rural or urban, life revolved around family. Even though the independent young woman was admired in the media, the assumption remained that she would settle down, becoming the 1920s version of the wife/mother/homemaker: modern and efficient, making use of scientific and business expertise. That model, of course, was remote from most female lives in Saskatchewan, and what impact it had is difficult to determine. Certainly, metropolitan currents were felt, such as for example the growing interest in birth control; even its advocates, however, saw it appropriately used only by married women. Since birth control was illegal, its use was largely subterranean,[24] but sometimes the topic received a public airing: the late 1920s saw a flurry of interest (continuing into the early 1930s); some discussion occurred in newspapers; and the topic became a lively one at United Farmers of Canada conventions, both at the women's section and general conventions. Among those who endorsed legalization were Zoe Haight, Violet McNaughton, and SOPHIA DIXON. Support diminished as religious, especially Roman Catholic, opposition surfaced. Divorce, too, became more common and now attainable in the provincial court system; but grounds were largely unchanged, and the stigma remained great.[25] Common were efforts to make women better homemakers by disseminating up-to-date household science information, and to improve upon motherhood. Included were government programs that provided minimal assistance to needy married women, and mothers' allowances that targeted indigent widows and dependent children.[26] Initial efforts to reduce the high infant and maternal mortality rates also expanded. Beginning in 1919–20, maternity grants assisted poor women who were remote from doctors, and by 1929–30 help was given to 1,112 mothers.[27]

As the 1920s decade neared its end, many Saskatchewan women of diverse backgrounds doubtless felt caught between old and new: modern ways of carrying out women's age-old roles vied with traditional ones, and new models beckoned. Cultural transformation emanating from metropolitan centres threatened traditional values, leading for example the still influential WCTU to feel at increasing odds with society. Often a worry for mothers was the movies: enticing, yet sometimes threatening—a danger to their children. Girl Guides and the CGIT provided welcome counter-influences. Concern about children had also brought into being the new Home and School Associations, with GRACE BLUE as a leading advocate. Present also was conflict over the new province's future as ethno-cultural tensions in polyglot Saskatchewan boiled over and women were caught up in the tensions: some were voices of the new, some of the old, seeking to keep the province British, perhaps supporting efforts like the Fellowship of the Maple Leaf, the Anglican Sunday School Caravan Mission led by Eva Hasell, or the recruitment of British domestic servants. Then, in the latter 1920s came the KU KLUX KLAN; women's involvement in it is an interesting question. Preoccupied with diverse cultural issues and the demands of daily life, one wonders whether a breakthrough like ETHEL CALDERWOOD's victory at the 1928 Olympics was a welcome diversion or a non-event for most women. As for sports generally, some younger urban women did continue their interest; the 1920s saw the spread of women's curling teams, and by decade's end an annual bonspiel had been established.

Cultural questions, and many other issues, took a back seat in the 1930s as economic survival became paramount. In that decade of making do, women were critical players. Urban women suffered—as wives, mothers, homemakers, and wage earners[28]—especially those already living in straitened circumstances.[29] Most still lived on farms, likely caught up in the vicissitudes of the wheat economy that dominated agricultural Saskatchewan, at the mercy of nature and international markets. Some left the province; others headed to new settlement areas where they attempted to start from scratch; still others tried their luck in urban centres. Most remained, even where conditions were at their worst in southern Saskatchewan, and experienced terrible burdens psychologically and materially. Impoverishment became widespread, and women struggled to maintain home and family. They made do with used clothing, charity food, closure or reduction of services, and even more inadequate health care; ironically, though, infant and maternal mortality rates lessened.[30] Usually hidden, moreover, are the stories of violence and abuse.

More women became politically active, participating in demonstrations or, more likely, joining political movements of leftist orientation. The movement with a future turned out to be the CO-OPERATIVE COMMONWEALTH FEDERATION, founded in 1932 and in which women's roles were circumscribed by conventional attitudes. Twenty or so women (out of over 130 delegates) were present at the first national convention, in July 1933, when the REGINA MANIFESTO was endorsed. In it women were given brief egalitarian lip service, but in practice were viewed as domestic creatures and auxiliary personnel. The need for able workers did occasionally provide new opportunities for Saskatchewan women: the "right-hand man" for leader George Williams, for example, was a woman, Georgina Mathers; an effective speaker like LOUISE LUCAS, or a capable organizer like Elsie Gorius was welcomed; Sophia Dixon even became an early member of the CCF National Council. Occasional female candidates ran; they were usually welcome only if the CCF candidate had little chance of success, as Gertrude Telford discovered when she sought nomination in Pelly constituency[31] (*see* WOMEN AND POLITICS, POST-SUFFRAGE TO THE 1970S). Interestingly, a once-bright female light in the CCF who had been expelled became a Saskatchewan first: the first woman from the west to sit in the House of Commons. This was DORISE NIELSEN, an English immigrant who had become radicalized during the 1930s; in 1940 she successfully ran as a United Progressive candidate in 1940 for North Battleford.

Women's involvement in the political sphere also included occasional election to city councils. HELENA B. WALKER, the LCW endorsed candidate, won a seat on the Regina city council in 1932; in 1937 Ella Muzzy was elected in Prince Albert, serving until 1942. As for Regina, intra-gender conflicts abounded in politics. In 1932, for example, there had been a second woman candidate: Mabel Hanway, no longer welcome in the LCW, had stood as a labour candidate. In the late 1930s, after the LCW ceased to endorse candidates, a League of Women Voters affiliate was launched by the Regina Business and Professional Women; its apparent initial objective was support for city council candidates that were acceptable to the establishment. As for the familiar women's organizations, they felt the impact of the DEPRESSION and suffered some membership decline, but remained active. Occasional new ones, largely branches of organizations headquartered elsewhere, were also established, in particular the BUSINESS AND PROFESSIONAL WOMEN'S CLUBS in Saskatoon (1930) and Regina (1933). As well, the aforementioned League of Women Voters emerged in Regina and lasted until the late 1950s.

There were occasional success stories for career-oriented women; admittedly they were rare, and usually emerged because of unusual circumstances. Of particular note was RUTH SWITZER MCGILL, a 1932 University of Saskatchewan Law School graduate, whose prominent legal and business career was doubtless assisted by her association with her father, founder of the Debenture Company of Canada. Willing to endure the long hours and poor pay of Regina College, HILDA NEATBY began her career as history professor in the mid-1930s. In Saskatoon MABEL TIMLIM was following an unusual path with her part-time studies and part-time teaching of economics at the University. Jean Murray began teaching there too, her salary paid by her father, the president. In 1936 in Moose Jaw, LYDIA GRUCHY became a Saskatchewan record-maker when she became the first woman to be ordained in a major denomination (the United Church). That career-oriented women faced obstacles and hostile receptions is certain, and occasionally discussion surfaces, as in the autobiography of another who established herself in 1930s, Dr. PHYLLIS L. STEELE, one of a dozen women doctors in the province.[32] Cultural endeavours continued to attract women, and one Saskatchewan product, EDNA JAQUES, gained national recognition: her poems, a celebration of ordinary daily life, were disdained by critics but beloved by average Canadians.

Before the Depression decade ended, war came again in September 1939. During the earlier anti-war movement, Saskatchewan women's voices had been raised, some of whom like Sophia Dixon were involved with the Women's International League for Peace and Freedom (founded during World War I). Some refused to jettison deeply held pacifist views: Gertrude Telford, for example, who was rewarded with an annual visit from the RCMP. Most women endorsed the war effort, as in World War I, and worked to ensure women's home front participation. They undertook tasks similar to those of 1914–18, and once again did so primarily through women's organizations. Some also took over normally male jobs. Others went into war industries, factories making munitions, planes, and other war materials—often moving to central Canada. A few worked making munitions in Regina, at the former GM plant; still others joined the military when the three services opened their doors, serving in auxiliary positions and thereby freeing more men for combat duty. Most remained in Canada, but some were posted overseas in non-combatant positions. Occasionally women became prominent: MARION GRAHAM, of Saskatoon, for example, one of the first women to enlist in the RCAF, became a squadron leader. The province also was home to the first woman of the First Nations to enlist in the army, Mary

Greyeyes of the Muskeg reserve. Saskatchewan women made a name for themselves in other ways. GLADYS ARNOLD, for example, who had started out as a secretary-turned-journalist at the *Leader-Post* from 1929 to 1935, became a passionate defender of the Free French. JOANNE BAMFORD FLETCHER got over 2,000 Dutch civilian prisoners out of Sumatra. On the lighter side, Saskatchewan produced about half of the fifty Canadian women who played in P.K. Wrigley's All-American Girls' Baseball League during the war years.

By war's end, the CCF government was in power: elected in 1944, it was to remain for twenty years. Women had campaigned both for and against the CCF, and parties once again directed appeals to women voters that emphasized how proposed programs would help shore up women's (family-oriented) concerns. In office, the CCF implemented numerous measures that impacted women as wives, mothers, and homemakers. It quickly established the Department of Social Welfare (November 1944), and subsequent changes to social welfare policies culminated in the Social Aid Act of 1959.[33] Sometimes the government built upon existing programs, as when it moved quickly to provide free health care services to recipients of Mothers' Allowances and their dependents, effective January 1945. Between 1945 and 1947, numerous changes were made to Acts affecting such matters as deserted wives and children. Health care for mothers and babies was a major concern. Infant and maternal mortality rates had already dropped considerably by 1944, and hospital births had risen from 55.5% by 1941 to 77.2% in 1945. In the early CCF years, controversy erupted over proposed implementation of nurse-midwives in remote areas: although several women did receive specialized training, the program remained limited in scope, and lay midwives were still used sometimes.

The introduction of MEDICARE in 1962 further alleviated the burdens of costly health care, but women were split on the issue and on the manner of handling proposed changes. A few Regina women, in fact, spearheaded the formation of the "Keep Our Doctors" committees, which quickly spread. Numbers of women actively supported the legislation, including, of course, CCF women: MARJORIE COOPER, CCF MLA, had introduced the bill and was a leading spokeswoman. Nurses themselves were divided, and the Saskatchewan Registered Nurses Association took no stand.[34] Ultimately, women and their families benefited from the expansion of tax-funded health care; those in cities and larger towns enjoyed the greatest accessibility.

Other government policies also affected women: growth of the government bureaucracy, for example, created a range of female jobs, mostly clerical. Better professional opportunities arose as well: the great expansion of health care services meant that nurses and nurses' aides were needed. The elaboration of social assistance measures provided some professional opportunities, as in the case of Mildred Battel, who became a prominent figure. She was a McGill graduate (1945), the first Saskatchewan woman to graduate as a professional social worker. Appointed assistant director of child welfare in the Department of Social Welfare in 1952, she became director two years later; she played an influential role in shaping policies and practices relating to child abuse, and also sought to get better treatment of, and respect for, unwed

RALPH VAWTER PHOTO/SASKATCHEWAN ARCHIVES BOARD R-A11592-1

Mildred Battel, director of child welfare, 1962.

mothers and babies. MARY ROCAN, who was a secretary to the Minimum Wage Board in the new Department of Labour, became assistant director of the Labour Standards Branch in the early 1950s; soon after the Liberal victory of 1964, she became founding Supervisor of the first Women's Bureau. Women in the arts benefited from the establishment of the Saskatchewan Arts Board, sometimes as paid employees, often as recipients of support.

This expansion of opportunities, however, was limited, occurring in an environment in which women were usually still seen as rightly playing subordinate roles in a male-dominated world. Sex discrimination, in fact, was not mentioned in the 1947 Bill of Rights, the first general law in Canada that prohibited discrimination. The 1945 amendment of the 1930 Public Service Act did repeal the ban on employment of married women except in special circumstances, stating that there should be no discrimination on grounds of sex, race, or religion; even so, a married woman could be employed only in certain circumstances. As for the 1947 Public Service Act, it made no specific references to women, married or single.

The CCF can claim no responsibility for advancing women in politics. As for elective office, in 1944 only two CCF candidates ran, BEATRICE TREW being the sole victor; the loser, GLADYS STRUM, was elected in the 1945 federal election and served one term (LOUISE LUCAS, a likely winner, dropped out of the federal race because of terminal cancer). In 1952, Marjorie Cooper became an MLA, winning a Regina seat and staying in office for the remainder of the CCF government. She was, in fact, one of the few (now NDPers) who kept their seats in 1964, and she retired in 1967. She offered a woman's perspective but, unlike Strum, who was a relatively outspoken feminist, her demeanour exuded 1950s stereotypes: feminine, soft-spoken, and family-oriented. Not all were satisfied with the near-absence of women candidates: Gertrude Telford, for example, who in 1959 expressed her displeasure with the CCF record and blamed both men and women.[35]

Well-established patterns of women's political behaviour continued during the postwar era. Most preferred auxiliary work, and the likeliest place to find a woman elected office-holder was in local government. City councils did see a few more women members. Saskatoon elected its first female council member, MARGARET HARRIS, in 1948; and Regina continued to have at least one female councillor, usually someone with a Council of Women connection, until 1955, after which no more were elected until 1967. In both cities, women candidates usually spoke of the housewife's perspective and were still likely to be perceived in terms of mothers/wives/homemakers. Beginning at mid-century, voters in a few smaller cities began occasionally to elect women councillors. For most women home and family remained central, and this emphasis permeated the CCF era. It was seen, for example, in left-oriented organizations like the Housewives Consumers' Association or the Saskatchewan Women's Co-operative Guild (founded in 1940), as well as in Dorise Nielson's *New Worlds for Women*, written in 1944 while still an MP (she had, like occasional others, also affirmed women's right to work, married or single).

How that domestic life was lived did vary, as always, according to factors such as locale, class,

W

Miss Saskatchewan Wheat Queen (centre) and two princesses, 1958.

and ethnicity. As well, the advent of television both reinforced and challenged conventional British-Canadian mores. Saskatchewan females, in general, followed patterns common elsewhere during the postwar era: more finished secondary or post-secondary studies; yet getting a husband was a major objective, and if "gotten," the importance of ensuring his graduation could spawn an organization like the PHT (Putting Hubby Through) Club at the University of Saskatchewan. Larger families became the norm during these baby-boom years, and motherhood was privileged; yet, women were seen as increasingly in need of direction to properly carry out their roles, and family and child experts became more important. For those whose marriages were difficult, escape was rare: although divorce rates increased, especially in the immediate postwar era, divorce was still frowned upon (in 1946, 505 divorces occurred, the highest number up to that time).[36]

Perhaps not surprisingly, the numerous women's organizations, urban and rural, long seen as an appropriate outlet for women, often remained attractive, still able to meet diverse needs. They were, however, in their Indian summer: after the war, membership in many bodies had increased, but in the course of the late 1950s and into the 1960s it tended to decline for many organizations. Even so, in 1960 the *Star-Phoenix* reported a list of over 150 groups in their Women's Page files (exclusive of church and lodge circles, or HOME AND SCHOOL Associations). Some organizations had undertaken invigorating new tasks: the Regina Council of Women, for example, turned its attention to the serious housing problem in postwar Regina; it long remained a major concern, and attracted capable activists like JACKIE HOAG. Many organizations, however, simply ceased to attract new members as new interests arose, although service clubs did seem to thrive.

Women continued to play an important role in the era's cultural developments, their interests often rooted in established organizational activities. Several arts centres opened: for example one in Regina Beach, in which Barbara Muir Barber (Mrs. Fred Barber) played a central role; she had long been active in the Women Artists' Association and had served as convenor of the LCW (Regina) Arts and Letters Committee. In Regina the Norman MACKENZIE ART GALLERY opened, its core the carefully husbanded (by the Regina Council of Women) collection of its namesake. Drama, music, and writing, with their many female supporters, grew; women were important not only on the new Saskatchewan Arts Board, as mentioned, but also on many community arts councils.

These were also decades when paid work enticed more women. Despite the fact that the glories of home, family, and children were being trumpeted, more women were joining the workforce, among them increasing numbers of married women with children old enough to be in school. Job opportunities in an agrarian province like Saskatchewan were, of course, limited; but they did exist–many, as noted, related to the expansion of the government bureaucracy. The traditional female profession, teaching, continued to provide jobs, demand outstripping supply as baby-boom children reached school age. In fact, the need for teachers led to gradual elimination of formal barriers to married women teachers. In some other jobs, too, marriage became less of a barrier to employment. Other opportunities arose in relatively professional areas: the expansion of library services, for example, created influential positions for women–married and single–like MARION SHERMAN, FRANCIS MORRISON, and Marjorie Dunlop. Occasionally other opportunities arose, sometimes in business. Most females who needed work, though, sought unskilled or semi-skilled jobs; the major departure from past practice was the de-emphasizing of domestic service in the immediate postwar period.

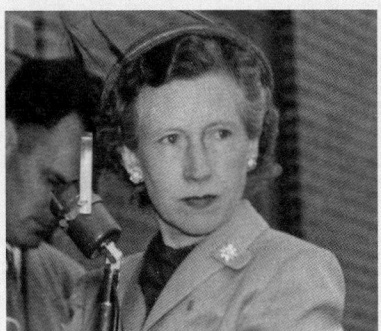

Above, Marion Sherman.

Right, Miss "Penny Powers" of the Saskatchewan Power Corporation addresses a group of about 100 farm women in the South Arcola Community Hall, August 1960.

Work gendering is clearly evident in this 1980 photo of a group of secretaries and their male supervisors.

Rural and farm women still constituted the majority of females after the war; but their numbers were declining, and by the end of the CCF era farm women had become a minority.[37] Rural or farm, the lives of girls and women were affected by many changes between 1944 and 1964. Beyond the provincial government's control, of course, were trends resulting in fewer and larger farms; but the CCF had as a central concern rural life, establishing for example the Royal Commission on Agricultural and Rural Life, and its policies did impact female lives. Construction of better roads, for example, increased mobility: now it was easier to enjoy the amenities of a nearby urban centre, perhaps the "big city," or to take an off-farm job. The massive rural electrification of the 1950s revolutionized the farm and the farmhouse itself, and "Penny Powers" was used to promote the use of electricity. Now electric stoves, washing machines, vacuum cleaners, refrigerators, and deep freezers became a part of farm life (whether it reduced farm women's labour or merely transformed it can be debated). However, farm homes frequently lagged behind urban homes in amenities, and many remained cramped, drafty places.[38] Farm or rural, women remained the backbone of social life, and their norm was unsung service in women's groups and auxiliary bodies.

By the mid-1960s a new era was beginning. Central was the resurgence of feminism during the decade, and its impact upon a new women's organization is illustrative. When the recently established VOICE OF WOMEN (VOW) arrived in Saskatchewan in 1961, it exemplified the traditional anti-war strain in women's thinking, one that included solicitude for children and affirmation of women's allegedly peaceful nature. Its immediate concerns were opposition to the military posturing of both sides in the Cold War and the threat of nuclear annihilation. Within a few years, however, VOW had also taken up women's rights issues and was among the organizations that presented briefs to the Royal Commission on the Status of Women. Responses to the recommendations of the subsequent report (1970) illustrated burgeoning feminist sentiments in many quarters. By the mid-1970s the new Advisory Council had Saskatchewan members, and within the province the Saskatchewan Action Committee on the Status of Women had been established. The pace of change, however, was too slow and the objectives too limited for many younger women who, often campus-based, had already established women's liberation groups (see FEMINISM:

CONSCIOUSNESS AND ACTIVISM SINCE THE 1960S and WOMEN'S MOVEMENT, 1970–2004).

The battles of the late 1960s and the 1970s seem distant now, but they wrought significant changes in female lives. Several developments were dependent upon federal action: legalization of birth control (1968); initial liberalization of abortion laws (1968, with subsequent changes); and easement of divorce laws (1967–68). Nevertheless, how things worked out depended upon local circumstances. As well, provincial-level changes affected areas like employment, with stimulus coming from the Women's Division (1964), later the Women's Bureau (1966), housed in the Department of Labour (see STATUS OF WOMEN OFFICE). Not until 1980 did significant changes begin to occur in the conventional understanding of married women's property rights (see LEGAL RIGHTS OF WOMEN). What happened in Saskatchewan, it should be emphasized, was rarely distinctive; one exception was the 1972 formation of the SASKATOON WOMEN'S CALENDAR COLLECTIVE.

Women made a few breakthroughs in politics, but have remained under-represented. So far only two women have been city mayors: IDA PETTERSON, from 1970 to 1976, in Estevan; and M. ISABELLE BUTTERS, from 1976 to 1982, in Weyburn. On the provincial level, more women have become MLAs: since the early 1990s there have been approximately ten at any given time. In 1982 the newly elected Progressive Conservative government named the first women to Cabinet: JOAN DUNCAN and Patricia Smith (see WOMEN AND POLITICS SINCE THE 1970S). As for women's organizations, once a source of women's influence (albeit limited), they have been overshadowed by complex economic, social, and cultural transformation. Membership fell in established organizations, urban and rural, as women took jobs, developed new interests and needs, or simply aged. Emergent organizations were likely to focus primarily upon interests of identifiable segments of women, for example: Aboriginal women's groups, IMMIGRANT, REFUGEE, AND VISIBLE MINORITY WOMEN OF SASKATCHEWAN, ELIZABETH FRY SOCIETY, or WOMEN ENTREPRENEURS OF SASKATCHEWAN. Although two-thirds of females are now classified as urban, Saskatchewan remains the most rural of the prairie provinces. Remaining farm women still work hard, and many work off-farm to help keep the farm intact; a growing minority are farm operators themselves (see WOMEN AND AGRICULTURE). Whether farm or rural, non-urban women find that services are unevenly distributed: the lioness's share is to be found in the provincial cities.

Women who are in the paid workforce, a growing percentage, continue to congregate in certain work categories, with perhaps fewer opportunities in face of downsizing and rationalization of work. Nevertheless, women are better represented than previously in professional categories such as law and medicine. As for business, about one-third of businesses are woman-owned and -operated (sometimes with a male partner), and special assistance programs are available. The businesses, though, are often small ones, and many doubtless help to keep the family farm afloat. Even now, there are relatively few female entrepreneurs like JACKIE HOAG, founder of Old Fashion Foods forty years ago. For many women life is difficult, and problems are still compounded by class and ethnicity. Aboriginal women face the most risks, but others are vulnerable, too. Women have borne the brunt of minimum wages lagging behind inflation, and of part-time work with its limited benefits and higher risks. Women and children rely most heavily on food banks, and, cutting across class and ethnic lines, women face increased hours of work: there is less time for family life, despite a growing emphasis upon its importance, for leisure, or for what remains of women's organizations.

NOTES

1. John Hawkes, *The Story of Saskatchewan and Its People*, 3 vols. (Chicago: S.J. Clarke Publishing Company, 1924), II, 865.

2. Although this essay contains numerous cross references, it does not attempt to cross reference all the women (or organizations) that appear in individual entries.

3. Georgina Taylor, "Grace Fletcher, Women's Rights, Temperance, and 'British Fair Play' in Saskatoon, 1885–1907," *Saskatchewan History* 46, no. 1 (1994): 3–21. For a discussion of early women in the Saskatoon area, see Jacqueline Bliss, "Seamless Lives: Pioneer Women of Saskatoon, 1883–1903," *Saskatchewan History* 43 (Autumn 1991): 94–100.

4. They can be identified by name in the manuscript censuses, including the now released special census of 1905.

5. See the following essays in David De Brou and Aileen Moffatt (eds.), *"Other" Voices: Historical Essays on Saskatchewan Women* (Regina: Canadian Plains Research Center, 1995): Lesley Erickson, "The Interplay of Ethnicity and Gender: Swedish Women in Southeastern Saskatchewan"; Mathilde Jutras, "'La Grande Nostalgie': French-Speaking Women and Homesickness in Early Twentieth-Century Saskatchewan"; Anna Feldman, "'A Woman of Valour Who Can Find?': Jewish-Saskatchewan Women in Two Rural Settings, 1882–1939."

6. Natural increase and family unit migration had largely resolved the problem.

7. British Canadians tended to ignore the fact that, when necessity required, their own women and girls did it.

8. The petition campaign had been originated by the *Grain Growers Guide*, and was supported by numerous settlers, female and male. It was also endorsed by numerous organizations and prominent individuals. Among the organizations were the Winnipeg Board of Trade, the Grain Growers of the three prairie provinces, the National Council of Women, the Canadian Women's Press Clubs, and the national WCTU board. Minister of the Interior Frank Oliver adamantly opposed proposed changes.

9. The total population in urban centres, defined in the censuses as incorporated centres with 500 or more people, was 9.2% in 1901, 13.2% in 1906, and 19% in 1911. From 1919–71, the definition referred to incorporated centres with 1,000 or more. See Appendix F, Rural/Urban Populations Trends in Saskatchewan, in John A. Archer, *Saskatchewan: A History* (Saskatoon: Western Producer Prairie Books, 1980), 360–61.

10. The following discussion, and subsequent ones, concerning female employment sometimes define job areas differently from census categories.

11. After 1912, however, White females could not work in Chinese-run restaurants (or other businesses). Legislation passed that year prohibited their employment by Orientals, and amendment the following year explicitly singled out Chinese employers. In new legislation of 1918–19 licensing provisions replaced the prohibition, and remained in force until 1969.

12. The Lady Brokers, listed in *Henderson's Directory* 1912, were Grace J. Wilkes and Jean A. Grant. The nursery was established in 1906, and Mrs. Marriott was apparently active from the start, took over after her husband's death in 1913, and was later assisted by her son.

13. Cathro also became prominent in women's organizations, and served on public school and library boards.

14. Examples of same-sex schools would be a convent school like St. Ann's or an institution like Regina's Sacred Heart Academy. St. Ann's, established in the mid-1880s in Prince Albert, was open to Roman Catholics and non-Roman Catholics. Sacred Heart Academy, founded in 1905, became an all-girls' school in 1910, and closed in 1969. A Roman Catholic school, it accepted non-Roman Catholics, and had boarding and non-boarding students. It was one that did attract a large number of students of German origin. Some schools came to be run by other denominations, for example St. Chad's, an Anglican institution that was established after World War I.

15. Sandra Rollings-Magnusson, "Hidden Homesteaders: Women, the State and Patriarchy in the Saskatchewan Wheat Economy, 1870–1930," *Prairie Forum* 24, no. 2 (Fall 1999): 171–83.

16. Since church affiliation so often functioned as a sign of community respectability and individual moral character, the depth of religious belief can be difficult to assess, but its presence is unquestionable.

17. An example was Mrs. Truesdale's serving as treasurer at Regina's First Baptist Church.

18. That the dominant churches did not meet all women's needs is suggested by the significant women's presence in the Salvation Army, an English import. The first Halleluiah Lassies appeared in Regina in the mid-1890s.

19. The new game of women's hockey quickly spread to "Saskatchewan," and teams were established in places like Prince Albert and Regina. The new game of basketball, adapted for women, also arrived, and the first team photograph dated from Weyburn High School, 1906. Schools, churches, and "Y"s all had leagues.

20. The government had already moved to address, or seemingly address, issues of women's rights. The Homestead Act, for example, dated from 1915; even with subsequent amendments, the law could be evaded. Other legal changes brought limited improvements.

21. Nadine Small, "The 'Lady Imperialists' and the Great War: The Imperial Order Daughters of the Empire in Saskatchewan, 1914–1918," in DeBrou and Moffatt (eds.), *"Other" Voices*, 76–93.

22. Strikes involving women, which were rare, occurred mainly in the late 1910s and early 1920s. See Christine Smillie, "The Invisible Workforce: Women Workers in Saskatchewan from 1905 to World War II," *Saskatchewan History* 39 (Spring 1986): 62–79.

23. An effort to produce a women's magazine that sought to respond to interests of the more comfortably placed, *The Western Woman and Rural Home*, produced in Govan, fizzled. It lasted 1923–26.

24. The Criminal Code did allow it if the public good was served. In the 1930s this proved to be an Achilles' heel in some cities.

25. In 1919 only three divorces were granted to Saskatchewan residents. Then came the changeover. Twenty divorces were granted in 1920. In 1921 there were fifty-nine divorces, then a drop until 1929 when a new high was reached: seventy-one. Grounds for divorce changed slightly in the mid-1920s: women no longer had to prove aggravated adultery.

26. Saskatchewan had been the second province to approve these mothers' allowances, which became effective in 1918.

27. This number jumped considerably—even the next year, 1930–31, saw 3,020 mothers assisted. Numbers continued to escalate, and this led to replacement of the grant program by a maternity package of layette, and supplies for mother. Numbers greatly dropped, but the program was criticized. The Maternity Grant program was reinstated in 1934–35, and the number of children who were born in hospitals again increased. The government perceived the program as a way to reduce mortality rates of mothers and infants, not as a relief measure. In 1938 the maternal death rate was 2.5 per 1,000, the lowest in Canada. The infant death rate was also the lowest—52 per 1,000 living births. By the end of decade, slightly over half of the births were in hospitals.

28. According to the November 29, 1932, issue of the *Leader-Post*, there were 483 women among the 1,729 reported as unemployed in three cities: Regina (147), Moose Jaw (102), and Prince Albert (59).

29. Theresa Healy, "Engendering Resistance: Women Respond to Relief in Saskatoon, 1930–1932," in DeBrou and Moffatt (eds.), *"Other" Voices*, 94–115.

30. Christa Scowby, "'I Am A Worker, Not A Drone': Farm Women, Reproductive Work and the *Western Producer*, 1930–1939," *Saskatchewan History* 48 (Fall 1996): 3–15. She argues that the farm women's identity was largely based on their work roles—productive, reproductive, and community. During this decade they redefined what it meant to be a wife, mother, and homemaker. She overstates her case.

31. She managed to secure nomination in the 1938 provincial election. Although she lost, she made a good showing, and sought nomination again. She failed to secure it, the victim of political infighting.

32. Phyllis L. Steele, *The Woman Doctor of Balcarres* (Hamilton: Pathway Publications, 1984).

33. Jim Pitsula, "The CCF Goverment in Saskatchewan and Social Aid, 1944–1964," in J. William Brennan (ed.), *"Building the Co-operative Commonwealth": Essays on the Democratic Socialist Tradition in Canada* (Regina: Canadian Plains Research Center, 1984), 205–25.

34. Marguerite E. Robinson's 1967 history of the organization, *The First Fifty Years*, studiously avoids reference to the topic.

35. Georgina M. Taylor, "'The Women … Shall Help to Lead the Way': Saskatchewan CCF-NDP Women Candidates in Provincial and Federal Elections, 1934–1965," in Brennan (ed.), *"Building the Co-operative Commonwealth"*, 141–60.

36. The following year saw 507 divorces, then numbers significantly dropped. In 1968, the last year before the revised legislation began to affect statistics, there were 384 divorces. In 1969 the number shot up to 880 (then dropped).

37. See Table, Rural/Urban Population Trends in Saskatchewan, in Archer, *Saskatchewan*, 360–61. In 1946 the rural and farm populations accounted for 74.9%, and in 1966, 51.0%. Farm population per se went from 53.3% to 29.3%.

38. In 1951 only 21% of farm homes were electrified. The electrification program began in 1949 with the Saskatchewan Electrification Act. By 1958 51,025 farms were electrified. See Saskatchewan, Royal Commission on Agricultural and Rural Life, *Farm Electrification*, Report no. 10 (1956). Report no. 11 dealt with *The Home and Family in Rural Saskatchewan*.

WOMEN'S MUSICAL CLUB OF REGINA. The Women's Musical Club of Regina (now Regina Musical Club) has had a lasting, significant effect upon Regina's cultural life. Organized in 1907 as the Women's Morning Musical Club, it was renamed the Women's Musical Club in 1909. Membership required referral by two Club members. For many years the members were mainly middle-class house-wives or, less often, professional music teachers. Talented and determined, these women shared a serious interest in music; they sought to provide opportunities for performance and to promote the enjoyment and appreciation of music. From the out-set, the Club was in contact with women's musical clubs from other centres across the prairies, exchanging both ideas and visits.

The Club's emphasis has been upon perform-ance. Its fortnightly meetings (actually hour-long recitals) were for members only. There were, how-ever, public performances in fall and spring as well as at Christmas, and occasional concerts with guest artists. The Club also gave countless young musi-cians the valuable experience of performing before a live audience, and offered medals and scholar-ships to skilled music students. Except for a brief hiatus during WORLD WAR I, the Club has endured. Its membership peaked after WORLD WAR II, briefly reaching 1,000 in 1950. When interest plummeted in the 1950s, men began to be admitted as associ-ate members. Today the Regina Musical Club offers to the public an annual series that features young performers.

Constance A. Maguire

FURTHER READING: Maguire, C.A. 2000. "'Concerts and Curtains': Darke Hall and The Women's Musical Club of Regina," *Façade* 12: 16; Women's Musical Club of Regina. Papers. R-347. Saskatchewan Archives Board. Regina.

WOMEN'S MUSICAL CLUB OF SASKA-TOON. In 1912 the Women's Musical Club of Saskatoon was formed to encourage the serious study of music; and it did just that for sixty-six years. Initially, membership was restricted to active mem-bers, willing to perform at Club meetings; by the 1950s, however, the Club admitted inactive mem-bers—women who would be willing to provide an audience for the performers. From the beginning, prospective active members not only needed a refer-ral from a Club member, but also were required to pass a rigorous audition. Although professional music teachers made up a greater proportion of members than in Regina, most members were mid-dle-class housewives, and all were classically trained musicians.

Seldom having more than forty members, the Club met in members' homes until 1939, after which Club members and their invited guests assem-bled in various public venues. Their regular meet-ings featured lectures and essays on musical topics, as well as performances. They covered a wide spec-trum of classical music, including new compositions (even some written by Club members). Twice a year the Club held Morning Musicales, public perform-ances by its members that were always well attend-ed. The Club also offered scholarships and prizes to promising, talented students. By 1978 the Club could no longer attract sufficient support; citing "changing times," it unanimously voted to disband.

Constance A. Maguire

FURTHER READING: Women's Musical Club of Saskatoon. Papers. B-105. Saskatchewan Archives Board, Saskatoon.

WOMEN'S ROYAL CANADIAN NAVAL SERVICE (WRCNS). Founded in 1942, the Women's Royal Canadian Naval Service (WRCNS) was established as part of the Royal Canadian Navy (RCN) to free trained male naval personnel for war service. Between 1942 and 1946, close to 7,000 women volunteered for service in the "WRENS," as they came to be known. These women served in Canada, the United States, England, Ireland, and Scotland. In Saskatchewan, WRENS served in the shore establishments, HMCS *Queen* and HMCS *Unicorn*. The WRCNS was demobilized in August 1946, but in 1951 the Canadian government again established a Women's Royal Canadian Naval Service in the Royal Canadian Naval Reserve. On February 1, 1968, the WRCNS, along with the RCN, was eliminated under the Canadian Forces Reorganization Act.

Peter Borch

FURTHER READING: Fletcher, M.H. 1989. *The WRNS: A History of the Women's Royal Naval Service*. Annapolis, Maryland: Naval Institute Press; Klein, Y.M. (ed.). 1997. *Beyond the Home Front: Women's Autobiographical Writing of the Two World Wars*. London: Macmillan.

WOMEN'S SHELTERS. Violence against women in intimate relationships, also known as domestic or family violence, is a serious problem: almost 30% of Canadian women indicate to researchers that they have experienced violence in a domestic relation-ship, and there is evidence that further domestic vio-lence goes unreported.

Women's shelters offer short-term accommoda-tion and support to women and children fleeing vio-lence. Shelters began to open more than thirty years ago in Saskatchewan, as the women's movement gained momentum in the early 1970s. Women were beginning to talk to each other about issues affect-ing them, including violence in their families and communities. It was through these discussions that they identified a need for women leaving abusive relationships to have a safe place to stay as well as the support of other women. Women's shelters—also commonly known as transition houses, interval houses, or temporary emergency shelters—operate much like a home setting. Women have their own bedroom for themselves and their children, but share bathroom, kitchen, and living areas with other shelter residents. Some shelters look just like a single-family residence from the outside, while oth-ers are in more institutional settings. Women's shel-ters normally do not charge a fee to their residents, since women leaving violent domestic relationships are usually in financial distress.

Shelters have staff on duty twenty-four hours a day; continuous availability is very important since women may need to leave an abusive situation at any time of the day or night. Unfortunately, there is not always room at a shelter, and a woman may be put on a waiting list until a space opens up. Shortage of space in shelters, and uneven geograph-ic access to shelters, remain problems for women needing safety and support immediately, when other options such as staying with family or at a hotel may not be safe or affordable.

Saskatoon was the first community in Saskatchewan, and one of the first in Canada, to establish a women's shelter. The opening of Saskatoon Interval House in 1973 was followed over the next five years by Wichihick Iskewak Safe House in Regina, Regina Transition House, and Moose Jaw Transition House. Since that time several additional shelters have opened in communities across the province, including Prince Albert, Yorkton, the Battlefords, Saskatoon, Regina, Swift Current, Meadow Lake, and Fort Qu'Appelle. During the 1970s and 1980s many of the shelters in Saskatchewan were funded by the provincial gov-ernment on a fee-for-service basis, supplemented by other grants and fundraising efforts. Fluctuating income from fees-for-service created financial insta-bility for shelters. Most shelter funding is now pro-vided through operating grants from the provincial Department of Community Resources and Employ-ment. A few shelters are funded in whole or in part by Indian and Northern Affairs Canada. Many shel-ters have also received capital improvement grants from federal government departments and agencies. In addition to receiving government grants, shelters do extensive fund raising, and rely significantly on volunteers to supplement staff resources and enhance programming.

When the first shelters opened in Saskatchewan and across the country, they were a reaction to an immediate need to keep women safe from violence. At first there was very little programming offered to women and children staying in shelters. While safe-ty has remained the most critical service, over time shelters have expanded their services to fit the vari-ety of needs of their residents. Many now offer serv-ices like child counseling and other children's pro-gramming, support groups for current and past clients, adult counseling services, abuse education, transportation, referrals, and advocacy. Shelter staff and volunteers are also active in communities, increasing public awareness and understanding of domestic violence issues.

The original shelter concept addressed the short-term needs of women leaving violent relationships. In some cases, longer-term support strategies are needed to meet the needs of women and children in these circumstances. There are now several longer-term housing facilities, called second-stage shelters, where women leaving emergency shelters can stay for several months in a safe and low-cost environment until they are ready or able to live in a less secure setting. Women's shelters are part of the range of programs and services to prevent family violence, to reduce the impact of family violence on women and children, and to help Saskatchewan communities maintain a safe and respectful environment for all people. *Amy Stensrud*

WOOD MOUNTAIN, village, pop 40, located SW of Assiniboia near the junction of Hwys 18 and 358. The Wood Mountain Plateau consists of flat-topped hills cut by treed coulees, rising some 400 metres above the surrounding plains. In the 1800s, Red River Métis established wintering camps in the area, calling it *Montagne de Bois* (Mountain of Wood) for the abundance of poplar trees in the otherwise barren region. After 1870 and the uprising at Red River, Métis families settled permanently in the area, and during the decade the Hudson's Bay Company and later the NWMP established posts south of the present village. The International Boundary Commission used the area for a supply depot early in the decade. The police pursued whisky traders and horse thieves in the region, and from 1876 to 1881 they monitored the over 5,000 Sioux and their leader, SITTING BULL, who had sought refuge in Canada after the Battle of the Little Big Horn. Large-scale ranching began in the district in the 1880s but by 1908 the unfenced rangeland was gradually being given over to homesteaders. In 1917, the SASKATCHEWAN PROVINCIAL POLICE force was created and the contract with the RNWMP was terminated, resulting in the closing of the Mounties' post at Wood Mountain in 1918. With the arrival of the CPR in 1928 the present Wood Mountain townsite developed, and on March 4, 1930, the village of Wood Mountain was incorporated. The community has never been particularly large; the population was 127 in 1931, and until the mid-1960s Wood Mountain averaged about 120 residents. Subsequently, however, the village began to decline, facing school closure, elevator closure, and rail line abandonment in the 1990s. Despite its small size, Wood Mountain remains an active community. A horticultural society maintains the regional park south of the community where an interpretive museum has been established. Near the

park, the NWMP post has been partially restored and there is a hill-top monument dedicated to Sitting Bull. The site is also the location of Canada's oldest continually running rodeo, which, as of the summer of 2005, will have been running for 115 years.
David McLennan

WOOD MOUNTAIN DAKOTA FIRST NATION. The Wood Mountain Reserve consists of 2,376.2 ha of rolling prairie near the village of Wood Mountain. The nomadic Dakota camped in the borderland between the United Stated and Canada in the mid-1800s, establishing a degree of permanency in the territory between JEAN-LOUIS LÉGARÉ's Wood Mountain trading post and Moose Jaw Creek by 1876. Joined by SITTING BULL in his flight from the US Cavalry, many of his people remained at Wood Mountain when he returned to the United States in 1881, supporting themselves through traditional subsistence and wage labour. On October 29, 1910, a temporary reserve was created for them near Wood Mountain, and although the Lakota never signed treaty with the Canadian government the Wood Mountain Reserve was recognized by an Order-in-Council on August 5, 1930. The band's thirty-seven founding families declined in number, in part from marrying into the surrounding non-First Nations community. There are 209 registered band members, only twelve of whom live on the reserve.
Christian Thompson

WOOD MOUNTAIN PLATEAU (49°14'N 106°23'W: Map sheet 72 G/1). Elevated to a maximum of 1,013 m, Wood Mountain is located close to the international boundary and approximately 30 km southwest of Assiniboia. Like the CYPRESS HILLS to the west, the southeastern portion of the Wood Mountain upland stood above the continental ice-sheet during the last GLACIATION, preserving Tertiary sands and gravels at higher elevations. Elsewhere, the uplands are covered with varying amounts of glacial drift. The plateau is deeply dissected by numerous gullies creating a landscape of coulees, separated by flat-topped hills. A prominent feature is Pinto Butte at the western end of the plateau. Most drainage is to the south, but some gullies drain northward into the Wood River and to lakes along the northern flank. When MÉTIS settlers occupied the area in the 1870s, it was well wooded with poplar and still had significant numbers of buffalo and other game. SITTING BULL and his people found temporary refuge there after fleeing the US army. Today the vegetation is dominated by native mixed-grass prairie on the uplands, with shrubs in the moist coulees.

Land use has undergone several changes. The hunting economy disappeared with the buffalo in 1879. JEAN-LOUIS LÉGARÉ, who built a trading post at Wood Mountain in 1870, introduced ranching to the

region. Homesteading did not begin until 1907. Much of the region is still rangeland, the amount of arable land being severely limited by topography and poor soils. The village of Wood Mountain (pop. 40) is located on the northern flank of the plateau. The site of the former NWMP post was designated a Provincial Historic Park in 1965. The East Bloc of the GRASSLANDS NATIONAL PARK lies around the Kildeer Badlands on the southwestern flank of Wood Mountain.
Marilyn Lewry

FURTHER READING: Poirier, T. (ed.). 2000. *Wood Mountain Uplands: From the Big Muddy to the Frenchman River.* Wood Mountain, Saskatchewan: Wood Mountain Historical Society.

WOOD MOUNTAIN–FORT QU'APPELLE TRAIL. The Wood Mountain–Fort Qu'Appelle Trail was a provisional supply route during the height of the fur trade. It was approximately 250 km in length and crossed vast expanses of southern prairie. From east to west it followed a general southwest direction from Fort Qu'Appelle, south of Regina, through the Dirt Hills ending in WOOD MOUNTAIN. The trail functioned as an important provisional route supplying Hudson's Bay Company posts southwest of Fort Qu'Appelle. Lebret missionaries also used the trail extensively, as it was their only access to numerous MÉTIS settlements. Chief SITTING BULL and his followers are reported to have used the trail when seeking refuge from American authorities in the late 19th century.
James Winkel

WOODPECKERS. Woodpeckers are members of the family Picidae, order Piciformes. The approximately 217 species are found in the Americas, Eurasia and Africa. Of the twenty-two species found in North America, twelve have been identified in Saskatchewan. Woodpeckers are characterized by their tree-climbing ability: stiff tail feathers (used to prop themselves on tree trunks); bracing feet with two long toes forward and two back; pointed bills with which they peel bark or excavate nest holes; and tongues which can be extended to an amazing length. During mating season, woodpeckers use their bills to drum on trees. They nest in holes excavated in live or dead trees. Generally indifferent to the presence of people, they often allow close approach as they search for grubs and insects or dig their nest chambers.

The Northern flicker (*Colaptes auratus*) is probably the best known provincial woodpecker; a large bird, it is often seen on the ground feeding on ants. There are two distinct subspecies: the yellow-shafted, golden yellow under the wings and tail; and the red-shafted of the extreme southwest, salmon-pink under wings and tail. A few remain over winter, especially where attracted to suet feeders. Hairy (*Picoides villosus*) and downy (*P. pubescens*)

ILLUSTRATION BY PAUL GERAGHTY/COURTESY OF THE ROYAL
SASKATCHEWAN MUSEUM

Pileated Woodpecker.

woodpeckers are common permanent residents throughout the wooded areas of the province. They look alike, both spotted with black and white, but the sparrow-sized downy is much smaller than the hairy. Black-backed (*P. arcticus*) and three-toed (*P. trydactylus*) woodpeckers are permanent residents of the boreal forest, generally found in trees killed by fire or insects. Never common, occasional individuals of both species turn up in the south during winter. The pileated woodpecker (*Dryocopus pileatus*), our largest woodpecker, is crow-sized with a flaming red crest; characteristic of the boreal forest, it has recently begun showing up farther south. The yellow-bellied sapsucker (*Sphyrapicus varius*), a migratory woodpecker, is common through most of the wooded areas of the province. The red-naped sapsucker (*S. nuchalis*), a close relative, is found only in the CYPRESS HILLS.

Four other species are either rare or erratic in Saskatchewan. Red-headed woodpeckers (*Melanerpes erythrocephalus*), striking black, white and red birds, nest sporadically in the southern third of the province. On rare occasions (six reports in the last forty years) Lewis's woodpecker (*M. lewisi*) strays across the prairies from the mountains of British Columbia. The red-bellied woodpecker (*M. carolinus*), a bird of eastern deciduous forests, has been noted only six times in Saskatchewan, and the even rarer Williamson's sapsucker (*S. thyroideus*) has been seen within the borders only twice, in 1965 and 1977.   *J. Frank Roy*

FURTHER READING: Alsop, J.P., III. 2002. *The Birds of Canada.* New York: Dorling Kindersley.

WORKERS' COMPENSATION. The Saskatchewan Workers' Compensation Board marks its 75th year in 2005. Like all such Canadian boards, the Saskatchewan Workers' Compensation Board is an administrative tribunal operating under the authority of the WORKERS' COMPENSATION ACT, 1979, a provincial statute. The first Saskatchewan no-fault workers' compensation legislation was passed in January 1929. Passage occurred within four weeks of the GARDINER government receiving the Anderson Royal Commission report recommending that Saskatchewan adopt the Meredith compensation system, already in place in Ontario, Nova Scotia, British Columbia, Alberta, New Brunswick, and Manitoba. Under the Meredith compensation model, civil liability laws for workplace injury were replaced by a statutory framework with five key features: no fault, collective employer liability, security of payment for injured workers, exclusive jurisdiction, and public administration by an independent body.

With a $25,000 start-up grant from the province, the new board was issuing benefits to injured workers, paying for injured workers' hospital care and x-rays, collecting employer assessments, and engaging in industrial accident prevention by the summer of 1930. The original tripartite governance structure—three board members representing government, workers, and employers—remains unchanged after seventy-five years. These full-time members, appointed by an Order-in-Council, fulfill three general responsibilities: interpreting and administering the compensation act through policy, supervising the Workers' Compensation Board administration, and acting as the final level of appeal. This structure acknowledges the founding principles of workers' compensation, based on a "historic compromise" between workers and employers which abolished the right of workers to sue in the courts for work injury or disease in exchange for an employer-funded compensation system.

The founding stakeholders' central role was further entrenched in 1945 when the DOUGLAS government added the Committee of Review section to the Act. Committees of Review have broad scope to study workers' compensation every four years. Every Committee of Review since the first in 1949 has submitted consensus recommendations by individuals representing Saskatchewan employers and organized workers. The 1978 Committee of Review was a pivotal influence on the BLAKENEY government's decision in 1979 to replace the medical pension system with the wage loss system. A wage loss system calculates loss of earnings from the work injury, whereas a pension system assigns a monetary value to each type of injury. Saskatchewan was the first province to take this step.

Over seven decades, the Saskatchewan Workers'

Compensation Board has mirrored the province's growing and diversifying economy. In its first year of operation the Board registered 4,476 employer accounts, collected $530,000 in employer assessments, and paid $401,000 in benefits on 3,969 injury claims.

In contrast, annual gross Board revenues in 2000-03 were $220 million. Typically, employer premiums accounted for 60%–80% of revenues. For the same period, injury claim expenditures (mostly wage loss replacement and health care treatment) ranged from $200-$240 million for nearly 40,000 claims. Projected liabilities rise each year for future injured worker benefits. These obligations reached $802 million in 2003, of which a total of 95% was set aside in investment funds.

Tribunals such as workers' compensation boards have administrative safeguards in place to correct adjudication errors. This appellate role has been filled since 1930 by the three Board members. In 1985, an intermediate appeal level, known as the Appeals Committee, was established by the Board. Together they respond to about 1,100 appeals each year. Many injured workers who lodge appeals are assisted by the Office of the Workers' Advocate. This independent office, the first of its kind in Canada, was created in 1973, expressly to aid claimants who challenged Board claim decisions.

Benefits for Saskatchewan injured workers and surviving dependents have grown more generous and comprehensive over seventy-five years. For example, between 1930 and the 1980s, the wage loss benefit has risen from 66% of gross earnings to the current level of 90% of take-home earnings. The funding of workers' compensation is the sole responsibility of employers, not the provincial government. Employer premiums, along with investment earnings, meet the costs of administering the compensation system. While the Board actively promotes injury prevention and safety to encourage fewer work accidents, premium levels are set to reflect current work injury and occupational disease costs. In Saskatchewan, average Workers' Compensation Board premium levels are typically among the lowest in Canada.

Workers' compensation stakeholders have high accountability expectations of the Board. Here, Saskatchewan is a pacesetter through the Board's regular appearances before legislators, public annual general meetings and Compensation Institutes, and the implementation of Committee of Review stakeholder recommendations. In 2003, the Board strengthened its accountability with the appointment of a past Saskatchewan deputy ombudsman as its first "fair practices officer." The office receives and investigates inquiries and concerns when injured workers and employers believe a policy, procedure, or practice has not been applied fairly.

The transition from economies dominated by

resources and manufacturing employment to the knowledge-based service economy is a significant factor in a lower injury rate and a changing injury mix for all workers' compensation jurisdictions. Specifically, soft-tissue (sprains and strains) injuries are now more prevalent than traumatic accident injury claims. Advancing medical knowledge has also established stronger occupational linkages to more diseases. Collectively, Saskatchewan workplaces post one of Canada's highest work injury rates. With the upward creep of health care costs, it will be important to reduce work injuries to help hold future compensation expenditure growth in check and reduce human suffering. Nothing is more important to workers' compensation, the Anderson Commission said, than the prevention of accidents. Except for an interlude ending in the 1990s, the Workers' Compensation Board has been active in injury prevention from its inception. An important element in injury prevention is firm-based experience rating. These financial incentives are designed to stimulate workplace safety and occupational health investments that reduce injury and occupational disease. Most recently, in 2003 the Board's strategic plan incorporated injury prevention to harness the efforts of WorkSafe Saskatchewan and workplace parties to achieve the goal of reducing work injuries by 20% by 2007.   *John Solomon*

FURTHER READING: Anderson, P.M. 1929. *Report of the Royal Commission Appointed to Enquire into Workmen's Compensation for Saskatchewan.* Regina: King's Printer; Saskatchewan Workers' Compensation Board. 1997. *The Story of Workers' Compensation in Saskatchewan.* Regina.

WORKERS' COMPENSATION ACT: *see* LEGISLATION IN SASKATCHEWAN

WORKERS' UNITY LEAGUE. When the GREAT DEPRESSION began battering the economy in 1930, Canadian workers were faced with catastrophic unemployment as well as declining wages and working conditions in many sectors among those fortunate enough to keep their jobs. Only a small number of workers were organized within their own specialties: the Trades and Labour Congress (TLC) was composed exclusively of international craft unions; the Canadian Congress of Labour (CCL) consisted of exclusively Canadian craft and industrial unions; and the Canadian Catholic Congress of Labour (CCCL) was limited almost entirely to Quebec. None of the federations had a strategy for dealing with the magnitude of the economic crisis; they were overwhelmed by the struggle to hold themselves together as they lost thousands of members to unemployment.

The inability of the mainstream trade unions to mount an effective intervention on behalf of work-

ing people left an organizational and political vacuum: the **WORKERS' UNITY LEAGUE** (WUL) would be an attempt to fill this vacuum. The WUL was organized in 1930, mainly by Communists and leftist allies in an attempt to provide a radical alternative to the mainstream trade union federations. Unlike conventional federations, the WUL organized and affiliated associations of unemployed, women, and other groups who were not technically trade unions in that they did not have employers with whom to bargain. The WUL organized in the mining, forestry and other resource industries, as well as among immigrant communities, which had not previously been organized. The WUL led many of the strikes in the 1930–35 period, with heavy resistance from employers and repression from the state, in the form of police attacks on strikers and demonstrations, imprisonment of activists, and deportation of immigrants. The repression reached a level never seen before or since over an extended period of time.

In Saskatchewan, the WUL was active in organizing miners under the auspices of the Mine Workers' Union of Canada (MWUC) in the Bienfait-Estevan coal fields, and the unemployed throughout the province; many of the latter affiliated to the National Unemployed Workers' Association (NUWA) in the cities and the Relief Camp Workers' Union (RCWU) in Dundurn relief camp. The MWUC temporarily succeeded in organizing miners around Beinfait in 1931, but was met by severe state repression. Three miners were killed and many injured by the RCMP, who dispersed a demonstration in the streets of Estevan on September 29, 1931 (*see* ESTEVAN COAL STRIKE). This was followed by an all-out attack against the union and its sympathizers, which went on for months. The union was smashed, with many leaders and activists imprisoned on trumped-up charges, deported, and blacklisted from the mines. There would be later attempts to organize the miners in the late 1930s and 1940s, and eventually they became a local of the United Mine Workers of America (UMWA). Today, the militants of 1931 are recognized as the pioneers of the local labour movement.

The NUWA provided a national focus to the unemployed movement in Saskatchewan, which participated in petitions, protests and demonstrations for improved relief systems and unemployment insurance. The RCWU also led a contingent from Dundurn relief camp to participate in the ON-TO-OTTAWA TREK when it reached Regina in 1935, and led a strike in the camp in 1935–36.

The WUL disbanded in 1935. Many of its former affiliates and individual members joined other federations. In the late 1930s and 1940s, many WUL veterans were active organizing industrial unions; they achieved unemployment insurance in 1941, and other pro-labour legislation in subsequent years. In

this sense, they were pioneers of what would become a greatly expanded House of Labour.

Lorne A. Brown

FURTHER READING: Brown, L. 1987. *When Freedom Was Lost: The Unemployed, the Agitator and the State.* Montreal: Black Rose Books; Endicott, S.L. 2002. *Bienfait: The Saskatchewan Miners Struggle of 31.* Toronto: University of Toronto Press; Waiser, B. 2003. *All Hell Can't Stop Us: The On-to-Ottawa Trek and Regina Riot.* Calgary: Fifth House.

WORKING FARM DOGS. Working farm dogs have specific roles as livestock guardians and herding dogs on Saskatchewan farms. The herding and guarding instincts are usually not both found in one dog. Working dogs constitute business investments for their owners and are different from the usual dogs found on most farmyards, which function primarily as companion animals for their owners and to warn of the approach of visitors to the yard. Herding dogs (also called stock dogs) are used to move livestock, primarily sheep and cattle, on pastures and in barnyards. Herding dogs are essential for sheep producers who have more than a handful of sheep. A well-trained dog is a huge asset to a livestock producer since a dog can replace several people when livestock need to be moved. Dogs are faster and can anticipate the behaviour of livestock more keenly than people, and they have the ability to intimidate livestock into moving for them. Some dogs instinctually herd animals from the front or head of livestock, and others from the rear or heel end.

The border collie is the predominant dog breed for herding, but other breeds such as blue heeler and Australian shepherd are used as well. Herding dogs have been selected for their herding instinct and have a high level of intelligence; their great desire to please their masters means that these dogs readily accept training. In Saskatchewan there is a well-developed network of herding dog breeders and trainers; herding dog enthusiasts compete with their animals in numerous stock dog competitions throughout western Canada.

Guardian dogs are effectively used to protect livestock from predators, which in Saskatchewan are primarily coyotes. Sheep are the most vulnerable of any domestic livestock because of their small size, and because the pastures which they graze night and day are also coyote habitat. Coyote predation has been one of the major reasons for the decline of the sheep industry in Saskatchewan since its peak in the 1930s and 1940s. The use of guardian dogs, which has only begun in the last twenty years in Saskatchewan, now provides an effective control of the coyote problem. The guardian dogs stay with the sheep twenty-four hours a day in the pasture or in the barnyard, through all seasons and all weather.

COURTESY OF AGRICULTURE AND AGRI-FOOD CANADA
Herding sheep.

The large dogs are part of the flock; they must grow up with sheep and have minimal human contact so that they become bonded with the sheep and not their owner. Though they are capable of killing coyotes, their presence intimidates coyotes to keep their distance. Numerous breeds of dogs, including Great Pyrenees, Komondor, Kuvasz, Akbash, and Maremma, are used as livestock guardians.

Harry Harder

WORLD WAR I AND SASKATCHEWAN. From August 4, 1914, when Britain's declaration of war brought Canada into World War I, two attitudes prevailed in Saskatchewan: one was a determination to defend all things British, and the second was an appreciation for jobs and wages which peace had not provided. Many of the first volunteer soldiers answered blood ties to the Empire: for example, of 68 Swift Current recruits in the first days of the war, 63 were British-born. But as seasonal work dried up later that fall, more volunteers came from other ethnic groups. Many unemployed responded to the $1.10 per diem provided to soldiers, as unemployment had risen since the end of western railroad expansion in 1912. Saskatchewan politicians, clerics and journalists asked the federal government to expand the armed forces *faster* to absorb all the unemployed. Soldiers received a warm send-off from a populace excited by the prospect of a short war. Scrambling to enlist, some Saskatchewan soldiers served in regiments mobilized in other provinces. The Princess Patricia Light Infantry (the Pats), one of the first Canadian units to reach France in December 1914, recruited veterans from across the country who had "no attachment to any militia"; as they were experienced, they were sent to the front with much less training. So many men from the

West enlisted with the Pats that they were often considered a prairie battalion by other units. Similarly, a rumour that Manitoba units would reach the fighting sooner prompted many Saskatchewan lads to join there.

Canada's military leadership re-shuffled all the units going overseas into numbered battalions. The 95th Saskatchewan (later Regina) Rifles and the 105 Fusiliers (later Saskatoon) both fought with the 11th Battalion of the Canadian Expeditionary Force (CEF), and in turn sent many reinforcements to the 5th Battalion CEF. The **NORTH SASKATCHEWAN REGIMENT** (later Prince Albert) and the **SOUTH SASKATCHEWAN REGIMENT** (later Weyburn) also received their marching orders in the fall of 1914. Moose Jaw's 27th Light Horse was called in early 1915. After the initial mobilization, recruiters were simply given blocks of numbers to assign. CEF battalions like the 65th and 96th battalions, mobilized in Saskatoon in 1916, were recruited there. Later the 28th, 46th, 68th, 152nd and 195th battalions all mobilized men from Saskatchewan, but province of origin was not considered important. Although records of the Saskatchewan units can be confusing or non-existent, their war experience proved remarkably uniform. Assembled at Valcartier Camp near Quebec City, they embarked for Britain and a few months' further training before joining other Canadian units fighting in the trenches in Flanders. Here their war abbreviates to a list of famous battles: Ypres (April–May 1915), Festubert (May 1916), Mount Sorel (June 1916), the Somme (July–November 1916), **VIMY RIDGE** (April 1917), Hill 70 (August 1917), Passchendaele (November 1917), Amiens (August 1918), and Valenciennes (November 1918).

The battle for Ypres, the gateway to the French

ports of Calais and Dunkirk, demonstrated the mettle of 1st Canadian Division when they were first to encounter chlorine gas and suffer casualties. But the headlong daylight rushes against machine-gun pillboxes, adopted by military leaders on both sides, meant that every battle had high casualty rates. The daily course of trench warfare also took a large toll. At the Somme in 1916 (600,000 Allied casualties), three Canadian divisions suffered 2,600 casualties *before* the main onslaught began.

Eventually the Somme, where 24,029 men from the four divisions of the Canadian Corps died for six miles of No Man's Land, changed the country's recruitment policy. Even before conscription was introduced in August 1917, the army command began breaking up units in training to rush the soldiers forward as replacements at the front. The **196TH WESTERN UNIVERSITIES BATTALION** was one of the casualties of this change. Led by **WALTER C. MURRAY**, president of the **UNIVERSITY OF SASKATCHEWAN**, they sought to recruit and train a special soldier "of the university type"—that is, British. Almost all male students were required to train, and as one student of agriculture explained to his mother: "They make you feel like two cents at the University if you don't enlist." The University of Saskatchewan outfitted some 200 men, but these efforts ceased after mid-1916 when the Brigade became replacements for other regiments. Another special unit, the 107th Battalion, mobilized many Aboriginal soldiers from Saskatchewan. Some of these Aboriginal units, with reputations for valour, were disbanded for fear they might be wiped out all at once.

By 1916, all Canadian infantry entered battle together as the Canadian Corps; after their hard-won victory at Vimy Ridge, they had one of their own as commander: General Arthur Currie. At home, however, divisions had deepened. Camps for "enemy aliens" opened across the prairies in October 1914 and eventually interned over 8,000—mostly Ukrainians (known as Ruthenians for that area of the Austro-Hungarian Empire). Along with conscientious objectors, Mennonites and Doukhobors, they were disenfranchised by the Wartime Elections Act of 1917, which included alien immigrants naturalized after 1902. Saskatchewan voted for the revamped Unity Government of Robert Borden in December 1917 largely out of support for conscription. However, the Military Services Act (August 1917), administered by local committees, continued to exempt conscripts in Quebec, but drafted the farmers' vital workers in Saskatchewan, where local committees were made up of, or influenced by, veterans. Farmers were further dismayed when agricultural exemptions were lifted in the spring of 1918 as German offensives produced even greater casualties.

Armistice on November 11, 1918, came as a surprise. A poor crop had signaled another hard year. Divisions over war and conscription, between

English and French Canadians, between Empire and immigrant, would continue for years.   *Scott Broad*

FURTHER READING: Giesler, P. 1982. *Valour Remembered: Canada and the First World War*. Ottawa: Government of Canada Veterans Affairs; Martin, W.M. 1919. *What Saskatchewan Has Done in the Great War*. Regina: J.W. Reid Government Printer; Thompson, J.H. 1978. *The Harvests of War: The Prairie West, 1914–1918*. Toronto: McClelland and Stewart.

WORLD WAR II AND SASKATCHEWAN.

When Canada declared war on Germany on September 10, 1939, the country was militarily unprepared; so too was Saskatchewan, although an attitude of grim determination left over from the **DEPRESSION** made up for lack of planning. Military spending had been trimmed to the bone during the hard years. When Nazi Germany over-ran Czechoslovakia in 1938, military appropriations doubled to $60 million, but Canada's standing army only consisted of 4,500 men at the onset of war. In Saskatchewan, militia units trained dutifully, although they lacked sufficient armaments and transport. Within a few weeks of the declaration of war two regiments, the **SASKATOON LIGHT INFANTRY** and the **SOUTH SASKATCHEWAN REGIMENT**, were mobilized. And in June 1940, another regiment, the Regina Rifles, mustered men from North Battleford, Prince Albert and Regina. The Saskatoon Light Infantry embarked for Europe in December 1939 with Canada's First Division. General **A.G.L. MCNAUGHTON**, a native of Moosomin, led the Division, which also included the Princess Patricia Canadian Light Infantry, a brigade laced with Saskatchewan recruits; indeed, volunteers from Saskatchewan could be found in many different units. The South Saskatchewan Regiment embarked in December 1940; the Regina Rifles followed on August 24, 1941.

However, most of the 70,000 military personnel from Saskatchewan joined other services. Uncounted thousands joined the Royal Canadian Navy and the Canadian Merchant Marine. Prairie boys, said to be adverse to the infantry because of grizzly stories of gas and trenches told by **WORLD WAR I** veterans, made excellent sailors: although not held by military discipline, the men of the Merchant Marine maintained Britain's lifeline throughout the prolonged Battle of the Atlantic. Targets of Germany's submarines, the merchant sailors suffered higher casualties than their Navy escorts. Saskatchewan also contributed many airmen to the war effort, and took part in training Allied air crews. Canada did not have its own air service until 1936; yet on December 17, 1939, the Canadian government signed the **BRITISH COMMONWEALTH AIR TRAINING PLAN**. At first the Training Plan relied on private flying clubs and their facilities; but training

EVERETT BAKER PHOTO/COURTESY OF THE SASKATCHEWAN HISTORY AND FOLKLORE SOCIETY

George Baker displays The *Leader-Post* headline declaring "Victory," May 7, 1945.

centres grew overnight, taking advantage of the wide open spaces around Regina, Saskatoon, Prince Albert, Weyburn, Davidson, Yorkton, Caron, Wilcox, Mossbank, and Dafoe. In 1940 the British organized a training scheme of their own and built aerodromes in Assiniboia, Estevan, Swift Current, North Battleford, and Moose Jaw over the following two years. Both training campaigns provided air crews for a prolonged air war in Europe. Allied forces ultimately dominated the skies thanks to their superiority in numbers of experienced personnel. Approximately 130,000 air crew trained on the prairies, more than 55% of them Canadians.

Air bases revitalized communities still mired in the Great Depression. Prices had dropped until wheat hit 70¢ per bushel in 1939. Farmers responded by raising more pork and beef, but they also began to demand programs for long-term security. Two trains chartered by the **SASKATCHEWAN WHEAT POOL** carried 400 farmers on a successful "March on Ottawa" in February 1942. In March the Liberal government in Ottawa raised the price of wheat to 90¢, and in December 1943 drew up a program of floor prices aimed at meeting farmers' demands. Soon thereafter, the provincial Liberal government introduced similar social security measures in health care and education; but the new thirst for public programs was not easily quenched. Concerned with another sort of security, in June 1940 the provincial government instituted the Saskatchewan Veterans Civil Security Corps by Order-in-Council. The Corps grew to 7,500 men, mostly Legion members. They

drilled against the eventuality of a German invasion, encouraged younger men to enlist, and guarded against subversion. Corps "intelligence officers" tried sacking ethnic German workers from jobs to make way for veterans; during the Conscription Plebiscite of April 1942, the Corps, under RCMP direction, also harassed Jehovah's Witnesses, Duokhobors, Mennonites, and other ethnic minorities.

Farmers experiencing labour shortages turned to mechanization, even though wartime measures made materials scarce. Northern Saskatchewan contributed metals needed for war—including the uranium used in the Manhattan Project, which produced the atomic bombs dropped on Japan. Meanwhile, the Canadian infantry suffered a long period of idleness, broken only by intensive training. A "lucky" few from Saskatchewan joined the 2,000 Canadians dispatched to save Hong Kong in November 1941; after three weeks of bitter combat, the survivors spent an arduous three years in Japanese POW camps. In Europe, Canadian infantry contributed to the defense of Britain, but their first fight came with the raid on Dieppe in August 1942. Unlike most of the 6,000 Allied infantry (including 5,000 Canadians) who were trapped on the beaches, the South Saskatchewan Regiment almost reached its objectives. Their commanding officer, Lt. Col. Cecil Merritt, became the first World War II **VICTORIA CROSS** recipient for valour during the evacuation from Dieppe's beaches. Captured with 1,900 other Canadians, he spent the rest of the war as a prisoner.

The Princess Patricia and the Saskatoon Light Infantry joined the Allied landing in Sicily in July 1943, and the invasion of Italy three months later. The 5,900 graves that stretch northward along the Italian peninsula tell the story of tenacious fighting against crack German units. These troops still held the top of the Italian "boot" when most Canadian units were transferred to the northern European front in February 1945. The South Saskatchewan Regiment and the Regina Rifles landed on Normandy's Juno beach on D-day, June 6, 1944. After putting up fierce resistance for two months in Normandy, German forces fell back to defensive positions on their own frontier and in the Low Countries. The Canadians were assigned the job of clearing ports on the English Channel. In doing so, they encountered tenacious German counter-attacks, particularly around the Belgian port of Antwerp. Liberating Antwerp shortened the Allies supply lines; they were almost immediately able to throw themselves against the imposing Sigfried Line and to reach the German industrial heartland along the Rhine. Once the Rhine was reached, the Canadians turned to liberate Holland. At war's end, the toll of the Saskatchewan dead read 3,880.   *Scott Broad*

FURTHER READING: Archer, J. 1980. *Saskatchewan: A History*. Saskatoon: Western Producer Prairie Books.

WOROBETZ, STEPHEN (1914–). Recognized for his exemplary service to both his province and country, the Honourable Dr. Stephen Worobetz was born in Krydor on December 26, 1914, and educated at the Universities of Saskatchewan and Manitoba. He served as a medical officer with the Canadian Army in **WORLD WAR II** and was awarded the Military Cross for his courageous actions during the Italian campaign. Following the war, he practiced as a family physician in Saskatoon and later completed post-graduate work in Winnipeg and Philadelphia to be a general surgeon. In 1970, Dr. Worobetz was the first person of Ukrainian origin appointed **LIEUTENANT-GOVERNOR** of Saskatchewan. He occupied the vice-regal post for six years and returned to the medical profession until his retirement in 1982. Dr. Worobetz's philanthropic work included the creation of the Stephen and Michelene Worobetz Foundation in 1989, which encouraged volunteerism and supported charitable organizations. For his dedication throughout the years, Dr. Worobetz received an honorary doctorate from the **UNIVERSITY OF SASKATCHEWAN** and was made an Officer of the Order of Canada in 1993. He received the Saskatchewan Order of Merit in 1999.

WRENS. Wrens (family *Troglodytidae*) are small, brown, secretive songbirds with raised, distinctively barred tails, which creep through vegetation looking for insects and fruit. They have short rounded wings

ILLUSTRATION BY PAUL GERAGHTY/COURTESY OF THE ROYAL SASKATCHEWAN MUSEUM

Marsh wren (*Cistothorus palustris*).

for quick and erratic flight. Their narrow heads and long slender bills are ideal for probing for food in deep crevices. Most species nest in cavities. The family is native to the New World, except for a single Eurasian species. There are seventy-nine wren species, nine of them in North America; five wren species breed in Saskatchewan. The house wren (*Troglodytes aedon*) is small, with drab grayish-brown plumage and very pale facial markings. Its incessant, cheerful babbling song is commonly heard in summer in southern Saskatchewan. It breeds in a variety of shrubby habitats. Its population has been increasing in Saskatchewan since 1960s. The winter wren (*Troglodytes troglodytes*) is tiny, short-tailed, and dark-coloured with a distinctive "eyebrow." It breeds in the old-growth mixed-wood and coniferous stands of the southern forest. The rock wren (*Salpinctes obsoletus*) breeds in badland areas, gravel pits and coal spoil piles in southern Saskatchewan. This wren is relatively large, has a long bill and pointed wings, and distinctive pale

F. LAHRMAN PHOTO/© SASKATCHEWAN ENVIRONMENT/ SKCDC, 2001. ECOSYSTEM IMAGE INFORMATION SYSTEM

House wren (*Troglodytes aedon*).

buffy tips on tail feathers. The sedge wren (*Cistothorus platenis*) is tiny and fairly short-tailed, and has a boldly streaked brownish back and crown. It breeds in wet tall grass meadows with scattered shrubs in the aspen parkland, boreal forest fringe, and northern edge of the grassland ecoregion in Saskatchewan. The marsh wren (*Cistothorus palustris*) is small and stocky, long-billed, and relatively brightly patterned with rufous rump and white eye stripe. It breeds in the reeds, bulrushes and cattails of permanent marshes of southern Saskatchewan.   *Robert Warnock*

FURTHER READING: Alsop, Fred J., III. 2002. *Birds of Canada*. New York: Dorling Kindersley.

WRIGHT, CLIFFORD (1927–). Recognized for his leadership in civic, provincial, and national affairs, Clifford Wright was born in Saskatoon in 1927 and was first elected to city council in 1966. During Wright's tenure as mayor of Saskatoon from 1976 to 1988, the city hosted the 1979 Western Canada Summer Games, celebrated its centennial in 1982, and saw the creation of Wanuskewin Heritage Park and the Meewasin Valley Authority. Wright entered federal politics in 1989 and as Treaty Land Commissioner, his recommendations helped amicably settle 120-year-old treaties. Awarded an honorary doctorate from the **UNIVERSITY OF SASKATCHEWAN** in 1988, Wright was appointed an Officer of the Order of Canada a decade later and received the Saskatchewan Order of Merit in 1999.

WYANT, GORDON (1914–). Gordon Wyant was born in Frankfurt am Main, Germany, on March 28, 1914. He received his MD from Bologna, Italy, in 1938. He moved from Loyola University, Chicago, to become the first head of Anesthesia at the new medical college in Saskatchewan from 1954 to 1981, and has been Professor Emeritus since. Wyant is a past president of the Canadian Anesthetists' Society and of the Defense Medical Association. He is the author of over 100 scientific publications. He was a member of the **UNIVERSITY OF SASKATCHEWAN** team which pioneered kidney transplants.

Wyant's military career began in 1941. He achieved the rank of lieutenant colonel and was commanding officer of the 20th medical company in the Royal Canadian Army Medical Corps. Dr. Wyant also served on diocesan and national synods in the Anglican Church.

Dr. Wyant has received the War Medal, the city of Saskatoon Certificate of Distinguished Community Service, and the Quality Improvement Award from the **SASKATCHEWAN MEDICAL ASSOCIATION** and the **COLLEGE OF PHYSICIANS AND SURGEONS OF SASKATCHEWAN**. He was made an Officer of the Order of Canada in 1992.   *Marc A. Baltzan*

WYERS, JAN (1888–1973). A self-taught artist of vernacular subjects from the village of Windthorst, Saskatchewan, Jan Gerrit Wyers' work was championed by the generation of well-educated artists emerging in Regina around 1960, and then again by the generation emerging in the 1970s. He was born at Emmer, a farming community within the municipality of Steenderen near Arnhem, in The Netherlands. He left home in 1913 and settled near Windthorst in 1916 as a farmer, a career from which he retired in 1960. A lifelong bachelor, Wyers' activities during the 1930s included bootlegging and patenting an animal trap. He took up painting later in the decade.

Wyers began exhibiting his work in provincial exhibitions in the 1950s, and in 1956 received an Award of Merit for the painting *The First Saskatchewan Harvest* in the annual exhibition of the **SASKATCHEWAN ARTS BOARD**. In 1959, the National Gallery of Canada included eight of his paintings in its exhibition *Folk Painters of the Canadian West*, which traveled extensively in Canada and the United States. That year, **RONALD BLOORE**, director of the **MACKENZIE ART GALLERY** purchased his *Good Old Thrashing Days* from this show for the gallery's permanent collection. In 1960, Bloore wrote an article on Wyers for the March 1960 issue of *Canadian Art* magazine, in which the painting was featured on the cover. Bloore and fellow artist **KENNETH LOCHHEAD** shared this interest in folk art; both belonged to a group of artists who achieved national stature for their modernist abstraction in the early 1960s as the **REGINA FIVE**.

Numerous articles kept the artist in the public eye during the 1960s. A few months after Wyers' death in Regina in 1973, the National Gallery of Canada mounted the comprehensive national survey exhibition of historical and contemporary folk art *People's Art: Native Art in Canada*, which included two of his works. Wyers worked from close observation, memory, and magazine or book illustrations. His subjects, which he repeated several times, were taken from everyday experience and included harvesting, horses in pasture, farmsteads, cats and dogs, and self-portraits. His strong and colourful paintings are a moving tribute to life on the prairies.

During the 1970s, the relationship intensified between folk artists and several contemporary artists from the Regina area, including **VIC CICANSKY**, **DAVID THAUBERGER**, and **JOE FAFARD**. This enthusiasm for folk artists stemmed from their straightforward expression of experiences of life on the prairies, and was a catalyst for their own vernacular expression. Wyers is remembered as a pioneer artist within a community of like-minded artists, rather than an isolated folk artist.

Andrew Oko

FURTHER READING: Bloore, R.L. 1960. "Jan G. Wyers," *Canadian Art* 17 (2): 60–65; Oko, A. 1989. *Jan Gerrit Wyers 1888–1973*. Regina: MacKenzie Art Gallery.

WYNYARD, town, pop 1,919, located on Hwy 16, immediately S of the **QUILL LAKES**. The first pioneers in the area were Icelanders who began arriving around 1904-05. These were soon followed by settlers of British, Ukrainian, and Polish origins. The community grew rapidly, reaching a population of 1,000 around 1930 and developing into the largest service centre in the surrounding agricultural district, which today produces wheat, barley, oats, canola, flax, lentils, and durum. The town has a diverse economy. It calls itself the "Chicken Capital of the World" because the Wynyard Division of Lilydale Poultry Products supplies chicken to all the Kentucky Fried Chicken outlets across western Canada. Metal fabrication, potassium sulphate, and fertilizer production are additional local industries. The Quill Lakes Interpretive Centre provides information on the significant migratory bird populations which frequent the area's marshes. The district attracts large numbers of bird watchers, as well as hunters. Wynyard Regional Park offers golfing and fishing for trout. Annual community events include Rodeo Week, the "Famous Chicken Chariot Races," and Thorrablot, an Icelandic Heritage Celebration. Wynyard has been twinned with the French town of Martres-de-Veyre since 1972, in recognition of a Wynyard soldier, **PETER DMYTRUK**, who served overseas in **WORLD WAR II**. Dmytruk was shot down over France and then served with the French Resistance until he was killed in December 1943, halting a raid against Martres-de-Veyre and likely saving many lives. A monument was built on the spot where he died. Over the years, residents of the two towns have exchanged a number of visits and have formed lasting friendships. Peter Dmytruk's story is recounted in the award-winning Saskatchewan book, *Their Names Live On.*

David McLennan

COURTESY OF THE FRANK CAMERON MUSEUM

Jack Teskey in his "Blue Cash" store, Wynyard. Teskey was known for his kindness; the Town of Wynyard named Teskey Crescent in his honour.

XYZ

YANKE GROUP OF COMPANIES. Founded in 1968, Yanke is a privately owned, Saskatoon-based transportation company offering a wide range of service options including freight forwarding, air cargo, international steamship line containers, inland rail, domestic double stack rail, full truckload dry van services, and temperature controlled services. Yanke serves all of Canada and forty-eight US states via road and intermodal rail transportation. The company's container port operations allow it to service fifty-six countries worldwide in international freight forwarding operations. Yanke employs over 600 people and has terminals in Vancouver, Calgary, Edmonton, Regina, Winnipeg, Brampton, Ontario and Point Clair, Quebec. The Yanke Group of Companies generate about $112 million worth of business each year. *Joe Ralko*

YELLOW GRASS, town, pop 422, located 25 km NW of Weyburn on Hwy 39. Yellow Grass is also located on the CPR **SOO LINE**, which runs from

DAVID MCLENNAN PHOTO

"Canada's Hot Spot" sign in the town of Yellow Grass.

Moose Jaw through Estevan and down through the USA. It was about the time that the line was built, in 1893, that the first settlers began to arrive in the Yellow Grass area. The early population was predominantly German, and the Yellow Grass post office was established in 1896. On July 22, 1903, Yellow Grass was incorporated as a village. The two-storey stone school house built that year is still standing; it currently houses the library, and was designated a heritage property in 1982. On February 15, 1906, Yellow Grass attained town status. The community developed as the main agricultural service centre between Weyburn and Milestone, and agriculture remains the basis of the area economy. Grains are the main crops grown, but in recent years there has been an increasing production of pulse crops. Yellow Grass, along with the town of Midale to the southeast, holds the record for having had the highest temperature ever recorded in Canada: on July 5, 1937, the mercury hit 45° Celsius (113° Fahrenheit). *David McLennan*

YELLOW QUILL FIRST NATION. Chief Yellow Quill and headmen Kenistin and Ne-Pin-awa adhered to **TREATY 4** on August 24, 1876, at Fort Pelly. In September 1881 a reserve was surveyed at Fishing and Nut Lakes; Chief Yellow Quill chose the Nut Lake Reserve, situated 8 km east of Rose Valley. Band members continued to trap, hunt and fish until the disappearance of fur-bearing and big game animals forced them to begin farming in the 1930s. They progressed quickly, and by the mid-1950s grain sales provided their primary source of income. The first school was built on the reserve in 1949. Following Yellow Quill's death, Farmer (born in 1887) became chief for life. The band successfully ratified a Treaty Land Entitlement Framework Agreement on September 23, 1992, and in 1997 purchased an office complex in downtown Saskatoon. While significant, this acquisition is only one of several economic activities the band currently has underway. The Yellow Quill First Nation is located 19 km northwest of Kelvington; 808 of the 2,409 band members live on their 5,923.3 ha of reserve land. *Christian Thompson*

YELLOWHEAD HIGHWAY. The Yellowhead Highway is a 2,875 km east-west highway connecting the four western Canadian provinces of British Columbia, Alberta, Saskatchewan and Manitoba. It is designated as Highway 16 for its entire length, and cuts northwesterly through Saskatchewan at Langenburg, Yorkton, Wynyard, Saskatoon, North Battleford and Lloydminster. It was officially opened in 1962, and completed in 1965. The Yellowhead Highway and pass are named after Pierre Hatsinaton (also recorded as Pierre Bostonais), an Iroquois trapper who had blonde hair: also known as Tête Jaune Cache, he was born in Quebec and

became a guide for the Hudson's Bay Company at the turn of the 19th century. Hatsinaton has been credited with blazing the Old North-West Trail—the forerunner of the Yellowhead Highway. *Daria Coneghan*

YORATH, CHRISTOPHER (1879–1932). Christopher J. Yorath, born in 1879, came from England in 1913 to become commissioner of Saskatoon. An engineer by training, Yorath had extensive experience in town planning, housing projects, electricity, roads, bridges, and drainage. Dedicated to fiscal responsibility, Yorath also acted as city treasurer, managing the city's finances through the turbulent war years. He continually created new schemes regarding the city's development: his original city plan, presented in 1913, included park space, civic areas, roads, tramways, as well as a "ring road"—a forerunner of today's Circle Drive. He also campaigned for paved roads, increased energy capacity, adequate housing, and rail line consolidation. During Yorath's tenure, there was considerable debate regarding the role and responsibilities of civic administrators versus civic politicians. Yorath defined his role as essentially a city manager, independent of city council; this attitude brought him into conflict with five-time mayor A. MacGillivray Young, who felt that Yorath was usurping mayoral rights and duties. He resigned in 1921 to become city commissioner for Edmonton, and later moved to Nanaimo, where he died in 1932. Both Yorath Island, south of Saskatoon, and Yorath Avenue in the Avalon area of Saskatoon were named in his honour. *Merle Massie*

YORK BOATS. York boats were first made at York Factory by the Hudson's Bay Company (HBC) for use in the fur trade. They were later made at inland

HBC trading posts, and had a competitive advantage over canoes for transporting furs and supplies along the river systems and particularly on large lakes. By the 1790s they were used extensively. York boats were about 12 m long and almost 3 m across, and could carry over 2,500 kg; the crew consisted of up to ten people. A sail was used when wind conditions were favourable on the lakes. York boats were heavy, required log-rolling portages, and had a short life span due to the rough conditions on the rivers. The HBC hired Orkney Island boat builders to work in the posts where these boats were made. York boats were no longer in use after the early 1920s. *Bob Ivanochko*

YORK FARMERS' COLONIZATION COMPANY. The York Farmers' Colonization Company was incorporated on May 12, 1882, with a capital of $300,000. Its purpose was to promote western settlement and make a profit with the sale of lands. Emissaries came to view an area near the Manitoba border in the North-West Territories in 1882 and were impressed by the richness of the soil and the wooded land. They purchased portions of six townships in the east-central part of the Provisional District of Assiniboia, naming the settlement "York Colony." Invitations went out to people in Ontario, Quebec, the Maritimes, British Columbia, England, Scotland, Ireland, and the United States. Several settlers came during 1882 and began planning for the next year; only four remained to spend the winter caring for a small herd of oxen. Surviving on rations and with the help of First Nations people, they welcomed the spring by journeying to Fort Ellice in Manitoba for supplies. Settlers began arriving and the company erected a hamlet, "York City," on the banks of the Little White Sand River. It opened for business, acting as a government agency

Replica of a York boat afloat on the Bigstone River at Cumberland House, August 1993.

Fly-over salute at Yorkton Service Flying Training School.

for assigning free homesteads, and selling land at $2 an acre.

By 1883, the CANADIAN PACIFIC RAILWAY main line had reached Whitewood, which became the stopping point from which settlers travelled to York Colony. The Company acquired more land, built a flour mill, constructed roads and bridges, and provided loans; it also arranged for stage coach service and ferry transportation across the QU'APPELLE RIVER, a vital crossing on the settlers' trail north from the CPR mainline. On January 1, 1884, the post office was officially opened as "Yorkton" to prevent confusion with York, Ontario. During the NORTH-WEST RESISTANCE, the Company lobbied Ottawa to protect its 164 settlers; a short-lived Fort Watson was erected, and a volunteer militia was organized. By 1888, the Company had complied with the terms of its agreement with the government. All along it had used political clout to have the Manitoba and North Western Railway extend its line westward, and finally in 1890 Yorkton moved 4 km south to its present site near the rail line. As large numbers of settlers arrived from many lands, the company continued to deal in real estate around Yorkton and southeastern Saskatchewan. In 1947 the last of its holdings was sold: the area known today as the Ravine Ecological Preserve. That same year the Company surrendered its Charter to the Secretary of State of Canada, and dissolution was granted on December 17.

Therese Lefebvre-Prince

YORKTON. Yorkton, pop 15,107, is located in northeastern Saskatchewan about 175 km NE of Regina, at the convergence of three main highways: No. 16 (the Yellowhead Route), No. 10 (to Regina), No. 9 (to the US border). The community is a regional service centre for the surrounding area, which is known for its rich agricultural land. When explorers and traders first came through the region,

they encountered the Assiniboine, Cree, Saulteaux, and Métis nations. In 1882 the YORK FARMERS' COLONIZATION COMPANY, a block settlement group from York County, Ontario founded York City about 4 km NE from the present-day city, on the banks of the Little White Sand River, a tributary of the Assiniboine. Settlers came from eastern Canada, Manitoba, the United States, England, Scotland, and Ireland. In 1884 a post office was established, and the settlement was renamed Yorkton to prevent confusion with York, Ontario.

In 1889 the railway was extended westward from Saltcoats to present-day Yorkton, 4 km south of the original colony. In order to be alongside the new railway line the colony moved to its present site, where it prospered; it was incorporated as a village in 1894, and as a town in 1900. The railway brought with it a major influx of Hungarians, Germans, Scandinavians, Russians, Belgians and Americans, as well as great numbers of Ukrainians and Doukhobors. These immigrants provided the community with a population boost, a new vitality, and culturally diverse institutions and festivities. Yorkton achieved city status in 1928, and is today the province's fifth largest city. It is a regional centre for retail and wholesale trade, health and government functions, and a variety of commercial services. Yorkton hosts many events throughout the year, including the internationally renowned YORKTON SHORT FILM AND VIDEO FESTIVAL.

Daria Coneghan

YORKTON SERVICE FLYING TRAINING SCHOOL. In order to participate in the BRITISH COMMONWEALTH AIR TRAINING PLAN (BCATP), which was established in Canada in 1939 at the onset of WORLD WAR II, Mayor Charles Peaker of Yorkton and other politicians, including the Liberal member of Parliament for the area, George W. McPhee, asked

the federal government to establish a flying training school near that city. Their bid was successful, and construction of facilities for the training station began in the spring of 1940, on a site a few kilometres north of Yorkton. Two relief stations were also built at the nearby communities of Rhein and Sturdee. The station at Yorkton was an impressive complex consisting of 40 buildings, including a large mess hall, a 35-bed hospital, and hangars to shelter some 200 planes.

By November 1940, work on the project had progressed to a sufficient stage to allow for an official opening on June 11, 1941. The first commanding officer of the station was Group Captain George R. Howsam. The station created a boom for Yorkton, bringing opportunities for the city to become closely involved with its airmen and airwomen. A hostess club was organized, with headquarters on the third floor of the old city hall, which provided a diversity of social events for military personnel and local citizens. Students came from all over Canada and the Commonwealth to perfect their flying skills. They flew North American Harvards and twin-engine Cessna Cranes—unfortunately not without a few fatal accidents. By the end of the war in 1945, an estimated 2,000 pilots had earned their wings at the Yorkton school.

Therese Lefebvre-Prince

YORKTON SHORT FILM & VIDEO FESTIVAL. The Yorkton Short Film & Video Festival has the distinction of being the longest-running festival of its kind in North America. The festival's mission is "to provide a forum to celebrate short film and video through recognition, presentation, and education." The festival was the brainchild of James Lysyshyn, a young National Film Board field officer stationed in Saskatchewan in 1947. That year, Lysyshyn presented his idea for a film festival to Yorkton's film council, and in 1950 the Yorkton International Documentary Film Festival became a reality. Entries for that first festival came from across Canada and from all corners of the world. The winning entries were initially chosen by the viewing public; however, since 1956 they have been decided by a panel of adjudicators comprised of members of the film industry. One of the first adjudicators, Frank Morris, thought Yorkton should have a grand prize symbolic of the festival; named for the wheat fields surrounding the city, that grand prize became known as the "Golden Sheaf."

In 1977, the international part of the competition was dropped, and the Yorkton Short Film Festival was born. The fifteenth festival in 1978 drew a record 250 entries. Until that time the festival had been held biannually, but due to such a successful year it was decided to make it a yearly event. With the addition of a video category in 1981, the festival took on its present name. It takes place during four days each spring. A wide variety of events of interest to both filmmakers and the general public are held throughout the city. Some of the more popular events include workshops, public/private screenings of entries, premieres, luncheons, banquet and awards ceremony, barbecue/ballgame, and golf tournament. The modern-day festival draws a yearly average of 375 entries, with a record 450 entries received in 2003.   *Linda Channing*

YOUNG CHIPEEWAYAN FIRST NATION (STONY KNOLL).

On August 23, 1876, Chief Chipeewayan and four headmen (Naa-poo-chee-chees, Wah-wis, Kah-pah-pah-mah-chatik-way, and Kee-yeu-ah-tiah-pim-waht) signed **TREATY 6** at Fort Carlton, and in 1879 a reserve was surveyed for them. When Chief Chipeewayan passed away in 1877, his son, Young Chipeewayan, became the hereditary chief and the Department of Indian Affairs adopted his name as the proper name for the band. In the difficult years that followed, the band was not able to sustain itself on its Stony Knoll Reserve as it attempted an economic and cultural transition to farming. Treaty pay lists from 1879 to 1885 disclose that band members were paid annuities at Battleford, Fort Walsh (Maple Creek), and Jack Fish Creek, and that their population dwindled. When the **NORTH-WEST RESISTANCE** took place, the Young Chipeewayan Band was considered to have taken part in insurrection, and annuity payments were withheld. By 1888 the Young Chipeewayan Band was no longer identified as a separate band; Young Chipeewayan himself was included on the Thunderchild treaty pay list. Over the next few years, the land formerly comprising Stoney Knoll Indian Reserve was deeded out to private purchasers. By 1889, all who had received treaty payments as members of the Young Chipeewayan Band had either died, been transferred to the treaty pay lists of other First Nations, or

disappeared. On June 17, 1982, Chief Alfred Snake requested on behalf of the Young Chipeewayan Band examination into a specific claim, but was rejected. In 1993 the Indian Claims Commission began an inquiry into the specific claim of the Stoney Knoll Indian Reserve, but the claim remains unsettled.   *Christian Thompson*

YOUNG MEN'S CHRISTIAN ASSOCIATION (YMCA).

The Young Men's Christian Association (YMCA) is an international charitable organization that promotes the development of individuals in spirit, mind, and body. Founded in London, England in 1844 by George Williams, the YMCA provided spiritual improvement for young men confronted by the temptations of modern urban life. The first North American association was established in Montreal in 1851 and a Canadian National Council was created in 1912.

Citizens of Regina founded a provisional YMCA in 1890. Activities were conducted in various downtown churches, halls, and homes until a permanent meeting place was built in 1908. Located on the corner of 12th Avenue and Cornwall Street, the city's first YMCA was partially destroyed by the **REGINA CYCLONE** of 1912. It was rebuilt and used until 1959 when a new facility was constructed on the corner of 13th Avenue and Smith Street, the association's current location. Renovated in 1976 and again in 1992, the YMCA became the Family YMCA of Regina in 1980.

Sources indicate that the YMCA of Saskatoon was established in 1905 while others suggest 1908. The Association operated out of temporary quarters until its first home opened in 1912. The facility, located on the corner of Spadina Crescent and 20th Street East, served as a convalescent hospital and vocational training school for returned soldiers from 1917 to 1920. The YMCA reoccupied the premises in September and remained there until its present facility at 25-22nd Street East opened in 1969. The YMCA serves over 6,000 children, youth, adults, and seniors annually.

The Moose Jaw YMCA was founded in 1905. It occupied the second floor of the Masonic Temple on Main Street North before moving to a permanent location on 23 Fairford Street East in 1909. In 1954, the men's organization joined with the city's Young Women's Christian Association to form the YMCA-YWCA of Moose Jaw. The combined Association's current facility at 220 Fairford Street East was opened in 1973.

Today the YMCA serves people of both sexes regardless of age, race, or religion. Although it is best recognized for its promotion of fitness and recreation, the YMCA also provides childcare, employment training, and adult education programs.

Holden Stoffel

FURTHER READING: Argan, William, with Paw Cowen and Gordon W. Staseson. 2002. Regina, *The First 100 Years: The History of Regina Told Through its Buildings and Monuments*. Regina: Leader-Post Carrier Foundation; *The City of Saskatoon, Municipal Manual 2004: Containing Facts and Figures About the City and its Various Departments*. Saskatoon: Office of the City Clerk.

YOUNG WOMEN'S CHRISTIAN ASSOCIATION (YWCA).

In the early 1900s, Saskatchewan women sought to establish the YWCA, a well-known urban-based evangelical Protestant organization that aimed to uplift and protect young women, especially those moving into the rapidly growing cities. Over the decades, the YWCAs have changed considerably, adapting to shifts in societal needs and in notions of womanhood. The first provincial YWCA was founded in Moose Jaw (1907). The Regina and Saskatoon YWCAs were first established in 1910; that in Prince Albert in 1912. In Regina the Local Council of Women played an instrumental role. In Saskatoon, Christ Church Women's Auxiliary and the Golden West chapter of the IODE were involved, but of central importance was an individual woman of independent means: Millicent Silcox. A Church of England deaconess, she had already begun Travellers' Aid work, meeting trains and providing lodging to young women; she continued this work under YWCA auspices. All four YWCAs did extensive Travellers' Aid Work, but their prime objective was to provide respectable, affordable quarters for young women who were coming into the cities to work or study. Programs and services proliferated under the guidance of paid staff and volunteer workers, the most extensive being in Regina and Saskatoon. The Saskatoon YWCA, for example, developed educational programs including classes in domestic science, dress-making, Bible study, first aid, current events, and English-language training. Employment assistance was often provided. Clubs proliferated, as did social events like teas; in time, dancing was allowed. Physical activities were always encouraged, and extensive sports programs also developed; camping became popular.

The YWCAs continued their work through the social disruption of the two world wars, the economic devastation of the 1930s, and the challenges of the postwar decades. Programs and services constantly adapted to the changing needs of young women and the community. The YWCA, for example, responded to the need for support services to new Canadians, and in the late 1970s extended a helping hand to Vietnam refugees. As well, YWCAs have addressed social issues such as the needs of women with disabilities, and violence against women. In the early 1980s Regina and Saskatoon YWCAs began to offer annual Women of Distinction Awards, and Prince Albert began to do so in 1990.

As of early 2005, Regina, Saskatoon, and Prince Albert still had YWCAs. In 2004 the combined YMCA/YWCA in Moose Jaw (which dated from 1954) became a YMCA Family Y.

Clara Bayliss and Lisa Dale-Burnett

FURTHER READING: YWCA. 1955. *Building Fellowship: A History of the YWCA in Saskatchewan.* Saskatoon: Modern Press; Wylie, C.O.T. 1989. "'God's Own Cornerstones, Our Daughters': The Saskatoon Young Women's Christian Association, 1910-1939." MA thesis, University of Saskatchewan.

YOUTH JUSTICE. The youth justice system has been developed as distinct from adult justice because young persons lack the maturity of adults, and therefore may need different responses to offending or anti-social behaviour, while still being held accountable. Youth justice and related issues are governed in Canada by federal legislation: the Youth Criminal Justice Act. According to this legislation, the objective of the youth justice system is to protect society through prevention of crime, rehabilitation and reintegration of young offenders, and imposition of meaningful consequences for offending behaviours. The youth justice system aims to achieve accountability for offending behaviour of youth through fair and proportionate responses that reinforce societal values, encourage the repair of harm done, and are respectful of gender, ethnic, cultural and linguistic differences, and of the special requirements of youth. Youth justice processes try to balance the rights of young people and victims and to inform and involve offending youth's parents as much as possible.

The provincial government is responsible for administering youth justice legislation and for making sure that youth justice programs and services are available in Saskatchewan. The Saskatchewan Department of Justice prosecutes offenses by youth under the Youth Criminal Justice Act and other statutes, while the Department of Corrections and Public Safety provides programs and services ranging from custody to community services. Other agencies such as health authorities, Aboriginal organizations, and community social service agencies are also involved in providing youth justice services. Police are usually the first agency involved in a youth justice situation. Where the situation warrants, the Crown Prosecutor is involved to determine what charges will proceed against a youth, to direct the matter to youth courts for disposition, or to propose alternatives to a formal court process such as victim/offender mediation. In Saskatchewan, a majority of alternative programs to youth court are delivered by non-government organizations, including Aboriginal organizations under contract with the provincial government. Youth in these "extra-judicial" programs are able to consult a lawyer, and may opt for more formal justice processes at any time.

In mediation, the offending youth and the victim try to come to an agreement to resolve the offense. For example, the youth might agree to do volunteer work for the victim or the community, make restitution, take counseling, or engage in any other activity acceptable to both parties. If the youth successfully completes the agreement, he or she is cleared of any further legal processes related to the offense. Some youth are required to go through a more formal youth court process. In most cases, youth will live in their normal home while the court process is underway. In other cases, youth may be detained or remanded in youth facilities until they make a court appearance. Whether or not a youth is detained depends on factors such as previous criminal involvement and assessment of the likelihood of attending court. Some youth are initially detained, but then are released with intensive supervision and support. If a youth court finds a youth guilty of charges, a youth worker or probation officer may be required to prepare a pre-sentence report that reviews the criminal and social history of the youth as well as any special needs or circumstances. Judges make sentencing decisions based on input from the Crown, the defence, the youth and his or her family, the victim, the community, and youth workers.

A number of possible sentences may be imposed. In minor cases, a reprimand may be considered sufficient. The judge can also order an absolute or conditional discharge, or impose a fine up to $1,000. The court may order the youth to compensate another person for loss, damage or injury, to make restitution to a property owner, to serve up to 240 hours community service, or to suffer other penalties or forfeitures. Additional conditions on behaviour such as probation may be applied with a level of supervision determined on the basis of a risk and needs assessment. A youth may also be required to attend specific programs on conditions set by the judge.

Where custody is ordered, there are two levels available: open custody and secure custody. Open custody is for youth that can be managed in the community. Secure custody is for youth assessed as a potential risk to the community. All custody orders include a period of supervision in the community. Some non-violent offenders who would otherwise be sentenced to custody may be ordered to serve all or part of their sentence in the community, subject to conditions which, if violated, result in custody. A special sentence may be applied by youth courts to serious violent young offenders, where the young person has been found guilty of murder, attempted murder, manslaughter, or aggravated sexual assault, has a psychological disorder, or has a pattern of repeated, serious, violent offenses. In these cases an individualized treatment plan will be developed for the young person while in custody.

Because most of the root causes of criminal behaviour lie outside the justice system, the youth criminal justice system itself has only a limited effect on the incidence of youth crime. Research points to background factors frequently associated with offending, such as poor school or work performance, parenting and other family issues, pro-criminal friends and attitudes, substance abuse, and anti-social behaviours. Research into effective interventions in youth justice systems suggests that an increase in punishment alone for young offenders is not effective in reducing criminal behaviour. The most effective way to reduce youth crime is to address the social and behavioral issues that contribute to criminal behaviour. Like other parts of the justice system, youth justice is evolving from a simple correctional response to a system that supports positive change and growth in communities and individuals, and thus helps to reduce the factors leading to criminal behaviour in youth.

Jim McIlmoyl

L. MARUSIAK PHOTO/SASKATCHEWAN ARCHIVES BOARD 81-1748-54

Russell Yuristy, September 1981.

YURISTY, RUSSELL (1936–). Russell Yuristy is well known for his surrealistic playground creations: these playful sculptures can be found across Canada and in the United States. However, he is not confined to three-dimensional works, but also expresses himself through painting, works in pen, pencil, pastels, and various printmaking techniques. Yuristy was born in Goodeve, Saskatchewan. In 1959, he received his BA with a major in English and creative writing from the **UNIVERSITY OF SASKATCHEWAN**. In 1962–63, he attended art classes there, and then completed an MSc in Art in 1967 at the University of Wisconsin in Madison. He taught drawing and painting at the University of Saskatchewan, Regina Campus from 1967 to 1971, and was also workshop coordinator for the Emma

Lake Artists' Workshops in 1969 and 1970. In 1971, Yuristy moved to Silton, Saskatchewan, where he purchased the old Roman Catholic Church on the main street. In Silton, Yuristy became the project leader of the Creative Playground Workshop, which saw the construction, sometimes in his backyard, of large animal playground structures. These structures were inspired by surrealistic drawings he had made of hollow animals.

In 1974, officials of Expo Canada commissioned Yuristy to design and build a wooden animal playground for Expo '74 in Spokane, Washington. The fair's theme of conservation and ecology matched his work perfectly because his playground structures use lumber mill rejects and recycled wood. Some of the pieces located on Canada Island include a giant crow and hornless moose. Children have approved of Yuristy's constructions, but adults have not always agreed. In 1977, there was an uproar over a structure in the shape of a giant buffalo built for the Swift Current Exhibition Centre; the original wooden structure, destroyed by vandals, was rebuilt in 1978 out of concrete and reinforced steel. Some of his other playground structures include a goose commissioned by the Wascana Centre Authority in Regina, and a beaver commissioned by the National Capital Commission in Ottawa. In 1994, he created a large aluminium sculpture titled *Switch Hitter* for Ottawa's Triple A Stadium.

Yuristy has also exhibited his paintings, drawings, and prints in numerous cities across Canada. He has had solo exhibitions at the Susan Whitney Gallery in Regina as well as in Montreal, Ottawa, and Lethbridge. In 1986, he left Saskatchewan for Ottawa. His works can be found at the National Gallery of Canada, Canada Council Art Bank, **MENDEL ART GALLERY, MACKENZIE ART GALLERY,** McDonald Corporation (Chicago), and Shaklee Corporation (San Francisco). *Julia Krueger*

ZAKRESKI, PETER E. (1939–). Peter Zakreski was born on June 28, 1939. Dedicated to the city of Saskatoon, he has received several awards for his community service and volunteering efforts. He helped coordinate the 1979 Western Canada Summer Games, the 1989 Jeux Canada Games and the 1991 World Junior Hockey Championships hosted by Saskatoon. Zakreski also served as an alderman for six years. He has been awarded the Canada 125 Medal, the University of Saskatchewan Alumni Humanitarian Award, and the Order of Canada in 2002.

ZEALANDIA, town, pop 111, located 19 km NE of Rosetown on Hwy 7. Settlers began arriving in the district in 1904–05—many traversing what was known as the Old Bone Trail, which ran southwestward from Saskatoon. The Zealandia post office was established in 1906, and with the construction of the

railway from Saskatoon to Zealandia en route to Rosetown in 1908, significant development at the townsite began. By 1910, four grain elevators lined the tracks in the community, and a good number of businesses had been established. In 1911, Zealandia acquired town status with a population of 264, the largest the community would ever have. The town's numbers significantly declined through the 1920s, and plummeted to 136 by 1936. The town recovered somewhat after **WORLD WAR II,** but by the early 1970s it once again was in decline. Today, little is left of the once-thriving business community, although there remains a plant which processes lentils, peas, and chickpeas for export. *David McLennan*

ZENON PARK, village, pop 231, located in the eastern parklands, 45 km NE of Tisdale. In the spring of 1910, French-Canadians who had been working as factory workers in Massachusetts and Rhode Island began arriving in the area. Poverty had driven them to the US, but the prospect of owning their own land brought them back to Canada, and then west. The townsite of Zenon Park was established in 1929 when the Canadian National Railway constructed a branch line north from Crooked River. The name of the community pays tribute to Zenon Chamberland, one of the first pioneers and the first postmaster of the new settlement. Today, the community remains predominantly French-speaking, although most residents are bilingual. Our Lady of the Nativity Roman Catholic Church, constructed in the summer of 1930 with local volunteer labour to replace the original 1913 church that was destroyed by fire earlier that year, has a very active congregation and has been designated a heritage property. The Zenon Park area economy is predominantly agriculture-based, but diverse: it includes honey production, organic seed-processing, alfalfa dehydration, seed production, herbs, and spices. *See also* **FRENCH SETTLEMENTS.** *David McLennan*

ZERO-EFFLUENT PULP MILL. A pulp mill at Meadow Lake, Saskatchewan, is the first in the world not to discharge any effluent or waste water into any nearby creek, river, stream or lake.

Millar Western Pulp (Meadow Lake) Ltd. operates the state-of-the-art manufacturing facility, which has an international reputation in the production and marketing of bleached chemi-thermo-mechanical pulp (BCTMP). With its advanced pulp processing and environmental control technology, the Meadow Lake pulp mill has helped set new standards for responsibility in the forest products industry. In 1989, the Crown Investments Corporation of Saskatchewan and Millar Western Industries of Edmonton formed a partnership to build the Meadow Lake mill; the two-line, totally chlorine-free BCTMP mill began operating in 1992. Since then, it has held a leading position in the global BCTMP sector in terms of environmental performance, market development, product quality, cost efficiency, and productivity. The mill now produces up to 325,000 air-dried metric tonnes (ADMT) of pulp annually, well above its initial design capacity of 240,000 ADMT.

Certified to the ISO 9001: 2000 standard for quality management and the ISO 14001 standard for environmental management, the Meadow Lake mill produces pulp from aspen, a hardwood tree that grows virtually everywhere in Saskatchewan. The facility produces seventeen different grades of pulp for specific paper and board end-use applications, and is in high demand around the world for its consistent quality and exceptional papermaking properties. It also continues to be recognized for its pioneering environmental technology. As a zero-effluent-discharge mill, the facility cleans and reuses its process waste water; this water recycling system not only eliminates the discharge of effluent to the environment, but also significantly reduces the mill's fresh-water intake compared to that of other BCTMP mills and conventional kraft mills. *Joe Ralko*

MARLOW ESAU PHOTO/COURTESY OF MILLAR WESTERN FOREST PRODUCTS LTD

The chlorine-free Millar Western Pulp (Meadow Lake) Ltd. bleached chemi-thermo-mechanical pulp mill at Meadow Lake is the world's first successful zero-effluent-discharge market pulp mill.

ZOOPLANKTON. Zooplankton (*zoo-* = animal; *plankton* = floating, drifting) comprise a diverse range of aquatic organisms in which many phyla are represented. They are dominated by four major groups that spend some or all of their life cycle in the water column of lakes and rivers. These include: protozoa (four phyla/subphyla and eleven classes: unicellular or colonial heterotrophic eukaryotes); rotifers or "wheel animals" (phylum Rotifera; two classes); and two sub-classes of Crustacea (phylum Arthropoda), the Cladocera and the Copepoda. The size range among freshwater zooplankton typically spans 20 micrometres to a few millimetres. They consume both living and non-living organic matter, some preying on other zooplankton, others on small algae, bacteria and detritus. Large-bodied cladoceran species (e.g., *Daphnia*) are particularly effective at grazing algae of suitable dimensions, and can be responsible for periodic high water clarity in otherwise turbid lakes. Other groups of animals may be found among the true zooplankton (or holo-plankton) from time to time, whether as life cycle stages, or from temporary benthic entrainment due to water mixing. These may include a few coelenterates (hydras, freshwater jellyfish), various larvae and adults of fish, insects (especially midges of the family Chaoboridae), trematode flatworms, annelid worms, gastrotrichs, ostracodes, water mites, and others.

Zooplankton play a crucial role in ecosystem function by transferring energy from lower to higher trophic levels in aquatic food webs. They are of great importance as food for many fish species, especially juvenile stages. For the crustacean zooplankton, keys and lists have been assembled for some Canadian provinces (notably Ontario, Alberta, and British Columbia), and for North America as a whole. Based on available Canadian province lists (covering both shield and prairie habitats), Saskatchewan should be home to more than fifty species in thirty genera of cladocerans, and more than fifty-four species in thirty-three genera of copepods. However, knowledge of zooplankton biogeography is spotty. The widely distributed or ubiquitous species are those with tolerance to a wide range of physical and chemical conditions. Other genera may be regionally or locally restricted due to narrower tolerance thresholds. Some groups produce desiccation-resistant cysts or have life stages that can remain viable out of water for periods of time, so that some zooplankton can colonize aquatic habitats—even temporary ones—rapidly. Transportation may occur by a variety of mechanisms, ranging from the water itself to aerial transport and hitch-hiking on animals. Water temperature, depth and current, oxygen, salinity, pH, alkalinity, and the types and abundance of algae and zooplankton predators are among the factors influencing the distribution of species. These base conditions vary with the type of rocks, soils, vegetation and drainages found across the landscape. The full range of inland water types can be found in Saskatchewan. On a broad scale, a transition of conditions extends from northern cold-water systems in the boreal Shield to cool and warm-water systems on the southern prairies. This cline of inland water types means that species occurrence and abundance within zooplankton are highly varied. For this reason a substantial zooplankton diversity exists within Saskatchewan. With few specialists working in this field, the presence of species described from similar habitats elsewhere may be slow to be confirmed. In other cases, particularly in the more obscure and globally less-studied fauna like the protozoa, perhaps some new types may yet be described. Also, species exotic to North America introduced among others by shipping ballast discharges and the aquaria industry will no doubt continue to appear, perhaps colonizing Saskatchewan waters in the future. *Ken Scott*

FURTHER READING: J.H. Thorp and A.P. Kovitch (eds). 1991. *Ecology and Classification of North American Freshwater Invertebrates.* San Diego: Academic Press; R.W. Wetzel. 2001. *Limnology.* San Diego: Academic Press.

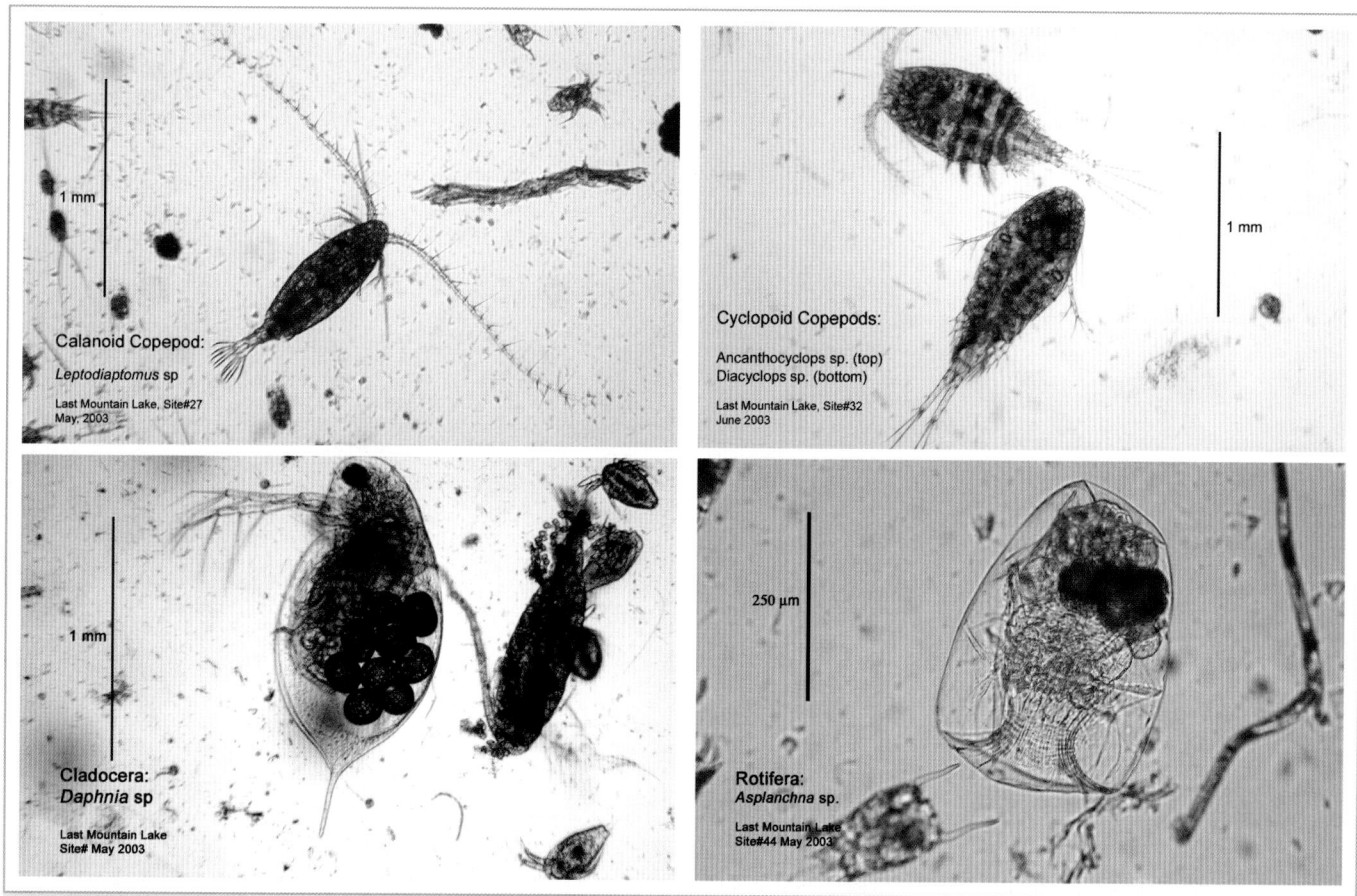

KEN SCOTT PHOTOS/COURTESY OF SASKATCHEWAN ENVIRONMENT

Common genera representing the following zooplankton groups: Calanoid copepods; Cyclopoid copepods, Cladocerans; Rotifers.

APPENDIX A:
CONTRIBUTING WRITERS

Kathy Abernethy
Janice Acoose
Stephen Acres
Marianne Gosztonyi
 Ainley
Shakeel Akhtar
David Akister
Robert Allan
Bob Allen
Raymond Ambrosi
Ted Amendt
Alan Anderson
Barrie Anderson
Don Anderson
Frederick Anderson
Jack Anderson
Leona Anderson
Robert Anderson
W.O. Archibold
Ved Arora
Michelle Arsenault
Bill Asikinack
Andrea Atkinson
Irene Attrux
Rick August
Cheryl Avery
E.H. Baergen
Donald A. Bailey
Bonnie Baird
Harold R. Baker
Linda Baker
Roger Bakes
Marc Baltzan
Cara Banks
Sabine Banniza
Bob Barkman
G. Dudley Barnett
Gordon L. Barnhart
Elaine Barrow
Bill Barry
Harvey Basi
Paul Baskey
Sandra Bassendowski
Dean Bauche
Clara Bayliss
Bob Beal
Sandra Beardsall
Greg Beatty
Tina Beaudry-Mellor
R. Glen Beck
Martin Beech
Paul Beingessner
Yale Belanger
Richard Belford
George Bell
Sandra Bellegarde
Melissa Bennett
Viola Bens
Jamie Benson
Marjorie L. Benson
Loleen Berdahl
Dan Beveridge
Beth Bilson
Sandra Bingaman
Ann Bishop

Frances Bitney
Don Black
Lauren Black
Mary Blackstone
Jim Blanchard
Sue Bland
John A. Boan
Merle Bocking
Rexford A. Boda
Trevor Boddy
David Boehm
June Bold
Michele Bonneau
Stephane Bonneville
Peter Borch
Marie-Ann Bowden
Joan Boyer
Ian Brace
Pat Brassard
Donna Braun
Gordon Bray
Mark Brigham
Scott Broad
Lorne Brown
M. Winifred Brown
Harold Bryant
M.W. Buckley
Darlene Bullard
Patricia Burke
Patrick Burns
John Burton
John Bury
David Butler-Jones
Victor Buyniak
Barb Byers
Rick Byrne
Peter J. Calhoun
Barb Cameron
Delee Cameron
Anne Campbell
Claire Campbell
Barb Cape
Gerry Carline
Svein Carlsen
Gary Carlson
Phyllis Carlson
Ron Carlson
W.J. Carlyle
Sarah Carter
Will Chabun
David Chandler
Linda Channing
Ellen Chapco
William Chapco
John Chaput
Nadine Charabin
Harvey Chatlain
Gail Chin
Doug Chisholm
Patrick Chopik
David Christensen
Deanna Christensen
Paul Cipywnyk
Henry Classen
Verne Clemence

Heather Cline
Patrick Close
Daniel Coleman
Terence Coleman
Anne Collins
Michael Collins
John Comrie
Damian Coneghan
Daria Coneghan
Karen Conway
Doug Cooney
Carol Cooper
Maryanne Cotcher
Mark Côté
Michael Cottrell
Bruce Coulman
Brian Cousins
Roy Crawford
Charlene Crevier
Ray Crone
Ronald C.C. Cuming
Doug Cuthand
Harry Dahl
Brenda Dale
Janice Dale
Lisa Dale-Burnett
Estelle d'Almeida
Dan Dattani
Wayne Davies
Kate Davis
Moira Day
W. Earle De Coteau
Dan de Vlieger
Bernard De Vries
Patricia Deadman
Marilyn Decker
Alice Derow
Gloria DeSantis
Garnet Dishaw
Leonard Doell
Brian Dojack
Derek Donais
Walter A. Donovan
Patrick Douaud
Keith Downey
Murray D. Drew
Otto Driedger
Deana Driver
John Duerkop
Tonya Duffy
Rose-Alma Dumont
Bruce Dyck
Erika Dyck
Ian Dyck
James H. Dyck
Susan Eaton
Patience Elabor-
 Idemudia
David R. Elliott
Doug Elliott
Kathryn Ellis
Jo-Ann Episkenew
Henry Epp
Linda Epstein
Michael Epstein

Pat Erhardt
Willie Ermine
Rick Espie
Trent Evanisky
Simon Evans
Joan Eyolfson Cadham
Brett Fairbairn
Sherry Farrell Racette
Barry Farrow
Daralyn Fauser
Joan Feather
Sergey Fedoroff
Sylvia Fedoruk
Mike Fedyk
Winter Fedyk
Murray Feist
Anna Feldman
Harold Fenske
C. Marie Fenwick
Gerald Filson
Gregory Fingas
Elyse Fisher
Colleen Fitzgerald
Bernard Flaman
Jan Fleming
Sandra Flood
Marianne Flory
Lorena Fontaine
R.J. Ford
Louise H. Forsyth
Pam Franklin
Murray M. Fraser
Malcolm French
Henry A. Friesen
Verner Friesen
Paul Fudge
Murray Fulton
Hartley Furtan
Patricia Gallagher
Verna Gallen
Joseph Garcea
Kay Garside
Gerald Gartner
David Gauthier
Krzysztof Gebhard
Patti Gera
Annie Gerin
Maria L. Gerritsen
Victor Gignac
Peter Gilmer
Gord Gilmour
Gordon Goddard
J. Kenneth Goldie
Lyn Goldman
Mike Gollop
Ken Goodwill
Martin Grajczyk
Cheri Gratto-Trevor
David Greenfield
Therese Greenwood
Nestor Gregoire
William Greuel
Harry Groenen
Dennis Gruending
John Gruszka

Bruce Guenther
Paul Guillet
William Gulka
Kathleen Gullacher
Walter Hader
Laurel Halladay
Elaine Hamm
U. Theodore Hammer
Margaret Hammond
Mossie Hancock
Miriam Handel
David Hanly
Harry K. Harder
Jim Harding
Claude-Jean Harel
Vernon L. Harms
Charles Harper
Tej Harrison
Regan Hart-Mitchell
Richard Harvey
David Hay
Michael Hayden
Alison Hayford
Elaine Hays
Richard Hazel
Heather Heavin
Gilles Hebert
Rachel Lea Heide
Donna Heimbecker
Gerald Heinrichs
Joan Helm
John Hemstad
Norman Henderson
Hugh Henry
Daryl H. Hepting
Bob Herbison
Al Hergott
Ross Herrington
Steve Hewitt
Daniel Hickey
Walter Hildebrandt
Bryan Hillis
Leonard Hines
Bob Hinitt
Jill Hobbs
Kate Hobin
Eugene Hodgson
George Hoffman
Susan Hogarth
Don Hoium
F.A. Holm
Maxine Holm
Jim Holmes
Ronald Hooper
Richard Hordern
William Hordern
Louis Horlick
Ken Horsman
C. Stuart Houston
Mary Houston
Carmen Howell
Pierre Hucl
Jeff Hudson
Raymond Huel
Victoria Hunchak

Gordon Hutchings
Fay Hutchinson
Gary Hyland
William Michael
 Ingledew
Robert Innes
L. Lee-Ann Irvine
Dan Ish
Bob Ivanochko
Richard Jack
Michael Jackson
Nicholas Jesson
Keith Jeworski
Anthony Jo
Noreen Johns
Doug Johnson
Faith Johnston
Gwen Jones
Lloyd Jones
Tim E.H. Jones
Patricia Joyce
Elizabeth Kalmakoff
Teresita Kambeitz
M.V. Kanchana
Krishan Kapila
Amy Karlinsky
Jay Kasperski
Lindy Kasperski
Michael Katz
Bob Kavanagh
Mike Kaytor
Orris Keehr
Michaela Keet
Anne Keffer
Don Kerr
William Kerr
Rose Ketchum
David Klatt
Frieda Esau Klippenstein
Louis Knafla
Murray Knuttila
Charles Kooger
Bohdan Kordan
Valerie Korinek
Frank Korvemaker
Denise Kouri
Joanne Kozlowski
Naomi Kral
Pat Krause
Caroline D. Krentz
Gerry Krochak
June Krogan
Julia Krueger
Tim B. Krywulak
Wendee Kubik
Joan Kuffner
Suren Kulshreshtha
Jake Kutarna
Patrick Kyba
P. Whitney Lackenbauer
Trish LaFontaine
Ron Laliberté
André Lalonde
Vinh-The Lam
Kathy Lang

Scott Langen
James E. Lanigan
Alex Lapchuk
Richard Lapointe
Paul Laverdure
Sylvain Lavoie
Gordon Lawson
Donald H. Layh
Joanna Leach
Therese Lefebvre Prince
Louise Legaré
Ann Leger-Anderson
Erin Legg
Phyllis Lerat
John Leszczynski
Marilyn Lewry
Roberta Lexier
Howard Leyton-Brown
Ken Leyton-Brown
Murray Little
Michael Littlewood
Steven Lloyd
Cheryl Loadman
Lowell Loewen
Timothy Long
Wayne Lorch
Ron Love
Ken Lozinsky
Yars Lozowchuck
Cathy Luciuk
Gerald Luciuk
Holly Luhning
Maureen Lux
Alex MacDonald
Robert Macdonald
Kristiana MacKenzie
I.S. MacLaren
Constance Maguire
Gregory Maillet
Colleen Malley
George Manz
Ann March
Gregory Marchildon
Terry Marner
Kim Marschall
Guy Marsden
David Marshall
Angela Martin
Lee-Ann Martin
Nancy Martin
Diane Martz
Helen Marzolf
Merle Massie
Maureen Matthews
Lesley McBain
Stephen McClatchie
Blair McClinton
John McCormick
Anne McDonald
Susanne McElhinney
Ken McGovern

Marcia McGovern
Alicia McGregor
Kirk McGregor
Jim McIlmoyl
Tom McIntosh
Gordon McKay
Robert McKercher
Ken McKinlay
Don McKinnon
Greg McKinnon
John McKinnon
Robert McLaren
David McLennan
Neal McLeod
Miriam McNab
James McNinch
Ray W. McVicar
Leona Meier
Lillian Mein
Stewart Mein
George Melnyk
Justin Messner
David Meyer
Herman Michell
Leanne Miles
Nick Miliokas
Ruth Wright Millar
David Miller
Marilyn Miller
Erin Millions
Isabelle Mills
Barbara Mitchell
George Mitchell
Janet Mitchell
Ken Mitchell
Ormond Mitchell
Rosella Mitchell
Brian Mlazgar
Faye Moen
Ben Moffat
Jeremy Mohr
Duane Mombourquette
Elizabeth Mooney
Jeremy Morgan
Ross Moxley
Theresa Mui
Kevin Murphy
Michael Murphy
Ian C. Nelson
Rob Nestor
Melanie Neuhofer
Paul M. Newton
Judy Nicholson
Don Nicks
N. Ole Nielsen
Richard Nieman
Ray Nixdorf
Jeff Noel
Marian Noll
Ken Norman
Dianne Lloyd Norton

Roger Nostbakken
Peter Novecosky
Jason Nystrom
Mike O'Brien
Bart Oegema
Andrew Oko
M. Rose Olfert
Owen Olfert
Lynn Oliver
Natalie Ostryzniuk
Donna Ottenson
Machiko Oya
Adriane Paavo
Glenn Padbury
Rupen Pandya
Theodosia Papirnik
Julie Parchewski
Jeremy Parnes
Lorena Patino
Alec Paul
Garry Paul
Lynden Penner
Susan Pentelichuk
Jeanette Pepper
Marion Perry
Judy Peters
Myrna Petersen
Carol Peterson
Peter W.B. Phillips
Rodolfo Pino
Brock Pitawanakwat
James Pitsula
Joseph Piwowar
Brian Porter
Stephen Porter
Jessica Pothier
Clare Powell
Marian Powell
Trevor Powell
Jocelyne Praud
Darren Prefontaine
Michael Pretes
David T. Priestly
Ken Probert
Merran Proctor
Tara Procyshyn
Nadia Prokopchuk
Garth Pugh
Bill Quine
Gail Quinney
Brett Quiring
David Quiring
Vernon Racz
Jay Rahn
Brian Rainey
Marie Raiwet
Joe Ralko
Jai Ram
Kavita Ram
Christine Ramsay
Al Ramsey

C. Rangacharyulu
Andrew Rathwell
Blaine Recksiedler
Pat Rediger
Robert E. Redmann
Mary Reeves
Ted Regehr
Joanne Reilly
Judy Reimer
Paula Jane Remlinger
Yuan Ren
Alun Richards
Neil Richards
Dan Ring
Joseph Roberts
Sheila Roberts
Carmen Robertson
Heather Robison
Ken Rodenbush
Keith Roney
Gladys Rose
George Rosenau
Alan M. Rosenberg
Rhonda Rosenberg
Emma Rousseau
Gordon Rowland
J. Frank Roy
Robert G. Roy
Wayne Roznowsky
Dale Russell
Nora Russell
Peter A. Russell
Camille D. Ryan
Mary Ryan
Gregory Salmers
Merv Samborsky
Margaret Sanche
Miguel Sanchez
James Sanheim
A. Margaret Sarjeant
David Sauchyn
Gail Saunders
Murray Sawatsky
Colleen Sawyer
Karen Schmidt
Shirley Schneider
Dorothea Schrader
Glenn Schwartz
Graham J. Scoles
Ken Scott
Lorne Scott
Diane Secoy
Bernard Selinger
Margaret M. Sharon
Leah Sharpe
R. Bruce Shepard
Eleanor Shia
Carl Shiels
Steven J. Shirtliffe
Tim Schowalter
Judith Silverthorne

Colette Simonot
Maureen L. Simpson
Braj Sinha
Kimberly Skakun
Dagmar Skamlova
Al Slinkard
Jim Slough
Laura Small
Alan R. Smith
Allan E. Smith
Colin Smith
David E. Smith
William Smythe
John Solomon
Juliana Soroka
Tanya Sosulski
Christine Sowiak
Kalburgi M. Srinivas
Mel Stauffer
Kathy Stedwill
Brenda Stefanson
Magdalen Stengler
Amy Stensrud
Ardith Stephanson
Terence Stevens
Fiona Stevenson
Sheila Stevenson
Iain Stewart
Van Stewart
Bob Stirling
Holden Stoffel
Boris Stoicheff
Blair Stonechild
Gary Storey
Richard St-Pierre
Maureen Strawson
Glenn Sutter
Ken Svenson
Robin Swales
Shelley Sweeney
Merv Switzer
Karen Tanino
Koozma J. Tarasoff
Doug Tastad
Alex Taylor
Cheryl Taylor
Doug Taylor
Georgina Taylor
Sylvestor Taylor
Karen Taylor-Browne
Philip Thacker
Stuart Thiesson
Joan Thomas
Michael Thome
Christian Thompson
Loraine Thompson
Bernard Thraves
Jane Thurgood Sagal
Theo Tibo
Dave Tickell
Brian Titley

Tracy Tomlinson
Gary Tompkins
Martha Tracey
Cheryl Troupe
Tara Truemner
Kevin Tunney
Dana Turgeon
R.T. Tyler
Mark Vajcner
Albert Vandenberg
Laurence Vigrass
William A. Waiser
Wally Waldman
Cliff Walker
Kathleen Wall
Susan Wallace
Crystal Wallin
Valerie Warder
Robert Wardhaugh
Wayne Wark
John Warnock
Robert Warnock
Jim Warren
Edwin Wasiak
Lorraine Waskowic
Douglas Waterer
Ailsa Watkinson
Robb Watts
Harlan Weidenhammer
Erin Weir
Stephen Weiss
Joyce Wells
Teresa Welsh
Simon Weseen
Elaine E. Wheaton
Donny White
Judy White
Alan Whitehorn
Lloyd Whitesell
Lee Whittington
Randy Widdis
Wanda Wiegers
C.M. Williams
Lucy D. Willis
Barry Wilson
James Winkel
Dianne Winkelman-Sim
Wojciech Wojtkowiak
Armin Wollin
Donna Woloshyn
Arok Wolvengrey
Karen Wright
Robert A. Wright
Garth Wruck
Dwayne Yasinowski
Xiang S. Yin
Alex Youck
Karen Zemlak
Li Zong

APPENDIX B:
ENTRIES BY SUBJECT AREA

Research for the *Encyclopedia of Saskatchewan* was undertaken under 19 theme areas—Aboriginal (which includes First Nations and Métis), Agriculture and Food, Arts and Culture, Business and Industry, Education, Geography, Health, History, Labour, Law and Justice (which includes Legislation), Military, Politics, Population (which includes Ethnic Bloc Settlements), Religion, Science and Technology, Social Policy, Sports, Transportation, and Women—each supervised by an Editorial Board member (see Acknowledgements on page xix). Three additional categories included were Communities, Saskatchewan Order of Merit recipients, and members of the Order of Canada. For readers interested in a particular theme (rather than a specific subject), the following list organized by theme area will be helpful. Some entries are listed here under more than one theme area.

Aboriginal (First Nations and Métis)

Aboriginal Artists, Contemporary
Aboriginal Artists, Traditional
Aboriginal Education
Aboriginal Education Policy
Aboriginal Fishing Rights
Aboriginal Friendship Centres of Saskatchewan
Aboriginal Health
Aboriginal Hunting Rights
Aboriginal Justice
Aboriginal Languages
Aboriginal Media
Aboriginal Peoples and the World Wars
Aboriginal Peoples of Saskatchewan Theme Essay
Aboriginal Population Trends
Aboriginal Reserve Agriculture to 1900
Aboriginal Spiritual Healing Lodge
Aboriginal Theatre
Aboriginal Veterans
Aboriginal Writers
Acoose, Paul
Ahenakew, David
Ahenakew, Edward
Ahenakew, Freda
Ahtahkakoop
Ahtahkakoop First Nation
Almighty Voice
Arcand, John
Batoche
Beardy's and Okemasis First Nation
Bellegarde, Perry
Big Bear (Mistahi-Maskwa)
Big Bear First Nation
Big Island Lake First Nation (Joseph Bighead)
Big River Cree First Nation
Birch Narrows Dene First Nation
Black Lake Denesuline First Nation
Brady, James Patrick
Brass, Eleanor

Brass, Oliver Johnson
Buffalo River Dene First Nation
Canoe Lake First Nation
Carry the Kettle First Nation
Chacachas First Nation
Chakastapaysin First Nation
Chartier, Clem
Claxton, Dana
Clearwater River Dene Band
Cote First Nation
Cowessess First Nation
Cree
Crowe, Roland
Cumberland House First Nation
Cummings, Nora
Dakota/Lakota
Daniels, Harry
Day Star First Nation
Decoteau, Alex
Deiter, Walter Perry
Denesuline (Dene)
Dumont, Gabriel
English River First Nation
Federation of Saskatchewan Indian Nations (FSIN)
First Nations Bank of Canada
First Nations Economic Development
First Nations Governance
First Nations Intergovernmental Relations
First Nations Land Claims
Fishing Lake First Nation
Flying Dust First Nation
Fond du Lac Denesuline First Nation
George Gordon First Nation
Goulet, Keith
Hatchet Lake Denesuline First Nation
Indian Policy and Early Reserve Period
Island Lake Band (Ministikwan Indian Reserve)
Jackson, Tom
James Smith Cree Nation
Kahkewistahaw Band
Kawacatoose First Nation
Keeseekoose First Nation
Kinistino First Nation

Lac La Ronge Indian Band
LaRocque, Joseph Z.
Lavallee, Mary Ann
Little Black Bear First Nation
Little Pine First Nation
Longman, Mary
Lucky Man Cree First Nation
Makwa Sahgaiehcan First Nation
McMaster, Gerald
Métis and Non-Status Indian Legal Issues
Métis Communities
Métis Culture and Language
Métis Education Métis Farms
Métis History
Métis Nation–Saskatchewan
Métis Women
Mistawasis First Nation
Montreal Lake Cree Nation
Moosomin First Nation
Morin, Gerald
Mosquito, Grizzly Bear's Head, Lean Man First Nations
Muscowpetung First Nation
Muskeg Lake Cree Nation
Muskoday First Nation
Muskowekwan First Nation
Nakota (Assiniboine)
Nekaneet Cree First Nation
Non-Status Indians
Norris, Malcolm
North-West Resistance
North-West Resistance and First Nations
Ocean Man First Nation
Ochapowace First Nation
Office of the Treaty Commissioner
Okanese Reserve
One Arrow First Nation
Onion Lake First Nation
Opekokew, Delia
Pasqua
Pasqua First Nation
Peepeekisis First Nation
Pelican Lake First Nation
Peter Ballantyne Cree First Nation
Peter Chapman First Nation
Pheasant's Rump Nakota First Nation

Piapot (1816-1908)
Piapot Cree First Nation
Poundmaker
Poundmaker Cree First Nation
Pratt, Charles Cowley
Red Earth First Nation
Red Pheasant First Nation
Reserves, Urban
Riel, Louis "David"
Sakimay First Nation
Sanderson, Sol
Saskatchewan Indian Cultural Centre
Saskatchewan Indian Gaming Authority (SIGA)
Saskatchewan Indian Institute of Technologies
Saulteaux
Saulteaux First Nation
Scrip
Shoal Lake First Nation
Sinclair, Jim
Sitting Bull
Standing Buffalo Dakota First Nation
Starblanket, Noel
Starblanket First Nation
Sturgeon Lake First Nation
Sweet Grass First Nation
The Key First Nation
Thunderchild First Nation
Tootoosis, Gordon
Tootoosis, John
Traditional Ecological Knowledge
Treaty Eight
Treaty Five
Treaty Four
Treaty Six
Treaty Ten
Trotchie, Clarence
Urban Aboriginal Population
Urban Reserves
Wahpeton Dakota Reserve
Wanuskewin Heritage Park
Waterhen Lake First Nation
White Bear First Nation
Whitecap Dakota First Nation
Witchekan Lake First Nation
Wood Mountain Dakota First Nation
Yellow Quill First Nation

Young Chipeewayan First Nation (Stony Knoll)

Agriculture and Food

Aboriginal Reserve Agriculture to 1900
Agricultural Implement Industry
Agricultural Marketing
Agricultural Markets and Trade
Agricultural Policy
Agriculture and Food Theme Essay
Agronomy
Aquaculture
Atkinson, Robert Roy
Barber, Clarence Lyle
Barley
Beef Farming
Beef Industry
Beekeeping
Bell, John Milton (Milt)
Brewing and Fermentation Industry
Brown, Jacob
Canadian Grain Commission
Canadian Wheat Board
Canaryseed
Canola
Cargill Limited
Centre for Studies in Agriculture, Law and the Environment (CSALE)
Chicken Farmers of Saskatchewan
Christensen, David A.
Community Pastures
Crawford, Roy Douglas
Crop Development Centre
Crop Pests
Dairy Farming
Dairy Industry
Downey, Richard Keith
Elliott, Moses
Farm Machinery and Equipment
Farm Movement (1901-1949)
Farm Organizations
Farming

Benedictines of St. Peter's Abbey
Bergthaler Mennonite Church
Beth Jacob Jewish Community
Bethany College
Bible Schools and Colleges
Briercrest Schools
Canadian Bible College/Canadian Theological Seminary
Canadian Catholic Organization for Development and Peace
Catholic Ministry to First Nations People
Catholic Shrines and Pilgrimages
Catholic Women's League (CWL) of Canada
Central Pentecostal College
Christian and Missionary Alliance Church
Christian Reformed Church in North America
Church of Jesus Christ of Latter-Day Saints (Mormons)
Church of the Nazarene
Congregation of the Most Holy Redeemer (Redemptorists)
Cree Cosmology
Cree Religious Ethos
Dakota/Lakota Spirituality
Daughters of Providence (Les Filles de la Providence, FDLP).
Denesuline Worldview
Doukhobor Philosophy
Evangelical Free Church of Canada
Evangelical Lutheran Church in Canada
Evangelical Mennonite Conference
Evangelical Mennonite Mission Conference
First Nations Religion: Overview
Franciscan Sisters of St. Elizabeth
Free Methodist Church
Hadassah - WIZO
Hai Duc Buddhist Pagoda
Hindu Communities
Hindu Temple, Regina
Hutterites
Knights of Columbus
Lutheran Church-Canada Central District
Lutheran Theological Seminary
Mennonite Central Committee Saskatchewan
Mennonite Church Saskatchewan
Mennonites
Multi-Faith Forum, Regina
Muslims
North American Baptists
Oblates of Mary Immaculate (OMI) Assumption Province
Oblates of Mary Immaculate (OMI) Saint Mary's Province
Obnova Club
O'Brien, Ann Gordon
Ogle, Father Robert
Old Colony Mennonite Church
Orthodox Churches

Pentecostal Assemblies of Canada
Pipe Ceremony
Prairie Centre for Ecumenism
Presbyterians
Regina Anti-Poverty Ministry
Regina Council of Churches
Regina Vineyard Christian Fellowship
Religion Theme Essay
Religious Society of Friends (Quakers)
Roman Catholic Cathedrals
Roman Catholic Congregations of Men Religious
Roman Catholic Congregations of Women Religious
Roman Catholic Dioceses and Bishops
Roman Catholic Missions in the North-West and Saskatchewan (19th-20th Centuries)
Roman Catholics
Salvation Army
Saskatchewan Conference of Mennonite Brethren Churches
Saskatoon Council of Churches
Saskatoon Jewish Foundation
School Sisters of Notre Dame
Sheptytsky Institute
Shiloh Assembly Church
Shir Chadash Synagogue
Shri Lakshami Narayana Temple
Sikhism
Sisters of Charity of Montreal (Grey Nuns)
Sisters of Charity of St. Louis
Sisters of Charity of the Immaculate Conception
Sisters of Loretto (Institute of the Blessed Virgin Mary)
Sisters of Mission Service
Sisters of Notre Dame d' Auvergne
Sisters of Our Lady of Sion (NDS)
Sisters of Our Lady of the Cross (Notre Dame de la Croix ndc)
Sisters of Our Lady of the Missions
Sisters of Providence of St. Vincent de Paul
Sisters of Service
Sisters of the Child Jesus
Sisters of the Presentation of Mary
Sisters Servants of St. Mary Immaculate
Smudging
Sri Sathya Sai Baba Organization in Saskatchewan
Sri Sri Rhadha Krishna Temple
St. Joseph's College
Sun Dance
Sweat-Lodge Ceremony
Synagogues
Taché, Alexandre-Antonin
Temple Beth Tikvah
Ukrainian Catholic Brotherhood
Ukrainian Catholic Women's League
Ukrainian Catholics
Ukrainian Sisters of St. Joseph of Saskatoon

Unitarian Fellowship in Saskatchewan
United Church of Canada
Ursulines (Order of St. Ursula, OSU)
Wat Buddhadhamma

Science and Technology

Accutrak
Agriculture Canada Research Stations
Airseeders
Algae
American Dipper
Amphibians
Aurora Borealis
Automated Teller Machines (ATM)
Bard, Frederick George
Bats
Beetles
Belted Kingfisher
Biodiversity
Biodiversity Action Plan
Biofiltration Water Treatment System
BiphasixTM
Birds
Bison
Blackbirds
Blakiston, Thomas Wright
Brown Creeper
Bugs (Order Hemiptera)
Buntings and Allies
Butterflies and Moths
Canadian Light Source
Carbon Dioxide Storage
Carnivores
Chickadees
Chimney Swift
Chronic Pain
Computer-Generated Plant Animation
Conservation
Conservation Agencies
Conservation Areas
Contraceptive Patch
Cormorants
Coupland, Robert Thomas
Covington, Arthur Edwin
Cranes
Crow Family
Cuckoo, Black-billed
Currie, Balfour
Deer
Doves and Pigeons
Dragonflies
Drummond, Thomas
Duck Family
Ecozones and Ecoregions
Edmunds, Frederic Harrison
Energy-Efficient Houses
Falcons
Finches
Fishes of Saskatchewan
Flowering Plants
Flycatchers
Follicular Waves
Forests
Fossil Record
Franklin, Sir John
Gardiner Dam
Gilroy, Doug
Grasshoppers
Grasslands National Park
Grebes
Grey Owl (Archibald Stansfield Belaney)

Grouse and Allies
Gulls and Terns
Hammer, Ulrich Theodore
Hares and Rabbits
Hawks and Eagles
Heavy Oil Upgraders
Herons
Herzberg, Gerhard
Horned Lark
House Sparrow
Houston, Clarence Stuart
Hummingbirds
Hydrogen Diesel Trucks
Hydrogen Production
Hymenopterans
Ibis
Katz, Leon
Kidney Re-transplant
Kinglets
Lahrman, Frederick William
Last Mountain Bird Observatory
Lattice Quantum ChromoDynamics (LQCD)
Leaver, Eric William
Ledingham, George Filson
Lichens
Loons
MacKay, Angus
Mackenzie, Chalmers Jack
Macoun, John
Mammals
M-DNA
Mineral Detection
Native Plant Society of Saskatchewan
Nature Saskatchewan
Nightjars
Nuthatch
Owls
Palliser Triangle
Pelican
Phosphate Innoculant
Pipits
Plant Root Simulator
Prairie Conservation Action Plan (PCAP)
Priestley, Isabel M.
Prince Albert National Park
Pronghorn
Rails
Rempel, Jacob G.
Reptiles
Richardson, John
Riegert, Paul
Rodents
Royal Saskatchewan Museum
Saskatchewan Conservation Data Centre
Saskatchewan Research Council
Saskatchewan Science Centre
Saskatchewan Wildlife Federation
SaskTel Fibre Optics
Schneider, William George
Science and Technology Theme Essay
Shorebirds
Shrews
Shrikes
Snow Rollers
Space Engineering Division
Space Shuttle Experiment
SPARRO Project
Sparrows, Native
Species at Risk
Spiders
Spinks, John William Tranter
Starlings
Sun-Dogs

Swallows
Synthetic Sugar
Tanagers
Taube, Henry
Thode, Henry George
Thrashers
Thrushes and Bluebirds
Titanic Rusticles
Trace Analysis Facility
Trees
Turkey Vulture
Van Cleave, Allan Bishop
Vireos
Warblers
Waxwings
Weigh-In-Motion Scale
Woodpeckers
Wrens
Zero-Effluent Pulp Mill
Zooplankton

Social Policy

Children
Community Economic Development
Community Social Services
Community Support for People with Intellectual Disabilities
Disability, Citizenship, and Public Policy
Early Childhood Development Programs
Economics and Development
Emergency Social Services
Employment Supports and Services
Families
Housing Policy
Income Security
Saskatchewan Institute of Public Policy
Social Assistance
Social Policy Theme Essay
Social Work
Sociology and Saskatchewan Development
Voluntary Sector
Women's Shelters
Workers' Compensation
Youth Justice

Sports and Recreation

Alexander, Jack
Baker, Mary
Baseball
Bentley Brothers, Douglas and Maxwell
Boldt, Arnold
Catherwood, Ethel
Clarke, Bill
Cleveland, Reggie
Competitive Games
Curling
Currie, Gordon
Dewar, Phyllis
Dojack, Paul
Donison brothers: Lee, Danny, and Sebastian 'Butch'
DuWors, Maureen (née Rever)
Figure Skating
Folk, Rick
Football
Francis, Emile
Genereux, George Patrick
Gerein, Clayton
Gillies, Clark

Rocanville
Roche Percee
Rockglen
Rose Valley
Rosetown
Rosthern
Rouleau
Saltcoats
Saskatoon
Scott
Shaunavon
Shellbrook
Sintaluta
Southey
Spiritwood
Springside
St. Walburg
Stanley Mission
Star City
Stoughton
Strasbourg
Sturgis
Swift Current
Tisdale
Turtleford
Unity
Uranium City
Vonda
Wadena
Wakaw
Waldheim
Wapella
Warman
Watrous
Watson
Wawota
Weyburn
White City
Whitewood
Wilkie
Willow Bunch
Wolseley
Wood Mountain
Wynyard
Yellow Grass
Yorkton
Zealandia
Zenon Park

Saskatchewan Order of Merit Recipients

Azevedo, Ted
Baldwin, Mildred
Bear, Angus
Bell, Carol Gay
Bothwell, George
Brandt, Elisabeth Pasztor
Brown, Jacob A.
Bunnie, Samuel
Campbell, Constantine
Carrier, Lorne
Carter, Roger
DePauw, Ronald
Dietrick, Lorne
Ferguson, Robert R.
Gallaway, Marguerite
Gathercole, Frederick J.
Green, John
Greyeyes, David
Hanson, Bill
Haughton, Willa
Hill, Frederick
Johnson, F.W.
McKercher, Margaret
McLeod, John
Morris, George
Ohlsen, Dieter

Olaski, Suzanne Claire
Pawson, Geoffrey
Pawson, Ruth
Pearsall, Victor
Petit, Claude
Phillips, Roger
Pinder, Ross
Rawlinson, Edward
Seifert, Lillian
Shumiatcher, Jacqui
Small, William
Staseson, Gordon
Sudom, Anna
Sutter, Christian
Tinney, Phyllis
Wagman, Fred
Wallman, Arthur
Worobetz, Stephen
Wright, Clifford

Order of Canada Recipients

Adams, Nancy
Black, Donald
Blake, Joyce
Bonneau, Solomon
Boucher, John B.
Buckwold, Sidney L.
Carr, Denny
Cennon, Jack
Chan, Ernest
Craig, Albert
Currie, Balfour
de Lint, Willem
Egnatoff, John G.
Gauley, David Eldon
Gervais, Alice
Gerwing, Alphonse Mathias
Gjesdal, Joseph Harvey
Gocki, Anthony J.
Goplen, Henrietta
Gordon, Percival H.
Hildebrand, Henry
Hudec, Margaret
Ingham, Anna Gertrude
Kartusch, Michael P.
Kettles, James G.
Kindrachuk, Michael John
Kirk, Lawrence E.
Kitagawa, Genzo
Knight, Doris
Koziak, Methodius
Kyle, Elva
Langan, Henry J.
Larre, Lucien
Lawrence, Thomas
Lee, Douglas A.
Leslie, E.C.
Lewry, Louis H.
Leyton-Brown, Myrl
MacKay, Harold
Marchildon, Arthur
McDougall, Médéric Zéphirin
McNab, Hilliard
Mitchell, Charles Stuart
Moran, Patrick Joseph
Mossing, Robert Lynn
Nixon, Howard R.
Opheim, Eloise E.
Peacock, Albert E.
Pine, Grace Davis
Pinsonneault, Ronald A.
Podiluk, Walter
Porteous, George
Renaud, André
Rezansoff, Paul J.
Roe, Jean A.

Rose, Gerald F.
Sandison, John Edgar
Sebestyen, Edmund Alexander
South, Gordon
Spence, Ahab
Stensrud, Howard
Stevenson, Lawrence H.
Terry, George
Thomas, Lewis H.
Thompson, Douglas
Thompson, W.P.
Wakabayashi, Arthur Tsuneo
Waskewitch, Gus
Wedge, James Balfour
Williamson, Robert G.
Zakreski, Peter E.

INDEX

This index includes only individuals who are referred to in the *Encyclopedia* but who do not have their own articles. In cases where an individual's name appears in more than one article, the article names are separated by a semi-colon.

A

Abbott, Edith: FREE METHODIST CHURCH
Abel, Sid: HOWE, GORDIE; HOCKEY
Aberhart, William: SOCIAL GOSPEL
Achtymichuk, George: CURLING
Acoose, Janice: METIS COMMUNITIES
Acoose, Madeleine (O'Soup): ACOOSE, PAUL
Acton, D.F.: SASKATCHEWAN SOIL SURVEY
Adams, Bob: TRACK AND FIELD
Adams, Gregg: FOLLICULAR WAVES
Adams, John: UNITARIAN FELLOWSHIP IN SASKATCHEWAN
Adams, John Quincy: UNITARIAN FELLOWSHIP IN SASKATCHEWAN
Adaskin, Harry, John and Gordon: ADASKIN, MURRAY
Ah-yah-tus-kum-ik-im-am, Chief (William Twatt): STURGEON LAKE FIRST NATION
Aich, Palok: MCNAUGHTON, VIOLET CLARA
Albani, Emma: MUSIC; OPERA
Albee, Edward: SASKATOON GATEWAY PLAYERS
Albulet, Steve: AIR AMBULANCE
Aldag, Roger: FOOTBALL
Alexiewich, John: UKRAINIAN LABOUR FARMER TEMPLE ASSOCIATION
Allan (Inspector): ALMIGHTY VOICE
Allende, Salvador: CHILEAN COMMUNITY
Allids, John: CHOIRS
Alloway, Lawrence: GODWIN, TED
Alype, Sister M.: SISTERS OF OUR LADY OF THE CROSS
Amyotte, Joe: MÉTIS NATION-SASKATCHEWAN
Anderson, Dr. J.F.C.: THOMPSON COMMITTEE
Anderson, Marian: OPERA
Anderson, Martha (Amundson): ANDERSON, MATHIAS S.
Anderson, Morris A.: MURRAY COMMISSION REPORT, 1988–90
Anderson, William: SALTCOATS
Andreasen, Gerda: HNATYSHYN, RAMON JOHN
Andrew, Bob: CITIZENS CONCERNED ABOUT FREE TRADE
Andrews, Arthur: FEDERAL GRAIN LTD.
Andrews, Nellie: WOMAN SUFFRAGE
Andrist, Rachel: OPERA
Anson, Adelbert: ANGLICAN CHURCH OF CANADA
Apisis, William (Chief): ENGLISH RIVER FIRST NATION
Appleby, Frank: FARM MOVEMENT
Appleby, Fred: ACOOSE, PAUL
Apseenes (Young Sweet Grass): SWEET GRASS FIRST NATION
Arcand, Emma, Jean-Baptiste and Victor: ARCAND, JOHN
Archange, Philomena: BRADY, JAMES PATRICK
Argue, Robert: CENTRAL PENTECOSTAL COLLEGE
Armstrong, Charles: SPORTS MEDICINE
Armstrong, Margaret: WOMAN SUFFRAGE
Armstrong, Nora: ARMSTRONG, GRACE; SASKATCHEWAN REGISTERED NURSES' ASSOCIATION
Arneson, Robert: FAFARD, JOSEPH
Arnett, Dr. G. Dudley: TUBERCULOSIS CONTROL
Arnot, David: OFFICE OF THE TREATY COMMISSIONER
Arya, Dr. Usharbudh: HINDU TEMPLE, REGINA
Ashfield, Chris: WHITEWOOD
Askenootow (Worker of the Earth): PRATT, CHARLES COWLEY

Asmundson, Gordon: CHRONIC PAIN
Atchison, Ron: FOOTBALL
Atelier, Julienne: FAFARD, JOSEPH
Atkinson, C.J.: SCOTT, THOMAS WALTER
Atkinson, Marion: STAPLES, R.J.
Attenborough, Richard: DE WALT, KEVIN
Attickasish (Little Deer): HENDAY, ANTHONY
Axtell, Don: TENNIS
Axworthy, Chris: CALVERT, LORNE ALBERT
Ayimâsis: BIG BEAR FIRST NATION; FROG LAKE MASSACRE
Aypaspik: FLYING DUST FIRST NATION
Azure, Isabella: DUMONT, MADELEINE

B

Babbitt, Annie Blanch: BULYEA, GEORGE
Babcock, Reverend Lotta: FREE METHODIST CHURCH
Back, George: KANE, PAUL
Badgely, Robin: WOLFE, SAM
Baerwald, Angela: FOLLICULAR WAVES
Bailey, Renata: TRACE ANALYSIS FACILITY
Bailie, H.D.: LABOUR AND CIVIC POLITICS
Baker, Terry: SASKATCHEWAN WHEAT POOL
Bakker, Sharon: 25TH STREET THEATRE
Balfour, James: MARTIN, WILLIAM MELVILLE
Banbury, Erwin and Robert: BEAVER LUMBER
Banting, Chris: MORRIS RODWEEDER STRIKE
Barbier (Abbé): FRENCH SETTLEMENTS
Barbier, Euphrasie: SISTERS OF OUR LADY OF THE MISSIONS (RNDM)
Barish, Solomon: JEWISH RURAL SETTLEMENTS
Barmby, Walter: BARMBY, MARJORIE
Barnett, Will: KNOWLES, DOROTHY; LOCHHEAD, KEN; MULCASTER, WYNONA
Barnhart, Gordon: SALTCOATS
Barr, George H.: UNIVERSITY OF REGINA
Barr, Reverend Isaac M.: BARR COLONY; ENGLISH SETTLEMENTS; UTOPIANISM
Barry, Bill: PLACE NAMES
Barrymore, Ethel: THEATRE
Bartman, Clara: UNITARIAN FELLOWSHIP IN SASKATCHEWAN
Barwell, Gordon: FOOTBALL
Baskin, Reg: COMMUNICATIONS, ENERGY AND PAPERWORKERS UNION OF CANADA
Bassaraba, Stefanka Molly: LENHARDT, MOLLY
Bastien, A.H. Rocan: FRENCH SETTLEMENTS; ROCANVILLE
Bateman, Captain Reginald: 196TH WESTERN UNIVERSITIES BATTALION
Bates, Lloyd: HIGH-ENERGY CANCER TREATMENT
Batty, Harold: AIR AMBULANCE
Baudemont, Frédérique: TROUPE DU JOUR, LA
Baudoux, Maurice: FRENCH SETTLEMENTS
Beamish, Mae: KENDERDINE, AUGUSTUS FREDERICK LAFOSSE
Beattie, Jessie Ann: GRASSICK, JAMES
Beaudry, Henry: ABORIGINAL ARTISTS, CONTEMPORARY
Bechard, Jerome: AIR SEEDERS
Beck, R.G.: HEALTH ECONOMICS
Beckett, Mel: SASKATCHEWAN ROUGHRIDERS
Beechy, Frederick William: BEECHY
Beet, Harry Churchill: VICTORIA CROSS: SASKATCHEWAN RECIPIENTS
Bégin, Monique: GOODWILL, JEAN CUTHAND
Behrens, Jack: OPERA
Belanger, Maureen: ABORIGINAL THEATRE

Belcourt, Emile: OPERA
Belding, Donna: CURLING
Bell, Alexander Graham: HOME AND SCHOOL; UNITARIAN FELLOWSHIP IN SASKATCHEWAN
Bell, Hubbard Mabel: HOME AND SCHOOL
Bell, Chelsey: CURLING
Bell, Keith: SAVAGE, CANDACE
Bell, Linda: HYLAND, GARY
Bell, Major William R.: TELECOMMUNICATIONS
Benjamin, Arthur: FLEMING, ROBERT JAMES BERKELEY
Bennett, R.B: ASELTINE, WALTER MORLEY; BENNETT BUGGY; EXPLORERS; MEDIA: NEWSPAPERS, ON-TO-OTTAWA TREK AND THE REGINA RIOT; TELEVISION AND RADIO; WEIR, ROBERT
Bentley (Mrs.): ROSS, SINCLAIR
Bentley-Fisher, Tom: 25TH STREET THEATRE
Bereskin, Abram: PLACE NAMES
Berg, Nathan: OPERA
Bergen, Dr. Arthur: INTERNATIONAL ROAD DYNAMICS
Berger, Philip: JEWISH RURAL SETTLEMENTS
Bernhardt, Sarah: THEATRE
Bérubé (Abbé): FRENCH SETTLEMENTS
Best, Dr. Charles H.: JACQUES, LOUIS BARKER
Bethune, Dr. Norman: MCLEAN, GRANT; MITCHELL, KEN
Betker, Jan: CURLING; SCHMIRLER, SANDRA
Beyer, Sisters Agnes and Petra: SCHOOL SISTERS OF NOTRE DAME
Beynon, Francis Marion: ORGANIZED FARM WOMEN IN THE WGG, THE UFC, THE SFU AND THE NFU; WOMAN SUFFRAGE
Birtsch, Molly: CANCER TREATMENT
Bjelajac, Nicolas: COWLEY, RETA
Black, Conrad: MEDIA: NEWSPAPERS, TELEVISION AND RADIO
Black, D. Lyall: GOODWILL, JEAN CUTHAND
Black, Henry: ELLISON, ALBAN CEDERIC; SASKATCHEWAN RELIEF COMMISSION
Blackett, George: CANADIAN BIBLE COLLEGE/CANADIAN THEOLOGY SEMINARY
Blackwell, Mary: SAUNDERS, CHARLES
Blais, Leo: ROMAN CATHOLIC DIOCESES AND BISHOPS
Blake, William: UNITARIAN FELLOWSHIP IN SASKATCHEWAN
Blakeney, Ann: VOICE OF WOMEN
Bland, Salem: BRONFMAN FAMILY
Blanket, Yellow Mud: TOOTOOSIS, JOHN BAPTISTE
Blewett, Duncan: PSYCHOLOGY
Bloch, Ernest: LEYTON-BROWN, HOWARD
Blue, A.M. (Monty): BLUE, GRACE E.
Boan, J.A.: HEALTH ECONOMICS
Bocking, D.H.: HISTORIANS AND HISTORIGRAPHY
Boda, Rexford: CANADIAN BIBLE COLLEGE/CANADIAN THEOLOGY SEMINARY
Bodard, Auguste: FRENCH SETTLEMENTS
Bodeutz, Petre: DANCE
Bold, June: SASKATCHEWAN HEALTH RESEARCH FOUNDATION
Bolt, Carol: GLOBE THEATRE
Booth, General William: SALVATION ARMY
Borden, Robert: TRANS-CANADA HIGHWAY; WILLOUGHBY, WELLINGTON BARTLEY
Boswell, W.G.: VETERINARY MEDICINE
Bothwell, Austin: BOTHWELL, JESSIE
Botkin, Jean: DANCE
Bottineau, Josephte: LÉGARÉ, JEAN-LOUIS
Boucher, Marie-Anne: DUPERREAULT, MARIE-ANNE

Saskatchewan at a Glance

ORIGIN OF THE NAME: From the Cree word, *kisiskâciwani-sîpiy* *("the river that flows swiftly")*, a reference to the area's major river.

AREA: Approximately 651,900 square kilometres (87.4% land, 12.6% water). Forests cover one-half of the province, agricultural land covers one-third, and fresh water covers approximately one-eighth (approximately 100,000 lakes, rivers and streams).

GEOGRAPHY: The only province in Canada whose borders are drawn without reference to natural features; bordered on the west by Alberta, on the north by the Northwest Territories and Nunavut, on the east by Manitoba, and on the south by North Dakota and Montana. The geographic centre of the province is 100 km north of Prince Albert. The major river systems are North and South Saskatchewan, Assiniboine and Churchill, all of which flow into Hudson Bay. The highest elevation is the Cypress Hills, at 1,392 m above sea level (higher than Banff).

TIME ZONE: Central Standard Time (CST) year-round (no Daylight Savings).

POPULATION: As of January 2005, the population was approximately 995,280 (urban 64%, rural 36%; female 51%, male 49%). There are 13 cities, 145 towns, 289 villages, 39 resort villages, 169 organized hamlets, 35 northern communities, and 296 rural municipalities in the province.

CLIMATE: Canada's "sunniest" province averaging between 2,000 to 2,500 hours of sunshine annually. The city of Estevan in the southeast leads the country with an average 2,540 sunshine-filled hours each year. The highest temperature (45.0°C) was recorded at Midale and Yellow Grass on July 5, 1937; the lowest temperature (-56.7°C) was recorded at Prince Albert on February 1, 1893.

GOVERNANCE: Saskatchewan became a province on September 1, 1905. The capital city is Regina. A democratic government is run according to the parliamentary system with an appointed Lieutenant-Governor representing the Crown, and an elected Legislative Assembly.

PROVINCIAL FLAG: Saskatchewan's official flag was adopted in 1969. It features the provincial shield of arms along with the floral emblem, the western red lily. The flag's upper half is green, representing Saskatchewan's northern forests; the lower half is gold, symbolizing the southern grain areas.

PROVINCIAL FLOWER: In 1941, the western red lily was chosen as the official flower of Saskatchewan. A protected species, this lily grows in moist meadows and semi-wooded areas.

PROVINCIAL BIRD: The sharp-tailed grouse was selected as the provincial bird emblem in 1945.

PROVINCIAL ANIMAL: The white-tailed deer was designated as the official provincial animal in 2001.

PROVINCIAL GRASS: In 2001, needle-and-thread grass was designated Saskatchewan's official grass. It is a native bunchgrass common to the dry, sandy soils of the Northern Plains.

PROVINCIAL MINERAL: Sylvite (potash) is Saskatchewan's official mineral.

PROVINCIAL SPORT: Curling was named Saskatchewan's official sport in 2001.